Congress and the Nation

Congress and the Nation

VOLUME X · 1997–2001

A REVIEW OF GOVERNMENT AND POLITICS

105th and 106th Congresses

CQ PRESS

A Division of Congressional Quarterly Inc.
Washington, D.C.

Printed and bound in the United States of America

06 05 04 03 02   5 4 3 2 1

⊚ The paper used in this publication meets the minimum require-
ments of the American National Standard for Information
Sciences—Permanence of Paper for Printed Library Materials,
ANSI Z39.48-1992.

Editor: David R. Tarr

Associate Editors: Gwenda Larsen, Ann O'Connor, Jon Preimesberger

Major Contributors: Adriel Bettelheim, John Felton, Martha V.
Gottron, David Hosansky, Ken Jost, Kerry Kern, David Masci,
Colleen McGuiness, Julie Rovner

Contributors: Carolyn Goldinger, Grace Hill, Melinda Nahmias,
Walter Oleszek, Ann O'Malley, Sally Ryman

Cover: Paul Pressau

Composition: BMWW, Baltimore, Md.

Index: Jan Danis

Library of Congress Catalog Number: 65-22351

ISBN: 1-56802-624-2
ISSN: 1047-1324

Editors' Note

Congress and the Nation Vol. X continues a series launched by Congressional Quarterly in 1965 with the publication of *Congress and the Nation Vol. I*, a 2,000-page reference book covering national government and politics from 1945 through 1964. Each of the succeeding volumes has covered governmental action during a four-year presidential term: *Congress and the Nation Vol. II*, 1965–1968; *Congress and the Nation Vol. III*, 1969–1972; *Congress and the Nation Vol. IV*, 1973–1976; *Congress and the Nation Vol. V*, 1977–1980; *Congress and the Nation Vol. VI*, 1981–1984; *Congress and the Nation Vol. VII*, 1985–1988; *Congress and the Nation Vol. VIII*, 1989–1992; *Congress and the Nation Vol. IX*, 1993–1996; and the current edition, *Congress and the Nation Vol. X*, 1997–2001.

With the publication of this volume, which covers the 105th and 106th Congresses, librarians, historians, political scientists, journalists, and students have ten editions spanning more than half a century of Congressional Quarterly's reporting on national government, elections, and public policy.

In compiling *Congress and the Nation Vol. X*, the editors at CQ Press have condensed legislative, presidential, and political coverage during the January 1997–January 2001 period into a 1,200-page volume. Chapters give an overview of the four years, with additional discussion of earlier events as needed, in addition to providing detailed chronologies of congressional action in major subject areas.

This volume focuses on the second presidential term of Bill Clinton but surveys his full eight years in office in many places to set the context for his last four years. Clinton's final term was an extraordinary four-year period, highlighted by his impeachment and acquittal in Congress—only the second time in history that a president faced an impeachment trial. With the inauguration of Clinton in 1993, both the White House and Congress were controlled by the Democratic Party for the first time since Jimmy Carter's presidency ended in 1981. It lasted just two years. The Republicans staged a huge upset in the 1994 midterm elections and won control of both houses of Congress for the first time in forty years. Republican control of Congress continued for the rest of Clinton's years in the White House. The deeply partisan divisions that arose in those six years dominated most of the political and legislative activity until Clinton left office in 2001.

Clinton, however, was more than just a survivor. In the aftermath of the 1994 GOP election victory, he looked to be a one-term president. But in 1996—with the economy humming, the massive federal deficit declining, and relative peace abroad—Clinton won reelection by a substantial margin. Republicans continued to control Congress as they also did after the 1998 off-year elections. But in both those congressional elections the

clear majority that voters had given the GOP in 1994 shrank to a point where for all practical purposes the national government was in delicate balance between the parties. As a result, both parties spent much of Clinton's second term positioning themselves in the voters' eyes for the 2000 national elections when there would be no incumbent in the White House. The upshot, particularly in the 106th Congress in 1999–2001, was plentiful posturing on both sides with congressional Republicans sending the president bills they knew he disdained and the president predictably vetoing them.

Both parties worked toward what they hoped would be a definitive decision by voters in 2000 in favor of their view of government. As often happens, the voters did not comply. In the most remarkable election of modern times, the presidency was settled in favor of a Republican, George W. Bush, only after the Supreme Court, in a divided 5–4 ruling, awarded him Florida's electoral votes in a bitterly contested race in that state. Even with the electoral victory, Bush lost the popular vote to his opponent, Vice President Al Gore, by half a million ballots. It was little better in Congress. Republicans retained control of the House of Representatives, but by only a few seats. The Senate, although divided evenly down the middle, 50–50, remained in nominal control of the GOP only because of the constitutional right of Bush's vice president, Richard B. Cheney, to cast a vote to break a tie. The stalemate may have reflected an electorate comfortable with a long unbroken stretch of economic prosperity that was unsure of the role it wanted government to play.

To be sure, Congress and the president collaborated on significant legislation, including a landmark agreement to balance the budget and cut taxes concurrently, a measure giving China the same trade status with the United States as that enjoyed by most other nations, and legislation reforming the huge financial services business. But many other important measures died, the victims of the unusually bitter partisanship that had characterized Washington for years—even before Clinton arrived—and at times seemed to make legislators unable to do more than jockey for momentary political advantage.

One catalyst for partisanship was President Clinton himself, who displayed a remarkable knack for frustrating Republican legislative and political goals after the GOP took control of Congress in 1995. But the president's strengths were compromised by personal conduct that even his partisans thought shabby and unbefitting a president. Revelations in early 1998 of Clinton's affair with a young White House intern gave Republicans a political opening to retaliate against the president by seeking his impeachment on charges of perjury and obstruction of justice. But instead of being driven from office, Clinton emerged at the end of the ordeal with his public support sur-

v

prisingly intact and his willingness to use a sharp veto pen as strong as ever.

Another catalyst in the partisanship of the period was a charismatic and fiery Republican from Georgia, Newt Gingrich, the man widely credited with engineering the GOP takeover of the House in the 1994 elections and a chief practitioner of a highly negative brand of politics based on discrediting the opposition. House Republicans rewarded Gingrich by making him Speaker in 1995, but his speakership would last only four years. After losing a series of confrontations with Clinton that contributed to Republican loss of seats in the House, the mercurial Gingrich announced in November 1998 that he was resigning from Congress. Although Republican legislators were no longer in awe of Gingrich, many saw his departure as yet another loss and embarrassment inflicted on the GOP by Clinton. The party was further embarrassed when Gingrich's anointed successor also resigned from Congress after a revelation of sexual infidelities in a bizarre echo of the charges the GOP had been hurling at the president.

Congress and the Nation Vol. X is a record of these and other congressional and presidential activities—from momentous events to routine extensions of federal programs. Readers seeking an overview of the period and the principal players will begin with Chapter 1, Politics and National Issues, which gives a legislative summary of each session of the 105th and 106th Congresses and a discussion of the 1998 and 2000 elections. The chapter forms a framework for the legislative chapters that follow.

Chapters 2 through 14, the legislative chapters on public policy, provide details on issues and legislation, descriptions of proposals and bills, succinct accounts of legislative and executive actions, lobbying activity, key votes on selected issues, and provisions of bills that became law. Chapters 15 and 16 examine Congress as an institution and the second term of the Clinton presidency.

HOW TO USE THIS BOOK

The **Summary Table of Contents** following this editors' note shows the overall organization of the book. The detailed **Table of Contents** *(p. ix)* provides an outline of each chapter as well as a listing of stories and sidebars included in the chapters. For a specific topic within a story, readers should consult the **Index** *(p. 1145)*. Throughout the book readers will find page references to related subjects on other pages (and to other volumes of *Congress and the Nation* for historical context). These page "flags" are designed to speed research across an array of subjects. Their use is particularly significant during the period of this volume because Congress often legislated in omnibus bills, covering a variety of topics in a single piece of legislation that *Congress and the Nation* treats in different chapters.

The **Appendix** *(p. 829)* contains supplementary material, including Senate and House key votes (highlighted in boldface in the legislative chapters) during the four-year period, with charts showing how each member voted; a glossary of congressional terms and an explanation of how a bill becomes law; lists of committee and subcommittee chairmen; biographical data on members of Congress between 1997 and 2001; profiles of cabinet members and other senior officials; controversial nominations; presidential vetoes; and major presidential speeches and messages to Congress as well as other important documents. In addition, the appendix includes extensive political charts, including presidential, House, Senate, and gubernatorial election returns for the period. Tables also record special elections and members who switched parties. Finally, the appendix provides a complete list of public laws enacted during the four years.

This volume has been prepared under the direction of editors at CQ Press, a division of Congressional Quarterly Inc. The chapters and the appendix were written or compiled by the contributors listed on page iv, many of whom have covered Congress for Congressional Quarterly and other Washington news organizations. CQ Press editors wish to express their thanks to these dedicated reporters and to editors and writers on the *CQ Weekly* and the *CQ Almanac* for their assistance in the preparation of this edition.

CQ Press Editors
April 2002

Summary Table of Contents

CHAPTER 1   Politics and National Issues   1

CHAPTER 2   Economic Policy   31

CHAPTER 3   Trade Policy   145

CHAPTER 4   Foreign Policy   171

CHAPTER 5   Defense Policy   233

CHAPTER 6   Transportation, Commerce, and Communications   313

CHAPTER 7   Environment and Energy   339

CHAPTER 8   Agricultural Policy   415

CHAPTER 9   Health and Human Services   427

CHAPTER 10   Education Policy   505

CHAPTER 11   Housing and Urban Aid   551

CHAPTER 12   Labor and Pension Policy   569

CHAPTER 13   Law and Justice   587

CHAPTER 14   General Government   731

CHAPTER 15   Inside Congress   755

CHAPTER 16   The Clinton Presidency   795

APPENDIX   829

INDEX   1145

Table of Contents

Tables and Figures   xix

CHAPTER 1   Politics and National Issues

Introduction   3

1997 Chronology
The Legislative Year   6
Congress in 1997   6
Congressional Leadership 1997–2001   7
The Political Year   8

1998 Chronology
The Legislative Year   10
Congress in 1998   10
The Political Year   11

1999 Chronology
The Legislative Year   15
Congress in 1999   15
The Political Year   17

2000 Chronology
The Legislative Year   19
Congress in 2000   19
The Political Year   20
Countdown in Florida   26

CHAPTER 2   Economic Policy

Introduction   33
Economic Leadership   34
Budget Surplus: A Goal Reached   39

The Federal Budget: Introduction   40

The Federal Budget: 1997–1998 Chronology   43
Fiscal 1998 Budget Resolution   43
Budget Law: A Brief History   44
A Budget Glossary   46
1997 Reconciliation Overview   48
1997 Reconcilation Package: Spending
Cuts   50
Budget Rules Extended through 2002   52
Balanced-Budget Amendment   56

Fiscal 1998 Appropriations   58
Fiscal 1999 Budget Resolution   60
Fiscal 1999 Omnibus Appropriations Bill   62
Line-Item Veto: A Failed Experiment   64
Other Fiscal 1999 Appropriations Bills   69

The Federal Budget: 1999–2000 Chronology   71
Fiscal 2000 Budget Resolution   71
Fiscal 2000 Appropriations   73
Other Fiscal 2000 Appropriations Bills   75
Fiscal 1999 Supplemental Appropriations   76
Budget Process Reform   77
Social Security "Lockbox"   78
Fiscal 2001 Budget Resolution   79
Fiscal 2001 Appropriations   81
Fiscal 2000 Supplemental Appropriations   84
Debt Reduction   85

Tax Policy: Introduction   87

Tax Policy: 1997–1998 Chronology   90
1997 Tax Cuts   90
Tax Credit Extensions   105
IRS Overhaul   106
Tax Record "Snooping" Prohibition   106

Tax Policy: 1999–2000 Chronology   110
Republican Tax Cut   110
1999 Tax Extenders   113
Marriage Status Tax Cut   113
Estate Taxes   115
Tax Cut Catchall Package   117
Corporate Income Earned Abroad   118
Telephone Tax Repeal   118
Retirement Savings Tax Incentives   119

Financial Regulation: Introduction   120

Financial Regulation:
1997–1998 Chronology   122
Financial Services Modernization   122
Key Rulings Expanded Bank Powers   123
Earlier Financial Services Reform
Attempts   124
Bankruptcy Overhaul   126
Credit Union Expansion   128

Securities Fraud Lawsuits   128
Interstate Banking   129
Coin Designs   129
Financial Regulation:
1999–2000 Chronology   130
Financial Services Modernization   130
Competing Interests: Who Wanted What   131
Penny Stocks   138
Commodities Law Overhaul   141
Bankruptcy Overhaul   142

CHAPTER 3   Trade Policy

Introduction   147
1997–1998 Chronology   151
China Trade Status   151
Trade Leadership   152
Fast-Track Authority   153
Export-Import Bank   156
Caribbean Trade   157
Hong Kong Trade Ties   158
Vietnam Trade Status   158
Other Trade-Related Bills   159
1999–2000 Chronology   160
China Trade Agreement   160
China Bill "Safeguards" Won Extra Votes for
Passage   162
China Trade Status   166
Export Administration Act   166
Vietnam Trade Status   167
Africa Trade Initiative   167
Steel Import Quotas   168
"Silk Road" Trade   169
Overseas Private Investment Corporation   169
Other Trade-Related Bills   169

CHAPTER 4   Foreign Policy

Introduction   173
1997–1998 Chronology   177
Kosovo Policy   177
Foreign Policy Leadership   179
China Policy   180
U.S.-China Summitry   183
1998 Aid Appropriations   183
1999 Aid Appropriations   186
Azerbaijan Aid Ban   187

State Department Authorization   189
1998 Middle East Summit   190
U.N. Debt Repayment   192
Foreign Policy Agencies   193
International Monetary Fund   194
Family Planning Funds   194
Russia Sanctions   195
Iraq Policy   196
Confrontations with Iraq   197
War Powers and Bosnia   198
Religious Persecution   198
Economic Sanctions   199
1998 Intelligence Authorization   200
1999 Intelligence Authorization   201
Mexico Certification   203
Diplomatic Immunity   203
1999–2000 Chronology   204
Kosovo Policy   204
China Policy   208
2000 Aid Appropriations   210
Debt Relief and the IMF   213
2001 Aid Appropriations   214
2000 Middle East Summit   216
State Department Authorization   217
U.N. Debt Repayment   219
Colombia Antidrug Aid   220
Russia Sanctions   221
Economic Sanctions   223
Elián González Controversy   225
2000 Intelligence Authorization   226
2001 Intelligence Authorization   227
2001–2002 Aid Authorization   228
Military Aid Authorization   229
HIV/AIDS Assistance   230
"Microenterprise" Aid   230
Peace Corps   230
Armenia Resolution   231
International Adoptions   231

CHAPTER 5   Defense Policy

Introduction   235
1997–1998 Chronology   239
1998 Defense Authorization   239
Defense Leadership   241
1998 Defense Appropriations   245
1998 Military Construction   250
Vetoed Provisions   252

1999 Defense Authorization   252
1999 Defense Appropriations   259
1999 Military Construction   263
Defense Assessments   263
Antimissile Defenses   265
Terrorism Policy   267
Chemical Weapons Treaty   268
"Understandings" Attached to Ratification
    Resolution   271
NATO Expansion   272
NATO Treaty Excerpts   272
Land Mine Treaty   274
Conventional Forces Treaty   274
Other Defense-Related Matters   275

1999–2000 Chronology   276
2000 Defense Authorization   276
2000 Defense Appropriations   283
House Challenges F-22—and Pentagon   286
2000 Military Construction   289
2001 Defense Authorization   290
2001 Defense Appropriations   296
2001 Military Construction   300
Nuclear Security   302
Security Breach Allegations at Labs   303
China Espionage Report   304
Antimissile Defenses   306
Antimissile Defense Chronology   307
Terrorism Policy   308
Test Ban Treaty   310
Treaty Provisions   311

CHAPTER 6   Transportation, Commerce,
and Communications

Introduction   315

1997–1998 Chronology   318
Surface Transportation Reauthorization   318
Amtrak   320
Commerce, Transportation, Small Business
    Leadership   320
Airline Ticket Taxes   321
FAA Reauthorization   321
Ocean Shipping   321
Product Liability   322
Tobacco Settlement   322
Baseball Antitrust Exemption   324
Patent Overhaul   324
Small Business Programs Reauthorization   324

Spectrum Auctions   325
Encryption Exports   326
Television Ratings   327
Internet Taxes   327
Digital Copyright   328
Internet Gambling   328
Online Pornography   329
Satellite Fees/Cable TV Rates   329
Cell Phone Fraud   329
"Slamming" Restrictions   330
Year 2000 Computer Glitch   330

1999–2000 Chronology   331
FAA Reauthorization   331
Truck Safety   332
Auto Safety   333
Steel, Oil, and Gas Subsidies   333
Fuel Efficiency Standards   333
Patent Overhaul   334
Copyright Infringement   334
Telephone Excise Tax   334
Internet Taxes   335
Electronic Signatures   335
Year 2000 Liability   336
Encryption Exports   336
Internet Domain Names   336
Internet Alcohol/Gambling   337
Internet Privacy   337
Satellite TV   338
Rural TV Subsidy   338

CHAPTER 7   Environment and Energy

Introduction   341

1997–1998 Chronology   345
"Dolphin-Safe" Tuna   345
Environment, Energy Leadership   347
National Wildlife Refuges   348
Endangered Species   349
Clean Air Act   351
"Superfund" Overhaul   352
Global Warming   354
Filming Fees at National Parks   356
Fish and Wildlife Foundation   356
Energy Conservation   356
Grazing Fees   356
Great Lakes   357
Hunting of Migratory Birds   358
National Park Operations   358

National Parks Projects   359

Texas Low-Level Waste Site   359

Nuclear Waste Storage   361

Nutria Eradication Program   363

Ocean Policy Panel   364

Salton Sea Rehabilitation   364

Uranium Cleanup   365

Vehicle Emissions   365

Antiquities Act   365

Utah Wilderness   366

Alaska Land Swaps   366

Minnesota Boundary Wilderness   367

Hells Canyon   367

U.N. Lands Designation   367

Forest Health   368

Debt Forgiveness   369

African Elephant Conservation Act   369

Fish and Wildlife Service Revenue   369

Underground Storage Tanks   370

American Heritage Rivers   370

Tennessee Valley Authority   370

1999–2000 Chronology   372

Florida Everglades, Water Projects   372

Conservation and Reinvestment Act   375

Alaska Development   379

Great Ape Protection   379

Coastal Water Quality Standards   380

Beached Marine Mammals   380

Bear Parts   381

Two New National Parks   381

California Water Project   381

Clean Air Act Rewrite   382

Clean Water Regulations   382

Coastal Barrier Resources   383

Coastal Zone Management Act   383

Controlling Bird Populations   384

Restoring Watershed Dams   385

Endangered Species Act   385

Estuary Restoration Program   386

Filming Fees at National Parks   387

National Forests   387

Subsistence Fishing   388

National Marine Sanctuaries   388

Methane Research   388

Migratory Birds   389

National Monuments   389

Gasoline Additive MTBE   390

Native Alaskan Lands   391

Northern Spotted Owl   392

National Ocean Policies   392

Fish and Wildlife Spending   392

Coral Reef Protection   393

Steller Sea Lions   393

Las Cienegas National Conservation Area   394

Route 66 Preservation   394

Roadless Areas   394

Salmon Project   395

Shark Protection   395

"Superfund" Overhaul   396

Forest Revenues   399

Low-Flow Toilets   400

National Discovery Trails   400

U.N. Lands Designation   401

Otay Mountain Wilderness   401

Las Vegas Airport   401

Sequoia National Park   401

Cat Island Refuge   402

Colorado River   402

San Rafael Swell   402

Lake Tahoe   402

California Monument   403

Oregon Land Exchanges   403

Oregon Wilderness   403

Conservation Areas   403

Electricity Deregulation   404

Nuclear Waste Storage   407

Strategic Petroleum Reserve   409

Energy Supplies   409

Security at Energy Department   410

Arctic National Wildlife Refuge   413

Coal Leases   413

Economic Sanctions Against Oil
    Producers   414

CHAPTER 8   Agricultural Policy

Introduction   417

1997–1998 Chronology   419

Grazing Fees   419

Agriculture Leadership   420

Dairy Recalls   420

Conservation Reserve Program   420

Sanctions   420

Crop Insurance, Food Stamps   421

Minority Farmers Legislation   422

Farm Tax Breaks   422

1999–2000 Chronology   424
    Dairy Pricing   424
    Crop Insurance   425
    Agriculture Exports   426

CHAPTER 9   Health and Human Services

Health and Human Services: Introduction   429

Health: 1997–1998 Chronology   432
    Medicare, Medicaid, Children's Insurance   432
    Health Leadership   435
    Medicare "Givebacks"   443
    Food and Drug Administration Overhaul   444
    Patients' Rights   454
    Abortion   455
    Hemophiliacs with HIV   459
    Assisted Suicide   459
    Human Cloning   459

Health: 1999–2000 Chronology   461
    Medicare "Givebacks"   461
    Medicare Commission   464
    Medicare Drug Benefit   465
    Patients' Rights   466
    Managed Care Bills Compared   469
    Disabled Workers' Insurance   470
    Breast and Cervical Cancer   471
    Abortion   472
    Unborn Victims of Violence   474
    Organ Transplants   475
    Assisted Suicide   477
    Health Policy Research Agency   477
    Medical Errors   478
    Medical Privacy   479
    Physician Antitrust   480
    Public Health, Bioterrorism   481
    Children's Health   482
    AIDS Program   483
    Drug "Reimportation"   483
    Minority Health   484
    Nursing Home Evictions   485

Human Services: 1997–1998 Chronology   486
    Welfare Law Revisions   486
    Head Start   491
    Adoption of Foster Children   493
    WIC, Child Nutrition   494
    Child Support Enforcement   495
    Inmate Benefits Restriction   495

Human Services: 1999–2000 Chronology   496
    Older Americans Act   496
    Post-Foster Care Aid   496

Veterans Affairs: 1997–1998 Chronology   497
    Omnibus Veterans Bill   497
    Veterans COLAs   498
    Loss of Burial Rights   498
    Disability Appeals   499
    Cost-Saving Programs   499
    Veterans Leadership   499
    Veterans Benefits   500
    Job Preference   500

Veterans Affairs: 1999–2000 Chronology   502
    Long-Term Health Care   502
    Appeals Aid   502
    Health, Education Benefits   502
    Veterans COLAs   503

CHAPTER 10   Education Policy

Introduction   507

1997–1998 Chronology   509
    Higher Education   509
    Education Leadership   510
    Vocational Education   513
    IDEA Reauthorization   515
    Bilingual Education   516
    Education Savings Accounts   518
    Budget Reconciliation   520
    National Testing   523
    Charter Schools   525
    Student Loans   526
    Block Grants   527
    Ed-Flex   527
    Education Vouchers   528
    Literacy   529
    School Resources Officers   530

1999–2000 Chronology   531
    Elementary and Secondary Education Act   531
    Ed-Flex   539
    Education Savings Accounts   544
    Financial Aid   546
    National Award for Arts Education   546
    Sex Offenders on Campus   547
    Historic Buildings   547
    Tuition for D.C. Students   547
    Department of Education Audit   548

National Academy   548

Students Abroad   549

CHAPTER 11   Housing and Urban Aid

Introduction   553

1997–1998 Chronology   555

Public Housing   555

Housing Leadership   556

Homeless Programs   561

HUD Cost Reductions   562

Mortgage Insurance   563

Home Ownership   563

1999–2000 Chronology   564

Community Development   564

Home Ownership   565

Affordable Housing for Elderly, Disabled   567

CHAPTER 12   Labor and Pension Policy

Introduction   571

1997–1998 Chronology   573

Job Training Overhaul   573

Employers and "Salting"   575

Labor Leadership   575

Compensatory Time   576

Work Safety Bills   577

Teamsters Probe   578

Workplace Teams   578

1999–2000 Chronology   579

Minimum Wage   579

Railroad Retirement   580

Stock Options   581

Pension Changes   581

Social Security Reform Proposals Generate
Little Agreement   582

Social Security Earnings Limit   583

Ergonomics Standards   584

Amish Work Exception   584

"Salting" Revisited   584

Attorney's Fees   585

CHAPTER 13   Law and Justice

Introduction   589

Law Enforcement: 1997–1998 Chronology   593

Juvenile Crime   593

Law Leadership   594

Gun Penalties   597

Safety Locks   598

Armored Car Employees   598

Concealed Weapons   598

Background Checks   599

Bounty Hunters   599

Bulletproof Vests   599

HIV Testing   600

Identity Theft   600

Witness Intimidation   601

Crimes Against the Disabled   601

Methamphetamine   601

Drug Prevention and Treatment   602

Antidrug Grants   602

Office of National Drug Control Policy   602

Prison Labor   603

Sex Offenders   603

Cemetery Vandalism   604

Civil Forfeiture   604

Antiterrorism   605

Money Laundering   605

Assisted Suicide   606

Arbitration   607

Bankruptcy Judges   608

Traffic Stops   608

Civil Rights Commission   608

Victims' Rights   609

Victim Impact Statements   609

Flag Protection   610

Religious Expression   611

Justice Department Reauthorization   613

Kennedy Assassination   613

Assaults on Federal Judges   613

Dispute Resolution   613

U.S. Marshals   614

Medals of Valor   614

Off-Duty Officers   614

Slain Officers   614

Volunteers   615

Affirmative Action   615

Supreme Court Volunteers   616

High-Tech Visas   616

Citizenship for Children Born Abroad   619

Immigration   619

Illegal Immigrants   620

Judicial Activism   620

Judicial Nominations   622

Lee Nomination   624

Fletcher Nomination   627

Law Enforcement: 1999–2000 Chronology   629
Crime Bill   629
Juvenile Justice   633
Gun Control   637
Hate Crimes   642
HIV Testing   644
Alternative Sentencing   644
Counterfeit Badges   644
Body Armor   645
Bulletproof Vests   645
Stalking   645
Antiterrorism   645
Unidentified Persons   646
War Criminals   646
Wiretapping   646
Child Abuse Programs   646
Child Molesters   647
Government Seizure of Civil Assets   647
Concealed Weapons   650
Police Athletic League Chapters   650
Overseas Crimes   650
Law Enforcement Animals   650
Animal Cruelty   650
Secret Service   651
College Aid for Slain Officers' Families   651
Racial Profiling   652
Railroad Officers   652
Federal Prison Industries   652
Prisoner Deaths   653
Prisoner Health Care   653
Transport of Prisoners   653
Law Enforcement Grants   654
Date Rape Drugs   654
DNA Evidence   654
Access to Electronic Information   655
Crimes Against Judges   656
Mental Health Courts   656
Missing Adults   656
National Center for Missing and Exploited Children   657
False IDs   657
Forensics   657
Federal Protective Service   657
Assisted Suicide   658
Religious Expression   660
Fetal Rights   661
Independent Counsel Law   662
Secret Evidence   663
Italian Americans   664
Asbestos Compensation   664

Flag Desecration   666
Victims' Rights   668
Federal Court System   669
Transferee Courts   669
H-1B Visas   670
Visa Fees   672
Immigration Relief   672
Orphaned Immigrant Siblings   673
Farmworker Visas   673
Nurses' Visas   674
Religious Worker Visas   675
Fraud Against the Elderly   675
Alien Smugglers   675
Border Controls   675
Citizenship for the Disabled   676
Deportations   676
Visa Reauthorization   677
Judicial Nominations   677
Recess Appointments   680
Waco Investigation   680
Clemency for FALN Members   681
Supreme Court: Introduction   684
Bush v. Gore   686
The Court of 1997–2000   689
Supreme Court Decisions, November 1996–June 2000   692
Business Law   692
Courts and Procedure   695
Criminal Law and Procedure   697
Due Process, Equal Protection   698
Double Jeopardy, Self-Incrimination   701
Search and Seizure   705
Election Law   707
Environmental Law   710
Family Law   710
Federal Government   710
First Amendment   714
Religion, Speech, and Press   715
Immigration Law   716
Individual Rights   716
Labor Law   721
Property Law   724
States   724
Torts   728

CHAPTER 14 General Government
Introduction   733
1997–1998 Chronology   736
2000 Census   736

Federal Rulemaking   737
Property Rights   737
NEA Funding   738
NEA Funding Ruling   738
Government Documents   739
Federal–D.C. Ties   739
Puerto Rico Status   740
Reagan National Airport   741
NASA Authorization   742
Glenn in Space   742
Space Station   743
Private Shuttles   744
NSF Authorization   744
NIST Reauthorization   745
NOAA Reauthorization   745
Human Cloning   745
Next Generation Internet   746
Energy Research and Development   746
Internet Addresses Ruling   746
EPA Research   747
Federal Invention Licensing   747

1999–2000 Chronology   748
2000 Census   748
Sampling Ruling   748
Federal Regulations Review   749
Rules Impact Analyses   749
Federal Subcontractors   749
Ethics Office Reauthorization   750
NEA Funding   750
Presidential Pay Raise   751
Presidential Commemoratives   751
Charity Postal Stamps   751
Martin Luther King Jr. Legacy   751
NASA Authorization   752
Space Station   753
Space Launches   754
Energy Research and Development   754

CHAPTER 15   Inside Congress

Introduction   757

Members and Procedures: 1997–1998
Chronology   759
Organization: 105th Congress   759
Gingrich Reprimand   761
Attempted Coup to Remove Gingrich   762
Ethics Probes   764
Rota Sentenced   764
House Ethics Overhaul   766
House Committee Funding   767

Physicians' Outside Income   767
Chief Administrative Officer   768
Members and Procedures:
1999–2000 Chronology   769
Organization: 106th Congress   769
House Audit   770
Ethics Probes   770
Senate Ethics Process   774
House Chaplain   775
POGO Contempt of Congress   775

Election Issues: 1997–1998 Chronology   776
Campaign Finance   776
Senate and House Campaign Finance Probes:
Cost Much but Produced Little   778
FEC Issue Ads Ruling   780
Term Limitations   783
California Term Limits   783
Landrieu Election   784
Sanchez Election   785

Election Issues: 1999–2000 Chronology   786
"527" PACs   786
Minority Districts Ruling   788
Campaign Finance   788
Voter Guides Ruling   790

Pay and Benefits: 1997–1998 Chronology   791
Congressional Pay   791
Gratuities Law Ruling   792

Pay and Benefits: 1999–2000 Chronology   794
Congressional Pay   794

CHAPTER 16   The Clinton Presidency

Bill Clinton's Second Term   797
The Economy   798
Domestic Policies   798
Presidential Nominations   799
Foreign Policy   800
Scandals and Pardons   804
Scandals and Charges Engulfed Clinton   805
Hillary Clinton: From First Lady to
U.S. Senator   806
Relationship with Congress   809
Clinton Vetoes: New Uses for an Old
Weapon   810

Clinton Impeachment   813
Unfolding of a Scandal   813
Johnson Impeachment   814
Starr Report   816
In Pursuit of Impeachment   818

Articles of Impeachment Considered by the
House   821

Wary GOP Leaders Criticize Iraq
Bombing   822

Senate Trial   823

Postimpeachment Developments   827

APPENDIX

Glossary of Congressional Terms   831

The Legislative Process in Brief   857

Key Votes

1997 Key Votes   865

1998 Key Votes   883

1999 Key Votes   899

2000 Key Votes   915

Congress and Its Members

Senate Membership in the 105th
Congress   935

House Membership in the 105th Congress   936

Membership Changes, 105th and 106th
Congresses   938

Senate Membership in the 106th Congress
939

House Membership in the 106th Congress   940

Members of Congress, 1997–2001   942

Congressional Committees, 105th and 106th
Congresses   951

Postelection Sessions   965

Senate Cloture Votes, 1917–2000   967

House Discharge Petitions since 1931   972

Congressional Apportionment,
1789–2000   973

The Presidency

Clinton Appointments   977

Presidential Vetoes   994

Selected Texts

The Presidency   999

President Clinton's Second Inaugural
Address   999

President Clinton's 1997 State of the Union
Address   1000

President Clinton's Address to the United
Nations   1006

President Clinton's 2000 State of the Union
Address   1008

Clinton Impeachment   1017

Clinton: "Critical Lapse in Judgment"   1017

Democratic Senators' Comments   1017

Independent Counsel's Report   1018

Articles of Impeachment   1020

Congress   1022

Rep. Newt Gingrich's Comments on Reelection
as House Speaker   1022

Excerpts of Findings in Gingrich Ethics
Case   1024

Election of Dennis Hastert as House
Speaker   1029

Campaigns and Elections   1032

Gore Discusses Fund-Raising Activities   1032

Attorney General Rejects Call for
Counsel   1035

Presidential Nominating Conventions,
1996   1037

Presidential Nominating Conventions,
2000   1039

Supreme Court's *Bush v. Gore* Decision   1046

Al Gore's Concession Speech   1055

George W. Bush's Acceptance Speech   1055

Political Charts

Summary of Presidential Elections,
1789–2000   1059

Victorious Party in Presidential Races,
1860–2000   1062

1996 Presidential Election   1064

1996 Electoral Votes   1065

2000 Presidential Election   1066

2000 Electoral Votes   1067

2000 Republican Convention Balloting   1068

2000 Democratic Convention Balloting   1069

Distribution of House Seats and Electoral
Votes   1070

Party Affiliations in Congress and the
Presidency, 1789–2001   1071

105th Congress Special Elections, 1997
Gubernatorial Returns   1073

1998 Elections Returns for Governor, Senate,
and House   1074

106th Congress Special Elections, 1999
Gubernatorial Returns   1081

2000 Elections Returns for Governor, Senate,
and House   1082

Results of House Elections, 1928–2000   1090

Governors, 1997–2001   1094

Public Laws

105th Congress—1997   1099

105th Congress—1998   1106

106th Congress—1999   1117

106th Congress—2000   1125

INDEX   1145

Tables and Figures

TABLES

Number of Public Laws Enacted, 1975–2000   11
Recorded Vote Totals   12
Age Structure of Congress   17
Presidential Vote by Region   21
Women in Congress, 1947–2001   28
Blacks in Congress, 1947–2001   29
Hispanics in Congress, 1947–2001   30
Deficit History, 1929–2000   36
Federal Budget, 1993–2000   41
Taxes and Other Revenues as Percentage of GDP, 1935–2000   91
U.S. Supreme Court Caseload   690
Congressional Pay History   794

FIGURES

A Look at the Economy, 1980–2000   37
Growth of Deficit and Debt   41
Federal Budget Receipts   88
Trade Balance   148
Outlays for International Affairs   174
Outlays for National Defense   236
Outlays for Transportation   316
Outlays for Natural Resources and Environment   342
Outlays for Energy   343
Outlays for Agriculture   418
Mandatory Outlays for Medicaid and Medicare   430
Outlays for Health   434
Outlays for Income Security   488
Outlays for Veterans Benefits and Services   498
Outlays for Education   508
Outlays for Community and Regional Development   554
Outlays for Social Security   572
Outlays for Law Enforcement   590
Outlays for Science, Space, and General Government   734

Congress and the Nation

CHAPTER 1

Politics and National Issues

Introduction   3

1997 Chronology   6

1998 Chronology   10

1999 Chronology   15

2000 Chronology   19

Politics and National Issues

The American voter was enamored with divided government in the waning years of the twentieth century. Whether it was infatuation or mainly indifference, it was the reality in Washington. Except for a few years, voters elected a president from one political party and gave control of at least one chamber of Congress to the other. Experts thought it was a passing phenomenon that would vanish when voters made up their collective mind about the role they preferred government to play in national life. It did not happen, not even by the 2000 general elections, which muddied the waters even more by revealing a nearly perfectly divided electorate.

This schizophrenic political mind characterized President Bill Clinton's second term and helped explain the seemingly endless battles between Republicans and Democrats. The sharp divisions actually had their roots in his first term but persisted through his entire second term. The antagonism played out in different ways and contributed to career-ending debacles of some members of Congress and to a record of legislative activity that was noteworthy more for its symbolic flying of partisan flags than actual accomplishments. Except for a few important pieces of legislation to which both sides pointed with pride, overall the final four years for Clinton were largely a wasteland of acrimonious warfare with his Republican adversaries on the Hill.

The stalemate may have reflected an electorate comfortable with a long unbroken stretch of economic prosperity but uncertain of the role it wanted its government to play.

To be sure, Congress and the president collaborated on significant legislation, including a landmark agreement to balance the budget and cut taxes concurrently, a measure giving China trade status with the United States equal to that enjoyed by most nations, and legislation reforming the huge financial services business that would permit the melding of banks, securities firms, and insurance companies. But many other important measures died, victims of the unusually bitter partisanship that had characterized Washington for years—even before Clinton arrived—and at times seemed to make legislators unable to do more than jockey for momentary political advantage.

One catalyst for the partisanship was the president himself, who displayed a remarkable knack for frustrating Republican legislative and political goals when the GOP took control of Congress in 1995 after riding high in the 1994 elections with promises of a conservative "Republican revolution" that would shrink government dramatically. But the president's strengths were compromised by his own personal conduct that even his partisans thought shabby and unbefitting a president. Revelations in early 1998 of an affair with a young White House female intern gave Republicans a political opening to retaliate against the president by seeking his impeachment on charges of perjury and obstruction of justice. But instead of being driven from office, Clinton emerged at the end of the ordeal with his public support surprisingly intact and his willingness to use a sharp veto pen as strong as ever.

Another catalyst in the partisanship of the period was a charismatic and fiery Republican from Georgia, Newt Gingrich, the man widely credited for engineering the GOP takeover of the House in the 1994 elections—for the first time since 1953—and a chief practitioner of a negative brand of politics based on discrediting the opposition. House Republicans rewarded Gingrich by making him Speaker in 1995. But after losing a series of confrontations with Clinton that contributed to Republican loss of seats in the House, the mercurial Gingrich announced in November 1998 that he was resigning from Congress. Although many Republican legislators were no longer fully in awe of Gingrich, many saw his departure as yet another loss and embarrassment inflicted on the GOP by Clinton. The party was further embarrassed when Gingrich's anointed successor also resigned from Congress after revelation of sexual infidelities in what was a bizarre echo of the charges the GOP had been hurling at the president.

For the remaining two years of Clinton's term, Republicans and Democrats were mainly intent on maneuvering for political advantage in the run-up to the 2000 presidential elections, in which there would be no White House incumbent, and congressional races for control of the House hung on a small number of districts. It was amply clear that elections—not enacting legislation—were at the top of the agenda of both parties. Neither side was willing to make the compromises necessary to enact the measures that both sides professed to support—including deeper tax cuts, new patients rights in dealing with managed care health plans, a prescription drug program for Medicare beneficiaries, expanded federal elementary and secondary education aid, and a higher minimum wage. Even the first budget surplus since 1969 did little to ameliorate the standoff. Both parties welcomed the advent of the surplus—and the projections for steadily larger increases—but then quickly fell to quarreling about what to do with it: tax cuts or spending priorities.

But to the consternation of both parties, the 2000 elections did not clarify matters and, if anything, left them more confused than ever. Republican George W. Bush of Texas won the White House, but only after a five-week-long dispute over recounting presidential ballots in Florida was ended when the Supreme Court effectively awarded Bush that state's decisive electoral votes. This gave Bush enough to win the electoral college vote, although Democrat Al Gore, Clinton's vice president, had won the popular vote. Republicans also held onto control of Congress but just barely. In the House the GOP had nine more seats than the Democrats, while the Senate was split fifty-fifty. Thus, for all practical purposes, divided government continued.

CLINTON, CONGRESS, AND CONFRONTATION

In retrospect the pivotal event shaping Clinton's relations with Congress in his second term was the Republican decision in late 1995 to challenge the president over the budget. Clinton and congressional Democrats successfully portrayed the Republicans as favoring cuts in popular programs such as Medicare to finance generous tax breaks for upper-income Americans. The showdown sparked two government shutdowns when spending bills languished in Congress, which the public blamed on Republicans. In the end both sides compromised but in the court of public opinion Clinton came out ahead. Considered by many a possible one-term president before the confrontation, Clinton handily won reelection in 1996, in part on the expectation that he would continue to check the more extreme impulses of congressional Republicans. The GOP just barely held its majority in the House.

The episode chastened both sides, at least momentarily, and led in early 1997 to a remarkable and totally unexpected bipartisan deal between Clinton and the GOP to eliminate the budget deficit within five years while still modestly cutting taxes. Even though the threat of a government shutdown never arose again, the 1995 showdown established the confrontational pattern between the two sides that was to be repeated, with minor variation, throughout the remainder of Clinton's term. *(Budget agreement, p. 43)*

For the Republicans, the most devastating confrontations came when they overreached. In 1997, for example, in an eerie repeat of the 1995 episode, GOP leaders tried to force Clinton to accept two controversial policy riders by attaching them to an important disaster relief bill. They believed that Clinton would back down from his veto threat or, alterna-

tively, that he would pay a high political price for vetoing badly needed flood aid for the Midwest. Clinton called their bluff, vetoing the legislation, and an angry public once again blamed congressional Republicans. The leadership quickly moved legislation without the riders.

House Republicans appeared to be overreaching once again when in 1998 they decided to push Clinton's impeachment. Despite clear opposition from the public and the near certainty that the Senate would not vote to remove the president from office, the House leadership spurned all attempts to mete out a lesser punishment and persisted in impeaching Clinton on one charge of perjury and one charge of obstruction of justice. Support was so weak in the Senate that the Republicans could not even muster a simple majority in favor of convicting the president on the perjury charge, let alone the two-thirds majority required. Senators split fifty-fifty on the obstruction of justice charge. *(Impeachment, p. 813)*

After the impeachment loss, Republicans did not again take such large risks of alienating the public. Instead they made the compromises necessary to ensure passage of annual spending bills while working to turn aside legislation that might give the Democrats a political advantage and highlighting proposals that advanced their political philosophy.

In 2000, for example, with GOP presidential candidate Bush leading in the polls and promising large tax cuts if elected, Republicans refused to compromise on two tax-reduction bills—one to eliminate a so-called "marriage penalty" tax and one to end the estate tax—even though compromising might have secured enough Democratic votes to enact the measures over Clinton's veto. Instead they used debate on the legislation and Clinton's veto to draw attention to an important campaign issue for the party, arguing that the tax cuts were a matter of fairness. Democrats, of course, also used these issues in their campaign rhetoric by arguing that GOP cuts were too broad and that the developing budget surplus should be used to shore up Social Security and reduce the national debt before going to tax reductions, a position that polls showed the public preferred.

For his part Clinton abandoned any lingering hopes of persuading Congress to accept his legislative initiatives. Although his annual State of the Union message always contained a laundry list of priorities, the administration seldom backed it up with detailed proposals. Instead Clinton skillfully used his veto power both to force GOP concessions on funding for programs they wanted to deny him or to block Republican legislation he opposed. Clinton vetoed thirty-seven bills in his eight years in office, all of them after Republicans took control in 1995. Fourteen of them were appropriations bills. Congress overrode only two of Clinton's vetoes. *(Vetoes, appendix, p. 994)*

Clinton also used his executive powers and executive branch regulations to implement some programs that did not require congressional action. For example, he protected a total of 4.6 million acres from development by designating them as national monuments. Attempts by western Republicans to limit Clinton's ability to make such declarations failed. Other examples of executive actions were Department of Health and Human Services regulations protecting medical record privacy after Congress failed to act and Labor Department rules requiring businesses to reduce worker injuries and disabilities caused by repetitive stress. (Congress overturned the labor regulations in 2001.)

INTERNAL DIVISIONS

Internal congressional divisions between the House and the Senate and within the GOP made for confrontations of their own. Conservative Republicans set the agenda in the House, often with the support of a handful of conservative Democrats. The House GOP leadership could use the chamber's tight procedural rules to stop challenges from moderates of either party. Conservatives did not hold the same sway in the Senate, in part because they lacked the votes and in part because the Senate's less rigid procedural rules allowed a determined minority of either party to block legislation.

By the same token, legislative initiatives backed by Democrats and moderate Republicans could be killed in the House. A Senate-passed gun control measure, for example, died in the House after GOP leaders made sure it was so loaded down with "poison pills" that even gun control supporters voted against it.

To an extraordinary degree, the controversies raised by these divisions were played out on the annual appropriations bills. The usual conflicts arose over competing spending priorities, which were exacerbated by tight budget caps adopted in 1997. Despite the growing surplus neither side was willing to abandon the caps for fear of being accused of squandering the surplus; Congress and the president finally agreed to raise them somewhat in 2000 but then proceeded with no apparent qualms to exceed even the higher numbers.

Traditionally legislators find spending bills convenient vehicles for unrelated controversial legislation that could not pass on its own, and the 105th and 106th Congresses were no exception. In addition, congressional leaders used the spending bills to carry agreements negotiated on other legislation that would have been blocked on a straight up-or-down vote. Such measures were protected when they were attached to conference reports on spending bills because Congress had to accept them in order to gain enactment of the annual appropriations. Perhaps the most extreme example occurred in 1998, when Congress packaged eight of the thirteen regular appropriations bills into a single $500 billion omnibus measure that also reorganized the government's foreign policy agencies and approved ratification of the international Chemical Weapons Convention, among other things. *(Omnibus bill, p. 62)*

As a result, many of the most important policy issues of the day—peacemaking efforts in the Middle East, peacekeeping efforts in the Baltic region, abortion restrictions at home and abroad, fuel efficiency standards in cars, incentives for hiring more teachers and police officers—were resolved, if at all, by the top GOP leadership negotiating with White House officials behind closed doors. Although the rank and file of both parties complained about being shut out of the deliberations, the leadership justified the process by arguing that a larger circle of participants would have made negotiating the necessary deals much more difficult, if not impossible.

A SUMMING UP

Although the second Clinton term played out on TV and in the press through images of an articulate and engaged president at battle with a variety of colorful and equally forceful personalities in Congress, underlying this personalization of conflict was a fundamental disagreement between the political parties, and their various factions, about the role of the federal government, and even about federalism itself.

After more than a half century of expanding and activist national government, the political tides were flowing toward a more conservative view of government and politics that favored Republicans and raised the role of the states to a much more prominent level. Although scholars and other observers welcomed development of more robust state government, the extent of this movement—and the remaining appropriate role for national government—deeply divided politicians, especially in Washington. Conservative Republicans such as Gingrich and his allies, who largely controlled the Republican Party, wanted to dramatically change the face of national government through such activities as deregulation of business, large tax cuts primarily to high-income individuals who they said were the risk takers that created jobs, elimination of entire federal agencies, and devolution to the states of a myriad of powers the government had assumed since the New Deal of Franklin Roosevelt. They were largely checkmated during Clinton's time in the White House, in part because of the president's political skills and in part because Americans were not entirely convinced of the wisdom of their program.

The 2000 elections provided no answers. The new Republican administration came into office, somewhat crippled by a controversial victory, but with no clear mandate and with the national government's role still at the center of debate. That was to change dramatically in less than a year after George W. Bush took the oath of office.

1997

The Legislative Year

Chastened by the results of the 1996 elections, the members of the 105th Congress returned to a more traditional style of legislating during 1997. The comfortable thirty-seven-seat majority held by House Republicans in late 1996 fell to just nineteen seats after the elections (227 Republicans, 207 Democrats, and one Independent). Senate Republicans gained two seats, for a total of fifty-five, but that was still far short of the sixty votes needed to block a filibuster, a tool Democrats had used successfully in the 104th Congress to blunt GOP initiatives.

As a result, the frenetic days of round-the-clock work that marked the GOP takeover of Congress in 1995 all but disappeared. Gone, too, was much of the bravado of a new Republican majority trying to cow the Democratic White House. Instead, Republican leaders in 1997 worked through the committee system to build majority coalitions—many of them bipartisan—to pass bills. Lawmakers looked more often for common ground with their adversaries rather than sticking to ideological purity.

Another casualty of the 1996 elections was the unquestioned authority of a few newly empowered leaders. In one of the sharpest contrasts with the 104th Congress, Speaker Newt Gingrich, R-Ga., the undisputed leader of the GOP "revolution" that swept Capitol Hill in 1995, saw his hold on power severely weakened. Intraparty bickering over whether to retain him as Speaker was a subtheme through much of the year, repeatedly distracting House Republicans.

Moderation and compromise in 1997 won Republicans what confrontation and inflexibility in earlier years had not. The most notable example was a landmark, bipartisan agreement to balance the budget by 2002 while providing the biggest tax cut since the Ronald Reagan administration—a goal that Republicans had found unattainable in the 104th Congress. The package extended caps on discretionary spending and made spending cuts in Medicare, the federal health insurance program for the elderly, and in Medicaid, the federal-state health program for the poor and disabled. The budget package also included a new program to help states provide health insurance to about half the nation's estimated ten million uninsured children.

GOP leaders also got all thirteen regular appropriations bills enacted before adjourning for the year, abandoning the take-it-or-leave-it strategy that had triggered two government shutdowns and hurt Republicans during their first two years in power.

Beyond that, however, the first session of the 105th Congress was not notably productive. Highlights included enactment of a long-stalled overhaul of the Food and Drug Administration aimed at speeding up the approval of new drugs and medical devices; a bailout of Amtrak, the nation's troubled passenger railroad; and a bill to expedite the adoption of abused and neglected children by making it easier for local authorities to remove children permanently from abusive homes.

Unable to complete work on an ambitious, six-year highway bill, legislators cleared a short-term extension of existing law to keep federal transportation money flowing to the states in the interim. Democratic-led efforts to overhaul campaign financing rules did not generate enough momentum to break through the procedural roadblocks erected by the GOP leadership.

On the foreign policy front, the Senate approved ratification of an international chemical and biological weapons treaty, to the distress of conservative Republicans, and the House let stand the administration's decision to renew China's most-favored-nation trading status.

By contrast, items that had been high on the conservative agenda generally fell by the wayside—further evidence that the GOP revolution was waning, weakened by Republican infighting and the continuing ability of the Democratic minority to stand together to block crucial initiatives. Conservatives failed to win approval for constitutional amendments to impose term limits on members of Congress (eleven versions failed to get the necessary two-thirds vote in the House) and to require a balanced budget (the Senate fell just short of a two-thirds majority March 4).

Social conservatives also met with defeat on a number of so-called wedge issues, including proposals to provide vouch-

---

CONGRESS IN 1997

The first session of the 105th Congress convened Jan. 7, 1997, and closed at 10:44 p.m. EST on Nov. 13, when the House adjourned *sine die*. The Senate had adjourned *sine die* hours earlier at 7:56 p.m.

The session lasted 311 days—thirty-five days longer than the last session of the 104th Congress. The Senate met on 153 days, the House on 132 days.

There were 5,568 bills and resolutions introduced during the 1997 session, compared with 2,759 in 1996 and 5,231 in 1995. A total of 153 bills cleared by Congress in 1997 became public law. President Clinton vetoed three bills (not counting line-item vetoes), one of which was overridden in 1998. *(Public laws, table, p. 11; presidential vetoes, p. 994)*

During the 1997 session, the House took 633 recorded votes, 179 more than in 1996. The Senate took 298 recorded votes, eight fewer than in 1996. (Totals do not include quorum calls.) *(Recorded votes, table, p. 12)*

CONGRESSIONAL LEADERSHIP 1997–2001

105th Congress

Senate

President Pro Tempore—Strom Thurmond, R-S.C.
Majority Leader—Trent Lott, R-Miss.
Majority Whip—Don Nickles, R-Okla.
Republican Conference Chairman—Connie Mack, R-Fla.
Republican Conference Secretary—Paul Coverdell, R-Ga.

Minority Leader—Tom Daschle, D-S.D.
Minority Whip—Wendell H. Ford, D-Ky.
Democratic Conference Secretary—Barbara A. Mikulski,
  D-Md.

House

Speaker—Newt Gingrich, R-Ga.
Majority Leader—Dick Armey, R-Texas
Majority Whip—Tom DeLay, R-Texas
Chairman of the Republican Conference—John A.
  Boehner, R-Ohio

Minority Leader—Richard A. Gephardt, D-Mo.
Minority Whip—David E. Bonior, D-Mich.
Chairman of the Democratic Caucus—Vic Fazio, D-Calif.

106th Congress

Senate

President Pro Tempore—Strom Thurmond, R-S.C.
Majority Leader—Trent Lott, R-Miss.
Majority Whip—Don Nickles, R-Okla.
Republican Conference Chairman—Connie Mack, R-Fla.
Republican Conference Secretary—Paul Coverdell, R-Ga.[1]

Minority Leader—Tom Daschle, D-S.D.
Minority Whip—Harry M. Reid, D-Nev.
Democratic Conference Secretary—Barbara A. Mikulski,
  D-Md.

House

Speaker—J. Dennis Hastert, R-Ill.
Majority Leader—Dick Armey, R-Texas
Majority Whip—Tom DeLay, R-Texas
Chairman of the Republican Conference—J.C. Watts Jr.,
  R-Okla.

Minority Leader—Richard A. Gephardt, D-Mo.
Minority Whip—David E. Bonior, D-Mich.
Chairman of the Democratic Caucus—Martin Frost,
  D-Texas

1. Coverdell died in July 2000. His position as conference secretary was filled by Kay Bailey Hutchison, R-Texas.

---

ers for private school education, create tax-free savings accounts for tuition, eliminate the National Endowment for the Arts, ban a controversial procedure that opponents dubbed "partial birth" abortion, and allow employers to offer compensatory time off instead of overtime pay. A House bill to end race and gender preferences by the government and its contractors was scuttled in committee.

President Clinton won a major political victory when a Republican attempt to force his hand on a veto threat backfired. Despite repeated veto threats from the White House, GOP leaders in June attached two controversial policy riders to a must-pass disaster relief bill. The leaders calculated that Clinton would back down from his veto threats or suffer the political consequences of holding up badly needed flood aid for the Midwest. Clinton vetoed the bill, and the public directed its anger at congressional Republicans for holding up the aid. Congress quickly sent the president a second aid bill without the riders, which Clinton immediately signed into law.

The president suffered some defeats, too. His most important loss was on renewal of fast-track authority to negotiate trade deals. Republicans supported the measure, but it was pulled from consideration in the House after labor

unions put heavy pressure on Democrats to vote no. Congress also refused to provide money Clinton had requested to underwrite a world currency stabilization program and to pay off U.S. debts to the United Nations, after the president infuriated conservatives by blocking legislation to ban U.S. aid for overseas organizations that performed or advocated abortions.

Clinton also lost several nomination battles with the Senate. His nominee for ambassador to Mexico, former Massachusetts Gov. William F. Weld, a Republican, was blocked, as was the nomination of Bill Lann Lee for assistant attorney general for civil rights. (Clinton subsequently appointed Lee as acting assistant attorney general.) Conservative objections also forced the Senate to postpone until 1998 a floor vote on the nomination of David Satcher for surgeon general.

Clinton made the first use ever of a new line-item veto law, striking individual items in nine appropriation bills and the two reconciliation bills. Although he used the power with relative caution, he provoked an angry bipartisan backlash when he struck thirty-eight projects from the military construction spending bill. Congress approved a bill overturning all thirty-eight of the line-item vetoes, but Clinton vetoed that as well. Congress overrode that veto in February 1998, one of only two vetoes overridden during Clinton's eight years in office. The line-item veto was also under attack in the Supreme Court, which had dismissed a challenge to the 1996 law without addressing the separation of powers issue underlying the measure.

The Political Year

Continuing their domination of elections held in the odd-numbered years of the 1990s, Republicans in 1997 won the bellwether gubernatorial races in New Jersey and Virginia, the mayoral races in New York and Los Angeles, and two of three special elections held to fill congressional vacancies. Three other congressional vacancies remained at year's end.

Other political events in 1997 included the resignation of Arizona's Republican Gov. Fife Symington, who was convicted Sept. 3, on seven counts of fraud stemming from his career as a real estate developer. He was succeeded Sept. 8 by Jane Dee Hull, another Republican, who had been Arizona's secretary of state. Hull was the second woman elevated to the Arizona governorship in nine years to replace a governor forced to resign in disgrace. The first was Rose Mofford, a Democrat, who served as governor from 1988 to 1991. She took the reins from Republican Evan Mecham, who had been impeached on charges of obstruction of justice and illegally lending state money to his car dealership.

Gubernatorial Elections

Republicans held on to their gubernatorial posts in New Jersey and Virginia, although New Jersey Gov. Christine Todd Whitman's opponent came within 27,000 votes of unseating her. In Virginia former state Attorney General James S. Gilmore III defeated Democratic Lt. Gov. Donald S. Beyer Jr., in the most expensive gubernatorial race in the history of the commonwealth.

Whitman took 47 percent of the vote against her Democratic opponent, James McGreevey, a state senator and mayor of Woodbridge Township, who tallied 46 percent of the vote. Her margin of victory was within about 600 votes of her margin in 1993, when she upset Democratic Gov. James J. Florio. Third-party candidates took the remaining votes.

Exit polls suggested that Whitman survived because just enough conservatives decided to stick with her despite her views on abortion and other social issues. Although McGreevey did a fair job of turning out party support, he was unable to claim as many independent voters as early polls had suggested he might. Whitman, meanwhile, was able to cut the usual Republican gender gap to almost nil. Although she did better among men than among women—as Republican candidates nearly always did—the difference was reduced to two percentage points. (She took 48 percent of the men's vote and 46 percent of the women's.)

The election was mostly a referendum on Whitman, as could be expected when an incumbent was on the ballot against a little-known challenger. The only elected woman governor in the nation and the only Republican to win a statewide contest in New Jersey since 1988, Whitman tried to highlight her successes, beginning with her 30 percent cut in income tax rates and the thriving state economy.

In Virginia, Gilmore, who had resigned as attorney general early in 1997 to devote all of his energies to his gubernatorial campaign, spent $10 million and was aided by $2 million in outside GOP money to win 56 percent of the vote. Beyer spent $8 million to win 43 percent of the vote. Beyer enjoyed little monetary help from his national party and had to borrow a reported $400,000 to keep his campaign running in the final days. Beyer, a millionaire car dealer, proved unwilling to pump large sums of family money into the campaign.

Virginia's turnout, at 48 percent, was its lowest of the modern era. But if the race failed to entice a majority of the registered voters, it was nonetheless a big victory for the GOP, marking the first time the Republicans had swept all the constitutional offices in Virginia—and the first time they had done so in any southern state since Reconstruction.

Gilmore's appeal was simple, calling for the abolition of the personal property tax on cars and trucks. By emphasizing the tax cut proposal in his advertising, Gilmore was able to break open what had been a closely contested race through most of the year. Gilmore even won in the populous northern Virginia suburbs, Beyer's geographical base. Those communities, where many residents commuted to work in Washington, D.C., were home to some of the highest car tax rates in the state.

Special Elections

Special elections were held in congressional districts in Texas (April 12), New Mexico (May 13), and New York (Nov. 4) following the death of one incumbent and the resignations of two others. The special elections yielded a net gain of one seat for the Republicans.

Texas state Rep. Ciro D. Rodriguez won a ticket to Washington April 12 with two-thirds of the vote in a runoff election in San Antonio. Rodriguez won the seat formerly held by Democrat Frank M. Tejeda, who died Jan. 30 of pneumonia, following treatment for a brain tumor. Rodriguez had dominated fourteen rivals in the first round of voting in the March 15 special election, but his 46 percent share of the vote fell short of the majority required to win the seat outright. In the runoff he defeated Juan F. Solis III, a former member of the city council, who had mounted an aggressive campaign in which he claimed the support of some members of Tejeda's family. Rodriguez was better known and better financed, however, and he promised to fight for education and to protect Social Security and other programs important in this largely Hispanic district.

In New Mexico, Republican Bill Redmond scored a head-turning, upset victory in the heavily Democratic Third Congressional District, left vacant when Democratic incumbent William B. Richardson resigned Feb. 13 to accept appointment as the U.S. representative to the United Nations. The early favorite in the special election, Democratic nominee Eric P. Serna, a member of the state's Corporation Commission, found himself dividing the district's usually Democratic vote with Carol A. Miller, the nominee of the Green Party, a rising force in state politics. Redmond won 43 percent, Serna 40 percent, and Miller 17 percent.

Redmond was unable to hold onto the seat in the 1998 general election, however. He lost to Democrat Thomas Udall, New Mexico's attorney general who was making his third try for a seat in the House.

In a special election scheduled to coincide with New York City's regular local election Nov. 4, Republican City Councilman Vito J. Fossella ran away from his Democratic opponent to claim the Staten Island seat vacated Aug. 1 by the resignation of Republican Rep. Susan Molinari. Molinari resigned to accept a job as an on-air personality with CBS-TV. Fossella won 61 percent of the vote to 39 percent for his Democratic rival, state Rep. Eric N. Vitaliano. Most polls had shown the race to be tight until mid-October, when the Republican National Committee weighed in with TV, ads attacking Vitaliano for having supported state income tax increases. Fossella was also lifted by the landslide reelection victory of New York City's Republican mayor, Rudolph W. Giuliani, who received more than 80 percent of the vote on Staten Island.

1998

The Legislative Year

The House and Senate took hundreds of votes in 1998, but history was likely to take note of just two: the House votes Dec. 19 to impeach President Clinton on charges of perjury and obstruction of justice. The votes were all the more dramatic for being taken as American bombers strafed Baghdad and other cities in Iraq in retaliation for Iraqi President Saddam Hussein's refusal to cooperate with United Nations weapons inspectors.

The two votes closed out a year in which the president's affair with former White House intern Monica Lewinsky and his denial under oath of a sexual relationship cast a long shadow over Washington. From the time the relationship was publicly revealed in January, the scandal was never far in the background for either the administration or Congress. Sometimes it took center stage, such as when Clinton went to Capitol Hill on Jan. 27 to deliver his State of the Union address, six days after the first reports of the Lewinsky affair. Although many pundits and legislators predicted that Clinton had finally used up his nine political lives, the president ignored the embarrassing reports and steadily delivered his legislative agenda.

At others times, the scandal seemed to take a back seat to initiatives facing floor votes or other pivotal decisions. But even then, the affair was a subtext affecting nearly every action Congress took. Time and again Republicans and Democrats, the powerful and the obscure, found themselves asked for their opinion on the president's conduct and possible punishments; the news media showed little interest in the details of regular legislation.

Congress had a hand in creating much of the quagmire in which it was trapped for the last half of the year, especially after the House voted Sept. 11 to release the salacious details of Independent Counsel Kenneth W. Starr's report on Clinton's behavior and Starr's conclusion that eleven counts of impeachable offenses could be upheld. That vote, which came before anyone in Congress had read the report or made an independent assessment of the evidence, significantly added to the frenzy that consumed much of Congress's energy late in the year. The report was followed by impeachment hearings in the House Judiciary Committee and then the impeachment itself in December.

The House Republican leadership's push to punish the president, despite clear signs from the public that it was opposed to impeachment, backfired in the November elections, when the GOP lost five House seats. The embarrassing setback prompted Newt Gingrich of Georgia, who had led the GOP takeover of the House in 1994, to resign as Speaker and announce plans to leave the House in 1999. The GOP embarrassment was not yet over, however. Just two days before the impeachment vote, Gingrich's designated successor, Robert L. Livingston of Louisiana, acknowledged that he had had extramarital affairs. During the impeachment debate on Dec. 19, Livingston said he would resign from the House and called on Clinton to follow his example—a call Clinton chose to ignore.

Before the elections, Republicans had assumed that voter displeasure with Clinton's behavior would help them gain seats in both the Senate and House. As a result they did not push a legislative agenda as strongly as they had in previous years. In any case, recurrent divisions within the party would have made it difficult to put forward a coherent agenda, even if leaders had tried. The GOP divided over issues ranging from transportation funding, to a ban on cloning, to military training for men and women in the same units. Democrats also split on some issues, namely, an education savings account plan in the Senate and the resolution to release the Starr report in the House.

The distractions and fractures, particularly among House Republicans, created a political vacuum that allowed the president and a few legislators to step in and win passage of legislation that would have likely met with defeat in the earlier, headier days of the Republican revolution. For example, Rep. Nita M. Lowey, D-N.Y., a family planning and abortion rights proponent, managed to obtain enough support to pass a provision requiring certain federal employee health plans to cover a full range of contraceptives.

Despite the disarray, Congress cleared consequential measures on foreign policy, transportation, education, and other matters. In April the Senate voted overwhelmingly to expand NATO's borders to include three former Warsaw Pact na-

---

CONGRESS IN 1998

The second session of the 105th Congress closed at 2:36 p.m. EST on Dec. 19, 1998, when the House adjourned *sine die.* The Senate had adjourned *sine die* at 2:33 p.m. on Oct. 21. The House had adjourned on Oct. 21 and returned on Dec. 17 for a lame duck session after the election to consider impeachment charges against President Clinton. *(Clinton impeachment, p. 813)*

Convened on Jan. 27, the session lasted 327 days—sixteen days longer than the first session. The Senate was in session on 143 days, the House on 119 days.

During the session a total of 3,573 bills and resolutions were introduced, compared with 5,568 in 1997 and 2,759 in 1996. A total of 241 bills became public law in 1998. President Clinton vetoed five bills. *(Public laws, table p. 11; presidential vetoes, p. 994)*

During 1998, the House took 533 recorded votes, 100 fewer than in 1997. The Senate took 314 recorded votes, sixteen more than in 1997. (Totals do not include quorum calls.) *(Recorded votes, table, p. 12)*

Number of Public Laws Enacted, 1975–2000

Year	Public Laws	Year	Public Laws
1975	205	1988	471
1976	383	1989	240
1977	223	1990	410
1978	410	1991	243
1979	187	1992	347
1980	426	1993	210
1981	145	1994	255
1982	328	1995	88
1983	215	1996	245
1984	408	1997	153
1985	240	1998	241
1986	424	1999	170
1987	242	2000	410

tions. And after a bitter battle, lawmakers provided $17.9 billion for the International Monetary Fund, in return for modest reforms by the global lender. With concerns over the budget deficit fading, Congress passed a $217.9 billion transportation bill that boosted spending on highways and mass transit by 40 percent. With little fanfare, Congress enacted a major reauthorization of the Head Start program. Lawmakers also agreed on a badly needed overhaul of federal public housing programs.

But the second session of the 105th Congress was perhaps more notable for what it did not do. For the first time since the modern budget process was established in 1974, Congress did not produce a fiscal budget resolution. House and Senate Republicans were simply unable to agree on a spending plan. The failure to agree on a budget was especially ironic because for the first time since 1969, the government ran a surplus rather than a deficit. The lack of a budget resolution slowed the appropriations process to a crawl, eventually forcing GOP leaders to cobble together a $500 billion, budget-breaking omnibus spending bill that wrapped together eight individual appropriations measures and served as the vehicle for much of the year's limited legislative output. Speaker Gingrich defended the huge catchall bill as a practical necessity, but Republican conservatives and moderates alike charged the leadership with caving in to Clinton.

Republican activists were equally galled when their hopes for a sizable tax cut evaporated because GOP leaders in the House and Senate could not agree on the numbers. In addition, Clinton scared many Republicans by calling on Congress to "save Social Security first" and not to use any of the budget surplus for major tax breaks.

The president lost a potent tool for helping to control congressional spending on June 25, when the Supreme Court ruled that the line-item veto enacted in 1996 was unconstitutional because it permitted the president to rewrite bills that he had already signed into law. The vote was 6–3. Clinton had used the line item veto in 1997, albeit sparingly. Nonetheless, Congress in February 1998 overrode his line item veto of several military construction projects.

Congress also failed to reach agreement on perhaps the most important domestic matter on its plate in 1998: implementation of the groundbreaking $368.5 billion agreement between tobacco companies and state attorneys general to combat teenage smoking. The legislation, which expanded well beyond the parameters of the original deal, died in the Senate when GOP conservatives objected to its sharply higher cigarette taxes and new bureaucracies. Late in the year the states reached a smaller but still sizable settlement that did not require congressional approval to be implemented.

Much to nearly everyone's surprise, the House approved a bill to reform campaign financing, but the measure met a predictable demise in the Senate. The House also approved a GOP-backed bill placing some restrictions on managed care health plans. But the Senate never addressed the issue as Republicans and Democrats squabbled over the parameters of the debate.

The most accurate assessment of the session may have been given by Gingrich in his last regular speech on the House floor. Defending the budget agreement against a cacophony of conservative criticism, Gingrich said that in a divided government, some compromises are necessary: "If we don't work together on the big issues, nothing gets done."

The Political Year

Four years after the voters gave Republicans control of both chambers of Congress for the first time in forty years, the GOP appeal seemed to be losing its edge. In the 1998 congressional elections, Democrats won a net gain of five seats in the House, the first time since 1934 that the party controlling the White House gained seats in the House in a midterm election. In the Senate the party breakdown remained the same, even though the Democrats had more seats to defend. The GOP held on to its large lead in the number of governorships, but the Democrats won the governorship of California for the first time in twenty years.

Senate Elections

Six seats switched parties in the Senate, but with the Democrats and Republicans each winning three, the Senate party breakdown remained the same, at fifty-five Republicans and forty-five Democrats.

Only three incumbents were defeated. In Illinois, Peter G. Fitzgerald, a Republican state senator, defeated incumbent Carol Moseley-Braun, a Democrat and the only African American in the U.S. Senate. Fitzgerald took 50 percent of the total vote to Moseley-Braun's 47 percent. Fitzgerald was a committed conservative, whose stance on social issues stood in sharp contrast to Moseley-Braun's. Fitzgerald opposed abortion in all instances except to save the life of the mother. He was also an ardent proponent of tax cuts and free market policies.

In New York, Democratic Rep. Charles E. Schumer decisively defeated incumbent Republican Alphonse M. D'Amato, 55 percent to 44 percent. Schumer not only raised the millions needed to defeat the well-financed chairman of the Senate Banking Committee, but he was also willing to take on D'Amato in a campaign that more often resembled a street fight than a reasoned debate on political issues. Schumer first went to the U.S. House in 1981, replacing Democratic Rep. Elizabeth Holtzman, who left the House to challenge D'Amato for the Senate.

The third incumbent to lose was North Carolina Republican Lauch Faircloth, who was ousted by Democrat John Edwards, a trial lawyer who was running for political office for the first time. Edwards took 51 percent of the vote to Faircloth's 47 percent. Edwards campaigned on a platform designed to appeal to both conservatives and liberals. He promised to fight crime by supporting the death penalty and to advocate local control of education at the same time that he embraced such core Democratic principles as saving Social Security, enacting a patient's bill of rights, and protecting the environment. Edwards also promised to be "flexible," saying that he was not going to Washington "with a bunch of programs in mind."

The other three turnovers were all for seats left open by the retirement of the incumbent. In Kentucky, Republican U.S. Rep. Jim Bunning squeaked by his Democratic House colleague Scotty Baesler to win the seat formerly held by Democrat Wendell H. Ford. A former professional baseball player and conservative Republican, Bunning defeated Baesler by half a percentage point. Ohio Gov. George V. Voinovich, a moderate Republican, won 57 percent of the vote to defeat Democrat Mary O. Boyle for the seat held by Democrat John H. Glenn Jr. Known for his ability to build alliances across political divides, Voinovich won praise from both Republicans and Democrats in his Senate campaign. And in Indiana, Democrat Evan Bayh, son of former Sen. Birch E. Bayh, trounced his Republican opponent Paul Helmke, the Republican mayor of Fort Wayne. In 1988 Bayh was the first Democrat elected as Indiana's governor in twenty years. He held the post for eight years, leaving in 1997 with a 79 percent approval rating. Bayh won 64 percent of the vote in the race against Helmke for the seat vacated by Republican Sen. Daniel R. Coats.

Two other freshman senators were elected, but no change in party occurred. In Arkansas, Democrat Blanche L. Lincoln defeated Republican Fay Boozman for the Senate seat left vacant by Democrat Dale L. Bumpers who retired. Lincoln's election kept the number of women serving in the Senate at nine. In Idaho, U.S. Rep. Michael D. Crapo, R, won the Senate seat held by Dirk Kempthorne, R, who won election as Idaho's governor.

House Elections

The net gain of five House seats for the Democrats brought the party breakdown to 223 Republicans, 211 Democrats, and one independent, the slimmest majority since

Recorded Vote Totals

Following are the recorded congressional vote totals between 1950 and 2000. The figures do not include quorum calls. The 95th Congress (1977–1979) took 2,696 recorded votes, the highest number for an entire Congress. The high for a single year was 1995, when 1,480 recorded votes were taken. That year was also the high mark for recorded votes in the House—867. The high for the Senate was 700 recorded votes in 1976.

Year	House	Senate	Total
1950	154	229	383
1951	109	202	311
1952	72	129	201
1953	71	89	160
1954	76	181	257
1955	73	88	161
1956	74	136	210
1957	100	111	211
1958	93	202	295
1959	87	215	302
1960	93	207	300
1961	116	207	323
1962	124	227	351
1963	119	229	348
1964	113	312	425
1965	201	259	460
1966	193	238	431
1967	245	315	560
1968	233	280[1]	513
1969	177	245	422
1970	266	422	688
1971	320	423	743
1972	329	532	861
1973	541	594	1,135
1974	537	544	1,081
1975	612	611	1,223
1976	661	700	1,361
1977	706	636	1,342
1978	834	520	1,354
1979	672	509	1,181
1980	604	546	1,150
1981	353	497	850
1982	459	469	928
1983	498	381	879
1984	408	292	700
1985	439	381	820
1986	451	359	810
1987	488	420	908
1988	451	379	830
1989	368	312	680
1990	511	326	837
1991	428	280	708
1992	473	270	743
1993	597	395	992
1994	497	329	826
1995	867	613	1,480
1996	454	306	760
1997	633	298	931
1998	533	314	847
1999	609	374	983
2000	600	298	898

1. This figure does not include one yea-and-nay vote that was ruled invalid for lack of a quorum.

1955. The Republican losses threw the GOP into disarray. Although Speaker Gingrich crowed at the fact that the GOP had won its third consecutive House election for the first time since the Great Depression, rank-and-file legislators blamed Gingrich for the party's losses. They said that the leadership's obsession with the possible impeachment of President Clinton and its attempt through a national advertising campaign to link all Democratic candidates to the presidential sex scandal was a major miscalculation.

Faced with a serious challenge to his leadership from Livingston, Gingrich announced on Nov. 6 that he was stepping down as Speaker and would resign his House seat. Little more than a month later, Livingston made his dramatic resignation announcement. Both men were replaced by Republicans in special elections in 1999, leaving the party lineup unaffected.

Despite the drama caused by the GOP losses, very few House seats were hotly contested in 1998. More than one-fifth of all House members—ninety-four out of 435—won election without major party opposition. Sixty of those uncontested races took place in the South. All but six incumbents—five Republicans and one Democrat—who ran for reelection held on to their seats. A sixth Republican incumbent had lost his seat in a primary election. Only nineteen legislators—ten incumbents and nine newcomers—won their seats with less than 52 percent of the vote.

The incumbents who lost on election day were in their first or second term. The five Republicans were Jon D. Fox, Pa.; Michael Pappas, N.J.; Bill Redmond, N.M.; Vincent Snowbarger, Kan.; and Rick White, Wash. The lone Democrat was Jay Johnson, Wis.

The lack of closely contested seats resulted in the lowest voter turnout since 1942, when the nation was in the midst of fighting World War II. In 1998, 33 percent of the voting-age population (excluding voters in the District of Columbia) cast ballots in House races.

State Elections

Republicans managed to hold on to the lion's share of governorships, losing a net of one. As a result of the election, Republicans held thirty-one governorships, Democrats seventeen, and independents two. One of the two independents was Jesse "The Body" Ventura, a former professional wrestler, who won the Minnesota race on the Reform Party ticket against Republican Norm Coleman and Democrat Hubert Humphrey III. The other independent was Angus King, who easily won reelection as Maine's governor.

Ventura seemed undaunted by his new and unexpected challenge. "I've jumped out of an airplane thirty-four times," he said. "I've dove 212 feet under water. I've done a lot of things that defied death. And this isn't defying death. It's just common sense and hard work."

Two sons of former President George Bush were elected governors in 1998. George W. Bush, the front-runner for the Republican presidential nomination in 2000, easily won reelection as governor of Texas, while his younger brother Jeb won the governorship of Florida. Jeb Bush had lost a bid for the governorship four years earlier. They were the first brothers to preside over two states simultaneously since Nelson and Winthrop Rockefeller held sway over New York and Arkansas in the late 1960s and early 1970s.

Jeb Bush's easy win over Democratic Lt. Gov. Kenneth H. "Buddy" MacKay put the GOP in control of both the Florida legislature and governorship. That would prove useful in the congressional redistricting to be undertaken after the 2000 Census. It would also prove critical to George W. Bush's presidential election in 2000. Florida's Republican administration certified George W. Bush the winner of the popular vote in the state, despite Democrats' insistence that thousands of disputed ballots be hand-counted. Ultimately the Supreme Court intervened to stop a recount of those disputed ballots in the state, giving George Bush Florida's 25 electoral votes and victory in the electoral college, even though Democrat Al Gore won the national popular vote by more than half a million votes. *(2000 presidential election, p. 21)*

Altogether in 1998 Republicans won formerly Democratic governors' mansions in Colorado, Florida, Nebraska, and Nevada, and held on to closely contested governorships in Illinois and Ohio. Democrats won formerly Republican governorships in Alabama, California, Iowa, and South Carolina, and retained an open seat in Georgia.

The Democratic win in California was considered a major prize if for no other reason than that California was expected to gain as many as five seats in the U.S. House after the 2000 Census. With Democrats controlling the governorship and the California legislature, the party had high hopes of drawing congressional lines to maximize its strength. Even with California in the Democratic column, however, Republicans still governed eight of the ten most populous states.

Republicans, however, lost ground nationwide in state legislative elections, losing a net of three legislative chambers. That put Democrats in control of fifty-three legislative chambers and Republicans in control of forty-five. (The unicameral Nebraska legislature was nonpartisan.)

Special Elections

Six special elections were held in 1998 to replace House members who had either died or resigned. None of the seats changed party. All six of the new members won reelection to a full term in the 1998 general elections.

Three of the special elections took place in California. Barbara Lee, D, easily won election to the Ninth District seat held by veteran House member Ronald V. Dellums, D, who resigned in February 1998. Lois D. Capps, D, won the Twenty-second District seat held by her husband, Walter Capps, D, who had died in October 1997. And Mary Bono, R, won the Forty-fourth District seat held by her husband, Sonny Bono, R, who died in a skiing accident in January 1998.

In New Mexico's First District, Republican Heather Wilson defeated Phillip J. Maloof to replace Rep. Steven H. Schiff, a Republican, who had died in March 1998. In New York's Sixth District, Democrat Gregory W. Meeks easily bested a field of candidates to win the seat vacated by Floyd H. Flake, also a Democrat, who resigned in November 1997 to focus on his ministry. And in Pennsylvania's First District, Democrat Robert A. Brady easily defeated his Republican opponent to win the seat left vacant after Thomas M. Foglietta, D, resigned in November 1997 to become U.S. ambassador to Italy.

1999

The Legislative Year

Although the Senate impeachment trial and acquittal of President Clinton was finished less than six weeks after the new Congress convened in January, the legacy of ill will left by the impeachment battle tainted the remainder of the session. The extraordinarily polarized climate in Congress was further exacerbated as both parties jockeyed for political advantage heading into the 2000 elections, in which control of the White House and both houses of Congress was at stake. With neither the Democratic president nor the Republican-controlled Congress in a cooperative mood, little of note was achieved during the first session of the 106th Congress.

Clinton was only the second president ever to be impeached. The first, Andrew Johnson, was also acquitted in a partisan atmosphere that perhaps even exceeded that in Washington in 1999. Clinton was never in any serious danger of being convicted on the impeachment charges of perjury and obstruction of justice brought by the House in connection with his affair with a former White House intern. To their chagrin, Republicans could not even rally a majority on either charge, let alone the two-thirds vote required by the Constitution for conviction. The Senate acquitted the president on the perjury charge, 45–55, and on the obstruction of justice charge, 50–50. *(Clinton impeachment, p. 813)*

Those votes seemed to add insult to injury to the GOP, particularly in the House, which was still suffering from the loss of five seats in the 1998 elections. House Speaker Newt Gingrich, R-Ga., had resigned when the election losses were blamed in large part on his insistence on pursuing Clinton's impeachment in the face of overwhelming evidence that the public was tired of the scandal and wanted their lawmakers to turn to other matters.

Many Republicans made little secret of their dislike for the president. "Nobody trusts him, Republican or Democrat," House Majority Leader Dick Armey, R-Texas, maintained.

After the Senate trial, the president and the Republican-led Congress showed even less inclination than in the past to try to compromise with each other. As a result, none of the major initiatives that Clinton outlined in his State of the Union—overhauling Social Security and Medicare, raising the minimum wage, tightening regulation of health maintenance organizations (HMOs), or raising tobacco-related revenue—became law. Few ever came up for a vote.

Failure to seek compromise also contributed to the defeat of the centerpiece of the GOP agenda—a ten-year, $792 billion tax cut plan. Republicans made it clear that the tax cut was a party-defining issue designed to appeal to their political base and not an invitation to negotiate. To their consternation, the voters hardly raised a ripple of public protest when Clinton vetoed the measure.

Ironically, the most significant legislative accomplishment of the session was a financial services overhaul bill that had been blocked for decades by differences among various sectors of the financial services industry as well as among members of Congress. The measure was enacted in 1999 only because key participants eventually agreed to compromise their differences. The new law altered the basic structure of the industry to allow banks, securities firms, and insurance companies to compete on one another's traditional turf.

The session's other achievements included enactment of a bill increasing Medicare reimbursements to health care providers and legislation granting extended federal health care benefits to the disabled when they returned to work. Congress also cleared a package extending several business tax breaks, legislation allowing satellite television providers to carry local stations' programming, and a measure cracking down on software piracy.

More often, however, the story in 1999 was one of process rather than progress, of maneuvering in an era in Washington when power between the parties was divided, congressional majorities were narrow, and civility was on the decline.

In a few important instances, House GOP leaders had to rely on their Senate counterparts to stop legislation they opposed. The House and Senate, for example, each passed bills designed to bolster the rights of people whose medical insurance was provided through managed-care plans. The House passed its more sweeping measure with a solid, bipartisan majority that the GOP leadership was unable to tamp down. The Senate vote to pass its narrower version was orchestrated by Majority Leader Trent Lott, R-Miss., and ran along party lines. The prospects for reconciling the differences between the two versions were remote.

Similarly, GOP leaders could not prevent the House from passing a bill aimed at changing the role of money in na-

---

CONGRESS IN 1999

The first session of the 106th Congress closed at 12:03 p.m. EST on Nov. 22, 1999, when the House adjourned *sine die*. The Senate had adjourned *sine die* at 8:49 p.m. on Nov. 19. Both chambers started the year on Jan. 6. The session lasted 321 days. The Senate met on 162 days, the House on 137 days.

During the session a total of 6,593 bills and resolution were introduced, compared with 3,573 in 1998 and 5,568 in 1997. A total of 170 bills were signed into law in 1999. President Clinton vetoed five bills. *(Public laws, table, p. 11; presidential vetoes, p. 994)*

During 1999 the House took 609 recorded votes, seventy-six more than in 1998. The Senate took 374 recorded votes, sixty more than in 1998. (Totals do not include quorum calls.) *(Recorded votes, table, p. 12)*

tional politics, but they were able to stop Senate legislation when supporters could not come up with the votes to overcome a threatened filibuster.

On gun control, the roles were reversed. A month after a shooting spree at a Littleton, Colo., high school killed fifteen people, the dam against new restrictions on firearms appeared to be breaking. The Senate passed, with Vice President Al Gore's tie-breaking vote, gun show regulations that the National Rifle Association emphatically opposed. The Senate then passed the underlying juvenile crime bill by a wide margin, suggesting that a new center on a long-polarized issue might have been found. But a month later, the House soundly defeated a package of more modest gun controls. To that end, Majority Whip Tom DeLay, R-Texas, employed a classic technique for stopping legislation: he arranged for enough "poison pills" that ardent fans and ardent foes of gun control alike found the final language objectionable.

Important measures were not always thwarted by parliamentary tactics or unbridgeable differences between the two chambers. The Senate's resounding rejection of a treaty to expand restrictions on nuclear testing may be remembered as one of Clinton's most embarrassing foreign policy setbacks.

Occasionally the White House was able to compromise with Congress. An example was an agreement to pay nearly $1 billion in back dues to the United Nations. Clinton had vetoed a similar bill in 1998 because it had contained provisions barring federal aid to international family planning groups that advocated abortion, and he vetoed the State Department appropriation bill in 1999 in part because it contained similar restrictions. As adjournment neared, however, and the United States came closer to losing its seat in the U.N. General Assembly for refusing to pay its bill, Clinton decided to negotiate. He agreed to accept compromise language on the abortion issue in return for provisions in an omnibus spending bill that would pay the U.N. debt as well as fund the United States' contribution to a global debt relief plan for the world's poorest countries.

On other foreign policy matters, both sides of the Capitol showed ambivalence about Clinton's military deployment in the Serbian province of Kosovo, although the messages Congress sent about what U.S. policy should be were somewhat muddied by anti-Clinton sentiments and unwillingness to go too far out on a limb. On a tie vote, the House rejected a symbolic resolution to endorse the air bombing campaign that Clinton had launched five weeks earlier. A month later, the Senate narrowly voted down an amendment to the annual defense authorization bill that would have required Clinton to obtain express congressional permission before deploying ground troops.

There was evidence of isolationism on trade as well. The protectionist sentiment displayed in March when the House voted by a two-to-one ratio to pass a bill restricting steel imports portended the standoff that came later in the year on proposals designed to stimulate trade with Africa and the Caribbean. At the same time, lawmakers showed growing impatience with the policy of trying to isolate Cuba. Although it was dropped in conference, the Senate lined up overwhelmingly behind an amendment to its fiscal 2000 agriculture spending bill that would have allowed food and medicine shipments to the island.

Social conservatives had a mixed record in 1999. Antiabortion forces opened a new offensive, ushering to passage in the House a measure to declare a fetus to be an "unborn child" and elevate its standing under federal law. Abortion rights groups said that would undermine the legal rationale for *Roe v. Wade*, the 1973 Supreme Court decision legalizing abortion. Abortion opponents also took heart when only fifty-one senators voted for nonbinding language endorsing that landmark ruling.

A vote on a measure to block an Oregon law permitting physician-assisted suicide forced the House to choose between the wishes of two GOP constituencies: those who advocated states' rights and those who said the right to life is paramount. The House sided with the latter group.

But social conservatives were rebuffed on an amendment to a juvenile crime bill that would have criminalized sales of explicitly violent or sexual material to young people. This time, the House sided with another longstanding constituency: retailers such as bookshop owners and video rental outlets, who teamed up with movie and music producers to stop the proposal.

Environmentalists, who had had some success playing defense against the GOP Congress, had none when they tried to play offense. The auto industry persuaded the Senate to reject an amendment to the transportation spending bill urging a reconsideration of automobile fuel-efficiency standards. And the House again sided with its public works promoters in their annual tussle with the budget hawks, defeating an amendment to strike from a bill language dedicating revenue from airline ticket taxes to aviation projects.

Both parties in both chambers gave solid backing to a measure giving localities greater latitude in spending federal education money. But the debate was filled with rancor because Democrats saw themselves as the education party and were loath to share the label with the GOP. When the Senate took up its version of the legislation, Democrats tried to make it a vehicle for their own education agenda, including the hiring of 100,000 new teachers. In the House, Democrats used a bill to create a new federal education block grant as their vehicle for funding the teachers. Although both efforts came up short, the votes were close enough to give Clinton incentive to push the teacher proposal in the year-end budget talks, and the provision made it into the omnibus spending bill for fiscal 2000.

House Speaker J. Dennis Hastert, R-Ill., had promised during his first year at the helm to bring "regular order" to the budget process, which he said meant enacting the thirteen annual appropriations bills by the time fiscal 2000 began on Oct. 1. Republicans were also determined to avoid repeating the previous year's endgame negotiations with the White House that yielded a mammoth spending package that both sides viewed as a victory for Clinton. The Republican strategy for 1999 called for moving spending bills one at a time, while honoring the discretionary spending caps imposed by the 1997 Balanced Budget Act and pledging not to dip into the Social Security surplus.

Hastert largely succeeded on the first goal, but after Clinton rejected five of the bills, negotiators began more than two weeks of talks over yet another omnibus measure. Despite taking every advantage of controversial scorekeeping and accounting tactics, the GOP was unable to meet its two other goals. The Congressional Budget Office said the GOP-passed spending bills exceeded the caps by $31 billion and dipped into Social Security surpluses by $17 billion.

Ultimately, the Republicans found themselves once again giving in to many of Clinton's spending goals to reach an agreement on the omnibus bill. Clinton obtained more than $5 billion in year-end add-ons and won funding for hiring new teachers and police officers, the release of back dues to the United Nations, and funding to purchase new federal lands. The GOP won a small across-the-board cut in discretionary spending, and northeastern lawmakers won a significant victory on dairy pricing policy.

Finally, although Republicans may have had a personal antipathy for Clinton, they apparently did not harbor such grudges against the office of the presidency itself. Both chambers agreed to double the next president's salary to $400,000 a year. A string of former White House officials representing every administration from Lyndon B. Johnson's to Clinton's said the low pay for the chief executive was holding down the pay of other federal officials and making public service less attractive to well-qualified people. The president's salary had been frozen at $200,000 a year since 1969.

The Political Year

Special elections were required in Georgia and Louisiana to fill seats left vacant after House Speaker Gingrich of Georgia and his would-be successor, Robert L. Livingston Jr., R-La., both resigned from Congress. On Nov. 6, 1998, just three days after Republicans lost a net of five seats in the House, Gingrich announced that he was giving up his Speakership and would resign from Congress officially on Jan. 3, 1999. He was succeeded by Johnny Isakson, R, a Georgia real estate executive who had served seven terms in the Georgia state house and later two terms in the state senate before being appointed chairman of the Georgia Board of Education in 1996. Isakson, who had run unsuccessfully for governor in 1990, won 65 percent of the vote in the Feb. 23, 1999, special election for Gingrich's seat.

At a party meeting Nov. 18, 1998, Republicans had elected Livingston their Speaker-designate. A month later, just two

Age Structure of Congress

Year	House	Senate	Total
1949	51.0	58.5	53.8
1951	52.0	56.6	53.0
1953	52.0	56.6	53.0
1955	51.4	57.2	52.2
1957	52.9	57.9	53.8
1959	51.7	57.1	52.7
1961	52.2	57.0	53.2
1963	51.7	56.8	52.7
1965	50.5	57.7	51.9
1967	50.8	57.7	52.1
1969	52.2	56.6	53.0
1971	51.9	56.4	52.7
1973	51.1	55.3	52.0
1975	49.8	55.5	50.9
1977	49.3	54.7	50.3
1979	48.8	52.7	49.5
1981	48.4	52.5	49.2
1983	45.5	53.4	47.0
1985	49.7	54.2	50.5
1987	50.7	54.4	52.5
1989	52.1	55.6	52.8
1991	52.8	57.2	53.6
1993	51.7	58.0	52.9
1995	50.9	58.4	52.2
1997	51.6	57.5	52.7
1999	52.6	58.3	53.7
2001	54.4	59.8	55.0

NOTE: Figures indicate the average ages of members at the beginning of each Congress from 1949 to 2001.

days before the House debate on articles of impeachment against President Clinton in connection with his affair with a White House intern, Livingston admitted that he had had extramarital affairs. During the Dec. 19 impeachment debate, he announced that he would not run for Speaker in the new Congress and that he would resign his seat early in the next session. Livingston officially resigned on Feb. 28, 1999, and was replaced by Republican David Vitter, an attorney who had served for seven years in the Louisiana state house. Vitter had come in a close second after former Gov. Dave Treen, R, in the May 1, 1999, special election for Livingston's seat, but he defeated Treen in the May 29 runoff election after capturing 51 percent of the vote.

On Nov. 16, California state senator Joe Baca, D, won a special election to fill the Forty-second District seat left vacant by the death of veteran Democratic Rep. George E. Brown Jr. Baca won the election with 51 percent of the vote after narrowly winning the Democratic primary in September. In that race, he defeated Brown's widow, Marta Macias Brown, by 518 votes. Baca won election to a full term in 2000, taking 60 percent of the vote against the same Republican candidate he had defeated in the special election.

Lincoln D. Chafee was appointed to fill the Senate seat left vacant when his father John H. Chafee died in October. The younger Chafee easily won the seat outright in the 2000 election.

Gubernatorial Elections

Three states held gubernatorial elections in 1999. Two incumbents were easily elected to second terms, while a party turnover occurred in the third state.

In Kentucky, Democrat Paul E. Patton was returned to the governor's mansion with 61 percent of the vote. He defeated Republican Peppy Martin, who won 22 percent, and Reform Party candidate Gatewood Galbraith, who took 15 percent of the vote.

In Louisiana, Republican Murphy J. "Mike" Foster won reelection with 62 percent of the vote. Foster was only the second GOP governor of the state in 122 years and the first to win two terms. He was sworn in for his second term down the street from the courtroom in which his predecessor, the flamboyant Edwin W. Edwards, D, was being tried on federal racketeering charges. Edwards was eventually convicted.

In Mississippi, Lt. Gov. Ronnie Musgrove, D, was the front-runner in a four-way race to succeed Republican Gov. Kirk Fordice, who was ineligible to run for a third term. When Musgrove failed to win a majority of the vote, the election for the first time was thrown into the state house, which voted overwhelmingly for Musgrove, 86–36. Fordice, the first GOP governor in the state in a century, had scandalized voters when he conducted a very public affair with a childhood sweetheart. So outraged were state legislators by his conduct that they refused to allow him to make the traditional final address to the legislature.

2000

The Legislative Year

Republican leaders opened the second session of the 106th Congress emphasizing new tactics rather than rolling out a fresh list of legislative priorities. They insisted they already knew what Americans wanted—lower taxes, restraint in the growth of government, and some tweaks in the laws affecting health care. They just needed to find a way during an election year to push their agenda through a narrowly divided Congress and get it signed by a Democratic president.

The strategy called for repackaging the tax cut proposals that President Clinton had rejected in 1999 in a way that would be more difficult for him to veto. GOP leaders also wanted to accelerate the appropriations process to avoid an end-of-session pileup of unfinished spending bills—a situation Clinton had used to his advantage in previous years to extract more spending from Congress. In the Senate, Majority Leader Trent Lott, R-Miss., had an additional goal: to protect endangered GOP incumbents from having to cast tough votes on controversial issues before the Nov. 7 elections. Democrats hoped to regain control of the Senate, where Republicans were defending nineteen of the thirty-four Senate slots to be elected in 2000. At the same time, Senate Democrats mastered the art of the filibuster and used it well, slowing work in the Senate to a crawl when they disagreed with the GOP leadership.

Although GOP leaders managed some success in executing their strategy, it did little to help them achieve their goals. The second session of the 106th Congress, like the first session in 1999, was a year of relatively modest legislative ambitions and even more modest accomplishments. With the possible exception of a bill giving permanent normal trading status to China, it was hard to argue that any of Congress's actions in 2000 carried much historic significance. There were the usual rumblings about checking the growth of entitlements, overhauling campaign finance laws, and improving access to health care. But Congress ignored or sidestepped more tough issues than it confronted and by the end of the year found itself in the all-too-familiar position of being almost entirely consumed by the struggle to finish its basic task—drawing up the federal budget. Moreover, it found itself returning after the elections for a lame-duck session to wrap up its work on spending bills.

Clinton's veto of the ten-year, $792 billion tax cut in 1999 left Republicans undaunted in 2000. Clinton had warned that he would reject large tax cuts that he claimed would jeopardize efforts to reduce the national debt, but Republicans calculated that the president would find it difficult to veto politically popular tax cuts if they were sent to him in bite-size pieces. They passed separate bills repealing estate taxes and the "marriage penalty" in the tax law. (The latter was a quirk in the federal income tax code that caused more than half of all married couples to pay more in income taxes than they would as two single people.) Clinton vetoed them both, saying he wanted a broader deal on taxes that would spell out the bottom line on revenue reductions. The House sustained both vetoes, and no deal on a broader tax bill ever emerged.

GOP leaders approached the fiscal 2001 appropriations process in much the same way, emphasizing strategy rather than compromise. Congress adopted the budget resolution by the April 15 deadline, and the House passed twelve of the thirteen regular appropriations bills before the August recess. But many of those measures ran into a wall in the Senate, where Lott balked at exposing his members to votes on gun control, abortion, and other "hot-button" proposals sure to be offered by Democrats as amendments. Despite Lott's best efforts, five Republican incumbents lost their Senate seats in the Nov. 7 elections. The GOP, however, picked up a Democratic seat, so the party's net loss in the Senate was four seats. A GOP seat also had been lost earlier in the year when a Democrat was appointed to fill the vacancy left by the death of Republican Paul Coverdell of Georgia in July.

In addition, both chambers ran into problems because the highly partisan budget resolution allowed only a tiny increase in discretionary spending—less than needed to keep pace with inflation. In the end, spenders would win out over savers, as moderate Republicans joined Democrats in pushing for budget-breaking levels of spending, much to the chagrin of fiscal conservatives who wanted to live within the budget.

Compounding their problems, GOP leaders occasionally were outflanked by opponents in floor battles. Advocates of overhauling campaign finance rules won a small but symbol-

---

CONGRESS IN 2000

The second session of the 106th Congress began on Jan. 24, 2000. The Senate adjourned *sine die* at 8:03 p.m. on Dec. 15, 2000. The House adjourned *sine die* at 8:41 p.m. the same day. The session lasted 326 days. The Senate met on 141 days, the House on 135 days.

During the session a total of 4,247 bills and resolutions were introduced, compared with 6,593 in 1999 and 3,573 in 1998. A total of 410 bills were signed into law in 2000. President Clinton vetoed seven bills, including one pocket veto. (*Public laws, table, p. 11; presidential vetoes, p. 994*)

During 2000, the House took 600 recorded votes, nine fewer than in 1999. The Senate took 298 recorded votes, 76 fewer than in 1999. (Totals do not include quorum calls.) (*Recorded votes, table, p. 12*)

ically important victory with the first change in federal election law in two decades. A defining moment came on the Senate floor, when opponents of the proposal were unable to sustain a point of order against it. After Senate adoption, party moderates pressured House leaders to take up a similar bill, and it passed overwhelmingly.

Another embarrassing moment in the Senate came when a conference report combining the appropriations bills for the legislative branch and the Treasury Department was rejected. GOP leaders had thought they had the votes to overcome a number of complaints lodged against the bill from both sides of the aisle.

The biggest foreign policy decision of the year, and arguably the most important action Congress took in 2000, was to declare China a permanent normal trading partner, which meant that the same tariff rates would apply to Chinese imports as to goods from most other U.S. trading partners. The opposition was strongest in the House, but Clinton teamed with his frequent nemesis, House Majority Whip Tom DeLay, R-Texas, to pull together a bipartisan coalition. Clinton had made the legislation a priority, and its passage solidified his legacy as a free-trade Democrat. It also meant the United States would support China's bid to join the World Trade Organization.

On other foreign policy matters, Congress agreed to boost the U.S. commitment to international debt relief. Congress also substantially expanded the scope of efforts to stem production of illegal drugs by approving $1.3 billion in emergency funds to fight drug-trafficking in South America, primarily in Colombia. The Senate rejected efforts to limit Clinton's authority to deploy peacekeeping troops in the Serbian province of Kosovo. Opponents warned that such limits would set a dangerous precedent for future commanders-in-chief. Republican presidential nominee (and the eventual winner of the election) George W. Bush largely avoided discussing matters pending in Congress, but he came out against efforts to scale back the president's authority to deploy troops.

Like other presidents in their final year in office, Clinton focused much of his activity on unilateral executive actions to put in place some of his legislative agenda that had been blocked in Congress. In particular, the administration issued new environmental protections affecting millions of acres of federal lands and new workplace safety rules that infuriated Republicans and business groups. After Congress failed to take action to protect the confidentiality of individual medical records, Clinton late in December issued medical record privacy rules drawn up by the Department of Health and Human Services.

GOP leaders were largely unsuccessful in their efforts to rein in their lame-duck rival. For example, the House included language in its Interior appropriations bill to limit the administration's ability to use national monument designations to restrict the uses of some federal lands, but the provision was stripped from the bill by an amendment on the floor. A similar amendment was rejected in the Senate as well. Late in the year Republicans said they would call on President-elect Bush to repeal many of the executive actions Clinton had taken.

Congress had relatively little to say about sensitive social issues in 2000. There were no substantive, decisive votes on gun control, abortion, or school choice. The Senate adopted a measure that would have expanded the definition of a hate crime to include offenses against gays and the disabled, but the language was later dropped in conference. Efforts to increase the minimum wage by $1 an hour surfaced and then sank, as Democrats and Republicans fought over whether it should be phased in over two years or three.

In health care policy, efforts to change the ground rules for managed care went nowhere. The House narrowly passed a Republican plan to provide prescription drug coverage under Medicare, but the Senate ignored the proposal.

In many ways, the disputes over social issues were framed in the debates over the budget, appropriations, and especially taxes. Republicans portrayed their unsuccessful efforts to eliminate the estate tax as a battle to protect family farmers and small business owners from the ruinous reach of the Internal Revenue Service, while Democrats and the White House argued that the GOP was pushing a tax break for the wealthiest Americans. The GOP also billed their effort to repeal the marriage penalty in the tax code as a way to help families. But Democrats responded that the plan was heavily tilted toward the wealthy and would slash taxes far more than necessary to fix the marriage penalty.

Both sides did agree to lift the limit on how much outside income retirees between ages sixty-five and sixty-nine could earn and still collect full Social Security benefits.

The biggest budget fight of the year, not surprisingly, was over education, an issue over which both parties were trying to claim dominion. The dispute was the primary cause of the lame-duck session. Republicans pushed for more block grants and local control, while Democrats pushed Clinton's proposals to target aid for hiring new teachers and for school construction. In the end, both sides got some, but not all, of what they wanted.

The Political Year

The federal and state elections of 2000 gave new meaning to the phrases "close vote" and "divided government." More than a hundred million votes were cast in the presidential election, in which the Democratic nominee, Vice President Al Gore, won the popular vote by half a million votes, but the Republican nominee, Texas Gov. George W. Bush, won the electoral college vote, and the presidency, with one vote to spare. Bush won the electoral college vote only after being declared the winner of Florida's disputed popular vote by 537 votes out of more than six million cast—and only after the Supreme Court stopped a hand recount of several thousand ballots by a vote of 5–4.

In the U.S. Senate, Republicans watched their 54–46 majority fade away to a 50–50 split, the first time since the election of 1880 that the Senate had been evenly divided. Because Bush's vice president, Richard B. Cheney, would serve as president of the Senate—and wield the tie-breaking vote—in the 107th Congress, the Republicans retained their voting majority. But the GOP was forced into negotiating an unprecedented power-sharing arrangement with the Democrats, and both sides would have to court support from the opposition to pass any controversial legislation.

A similar situation prevailed in the House, where the Republicans lost a net of two seats, ending the election with a 221–212 edge over the Democrats, with two independents. It was the most closely divided the House had been since the election of 1952, and, as in the Senate, the leadership of both parties would most likely have to forge compromises with some members from the other side of the aisle to accomplish anything of significance.

In the nation's state capitols, Republicans continued to dominate governorships, holding twenty-nine to the Democrats' nineteen. Two states had independent governors. But state legislatures were closely divided, with the Republicans controlling both chambers in eighteen states, Democrats controlling both in sixteen states, and the control divided between the parties in fifteen. One state, Nebraska, was nonpartisan.

"It is safe to say that never in our history have we ever had a partisan balance across the country as even as this," Norman Ornstein, resident scholar at the American Enterprise Institute, said, at a Nov. 9 forum.

The Presidential Election

The last presidential election of the twentieth century was also the century's most extraordinary. The Nov. 7 election left Gore and his running mate, Connecticut Sen. Joseph I. Lieberman, the clear winners of the national popular vote, but they were three votes short of the 270 needed under the Constitution to win the electoral college and thus the presidency. Bush and Cheney had 246 electoral votes coming out of the election. In doubt were Florida's 25 electoral votes, which would provide the margin of victory. There Bush had a slim advantage, and for five weeks lawyers and partisans for the two sides clashed in the courts, at local elections headquarters, and even in the streets.

Throughout the ordeal, the nation and world watched as election workers peered at ballots looking for signs of voter intent, and as judges struggled with Florida's sometimes conflicting laws to determine the state legislature's intent. The situation was the closest the United States had come to a constitutional crisis over a presidential election since 1876, when an election dispute dragged on for months and was finally resolved by a contentious vote of a special electoral commission.

Ultimately Florida's Republican administration, headed by Gov. Jeb Bush, certified his brother as the popular vote

Presidential Vote by Region

Democrat Al Gore, who won the national popular vote by more than 500,000 votes, gained his largest support in the East and in California. Republican George W. Bush, who won the electoral vote to become president, dominated in the South, where he won his own home state of Texas as well as Gore's home state of Tennessee. Bush also carried all the Mountain West states, except New Mexico. The Midwest was more evenly split between the two parties, with Bush winning the popular vote in the region, while Gore won more electoral votes.

	1996				
	Popular vote			Electoral vote	
Region	Clinton	Dole	Perot	Clinton	Dole
East	55%	34%	9%	127	0
Midwest	48	41	10	100	29
South	46	46	7	59	104
West	48	41	8	93	26
National	49	41	8	379	159

	2000				
	Popular vote			Electoral vote	
Region	Gore	Bush	Nader	Gore	Bush
East	56%	39%	4%	117[1]	9
Midwest	48	49	3	68	61
South	43	55	1	0	163
West	48	46	4	81	38
National	48	48	3	266[1]	271

1. A Democratic elector from the District of Columbia withheld her electoral vote to protest lack of voting representation for the District in Congress.

winner in Florida, raising his nationwide electoral vote total to 271—one more than he needed to win. Gore contested the election in Florida state court on grounds that the state had stopped the recounts prematurely, leaving thousands of machine-processed ballots unsubjected to the scrutiny of human eyes in a hand recount. The state Supreme Court allowed the hand count to go forward. But, in the end, a sharply divided U.S. Supreme Court issued a highly controversial ruling that halted the Florida count and effectively decided the election in Bush's favor. With no viable alternative remaining, Gore conceded on Dec. 13, a day after the Supreme Court ruling was announced.

It was the first time that the outcome of a presidential election had been contested in the courts; the first time that the U.S. Supreme Court had taken up a lawsuit—this one brought by Bush—related to a presidential election; and the first time the Court had gone against its traditional states' rights principles to overturn a state judiciary in such a matter. And in a historic election studded with anomalies, "firsts," and ironies, the Court for the first time immediately released audio tapes of its hearings on the suit, *Bush v. Gore*. Some constitutional scholars said that the Court should not have intervened in a political situation and that its 5–4 vote in the case weakened the Court's credibility and authority.

The tumult focused new attention on proposals to abolish or reform the electoral college system. It also brought to light the need to modernize the problem-prone voting systems still in use in Florida and many other states. And it exposed serious flaws in the technology that broadcast media relied on to project election results minutes after the polls have closed.

In the midst of the uproar, Cheney experienced his fourth (and apparently mild) heart attack. Doctors at George Washington University Hospital in Washington used angioplasty to install a stent, an expandable metal tube, in Cheney's heart to open a blocked artery. Within a few days Cheney was back on the job as head of Bush's transition team.

Bush's victory marked the fourth time in U.S. history that the popular vote loser gained the presidency. The first such election, in 1824, was won by John Quincy Adams, who, similar to Bush (son of former president George Bush), was the son of a president, John Adams. Although Andrew Jackson won the 1824 popular vote, none of the four candidates received the required electoral vote majority, and the House of Representatives decided the election in Adams's favor.

The second contested presidential election, in 1876, was more analogous to the Bush-Gore dispute in that it too involved charges of irregularities in the election process. New York Democrat Samuel J. Tilden won the national vote against Ohio Republican Rutherford B. Hayes, but controversies over the popular votes in three southern states, including Florida, led to rival sets of electoral vote results being sent to Congress from the three states. Lacking a procedure for resolving the dispute, Congress formed a bipartisan special commission, including Supreme Court justices, which gave the votes to Hayes in return for concessions to the South. Hayes thereby won the presidency by a single electoral vote.

In 1887 Congress enacted the Electoral Vote Count Act, specifying procedures for settling electoral vote disputes. One year later Republican Benjamin Harrison won the 1888 presidential election even though Democrat Grover Cleveland received more popular votes. The 1887 act did not come into play, however, because Harrison decisively won the electoral college vote, 233 to 168.

Although Gore's lead in the national popular vote was slim—537,179 votes out of 105,396,627 cast for all presidential candidates—the vote was even closer in the 1960 and 1968 presidential elections. In 1960 John F. Kennedy led Richard Nixon by 118,574 votes; in 1968 Nixon beat Hubert H. Humphrey by 510,314 votes. But the winners of the popular votes in those elections also won the electoral college vote decisively.

Had the Supreme Court not intervened in 2000, it was conceivable that Florida might have sent competing sets of electors' votes to Congress. Although that did not happen, the rules of the 1887 act thwarted efforts by some House members to challenge Florida's electoral votes. In one of the ironies of the election, it fell to Gore as Senate president to reject his supporters' objections and certify Bush as the winner of the electoral college vote.

THE NOMINATIONS

The prolonged dispute over Florida's crucial vote overshadowed all other aspects of the 2000 presidential election, including a rather lackluster primary season dominated throughout by Gore on the Democratic side and Bush on the GOP side. Both men locked up their nominations early, despite some strong opposition, primarily from Arizona Sen. John McCain against Bush and former New Jersey Sen. Bill Bradley against Gore.

Bush entered the race in early 1999 and quickly established himself as the favorite of the Republican establishment and its campaign donors. Without a sitting Democratic president to compete against, a dozen hopefuls were attracted to the contest for the GOP nomination. But even before the kickoff Iowa caucuses in January 2000 half of the field dropped out, including former vice president Dan Quayle, former Tennessee governor Lamar Alexander, and Elizabeth Dole, head of the Red Cross and wife of 1996 nominee Bob Dole, who said she was unable to compete with Bush's fundraising prowess. Conservative commentator Pat Buchanan, a past candidate, decided instead to seek the Reform Party nomination.

By early February Bush and McCain remained the only serious contenders. McCain upset Bush in the New Hampshire and Michigan primaries, but Bush went on to win a cluster of March 7 primaries and enough convention delegates to clinch the nomination.

McCain, a former Vietnam prisoner of war and cosponsor of bipartisan campaign finance reform legislation, was perceived as a moderate despite his solid conservative voting record in the Senate. This, and his penchant for bluntness, appealed to many non-Republicans, who could vote in the growing number of open or semi-open GOP primaries. In all, McCain defeated Bush in seven of the eighteen primaries he entered. But McCain eventually endorsed Bush and was the only member of Congress accorded a prime-time speaker's slot at the party's nominating convention in Philadelphia.

For Gore, the nomination challenge from Bradley was short and sweet. Bradley failed to win a single primary and dropped out of the race in early March. In a speech to the Democratic Convention at Los Angeles, Bradley expressed his support for Gore.

After the conventions Gore, more so than Bush, faced a vote-siphoning threat from the Green Party candidate, consumer advocate Ralph Nader, who received almost 1 percent of the presidential vote in 1996 and was aiming for 5 percent in 2000—a level that would ensure federal campaign funding for the Greens in the 2004 election. Although Republican swing votes were unlikely to switch to corporation-basher Nader, disaffected liberals who supported Bradley found Nader an attractive alternative.

THE REPUBLICAN CONVENTION

The Republican Party met July 31–Aug. 3 in Philadelphia at the First Union Center, where delegates named Bush the party's standard-bearer for 2000, with his proud father, the former president, applauding the party's choice. The senior Bush lost to Democrat Bill Clinton in 1992; after eight years of Democratic control, the younger Bush was now trying to deny the Democrats another four years in the White House, this time with Clinton's vice president at the helm.

The overriding difference between the election of 1992 and the election of 2000 was, as the Clinton-Gore strategists put it during the earlier election campaign, "the economy, stupid." Where the senior Bush was washed out of office in a sea of red ink, Gore was riding a crest of unprecedented prosperity and federal budget surpluses. The year 2000 was a time of plenty that both parties sought to exploit.

In their acceptance speeches, Bush and Cheney, his running mate, assailed the Democrats for failing to take advantage of the opportunities of an overflowing treasury. "For eight years the Clinton-Gore administration has coasted through prosperity," Bush said. "So much promise to no great purpose. Instead of seizing this moment, the . . . administration has squandered it."

Similarly, the party's 32,000-word platform was replete with references to prosperity and ways to use it, chiefly through tax cuts, which Bush said would benefit all taxpayers and not just the rich.

With all of his competitors eliminated during the primaries, Bush's nomination was strictly a formality. For the vote, the convention planners used a novel "rolling roll call" that took several days. Bush and Cheney won the votes of all 2,066 delegates.

In keeping with the convention's themes of unity and inclusion, there were no floor fights on rules or on platform planks. Averting one such fight, the rules committee rejected, 66–33, the so-called Delaware plan to limit the GOP presidential primary schedule to four months, with smaller states voting first. The Republican National Committee approved the plan, but big states objected that it would weaken their strength in the delegate-selection process.

A floor fight over the issue of abortion was also avoided. Moderates tried unsuccessfully to remove platform language supporting a constitutional ban on abortion, fearing that it would hurt GOP candidates, especially among women voters. Bush told the delegates that as president he would sign a ban on partial-birth abortion if Congress sent him one.

Although only 4 percent of the delegates were black, the convention gave prominent roles to minorities, and to women as well. Retired general Colin L. Powell, an African American, gave the keynote speech. Among other speakers were the nominee's wife, Laura, as well as Hispanics and a gay House member, James T. Kolbe of Arizona. As Kolbe spoke, several Texas delegates removed their cowboy hats and bowed their heads to show, as one put it, that they were not "condoning perversion."

The platform reaffirmed the party's opposition to homosexuality in the military, but in other ways it reflected Bush's self-described "compassionate conservatism." Missing from its pages were past GOP calls for eliminating the Education and Energy Departments and federal agencies supporting the arts and humanities. Added was a new women's health section supporting more research on diseases that affect women disproportionately. In a softened stance on immigration, the document also welcomed "New Americans."

THE DEMOCRATIC CONVENTION

Declaring himself "my own man," Gore stepped from the shadow of Bill Clinton and accepted the Democratic Party's nomination for president on the final night of the party's Aug. 14–17 convention at Los Angeles's Staples Center.

Reinforcing the independence he sought to portray, Gore earlier had taken a gamble unprecedented in American politics. In choosing Lieberman as his running mate, Gore made him the first Jew to run on a major party's national ticket. Besides being of a religious minority, Lieberman had at times broken with his party on economic issues and had sternly rebuked Clinton for his sexual affair with Monica Lewinsky. The convention delegates enthusiastically applauded Gore's choice, giving the Gore-Lieberman ticket their unanimous approval.

Gore used his acceptance speech to try to allay many of the concerns that had been troubling his candidacy, including fallout from Clinton's personal scandals, the defections to Nader among the liberal wing of the party, and his own shortcomings as a campaigner. He associated himself with the administration's achievements as the "partner of a leader who moved us out of the valley of recession and into the longest period of prosperity in American history." But he also quietly distanced himself from the moral misbehavior in office that led to Clinton's impeachment and Senate trial. "I want you to know me for who I truly am," Gore told the convention as he spoke about the values instilled in him by his parents—"faith and family, duty and honor, and trying to make the world a better place."

Aligning himself with the progressive tradition of the Democratic Party, he promised to stand up for working families against "powerful interests." Seeking to deflect criticism that he did not have the same rapport with the voters as Bush, Gore said the presidential election was "more than a popularity contest" and that he was there to "talk seriously about the issues" because the voters "deserve to know specifically what a candidate proposes to do."

Clinton himself recognized Gore's need to shake loose the moral baggage of the president he had served for eight years. In a farewell speech to the convention on Aug. 14, Clinton praised Gore's character as an adviser, leader, and champion of ordinary Americans. Choosing Gore as his vice president, Clinton said, was "one of the very best decisions of my life."

On Aug. 15 the convention adopted the Democratic Party platform by voice vote without dissent, a remarkable display of unity for a party known in the past for its fractiousness. It was the third Democratic platform in a row in which the party turned away from its liberal New Deal roots to a more centrist philosophy that called for economic growth, personal responsibility, family vitality, law and order, and military readiness.

The platform and Gore's acceptance speech stressed the prosperity and budget surpluses achieved during Clinton's two terms. Gore pledged to continue balancing the budget while delivering "the right kind of tax cuts." The Bush kind, he said, would benefit the wealthy and leave little to pay down the national debt or meet the needs of poor and working families. "They're for the powerful," Gore said of Bush and Cheney. "We're for the people."

THE CAMPAIGN

With polls continuing to show the electorate almost evenly divided, the major party race settled down to basically a personality contest between two Ivy Leaguers—Gore (Harvard) and Bush (Yale). Gore was a serious and intelligent man with a mastery of policy detail. He had served in the House and Senate before being selected as Bill Clinton's running mate in the 1992 race, in which the Democrats turned Bush's father out of the White House after only a single term. Gore was said to be charming and persuasive in small gatherings, but in campaign appearances, he often came across as wooden, his speeches delivered in a monotone with little of the spark that energized crowds. Occasionally Gore was perceived as overbearing or patronizing.

In contrast, Bush projected amiability and in general seemed more comfortable than Gore when working a crowd, often speaking in the generalities and campaign platitudes that voters seemed to find reassuring. Bush's nomination was a remarkable political achievement for a man who had entered politics only six years earlier and who had a reputation for having an uninquiring mind, uninterested in the details of policy. Not since World War II hero General Dwight D. Eisenhower was elected in 1952 had a presidential nominee of either major party had so little political experience. Detractors said that Bush would never have won the nomination had he not been his father's son.

Both candidates took a lot of negative press and ribbing from late-night comedians about their speaking habits—Bush for malapropisms and Gore for exaggerations. Bush, for example, in one off-hand statement derided people who regard Social Security as "some kind of federal program," which of course it was. Gore's most ridiculed statement was about his purported claim of "inventing" the Internet. What he actually said on a CNN program, however, was: "during my service in Congress I took the initiative in creating the Internet"—referring to his sponsorship of legislation that funded the early development of the technology. Despite the alleged "liberal bias" of the news media, a preconvention study by the Pew Research Center and the Project for Excellence in Journalism found that most news coverage portrayed Gore as an exaggerator or as scandal tainted (for his role in the Democrats' 1996 fund-raising practices), while

Bush was usually referred to more positively as "a different kind of Republican."

From the outset, the election was Gore's to lose. It has been almost axiomatic that the party in power retains the White House in times of peace and prosperity. With Clinton ineligible to succeed himself, Gore stood to inherit the advantage of running on Clinton's successes, especially an economy that had gone from record federal deficits to record surpluses, which opened the prospect of retiring the $3.7 trillion national debt while safeguarding Social Security, Medicare, and other popular but expensive social programs. Clinton could also claim legislative successes in welfare reform and the North American Free Trade Act as well as foreign policy efforts in Bosnia, Kosovo, Northern Ireland, and the Middle East.

Despite his high job approval ratings, Clinton himself was perhaps Gore's biggest handicap. Bush and other Republican candidates tried to saddle Gore with the sins of the Clinton administration, particularly Clinton's December 1998 impeachment for lying under oath about his affair with Monica Lewinsky when she was a White House intern. The Republicans' strategy was to run against "Clinton-Gore" rather than against Gore alone—even though Gore's marital fidelity was not at issue. *(Clinton impeachment, p. 813)*

Conservative congressional Republicans had never forgiven Clinton for defeating their effort to remove him from office through the impeachment process. In November 1998, with impeachment looming, Clinton had become the first president since Franklin D. Roosevelt in 1934 to gain House seats at a midterm election. He made a net gain of five seats and got rid of his nemesis, Speaker Newt Gingrich, who resigned from Congress in reaction to the GOP setback. The Speaker-designate, Robert L. Livingston of Louisiana, also resigned after admitting extramarital affairs. Then, in a political twist of the knife, Clinton handily won acquittal from the Senate in his impeachment trial.

In the 2000 campaign, however, neither the Republicans nor the Democrats openly raised the "character" issue. But Gore's need to distance himself from Clinton's indiscretions was implicit in his choice of Lieberman as his running mate. Lieberman was known for speaking out on moral issues and family values. Although he voted in the Senate to acquit Clinton, Lieberman had publicly taken the president to task for his dalliance with Lewinsky. On the Republican side, Bush's frequent pledges to "restore the honor and dignity" of the presidency also were a thinly veiled reference to impeachment.

Some Gore supporters felt that he perhaps distanced himself from Clinton too much, thereby sacrificing the opportunity to take his share of the credit for the booming economy and other positive aspects of the Clinton legacy. Clinton himself was said to feel "underused" by the Gore campaign. By the final weeks of the campaign Gore became less reluctant to run on Clinton's record, but it was too late to make much of an impression on undecided voters.

With the cold war over and most people better off than they were eight years earlier, traditionally Democratic pocketbook and social issues dominated the campaign—Social Security, education, health care, abortion rights, gun control. The huge federal surpluses fueled the money issues, with Bush pushing for tax cuts and heavier outlays for antimissile research and development. Gore pledged a "lockbox" for Social Security and criticized Bush's concept of allowing workers to divert part of their trust fund contributions to private investment accounts.

In the primary campaign, Bush raised almost $100 million, mostly from individuals, allowing him to decline federal grants and the spending limits that went with them. The Gore campaign accepted federal funding for the primaries. Both candidates received federal funding for their general election campaigns.

THE LONG ELECTION "NIGHT"

Problems with the crucial Florida vote erupted almost immediately on election day 2000. Voters in Palm Beach County reported difficulties with an unusual "butterfly" punch-card ballot. Some Democratic voters there thought that they had inadvertently voted for Reform Party nominee Pat Buchanan instead of for Gore. In some of the other twenty-four counties using outmoded punch-card systems, but with regular ballot forms, voters said they were unable to punch out the hole for the candidate of their choice.

Within hours, as news of the problems spread, people around the world became familiar with the obscure noun *chad*, singular or plural, meaning the tiny piece of paper that is pushed out in a punch-card system. If the chad is only dented (dimpled) or partially dislodged, the voting machine may not register the punch as a vote. Therein lay the basis for much of the contention in the days and weeks that were to follow.

Another serious problem emerged shortly after the polls began to close on the East Coast, this one having to do with the system—based on exit polling—devised by the news media to project election winners before the votes are counted. The system is uncannily accurate, but its worst and most embarrassing mistake happened at 7:47 p.m. EST when the broadcast networks, using Voter News Service (VNS) data, projected Gore as the winner in Florida. People were still voting in Florida's western panhandle, in the central time zone, when the election was called for Gore. A short time later, the networks retracted and said Florida was too close to call. *(Countdown in Florida, box, p. 26)*

In the early hours of Nov. 8 the news reports put Bush ahead. Gore called Bush from Nashville and told him he was prepared to concede. Later, after being advised that there might be a recount in Florida, Gore called again to Bush in Austin. "You mean you're retracting your concession?" a surprised Bush reportedly asked. "You don't have to get snippy about it," Gore is said to have replied.

Besides leading nationwide in the popular vote, Gore outside of Florida led in the electoral college vote, 267 to 246. The entire 2000 presidential election therefore hung on the final results of the popular vote in Florida, which would determine the winner of the state's 25 electoral votes.

The close election in Florida triggered an automatic machine recount, showing Bush ahead by about three hundred votes. But the Gore camp focused on the thousands of votes that the machines rejected as "undervoted," showing no vote for president, or "overvoted," showing more than one vote for presidential candidates. Only a manual count of those ballots could discern votes that the machines could not detect, Gore lawyers argued. The Democrats' war cry became, "Every vote counts; count every vote."

In what may have been a tactical mistake, Gore did not request an immediate statewide revote or recount. Instead his lawyers fought to keep hand counts going where Gore was picking up votes, in mostly Democratic counties such as Broward, Miami-Dade, and Volusia, and in Palm Beach County where the butterfly-ballot had recorded an unlikely 3,407 votes for Pat Buchanan, three times more than he received elsewhere in the state. Buchanan himself said it appeared he received votes meant for Gore. Just as fiercely, the Bush forces fought to stop the hand counts. They argued that the votes had been legally counted and recounted, including military and other absentee ballots that favored Bush, and that the canvassers had no uniform standards for gauging the difference between a vote and a nonvote on a punch-card ballot. Allowing more time for recounts, they said, would be changing the rules after the game started.

Both sides assembled high-powered legal teams, each headed by a former secretary of state, James A. Baker III for Bush and Warren M. Christopher for Gore. Both served as above-the-fray spokesmen while the trench warfare fell chiefly to Barry Richard of Tallahassee for Bush and David Boies of New York for Gore. U.S. Supreme Court arguments for Bush were presented by Washington attorney Theodore Olson and for Gore initially by Laurence Tribe of Harvard Law School and later by Boies.

But it was a race against the calendar, and Katherine Harris was the timekeeper. Harris, Florida's secretary of state and former cochair of Bush's campaign in the state, announced Nov. 13 that counties had until the following day, the date set in state law, to submit their returns, without any manual recount figures. Lawsuits stayed Harris's hand, however, and the manual counts proceeded by fits and starts until Sunday, Nov. 26, under an extension granted by the seven-member Florida Supreme Court, made up mostly of Democratic appointees. That evening Harris ceremoniously "certified" Bush as the Florida winner by 537 votes out of more than six million cast.

The battle was by no means over, however. Gore formally contested the election and Bush meanwhile had protested the deadline extension to the U.S. Supreme Court, which

COUNTDOWN IN FLORIDA

Nov. 7, 2000

Election in Florida too close to call, with Republican George W. Bush holding narrow lead. TV networks retract premature reports declaring Democrat Al Gore winner of state's twenty-five electoral votes.

Nov. 8–10

Gore calls Bush to concede early Nov. 8, then calls back to withdraw concession. Gore seeks Florida hand recounts in four largely Democratic counties. Bush has unofficial 1,784-vote lead Nov. 9. All but one of Florida's sixty-seven counties complete machine recount required by state law; Bush lead falls to 327 votes.

Nov. 11–14

Broward, Miami-Dade, Palm Beach, and Volusia Counties undertake manual recounts requested by Gore; federal court rejects Bush bid to block hand counts Nov. 13; Volusia finishes recount Nov. 14.

Nov. 13

Florida Secretary of State Katherine Harris says she will enforce state law deadline of Nov. 14 for counties to submit returns and will not include manual recounts; election boards in Volusia and Palm Beach Counties ask state court judge to overturn deadline.

Nov. 14–16

Leon County Circuit Judge Terry P. Lewis says Harris must justify her position on deadline; Harris reaffirms decision Nov. 15; Lewis hears new round of arguments Nov. 16.

Nov. 17

Lewis upholds Harris's decision to disregard manual recounts, but Florida Supreme Court bars certification of state results pending oral arguments on Nov. 20; federal appeals court rejects Bush suit over manual recounts.

Nov. 18

Bush lead grows to 930 votes with absentee ballots; Bush campaign criticizes Democrats for challenging absentee votes from military.

Nov. 21

Florida Supreme Court rules manual recounts must be included in presidential race if submitted to Harris by 5:00 p.m. Sunday, Nov. 26.

Nov. 22–24

Bush running mate Richard B. Cheney has heart attack, leaves Washington hospital two days later after surgery to insert stent in artery. Shouting, fist-waving crowd, including Republican congressional aides, tries to enter private room where Miami-Dade has resumed recounts. County stops recount, pleading too little time and denying intimidation by the demonstrators. State Supreme Court rejects Nov. 23 Gore suit to force Miami-Dade to resume counting. U.S. Supreme Court agrees to hear Bush appeal of Florida Supreme Court action allowing extended deadline for certifying presidential race.

Nov. 25–26

Manual recounts: Broward finishes Nov. 25; Palm Beach falls just short of completion Nov. 26. Harris announces Nov. 26 that state elections canvassing board certifies Bush as winner by 537-vote margin; Bush claims victory, says he and Cheney are "honored and humbled" to have won Florida's electoral votes.

heard the arguments Dec. 1. In Tallahassee, after hearing two days of televised testimony, Leon County Circuit Judge N. Sanders Sauls ruled that Gore failed to prove the need for manual recounts. Gore's witnesses had testified that "chad buildup" and poorly maintained equipment could prevent voters from cleanly punching out a machine-read ballot. Gore received another setback the same day, Dec. 4, when the U.S. Supreme Court returned the deadline-extension case to the Florida high court for clarification.

Gore scored a short-lived victory Dec. 8 when the Florida court by a 4–3 vote ordered a resumption of the hand counts, only to have the U.S. Supreme Court halt them the following day, pending its decision in *Bush v. Gore.* In its 5–4 decision, handed down Dec. 12, the Court majority ruled for Bush that the lack of uniform standards for manual recounts denied "equal protection of the laws" to Florida voters. The Court split along ideological lines in the unsigned decision. In the majority were conservatives William Rehnquist, Antonin Scalia, Clarence Thomas, Anthony Kennedy, and Sandra Day O'Connor. Dissenting were liberals or moderates Stephen Breyer, Ruth Bader Ginsburg, David Souter, and John Paul Stevens.

The Court action left 42,000 Florida undervotes unexamined, including 35,000 from the punch-card counties, but it effectively resolved the 2000 presidential race and possibly averted a constitutional crisis that might have arisen had the dispute resulted in Florida's sending two sets of electoral votes to Congress. The state legislature had already designated a slate of electors committed to Bush. Faced with a hopeless situation, Gore folded his campaign and conceded Dec. 13. "Let there be no doubt," Gore said, "while I strongly disagree with the Court's decision, I accept it. . . ." And he called on the American people to unite behind the next president, George W. Bush.

Nov. 27–29

Gore formally contests the Florida election Nov. 27. He sues in Leon County Circuit Court, in Tallahassee, claiming the number of legal votes "improperly rejected" and illegal votes counted in Nassau, Palm Beach, and Miami-Dade Counties is enough to change outcome. Judge N. Sanders Sauls orders ballots brought to Tallahassee for possible counting. More than one million ballots are trucked with police escort to the state capital.

Dec. 1

U.S. Supreme Court hears Bush appeal of deadline extension. Florida justices refuse to order revote requested in Palm Beach County because of controversial "butterfly ballot" used there.

Dec. 2–3

Judge Sauls hears testimony on whether 13,000 ballots from Miami-Dade and Palm Beach Counties should be manually counted. Both sides call witnesses on reliability of punch-card voting systems.

Dec. 4

Sauls rejects Gore's request for manual recount and refuses to decertify Bush as winner. U.S. Supreme Court asks state high court to explain its Nov. 21 action allowing manual recounting and extending deadlines.

Dec. 8–9

Florida justices order hand count of ballots on which machines found no vote for president. U.S. Supreme Court halts the hand counts the next day.

Dec. 10–11

U.S. Supreme Court receives briefs and hears arguments in *Bush v. Gore.*

Dec. 12

U.S. Supreme Court splits 5–4 in ruling for Bush against further hand counts. Florida legislature convenes special session to meet the federal deadline for designating presidential electors. Twenty states miss the deadline by a few days.

Dec. 13

Gore concedes election, congratulates Bush, and jokingly adds "and I promised him that this time I wouldn't call him back."

Dec. 18

Presidential electors meet in state capitals to cast votes. One District of Columbia elector, Barbara Lett-Simmons, withholds her vote from Gore in protest of D.C.'s lack of representation in Congress. Final electoral vote tally is 271 for Bush, 266 for Gore with one abstention.

Jan. 6, 2001

Congress meets in joint session to count electoral votes. As Senate president, Vice President Gore presides over his own defeat. Twenty Gore supporters, mostly Congressional Black Caucus members, try to block Florida's votes, but Gore rejects each representative's written objection because none has also been signed by a senator as the 1887 Electoral Vote Count Act requires.

Jan. 20

Inauguration of Bush as president and Cheney as vice president. Protests, largely nonviolent, mar—but do not disrupt—the inaugural parade.

When the presidential electors met in their states Dec. 18 to cast their ballots, one District of Columbia elector withheld her vote from Gore in protest of the District's lack of representation in Congress. This reduced Gore's electoral vote total to 266 against 271 for Bush. Gore received 51.0 million votes (48.4 percent) to 50.5 million (47.9 percent) for Bush. Gore's lead in the popular vote was 537,179. Nader's 2.9 million votes amounted to 2.7 percent of the total. Buchanan received less than 1 percent with 449,077 votes.

An embarrassing loss to Gore was his own state of Tennessee and its eleven electoral votes. Had he won there he would have had an electoral vote majority and the Florida vote would have been irrelevant.

Several Democrats publicly blamed Nader for costing Gore the election. Nader drew more than 97,000 votes in Florida. Had he withdrawn from the race before the election, as many Democrats had prevailed upon him to do, enough voters might have switched from Nader to Gore to have given the state's electoral votes to the Democrats and averted the ballot dispute. According to elections specialist Rhodes Cook, however, Buchanan's presence in the race may have offset any harm Gore suffered from Nader's presence in the race. In four states with a total of thirty electoral votes—Iowa, New Mexico, Oregon, and Wisconsin—the number of votes cast for Buchanan exceeded Gore's margin of victory in those states. In addition to Florida, Nader's vote was greater than Bush's margin of victory in New Hampshire as well as Florida, for a total of twenty-nine electoral votes. So Cook concluded that the effect of the two third-party candidacies on the electoral votes was "essentially a wash."

Senate Elections

Had the presidential election not been so close, public attention would have been riveted by the Senate elections. Not only did the Senate end up evenly divided between the two parties, but for the first time ever a sitting First Lady stood for election to public office, and a popular Democratic governor ousted a Republican freshman even though the Democrat had died shortly before the election.

Republicans were stunned by their losses in the Senate, where the GOP was defending nineteen seats to the Democrats' fifteen. Five Republican incumbents lost their seats, and the GOP picked up only one of four open Democratic seats, while the Democrats lost only one incumbent and picked off the one open Republican seat. Only once before had an election resulted in a Senate equally divided between the two major parties. The election of 1880 produced a Republican president, James Garfield, and a Senate of thirty-seven Republicans, thirty-seven Democrats, and two independents.

The most dramatic Democratic victory came in Missouri where Gov. Mel Carnahan, who had died in a plane crash three weeks before the election, outpolled freshman Republican incumbent John Ashcroft. The race had been close before the accident, and Carnahan's death placed Ashcroft in the awkward position of running against a dead man and his widow, Jean, who had agreed to take Carnahan's place in the Senate if he won the election. Although some Republicans talked of challenging the election, Ashcroft said the day after the election that he would not contest it or support anyone who did, and the GOP agreed to honor that concession. President-elect Bush subsequently chose Ashcroft as his attorney general.

In two other races the contest was so close that the outcome was not known immediately. In Michigan, Democratic Rep. Debbie Stabenow eked out a narrow margin over freshman Republican Sen. Spencer Abraham, who was later named secretary of energy. In Washington state, former Rep. Maria Cantwell, a Democrat, was declared the victor over three-term Republican Sen. Slade Gorton. Gorton conceded on Dec. 1 after a recount gave Cantwell a lead of about 2,200 votes.

The other losing Republicans were five-term GOP Sen. William V. Roth Jr. of Delaware, and freshman Sen. Rod Grams of Minnesota. Roth was defeated by Democrat Thomas R. Carper, the state's popular two-term governor who had also served ten years in the House (1983–1993). Grams lost to former state auditor and department store heir Mark Dayton, who pumped nearly $12 million of his own money into the race. Democrats also won the open seat being vacated by retiring Republican Sen. Connie Mack of Florida, when Democratic state Insurance Commissioner Bill Nelson beat Republican Rep. Bill McCollum for the seat. McCollum was best known as a House manager during the impeachment trial of President Clinton in 1999. Nelson had served in the U.S. House from 1979 to 1991.

Women in Congress, 1947–2001

Congress		Senate	House
80th	(1947–1949)	1	7
81st	(1949–1951)	1	9
82nd	(1951–1953)	1	10
83rd	(1953–1955)	3	11
84th	(1955–1957)	1	15
85th	(1957–1959)	1	15
86th	(1959–1961)	1	16
87th	(1961–1963)	2	18
88th	(1963–1965)	2	12
89th	(1965–1967)	2	11
90th	(1967–1969)	1	11
91st	(1969–1971)	1	10
92nd	(1971–1973)	2	13
93rd	(1973–1975)	0	16
94th	(1975–1977)	0	17
95th	(1977–1979)	2	18
96th	(1979–1981)	1	16
97th	(1981–1983)	2	21
98th	(1983–1985)	2	22
99th	(1985–1987)	2	23
100th	(1987–1989)	2	23
101st	(1989–1991)	2	28
102nd	(1991–1993)	3	28
103rd	(1993–1995)	7	47
104th	(1995–1997)	9	48
105th	(1997–1999)	9	54
106th	(1999–2001)	9	56
107th	(2001–2003)	13	60

NOTE: Totals are for an entire Congress. They include women elected in general and special elections as well as those who were appointed to office. Members sworn in after the adjournment of a Congress are not counted in the total for that Congress. House totals exclude nonvoting delegates. Totals for the 107th Congress are through Dec. 31, 2001.

The Republican gains were in Virginia, where former GOP Gov. George F. Allen ousted Democratic Sen. Charles S. Robb, and Nevada, where former GOP Rep. John Ensign (1995–1999) defeated Democratic Las Vegas lawyer Ed Bernstein for the seat being vacated by retiring Democrat Richard H. Bryan. Ensign had lost a 1998 Senate bid against Democratic Sen. Harry Reid by just 428 votes.

Perhaps the most closely watched race, however, was in New York, where First Lady Hillary Rodham Clinton was running for the seat being vacated by retiring Democratic Sen. Daniel Patrick Moynihan. Clinton, the first sitting presidential spouse ever elected to office, had expected to run against New York City's Republican Mayor Rudolph W. Giuliani. In May Giuliani announced that he had prostate cancer and would not seek the Senate seat, and the state GOP quickly nominated Rep. Rick A. Lazio to take Giuliani's place. Clinton defeated Lazio 55 percent to 43 percent, in large measure by drawing unusually high support in upstate New York, which traditionally supported Republicans.

The election of three freshman women—Clinton, Cantwell, and Stabenow—together with the appointment of Jean Carnahan to her husband's seat meant that thirteen women would sit in the Senate in the 107th Congress, the most in Senate history.

Another notable race occurred in New Jersey, where former Wall Street CEO John Corzine, a Democrat, spent $60 million of his own money on his campaign. His Republican opponent, Rep. Bob Franks, whittled down Corzine's once wide lead by charging that Corzine was trying to buy the election. But with only about $6 million to spend, Franks could not compete over the airwaves with Corzine, who narrowly won the seat being vacated by retiring Democratic Sen. Frank R. Lautenberg.

House Elections

Republicans withstood an aggressive Democratic attempt to win control of the U.S. House, losing a net of only two seats. The election resulted in a party lineup of 221 Republicans, 212 Democrats, and two independents. The last time the House was so closely divided was after the 1952 election, when the GOP also held the majority. (Democratic Rep. Julian Dixon of California died on Dec. 8, leaving the major party lineup at 221–211, but Democrats were expected to win a special election in 2001 to fill the vacancy.)

The 2000 election marked the first time since 1924 that the GOP had won a majority of the House seats in four consecutive elections. But it was also the third straight election that the party had lost seats. After losing a net of fifty-two seats and control of the House in 1994, Democrats gained nine seats in 1996 and five seats in 1998.

Democrats had expected a better showing. Republicans had to defend twenty-six of the thirty-five seats left open by incumbents who retired, sought other office, or were defeated in primary elections. But the Democrats were able to capture only six open Republican seats, a gain that was nullified when Republicans captured six of the nine open Democratic seats. "We lost a lot of very close races," said David Plouffe, executive director of the Democratic Congressional Campaign Committee, in his interpretation of why the party failed to regain control of the House.

As usual, incumbents in both parties fared well. Of the 403 House members who sought reelection, three lost in the primaries and six lost in the general election, an incumbent retention rate of 97.8 percent. Two of the six incumbents to lose their seats in the general election were Democrats who had not been thought to be in serious trouble until late in the campaign. In Connecticut's Second District, Rep. Sam Gejdenson lost his bid for an eleventh term to Republican state Rep. Rob Simmons, while four-term Democratic Rep. David Minge lost his race in Minnesota's Second District to Republican businessman Mark Kennedy.

Three of the four Republican incumbents to lose in the general election were from California. Two-term Rep. James E. Rogan lost to Democratic state senator Adam Schiff in a race in which the candidates spent more than $11 million combined. Republicans said Rogan's defeat was attributable to the Democratic trend in the Twenty-seventh District and not to Rogan's role as a House manager in the politically

Blacks in Congress, 1947–2001

Congress		Senate	House
80th	(1947–1949)	0	2
81st	(1949–1951)	0	2
82nd	(1951–1953)	0	2
83rd	(1953–1955)	0	2
84th	(1955–1957)	0	3
85th	(1957–1959)	0	4
86th	(1959–1961)	0	4
87th	(1961–1963)	0	4
88th	(1963–1965)	0	5
89th	(1965–1967)	0	6
90th	(1967–1969)	1	5
91st	(1969–1971)	1	10
92nd	(1971–1973)	1	12
93rd	(1973–1975)	1	15
94th	(1975–1977)	1	16
95th	(1977–1979)	1	16
96th	(1979–1981)	0	16
97th	(1981–1983)	0	18
98th	(1983–1985)	0	21
99th	(1985–1987)	0	21
100th	(1987–1989)	0	23
101st	(1989–1991)	0	24
102nd	(1991–1993)	0	26
103rd	(1993–1995)	1	39
104th	(1995–1997)	1	38
105th	(1997–1999)	1	38
106th	(1999–2001)	0	37
107th	(2001–2003)	0	37

NOTE: Totals are for an entire Congress. They include blacks elected in general and special elections as well as those who were appointed to office. Members sworn in after the adjournment of a Congress are not counted in the total for that Congress. House totals exclude nonvoting delegates. Totals for the 107th Congress are through Dec. 31, 2001.

unpopular impeachment trial of President Clinton in early 1999.

In California's Thirty-sixth District, Democrat Jane Harman narrowly edged out freshman Republican Steven T. Kuykendall to reclaim the seat she had held from 1993 to 1999, when she retired to make an unsuccessful run for governor. In the Forty-ninth District, Democratic state Rep. Susan David defeated three-term Republican Brian P. Bilbray.

The fourth Republican incumbent to lose was Jay Dickey, who represented Arkansas's Fourth District. President Clinton, who was born and raised in that district, campaigned for Dickey's opponent, Democratic state senator Mike Ross, who won with 51 percent of the vote.

Reinforcing the presence of an evenly divided electorate, twenty-five House races were decided by less than 52 percent of the vote in their district. That number was larger than in 1998 but still minuscule in comparison with the hundreds of House races that were won in 2000 with little or no competition at all.

The number of African Americans and Hispanics in the House stayed the same, at thirty-seven and nineteen respectively. The number of women in the House increased by four, to a total of sixty.

Hispanics in Congress, 1947–2001

Congress		Senate	House
80th	(1947–1949)	1	1
81st	(1949–1951)	1	1
82nd	(1951–1953)	1	1
83rd	(1953–1955)	1	1
84th	(1955–1957)	1	1
85th	(1957–1959)	1	1
86th	(1959–1961)	1	1
87th	(1961–1963)	1	2
88th	(1963–1965)	0	3
89th	(1965–1967)	1	4
90th	(1967–1969)	1	4
91st	(1969–1971)	1	5
92nd	(1971–1973)	1	6
93rd	(1973–1975)	1	6
94th	(1975–1977)	1	6
95th	(1977–1979)	0	5
96th	(1979–1981)	0	6
97th	(1981–1983)	0	7
98th	(1983–1985)	0	10
99th	(1985–1987)	0	11
100th	(1987–1989)	0	11
101st	(1989–1991)	0	11
102nd	(1991–1993)	0	11
103rd	(1993–1995)	0	17
104th	(1995–1997)	0	17
105th	(1997–1999)	0	18
106th	(1999–2001)	0	19
107th	(2001–2003)	0	19

NOTE: Totals are for an entire Congress. They include Hispanics elected in general and special elections as well as those who were appointed to office. Members sworn in after the adjournment of a Congress are not counted in the total for that Congress. House totals exclude nonvoting delegates. Totals for the 107th Congress are through Dec. 31, 2001.

State Elections

Elections for governors and state legislatures were particularly important in 2000 as the two parties jockeyed for position in the redistricting that would occur as a result of the 2000 Census. Republicans continued to dominate the nation's governor's mansions, holding twenty-nine governorships to the Democrats' nineteen. Two states, Maine and Minnesota, were governed by independents. Republicans controlled eighteen state legislatures to the Democrats' sixteen, while control was divided in fifteen states. Nebraska's unicameral legislature was nonpartisan. The Democrats had controlled both chambers in twenty states after the 1998 elections, the Republicans seventeen.

Only eleven states had gubernatorial races in 2000. Party control of a governorship changed only in West Virginia, where Democratic Rep. Bob Wise defeated Republican Gov. Cecil H. Underwood. The elections also produced a record number of female governors: five women were slated to become chief executives of their states, and Sila Calderon was elected to govern in Puerto Rico. One of those women, Gov. Christine Todd Whitman, subsequently resigned her seat to become head of the Environmental Protection Agency in the Bush administration. But the number of female governors went back up to five early in 2001, when Jane Swift, the Republican lieutenant governor of Massachusetts, became acting governor after President Bush named Gov. Paul Celucci as his ambassador to Canada.

Ballot initiatives around the country presented voters with some of the contentious issues that Congress had been avoiding. Almost half of the seventy-one statewide initiatives on ballots around the country were approved on Nov. 7. Among the notable initiatives adopted were those in Colorado and Oregon to require background checks of would-be gun purchasers at gun shows. Voters in Nebraska and Nevada supported bans on same-sex unions, while voters in Maine voted down a proposal to ban discrimination based on sexual orientation. Maine voters also rejected an assisted suicide measure. Voters in California and Michigan turned aside school voucher measures.

Special Election

Only one special election was required in 2000 and that was to fill the vacancy left by the death of Sen. Paul Coverdell of Georgia. A highly regarded Republican as well as an adroit inside player, Coverdell died on July 18 of complications following a cerebral hemorrhage. Coverdell first won election to the Senate in 1992 and gained a second term in 1998.

In addition to losing a well-loved colleague, Senate Republicans also lost a Senate seat. On July 24 Georgia Democratic Gov. Roy Barnes appointed Democrat Zell Miller, a former two-term Georgia governor (1991–1999), to fill the seat until a special election, scheduled for Nov. 7, coincident with the general election, could be held to fill the seat for the remaining four years of Coverdell's term. Miller, a moderate and one of Georgia's most popular politicians, won that special election, beating former Republican Sen. Mack Mattingly (1981–1987) 58 percent to 38 percent.

CHAPTER 2

Economic Policy

Introduction	33
The Federal Budget	40
Tax Policy	87
Financial Regulation	120

Economic Policy

Bill Clinton had the good fortune to be president during almost the entire ten-year run of the longest economic expansion in American history. Clinton argued, of course, that luck was only part of the equation, and that his government's budgetary and economic policies provided a solid basis for the expansion. The president's detractors in the Republican Party instead gave the credit to the American public and business community, as well as to the monetary policies of the Federal Reserve Board, headed by Republican Alan Greenspan. The voters apparently sided with Clinton in 1996, returning him to office for a second term, making him the first Democrat to serve two full terms in his own right since Franklin Delano Roosevelt a half century earlier.

In 2000, however, that history of economic growth was not enough to power Clinton's designated successor, Vice President Al Gore, into the White House. George W. Bush, who squeaked into the presidency by the thinnest of margins, was left to face a recession that officially began in the second quarter of 2001 and deepened later in the year. Bush thus followed his father as the second President Bush in ten years to preside over a recession.

A DECADE OF ECONOMIC GROWTH

Officially, the economic expansion of the 1990s began in the second quarter of 1991 after a brief one-year recession. Some aspects of the recession, such as rising unemployment, continued well into 1992, however, giving Clinton a powerful political argument in that election year against the first President Bush.

By February 2000, the expansion had been under way for 107 months, making it the longest in U.S. history. The previous record holder had been the 106-month-long expansion of 1961–1969, part of which was sustained by spending during the Vietnam War. Clinton thus became the first president since Lyndon B. Johnson (1963–1969) who could say a recession had not occurred while he was in office. At the end of Clinton's presidency the expansion had lasted for 118 months.

During Clinton's tenure in the White House economic growth averaged 4.0 percent per year compared with an average growth of 2.8 percent during the expansion of the 1980s. The high point was in 1997 and 1998 when the economy expanded by 4.4 percent (as measured by the "real," or inflation-adjusted, gross domestic product), but the growth slowed considerably in 2000, to just 3.4 percent. Most of the slowdown occurred in the second half of 2000 when business investment (especially in high-technology equipment and software) declined sharply.

As his second term ended Clinton could (and often did) point to a long list of superlatives about the U.S. economic performance while he was in office. Among the figures he most often cited: more than 22.5 million jobs were created, 92 percent of which were in the private sector; the median family income increased by more than $6,000, to $48,950; unemployment fell to the lowest level in more than thirty years, to 4.0 percent in 2000; inflation averaged just 2.5 percent during Clinton's presidency, the lowest rate since the early 1960s; the poverty rate declined to a three-decade low of 11.8 percent by 1999; and the rate of home ownership among Americans reached a record high of nearly 67.7 percent in late 2000. The federal government's budget deficit, which had reached $290 billion the year before Clinton took office, fell sharply during the 1990s and turned into a large surplus by fiscal 1998.

For most Americans, these figures touted by Clinton were less important than the fact that they felt more prosperous than they had in many years. During the economic boom of

REFERENCES

Discussion of economic policy for the years 1945–1964 may be found in *Congress and the Nation Vol. I*, pp. 337–458; for the years 1965–1968, *Congress and the Nation Vol. II*, pp. 119–182, 253–305; for the years 1969–1972, *Congress and the Nation Vol. III*, pp. 53–145; for the years 1973–1976, *Congress and the Nation Vol. IV*, pp. 49–149; for the years 1977–1980, *Congress and the Nation Vol. V*, pp. 205–287; for the years 1981–1984, *Congress and the Nation Vol. VI*, pp. 27–120; for the years 1985–1988, *Congress and the Nation Vol. VII*, pp. 27–136; for the years 1989–1992, *Congress and the Nation Vol. VIII*, pp. 31–161; for the years 1993–1996, *Congress and the Nation Vol. IX*, pp. 31–148.

ECONOMIC LEADERSHIP

Holders of the top positions in the government's five key economic and budget policy agencies engaged in a game of musical chairs during President Bill Clinton's presidency, with fifteen different occupants of those posts. But there was more stability than those numbers might indicate. Some officials served in more than one post, and the two most visible positions were held for most of Clinton's eight years by two men who were widely respected in both the financial and political worlds: Robert E. Rubin served as Treasury secretary from January 1995 until June 1999 (after serving earlier as head of Clinton's National Economic Council), and Alan Greenspan continued his long tenure, throughout Clinton's presidency, as chairman of the Federal Reserve Board of Governors. The presence of Rubin and Greenspan, along with others, led many observers to argue that Clinton's economic team was the strongest group of officials in his administration. Lesser-known officials held some critical economic posts at the end of Clinton's tenure, but by then most major decisions on economic matters had already been made and the economy was humming along in a record-breaking expansion. *(Clinton's first-term economic team, Congress and the Nation Vol. IX, p. 32)*

Treasury Department

Clinton's first Treasury secretary was former Senator Lloyd M. Bentsen, a Texas Democrat who had chaired the Finance Committee and was Democratic nominee for vice president in 1988 (when Michael Dukakis lost to George Bush). Bentsen served during 1993 and 1994 and provided the new president—who himself had no Washington experience—with an important degree of credibility on Capitol Hill. Bentsen was succeeded in January 1995 by Rubin, a former cochairman of the Goldman Sachs investment firm who commanded deep respect on Wall Street, among international financial circles, and in Congress.

Rubin returned to private life in 1999 and was succeeded by Lawrence H. Summers, who had been deputy secretary since August 1995 and undersecretary for international affairs from 1993 to 1995. Summers was a former chief econo-

mist at the World Bank and an economics professor at Harvard. Summers also was viewed in the financial markets and in Congress as a strong and knowledgeable figure, although his often-brash style made him a somewhat more controversial figure than Rubin had been.

Federal Reserve Board of Governors

Since 1987 the powerful Federal Reserve Board (Fed) had been pretty much a one-man show, and the same man remained in place all during Clinton's presidency. Greenspan, whose murky verbiage may have contributed to his oracle-like stature in the financial world, was first named Fed chairman in 1987 by President Ronald Reagan. President George Bush reappointed him to a second term, and Clinton had two opportunities, in 1996 and 2000, to reassure the financial markets by keeping Greenspan in place.

Greenspan's reappointments were not without controversy. In both 1996 and 2000, some congressional Democrats argued that the Republican Fed chairman had been too quick to raise interest rates to head off the prospect of inflation. The Fed had raised interest rates in 1994–1995 and again in 1999–2000, in both cases because Greenspan was concerned that an overheated economy might become inflationary. The latter round of action by the Fed had helped push real interest rates to their highest levels in fifteen years. Despite such criticisms, the Senate confirmed Greenspan by wide margins on both occasions: by a 91–7 vote in June 1996 and by an 89–4 vote in February 2000.

A relatively large cast of economic experts served with Greenspan on the seven-member Fed board during the Clinton years. Four people served as vice-chairman: David W. Mullins Jr., a holdover appointed by Bush who served until February 1994; Alan S. Blinder, a former Princeton University professor, whom Clinton appointed in 1994 and who served until February 1996; Alice M. Rivlin, a veteran Washington insider who had been director of the White House Office of Management and Budget (OMB) and who served in the Fed until July 1999; and, finally, Roger W. Ferguson Jr., a former partner of the international consulting firm McKinsey and

the 1990s Americans invested heavily in the stock market through pension funds and direct investments. With interest rates low they purchased more luxurious homes. As a result, millions saw their net worth soar to unimaginable highs. Gas prices were low, so Americans bought bigger cars, especially gas-guzzling sport utility vehicles. Clothing and electronic products imported from overseas were relatively inexpensive because of the strong dollar and reduced tariffs.

A "NEW ECONOMY"?

The Clinton administration proclaimed in 2000 that information technology (computers, software, the Internet,

and related services) had helped transform the overall U.S. economy into a "new economy" that was fundamentally different from the old manufacturing-based economy. The high-tech sector remained a relatively small part of the economy, accounting for only about 8.3 percent of gross domestic product in 2000, according to the White House. But that sector was responsible for nearly one-third of all growth in output during the last half of the 1990s.

The very features of the economy during the decade—high growth rates coupled with low unemployment and low inflation—justified the use of the term "new economy," the White House said.

Co., whom Clinton had first appointed to the Fed board in 1997. Ferguson's term as vice-chairman was scheduled to run until October 2003.

Clinton made two other appointments to fill vacancies on the Fed board. In 1996 he appointed Lawrence H. Meyer, a prominent economic forecaster, for a term expiring in January 2002; and in 1997 he appointed Edward Gramlich, dean of the School of Public Policy at the University of Michigan, to a term expiring in January 2008.

The Senate approved all of Clinton's nominations to the Fed board by wide (usually unanimous) margins, except for that of Rivlin. As White House budget chief she had angered many Republicans during budget battles between the Clinton administration and Congress. The Senate confirmed her nomination on June 20, 1996, by a vote of 57–41, with all the "no" votes coming from Republicans.

Office of Management and Budget

Rivlin may have been one of Clinton's most combative budget directors but she certainly was not his only one. Four people served in that key post during Clinton's presidency.

Leon E. Panetta, a California Democrat who had chaired the House Budget Committee while in Congress, was Clinton's first budget director. A moderate who was highly respected in both parties on Capitol Hill, Panetta played a key role in establishing the president's central priority of reducing the budget deficit. Panetta moved to the White House as Clinton's chief of staff in July 1994 and was succeeded at OMB by Rivlin, who had been his deputy. Rivlin had served as the first director of the Congressional Budget Office during the 1970s and later was a fellow at the Brookings Institution.

When Rivlin left her post to go to the Federal Reserve Board in 1996, Clinton named as her successor Franklin D. Raines, then vice-chairman of the Federal National Mortgage Association (Fannie Mae). Raines served for nearly two years then returned to Fannie Mae as chairman-designate in May 1998. Clinton then appointed Raines's deputy at OMB, Jacob J. Lew, to take the top post. A former congressional aide and Washington attorney, Lew served as OMB chief through the end of Clinton's presidency.

National Economic Council

Shortly after taking office, Clinton created a new entity in the White House called the National Economic Council. Clinton described the council, which was to coordinate economic policy within the administration, as a counterpart to the National Security Council, the staff of which coordinated defense and foreign policy. Many Washington observers suggested that the council could diminish the role of a venerable White House institution, the Council of Economic Advisers (CEA), which many presidents had used as a sort of economic think tank.

Rubin was the first head of the National Economic Council, and his personal stature gave the new office a degree of credibility. Rubin served in the post until he became Treasury secretary in January 1995. His successor was Laura D'Andrea Tyson, who had been head of the Council of Economic Advisers. Tyson served through the rest of Clinton's first term, then resigned and was succeeded by her deputy, Gene B. Sperling, who served throughout the second term. Sperling was one of the few senior White House officials who served the entire length of Clinton's presidency.

Council of Economic Advisers

The three-member CEA had a host of occupants during Clinton's two terms, including four different chairmen. Tyson, a former economics professor at the University of California at Berkeley, was the first to lead the CEA, serving until she moved over to the National Economic Council in February 1995. She was succeeded by Joseph E. Stiglitz, a council member since 1993; he was on leave from Stanford University, where he had been a professor of economics.

Stiglitz left the council in 1997 to become chief economist at the World Bank. As his successor, Clinton appointed Janet Yellen, a former economics professor at the University of California at Berkeley, who had been a member of the Board of Governors of the Federal Reserve system since 1994. Yellen served two years and was succeeded in 1999 by Martin N. Baily, a former principal at McKinsey and Co. He served as chairman through the end of the administration.

Except for brief moments in 1995 and 1996 the nation's unemployment rate headed in just one direction during Clinton's presidency: down. When Clinton took office in January 1993 the annual unemployment rate stood at 7.5 percent, its highest level since 1984 when the country was just beginning to emerge from the 1982–1983 recession. In real terms that rate meant that about 10 million people who wanted jobs were without them. The unemployment rate started on its downward path early in 1993 and dropped below 6 percent in 1996, fell below 5 percent in 1997, and briefly dipped below 4 percent in 2000. By the end of Clinton's presidency, the un-

employment rate had been under 5 percent for forty consecutive months, a modern-day record.

The surging economy helped all Americans find jobs, even those historically left behind during many other periods of prosperity. The unemployment rate for blacks was cut in half, from about 14 percent at the start of 1993 to 7.3 percent in late 2000, and for Hispanics the rate fell from just under 12 percent in early 1993 to 5 percent in late 2000. In both cases, the 2000 unemployment rates were historic lows.

Inflation—periodically the scourge of the U.S. economy since the early 1970s—all but disappeared as a significant

Deficit History, 1929–2000

(Fiscal years in billions of dollars)

Fiscal Year	Receipts	Outlays	Surplus or Deficit (−)
1929	3.9	3.1	0.7
1933	2.0	4.6	−2.6
1939	6.3	9.1	−2.8
1940	6.5	9.5	−2.9
1945	45.2	92.7	−47.6
1950	39.4	42.6	−3.1
1955	65.5	68.4	−3.0
1960	92.5	92.2	0.3
1965	116.8	118.2	−1.4
1969	186.9	183.6	3.2
1970	192.8	195.6	−2.8
1975	279.1	332.3	−53.2
1980	517.1	590.9	−73.8
1981	599.3	678.2	−79.0
1982	617.8	745.8	−128.0
1983	600.6	808.4	−207.8
1984	666.5	851.9	−185.4
1985	734.1	946.4	−212.3
1986	769.2	990.5	−221.2
1987	854.4	1,004.1	−149.8
1988	909.3	1,064.5	−155.2
1989	991.2	1,143.7	−152.5
1990	1,032.0	1,253.2	−221.2
1991	1,055.0	1,324.4	−269.4
1992	1,091.3	1,381.7	−290.4
1993	1,154.4	1,409.5	−255.1
1994	1,258.6	1,461.9	−203.3
1995	1,351.8	1,515.8	−164.0
1996	1,453.1	1,560.6	−107.5
1997	1,579.3	1,601.3	−22.0
1998	1,721.8	1,652.6	69.2
1999	1,827.5	1,701.9	125.5
2000	2,025.2	1,788.8	236.4

SOURCE: Executive Office of the President, Office of Management and Budget, *Budget of the United States Government, Fiscal Year 2003, Historical Tables* (Washington, D.C.: Government Printing Office, 2002), Table 1.1.

issue during the Clinton years. The "core" inflation rate (the Consumer Price Index excluding volatile energy and food prices), which had been well above 5 percent on an annual basis during most of the 1980s, fell to about 3.5 percent during 1993 and never again rose above that level through 2000. The broader measure of inflation including energy and food prices fell below 2 percent from late 1997 through 1999 when oil prices slumped dramatically but then jumped back up to about 4 percent in 2000 when oil prices surged briefly.

Another key indicator of the new economy was the sustained growth in productivity during the decade—a trend made possible largely by the increasing computerization of most business sectors. From 1993 to 2000, output per hour in the nonfarm business sector (a principal measure of productivity) grew at an annual average of 2.3 percent; that compared to an average of 1.4 percent during the previous two decades, according to the president's economic report in January 2001.

FISCAL POLICY

In his first year in office Clinton adopted an economic strategy focused on reducing the federal government's budget deficit in hopes of bringing down interest rates and thus encouraging private investment that would stimulate the economy. Two other central aspects of Clinton's strategy were increased federal spending on education and research and opening international markets to expanded trade. Despite numerous political battles Clinton met or exceeded his expectations in cutting the budget deficit and promoting trade; his plans to boost federal spending in key areas were less successful because of resistance in Congress.

Clinton's first step was to persuade the then-Democratic controlled Congress in 1993 to adopt a package of budget cuts and tax increases (PL 103-66). That approach ran counter to classical economic theory, which argued that cutting government spending and raising taxes just after a recession would harm the prospects for economic growth. Republicans objected to Clinton's plan and unanimously refused to vote for it, not on theoretical grounds but simply because it raised taxes. But Democrats went along with Clinton, adopting his budget plan in 1993. That move demonstrated to financial markets that the new president was serious about curbing the chronic budget deficit, and it contributed to a steady decline in interest rates. The president's tax increases were less popular with the voters, however, and they turned Congress over to Republican control in the 1994 elections.

Another defining moment on fiscal policy came at the end of 1995 when Clinton and the new Republican leadership in the House went to the mat over spending issues, forcing a series of brief closings of most government agencies. Clinton emerged with a political victory from that encounter and went on to win a second term in 1996. During the rest of his presidency he skillfully used his veto power to force many of his spending priorities through Congress. A final budget-reduction accord (PL 105-33) between Clinton and Congress in 1997 set the stage for a surplus in fiscal year 1998, the first in nearly three decades.

The new era of budget surpluses spawned another dispute between the president and Republican leaders in Congress: how to "spend" the surplus. Clinton's suggested priorities were "saving" the financially troubled Social Security system and paying off the national debt, which stood at about $5.5 trillion. Congressional Republicans pressed instead for tax cuts for individuals and businesses. Public opinion polls showed that the voters generally sided with Clinton and Congress eventually set aside much of the early surpluses to pay off the debt. During fiscal years 1998–2000, the government bought back $363 billion in debt, saving tens of billions of dollars in long-term interest.

In retrospect, most economists agreed that Clinton's determination to stick with his fiscal policies almost certainly contributed to the economic expansion of the 1990s, even if it was not fully responsible.

A Look at the Economy, 1980–2000

Economic Growth...

Annual Percentage Change

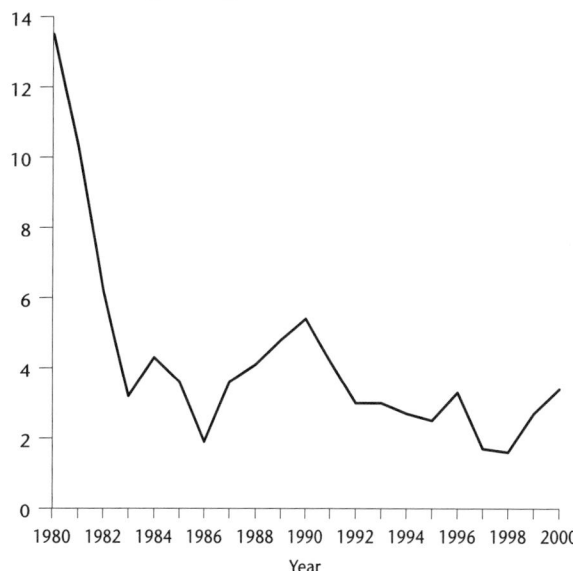

... showed a bigger decline in the 1981–1982 recession than in the shorter 1980 and 1990–1991 recessions. Recovery was sharp after the 1981–1982 recession, although not as prolonged as the robust recovery during the nine years from 1992–2000.

Growth: Annual changes in the gross domestic product (GDP).

SOURCE: Commerce Department, Bureau of Economic Analysis.

Inflation...

Annual Percentage Change

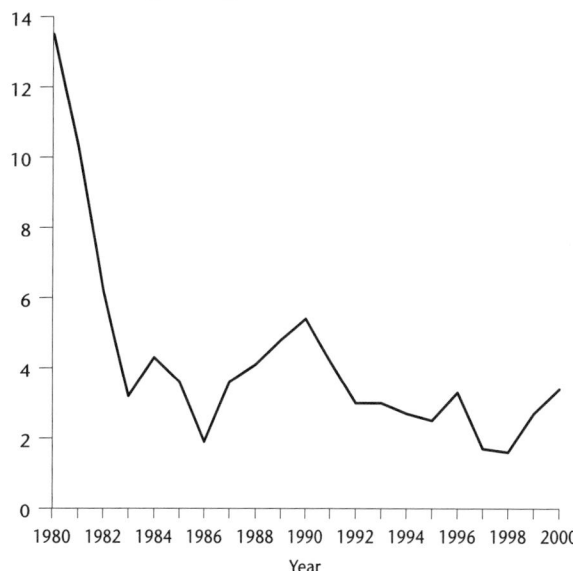

... reached historically high levels before the 1980 and 1981–1982 recessions began. The consumer price index did not hit similar peaks before the 1990–1991 recession and has showed tame increases since.

Inflation: Annual change in the consumer price index for all urban consumers, expressed as an annual average rate.

SOURCE: Labor Department, Bureau of Labor Statistics.

Unemployment...

Annual Percentage Average

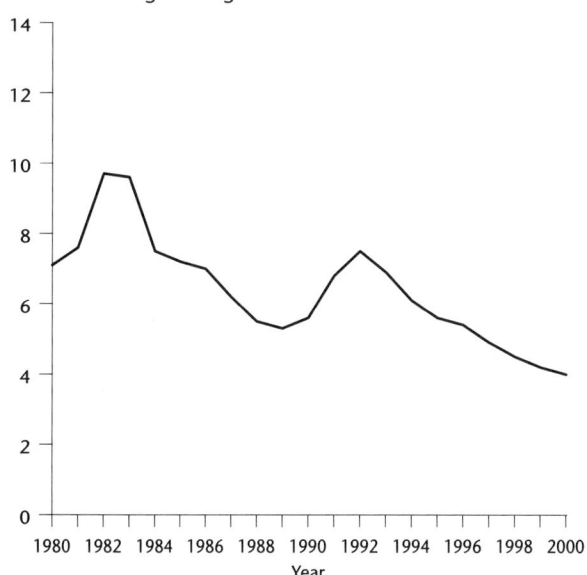

... surged during all three recessions of the past two decades and remained high for a time in the years following each one. Since 1992, the jobless rate has been on a steadily declining path as the economy expanded.

Unemployment: Annual rate of unemployment for all civilian workers (does not include the military).

SOURCE: Labor Department, Bureau of Labor Statistics.

Interest Rates...

Annual Percentage Average

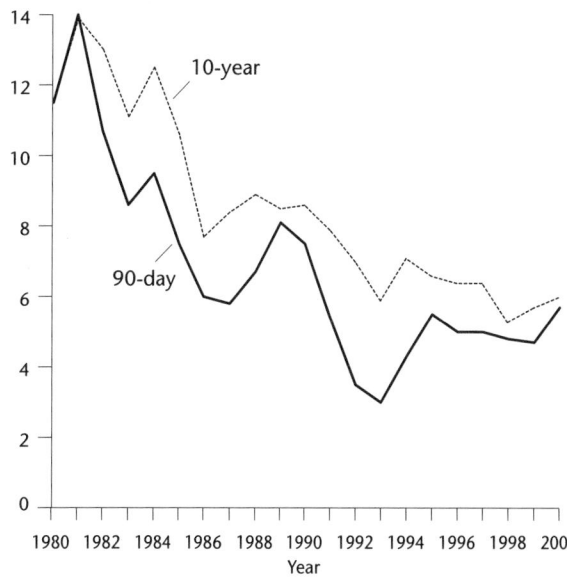

... on long- and short-term Treasury securities fell in 1993 to their lowest levels in almost twenty years, as the economy recovered slowly from the 1990–1991 recession. Since then rates rose modestly until another slight dip in 1998.

Interest rates: Annual average for new issues of 90-day Treasury bills and 10-year Treasury notes, adjusted for constant maturities.

SOURCE: Treasury Department.

MONETARY POLICY

One of many direct benefits of low inflation during the 1990s was a dampening of interest rates to levels that had been inconceivable just a decade earlier. The Federal Reserve Board, which controls the nation's money supply, generally kept interest rates low during Clinton's years in office. Responding to that policy, and to declining budget deficits after 1993, the financial markets curbed returns on Treasury bills and commercial bonds. Consumer loans, such as mortgages and new-car financing, fell to their lowest rates since the mid-1970s.

The Fed, as the Federal Reserve was commonly called, had kept a tight grip on monetary policy during much of the 1980s because of concerns about inflation. The so-called "overnight" rate on loans between banks dipped below 6 percent only once during that decade (in the fall of 1986) and hovered around 9 percent during the late 1980s. When the economy began slipping into recession toward the end of 1989 the Fed gradually eased its policy, allowing the overnight rate to fall below 3 percent early in 1993 for the first time since the early 1960s.

Then in 1994 Federal Reserve Board Chairman Greenspan and his colleagues, concerned that the economy might overheat, glimpsed signs of inflation that were not evident to anyone else and gradually boosted interest rates seven times, until the overnight rate reached 6 percent in February 1995. Inflation did not appear and the Fed gradually relaxed its policy during the next four years.

Other interest rates stayed low during most of the Clinton years. Returns on ten-year Treasury bills averaged 6 percent, or even less, from 1995 through 2000, and returns on investment-quality commercial bonds ranged between 6.5 percent to 7.5 percent in that period. Rates on thirty-year home mortgages, which had ballooned to well over 10 percent throughout the 1980s, fell to much more affordable levels of 7 percent to 8 percent during the late 1990s.

The Fed's concerns about inflation arose again in 1999, when energy and food prices began creeping up. In response the Fed began a new series of six interest rate increases that stretched through May 2000, when the federal funds rate reached 6.5 percent; that move in turn pushed real (inflation-adjusted) interest rates to their highest levels in fifteen years.

Responding to increasing signs of an economic slowdown, the Fed lowered the federal funds rate by one-half percentage point on Jan. 3, 2001. It was the first of a series of interest rate cuts that would continue all through 2001.

THE STOCK MARKET

For much of the 1990s, the U.S. stock markets seemed to defy gravity, and possibly common sense, as they soared higher and higher in tandem with the economy. All major stock indexes reached record highs in late 1999 and early 2000. The Dow-Jones Industrial Average of thirty major blue chip stocks reached a high of 11,497 and the Standard and Poor's index of 500 stocks topped out at 1,469. Most spectacular of all, the NASDAQ index (heavily weighted with high-technology stocks) soared by 86 percent during 1999 and reached a peak of 4,696 in February 2000. According to government statistics, the total market value of U.S. stock holdings was $17 trillion at the end of 1999, an increase of $10 trillion in just four years.

The bull market was driven in large part by optimism about the future of the high-technology industry, which in turn was based on the spectacular growth in use of the Internet during the decade. By 1998 and 1999, it often appeared that anyone claiming knowledge of computers and with a business plan mentioning the Internet could secure millions of dollars in financing, either through venture capitalists or through public stock offerings. Shares in companies that could not demonstrate even a remote prospect of turning a profit often sold for astronomical prices on Wall Street as investors rushed onto the high-tech bandwagon before it was too late. A notable example was Priceline.com, a money-losing promoter of discount air travel and other consumer services, which at one point in 1999 had a stock market valuation greater than the combined worth of the airlines whose tickets it was selling. Thousands of "dot-com millionaires" became the country's *nouveau riche*; most prominent among them was Microsoft Corp. cofounder Bill Gates, who by the late 1990s had a paper worth in the tens of billions of dollars and was generally considered to be the world's richest person. Millions of average Americans also benefited from the stock market, as the growing value of pension funds and personal investments created a "wealth effect" that made them more willing to spend, and that spending in turn fueled economic growth.

The high-tech bubble burst early in 2000 as a result of several factors. One was a federal district court ruling that Microsoft had violated U.S. antitrust law and should be broken into two components. Another was a growing realization among some stock market analysts that many high-tech companies were unlikely to become profitable anytime soon. Yet another factor was that businesses and governments had invested heavily in new computers and software during the late 1990s in hopes of avoiding the so-called "millennium bug"—the prospect that data processing systems built during the 1960s to 1980s would simply stop working on Jan. 1, 2000. Once that danger was past, many companies and individuals called a halt to their spending on computer systems, leaving the high-tech industry with enormous inventories of unwanted goods.

The stock markets began falling in March and April 2000, then staged a modest recovery during the summer months, only to fall again starting in October when dozens of companies reported decreased earnings for the third quarter. By the end of that year every major sector of the high-tech industry had suffered a severe drop on Wall Street. Stocks of Internet-based companies were hardest-hit, falling more than 66 percent on average, according to the Bloomberg financial news service. The NASDAQ index dropped 48 percent from its peak during 2000. So-called "old economy" stocks also fell, but not as much. The Dow Jones average dropped by 6.2 percent during 2000, and the Standard and Poor's index fell by 10.1 percent.

THE GLOBAL ECONOMY

The U.S. economy did not surge in a vacuum. In fact, most economists agreed that the performance of the economy was directly related to, and in turn affected, developments in the rest of the world. U.S. economic growth helped fuel growth in many other countries, largely because Americans spent billions of dollars buying clothes, computers, and other imported products. Moreover, American corporations invested billions of dollars overseas, just as foreign companies pumped large amounts into the U.S. economy. These expenditures were all part of an overall trend that came to be known during the Clinton years as "globalization"—a term that sought to describe the growing interdependence of the world's economies.

Globalization was in part the result of policy choices by governments in the United States and other countries. Since the late 1940s most countries, including the United States, had actively promoted foreign trade through such steps as reducing tariffs and minimizing restrictions on foreign investment. These moves reached a high point in the early 1990s with the successful conclusion of the "Uruguay Round" of international trade talks; that round established the World Trade Organization and fostered interest in regional free-trade zones, including the North American Free Trade Agreement (NAFTA) among Canada, Mexico, and the United States. (Trade policy, p. 145)

Such policy decisions by governments helped spark a boom in trade and private investment during the 1990s. Between 1993 and 1999, the annual volume of U.S. exports jumped from $456.8 billion to $684.3 billion (an increase of nearly 50 percent), and imports rose from $589.4 billion to $1.03 trillion (an increase of nearly 75 percent). During that same period, private American investments overseas more than doubled in value (to $441 billion), while private foreign investments in the United States more than tripled (to $710 billion). More goods and money entered the United States than went overseas because Americans had plenty of money to spend on imported goods, and a strong dollar made the United States a safe and attractive place for foreigners to invest their money.

A handful of other countries also enjoyed unrelenting economic growth during the decade, most notably China, which benefited from a surge of trade and investment as it replaced communist dogma with free-market economic principles. But Japan and Germany, the world's second- and third-largest

BUDGET SURPLUS: A GOAL REACHED

The federal government in 1998 recorded its first budget surplus since 1969, and the event tied lawmakers in knots as they tried to decide what to do with it. In the end, a $69.2 billion fiscal 1998 surplus ended up in the bank, taking a nibble out of the $5.5 trillion national debt. (Surplus, p. 36)

President Bill Clinton announced the official surplus on Oct. 28. Only a year earlier, Clinton and GOP lawmakers thought it would take until 2002 for their budget pact (PL 105-33) to produce balance, much less such a large surplus.

But the booming economy produced an impressive surge in tax revenues, which were largely responsible for a surplus that only the most optimistic economists had foreseen. Reduced spending for "safety net" programs such as welfare and food stamps contributed to the favorable numbers, but to a lesser extent.

The budget picture brightened steadily all year, sometimes leaving Republican leaders, especially in the House, uncertain about what to do with the unexpected funds. When they tried to cut taxes, Clinton easily blocked their plans with the potent political argument that any tax cuts should wait until Social Security was reformed and put on a sound financial footing to meet the needs of retirees in the first decades of the twenty-first century.

Clinton and the Republicans did collaborate late in the year on a $21 billion emergency supplemental spending package financed largely by the surplus. It was added to the fiscal 1999 omnibus appropriations bill (HR 4328—PL 105-277). (Emergency spending, p. 62)

Although both the White House Office of Management and Budget and the Congressional Budget Office projected steadily increasing budget surpluses into the next century, economists cautioned that an economic downturn or other unexpected event could reverse the budget picture. In a nearly $9 trillion economy, small changes could produce wild swings in surplus or deficit projections.

economies, remained sluggish, and a financial crisis that started in East Asia in 1997 spread the following year to Russia and other former Soviet bloc countries, and also to South America, including Argentina and Brazil. The strength of the U.S. economy moderated the impact of those crises: U.S. aid, through the International Monetary Fund, helped stabilize the affected countries while they recovered, and American consumers kept buying the goods those countries produced.

Chronology of Action on Economic Policy: The Federal Budget

Introduction

A generation-long era of federal budget deficits came to an end in 1998 when the government showed a surplus of $69.2 billion for the fiscal year ending Sept. 30. It was the first surplus of any kind since 1969 and the largest as a percentage of the overall size of the U.S. economy—the gross domestic product—since 1956.

President Bill Clinton announced the official surplus on Oct. 28. Only a year earlier, Clinton and Republican lawmakers who controlled Congress thought it would take until 2002 for a budget agreement they negotiated to produce balance much less such a large surplus. But the booming economy of the 1990s produced a dramatic increase in tax revenues that pushed government ledgers into surplus. As is normal during economic good times, reduced spending for "safety net" programs such as welfare and food stamps also helped, but these lower expenses contributed to the favorable numbers to a lesser extent than surging tax revenues.

In technical terms the federal government's actual operating budget for fiscal 1998 ran a deficit of $30 billion, according to the Congressional Budget Office, but a combined $99 billion surplus in the "off-budget" Social Security and Postal Service accounts masked that shortfall. The following year, fiscal 1999, the operating budget itself came into surplus of $700 million. *(Table, p. 41)*

YEARS OF DEFICITS

Until 1998 the federal government's books had dripped red ink for nearly three decades. The last budget surplus was $3.2 billion for fiscal year 1969, made possible by a 10 percent income tax surcharge used by President Lyndon Johnson (1963–1969) to help pay for the Vietnam War. Deficits were small during the administrations of Richard Nixon (1969–1974) and his successor Gerald R. Ford (1974–1977). They grew starting in fiscal 1975 when petroleum prices rose dramatically following a 1973 oil embargo by petroleum producing nations in the Middle East following renewed Arab-Israeli conflict. The oil price rise contributed to the na-tion's worst economic downturn since the Great Depression. Through the presidency of Jimmy Carter (1977–1981), when inflation was the greatest economic challenge, deficits averaged around $50 billion annually. Although a large amount of money it remained manageable when compared with the size of the overall economy.

During Ronald Reagan's presidency (1981–1989) government deficit spending accelerated dramatically. Reagan in 1981 prodded Congress to enact the biggest tax cut in U.S. history, arguing that the move would stimulate the economy. At the same time, expenditures shot up because of the president's large increases in defense outlays and the inability of the White House and Congress to agree on methods to restrain other areas of federal spending. The annual deficit crept over $100 billion in 1982 and over $200 billion in 1983 before leveling off at around $150 billion during the economic expansion in the remaining Reagan years. A recession in the middle of George Bush's presidency (1989–1993) pushed the deficit to previously unimagined heights: a record $292 billion in fiscal

REFERENCES

Discussion of federal budget policy for the years 1945–1964 may be found in *Congress and the Nation Vol. I*, pp. 387–395; for the years 1965–1968, *Congress and the Nation Vol. II*, pp. 127–140; for the years 1969–1972, *Congress and the Nation Vol. III*, pp. 63–75; for the years 1973–1976, *Congress and the Nation Vol. IV*, pp. 57–81; for the years 1977–1980, *Congress and the Nation Vol. V*, pp. 211–230; for the years 1981–1984, *Congress and the Nation Vol. VI*, pp. 33–61; for the years 1985–1988, *Congress and the Nation Vol. VII*, pp. 33–74; for the years 1989–1992, *Congress and the Nation Vol. VIII*, pp. 37–86; for the years 1993–1996, *Congress and the Nation Vol. IX*, pp. 37–82.

Federal Budget, 1993–2000

(Fiscal years in billions of dollars)

Year	Revenues	Outlays	On-Budget	Social Security	Total[1] Surplus (Deficit)	Public Debt
1993	$1,154.4	$1,409.5	–$300.5	$46.8	–$255.1	$3,248.8
1994	1,258.6	1,461.9	–258.9	56.8	–203.3	3,433.4
1995	1,351.8	1,515.8	–226.4	60.4	–164.0	3,604.8
1996	1,453.1	1,560.6	–174.1	66.4	–107.5	3,734.5
1997	1,579.3	1,601.3	–103.4	81.3	–22.0	3,772.8
1998	1,721.8	1,652.6	–30.0	99.0	69.2	3,721.6
1999	1,827.5	1,701.9	1.8	124.7	125.5	3,632.9
2000	2,025.2	1,788.8	86.6	151.8	236.4	3,410.1

1. Includes surplus (deficit) for the U.S. Postal Service.

SOURCE: Congressional Budget Office, *The Budget and Economic Outlook: Fiscal Years 2003–2012* (Washington, D.C.: Government Printing Office, 2002), Table F-1.

1992. Projections at the time put future deficits at $400 billion or more without significant spending cuts or tax increases.

President Clinton had the good fortune to take office in 1993 just as the recession was ending and the economy was beginning the longest uninterrupted period of growth in the nation's history. The economic boom generated the tax revenues that steadily whittled away at the deficit, even as Clinton and Congress struggled to restrain spending. Congress in 1993 enacted a $500 billion deficit-reduction plan of spending cuts and tax increases developed by Clinton and the Democrats, who at that time had the majority on Capitol Hill. Arguing that the plan would send the economy into decline not a single Republican voted for it. Clinton later gleefully claimed that the 1993 legislation helped stimulate the economy in the 1990s and thus contributed significantly to the government surplus that materialized in 1998.

By the time Clinton's second term began in 1997 many dramatic events had occurred in Washington, none more so than the Republican off-year election victories in 1994 that gave the GOP full control of Congress for the first time since 1953. The Republicans, led by zealous conservatives in the House and backed by a phalanx of similarly minded troops who had been swept into office in 1994, set out to make fundamental changes in the size and character of the federal government. In their zeal to shrink its size and retract what they saw as its overreaching activism they misjudged both the political skills of President Clinton and the public's general preference for the government as it had become.

Growth of Deficit and Debt

Deficit Rose and Fell, Becoming a Surplus...

Deficit as Percentage of GDP

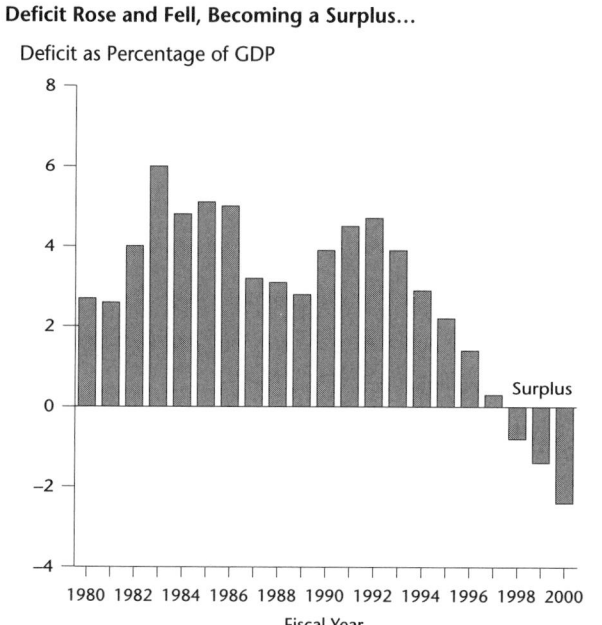

...As Debt Rose Steadily Before Falling

Debt as Percentage of GDP

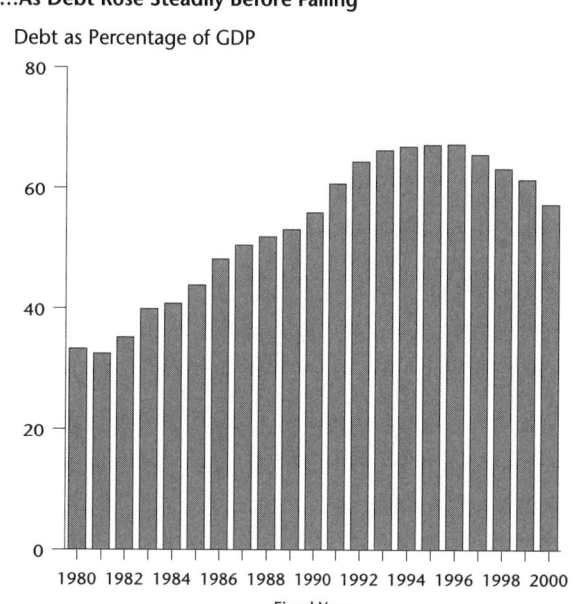

The federal deficit responded periodically during the 1980s to efforts to control it. Measured against the performance of the economy as a whole, the deficit rose in the years just after the 1990–1991 recession to 4.7 percent of gross domestic product (GDP). Then, with the economy rebounding and the Clinton administration's budget-cutting efforts having some success, the deficit began to fall dramatically reaching a surplus in 1998, the first in nearly three decades. Meanwhile, the total federal debt (including that portion owed to the Social Security trust funds) rose inexorably during the 1980s and early 1990s. The debt as a share of the economy more than doubled from about 33 percent of GDP in 1980 to 67.3 percent in 1996, before falling to 57.3 percent in 2000.

SOURCE: Office of Management and Budget, *Historical Tables, Budget of the United States Government: Fiscal Year 2002* (Washington, D.C.: U.S. Government Printing Office, 2001), Tables 7.1 and 15.6.

The ensuing battles, which the Republicans mostly lost in fact and in the realm of public opinion, contributed to Clinton's overwhelming reelection in 1996 and the loss of a number of GOP congressional seats, even though the party retained control of Congress. Thus the stage was set for the fully unexpected accommodations the two parties made early in Clinton's second term that produced the structure for long-range budget savings. Although the outcome—an end to budget deficits—was pushed along by the unprecedented prosperity of the 1990s that saw tax revenues soar, the acceptance by both parties of achieving budget discipline proved to be a primary legacy of the odd combination of a liberal Democrat in the White House and a conservative majority on Capitol Hill.

Once the budget came into surplus, however, Clinton and lawmakers engaged in extraordinary contortions to use some of the excess for priority projects while still staying within the letter—if not the spirit—of the budget law. "Emergency" spending and other accounting sleight of hand were routinely employed in the last three years of Clinton's presidency to justify appropriations that were consistently higher than the spending caps put in place in 1997.

Moreover, the problems of passing authorizing legislation were so great in the closely divided Congress that leaders began lumping everything into must-pass spending bills. Among the major pieces of authorizing legislation cleared as part of a spending bill were a reorganization of several foreign policy agencies, the reauthorization of the State Department, and a measure implementing the Chemical Weapons Convention. The spending bills also became magnets for thorny legislative riders, including funding international family planning agencies that advocated abortion, paying back dues to the United Nations, lifting some economic sanctions on Cuba, and raising the minimum wage.

Clinton, who lacked the votes in Congress to get his own legislative program passed, took full advantage of the divisions on Capitol Hill. He resorted to frequent use of the veto to block what he considered to be the worst excesses of the Republicans and to force GOP leaders to give him some of his priorities in return for his acceptance of some of theirs. In his last four years as president Clinton vetoed eight spending bills, all of which forced the congressional leadership to compromise with the president on spending priorities.

The result was a convoluted legislative process where negotiations between a few GOP leaders and the White House covered a wide range of issues across many different bills. In one case negotiations reopened legislation that had already been cleared but not sent to the president. In a couple of instances legislation was so controversial that the GOP leadership skipped floor action in one chamber and took the measure directly to conference with the other chamber. The first time rank-and-file lawmakers considered the legislation on the floor was during debate on the conference report, which was filed only hours before the vote. Democrats and Republicans alike derided the process but most acknowledged it was the only way that legislation in the intensely partisan 105th and 106th Congresses could be passed.

1997–1998

The central achievement of the 1997 congressional session for both Republicans and Democrats was a deal to balance the U.S. government's budget, a goal that had eluded Washington policy makers for more than a quarter century. The successful negotiations were propelled by a new and unusual spirit of compromise and a booming economy that was driving tax revenues higher than almost anyone had predicted. The historic agreement between President Clinton and the Republican Congress was outlined in principle in the fiscal 1998 budget resolution and then written into law with the passage of two reconciliation bills setting limits or "caps" on discretionary spending through fiscal 2002 and making changes in the tax code, including some tax cuts long sought by Republicans.

The agreement enabled Congress to clear each of the thirteen regular appropriations bills in 1997 without resorting to an omnibus spending measure. The agreement also undercut efforts by Republican conservatives to obtain approval of a constitutional amendment requiring a balanced budget. For the third year in a row, a proposed balanced-budget amendment died in the Senate.

But by the time Congress adjourned in November 1997, the bonhomie and bipartisanship surrounding the budget deal were fading in the face of partisan disputes over policy riders on some of the spending bills and on other controversial legislation. Clinton and Congress would never recover the spirit of compromise that existed in the first few months of that year.

In 1998 Congress failed to produce a budget resolution for the first time since the modern budget process was established in 1974. House and Senate Republicans were simply unable to agree on a spending or tax cut plan. The failure was all the more ironic because for the first time in three decades, the federal budget posted a surplus—well ahead of the schedule written into law in 1997.

The lack of a budget resolution, coupled with the distraction from GOP-led impeachment proceedings against President Clinton, slowed the appropriations process to a crawl in 1998. *(Impeachment, p. 813)*

Eventually GOP leaders were able to cobble together a $500 billion, budget-busting spending bill that incorporated eight individual appropriations measures into one massive omnibus piece of legislation and served as the vehicle for much of the year's limited legislative output. Republicans were forced to give into Clinton on some of his most cherished spending priorities, including funding to start a new program to hire teachers and to support the International Monetary Fund. GOP leaders also won funding for some of their priorities, included $1 billion for an antimissile defense program. But conservative Republicans were incensed that— as they saw it—their leaders had "caved in" to the president.

The 105th Congress also witnessed the first and possibly the last use by a president of the line-item veto. Legislation that allowed the president to delete individual items in spending and tax bills was signed into law in 1996 and took effect on Jan. 1, 1997. The line-item veto authority, sought by presidents for more than 100 years, had been a main goal for Republicans after they took control of Congress in 1995. Clinton used the new authority for the first time in August 1997, and the action was immediately challenged in federal court. The following June the Supreme Court ruled that the line-item veto was unconstitutional. *(Court decision, pp. 64, 714)*

Fiscal 1998 Budget Resolution

Building on a strong economy and two earlier rounds of deficit reduction, President Clinton and the Republican majority in Congress struck an historic agreement in 1997 to balance the budget in five years, while cutting taxes and increasing spending for selected administration priorities such as children's health care.

The fiscal 1998 budget resolution (H Con Res 84) aimed to reduce the deficit by $204.3 billion over five years, including $115 billion in savings from Medicare. The reduction was projected to produce a small surplus of $1.3 billion in fiscal 2002, eliminating the federal budget deficit for the first time since 1969. The resolution also provided for $85 billion in net tax cuts, a $16 billion children's health care initiative, restoration of Supplemental Security Income (SSI) and other benefits for disabled legal immigrants, and increases in domestic appropriations, at least in the short term. The resolution did not require the president's signature and did not have the force of law, although Congress's rules required it to abide by the resolution's broad outlines. *(Budget law, box, p. 44; budget glossary, box, p. 46)*

The bipartisan agreement was a major breakthrough after more than two years of bitter partisan fighting over the budget. Republicans won both the House and Senate in the 1994 elections, giving the GOP control of Congress for the first time in forty years. On taking power in January 1995 they were determined to make a balanced budget and tax cuts their vehicle for reshaping the federal government. But they had underestimated Clinton's will and political skills, which he used with great ability to stymie them. By the time they conceded defeat in budget talks that dragged into 1996, Republicans had triggered two shutdowns of almost all federal offices, essentially closing down the government for brief periods that brought them a drubbing in public opinion polls. The residue of those battles, including Clinton's 1996 reelection and the loss of Republican House seats in that election, was a deep bitterness that seemed likely to poison the rela-

BUDGET LAW: A BRIEF HISTORY

The federal government did not operate under a budget during its first 130 years, as each agency pressed its own spending request on Congress. Then, with passage of the Budget Act of 1921, Congress acknowledged that it needed better control of what was becoming an increasingly complex process. The 1921 act gave the president the statutory responsibility to send Congress an annual budget. The Bureau of the Budget—later renamed the Office of Management and Budget in 1970—was created as a clearinghouse for agency budget requests, and the General Accounting Office was formed as Congress's first attempt to strengthen its oversight of spending.

During the next sixty years, as the role of the federal government expanded and its budget grew steadily larger, Congress enacted four major laws in the years listed below to revamp the budget process:

• **1946.** Congress was required to approve a concurrent resolution setting an annual ceiling on spending, and a Joint Budget Committee—the entire House Appropriations and Ways and Means and Senate Appropriations and Finance Committees—was created to prepare the resolution. The process was abandoned as unwieldy three years later.

• **1974.** The main tenets of the current budget process were set under a law (PL 93-344) creating the Congressional

Budget Office and the House and Senate Budget Committees. Those panels were directed to review the effect of legislation on federal expenditures and to draft two concurrent budget resolutions, in the spring and the fall. The fall resolution was informally dropped in the early 1980s. The law also set the ground rules for reconciliation, the process by which tax laws and spending programs are changed to conform to targets set by the budget resolution.

• **1985.** Enacted in hopes that it would staunch the record federal budget deficits, the Gramm-Rudman-Hollings Act (PL 99-177) created an automatic deficit reduction tool called sequestration—across-the-board spending cuts—to be triggered when Congress and the president failed to meet an annual deficit target. The law also mandated that any increase in spending be offset with either spending cuts or revenue increases.

• **1990.** A deficit reduction law (PL 101-508) set annual caps for three fiscal years on discretionary appropriations for domestic, defense, and international programs. It also subjected taxes and entitlements to pay-as-you-go procedures, which required all tax cuts, new entitlement programs, or expansions of existing entitlements to be offset by additional taxes or by cuts in existing entitlement programs. The spending caps were revised and extended in 1993 and 1997.

---

tionship indefinitely. *(1995–1996 budget battles, Congress and the Nation Vol. IX, p. 71)*

To reach accommodation in 1997, both sides relinquished some fervently held positions. The budget deal gave Republicans tax and spending cuts, albeit much smaller than they initially demanded. The agreement did not contain the radical overhaul of entitlement programs, the elimination of entire cabinet departments, or the stringent lowering of spending levels for domestic programs that the GOP had refused to bargain away in 1996.

At the same time, Clinton agreed to tax cuts for higher income individuals, only four years after the new president pushed through a major tax increase on this same group to cope with a rapidly enlarging budget deficit. The 1997 agreement gave the president limited money for selected priorities, but it also accelerated a trend toward squeezing domestic spending.

As passed by both chambers in early June, the fiscal 1998 budget resolution (H Con Res 84) set the overall limit for the thirteen regular fiscal 1998 appropriations bills at a total of $526.9 billion in budget authority for discretionary spending, up about 3 percent from fiscal 1997. It did not set individual spending levels for the thirteen bills, however, a fact that virtually guaranteed fights between the president and Congress over several of the measures. *(Fiscal 1998 appropriations, p. 58)*

H Con Res 84 also contained instructions for writing two separate reconciliation bills—legislation designed to reconcile tax and spending policy with deficit-reduction goals. The first was to be written by Congress's authorizing committees to cut spending in various entitlement programs such as Medicare. The second, the responsibility of the tax-writing committees, was supposed to produce tax cuts that matched those in the budget deal. *(Spending bill, p. 50; tax cuts, p. 90)*

The White House had insisted on splitting the reconciliation process in two so that Democrats could vote for balancing the budget but against tax cuts if they felt the tax bill was excessively tilted toward wealthy taxpayers. That strategy also preserved White House leverage over the shape of the tax cuts without also killing the balanced-budget package.

RESOLUTION HIGHLIGHTS

In its final form, H Con Res 84 included the following major elements:

• **Deficit reduction.** The deficit was slated to disappear in fiscal 2002, although it was projected to increase in the short term because the effects of the tax cuts would be felt more quickly than the effects of the spending cuts. About half the net tax cuts would come in the last two years of the five-year package, while more than 70 percent of the net spending cuts were deferred to those last two years.

• **Taxes.** The only two absolute numbers in the tax portion of the budget resolution were net cuts of $85 billion over five years and $250 billion over ten years. (The gross cuts in the first five years were expected to be $135 billion, $50 billion of which was to be offset by revenue raisers, including extension of a tax on airline tickets.)

Two letters from the GOP leadership to the White House set out several other points of understanding. The first letter stated that the cuts would include a permanent, broad-based capital gains tax cut, a $500-per-child tax credit, expanded individual retirement accounts (IRAs), a reduction in the estate tax, and "roughly" $35 billion over five years to help middle-income families pay postsecondary education costs, a key Clinton initiative. Also mentioned, although less securely guaranteed, were a welfare-to-work tax credit, capital gains tax relief for home sales, tax incentives for businesses to clean up environmentally damaged areas, and tax incentives for the District of Columbia.

The second letter said that the Joint Committee on Taxation would consult with the Treasury Department on how to estimate the cost of the tax provisions. In the past, the committee and the department had disagreed, especially on how to score capital gains tax cuts.

• **Medicare.** The agreement assumed $115 billion in net savings over five years from Medicare, the health insurance program for the elderly and disabled. About $100 billion of the savings was expected to come from reductions in reimbursement rates for providers such as hospitals, doctors, and health maintenance organizations. Medicare beneficiaries were expected to make up the remaining $15 billion through an increase in the monthly premiums for the Part B portion of Medicare, which covered outpatient doctor visits. Low-income beneficiaries were protected from higher premiums by the addition of $1.5 billion in spending to subsidize their costs. *(Medicare, pp. 429, 432)*

Four new benefits were included in the resolution: colorectal screenings, mammograms, diabetes self-management, and preventive vaccinations.

• **Medicaid.** Spending on health care for the poor and disabled was to be reduced by a net of $13.6 billion over five years. The savings were to come largely from reducing reimbursements to hospitals. *(Medicaid, pp. 429, 432)*

• **Welfare.** The agreement included a key Clinton initiative—restoring SSI and Medicaid benefits for disabled legal immigrants who had entered the country before Aug. 23, 1996. The benefits had been terminated as part of the 1996 welfare overhaul law (PL 104-193). Under the agreement, those disabled legal immigrants who entered the country after Aug. 22, 1996, and were on the rolls before June 1, 1997, would also be eligible. The cost of restoring the benefits was $9.7 billion over five years. *(Legal immigrants, p. 619)*.

Negotiators also agreed to restore $1.5 billion over five years in food stamp spending. The welfare law had cut the amount for food stamps by $23 billion over five years. *(Welfare overhaul, Congress and the Nation Vol. IX, p. 578)*

• **Children's health.** Clinton also won guarantees that Congress would spend $16 billion over the first five years to insure up to 5 million children whose parents were too poor to purchase health insurance. The resolution also guaranteed funding at Clinton's requested levels for several top-priority programs, including the National Institute of Standards and Technology; bilingual and immigrant education; an increase in Pell grants, which aided low-income college students; child literacy initiatives; Head Start; national parks, including the Everglades Restoration Fund; the Bureau of Indian Affairs' tribal priority allocations; training and employment services, including Job Corps; and the Violent Crime Reduction Trust Fund.

CLINTON'S FISCAL 1998 BUDGET

Clinton's $1.96 trillion budget for fiscal 1998, sent to Capitol Hill on Feb. 6, 1997, laid down a White House marker for budget negotiations and showed how much distance still had to be crossed before the two sides had an agreement. By GOP lights, Clinton's budget still proposed to spend too much, cut taxes too little, and achieve only about half the deficit reduction needed to meet the Republicans' goal of balancing the budget by 2002. But after the politically disastrous battles in 1995 and 1996, Republicans were looking for a deal.

Using the more optimistic projections of the Office of Management and Budget, Clinton proposed to balance the budget by fiscal 2002 with a net deficit reduction of $252 billion. In contrast, GOP budget writers, using Congressional Budget Office (CBO) projections, said it would take at least $435 billion over five years to reach a balanced budget by fiscal 2002.

Clinton proposed $98.4 billion in gross tax cuts over five years, including a $500-per-child tax credit and a capital gains break on the sale of a principal residence. More than a third of the proposed tax cuts—$38.4 billion over five years—was aimed at helping families send their children to college. Clinton called for offsetting all but $22.4 billion of the lost revenue by extending expiring taxes and ending a variety of corporate tax breaks.

Republicans wanted gross tax cuts twice as big as Clinton's and net tax cuts as much as six or seven times as large—between $120 billion and $150 billion.

On specific areas, Clinton called for restoring about $18 billion of the $54.6 billion in savings expected from the 1996 welfare reform law (PL 104-193), much of it to overturn the ban on an array of federal social services to legal immigrants. He also called for new spending of $3.6 billion, chiefly to get welfare recipients into jobs. In addition to the requested education tax credits, Clinton requested significant spending increases for selected education programs, including school modernization, student loans, remedial education for low-income students, and a new program to promote reading. He also called for increased spending on health care for children.

A BUDGET GLOSSARY

Appropriations. The process by which Congress provides budget authority, usually through the enactment of thirteen separate appropriations bills.

Budget authority. The authority for federal agencies to spend or otherwise obligate money, accomplished through enactment of appropriations bills.

Budget outlays. Money that is actually spent in a given fiscal year, as opposed to money that is appropriated for that year. One year's budget authority can result in outlays during several years, and the outlays in any given year result from a mix of budget authority from that and other years.

Discretionary spending. Programs that Congress can finance as it chooses through appropriations (usually within the parameters set by authorization bills). With the exception of paying entitlement benefits to individuals and interest on the national debt (see mandatory spending), almost everything the government does is financed by discretionary spending. Examples include all federal agencies, Congress, the White House, the federal courts, the military, and activities from space exploration to child nutrition. About a third of all federal spending falls into this category.

Fiscal year. The budget year, which runs from Oct. 1 of one year to Sept. 30 of the next.

Mandatory spending. Spending on programs—made up mostly of entitlements—whose eligibility requirements are written into law. Anyone who meets those requirements is entitled to the money until Congress changes the law. Examples include Social Security, Medicare, Medicaid, unemployment benefits, food stamps, and federal pensions.

Another major category of mandatory spending is the interest paid to holders of federal government bonds. Social Security and interest payments are permanently appropriated. Although budget authority for some entitlements is provided through the appropriations process, appropriators have little or no control over the money. Mandatory spending accounts for about two-thirds of all federal spending.

Pay-as-you-go rule (PAYGO). This rule requires that all tax cuts, new entitlement programs, or expansions of existing entitlement programs be budget-neutral—offset either by additional taxes or cuts in existing entitlement programs.

Reconciliation. The process by which tax laws and spending programs are changed, or reconciled, to reach outlay and revenue targets set in the congressional budget resolution. Established by the 1974 Congressional Budget Act, it was first used in 1980.

Rescission. The cancellation of previously appropriated budget authority. This is a common way to save money that already has been appropriated. A rescissions bill must be passed by Congress and signed by the president (or enacted over his veto), just as an appropriations bill.

Revenues. Taxes, customs duties, some user fees, and most other receipts paid to the federal government. Some receipts and user fees show up as "negative outlays," however, and do not count as revenue.

Sequester. The cancellation of spending authority as a disciplinary measure to stop spending above the preset limits. Appropriations that exceed annual spending caps can trigger a sequester that would cut all appropriations by the amount of the excess. Similarly, tax cuts or new or expanded entitlement spending programs that are not offset under pay-as-you-go rules would trigger a sequester of nonexempt entitlement programs.

Signaling a desire for a truce with Republicans on Medicare, Clinton proposed cutting projected spending for the program by $100 billion over five years, mostly by reducing payments to health care providers. He also called for a $9.3 billion cut in projected spending for Medicaid, the federal-state health care program for the poor, mostly by limiting federal contributions to states to a set amount per beneficiary. Together the projected savings from Medicare and Medicaid accounted for 43 percent of the deficit reduction called for in Clinton's budget.

DRAMATIC TURNAROUND

Several factors led both sides to set aside their differences, at least temporarily, and seek a bipartisan budget accord in 1997. Congressional Republicans were dealing with a smaller majority in the House and the realization that the Democrats would control the White House for another four years. Republicans had promised voters both a balanced budget and tax cuts but they were sensitive to charges that they could achieve their goals only by gutting critical federal programs, the same attacks that had hurt them so badly in 1995–1996.

GOP leaders also worried that internal party splits over spending and taxes could lead them into chaos if they had to pass a budget on their own. Fights already were brewing between House and Senate Republicans over appropriations and among Republicans in both chambers over whether to delay the promised tax cuts until the budget was in balance.

Clinton meanwhile was searching for a landmark achievement to help define his second term and to divert attention from ongoing investigations into his and other Democrats' alleged campaign financing irregularities. Administration officials also said that Clinton had come to believe that concluding a budget deal with Republicans offered a compelling long-term strategy for Democrats. Clinton was said to believe that to prosper politically in the twenty-first century, the Democrats needed to demonstrate that they were the party of fiscal responsibility rather than—as their critics had long charged—a party of "tax and spend."

The two sides jockeyed back and forth for position on various issues for several weeks before beginning intense negotiations the week of April 7. Both sides had to work as hard on holding their own forces together as finding accommodation with the opposing side. In the Senate conservative Republicans were pushing their leaders to hold firm to core GOP principles on taxes and spending, while moderate Republicans were threatening to join forces with moderate Democrats if a deal fell apart. In the House, budget writers were torn between insisting on a budget deal that would appeal to the vast majority of House Republicans or writing a more bipartisan one that could run into trouble from conservatives on the floor.

For his part Clinton was gradually alienating liberal Democrats as he moved his tax cuts and spending plans closer to the Republican position. At one point, 109 Democrats wrote the president warning him not to hold defense harmless while cutting domestic spending. In meetings at the White House, Clinton promised not to walk away from Democratic priorities. But he also said forcing the Republicans to write their own budget would only make it tougher to reach agreement.

The tension eased somewhat on May 1, when the CBO projected that the fiscal 1997 deficit would be nearly $50 billion lower than previous estimates and that higher-than-expected income tax receipts gave negotiators an extra $114 billion in revenue over the five-year period. The negotiators used the windfall to make changes designed to appeal to disaffected legislators. They set aside $64 billion of the extra revenue to lower the projected deficit in coming years, a move that pleased fiscal conservatives. Another $24 billion was used to eliminate the need for legislation mandating a reduction in the Consumer Price Index (CPI). The reduction would have made a large dent in the deficit, but it would also have lowered the annual cost-of-living increase in Social Security benefits. The rest was used to jettison some of the spending cuts in the plan that Democrats objected to the most, including the per capita cap on Medicaid funding, and to fund extra spending for Clinton's priorities. On May 2 negotiators announced that they had reached agreement.

The bargaining was hardly finished, however. Within a week, congressional and White House negotiators were arguing over exactly what it was they had agreed to. Disputes arose over the size and composition of the tax cuts, which programs would receive new spending, and how to make the deficit drop steadily until the budget was balanced in 2002. Negotiations stalled repeatedly when one side put down on paper its version of the verbal agreement only to have opponents insist that specific items had never been approved.

On May 15 negotiators finally presented a written version of the accord that would be used as the basis of the budget resolution. In twenty-four pages they spelled out details of the more than $33 billion Clinton won in restored or new spending. The talks also produced the two letters from the GOP leaders committing the Republicans to support "roughly $35 billion" for Clinton's education tax cuts and credits and pledging that the tax cut package "shall not cause costs to explode in the out years."

COMMITTEE ACTION

Just hours after the bargaining concluded late on May 15, the House Budget Committee approved a draft resolution that reflected the bipartisan deal. The vote on the measure was 31–7, later introduced as H Con Res 84 (H Rept 105-100).

Voting along party lines each time, the committee rejected eleven Democratic amendments aimed at ensuring that the tax benefits would benefit people of all income levels, that the revenue losses would not balloon after five years, and that several domestic programs would be added to the list of priorities that both sides had already agreed to protect.

A virtually identical budget sailed through the Senate Budget Committee in less than three hours May 19, winning approval on a 17–4 vote. The committee turned aside four amendments, including one that would have lowered defense spending by about $17 billion and allowed the money to be used on nondefense programs.

HOUSE ACTION

After eleven hours of debate that ran past 3 a.m. on May 21, the House gave overwhelming approval to the budget resolution. The **key vote was 333–99 (R 201–26; D 132–72; I 0–1).** Democrats delivered enough votes to satisfy Clinton's vow to back the deal only if it had the support of more than half his party's caucus; 64 percent—nearly two-thirds—of the House Democrats voted for the resolution. *(1997 key votes, p. 865)*

The potential shallowness of support for the deal was underscored by a challenge mounted by Transportation and Infrastructure Chairman Bud Shuster, R-Pa., whose alternative budget was narrowly defeated on a 214–216 vote. Shuster's budget would have reduced both spending and tax cuts to get another $12 billion for roads, bridges, and other transportation projects. Shuster's amendment won the support of three-fourths of the House Democrats, despite pressure from the White House to vote against it. The amendment was defeated only after GOP leaders pleaded with their members to put the balanced-budget deal ahead of their concerns for specific road and bridge projects.

Four other alternative budgets were offered during the debate; all four were rejected. Three of them, including one sponsored by the Congressional Black Caucus, would have rearranged spending priorities, eliminated or delayed the tax cuts, and paid for the additional spending by cutting defense programs. The fourth, offered by the Conservative Action Team, would have doubled the size of the tax cuts and paid for them by making deeper cuts in non-defense discretionary funding.

SENATE ACTION

More than fifty amendments spread across four days of Senate debate May 20–23 highlighted nearly all the ways members of both parties disliked the bipartisan budget deal. But in the end, the Senate left the budget virtually unchanged, approving it May 23 by a **key vote of 78–22 (R 41–14; D 37–8).** Just fourteen Republicans and eight Democrats voted against the resolution; forty-one Republicans and thirty-seven Democrats voted for it. *(1997 key votes, p. 865)*

Ironically, a chief theme during the four days of debate was that the deal offered too little new spending. Republicans and Democrats alike tried to wring out more money for children without health insurance, highway projects without sufficient funding, and other bipartisan projects.

The most severe test came on an amendment by Orrin G. Hatch, R-Utah, and Edward M. Kennedy, D-Mass., to raise the tax on cigarettes by 43 cents a pack and divide the proceeds between deficit reduction ($10 billion) and additional health insurance coverage for uninsured children ($20 billion). The amendment was nearly irresistible to members from both parties but Majority Leader Trent Lott, R-Miss., threatened to pull the resolution from the floor if it looked as if the amendment would be adopted, and although the president did not speak publicly on the issue, a White House spokesman made it clear that Clinton did not want the amendment at the expense of losing the resolution. In the end, the Senate voted 55–45 to table, or kill, the amendment, with eight Democrats voting to table, offsetting eight Republicans who voted to preserve the amendment.

FINAL ACTION

After returning from the Memorial Day recess, House and Senate conferees met briefly June 4 to resolve the relatively minor differences between the two chambers' resolutions. The House approved the conference report (H Rept 105-116) June 5, 327–97. The Senate acted just hours later, approving the conference report, 76–22. That completed work on the budget resolution, which did not require the president's signature.

1997 Reconciliation Overview

With flags flying and a military band playing, President Bill Clinton on Aug. 5, 1997, signed a pair of budget reconciliation bills that promised to eliminate the federal deficit by 2002, while providing substantial tax cuts over five years and expanding access to health care for children. Together with Republican lawmakers, veterans of some of the bitterest budget battles in recent memory, Clinton heralded the bills as a victory for bipartisanship.

Congress had cleared the separate spending and tax reconciliation bills with relative ease on July 31, following intense negotiations that lasted throughout July.

The spending bill—officially the Balanced Budget Act of 1997 (HR 2015—PL 105-33)—was expected at the time to result in gross spending cuts of $263 billion over five years. More than half that total—$140 billion—came from extending caps on discretionary spending, the money over which

congressional appropriators had annual authority. The remaining cuts resulted mainly from reductions in Medicare and Medicaid, and from revenues from auctioning portions of the electromagnetic spectrum and from increasing the federal tax on cigarettes. *(Provisions, pp. 50, 53)*

The spending cuts were partly offset by $33 billion in new spending sought by Clinton and the Democrats for a children's health insurance initiative and to restore some cuts made in the 1996 welfare reform legislation (PL 104-193). The bill also continued "pay-as-you-go," or PAYGO, rules for entitlement and tax changes and increased the statutory ceiling on the federal debt.

The tax bill—dubbed the Taxpayer Relief Act of 1997 (HR 2014—PL 105-34)—promised net cuts of $95 billion over five years and $275 billion over ten years. The most costly item was a $500-per-child tax credit targeted at the middle class. The tax cuts were partially offset by a set of revenue raisers, including the renewal and restructuring of airline ticket taxes and fees, projected to bring in $33.2 billion over five years. *(Tax bill, p. 90)*

Although it was not the revolution Republicans had hoped for, the legislation capped the drive to balance the budget and cut taxes that had propelled the GOP since the party took over Congress in 1995. The bills also marked one of Clinton's greatest legislative triumphs. His team left the bargaining table with more of what he wanted on the details than most in Congress had expected. These included the scope of the child tax credit, a new children's health initiative, new and expanded education tax incentives, and restoration of welfare benefits for disabled legal immigrants. He also managed to block the adoption of programs he opposed, including plans to index capital gains taxes to inflation and to establish means testing for the deductibles seniors pay for Medicare Part B outpatient services.

Bipartisan agreement on a budget reconciliation plan was possible only because of the politically wrenching antideficit battles of 1990 and 1993 and because of a roaring economy that was producing revenue greater than anyone had anticipated. *(1990 deficit debate, Congress and the Nation Vol. VIII, p. 37; 1993 debate, Congress and the Nation Vol. IX, p. 44)*

Budget purists found the final product lacking because it put off until later the tough choices needed to address the crisis that would occur when the baby boom generation began to retire and claim Social Security and Medicare benefits. Although the Senate had voted to increase the eligibility age for Medicare coverage and take other dramatic cost-saving steps, the final bill did none of that but instead created another study commission to look into the problem.

The pact was also criticized for relying, first, on predictions that there would be no recession in the next five years; second, on discretionary spending caps that would not really bite until after the 2000 presidential elections; and third, on one-time (and perhaps illusory) savings from auctions of the electromagnetic spectrum. But for the overwhelming majority in Congress, which had been obsessed with the budget deficit since the 1980s, such long-term concerns were secondary to getting the deficit monkey off its back.

BACKGROUND

The two bills grew out of bipartisan budget talks in the spring, primarily between congressional Republicans and the White House, that culminated in an agreement to balance the federal budget by 2002. Although much remained to be nailed down, that agreement marked a dramatic shift from the earlier rancorous, partisan warfare over the budget. When the Republicans took control of Congress in 1995, at the beginning of the 104th Congress, they vowed to eliminate the deficit, then about $200 billion, by 2002. To that end they planned to cut projected spending by $894 billion over seven years, while also cutting taxes by $245 billion.

Republicans ended the 104th Congress far short of their goal. They could point to only two principal areas of savings: $49 billion from reduced domestic appropriations and $55 billion expected from the 1996 overhaul of the federal welfare laws. Although they reframed the debate—Clinton and even most liberal Democrats agreed on the goal of a balanced budget—Republicans lost the political battle by refusing to accept incremental gains and instead forcing two disruptive shutdowns of much of the federal government. *(Congress and the Nation Vol. IX, p. 72)*

In the 1996 elections, Democrats depicted the GOP as a threat to the future of Medicare. Voters handed Clinton a second term in the White House and left Republicans in control of Congress, although reducing their margins in the House. As the 105th Congress began, both parties read the split electoral decision as a mandate for bipartisanship. The vigorous growth of the economy provided a strong tailwind, giving both sides an opportunity to balance the budget with relatively little pain.

Full-fledged negotiations began in the spring. An initial agreement was reached in May, some of which was put into writing two weeks later. But many of the details were left to be filled in by lawmakers writing bills that would implement the deal. The next step came in June, when legislators adopted a bipartisan fiscal 1998 budget resolution (H Con Res 84) that reflected the budget agreement. *(Budget resolution, p. 43)*

The resolution, which received final approval June 5, called for two reconciliation bills, so named because they were intended to reconcile spending and tax policies with balanced-budget goals. One was designed to cut taxes, the other to reduce spending so as to balance the budget and finance the tax cuts. Authorizing committees in the House and Senate were assigned to contribute pieces of the two bills, which were then assembled by the House and Senate Budget Committees into two bills for floor action.

CONGRESSIONAL ACTION

Both chambers easily passed versions of the spending and tax bills the week of June 23. In the House, the two measures moved on separate tracks, accompanied by highly partisan

negotiations over possible changes. The spending bill passed 270–162, with only seven Republican "no" votes; Democrats opposed the bill by a margin of about three to one. The vote on the tax bill was even more partisan. It passed 253–179, with just one Republican opposed and only 27 Democrats voting for it.

By contrast a bipartisan tone prevailed in the Senate as it worked through the two bills. The spending bill passed 73–27, with just three GOP defections. Democrats, deeply divided over proposals for Medicare means testing among others, split almost evenly, with twenty-one in favor and twenty-four opposed. On the tax bill, which passed 80–18, Senate Republicans held all but four of their own. Democrats were still divided, but less so: twenty-nine voted "yes," while fourteen voted "no."

Despite all the talks that had already gone on, several highly emotional issues still had to be resolved by a House-Senate conference. Among them were whether to require high-income seniors to pay bigger Medicare deductibles on medical bills and whether to raise the eligibility age for the health care program. Another Senate-added provision was also at issue: whether to retain a 20-cent increase in the federal per-pack cigarette tax. Other thorny issues concerned the scope of child tax credit and SSI payments for legal immigrants, the shape of the new education tax incentive programs and child health initiative, and the size of the capital gains and estate tax cuts.

But the possibility of bringing the federal budget into balance for the first time since 1969 and at the same time producing the most sweeping tax cuts since Ronald Reagan came into office in 1981 propelled Republicans into the conference with a degree of flexibility that would have seemed unthinkable just two years earlier. Clinton, too, had an enormous stake in a successful outcome. His initiatives to increase spending on domestic priorities including child health care and education tax credits hung in the balance.

Little happened during the first few days as Republican leaders debated their strategy. Finally House Speaker Newt Gingrich, R-Ga., and Senate Majority Leader Trent Lott, R-Miss., decided to exclude Democratic lawmakers and the White House from negotiations and draw up a unified House-Senate GOP position on the two bills. The result was a negotiating stance that staked out hard-line positions on the most emotional issues.

But when the GOP leaders began serious negotiations with the White House the week of July 23, the Clinton administration showed no signs of backing down from its position, and the Republicans began to make concessions.

Several factors worked in the president's favor. As their self-imposed deadline to complete the two bills before the August recess approached, Republicans were feeling more pressure than the Democrats. Moreover, Clinton was enjoying a wave of popularity, with a record 64 percent approval rating in the Washington Post/ABC News poll. Public opinion surveys indicated he was winning the public relations war over whether the GOP-drafted tax plans gave too much tax relief to high-income taxpayers and not enough to the middle class.

At the same time, House GOP leaders were reeling from the stunning and highly publicized revelation of a plot within their ranks to topple Gingrich. Republicans across the spectrum were anxious to get beyond the embarrassment of the aborted coup and deliver tax cuts and a balanced budget to their constituents. *(Gingrich, p. 762)*

After working through a weekend, Gingrich and Lott and the White House negotiators emerged with agreements on both bills, and final passage occurred just days later in both the House and Senate.

On July 30 the House adopted the conference report on the spending bill, 346–85, after a ninety-minute debate, with much of the opposition coming from liberal Democrats and tobacco-state lawmakers opposed to the increase in the cigarette tax. Moving with rare dispatch, the Senate cleared the spending bill July 31, 85–15. Lawmakers in both parties and both chambers voted for the conference report on the tax bill July 31 by overwhelming margins. In the House, the tally was 389–43, with just one Republican opposed. In the Senate, the vote was 92–8, with all eight "nay" votes cast by liberal Democrats.

1997 Reconciliation Package: Spending Cuts

After months of balanced-budget negotiations, Congress and the White House agreed on a huge package of spending cuts that promised to reduce the net federal deficit by $127 billion over five years. Called the Balanced Budget Act of 1997, the measure (HR 2015—PL 105-33) was cleared by Congress on July 31. President Clinton signed it into law, along with a companion tax reconciliation bill, at a White House ceremony Aug. 5. Together the bills were expected to result in a balanced federal budget by 2002, while allowing for significant tax cuts.

Gross spending reductions totaled $263 billion over five years, split about evenly between entitlement programs ($122 billion) and discretionary appropriations (about $140 billion). The biggest savings—$115 billion over five years— came from Medicare, the government-subsidized health insurance program for the elderly. The bill also cut projected Medicaid spending, authorized new auctioning of portions of the broadcast spectrum, and affected programs ranging from student loans to housing and veterans' benefits.

The hard bargaining required to produce the bill yielded rewards for both sides. Clinton carried the day on restoring benefits to legal immigrants who were in the country when the 1996 welfare overhaul law (PL 104-193) was signed. He also won inclusion of a new children's health care initiative, funded in part by an increases in the federal tax on cigarettes.

Republicans won spending cuts large enough to deliver on their promise to both balance the budget and provide hefty tax reductions. They also won inclusion of a pilot program for 390,000 seniors to purchase "medical savings accounts."

BILL HIGHLIGHTS

The spending cut package contained the following highlights:

• **Medicare.** The bill cut the projected growth of the Medicare program by 12 percent, or $115 billion, over five years, primarily by reducing payments to doctors, hospitals and other health care providers. It also increased Medicare Part B premiums, which paid for doctor visits and other outpatient services. *(Medicare-related provisions, p. 432)*

At the same time, the bill provided for Medicare to cover more preventive tests, including prostate screenings, bone density tests, blood testing and diet counseling, for beneficiaries needing them.

Although the changes were the most extensive made in the Medicare program since it began in 1965, the final bill did not include key structural changes endorsed by the Senate. That chamber wanted to increase the eligibility age for Medicare gradually from sixty-five to sixty-seven, require wealthier seniors to pay a higher Medicare premium, and require beneficiaries to pay a $5 copayment for each home health care visit. These proposals, which addressed the program's long-term financial problems, were deemed too controversial by both the House and the administration.

• **Medical savings accounts.** The bill created a pilot program to allow about 390,000 people to use new medical savings account instead of traditional Medicare to pay for health expenses.

• **Medicaid.** The bill reduced projected spending on Medicaid, the government-backed health insurance program for the poor, by about $10.4 billion over five years. Most of the savings came from reducing payments to states for hospitals that served a disproportionate share of low-income patients. Additional savings were achieved by giving states more flexibility in setting provider payment levels. The bill repealed the so-called Boren Amendment, which required state Medicaid programs to pay hospitals and nursing homes a "reasonable and adequate" rate.

The bill also established a $1.5 billion block grant to states to help low-income Medicaid enrollees pay their Part B Medicare premiums.

• **Children's health initiative.** The bill provided $23.4 billion to expand health coverage to uninsured children. The costs were partially offset by a 15-cents-per-pack increase in the federal cigarette tax. States were given flexibility to determine eligibility for the programs, although it was generally limited to children from families with incomes of 200 percent of the poverty level or less.

States could decide to expand their Medicaid programs, provide health insurance programs for these children, use up to 10 percent of their funds for direct services to children, or draw up some combination of these options. Some of the money could go to hospitals and other health care providers, but most had to be used to pay for insurance.

• **Welfare.** Legal immigrants who were in the United States on Aug. 22, 1996, the date the 1996 welfare overhaul bill was signed into law, were made eligible for Supplemental Security Income (SSI) cash benefits for the low-income aged and disabled, whether they were disabled then or became disabled later. Without the change, all noncitizens would have been removed from the SSI rolls Oct. 1, 1997. *(Welfare provisions, p. 486; 1996 welfare overhaul, Congress and the Nation Vol. IX, p. 578)*

HR 2015 also continued Medicaid coverage for disabled children who lost their SSI benefits because of eligibility changes contained in the welfare law. It created a fund worth $3 billion to help states place long-term welfare recipients into the workforce in fiscal 1998 and 1999. The final bill did not include controversial House provisions that would have exempted recipients in certain "workfare" positions from the federal minimum wage law. The bill did increase spending by a total of $1.5 billion over five years for food stamps and employment and training benefits for people who might otherwise have lost their eligibility under the welfare overhaul law.

• **Spectrum auction.** The bill raised a total of $21.4 billion over five years by extending and expanding the authority of the Federal Communications Commission to auction portions of electromagnetic spectrum, including portions returned by television broadcasters after they converted to digital broadcasts. *(Spectrum auction, p. 325)*

• **Caps on discretionary spending.** Budget enforcement provisions in the bill extended existing caps on appropriated spending through 2002, for an estimated five-year savings of $140 billion.

• **Other deficit reduction.** The final legislation included the following additional savings and revenue over five years:

  • $2.7 billion in savings by reducing spending on veterans' programs.

  • $4.8 billion in savings by increasing federal agency and federal employee contributions to federal employee retirement plans.

  • $1.8 billion in savings from changes in federal student loan programs. *(Student loans, p. 526)*

  • $1.8 billion in savings from replacing the Federal Housing Administration's foreclosure relief program and reducing subsidies in the Section 8 rental housing program. *(Housing, pp. 553, 562)*

  • $736 million in increased revenues from extending vessel tonnage fees, selling Governor's Island in New York Harbor, and selling air rights over tracks behind Washington's Union Station.

• **Debt limit.** In a little noticed provision, the bill also increased the statutory limit on the public debt from $5.5 trillion to $5.950 trillion. Under then-current estimates, that was considered sufficient to last until Dec. 15, 1999.

BACKGROUND

The broad parameters for the tax and spending bills had been set in the bipartisan budget deal reached in May and refined in the fiscal 1998 budget resolution (H Con Res 84) cleared June 5. The budget resolution instructed eight committees each in the House and Senate to contribute pieces to the spending cut bill, with the most significant responsibility assigned to the House Ways and Means Committee and the Senate Finance Committee. The Budget committees in both chambers would then stitch together the pieces produced by the individual panels.

In many cases, work on the spending cuts proceeded smoothly. The Ways and Means Committee, for example, approved provisions restructuring Medicare with only three dissenting votes. But in areas such as welfare and children's health, House Republicans adopted positions that drew objections from the administration. Senate action proceeded on a more bipartisan basis.

HOUSE ACTION

The House Budget Committee worked into the evening June 20 before approving its version of the spending cuts (HR 2015—H Rept 105-149) 25–5. The markup convened after a day of negotiations involving the committee chairman, ranking Democratic member, and administration officials over the changes that would be made to the bill on the floor. The administration objected to several committee provisions, including:

• A provision that limited SSI payments only to legal immigrants who were already receiving the benefits in August 1996 when the welfare overhaul bill was cleared. The administration wanted legal immigrants to be eligible for the payments whenever they became disabled.

• The House version of the children's health initiative. Democrats said it would cover only half of the nation's 10 million uninsured children and did not have enough protections to ensure that the money would be used for its intended purpose.

• A provision that would effectively revoke a Labor Department directive requiring states to pay the minimum wage to workfare beneficiaries—welfare recipients who were required to work in public or nonprofit jobs as a condition of receiving welfare benefits.

• A decision not to help low-income people pay higher Medicare premiums for doctor visits. Democrats said by failing to include funding for that purpose, the Republicans were reneging on the original budget agreement.

Negotiations continued even after the committee had approved the bill, and those changes were incorporated into HR 2015 when the House adopted a "self-executing" rule (H Res 174) that allowed the tax and spending reconciliation bills to come to the floor. Among the changes were provisions to add funds to help low-income beneficiaries pay for Medicare Part B premiums, increased access to new health

BUDGET RULES EXTENDED THROUGH 2002

As part of the spending reconciliation bill (HR 2015—PL 105-33) Congress in 1997 extended through 2002 a set of rules first enacted in 1990 to help lawmakers curb the growing federal deficit. Those rules imposed spending cuts if Congress failed to abide by specific limits on discretionary spending or if it changed the tax code or mandatory programs in ways that resulted in a net increase in the deficit.

Before those rules were extended, however, House Republican leaders had to fend off an attempt by a group of conservative "budget hawks" to enact tough new rules that would force Congress to achieve its stated goal of erasing the budget deficit by 2002.

Their plan was to use the levels set in the fiscal 1998 budget resolution (H Con Res 84) to create annual statutory caps on spending for entitlement programs, such as Medicare and Medicaid, as well as a floor for revenues and a limit on the total deficit. If those limits were breached, Congress and the White House would have until Dec. 15 of a given year to find a way to make up the difference. If they failed certain automatic steps would kick in to ensure that the limits were met.

The leaders of the group first sought a hearing for their proposal by threatening to defeat the rule under which the spending and tax reconciliation bills would be brought to the House floor. The House Rules Committee initially rejected the demand but when it learned that the rule was in serious trouble of failing on other issues the committee relented and promised to allow a separate vote. The GOP leadership agreed to allow a separate floor vote on the budget enforcement proposal.

The proposal came back to the House floor on July 23, 1997, as HR 2003, and was soundly defeated by a vote of 81–347. Republicans objected because the proposal might slow down their plans for future tax cuts. Moreover, legislators from both parties said the implications of the proposed rule for key programs such as Social Security and veterans benefits were unclear.

care coverage for children, and a modification of the workfare provisions so that only cash welfare benefits and food stamps would be counted toward compensation. House Republicans had wanted to count all federal welfare benefits as part of compensation for minimum wage purposes.

Also included in the rule was a set of budget enforcement procedures that extended caps on discretionary spending and so-called PAYGO rules through fiscal 2002. Under PAYGO, congressional action to cut taxes or expand entitlement spending must be offset by tax increases or entitlement cuts.

A small bipartisan group of deficit hawks threatened to defeat the rule for floor consideration of the reconciliation bills if they were not allowed to offer an amendment containing stricter budget enforcement rules. Republican leaders persuaded them to back off in exchange for a separate vote on their bill. When the rule came to the House floor on June 25, it was adopted, 228–200. The separate bill (HR 2003) was subsequently defeated. *(Budget rules, box, this page)*

After the rule was adopted the House passed the spending reconciliation bill by a vote of 170–162. No Democratic amendments were allowed. Although the changes incorporated through the rule did not address all of the Democrats' concerns, they represented enough of a good faith effort to win the votes of 51 Democrats.

SENATE ACTION

The Senate Budget Committee approved its own version of the spending reconciliation bill (S 947) on June 20 by a vote of 18–3. The panel made no changes to the provisions it received from the eight Senate committees, and it issued no written report.

The heart of the Senate bill, and the provisions that set it off from both the House version and the administration wishes, was a radical restructuring of the Medicare program. Under the proposal added by the Finance Committee, the annual deductible for Medicare's Part B outpatient services would be linked to incomes, with wealthier seniors paying higher deductibles. The proposal also would raise the eligibility age for Medicare gradually to sixty-seven, from sixty-five, and require a $5 copayment for some home health care services.

When the bill came to the Senate floor, liberal Democrats moved to eliminate the Medicare restructuring proposals but their efforts were voted down by surprisingly large margins. On June 24, the Senate tabled (killed), 59–41, an amendment by Democrats Edward M. Kennedy, Mass., and Paul Wellstone, Minn., to remove the $5 copay requirement. The Senate then voted 62–30 to waive the so-called Byrd rule, which barred extraneous material in reconciliation bills, to retain the proposed increase in the Medicare eligibility age. Finally, senators voted 70–30 to kill an attempt by Kennedy to eliminate means testing for Medicare Part B deductibles.

In a victory for the administration, the Senate June 25 approved by voice vote an amendment that would make legal immigrants in the country on Aug. 22, 1996, eligible for SSI payments, no matter when they became disabled.

The Senate then passed its version of the spending reconciliation bill by a vote of 73–27. It subsequently agreed by voice vote to pass HR 2015, after substituting the Senate text. The vote reflected the bill's bipartisan support in the Senate, as well as the uncomfortable splits it created in the Democratic ranks: twenty-one Democrats voted for the bill; twenty-four voted against it.

CONFERENCE, FINAL ACTION

The House-Senate conference on the bill proceeded slowly at first, with Republicans soon retreating behind closed doors to work out a unified House-Senate GOP position to take to Clinton.

Serious negotiations with the White House began July 24. Republicans at first took a hard line, rejecting for example, proposals to allow SSI benefits to legal immigrants who became disabled after the welfare overhaul law was enacted in 1996. That position was the only one in the spending reconciliation bill to draw an explicit veto threat.

But Republicans knew they would have to make concessions if they were to reach their goal of getting a bill enacted before the August recess—particularly given Clinton's rising popularity ratings in the polls and the discord in their own ranks evidenced by the recent coup attempt against House Speaker Newt Gingrich, R-Ga. Republicans started making concessions in weekend talks July 26–27 that finally produced an agreement on July 28.

The House adopted the resulting conference report (H Rept 105-217) on July 30 by a vote of 346–85. The Senate cleared the bill, 85–15, the following day. The legislation was signed by President Clinton Aug. 5, 1997 (PL 105-33).

MAJOR PROVISIONS

HR 2015—PL 105-33 included a variety of provisions extending across many subjects. Major provisions listed below deal with budgeting issues, the District of Columbia, and certain civil service–related matters. Provisions on Medicare, Medicaid, welfare, and spectrum sales are found in the appropriate chapters with page references listed below.

In budgeting provisions HR 2015 extended two key mechanisms for enforcing budget limits established by the 1990 budget law (PL 101-508). The rules, which had been renewed in 1993, had been scheduled to expire at the end of fiscal 1998. The bill also updated and revised the Congressional Budget and Impoundment Control Act (PL 93-344), which had been amended numerous times since it became law in 1974. Most provisions involved technical changes and corrections, elimination of redundancies, and revisions to reflect evolution in budget practices.

Budget Enforcement

• **Discretionary spending caps.** Extended limits on discretionary spending—the money provided annually through the appropriations bills—through 2002. The limits applied to both budget authority and outlays. As before, they were enforceable through sequestration—automatic across-the-board cuts in nonexempt discretionary programs.

The White House could adjust the annual caps to account for emergency appropriations and differences between the Congressional Budget Office (CBO) and the White House Office of Management and Budget (OMB) in estimating outlays, as under existing law. The caps could also be raised if legislation were enacted to provide funding for the International Monetary Fund, international arrearages in United Nations dues and other accounts, and efforts to curb fraud in the earned income tax credit program, which provided tax relief for low-income workers. But the caps could no longer be adjusted for inflation or for differences between CBO and OMB in estimating budget authority.

Separately, the chairmen of the House and Senate Budget Committees could adjust budget levels set forth in the annual budget resolution to reflect certain action on legislation, generally mirroring adjustments made by the president in discretionary caps.

• **'Firewalls.'** Revived and modified "firewalls" separating specific discretionary spending accounts. Those barriers, first set up under the 1990 law and since expired, had separated domestic, defense, and international accounts; only those accounts within the subcategory that was breached were subject to a sequester. The effect was to prevent Congress from cutting defense to pay for extra domestic spending, or vice versa.

The new firewalls separated defense and non-defense discretionary spending in fiscal 1998 and 1999. In fiscal years 2000, 2001, and 2002, all discretionary spending would be in a single category.

In addition, the bill incorporated into the budget rules caps on discretionary spending for crime prevention enacted under the 1994 crime law (PL 103-322). Those limits were effective from fiscal 1998 through 2000.

The bill extended the caps as follows (in billions of dollars):

Fiscal Year	Spending Category	Budget Authority	Outlays
1998	Defense	$269.0	$269.8
	Nondefense	252.4	282.9
	Violent crime reduction	5.5	3.6
1999	Defense	271.5	266.5
	Nondefense	255.7	287.9
	Violent crime reduction	5.8	5.0
2000	Discretionary	532.7	558.7
	Violent crime reduction	4.5	5.6
2001	Discretionary	542.0	564.4
2002	Discretionary	551.1	560.8

• **PAYGO rules.** Extended through 2002 pay-as-you-go rules, known as PAYGO, for legislation affecting direct or mandatory spending or revenues. Under PAYGO, the cost of any new or expanded entitlement program or any tax cut had to be offset by cuts in other entitlement spending or by tax increases. A sequester was triggered if the net effect of tax and entitlement legislation was to increase the deficit.

Any sequestration was to be evenly divided between nonexempt defense accounts and nonexempt nondefense accounts. Exempt accounts included Social Security, veterans' programs, net interest payments on the debt and programs for low-income people. Sequestration of many other programs was governed by limitations, special rules, and exceptions; for example, any sequestration of Medicare was limited to a 4 percent cut.

Extended PAYGO enforcement procedures through fiscal 2006. Any legislation enacted through 2002 was subject to PAYGO rules and enforcement by sequester for five years. (The goal was to prevent Congress from passing legislation that met PAYGO requirements before 2002 but resulted in a deficit afterward.)

PAYGO applied only to legislative changes—for example the creation of a new entitlement program or the expansion of an existing one. It did not cover factors considered outside Congress's control such as a recession.

Budget Act Amendments

• **Budget resolution.** Required Congress's annual budget resolution to cover a minimum of five years, making permanent a temporary five-year requirement—set to expire at the end of fiscal 1998—enacted as part of the 1990 budget law. The House and Senate Budget Committees could recommend that the budget resolution cover a longer period.

• **Appropriations allocations.** Changed the procedure for providing contingent budget allocations to the House Appropriations Committee in the event that a budget resolution was not adopted by the April 15 deadline. Such contingent allocations were to be based on the discretionary spending limits in the prior year's budget resolution, instead of those in the president's budget.

• **Senate task force.** Provided for the appointment of a six-member bipartisan task force to study Senate floor procedures for considering the budget resolution and budget-reconciliation bills. This responded to criticism that senators sometimes voted on numerous amendments—with very little debate—during so-called vote-a-thons after the time for debate had expired.

Debt Limit

• The bill increased the statutory limit on the national debt from $5.5 trillion to $5.95 trillion. The increase was expected to provide sufficient borrowing authority for the federal government until approximately Dec. 15, 1999.

Medicare and Medicaid

The bill included some of the most significant alterations to Medicare, the federal health insurance program for the elderly and disabled, since the program was created in 1965. Among other things, the bill broadened the options available to seniors to include several managed care alternatives, such as preferred provider organizations and provider-sponsored organizations. It also allowed up to 390,000 seniors to open medical savings accounts, which could be used for qualified medical expenses but had to be coupled with high-deductible health insurance plans to pay for catastrophic illnesses.

The changes in Medicaid, the federal-state health insurance program for the poor, gave states more flexibility to put enrollees in managed care. The bill also reduced so-called disproportionate share payments from the federal government that helped states care for the poor or uninsured. *(Medicare and Medicaid legislative details and provisions, pp. 429, 432)*

Welfare

HR 2015 also included extensive provisions dealing with welfare law, including food stamps, welfare-to-work grants, temporary assistance for needy families, supplemental security income, and aid to legal immigrants. *(Aid to legal immigrants, pp. 421, 486, 488)*

District of Columbia

The bill made the most far-reaching changes to the federal government's relationship with its capital city since Congress granted home rule to the District of Columbia in 1973. The initiatives were expected to cost the federal government $928 million over five years, lifting a sizable financial burden from a city chronically in the red. *(Federal–D.C. ties, p. 739)*

The following are major provisions affecting the District:

• **Pension liability.** Resumed federal responsibility for a costly pension plan for city teachers, police, and firefighters who retired by June 30, 1997. The federal government had transferred responsibility for the fund to the District in a 1979 law (PL 96-122). At that time the fund had unfunded liabilities of $1.9 billion. That liability had grown to $4.8 billion by fiscal 1997, about the same amount as the District's total annual budget.

Under the bill, pension payments for city workers were to come from a federal trust fund run by the Treasury Department. The bill left the District with $1.275 billion from its old pension fund to start another plan for teachers, police, and firefighters who retired or became disabled after June 30.

• **Management changes.** Required a federally created control board overseeing the city's finances to hire, no later than thirty days after enactment of the bill, consultants to develop management overhaul plans for nine city departments: Administrative Services, Consumer and Regulatory Affairs, Corrections, Employment Services, Fire and Emergency Medical Services, Housing and Community Development, Human Services, Public Works and Public Health.

The bill declared vacant the director positions for those departments, which meant that incumbent department heads had to be reappointed or replaced. It made mayoral appointments to head those departments subject to an affirmative vote of a financial control board created by the federal government in 1995. The control board could appoint a department head if the mayor did not act within thirty days of a vacancy. It also gave the board the power to remove any department head.

The fiscal 1998 spending bill for the District of Columbia (HR 2607—PL 105-100) clarified that the city council could veto mayoral appointments to head the nine departments.

• **Penal system transfer.** Required that the District's Lorton Prison complex in northern Virginia be closed no later than Dec. 31, 2001. All prisoners were to be transferred by Oct. 1, 2001, to a facility operated by or under contract to the Federal Bureau of Prisons. The District was required to provide for the prisoners at Lorton until it closed, or until the last prisoner had been moved.

The Bureau of Prisons was required to house at least 2,000 District inmates in private prisons by Dec. 31, 1999, and at least 50 percent of District inmates in such facilities by Sept. 30, 2003. The Bureau of Prisons was authorized to buy land and contract to build a new facility for felony inmates, but the bill specified that no facility could be built on the Lorton site or surrounding Lorton lands.

The bill transferred the highly desirable land occupied by the Lorton Prison complex to the Interior Department, with the exception of two small pieces that were to go to the Fairfax County Water Authority and the Fairfax County Parks Authority. It was unclear what would eventually happen to the rest of the land. Some Virginians wanted it to become a park, but others hoped to use it for housing or retail developments.

• **Truth in sentencing.** Established a seven-member commission led by a Justice Department nominee to recommend changes to make the District's criminal code comparable to federal truth-in-sentencing laws for felonies. Such laws required inmates to serve out the majority of their prison terms. The recommendations, due within 180 days of the bill's enactment, would be transmitted to the city council and to the D.C. Superior Court. If the commission failed to make a recommendation or the council failed to act on it within 270 days of the bill's enactment, the attorney general could promulgate regulations to change the District code.

• **Parole.** Required the U.S. Parole Commission to assume authority to grant and deny parole to District offenders within one year after the bill's enactment.

• **Reorganizing criminal justice.** Required the attorney general, in consultation with the chair of the control board and the mayor, to appoint a trustee to reorganize pretrial and defense services, parole, and probation. The bill created an Offender Supervision, Defender, and Courts Services Agency to supervise those on parole, probation, or early release. Pretrial and public defender services would also be provided by the agency. The director would be appointed by the president.

• **Courts transfer.** Established separate federal appropriations for the D.C. Superior Court, the D.C. Court of Appeals and the D.C. Court System to be made through the State Justice Institute. Lawmakers later determined that the institute was too small to handle the duty. The fiscal 1998 spending bill (HR 2607—PL 105-100) for the District of Columbia transferred responsibility for the appropriations to OMB.

The bill also set up a new retirement plan for judges and their survivors, encompassing money the judges and the District government had put into the D.C. Judges' Retirement Fund. Under the bill, nonjudicial employees of the courts were to be treated as federal employees for purposes of retirement.

• **Crime studies.** Authorized funds to set up a District institute or corporation to study and implement demonstration projects on preventing and solving crimes and punishing offenders.

• **Penalty for blocking bridges.** Instituted fines of $1,000 to $5,000 and prison terms of up to thirty days for anyone "knowingly and willfully" obstructing a bridge between the District and Virginia. "Janitors for Justice," a group made up mostly of Service Employees International Union members, had blocked the 14th Street Bridge several times in the mid-1990s to picket for better working conditions. Their protest angered many commuters who were tied up for hours in traffic jams.

• **Garnisheeing wages.** Allowed private entities, such as businesses, and public entities, such as child support enforcers, to garnishee the wages, retirement benefits, or disability pay of city workers. For decades the federal government had shielded its workers from collections for alimony or other debts; and before Home Rule, District employees were part of the federal workforce. After the city gained autonomy, it continued to shield employees from collectors, even when the federal government dropped that policy in the mid-1990s.

• **Collecting taxes.** Allowed the District's chief financial officer to contract with a private entity to collect the District's taxes.

• **Financing debt.** Authorized the District government to borrow from the federal Treasury up to $300 million for a ten-year term to pay down the city's $500 million accumulated operating deficit. The loans would incur the standard Treasury interest rate at the time.

• **Other financing.** Authorized the city council to issue general obligation bonds and taxable or tax-exempt revenue bonds to finance capital projects. The Home Rule Act of 1973 had restricted the District's ability to sell bonds for many purposes, including economic development.

• **Federal payment.** Repealed requirements that the federal government provide an annual payment to the city, but authorized a $190 million payment in fiscal 1998, an amount enacted in the subsequent appropriations measure. Because of federal requirements that limited the District's earning potential—for example, by limiting the height of buildings and exempting some groups from local property taxes—the bill authorized unspecified sums to be appropriated in subsequent years.

• **Balancing the budget.** Required that the District balance its city budget in 1998, one year earlier than required by the 1995 law (PL 104-8) that created the control board.

• **Writing the budget.** Removed several cumbersome federal requirements on how the mayor, city council, and financial control board had to interact when writing the District's annual budget. If the three entities agreed on a budget, the bill allowed them to submit it to Congress and the president.

• **Regulatory overhaul.** Required the control board to complete within six months of bill enactment a review of the District's regulations, particularly permit and application processes. The board's recommendations, which the bill said should focus on regulations that "unnecessarily and inappropriately impair economic development," were to be submitted to the mayor, city council, and Congress. The control board could implement the recommendations, but it was required to consider the views of the city council and mayor.

• **Clean air fee.** Wiped from the District code a 1994 ordinance assessing a "clean air" fee on federal employees who parked in federal lots in the District.

• **Utility mergers.** Eliminated a requirement that Congress approve mergers involving District utility companies.

Civil Service Pensions

Federal departments and federal employees were required to contribute more to their pension and disability plans, saving the Treasury $5.94 billion over five years. Provisions in the bill included the following:

• **Pension contributions.** Required federal agencies to increase their contributions to the Civil Service Retirement System (CSRS) by $2.9 billion, or about 1.5 percent, beginning Oct. 1, 1997, and continuing through Sept. 30, 2002. Only the Postal Service and the Metropolitan Washington Airports Authority were exempt from the increase.

Workers participating in CSRS or the Federal Employees Retirement System (FERS)—the other retirement plan—were required to pay $1.8 billion more, increasing their existing contributions by about 0.5 percent by 2001.

The bill prohibited agencies from decreasing their contribution to FERS in light of employees' increased contributions.

• **Health benefits.** Established a permanent formula for calculating the amount the government would contribute for employees and their families under the Federal Employees Health Benefits Program. The existing formula was set to expire in 1999.

The bill required the Office of Personnel Management to calculate the rate by Oct. 1 of each year. Under the formula, the government would pay a "weighted average" based on the number of subscribers in specific health insurance plans. The government would contribute 72 percent of that average. However, the provision stipulated that the government could not pay more than 75 percent of a plan's premium.

Without the changes, federal employees and retirees would have faced an average premium increase of $276 a year, according to the Senate Governmental Affairs Committee.

• **Injured postal workers.** Ended an annual payment to the Postal Service of about $35 million to compensate workers injured before the Post Office Department became the quasi-independent Postal Service in 1970. Instead, the Postal Service had to use its own revenue to pay these claims.

Broadcast Spectrum Sales

Lawmakers looked to an invisible but lucrative government commodity to help reduce the deficit. CBO estimated that the government would take in $21.4 billion through 2002 from the auction of electromagnetic spectrum, the airwaves used to carry the signals for communications such as cellular telephones, radio, and television. The legislation broadened and extended the authority of the Federal Communications Commission (FCC) to auction spectrum. *(Background and legislative action, p. 325)*

Other Provisions

• **Petroleum reserve.** Anticipated raising $13 million through 2002 by allowing foreign governments to lease unused space in Louisiana salt caves that stored the nation's Strategic Petroleum Reserve. Key members of the Senate Energy and Natural Resources Committee approved the change in May after securing a commitment from budget writers that those foreign leases would be used after 2002 to restock the depleted, 564-million barrel reserve.

• **Transportation.** Ordered the sale of Governor's Island, the site of a Coast Guard base, by 2002 to raise an estimated $500 million. The bill also ordered the sale of 16 acres of air rights over tracks behind Washington's Union Station for $40 million. And it extended vessel tonnage fees, which expired in 1998, through 2002, to raise an estimated $245 million.

Balanced-Budget Amendment

Advocates of a constitutional amendment to require a balanced federal budget had their hopes dashed once again in 1997 as two Senate Democrats switched their positions to defeat the proposal. It was the third time in three years that the Senate had fallen just short of the two-thirds vote needed to pass a constitutional amendment.

The potential impact of the amendment on Social Security, the issue that had killed the amendment in previous years, was a critical factor in the 1997 vote. Two other factors also undercut the Republican led-drive for the amendment. First was the expectation that Congress and President Clinton would reach agreement on balancing the budget on their own later in the year. Second was the booming economy, which led to expectations of declining budget deficits. *(Budget resolution, p. 43)*

The amendment (S J Res 1, H J Res 1) would have required a balanced budget by fiscal 2002 or two years after ratification by three-fourths of the states, whichever came later. A three-fifths supermajority vote in both the House and Senate would have been required to waive the balanced-budget requirement as well as to raise the national debt.

Although the makeup of the Senate after the 1996 elections suggested the measure would pass the chamber with 68 votes, the count stalled at 66, just one vote short of the 67 required. Democrats Robert G. Torricelli of New Jersey and Tim Johnson of South Dakota, both of whom had voted for an identical amendment when it passed the House in 1995, switched to "nay" and the amendment died.

Even had the amendment passed in the Senate, however, supporters would have had difficulty getting it through the House. Democratic gains in the 1996 elections had given hope to the amendment's opponents that they might be able to kill the measure, which had passed the House in 1995 with a dozen votes to spare. Labor unions lobbied hard against the proposal, and whip counts showed amendment supporters perhaps a dozen votes shy in the House.

Republican leaders in the House indicated privately that they were in no hurry to force members to cast a potentially uncomfortable vote related to Social Security unless the Senate acted first. When the Senate killed the amendment, it was shelved in the House.

BACKGROUND

The idea of amending the Constitution to require a balanced budget had been raised frequently since the early 1980s. Support had built gradually as frustration mounted over the seemingly permanent budget deficit and the resulting $5.3 trillion national debt.

When Republicans took control of the House in 1995, the centerpiece of their ambitious agenda was passage of a balanced-budget amendment. Shocked at their loss of control for the first time in forty years, Democratic leaders did not mount a fight, and on Jan. 26, 1995, the House approved the amendment by an overwhelming vote of 300–132.

By contrast, both sides knew the Senate vote would be close. Majority Leader Bob Dole, R-Kan., presidential hopeful and lead sponsor of the Senate resolution, had a huge stake in securing a two-thirds majority in favor of the amendment. Dole held off final balloting for two days while he scrambled to find a sixty-seventh vote, but he was unable to pry one loose. After Dole switched his vote to "no" to preserve his ability to call for a revote later in the session the final tally on March 2 was 65–35.

Dole tried again in 1996, primarily to emphasize his credentials as a budget hawk before he resigned from the Senate in June to run full-time for president. The amendment failed June 6 on a 64–35 vote. (*Congress and the Nation Vol. IX, pp. 62, 80*)

ARGUMENTS PRO AND CON

The central argument in favor of the amendment was compellingly simple: nothing short of a constitutional mandate would reverse the chronic inability of Congress and the president to stop deficit spending. Arguments against the amendment included opposition to writing fiscal policy into the Constitution and concerns that the amendment would allow federal judges to make budget decisions. But the key concern about the amendment stemmed from its alleged effect on Social Security.

Under existing law, the Social Security trust funds were officially "off budget," but the surpluses they were piling up to cover benefits once baby boomers started to retire were being counted toward bringing the overall deficit into balance. Opponents argued that the proposed amendment would enshrine this practice in the Constitution. They further warned that when the surpluses began to dry up, as they were expected to do around 2019, the balanced-budget amendment would force Congress to reduce Social Security benefits or raise payroll taxes to finance other government programs.

Amendment supporters countered that the Social Security issue was purely a political fig leaf to justify a "no" vote on the amendment. Most budget analysts agreed with the GOP that the opposition's arguments on Social Security were disingenuous but Democrats had a potent weapon in the political battle. Moreover, leading conservative voices, such as Federal Reserve Board Chairman Alan Greenspan and the editorial board of the *Wall Street Journal,* opposed the amendment on the grounds that economic policy should not be conducted through the Constitution.

SENATE ACTION

The Senate Judiciary Committee got started quickly in the 105th Congress, approving the GOP version of the balanced-budget amendment Jan. 30, 1997, by a vote of 13–5 (S J Res 1—S Rept 105-3). Republicans generally acted as a bloc during the markup to defeat several Democratic amendments, including a wide-ranging proposal by Dianne Feinstein, D-Calif., that would have rewritten the proposal to cover all of the opposition's concerns about the amendment. The Feinstein amendment was defeated on a party-line vote of 8–9.

The measure went to the Senate floor Feb. 5 with every Republican pledged to vote for it. But GOP leaders were unable to win over all of the 12 Democratic votes they needed to prevail. When the Senate finally acted on March 4, supporters fell one vote shy of the two-thirds majority needed to pass a constitutional amendment. The amendment was defeated on a **key vote of 66–34 (R 55–0; D 11–34).** (*1997 key votes, p. 865*)

During the month the amendment was on the floor, attention focused on four undeclared Democratic freshmen who had either voted for the amendment as House members or promised during their election campaigns to support it. One by one they announced their position. Max Cleland of Georgia was first, announcing on Feb. 14 that he would vote for the amendment. On Feb. 20 Johnson announced that he would vote "no" because of concern about the potential effect on Social Security. On Feb. 25 Mary Landrieu of Louisiana announced that she would keep her campaign promise to vote for the amendment. That left the deciding vote to Torricelli, a Democratic loyalist who had voted three times for a virtually identical amendment in the House and who had also supported it during a nasty Senate campaign. In a dramatic announcement Feb. 26, Torricelli said he would vote "no," dooming the amendment

At the end of the roll call March 4, Majority Leader Trent Lott, R-Miss., declined to switch his vote to "no," which would have permitted him to call up the amendment at any time for a revote. To have switched would have interfered with the GOP message that all fifty-five Senate Republicans had supported the measure, and its defeat came at the hands of Democrats who broke campaign promises that they would back the amendment.

Throughout the month-long debate, Republicans consistently voted down Democratic amendments. The closest vote came on an amendment by Harry Reid, D-Nev., to exclude the Social Security trust funds from the amendment's reach. The amendment was tabled (killed) Feb. 25 on a straight party-line vote, 55–44.

HOUSE ACTION

The House Judiciary Committee took up an identical resolution on Feb. 5, the same day that the Senate began floor debate. But Chairman Henry J. Hyde, R-Ill., abruptly adjourned the markup after only two hours or debate and no votes. Hyde acted after it appeared that he lacked the votes in committee to block a Democratic amendment exempting Social Security.

Although House leaders thought briefly about trying to resurrect the amendment after the Senate vote, they abandoned the idea in the face of whip counts that showed them to be about ten votes short of the necessary two-thirds majority. Faced with pessimistic vote counts, the leadership shelved that plan and turned instead to the bipartisan budget talks with the president.

Fiscal 1998 Appropriations

Abandoning the take-it-or-leave-it strategy that triggered two government shutdowns and hurt Republicans during their first two years in power, GOP leaders in 1997 succeeded in getting all thirteen regular appropriations bills enacted before adjourning for the year. Even so, disputes over partisan policy riders stalled work on four of the fiscal 1998 spending bills until November, requiring a string of six temporary appropriations bills, or continuing resolutions, to keep the government operating in the interim. The last two spending bills were cleared Nov. 13, the last day of the session.

Earlier in the year, Republicans staged an ill-conceived showdown with the White House over a fiscal 1997 supplemental appropriations bill that seemed to signal they had learned little from their disastrous confrontations with Clinton in 1995–1996.

Despite repeated White House veto threats, GOP leaders added several controversial policy riders to a must-pass supplemental bill (HR 1469), which contained badly needed disaster aid for victims of spring flooding in the upper Midwest. Republicans calculated that the president would be forced either to sign the bill, including the objectionable riders, or to pay the political price for vetoing the disaster relief.

But with flood victims desperate for federal help and nightly newscasts highlighting the story, the GOP strategy backfired. Bogged down by disputes over the unrelated provisions, lawmakers did not finish work on the bill until June 5. True to his word, President Clinton vetoed it June 9. The president blamed GOP leaders for weighing the bill down with "contentious issues totally unrelated to disaster assis-

tance, needlessly delaying essential relief." Opinion polls showed that the public was also blaming the Republicans for the slowdown in disaster relief.

Republican leaders decided to cut their losses and send Clinton a clean flood relief bill that he would sign. On June 12 the House passed a bill (HR 1871) stripped of virtually all controversial riders on a 378–74 vote. Nearly the entire GOP leadership voted "no." The Senate cleared the bill, 78–21, also on June 12, and Clinton signed it into law (PL 105-18) the same day.

As cleared, the bill appropriated $8.9 billion in fiscal 1997 supplemental spending to provide emergency relief from natural disasters and to finance peacekeeping operations in Bosnia and enforcement of the no-fly zone over Iraq.

THE REGULAR BILLS

Work on the thirteen regular fiscal 1998 appropriations bills went into high gear in September, following a summer spent largely on completing a pair of massive budget reconciliation bills. Just four of the thirteen spending bills cleared by Sept. 30, the end of fiscal 1997, with a fifth completed the next day. The following are summaries of the five bills:

• Defense (HR 2266—PL 105-56). The final defense spending bill provided $247.7 billion for defense programs ranging from salaries and maintenance to research and weapons procurement. The total was about $3.8 billion more than Clinton had requested. The president was able to turn aside efforts to restart production of the B-2 stealth bomber and to bar U.S. peacekeepers in Bosnia after June 30, 1998.

• Energy and Water Development (HR 2203—PL 105-62). The bill appropriated $21.1 billion for politically popular water projects and for energy and nuclear weapons programs. The total was $1.9 billion less than President Clinton had requested and about $160 million less than was appropriated for fiscal 1997.

• Legislative Branch (HR 2209—PL 105-55). Under pressure to show self-discipline in spending on itself, Congress agreed to operate with only a slight increase in its funding for fiscal 1998. The $2.25 billion appropriated was only 2 percent higher than the $2.17 billion approved in fiscal 1997.

• Military Construction (HR 2016—PL 105-45). The first appropriations bill of the season, this measure drew overwhelming support in both chambers because it was devoted to construction and repair projects at military bases in nearly all of the fifty states. As cleared the measure provided $9.2 billion—$800 million more than Clinton had requested but still $610 million less than appropriated in fiscal 1997. Nonetheless, this was the first appropriations bill on which the president exercised his newly granted line-item veto, canceling thirty-eight projects totaling $287 million. (Clinton earlier had used his line-item veto to kill three provisions in the reconciliation bills.) Congress overrode the line-item vetoes for the military construction bill in 1998. (*Line-item veto, p. 64; Clinton vetoes, appendix, p. 994*)

• Treasury, Postal Service, General Government (HR 2378—PL 105-61). Congress approved spending of $25.6 billion in fiscal 1998 for the Treasury Department, Postal Service, and general government, but only after dropping a controversial Senate provision that would have blocked a scheduled cost-of-living pay increase for lawmakers. Some members in both chambers had argued that Congress should not take a pay raise until the federal budget deficit was erased, which was expected to happen in 2002.

Four more spending bills were completed by the end of October. The following are summaries of those four:

• Agriculture (HR 2160—PL 105-86). Congress approved $49.7 billion in spending for agriculture programs, about $4 billion less than was appropriated in fiscal 1997. The bill also included $34 million for a program to curb underage smoking, but both chambers rejected efforts to cut federal support for crop insurance and disaster assistance for tobacco growers.

• Interior (HR 2107—PL 105-83). Congress agreed on $13.8 billion for the Department of Interior and several related agencies. The measure almost foundered in the House over the future of the National Endowment for the Arts, an agency that made grants to local arts organizations and that had been the target of GOP conservatives for several years. The House version approved no funding for the agency, but the Senate approved $100 million, and House-Senate conferees settled on $98 million, about the same amount as appropriated in fiscal 1997.

• Transportation (HR 2169—PL 105-66). The fiscal 1998 transportation spending bill provided a record $42.2 billion for highways, highway safety, and transit. That amount was well above the $38.1 billion appropriated in fiscal 1997 and the president's request of $40.2 billion. Clinton subsequently used the line-item veto to cancel three projects worth a total of $6.2 million. (*Line-item veto, p. 64; Clinton vetoes, appendix, p. 994*)

• VA, HUD, Independent Agencies (HR 2158—PL 105-65). A fight among Republicans over the troubled Section 8 subsidized housing program for low-income families, the elderly, and the disabled delayed final action on the spending measure for veterans, housing, environmental and space programs. The final version appropriated a total of $90.7 billion for the Department of Veterans Affairs, the Department of Housing and Urban Development, and seventeen independent agencies, including the Environmental Protection Agency, National Aeronautics and Space Administration, National Science Foundation, and Federal Emergency Management Agency. Clinton subsequently used his line-item veto authority to cancel seven projects worth $14 million. (*Line-item veto, p. 64; Clinton vetoes, appendix, p. 994*)

That left four bills that had been snagged all along over controversial policy issues: Foreign Operations (abortion and family planning); District of Columbia (vouchers for private schooling); Labor, Health and Human Services, and Educa-

tion (national student testing); and Commerce, Justice, and State (census sampling).

With the exception of Clinton's plan for voluntary national student testing, each of these issues had been hashed out before, mostly to the dissatisfaction of conservatives, who insisted on renewing the battles. That dismayed House Appropriations Committee Chairman Robert L. Livingston, R-La., who was determined to avoid having to bundle unfinished spending measures into a year-end omnibus appropriations bill. Twice before, Clinton had used such circumstances to maximize his leverage and force Republicans to accede to his priorities. This time the two sides essentially fought to a draw. The following are summaries of those four bills:

• Commerce, Justice, State, Judiciary (HR 2267—PL 105-119). On the census, the final bill allowed the president to go forward with his plan to use statistical sampling in addition to traditional methods of counting the population, but Republicans won the right to an expedited court challenge of the procedure. The cleared bill appropriated a total of $31.8 billion, more than half of it for law enforcement programs, none of which were controversial.

• District of Columbia (HR 2607—PL 105-100). The student voucher plan, aimed at sending 2,000 low-income District children to private or suburban schools, was pushed by House Republican leaders, but they agreed to drop the plan after Senate Democrats made it clear they would filibuster any effort to add a similar provision to the Senate version. The final bill appropriated $855 million for the District, most of it for federal agencies that were assuming responsibility for much of the city's services. (*Federal–D.C. ties, p. 739*)

• Foreign Operations (HR 2159—PL 105-118). House conservatives also backed down from their insistence on a provision that would have banned funds for family planning groups that promoted, performed, or advocated abortion abroad even if they used their own money. The victory cost Clinton two other key priorities—a plan to pay off back debts to the United Nations and a proposed $3.5 billion commitment to help underwrite an International Monetary Fund program to deal with global financial crises. In addition, the cherished plans of Senate Foreign Relations Committee Chairman Jesse Helms, R-N.C., to restructure foreign policy agencies and revamp the United Nations were stalled by the same imbroglio over abortion. (*State Department authorization, pp. 189, 193*)

The deletion of the proposed funding for the IMF accounted for most of the difference between the $16.9 billion that Clinton requested and the $13.2 billion that Congress agreed to appropriate.

• Labor, Health and Human Services, Education (HR 2264—PL 105-78). For the first time in three years, Congress cleared a stand-alone spending bill for the Departments of Labor, Education, and Health and Human Services, appropriating a total of $276.9 billion; less than a third of the total—$80.4 billion—was for discretionary spending. Despite protracted negotiations, President Clinton was forced to give way on his national voluntary testing plan, which was under attack from conservatives, who worried it would mean federal intrusion into local school systems, and from black and Hispanic lawmakers, who said it would further stigmatize schools in low-income areas.

Fiscal 1999 Budget Resolution

For the first time since the modern congressional budget process was established in 1974, Congress in 1998 failed to agree on a budget resolution for the coming fiscal year. The House and Senate passed dramatically different versions and never even began formal negotiations to work out the differences, which principally involved the size of a proposed tax cut and the consequent spending cuts needed to offset the revenue loss.

Other than the yearly lump-sum allocation to the appropriations committees, which control one-third of the budget, the annual budget resolution was nonbinding. Failure to pass a resolution left in place the blueprint set down in 1997, when President Clinton and the Republican Congress agreed on a five-year plan to balance the budget and cut taxes.

Although it did not produce a finished product, the debate over the budget in 1998 offered both parties an opportunity in an election year to lay out their competing ideas about the role of government. Clinton and the Democrats argued for increased federal "investments" in education, health care, scientific research, and several other domestic programs that appealed to large numbers of voters. Clinton's plan to use any budget surpluses to bolster Social Security was also popular with the voters. For their part, Republicans argued for smaller government and large tax cuts, including elimination of the so-called "marriage penalty" that left about half of all married couples paying more in taxes than they would have as two individual taxpayers.

CLINTON BUDGET REQUEST

Buoyed by steadily increasing tax revenues, President Clinton won a political coup Feb. 2 when he sent Congress not only the first balanced budget in three decades, but also a seemingly pain-free plan to boost spending by as much as $114 billion over five years while running a $219 billion surplus. Although the plan relied heavily on creative accounting and some unlikely legislative luck, its voter appeal sent Republicans scrambling to come up with an alternative.

Overall, Clinton's budget proposal called for $1.73 trillion in spending in fiscal 1999, up 3.9 percent from 1998. Spending would grow at about 2.9 percent a year, reaching $1.95 trillion by fiscal 2003. Social Security, Medicare, and Medicaid accounted for much of the increased spending. But Clinton also proposed new spending for child care, additional teachers to reduce class size, and a myriad of other domestic and defense programs.

The Clinton budget proposed to offset the new spending with $129 billion in new revenues over five years. About half of that ($66 billion) was projected to come from the proceeds of a legal settlement between state governments and tobacco companies that needed congressional approval to take effect. Support for the settlement in Congress was never assured, and the settlement died in June in the Senate, killing any chances that the federal government would receive the projected revenues. (*Tobacco settlement legislation, p. 322*)

Clinton also called for $24.9 billion in tax cuts over five years, including increases in the child care tax credit and monies to promote energy efficiency and to subsidize school construction bonds. To offset these tax cuts, Clinton proposed closing thirty-nine tax loopholes. The budget projected this action would raise $23 billion, but Republicans quickly pointed out that about half of that amount came from tax breaks that Congress had refused to eliminate in the past.

In a politically shrewd move, the administration proposed to "reserve" budget surpluses to "save Social Security first." In actuality, the administration would use the surplus to pay down the national debt. Reducing the debt, especially the portion held by the public, would put downward pressure on interest rates and strengthen the government's overall financial health, making it less costly to issue new debt in the future to pay off the bonds in the Social Security trust funds. Although some lawmakers said the administration was disingenuous in describing buying down debt as protecting Social Security, the proposal, at least initially, forced Republicans to back away from plans to use any surplus to finance tax cuts.

SENATE ACTION

The Senate Budget Committee approved a draft budget resolution (S Con Res 86—S Rept 105-170) March 18 on a 12–10 party-line vote. The resolution hewed closely to the balanced-budget accord Clinton and Congress reached in 1997. The Senate plan anticipated a $1.73 trillion federal budget in fiscal 1999, surpluses beginning in 1998 and totaling $147 billion over five years, and no new net tax cuts, although it would permit $30 billion in such cuts over five years, provided they were paid for with spending offsets or new revenues.

The only major deviation from the 1997 budget resolution was the GOP plan to provide $18.5 billion in additional outlays for highway construction over five years. The resolution would permit the Senate Appropriations Committee to use $19 billion in offsets from the mandatory spending side of the federal ledger to pay for the new highway spending. Appropriators often claimed cuts in mandatory spending programs to finance new discretionary spending but never to the degree anticipated in the fiscal 1999 budget proposals offered by Clinton and the Senate Budget Committee.

To parry Clinton's move to use tobacco money to finance new domestic spending programs without breaking the spending caps, the Republican bill proposed to deposit any tobacco settlement revenues into the Medicare trust fund that pays hospital bills. GOP Senate leaders cast the maneuver as vital to saving the financially troubled federal health care program for the elderly. But even some Republicans on the Budget Committee all but acknowledged that the real purpose of the move was to provide a politically potent counter to Clinton's popular spending plans—just as he had stymied Republican plans for tax cuts with his call to "save Social Security first."

Despite a week of sometimes heated debate, the Senate made no substantive changes in the committee version of S Con Res 86, passing it on April 2 on a nearly party-line vote of 57–41. The only serious challenge to the resolution came from a group of conservatives, led by John Ashcroft, R-Mo., who attacked the plan for doing nothing to advance Republicans principles such as cutting government and reducing taxes. The group initially threatened to oppose the measure if it were not changed significantly, raising the possibility that the resolution might not pass if Democrats held ranks.

The group of conservatives ultimately agreed to back the resolution after winning assurance from the GOP leadership that the final version of the budget resolution that emerged from a House-Senate conference would permit additional tax cuts, allow consideration of a budget reconciliation bill to resolve tax and spending policy issues (S Con Res 86 did not provide for a reconciliation bill), and try to ease the marriage penalty.

HOUSE ACTION

The dilemma for John R. Kasich, R-Ohio, chairman of the House Budget Committee, was to draft a budget resolution that could win support from both the conservative tax-cutting wing of the GOP and the moderate wing who were content with the spending and tax levels spelled out in the 1997 budget accord. With just an eleven-seat GOP majority and little help, if any, expected from Democrats, Kasich and Republican leaders faced a difficult task.

Kasich's original plan called for $154 billion in spending cuts over five years to finance a combination of lower taxes and less government. The list of proposed cuts received a chilly reception from Republican moderates, who objected to reductions in favored programs such as education; from the Senate and the Clinton administration, who said the plan violated the terms of the 1997 budget accord in which Clinton agreed to a GOP-driven tax cut in exchange for higher domestic spending; and from the House's Conservative Action Team, a group of about forty members who insisted on a five-year tax cut of $100 billion or more. In addition, Republicans on the House Appropriations Committee were dismayed at Kasich's plan to cut discretionary spending below the already tight budget caps, arguing that such a move was politically undoable, especially in an election year.

Kasich quickly scaled his plan back to $101 billion in spending and tax cuts, but that did little to overcome objec-

tions from House GOP moderates. So Kasich retreated to a third plan, which still recommended $101 billion in spending cuts but left it up to the policy-making committees to determine where those cuts would come.

As approved by the House Budget Committee May 20 on a party-line vote of 22–16, the nonbinding House budget resolution (H Con Res 284—H Rept 105-555) would cut nondefense discretionary spending by $46 billion over five years, a reduction of 3.5 percent under the budget caps that appropriations subcommittees were already trying to breach. Mandatory spending programs would face cuts totaling $54 billion over five years, although many of the reductions most likely to be enacted had already been earmarked to pay for a massive highway construction bill.

The House passed the budget blueprint June 5 by a vote of 216–204—a tally that required an all-out drive by GOP leaders, who encountered significant resistance from moderates, appropriators, and deficit hawks. To muster the votes necessary to pass the resolution, House GOP leaders promised moderates that the final version of the resolution would be scaled back—a promise directly opposed to one made by Senate GOP leaders to conservative senators to seek larger tax cuts, on the order of those in the House resolution.

FINAL ACTION

No further legislative action was taken on the resolution, which died at the end of the session. Seeming irreconcilable differences within the Republican ranks prevented the House and Senate versions of the budget resolution from ever going to a formal conference. Kasich, Senate Budget Committee Chairman Pete V. Domenici, R-N.M., and other GOP leaders met informally to explore the potential for compromise but quickly found the two sides were still far apart. An upward surge in projections for a budget surplus—to $1.6 trillion over the next ten years—only served to deepen the differences. House Republican leaders were intent on advancing a bill that would provide as much as $167 billion in tax relief over five years and $700 billion over ten years. Moderate and conservative GOP senators alike attacked the plan as bad politics and bad policy, arguing that Social Security had to be fixed before tax cuts were made—as proposed by the president.

Budget process rules would allow Senate Democrats to kill any attempt to use the surplus to cut taxes, but not before they and Clinton hammered away at Republicans on Social Security. House Republicans were frustrated because they believed that tax cuts were a winner with voters and that unless taxes were cut, Congress and Clinton would devote the surplus to new spending programs.

Any slim possibility that a compromise on the matter could be reach disappeared altogether by September when the House voted to begin an impeachment inquiry of the president on charges that he had committed perjury and obstructed justice in an attempt to cover up an affair with a White House intern. (Impeachment, p. 813)

Fiscal 1999 Omnibus Appropriations Bill

After a year-long confrontation between the White House and the House Republicans in 1998, election-year deadline pressure pushed eight of the thirteen appropriations bills for the year into an omnibus spending measure for fiscal 1999 (HR 4328—PL 105-277) that broke through budget caps set in 1997.

The measure incorporated the spending bills for Agriculture, Commerce-Justice-State, District of Columbia, foreign operations, Interior, Labor-HHS-Education, Transportation, and Treasury-Postal Service. The bill also served as a vehicle for writing several policy-setting pieces of legislation into law.

The measure, which appropriated approximately $500 billion, cleared Oct. 21 after more than a week of negotiations between top GOP leaders and White House officials, led by soon-to-retire Chief of Staff Erskine Bowles. Despite Clinton's perceived weakness—caused by the pending impeachment inquiry over charges that he lied to cover up an extramarital affair—the administration was able to extract numerous spending and policy concessions, including $1.2 billion for Clinton's initiative to subsidize the hiring of 100,000 new teachers and his full $17.9 billion request for the International Monetary Fund. The omnibus bill also contained $21 billion in supplemental spending for such items as Bosnia peacekeeping, antiterrorism efforts, and federal computer upgrades.

Republicans, who had suffered at the polls in 1996 after their refusal to cooperate with the president led to two temporary shutdowns of the federal government, were eager to obtain the president's signature on the mammoth bill before going home to campaign in the 1998 elections. They conceded one spending demand after another and dropped many of the conservative policy "riders" that had blocked agreement on the original appropriations bills. In return, Republicans won a boost in defense spending and some riders, such as an extended ban on taxpayer-funded needle-exchange programs and continued curbs on Clinton's national educational testing initiative.

Nonspending bills attached to the omnibus spending bill included legislation to extend tax credits, a reorganization of U.S. foreign policy agencies, an increase in the number of visas for high-tech workers, new curbs on minors' access to pornography on the Internet, a moratorium on Internet taxes, and implementation of the recently ratified Chemical Weapons Convention.

A TURBULENT YEAR

The bill's passage capped a turbulent year for appropriations. House GOP leaders, aiming to placate conservatives, insisted that appropriators write Republican-tilting bills instead of the bipartisan measures that passed in 1997 in the wake of that year's budget deal. The result was a stormy summer and numerous differences—not only between Republicans and the White House but also among Republicans. The Senate wrote bipartisan bills that used accounting devices, such as "emergency" spending that does not count against budget caps, to pump more money into the bills. But Democrats politicized debate on several bills, and four of the appropriations measures failed to pass the Senate.

The sometimes chaotic negotiations over the omnibus bill produced a bloated measure that conservatives and budget hawks loathed in a process that no one was willing to defend: decisions made by senior White House aides in a room with a small group of lawmakers. Democratic legislators felt shut out of the process but they won concessions that they would not have obtained had all thirteen appropriations bills been negotiated individually and sent separately to the White House.

NO GUIDELINES

The omnibus appropriations bill was probably the logical outcome in a year when neither Clinton nor lawmakers displayed much enthusiasm for debating budget and tax issues. After sending Congress a budget in February Clinton pressed other issues, such as health insurance changes, a campaign finance overhaul, and antismoking legislation, each of which died. (*Children's health insurance, pp. 433, 438; campaign finance, pp. 776, 778*)

For all their talk of cutting taxes, Republicans never tried to piece together a realistic tax reduction package. The House managed to pass an $80 billion tax cut bill (HR 4579) on Sept. 26, 1998, on a 229–195 party-line vote, but Senate GOP leaders could not muster a simple majority to pass it, much less reach the 60 votes needed to overcome Democratic parliamentary maneuvers. They never took up the House measure. (*Tax cut, p. 105*)

Nor was Congress able to pass a 1998 budget resolution—the blueprint that was supposed to serve as the guideline for subsequent action on spending and taxes. It was the first time since passage of the 1974 budget act (PL 93-344) that Congress failed to pass such a resolution. (*1999 budget resolution, p. 60*)

Meanwhile, lawmakers of both parties found opportunities to spend more money. They relied not only on the emergency spending loophole and accounting tricks to get around the spending caps contained in the 1997 tax- and deficit-cutting resolution but also on a growing budget surplus. Clinton's February budget predicted small surpluses heading into the next century. But by the time summer arrived surplus projections had surged and, to no one's surprise, lawmakers started making plans to spend some of it. Given those circumstances, said Robert D. Reischauer, a senior fellow at the Brookings Institution and former director of the Congressional Budget Office, "the fact that Congress has abandoned the [budget] discipline to the tune of $10–$20 billion should probably be viewed as about as good as one could expect."

CONGRESSIONAL ACTION

Talks on the omnibus bill began Oct. 7 after disagreements among Republicans and between them and the White House prevented eight appropriations bills from being enacted before the new fiscal year began on Oct. 1. The negotiations moved slowly as Democrats in Congress, who were generally closed out of direct negotiations, pressured Bowles to play hard ball. As negotiations dragged on, Democrats took delight in having a forum for their election year agenda.

The negotiations involved virtually every legislative item that had any life in it. Proposals were floated, shot down, and floated again. At one point, tax lobbyists were pessimistic about the fate of a popular measure (HR 4738) to extend expired tax breaks such as the research and development tax credit. But the $9.2 billion measure was inserted at the last minute, even though adding it to the omnibus bill amounted to treading on the well-guarded turf of the tax-writing House Ways and Means and Senate Finance Committees.

The epicenter of the talks was the office of House Speaker Newt Gingrich, R-Ga., where under the watchful eye of the speaker's famed Tyrannosaurus Rex dinosaur head, Bowles, Office of Management and Budget Director Jacob Lew, and other members of the White House negotiating team wrangled for days with Republicans. Shuttling back and forth from the "dinosaur room" to the office of Senate Minority Leader Tom Daschle, D-S.D., and House Minority Leader Richard A. Gephardt, D-Mo., Bowles attracted hordes of reporters eager for any hint of progress.

Inside the room, hundreds of big and small deals were cut. Often a deal that everyone thought was settled was reopened in negotiating still other deals. In the aftermath, staff aides responsible for drafting precise bill language lamented that in many cases negotiators had not put the deals in writing nor determined who would provide the legislative text. The result was a sixteen-inch, forty-pound, nearly 4,000-page measure that was far bigger and stuffed with more extraneous provisions than Democratic Congresses had ever delivered to Republican presidents Ronald Reagan or George Bush.

To Speaker Gingrich, the omnibus bill and the process that had spawned it were the price of having government divided between Republicans in Congress and a Democrat in the White House. But many Republicans, especially among those first elected in the Republican takeover of 1994, disagreed. "At a time when we are dealing with a weakened president . . . you would think that our leadership, who professed to be conservatives leading this [Republican] revolution, could stand tough within that budget cap and stay true to the commitment we came to and came here for in 1994," said conservative Rep. John W. Christensen, R-Neb. "We have failed in this process."

Gingrich responded to such allegations in a passionate speech closing floor debate on the bill: "The fact is there is a liberal Democrat in the White House . . . . And there are things that he wants in order to sign a bill, and that is legitimate and a part of precisely what the Founding Fathers established: a balance of power."

Still, no one took pride in a process that produced a take-it-or-leave-it vote on a massive piece of legislation that virtually no one had read and on which decisions were made by very few people. "I am not going to defend the process. I hate

the process," said House Appropriations Committee Chairman Robert L. Livingston, R-La.

Despite misgivings about the process and reservations about the new spending, Congress easily cleared the bill. The House adopted the conference report on HR 4328 (H Rept 105-825) Oct. 20 on a **key vote of 333–95 (R 162–64; D 170–31; I 1–0).** GOP leaders in the Senate had hoped to clear the bill by voice vote, but several dissatisfied senators demanded a recorded vote to register their opposition. The Senate nonetheless easily cleared HR 4328 Oct. 21 by a **key vote of 65–29 (R 33–20; D 32–9).** Clinton signed the measure the same day. *(1998 key votes, p. 883)*

PROVISIONS

As cleared, the omnibus appropriations bill (HR 4328—PL 105-277) represented the largest single legislative measure in recent history. The vehicle for the bill was the House- and Senate-passed Transportation appropriations bill to which conferees added their agreements on the seven other appropriations measures. Altogether appropriations for the departments and agencies covered by the eight regular spending bills amounted to $487 billion. In addition, the package included $20.8 billion in supplemental "emergency" fiscal 1999 funds, offset by $2.6 billion in spending reductions, and it enacted several other nonrelated matters. Following are highlights from the measure.

Agriculture

HR 4328 provided $55.9 billion in fiscal 1999 for the Agriculture Department and related agencies. It also included $5.9 billion in emergency payments to farmers and $1 billion in tax cuts to address the farm financial crisis. Clinton had vetoed the regular agriculture appropriations bill (HR 4101) on Oct. 7 because he said it failed to deal adequately with the farming crisis.

The omnibus spending bill did not contain a provision prohibiting the Food and Drug Administration from approving abortion drugs such as RU-486. The House had included such a prohibition in the original version of the agriculture spending bill, but it was dropped in the conference on that bill.

Commerce-Justice-State

HR 4328 provided a total of $33.7 billion in fiscal 1999 for the Commerce, Justice, and State Departments; the federal judiciary; and related agencies. But in an unusual twist, the agreement stipulated that all funding under the bill would expire on June 15, 1999, unless and until separate legislation was enacted specifying whether the Census Bureau could use statistical sampling to augment the traditional headcount during the 2000 census. The deadline was intended to give the Supreme Court enough time to rule on the legality and constitutionality of statistical sampling. *(Sampling controversy, pp. 733, 736)*

Republicans generally opposed statistical sampling because they said it violated both the law and the Constitution,

LINE-ITEM VETO: A FAILED EXPERIMENT

The long-sought line-item veto, which gave the president authority to veto individual items in appropriations bills, had a short and tumultuous life before being declared unconstitutional by the Supreme Court in June 1998. The Court's ruling ended a brief experiment intended to strengthen the president's hand in curbing the congressional spending appetite. Proponents of a line-item veto said they would try to find another way to resurrect the idea, but the advent of a budget surplus in 1998 undermined the political urgency that had originally impelled Congress to transfer part of its spending power to the president.

The governors of forty-four states had some form of line-item veto power, enabling them to cancel individual items in spending bills without having to veto the entire measure. Although numerous presidents since Ulysses S. Grant (1869–1877) had sought similar line-item veto authority, the idea did not gain any measurable support in Congress until budget deficits began to burgeon under the presidency of Ronald Reagan (1981–1989). Republican candidates for the House of Representatives made the line-item veto a cornerstone of their "Contract with America" platform in 1994. When the GOP won control of Congress in that year's election they made good on their pledge by enacting a version of the line-item veto in 1996. *(Congress and the Nation, Vol. IX, p. 78)*

Even before the Supreme Court invalidated the line-item veto it had become clear that the procedure, by itself, was not likely to be a cure-all for chronic budget deficits. Although opponents had said the line-item veto transferred too much power to the president, President Bill Clinton, who had embraced enactment of the veto with enthusiasm, used the new authority sparingly, especially after his first vetoes provoked both howls of protest from Congress and the constitutional challenge to the transfer of power. Nor was there any evidence that the prospect of a line-item veto curbed legislators' penchant for "pork-barrel" projects that benefited their constituencies. Supporters had argued that curbing such spending was the primary reason for enacting the line-item veto in the first place. *(Supreme Court decision, p. 714)*

Enhanced Rescissions

The line-item veto enacted in 1996 (PL 104-130) was not a true line-item veto, which would have allowed the president to strike individual items or lines or words from bills that he wanted to sign. Because the Constitution required the president to accept or reject bills in their entirety, a true line-

item veto would have required a constitutional amendment, which was considered politically infeasible.

Instead Republicans crafted a complex procedure, called the "enhanced rescission." A rescission was a procedure dating from the 1974 budget control law allowing a president to tell Congress that he was planning not to spend certain sums that had been appropriated. Congress could overturn a rescission by passing disapproval legislation by a majority vote. Under the new "enhanced rescission" procedure, Congress would pass its normal appropriations bills and send them to the president for his signature. Within five days after signing a spending bill, the president could, in effect, "cancel" individual spending items, as well as narrowly focused tax breaks and new entitlement programs. To restore the spending or tax provision, Congress could pass a "disapproval" bill within thirty days. Such a bill would itself be subject to a presidential veto, which Congress then could overturn but only by mustering a two-thirds vote of both chambers as the Constitution requires for a veto override.

Led by Robert C. Byrd, D-W.Va., a dogged defender of congressional powers and prerogatives, a handful of members of Congress filed a legal challenge to the veto law on Jan. 2, 1997, the day after it took effect and before it had been used. The legislators argued that the new law gave the president the power to change or amend a law after he had signed it, in violation of Article I of the Constitution, which vested in Congress all legislative power to write and amend laws. On June 26, 1997, the Supreme Court threw out that challenge on procedural grounds. In its 7–2 decision in *Byrd v. Raines*, the Court ruled that the legislators did not have standing to sue because they had not been harmed personally by use of the veto.

Clinton's Exercise of the Veto

Although the line-item veto law went into effect on Jan. 1, 1997, Clinton did not use it until Aug. 11, when he "canceled" two narrowly targeted tax breaks and a "direct spending" provision to help the state of New York finance its Medicaid program, provisions contained in the twin tax and spending reconciliation laws (PL 105-33; PL 105-34). In exercising the line-item veto in these three instances, Clinton ignored advice to wait and use the veto against appropriations measures where legal analysts said he would be on more solid constitutional ground. Clinton's political advisers reportedly carried the day, arguing that Clinton had to use this opportunity in advance of the appropriations season to demonstrate his willingness to use the new veto power.

On Oct. 6, Clinton outraged members of Congress when he canceled thirty-eight projects worth $287 million from the $9.2 billion fiscal 1998 military construction spending bill (HR 2016—PL 105-45). Several legislators who had voted for enactment of the line-item veto quickly changed their position. "I feel like I need to eat a little crow," said one.

On eight subsequent appropriations bills sent to him in 1997, Clinton used the new tool with a lighter hand, vetoing forty-three additional projects totaling less than $200 million. He appeared uneasy at the prospect of alienating members whose votes he needed for a major fast-track trade negotiating authority bill (HR 2621), which ultimately failed. The president limited his vetoes to projects that appeared difficult to defend, such as a $1.9 billion project to dredge a Mississippi lake for a private marina and conference center. *(Fast-track authority, p. 153)*

Congressional Challenge

Despite their grumbling, lawmakers challenged only Clinton's veto of the thirty-eight military construction projects. From the outset, angry appropriators ignored offers from the White House to cooperate in redrafting some of the vetoed provisions. Instead, the Senate on Oct. 30 passed a bill (S 1292) disapproving all but two of the vetoes. The **key vote was 69–30 (R 42–12; D 27–18)**, a two-vote cushion over the two-thirds majority the Senate would need to override a veto of the bill. *(1997 key votes, p. 865)*

House appropriators initially signaled their disinterest in challenging the president, hinting they might instead try to restore the military construction funding through a supplemental appropriations bill. The Senate vote, however, emboldened the House to pass a measure (HR 2631) on Nov. 8, disapproving of all thirty-eight vetoes. The vote was 352–64. The Senate agreed to the House bill the next day, clearing it by voice vote.

As expected, Clinton vetoed the new bill Nov. 13, just as the House adjourned for the year. When Congress returned in 1998, the House voted to override Clinton's veto Feb. 5 on a **key vote of 347–69 (R 197–23; D 149–46; I 1–0)**. The Senate cleared the measure (PL 105-159) restoring funding for the military construction projects Feb. 25 on a 78–20 vote. It was one of just two Clinton vetoes that Congress over-rode; the other was a 1995 law (PL 104-67) to curb securities fraud litigation. *(1998 key votes, p. 883; Clinton vetoes, p. 810 and appendix, p. 994; 1995 law, Congress and the Nation, Vol. IX, p. 142)*

Constitutional Challenge

The successful court challenge to the line-item veto came from Clinton's first use of it: his vetoes of provisions to help New York state finance its Medicaid program and to give a capital gains tax break to farmer-owned cooperatives. Plaintiffs claiming they had been harmed by these two vetoes included New York City, its hospital system, and hospital workers, and the Snake River Potato Growers Inc. in Idaho. The cases of *Clinton v. City of New York* and *Snake River Potato Growers Inc. v. Rubin* were subsequently consolidated to help ensure that at least one plaintiff would have standing under the Constitution.

On Feb. 12, 1998, U.S. District Court Judge Thomas F. Hogan, in Washington, ruled in favor of the plaintiffs, declaring the veto law was unconstitutional. Hogan's ruling went straight to the Supreme Court for review. In a 6–3 ruling on June 25, the high court struck down the line-item veto law as violating Article I, Section 7 of the Constitution, which established the procedure for the enactment of laws, and Article I, Section 1, which defined the separate powers of the three branches of government.

Writing for the majority, Justice John Paul Stevens said: "If the Line-Item Veto Act were valid, it would authorize the president to create a different law—one whose text was not voted on by either House of Congress or presented to the president. If there is to be a new procedure in which the president will play a different role in determining the final text of what may 'become a law,' such change must come not by legislation but through . . . [constitutional] amendment."

In a statement, Clinton called the Court's decision "a defeat for all Americans." Overturning the veto had deprived presidents of "a valuable tool for eliminating waste in the federal budget," he said. In contrast, James W. Dyer, staff director of the House Appropriations Committee, may have reflected the sentiment of many members of Congress when he said: "This is a law that really did not make a significant contribution to reducing the deficit and was poorly handled to the point it was an embarrassment to the administration and the Hill both."

which required actual head counts and because they feared it could open the census to political manipulation and error that could lead to congressional district alignments more favorable to Democrats. Democrats, including President Clinton, and most professional statisticians favored statistical sampling as a more accurate way to count people often missed by a traditional head count, including those who do not speak English, rural and urban poor, and those who were not comfortable dealing with census takers.

The original House bill (HR 4276—H Rept 105-636), which passed Aug. 6, 225–203, would have cut of funding on March 31, 1999, if an agreement had not been reached, but only for the Census Bureau. The Senate bill (S 2260—S Rept 105-235), passed July 23, 99–0, did not address the issue.

The omnibus spending bill also provided $475 million in U.S. back payments to the United Nations, but the bill required that U.N. funding could not be released until it was approved in separate legislation, and until the U.S. share of U.N. funding was reduced to 22 percent from its current level of 25 percent. Congress had cleared a measure (HR 1757) that would have paid off all of the U.S. debt to the United Nations but Clinton vetoed it on Oct. 21—the same day he signed the omnibus spending bill—because it contained antiabortion restrictions on international family planning aid. *(Antiabortion restrictions, p. 189)*

HR 4328 also contained provisions requiring federal prosecutors to follow the prosecutorial guidelines of the state in which they work. Dropped from the omnibus bill were provisions passed by the House that would have created a new set of federal ethical guidelines to be followed by all federal prosecutors, including independent counsels, such as Kenneth W. Starr, whose investigation of President Clinton led to the president's impeachment. The provisions had been sponsored by Joseph M. McDade, R-Pa., who had been the subject of a six-year probe into allegations of bribery, of which he was acquitted in 1996. *(Impeachment, p. 813)*

District of Columbia

The House passed its original spending bill for the District of Columbia (HR 4380—H Rept 105-670) on Aug. 7 by a vote of 214–206, after Republicans pushed through several legislative riders that Democrats criticized. Wary of the controversy surrounding the measure, Senate leaders never brought their version of the bill (S 2333—S Rept 105-254) to the floor.

The omnibus spending bill left out several of the House-passed riders, including one that would have prohibited unmarried couples in the District from adopting a child and another that would have required new District employees to live in the District of Columbia. It did incorporate two controversial House-passed provisions. One would have prohibited public funding of any needle exchange program for drug addicts in the District. Advocates of such programs said they

helped stem the transmission of AIDS, but opponents said they encouraged drug use. The second provision prohibited the District from joining in any civil action against major tobacco companies. The District would thus not be permitted to participate in any suits brought by the states to recover Medicaid and other costs that might be determined to be attributable to tobacco use.

Foreign Operations

The omnibus fiscal 1999 spending bill appropriated $12.8 billion for foreign aid and export assistance, $750 million less than the president requested. The final version largely resembled the House-passed version of the foreign operations appropriations bill (HR 4569—H Rept 105-719) except for two key provisions. Unlike the House version, HR 4328 did not contain the antiabortion restrictions on international family planning funding. HR 4328 also contained the full $17.9 billion the administration had requested for the International Monetary Fund (IMF), including $14.5 billion in credit that Clinton wanted to help replenish funds depleted by financial crises in Asia, Mexico, and Russia. The original Senate bill (S 2334—S Rept 105-255), but not the House bill, had contained the $14.5 billion appropriation. The omnibus spending bill stipulated that none of the funds could be released to the IMF until the Treasury secretary and the Federal Reserve chairman had certified to Congress that the IMF had made certain specific reforms. *(IMF, p. 188)*

HR 4328 provided $3 billion in aid for Israel and $2.1 billion for Egypt. For the first time since the signing of the Camp David accords between Israel and Egypt in March 1979, it cut economic assistance to the two countries as part of a ten-year phaseout of U.S. economic aid. For the first time in twenty years, Congress appropriated no military financing assistance for either Greece or Turkey. The agreement earmarked $35 million for the purchase and shipment of fuel oil to North Korea but restricted those payments until the president certified that North Korea was making progress toward ending its nuclear and ballistic missile programs. The president could waive certification if he determined that doing so was in the best interests of national security. *(North Korea aid, p. 189)*

Interior

The omnibus agreement appropriated a total of $14.1 billion in fiscal 1999 for the Interior Department and related agencies, $616 million more than the House-passed bill (HR 4193—H Rept 105-609) but $163 million less than the president's request. The Senate never passed its bill (S 2237—S Rept 105-227); it was pulled from the floor Sept. 16 after it had become mired in nongermane amendments.

White House negotiators were able to pry loose $1.7 billion for the president's Clean Water Action Plan, a five-year initiative to address problems caused by agricultural and storm water runoff; $328 million for the Land and Water

Conservation fund, the government's primary tool for acquiring land that was ecologically important and threatened; and $1 billion for climate change initiatives, with most of the money going for research on energy efficiency and renewable energy. The latter provision was controversial because it was linked to the Kyoto treaty on global warming, which was highly unpopular in Congress. *(Kyoto treaty, p. 354)*

The White House said most of the environmental riders that had drawn strong administration objections during consideration of the regular spending bill had been removed or minimized. Among them were a plan that would have dismantled the Columbia Basin Ecosystem Management Plan, a novel, seven-state agreement to protect endangered salmon while allowing property owners more use of their land.

To the relief of environmentalists, negotiators also deleted riders that would have allowed construction of a single-land gravel road through Alaska's Izembek National Wildlife Refuge and allowed additional logging in the Tongass National Forest. Also eliminated was a $50 million annual subsidy to timber companies logging on federal land. The final bill still contained several items that left environmental groups disappointed, including provisions to allow additional logging in three national forests in California and to renew automatically grazing leases on some public lands. *(Roadless areas, p. 394)*

Labor-HHS-Education

Disputes were so numerous and the underlying policy disagreements so fundamental that neither the House nor the Senate passed a regular spending bill for the Labor, Education, and Health and Human Services departments in 1998. With no floor action in either chamber, Republicans were in a weak bargaining position during negotiations over the omnibus bill. The administration won numerous victories as a result.

One of the most significant gains for the White House was an appropriation not included in either of the original House or Senate bills—$1.2 billion as a first installment on the administration's proposal to hire 100,000 teachers in the next seven years to reduce class sizes in the first three grades. The agreement also provided $260 million for a literacy initiative proposed by the administration but not funded in either chamber's bill. The deal also reinstated funding for the summer jobs program at the fiscal 1998 level of $871 million and provided $1.1 billion for the Low-Income Home Energy Assistance Program, two of the president's top priorities. The House committee bill (HR 4274—H Rept 105-635) had cut all funding for these two programs.

Other agencies that won large funding increases included the National Institutes of Health, which got a 15 percent increase of nearly $2 billion, and the Ryan White AIDS programs, which received a 24 percent increase ($262 million).

The final bill did not include a controversial provision that would have required parental consent before a minor child could obtain contraceptive drugs or devices from federally funded family planning clinics. Conservatives were pleased, however, that the bill banned federal funding for needle exchange programs and for the creation of human embryos for research purposes. The measure also banned the use of federal education funds to develop, plan, or administer any national education test unless explicitly authorized by law. In addition, it imposed a moratorium on implementation of controversial regulations creating a national system for allocating hearts, kidneys, and other organs donated for transplant.

Overall, the bill provided about $290 billion in spending for health, education, and labor programs. The majority of the spending was for entitlement programs. Discretionary spending totaled $83.2 billion, up from $81.1 billion. The Education Department increased by nearly $3.5 billion, and education funding exceeded Clinton's original budget request.

Transportation

The House and Senate versions of the regular transportation spending bill were not far apart on spending levels and contained relatively narrow differences on other issues. As a result, transportation appropriators hoped that a conference version could be kept separate from the omnibus spending bill that was certain to be negotiated at the end of the session. Instead the transportation bill became the underlying vehicle for the massive spending measure.

In its final form HR 4328 provided $47.0 billion for federal transportation programs, 12 percent more than was appropriated in 1997 and 9 percent more than the administration had requested. About 70 percent of the funding was earmarked for highway, highway safety, and mass transit programs. Those amounts conformed to the levels laid out in the six-year surface transportation law enacted earlier in the year. Lawmakers increased funding in some areas, however, including adding $75 million for President Clinton's welfare-to-work initiative—$25 million more than guaranteed—to help low-income workers commute to jobs. *(Transportation law, p. 318)*

Controversial riders inserted in the final bill included a freeze on new corporate average fuel economy (CAFE) standards for automobiles and several waivers of environmental reporting requirements for three specific road projects. One controversial rider that was dropped from the final bill would have transferred the Office of Motor Carriers, which regulates long-haul carriers, from the Federal Highway Administration to the National Highway Traffic Safety Administration. The transfer was aimed at toughening truck safety inspections. *(CAFE standards, p. 333)*

The omnibus bill included a six-month reauthorization of the Federal Aviation Administration that was intended to force debate in early 1999 on controversial proposals to nurture airline competition at four crowded airports in Washington, D.C., Chicago, and New York.

Treasury-Postal Service

The Treasury-Postal Service appropriations bill, traditionally one of the more nettlesome of the regular spending measures, ran true to form in 1998. But the problems the bill encountered were primarily because of its legislative provisions rather than its funding levels. The version incorporated into the omnibus bill appropriated a total of $26.8 billion for the Treasury Department, Postal Service, Executive Office, and general government functions. It included provisions requiring federal employee health plans that cover prescription drugs to cover a full range of contraceptives, and it permitted about 50,000 Haitian refugees to remain permanently in the United States.

The provision on contraceptives was one of the last issues to be resolved in the top-level negotiations over the omnibus spending bill. The final version specifically exempted five religious health plans from the requirement, along with individual doctors who refuse to prescribe contraceptives because their use would be contrary to their religious beliefs or moral convictions. The measure also barred the use of any funds in the bill to pay for abortions under federal employee health benefit plans, except if the life of the woman was endangered or in cases of rape or incest. (*Provisions, p. 458*)

The bill also provided a 3.6 percent cost-of-living adjustment for all federal employees except members of Congress, federal judges, and high executive officials, who were barred from receiving the inflation adjustment. A provision that would have placed term limits on the top two staff officials at the Federal Election Commission (FEC) was dropped from the final bill. Introduced in the Senate by Republican Mitch McConnell, Ky., the provision was vigorously opposed by Democrats who charged that it was intended to stifle the FEC's scrutiny of "soft money" donations, which are largely unregulated contributions to political parties.

Supplemental Appropriations

HR 4328 appropriated $20.8 billion in supplemental spending in fiscal 1999 in a package that blended priorities of the administration with those of the Republicans. Under budget-writing rules on Capitol Hill, supplemental spending requests must be designated as "emergency" spending or counted against budget caps set most recently in the 1997 spending reconciliation bill (PL 105-33). Usually such spending was for genuine emergencies such as natural disaster aid. But with appropriators already struggling to stay within the caps, estimates of future budget surpluses rising rapidly, and tough negotiations over myriad spending items, the level of emergency spending exploded.

In addition to $5.9 billion in emergency farm aid, the omnibus spending bill included $6.8 billion in supplemental funds for the Defense Department, including a $1.9 billion administration request to continue U.S. participation in peacekeeping forces in Bosnia and $1 billion for ballistic missile defense programs; $2.4 billion in antiterrorism activities;

$1.5 billion for emergencies related to Hurricane George and other disasters; and $3.4 billion to help the federal government deal with the year 2000 (Y2K) computer problem.

Other Provisions

The omnibus bill contained several other legislative programs that had been debated in the context of one regular spending bill or another. Among the most important of these were the following:

- **Tax extenders.** The agreement extended, generally for one year, several expiring tax breaks at a cost of $9.2 billion over nine years. The extensions were fully offset by other changes in the tax code. (*Tax breaks, p. 106*)

- **Visas for high-tech workers.** The agreement increased the number of visas for foreign skilled workers and professionals—known as H-1B visas—from 65,000 in fiscal 1998 to 115,000 in both fiscal 1999 and fiscal 2000. The measure required all companies hiring H-1B workers to state that they had not laid off or otherwise displaced U.S. workers with substantially equivalent qualifications. (*High-tech visas, p. 616*)

- **Medicare home health care payments.** In a boost for Medicare patients at risk of losing their home health care, negotiators increased reimbursements for such care by $1.7 billion. Providers had said that the reimbursement formula adopted in the 1997 spending reconciliation bill was driving many of them out of business and forcing others to deny service.

- **Internet tax moratorium.** The agreement imposed a three-year moratorium on new taxes on Internet access and online services. It also created a nineteen-member commission to study whether electronic commerce should be taxed. (*Internet tax, p. 327*)

- **Internet access to pornography.** The agreement made it illegal for commercial Internet Web sites to offer material considered "harmful to minors" unless the operator of the Web site restricted access by minors through an adult-verification system, such as use of a credit card, debit card, adult access codes, or adult personal identification number. The provisions were similar to those contained in a House-passed bill (HR 3783—H Rept 105-775). (*Internet safeguards, p. 329*)

Another provision required the Federal Trade Commission to establish rules requiring commercial Web sites to obtain parental consent before collecting and using any personal information from children that visit that Web site.

- **Foreign affairs agencies reorganization.** The agreement contained provisions of HR 1757 reorganizing U.S. foreign policy agencies. President Clinton was expected to veto HR 1757 because it carried a controversial provision imposing antiabortion restrictions on international family planning aid. (Clinton did veto HR 1757 on Oct. 21, the same day that he signed the omnibus spending bill.) The omnibus agreement directed a major reorganization of U.S. foreign policy agencies, including elimination of the Arms Control and Disarmament Agency, the U.S. Information

Agency, and certain functions of the Agency for International Development and consolidated their functions into the State Department. *(Reorganization, p. 193)*

• **Chemical Weapons Convention.** The agreement amended U.S. law to implement the Chemical Weapons Convention, which outlawed the development, use, or stockpiling of chemical weapons and established an international agency to conduct inspections and collect data to verify compliance. The United States was in technical violation of the treaty until it passed implementing legislation. The Senate had passed the implementing legislation (S 610) on May 23, 1997, a month after ratifying the treaty, but the measure languished for months in the House, where GOP leaders eventually attached it to a separate bill (HR 2709) aimed at punishing overseas companies and research laboratories, primarily in Russia, that provided missile technology to Iran. Republicans hoped the move would force Clinton to agree to economic sanctions against Iran that he opposed. Instead, Clinton vetoed the Iran sanctions bill, and with it the treaty-implementing provisions. *(Iran sanctions, p. 199)*

Other Fiscal 1999 Appropriations Bills

Only five of the thirteen regular fiscal 1999 appropriations bills were enacted on their own in 1998, and only one of those—military construction—was passed on time and unencumbered. The spending bill for the departments of Veterans Affairs (VA) and Housing and Urban Development (HUD) became the vehicle for an overhaul of public housing policy and nearly foundered over two other unrelated policy riders. Three spending bills—Defense, Legislative Branch, and Energy and Water—passed after last-minute or controversial provisions were transferred to the omnibus appropriations bill (HR 4328—PL 105-277).

DEFENSE

HR 4103 (PL 105-262) appropriated $250.5 billion for defense in fiscal 1999, in line with the budget caps set in 1997 (PL 105-33) and with the president's request. But House-Senate conferees left out $400 million for spare parts and repairs after President Clinton announced that he would ask for at least $1 billion in supplemental spending for just such items in the name of combat readiness. HR 4103 also did not include a $1.9 billion request for peacekeeping operations in Bosnia. The emergency supplemental added to the omnibus spending bill contained the full request for Bosnia and $1.3 billion for combat readiness.

ENERGY AND WATER

A dispute between the House and the Senate over the federal subsidy for nonpower activities of the Tennessee Valley Authority (TVA) was resolved one way in the regular Energy and Water appropriations bill (HR 4060—PL 105-245) but reversed in the omnibus bill. As it had in 1997, the House provided no money for the TVA subsidy, which funded such activities as flood control, navigation, dam maintenance, and environmental initiatives. Unlike in 1997, the House prevailed in conference, when Senate negotiators agreed to drop their provision appropriating $70 million for the subsidy. *(TVA, p. 370)*

Instead the senators turned to the emergency supplemental, where they succeeded in adding $50 million for the TVA subsidy. Lawmakers from Tennessee and adjacent states, as well as Vice President Al Gore, a Tennessee native, supported a continuation of the funding, defending it against charges that the federal government should not be offering financial support to an electricity producer.

The supplemental appropriations also included funding for several other energy and water development projects, much of it in emergency funding to help Russia. It included $200 million to dispose of fifty tons of Russian nuclear weapons-derived plutonium and $325 million to buy nuclear weapons-derived uranium.

LEGISLATIVE BRANCH

Little controversy surrounded passage of the regular spending bill for the legislative branch (HR 4112—PL 105-275). The legislation included a 12 percent increase for the Capitol Police, in the wake of the deaths of two officers in a July 24, 1998, shooting in the Capitol. But $207 million for additional security improvements requested by the police and congressional leaders, including the construction of a visitors' center, was treated as "emergency" supplemental funding in the omnibus spending bill.

VA-HUD

Riders to overhaul public housing programs, establish patients' rights under managed health care plans, and prohibit the administration from implementing the Kyoto global warming treaty it had negotiated nearly sunk the regular VA-HUD spending bill (HR 4194—PL 105-276).

The move to add the public housing overhaul to the spending bill touched off a contentious debate on the House floor. Appropriators believed that inclusion of the languishing and controversial housing legislation would delay enactment of the spending bill. The House nonetheless adopted the amendment by a 230–181 vote, and both House and Senate conferees agreed that attaching the authorizing legislation to the spending bill was the only way to get it passed. A separate "subconference" of leaders on the Banking Committees' housing subcommittees worked out the differences between the two chambers on the housing reform, and it was incorporated into the final version of the spending bill. *(Housing reform, p. 553)*

In the Senate, consideration was delayed for more than a week as Democrats tried to attach the unrelated patients' rights legislation. Senate Minority Leader Tom Daschle, D-S.D., said the move was necessary because Republicans would not agree to an open debate on health care. Daschle had failed in several earlier attempts to add the Democrats' managed care bill to other must-pass legislation, and this effort similarly failed. He eventually withdrew the amendment.

Another significant obstacle to the bill's passage involved an effort to prevent the Environmental Protection Agency (EPA) from attempting to implement that Kyoto Protocol, an international agreement to reduce global warming that the Clinton administration had endorsed in December 1997. The treaty was highly unpopular in both chambers of Congress, and the Senate was considered highly unlikely to ratify it. Not wishing to take any chances, however, treaty opponents in both chambers wanted to ensure that the administration could not implement the treaty through regulatory action.

The language agreed to by conferees prohibited the use of funds "to propose or issue rules, regulations, decrees or orders for the purpose of implementation of the Kyoto Protocol." Report language made it clear that the provision was intended to bar actions related solely to implementing the Kyoto treaty and was not intended to prevent the EPA from carrying out activities already authorized in other laws. *(Kyoto treaty, p. 354)*

1999–2000

Adapting to the politics of a budget surplus was perhaps the biggest challenge facing both political parties during the 106th Congress in 1999 and 2000. Despite the requisite calls from Republicans and the White House for high-minded bipartisanship, both sides quickly dug in for a battle over use of the rapidly enlarging surplus, fully aware that they were setting the stage for the important 2000 elections in which control of the White House and Congress was up for grabs.

With Democrats and Republicans promising to reserve a large portion of the surplus to pay down the public debt, the controversy quickly came down to taxes. In 1999 and 2000 Republicans spent much of the legislative year pushing expensive tax cut packages through Congress, only to have them vetoed by President Clinton. The exercise gave Democrats and Republicans ample opportunity to define their political philosophies for the voters, but it also pushed congressional action on spending bills late in the legislative year and exacerbated partisan tensions. *(Tax controversies, pp. 87, 110)*

In 1999 Congress quickly passed a nonbinding budget resolution that allowed for the GOP's massive tax cut while holding to the tight spending limits established in 1997. But action on appropriations was slow, in part because legislators were waiting to see how the tax legislation would play out and in part because Clinton rejected five of the spending bills. Once again, Congress was forced to draw up an omnibus spending bill, in which Republicans gave Clinton more funding for his priorities than they would have liked and agreed to drop some policy riders he opposed. Republicans claimed victory by arguing that they had denied the president billions in spending demands. Nevertheless, total discretionary spending in 1999 exceeded the budget caps by an estimated $31 billion.

Clinton and Congress repeated the scenario in 2000: quick passage of a budget resolution, slow work on spending bills while the conflict over tax cuts played out, and then the hammering out of a compromise omnibus spending resolution at the end. In 2000, however, the spending battle slid over into a lame duck session that was not completed until mid-December, after the disputed presidential election was resolved in favor of Republican George W. Bush. Bush's election cost Clinton some bargaining leverage, and he perhaps did not win as much as he had in earlier years. But with both parties eager to spend money on programs favored by the voters, total discretionary spending in 2000 exceeded the budget caps by an estimated $34 billion.

Efforts by conservative Republicans in both 1999 and 2000 to ensure that the surplus would not be used on federal spending programs came to naught. In the so-called "lockbox" debate of 1999, Senate Democrats successfully filibustered legislation passed by the House that would have made it politically difficult for Congress to use any surplus in the Social Security funds to finance federal spending programs.

Although the Democrats were essentially protesting GOP procedural moves that barred them from offering amendments to the measure, Republicans took great delight in chiding them for opposing a plan to protect Social Security. In 2000 the House repeatedly approved legislation to preserve the surplus for paying down the deficit, but the Senate never took action.

Fiscal 2000 Budget Resolution

For only the fourth time since 1974, when the current budget procedures were put in place (PL 93-344), Congress met the statutory deadline for passing its budget. But adoption of the blueprint (H Con Res 68) provided only a few clues about the ultimate fate of an unexpectedly large surplus that the booming economy dropped in the laps of President Clinton and his congressional rivals. Debate on the measure gave lawmakers of both parties an opportunity to showcase their competing plans for the surplus.

For Republicans the focus was on cutting taxes, reducing the national debt, and abiding by "caps" on discretionary spending, the approximately one-third of the federal budget that Congress must appropriate every year to finance day-to-day government operations. (The remainder goes largely to entitlement or other programs where payments must be made by law or cannot be refused for other reasons.) Democrats agreed with Republicans on debt reduction but they countered with proposals to use part of the estimated $2.6 trillion surplus over the next decade to shore up the Social Security and Medicare trust funds, while increasing spending for domestic programs such as education and health care.

Initially, GOP congressional leaders considered raising the budget caps that had been set under the 1997 balanced-budget agreement (PL 105-33). Those caps had been broken the very next year, when Clinton and Congress in 1998 negotiated a year-end omnibus spending bill for fiscal 1999 (PL 105-277). But after prominent Democrats such as Senate Minority Leader Tom Daschle of South Dakota said lawmakers should live within the caps, those efforts fell apart.

Instead, Republicans crafted a budget resolution that was aimed chiefly at paving the way for a big tax bill. The measure provided for a tax cut of $142 billion from 2000 through 2004, ballooning over the next five years to a total of $778 billion over ten years. (The budget blueprint was extended for ten years for the first time, instead of the customary five, so that Republicans could lay claim to the long-term surpluses in the second five years of the plan.)

Democrats and even many Republicans said the GOP budget blueprint called for untenable cuts in discretionary spending programs such as education, scientific research, and housing. Just to maintain discretionary appropriations at a "freeze" level, appropriators said, would require breaking the caps by about $17 billion. Virtually no one believed such cuts could be achieved in an era of surging surpluses.

In the end the conventional wisdom turned out to be right. Republicans passed a $792 billion tax cut stretching over ten years, which Clinton promptly vetoed. Congress and Clinton then teamed up to exceed the 1997 budget caps by more than $30 billion, according to the Congressional Budget Office. (*Tax cut, p. 110*)

CLINTON BUDGET REQUEST

President Clinton's budget request for fiscal 2000 was as much a political document as was the eventual Republican budget resolution. The president's budget was filled with a panoply of new spending and targeted tax cuts that he proposed to finance with an array of politically difficult tax increases, tax loophole closings, accounting gimmicks, and new fees and savings.

Even as he asked for $213 billion in new spending over five years, Clinton wrapped himself in the cloak of fiscal discipline by insisting that most of the projected surplus—about $827 billion over the next five years—be dedicated to buying down the debt. To make that proposal more politically palatable, he tied debt reduction to the enormously popular retirement and health insurance programs for senior citizens by proposing to deposit Treasury bonds worth 62 percent of the surplus into Social Security and 15 percent into Medicare. Clinton also proposed to devote 12 percent of the surplus to establish Universal Savings Accounts, an administration plan for federally subsidized retirement accounts to supplement Social Security.

Overall, Clinton's budget called for $1.77 trillion in spending in fiscal 2000, a $39 billion increase (2.2 percent) over fiscal 1999. Almost all of the increase, $35 billion, would go to mandatory entitlement programs, including Social Security, Medicare, and Medicaid grants to states. Clinton proposed $18 billion in discretionary spending above the fiscal 2000 spending caps set by the 1997 balanced-budget act. To stay within the spending limits, Clinton claimed offsetting savings or revenue increases—such as a 55-cents-per-pack increase in cigarette taxes—that Congress was highly unlikely to enact. The president also proposed a "tobacco recoupment policy" to claim from the states $16 billion through 2004 from settlement of their lawsuit against the tobacco companies. The $16 billion represented the portion of Medicaid that the federal government spent on tobacco-related health care for Medicaid patients.

Starting in fiscal 2001 and assuming passage of an overhaul of Social Security, Clinton proposed raising the budget caps and spending $26 billion of the surplus in additional appropriations; such surplus-financed spending would total $138 billion from fiscal 2001 through 2004. In addition, Clinton proposed $21.8 billion in new mandatory entitlement spending over the next five years, focusing on child care subsidies and expanded health care. The budget antici-

pated that the initiative would be financed through offsetting savings.

The single biggest beneficiary of Clinton's new spending would be the Department of Defense, whose budget would steadily rise from $262 billion in fiscal 2000 to $300 billion in fiscal 2004.

In lieu of a big tax cut, Clinton proposed $33 billion over five years in targeted tax cuts, such as greater tax credits for child care and new tax credits for long-term care, energy efficiency, and the subsidizing of school construction bonds. These cuts were to be funded by $33 billion in tax hikes and loophole closures, including a major assault on corporate tax shelters designed to raise $7.2 billion over five years.

The Clinton administration made the budget add up by violating budget rules, chiefly by using proposed new taxes to pay for discretionary spending. Clinton also claimed for the Pentagon $2.9 billion in mandatory savings that would flow from previously enacted bills. An additional $2.6 billion came by claiming spectrum auction revenues in fiscal 2000 that would not actually be received until fiscal 2001 and 2002.

CONGRESSIONAL ACTION

Republicans immediately lambasted Clinton's budget plan as being full of funny numbers, phony assumptions, and politically dead proposals. But the Republican plan also had its share of hard-to-believe assumptions, namely, that Congress would abide by the discretionary spending caps that it set in 1997.

H Con Res 68, written largely by Senate Budget Committee Chairman Pete V. Domenici, R-N.M., and passed by both chambers with only minor differences, dedicated to tax cuts almost $800 billion over ten years in "on-budget" surpluses—those that do not depend on surplus Social Security revenues—while reserving the estimated $1.8 trillion Social Security surplus for reducing the national debt. The plan also increased funding for education above Clinton's request and significantly raised Pentagon spending for the first time since President George Bush was in office (1989–1993).

The plan also hewed to the exceedingly tight caps on discretionary appropriations. As a result, Senate and House appropriators would be forced to cut about $20 billion from nondefense appropriations, a task that many Republicans did not believe could be done.

Nonetheless, the House Budget Committee approved H Con Res 68 (H Rept 106-73) March 17 on a party-line vote of 22–18. The Senate Budget Committee approved an almost identical plan (S Con Res 20—S Rept 106-27) the next day on a 12–10 vote.

The House adopted H Con Res 68 on March 25 by a 221–208 vote. House Speaker J. Dennis Hastert, R-Ill., had to defuse a minor crisis when Transportation Committee Chairman Bud Shuster, R-Pa., threatened to scuttle the resolution unless he won an amendment to reserve for airport projects $50 billion over ten years in unspent aviation taxes, instead of devoting them to tax cuts. Shuster ultimately dropped his amendment in exchange for a pledge of speedy floor action on his bill (HR 1000), which would devote all the money in the aviation trust fund to airport projects. Hastert agreed to let Shuster bring up the measure without finding offsetting spending cuts that would otherwise be required under budget rules. *(Aviation trust fund, p. 331)*

The House easily defeated two Democratic alternatives to the budget resolution. By a vote of 134–295, the House rejected a plan drafted by moderate-to-conservative "Blue Dog" Democrats that would have devoted all of the Social Security surplus and half of all on-budget surpluses to reducing the national debt. The remainder of the on-budget surpluses would be evenly divided between tax cuts and new spending. By a vote of 173–250, the House then killed the mainstream Democratic alternative, which would have blocked tax cuts or new spending until legislation was enacted addressing the solvency of the Social Security and Medicare trust funds.

The Senate passed its version of the budget on March 25, after a two-day debate which left the committee version largely intact. The only substantive changes were the adoption of Democratic amendments to add $2 billion in fiscal 2000 for veterans' health care and to pare the tax cut by $10 billion over ten years to finance additional child care block grants.

Republicans killed numerous other Democratic amendments, including ones to delay tax cuts until Social Security and Medicare were fixed, increase agricultural subsidies, devote much of the surplus to Medicare, add funding for education, and express Senate support for raising the minimum wage by $1 by September 2000, to $6.15 an hour.

With few differences between the two versions, conferees acted quickly, and the House adopted the conference report (H Rept 106-91) April 14 on a vote of 220–208. The Senate followed suit, 54–44 on April 15, the statutory deadline for completing action on the annual budget resolution. The president did not need to act on the nonbinding resolution.

Fiscal 2000 Appropriations

In 1999 the new Speaker of the House, J. Dennis Hastert, R-Ill., began his tenure vowing to return to "regular order" and to pass all thirteen of the annual spending bills separately, avoid year-end negotiations over an omnibus bill, and leave Social Security surpluses untouched. Hastert was trying to avoid the situation that developed in 1998, when after months of attempts to deny or reduce spending for programs high on President Clinton's priority list, Republicans gave in to most of the president's requests. The result was a $500 billion omnibus spending bill that incorporated eight of the thirteen regular appropriations bills and broke the budget caps on overall spending set by the 1997 balanced-budget act (PL 105-33).

Hastert largely succeeded on the first goal but after Clinton vetoed four of the regular spending bills and threatened to veto a fifth, negotiators began more than two weeks of talks over yet another omnibus measure. The basis for the omnibus bill was a spending measure for the District of Columbia (HR 3194), a new version of spending legislation that Clinton had already vetoed twice. To that bill were added the spending bills for foreign aid (HR 3422); and the departments of Interior (HR 3423); Commerce, Justice, and State (HR 3421); and Labor, Health and Human Services, and Education (HR 3424).

In the negotiations, the president was able to win an additional $6.5 billion for high-priority items, including funds to hire more teachers and police officers, implement the Wye River Peace accords between Israel and the Palestinian Authority, provide debt relief for the world's poorest countries, and acquire land for conservation purposes. In return, Republicans won greater flexibility in the use of federal education funds; higher overall spending than requested for education, defense, veterans' health care, and health research; and, perhaps most important, an across-the-board spending cut intended to prevent the federal government from spending any of the Social Security trust fund surplus in fiscal 2000 on other government programs.

Despite that last provision, the Congressional Budget Office estimated that the appropriations bills enacted for fiscal 2000 would require about $17 billion of the Social Security surplus. Altogether, the fiscal 2000 spending bills exceeded the spending caps set in 1997 by about $30 billion.

OMNIBUS SPENDING BILL

Total fiscal 2000 spending in the five bills that made up the omnibus spending bill tallied $385 billion. The bill also included provisions that offset spending by about $7 billion. One of the offsets was a 0.38 percent across-the-board cut in most discretionary spending accounts. The bill also served as a vehicle for year-end deals to provide northeastern lawmakers a big win on dairy policy, ease Medicare cuts enacted in 1997, boost the satellite television industry, and reauthorize the State Department.

The House adopted the conference report on the omnibus measure (HR 3194—H Rept 106-479) Nov. 18 by a 296–135 vote. The Senate cleared the bill, 74–24, on Nov. 19, and President Clinton signed it on Nov. 29 (PL 106-113). Following are highlights from that bill.

Labor-HHS-Education

The House Appropriations Committee reported a Labor-HHS-Education spending bill (HR 3037—H Rept 106-370) that was so burdened by controversy the GOP leadership decided not to bring it to the floor. Instead they "preconferenced" the committee-reported bill with the version passed by the Senate and attached the resulting agreement to the conference report on the second District of Columbia bill (HR 3064). Both chambers adopted the conference report on HR 3064 (H Rept 106-419) by narrow margins: the House vote was 218–211, and the Senate vote was 49–48.

Clinton vetoed HR 3064 on Nov. 3 for several reasons. One of the more important was that the bill did not ensure that the funds appropriated for hiring new teachers to reduce class size would actually be used for that purpose. The president also objected to a 0.97 percent across-the-board cut in all discretionary fiscal 2000 spending.

The final version of the Labor-HHS-Education portion of the omnibus spending bill provided $328.2 billion before scorekeeping adjustments were made, $1.4 billion more than the vetoed bill. Most of the increase, $1 billion, was designated for education programs. Negotiators agreed to appropriate $1.3 billion for the president's program to hire 100,000 new teachers, only $100 million less than the president had requested. The final version also raised the amount of the hiring funds that could be used for professional development of already-hired teachers to 25 percent, from 15 percent. Certain schools with high numbers of uncertified teachers could use all of the funds for professional development.

The bill also increased the appropriation for the National Institutes of Health by 15 percent over fiscal 1999 levels, to $17.9 billion. It continued existing bans on using any funds in the bill to create human embryos for research purposes or to fund needle exchanges for drug addicts to prevent the spread of AIDS. It also lifted a moratorium, enacted in the fiscal 1999 omnibus spending bill, on implementation of a national system of allocation of human organs for transplantation. (Organ transplants, p. 475)

Commerce-Justice-State

President Clinton vetoed the first appropriations bill (HR 2670) for the departments of Commerce, Justice, and State, the federal judiciary, and fourteen agencies, complaining that it did not provide enough for his priorities and could have jeopardized the U.S. seat in the United Nations General Assembly. Negotiators than drafted a second bill that split the difference between Republican and presidential wishes.

Clinton claimed as his biggest domestic policy victory in the bill its $595 million for the Community Oriented Policing Services program, created under the 1994 anticrime law (PL 103-322) to fulfill Clinton's 1992 election campaign pledge to boost local police rolls by a total of 100,000 officers. The vetoed spending bill provided only about half that amount; the $595 million was still only half of what he requested. Republicans claimed victory here too because they insisted on directing $523 million to the Local Law Enforcement Block Grant. The president had requested no funding for this item.

One of the last items settled by negotiators allowed the State Department to send $926 million to the United Nations, thereby making good on years of back dues. In return, Clinton agreed to support legislation (HR 3427), also rolled into the omnibus package, that revived some abortion restrictions on international family planning assistance. The controversy over the back dues and the abortion restriction had delayed reauthorization of the State Department for several years. (State reauthorization, p. 217)

A Senate provision that would have allowed federal prosecution of hate crimes motivated by a victim's sexual orientation, gender, or disability was dropped at the insistence of Republican negotiators from both the House and Senate.

A Supreme Court ruling in January that resolved a controversy over how to conduct the 2000 census put an end to the disputes that had tied the Commerce-Justice-State spending bill in knots in 1997 and 1998. In 1999 all sides agreed to give the Census Bureau all $4.5 billion it requested to conduct the census. (Census, pp. 736, 748)

Interior

After weeks of threats, cloistered negotiation, and frantic compromise, Congress included $14.9 billion in fiscal 2000 spending for the Interior Department in the omnibus appropriations package. The final product marked a clear victory for the Clinton administration, which was able to add money for its Lands Legacy initiative and to delete or substantially neutralize a series of policy riders it opposed. The original Interior spending bill (HR 3423) had cleared both chambers but was never sent to the president, who had threatened to veto it.

In the final negotiations, Clinton won $470 million for his priority Lands Legacy program, aimed at acquiring and conserving environmentally and culturally significant land threatened by development. The amount was a third less than Clinton had requested but the original bill had set aside only $266 million for this purpose.

Among the contentious items added during Senate consideration of the spending bill were riders on mining waste, grazing permits, and oil drilling on public land. The administration strongly objected to a proposed moratorium on implementation of a new Interior Department royalty formula for oil extracted from public lands, claiming that failure to use the new formula would allow companies to underpay the government by at least $68 million annually. The final version allowed implementation of the new rules after March 15, 2000.

Another issue that attracted attention from environmentalists concerned mining waste. The House voted overwhelmingly to include language supporting an Interior Department ruling that required mining operations to limit waste sites on public lands to five acres. The department said the restriction would protect public lands from being scarred and polluted by the mining companies, but the mining industry said that it could not operate under such tight restrictions. The Senate sided with the industry, adopting language that would nullify the ruling altogether. The final version allowed the limitation to take effect but exempted mining claims approved before November 1997.

Also over environmentalists' objections, the Senate approved language that would renew expiring grazing permits under the same terms and conditions as the old permits. Environmental groups argued that the provision would undercut efforts to add environmental protections to the permits, which allowed ranchers to graze their livestock on federal land. The final version provided that the new permits could be canceled or modified after the required environmental impact analyses were completed.

Foreign Operations

A last-minute compromise on debt relief for poor nations allowed Congress to finish the $15.3 billion fiscal 2000 foreign operations spending bill. *(2000 aid appropriations, p. 210)*

With congressional Republicans determined to hold down foreign aid spending as part of their overall budget plan and the White House equally intent on funding some key foreign policy initiatives, the foreign operations had become a major battleground in the fiscal 2000 budget wars.

The conference report on the first foreign aid bill (HR 2606) was nearly $2 billion below Clinton's initial request and did not include another $1.8 billion he sought to help Israel, Jordan, and the Palestinian Authority implement the 1998 Wye River peace agreement. The low spending level prompted Clinton to veto the bill on Oct. 18. *(Wye River agreement, pp. 190, 210)*

Republicans then backed down and moved a new bill (HR 3196) that included the $1.8 billion for the Wye River agreement, plus another $800 million for various recipients, including the World Bank and republics of the former Soviet Union. Negotiators removed the last sticking point in mid-November with an agreement to allow the International Monetary Fund to use a rise in the value of the gold it holds in storage toward its share of an international package to finance debt forgiveness of some of the world's poorest developing countries. The bill also provided $123 million in bilateral debt relief to these countries. *(Debt relief, p. 213)*

At the last minute, GOP leaders appeased antiabortion members by attaching restrictions on family planning assistance to the bill, a move that cleared the way for the stalled Commerce-Justice-State appropriations bill as well as the State Department authorization measure. The compromise provision, which would expire at the end of fiscal 2000, barred any of the $385 million in U.S. international family assistance for organizations that perform abortions (except in cases of rape or incest or when the life of the mother is in danger) or that lobby to change abortion laws or government policies in other countries. Clinton could waive the restriction, but a waiver would trigger a shift of $12.5 million in family planning aid to an account for child survival and disease prevention. *(Family planning, p. 214)*

State Department Reauthorization

The omnibus bill also included a two-year reauthorization of the State Department. In addition to repayment of the U.S. debts to the United Nations, this measure also authorized $4.5 billion over five years to improve security at U.S. embassies in the wake of the 1998 terrorist bombings in Kenya and Tanzania.

Policy Riders

Among the policy riders attached to the omnibus spending bill that were not directly related to any of the spending measures that composed it were the following:

• An agreement worked out between Senate, House, and White House negotiators that would give hospitals, nursing homes, home health care agencies, and other health care providers relief from cuts in Medicare payments that were enacted in the 1997 balanced-budget law. The changes in the 1997 law reduced Medicare outlays by about twice the amount anticipated and led to an outcry from health care providers. *(Medicare relief, p. 461)*

• Most of the provisions of the conference report on HR 1554, which allowed satellite television companies to deliver local broadcast stations in cities across the country, matching the services provided by rival cable television systems. Dropped from the final version because of Senate objections was language that would have authorized $1.25 billion in loan guarantees for satellites to improve service for rural viewers. *(Satellite TV, p. 338)*

• An overhaul of the patent process, which established the U.S. Patent and Trademark Office as an independent agency, reduced patent filing and maintenance fees, and made a number of other changes. *(Patent overhaul, p. 334)*

• An extension of the Northeast Interstate Dairy Compact for two years. The agreement blocked the Agriculture Department from revising federal dairy pricing policy to make the system more market-oriented. Opponents of the compact, namely farmers and lawmakers from the upper Midwest states, had kept the extension out of the regular farm spending bill. *(Dairy pricing, p. 424)*

Other Fiscal 2000 Appropriations Bills

Eight of the thirteen regular appropriations bills were passed as stand-alone bills. Four of them were relatively noncontroversial: legislative branch (HR 1905—PL 106-57), cleared Aug. 5; military construction (HR 2465—PL 106-52), cleared Aug. 3; transportation (HR 2084—PL 106-69), cleared Oct. 4; and Veterans Affairs-Housing and Urban Development (HR 2684—PL 106-74), cleared Oct. 15.

The other four cleared but only after controversies that threatened to scuttle the appropriations at one stage or another were resolved. Highlights from those debates follow:

AGRICULTURE

The regular agricultural appropriations bill (HR 1906—PL 106-78) was controversial both for what it did and did not contain and for the way it was negotiated. The final version contained a record-breaking $8.7 billion in relief to farmers who had been hurt by low commodity prices, bad weather, and barriers to overseas markets. Despite its unprecedented size, many members said the relief package still fell short of what was needed. Another $576 million in emergency assistance was included in the fiscal 2000 omnibus spending measure (HR 3194—PL 106-113).

Aside from the relief money, two controversial provisions—on dairy pricing and the removal of sanctions on food and medicine exports to Cuba—were not included in the final measure. But they attracted considerable attention during floor debate, where several members also complained that the House and Senate leadership had made decisions on the issues in private talks after the conference committee was suspended.

New England members sought language to extend the Northeast Dairy Compact, which gave farmers in the northeast higher prices for their milk. Lawmakers from the upper Midwest kept the extension out of the agriculture spending bill, but it was included in the omnibus. (*Dairy pricing, p. 424*)

Various farm-state members also sought unsuccessfully to lift sanctions on food and medicine sales to Cuba and a handful of other nations, arguing that the embargo hurt American farmers without achieving its foreign policy goals. The matter was dropped after House conservatives opposed the move. (*Cuba sanctions, p. 224*)

DEFENSE

The $267.8 billion defense appropriations bill for fiscal 2000 (HR 2561—PL 106-79) added $4.5 billion to President Clinton's budget request. It was cleared on Oct. 14 after House and Senate conferees agreed to allow the Air Force to buy additional F-22 fighter planes, an expenditure the House had originally rejected. Conferees also required additional testing before full-scale production of the plane could begin. Despite initial hints of a veto, Clinton on Oct. 25 signed the measure, which provided the first significant defense spending increase since 1985 and the largest military pay raise since 1981. (*F-22 debate, p. 286; pay raise, p. 283*)

ENERGY AND WATER

The relatively noncontroversial energy and water spending bill (HR 2605—PL 106-60) was one of only four regular spending bills to clear before the start of fiscal 2000. The final version appropriated $21.3 billion for the Energy Department and water projects managed by the Interior Department and the Army Corps of Engineers. That amount was $2.6 million more than the Senate passed, but $1.1 billion more than the House had approved. The House had withheld $1 billion in funding for the Energy Department's nuclear weapons programs in an effort to force the department either to restructure them or to establish an independent agency to oversee them. Senate Republican Pete V. Domenici, who was chairman of the Appropriations Subcommittee on Energy and Water and whose state of New Mexico was home to two of the department's nuclear weapons laboratories, held up action on the conference report until House leaders agreed to the higher funding level. A restructuring of the weapons programs was included in

the fiscal 2000 defense authorization act. (*Nuclear weapons program, p. 276*)

TREASURY-POSTAL SERVICE

President Clinton signed the $28.2 billion fiscal 2000 spending bill for the Treasury Department, Postal Service, and general government agencies (HR 2490—PL 106-58) Sept. 29. The bill doubled the pay of the next president, bringing it up to $400,000 a year. The first presidential pay increase in three decades drew bipartisan support in Congress and from high-ranking officials in previous administrations. (*Presidential pay, p. 751*)

The bill was silent on congressional pay, allowing an automatic annual pay increase to take effect. The Treasury bill traditionally had been the vehicle for blocking the increase during the years when the government was running a deficit. (*Congressional pay, p. 791*)

The most contentious fights came not over spending but on an unsuccessful attempt by House Democrats to add gun control amendments in the wake of school shootings in Littleton, Colorado, and Conyers, Georgia. Efforts by House conservatives to cut proposed funding for the Internal Revenue Service led to another partisan fight and to a one-vote margin of victory for the bill on the floor. But the cuts were restored in conference, and the final bill won by comfortable margins in both chambers. (*Gun control, pp. 597, 637*)

Fiscal 1999 Supplemental Appropriations

Repeating the pattern of recent years, Congress in 1999 cleared a substantial fiscal 1999 supplemental appropriations bill just months into the new session. The $14.5 billion measure (HR 1141—PL 106-31) included $10.9 billion in funding related to operations in Kosovo, emergency funds for disaster relief from Hurricanes Mitch and Georges, and funding to back loans for U.S. farmers hurt by persistently low commodity prices.

As initially passed by both the House and Senate, HR 1141 contained supplemental funding only for disaster aid and loan support. The House version (H Rept 106-64), passed on March 24 by a vote of 220–211, appropriated $1.3 billion—offset by $1.1 billion in rescissions from other programs, primarily one to back up international lending programs and another to diminish Russian nuclear capacity. Democrats almost uniformly opposed cuts in those programs and voted against passage after losing on an amendment to remove the offsets. The Senate bill, which contained $2.4 billion in supplemental funding, was passed by voice vote on March 25.

Shortly after the House and Senate votes, the Clinton administration asked for another $6 billion to help pay for NATO's massive bombing campaign of Yugoslavia, designed to stop escalating Serbian violence against ethnic Albanians in the Serbian province of Kosovo. Although many Republicans in Congress were dubious about the bombing campaign, they viewed the new request as an opportunity to bolster what they considered to be dangerously underfunded defense readiness accounts. By providing additional defense spending in the fiscal 1999 supplemental, House Republicans hoped to ease the crunch that was expected when the fiscal 2000 defense appropriations bill (HR 2561—PL 106-79) ran up against the budgetary caps imposed by the 1997 balanced-budget law (PL 105-33). *(Kosovo war, pp. 177, 204)*

On May 6, the House passed, 311–105, a second supplemental bill (HR 1664—H Rept 106-125) containing $13.1 billion in funding for the Kosovo crisis and other programs. By the time conferees met on HR 1141, most of the main Kosovo and defense funding questions had been settled, and conferees shifted the Kosovo funding from HR 1664 to HR 1141.

Negotiations on HR 1141 threatened to break down over a series of Senate "riders" that House leaders pledged to oppose. Chief among these was a provision by Democrat Robert C. Byrd of West Virginia to establish a $1 billion loan guarantee program for U.S. steel producers hurt by rising steel imports. Only after a pledge by House leaders to bring the loan guarantee measure to the House floor as a freestanding bill did Senate conferees agree to drop Byrd's provision. The Senate in June incorporated Byrd's loan guarantee provisions into HR 1664, which both chambers cleared and the president signed (PL 106-51).

The final version included $10.9 billion for military operations in Kosovo and other defense spending, including $1.8 billion for an increase in military pay and retirement benefits. The bill also provided $1.1 billion for international economic, refugee, and disaster assistance related to Kosovo, $687 million for recovery efforts in Central America and the Caribbean associated with Hurricanes Mitch and Georges, $574 million to support loans to U.S. farmers hurt by persistently low crop prices, and $900 million for tornado victims in Oklahoma and Kansas.

All but $1.7 billion of the bill's funding was declared "emergency" spending, avoiding the need for offsetting cuts in other fiscal 1999 discretionary accounts. The bill instead relied on the projected budget surplus for the bulk of its funding.

The House adopted the conference report (H Rept 106-143), 269–158, on May 18. The Senate cleared the bill, 64–36, on May 20, and President Clinton signed it into law on May 21, 1999.

Budget Process Reform

In the face of widespread opposition among Democrats and reservations among some Republicans, efforts in the House and Senate to overhaul the congressional budget process made little headway during the 106th Congress. The House resoundingly defeated a reform measure in 2000. The Senate never acted on one measure, calling for a two-year budget cycle, reported from committee (S 92—S Rept 106-

12) in 1999, while a second measure (S 557—S Rept 106-14), dealing with emergency supplementals, became the vehicle for a failed effort to protect Social Security surpluses. As a result, Congress, awash in surplus revenue, would continue to operate with an aging set of budget rules designed in an era of deficit spending.

Advocates of changing the way congressional fiscal policy was set generally agreed that less time should be devoted to budgeting and appropriations and more time to program oversight. But Appropriations Committee members in both chambers and both parties viewed some of the key provisions in the House and Senate bills as robbing them of their power, while other opponents said the measures would transfer too much power to the executive branch.

HOUSE ACTION

In the House, the budget reform measure (HR 853—H Rept 106-198, Pts. 1–3) was reviewed by three committees: Budget, which approved it June 17, 1999, on a 22–12 vote; Appropriations, which on June 22 deleted the one provision it had jurisdiction over and then agreed by voice vote to send the bill forward with a recommendation that it be voted down; and Rules, which approved it by voice vote June 23.

The specific provision that the Appropriations Committee objected to would have created automatic continuing resolutions (CRs), the stopgap spending measures that keep the government running whenever the appropriations process is not completed by the Oct. 1 start of a new fiscal year. The provision was designed to wrest from the president much of the leverage that he has to negotiate spending deals at the end of the appropriations process. It was also designed to avoid future government shutdowns such as the two in 1995 that occurred when Republicans tried to strong-arm President Clinton into accepting their budget plan by refusing to pass a CR. When Clinton refused, major parts of the government shut down temporarily and voters blamed Republicans in the 1996 elections. *(Government shutdowns, Congress and the Nation, Vol. IX, p. 72)*

Members of the Appropriations panel said an automatic CR would shift power to those defending the status quo and would permit a minority in the Senate to stall any appropriations bill and therefore block any funding changes. In effect, they said, the budget could be put on autopilot. Some members noted that an automatic CR would deny lawmakers the opportunity to earmark money for specific projects or favored programs.

The following are other provisions of HR 853:

• Give the annual budget resolution, currently a nonbinding "concurrent" resolution of both chambers, the force of law by making it a "joint" resolution, requiring the president's signature.

• Ease the current pay-as-you-go (PAYGO) budget rules to permit budget surpluses not generated by Social Security to be used for tax cuts or new entitlement spending. Under existing law, all tax cuts had to be financed with cuts in mandatory spending or new revenues. Violations of the PAYGO rules required the president to impose an across-the-board sequester of mandatory spending. Democrats objected to this change because it would remove a major procedural roadblock to Republican efforts to cut taxes.

• Create a reserve fund for supplemental spending for natural disasters and other emergencies and tighten the definition of "emergency" to make it more difficult for nonurgent items to be funded with such money.

• Significantly weaken the Senate's "Byrd rule" (named after Robert C. Byrd, D-W.Va.) which requires 60 votes to retain nonspending items in budget "reconciliation" bills, the vehicles used for reconciling tax and spending decisions with the budget targets.

• Create a complicated "lockbox" procedure to ensure that cuts from appropriations bills made on the floor are not restored to other appropriations accounts later in the process.

HR 853 came to the House floor on May 16, 2000. In an attempt to overcome objections by appropriators, Republican leaders had removed from HR 853 some of the proposals that had engendered the most opposition. The most controversial of these was the automatic CR, and an amendment to restore it to the bill was rejected 173–236.

The House also rejected, 201–217, an amendment calling for a two-year budget cycle. Although the White House supported this provision, which was also contained in the Senate measure, Democrats were concerned that it would undermine their leverage in persuading agencies to change their policies or practices.

The House then went on to defeat the legislation altogether, by a resounding vote of 166–250. Only twelve Democrats supported the measure, while sixty-three Republicans opposed it. Of the sixty members of the Appropriations panel, only nine Republicans voted for passage; no Democrats supported it.

Social Security "Lockbox"

A bill that supporters said would put surplus Social Security revenues into a protected "lockbox" passed in the House in 1999 but ran into a Democratic filibuster in the Senate. The impasse in the Senate was welcomed by the Republicans who delighted in chiding Democrats for filibustering to death a bill aimed at making it more difficult to "raid" Social Security surpluses for new spending.

The great lockbox debate of 1999 began as congressional Republicans sought to use Social Security as a political wedge to advance their budget and tax goals while winning political points at the expense of the Democrats. With surplus projections far surpassing previous estimates, the federal government in fiscal 2000 would no longer have to borrow from Social Security reserves to pay for other government programs—provided lawmakers could curb their appetites for spending programs and tax cuts. The

lockbox bills aimed to make it more difficult for lawmakers to cast votes to "spend" Social Security surpluses.

SENATE PLAN

The idea originated in the Senate, where Budget Committee Chairman Pete V. Domenici, R-N.M., crafted a plan to "protect" Social Security by ratcheting down the limit on the publicly held national debt each year by the amount of the Social Security surplus. But Finance Committee Chairman William V. Roth Jr., R-Del., opposed the measure, saying it could provoke a first-ever default on the national debt.

Because of Roth's objection and because Finance had jurisdiction over the matter, the measure came to the floor as an amendment to a bill (S 557) to make it more difficult to put funding for nonemergencies into emergency supplemental appropriations measures. The lockbox measure also required 60 Senate votes to pass any bill that would spend the Social Security surplus. Existing Senate rules already posed that hurdle for tax bills.

The Clinton administration opposed the Domenici plan. Treasury Secretary Robert E. Rubin agreed that the plan could provoke a debt crisis. Moreover, he warned, if the government breached the debt limit, distribution of Social Security benefit checks might be hindered. Rubin said he would urge the president to veto the bill if it came to him with the debt limit provisions.

The measure was briefly debated on the Senate floor on April 20, and Republicans turned to other matters before losing a cloture vote on April 22. The vote to limit a Democratic filibuster and proceed to the lockbox measure was 54–45, short of the 60 votes required for cloture. Roth was the only Republican to oppose cloture; no Democrats supported the motion. A second cloture vote failed on April 30 by a vote of 49–44; again Roth was the only Republican voting against limiting debate.

HOUSE ACTION

In the House, opposition from House Ways and Means Committee Chairman Bill Archer, R-Texas, killed any prospect for the Senate bill and its public debt reduction component. Instead the House overwhelmingly passed HR 1259 (no report), a measure that sought to establish points of order in both chambers against any bill that "spent" the surplus generated by Social Security for new spending or tax cuts.

HR 1259 passed on May 26 by a vote of 416–12, after a sparsely attended debate during which bill proponents exaggerated the potential effectiveness of their "lockbox." Bill sponsor Wally Herger, R-Calif., for example, said the bill "locks up the Social Security surpluses and allows them only to be used for Social Security and Medicare reform."

In fact, the bill did not bar the use of the Social Security surpluses to help pay for other programs but only made it politically more difficult to vote for measures that do so.

While acknowledging that fact, some supporters said HR 1259 nevertheless set a barrier that would be hard for lawmakers to cross. Democrats voted for the bill even as they dismissed it as toothless. "If members want to save Social Security, bring out a bill that saves Social Security," said Rep. David R. Obey, D-Wis. "Do not bring out something which ought to be labeled the No. 1 legislative fraud of the year." Democrats also noted that Republicans only days before had waived similar points of order that already existed to fund nonemergency programs in an "emergency" supplemental appropriations bill, thus avoiding the budget caps on spending without making offsetting spending cuts or tax hikes. That meant the programs were effectively paid for with the budget surplus. *(1999 supplemental appropriations, p. 76)*

SENATE ACTION

Although the Senate was expected to approve the House-passed measure, an impasse over both HR 1259 and S 557 developed when Senate Majority Leader Trent Lott, R-Miss., used once rarely employed procedural devices to block floor amendments. Minority Leader Tom Daschle, D-S.D., had mounted successful filibusters every time his forty-five member caucus was barred from offering amendments, and this bill was no exception.

On June 15 a motion to invoke cloture and take up the Senate bill failed, 55–44. The next day Democrats again denied cloture, 55–44, this time on the weaker House-passed bill. Finance Committee Chairman Roth voted with his colleagues on this bill because it did not contain the provision requiring the public debt to be lowered. A fifth and final attempt to obtain cloture, again on the Senate bill, failed on July 16. The vote was 52–43.

Fiscal 2001 Budget Resolution

Republicans in early 2000 pushed through Congress a fiscal 2001 budget resolution (H Con Res 290) with a discretionary spending limit that exceeded the statutory caps yet was still so tight that even some Republicans warned that the party was setting itself up for failure. By fall, it was clear just how far from reality the budget had been. Appropriations for fiscal 2001 overshot the $600.3 billion ceiling by a cumulative $34.2 billion. *(2001 appropriations, p. 81)*

The pressure to spend came from President Clinton, congressional Democratic leaders, and the rank and file in both parties who wanted to push parochial interests in an election year. The growing budget surplus made calls for new spending difficult to deny, further eroding Congress's already weakening fiscal restraint.

Congress never expected to make the drastic spending cuts necessary to meet the spending limit of $541 billion set for fiscal 2001 by the 1997 balanced-budget act (PL 105-33). That law was intended to achieve a balanced budget by fiscal 2002. But the surging economy produced additional tax revenues that erased the debt in 1998, well ahead of schedule. Lawmakers had already made it clear, during action on the appropriations bills in 1998 and 1999, that they were unwilling to hew to bare-bones spending limits enacted to reduce a deficit that no longer existed, especially if deep cuts in popular domestic programs were involved.

Estimates of the surplus only grew more optimistic as the year 2000 went on. The $1.86 trillion budget request Clinton sent to Congress on Feb. 7 projected that the cumulative surplus for fiscal 2001–2010 would total $2.9 trillion (most of it in the Social Security and Medicare trust funds), assuming discretionary spending were to grow at the rate of inflation. In July the White House raised the cumulative projection to $4.2 trillion and estimated the fiscal 2001 "on-budget" surplus (excluding the surplus in the Social Security trust funds) would be $79 billion.

The budget resolution's $600.3 billion limit on discretionary spending was $14.3 billion above a freeze at the fiscal 2000 level and $6.7 billion less than would be spent if discretionary spending kept pace with the rate of inflation, according to the Congressional Budget Office (CBO).

Although conservative Republicans in both chambers challenged the budget resolution for not abiding by the 1997 spending caps, it was adopted on nearly straight party-line votes and by the statutory April 15 deadline for the second year in a row. As a congressional resolution, it did not require the president's signature and did not have the force of law.

The GOP tax cut provided for in the budget was never enacted. The resolution provided for two reconciliation bills to implement no more than $150 billion in tax cuts over five years. Clinton vetoed the first bill (HR 4810), which cut taxes for married couples by $90 billion over five years, and the House sustained the veto. Retirement savings incentives at the heart of the second reconciliation bill (HR 5203) were included in a wrap-up tax package (HR 2614) worth $240.4 billion over ten years. That bill died in the Senate. *(Tax bills, pp. 113, 117)*

CLINTON BUDGET REQUEST

The president's fiscal 2001 budget request, released on Feb. 7, 2000, signaled the formal beginning of the eighth and final budget confrontation between Clinton and Congress. It also gave the president one last opportunity to leave his imprint on government spending priorities. Clinton asked for the largest increase in discretionary spending in the history of the Education Department, the creation of a new entitlement in the form of prescription drug coverage for Medicare beneficiaries, and an end to the spending caps that Congress had tried but failed to live within in 1998 and 1999.

As it had in previous years, the budget proposed to prohibit the use of Social Security surpluses for boosting domestic spending or deeply cutting taxes. Clinton called for some limited tax cuts, however, including measures to ease the "marriage penalty" quirk in the tax code—a priority for

Republicans—and to spur investments in areas that were not benefiting from the economic boom.

Overall, the Clinton administration projected fiscal 2001 revenues of $2.02 trillion and spending of $1.84 trillion, for a surplus of $184 billion, all but $9 billion of which would be generated by the Social Security trust funds. The president proposed increasing discretionary spending by 3.9 percent above the current level—which would be slightly more than one parentage point above the expected rate of inflation. The fiscal 1999 appropriations laws raised discretionary spending by 7 percent above fiscal 1998 levels; the fiscal 2000 laws raised the figure another 3.5 percent.

By tying growth in discretionary spending to the expected pace of inflation, the administration proposed raising the caps on statutory spending enacted in the 1997 budget-balancing act from $542 billion to $614.3 billion in budget authority in fiscal 2001, and from $551.1 billion to $625.5 billion in fiscal 2002. The 1997 law did not set caps beyond the end of 2002. In its analysis of the budget request, the CBO calculated that Clinton's discretionary programs actually added up to $625 billion, thereby exceeding his own proposed spending caps by more than $10 billion.

Clinton earmarked about half of his request for discretionary spending for the Defense Department: $306.3 billion in new budget authority, a 4.1 percent increase above fiscal 2000. Other major discretionary spending requests included $61.5 billion for education, training, and social services, and $41.3 billion for "income security," including food stamps and special nutrition assistance programs for women and children. Clinton also proposed creating a Medicare prescription drug cost-sharing program, beginning in fiscal 2002, which the administration projected would cost $605 billion over five years. (*Prescription drug program, p. 465*)

Clinton's budget called for cutting taxes by $350.3 billion over ten years. His plan for fixing the marriage penalty accounted for $44 billion of that total, while another $40 billion would be used to adjust the alternative minimum tax and reduce its impact on middle-income families with children. A series of offsetting tax increases and closures in corporate tax loopholes would create a net ten-year tax cut of $168.6 billion, according to the administration. It seemed doubtful, however, that Congress would agree to many of the proposed tax increases, including a 30-cents-per-pack increase in cigarette taxes.

CONGRESSIONAL ACTION

The GOP leadership in both chambers faced the same problem: the spending levels in the resolution were barely big enough to keep appropriators happy but were not small enough to avoid alienating a potentially pivotal number of the most fiscally conservative Republican legislators.

In the House, days of delicate negotiations and deal-cutting paid off, when the House March 24 passed the budget resolution (H Con Res 290—H Rept 106-530) on a 211–207 vote. Only five Republicans cast "no" votes, while only two Democrats voted for the resolution, which called for no more than $596.5 billion in discretionary funding in fiscal 2001 and at least $150 billion in tax cuts over five years.

As was customary, House leaders allowed several factions to offer alternative budgets. Each was soundly rejected. The closest vote came on the Democratic alternative, which would have reserved more of the surplus for paying down the debt and avoided cutting social programs. To accomplish that, the plan would have permitted only $50 billion in tax cuts over five years. The plan was rejected, 184–233.

The Senate adopted its version of the budget resolution (S Con Res 101—S Rept 106-251) April 7 by a vote of 51–45. It called for approximately $601 billion in discretionary spending, about $4 billion more than the House version. The increase was for additional defense spending.

A quarrel between GOP conservatives and Senate appropriators delayed Senate passage of the resolution for several days. Fiscal conservatives led by Phil Gramm, R-Texas, had insisted on several provisions that would require 60-vote super-majorities in the Senate to exceed the resolution's discretionary spending limits. Gramm had used his leverage in the Budget Committee, where Republicans had a narrow 12–10 majority, to insist that the provisions be included in the resolution sent to the floor.

But when the bill reached the floor, Appropriations Committee Chairman Ted Stevens, R-Alaska, balked and prepared to offer floor amendments that would have deleted the restraints. Had he succeeded, Gramm and perhaps others would have opposed the resolution, imperiling its adoption on the floor. A compromise reached on April 6 kept the provisions in the bill but relaxed them somewhat by applying them primarily to nondefense spending. Although Stevens made it clear he was not happy with the compromise, he went along with the deal to get the budget resolution passed so that work could begin on annual spending bills.

Before passing the resolution, the Senate took up a host of controversial but nonbinding policy statements, ranging from gun violence to an increase in the minimum wage. Many were adopted on voice vote; others were defeated or ducked with the offering of less controversial substitutes. Senators of both parties voted to delete an unpopular proposal to cut the federal gas tax by 4.3 cents a gallon. Senators were loath to cut off a source of funding for transportation projects across the nation. By a narrow vote, of 51–49, the Senate did retain a perennially controversial proposal to open the Arctic National Wildlife Refuge to oil drilling. Separate legislation would be required to enact the proposal. Senators also rejected, 45–55, a Democratic budget alternative that closely tracked Clinton's budget.

Conferees quickly reconciled the differences between the two versions of the resolution. In its final version the resolution allowed $600.3 billion in discretionary spending in fiscal 2001—$310.8 billion for defense and $289.5 billion for nondefense programs. It also authorized two reconciliation bills to be drafted outlining as much as $150 billion in tax cuts over five years—$11.6 billion of it in fiscal 2001—plus a $25 billion reserve fund that could be used for additional tax cuts. Tax cuts considered under the authority of reconciliation instructions enjoyed procedural protections that were particularly important in the Senate, where such bills were not subject to filibuster. In addition, any upward revisions in the non-Social Security surplus projected by the CBO would be used for tax reduction, at the discretion of the budget committee chairmen.

The budget resolution also set aside as much $40 billion over five years to finance Medicare reform or a program to provide prescription drug coverage for seniors. The Senate also adopted a permanent 60-vote point of order against "emergency" nondefense spending.

On April 13, 2000, the House adopted the conference report on the budget resolution (H Rept 106-577) by a vote of 220–208, with five Republicans who voted against the measure offset by six Democrats who voted for it. Several hours later, the Senate passed it on a **key vote of 50–48 (R 50–4; D 0–44),** with four Republicans joining a united Democratic front in opposition. *(2000 key votes, p. 915)*

Fiscal 2001 Appropriations

Congress was unable to avert its annual pileup of overdue appropriations bills at the end of 2000. With election-year partisanship at fever pitch, the fiscal 2001 appropriations impasse spilled into a lame-duck session that lasted until mid-December, when an omnibus package was used to close the books on four spending bills and move other unrelated legislation.

Republicans claimed victory by arguing that in the final weeks of negotiations, they had curtailed billions in White House spending demands. Still, Congress ended up appropriating about $635 billion for all discretionary spending programs in fiscal 2001—$10 billion more than the president requested at the beginning of the year and about $35 billion more than the limit imposed by the fiscal 2001 budget resolution (H Con Res 290) set at the beginning of the year, and $94 billion more than the limits set by the 1997 balanced-budget law (PL 105-33).

When Congress passed H Con Res 290 lawmakers on both sides of the aisle had warned that its tight spending restraints—it called for a less-than-inflation increase in discretionary spending to no more than $600.3 billion—would doom any chance of clearing realistically funded bills that President Clinton would sign. The critics were right. Republicans tried to hold the line on spending but when it became clear the budget resolution's spending limit would be ignored members of both parties began to pad the spending bills with hundreds of special projects.

With both Republicans and Democrats equally eager in an election year to push for big increases for education, health research, and other popular social programs, the tab rose to far above Clinton's initial request of about $625 bil-

lion, a total Republicans had blasted as recklessly excessive at the time.

The biggest budget fight of the year was over education. The dispute was the primary cause of the lame-duck session. Republicans pushed for more block grants and local control, while Democrats backed Clinton's proposals to target funds to hire new teachers and to support school construction. In the end both sides got some, but not all, of what they wanted.

To avoid other fights, especially those that might allow Democrats to score political points in an important election year, Republican leaders resorted to some unusual procedural moves. The Treasury-Postal Service spending bill was a prime example. After the House unexpectedly adopted controversial floor amendments aimed at loosening enforcement of trade sanctions against Cuba and Senate Democrats promised a floor fight over gun control, GOP leaders decided to add a negotiated version of the bill to the relatively noncontroversial legislative branch spending bill. That move avoided Senate debate on a stand-alone Treasury-Postal Service measure, but it also infuriated Democrats and some Republicans in both chambers. The conference report on the combined legislative branch-Treasury-Postal Service did not clear until Oct. 12.

Even though the White House had signed off on the final package, including additional funding for the Internal Revenue Service (IRS), which was added to the Transportation spending bill, Clinton vetoed the measure, saying that appropriations for Congress and the White House, covered by the bill, should not go forward when much of the rest of the appropriations process was still in gridlock. The president specifically cited his disappointment at failing to reach a deal with Republicans on unrelated legislation to provide tax breaks for school construction and to implement proposed regulations to reduce repetitive stress injuries in the work place. When those issues were resolved after the election, the spending bills for the legislative branch and Treasury-Postal Service were attached to the omnibus spending bill and cleared virtually unchanged from the vetoed version.

OMNIBUS SPENDING BILL

President Clinton did not have to retreat often during his six years of budgetary battle with a Republican Congress. But when Republican Gov. George W. Bush emerged as the presidential victor on Dec. 12, 2000, after five weeks of legal challenges over ballots cast in Florida, Republicans were able to force an array of concessions from Clinton during final negotiations on an omnibus spending measure for fiscal 2001. *(2000 elections, p. 21)*

The deal was written into the conference report for the fiscal 2001 appropriations bill covering the departments of Labor, Health and Human Services, and Education (HR 4577—PL 106-554), and included two other measures—for the legislative branch and for the Treasury Department and Postal Service—that Clinton had vetoed before the election. It also made changes to a bill for the departments of Commerce, Justice, and State that had previously been cleared by both chambers but never sent to the president.

Negotiators had worked out most of their differences on the massive Labor-HHS-Education spending bill before the elections. But continuing disagreements over the administration's intention to implement new regulations dealing with repetitive stress injuries in the workplace, and immigration provisions contained in the already-cleared Commerce-Justice-State spending bill prevented final agreement before the elections.

Republican concern about the repetitive stress injury regulations eased somewhat after Bush was declared the president-elect, and the administration softened its demands for amnesty for about 1 million illegal immigrants. Negotiators still had to respond to several hundred requests from members for spending for special projects and to an attempt by Sen. Ted Stevens, R-Alaska, to block the administration's plans to restrict pollock and cod fishing in Alaska to protect the endangered Steller sea lion, which feeds on the fish. Negotiators completed the measure on the afternoon of Dec. 15 and took the conference report directly to the House, which adopted it by a vote of 292–60; the Senate cleared it later that day by voice vote.

Overall, the package appropriated about $384 billion, including $127 billion in discretionary funding. That was about $5 billion less than Clinton had won in agreements negotiated earlier in the year. It also included several pieces of authorizing legislation that Congress had been unable to complete, including a bill (HR 4541) extending the Commodity Futures Trading Commission and reforming the regulation of futures markets, a measure reauthorizing the Small Business Administration, and the "Even Start" family literacy programs.

Following are highlights from the omnibus appropriations bill.

Labor-HHS-Education

The final package boosted spending for federal education programs by a record $6.5 billion, an 18 percent increase over the fiscal 2000 funding level and the largest increase since the Education Department was created in 1979. The measure provided $1.6 billion for the president's initiative to hire 100,000 new teachers to help reduce class sizes and $1.2 billion for school renovation grants. It also provided $7.4 billion for education programs for children with disabilities, $1.1 billion more than the president requested.

HR 4577 appropriated $20.3 billion for the National Institutes of Health (NIH), $2.6 billion more than the fiscal 2000 appropriation, and $1.5 billion more than the administration requested. The measure also established the National Center for Minority Health and Health Disparities within NIH.

The omnibus agreement did not include a House provision in the Labor-HHS-Education spending bill that would

have prohibited the Occupational Safety and Health Administration (OSHA) from implementing or enforcing its proposed regulations designed to limit injuries or disabilities to workers from performing repetitive tasks. The provision became moot when OSHA published the rule after GOP negotiators rejected a White House offer to delay its enforcement until the next president took office.

Commerce, Justice, State

Although the original Commerce, Justice, and State spending bill gave Clinton nearly all the fiscal 2001 spending he requested, it remained under a veto threat because it did not include a set of immigration provisions he had also wanted. The final agreement on the omnibus spending measure gave him some of what he wanted, but a broad provision granting about 1 million illegal immigrants amnesty was denied. *(Immigration, p. 672)*

In other action, the omnibus bill dropped from the Commerce-Justice-State funding bill a provision that would have prohibited imports of so-called conflict diamonds—stones that were mined and sold to fund war—from several African countries, as well as provisions, known as "Amy Boyer's Law," intended to protect Social Security numbers from being sold over the Internet. Critics, which included Boyer's family, the administration, and privacy groups, said the legislation contained too many exemptions and loopholes to be effective. (Amy Boyer was a twenty-year-old New Hampshire dental assistant who was killed in October 1999 by a person who had bought her Social Security number from an Internet information broker.)

Policy Riders

Among the policy riders added to the omnibus spending measure were the following:

• Provisions to increase Medicare payments to hospitals, managed care organizations, nursing homes, and other health care providers, thereby easing cuts in Medicare payments made by the 1997 balanced-budget law. It was estimated that the giveback would increase Medicare spending by about $35 billion over five years. Congress approved $16 billion in Medicare givebacks in fiscal 2000. *(Medicare givebacks, p. 461)*

• Tax breaks and other economic incentives worth $25.9 billion to encourage business investment and job creation in economically depressed urban and rural communities. This program had been a high priority for Clinton but was passed only because it was also a high priority for House Speaker J. Dennis Hastert, R-Ill.

• A one-year delay in federal restrictions on fishing in the habitat of the endangered Steller sea lion.

• A requirement that schools and libraries that receive federal subsidies for Internet connections install Internet filtering software to prevent students from viewing pornography or other harmful material on school and library computers.

REGULAR FISCAL 2001 APPROPRIATIONS

Although they did not become part of the omnibus spending bill, most of the other appropriations measures got caught up in the end-of-year negotiating between Republicans and the White House. Only the Defense and military construction spending bills cleared before the Oct. 1 beginning of fiscal 2001. Following are highlights from the regular appropriations bills for fiscal 2001:

Agriculture

Lawmakers grudgingly resolved their differences on the fiscal 2001 agriculture appropriations bill (HR 4461—PL 106-387) that had been stalled for months by controversies over drug reimportation and provisions to ease economic sanctions against Cuba and other countries. They added $3.6 billion in emergency aid to farmers before sending the $78.5 billion bill to President Clinton, who signed it Oct. 28.

The House was treated to fiery rhetoric reminiscent of the cold war era after farm-state Republicans added language by Rep. George Nethercutt, R-Wash., to remove sanctions on food and medicine exports to Cuba, Iran, Libya, North Korea, and Sudan. Democrats joined many of the GOP rank and file in forcing a showdown with conservative Republican House leaders, most notably Majority Whip Tom DeLay, R-Texas, and Cuban-born Republican Reps. Lincoln Diaz-Balart and Ileana Ros-Lehtinen of Florida, who staunchly opposed improving ties with the communist regime of Fidel Castro. After months of negotiations—some of which played out during the dispute over repatriating seven-year-old Elián Gonzalez—the sides compromised, allowing exports but barring public or private U.S. financing of Cuban agricultural purchases. The bill also contained what amounted to a one-year ban on Americans traveling to Cuba. (Cuba sanctions, p. 224)

Concern over rising prescription drug prices led to language in the bill allowing pharmacists and drug wholesalers to reimport U.S. prescription drugs that were sold abroad for less than they cost in the United States. Previously only drug manufacturers could reimport the products. Republicans saw the provision as preferable to creating a defined Medicare drug benefit, although Democrats charged that drug manufacturers could exploit the language to keep drug prices high. (Prescription drugs, p. 483)

Conferees accepted an amendment by Sen. Robert C. Byrd, D-W.Va., to redirect tens of millions of dollars in antidumping duties assessed on foreign companies to "injured parties" in the United States. Byrd said the provision would help agricultural interests, while opponents said it was aimed more at aiding steel companies and their unions.

Energy-Water

A controversy over federal management of the Missouri River caused President Clinton to veto the first energy-water spending bill for fiscal 2001. The administration supported a new plan for managing the flow of water from dams on the river by releasing more in the spring to improve the habitat of fish and birds and releasing less in the summer. Downstream senators, most of them Republican, complained that the new plan would limit barge traffic and could cause spring floods. They inserted language to block the new plan from taking effect, hoping that pressure from Missouri in an election year would keep Clinton from vetoing the bill.

Although the House voted to override the veto, the Senate did not have the two-thirds majority required for an override. Instead Congress passed a new spending bill (HR 5483) that did not include the blocking language, and that bill was incorporated by reference into the spending bill for the departments of Veterans Affairs and Housing and Urban Development (HR 4635—PL 106-377).

Foreign Operations

Eager to avoid an election-year confrontation with President Clinton, congressional Republicans yielded to his demands on major issues and cleared a fiscal 2001 foreign aid spending bill that provided $435 million in debt relief for the world's poorest nations and lifted abortion restrictions on international family planning aid. Clinton signed the measure (HR 4811—PL 106-429) on Nov. 6.

The decision to lift the abortion restrictions was a major concession for Republicans, who had won inclusion of the language in 1999 after a multiyear battle with the White House. Republicans wanted to extend the abortion restrictions for another year but backed down when Clinton threatened a veto. (Family planning, pp. 210, 214)

Interior

After lengthy negotiations over the level of spending on public lands programs, Congress cleared the $18.8 billion Interior Department spending bill for fiscal 2001 (HR 4578—PL 106-291) on Oct. 5, and President Clinton signed it Oct. 11. The negotiations between appropriators and the White House led to the creation of a protected six-year, $12 billion discretionary fund devoted to land conservation, preservation, and maintenance. The program, a victory for the administration, was a compromise for a larger, permanent lands conservation program that had been blocked in the Senate. (Land conservation, p. 375)

Negotiators added $3 billion to the spending measure, including $1.2 billion for land conservation and $1.6 billion in emergency spending for forest firefighting and prevention in the wake of a devastating wildfire season. Those additions increased the spending in the bill to $3.9 billion more than was appropriated in fiscal 2000 and $2.4 billion more than Clinton had requested.

Although it was typically a magnet for partisan environmental policy disagreements, the Interior spending bill emerged from the House and Senate floors relatively free of riders. Democrats in both chambers defeated GOP attempts to attach language limiting Clinton's ability to declare national monuments, a designation that halted virtually all commercial development of the land and that was intensely opposed by Western lawmakers. In the House the amendment was defeated on a **key vote of 187–234 (R 177–38; D 9–195, I 1–1)**. In the Senate, the amendment was defeated 49–50. Republicans also backed down from riders that would have blocked administration regulations curbing recreation and road-building on public lands. *(2000 key votes, p. 915; national monuments, p. 389)*

Transportation

Congress cleared a $58 billion fiscal 2001 Transportation spending bill (HR 4475—PL 106-346) that significantly increased funding for highways and airport construction, including hundreds of last-minute projects, and that struck compromises on several highway safety issues that the Clinton administration had made a priority.

Chief among the safety issues was a provision setting the national standard for drunken driving at a blood alcohol content of 0.08. A national standard had never been established. Eighteen states had adopted the 0.08 standard but most other states had a 0.10 standard. As adopted in the Senate states that did not comply with the national standard would be denied federal highway funds. After intense lobbying by alcohol and restaurant associations, conferees agreed to delay the sanctions until 2004.

The Senate also agreed to an amendment that would block the administration from proceeding on new rest regulations for truck and bus drivers. The final version barred the Transportation Department from issuing a final regulation on the length of truckers' work shifts in fiscal 2001. The Senate also added language, requested by the auto industry, blocking federal rollover ratings of new vehicles. Conferees agreed to allow the rollover testing program to go forward while the National Academy of Sciences (NAS) studied the issue. The final bill also contained a Senate provision that barred the Transportation Department from updating for another year Corporate Average Fuel Efficiency (CAFE) standards but directed the NAS to study the impact of the standards. *(CAFE standards, box, p. 333)*

The Transportation spending bill was also the vehicle for carrying the compromise that resolved disputes over the Treasury-Postal Service bill, which Clinton had vetoed. After negotiators agreed to include an additional $216 million for improved customer service and enforcement at the IRS and $37 million for counterterrorism programs in the Transportation bill, the Treasury-Postal Service spending bill was incorporated into the omnibus spending bill.

VA-HUD

The spending bill for the departments of Veterans Affairs (VA) and Housing and Urban Development (HUD), similar to several other spending bills in fiscal 2001, took an unusual path to enactment. After Clinton threatened to veto the House-passed version (HR 4635) because it cut off funds for AmeriCorps, the volunteer service program he had pushed to enactment in 1993 (PL 103-82), and provided too little funding for housing, environmental protection, space, and the National Science Foundation, Republican leaders decided not to take the bill to the Senate. Instead, House and Senate appropriators and administration officials negotiated for three weeks on a compromise version. The Senate then approved HR 4635 after amending it to incorporate the compromise, after which a formal conference committee was convened to issue a report spelling out the deal. Both the House and Senate adopted the conference report by wide margins on Oct. 19, and the president signed the bill (PL 106-377) on Oct. 27.

The key points in the compromise were decisions to spend $435 million in unspent fiscal 2000 low-income housing funding to provide 79,000 new Section 8 housing subsidy vouchers; to give AmeriCorps a 21 percent increase, to $434 million; and to limit the duration of restrictions included in the House bill on enforcement of interim water pollution standards for arsenic, dredging of waterways to remove hazardous wastes, and enforcement of new air pollution standards for ozone.

The conference report also carried the revised version of the fiscal 2001 energy and water appropriations bill, shorn of a Missouri River management provision that had prompted Clinton to veto the initial version.

Fiscal 2000 Supplemental Appropriations

Congress cleared an $11.2 billion package of supplemental fiscal 2000 appropriations June 20, 2000, with three-fourths of the fiscal year already completed and in a highly unusual procedure that left some GOP members complaining that their leadership was cramming the bill down their throats. The package—containing funding primarily for defense, disaster relief, and a new initiative to stem Colombia's narcotics trade—was added to the conference report on the military construction spending bill for fiscal 2001 (HR 4425—PL 106-246), the first of the thirteen regular appropriations measures to clear. The unusual method for advancing the supplemental was insisted upon by Senate Majority Leader Trent Lott, R-Miss., who refused to let the Senate consider a stand-alone measure for fear its price tag would balloon. Lott's tactic may have worked. The $11.2 billion was more than double the president's request but $2 billion less than the House had approved.

The supplemental bill's odd path to passage began on Feb. 7, when President Clinton sent to Congress his fiscal 2001 budget request that included a request for $4.4 billion in supplemental budget authority for fiscal 2000. Almost half the request was to replenish Pentagon accounts tapped to pay for the 6,200 U.S. soldiers in the NATO peacekeeping force in Kosovo. The second biggest request, $1.3 billion, was to fund a new program of aid to the Colombian government to combat drug barons and the leftist guerrillas who aided them, a cause embraced by both Clinton and House Speaker J. Dennis Hastert, R-Ill. Clinton added to his request several times in the ensuing weeks, bringing it to a total of $5.5 billion.

The price tag escalated quickly after that. The bill approved by the House Appropriations Committee on March 9 (HR 3908—H Rept 106-521) totaled $9.1 billion. When the House passed it three weeks later, on March 30, by a vote of 263–146, the total was $13.2 billion. In addition to the president's request, the House added $4 billion to bolster Pentagon arms procurement, maintenance, and health programs and $1.2 billion in additional disaster relief.

The supplemental was halted in the Senate, where Lott refused to bring a stand-alone bill to the floor. He said he did not want to devote scarce floor time to a debate that could last for weeks as senators tried to add extra funding for their pet projects. Lott also feared that the bill's price tag would balloon even further in such a debate.

Instead he pressed the Senate Appropriations Committee to spread about $8 billion in supplemental spending among the first three fiscal 2001 appropriations measures they marked up—agriculture, foreign operations, and military construction.

But work on the three underlying spending bills was delayed by problems not related to the supplemental. The agriculture bill was slowed by debate over lifting restrictions on the sale of food and medicine to Cuba and certain other countries. The foreign operations spending bill was an annual target for battles between Clinton and conservative Republicans over foreign aid levels, population control, and other provisions.

Even the usually noncontroversial military construction spending bill was in some trouble as a result of an amendment added in the Senate Appropriations Committee to end the deployment of U.S. troops as peacekeepers in Kosovo on July 1, 2001, unless Congress authorized an extension. In the House, a floor amendment to withhold half of the $2.1 billion supplemental funding for Kosovo until Europe did more to assist in the mission was voted down by a 200–219 vote, indicating that substantial numbers of lawmakers in both chambers were concerned about the U.S. presence in that unstable region. *(Kosovo debate, p. 204)*

Delay on the regular spending bills meant that many "emergency" needs went unmet for many weeks. The Pentagon warned that if its share of the supplemental was not guaranteed by the end of June, it would be forced to cancel training exercises and maintenance projects, the accounts that had been tapped to finance the Kosovo mission. The delay was also allowing time for congressional skepticism about the Colombia initiative to grow. Many lawmakers were expressing concerns that the United States was getting too involved with an unstable government and that the antinarcotics plan was unfocused, incomplete, and incapable of being implemented. At the same time, the supplemental package was attracting a host of special projects of the sort that Lott had hoped to deter. *(Colombia antinarcotics program, p. 220)*

By mid-May, both the House and Senate had passed versions of the military construction bill and Lott came under pressure from GOP House leaders to add all the supplemental funds to that bill during conference. Although he at first expressed reluctance, Lott relented at a meeting of GOP leaders on June 22.

The final $11.2 billion package was assembled with speed and unusual secrecy, mostly by the top four members of the Appropriations Committees. The biggest items were $2 billion to replenish the Pentagon accounts used for the Kosovo mission; $1.6 billion to pay higher-than-expected military fuel bills; $1.3 billion for unfunded military health programs; $1.3 billion to battle drug smugglers in Colombia and other South American countries; $1 billion in disaster aid; and $700 million for the Coast Guard, mostly for new equipment. Another $5.5 billion emergency relief package for farmers hurt by low commodity prices had already been attached to a crop insurance subsidy law (HR 2559—PL 106-224) that Congress passed earlier in June. *(Crop insurance, pp. 421, 425)*

GOP leaders limited the appropriators to allocating $200 million in other earmarks, most of it going to senior lawmakers. These included such items as $25 million for a convention center in Youngstown, Ohio, $25 million for a Customs Service firearms training facility in West Virginia, and $12 million for hospital improvements and economic development grants for Libby, Montana. An attempt by Senate Republicans to prevent the Justice Department from receiving money from other agencies to press its lawsuit against tobacco companies was rebuffed, as was an attempt Sen. Judd Gregg, R-N.H., to win extension of a biotechnology drug patent held by Columbia University, his alma mater, that netted the school as much as $100 million a year. The measure also voided more than $4 billion in scorekeeping adjustments that had artificially deflated overall fiscal 2000 spending by shifting the spending into fiscal 2001.

Less than an hour after the conference report was formally filed, the House adopted it 306–110, the night of June 29. The Senate cleared the bill by voice vote the next afternoon, and Clinton signed it into law on July 13.

Debt Reduction

Five times during the 2000 session, House Republicans won passage of measures to commit slices of the federal surplus to debt reduction. Democrats called the bills meaningless but voted for them anyway. The Senate ignored all five bills.

The debate began when President Clinton applied the term "lockbox" to his proposal to retire the publicly held national debt, which then stood at $3.6 trillion, by 2013—a pledge Vice President Al Gore renewed repeatedly throughout his presidential campaign. House Republicans promised to pursue policies that would at least match that timetable.

Much of the debate was merely election-year posturing as both parties tried to portray themselves as guardians of the public purse while accusing the other party of fiscal irre-sponsibility. But the legislation also enabled GOP leaders to allay concerns among conservative Republicans upset that Republicans in both 1998 and 1999 had agreed to break the budget spending caps in order to get President Clinton to sign off on the annual spending bills.

The first GOP effort to save the surplus for debt reduction (HR 4601—H Rept 106-673, Pt. 1) was the most modest. It would have allocated to debt reduction any portion of the fiscal 2001 "on-budget," or non-Social Security, surplus above $24.4 billion. The House passed HR 4601 on June 22, 419–5. A second bill (HR 3859—no report), passed the same day by a vote of 420–2, would have reserved Social Security and Medicare trust fund surpluses for debt reduction as well. A month later, on July 18, the House passed a bill (HR 4866—no report), 422–1, to allocate $25 billion of the fiscal 2001 surplus to debt relief.

By midyear, fiscally conservative Republicans were grow-ing nervous about the budget-breaking spending totals that were working their way through the fiscal 2001 appropria-tions process, and they were threatening to vote against spending bills that were too heavily funded.

In response, GOP House leaders in September rolled out a so-called "90–10" debt reduction plan, which specified that 90 percent of the cumulative fiscal 2001 surplus would go to paying down the national debt. The remaining 10 percent—about $28 billion, based on the most recent fiscal 2001 pro-jections—could be used for a combination of tax cuts and spending increases, and party leaders said they likely would split it evenly between the two priorities. While Republican

leaders trumpeted the debt reduction aspect of their plan, it actually amounted to a blueprint for allowing a big increase over the budget in spending for fiscal 2001. To further ap-pease conservatives, GOP leaders also promised to attach debt-reduction riders to the remaining appropriations bills, thereby setting aside specific amounts of surplus funds for debt relief with each corresponding spending bill approved.

The GOP strategy worked. Conservative Republicans liked the 90–10 plan and the debt-reduction riders. Demo-crats said the GOP plan was a meaningless gimmick. Surplus funds were automatically used to pay down the public debt, they argued, so the way to reduce the debt was simply not to spend the money. Still Democrats glibly endorsed the mea-sure, saying it amounted to a symbolic repudiation of the Republicans' own large tax cuts proposed earlier in the year, since the 90–10 plan could not accommodate them. *(Tax cuts, p. 110)*

The 90–10 plan passed overwhelmingly—twice. The first measure (HR 5173—H Rept 106-862, Pt. 1) was passed on Sept. 18 by a **key vote of 381–3 (R 191–0; D 188–3; I 2–0).** The second measure (HR 5203) was the second reconcilia-tion bill of the year and combined the debt reduction lan-guage with a package of expanded tax breaks for retirement savings. It passed on Sept. 19, by a vote of 401–20. *(2000 key votes, p. 915; retirement tax breaks, p. 119)*

Senate Republicans endorsed the 90–10 idea but never moved companion legislation. GOP leaders said they viewed the plan as a guide for the coming spate of deal-cutting on fiscal 2001 spending bills rather than as a legislative vehicle. *(2001 appropriations, p. 81)*

Chronology of Action on Economic Policy: Tax Policy

Introduction

With one major exception, debate about tax policy in President Bill Clinton's second term from 1997 to 2001 followed substantially the same pattern: the Republican leadership pushed large tax cuts through Congress while making little effort to accommodate Democratic demands or to court Democratic support. As a result Republicans were unable to muster the votes necessary to override the inevitable Clinton vetoes.

The legislative failures, however, did not appear to trouble Republicans who seemed as eager to define a major philosophical difference between the two parties as to enact legislation and share credit with Clinton and the Democrats.

The exception came in 1997. In a rare display of bipartisanship Congress passed and Clinton signed legislation cutting taxes by $96 billion over five years. The measure was part of a package Congress and Clinton negotiated to eliminate the federal budget deficit within five years while still easing taxes. In fact, the continuing vigor of the economy erased the budget deficit well ahead of that schedule as tax revenues continued to pour in to the federal coffers. In 1998 the federal budget showed the first surplus since 1969, albeit a small one. During the next two years the estimated size of the surplus grew exponentially, posing the inevitable question of how the money should be spent. *(Deficit history, table, p. 36)*

Democrats and Republicans easily agreed that a portion of the surplus should go to pay down the public debt and shore up the Social Security system. But then they parted ways. The president and most Democrats advocated using the surplus primarily for those purposes. Most Republicans argued for larger tax reductions. Neither side budged from its position for the next three years.

1997 TAX REDUCTION

The $96 billion tax cut package enacted in 1997 was modest beside the $600 billion tax reduction Republicans crusaded for after winning control of Congress in the 1994 elections. In fact, the final number was not significantly more than the net five-year, $75 billion figure Clinton offered before budget negotiations fell apart at the end of 1995. *(Fiscal 1996 budget negotiations, Congress and the Nation Vol. IX, p. 70)*

Nonetheless, the package fulfilled several GOP promises including a $500-per-child tax credit, the largest reduction in capital gains tax rates since 1981, a significant increase in the tax exemption for estates, and an expansion of tax-sheltered individual retirement accounts. Correspondingly, Clinton won new tax incentives for education and shaped the child tax credit to the advantage of most working poor families including those who were too poor to owe any income tax.

The bipartisanship behind the historic 1997 deficit reduction and tax cut package was a direct outgrowth of the 1995 budget fight, in which House Republican leaders, newly in control, tried to force the president to accept their spending and tax plans. The battle was a standoff but led to two brief and unpopular government shutdowns that embarrassed Republicans. The public blamed the GOP, not Clin-

REFERENCES

Discussion of tax policy for the years 1945–1964 may be found in *Congress and the Nation Vol. I*, pp. 397–442; for the years 1965–1968, *Congress and the Nation Vol. II*, pp. 141–182; for the years 1969–1972, *Congress and the Nation Vol. III*, pp. 77–96; for the years 1973–1976, *Congress and the Nation Vol. IV*, pp. 83–106; for the years 1977–1980, *Congress and the Nation Vol. V*, pp. 231–251; for the years 1981–1984, *Congress and the Nation Vol. VI*, pp. 63–82; for the years 1985–1988, *Congress and the Nation Vol. VII*, pp. 75–107; for the years 1989–1992, *Congress and the Nation Vol. VIII*, pp. 87–112; for the years 1993–1996, *Congress and the Nation Vol. IX*, pp. 83–107.

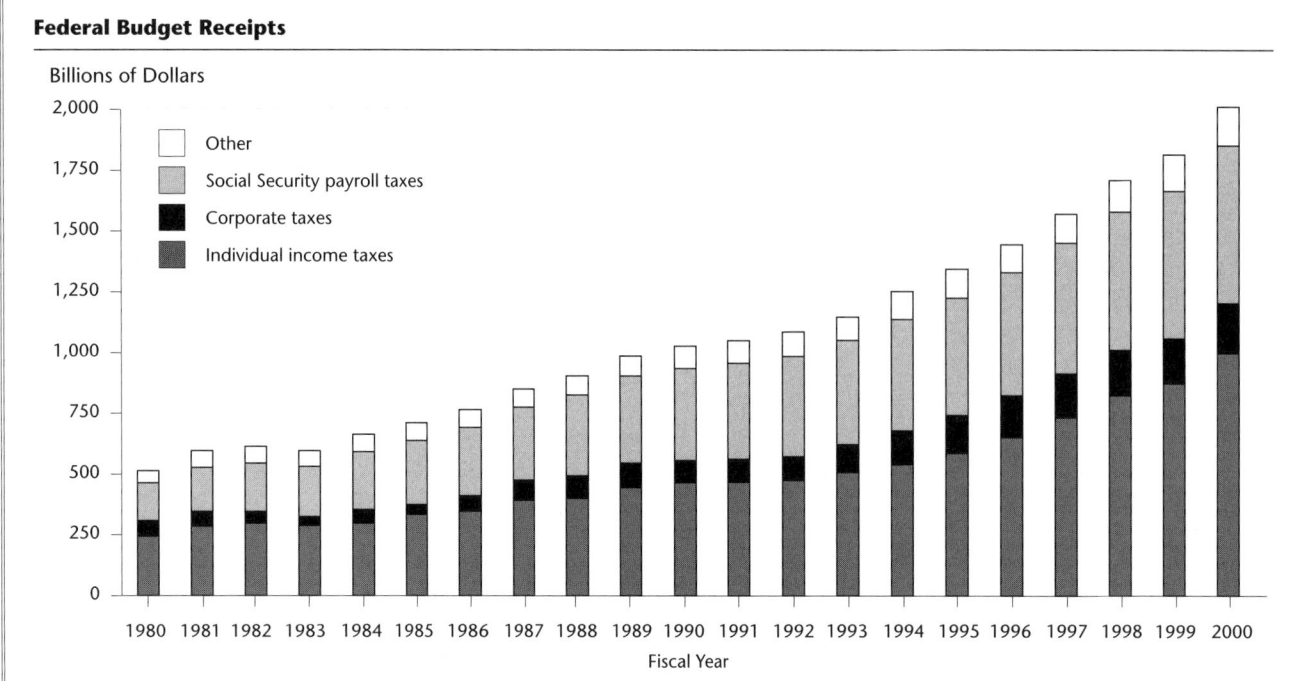

Federal Budget Receipts

Billions of Dollars

Other
Social Security payroll taxes
Corporate taxes
Individual income taxes

Fiscal Year

SOURCE: Office of Management and Budget, *Historical Tables, Budget of the United States Government: Fiscal Year 2002* (Washington, D.C.: U.S. Government Printing Office, 2001), Table 2.1.

ton, which contributed to the loss of nine Republican seats in the House in the 1996 elections. Legislators agreed that voters were warning both parties to take a more cooperative stance.

The fragile bipartisanship displayed in 1997 began to unravel in 1998. Anticipating the first budget surplus since 1969, Clinton in his State of the Union address urged Congress not to spend the surplus "until we have taken all the necessary measures to strengthen the Social Security system for the twenty-first century." Clinton's call to "save Social Security first," which he repeated again and again during the next three years, was politically popular as was his call to pay down the publicly held debt that peaked at $3.8 trillion in fiscal 1997. Opinion polls consistently showed that the American public preferred debt reduction to tax reduction.

As a result many moderate Republicans, particularly in the Senate, joined Democrats in opposing GOP plans to use the surplus for tax cuts. They also were unwilling to make the spending cuts in domestic programs that major tax reductions would have dictated.

Despite that opposition, House leaders pushed ahead in the fall of 1998 with a comparatively modest tax cut bill with clear political appeal: it would have altered tax laws that required some married couples to pay more taxes than they would have as single individuals; cut taxes for farmers and the self-employed; and provided new tax incentives for investment in low-income areas. It passed the House on a near

party-line vote, which meant a Clinton veto almost certainly would not be overridden. The measure never came to the floor in the Senate.

SPENDING THE SURPLUS

The Republican-led effort to impeach Clinton and remove him from office in late 1998 on charges that he had lied under oath to cover up an affair with a White House intern shattered any incentive the GOP might have had to negotiate a tax reduction with the president. With surplus projections rising steadily, the Republican leadership in 1999 decided the time was ripe to push for a large income tax cut. Even if President Clinton vetoed the legislation, as he promised to do, the GOP leadership calculated that congressional passage of a bill, largely on Republican votes, would highlight for the 2000 presidential elections a major difference between the two political parties.

Tax cuts are "the defining difference between Republicans and Democrats," Bill Archer, R-Texas, chairman of the House Ways and Means Committee, said in July 1999 as the committee began to mark up the largest tax cut bill since 1981. "Democrats believe the government can spend money more effectively and more wisely than people can spend their own money. We believe people can spend their money more wisely. . . . That is the issue that is before us. . . ."

Despite initial misgivings among moderate GOP members about its size, the Republicans in 1999 went on to pass a

$792 billion tax measure providing for across-the-board cuts in tax rates, an end to the marriage status differentiation in tax law (which its critics labeled a "marriage penalty"), elimination of estate taxes, and a cut in individual capital gains tax rates, as well as many lesser tax breaks. Democrats called it a sop to the wealthy and voted nearly unanimously against it, again denying the GOP the votes they needed to override Clinton's veto. To Republican dismay, Clinton's veto barely raised the public eyebrow, according to public opinion polls.

In 2000 the GOP leadership decided to keep the political spotlight on the tax issue but took a different tack, breaking into separate bills two smaller components that had broad public support. More Democrats voted for these measures that eliminated the marriage status laws and the estate tax. But after Clinton vetoed both bills, pressure from party leaders persuaded some Democrats to reconsider, allowing both vetoes to be sustained.

Although a few Republicans held out hope for a possible compromise on the issue before the end of the session, Republican leaders made it clear that they were not interested in anything less than repeal, especially because the Republican presidential nominee, Gov. George W. Bush of Texas, supported large tax cuts. "We've carried it as far as we can go this year," House Majority Leader Dick Armey, R-Texas, told reporters on Sept. 7. "If we don't have it now, we'll have it within the first six months of the Bush presidency."

1997–1998

Republicans won a sizable down payment on their plans to cut the federal tax burden with passage of the tax reconciliation bill of 1997. That bill called for net tax cuts of $96 billion over five years, including cuts in the capital gains tax long sought by the GOP. But in 1998 quarrels between House and Senate Republicans over how to use the budget surplus prevented adoption of the nonbinding budget resolution for the first time since 1974 when the modern budget process was adopted and doomed a House measure making additional tax cuts. At the end of the year lawmakers had barely managed to pass a modest measure extending a number of traditional tax breaks.

Congress in 1998 had better luck with a measure overhauling the Internal Revenue Service. The legislation grew out of widespread complaints of taxpayer harassment and other abuses by IRS agents.

1997 Tax Cuts

As a direct result of the bipartisan balanced-budget agreement reached in May, Congress in 1997 cleared the deepest tax cut since 1981 (HR 2014—PL 105-34). As approved overwhelmingly by both chambers on July 31 and signed into law by President Clinton on Aug. 5, the measure represented a compromise between Republicans, who wanted to cut individual and corporate tax rates, and Democrats, who were intent on aiding low- and middle-income workers and families. The biggest benefits in the measure went to those who had children, sought higher education, had capital gains on investments, or wanted to save for retirement.

The tax-reduction bill was one of a pair of budget reconciliation measures that aimed to eliminate the federal deficit by the year 2002 while providing significant tax cuts. That overarching goal, and some of the details for getting there, had been agreed to during lengthy bipartisan negotiations that culminated in a balanced-budget accord announced May 2. Legislators, however, were unable to come to agreement on the tax cut plan without exceeding the parameters agreed to in May. The price tag was $96 billion in net tax cuts during the first five years, growing to $275 billion over ten years. The original agreement was for $85 billion in net cuts in the first five years and $250 billion over ten years. *(Budget resolution, p. 43; reconciliation, pp. 48, 50)*

The tax and spending reconciliation bills moved through Congress in tandem, although by all accounts the tax package was the more difficult of the two to complete. It ultimately succeeded because it gave major victories to both sides. Republican gains included the largest reduction in capital gains rates since 1981, a $500-per-child tax credit, a significant increase in the tax exemption for estates, and an expansion of tax-sheltered Individual Retirement Account (IRA) savings plans.

Clinton and his Democratic allies won hefty new tax incentives for higher education, and they managed to shape the $500-per-child tax credit to make it available to most working poor families including some too poor to owe any income taxes.

Gross tax cuts in the final package were about $152 billion over five years with an offset of $56 billion in tax increases, according to estimates by the Joint Committee on Taxation. Over 10 years, the gross tax cut was projected to be $401 billion with $126 billion in offsetting tax increases.

TAX BILL HIGHLIGHTS

Major elements of the tax portion of the reconciliation bill included:

Child Tax Credit

A $500-per-child tax credit ($400 per child in 1998) for families with children under age seventeen. The full credit would be available to single filers with up to $75,000 in adjusted gross income and married couples with up to $110,000. The credit was partially refundable to low-income families with three or more children, which meant that the parents could receive the credit as a payment even if they owed no income tax. The child tax credit accounted for more than half the bill's gross five-year tax cuts; making it more available to low-income families was the main factor increasing the overall size of the tax bill.

Education

The bill contained eleven education tax incentives, including the following:

• **HOPE tax credit.** The bill allowed a nonrefundable HOPE tax credit of as much as $1,500 per student for each of the first two years of college. Joint filers with up to $80,000 in adjusted gross income ($40,000 for single filers) would be eligible for the full credit.

• **Lifetime learning credit.** The bill established a nonrefundable lifetime learning credit worth up to $1,000 a year through 2002, rising to a maximum of $2,000 a year after that. The credit could be used for the second two years of college, for graduate and postgraduate education, and for any formal education after that.

• **A new education savings account.** Individuals could make nondeductible contributions of up to $500 per child per year and withdraw the principal and interest earnings tax free to help pay for a child's college or graduate education.

• **Penalty-free withdrawals.** The bill allowed penalty-free withdrawals from all IRAs for education expenses.

Capital gains

A cut in the maximum individual tax rate on capital gains from 28 percent to 20 percent for investments held for more

Taxes and Other Revenues as Percentage of GDP, 1935–2000

Fiscal year	Individual income	Corporate income	Social insurance	Excise	Other	Total
1935	0.8	0.8	—	2.1	1.6	5.2
1940	0.9	1.2	1.8	2.0	0.7	6.8
1945	8.3	7.2	1.6	2.8	0.5	20.4
1950	5.8	3.8	1.6	2.8	0.5	14.4
1955	7.3	4.5	2.0	2.3	0.5	16.6
1960	7.8	4.1	2.8	2.3	0.8	17.8
1965	7.1	3.7	3.2	2.1	0.8	17.0
1970	8.9	3.2	4.4	1.6	0.9	19.0
1975	7.8	2.6	5.4	1.1	1.0	17.9
1980	8.9	2.4	5.8	0.9	1.0	18.9
1981	9.3	2.0	6.0	1.3	0.9	19.6
1982	9.2	1.5	6.2	1.1	1.0	19.1
1983	8.4	1.1	6.1	1.0	0.9	17.5
1984	7.8	1.5	6.2	1.0	0.9	17.4
1985	8.1	1.5	6.4	0.9	0.9	17.7
1986	7.9	1.4	6.5	0.7	0.9	17.5
1987	8.4	1.8	6.6	0.7	0.9	18.4
1988	8.0	1.9	6.7	0.7	0.9	18.1
1989	8.2	1.9	6.6	0.6	0.9	18.3
1990	8.2	1.6	6.6	0.6	1.0	18.0
1991	7.9	1.7	6.7	0.7	0.9	17.8
1992	7.7	1.6	6.7	0.7	0.9	17.5
1993	7.8	1.8	6.5	0.7	0.8	17.6
1994	7.8	2.0	6.6	0.8	0.8	18.1
1995	8.1	2.1	6.6	0.8	0.9	18.5
1996	8.5	2.2	6.6	0.7	0.8	18.9
1997	9.0	2.2	6.6	0.7	0.8	19.3
1998	9.6	2.2	6.6	0.7	0.9	19.9
1999	9.6	2.0	6.7	0.8	0.9	20.0
2000	10.3	2.1	6.7	0.7	0.9	20.8

NOTE: The Social Insurance category includes Social Security, Medicare, railroad and other retirement programs, and unemployment insurance. The Other category principally includes estate and gift taxes and customs duties.

SOURCE: Office of Management and Budget, *Historical Tables, Budget of the United States Government: Fiscal Year 2003* (Washington, D.C.: U.S. Government Printing Office, 2002), Table 2.3.

than eighteen months, dropping to 18 percent after 2000 for assets held for at least five years. (The eighteen-month holding period was further reduced in separate legislation to twelve months.) In addition, the bill provided a capital gains tax exemption for profits from the sale of a primary residence. Single filers could exempt up to $250,000; couples filing jointly could exempt up to $500,000.

IRAs

A new "back-loaded" retirement savings account, known as the "Roth IRA" after its chief sponsor, Senate Finance Committee Chairman William V. Roth Jr., R-Del. Contributions were not tax deductible but the principal and earnings could be withdrawn tax free after five years if the holder was age 59½, disabled or deceased, or the money was used for a first-time home purchase. Taxpayers with adjusted gross incomes up to $100,000 could convert their existing IRAs to Roth IRAs after paying taxes on the funds.

The bill also increased the existing income limit for individuals making tax-free contributions to traditional IRAs and it allowed penalty-free withdrawals to finance a first home or for educational purposes.

Estate Tax

A gradual increase in the amount exempt from gift and estate taxes from $600,000 to $1 million by 2007 and an immediate increase to $1.3 million in the exemption for family farms and businesses. The gift tax exclusion of up to $10,000 to any number of recipients was indexed for inflation after 1998.

Corporate Alternative Minimum Tax

Repeal of the corporate alternative minimum tax (AMT) for small businesses and a faster depreciation schedule for large businesses. The AMT was designed to ensure that even corporations that did not owe regular income taxes still paid some tax. The AMT was used only when a business's alternative minimum tax liability exceeded its regular tax liability.

Gasoline Tax

Repeal of a requirement that 4.3 cents per gallon in federal gasoline taxes go to deficit reduction. Instead the money, along with the rest of the gasoline tax, was dedicated to the Highway Trust Fund.

Airline Ticket Tax

Reduction of the tax on domestic airline tickets from 10 percent to 7.5 percent. The bill added a new per-passenger fee for each flight segment—$1 per segment in 1998 rising to $3 in 2002. Also the existing $6 departure tax on international flights was replaced with a $12 tax on both arrivals and departures.

HOUSE COMMITTEE ACTION

The central actor in the House tax debate was Ways and Means Committee Chairman Bill Archer, Texas, a conservative Republican who had blocked House Budget Committee members from settling many of the tax issues during negotiations on the budget resolution by insisting that his committee retain its jurisdiction over the tax provisions.

Archer announced the details of his tax cut plan on June 9, immediately provoking an outcry from members of his party as well as from Democrats. Even before the markup began on June 12, Republican leaders vetoed Archer's plan to repeal the corporate AMT outright and to cover the costs by raising the exemption on estate taxes less than its advocates wanted. Lobbyists for a host of small business and farming organizations immediately launched a campaign aimed at forcing Archer to rewrite those portions of the bill. GOP leaders successfully prevailed on the chairman to confine the AMT repeal to corporations with gross receipts of less than $5 million a year and to accelerate the estate tax cut.

Rural Republicans, who supported the increase in the estate tax, also balked at Archer's proposal to terminate the tax credit for ethanol, a fuel made from corn. A bipartisan effort to amend the bill to restore the ethanol tax credit failed during the markup 17–21.

Republicans helped Democrats kill another Archer proposal, this one to levy income taxes on all commercial businesses run by Native American tribes. Traditionally Native American tribes, which were considered sovereign nations, were not subject to income taxes. According to Joint Tax Committee analysts, 80 percent of the revenues from Archer's proposal would have come from a tax on gambling income. Lawmakers whose states had private casinos or riverboat gambling had complained that it was unfair to tax that income while exempting income from tribal-owned casinos. Led by J. D. Hayworth, R-Ariz., whose state had one of the largest Native American populations in the country, the committee eliminated Archer's proposal on a 22–16 vote

with seven Republicans joining all of the committee Democrats in support of Hayworth.

For their part Democrats complained that Archer had violated the spirit if not the letter of the balanced-budget agreement. "Every part is skewed against low-income people," said Charles B. Rangel, N.Y., the ranking Democrat on Ways and Means. "I don't find any violation of what was put down in the [budget] agreement, it's just that he pushed this envelope as far to the right as he could."

A Democratic alternative that had Clinton's endorsement and the backing of the full Democratic caucus from the most liberal to the most conservative party members had many of the same elements as the GOP bill—a per-child tax credit, a capital gains tax cut, education tax breaks, estate tax relief, and expanded IRAs—but every provision was designed to give the maximum tax benefit to low- and middle-income workers and their families. For example the Democrats' version of the $500-per-child tax credit was limited to couples with adjusted gross incomes of less than $75,000 instead of the $110,000 in the GOP bill. The capital gains cut, with a top rate of 18 percent, was restricted to the first $600,000 in gains over a lifetime.

The Democratic alternative was rejected on a straight party-line vote. The committee then approved HR 2014 22–16 with no Democrats voting for it. That vote brought to a close an acrimonious markup that began on June 12 and ran into the predawn hours of the following day. As approved the Ways and Means package proposed to cut taxes by $133 billion over five years, offset by $48 billion in tax increases, for a net tax cut of $85 billion—the target set in the budget resolution. The offsetting revenues came primarily from a controversial plan to restructure and expand excise taxes on airline tickets.

Because the measure was a budget reconciliation bill the job of reporting it to the floor fell to the House Budget Committee. That panel agreed 20–12 on June 20 to send the bill to the full House (H Rept 105-148).

HOUSE FLOOR ACTION

The House passed HR 2014 June 26 on a 253–179 vote. Only 27 Democrats voted for the tax cut bill—the same number that voted for the GOP's Contract with America tax-cut bill in 1995. Only one Republican voted against the tax cut.

Archer overcame many of the earlier GOP criticisms by agreeing to several modifications that were incorporated into the bill as part of the rule for floor debate (H Res 174). Foremost among the changes, Archer agreed to retain the tax credit for ethanol. He also agreed to modify the per-child and dependent care tax credits so that joint taxpayers with adjusted gross incomes under $60,000 could claim both credits in full.

That change was still not enough to satisfy Democrats who said the bill was skewed in favor of the wealthy. A Democratic substitute offered by Rangel—the only amendment allowed under the rule—was defeated on a near party-line vote 197–235. As they had in committee Democrats sought to limit the tax cuts that would go to higher-income investors and to limit the per-child tax credit to less wealthy families and to make it fully refundable to working families still too poor to owe any taxes.

Barred by the rule from offering a separate amendment, conservative "Blue Dog" Democrats led by Collin C. Peterson of Minnesota, offered a motion to recommit the bill to committee with instructions to target the capital gains tax reduction on investors who held the assets for longer periods as well as to increase the amounts exempt from estate taxes. The motion was defeated 164–268 with both liberal Democrats and a majority of Republicans opposing it.

SENATE COMMITTEE ACTION

In contrast to the sharp wrangling over the House bill the Senate Finance Committee approved a bipartisan draft bill June 19 by a vote of 18–2. Every Democrat voted for the measure; the "no" votes came from two conservative Republicans, Don Nickles of Oklahoma and Phil Gramm of Texas, who objected to provisions raising the tobacco tax and increasing spending for child health.

The bill, which chairman Roth subsequently introduced as S 949 (S Rept 105-33), provided for $77 billion in net tax cuts over five years. That was $8 billion less than the $85 billion allowed in the budget resolution and approved by the House (although S 949 did meet the $135 billion in gross cuts allowed by the budget resolution). The net ten-year tax cut, similar to that in the House bill, was roughly $250 billion.

The bipartisan bill came out of a freewheeling markup that surprised just about everyone. When committee members met behind closed doors to winnow the 110 amendments that senators wanted to add to the measure, they were expected to return in a couple of hours with a few modifications. But as the hours dragged on and the ranks of lobbyists outside the committee room swelled to more than 200, it was clear that more than minor changes were being discussed. At one point most of the committee staff was even asked to leave the room.

When the senators emerged eight hours later they unveiled a bipartisan deal that called for nearly doubling the federal tax on cigarettes from 24 cents a pack to 44 cents. The resulting revenue—as much as $15 billion over five years according to initial estimates—allowed for horse-trading in several other areas.

About half the money was targeted for new block grants to states for children's health care. Nearly $3.5 billion was used to reduce the ticket tax on international flights that Roth had included in the draft bill. About $800 million went to boost the capital gains tax break for real estate and $3 billion was used to increase the number of working poor families who would be eligible for the $500-per-child tax credit.

Another significant amendment added during the closed session proposed taking the 4.3 cents-per-gallon gas tax that had been dedicated to deficit reduction since 1993 and depositing it into the Highway Trust Fund. A laundry list of twenty-eight special-interest amendments requested by Finance Committee members also was added to the bill.

The Finance Committee deal came together as a result of a combination of virtually unforeseen forces. Chief among them was the intense lobbying by the seven major airline companies for a reduction in the proposed ticket tax and by the real estate industry for a bigger capital gains tax break. Because nine proposed amendments called for raising the cigarette tax to offset reduced taxes on real estate, estates, and other items, it seemed clear that similar amendments would be raised on the Senate floor. According to one committee member, the panel thus made the simple calculation that they would rather control how the revenue was spent.

Republican Orrin G. Hatch of Utah pushed the proposal to put some of the revenue into children's health care, warning colleagues that Democrats would pillory them if they raised the tobacco tax but did nothing for children.

SENATE FLOOR ACTION

The Senate took up the tax bill June 27, one day after the House had acted, and passed it 80–18 with 29 Democratic votes. (The Senate voted on HR 2014 after substituting the amended text of its own bill.)

Senate GOP leaders worked to bury amendments from their own ranks that threatened to undermine the committee bill. They also were able to turn aside all important amendments offered by Democrats. These included a substitute amendment that would have made the child credit refundable, targeted a sizable portion of the capital gains tax cuts to investments in small and start-up companies, and created a special estate tax exemption for family-owned businesses and farms. The amendment failed 38–61. Of the seven Democrats voting against it six were Finance Committee members who felt bound to resist all efforts to change the committee package.

Also defeated were two attempts to restrict the capital gains tax break, an amendment to index the capital gains tax cuts to inflation, and two amendments to raise the tobacco tax even higher than the committee had proposed.

CLINTON WEIGHS IN

In anticipation of a House-Senate conference on the bill President Clinton released a revised tax cut plan of his own on June 30. Although Clinton had previously criticized both the House and Senate tax bills in detail this was the administration's first comprehensive proposal since the president submitted his fiscal 1998 budget to Congress on Feb. 6.

The White House proposal tracked closely most of the elements in the House and Senate Democratic proposals. It also included versions of several primary GOP proposals including a capital gains tax cut and a significant reduction in estate taxes for small businesses and farms. Following are the principal differences between the Clinton proposal and the competing House and Senate versions:

• **Child tax credit.** Clinton left this provision of his original tax cut package largely unchanged. He called for a $400-per-child tax credit in 1998, rising to $500 in 1999 and indexed for inflation thereafter. It was to be available for children under seventeen with the age limit rising to nineteen after 2002.

Clinton wanted the full credit to be available until 2000 to families with adjusted gross incomes of up to $60,000, phasing out completely for those making more than $75,000. After 2000, the respective income thresholds would rise to $80,000 and $100,000. The House and Senate versions proposed to make the credit available to single taxpayers with up to $75,000 a year in adjusted gross income and to couples with up to $110,000 a year.

Unlike the congressional plans Clinton wanted to make the credit partially refundable. Taxpayers too poor to owe any income tax would still qualify for the credit depending on whether they also received the earned-income tax credit (EITC). If they received the EITC and it did not fully offset their payroll tax liability, the per-child tax credit could be used to eliminate the remaining portion of their tax liability.

• **Capital gains.** Clinton proposed a top effective capital gains tax rate for individuals of 27.7 percent. This was only a slight drop from the existing top rate of 28 percent. Those in the 28 percent income tax bracket would receive an effective capital gains tax rate of about 20 percent while those in the 15 percent bracket would qualify for a capital gains rate of roughly 11 percent.

Both the House and Senate bills aimed to reduce the top rate to 20 percent (10 percent for those in the 15 percent bracket). The House also wanted to index capital gains to inflation. Clinton's plan, similar to the Senate bill, proposed no capital gains tax relief for corporations. The House called for a cut in those taxes.

• **Education.** Similar to the House and Senate bills Clinton included numerous education-related tax incentives but two of them accounted for most of the revenue loss: a HOPE tax credit and a tuition tax credit. The HOPE credit would be available for two years of a student's educational costs and would be worth up to $1,500 a year. After 2002 the maximum credit would increase to $2,000. The full credit would be available to couples with adjusted gross incomes of up to $80,000 and phase out completely for taxpayers with incomes of more than $100,000. Both the House and Senate proposals contained a similar credit.

Neither version, however, contained Clinton's second proposed credit—a 20 percent tuition tax credit for third- and fourth-year college students, graduate students, and workers returning to school. The credit would be worth up to $1,000 through 2002, increasing to $2,000 thereafter. The

tuition tax credit would be available for taxpayers of the same income levels as the HOPE credit.

Similar to the House and Senate bills, Clinton called for penalty-free withdrawals from IRAs for undergraduate, vocational, and graduate education expenses. Clinton also proposed that families receiving the child tax credit could put the money into a special IRA along with a $500 after-tax contribution of their own. Interest and principal could be withdrawn tax-free if the money was used for education, purchase of the child's first home, or the taxpayer's retirement.

• **Tobacco tax.** Clinton endorsed the 20-cent per-pack increase in tobacco taxes that was part of the Senate bill, but he wanted to put all of the revenue into a trust fund for children's health care. The Senate wanted to use some of the revenue to offset other tax breaks. The House bill contained no similar provision.

• **Estate taxes.** Although Clinton had initially proposed only minor changes in estate tax payment schedules, his new plan would allow family-owned businesses and farms to exempt an additional $900,000 in value. Under existing law heirs other than spouses could avoid taxes on the first $600,000. Clinton did not propose increasing the exclusion from estate and gift taxes for individuals, a plan strongly supported by many congressional Republicans. The House and Senate bills sought to increase the existing $600,000 exemption gradually to $1 million over about nine years.

• **Alternative minimum tax.** Unlike the congressional bills Clinton did not propose any reduction in the alternative minimum tax.

CONFERENCE ACTION

Republican leaders spent much of the four-week period following passage of the House and Senate bills trying to get their own house in order. In sessions that began July 18 and finished July 23 they met among themselves to develop a measure that their members could support and that the president could sign.

Clinton kept up the pressure, at one point inviting top congressional negotiators to the White House for direct talks. He also said he would veto any bill that indexed capital gains, did not make the per-child tax credits refundable to low-income families, and did not contain education tax incentives similar to those he had proposed.

Initially Republicans took a hard line, embracing the very elements of the bill that Clinton had said were unacceptable. The strong GOP reluctance to make big concessions left some White House officials astonished. Why, they asked, would the Republicans not give up indexing when they could still get a lower capital gains tax rate, the child tax credit, and a cut in estate taxes, all proposals from their Contract with America?

But House GOP leaders faced a complicated task. They were just recovering from an aborted coup attempt against House Speaker Newt Gingrich, R-Ga., fueled by conservative angst over what the Speaker might give away to Clinton. GOP leaders were thus anxious to prove that they had fought hard for the House version of the bill. They also had to figure out how to hold or replace a bloc of fifteen to twenty Republicans from tobacco-growing states whose support was tied to the fate of the tobacco tax. The turmoil over Gingrich also was interfering with the leadership's ability to get firm vote counts on the different options.

The final round of give and take on the bill began July 25 with intensive meetings in the office of Gingrich or Lott attended by top administration officials. In one of the most obvious trade-offs the administration accepted the Republican demand to lower the top capital gains tax rate to 20 percent in return for Republican agreement to give up indexing gains to inflation. In another obvious trade-off Republicans agreed to make the child tax credit refundable to low-income families who paid only payroll taxes, not income taxes. In return Clinton agreed to the Republicans' higher income levels of $75,000 for a single taxpayer and $110,000 for a couple.

Clinton won the $35 billion in education tax breaks that he had insisted on, including his HOPE credits, but the GOP shaped some of the finer points. In return the GOP won essentially what it wanted regarding estate taxes: an increase to $1 million (over ten years), from $600,000 in the amount exempted from inheritance taxes as well as an additional exemption that brought the total allowable for small businesses and family farms to $1.3 million. The House also won repeal of the corporate alternative minimum tax for small businesses and faster depreciation for large corporations. Proposals in both bills to increase the amount exempt from the individual AMT were dropped.

Conferees agreed to the House proposal to restructure the taxes on domestic airline tickets, moving to a 7.5 percent ticket tax combined with a per-passenger tax on each segment of a flight. The final version also raised the international departure tax and augmented it with an arrival tax. The White House did not object to the compromise.

Conferees agreed to a lower increase in the tobacco tax than the Senate had originally approved—10 cents per pack in 2000 rising to 15 cents in 2002—and moved the provision to the conference report on the separate spending reconciliation bill where it was used in part to pay for children's health programs.

Lott tried unsuccessfully to put off the issue, arguing that Congress should not increase cigarette taxes while it was considering a settlement between the tobacco industry and forty state attorneys general that had been announced June 20. The states had sued the tobacco industry to recover state Medicaid funds spent on tobacco-related illness. Tobacco firms did persuade GOP leaders—with the apparent acquiescence of the White House—to reduce the amount of the proposed settlement ($368.5 billion over twenty-five years) by the amount raised by the higher cigarette tax. The provision, which was quietly inserted just hours before the bill was printed, was subsequently repealed during consideration of the spending bill for the departments of Labor, Health and Human Services, and Education, and the settlement ultimately fell apart when Congress failed to act on it. *(Tobacco settlement, p. 322)*

Clinton issued a last-minute veto threat, not over tax policy but over a provision inserted in the Senate bill that would have allowed taxpayers to use their IRAs to pay tuition at private and parochial elementary and secondary schools. GOP leaders said they would not drop the provision unless the president put his veto threat in writing. He did and the provision was dropped.

FINAL ACTION

Lawmakers in both parties and both chambers voted for the conference report (H Rept 105-220) July 31 by overwhelming margins. In the House the vote was 389–43 with just one Republican opposing it. In the Senate the vote was 92–8; all eight "nay" votes were cast by Democrats. The Democratic dissenters' main argument against the bill was that it was still tilted too much in favor of higher-income Americans. President Clinton signed HR 2014 into law on Aug. 5, 1997 (PL 105-34).

MAJOR PROVISIONS

The major provisions below are those that were expected to raise more than $100 million in revenue over ten years or cost the Treasury that much in lost revenues, according to the Joint Tax Committee. The list also includes a handful of significant provisions that involved a smaller tax gain or loss.

Family, Education Tax Cuts

• **Child credit.** Families with children under age seventeen could take a $400-per-child tax credit starting in 1998, rising to $500 per child in 1999. Grandparents could claim the credit if they claimed the child as a dependent on their tax form.

The tax credit began to phase out for single taxpayers with adjusted gross annual incomes of more than $75,000 and for couples with incomes of more than $110,000. The maximum child credit available to the taxpayer ($500 times the number of qualifying children) was reduced by $50 for each $1,000 that the taxpayer's adjusted gross income exceeded the threshold amounts. The more children a family had the higher the income level at which the tax credit phased out entirely. For instance a couple with an income of $150,000 and five qualifying children would still be eligible for a $500 credit.

Low-income families that were eligible for the EITC (generally those with incomes of $30,000 a year or less) could take the child credit before they figured their earned-income credit. If the child credit exceeded a taxpayer's regular tax liability the taxpayer was required to calculate whether the tax liability plus the employee share of federal payroll taxes exceeded the earned-income credit. If so the new law provided that the amount by which the child credit exceeded the amount calculated above was refundable to the taxpayer. This applied only to taxpayers with three or more children.

Effective date: Jan. 1, 1998. Estimated cost: $85 billion over five years and $183.4 billion over ten years.

Education Incentives

• **HOPE college tax credit.** Taxpayers could receive a nonrefundable credit of up to $1,500 per student for each of the first two years of college. The credit could be applied to 100 percent of the first $1,000 of tuition and fees and 50 percent of the next $1,000 in costs. The credit could not be claimed against the purchase of books or the cost of student activities. The credit would be indexed for inflation starting in 2002.

A single taxpayer would be eligible for the full credit if his or her adjusted gross annual income was less than $40,000; the ceiling for joint filers was $80,000. The first taxable year in which the income limits would be adjusted for inflation was 2001.

• **Lifetime learning credit.** For the second two years of college, or for graduate and postgraduate education and thereafter, a lifetime tax credit was available equal to 20 percent of up to $5,000 in tuition and related school expenses; after 2002 the credit would be equal to 20 percent of up to $10,000. Taxpayers would be eligible for the full credit if their adjusted gross annual incomes were less than $40,000 for single filers and $80,000 for joint filers. The first taxable year in which the income limits could be increased to reflect inflation was 2001.

Effective date for both the HOPE credit and the lifetime learning credit: Dec. 31, 1997. Estimated cost of both: $31.6 billion over five years and $76 billion over ten years.

• **Education savings accounts.** Modeled on individual retirement accounts (IRAs), these accounts allowed taxpayers to make nondeductible contributions of up to $500 per year for each child under age eighteen. The principal and interest could be withdrawn tax free at any time to help pay for a child's college or graduate education. Virtually all taxpayers—except those with incomes in the top 3 percent or so—were eligible to make use of the accounts. The adjusted gross annual income limit for single filers was $95,000; for joint filers, $150,000.

Any balance remaining in an education account at the time a beneficiary reached 30 years of age had to be distributed and the earnings portion of such a distribution would be subject to tax and to an additional 10 percent penalty.

Each year, for each student, the taxpayer could choose either the HOPE credit, the lifetime learning credit, or a tax-free distribution from an education savings account.

Effective date: Dec. 31, 1997. Estimated cost: $3.9 billion over five years and $14.2 billion over ten years.

• **Penalty-free IRA withdrawals.** Penalty-free withdrawals could be made from all IRAs for undergraduate, postsecondary vocational, and graduate education expenses.

Effective date: Dec. 31, 1997. Estimated cost: $812 million over five years and $1.7 billion over ten years.

• **Student loan interest deduction.** A deduction of up to $1,000 was permitted for interest payments on student loans starting in 1998 and rising to $2,500 in 2001. The deduction was available to individual taxpayers with adjusted gross annual incomes of up to $40,000 and couples with incomes of up to $60,000. Income ranges would increase for inflation after 2002. (This provision largely reversed a provision of the 1986 tax act, which disallowed the deduction of personal interest, including student loan interest.)

Effective date: Dec. 31, 1997. Estimated cost: $690 million over five years and $2.4 billion over ten years.

• **Deduction for state programs.** Deductions for state-sponsored prepaid tuition programs and other state savings programs were expanded to include the costs of room and board in addition to tuition.

Effective date: Dec. 31, 1997. Estimated cost: $533 million over five years and $1.5 billion over ten years.

• **Employer assistance exemption.** The law extended through May 31, 2000, the exemption from taxation of employer-provided educational assistance for undergraduates. The exclusion had previously applied to graduate as well as undergraduate education but the 1996 small-business tax bill (PL 104-188) limited the exemption to undergraduate courses beginning after June 30, 1996.

Estimated cost: $1.2 billion over five years.

• **School bonds tax credit.** The bill made it easier for public schools in qualified zones—generally impoverished neighborhoods—to form partnerships with corporations to provide job training. The school districts could borrow money and pay only 50 percent of the present value of the loan: half the total interest payments due over the term of the loan plus the principal. The government would pay the lender, such as a bank or insurance company, the other 50 percent.

Corporations would have to make an investment in the school worth at least 10 percent of the value of the bond. All investments had to be in schools in designated "enterprise zones" or in areas where at least 35 percent of the students qualified for the school lunch program. Up to $400 million of "qualified zone academy bonds" could be issued in 1998 and $400 million in 1999. The bonds could be issued by a state or a local unit of government.

Effective date: Dec. 31, 1997. Estimated cost: $172 million over five years and $408 million over ten years.

• **Corporate computer contributions.** Companies became eligible for an income tax deduction when they contributed new or unused computers, computer printers, and computer technology such as software to educational organizations with students in kindergarten through twelfth grade. The provision was effective from Jan. 1, 1998, until Jan. 1, 2001.

Estimated cost: $225 million over five years.

• **Nonprofit bond limit.** Nonprofit entities—those organized under section 501(c)(3) of the tax code—were allowed to issue an unlimited amount of tax-exempt bonds. Interest paid on the bonds was not subject to federal tax.

The provision repealed a policy in place since the 1986 tax act, which placed a $150 million cap on the amount of tax-exempt debt that each nonprofit entity could issue. However, any bonds above the prior cap could only be issued for new projects, not to help finance existing projects. The provision was expected to be used primarily by universities and nursing homes.

Effective date: Aug. 5, 1997. Estimated cost: $315 million over five years and $962 million over ten years.

- **School construction bonds.** Government units (such as a school district) that were classified as "small issuers" of tax-exempt bonds because their issues were worth $5 million or less could issue an additional $5 million in bonds to finance public school capital expenditures. The issuer could sell the bonds months before the building project got under way and invest the bond proceeds until needed without having to rebate the earnings to the federal government. Larger issuers had to rebate the earnings.

Effective date: Dec. 31, 1997. Estimated cost: $36 million over five years and $199 million over ten years.

Capital Gains

The bill created a new rate structure for taxes on individual capital gains—profits from the sale of stocks or other investments—giving progressively lower rates for assets held for longer periods of time.

- **Tax rate changes.** The new law
  - Reduced the top individual tax rate on capital gains from 28 percent to 20 percent. To qualify, assets had to be held for more than eighteen months. For individuals in the 15 percent tax bracket the new top rate was 10 percent.
  - Reduced the top rate to 18 percent for assets purchased after 2000 and held for at least five years. Taxpayers with assets bought before 2000 could pay a "tollgate tax" at the 20 percent rate on the gain on their assets up until 2000 and then take advantage of the 18 percent rate.
  - Retained the existing top rate—28 percent (15 percent for individuals in the 15 percent bracket)—for assets held for at least twelve months but not more than eighteen months. Collectibles such as art and antiques would continue to be taxed at this rate regardless of how long they were held.
  - Taxed short-term gains—those on assets held for less than twelve months—at ordinary income rates, which could go as high as 39.6 percent.
  - Taxed profits from investments in real estate (so called real estate recapture) subject to the capital gains tax at a 25 percent rate.

Effective date: retroactive to May 7, 1997. Estimated cost: $123 million increase in revenues over five years but a loss of $21.2 billion over ten years.

- **Primary residence exclusion.** The new law eliminated capital gains taxes on profits from the sale of a primary residence that netted the seller up to $250,000 for individual taxpayers and $500,000 for couples. The law erased a taxpayer's prior ability to take the profit from the sale of one house and put it immediately into the purchase of another house that was equal or greater in cost without paying tax on the gain. Also eliminated was the $125,000 exclusion for the sale of a principal residence for those 55 or older.

Effective date: May 6, 1997. Estimated cost: Negligible.

- **Rollover of small-business stock gain.** In a step designed to spur venture capital investment, the bill expanded a 1993 provision that provided individuals a 50 percent exclusion for gains from the sale of certain small-business stock. The stock had to have been acquired when the company first issued it. The amount of gain eligible for the 50 percent exclusion was the greater of ten times the taxpayers' tax basis in the stock or $10 million.

Previously a corporation could not qualify as a small business if its gross assets exceeded $50 million. The new law doubled that threshold to $100 million. An individual could roll over the gain from the sale of such stock tax-free so long as the proceeds were used to purchase qualified small business stock.

Effective date: the increase in the size of eligible corporations was effective Aug. 5, 1997. The remaining provisions applied to stock issued after Aug. 10, 1993, the original effective date of the small business provision.

Individual Retirement Accounts

The law provided for two new types of individual retirement accounts. One was the education savings account (see above). The other was the "backloaded" Roth IRA, named for its chief sponsor, Sen. William V. Roth Jr., R-Del. The law also changed the rules for traditional tax-deferred IRAs, which allowed taxpayers to save pretax dollars and withdraw them at retirement.

- **Roth IRA.** Single filers with adjusted gross annual incomes up to $95,000 and joint filers with incomes up to $150,000 could make after-tax contributions to a Roth IRA ($2,000 for individuals, $4,000 for couples). Individuals making up to $110,000 and couples making up to $160,000 could make partial contributions.

Although contributions to the Roth IRA were not tax deductible, both the interest and principal could be withdrawn tax free if the account had been open for five years and the account holder was age 59½, was disabled or deceased, or was withdrawing the money for a first-time home purchase. The contributions to a Roth IRA could be withdrawn early without penalty.

Taxpayers with adjusted gross annual incomes under $100,000 could convert all or part of the funds they had accumulated in a traditional tax-deferred IRA to a Roth IRA. The withdrawals (pretax contributions and earnings) were subject to income tax at the time of the rollover but there was no penalty. If the rollover was done before Jan. 1, 1999, the tax could be spread over four years.

Future earnings could be withdrawn tax free after five years as long as the distribution was used for a first-time home purchase or the individual was 59½, disabled, or deceased.

• **Tax-deferred IRA.** Previously taxpayers who participated in employer-sponsored retirement plans had to have relatively low adjusted gross incomes—less than $25,000 for single filers and less than $40,000 for couples—to make a fully deductible $2,000 annual contribution to an IRA.

The new law increased the income limits by $5,000 for single filers and by $10,000 for joint filers in 1998, and by $1,000 each year thereafter through 2002. After that the limits would gradually rise to $50,000 for single filers and $80,000 for joint filers. The new law also allowed penalty-free withdrawals to finance a first-time home purchase or for educational purposes.

Beginning in 1998 a spouse who was not an active participant in an employer-sponsored plan could make a fully deductible IRA contribution up to $2,000 if the couple's adjusted gross income was less than $150,000—even if the other spouse was covered by a retirement plan at work.

Effective date for all IRA provisions: Dec. 31, 1997. Estimated cost of all IRA provisions: $1.8 billion over five years and $20.2 billion over ten years.

Other Tax Deductions

• **Home office deduction.** The new law expanded the deduction for home offices to cover taxpayers who worked outside the home but did their billing, administrative work, and management from their home offices. The deduction was available as long as the office was the taxpayer's principal place of business, defined as the place where the taxpayer "conducts substantial administration or management of the trade or business."

The provision overturned a 1993 U.S. Supreme Court decision (*Commissioner v. Solliman*) that disallowed a deduction for an anesthesiologist who went from hospital to hospital but had no office in those places and did his billing from a home office.

The new law allowed the deduction even for people who had an office outside the home but chose not to do their administrative and management work there. This could apply, for instance, to independent contractors who were consultants, free-lance writers or editors, or shopkeepers who sold merchandise in a store but kept their accounts in an office at home.

Estimated cost: $880 million over five years and $2.4 billion over ten years.

• **Self-employed health insurance.** The deductibility of premiums paid by the self-employed was increased to 100 percent by 2007. Previously it was to have been increased to 80 percent by 2006. Estimated cost: $383 million over five years and $3.5 billion over ten years.

• **Charitable mileage deduction.** Taxpayers who used personal vehicles for charitable purposes (such as delivering meals to homebound people) could deduct 14 cents per mile, an increase from the previous 12 cents per mile deduction.

Effective date: Jan. 1, 1998. Estimated cost: $247 million over five years and $621 million over ten years.

Corporate Alternative Minimum Tax

• **Depreciation conformity.** For all businesses the depreciation adjustment under the alternative minimum tax (AMT) was altered to make it the same as depreciation under the regular tax system. That meant a shorter life for all property taxed under the AMT and sharply reduced the AMT liability of those firms that were subject to it.

The AMT was designed to ensure that even corporations that did not owe regular income taxes still paid some tax. The AMT was used only when a taxpayer's alternative minimum tax liability exceeded the regular tax liability. The corporate AMT was 20 percent on alternative minimum taxable income in excess of a phased-out $40,000 exemption.

Effective date: Jan. 1, 1998. Estimated cost: $6.8 billion over five years and $18.3 billion over ten years.

• **Small business exemption.** Businesses with average gross annual receipts of less than $5 million were no longer subject to the AMT.

Effective date: Jan. 1, 1998. Estimated cost: $577 million over five years and $762 million over ten years.

• **Farmer installment method repealed.** The new law allowed farmers to defer counting the income on sales of crops and other products from the year in which the product was sold until the following year without incurring any additional alternative minimum tax liability. Previously deferred sales were counted as preference items for minimum tax purposes, which increased farmers' minimum tax liability. It had been unclear since 1986 how the deferral law applied to farmers; after wrangling with the IRS farmers asked Congress to clarify that deferral of income from crop sales was permissible.

Effective date: retroactive to tax year 1987. Estimated cost: $811 million over five years and $872 million over ten years.

Estate and Gift Taxes

• **Estate and gift tax credit increase.** Since 1976 the tax on gifts (given during the donor's lifetime) and estates (transferred at death) had been unified with a single graduated rate for the cumulative transfers made by a taxpayer during his lifetime and at death. Under existing law $600,000 was effectively exempt from the estate and gift tax rate, which began at 37 percent and reached a maximum of 55 percent.

The new law increased the amount of an estate that was exempt from the federal estate tax from $600,000 to $1 million. The schedule for the exemption rose gradually and erratically with just $100,000 of the increase occurring before 2003. The exemption would increase to $625,000 in 1998, to $650,000 in 1999, and to $675,000 in 2000 and remain at that level in 2001. Then it would jump to $700,000 in 2002 and remain at that level in 2003, to $850,000 in 2004, to $950,000 in 2005, and finally to $1 million in 2006.

• **Gift tax exclusion.** Previously a benefactor could give $10,000 per year to any number of recipients without paying tax on the gift or affecting his total estate tax exemption. The new law indexed the $10,000 exclusion for inflation after 1998.

• **Generation-skipping tax exemption.** Existing law allowed a grandparent to transfer up to $1 million to a grandchild whose parent was dead without paying a generation-skipping tax on the gift. The bill indexed this exemption for inflation after 1998.

• **Special use valuation.** So-called special use valuation allowed farmers to value their property at its current value rather than its highest and best-use value and reduce the total value of their property for estate tax purposes by up to $750,000. The bill indexed this exemption for inflation after 1998.

Effective date: Jan. 1, 1998. Total estimated cost: $5.9 billion over five years and $33.1 billion over ten years.

• **Family farms and small businesses exemption.** A new estate tax exemption of $700,000 was created for family farms and family-owned businesses starting in 1998. However in future years as the unified credit rose to $1 million (see above) the family business exemption would fall to $300,000. In any given year the combination of the unified credit and the exemption for family-owned farms and businesses was to equal $1.3 million.

To be eligible for the exemption, 50 percent of the business had to be under the ownership of one family; alternatively 70 percent could be under the ownership of two families or 90 percent under the ownership of three families. In addition, an heir had to participate in the management of the business for five years out of any eight-year period in the ten years after the death of the previous owner. (An heir also had to be a relative of the previous owner, such as a child, spouse, or lineal descendent.) In addition, the business had to constitute at least half of the previous owner's estate in order to qualify for the exemption.

If the heir decided to withdraw from material participation in the business within ten years of the previous owner's death, the estate tax benefit would be subject to recapture, meaning that the IRS could assess the taxpayer for the difference between the estate taxes paid and the estate tax that would have been paid if there had been no exemption.

Estimated cost: $5.9 billion over five years and $33.1 billion over ten years.

• **Installment payments.** Closely held businesses and family farms had been able to pay estate taxes on an installment plan over fourteen years with an especially low interest rate. Under the bill, the interest rate was reduced from 4 percent to 2 percent. However the interest was no longer deductible for estate or income tax purposes.

Effective date: Jan. 1, 1998. Estimated cost: $84 million over five years and $349 million over ten years.

• **Permanent conservation easement exclusion.** If a permanent easement was put on a piece of land, meaning that it could not be subdivided for development purposes, then the executor of an estate could exclude from tax 40 percent of the value of the land so long as the exclusion was not in excess of $1 million. To qualify for the exclusion the land had to be within twenty-five miles of a metropolitan area or within ten miles of an Urban National Forest; it also had to have been owned by the person who died or a member of his family during the preceding three years.

Effective date: Jan. 1, 1998. Estimated cost: $82 million over five years and $349 million over ten years.

• **Limit on gift reevaluation.** This provision halted the occasional practice by the IRS of revaluing (and in some cases increasing the imputed value of) a taxpayer's gifts after he or she died.

Effective date: Aug. 5, 1997. Estimated cost: $81 million over five years and $310 million over ten years.

Expiring Tax Provisions

• **Research tax credit.** The research and development tax credit was extended for thirteen months—from June 1, 1997, to June 30, 1998. The credit was equal to 20 percent of a company's research expenditures; if the company gave a grant to a university to do basic research, a portion of that expenditure was eligible for the tax credit.

Estimated cost: $2.24 billion over five years and $2.27 billion over ten years.

• **Stock donated to private foundations.** The bill extended for thirteen months—from June 1, 1997, to June 30, 1998—a provision that allowed taxpayers who gave stock to charitable organizations to deduct not only their basis in the stock but also any capital gain.

Estimated cost: $112 million over five years and $112 million over ten years.

• **Work opportunity tax credit.** The law extended for nine months the credit for employers who hired workers from one of seven needy groups and added one new group: Supplemental Social Security recipients. The other groups included people trying to get off welfare, high-risk youths, qualified veterans, and qualified ex-felons.

Estimated cost: $383 million over five years and $385 million over ten years.

• **Orphan drug tax credit.** The bill made permanent a 50 percent tax credit for qualified clinical testing expenses incurred in testing of certain drugs for rare diseases or conditions. Rare diseases and conditions were defined as those that affected fewer than 200,000 people nationwide, or more than 200,000 but for which there was no reasonable expectation that businesses could recoup the costs of developing a drug for such disease from U.S. sales.

Effective date for clinical testing expenses incurred: May 31, 1997. Estimated cost: $152 million over five years and $346 million over ten years.

District of Columbia

• **Enterprise zone.** Most of the nation's capital was included in an enterprise zone created under the bill. The zone included those census tracts that had been in Washington's enterprise community (portions of Anacostia, Mt. Pleasant, Chinatown, and the easternmost part of the District) and all other census tracts where the poverty rate was more than 20 percent. Employers who moved there were eligible for a 20 percent wage credit, increased expensing, and expanded tax-exempt financing.

Effective date: Jan. 1, 1998, through Dec. 31, 2002. Estimated cost: $539 million over five years and $582 million over ten years.

• **Zero-percent capital gains rate.** Capital gains on sales of business property in such neighborhoods were reduced to zero if the property was held for at least five years.

Effective date: Jan. 1, 1998, through Dec. 31, 2002. Estimated cost: $73 million over five years and $502 million over ten years.

Welfare to Work

• **Wage credit.** The bill offered a wage credit to employers who hired former welfare recipients. The credit was worth 35 percent of the first $10,000 in wages in the first year of employment and 50 percent on $10,000 of wages in the second year of employment. The maximum credit was $8,500 per qualified employee.

Effective for wages paid or incurred from Dec. 31, 1997, through April 30, 1999. Estimated cost: $99 million over five years and $106 million over ten years.

Excise Taxes

• **Gas tax and Highway Trust Fund.** Revenue from a 4.3-cents-per-gallon federal tax on gasoline, motor fuels, and diesel was channeled into the Highway Trust Fund instead of the general fund. The 4.3-cents-per-gallon tax was only a portion of the total 18.3-cents-per-gallon federal tax; it was added in 1993 as part of President Clinton's deficit-reduction plan. Although the change had no overall effect on government revenues, it limited the money available in domestic accounts for nonhighway trust fund spending.

Effective date: Oct. 1, 1997. Estimated cost: None.

• **Alternative fuels excise tax.** The bill equalized the taxation of alternative fuels so that it was based on their energy content. The result was a tax cut for propane, liquefied natural gas, and methanol.

Effective date: Oct. 1, 1997. Estimated cost: $82 million over five years and $186 million over ten years.

• **Vaccine excise rates.** The tax paid by manufacturers of vaccines was leveled so that all vaccines would be taxed at the same rate of 75 cents per dose. Combination vaccines, such as measles, mumps and rubella (MMR) vaccines, would be taxed at 75 cents times the number of components in the combined vaccines; the tax on MMR would be $2.25 per dose.

In addition three new vaccines were made subject to the tax: haemophilus influenza, hepatitis B, and chicken pox.

Amounts equal to the revenues from the tax were deposited in the Vaccine Injury Compensation Trust Fund to finance awards to individuals who suffered certain injuries following administration of the taxable vaccines.

Effective for vaccines purchased after Sept. 30, 1997. Estimated cost: $74 million over five years and $146 million over ten years.

Brownfields

• **Deduction.** Under the bill a business could deduct the cost of cleaning up environmental contamination in so-called brownfields sites in targeted areas. Such sites were not hazardous enough to come under superfund but had been certified by a state environmental agency to contain or potentially contain a hazardous substance. A targeted area was an empowerment zone or enterprise community or any census tract with a 20 percent or greater poverty rate.

The deduction could be taken starting in the year after the date of enactment and it expired on Jan. 1, 2001. However, if the property was sold or disposed of before the environmental cleanup was complete, the taxpayer would have to include the prior deductions as income.

Effective date: For expenses in taxable years ending after Aug. 5, 1997. Estimated cost: $417 million over five years and $352 million over ten years.

Empowerment Zones

• **Two new urban zones.** The bill provided for the creation of two new urban empowerment zones in addition to the six created under the 1993 budget-reconciliation act (PL 103-66). The new zones had to be designated within 180 days.

The existing urban zones were in New York City, Baltimore, Atlanta, Philadelphia-Camden, Detroit, and Chicago. Qualified businesses located in the zones were eligible for special tax incentives, such as a credit for wages paid to zone residents, additional expensing and special tax-exempt financing.

• **Additional zones.** The new law also authorized the creation of twenty additional empowerment zones—fifteen in urban areas and five in rural areas. The zones would have a range of incentives similar to those enjoyed by existing empowerment zones although businesses would not be eligible for the work opportunity tax credit, which offset the cost of hiring employees. The new brownfields deduction would be available in all the new empowerment zones.

The zones had to be designated before 1999; the designations generally would remain in effect for ten years.

Effective date: Aug. 5, 1997. Estimated cost: $717 million over five years and $1.2 billion over ten years.

Other Domestic Provisions

• **Inventory accounting estimates.** Targeted at large retailers, manufacturers, and other businesses with significant tangible inventories, this provision clarified that estimates of inventory shrinkage—because of breakage, undetected theft, and bookkeeping errors—would be considered valid even if they were not taken at the end of the year but were based on physical estimates earlier in the year and adjusted at year's end. A complex formula was set up specifically for retailers who had recently tangled with the IRS in a number of cases involving inventory shrinkage estimates.

Effective date: Aug. 5, 1997. Estimated cost: $103 million over five years and $268 million over ten years.

• **Treatment of workers' compensation.** The tax treatment of workers' compensation payments was brought into conformity with the treatment of structured settlements in personal injury cases. Such payments were tax-exempt because the injured party was being compensated for loss, not realizing a gain.

Effective date: Aug. 5, 1997. Estimated cost: $27 million over five years and $164 million over ten years.

• **Income averaging for farmers.** The new law set up a formula for farmers so that they were taxed annually based on their average income over a three-year period. Income averaging, which generally reduced a taxpayer's liability, had been repealed for all taxpayers by the 1986 act.

Effective date: Dec. 31, 1997, through tax year 2000. Estimated cost: $161 million over five years.

• **Business meals deduction.** The bill increased from 50 percent to 80 percent the deduction for meals taken while a person subject to the Department of Transportation hours-of-service limitations was away from home during a period of duty or incident to a period of duty. The increased deduction was to be phased in over eleven years with the first increase taking effect in 1998.

Effective date: Jan. 1, 1998. Estimated cost: $138 million over five years and $600 million over ten years.

Foreign Business Provisions

• **Foreign sales of computer software.** Profits on computer software sold for reproduction through a foreign sales corporation to overseas buyers were tax exempt under the bill. This was the same tax benefit received by other products sold through a foreign sales corporation.

Software giants Microsoft and Oracle were the two companies that pushed hardest for the provision, but numerous other computer software companies were expected to take advantage of it.

Effective for software licenses after Dec. 31, 1997. Estimated cost: $568 million over five years and $1.7 billion over ten years.

• **Passive foreign investment asset valuation.** The new law drew a brighter line between passive foreign investment companies (PFICs) and controlled foreign corporations (CFCs), making it easier for some overseas subsidiaries of U.S. firms to qualify as CFCs.

Under the law a PFIC (such as a foreign mutual fund) taxed a U.S. investor on earnings whereas a shareholder of a CFC was not taxed until the income was repatriated. A PFIC was any company in which either 75 percent or more of its gross income was passive (from investments) or 50 percent or more of the fair market value of its assets consisted of assets that produced passive income.

Another section of the provision, sought by Amway, allowed foreign subsidiaries of publicly traded U.S. companies to be defined as PFICs only if their assets met the fair-market value test. This ensured that they would continue to be classified as CFCs, which was preferable from a tax standpoint.

Effective date: Jan. 1, 1998. Estimated cost: $124 million over five years and $280 million over ten years.

• **Tax credit on interests in foreign joint ventures.** The foreign tax credit system was streamlined for U.S. firms that owned between 10 percent and 50 percent of the stock of a joint venture with an overseas firm. Previously a U.S. company had to apply a separate foreign tax credit against dividends received from each venture; some firms had hundreds of such ventures. This provision allowed U.S. firms to combine their dividends and their offsetting credits instead of calculating each one individually.

Effective date: Jan. 1, 2003. Estimated cost: $982 million over ten years.

• **Income of U.S. citizens overseas exempted.** The bill increased from $70,000 to $80,000 the amount of annual income that a U.S. citizen working overseas could earn without paying U.S. income tax. The increased exemption was to be phased in at a rate of $2,000 per year starting in 1998. The exemption was designed to offset the tax that U.S. citizens paid to the country where they were residing. The provision was strongly supported by multinational companies that had foreign subsidiaries or subcontracted with overseas companies that employed U.S. citizens.

Estimated cost: $244 million over five years and $801 million over ten years.

Amtrak

The imperiled passenger railroad system was granted a refund—known as a net operating loss carry-back—on taxes paid by the predecessor railroad lines that merged their passenger operations in 1971 to form Amtrak. However the tax break was contingent on the company embracing management changes that had to be ratified by Congress in a separate bill. (An Amtrak restructuring bill was signed into law Dec. 2, freeing the $2.3 billion that had been set aside.)

Estimated cost: $2.3 billion over five years.

Excise and Employment Taxes

• **Airline ticket tax.** Under the new law the existing 10 percent tax on domestic airline tickets was reduced to 9 percent in fiscal 1998, 8 percent in fiscal 1999, and 7.5 percent in 2000. A new per-passenger tax was imposed on each segment of a domestic flight beginning at $1 in fiscal 1998, gradually increasing to $3 in fiscal 2002 and then changing to reflect inflation based on the Consumer Price Index (CPI). Flights to small airports in isolated rural areas were exempt from the segment tax.

The tax on international departures was increased from $6 to $12, and a new $12 tax was imposed on international arrivals with those taxes indexed to the CPI beginning in January 1999. The bill kept the existing $6 tax on flights to

Alaska and Hawaii, but indexed it to the CPI beginning in 1999. It also imposed a 7.5 percent tax on purchases of frequent-flier miles by credit card companies and others. Taxes on air cargo and aviation fuel were extended.

Estimated revenue: $33.2 billion over five years and $79.7 billion over ten years.

• **Tax on kerosene.** The bill required that kerosene be taxed when it was removed from the terminal where it was stored unless it was indelibly dyed and destined for a nontaxable use such as home heating fuel or aviation fuel. Similar to diesel fuel, kerosene was supposed to be taxed at the wholesale level when it was destined for use as a transportation fuel. However, the IRS had had problems enforcing the taxation in the case of kerosene because previously there had been no dying requirement.

Effective date: July 1, 1998. Estimated revenue: $226 million over five years and $461 million over ten years.

• **Leaking underground tanks.** The bill reinstated the 0.1 cent per gallon excise tax on gasoline, diesel fuel, special motor fuels, aviation fuels, and inland waterway fuels through March 31, 2005. The tax revenue was used to help gas stations convert to new nonleaking tanks.

Effective date: Oct. 1, 1997. Estimated revenue: $645 million over five years and $983 million over ten years.

• **Excise tax on prepaid phone cards.** The bill specified that phone cards were subject to the 3 percent telephone excise tax. In theory the cards were already subject to the tax, but there had been confusion as to whether the tax was supposed to be levied by the retailer selling the card or by the communications company that sold the service. The bill required that the tax be built into the face value of the card and be charged by the communications service provider (the company that bought time from the owners of the telephone lines).

Effective date: Aug. 5, 1997. Estimated revenue: $193 million over five years and $684 million over ten years.

• **Excise tax on trucks and truck tires.** The bill consolidated the taxes on trucks and truck tires. Previously the truck tax was based on the selling price, but the buyer was allowed to subtract the value of the tires in determining the price of the truck and then pay a tax on the tires that was based on weight.

Effective on sales after Dec. 31, 1997. Estimated revenue: $452 million over five years and $979 million over ten years.

• **Federal unemployment surtax extended.** The bill extended through Dec. 31, 2007, the existing federal unemployment surtax of 0.2 percent on the first $7,000 paid annually by covered employers to each employee. In addition to the temporary 0.2 percent surtax, which was first enacted in 1976, there was a 0.6 percent permanent federal unemployment tax (FUTA). The revenue went to finance administration of the system, half of the federal-state extended-benefits program, and a federal account for state loans. The provision also allowed more money to accumulate in the federal unemployment trust fund.

Effective date: Jan. 1, 1999. Estimated savings: $6.4 billion over five years and $6.7 billion over ten years.

Individual Tax Simplification

• **Standard deduction for dependents.** The bill increased slightly the allowable standard deduction for dependents both under the regular tax system and the alternative minimum tax system.

Effective date: Tax years after Dec. 31, 1997. Estimated revenue: $146 million over five years and $327 million over ten years.

• **Estimated tax.** Existing law required individual taxpayers to make up any income taxes that they owed beyond what was withheld from their paychecks by making quarterly estimated payments. If the remaining tax liability was $500 or more the taxpayer was fined. The new law increased the *de minimis* threshold for estimated tax payments to $1,000.

Effective for tax years after Dec. 31, 1997. Estimated revenue: $208 million over five years and $326 million over ten years.

Corporate Operations, Financial Products

• **Gain on certain stock positions.** The bill specified that profits from certain transactions that were economically equivalent to an outright sale—such as the practice known on Wall Street as "selling short against the box"—be treated as sales that could be taxed as a capital gain.

Effective date: June 8, 1997. Estimated revenue: $708 million over five years and $1.2 billion over ten years.

• **Losses from certain property terminations.** The bill required that any loss resulting from the termination of a capital asset—for example when a bond was paid off—be treated as a capital loss for tax purposes. Previously such losses could be treated as ordinary losses, deductible against ordinary income; that was more advantageous than a capital gains loss because ordinary income was taxed at a higher rate than capital gains. In addition, a capital loss was limited to $3,000 a year and was netted against capital gains.

Effective date: June 8, 1997. Estimated revenue: $117 million over five years and $242 million over ten years.

• **Interest of debt obligations.** This provision was primarily designed to force credit card companies to include in their taxable income the interest they expected to receive from credit card debt. Companies rarely received all the interest they were owed, because a portion of credit bills went unpaid and had to be written off. Previously credit card companies could defer taxes on the interest until it was paid by borrowers. The new law required them to estimate how much they would ultimately receive and include it as taxable income.

Effective date: Jan. 1, 1998. Estimated revenue: $1.3 billion over five years and $1.9 billion over ten years.

• **Interest deduction on certain debt instruments.** The bill required that when a corporation issued a financial instrument that was payable in stock when it was redeemed the issuer could not deduct interest earned on the instrument. This was designed to limit the tax advantage for certain types of exotic financial instruments that were being called "debt" but had the characteristics of equity.

Effective for transactions after June 8, 1997. Estimated revenue: $148 million over five years and $469 million over ten years.

• **Tax treatment of certain extraordinary dividends.** Large one-time dividends resulting from corporation-to-corporation transactions had to be recognized as capital gains for tax purposes. Previously corporations could take so-called dividend-received deductions, which were worth 70 percent of the total dividend, and pay tax on the balance.

Effective date: Sept. 13, 1995. Estimated revenue: $68 million over five years and $375 million over ten years.

• **Certain distributions of corporation stock.** Triggered by several highly publicized transactions in which corporations effectively sold a trade, business, or subdivision without paying tax, this provision (Morris Trust provision) required that when a company spun off a subsidiary gain was recognized and the company paid tax on the transaction.

Effective for acquisitions of stock that occurred after April 16, 1997. Estimated revenue: $1.1 billion over five years and $1.5 billion over ten years.

• **Holding period for dividends-received deduction.** The dividends-received deduction was limited to those corporate taxpayers who held stocks that carried a genuine risk of loss on the investment. Corporate investors in stock could deduct 70 percent of the value of dividends received. Previously there were some financial products that allowed corporate investors to buy stock but for much of the holding period hedge the risk that usually accompanied equity investment and still take the dividend deduction.

Effective for dividends received or accrued thirty days after the date of enactment with exceptions for stock held on June 8, 1997. Estimated revenue: $71 million over five years and $156 million over ten years.

• **Registration of corporate tax shelters.** The bill tightened rules for registering confidential tax shelters including a requirement that shelters be registered one day after they were first offered to potential investors.

Effective as soon as Treasury issued regulations. Estimated revenue: $170 million over five years and $392 million over ten years.

• **Certain preferred stock treated as "boot."** The bill required that in certain corporate transactions, such as reorganizations, in which stockholders exchanged equity for preferred stock, any gain be recognized and taxed at the preferred stocks' fair market value. There were numerous exceptions, such as for a taxpayer who exchanged one type of preferred stock for a comparable type of preferred stock and for recapitalization of a family-owned business.

Effective for transactions after June 8, 1997. Estimated revenue: $194 million over five years and $248 million over ten years.

IRS Authority

• **Tax return information for veterans' programs.** The bill permanently extended the right of the IRS to disclose certain information about self-employment and other areas to the Department of Veterans Affairs so that it could accurately determine benefit amounts for needs-based pensions, health care, and other programs.

Effective date: Oct. 1, 1998, through Sept. 30, 2003. Estimated revenue: $116 million over five years and $152 million over ten years.

• **IRS levy on benefits.** The IRS was allowed to place a continuous levy on nonmeans-tested federal benefits such as Social Security if a taxpayer failed to pay his tax bill. A levy allowed the IRS to seize or sell nonexempt taxpayer property to satisfy tax obligations. The levy would go into effect 10 days after notice and demand for payment by the IRS. In addition, the Treasury secretary was authorized to place a continuous levy on workers' compensation payments, annuity or pension payments under the railroad retirement act and the railroad unemployment insurance act, unemployment benefits, and public assistance benefits.

Effective date: Aug. 6, 1997. Estimated revenue: $1.3 billion over five years and $1.8 billion over ten years.

Earned-Income Tax Credit (EITC)

• **EITC compliance.** Complaints about fraud and inaccuracy in the EITC system prompted Congress to enact a series of measures designed to clamp down on the problem.

Effective date: Dec. 31, 1996. Estimated savings: $88 million over five years and $193 million over ten years.

• **Change in gross income eligibility.** Taxpayers were required to include tax-exempt interest and nontaxable distributions from pensions, annuities, and IRAs when calculating their adjusted gross income for EITC eligibility purposes. In addition, 75 percent of losses from a business such as a small family-owned firm had to be disregarded when calculating adjusted gross income.

Effective date: Dec. 31, 1997. Estimated savings: $312 million over five years and $788 million over ten years.

• **Federal case register data.** By Oct. 1, 1999, the secretary of the Treasury Department was required to have access to the registry at the Department of Health and Human Services of all child support orders and the Social Security numbers of all children covered by the orders. It was anticipated that the IRS could use the Social Security numbers to identify questionable claims for the EITC, the dependent exemption, and other tax benefits before the refunds were paid out.

Effective date: Aug. 5, 1997. Estimated savings: $30 million over five years and $350 million over ten years.

• **Workfare wages not counted as income.** Wages received by former welfare recipients as part of "workfare" programs would not be qualified as wages for the purpose of qualifying for the EITC.

Effective date: Aug. 5, 1997. Estimated savings: Negligible.

Other Provisions

• **Repeal of grandfather rules.** Under the law passed in 1986, a nonprofit organization could not be exempt from tax if a substantial aspect of its work included providing commercial insurance. There was a partial exception for Blue Cross/Blue Shield organizations. The bill overturned the exception for two other companies: Mutual of America, which was established to handle pension plans for social workers, and Teachers Insurance Annuity Association—College Retirement Equity Fund, which handled the pension business of college teachers.

Effective date: Dec. 31, 1997. Estimated revenue: $450 million over five years and $1.2 billion over ten years.

• **Foreign tax credits holding period.** The bill required shareholders that received dividends from foreign corporations to hold the stock for at least sixteen days for common stock and forty-six days in the case of preferred stock before receiving foreign tax credits for foreign income taxes paid on the dividend. Previously there was no holding period, which led taxpayers who could not use the foreign tax credits (for instance because they were tax-exempt entities) to engage in transactions that involved trading the dividends to taxpayers who could use the foreign tax credits. The provision aimed to limit those practices.

Effective for dividends paid or accrued thirty days or more after the date of enactment, Aug. 5, 1997. Estimated revenue: $230 million over five years and $552 million over ten years.

• **Parking or cash compensation.** Employers gained the option of offering employees either tax-free parking worth up to $165 a month or taxable cash compensation equivalent to that amount. The aim was to give employers and employees more choice, reward people for taking public transportation, and give the government the potential to raise some revenue: if the employee took the cash it would be taxed.

Effective date: Dec. 31, 1997. Estimated revenue: $46 million over five years and $118 million over ten years.

• **Basis recovery method.** The bill created a new formula that reduced the amount of a pension annuity excludable from income when the annuity was a joint and survivor annuity as opposed to a single life annuity.

Effective date: Dec. 31, 1997. Estimated revenue: $30 million over five years and $130 million over ten years.

• **Suspense accounts for family farm corporations.** The bill tightened accounting rules that had allowed primarily large farms to effectively defer paying taxes for years. The new rules prohibited so-called suspense accounts; those farms that had them were required to phase them out, paying tax on the money in them over twenty years.

Effective date: June 8, 1997. Estimated revenue: $170 million over five years and $377 million over ten years.

• **Two-year carry-back and twenty-year carry-forward.** The bill reduced from three years to two years the amount of time that a taxpayer could carry back a net operating loss but extended the amount of time it could be carried forward to twenty years from fifteen years. Estimated revenue: $1.1 billion over five years and $1.7 billion over ten years.

• **Company-owned life insurance.** Further restrictions were placed on deductions for life insurance contracts. The provision arose after it became public that some large mortgage companies planned to sell their contracts to borrowers. The tax treatment of life insurance contracts had been sharply curtailed in 1996 following widespread reports that corporate investors were avoiding tax on the contract's inside buildup.

Effective date: June 8, 1997. Estimated revenue: $500 million over five years and $2.2 billion over ten years.

• **Basis allocation rules for distributee partners.** The bill tightened rules governing the allocation of the assets of a partnership when the partnership was sold to eliminate disguised sales made through partnerships.

Effective date: Aug. 5, 1997. Estimated revenue: $249 million over five years and $581 million over ten years.

• **Appreciation requirement eliminated.** The substantial appreciation requirement for inventory of a partnership was eliminated. Partnerships could no longer exempt the first 20 percent of inventory appreciation; all inventory appreciation had to be taxed as ordinary income. This provision applied only to individuals with partnership interests and affected the tax consequences only of the inventory. Any appreciation in the partnership shares would be taxed as a capital gain.

Effective date: Aug. 5, 1997. Estimated revenue: $316 million over five years and $760 million over ten years.

• **Income forecast method restricted.** The provision limited use of the income forecasting method of calculating depreciation to the types of products for which it was designed—such as movies, books, and other intellectual property whose value was not affected by the passage of time in the same way as other durable goods. This depreciation method was not to be used for other leased property.

Effective date: Dec. 31, 1997. Estimated savings: $248 million over five years and $352 million over ten years.

• **Property losses.** The bill specified that a taxpayer who involuntarily lost property (such as a small-business owner whose store burned down) had to acquire replacement property from an unrelated party, meaning not a relative. Property replaced as a result of such an involuntary conversion was not subject to tax if the replacement property was more valuable than the original property. However if the replacement property was acquired from a relative—a spouse, sibling, or parent—it could be a way of avoiding tax.

Effective for involuntary conversions occurring after June 12, 1997. Estimated savings: $30 million over five years and $115 million over ten years.

• **General business credit.** The bill limited to one year the length of time that all general business credits could be carried back and extended from fifteen years to twenty years the length of time the credits could be carried forward. The credits covered by the bill included, but were not limited to, the empowerment zone credit, energy credit, reforestation credit, alcohol fuels credit, and the low-income housing credit.

Effective date: Dec. 31, 1997. Estimated savings: $471 million over five years and $527 million over ten years.

• **Installment sales grandfather rules repealed.** An exception in the 1986 tax overhaul that allowed farm machinery manufacturer John Deere and major automakers to use the installment sales method of accounting was ended. The installment sales method allowed those companies to avoid recognizing the sale of a vehicle until the dealer sold it and paid them for it, similar to a consignment sale. The exception was put in place when John Deere was in dire straits.

Effective date: Dec. 31, 1998. Estimated savings: $353 million over five years and $507 million over ten years.

Miscellaneous Revenue Reductions

• **Unrelated business income tax.** The new law repealed unrelated business income tax on an employee stock ownership plan (ESOP) that was a shareholder in a subchapter S corporation. The bill exempted ESOPs from paying income tax on the distributions from a subchapter S corporation until the ESOP distributed the income to the ESOP participants.

Effective date: Dec. 31, 1997. Estimated cost: $149 million over five years and $400 million over ten years.

• **Limit employer stock in 401(k) plans.** The bill restricted the amount of company stock that an employer could hold in a 401(k) retirement plan to 10 percent of the assets derived from employees' elective deferrals.

Effective date: Aug. 5, 1997. Estimated cost: Negligible.

• **Limit for defined-benefit plans.** Businesses were allowed to increase the funding of their defined-benefit pension plans beyond the existing full-funding limit, which was defined as the lesser of a plan's accrued liability or 150 percent of the current liability. Under the act plans could be funded up to 155 percent of liability beginning in 1999, up to 160 percent beginning in 2001, up to 165 percent beginning in 2003 and up to 170 percent in 2004 and thereafter. When corporations contributed to employee pension plans they did not have to count the money as part of their taxable income.

Effective date: Dec. 31, 1997. Estimated cost: $48 million over five years and $164 million over ten years.

• **Limits for state and local plans.** Under the bill state and local employees could credit previous pension participation in other states or in the private sector toward their current state or local government retirement plan. Employees were given the chance to buy into their new employer's plan by making a contribution equal to the amount that they would have paid if they had worked the requisite number of years.

Previously people were prohibited from contributing the lesser of $30,000 or 25 percent of their annual salary at any one time to a state or local plan. That created a problem for some workers such as public school teachers who had taught for five years in a private school and then went to teach in the public school system. Many teachers were reaching retire-

ment age only to discover that they could not retire with a pension. While they could theoretically buy into the state or local plan they could not do so all at once because of the cap on contributions. This provision raised the cap to $30,000 or a maximum annual pension benefit of $125,000.

Effective date: Dec. 31, 1997. Estimated cost: $111 million over five years and $246 million over ten years.

• **Investment company limitation repealed.** The new law repealed the 30 percent gross income limitation for regulated investment companies. Aimed at giving mutual funds more flexibility this provision allowed mutual funds to get more than 30 percent of their income from stocks and bonds held for less than three months without losing preferential tax status. Under preferential status tax liability passed through to the shareholders and the mutual fund effectively paid no corporate tax.

Effective date: Dec. 31, 1997. Estimated cost: $138 million over five years and $408 million over ten years.

Trade

• **Generalized system of preferences.** To spur economic development around the world Congress in 1974 began granting the president authority to extend duty-free treatment to imports from countries designated as developing nations. That authority had last expired on May 31, 1997. The law reauthorized the program from June 1, 1997, through June 30, 1998. Estimated cost: $378 million over five years.

Tax Credit Extensions

Republican leaders began 1998 hoping to enact a major tax cut on the order of $100 billion over five years. By the time Congress adjourned in late October the GOP had barely won passage of a $9.2 billion measure that extended expiring tax credits and accelerated a health insurance deduction for the self-employed.

President Clinton set the tone for the year in his State of the Union message in which he urged lawmakers to leave the projected budget surplus untouched until the government could ensure the long-term solvency of the Social Security Trust Fund. His simple refrain, "Save Social Security first," resonated powerfully with the electorate, leaving would-be tax cutters unsure how to proceed.

In the months following the January speech GOP leaders vacillated between challenging Clinton directly by taking up a major tax cut or assembling a comparatively minor package offsetting any tax cuts with revenue raisers. The conflict doomed efforts to agree on a budget resolution because Republicans could not bridge the gap between a House plan to cut taxes by $101 billion over five years and the Senate version that made no net cuts. *(Budget resolution, p. 60)*

Giving up on a budget blueprint, the House Sept. 26 passed an $80.1 billion five-year tax cut (HR 4579—H Rept 105-739). Designed for maximum political appeal, the plan would have reduced taxes for certain married couples, farmers, and the self-employed; granted deductions for interest on savings accounts; and provided new tax incentives for businesses in designated low-income areas. Although Democrats praised many of the bill's provisions, they opposed it overall, arguing that Congress should not tap into the projected budget surplus until Social Security had been put on a sound footing. House passage was on a largely partisan 229–195 vote. All but nineteen Democrats present voted against the bill, as did eleven Republicans.

Most Senate Democrats and a few moderate Republicans opposed the House measure, also arguing that any budget surplus should first go to Social Security. Unable to round up a 51-vote majority, let along the 60 votes needed to cut off a filibuster, and not wanting to allow President Clinton to win political points by vetoing a bill, Senate Majority Leader Trent Lott, R-Miss., declined to bring the measure to the Senate floor.

The business community, however, continued to press lawmakers to salvage one piece of the bill: a plan to extend expired tax credits including one for corporate research and development. The House swiftly worked up a nine-year, $9.2 billion plan (HR 4738—H Rept 105-817), passing it by voice vote on Oct. 12.

The Senate Finance Committee responded with an informal $8.5 billion package to extend additional tax credits but for shorter periods of time. Unable to reach agreement on a stand-alone tax bill, leaders merged elements of the House and Senate plans and added them to the omnibus spending bill (HR 4328—PL 105-277), which cleared Congress on Oct. 21. (1998 omnibus spending bill, p. 68)

The final tax credit provisions extended, generally for one year, eight expiring tax and trade provisions designed to benefit people who contribute stock to private foundations, U.S. shareholders of foreign corporations, and employers of disadvantaged workers. The plan also granted the self-employed a 100 percent deduction for health insurance premiums beginning in 2003; allowed taxpayers to claim personal credits, such as the child tax credit, without facing an additional alternative minimum tax; and increased the cap on private activity bonds to help local governments fund various projects. The $9.2 billion plan was offset by several revenue raisers, including the closing of a loophole for real estate investment trusts.

IRS Overhaul

Horror stories of harassment and abuses by federal tax agents led to passage in 1998 of legislation to overhaul the Internal Revenue Service (IRS). The measure (HR 2676—PL 105-206) was designed to give taxpayers more rights and protections in their dealings with the tax collection agency. It shifted the burden of proof from the taxpayer to the IRS in certain cases, curbed some penalties and interest charges, allowed taxpayers to sue the government for damages if IRS personnel disregarded tax laws, and made it easier for a joint

TAX RECORD "SNOOPING" PROHIBITION

Congress in 1997 cleared a bill (HR 1226—PL 105-35) making it a crime for IRS employees to snoop through tax returns and other records. Under the legislation IRS workers risked a misdemeanor charge for "browsing" through tax records of cases they were not authorized to review. Anyone convicted could face up to one year in prison and a $1,000 fine. In addition, taxpayers whose records had been unlawfully accessed would be notified by the IRS after an employee was convicted and could then seek civil damages from the employee.

The House Ways and Means Committee approved the measure by voice vote April 9 (H Rept 105-51). The House passed the bill on tax filing day, April 15, by a vote of 412–0. The Senate passed a similar bill (S 522) the same day by a vote of 97–0, but that version had additional provisions that were not in the House bill. Senate sponsors later agreed to drop the extra provisions in favor of the House bill, and the Senate then cleared the measure by voice vote July 23. President Clinton signed the bill Aug 5.

filer to be exempt from liability for the tax mistakes of his or her spouse.

Despite years of complaints from taxpayers about heavy-handed tactics by the IRS, overhaul efforts got off to a slow start in the 105th Congress. A bipartisan task force issued a 190-page report in June 1997 that recommended sweeping changes. The Clinton administration opposed many of the recommended changes, however, and little happened until September when the Senate Finance Committee held hearings at which many taxpayers described incidents of IRS abuse. The high-profile hearings produced a torrent of negative publicity that forced the Clinton administration to support the overhaul effort. The House quickly passed its version of the legislation in the final days of the session.

Despite pressure from Senate Democrats, a handful of Republicans, and President Clinton to clear the legislation in time for the 1998 tax season, Senate Republican leaders opted to hold another round of hearings in early 1998 at which more abuses were detailed. Although the hearings confirmed the need for corrective action, the Republican leadership was criticized for using the hearings to discredit federal tax laws as part of their strategic plan to enact large tax cuts. Critics also said GOP leaders were using the hearings to stimulate political fund-raising. Lawmakers from both parties said it was time to put aside the political motives and move ahead with the long-delayed legislation. Even so, several more months passed before both chambers approved a compromise measure by overwhelming margins in midyear.

BACKGROUND

The drive to overhaul the IRS began on June 25, 1997, when a congressionally created bipartisan commission issued a set of fifty-two recommendations after a year of hearings and debate. The National Commission on Restructuring the Internal Revenue Service was cochaired by Republican Rep. Rob Portman of Ohio and Democratic Sen. Bob Kerrey of Nebraska. The primary recommendation was shifting IRS oversight from the Treasury Department to an independent board of governors, which would include people from the private sector.

The commission report was immediately endorsed by GOP leaders but opposed by the Clinton administration. Treasury Secretary Robert E. Rubin said that appointing business leaders to the board would give the appearance, if not the reality, of a conflict of interest with IRS tax policies. Rubin insisted that the administration had already initiated management changes at the IRS, including establishment in 1996 of an oversight board with members drawn from the government. The Clinton administration wanted to make that board permanent.

Supporters of the Kerrey-Portman recommendations argued that private-sector expertise was needed to address strategic modernization and customer service issues dogging the IRS and that government officials with short tenures would not offer the continuity or independence needed to curb abuses within the agency.

SENATE HEARINGS

The administration was forced to drop its opposition to the IRS overhaul after the Senate Finance Committee held three days of hearings Sept. 23–25 when four taxpayers told of being harassed by IRS agents and seven active and former IRS employees said the agency's culture endorsed improper tactics. One revenue agent testified that "egregious tactics" were used with the support of supervisors "to extract unfairly assessed taxes from taxpayers, literally ruining families, lives, and businesses—all unnecessarily and sometimes illegally."

The hearings culminated in an extraordinary public apology from acting IRS Commissioner Michael P. Dolan, who promised rapid reforms. Still Dolan and other IRS officials defended the IRS's overall record. In 1996 the agency collected nearly $1.5 trillion from 209 million tax returns. Of those returns, just 1.4 percent were audited, and only 3.8 percent of the audited returns resulted in penalties.

HOUSE ACTION

After the hearings, action shifted from the Senate to the House where the Ways and Means Committee Oct. 22 reported a restructuring bill (HR 2676—H Rept 105-364) by a vote of 33–4. A day earlier House Minority Leader Richard A. Gephardt, D-Mo., announced that he would support the restructuring measure. An hour later the administration followed with a more tepid endorsement when Rubin called the

legislation "workable." The House passed the bill Nov. 5 by an overwhelming vote of 426–4 with no amendments.

SENATE ACTION

The bill approved by the Senate Finance Committee March 31, 1998, on a 20–0 vote (S Rept 105-174) was considerably broader in scope and more expensive than the version approved by the House. The major difference was a provision in the Senate bill that would generally make the liability of spouses proportionate to their individual incomes, meaning that a spouse with a low income would not be liable for taxes on income earned by the other spouse. Under current law spouses who signed a joint tax return were each responsible for the accuracy of the return and the full tax liability.

The provision was estimated to cost $5.2 billion over ten years, which would be offset by allowing taxpayers older than 70½ years to convert a portion of their traditional individual retirement accounts to Roth IRAs beginning in 2005. (Named for Senate Finance Chairman William V. Roth Jr., R-Del., Roth IRAs were authorized in 1997; they differ from traditional IRAs in that taxes are not deferred on contributions to a plan but principal and interest earned is nontaxable when withdrawn at retirement. Taxes are deferred on contributions to regular IRAs but retirement benefits, including interest earnings, are then taxed as regular income.) Under the offset plan, taxes would have to be paid on amounts moved from a traditional to a Roth IRA at the time of the transfer.

The provision was expected to raise $8 billion by 2007 but would cost the Treasury more than $45 billion over twenty years because of the tax break on interest earnings. Although Democrats objected to the scheme, they did not try to block the bill over the issue, which demonstrated the potency of the IRS overhaul as a political issue in an election year. The Senate adopted several noncontroversial amendments by voice vote before passing HR 2676 by a 97–0 vote on May 7.

FINAL ACTION

The House adopted the conference report (H Rept 105-599) on the bill June 25 by a 402–8 vote; the Senate cleared it July 8 by a vote of 96–2. Clinton signed the measure on July 22. The final version of the bill retreated somewhat from the Senate version but was still considerably broader than the original House version. It also contained several provisions that had not been in either the House or Senate versions, including a controversial tax break on capital gains.

The final version of the bill restructured the IRS, creating a board within the Treasury Department to oversee IRS administration and management of the U.S. tax code. The bill outlined a number of new offenses for which IRS employees would be fired, including falsifying or destroying documents to cover up mistakes, and made it a felony for executive branch officials to use IRS audits for political purposes.

Congress had already enacted, in 1988 and 1996, two so-called Taxpayer Bill of Rights. HR 2676 expanded on those laws by shifting the burden of proof in tax court proceedings from individual taxpayers and small businesses to the IRS and also made it significantly easier for a joint filer to claim "innocent spouse" status when the IRS finds that his or her spouse had made mistakes on a tax return. *(1988 Taxpayer Bill of Rights, Congress and the Nation Vol. VII, p. 105; 1996 Taxpayer Bill of Rights, Congress and the Nation Vol. IX, p. 104.)*

The most significant provision added during the House-Senate conference reduced from eighteen months to twelve months the time a taxpayer is required to hold investments before selling them to qualify for a reduced, 20 percent tax rate on the profits.

The final bill also included a totally unrelated provision that changed the nomenclature for the trade concept known as "most favored nation." The term applied to agreements equalizing trade benefits between nations. HR 2676 gave it the more direct name of "normal trade relations." *(Trade provision, p. 109)*

MAJOR PROVISIONS

Oversight Board

Created an oversight board within the Treasury Department to oversee IRS administration, management, conduct, direction, and supervision of the execution and application of the tax code but without responsibility for federal tax policy or IRS enforcement activities. Ordered creation of organizational units to assist particular groups of taxpayers with similar needs.

Directed the board to review: IRS strategic plans, performance standards, and annual and long-range goals; IRS operational functions; the IRS commissioner's selection; plans for major reorganization of the agency; and the IRS's annual budget.

Specified a board of nine persons, six of whom are not federal employees and would serve no more than two five-year terms, plus the Treasury secretary, the IRS commissioner, and an individual from a union representing a substantial number of IRS employees. Specified members would be appointed by the president and confirmed by the Senate.

Discipline of IRS Employees

Required the IRS to fire an employee for perjury; falsifying or destroying documents; willful failure to obtain approval to seize a taxpayer's assets, including a home; assault or battery on a taxpayer or other IRS employee; violations of IRS rules for the purpose of retaliating against a taxpayer or other IRS employee; or violations of the civil rights of a taxpayer.

Office of Taxpayer Advocate

Specified that the taxpayer advocate be appointed from three individuals recommended by the oversight board. Reaffirmed existing-law functions of the advocate and added certain new monitoring duties. Created a system of local taxpayer advocates reporting to the national taxpayer advocate.

Required the national advocate to submit two annual reports to the House and Senate tax-writing committees including information on areas of tax law that impose significant compliance burdens on taxpayers or the IRS.

Politically Motivated Audits

Made it a felony for executive branch officials to use IRS audits for political purposes and modified existing law to clarify that the prohibition applied to direct or indirect requests for IRS audits. Established three exceptions: a request made to a specified person (executive branch employee) by a taxpayer or a taxpayer's representative; requests for disclosure of tax returns made in accordance with applicable law; and requests by the Treasury secretary resulting from implementation of a change in tax policy.

Electronic Filing and Access

Stated the policy of Congress to promote paperless filing and set a goal of limiting paper returns to 20 percent of all tax returns by the year 2007. Directed the Treasury secretary to eliminate barriers to and provide incentives for electronic filing.

Directed the IRS to develop procedures to eliminate the need to file a paper form with a signature and to allow signatures to be accepted digitally or in another electronic form. The bill would clarify that such "alternative signatures" are treated legally as signatures. Required the IRS to establish by 2007 a means by which taxpayers who file their tax returns electronically could access their accounts electronically.

Taxpayer Rights

Expanded existing taxpayer rights by shifting to the IRS the burden of proving the validity of tax liability in disputes dealing with income, estate, and gift taxes that come before the U.S. Tax Court. (Existing law required taxpayers to prove the invalidity of an IRS claim.) Required the shift in burden of proof if the taxpayer has cooperated with the IRS by providing access to witnesses, information, and documents within the control of the taxpayer.

Innocent Spouse Relief

Expanded the ability of a joint filer to claim "innocent spouse" status when the IRS finds that his or her spouse made mistakes on a tax return. Limited a spouse's tax liability to the proportion of the couple's income for which the spouse is responsible for those spouses who are no longer married, are legally separated, or have been living apart for at least twelve months. Authorized a tax court with jurisdiction to review any IRS denial of, or failure to rule on, an application for innocent spouse relief.

Civil Damages for Negligence

Expanded existing law to allow a taxpayer to sue the federal government for up to $100,000 in civil damages caused by IRS employees who "negligently" disregard provisions of the tax code, in addition to suits currently allowed when an IRS employee "recklessly" or "intentionally" disregards a provision.

Taxpayer Audits and Collections

Defined circumstances that the taxpayer advocate must consider when issuing a "taxpayer assistance order" that, for example, would release property of the taxpayer that has been levied upon or require the IRS to cease action against the taxpayer. Prohibited the IRS from seizing residences to satisfy unpaid tax liabilities of less than $5,000, and prohibited the IRS from seizing a taxpayer's home without a court order.

Congressional Oversight

Required the Joint Committee on Taxation to review all requests (other than requests by the chairman or ranking member of a committee or subcommittee of Congress) for investigations of the IRS by the General Accounting Office (GAO), and approve such requests when appropriate. Required annual joint meetings by senior congressional members on the financial, appropriations, and oversight committees to review IRS strategic plans and budgets. Required the Joint Committee on Taxation to submit an annual report to the standing congressional tax committees on the overall status of the federal tax system, together with recommendations on possible simplification proposals.

Complexity Analysis

Required the Joint Committee on Taxation, in consultation with the IRS and the Treasury Department, to provide a "tax complexity analysis" for tax legislation that identifies provisions that add significant complexity or simplification to tax law.

Capital Gains Holding Period

Reduced from eighteen months to twelve months the time a taxpayer is required to hold investments before selling them to qualify for the lower 20 percent tax rate on the profits (capital gains). (Earlier tax legislation—PL 105-34—reduced the maximum tax rate on capital gains from 28 percent to 20 percent for investments held at least eighteen months.)

Employer-Provided Meals

Clarified that meals provided on the employer's premises, for the convenience of the employer, where more than half of the employees receive the meal, would not be taxable to the employees and would be fully deductible to the employer.

Most Favored Nation Name Change

Changed the language in trade law regarding "most favored nation" trade status to "normal trade relations."

1999–2000

Apparently calculating that they would win valuable political points even if they did not succeed in passing any legislation, Republicans in the 106th Congress decided to go for broke in their pursuit of their longtime goal of drastically reducing taxes. In 1999, with little Democratic support, they passed a measure that would have slashed taxes by $792 billion over ten years. When Clinton vetoed the bill, as he had promised he would, Republicans in 2000 stripped out two of the more popular tax cuts—elimination of the marriage status differentiation and a gradual end to estate taxes—and passed them as individual bills. Although those measures drew more Democratic support, Clinton still vetoed them and the GOP was unable to override him.

Congress did pass a measure changing the tax code on income earned abroad to avoid a threatened trade war with the European Union. But several other tax cuts and tax breaks fell by the wayside in the rush to adjourn before the presidential elections in November.

Republican Tax Cut

Seeking an issue to define philosophical differences between the two major political parties, Republican leaders pushed a $792 billion tax cut (HR 2488) through Congress in 1999 despite public indifference, near-unanimous Democratic opposition, and President Clinton's repeated promise to veto the measure.

The final version of the bill, which Clinton vetoed Sept. 23, called for a broad-based cut in personal income taxes, provided relief to married couples who pay more in income taxes than they would have if they filed separately, phased out gift and estate taxes, and cut individual (but not corporate) capital gains taxes, among other provisions. It would have been the largest single tax cut measure enacted since 1981, when Congress passed a $749 billion tax cut at the urging of newly elected President Ronald Reagan. *(Reagan tax cut, Congress and the Nation Vol. VI, p. 65)*

The tax cut legislation was an outgrowth of the debate about how to allocate budget surpluses, which in early 1999 were projected to be more than $800 billion over five years. Although both parties agreed that more than 60 percent of the surplus should be used to bolster Social Security, Republicans wanted to devote much of the rest to tax cuts whereas Clinton wanted to use nearly 90 percent of the surplus to shore up Social Security and Medicare and the remainder to raise the budget caps on discretionary spending. Clinton proposed only modest targeted tax cuts.

Republican congressional leaders had little inclination to compromise with the president on an issue that one House member called the "meat and bones of the party." Nor did they have much hope in the closely divided Congress of passing their massive tax cut over the president's certain veto. Nonetheless, GOP leaders felt obliged to push for a tax reduction to highlight a fundamental difference between the two parties that could prove useful in the 2000 elections, where Republicans hoped to beef up their slim majorities in the House and Senate and gain control of the White House.

Although a large tax cut was avidly backed by the GOP's core supporters, opinion polling consistently showed that Clinton's plea to "save Social Security first" had more appeal to the public, which also preferred to use the surplus to increase spending on defense and social programs such as education and health care. As a result Republicans had trouble drumming up public support for their bill, allowing the president to veto it without political injury.

Clinton did just that on Sept. 23, citing his "profound differences" with the "extreme approach" taken by Republicans. Not only would the legislation give tax cuts to the wealthiest Americans, Clinton said, it would deny average Americans the benefits of debt reduction, including lower interest rates, low inflation, low unemployment, and continued economic growth. No attempt was made to override the veto.

In his fiscal 2000 budget, presented to Congress Feb. 1, Clinton had proposed $32.6 billion in targeted tax breaks and credits, such as credits to taxpayers to help care for disabled or elderly relatives, to pay for day care expenses, and to defray the costs of staying at home to rear infants or of installing energy-saving devices in their homes. The costs of these tax cuts would be covered by closing or restricting corporate tax shelters and tweaking the tax code to extract more revenues from wealthy taxpayers and businesses.

HOUSE ACTION

Although several Republican tax cut plans were bandied about early in 1999 GOP leaders were wary of pushing a large tax cut for which the public was not clamoring so soon after the unpopular impeachment trial of President Clinton. They thus decided to put off any serious action until the budget resolution had passed. *(Clinton impeachment and acquittal, p. 813)*

With the budget resolution in place by mid-April and projections of even higher budget surpluses, Republicans decided to move. In the House the Ways and Means Committee began to work on a plan drawn up by Chairman Bill Archer, R-Texas, on July 13. As introduced, HR 2488 would reduce income tax rates by 10 percent across the board over ten years; ease but not eliminate the so-called marriage penalty, in which some married couples pay more in income taxes than they would if they had remained single; lower tax rates on capital gains from the sale of real estate, stocks, and other investments; and phase out inheritance taxes over ten years.

The committee defeated several Democratic attempts to trim back the Archer bill and redirect the tax cuts including a proposal to cut $375 billion to use for a Medicare benefit covering prescription drugs, as proposed by the president. All were defeated on party-line votes. The committee also accepted several GOP amendments to target tax breaks at specific industries, such as timber and oil and gas, before approving the bill 23–13 on July 14.

The House passed HR 2488 on July 22 but only after GOP moderates forced GOP leaders to accept a compromise that conditioned the bill's 10 percent cut in tax rates on achieving promised levels of savings elsewhere in the budget. The moderates, fifteen to twenty in number, were concerned that without modification the tax cut would eat up almost all the surplus not generated by Social Security taxes over the next decade. They wanted more of that money available for deficit reduction, Social Security and Medicare reforms, and additional discretionary spending programs.

Archer reluctantly agreed to a compromise that conditioned most of the proposed 10 percent tax rate cut on whether interest payments on the national debt went up or down. The first 1 percent of the rate cut would automatically take effect in 2001. Additional cuts scheduled to start in 2004 would go into effect only if the annual interest expense on the debt was going down. All but four moderate Republicans voted for this compromise.

In addition Archer scaled back his original $864 billion bill to $792 billion, the size of the Senate Finance Committee proposal and the amount set forward in the budget resolution (H Con Res 68). The cut was made ostensibly to placate moderates, but it would have been made in any event because of Senate rules that allow opponents to block any tax cut bill that exceeds the budget resolution's figure. The cost savings in HR 2488 came in part from delaying the phase-in of the tax rate cut.

With the rebellion by moderate Republicans quelled, remaining House action on the bill was anticlimactic. Republicans easily turned back a $250 billion Democratic substitute that would have eased the marriage penalty, increased per-child tax credits, subsidized state and local school construction bonds, and permanently extended the research and development tax credit and other expiring tax credits. The Democratic alternative failed, 173–258.

The House then passed the bill on a **key vote of 223–208 (R 217–4; D 6–203; I 0–1).** Democrats stayed unified in their opposition to the bill, surprising some Republicans who had predicted that up to two dozen would vote for it. The approval was a major victory for House Speaker J. Dennis Hastert, R-Ill., who had staked his young Speakership on the bill. Losing the vote would have been a political debacle both for Hastert and the party. *(1999 key votes, p. 899)*

SENATE ACTION

In the Senate, Finance Committee Chairman William V. Roth Jr., R-Del., drafted a bill (S 1429—S Rept 106-120) that sought to walk a fine line between the two wings of the Republican Party. The measure's main component, for example, cut the lowest income tax rate bracket from 15 percent to 14 percent, at an estimated cost of $216 billion in lost revenue over ten years. That approach appealed to moderates concerned about helping those with lower incomes, whereas conservatives generally preferred an across-the-board cut similar to the one in the House bill. At the July 21 markup two attempts by conservative Republicans to shift more of the tax cuts toward the middle class and wealthy taxpayers failed when three Republican moderates, including Roth, voted with the Democrats in opposition.

The Senate bill differed from the House version in several other respects as well. For example, S 1429 virtually eliminated the marriage penalty by allowing married couples to file separate schedules on a joint basis, at an estimated cost $112 billion over ten years. Conservatives tended to favor that version rather than the House bill, which would have only eased the marriage penalty by increasing the standard income tax deduction for married couples filing jointly from $7,200 to $8,600, double that of a single taxpayer.

In other provisions S 1429 increased the annual amount that could be contributed to all individual retirement accounts to $5,000, from $2,000, and it permanently extended the research and development tax credit.

The bill also contained a controversial provision to evade the so-called Byrd rule, which requires a supermajority of sixty votes to pass tax cut measures that are not offset by spending cuts or revenue increases. In addition to the normal sunset bill, which stipulated that the legislation would expire and taxes revert to current levels after Sept. 30, 2009, unless future Congresses took action to extend them, S 1429 contained a provision that negated the sunset provision by restarting the tax code changes on Oct. 1, 2009.

When Democrats began to argue that the bill would cost trillions of dollars after 2009, Senate Majority Leader Trent Lott, R-Miss., issued a point of order against the provision extending the tax cuts beyond September 2009. Had he not done so Democrats could have filed a point of order against the entire bill, jeopardizing its passage. On July 28 Roth lost a motion to waive Lott's point of order, 51–48; 60 votes were required for Roth's motion to pass.

The Senate voted on more than twenty amendments over twenty hours of debate, most of them centered on Democratic attempts to divert some of the anticipated surplus toward such programs as Medicare and education and Republican attempts to make the tax cuts larger. Nearly all efforts failed including the Democratic substitute that would have cut taxes by $290 billion over ten years. The most important to succeed was an amendment to make the standard deduction for married couples double that of singles and to phase in that change beginning in 2001. That amendment, which strengthened the marriage differentiation provisions in the Senate bill, had been sought by conservative religious groups, such as the Christian Coalition.

During debate on the amendments, the Senate GOP held together easily. Although several moderates expressed concern that the bill might use up too much of the non-Social

Security budget surplus on tax cuts, only two Republicans voted against it. Democratic Minority Leader Tom Daschle, S.D., had a much harder time keeping his colleagues in the fold. Four Democratic senators voted for the GOP version on final passage. They had supported an alternative $500 billion tax cut that was also favored by some GOP moderates. But it was withdrawn after GOP leaders and President Clinton made it clear they preferred to treat the tax cut debate as a partisan political issue rather than try to find a compromise position. The Senate then passed the bill on July 30 in a **key vote of 57–43 (R 52–2; D 4–41; I 1–0).** *(1999 key votes, p. 899)*

CONFERENCE, FINAL ACTION

With Republicans eager to tout a GOP tax cut bill to constituents during the August recess, the conference to negotiate the differences between the two versions of the legislation went quickly. Conferees were appointed Aug. 2 and, with hands-on participation by party leaders, an agreement was announced on Aug. 3. Lott, a member of the Finance Committee, and House Majority Leader Dick Armey, R-Texas, who did not sit on the Ways and Means Committee, were both conferees.

The final measure compromised on the main differences between the House and Senate versions by agreeing to reduce each of the five tax rate brackets by 1 percentage point by 2005. The Senate bill would have reduced the rate only for the lowest bracket; the broader House bill would have cut tax rates by 10 percent across the board by 2009. Although the final version did not include the Senate provision allowing married couples to file a joint return with separate schedules, it did raise the standard deduction for married couples to double that for single filers and contained other provisions to ease the marriage disparity.

Other provisions eliminated estate and gift taxes; phased out the individual alternative minimum tax; cut individual, but not corporate, capital gains taxes; increased allowable contributions to individual and other retirement accounts; and provided tax breaks to several specific industries and corporations.

After GOP conferees reached agreement the evening of Aug. 3, Lott and others reopened the bill Aug. 4 and inserted provisions to attract votes from moderate Senate Republicans. Among those provisions were $4 billion to give a bigger tax benefit to couples who qualified for the earned-income tax credit (EITC) and $4 billion to allow states to issue more low-interest bonds to developers of housing for the poor. More tax credits for child and dependent care were also inserted.

Those concessions helped win support of some GOP moderates, but the Senate cleared the conference report (H Rept 106-289) Aug. 5 by only one vote 50–49. Four Republicans joined all the Democrats, including the four that had voted for the Senate version of the bill, to oppose the final version. The four Democrats said the final bill was too weighted toward the House version, which they said gave

too many tax cuts to businesses and well-off individuals. The House had adopted the conference report a few hours earlier on a vote of 221–206.

BILL HIGHLIGHTS

As cleared by Congress and vetoed by the president, HR 2488 would have cut taxes by $792 billion between 1999 and its expiration in 2009.

• **Broad-based income tax cut.** Reduced each of the five income tax brackets by 1 percentage point by 2005. Expanded the lowest bracket in 2006 allowing single filers and heads of households to earn $3,000 more than existing limits—$25,750 and $34,550 in 2000, respectively—and still file in the lowest bracket.

• **Marriage status.** Beginning in 2001, gradually raised the standard income tax deduction for married filers to $8,600, double that of an individual taxpayer. Increased the amount that a married couple could earn annually and still file under the lowest income tax bracket.

• **Alternative minimum tax.** Allowed taxpayers subject to the alternative minimum tax (AMT) to claim personal credits, such as the $500-per-child tax credit, against their taxes, beginning in 2005. (The AMT was a parallel tax system intended to ensure that no one avoided income taxes.)

• **Estate taxes.** Eliminated estate, gift, and generation-skipping taxes over a period ending in 2009. Repealed laws that effectively set beginning tax rates for estates at 38 percent, thereby setting initial tax rates for estates worth more than $650,000—the threshold for estate taxes—at 18 percent.

• **Health care.** Allowed self-employed taxpayers and those whose employers paid no more than 50 percent of health care insurance premiums to deduct 100 percent of their premiums from income taxes. Allowed persons who cared for an elderly relative in their home to exempt about $2,750 from taxes beginning in 2000.

• **Retirement.** Increased tax-preferred contributions limits for individual retirement accounts (IRAs) from $2,000 to $5,000 by 2008 reverting to $2,000 in 2009. Allowed couples making as much as $200,000 annually to convert standard IRAs, in which contributions are not taxed but withdrawals are, to Roth IRAs, in which contributions are taxed but withdrawals are not.

• **Capital gains.** Reduced individual (but not corporate) capital gains tax rates of 20 and 10 percent, based on a taxpayer's income, to 18 percent and 8 percent, respectively. Indexed capital gains for inflation beginning in 2000.

• **International taxes.** Allowed U.S. companies to deduct interest expenses incurred in foreign businesses of which they owned more than 50 percent (existing law required 80 percent ownership).

• **Other provisions.** Increased allowable contributions to 401(k)s and other retirement accounts. Increased to $2,000 from $500 the limit on contributions to Education IRAs, renamed Education Savings Accounts.

1999 Tax Extenders

Surging budget surpluses allowed Congress in 1999 to extend a set of expiring tax credits and other tax breaks for at least two years. But the legislation, usually on Congress's annual "must-pass" list, nearly succumbed to partisan wrangling before being cleared in the final days of the session.

Action on the so-called "extenders" began in September after President Clinton vetoed the GOP's $792 billion tax bill (HR 2488) on Sept. 23. GOP leaders immediately decided to try to use a portion of the projected budget surplus to grant long-term extensions of expiring tax provisions.

The House measure (HR 2923—H Rept 106-344), approved by the Ways and Means Committee Sept. 24 on a 23–14 vote, extended for five years the research and experimentation tax credit, which generally benefited high-tech, biotechnology, and manufacturing companies. It also allowed millions of taxpayers subject to the alternative minimum tax (AMT) to continue claiming personal tax credits, such as the $500-per-child credit enacted in 1997. The AMT was a parallel tax system designed to ensure that taxpayers were not able to wipe out all tax liability through deductions and credits. HR 2923, which also extended several other existing tax credits, was expected to cost $23.3 billion over five years; that revenue loss was to be covered with offsetting changes in other parts of the tax code only in fiscal 2000.

The Senate measure (S 1792—S Rept 106-201), which the Senate passed on Oct. 29 by voice vote, was much narrower than the House version. It extended all of the expiring tax provisions only through Dec. 31, 2000, and cost $8.5 billion over ten years. Moreover, all revenue losses would be offset with other changes to the tax code. This version was approved by the Senate Finance Committee Oct. 20, after Chairman William V. Roth Jr., R-Del., agreed—in the face of opposition from committee members of both parties—to abandon a version that more closely resembled the House measure.

With the session drawing to a close, the chairmen and ranking members of the House and Senate tax-writing committees, together with administration officials, agreed on a compromise package that extended the research and development credit for five years, extended twelve other tax credits through Dec. 31, 2001, and allowed taxpayers using the alternative minimum tax to claim personal tax credits. The bill's $21 billion cost over ten years was partially offset with $2.9 billion in other changes to the tax code. The White House and congressional Democrats had been pushing to offset the entire measure, but they dropped any significant opposition after Republicans agreed to extend a set of provisions that Democrats wanted.

The extension measure encountered one last hurdle before it was cleared. Because the House had never passed its version of the bill, GOP leaders decided to add the agreed-upon version to a pending conference report on legislation (HR 1180) dealing with health benefits for workers with dis-abilities. That measure nearly foundered over procedural difficulties in the Senate and a last-minute controversy over organ donations. With those problems cleared away the House approved the conference report on HR 1180, 418–2, on Nov. 18. The Senate cleared the measure Nov. 19 on a vote of 95–1. President Clinton signed HR 1180 (PL 106-170) on Dec. 17. *(Health benefits for disabled workers, p. 470)*

Marriage Status Tax Cut

Republicans in 2000 were unswerving in their push to cut taxes for married couples, but their unwillingness to negotiate the details with President Clinton or congressional Democrats meant the proposal served only as a campaign issue. Clinton vetoed the GOP bill and the House sustained the veto.

The marriage status issue was one of a series of targeted tax bills that Republican leaders decided to advance in 2000 after Clinton vetoed their $792 billion tax package in 1999. Republicans had used that measure primarily to highlight the differences between the two parties on tax policy. When it failed to generate much enthusiasm among voters GOP leaders decided to take up individual tax cuts that had clear public support. The marriage status provision seemed a good choice because it affected more than half of all married couples at all income levels. *(1999 tax cut, p. 110)*

Both parties began the year agreeing in principle that the marriage status issue should be addressed. Clinton proposed a plan in his fiscal 2001 budget that would have cost $44 billion over ten years to alleviate the disparity, which referred to operation of parts of the federal income tax code that caused a majority of married couples to pay more in income taxes than they would as two single people. Republicans favored a more expensive package that not only would have reduced the tax for the estimated 24.8 million couples who paid the higher amount—generally those in which the husband and wife have similar incomes—but also would have given tax breaks to the 21 million couples who were paying less in federal taxes than they would as two single people. These were mainly couples with one spouse who did not work or who earned much less than the other spouse.

The legislation followed a tortuous path through Congress. The first version (HR 6) was passed in the House early in the year but blocked in the Senate when GOP leaders could not gather the necessary votes to cut off a filibuster. A second version (HR 4810) was then given expedited consideration under the reconciliation instructions in the fiscal 2001 budget resolution (H Con Res 290). Clinton offered to sign the bill if Republicans would adopt his plan to have Medicare cover senior citizens' prescription drug costs, but the GOP rejected the trade. *(Budget resolution, p. 79)*

With protection from a filibuster and other delaying tactics conferred by its reconciliation status, the bill was passed in both chambers relatively easily, although not by enough votes to override Clinton's veto. In his veto message Clinton said the bill cost too much and would benefit wealthier couples disproportionately. A House attempt to override the veto failed.

The vetoed bill would have cost $90 billion over five years and $292 billion if kept on the books for ten years. It would have allowed married couples filing jointly to claim a standard deduction twice that of singles. Taxable income in the lowest (15 percent) income tax bracket for married couples would have been expanded to twice the corresponding bracket for singles. Married couples filing jointly could have continued using certain nonrefundable tax credits to offset their tax liability even if they were subject to the alternative minimum tax, the system designed to prevent the wealthy from avoiding all tax liability. In addition, lower-income couples would have been allowed to earn up to $2,000 more annually while still qualifying for the earned-income tax credit (EITC), which enhances or provides refunds for the working poor.

HOUSE ACTION

Partisanship on the measure began almost as soon as the congressional session got under way. Even before the president's fiscal 2001 budget proposals had been released and work on the congressional budget resolution had begun the House Ways and Means Committee Feb. 2 approved a measure (HR 6—H Rept 106-493) on a straight party-line vote of 23–13. The bill sent to the House floor had three parts. First, beginning in 2001, it increased the standard deduction for married couples to double that of single individuals; under existing law it was 60 percent higher.

Second, HR 6 gradually expanded the limit on couples' income taxed at the lowest marginal rate—15 percent—to twice that for individuals. The change would be phased in between 2003 and 2008. On returns for 2000 the lowest bracket would apply to the first $43,850 of a married couple's taxable income and the first $26,250 of a single person's taxable income. Bracket limits would be adjusted annually for inflation.

Third, HR 6 increased by $2,000 the income levels making married couples eligible for at least some EITC.

Committee Democrats objected to the bill because it was being moved before Congress even considered the fiscal 2001 budget resolution, which would lay out the spending, tax, and entitlement priorities for the year. They also objected to the increase in the 15 percent tax bracket, arguing that it would primarily benefit the wealthiest taxpayers because more of their income would be taxed at the lowest rate. They further argued that the bill would provide tax relief not only to couples who paid more because of their marriage status but also to those couples who paid less.

When the bill reached the House floor on Feb. 10, Democrats took up Clinton's theme, stressed throughout his Feb. 7 budget package, that Social Security, Medicare, and the national debt should be addressed before tax cuts. The president's budget proposed tax relief only for those couples that actually faced higher taxes from their marriage status. A

Democratic alternative to provide $95 billion in marriage status relief over ten years, conditioned on administration certification that steps had been taken to ensure the solvency of Social Security and Medicare and the elimination of the public debt, was rejected 192–233.

The vote for the bill was 268–158. Although few Democrats spoke in favor of the bill during floor debate forty-eight of them—nearly a quarter of the caucus—voted for the measure. Most were from marginally Democratic districts or were running for higher office. No Republican voted against the bill.

SENATE ACTION

Although Senate Republicans were initially less enamored with the idea of trying to pass a stand-alone bill dealing only with the marriage status, they changed their minds after the House GOP bill won some Democratic support and glowing media coverage. On March 30 the Senate Finance Committee approved S 2346 by an 11–9 party-line vote. The Republican draft followed the outlines of the House version but was more generous in some areas, giving more tax relief to married couples at the higher end of the income scale and making more couples eligible for the EITC. Its total cost was estimated at $248 billion over ten years.

The Senate version also provided $45 billion in relief over ten years to taxpayers who pay the alternative minimum tax (AMT), a provision in the tax code that ensured that higher-bracket taxpayers paid some taxes regardless of the number of deductions and credits they claimed. As incomes rose during the 1990s, more and more taxpayers had been hit by the AMT and had lost deductions such as the $500-per-child tax credit.

A more modest Democratic proposal that would have allowed married couples to file as if they were two single people failed on a 9–11 party-line vote.

Majority Leader Trent Lott, R-Miss., scheduled the measure for floor action the week of April 10, timing it to coincide with the April 17 income tax filing deadline for maximum political impact. Minority Leader Tom Daschle, D-S.D., mounted a Democratic filibuster in protest of Lott's decision not to permit Democratic floor amendments on the measure. Twice on April 13 and again on April 27, Lott was unable to muster the sixty votes needed to invoke cloture (cut off debate). The votes on April 13 were both 53–45; on April 27, 51–44. After the third attempt at cloture failed, the majority leader withdrew the bill and urged the Finance Committee to attach marriage status and other tax relief measures to one of the year's reconciliation bills, which were protected from certain types of amendments and open-ended debate.

LEGISLATIVE ACTION ON SECOND BILL

The marriage tax issue came back to Congress in late June, after the House and Senate agreed to a budget resolution (H Con Res 290) for fiscal 2001 that called for two tax-cutting reconciliation bills. On June 28 the Senate Finance

Committee approved the first of the two reconciliation bills on a party-line vote of 10–5. S 2839 contained the same marriage tax provisions as the March version that had died except that it was limited to five years, rather than ten, to conform with the budget resolution. The five-year cost of the bill was estimated at $55.6 billion.

Finance Committee Chairman William V. Roth Jr. also spurned a compromise President Clinton had offered earlier in the day: his approval of the GOP marriage tax bill in return for GOP support for adding a prescription drug benefit to Medicare. At the beginning of the markup Roth pledged to take up a drug benefit bill separately and to work with the Democrats on drafting it.

Before the Senate took up the bill on the floor the House repassed a marriage tax bill on July 12 by a vote of 269–159. Again, 48 Democrats voted with the Republicans to pass the bill (HR 4810), which was virtually the same as HR 6 except that it was limited to five years rather than ten.

Before passing the bill the House voted down a Democratic alternative, 198–228. It also rejected, 197–230, an attempt by the Democrats to attach language ensuring Clinton's signature on the marriage bill if Congress agreed to his plan to create a Medicare prescription drug benefit.

Senate debate on its version of the legislation began July 14 under reconciliation rules, which allowed no more than twenty hours of debate and prohibited consideration of non-germane amendments. The Senate debated several dozen amendments and adopted several including one that would have allowed self-employed taxpayers to deduct 100 percent of their health care premiums retroactive to the end of 1999. Before voting on the bill, however, the Senate agreed to a motion by Majority Leader Lott to send the bill back to the Finance Committee with instructions to return it immediately to the floor with all amendments removed. The motion was adopted, 54–45 on July 18 and the Senate then passed the bill, 61–38, with eight Democrats voting for passage and one Republican voting against it.

Concerned about Democratic arguments that the measure was weighted too heavily toward the well-to-do, House and Senate GOP conferees agreed July 19 to the House provision expanding only the amount of taxable income subject to the 15 percent income tax rate. The Senate version expanded the income subject to the 28 percent rate as well. Senators also agreed to the less generous House provisions for working poor couples, allowing them to make $2,000 more annually and still qualify for the EITC. The Senate allowed such couples to earn $2,500 more annually. Buoyed by forecasts of higher surpluses conferees also decided to begin phasing in the tax cuts in 2000, one year earlier than had originally been planned. That raised the five-year cost of the bill significantly, to $89.8 billion from $50.7 billion in the House version and $55.6 billion in the Senate version. Democratic conferees said they were excluded from the negotiations.

Mindful of the coming elections, unusually large numbers of Democrats in both chambers voted to adopt the con-

ference report on HR 4810 (H Rept 106-765). The vote in the House on July 20 was 271–156 with 51 Democrats voting for the final version. The Senate adopted the report July 21 on a **key vote of 60–34 (R 53–1; D 7–33)**. *(2000 key votes, p. 915)*

Both votes were well short of the two-thirds necessary to override a veto, however, which Clinton issued on Aug. 5. On Sept. 13 the House fell sixteen votes short of an override, sustaining the veto by a vote of 270–158. Only a week earlier the House had failed to override Clinton's veto of a GOP bill (HR 8) to eliminate the estate tax.

Estate Taxes

The Republican bid to repeal the combined tax on estates and gifts advanced rapidly once farmers, minority business owners, and other constituency groups joined together to support the effort. As a result, even many traditional liberals backed some cut in the tax. But with bill sponsors refusing to accept anything less than an outright repeal, President Clinton followed through on his promise to veto the measure, and the House failed to override his decision.

The estate tax was enacted in 1916 to help finance World War I and to stem the consolidation of wealth in families with vast ownership of stocks and bonds that accompanied rapid industrial growth in the late nineteenth century. The top rate then was 10 percent but by the time the United States entered World War II in 1941 it had climbed to 77 percent. In 1976 Congress cut the top rate to 70 percent (PL 94-455) and in 1981 it voted to further lower that rate to 50 percent over four years (PL 97-34). *(Congress and the Nation Vol. IV, p. 99; Vol. VI, p. 69)*

Subsequent Congresses delayed that cut, however, and in 1993 created a 55 percent top rate (PL 103-66). Four years later, in 1997, Congress increased the threshold for estates subject to taxation to $1 million by 2006. Another provision gave an additional exemption to family farms and closely held family businesses. Both groups would not be subject to the tax until their estates topped $1.3 million. *(1993 law, Congress and the Nation Vol. IX, p. 87; 1997 law, pp. 91, 98)*

After Republicans took control of Congress in 1995 business and farm groups pressed for a repeal of the tax, although at the outset many of their members viewed the prospects as unlikely. A gradual phase out of the estate tax was included in the tax cut that Republicans passed and Clinton vetoed in 1999. When GOP leaders were deciding which tax cuts to pursue as stand-alone bills in 2000, the estate tax and the marriage status tax seemed most likely to have broad political appeal. Baby-boomers were inheriting ever more valuable estates from their parents, more farmers and business owners found themselves paying for estate planning, and a surging stock market led many people to believe that their own estates—or those they stood to inherit—were worth more than ever. Republicans reasoned that in an election year Clinton might be persuaded to sign the popular tax cut bill. If he vetoed it, the GOP would have a useful political issue in the presidential election campaign.

In addition to phasing out the estate tax over ten years, the legislation would have eliminated a tax on gifts worth more than $10,000 and rid the code of the generation-skipping tax, a levy imposed on trust funds and other gifts generally set up for grandchildren. In exchange for this relief the bill would have raised capital gains taxes on some persons who sold an inherited asset. The bill's cost was estimated at $104 billion over the ten-year life of the phase out and $75 billion a year after that.

HOUSE ACTION

Although little had changed to indicate that Clinton might drop his past opposition to a repeal of the estate tax, a coalition of some 200 trade groups sparked bipartisan support in the House where a bill (HR 8) sponsored by Jennifer Dunn, R-Wash., and John Tanner, D-Tenn., attracted 241 cosponsors including 45 Democrats. Supporters said the estate tax had become a heavy burden on family-owned farms and businesses who were spending billions of dollars each year on estate planning costs, money that would be better spent expanding their businesses, hiring new employees, or providing benefits such as health insurance. They also pointed to cases where they said the sudden death of a principal owner had forced heirs to sell the businesses to pay the estate taxes. Several minority chambers of commerce lobbied for the repeal, claiming that the tax was hurting the creation of wealth in black and Hispanic communities.

Although supporters of repeal decried what they described as the inherent unfairness of the tax, opponents said the facts painted a different picture in asserting that repeal would primarily benefit the wealthiest Americans. According to statistics from the Joint Committee on Taxation about 58,000 estates paid the tax each year, less than 2 percent of all estates. Of the estates affected by the tax only 10 percent were valued at more than $5 million and they generated about half of the $30 billion raised by estate and gift taxes every year. Moreover, the Treasury Department estimated that of the 58,000 payers of estate taxes each year about 6 percent had inherited farms and about 3 percent small businesses. Opponents of repeal, primarily Democrats, also argued that the high cost of repeal in terms of lost revenue could have a catastrophic impact on the federal budget.

During the markup of HR 8 in the House Ways and Means Committee, ranking Democrat Charles B. Rangel, N.Y., and Benjamin L. Cardin, D-Md., offered a substitute amendment they said would cost about $15 billion over ten years and would be acceptable to the White House. Instead of an outright repeal, the substitute raised the threshold for qualifying for the tax to $4 million from the current $650,000 and would cut the tax rate by 20 percent. Committee Republicans dismissed the idea as insufficient and it was defeated 12–21, largely along party lines. The committee then approved HR 8 (H Rept 106-651), 24–11 on May 25.

When the bill came to the House floor on June 9, Democrats again offered their substitute, which was rejected on a vote of 196–222. The House then passed HR 8 on a **key vote of 279–136 (R 213–0; D 65–135; I 1–1)**, more than the two-thirds necessary to override an anticipated vote. *(2000 key votes, p. 915)*

SENATE ACTION

The large House margin in favor of repeal renewed interest in the Senate where GOP leaders had been reluctant to bring a bill to the floor for fear it would fall victim to a filibuster, just as the Republican bill to eliminate the marriage status tax had in April. On July 13 HR 8 was taken up on the Senate floor where under an unusual agreement between the two parties debate lasted less than two full days. In that time period the Senate considered nineteen amendments but all were defeated, held to be out of order under Senate budget rules, or wiped out in an procedural move. Among the defeated amendments was a Democratic alternative similar to the one rejected by the House. The Senate defeated its version of the amendment 46–53.

Among the five amendments that were accepted were measures to repeal the excise tax on telephone service and to increase the tax breaks given to contributions to pension plans, both of which were also considered as stand-alone bills. All the accepted amendments were stricken from the bill when the Senate adopted 53–45 a motion by Majority Leader Trent Lott, R-Miss., which sent the bill to the Finance Committee and returned it immediately to the Senate floor absent any amendments. The Senate then cleared HR 8 on June 18 by a vote of 59–39, eight votes short of the two-thirds majority needed for an override. *(Phone excise tax, p. 118; pension tax breaks, p. 119)*

Finance Committee Chairman William V. Roth Jr., R-Del., said the procedure stripping the bill of its amendments was necessary to expedite the measure's delivery to the White House. Otherwise the few amendments would have required another vote by the House or conference committee negotiations. Those delays likely would have kept the bill off Clinton's desk until after the Republican National Convention in early August. Republicans, hoping to turn Clinton's expected veto to their political advantage, wanted to force the president to act on a completed bill immediately before or during the convention.

CLINTON VETO

During Congress's August adjournment, HR 8 fell to Clinton's pocket veto. But in an Aug. 31 message Clinton said he was also returning the measure to Congress without his signature to make clear that he had vetoed the repeal. In his message Clinton said HR 8 was "fiscally irresponsible," providing "a very expensive tax break for the best-off Americans while doing nothing for the vast majority of working families."

On Sept. 7 the House fell fourteen votes short of the two-thirds majority needed to overturn the veto. The vote was

274–157 in favor of the override with four members not voting. Thirteen Democrats who had voted for repeal in June voted against an override. Some said that although they believed the estate tax was too onerous, they had supported the initial bill only in the hope that it would lead to a compromise on something less than repeal.

Although a few Republicans held out hope for a possible compromise on the issue before the end of the session, Republican leaders left no doubt they were interested only in full repeal, especially because the Republican presidential nominee, Gov. George W. Bush of Texas, supported repeal.

Tax Cut Catchall Package

With their main tax proposals—a tax cut for married couples and repeal of the estate tax—stopped by presidential vetoes, Republicans in 2000 fell back on a package of other tax bills, many of which had garnered bipartisan support earlier in the year. But that bill died too in the lame-duck session although pieces of it were attached to other legislation and passed in the waning hours of the 106th Congress.

The package (HR 2614) included bills to:

• Increase tax incentives for retirement savings (HR 1102).

• Establish new tax breaks for investments in struggling urban and rural communities (HR 4923; S 3152).

• Increase the minimum wage by $1 an hour over two years and provide tax breaks to the retailers, restaurateurs, and others most likely to have to pay the increased wage (HR 833; HR 3081).

• Repeal a tax break for exporters that ran counter to World Trade Organization (WTO) rules.

For a time the retirement savings bill seemed a likely vehicle to carry the tax package. As passed by the House on July 19, HR 1102 increased contribution limits for tax-sheltered individual retirement accounts and tax-deferred 401(k) pension plans, expanded eligibility for IRAs, and made pensions more portable. The Senate Finance Committee approved an amended version Sept. 7 and gave the bill special protection from amendment in the Senate by making it the second of two budget reconciliation bills allowed under the fiscal 2001 budget resolution. *(Retirement savings bill, p. 119)*

By then House leaders were stressing the party's interest in debt reduction in the wake of Clinton's vetoes of their main tax bills, and they were hesitant to make retirement savings the exclusive focus of the second reconciliation bill. On Sept. 19 the House passed its own reconciliation bill (HR 5203) combining HR 1102 with a proposal to dedicate 90 percent of the fiscal 2001 budget surplus to debt reduction.

In late October with the fate of the tax measures dependent on resolving disagreements between Republicans and the White House on education and health care issues, GOP leaders decided to attach the tax package and the two-year minimum wage increase to HR 2614, which had already been passed by both chambers. Leaders also attached a plan to add about $30 billion over five years in reimbursements to some Medicare health providers and a bill that would have overturned an Oregon law permitting doctor-assisted suicide, two proposals that Clinton and many congressional Democrats opposed. Clinton also was disappointed that GOP leaders did not include a provision creating a new tax credit for school construction and repairs, which he had said was the price for any tax bill. Instead GOP leaders agreed to expand an existing school bond program to help in school construction, a plan that seemed to please hardly anyone. Clinton, congressional Democrats, and moderate Republicans said it would not do enough, while conservative Republicans said the issue should not have been addressed at all.

The House adopted the conference report on HR 2614 (H Rept 106-1004) on Oct. 26 by a vote of 237–174. In the Senate, however, where most Democrats were lined up against the bill and Democrat Ron Wyden of Oregon was filibustering to protest the assisted suicide provision, Senate Majority Leader Trent Lott, R-Miss., postponed consideration of the conference report until after the Nov. 7 election.

Instead the Senate passed a separate bill (HR 4986) to restructure taxes on income earned abroad in hopes of satisfying the WTO. House leaders resisted, hoping to use the tax code fix, a high priority for U.S. businesses, to drive the broader bill to enactment. When they finally relented Nov. 14, clearing the separate bill on foreign income, it signaled the death knell for the catchall bill, which did not come up again in the lame duck session. *(Overseas income, p. 118)*

Instead negotiators agreed on Dec. 11 to rescue the community renewal package from HR 2614 and add it to the conference report for the fiscal 2001 Labor, Health and Human Services, and Education appropriations bill (HR 4577), which became the omnibus spending bill for the year. In addition to the community renewal package, Clinton had appealed to GOP leaders to include the minimum wage increase and expansions of Medicaid, including a provision to let the parents of children with disabilities buy coverage (S 2774), in the omnibus spending measure. The congressional leaders in essence told Clinton to pick his favorite. "Republicans are willing to give him a sugar plum but not three sugar plums," a GOP leadership aide familiar with the talks said at the time. *(Omnibus spending bill, p. 81; community renewal, p. 564)*

Negotiators also added the compromise on school construction bonds to HR 4577 along with ten other, mostly technical tax provisions. A bill (HR 3594—PL 106-573), passed by the House on Dec. 14 and cleared by the Senate on Dec. 15, repealed a 1999 law (PL 106-170) that required business owners who sold their company in installments to pay all capital gains within the first year of the sale.

Increased tax incentives for retirement savings and an increase in the minimum wage were never enacted. Nor was the ban on Oregon's assisted-suicide law. *(Minimum wage, p. 579; assisted-suicide ban, p. 477)*

Corporate Income Earned Abroad

Under pressure from the White House and leaders of the nation's largest corporations to avert a trade war with Europe, Congress Nov. 14 cleared a measure (HR 4986—PL 106-519) to repeal a tax break for exporters. The World Trade Organization (WTO) had ruled that the tax break was an unfair subsidy and given the United States until Oct. 1, a deadline that it later extended, to correct the matter.

Failure to pass (HR 4986) would have allowed the European Union to retaliate by imposing tariffs worth about $4 billion on U.S. goods sold in Europe. Despite that threat and heavy lobbying by affected corporations, Congress nearly failed to clear the bill. Initially delayed in the Senate, the measure became a pawn in a House-led GOP effort to force President Clinton and congressional Democrats to accept a broad tax-cut bill. With future control of the White House still uncertain in the first weeks after the 2000 elections, interest in passing a multifaceted tax cut waned and Congress quickly finished action on HR 4986. *(Catchall tax bill, p. 117)*

THREAT OF TRADE WAR

The tax break that Congress repealed (PL 98-369) had been enacted in 1986. It allowed U.S. companies to set up subsidiaries, known as foreign sales corporations and usually located in tax havens such as the Virgin Islands or Barbados, to manage their export business. The law further exempted a portion of the earnings of these subsidiaries from U.S. income taxes so long as at least 50 percent of the components in the exports were made in the United States. The administration said that the tax break allowed about 7,100 U.S. exporters to shield from taxes a total of about $4 billion in earnings annually.

In 1999 a WTO panel agreed with a complaint lodged by the European Union that the tax breaks constituted an unfair government subsidy to certain U.S. exporters. On Feb. 24, 2000, a WTO appellate panel upheld that decision and gave the United States until Oct. 1 to comply with the ruling. If it did not, the European Union could announce the sanctions it planned to place on U.S. goods entering its fifteen-member nations.

HOUSE ACTION

The House Ways and Means Committee approved HR 4986 (H Rept 106-845) by a 34–1 vote on July 27. The measure, which had been drafted in collaboration with the Treasury Department, repealed the offending sections of the 1986 law and replaced them with a much broader exemption for all foreign-source income, both from exports and from goods manufactured abroad so long as a majority of the value of the product or service was derived from U.S. components or labor. The broader exemption was projected to cost the Treasury an additional $1.5 billion between 2001 and 2005.

After the bill was approved in committee but before it came to the floor Ways and Means Committee Chairman Bill Archer, R-Texas, restored a provision of existing law, cut in the original draft, that allowed companies with overseas sub-

sidiaries to claim a tax deduction on dividends from foreign subsidiaries. The prime beneficiary of that provision was Caterpillar Inc., the world's largest manufacturer of construction and mining equipment and one of the leading U.S. exporters.

The bill then came to the House floor on Sept. 13 under suspension of the rules, a procedure that prohibited floor amendments, limited debate, and required a two-thirds majority vote for passage. The vote on passage was 315–109. A handful of liberal Democrats criticized the measure as corporate welfare. At a minimum, they argued, the tax exemption should not apply to income earned overseas on tobacco sales or on U.S. drugs sold abroad at prices more than 5 percent below U.S. prices.

SENATE ACTION

The Senate Finance Committee approved its version of the bill (S Rept 106-416) by voice vote on Sept. 19 after deleting the Archer provision continuing tax deductions on dividends from foreign subsidiaries. Sen. Charles E. Grassley, R-Iowa, said the provision would further annoy the European Union, which had mentioned that particular provision in its complaint against the United States.

The Senate did not take up HR 4986 floor until Nov. 1 when it passed the measure. In the intervening weeks House Republican leaders decided to add the substance of the bill to a catchall package of tax cuts and policy initiatives (HR 2614) it was hoping to push through Congress at the end of the session. After the Senate passed HR 4986, the House refused to clear the measure, arguing that breaking it away from the catchall package would weaken the incentive for members to support the broader legislation.

When the muddled results of the 2000 elections failed to spur any interest in clearing the tax-cut package, GOP House leaders relented. The House agreed to the Senate version of HR 4986 on Nov. 14 by a vote of 316–72 clearing the measure, which President Clinton signed into law on Nov. 15.

It was unclear whether the new law would satisfy the European Union. When U.S. and European negotiators agreed in late September to move the deadline for U.S. compliance to Nov. 1, the European negotiators indicated displeasure with some aspects of HR 4986 including its provision limiting the tax exemption to goods that were at least 50 percent American-made.

Telephone Tax Repeal

Despite broad support from both parties legislation to repeal the 3 percent federal excise tax on telephones died in 2000 as the session came to a close. The tax, first enacted in 1898 to help finance the Spanish-American War, was widely regarded as archaic and regressive.

By an overwhelming vote of 420–2 the House on May 25 passed a measure (HR 3916—H Rept 106-631) that would phase out the levy over three years at an estimated cost in lost revenue of $19.9 billion. Democrats and Republicans alike said the tax was a burden on the poor that could widen the so-called digital divide and further limit access to the Internet by disadvantaged Americans.

The Senate Finance Committee approved an amended version of the bill (S Rept 106-328) on June 14 that would repeal the tax in full on all phone bills after Aug. 31, 2000, at an estimated cost of $24.2 billion.

The repeal was supported by telecommunications companies and small business and minority groups. But the White House was lukewarm to the idea, saying a repeal should not be put before other budget priorities such as shoring up Medicare and Social Security. The administration also said it wanted to see the entire Republican tax package for the year before deciding whether to accept any one piece.

Uncertain about the fate of their other tax proposals, GOP leaders folded the House version of the phone tax repeal into the conference report on the fiscal 2001 legislative branch appropriations measure (HR 4516—H Rept 106-796), to which the Treasury-Postal Service appropriations had already been added. The House then adopted the conference report Sept. 14, and, after first rejecting it, the Senate cleared HR 4516 on Oct. 12.

On Oct. 30 President Clinton vetoed the appropriations bill, saying he could not "in good conscience sign a bill that funds the operations of the Congress and the White House before funding our classrooms, fixing our schools, and protecting our workers." Clinton was referring to the collapse of negotiations on unrelated legislation to provide tax breaks for school construction and to implement proposed work safety rules aimed at reducing repetitive stress injuries. Although the legislative, Treasury, and Postal Service appropriations were eventually incorporated into an omnibus spending bill that Clinton did sign, that legislation did not include a repeal of the telephone excise tax. (*Omnibus spending bill, p. 81*)

The original 1 percent telephone tax had been imposed on long-distance service at a time when telephones were a luxury. Congress repealed it in 1902 but brought it back to help pay for World War I. The tax was repealed again in 1924 but resurrected in 1932 during the Great Depression. In 1941 the tax was extended to general local service to help pay for World War II. The levy was increased to 3 percent in 1982 and made permanent in 1990 as part of efforts to balance the federal budget.

Retirement Savings Tax Incentives

The House in 2000 twice passed legislation to increase tax incentives for retirement savings, but the measure got caught in a late-session tangle over a package of tax breaks and the Senate never acted on it. In 1999 President Clinton had vetoed a similar retirement savings package as part of the 1999 $792 billion tax cut package (HR 2488).

The measure that was marked up by the House Ways and Means Committee (HR 1102—H Rept 106-331, Pt. I)

had broad bipartisan support; half of its 181 cosponsors were Democrats. Despite the 1999 veto, lawmakers were interested in doing something to stimulate saving for retirement. According to the measure's chief sponsor, Rob Portman, R-Ohio, half of the national work force, or 70 million people, had no pension coverage. Congressional restrictions on pension plans had contributed to a decline in the number of businesses that offered traditional plans to 45,000 in 1997, down from 114,000 a decade earlier. Moreover, Congress had reduced tax benefits for retirement savings or held them unchanged in recent years as a means of increasing federal revenue.

As passed by the House July 19, by a vote of 401–25, HR 1102 would increase the annual contribution limit to a tax-free individual retirement account (IRA) from $2,000 to $5,000 by 2003, with an annual $500 increase in the limit after that. It would increase the annual limit on salary reduction contributions to tax-deferred 401(k) pension plans from $10,500 to $15,000 by 2005.

To help those close to retirement age and those, such as stay-at-home mothers who had been out of the workforce for any period of time, the bill included "catch-up" provisions. Those older than fifty could contribute an additional $5,000 each year to their IRAs beginning in 2001 and another $5,000 each year to their contribution to a 401(k) plan.

The bill would allow workers to take their pension benefits with them when changing jobs and allow workers to become vested in their pension plans in three years, rather than five permitted under existing law. The bill would cost the Treasury $16.1 billion in lost revenue over five years.

Charging that the bill did little to help low-income workers, Democrats offered an alternative adding to the core provisions of HR 1102 a refundable tax credit of up to 50 percent of annual contributions to an IRA or 401(k) plan, phased out for individuals with adjusted gross incomes above $80,000, plus tax relief for small businesses that set up pension plans. The House rejected that amendment on July 19 by a nearly party-line vote of 200–221. The House then passed HR 1102, 401–20.

The Senate Finance Committee on Sept. 7 unanimously approved a version of HR 1102 (S Rept 106-411) that closely paralleled the Democratic alternative in the House. To protect it from Senate amendment the committee also made HR 1102 the second of two budget reconciliation bills allowed under the fiscal 2001 budget resolution. The full Senate never acted on that measure, however. In late October it was incorporated into a tax package (HR 2614), which the House approved on Oct. 26, but which never came up in the Senate.

Meanwhile, by mid-September Clinton had vetoed the GOP's two main tax bills—a tax cut for married couples and elimination of the estate tax—and House leaders were stressing the party's interest in deficit reduction. On Sept. 19, the House passed its own reconciliation bill (HR 5203), which combined its version of HR 1102 with a proposal to dedicate 90 percent of the fiscal 2001 budget surplus to debt reduction. That bill never advanced in the Senate and died at the end of the session. (*Debt reduction, p. 85*)

Chronology of Action on Economic Policy: Financial Regulation

Introduction

Technological advancements and competitive pressures in the financial industry and booming economic times converged in President Bill Clinton's second term to allow modernization of the nation's banking laws. Reform had eluded Congress for years even in the face of wide agreement that the half-century-old U.S. financial institution laws were outdated. The legislation erased the legal barriers preventing banks from fully engaging in the securities and insurance businesses and was expected to change the face of the nation's financial services industry.

In separate action Congress modernized the Commodities Exchange Act to clarify the regulatory status of several new financial products that were traded on the world's commodities exchanges.

The nation's financial industry had been operating under a set of laws enacted in the wake of widespread bank failures during the Great Depression in the 1930s even though the financial world had changed dramatically since those days. With new computing and communications technology by the 1990s, businesses and consumers could use an array of devices such as automated teller machines, telephones, and computers to conduct much of their financial business at electronic speed. The ability to move money electronically broke down international investment borders as well as the boundaries between different types of financial institutions.

Companies began to offer hybrid products—such as mutual funds with check-writing options or savings accounts that resembled insurance annuities—that did not fit well into the old definitions of banking. The movement of money also changed the competitive dynamics among different types of financial institutions. As more money flowed out of banks and into mutual funds and other investments, bank holding companies began offering services such as limited insurance policies to retain their share of the financial marketplace.

Securities firms expanded by offering banking services such as checking accounts. Insurance companies laid the groundwork to set up thrift associations, thereby competing

for savings accounts. And commercial giants such as General Electric offered credit cards and brokerage services.

Although it was widely acknowledged that the banking laws were outmoded, efforts to rewrite them in 1988 and 1991 failed. Different sectors of the financial industry profoundly disagreed over the shape of new regulations. Moreover, Congress and the financial world were still dealing with the aftermath of the 1980s financial debacle in which thousands of savings and loan associations went broke, requiring a multibillion dollar government bailout. Few in government, or out, had the political stamina to tackle a major overhaul of the entire financial industry. (*S&L failures, Congress and the Nation Vol. VII, p. 120*)

When President Clinton began his first term in 1993, the experiences of past failures to rewrite the financial services laws were fresh in the minds of lawmakers, administration officials, and industry groups alike. Although the economy was beginning to rebound from the 1990–1991 recession there was little urgency within the industry or Congress to

REFERENCES

Discussion of financial regulation legislation for the years 1945–1964 may be found in *Congress and the Nation Vol. I*, pp. 337–386; for the years 1965–1968, *Congress and the Nation Vol. II*, pp. 253–279; for the years 1969–1972, *Congress and the Nation Vol. III*, pp. 135–145; for the years 1973–1976, *Congress and the Nation Vol. IV*, pp. 107–117; for the years 1977–1980, *Congress and the Nation Vol. V*, pp. 253–265; for the years 1981–1984, *Congress and the Nation Vol. VI*, pp. 83–93; for the years 1985–1988, *Congress and the Nation Vol. VII*, pp. 109–136; for the years 1989–1992, *Congress and the Nation Vol. VIII*, pp. 113–161; for the years 1993–1996, *Congress and the Nation Vol. IX*, pp. 109–148.

tackle the difficult problem of rationalizing an obsolete regulatory system.

CHANGING MOMENTUM

The momentum began to change, albeit slowly, after Republicans took control of Congress in 1995. Rep. Jim Leach, R-Iowa, the new chairman of the House Banking Committee, began to push for legislation that would allow banks to offer a full range of financial services. Although that effort initially failed, he persisted and the House in 1998 passed an overhaul bill for the first time, only to see it die in the Senate.

When the 106th Congress convened in January 1999, the dynamics both in Congress and in the industry had shifted in favor of the legislation. Even though lenient regulators had blurred lines separating financial services, many elements of the industry were still chafing under remaining restraints and legal uncertainties that prevented them from taking full advantage of opportunities. Large banks, for example, wanted to merge with brokerages and insurance companies to better compete with overseas financial conglomerates in world markets. Industry lobbyists also had reached agreement on many issues that previously divided them. Thus many powerful industry forces began to work for passage of the legislation rather than against it. *(Earlier reform attempts, box, p. 124)*

But the most significant change may have been the elevation of Sen. Phil Gramm, R-Texas, from a relatively obscure member of Congress to chairman of the Senate Banking Committee. Gramm had filibustered the House bill to death in 1998. In 1999 he shepherded a bill through the Senate by early May. Although his measure differed substantially from the version passed by the House in July and drew repeated veto threats from the president, Gramm never walked away from the table. In the end, and under pressure from his own leadership and the industry, he made the concessions necessary to win final passage and White House approval.

PRIVACY PROTECTION, BANKRUPTCY PROTECTION

A side issue that nearly derailed the financial services overhaul and that was likely to plague future Congresses was protection of consumer privacy. This was a central issue not only in the financial services industry but in numerous other legislative arenas, including rapidly expanding use of the Internet and access to medical records. Consumer groups and their congressional allies had long wanted to curtail companies' ability to sell or trade customer data. Pointing to technology's potential intrusiveness consumer groups argued that limitations were necessary to prevent the abuse and misuse of personal information. But businesses warned that their ability to cross-market their products, detect fraud, and perform routine transactions would be hurt by restrictions on information-sharing.

A push in the House to add privacy protection to the bank overhaul bill gained impetus early in 1999 when the head of U.S. Bankcorp defended his company's practice of selling information about customers' account balances, telephone numbers, addresses, and credit card purchases to an outside marketing firm by saying that such sales were "an industry-wide practice." Consumer groups pointed to that admission and other incidents to force the financial industry to accept language in the overhaul bill that required banks to disclose their information-sharing policies with customers and give consumers the right to opt out of the practice with unaffiliated third parties. Consumer advocates said that language did not go far enough and promised that they would continue to push for stiffer restrictions.

Another volatile issue certain to haunt future Congresses was revision of the country's personal bankruptcy laws. Unrelenting pressure from credit card companies and other creditors and a widespread impression that the system was being abused led to passage of a measure making it more difficult for people to declare bankruptcy and avoid paying their debts even when they could afford to do so. The number of bankruptcy filings had jumped from under 300,000 a year in the mid-1980s to about 1.4 million in 1997. President Clinton pocket-vetoed that measure at the end of 2000, however, and it did not become law during his time in office.

Although the legislation passed with bipartisan support, liberal Democrats and consumer groups opposed it because they said it was too weighted toward creditors. They argued that credit card companies deserved much of the blame for the increase in personal bankruptcy filings, because they granted too much credit to unqualified customers and enticed others to buy more goods and services on credit than they could afford. In his veto message, Clinton indicated that he agreed with this view. But he specifically objected to a provision that would allow well-off debtors to hide their wealth in expensive homes.

1997–1998

For the first time the House voted to pass legislation repealing decades-old laws that prevented banks, securities firms, and insurance companies from merging. But a filibuster in the Senate forced the GOP leadership there to pull the legislation from floor consideration. Nonetheless, the House action renewed hopes that Congress might, after many failed attempts, be close to approving the measure long-sought by the financial services industry.

In other action, Congress began to debate legislation seeking to reduce the large number of personal bankruptcy cases filed in the United States. The measure was derailed in 1998 by disagreements between the White House and the credit industry but it appeared likely that Congress would resume deliberations in the 106th Congress. Lawmakers passed a number of less extensive measures dealing with banks and other financial services, including one that would allow credit unions to expand.

Financial Services Modernization

Despite an unprecedented agreement between the banking and insurance industries, Congress was once again unable to clear legislation to overhaul the financial services industry. The bill (HR 10) would have revised the 1933 Glass-Steagall Act and other laws that separated the banking, insurance, and securities industries.

As passed by the House and approved by the Senate Banking, Housing and Urban Affairs Committee, the measure removed restrictions on affiliations between the three financial services industries and allowed the creation of financial holding companies through which banks could underwrite and sell insurance and securities, and insurance companies and brokerage houses could acquire banks.

Strongly supported by securities and insurance groups, the House legislation was largely opposed by banks that were already offering many securities and insurance services under court and regulatory decisions. The bill passed in May 1998 by a single vote and only after House Speaker Newt Gingrich, R-Ga., pressured a handful of Republicans to vote "aye." It was the first time that the House had passed an overhaul of the Glass-Steagall Act.

Senate consideration of the bill quickly bogged down as conservative Republicans led by Phil Gramm, R-Texas, fought the bill's Community Reinvestment Act requirements. Failure to resolve that issue effectively killed the bill for the 105th Congress. But even had a compromise been reached other serious disagreements—within and among the various interest groups, between the financial industry and consumer groups, and between federal regulators—remained.

BACKGROUND

The Glass-Steagall Act, enacted in the midst of the Great Depression, was intended to stabilize the banking industry after widespread bank failures and to prevent similar failures in the future. It erected barriers between the banking and securities industries, and the 1956 Bank Holding Company Act imposed barriers between banking and insurance activities.

In the succeeding decades, innovations both in technology and in the types of financial products offered began to blur these barriers, and a series of rulings by courts and federal regulators further muddied the waters. (Key rulings, p. 123)

All sides generally agreed that the Glass-Steagall Act was outmoded and that banks, insurance companies, and securities firms should have the right to enter each others' business, with appropriate safeguards for the deposit insurance system. The central question—the extent to which banks, securities firms, and insurance companies should be able to affiliate with each other and with commercial firms—invited intense controversy, however.

Industry divisions had caused the demise of several previous attempts by Congress to deal with the situation. Democrats tried but failed to muster a consensus for change in 1988 and 1991. (Congress and the Nation Vol. VII, p. 114; Vol. VIII p. 136)

The Republican-led 104th Congress in 1995–1996 did no better despite determined efforts by Jim Leach, R-Iowa, in his first term as chairman of the House Banking Committee. Leach struggled for more than a year to bring an ambitious rewrite of banking law to the House floor, repeatedly redrafting a bill in his search for a legislative mix that would suit various industry groups in the financial services sector. (Congress and the Nation Vol. IX, p. 133)

But the redrafts did not sufficiently ease the opposition from banks, which objected to language curbing the ability of federal regulators to expand bank powers to sell certain insurance products. In March 1996 the Supreme Court confirmed the ability of national banks to sell insurance from small towns without interference from state regulators, a ruling that gave banks what they wanted without having to seek approval from Congress.

Also bedeviling Leach's efforts was the indifference of Senate Banking Chairman Alfonse M. D'Amato, R-N.Y. Publicly, D'Amato said he would mark up a bill once the House acted. But he was confident that Leach would fail and made no preparations to act. D'Amato's inaction reinforced the belief among House leaders that the bill had no chance to become law, which made them were reluctant to require members to cast politically uncomfortable votes.

Nor did the Clinton administration display any interest in advancing the bill. And, roiling the waters, the Comptroller of the Currency waged a behind-the-scenes war against the measure, which would have shifted some regulatory authority from his agency to the Federal Reserve.

After the legislation stalled in 1996, regulators issued new rulings that further strengthened the market position of

KEY RULINGS EXPANDED BANK POWERS

With Congress deadlocked for years over banking legislation, regulators and judges stepped into the breach with a series of decisions that expanded the reach of banks—sometimes over the objections of insurers and securities firms. Following is a summary of major regulatory and court decisions affecting the banking industry since 1986:

1986. The Office of the Comptroller of the Currency issued a letter permitting banks to sell insurance nationwide. The comptroller based the decision on a provision of the National Bank Act of 1916 that authorized national banks located in towns of 5,000 or fewer residents to sell insurance.

However, the 1916 provision did not explicitly state whether banks could sell insurance outside those small towns, a subject that had been the subject of considerable debate. For years before the comptroller acted national banks had been restricted to selling insurance in small towns and surrounding rural areas where insurance might not be readily available.

1987. The Federal Reserve authorized bank holding companies to engage in limited securities activities. It allowed the companies' subsidiaries to receive up to 5 percent of their gross revenue from underwriting and dealing in securities such as commercial paper and municipal revenue bonds.

1989. The Federal Reserve expanded the activities of the bank holding company subsidiaries, allowing them to derive up to 10 percent of their revenues from securities underwriting. Large bank holding companies were permitted to engage in longer-term corporate debt securities.

1991. The Federal Reserve authorized foreign banks to underwrite securities in the United States directly through subsidiaries instead of through a subsidiary of a holding company as required of domestic banks.

1993. Upholding the interpretation of the Comptroller of the Currency, a federal judge in Washington, D.C., ruled in a case brought by the Independent Insurance Agents of America that banks could indeed sell insurance from towns of 5,000 or fewer residents. The insurance agents decided not to appeal the decision to the Supreme Court, but the issue continued to spawn various legal and regulatory disputes.

1995. Amid debate over whether certain products should be defined as insurance or banking, the Supreme Court ruled that annuities were a banking product and could be sold by banks. Insurers had contended that annuities involved the pooling of risk and therefore should be regulated as insurance products.

1996. In a landmark decision, *Barnett Bank v. Nelson,* the Supreme Court ruled that banks could sell insurance from offices in small towns, even in states that had laws prohibiting such sales. The ruling overrode a Florida law barring affiliations between banks and insurance agents.

In separate action in 1996, the Federal Reserve issued a series of rulings greatly expanding the ability of bank holding companies to underwrite securities. It increased the amount of gross revenues that a bank subsidiary would derive from securities activities to 25 percent from 10 percent. It also eased "prudential limitations," or firewalls, between bank holding companies and their bank and securities subsidiaries, allowing bank directors, officers, or employees to serve on the board of the securities subsidiary so long as they did not constitute a majority. The rulings cleared the way for bank holding companies to acquire major securities firms in a series of takeovers.

banks. Particularly important was a Federal Reserve Board rule easing restrictions on the securities activities of banking companies. That set the stage for a major merger, announced in early 1997, between Bankers Trust New York Corp., the seventh-largest U.S. banking company, and Alex Brown Inc., a major regional brokerage based in Baltimore. The planned merger was the biggest breach of the Glass-Steagall walls to date.

ADMINISTRATION PROPOSAL

With the financial services industry showing little interest in overhaul legislation, the Treasury Department issued a long-awaited proposal in June 1997 that sent some of the most contentious issues to Congress. Under the plan, banking companies would be allowed to engage in a full range of insurance and securities underwriting and sales activities, either as subsidiaries of a bank or as affiliates within a holding company. Insurance companies and agents immediately opposed that provision, claiming it gave too much control to federal regulators at the expense of state insurance regulators. (Insurance products had traditionally been regulated at the state level.)

On the controversial issue of mergers between banks and commercial companies, Treasury offered two options. The first option allowed a limited portion of a bank holding company's revenues to come from nonfinancial activities. The administration backed away from that option after consumer groups, labor unions, and small banks said it would lead to a dangerous concentration of financial power and make it more difficult for average citizens to get loans.

The other Treasury option blocked any commercial activities by banking companies although such activities could be carried out through a special class of thrift affiliates that could only accept deposits of $100,000 or more and would not carry deposit insurance. But in a politically nettlesome requirement these "wholesale" financial institutions would be subject to the Community Reinvestment Act, which pressured banks to lend in underserved communities.

EARLIER FINANCIAL SERVICES REFORM ATTEMPTS

The Glass-Steagall Act of 1933 separated the commercial and savings bank industries from investment banking and prohibited banks from underwriting or selling securities. After enactment support grew for regulation of bank holding companies to prevent bank monopolies. President Franklin D. Roosevelt requested such legislation in 1938 and bills to regulate holding companies were introduced in nearly every Congress until the Bank Holding Company Act of 1956 (PL 84-511) became law.

The law defined holding companies as those with at least a 25 percent share of two or more banks. It limited their activity to the ownership and management of banks and prevented them from controlling assets in nonbanking enterprises including insurance. Certain companies were exempt, however, including one-bank holding companies, some long-term investment trusts, and certain registered investment companies.

Between 1965 and 1996 Congress tried repeatedly and, for the most part unsuccessfully, to amend the two laws. Following are summaries of the legislative efforts to relax the banking restrictions contained in the 1933 and 1956 laws:

1965–1966. The House passed legislation in 1965 that sought to eliminate virtually all exemptions from the 1956 law including its exemption for one-bank holding companies. The bill was signed in 1966 (PL 89-485), but by then it contained Senate-passed provisions to restore many exemptions including the one for one-bank holding companies.

1969–1970. At President Richard Nixon's request the House in 1969 and the Senate in 1970 passed a measure (PL 91-607) to extend the 1956 law to one-bank holding companies.

1978. Amendments to the 1956 law to allow bank holding companies to engage in limited insurance activities were included in an omnibus financial services bill. But the House failed to complete work on the holding company provisions before the bill became law (PL 95-630).

1980. The House passed a bill to restrict certain bank holding companies from acting as insurance agents. Similar legislation never reached the Senate floor. Congress did clear legislation (PL 96-221) that removed most federal regulatory distinctions between commercial banks and savings and loans. The measure permitted the financial institutions to diversify the services they offered, gradually lifted the interest rate ceilings that prevented financial institutions from paying the going market rate on savings deposits, and dismantled federal regulations that had locked banks and thrifts into limited loan portfolios and kept them from competing effectively with high-yielding investment opportunities such as money market funds.

1983. President Ronald Reagan proposed that banks be permitted to engage in securities, insurance, and real estate activities. But legislators had little incentive to act because it was widely believed that a repeal of Glass-Steagall would adversely affect constituents in every congressional district.

1984. Legislation was introduced in the House to close loopholes in the 1956 law including requiring banks to divest themselves of their nonbanking activities within two years, but it never reached the floor. The Senate passed legislation to allow bank holding companies to form subsidiaries to underwrite mortgage-backed securities and municipal bonds.

1987. A law to bail out the Federal Savings and Loan Insurance Corporation (PL 100-86) also amended the 1956 law to close loopholes in nonbanking activities through which some retailers and financial houses had opened limited banking operations.

1988. The Senate passed a bill to repeal portions of the Glass-Steagall Act to allow banks to engage in securities dealings while restricting insurance activities. Two House committees approved a similar bill but could not compromise on jurisdiction issues.

1991. The House rejected a bill to repeal parts of Glass-Steagall and to allow banks to open branch offices nationwide. The Senate passed a bill overhauling the deposit insurance system only after the Glass-Steagall language was stripped on the floor.

1995–1996. A bill to deregulate the financial services industry, including Glass-Steagall changes, failed to reach the House floor in 1995 after opposition from banks and others persuaded leaders to shelve it. The bill was redrafted several times in 1996, but banks continued to oppose it because it included restrictions on selling insurance. Bill sponsors lost hope after it became clear that House leaders would not allow floor action.

HOUSE ACTION

Congressional action in 1997 began in the House Banking and Financial Services Committee where Chairman Leach again took the lead in pushing overhaul legislation. After a four-day markup the committee on June 20 approved HR 10 (H Rept 105-164, Pts. I and II) by just two votes, 28–26.

The measure was nearly scuttled several times by opposition from one special interest or another. Leach attested to the contentiousness of the debate when he said that he might not vote for the bill because of amendments added in committee, over his objections, that would allow banks and commercial companies to affiliate. Supporters of the amendments said such cross-ownership was necessary to allow financial institutions to be competitive. Leach and other opponents contended that such affiliations would allow a small number of companies to dominate financial services markets. They also argued that it could create conflicts of interest, with banks providing credit to commercial affiliates regardless of their soundness.

The Banking Committee shared jurisdiction over financial regulation with the House Commerce Committee, which faced a similarly complex jigsaw puzzle of competing interests. The committee repeatedly postponed action on the measure while its leaders struggled to find enough support to move the bill forward. The Commerce Committee eventually approved its version of HR 10 (H Rept 105-164, Pt. III) on Oct. 30, 1997, by a surprisingly wide margin, 33–11.

After the Commerce Committee finished its work, Republican Conference Chairman John A. Boehner, R-Ohio, brought together senior Democrats and Republicans on the Banking, Commerce, and Rules Committees to try to move a consensus version of the bill through the Rules Committee. But the versions passed by the two House committees clashed over basic issues. In addition to taking different approaches on allowing partial mergers between financial firms and commercial companies, the two versions differed on the extent to which bank sales of insurance and securities would be regulated and on elimination of the federal thrift charter.

Rules Committee Chairman Gerald B. H. Solomon, R-N.Y., and senior Commerce Committee Democrat John D. Dingell, Mich., both of whom were close to insurance interests, pressed for strict limits on bank sales of insurance—a position opposed by Leach and other bank allies on the Banking Committee. Commerce Committee members also supported efforts to step up regulations on bank sales of securities, despite objection from Banking Committee members.

Talks collapsed shortly before the end of the session when Commerce Committee members failed to attend a scheduled meeting. House leaders vowed to continue pressing for consensus early in 1998.

The legislation gained new impetus in early March 1998 when House GOP leaders announced a compromise between the two committee versions. The compromise generally kept large commercial conglomerates out of the banking business. Consumer organizations argued that such "merchant banks" on a broad scale could limit credit only to those companies in which they owned a stake, limiting the growth of competitors if the number of traditional financial institutions dwindled significantly. Most of the world's developed countries have such merchant banking systems.

The compromise allowed firms to establish financial holding companies to acquire banks but only 15 percent of the companies' annual gross revenues could come from commercial holdings. That provision was expected to allow securities and insurance firms to buy banks but to bar most commercial firms from the field. Banks could establish holding companies to buy securities and insurance firms but their commercial activity could not exceed 5 percent of the holding company's consolidated annual gross revenue.

In addition, the bill would shut down the unitary thrift charter. The charter allowed commercial companies to acquire a single savings institution, which banks said amounted to allowing commercial firms to own banks. "There is nothing to prevent GE . . . from buying one of the largest regional banks and running it as a thrift," said a representative of the American Bankers Association.

Securities and insurance groups generally supported the compromise, as did a few large banks, such as BancOne and NationsBank, who said the measure would improve their ability to compete with foreign banks. Most banks and bank associations opposed the measure although not always for the same reasons, and the thrift industry was also opposed. Both sides brought strong lobbying campaigns to bear on House members.

In an effort to drum up support for the bill GOP House leaders added a popular bill (HR 1151) reversing a February Supreme Court decision that stopped credit unions from expanding their membership. Leaders also tinkered with the thrift provisions to appease savings and loans and they agreed to allow some amendments from the floor.

But when they tried to bring HR 10 to the floor March 31, they met a phalanx of opposition from Republicans and Democrats alike, who expressed everything from technical concerns about the legislation to fears that the bill would lead to too much or too little industry consolidation. Members were also angered by the decision to combine HR 10 and the credit union bill. Leaders decided to pull HR 10 from the floor and allow the credit union bill to be considered on its own. It passed quickly on April 1 with only eight dissenting votes. *(Credit union bill, p. 128)*

HR 10 still faced uncertain prospects when it came back to the House floor on May 13, 1998. By large margins, the House rejected two amendments, dealing with the structure and regulation of financial firms, that leaders had said would kill the bill. The House did adopt, 229–193, an amendment by Leach and two others to prevent financial holding companies from owning commercial businesses.

In a suspenseful moment, the House then passed HR 10 but only by a single vote and only after House Speaker Newt Gingrich, R-Ga., prevailed on a half dozen members either to vote "aye" or to change their vote from "nay" to "aye." Both parties were fractured by the **key vote of 214–213 (R 153–73, D 61–139, I 0–1)**, with Republicans supporting it by a margin of about two-to-one and Democrats opposing it by about the same margin. *(1998 key votes, p. 883)*

The slim success prompted many opponents to label it a "hollow victory" because Senate Banking Committee Chairman D'Amato had pledged to take financial reform up only if it received broad bipartisan support in the House. Boehner disagreed. "Given the House's history of refusing to even bring such bills to the floor" in the past, he said, "a one-vote victory looks like a landslide."

SENATE ACTION

Despite skepticism that the vote would spur Senate action on the bill, D'Amato, who was facing a tough reelection battle in 1998 that he would eventually lose, decided to move ahead on HR 10. D'Amato was prepared to begin markup of his version of HR 10 on Sept. 3 but postponed the meeting after Republican Sen. Phil Gramm of Texas insisted on an amendment removing provisions that would apply the 1977 Community Reinvestment Act (CRA) to the new financial giants that would be created under HR 10. The CRA required federal regulators to take into account a bank's lending record to all segments of its community when determining whether to approve an application for a new branch, merger, or other endeavor.

Gramm and his allies on the issue had long complained that the reinvestment requirements amounted to legalized extortion. Most Democrats argued, however, that the reinvestment act was key to ensuring that minority communities had access to financial services.

D'Amato rescheduled the markup for Sept. 11 after committee members reached a compromise on the issue. Gramm did not support the compromise but decided against trying to amend the compromise when it became clear that even ardent opponents of reinvestment would vote against him to keep the bill alive. The committee then approved its version of HR 10 (S Rept 105-336) by a vote of 16–2.

But the measure did not advance any further. Gramm and his supporters first delayed floor action on the bill and they then slowed Senate debate to a crawl. With little time remaining in the session, and several unresolved issues remaining in addition to the reinvestment law controversy, Senate Majority Leader Trent Lott, R-Miss., pulled the measure from the floor. *(1999 action, p. 130)*

Bankruptcy Overhaul

Banks and other creditors began a formidable lobbying campaign in 1997 aimed at revamping federal personal bankruptcy laws and making it more difficult for consumers to walk away from their debts. The effort was derailed, at least temporarily, in 1998 when GOP congressional leaders were unable to find a compromise that would satisfy Senate Democrats and the Clinton administration, on one side, and the creditors who sought the legislation, on the other.

BACKGROUND

The increased attention was the result of the skyrocketing rate of bankruptcies across the country. A record 1.4 million Americans were expected to declare bankruptcy in 1997—more than double the number of a decade earlier—leaving unpaid bills worth more than $40 billion. Lenders said the write-offs were costing the average household more than $400 a year in the form of higher interest rates and merchandise prices.

No one could pinpoint the precise reason for the increase in bankruptcies, although analysts pointed to increased consumer lending, a reduction in the public stigma attached to bankruptcy, job insecurity, the growth of legalized gambling, and aggressive advertising by bankruptcy lawyers. In addition,

a substantial portion of consumer bankruptcies—one in five, by some estimates—were declared by small-business owners who lost their savings when their companies foundered.

Whatever the causes, the delinquency rate had reached more than one bankruptcy for every 100 households, and both creditors and taxpayers were beginning to feel the pinch. Creditors warned that the billions of dollars in losses were forcing them to tighten their lending policies and raise their interest rates. Bank credit card companies were bracing for about $10 billion in bankruptcy-related losses in 1997, according to a spokesperson for Visa U.S.A. Credit unions, diversified financial companies such as American Express, and retailers that sold on credit were also losing billions.

Annual consumer debt topped $1 trillion in 1997 (although a portion of that included credit card balances that were paid off in full every month) and the economy had become so oriented toward credit that certain transactions, such as renting a car or reserving a hotel room, were difficult to conduct without a credit card.

A coalition of banks, credit card companies, retailers, and other lenders blamed the surge in bankruptcies on laws that made it easy to file for bankruptcy, coupled with a relaxed societal attitude toward financial delinquency. They pressed Congress to tighten the bankruptcy code so that people who had money could not escape their debts, steps lenders said might enable them to recover several billion dollars each year. Topping the list of lobbyists working on their behalf were former Democratic Sen. Lloyd Bentsen of Texas, who had served as chairman of the Senate Finance Committee and President Clinton's first Treasury secretary, and Haley Barbour of Mississippi, former head of the Republican National Committee.

On the other side, bankruptcy lawyers and many consumer groups generally defended existing bankruptcy law, saying the chief problem was the reckless marketing of credit. They denounced credit card companies for mailing as many as 2.8 billion solicitations a year to potential cardholders and they warned that the proposed bankruptcy changes amounted to "the next step before debtors' prison."

NATIONAL COMMISSION

The debate on the issue kicked off Oct. 20, 1997, when the National Bankruptcy Review Commission, created by Congress in 1994 to recommend changes to the bankruptcy code, presented its findings. The nine-member panel presented a list of 172 relatively modest recommendations. It did not take up the issue of requiring consumers with money to repay their debts. *(Congress and the Nation Vol. IX, p. 347)*

The commission, which split 5–4 on some issues, recommended that the federal government adopt uniform exemptions for assets in bankruptcy cases to prevent debtors from targeting a state and sinking thousands of dollars into a protected asset, such as a house or a racehorse. The commission also recommended a bar on "reaffirmations" of certain kinds of debt, in effect prohibiting lenders from working with a borrower outside the bankruptcy process to recover assets. It said debtors should be limited to no more than two bankruptcy filings every six years to prevent debtors from repeatedly filing to evade debt. It also proposed that student loans be treated as dischargeable debts similar to any other loan.

CONGRESSIONAL ACTION

Bipartisan majorities in both the House and Senate were in favor of doing something to stem a record number of personal bankruptcies, but Republicans and a number of moderate Democrats argued that debtors who could afford it should be required to pay back their debts. More liberal Democrats said that the real problem lay with banks and other lenders that aggressively and recklessly marketed credit cards. An oft-repeated example during debate were ATM machines conveniently located in or near gambling casinos.

Prospects for the bankruptcy overhaul looked uncertain from the outset because the main provisions in the Senate and House bills differed substantially.

The Senate bill (S 1301—S Rept 105-253), sponsored by Charles E. Grassley, R-Iowa, tweaked the existing system to give bankruptcy judges another reason to move a debtor from Chapter 7, which absolves any debt remaining after liquidation of the debtor's nonessential assets, into Chapter 13, which restructures debt so that the debtor can pay off bills in three to five years. Under the bill, a debtor's ability to pay 30 percent or more of unsecured debts, such as credit card balances, would constitute a reason to move a case to Chapter 13. The Senate passed its version Sept. 23, 1997, on a vote of 97–1.

The House passed its bill (HR 3150—H Rept 105-540, Pts. I-IV) June 10, on a vote of 306–118. Sponsored by George W. Gekas, R-Pa., HR 3150 set up a stricter system for determining who could file for Chapter 7 protection. Under that bill, a person who earned the median income or more—about $51,000 for a family of four—and could pay off at least 20 percent of unsecured debt would be precluded from Chapter 7 protection. Such debtors would have to file under Chapter 13 or work out their debts privately.

Grassley, Gekas, and other Republicans reached a compromise requiring debtors to file under Chapter 13 if they had an above-median income and could pay off at least 25 percent of their unsecured loans over five years. The House easily passed the conference report (H Rept 105-794), 300–125 on Oct. 9. But Democrats, including Sen. Richard J. Durbin of Illinois, a cosponsor of the original bill, said they had been left out of the decision making and opposed the conference report. Durbin was particularly angry with a conference decision to delete several of his consumer protection amendments that had been adopted on the Senate floor. After the Clinton administration made it clear the president would veto the conference version of HR 3150 the Senate took no further action on the bill and it died at the end of session.

Republicans then tried to find a place for the measure in the omnibus spending bill (HR 4328—PL 105-277), generally regarded as must-pass legislation. But that effort died when the Clinton administration insisted on changes to the means test that creditors said they could not accept. *(2000 action, p. 142)*

MAJOR ISSUES

Philosophical and political differences over bankruptcy overhaul became apparent as soon as the House and Senate Judiciary committees began considering the issue. Most Republicans and moderate Democrats agreed that Chapter 7 of the bankruptcy code, which allowed people to walk away from most unsecured debts, should be available only to those who truly could not pay their bills. They argued that the ease and benefits of declaring bankruptcy had worn away the stigma that used to be attached to filing for bankruptcy. With a quick trip to bankruptcy court, they said, a person could erase quantities of credit card debt, leaving creditors and other consumers to pick up the tab. The solution, Gekas, Grassley, and others argued, was to make bankruptcy less attractive and to establish safeguards to prevent abuses of the system.

But liberal Democrats argued that credit card companies should also be held responsible for the surge in personal bankruptcy filings because of their aggressive marketing techniques and reckless lending practices. Some Democrats also objected to the Republican-sponsored means tests, because they would not allow judges to take individual situations into account when determining whether a person could file under Chapter 7 or not. For example, they said, many people entered bankruptcy reluctantly, pushed there by illness, job loss, or divorce. Although both chambers eased their respective means test before passing their bills, Democrats said the bills still did not go far enough.

Another major point of contention concerned the amount of home equity that bankruptcy filers could shield from creditors. Most states capped such exemptions at $40,000 but five states had no cap at all. Two of the states, Florida and Texas, had reputations as havens for well-heeled debtors who moved to the state, bought a mansion, and then filed for bankruptcy, knowing their investment was safe from creditors.

The Senate version capped the homestead exemption at $100,000. A similar provision was added in the House Judiciary Committee before it approved the bill, 18–10, May 14 in a largely party-line vote. During floor debate on the bill June 10, the House adopted, 222–204, an amendment by Gekas that eliminated the $100,000 cap. Instead, it required filers to have lived in a state for a year before the new state's home exemption would apply. If a debtor declared bankruptcy before meeting the residency requirement, the homestead exemption from the former state would apply.

Republicans left Democrats out of the final negotiations on the conference agreement, which struck a middle ground between the more stringent and rigid means testing requirements in the House version and the broader discretion given to judges in the Senate version. Similar to the House version, the conference agreement did not cap the homestead exemption but it did lengthen to two years the period that a resident would have to live in a state before claiming the exemption.

But Senate Democrats were miffed about being left out of the final negotiations. Durbin, a sponsor of the original Senate bill who grew increasingly uneasy with the measure at each stage of the legislative process, was particularly disturbed that Republican conferees had dropped several of the debtor protections he had added during Senate floor consideration.

Credit Union Expansion

President Clinton on Aug. 7, 1998, signed into law a bill (HR 1151—PL 105-219) to allow credit unions to continue expanding their membership bases. The legislation effectively overturned a Supreme Court decision on Feb. 25 holding that credit unions and their federal overseer, the National Credit Union Administration, had overstepped legal bounds in seeking new members who did not have a common employer, organization, or geographic ties to the chartering organization.

Credit unions organized a grassroots campaign to persuade Congress to overturn the Court ruling, warning that it would force 20 million people out of credit unions. The nation's 11,500 credit unions enrolled about 70 million members. As introduced, the legislation had broad bipartisan support in the House. Both House Speaker Newt Gingrich, R-Ga., and Minority Whip David E. Bonior, D-Mich., signed onto the original version.

But banks vigorously opposed the bill. The industry said it would not try to force credit unions to expel existing members but argued that continued expansion was unfair because credit unions enjoyed a nonprofit and tax-exempt status that gave them a competitive advantage over banks when it came to interest rates on loans and savings accounts. Credit unions countered that their members paid taxes and that, unlike banks, credit unions were run to benefit their members, not investors.

The credit unions eventually won the argument. The final version of the legislation allowed credit unions to continue accepting members from an unrelated group as long as the number of potential members in that group was fewer than 3,000.

The House Banking Committee approved HR 1151 (H Rept 105-472) March 26 by voice vote. As a sop to the banks, the House Banking and Financial Services Committee added a provision that would have made credit unions subject to provisions similar to those in the 1977 Community Reinvestment Act (PL 95-128), which required banks to make loans to low-income and minority neighborhoods in their communities. Banks that did not make such loans stood to be rejected when applying to federal regulators for a merger, new branch, or other endeavor requiring federal approval.

The House passed HR 1151 April 4 by a 411–8 vote under suspension of the rules after House Republican leaders were forced to decouple it from a broader bill (HR 10) to overhaul regulation of the nation's financial institutions.

The Senate Banking, Housing and Urban Affairs Committee approved HR 1151 (S Rept 105-193) on April 30. When the bill reached the Senate floor on July 28, Phil Gramm, R-Texas, a vehement opponent of the 1977 reinvestment law, sought to remove the provision applying it to credit unions. A motion to table (kill) Gramm's amendment was rejected, 44–50, and the Senate then adopted the Gramm amendment by voice vote.

The Senate did table another amendment that had drawn a veto threat from President Clinton. Offered by Richard C. Shelby, R-Ala., the amendment would have lifted the community reinvestment requirements on banks with less than $250 million in assets. The Senate tabled the amendment 59–39. Controversy over the Community Reinvestment Act was a major factor in killing legislation overhauling regulation of the nation's financial institutions. (*Financial overhaul, p. 122*)

Once the Shelby amendment was killed the Senate easily passed the bill, 92–6. Despite some Democratic objections, the House approved the Senate version of the bill by voice vote on Aug. 4. President Clinton signed the legislation on Aug. 7.

Securities Fraud Lawsuits

Congress cleared a measure (S 1260—PL 105-353) Oct. 13, 1998, that was intended to cut down on class-action lawsuits against companies whose earnings did not meet expectations. The measure closed a loophole in a 1995 law (PL 104-67) that was aimed at stemming what sponsors believed to be a growing number of class-action lawsuits against publicly traded companies with volatile stocks, such as many high-technology firms. The 1995 law, which was passed over President Clinton's veto, tightened standards for bringing class-action suits alleging securities fraud in federal court but did not address standards in state courts. As a result, a handful of law firms shifted their efforts to state courts. (*Congress and the Nation Vol. IX, p. 142*)

S 1260, which the White House supported, moved all securities fraud class-action suits involving fifty or more parties to federal courts. In addition, fifty or more securities fraud cases filed separately in the same state court and involving "common questions of law" could be consolidated and moved to federal court. The bill also allowed state and local governments, including state pension plans, to continue filing securities fraud class-action suits in state courts as long as all the plaintiffs were government entities.

Although a handful of Democrats opposed the legislation because they said the tougher federal standards would prevent small investors who thought they had been defrauded from seeking redress, the legislation was approved easily. The Senate passed S 1260 (S Rept 105-182) 79–21 on May 13. The House passed S 1260 340–83 on July 22 after substituting the language of its version (HR 1689—H Rept 105-640). The differences in the two versions of the bill were easily resolved and the conference report (H Rept 105-803) was cleared on Oct. 13 after the Senate adopted it by voice vote and the House adopted it on a vote of 319–82. President Clinton signed it on Nov. 3, 1998.

Interstate Banking

Legislation clarifying whether the home state or the host state should regulate branches opened by out-of-state banks was signed into law (HR 1306—PL 105-24) on July 3, 1997. Under a 1994 interstate banking law (PL 103-328) both state-chartered and federally chartered national banks could open branches in states other than their own. But the law was unclear on whether the new branches were to be regulated by officials in the bank's home state or the state in which the branches were located.

Under the 1994 law the branches of state-chartered banks opened in other states were supposed to be regulated by and have the same powers as the state-chartered banks of the host state. In some states, however, existing regulations gave greater powers to national banks. As a result some state-chartered banks wishing to branch into these states had switched to national charters to take advantage of the additional powers. These conversions raised concerns that other state-chartered banks would do the same thing thereby weakening the nation's dual banking system, which gave the banks the option of operating and being regulated under either federal banking rules or separate state rules.

At the time forty-three states had so-called "wild card" or "parity" laws that granted state-chartered banks the same powers enjoyed by national banks. The 1997 legislation was intended to address the discrepancy in regulation that oc-curred in the remaining seven states. The legislation charged the state hosting the branch with regulating it in most instances. If the law of the host state did not apply to a branch of an out-of-state bank, the branch was to be governed under the law of its home state.

The bill was passed in the House on May 21 by voice vote under suspension of the rules. The Senate passed the measure by voice vote on June 12, along with several technical amendments. The House accepted the changes on June 24 by voice vote, clearing the bill. President Clinton signed the legislation July 7.

Coin Designs

Legislation requiring the U.S. Mint to strike new quarters commemorating each of the fifty states was signed into law Dec. 1, 1997 (S 1228—PL 105-124). The measure did not alter the front of the quarter, which featured a profile of George Washington, but the eagle on the back was to be replaced with a different design honoring each state. The bill required the Mint to issue five versions of the new quarter each year for ten years, beginning in 1999, with the states honored in the order that they entered the Union. The legislation also called on the Treasury Department to create and design a gold-colored dollar coin to replace the Susan B. Anthony dollar, which was minted from 1979 to 1981.

The bill began in the Senate Banking, Housing and Urban Affairs Committee, which approved it by voice vote Oct. 23. The full Senate passed it by voice vote on Nov. 9. The House passed the measure by voice vote Nov. 13, after approving a companion bill (HR 2414) on Sept. 23, by a vote of 413–6. House passage of the Senate bill cleared the legislation.

1999–2000

One of the few legislative areas in which the 106th Congress exhibited bipartisanship was in the field of financial regulation. In 1999 Congress, the White House, and the financial services industry finally reached a consensus that had eluded them for decades, passing a measure that swept away the legal barriers separating banking, insurance, and securities activities. Enactment of that legislation was one of the most notable achievements of both the 106th Congress and Clinton's second term of office.

Congress followed up in 2000 with legislation overhauling the Commodities Exchange Act, which had failed to keep pace with new financial products. Experts had warned that the United States might lose business to exchanges overseas unless the law was updated. Congress also passed a bill aimed at stemming the numbers of people who declared bankruptcy and walked away from their debts even when they could afford to repay at least a portion of them. President Clinton, however, pocket-vetoed that bill at the end of the session.

Financial Services Modernization

After decades of failed efforts, Congress in 1999 passed and President Clinton signed a historic overhaul of the laws governing the financial services industry. Although the issue drew scant public attention, it was likely to have a substantial impact on the banking, insurance, and securities services used by most Americans and ranked as one of the key legislative achievements of Clinton's second term.

The measure (S 900—PL 106-102) repealed laws restricting cross-ownership among banks, brokerages, and insurers and established a new regulatory framework for maintaining the safety and stability of the financial industry. The bars on cross-ownership had been enacted during the Great Depression of the 1930s in the belief that they would help stem future financial failures. The 1933 Glass-Steagall Act erected barriers between the banking and security industries, and the 1956 Bank Holding Company Act imposed barriers between banking and insurance activities.

The development of new financial services in the late twentieth century combined with advances in computer and communications technology to make these laws increasingly outdated. A consensus began to develop in Congress that widespread financial collapse could be averted under less onerous restrictions. Supporters of modernization also argued that repealing the barriers would improve customer service by offering one-stop shopping for financial products and would help U.S. financial institutions better compete in the growing global financial markets.

Recent court and regulatory decisions had already eroded the barriers among the industries, allowing some cross-sector affiliations to proceed. Still, the financial industry wanted new laws explicitly repealing the barriers and providing guidance for future consolidation.

Overhaul efforts had foundered repeatedly in previous Congresses as various industry sectors fought among themselves over the details. In 1999 the competing interests in financial services generally put aside their differences and united to get a bill enacted. They repeatedly applied heavy pressure on GOP leaders to keep the measure moving. *(Competing interests, box, p. 131)*

The chief congressional players were Rep. Jim Leach, R-Iowa, and Sen. Phil Gramm, R-Texas, each chairman of his chamber's Banking Committee. The two approached the issue with different leadership styles and the bills that initially emerged from the two chambers differed dramatically.

In 1995 and 1996 Leach, in his first term as committee chairman, struggled to bring an ambitious rewrite of banking laws to the floor but his efforts were to little avail. He had more success in 1998 when he helped persuade the House to pass a financial services reform bill. Although the measure carried by only a single vote the effort represented the first time that the House had put itself on record as being in favor of financial service reforms. In 1999 Leach worked hard to win Democratic support for his bill (HR 10), seeking bipartisan consensus at every turn while trying to avoid divisive partisan provisions. *(1997–1998 action, p. 122)*

Gramm took a more partisan approach. In 1998 his objections to the 1977 Community Reinvestment Act (PL 95-128), an antiredlining law intended to force banks to make loans in low-income areas, helped kill the reform bill in the Senate. In 1999 Gramm again insisted on provisions easing compliance requirements for banks. Democrats, the White House, and community groups vehemently opposed those provisions. The Senate bill passed on a party-line vote in committee and with only one Democratic vote on the floor. In conference negotiations Gramm made concessions on the reinvestment act that eventually helped seal a bipartisan agreement.

Privacy provisions were another partisan flash point. In the final version Democrats succeeded in placing some new restrictions on the ability of financial services companies to transfer customer data to third parties. Republicans, backed by the industry, fought off Democratic efforts to impose more sweeping privacy measures opposed by the financial services industry.

Several other difficult provisions divided members of Congress although not necessarily along partisan lines. For example, conferees haggled over whether savings and loans, also known as thrifts, should be barred from affiliating with commercial firms. Conferees eventually decided to bar such mergers in the future, although existing affiliations would be allowed to continue.

Another key turning point for the bill was an agreement between the Treasury Department and the Federal Reserve

COMPETING INTERESTS: WHO WANTED WHAT

Previous congressional efforts to overhaul financial services regulation foundered largely because industry groups, consumer organizations, and regulators could not agree on the details. By 1999 these groups were more willing to compromise to get a bill passed, but each retained specific interests they worked diligently to protect. Following is a description of major interest groups and their positions on the issue as the House and Senate began considering legislation in 1999:

• **Banks.** Large banks wanted the legislation to allow consolidation of financial services. Smaller banks, with less capacity to develop other financial services, feared being at a competitive disadvantage. All banks wanted the legislation to scale back unitary thrifts (savings and loan associations), which banks regarded as competitors with unfair advantages.

Banks generally preferred federal oversight of their insurance and securities activities instead of operating under state rules and regulations that could vary widely. At the federal level, banks wanted bank regulators rather than the Securities and Exchange Commission (SEC) to oversee banks' securities activities.

• **Insurance.** State insurance agents and regulators wanted state oversight of bank insurance activities. State regulators said they could best protect consumers because most insurance activities already were regulated by states. Insurance agents feared that less rigorous federal controls might give banks a competitive edge. Insurance companies took a different view, preferring that federal authorities have a substantial role in regulating bank insurance activities.

• **Securities.** State securities regulators who shared regulatory chores with the SEC wanted this dual oversight to extend to bank securities activities. Banks wanted to report solely to banking regulators. The SEC opposed giving federal banking regulators primary oversight of banks' securities activities.

• **Consumer groups.** Consumer groups wanted privacy protections to prevent subsidiaries of financial conglomerates from sharing personal financial data among themselves or selling the data to third parties. The financial industry opposed the privacy protections. Consumer groups also wanted to protect and expand the 1977 Community Reinvestment Act, which set standards for lender activities in distressed community areas, and they wanted state oversight of insurance because they believed state regulators were more friendly to consumers than federal regulators.

• **Federal regulators.** The Federal Reserve and the Treasury Department disagreed over how financial conglomerates should be structured and thus which agency would regulate them. The Federal Reserve regulated bank holding companies while the Treasury regulated banks and bank subsidiaries.

(Fed) on how the new financial conglomerates would be structured and who would regulate them. The White House had threatened to veto the bill if Treasury's demands were ignored, but many legislators were reluctant to pass a bill over the objections of Fed Chairman Alan Greenspan. The two agencies settled their long-running feud during conference negotiations by agreeing to a framework in which both agencies would continue to play strong banking oversight roles.

KEY ELEMENTS

The final version of the bill contained the following key elements:

• **Structure and regulatory oversight.** Banks generally would be allowed to operate most financial services, except insurance underwriting and real estate development, as subsidiaries. The total assets of a bank's subsidiaries, however, could not exceed $50 billion or 45 percent of the bank's assets, whichever was less. The provision was a compromise worked out by the Fed, which regulated bank holding companies, and the Treasury Department, which monitored banks and subsidiaries that were not part of a holding company. The Fed had argued that financial conglomerates should be required to keep nonbank affiliates at arm's length by organizing them as affiliates under a holding company. The Treasury Department insisted that the banks be allowed to organize nonbanking financial activities as subsidiaries.

• **Regulation of insurance and securities.** Insurance and securities activities would continue to be monitored by their respective state and federal regulators even if the activities were conducted by a bank affiliate or subsidiary. Exceptions would be made for some traditional bank activities, such as trust management, which would continue to be overseen by bank regulators. The Senate version would have placed more securities functions under the review of bank regulators rather than the Securities and Exchange Commission (SEC).

• **Thrifts.** The final version forbade new and existing thrift institutions from affiliating with commercial firms. Opponents of affiliation argued that mixing banking and commerce not only placed the financial industry at risk but could be anticompetitive if thrifts refused to grant loans to potential competitors of their commercial affiliates. Banks also complained that existing thrifts had an unfair advantage because under existing law they were allowed to affiliate with commercial firms whereas banks were not.

• **Wholesale financial institutions.** The final version allowed the creation of a new type of bank called a wholesale financial institution, or "woofie" for its acronym WFI. These institutions would not be as heavily regulated as regular banks and their deposits would not be federally insured. They would require a minimum deposit of $100,000 and would be geared to the needs of institutional and large individual investors. These institutions could not be affiliated with federally insured banks and the Community Reinvestment Act would not apply to them.

• **Privacy.** Banks were required to develop written privacy policies, disclose them conspicuously to customers, and allow customers to opt out of information-sharing with unaffiliated third parties. Banks would not be required to allow consumers to opt out of joint marketing agreements with other financial institutions. Small banks requested that exception, arguing that without it they would be at a competitive disadvantage because large banks were more likely to have inhouse affiliates that could participate in cross-marketing projects. Republicans thwarted Democratic efforts to pass stronger privacy measures including an amendment that would have allowed customers to opt out of all of the bank's information-sharing arrangements.

The bill also made "pretext" calling a crime. Pretext calling was the practice of using false information or deceptive tactics to gather personal information about a bank's customers. Exceptions were made for law enforcement activities and attempts to collect child support payments.

• **Community Reinvestment Act (CRA).** An antiredlining law, the Community Reinvestment Act required banks to document efforts to invest in all segments of their communities. HR 10 applied these same requirements to the new financial conglomerates that would be created but reduced the number of reinvestment reviews by federal regulators for most banks with less than $250 million in assets unless they sought to merge, establish a new branch, or relocate. Banks would have to have satisfactory reinvestment ratings to expand into insurance or security activities.

A "sunshine" requirement required banks and community groups to disclose deals in which a bank offered grants or loans to a community group in return for the group's support of its reinvestment activities. Critics of reinvestment requirements said the confidential agreements allowed community groups to abuse the law by making deals with banks eager to avoid challenges to their expansion plans.

SENATE COMMITTEE ACTION

The Senate Banking, Housing, and Urban Affairs Committee March 6 approved legislation (S 900—S Rept 106-44) to overhaul the financial services industry in a markup that was partisan from the outset. Republicans held together on two 11–9 party-line votes, rejecting a Democratic-supported overhaul proposal offered by ranking Democrat Paul S. Sarbanes of Maryland and then approving the measure drafted largely by committee Chairman Gramm. Gramm had taken over the committee at the beginning of the year after former Chairman Alfonse M. D'Amato, R-N.Y., lost his bid for reelection.

The most contentious issue of the day, however, was an amendment by Richard C. Shelby, R-Ala., to exempt nonurban banks with less than $100 million in assets from the 1977 Community Reinvestment Act. The amendment passed 11–9 with one member of each party switching sides. Democrats warned that Republican insistence on scaling back community reinvestment laws would kill any chance of shaping a bill that President Clinton would sign. The CRA supporters included community groups across the nation, who said the law had helped revitalize neighborhoods by prodding banks to look for investment opportunities in poor neighborhoods. Republicans said the act had created heavy paperwork requirements that were particularly burdensome for small banks.

SENATE FLOOR ACTION

Partisan rancor characterized the three-day Senate debate on S 900, which passed the committee bill with only minor changes on May 6. The vote was 54–44, with only one senator, Ernest F. Hollings, D-S.C., crossing party lines to vote for the bill.

The issue claiming the largest portion of the Senate debate was the CRA. In addition to exempting nonurban banks with assets under $100 million from complying with the act, S 900 also made it more difficult for community groups to challenge a bank's reinvestment record if it had been in compliance with the law for the past three years. Two Democratic attempts to amend these provisions failed on near party-line votes. An amendment to strip the bill of its reinvestment provisions was tabled (killed) 52–45. A Sarbanes substitute for S 900, which would have deleted the reinvestment provisions, among other changes, was also tabled, 54–43.

A squabble among Republicans over how to structure the new financial conglomerates nearly derailed the bill. Gramm's bill generally adhered to a position advocated by Fed Chairman Greenspan requiring nonbanking financial activities, such as insurance and securities underwriting, to be conducted separately from bank operations under the umbrella of a holding company. The Fed was responsible for regulating bank holding companies.

The Clinton administration, most Democrats, and some Republicans favored giving banks the option of operating nonbanking activities through bank subsidiaries, which were regulated by the Treasury Department, and Clinton had threatened to veto legislation that did not allow the subsidiary structure. Shelby introduced an amendment to allow the subsidiary structure, which was favored by many large banks but not generally by smaller ones. Shelby said the subsidiary structure was more flexible and would make U.S. banks more competitive globally without endangering the banking system.

Gramm disagreed with his Republican colleague, saying federally insured bank operations must be separated from other financial services to ensure banking system safety. He added that he would pull S 900 from the floor if the Shelby amendment was adopted. It was tabled 53–46 with six Democrats and seven Republicans crossing party lines.

In other action, the Senate adopted an amendment by voice vote that would prohibit commercial companies from buying existing unitary thrifts.

HOUSE COMMITTEE ACTION

In the House the overhaul legislation (HR 10) was referred to both the Banking and Financial Services Committee and the Commerce Committee. Although the two committees won broad bipartisan support for the measure, the two versions differed substantially.

The Banking Committee acted first. After a grueling three-day markup, held March 4, March 10, and March 11, it approved the measure 51–8. Committee Chairman Leach painstakingly steered the panel through a minefield of partisan pitfalls and veto-triggering amendments to produce a bill that had members of both parties clapping and backslapping after committee approval.

As in the Senate markup the CRA figured prominently in the committee's deliberations. The House bill would extend reinvestment requirements to banks included in the new financial conglomerates, and Leach and ranking Democrat John J. LaFalce, N.Y., turned back efforts both to extend and to scale back the reinvestment requirements.

The other major controversy concerned privacy. The issue arose at the March 10 meeting, when Jay Inslee, D-Wash., offered an amendment that, among other things, would require banks to notify customers if they planned to release information about their depository transactions, such as check-writing habits, to third parties. Customers would then have thirty days to inform the bank that they did not want the information disclosed.

Leach said he shared Inslee's concerns but argued that the issue was complicated and needed to be considered more thoroughly. Instead of withdrawing his amendment as Leach had suggested, Inslee came back the next day with a revised privacy amendment that had bipartisan support. Leach countered with his own privacy amendment, coauthored with Bruce F. Vento, D-Minn., that would require banks to inform consumers of their information-sharing practices but would not give consumers the right to opt out of the disclosures. Although several members said they were uneasy with the last-minute nature of both amendments the committee agreed to the Leach-Vento privacy provisions 34–22.

On another controversial issue, Ken Bentsen, D-Texas, succeeded in an effort to relax a provision in HR 10 relating to unitary thrifts. Unitary thrifts were insured federal savings institutions that functioned similar to banks and were allowed to affiliate with commercial firms. Banks, which were barred from commercial affiliations, saw this as giving thrifts an unfair competitive edge. Leach and many other legislators believed that mixing banking and commerce was problematic

and perhaps dangerous and supported language prohibiting new thrifts from affiliating with commercial companies.

However there were splits within both parties over whether the same prohibition should be applied to existing thrifts. As drafted HR 10 prohibited all thrifts from affiliating with commercial firms. Arguing that it was unfair to change the rules, Bentsen offered an amendment allowing thrifts already in existence to continue to affiliate with commercial firms. His amendment was approved 29–26.

The House Commerce Committee approved its version of the bill by voice vote on June 10. In major differences with the Banking Committee bill, the Commerce measure prohibited the sale of existing thrifts to commercial firms, required financial services companies to give consumers the right to opt out of information-sharing among affiliates and third parties, and required banks to conduct their insurance and securities activities through affiliates under the umbrella of a holding company, rather than through subsidiaries.

The privacy provisions, pushed by Rep. Edward J. Markey, D-Mass., would curtail businesses' ability to sell and share data about their customers. Markey and other Democrats said the financial services industry stood to make billions of dollars from consumer databases that contain everything from Social Security numbers to information about check-writing habits.

The provisions were immediately opposed by the financial services industry, which claimed that the privacy protections would have unintended consequences that could hurt their ability to serve customers. The debate over the issue put Republicans who supported the industry in a difficult position because they were also aware that the public was growing increasingly concerned about privacy. The original Markey amendment allowed consumers to opt out of information-sharing both among affiliates of the same financial services company and with unaffiliated third parties. An amended version requiring the "opt-out" provision only for information-sharing with third parties was agreed to by voice vote.

In one important area, however, the Banking and Commerce versions were the same: both would apply the community reinvestment provisions to new financial services conglomerates.

Over the next several weeks House leaders worked to reconcile the two committee versions in a way that both committees could live with. The reconciled version of HR 10 sided with the president rather than the Fed chairman in agreeing to allow subsidiaries for financial services except insurance underwriting and real estate development. It also decided to go with the weaker Banking Committee language on privacy, which required only that consumers be notified of information-sharing; it did not include the Commerce Committee's opt-out provision.

On the issue of whether existing thrifts could continue to affiliate with commercial firms, House leaders opted for a compromise that would allow them to do so only with the approval of the Fed. Because the Fed had historically opposed any mixing of banking and commerce, it was unclear what this provision would mean for thrifts.

HOUSE FLOOR ACTION

The bipartisan support for HR 10 continued on the House floor, where the measure was adopted July 1 on a **key vote of 343–86 (R 205–16; D 138–69; I 0–1).** Of the 343 members who voted for the bill, 130 had voted "no" in 1998 when the predecessor to HR 10 (also numbered HR 10) passed by only one vote. Seventy-four of those who changed their position were Democrats, including Minority Leader Richard A. Gephardt, Mo., and Minority Whip David E. Bonior, Mich. Democrats said factors in their change of heart included the addition of privacy protection provisions, administration preference for HR 10 over the Senate version, and larger consensus within the financial services industry on the shape of an overhaul bill. *(1999 key votes, p. 899)*

Before the vote on passage, the House voted 427–1 to strengthen the privacy provisions by requiring financial services companies to give consumers the opportunity to opt out of information-sharing arrangements with third parties. Although Markey said he was disappointed that he was not allowed to offer an even stronger amendment that would have allowed consumers to opt out of information-sharing among financial services affiliates, House leaders agreed that the "opt-out" for third parties was the best the Democrats could do without provoking widespread industry opposition to the bill. The near-unanimous support for the amendment and the strong support for the overall bill put the House in a formidable position as it entered conference negotiations with the Senate. The Senate version of the bill contained no privacy provisions.

The vote on passage belied underlying dissatisfaction with elements of the measure. Democrats tried to rally their entire caucus against the rule that Republican leaders had crafted because it allowed only eleven amendments, leaving Democrats fuming over items excluded from consideration. They were particularly irate about the exclusion of an amendment to preempt state insurance laws and ban insurance "redlining," the practice of refusing to sell insurance in specific geographic areas, usually poor neighborhoods. The provision had been approved by the Banking Committee but stripped by the Rules Committee. The rule was adopted 227–103 with six Democrats defecting to support it.

At the end of the debate Democrats made a final push to reinsert the amendment along with two proposals to strengthen the privacy provisions. The move was defeated 198–232.

CONFERENCE AND FINAL ACTION

House-Senate negotiations on a final bill were lengthy and contentious and succeeded largely because the financial services industry kept steady pressure on negotiators to reach agreement. Banks, brokerages, and insurance interests were unwilling to let the legislation die, particularly because it represented the first time that an overhaul measure had ever passed both chambers of Congress.

As they had been throughout, the chief strategists were Leach and Gramm. Leach had watched in frustration as previous overhaul plans evaporated despite his painstaking efforts to craft bipartisan agreements. House rules that forced him to relinquish his chairmanship of the Banking Committee at the end of the 106th Congress gave additional urgency to his efforts to pass the most sweeping financial services legislation in decades.

As the new chairman of the Senate Banking Committee, Gramm was operating under a different set of responsibilities than had governed his past actions. Instead of playing spoiler over pet issues of his own, he found himself under heavy pressure from the GOP leadership to get a bill passed. Although he stuck to his guns until the final hour and won some of what he wanted on the controversial community reinvestment provisions, Gramm ended up agreeing to a finished product that was far different from the legislation he set before his committee at the beginning of the year.

The House-Senate conference got off to a bumpy start when a procedural problem delayed action. Once that was resolved negotiators meeting in open session in September resolved several noncontroversial and technical differences. But the conference threatened to break up several times when controversial issues came up for discussion.

On Sept. 29 Gramm suggested that he, Leach, and House Commerce Committee Chairman Thomas J. Bliley, R-Va., retreat behind closed doors to hammer out the necessary compromises. Otherwise, Gramm said, it was unlikely that the conference would ever reach agreement. Leach balked at the proposal, preferring to maintain bipartisan support by negotiating the issues point by point in open session. Sensing that the momentum behind the measure might slip as Congress moved closer to adjournment, the financial industry put pressure on House Speaker J. Dennis Hastert, R-Ill., and Senate Majority Leader Trent Lott, R-Miss., to keep negotiations moving. Under pressure Leach reluctantly agreed to Gramm's plan and the three chairmen revealed their closed-door compromise on Oct. 12.

When the full conference committee reconvened on Oct. 14, two of the more contentious issues had been resolved. Conferees agreed to a provision that allowed thrifts already affiliated with commercial firms to continue that affiliation but prohibiting any more from taking place. And the Treasury Department and the Fed announced that they had reached agreement to allow banks to operate most financial services, except insurance underwriting and real estate development, as subsidiaries regulated by the Treasury Department. Gramm, who preferred the holding company concept originally backed by the Fed, said he would support anything that Fed Chairman Greenspan endorsed.

Those agreements left two issues unresolved: privacy and community reinvestment.

The question of whether the Senate would agree to any privacy provisions appeared to be resolved early on when Republican Shelby announced that he supported even stronger provisions than the House had approved. After wrangling for hours over the issue, conferees settled Oct. 18 on provisions similar to those passed in the House. The measure called for banks to develop written privacy policies and disclose them conspicuously to customers. Banks also had to give customers the right to opt out of information-sharing with unaffiliated third parties. An exception was made for joint marketing agreements with other financial institutions. The White House quickly endorsed those provisions, drawing complaints from Democrats who had fought for stronger measures and said they felt abandoned by the administration.

That left only the community reinvestment provisions unresolved. Although the three committee chairmen had modified the Senate CRA provisions, dropping the exemption for small nonurban banks, the White House still objected to the language, particularly provisions that reduced the frequency of reinvestment regulatory exams for many small banks and that required disclosure of deals in which banks offered grants or loans to a community group in exchange for the group's support of the bank's reinvestment activities. Gramm insisted that the community groups provide detailed reports on how they spent the grants or loans.

Marathon talks among Gramm, Treasury Secretary Lawrence H. Summers, and other White House officials produced an agreement in principle Oct. 22. But hammering out the final text of the bill and report language proved daunting. Republican and Democratic House staff aides said Gramm caused problems by seeking language that veered away from the Oct. 22 agreement. Gramm said it was the White House that was trying to renege on the spirit of the agreement.

Eventually, the final version of S 900 was completed and emerged from conference with broad bipartisan support. In the House thirty-eight of the forty-six conferees signed the report (H Rept 106-434). All but two of the twenty Senate conferees signed it. Shelby and Richard H. Bryan, D-Nev., opposed it because they said its privacy protections were inadequate.

Both chambers overwhelmingly adopted the conference report on Nov. 4. The Senate acted by a **key vote of 90–8 (R 52–1; D 38–7).** The House cleared the measure 362–57 for President Clinton, who signed it on Nov. 12, 1999 (PL 106-102).

MAJOR PROVISIONS

The following are major provisions of the bill.

Laws Repealed

• **The 1933 Glass-Steagall Act.** Repealed prohibitions on affiliations between the banking and securities industries.

• **The 1956 Bank Holding Company Act.** Repealed prohibitions on affiliations between the banking and insurance industries.

Structure and Oversight

• **Shared bank jurisdiction.** Provided that the Fed and the Treasury Department would continue to share oversight of national banks: the Fed for bank holding companies and new financial holding companies created under the law and the Treasury Department as primary regulator of national banks.

• **Functional regulation.** Specified that each affiliate or subsidiary of a financial conglomerate would be regulated by its "functional" regulator: banks by banking regulators, securities affiliates by the Securities and Exchange Commission (SEC), and insurance companies by state insurance regulators.

• **Safeguards.** Authorized federal banking regulators to restrict relationships and transactions among insured banks and their affiliates or subsidiaries if needed to avoid conflicts of interest or to enhance the financial stability of banks and the general banking system.

Subsidiary Activities and Oversight

• **Bank and bank subsidiary activities.** Allowed national banks to engage in, directly or through an operating subsidiary, activities that are "financial in nature or incidental to a financial activity." Specified that the Treasury would supervise bank activities and functional regulation, as discussed previously, would apply to operations of individual bank subsidiaries.

• **Exceptions to allowable bank subsidiary activities.** Prohibited banks or bank subsidiaries from conducting the following activities: insurance or annuity underwriting, insurance company portfolio investments, real estate development, real estate investment, and merchant banking activities. (Companies engaging in such activities had to establish financial holding companies and organize activities as affiliates rather than as subsidiaries. However, subsidiaries could conduct merchant banking activities after five years if the Treasury and the Fed approved.)

• **Subsidiary requirements.** Required parent national banks and all affiliated banks to be well-capitalized and well-managed before financial activities could be conducted through a subsidiary. Required the parent bank to obtain Treasury Department approval before initiating any eligible activity through subsidiaries, and specified that the consolidated total assets of all subsidiaries of any single bank could be no more than $50 billion or 45 percent of the assets of the parent bank, whichever was less.

• **Large bank limitations.** Permitted the largest 100 banks in the nation by total asset size to conduct securities underwriting activities in subsidiaries only if the parent bank met certain debt rating requirements.

Holding Company Activities and Oversight

• **Other financial activities.** Allowed financial holding companies, in addition to banking, insurance, and securities activities, to engage in activities that are "financial in nature," incidental to activities that are financial in nature, or complementary to such activities. (The provision significantly expanded previous law, which limited bank affiliates to activities "closely related to banking.") Specified that investment advisory activities, merchant banking, and insurance company portfolio investments are financial in nature. Empowered the Fed, with Treasury Department concurrence, to define and authorize other eligible activities.

• **Limits on Fed oversight.** Prohibited the Fed from examining functionally regulated nonbank affiliates unless it has reasonable cause to believe the affiliate is engaged in activities that pose a material risk to an insured bank. Prohibited the Fed from imposing capital adequacy rules, guidelines, or other requirements beyond those already required by the affiliates' functional regulators. Limited the reach of the Fed's "source of strength" doctrine, which states that affiliates of insured banks may be considered part of the bank's enterprise with responsibility for financially supporting the institution. Allowed the SEC and state insurance regulators to prevent the Fed from compelling securities, investment advisers, and insurance affiliates to provide funds to an undercapitalized insured bank affiliate.

• **Fed enforcement of nonbank affiliates.** Barred the Fed from enforcement action against a nonbank affiliate unless it was needed to prevent or redress a practice that poses a material risk to the financial soundness of an affiliated bank or the U.S. or international payments systems, and only if it was not possible to guard against such risk through requirements imposed directly on the bank. (In overseeing nonbank affiliates, the Fed generally had to rely on reports from the affiliates and on examinations conducted by other regulators.)

• **Prohibited activities.** Prohibited banks from affiliating with commercial nonfinancial entities, such as retail or manufacturing businesses.

• **Exceptions to prohibited activities.** Allowed securities and insurance firms that already owned, or were affiliated with, commercial nonfinancial companies to affiliate with banks under a financial holding company if they were engaged in commercial activities as of Sept. 30, 1999, as long as the commercial activities made up 15 percent or less of the company's gross revenue. Specified that such commercial activities could not be expanded and would have to be terminated or divested within ten years of the bill's enactment. Allowed firms that owned or were affiliated with companies engaged in commodities trading or investments to affiliate with banks under a holding company if they were engaged in such commodity activities as of Sept. 30, 1997, and if such commodity activities made up 5 percent or less of the company's total assets. (The measure did not require divestiture of these activities but it prohibited cross-marketing of banking and commodities products.)

Community Reinvestment Act

• **Existing law.** Preserved existing requirements of the 1977 Community Reinvestment Act (PL 95-128) intended to spur loans in low-income areas by requiring banks to document their efforts to make loans in all areas where they collect deposits. (Banks seeking to merge or open new branches must have reinvestment ratings of satisfactory or better.)

• **New affiliations.** Required banks to have a satisfactory or better reinvestment rating before they could affiliate with securities and insurance firms, and prohibited holding companies that have a bank with an unsatisfactory reinvestment rating from engaging in new financial services activities until the bank achieved a satisfactory rating.

• **"Sunshine" provision.** Required public disclosure of any agreements made between banks and community groups involving more than $10,000 in grants or $50,000 in loans when the agreement was made in connection with the bank fulfilling its Community Reinvestment Act (CRA) requirements. Specified that the requirement applied only to parties that commented or testified about or otherwise contacted the bank about the CRA.

• **Disclosure of expenditures.** Required groups receiving funds under a CRA agreement with a bank to submit a detailed, itemized list reporting how the funds were used, including salaries, administrative expenses, travel, entertainment, consulting fees paid, and any other categories required by the banking regulator. Allowed community groups to submit their annual reports directly to the bank, which had to forward them to banking regulators.

• **Reduced regulatory reviews.** Reduced the frequency of CRA reviews for rural and small banks with less than $250 million in assets that have good CRA records. Limited CRA regulatory reviews to every five years for such banks that have "outstanding" CRA ratings and every four years for banks that have "satisfactory" ratings. Specified that banks would remain subject to CRA reviews whenever they propose to open a new branch or merge, and allowed banking regulators to conduct reviews more or less frequently if they had reasonable cause.

• **Studies required.** Directed the Treasury Department, in consultation with federal banking agencies, to study the extent to which services are being provided as intended by the CRA including services in low- and moderate-income neighborhoods and for people of moderate means. Required the Fed to conduct a comprehensive study on the default rates, delinquency rates, and profitability of loans made by banks in complying with the CRA.

Privacy

• **Disclosure.** Required financial institutions to disclose clearly and conspicuously their policies regarding the sharing of customer information with other institutions. Specified that these disclosures must describe the type of customer information collected, the institution's policies and practices for sharing information with both affiliated institutions and nonaffiliated third parties, and policies for protecting the confidentiality and security of customer information. Required such disclosures be made to every new customer and to all existing customers at least once a year.

- **Opt-out requirement.** Required banks to allow consumers to opt out of their information-sharing arrangements with unaffiliated third parties but did not require companies to let consumers opt out of information-sharing with affiliates or subsidiaries.

- **Opt-out exception for marketing agreements.** Provided that banks were not required to let consumers opt out of information-sharing with third parties made in association with a financial institution's joint marketing agreement provided the institution disclosed the arrangement with its customers and the third party agreed to keep the customer information confidential. Prohibited financial institutions from disclosing a customer's bank account or credit card number or means of accessing such accounts to third parties for purposes of telemarketing, direct mail marketing, or electronic mail marketing.

- **Additional opt-out limitations.** Barred consumers from opting out of information-sharing associated with the processing of consumer-initiated transactions, maintaining consumer accounts, or complying with consumer reporting requirements, legal requirements, or law enforcement investigations.

- **Privacy rules.** Required federal banking regulators, the Treasury Department, the SEC, and the Federal Trade Commission (FTC), in consultation with state insurance authorities, to establish standards to ensure the security and confidentiality of customer financial records and information and to protect against unauthorized access and use of such information. Required each agency to conduct its own rule-making but required agencies to coordinate with one another and, to the extent possible, make their regulations consistent.

- **Privacy study.** Required the Treasury Department to conduct a study of information-sharing practices among financial institutions and their affiliates. Specified that among the matters to be examined were (1) the purposes for which confidential consumer information is shared and the potential benefits of sharing for financial institutions and for customers; (2) the potential risks to consumer privacy by sharing; (3) the adequacy of existing laws to protect privacy; and (4) the adequacy of security protections for shared information. Required that the study explore the feasibility of approaches to privacy, including opt-out and opt-in policies that allow customers to control whether their confidential information can be shared with affiliates and third parties.

- **State privacy laws.** Established a floor, rather than a ceiling, for consumer privacy protection by allowing states to enact more stringent privacy provisions than those established in federal law.

Privacy and Fraud

- **Pretext calling.** Made illegal the practice of obtaining or attempting to obtain confidential information about a customer from a financial institution by fraudulent or deceptive means or to request that another person obtain such information knowing that it will be done in a fraudulent manner. Established criminal fines and imprisonment up to five years with penalties doubled for certain aggravated cases.

- **Pretext calling exceptions.** Provided exceptions to pretext calling prohibitions for certain law enforcement activities, for financial institutions that are testing their internal security procedures, for investigations of allegations of improper conduct by employees, for insurance companies and agents investigating insurance fraud or other misconduct, and for state-licensed private investigators authorized by a court to help collect delinquent court-ordered child support payments.

Automated Teller Machine Fees

- **Disclosure.** Required banks and other operators of automated teller machines (ATMs) to disclose prominently whether a user of a machine will be charged a fee if the person is not a customer of the bank or other ATM operators. Required this must be done both through a sign on the ATM and a notice either on the ATM's screen or on a slip of paper dispensed by the machine. Required the disclosures to specify the amount of the surcharge and must provide the consumer with the opportunity to refuse the fee and cancel the transaction.

- **GAO study.** Required the General Accounting Office (GAO) to study the feasibility, costs, benefits to consumers, and competitive impact of requiring ATM operators to disclose to customers ATM fees that are being charged by the customer's bank.

Thrift Holding Companies

Prohibited new and existing savings and loans, also known as thrifts, from affiliating with commercial activities but allowed existing thrift-commerce affiliations to continue including pending affiliations in which an application was filed on or before May 4, 1999.

SEC Regulation

- **Banks as brokers and dealers.** Repealed the broad exemption for banks from regulation under federal securities laws, thereby providing for functional regulation of bank securities activities by the SEC. Extended SEC regulation of securities to the securities activities of banks by amending the definitions of "broker" and "dealer" under the 1934 Exchange Act to include banks. (Subjecting banks to federal securities regulation required banks either to register as securities broker-dealers or to move their securities activities out of banks and into registered securities affiliates or subsidiaries.) Exempted specified types of bank securities activities allowing banks to continue those activities without registering as broker-dealers.

- **Exempted securities activities.** Exempted certain bank securities activities from SEC broker-dealer regulation including third-party brokerage arrangements in which a registered broker or dealer offers services on or off bank premises but away from bank deposit-taking activities. Exempted other activities: traditional bank trust activities provided the bank receives no brokerage commissions and does not solicit brokerage business; transactions in commercial paper, bankers acceptances, commercial bills, and municipal and other exempted securities; certain stock purchase plans such as those made in connection with 401(k) plans and dividend reinvestment plans as long as the bank does not solicit transactions or provide investment advice on those transactions; and sweep accounts in which banks invest customers' deposits in registered money market funds.

- **Exemption for low-volume securities activities.** Exempted from SEC broker-dealer regulation banks that perform fewer than 500 securities transactions per year of any kind.

- **Exemption for private placements.** Allowed banks to perform private placements (nonpublic securities sales made to certain large investors) with "qualified investors" without SEC broker-dealer regulation. Classified individuals and corporations as qualified investors for all private placements, except for asset-backed securities and loan participations, if they have at least $25 million in investments, up from $10 million previously.

- **Mutual fund oversight.** Ended the exemption from the 1940 Investment Advisers Act for banks that sell mutual funds or advise mutual fund companies, thereby authorizing SEC oversight of such bank activities. (Banks that advise mutual fund companies must register with the SEC as investment advisers and are subject to SEC examination of their mutual fund activities. If a bank established a separately identifiable department within the bank to act as the investment adviser only that department would be required to register with the SEC.)

- **Disclosure of mutual fund risk.** Required banks that sell mutual funds to disclose clearly to customers that such investments are not federally insured or otherwise guaranteed.

- **Investment trust requirements.** Required the SEC to issue rules on the conditions under which a bank or bank officer may serve as custodian of the assets of an affiliated management investment company or unit investment trust. Placed restrictions on loans and other transactions between a bank and an affiliated investment company and it limited the ability of bank officers to serve on the board of such affiliated companies.

- **Oversight of new products.** Empowered the SEC to determine if future "hybrid" products developed by banks are securities subject to SEC regulation. Required the SEC, before initiating a rulemaking process, to seek the concurrence of the Fed and consider the history and purpose of the hybrid product and the likely impact that regulating the product as a security would have on the banking industry. Specified that if the Fed opposed an SEC rule declaring a hybrid to be a security the measure would receive an expedited review in the U.S. Court of Appeals.

- **Securities holding companies.** Allowed securities holding companies to be voluntarily supervised by the SEC. (Previously such holding companies, which may include other fi-

---

PENNY STOCKS

To head off virtually certain congressional action, the New York Stock Exchange voted on June 5, 1997, to begin pricing stocks by the penny rather than in eighths of a dollar as they had been for more than a century. The exchange said the change would occur "as soon as the essential systems are in place." All stocks on the New York Stock Exchange began to be denominated in pennies on Jan. 29, 2001.

Legislation to force the change had been moving through the House, but sponsors pulled the bill (HR 1053) after the stock exchange acted. The bill had been opposed by the brokerage industry, which made its profits from the eighth-of-a-dollar (12.5 cent) spread between each price point. Michael G. Oxley, R-Ohio, chairman of the House Subcommittee on Finance, said every penny by which the 12.5 cent spread was narrowed would collectively benefit investors by $1 billion or more a year.

---

nancial and nonfinancial affiliates as well as securities firms, were not subject to overall regulation. The voluntary SEC oversight of the entire holding company was intended to enhance the ability of certain U.S. investment bank holding companies to do business in foreign nations that require consolidated holding company supervision.)

- **Limitations on voluntary SEC oversight.** Specified that the voluntary SEC oversight would apply only to securities holding companies that do not include an insured depository institution. (All holding companies that include insured banks are automatically subject to regulation by the Fed.)

Bank Insurance Activities

- **State regulation of insurance.** Reaffirmed the 1945 McCarran-Ferguson Act (PL 79-15) that made the insurance industry subject to regulation by the states, not the federal government, and provided that no person or entity may underwrite or sell insurance in a state unless licensed by that state. (*Congress and the Nation Vol. VII, p. 399*)

- **Insurance products defined.** Defined "insurance" to help delineate which products are to be regulated as bank products and which are to be regulated by states as insurance. Defined insurance products as anything regulated by a state as insurance as of Jan. 1, 1999, including annuities. Provided that future bank products will be classified as insurance if they are based on certain insurance concepts and are regulated by the state as insurance. Specified that products based on core banking products—such as deposits, loans, trusts, derivatives and guarantees—would be treated as banking products unless treated as insurance for tax purposes by the IRS.

- **Dispute resolution.** Established a dispute resolution process when federal bank and state insurance regulators disagree over the status of a product under which either the banking or the insurance regulator may file a review petition directly to the U.S. Court of Appeals, bypassing U.S. district courts. Required the appeals court to examine the case's merits under both state and federal law, consider the nature and history of a product and its regulation, and make a decision within sixty days, without deference to the opinion of either the state or federal regulator. (Courts previously deferred to the opinion of the Office of the Comptroller of the Currency (OCC) in disputes concerning bank products. Court decisions could be appealed to the Supreme Court.)

- **Restrictions on bank insurance underwriting.** Prohibited national banks and their subsidiaries from underwriting insurance except for products that national banks were underwriting as of Jan. 1, 1999, or those the Office of the Comptroller of the Currency had authorized banks to underwrite as of that date. Made clear that, generally, any insurance underwriting had to be conducted by insurance affiliates of banks under a financial holding company.

- **Title insurance restrictions.** Prohibited national banks or their subsidiaries from underwriting or selling title insurance in most instances. Allowed national banks and subsidiaries to sell title insurance if a state allowed state banks to sell this coverage but only to the same extent and manner as allowed for state banks. Allowed existing title insurance activities by banks and subsidiaries to continue although such activities (including both underwriting and sales) had to be moved out of the bank or subsidiary to an insurance affiliate, if one existed.

- **Consumer protections.** Required federal banking regulators to develop consumer protection rules to govern the sale of insurance by banks including: antitying and anticoercion rules that prohibit banks from misleading consumers into believing that a loan or extension of credit is conditional on the purchase of insurance; disclosure rules requiring that consumers be told orally and in writing that the insurance product is not FDIC-insured, that there may be an investment risk involved, and that the product may lose value (in the case of variable annuities); guidelines on the extent to which insurance transactions should be conducted in a location away from where bank deposits are made; consumer grievance procedures to address customer complaints; and a prohibition on discriminating against victims of domestic violence in providing insurance.

Preemption of State Insurance Laws

- **Preemption of state affiliation laws.** Provided that insurance is to be regulated by the states but specifically preempted state laws and rules that prevent or restrict affiliations between banks and insurance companies. Allowed state laws that regulate the "business side" of insurance (rather than sales, solicitation, or cross-marketing activities) to continue and state regulators to prohibit affiliations for managerial or

solvency reasons. Authorized state insurance regulators to gather certain information from parties proposing to acquire or merge with an insurance company to ensure that capital requirements for the company will be met and maintained. Preempted state laws that restrict the ability of banks and bank subsidiaries or affiliates to sell, solicit, or cross-market insurance by codifying the standard set by the Supreme Court in a 1996 decision, *Barnett Bank v. Nelson*, that held that no state laws or rules can "prevent or significantly interfere" with the rights of a national bank to engage in insurance sales or solicitation activities under federal banking law.

- **Court guidelines for review of state insurance laws.** Reaffirmed existing practice that, in the case of state laws enacted before Sept. 3, 1998, the court in deciding whether the state law meets the *Barnett* standard must defer to the opinion of the federal bank regulator. Specified that the court must not defer to the opinion of either state or federal regulators for state laws enacted on or after Sept. 3, 1998, but must consider four nondiscrimination tests spelled out in the legislation.

- **"Safe harbors" for state insurance regulation.** Specified thirteen kinds of state insurance sales laws that are protected and may not be preempted regardless of when they were enacted including the following: state laws prohibiting banks from requiring customers to obtain coverage from an affiliated insurance company if insurance is required when taking out a loan; requiring banks to provide written disclosures to customers that they may obtain insurance from third parties; prohibiting banks from charging fees for handling third-party insurance policies; prohibiting advertising or other materials that could lead customers to believe that bank loans or insurance policies are government-backed, and requiring written disclosures stating that such policies are not federally backed; prohibiting insurance brokerage fees or commissions for unlicensed personnel; prohibiting the release of certain insurance information on customers; and requiring credit and insurance transactions to be completed through separate documents.

Uniform Insurance Licensing

- **New standards and reciprocity.** Urged states to enact laws creating uniform state licensing standards that will provide reciprocity for licensed insurers to operate in other states. (States followed different licensing and other requirements, which made it difficult and expensive for insurance agencies to sell in different locations.)

- **Creation of federal standards.** Provided, if a majority of states fail to enact uniform licensing standards and reciprocity laws within three years, a private, nonprofit corporation called the National Association of Registered Agents and Brokers (NARAB) would be created to develop uniform standards to be applied on a multistate basis, preempting state licensing requirements. Requires that NARAB be created under the direction of the National Association of Insurance Commissioners (NAIC), the association of state insurance regulatory bodies. Specified that insurance agents and brokers who join NARAB would be allowed to work in any state, with NARAB's licensing requirements overriding state requirements. Preserved, nevertheless, the rights of states to license insurance agents and brokers but those state requirements would apply only to state-licensed agents and brokers and not to NARAB members.

Federal Home Loan Bank Changes

• **Thrift membership.** Made membership in the Federal Home Loan Bank (FHLB) system voluntary. (The system provides low-cost loans to local lenders for use in providing home mortgages. Previously, federally chartered thrifts were required to join the system but state-chartered savings and loans were voluntary members.)

• **Participation requirements eased.** Changed existing law to no longer require small banks and thrifts to have at least 10 percent of their assets in mortgages or mortgage-backed securities to obtain FHLB advances.

• **Mission expanded.** Expanded the mission of the home loan bank system by allowing small thrifts and banks with less than $500 million in assets to obtain advances for use in funding small businesses and small farms. Allowed these institutions to pledge secured loans they previously made for eligible activities as collateral for such FHLB advances.

• **Management changes.** Set the terms for both elected and appointed FHLB bank directors at three years. (Previously elected directors served two years and appointed directors served four.)

'Limited-Purpose' Banks

Lifted certain restrictions on cross-marketing and other activities for so-called limited-purpose banks. Allowed limited-purpose banks to cross-market products of affiliates and expanded the types of overdrafts such banks may incur on behalf of an affiliate. (These federally insured limited-purpose banks, owned by major financial and commercial firms, either accept demand deposits or make commercial loans, but not both.)

Special Thrift Fund Eliminated

Eliminated a special reserve fund to augment the Savings Association Insurance Fund (SAIF) that was created under the 1996 Deposit Insurance Act (PL 104-208). (The reserve fund was intended to back up the SAIF and further protect taxpayers from thrift bailouts. It was established Jan. 1, 1999, using $1 billion in SAIF deposits that exceeded the SAIF's designated reserve ratio of 1.25 percent of estimated insured deposits. Critics of the reserve fund contended that it would be better to make these funds available to the regular SAIF account.)

Microenterprise Technical Assistance

• **New grant program.** Established a new grant program to fund local nonprofit microenterprise development organizations and programs that help low-income and disadvan-

taged entrepreneurs. Specified that grants could be provided to eligible organizations to provide training and technical assistance to entrepreneurs interested in starting or expanding businesses, to enhance the capacity of other organizations to serve low-income and disadvantaged entrepreneurs, and to support research and development of better training and technical assistance programs. Required local organizations to match $1 for every $2 in federal assistance provided and specified that at least 50 percent of federal grant funding must be used to benefit people with extremely low incomes, defined as families living at 150 percent of the poverty line or below.

• **Grant funding authorized.** Authorized $15 million a year through fiscal 2003 for the program, which would be administered by the Small Business Administration.

Miscellaneous Provisions

• **Bank municipal bond activities.** Authorized national banks to underwrite, purchase, and deal in municipal bonds.

• **Plain language.** Required federal banking agencies to use plain language in all rulemaking proposals published in the *Federal Register* after Jan. 1, 2000.

• **Interest rate cap exemption.** Allowed local banks in states in which interest rates are capped to charge higher rates equal to those charged by an interstate bank that branches into the state.

• **Name rights.** Permitted existing thrifts that convert to national or state banks to keep the word "federal" in their names.

• **Bank board changes.** Amended utility law to permit officers and directors of public utilities to serve as officers or directors of banks, trust companies, or securities firms.

• **Reserve bank audits.** Required the Fed to contract for independent annual audits of the financial statements of each Federal Reserve Bank, as well as of the board itself.

• **Foreign bank powers expanded.** Allowed a federal or state agency of a foreign bank to upgrade to a branch with the approval of the appropriate chartering authority and the Fed.

• **Grand jury access for state banks.** Authorized U.S. attorneys to seek court orders to provide state banking regulatory agencies with access to certain grand jury material, thereby giving state agencies parity with federal bank regulatory agencies.

Additional Studies

• **Federal Reserve.** Required that the GAO study the conflict of interest faced by the Fed between its role as a primary regulator of the banking industry and its role as a vendor of services to the banking and financial services industry.

• **Treasury Department.** Required the Treasury Department to study the extent to which credit is provided to small businesses and farms as a result of this legislation.

• **"S" corporations.** Required the GAO to study the implications of revising rules concerning "S" corporations to allow greater access by community banks to S corporation treatment. (An S corporation receives tax treatment similar to a partnership.)

Commodities Law Overhaul

A wide-ranging rewrite of the Commodity Exchange Act that governs commodities trading was attached to the fiscal 2001 omnibus spending bill (HR 4577—PL 106-554) at the end of 2000 after negotiators reached a last-minute deal on a key provision. The legislation reauthorized the Commodity Futures Trading Commission (CFTC), provided "legal certainty" to over-the-counter derivatives and allowed trading of futures of a single stock.

Key lawmakers in the House and Senate, backed by Treasury Secretary Lawrence H. Summers and Federal Reserve Chairman Alan Greenspan, pressed for the legislation, warning that failure to act would drive business overseas, mostly to European financial exchanges. The global market for derivatives was estimated at $88.2 trillion in 1999 by the Bank for International Settlements in Switzerland. The potential loss to the U.S. market made the legislation one of the most heavily lobbied measures of the year.

BACKGROUND

The Commodity Exchange Act was first enacted in 1936 to regulate the commodity exchanges where farmers and food processors traded physical commodities such as corn, sugar, and pork bellies, and entered into futures contracts to lock in favorable prices and avoid market fluctuations. In 1974 Congress created the CFTC to regulate the futures markets, which had evolved into highly sophisticated investments, known as derivatives, tied to such financial yardsticks as stock indexes, interest rates, and currency exchange rates. Another sophisticated financial instrument was the over-the-counter (OTC) derivative, an unregulated, privately negotiated derivative contract between two parties that was not traded on an exchange. Large institutions typically used "swaps" to hedge against risk. A corporation, for example, might use a swap with a bank to lock in the interest rate on a loan, much the way homeowners lock in rates on their mortgages.

Congress last reauthorized the CFTC in 1995 (S 178—PL 104-9), extending it through June 30, 2000. But that law did nothing to clarify the legal status of OTC derivatives. The U.S. OTC derivatives market had been unsettled since 1998 when the CFTC proposed a study on whether the unregulated OTC derivatives should be regulated by the CFTC. Investors and the commodity exchanges worried that regulation would unintentionally make existing OTC contracts unenforceable and enable participants to walk away from billions of dollars of commitments, creating the potential for the futures markets to crash. (*1995 authorization, Congress and the Nation Vol. IX, p. 505*)

Complicating the "legal certainty" issue was a political issue on whether to lift the prohibition on writing futures contracts based on individual stocks and bonds. That ban was written into the 1982 reauthorization of the Commodity Exchange Act (PL 97-444) because the CFTC, which oversees futures markets, and the Securities and Exchange Commission (SEC), which regulates securities products, could not resolve a jurisdictional dispute. Eighteen years later the two agencies were still in discord over the issue.

The Chicago Board of Trade, the Chicago Mercantile Exchange, and other commodities exchanges worried that a continuing ban on single-stock futures would drive the business overseas, arguing that such futures would allow investors to hedge against price declines in stocks they own just as they do for commodities. The New York Stock Exchange, other stock exchanges, and securities dealers countered that trading of single-stock futures would siphon business away from their exchanges and inject a new element of speculation and volatility into the stock markets.

CONGRESSIONAL ACTION

Jurisdictional issues also complicated the matter in the House, where three separate committees—Agriculture, Banking, and Commerce—each held hearings and produced their own versions of the bill (HR 4541—H Rept 106-711, Pts. I, II, III). The measure was then delayed for several weeks while the SEC and CFTC continued to negotiate their jurisdictional differences over single-stock futures. On Sept. 14 the two agencies announced they had settled their feud by agreeing to share oversight of the products. With the agreement in place the three House committee chairmen were able to blend their three versions into a compromise (H Rept. 106-711, Pt. IV) that resembled the original Agriculture panel version written by Thomas W. Ewing, R-Ill. The House passed HR 4541 on Oct. 19, 2000, by a vote of 377–4 under suspension of the rules.

Action in the Senate was blocked by Phil Gramm, R-Texas, chairman of the Senate Banking, Housing and Urban Affairs Committee, who was concerned about the language clarifying the legal status of swaps. That issue was not resolved until meetings the week of Dec. 4 between representatives of Chicago's big commodities exchanges and the senator. Once that compromise had been worked out and reviewed by the three House committees, House and Senate leaders agreed to attach a new version of HR 4541 to the pending omnibus spending bill (HR 4577).

The House adopted the conference report on HR 4577 (H Rept. 106-1033) on Dec. 15 by a vote of 292–60. The Senate cleared the bill by voice vote later that day, and President Clinton signed it on Dec. 21.

MAJOR PROVISIONS

As signed into law, the Commodity Futures Modernization Act:

• Specifically exempted OTC derivatives from regulation by the CFTC, thereby providing legal certainty and enforceability by ensuring that those contracts would not come under regulation.

Under the measure OTC derivatives generally would be exempt from CFTC regulation if the contracts were based on nonagricultural commodities and if they were negotiated privately between institutions or sophisticated investors that have high net worths. Any contract traded in an open exchange where multiple bids were solicited and accepted would be subject to CFTC regulation. The CFTC was also given limited authority over OTC derivatives based on energy products (such as oil or natural gas) or metals (gold, silver, and so forth).

• Specifically exempted numerous banking products from CFTC regulation including bank swap agreements. Established guidelines under which the SEC may take enforcement action against individuals who engage in fraud or manipulation involving equity-based swaps.

• Allowed the trading of futures contracts that were based on an individual stock or on a narrow index of stocks, which had been prohibited under existing law. Gave the Fed responsibility for harmonizing margin (down payment) requirements and tax treatment of stock options and single-stock futures. (Stock options were subject to larger margins and less favorable tax treatment than futures contracts under existing law.)

• Codified recent CFTC reforms creating three separate tiers of regulation for futures contracts based on the type of futures being traded and the sophistication of the investors. Exchanges for ordinary investors would be permitted to set and enforce their own rules, provided that the market met certain minimum standards and adhered to eighteen core principles spelled out in the bill. Required all futures contracts based on agricultural commodities to be traded on these markets.

Separate markets with even less regulations could be established for the trading of more complex derivative instruments with participation limited to institutions and sophisticated investors.

All clearinghouses, systems, or organizations used to track trades would be regulated by the CFTC or by another federal financial services regulator.

Bankruptcy Overhaul

President Clinton pocket-vetoed a major overhaul of the nation's bankruptcy laws Dec. 19, 2000. Congress had cleared the measure, a top priority for the credit industry, Dec. 7.

The main thrust of the measure was to slow the surge in personal bankruptcy filings by limiting the use of Chapter 7, which allows cancellation of debts beyond those that can be repaid after nonessential assets are liquidated. The bill would have required debtors who exceeded a specific means test to file under Chapter 13, which requires repayment of personal debt over three to five years. The final version also contained provisions requiring credit card companies to make information on interest rates and other terms of the card easier for consumers to understand.

Proponents of the legislation, which was passed with bipartisan support in both the House and Senate, said the existing bankruptcy law, together with a relaxed societal attitude toward financial delinquency, made it too easy for many

debtors to walk away from their obligations. They insisted that the legislation was a fair and reasonable way to curb egregious abuses of the system.

Liberal Democrats, backed by consumer advocates, argued that the bill was too weighted toward creditors, who they said bore a large share of the responsibility for the problem because of aggressive marketing campaigns and reckless lending practices that encouraged consumers to incur debt at high interest rates. They were particularly critical of issuers of credit cards and other unsecured debts who granted excessive lines of credit to unqualified consumers and lured consumers into high-interest debts by offering low introductory interest rates, payment options that were too small to reduce principal balances, and other practices designed to raise lender profits.

Although Clinton indicated that he too thought the measure was weighted too heavily toward the interests of creditors, he cited two specific reasons for his veto. The first was a provision that allowed wealthy debtors to shield most, if not all, of their home equity from creditors. Clinton said the so-called "homestead exemption" was unfair not only to creditors but also to less wealthy debtors who had no similar protections and could be forced to live frugally while paying off at least a portion of their debts. Clinton also objected to the deletion of an amendment, added on the Senate floor but dropped during final negotiations, that would have barred violent antiabortion protesters from seeking bankruptcy to avoid fines and court judgments.

The Senate bill also contained an increase in the minimum wage and an offsetting package of tax sweeteners for businesses. Those controversial provisions were dropped from the final version of the bill.

The legislation was prompted by a relatively sudden increase in filings for personal bankruptcy in the United States. About 1.4 million people filed in 1997 compared with about 285,000 in 1984. About 70 percent of those filed under Chapter 7 of the bankruptcy code. The credit industry lobbied hard for legislation that would steer more people away from Chapter 7 and toward Chapter 13 filings so that creditors would have a better chance of recouping at least some of their losses.

Congress had come close to enacting a bankruptcy overhaul bill in the 105th Congress. That effort failed at the eleventh hour when Republicans were unable to fashion a compromise measure that would satisfy Senate Democrats, the Clinton administration, and consumer groups on the one hand and the credit industry on the other. *(1997–1998 action, p. 126)*

HOUSE ACTION

Using the agreement that had stalled in 1998 as a starting point the House got off to a fast start on bankruptcy overhaul, passing a bill (HR 833) on May 5, 1999, by a veto-proof vote of 313–108. The House Judiciary Committee approved the reform bill (H Rept 106-123, Pt. I) on April 28 on a vote of 22–13 with Barney Frank, D-Mass., voting "present."

As passed by the House, the bill would require courts to transfer debtors from Chapter 7 to Chapter 13 if it was determined that they could pay at least $100 a month of unsecured debts, such as credit card balances, after they had paid attorney fees, monthly living costs, a minor child's tuition, all secured debts such as mortgages, and any unsecured debts given priority by the court.

Trustees would consider a person's ability to pay for sixty months. Thus, applicants judged likely to have $6,000 or more in disposable income over the five-year period would be moved into Chapter 13. An exception to this means test would be made for filers earning the median income or less for their geographic region (in 1999 about $50,000 for a family of four). These debtors could file under Chapter 7 even if they had some disposable income. But the bill also made it harder for debtors to nullify certain debts. Filers would have to continue to pay some credit card debts, a requirement that did not exist under existing law, and bankruptcy trustees could not reduce the amount a filer owed on a secured debt, such as a car acquired within five years of filing for bankruptcy.

The bill also capped the homestead exemption for bankruptcy filers at $250,000 and, in a bow to those states with no caps, allowed states to opt out of the restriction. Although most states capped homestead exemptions at about $50,000, five states—Florida, Iowa, Kansas, South Dakota, and Texas—placed no limits on the amount of home equity a debtor could shelter from creditors. Democrats frequently cited Florida and Texas as the two major havens for people seeking to shelter assets from creditors.

During five days of markup in the House Judiciary Committee in April, Democrats—often with support from Republican Chairman Henry J. Hyde of Illinois—tried to ease the impact of the means test on debtors and require consumer protections against credit card marketing practices, all to little avail. Among the amendments that failed in committee was one that would have exempted Social Security benefits from the means test. A similar amendment offered on the floor as part of a procedural motion passed by voice vote. The full House also accepted amendments requiring credit card issuers to make certain disclosures about interest rates and minimum payments in their solicitations.

For the most part, however, Republicans, joined by moderate Democrats, rejected amendments their sponsors said would better balance the reforms between debtors and creditors. A substitute amendment by Jerrold Nadler, D-N.Y., to ease many of the restrictions on debtors in the bill was rejected on the House floor by a vote of 149–272. An amendment by Hyde and John Conyers Jr., D-Mich., to give judges more discretion in determining a debtor's monthly expenses was rejected, 184–238. Hyde offered the amendment because he said the standards in the bill would require too much of a filer's resources for debt repayment. "What will debtors, their spouses, and their children be able to live on?" he asked. Republicans, led by bill sponsor George W. Gekas, Pa., countered that HR 833 provided sufficient protection for the poor while preventing debtors who could afford to repay some of their debts from abusing the system.

SENATE ACTION

The Senate Judiciary Committee approved its overhaul measure (S 625—S Rept 106-49) April 27, 1999, by a vote of 14–4. But the committee left unresolved several difficult issues, including Democratic efforts to soften the means test, to require more thorough disclosure of terms by credit card companies, and to bar violent protestors at abortion clinics from using the bankruptcy law to avoid paying related fines and court fees. Committee Chairman Orrin G. Hatch, R-Utah, persuaded Democrats to withdraw several contentious amendments in hopes that compromises could be worked out before the measure reached the Senate floor. Other amendments were defeated with a pledge from Republicans to search for compromise.

S 625 did not reach the Senate floor until Nov. 4 where it quickly became loaded down with a raft of controversial amendments, including a Republican plan to increase the minimum wage by $1 over three years together with tax sweeteners to businesses worth $18.4 billion over five years. Republicans killed a Democratic alternative of a $1 increase over two years offset by $9.5 billion in tax cuts. (*Minimum wage, p. 579*)

Congress adjourned for the year with several controversial amendments to the bankruptcy reform bill still pending. These were quickly resolved on Feb. 2, 2000, when the Senate renewed debate on the measure. Amendments to prevent gun manufacturers from using bankruptcy to get rid of debts arising from lawsuits against them was defeated, 29–68. An amendment to protect debtors from eviction during bankruptcy proceedings was tabled (killed) 53–44.

Republicans averted a showdown with the Democrats over an amendment by Charles E. Schumer, D-N.Y., to prevent violent protestors of abortion clinics from avoiding paying court fines or fees by filing for bankruptcy. Republican leaders initially opposed the amendment but when they found that some Republicans wanted an opportunity to vote against violence at abortion clinics and that Vice President Al Gore would be present to break a tie vote, they changed their strategy and urged Republicans to vote for the amendment. Majority Leader Trent Lott, R-Miss., said he was not willing to hand Gore a chance to make political points in his presidential campaign against likely Republican nominee George W. Bush. "We'll never let him cast another tie-breaking vote again," Lott said. The Schumer amendment passed, 80–17. The Senate then passed its version of the bankruptcy reform bill, 83–14.

FINAL ACTION; VETO

The bill passed by the Senate was generally less restrictive than the House version. It required bankruptcy cases to be handled under Chapter 13 if debtors earned more than the median wage and could afford to pay back $15,000 or 25 percent of their debt, whichever was less, over five years. The

House bill required debtors to file under Chapter 13 if they could pay back $6,000 over five years. The Senate bill capped the homestead exemption at $100,000 and included several consumer protections that were not contained in the House version. It also included the abortion protestors amendment as well as language that would have given creditors broad authority to tap into individuals' pension funds to collect outstanding debt.

But the biggest problem facing lawmakers was the venue for settling these differences. House members could object to a formal conference with the Senate because the Senate bill contained revenue measures—namely, the business tax breaks adopted in conjunction with an increase in the minimum wage—in violation of the constitutional requirement that the House act first on revenue measures.

After months of internal debate House and Senate Republicans agreed among themselves to a draft conference report that resolved many of the differences between the two versions. In a significant move, Senate leaders agreed to set aside the amendment raising the minimum wage and cutting taxes; that amendment alone would have invoked a certain presidential veto.

The Republican compromise was then subjected to more negotiations with the Democrats and the White House before being finalized. To get around procedural hurdles, Senate and House leaders took a long-dormant bill (HR 2415) dealing with embassy security that had been passed, in different forms, by both chambers, deleted its text, and inserted the compromise provisions of the bankruptcy bill.

In its new form HR 2415 required debtors who earned more than the median wage and who were able to repay $10,000 or 25 percent of their debts over five years, whichever was less, to file for bankruptcy under Chapter 13 rather than under Chapter 7. The measure capped the homestead exemption at $100,000 but then applied the cap only to homes that had been purchased within two years of a bankruptcy filing. The bill also made permanent bankruptcy protections for family farmers.

Omitted from the final version of the bankruptcy measure was the prohibition on bankruptcy relief for violent protestors at abortion clinics. The final version also dropped the Senate provision that would have allowed creditors to tap into debtors' tax-exempt retirement savings and education savings accounts.

The House then adopted its conference report on the bankruptcy reforms (H Rept 106-970) by voice vote on Oct. 14. Senate opponents of the bill mounted a filibuster against the conference report. After a motion to invoke cloture and cut off debate was defeated Nov. 1 by a vote of 53–30, 7 votes short of the 60 needed for cloture, Senate leaders put off further action on the measure until after the 2000 elections.

When Congress reconvened for a lame-duck session, the political landscape had changed significantly. The Senate in the 107th Congress would be evenly divided between the two parties, and both sides agreed that passage of a bankruptcy bill under those conditions would be extremely difficult. Although President Clinton was certain to veto the bankruptcy legislation the credit industry and their supporters calculated that Congress might have time to override the veto before the 106th Congress drew to a close. The gamble was whether Congress would adjourn before the president acted. If it did he could simply pocket-veto the measure, denying Congress the opportunity to attempt an override.

And that is what happened. On Dec. 7 the Senate cleared the conference report, by a vote of 70–28, enough to override a veto. Congress then adjourned Dec. 15, and President Clinton pocket-vetoed HR 2415 on Dec. 19. Privately, Democrats attributed the strong vote in favor of the conference report to the widespread sentiment that Congress would be denied the opportunity to attempt an override.

CHAPTER 3

Trade Policy

Introduction   147

1997–1998 Chronology   151

1999–2000 Chronology   160

Trade Policy

The eight years of Bill Clinton's presidency from 1993 to 2001 coincided with a trend that came to be known as "globalization": the growing importance of trade and investment between and among countries. By the late 1990s the world was bound together by commerce to an extent unprecedented in history. The international trade in goods, services, and intellectual property was at an all-time high, and corporations and individuals were putting an increasingly large share of their capital into foreign countries.

Globalization resulted from a convergence of numerous trends during the late twentieth century, including the collapse of communism in eastern Europe and the former Soviet Union between 1989 and 1991; a move toward capitalism in communist China, the world's most populous country; the adoption of free market economic principles in many developing countries that had tried socialism since the 1960s; the rise of regional "free trade" zones, particularly in Europe, North America, and South America; the growing importance of computers, the Internet, and related high-tech devices, both as items of trade and as the means of sharing information across international borders; the dramatic reduction, during the latter part of the twentieth century, of tariffs, quotas, and other barriers to trade and investment; and the launching in 1995 of the World Trade Organization (WTO) as a global arbiter of trade agreements.

As the world's largest economy, the United States participated in all these trends and was the most important engine for globalization. The U.S. economic expansion that started in 1991 and continued through the rest of the decade helped fuel growth and trade throughout the world. The American appetite for foreign-made consumer goods also provided a vital cushion against problems elsewhere, among them Japan's chronic economic sluggishness during the decade, a Mexican financial crisis of 1994–1995, and an international financial crisis in 1997–1998 that started in East Asia and spread to Argentina, Brazil, Russia, and other "emerging market" countries.

Washington also participated in, and was a major factor in promoting, international agreements to reduce barriers to trade. Among the principal achievements of President Clinton's first term were the negotiation and congressional approval of the North American Free Trade Agreement (NAFTA) that eliminated most trade barriers among Canada, Mexico, and the United States; and the Uruguay Round of the General Agreement on Tariffs and Trade (GATT), which reduced many tariffs and trade quotas worldwide and created the WTO. One of the most important accomplishments during Clinton's second term was the negotiation of a permanent trade agreement between the United States and China. Congress approved that agreement in 2000.

Despite its clear benefits, especially for the industrialized countries, globalization became increasingly controversial as its importance grew. In the United States, Clinton's presidency began and ended with divisive congressional debates over trade agreements. The 1993 congressional action to approve NAFTA was one of the most contentious political battles of Clinton's first term, and the 2000 debate over the China agreement played a comparable role in his second term.

Free trade and globalization had many advocates—especially corporations, financiers, and economists, but also many critics. Labor unions in the United States and other industrialized countries argued that globalization meant the transfer of millions of industrial jobs to developing countries where pay and labor standards were lower. Environmental advocates asserted that developing countries generally had weak regulations to guard against air and water

REFERENCES

Discussion of trade action for the years 1945–1964 may be found in *Congress and the Nation Vol. I*, pp. 187–207; for the years 1965–1968, *Congress and the Nation Vol. II*, pp. 49–116; for the years 1969–1972, *Congress and the Nation Vol. III*, pp. 119–134; for the years 1973–1976, *Congress and the Nation Vol. IV*, pp. 125–137; for the years 1977–1980, *Congress and the Nation Vol. V*, pp. 267–276; for the years 1981–1984, *Congress and the Nation Vol. VI*, pp. 95–112; for the years 1985–1988, *Congress and the Nation Vol. VII*, pp. 139–166; for the years 1989–1992, *Congress and the Nation Vol. VIII*, pp. 165–200; for the years 1993–1996, *Congress and the Nation Vol. IX*, pp. 151–184.

Trade Balance

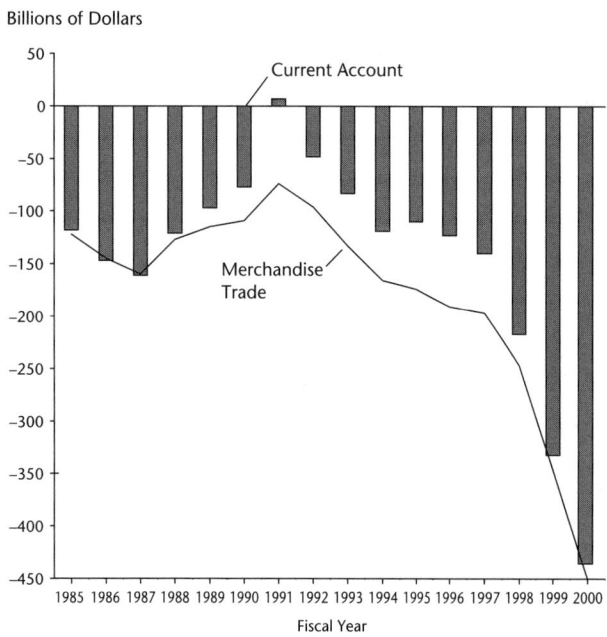

SOURCE: Office of Management and Budget, *Economic Report of the President 2001* (Washington, D.C.: U.S. Government Printing Office, 2001), Table B-103.

pollution by industry. For these and other critics, including some religious leaders and human rights organizations, globalization meant a "race to the bottom": an aggressive drive by multinational corporations to maximize profits by shifting industrial production wherever costs were lowest, regardless of the impact on workers and their families.

Antiglobalization protests became common during the late 1990s, usually in conjunction with major international gatherings of finance and trade executives, such as the annual meetings of the World Bank and International Monetary Fund. The high point of the antiglobalization movement may have come during the 1998 WTO meeting in Seattle, which was called to initiate a new round of negotiations to reduce trade barriers. Thousands of protesters gathered outside the WTO conference center, drawing unprecedented international attention to their complaints about negative consequences of globalization. The protests contributed to, but were not directly responsible for, the WTO's failure to decide on an agenda for its trade negotiations. That failure resulted mainly from continuing disagreements over how to reduce barriers to agricultural trade, which for many countries, including the United States, was one of the most sensitive topics on the trade agenda because of the political influence of farmers.

FAST-TRACK DEBATE

Even before the tumultuous WTO meeting, antiglobalization fervor contributed to one of the most embarrassing legislative defeats of Clinton's presidency involving a procedure known as "fast track." Under this procedure, in use for the previous two decades, Congress was limited to voting up-or-down on trade agreements negotiated by the president and his representatives. With fast track, U.S. negotiators and their counterparts from other countries could be reasonably certain that Congress would not try to amend a trade agreement after it was signed, thus forcing new rounds of negotiations.

Congress last approved fast track in 1993, enabling Clinton to negotiate the final stages of the long-running Uruguay Round under GATT, but then allowed the procedure to expire. Clinton made a modest effort in 1995 to regain fast-track authority but was rebuffed by Republicans in Congress who had won control of both House and Senate in the 1994 elections. The GOP leaders refused to give Clinton any authority to negotiate environmental and labor standards for U.S. trade, which were priorities for most Democrats.

After his reelection in 1996 Clinton again sought fast-track authority in 1997, only to encounter resistance from both parties on Capitol Hill. Angered that NAFTA had seemed to result in the loss of U.S. industrial jobs to Mexico, many Democrats opposed giving Clinton unfettered authority to negotiate future trade agreements. Republicans, despite their general support for free trade, continued to fear that Clinton would give in to pressure from unions and environmental groups for tough labor and environmental standards on U.S. trade. Faced with this resistance, Clinton delayed making an all-out push for fast-track authority until the fall of 1997. The president found strong support for his position in the Senate (where free-trade sentiment traditionally was strong) but organized labor mounted a vigorous campaign against him in the House. Faced with the likelihood that only a small number of Democrats would support the president, House GOP leaders in November shelved the fast-track legislation without bringing it to a floor vote.

The move marked one of the gravest defeats for any president on trade legislation in many years. Perhaps more important for the long term, House reluctance to approve fast-track authority illustrated the growing uncertainty in the nation about the benefits of globalization and free trade. Congressional reluctance to grant fast-track authority also contributed to a delay in long-awaited negotiations toward a Free Trade Area of the Americas, which would cover nearly all countries in the Western Hemisphere. Clinton made no move after 1997 to stimulate those negotiations, and his successor was certain to face difficulty in the talks unless he convinced Congress to provide fast-track authority.

TRADE WITH CHINA

Clinton's second term brought the beginning of a new economic relationship between the United States and China. Since the thawing of relations between the two nations during the 1970s trade had grown dramatically but mostly in a one-way direction with Americans buying $3 or $4 worth of Chinese goods for every $1 they sold to China.

Although Americans clearly liked low-cost consumer goods from China, American politicians and special interest groups argued that U.S.-China commerce strengthened the communist regime in Beijing, which continued to be one of the most repressive in the world. Throughout the 1980s and 1990s, congressional critics of China had an opportunity every year to focus attention on that country's policies on human rights, religious freedom, and other issues. The opportunity arose because of a provision in the 1974 Trade Act (PL 93-618), known as the Jackson-Vanik amendment, that allowed the president to accord normal trade status to communist nations only one year at a time. This provision gave Congress the opportunity to overturn a presidential grant of normal trade status (previously known as "most favored nation" status). Critics never came close to having enough votes to block China's trade status but they mounted annual debates in the House that continued through Clinton's second term.

By 2000, however, the China trade issue had reached a new level. The Clinton administration and Chinese leaders in late 1999 concluded a permanent agreement that reduced most remaining trade barriers between the two countries and that cleared one of the last remaining hurdles to China's membership in the WTO. The agreement was subject to congressional approval, in large part because it would exempt China from the Jackson-Vanik provision.

The main battle occurred in the House, where the China accord became a proxy for ideological disputes over globalization as well as older issues concerning Beijing's communist practices. The issue became the most hard-fought legislative battle at the end of Clinton's presidency outside of the Republican impeachment effort aimed at the president in the latter part of 1998.

Clinton entered into an uncommon alliance with conservative Republicans and big-business groups that favored the China agreement. The opposition featured an equally odd alliance of conservatives and liberals from both parties, labor unions, religious leaders, human rights groups, and environmental activists. After much vituperative rhetoric on both sides and the expenditure of millions of dollars by lobbyists, the House approved legislation on the trade accord by a comfortable margin in May 2000. After Senate Republican leaders delayed action for several months, the Senate gave overwhelming approval in September.

OTHER TRADE ISSUES

Congress spent little time or political energy dealing with other trade matters during the second Clinton term, reflecting the overall difficulty of reaching consensus on contentious matters amid the high level of partisan rancor in Washington.

One matter that was resolved in 2000, after nearly two years of consideration, was Clinton's proposal for trade preferences for sub-Saharan Africa. Clinton had called for a broad reduction in U.S. tariffs and quotas on imports from Africa, arguing that the continent's impoverished nations needed more "trade, not aid." Sympathy for the plight of Africa was strong on Capitol Hill but so was concern that cheap imports from the region could hurt some U.S. producers. In the end, Congress approved legislation that temporarily eliminated U.S. tariffs on some, but not all, imports of clothing and textiles from sub-Saharan Africa. Continuing a process that had been underway for nearly two decades, the bill eliminated tariffs on most clothing imports from Caribbean and Central American countries.

During the last Clinton years Congress also signaled a willingness to expand economic relations with Vietnam, the communist country that had been an enemy during the Vietnam War of the 1960s and 1970s. Clinton in 1994 lifted a broad economic embargo that Washington had imposed against Vietnam as a consequence of the war, and in 1997 he began negotiations toward a formal U.S.-Vietnam trade agreement. As those negotiations were under way, Clinton in 1998 offered Vietnam normal trade status, which was subject to congressional review. Efforts to overturn that status were defeated in the House that year and again in 1999 and 2000. U.S. and Vietnamese officials completed a permanent trade agreement in 1999 and signed it in 2000.

THE TRADE DEFICIT: A NEW TWIST

A remarkable feature of U.S. debates over trade policy in the late 1990s was the relative lack of concern about the country's mounting trade deficit. The United States had run a deficit in its trade with other countries in goods and services every year since 1982. The deficit rose sharply through the 1990s, from $35.7 billion in 1992 to $264.9 billion in 1999. A broader gauge of U.S. trade, which included goods, services, investment income, and money transfers (collectively called the "balance on current account"), showed a somewhat larger deficit growth, from $47.7 billion in 1992 to $331.5 billion in 1999.

In the past, the trade deficit had been a source of concern among many economists and politicians, one of several indications that perhaps Americans were spending beyond their means. The deficit also sparked worries in the United States about the consequences of free trade. Representatives of labor unions and some businesses hurt by low-cost imports argued that Americans were buying too many foreign goods and investing too much money in other countries rather than at home. "Buy American" became a slogan that summarized these concerns and promised a response to them.

But as the trade deficit widened to previously unimaginable levels in the late 1990s, the volume of complaints about it appeared to diminish. There were several explanations for this seemingly contradictory trend. Most important, the trade deficit was a reflection of U.S. economic strength during the decade, especially in comparison to many other countries. Americans prospered during the 1990s, spending record amounts of money buying goods from foreign countries and

investing record amounts in those nations. A strong economy also meant a strong dollar, and a strong dollar made
U.S. exports relatively expensive and foreign imports relatively inexpensive. Low-cost foreign goods helped keep inflation in check and meant that clothing, computers, and many
other products were relatively cheaper in the 1990s than a
decade earlier. A strong dollar also made foreign travel
cheaper for Americans, millions of whom happily deposited
their dollars in Britain, France, the Caribbean, and other vacation spots.

Moreover, the trade deficit remained tiny compared with
the overall U.S. economy, averaging less than 2 percent of the
country's gross domestic product during most of the decade.
The trade deficit had been larger, relative to the total economy, during the 1980s, in part because the U.S. government
borrowed billions of dollars from lenders in Japan and other
countries to finance its enormous recurring budget deficit.
The federal budget deficit began to decline during the Clinton years, and foreigners—still wanting to put their money
in the United States—began investing more heavily than ever
before in U.S. businesses. This foreign investment helped
American businesses grow and become more productive and
ultimately more competitive but it contributed to the growing current account deficit.

Chronology of Action on Trade

1997–1998

Congress took little action on trade issues during the 105th Congress, in contrast to the early years of President Bill Clinton's first term, when debates over the North American Free Trade Agreement (NAFTA) and the Uruguay Round of the General Agreement on Tariffs and Trade (GATT) were at the top of the Capitol Hill agenda.

The most significant congressional action on trade was inaction: the failure in the House of Clinton's request for "fast-track" authority in negotiating future trade agreements. With this authority in place, Congress would give up its right to amend trade agreements, giving U.S. negotiating partners some assurance that a deal would not unravel once it reached Congress. Congress had allowed the authority to lapse in 1994, and Clinton delayed seeking its renewal until 1997. By then, it was too late. Republican mistrust of Clinton, and anger among Democrats about the consequences of NAFTA, undermined support for broad new trade deals.

The House also debated in 1997 and 1998, but did not approve, resolutions to deny "most favored nation" trade status (later changed to "normal trade relations") for China. House debates on China's trade status had become an annual occurrence since the 1980s.

China Trade Status

As it had done annually during most of the 1990s, Congress in both 1997 and 1998 rejected efforts by a broad coalition of conservatives, liberals, human rights activists, labor unions, and religious groups to deny favorable trade status for China. Also as usual, nearly all the action took place in the House where the interested groups used the annual trade debate as a forum for denouncing the Chinese communist government. *(U.S. China policy, pp. 180, 208)*

BACKGROUND

Most-favored-nation (MFN) trade status entitles countries to the lowest-available tariffs on goods and services exported to the United States, provided that those countries re-

ciprocate on the goods and services they import from the United States. The designation was changed in 1998 to "normal trade relations," a name that more closely reflected actual practice. *(Provisions, p. 165)*

In addition to low tariffs, U.S. firms could obtain loans, loan guarantees, and political risk insurance from the Export-Import Bank, the Overseas Private Investment Corporation, and the Agriculture Department for exports to and investments in countries with MFN status.

Under the Jackson-Vanik amendment to the 1974 Trade Act (PL 93-618), China and other communist countries were eligible for most-favored-nation trade status only on a year-to-year basis, as determined by the president. In theory, Congress could reject the trade status for any communist country by passing a joint resolution of disapproval within ninety days of the president's determination. But to do so, Congress would have to override an almost certain presidential veto, a step requiring a two-thirds vote in both houses.

President Jimmy Carter first extended MFN status to China in 1979, the same year diplomatic relations were established between Washington and Beijing. Resolutions to overturn that status were introduced in the House in 1982 and 1983 but not adopted. The Chinese government's brutal crackdown on prodemocracy demonstrators in Beijing's Tiananmen Square in June 1989 heightened criticism of the government worldwide and led to the annual series of debates in Congress on China's MFN status, starting in 1990. Critics of China used the annual presidential determination on China's MFN status as an opportunity to raise concerns about issues ranging from repression of human rights to the country's controversial one-child-per-family population control policy. The House considered resolutions to overturn China's trade status in 1990, 1991, and 1992 but the Senate did not.

By the late 1990s, as U.S.-China trade grew in economic importance and the Tiananmen Square killings faded into history, the debate had become an annual ritual with a known outcome: opponents never came close to overturning

China's trade status but their heated rhetoric about Beijing often roiled U.S.-China relations. *(1995–1996 action, Congress and the Nation Vol. IX, p. 178)*

1997 HOUSE ACTION

The 1997 debate over China's trade status featured some new elements, the most important of which were allegations that China tried to buy influence in the 1996 elections through campaign donations. Leading religious conservatives also raised concerns about reports of government mistreatment of missionaries in China.

President Clinton started the annual debate on May 19, announcing that he would once again renew Beijing's trade status. Opponents across a broad range of ideological and other interests promptly introduced legislation in the House (H J Res 79) to overturn Clinton's determination. The House Ways and Means Committee on June 18 overwhelmingly backed Clinton's position. By a vote of 34–5, the panel sent H J Res 79 to the floor but with a recommendation (H Rept 105-140) strongly recommending that it be defeated. Some committee members said there was much Chinese conduct to criticize but U.S. businesses and strategic interests would suffer if normal trading relations were halted. Bill Archer, R-Texas, Ways and Means chairman, said ending MFN would cost the United States bargaining power on human rights and other issues with China.

Jim Bunning, R-Ky., adamantly disagreed, arguing that trade had given the United States little leverage over China. Bunning was the only Ways and Means Republican to vote in favor of ending MFN; he was joined by four Democrats. The House handily rejected the resolution on June 24, 1997, by a vote of 173–259. Although the outcome disappointed MFN opponents, they did get 32 more votes than in 1996 when an identical resolution received 141 votes.

As usual, the issue caused numerous splits among traditional allies in the House. For example, some conservative Republicans voted to deny China's trade status, while others supported it. The bitterness of the debate was underscored by Dana Rohrabacher, R-Calif., a conservative who said after the vote: "My hands are clean. I have not been shaking hands with butchers." But Majority Whip Tom DeLay, R-Texas, a fellow conservative, sided with the Clinton administration in arguing that trade was the key element of the U.S.-Chinese relationship. "Washing our hands of China is simply irresponsible," he said. "Let us not impose a false isolation on China that diminishes our influence and hurts the very people we want to help."

Minority Leader Richard A. Gephardt, D-Mo., a frequent critic of U.S. trade policy and a potential presidential candidate in 2000, joined conservatives in opposing the MFN extension. In an emotional floor speech, he said the United States had a moral obligation to look past China's immense economic potential and focus on its suppression of political and religious liberties. "This country is not just about business," he said. "This country is about an idea, a moral belief

---

TRADE LEADERSHIP

President Clinton had a relatively stable leadership for trade matters during his eight years in office. Two people, Mickey Kantor and Charlene Barshefsky held the position as U.S. trade representative, each for about four years.

Kantor, Clinton's trade chief during his first term, came to the office after acting as national chairman of the 1992 Clinton-Gore campaign and head of President-elect Clinton's transition team. Although Kantor, a former corporate lawyer in Los Angeles, had little experience in international trade he received high marks as a negotiator during his term. After Commerce Secretary Ronald Brown was killed in a plane crash on a trade mission to Croatia in April 1996, Clinton named Kantor to take over the helm at the Commerce Department. He also named Deputy U.S. Trade Representative Charlene Barshefsky to be Kantor's acting replacement at the trade office. Barshefsky remained the acting U.S. trade representative for the duration of the year.

On Dec. 13, 1996, Clinton nominated Barshefsky to be the permanent trade representative. To assume the job, however, Barshefsky needed a waiver from both chambers of Congress because of provisions in a 1995 lobbying law (PL 104-65) that barred anyone who had advised a foreign government from becoming the permanent U.S. trade representative. As a lawyer in private practice Barshefsky had briefly advised the government of Canada and the province of Quebec in a trade dispute. The Senate passed the waiver, 98–2, on March 5, the same day it confirmed Barshefsky. Wayne Allard, R-Colo., and Majority Leader Trent Lott, R-Miss., cast the two "no" votes. The House cleared the waiver legislation by voice vote on March 11. Barshefsky was sworn in on March 17, a day after President Clinton signed the waiver (S J Res 5—PL 105-5). She remained in the post through the end of the Clinton administration. *(Background, cabinet profiles, p. 984)*

---

that every human being in the world is created with liberty and freedom."

One question on the minds of many members was how the Chinese government would handle its new responsibilities over Hong Kong. Great Britain, which had ruled Hong Kong as a colony since the late 1800s, was scheduled to return the territory to Beijing's control on July 1, 1997. House Speaker Newt Gingrich, R-Ga., had flirted with the idea of extending MFN to China for only three to six months to enable Congress to assess Beijing's governance of the territory. But Britain's last governor of Hong Kong, Chris Patten, essentially nixed that approach, warning in a May letter to Gingrich that any prospect of cutting off China's MFN status would "jeopardize rather than reinforce Hong Kong's way of life." *(Hong Kong trade, p. 158)*

1998 HOUSE ACTION

The House debate in 1998 on China's MFN status covered familiar ground, including Beijing's human rights abuses and alleged attempts to influence the 1996 U.S. elections. In addition, critics voiced concern about CIA reports that China was continuing to provide missile technology to Pakistan, which in May had tested nuclear weapons for the first time in response to similar tests by India, its long-time rival. In addition, congressional investigators were examining charges the Clinton administration had jeopardized national security by allowing Loral Space and Communications Ltd. to launch a commercial satellite on a Chinese rocket. The company's chairman, Bernard Schwartz, was the largest individual contributor to Democrats during the 1996 election cycle. *(China policy, p. 180)*

These and other issues generated controversy on Capitol Hill in the spring as President Clinton prepared for a nine-day trip to China in late June. Some Republicans demanded that Clinton cancel his trip, reminding him that during his 1992 presidential campaign he had denounced President George Bush for "coddling tyrants" in Beijing.

Such arguments carried little weight in the House Ways and Means Committee, long a center of support for increased U.S. trade. On June 25, the day that Clinton arrived in Beijing, the committee supported Clinton's decision to extend the China trade status for another year. The committee acted by voice vote, urging the full House to reject a resolution (H J Res 121—H Rept 105-638) that sought to overturn China's trade status.

Upon his return to Washington, Clinton declared his China trip an unqualified success, arguing that he had built up good will with the Chinese leaders and had pressed them on human rights and other issues of concern among Americans. Even House Speaker Gingrich, one of Clinton's sharpest critics in Congress, acknowledged that the president had done "a good job" in China. "I think if you reach out to a billion people and talk about open markets and expand the zone of freedom on the planet, that's a pretty good investment for the world." But other Republicans were unswayed. "A verbal joust doesn't change Chinese policies or the repressive crackdown on the Chinese people," said Sen. Tim Hutchinson, R-Ark.

The full House took up the MFN disapproval resolution on July 22, the same day that Clinton signed into law unrelated legislation (HR 2676—PL 105-206, devoted mainly to reforms in the Internal Revenue Service) that changed the name of the trade status from MFN to "normal trade relations." The House debate echoed rhetoric of previous years and the outcome was similar. The resolution (H J Res 121) was rejected 166–264; proponents of the resolution received seven fewer votes than the previous year. *(1999–2000 action, p. 166; China trade agreement, p. 160)*

Fast-Track Authority

President Clinton suffered a major political and foreign affairs setback late in 1997 when House Democrats and their allies in organized labor denied him a renewal of "fast-track" authority for newly negotiated trade agreements. The Senate demonstrated strong support for the president's request but Clinton averted an outright defeat in the House only when Republican leaders shelved a scheduled vote on it. After that failure Clinton made no other effort during his second term to secure the authority, which Congress had given to every other president since Gerald R. Ford in the 1970s. The House rejected the measure (HR 2621) outright in 1998 but that vote was more a reflection of preelection partisan squabbling than a measure of sentiment on trade issues.

Clinton's defeat on the issue almost certainly contributed to his decision not to press for multinational negotiations on a proposed Free Trade Area of the Americas, which would create a free-trade zone for all thirty-four countries in the Western Hemisphere except Cuba. Clinton did pursue and obtain controversial trade agreements with China in 1999 and with Vietnam in 2000. *(China trade agreement, p. 160; Vietnam agreement, p. 167)*

In addition to its impact on potential trade agreements, the failure of fast track illustrated Clinton's ambivalent position among Capitol Hill Democrats, who should have been his closest allies. House Minority Leader Richard A. Gephardt, D-Mo., the Democrat nominally charged with shepherding the president's legislative agenda through the House, led the opposition to fast-track authority. His position reflected organized labor's strong opposition to many aspects of growing international trade and Gephardt's close ties to labor.

Fast-track authority guaranteed that, once the president submitted a trade agreement to Congress, lawmakers would take an up-or-down vote within ninety days, with no amendments allowed. Without such restrictions, foreign countries were reluctant to undertake serious trade negotiations with the United States for fear that members of Congress would force a second round of bargaining to obtain concessions beneficial to their states or districts. Unlike treaties, which have to be approved only by the Senate, trade agreements are subject to approval by a majority vote in both houses of Congress.

The most recent extension of fast-track authority had expired at the end of 1994, the year that Republicans won control of both houses of Congress. Clinton delayed submitting a request for renewal of the authority until September 1997. In the meantime, the number of members of Congress who advocated free-trade positions had declined. Moreover, the early years of experience with the North American Free Trade Agreement (NAFTA), approved by Congress in 1993, had been disappointing from the point of view of U.S. labor unions and environmental groups, both influential among Democrats. Representatives of those organizations argued that NAFTA had led to the transfer of thousands of manufacturing jobs from the United States to Mexico, where labor and environmental standards were weaker. In many ways, congressional action on the fast-track authority became a referendum on NAFTA.

BACKGROUND

As of 1997, Clinton and congressional leaders had been negotiating on and off for nearly three years on the details of a plan to renew fast-track authority. The impasse was over reconciling competing claims: Republicans insisted that any future trade negotiations focus strictly on trade issues (such as tariffs and market access) while Democrats wanted labor and environmental standards addressed in the "core" of any trade agreement, thus making them enforceable by trade sanctions. *(1995–1996 action, Congress and the Nation Vol. IX, p. 178)*

House Speaker Gingrich signaled in April 1997 that the Republican Party was open to a compromise on the matter but the president put off action until fall while he worked with Congress on legislation to create a balanced budget. Clinton's hesitation frustrated free-trade supporters, especially in the Senate, who argued that the measure needed an all-out push by the administration, preferably during the summer months before the rush to adjournment. Clinton did announce in July that he had assembled a team of private-sector, cabinet, and subcabinet representatives to draft a fast-track bill and push it through Congress in September and October.

Clinton officially began his campaign for renewed fast-track authority on Sept. 10. But instead of offering a detailed request, the White House event amounted to little more than a pep rally. In deference to Senate Minority Leader Tom Daschle, D-S.D., and others who complained that they had not been adequately consulted as the administration prepared to unveil its bill, Clinton delayed revealing any specifics.

In his speech, Clinton vowed to "continue to seek even further adherence around the globe to fundamental worker rights and environmental protection, as we have for decades." Clinton said he firmly believed that trade was essential to sustaining the economic expansion that helped him win reelection in 1996. "Every trade agreement we will reach will tear down barriers to our goods and services, and that is good for America," he said.

When Clinton went to the Capitol on Sept. 16 to unveil the details of his plan, he immediately ran into a skeptical, and sometimes hostile, caucus of House Democrats who said the bill did not put enough emphasis on labor and environmental issues. The Democrats were emboldened by labor unions, which had launched a major campaign against the measure. The union lobbying was intense and personal. Many Democrats, especially freshmen who had yet to face a key trade vote, owed their seats in large part to labor-financed campaigns. The AFL-CIO vowed a $1 million advertising campaign to whip up voter sentiment in the districts of undecided members.

Opinion polls indicated that the public was skeptical of free-trade agreements in general. The surveys also showed that the public, by a wide margin, supported the Democrats' idea of using trade agreements to try to protect the environment and raise labor standards in other countries.

In his proposal, Clinton had included language encouraging the negotiation of trade agreements that would require "trade-related" labor and environmental improvements. But that attempt to win support, or at least reduce opposition, from labor unions and environmental groups caused problems for Clinton among those who normally would support fast-track authority. Republicans complained that such requirements cold impede trade. In addition, they argued that the language could, at least in theory, give the president license to negotiate trade deals that would change U.S. environmental and labor laws. Sen. Phil Gramm, R-Texas, normally a staunch advocate of free trade, called Clinton's proposal "totally and absolutely unacceptable."

From the outset, it was widely recognized that the fate of Clinton's proposal would be decided in the House, where opposition was strongest among Democrats. The Senate traditionally had been more friendly to trade initiatives.

1997 SENATE ACTION

By the time the Senate Finance Committee marked up its version of the fast-track bill on Oct. 1, 1997, most senators' concerns had been mollified. Members met first behind closed doors with U.S. Trade Representative Charlene Barshefsky and then approved the measure (S 1269—S Rept 105-102) by voice vote in a public markup session that lasted less than a minute. Only Kent Conrad, D-N.D., voted "no."

The committee bill said labor and environmental issues should be considered during trade negotiations but only to the extent needed to prevent trading partners from lowering their standards to boost exports. Also, any such agreements could not restrict U.S. autonomy. In addition, the GOP-drafted bill proposed to narrow the scope of issues that could be added to bills eligible for fast-track treatment. Under previous fast-track rules, anything deemed "necessary or appropriate" to implement an agreement was allowed. The committee bill proposed tightening that to include only provisions that would be "necessary to implement such agreement" or "otherwise related to the implementation, enforcement . . . and are directly related to trade."

For their part, committee Democrats won a two-year extension of trade assistance programs that would help workers and companies who lost jobs and business to foreign competitors. Funding was to come from a $5 surcharge on airline and ship passengers arriving from Canada, Mexico, and the Caribbean. Also included was language requiring that the administration consult with Congress before initialing any trade agreements, typically the time when the most controversial items in the negotiations were added or dropped.

Administration officials wanted the Senate to take up the bill quickly, on the theory that a big vote for it in that chamber would provide momentum in the House. But the Senate did not act during October, when proponents and opponents were preparing for action in the House. In back-to-back votes early in November, the Senate demonstrated that the measure had a filibuster-proof level of support. The first vote came Nov. 4 on a move to invoke cloture (thus heading off a filibuster). The margin was surprisingly large on a **key vote of 69–31 (R 43–12; D 26–19)** and was taken as a sign that the Senate would be able to pass the legislation. *(1997 key votes, p. 865)*

The next day, Nov. 5, the Senate agreed by a similar margin, 68–31, to proceed to floor consideration of the bill. But then the Senate stopped and waited for the House to act.

1997 HOUSE ACTION

Clinton's problems in the House were evident at a Ways and Means Trade Subcommittee hearing Sept. 30, 1997. Top Democratic supporter Robert T. Matsui, D-Calif., warned that fast track "is in deep trouble at this particular time." Speaker Gingrich echoed the sentiment, saying: "I do not today see the votes to pass fast track."

According to vote counters on both sides, House passage required 60 to 80 Democratic votes in addition to those of 150 or so Republicans. Both sides were well short of their respective goals at that point. Representatives of each party blamed the other. Republicans said Clinton had not been active enough on the issue and had been afraid of antagonizing labor unions. Democratic supporters, such as Matsui, contended that business interests were not doing enough to line up support among their allies.

As in the Senate committee markup, the stage was set for action in the full Ways and Means Committee by a round of last-minute negotiations between committee leaders and the office of the trade representative. Those talks resolved an expected collision between the administration and committee chairman Bill Archer, R-Texas.

Archer had produced an initial draft that the administration opposed on three counts: the negotiating authority was too narrow in scope; the White House disagreed with the way labor and environmental issues were addressed; and language governing the issues that could be included in the implementing legislation was too strict. When Archer learned that his first draft was not going to receive administration support or any Democratic votes, he gave ground. The administration said the resulting bill, though it used different language, closely tracked the Senate Finance measure.

Like the Senate version, it allowed for labor and environmental issues to be part of fast-track trade deals when they were directly related to trade. Both bills said the president would be free to pursue those issues in the International Labor Organization and the World Trade Organization but that any "side agreements" would be subject to the normal legislative process—in other words, open to amendments and vulnerable to Senate filibusters.

The Ways and Means Committee approved its version of the bill on Oct. 8 by a vote of 24–14 (HR 2621—H Rept 105-341, Pt. 1). But the most closely scrutinized factor—how many Democrats supported the measure—provided an ominous signal to the White House. Only four of the panel's sixteen Democrats voted for the bill despite a personal push by Clinton who met with about half of them on the eve of the markup. Before the session, Clinton had the support of Democrats Matsui and John Tanner of Tennessee. The president's pleas brought over only two more: Jim McDermott of Washington and William J. Jefferson of Louisiana. The tepid show of Democratic support rankled Republicans, some of whom clearly were not happy in the role of defending a Clinton priority. "If this is such an important issue for the president, why is it he could only get four votes?" remarked Jim Nussle, R-Iowa.

Clinton, who left Oct. 12 for a seven-day visit to three South American countries to talk about trade, hailed the panel's action. But Archer echoed the sentiments of other House Republican leaders, who said they still wanted 80 to 90 Democratic votes when and if fast track came to the floor. Such a tally was all but impossible, however. Democratic vote counters said the maximum number of Democratic votes for the bill was 70 and that number could be reached only if nothing changed. Republican leaders later lowered their demand to 70 Democratic votes.

Democratic supporters of the legislation, with the vote count on their side stalled and undecided members dribbling into the opponents' camp, pleaded for a do-or-die vote in hopes of pushing some undecided party members into their column. That put pressure on Republican leaders, who did not want to be blamed for killing the measure because of a failure to schedule a vote. House leaders agreed on Oct. 29 to schedule a floor vote before Congress adjourned for the year and picked Nov. 7 as the date. Once a vote was scheduled, the White House mounted a furious push, extending to undecided Democrats the best it had to offer, including promises of presidential visits to their districts to help raise funds before the 1998 elections. On Nov. 5 Clinton unveiled a $4 billion package for job retraining and other aid to communities that lost jobs to trade. Less than half the money represented increases in future funding; the rest was already anticipated. The following day Clinton flew to Texas for the dedication of the presidential library of his predecessor, George Bush. Former presidents of both parties joined Clinton in pushing for fast-track renewal. "We hope and pray you get the votes tomorrow," Republican Gerald R. Ford (1974–1977), said. Clinton hurried back to Washington to work the phones and visit with lawmakers. But by late that evening the count of Democratic supporters was stuck in the low 40s, a figure that would require Republicans to deliver more than 170 votes to pass the bill.

With the White House still unable to count enough votes by Friday, Nov. 7, House leaders at Clinton's request pushed the vote past the weekend. Clinton's frustration was evident Nov. 7 at his third news conference on fast track in as many days. "This is a no-brainer on the merits," he told reporters. The all-out lobbying blitz continued into Monday, Nov. 10.

House Republicans produced more votes on their side than had been promised but Clinton was still unable to move enough Democrats to clinch the victory. Clinton's aides said he drew the line when several swing members demanded concessions on unrelated bills that were also in danger in the session's final hours. Rather than allow fast track to be defeated, Clinton and Gingrich shelved the bill on Nov. 10. Gingrich later said the bill was "about eight votes" short of a majority.

Gephardt, who had led the opposition, said he was willing to work with Clinton to draft a new bill for consideration in 1998. But key supporters expressed skepticism that fast track had any future while Clinton remained president. "After all this massive effort, after the Senate doing its part, and after all the work that went into trying to get the votes in the House, I don't see it happening at this point," Senate Majority Leader Trent Lott, R-Miss., said. "So it would appear to me that it's dead."

1998 SENATE ACTION

Despite Lott's prediction, Republicans in both chambers revived the fast-track issue in 1998, more as a way of demonstrating splits in Democratic ranks during an election year than as a serious effort to pass legislation. In contrast to the bruising battles of 1997, Clinton played only a minor role during 1998. In July, his spokesperson, Mike McCurry, called the Republican action "political mischief-making." Even if Clinton had been inclined to tackle the issue again, his political strength was sapped during the year by the sex-and-lies scandal that led to his impeachment. *(Impeachment, p. 813)*

The Senate Finance Committee opened the 1998 deliberations on trade issues on July 21 by approving a broad measure (S 2400—S Rept 105-280) combining fast track with several other trade measures. The vote was 18–2, with only Conrad and Carol Moseley-Braun, D-Ill., voting "no." Committee chairman William V. Roth, R-Del., sought to expand the debate beyond fast track. He included in the bill an array of trade items with support from various factions in Congress. The most prominent was an initiative to promote trade with forty-eight nations of sub-Saharan Africa. "We feel by putting this package together we improved the chances of getting it all approved," Roth said.

In its markup, the committee rejected two amendments related to fast track that were offered by Conrad, an opponent. One, rejected 6–14, would have required the administration to consider the potential economic consequences of trade agreements and allowed the United States to renegotiate agreements that had adverse effects. The other, rejected 4–16, would have required the president to assess the currency stability of other parties to any agreement negotiated under fast-track authority.

The bill included several other trade-related provisions, including one that would allow Caribbean and Central American nations covered by the 1983 Caribbean Basin Initiative to export some products, such as canned tuna, petroleum, and some textiles, to the United States free of duties and quotas. *(Caribbean trade, p. 157)*

Despite the strong committee vote for the bill Senate leaders did not bring the measure to the Senate floor in the remaining months of 1998.

1998 HOUSE ACTION

With crucial midterm elections looming, and with Clinton battling a drive for his impeachment, House Republicans decided in September to bring the fast-track bill (HR 2621—H Rept 105-341, Pt. 1) to the floor for the vote that had been shelved the previous November. The apparent Republican strategy was to demonstrate divisions within the Democratic Party and to give Republicans on either side of the issue an opportunity to cast votes that might be popular with voters back home. In that partisan context, the fast-track bill failed Sept. 25 on a vote of 180–243 with 71 Republicans voting against the bill and 151 in favor.

House action on the bill came as the world was still reeling from the effects of the 1997–1998 Asian financial crisis. Russia in August had been forced to default on some of its debt and Argentina and Brazil had been battered in the financial markets. Supporters of fast track appealed to Speaker Gingrich to avoid a vote, saying in a letter that the certain defeat of the bill "will send further shock waves to already fragile world markets." But Gingrich brushed such concerns aside and blasted the Democratic Party for its divisions. "It is sad to see the partisan politics of the unions and the Democratic Party, and yes, this [measure] may go down," he said. "But if this goes down and we end up in a steep worldwide recession, some of us will have the comfort of knowing we cast the right vote."

Among the majority voting "no" was Matsui, the leading supporter of fast track among Democrats. Matsui angrily denounced Gingrich's maneuver, which he said "shows a disdain for the legislative process and it threatens to disrupt international markets and quite possibly our national economy." Despite that prediction, international financial markets were not roiled by the House vote. Experts said investors had not taken the House action seriously. But, paradoxically, some observers said the vote ultimately might improve the chances for fast-track legislation by demonstrating that it was needed to overcome Congress's tendency to become bogged down in partisan wrangling over trade matters.

Export-Import Bank

Congress in 1997 agreed to a four-year reauthorization (S 1026—PL 105-121) for the Export-Import Bank, an independent federal agency established in 1945 to help finance foreign purchases of U.S. goods through low-interest direct loans, loan guarantees, and export credit insurance.

Previous authorization for the bank had expired on Sept. 30, 1997; the bill extended it to Sept. 30, 2001. The legislation did not include a specific funding level, leaving that up to the appropriations committees.

Some lawmakers were critical of the Ex-Im Bank (as it was commonly known), calling its activities "corporate welfare." On the other side, proponents argued that the bank was essential to helping U.S. firms compete with foreign companies that received significant export assistance from their governments. House sponsor Michael N. Castle, R-Del., said the reauthorization would help ensure that U.S. businesses and workers "are able to compete and win against subsidized foreign competition in today's global market."

SENATE ACTION

The Senate version of the bill, sponsored by Rod Grams, R-Minn., began in the Banking Committee, which approved it, 16–0, on July 31 (S 1026—S Rept 105-76). The Senate passed the bill by voice vote on Sept. 16. The committee approved, 17–0, an amendment by Michael B. Enzi, R-Wyo., directing the bank to do more to inform small and rural companies about its programs. Enzi withdrew a second amendment that would have required the bank to give preferences to companies that did not regularly use the bank's services.

HOUSE ACTION

The House Banking Committee approved the Ex-Im bill (HR 1370—H Rept 105-224) by voice vote on July 9. The panel approved two amendments sponsored by Bernard Sanders, I-Vt. One, adopted by voice vote, required that the bank have at least two labor representatives on its advisory committee. The second, approved 24–19, directed the bank to ensure that preference be given to assisting firms with a commitment to investment and creating jobs in the United States.

The House passed the bill Oct. 6 by a vote of 378–38, then inserted the text into S 1026 and passed that bill by voice vote.

The House first agreed to amendments to:

• Prohibit bank subsidies of exports to Russia if that country transferred missile systems to China. The amendment, sponsored by Gerald B. H Solomon, R-N.Y., was approved by voice vote.

• Bar Ex-Im Bank financial assistance to companies that employed child labor. Offered by Bruce F. Vento, D-Minn., the amendment was approved by voice vote.

• Give preference to U.S. companies seeking help for operations in China that avoided the use of child or prison labor; avoided discrimination based on religion, race, or gender; and, in general, respected human and worker rights. Offered by Lane Evans, D-Ill., the amendment was adopted by a vote of 241–182.

• Change the name of the bank to the United States Export Bank. Offered by John LaFalce, D-N.Y., the amendment was adopted 362–56.

CONFERENCE, FINAL ACTION

House and Senate negotiators reached agreement on the bill on Nov. 7. The Senate adopted the conference report (H Rept 105-392) by voice vote on Nov. 8, and the House cleared the bill on Nov. 9, also by voice vote. Senate conferees balked at the House-passed proposal to change the bank's name, and the proposal was dropped.

Conferees also decided, by an 8–2 vote, to modify the House-passed provision to prohibit the bank from subsidizing exports to Russia if that country transferred missile systems to China. The new language applied only to the sale of SS-N-22 antiship missile systems. It also required the president to certify that the transfer had occurred and that it posed "a significant and imminent threat to the United States" before the subsidies could be banned.

The bill included a provision stating that it was U.S. policy to foster the expansion of exports, thereby contributing to a commitment to reinvestment and job creation in the United States. The bill also added child labor to the list of human rights abuses that could serve as a basis for the president to deny Ex-Im credits. President Clinton signed the bill (PL 105-121) into law on Nov. 26, 1997.

MAJOR PROVISIONS

In addition to the overall reauthorization, the bill included provisions to:

• Reauthorize the Tied-Aid Credit Fund for four years. Tied-aid grants were paired with traditional export financing by the bank to encourage foreign purchasers to buy U.S. goods and services. The program was designed to counter similar tied-aid programs of nations such as Japan, Germany, and France.

• Extend the Ex-Im Bank's authority to help finance the export of nonlethal defense articles.

• Establish an assistant general counsel for administration at the Ex-Im Bank to deal with ethics issues, and a new advisory committee to facilitate U.S. exports to sub-Saharan Africa.

• Require that two labor representatives be included on the bank's advisory committee, and require the bank to design an outreach program for companies that had never used its services.

• Deny export financing for sales to the Russian government or military if that country transferred SS-N-22 antiship missile systems to China. The SS-N-22 reportedly was the world's fastest and most dangerous cruise missile, with versions launched by planes and submarines.

• Create an advisory committee to recommend ways to increase exports to sub-Saharan Africa.

Caribbean Trade

The House on Nov. 4 defeated a bill (HR 2644) intended to expand trade preferences for goods imported from twenty-six Caribbean and Central American countries. The measure was rejected by a **key vote of 182–234 (R 136–83: D 46–150; I 0–1)**. *(1997 key votes, p. 865)*

Congress in 2000 approved some of the trade benefits that had been included in HR 2644. The chief benefit was the elimination of tariffs on imports of many clothing and textile items from the region; it was included in a broader measure (HR 434—PL 106-200) that also provided some trade benefits for sub-Saharan Africa. *(Africa trade initiative, p. 167)*

The bill defeated in 1997 would have given preferential tariff and quota treatment, equivalent to that accorded Mexico under the North American Free Trade Agreement (NAFTA), to specific products from nations that were part of the Caribbean Basin Initiative (CBI). The CBI, launched by President Ronald Reagan in 1983, provided preferential access to U.S. markets as a way of encouraging economic development and political stability in the region. CBI trade benefits were made permanent in 1990. *(1983 action, Congress and the Nation Vol. VI, p. 106; 1990 action, Congress and the Nation Vol. VIII, p. 180)*

HR 2644 was intended as temporary relief, lasting for fourteen months or until the Caribbean countries joined NAFTA or a proposed hemisphere-wide Free Trade Area of the Americas. The bill included a statement that it was U.S. policy to include these Caribbean countries in NAFTA or a comparable free-trade agreement at the earliest possible date.

The relief would have applied to such products as textiles, apparel, canned tuna, petroleum and petroleum products, footwear, handbags, and luggage, which did not receive duty-free treatment under the CBI. The projected cost was $243 million in lost revenue in fiscal 1998–1999, to be offset by tightening deductions for employment severance pay.

The bill originated in the House Ways and Means Committee, which approved it by voice vote on Oct. 9 (H Rept 105-365). But when the bill reached the floor opponents argued that Caribbean exports had increased since NAFTA took effect and continued to outstrip Mexican exports in some key sectors. U.S. imports of textile and apparel goods, including finished products made from U.S.-supplied materials, totaled $6.1 billion from Caribbean countries in 1996, compared with $3.6 billion of such goods from Mexico. Some lawmakers also complained that the expanded Caribbean bill included fewer safeguards than NAFTA required of Mexico. They noted, for example, that the bill did not require sanctions against exporters that used sweatshops or child labor. Other opponents argued that NAFTA had cost U.S. jobs and that expanding Caribbean preferences would only aggravate those losses.

The House had approved identical CBI provisions earlier in 1997 as part of a tax-reconciliation bill (HR 2014), but they were dropped in conference at the insistence of the Senate, which had not yet considered them. As negotiations on the final tax bill were reaching a conclusion, the White House made a last-minute attempt to win inclusion of the CBI proposal but was unsuccessful. *(Tax reconciliation, p. 48)*

Hong Kong Trade Ties

Hong Kong was allowed to maintain separate economic and trade offices in the United States after July 1, 1997, when Great Britain, which held it as a colony since the late 1800s, handed the territory back to China. Congress authorized that step in a bill that President Clinton signed into law on June 27 (S 342—PL 105-22). The Beijing government promised to accord Hong Kong substantial economic and political autonomy. Located on the southeast China coast, Hong Kong had developed one of the most successful economies in East Asia based on financial services and trade.

The measure prevented Hong Kong trade offices in the United States from coming under the control of the Chinese embassy in Washington. It also ensured that, following the reversion, Hong Kong civil servants working in those offices would be accorded the same status as officials with international organizations.

The trade office provisions originally were part of a broader bill (HR 750) that also would have authorized the president to reconsider the special status that Hong Kong enjoyed in a variety of areas, including trade and law enforcement, if China moved to restrict the territory's autonomy. The House passed that bill March 11 by a vote of 416–1, with Ron Paul, R-Texas, casting the only dissenting vote. It had been approved by the International Relations Committee on March 6.

The Senate on May 20 passed a narrower bill (S 342, no written report), which focused on the economic and trade offices. The bill passed on a voice vote after no debate. The House accepted that version on June 17, also by voice vote, clearing it for the president.

Vietnam Trade Status

The House in 1998 supported President Clinton's effort to improve trade relations with Vietnam. By a vote of 163–260 on July 30, the House rejected a move (H J Res 120—H Rept 105-653) to deny favorable trade status for Vietnam. The vote was the latest in a series of actions during the 1990s to improve relations between Washington and Hanoi, which had been on the opposing sides of the Vietnam War during the 1960s and early 1970s.

Clinton in 1994 had lifted a wide-ranging trade embargo against Vietnam. That move was largely a reward to Hanoi for cooperating with U.S. efforts to locate the remains of American servicemen who were killed or missing during the war. A year later, Clinton established formal diplomatic relations with the communist government of Hanoi, which was introducing elements of capitalism into its economy. Trade between the United States and Vietnam grew rapidly, from $224 million in 1994 to $948 million in 1996. Then in 1997 the two countries began negotiations toward a comprehensive trade agreement; a final agreement was reached in 2000.

With the trade talks under way, Clinton on March 9, 1998, determined that Vietnam should be eligible for most-favored-nation (MFN) trade status. That status entitled countries to the lowest-available tariffs on goods and services exported to the United States, provided that those countries reciprocate on the goods and services they import from the United States. The designation was changed later in 1998 to "normal trade relations," a name that more closely reflected actual practice. In addition to low tariffs, U.S. firms could obtain loans, loan guarantees, and political risk insurance from the Export-Import Bank, the Overseas Private Investment Corporation, and the Agriculture Department for exports to and investments in countries with MFN status.

Under the Jackson-Vanik amendment to the 1974 Trade Act (PL 93-618), communist countries such as Vietnam were eligible for MFN trade status only on a year-to-year basis, as determined by the president. In theory, Congress could reject the trade status for any communist country by passing a joint resolution of disapproval within ninety days of the president's determination. But to do so, Congress would have to override an almost certain presidential veto, a step requiring a two-thirds vote in both houses.

For technical reasons, Clinton's initial MFN designation for Vietnam ran for only four months. On June 3, 1998, Clinton granted the status for a full year, effective on July 3, 1998. On June 3, Rep. Dana Rohrabacher, R-Calif., a long-time opponent of trade relations with communist countries, introduced legislation (H J Res 120) to overturn Clinton's determination granting MFN status to Vietnam. By a voice vote on July 1 the House Ways and Means Committee sent the resolution to the House floor with a recommendation that it be defeated.

During House debate on the measure on July 30, Rohrabacher and other critics of the trade status insisted that Vietnam had not done enough to deserve improved relations with the United States. Specifically, they charged that Hanoi had not fully accounted for U.S. soldiers missing since the Vietnam War ended in 1975. Opponents also said that U.S. government financing for exports to Vietnam represented "corporate welfare for communists," especially given what the critics said was Hanoi's poor record of economic management. Supporters of Clinton's policy said Hanoi had stepped up its efforts to determine the fate of servicemen missing since the war, and they argued that closer relations between the two countries were in the U.S. national interest. The House rejected the resolution by a voice of 163–260, a margin similar to the vote three days earlier rejecting a comparable effort by Rohrabacher to deny the favorable trade status for China. *(1999–2000 action, p. 167)*

Other Trade-Related Bills

The 105th Congress considered several other bills dealing with trade matters in 1997 and 1998, including the following.

GENERALIZED SYSTEM OF PREFERENCES

Congress in 1997 extended the Generalized System of Preferences (GSP) from June 1, 1997, through June 30, 1998, as part of the tax bill (HR 2014—PL 105-34) enacted on Aug. 5 in connection with the year's budget-reconciliation package. GSP provided duty-free status to products imported from developing nations with the aim of spurring economic growth in those countries. The most recent extension had expired on May 31. Congress in 1998 further extended GSP through June 30, 1999, as part of an omnibus appropriations bill for fiscal 1999 (HR 4328—PL 105-277). *(1999 action, p. 169)*

OVERSEAS PRIVATE INVESTMENT CORPORATION

Congress in 1997 agreed to reauthorize the Overseas Private Investment Corporation (OPIC) for two years as part of the fiscal 1998 foreign operations appropriations bill. OPIC provided loan guarantees and political risk insurance for U.S. companies operating abroad. The spending bill, signed into law by President Clinton on Nov. 26 (HR 2159—PL 105-118) reauthorized OPIC operations and raised OPIC's combined statutory ceiling for financing and risk insurance from $23 billion to $29 billion. The measure also provided $60 million for OPIC direct and guaranteed loans, and $32 million in administrative expenses. *(1994 action, Congress and the Nation Vol. IX, p. 177; 1999–2000 action, p. 169)*

INDIA, PAKISTAN SANCTIONS

Responding primarily to U.S. agricultural interests, Congress in 1998 authorized President Clinton to waive some of the economic sanctions he had been required to impose against India and Pakistan after both countries tested nuclear weapons in May of that year. The sanctions had been required by an Arms Export Control Act provision in the 1994 State Department authorization bill (PL 103-263). The Arms Export Control Act required the president to impose trade and credit sanctions against countries that tested nuclear weapons.

The nuclear testing in India and Pakistan caused worldwide concern because the countries were long-time enemies that had fought several wars and were engaged in an ongoing dispute over the region of Kashmir. But the U.S. farm lobby opposed banning food exports for foreign policy reasons. In response to such concerns, the Senate in July adopted an amendment to the fiscal 1999 agricultural appropriations bill (HR 4101) allowing the president, for one year, to waive the sanctions against India and Pakistan so that both countries could continue receiving shipments of U.S. food and other humanitarian supplies. The president could not waive bans on other types of exports to those countries, including military items. The waiver was included in the House-Senate conference version of the bill (H Rept 105-763) and the entire agriculture bill was then folded into an omnibus fiscal 1999 appropriations bill (HR 4328—PL 105-277). *(1999 action, p. 169; omnibus bill, p. 62)*

1999–2000

Congress had not had a major debate over trade policy since 1994 when it approved an international trade deal creating the World Trade Organization but it made up for lost time in 2000 with a hotly contested debate over a permanent trade agreement with China. After several years of negotiations, the Clinton administration and Chinese officials had signed an agreement in November 1999 intended to normalize two-way trade.

Clinton said the deal was good for the United States because it would open China's closed market to American goods and services. Eager to make the 1.2 billion Chinese their customers, American businesses heartily agreed. But labor unions, human rights organizations, and other groups strongly opposed the agreement, arguing that China remained a repressive society and that imports of cheap consumer products from China were putting Americans out of work.

Commercial arguments carried the most weight on Capitol Hill. The House approved the trade deal in June by a surprisingly comfortable margin, and the Senate followed suit in September.

Congress in 2000 also approved significant legislation intended to bolster the textile and apparel industries in Caribbean and Central American nations and to help develop those industries in sub-Saharan Africa.

China Trade Agreement

Congress in 2000 took one of its most important economic and foreign policy steps in many years by approving permanent normal trade relations between the United States and China. This was a key element of a landmark trade agreement between the nation with the world's largest economy and the nation with the world's largest population. It helped clear the way for China's membership in the World Trade Organization (WTO). Over time, the accord was expected to boost U.S. exports to China.

President Clinton lobbied hard for approval of the China agreement, making it his chief legislative priority on Capitol Hill during his last full year in office. The political battle over the issue centered in the House where a coalition of conservative Republicans and liberal Democrats opposed closer relations with the communist government of China. House approval had been uncertain for several months after the trade deal was signed in November 1999. But a strong lobbying campaign by business interests, especially agriculture and high-technology sectors, helped push legislation approving the deal through the House by a surprisingly large margin in May. Political gridlock delayed action in the Senate for four months, but that chamber ultimately gave its approval in September. Clinton signed the measure into law in October. Both presidential candidates, Democrat Al Gore

and Republican George W. Bush, had supported the bill and pledged to pursue expanded international trade if elected. *(China policy, p. 208)*

BACKGROUND

Signed in Beijing on Nov. 15, 1999, the U.S.-China trade agreement had two main purposes: it normalized trade between the two countries, making it easier for each to sell goods and services to the other, and it gave U.S. approval for China to enter the WTO.

The agreement was the result of several years of negotiations made possible by the general improvement in relations since the 1970s between two countries that had been on opposite sides of the Korean War and the cold war. U.S.-China trade had grown rapidly during the 1980s and 1990s but by the late 1990s had primarily become a one-way street, with China selling much more to the United States than it bought in return. The principal reasons were that the American market was more open to foreign trade than was the Chinese market and the United States was a very wealthy country with an enormous appetite for low-cost consumer goods produced by China while China was still a poor country unable to afford large quantities of the goods and services sold by the United States. The trade agreement removed most of China's legal and administrative barriers to imports from the United States, thus making possible a more equal balance in two-way trade.

China first sought to join the General Agreement on Tariffs and Trade (GATT), the predecessor to the WTO, in 1986 when Beijing began transforming the economy from pure communism to a mixture of communism and capitalism. Since the formation of the WTO in 1995 China had made membership in that body one of its main economic and foreign policy objectives. The WTO monitored compliance with trade agreements, and membership in it generally was considered vital for any country's long-term economic growth. As of early 1999 China's main hurdle to WTO membership was its lack of permanent trade agreements with the United States and the European Union, respectively the first- and second-largest markets in the world. China completed its agreement with the European Union on May 19, 2000—five days before the crucial House vote—and won formal approval for WTO membership in late 2001.

U.S.-CHINA TRADE AGREEMENT

In general, the 1999 U.S.-China agreement reduced tariffs and nontariff barriers (such as quotas and other restrictions) on the trade in goods and services between the two countries. Because China had imposed more of these barriers in the past than had the United States, the agreement was expected to generate a bigger boost in U.S. exports to China than vice versa.

Much of the agreement dealt with trade in agricultural goods, an important aspect of U.S. trade that had been stymied in China by government restrictions. China agreed to reduce its tariffs on key U.S. food products (such as beef, cheese, grapes, pork, poultry, and wine) from 31.5 percent to 14.5 percent by 2004. China also agreed to allow private trade in agricultural products for the first time (previously, all such trade had to be conducted by government entities) and to eliminate government subsidies on exports of its agricultural products. By encouraging U.S. food imports, these elements of the trade agreement were expected to have a negative effect on China's inefficient, low-technology agricultural sector, a factor that heightened resistance to the agreement within China.

The agreement reduced China's tariffs on U.S. industrial products from an average of 24.6 percent to 9.4 percent by 2005. Tariffs on goods that the United States considered to be "priority products" (such as chemicals, medical equipment, paper, and wood) would be reduced even further. China would eliminate all tariffs on U.S.-made computers, semiconductors, and telecommunications equipment by 2005; previously, China's tariffs on these items had averaged 13.3 percent. Finally, China agreed to reduce numerous restrictions on operations by U.S. banks, insurance companies, telecommunications providers, and other service firms.

One aspect of the trade deal had a direct impact on Congress: once China joined the WTO it would achieve "permanent normal trade relations" with the United States, a status that would exempt it from the provisions of the Jackson-Vanik amendment to the 1974 Trade Act (PL 93-618). Jackson-Vanik stipulated that no communist nation could be eligible for "most favored nation" trade status (later changed to "normal trade relations") with the United States unless the president certified annually to Congress that it allowed its citizens to emigrate freely. Congress could overturn the president's action by passing a joint resolution. Jackson-Vanik originally was intended to force the Soviet Union to allow free emigration by Jews but during the 1980s and 1990s congressional critics of China used the law as the basis for annual debates about Beijing's suppression of human rights. The Jackson-Vanik issue thus became a focal point of the congressional debate over the China trade deal. *(China trade status, pp. 151, 166)*

PREDEBATE MANEUVERING

President Clinton on March 8, 2000, submitted proposed legislation to Congress implementing the U.S.-China trade agreement. Clinton formally began his lobbying campaign at a White House ceremony on May 9 featuring former presidents Gerald R. Ford and Jimmy Carter and a host of other dignitaries including former secretary of state Henry A. Kissinger and Minnesota Gov. Jesse Ventura. Opponents held a news conference on the same day featuring actress Goldie Hawn.

Clinton's proposal prompted the onset of one of the most intense lobbying campaigns of the 106th Congress. House Minority Whip David E. Bonior, D-Mich., led the congressional opposition and predicted the vote would be close enough that one or two members could make the difference. Organized labor mounted an aggressive lobbying campaign against the China bill; its prime argument was that China used slave labor to produce many export products and refused to allow independent labor unions. Religious and human rights groups also argued that China's government was one of the most repressive on Earth, one that should not be rewarded with the political and economic favors of increased trade with the United States.

At the same time, business leaders initiated a multimillion-dollar advertising campaign on behalf of the trade deal. The business campaign was led by the Chamber of Commerce of the United States, which argued that the trade agreement would help open China's huge market to U.S. exports. The Business Roundtable, a group of executives from large corporations, said it planned to spend $10 million on advertisements and lobbying in support of the bill.

From the outset, the principal political question was the number of House Democrats who would vote for the China trade measure. Republican leaders assumed that they could provide most of the 218 votes needed to ensure passage in the 435-member House but they insisted that the White House produce between 85 to 90 Democratic votes in favor. As of early May, administration officials said they could count on only 30 to 40 votes among the 211 Democrats in the House. It was generally assumed that a strong majority would vote for the legislation in the Senate, which traditionally had a higher percentage of members with protrade, internationalist outlooks.

A few House centrists began to seek an option other than "yes" or "no." Sander M. Levin, D-Mich., and Doug Bereuter, R-Neb., explored ways to hold China accountable for its actions on human rights, compliance with trade rules, and other issues. As the vote drew near, they came together with a proposal to establish a joint congressional-executive branch commission to monitor China's actions and report to Congress. When Republican leaders agreed to attach the plan to the China bill, approval was assured. Party whips said the Levin-Bereuter package had won over as many as 30 votes. The China bill ultimately passed by 40 votes. *(China bill "safeguards," box, p. 162)*

Another key step was an agreement between Clinton and House Speaker J. Dennis Hastert, R-Ill., on a package of legislation to help impoverished inner cities and rural areas through tax cuts and other development incentives. The agreement, which coupled political and legislative priorities of both leaders, was one of the most significant bipartisan developments in recent years. Commerce Secretary William M. Daley acknowledged in a press briefing on May 23 that the timing of the deal was no coincidence. He said there was a strong desire "by a number of members, especially minority members, that as we move forward with trade, we address some of the difficult areas of our nation."

CHINA BILL "SAFEGUARDS" WON EXTRA VOTES FOR PASSAGE

When the House passed the bill (HR 4444) in 2000 to normalize trade relations with China much of the credit for bringing the crucial bloc of lawmakers on board went to two low-key intellectuals of the House. Sander M. Levin, D-Mich., and Doug Bereuter, R-Neb., spent months crafting language to address concerns about enhancing the trade status of a nation with a record for human rights violations, labor abuses, and military posturing. When they unveiled it on May 19 ranking Republicans announced that they intended to make the proposal part of the China bill on the House floor. Several wavering lawmakers said that new language would ensure their "yes" votes. "It makes the vote substantially easier," said chief deputy majority whip Roy Blunt, R-Mo.

Bill supporters, particularly Democrats, had long said provisions addressing specific China issues would ease passage by securing as many as forty votes and shore up others whose support was only tentative. At the May 19 news conference two previously undeclared members—Diana DeGette, D-Colo., and John J. LaFalce, D-N.Y.—said they would now vote "yes." Jim DeMint, R-S.C., suggested he would do so as well. And Tom Sawyer, D-Ohio, and Asa Hutchinson, R-Ark., said the language had eased their affirmative decisions.

One major proposal by Levin and Bereuter that the Ways and Means Committee added to the bill sought to protect U.S. industry and agriculture against potential "surges" of low-cost imports from China. A series of other proposals on human rights, labor rights, and other issues were appended to the bill as part of the rule (H Res 510) drafted by the Rules Committee for House action on the measure. The core proposal was for a twenty-three-member panel, composed of members appointed by Congress and the president and with a full-time staff, that would monitor human rights, labor standards, and religious freedoms in China. The panel would report to Congress at least annually, and the House International Relations Committee would be required to hold a hearing on that report. *(Other provisions, p. 165)*

Opponents insisted, as they had for months, that the plan was no more than a "fig leaf" that would effect no change in China. "That is a feel-good amendment, that is a let's-get-a-couple-more-votes amendment," said Bob Ney, R-Ohio.

House minority whip David E. Bonior, D-Mich., also pointed to recent cases in which Congress ignored the recommendations of commissions it created, most recently a panel on religious persecution and human rights that recommended against permanent normal trade status for China. That, Bonior said, was a sign that Congress also would ignore the panel that Levin and Bereuter sought to create.

The administration also sought to address local priorities for individual members who were wavering on the China issue. Democrat Robert E. "Bud" Cramer agreed to support the bill after the Commerce Department promised to reconsider a plan to close a national weather station in his tornado-prone Alabama district. And Democratic Caucus Chairman Martin Frost of Texas supported the bill after the Northrop Grumman Corp., a major defense contractor, signaled that it would stay put in Dallas after reaching agreements with the Navy and the city.

Of particular importance was the ultimate position of influential New York Democrat Charles B. Rangel, a senior member of the Congressional Black Caucus and the ranking Democrat on the Ways and Means Committee. Rangel announced on May 16 that he would vote for the bill, a move that helped win significant support from his colleagues among the New York delegation, within the Black Caucus, and on the Ways and Means panel.

The deep partisan divisions in Washington were put on hold in the days surrounding the House debate. Majority Leader Dick Armey, R-Texas, who normally prized his role as a Clinton nemesis, said at a May 24 news conference that he was "proud of the effort the president made" in support of the bill. Most striking of all was the close cooperation between the White House and House Majority Whip Tom

DeLay, R-Texas, one of the most partisan Republicans on Capitol Hill and the man generally credited as the chief strategist behind the 1998 House impeachment of Clinton.

At the start of 2000, proponents of the China trade initiative feared that Clinton would back away from the bill to aid Vice President Al Gore, who was caught between his loyalty to the administration and his desire for union support on his bid for the presidency. Instead, Clinton spent much of his available time early in the year lobbying undecided Democrats. Robert T. Matsui of California, the main Democratic vote-counter in the House, said that many to whom Clinton paid the most attention ultimately voted for the bill.

2000 COMMITTEE ACTION

The two committees with jurisdiction over the China legislation, Senate Finance and House Ways and Means, both approved it on May 17 by overwhelming margins, giving the measure powerful momentum. The Senate panel acted first, approving its version (S 2277—S Rept 106-305) on an 18–1 vote. The House committee acted a few hours later, approving its version (HR 4444—H Rept 106-632) on a 34–4 vote. The action was not particularly suspenseful in either committee. Each committee enjoyed sole jurisdiction over trade in its chamber, and both tended to be far more attentive to the needs of commerce than most other congressional committees.

One key to the wide margin in the Ways and Means Committee was the inclusion of a provision drafted by Levin and Bereuter that aimed to stem the negative effects on specific U.S. industries of a potential "surge" of Chinese imports. This provision codified language in the underlying U.S.-China trade agreement by allowing the president to raise tariffs and quotas on the excess volume of goods. Steel producers and farmers were considered the American businesses most likely to be affected by any surge in Chinese products because their bottom lines often were closely linked to the price of imports. Ways and Means approved the Levin-Bereuter proposal by voice vote; the proposal was offered as an amendment by committee chairman Bill Archer, R-Texas.

The House Rules Committee on May 23 added to the bill other provisions of the Levin-Bereuter proposal for a commission to monitor Chinese actions on human rights and other issues. As part of its rule (H Res 510) for floor consideration of the bill the Rules Committee also added a $99 million authorization for news broadcasts into China; this proposal had been a priority of undecided John Edward Porter, R-Ill., who then announced support for the trade bill.

The Finance Committee bill had none of the Levin-Bereuter provisions. Senate Majority Leader Trent Lott, R-Miss., who favored the China agreement, made clear that he disliked the antisurge provision but he also said: "I think we shouldn't jump to conclusions before we see what they do" in the House. Max Baucus, a Democrat from the agricultural state of Montana, and Orrin G. Hatch, a Republican from steel-producing Utah, sent a letter to Senate colleagues May 16 seeking support for the antisurge language should it reach the Senate.

In its deliberations, Ways and Means considered, but did not adopt, three other amendments. One, by Benjamin Cardin, D-Md., was ruled nongermane. It aimed to strengthen U.S. trade law to make it easier for manufacturers such as steelmakers to prove that foreign products had been dumped on the U.S. market ("dumping" is the exporting of products at below-market prices in hopes of gaining increased market share), and called on the administration to raise tariffs and quotas on imported products.

Two amendments offered by Pete Stark, D-Calif., were defeated. The vote was 10–28 against one amendment to preclude the president from granting normal trade status to China unless Taiwan were allowed into the WTO before or at the same time as China. Stark's other amendment, defeated 6–16, would have required China and the United States to reach agreement on banning the import of AK-47 machine guns and similar weapons made in China. Administration officials said that provision was unnecessary because Clinton already had signed an executive order banning such imports.

The Senate committee considered no amendments to the bill, and instead devoted much of its deliberations to congratulatory comments about the historic nature of the vote before them. Phil Gramm, R-Texas, said that a chance to vote on such a measure, which he said could bring China "back from the dark side," was something senators lived for when they were kissing babies, shaking hands, and considering legislation over which they were "bored to tears" much of the rest of their careers.

The lone "no" vote in the Senate panel came from James M. Jeffords, R-Vt., who passionately described China's suppression of rights in Tibet.

2000 HOUSE ACTION

By the time the full House considered the China trade bill (HR 4444) on May 24 it was clear that passage was likely but the margin remained uncertain. The Levin-Bereuter amendments, coupled with sustained lobbying by business interests and not-so-subtle deal-making by the White House, had ensured that at least 150 Republicans and 70 Democrats would support the bill, enough to give it a slight majority.

The first test came on adoption of the rule for House consideration of the bill. The rule was crucial because it attached to the bill the Levin-Bereuter plan for a legislative-executive commission that would report on human rights and other developments in China. The rule was adopted by a wide margin, 294–136.

Opponents tried to make passage of the bill more difficult by offering a motion to recommit it to the Ways and Means Committee with a requirement that the committee add language saying China's permanent normal trade status would be revoked if it attacked or blockaded Taiwan. China regarded Taiwan as a "renegade" province and had recently threatened military action against it. The proposal was designed to make the China vote more difficult for Republicans (many of whom had strong commitments to Taiwan), but it was defeated 178–258—providing a clear indication that the underlying bill would pass.

Passage of HR 4444 come on a **key vote of 237–197 (R 164–57; D 73–138; I 0–2),** 19 votes more than were necessary for a majority. *(2000 key votes, p. 915)*

Supporters praised the bipartisan cooperation that had made passage possible, and Clinton described the vote as "an historic step toward continued prosperity in America, reform in China, and peace in the world." If the Senate followed suit, he said, the China agreement "will open new doors of trade for America and new hope for change in China." Opponents clearly were frustrated by their failure. "The burden is now on members of Congress who voted for this legislation and on the president of the United States to produce some results," said Nancy Pelosi, D-Calif., a leading opponent.

After the vote, Democrats began trying to reunite the party. Levin said he agreed with bill opponents that the next president would have to address labor and environmental standards before he would win congressional approval for "fast-track" authority to negotiate further trade agreements. That authority, which requires Congress to vote up or down on trade agreements the president negotiates, expired in 1994 and Clinton had been unable to win it back. *(Fast track, p. 153)*

The day after the vote, Clinton called Bonior and Minority Leader Richard A. Gephardt, D-Mo., who had opposed the bill, to the White House to discuss proposals to provide Medicare coverage for prescription drugs for senior citizens, a priority issue for Democrats.

2000 SENATE ACTION

Expectations in Washington that House passage of the bill would be followed by quick action in the Senate were dashed during late May and early June when Senate Majority Leader Lott made it clear that he was in no hurry to hand another political victory to Clinton. Lott said he objected to some of the amendments, such as the Levin-Bereuter proposals that had eased House passage of the bill, and indicated he was inclined to send the House bill to committee instead of directly to the Senate floor. Moreover, some senators appeared to view the China bill as a possible means of forcing action on unrelated matters, such as the long-pending measures to overhaul campaign finance laws.

The minority of senators who opposed the bill, generally the most liberal and the most conservative lawmakers, also begin preparing hostile amendments. Paul Wellstone, D-Minn., planned to focus efforts on monitoring human rights, labor rights, and environmental conditions in China. Foreign Relations Committee Chairman Jesse Helms, R-N.C., predicted "robust" Senate deliberations into Chinese prison labor, religious persecution, human rights abuses, proliferation of nuclear weapons, and military threats to Taiwan. "We are going to have a debate, Mr. Clinton. And we are going to have votes, perhaps uncomfortable votes, on a range of issues relating to China," Helms said.

Perhaps the greatest threat to expeditious Senate action was a proposal (S 2645) by Robert G. Torricelli, D-N.J., and Fred Thompson, R-Tenn., to set up an annual presidential review of China's record in supplying nuclear weapons and technology to nations that may not be friendly to the United States, especially North Korea, and to require the president to take action if he determined that such transfers were taking place. Torricelli and Thompson said they might attempt to attach their proposal to the China trade bill, a step that, if successful, would force the issue back to the House for another contentious debate. In addition, Appropriations Committee Chairman Ted Stevens, R-Alaska, who favored the China bill, said Senate action on it should be delayed until after Congress had passed and Clinton had signed all thirteen appropriations bills for the coming fiscal year. With those types of maneuvers under way, Lott announced on June 12 that he would delay Senate consideration of the China trade bill. "Senators have strong feelings on all sides, and some of them are going to insist on offering amendments," he told reporters. "And I just think if we rush to it we could . . . take something that probably is going to pass overwhelmingly and get it tangled up in a way that would be counterproductive."

Administration officials and Senate Democratic supporters of the China bill urged Lott not to delay floor action. Joe Lockhart, Clinton's spokesperson, said on June 13 that Lott would be "making a huge mistake if he decided to use an issue of this importance to play politics."

While the bill awaited debate in the Senate, Clinton on June 2 declared another one-year extension of normal trade relations status for Beijing. The House on July 18 rejected, 147–281, a resolution (H J Res 103) to overturn Clinton's decision. *(China trade status, p. 166)*

After a summer during which it focused its attention on other business, the Senate took up the House version of the China trade bill (HR 4444) on Sept. 5, just after the annual Labor Day recess. With an estimated three-fourths of the 100 senators committed to supporting the bill the only question was whether the Senate would adopt amendments that would force the measure back to the House. Supporters argued that such a move would endanger the bill, in part because some House Democrats who had voted for it in May might change their positions now that the November elections were approaching. Finance Committee Chairman William V. Roth Jr., R-Del., put the argument this way: "Bluntly, a vote to amend is a vote to kill this bill and, with it, any chance that U.S. workers, farmers, and businesses will benefit from China's accession to the WTO."

A strong majority of senators clearly accepted that line of reasoning and pledged to oppose any amendments, even ones they might otherwise support. Among those frustrated by this stance was Robert C. Byrd, D-W.Va., a former majority leader who saw himself as a defender of the prerogatives of the Senate and its members. Complaining that senators had taken a "blood oath" to vote against amendments, Byrd tore into his colleagues for abandoning their cherished right to amend legislation sent to them by the House. "What is the Senate coming to when the Senate engages in that kind of charade?" he asked. "Senators ought to bow their heads in shame." Byrd offered an amendment aimed at promoting the use of "clean coal" technology in China but admitted he was "utterly wasting my time." The 32–64 vote against the amendment proved him correct.

Opponents of the trade bill dominated much of the Senate debate, which was notable for its lack of passion and suspense. Helms was among the few senators using strong language, blasting China's human rights record, its hostility toward Taiwan, and its sales of nuclear weapons technology to countries such as Pakistan.

The Senate repeatedly rejected amendments during the first two weeks of September before encountering the only one that was given even a remote chance of adoption: a reworked version of the Thompson-Torricelli measure calling for sanctions against China if it was found to be sending weapons of mass destruction to other nations. In an unsuccessful bid to accommodate the White House, the two senators had redrawn their proposal during the summer to apply to all key suppliers of such weapons—not just China—and making sanctions against those countries discretionary rather than mandatory. The new proposal also would have required the president to impose nontrade-related sanctions on individuals, companies, and groups found to be spreading weapons of mass destruction.

Despite their efforts at compromise, Thompson and Torricelli were forced to watch their amendment fail on Sept. 13, when the Senate tabled it by a **key vote of 65–32 (R 30–23; D 35–9).** "I was hoping we could get into the 40s rather than the 30s," Thompson said afterward, tacitly acknowledging that the proposal never posed a true threat to the China bill. "Clearly, the no-amendment strategy is working for them." *(2000 key votes, p. 915)*

The failure of the amendment underscored how difficult it had been for Republicans worried about China's danger to U.S. national security to make their voices heard over those more concerned with promoting commerce. Although senior GOP lawmakers had condemned the administration for using the term "strategic partnership" to characterize U.S.-China relations they also had heeded the warning of the party's business allies not to stir up any anti-China sentiment. Thompson pointed to recent intelligence reports of increasing Chinese exports of weapons of mass destruction as evidence that Congress should hold the government in Beijing accountable. Opponents questioned whether unilateral U.S. sanctions would prove effective against China. Because few, if any, other countries were likely to follow the U.S. lead in punishing China the effect would be to put American companies at a competitive disadvantage, they argued.

The Senate rejected seventeen other amendments, among them proposals:

• By Helms, to require the president to certify to Congress that China had made strides in improving a range of human rights, including dismantling labor camps, opening access to Tibet, and releasing those imprisoned for political or religious reasons. Rejected 32–63.

• By Robert C. Smith, R-N.H., who offered three proposals to require the congressional-executive branch commission created in the bill to monitor China's cooperation with U.S. goals on human rights issues, such as reducing the harvesting of internal organs from prisoners. Defeated 29–66.

• By Wellstone, to require the president to certify that China was not exporting goods made with prison labor. Defeated 29–68.

The Senate gave final approval to the bill by a vote of 83–15 on Sept. 19. The "yes" vote was slightly higher than most predictions at the outset of debate two weeks earlier. Eight of the 55 Republicans and 7 of the 45 Democrats voted against the bill. Two Democrats were absent: Joseph Lieberman, of Connecticut, who was campaigning as his party's vice-presidential candidate, and Daniel Akaka of Hawaii.

President Clinton signed the trade measure into law on Oct. 10, 2000.

MAJOR PROVISIONS

The centerpiece of HR 4444 (PL 106-286) was language making permanent the "normal trade relations" status that the United States had accorded to China on an annual basis and effectively approving the U.S.-China trade agreement signed in November 1999. Following are major provisions of the bill:

• **Normal trade relations.** The bill authorized the president to exempt China from the Jackson-Vanik amendment to the 1974 Trade Act (PL 93-618) and to extend permanent, nondiscriminatory treatment to Chinese goods and services once China was accepted into the WTO. Under Jackson-Vanik, normal trade relations (previously known as most-favored-nation status) could be extended to most communist countries only for one year at a time.

• **Presidential certification.** Before granting permanent normal trade status to China the president would have to certify to Congress that the terms for China's entry into the WTO were as rigorous as those agreed to in the November 1999 U.S.-China trade agreement

• **Antisurge safeguards.** The president was given authority to increase tariffs and quotas on Chinese imports to provide relief to specific U.S. industries and workers in response to instances when the U.S. International Trade Commission found that a surge in Chinese imports threatened to disrupt the U.S. market.

• **Human rights and labor commission.** A twenty-three-member commission, appointed by Congress and the president, was created to monitor human rights and labor issues in China. The commission would submit an annual report of its findings on internationally recognized freedoms, such as freedom from torture and from being jailed for political views or advocacy of human rights; freedom from arbitrary arrest, detention, or exile; the right to a fair public trial by an independent tribunal; freedom of choice in employment; and freedom of religion. The House International Relations Committee would be required to hold a hearing on the findings within thirty days of receiving them and could draft legislation to follow up on the panel's recommendations no later than sixty days after receiving the report.

• **WTO compliance.** The Office of U.S. Trade Representative was required to issue an annual report on China's compliance with multilateral and bilateral trade agreements. The World Trade Organization (WTO) would be urged to carry out an annual review of China's compliance.

• **Forced labor.** An interagency task force, headed by the Treasury Department, was created to monitor imports and promote effective enforcement of U.S. laws barring goods made in China with forced or prison labor.

• **Trade pact enforcement.** Federal agencies would receive additional resources to monitor and enforce trade agreements with China and other nations.

• **Technical assistance.** The Commerce, Labor, and State Departments were directed to provide training and technical assistance to help China develop its labor and commercial laws.

• **Taiwan.** The bill expressed the sense of Congress that the WTO should accept Taiwan as a member at the same time China joined.

• **Radio Free Asia, Voice of America.** The bill authorized $99 million in fiscal year 2001 for Radio Free Asia and the Voice of America to expand broadcasts to China and neighboring countries.

China Trade Status

In a run-up to the following year's debate over a landmark trade agreement between the United States and China the House in July 1999 rejected a move to deny normal trading status to China. The action was the latest of an annual series of House debates about China centering around the temporary, one-year extension of favorable trading status for China. Congressional approval in 2000 of a permanent U.S.-China trade agreement, coupled with China's expected entry into the World Trade Organization, ultimately would make the annual debates unnecessary. *(1997–1998 action, p. 151; China trade agreement, p. 160)*

1999 HOUSE ACTION

The 1999 debate occurred in the context of a downturn in relations between Washington and Beijing. A special House committee had reported in late 1998 that China might have acquired information useful for its nuclear weapons program as a result of espionage at U.S. weapons laboratories. Then in May NATO warplanes bombed the Chinese embassy in Belgrade during the alliance's campaign to force the Yugoslav military out of Kosovo. The Clinton administration insisted that the bombing was accidental but Chinese authorities for months refused to accept that claim, demanding compensation for damages and punishment of those responsible for the bombing. *(Embassy bombing, p. 226)*

President Clinton on June 3 submitted to Congress his determination that China should continue to receive normal trade status from the United States (formerly known as most-favored-nation status) for another year. Rep. Dana Rohrabacher, R-Calif., immediately introduced legislation (H J Res 57) to overturn Clinton's determination. The House Ways and Means Committee reported (H Rept 106-262) the resolution on July 1, by voice vote, with a recommendation that the House reject it. The full House debated the measure on July 27 and ultimately rejected it, 170–260—a margin similar to the House vote in 1998. Because both chambers had to vote to disapprove continuation of normal trade status, the House action ended the matter for the year.

As in most previous years, the House debate centered on human rights abuses in China. Rohrabacher and other critics castigated Beijing for repression of religion and political dissent. Supporters of the trade status argued that the United States could best influence events in China through trade and diplomacy.

Although the vote was not close, members on both sides of the issue said the margin offered no clue as to the outcome of the anticipated debate on extending permanent normal trade status to China. "A permanent vote is much more difficult," said Robert T. Matsui, D-Calif., a prominent proponent of free trade. U.S. and Chinese representatives signed a permanent trade agreement on Nov. 15, 1999, and Clinton said he would submit the deal to Congress for approval in 2000.

2000 HOUSE ACTION

Even with pending congressional approval of permanent trade status for China in 2000, any change in status would not take effect until China entered the World Trade Organization, a step not expected until late 2001 or early 2002. In the meantime yet another extension of China's temporary trade status was necessary. Clinton on June 2, 2000, sent Congress his determination to issue such an extension, to be effective from July 2000 to July 2001. Rohrabacher then introduced legislation (H J Res 103) to overturn Clinton's determination. By voice vote on July 13 the Ways and Means Committee ordered the resolution reported to the House with an unfavorable recommendation (H Rept 106-755). The full House rejected Rohrabacher's resolution on July 18 by a vote of 147–281. The margin was the widest of any vote on the China trade issue since 1996 when opponents garnered only 141 votes to deny the status to China.

Export Administration Act

With Congress at an impasse over legislation regulating high-technology exports, lawmakers in October 2000 cleared a one-year, stopgap bill (HR 5239—PL 106-508) to govern the export of products with military as well as commercial applications. President Clinton, whose administration had appealed for legislation on the matter, signed the bill into law Nov. 13.

High-tech exports had been covered by the Export Administration Act (PL 96-72), the most recent version of which expired in 1994. Congress was unable to agree on an extension, and for six years thereafter Clinton had regulated exports of sensitive "dual-use" technology (including such items as supercomputers) through executive orders and waivers. Interest in reauthorizing the act was revived after allegations in 1998 that China had improved its long-range missiles with technology gleaned from the launching of U.S. commercial satellites.

The Export Act had established federal policy for licensing the export of nearly 2,400 dual use items, including high performance computers and software. It included penalties for companies and individuals who violated the act. *(1994 action, Congress and the Nation Vol. IX, p. 174)*

The Senate Banking, Housing, and Urban Affairs Committee unanimously approved a comprehensive authorization bill (S 1712—S Rept 106-180) in September 1999. But several Senate committee chairmen blocked floor action, citing national security and jurisdictional concerns. The committee bill would have reduced the number of products restricted for export abroad while raising the penalties for violations of export restrictions. A central issue before the Senate was whether high-tech exports should be regulated primarily by the Commerce, Defense, or State Departments, each of which presumably would bring a different perspective to bear on the question of how tightly the government should control such trade. It was widely assumed that the Commerce Department would want to promote exports as much as possible, that the Defense Department would seek to curtail exports of items with military applications, and that the State Department would focus on using exports to advance U.S. foreign policy interests.

Several efforts to draft a compromise version of the bill stalled in the Senate during 2000. In the meantime, the Clinton administration pressed for congressional action, arguing that U.S. competitiveness in the worldwide market for high-technology products was hampered by uncertainty resulting from the absence of legislation. Some members of Congress also argued that the president lacked sufficient authority to penalize companies that improperly exported high-technology items.

The House on Sept. 25, 2000, passed legislation (HR 5239—PL 106-508) to increase penalties for companies and individuals that violated U.S. rules on export of dual-use items. The bill would have increased fines for corporate violations of the original Export Administration Act from the existing $50,000 to $500,000, or five times the value of the exports. For individuals, the fines would be $250,000, or five times the export value.

The Senate took up the House bill on Oct. 11 and decided on a simpler step: it discarded the new penalty provisions and substituted language extending the expired Export Administration Act for a one-year period. Sen. Michael B. Enzi, R-Wyoming, advocating the temporary measure, said the country "needs comprehensive reform of its export control system" but he acknowledged that there was not yet a consensus on such a broad approach. A stop-gap measure "keeps the pressure on" Congress to reach agreement, he said.

The Senate passed the temporary measure by voice vote and sent it back to the House, which cleared it by voice vote on Oct. 30. President Clinton signed the legislation on Nov. 13, 2000.

Vietnam Trade Status

The House in 1999 and 2000 overwhelmingly rejected efforts by some members to block favorable trade status for Vietnam. The votes generally were viewed as indicating that Congress probably would approve a formal trade agreement, signed in 2000, between the United States and Vietnam. *(1998 action, p. 158)*

Following a series of steps in the 1990s to improve relations with Vietnam President Clinton in 1998 extended "most-favored-nation" trade status (later renamed "normal trade relations") to Vietnam. That move reduced the tariffs on Vietnamese exports to the United States (and vice versa)

and made American companies doing business in Vietnam eligible for U.S. government loans and guarantees. An attempt by opponents of improved relations with Vietnam to overturn Clinton's action failed in the House in July 1998 by a vote of 163–260.

Under the 1974 Trade Act (PL 93-618) Clinton could extend Vietnam's normal trade status only on a year-to-year basis, subject to a congressional veto. Clinton on June 3, 1999, announced that he would renew the status for another year. On June 9, Rep. Dana Rohrabacher, R-Calif., introduced H J Res 58 to overturn Clinton's action. The House Ways and Means Committee opposed the resolution by voice vote on July 1, sending it to the House floor with a negative recommendation (H Rept 106-282). The House on Aug. 31 rejected the resolution 130–297.

By 1999, two-way trade between the United States and Vietnam had reached $946 million, according to State Department figures. The trade balance was in Vietnam's favor; in that year, Vietnam exported $655 million worth of goods to the United States and imported $291 million worth of U.S. goods. U.S. investments in Vietnam, which had grown rapidly during the mid-1990s, slowed in the latter part of the decade. In 1999 U.S. companies invested about $120 million in Vietnam.

In 2000, as U.S. and Vietnamese diplomats were putting the final touches on a permanent trade agreement between the two countries, Rohrabacher and other critics made another attempt to block normal trade status for that country. Rohrabacher on June 6 introduced H J Res 99 to overturn Clinton's granting of normal trade status to Vietnam for the 2000–2001 period. Again, the Ways and Means Committee opposed that resolution (H Rept 106-794), and the full House rejected it by a wide margin, 91–332, on July 26.

Just two weeks before that House vote, on July 13, U.S. and Vietnamese officials formally signed the long-awaited bilateral trade agreement giving Vietnam permanent normal trade status. Clinton praised the agreement in a statement: "From the bitter past we plant the seeds of a better future," he said. "This agreement is one more reminder that former adversaries can come together to find common ground." The accord was subject to congressional action, expected in 2001 or 2002.

Africa Trade Initiative

Two years after President Clinton first asked for it Congress in May 2000 approved legislation offering limited trade concessions for low-income countries in sub-Saharan Africa, the Caribbean, and Central America. The trade bill (HR 434—PL 106-200) fell far short of the sweeping "free trade" measures that some African leaders long had hoped for but it did offer a promise that some countries in the region could substantially boost their exports to the United States. It was the first major legislation in six years to expand U.S. trade.

Clinton had requested legislation in 1998 including the forty-eight-nation region of sub-Saharan Africa under the "generalized system of preferences," which allows some products from developing countries to be exported duty-free to the United States and other industrialized countries. The president and his aides promoted the idea of stimulating the economies of some of the world's poorest economies through trade rather than foreign aid. The final bill, however, was restricted primarily to supporting the apparel industry in the Caribbean and Central America and promoting the development of such an industry in sub-Saharan Africa. *(Caribbean trade, p. 157)*

The House approved a version of Clinton's request (HR 1432) in March 1998 but the measure was blocked in the Senate by senators from southern states with important textile and clothing industries; representatives of those industries feared an influx of inexpensive goods from Africa.

The Clinton administration revived the issue again early in 1999 but it took nearly a year for final action. The House passed an Africa trade measure (HR 434) on July 16, 1999, by a vote of 234–164 and the Senate approved a heavily amended version on Nov. 3, 1999, by voice vote. The measure stalled in conference committee, however, until Clinton pressed for action early in 2000 in hopes of creating a pro-trade environment for the crucial vote on a U.S.-China trade agreement. The House-Senate conference report on HR 434 (H Rept 106-606) was filed on May 4, 2000, and adopted by the House that same day on a 309–110 vote. The Senate cleared the bill for the president by a 77–19 vote on May 11. President Clinton signed the bill on May 18.

MAJOR PROVISIONS

For African countries the most important provision of the bill eliminated, for eight years, quotas and tariffs on U.S. imports of clothing made from African-made fabrics and yarns. This provision would remain in effect so long as the imports from Africa did not initially exceed 1.5 percent of all U.S.-imported apparel and 3.5 percent of the national total during the eight-year period of the bill. The Clinton administration estimated that this provision, if fully used, could boost African clothing exports to the United States from about $250 million a year to as much as $4.2 billion annually.

The bill also eliminated, for a four-year period, quotas and tariffs on African clothing made from fabrics produced outside Africa or the United States so long as the annual per capita income of the African country where the clothing was made did not exceed $1,500. That provision would enable African manufacturers to import low-cost fabric from Asian countries, convert it into finished clothing, and export the product to the United States duty-free. The provision was intended to encourage investments in clothing manufacturing facilities in Africa's poorest countries. U.S. apparel manufacturers pressed for the time limit on this provision.

Apparel made in Africa from U.S.-origin fabrics or yarns could be imported into the United States free of any duties, quotas, or other restrictions.

U.S. government officials and representatives of importing firms said they expected the primary beneficiaries of the bill, at least initially, would be South Africa and the island nation of Mauritius, both of which had well-established clothing manufacturers. The bill established eligibility criteria that effectively ruled out countries that were dictatorships and were not moving toward market economies governed by the rule of law.

Clinton on Oct. 2 signed a proclamation designating thirty-four sub-Saharan countries as being eligible for the bill's provisions; among the major countries excluded from that list were the Democratic Republic of Congo (formerly Zaire), the Ivory Coast, and Zimbabwe. The Congo was embroiled in a major civil war and the Ivory Coast and Zimbabwe were both undergoing severe political turmoil. Clinton included war-torn Sierra Leone on the list of eligible countries but delayed the effective date until the U.S. special trade representative determined that the country fully met the bill's provisions.

The bill also offered duty-free treatment for most imports of apparel manufactured in Caribbean and Central American nations. In other provisions, the bill lowered tariffs on imports of high-quality wool used by U.S. suit manufacturers and increased the types of retaliation the United States could take in trade disputes with other countries. The latter provision was aimed at the European Union, which had imposed restrictions on imports of U.S. beef treated with hormones and bananas marketed by U.S. companies.

In addition the bill extended permanent normal trade relations status to Albania and Kyrgyzstan, two formerly communist countries. Both had been receiving annual waivers from the Jackson-Vanik amendment to the 1974 Trade Act (PL 93-618), which limited U.S. trade relations with communist nations unless they allowed free emigration of their citizens. The United States had signed permanent trade agreements with both countries during the 1990s.

Steel Import Quotas

The House overwhelmingly passed a bill (HR 975—H Rept 106-52) to impose quotas on steel imports but the measure died when the Senate failed to invoke cloture (limit debate) on taking up the measure. The legislation was pushed in the House by representatives from steel-producing districts who were reacting to several steel company bankruptcies and layoffs of thousands of steel workers. The legislation would have required the president to impose quotas on steel imports within sixty days of passage of the legislation.

The House passed the bill on March 17 by a **key vote of 289–141 (R 91–128; D 197–13; I 1–0)**. The wide margin of victory came as a surprise to its supporters; the bill had been reported adversely by the Ways and Means Committee and was opposed by the Clinton administration. Clinton's opposition as well as opposition from agricultural interests, which feared countries would retaliate against them for steel quotas, doomed the bill in the Senate, however. On June 22 the

Senate defeated a motion to invoke cloture on taking up the bill by a vote of 42–57, well short of the sixty votes required for the motion to pass. The Senate may also have felt that it had done enough for the industry because it had just voted for $1 billion in loan guarantees to beleaguered steel companies (HR 1664—PL 106-51). *(1999 key votes, p. 899)*

"Silk Road" Trade

As part of an omnibus fiscal 2000 appropriations bill cleared in November 1999 (HR 3194—PL 106-113) Congress approved legislation intended to prove economic cooperation and U.S. trade along the historic "silk road" trade route in Central Asia and the South Caucasus region. The bill provided no new funds but redirected some previously appropriated aid for former Soviet states in the Balkans and eastern Europe. Nations that would benefit from the bill included the former Soviet republics of Armenia, Georgia, Kazakhstan, Kyrgyzstan, Tajikistan, Turkmenistan, and Uzbekistan. Sponsors said those nations represented a national security priority for the United States because of their proximity to Russia, China, Iran, Afghanistan, and Turkey. Several of the nations also held enormous reserves of oil and natural gas, some of which was being tapped by U.S. energy companies. *(Foreign operations appropriations bill, p. 210)*

The most controversial issue in the "silk road" measure had been an effort by some legislators to allow the president to waive a 1992 ban (included in PL 102-511) on direct U.S. aid to Azerbaijan. Congress had imposed the ban to protest Azerbaijan's blockade of its principal enemy, land-locked Armenia. The two nations fought a war in the early 1990s over Nagorno-Karabakh, a region of Azerbaijan with a majority Armenian population. Armenia seized control of most of the area and a Russian-mediated cease-fire had been in effect since 1994. Congress later loosened the aid restriction to allow trade-related assistance to Azerbaijan but during its consideration of the "silk road" legislation the Senate in June rejected by a 53–45 vote an attempt to give the president authority to waive the ban entirely.

Overseas Private Investment Corporation

Congress in November 1999 extended the authority for the Overseas Private Investment Corporation (OPIC) after the House soundly rejected a move to close the agency. OPIC provided loan guarantees and political risk insurance for U.S. companies operating abroad. The authority was included in the fiscal 2000 foreign operations appropriations bill (HR 3422), which was incorporated into omnibus spending legislation (HR 3194—PL 106-113). *(1997 action, p. 159)*

HOUSE ACTION

The House action came on Aug. 2 as the chamber was debating its original version of the foreign operations bill (HR 2606). Robert E. Andrews, D-N.J., offered an amendment to prevent OPIC from insuring new U.S. investments in developing countries or making any additional loans. Andrews and other critics said OPIC was providing large corporations with insurance they could obtain from the private sector. And they warned that the U.S. government could be liable for billions of dollars of bad loans or insurance payments if OPIC-guaranteed investments went sour. OPIC defenders said the agency had supported the expansion of U.S. industries into new markets and that it provided a service that could not be obtained commercially.

OPIC opponents had prevailed in the House in 1996 when that chamber voted 260–157 to reject legislation reauthorizing the agency. Even so OPIC was kept in business that year as part of the foreign operations provisions of an omnibus appropriations bill (PL 104-208).

In the meantime businesses that relied on OPIC financing and guarantees launched a major lobbying effort among House members, arguing that the agency helped guarantee jobs in many of their districts. As a result, the House overwhelmingly rejected Andrews's amendment 315–103; among those voting against the amendment were 107 members who had opposed continuing the agency just three years earlier.

Congress in 2000 again extended authority for OPIC as part of the fiscal 2001 foreign operations appropriations bill (HR 4811—PL 106-429).

Other Trade-Related Bills

The 106th Congress considered several other bills dealing with trade matters in 1999 and 2000 including the following.

GENERALIZED SYSTEM OF PREFERENCES

Congress in 1999 extended the Generalized System of Preferences (GSP) through Sept. 30, 2001, as part of a bill expanding the availability of health care coverage for working people with disabilities (HR 1180—PL 106-170). President Clinton signed the measure on Dec. 17. A previous extension of GSP had expired on June 30. GSP provided duty-free status to products imported from developing nations with the aim of spurring economic growth in those countries. *(1997 action, p. 159)*

ECONOMIC SANCTIONS REFORM

Congress in 1999 considered, but took no final action on, several proposals to reform the use of economic sanctions to achieve foreign policy goals. Numerous laws enacted by Congress since World War II had authorized—and in some cases required—the president to impose trade embargoes and other forms of economic sanctions against other countries for various foreign policy reasons. Among the targets had been communist countries, countries that tested nuclear weapons or exported ballistic missile systems and countries that engaged in systematic violations of human rights. Critics argued that many of these sanctions had failed to achieve satisfactory foreign policy goals and U.S. companies complained that sanctions had hurt U.S. commercial interests.

Both chambers passed legislation during the year that would have limited the use of food and humanitarian goods (such as medicines) in economic sanctions. The House on June 15 passed a bill (HR 17—H Rept 106-154) that would have established a procedure for Congress to overturn any agricultural embargo the president imposed against another country.

The Senate on Aug. 4 adopted an amendment, sponsored by John Ashcroft, R-Mo., to the fiscal 2000 agriculture appropriations bill (S 1233) to eliminate virtually all restrictions on the export of medicine and agricultural products unless specifically authorized by Congress in a joint resolution. Among other things the Senate provision would have weakened the longstanding U.S. trade embargo against Cuba. But House-Senate conferees in November stripped the Ashcroft amendment from the final version of the agriculture bill (HR 1906—PL 106-78). *(Economic sanctions, p. 223)*

INDIA, PAKISTAN SANCTIONS

A year-and-a-half after India and Pakistan both tested nuclear weapons—raising the prospect of nuclear conflict in South Asia, one of the world's most unstable regions—Congress in late 1999 gave the president permanent authority to lift all sanctions the United States had imposed against both countries. The sanctions had been required by an Arms Export Control Act provision of the 1994 State Department authorization bill (PL 103-263). The Arms Export Control Act required the president to impose trade and credit sanctions against countries that tested nuclear weapons.

Congress in 1998 had allowed the president, for just one year, to allow exports of food and humanitarian supplies to India and Pakistan despite the sanctions. *(1998 action, p. 159)*

Then in 1999 Congress broadened the waiver authority, giving the president the permanent power to waive all economic sanctions against the two countries if he determined that doing so would be in the "national security interest" of the United States. In particular Congress suggested that any sanctions imposed on those nations be targeted only against companies and agencies directly involved in nuclear weapons or ballistic missile programs. The waiver authorization was included in the fiscal 2000 defense appropriations bill (HR 2561—PL 106-79) signed by President Clinton on Oct. 25, 1999. Congress put one limit on the waiver authority, however, saying that the president would have to reimpose sanctions against either India or Pakistan if it again exploded a nuclear weapon. *(India, Pakistan sanctions, p. 223)*

CHAPTER 4

Foreign Policy

Introduction   173

1997–1998 Chronology   177

1999–2000 Chronology   204

Foreign Policy

During Bill Clinton's presidency, the post–World War II maxim that politics should stop at the water's edge seemed little more than a vestige of a bygone era of bipartisanship and good will. The bitter partisan clashes and pervasive mistrust that would culminate in his impeachment were seen repeatedly in congressional debates on his foreign policy.

Yet, in the end, President Clinton usually managed to get about what he wanted. There were compromises and temporary setbacks, but outright defeats for the White House were a rarity. When powers of persuasion failed to work, the power of the presidential veto was put into play.

Clinton presided over a NATO air campaign to end ethnic violence in the Serbian province of Kosovo, while members of the House were still debating the wisdom of such an undertaking. Clinton advanced his policy of engagement with China, despite an uproar over allegations of Chinese nuclear espionage. Clinton got congressional approval of a plan to repay U.S. debts to the United Nations, overcoming conservative disdain for that organization. Clinton persuaded members with little use for foreign aid to agree to forgive the debts of the world's poorest nations. When he did not get the foreign aid he wanted, he let his veto pen underscore his message to try again, and Congress did. After Congress first approved mandatory sanctions against Russia for transferring weapons technology to Iran, Clinton held out for—and got—discretionary authority. He won billions of dollars in new credit for the International Monetary Fund (IMF), while giving little in return to IMF critics on Capitol Hill. He worked with Republican leaders to underwrite a new antinarcotics initiative in Colombia and neighboring Latin American countries, despite the misgivings of liberal critics.

Of course, not everything went Clinton's way. He suffered a humiliating defeat when the Senate rejected one of his top foreign policy goals, a nuclear test ban treaty. He was forced to go along with a plan of Senate Foreign Relations Committee Chairman Jesse Helms, R-N.C., to reorganize the foreign policy bureaucracy. Clinton's annual battle with Congress over abortion restrictions on international family planning could best be described as ending in a draw, sometimes going Clinton's way, sometimes not. A bipartisan majority gave him legislation easing the long-standing trade embargo against Cuba, but a group of powerful conservatives diluted it with some additional restrictions. His nominee for ambassador to Mexico, former Massachusetts Gov. William F. Weld, a Republican, never got a hearing before the Foreign Relations Committee, but, then, more than a few senior Democrats were said to be secretly rooting for Helms, Weld's chief antagonist, anyway.

Through it all, the disdain Republicans harbored for Clinton and his foreign policy was palpable. Highly vocal critics questioned the competency of his leadership and the coherence of his policies. Criticism heightened at the time of the Monica Lewinsky sex scandal, as members voiced their opinion that the scandal was eroding the credibility of Clinton and his foreign policy team at home and abroad. A particularly bitter exchange took place when Clinton ordered air attacks on Iraq on the eve of the scheduled House debate on his impeachment. Some members speculated aloud whether the motives of the commander in chief had been political rather than military, a charge denied by the White House.

OVERSEAS DEPLOYMENTS

With the end of the cold war in 1989, many of the religious, political, and ethnic conflicts that had been obscured

REFERENCES

Discussion of foreign policy for the years 1945–1964 may be found in *Congress and the Nation Vol. I*, pp. 91–232; for the years 1965–1968, *Congress and the Nation Vol. II*, pp. 49–116; for the years 1969–1972, *Congress and the Nation Vol. III*, pp. 853–948; for the years 1973–1976, *Congress and the Nation Vol. IV*, pp. 847–912; for the years 1977–1980, *Congress and the Nation Vol. V*, pp. 31–95; for the years 1981–1984, *Congress and the Nation Vol. VI*, pp. 123–197; for the years 1985–1988, *Congress and the Nation Vol. VII*, pp. 169–251; for the years 1989–1992, *Congress and the Nation Vol. VIII*, pp. 203–297; for the years 1993–1996, *Congress and the Nation Vol. IX*, pp. 187–250.

Outlays for International Affairs

Billions of Dollars

NOTE: Data for 2001 are estimated.

SOURCE: Office of Management and Budget, *Historical Tables, Budget of the United States Government: Fiscal Year 2002* (Washington, D.C.: U.S. Government Printing Office, 2001), Table 3.2.

by the competition between the United States and Soviet Union started to erupt. The White House and Congress wrestled with how—or whether—the United States, as the world's dominant power, should respond to these global hotspots. What kind of conflict, crisis, or suffering would warrant U.S. intervention?

Debates on this question spotlighted Republicans' deep distrust of Clinton's stewardship of the military. The president had made no friends among the military's loyal supporters on Capitol Hill with his youthful avoidance of military service during the Vietnam War and his unsuccessful attempt at the outset of his administration to allow openly gay persons to serve in the military.

Military deployments during Clinton's first term—in Somalia, Haiti, and Bosnia—only deepened his critics' suspicions. Members questioned the value of the overseas missions and warned of potential casualties, high costs, and the corrosive effect they were having on military readiness for more traditional conflicts. The debate raged anew in Clinton's second term when the president led the NATO campaign against ethnic violence in Kosovo.

But for all the clamor over successive congressional challenges to various deployments, Clinton yielded only once—in 1994, he abandoned the effort to build social order in Somalia because of the firestorm of opposition generated by the death of eighteen U.S. soldiers during an October 1993 operation. The inability of congressional critics to significantly restrict controversial deployments reflected a fundamental fact of American political life unchanged by three

decades of political agitation: except under the most extraordinary circumstances, the president had a free hand to dispatch forces abroad. And once troops were in the field, Congress was unlikely to compel their return.

The years of sparring between Clinton and Congress over military operations in the former Yugoslavia may have made those facts more obvious.

Congress was divided on the question of intervening in Kosovo and on Clinton's handling of the crisis. Members urged action in Kosovo when Clinton appeared hesitant and counseled restraint as Clinton moved toward military involvement. When the administration attempted to negotiate an end to the crisis in late 1998 and avoid military airstrikes, skeptical GOP members, including supporters of U.S. action in the region, stepped up their criticism. One leading Republican in the Senate publicly called the administration's policy indecipherable, another predicted it would lead to disaster, and yet another insisted that the administration had no plan at all.

The president certainly would have preferred the enthusiastic backing of Congress, but he was not deterred by the lack of it. His critics pointed out that President George Bush had obtained congressional approval before launching the Persian Gulf War against Iraq in 1991. But in a 1998 memoir, Bush had said what many observers long had assumed: he would have begun the attack with or without congressional approval.

Clinton took the same position as his predecessor. He was unfazed when the House in April 1999 rejected on a tie vote a Senate-passed resolution that would have authorized NATO airstrikes against Serbian forces in Kosovo. The bombing campaign was then in its fifth week. On the other hand, the House vote also indicated that members felt no compulsion to voice support for a mission they opposed merely because U.S. troops already were in the field.

A GOP attempt in the Senate in 2000 to force Clinton to withdraw U.S. peacekeeping troops unless Congress authorized their continued deployment went the way of previous attempts to challenge the administration's deployments in Bosnia and Kosovo: it was defeated. On the House side, a provision that potentially could have forced a withdrawal from Kosovo if the NATO allies were not shouldering their fair share of the peacekeeping burden was approved but later dropped in conference.

In the end, Clinton got the kind of support from Capitol Hill he needed: Congress appropriated the funds for the air campaign, the peacekeeping deployment that followed, and the beginning of the reconstruction of Serbia.

POLICY CHALLENGES

Administration efforts to forge new relationships with China and Russia faced a number of challenges, not the least of which was garnering support on Capitol Hill.

Few relationships were more sensitive—or more important—than that between the world's dominant power and the world's fastest rising power, the United States and China. Experts believed China posed the single greatest challenge to a smooth U.S. foreign policy, largely because of the many facets of the relationship between the two countries: trade, human rights, nuclear nonproliferation, and Taiwan.

Clinton pursued his policy of engagement with China against a backdrop of congressional investigations and outrage over allegations that his administration had allowed China to acquire U.S. missile technology and that China was just plain stealing U.S. nuclear weapons secrets. Reports of human rights abuses, of increased exports of weapons of mass destruction, and of threatening actions toward Taiwan did not help him make his case. Yet, the importance of China as a trading partner ensured that Congress would not block normal trade relations between the two nations. The annual fight over the trade issue was finally ended in 2000 when, in one of the most significant debates of the 106th Congress, lawmakers went along with the administration's proposal to make the trade relationship permanent.

A number of issues troubled U.S. relations with Russia but none as significant as U.S. plans for a nationwide defense against ballistic missiles. Strong pressure from Capitol Hill and the test firing of a missile by North Korea convinced Clinton to develop a system to protect the United States against a small number of missiles fired by a rogue state. But if such a system was to be deployed, the United States would have to either abrogate the 1972 Anti-Ballistic Missile Treaty or win Russia's approval to amend the ABM treaty. Russian officials at that time remained committed to the treaty and were reluctant to change it. On Capitol Hill, conservative lawmakers expressed little confidence that the Clinton administration would negotiate a tough deal with Russia.

Other tensions in U.S.-Russian relations included complaints about widespread human rights violations by the Russian military in the bloody war in the separatist region of Chechnya; investigations into corruption and money laundering by Russian officials; anger about Russian intransigence on the U.N. Security Council, particularly regarding Iraq; and Russia's failure to carry out substantial economic reforms.

The 105th Congress issued a sharp rebuke of Russia for its transfer of missile technology and arms to Iran by passing a mandatory sanctions bill. Clinton vetoed that bill but went along with legislation granting discretionary sanctions authority passed in the next Congress. Provisions limiting aid to Russia were tacked on to foreign aid bills because of a range of behavior Republicans considered inimical to U.S. interests, including the war in Chechnya.

Republican criticism of administration policies toward Russia was also viewed, at least by Democrats, as an effort to diminish Vice President Al Gore's foreign policy reputation as he went into the fall 2000 presidential campaign against Texas Gov. George W. Bush, the Republican candidate. Gore's overseas specialty had been U.S. relations with Russia. A task force set up by House Speaker J. Dennis Hastert, R-Ill., issued a report critical of administration policy toward Russia. House Republican Policy Committee Chairman Christopher Cox of California denied that the report was merely an election-year document, but he did acknowledge that its fundamental purpose was to offer a contrast between Republican policies and what his party saw as the failures of Clinton and Gore.

ABORTION RESTRICTIONS

For years Clinton fought with social conservatives over one of his first acts as president: the lifting of abortion restrictions on international family planning assistance. Under a policy first pronounced by President Ronald Reagan at a U.N. population conference in Mexico City in 1984 and continued by the George Bush administration, U.S. aid had been prohibited for international groups that performed or promoted abortions. The so-called Mexico City policy had been vehemently opposed by Clinton and many Democrats on Capitol Hill, so the new president in January 1993 overturned it, setting off a protracted struggle with Congress with significant ramifications. Indeed, during Clinton's second term, the abortion issue proved to be one of the biggest stumbling blocks in legislating his foreign policy priorities.

In 1997 conservatives were forced to back away from their demands that the Mexico City policy be reinstated during debate on the annual foreign aid funding bill. But they took "hostages," blocking proposals to repay U.S. debts to the United Nations, to consolidate several foreign policy agencies, and to extend additional credit to the International Monetary Fund. The U.N. repayment and foreign policy reorganization plans had been the result of delicate negotiations by Senate Foreign Relations Committee Chairman Helms, the committee's ranking Democrat, Joseph R. Biden Jr. of Delaware, and the administration.

Clinton vetoed a two-year State Department authorization bill the next year because of the abortion restrictions. Funding for the U.N. debt was left out of an omnibus funding bill at the end of the session because Republicans continued to tie it to the abortion issue. The reorganization and IMF credit plans, however, made it through this time.

In 1999 Clinton decided to pay the price—he accepted the abortion restrictions to win approval of the U.N. debt repayment plan. The fact that the United States was on the brink of losing its seat in the U.N. General Assembly because of its debt weighed heavily on his decision. There were, however, strings attached to the U.S. agreement to settle its bill. The United Nations would have to make certain reforms and also reduce the U.S. share of the U.N.'s budget and peacekeeping costs.

The following year it was the Republicans' turn to back down. In order to avoid an election-year confrontation with Clinton, they heeded his veto threat and removed the restrictions from the annual aid bill and approved increased funding for international family planning. But they attempted to have the last word by delaying release of the money until after Clinton left office. They were hopeful that a Republican sympathetic to their cause would be in the White House by then.

FOREIGN AID

Foreign aid continued to have a tough time of it. During the cold war, a coalition of security-minded conservatives and humanitarian-minded liberals made foreign spending a relatively easy sell. Congress simply allocated more international spending according to political goals. Countries friendly to the United States and hostile to the Soviet Union benefited from American generosity. But foreign aid was never broadly popular, and after the fall of the Berlin Wall in 1989, many lawmakers did not consider much of it necessary.

Republicans favored military assistance and antinarcotics programs over development aid, considering them adjuncts to the defense budget. Democrats, on the other hand, still favored increased spending on development assistance, environmental initiatives, and support for United Nations agencies. Attempts in the 105th and 106th Congresses to bridge the gap between the two sides produced more than a few raucous debates and angry stalemates.

Indeed, foreign aid was such a divisive issue that Congress had been unable to approve a foreign assistance authorization bill since 1985. Programs continued to be funded through the annual foreign operations appropriations bill, however. But that had important institutional consequences. The authorizing committees—Senate Foreign Relations and House International Relations—lost much of their influence to the Appropriations panels, which were able to muscle through their spending bills, even if one of them included foreign aid.

Nonetheless, the appropriations bills still provoked some heated battles, as the fight over international family planning assistance, IMF credit, and U.N. debt repayment illustrated.

Other administration aid proposals stirred controversy as well. Clinton vetoed an aid funding bill in 1999 because the GOP, anxious to hold down spending as part of their overall budget plan, left out several of his top priorities. Among them was money to help Israel, Jordan, and the Palestinian Authority implement a 1998 Middle East peace agreement. Clinton got what he wanted on a second try.

Clinton's plans to join with other prosperous countries in forgiving the debts of the world's poorest countries also came under fire on Capitol Hill. Opponents argued that it would not work unless the third world countries changed the way their governments were run. But, with a boost from such supporters as Pope John Paul II and rock star Bono, debt relief received congressional approval. Money was provided for the United States to forgive debts and authorization was given to the International Monetary Fund to revalue some of its gold reserves to fund additional debt relief.

A proposal to provide aid to Colombia and some of its Latin American neighbors to fight narcotics trafficking enjoyed a rare distinction: bipartisan support. In fact, Republican House Speaker Hastert was probably the most enthusiastic supporter of this major new foreign policy commitment. Some critics worried about the power of right-wing paramilitary groups in Colombia, while others were concerned that the United States might be drawn into the conflict in Colombia, but attempts to cut back on the aid were defeated.

Bipartisan support was also given to a new international trust fund to fight the spread of AIDS. Senate Foreign Relations Committee Chairman Helms called the authorization one of the most important pieces of international humanitarian legislation that Congress had passed in years.

Chronology of Action on Foreign Policy

1997–1998

The White House clashed repeatedly with the Republican-controlled 105th Congress over foreign policy priorities. In the end, President Clinton chalked up some significant wins, but most had not come easily or without a price.

Skeptical lawmakers, particularly Republicans, kept a watchful eye on the development of U.S. and NATO policy toward the troubled Serbian region of Kosovo. The advice members offered was mixed, sometimes pushing for military action and sometimes advocating a diplomatic solution.

Congress went along with the administration's decision to renew regular trading status for China but remained sharply critical of Clinton's policy of engagement with China. Investigations were launched into whether administration policies had resulted in the transfer of missile technology to China and whether China had engaged in nuclear espionage in the United States.

Some of the heated exchanges between Clinton and members of Congress were not simply over the merits of Clinton's foreign policy proposals. Key parts of his agenda also became bargaining chips for members seeking to reinstate abortion restrictions on international family planning aid. Those restrictions, first pronounced by President Ronald Reagan and continued by President George Bush, had been repealed by Clinton within days of his inauguration in 1993. Reversing Clinton's action had been a top goal of conservatives ever since.

House conservatives ultimately were forced to back down from their demands for abortion restrictions but not before holding hostage several key initiatives sought by Clinton and Senate Republicans. Action was blocked in 1997 on proposals to repay most U.S. debts to the United Nations, to reform the foreign policy bureaucracy, and to underwrite an International Monetary Fund (IMF) currency stabilization program. The plans to repay the U.N. debt and to reorganize foreign policy agencies were the result of a carefully crafted trade-off engineered by the administration, Senate Foreign Relations Committee Chairman Jesse Helms, R-N.C., and ranking committee Democrat Joseph R. Biden Jr., Del.

The standoff continued in 1998. A State Department authorization bill linking repayment of the U.N. debt and the agency reorganization with abortion curbs fell to a presidential veto. A foreign aid spending bill also stalled after the House attached antiabortion language and approved substantially less than requested for the IMF.

Late in 1998 House conservatives relented and agreed to the agency reorganization plan, as well as the president's IMF request. But they continued to link the U.N. repayment plan with abortion restrictions and that issue would have to wait until the next Congress for enactment.

Clinton won a big victory in 1997 when the Senate approved an international chemical and biological weapons treaty despite the strong opposition of conservative Republicans. Approval, however, had cost the White House major concessions, including agreement to Helms's demand that the foreign policy agencies be restructured. *(Chemical weapons treaty, p. 268)*

Congress attached a bill implementing the chemical weapons treaty to separate legislation aimed at punishing overseas companies and research labs, primarily in Russia, that provided missile technology to Iran. Republicans hoped the move would force the president to agree to economic sanctions he opposed, but it triggered a veto instead. The implementing legislation was later passed separately.

Legislation authorizing the use of sanctions to combat religious persecution abroad—another top priority for conservatives—was enacted. Although the final bill had been significantly watered down, it still had the support of conservatives because it spotlighted the issue.

Kosovo Policy

The United States and its NATO allies spent much of 1998 seeking an end to ethnic violence in the Serbian province of Kosovo. As diplomatic and economic pressures were applied and military action considered, members of Congress weighed in on various policy options. The signals they sent were sometimes mixed. After urging the White House to take action in the troubled region earlier in the year, some members expressed doubts about President Clinton's policies as the likelihood of military action increased.

BACKGROUND

The situation in Kosovo was the latest chapter in that region's history of ethnic fighting and upheaval.

Despite fundamental religious, language, and cultural differences across the region, a pan-Slavic kingdom that would become known as Yugoslavia had been carved out at the end of World War I. This in turn became the Federal Republic of Yugoslavia—consisting of the six republics of Serbia, Montenegro, Bosnia, Croatia, Macedonia, and Slovenia—at the end of World War II. The disparate grouping held together until the early 1990s, thanks to a dictatorial monarchy after World War I and communist control after World War II.

But things started to unravel in the 1980s with the death of Joseph Broz Tito, Yugoslavia's leader since World War II, and the emergence of Slobodan Milosevic as the leader of Serbia. To further himself politically, Milosevic fomented Serbian nationalism by calling for a "Greater Serbia" that would include parts of the neighboring republics inhabited by Serbs.

The collapse of communism in 1989 accelerated Yugoslavia's disintegration. Croatia, Slovenia, and Macedonia declared their independence in 1991, and Bosnia seceded in 1992. The Yugoslav army, dominated by Serbia, waged all-out wars on Croatia and Bosnia but lost. The Bosnia conflict was particularly brutal as Yugoslavian and Bosnian Serb forces committed numerous atrocities against ethnic Muslims and Croats in Bosnia. Their attempts to carve out Serb-held areas by expelling or killing Muslims and Croats gave rise to the term "ethnic cleansing." (*Congress and the Nation Vol. IX, pp. 197, 224*)

Kosovo had been an autonomous province of Serbia until 1989, when Milosevic, in another move to fan the fires of Serbian nationalism, revoked Kosovo's autonomy and placed the overwhelmingly Albanian Muslim population under the authority of his government in Belgrade. Milosevic's move against Kosovo set off a decade of turmoil that in time exploded into open warfare between Milosevic's Serbian forces and ethnic Albanian insurgents.

Attempts by ethnic Albanians, who comprised 90 percent of Kosovo's population, to break away from Belgrade's control and become a separate republic were met with repression and human rights abuses by the Milosevic regime. Ethnic Albanians saw their assembly dissolved and their cultural institutions suppressed. They were denied jobs and the right of ownership.

The ethnic Albanians responded at first with nonviolent resistance but then a rebel force known as the Kosovo Liberation Army began armed hostilities. Attacks on Serb state officials and police led to counterinsurgency moves by the Serb police and Yugoslav military. In early 1998 reports of Serb forces burning houses, destroying villages, and executing ethnic Albanians fueled fears of a wider conflict and of renewed ethnic cleansing in the troubled Balkan region. The violence set in motion a massive displacement of Kosovo's civilian population as ethnic Albanians either fled or were forced to leave their homes. Refugees began to flow into neighboring countries.

As the situation in Kosovo rapidly deteriorated, the international community searched for a peaceful solution to the crisis. The United Nations established an arms embargo against Yugoslavia. The United States and other Western countries reimposed sanctions on Yugoslavia. The United States tried shuttle diplomacy in an attempt to end the bloodshed.

But a ceasefire proved elusive and by mid-1998 NATO military planners were readying strike plans against Serbian forces. In September NATO ordered its members to prepare air and naval forces that could be used for an escalating series of military actions—from a salvo of cruise missiles to large-scale bombing.

As NATO made its preparations, the United States kept up its diplomatic offensive. On Oct. 12 the U.S. special Balkan envoy, Richard C. Holbrooke, announced that an agreement had been reached with Milosevic. The deal called for sending 2,000 international inspectors to Kosovo and for overflights by NATO aircraft to monitor the withdrawal of Serb forces and to deter further violence. It also called for the return of refugees and for meaningful negotiations toward Kosovo's autonomy.

Milosevic was given until Oct. 27 to comply with the agreement or face the possibility of air strikes. When Serbia withdrew more than 4,000 troops hours before the deadline, NATO decided to put off military action while it monitored Serbian compliance with the other aspects of the agreement.

But the violence continued and several months into 1999 diplomatic efforts again stalled. At that point NATO made good on its threats. (*Kosovo war, p. 204*)

CONGRESSIONAL ACTION

When President Clinton sent U.S. troops to Bosnia in 1995 as part of a NATO-led peacekeeping force, he had to convince a reluctant Congress. But, by mid-1998, the roles appeared reversed. Some lawmakers were pushing Clinton to consider deploying U.S. troops as part of a NATO-led force to contain ethnic violence in Kosovo, while the administration was publicly expressing doubts.

The shift was particularly strong among Republicans, reflecting both a change in attitude about the Bosnia mission as well as an unusual bipartisan commitment to defend Kosovo that dated back to the Bush administration. In a late 1992 statement, President George Bush and President-elect Clinton had warned of U.S. military action if Milosevic used force in Kosovo.

Former Senate Majority Leader Bob Dole, R-Kan. (House, 1961–1969; Senate, 1969–1996), who was serving as chair-

FOREIGN POLICY LEADERSHIP

Secretary of State

Madeleine K. Albright was confirmed as President Clinton's secretary of state on Jan. 22, 1997, by a Senate vote of 99–0. She was the first female to serve in that office. Albright, who previously was the U.S. representative to the United Nations, succeeded Warren Christopher, who resigned after serving in the first Clinton administration. Albright was warmly received by the Senate Foreign Relations Committee during her confirmation hearings, but committee chairman Jesse Helms, R-N.C., said his support for Albright should not be construed as support for Clinton's foreign policy. While Albright was cautious in her policy pronouncements, she pledged to work with the committee on a plan to reorganize the foreign affairs bureaucracy, a cherished goal of Helms. *(Cabinet profiles, p. 981)*

CIA Director

George J. Tenet was confirmed as director of Central Intelligence by a voice vote of the Senate on July 10, 1997, four months after he was nominated and nearly eight months after the job fell vacant. President Clinton's first choice, former national security advisor Tony Lake, abruptly withdrew his nomination after it became caught up in partisan controversy over White House and Democratic fund-raising practices. *(Controversial nominations, p. 985)*

Tenet's nomination was warmly received by the Senate Intelligence Committee, where he had served as staff director from 1988 to 1993. After leaving the committee staff, he went to the National Security Council, where he served as Lake's senior director for intelligence. He became deputy director of Central Intelligence in 1995 and then served as acting director after CIA Director John M. Deutch resigned in December 1997.

During hearings before the Intelligence Committee, Tenet was questioned about how he would lead the nation's intelligence community in the post–cold war era and what reforms he believed were still needed in the wake of the 1994 Aldrich

H. Ames spy scandal, one of the most devastating in the CIA's history. The panel approved the nomination after the Justice Department completed an inquiry into Tenet's failure to disclose until 1994 some holdings he had inherited in 1983. Tenet apparently had been unaware of the holdings and the Justice Department determined there was no need for an independent counsel to look into the matter further. *(Tenet profile, p. 983)*

U.N. Representative

Bill Richardson, who succeed Madeleine Albright as U.S. representative to the United Nations, was confirmed on Feb. 11, 1997, by a Senate vote of 100–0. He had served as a Democratic representative from New Mexico from 1983 until he resigned to become the new U.N. ambassador. He served in the U.N. post until August 1998 when he became secretary of energy.

Richardson was succeeded as U.S. representative by Richard C. Holbrooke but only after a fourteen-month struggle. Holbrooke, former U.S. ambassador to Germany, former assistant secretary of state for European and Canadian Affairs, and the key negotiator of the 1995 Dayton peace accords for Bosnia, was confirmed by an 81–16 vote of the Senate on Aug. 5, 1999. Between Clinton's announcement in June 1998 that he intended to nominate Holbrooke and the Senate vote, Holbrooke had undergone an eight-month administration investigation, a four-month investigation by the Senate Foreign Relations Committee, four hearings before that panel, and more than a month of holds on the nomination by senators who wanted to pressure the administration on unrelated issues. Clinton had submitted the nomination to the Senate on Feb. 10, 1999, upon completion of a Justice Department inquiry into allegations that Holbrooke had violated federal ethics rules by improperly trading on his government contacts after leaving the State Department in February 1996 to become vice chairman of CS First Boston. Holbrooke paid a civil fine, while still denying the charges.

man of the International Commission on Missing Persons in Bosnia, was in the forefront of those urging the administration to take bolder action in Kosovo.

By the fall of 1998, however, lawmakers, particularly Republicans, were sounding more cautious—and more skeptical—about administration policy. They questioned potential military moves and proposed diplomatic solutions. Senate Majority Leader Trent Lott, R-Miss., even wondered aloud why the administration had suddenly decided to take action so close to the November congressional elections after months of waiting.

Both chambers approved Kosovo-related resolutions during 1998. On March 18, the House and the Senate adopted resolutions condemning violence against the ethnic Albanians in Kosovo by Serbian authorities. The House approved H Con Res 235 by a 406–1 vote and the Senate approved S Con Res 85 by a vote of 98–0. On Sept. 23, the House adopted another resolution (H Con Res 315) condemning Serbian atrocities in Kosovo by a vote of 410–0. The two chambers also approved resolutions (S Con Res 105 and H Con Res 304) expressing the sense of Congress that the United States should declare there to be probable cause that Milosevic had committed war crimes and genocide. The Senate adopted its resolution by voice vote July 17 and the House adopted its resolution by a vote of 369–1 on Sept. 14, before approving S Con Res 105 by voice vote.

Congress also included in the fiscal 1999 omnibus spending bill (HR 4328—PL 105-277), which cleared in October, a provision writing into law economic sanctions against Serbia. In an effort to isolate Milosevic, the bill lifted sanctions against Montenegro, the junior partner in the Federal Republic of Yugoslavia. It also called for U.S. export agencies to promote trade with Montenegro. The administration argued, and lawmakers generally agreed, that Montenegro should be rewarded for steering a more peaceful and democratic course than Serbia.

China Policy

The Clinton administration's policy of engagement with China came under heavy fire on Capitol Hill during the 105th Congress. Although Congress did agree to extend China's trade status, allowing Beijing the same tariff treatment as nearly all other nations, it took aim at a number of other targets. *(China trade, p. 151)*

A major fight erupted over Clinton's easing of restrictions to allow U.S. companies to launch their satellites aboard inexpensive Chinese rockets. At one point, nearly a dozen congressional committees were investigating whether Clinton's action had allowed Beijing to acquire missile technology that could be used against the United States and whether campaign contributions had helped influence the president's decision to waive tough export controls.

By the end of 1998 a special House investigating committee had concluded that China had engaged in a "serious and sustained" pattern of efforts to acquire sensitive U.S. technology stretching back two decades. It would be another five months before the panel's final report was made public, and by that point Congress was in an uproar over allegations of nuclear espionage by the Chinese. *(Nuclear security, p. 302)*

But, without waiting for the various committees to report, Congress took steps in the fiscal 1999 defense authorization bill (HR 3616—PL 105-261) to hinder the potential transfer of missile technology to China by shifting responsibility for licensing from the Commerce Department back to the State Department where it had been prior to 1996. Both chambers approved additional China policy directives during consideration of the defense bill. *(1999 defense authorization, p. 252)*

Critics of China found other avenues to express their frustration with Beijing. In late 1997 the House passed a series of bills assailing the communist regime on a variety of fronts, including its human rights record, policy toward Taiwan, and military weapons and technology sales to countries that supported terrorism. Both the House and Senate attacked China's human rights record in measures approved in 1998.

CONGRESSIONAL INVESTIGATIONS

Allegations that Clinton, in his eagerness for more trade and better relations with Beijing, allowed China to acquire sensitive missile technology touched off investigations by eleven congressional committees and subcommittees. Among them was the specially created House panel, the Select Committee on U.S. National Security and Military/Commercial Concerns with the People's Republic of China. The committee, chaired by Christopher Cox, R-Calif., was set up by H Res 463, which the House passed by a vote of 409–10 on June 18. H Res 463 had been reported by the House Rules Committee on June 16 (H Rept 105-582).

The focus of the investigations included:

• Clinton's February 1998 decision to allow Loral Space and Communications to launch a satellite on a Chinese rocket even after he was warned the company might have violated national security in a previous launch. Republicans alleged the Loral decision was influenced by large campaign contributions to the Democratic Party from former Loral chairman Bernard L. Schwartz.

• Clinton's decision in 1996 to shift the licensing of all satellite exports from the State Department to Commerce.

The committees also were forced to confront a series of other issues including the approach the United States should take toward China, the role of foreign money in U.S. campaigns, the adequacy of export controls, the proliferation of weapons to countries such as Pakistan and Iran, and U.S. space policy.

Background

The communications revolution produced a boom in satellites for telephone and computer communications and television transmission. Since two of every three satellites were built in the United States, companies such as Hughes Space and Communications and Loral prospered.

U.S. companies that launched satellites, such as Boeing and Lockheed Martin, also benefited. But the demand for rockets and launching pads in time outstripped the domestic supply, and the market share of U.S. companies fell from complete domination two decades earlier to 40 percent in 1998.

Changes in U.S. government policy also had an impact on the launch business. Until 1984, all U.S.-built satellites were launched on U.S. aircraft, principally the space shuttle. But after the 1986 explosion of the space shuttle *Challenger,* in which seven astronauts were killed, President Ronald Reagan for more than two years banned all commercial cargo aboard the shuttle and then limited private payloads to those that could not be launched on other vehicles.

Eager to get their wares into space, satellite makers clamored to be allowed to launch their products on China's Long March rockets, which were both available and cheaper than U.S. or European launch providers.

In 1988 Reagan agreed, as long as the launches were approved by the State and Defense Departments and included a series of safeguards. His decision was sealed in a bilateral agreement allowing China to launch no more than nine satellites between 1989 and 1994, a deal later extended to eleven more satellites by 2001.

The policy was temporarily derailed by the June 1989 Tiananmen Square massacre of hundreds of students and other prodemocracy demonstrators by the Chinese army. In its wake, President George Bush suspended satellite sales to China, a ban that was eased late that year.

Congress in the fiscal 1990–1991 State Department authorization bill (PL 101-246), which cleared in early 1990, banned the practice of launching satellites in China and the export to China of material on the State Department's munitions list, which included some satellite-related equipment. The president could issue waivers for individual satellite launches that he considered in the national interest. Manufacturers would have to obtain an export license from the State Department for each overseas launch. (*Congress and the Nation Vol. VIII, p. 250*)

As Bush prepared to leave office in 1992, his administration drafted a policy allowing the Commerce Department, with little input from State or Defense, to license the export of satellites devoid of technology that could have military use. The transfer of authority took place in 1993, the first year of the Clinton administration.

At the urging of the Commerce Department, Clinton in 1996 authorized the transfer of licensing authority for dual-use satellites—those with both military and civilian applications—from State to Commerce but with a new set of safeguards said to ensure the continued role of State and the Pentagon in the decision-making process.

These policy changes took place against a backdrop of U.S. concern over Chinese exports of missile technology to Pakistan and Iran. Twice, from 1991 to 1992 and from 1993 to 1994, the State Department prohibited exports of U.S.-made satellites to China because Beijing exported technology for Pakistan's effort to develop a nuclear arsenal. The sanctions cost U.S. satellite manufacturers hundreds of millions of dollars in business that went to European firms.

Subsequently, U.S. companies lobbied for the shift of control over satellite exports to Commerce. Under Commerce Department rules, China had to transfer entire missiles or major missile components, rather than missile technology, to trigger a cutoff of U.S. exports.

Questions Raised

Satellite export rules probably would have stayed off the public radar had it not been for two launch accidents. A Long March rocket carrying a Hughes satellite exploded in January 1995 and another carrying a Loral satellite crashed after launch in February 1996. There were investigations into the actions taken by both companies in the aftermath of the accidents, but it was Loral's actions that caught Congress's attention. Indeed, a 1997 Pentagon report concluding that Loral's actions after the 1996 crash had damaged national security was at the heart of the congressional investigation.

In the wake of the crash, a committee of U.S. and European experts met in Beijing and in California to determine the cause of the crash. Because the satellite contained "militarily sensitive technologies" someone from the Defense Department was to monitor all such meetings but no one from Defense attended. The group also was supposed to get government clearance for any correspondence that might help China's missile program. But as Loral officials acknowledged, before a final report was sent to U.S. government officials, a preliminary version was faxed to Chinese officials.

Loral officials soon confessed their error to the State and Defense Departments and the Justice Department opened an investigation.

According to *The New York Times*, Pentagon officials determined that if they had seen the report first, they would not have cleared information that Loral provided China regarding its guidance and flight control systems and suggestions for diagnostic techniques that could be used to determine flaws in the launch vehicle. China's Long March rockets were virtually identical to its ballistic missiles, the Pentagon said, so the information would prove valuable to its military efforts. CIA officials, however, disagreed in their own report, saying the technology used in the commercial rockets did not lend itself to ballistic missiles.

Claims that the technology transfers, if they occurred, damaged national security rested on China's increasing ability to launch sophisticated satellites without incident and on the close relationship between conventional rockets and nuclear missiles.

As prosecutors worked on the case, Loral launched a previously licensed satellite on a Chinese rocket in 1997, then sought another presidential waiver to launch a satellite. Clinton approved the launch in February 1998, despite the Justice Department reportedly saying that the waiver could hamper any prosecution of the company.

Political Overtones

Congressional investigators focused primarily on the Loral case not only because of the Pentagon report but also because of its political overtones.

Schwartz was the single largest contributor of campaign cash in the 1995–1996 election cycle, and his money overwhelmingly went to Democrats. By the time the congressional investigations were getting underway, Schwartz had already contributed about $400,000 to Democrats in the 1997–1998 cycle.

Investigators were also looking into another campaign finance tie. Johnny Chung, a key figure in a Justice Department investigation of illegal foreign campaign contributions in the 1996 election, claimed that he had acted as a conduit for money given to him by the daughter of a top Chinese government official to make political contributions to the Democrats. The woman was an executive of a state-run aerospace company whose subsidiary ran the commercial launch business. Both the executive and the Chinese government denied the claim, but the Democratic National Committee later returned the money Chung contributed because of questions about its source. *(Campaign finance probes, box, p. 778)*

Findings

Although at the outset a number of committees were investigating various aspects of U.S.-China policy, as time wore on and the White House sex scandal took precedence, the work largely fell to the Senate Intelligence Committee and the special House committee.

Reports from those two committees were not released until mid-1999. However, a preview of the House panel's report emerged in late 1998. According to panel aides, the committee had concluded December 30 that China had successfully orchestrated an effort to steal U.S. military secrets, often under the guise of commercial transactions, for more than two decades. But the unanimous bipartisan report reportedly also found that—despite Republican lawmakers' initial suspicions—illegal Chinese campaign contributions to the Democratic Party did not play a key role in the surreptitious technology transfers. *(1999 committee reports, p. 208)*

OTHER ACTION

Although the technology transfer issue was the main focus of the heated debate over U.S.-China relations, members expressed their views on China and U.S. policies toward it in a number of other areas.

1997 Action

The House passed nine China-related bills in early November 1997 by overwhelming majorities. Several factors contributed to the lopsided support for the package. A summit meeting between Clinton and Chinese President Jiang Zemin had ended October 30, so the votes did not threaten to upstage it. The Senate was considered unlikely to act on the legislation before adjournment, which made it a free vote. And a number of the bills were merely nonbinding resolutions that lacked the force of law. All those factors combined to give members a relatively painless way to send a message on human rights, weapon sales, and Taiwan, while continuing to support trade relations with China.

The bills included:

• HR 2358 (H Rept 105-305), a bill to fund more personnel to monitor human rights in China, became the vehicle for a floor amendment aimed at the centerpiece of the U.S.-China summit, an agreement to certify that China was in compliance with the 1985 nuclear cooperation agreement and thus allow the sale of U.S. nuclear equipment to China. In return, China had assured the president that it would discontinue its export of technology that enabled countries such as Iran and Pakistan to develop missiles and other weapons. The House on Nov. 5 adopted, 394–29, an amendment to revise the law (PL 99-183) implementing the nuclear cooperation agreement by extending from thirty to 120 days the time Congress had to review a certification of Chi-

nese compliance with nuclear nonproliferation statutes. HR 2358 was then passed by a vote of 416–5. *(Congress and the Nation Vol. VII, p. 207)*

• HR 967 (H Rept 105-309), the most controversial of the bills, was a proposal to deny U.S. visas to Chinese officials, with some exceptions, who headed government-created religious organizations or who implemented policies that persecuted religious minorities. The House International Relations Committee considered the bill on three separate days before approving it. The House passed the bill Nov. 6 by a vote of 366–54.

• HR 2386 (H Rept 105-308), another bill that prompted fierce debate, required the secretary of defense to study the feasibility of constructing a theater ballistic missile defense that could protect Taiwan. The bill expressed the sense of Congress that the president—if requested by Taiwan and in accordance with the results of the study—should transfer to Taiwan appropriate defense articles or services under the foreign military sales program for the purpose of operating a local-area ballistic missile defense system. The House passed the bill Nov. 6 by a vote of 301–116.

• H Res 188 (H Rept 105-304) urged the president to impose sanctions on China for transferring C-802 cruise missiles to Iran in violation of the 1992 Iran-Iraq Arms Non-Proliferation Act (PL 102-484). In 1996 Chinese companies had delivered more than sixty of the missiles to Iran for use by its navy. H Res 188 was adopted Nov. 6 by a vote of 414–8.

• HR 2195 (H Rept 105-366), passed Nov. 5 by a vote of 419–2, authorized funds to enforce an existing ban on importing products made with prison labor.

• HR 2570, passed 415–1 on Nov. 6, condemned the actions of most Chinese officials involved in compulsory abortion or sterilization and proposed denying them visas for entry into the United States.

• HR 2605, passed 354–59 on Nov. 6, directed the president to instruct U.S. officials at international financial organizations to oppose below-market loans for China.

• HR 2647, passed 408–10 on Nov. 7, authorized the president to monitor, restrict, seize the assets of, and ban companies in the United States associated with China's army.

• HR 2232 (H Rept 105-303), passed 401–21 on Nov. 9, authorized funding for Radio Free Asia, a nongovernment outlet that broadcasted in seven Asian languages and English. The bill, the only one of the nine on which the Senate acted, was reported (no written report) by the Senate Foreign Relations Committee on May 27, 1998.

1998 Action

Members again found legislative vehicles for registering their views on U.S. policy toward China.

• S Res 187, adopted 95–5 March 12, and H Res 364, adopted 397–0 March 17, urged the president to introduce and support a United Nations resolution condemning China's human rights practices at the 54th session of the U.N. Commission on Human Rights, which was meeting the week of

U.S.-CHINA SUMMITRY

Chinese President Jiang Zemin traveled to the United States in October 1997 for the first official visit by a Chinese head of state in twelve years. It was also the first official summit since the 1989 crackdown in Tiananmen Square.

The high point of the summit was an agreement by Clinton to certify that China was in compliance with the 1985 nuclear cooperation agreement. The administration received assurances that Beijing would stop selling technology to countries such as Iran and Pakistan that were trying to develop nuclear weapons. But some in the Senate remained wary of China's promises. Foreign Relations Committee Chairman Jesse Helms, R-N.C., and Intelligence Committee Chairman Richard C. Shelby, R-Ala., had said in an Oct. 27 letter to Clinton that they wanted to review all written texts of any nuclear agreements, all intelligence reports and data on Chinese proliferation since Jan. 1, 1986, as well as any intelligence on Chinese diversion of U.S. technology.

During Jiang's visit he also met with fifty-five members of the House and Senate, including all the members of the leadership except for House Republican Whip Tom DeLay, Texas, who stayed away to protest China's treatment of religious minorities. At the meeting Jiang appealed for restraint by the United States and particularly by Congress. Lawmakers in turn peppered the Chinese leader with pointed questions on everything from religious persecution to compulsory abortion. After Jiang's departure, the House approved a series of bills chastising China on various issues. (*China resolutions, p. 182*)

President Clinton traveled to China in June 1998. His trip came as Congress pressed forward with several investigations into allegations tying China to breaches of national security and campaign finance rules. Lawmakers also began their annual debate over the president's decision to renew regular trade relations with China.

But Senate Democrats succeeded in blocking several Republican amendments to the fiscal 1999 defense authorization bill that they said were designed mainly to undermine Clinton on the eve of his trip and would violate the time-honored tradition that Congress close ranks behind a president when he is abroad. The amendments would have condemned Chinese human rights abuses and required a tougher U.S. stance toward Beijing's bids for international stature and financial assistance. At the Democrats' insistence, the amendments were withdrawn. (*1999 defense authorization, p. 252*)

After Clinton's return, both chambers took an indirect jab at remarks Clinton made during his trip on U.S. policy on Taiwan. (*Taiwan resolutions, this page*)

Clinton's China trip included an unprecedented televised appearance by a U.S. president.

March 16 in Geneva. The unanimous rebuke in the House came several days after administration officials had announced that they would break with their past policy and no longer seek to condemn China at the U.N. conference. They pointed to what they described as significant, positive strides that Beijing had made on human rights in the last year. In particular, the administration cited China's March 12 decision to sign the International Covenant on Civil and Political Rights, thereby promising to respect freedom of religion, thought, conscience, and expression. The administration also applauded Beijing's decision to release a prominent dissident and to pursue judicial reforms. But Democratic and Republican lawmakers said that Beijing's human rights record had not changed enough to justify the change in policy. Moreover, they said that China was unlikely to live up to its new commitments.

• H Con Res 285, adopted by the House 305–116 June 4, urged the president not to attend a welcoming ceremony in Tiananmen Square when he visited China later that month.

• S Con Res 107, adopted by a Senate vote of 92–0 July 10, and H Con Res 301, adopted by a House vote of 390–1 July 20, reaffirmed U.S. support for Taiwan as stipulated in the 1979 Taiwan Relations Act (PL 96-8). The 1979 act acknowledged Beijing as the legitimate government of China but expressed a U.S. commitment to aid Taiwan's defense and ensure that its future was decided by peaceful means. It called for Taiwan's membership in international financial institutions such as the World Bank and International Monetary Fund. (*Congress and the Nation Vol. V., p. 65*)

The resolutions were aimed at comments Clinton had made in his June visit to China. The president largely restated U.S. policy that Taiwan was part of China but should only rejoin the mainland in a peaceful settlement. But the president had used more explicit words than were usually used in the carefully constructed policy of "strategic ambiguity."

• S 2132, the Senate version of the fiscal 1999 defense appropriations bill, was amended by voice vote July 30, to deny U.S. visas to officials of foreign governments directly involved in implementing policies of religious persecution, forced abortion or sterilization, or female genital mutilation. The amendment, primarily aimed at Beijing, was dropped in conference on the final bill (HR 4103). (*1999 defense appropriations, p. 259*)

1998 Aid Appropriations

Congress in 1997 cleared legislation (HR 2159—PL 105-118) appropriating $13.2 billion for foreign aid and related programs in fiscal 1998. The total appropriation was significantly smaller than the $16.9 billion requested by President Clinton but about $880 million more than was appropriated the previous year.

For the third consecutive year, a dispute over abortion restrictions on international family planning funds delayed completion of the foreign operations spending bill until the final days of the session. At issue was a House-passed provision barring funds for family planning groups that promoted, performed, or advocated abortions abroad, even if they used their own money. It would have, in effect, reinstituted the so-called Mexico City policy from the Reagan and Bush administrations that Clinton had repealed when he came into office. The provision faced strong opposition in the Senate and a presidential veto threat. Similar restrictions had delayed release of fiscal 1997 family planning funds until early in 1997. *(Background, p. 195)*

When appropriators from both chambers proved unable to resolve the controversy, the Republican leadership proposed stripping away the restrictions, funding the groups at the fiscal 1997 level of $385 million, and providing the money at a rate of 8 percent per month. That cleared the way for final passage on the day Congress adjourned.

The decision to yield to the White House came at a price, however. Conservative House Republicans, forced to compromise on the family planning provision, blocked three unrelated items sought by the administration and Senate Republicans: payment of most U.S. debts to the United Nations, $3.4 billion for the International Monetary Fund (IMF), and consolidation of some foreign policy agencies. *(United Nations dues, p. 192; IMF, p. 194; Foreign policy agencies, p. 193)*

The abortion language even became a bargaining chip in Clinton's unsuccessful effort to secure votes for legislation giving him fast-track trade authority. *(Fast track, p. 153)*

SENATE ACTION

The Senate passed its foreign operations funding bill (S 955) on July 17, 1997, by a vote of 91–8. The bill had been reported by the Senate Appropriations Committee (S Rept 105-35) on June 24.

S 955 provided the administration with just about everything it sought. The bill recommended $16.9 billion in new budget authority, including a one-time $3.5 billion appropriation to underwrite the U.S. share of a new IMF loan account aimed at preventing massive currency fluctuations. While the size of the commitment to the IMF raised eyebrows in the House and Senate, it was actually a swap of assets with the IMF, backed by the IMF's gold reserves. The administration said the $3.5 billion appropriation would entail no new outlays—actual spending—and would not add to the deficit.

During consideration by the Senate Appropriations Subcommittee on Foreign Operations, Chairman Mitch McConnell, R-Ky., stirred a furor by eliminating a long-standing provision earmarking a minimum of $2.1 billion in military and economic aid for Egypt. He said the action was intended to signal U.S. disfavor with Egypt's failure to live up to its 1979 peace agreement with Israel. But the full Appropriations Committee agreed to restore the earmark during floor debate.

When the bill reached the floor, the only major foreign policy debate was over an amendment offered by John McCain, R-Ariz., and Christopher J. Dodd, D-Conn., to suspend the annual narcotics certification process for foreign countries for two years and develop a multilateral approach to stemming the spread of illicit drugs. The question of scrapping the certification process had been vigorously debated after Clinton had certified earlier in the year that Mexico had cooperated fully, despite incidents highlighting the failure of Mexico's counter-narcotics efforts. The McCain-Dodd amendment, however, was defeated 38–60, on July 16. *(Mexico decertification attempts, p. 203)*

The Senate earlier that day adopted, 95–4, an amendment by Gordon H. Smith, R-Ore., to cut off aid to the Russian government if it enacted a pending plan that Smith said would result in discrimination against religious minorities. With less fanfare, the Senate agreed by voice vote to expand the bill's prohibitions on aid to Russia if that country aided Iran's nuclear development program, to include selling ballistic missiles to Iran.

A nonbinding amendment by Tim Hutchinson, R-Ark., to deny Beijing most-favored-nation trade status was rejected 22–77 on July 17. *(China MFN, p. 151)*

HOUSE ACTION

The House passed a $12.3 billion version of the foreign operations funding bill (HR 2159) by a vote of 375–49 on Sept. 4. The Senate passed HR 2159 by voice vote the next day, after substituting the text of S 955. HR 2159 had been reported by the House Appropriations Committee (H Rept 105-176) on July 14.

The House-approved total was considerably less than Clinton had requested or the Senate approved. The biggest difference was the House bill's omission of the $3.5 billion for the IMF.

But differences over funding levels took a back seat when compared to the battle over a House amendment barring aid to family planning groups that used their own money to subsidize abortion overseas.

On Sept. 4, the House approved, 234–191, an amendment by Christopher H. Smith, R-N.J., barring the aid except in cases of rape, incest, or danger to the life of any woman. The amendment also barred funding for any foreign organization that lobbied for or against abortion, and for the U.N. Population Fund unless it ceased all activities in China.

Before voting on Smith's amendment, the House narrowly rejected a bipartisan substitute offered by Nancy Pelosi, D-Calif., and Benjamin A. Gilman, R-N.Y. The substitute, defeated by a **key vote of 210–218 (R 38–185; D 171–33; I 1–0),** would have allowed funding for groups that did not "promote abortion as a method of family planning," even if they actually performed abortions. *(1997 key votes, p. 865)*

CONFERENCE, FINAL ACTION

With the exception of the abortion amendment, House and Senate negotiators ironed out virtually all their differences in less than three hours. Conferees agreed to a $13.2 billion appropriation after working out compromises on significant stumbling blocks such as aid to Jordan and assistance for the former states of the Soviet Union.

Angered by Israel's refusal to guarantee that it would contribute toward aid to Jordan, members of the House Appropriations Committee had put a hold on $75 million that Israel was scheduled to receive from the United States under a just-expired continuing resolution (H J Res 94—PL 105-46). The resolution provided stop-gap funding for departments whose regular funding was covered by unfinished appropriations bills. But once Israel indicated it would pay its $50 million portion, the hold was lifted and conferees were able to meet and agree on the aid package. The bill provided $225 million in assistance to Jordan, including the $50 million contribution from Israel and $50 million from Egypt. Israel received its customary $3.1 billion in U.S. assistance and Egypt $2.1 billion.

Negotiators trimmed Clinton's request for the former Soviet states by $130 million, leaving $770 million. They reserved $250 million of the money for the troubled southern Caucasus region, including $52.5 million to promote peace between Armenia and its neighbors, among them Azerbaijan. The bill continued a ban on direct government-to-government aid to Azerbaijan, but it exempted political risk insurance provided by the Overseas Private Investment Corporation (OPIC) to U.S. companies investing in that country, as well as various economic development efforts.

The conference report also set restrictions to discourage Russian transactions with Iran. In addition, conferees agreed on a version of the provision sponsored by Sen. Smith barring aid to Russia if it implemented recently passed laws discriminating against religious minorities.

After weeks of delay and with the pressure to adjourn increasing, Republican leaders circulated a proposed compromise on the abortion dispute. The leadership essentially proposed to codify the restrictions on funding for international family planning groups, including the ban on lobbying. The president could have waived the restrictions, but then funding would have been limited.

All the Senate Republicans signed the conference report, but two moderate House Republicans and the Democratic conferees from both chambers refused. The GOP leadership tried to make the package more appealing by attaching some provisions long sought by the White House that were languishing in a conference on the 1998–1999 State Department authorization bill (HR 1757) because of a similar House-passed provision on abortion and family planning.

The package included the consolidation of several foreign policy agencies, repayment of U.S. debts to the United Nations, and the $3.5 billion for the IMF. *(State Department authorization, p. 189)*

Agreement could not be reached and so, with the date for adjournment looming, GOP leaders finally yielded to Clinton and approved overseas family planning aid without abortion restrictions. But the carrots dangled in front of the Democrats were dropped as well. Administration pleas to the GOP to relent on the IMF and U.N. funding proved unsuccessful.

In the waning hours of the session, a Republican attempt to bundle the remaining spending bills together with the IMF and U.N. money, State Department reorganization, and a version of the restriction on family planning aid was abandoned in the face of strong Democratic opposition and the possibility of a defeat in the House.

The House adopted the conference report (H Rept 105-401), 333–76, early on the morning of Nov. 13. The Senate cleared the bill by voice vote later that day. Clinton signed it Nov. 26.

MAJOR PROVISIONS

As signed into law, HR 2159 appropriated $13.2 billion for foreign aid and related programs in fiscal 1998. This included $1.65 billion in multilateral aid, $7.6 billion in bilateral aid, $3.38 billion in bilateral military aid, and $583 million in export assistance.

Major provisions of the bill:

Middle East

Earmarked $3.1 billion in aid for Israel, $2.1 billion for Egypt, and $225 million to Jordan.

Palestinians

Barred aid to the Palestinian Authority in the West Bank and Gaza unless the president determined that providing the money was in the interest of U.S. national security.

Former Soviet Union

Appropriated $770 million for the former Soviet republics, including $225 million earmarked for Ukraine and $250 million for the southern Caucasus ($70 million for refugee-related aid, $87.5 million for Armenia, and $92.5 million for Georgia). Half of the aid to Ukraine was to be withheld and released after four months if the secretary of state certified that Kiev had undertaken economic reforms. (Secretary of State Madeleine Albright made that certification in April 1998.)

The bill withheld 50 percent of the aid to Russia unless it ended its practice of sharing sensitive military technology with Iran, a provision the president could waive. Also, aid to Russia was to be cut off unless the president certified that no law or regulation discriminating against religious groups had been implemented.

The bill urged the Export-Import Bank to suspend all transactions with Gazprom, the largely state-owned Russian company, which was helping Iran in a $2 billion project to develop offshore natural gas deposits.

Turkey, Greece

Provided a total of $105 million in loans to Greece and $150 million in loans to Turkey.

Cambodia

Prohibited any funds from being made directly available to the new regime in Cambodia, except for election monitoring, humanitarian aid, and de-mining activities.

North Korea

Included $30 million as requested to purchase and ship fuel oil to North Korea as part of a 1994 agreement intended to reduce that country's need for nuclear power plants. (Congress and the Nation Vol. IX, p. 221)

Development Aid

Appropriated $1.2 billion for general development assistance, such as agriculture, rural development, and basic education programs. In addition, it provided $650 million for a child survival and disease fund created under the fiscal 1997 spending bill.

Family Planning

Provided $385 million for family planning organizations, which was to be disbursed at a rate of 8 percent a month.

The bill provided $25 million for the United Nations Population Fund (UNFPA) but barred the use of any of that money for activities in China. If the secretary of state reported UNFPA had budgeted money for activities in China, an equal amount was to be withheld from the U.S. contribution after March 1, 1998.

1999 Aid Appropriations

Congress in 1998 approved $31.6 billion in appropriations for foreign operations in fiscal 1999, as part of an omnibus spending bill (HR 4328—PL 105-277). The final bill included regular appropriations of $12.8 billion for foreign aid and export assistance, $17.9 billion in credit for the International Monetary Fund (IMF), and $539 million in debt payments to multilateral development banks. It contained another $399 million in "emergency" supplemental funding.

Agreement on the bill had come after more than a year of wrangling over foreign policy priorities. In the end, GOP leaders in Congress agreed to President Clinton's demands for credit for the IMF to replenish coffers depleted by financial crises in Asia, Russia, and elsewhere, albeit with strings attached. The $12.8 billion foreign aid funding level was $750 million less than Clinton had requested, but Congress

did agree to stepped-up aid to Russia and other former Soviet republics.

Abortion-related restrictions on international family planning funds were also dropped from the final bill, although funding limits approved the previous year were retained. The foreign aid legislation had been an annual battleground over the issue of abortion since 1995. (1998 aid appropriations, p. 183)

For the first time since the signing of the Camp David Accords between Israel and Egypt in March 1979, economic assistance to the two countries was cut. The reduction was part of a ten-year plan to phase out U.S. economic aid to Israel and reduce by 50 percent aid to Egypt. HR 4328 provided $3 billion in aid for Israel and $2.1 billion for Egypt.

And for the first time in twenty years, the foreign aid bill provided no military financing assistance to either Greece or Turkey.

SENATE ACTION

The Senate on Sept. 2, 1998, passed, 90–3, a fiscal 1999 foreign operations spending bill (S 2334) appropriating $12.6 billion for foreign aid and export assistance, $17.9 billion in additional credit for the IMF, and $311 million for repayments to multilateral institutions. The Senate Appropriations Committee had reported S 2334 (S Rept 105-255) on July 21.

The Senate bill included President Clinton's full request for credit for the IMF, whose coffers had been depleted by bailouts for several Asian nations and Russia. An attempt by Sen. John Kyl, R-Ariz., to place binding restrictions on the IMF money was tabled (killed) by a 74–19 vote during floor debate. The Senate had approved the IMF package earlier in 1998 as part of a fiscal 1998 supplemental spending bill (S 1768), but it was stripped out in conference on the final version of the supplemental (HR 3579—PL 105-174).

Although S 2334 included Secretary of State Madeleine K. Albright's top objective—IMF funding—she recommended that the president veto the measure because it fell about $1 billion short of his budget request. The bill, for example, reduced Clinton's request for aid to the states of the former Soviet Union from $925 million to $740 million. The administration also suffered setbacks on several policy issues.

Senators reacted sharply to North Korea's Aug. 31 test launch of a medium-range missile that passed over northern Japan, as well as to recent revelations that Pyongyang might be building a nuclear reactor in violation of a 1994 agreement with the United States. A July 7 General Accounting Office report said that North Korea had refused full access to its nuclear sites, making it difficult to determine if the country had hidden enough plutonium to build nuclear bombs.

Sen. John McCain, R-Ariz., offered an amendment to condition the $35 million allocated in S 2334 to the Korean Peninsula Energy Development Organization on a presidential certification that North Korea had halted its nuclear program or a waiver by the president on national security

AZERBAIJAN AID BAN

Attempts in 1998 to repeal a six-year ban on direct aid to Azerbaijan, an oil-rich, former Soviet republic on the Caspian Sea in Central Asia, proved futile.

Since the break-up of the Soviet Union, Azerbaijan and neighboring Armenia had been locked in a fight over the largely Armenian enclave of Nagorno-Karabakh. Although Armenian troops had occupied the enclave for several years, U.S. and Azeri officials said it was legally part of Azerbaijan. The predominantly Muslim state of Azerbaijan had instituted a blockade of the mostly Orthodox Armenia in an effort to win back the disputed enclave. A ceasefire had held since 1994, but attempts by the United States, France, and Russia to broker a settlement had failed.

Secretary of State Madeleine K. Albright and other Clinton administration officials argued that the aid restrictions had hurt the ability of the United States to act as an honest broker in the dispute. They and other supporters of lifting the restrictions, particularly U.S. oil companies, argued that the ban hindered U.S. efforts to persuade Azerbaijan and other Caspian Sea countries to ship their oil through a Western-oriented pipeline to Turkey rather than through Iran or Russia. It was estimated that there was as much as $4 trillion worth of oil in the region, second only to the Persian Gulf.

More than a dozen U.S. oil companies had invested more than $35 billion in Azerbaijan alone.

But longtime supporters of Armenia and Armenian-American interests said that the change would reward a government in Azerbaijan that was corrupt and had engaged in ethnic cleansing. They said that the 1992 law (PL 102-511) had taken the appropriate stance by cutting off direct aid to the Azerbaijan government unless it stopped blockading Armenia.

Senate advocates of lifting the aid ban, led by Sam Brownback, R-Kan., shelved their plans to amend the fiscal 1999 foreign operations bill (S 2334) when it became apparent there were not enough votes. Repeal language was included in the House Appropriations Committee's version of the bill (HR 4569) but it was deleted on the House floor. Brownback was also the lead sponsor of the Silk Road Strategy Act (S 1344—S Rept 105-394), which would have lifted the ban as part of a broader U.S. strategy to upgrade relations with eight nations in central Asia and the Caucasus. But that bill went no further after the Senate Foreign Relations Committee reported it Oct. 9, 1998. (The Silk Road was the ancient trade route that wound through the region connecting China with the Mediterranean.)

---

grounds. The energy organization had been set up in 1994 to funnel international money into the construction of two light-water nuclear reactors in North Korea and into deliveries of heavy fuel oil to meet North Korea's needs, in return for that country's pledge to freeze and dismantle its nascent nuclear weapons program and the reactors that fed it. An attempt to table McCain's amendment failed, 11–80, and McCain's amendment was subsequently adopted by voice vote.

The Senate action on the Korean energy organization marked the end of administration plans to win increased funds to compensate for lower than expected contributions from other nations.

The White House also suffered a setback to its counterproliferation policy when a test vote indicated less than overwhelming support for the Comprehensive Nuclear Test Ban Treaty (Treaty Doc 105-28).

For months the administration had urged the Senate to take up the treaty, but Foreign Relations Committee Chairman Jesse Helms, R-N.C., had blocked its consideration, saying it could not be verified or enforced. *(Test ban treaty, p. 310)*

As a test vote, Arlen Specter, R-Pa., introduced an amendment that would authorize $29 million to fund an international commission laying the groundwork and installing technical equipment to monitor compliance with the treaty. On Sept. 1 the Senate adopted the amendment, 49–44, far

short of the two-thirds majority needed to approve the treaty itself.

The White House lost in its effort to lift the six-year-old restrictions on U.S. aid to Azerbaijan, an oil-rich country beside the Caspian Sea in Central Asia. Azerbaijan and neighboring Armenia were locked in a struggle over the enclave of Nagorno-Karabakh. Sen. Sam Brownback, R-Kan., had intended to push for lifting the restrictions but his proposal did not have enough backers. Members were reluctant to take on the formidable Armenian-American lobby in an election year. *(Azerbaijan aid ban, box, this page)*

HOUSE ACTION

The House passed its version of the fiscal 1999 foreign operations bill (HR 4569) by a vote of 255–161 on Sept. 17. The House Appropriations Committee had reported the bill (H Rept 105-719) Sept. 15.

An antiabortion provision and the omission of much of the administration's request for the IMF triggered a veto threat. As passed, HR 4569 appropriated $12.5 billion for foreign aid and export assistance, $3.4 billion for the IMF, and $352 million in debt payments to the international development banks.

During committee consideration, Appropriations Chairman Robert L. Livingston, R-La., had urged members to hold off approving the additional $14.5 billion in credit for the IMF until the administration first agreed to a requirement that the IMF conduct its operations with greater openness and accountability. He noted that Russia's chief negotiator with the IMF had recently boasted that he had "conned" the fund out of billions of dollars in loans by lying about the extent of his country's financial problems.

The administration suffered another setback when the committee added antiabortion restrictions. The provision would have reinstated a policy of the Reagan and Bush administrations banning aid to international family planning groups that performed, lobbied for, or otherwise advocated abortion, even if they used their own money. In a relaxation of the Reagan/Bush standard, the president would have been allowed to waive the section of the bill related to groups that performed abortions. But if he did, spending on family planning programs would be limited to $356 million a year, $29 million below current spending.

The House bill slashed Clinton's $925 million request for aid to the former Soviet republics to $590 million.

On the question of energy assistance for North Korea, the House went further than the Senate by following Japan's lead and cutting off all aid to the Korean Peninsula Energy Development Organization. The action came as the State Department announced a resumption in talks with North Korea on its missile and nuclear programs and pledged to send several hundred thousand tons of fuel oil to Pyongyang. U.S. officials reportedly also were considering stepped-up food aid.

The House Appropriations Committee had voted to lift the ban on direct aid to Azerbaijan, but that decision was reversed when the bill reached the House floor. By a vote of 231–182 on Sept. 17, the House adopted a John Edward Porter, R-Ill., amendment eliminating the repeal provision.

But little else was changed during the floor debate. Democrats said the rule governing debate had effectively prevented them from making their case on other contentious issues. The rule had been adopted 229–188.

CONFERENCE, FINAL ACTION

The House adopted the conference report on HR 4328 (H Rept 105-825) by a vote of 333–95 on Oct. 20. The Senate cleared the bill, 65–29, on Oct. 21, and Clinton signed it that same day.

In the final bill the Clinton administration won congressional backing for some of its key foreign policy priorities, including nearly $18 billion in credit for the IMF and almost $1 billion for countries of the former Soviet Union. But the long-standing dispute over abortion derailed another top goal: getting Congress to support paying off nearly $1 billion in debts to the United Nations.

The mixed results highlighted continued Republican reluctance to participate in multilateral organizations, and the key role business groups and religious conservatives played in determining how the GOP approached foreign policy issues.

GOP resistance to extending additional credit to the IMF had been worn down as influential business and farm groups pressed Republican leaders to approve the credits, saying they were essential to reviving American farm and other exports to economies damaged by the global financial crisis.

House Majority Leader Dick Armey of Texas and other Republicans who had opposed the IMF credits still claimed victory on the issue, saying the U.S. contribution would be conditioned on major developing countries approving a series of changes in the IMF. But diplomats, IMF officials, and congressional aides said Armey's triumph was somewhat illusory, because most of the "conditions" required the IMF to do things it already was doing.

In accepting the IMF credits, Republican leaders agreed to cut the link between the IMF funds and the GOP attempt to reimpose Reagan and Bush era abortion restrictions on international family planning aid. The conference report retained fiscal 1998 provisions allowing limited international family planning aid without the Reagan/Bush restrictions. The bill cut off money for the United Nations Population Fund because of that group's involvement with China and its sometimes coercive efforts to limit families to one child.

House GOP leaders continued to condition payment of U.S. debts to the United Nations on adoption of the antiabortion restrictions, despite administration and Senate opposition. Democrats failed in their attempts to include in the omnibus bill $200 million in U.N. dues, along with proposed reforms of the international organization and a reorganization of U.S. foreign affairs agencies.

Conferees agreed to give the administration more money for countries of the former Soviet Union, particularly Russia. Clinton had sought $925 million, but the figure dropped as low as $590 million in the House-passed bill. With White House officials worried about the state of the Russian economy and the political survival of Russian President Boris Yeltsin, the administration persuaded conferees to allocate $847 million to the region.

The final bill included money for the Korean energy organization, as long as certain conditions were met. It also contained funding for the Global Environmental Facility, a controversial program administered by the World Bank that the House had cut.

MAJOR PROVISIONS

As signed into law, HR 4328, the omnibus appropriations bill, provided $31.2 billion in regular fiscal 1999 appropriations, including $19.5 billion for multilateral aid, $7.6 billion in bilateral aid, $3.4 billion in bilateral military aid, and $656.5 million for export assistance.

The bill also included an additional $399 million in "emergency" supplemental funds for the child survival fund, aid to the former Soviet states, counter-narcotics, and Africa embassy bombing-related costs.

Major provisions of the bill:

International Monetary Fund

Provided $17.86 billion in credit for the International Monetary Fund but set certain conditions, most of which the IMF was already doing:

• Countries facing a run on their currencies because of balance-of-payments problems and a loss of market confidence could be offered only short-term loans that would have to be repaid within one to two-and-a-half years at a rate 3 percent above the average market rates in five major industrialized countries. (The IMF had already established this condition when it set up the Supplemental Reserve Facility in December 1997.)

• Countries that received loans would have to eliminate subsidized loans and treat foreign lenders on a par with domestic creditors.

• More public information about the IMF's loans and operations would have to be made available.

• A temporary bipartisan advisory commission would have to be established to examine the future role and responsibilities of international financial institutions—the IMF, the World Trade Organization, and the Bank for International Settlements.

• Creation of a permanent international advisory committee of elected members of national legislatures was recommended.

Former Soviet Union

Appropriated $847 million for aid to the former Soviet republics, including $46 million in emergency supplemental funds.

Of this, $195 million was earmarked for Ukraine and $228 million provided for the southern Caucacus, of which $84.4 million was earmarked for Georgia and $79.9 million for Armenia and $40 million was set aside as an initial peace dividend if Armenia and Azerbaijan were able to settle their long-standing conflict over Nagorno-Karabakh.

The bill continued certain conditions on aid to Russia and Ukraine established the previous year. Half of U.S. aid to Russia was to be withheld until that country ended its nuclear and ballistic missile cooperation with Iran, unless waived by the president. Aid to Russia was to be cut off, unless the president certified that the Russian government had implemented no law or regulation discriminating against religious groups.

The bill provided $10 million for Turkmenistan, largely to develop a pipeline to carry natural gas across the Caspian Sea instead of through neighboring Iran.

North Atlantic Treaty Organization

Provided $30 million in military aid to help integrate new NATO members Poland, Hungary, and the Czech Republic into the alliance.

The bill also provided $15 million to help the Baltic states of Latvia, Lithuania, and Estonia make their militaries more compatible with those of NATO, in hopes of joining the alliance in the future.

Middle East

Provided $3 billion in aid for Israel and $2.1 billion for Egypt. The bill began a ten-year plan to phase out economic assistance to Israel and cut aid to Egypt by 50 percent.

The bill provided $150 million in U.S. aid to Jordan and $7 million to Tunisia, both for supporting the Middle East peace process.

North Korea

Provided $35 million for the Korean Peninsula Energy Development Organization. The money would be available in two phases and would be subject to certain presidential certifications regarding North Korea's progress toward ending its nuclear and ballistic missile programs. The certification requirements could be waived in national security interests. The bill required the appointment of a senior presidential envoy to review U.S. policy toward North Korea.

World Bank Program

Provided $193 million for the Global Environment Facility.

Family Planning

Provided $385 million for family planning organizations, which was to be disbursed at a rate of 8 percent a month.

The bill cut off funding for the United Nations Population Fund.

FISCAL 1999 SUPPLEMENTAL

Although intended primarily as a measure to fund U.S. military operations in Kosovo, a fiscal 1999 supplemental appropriations bill (HR 1141—PL 106-31) also included, among other things, foreign aid provisions. HR 1141 was signed into law May 21, 1999.

In addition to its $5 billion for military operations in Kosovo, the bill appropriated $1.1 billion for refugee, disaster, and economic assistance to address the crisis in Kosovo.

HR 1141 also included long-delayed aid to Central American nations hit by Hurricanes Mitch and Georges in 1998, appropriating $687 million in emergency funds.

Also appropriated was $100 million in economic support and foreign military financing for Jordan in conjunction with that nation's participation in the Wye River peace accords. President Clinton had wanted Congress to accelerate aid to Jordan in advance of the broader Wye River aid package in order to buoy Jordan after the death of King Hussein. Clinton had requested $300 million.

State Department Authorization

Congress in 1998 cleared a two-year $12.8 billion State Department authorization bill (HR 1757) containing a delicate compromise on the payment of U.S. debts to the United Nations and consolidation of several foreign affairs agencies. But President Clinton vetoed the measure because of House-passed abortion restrictions on international family planning aid.

The core of the Senate version had been an elaborate trade-off put together in the summer of 1997 by Senate Foreign Relations Committee Chairman Jesse Helms, R-N.C.;

1998 MIDDLE EAST SUMMIT

Commitments made by President Clinton to seal the Oct. 23, 1998, interim peace agreement between Israel and the Palestinians raised a number of concerns among congressional Republicans.

After a marathon nine-day summit at the Wye River conference center in Maryland with Israeli Prime Minister Benjamin Netanyahu and Palestinian Authority Chairman Yasser Arafat, Clinton pledged:

• Increased U.S. assistance for Israel to meet the security costs of moving forces out of the West Bank and for the Palestinians to meet the costs of development.

• An unusually public role for the CIA in monitoring the success of the accords and reviewing the security situation on both sides.

• A review of the case of Jonathan Jay Pollard, a former U.S. Navy intelligence analyst sentenced to life imprisonment in 1987 for selling top-secret material to Israel.

Under the land-for-peace agreement, Israel was to pull back from 13 percent of occupied parts of the West Bank and hand over another 14 percent then jointly controlled with the Palestinians. All told, the Palestinians were slated to control 40 percent of the West Bank.

In return, the Palestinians agreed to clamp down on terrorism, reduce the size of their police force, and delete twenty-six clauses from the Palestine Liberation Organization charter calling for the destruction of Israel.

Some Republicans on Capitol Hill questioned whether Clinton's promises were a campaign ploy coming just two weeks before congressional elections. Sonny Callahan, R-Ala., chairman of the House Foreign Operations Appropriations Subcommittee, said he could not support spending any more for Israel or the Middle East. Senate Intelligence Committee Chairman Richard C. Shelby, R-Ala., said he found the more public role proposed for the CIA troubling. And GOP leaders and others all questioned Clinton's agreement to review the Pollard case, firing off a letter to the president Oct. 27 saying that Pollard had deserved his life sentence and should not be pardoned.

Congress in the fiscal 2000 foreign operations spending bill (PL 106-113) agreed to appropriate $1.8 billion over three years to assist Israel, Jordan, and the Palestinian Authority in implementing the Wye River agreement. An earlier version had been vetoed, in part because it did not contain money for the peace accord. *(2000 aid appropriations, p. 210)*

---

the panel's ranking Democrat, Joseph R. Biden Jr. of Delaware; and administration officials. Helms agreed to allow payment of almost $1 billion in U.S. debts to the United Nations, while the administration pledged to insist on U.N. reforms and a reduction in the U.S. share of the U.N. budget and peacekeeping costs. The administration also agreed to merge several foreign affairs agencies into the State Department—the U.S. Information Agency (USIA), the Arms Control and Disarmament Agency (ACDA), and parts of the Agency for International Development (AID). *(United Nations dues, p. 192; foreign policy agencies, p. 193)*

But the carefully laid plans started to unravel when House conservatives attached controversial provisions to reinstate portions of a policy, first pronounced by President Ronald Reagan at a U.N. population conference in Mexico City in 1984 and continued by the George Bush administration, that banned U.S. aid to family planning groups that used their own funds to perform or advocate abortions or that lobbied foreign governments on the issue. The president would have been allowed to waive some restrictions but then would have had to settle for less family planning aid.

The so-called Mexico City policy was vehemently opposed by the Clinton administration and many Democrats on Capitol Hill. One of Clinton's first acts as president in January 1993 was to overturn the policy. *(Background, Congress and the Nation Vol. IX, box, p. 209)*

But Republicans over time managed to move HR 1757 through conference. After an easy victory in the House and a narrow approval in the Senate, Republican leaders held on to the conference agreement for six months before sending it to the White House. When they finally did, Clinton promptly vetoed the bill.

In the end, the foreign affairs reorganization and several other key provisions were included in an omnibus spending bill signed by Clinton (HR 4328—PL 105-277). Only the U.N. debt funds were left out, as Republicans continued to tie them to the antiabortion restrictions. A U.N. repayment plan was ultimately enacted in 1999 as part of the fiscal 2000 omnibus spending bill (HR 3194—PL 106-113). *(1999 action, p. 217)*

HR 1757 would have authorized $6.1 billion for fiscal 1998 and $6.7 billion for fiscal 1999.

HOUSE ACTION

The House passed HR 1757 by voice vote on June 11, 1997.

The House International Relations Committee had reported a broader version of the bill (HR 1486—H Rept 105-94) on May 9. That bill had combined the State Department authorization with a two-year authorization of foreign aid programs, bringing the bill's total to $32.4 billion, including about $20.1 billion for foreign assistance. Benjamin A. Gilman, R-N.Y., the committee chairman, saw the combined package as offering the best hope for getting a foreign aid authorization bill enacted for the first time since 1985.

Gilman also assiduously courted the administration and panel Democrats. The result was a high degree of bipartisanship that contrasted sharply with the previous Congress, when Gilman and other committee Republicans rammed through a partisan bill slashing funds for international programs and challenging Clinton's foreign policy. *(Congress and the Nation Vol. IX, p. 228)*

But in an unusual move, House Republican leaders jettisoned the committee-approved bill in favor of HR 1757, a hastily drafted measure designed to draw support from conservative Republicans. The new $12.2 billion bill included the committee provisions on the State Department and related agencies, but it dropped nearly all the foreign aid authorization.

The move by GOP leaders to scuttle HR 1486—a decision enforced by the Rules Committee during a contentious session on June 3—was a rebuke of Gilman's leadership and drew heavy criticism from Democrats. But Republicans insisted that the original bill faced certain defeat largely because it was too generous to the administration. "It was obvious this would never pass the House," Rules Committee Chairman Gerald B. H. Solomon, R-N.Y., said of Gilman's bill.

The action, which marked another in a string of setbacks for the International Relations Committee, came at the behest of senior members of the House Appropriations Committee, who used blunt language in demanding that GOP leaders completely restructure the bill. They charged that the International Relations Committee had essentially punted to the appropriators a number of tough policy issues. They also objected to the high spending levels in the bill, saying it was almost a carbon copy of the administration request.

The new bill directed a reorganization of the foreign policy agencies along the lines agreed to by the Clinton administration, but an amendment by Lee Hamilton, D-Ind., to give the president broader latitude in carrying out the consolidation plan failed, 202–224, on June 4.

The bill still did not include authorization for back payments to the United Nations. It did contain many of the foreign policy provisions from the committee bill, including funding to move the U.S. embassy in Israel to Jerusalem and the requirement that government publications refer to Jerusalem as the capital of Israel.

In a reprise of struggles from previous years, the House on June 5 adopted, 232–189, an amendment by Christopher H. Smith, R-N.J., banning all funding for international organizations that used their own funds to promote or perform abortions and barring aid to the United Nations Population Fund unless it terminated all activities in China, whose government had been widely condemned for its policies of forced abortion and sterilization. The House earlier had rejected, 200–218, an attempt to weaken Smith's amendment by reducing but not ending funding for the U.N. agency if it continued to operate in China.

The House considered a series of amendments before passing HR 1757 on June 11. The House then passed, also by voice vote, a second bill (HR 1758) endorsing the expansion of NATO to include the emerging democracies of central and eastern Europe and added it to HR 1757.

SENATE ACTION

The Senate passed HR 1757 by a vote of 90–5 on June 17, 1997, after substituting the text of its two-year, $12 billion State Department authorization bill (S 903). S 903 had been reported by the Senate Foreign Relations Committee on June 13 (S Rept 105-28).

The Senate bill included the deal struck by Helms and Biden on paying off most U.S. debts to the United Nations. It also included Helms's plan to consolidate foreign affairs agencies.

The Helms-Biden agreement provided for payment over three years of $819 million in back debts to the United Nations, but only if that organization took a number of actions, including reducing the U.S. share of its budget. Like the House bill, S 903 proposed consolidating the arms control agency and USIA, along with parts of AID, into the State Department. But it went further by seeking to fold more of AID into State and requiring that foreign aid be funded through the State Department rather than through AID. The House bill adhered more closely to Clinton's approach.

With the Helms-Biden deal in place, the bill sailed through the Senate. The only challenge to the U.N. provision came from Indiana Republican Richard G. Lugar, who found himself in the unenviable position of trying to derail an initiative backed by leading conservatives, Biden, and the administration. Lugar charged that the bill would force the U.N. into humiliating concessions and would fall far short of fully funding the U.S. debts to that organization. But his amendment to eliminate conditions on the payment plan was defeated, 25–73, on June 17.

Biden and Helms also teamed up on June 17 to quash an amendment by Russell D. Feingold, D-Wis., to put U.S.-government broadcasting operations, such as Radio Free Europe and the recently established Radio Free Asia, into the State Department, along with USIA. The proposal was rejected, 21–74.

As the bill headed into conference, the big question was whether Helms's imprimatur would be sufficient to win over the many hard-core U.N. opponents in the House.

CONFERENCE, FINAL ACTION

The conference on HR 1757 opened in late July 1997, but no agreement was reached before Congress adjourned for the year. Conferees could not find a way past the stubborn abortion dispute, which was also paralyzing work on the foreign operations spending bill. The House Republican leadership and a majority of GOP members made it clear they did not intend to budge on either bill. The House voted 233–194 on Oct. 7 to instruct conferees on the appropriations bill to insist on the abortion restrictions. On Oct. 8, the House voted 236–190 to give the same instruction to House conferees on the State Department bill. An attempt by Helms and Biden to attach the U.N. repayment and foreign policy agency consolidation plans to the spending bill failed.

In November House Republican conservatives refused to let the State Department bill move forward—as well as a $3.5 billion authorization for the International Monetary Fund—while the abortion impasse remained.

The Clinton administration made little or no effort to negotiate on the dispute. But House Speaker Newt Gingrich, R-Ga., and Helms revived the dormant State Department bill in early 1998. Gingrich instructed the reluctant Gilman to resuscitate the authorization conference with Republicans only. GOP senators, including Helms, had their doubts, but they eventually relented.

Several weeks of talks produced a conference report on March 10, 1998 (H Rept 105-432). When faced with the opposition of conferee and GOP moderate Jim Leach, R-Iowa, who favored more money for the United Nations and opposed restrictions on family planning funds, Gingrich pulled Leach off the conference committee and replaced him with a Republican willing to sign the report.

The Republican-only conference report provided for the United States to repay $819 million over fiscal years 1998–2000 in back dues to the United Nations while forgiving $107 million the organization owed the United States, mostly for peacekeeping. In return, the United Nations would have to reduce the U.S. share of its regular budget and peacekeeping budget.

The arms control agency and USIA were to be abolished and, along with some functions of AID, absorbed by the State Department.

Under the bill, for the first time, the Mexico City restrictions on international family planning aid would be written into law. No aid would be given to overseas family planning groups that used their own money to perform abortions or that lobbied against abortion laws in other countries. The president would be allowed to waive the section of the bill related to groups that performed abortion, but if he chose to exercise that authority, the result would be a permanent spending cap of $356 million for family planning in any fiscal year, $29 million less than the level at that time. The president had no waiver authority on lobbying.

The conference bill also included items that were popular with various ethnic groups and were included to gain support from Republicans who opposed the abortion provision. Among them were authorizations to move the U.S. embassy in Israel from Tel Aviv to Jerusalem, to state support for the expansion of NATO, to fund efforts to undermine the regime of Iraqi President Saddam Hussein, and to contribute to an international fund for Ireland with the aim of helping businesses eliminate religious-based discrimination in recruitment and employment.

House approval of the long-delayed conference report for HR 1757 came on an anticlimactic voice vote March 26. An earlier vote of 234–172 on the rule for debate had told Democrats they did not have the votes to defeat the conference report. Hamilton, the Democratic floor manager for the bill, decided that a recorded vote would only force antiabortion Democrats to vote against their beliefs or against President Clinton. Also, some Democrats were absent from the floor, accompanying Clinton on a trip to Africa.

The Senate on April 28 narrowly adopted the conference version of HR 1757 by a 51–49 vote.

VETO

Republican leaders took the unusual step of holding on to HR 1757 for nearly six months before sending it to the White House in hopes of changing Clinton's mind about a threatened veto. They tried to persuade him that the bill offered the only opportunity of accomplishing the White House priority of paying off U.S. debts to the United Nations.

But the delay and their arguments were to no avail. Clinton's veto came on Oct. 21 just hours after the bill arrived. The president said the bill "threatened our leadership in the world community by tying our payment of dues to the United Nations and other international organizations to these unrelated family planning issues."

U.N. Debt Repayment

A plan to pay off nearly $1 billion in U.S. debts to the United Nations fell victim in the 105th Congress to a dispute between Congress and the White House over abortion restrictions on international family planning aid. The repayment plan was the centerpiece of a State Department authorization bill (HR 1757) that President Clinton vetoed in 1998 because of the abortion provision.

The plan had been negotiated by Senate Foreign Relations Committee Chairman Jesse Helms, R-N.C., and Joseph R. Biden Jr. of Delaware, the panel's ranking Democrat. It provided for the United States to pay over fiscal years 1998–2000 $819 million in back dues to the United Nations while forgiving $107 million the organization owed the United States, mostly for peacekeeping. In return, the United Nations had to reduce the U.S. share of its budget.

The debts had accumulated over two decades for a variety of reasons. The United States had fallen behind almost $300 million in contributions to the U.N.'s regular budget because Congress, in a series of bills, ordered the administration to withhold the money. The United States also owed the United Nations almost $1 billion for peacekeeping operations in Somalia, Bosnia, and other places. The Clinton administration disputed about $250 million of those, partly because a 1994 law (PL 103-236) blocked the United States from paying more than a quarter of the peacekeeping budget, even though other U.N. members had never agreed to reduce the U.S. share below 31 percent.

All told, the Clinton administration acknowledged about $1 billion in debt. Members of Congress put the total lower. In April 1997 Helms, Biden, and Bill Richardson, who at the time was the U.S. representative to the United Nations, worked out the deal to repay $819 million and demand sweeping management overhauls, including a reduction in the U.S. share of the regular and peacekeeping budgets.

Senate passage was virtually assured once Helms, a fierce critic of the United Nations, gave his seal of approval. Helms's support made the bill palatable for other GOP conservatives, many of whom were normally leery of voting for any funds for the United Nations. The only challenge to the U.N. provision came from Indiana Republican Richard G. Lugar, who contended that the United States had an obligation to pay its debts fully to the organization without imposing conditions. Failing to do so, he said, would weaken the U.N. and strain relations with U.S. allies in Europe. But Lugar's amendment to eliminate conditions for payment of the debt was easily defeated, 25–73, on June 17, 1997. The bill was passed later that day.

When HR 1757 returned to the House, Republicans, already cool to the United Nations, insisted on tying the bill to legislation denying U.S. family planning funds to groups that advocated abortion or changes in abortion policies overseas.

After the House refused to back down, Helms and Biden persuaded appropriators to include the repayment plan in a compromise version of the foreign operations spending bill (HR 2159). But that bill also was caught up in the battle over abortion restrictions. In the final days of the 1997 session, GOP leaders dropped the abortion language in order to get the spending bill enacted. Forced to back down on the abortion issue, conservative House Republicans then rejected, among several things, the plan to repay U.N. debts.

Efforts to enact the repayment plan then reverted to the State Department authorization bill. Congress sent Clinton the conference bill containing both the U.N. debt payment and the abortion restrictions in October 1998, after holding on to it for six months. The president vetoed HR 1757 within hours of receiving it. (State Department authorization, p. 189)

Several of the bill's key provisions were included in an omnibus spending bill signed by Clinton (HR 4328—PL 105-277) but not the U.N. funds. Republicans continued to tie them to the antiabortion restrictions.

There was some concern that the United States could lose its seat in the U.N. General Assembly under Article 19 of the U.N. Charter. That provision denied membership to any U.N. country that ran debts equivalent to two years of assessments for peacekeeping and regular U.N. operations. But the United States avoided violating Article 19, when Congress approved a last-minute appropriation as part of the fiscal 1999 omnibus spending bill (PL 105-277).

A repayment plan was finally enacted into law (HR 3194—PL 106-113) in 1999. (1999 action, p. 219)

Foreign Policy Agencies

Congress in 1998 cleared legislation (HR 4328—PL 105-277) reorganizing the United States' foreign policy agencies. The plan merged the U.S. Information Agency (USIA), the Arms Control and Disarmament Agency, and parts of the Agency for International Development (AID) into the State Department.

The reorganization had been included in the fiscal 1998–1999 State Department authorization bill (HR 1757), but when that bill was vetoed, the plan was attached to HR 4328, the fiscal 1999 omnibus spending bill. (State Department authorization, p. 189; funding bill, p. 62)

Senate Foreign Relations Committee Chairman Jesse Helms, R-N.C., had pushed the hardest for revamping the foreign policy apparatus. The agency consolidation originally had been a Democratic idea. Hoping to head off deep cuts in his department's budget by the Republicans, Secretary of State Warren Christopher first proposed merging the three independent agencies into the State Department in January 1995. Vice President Al Gore's National Performance Review, however, concluded that the agencies functioned better separately. But Helms disagreed and several months later unveiled his version of the consolidation, calling for folding all three of the foreign policy agencies into State. His proposal set off a yearlong battle with the Clinton administration and, although scaled back to require the consolidation of only one of the agencies with State, remained unacceptable to the White House. It was one of the key reasons for a veto of the fiscal 1996–1997 State Department authorization bill. (Congress and the Nation Vol. IX, p. 228)

But when the 1996 elections left Clinton still facing a Republican majority on Capitol Hill, administration officials concluded that some type of reorganization was needed in return for Helms's cooperation on other issues. In April 1997 Clinton announced a reorganization plan to fold the arms control agency and USIA into the State Department, while allowing AID to remain a separate agency but under the oversight of the secretary of state. The president signed off on the proposal on the same day that Helms agreed to let a long-stalled chemical weapons treaty reach the Senate floor. Both sides denied that there was an explicit linkage between the two developments. (Chemical weapons treaty, p. 268)

Helms and Sen. Joseph R. Biden Jr. of Delaware, ranking Democrat on the Foreign Relations Committee, incorporated the broad outlines of the plan in HR 1757, the State Department authorization bill that the Senate passed overwhelmingly on June 17, 1997. The House on June 11 had passed its version of the bill, containing a reorganization plan that adhered more closely to Clinton's approach. The Helms-Biden plan went further by seeking to fold more of AID into State and requiring that foreign aid be funded through the State Department rather than through AID.

The final version included in the vetoed State Department bill and the omnibus funding bill abolished the arms control agency by April 1, 1999, and USIA by Oct. 1, 1999, and transferred the functions of the two agencies to the State Department. The measure mandated the reorganization of AID by April 1, 1999, and transferred its press office and certain administrative functions to the State Department. AID was placed under the direction of the secretary of state. HR 4328 was signed into law Oct. 21, 1998, the same day Clinton vetoed the State Department bill.

International Monetary Fund

President Clinton's request for $17.9 billion in credit for the International Monetary Fund (IMF) sparked a yearlong battle in 1998 over issues as far-ranging as the global economy and overseas abortion policy. Under pressure from the business community, a reluctant Congress approved the entire amount as part of an omnibus appropriations bill (HR 4328—PL 105-277) that cleared shortly before adjournment.

BACKGROUND

The IMF package consisted of two parts: $3.4 billion for a new $25 billion IMF lending program aimed at preventing massive currency fluctuations and $14.5 billion for a more controversial dues increase to replenish the IMF's coffers.

The administration said the $3.4 billion appropriation would entail no new outlays—actual spending—and would not add to the deficit but instead would involve a swap of assets with the IMF, backed by the IMF's gold reserves. The $14.5 billion for the increase in U.S. dues would not all necessarily leave the Treasury but was to be available to the IMF as needed.

Each of the 182 members of the IMF contributed a certain sum—known as a quota subscription—from which the IMF could draw money to lend to members in financial difficulty. These quotas also formed a basis for determining how much the contributing member could borrow from the IMF and how many votes it would have in the IMF's complicated voting system. In December 1997 the executive board of the IMF proposed a 45 percent increase in the pool of money formed by members' quotas, from $196 billion to about $287 billion. The proposed increase was partly in response to a crisis in east Asia where the IMF was loaning nations more than $100 billion. Another recent drain on the IMF's coffers had occurred in 1995, when the IMF extended more than $17 billion in credit to Mexico and $6.2 billion to Russia.

LEGISLATIVE ACTION

The legislative battle over Clinton's IMF request formally started when the House Banking and Financial Services Committee on March 18, 1998, reported a bill (HR 3114—H Rept 105-454) providing the full $17.9 billion in funding, along with general language to revamp IMF lending policies. But Republican leaders never brought that measure to the floor.

The Senate, friendly turf for trade and international commerce measures, approved funding with some conditions in a fiscal 1998 supplemental spending measure (S 1768—S Rept 105-168) that was reported March 17. The IMF credit was approved by a **key vote of 84–16 (R 41–14; D 43–2)** on March 26. But the House Appropriations Committee took a different tack, splitting off the funding into a separate measure (HR 3580—H Rept 105-470) that was reported March 27 but never made it to the floor. The Senate-approved IMF funding was stripped out in a House-Senate conference on the final supplemental funding bill (HR 3579—PL 105-174), saving the debate for the fiscal 1999 foreign operations spending bill. *(1998 key votes, p. 883)*

For much of the spring and summer, the IMF funding appeared to hang in the balance. Business and farm lobbyists joined the administration in a major lobbying campaign, contending the money was necessary to stabilize overseas economies. But House Majority Leader Dick Armey, R-Texas, and other conservatives assailed the IMF for interfering with free markets, and liberals criticized it for pressuring nations to slash social and environmental programs.

The Senate, spurred by the decline of markets around the globe, included the full funding in its version of the foreign operations bill (S 2334). During debate on the bill Sept. 2, GOP Sen. John Kyl of Arizona proposed that the IMF receive the additional funds only if it agreed to require all borrowing countries to abide by international trade agreements, to stop directing loans or subsidies to favored companies or institutions, and to ensure that U.S. creditors receive the same treatment in bankruptcy proceedings as their own creditors. S 2334 urged the IMF to adopt such requirements but did not compel it to do so. Kyle's amendment was tabled (killed), 74–19.

The House put just $3.4 billion in its version of the foreign operations bill (HR 4569) and attached a provision to impose abortion restrictions on international family planning aid—a provision strongly opposed by the administration.

Unable to resolve their differences on a stand-alone bill, GOP leaders buckled under the administration and business community pressure. In the final days of the session, they agreed to drop the abortion language and include the full $17.9 billion in the omnibus appropriations bill (HR 4328). Congress attached conditions to the funding, but the language was of little importance because the IMF was already doing what the legislation required. *(1999 aid appropriations, p. 186)*

Family Planning Funds

Congress in early 1997 approved a resolution (H J Res 36—PL 105-3) authorizing the release of $385 million in previously appropriated international family planning aid. The funds had been part of the fiscal 1997 foreign operations appropriations bill (PL 104-208), but their release had been delayed because of a dispute over the emotionally charged issue of abortion.

An intricate compromise reached in 1997 required a presidential report and congressional approval of their release. (*Congress and the Nation Vol. IX, p. 234*)

BACKGROUND

Since 1973, U.S. law had prohibited the government from directly paying for abortions overseas. But antiabortion forces in Congress also opposed aiding overseas family planning groups that used non-U.S. money to advocate or perform abortions.

The battle in recent years had revolved around efforts by abortion opponents to reinstate the so-called Mexico City policy of the Reagan and Bush administrations, which denied U.S. funds to population planning groups that performed or advocated abortions, even if the groups used their own money for the procedure. The Mexico City policy, named for the site of a 1984 world conference on population where it was first formulated, had remained in effect until January 1993, when newly elected President Clinton signed an executive memorandum revoking it.

Efforts to restore the restrictions stalled action on the fiscal 1997 foreign operations bill. Under the deal that allowed the bill to clear, Republican leaders agreed to drop the abortion restrictions if the White House accepted severe funding limitations. The bill cut the funding request by $79 million and provided that the $385 million approved would not be available until July 1, 1997, after which no more than 8 percent of the funds, about $31 million, could be spent a month. The deal also required the president to report to Congress by Feb. 1, 1997, on the impact of the delay in releasing the funds. If he found a negative impact, the funds could be released beginning March 1—but only after Congress approved the release by a joint resolution of approval no later than Feb. 28.

On Jan. 31, 1997, Clinton reported his negative findings to Congress, triggering a vote on release of the funds.

LEGISLATIVE ACTION

The House passed H J Res 36 by a vote of 220–209 on Feb. 13. The Senate passed the resolution, 53–46, on Feb. 25, clearing it for the president's signature Feb. 28.

The vote was a rare defeat in the House for abortion opponents, who had mounted an intensive campaign to kill the measure because it included no abortion restrictions. Their setback was only partly ameliorated by the opportunity on Feb. 13 to cast a vote on a separate bill (HR 581) to deny funds to overseas groups that used private money to perform or promote abortions. That bill passed, 231–194, but the Senate did not take it up.

Russia Sanctions

Legislation (HR 2709) aimed at halting the transfer of sophisticated missile technology to Iran cleared Congress in 1998 but was vetoed by President Clinton. The bill would have imposed tough economic sanctions on overseas companies and research institutes, mainly Russian, that provided arms technology to Iran, unless waived on national security grounds.

The legislation stemmed from congressional anger over widespread, credible reports that Russian state-owned companies had transferred high-strength metals, other exotic materials, and technical assistance that Iran was using to extend the range of its Scud missiles far enough to threaten Israel and U.S. forces in the Middle East. Bill supporters argued that the Clinton administration was unwilling to challenge Russia and enforce existing sanctions aimed at punishing those who dealt with Iran.

Since 1980 the United States had maintained an almost total ban on trade and financial dealings with Iran, originally because of its seizure of the U.S. embassy and fifty-two hostages in Tehran on Nov. 4, 1979, and later due to its support of international terrorism.

With the support of pro-Israel groups, HR 2709 sailed through the House in 1997 and the Senate in 1998. In an attempt to induce Clinton to sign the Iran sanctions measure, House GOP leaders attached to it a bill (S 610) to implement the global treaty banning chemical weapons that the Senate ratified in 1997. Until such implementing legislation was enacted, the United States was in violation of the pact. (*Chemical weapons treaty, p. 268*)

But Clinton rejected the bill, saying that it would undermine his administration's efforts to maintain good relations with Russia and to reach out to Iran. A move to override the veto stalled after the administration announced its own steps against seven Russian companies and laboratories.

Legislation (HR 1883—PL 106-178) authorizing, but not requiring, the president to impose sanctions against entities transferring major weapons technology to Iran was finally enacted in 2000. Provisions implementing the chemical weapons treaty were added in 1998 to the omnibus fiscal 1999 spending package (HR 4328—PL 105-277). (*Sanctions legislation, p. 199*)

HOUSE ACTION

The House passed HR 2709 by voice vote Nov. 12, 1997. The House International Relations Committee had reported the bill Nov. 4 (H Rept 105-375).

Like a similar Senate bill (S 1311), the House bill contained a provision to require the administration to publish periodic reports identifying companies or research institutes that, according to "credible reports," had transferred, or attempted to transfer, prohibited missile-related technology to Iran since August 1995. That was the date Russia joined the Missile Technology Control Regime, an international pact to prevent the proliferation of ballistic missile technology. Though the legislation did not specifically mention Russia, the companies and labs more frequently cited were all Russian. Specific economic sanctions, including a prohibition on any U.S. economic assistance, would be levied for at least two years against any organization violating the ban. HR 2709 allowed the president to waive the required sanctions on national security grounds, but the Senate bill had no such waiver.

A key administration objection to both bills was that the sanctions would be triggered by "credible information" of a violation. Other laws that used economic sanctions to discourage weapons proliferation required sanctions only if a "preponderance of the evidence" indicated a violation. The administration argued that the bill was inflexible in that it would apply equally to minor and major transfers. Opponents also objected to the bill being retroactive, saying that organizations would have no incentive to refrain in the future if they were to be subject to mandatory sanctions for past actions.

Spurred by published reports of technology transfers and Israeli warnings about the threat that new missiles would pose to Israel, the House moved quickly on the legislation. Both House Speaker Newt Gingrich, R-Ga., and Minority Leader Richard A. Gephardt, D-Mo., were among more than 100 House cosponsors of the bill and passage came easily.

SENATE, FINAL ACTION

Despite a veto threat, the Senate passed HR 2709 by a vote of 90–4 on May 22, 1998. The Senate had been posed to take up the bill moments before Congress adjourned Nov. 13, 1997, but Democrats, heeding Clinton's veto threat, had blocked floor consideration of the bill.

The proposal, however, had strong bipartisan backing in the Senate. S 1311, the companion bill, had eighty-four cosponsors.

In an attempt to make the bill more palatable for the White House, the Senate adopted by voice vote an amendment by Carl Levin, D-Mich., to move the effective date from Aug. 8, 1995, to Jan. 22, 1998.

The House on June 9 voted 392–22 to accept the Senate amendment and thus clear HR 2709.

VETO

President Clinton vetoed HR 2709 on June 23. In his veto message, he said the bill would have made it harder to work with Russia on a range of issues, including nuclear proliferation and law enforcement. He discounted his ability to waive sanctions on national security grounds. The White House also said it did not want to undermine Secretary of State Madeleine K. Albright's recent overture to Iran's moderate president, Mohammad Khatami.

Clinton's decision drew bipartisan criticism on Capitol Hill. Having cleared both chambers by far more than a two-thirds majority, the legislation seemed headed for an override. But House Republicans decided to put off an override attempt after the administration announced July 15 it was taking steps to punish seven Russian companies and labs for possible aid to Iran's missile program. The Russian government was also said to be investigating the same organizations, as well as two others, and to have pledged to finish drafting a law to tighten export controls.

OTHER LEGISLATION

The GOP majority took a step toward punishing Russia in legislation the president did sign on Nov. 26, 1997, the fiscal 1998 foreign operations spending bill (HR 2159—PL 105-118). *(1998 aid appropriations, p. 183)*

The bill contained a provision that would withhold 50 percent of aid to Russia if it failed to stop sharing sensitive military technology with Iran. The president could waive the provision if he notified Congress that the aid was in U.S. national security interests and that Russia was taking steps to curtail the transfer of technology to Iran.

In other action, the House on Aug. 3, 1998, voted 405–13 to pass legislation (HR 3743) to prevent the International Atomic Energy Agency from using U.S. money to aid nuclear power plant programs in Iran. The bill would have affected only a small portion of U.S. contributions to the agency. There was no further action.

Iraq Policy

A turbulent year for U.S.-Iraq relations—and for the executive-congressional tug-of-war over what U.S. policy toward Iraq should be—culminated in late 1998 in several days of air attacks on Iraq for that country's refusal to allow inspection of its suspected weapons facilities.

The attacks commenced on Dec. 16, 1998—the eve of the scheduled House debate on articles of impeachment against President Clinton—triggering an outcry from some key Republicans who questioned the president's motives for launching the military attack at that time. But the White House insisted that military—not political—considerations dictated the timing.

The open distrust that had erupted was a blow to the post–World War II custom of separating politics and foreign policy. That tradition, in the oft-quoted maxim of Sen. Arthur Vandenberg, R-Mich. (1928–1951), was necessary to "unite our official voice at the water's edge."

CONGRESSIONAL RESPONSE

Clinton emphatically denied any political motivation in the December attacks on Iraq. He said military action was prompted by a Dec. 15 report from chief U.N. weapons inspector Richard Butler that Iraqi President Saddam Hussein had broken his promise to allow inspection of suspected nuclear, chemical, and biological weapons factories. If the United States had failed to respond, the president said, the credibility of U.S. power would have been destroyed. Military planners were said to have underscored the importance of the element of surprise and of acting quickly before the Muslim holy month of Ramadan began Dec. 19.

However, some of Clinton's more vocal critics compared the Iraqi mission to *Wag the Dog*, the 1997 movie in which aides to a fictional president manufactured a war to deflect attention from a sex scandal. The comparison had first surfaced in August 1998, when Clinton ordered missile strikes against suspected terrorist sites in Afghanistan and Sudan

CONFRONTATIONS WITH IRAQ

- **1991**. U.S. and allied forces drive Iraqi army from Kuwait in Operation Desert Storm. *(Congress and the Nation Vol. VIII, p. 299)*
- **1993**. Allied planes strike Iraq after alleged cease-fire violations; missiles later destroy Iraqi intelligence headquarters, retaliating for alleged plot to kill former President George Bush. *(Congress and the Nation Vol. IX, p. 223)*
- **1994**. Iraqi troops threaten Kuwait but pull back when U.S. forces are sent to Persian Gulf.
- **1996**. Iraqi forces capture Kurdish "safe haven" in northern Iraq. U.S. forces fire cruise missiles at military targets in Iraq. United Nations allows Iraq to sell limited amounts of oil to purchase humanitarian goods ("oil-for-food program"), easing the nearly total trade embargo imposed in 1990. *(Congress and the Nation Vol. IX, p. 249)*
- **1997**. U.N. weapons inspection teams withdrawn after Iraq expels U.S. members; teams return after Russian mediation.
- **Jan.–Feb. 1998**. Allies threaten air strikes after Iraq blocks some weapons inspections; U.N. Secretary General Kofi Annan mediates a deal.
- **Oct.–Nov. 1998**. Iraq says it will no longer cooperate with inspections; U.S. air strikes called off at the last minute when Iraq agrees to cooperate.
- **Dec. 1998**. U.N. inspectors report that Iraq is blocking inspections; Clinton launches air strikes.

three days after admitting he misled the public about an "inappropriate" relationship with former White House intern Monica S. Lewinsky. *(White House scandal, p. 813)*

Still, many Republicans lined up behind Clinton's decision to bomb Iraq. Some members of both parties had been critical of the White House in November for calling off air strikes after Saddam agreed to cooperate with United Nations arms inspectors.

Republicans disagreed among themselves about whether using air attacks to diminish Iraq's ability to produce such weapons would ultimately prove successful. Many also called for a tougher strategy to force Saddam out of power.

Congressional support for a tough U.S. stance toward Iraq was demonstrated by a 417–5 House vote Dec. 17 in favor of a resolution (H Res 612) supporting U.S. forces engaged in the attacks and calling for Saddam's ouster and the installation of a democratic government in Baghdad. There was no action in the Senate, which was not in session.

RESOLUTION FALTERS

The Senate earlier in the year had approved a nonbinding resolution (S Con Res 78) urging the president to press for a United Nations–sponsored tribunal to indict and try Saddam for genocide and crimes against humanity. The resolu-

tion had been reported by the Senate Foreign Relations Committee (no written report) on March 3, 1998, and was adopted by the full Senate on March 13 by a vote of 93–0.

That vote came about a month after the Senate had failed to act on a resolution (S Con Res 71) that would have supported U.S. military action over Iraq's refusal in February to allow U.N. inspections. Congressional leaders had been unable to muster the overwhelming support for the resolution they believed was necessary and therefore did not bring it up for consideration.

Some Democrats were concerned that a broadly written resolution might be interpreted by the administration as a blank check for continuing military action. The 1964 Tonkin Gulf resolution that essentially gave the executive branch a blank check to wage the Vietnam War was never far from some members' minds. *(Congress and the Nation Vol. III, p. 946)*

But it was Republican annoyance with Clinton's strategy that escalated to open criticism of the administration and doomed the resolution. Republicans questioned the White House plan to use military force to contain Saddam and prevent him from rebuilding his weapons of mass destruction rather than finding the means to remove him from power. They wondered aloud about the reluctance of U.S. allies, especially Saudi Arabia and other Arab nations, to support a strike against Iraq. They also pressured the administration for answers on how it would pay for any military operation.

Clinton had not requested the resolution—Senate Majority Leader Trent Lott, R-Miss., and House Speaker Newt Gingrich, R-Ga., had drafted it on their own—and while the administration said it welcomed the effort, it did not believe it was necessary. The resolution Congress passed seven years earlier on the eve of the Persian Gulf War (PL 102-1) was considered sufficient authority for any military strike against Iraq. Moreover, Clinton, during his tenure, had never felt the need to ask for congressional authorization before dispatching military forces. *(Persian Gulf War, Congress and the Nation Vol. VIII, p. 309)*

OTHER ACTION

Lawmakers found other ways to express their views on U.S. policy toward Iraq and to keep up pressure on Clinton to take action against the Iraqi regime.

Both chambers approved a resolution (S J Res 54—PL 105-235) declaring that Iraq had repeatedly broken its promises on weapons inspections. The resolution cataloged a long list of Iraq's alleged violations since the Persian Gulf War ended in 1991. S J Res was reported by the Senate Foreign Relations Committee (no written report) July 27, 1998, and was passed by voice vote of the Senate on July 31. The House passed it Aug. 3 by a vote of 407–6 and the president signed it Aug. 14.

The 1999 intelligence authorization (HR 3694—PL 105-272) authorized enhanced covert operations against Iraq. *(1999 intelligence authorization, p. 201)*

Another bill, the "Iraq Liberation Act" (HR 4655—PL 105-338), authorized up to $97 million for defense services, military education, and training for democratic organizations in Iraq and up to $2 million to support radio and television broadcasts to Iraq by those organizations. The House passed HR 4655 by a vote of 360–38 on Oct. 5 and the Senate cleared the bill by voice vote Oct. 7. Clinton signed the bill Oct. 31, but administration officials and Marine Corps Gen. Anthony C. Zinni, the top U.S. commander in the Middle East, warned that none of the existing Iraqi opposition groups were strong enough to unify Iraq.

GOP leaders in September invited former U.N. weapons inspector Scott Ritter to testify before a joint hearing of the Senate Armed Services and Foreign Relations committees. Ritter told members that the Clinton administration had undercut efforts to uncover Iraq's chemical, biological, and nuclear weapons. He criticized U.S. and United Nations officials for not confronting Saddam and said he had resigned his post in August in frustration over the process and policy of weapons inspections. Democrats said the administration had little choice but to carefully choose when to confront Iraq, since other U.N. Security Council members did not support inspections and Congress had been unwilling to endorse unilateral military action.

War Powers and Bosnia

An attempt to turn the U.S. deployment in Bosnia into a test case of the constitutionality of the 1973 War Powers Resolution failed in 1998. The House on March 18 rejected, 193–225, a resolution (H Con Res 227) calling for the removal of U.S. troops from Bosnia, unless Congress voted to authorize their presence. The House International Relations Committee had reported H Con Res 227 adversely (H Rept 105-442) March 13.

Congress's failure to pass the resolution offered by Rep. Tom Campbell, R-Calif., followed a quarter of a century in which lawmakers and the White House had sidestepped a court test of the 1973 law. Congress had approved the War Powers Resolution (PL 93-148), over President Richard Nixon's veto, with the contention that its constitutional power to declare war had been undermined by undeclared conflicts in Korea and Vietnam. *(Congress and the Nation Vol. IV, p. 849)*

The 1973 law required Congress to authorize the use of U.S. forces or to declare war within sixty days of an overseas deployment. Without such approval, the president would have to withdraw troops within thirty more days. It also permitted Congress—through the use of a procedure known as a legislative veto—to force withdrawal of troops at any time through passage by both chambers of a concurrent resolution. Every president since its enactment has called the resolution unconstitutional and a 1983 Supreme Court decision barred Congress from using legislative vetoes.

Nonetheless, Congress had shied away from proposals to repeal the law and instead used threats to invoke the War Powers Resolution to force changes in administration policy in trouble spots from Lebanon to Somalia.

On Bosnia, lawmakers had rejected several opportunities to prevent deployment of U.S. forces or to require their withdrawal since the initial deployment in 1995. *(Congress and the Nation Vol. IX, p. 224)*

In the fiscal 1998 defense appropriations bill (HR 2266—PL 105-56), Congress allowed Clinton to extend the mission beyond June 1998, as long as he told Congress why and for how long. *(1998 defense appropriations, p. 245)*

Religious Persecution

Congress in 1998 cleared legislation (HR 2431—PL 105-292) authorizing the use of sanctions to combat religious persecution overseas. HR 2431 gave the president authority to impose diplomatic and economic sanctions against countries that consistently permitted or endorsed attacks against religious believers. The sanctions were to expire after two years if not reauthorized and could be waived in the national interest or if they encouraged a backlash against members of a persecuted group.

The legislation was a top priority of religious conservatives, but it was watered down considerably from the original proposal because of the concerns of business groups over its impact on trade and of the State Department over its effect on overseas relations.

HOUSE ACTION

The House approved HR 2431 by a vote of 375–41 on May 14, 1998. The bill had been reported by the House International Relations Committee April 1, 1998 (H Rept 105-480, Pt. I), by the House Ways and Means Committee May 8 (Pt. II), and by the House Judiciary Committee May 8 (Pt. III).

House passage marked a victory not only for the bill's author, Frank R. Wolf, R-Va., who had labored to move the bill through the three committees and onto the House floor, but also for religious conservatives, who felt their agenda had been neglected by Republican leaders.

Despite the lopsided vote, House debate on the measure was contentious. Supporters cast the House vote for passage as a supreme moral choice. Critics complained the bill would give victims of religious persecution more protections than those who suffered because of their race or ethnicity. Opponents also said the measure would endanger U.S. diplomatic interests and commerce in countries such as Pakistan and Indonesia. But the bill's defenders said such concerns paled in comparison to defending a basic moral principle.

HR 2431 had undergone substantial revision as it worked its way through the House. As proposed by Wolf and Sen. Arlen Specter, R-Pa., in late 1997, the bill would have created a White House office to monitor religious persecution and impose tough sanctions on violators. The president could have waived sanctions only in the interest of U.S. national security. The bill also would have increased the importance of religious persecution as a criterion for U.S. asylum.

The House International Relations Committee took the first cut at the bill, giving the State Department control over monitoring and agreeing to delete references in the bill to specific countries, with the exception of Sudan, which was singled out because of its "holy war" against Christians in the southern half of the country, including murder, crucifixions, torture, and slavery. The panel had delayed consideration for six months while members tried to iron out differences.

When the Ways and Means Committee took up the bill, it voted to strip out the provisions banning trade with and investment in Sudan. Critics said such sanctions would not stem persecution and would harm other interests. After removing the Sudan provisions, the panel took the unusual step of voting out the bill without a recommendation to the House. Acting that same day, the House Judiciary Committee effectively gutted the asylum and refugee portion of the bill by deleting an important provision that would have automatically granted members of persecuted religious groups an asylum hearing, thus exempting them from provisions of a 1996 immigration law (PL 104-208) that required them to first prove a "credible fear" of persecution or face deportation.

SENATE ACTION

The Senate passed HR 2431, 98–0, on Oct. 9, 1998, after substituting the text of S 1868. Although the House bill had been significantly revised, it was still considered too strong for the Senate. Majority Whip Don Nickles, R-Okla., produced his own measure (S 1868), which was watered down further before final passage and enactment.

After months of behind-the-scenes negotiations, Senate Republicans had agreed on a version designed to minimize tensions with countries not considered major offenders. Decisions on sanctions were left largely to the president, with the standard for waiving sanctions broadened from on the grounds of national security to "in the national interest." The latter change, plus other alterations, brought more Democrats on board, including President Clinton, who earlier had threatened to veto the legislation.

FINAL ACTION

The House agreed to the Senate version of HR 2431 by voice vote Oct. 10, clearing the bill for the president. Representative Wolf had agreed to allow the House to consider the Senate-passed bill to avoid convening a conference committee to reconcile the two measures. Although the bill was far less stringent than the original proposal, religious conservatives supported it because it brought high-level attention to the issue of religious persecution.

Clinton signed the bill into law Oct. 27, but he stressed that because some of the provisions "infringe on the authority vested by the Constitution solely with the President," he would interpret the measure in a fairly narrow manner. The president, for example, said that his constitutional responsibility to conduct foreign policy was undermined by a portion of the bill that required him to undertake negotiations with foreign countries before imposing economic sanctions and to disclose to Congress diplomatic communications on those meetings.

MAJOR PROVISIONS

As signed into law, HR 2431 (PL 105-292):

• Created an ambassador-at-large to monitor and promote religious freedom in other countries.

• Created a ten-member autonomous commission to monitor progress and advise Congress on efforts to counter religious persecution. The commission would have to be reauthorized every four years.

• Required the State Department to produce annual reports examining religious freedom in countries around the globe.

• Required the president once a year to list "countries of concern" that warranted sanctions.

• Authorized the president to invoke diplomatic and economic sanctions against countries that consistently permitted or endorsed attacks against religious believers. The sanctions would expire after two years if not reauthorized.

• Allowed the president to waive any sanctions if the president determined that a waiver would further the purposes of the act, the sanctions were no longer needed because persecution had ended in the country, or the sanctions were not in the national interest.

Economic Sanctions

The 105th Congress displayed conflicting views on the use of unilateral economic sanctions as a tool to punish and pressure countries that had violated U.S. interests or values.

1997 ACTION

The House in 1997 passed a bill (HR 748) to further limit U.S. trade with countries that supported terrorism. It would have eliminated the executive branch's right to make exceptions to a 1996 law (PL 104-132) that barred financial transactions between U.S. citizens and companies and countries that supported terrorism. The State Department listed Cuba, Libya, North Korea, Iran, Iraq, Syria, and Sudan as terrorist-sponsoring countries.

The 1996 law had included an exception designed to exempt routine diplomatic transactions. But bill sponsor Bill McCollum, R-Fla., argued that the Treasury Department had broadened that exemption to create "a loophole big enough to drive a car bomb through." The Clinton administration had made exceptions for Syria and Sudan.

Opponents of the bill said HR 748 would go too far in ending financial transactions and could harm the Middle East peace process by strengthening sanctions against Syria, a key player in the region.

The House Judiciary Committee reported the bill (H Rept 105-141) on June 21, 1997, and the House passed it July 8 by a 377–33 vote. There was no further action on HR 748.

The Senate had included similar language in its version of the State Department authorization bill (HR 1757), but that bill was vetoed.

1998 ACTION

During Senate consideration of the agriculture appropriations bill (S 2159) in 1998, Sen. Richard G. Lugar, R-Ind., offered an amendment to force a cost-benefit analysis of any future sanctions and to place a two-year limit on any sanctions unless they were renewed by Congress. Lugar's amendment was tabled (killed) by a **key vote of 53–46 (R 27–28; D 26–18)** on July 15. *(1998 key votes, p. 883)*

In other action on S 2159, the Senate by voice vote adopted a Christopher J. Dodd, D-Conn., amendment barring sanctions on food and medicine, after rejecting a motion to table it by a 38–60 vote. But then the Senate agreed by voice vote to a proposal by Robert F. Torricelli, D-N.J., to retain such sanctions for terrorist nations. The Senate rejected, 30–67, a motion to table Torricelli's amendment. In the end, however, the provision was dropped in conference on the bill.

Nonetheless, opposition to the use of sanctions appeared to be on the rise. Sanctions were viewed by many as an appealing alternative to diplomacy or military force. But with Asia's economic crisis already hurting U.S. exports and India and Pakistan's explosion of nuclear bombs in May 1998 showing the limited deterrence of sanctions, others were questioning the usefulness of such economic weapons.

The grassroots politics of sanctions also was changing. Where opposition from business and trade groups had been weak and unorganized in the past, now more than six hundred companies had joined a powerful coalition, USA Engage, whose major mission was to end unilateral trade sanctions. Joining the effort were agricultural groups and farm state lawmakers who saw a repeal of sanctions as one way to boost sagging farm prices.

A consensus also was developing among mainstream foreign policy think tanks that comprehensive, unilateral sanctions generally had little effect on other countries' behavior but cost U.S. companies as much as $20 billion a year.

India, Pakistan Sanctions

The limitations of sanctions became apparent after India's and Pakistan's nuclear tests, according to proponents of change. Under the Glenn Amendment—named for Sen. John Glenn, D-Ohio—of the 1994 Arms Export Control Act (PL 103-236), Clinton had to impose a wide range of sanctions on the two nations. Many in Congress and the executive branch said the sanctions had made it more difficult to contain the budding south Asian arms race and had driven Pakistan toward bankruptcy. *(PL 103-236, Congress and the Nation Vol. IX, p. 212)*

Some of the sanctions on India and Pakistan were lifted in November 1998, after the fiscal 1999 omnibus appropriations bill (HR 4328—PL 105-277) gave the president the power to ease some economic sanctions for up to one year.

Earlier 1998 legislation (S 2282—PL 105-194) had temporarily lifted loan sanctions hampering exports of medicine and farm products to India and Pakistan. The legislation exempted through Sept. 30, 1999, Agriculture Department aid for the purchase of food, fertilizer, medicines, and medical equipment from the ban in PL 103-236 on U.S. government credit, guarantees, or other financial assistance to countries involved in the transfer or use of nuclear explosive devices. The Senate had passed S 2282 by a 98–0 vote on July 9 and the House passed an amended version by voice vote July 14. The Senate agreed to the House version by voice vote on July 14 and the president signed it later that day. The measure had been rushed through Congress so U.S. farmers could bid July 15 on a wheat sale to Pakistan. They won the contract.

Task Force

Senate Majority Leader Trent Lott, R-Miss., in 1998 appointed a bipartisan task force to study sanctions, but the group reportedly deadlocked on the issue.

1998 Intelligence Authorization

Congress in 1997 authorized an estimated total of nearly $27 billion for the activities of the Central Intelligence Agency (CIA), the National Reconnaissance Office, and other intelligence-related organizations in the fiscal 1998 intelligence authorization bill (S 858—PL 105-107). A controversial whistleblower provision was dropped from the final bill under President Clinton's threat of a veto.

During consideration of the bill, Congress had, as usual, kept secret the total amount authorized. But in October 1997 Director of Central Intelligence George J. Tenet revealed that $26.6 billion had been spent in fiscal 1997. With what was said to be a 1.4 percent increase in fiscal 1998, that translated into a bottomline of nearly $27 billion. The guesswork ended in April 1998 when Tenet revealed that the fiscal 1998 intelligence budget had been $26.7 billion.

BACKGROUND

The effort to reduce secrecy came from several fronts in 1997.

Tenet's Oct. 15 revelation had been prompted by a lawsuit, filed May 19, by the Federation of American Scientists, demanding disclosure of the total amount spent annually on intelligence programs. The suit, filed in U.S. District Court in Washington, D.C., claimed the CIA was violating the Freedom of Information Act by refusing to reveal the overall budget figure. Although the Clinton administration and several blue-ribbon commissions had supported disclosure of the overall budget figure, Congress had resisted. Some feared that it would lead to disclosure of the amount spent on specific activities. Tenet said decisions on disclosing spending totals in the future would be made on a case-by-case basis.

On another front, a congressional commission led by Sen. Daniel Patrick Moynihan, D-N.Y., issued a report March 4 concluding after a two-year study that the government kept too many secrets and the practice should be reined in. The twelve-member Commission on Protecting and Reducing Government Secrecy recommended legislation to set government-wide standards for classifying documents when there was a "demonstrable need" to protect the material, a timetable for declassifying documents, and an office, probably at the National Archives, to coordinate the process.

But members acknowledged that enacting such a law would be difficult, since government secrecy was historically the prerogative of the president, as commander in chief. Clinton had set his own guidelines for classifying documents in an executive order in April 1995.

LEGISLATIVE ACTION

The Senate passed S 858, 98–1, on June 19, 1997. The bill had been reported by the Senate Intelligence Committee (S Rept 105-24) on June 9 and by the Senate Armed Services Committee (no written report) on June 18.

Passage came easily, despite a veto threat. What upset the administration was a provision to require the president to make clear to federal employees or contractors that it was not illegal for them to disclose classified information to a member of Congress if the information showed evidence of criminal wrongdoing, if a false statement had been made to Congress, or if there was evidence of a gross waste of funds or abuse of authority. The White House said the provision was an unconstitutional violation of the president's authority to protect national security and other privileged information. The provision stemmed from concern over a letter sent in late 1996 by the director of Central Intelligence to the State Department admonishing an employee who revealed to Sen. Robert G. Torricelli, D-N.J., classified information linking a CIA informant to the murder of an American and the disappearance of a rebel leader in Guatemala. Torricelli had made the information public in 1995. The State Department employee lost his top security access. *(Congress and the Nation Vol. IX, p. 243)*

An amendment by Torricelli calling for disclosure of the bill's spending total stirred the only controversy during Senate consideration of S 858. The amendment was rejected on a 43–56 vote June 19.

The House passed its version of the intelligence bill (HR 1775) by voice vote July 9. HR 1775 had been reported by the House Intelligence Committee (H Rept 105-135) on June 18. The House passed S 858 by voice vote on July 17, after substituting the text of HR 1775.

The House rebuffed two attempts during floor debate July 9 to cut spending across the board. An amendment by Bernard Sanders, I-Vt., to cut most funding based on fiscal 1997 levels by 5 percent was rejected 142–289. Lawmakers defeated, 182–238, an attempt by Barney Frank, D-Mass., to reduce intelligence spending to the level requested by Clinton.

Members also defeated, 192–237, an amendment by John Conyers Jr., D-Mich., to make public the total amount spent on intelligence activities.

FINAL ACTION

The Senate adopted the conference report (H Rept 105-350) by voice vote Nov. 6 and the House cleared it the next day on a 385–36 vote. Final approval of the bill had been delayed for weeks because the Intelligence committee leaders in both chambers had agreed to hold it back while differences were worked out on the separate defense authorization bill (HR 1119—PL 105-85), which traditionally moved first. The president signed the bill Nov. 20.

Clinton's approval had been assured when conferees agreed to drop the Senate's whistleblower provision. A narrower version of the proposal was enacted into law in 1998. *(1999 intelligence authorization, this page)*

Conferees also rejected a House provision that would have abolished the Defense Airborne Reconnaissance Office, deferring instead to the defense authorization bill, which sought to scale back the agency.

The final bill included language directing the secretary of state to provide as much information as possible to families of Americans abused, tortured, kidnapped, or killed overseas, as long as the disclosure did not jeopardize national security or an ongoing criminal investigation.

Another provision required the directors of Central Intelligence and the FBI to report on China's intelligence activities directed against or affecting the United States.

1999 Intelligence Authorization

Congress in 1998 approved an increase in spending for the Central Intelligence Agency (CIA), the National Reconnaissance Office, and other intelligence agencies, as part of the fiscal 1999 intelligence authorization bill (HR 3694—PL 105-272). The bill also included provisions giving enhanced wiretapping authority to federal law enforcement agencies and protection to employees who used classified data to blow the whistle on problems in intelligence agencies.

Although the bill's funding levels were classified, HR 3694 was said to raise the amount allocated slightly above the previous year's total of $26.7 billion. Director of Central Intelligence George J. Tenet had revealed the fiscal 1998 spending figure in April 1998. His announcement marked the second year in a row that the bottomline of the intelligence budget had been made public. *(1998 intelligence authorization, p. 200)*

BACKGROUND

In an era with no single ominous threat overseas, Congress continued to focus on redefining the role that U.S. intelligence agencies should play. To this end, the fiscal 1999 intelligence authorization bills in both chambers attempted to address "real-world threats"—proliferation of weapons of mass destruction and missile technology among rogue nations, as well as terrorism, narcotics, counter-espionage, and even computer hackers.

After years of focusing on the communist threat, the CIA was said to be short of linguists and specialists in areas other than former cold war enemies. The House and Senate bills added funds for critical personnel areas and to revitalize clandestine espionage programs.

LEGISLATIVE ACTION

The House passed its fiscal 1998 intelligence authorization bill by voice vote May 7. HR 3694 had been reported by the House Intelligence Committee (H Rept 105-508) on May 5.

The Senate passed HR 3694 by voice vote June 26, after substituting the text of its bill (S 2052). S 2052 had been reported by the Senate Intelligence Committee (S Rept 105-185) May 7.

The Senate bill included provisions of a separate bill (S 1668) to provide protections for employees who used classified data to reveal fraud or other problems in intelligence agencies. The issue stemmed from congressional furor over a letter the CIA sent in 1996 to the State Department chastising a State Department employee, Richard A. Nuccio. In 1995 Nuccio had told Sen. Robert G. Torricelli, D-N.J., then a House member, about classified information linking a CIA informant to the death of an American innkeeper and the disappearance of a rebel leader in Guatemala. Nine former and current CIA employees eventually were punished for unprofessional behavior and failure to inform Congress of human rights abuses in Guatemala. But Nuccio lost his top security access, which hampered his ability to carry out his job. He left the State Department for a job as a senior adviser to Torricelli but then was thwarted in his effort to retain his separate top secret clearance. *(Congress and the Nation Vol. IX, p. 243)*

The Senate had pushed for including whistleblower protections in the fiscal 1998 intelligence authorization (S 858—PL 105-107), but the provisions were dropped from the final bill to avoid a presidential veto. Both chambers vowed to take up the issue in the next session.

An overwhelming majority of the Senate approved similar provisions in 1998. On March 9, by a 93–1 vote, the Senate passed S 1668 to direct the president to inform employees of intelligence agencies that they could disclose information to members of Congress on the relevant oversight committees about any violation of law, false statement to Congress, or other abuse. S 1668 had been reported by the Senate Intelligence Committee (S Rept 105-165) on Feb. 23.

Supporters said the legislation was necessary because the Whistleblowers Protection Act (PL 101-12) did not cover employees of the nation's intelligence agencies. Workers who disclosed information to Congress could face various sanctions, ranging from a reprimand to termination of security clearance to firing, the Intelligence Committee said in its report. But the administration insisted the bill was unconstitutional, arguing that it would usurp the executive branch's authority to decide what sensitive information should be shared with the legislative branch. *(PL 101-12, Congress and the Nation Vol. VIII, p. 862)*

The House Intelligence Committee reported its version of the whistleblower legislation (HR 3829—H Rept 105-747, Pt. I) on Sept. 25. The House bill provided for an employee to take a complaint to the CIA inspector general, who would determine if the information was credible. If so, the inspector general would report it to the CIA director, who would then send it to the congressional Intelligence committees.

HR 3829 was not taken to the floor and instead, since the Senate had attached its bill to the intelligence authorization bill, the issue was dealt with in the conference on that legislation. The House approach ultimately prevailed.

FINAL ACTION

The House adopted the conference report on HR 3694 (H Rept 105-780) by a vote of 337–83 on Oct. 7. The Senate cleared the conference report the next day by voice vote. President Clinton signed it into law Oct. 20.

Conferees restored cuts made in the Senate version of the bill that had drawn protests from the Clinton administration. Senators said they tried to cut only low-priority items, but the Office of Management and Budget said the Senate cuts "could have severe near- and long-term effects on the ability of the intelligence community to provide battlefield support."

The conference agreement largely left intact the House version of the whistleblower legislation. Under the bill, employees who witnessed or were informed of fraud or other violations in intelligence agencies were to report the complaint to the CIA inspector general, who would be required within fourteen days to determine the credibility of the complaint. If the complaint was subsequently referred to the CIA director, the director would have one week to determine its credibility and forward it to the House and Senate Intelligence committees.

Another big controversy arose over the ability of law enforcement officials to conduct roving wiretaps, which follow a person from phone to phone, to combat terrorism. Under existing law, authorities seeking such a wiretap had to show that the target was changing phones with a criminal intent to evade a tap, a standard considered difficult to meet. The conference bill removed the need to consider the individual's motive. The provision drew protests from civil liberties groups as well as from House conservatives led by Bob Barr, R-Ga. But the House defeated Barr's motion to send the bill back to conference and strip the wiretap language, 148–267.

The conference bill included funding authority for enhanced covert operations against Iraq. Lawmakers had recently stepped up pressure on Clinton to take action against the regime of Iraqi dictator Saddam Hussein.

The intelligence bill also renamed CIA headquarters in Langley, Va., for former President George Bush, the agency's director from January 1976 to January 1977.

Mexico Certification

The Senate blocked attempts in 1997 and again in 1998 to overturn President Clinton's certification of Mexico as an ally in the fight against narcotics.

Under a 1986 law (PL 99-570), the president must reduce U.S. aid by 50 percent and oppose loans from international financial agencies for any country that is a major source or transit route for narcotics, unless he certifies to Congress that the country has "fully cooperated" with antidrug efforts. After the certification, Congress has thirty days to disagree by a joint resolution of both houses. *(Congress and the Nation Vol. VII, p. 723)*

Mexican counter-narcotics efforts came under scrutiny in early 1997 because the country's leading antidrug agent was arrested for taking bribes from one of Mexico's largest drug cartels. However, in numerous briefings with lawmakers, senior administration officials argued that taking a hardline would inflame nationalism in Mexico, triggering a backlash that would undermine bilateral efforts to crack down on the drug trade. Critics countered that any step short of decertification would permit the United States and Mexico to continue a "silent conspiracy" in which both nations falsely claimed that progress was being achieved in the drug war.

When a resolution to decertify Mexico was reported out of the House International Relations Committee (HJ Res 58—H Rept 105-10) on March 10, 1997, it seemed likely to pass in both chambers with bipartisan support. But House Republican leaders forced major changes that alienated Democrats. The GOP amendment, adopted on a largely party-line vote of 212–205, gave Mexico ninety days to drastically upgrade its antidrug cooperation with the United States or be decertified. It also included a lengthy preamble criticizing every office involved in implementing the admin-istration's antidrug strategy. The House passed the amended resolution on March 13 by a 251–175 vote.

After weeks of debate and dispute, the Senate on March 20 by a 94–5 vote adopted a bipartisan amendment to HJ Res 58 that had the administration's blessing. It required the president to report to Congress by Sept. 1, 1997, on whether Mexico had made "significant and demonstrable progress" in several areas. The Senate then adopted the underlying resolution by voice vote. There was no further action on HJ Res 58.

The dispute over certification was renewed in 1998, when President Clinton again certified Mexico as fully cooperating in the war on drugs. But the Senate on March 26, 1998, by a vote of 45–54, rejected a resolution (SJ Res 42) to overturn Clinton's decision. Opponents of SJ Res 42 insisted that the Mexican government had become measurably more cooperative in the past year and that decertification would be counterproductive.

Diplomatic Immunity

Congress cleared legislation (S 759—PL 105-375) in 1998 requiring the State Department to report to Congress each year the number of people with diplomatic immunity who were suspected of committing a serious criminal offense. Such an offense was defined as any felony under federal, state, or local law, as well as driving under the influence or reckless driving.

The bill stemmed from a 1997 incident in Washington, D.C., in which a sixteen-year-old Maryland girl was killed in an accident involving a diplomat from the former Soviet Republic of Georgia. Georgia subsequently waived immunity for the diplomat, who pleaded guilty and was sentenced to prison.

S 759 was reported by the Senate Foreign Relations Committee (no written report) Nov. 4, 1997, and passed by voice vote of the Senate Nov. 8. It was cleared by voice vote of the House the following year on Oct. 14, 1998, and signed into law Nov. 12.

1999–2000

President Clinton's foreign policy agenda had a bumpy ride through the 106th Congress.

The congressional response to Clinton's policy on the ethnic violence in the Serbian province of Kosovo was ambivalent at best. On a tie vote, the House rejected a symbolic Senate-passed resolution to endorse the air bombing campaign that the United States and its NATO allies had launched five weeks earlier. But that same day the House also rejected a resolution ordering the withdrawal of U.S. forces. A month later, the Senate narrowly rejected a move to require Clinton to get express congressional permission before deploying ground troops. Yet, as divided as Congress was on Kosovo, in the end it gave Clinton the money he wanted for the air campaign, a peacekeeping deployment, and the beginning of the reconstruction of Serbia.

The White House suffered an embarrassing setback when the Senate rejected a top foreign policy priority of Clinton's—a nuclear test ban treaty. The partisan divide on Capitol Hill was reflected in the vote: all but one Democrat voted for the treaty but only four Republican senators joined them. *(Test ban treaty, p. 310)*

Congress, however, handed the president a major victory when it made normal trade relations with China permanent. House approval had not come easily. *(China trade, p. 160)*

The running battle between Clinton and House conservatives over abortion restrictions on international family planning aid continued in the 106th Congress. Clinton agreed in 1999 to accept the restrictions as the price for congressional approval of a plan to repay U.S. debts to the United Nations. But the following year it was Congress's turn to back down, as it yielded to the president's demands for money to provide debt relief for the world's poorest nations and for a lifting of the abortion restrictions. Members, however, would back down only so far—the increased funding approved for international family planning was to be available a month after Clinton left office. It was conservatives' fondest hope that a Republican would be in the White House by then and abortion restrictions would be reinstated.

Congress approved a major new foreign policy commitment when it agreed to underwrite an antidrug campaign in Colombia and neighboring countries. The initiative was strongly supported by Clinton and the GOP leadership on Capitol Hill.

It took a presidential veto to bring Congress around to supporting several key administration priorities in an aid appropriations bill, including funding to help Israel, Jordan, and the Palestinian Authority implement the 1998 Wye River peace agreement.

Conservatives in both houses fought mightily against any easing of the long-standing U.S. trade embargo on Cuba. Congress ultimately agreed to allow shipments of food and medicine to Cuba, although financing of agricultural pur-chases was barred and the existing ban on travel to Cuba was written into law. The decision to ease the embargo came during a high-profile battle over whether a young Cuban boy found shipwrecked off the coast of Florida should stay in the United States or be returned to his father in Cuba.

Congress also gave the president authority to waive certain sanctions imposed on India and Pakistan in 1998 after both nations tested nuclear weapons. Lawmakers, on the other hand, approved legislation authorizing sanctions to punish Russia for transferring weapons technology to Iran.

The annual intelligence authorization bill seemed an unlikely candidate for a presidential veto, but that was exactly what happened when members attached a provision establishing criminal penalties for leaking classified information. The language, which critics said would have a chilling effect on whistleblowers and the First Amendment, was dropped from a revised bill.

Kosovo Policy

The United States and its NATO allies in 1999 launched airstrikes against the Serbian forces of Yugoslav President Slobodan Milosevic to halt escalating ethnic violence in the Serbian province of Kosovo. The air campaign came after diplomatic efforts, economic pressures, and threats of military action failed to persuade Milosevic to stop the repression of ethnic Albanians in Kosovo.

The response from Capitol Hill was mixed, reflecting divisions in both parties over the direction U.S. policy should take. Lawmakers debated the wisdom of the Kosovo mission virtually up to the time the airstrikes began, and beyond. The Senate endorsed the NATO air operation the day before it began, but the House refused to approve it even after it was underway. Congress declined to limit President Clinton's authority either to send U.S. ground forces to Kosovo as part of a NATO-led peacekeeping force or to keep them there once they had been deployed.

Still, some members, particularly Republicans, kept up a chorus of criticism of Clinton's policy throughout the 106th Congress. In the end though, Congress appropriated the funds needed for the air campaign, the peacekeeping deployment, and the beginning of the reconstruction of Serbia.

KOSOVO CRISIS

Milosevic's 1989 attempt to fire up Serbian nationalism by revoking Kosovo's long-standing status as an autonomous province within Serbia set off a decade of upheaval. Attempts by ethnic Albanians, who made up 90 percent of Kosovo's population, to free themselves of Serbian domination only invited further repression. Milosevic's policy of "ethnic cleansing," in which Serbs forced ethnic Albanians out of parts of Kosovo, provoked international outrage. Hundreds of thousands of people were displaced. *(Background, p. 178)*

The United States and its Western allies attempted to negotiate a settlement to the Kosovo crisis at peace talks in Rambouillet, France, in early 1999. After Milosevic refused to sign an interim agreement, the NATO allies launched airstrikes on March 24. Milosevic's forces responded with an intensified ethnic cleansing campaign.

The number of ethnic Albanians who either fled or were driven out of their homes reached levels of staggering proportions. By one estimate, 1.6 million people—90 percent of the Kosovar Albanian population—left their homes from March 1998 to June 1999, with the majority said to have left during the NATO air campaign. Nearly 800,000 were thought to have fled to neighboring Albania, Macedonia, Montenegro, and Bosnia—countries ill-equipped for such a massive influx of refugees.

The air war dragged on for seventy-eight days, as NATO planes and missiles attacked military and economic targets, including key government installations in the Yugoslavian capital of Belgrade. On June 3, the Serbian Parliament and Milosevic approved the outlines of a peace plan previously endorsed by NATO and Russia, and a week later the NATO airstrikes were suspended.

The plan had been worked out in parallel negotiations between Russia and Yugoslavia, and Russia and NATO members. It called for the return of ethnic Albanians to Kosovo under the protection of an international peacekeeping force. Once they returned, the refugees were to be guaranteed substantial autonomy within Kosovo, under United Nations auspices. Serbia agreed to pull all of its military and police forces out of Kosovo before other steps began. If Belgrade adhered to the peace plan, a small, largely symbolic contingent of forces was to be allowed to return to guard Serbian monasteries and other cultural sites in Kosovo. The allies also promised the rebel Kosovo Liberation Army would be demilitarized. An estimated 7,000 Americans were expected to participate in the 50,000-member peacekeeping force.

Despite losing his bid for Serbian supremacy and provoking NATO's destructive air assault on his country, Milosevic managed to stay in power for more than a year. In the fall of 2000, however, he faced a popular uprising and had to step down. After apparently losing Yugoslavia's Sept. 24 presidential election, Milosevic had insisted that, although the official results showed him running behind Vojislav Kostunica, his opponent had not won an outright majority and there would have to be a runoff election Oct. 8. Kostunica, on the other hand, claimed to have won far more than 50 percent of the vote, an assessment shared by Washington. The people of Yugoslavia agreed as well and, in a peaceful, lightning-fast revolt in the streets of Belgrade, they drove Milosevic from power.

1999 ACTION

As members of Congress debated strategy options in the Balkans, they once again were contemplating the larger, institutional question of what Congress's role should be in decisions to deploy U.S. troops overseas. And once again they found there were no easy answers.

Peacekeeping Role

On March 11, 1999, the House approved a resolution (H Con Res 42) supporting the deployment of U.S. armed forces to Kosovo as part of a NATO peacekeeping operation implementing a peace agreement.

It was a mixed victory for the White House. The administration had won enough support from Republican moderates and human rights backers for the House to adopt H Con Res 42 by a 219–191 vote. However, President Clinton and Secretary of State Madeleine K. Albright had asked the House leadership to postpone action while delicate peace negotiations were under way between the warring parties in Kosovo.

House Speaker J. Dennis Hastert, R-Ill., rebuffed that request. He noted that the British and German parliaments had recently voted on the issue. Plus, he told reporters that he did not want to repeat the pattern of recent years, when Congress expressed its opinion only after troops had been deployed, making it difficult to oppose the mission without harming military morale. While even some Democrats congratulated Hastert for forcing Republicans to take more responsibility for foreign policy decisions, Minority Leader Richard A. Gephardt, D-Mo., had urged his colleagues to defeat the rule allowing debate on the resolution to proceed. But the rule was approved, 218–201.

The biggest fight came over an amendment by Tillie Fowler, R-Fla., that would have prohibited the deployment of U.S. ground forces to Kosovo. Fowler and other Republicans argued that such deployments hurt morale and the military's ability to retain trained troops. "American soldiers have been trained to be warriors, not baby sitters," said House Majority Whip Tom DeLay, R-Texas, who helped press Hastert into taking up the resolution. Other critics said intervening in Kosovo would be unjustified under international law because the province was in Serbia, a sovereign country. But with the help of some key Republicans, such as International Relations Committee Chairman Benjamin A. Gilman of New York and Judiciary Committee Chairman Henry J. Hyde of Illinois, Democrats were able to defeat the Fowler amendment, 178–237.

By voice vote the House adopted an amendment requiring details on the deployment and how it would be paid for, as well as requiring that U.S. forces serve under a U.S. military commander. Another amendment authorizing the deployment when a "fair and just" peace agreement had been reached and limiting a U.S. deployment to 15 percent of the total peacekeeping force was also approved by voice vote.

NATO Airstrikes

President Clinton's last-minute lobbying persuaded a majority in the Senate to support the NATO operation, but the debate that preceded the March 24 onset of airstrikes revealed the fundamental apprehension of most lawmakers about the mission. No one was certain what the next step would be if the airstrikes failed to cow Milosevic into signing a peace accord. Most members appeared adamant that U.S. ground troops should not be sent to wage war in Kosovo if the airstrikes were not sufficient, although they skipped several opportunities to put such restrictions into law.

Other concerns were raised as well. Many senators acknowledged the potential loss of life among Kosovo's ethnic Albanians, but they questioned whether U.S. national interests justified stepping into a Balkan province unknown to most Americans. They pointed out that the situation in Kosovo was far from the only humanitarian crisis in the world that could merit U.S. intervention. Members also voiced concern that the administration was stretching NATO's mission. The bombing marked the first time that the transatlantic alliance had conducted an offensive military operation against a sovereign state.

Clinton sought to reassure congressional critics in a prime-time televised speech to the nation March 24, saying, "I do not intend to put our troops in Kosovo to fight a war." But he stressed the need to protect innocent people from the military offensive in Kosovo and to prevent a wider war in Europe. "Imagine what would happen if we and our allies instead decided just to look the other way as these people were massacred on NATO's doorstep. That would discredit NATO, the cornerstone on which our security has rested for 50 years now," Clinton said.

Clinton met with dozens of lawmakers from March 19 through March 23, the day the Senate adopted, 58–41, a bipartisan resolution (S Con Res 21) in support of the airstrikes.

The House on March 24 adopted, 424–1, a resolution (H Res 130) backing the personnel involved in the air attacks but waited a month before taking up S Con Res 21. In the meantime, it approved two other measures. HR 1376, giving U.S. troops taking part in the operation an additional six months to file their tax forms and a tax exemption for their combat pay, was reported by the House Ways and Means Committee (H Rept 106-90) on April 13 and passed by the full House, 424–0, April 15. The Senate passed it, 95–0, later that day and Clinton signed it April 16 (PL 106-21), even though he had already granted the breaks by executive order April 13. Also on April 15, the House adopted by voice vote a resolution (H Con Res 83) demanding the release of three Americans captured earlier that month by Serb forces.

In late April the House debated Clinton's strategy in Kosovo—but found no strategy of its own. It demanded congressional approval for sending ground troops but neither endorsed nor condemned the ongoing NATO air campaign against Yugoslavia.

After five weeks of NATO planes pounding targets in Serbia, congressional leaders had not been eager to debate Clinton's policy or, as some GOP lawmakers had taken to calling it,

"Clinton's war." But Rep. Tom Campbell, R-Calif., by invoking a section of the 1973 War Powers Resolution (PL 93-148) that required expedited congressional consideration of war-related measures, forced the House to take up two resolutions—H Con Res 82, ordering a withdrawal of U.S. forces, and H J Res 44, declaring war on Yugoslavia. Two others were added to the agenda to give members a broader policy choice—S Con Res 21, to authorize the current air operations, and HR 1569, to require authorization for any ground troops.

At a White House meeting April 28 with a bipartisan group of Senate and House leaders, Clinton insisted that he had no plans to use troops and that he would consult with Congress before committing them. However, like all his recent predecessors, he refused to be bound by Congress on this point. Minutes before the House voted on HR 1569, Clinton's assurances, embodied in a letter to Speaker Hastert, were circulated to all members. However, some administration allies said this came too late to make a difference.

In the end, the only one of the measures to pass was HR 1569. The House approved it, 249–180, on April 28. The Senate did not take up the bill.

Both H Con Res 82 (H Rept 106-116) and H J Res 44 (H Rept 106-115) had been reported unfavorably by the House International Relations Committee on April 27. The next day the full House rejected H Con Res 82 by a vote of 139–290 and H J Res 44 by a vote of 2–427. And then the House rejected, by a tie vote, the Senate-passed endorsement of the air war. S Con Res 21 was defeated by a **key vote of 213–213 (R 31–187; D 181–26; I 1–0).** *(1999 key votes, p. 899)*

"All Necessary Force"

In effect, the War Powers Resolution forced action on a Kosovo-related resolution in the Senate as well. S J Res 20 would have authorized the president to use "all necessary force" to achieve NATO's goal of forcing the Serb-dominated government of Yugoslavia to halt its persecution of Kosovar Albanians. The resolution was designed by a bipartisan group, led by John McCain, R-Ariz., to express support for NATO to begin planning how it would use ground troops to occupy Kosovo in case the bombing campaign did not stop Milosevic. Although it did not mention the War Powers Resolution, the Senate parliamentarian ruled that S J Res 20 fit the criteria for triggering the War Powers Resolution's expedited procedures.

Senate Majority Leader Trent Lott, R-Miss., was one of many Republicans who did not want either to endorse what they saw as a badly flawed Clinton policy or to cast a vote that could be taken as encouragement by the Milosevic regime. But negotiations to postpone action on the McCain proposal broke down, leaving the Senate on the procedural autopilot set by the War Powers Resolution. Under the timetable, the McCain resolution would have been discharged from the Foreign Relations Committee on May 1, if the panel had not reported the measure by then. The panel reported the resolution (no written report) on April 30.

On May 4 the Senate voted 78–22 to table, or kill, S J Res 20. The tabling motion was backed by both Republican and Democratic leaders, who saw the measure as premature.

Kosovo Funding

The House on May 6 rejected an amendment to a fiscal 1999 supplemental appropriations bill (HR 1664) that would have put teeth into the position the House had taken only a week earlier when it passed HR 1569, requiring congressional authorization for the use of ground troops in Kosovo. This time, the House rejected, 117–301, an amendment by Ernest Istook, R-Okla., that would have barred the use of any funds in the supplemental bill for an invasion of Yugoslavia by U.S. ground troops. Voting "nay" on the Istook amendment were one hundred Republicans and twenty-eight Democrats who had voted for HR 1569. There was concern that Istook's amendment would delay the bill and send a signal to Milosevic that he would not have to worry about a land war.

To avoid a lengthy debate over Kosovo, Senate leaders attached money for the air war to an earlier fiscal 1999 supplemental appropriations bill that was already in conference. The final $14.6 billion measure (HR 1141—PL 106-31), which cleared May 20, included about $5 billion for Kosovo military operations and $1.1 billion for Kosovo humanitarian assistance.

The Senate rejected several attempts to limit Clinton's military options during debate on the fiscal 2000 defense authorization bill (S 1059). On May 25, by a **key vote of 52–48 (R 17–38; D 35–10),** the Senate tabled, or killed, an amendment by Arlen Specter, R-Pa., that would have barred the deployment of U.S. ground troops, except for peacekeeping forces, in Kosovo unless Congress authorized the operation. Specter, who said that Clinton might persuade him to vote for such an authorization, cast the issue as one more round in the twenty-five-year effort to give Congress more control over whether U.S. forces should be sent into combat. The next day the Senate voted 77–21 to table an amendment by Robert C. Smith, R-N.H., that would have cut off any funds for military operations in Yugoslavia—including NATO's bombing campaign—on Oct. 1 unless Congress authorized the mission. *(1999 key votes, p. 899)*

During consideration of its version of the defense authorization (HR 1401), the House on June 10 adopted, 270–155, an amendment by Ike Skelton, D-Mo., to eliminate from the bill a provision that would have barred Clinton from using any funds authorized by the bill either for the air war against Yugoslavia that was under way when the bill was drafted in May, or for a peacekeeping operation in Kosovo. When the House took up Skelton's amendment, as Yugoslav forces were beginning to pull out of Kosovo and NATO troops were preparing to move in, Democrats contended that the committee's ban would pull the rug out from under U.S. forces just when their efforts had succeeded. Leading House Republicans agreed to support the motion to kill the amendment only after Clinton promised in writing that he would seek supplemental appropriations to pay for the Kosovo operation.

The final version of the defense authorization (S 1059—PL 106-65) required the president to request a supplemental appropriation to pay for the deployment of U.S. forces in Kosovo. *(2000 defense authorization, p. 276)*

Because of Clinton's pledge to seek a separate appropriation, the regular fiscal 2000 defense appropriations bill (HR 2561—PL 106-79) contained no funds for the Kosovo deployment. The final bill did include a Senate provision—a Don Nickles, R-Okla., amendment adopted by voice vote June 8—barring any reconstruction aid to Serbia as long as Milosevic remained in power. *(2000 defense appropriations, p. 283)*

The fiscal 2000 foreign operations spending bill, included in the fiscal 2000 omnibus funding bill (HR 3194—PL 106-113), included a ban on aid to Serbia. The ban did not apply to Kosovo or Montenegro or to efforts to promote democracy. *(2000 aid appropriations, p. 210)*

2000 ACTION

Congress continued in 2000 to grapple with questions about U.S. policy in Kosovo—and about what role Congress should play in setting that policy.

Kosovo Funding

Congress appropriated $2.2 billion in 2000 to replenish Defense Department accounts used to pay for approximately 6,200 U.S. soldiers in the NATO peacekeeping force in Kosovo, 1,000 support personnel in neighboring countries, and enforcement of international sanctions against Yugoslavia. The money was part of a supplemental fiscal 2000 appropriations package that was attached to the fiscal 2001 military construction appropriations bill (HR 4425—PL 106-246). *(2001 military construction, p. 300)*

Congress had been under intense pressure to approve the funding for the Kosovo deployment because the money had already been borrowed and spent from military training budgets. If Congress had not come through, some training exercises would have been canceled. Nevertheless, congressional frustration with the Kosovo mission was rising. A bloc of Republicans had been skeptical of the operation from the outset, and even some of the mission's supporters were decrying the failure of European allies to fulfill their pledges to provide police officers to keep order in the province and to provide funds for economic reconstruction. But during consideration of its version of the supplemental spending bill (HR 3908), the House on March 30 rejected, 200–219, an amendment offered by Budget Committee Chairman John R. Kasich, R-Ohio, that would have withheld half of the Kosovo funds until Europe did more to assist in the mission. Opponents said that such a move would be tantamount to a U.S. withdrawal from the area.

On the Senate side, the Kosovo funding was added to that chamber's fiscal 2001 military construction appropriations bill (S 2521), along with a committee amendment authored by Robert C. Byrd, D-W.Va., that would have ended the deployment of U.S. troops as peacekeepers in Kosovo on July 1, 2001, unless Congress authorized an extension. It also would have conditioned a quarter of the fiscal 2000 funds on a presidential certification that European countries were assuming specified shares of the costs in Kosovo. The amendment alarmed the White House, the Pentagon, and some Senate Democrats. It also was criticized by Texas Gov. George W. Bush, the presumed Republican presidential nominee. On May 18 the full Senate, by a **key vote of 53–47 (R 15–40; D 38–7),** struck the Kosovo amendment from the bill. *(2000 key votes, p. 915)*

The issue of whether the NATO allies were paying their share of the costs also surfaced during House consideration of the fiscal 2001 defense authorization bill (HR 4205—PL 106-398). On May 17 the House adopted, by a **key vote of 264–153 (R 195–18; D 67–135; I 2–0),** another Kasich amendment that potentially could have forced the withdrawal of U.S. troops from Kosovo if the president had not certified by April 1, 2001, that European allies were paying a fair share of costs in Kosovo. The House provision, which could have been waived by the president for six months in case of a military crisis or if Congress approved a longer deployment, was dropped in conference. *(2001 defense authorization, p. 290; 2000 key votes, p. 160)*

Aid Bills

Sensing a chance to bring U.S. troops home from the Balkans, members of Congress closed ranks behind President Clinton's efforts to get Milosevic to step down after he apparently lost his Sept. 24 bid for reelection. The next day the House passed by voice vote legislation (HR 1064) to strengthen groups opposed to Milosevic, codify sanctions against his regime, and lay the groundwork for a change of power in Belgrade. Although the Senate had passed similar legislation (S 720—S Rept 106-139) on Nov. 4, 1999, HR 1064 ground to a halt in the Senate. Some lawmakers, led by Republican Policy Committee Chairman Larry E. Craig of Idaho, objected that by writing some existing sanctions into law, the bill might make it too difficult for the White House to eventually lift sanctions on a new government after Milosevic departed. Craig said the Serbian-American community was very divided on the bill, particularly on the issue of sanctions and whether the legislation should condition aid on Milosevic being turned over to the International Criminal Tribunal at The Hague, which had indicted him. The bill would have allowed the president to waive many of the sanctions for a post-Milosevic government.

Both the House and Senate approved foreign aid funding bills while Milosevic was still in power. Those bills called for banning aid to Serbia and effectively requiring the United States to oppose loans from international financial institutions as long as Yugoslavia harbored Milosevic. The conference version (HR 4811—PL 106-429), which cleared after

Milosevic was ousted, gave Serbia $100 million in aid, but only if the president certified by March 31, 2001, that the new Yugoslav government was cooperating in bringing accused war criminals such as Milosevic before the war crimes tribunal. The bill also required the new government to implement policies respecting human and minority rights and the rule of law. *(2001 aid appropriations, p. 214)*

China Policy

U.S.-China relations remained tumultuous in the 106th Congress. Yet, despite seemingly insurmountable obstacles, President Clinton's policy of engagement stayed, more or less, on track.

Members of Congress expressed outrage over everything from China's alleged attempts to steal U.S. nuclear secrets to its ongoing threat to Taiwan to its record on human rights. But, in the end, Congress in 1999 again renewed normal trade relations with China and in 2000 went along with the administration's proposal to permanently normalize trade relations with China. *(Nuclear security, p. 302; China trade, p. 160)*

1999 ACTION

Both chambers adopted measures urging the Clinton administration to push for a resolution at the annual meeting in Geneva of the U.N. Human Rights Commission, March 30–April 30, that would call on China to end its human rights abuses. The Senate adopted S Res 45 by a vote of 99–0 on Feb. 25, 1999, and the House adopted H Con Res 28 by a 421–0 vote March 11.

The House May 25 adopted, 418–0, a resolution (H Res 178) condemning the Chinese government for continuing human rights abuses. It called on China to release political dissidents imprisoned because of their participation in the 1989 demonstrations in Tiananmen Square and to investigate the ensuing violence with the goal of bringing those responsible to justice. Following the death of the Communist leader Hu Yaobang on April 15, 1989, thousands of protesters throughout China had begun pressing for democratic reforms. Demonstrations were abruptly and violently halted on June 3 and 4, 1989, by government forces. Human rights groups estimated that scores of people were killed in Tiananmen Square and countless more throughout China imprisoned.

Also on May 25, a House report was released detailing China's alleged attempts over several decades to steal highly classified information from the Energy Department's nuclear weapons laboratories. The report unleashed a torrent of ill will toward China, with some lawmakers saying it was a rationale for a fundamental reexamination of relations with China. House International Relations Chairman Benjamin A. Gilman, R-N.Y., called the Clinton administration's policy of "strategic partnership" with China "naive and misguided" in the wake of the report's revelations.

But other members foresaw little dramatic change in relations between the two countries. "There's too much need, too much at stake," said Joseph R. Biden Jr. of Delaware, the Senate Foreign Relations Committee's ranking Democrat. "You can't ignore a billion people, and they can't ignore us."

Chinese officials denounced the House report as an inaccurate and misguided attempt to demonize their country. Their comments, coming three weeks after the May 7 accidental U.S. bombing of China's embassy in Belgrade during NATO's air campaign against Serbia, further poisoned relations between the two nations. *(Details, 2000 intelligence authorization, p. 226)*

In response to the House report, Congress approved a plan to restructure the Energy Department's nuclear weapons programs as part of the fiscal 2000 defense authorization bill (S 1059—PL 106-65) signed into law Oct. 5. The bill also contained provisions requiring closer monitoring of U.S. satellite launches in China and prohibiting some U.S.-Chinese military exchanges. *(2000 defense authorization, p. 276)*

Concern over China's human rights abuses hung heavily over the annual ritual of renewing China's trade relations with the United States. With the Chinese government's decision in July 1999 to outlaw a nonpolitical meditation movement known as Falun Gong and issues such as religious persecution still unresolved, members of both parties on Capitol Hill argued that U.S. "engagement" with China had failed. But other members who saw trade as the best way to promote political and economic change in the world's most populous nation won the argument. A resolution (H J Res 57) to deny China normal trade status was rejected in the House, 170–260, July 27.

The debate was far from over. U.S. and Chinese negotiators reached an agreement Nov. 15 that called for China to slash tariffs and open a wide range of markets in order to join the World Trade Organization after thirteen years of trying to gain entry. In return, the United States would grant China permanent trade relations, a pledge that assured an even tougher battle in Congress in 2000.

The issue of human rights abuses in China surfaced elsewhere. The fiscal 2001 State Department authorization bill, enacted as part of the fiscal 2000 omnibus spending bill (HR 3194—PL 106-113), included several provisions on the topic. The bill stated Congress's concurrence in the State Department's 1998 findings that the Chinese government had committed "widespread and well-documented human rights abuses." The bill earmarked funds for additional U.S. personnel in China to monitor political and social conditions, with particular emphasis on human rights. The bill also established a prisoner information registry to monitor the treatment of political prisoners, as well as prisoners of conscience and prisoners of faith.

U.S. policy toward Taiwan provoked fierce rhetoric, as Taiwan's supporters on Capitol Hill criticized Clinton's "one China" policy and pushed the White House to urge China to renounce the use of force against Taiwan. While supporting the idea that Taiwan and China were part of one country, the

United States had not specified under whose control they fell—a diplomatic maneuver that allowed U.S. negotiations with both governments to continue. On March 23, the House adopted, 429–1, a resolution (H Con Res 56), reaffirming the U.S. commitment to the 1979 Taiwan Relations Act (PL 96-8), which allowed the United States to supply Taiwan with resources to defend itself. *(Congress and the Nation Vol. V, p. 65)*

2000 ACTION

Congress in 2000 approved legislation (HR 4444—PL 106-286) to permanently grant China the same trade status enjoyed by most of the United States' trading partners. But key problems in U.S.-China relations were raised in both chambers' debates.

House passage was eased by the addition in committee of language addressing concerns about enhancing the trade status of a nation with a record for human rights violations, labor abuses, and military posturing. The proposal, crafted by Sander M. Levin, D-Mich., and Doug Bereuter, R-Neb., among other things, created a twenty-three-member panel with a fulltime staff to monitor human rights in China, including labor standards and religious freedom, and report annually to Congress and the president. It also established an interagency task force to monitor the import of products made with forced or prison labor and to take steps to enforce the U.S. ban on such products. The provisions remained in the final bill.

The issue of China's role in supplying weapons of mass destruction surfaced in the Senate debate on HR 4444. Fred Thompson, R-Tenn., and Robert G. Torricelli, D-N.J., had introduced legislation (S 2645) to require the president to punish the Chinese government or individual Chinese companies found to be supplying such weapons or components to other nations. In an attempt to accommodate White House objections, the two modified their proposal to apply it to all key suppliers of such weapons, not just China, and to make sanctions discretionary instead of mandatory. But a motion to attach it as an amendment to HR 4444 was tabled, or killed, by a **key vote of 65–32 (R 30–23; D 35–9)** on Sept. 13. The administration had opposed all changes out of fear that returning HR 4444 to the House for approval of Senate changes could doom it so late in the session. No action was taken on S 2645. *(2000 key votes, p. 915)*

Congress in 2000 approved a one-year extension (HR 5239—PL 106-508) of a law governing the export of products with both military and commercial uses. Interest in reauthorizing the Export Administration Act (PL 96-72), which expired in 1994, had been revived after the controversy erupted in the 105th Congress over whether China had acquired missile technology while launching U.S. commercial satellites. *(Export Administration Act, p. 166; 1997–1998 China policy, p. 180)*

Early in 2000 the House passed legislation (HR 1838) to strengthen U.S. military ties with Taiwan. But the White

House, threatening a veto, insisted that it would undermine stability in Asia and diminish Taiwan's security. HR 1838 was reported by the House International Relations Committee (H Rept 106-423) on Oct. 28, 1999, and was passed by the full House, 341–70, on Feb. 1, 2000. The Senate did not act on the bill.

2000 Aid Appropriations

Congress in 1999 cleared a $15.3 billion foreign operations spending bill as part of the fiscal 2000 omnibus appropriations bill (HR 3194—PL 106-113).

With congressional Republicans determined to hold down foreign aid spending as part of their overall budget plan and the White House equally intent on funding some key foreign policy initiatives, the aid bill had become a major battleground in the fiscal 2000 budget wars. President Clinton vetoed an earlier version (HR 2606) that had appropriated $2.6 billion less than the final bill and omitted several of his key priorities, including funding to help Israel, Jordan, and the Palestinian Authority implement the 1998 Wye River peace agreement. *(Middle East summit, box p. 190)*

Republicans finally backed down and Congress moved a revised bill (HR 3196) that contained the $1.8 billion requested for the Wye River agreement, as well as funding for such Clinton priorities as a program to find work for Russian nuclear scientists to help stop any "brain drain" to unfriendly countries and assistance to help some of the world's poorest nations restructure debts they owed the United States.

In an attempt to wage the aid battle on budgetary terms alone, House Republicans had tried to steer clear of policy disputes, particularly the perennial stumbling block of restrictions on family planning assistance. They had removed a restriction on a U.S. contribution for the United Nations Population Fund (UNFPA). Critics accused the fund of helping finance compulsory abortions in China. But at the last minute, GOP leaders appeased antiabortion members by attaching restrictions on assistance to other international family planning groups. Clinton's acceptance of the restrictions paved the way for enactment of a plan to repay U.S. debts to the United Nations as part of the fiscal 2000–2001 State Department authorization bill. That measure also was incorporated into the omnibus funding bill. *(State Department authorization, p. 217)*

VETOED BILL

House and Senate Republicans—facing nearly solid Democratic opposition—narrowly cleared the first version of the aid bill (HR 2606). GOP leaders had united party members with warnings that their budget strategy and even their House majority hung in the balance. They insisted that Clinton's foreign policy goals could only be achieved by dipping into the Social Security surplus.

But Clinton vetoed the bill, denouncing its $12.7 billion total as too low and another chapter in the slide by Republicans toward isolationism. Only days earlier the Senate had rejected the Comprehensive Test Ban Treaty. *(Test ban treaty, p. 310)*

Senate Action

The Senate passed a $12.7 billion aid bill (S 1234) on June 30, 1999, by a lopsided 97–2 vote. The bill had been reported by the Senate Appropriations Committee (S Rept 106-81) on June 17.

S 1234 authorized $535 million for postwar reconstruction in the Balkan region but none of it was to go to Serbia as long as Yugoslav President Slobodan Milosevic remained in power. Administration officials complained that the provision gave them no flexibility and could also unintentionally force the United States to impose sanctions on neighboring states that provided humanitarian assistance to Yugoslavia. During floor action, the Senate adopted, by voice vote, a Jesse Helms, R-N.C., amendment incorporating central provisions of his legislation (S 720) to authorize $100 million over the next two fiscal years to aid democratic forces opposed to Milosevic. (Subsequently, S 720 was reported by the Senate Foreign Relations Committee (S Rept 106-139) on Aug. 5, 1999, and passed by voice vote of the Senate on Nov. 4.)

S 1234 did not authorize the $500 million the president requested for fiscal 2000 to buttress the 1998 Wye River peace accords. It also did not include funds for a program aimed at halting the brain drain of Russian weapons scientists to unfriendly states such as Iran, Iraq, or North Korea, but the Senate approved nonbinding language calling for the money to be added in conference.

The closest vote of the daylong debate June 30 came on an attempt by Sam Brownback, R-Kan., to change U.S. policy toward Azerbaijan, which for a decade had been locked in a struggle with neighboring Armenia over the enclave of Nagorno-Karabakh. U.S. energy companies had invested heavily in the oil-rich region of the former Soviet Union between the Caspian Sea and the Caucasus Mountains, and they favored closer ties with Azerbaijan. *(Azerbaijan aid ban, box, p. 187)*

Brownback proposed allowing the president to waive a ban on most direct U.S. assistance to Azerbaijan—the only former Soviet republic under such limitations. The attempt came as part of a broader amendment that incorporated Brownback's "Silk Road" bill (S 579—S Rept 106-45), which had been reported by the Senate Foreign Relations Committee May 11. S 579 was designed to encourage political and economic reform, economic development, and the settlement of conflicts in the Caspian region. The Senate ultimately adopted Brownback's amendment by voice vote but first agreed, 53–45, to a second-degree amendment by Mitch McConnell, R-Ky., and Spencer Abraham, R-Mich., to delete the change in policy toward Azerbaijan.

Lawmakers also squared off on an amendment by Christopher J. Dodd, D-Conn., that would have allowed Americans to freely travel to and from Cuba by barring the president from regulating or prohibiting such travel. But Cuba's traditional supporters in Congress said that Cuban leader Fidel Castro's recent crackdown on overseas trips showed that U.S. policy, written into law (PL 104-114) in 1996, should be maintained. Clinton earlier in 1999 had chosen to continue the long-standing embargo on U.S. trade with Cuba but allowed increased exchanges, including additional flights to the island. Dodd's amendment was tabled (killed), 55–43. *(1996 law, Congress and the Nation Vol. IX, p. 237; 2000 action, economic sanctions, p. 223)*

House Action

The House passed a $12.6 billion aid bill (HR 2606) by a 385–35 vote on Aug. 3. The bill had been reported by the House Appropriations Committee (H Rept 106-254) on July 23.

Like the Senate bill, HR 2606 did not take full account of the amount the administration was expected to request later in the year for long-term reconstruction in the Balkans, including Kosovo. Nor did either bill take account of additional funding that the administration was seeking for aid to Colombia, countries engaged in the Middle East peace process, or very poor countries seeking debt relief.

But the biggest obstacle to a compromise on the legislation was posed by the House bill's abortion restrictions on international family planning assistance. The House on July 29 adopted two substantially different amendments on family planning aid.

The House rebuffed attempts by abortion rights supporters to use an amendment offered by James C. Greenwood, R-Pa., as a substitute for one offered by Christopher H. Smith, R-N.J. Instead the House adopted, 256–172—largely along party lines—a debate rule that allowed members to vote on both.

The House first adopted, 228–200, Smith's amendment prohibiting aid to international family planning groups that performed abortions—except where the life of the mother was in danger or in cases of rape or incest—or that violated antiabortion laws in other countries or tried to change those laws. The amendment reinstated part of the so-called Mexico City policy of Presidents Ronald Reagan and George Bush, a policy named for a 1984 world conference on population where it was first espoused. Clinton had rescinded the restrictions in 1993 and had made opposition to their reinstatement a cornerstone of his foreign policy.

Greenwood's amendment, adopted next by a 221–208 vote, prohibited the use of U.S. aid by international groups to promote abortion as a means of family planning or to lobby for or against abortion. Such groups would be required to certify that they would use the U.S. funds to reduce the incidence of abortion. But they would be free to do what they wished with non-U.S. funds. Greenwood contended that his provision, unlike the Smith amendment, would likely survive a conference committee.

A conference committee would also have to deal with the House's adoption July 29, on a 230–197 vote, of an amendment by Joe Moakley, D-Mass., cutting off foreign operations funding for military training conducted at the Army's School of the Americas at Fort Benning, Georgia. No such provision was in the Senate bill. The House action, even if supported in conference, would not close the school, since most of its funding came from the defense appropriations bill. Critics said the graduates of the military school included some of the most notorious violators of human rights in Central and South America. But supporters, including top Pentagon officials, contended that most of its graduates had promoted democracy and battled the drug trade at home.

On Aug. 2, the House rejected, 103–315, an amendment by Robert E. Andrews, D-N.J., to prevent the Overseas Private Investment Corporation (OPIC) from insuring new investment in developing countries or making additional loans. Critics said OPIC was providing large corporations with insurance that could be obtained in the private sector and they warned that the U.S. government could be liable for billions of dollars of bad loans or insurance payments if OPIC-guaranteed investments went sour.

But OPIC's defenders said the agency had supported the expansion of U.S. industries into new markets and that it provided a service that could not be obtained commercially. Moreover, they maintained that U.S. companies would be at a disadvantage in the global marketplace since most major U.S. competitors had such services. In 1996, OPIC's supporters had lost the fight when the House voted 260–157 to reject legislation reauthorizing the agency. It was continued thanks to funding in the fiscal 1997 foreign operations spending bill, part of an omnibus spending bill (PL 104-208). *(Congress and the Nation Vol. IX, p. 236)*

Conference, Veto

The House adopted the conference report on HR 2606 (H Rept 106-339) by a vote of 214–211 on Oct. 5. The Senate cleared it, 51–49, the next day.

The $12.6 billion total that conferees agreed on did not include billions more that Clinton had requested or was expected to request for such items as debt relief or the Middle East peace accord. House Republicans agreed to strip out $100 million they had previously set aside for Jordan on the assumption that there would be a supplemental appropriations bill that would include much of what Clinton had pledged to Israel, Jordan, and the Palestinians.

Republicans insisted that they could not yield to Clinton's demands for more foreign aid spending because they would be forced to break the caps from the 1997 balanced budget agreement (PL 105-33). To some fiscal conservatives, the final bill was already too expensive. *(1997 Balanced Budget Act, p. 48)*

House conferees agreed to drop the provision cutting off funding for the School of the Americas. House Appropriations Committee Chairman Sonny Callahan, R-Ala., said that Army officials had indicated they would shift all funding for the school to the defense budget and that would have meant a loss of jurisdiction over foreign military training programs for his committee.

House abortion restrictions on international family planning aid once again proved to be the major stumbling block for conferees. Callahan offered a compromise that attempted to bridge the gap between the slight antiabortion majority in the House and the majority of senators opposed to further abortion restrictions on such assistance. He proposed retaining the language in the fiscal 1999 omnibus spending law (PL 105-277), which permitted the president to spend $385 million a year on international family planning aid but omitted restrictions supported by social conservatives that would have restored antiabortion policies of the Reagan and Bush administrations. At the same time, Callahan tried to appease abortion opponents by proposing to drop a $25 million contribution to UNFPA that had been approved by both chambers. The House had agreed to reauthorize the contribution for fiscal 2000 after eliminating it for the previous year. But Senate conferees rejected the proposal to drop UNFPA funds.

House GOP leaders yielded to Senate demands to renew the UNFPA funds but then faced an uphill battle to marshal enough votes in the House for the conference report. House Democratic leaders, eager to shoot down one of the Republicans' spending bills, seized on the lack of Wye River funds as a reason for voting against the measure. But Republican leaders wanted to hold off on the Wye River spending because it would undermine their budget strategy. They insisted that to attempt to fund it in fiscal 2000 would mean using money set aside for Social Security.

Short of votes, House GOP leaders began wooing Republicans who had previously opposed the measure. The horse-trading even included concessions to northeastern lawmakers worried about dairy pricing included in the fiscal 2000 agriculture appropriations conference report (HR 1906—H Rept 106-354), which the House adopted Oct. 1.

Republican leaders' arguments that passage of the legislation was essential for maintaining budget discipline finally won enough votes in both chambers to clear the conference report.

On Oct. 18, Clinton carried out his threat to veto the bill.

REVISED BILL

The House passed a revised fiscal 2000 foreign operations funding bill (HR 3196) on Nov. 5 by a vote of 316–100 but that bill stalled in the Senate. A new foreign operations bill (HR 3422) was incorporated into the conference report on the fiscal 2000 omnibus appropriations bill (HR 3194—H Rept 106-479), which the House adopted, 296–135, on Nov. 18 and the Senate cleared, 74–24, on Nov. 19. President Clinton signed HR 3194 on Nov. 29.

After Clinton's veto of the initial foreign aid bill, Republicans quickly gave in to most of Clinton's demands for higher foreign aid spending. GOP leaders agreed to $2.6 billion in additional aid, including more money for the Middle East, the former Soviet Union, and the World Bank.

Republicans said they agreed to the compromise in an effort to wrap up the overall budget talks. White House budget director Jack Lew reportedly had promised that once foreign aid was settled, everything else could be settled quickly. Republicans initially had hoped to add just the $1.8 billion for the Wye River peace agreement but in the end had to include another $799 million to get enough Democrats on board to pass HR 3196.

That bill then stalled in the Senate. Several Senate Democrats blocked attempts to pass it by voice vote in order to use the bill as leverage in winning support on other issues. Also hindering HR 3196 was a debt relief dispute, which Clinton administration officials and Republican leaders were working on behind closed doors in hopes of producing a final bill in a future House-Senate conference.

Lawmakers had already agreed to the administration's request to forgive nearly all the bilateral debt owed to the United States by the poor countries. It was also agreed that discussions on an additional $1 billion in multilateral debt relief over four years Clinton requested would be put off until the following year. But a dispute emerged over a somewhat esoteric policy change that would allow the IMF to revalue its gold reserves in order to finance its portion of the debt relief package. *(IMF gold reserves, box, p. 213)*

Despite protests from House Majority Leader Dick Armey, R-Texas, and others, House Speaker J. Dennis Hastert, R-Ill., largely conceded to the administration as part of a broad agreement that allowed the IMF to proceed with the plan. Authorization was included in a miscellaneous appropriations bill (HR 3425), which was also rolled into the omnibus funding bill. In return, Armey received a number of commitments, which he said would further open up the often secretive IMF to international scrutiny. Most importantly, he said, the compromise would require the IMF to publish its budget for the first time.

As details of the foreign aid spending bill were being negotiated, White House officials and congressional Republicans were also trying to reach a compromise on paying nearly $1 billion in U.S. debts to the United Nations as part of a State Department authorization bill. The perennial linkage of the U.N. debt repayment issue with abortion restrictions on international family planning aid had triggered several Clinton vetoes in the past and seemed likely to do so again.

However, Clinton was eager to curtail anti-American sentiment at the United Nations because of the debts and had told Hastert that he would like to reach a compromise with congressional Republicans. Lawmakers said Clinton changed his mind largely because he was running up against two deadlines:

• U.N. rules would have forced the United States to give up its seat in the U.N. General Assembly if Congress did not pay at least $111 million of the money owed the world body.

• It was the last year, under the 1997 balanced-budget law (PL 105-33), that such spending could be written off as "emergency spending" without offsetting budget cuts.

DEBT RELIEF AND THE IMF

A somewhat arcane dispute over the use of the gold reserves of the International Monetary Fund (IMF) complicated the final round of negotiations on the fiscal 2000 foreign operations appropriations bill.

The dispute centered on U.S. support for an IMF proposal on how to finance part of a debt-relief plan agreed to by President Clinton and the leaders of other wealthy nations at a summit in Cologne, Germany, in June 1999. That plan would forgive $27 billion in foreign debt owed by some of the world's poorest countries. Under the plan, wealthy nations were supposed to forgive bilateral debt owed by the poor countries and to contribute to a pool that would help write off some of the money the poor countries owed to multilateral agencies such as the IMF and the World Bank. At the same time, those agencies were supposed to use some of their own resources to write off a portion of the debt.

IMF officials earlier in 1999 planned to sell some of its gold reserves to finance their portion of the debt relief. The gold stores, contributed by the United States and other IMF members, had rarely been tapped but had been held in reserve in case IMF loans were not repaid. IMF officials had considered the sale as a way of capturing some of the difference between how the gold deposits were valued on the IMF's books—about $47 per ounce, the price at which it was acquired decades earlier—and its current market price of close to $300 an ounce. The IMF, which had more than 100 million ounces of gold, was considering selling about 10 million ounces, which was expected to yield $2 billion to $3 billion for debt relief.

Under IMF rules, the U.S. government had an effective veto over gold sales, and U.S. law required prior congressional approval. The United States had agreed to such sales in the past, such as in the late 1970s when the IMF sold gold to help poor countries. But the proposed sales in 1999 produced protests on Capitol Hill, where lawmakers feared it would further weaken gold prices.

When the gold sale option was rejected, IMF officials hit upon an accounting maneuver that would similarly tap the difference between the market value of the gold and its value on the IMF's books, without requiring an open market sale of the gold.

Acting through a complicated series of sales and purchases among member countries, the maneuver would revalue the gold on the IMF's books at market prices. That boost in assets would allow the IMF to write off some debt from poor countries at the same time, without affecting its balance sheet.

IMF critics on Capitol Hill, especially House Majority Leader Dick Armey, R-Texas, still objected, arguing that those profits should flow to IMF members, such as the United States, which had deposited the gold and that the IMF should find other sources to finance its portion of the debt relief package. But in the end Congress agreed to let IMF proceed with their new plan in a miscellaneous appropriations bill (HR 3425), which was included in the fiscal 2000 omnibus appropriations bill (HR 3194—PL 106-113).

Under the plan, the United States would support freeing up about $3.1 billion for debt relief by revaluing 12.5 million ounces of gold. Almost two-thirds of the funds would become available immediately for debt relief, while Congress would have to vote the next year to reauthorize the remainder, which it did in the fiscal 2001 foreign operations funding bill (HR 4811—PL 106-429). *(2001 aid appropriations, p. 214)*

Lawmakers also said Clinton had more leeway to negotiate on abortion than the previous year, when his impending impeachment trial in the Senate made him loath to anger women's groups.

A compromise was reached providing for repayment of the U.N. debt as part of the State Department bill and attaching abortion restrictions to family planning aid in the foreign operations bill.

Both advocates and opponents of the new abortion restrictions acknowledged that they would have little practical effect. But both sides also agreed that writing the provisions into statute, rather than executive order, would set an important precedent. They also said that even though the restrictions were only for ten months, such "temporary" prohibitions can have a long life.

The revised bill gave the administration a freer hand in some areas. Most importantly, it dropped many of the original bill's restrictions on military and economic assistance to Indonesia, which had been inserted by Sen. Patrick J. Leahy, D-Vt. The vetoed bill would have cut off nearly all U.S. aid in retaliation for the Asian nation's violent treatment of the province of East Timor, which had voted for independence. However, after the conference report on that bill was written, Indonesia had undergone major changes. East Timor had been granted independence and a new Indonesian government had been elected and warmly welcomed by Congress and the White House. Moreover, business groups and pro-business lawmakers pressed to see the restrictions dropped, calling them an affront to a major trading partner. The new bill permitted aid but made military assistance contingent on a presidential determination that, among other things, the Indonesian government and armed forces were cooperating with investigations of human rights violations and with the international peacekeeping force deployed in East Timor.

MAJOR PROVISIONS

As signed into law, HR 3194, the omnibus appropriations bill, appropriated $15.3 billion for foreign aid and related programs in fiscal 2000. This included $599 million for export and investment assistance, $8.43 billion for bilateral economic aid, $4.99 billion for military assistance, and $1.3 billion for multilateral economic assistance.

Major provisions of the bill:

Middle East

Provided $2.88 billion in aid for Israel and $2.035 billion for Egypt. The bill also earmarked $225 million for Jordan.

The bill appropriated $1.8 billion over three years to help Israel, Jordan, and the Palestinian Authority implement the 1998 Wye River peace accords. The funds were designated "emergency" spending not subject to budget limits or offsets.

Former Soviet Union

Appropriated $839 million for aid to the republics of the former Soviet Union. Of this, $241 million was set aside for a program to find work for Russian nuclear scientists to help stop any "brain drain" to unfriendly countries.

Family Planning

Barred any of the bill's $385 million in U.S. international family planning assistance for organizations that performed abortions—except in cases of rape, incest, or where the life of the woman was in danger—or lobbied to change abortion laws or government policies in other countries. The president could waive this restriction for up to $15 million but that would trigger a shift of $12.5 million in family planning aid to an account for child survival and disease prevention. The restrictions applied only through fiscal 2000.

The bill provided $25 million for the United Nations Population Fund (UNFPA), but none of the money would be made available if UNFPA funded abortions nor could it be used for a program in China. Moreover, if the secretary of state reported UNFPA had budgeted money for activities in China, an equal amount was to be withheld from the U.S. contribution after March 1 for the remainder of that fiscal year.

Balkan Assistance

Appropriated $535 million for Balkan reconstruction, including $150 million for Kosovo. Use of any funds in the bill for Serbia (other than for Kosovo or Montenegro, or to promote democratization) was prohibited.

North Korea

Provided $35 million for the Korean Peninsula Energy Development Organization. The money would be available in two phases and would be subject to certain presidential certifications regarding North Korea's progress toward ending its nuclear and ballistic missile programs. The certification requirements could be waived in national security interests. *(1999 aid appropriations, p. 186)*

Silk Road

Incorporated legislation aimed at developing closer economic ties to former Soviet republics in Central Asia and the Caucasus. *(See Silk Road trade, p. 169.)*

Debt Relief

Appropriated $123 million to help some of the world's poorest nations restructure debts they owed the United States.

World Bank Program

Provided $35.8 million for the Global Environment Facility.

Iraqi Opposition

Appropriated $10 million to support efforts to bring about a political transition in Iraq, of which not less than $8 million was to go to Iraqi opposition groups for their political, economic, humanitarian, and other activities.

2001 Aid Appropriations

Congress in 2000 cleared a $14.9 billion fiscal 2001 foreign operations spending bill (HR 4811—PL 106-429).

Eager to avoid an election-year confrontation with President Clinton, congressional Republicans yielded to his demands on key issues, including providing debt relief for the world's poorest nations and lifting abortion restrictions on international family planning aid. The bill also increased funds for Russia and other former Soviet republics, for international efforts to combat HIV/AIDS, and for the Global Environment Facility, a multilateral program that provided grants to developing countries for environmental initiatives. Aid was provided to Serbia's new government, as long as officials there cooperated with an international war crimes tribunal and respected human rights.

In the most controversial spending item, Congress agreed to fund Clinton's $435 million request for third world debt relief and included language allowing, as it had the previous year, the International Monetary Fund to use money from a revaluation of its gold reserves for additional debt forgiveness. *(Debt relief and the IMF, box, p. 213)*

But the largest concession was on the family planning aid. House GOP leaders had wanted to extend abortion-related restrictions contained in the fiscal 2000 foreign aid bill (PL 106-113), but Clinton threatened to veto legislation that included any such restrictions. Conferees eventually backed down and approved increased funding. However, the final bill prohibited spending the money until Feb. 15, 2001, a month after Clinton would leave office. *(2000 aid appropriations, p. 210)*

SENATE ACTION

The Senate, by a 95–4 vote on June 22, 2000, ordered its version of the foreign aid spending bill (S 2522) engrossed and read for a third time. But it did not proceed to final passage. Instead, the Senate on July 18 incorporated it into the House-passed bill (HR 4811) and passed that bill by voice vote. The bill had been reported by the Senate Appropriations Committee (S Rept 106-291) on May 9.

The Senate version included $13.4 billion for fiscal 2001, plus about $1.3 billion in supplemental fiscal 2000 money. The supplemental funds included $934 million in emergency drug-fighting aid that was to flow to Colombia and other South American countries. The House had passed a separate supplemental appropriations bill in March that contained $1.7 billion in aid to Colombia and its neighboring countries. However, Senate Majority Leader Trent Lott, R-Miss., insisted that all fiscal 2000 emergency funds be incorporated into regular fiscal 2001 spending bills, despite pleas from House Speaker J. Dennis Hastert, R-Ill., and the Clinton administration to move quickly on the Colombia funds.

Conflicting views on the Colombia aid question surfaced during the foreign aid debate, but the money remained in the Senate bill after an attempt to slash the funding was soundly defeated. Ultimately, however, the Colombia antidrug funds, along with the rest of the fiscal 2000 supplemental appropriations, were attached to a military construction spending bill (HR 4425—PL 106-246) that cleared June 30. *(Colombia antidrug aid, p. 220)*

While claiming victory on the Colombia funds, the administration was still dissatisfied with several elements of the Senate version. The bill's $13.4 billion total for fiscal 2001 was about $1.7 billion less than Clinton requested.

Clinton's request for $435 million over two years for debt relief for the world's poorest countries was cut by the Senate to $75 million in fiscal 2001. His request for $210 million in supplemental spending for debt relief for fiscal 2000 also was not included in the supplemental measure (PL 106-246). Administration officials were concerned that Congress's unwillingness to provide debt relief would unravel a $27 billion agreement by Clinton and the leaders of other prosperous countries at a summit in Cologne, Germany, in June 1999. Clinton had pledged that the United States would contribute $600 million as part of the effort. Congress had reluctantly provided $123 million in debt relief in the fiscal 2000 foreign operations spending bill, which was incorporated in the omnibus spending bill (HR 3194—PL 106-113). *(2000 aid appropriations, p. 210)*

The administration also objected to the funding level for peacekeeping in the Balkans and various conditions the Senate bill imposed on aid to Kosovo and Russia.

HOUSE ACTION

The House passed its $13.3 billion version of the foreign operations appropriations bill (HR 4811) by a 239–185 vote on July 13. The House Appropriations Committee had reported HR 4811 (H Rept 106-720) on July 10.

Administration officials had said they would recommend the president veto the House committee version of the bill if sent to him because of the funding level and policy disputes.

But Democrats managed to win approval of several amendments on the House floor that they thought might put the White House in a better negotiating position.

Most significantly, in a drawn-out, dramatic **key vote of 216–211 (R 26–194; D 189–16; I 1–1)** on July 13, Democrats won adoption of an amendment by Maxine Waters, D-Calif., to increase the U.S. contribution to the multilateral fund that would forgive some of the debts that poor countries owed to international financial institutions. The amendment increased debt relief by $156 million, bringing total funding for the multilateral debt relief in fiscal 2001 up to Clinton's request of $225 million. *(2000 key votes, p. 915)*

The boost in debt relief funds was seen as a victory for the Congressional Black Caucus, which had ardently supported it. The caucus scored another victory, when the House approved, 267–156, a Barbara Lee, D-Calif., amendment to shift $42 million from other accounts to programs to combat HIV/AIDS, primarily in Africa. The House, by voice vote, also adopted an amendment by Brad Sherman, D-Calif., to shift $10 million into AIDS prevention and research.

Republicans succeeded in including some provisions opposed by most Democrats, including antiabortion language. By a vote of 206–221, the House defeated a James C. Greenwood, R-Pa., amendment that would have removed abortion-related restrictions on international family planning aid. As approved by the House, HR 4811 retained restrictions from the fiscal 2000 omnibus spending law. Clinton had reluctantly agreed to those provisions in 1999 as part of a broader compromise, but administration officials were urging a veto if they were continued in the fiscal 2001 bill.

Republicans took aim once again at the Clinton administration's effort to improve relations with North Korea. The House adopted, 298–125, an amendment by Doug Bereuter, R-Neb., to bar the federal government from indemnifying U.S. companies that supplied parts for nuclear power plants built in North Korea, but the provision was dropped in conference. The House had attached a similar amendment, offered by Christopher Cox, R-Calif., to its fiscal 2001 defense authorization bill (HR 4205) by a vote of 334–85 on May 18, but it, too, was dropped from the final bill. Three days earlier, on May 15, the House had passed, 374–6, a bill (HR 4251) blocking the transfer of U.S. nuclear material or technology to North Korea unless Congress enacted a joint resolution confirming that North Korea had complied with international nonproliferation accords. There was no further action on HR 4251. A similar provision mandating congressional approval for any nuclear transfer to North Korea had been dropped from a State Department authorization bill (HR 3194—PL 106-113) in 1999. *(2001 defense authorization, p. 290; State Department authorization, p. 217)*

CONFERENCE, FINAL ACTION

The House agreed to the conference report (H Rept 106-997) on Oct. 25 by a vote of 307–101. The Senate cleared HR

4811 later that day by a vote of 65–27. Clinton signed it into law Nov. 6.

After months of delay over debt relief, family planning, and aid to Russia, congressional negotiators gave the president most of what he had requested in October—three months after the Senate and House had passed their original bills. The final bill appropriated $14.9 billion, well above the Senate- and House-passed versions. At the insistence of Senate Republican appropriators, conferees agreed to include language raising the fiscal 2001 cap on overall discretionary spending established in the fiscal 1997 budget agreement (PL 105-33) from $541 billion to as much as $640 billion.

Each year since 1997, the major stumbling block to a deal on the foreign operations bill had been abortion-related restrictions on family planning aid. In 2000 conferees essentially gave abortion-rights advocates what they sought—but blocked the executive branch from spending the money until the month after Clinton left office. Supporters of the aid agreed to the stipulation because there was enough money in the pipeline for the groups to use until then. Opponents, on the other hand, were hoping that Texas Gov. George W. Bush would be elected president and would reinstate restrictions on use of the money.

Conferees agreed to fund Clinton's $435 million request for Third World debt relief and included language allowing the International Monetary Fund to revalue some of its gold reserves for additional debt forgiveness. Debt-relief supporters attributed the increased funding to a persistent campaign that included appeals from Pope John Paul II and Irish singer Bono of the rock group U2. Some religious groups considered debt forgiveness a part of the Year of Jubilee called for in the Bible every fifty years. Some Republicans, however, expressed doubt that the debt relief plan would work because it did not call for changes in the way governments in such countries were run. Conferees did agree to a two-year moratorium on some loans made by international banks from a fund—that the United States contributed to—for heavily indebted countries.

In an attempt to encourage Yugoslavia's new government, the bill provided as much as $100 million in aid to Serbia if officials there cooperated with an international war crimes tribunal and respected human rights.

The final bill included more aid to former Soviet states—$810 million—than the House and Senate versions, but it imposed some detailed conditions and instructions on how the money was to be spent.

Clinton scored significant gains in funding for the World Bank and other international financial institutions, notably unpopular in Congress and particularly in the House. The bill more than doubled what the House and Senate voted to spend on the Global Environment Facility.

MAJOR PROVISIONS

As signed into law, HR 4811 appropriated $14.9 billion for foreign aid and related programs in fiscal 2001. This included $741 million for export assistance, $9.06 billion for

---

2000 MIDDLE EAST SUMMIT

Middle East peace talks mediated by President Bill Clinton at Camp David, Md., in July 2000 failed to produce a peace agreement between Israel and the Palestinian Authority.

In the aftermath, Palestinian Authority President Yasser Arafat threatened to unilaterally declare a Palestinian state on Sept. 13 in the absence of a peace agreement. The Palestinians controlled a patchwork of land in the Gaza Strip and the West Bank. The authority had limited self-rule but depended on Israel for many of its services.

Sept. 13 passed with no declaration, but Arafat had not rescinded the threat. On Sept. 27 the House passed legislation (HR 5272) that would have punished the Palestinian Authority if it unilaterally declared an independent state. The measure, passed 385–27, would have directed the president to downgrade diplomatic relations with the Palestinian Authority in such an event, and would have barred U.S. funds from being spent to help the authority gain official recognition. Supporters of the bill said the bill was necessary to pressure the Palestinians to continue the peace negotiations as high-level talks restarted.

---

bilateral economic aid, $3.76 billion for military assistance, and $1.33 billion for multilateral aid.

Major provisions of the bill:

Middle East

Provided $2.8 billion in economic and military aid for Israel, $1.99 billion for Egypt, and $226 million for Jordan.

The bill set up a mechanism for Egypt to receive its military aid by Oct. 31, 2000 (or within thirty days of the bill's enactment), so it could be put in a special account where it would earn interest during the year. Israel for some time had been receiving its military and economic aid at the beginning of the fiscal year.

Former Soviet Union

Appropriated $810 million in aid to former Soviet states. Russia was to receive about $202 million, excluding nuclear safety programs. Russia could lose 60 percent of the aid if it sent weapons technology to Iran or blocked a war crimes investigation in Chechnya, and Russia could lose all of the aid if it discriminated against religious groups.

Family Planning

Appropriated $425 million for international family planning programs, but the funds could not be spent until Feb. 15, 2001.

The bill provided $25 million for the United Nations Population Fund (UNFPA), but none of the money would be made available if UNFPA funded abortions nor could it be used for a program in China. If the secretary of state reported that UNFPA had budgeted money for activities in China, an equal amount was to be withheld from the U.S. contribution after March 1 for the remainder of that fiscal year.

Balkan Assistance

Appropriated $100 million in aid but only if the president certified that the new Yugoslav government was cooperating in bringing accused war criminals before the International Criminal Tribunal at The Hague and was implementing policies respecting minority rights and the rule of law.

Debt Relief

Appropriated $435 million for Third World debt relief.

The bill also allowed the International Monetary Fund to use up to $800 million from a revaluation of its gold reserves for additional debt forgiveness.

North Korea

Provided $55 million for the Korean Peninsula Energy Development Organization. The money would be available only if the president certified progress toward ending North Korea's nuclear and ballistic missile programs. The certification requirements could be waived in national security interests.

World Bank Program

Provided $108 million for the Global Environment Facility.

Yemen

Provided $4 million to the Arabian Peninsula country of Yemen to spend on counterterrorism training and investigations. The bill required that the money be withheld until the FBI reported to Congress that Yemen's government was fully cooperating with the investigation of the Oct. 12, 2000, bombing of the U.S. Navy destroyer *Cole* in the Yemeni port of Aden.

HIV/AIDS, TB Assistance

Provided $315 million to combat HIV and AIDS infection and $60 million to fight tuberculosis.

Iraqi Opposition

Appropriated $25 million to support activities of Iraqi opposition groups, of which not less than $12 million was to be used for humanitarian assistance.

State Department Authorization

Congress in 1999 cleared a two-year State Department authorization as part of the fiscal 2000 omnibus appropriations bill (HR 3194—PL 106-113). The measure authorized $6 billion in fiscal 2000 and "such sums as may be necessary" for fiscal 2001.

The final bill permitted the repayment of U.S. debts to the United Nations, after a compromise was reached on abortion restrictions. The abortion issue had bedeviled foreign policy committees and the White House since 1997, when Rep. Christopher H. Smith, R-N.J., a leader of antiabortion forces, persuaded House Republican leaders to link the repayment of U.S. debts to the United Nations to the restoration of some abortion restrictions on international family planning aid. Presidents Ronald Reagan and George Bush had imposed such restrictions by executive order, but President Clinton lifted them in 1993 as one of his first acts in office. (*United Nations debt, pp. 192, 219*)

Clinton had vetoed a State Department authorization bill in 1998 because of a linkage between abortion restrictions and U.N. debt repayments. This "unacceptable linkage" was also one of the main reasons for his veto of the fiscal 2000 Commerce-Justice-State appropriations bill (HR 2670) in 1999. Restrictions on aid to international family planning groups ultimately were included in the fiscal 2000 foreign aid funding bill, which also was folded into PL 106-113. (*State Department authorization, p. 189; 2000 aid appropriations, p. 210*)

The final bill authorized $4.5 billion over five years to improve security at U.S. embassies in the wake of the 1998 terrorist bombings in Kenya and Tanzania that killed more than 250 people and injured more than 5,500. A State Department review committee formed after the bombings had recommended that the administration spend an average of $1.4 billion a year over the next decade to upgrade embassies. The panel, headed by retired Adm. William J. Crowe Jr., a former chairman of the Joint Chiefs of Staff, criticized Congress and the executive branch for failing to fully implement recommendations of a 1985 commission that had called for revamping hundreds of missions worldwide to minimize terrorist threats. Congress in 1986 had authorized a $2.4 billion embassy security program, but that was still $2 billion less than the Reagan administration's request. (*Congress and the Nation Vol. VII, p. 202*)

SENATE ACTION

The Senate passed its version of the State Department authorization (S 886) on June 22, 1999, by a vote of 97–2. On Aug. 3, it passed the House version (HR 2415) by voice vote, after substituting the text of S 886. The Senate Foreign Relations Committee had reported S 886 (S Rept 106-43) on April 27.

S 886 authorized $6.4 billion in fiscal 2000 and $6 billion in fiscal 2001.

The heart of the bill was a compromise between Senate Foreign Relations Committee Chairman Jesse Helms, R-N.C., ranking Democrat Joseph R. Biden Jr. of Delaware, and Secretary of State Madeleine K. Albright over repaying U.S. debts to the United Nations. Under the plan, the United States was to repay $819 million over three years and another $107 million would be forgiven. In order to receive the money, the United Nations would have to agree to institute a number of reforms. The most important would lead to a reduction in the U.S. share of the U.N. budget from 25 percent to 20 percent and a cut in the U.S. portion of the peacekeeping budget from 31 percent to 25 percent.

Since the provisions were originally drafted in 1997, U.S. relations with the United Nations had nose-dived. At the same time, U.N. Secretary General Kofi Annan had carried out his own reform effort. The results had been a growing resistance to U.S. demands, something Helms tacitly acknowledged by backing off from some earlier demands. Most important, the bill allowed the administration to waive the requirement that the debts could be paid off only if the U.S. share of the U.N. budget was reduced.

Aside from the U.N. issue, the other key initiative in the Senate bill was a provision calling for spending $3 billion over five years to enhance security at U.S. embassies overseas.

Several provisions were designed to bolster Israel's claim to Jerusalem as the permanent capital of Israel. In particular, the bill authorized $50 million a year in fiscal 2000 and 2001 to build a new U.S. embassy in Jerusalem. The embassy at the time was in Tel Aviv, in order not to prejudice negotiations over Jerusalem's final status.

HOUSE ACTION

The House passed its authorization bill (HR 2415) by voice vote July 21. The House International Relations Committee had reported an earlier version (HR 1211—H Rept 106-122) on April 29.

Anticipating battles on the highly charged issues of aid to North Korea and the United Nations Population Fund (UNFPA), House leaders had sought to minimize the potential for other conflict by bringing a new, otherwise noncontroversial bill, HR 2415, to the floor instead of HR 1211. Left out of the new bill were dozens of provisions setting specific authorizations for the bill's programs. That not only freed the legislation from several potential conflicts but also lowered its overall cost, from $7.6 billion to $2.4 billion. Of that, $1.4 billion was to upgrade security at U.S. missions overseas. International Relations Committee Chairman Benjamin A. Gilman, R-N.Y., already had scaled back the bill's cost by making it a one-year authorization rather than a two-year bill.

The House panel ignored a State Department plea to include funds in the bill to repay U.S. debts to the United Nations. Instead, ranking Democrat Sam Gejdenson of Connecticut said he and Gilman planned separate legislation for debt repayment. Although the U.N. funds normally would be in the authorization bill, the two committee leaders were eager to keep them separate, because Smith, the chairman of the International Operations and Human Rights Subcommittee, was likely to add antiabortion language to any bill that provided the U.N. funds.

In order to speed passage of the bill, Gejdenson and Smith agreed to thrash out the U.N. debt issue and aid to international family planning organizations in a future House-Senate conference instead of during the floor debate. But House members did adopt controversial amendments on aid to the U.N. family planning agency and to North Korea.

Smith offered an amendment to eliminate from the bill a $25 million U.S. contribution to UNFPA, unless the organization ended its programs in China. Smith argued that the funds indirectly supported coercive abortion and sterilization in China. But before Smith's amendment was considered, it was modified by a Tom Campbell, R-Calif., amendment that permitted the contribution to the population fund but would deduct from the $25 million total any money that the fund spent in China. The House on July 20 adopted Campbell's second-degree amendment by a 221–198 vote and then the revised Smith amendment by voice vote.

On July 21 the House adopted, 305–120, an amendment by Gilman and Edward J. Markey, D-Mass., giving Congress a greater say over Clinton's policy toward North Korea. The amendment would have prevented any U.S.-North Korea agreement on nuclear cooperation from taking effect until the president certified and Congress adopted a joint resolution agreeing that North Korea had complied with international nonproliferation accords. In particular, the amendment required North Korea to implement a 1994 bilateral agreement with the United States to freeze its nuclear weapons program and allow international inspections before receiving international aid. Markey said North Korea had consistently violated the 1994 accord as well as other nonproliferation agreements. He also noted that U.S. intelligence officials believed the North Korean regime had provided nuclear and missile technology to other countries and was preparing to test a missile capable of hitting the West Coast of the United States. *(1994 agreement, Congress and the Nation Vol. IX, pp. 221, 247; 1999 aid appropriations, p. 186)*

CONFERENCE, FINAL ACTION

A new version of the State Department authorization bill (HR 3427) was folded into the omnibus funding bill, HR 3194. (The earlier State Department authorization bill, HR 2415, however, lived to see another day. In 2000 the text of the long-dormant bill was deleted and a bankruptcy overhaul bill was inserted in its place.)

On Nov. 18 the House agreed to the conference report (H Rept 106-479) on HR 3194 by a vote of 296–135 and the Senate agreed to it, 74–24. It was signed into law Nov. 29.

The conference agreement took the Senate's lead and authorized State Department and related agencies' activities for fiscal years 2000 and 2001, as opposed to the House's recommendation for a one-year authorization. The measure authorized $4.5 billion to upgrade security at overseas missions.

Once a compromise on abortion restrictions was reached in the fiscal 2000 foreign operations spending bill (HR 3422), which was also included in the omnibus spending bill, conferees reached agreement on the repayment of U.S. debts to the United Nations. The Helms-Biden plan was incorporated into the bill.

House-Senate negotiators avoided another battle by dropping the provision dealing with the recognition of Jerusalem as Israel's capital. Also eliminated was the requirement that Congress adopt a joint resolution approving a presidential certification of North Korea's compliance with nuclear nonproliferation accords.

Conferees put off an effort to provide as much as $1.6 billion in aid to Colombia and neighboring nations in South America over the next three years to counter narcotics traffickers who were often protected by a growing guerrilla insurgency.

Negotiators also postponed a decision on what to do with billions of dollars in Iraqi assets that had been frozen in U.S. banks since the Persian Gulf War in 1991. The House bill had included a provision that would have given U.S. Gulf War veterans first claim on the frozen assets. The Lloyd Doggett, D-Texas, amendment had been adopted by a 427–0 vote on July 21. But Helms objected to the provision on the grounds that it would disadvantage U.S. companies, including tobacco companies, and U.S. government agencies, particularly the Commodity Credit Corporation, that were owed money by Iraq. As a possible compromise, Helms proposed giving the veterans legal standing in any settlement, which would give them an opportunity, but no guarantee, of gaining a share of the assets. But the clock was running out and consideration of the issue was postponed.

MAJOR PROVISIONS

As signed into law, major provisions of the State Department authorization in HR 3194:

Funding

Authorized $6 billion in fiscal 2000 and "such sums as may be necessary" for fiscal 2001; the second year's spending was expected to be 15 percent higher than the first year's.

U.N. Debt Repayment

Authorized payments totaling $819 million over three years to repay the U.S. debt to the United Nations: $100 million in fiscal 1998 funds, $475 million in fiscal 1999 funds, and $244 million in fiscal 2000 funds. Another $107 million owed by the United Nations to the United States for peacekeeping was authorized to be applied to the U.S. debt.

In return, the United States demanded reforms at the United Nations. The most important were to reduce the U.S. share of the regular U.N. budget and several specialized U.N. agencies from 25 percent to 20 percent and the U.S. share of the peacekeeping budget from 31 percent to 25 percent. The bill allowed the secretary of state to waive the 20 percent ceiling requirement.

International Peacekeeping

Authorized appropriations of $500 million in fiscal 2000 and such sums as may be necessary in fiscal 2001 for international peacekeeping activities under United Nations auspices.

Embassy Security

Authorized a total of $4.5 billion over five years—$900 million in each of fiscal years 2000–2004—to upgrade security at U.S. missions abroad.

U.N. Population Fund

Authorized $25 million for the U.N. Population Fund (UNFPA) in each of fiscal years 2000 and 2001 but set conditions. The money would not be available if UNFPA funded abortions. None of the U.S. money could be used for activities in China. An amount equal to what the secretary of state reported UNFPA was spending in China was to be withheld from the U.S. contribution after March 1 for the remainder of that fiscal year.

North Korea

Prohibited any agreement for nuclear cooperation between the United States and North Korea from taking effect, until the president determined and reported to Congress that North Korea was meeting certain conditions. These included complying with the 1994 agreement with the United States, allowing International Atomic Energy Agency inspections, and having no nuclear weapons program.

Refugee Assistance

Authorized $750 million for migration and refugee assistance in each of fiscal years 2000 and 2001.

U.N. Debt Repayment

Congress in 1999 agreed to a plan to repay nearly $1 billion in U.S. debt to the United Nations, as part of the fiscal 2000 omnibus spending bill (HR 3194—PL 106-113).

Under the plan, the United States would repay $819 million: $100 million in fiscal 1998 funds, $475 million in fiscal 1999 funds, and $244 million in fiscal 2000 funds. In addition, the United States would forgive $107 million that the United Nations owed the United States for peacekeeping.

In order to receive the money, however, the United Nations would have to agree to institute a number of reforms. The most important would lead to a reduction in the U.S. share of the U.N. budget and the budget for certain U.N. specialized agencies (Food and Agriculture Organization, International Labor Organization, and World Health Organization) from 25 percent to 20 percent and a cut in the U.S. portion of the peacekeeping budget from 31 percent to 25 percent. After notifying and consulting with the appropriate congressional committees, the secretary of state could waive the requirement for a 20 percent ceiling for the regular U.N. budget and the designated agencies by fiscal 2000.

The plan had been negotiated by Senate Foreign Relations Committee Chairman Jesse Helms, R-N.C., ranking Democrat Joseph R. Biden Jr. of Delaware, and Secretary of State Madeleine K. Albright. A similar Helms-Biden agreement had fallen to a presidential veto in 1998, after being combined in a State Department authorization bill with abortion restrictions on international family planning assistance. *(Background and 1997–1998 action, p. 192)*

In 1999 the Senate again included the Helms-Biden package in its State Department authorization bill (S 886), but key lawmakers in the House decided against including the plan in their version (HR 2415) in order to avoid likely efforts to link the issue once again with antiabortion language. They preferred instead to tackle the issue later in a House-Senate conference. President Clinton vetoed an appropriations bill for the departments of Commerce, Justice, and State (HR 2670) on Oct. 25, 1999, citing the bill's "unacceptable linkage" between funds for the U.N. repayment and antiabortion restrictions as one of the main reasons.

When it looked as if the State Department authorization bill would stall if a conference was convened, it, along with the Helms-Biden plan, was attached to the omnibus funding bill and enacted into law. Approval was made possible by an agreement to include abortion restrictions in the fiscal 2000 foreign operations funding bill, which also was part of PL 106-113. *(2000–2001 State Department authorization, p. 217; 2000 aid appropriations, p. 210)*

Colombia Antidrug Aid

Congress in 2000 approved $1.3 billion for a new initiative to stem the narcotics trade in Colombia and neighboring Andean countries. The supplemental aid was attached to the fiscal 2001 military construction spending bill (HR 4425—PL 106-246), the first of the year's appropriations bills to clear.

President Clinton and lawmakers from both parties, led by House Speaker J. Dennis Hastert, R-Ill., sought to shore up the government of Colombian President Andres Pastrana, which was under siege from left-wing guerrillas, right-wing paramilitaries, and drug lords. The $1.3 billion was approved after a long debate over the mix of military and economic aid and the appropriate level of assistance to Colombia's national police.

Some liberals wanted tighter human rights restrictions on aid, complaining that Colombia's military had cooperated with right-wing paramilitary groups. The final bill included some restrictions that could be waived by the president, which Clinton for the most part did in August 2000.

Other critics worried that the United States would be drawn into the conflict in Colombia.

BACKGROUND

Colombia had been under increasing pressure from guerrillas who were allegedly financing their operations from drug profits. In 1999 Colombian President Pastrana proposed a $7.5 billion "Plan Colombia" to combat the guerrillas and drug traffickers, including $1.5 billion in U.S. aid over three years.

Supporters in Congress warned of an impending disaster and urged quick administration action to avert the creation of a "narcostate" in South America. But administration officials delayed partly to have a bargaining chip in budget negotiations and partly because of disputes between the Pentagon, State Department, and other agencies over the nature of an aid package. Republican congressional leaders also were more interested in keeping their pledge not to tap the Social Security surplus than in appropriating the funds in 1999, saying there was enough money to tide over Colombia until 2000 when the aid could be included as part of a supplemental spending bill.

In his Feb. 7, 2000, budget message, Clinton requested $955 million as the first installment in a two-year package of $1.3 billion in economic and military aid to Colombia and other Andean nations for antidrug efforts. The money was requested as emergency supplemental funding so that it would be exempted from the strictures of the 1997 balanced-budget law (PL 105-33). Under the 1997 law, nonemergency spending was subject to budget caps, and expenditures that exceeded those caps had to be offset.

Clinton said that money appropriated for fiscal 2000 would be focused on enhancing drug interdiction and enforcement in Colombia's southern jungles, which by then were largely controlled by guerrillas. Meeting a key congressional demand, the plan also called for a significant portion of the funds to be dedicated to enhancing the mobility of Colombia's counternarcotics military and police officers, including the purchase of Black Hawk and Huey helicopters. In line with Pastrana's "Plan Colombia," the proposal also called for funds for economic development, protection of human rights, and judicial reforms.

LEGISLATIVE ACTION

The House on March 30, 2000, approved, 263–146, an emergency supplemental appropriations bill (HR 3908) that included $1.4 billion for counternarcotics assistance to Colombia and neighboring areas. (The bill also contained nearly $300 million for U.S. antidrug efforts.) HR 3908 had been reported by the House Appropriations Committee (H Rept 106-521) on March 14.

During the House floor debate, members of both parties expressed concerns about expanding U.S. involvement in the efforts to control narcotics exports from Colombia and warned that the United States could be entering a quagmire. But Speaker Hastert noted that the United States had helped curb drug production in Peru without getting into a protracted affair involving U.S. troops. He also argued that the police force in Colombia was a credible partner in the fight against drugs but did not have the resources to do the job.

The House defeated all attempts to cut the counternarcotics aid. On March 29, by a vote of 186–239, the House rejected a David R. Obey, D-Wis., amendment to cut $552 million from the antidrug allocation and allow for expedited consideration of the funding in July. Later that day the House rejected, 158–262, a Jim Ramstad, R-Minn., amendment that would have cut all the counternarcotics funding from the bill. Obey and other Democrats complained bitterly that Republicans had refused to allow Nancy Pelosi, D-Calif., to offer an amendment that would add funds for domestic drug treatment to the supplemental.

On the Senate side, Majority Leader Trent Lott, R-Miss., decided to quash the fiscal 2000 supplemental spending bill and instead add needed funds to various fiscal 2001 appropriations measures. Supplemental spending bills tended to become bloated, slow-moving targets for legislators looking to find homes for their pet projects. Lott argued that his piecemeal approach would be a cleaner, more fiscally responsible way to encourage prompt action on fiscal 2001 spending while limiting fiscal 2000 extras. But the appropriations process is rarely easy or predictable. And in the end the supplemental funding was pulled together and attached to the first funding bill to pass both chambers, the fiscal 2001 military construction appropriations bill (HR 4425).

In the meantime the Senate had taken up the Colombia aid issue primarily as part of the fiscal 2001 foreign operations appropriations bill (S 2522—S Rept 106-291) and to a lesser extent the fiscal 2001 military construction appropriations bill (S 2521—S Rept 106-290). Those bills, reported by the Senate Appropriations Committee May 9, together appropriated about $1.1 billion for Plan Colombia and related items. About $934 million of that total was in S 2521.

During debate on the foreign operations bill, Lott June 21 argued that the funds were needed to slow the flow of drugs to the United States that were "poisoning our children." Colombia was the predominant source of cocaine smuggled into the United States.

But Patrick J. Leahy of Vermont, the ranking Democrat on the Foreign Operations Appropriations Subcommittee, derided U.S. help to "Plan Colombia." Leahy said June 20: "Nobody can say what they expect this to cost, what we can expect to achieve, in what period of time, how intensifying a war that cannot be won will lead to peace, or what the risks are to hundreds of American military and civilian personnel in Colombia."

However, as in the House, proposals to cut back on the aid were defeated in the Senate. A Paul Wellstone, D-Minn., amendment that would have transferred to U.S. drug treatment programs $225 million slated for programs to train two additional antidrug battalions in Colombia's military and provide supporting equipment was tabled, or killed, 89–11, on June 21. Next a Slate Gorton, R-Wash., amendment to cut the aid to $200 million was defeated by a **key vote of 19–79 (R 13–41; D 6–38)**. *(2000 key votes, p. 915)*

As soon as the Senate finished voting on S 2522 on June 22, key aides said negotiators on HR 4425, the military construction bill already in conference, had settled on $1.3 billion in emergency funding to fight drugs in Colombia and neighboring countries. The bill also included conditions on the aid, which could be waived on national security grounds. The House adopted the conference report on HR 4425 (H Rept 106-710) by a vote of 306–110 on June 29 and the Senate cleared it by voice vote on June 30. President Clinton signed the bill July 13.

MAJOR PROVISIONS

As signed into law, HR 4425 appropriated $1.3 billion in emergency funding for antidrug programs in Colombia and neighboring countries in fiscal 2000 and 2001.

The bill placed a number of conditions on the aid but permitted the president to waive them if it was in the national security interest. Among the conditions, the secretary of state was to certify to the appropriate congressional committees that:

• The president of Colombia had directed that Colombian armed forces personnel alleged to have committed gross violations of human rights would be brought to justice in Colombia's civilian courts.

• The commander general of the Colombian armed forces was promptly suspending from duty any Colombian armed forces personnel alleged to have committed gross violations of human rights or to have aided or abetted paramilitary groups.

• The Colombian armed forces were cooperating fully with civilian authorities in investigating, prosecuting, and punishing in the civilian courts personnel alleged to have committed gross violations of human rights.

• The government of Colombia was vigorously prosecuting in the civilian courts the leaders and members of paramilitary groups and Colombian armed forces personnel who were aiding and abetting those groups.

• The government of Colombia had agreed to and was implementing a strategy to eliminate Colombia's total coca and opium poppy production by 2005.

• The Colombian armed forces were developing and deploying in their field units a Judge Advocate General Corps to investigate Colombian armed forces personnel for misconduct.

The legislation also made applicable to the Colombian aid program several existing provisions of law barring aid to any unit of a foreign country's security forces that had committed gross violations of human rights. Known as the "Leahy Amendments" for their chief sponsor, Senator Leahy, such provisions had been in force for several years and had last been extended in the fiscal 2000 foreign operations appropriations bill (PL 106-113) and the fiscal 2000 defense appropriations bill (PL 106-79).

HR 4425 placed a cap of 500 U.S. military personnel and 300 U.S. civilian contractors in Colombia supporting the antidrug plan, unless Congress passed a joint resolution approving a presidential request that the cap be lifted. The cap could be waived once if U.S. armed forces were involved in or were about to be involved in hostilities.

Russia Sanctions

Congress in 2000 cleared several measures aimed at punishing Russia for actions troubling to the United States, including the transfer of weapons technology to Iran.

HR 1883 (PL 106-178) authorized the president to impose economic sanctions against any country, company, or individual that knowingly transferred items, information, or sensitive technology that Iran could use to develop weapons of mass destruction. It also allowed the president to withhold subsidies to Russia for its share of the International Space Station, unless Russia showed a commitment to nonproliferation. A 1998 bill requiring sanctions unless they were waived on national security grounds had been vetoed. This time language was added clarifying that the sanctions were authorized but not required. *(1997–1998 action, p. 195)*

The fiscal 2001 foreign aid spending bill (HR 4811—PL 106-429) also included a provision cutting aid to Russia by 60 percent if it sent weapons technology to Iran, blocked a war crimes investigation in its war-torn, separatist region of Chechnya, or violated the treaty on conventional forces in Europe.

Other measures passed the House but did not come up in the Senate, including a bill (HR 4022) to tie any rescheduling or cancellation of Russia's debts to its halting the sale of anti-ship missiles to China, and another (HR 4118) to forbid the debt restructuring unless Russia closed an intelligence facility in Cuba.

BACKGROUND

The legislative push by Congress was sparked by concerns about Iran's growing capability, with the help of Russian scientists, to launch ballistic missiles that could reach Israel, the Arabian peninsula, and Europe. Although the Clinton administration contended that Moscow was making progress in controlling proliferation, Congress disagreed. In the words of Senate Majority Leader Trent Lott, R-Miss., members wanted to send "a clear message to Russia that they must do more."

The legislative effort had broad bipartisan support. Nevertheless, it also was seen as part of an attempt by Republicans to diminish Vice President Al Gore's foreign policy reputation as he went into the fall 2000 presidential campaign against Texas Gov. George W. Bush. Gore's foreign policy portfolio included co-chairing a binational commission on U.S.-Russian relations with a series of Russian prime ministers.

Republican lawmakers such as Senate Foreign Relations Committee Chairman Jesse Helms of North Carolina largely blamed the White House for a range of Russian behavior they considered inimical to U.S. interests—the war in Chechnya, the sale of arms to China, and loans to Yugoslav President Slobodan Milosevic. They said the White House had been too cozy with the Kremlin.

Helms in mid-2000 blocked Senate action for a month on thirteen ambassadorial nominees his committee already had approved, seeking to force the administration to take a tougher line toward Russian president Vladimir V. Putin's government. He lifted the holds in late July after administration assurances that its support for Russia's efforts to write off old Soviet-era debts would be tied to steps for a peaceful solution in Chechnya and a cutoff of Moscow's support for Milosevic. The debts to the United States totaled about $485 million, some of which dated back to the Lend-Lease payments of World War II.

House GOP leaders in September released a report critical of the Clinton administration's and particularly Gore's handling of U.S. policy toward Russia.

SANCTIONS BILL

HR 1883 was passed by a 419–0 vote of the House on Sept. 14, 1999. The bill had been reported by the House International Relations Committee (H Rept 106-315) earlier that day.

House action had been delayed at the behest of the administration and Israeli officials. Clinton administration officials contended that Russia was taking steps to check the spread of weapons and that the legislation might undercut Russia's recent reforms on technology transfers. Israeli officials also feared the bill might deter Russia from limiting technology transfers to Iran. In addition, NASA officials objected to the provision withholding subsidies for Russia's contribution to the space station. NASA in 1998 had proposed sending Russia $650 million for goods and services related to space station construction.

Before taking up the bill in September, lawmakers made several changes, including eliminating one of the reporting requirements and giving the president greater latitude in imposing sanctions. But the administration still opposed the bill and threatened to veto it.

However, Senate sponsors proposed a manager's amendment with modest changes that eased the administration's concerns. The added language clarified further that the bill would authorize, but not require, the president to impose the sanctions. The Senate then passed its amended version by a 98–0 vote on Feb. 24, 2000.

Senate passage of the bill came on the heels of a substantial reformist victory in Iran's parliamentary elections in February. Lott said the bill should strengthen the reformers while warning Iran's Islamic fundamentalists that the United States remained concerned about the country's quest for long-range missiles. Other lawmakers expressed hope that the election could lead to improved U.S.-Iranian relations. For two decades, the United States had maintained an almost total ban on trade and financial dealings with Iran, originally because of its 1979 seizure of the U.S. embassy in Tehran and later because of its support of terrorism.

The House accepted the Senate version by a 420–0 vote on March 1 and the president signed it March 14.

As enacted, the bill required the president every six months to inform Congress of any countries, organizations, companies, or individuals which, according to "credible information," had transferred to Iran technology related to missiles or other nuclear, chemical, or biological weapons. The president was authorized to impose penalties, such as economic sanctions or a cutoff of U.S. military aid, unless the foreign government already had punished those involved. If the president chose not to impose sanctions, he would have to explain why to Congress. The bill also withheld pending U.S. aid to the Russian Aviation and Space

Agency unless Russia made it national policy to eliminate nuclear proliferation and the space agency showed that it had not allowed anyone to transfer sensitive technology to Iran.

AID BILL

Both chambers attached tough conditions on aid to Russia as part of the fiscal 2001 foreign operations appropriations bill (HR 4811). *(2001 aid appropriations, p. 214)*

During consideration of its version (S 2522), the Senate adopted a Helms amendment by voice vote June 21, 2000, that precluded any debt forgiveness or rescheduling, trade financing, or loans from international financial institutions to Russia until the Kremlin stopped providing aid to the Milosevic government. The amendment also cut aid to Russia by an amount equal to that which the Kremlin had loaned to the Milosevic government. The president could waive the restrictions on the grounds of national interest.

In addition, a provision included in S 2522 by Mitch McConnell, R-Ky., chairman of the Foreign Operations Appropriations Subcommittee, made aid to Russia conditional on Kremlin cooperation with international efforts to investigate alleged human rights violations and to provide humanitarian help in Chechyna.

The House version (HR 4811) tied aid to Russia to its movement of troops out of areas flanking Chechnya, which the House said violated the 1990 Conventional Forces in Europe Treaty. That treaty was amended in 1997. *(1997 amendment, p. 274)*

Both the Senate and House bills continued an existing provision that made nearly half of government-to-government assistance to Russia conditional on an end to the Kremlin's cooperation with Iran's ballistic missile program.

The final bill (PL 106-429) stipulated that Russia could lose 60 percent of U.S. aid if it sent weapons technology to Iran, blocked a war crimes investigation in Chechyna, or violated the conventional forces treaty, and could lose all of the aid if it discriminated against religious groups.

OTHER LEGISLATION

In other action, the House International Relations Committee June 12 reported and the full House July 19, 2000, passed, 275–146, a bill (HR 4118—H Rept 106-668) to forbid debt restructuring unless Russia closed its intelligence facility at Lourdes, Cuba. The president could waive the requirement under certain conditions. Arguing against the legislation, administration officials said Russia needed the facilities to monitor U.S. compliance with arms control accords. They said questioning Russia's right to the site could undermine the Kremlin's willingness to permit the United States to conduct similar monitoring. House Intelligence Committee Chairman Porter J. Goss, R-Fla., attacked that logic, questioning why the facility was needed in light of claims by the administration, citing Gore in particular, that it had achieved a special relationship of trust with Russia.

The House International Relations Committee June 12 reported and the full House Oct. 3 passed by voice vote a bill (HR 4022—H Rept 106-667) to prevent the president from rescheduling Russia's debt unless Moscow stopped selling SSN-22 Moskit antiship missiles to China. The bill allowed the president to waive the restrictions on national security grounds. Dana Rohrabacher, R-Calif., who sponsored the bill, had said earlier that by the end of April, China was expected to purchase the first eight Moskit missiles, which traveled at supersonic speeds and could evade advanced countermeasures. The missiles were to be mounted on a destroyer that Russia had already sold to China. Rohrabacher contended that the missile had been developed for the sole purpose of destroying American warships.

Economic Sanctions

The 106th Congress and the White House took significant steps toward easing unilateral economic sanctions overseas. Complaints from business and agricultural groups that selective U.S. export sanctions were depriving them of overseas markets provided strong impetus for the actions.

In 1999, in the fiscal 2000 defense appropriations bill (HR 2561—PL 106-79), Congress gave President Clinton authority to waive sanctions imposed on India and Pakistan in 1998 after both nations tested nuclear weapons. He had been given temporary authority previously, but this time, under PL 106-79, there was no time limitation.

After a fiery debate in 2000, Congress cleared a fiscal 2001 agricultural appropriations bill (HR 4461—PL 106-387) that included a provision lifting food and medicine sanctions first imposed on Cuba in 1962. The language applied to Libya, North Korea, Iran, and Sudan as well. But as part of the tradeoff for the easing of humanitarian sanctions, public or private financing of Cuban agricultural purchases was barred and an existing ban on travel to Cuba was written into law.

INDIA, PAKISTAN

Clinton had imposed trade and credit sanctions on India and Pakistan after they exploded nuclear weapons in May 1998. His action was required by the Arms Control Export Act contained in the 1994 State Department authorization bill (PL 103-236).

But some lawmakers argued that sanctions hurt American farmers and businesses and did little to deter foreign nations from developing nuclear weapons. Twice in 1998 Congress gave the president authority to temporarily ease various sanctions. *(1998 action, p. 199)*

The House on June 15, 1999, passed by voice vote a bill (HR 973) to extend the president's authority to waive certain economic and military assistance sanctions against India and Pakistan for another year, until September 2000. A one-year waiver also was included in the fiscal 2000 State Department authorization bill (HR 2415) the House passed July 21. The

Senate included a five-year waiver in the fiscal 2000 defense spending bill (S 1122) it passed June 8. Both chambers agreed on giving the president a waiver with no time limit as part of HR 2561, the defense spending bill signed into law Oct. 25 (PL 106-79).

The president quickly waived a number of the sanctions on India but comparatively few of the sanctions on Pakistan. That country's military coup in October 1999 triggered a ban on foreign aid under provisions of the annual foreign operations appropriations bill. Congress in 2000 did agree to an exception for assistance for basic education programs in Pakistan as part of the fiscal 2001 aid spending bill (HR 4811—PL 106-429).

CUBA, OTHER NATIONS

Efforts to end sanctions on food and medicine finally proved successful late in the 106th Congress but only after an all-out battle over the U.S. trade embargo against Cuba.

Cuba Embargo

In an effort to topple Cuban leader Fidel Castro and end his communist regime, the United States had imposed a unilateral trade embargo in 1962. For decades the embargo proved ineffective because of assistance given to Cuba by its communist allies. However, with the fall of communism in the Soviet Union and eastern Europe in the early 1990s, Cuba lost its support system and its economy plummeted. Hoping to take advantage of the situation, the United States twice tightened its embargo, in 1992 (PL 102-484) and again in 1996 (PL 104-114). The 1996 law also wrote the embargo into law, which meant that the president no longer had the authority to lift or ease the embargo by executive order or regulation but instead would need congressional approval. (Congress and the Nation Vol. VIII, p. 295; Vol. IX, p. 237)

The president still had some maneuvering room, albeit limited. On Jan. 5, 1999, Clinton unveiled several small steps to increase contacts with Cuba. His decision to ease restrictions on travel, mail, and financial transfers, and to allow the sale of food and agricultural products to certain nongovernment groups won support from key lawmakers in both parties, although it prompted criticism from others who thought the measures went either too far or not far enough.

The president, however, stopped short of backing a call from eighteen senators, led by Armed Services Committee Chairman John W. Warner, R-Va., for an independent national commission to review U.S. policy toward Cuba. Clinton reportedly turned down the commission idea because of concern about criticism from Cuban-American groups and the political impact such a move would have on Vice President Al Gore, who had recently announced that he would run for president in 2000.

Clinton on April 28 issued an executive order easing sanctions on the sale of food and medicine to Iran, Libya, and Sudan but retained existing restrictions on sales to Cuba as well as North Korea and Iraq.

Unsuccessful Attempts

The near unanimous support on Capitol Hill for Clinton's April executive order was a good indicator of the growing support for the easing of economic sanctions, especially those on humanitarian goods.

The House by voice vote on June 15, 1999, passed a bill (HR 17) to give Congress authority to approve or disapprove agricultural trade sanctions. The bill had been reported by the Agriculture Committee May 20 (H Rept 106-154, Pt. I) and by the House International Relations Committee June 14 (Pt. II). The Senate did not act on HR 17.

The Senate, however, did take up the issue during debate on its fiscal 2000 agriculture appropriations bill (S 1233). On Aug. 4, 1999, senators adopted by voice vote an amendment by John Ashcroft, R-Mo., that would have lifted virtually all existing and future sanctions from exports of food and medicine, unless authorized by Congress in a joint resolution. Foreign Relations Committee Chairman Jesse Helms, R-N.C., who opposed any easing of the U.S. embargo on trade with Cuba, tried to ward off Ashcroft's proposal. He and Robert G. Torricelli, D-N.J., argued that the amendment would hurt U.S. efforts to punish nations such as Cuba and North Korea that allegedly supported terrorism. It also would have severely weakened PL 104-114, the 1996 law, which Helms cowrote. But Helms's motion to table (kill) the Ashcroft amendment had been rejected by a **key vote of 28–70 (R 17–36; D 10–34; I 1–0)** on Aug. 3. (1999 key votes, p. 899)

To highlight the Senate's action on S 1233, two key farm state Democrats—Senate Minority Leader Tom Daschle of South Dakota and Byron L. Dorgan of North Dakota—traveled to Havana to meet with Castro and other Cuban officials in August. Daschle was the highest-level U.S. official to visit Cuba in years.

The Senate-approved provision, however, provoked an uproar from Cuban-American lawmakers in the House and ultimately was dropped during the House-Senate conference on the final agricultural spending bill (HR 1906—PL 106-78).

Sanctions Eased

The issue reappeared during consideration of the fiscal 2001 agriculture appropriations bill (HR 4461—PL 106-387). The predictably heated debate over easing sanctions against Cuba came in the midst of a dispute over repatriating Cuban shipwreck victim Elián González and triggered rhetoric reminiscent of the cold war era. (Elián González controversy, box, p. 225)

As reported by the House Appropriations Committee May 16, 2000, HR 4461 (H Rept 106-619) contained an amendment offered by George Nethercutt, R-Wash., lifting medical and agricultural sanctions on a handful of nations, including Cuba. Floor action was delayed for more than a month as farm-state lawmakers and House GOP leaders argued over the provision. The leaders were intent on keeping the sanctions in place but could not muster enough votes to overcome a coalition of Democrats and farm-state Republi-

ELIÁN GONZÁLEZ CONTROVERSY

The story of a young Cuban boy found shipwrecked off the coast of Florida on Thanksgiving Day 1999 captivated the nation. But the heartwarming story soon gave rise to a debate over Elián González's fate that would play out on the nightly news, in the halls of Congress, on the streets of Miami's Little Havana, in federal agencies and the courts, and even in the 2000 presidential campaign.

Elián González was six at the time he was found floating in an inner tube in the ocean. His mother and some of the other passengers had drowned when their boat sank while they were attempting to flee Cuba and come to the United States. Following his rescue, Elián went to stay with relatives in Miami. But his father back in Cuba pressed for his return. The U.S. Immigration and Naturalization Service (INS) ruled Jan. 5, 2000, that Elián's father had the sole legal authority to make decisions for the boy and said Elián should be returned to Cuba to be with his father. President Clinton and Attorney General Janet Reno supported the decision.

The ruling, however, angered the Cuban-American community in Miami, as well as Cuban leader Fidel Castro's strongest foes on Capitol Hill. GOP leaders and Florida Republicans in Congress called for making Elián a citizen so he could remain in the United States. But there was great division within the GOP on the question. In the end, the proposal foundered largely because most lawmakers believed Elián belonged with his father. Subsequent proposals that Elián—his immediate family, too, according to the provisions of a Senate bill—be given permanent residency status in the United States also went nowhere.

The federal courts upheld the INS decision. When the Miami relatives failed to give up Elián, the INS on April 22 staged an armed raid to remove him and reunite him with his father, who had traveled to the United States. The move by the INS—which resulted in a sensational photograph showing a Border Patrol agent brandishing an automatic weapon in front of Elián—initially triggered outrage from Republicans, but the reaction quickly toned down with the promise of brief hearings into whether the agents used excessive force. The Justice Department defended the armed action, saying it had information indicating that guns might be in or around the Miami house. After the Supreme Court on June 28 refused to hear a final appeal, Elián and his father departed for Cuba.

Elián's fate had been decided, but the future of the Cuban-American community and its formidable political clout was not as certain. Cuban-Americans comprised a vocal minority that had long been accustomed to getting what it wanted from politicians eager to compete for the state's twenty-five electoral votes and the blessing of an influential Washington lobby. The community for decades had enjoyed widespread support for its passionate stance against communism and Castro's authoritarian regime. But public opinion on Elián's fate fell squarely against the community. And as the increasingly complex politics of the Elián case began spilling over into the heated battle over whether to ease the trade embargo against Cuba, some thought the Cuban-American community could lose more than Elián, as the American public absorbed television images of protesters pushing past police barricades toward the Little Havana home of Elián's relatives. *(Economic sanctions, p. 223)*

---

cans who favored the language on humanitarian grounds and because it would open new export markets. Supporters claimed those markets would be worth about $7 billion per year. The two sides reached a compromise on the provision and agreed to allow the language to be removed from the bill on a point of order and inserted later in the House-Senate conference report on the bill.

The compromise lifted food and medicine sanctions against Cuba, Libya, North Korea, Iran, and Sudan. It also made it more difficult for future presidents to impose embargoes on food and medicine without the consent of Congress. To gain the support of powerful Castro critics such as House Majority Whip Tom DeLay, R-Texas, the amendment also barred public and private U.S. financing of Cuban agricultural purchases and wrote into law restrictions on travel to Cuba that previously had been implemented by executive order.

The Senate version (S 2536—S Rept 106-288) also lifted humanitarian sanctions but without the same financing conditions or restrictions on travel to Cuba. The Senate Appro-

priations Committee reported S 2536 on May 10 and the full Senate passed HR 4461, 79–13, on July 20, after substituting the text of S 2536.

President Clinton, congressional Democrats, and some Republicans criticized the add-ons but in the end went along. The House adopted the conference report (H Rept 106-948), 340–75, on Oct. 11 and the Senate cleared the bill, 86–8, on Oct. 18. Clinton signed the agriculture spending bill into law Oct. 28 (PL 106-387).

In other action, the House on July 20 had attached several provisions easing restrictions on Cuba to its version of the fiscal 2001 Treasury-Postal Service appropriations bill (HR 4871). The controversial amendments were dropped from the final spending bill (HR 4577—PL 106-554), but at the time of their adoption Nethercutt said the votes would add momentum to his efforts on HR 4461. One amendment, offered by Mark Sanford, R-S.C., and adopted 232–186, would have blocked funding for enforcing restrictions on travel to Cuba. The other, offered by Jerry Moran, R-Kan., and adopted 301–116, would have blocked funding to enforce restrictions on the export of medicine and food to Cuba. The House, however, rejected by a 174–241 vote, an amendment by Charles B. Rangel, D-N.Y., that would have ended enforcement of the economic embargo of Cuba.

2000 Intelligence Authorization

Congress in 1999 boosted spending for intelligence activities in the fiscal 2000 intelligence authorization bill (HR 1555—PL 106-120). The legislation covered the intelligence-gathering activities of eleven agencies, including the Central Intelligence Agency.

Spending levels in the bill were classified, but sources said the measure authorized a 2.4 percent increase over President Clinton's request. The last year in which the administration made spending figures public for intelligence and security-related activities was 1998, when officials announced that the fiscal 1998 budget was $26.7 billion. *(1998 intelligence authorization, p. 200)*

The final bill contained a provision, added in conference, to impose economic and financial sanctions on international drug kingpins. That provision, along with disputes over funding for classified satellite programs, had held up conference action on HR 1555 for months.

Allegations that Chinese spies had stolen sensitive nuclear weapons data from the Department of Energy's nuclear weapons laboratories affected legislative action as well. Senate Republicans initially sought to attach to the intelligence bill provisions to tighten oversight of the department's nuclear weapons programs, but the matter was handled in the defense authorization bill (S 1059—PL 106-65) instead. *(Nuclear security, p. 302)*

LEGISLATIVE ACTION

The House passed HR 1555 by voice vote on May 13, 1999. The House Intelligence Committee had reported the bill (H Rept 106-130) on May 7.

House floor debate was dominated by talk of NATO's accidental bombing on May 7 of the Chinese embassy in Belgrade, in which three Chinese journalists were killed. The bombing prompted apologies from President Clinton and other administration officials who candidly acknowledged that the CIA and the National Imagery and Mapping Agency, using outdated maps, had incorrectly identified the building as belonging to the Yugoslav government.

Angry Chinese officials demanded an investigation and remained deeply suspicious that their building was deliberately targeted. The incident sparked several days of demonstrations in Beijing, leading some congressional Republicans to rebuke China for using the bombing mistake to stir up anti-U.S. sentiment.

House Intelligence Committee Chairman Porter J. Goss called the mistake a "predictable outcome of stretching our finite resources too thin." Although the amount authorized

by the bill was classified, Goss said that it was what the intelligence community could absorb that year. He cautioned that intelligence programs were in the midst of a rebuilding that likely would take several more years.

The House rejected, 68–343, a Bernard Sanders, I-Vt., amendment limiting the bill's authorization to the fiscal 1998 level and requiring a report from the Director of Central Intelligence on, among other things, the mapping failures that led to the Chinese embassy bombing.

To deal with the allegations that Chinese spies had stolen U.S. technology secrets, HR 1555 was said to provide more money for FBI counterintelligence, computer security, foreign nuclear weapons analysis, and foreign language training of intelligence officials.

The Senate passed HR 1555 by voice vote July 21 after substituting the text of its version (S 1009). The Senate Intelligence Committee had reported S 1009 (S Rept 106-48) on May 11 and Senate Armed Services had reported it (no written report) on June 8.

The Armed Services Committee had added to the bill several initiatives to deal with the alleged Chinese espionage. Further changes were made when the bill reached the floor. After months of wrangling, the Senate and the White House finally agreed on the creation of a nuclear security agency within the Energy Department. The plan, offered as an amendment by Jon Kyl, R-Ariz., was adopted by a 96–1 vote. *(Nuclear security agency plan, p. 302)*

FINAL ACTION

The House adopted the conference report on HR 1555 (H Rept 106-457) by voice vote on Nov. 9. The Senate approved it by voice vote on Nov. 19 and Clinton signed HR 1555 into law Dec. 3.

Senate action had been delayed because of concerns by Carl Levin, D-Mich., over the provision targeting drug kingpins that was added in conference. The provision required U.S. officials to release an annual list of individuals who played a significant role in international narcotics trafficking. Those on the list would have their U.S. assets frozen and would be barred from entering the United States. Any individuals or businesses in the United States having dealings with those on the list could face penalties of up to ten years in prison and $10 million in fines. Although the House had approved the anti-drug provision as a separate bill (HR 3164) on Nov. 2 by the overwhelming vote of 385–26, Senate conferees agreed to include the measure in the intelligence bill.

But Levin and a handful of other Democrats feared it would allow officials to take property without due process of law and would presume people to be guilty by association with alleged drug kingpins. Levin asked Treasury officials to provide him with a legal opinion on whether U.S. citizens could contest having their assets frozen. Treasury Department officials told Levin that although the provision would foreclose claims under the federal Administrative Procedure

Act of 1946, citizens would have other ways to mount a legal challenge. But Levin said such challenges would have to be made on constitutional grounds and that he planned to introduce legislation restoring the original due process language. House and Senate conferees included in HR 1555 a provision establishing a congressionally appointed commission to review the issue.

The final bill also authorized creation of a commission to conduct an independent review of the National Reconnaissance Office—the Defense Department agency that handled space-borne reconnaissance—to ensure that the intelligence community acquired the best possible satellite collection systems.

The Senate had used the intelligence bill as a vehicle for addressing security lapses at the Energy Department's nuclear weapons laboratories. But all of the Energy-related language was stripped out in conference and included in the fiscal 2000 defense authorization bill.

2001 Intelligence Authorization

Congress in 2000 cleared a revised fiscal 2001 intelligence authorization bill (HR 5630—PL 106-567), after President Clinton vetoed an earlier version because of a provision establishing criminal penalties for leaking classified information.

The authorization levels in HR 5630, which covered the Central Intelligence Agency and other intelligence-gathering agencies, were classified. However, published reports put the previous year's figure in the range of $30 billion and in fiscal 1998—the last time the administration made intelligence-related spending figures public—the total was $26.7 billion. *(1998 intelligence authorization, p. 200)*

The issue of information leaks had entangled the normally noncontroversial intelligence bill. The provision in the original bill (HR 4392) would have made almost all unauthorized and willful disclosures of classified information, whether or not they jeopardized national security, a felony punishable by up to three years in prison. Supporters said the language was narrowly drawn and had the backing of the Justice Department. Critics, including many Democrats and news organizations, said it would silence whistleblowers and undermine the First Amendment. In vetoing the bill, Clinton said the provision might "unnecessarily chill legitimate activities that are at the heart of a democracy."

LEGISLATIVE ACTION

The House passed HR 4392 by voice vote May 23, 2000. The House Intelligence Committee had reported the bill (H Rept 106-620) on May 16.

Lawmakers said the bill would raise spending for intelligence activities significantly—6.6 percent above the previous fiscal year's level. Much of the additional spending was to be used to modernize equipment at the National Security Agency (NSA), the super-secret arm of the intelligence community that used satellites and other equipment to intercept, process, and analyze electronic signals. The bill also called for NSA to restructure its operations to better handle the rapid technological changes in signals intelligence. The committee report said the agency "cannot remain split into multiple, separate collection 'stovepipes.' " Instead, it said, the agency "must be organized and operated as a single, cohesive enterprise."

Published reports said NSA had an annual budget of about $3.6 billion. The agency had been the subject of worldwide news media reports that accused it of spying on U.S. citizens and providing intelligence data to U.S. companies, among other things. Director of Central Intelligence George J. Tenet and NSA's director, Air Force Lt. Gen. Michael V. Hayden, strongly denied the allegations April 12 at a rare public hearing of the House Intelligence Committee.

During floor debate May 23, House members rejected, 175–225, an amendment by Tim Roemer, D-Ind., that would have required declassifying the costs of intelligence-gathering activities for the previous year.

The Senate passed HR 4392 by voice vote Oct. 2 after substituting the text of its own measure (S 2507). The Senate Intelligence Committee had reported S 2507 (S Rept 106-279) on May 4 and the Senate Armed Services Committee reported it (S Rept 106-325) on June 29.

Like the House bill, S 2507 placed special emphasis on NSA. An advisory group to the Senate Intelligence panel had concluded that the agency was in dire need of modernizing its technology infrastructure.

Senate floor action had been delayed, in part, by the bill's attempt to resolve a controversy over a provision in the fiscal 2000 intelligence authorization bill (PL 106-120) that imposed financial sanctions on international drug kingpins. Some senators, led by Carl Levin, D-Mich., worried that the provision would allow officials to take property without due process of law. Therefore, the 2001 bill included a provision stating that U.S. citizens would still have the power to challenge a decision blocking them from using property. Some House members, however, said they did not want to make any legislative changes until a commission set up in the previous year's law had completed its review of the matter. *(2000 intelligence authorization, p. 226)*

The Senate bill also included a controversial provision to criminalize leaks of classified information. Lawmakers had become increasingly concerned over the amount of classified information leaked to the news media. Under existing law, government employees faced felony charges if they released material that harmed national security. The Senate bill would have made almost all other unauthorized and willful disclosures of classified information a felony punishable by up to three years in prison.

FINAL ACTION, VETO

First the Senate and then the House adopted the conference report on HR 4392 (H Rept 106-969) by voice vote Oct. 12. The president vetoed the bill Nov. 4.

House approval had come after an unusually heated debate on whether the classified-information language would silence whistleblowers and undermine the First Amendment. The other disputed Senate provision, clarifying the drug kingpin law, had been dropped in conference.

The provision on classified information was backed by the CIA and the Justice Department, and the Clinton administration had not objected when it was first included in the intelligence bill. White House officials, however, became increasingly concerned about its implications after the legislation cleared Congress.

News organizations and some lawmakers mounted a last-minute lobbying campaign against the provision. They contended that it was so broad it would threaten the freedom of journalists to publish important information and it would conflict with existing laws protecting government whistleblowers.

Some critics suggested a compromise—a one-year delay in implementing the provision to give Congress time to assess its implications. Supporters of the provision said concerns over its effects on press freedom were unjustified. They said it should become law immediately to curtail what they described as a growing flood of government secrets leaked to the news media.

Clinton sided with the critics and vetoed the bill. In his veto message, Clinton criticized the provision as "badly flawed" and "overbroad." He also noted that it had not been discussed at public hearings before being included in the Senate version of the bill.

The president's veto led Senate Intelligence Committee Chairman Richard C. Shelby, R-Ala., to angrily accuse opponents of the provision of mischaracterizing what it would do and overstating the harm it would cause.

REVISED BILL

The House stripped out the disputed provision and passed an otherwise identical bill, HR 5630, by voice vote Nov. 13. The Senate passed an amended version of HR 5630 by voice vote Dec. 6. The House agreed to the Senate amendment and cleared the bill by voice vote Dec. 11. The president signed it into law Dec. 27.

In accepting the Senate version, the House agreed to drop a provision that would have allowed the National Reconnaissance Office (NRO) to negotiate and manage its own contracts for launching spy satellites without help from the Air Force. The NRO had lost several satellites and the House Intelligence Committee contended that many of its problems could be improved by streamlining the contracting process and eliminating bureaucratic turf battles.

Although the House provision had been agreed to in the conference on the earlier bill, the Senate adopted a Wayne Allard, R-Colo., amendment to the second version striking the satellite language. Allard aides said the senator viewed the provision as a dramatic shift from existing practice and

wanted more time to study the idea. That sent the measure back to the House, where angry Intelligence Committee Republicans initially refused to let the bill clear by unanimous consent. They reluctantly relented, clearing the bill.

A bipartisan study commission, set up by the fiscal 2000 intelligence authorization (PL 106-120), had concluded in a report released in November that bureaucratic changes were needed at the NRO. The commission recommended that an Office of Space Reconnaissance be established as a semi-autonomous agency within the NRO.

2001–2002 Aid Authorization

A Senate attempt in 2000 to resurrect the long-dormant foreign aid authorization bill failed, after a bill (S 2382) stalled in committee and never made it to the floor. However, several components of S 2382 were enacted separately, including bills authorizing foreign military and nonproliferation assistance (HR 4919—PL 106-280), programs to combat AIDS (HR 3519—PL 106-264), and assistance to small businesses (HR 1143—PL 106-309).

Because of declining congressional support for foreign aid and bitter disagreements over policy, Congress had not fully authorized the aid program since 1985 (PL 99-83). The last sustained attempt was in 1993, when the House passed a measure that the Senate failed to consider. A House committee bill in 1997 was swallowed by a State Department authorization measure drafted by House leaders. *(1993 action, Congress and the Nation Vol. IX, p. 202; 1997 action, p. 183)*

As a result, members of the House and Senate foreign affairs committees had lost much of their influence to appropriators who fashioned the annual foreign operations spending bills. In 2000, in an effort to reclaim territory, Senate Foreign Relations Committee Chairman Jesse Helms, R-N.C., and ranking Democrat Joseph R. Biden Jr. of Delaware introduced S 2382 to authorize the bulk of foreign aid spending while avoiding such politically vulnerable programs as basic development assistance and aid to Russia.

The Senate Foreign Relations Committee reported S 2382 (S Rept 106-257) on April 7, 2000. But Senate Banking Committee Chairman Phil Gramm, R-Texas, asserted his prerogative to have his committee examine the foreign aid bill before it went to the Senate floor. Gramm, a critic of the International Monetary Fund (IMF), then insisted that the administration agree to major changes in the way the IMF did business before he would allow the authorization to go forward. "No reform, no bill," Gramm said. The bill would have authorized the IMF to provide debt relief to some of the world's poorest nations by profiting from transactions involving the revaluation of some of its gold reserves. *(Debt relief and the IMF, box, p. 213)*

As a compromise, Helms offered to introduce jointly with Gramm an amendment on the Senate floor calling for broader changes at the international financial institutions, but to no avail. Some lawmakers said that Gramm was holding up the debt relief legislation to force Helms to side with him in a dispute over a proposed reauthorization of the Export Administration Act (S 1712), although his committee denied the charge. *(Export controls, p. 166)*

Frustrated by Gramm's decision to hold up S 2382, Helms decided in late June to split the measure into four bills and try to advance them separately to the Senate floor. Helms's action was endorsed by the rest of his committee.

The new bills were to provide debt relief for poor countries; authorize more money to combat HIV/AIDS, tuberculosis, and other diseases; authorize an increase in U.S. military assistance overseas; and authorize a program of small loans to budding entrepreneurs in developing countries. The first of these—debt relief—was included in the fiscal 2001 foreign operations appropriations bill (HR 4811—PL 106-429). The others were enacted as separate authorization bills. *(2001 aid appropriations, p. 214; HIV/AIDS assistance, p. 230; 2001–2002 military aid, this page; "Microenterprise" aid, p. 230)*

Another section that would have promoted democracy in Serbia was passed by the House (HR 1064) but stalled in the Senate, although that chamber had passed similar legislation (S 720) the previous year. *(Kosovo policy, p. 204)*

Military Aid Authorization

Congress in 2000 cleared legislation (HR 4919—PL 106-280) authorizing $3.8 billion in fiscal 2001 and $3.9 billion in fiscal 2002 for foreign military aid and military training, antiterrorism, nonproliferation, and export control assistance.

Congress had not fully authorized these programs since 1985, the last time it passed a free-standing foreign aid bill (PL 99-83). Instead, the programs had been funded through the annual appropriations bills. *(2001–2002 aid authorization, p. 228)*

HR 4919 took steps to make it easier to export defense-related technology to friendly countries, as long as certain conditions were met that would guard against defense items being re-exported to unfriendly nations. In May 2000 the Clinton administration had threatened to end Canada's sixty-year exemption from military export licensing after U.S. equipment sold to Canada was found in Iran and China. Canada said the hardware was outdated. The United States and Canada signed an agreement in June to restore about 80 percent of the exemption after Canada agreed to change its export control laws. HR 4919 would apply to other close U.S. allies, such as Great Britain and Australia.

To make it easier for U.S. companies to launch satellites from countries other than China, HR 4919 shortened the review period for licenses to launch satellites from several former Soviet republics.

The bill also met a key goal of Senate Foreign Relations Committee Chairman Jesse Helms, R-N.C., by increasing military aid and training for countries outside the Middle East. At the time, Israel, Egypt, and Jordan were receiving 98 percent of U.S. military assistance, according to committee reports on HR 4919.

LEGISLATIVE ACTION

The House passed HR 4919 by voice vote on July 24, 2000. The Senate passed HR 4919 by voice vote on Sept. 7, after substituting the text of its own bill (S 2901). The Senate Foreign Relations Committee had reported S 2901 (S Rept 106-351) on July 20.

The House adopted the conference report (H Rept 106-868) by a vote of 396–17 on Sept. 21 and the Senate cleared it by voice vote the next day. The president signed HR 4919 on Oct. 6.

MAJOR PROVISIONS

As signed into law, HR 4919 authorized $3.55 billion in fiscal 2001 and $3.63 billion in fiscal 2002 for foreign military and related assistance; $55 million in fiscal 2001 and $65 million in fiscal 2002 for international military education and training; $129 million in fiscal 2001 and $142 million for fiscal 2002 in nonproliferation and export control assistance; and $72 million in fiscal 2001 and $73 million in fiscal 2002 for antiterrorism assistance.

Major provisions of the bill:

Military Exports

Allowed close U.S. allies, such as Britain and Australia, to largely bypass U.S. export law's cumbersome licensing process for the purchase of defense items, provided those nations signed binding agreements with the United States to adopt export controls at least comparable to those of the United States.

Satellite Launches

Shortened from thirty to fifteen days the congressional review period for licenses to export satellites for launching in Russia, Ukraine, and Kazakhstan.

Middle East

Authorized about $2 billion for Israel and $1.3 billion for Egypt for military aid in each of fiscal 2001 and 2002. Both countries were to receive their aid near the start of the fiscal year in order to benefit from the interest earnings. Israel was allowed to continue to spend about one-quarter of its military aid on Israeli-made weapons, while other aid recipients had to buy U.S.-made products.

Other Recipients

Provided $99 million more in fiscal 2002 for countries other than Israel, Egypt, and Jordan.

The measure specified $35.4 million in fiscal 2001 and $42 million in fiscal 2002 for military aid and training programs for new NATO members Poland, Hungary, and the Czech Republic. It also set aside significant military aid and training funds for NATO aspirants such as Romania, Bulgaria, and Estonia.

Antiterrorism and Nonproliferation

Authorized for the first time a number of counterproliferation programs, including antiterrorist efforts and programs to prevent the spread of advanced weapons and technology from the former Soviet Union.

Participants in Training Programs

Authorized tracking the performance of military training program graduates, including any human rights abuses or criminal activity, in order to assess the effectiveness of the programs for foreign military personnel—such as the Army's School of the Americas.

HIV/AIDS Assistance

Congress in 2000 cleared legislation (HR 3519—PL 106-264) authorizing assistance to bolster the global fight against AIDS.

As enacted, HR 3519 authorized $300 million a year in fiscal 2001 and 2002 in bilateral aid for ongoing HIV/AIDS programs worldwide. Of the amount, 65 percent would be specifically authorized for nongovernmental organizations, including religious groups. Also, 20 percent of the U.S. bilateral funding was to be set aside for helping orphans in Africa, including the growing number of AIDS orphans.

In addition, the bill required the Treasury secretary to negotiate with the World Bank for an international AIDS trust fund that the bank would administer through its International Bank for Reconstruction and Development. Money from the fund would be used for education, prevention, and treatment programs to combat the spread of HIV and AIDS. The bill authorized $150 million a year for fiscal 2001 and 2002 for the trust fund.

HR 3519 also authorized a total of $120 million for fiscal 2001 and 2002 for tuberculosis prevention and treatment.

The final version largely incorporated legislation (S 2845—S Rept 106-336) introduced by Senate Foreign Relations Committee Chairman Jesse Helms, R-N.C., and reported by his committee July 11, 2000. Helms called the bill one of the most important pieces of international humanitarian legislation that Congress had passed in years. It had originally been part of a broader foreign aid authorization bill (S 2382) that had stalled in the Senate Banking Committee. *(2001–2002 aid authorization, p. 228)*

The original House bill would have authorized $100 million a year for fiscal 2001 to 2005 for the trust fund. HR 3519 was reported by the House Banking and Financial Services Committee (H Rept 106-548) March 28 and passed by voice vote of the full House May 15. The Senate passed

the bill by voice vote July 26, after substituting its version. The House agreed to the amended Senate version July 27, clearing the bill by voice vote. President Clinton signed it into law Aug. 19.

"Microenterprise" Aid

Congress in 2000 cleared legislation (HR 1143—PL 106-309) authorizing $155 million a year in fiscal 2001 and 2002 for small loans for "microenterprises"—businesses with ten or fewer employees—in developing countries. Such loans, usually only several hundred dollars apiece, were designed to help poor people start their own businesses.

HR 1143 had been reported by the House International Relations Committee (H Rept 106-82) on April 12, 1999, and passed by voice vote of the full House April 13. The Senate Foreign Relations Committee reported its version (S 2844—S Rept 106-335) on July 11, 2000. The Senate passed an amended version of HR 1143 by voice vote on Oct. 3. The House agreed by voice vote Oct. 5, clearing the bill for the president, who signed it Oct. 17.

Peace Corps

Congress in 1999 cleared a four-year reauthorization (HR 669—PL 106-30) of the Peace Corps that would allow the thirty-eight-year-old agency to expand to 10,000 volunteers by 2003 if Congress appropriated the money.

The measure authorized $270 million for the Peace Corps in fiscal 2000—President Clinton's budget request and a 12 percent increase over the previous year. Congress, however, cut the authorization by $25 million in its fiscal 2000 omnibus appropriations bill (HR 3194—PL 106-113). HR 669 also authorized $298 million for fiscal 2001, $327 million for fiscal 2002, and $365 million for fiscal 2003.

The goal of once again fielding 10,000 Peace Corps volunteers—who were sent overseas for two years to work on educational, agricultural, health, environmental, urban planning, or small business development projects—was first voiced by President Ronald Reagan and enacted into law (PL 99-83) in 1985. The goal was later endorsed by Clinton. Despite broad bipartisan support on Capitol Hill, the agency had not been able to afford that many volunteers since the 1960s. The agency, founded in 1961 during the early days of John F. Kennedy's presidency, peaked at 15,556 volunteers in 1966, then plummeted through the 1970s, finally bottoming out at 4,219 in 1987. It had about 6,700 volunteers in 1999.

HR 669 was reported by the House International Relations Committee (H Rept 106-18) on Feb. 16, 1999, and passed by a 326–90 vote of the House on March 3. The Senate Foreign Relations Committee reported the bill (S Rept 106-46) on May 11 and the Senate cleared it by voice vote May 12. It was signed into law May 21.

Armenia Resolution

At President Clinton's request, the House canceled a floor vote set for Oct. 19, 2000, on a nonbinding resolution (H Res 596) that called on the president to characterize as genocide a mass killing of Armenians nearly a century earlier. The administration viewed the resolution as a threat to U.S. relations with Turkey.

H Res 596, reported Oct. 4 by the House International Relations Committee (H Rept 106-993), stated that the Ottoman Empire committed genocide against ethnic Armenians from 1915 to 1923, resulting in the deaths of more than 1.5 million people. Turkey, which rose from the ashes of the Ottoman Empire in 1923, strenuously rejected that characterization, insisting that the Armenians died as a consequence of broader fighting in World War I. A committee amendment clarifying that the Ottomans, not modern Turkey, were at fault failed to defuse the controversy.

In a letter to Speaker J. Dennis Hastert, R-Ill., Clinton warned that any action could affect national security. A vote on the resolution "could have far-reaching negative consequences for the United States," Clinton said. The president pointed to continuing tensions in the Middle East and said the resolution "could undermine efforts to encourage improved relations between Armenia and Turkey."

Similar measures had been blocked for the past twenty years, but Hastert had helped push H Res 596 forward in 2000. Democrats claimed that it was because he wanted to help the reelection campaign of embattled GOP Rep. James E. Rogan, whose southern California district was home to a large population of Armenian-Americans. (Rogan was defeated in November 2000.)

Some members questioned why the Armenians should be singled out for recognition, and not the victims of more recent slaughters in Cambodia and Rwanda.

International Adoptions

The Senate approved the ratification of an international treaty on adoptions after Congress reached agreement on legislation (HR 2909—PL 106-279) to implement the pact in the United States.

The Hague Convention on Protection of Children and Cooperation in Respect of Intercountry Adoption (Treaty Doc 105-51) aimed to ensure that international adoptions took place in the best interests of the child, that countries cooperated to prevent child abductions and trafficking, and that adoptions adhered to basic standards.

BACKGROUND

Families in western Europe, North America, Israel, and Australia had adopted 20,000 children from developing countries and eastern Europe since the early 1980s. Americans were said to adopt four out of five children placed through international adoption.

But in some cases the adoptions had produced a backlash, including accusations of exorbitant fees, kidnapping, baby smuggling, and a lack of information about the children's medical and psychological conditions. Supporters of the international adoption pact said this had led a number of countries, including Russia, Romania, and Guatemala, to suspend overseas adoptions until safeguards could be put in place.

The treaty, signed by the United States in 1994, had been submitted to Congress on June 11, 1998.

LEGISLATIVE ACTION

The Senate Foreign Relations Committee reported its version of the implementing legislation (S 682—S Rept 106-276) on April 27, 2000. The House International Relations Committee reported HR 2909 (H Rept 106-691) on June 22 and the full House passed the bill by voice vote July 18. The Senate passed an amended version of HR 2909 by voice vote July 27. The House further amended the bill and passed it by voice vote Sept. 18. The Senate cleared HR 2909 by voice vote Sept. 20 and President Clinton signed it Oct. 6.

The Senate also approved the adoption pact by voice vote Sept. 20. The Senate Foreign Relations Committee had reported the treaty (S Exec. Rept 106-14) on April 27.

Senate Foreign Relations Committee Chairman Jesse Helms, R-N.C., one of the key movers in winning approval of the treaty, had held up the implementing legislation in 1999 to ensure that the State Department would be given primary jurisdiction over the international adoption program. He argued that the State Department was better placed to monitor adoption agencies overseas. The House International Relations Committee had wanted the Department of Health and Human Services to have the main responsibility but gave in to Helms and cosponsor Mary L. Landrieu, D-La.

The bill was further delayed by social conservatives in the House, led by Christopher H. Smith, R-N.J., who feared that the treaty and implementing legislation were not strict enough in setting rules on who could adopt and which agencies could be involved in the process. In particular, they worried that the bill could undermine state and foreign laws governing the potential pool of adoptive parents, such as laws that prohibited or restricted adoptions by gay adults. Smith and others eventually agreed to compromise language allowing foreign countries to review "home studies" that screened potential adoptive parents.

## CHAPTER 5

Defense Policy

Introduction	235
1997–1998 Chronology	239
1999–2000 Chronology	276

Defense Policy

President Clinton's defense policy never lacked for critics on Capitol Hill. Conservatives found his defense budgets too stingy, his overseas missions too costly, his antimissile defense proposal too limited. Whatever the policy, more often than not they would find fault with it.

But this was nothing new. Indeed, it had been that way from the outset. Clinton's youthful maneuvering to avoid military service in the Vietnam War had put defense-minded members on high alert before he ever set foot in the White House. His unsuccessful attempt early in his presidency to allow gays to openly serve in the armed forces only hardened their early suspicions. His paring of defense budgets while deploying U.S. forces on humanitarian and peacekeeping missions around the globe heightened the chorus of criticism during his first administration. But, in the end, Clinton—and his defense policies—for the most part had prevailed.

The situation was much the same in Clinton's second administration. If anything, the divide with his critics widened. The spectacle of key Republicans questioning whether their commander-in-chief's decision to bomb Iraq on the eve of scheduled House impeachment proceedings was politically motivated starkly illustrated the depth of animosity and distrust conservatives harbored toward Clinton.

The president's selection of a Republican, former Sen. William S. Cohen of Maine, to lead the Defense Department in his second term did little to allay conservatives' concerns, even though Cohen himself had at times been a vocal critic of Clinton's policies.

Defense-minded members of Congress kept up a barrage of criticism of Clinton's defense budgets. They managed to make incremental increases and finally, with the help of the Joint Chiefs of Staff, won a promise from the White House of larger increases in the years ahead. But, thanks to the budget caps that Congress and the White House had agreed to in 1997, Clinton's budgets stayed largely intact.

The commitment of U.S. airpower to halt ethnic violence in the Serbian province of Kosovo and of U.S. ground troops to participate in a peacekeeping force there set off another round in the debate over the proper use of U.S. military power and whether overseas missions were taking too great a toll on military readiness. But, when the debate was over, the mission went forward.

Few issues were closer to the hearts of conservatives than nationwide antimissile defense. For years—decades—they had been pushing for a system that would protect the United States from enemy missiles. Although the enemy had changed over time, conservatives' zeal had not. The backing for such a system widened and the pressure on the Clinton White House mounted amid reports of missile advances by radical regimes. Congress insisted that Clinton commit to deploying a system once it was feasible. The president agreed, but the final go-ahead would still be the president's call to make.

BUDGETING FOR DEFENSE

The post–cold war drop in defense spending had begun in the last two years of a Republican administration, that of George Bush, and continued during much of the Clinton presidency. The U.S. defense budget, which was at least 5 percent of the gross national product during most of the cold war, had declined to about 3 percent by 2000.

Defense hawks of both parties contended that Clinton had undermined military readiness with defense budgets that were too small and a military workload that was too ambitious. But his supporters asserted that the U.S. defense budget far outstripped that of any other nation and that the

REFERENCES

Discussion of defense policy for the years 1945–1964 may be found in *Congress and the Nation Vol. I*, pp. 237–334; for the years 1965–1968, *Congress and the Nation Vol. II*, pp. 827–890; for the years 1969–1972, *Congress and the Nation Vol. III*, pp. 191–252; for the years 1973–1976, *Congress and the Nation Vol. IV*, pp. 153–197; for the years 1977–1980, *Congress and the Nation Vol. V*, pp. 125–176; for the years 1981–1984, *Congress and the Nation Vol. VI*, pp. 201–257; for the years 1985–1988, *Congress and the Nation Vol. VII*, pp. 273–340; for the years 1989–1992, *Congress and the Nation Vol. VIII*, pp. 335–412; for the years 1993–1996, *Congress and the Nation Vol. IX*, pp. 253–323.

Outlays for National Defense

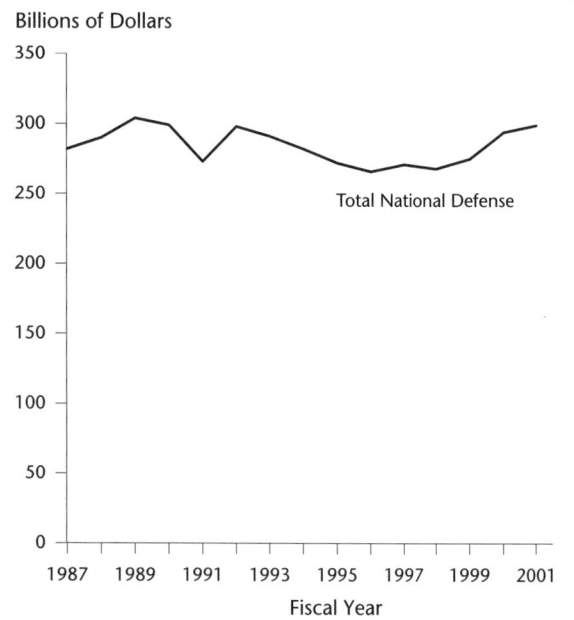

Billions of Dollars

Total National Defense

Fiscal Year

NOTE: Data for 2001 are estimated.

SOURCE: Office of Management and Budget, *Historical Tables, Budget of the United States Government: Fiscal Year 2002* (Washington, D.C.: U.S. Government Printing Office, 2001), Table 3.2.

military could meet its goal of being capable of fighting two major regional wars at the same time.

Efforts to increase military spending were stymied, in large part, by assurances of the Joint Chiefs that they could live within Clinton's budgets, despite the wish lists of "unfunded priorities" they had been sending Congress every year since the Republicans took control in 1995. The issue seemed to be moot after the 1997 balanced-budget agreement set caps on spending. An increase in defense spending would have required a decrease in domestic spending—a politically unacceptable alternative for both federal branches.

An ever ingenious Congress, however, did find ways to make modest increases totaling, on average, about $6 billion in each of the five years after the Republican takeover. The gimmick of choice was "emergency spending," which was exempt from the budget caps. Funds that at one time went for true emergencies, such as cleanup efforts after a natural disaster, were now being used for ongoing overseas deployments, a military pay raise, and routine operating expenses. Even Clinton found the emergency-spending route a convenient way to replenish accounts depleted by overseas deployments.

But the clamor for still greater increases continued, and, in time, the military leaders joined in. In the fall of 1998, the Joint Chiefs of Staff went to Capitol Hill and launched a public campaign to beef up future Pentagon budgets, warning that the quality of the nation's armed forces had begun to decline. Without a clear political commitment, in the form of stepped-up defense spending, several service chiefs said

the military could deteriorate within five years into the ineffectual "hollow force" of the late 1970s.

Their message was heard in the White House. Clinton agreed to "the first, sustained, long-term increase in defense spending in a decade"—a series of annual increases in projected Pentagon purchasing power that would total $110 billion through fiscal 2005.

The Joint Chiefs and defense experts in both parties called for even greater increases than Clinton proposed. But the budget caps were still in place and any increase in defense spending would have to be offset in the domestic column.

Even by 2000 when the budget surplus was ballooning, proposals for broader increases faced all but insurmountable obstacles. Clinton and GOP leaders had taken off the table tens of billions of dollars of the projected Social Security surplus. Clinton first used this pledge to shoot down Republican hopes of parlaying the projected surplus into a large tax cut. With their priority thus stymied, Republicans used the same promise on Social Security to sharply reduce the amount Clinton could use to fund new initiatives. Clinton, meanwhile, submitted a request that was several billion dollars larger than he had projected a year earlier. This, in turn, reduced the pot from which any congressional defense increase would have come.

The decisive factor in the political equation driving the defense budget, however, was that a significant group of congressional Republicans placed a higher priority on holding down federal spending and cutting taxes than on increasing funds for defense. Although these deficit hawks probably were outnumbered by defense hawks, they could still join with the Democrats to torpedo any budget that subordinated their priorities to defense—particularly in the House, with its very narrow GOP majority.

Congress rejected out of hand the administration's proposal to close more military bases to free up more money for procurement priorities. Most members found the prospect of closing bases in their home states and districts politically distasteful. Moreover, many Republicans were convinced that Clinton had improperly manipulated the last round of base closings, in 1995, to save jobs in vote-rich Texas and California.

BOLSTERING MORALE

When the Joint Chiefs made their case for greater defense spending, they cited pay and pensions as their most urgent problems. They hoped that changes in those areas would improve their ability to recruit and retain military personnel.

It was an article of faith in the military that since 1981—the last time there was a major increase—military pay had improved at a slower rate than private-sector wages, creating a pay gap of 13.5 percent. Clinton's plan promised to narrow that gap with a series of annual pay raises that slightly exceeded the rate at which private-sector wages increased.

Although some analysts challenged the notion that any pay gap existed, top military leaders lent their authority to the argument and the debate in 1999 focused on whether the president's proposed raise for the following year was large enough. Apparently it was not—Congress bumped it up from 4.4 percent to 4.8 percent, for the largest pay raise since the 1981 hike. Changes also were made in pension benefits, as well as recruitment and retention incentives.

Emboldened by forecasts of a growing budget surplus, a formidable coalition of retirees, the Joint Chiefs, and members of both parties pushed into law in 2000 a new, permanent health entitlement for career military retirees. The anticipated price tag was $60 billion during the first ten years. Again, proponents argued that when retirees complained they were not getting the health care they had been promised, it hurt recruitment and retention.

SETTING PRIORITIES

After pay and pensions, the service chiefs said additional funds were needed to attack the root causes of the readiness crunch by fielding more modern equipment that would break less often and be easier and cheaper to maintain. What exactly that equipment would be was the subject of much debate. Pentagon officials lobbied hard for a new generation of weapons, but their critics contended that the services planned to spend too much money on weapons that were unnecessarily sophisticated for the post-Soviet world.

Early in Clinton's second administration, two studies offered the White House and Congress conflicting assessments and recommendations on the nation's long-term defense needs. The Pentagon's Quadrennial Defense Review, a six-month assessment of future defense needs and plans, essentially endorsed the status quo. The review called for retaining most of the existing forces, missions, and strategies. As such, it reaffirmed the main elements of Clinton's defense program, including the goal of being able to fight and win two major wars in widely separated regions but overlapping in time—for example, in the Persian Gulf and the Korean peninsula.

In presenting his department's review to Congress in spring 1997, secretary Cohen restated the conclusion, reached nearly two years earlier by Joint Chiefs of Staff Chairman Gen. John M. Shalikashvili, that the Pentagon's annual procurement budget would have to reach $60 billion, a climb of some $15 billion, in order to fund necessary high-tech weapons. Cohen warned against making major cuts in plans to buy those sophisticated new weapons or in force structure—the number of combat divisions, warships, and fighter squadrons.

In December 1997 Congress heard from a blue-ribbon commission it had set up to review the quadrennial defense study and offer recommendations. The commission's report provided a sharp contrast with the Pentagon's thinking. The panel questioned Pentagon plans to improve the armored divisions and fighter squadrons that swept aside their Iraqi opponents in the 1991 Persian Gulf War, saying those forces would be less relevant against future threats. It recommended

developing forces that could be quickly dispatched to overseas trouble spots and that would be less vulnerable once there to chemical or biological weapons. It also called for the Pentagon to devote more effort to preparing for attacks on U.S. soil, including terrorist strikes using nuclear, chemical, and biological weapons. Yet, to the dismay of conservatives, it recommended deferring deployment of a nationwide antimissile defense system until warranted by a specific threat.

The panel also took exception to the administration's two-war scenario. While conceding that U.S. forces needed to remain capable of dealing with major conflicts in Korea and the Persian Gulf, it warned that the two-war strategy was counterproductive in the long run because it gave the armed services a rationale for spending money to beef up for traditional wars that were unlikely to happen. Instead, the commission contended, the military should be developing equipment and methods that would be needed to face the nontraditional threats that were likely to confront the country in the future.

While acknowledging that the services were considering these types of changes, the panel recommended putting more money into their efforts. It called on the Army, for example, to accelerate its two-stage plan that called for initially equipping existing forces with new and upgraded weapons and then beginning the transition from that modernized force to a radically redesigned force. That new force would consist of smaller, more agile combat units equipped with weapons that were lighter and more easily transported.

Members of Congress seemed to embrace the recommendations of both the quadrennial report and the blue-ribbon panel. They continued to fund the Pentagon's requests for big-ticket items that evolved during the forty-year standoff with the Soviet Union—heavy tanks, huge aircraft carriers, and supersonic jets—but they also put more money into the military's modernization efforts. Items made in the home states or districts of prominent members also retained their appeal.

But in 1999 the chairman of the House Defense Appropriations Subcommittee decided to confront the military on the hard choices it faced. Chairman Jerry Lewis, R-Calif., convinced first his subcommittee, then the full Appropriations Committee, and ultimately the House to turn down the funding request for the Air Force's premier procurement program, the F-22 fighter plane.

Lewis had chosen his target carefully. The F-22, on the cusp of production, offered him both the leverage to force a showdown with the Pentagon and, he insisted, an illustration of the way a handful of big-ticket items crowded other programs out of the budget. Lewis and his supporters were concerned that the military, while complaining that it did not have enough money for spare parts, maintenance, and personnel, was still going forward with three different air-superiority fighter planes. They contended that the Pentagon's long-range spending plans were based on highly optimistic budget projections, given the competing pressures of tax cuts and domestic spending. Moreover, they insisted, a super-sophisticated aircraft such as the F-22 no longer made sense in the post–cold war era and only shortchanged personnel programs and equipment more relevant to a changed world.

Lewis's move jolted the military establishment and its supporters into action. They effectively restored funding for the F-22, although additional testing was required. But Lewis and others insisted that they had achieved their goal of putting the Pentagon on notice that other high-priced weapons programs would be receiving the same critical scrutiny in the future.

SHIELDING A NATION

Of all the issues facing Washington policy makers, few were as divisive as the question of antimissile defense. Conservative defense activists had argued for two decades that the country should protect itself from missiles if it could. It made no sense to them that the United States had no way to destroy even a missile launched by mistake. Former President Ronald Reagan and his advisers had envisioned an umbrella of ground-based rockets and satellite lasers—derided by critics as "star wars."

Pressed by Republicans to increase funding for antimissile defense, Clinton had agreed in 1996 to spend the next three years developing a more limited system that could be ready for deployment by 2003—if the decision was made to proceed. Clinton proposed a system that would take out a handful of incoming warheads—an errant missile, for instance, or missiles fired by radical regimes in North Korea or the Middle East. Conservatives regarded the proposal as too puny and argued that it was more political than military—designed to shield Democrats from charges that they were soft on defense.

Many congressional liberals feared that even the limited defense Clinton planned could spark a nuclear arms race around the globe, as other countries rushed to build more bombs and offensive missiles, design more sophisticated warheads and decoys, and even tinker with missile defenses of their own.

Liberal critics also feared a missile defense system could upset the balance of power with Russia. The cornerstone of U.S.-Soviet nuclear relations, inherited by Russia, was the 1972 Anti-Ballistic Missile (ABM) Treaty, which specifically banned national missile defenses, because two superpowers defenseless against attack were less likely to strike each other. Even the limited defense system Clinton was planning would

have required changes in the treaty, which Russian officials had so far rejected.

Still, liberals were reluctant to challenge the program head-on. The antimissile program had gained political momentum in the summer of 1998, when a commission chaired by former—and future—Defense Secretary Donald H. Rumsfeld warned that countries such as North Korea and Iran could have missiles capable of reaching the U.S. mainland within five years. A few weeks later, North Korea tested a missile nearly powerful enough to carry a small warhead to Alaska or Hawaii.

The report and North Korea's test changed the dynamics of the debate. The following year Congress passed legislation calling for the deployment of a nationwide defense when it was "technologically feasible." Although Clinton was reluctant to commit to deploying a system until he had something that worked, he faced certain defeat if he opposed the bill. He signed it into law, after several face-saving amendments were added.

But test failures slowed progress on the system, and there was concern that it could be easily flummoxed by relatively simple decoys. Some GOP lawmakers balked at any hint of a slowdown by Clinton because they did not believe he was committed to the program's success. Sen. Gordon H. Smith, R-Ore., voiced the conservative view in a May 2000 discussion of arms control and antimissile defenses between Russian and American lawmakers. "President Clinton does not enjoy the trust of the United States Senate when it comes to arms control or military matters," he said.

That view had been apparent in 1997 when the conservatives' price for scheduling action on the chemical weapons treaty included Clinton's agreement to submit to the Senate any changes in the ABM treaty. Their disdain was also abundantly clear in the political maneuvering that surrounded the Senate's rejection of the Comprehensive Test Ban Treaty in 1999, a major defeat for Clinton and a big win for the conservatives.

Clinton did not improve his standing with conservatives when he announced late in his presidency that he would leave to his successor the decision of whether or not to deploy a national missile defense system. The president cited technical problems and diplomatic opposition. The decision drew a mixed—and predictable—reaction on Capitol Hill. Conservative Republicans saw it as misguided, while Democrats and some Republicans endorsed the decision. And so it went in the closing months of the Clinton presidency, much like the earlier months and so many in between.

Chronology of Action on Defense

1997–1998

President Clinton's defense budgets were a perennial target for his Capitol Hill critics. They accused the commander-in-chief of undermining national security by reducing the size of the military too much, sending it overseas too often, and cutting its budget too much. But the decision by Republican leaders to make deficit reduction their top priority in the 105th Congress put the brakes on the hefty increases Congress had been making in Clinton's budgets.

The 1997 bipartisan balanced-budget agreement placed annual ceilings on the overall defense budget. Despite grumbling from defense hawks, the 105th Congress managed to stay within those fiscal constraints in its annual defense authorization and appropriations bills. However, members increasingly found "emergency" supplemental appropriations bills a convenient way to add to Pentagon accounts without bumping up against the budget ceilings. The White House was not opposed to that route either, at least when it came to financing peacekeeping efforts abroad.

Although the budget agreement had preempted efforts to substantially increase the defense budget in the 105th Congress, critics continued to voice their concerns about the toll it was taking on military readiness, modernization, and morale. In time, top military officers joined the debate. Pentagon leaders initially had voiced confidence they could live with the pared-down budgets, but by the summer of 1998 they were calling for substantial increases over the budget ceilings in the future. That fall Clinton bowed to the pressure and agreed to future increases.

Congress had received two reports in 1997 with contrasting views on how those budgets should be spent. The Pentagon's Quadrennial Defense Review basically reaffirmed existing strategies and missions, while Congress's review panel recommended spending less on existing forces and focusing more on the kinds of weapons and tactics that would be needed in the future.

Although overall defense spending totals were no longer on the table, the defense bills still provided a venue for contentious policy debates, ranging from a parochial feud over Air Force maintenance depots to restrictions on overseas peacekeeping missions to the question of whether male and female recruits should be trained together.

Despite all the budget and policy battles, Congress and the White House occasionally found common ground. A treaty to expand NATO to include Poland, Hungary, and the Czech Republic enjoyed strong support at both ends of Pennsylvania Avenue. But, though the pact was approved by far more than the required two-thirds vote, some of the treaty's important backers indicated that they would be opposed to further expansion of NATO any time soon.

The Senate also gave its approval to a treaty to ban chemical weapons. It was a big win for Clinton, but Senate Foreign Relations Chairman Jesse Helms, R-N.C., and the GOP leadership exacted some concessions before moving the treaty to the floor. Among the trade-offs was the president's agreement to reform the foreign policy bureaucracy, a top goal of Helms's, and to submit to the Senate for its approval any changes he negotiated in the 1972 Anti-Ballistic Missile Treaty and the 1990 Conventional Forces in Europe Treaty.

1998 Defense Authorization

Congress in 1997 cleared a $268.3 billion fiscal 1998 defense authorization. The final bill (HR 1119—PL 105-85) authorized $2.6 billion more than President Clinton had requested.

HR 1119 had been delayed for months in conference because of a parochial feud over Air Force maintenance depots. By the time agreement was reached, the spending authority provided by HR 1119 had largely been superseded by the fiscal 1998 defense appropriations bill already signed into law (HR 2266—PL 105-56). But the authorizing committees' fear of being marginalized in the congressional debate over military policy, coupled with the Pentagon's eagerness for authorization for, among other things, a military pay raise, drove conferees to an agreement.

The controversy over maintenance depots had been set off by Clinton's 1995 announcement that thousands of jobs at two depots in California and Texas that had been targeted for closure would be saved by having private contractors take them over. Clinton's proposal, seen by critics as a political move to win support in two key electoral states, produced angry protests from lawmakers representing the three remaining Air Force depots, located in Georgia, Oklahoma, and Utah, which had anticipated picking up work from the closing depots. Agreement was finally reached in conference on provisions aimed at steering maintenance work to those three depots. The dispute helped sink a request by the administration that the bill authorize two more rounds of base closings.

The final bill authorized funding for the B-2 stealth bomber, built to evade detection and pierce Soviet air defenses, but left it up to the president to decide whether to use the money to gear up for buying additional planes or to repair and upgrade the B-2s already in service. Reopening the production lines seemed unlikely at that time, with senior Air Force leaders insisting that future budgets could not absorb more of the $750 million planes.

On the issue of U.S. troops in Bosnia, which had lain dormant for most of the year, the bill called for U.S. operations to end June 30, 1998, the last deadline that had been set by Clinton. But the bill also allowed the president to waive the deadline, which he subsequently did.

CLINTON BUDGET

The fiscal 1998 budget Clinton sent to Congress on Feb. 6, 1997, called for $265.7 billion in new budget authority for defense-related programs.

The reception on Capitol Hill was predictable. Throughout Clinton's first term, Republican defense experts had criticized Clinton's defense requests as inadequate. This year was no exception. Indeed, authorizing committee members of both parties were particularly unhappy that, once again, the administration was deferring a long-promised upturn in the budget for weapons procurement, which had declined about 70 percent in inflation-adjusted terms since 1985.

In 1996 Clinton had projected a $45.5 billion procurement request for fiscal 1998; his actual request was $42.9 billion. On paper, however, the administration remained committed to reaching, by fiscal 2001, the $60 billion procurement budget that Joint Chiefs of Staff Chairman Gen. John M. Shalikashvili had wanted to reach in fiscal 1998.

Although the draw-down in active-duty military personnel begun a decade earlier was to have been all but completed in fiscal 1997, the president's budget request assumed a further reduction of 21,000 from the Navy and Air Force. A senior Pentagon official said the services had decided on the additional cuts to gain more money for weapons modernization. Clinton's projected fiscal 1998 personnel ceiling of 1.43 million was about 14,000 below his planned personnel floor and conflicted with House-sponsored provisions in each of the two previous defense authorization bills barring the Defense Department from going below the planned personnel level. The active-duty military had been cut by about one-third from its post-Vietnam peak of 2.17 million.

The $93.2 billion request for operations and maintenance in fiscal 1998 was $5.1 billion higher than Clinton had projected in 1996. That cost increase, in turn, was largely to blame for the continuing slippage in the administration's often-promised upturn in Pentagon procurement funding.

Clinton's budget request continued the Pentagon's enthusiastic investment in the information revolution as a core element of future combat capability. Each of the services hoped to link not only its major weapons, but its supply units and, in the Army's case, even individual soldiers to an electronic web to provide "battlefield awareness"—a commonly shared map of friendly and enemy units that would allow U.S. commanders to strike the enemy at its weakest points.

Advocates of increased defense spending were hopeful that change was on its way when a Republican, former Sen. William S. Cohen of Maine, took over as defense secretary in 1997. Those hopes hinged on two long-term assessments of U.S. defense policy that were to be released during the year: the Pentagon's in-house Quadrennial Defense Review and the work of the congressionally mandated National Defense Panel. But Cohen's recommendations, announced in May and rooted in the Quadrennial Review, were to retain most of the Pentagon's existing forces, missions, and strategies and to modernize the military with money cut from defense programs traditionally held sacred on Capitol Hill: military bases, civilian maintenance and administrative jobs, and the National Guard and reserves. (Defense leadership, box, p. 241; defense reviews, p. 263)

BUDGET RESOLUTION

Although defense hawks were dissatisfied with Clinton's budget request, they were constrained by their leaders' commitment to eliminating the deficit.

Congressional leaders reached a budget agreement with the White House in May that included a fiscal 1998 ceiling of $268 billion for defense. The agreement, which aimed to balance the budget by 2002, was written into the fiscal 1998 budget resolution (H Con Res 84) that passed both chambers with bipartisan support in June. The defense total was $2.6 billion above what Clinton requested, but that increase was a relative pittance compared with the $11 billion that the defense committees had added to Clinton's fiscal 1997 defense budget request. (Budget resolution, p. 43)

Republican defense experts contended that the resulting Pentagon budget would be too tight to allow the military to stay in fighting trim and modernize its arsenal while maintaining the high pace of overseas deployments that Clinton had approved.

HOUSE COMMITTEE ACTION

The House National Security Committee reported its $268.3 billion version of the defense bill (HR 1119—H Rept 105-132) on June 16.

The committee ignored Secretary Cohen's recommendations that Congress authorize two additional rounds of base closings—a key element of the Quadrennial Defense

DEFENSE LEADERSHIP

The Senate on Jan. 22, 1997, approved, 99–0, the nomination of former Republican senator William S. Cohen of Maine to be secretary of defense in the second Clinton administration. Cohen had been questioned by his former colleagues on the Armed Services Committee and approved by the panel 18–0 earlier that day. *(Background, cabinet profiles, p. 979)*

Senate approval came after a brief debate in which senators lauded their just-retired colleague as a thoughtful and independent-minded voice for bipartisanship in defense policy. Cohen was the only Republican to join the Clinton cabinet.

Though one of the Senate's most liberal Republicans on domestic issues, Cohen's stance on defense questions was solidly in the GOP mainstream. A member of the Armed Services Committee for his entire eighteen-year Senate career (1979–1997), Cohen had been critical of President Clinton on many policy issues, including the president's 1996 extension of the Bosnia mission without seeking congressional authorization and his 1995 veto of legislation that would have accelerated deployment of a nationwide antimissile defense system. Cohen had consistently supported higher military budgets than his Democratic colleagues or the administration. But he assured the panel that he could be an effective member of the Clinton administration with his record of building consensus and forging compromise.

Cohen replaced William J. Perry, who said he was leaving the post to have more time to spend with his grandchildren. *(Congress and the Nation Vol. IX, p. 259)*

Gen. Henry H. Shelton won voice vote approval from the Senate on Sept. 16, 1997, to succeed Gen. John M. Shalikashvili as chairman of the Joint Chiefs of Staff. Shalikashvili's term concluded at the end of September.

The Senate Armed Services Committee had approved the nomination on Sept. 9, following a hearing in which members of both parties lauded the thirty-three-year Army veteran. Shelton was the third Army officer in a row to serve in the top Pentagon spot and the first chairman whose military career was rooted in the special forces—elite units trained for missions of clandestine reconnaissance, guerrilla warfare, and quasi-political dealings with foreign military forces and local populations. As such, his experience in the top ranks was heavily weighted toward combat assignments rather than staff offices. During the confirmation hearing, Georgia Democrat Max Cleland said Shelton's background and experience would be useful in dealing with threats to U.S. security from terrorists, rogue states, and drug cartels.

Clinton initially offered the chairmanship to Air Force Gen. Joseph W. Ralston, the vice chairman of the Joint Chiefs. Ralston withdrew from consideration after it was disclosed that he had been involved in an adulterous affair in the early 1980s. In May 2000 Ralston succeeded Army Gen. Wesley K. Clark as commander in chief of U.S. forces in Europe and as NATO's top military commander.

Review—and that it eliminate a requirement that at least 60 percent of depot maintenance—major overhauls of ships, planes, engines, and other items—be carried out by Pentagon-owned facilities. Not only were base closings politically unpalatable, but many lawmakers complained that Clinton had manipulated the 1995 round for political gain with his proposal that private contractors take over the work of the depots slated for closure—McClellan Air Logistics Center in Sacramento, Calif., and Kelly Air Logistics Center in San Antonio, Texas. The committee bill included a provision to bar the assignment of any Air Force maintenance work to private contractors operating the California or Texas sites. On the ratio of public to private maintenance work, the bill contained a provision making the application of the 60 percent requirement more restrictive. *(1995 base closings, Congress and the Nation Vol. IX, p. 319)*

Clinton had requested $22 million to continue shutting down the production line for the giant, radar-evading B-2 bomber. The committee decided to add $331 million more, for a total of $353 million, and use the funds to restart production and purchase components for nine more planes.

The committee also agreed to authorize $1.3 billion to buy as many as twelve F/A-18 "E" and "F" planes—enlarged versions of the "C" and "D" models then in service. The Navy had requested $2.1 billion. After vigorous lobbying by the Navy and prime contractor McDonnell Douglas, the panel rejected an attempt to reduce the number of newer models purchased and add in some of the older models.

The committee bill authorized the $2.1 billion requested to continue developing the Air Force's F-22 fighter and cut $31 million from the $924 million requested to develop the Joint Strike Fighter, slated to replace jets of 1970s vintage beginning in 2008.

The committee approved a $2.6 billion request for the first of a new class of nuclear-powered submarines but rejected one member's proposal to add $345 million to begin buying components of a nuclear-powered aircraft carrier slated to replace the oil-fueled *Kitty Hawk* in 2008, when that ship would be forty-seven years old. The Navy planned to begin requesting money for the new carrier in fiscal 2000.

Although their bill added hundreds of millions of dollars to accelerate development of several antimissile defense programs, committee members did not seek to force deployment of a nationwide defense by 2003, a requirement that Clinton had strongly resisted and cited as grounds for vetoing the defense authorization bill in 1995. *(1995 action, Congress and the Nation Vol. IX, p. 316)*

HOUSE FLOOR ACTION

The House passed the $268.3 billion defense authorization bill June 25 by a vote of 304–120.

Lawmakers on June 19 rejected, 89–332, a proposal by Bernard Sanders, I-Vt., that would have cut the authorization by 5 percent—a reduction of $13.4 billion. And National Security Committee members made clear that their recommended additions to Clinton's budget request were only a down payment on making up what the Pentagon itself described as a $15 billion annual shortfall in the weapons procurement budget.

The House on June 24 challenged the administration on Bosnia, voting 278–148 to adopt an amendment by Steve Buyer, R-Ind., to require a pullout of U.S. troops in Bosnia by June 30, 1998—Clinton's announced deadline for a pullout. But the House rejected by a **key vote of 196–231 (R 174–49; D 21–182; I 1–0)** a Van Hilleary, R-Tenn., substitute amendment setting the deadline at Dec. 31, 1997, with a proviso that Clinton could ask Congress to approve a six-month extension to June 30, 1998. It was the first significant congressional action on the subject since Clinton announced, shortly after his reelection, that U.S. forces, numbering about 8,000 in mid-1997, would remain in the Balkans through June 1998—eighteen months later than he had stipulated when he dispatched the troops to Bosnia in late 1995 as part of a NATO-led peacekeeping force. *(1997 key votes, p. 865; Bosnia policy, Congress and the Nation Vol. IX, p. 224)*

The debate over the future of the B-2 bomber continued on the floor of the House. Members on June 23 rejected, 209–216, an amendment by Ronald V. Dellums of California, the ranking Democrat on the National Security Committee, Budget Committee Chairman John R. Kasich, R-Ohio, and Mark Foley, R-Fla., to restore the requested $22 million to shut down B-2 production, while sweetening the deal by earmarking the extra $331 million added in committee to buy equipment for National Guard and reserve units. Citing an estimate by the Congressional Budget Office (CBO), Dellums and his allies contended that it would cost $27 billion to buy the nine additional planes and operate them for twenty years, money that would have to be squeezed out of other programs. National Security Committee Chairman Floyd D. Spence, R-S.C., argued that the Pentagon's public opposition to additional B-2s was the result of White House political pressure.

An attempt by Terry Everett, R-Ala., to strike the bill's provision barring Air Force maintenance contracts with private firms at the depots in Texas and California was rejected, 145–278, on June 23.

On June 19 the House rejected, 196–224, a Jane Harman, D-Calif., amendment to repeal a law barring female members of the armed services or female dependents overseas from obtaining abortions in U.S. military hospitals, even if the procedures were paid for privately. Harman's amend-

ment had been defeated during committee consideration as well.

For the second year, the House rejected, by a narrow margin, an effort to use the so-called Nunn-Lugar program as a lever on Russian policy. The program—named for its sponsors, former Sen. Sam Nunn, D-Ga. (1972–1997), and Sen. Richard G. Lugar, R-Ind.—was aimed at helping former Soviet states dismantle their nuclear and chemical warfare arsenals. The Clinton administration requested $382 million for the program. The committee version of the bill offered $285 million, of which $181 million was earmarked for Russia.

Dana Rohrabacher, R-Calif., proposed cutting off the funds for Russia if that country sold any SS-N-22 antiship cruise missiles to China. Rohrabacher and his allies warned that such missiles in China's arsenal might pose a grave threat to a U.S. fleet defending Taiwan. The danger would be more widespread, they said, if China, in turn, transferred the missiles to other countries hostile to the United States. Opponents of the amendment contended that the reduction in former Soviet weaponry fostered by the Nunn-Lugar funding more than offset the increased threat from the cruise missiles. The House initially adopted Rohrabacher's amendment, by a vote of 215–206, on June 23 but then overturned the result on June 25 when the House rejected the amendment, 204–219.

By a vote of 332–88, the House on June 19 adopted an amendment offered by Spence and Dellums requiring approval by the secretaries of state, defense, commerce, and energy and the director of the Arms Control and Disarmament Agency of any sale of high-powered supercomputers to a country suspected of fostering the spread of nuclear weapons.

SENATE COMMITTEE ACTION

The Senate Armed Services Committee reported its version of the $268 billion defense bill (S 936—S Rept 105-29) on June 18.

Similar to their House counterparts, Senate authorizers restricted Pentagon use of private contractors for maintenance work and rejected the idea of additional base closings. The panel turned down a proposal by senior Democrat Carl Levin of Michigan to replace the bill's outright ban on privatizing overhaul work at the former Kelly and McClellan Air Force bases with a competitive system for the remaining depots and private contractors. However, the Senate bill included a proposal, not in the House version, to lower from 60 percent to 50 percent the amount of maintenance that would have to be performed in government-owned depots. And the committee came within a single vote of approving Cohen's request for two additional rounds of base closings. An amendment to that effect was rejected by a tie vote of 9–9.

The Senate panel also agreed with the House in authorizing the $2.6 billion requested for the first of a new class of nuclear-powered submarines. But it was sharply at odds with the House over B-2 production, the timetable for funding a new aircraft carrier, and the number of Aegis destroyers to be funded in fiscal 1998. The Senate authorizers included a provision specifically barring production of additional B-2 planes and added to the bill $345 million to start buying components of a new aircraft carrier. They also added to the administration's $2.7 billion request for three Aegis destroyers another $720 million for a fourth destroyer.

SENATE FLOOR ACTION

The Senate passed S 936 on July 11 by a vote of 94–4 and then passed HR 1119 by voice vote, after substituting the text of its bill.

Faced with the prospect of authorizing additional rounds of base closures in 1999 and 2001, the Senate voted instead to study how much had been saved by the four rounds in 1989, 1991, 1993, and 1995. The four senators whose amendment had been defeated in committee—Republicans John McCain of Arizona and Daniel R. Coats of Indiana and Democrats Levin of Michigan and Charles S. Robb of Virginia—tried again when S 936 reached the floor. Their amendment would have authorized new closures under the rules enacted to govern the four earlier rounds—a commission designed to insulate the process from political influence. But the Senate on July 9 approved, 66–33, a substitute offered by Byron L. Dorgan, D-N.D., requiring the Pentagon to report to Congress on the costs and savings of the previous closures and recommend whether further base closings were needed. Dorgan and others cited reports by the General Accounting Office (GAO) and the CBO that the estimated savings from the previous base closings could not be verified. This, along with members' fears that their states would lose jobs and their contention that Clinton had meddled in the 1995 round for political reasons, accounted for the lopsided vote. *(Previous closings, Congress and the Nation Vol. VIII, pp. 353, 393; Congress and the Nation Vol. IX, pp. 288, 319)*

Only a few senators debated an amendment dealing with the continued deployment of U.S. troops in Bosnia. The language that was ultimately approved by voice vote merely expressed an opinion that U.S. troops should be withdrawn on the date Clinton had already set. Administration officials warned that the president would veto any effort to write the date into law.

By a vote of 72–27 on July 10, the Senate gutted an amendment by Thad Cochran, R-Miss., and Richard J. Durbin, D-Ill., that would have tightened government controls on the export of relatively sophisticated computers to certain countries, including Russia and China. The debate was sparked by several recent cases in which such computers had wound up in the hands of those countries' military organizations. The Senate substituted for the Cochran-Durbin language a proposal by Republican Rod Grams of Minnesota requiring a GAO study of the national security risks posed by the sale of certain types of computers. It then adopted the revised amendment by voice vote.

In other action, the Senate by voice vote adopted a Lugar proposal to increase by $135 million the amount to be authorized for Nunn-Lugar and related programs. The amendment would bring the authorization up to $668 million, the amount requested.

Similar to the House, the Senate defeated an attempt to repeal the law barring female service members or dependents from obtaining privately funded abortions in U.S. military hospitals overseas. The amendment, offered by Patty Murray, D-Wash., was rejected, 48–51, on July 10.

CONFERENCE ACTION

The House adopted the conference report (H Rept 105-340) Oct. 28 by a vote of 286–123. The Senate agreed to the report Nov. 6 by a vote of 90–10, clearing the measure for the White House.

The bill cleared nearly four months after it had been sent to conference, when lawmakers finally broke the logjam created by the dispute over maintenance depots. At the insistence of members representing the three remaining Air Force depots, in Georgia, Oklahoma, and Utah, the final bill included language aimed at nullifying any price advantage private companies would have over government depots. But the compromise also included the Senate provision reducing the proportion of work that had to be done at government depots from 60 percent to 50 percent.

The conference report tracked the defense appropriations bill (HR 2266) on the B-2 controversy, giving the president discretion to decide whether to expand the existing fleet of twenty-one stealth aircraft with the funds authorized.

The final bill implicitly acknowledged that Congress could not block Clinton from continuing U.S. participation in the peacekeeping mission in Bosnia. While barring the use of funds for U.S. troops in Bosnia after June 30, 1998, the measure also allowed the president to waive the prohibition. The conference report expressed the sense of Congress that European members of NATO, whose troops outnumbered U.S. forces in Bosnia and made up the bulk of the 32,000 peacekeepers, should provide all ground combat troops after June. Major European allies insisted they would pull their troops out of Bosnia if U.S. ground forces were withdrawn, in which case the brutal civil war almost certainly would reignite.

In the wake of scandals and reports of sexual harassment in the services, particularly in training, the bill created a congressional commission to review the adequacy of recruit training and the services' policies on whether male and female recruits should train together. The Marine Corps was the only branch that still segregated the sexes in training.

In signing the bill on Nov. 18, Clinton reiterated his concerns over the spending level and the language on maintenance depots, but he said the Pentagon had indicated it could conduct competition in the future between public and private maintenance facilities. The president also vowed to seek legislation in 1998 to overturn provisions in the bill that would tighten controls on the export of supercomputers to certain countries, including Israel, Russia, and China.

MAJOR PROVISIONS

As signed into law on Nov. 18, 1997, HR 1119 authorized $268.3 billion in defense spending in fiscal 1998, $2.6 billion more than requested.

The following are major provisions of HR 1119.

Personnel Issues

• Authorized, as requested, a ceiling of 1.43 million for the active-duty military, nearly 21,000 fewer than in fiscal 1997. But conferees rejected a House-passed provision that would have suspended for one year a program that allowed service members to retire, with a reduced pension, after only fifteen years of service instead of the usual twenty. This was part of an unsuccessful effort by the House to freeze the active-duty level.

• Authorized a National Guard and reserve of about 895,000, slightly smaller than had been requested. The most important element of the change was a cut of 5,000 from the Army National Guard, resulting in an authorized force of 362,000 instead of the 367,000 requested. The reduction, expected to save $22 million, was intended as a first step toward cuts recommended by the Pentagon's Quadrennial Review.

Lobbyists for the National Guard complained that the conferees did not make a similar reduction in the Army's active-duty personnel ceiling recommended in the review.

Supporters of the National Guard were dealt another blow when the conferees rejected a Senate-passed proposal to add a four-star general to the Joint Chiefs of Staff to represent the Guard and reserves. The White House and the Pentagon strongly opposed the proposal, saying it would violate the 1986 law (PL 99-433) that reorganized the military's high command. Instead, the conferees approved the appointment of two-star generals to advise the Joint Chiefs—one representing the services' reserve components and the other representing the Guard.

Though disappointed, the private National Guard Association of the United States expressed satisfaction that debate on the issue had alerted members of Congress to the Guard's needs. While Clinton requested $969 million for Guard and reserve equipment, the conferees added another $1.2 billion for a total of $2.2 billion.

• Authorized the 2.8 percent increase in basic pay for military personnel that Clinton requested.

The final bill also consolidated several housing and food allowance programs to boost total compensation. For example, service personnel not living in barracks or on ships had been reimbursed for part of their food and housing by a complex set of cash allowances. The conference report consolidated those payments into a housing allowance indexed to local housing costs and a "subsistence" allowance indexed to food costs.

• Included provisions intended to tighten the services' screening of prospective recruits' medical fitness. It also directed the secretary of defense to provide incentives for recruits to improve their physical fitness before they enlisted.

• Included two provisions intended to cut costs by reducing the number of military and civilian employees in administrative jobs. One required a 25 percent reduction over the following five years in the number of people assigned to headquarters units—a cut of about 12,500 personnel—while the other required a reduction in fiscal 1998 of 25,000 employees from the number assigned to acquisition jobs, though the secretary of defense could soften the cut to 10,000.

• Created a congressional commission to review the adequacy of recruit training and the services' policies on mixed-gender training.

• Included a provision intended to raise the standards for drill sergeants, including requiring psychological screening of all prospective drill sergeants.

Antimissile Defense

• Authorized $4.08 billion for antimissile research and procurement—$653 million more than the administration initially requested but only $382 million more than the amended request it subsequently submitted. The total included $978 million for nationwide missile defense, $406 million for the Army's Theater High-Altitude Area Defense (THAAD), and $345 million for the Navy's "Upper Tier" system. *(Antimissile defense, p. 265)*

Ground Combat

• Authorized without change the funding requests for several Army programs to upgrade existing weapons and develop others from scratch. All were to be linked in a web of digital communications that would give tank commanders, helicopter pilots, and individual soldiers a shared map of the battlefield.

The final bill authorized $595 million to upgrade M-1 tanks with larger cannon, night-vision equipment, and digital links; $512 million to equip missile-armed Apache helicopters with the Longbow target-finding radar; and $282 million to continue developing the new, smaller Comanche armed helicopter.

• Added to Clinton's budget $209 million for Army and Marine Corps trucks, ranging in size from jeep-like "Humvees" to huge low-boy tractor-trailers designed to carry seventy-ton tanks.

Air Combat

• Authorized $331.2 million for the B-2 bomber, which the president could use either to purchase additional B-2 bombers or to modify and repair the existing fleet of twenty-one of the stealth aircraft.

• Made only minor changes in the budget request for all three of a new generation of combat jets slated to enter service over the next decade, providing:

  • $2.2 billion to gear up for production in 1999 of the Air Force's F-22 fighter.

  • $2.1 billion to buy twenty of the Navy's F/A-18 E and F jets.

  • $946 million to continue developing the Joint Strike Fighter.

• Authorized funds beyond those requested to buy more of the fighters already in production:

- $226 million for five Air Force F-15s, an increase of two planes ($67 million) over the request.
- $66 million for three smaller F-16s that were not requested.

Naval Combat

- Authorized $3.4 billion for four destroyers equipped with the Aegis antiaircraft system. Though the administration initially asked for $2.7 billion for three Navy destroyers, senior administration officials had agreed with Senate Majority Leader Trent Lott, R-Miss., months earlier to accept an additional $720 million for a fourth ship. The ships were to be built in Bath, Maine, by General Dynamics and in Pascagoula, Miss., by Litton Industries.
- Authorized, as requested, $2.6 billion for a new class of nuclear-powered submarines—$2.3 billion for the first submarine and $285 million for components to be used in future ships of this type. The bill permitted two companies—the Electric Boat Corporation in Connecticut and the Newport News Shipbuilding and Dry Dock Company in Virginia—to team up to build the subs.
- Authorized the $1.6 billion requested to give the twenty-two-year-old aircraft carrier *Nimitz* a three-year overhaul.
- Added to the budget request down payments on two ships—$100 million for an amphibious landing transport to be built in Louisiana and $16 million for an oceanographic research ship to be built in Mississippi.
- Authorized only $50 million to begin work on the nuclear-powered aircraft carrier that would be built at Newport News in Virginia instead of the $345 million that carrier supporters had sought.

Although the administration requested $90 million to begin designing a new, smaller and cheaper carrier, the conferees reduced that to $12 million while adding $17 million to perfect new technologies for the *Nimitz* class.

- Included only $35 million of the $150 million the Pentagon had requested to develop a so-called arsenal ship, a highly automated vessel with a small crew and hundreds of guided missiles. (The Navy canceled the project late in October 1997, partly for want of congressional support.)
- Added $115 million to the $132 million requested to develop and begin deploying the Navy's "cooperative engagement system"—a digital communications network intended to link the radar of all the ships and planes in a fleet.

Air and Sea Transport

- Authorized the $1.9 billion requested for nine C-17 wide-body cargo jets and the $581 million requested to buy two additional cargo ships intended to carry tanks and other heavy combat equipment for Army units headed to distant trouble spots.

Pentagon Purchasing

- Included, with minor changes, a Senate provision increasing from $250,000 to $340,000 the amount a defense

contractor could charge the Pentagon for salaries of its top five executives.

- Included a House-passed provision making permanent a section of the fiscal 1997 defense appropriations bill (PL 104-208) that limited Pentagon reimbursement to contractors for the cost of mergers—$1 for every $2 the Pentagon saved because the merger lowered prices.
- Repealed a law requiring that all weapons contracts include warranties. The GAO reported that the warranties cost $271 million annually and provided little return.
- Required the Pentagon to ensure that, by the start of fiscal 2001, 90 percent of all purchases of less than $2,500 be made by government credit card. The credit card procedure was intended to replace time-consuming red tape for routine purchases, such as office supplies. But midlevel managers had been slower to adopt the new streamlined procedures than its proponents had hoped.

Maintenance Depots

- Required private companies using two closed Air Force maintenance depots in California and Texas to include in their bids the market cost of the facilities, thus nullifying any price advantage over the government depots, which were required to "charge" the Air Force a high enough price to cover their own costs.
- Reduced the proportion of heavy maintenance work that had to be done at government depots from 60 percent to 50 percent, thereby helping the private companies.
- Expanded the definition of "depot maintenance," thus enlarging the pool of work from which the government depots were guaranteed the smaller share.

Other Provisions

- Barred the use of funds for U.S. operations in Bosnia after June 30, 1998. However, the president could waive the prohibition if he notified Congress at least forty-five days in advance of the deadline and provided a strategic rationale for his decision along with a projection of the size, duration, mission, cost, and "exit strategy" of the extended deployment. The conference report expressed the sense of Congress that European members of NATO should provide all ground combat troops after June.
- Gave the secretaries of state, defense, commerce, and energy, and the director of the Arms Control and Disarmament Agency ten days to review and decide whether to require an export license for the sale of high performance computers to certain countries. The president could change the definition of computers covered by the requirement, which Congress would then have 180 days to review.

1998 Defense Appropriations

Congress in 1997 cleared a $247.7 billion fiscal 1998 defense appropriations bill. Although the final bill (HR 2266—PL 105-56) appropriated about $3.8 billion more than President Clinton had requested in his February budget, it fell within the funding levels the White House and Congress subsequently agreed on in the spring. The president signed the measure into law, after Congress backed down on provisions aimed at restarting production of the B-2 stealth bomber and barring U.S. peacekeepers in Bosnia after June 1998.

Combined with funds provided in two other appropriations bills—$9.2 billion in the military construction bill (HR 2016—PL 105-45) and $11.5 billion in the defense sections of the energy and water measure (HR 2203—PL 105-62)—HR 2266 brought overall defense spending to just over $268 billion, the amount allowed under the bipartisan budget agreement reached by Clinton and Congress in May and embodied in Congress's fiscal 1998 budget resolution (H Con Res 84). Less than a week after signing the bill, Clinton used his line-item veto authority to strike thirteen projects for a savings of $144 million. *(1998 energy appropriations, p. 58; 1998 military construction appropriations, p. 250)*

HR 2266 was enacted more than a month before the fiscal 1998 defense authorization (HR 1119—PL 105-85). However, in deciding how to allocate the Pentagon funds, the appropriations committees had worked closely with the authorizing panels, which had established themselves as arbiters of defense policy. In each chamber, the committees had long-since worked out methods of getting along, accommodating each other's top priorities so that the appropriations bills typically conformed to the authorizing legislation in most important respects. *(1998 defense authorization, p. 239)*

On both bills, Congress avoided a showdown with the administration when it agreed to provide the president with discretionary authority over the use of funds for the B-2 stealth bomber and the withdrawal of U.S. peacekeeping troops in Bosnia.

SENATE ACTION

The Senate passed its version of the defense spending bill (S 1005) by a vote of 94–4 on July 15, 1997. The Senate Appropriations Committee had reported the bill (S Rept 105-45) on July 10.

S 1005, which appropriated $3.3 billion more than Clinton had requested, was passed after two days of low-key debate. Having just spent the better part of a week on the companion defense authorization bill, senators seemed to have little taste for lengthy consideration.

Similar to the defense authorization bill, S 1005 sought to accelerate some weapons programs without challenging Clinton's basic defense plan. The Senate Appropriations Committee, for example, added $440 million for two additional C-17 wide-body cargo jets, for a total of eleven. Clinton had requested, and the Senate Armed Services Committee had approved, nine of the planes for a total of $1.9 billion. The Appropriations panel also approved an additional $720 million for a fourth Navy destroyer equipped with the Aegis antiaircraft system, in addition to the $2.7 billion requested and approved by the Armed Services Committee for three of the ships. Funding of $345 million was

added for components to be used in a new carrier, although the schedule called for initial components to be purchased in fiscal 2000 and the bulk of the money for the carrier to be appropriated two years later.

The most significant cut in the bill, compared with the Senate authorization measure, was a reduction of $65 million in the $292 million requested for Trident II submarine-launched ballistic missiles. That would have bought only five of the seven missiles requested and approved by the authorization bill.

There were few changes in the bill on the Senate floor. The Senate adopted by voice vote amendments requiring the secretary of defense to report to Congress on the anticipated cost to the United States of admitting Poland, Hungary, and the Czech Republic to NATO and expressing the sense of Congress that the U.S. share of NATO's costs should not increase. The Pentagon had said the expansion was expected to cost the United States about $2 billion over the following decade, but other estimates were much higher. *(NATO expansion, p. 272)*

Critics of the use of U.S. troops in Bosnia warned that NATO's action July 10 seizing alleged war criminals in Bosnia for the first time, smacked of "mission creep"—taking on a new role without adequate consideration of the increased risks. The Senate gave voice approval to an amendment calling on the administration to consult on NATO involvement in such efforts.

John McCain, R-Ariz., tried to eliminate from the bill a complex section written by Daniel K. Inouye of Hawaii and apparently designed to benefit a U.S.-flag cruise ship line operating only among the Hawaiian Islands—American Hawaii Cruises, owned by American Classic Voyages Co. of Chicago. McCain dropped his amendment when Inouye, the senior Democrat on the Defense Appropriations Subcommittee, agreed to language stipulating that none of the funds provided by the bill would actually be used to build a cruise ship.

In other action, the Senate approved by voice vote an amendment by Appropriations Chairman Ted Stevens, R-Alaska, to restore $60 million that his committee had cut from the administration's $382.2 million request for the so-called Nunn-Lugar program. Named for its sponsors, former Sen. Sam Nunn, D-Ga. (1972–1997), and Sen. Richard G. Lugar, R-Ind., the program was aimed at helping former Soviet states dismantle their nuclear and chemical warfare arsenals.

HOUSE ACTION

The House passed HR 2266 by a vote of 322–105 on July 29. The House Appropriations Committee had reported the $248.3 billion appropriations bill (H Rept 105-206) on July 25.

Disregarding threats of a presidential veto, the Appropriations panel had included provisions setting a firm deadline for the withdrawal of U.S. troops from Bosnia and laying the groundwork for buying more B-2 stealth bombers.

The Bosnia provision, which the House had also added to the companion defense authorization bill in June, proposed to bar the use of funds for U.S. ground troops in Bosnia after June 30, 1998. That was the date Clinton himself had set for removing U.S. troops from the war-torn country, where they served as the backbone of a NATO-led peacekeeping force, but the administration vehemently opposed locking it in by law.

In another controversial move, House appropriators added $331 million to Clinton's budget for stepped-up B-2 production—buying components and gearing up subcontractors in preparation for buying nine more bombers, in addition to the twenty-one planes previously funded.

As usual, the funding bill closely tracked the House version of the defense authorization bill, with most of the added funding going to weapons development and production programs. One of the few dramatic departures from the authorization bill was the inclusion of the $2.1 billion requested for twenty F/A-18 E and F model Navy combat jets. The House version of the authorization bill included only $1.35 billion for the planes.

When the bill reached the floor, the committee's ranking Democrat, David R. Obey of Wisconsin, proposed taking the extra $331 million that had been added for B-2 funding and using it largely for deficit reduction, with small amounts going to accelerate an upgrade of midair refueling tankers and to pay for breast cancer research. His amendment was rejected, 200–222, on July 29.

On the broader question of defense funding, the House rejected, 137–290, an amendment cosponsored by Christopher Shays, R-Conn., and Barney Frank, D-Mass., that would have cut the bill's overall spending by $3.9 billion, essentially freezing it at the fiscal 1997 level.

The House rejected by voice vote an amendment by Jerrold Nadler, D-N.Y., designed to delay production of the Air Force's F-22 fighter for seven years. Nadler's amendment would have cut $420 million from the $2.1 billion in the bill for F-22 development. The Air Force argued that the new plane, with its stealth design, was essential if U.S. pilots in future wars were to have a technological edge. But Nadler cited an analysis by the General Accounting Office, concluding that the F-15 would beat all comers at least through 2010, thus allowing the slowdown he proposed for the F-22.

CONFERENCE ACTION

The House adopted the conference report on HR 2266 (H Rept 105-265) Sept. 25 by a vote of 356–65. The Senate cleared the bill later the same day, 93–5. The bill added $3.8 billion to Clinton's original request, but House and Senate conferees agreed to drop provisions he strongly opposed.

The final bill included a total of $331 million for B-2 related spending, $157 million above the president's request, but it did not require him to spend the money to begin buying additional planes, as the House had wanted. The administration had warned that, if it came to a showdown, Clinton would either veto the entire defense appropriations bill or use his line-item veto authority to knock out the money for new B-2s.

HR 2266 required that funds for deployment of U.S. peacekeepers in Bosnia be cut off after June 30, 1998, but it allowed Clinton to waive that limit if he told Congress in advance why he planned to leave troops in the war-town Balkan country and for how long. In the brief debate that preceded the Senate's adoption of the conference report, some members decried the deepening involvement of U.S. troops in an effort to rebuild the Bosnian state. But the administration insisted that without continued U.S. involvement the conflict would resume, potentially leading to a wider war in southeastern Europe.

Tight budget limits squeezed out some proposals for additional spending. Conferees dropped a House attempt to add funds to arm and upgrade some Army Kiowa scout helicopters, a program Congress had kept alive for years over Pentagon objections. They also dropped the $419 million Senate proposal to buy two more C-17 cargo planes than requested and approved only $50 million of the $345 million the Senate had added to begin work on a $5 billion aircraft carrier.

Reprising what had become a stock feature of the annual congressional defense debate, the Republican majority made a point of trimming a handful of relatively small programs that were among Clinton's signature Pentagon initiatives. For example, conferees approved $125 million of the $225 million requested to develop "dual-use" technologies that would have both military and commercial application and $47 million of the $80 million requested for overseas humanitarian missions.

As late as the day the conference report was filed with the House, administration officials were demanding that conferees reopen some of these issues to give Clinton more of what he wanted, but their demands were refused. Conferees did accommodate Clinton on one politically charged program: they approved the entire $382 million requested for the Nunn-Lugar program.

And, as always, the conferees funded some congressional initiatives that were blessed with particularly influential patrons, for example:

• As they had for years, conferees added money to buy C-130 Hercules cargo planes that were not requested by the administration. This year, the add-on came to $479 million for eight of the planes, which were built in a Marietta, Ga., plant just a short distance from the district of Republican House Speaker Newt Gingrich.

• In addition to the $2.7 billion requested for three Navy destroyers to be built by commercial shipyards in Maine and Mississippi, the conferees approved $720 million for a fourth ship, to be built in Republican Senate Majority Leader Trent Lott's home state of Mississippi.

• Conferees also added $16 million as a down payment on an oceanographic research ship to be built in Mississippi and $100 million to begin work on a second amphibious transport ship, known as an LPD, to be built in New Orleans, just outside the district of House Appropriations Committee Chairman Robert L. Livingston, R-La.

• Inouye got $35 million—instead of the $10 million Clinton requested and the House had approved—to continue removing unexploded bombs from a Hawaiian island used as a Navy target range. Likewise, conferees accepted Inouye's provision that apparently granted a U.S.-flag cruise line operating only in Hawaii a monopoly on business among the state's islands.

MAJOR PROVISIONS

As signed into law by President Clinton on Oct. 8, HR 2266 appropriated $247.7 billion for defense programs ranging from salaries and maintenance, to research and weapons procurement. The total was about $3.8 billion more than Clinton had requested in his Feb. 6 budget but complied with the balanced-budget agreement reached in May.

Major provisions of HR 2266 are the following.

Personnel and Operations

• Provided for an active-duty force of 1.43 million members, about 21,000 fewer than the fiscal 1997 level and essentially the number Clinton requested.

Conferees dropped a Senate initiative that would have cut an additional 10,000 members from the Army, at an estimated savings of $266 million. Also rejected was a House initiative that would have suspended for one year a program under which service members were allowed to retire, with a reduced pension, after only fifteen years of active-duty service instead of the usual twenty.

• Set for reserve and National Guard forces a personnel level of nearly 893,000, nearly 1,000 members more than the budget assumed.

• Added $369 million to the $6.3 billion Clinton requested for major overhauls of ships, aircraft, and vehicles. The bill also added $725 million to the $4.1 billion that was sought to repair and maintain facilities.

• Appropriated an additional $622 million to cover the cost of Navy and Air Force flight operations, in response to the administration's acknowledgment that it had miscalculated in its February budget request. Conferees covered the cost of this and other readiness-related add-ons by levying a 1.5 percent across-the-board reduction in all procurement and research programs covered by the bill.

• Added about $30 million to cover the cost of moving Army battalions to the huge computer-monitored, mock-combat range at Fort Irwin, in California's Mojave Desert.

• Set aside more than $100 million to cover the personnel and operating costs of keeping intact some aerial units Pentagon budget-writers wanted to downsize or eliminate, including:

   • $57 million to keep in service all ninety-four remaining B-52 bombers, including $10 million for modifications.

   • $25.2 million to prevent a cutback in the size of Air National Guard and Air Force Reserve C-130 squadrons.

• $1 million to keep operating a squadron of C-130 "hurricane hunters" based at Keesler Air Force Base in Mississippi. Repeated Air Force efforts to slough off this mission on some other agency had been stymied by Gulf Coast legislators.

• $30 million to continue operating a few SR-71 long-range, high-speed spy planes, which were retired by the Air Force in 1990 and put back into service by orders of Congress.

Missiles and Antimissile Defense

• Accepted the Senate proposal to slow the production of Trident II submarine-launched, nuclear-armed missiles, to allow for the possibility that future arms control agreements might render additional missiles superfluous. The bill provided $227 million for five missiles, a reduction of $65 million (two missiles) from the request.

• Appropriated $4.18 billion for antimissile defense programs. The president's February budget requested just over $3.4 billion, including $504 million to develop a system intended to protect U.S. territory against a handful of missiles that might be acquired surreptitiously by a rogue state. In May, as a result of the Pentagon's Quadrennial Review, the administration requested an additional $474 million for the national territory defense. Conferees approved the entire $978 million for nationwide defense.

Among the major changes the conferees made to the antimissile programs were approval of:

   • $406 million of the $556 million requested for the Army's Theater High-Altitude Area Defense (THAAD).

   • $410 million instead of the $195 million requested for a long-range "theater-wide" antimissile version of the Navy's ship-launched Standard missile.

   • $98 million to continue development of a laser-armed antimissile satellite.

Ground Combat

• Appropriated the $157 million requested by the Army for continued development of a digital communications network.

• Appropriated without change funds requested for several major weapons programs in which these digital links were to be embedded, including: $595 million to upgrade M-1 tanks with digital links, a larger cannon and improved night-vision equipment; $324 million to continue developing the Crusader mobile cannon; $512 million to equip missile-armed Apache helicopters with the Longbow target-finding radar; and $282 million to continue development of the Comanche "scout" helicopter.

Conferees rejected a House initiative that would have added $157 million to continue upgrading existing Kiowa scout helicopters with new, target-finding electronics.

• Appropriated an additional $210 million for upgraded Bradley troop carriers, mobile cannon and armor-plated ammunition carriers, all of them designated for the National Guard. This was in addition to the $653 million added to the bill to procure other equipment for National Guard and reserve units.

Air Combat

• Provided a total of $331 million for B-2 related procurement—$157 million more than requested—but left the president free to spend that money to upgrade and repair the twenty-one B-2s previously funded. The House had fought to add $331 million to begin gearing up production of nine more of the radar-evading stealth bombers.

• Appropriated, with minor changes, the amounts requested for all three of a new generation of combat jets slated to enter service over the following decade, including $2.1 billion to gear up for production in 1999 of the Air Force's F-22 fighter; $2.1 billion to buy twenty F/A-18 E and F model planes, larger versions of the F/A-18s that were being used as both fighters and bombers; $957 million to continue developing the Joint Strike Fighter, slated to replace Navy, Marine Corps, and Air Force jets of 1970s-vintage beginning in 2008.

• Appropriated funds to continue production of two Air Force fighters already in service: $226 million for five F-15s built in St. Louis by McDonnell Douglas—$67 million and two planes more than requested; $83 million for three additional Fort Worth-built Lockheed Martin F-16s, none of which were requested.

Naval Combat

• Appropriated the $2.7 billion requested for three Navy destroyers to be built by commercial shipyards in Maine and Mississippi and added $720 million for a fourth ship, to be built in Mississippi. The Pentagon had agreed to the fourth ship after Senate Majority Leader Lott objected when a team of companies that included a Litton Industries facility in his home state of Mississippi lost a competition to build a fleet of amphibious transport ships, known as LPDs.

• Included $2.3 billion for the first of a new class of nuclear-powered submarines and authorized the two commercial shipyards that built nuclear subs for the Navy to collaborate on construction of the new class.

• Included the $1.6 billion requested for a three-year overhaul and nuclear refueling of the carrier USS *Nimitz*, commissioned in 1975.

• Approved only $50 million of the $345 million the Senate had added to begin buying components for a new aircraft carrier to be built by Newport News Shipbuilding and Dry Dock near Norfolk, Va. The Pentagon had not scheduled initial funding for the components until 2000, with the bulk of the money slated for inclusion in the fiscal 2002 budget.

• Approved $213 million instead of the $139 million requested for the Navy's "cooperative engagement capability"—the fleet's counterpart to the Army's digital network links.

Air and Sea Transport

• Appropriated the $1.9 billion requested to buy nine C-17 wide-body cargo jets, dropping the Senate proposal to buy two more.

• Appropriated $627 million for seven V-22 Ospreys, a hybrid airplane/helicopter the Marine Corps planned to use as a troop carrier, an increase of $155 million and two aircraft above Clinton's request.

• Included, under prodding by Army Chief of Staff Gen. Dennis L. Reimer, $650 million for two large, high-speed cargo ships intended to carry tanks and other heavy combat equipment for Army units deploying to distant trouble spots.

Other Provisions

• Cut off funding for U.S. peacekeeping forces in Bosnia after June 30, 1998, unless the president reported to Congress no later than May 15, 1998, that a continuation of the deployment was in the national security interests of the United States and specified the reasons, number of U.S. military personnel involved, expected duration, exit strategy, and costs.

• Appropriated about $10.4 billion—slightly more than was requested—for the Pentagon's health care system. This included $13 million to continue operating the armed services' medical school in Bethesda, Md., a perennial target of budget cutters.

LINE-ITEM VETO

Still smarting from Congress's outrage over thirty-eight projects he eliminated from the fiscal 1998 military construction bill (HR 2016), Clinton used his line-item veto sparingly on HR 2266. Acting on Oct. 14, he cancelled just thirteen items totaling $144 million. *(1998 military construction, p. 250)*

The White House initially complained that Congress had added 750 unrequested projects totaling $11 billion to the bill. In the end, the president vetoed less than 2 percent of those items, most of them research or science projects. "I think what I did today was responsible and quite restrained," Clinton said.

The vetoed projects reflected a post–cold war world of shrinking defense budgets and the difficulty many members of Congress had in letting go of popular but costly weapons.

For instance, Clinton struck $39 million that Congress had appropriated for the SR-71 Blackbird spy plane that had been retired by the Air Force but revived by Congress even though the plane's mission had been largely taken over by satellites. Clinton also vetoed $37.5 million in research for a system to shoot down satellites (he had been trying to end the program since 1993) and $30 million for the Clementine program to track and intercept asteroids in space. The program had its origins in President Ronald Reagan's Strategic Defense Initiative of the 1980s that envisioned a space-based defense against missiles.

Five of the thirteen projects vetoed had been in neither the House nor the Senate versions of the defense spending bill but were added during the final negotiations. After the Supreme Court ruled in June 1998 that the president's new line-item veto powers were unconstitutional, however, the Office of Management and Budget announced that all funding that had been vetoed using the voided 1996 law would be restored.

1997 SUPPLEMENTAL BILL

Congress reimbursed the Pentagon for peacekeeping operations in Bosnia as part of a fiscal 1997 supplemental spending bill (HR 1871—PL 105-18) that was signed into law June 12, 1997. A virtually identical bill had been vetoed just three days earlier because of controversial policy provisions Republicans had attached despite White House warnings of a veto.

HR 1871 replenished $1.7 billion in Pentagon accounts that had been tapped for the Bosnia peacekeeping mission and to enforce a no-fly zone over Iraq. The bill's rescissions (cuts) in unspent budget authority included $1.9 billion in military funding.

1998 SUPPLEMENTAL BILL

Congress approved nearly $2.9 billion in defense spending as part of a fiscal 1998 supplemental spending bill (HR 3579—PL 105-174) that was signed into law May 1, 1998. The military spending included $1.3 billion for U.S. operations in the Middle East related to Iraq and $479 million for the Bosnia peacekeeping mission. There were no offsetting spending cuts in the Pentagon budget.

1998 Military Construction

Congress in 1997 cleared and President Clinton signed into law a seemingly routine $9.2 billion fiscal 1998 military construction appropriations bill (HR 2016—PL 105-45). But after the president decided to use his newly acquired line-item veto power on the bill, nothing about it was routine.

HR 2016 had faced little opposition on Capitol Hill, drew overwhelming support in both chambers, and was the first of the thirteen regular appropriations bills to be cleared by Congress. Clinton signed it into law Sept. 30, making it the only appropriation bill to be enacted before the start of the new fiscal year.

The low profile was typical of the annual military construction bill, which was devoted to construction and repair projects at military bases in almost all fifty states, including National Guard and reserve installations. HR 2016 appropriated nearly $3.9 billion for family housing, $3.4 billion for military construction projects, and $2.1 billion for base-closure costs.

The bill, however, appropriated $800 million more than the administration requested and contained funding for a number of projects that had not been requested by the Pentagon. That, together with the fact that it was the first spending bill to arrive on the president's desk, earned it another first: it was the first fiscal 1998 appropriations bill to become a target of the line-item veto. Clinton "canceled" thirty-eight individual items in the bill totaling $287 million.

Using procedures laid out in the line-item veto law, lawmakers attempted to restore all thirty-eight projects by clearing a separate bill (HR 2631) disapproving the president's actions. Clinton, in turn, vetoed the disapproval bill. But Congress had the last word: in 1998 both chambers voted to override that veto, thereby enacting HR 2631 into law (PL 105-159) and restoring the construction projects. Later that year the Supreme Court ruled that the line-item veto was unconstitutional. *(Line-item veto ruling, p. 714)*

LEGISLATIVE ACTION

HR 2016 never took more than fifteen minutes to mark up at the subcommittee or committee levels, drew no germane amendments, and faced only scattered opposition from deficit hawks, such as Sen. John McCain, R-Ariz., who called for Clinton to use his line-item veto to trim unrequested spending.

The House passed the $9.2 billion spending measure July 8, 1997, by a lopsided vote of 395–14. The House Appropriations Committee had reported it (H Rept 105-150) June 24.

The House version appropriated about $800 million more than requested. Much of the increase came in the area of family housing and so-called quality-of-life improvements, such as day care centers and medical facilities, considered necessary to maintain morale among the all-volunteer forces. Before the markup by the full committee, Franklin D. Raines, director of the White House's Office of Management and Budget (OMB), objected to ninety-four projects in the bill that had not been requested. But, in a time of declining spending, the military construction bill remained a place where lawmakers could reward their districts with earmarked spending.

Base closure decisions sparked the sharpest disagreement on the House floor. Bill McCollum, R-Fla., offered an amendment to prevent the Navy's Nuclear Power Propulsion Training Center from moving from Orlando, Fla., to Charleston, S.C., as ordered by the 1995 commission on base closures. But action on the amendment was blocked when a point of order that McCollum was trying to legislate on a spending bill was sustained.

The Senate passed its $9.2 billion version of the bill July 22 by a vote of 98–2. The Senate Appropriations Committee had reported HR 2016 (S Rept 105-52) on July 17.

The White House objected to 103 unrequested projects in the Senate bill. During that chamber's debate, McCain attacked several unrequested projects, maintaining that the reason these "low-priority" items were being funded was to "provide economic benefit to certain states." McCain and fellow Arizona Republican Jon Kyl were the only senators to oppose HR 2016.

CONFERENCE ACTION

The House adopted the conference report (H Rept 105-247) by a vote of 413–12 on Sept. 16. The Senate cleared the bill the next day, 97–3.

House and Senate appropriators had taken less than ten minutes to agree on a final version. The bottom lines of their respective versions had differed by only $100,000, although conferees still had to reconcile spending on about 200 projects. The single biggest difference was in what had been allocated for National Guard and reserve military construction projects: the House bill provided $328 million and the Senate bill proposed $569 million. Appropriators essentially split the difference when it came to totaling the major funding accounts.

MAJOR PROVISIONS

As signed into law by President Clinton on Sept. 30, HR 2016 provided $9.2 billion in fiscal 1998 for military infrastructure costs at home and abroad—$800 million more than requested. The bill paid for on-base housing for the nation's military force, as well as for day care and medical centers. It also covered the U.S. share of NATO infrastructure investment and the costs associated with base closures, such as environmental cleanup.

• **Family housing.** The bill's largest account was $3.87 billion for family housing, approximately $203 million more than Clinton had wanted. The House version would have appropriated $3.95 billion and the Senate version, $3.82 billion.

• **Military construction.** The final bill provided $3.36 billion for military construction projects, including $461 million for National Guard and reserve projects and $153 million for NATO infrastructure. The administration had requested a total of $2.65 billion, of which $173 million was to go to National Guard and reserve projects and $176 million to NATO. The House bill would have appropriated a total of $3.18 billion and the Senate bill, $3.33 billion.

• **Base closures.** The final bill followed the administration's request in providing $2.06 billion for base-closure and realignment costs, bringing to $17.8 billion the total cost for base closings since the first commission met.

• **Grand total.** Spending approved for the various categories added up to $9.29 billion, but revised economic assumptions reduced the overall total to $9.18 billion.

LINE-ITEM VETO

Declaring that "the old rules have, in fact, changed," Clinton on Oct. 6 used his powers under the 1996 line-item veto law (PL 104-130) to strike thirty-eight items from the bill. (*Line-item veto law, Congress and the Nation Vol. IX, p. 78; vetoed provisions, box, p. 252*)

Clinton avoided picking and choosing from among political friends and enemies, simply signing one of several option papers presented by OMB analysts. Clinton loyalists such as Rep. Steny H. Hoyer, D-Md., and Senate Minority Leader Tom Daschle, D-S.D., felt the lash of the vetoes, as did several senior appropriators such as Sen. Robert C. Byrd, D-W.Va., Rep. John P. Murtha, D-Pa., and Sen. Pete V. Domenici, R-N.M.

Clinton said he had made "tough calls involving real money and hard choices," but he pointedly did not describe the projects as wasteful or unnecessary. For one thing, thirty-two of the projects he struck down were included in long-range Pentagon plans. He said he vetoed projects that met three criteria: they were not requested in his fiscal 1998 budget; there had not been enough design work done on them to ensure that construction could begin in 1998; and they would not "substantially improve the quality of life of military service members and their families."

Congressional Response

The vetoes set off a furor in Congress. Members were genuinely stunned to find military construction projects in their districts on the chopping block. Among the most common complaints was the lack of advance notification, which would have allowed members to fight for cherished projects.

Lawmakers also wanted to discourage the White House from making wide use of the line-item veto on other spending bills—particularly those for the Pentagon and for energy and water development, both of which were packed with unrequested congressional pet projects.

Those involved in crafting the bill insisted that they had only included projects that met certain tests, such as being included in the annual defense authorization bill and being construction-ready by the end of the fiscal year. OMB subsequently acknowledged that some of the vetoes had been based on erroneous information and the White House offered to negotiate a solution.

But Congress moved ahead on legislation to reverse the president's vetoes. The Senate Appropriations Committee on Oct. 23 reported a bill (S 1292—no written report) restoring thirty-four of the vetoed projects. On Oct. 30 the Senate passed a revised version restoring thirty-six projects. The bill was approved by a **key vote of 69–30 (R 42–12; D 27–18)**, giving sponsors a two-vote cushion over the two-thirds majority need to override the president's promised veto. The day of the Senate vote, the White House said it had used erroneous data as the basis for vetoing eighteen items and reiterated its offer to work with Congress on restoring the vetoed projects. (*1997 key votes, p. 865*)

On Nov. 8, the House voted 352–64 in favor of its bill (HR 2631) overturning all thirty-eight of the line-item vetoes. To avoid convening a House-Senate conference to reconcile differences, the Senate cleared the House bill by voice vote Nov. 9. "Make way for liberty!" crowed Byrd, who had led the fight against granting the president line-item veto power in 1996.

On Nov. 13 Clinton vetoed HR 2631. With the first session of the 105th Congress winding to a close, members did not have time to attempt an override of that veto before adjournment, but the veto-proof majorities for the bill in both chambers indicated that an override attempt in the second session would be successful.

And it was. The House voted to override Clinton's veto of HR 2631 by a **key vote of 347–69 (R 197–23; D 149–46; I 1–0)** on Feb. 5, 1998. On Feb. 25, the Senate approved the override by a vote of 78–20 and HR 2631, restoring all thirty-eight projects, was enacted into law (PL 105-159) without the president's signature. (*1998 key votes, p. 883*)

VETOED PROVISIONS

Following are the thirty-eight projects totaling $287 million that President Clinton struck from the fiscal 1998 military construction appropriations bill (PL 105-45), beginning with the eight most expensive ($10 million and above).

Most Expensive Projects

• Norfolk Naval Shipyard, Portsmouth, Va. $19.9 million to speed up refurbishment work due to begin after the turn of the century, including construction of a new high-tech maintenance wharf large enough to hold two *Arleigh-Burke* class destroyers.

• Mayport Naval Station near Jacksonville, Fla. $17.9 million for dredging work and pier improvements to make way for eight destroyers expected to make Mayport their home port by fiscal year 2000.

• Fort Carson Rail Yard, Fort Carson, Colo. $16 million for the first phase of an upgrade that included building a state-of-the-art trackside warehouse at the World War II–era rail yard.

• Dyess Air Force Base, Abilene, Texas. $10 million to start building a new operations facility for the 13th Bomb Squadron, an 800-member B-1B squadron scheduled to be moved to Dyess in 2000.

• Camp Williams, Utah. $12.7 million to build facilities for an Army Reserve maintenance shop that was moving from its existing location at Fort Douglas, in Salt Lake City, to Camp Williams in order to make room for part of the Olympic Village slated for construction for the 2002 Salt Lake winter games.

• Coronado Naval Amphibious Base, San Diego. $10.1 million for two new buildings for the EOD (Explosive Ordnance Disposal) Unit at Coronado, which was working out of nine crumbling buildings that did not conform to fire and safety codes.

• Kirtland Air Force Base, Albuquerque, N.M. $14 million to replace a 1950s-era building that housed the Theater Air Command and Control Simulation Facility (TACCSF)—one of the military's most advanced combat simulators, which allowed missile crews, pilots, and command and control personnel to practice real-world combat situations.

• Johnstown, Pa. $14 million to build a new training center and hangar to replace cramped and dilapidated quarters used by an air reserve unit, Marine Wing Support Squadron 474.

Other Canceled Projects

• California: Fort Irwin. $2.7 million for a new helicopter landing pad and radio relay rooms for the Live Fire Command and Control Facility.

• California: Fort Irwin. $8.5 million for a twenty-four-bay wash facility for wheeled and tracked vehicles.

• California: Marine Corps Reserve Center, Pasadena. $6.7 million to demolish an old reserve center and build a new one for the 4th Light Anti-Air Defense Battalion.

• Florida: Whiting Field. $1.3 million to extend one runway and clear land for another to accommodate Beech MKII training aircraft due to arrive in fiscal 2002.

• Georgia: Moody Air Force Base. $6.8 million to build new support facilities for combat search and rescue and pararescue training operations relocating from Patrick Air Force Base in Florida.

• Hawaii: Fort Derussey. $9.5 million to provide new space for the Asian Pacific Center, which educated military and civilian officials on Asian-Pacific security issues.

• Idaho: Mountain Home Air Force Base. $9.2 million to build a new B-1B aviation electronics test and repair shop for the Air Expeditionary Wing.

1999 Defense Authorization

Congress in 1998 cleared legislation authorizing $270.5 billion for defense programs in fiscal 1999, about $400 million less than President Clinton had requested. The final bill (HR 3616—PL 105-261) also authorized $1.9 billion in emergency funding for peacekeeping operations in Bosnia.

HR 3616 made few significant changes in the administration's proposed defense program. The balanced-budget law passed in 1997 (PL 105-33) preempted serious debate over the size of the fiscal 1999 budget until after Congress had all but completed work on the annual authorization bill. Clinton in February had requested $271 billion for the Defense Department and defense-related programs conducted by the Department of Energy—essentially, the maximum allowed under a defense budget cap set by the budget law. At the same time he requested the $1.9 billion to continue the de-

ployment of U.S. troops in Bosnia but asked Congress to approve the Bosnia money as emergency funding, which would make it exempt from the budget cap. *(1997 balanced-budget law, p. 48)*

By September—shortly before Congress cleared the authorization measure—it had become clear Clinton would send Congress a supplemental fiscal 1999 funding request totaling at least $1 billion in an effort to stem growing problems with military morale and combat readiness. But that prospect had no impact on final negotiations over the authorization bill. *(1999 supplemental, p. 76)*

HR 3616 was the venue for the year's most contentious defense policy debate on Capitol Hill: an unsuccessful effort by conservative Republicans to make the armed services train male and female recruits in separate units. In the wake of sex scandals at some Army bases, an outside advisory panel chaired by former Kansas Republican Sen. Nancy

- Idaho: Mountain Home Air Force Base. $3.8 million to build a new facility for planning, and to brief and critique combat crews at the F-15C Squadron Operations Facility.
- Indiana: Crane Naval Surface Warfare Center. $4.1 million for a new support facility for chemical and biological warfare detection devices aboard ships.
- Indiana: Grissom Air Reserve Base. $8.9 million to build a new civil engineer complex, which would include maintenance shops, storage, and a roads and grounds facility.
- Kansas: McConnell Air Force Base. $2.9 million to build a transportation complex to include vehicle operations and parking facilities.
- Kentucky: Fort Campbell. $9.9 million for a vehicle maintenance shop and storage for a forward support battalion and a combat support hospital.
- Kentucky: Fort Knox. $7.2 million to modify a rifle range to new standards, with twenty-eight firing lanes.
- Maryland: St. Inigoes Naval Electronic Systems Engineering Activity. $2.6 million to build more hangar space for maintenance of unmanned aircraft.
- Montana: Malmstrom Air Force Base. $4.5 million to update kitchen facilities and add storage space for the airmen's dining facility.
- Nevada: Nellis Air Force Base. $2.0 million to build a larger facility to inspect, assemble, and test explosive munitions used by training aircraft.
- New Mexico: White Sands Missile Range. $6.9 million to repair launch facilities for the Patriot, Stinger, Chaparral, and HAWK missiles, and for the Multiple Launch Rocket System and Army Tactical Missile Systems.
- New York: Fort Drum. $9.0 million to replace existing aerial target ranges.
- New York: Niagara Falls International Airport. $2.1 million to replace two older buildings that housed a readiness office and combat arms training.
- North Carolina: Fort Bragg. $7.9 million to construct part of a training complex for military operations in urban terrain, with thirty-two buildings, streets, parking, and a bridge.
- Pennsylvania: U.S. Army Reserve Center, Oakdale. $6.0 million to build a new facility for training in communications security and medical systems.
- South Carolina: Leesburg Training Site, Eastover. $3.8 million to replace a 4,200-square-foot battle simulation center with a new one eleven times as large.
- South Dakota: Rapid City. $5.2 million to provide new support facilities for UH-1 and C-12 aircraft, used by the 1085th Medical Air Ambulance Company, including a hangar, and classroom and maintenance facilities.
- Tennessee: Arnold Air Force Base. $9.9 million to replace an old air dryer facility and support another testing facility for the new F-22 and Joint Strike Fighter.
- Texas: Fort Bliss. $7.7 million to expand areas for ammunition and other storage, and to build an oil dispensing facility.
- Texas: Laughlin Air Force Base. $4.8 million to build new facilities for painting T-1A, T-37, and T-38 aircraft.
- Virginia: Norfolk Naval Air Station. $4.0 million to build a new air traffic control facility and radar tower.
- Virginia: Yorktown Naval Weapons Station. $3.3 million to build an earth-covered storage facility for Tomahawk missiles.
- West Virginia: Camp Dawson. $6.8 million to expand facilities including administrative, training, exercise, and storage space for several Army National Guard units.
- Wisconsin: Mitchell Air Reserve Station, Milwaukee. $4.2 million to replace an older, smaller aerial port training facility.

Kassebaum Baker (1978–1997) recommended in December 1997 that recruits be segregated by sex in their smallest training units, and that they be housed in separate barracks. This drew strong objections from the armed services, with the exception of the Marine Corps that already followed the suggested policies. The final bill required only separate housing, although it included a nonbinding expression by the House that men and women also should train in separate units.

Among the changes the bill made in administration policy was to set the annual military pay raise at 3.6 percent, instead of the 3.1 percent Clinton proposed.

HOUSE COMMITTEE ACTION

The House National Security Committee reported its $270.8 billion version of the defense authorization bill (HR 3616—H Rept 105-532) on May 12, 1998. The bill did not include Clinton's request for the extra $1.9 billion in emergency funding for the Bosnia mission, stipulating instead that no more than $1.9 billion from the regular authorization could be spent for that purpose.

The House committee decided that military recruits should be housed and trained separately to prevent sexual harassment and distraction. The chiefs of the military services other than the Marine Corps strongly objected to such a course and Defense Secretary William S. Cohen in June announced that they could continue joint training, as long as men and women lived on separate floors of recruit barracks. The House bill required the services to begin training men and women separately and to house them in different barracks starting in April 1999, with the conversion to be completed by October 2001. The committee even threw in $8 million for new locks and barricades for existing barracks.

The House panel ignored the administration's request for another round of military base closings. Cohen and top military officers insisted that to modernize their forces within the stringent budget limits, they should close facilities no longer needed by an active-duty military that was one-third smaller than in the mid-1980s. Large cutbacks had been made between 1988 and 1995 under independent commissions set up by Congress. Support for that approach collapsed after critics accused Clinton of manipulating some of the 1995 closures for political gain. *(1998 defense authorization, p. 239)*

The committee bill repealed a provision enacted in 1996 (PL 104-107) limiting the use by U.S. forces of antipersonnel land mines, beginning in 1999. That law was one of several initiatives in a long-running campaign led by Sen. Patrick J. Leahy, D-Vt., and Rep. Lane Evans, D-Ill., to outlaw antipersonnel mines, which had been scattered by the millions in dozens of countries where they killed and maimed noncombatants—often children.

But Pentagon officials contended that U.S. land mines did not contribute to that problem, because all of them had battery-powered fuses and either self-destructed within a few days of being deployed or ran out of power within several weeks. They insisted that such mines were essential to deter North Korean troops poised within artillery range of South Korea's capital. Although the 1996 legislative ban exempted mines in the Korean De-Militarized Zone, the Pentagon wanted to be able to use them outside that four-kilometer-wide strip. *(Congress and the Nation Vol. IX, p. 231; land mine treaty, p. 274)*

As in the past, the House panel rejected a proposal to lift a ban on abortions at U.S. military hospitals overseas.

HOUSE FLOOR ACTION

The House passed its nearly $271 billion defense authorization bill by a vote of 357–60 on May 21.

House members had drafted several highly controversial amendments that would have reduced the total authorization by more than $2 billion, ended the Bosnia mission, and eliminated the National Security Committee provision requiring separation of men and women in basic training. But, by a vote of 304–108, the House on May 20 adopted a rule governing floor debate that did not allow any of those three amendments to be offered.

China Amendments

Most of the floor debate centered on amendments inspired by reports that China had improved its nuclear-armed missiles with technical know-how acquired from launching U.S. commercial satellites.

Because China charged less to launch satellites than U.S. or other overseas companies—as little as $25 million a trip—U.S. satellite makers had a powerful incentive to deal with China. But because a civilian communications satellite could cost several hundred million dollars, the companies and insurers had a stake in the reliability of China's launch rocket.

U.S. government licenses, under which American firms were allowed to send satellites to China for launch, restricted the information that company officials were allowed to pass along to Chinese officials. The licenses also required that Chinese access to the satellites themselves be tightly limited. However, the restrictions on satellite technology transfer had become less stringent in 1996, when Clinton moved the regulation of launch deals from the State Department to the Commerce Department.

The case at the heart of the congressional furor began in February 1996, when a Chinese rocket crashed while trying to launch an Intelsat satellite built by Loral Space & Communications and destined for use by media mogul Rupert Murdoch's News Corp. and cable TV giant Tele-Communications Inc. In the ensuing investigation, a non-Chinese outside review team concurred in the Chinese findings as to the cause of the accident. Loral conceded that the review team violated company policy by reporting the team's findings to the Chinese before consulting the appropriate State Department officials. The company insisted that no U.S. law was violated and that U.S. security was not harmed.

However, the Justice Department began an investigation into whether export control laws were violated and some critics argued that even affirming China's diagnosis of so mundane a problem as a loose electrical connection improved the reliability of China's nuclear missiles as well as its satellite launchers. "We don't want Chinese missiles to be reliable," said Rep. Duncan Hunter, R-Calif. "When the guillotine is over our head and it's sticking, we don't say 'I think I see your problem.' "

On May 20 the House adopted four GOP-sponsored amendments on China. Some senior Democratic defense specialists in the House warned that the amendments would complicate relations with China and handicap U.S. satellite companies in the face of international competition. But most Democrats laid low during the debate and supported the amendments. The amendments were:

• By National Security Committee Chairman Floyd D. Spence, R-S.C., and International Relations Committee Chairman Benjamin A. Gilman, R-N.Y., expressing the sense of Congress that business interests must not be placed above national security interests and that, during his visit to China in June, Clinton should not negotiate any of several proposed agreements that would liberalize existing limits on the transfer of satellite or missile technology to China. Agreed to 417–4.

• By Doug Bereuter, R-Neb., prohibiting any "U.S. person" from participating in any analysis of a failure by a Chinese rocket to launch a U.S.-built satellite. Agreed to 414–7.

• By Joel Hefley, R-Colo., prohibiting any export to China of missile equipment or technology. In effect, this amendment would have eliminated the president's existing authority to waive the general prohibition, subject to certain conditions. Agreed to 412–6.

• By Hunter, prohibiting any transfer to China of satellites, including transfers for the purpose of using Chinese launchers. Agreed to 364–54.

In other action, a special House investigating committee in 1998 concluded that there had been a concerted effort on China's part to acquire U.S. technology. The House found other avenues as well to voice its views on China. *(China policy, p. 180)*

Other Amendments

The House also weighed in on the export of civilian nuclear reactors and related technology. By a vote of 405–9 on May 21, it adopted a Gilman amendment requiring detailed reports to Congress before the Energy Department approved any proposed nuclear sale to a country other than the major traditional allies. Gilman indicated that he had India in mind when he wrote the amendment.

In an annual test of strength for opposing sides in the war over abortion rights, the House on May 20 rejected 190–230 an amendment by Nita M. Lowey, D-N.Y., that would have repealed the law barring female members of the armed forces or female military dependents overseas from obtaining abortions in U.S. military hospitals abroad, even if the procedure was paid for privately. The proposal had been defeated during committee consideration as well.

SENATE COMMITTEE ACTION

The Senate Armed Services Committee reported on May 11 its version (S 2057—no written report) authorizing $270.6 billion for military spending. In addition, the bill authorized the requested $1.9 billion in emergency funding for the Bosnia operation, but the committee planned to reconvene and review the issue before its bill reached the floor, leaving open the possibility of proposing conditions on the money.

Unlike its House counterpart, the Senate panel prohibited any change in the existing policy allowing mixed gender training until a basic training commission established by the fiscal 1998 defense authorization bill (HR 1119—PL 105-85) issued its report. S 2057 extended the due date for that report from September 1998 until March 1999.

The Senate committee turned down Clinton's request for more base closures, rejecting an amendment to establish a new base closing commission and another amendment to create a commission to review the previous base-closing process and recommend changes.

The Senate bill was silent on the issue of antipersonnel land mines.

The committee added to the bill's authorizations $50 million to buy components for a helicopter carrier for the Marines to be built by Litton Industries in Pascagoula, Miss., the hometown of Senate Majority Leader Trent Lott, R-Miss. There were already seven of these ships either in service or under construction, the newest of which, funded in fiscal 1996, cost upwards of $1.3 billion. Rather than building another one, the Navy had planned to overhaul an older ship for $1 billion. Litton, Mississippi's largest private employer, would not necessarily have won that refurbishing contract.

Members of both the Senate and House authorizing panels complained that the Pentagon was short-changing military retirees who had been assured when they enlisted that they and their dependents would be eligible for lifetime medical care in the military medical system. Base closures and reductions in the size of the services' medical staffs had made it more difficult for many retirees and dependents to obtain such care. The Senate committee added $60 million annually in each of the next three years for three pilot programs intended to test alternative methods of improving health care for military retirees over age sixty-five. The House committee could not find the funds to pay for any pilot programs but told the Pentagon to come up with a plan.

SENATE FLOOR ACTION

On June 25 the Senate first passed S 2057 by vote of 88–4 and then passed HR 3616 by voice vote after substituting the text of its bill.

During its consideration, the Senate spent little time debating the spending in the bill, focusing instead on such heated topics as Bosnia, China, mixed-gender housing and training, and future base closings. The Senate took up the authorization bill for two days in mid-May but then put it aside for a month while it considered other legislation.

Bosnia Deployment

Senior Armed Services members hoped to use that intervening month to work out with the Pentagon a compromise amendment defining the role of U.S. troops in Bosnia and thereby avoid a showdown over more contentious proposals.

President Clinton's decision late in 1997 to drop any deadline for ending the deployment of U.S. troops in Bosnia was strongly opposed by some members of Congress, who insisted that European NATO members should provide the combat troops who policed the Bosnian ceasefire on a day-to-day basis. The critics contended that the U.S. role in Bosnia should emphasize intelligence-gathering, communications, and transportation missions for which U.S. forces were uniquely equipped, as well as the provision of a combat reserve force stationed outside Bosnia but close enough to be quickly moved into the country should trouble erupt. The administration countered that the roughly 8,000 U.S. troops in Bosnia constituted about one-fourth of the international force.

Other lawmakers were less critical of the Bosnia deployment because peace appeared to be taking hold there. In the end, the Senate on June 24 adopted, 90–5, a nonbinding amendment by Armed Services Committee Chairman Strom Thurmond, R-S.C., expressing the sense of Congress that U.S. combat troops should be withdrawn from Bosnia "within a reasonable period of time." The Senate tabled (killed), by a vote of 65–31, an amendment by Robert C. Smith, R-N.H., that would have prohibited funding for U.S. ground troop deployment in Bosnia if both houses of Congress did not vote by March 31, 1999, on legislation authorizing the deployment to continue.

Sex-Integrated Training

After Bosnia, the Senate turned to another controversial issue: the question of whether men and women in the military should have separate housing and training.

Sam Brownback, R-Kan., offered an amendment that would have required the Pentagon to house male and female recruits in separate barracks during basic training. That proposal was overridden by a second-degree amendment offered by Olympia J. Snowe, R-Maine, and Max Cleland, D-Ga., reaffirming the provision in the bill that would have prohibited any immediate change in existing policy under which Navy and Air Force recruits and Army recruits headed for noncombat units were housed on different floors or in different wings of the same barracks. The Snowe-Cleland amendment was adopted on June 24 by a vote of 56–37, after which the amended Brownback amendment was adopted by voice vote.

On June 25, by a **key vote of 39–53 (R 31–21; D 8–32)**, the Senate rejected an amendment by Robert C. Byrd, D-W.Va., that would have required separate barracks and separate training units for male and female recruits. *(1998 key votes, p. 883)*

China Policy

Senate Democrats blocked several Republican amendments they said were designed mainly to undermine Clinton on the eve of a nine-day China visit. The amendments, offered by Tim Hutchinson, R-Ark., would have condemned Chinese human rights abuses and required a tougher U.S. stance toward Beijing's bids for international stature and financial assistance. Another amendment would have transferred from the Commerce Department to the State Department licensing authority for the shipment of U.S.-built satellites to China.

Hutchinson insisted that, by emphasizing the importance of human rights policy, his amendments would strengthen Clinton's hand in talks with Chinese leaders. But Democrats said that his proposals would violate the time-honored tradition that Congress close ranks behind a president when he is abroad.

Minority Leader Tom Daschle, D-S.D., threatened to bring work on the authorization bill to a standstill unless the China amendments were dropped. After some inconclusive procedural sparring, Hutchinson withdrew the amendments in return for a commitment that later in the year the Senate would debate a House-passed bill (HR 2358) that incorporated several of his proposals. HR 2358, however, never was considered in the Senate. *(China policy bill, p. 182)*

Earlier in its consideration of S 2057, the Senate had approved several China-related proposals by Hutchinson. On May 14, the Senate adopted by voice vote an amendment requiring the president to publicly identify companies controlled by the Chinese Army that did business in the United States. A motion to table (kill) the amendment had been rejected 24–76. Also adopted by voice vote was a Hutchinson amendment requiring a report on imports produced by prison labor or forced child labor.

Base Closings

The administration's only major policy defeat was the Senate's approval June 25, by a vote of 48–45, of an amendment by James M. Inhofe, R-Okla., to tighten the existing limits on the Pentagon's ability to close or scale down military bases without congressional approval. The vote was yet another reflection of congressional anger that the White House had interfered in the 1995 base-closing process to save jobs in the vote-rich states of California and Texas.

Other Amendments

By a vote of 44–49, the Senate on June 25 rejected an amendment by Patty Murray, D-Wash., to repeal a ban on female service members or military dependents stationed overseas from obtaining abortions in U.S. military hospitals abroad, even if the procedure was paid for with private funds.

The Senate adopted by voice vote a Thurmond amendment to authorize a 3.6 percent military pay raise instead of the 3.1 percent increase requested. The higher pay raise was in the House bill as well.

Senators agreed by voice vote to another Thurmond amendment giving the president authority to waive the one-year moratorium on the use of antipersonnel land mines.

CONFERENCE ACTION

The House adopted the conference report on HR 3616 (H Rept 105-736) on Sept. 24 by a vote of 373–50. The Senate agreed to it 96–2 Oct. 1, clearing the bill for the president.

Brushing aside objections from some social conservatives, conferees approved language keeping men and women together in basic training. Because the Senate had voted against separate units by a large margin, the final report included only a nonbinding expression by the House that basic training should be separate. The bill also included a provision requiring that permanent walls separate male and female recruits in barracks.

Conferees delayed a contentious decision on the production of tritium, an ingredient in enhancing nuclear weapons explosions. Although the administration had planned to decide by the end of the year where to produce tritium, conferees delayed a decision for one year.

The conference agreement transferred jurisdiction over the licensing of satellite exports from the Commerce Department to the State Department. The State Department had

had responsibility for satellite controls until it was switched to Commerce in 1996, after Commerce officials argued that technology once judged to have military characteristics was widely available commercially.

As had been routine for years, both versions of the bill had added several hundred million dollars to buy various versions of the C-130 cargo plane built by Lockheed Martin in Marietta, Ga. The administration had requested one plane, the House had wanted eight, and the Senate had approved five. In the end, conferees authorized seven, including four for the National Guard and reserves and two for the Marine Corps.

Conferees also included the $50 million down payment on another helicopter carrier that the Senate had added to the bill. The House had included $10 million for the project in its bill.

MAJOR PROVISIONS

As signed into law by the president on Oct. 17, 1998, HR 3616 authorized $270.5 billion in defense spending in fiscal 1999, $406 million less than requested. The bill also included $1.86 billion for U.S. troops in Bosnia, funding that had been requested and approved as emergency spending and, therefore, was exempt from the defense budget ceiling set by the 1997 balanced-budget law (PL 105-33).

Major provisions of HR 3616 are the following.

Personnel Issues

• Authorized, as requested, an active-duty force of slightly fewer than 1.4 million personnel, a reduction of nearly 36,000 from the fiscal 1998 level. The House bill had made a cut only about two-thirds that large.

• Authorized a National Guard and reserve force of more than 885,000—roughly what Clinton requested but nearly 10,000 fewer than the previous year.

• Authorized—to help recruiters in an increasingly difficult market—$36 million more than Clinton requested for advertising; $22 million more for bonuses paid to recruits who signed up for critical or hard-to-fill jobs; and $20 million more than was requested for education benefits, a prime recruiting incentive.

• Authorized a 3.6 percent increase in basic pay for military personnel in fiscal 1999 rather than the 3.1 percent requested by Clinton. The increase was initiated by the House, agreed to by the Senate, and ultimately accepted by the administration.

• Ordered the Pentagon to test options for improving medical care for military retirees age sixty-five and older. Because those people were eligible for Medicare, they were receiving only limited coverage from the Pentagon's health care system. That had become a very sore point not only with the large population of military retirees but also with active-duty personnel nearing the time when they typically decided whether to make the military a career.

The conference report authorized:

• A three-year program, conducted in at least six locations, allowing retirees and their families to participate in the relatively generous health insurance program available to civilian federal employees.

• A test program in two locations for using the Pentagon's Tricare dependent medical insurance program to supplement Medicare coverage for retirees, along the lines of commercially available "Medi-gap" supplemental insurance.

Readiness and Facilities

• Required that a more accurate readiness reporting system be implemented by Jan. 15, 2000. Conferees said this was necessary because of contradictions between the Pentagon's official assessment that military forces remained fully combat ready and the growing consensus among top officials that the military was under a heavy strain from budget cuts and the workload.

• Authorized modest increases to several budget accounts to shore up readiness in the meantime. These included:

• $5.9 billion—$151 million more than Clinton requested—for the routine overhaul of ships, planes, and vehicles and their engines and electronic gear.

• $3.9 billion—$296 million more than requested—for maintenance of barracks and operational facilities.

• $155 million over the request for spare parts to keep Navy and Air Force planes flying, and $178 million more for day-to-day operating costs of military bases.

• Authorized for military facilities and family housing $8.6 billion, $666 million more than Clinton requested. Of the increase, $301 million was specified for National Guard and reserve units.

Antimissile Defense

• Authorized $3.55 billion for ballistic missile defense, $51 million less than requested, even though Republicans had been pressing Clinton to accelerate the deployment of antimissile defenses.

Among the most controversial projects were:

• Development of a system to protect U.S. territory against a relatively small number of missiles. The bill authorized Clinton's request for $951 million.

• The Army's Theater High-Altitude Area Defense (THAAD) system, intended to protect troops and allies abroad from long-range missiles. The conference report authorized $527 million, $294 million less than Clinton asked. Although all five of the system's flight tests had failed, the conferees urged Pentagon managers not to overreact to those failures but to redouble their efforts to make the program work.

• The Navy's long-range antimissile system, a counterpart to THAAD. The conferees authorized $310 million, which was $120 million more than requested.

• The Army's battlefield antimissile system, called MEADS. The conferees approved only $24 million of the $43 million requested. Moreover, they included in the bill a provision barring the use of those funds until the defense secretary certified to Congress that the program would be funded in future Pentagon budgets.

• A laser-armed antimissile satellite. The bill authorized $188 million, double the amount requested.

• Authorized $235 million of the $292 million requested for an antimissile laser to be carried by a large cargo plane. The Air Force was developing this project separately from the antimissile defense program.

Nuclear Weapons

• Authorized $12 billion for defense-related programs of the Energy Department, $330 million less than Clinton requested. Included in that was $177 million—$20 million more than requested—for production of tritium, a radioactive form of hydrogen gas used to boost the explosive power of nuclear weapons. Because tritium loses its punch in twelve years and had not been produced since 1988, the administration was trying to decide between two methods for producing more of the gas.

The House version of the defense bill included a provision that, in effect, would have forced the administration to build a new tritium production facility at the Savannah River Site in South Carolina. The conferees dropped that provision, adding one that would defer for at least one year the selection of a tritium production plant.

Ground Combat

• Underwrote the Army's plan to modernize its existing forces with high-tech communications links while developing a new generation of combat gear for a more agile combat force after about 2010. The Army had unveiled June 9 the outlines of its plan for a slimmer Army in the years ahead that would rely more on electronics and updated weapons for greater mobility.

The final bill authorized $676 million to continue upgrading M-1 tanks with larger cannon, improved night-vision equipment, and digital links; $612 million to equip missile-armed Apache helicopters with digital links and the Longbow target-finding radar; and $391 million to continue developing the new, smaller Comanche armed helicopter.

Air Combat

• Authorized, with few changes, the Pentagon's plan to fund three major jet fighter programs, including:

• $771 million for two of the Air Force's F-22 fighter and components to be used in future planes, plus $1.58 billion to continue flight testing the stealthy F-22. After the administration objected to a Senate provision barring additional production funds until at least 4 percent of the test flight program had been completed, conferees kept the restriction in the final bill but added language allowing the president to waive the restriction.

• $2.8 billion to buy thirty of the Navy's F/A-18 E and F jets.

• $935 million to continue developing the Joint Strike Fighter.

• Authorized $276 million to improve the Air Force's fleet of twenty-one B-2 stealth bombers—$86 million more than requested—but there was no repeat of past battles over expanding the fleet. In a March 1998 report to Congress, an independent commission had recommended against further planes because of the cost.

• Added $25 million for one unrequested F-16. The House bill would have funded two of the fighter jets.

Naval Combat

• Authorized the $2.68 billion requested for three destroyers equipped with the Aegis antiaircraft system.

• Authorized the $2 billion requested for a new class of attack submarine—$1.5 billion for one sub and the rest to purchase components to be used in future subs.

• Authorized the $125 million requested for components of a nuclear-powered aircraft carrier designated CVN-77. Most of the ship's $4.6 billion cost was slated for inclusion in the fiscal 2001 budget.

Air and Sea Transport

• Authorized the $2.9 billion requested for thirteen wide-body, C-17 cargo jets plus components for future purchases.

• Authorized $743 million to buy eight V-22 Ospreys, hybrid airplane/helicopters used by the Marine Corps. The budget requested, and the Senate approved, seven aircraft, but the House added an additional plane.

• Authorized the $639 million requested for a ship designed to carry 700 Marines, their equipment, and landing craft.

• Authorized $50 million for advance purchases of components to be used in a helicopter carrier that could cost upward of $1.3 billion. Conferees said that the ship, which would be built by Litton Industries in the hometown of Senate Majority Leader Lott of Mississippi, would replace an older helicopter carrier for which the Navy had planned a $1 billion overhaul.

National Guard and Reserves

• Provided, as usual, more equipment to National Guard and reserve units than the Pentagon requested. The conferees approved $745 million for the Guard and reserves, in addition to the $1.36 billion worth of gear that was earmarked for them in Clinton's budget request.

The largest single addition was $306 million for four C-130 cargo planes. The conferees also approved $112 million for two tanker versions of the C-130 for the Marine Corps. In all, the conference report authorized $453 million for seven C-130s, all of which would be built by Lockheed Martin in Marietta, Ga., adjoining the district of House Speaker Newt Gingrich, R-Ga. The administration had requested $64 million for one aircraft.

China and U.S. Security

• Included several provisions added by the Senate because of allegations that China had improved its long-range missiles with technology gleaned from launching U.S.-made satellites.

The most significant of the provisions transferred authority over satellite export controls from the Commerce Department to the State Department. Clinton had moved the authority to Commerce in 1996 at the urging of satellite manufacturers, who complained that the State Department took too long deciding on transfers.

The conference report also included a provision barring the secretary of the Navy from leasing a former Navy base in Long Beach, Calif., to a Chinese government-owned shipping line.

Other Provisions

• Repealed a one-year moratorium on the use of antipersonnel landmines that was slated to go into effect, with some exemptions, in February 1999.

• Included a nonbinding provision expressing the sense of the House that the president and secretary of defense should adhere to the standard of "exemplary conduct" required of military commanders.

1999 Defense Appropriations

Congress in 1998 cleared a $250.5 billion defense appropriations bill for fiscal 1999. President Clinton dropped his veto threat and signed the bill into law (HR 4103—PL 105-262), after the conference committee cut a House provision that would have required the president to obtain congressional authorization before sending U.S. forces on an offensive military operation.

Combined with funds in two other appropriations bills—$8.45 billion in the military construction appropriations bill (HR 4059—PL 105-237) and $11.9 billion in the energy and water appropriations bill (HR 4060—PL 105-245)—HR 4103 brought overall defense spending to about $271 billion. That was within the $271.5 billion limit the 1997 balanced-budget law (HR 2015—PL 105-33) had set for the total defense budget for fiscal 1999.

HR 4103 appropriated $488 million less than Clinton requested, a reduction that largely reflected a shift of funds out of the defense bill and into the separate military construction bill rather than an attempt at a defense cutback. On the contrary, defense-minded members had contended that Clinton's budget was too tight and the services' combat readiness was eroding as a result.

But there was no serious effort to add money to the defense budget request until September. By then work on the defense appropriations measure was all but wrapped up, but Congress knew that it would have another chance to increase the defense budget because Clinton had submitted a request for fiscal 1999 supplemental appropriations that included defense items. Because Clinton's supplemental request in-cluded $1 billion for spare parts, equipment overhauls, and other readiness-related purposes, conferees on HR 4103 left out of their final bill at least $400 million for spare parts and repairs, using the money instead to fund other priorities.

The supplemental defense spending approved by Congress ultimately totaled about $9 billion and included Clinton's request for $1.87 billion in emergency funding for U.S. peacekeeping forces in Bosnia. The Senate had included the Bosnia money in its version of HR 4103, but the House had refused to do so. The supplemental appropriations were included in an omnibus spending bill (HR 4328—PL 105-277).

HOUSE ACTION

The House passed its $251 billion version of the defense appropriations bill on June 24 by a vote of 358–61. The House Appropriations Committee had reported HR 4103 (H Rept 105-591) on June 22.

The House-passed bill cut more than $2.2 billion from Clinton's overall proposed budget total, primarily by omitting the $1.9 billion Clinton had requested for the continued deployment of U.S. troops in Bosnia. Deficit-minded members balked at the president's request that the money be declared emergency funding and, therefore, exempt from the budget caps. Plus, many members of Congress were frustrated that Clinton, having sent troops into Bosnia without congressional approval, had twice ignored his own deadline for withdrawing them and now refused to set a date at all.

The House Appropriations Committee, however, did approve $1.6 billion in emergency funding to help the Pentagon improve the security of its computer systems and solve the Year 2000 problem. But, after budget conservatives objected to what they considered a circumvention of the 1997 budget agreement's caps, House Republican leaders decided to remove the $1.6 billion from the bill. By a near party-line vote of 221–201 on June 24, the House adopted the rule governing debate on HR 4103 that included language stripping the money from the bill.

House appropriators made a number of changes in the budget Clinton submitted, adding $3 billion for programs and projects it liked better than his. One of the costliest examples of this was the addition of $422 million for another seven C-130 cargo planes beyond the one Clinton had requested. The plane was built by Lockheed Martin in Marietta, Ga., near the district of Speaker Newt Gingrich, R-Ga. A large portion of the money spent on congressional initiatives—$1.4 billion—was aimed at beefing up maintenance of facilities and equipment rather than to buy products.

The cost of those added programs was more than offset by cuts in other parts of the defense budget request. Cuts in major weapons systems included $406 million from the $822 million requested for the Theater High-Altitude Areas Defense (THAAD), an antimissile program that had failed in several tests, and $220 million from the $2.8 billion requested for F/A-18 "E" and "F" model Navy fighter jets. But most savings in the bill would come from price reductions since the budget was drafted and from several efficiency measures that the committee insisted would have no negative impact on Pentagon operations.

Although it had triggered a veto threat from the administration, there was no floor debate on a provision in the bill to bar the use of funds for U.S. forces to conduct offensive military operations unless authorized by Congress pursuant to its constitutional authority to declare war. The amendment, sponsored by David E. Skaggs, D-Colo., had been added during committee consideration by a 30–25 vote. Skaggs had added a similar provision to the House version of the fiscal 1998 supplemental spending bill (HR 3579—PL 105-174), but it was dropped in conference.

HR 4103 included the president's request for a 3.1 percent military pay raise. House appropriators thus disregarded the provision of the House-passed defense authorization bill (HR 3616—PL 105-261) calling for a 3.6 percent pay increase. *(1999 defense authorization, p. 252)*

SENATE ACTION

The Senate passed a $252 billion version of HR 4103 by vote of 97–2 on July 30. The Senate Appropriations Committee had reported its defense spending bill (S 2132—S Rept 105-200) on June 4.

During floor action on the bill, the Senate decisively rejected a challenge to Clinton's deployment of U.S. troops in Bosnia. Early in 1998, Republican Kay Bailey Hutchison of Texas, one of the most prominent critics of the Bosnia deployment, and senior Appropriations Committee Democrat Robert C. Byrd of West Virginia had begun floating legislative proposals designed to ratchet down the number of personnel in Bosnia.

When the Appropriations Committee approved the defense bill, it omitted the requested funds for the Bosnia mission, pending a test of Senate sentiment on the issue. But shortly after taking up the bill on July 30, the Senate adopted, by voice vote, an amendment by Appropriations Committee Chairman Ted Stevens, R-Alaska, that added the $1.9 billion and designated it as emergency funding.

Hutchison then offered an amendment to require the Pentagon to reduce the roughly 6,700-member U.S. force in Bosnia at that time to 5,000 troops by Oct. 1, 1999. She argued that the Bosnia mission was sapping morale and combat readiness out of proportion to its significance to U.S. national security, and that U.S. allies in Europe should carry a greater share of the burden. But Defense Secretary William S. Cohen and Joint Chiefs of Staff Chairman Gen. Henry H. Shelton weighed in with a letter strongly opposing the amendment, insisting that military commanders needed the ability to determine how many troops were necessary for the mission. They warned that a mandate from Congress to cut the number of troops in Bosnia "would invite heightened intransigence and extremism" from those in Bosnia opposed to the U.S.-sponsored peace process. The amendment was rejected, 68–31.

Opponents of the Bosnia mission lost another fight when the Senate rejected, 84–15, an amendment by Richard J. Durbin, D-Ill., that would have barred the use of U.S. forces for offensive military operations unless authorized by Congress. Coming as it did amid warnings that Clinton might soon send additional troops to keep the peace in Kosovo, a restive province of Serbia, the Senate vote bespoke grudging acquiescence in Clinton's use of military force in the Balkans rather than enthusiastic support.

The Senate did approve by voice vote several amendments with a bearing on Balkan operations, including one by Pat Roberts, R-Kan., requiring the president to report certain information to Congress if he deployed U.S. troops elsewhere in the former Yugoslavia or in neighboring Albania or Macedonia.

The Senate adopted by voice vote an amendment by Tim Hutchinson, R-Ark., to deny U.S. visas to officials of foreign governments directly involved in implementing policies of religious persecution, forced abortion or sterilization, or female genital mutilation. As originally offered, the amendment was aimed at Chinese officials involved in religious persecution or forced population control. A motion to table (kill) the proposal was rejected, 29–70, but by a vote of 99–0 the scope of the amendment was broadened so that it would not apply to just Chinese officials.

The Senate approved by voice vote a 3.6 percent military pay raise instead of the requested 3.1 percent in the House bill.

The only amendment specifically aimed at a major weapons system was an effort by Russell D. Feingold, D-Wis., to cut $220 million from the $2.8 billion requested for thirty F/A-18 E and F model jet fighters. The amendment was tabled (killed), 80–19.

CONFERENCE ACTION

The House adopted the conference report (H Rept 105-746) on Sept. 28 by a vote of 369–43. The Senate cleared the bill the next day by a vote of 94–2.

The final bill appropriated nearly $500 million less than Clinton requested. Anticipating Clinton's supplemental budget request, House-Senate conferees left out some funds that both chambers had planned to add to his budget request. For example, the conference report included no additional funding for aircraft spare parts, even though both chambers had approved extra funds for that purpose. Similarly, the conference report added much less for equipment overhauls than Congress typically supplemented.

As usual, conferees found a couple of billion dollars for members' pet projects, including $400 million for six C-130 cargo planes. Some of the projects were paid for with across-the-board cuts in the budget request that conferees said reflected changing economic conditions, including lower-than-anticipated inflation, lower fuel prices, and a stronger dollar.

Conferees dropped several controversial policy amendments, including the Skaggs amendment, which had triggered a veto threat from the administration, and the modified Hutchinson amendment. The conference report included, in modified form, the Roberts amendment requiring the president to report to Congress before deployment of U.S. forces to Yugoslavia, Albania, or Macedonia, but the provision could be waived.

Conferees followed the lead of the Senate and approved the higher military pay raise.

MAJOR PROVISIONS

As signed into law Oct. 17, 1998, HR 4103 appropriated $250.5 billion for fiscal 1999, $488 million less than Clinton requested in regular defense spending. The bill did not include the $1.86 billion requested in emergency funding for the Bosnia mission.

Major provisions of HR 4103:

Personnel Issues

• Added $202 million to the budget request for a 3.6 percent military pay raise, instead of the 3.1 percent pay increase in the budget request. The administration now supported the larger raise.

• Included a provision, sponsored by C. W. Bill Young, R-Fla., chairman of the House Appropriations National Security Subcommittee, requiring the Pentagon to review the adequacy of overall military compensation and include any recommendations for change in the fiscal 2000 budget request. The conferees warned that the dissatisfaction many in the military felt with their pay and quality of life included a perception that key fringe benefits, such as pensions and medical care, were being eroded by the budget squeeze.

Operations and Readiness

• Added $455 million to reduce the backlog of buildings overdue for maintenance and repair; of this, all but $5 million was specified for quality-of-life projects such as improvements to barracks.

• Added $300 million to the bill for operating costs of military bases, a budget account that routinely was short-changed in budget requests.

• Ordered a report detailing the criteria that would be used to decide which jobs could be contracted out to the private sector. The conferees expressed "significant concern" over the impact on military readiness of Defense Secretary Cohen's plan to save $6 billion a year by allowing private contractors to bid on jobs at military bases that were performed by 150,000 civilian federal employees.

In some cases, the conferees' skepticism went further: they demanded three months' notice before the Pentagon took steps to privatize jobs at three Army arsenals in Arkansas, Illinois, and New York. They also added $21 million to the budget request to forestall a planned reduction in civilian jobs at

a Marine Corps maintenance depot in Barstow, Calif., a city represented by Republican and House Appropriations Committee member Jerry Lewis.

Antimissile Defense

• Appropriated $3.46 billion of the $3.6 billion requested for the Pentagon's antimissile defense program, including:

   • $445 million of the $822 million Clinton requested for the Army's THAAD system, intended to protect U.S. troops and allies overseas against long-range missiles. All five THAAD flight tests had failed.

   • $951 million, as requested, to continue developing a system that would protect U.S. territory against a small number of attacking missiles.

   • $338 million, $148 million more than requested, to continue developing a long-range, Navy antimissile system.

   • $74 million more than the $59 million requested to accelerate development of a satellite armed with an antimissile laser.

• Appropriated $267 million of the $292 million requested for an Air Force effort to mount an antimissile laser in the nose of a Boeing 747 cargo jet. This was not part of the antimissile program's budget.

Ground Combat

• Appropriated $368 million, as requested, to continue developing the Comanche stealth helicopter and $317 million for the Crusader mobile cannon, thus keeping on track the Army's top two weapons priorities.

• Appropriated $673 million to continue upgrading M-1 tanks with larger cannon, improved night-vision equipment, and digital links.

• Appropriated $612 million to equip missile-armed Apache helicopters with digital links and the Longbow target-finding radar.

Air Combat

• Made only minor changes in funding requests for the Pentagon's three major combat airplane programs, appropriating:

   • $581 million—$14 million less than requested—for the first two production-line versions of the Air Force's F-22 fighter and $190 million for components for future planes, plus $1.58 billion to continue developing the aircraft;

   • $2.88 billion for thirty F/A-18 E and F model Navy fighters, a reduction of $15 million from the budget request;

   • $927 million to continue developing the Joint Strike Fighter, intended to be built in three versions to replace 1970s-vintage planes being used by the Navy, Air Force, and Marine Corps. This was an increase of almost $8 million above the request.

• Halved what the House bill included for several aircraft programs: $30 million for a single Air Force F-16 fighter instead of two for $60 million; $50 million of the $86 million the House added for upgrading B-2 stealth bombers; and $36 million for components in case the Pentagon decided to buy another Joint STARS radar plane—the House had wanted $72 million for components of two planes.

Naval Combat

• Appropriated $2.67 billion for three Navy destroyers equipped with the Aegis antiaircraft system, $5 million less than was requested.

 • Appropriated as requested:

  • $1.5 billion for a new nuclear-powered submarine, plus $505 million for the nuclear reactor and other components to be used in another sub slated for funding in fiscal 2001.

  • $275 million to refuel one of the nuclear-powered carriers already in service, plus $125 million for components to be used in a new carrier—the tenth ship of the *Nimitz* class. Most of the $4.6 billion cost would be included in the fiscal 2001 budget.

• Included only $105 million of the roughly $180 million requested to design a new aircraft carrier—cheaper to operate than the *Nimitz* class—the first of which would enter service in 2013.

• Appropriated the $85 million requested to design a new destroyer.

• Appropriated $278 million instead of the $179 million requested to continue developing and installing in warships a "cooperative engagement capability"—a digital communications network over which all the ships and planes in a force could exchange data about the location of enemy units.

Air and Sea Transport

• Appropriated the $2.6 billion requested for thirteen C-17 wide-body cargo jets.

• Appropriated $611 million for seven C-22 Osprey tilt-rotor aircraft to be used by the Marines as troop carriers. The House bill had added $86 million for an eighth.

• Appropriated the requested $639 million for a transport ship to carry a Marine Corps landing force and a cargo ship to carry the tanks and other equipment of a U.S.-based Army unit.

• Added $45 million to the administration's budget request for components that would be used by Litton Industries to build a new helicopter carrier in Pascagoula, Miss., the hometown of Senate Majority Leader Trent Lott, R-Miss. The Navy had seven of these ships, the newest of which cost $1.3 billion. This seemingly minor addition lay the groundwork for a major additional cost in some future budget. The new carrier would replace an older ship the Navy had planned to refurbish at the cost of about $1 billion.

Balkans Provision

• Barred the deployment of U.S. forces to Yugoslavia, Albania, or Macedonia—other than the small observation force already in Macedonia—unless the president sent Congress a report outlining the anticipated scope, duration, and cost of the mission. The provision allowed the president to waive the reporting requirement in an emergency.

FIRST 1999 SUPPLEMENTAL BILL

Congress approved more than $8 billion in fiscal 1999 supplemental emergency funding for defense-related items as part of an omnibus appropriations bill (HR 4328—PL 105-277) that was signed into law Oct. 21, 1998. The bill overall included nearly $21 billion in supplemental funding.

President Clinton had requested about $4.5 billion for defense, but by the time Congress finished the defense spending had reached $8.26 billion. Of that total, $7.7 billion was for the Department of Defense and $525 million for the Department of Energy.

Passage of the bill marked the first time since 1985 that the Pentagon received an inflation-adjusted budget increase. GOP leaders cited the additional funding to buttress their argument that Clinton had undermined national security by reducing the size of the military too much, sending it overseas too often, and cutting its budget too much.

Sources said money in the bill would also address recommendations from two independent panels that examined national security matters.

• The first panel, chaired by retired Adm. David Jeremiah, looked into the CIA's failure to predict nuclear tests by India in May 1998. The Jeremiah panel in a June report identified a series of structural weaknesses, including a lack of trained and skilled analysts to sift through intelligence data, a shortage of human agents on the ground, and a lack of coordination between different agencies.

• The other panel, led by former Ford administration defense secretary Donald H. Rumsfeld (who would take the same post again in 2001 in the George W. Bush administration), warned in July 1998 that foreign governments were becoming increasingly adept at concealing nuclear missiles and nuclear, biological, and chemical weapons programs from satellites and other intelligence gathering.

Defense spending in HR 4328 included: $1.3 billion for military readiness, $1.86 billion for operations in Bosnia, $1.5 billion for intelligence spending, $1 billion for antimissile defense, $529 million for antiterrorism, $469 million for disaster-related repairs, $2 million for a defense health program, $1.1 billion for Year 2000 computer fixes, and $42 million for drug interdiction. The bill also provided $525 million for an Energy Department program to assist Russia dispose of nuclear material. (The total was reduced by $67 million because of savings from reduced fuel prices.)

The bill also included emergency funding for U.S. embassy security and farm relief.

SECOND 1999 SUPPLEMENTAL BILL

Congress approved a second fiscal 1999 supplemental spending bill (HR 1141—PL 106-31) the following year. President Clinton signed it into law May 21, 1999.

In response to Serb assaults against ethnic Albanians in the Serbian province of Kosovo, NATO had begun a massive bombing campaign at the end of March against Yugoslav forces. The administration subsequently requested $5 billion to pay for the NATO military operation along with $453 million for operations against Iraq. *(Kosovo policy, pp. 177, 204)*

Many Republicans viewed the new request as an opportunity to once again bolster defense readiness accounts. By providing additional emergency spending in the fiscal 1999 supplemental—including the first of a multiyear pay increase for military personnel—House Republicans hoped to ease the "cash crunch" when fiscal 2000 appropriations ran up against the budgetary caps set in 1997.

The final bill included $10.9 billion in defense-related funding—the $5.5 billion Clinton requested, plus another $5.4 billion added by Congress. In addition to the funds for Kosovo and Iraq operations, the bill appropriated: $2.35 billion for spare parts, maintenance, operating costs, and recruiting; $1.84 billion for a 4.8 percent increase in military pay and pensions; $550 million for procurement; $475 million for military construction; and $200 million for the Coast Guard.

1999 Military Construction

Congress in 1998 cleared an $8.45 billion fiscal 1999 military construction appropriations bill (HR 4059—PL 105-237).

HR 4059 provided $666 million more than President Clinton requested but $759 million less than the fiscal 1998 level, an 8 percent decline. During action on the bill, members of both parties lamented the spending constraints imposed by the 1997 balanced-budget agreement (PL 105-33).

HR 4059 had sailed through Congress with minimal debate and was the only appropriations bill signed into law by the Oct. 1 start of the fiscal year. The ease of enactment was not surprising for what was typically the least controversial of the thirteen annual spending measures. It provided a stark contrast to the previous year's battle triggered by Clinton's decision to use his short-lived line-item veto authority—an action Congress decisively reversed. *(1998 military construction, p. 250)*

Emergency supplemental funding for military construction projects subsequently brought the overall total appropriated for fiscal 1999 to $9.1 billion.

LEGISLATIVE ACTION

The House passed, 396–10, an $8.2 billion military construction bill on June 22, 1998, with almost no debate and without amendments. The House Appropriations Committee had reported the bill (H Rept 105-578) on June 16.

The Senate passed an $8.48 billion version on June 25 by voice vote. The Senate Appropriations Committee had reported its version (S 2160—S Rept 105-213) on June 11.

Both the House and Senate versions added money for new family housing and improvements to existing units. But the biggest increases were for construction projects. As in the past, Appropriations Committee members took special interest in the military construction needs of their states.

CONFERENCE ACTION

The House adopted the conference report (H Rept 105-647) by a vote of 417–1 on July 29. The Senate cleared the bill by a vote of 87–3 on Sept. 1. President Clinton signed the bill into law Sept. 20.

Conferees had quickly reached agreement on a final version. The conference bill provided $216 million more than the House bill but remained $31 million below the Senate version. Nearly half of the $666 million added to Clinton's budget request was for the National Guard and reserves.

MAJOR PROVISIONS

- **Family housing.** The bill's largest account was $3.54 billion for family housing, approximately $64 million more than Clinton had wanted. The House version would have appropriated $3.5 billion and the Senate version, $3.58 billion.
- **Military construction.** The final bill provided $3.27 billion for military construction projects, including $480 million for National Guard and reserve projects and $154 million for NATO infrastructure. The administration had requested a total of $2.57 billion, of which $180 million was to go to National Guard and reserve projects and $185 million to NATO. The House bill would have appropriated a total of $2.99 billion and the Senate bill, $3.16 billion.
- **Base closures.** The final bill provided $1.63 billion for base-closure and realignment costs. Both the House and Senate had approved the $1.73 billion Clinton had requested, but conferees reduced it by $100 million.

SUPPLEMENTAL APPROPRIATIONS

The fiscal 1999 omnibus appropriations bill (HR 4328—PL 105-277), enacted Oct. 21, 1998, contained $209 million in emergency supplemental funding for military construction needed to repair damage resulting from monsoons in Korea and Hurricanes Georges and Bonnie. The fiscal 1999 supplemental appropriations bill (HR 1141—PL 106-31), enacted May 21, 1999, included $475 million for unrequested military construction projects overseas. These additions brought the total fiscal 1999 appropriation for military construction to $9.1 billion.

Defense Assessments

Congress received two reports in 1997 assessing the nation's long-term defense needs. The Pentagon's Quadrennial

Defense Review, a six-month assessment of future defense needs and plans, was presented to Congress in May. A commission of defense specialists set up by Congress to review the Pentagon study issued its report in December.

The Pentagon study took a more conventional approach, focusing on strengthening existing forces against known threats. The outside study, on the other hand, recommended more long-range planning to anticipate future threats both at home and abroad, including those from unconventional weapons and terrorism.

Meanwhile, in an effort to find more money for weapons modernization, Defense Secretary William S. Cohen in November announced a series of plans that were aimed at making Pentagon operations cheaper and more agile.

QUADRENNIAL DEFENSE REVIEW

The Pentagon's review concluded that it was necessary to retain most of the existing forces, missions, and strategies, and to modernize the military with money cut from defense programs traditionally held sacred on Capitol Hill—military bases, civilian maintenance and administrative jobs, and the National Guard and reserves.

The study reaffirmed the main elements of President Clinton's defense program, including the goal of being able to fight and win two major wars in widely separated regions but overlapping in time—for example, in the Persian Gulf and on the Korean peninsula. It was also assumed that the United States would continue to deploy about 100,000 personnel in Europe and the western Pacific and continue to participate in peacekeeping missions, international training exercises, and other nonwar missions.

But, during appearances May 20 and May 21 before the Senate Armed Services and the House National Security committees, Cohen also reaffirmed the conclusion, reached nearly two years before by Joint Chiefs of Staff Chairman Gen. John M. Shalikashvili, that to fund necessary high-tech weapons, the Pentagon's annual procurement budget would have to reach $60 billion, a climb of some $15 billion.

Cohen told the committees that it would be too risky to make major cuts in force structure—the number of combat divisions, warships, and fighter squadrons—or in plans to buy high-tech weaponry. Some critics had called for canceling one or more of the new generation of weapons still on the drawing board or entering production. Key targets were the three fighter jet programs on which the Air Force, Navy, and Marine Corps planned to spend more than $300 billion. But the review concluded that canceling any of those programs—the Air Force F-22, the Navy F/A-18 E and F, or the tri-service Joint Strike Fighter—would not be prudent.

Instead, Cohen told the committees, the lion's share of the money should come from a new round of base closings, a push to contract out administrative functions to private companies, and additional cuts in the National Guard and reserves. Cohen and his top aides contended that the Pentagon had cut its overall size and its operating force by about one-third in the past decade while reducing the number of bases by only 18 percent.

Some defense policy analysts complained that the defense review was merely a bureaucratic effort to preserve the status quo, and that the Pentagon had squandered an opportunity to radically reorganize its forces at a time when the country was relatively free of any major, imminent threat.

But the outside critics' objections did not appear to resonate with the two defense committees. Indeed, the most significant challenge to Cohen's plan came from House Republicans who complained that the defense review would inhibit public debate on the size of the defense budget because Cohen had insisted that its recommendations conform to defense budgets of no more than $250 billion, plus inflation.

DEFENSE REVIEW PANEL

The blue-ribbon commission set up by Congress concluded in a Dec. 1 report that the Pentagon should spend less money fine-tuning its existing forces and more on the weapons and tactics the nation might need in the coming twenty years. Created under the fiscal 1997 defense authorization bill (PL 104-201), the nine-member panel was headed by Philip A. Odeen, president and CEO of BDM International Corp., a defense consulting and research firm. Odeen had held key positions in the Defense Department and on the National Security Council staff. The other eight members were retired senior military officers or veteran defense analysts.

The commission warned that Pentagon plans to improve the armored divisions and fighter squadrons that swept aside their Iraqi opponents in the 1991 Persian Gulf War would be less relevant against threats that could develop in the next two decades. The report said that the Clinton administration's two-war scenario was feasible with existing forces but counterproductive for the long run. According to the analysis, the two-war plan would give the services a rationale for spending money to beef up for traditional wars that were unlikely to happen, rather than developing the equipment and methods that would be needed to face the nontraditional threats that were likely to confront the country in the future.

To cope with such threats, the commission recommended developing forces that could be sent more quickly to distant trouble spots and, once there, be less vulnerable to chemical or biological weapons. The panel also recommended that the Pentagon devote more effort to preparing for attacks on U.S. territory, including terrorist strikes using nuclear, chemical, and biological weapons.

To the dismay of conservatives pressing for the early deployment of a nationwide defense against ballistic missiles, however, the panel endorsed the administration's plan to develop such a system but defer deployment until it seemed warranted by a specific threat.

The commission called for spending $5 billion to $10 billion annually for the proposed new forces and recommended getting that money by closing additional military bases and relying on private contractors instead of federal employees and military personnel for administrative and maintenance work. Without such cutbacks in overhead costs, the panel warned, the Pentagon would have to cancel major weapons programs or disband some of its forces.

The commission acknowledged that the services were considering the types of changes it recommended, but it said the financial follow-through was too skimpy. The advisory panel called on the services to conduct large-scale exercises to test some of their novel concepts and to push ahead with those that showed promise.

COST-CUTTING PLAN

On Nov. 10 Cohen announced a plan to cut operating costs at the Pentagon by $6 billion a year, thereby providing more money for weapons modernization. Nearly half the anticipated savings—$2.8 billion—was to come from two more rounds of base closings that would require legislative authorization. Congress had brushed aside Cohen's proposal for new rounds of base closings in 1999 and 2001 as part of the fiscal 1998 defense authorization bill (HR 1119—PL 105-85). Cohen's new plan put off the dates until 2001 and 2005, making it potentially more palatable by giving states time to absorb the economic impact of closures and deferring any new base closure decisions until after Clinton left office. Many members felt that Clinton had meddled improperly in the last base-closing rounds in 1995 for political gain. *(1998 defense authorization, p. 239)*

Most of the rest of Cohen's streamlining was to be accomplished without legislation, for an annual savings of about $3.2 billion. However, more than three-quarters of that amount—$2.5 billion—was to come from another proposal likely to draw congressional opposition: allowing private contractors to bid against Pentagon agencies over the following five years in such areas as payroll management, personnel services, leased property management, and drug testing. Members of Congress representing significant numbers of federal employees typically opposed contracting out large numbers of jobs, warning that once the federal government lost its trained workforce, the private company that won the competition had great leverage to raise its price for renewing the contract.

Antimissile Defenses

The 105th Congress voted for increased funding for the Pentagon's antimissile defense programs in fiscal 1998 and 1999. But Senate Republican proposals to mandate the deployment of a national defense shield by 2003 (S 7) or to call for deployment of such a system when it was technologically feasible (S 1873) never reached the floor.

The Pentagon was part way through a three-year program to develop a national missile defense program, which was intended to protect U.S. territory from an attack by a limited number of missiles. Development of the program was to be completed by 2000, when President Clinton was to decide, based on the system's performance and the world situation, whether to deploy it by 2003.

Republican critics wanted to move faster. Delaying the decision, they contended, created uncertainty in the minds of government officials and contractors.

Beyond the feasibility of a system, the United States still faced the thorny issue of how to mesh national antimissile defenses with the 1972 Anti-Ballistic Missile (ABM) Treaty, which imposed stringent limits on the deployment of missile defenses protecting either U.S. or Russian territory.

In addition to the national missile defense system, the United States was also developing so-called theater antimissile defenses, intended to protect U.S. forces or allies in distant theaters of military operations instead of protecting U.S. territory. Concerns about advances in Iranian and North Korean missile programs spurred members to seek additional funding for the Pentagon in 1998.

BACKGROUND

Since 1983 when President Ronald Reagan launched his effort to develop a nationwide missile defense—officially the Strategic Defense Initiative (SDI) and derisively nicknamed "Star Wars" by its critics—most Republicans had taken the view that missile defenses should be fielded as quickly as was technically possible. *(Congress and the Nation Vol. VI, p. 253; chronology since 1946, box, p. 307)*

They argued that ballistic missiles, possibly armed with chemical or biological weapons were, or soon would be, in the hands of so-called rogue states. Such states, they warned, might well disregard the horrible logic of deterrence that kept U.S.-Soviet relations eerily stable for decades even though each country had thousands of nuclear missile warheads aimed at the other.

Republicans tried unsuccessfully to arouse public interest in the issue during Clinton's first term. Late in 1995, Clinton vetoed the first version of the annual defense authorization bill because it would have required a nationwide antimissile defense by 2003. The veto was sustained, and there was no public outcry. *(Congress and the Nation Vol. IX, p. 316)*

A House GOP effort to pass a separate bill embodying the 2003 deadline collapsed when higher-than-anticipated estimates of the program's cost spooked budget-minded GOP deficit hawks. Senate action was blocked that year by a Democratic filibuster. An attempt to make it an issue in the 1996 presidential campaign fizzled.

Although the call for an antimissile defense gained little political traction outside the ranks of Republican activists, the party's leading defense specialists remained passionately committed to the effort, albeit as a ground-based system rather than the space-based defense envisioned by Reagan.

The Clinton administration put more emphasis on trying to head off potential missile threats by diplomatic means, including arms control agreements. In particular, White House officials contended that missile defense programs should not unnecessarily disrupt the ABM Treaty.

Opponents of missile defense, in Washington and abroad, argued that such a system would undermine the policy of mutual deterrence—embodied in the ABM Treaty—that had helped the world survive the cold war face-off between the United States and the Soviet Union without a single nuclear weapon being fired. Building a missile defense system, they said, would encourage current and future nuclear powers to build as many offensive weapons as possible to overcome or evade any U.S. defenses.

Clinton's strategy was to develop a system to protect the United States from a small number of missiles that might be fired by mistake or by a rogue state, but that would not be effective against a massive Russian attack. At the same time, he wanted to negotiate with Russia for changes in the ABM Treaty that would allow either country to have such a small-scale defense.

Administration officials said the ABM Treaty remained vital, reassuring Russia that its nuclear deterrent against the United States was still effective. Such reassurance was essential, they said, if the Russian legislature (the Duma) was to ratify the pending START II treaty slashing the number of U.S. and Russian nuclear warheads on long-range weapons. (The Duma agreed to the START II treaty in April 2000 but with conditions many Republicans found unacceptable, including continued adherence to the ABM Treaty.)

Those who wanted to build a missile defense system contended that the end of the cold war already had eroded the value of mutual deterrence between the United States and Russia. Weapons and technology, they said, were spreading to North Korea, Iran, Iraq, and Libya and could go farther, leaving the United States and its allies open to blackmail by just the threat of a nuclear attack.

Republicans complained that Democrats' deference to the ABM Treaty was a prescription for inaction or worse. They said it had led the Clinton administration to soft-pedal evidence of emerging missile threats. Although the treaty did not limit theater defenses, GOP critics insisted that the Pentagon had "dumbed down" the Army's Theater High-Altitude Area Defense (THAAD) and other theater defenses less they be so capable that they might duplicate the role of a national missile defense system and thus circumvent the treaty's limits.

ANTIMISSILE FUNDING

Congress in 1997 authorized a total of $4.08 billion for missile defense—$382 million more than Clinton's revised request—as part of the fiscal 1998 defense authorization bill (HR 1119—PL 105-85). Included in that was the $978 million requested to continue developing a nationwide defense system. The companion defense appropriations bill (HR 2266—PL 105-56) provided a total of $4.18 billion, including the same amount authorized for nationwide defense.

(1998 defense authorization, p. 239; 1998 defense appropriations, p. 245)

Congress provided an additional $179 million for antimissile defense as part of a fiscal 1998 supplemental appropriations measure (HR 3579—PL 105-174) signed into law May 1, 1998. These funds were intended to boost the ability of existing U.S. and Israeli antimissile weapons to deal with new Iranian and North Korean missiles.

In 1997 Israeli and U.S. intelligence agencies reported that Iran might, within a year, deploy a ballistic missile called Shahab-3 with a range sufficient to reach targets in Israel, Turkey, and Saudi Arabia. The United States also was caught off guard in 1997 when North Korea's No Dong 1 missile was deployed unexpectedly soon after its first test firing. Both of these missiles flew farther and faster than Iranian and North Korean missiles already in service.

Congress in 1998 authorized a total of $3.55 billion for missile defense—$51 million less than requested—in the fiscal 1999 defense authorization bill (HR 3616—PL 105-261). The bill authorized the $951 million requested for national missile defense, as did the companion defense appropriations bill (HR 4103—PL 105-262). The appropriations bill provided a total of $3.46 billion for antimissile defense. Republicans succeeded in adding another $1 billion to antimissile defense programs in the fiscal 1999 omnibus spending package (HR 4328—PL 105-277). *(1999 defense authorization, p. 252; 1999 defense appropriations, p. 259)*

ANTIMISSILE DEPLOYMENT

On April 30, 1997, the Senate Armed Services Committee reported a bill (S 7—S Rept 105-15) requiring the development and deployment of a national missile defense system by 2003 and directing the president to seek changes in the ABM Treaty. There was no further action on the bill, which had been introduced by Senate Majority Leader Trent Lott, R-Miss., and cosponsored by twenty-eight other Republicans.

The Armed Services Committee tried again the following year. This time the panel approved legislation (S 1873) calling for, but not requiring, a national defense against ballistic missiles "as soon as is technologically possible." S 1873, reported (S Rept 105-175) by the committee April 24, 1998, would have repudiated Clinton's plan to wait until 2000 before deciding whether to deploy.

Democratic filibusters twice blocked floor debate on S 1873. The first motion to invoke cloture, thus limiting debate, was rejected on May 13 by a vote of 59–41—one vote shy of the sixty votes needed to shut off debate. A second cloture motion was defeated by another 59–41 vote on Sept. 9.

Advocates of a national defense system had hoped to gain political advantage from a July 15, 1998, report by a congressionally mandated bipartisan commission of experts, chaired by Ford administration Defense Secretary Donald H. Rumsfeld. (Rumsfeld became defense secretary once again in 2001 in the George W. Bush administration.)

The panel warned that the United States might have little or no warning before hostile countries fielded ballistic missiles able to reach U.S. territory with nuclear, chemical, or biological warheads, and that hostile countries such as North Korea might have this missile capability within five years— much sooner than U.S. officials had estimated. Governments were becoming more adept at concealing missiles and weapons programs from prying satellites and other intelligence gathering, the commission said, and it was easier for them to obtain foreign help in developing or acquiring the technologies.

But Clinton's policy had been powerfully buttressed by a strong endorsement from the Joint Chiefs of Staff. The military chiefs' view had been expressed by their chairman, Gen. Henry H. Shelton, in an April 24, 1998, letter to James M. Inhofe, R-Okla. Inhofe, who chaired the Senate Armed Services Committee's Subcommittee on Readiness, had asked the Joint Chiefs to comment on the Rumsfeld report.

Writing on behalf of all the chiefs, Shelton endorsed the current plan of developing a defense by late 1999 and deciding in 2000 whether it should be deployed. He acknowledged that there was some risk that an adversary could acquire a long-range missile without being detected, but said the chiefs regarded this as unlikely. *(1999 action, p. 306)*

Terrorism Policy

The debate on U.S. policy on terrorism was renewed in the wake of the 1998 bombings of two U.S. embassies in Africa and retaliatory U.S. missile strikes. More than 250 people had been killed and more than 5,500 injured in the Aug. 7 bombing attacks on the embassies in Nairobi, Kenya, and Dar es Salaam, Tanzania. Twelve Americans were killed, all in Nairobi. In response, the United States on Aug. 20 launched missile strikes against targets in Afghanistan and Sudan.

U.S. RESPONSE

President Clinton cited "convincing evidence" that the Afghan bases had been involved in preparation for the embassy bombings. Clinton and other officials said the Sudan site was linked to exiled Saudi dissident Osama bin Laden and was used to process material used in making chemical weapons. Some foreign critics decried the missile attacks, contending that the site in Khartoum, Sudan, was a pharmaceutical plant that had nothing to do with chemical weapons.

Director of Central Intelligence George J. Tenet, Defense Secretary William S. Cohen, and other administration officials briefed lawmakers in secret Sept. 1–2 on the reasons for the U.S. strikes. Several senators who attended the classified briefings said the administration made a compelling case for both the missile attacks and the choice of targets.

Administration officials declined to say whether bin Laden was personally targeted, but some senators said that planners did have advance information the terrorist leader was at one of the camps. Bin Laden had warned of a war against the United States and issued an edict declaring that Americans should be killed.

Discussions were underway within the administration on how much to request for security upgrades at U.S. embassies. The funding was approved in 1999. But many lawmakers agreed that the fight against terrorism would take more than money and would require more than missile attacks. *(State Department authorization, p. 189)*

In May Clinton had issued a presidential order establishing within the National Security Council an Office of National Coordinator for Security, Infrastructure Protection and Counterterrorism, intended to oversee programs to combat chemical and biological weapons and attacks on computer systems and other critical networks.

Some Republicans, however, questioned whether the administration was doing an effective job of coordination. They had also expressed concern that the new approach shifted too much control away from the FBI.

LEGISLATION

In 1996 Congress had passed a modest antiterrorism bill (PL 104-132) in response to the bombing of a federal building in Oklahoma City a year earlier. The new law included provisions intended to block suspected terrorist groups from raising money in the United States and to turn away suspected terrorists at the border. It also authorized $1 billion over four years for the FBI and other agencies. *(Congress and the Nation Vol. IX, p. 727)*

But the law did not include the primary law enforcement tools that Clinton had sought: authority for federal agents to conduct multipoint wiretaps that could follow a person rather than a phone, and the use of chemical identifiers, known as taggants, in gunpowder. Conservative House Republicans, mistrustful of the federal government, rejected the wiretapping and chemical tracer provisions despite pleas from law enforcement officials.

Later in 1996, after a terrorist bombing killed nineteen U.S. service members at a Saudi Arabian air base, Congress authorized additional funding and procedures to combat and respond to domestic terrorist attacks (PL 104-201). The initiative included a program that called for training authorities in 120 cities over five years to respond to a chemical, biological, or nuclear incident. *(Congress and the Nation Vol. IX, pp. 308, 312)*

The fiscal 1998 funding bill for the departments of Commerce, Justice, and State and the federal judiciary (HR 2267—PL 105-119) instructed Attorney General Janet Reno to develop an antiterrorism plan. The plan was submitted to Congress in January 1999. And in the fiscal 1999 omnibus appropriations law (HR 4328—PL 105-277), Congress in 1998 set up a National Commission on Terrorism, which issued its report in June 2000. *(Terrorism policy, p. 308)*

The Senate in 1998 passed legislation (S 2536) to strengthen U.S. laws to fight terrorism, but the House did not act on the bill. *(Antiterrorism, p. 605; 1999–2000 action, p. 308)*

Chemical Weapons Treaty

The Senate in 1997 approved the ratification of the 1993 Chemical Weapons Convention—a treaty banning the development, production, sale, use, or stockpiling of chemical weapons. But Congress did not clear legislation to implement the pact (HR 4328—PL 105-277) for another year and a half.

Senate approval of the resolution of ratification of the chemical weapons ban (S Res 75) was a big win for President Clinton, who had faced determined opposition from GOP conservatives, but the victory came at a hefty price in concessions on collateral issues.

The Senate added to the resolution twenty-eight "understandings," which had been negotiated between Foreign Relations Committee Chairman Jesse Helms, R-N.C., and senior panel Democrat Joseph R. Biden Jr. of Delaware, limiting the treaty's reach. Biden and other treaty supporters managed to defeat five additional provisions backed by Helms that they said would render the Chemical Weapons Convention useless.

In addition, the treaty gave Senate Majority Leader Trent Lott, R-Miss., an opportunity to exact some key agreements from the Clinton administration in return for putting the treaty on the Senate agenda. As part of the deal with Helms and Lott, the Clinton administration agreed to restructure the nation's foreign policy agencies, a top Helms goal. Clinton also agreed to submit to the Senate as treaty amendments the changes he had negotiated with Russia to the 1972 Anti-Ballistic Missile (ABM) Treaty and the 1990 Conventional Forces in Europe Treaty. *(Foreign policy agencies, p. 189)*

The Senate passed implementing legislation a month after approving the treaty, but the measure languished for months in the House. GOP leaders at one point attached it to a bill authorizing sanctions against entities providing missile technology to Iran, but Clinton vetoed that bill. The chemical weapons bill finally was enacted as part of an omnibus spending bill that cleared late in the 1998 session.

BACKGROUND

The chemical weapons treaty, signed in 1993, was designed to outlaw the development, production, transfer, stockpiling, or use of chemical weapons for the battlefield. Negotiated by the Reagan and Bush administrations, the pact was signed by President George Bush shortly before he left office. *(Congress and the Nation Vol. IX, p. 293)*

The Senate Foreign Relations Committee approved the treaty (Treaty Doc 103-21) by a 13–5 vote on April 25, 1996, and reported it, along with seven conditions and eleven declarations, on April 30. The committee filed its report (Exec

Rept 104-33) on Sept. 11 and a floor vote was to be taken within a few days. But the Clinton administration asked for a deferral at the last minute after a vigorous campaign by Helms, Sen. Jon Kyl, R-Ariz., and other GOP conservatives made it doubtful that the resolution of approval would pass by the two-thirds majority required for a treaty.

The biggest factor in derailing the treaty was the opposition of beleaguered GOP presidential candidate and former majority leader Bob Dole of Kansas, who spelled out his objections in a Sept. 11 letter to Lott. A number of uncommitted Republican senators then rallied around Dole.

The critics also got a last-minute boost from the unexpected intervention of the National Federation of Independent Business (NFIB). The potent small-business lobby warned that the treaty's reporting and inspection requirements might burden its 600,000 members. Its position came as a surprise to treaty proponents because the pact had been vigorously supported from the outset by the Chemical Manufacturers Association, whose members expected to bear the brunt of the treaty's reporting and inspection requirements.

In 1997, however, NFIB changed its stance, concluding from new information it had been given that the treaty posed no risk of inundating small businesses with paperwork and regulation. A spokesman said the group's earlier statement had been mischaracterized as opposing the treaty when it had actually been an expression of concern.

PRELIMINARIES

In his Feb. 4, 1997, State of the Union address, Clinton called for the Senate to approve the treaty by April 29, the date on which the agreement was to become legally binding. Unless the United States ratified the pact by then, he warned, U.S. officials would play no role in the international inspection agency that was to be established to monitor compliance.

In March Lott assured Democrats that he planned to bring the treaty to the floor after the spring recess, but he would not commit himself to a vote before April 29. Such an explicit commitment would have brought Lott into a head-on collision with Helms, who had been pressuring the majority leader since January to act first on Republican foreign policy priorities that had been blocked by the Clinton administration before taking up the treaty.

Moreover, Helms also said the starting point for resuming consideration of the chemical weapons treaty should be a series of reservations he had drafted in April 1996, some of which had been rejected by his own Foreign Relations Committee. The reservations included language that was seen as effectively ruling out U.S. approval of the treaty.

Senate Hearings

Helms kicked off hearings in April with three former defense secretaries who were opposed to the treaty—James R. Schlesinger, who served under Presidents Richard M. Nixon and Gerald R. Ford; Donald H. Rumsfeld, who served in the

CHEMICAL WEAPONS TREATY

The Chemical Weapons Convention, signed in 1993, banned the use of chemical weapons in combat under all circumstances, including as a means of retaliation against chemical attack. Though the Geneva Protocol of 1925 banned the use of chemical weapons, many countries that ratified that pact nevertheless reserved the right to retaliate in kind if they were subjected to a chemical attack.

The 1993 treaty also prohibited the development, production, purchase, or stockpiling of chemical weapons for battlefield use. It did not outlaw "riot-control agents"—nonlethal irritants such as tear gas—for domestic use in law enforcement. It did, however, prohibit use of such chemicals in combat against enemy troops.

The pact prohibited any signatory from helping any other state—whether or not it had signed the treaty—to engage in any of the prohibited activities. It also required signatory countries both to cut off the sale of certain chemicals to countries that did not sign and to enact criminal penalties against private citizens who attempted to frustrate the treaty's aims.

Each signatory country was to report to a newly created monitoring agency—the Organization for the Prohibition of Chemical Weapons—any chemical weapons in its possession, any transfers of chemical weapons into or out of its territory, and any facilities on its territory that had been or could have been used to produce chemical weapons.

This organization and the forty-one-nation Executive Council that governed it were established once the treaty went into force April 29, 1997.

Verification Procedures

To check on compliance, agency inspectors were empowered to periodically inspect declared chemical weapons sites and industrial facilities with a significant potential for producing chemical weapons.

The treaty took into account the fact that many chemicals used in commercial manufacturing also could be used to manufacture chemical weapons. The severity of the treaty's restrictions and the intrusiveness of verification procedures for any such facility varied with the degree to which its chemical products could be used for prohibited purposes and with the volume of such chemicals used annually by each plant.

Any signatory could request on short notice a "challenge inspection" by the international agency of any site in any other country. However, the request could be denied if three-quarters of the forty-one countries on the Executive Council deemed it frivolous, abusive, or aimed at activities beyond the treaty's scope.

The inspectors were allowed to sample production lines, effluents, and soil for evidence of prohibited activities. To protect military or commercial proprietary secrets, officials at a challenged facility were allowed to turn off computers and shroud sensitive instrument displays.

Ford administration; and Caspar W. Weinberger, from the Reagan years. Their sentiments were echoed by a letter from a fourth former Pentagon chief, Dick Cheney, who served in the Bush administration.

The critics hammered at the fact that some pariah nations were not party to the treaty. They contended that the treaty's vaunted verification procedures would be intrusive enough to put trade secrets of U.S. companies at risk but still would not catch cheaters because it was relatively easy to make chemical weapons. They insisted that the treaty was worse than useless because, by collaborating in the international agency that would be set up to verify the treaty, the United States would expose to other governments critical information about how it obtained and analyzed intelligence, thus helping them work out methods to evade U.S. detection. Moreover, they argued, some of the treaty's provisions would undermine existing efforts to limit the spread of chemical weapons technology.

The case for the treaty was argued in the hearings by Secretary of State Madeleine K. Albright and a panel of former national security officials, including retired Lt. Gen. Brent Scowcroft, national security adviser under Bush.

The proponents' point of departure was that the United States had decided to dispose of its own chemical weapons and that approving the treaty as it was would give Washington a useful, if limited, tool for leverage on other governments to do the same. Even with some notorious chemical users outside the treaty, Scowcroft argued, the fact that more than 160 countries had signed the pact created powerful international pressure against chemical weapons. As for the treaty's net effect on U.S. intelligence, retired Adm. Elmo Zumwalt, a former chief of naval operations who was a member of the president's Foreign Intelligence Advisory Board, insisted that the gains would outweigh any losses. And the administration and treaty supporters contended that the critics were misreading the treaty in making their claims that several articles would undermine existing efforts to curtail chemical weapons technology.

The Deal

On April 10, Lott outlined elements of a deal to bring the treaty to the floor. The Senate would first debate a separate bill (S 495) by Kyl that would enact as U.S. law some provisions of the Chemical Weapons Convention. Kyl's bill was designed to provide political cover for Republicans who wanted to oppose the treaty but were leery of being seen as voting against a pact billed as banning poison gas.

The Senate would then take up the resolution approving ratification of the treaty (S Res 75). In addition to adopting "understandings"—modifications to the approval resolution—on which compromise language had been reached, the Senate would debate and vote on a small number of understandings that treaty supporters vehemently opposed as "killer amendments." During weeks of arduous negotiations, Helms and Biden had managed to reach accord on twenty-eight of the thirty-three amendments, or understandings, that Helms had included in S Res 75. As part of his price for agreeing to the floor vote on the treaty, Helms insisted that the Senate first vote individually on each of the remaining five amendments. (Understandings, box, p. 271)

On April 17 the Senate passed Kyl's bill, 53–44. Though the measure had little chance of enactment—and, indeed, it went no further—some treaty supporters worried that Republicans who voted for it might find it easier to oppose the treaty.

That same day, Clinton signed off on the plan to consolidate several foreign affairs agencies. Although Helms's aides insisted there was no quid pro quo, the deal was reported after Helms dropped his objection to the April 24 date for a vote on the chemical weapons pact.

TREATY APPROVAL

The Senate adopted the resolution of ratification, S Res 75, on April 24 by a **key vote of 74–26 (R 29–26; D 45–0).** (1997 key votes, p. 865)

On the morning of the vote, Lott had wrung one final concession from Clinton—a letter in which the president promised that the United States would withdraw from the treaty if two contentious sections of the pact ever allowed unfriendly nations to acquire chemical weapons or compromised U.S. security. Nonetheless, Lott's support for the treaty enraged conservative activists.

When the Senate began debate April 23, it gave voice vote approval to the twenty-eight provisos that Helms and Biden had agreed on. The following day, the Senate adopted amendments by Biden deleting the five contested understandings attached by Helms.

Those five were:

• **Treaty renegotiation.** The language emphasized most strongly by treaty opponents would have barred ratification until the treaty was renegotiated to revise two sections: Article X, which allowed signatories to obtain antichemical defense technology, and Article XI, which affirmed the right of nations to conduct international trade in chemicals. The Senate deleted it by a vote of 66–34.

Treaty critics argued that the articles would have the unintended effect of helping rogue nations to circumvent export controls and obtain advanced chemical weapons, while learning how to circumvent U.S. antichemical defenses.

Treaty supporters dismissed the argument as a willful misreading of the treaty, but they had agreed to two understandings, which Helms accepted. One stated that the requirement to provide defensive aid could be met by providing medical antidotes. The other stated that the United States and all other major chemical exporters agreed that the treaty was consistent with the Australia Group, the voluntary consortium through which these countries regulated chemical exports to potential misusers.

The view of Lott and some other Republicans that the understandings were not enough had led to Clinton's letter the morning of the vote.

• **Ratification by pariah states.** A second Helms proviso would have barred formal U.S. ratification until the pact was ratified by several countries hostile to U.S. interests and known to have chemical weapons. It was deleted, 71–29.

• **Russian compliance.** Another would have barred U.S. ratification until Russia ratified and complied with two older chemical weapons agreements. The amendment was deleted, 66–34.

• **Detection of violations.** A fourth amendment would have required the president to certify that U.S. intelligence agencies had "high confidence" that they could detect within a year if a country acquired a metric ton or more of a chemical weapons agent, and that U.S. agencies also could detect a pattern of minor violations over time. The administration conceded that it could not meet that standard but insisted that it would be able to detect a systematic effort by an adversary to equip its army to wage chemical warfare. This amendment was deleted by a vote of 66–34.

• **Barring certain inspectors.** The fifth disputed amendment would have required the president to bar from inspections on U.S. territory employees of the international verification agency who were nationals of China or certain other countries that had violated U.S. policy against nuclear proliferation. It was deleted, 56–44.

IMPLEMENTING LEGISLATION

The Senate passed legislation (S 610) to implement the Chemical Weapons Convention by voice vote on May 23, 1997. The Senate Judiciary Committee had reported the bill (no written report) the previous day.

The House attached the implementing legislation to an unrelated bill (HR 2709) aimed at punishing overseas companies and research labs, primarily in Russia, that provided missile technology to Iran. The bill was passed by voice vote on Nov. 12. Republicans hoped the move would force Clinton to agree to economic sanctions he opposed. (Russia sanctions, p. 195)

The Senate went along with the GOP plan, but the White House would not. The Senate passed an amended version of HR 2709 on May 22, 1998, by a vote of 90–4. The House accepted the changes and cleared the bill by a 392–22 vote June 9. And Clinton vetoed it on June 23.

Finally, in the days leading up to adjournment in October, House GOP leaders included the chemical weapons pro-

"UNDERSTANDINGS" ATTACHED TO RATIFICATION RESOLUTION

Negotiations on the ground rules for Senate debate on the Chemical Weapons Convention focused, in part, on thirty-three "understandings" that Senate Foreign Relations Committee Chairman Jesse Helms, R-N.C, wanted attached to the resolution (S Res 75) approving ratification of the pact. Helms, ranking committee Democrat Joseph R. Biden Jr. of Delaware, and the White House reached agreement on twenty-eight of those provisos.

Although the understandings did not amend the treaty itself—something prohibited by the treaty's own terms—they declared the U.S. interpretation of some treaty provisions and, in some cases, imposed legally binding obligations on U.S. officials.

Most of the understandings were relatively noncontroversial. Others were not. Following were some of the more challenging issues to confront the negotiators:

Use of Tear Gas

One particularly thorny issue that was settled at the end of the bargaining focused on the extent to which the treaty restricted use by military forces of tear gas and other, nonlethal riot-control agents. The treaty recognized a distinction between such irritants and chemical weapons. However, it barred the use of riot-control agents as weapons of war.

Early in the negotiations that led to the treaty, the Ford administration had defined this distinction in Executive Order 11850. The order cited four examples of circumstances in which the use of tear gas should be permissible under the treaty, for the sake of avoiding unnecessary loss of life: to subdue rioting enemy prisoners of war (POWs), to protect supply convoys from riots and guerrilla attack, to help rescue a U.S. pilot from enemy troops or a POW from behind enemy lines, and to incapacitate civilians being used as human shields by enemy troops.

In 1994 the Clinton administration revised the policy, concluding that the treaty would ban the use of tear gas in two of the four illustrative cases: rescuing a downed pilot and dealing with "human shield" tactics. The Joint Chiefs of Staff said that while they preferred the earlier interpretation, they still supported the treaty.

The administration ultimately accepted an understanding that reiterated the Ford administration interpretation that the treaty would not bar the use of tear gas in any of the four cases.

Snap Inspection Warrants

A second contentious issue on which Helms and the treaty's supporters reached agreement late in negotiations concerned the extent to which U.S. courts could protect companies targeted for surprise inspection by the international organization set up to verify the treaty.

Although most of the verification provisions focused on designated military or industrial sites, the treaty also allowed any country to request a "challenge inspection" of any site, to be conducted on five days' notice.

To trigger such an inspection, a country did not immediately need to identify the specific site to be inspected and needed to identify in only general terms the basis for requesting the inspection. The inspection then would occur unless three-fourths of the members of the verification organization's forty-one-country executive committee decided within twelve hours that the request was frivolous.

Treaty opponents argued that this procedure would lend itself to industrial espionage conducted under color of verifying compliance with the chemical weapons ban. Moreover, they argued, it would make a mockery of a U.S. company's right, under the Fourth Amendment to the Constitution, to freedom from "unreasonable searches and seizures."

At U.S. insistence, the treaty also included a provision requiring that inspections in any country be conducted in accord with that country's constitutional protections on searches and seizures. The treaty allowed officials at a challenged site to hide any equipment or information they deemed sensitive.

But Biden, Helms, and the administration went further and agreed to an understanding that barred challenge inspections of privately owned facilities unless either the targeted company did not object or the U.S. government secured a criminal search warrant. To obtain such a warrant, the government would have to present evidence showing "probable cause" to believe that the treaty was being violated at a specific site, to which the search would be limited.

Other Compromises

Three other provisions agreed on in the final days of the negotiations provided that:

- **Analyzing samples.** Chemical samples collected from U.S. sites by treaty inspectors could only be analyzed in U.S. laboratories. This was in answer to the critics' argument that samples collected to verify that a factory was not making forbidden chemicals could also be used, in violation of the treaty, to ferret out military or commercial secrets.
- **Waiver of immunity.** If an employee of the international verification organization were to compromise secret information gained as a result of an inspection, the president would demand that the employee's treaty-guaranteed immunity from U.S. legal jurisdiction be waived. Until the organization waived that immunity, the United States would withhold 50 percent of its annual payment to the organization.
- **U.S. payments.** The annual U.S. payment to the treaty organization would be limited to $25 million, unless Congress approved a presidential request for a higher payment.

visions in the omnibus spending bill (HR 4328), which Clinton signed into law on Oct. 21.

The implementing legislation authorized the president to issue regulations applying the treaty's prohibitions to anyone in the United States and to U.S. citizens anywhere in the world. It also established a legal framework for compliance inspections.

Proponents were troubled by some of the law's provisions, including restrictions giving the president the right to block surprise inspections on national security grounds as well as require that no chemical samples leave the United States for testing.

NATO Expansion

The Senate in 1998 voted in favor of admitting Poland, Hungary, and the Czech Republic into the North Atlantic Treaty Organization (NATO). The Senate's bipartisan vote of 80–19 to amend the 1949 North Atlantic Treaty and admit the three Central European nations was far larger than the two-thirds majority required.

These were the first new members of NATO since Spain was accepted in 1982. But, despite the Senate's strong vote for their admission, several senators warned against adding more former eastern European bloc nations to the alliance any time soon. The Senate rejected an amendment that would have barred further expansion for three years, but some strong proponents of admitting Poland, Hungary, and the Czech Republic voted for the amendment as well.

The three countries formally joined NATO in March 1999, after receiving the approval of the sixteen existing members. In giving that approval, NATO members, including the United States, were agreeing to defend the former Warsaw Pact nations from attack, just as they had agreed to defend western Europe.

The total cost of beefing up alliance-wide communications networks and selected bases, through which the three new members could receive reinforcements if they were under attack, was estimated at $1.5 billion over ten years, according to a NATO analysis that the Pentagon endorsed in February 1998. This did not include the much larger amount the three countries would have to spend to modernize their forces and make them operationally compatible with other NATO members.

Critics had warned that admitting the three countries would poison relations with Russia, divert the attention of the three countries from economic reform to military issues, and overextend U.S. military commitments.

But the Clinton administration argued that the NATO security umbrella needed to extend eastward, not to meet any specific military threat but to fill a power vacuum in central Europe. Proponents said the expansion would provide a path toward a more united, democratic, and prosperous Europe.

NATO TREATY EXCERPTS

Following are excerpts from the North Atlantic Treaty, signed April 4, 1949, in Washington, on the requirements for mutual defense and the method for adding new members:

Article 2

The Parties will contribute toward the further development of peaceful and friendly international relations by strengthening their free institutions, by bringing about a better understanding of the principles upon which these institutions are founded, and by promoting conditions of stability and well-being. They will seek to eliminate conflict in their international economic policies and will encourage economic collaboration between any or all of them.

Article 5

The Parties agree that an armed attack against one or more of them in Europe or North America shall be considered an attack against them all and consequently they agree that, if such an armed attack occurs, each of them, in exercise of the right of individual or collective self-defence recognised by Article 51 of the Charter of the United Nations, will assist the Party or Parties so attacked by taking forthwith, individually and in concert with the other Parties, such action as it deems necessary, including the use of armed force, to restore and maintain the security of the North Atlantic area* . . .

Article 10

The Parties may, by unanimous agreement, invite any other European State in a position to further the principles of this Treaty and to contribute to the security of the North Atlantic area to accede to this Treaty . . .

Article 11

This Treaty shall be ratified and its provisions carried out by the Parties in accordance with their respective constitutional processes . . .

---

*The area was later expanded with the addition of Turkey, Greece, Spain, and West Germany.

BACKGROUND

The Clinton administration built support for the expansion slowly and carefully. Sentiment to expand had been growing for some time. Clinton had told the Polish legislature in 1994 that the question of NATO's expansion was "not if, but when." During the 1996 presidential campaign, GOP nominee Bob Dole's only objection to Clinton's handling of the issue was that he was moving too slowly.

Both chambers of Congress had, since 1994, cast non-binding votes in favor of expanding the alliance. Congress also had authorized modest amounts of military aid to several eastern European nations to prepare them for the eventual transition to NATO. (*Congress and the Nation Vol. IX, p. 319*)

NATO leaders agreed at a July 1997 summit in Madrid to extend the invitation to the three former Soviet satellites. In opting to invite just three new members, as Clinton had insisted, the NATO allies rejected the approach backed by France and other European nations that had wanted to also extend invitations to Romania and Slovenia. French President Jacques Chirac had argued that admitting those two nations would bring needed stability to the Balkans. But Clinton, with a strong assist from British Prime Minister Tony Blair, succeeded in limiting the initial round of invitees to three.

The only serious U.S. opposition before the Madrid summit had come from an ideologically diverse group of nearly fifty former government officials and foreign policy scholars, including former Democratic Sen. Sam Nunn of Georgia (1972–1997) and Reagan administration arms control negotiator Paul Nitze. In a June 1997 letter to Clinton, the group called the enlargement of NATO "a policy error of historic proportions" and warned that expanding the alliance would create new divisions in Europe, inflict huge financial costs on the United States, and sow resentment in Russia.

But the Clinton team had been dealt a strong political hand on the issue and played it skillfully. The campaign to sell the concept at home was headed up by Jeremy Rosner, who joined the State Department from the Carnegie Endowment for International Peace, where he had been analyzing NATO issues since leaving Clinton's National Security Council staff in 1994.

For nearly a year, Rosner led the administration's lobbying effort, rounding up support for the three invited countries from veterans, labor, and ethnic organizations. Secretary of State Madeleine K. Albright and Defense Secretary William S. Cohen, both of whom were steeped in NATO issues, and Clinton himself pressed the case for admitting the three countries. Albright and Cohen made rare joint appearances on Capitol Hill to push for approval.

Senate support for the proposal began to jell in the summer of 1997, when Majority Leader Trent Lott, R-Miss., announced his backing for the effort. Senate Foreign Relations Committee Chairman Jesse Helms, R-N.C., signed on once Albright assured him in October 1997 that Russia would gain no significant influence over NATO's deliberations as the result of a consultation arrangement that was established to ease Moscow's concern over the expansion.

Facing an uphill fight from the beginning, opponents of expansion never gained political momentum. For example, their warning that expansion would undermine relations with Russia was stymied by the Russian government's acquiescence to the first round of invitations.

LEGISLATIVE ACTION

The Senate voted, 80–19, on April 30, 1998, to adopt the resolution of ratification of three amendments, or protocols, to the 1949 North Atlantic Treaty to allow the admission of Poland, Hungary, and the Czech Republic to NATO (Treaty Doc 105-36). A two-thirds vote of approval was necessary because the Senate was acting on amendments to a treaty.

The Senate Foreign Relations Committee had backed the resolution by a vote of 16–2 on March 3. The resolution was formally reported by the committee March 6 (Exec Rept 105-14).

The committee attached seven declarations and four conditions to the resolution. One condition required the president to consult with the Senate on NATO's revision of its "strategic concept," a process that was under way. Another condition required the president to reaffirm that the agreement negotiated in 1997 between NATO and Russia did not give Moscow a veto over NATO actions. Still another required the president to report periodically to the Senate on whether other NATO members were paying a fair share of alliance costs.

A group of eight Republicans and eight Democrats asked Majority Leader Lott to delay floor action until after June 1. They argued that too few senators had focused on the issue and that too many questions about the cost and implications were unanswered. But Lott rejected their request. The Senate debated it for several days in mid-March and then resumed consideration in late April.

During the floor debate, the Senate sent NATO a clear signal not to rush into inviting more former eastern bloc nations to join. The sentiment was reflected in the vote on an amendment by John W. Warner, R-Va., that would have barred membership invitations to additional countries for three years. The amendment was rejected by a **key vote of 41–59 (R 24–31; D 17–28)** on April 30, but the "ayes" included some strong proponents of admitting Poland, Hungary, and the Czech Republic, such as Helms. (*1998 key votes, p. 883*)

The Senate considered a number of other amendments. Republicans who opposed the deployment of U.S. forces in Bosnia tried to use the resolution to ensure that a revised overall NATO strategy that was being drafted at that time would not lead to more peacekeeping commitments beyond the territory of NATO members. But an amendment by John Ashcroft, R-Mo., requiring that NATO's mission remain focused on the defense of members' territory was tabled (killed), 82–18, on April 30. Also that day an amendment by Jeff Bingaman, D-N.M., barring ratification until NATO agreed on a new strategy was rejected, 23–76.

Two amendments to block ratification until Congress voted to authorize the U.S. deployment in Bosnia were rejected as well on April 30. One amendment by Larry E. Craig, R-Idaho, was rejected 20–80 and another by Robert C. Smith, R-N.H., was rejected 16–83.

The Senate on April 28 defeated, 24–76, an amendment by Tom Harkin, D-Iowa, limiting to no more than 25 percent the U.S. share of NATO assistance to help the three new members fit into the alliance's military structure.

The Senate did accept by voice vote amendments by Ted Stevens, R-Alaska, requiring congressional authorization of any U.S. spending related to NATO enlargement and urging the president to propose a gradual reduction of the U.S. share of NATO's budget.

An amendment by Kay Bailey Hutchison, R-Texas, delaying ratification until the administration proposed to NATO a formal process to resolve international disputes involving alliance members was rejected, 37–62, on April 29.

Daniel Patrick Moynihan, D-N.Y., proposed delaying NATO membership for the three countries until they were admitted to the European Union, but his amendment was defeated, 17–83, on April 30. Later that day an amendment by Kent Conrad, D-N.D., urging the administration to try to negotiate a reduction in the Russian arsenal of short-range nuclear weapons was rejected, 16–84.

Land Mine Treaty

President Clinton announced in September 1997 that the United States would not sign a treaty to outlaw antipersonnel land mines, though a majority in the Senate had expressed support for a ban. International negotiations on a treaty had begun earlier that month in Oslo, Norway. The United States, which joined the negotiations belatedly, had tried unsuccessfully to win two exemptions from the general ban—one to allow the use of antipersonnel mines in Korea and the other to allow the United States to continue packaging antipersonnel mines with its antitank mines to make it harder for enemy troops to remove the antitank mines.

In hopes of putting pressure on Clinton to sign the mine ban treaty, Reps. Jack Quinn, R-N.Y., and Lane Evans, D-Ill., had introduced a bill (HR 2459) in September to unilaterally ban new U.S. deployments of antipersonnel mines beginning in 2000. The bill would have allowed the president to waive the ban in the case of antipersonnel mines in Korea. Companion legislation (S 896) had been introduced in June in the Senate by Patrick J. Leahy, D-Vt., and Chuck Hagel, R-Neb., with fifty-five other senators.

But there was no further action on either bill and they did not win over Clinton. Negotiations concluded in Ottawa, Canada, in December 1997 and the treaty entered into force in March 1999, without the United States among the signatories.

BAN SUPPORTERS

For five years, Leahy, Evans, and an alliance of the Vietnam Veterans of America Foundation and other groups had fought to promote a ban on antipersonnel mines because of the toll they took on noncombatants, often years after the end of the war in which the mines were sown.

Leahy and his allies, including private international organizations such as the International Red Cross, argued that the relatively inexpensive mines were particularly heinous because of their indiscriminate harm to civilians. The U.S. government estimated that some 100 million mines were scattered around sixty-four countries, where they killed and maimed more than 25,000 persons annually.

Leahy in 1996 had engineered the enactment of a one-year moratorium on most uses of antipersonnel mines (PL 104-107). The ban was to go into effect in 1999, but Congress repealed it in 1998. *(1999 defense authorization, p. 252)*

PENTAGON OPPOSITION

The Army vehemently opposed a total ban and insisted on the two exceptions. They argued for the use of antipersonnel mines by the 37,000 U.S. personnel who stood guard with 550,000 South Koreans against a North Korean army of 900,000 that was within artillery range of Seoul, the capital of South Korea.

They also insisted on the need to couple antipersonnel mines with antitank mines to keep enemy troops from eliminating the antitank mines. The antipersonnel mines in the U.S. mixed systems were smart mines that automatically disarmed after a short period.

Clinton stuck with the Pentagon on the issue but did agree in August 1997 to drop a demand that self-destructing mines outside Korea be exempted. Thus, the Pentagon agreed to scrap more than eight million smart antipersonnel mines.

When he announced Sept. 17 that the United States would not sign the treaty, Clinton ordered the Pentagon to develop alternatives that would allow it to dispense with the use of antipersonnel mines after 2003, except in Korea for another three years. His order did not affect mixed systems.

Conventional Forces Treaty

The Senate agreed unanimously in 1997 to allow Russia to keep more weapons on its Baltic and Caucasian frontiers under the 1990 Conventional Forces in Europe (CFE) Treaty. The CFE Treaty amendment, which increased the numbers of tanks, cannons, and other heavy weaponry Russia was allowed to deploy, was approved 100–0 on May 14.

However, the unanimous vote masked a controversy over an unrelated provision pertaining to the separate 1972 U.S.-Soviet treaty limiting antiballistic missile (ABM) defenses.

Limits in the CFE treaty on Soviet deployments in the flank areas of the Baltic and Caucasian frontiers had been divided between Russia and Ukraine after the Soviet Union dissolved. But Russia complained that it was allowed too few weapons in its turbulent territory north of the newly independent Caucasian republics of Georgia and Azerbaijan, a requirement it flatly refused to meet. *(1990 treaty, Congress and the Nation Vol. VIII, p. 384)*

In May 1996 the thirty countries participating in the CFE Treaty, including the United States, agreed to amend the treaty to allow Russia to keep more weapons on the flank but also allow more inspections to guard against any threatening buildup.

Because this was an amendment to a treaty, it required the approval of a two-thirds majority of the Senate. The Senate Foreign Relations Committee approved a resolution of ratification (Treaty Doc 105-5) May 8, 1997, on a 17–0 vote and reported it (Exec Rept 105-1) the next day.

The committee attached fourteen conditions to the resolution of ratification, including one requiring the president to obtain Senate approval for a proposed agreement to make former Soviet republics parties to the ABM treaty. The Clinton administration had signed such an agreement in September 1997 but had not submitted it to Congress. Conservative Republicans, who saw the ABM treaty as an obstacle to deployment of a nationwide antimissile defense system, feared that having more countries than just Russia involved in the treaty would make it harder to negotiate a more liberal limit on antimissile systems.

The White House maintained that the president had the power to decide, without Senate approval, which countries inherited the Soviet obligations under the ABM pact. But a May 15 deadline for approving the CFE amendment gave Republicans enough leverage to press Clinton into accepting the rider.

Other Defense-Related Matters

SEXUAL HARASSMENT

Responding to studies that found widespread sexual harassment in the Army, senior Army leaders on Sept. 11, 1997, announced an "action plan" aimed at requiring more careful screening of prospective drill instructors and other soldiers who had contact with new recruits. Also, recruits' basic training curriculum was to be expanded from eight to nine weeks with the additional time allocated for instruction in ethics and moral values. The plan also called for more extensive training of all Army leaders in human relations.

The Army acted based on a report by a panel of senior Army officers and civilians, as well as a separate study conducted by the Army's inspector general. Many of the problems diagnosed by those reports, as well as several of the remedial steps, paralleled findings and recommendations of a three-member task force of the House National Security Committee, led by Steve Buyer, R-Ind.

SEXUALLY EXPLICIT MATERIAL

A federal district judge in New York ruled Jan. 22, 1997, that legislation enacted in 1996 barring the sale or rental of sexually explicit magazines or videos on military bases was unconstitutional. The ban, a provision of the fiscal 1997 defense authorization bill (PL 104-201), had been sponsored by Rep. Roscoe G. Bartlett, R-Md.

1999–2000

President Clinton sent the 106th Congress the first of his promised annual increases in the defense budget. He had agreed to larger defense budgets in 1998 under heavy pressure from congressional defense hawks and senior Pentagon leaders. Critics contended that the administration's spending plans were too stingy, given the large forces being sent overseas on peacekeeping and other missions.

However, there was still the nettlesome question of where the money would come from. The 1997 balanced-budget law set ceilings on spending, and so it appeared that any increase in defense spending would have to be offset by cuts in domestic spending. Congress had balked at significant additional domestic cuts, and GOP fiscal conservatives had dug in to support the spending caps.

Both the White House and Congress resorted to budget gimmicks in an attempt to get around the budget caps. Congress rejected Clinton's proposal to pay for military construction projects incrementally instead of following the usual practice of paying the full cost up front. But members found plenty of their own accounting maneuvers to finesse the differences between the caps and the spending increases.

Congress also approved new health benefits for military retirees that would have a major effect on future budgets. The program—enacted as an entitlement that would not be subject to annual appropriations—was expected to cost $60 billion over the first ten years. But advocates of the program insisted that it was the right thing to do for people who had spent their career in the military and been promised such benefits. Estimates of mounting budget surpluses made it much easier for lawmakers to back the proposal.

Congress rejected requests for new rounds of military base closures, which the administration touted as important cost-saving measures. Many Republicans were still angry over what they considered to be Clinton's manipulation of the last round of base closings for political purposes.

Defense battles during the 106th Congress went far beyond budget numbers. The Senate handed the president a major defeat when it rejected the Comprehensive Test Ban Treaty. GOP leaders had caught Democrats by surprise when they suddenly scheduled the treaty for floor action. In the past, moderate Republicans had joined with Democrats to approve ratification of arms control agreements, but many of those same moderates had serious doubts about the test ban treaty. Once treaty backers realized this, they scrambled to get the treaty off the Senate's calendar to avoid its outright rejection, but several conservatives refused to stop the debate.

In the wake of allegations of China's attempts to steal classified information on nuclear weapons technology, Congress and the White House grappled with how to protect the Energy Department's nuclear weapons laboratories from espionage. Agreement finally was reached on establishing a new semiautonomous administration within the Energy De-

partment, but only after a protracted debate and clashes with Energy Secretary Bill Richardson.

Clinton had little choice but to sign a bill declaring U.S. intent to deploy an antimissile defense system as soon as it was technologically feasible. He had resisted similar legislation in the past, but Democratic support had eroded in the face of reports of missile advances by countries such as North Korea and Iran.

2000 Defense Authorization

Congress in 1999 approved $288.8 billion in defense spending for fiscal 2000. The defense authorization bill (S 1059—PL 106-65) added $8.3 billion to President Clinton's budget request.

S 1059 cleared only after a protracted standoff between Energy Secretary Bill Richardson and the Republican-led Congress over provisions intended to improve security at the Energy Department's nuclear weapons laboratories. Richardson had argued that the bill's proposed reorganization of the department's nuclear weapons programs under a new National Nuclear Security Administration would undermine his authority, but in the end he dropped his call for Clinton to veto the bill. The reorganization was among the initiatives taken by Congress in response to reports of widespread Chinese efforts to obtain U.S. military secrets and subsequent revelations of lax security at the Energy Department. (*Nuclear security, p. 302*)

More than a third of the funds Congress added—$3.1 billion—resulted from a bookkeeping dispute with the White House. Instead of following the usual practice of requesting the full amount needed for military construction projects that were scheduled to begin in fiscal 2000, Clinton tried to hold down the size of budget outlays by deferring funds that would not be spent during the year. It was clear from the start that Congress would not go along, and lawmakers added the total cost of such projects to S 1059 as well as the military construction appropriations bill (HR 2465—PL 106-52).

Congress also added money for several major weapons programs. The largest was $375 million for components of a helicopter carrier for the Marine Corps. The remaining cost of the ship—about $1.1 billion—was to be in the fiscal 2001 budget. The ship was to be built by Litton Industries in Pascagoula, Miss., hometown of Republican Senate Majority Leader Trent Lott, who vigorously promoted its inclusion in the fiscal 2000 budget. The Navy had planned to include funds for the ship in the fiscal 2004 and 2005 budgets, but Litton argued that buying it earlier would reduce the price to $1.5 billion from $2.3 billion.

Defense authorizers sought to foster innovation in the services, but they did not go as far as the House appropriators who canceled the Air Force's F-22 fighter in their version of the fiscal 2000 defense appropriations bill (HR 2561) as a way of making the services take a closer look at their big-ticket weapons programs. Instead, the authorizers proposed accelerating the purchase of some high-tech weapons already in service and agreed to authorize more money for research and development. Several provisions in the final bill were aimed at encouraging innovative thinking in the military and among defense contractors.

The bill's most significant policy initiative was a package of military pay and pension increases aimed at attracting new recruits and holding on to experienced personnel. The pay raise was the largest in eighteen years.

Both the House and Senate rejected efforts to include in the bill a requirement that Clinton seek congressional approval before sending forces into the Serbian province of Kosovo. Critics of the administration warned that a war with Serbia over Kosovo—which was brewing as the bills were drafted and had started by the time they were debated—would undermine the combat readiness of U.S. forces by draining funds needed for training, maintenance, and modernization. GOP skepticism of Clinton was underscored when leading House Republicans insisted that he put in writing a promise to seek supplemental appropriations to pay for the Kosovo operation before they would join Democrats to kill the anti-Kosovo provision in the House bill.

In addition to challenging the administration on its plans for Kosovo, Congress cut funding for air and naval patrols of Iraq and peacekeeping operations in Bosnia, citing the Pentagon's decision to greatly reduce U.S. forces in Bosnia as justification. The bill also set a date for ending the deployment of U.S. troops in Haiti, underscoring GOP complaints that Clinton had been sending too many military forces abroad.

In another swipe at Clinton, Congress rejected his request to include authority for two additional rounds of base closings.

SENATE COMMITTEE ACTION

The Senate Armed Services Committee reported its $288.8 billion fiscal 2000 defense authorization bill (S 1059—S Rept 106-50) on May 17, 1999.

As had been true each year since the GOP took control of Congress in 1995, most of the funds added to the president's request were scattered across an array of accounts for such routine items as spare parts, maintenance, and a military pay raise of 4.8 percent instead of the 4.4 percent increase that Clinton proposed. The panel's largest addition to Clinton's weapons request was the $375 million to continue work on a new helicopter carrier.

The committee added several provisions intended to better protect secrets at Energy Department laboratories.

Another addition was a provision barring the administration from reducing the number of long-range nuclear weapons in the U.S. arsenal until Russia ratified the 1993 START II treaty. This time, however, the committee worded its provision so that the Navy could reduce from eighteen to fourteen the number of *Ohio*-class submarines that were used to carry Trident nuclear-armed missiles. The Navy wanted to retire the four oldest subs to save money, but the committee added $13 million to Clinton's request to study the feasibility of converting the four ships to carry hundreds of conventionally armed cruise missiles.

Despite a renewed push by Defense Secretary William S. Cohen and the Joint Chiefs of Staff for the expedited procedure that had been used four times since 1988 to close surplus military bases, the committee rejected two such proposals. While acknowledging that more bases needed to be closed, Armed Services Chairman John W. Warner, R-Va., said Congress would not authorize another round now because of widespread suspicions that Clinton manipulated the last round, in 1995, to save jobs in vote-rich California and Texas. But senior committee Democrat Carl Levin of Michigan said the effort was failing because Majority Leader Lott and Minority Leader Tom Daschle, D-S.D., both opposed it.

SENATE FLOOR ACTION

The Senate passed S 1059 by a vote of 92–3 on May 27, after a four-day debate that ranged across such contentious issues as nuclear security, the U.S. role in the Balkans, base closings, and abortion.

The debate was dominated by reaction to the release May 25 of a bipartisan House report critical of lax security at the Energy Department's nuclear weapons laboratories and at U.S. commercial satellite launches in China. Faced with the dual threat of a Democratic filibuster and a presidential veto, Republicans dropped the most far-reaching of several amendments designed to tighten up security at the facilities. But the Senate adopted, by voice vote, a watered-down amendment by Lott that was designed to strengthen export control laws, improve counterintelligence, and require closer monitoring of satellite launches and better notification to Congress of security breaches.

Another major stumbling block for the bill was removed when the Senate rejected efforts to limit Clinton's military options in Kosovo. The key Senate battle on U.S. policy in Kosovo came on an amendment by Arlen Specter, R-Pa., that would have barred the deployment of U.S. ground troops in that Serbian province unless Congress authorized the operation. The prohibition would not have applied to troops sent to police a peace agreement between the Serb-dominated government of Yugoslavia and the ethnic Albanians who made up a large majority of the Kosovar population until hundreds of thousands were driven into neighboring countries.

Clinton, who insisted he had no intention of sending ground troops into Kosovo, had assured congressional leaders that he would consult with Congress before making such a move. However, as every other president has since Congress enacted the War Powers Resolution of 1973 (PL 93-148) over President Richard M. Nixon's veto, Clinton refused to be bound by any congressional vote against a given deployment. *(1973 resolution, Congress and the Nation Vol. IV, p. 849)*

Specter's amendment was tabled (killed) by a **key vote of 52–48 (R 17–38; D 35–10)** on May 25. *(1999 key votes, p. 899)*

The next day the Senate tabled, by a vote of 77–21, an amendment by Robert C. Smith, R-N.H., that would have cut off any funds for military operations in Yugoslavia—including NATO's U.S.-led bombing campaign—on Oct. 1, 1999, unless Congress authorized the mission. Pat Roberts, R-Kan., a critic of the administration's involvement in Kosovo, offered an amendment in an unsuccessful effort to force a debate on the broader issue of whether U.S. forces should be engaged in such missions. Roberts's nonbinding amendment urged the president to seek Senate ratification of NATO's new "strategic concept," which was adopted at NATO's April 1999 summit, if he certified that it entailed new U.S. commitments. The amendment was agreed to on May 25 by a vote of 87–12, after the administration indicated it could live with it because, in its view, there were no new commitments.

An amendment calling for more base closings, sponsored by John McCain, R-Ariz., and Levin, was rejected, 40–60, on May 26. Because many Republicans contended that Clinton had improperly manipulated the last round in 1995, to save jobs in California and Texas, McCain and Levin noted that their amendment would not begin a new round until 2001, after Clinton left office. However, chairman Warner insisted that Clinton had poisoned the well on the issue, for the time being.

Another emotionally charged battle the administration lost came on an amendment by Olympia J. Snowe, R-Maine, and Patty Murray, D-Wash., that would have allowed women stationed with the armed forces overseas and female dependents to obtain abortions in local U.S. military hospitals, provided they paid for the procedure. The amendment was tabled 51–49 on May 26.

As had been typical of the defense authorization debate for years, few amendments came up that had a significant impact on major weapons. One that did, by Russell D. Feingold, D-Wis., would have capped Navy spending in fiscal years 2000–2004 for F/A-18 "E" and "F" jets at the projected cost of $8.8 billion. After that amendment was tabled, 87–11, on May 27, the Senate adopted by voice vote a Feingold amendment requiring the secretary of defense to certify that the plane was performing adequately.

On May 26 the Senate tabled, 56–44, an amendment by Bob Kerrey, D-Neb., that would have eliminated a provision to prevent the Pentagon from reducing the number of nuclear warheads deployed on long-range missiles and bombers unless Russia ratified the START II treaty.

HOUSE COMMITTEE ACTION

The House Armed Services Committee reported its $288.8 billion version of the fiscal 2000 defense authorization (HR 1401—H Rept 106-162) May 24. Some of the committee's specific additions to Clinton's budget request reflected shortfalls highlighted by the air war against Yugoslavia. But, as in the Senate bill, most of the added funds were spread across a wide range of accounts, reflecting the view of most Republicans, and many Democrats, that the president had run down U.S. forces by giving them too few dollars and too many missions.

The panel's generally collegial, nine-hour markup session was punctuated by two contentious battles:

• On a near party-line vote, the committee rejected a Democratic effort to eliminate a provision barring Clinton from using funds authorized by the bill to pay for military operations in Yugoslavia, including the possible use of ground troops in Kosovo.

Democrats complained that the provision would encourage Yugoslav President Slobodan Milosevic to hold out against the U.S.-led NATO airstrikes. Republicans insisted that the prohibition was needed to make Clinton seek supplemental funding for military operations in Yugoslavia and, they argued, stop him from undermining combat readiness by dipping into other Pentagon accounts to pay those costs.

An emergency supplemental appropriations bill (HR 1141—PL 106-31) was signed into law May 21, but that bill would fund operations only through fiscal 1999, which would end Sept. 30, 1999.

• In a series of votes, the committee liberalized one restriction on abortions in military hospitals overseas but turned back an effort to repeal the general ban. The fiscal 1996 defense authorization law (PL 104-106) had barred female service members or military dependents stationed overseas from obtaining abortions in U.S. military hospitals abroad, even if they paid for the procedure, except in cases where the pregnancy threatened the woman's life. The committee bill modified the exemptions to include cases of forcible rape and incest that were reported to a law enforcement agency. Steve Buyer, R-Ind., who offered the modifying amendment, said the language was intended to prevent fraudulent claims of rape by women seeking a government-funded abortion and to exclude cases of statutory rape. *(1996 law, Congress and the Nation Vol. IX, p. 294)*

HOUSE FLOOR ACTION

The House passed HR 1401 by a vote of 365–58 on June 10. On June 14 the House passed S 1059 by voice vote, after substituting the text of HR 1401.

The two-day debate was dominated by the Republican theme that Clinton was undermining U.S. forces with budgets that were too small and an agenda that swamped them with peacekeeping and humanitarian missions peripheral to national security interests.

The key battle over Clinton's peacekeeping policy came June 10 on an amendment by Ike Skelton, D-Mo., to eliminate the provision barring Clinton from using any funds authorized by the bill either for the air war against Yugoslavia that was under way when the bill was drafted in May, or for a peacekeeping operation in Kosovo. With Yugoslav forces beginning to pull out of Kosovo and NATO troops preparing to move in, Democrats contended that the provision would pull the rug out from under U.S. forces just when their efforts had succeeded. But Republicans would not relent until Clinton put in writing his promise to seek supplemental funding to pay for the Yugoslavia deployment. Once he did, Armed Services Chairman Floyd D. Spence of South Carolina and seventy-six other Republicans threw their support to Skelton, whose amendment was adopted, 270–155.

The House challenged Clinton on a related issue as well, when it adopted an amendment offered by Porter J. Goss, R-Fla., that would force him to withdraw by the end of 1999 U.S. troops still in Haiti. It had been more than four years since U.S. military intervention had forced a military junta from power in Haiti. Though fewer than 500 active-duty U.S. troops remained in Haiti, most Republicans considered their presence an example of the type of humanitarian mission, peripheral to U.S. security, on which they contended that Clinton was frittering away military strength. Their opposition gained strength early in 1999 when Marine Corps Gen. Charles E. Wilhelm, commander of U.S. forces in Latin America, recommended withdrawing the troops from Haiti because growing domestic turmoil in the country put them at risk. The Goss amendment, which allowed periodic U.S. deployments in Haiti so long as they did not amount to a continuous presence, was adopted 227–198 on June 9. *(Haiti intervention, Congress and the Nation Vol. IX, p. 195)*

But the large majority that rejected another amendment suggested that House opposition to U.S. deployments abroad did not extend to traditional missions in Europe. By a vote of 116–307 on June 10, the House rejected an amendment by Christopher Shays, R-Conn., and Barney Frank, D-Mass., that would have reduced the number of U.S. troops stationed in Europe from 100,000 to 25,000 by fiscal 2002.

Responding to reports of Chinese espionage at U.S. nuclear weapons laboratories, the House on June 9 adopted, 428–0, an amendment by Christopher Cox, R-Calif., and Norm Dicks, D-Wash., to tighten secrecy at the labs and in the handling of U.S.-built satellites sent to China for launching. The amendment incorporated several recommendations of a bipartisan House commission led by Cox and Dicks, including a temporary moratorium on visits to the labs by citizens of certain potentially hostile countries. But the House rejected, 159–266, an amendment by Jim Ryun, R-Kan., that would have imposed a two-year moratorium on lab visits by those from certain countries.

The only China-related amendment to spark a debate was a proposal by Majority Whip Tom DeLay, R-Texas, to sharply curtail visits by Chinese military officers to U.S. installations. Senior U.S. officers argued that such exchanges fostered Chinese respect for U.S. military power. But DeLay and his allies said that the Clinton administration had pressured the services to give Chinese officials too much access to U.S. tech-

nology and tactics. DeLay's amendment was adopted, 284–143, on June 9.

By a vote of 203–225 on June 9, the House rejected an amendment by Carrie P. Meek, D-Fla., to permit privately funded abortions in overseas military hospitals.

CONFERENCE ACTION

The House adopted the conference report on S 1059 (H Rept 106-301) by a vote of 375–45 on Sept. 15. The Senate agreed to it by a vote of 93–5 on Sept. 22, clearing the bill for the president.

House and Senate conferees had hundreds of issues to resolve but none as controversial as a GOP proposal to add to the conference bill a plan to create a National Nuclear Security Administration within the Energy Department to oversee all weapons-related activities. *(Nuclear security, p. 302)*

Three Republican senators in May had offered a proposal to restructure the Energy Department's weapons programs as an amendment to S 1059, but they withdrew the amendment after Energy Secretary Richardson objected. The senators then redrafted the amendment to conform to the recommendations of the President's Foreign Intelligence Advisory Board, which concluded in a report released June 15 that the Energy Department had had a "cavalier attitude" toward security.

After Richardson reluctantly endorsed the concept of a separate agency within his department, the Senate approved the restructuring plan, 96–1, as an amendment to the fiscal 2000 intelligence authorization bill (HR 1555). But then defense conferees decided that their bill was the proper place to deal with the restructuring because of the House Armed Services Committee's jurisdiction over nuclear weapons.

House conferees initially came up with a draft plan that was even stronger than the one the Senate had passed, but, under the threat of a veto, the plan was revised. Richardson still was not happy and was said to be prepared to recommend a presidential veto because he feared the provisions would undermine his authority.

Some Democrats on the Senate Armed Services Committee refused to sign the conference report because of similar concerns. They said they were undecided about whether to vote for the report when it came to the Senate floor. Among them was Levin, the ranking Democrat on Senate Armed Services.

In the end only five senators—all liberal Democrats—opposed adoption of the conference report. Even Levin voted in favor of the report. He said he supported the military pay raise and other defense initiatives contained in the bill, and that he had concluded the Energy reorganization might be workable.

Before the House agreed to the conference report, a motion by John D. Dingell, D-Mich., to eliminate the Energy Department provisions was rejected, 139–281.

In the days leading up to the Senate vote, Richardson tried to highlight the administrative reforms he had made in security at his agency. But after both chambers adopted the conference report on the popular defense bill by overwhelming majorities, he reversed course and announced Sept. 26 that he would no longer oppose the bill.

MAJOR PROVISIONS

As signed into law by President Clinton on Oct. 5, 1999, S 1059 authorized $288.8 billion in defense spending in fiscal 2000, $8.3 billion more than requested.

Major provisions of S 1059 are the following:

Personnel Issues

• Authorized for fiscal 2000 an active-duty force of 1.39 million personnel, a reduction of more than 10,000 from the previous fiscal year. The fiscal 2000 ceiling was slightly larger than Clinton requested, with most of the increase aimed at providing more Marine guards at U.S. embassies.

• Included a number of items aimed at improving recruiting and retention of military personnel:

• **Pay raise.** Authorized a 4.8 percent raise in basic pay, rather than the 4.4 percent Clinton requested. The higher increase was in both the House and Senate bills.

The conference report deducted from Clinton's budget request the $1.8 billion cost of a 4.4 percent raise, because it was paid for in the supplemental appropriations bill (PL 106-31) enacted in May. Because those were emergency funds, they did not count against the spending cap set by the 1997 balanced-budget act. The 0.4 percent additional pay raise required another $156 million.

The conference report also mandated that future annual pay raises through 2006 be 0.5 percent larger than the increase in private-sector wages, as measured by a government survey.

Both versions of the bill had approved the administration's request for additional targeted raises of up to 5.5 percent for mid-career officers and enlisted personnel.

• **Pension changes.** Replaced a 1986 law (PL 99-348) that reduced pensions for service members retiring after twenty years of active duty, from 50 percent of basic pay to 40 percent for those who joined up beginning in 1986. Members would have a choice: they could retire under the 50 percent formula or stay with the 40 percent pension, in which case they would receive a $30,000 lump-sum payment after fifteen years of service.

Because the change was expected to save money, the conference report offset some of its add-ons by trimming $161 million from the personnel budget. Conferees cut an additional $270 million from the total authorized on grounds that the services would start the fiscal year with fewer personnel than the budget assumed.

• **Military 401(k).** Authorized military personnel to contribute up to 5 percent of their pretax basic pay to a tax-sheltered investment fund, similar to civilian 401(k) plans. This option was to be available only if Congress in 2000 offset the loss in federal revenue elsewhere.

As a retention incentive, the Pentagon would have discretion to match such contributions, as many private companies did.

• **Pay raise for generals.** Provided a hefty pay raise to the services' 150 highest-ranking officers, who held the ranks of general, admiral, lieutenant general, or vice admiral, by raising the $110,700 limit on military pay. The limit was set to keep military officers from making more than their civilian bosses.

The bill increased the pay cap to $125,900, so pay for the thirty-five generals and admirals would climb to that level, while pay for the next tier of senior officers would increase to nearly $120,000, the full amount provided by the Pentagon's pay formula.

• **Recruiting benefits.** Added $225 million to the budget request to accelerate the transition to more liberal military housing allowances. But several Senate-passed provisions that would have provided more GI Bill education benefits were dropped.

The final bill renewed authority for enlistment and reenlistment bonuses and extra pay for personnel in key, hard-to-fill specialties. It also increased some existing bonuses and created new ones, such as a bonus for lawyers and Navy officers specializing in surface warfare.

It added $71 million to the amount requested for recruiting and advertising, and increased from $150 to $200 the monthly stipend for college students enrolled in senior ROTC programs. It also added $32 million to Clinton's request for high school ROTC programs, from which 40 percent of the graduates eventually joined the service.

In their report, the conferees urged the Pentagon to review the medical and physical standards for joining the services, with an eye to easing the requirements.

The measure directed the Army to test a program allowing recruits to defer the start of their full-time service for up to two years and collect a stipend while they completed college or technical training.

To better understand why military personnel were leaving, the conferees directed the Pentagon to survey all those departing between Jan. 1 and June 30, 2000.

Addressing one likely reason—long overseas deployments—the conferees approved a slightly revised version of a Senate-passed provision to require a general or admiral to approve any deployment of military personnel for more than 220 days in a year and to give anyone deployed away from home for more than 250 days in a year a bonus of $100 for each day beyond the 250. Each service chief could suspend this provision, for his service, on grounds of national security.

Operations and Readiness

• Added, as had been customary in recent years, funds to budget accounts Congress deemed particularly relevant to combat readiness, including:

- $868 million more than the $5.2 billion Clinton requested for facilities maintenance;
- $380 million more than the $13.8 billion requested for day-to-day base operating costs;
- $184 million more than the $7.3 billion requested for equipment overhauls; $145 million more than the $1.3 billion requested for aircraft spare parts; and $110 million more to amounts requested for major combat training ranges.

Peacekeeping Missions

- Included several provisions related to peacekeeping missions that reflected the view of many lawmakers that far-flung peacekeeping missions had undermined the combat readiness of U.S. forces:
- **Persian Gulf, Balkans.** Cut $508 million from the $2.4 billion Clinton requested for operations in the Persian Gulf and the Balkans. The conferees justified the cut by citing the Pentagon's decision to greatly reduce the number of U.S. troops deployed in Bosnia.

  To prevent the cost of operations in Bosnia or Kosovo from siphoning funds from training and maintenance, the conference report required the president to request a supplemental appropriation to pay for the deployment of U.S. forces in Kosovo and for any costs of the Bosnia mission in excess of the $1.82 billion Clinton requested.

  The Pentagon also was required to report on how severely deployments in the Balkans would affect the avowed goal of having U.S. forces ready to win nearly simultaneous wars, for instance in Korea and the Persian Gulf.
- **Haiti withdrawal.** Terminated by May 31, 2000, the deployment of U.S. forces in Haiti, a mission that began in 1994.

Antimissile Defense

- Authorized nearly $3.7 billion for the antimissile defense program, about 9 percent more than the $3.3 billion Clinton sought. But the real debate in 1999 over antimissile defenses was waged on separate legislation (HR 4—PL 106-38) rather than the defense authorization bill. *(Antimissile defenses, p. 306)*

Ground Combat

- Reflected the dilemma lawmakers faced in wanting to upgrade current weapons while encouraging faster development of new arms.
- Authorized $636 million, as Clinton requested, to upgrade early-model M-1 tanks with larger cannon and digital communications links, rejecting the Senate's proposed $28 million increase. But to the $309 million the administration requested to modernize early-model Bradley troop carriers, the bill authorized another $72 million to add improved night-vision equipment and other upgrades for older Bradleys assigned to National Guard units.

At the same time, following the lead of the House, the bill authorized an additional $12 million beyond the $65 million requested to develop a future combat vehicle that would weigh much less than the seventy-ton M-1 tank. That was intended to make it much easier to quickly deploy U.S. forces to distant trouble spots. The conferees ordered the Pentagon to come up with a plan for such a radically new combat vehicle that would be ready to go into development by 2007.

- Included House and Senate additions to the Clinton budget request for the Army's current and future armed helicopters. To the $765 million requested to equip tank-hunting Apache helicopters with Longbow ground-target radar, the final version of the bill authorized an additional $45 million to replace obsolete electronic components. It authorized $56 million more than the $427 million Clinton requested to accelerate development of the Comanche scout helicopter.
- Authorized the $344 million Clinton requested to develop the Crusader mobile cannon, criticized by some for its seventy-ton bulk. But the bill also added $31 million to accelerate development of a much lighter artillery rocket launcher that could be deployed in the Air Force's hundreds of C-130 cargo planes.

Air Combat

- Authorized, as requested, $1.9 billion in production funds for the F-22 fighter and $1.2 billion to continue developing the plane.

  The bill did not authorize the purchase of additional F-15 fighters, something that had been included in both House and Senate versions of the defense appropriations bill. The House Appropriations Committee said the F-15 was a cheaper alternative to the F-22. *(2000 defense appropriations, p. 283)*
- Authorized the administration requests for $253 million to buy ten F-16 fighters for the Air Force and $2.7 billion to buy thirty-six F/A-18 E/F jets for the Navy.
- Authorized $507 million, $30 million more than requested, to continue developing the Joint Strike Fighter, slated to enter service in about 2007 as a lower-cost complement to the F-22.
- Authorized $314 million, $112 million more than requested, to develop improvements to the B-2 stealth bomber. It also authorized $15 million more than the $32 million requested to develop improvements in the 1960s-vintage B-52 fleet, which the Air Force expected to soldier on for nearly four more decades.
- Authorized $25 million more than the $161 million requested to upgrade the aging fleet of Prowler radar-jamming planes.
- Authorized the $282 million requested for a fourteenth J-STARS ground-surveillance plane, a converted jetliner with radar that can track ground vehicles more than 100 miles away, and added $46 million for components to be used in a fifteenth plane, to be funded in fiscal 2001. The bill also added $48 million to the $131 million requested to improve

the J-STARS radar and $25 million more than the $82 million requested for mobile terminals on which ground commanders could view J-STARS data.

Naval Combat

• Authorized the requested $2.7 billion for three Aegis destroyers.

• Authorized the requested $748 million for components to be used in new submarines, to be funded in future years.

• Authorized the requested $752 million for components to be used in a nuclear-powered aircraft carrier, most of the funds for which will be included in the fiscal 2001 budget.

• Authorized the amounts requested to continue designing two new classes of warships: $195 million for a carrier, the first of which would be funded in fiscal 2006, and $270 million for a new destroyer intended to save money by using a crew of fewer than 100, about one-third the number aboard existing destroyers.

The new destroyers, the first of which was slated for funding in fiscal 2004, were intended to strike land targets up to 150 miles away with guided missiles and rocket-boosted cannon shells that used Global Positioning Satellite signals to steer to their targets. The bill authorized $15 million more than the $102 million requested to develop these land-attack weapons.

• Incorporated a Senate initiative that would add $13 million to plan for equipping four large missile-launching submarines to carry 132 Tomahawk missiles apiece instead of the twenty-four nuclear-armed Trident missiles they currently carried.

Air and Sea Transport

• Added $252 million for four Lockheed Martin C-130s, planes equipped to refuel Marine aircraft in midflight. No funds had been requested.

• Authorized $990 million for a dozen V-22 Osprey tilt-rotor aircraft—an increase of two aircraft and $123 million over the president's request—plus $50 million for advanced procurement.

• Added $157 million and twelve aircraft to the $511 million requested for twenty-eight H-60 helicopters built by United Technologies' Sikorsky division in Stratford, Conn.

• Authorized $127 million, $56 million more than was requested, to modernize the Army's fleet of Chinook cargo helicopters, an increase that was one of the Army's top priorities. The upgrade project was run jointly by Boeing's helicopter division in Philadelphia and by Allied Signal in Phoenix.

• Added, as the Senate had, $375 million for components to be used in a helicopter carrier designed to carry up to 2,000 Marines. The House bill would have authorized $15 million. The ship would be built by Litton Industries in Pascagoula, Miss. The authorization left about $1.1 billion of the ship's cost to be covered by future budgets. The Pentagon had planned to begin funding the ship in fiscal 2004. But an earlier start was avidly desired by the Marines, the Mississippi congressional delegation, and Litton, which said the

faster timetable would cut $780 million from the ship's projected $2.3 billion price tag.

• Authorized $80 million, which Clinton had not requested, to begin work on a high-speed cargo ship.

• Authorized $1.5 billion for two transport ships to carry Marine landing forces.

• Added $26 million to the $95 million requested to develop an amphibious troop carrier that could haul Marines ashore at 30 mph, four times as fast as the Marines' existing vehicle.

U.S.-Russia Cooperation

• Authorized $476 million, the amount requested, for Cooperative Threat Reduction. This was the Pentagon's portion of the so-called Nunn-Lugar program intended to help Russia and other former Soviet republics dispose of nuclear, chemical, and biological weapons. The program was named for its original sponsors, Sens. Sam Nunn, D-Ga. (1972–1997), and Richard G. Lugar, R-Ind.

But the conferees challenged an important aspect of the program by barring the use of Nunn-Lugar funds for construction of a storage facility in Russia to hold chemical weapons. The $130 million requested for the storage site was allocated to other projects.

As requested, $145 million was approved for the Energy Department's Nunn-Lugar initiatives aimed at helping former Soviet states secure their stockpiles of nuclear material from theft. But the conferees agreed to authorize only $40 million of the $60 million requested for two other Energy Department programs aimed at getting Russia's nuclear weapons workers employed in commercial activities.

China and U.S. Security

• Authorized the creation of a National Nuclear Security Administration within the Energy Department to oversee all weapons-related activities. The reorganization was in response to revelations about security lapses that apparently allowed China to obtain secrets from U.S. nuclear weapons laboratories.

• Included additional provisions triggered by allegations that China had tried to obtain militarily useful information. Among these were provisions that:

• Prohibited U.S.-Chinese military exchanges that would "inappropriately" expose certain U.S. military capabilities.

• Required an annual report on the transfer of militarily significant U.S. technology to China, Russia, or terrorist states.

• Required the president to notify Congress of any alleged violation of export control laws by U.S. companies having their satellites launched from China.

Other Provisions

• Included several provisions aimed at encouraging innovative thinking in the military and among defense contractors, including proposals to:

- Require a quadrennial Pentagon report to Congress on new warfare concepts.

- Add $10 million to the $42 million the administration requested for multiservice exercises to test new concepts.

- Require the Pentagon to consider whether changing the rules on profit margins for defense contracts might encourage greater innovation by contractors.

- Allow the Pentagon to spend as much as $10 million annually on cash prizes to companies that developed promising military technologies.

• Expanded Arlington National Cemetery, which was projected to fill its existing burial plots by 2025, by adding forty-four acres of adjacent Defense Department property.

• Required the armed services to provide, on request, at least a two-person honor guard for a veteran's funeral.

• Gave top Pentagon officials the final say over whether the Defense Department would be required to surrender to other users portions of the radio-frequency spectrum that had been reserved for defense use.

2000 Defense Appropriations

Congress in 1999 approved a $267.8 billion defense appropriations bill (HR 2561—PL 106-79) for fiscal 2000, $4.5 billion more than President Clinton's budget request. Despite initial hints of a veto, Clinton signed the measure, which provided the first significant defense spending increase since 1985 and the largest military pay raise since 1981.

HR 2561 cleared after House and Senate conferees agreed to allow the Air Force to buy additional F-22 jet fighters—which the House had rejected—but also to require more testing before full-scale production of the plane could begin. The F-22 was intended by the Air Force to be its premier fighter in the next few decades and the debate over its future was easily the most contentious issue conferees faced.

Combined with funds in two other appropriations bills—$8.4 billion in the military construction appropriations bill (HR 2465—PL 106-52) and $12 billion in the energy and water appropriations bill (HR 2605—PL 106-60)—HR 2561 brought overall defense spending in fiscal 2000 to about $288 billion. Congress had approved a $288.8 billion fiscal 2000 defense authorization bill (S 1059—PL 106-65). *(2000 defense authorization, p. 276)*

It had been clear from the start that Congress would add billions to Clinton's defense budget request despite increasingly tight budget caps set by the 1997 balanced-budget law (HR 2015—PL 105-33). In the end Congress simply finessed the spending squeeze with budget gimmicks that exempted $21 billion in defense spending from the budget caps, allowing the House and Senate to increase outlays for domestic programs by the same amount.

As usual, the bill made hundreds of additions to Clinton's funding request for projects of local interest to lawmakers. Most of the add-ons involved small amounts of money but not all of them. The White House was particularly critical of a $375 million addition to begin work on a helicopter carrier that would be built by Litton Industries in Pascagoula, Miss., hometown of Republican Senate Majority Leader Trent Lott. The Navy had planned to request funds for the ship beginning in 2004, but Litton said the price would drop from $2.3 billion to $1.5 billion if Congress funded it in 2000.

HR 2561 did not include funds to pay for U.S. forces serving with the NATO-led peacekeeping mission in the Serbian province of Kosovo. During negotiations on the defense authorization bill, Republicans had insisted that the president request a supplemental appropriation to cover that operation, which was expected to cost several billion dollars.

SENATE ACTION

The Senate passed a $264.7 billion fiscal 2000 defense appropriations bill (S 1122) by a vote of 93–4 on June 8, 1999. The Senate Appropriations Committee had reported S 1122 (S Rept 106-53) on May 25.

The bill added about $1.4 billion to Clinton's budget request. Originally it would have topped Clinton's request by $4.5 billion. But the Appropriations Committee sliced $3.1 billion from the defense bill and allowed the Pentagon to make up the loss with money from the fiscal 1999 supplemental bill (HR 1141—PL 106-31) enacted in May. Using fiscal 1999 money gave the committee more fiscal 2000 funds to allocate to other appropriations bills without breaching the 1997 budget caps.

The Senate bill made relatively few major changes in Clinton's requests for major weapons programs. But among the significant increases was $500 million added in committee for components for the helicopter carrier to be built by Litton.

Although S 1122 included no funds to pay for U.S. peacekeepers in Kosovo, the appropriations bill did not pass free of Kosovo-related provisions. During floor action on the bill, the Senate adopted by voice vote an amendment by Majority Whip Don Nickles, R-Okla., that would bar the use of funds to reconstruct Yugoslavia—battered by nearly three months of U.S.-led NATO airstrikes—while Slobodan Milosevic remained the country's president. Also winning voice vote approval was an amendment by Judd Gregg, R-N.H., to bar the use of Kosovar refugee relief funds contained in the supplemental bill for Balkan economic reconstruction unless authorized by Congress.

In what had become a regular feature of appropriations debates, the Senate on June 8 rejected, 16–81, an effort by John McCain, R-Ariz., to transfer billions of dollars from members' pet projects to the sections of the Pentagon's budget that had been cut by the Appropriations Committee. Committee chairman Ted Stevens, R-Alaska, and ranking Democrat Daniel K. Inouye of Hawaii—who both unabashedly shoehorned projects for their states into the annual defense bill—insisted that many parochial initiatives merely give local communities relief from problems created by the Pentagon in the first place.

The most heated dispute in the otherwise flaccid debate on S 1122 surrounded an amendment to eliminate a provision authorizing the Air Force to sign a long-term lease for six Gulfstream V executive jets for use by senior generals and admirals who commanded U.S. forces. The amendment, offered by Democrats Barbara Boxer of California and Tom Harkin of Iowa, would have required instead that the Pentagon do an analysis of alternative ways to provide transportation for those officers, who frequently traveled long distances. Opponents of the amendment argued that the Gulfstreams would be cheaper than the larger and older jetliners then in use. The amendment was tabled (killed), 66–31, on June 8.

The amendment with the largest budgetary impact, sponsored by Christopher S. Bond, R-Mo., added $220 million to the bill to buy four F-15E jet fighters, built by The Boeing Co. The Air Force had not requested additional copies of the plane, but the company had said it might have to lay off workers at its St. Louis plant because of dwindling overseas sales. Bond's amendment, adopted by voice vote, was offset by cuts in other items in the bill.

The Senate also adopted by voice vote a Sam Brownback, R-Kan., amendment to suspend for five years economic sanctions imposed on India and Pakistan after they each conducted nuclear test explosions in 1998.

HOUSE ACTION

The House passed its $268.7 billion version (HR 2561) of the defense spending bill on July 22 by a vote of 379–45. The House Appropriations Committee had reported the bill (H Rept 106-244) July 20.

California Republican Jerry Lewis, in his first run as chairman of the House Defense Appropriations Subcommittee, had jolted the Pentagon on July 12 when he persuaded his panel in a closed-door markup not to buy the F-22 fighter plane, the Air Force's premier procurement program. As Air Force generals fanned out across Capitol Hill to save the jet, the full House Appropriations Committee endorsed Lewis's decision.

President Clinton had requested $1.8 billion to buy the first six production F-22s. Lewis's subcommittee decided to divert the money to other uses, including older-model planes and pilot incentives, while approving the requested $1.2 billion for F-22 research and development.

The Air Force insisted that the F-22 was needed to ensure U.S. pilots an edge over adversaries who may be flying modern jets that were becoming available in the international market. But Lewis said the air war against Yugoslavia had shown there was no need for such an advanced aircraft, because two similar planes—the Joint Strike Fighter and the F-18E/F—were being developed.

Lewis and other members were also concerned that the military, while complaining that it did not have enough money for spare parts, maintenance, and personnel reten-

tion, was pouring money into three different air-superiority fighter planes. *(F-22 controversy, box p. 286)*

Some of the $1.8 billion the bill denied for new F-22s was parceled out for needs the Defense Appropriations Subcommittee said the Air Force had underfunded in its zeal for the F-22, including bonuses to stem the exodus of pilots from the Air Force, various air reconnaissance programs, and tanker versions of the C-130 cargo plane. The money also was to go for five F-16s in addition to the ten requested and eight F-15s, of which the administration requested none.

When the bill reached the floor, Bob Barr, R-Ga., offered an amendment to restore the procurement funds for the F-22, but he withdrew the amendment before it came to a vote. The issue was sent on to a House-Senate conference, where there appeared to be little chance the Senate would agree to halt the program.

Also missing from the House bill was funding for the helicopter carrier for which the Senate bill had added $500 million. The Senate passed HR 2561 by voice vote July 28, after substituting the text of its bill.

CONFERENCE ACTION

The House adopted the conference report (H Rept 106-371) by a 372–55 vote on Oct. 13. The Senate cleared the bill, 87–11, the next day.

Going into conference, the two bills were—at least, on paper—about $4 billion apart in their total appropriations. But those figures exaggerated the practical difference in spending because, in addition to the new budget authority, the Senate bill had allowed the Pentagon to use $3.1 billion from the fiscal 1999 supplemental bill, thereby freeing up more fiscal 2000 funds for the other appropriations bills. House conferees, however, insisted that most of the supplemental funds were needed to pay for military operations earlier in 1999 against Serbia.

Conferees ultimately reached agreement on a bill appropriating $267.8 billion in new budget authority for the Defense Department. In the process Republican leaders, using an array of budget gimmicks, came up with $21 billion that could be allocated to other appropriations bills.

The $21 billion in accounting changes reduced the outlays that would be counted against the spending caps set by the 1997 balanced-budget law (PL 105-33). GOP leaders had used similar tactics recently to exempt billions of dollars in other appropriations bills from the spending caps. But the breadth of the defense bill scorekeeping maneuvers was impressive:

• $7.2 billion in budget authority was designated emergency spending, as was $1.8 billion in budget authority to pay for most of the military's annual pay raise. Most of the pay raise funds were not included in the bill at all, but rather were drawn from the fiscal 1999 supplemental appropriations bill (PL 106-31). All told, this exempted at least $6.6 billion in fiscal 2000 outlays from the budget caps.

• The bill assumed that a Federal Communications Commission auction of broadcast frequencies would net the government $2.6 billion, which was to be turned over to the Pentagon to offset that amount of budget authority and outlays in the bill. The Congressional Budget Office (CBO), however, predicted that the auction would be delayed and would net less money.

• Congress ordered CBO to reduce its estimate of the bill's outlays by an additional $10.5 billion, on the premise that the Pentagon would spend the money more slowly than CBO assumed.

• The bill ordered the Pentagon to slow the rate at which it paid contractors, reducing outlays by $1.2 billion. David R. Obey of Wisconsin, ranking Democrat on the House Appropriations Committee, called this provision the "government deadbeat amendment." He said, "It will raise the cost of those contracts down the line, and, in the end, the taxpayers will pay for this foolishness." But the provision remained in the final conference bill.

Despite such complaints, the conference report drew few objections. Conferees had solved the most contentious issue with a compromise on the F-22 fighter, agreeing to spend $1 billion that could be used to begin work on up to six planes, though more testing was required.

House opposition to the F-22 was a rare challenge to a major Pentagon program. In most cases, lawmakers were adding, rather than cutting, defense funds, particularly for their own favored projects. For instance, conferees agreed with the Senate to add $375 million as partial payment for the helicopter carrier to be built in Senate Majority Leader Lott's hometown. But most of the add-ons involved much smaller amounts, one of the most modest being $250,000 to help conserve a cemetery at Fort Atkinson, Neb., an Army post in the 1820s.

MAJOR PROVISIONS

As signed into law on Oct. 25, 1999, HR 2561 appropriated $267.8 billion for fiscal 2000 military spending, of which $7.2 billion was designated as "emergency" defense spending. President Clinton had requested $263.3 billion.

Major provisions of HR 2561:

Personnel Issues

• Appropriated $73.9 billion for military pay and benefits, a net increase of $171 million over Clinton's request. The bill included some cuts as well as additions designed to improve recruiting and the retention of experienced personnel. Pentagon officials said the booming economy was the main reason the services had had trouble meeting their recruiting and retention goals. But they also said that the picture was improving because service personnel who were deciding whether to reenlist had become increasingly confident that Congress not only would approve a pay raise and other Clinton initiatives, but would sweeten the pot.

• Included a 4.8 percent military pay raise rather than the 4.4 percent increase Clinton requested and provided $165 million to fund the difference.

• Included scaled-down versions of other retention incentives the House had approved, and added to Clinton's request:

• $100 million to accelerate a more generous housing allowance for those who lived off base.

• $110 million for higher bonuses to stem the exodus of Air Force pilots.

• Added $162 million to Clinton's request for bonuses to those who enlisted or reenlisted in essential and hard-to-fill specialties.

• Provided $105 million more than the $784 million Clinton requested for recruiting and advertising.

• Added $35 million to Clinton's budget for high school ROTC programs. The services said that while these programs were not avowedly recruiting efforts, many graduates wound up joining the military.

• Added $7 million to fund an Army program that allowed junior college students to defer the start of active-duty service for up to two years and collect a stipend while they completed their education.

• Offset these congressional add-ons partly with cuts in Clinton's personnel budget, including reductions of:

• $219 million because the services started the fiscal year with nearly 10,000 fewer active duty personnel than the budget assumed.

• $136 million because of near-term savings in the military pension system. Clinton and Congress had agreed to essentially repeal a 1986 law (PL 99-348) that reduced pensions for those retiring after twenty years. But the retirement package written on Capitol Hill and enacted as part of the companion defense authorization bill (PL 106-65) would be cheaper than the administration's formula.

Operations and Readiness

• Appropriated $92.2 billion for day-to-day operations, maintenance, and training, $967 million more than Clinton requested, but $1.45 billion less than the House approved. It was $340 million more than the Senate version of the bill.

• With the intention of improving morale and combat readiness, added to Clinton's budget request:

• $289 million for spare parts.

• $222 million for overhauls of ships, planes, vehicles and other equipment.

• $223 million for routine base operations.

• $362 million for facilities maintenance.

• Partly offset, as in the past, those additions with cuts to Clinton's request which, the Appropriations Committees insisted, would have no effect on the services' combat readiness. The largest of these—$171 million—was because the dollar's strength would reduce the cost of supplies and ser-

HOUSE CHALLENGES F-22—AND PENTAGON

The House Defense Appropriations Subcommittee sent the Pentagon and its supporters on Capitol Hill reeling in 1999, when it challenged Air Force plans to begin buying the F-22 fighter plane. The F-22 was the centerpiece of Air Force plans to retain air superiority through the first few decades of the twenty-first century. But critics contended that the plane was too costly and unnecessarily complex and that it was soaking up funds needed by more essential but less glamorous Air Force programs.

During action on the fiscal 2000 defense appropriations bill (HR 2561), the subcommittee, at the urging of its chairman, California Republican Jerry Lewis, approved the requested $1.2 billion in research and development funding for the plane but denied the $1.9 billion requested to buy the first six production F-22s. The subcommittee's decision was backed by the full Appropriations Committee and remained in the bill approved by the full House.

But the F-22 was not without friends—powerful friends. Among them were President Clinton, Defense Secretary William S. Cohen, Air Force leaders, prime contractor Lockheed Martin Corp., and members of the Georgia, Texas, Connecticut, and Washington state congressional delegations whose states had a stake in the project.

There was no recent precedent for either the House or the Senate trying to kill off a major defense program that had come this close to production. F-22 supporters were determined to not let the attempt succeed and so was the Air Force, as its generals descended on Capitol Hill to save the jet.

Subcommittee Strategy

The House Defense Appropriations Subcommittee had a history of taking strong steps to get the Pentagon's attention,

but the F-22 decision seemed to go deeper. Chairman Lewis was after larger issues than one fighter jet.

Lewis picked this fight, blindsiding the Pentagon, to goad the Clinton administration and Congress into resolving what he and the committee insisted were fundamental problems in the Pentagon's long-term plans—problems, they said, that were typified by the stealthy fighter plane.

For one thing, they contended, the armed services' long-range spending plans were affordable only with highly optimistic assumptions that future defense budgets would increase, despite pressure to reduce taxes and increase domestic spending.

Compounding this mismatch between plans and budgets, the critics said, was the continued insistence of the military services on developing highly sophisticated weapons, designed to overpower Soviet forces that no longer existed, while short-changing personnel programs and equipment more relevant to the post–cold war world.

The Pentagon's mismatch of plans and budget was exemplified, they said, by the services' plans to spend about $340 billion over the next two decades on three fighter jets:

- The enlarged version of the Navy's F/A-18, already in production.
- The F-22, slated to enter service in numbers late in the next decade.
- The Joint Strike Fighter, three versions of which were slated for production late in the next decade to replace several types of planes dating from the 1970s.

Lewis argued that the air war against Yugoslavia showed there was no need for such an advanced aircraft as the F-22. He maintained that the F-15, with upgrades, could defeat any plane U.S. pilots were likely to face in the next couple of

vices purchased overseas. The conference report made other routine cuts as well.

Overseas Operations

- For operations in Bosnia and Iraq, the bill provided $1.7 billion of the $2.4 billion requested. Conferees said the $665 million reduction could be offset with funds left over because the air war against Serbia was halted before the end of fiscal 1999. The bill did not include money for fiscal 2000 operations in Kosovo, which Clinton has promised to ask for in a supplemental.
- Prohibited any reconstruction aid to Serbia as long as Yugoslavia President Slobodan Milosevic remained in power.

U.S.-Russia Cooperation

- Appropriated $461 million of the $476 million requested for the so-called Nunn-Lugar program to help Rus-

sia and other former Soviet states dispose of their nuclear, chemical, and biological weapons, and the long-range missiles and bombers that could carry them.

However, the bill had a greater impact on the program than the relatively small reduction suggested: it denied the $130 million requested to continue building a chemical weapons destruction facility in Russia and the $20 million requested for modifying three Russian reactors used to generate power to make it harder to use them to build nuclear weapons. The funds requested for those projects were parceled out to other parts of the Nunn-Lugar program.

Post–Cold War Missions

- Required reports from the Pentagon on how well U.S. forces were matched with the new missions they had been taking on since the end of the cold war, including:

decades, until the less-expensive Joint Strike Fighter entered service. Critics put the F-22's average cost at nearly $200 million apiece for a planned fleet of 339 planes.

Lewis and others said that the House position would provide a "pause" to let Congress and the Pentagon ponder whether the plane fit into projected future defense budgets, in light of competing requirements.

Pentagon Response

Secretary Cohen and other F-22 supporters insisted the House committee grossly underestimated the quality of the weaponry that U.S. pilots might confront a decade or more from then. No feasible modifications to the F-15, designed in the late 1960s, could give it an edge on fighters and antiaircraft missiles already on the international arms market or likely to become available, they contended.

The F-22 was intended to ensure combat domination with a combination of radar-evading "stealth," high speed for sustained periods, and a web of electronic sensors knitted together to give the pilot a comprehensive picture of the combat situation. The Joint Strike Fighter was intended to be slower and less stealthy than the F-22. Moreover, it would depend on technology being developed for the F-22.

Cohen and others said critics' nearly $200 million price tag was inflated, because it included for each plane a proportionate share of the $20 billion spent thus far to develop the aircraft. The only cost that was relevant to the Pentagon's future budget squeeze, supporters argued, was the price of buying the planes once they had been developed—a price they anticipated to be about $120 million apiece.

The Air Force and Lockheed Martin waged a strenuous lobbying effort to overturn the House action. They insisted that any significant reduction in the fiscal 2000 procurement request would be fatal to the program, because it would increase the cost of each plane.

Conference Compromise

Conferees on the bill resolved the controversy by denying the requested $1.9 billion to procure the first six planes and providing instead $1 billion in additional research and development money to build six planes that would be used for some of the additional testing the bill required.

F-22 supporters said the funds provided would keep the program on track, allowing the Air Force to begin production of additional planes. They contended that, practically speaking, the six test planes would be the six planes the Air Force had requested. Using research funds rather than production funds to pay for the planes was "not consequential," Senate Appropriations Committee member Kay Bailey Hutchison, R-Texas, said Oct. 6. Hutchison was a staunch F-22 support whose state had a major Lockheed Martin facility in Fort Worth.

But House subcommittee Chairman Lewis insisted that House conferees had achieved their aim because the conference report required the Air Force to conduct additional testing before committing to full-scale production of the aircraft.

Lewis and senior House subcommittee Democrat John P. Murtha of Pennsylvania said Oct. 7 that their skepticism about the F-22 foreshadowed the type of critical scrutiny their panel would give other high-priced weapons programs in the future.

• A report analyzing U.S. airstrikes against Iraq in December 1999 and NATO's war with Yugoslavia over the province of Kosovo, with attention to the effectiveness of U.S. forces and of NATO's command structure.

• A report reviewing the Pentagon's plans to modernize and expand its inventory of electronic warfare planes, such as the Prowler radar jammers. Defense officials said there was such high demand for the limited number of these craft that planes and crews were wearing out.

• In their statement on the compromise bill, conferees expressed particular concern that the Air Force's small fleet of aging U-2 reconnaissance planes might be worn out before a replacement entered service. The bill added $19 million for U-2 upgrades.

• A quarterly report on the costs the military incurred supporting resolutions of the United Nations Security Council and a report on Washington's efforts to persuade the United Nations to reimburse the United States for these costs.

Antimissile Defense

• Appropriated nearly $3.6 billion for the ballistic missile defense organization, including $837 million for a national missile defense system. Clinton had requested $3.3 billion, including the $837 million for national missile defense.

The bill appropriated another nearly $1.1 billion for related programs, as compared to the $956 million requested.

Ground Combat

• Appropriated $467 million, $40 million more than requested, to continue developing the Comanche stealth helicopter and $268 million of the $344 million requested to continue developing the mobile, long-range Crusader cannon. The Army touted the Crusader's unprecedented combat versatility, but critics argued that its fifty-five-ton weight compounded the Army's existing problems in deploying forces abroad.

• Appropriated the requested $636 million to continue upgrading M-1 tanks with larger cannon, improved night-vision equipment, and digital links.

• Appropriated $789 million to equip missile-armed Apache helicopters with digital links and the Longbow target-finding radar.

• Added $10 million to the budget for work on a new combat vehicle and $31 million to accelerate development of a compact artillery rocket launcher small enough to fit in a C-130 cargo plane.

Air Combat

• Appropriated $2.5 billion, mostly for research and development of the F-22 jet fighter. This included the $1.2 billion Clinton requested for research and development of the aircraft, but instead of the $1.9 billion he requested to start buying the aircraft, another $1 billion was added to the research and development column. Of that $1 billion, $725 million could be used to start work on as many as six planes that would be designated for some of the additional testing the bill required and $277 million would go for components to be used in ten additional F-22s. The remaining $300 million was to go in a reserve fund to cover the cost of killing the program if Congress or the Pentagon decided to do so.

• Appropriated $275 million for five Boeing F-15 fighters and $25 million for components of additional F-15s to be funded in fiscal 2001. The administration requested no F-15s. The Senate would have added $220 million for four, while the House would have added $440 million for eight.

• Appropriated $246 million to buy ten Lockheed Martin F-16s, for which the administration had requested $253 million. The House had added to that request $98 million for five additional F-16s.

• Appropriated $2.7 billion for thirty-six Boeing F/A-18 E and F model ground attack planes requested for the Navy.

• Appropriated $492 million—$15 million more than requested—to continue developing the Joint Strike Fighter, slated to enter service with the Navy, Air Force, and Marine Corps late in the next decade.

• Added $104 million to continue a long-running program to equip 1960s-vintage midair refueling tankers with more reliable and more powerful engines.

• Included $60 million for new engines for two tankers that had been modified into electronic eavesdropping planes.

• Included $240 million instead of the $161 million requested to upgrade the fleet of 1970s-vintage Prowler radar-jamming planes.

• Appropriated $293 million to buy one Joint STARS radar plane and components for a second one to be purchased in fiscal 2001. The House bill would have provided $468 million to buy two of the planes, which were converted jetliners able to find ground targets 150 miles away. The Clinton administration had requested $280 million for one plane.

Naval Combat

• Appropriated $2.7 billion for three destroyers equipped with the Aegis antiaircraft system.

• Appropriated $748 million for components of a nuclear-powered submarine slated for inclusion in the fiscal 2001 budget.

• Appropriated $752 million to be used in a nuclear-powered aircraft carrier, for which the administration planned to request about $4 billion in the fiscal 2001 budget.

Air and Sea Transport

• Appropriated $375 million as partial payment for the helicopter carrier to be built in Mississippi. The Navy had planned to buy components for the ship in fiscal 2004, with the bulk of the funding to be requested in 2005. But the contractor said the price would drop from $2.3 billion to $1.5 billion if Congress funded the vessel immediately. This was the largest single increase in the conference report.

• Added $320 million for a "roll on/roll off" cargo ship for trucks and other vehicles of a U.S.-based combat unit. Likely candidates for the contract were National Steel and Shipbuilding Co. in San Diego, a subsidiary of General Dynamics, and Avondale Industries in New Orleans, recently purchased by Litton Industries.

• Appropriated, as requested, $1.5 billion for two ships to carry Marine amphibious landing forces. Avondale and General Dynamics's Bath Iron Works subsidiary built these vessels.

• Authorized the Air Force to sign a multiyear contract to buy sixty additional C-17 cargo planes, beyond the 120 that were planned, provided the additional planes were at least 25 percent cheaper than those being purchased under the existing contract. This provision may have had the greatest long-term budgetary impact of all of the bill's provisions.

• Appropriated, similar to the Senate version, $153 million for two Lockheed Martin C-130 cargo planes, neither of which Clinton requested. The House had added $564 million for eight of the planes, which long had been popular with Congress.

• Appropriated $977 million for twelve V-22 Osprey tilt-rotor planes, built by Boeing's Vertol division in Pennsylvania and Textron's Bell Helicopter division in Fort Worth. The administration had requested $867 million for ten aircraft, plus $50 million to fund advance procurement.

• Added $116 million for eleven additional H-60 helicopters, on top of the $510 million requested for twenty-eight of the aircraft, built in Connecticut by the Sikorsky division of United Technologies Corp.

Other Provisions

• Authorized the president to waive a section of the 1994 Arms Export Control Act (PL 103-236) that required the automatic imposition of sanctions on India and Pakistan, after those countries conducted nuclear test explosions in 1998. *(Economic sanctions, p. 223)*

• Prohibited the use of any defense funds to aid North Korea, unless specifically approved by Congress.

• Added $630 million for medical research and treatment projects not requested, including $175 million for breast cancer research and $75 million for prostate cancer research.

• Allowed the Pentagon to lease, as requested, six Gulf-stream V executive jets for its top commanders. The bill also approved buying one 737 that the administration requested.

• Ordered the General Accounting Office, an investigative arm of Congress, to study the military's controversial anthrax immunization program, including its effect on military morale, retention, and recruiting.

2000 Military Construction

Congress in 1999 cleared an $8.37 billion fiscal 2000 military construction appropriations bill (HR 2465—PL 106-52). Although the military construction measure was typically the least controversial of the thirteen annual spending measures, the administration touched off a debate in 1999 by attempting to defer spending on some projects. Clinton's plan called for paying for construction projects incrementally instead of following the usual practice of authorizing and appropriating the total cost of a project, even when the budget authority would be spent as outlays over a period of several years.

Pentagon officials explained the "split funding" approach as a one-time action intended to make more funds available within the spending limits set by the 1997 balanced-budget law (PL 105-33). Under their incremental approach, Congress would have appropriated only what was to be spent in fiscal 2000—$5.4 billion—instead of the total, multiyear cost of projects: $8.5 billion. The proposal allowed Clinton to save $3 billion in his budget.

But it went nowhere on Capitol Hill. Members of both parties criticized the approach, with some contending that it would delay construction of essential projects. In the end, Congress provided $125 million less than the $8.5 billion cost of the projects.

The final bill allocated $4 billion for military construction, 15 percent more than Clinton's $3.5 billion request. But Congress more than compensated for that increase with cuts in the requests for funding for NATO construction and for base closings.

Congress approved $8.45 billion in regular military construction appropriations for fiscal 1999 and another $684 million in emergency supplemental funding. *(1999 military construction, p. 263)*

1999 LEGISLATIVE ACTION

The Senate passed its $8.27 billion military construction funding bill (S 1205) by a 97–2 vote on June 16, 1999. The Senate Appropriations Committee had reported the bill (S Rept 106-74) June 10.

The Senate made clear its intent to follow tradition when it came to the construction spending bill—it rejected the incremental-funding proposal out of hand and added millions for projects that had not been requested. Continuing his crusade against such unrequested additions to appropriations bills, John McCain, R-Ariz., issued a statement complaining that the add-ons reflected parochial interest rather than military priorities. But McCain was one of only two senators to vote "nay" on final passage.

The House passed its $8.49 billion version (HR 2465) by a vote of 418–4 on July 13. The House Appropriations Committee had reported the bill (H Rept 106-221) on July 2.

House members joined the Senate in spurning the administration's request for incremental funding. The bill was passed with little debate, with the four dissenting votes coming from lawmakers who protested what they considered unnecessary spending. But many lawmakers lamented that there was not enough money for a backlog of new housing projects and upgrades of existing facilities.

The Senate passed HR 2465 by voice vote July 14, after substituting the text of its bill.

CONFERENCE ACTION

The House adopted the conference report (H Rept 106-266) by a vote of 412–8 on July 29. The Senate cleared the bill by voice vote Aug. 3. President Clinton signed it into law Aug. 17.

Conferees agreed on a bill providing $8.37 billion in new budget authority—$125.7 million less than the House bill but $100.2 million more than the Senate version (S 1205). Compared with the fully funded Clinton budget—and not the incremental-approach version—the final bill appropriated $125.3 million less.

MAJOR PROVISIONS

• **Military construction.** The final bill reduced the amount for general construction to $4 billion, $187.2 million less than the House bill and $135.3 million less than the Senate version, but it still was $530.8 million more than the full Clinton request. Construction for active duty forces was cut, while the total for National Guard and reserve projects was $198.7 million higher than the House bill and $56.9 million more than in the Senate version.

In addition, the bill provided $81 million for the U.S. share of NATO construction, less than half the $191 million Clinton requested and $19 million less than the Senate bill included, but the same amount as the House bill.

• **Family housing.** The bill provided $3.6 billion, $64.8 million more than Clinton's budget. The total was $13.9 million more than the House bill and $10 million more than the Senate. Concerned by reports that both the Navy and Air Force had used operations and maintenance funds to improve housing for flag and general officers, the report included statutory language to prohibit the practice.

• **Base closures.** The bill appropriated $672 million for base closure and realignment costs, substantially less than Clinton's budget request of $1.28 billion. Both the Senate and House bills had included nearly $706 million.

2001 Defense Authorization

Congress in 2000 approved $309.9 billion in defense spending for fiscal 2001. The defense authorization bill (HR 4205—PL 106-398) added $4.6 billion to President Clinton's budget request.

Defense hawks of both parties contended that Clinton had undermined combat readiness with defense budgets that were too small and a military workload that was too ambitious. However, as it had done in the five previous years of Republican control on Capitol Hill, Congress exceeded Clinton's fiscal 2001 defense budget request only modestly—about 1.5 percent, much of it spread over dozens of smaller programs.

But rising estimates of the federal budget surplus for fiscal 2001 and beyond emboldened conferees to approve health benefits for military retirees that would have significant impact on future budgets. HR 4205 created a new, permanent retiree health entitlement that was expected to cost $60 billion over the first ten years. The bill also allowed most retirees to obtain low-cost prescriptions. The health care provisions were rooted in the argument by retirees that they were promised lifetime care for themselves and their dependents in return for a full career—at least twenty years—on active duty.

Of the money added to Clinton's fiscal 2001 budget, about $2.6 billion was for procurement and development, including nearly $800 million more for the Army's effort to transform itself into a lighter force, able to move overseas more quickly. There had been widespread complaints that it took too long for Army units to reach the Balkans during the Kosovo crisis in mid-1999 and that once there, some of the equipment was too unwieldy to operate in the mountainous terrain.

Conferees included several provisions intended to assert more congressional control over how U.S. nuclear secrets were protected, including expanded polygraph testing of Energy Department workers in sensitive jobs.

HR 4205 was delayed for several weeks until agreement was reached on the health care initiative as well as a compensation program for nuclear weapons workers exposed to radioactive and other toxic substances.

HOUSE COMMITTEE ACTION

The House Armed Services Committee reported its $309.9 billion fiscal 2001 defense authorization bill (HR 4205—H Rept 106-616) on May 12, 2000.

The panel expected the bill to win broad support, thanks to an increase of about $4.5 billion above Clinton's defense budget request, a 3.7 percent military pay raise, a new retire-

ment savings plan, and new health benefits for military retirees. Still, members of the Military Procurement Subcommittee lamented that there was not more money to modernize military equipment. Pentagon officials and defense analysts estimated that the procurement shortfall over the next several years would range from $15 billion to $100 billion.

The committee expressed Congress's strong desire for the Pentagon to slow down its plans for developing the Joint Strike Fighter. The Navy, Marine Corps, and Air Force planned to buy different versions of the plane beginning in 2008 to replace various planes of Vietnam War–era design. Plans called for spending about $200 billion to develop and buy 3,000 planes.

The Joint Strike Fighter was the most advanced of three air-superiority warplanes the Pentagon wanted to buy. The others were the Air Force's F-22, which some House appropriators had tried to block the previous year, and the F/A-18 E and F model Super Hornets for the Navy and Marine Corps, the closest of the three to production. *(F-22 controversy, box p. 286)*

The Defense Department had awarded contracts of more than $2 billion each to Boeing Co. and Lockheed Martin Corp. to develop concept planes for the Joint Strike Fighter. The department had planned to award a contract for engineering and manufacturing development to one of the companies by April 2001. But, according to the General Accounting Office (GAO), neither company would have critical technology ready in time to support the plane's next phase of engineering and manufacturing development. The GAO recommended that the Pentagon consider allowing the technology to catch up.

And, despite continued support for the Joint Strike Fighter, some lawmakers expressed unease about the price at the same time the Pentagon was pursuing the two other advanced fighters.

But the Armed Services Committee did find money to buy more F-15 and F-16 fighters—a priority for many House members—although none had been requested. About $200 million was shifted from the F/A-18 E and F request to pay for them.

The House bill challenged an agreement Clinton was attempting to implement on the status of the Puerto Rican island of Vieques, where the Navy had recently resumed training exercises. Exercises had been suspended for about a year after a Puerto Rican security guard working for the Navy was killed on the island by an errant bomb in April 1999. That event became a lightning rod for protests against noise, environmental destruction, and health concerns caused by the bombing.

Under the agreement Clinton reached with Puerto Rican Gov. Pedro Rossello, the Navy would transfer land at the western end of the island that was not used for bombing and provide $40 million in assistance up front before the residents of the island held a referendum sometime in the next two years on whether the Navy should stay or go. If residents voted the Navy out, the service would have to leave by May 2003. If the Navy was permitted to stay, it could resume bombing, but the federal government would provide an additional $50 million in assistance and ensure that live-fire training occurred no more than ninety days each year. The House committee bill did not require a referendum and authorized the initial $40 million payment only if the president certified that the Navy would resume all training, including live bombing, "without interference."

In other action, the House committee voted to limit the number of U.S. troops serving in Colombia to no more than 500 at a time.

For the second straight year, defense authorizers included language to prohibit any money from being used to plan, design, or build a chemical weapons destruction plant near Shchuch'ye in Russia's Ural Mountains. The administration had been pushing funds for the plant as part of an initiative enacted in 1991 (PL 102-228) to help Russia safeguard and destroy its nuclear, chemical, and other weapons. But some Republicans said the money should be going to enhance security at weapons sites in Russia. *(PL 102-228, Congress and the Nation Vol. VIII, p. 262)*

The House committee approved an amendment to bar the Navy from spending any money to assign women to its submarines. The panel defeated two amendments during its markup that would have loosened restrictions on abortions for female military personnel or family members.

HOUSE FLOOR ACTION

The House passed a $309.98 billion version of HR 4205 on May 18 by a vote of 353–63. The bill was $4.6 billion more than Clinton requested, but many lawmakers repeated their concern that the Pentagon needed even more money for such critical programs as modernization and procurement.

The two-day debate covered a wide range of issues, including the U.S. peacekeeping mission to Kosovo, export of high-performance computers, benefits for military retirees, and the dispute over Navy bombing on the Puerto Rican island of Vieques.

By a **key vote of 264–153 (R 195–18; D 67–135; I 2–0)**, the House on May 17 adopted an amendment by Budget Committee Chairman John R. Kasich, R-Ohio, to force the withdrawal of U.S. forces from Kosovo unless the president certified to Congress by April 1, 2001, that NATO countries were fulfilling their promise to aid the province. The provision could have been waived under certain circumstances. The House in March had rejected a similar Kasich amendment to the fiscal 2000 supplemental appropriations bill (HR 3908). And on the other side of Capitol Hill, the Senate on May 18 removed an amendment to its fiscal 2001 military construction appropriations bill (S 2521) that would have required a pullout by July 1, 2001, unless Congress authorized the mission. *(2000 key votes, p. 915; 2000 supplemental, p. 84; 2001 military construction, p. 300)*

One of the most popular floor amendments, offered by Rules Committee Chairman David Dreier, R-Calif., shortened the period for congressional review of high-performance computer exports from 180 days to sixty. The change was strongly backed by technology companies that contended the six-month review period was costing them business. The six-month time frame had been established in the fiscal 1998 defense authorization law (HR 1119—PL 105-85). It allowed for congressional review of administration changes to regulations governing computer exports to countries that posed the greatest risk to U.S. national security. Dreier's amendment was adopted 415–8 on May 18. *(1998 defense authorization, p. 239)*

By a **key vote of 406–10 (R 207–9; D 197–1; I 2–0)** on May 18, the House adopted an amendment by Gene Taylor, D-Miss., to allow military retirees over age sixty-five to obtain health care at military hospitals and clinics, with Medicare reimbursing the Defense Department for 95 percent of the cost. Under existing law, those retirees had to switch from the Defense Department's HMO-style health plan, called Tricare, to Medicare, where they lost some benefits such as prescription drug coverage. The House bill would have allowed older retirees to participate in the Tricare mail-order drug program and pharmacy network. Taylor's proposal broadened to the entire nation what was then a limited pilot program for Medicare subvention. *(2000 key votes, p. 915)*

But Steve Buyer, R-Ind., chairman of the House Armed Services Subcommittee on Military Personnel, said Medicare subvention was too expensive and needed to be tested further, along with other demonstration programs, before Congress committed to a long-term plan. Buyer's substitute proposal to expand the program but reauthorize it only through 2003 was rejected, 95–323.

In dealing with Vieques, lawmakers narrowly backed Clinton's proposal to transfer land on the western end of the island in accordance with the agreement negotiated with the Puerto Rican government. An amendment allowing the transfer, offered by House Armed Services ranking Democrat Ike Skelton of Missouri, was adopted, 218–201, on May 18.

On another contentious issue, the House on May 18 defeated, 204–214, an amendment by Joe Moakley, D-Mass., that would have closed the U.S. Army School of the Americas. The school, at Fort Benning, Ga., the Army's main infantry training base, received about $15 million a year from the federal government to train Latin American military graduates. Critics said that some of its graduates had violated human rights at home and insisted that changing the school's name and revising its curriculum to focus on human rights and democratic values, as HR 4205 required, would not resolve the problem. The House in 1999 had voted to cut off the foreign aid portion of funding for the school, but House leaders backed down when Senate appropriators threatened to shift all funding for the school to the defense budget. *(2000 aid appropriations, p. 210)*

The House on May 18 also rejected, 195–221, an amendment by Loretta Sanchez, D-Calif., that would have allowed women in the military and dependents to obtain abortions at overseas military hospitals if they used private funds.

SENATE COMMITTEE ACTION

The Senate Armed Services Committee reported its $309.8 billion fiscal 2001 defense authorization bill (S 2549—S Rept 106-292) on May 12, the day the House committee reported HR 4205. Like their House counterparts, Senate authorizers were satisfied that their bill would help reverse a decade of declining defense budgets while giving the military another pay increase and improving medical care for military retirees.

But the path of the two bills likely would be complicated by language the Senate panel added to curtail Energy Secretary Bill Richardson's authority over the National Nuclear Security Administration. Despite strong opposition from Richardson, Congress had created the new agency in 1999 to improve the security and accountability of the Energy Department's nuclear weapons programs as a remedy for apparent security lapses that might have allowed China to obtain secret material from weapons labs. *(Nuclear security, p. 302; 2000 defense authorization, p. 276)*

S 2549 included a provision prohibiting paying a salary to anyone serving in the same position in the Energy Department and in the nuclear agency—a procedure known as "dual-hatting"—and another provision removing the energy secretary's authority to make any organizational changes to the new agency. Senate Republicans contended that the changes were necessary because Richardson had not followed their intentions in submitting an implementation plan for the new agency earlier in 2000.

S 2549 also differed from HR 4205 in that it essentially authorized the president's request regarding Vieques. The Senate bill did not include money for F-15 or F-16 fighters but did add $460 million in advance procurement for the $1.5 billion helicopter carrier that would be built in Republican Senate Majority Leader Trent Lott's hometown of Pascagoula, Miss. HR 4205 had only $10 million for the helicopter carrier.

The Senate Armed Services Committee used its authorization bill to challenge some of the armed services' modernization plans and to prod the Pentagon into a more active transformation of forces to better meet the threats of the post–cold war world. Senate authorizers agreed with the House that plans for the Joint Strike Fighter should move ahead at a slower pace but the Senate bill put greater emphasis on developing radically new lightweight combat vehicles and more remote-controlled tanks and bombers to minimize the risk to U.S. personnel.

Similar to the House bill, S 2549 prohibited any money being used for the Russian chemical weapons destruction plant.

SENATE FLOOR ACTION

The Senate passed HR 4205 by a 97–3 vote on July 13, after substituting the text of its $309.8 billion version (S 2549).

During more than a month of intermittent debate, Armed Services Committee Chairman John W. Warner, R-Va., and other Republicans managed to keep the legislation largely free of controversial amendments—but not entirely.

After a spirited debate, the Senate on June 7 voted 51–47, largely along party lines, to allow the president to make unilateral arms reductions only after the Pentagon completed a review of nuclear weapons status, which was unlikely until late 2001 after Clinton had left office. The provision, offered by Warner, replaced the language in an amendment by Bob Kerrey, D-Neb., that would have given Clinton a free hand on nuclear arms reductions by removing an existing limit. The amended Kerrey amendment was subsequently adopted by voice vote.

For the past four years, the Armed Services Committee had included a provision in its authorization bill preventing the Pentagon from reducing the number of nuclear warheads on long-range missiles and bombers. The language initially was added in hopes of pressuring Russia to ratify the START II arms reduction agreement. Although the lower house of the Russian parliament, the Duma, did agree to the treaty in April 2000, Warner argued that the Duma had attached conditions that would be unacceptable to the Senate.

The Senate voted 96–1 on June 7 to accept a Warner amendment allowing military retirees sixty-five and older to participate in two health care plans for retirees and their dependents. But the Senate refused to waive a budget point of order against a Democratic proposal—an amendment by Tim Johnson of South Dakota—to further expand retirees' health care options to the same plan as civilian federal workers. The 52–46 vote was eight short of the required three-fifths majority. The Congressional Budget Office estimated that Johnson's plan would have cost $92 billion over ten years, while Warner's was estimated to cost $40 billion over the same period.

For the second straight year, senators rejected, 35–63, an attempt by Armed Services ranking Democrat Carl Levin of Michigan and Republican John McCain of Arizona to authorize additional base closures—in this case two new rounds the Pentagon said would save money. Although a new round of base closures would not have taken place until Clinton left office, Warner and others said they should not tie the hands of the next president by forcing him to close military bases.

On June 20 the Senate tabled (killed), 50–49, an amendment offered by Patty Murray, D-Wash., and Olympia J. Snowe, R-Maine, to allow service women stationed overseas and female dependents to obtain abortions in U.S. military hospitals, provided they paid for the procedure.

The Senate also tabled, 59–41, a Christopher J. Dodd, D-Conn., amendment to establish a bipartisan commission to examine U.S.-Cuba relations.

Shortly before final passage on July 13, the Senate tabled, by a **key vote of 52–48 (R 52–3; D 0–45)**, an amendment by Richard J. Durbin, D-Ill., calling for additional testing of a proposed national missile defense system to ensure that it would work against decoys and other countermeasures. The

Senate also voted, 81–18, to table a Russell D. Feingold, D-Wis., amendment terminating the Trident II submarine-launched missile. *(2000 key votes, p. 915)*

The Senate on July 12 followed the lead of the House in adopting, 86–11, an amendment to shorten the period for congressional review of export rules for high-performance computers from 180 days to sixty. The amendment was offered by Robert F. Bennett, R-Utah, and Harry Reid, D-Nev.

Work on the bill was slowed at times by debate on controversial amendments unrelated to defense. The Senate on June 8 tabled, 51–48, a proposal by Tom Daschle, D-S.D., and Edward M. Kennedy, D-Mass., to attach to the defense bill a version of the House bill on patients' rights in managed health care plans. The Senate adopted by voice vote an amendment by McCain requiring Section 527 political organizations to disclose their fund-raising and spending activities, after a procedural attempt to block the amendment failed by a **key vote of 42–57 (R 41–14; D 1–43)** on June 8. A Kennedy amendment to expand the definition of federal hate crimes was added to the bill June 20 by a **key vote of 57–42 (R 13–41; D 44–1)**. *(Managed care, p. 466; campaign finance, p. 786; hate crimes, p. 642; 2000 key votes, p. 915)*

CONFERENCE ACTION

The House adopted the conference report on HR 4205 (H Rept 106-945) by a 382–31 vote on Oct. 11. The Senate cleared the bill, 90–3, the following day.

Senate approval came only hours after the U.S. Navy destroyer *Cole* was severely damaged by a suicide bombing attack in the Port of Aden, in the Arabian Peninsula nation of Yemen. As many as seventeen of the ship's 350-member crew were feared dead. In addition to expressing condolences to the victims' families, lawmakers said the incident illustrated the broad range of threats that U.S. forces confronted. Critics of the president also said the incident underscored their contention that Clinton had undermined military effectiveness with his budget cuts and overseas missions.

Brushing aside congressional budget limits, conferees added expanded medical benefits for retired military personnel and their dependents that were estimated to cost nearly $60 billion over the next ten years. Although large majorities of the House and Senate Armed Services committees strongly supported the concept of providing lifetime medical care to military retirees, disagreements over how far to push the effort that year made it one of the last issues to be settled in the conference negotiations.

In the end, conferees decided to create a new entitlement program requiring mandatory annual funding not subject to the appropriations process. Making the retirees' benefit a mandatory spending program would buffer the program from any future pressure to cut the budget. Retirees' health benefits would not compete against such things as new weapons programs or combat training in the Pentagon's annual budget process. With budget discipline deeply eroded by ballooning estimates of the federal surplus, Rep. Buyer had publicly floated the idea of an entitlement program in

September while the bill was in conference, in hopes of putting pressure on the Senate.

Senate Armed Services Chairman Warner initially resisted the entitlement idea, fearing that it would be knocked out by a budgetary point of order when the conference report went to the Senate floor for approval. But he finally concluded that the retirees' health care proposals had such wide support he would be able to muster the 60 votes needed to waive the point of order. And, indeed, he did. When Sen. Kerrey of Nebraska raised a point of order that the costs of the health program would exceed the amount allowed for mandatory spending in the congressional budget resolution, the Senate voted 84–9 to waive it.

In other action, conferees agreed to create a program to compensate thousands of Energy Department workers exposed to dangerous levels of radiation and other toxic substances during the cold war. The compensation packaged was close to the original Senate plan written by Fred Thompson, R-Tenn., and Jeff Bingaman, D-N.M. Negotiators estimated that the agreement would cost about $1.8 billion over five years. House GOP leaders originally sought to pull the provision from the bill, calling it a costly entitlement that could drain other spending, but they relented after a bipartisan group of lawmakers objected. The inclusion of the compensation language in the final defense bill was a rare victory for Energy Secretary Richardson, who had been under fire in recent months for his agency's handling of security at nuclear weapons labs and the Clinton administration's oil policies.

Conferees dropped the House bill's Kosovo provision and the Senate's hate crimes provision. McCain's campaign finance proposal had ceased to be a contentious issue in the defense conference after both chambers in June passed a stand-alone bill containing similar language.

MAJOR PROVISIONS

As signed into law Oct. 30, 2000, HR 4205 authorized $309.9 billion, $4.6 billion more than requested.

Major provisions of HR 4205:

Personnel Issues

• Authorized the 3.7 percent military pay raise Clinton requested, effective Jan. 1, 2001. The raise was one half of 1 percent more than the average increase in private-sector pay, as measured by a government index.

• Authorized higher raises for senior sergeants and petty officers, at a cost of $88 million.

• Authorized the Pentagon to increase the housing allowance for personnel who did not live in government quarters, with the aim of covering all housing costs by 2005. As a step in that direction, the bill authorized $25 million more than the administration requested for housing allowances.

• Authorized additional pay of up to $500 a month to assist personnel who qualified for food stamps.

• Authorized $105 million more than Clinton requested for recruiting and retention, $84 million of which was for enlistment and reenlistment bonuses.

• Authorized a $50 increase in the $200 monthly stipend paid to senior ROTC cadets, in hopes of making that program more attractive to college students. It also added $14 million to the amount Clinton requested for high school ROTC, which the services regarded as a valuable recruiting tool.

Retirees' Health Care

• Created a new entitlement program of health benefits for military retirees. Those who had served at least twenty years on active duty and their dependents would be allowed to remain in the Pentagon's medical care and insurance system for life instead of having to rely on Medicare after they turned sixty-five. Most retirees would also be allowed to buy prescription drugs through a military system. The program, which required mandatory annual funding not subject to the appropriations process, was expected to cost $60 billion over the first ten years.

Antimissile Defense

• Authorized nearly $4.8 billion for the ballistic missile defense. The administration had requested $4.5 billion.

Clinton's request included $1.8 billion to continue developing a system that would be deployed in Alaska to protect U.S. territory from a small number of attacking missiles. Clinton had been expected to decide in the fall of 2000 whether to begin building the project, but in September he deferred the decision for his successor, contending that test failures had left too many questions unanswered for him to make a decision before he left office. The final defense bill added $135 million to Clinton's request for his national missile defense project.

The bill also authorized $80 million more than the $383 million Clinton requested to continue developing a long-range antimissile system based on ships. Some Republicans contended that this Navy Theater-Wide system could be upgraded relatively quickly and cheaply to a limited national missile defense shield. Critics said it would take much longer and cost much more.

• Authorized $1 billion for related missile defense programs. This included the requested $241 million for the Space-Based Infra-Red System, Low-altitude (SBIRS-Low), a program to develop satellites that could track missile warheads as they sped through space. The bill transferred the program from the Air Force to the Ballistic Missile Defense Organization in 2002.

The House version of the defense bill would have transferred from the Air Force to the missile defense organization a program to mount an antimissile laser in the nose of a wide-body jet transport. Supporters of this airborne laser complained that, similar to SBIRS-Low, the program was getting shortchanged by Air Force leaders more interested in funding the F-22 fighter. Defense conferees left the airborne laser in the Air Force budget but required the service to obtain the consent of the missile defense organization before

making any changes in the project's budget, schedule, or specifications.

The conference report also authorized $85 million more than the $149 million Clinton requested for the laser program, thus reversing an Air Force decision to slow the program for budget reasons. The resulting authorization—$234 million—would keep the project on schedule to try to shoot down a target missile in 2003.

Ground Combat

• Authorized about $1.8 billion for the Army's effort to field a new, medium-weight force able to move overseas more quickly, a concept that had become popular on Capitol Hill. This was about $800 million more than requested. The conference bill added $600 million to buy new, lighter equipment for the Army's "transformation" and another $196 million for the Army's research and development account for this program.

While strongly endorsing its goal, the conference report raised questions about the Army's plan to jump-start its transformation by equipping some brigades in the near term with off-the-shelf armored vehicles while it pursued the technological breakthroughs needed to build a twenty-ton light tank that could do the job of the existing seventy-ton M-1.

If the Army selected an "interim armored vehicle" other than an upgraded version of United Defense's M-113 troop carrier, some 17,000 of which the service already owned, the bill required the Army to give Congress a comparison of the cost and operational effectiveness of the new vehicle and the one already in service. The bill also required the new interim units to be tested in mock combat against armored tank units.

• Authorized $25 million to develop robot ground combat vehicles and $75 million to develop robot airplanes to attack especially dangerous targets. The Senate version of the bill included an initiative by Senate Armed Services Chairman Warner that would have authorized twice as much to work on the air and ground robots.

Air Combat

• Authorized $2.5 billion to continue production of the Air Force's new Lockheed Martin F-22 fighter, as Clinton requested.

• Authorized $2.9 billion—slightly more than Clinton asked for—to continue building the Navy's Boeing F/A-18 E and F model fighters.

• Authorized $689 million—$168 million less than Clinton requested—to continue developing the Joint Strike Fighter, which would be built in versions for use by the Navy, Air Force, and Marine Corps. Top Pentagon leaders had objected to the cut, but both Armed Services panels insisted that the Defense Department was pushing the program too fast.

• Authorized a total of $118 million above Clinton's request to develop long-range, precision-guided "smart" bombs and cruise missiles. About two-thirds of that amount was for an effort to capitalize on the fact that satellite-guided bombs already in service were so accurate that they carried much more explosive power than was needed to destroy many types of targets. If the weapons could be made smaller, one plane could carry more bombs and thus could hit more targets.

• Added $150 million for two Boeing F-15 fighters, built in St. Louis, Mo., and $52 million for two Lockheed Martin F-16s, built in Fort Worth, Texas. No F-15s or F-16s had been requested.

Naval Combat

• Authorized basically what the administration requested for new warships: $4 billion for a *Nimitz*-class carrier, $3.2 billion for three destroyers equipped with the Aegis antiaircraft system and components of future ships, and $1.7 billion for a nuclear-powered submarine and components of future subs.

• Authorized the $274 million Clinton requested to continue designing a new carrier that would be included in the 2006 budget, and $540 million—$10 million less than Clinton requested—to continue designing a new destroyer slated for the 2005 budget. Both new classes were expected to be cheaper to operate because they would have smaller crews.

• Required the Navy to give Congress thirty days' notice before assigning women to duty on submarines or beginning any design work or ship modifications intended to accommodate women as members of sub crews. The House version of the bill would have required a 120-day waiting period after notification.

At that time, submarines were the only class of major Navy ships to which women were not assigned, an exception based on the difficulty of assuring privacy in the cramped accommodations of a sub. House Armed Services Committee member Roscoe G. Bartlett, R-Md., had sponsored the House-passed version of the restriction after Navy Secretary Richard Danzig made a speech criticizing the "men only" policy for submarines.

Sea and Air Transport

• Added $460 million as a down payment toward the $1.5 billion cost of a helicopter carrier to be built by Litton Industries in Pascagoula, Miss.

• Authorized the $1.5 billion Clinton requested for two other ships also intended to carry Marine Corps combat units to their landing sites. The companion defense appropriations bill (PL 106-259) provided only $561 million to begin work on these two ships (designated LPD-17s). *(2001 defense appropriations, p. 296)*

• Added $209 million for sixteen H-60 helicopters, in addition to the $495 million Clinton requested for twenty-five of the craft, which were built in Connecticut by United Technologies' Sikorsky division.

• Added $165 million for two Lockheed Martin C-130s, built in Marietta, Ga., in addition to the $363 million requested for four of the planes.

Long-Range Planning

• Required the Pentagon to draw up several long-range plans in hopes of stimulating a debate that might generate support for more defense spending in the future, including:

• A plan to sustain U.S. nuclear forces as existing missiles, bombers, and missile-launching submarines reached the end of their useful life.

• An analysis of the military airlift fleet, a study likely to conclude that more planes were needed.

• A study of aerial reconnaissance, which likely would conclude that more radar picket planes and electronic eavesdroppers were necessary.

Weapons of Mass Destruction, Terrorism

• Authorized $443 million, $15 million less than Clinton requested, for the Nunn-Lugar program to help former Soviet republics dispose of nuclear, chemical, and biological weapons and the missiles and bombers that could deliver them.

While the bill would allow slightly more than requested for some Nunn-Lugar projects, conferees rejected $35 million Clinton requested to continue construction of a facility designed to destroy chemical weapons.

• Authorized the Defense and Energy Departments to study methods of destroying stockpiles of nuclear, chemical, and biological weapons buried deep underground. Antinuclear activists warned that this was a foot in the door for future efforts to develop and test very small nuclear weapons intended to destroy such targets, thus derailing efforts to secure a global ban on nuclear weapons tests.

• Included several provisions intended to help the government respond to terrorist acts on U.S. territory. It authorized $16 million more than Clinton requested to increase from twenty-seven to thirty-two the number of National Guard teams trained to help local police, fire, and emergency medical personnel deal with suspected nuclear, chemical, or biological weapons attacks.

• Required the secretary of defense to designate one assistant as his principal adviser on counterterrorism, responsible for coordinating the Defense Department's preparation to deal with terrorism.

• Established a commission of outside experts to examine the vulnerability of the U.S. electronic infrastructure to electromagnetic pulses—powerful radio waves that could be caused by a high-altitude nuclear explosion. Rep. Bartlett had warned for some time that a hostile country with only a handful of long-range, nuclear-armed missiles might get the most leverage out of them by trying to cripple U.S. communications and electronics by such an attack.

• Required the president to prepare a report on the country's preparedness to deal with the threat of biological terrorism. It also required the secretary of defense and the director of central intelligence to prepare an intelligence estimate assessing that threat.

Energy Department

• Created a new federal entitlement program for Energy Department workers exposed to radiation and toxic materials at nuclear weapons plants during the cold war. Injured workers would receive a $150,000 payment and medical care. Existing payments for Navajo uranium miners exposed to radiation would be increased from $100,000 to $150,000, and they would be offered medical care.

• Prohibited the energy secretary and Energy Department employees from serving in the same positions in both the Energy Department and the new National Nuclear Security Administration, a practice known as "dual-hatting."

• Required the Energy Department to polygraph all employees with access to "sensitive compartmented information"—the highly classified intelligence data produced under the CIA's supervision. The energy secretary could waive the polygraph requirements for employees on a one-time basis but could not grant a waiver on the grounds that polygraphing would hurt science at any of the labs.

Defense conferees added to the scope of polygraph questions as well, including a requirement that employees be asked if they had caused "deliberate damage to or malicious misuse of" a government information system.

Other Provisions

• Converted the Army's controversial School of the Americas into the Defense Institute for Hemispheric Security Cooperation. A board of overseers was to include representatives from religious organizations and human rights groups that had complained the institution's curriculum did not sufficiently emphasize to military officers from Latin American countries the importance of civilian control and the rule of law.

• Codified an agreement between the Pentagon and the governor of Puerto Rico over how to settle the future of the Navy bombing range on the island of Vieques, which many Puerto Ricans wanted to see closed. The bill authorized $40 million in economic assistance to Vieques with the provision that an additional $50 million would be turned over if the island's residents approved, in a referendum, the continued use of live ammunition on the firing range.

• Authorized—with conditions—a $6.9 billion contract to privatize all Navy and Marine Corps communications, including telephone, video, and computer services. Eventually, Electronic Data Services, which won the contract, would replace about 200 in-house networks that were maintained by nearly 2,000 Navy civilians. After a first phase of the contract was completed, covering about 45,000 work stations (15 percent of the total network), the bill required a complete evaluation of how well the contract was working before more jobs were converted. The bill also barred privatizing communications networks at Navy shipyards and aircraft repair depots and at Marine Corps installations during 2001.

• Expressed the sense of Congress that three officers held responsible for disasters that befell U.S. forces during World War II were, in fact, innocent. The bill called for the exonera-tion of Capt. Charles McVay III, captain of the cruiser *Indianapolis*, sunk by a Japanese submarine in July 1945. It also called for posthumously restoring the ranks of the Navy and Army commanders in charge of defending Hawaii when Japanese forces attacked Pearl Harbor—Adm. Husband E. Kimmel and Lt. Gen. Walter C. Short—who were demoted after the attack.

2001 Defense Appropriations

Congress in 2000 approved a $289.6 billion defense spending bill (HR 4576—PL 106-259) for fiscal 2001, $5.1 billion more than President Clinton requested. To avoid breaking spending limits set by the annual budget resolution, conferees designated $1.8 billion of the increase as fiscal 2000 emergency spending.

Combined with funds in two other appropriations bills—$8.8 billion in the military construction appropriations bill (HR 4425—PL 106-246) and $13.7 billion in the energy and water appropriations bill (HR 4635—PL 106-377)—HR 2561 brought overall defense spending in fiscal 2001 to about $310 billion.

Though projected budget surpluses were ballooning by the time the annual defense appropriations bill was being written, Republican defense hawks found themselves in a political bind. Clinton and GOP leaders had ruled out the growing Social Security surplus for discretionary spending, so the defense appropriations subcommittees were having to compete with domestic priorities for a more limited supply of extra funds. A relatively small but deeply committed band of fiscal conservatives threatened to torpedo any proposal that sacrificed tax cuts to fund defense increases.

The decision to designate almost a third of the increased spending as fiscal 2000 emergency appropriations was a thinly disguised ruse: the bill was cleared with little more than two months left in fiscal 2000 and the "emergency" spending was intended to pay for routine maintenance and peacekeeping operations that had been going on for some time.

As usual, the final bill was studded with projects of special interest to influential lawmakers. The largest was the addition of $460 million for components of a helicopter carrier to be built by Litton Industries in Pascagoula, Miss., the hometown of Republican Senate Majority Leader Trent Lott. The Pentagon had not planned to request most of the money for the $1.5 billion ship until 2005, but the contractor and the Navy insisted that earlier funding would save hundreds of millions of dollars.

The bill also added $400 million to continue producing F-15 fighters at Boeing Co.'s plant in St. Louis, a priority for Republican Sen. Christopher S. Bond, an Appropriations Committee member, and Democratic House Minority Leader Richard A. Gephardt, both of Missouri. Clinton had not requested any of the aircraft.

The bill funded the 3.7 percent military pay raise the president requested and added $200 million to cover the cost of a program in the companion defense authorization bill (HR 4205—PL 106-398) to give most military retirees access to low-cost prescription drugs. *(2001 defense authorization, p. 290)*

The bill nearly doubled—to $1.6 billion—what Clinton requested for the Army's long-term effort to make its combat units lighter and thus easier to deploy overseas. It provided the $3.9 billion Clinton requested to continue flight testing the Air Force's F-22 fighter and to buy ten more of the planes built by Lockheed Martin.

HOUSE ACTION

The House passed a $288.5 billion defense appropriations bill (HR 4576) on June 7, 2000, by a vote of 367–58. The House Appropriations Committee had reported the bill (H Rept 106-644) on June 1.

HR 4576 provided about $4 billion more than President Clinton requested, and the White House was not pleased. Besides complaining in general that the bill would increase defense spending at the expense of domestic programs, the Office of Management and Budget (OMB) also objected to some of the ways the bill would allocate money.

The bill's single most expensive initiative was the addition of more than $1 billion to accelerate the conversion of some Army combat units to "medium-weight" forces that would have more staying power than lightly armed airborne units but could be deployed more quickly than armored forces equipped with seventy-ton tanks. In its report, the Appropriations Committee had blasted the Pentagon's civilian leaders for underfunding the Army's "transformation," which, the panel insisted, could be completed in half the time if the service was given more money. But OMB insisted that Clinton's budget was adequate enough for the Army to begin the shift.

In stark contrast to the previous year, House appropriators did not interfere with the Air Force's plans to continue developing the controversial Lockheed Martin F-22 fighter. HR 4576 provided the requested $2.1 billion in fiscal 2001 to buy ten planes, as long as the Air Force met certain testing requirements before production began. House Defense Appropriations Subcommittee Chairman Jerry Lewis, R-Calif., who had challenged the F-22 in 1999 as unnecessarily expensive and sophisticated, said he was optimistic the testing goals could be met. *(F-22, box, p. 286)*

Still, the F-22 accounted for a sizable part of the floor debate on HR 4576. The House defeated, by voice vote, an amendment by Peter A. DeFazio, D-Ore., that would have sliced $930 million from the $2.1 billion. DeFazio and other Democrats said the plane's technology still had not been proven to a point that would justify starting up the F-22 production line to build the requested ten planes.

The House bill did put the brakes on another controversial new tactical aircraft program, the more advanced Joint Strike Fighter. Similar restrictions had been added to the companion defense authorization bill, reflecting a concern among lawmakers that the Pentagon was moving too quickly to select one of two competing designs for the plane—by

Boeing and Lockheed Martin Corp.—and then begin gearing up for its production. HR 4576 added funds for the testing phase, delayed the selection of the winning company until June 2001—about three months later than planned—and cut funding to begin building prototype aircraft. All told, the House bill provided $707 million for the fighter, about $150 million less than requested.

At the urging of Missouri lawmakers, the House Appropriations Committee had added the $400 million to buy five F-15 fighters, which were manufactured in St. Louis.

In committee and on the floor, members revisited longstanding concerns over a national antimissile defense system, for which the bill appropriated the $1.7 billion the administration requested. Several Democratic lawmakers argued during the floor debate that the proposed missile defense system was too costly and not technologically sound and would violate international arms control agreements. But the House defeated, by voice vote, an amendment by John F. Tierney, D-Mass., to cut $75 million set aside to begin constructing the system. The amendment would have used that money instead to help pay for a prescription drug benefit for military retirees.

The House also rejected by voice vote an amendment by Dennis J. Kucinich, D-Ohio, that would have cut 10 percent from the missile defense appropriation and used it for military health care instead.

SENATE ACTION

The Senate passed HR 4576 by a vote of 95–3 on June 13, after substituting the text of its $287.6 billion defense appropriations bill (S 2553). The Senate Appropriations Committee had reported S 2553 (S Rept 106-293) on May 12.

The Senate bill appropriated about $900 million less than the House-passed version, but lawmakers anticipated few problems in reconciling the two bills. Among their differences was the amount they would add for the Army's plan to transform itself into a lighter, more mobile fighting force. Clinton's budget request included $537 million to begin equipping the first interim brigade of about 4,000 troops. The Senate bill added $100 million to the requested amount, but the House bill was more generous, adding $283 million to complete the equipping of the first brigade, plus $800 million to equip a second one.

The Senate bill added $460 million to continue work on a helicopter carrier that would be built in Senate Majority Leader Lott's hometown in Mississippi. Although the House bill included no funds for the ship, it was nearly a foregone conclusion that the conference report would include the funding, which was ardently supported by Lott and fellow Mississippi Republican Sen. Thad Cochran, a member of the Appropriations Committee. Conversely, although the Senate bill did not have the $400 million the House had added at the urging of Missouri lawmakers to keep the production lines going at Boeing's F-15 plant in St. Louis, Senate Appropriations Committee Chairman Ted Stevens, R-Alaska, said he expected the F-15s to be in the final bill.

Similar to the House, the Senate insisted that the Pentagon slow down its timetable for choosing between two competing designs for the Joint Strike Fighter. The Senate bill appropriated about $53 million less than the House bill for the program. OMB warned that the cuts proposed by the two bills would disrupt the program.

The Senate debate was largely devoid of controversy. This was partly because of the appropriators' determination to keep out extraneous amendments by invoking a rule that barred authorization language on spending bills. As a result, some of the amendments that senators tried to offer to the spending bill were directed instead at the more controversial authorization bill. In addition, the relatively large pot of money available for the military in fiscal 2001 left all sides able to avoid serious disputes.

However, in what had become an annual ritual, Armed Services Committee member John McCain, R-Ariz., the Senate's most persistent critic of what he considered wasteful spending, took to the floor before passage to deride some of the projects that lawmakers added.

Among the amendments considered by the Senate was one that would have removed permission for the Navy, Marine Corps, and Army to each lease three executive jets to transport top-level officials. Democratic sponsors Barbara Boxer of California and Tom Harkin of Iowa wanted to limit the military's leasing of such aircraft, which they said was unnecessarily lavish. But Appropriations Chairman Stevens, who also chaired the Defense Subcommittee, said the services needed the flexibility to decide if it was more efficient and cost-effective to lease or buy the jets. The amendment was rejected 65–32 on June 13.

Senators also voted, 83–15, on June 13 to table (kill) an amendment by Paul Wellstone, D-Minn., that would have deleted $1 billion of the bill's $58 billion allocation for procurement and transferred the money to education programs for poor and disadvantaged children.

CONFERENCE ACTION

The House adopted the conference report on HR 4576 on July 19 by a vote of 367–58. The Senate cleared the bill, 91–9, on July 27.

The final bill gave the Defense Department $5.1 billion more than President Clinton requested, which was a larger increase than anticipated by the congressional budget resolution (H Con Res 290). Rather than openly flout the budget caps in that document, House and Senate conferees—including some of the Pentagon's most powerful political allies—camouflaged more than a third of the increase as emergency supplemental funding for fiscal 2000 and, therefore, exempt from the budget limits. But, with little more than two months left in fiscal 2000, there was little chance that any significant amount would be spent before the new fiscal year began. Moreover, the supposed "emergency" money was destined for routine maintenance and ongoing operations in Bosnia, Kosovo, and the Persian Gulf.

Conferees had no major disputes to settle this time around, unlike the previous year's conflict over procurement of the F-22 advanced fighter jet. To the Pentagon's chagrin, the fiscal 2001 agreement largely reflected decisions by both chambers to reduce funding for the Joint Strike Fighter and delay the construction of prototype airplanes.

The final bill made few significant cuts in the administration's budget request, while providing some important increases. For instance, in addition to funding a requested 3.7 percent military pay raise, the bill added $200 million to subsidize prescription drugs for military retirees over sixty-five. The House bill would have added $94 million and the Senate bill, $137 million, but conferees essentially accepted OMB's estimate that it would cost $200 million, but by the back door—the final bill included $100 million for fiscal 2001 and another $100 million in fiscal 2000 funds.

Following the lead of the House, conferees roughly doubled—to $1.6 billion—the amount that would be appropriated for the Army's plan for a lighter, more mobile force.

As usual, the final conference bill was studded with hundreds of add-ons sponsored by House and Senate members. Some of these were substantial, such as the helicopter carrier and the F-15s, but most were more modest. Still, conferees accommodated more members' initiatives for procurement and research and development programs than they could fit into the total spending, even with creative accounting. So they added a provision reducing the amount available to each of the special programs by seven-tenths of one percent, cutting the cost of the bill by $705 million.

When the Senate took up the conference report, Sens. Phil Gramm, R-Texas, and McCain objected that conferees had added $7 billion for projects not included in the Pentagon's budget request. Gramm was particularly critical of accounting gimmicks that conferees used to circumvent congressional spending limits, such as designating some of the money as emergency funding. He lamented that members could not resist spending the rapidly rising federal budget surplus. "[T]he surplus is literally burning a hole in our pockets," he said. And McCain blasted the bill as "a disgrace" for spending what was ostensibly Pentagon money on nondefense projects while the armed services, he said, remained overworked and underequipped.

MAJOR PROVISIONS

As signed into law Aug. 9, 2000, HR 4576 appropriated $289.6 billion for fiscal 2001 military spending, of which $1.8 billion was designated as emergency supplemental funding for fiscal 2000. President Clinton had requested $284.5 billion.

Major provisions of HR 4576 were the following:

Personnel Issues

• Provided $75.8 billion for overall military personnel costs in fiscal 2001, $46 million more than Clinton requested. But that paper increase was more than offset by another provision of the bill that cut the personnel accounts by $392 million because of currency fluctuations overseas.

• Added $200 million to subsidize prescription drugs for military retirees over age sixty-five—by far the most significant change the conferees made in the personnel budget. The program was created, as expected, by the final version of the companion defense authorization bill (HR 4205—PL 106-398).

The House bill had included $94 million for the new benefit and the Senate bill $137 million. While applauding the initiative, the administration warned that it probably would cost $200 million. In response, the conferees appropriated $100 million for the pharmacy benefit outright and provided another $100 million as an emergency fiscal 2000 appropriation, which could be spent if the president requested it.

• Included the administration's proposed 3.7 percent military pay raise for fiscal 2001.

• Added $50 million to the Navy's recruitment and retention budget for fiscal 2000. The Navy, as with most of the services, had lost many highly trained technical personnel to the booming civilian economy.

• Cut $244 million from Clinton's personnel funding request on grounds that the services would start the fiscal year with about 3,500 fewer members than the budget request assumed. But that reduction was offset by several additions, including $82 million for reenlistment bonuses, $31 million for housing cost allowances, and a total of $160 million, divided between the personnel and operations accounts, to keep units in service that the Clinton administration wanted to abolish.

Operations and Maintenance

• Provided $96.9 billion for operations and maintenance, $610 million more than Clinton requested. The bill also included $529 million in fiscal 2000 supplemental funds added to pay for equipment overhauls, facilities maintenance, and spare parts.

But other sections of the conference report cut $1.6 billion from the amount the bill appeared to appropriate for operations and maintenance. Taking all those adjustments into account, the conference report gave the Pentagon $450 million less than Clinton requested for operations and maintenance.

• Added $65 million to compel the Air Force to retain all ninety-four B-52 bombers that were still intact. The service had tried for several years to mothball part of the fleet but had been blocked by the senators from North Dakota, where about half of the big planes were based at Minot.

Overseas Operations

• Included $3.9 billion to pay for military operations in the Balkans and the Persian Gulf, $162 million less than Clinton requested. Of the amount approved, $1.1 billion was converted into fiscal 2000 emergency supplemental spending.

• Cut $9 million from the administration's request for $65 million to pay for sending U.S. forces on disaster relief and humanitarian missions overseas. OMB insisted that such operations paid off in both diplomatic goodwill and useful training for U.S. forces. Critics complained that funding for these missions had risen faster than funding for regular combat training.

U.S.-Russia Cooperation

• Included $443 million of the $458 million Clinton requested for the so-called Nunn-Lugar program to help Russia and other former Soviet republics dispose of nuclear, chemical, and biological weapons.

But that relatively minor reduction in funds obscured a major challenge to administration policy: following the lead of the House, the conferees denied the $35 million Clinton requested to continue building a chemical weapons destruction plant near the Russian city of Shchuch'ye. The administration insisted that the proposed facility would eliminate a large stockpile of small, easily smuggled nerve gas weapons stored at the site. But the House Armed Services Committee had blocked Nunn-Lugar spending for the project, arguing that other countries were not contributing enough to the project and that Russia could not afford to operate the facility even if it were built.

Conferees added $25 million to Clinton's budget request to scrap aging Russian nuclear-powered submarines.

Antimissile Defense

• Appropriated $4.8 billion for ballistic missile defense, including nearly $1.9 billion for a national missile defense system. Clinton had requested $4.5 billion, of which $1.74 billion was intended for national missile defense.

The bill appropriated another nearly $1.1 billion for related programs, as compared to $984 million requested.

Ground Combat

• Appropriated $1.6 billion for the Army's plan to make its forces lighter and thus more easily deployable to distant trouble spots. The key was developing a new type of tank that would weigh about one-third as much as the seventy-ton M-1. The Army wanted to have it by about 2012. As an interim step, Chief of Staff Gen. Eric K. Shinseki wanted to equip several 4,000-person brigades with lightweight combat vehicles already in production for U.S. and foreign forces.

Clinton requested $537 million to begin equipping the first of these brigades. The conference report added $320 million to finish equipping that first brigade, $500 million to begin equipping a second brigade, and $46 million to accelerate development of the new, light-weight combat vehicle. The latter increase was more than offset by the conference report's elimination of $69 million Clinton requested for a joint U.S.-British project to develop a lightweight, high-tech reconnaissance vehicle.

• Appropriated the $355 million requested by the Army to continue developing the Crusader self-propelled cannon. The Army was trying to reduce the Crusader's weight from fifty-five tons to forty tons. Conferees ordered the Army to conduct a study of how the weapons would fit into the planned lightweight Army forces of the future.

Air Combat

• Appropriated $689 million for the so-called Joint Strike Fighter, intended to enter service late in the decade as a replacement for several 1970s-vintage jets used by the Navy, Air Force, and Marine Corps. Clinton had requested $857 million. The conference bill slowed the Pentagon's timetable for choosing between two competing designs for the advanced aircraft. Not even a last-minute appeal by the Pentagon shook conferees from their conviction that the program was likely to slip by at least three months, enough to warrant the reduction in the funding.

• Appropriated the $3.9 billion Clinton requested to continue testing and initial production of the Air Force's F-22 fighter, including funds for ten planes.

• Appropriated $2.9 billion, $42 million less than requested, for the F/A-18E/F Hornet fighter.

• Appropriated $400 million for five F-15s built by Boeing in St. Louis, Mo., and $122 million for four F-16s built by Lockheed Martin in Fort Worth, Texas. Neither aircraft had been requested.

Naval Combat

• Appropriated $292 million of the $305 million Clinton requested to continue designing the DD-21 class of destroyers, the first of which was slated for funding in fiscal 2005.

• Appropriated $3.2 billion for three destroyers equipped with the Aegis antiaircraft system and components of similar ships to be funded in future budgets.

• Appropriated $1.7 billion for a new attack submarine and components of future subs.

Air and Sea Transport

• Added $460 million to Clinton's request to continue work on a helicopter carrier that would be built by Litton Industries in Pascagoula, Miss. The Pentagon had not planned to request the bulk of the funds for this $1.5 billion ship until 2005. However, the Navy and the contractor insisted that earlier funding would reduce the cost by hundreds of millions of dollars.

• Appropriated $561 million of the $1.5 billion the administration requested to buy components of two amphibious transport ships, which carried Marines, tanks, and cargo to landing sites. The administration had requested $1.5 billion for two of the ships, but the Senate Appropriations Committee had slashed the request, complaining that prices had risen and delivery dates had slipped for previously funded ships of this type (the LPD-17 class).

• Appropriated $2.8 billion to continue production of the C-17 cargo jet, just $50 million less than requested.

However, conferees followed the Senate's lead and removed the C-17 funds from the Air Force procurement account and put them in a separate revolving fund for long-range airlift. This was intended to make it harder for Air Force leaders to raid the C-17 budget to shore up the accounts for fighter jets.

• Appropriated $528 million for six of Lockheed Martin's cargo workhorses, the Georgia-built C-130 cargo plane configured for various missions. The administration had requested $363 million for four. The House had approved five and the Senate six.

• Appropriated $710 million for forty-one H-60 helicopters of various models. The administration had requested $495 million for twenty-five H-60 helicopters built in Connecticut by the Sikorsky division of United Technologies, different versions of which were used by the Army and Navy. The House added funds to buy more of the Army's troop-carrier version while the Senate added funds to buy more of the types used by both services.

2001 Military Construction

Congress in 2000 cleared an $8.8 billion fiscal 2001 military construction appropriations bill (HR 4425—PL 106-246). The bill also served as the vehicle for $11.2 billion in fiscal 2000 supplementary spending.

The military construction measure, which funds the construction of barracks, family housing, and other facilities on military bases, is typically the first and least divisive of the thirteen annual spending bills to become law. And, for awhile, HR 4425 seemed to be following the usual track, headed for early enactment.

However, progress slowed to a crawl, after Republican leaders decided to make the construction funding bill the vehicle for supplemental funds, including money to repay the Pentagon for U.S. peacekeeping operations in Kosovo. Things became even more complicated when critics of the Kosovo mission moved to limit the U.S. deployment in Kosovo, during Senate action on the bill. It took until the end of June for a compromise bill to emerge from Congress.

The final bill appropriated $800 million more for military construction than President Clinton had requested. It included $4.2 billion for general construction and $3.6 billion for family housing.

The supplemental package included, among other things, the funds to cover the cost of peacekeeping operations in Kosovo, antidrug aid to Colombia, and disaster assistance at home and abroad. *(2000 supplemental appropriations, p. 84; Colombia antidrug aid, p. 220)*

2000 LEGISLATIVE ACTION

The House passed an $8.6 billion military construction bill on May 16, 2000, by a vote of 386–22. The House Appropriations Committee had reported HR 4425 (H Rept 106-614) on May 11.

The Senate passed its $8.6 billion version of HR 4425 by a vote of 96–4 on May 18, after substituting the text of its bill

(S 2521). The Senate Appropriations Committee reported S 2521 (S Rept 106-290) on May 9.

The Senate Appropriations panel by a vote of 23–3 had attached to its bill an amendment offered by ranking Democrat Robert C. Byrd of West Virginia to end the deployment of U.S. troops as peacekeepers in Kosovo on July 1, 2001, unless the president requested and Congress authorized an extension. Byrd had the support of Senate Appropriations Committee Chairman Ted Stevens, R-Alaska, and Senate Armed Services Committee Chairman John W. Warner, R-Va.

But, with senior Clinton advisers threatening to recommend a veto if the Kosovo amendment remained in the bill, the Senate struck it from the bill on May 18 by a **key vote of 53–47 (R 15–40; D 38–7).** Senate passage of HR 4425 was also delayed by an unrelated debate over gun control. *(2000 key votes, p. 915; Kosovo policy, p. 204)*

Although the bills passed by the House and Senate had an identical bottom line for fiscal 2001, they did differ on how some of the money would be allocated. Plus, the Senate version included $4.7 billion in fiscal 2000 supplemental spending for the Kosovo mission, other defense projects, and drug interdiction.

President Clinton had requested about $5.5 billion in supplemental funding. The House on March 30 passed, 263–146, a $13.2 billion fiscal 2000 supplemental bill (HR 3908—H Rept 106-521), but Senate Majority Leader Trent Lott, R-Miss., refused to bring the supplemental funding to the floor as a stand-alone bill. He wanted to avoid both the time such a bill would take up and the add-ons the bill would attract. Instead, he pressed Senate appropriators to spread about $8 billion in supplemental spending among the first three fiscal 2001 appropriations measures they marked up, hoping that would spur those bills to early completion. One of those was the military construction bill.

But things did not go according to Lott's plan. After four months of false starts and delays, Congress found itself under extraordinary pressure to replenish the military readiness accounts that had been tapped to finance the U.S. forces in Kosovo. The Pentagon said that, if its share of the supplemental was not guaranteed for delivery by the end of June, it would be forced to cancel training exercises and maintenance projects. Lott relented and the supplemental funds were pulled together in a package in HR 4425.

CONFERENCE ACTION

The House adopted the conference report on HR 4425 (H Rept 106-710) by a vote of 306–110 on June 29. The Senate cleared the bill by voice vote June 30. President Clinton signed the bill into law July 13.

House and Senate appropriators said the Pentagon was not planning to invest enough in upkeep and construction of military facilities, but they were hard-pressed to come up with additional spending. The fiscal 2001 military construction bill provided $8.8 billion, which was $459.9 million more than enacted for fiscal 2000—a 5.5 percent increase—

and $800 million more than President Clinton requested for fiscal 2001.

Conferees added $11.2 billion in fiscal 2000 supplemental spending, which Congress declared emergency appropriations not subject to any budget limits.

MAJOR PROVISIONS

• **Military construction.** The final bill provided $4.2 billion for general construction, about $1 billion more than Clinton requested. The House bill had provided $3.7 billion and the Senate bill, $3.8 billion.

The bill included Clinton's request for $85 million to begin construction related to a national missile defense system, though the White House had not decided whether such a system, still in development, should be deployed.

Also in the bill was $90 million more than Clinton requested for building and modernizing military barracks, including several projects the House and Senate specified. The conferees added $11.9 million to Clinton's request for classroom additions at overseas bases to lower pupil-teacher ratios and increase the number of full-day kindergartens. The bill also increased, from $17 million to $43 million, the administration's request for building and improving day care centers. With the percentage of married military personnel rising, the Defense Department at that time was running 800 child care centers.

In addition to the $4.2 billion for general construction, the final fill appropriated $172 million for the U.S. share of NATO construction. Clinton had requested $190 million.

• **Family housing.** The bill provided $3.6 billion for military family housing, which was in dismal shape at many bases. That figure was substantially the same as the past two fiscal years and $124.7 million more than Clinton requested. Most of the extra funds were for new housing; the bill funded the president's request for operating and maintaining existing housing.

Congress had encouraged the Pentagon to experiment with privatizing military housing, but the conferees said the Army was spending "excessive amounts" to support contractors developing such proposals. The conferees wanted quarterly reports on such spending.

• **Base closures.** HR 4425 appropriated $1 billion for base closure and realignment costs. President Clinton had requested about $1.2 billion.

• **Supplemental spending.** The $11.2 billion supplemental package appropriated $6.4 billion for the Defense Department, including $2 billion to replenish accounts tapped for U.S. participation in the international peacekeeping force in Kosovo; $1.6 billion to pay higher military fuel bills; $1.3 billion for unfunded military health programs; $358 million for military personnel; $504 million to enhance readiness; $148 million for disaster-related repairs to U.S. bases; and $125 million for Patriot missile tests.

Other items in the supplemental package included $1.3 billion for an antidrug initiative in Colombia and other South

American countries; $1 billion in disaster aid; and $700 million for the Coast Guard, mostly for new equipment.

The measure voided more than $4 billion in scorekeeping adjustments that had artificially deflated overall fiscal 2000 spending by shifting the spending into fiscal 2001. By abandoning that gimmickry, appropriators were able to free up more money for the fiscal 2001 cycle.

Nuclear Security

A plan to restructure the Energy Department's nuclear weapons programs by putting them under a new agency within the department was enacted in 1999, as part of the fiscal 2000 defense authorization bill (S 1059—PL 106-65).

The creation of the new weapons agency represented the most far-reaching congressional response to a bipartisan House committee's report detailing China's alleged attempts to steal highly classified information from the Energy Department's nuclear weapons laboratories. The report confirmed a stream of earlier newspaper revelations that China had used a network of spies, front companies, and visitors to the United States to obtain military secrets and other technology. The report contained thirty-eight recommendations, including tightening security at the department's labs.

The release of the committee's findings was followed by a stinging report from the President's Foreign Intelligence Advisory Board, which detailed the Energy Department's lax security measures.

Some Republicans called for having the Defense Department assume the management of the nuclear weapons program, while others supported having a new agency entirely separate from the Energy Department, functioning in a manner similar to NASA. But most members believed that the agency should remain within—but insulated from—the Energy Department's normal bureaucracy. They ultimately agreed on the creation of a nearly autonomous National Nuclear Security Administration within the Energy Department, whose administrator would report to the energy secretary.

GOP negotiations with the administration, particularly Energy Secretary Bill Richardson, over the legislation had been stormy and protracted. In the end, Richardson only reluctantly backed down from his threat to recommend that President Clinton veto the bill. But the confrontations were not over, as the debate over the administration's implementation of the new law made abundantly clear.

BACKGROUND

Congress had begun investigating the Clinton administration's dealings with China after reports that two satellite companies—Loral Space & Communications Ltd. and Hughes Electronics Corp.—might have compromised national security in helping Beijing determine the causes of rocket failures in 1995 and 1996. *(China policy, p. 208)*

A number of standing committees launched investigations into various aspects of U.S. relations with China. In addition, the House on June 18, 1998, by a vote of 409–10, created the Select Committee on U.S. National Security and Military/Commercial Concerns with the People's Republic of China (H Res 463). Christopher Cox, R-Calif., was named to chair the panel.

Cox Report

By the end of 1998 the committee had concluded that China had made a concerted effort to steal U.S. military secrets and technology. The long-awaited declassified version of the committee's report—a 1,016-page, seven-and-a-half pound document in three volumes, complete with color photographs—was released on May 25, 1999.

The panel found that China's attempts to obtain nuclear secrets and other military technology over several decades had given it "design information on thermonuclear weapons on par with our own."

The thefts occurred at least as early as the late 1970s, according to the report, with significant secrets stolen in the mid-1990s and espionage was "almost certainly" continuing at the present time. It also said China had "stolen or otherwise illegally obtained" U.S. missile and space technology that had improved its military and intelligence capabilities.

The report of the bipartisan panel contained thirty-eight recommendations, including tightening export control laws, strengthening counterintelligence at the Department of Energy, sharpening oversight of U.S. satellite launches in China, improving the domestic U.S. space launch industry, and requiring more prompt notification of future security lapses to Congress and the executive branch. *(China espionage report, box, p. 304)*

President Clinton echoed earlier statements by administration officials that, by and large, the recommendations were acceptable and said the administration was in the process of implementing most of them.

Congress had already taken steps in the fiscal 1999 defense authorization bill (HR 3616—PL 105-261) to tighten control over U.S. satellite launches overseas by shifting responsibility for licensing from the Commerce Department back to the State Department where it had been prior to 1996. *(1999 defense authorization, p. 252)*

Rudman Report

Clinton in March 1999 had asked his own Foreign Intelligence Advisory Board to study Energy Department security. The board, chaired by former Sen. Warren B. Rudman, R-N.H. (1980–1993), concluded in a report released June 15 that the Energy Department had "a cavalier attitude" about security at its nuclear weapons laboratories.

In unusually blunt language, the report said reorganizing the department "is clearly warranted to resolve the many specific problems with security and counterintelligence in the weapons laboratories, but also to address the lack of accountability that has become endemic throughout the entire department." The board recommended creating either a

SECURITY BREACH ALLEGATIONS AT LABS

The uproar over security at the nation's nuclear weapons laboratories was fanned further by several well-publicized cases of alleged security breaches.

Wen Ho Lee

The case of Wen Ho Lee, a Los Alamos National Laboratory scientist suspected of providing nuclear weapons data to China, set off security alarms—and investigators—on Capitol Hill. Lee had been fired from his job in March 1999 in the wake of revelations that China had obtained classified information on how nuclear warheads worked. He had first come under suspicion of having contact with foreign nuclear scientists in 1988.

In a report released Aug. 5, 1999—in the midst of the wrangling in Washington over the Energy Department's weapons labs—the Senate Governmental Affairs Committee accused the FBI, Justice Department, and Energy Department of bungling the investigation of Lee. Among the committee's findings was that Lee had signed a waiver four years earlier that might have allowed his computer to be monitored, but that Energy and FBI investigators had not learned of the waiver until 1999.

Lee was arrested and charged in December 1999 in a fifty-nine-count indictment for downloading classified material from a secured computer to unsecured computer tapes. He denied any wrongdoing. Lee was jailed until September 2000 when he pleaded guilty to a single felony charge of unlawfully collecting and keeping classified information related to the national defense.

Lee's release was an embarrassing setback for the Clinton administration. Angry GOP senators promised more hearings on the Justice Department's handling of the Lee case. Democrats, however, said Republicans did not acknowledge the possibility that congressional overreaction had played some role in shaping events on the case.

At a joint hearing of the Senate Judiciary and Select Intelligence committees on Sept. 26, 2000, senators criticized Attorney General Janet Reno and FBI Director Louis J. Freeh for their handling of the case. Intelligence Committee Chairman Richard C. Shelby, R-Ala., questioned the "apparent imbalance between the serious charges against Dr. Lee and the leniency of the sentence agreed to in the plea agreement."

But Reno, who had been accused by ethnic advocacy groups of focusing the investigation on Lee because he was of Chinese descent, defended her department's handling of the case. She said of Lee, "He committed a very serious, calculated crime and he pleaded guilty to it."

Missing Hard Drives

Members of Congress were angered further in 2000 by the disappearance for more than a month of two top-secret computer hard drives at the Los Alamos National Laboratory. The hard drives turned up June 16 within the same general secured area in which they had been stored, indicating they may have been misplaced, but Los Alamos executives placed six employees on leave and began administering polygraph tests to scientists with access to the secrets.

Although employees at the lab had discovered hard drives missing May 7 from their storage place in a heavily guarded vault at the New Mexico facility, they waited more than three weeks to notify top lab officials. During much of that time, the lab was evacuated because of a nearby forest fire.

While the search continued, Energy Secretary Bill Richardson announced that former Sen. Howard H. Baker Jr., R-Tenn. (1967–1985), and former Rep. Lee H. Hamilton, D-Ind. (1965–1999), would conduct an independent assessment of the incident. The move did little to pacify lawmakers, who rebuked Richardson for declaring earlier in 2000 that security at the three labs was under control.

---

semiautonomous security agency within the department or a completely separate agency similar to NASA to run the weapons program.

The intelligence board accused both Congress and the Clinton administration of resorting to "simplification and hyperbole" on security issues within recent months.

Richardson Response

In response to the revelations, Energy Secretary Richardson had unveiled a series of reforms to improve security. On June 16 he announced that retired Air Force Gen. Eugene E. Habiger would be his agency's "security czar" as director of a new Office of Security and Emergency Operations. But even though the Foreign Intelligence Advisory Board's report had

praised Richardson for his attention to the security problem, it had concluded that creating such a position would not be enough to end the agency's enduring resistance to change.

Several Republicans agreed that a stronger legislative response was needed.

1999 LEGISLATIVE ACTION

The Cox report triggered immediate cries for action on Capitol Hill and produced a wave of proposed solutions. But initial hopes of establishing a bipartisan consensus that might mirror the spirit in which the Cox committee had operated proved elusive in both chambers. GOP attempts in the House and Senate to amend pending defense bills to tighten security stalled May 27 after Democrats objected.

CHINA ESPIONAGE REPORT

Major findings and recommendations in the 1999 report of the special House committee set up to investigate China's acquisition of U.S. technology included:

• "The People's Republic of China has stolen design information on the United States' most advanced thermonuclear weapons."

• "Elements of the stolen information ... will assist [China] in building its next generation of mobile ICBMs, which may be tested this year ... [and] could have a significant effect on the regional balance of power."

• "Security at our national nuclear weapons laboratories does not meet even minimal standards."

Key Recommendations

• The Energy Department should implement as quickly as possible and then sustain an effective counterintelligence program.

• Key agencies should assess the national security risks of continued scientific exchange programs between the United States and China that involve the national laboratories.

• Congress should examine whether the Energy Department should remain in charge of nuclear weapons development and maintenance.

• The United States should insist that China adhere to and abide by the Missile Technology Control Regime, a multilateral pact to limit the spread of missile technology.

• The United States should work to establish new, binding international controls on technology transfers and improve the tracking of technology.

• The State Department should have the sole authority, and adequate resources, to license the export of satellites.

• Congress should give the satellite industry tax credits to cover licensing costs.

• The Defense Department should arrange for security at overseas launches of U.S. satellites.

• Export-control laws should apply to communications among satellite manufacturers, buyers, and insurance companies.

• Congress should pass legislation to stimulate expansion of the U.S. space launch industry.

• The Energy and Defense Departments should review the national security implications of exporting high-performance computers to China. Legislation should grant export licenses only with the condition that China disclose the end-user of each machine.

• Congress should reenact the Export Administration Act, which expired in 1994. The most sensitive technologies should be subject to more extensive review. Licensing for others should be streamlined. *(Export Administration Act, p. 166)*

• U.S. companies with national security interests should notify the government of mergers with foreign-controlled companies.

• Congress should enact legislation requiring the Justice Department to share national security information with other, concerned federal agencies.

• U.S. agencies should conduct a broad intelligence analysis of China's aims, goals, and objectives in acquiring technology.

House Action

In the House, Republican leaders on May 27 abruptly pulled from the floor the rule governing debate on the fiscal 2000 defense authorization bill (HR 1401). The move came after Norm Dicks of Washington, the Cox committee's ranking Democrat, joined party colleagues in arguing that the rule would not allow consideration of a proposed amendment stemming from the report and intended to shore up security at the nuclear weapons labs. The rule, however, did contain proposed GOP amendments offered in reaction to the Cox report.

But on June 9 the House put aside its partisan differences and adopted, 428–0, an amendment to the defense bill that sought to bolster security and counterintelligence measures at the nuclear weapons labs while implementing stricter satellite export and launch guidelines to avert illegal technology transfers. The amendment was sponsored by Cox and Dicks.

The House also adopted, by voice vote, a series of amendments aimed at addressing Energy Department policies in response to the Cox committee's report, including a proposal to establish a counterintelligence polygraph program for agency employees with access to high-risk programs or information.

At the same time, the House rejected, 159–266, an amendment by Jim Ryun, R-Kan., to impose a two-year moratorium on scientific exchanges at the weapons labs. Administration officials strongly opposed the amendment because they said it would harm international cooperation. And many Democrats said that temporary moratorium language in the Cox-Dicks amendment was sufficient.

House Armed Services Chairman Floyd D. Spence, R-S.C., had planned to offer an amendment to the defense bill to have the Defense Department study taking over nuclear weapons maintenance but withdrew his proposal and supported the Cox-Dicks amendment.

Senate Action

On the other side of the Capitol on May 27, Sen. Jon Kyl, R-Ariz., offered an amendment to the Senate's fiscal 2000 defense authorization bill (S 1059) to reorganize the Energy Department's Office of Defense Programs and create a new agency to oversee nuclear weapons production. The latter was to function as a separate "stovepipe" within the department, insulated from normal bureaucracy and procedures and accountable directly to the energy secretary. But the proposal faced strong opposition from Richardson, who threatened to recommend a veto if it was included in the defense bill.

After Senate Democrats threatened a filibuster over the Kyl amendment, Senate Majority Leader Trent Tott, R-Miss., called a break for negotiations that stretched into several hours. Eventually, he announced that the proposal would be offered as an amendment to the fiscal 2000 intelligence authorization bill (S 1009). Lott did persuade senators to pass, by voice vote, a relatively modest amendment to the defense bill to strengthen U.S. export control laws, increase counterintelligence training, and require greater monitoring of satellite launches and better notification to Congress of security breaches.

As Senate Republicans prepared to offer their amendment to the intelligence bill in June, Richardson continued to oppose the plan. He insisted the plan would hinder or reverse his recent administrative changes and would undermine his authority. He said he saw no need for "a new fiefdom" within the department.

To accommodate Richardson, Kyl and other Republicans twice reworked their draft amendment, adding a number of changes aimed at clarifying the authority of the energy secretary. But Richardson and some Democrats said the amendment continued to raise concerns, leading Kyl to predict that an agreement might not be reached before the intelligence bill went to the Senate floor. Republicans had hoped that the June 15 report of the Foreign Intelligence Advisory Board would give them the momentum to initiate rapid changes at the Energy Department.

In an escalation of the clash between the two sides, Kyl joined Sens. Pete V. Domenici, R-N.M., and Frank H. Murkowski, R-Alaska, in issuing a harshly worded statement June 25 charging that their efforts "are being politicized and resisted by the Department of Energy at the expense of national security."

But a month later, when the Senate took up the House version of the intelligence authorization bill (HR 1555), the partisan rancor had disappeared. By a 96–1 vote on July 21, senators agreed to create an Agency for Nuclear Stewardship to oversee weapons programs within the Energy Department. Immediately after the intelligence bill passed, Richardson issued a statement calling the Senate's action "a good start." He said, "I believe it's critical that we pass legislation this year to codify reforms and accelerate security and coun-

terintelligence improvements." He said he hoped the Senate provision could be clarified in conference.

Richardson had relented and endorsed a legislative fix in order to avoid facing even more drastic alternatives, such as an independent nuclear programs agency organized like NASA. And Republican senators had pushed for a broad bipartisan vote in favor of creating the new agency to give the Senate leverage in conference with the House.

During action on the bill, Jeff Bingaman, D-N.M., negotiated with Republicans to win voice vote approval of three amendments that he said would enable the new agency to function within the department without interfering with nonnuclear weapons research being done at the weapons labs. Bingaman's state was home to two weapons labs, Sandia and Los Alamos, which did significant amounts of nonweapons work.

An amendment by Carl Levin, D-Mich., to ensure that the energy secretary would retain the authority to develop department-wide policy was rejected, 44–54. In the end, however, several of Levin's concerns were addressed in the final bill and he hoped the rest would be addressed in conference.

But when the intelligence bill went to conference, all of the Energy Department-related language was stripped out and the debate returned to the defense authorization bill.

CONFERENCE, FINAL ACTION

Defense conferees decided that the defense authorization bill was the appropriate place to deal with the question of nuclear security and not the intelligence authorization bill.

Despite resistance from House Commerce Committee members who wanted a stand-alone bill dealing with the issue, House defense conferees drafted an initial proposal that was much stronger than what the Senate had passed. The proposal, however, drew a veto threat from Office of Management and Budget Director Jack Lew, who said in a July 29 letter that it did not provide the energy secretary with enough authority.

Working against the clock as the August recess approached, conferees crafted another version. Levin, the ranking Democrat on Senate Armed Services, said it was still inadequate. In particular, he said it appeared to duplicate counterintelligence functions, while not permitting the energy secretary direct control over the employees of the new agency, only its administrator. Although Richardson was threatening to recommend a veto and several Senate Democrats, including Levin, refused to sign the conference report, the bill was reported out of conference.

Before adopting the conference report, the House rejected, 139–281, a procedural motion by John D. Dingell, D-Mich., that would have eliminated the Energy Department provisions. Besides warning that the proposed changes would dangerously insulate the nuclear weapons program from outside review, Dingell complained that the provisions had been added to the conference report with no debate in either the House or Senate and with no opportunity for other committees with jurisdiction over the Energy Department to weigh in. Dingell was the ranking Democrat on the Commerce Committee. Among the five Republicans backing Dingell's motion were Commerce Committee Chairman Thomas J. Bliley Jr. of Virginia and Science Committee Chairman F. James Sensenbrenner Jr. of Wisconsin.

Despite Richardson's vehement opposition, both chambers adopted the defense conference report (H Rept 106-301) by overwhelming majorities. The House approved the report on Sept. 15 by a vote of 375–45. The Senate cleared it on Sept. 22, 93–5.

After those votes, Richardson relented and on Sept. 26 announced that he would no longer oppose the bill.

REORGANIZATION PLAN

As signed into law on Oct. 5, 1999, S 1059:

• Created a new National Nuclear Security Administration. The new agency would be within the Department of Energy but insulated from it except through its administrator, who would report to the energy secretary. The administrator would be an undersecretary of energy for nuclear security who would be subject to Senate confirmation.

The agency was to be responsible for nuclear weapons development, defense activities to prevent the spread of nuclear weapons, and the disposition of fissionable material.

• Established new Energy Department offices of counterintelligence and intelligence. In addition, it directed the national nuclear security administrator to set up a separate counterintelligence program at each weapons laboratory or weapons production site.

• Made many of the organizational provisions of the law effective March 1, 2000.

ONGOING DEBATE

But passage of the legislation did not end the protracted dispute between the administration and Congress over nuclear weapons oversight. Republicans were incensed when Clinton ordered Richardson to act as head of the new agency and to assign current Energy Department managers to run its supposedly independent operations. Richardson had persuaded Clinton to allow him to assume the duties at the new agency until lawmakers could make some "very modest modifications" that he suggested in the new law.

A number of Republican senators lashed out at Richardson and the administration, accusing them of flouting Congress's intentions. Some senators advocated cutting Richardson's travel budget or forbidding him to take on the new role. But Democrats said it would be premature to punish Richardson, noting that most of the law's provisions did not take effect until March 2000.

Republicans were angered further in January 2000 when Richardson sent his blueprint for restructuring the department to accommodate the new agency. The lawmakers said the secretary's proposal to allow some current employees to also hold jobs within the new agency—an approach known as "dual hatting"—went beyond Congress's intent and would hamper the changes they said were badly needed.

Richardson told the House Armed Services Committee March 2 that eighteen of the new administration's 2,000 employees would be dual-hatted. He said such an approach complied with the law and would ensure the smooth functioning of the agency as well as the entire department.

Congress was heartened by the administration's selection in early 2000 of Air Force Gen. John A. Gordan, the deputy director of central intelligence, to be administrator of the new agency. Gordan was confirmed by the Senate June 14, 2000, by a vote of 97–0.

Congress included in the fiscal 2001 defense authorization bill (HR 4205—PL 106-398) language barring dual-hatting within the Energy Department and the new agency. The law also required broader polygraphing of Energy Department employees in sensitive positions. (2001 defense authorization, p. 290)

Antimissile Defenses

Legislation declaring it to be the policy of the United States to deploy a national antimissile defense system "as soon as is technologically feasible" was signed into law in 1999 (HR 4—PL 106-38).

Democrats had blocked a similar bill in the previous Congress. But the campaign for antimissile defenses had gained momentum since then because of growing evidence that North Korea and other potentially hostile states were developing long-range ballistic missiles. The policy of deploying a system that could shoot down a small number of attacking missiles launched at U.S. territory by a rogue nation was gaining support among Democrats.

Facing certain defeat if it opposed the legislation this time, the White House dropped its opposition after the Senate adopted two face-saving amendments declaring that the antimissile program would be subject to annual authorization and appropriations, and stipulating that the United States would continue negotiating reductions in Russian nuclear forces.

President Clinton previously had opposed any requirement that an antimissile system be fielded, saying he wanted to wait until June 2000 before making such a decision based on an assessment of threats. The administration and many Democrats had shied away from rushing a decision partly because they feared it could violate the 1972 Anti-Ballistic (ABM) Treaty with Russia, necessitating amendments to the agreement or a possible U.S. withdrawal from the treaty.

SENATE ACTION

The Senate Armed Services Committee on Feb. 12, 1999, reported legislation (S 257—S Rept 106-4) calling for deployment of an antimissile defense system "as soon as is technologically possible." An amended version was passed on March 17 by an overwhelming vote of 97–3.

ANTIMISSILE DEFENSE CHRONOLOGY

• **1946–1969.** The United States and the Soviet Union developed and deployed limited antimissile systems using explosive warheads. The U.S. weapons were dismantled in 1969; the Soviets kept theirs to defend Moscow.

• **1972.** The United States and the Soviet Union signed the Anti-Ballistic Missile (ABM) Treaty restricting each nation to two sites of 100 interceptors, later cut to one site.

• **1983–1984.** President Ronald Reagan launched a Strategic Defense Initiative (SDI) to explore land-based and space-based missile defense systems. Critics dubbed the program "Star Wars."

• **1987.** U.S. scientists began work on "Brilliant Pebbles," a plan to sow thousands of miniature satellite/interceptors in Earth orbit to be activated in case of attack. The program was later absorbed into broader research.

• **1991.** President George Bush changed the focus of SDI to defense against limited missile attacks, such as a mistaken launch.

• **1993.** The Clinton administration put more emphasis on military theater missile defense than national missile defense.

• **1998.** A special commission reported that North Korea, Iran, and Iraq could have a missile that would threaten the U.S. mainland within five years, sooner than expected. North Korea tested a medium-range missile over the Pacific.

• **1999.** Congress passed and President Clinton signed legislation (PL 106-38) declaring U.S. policy to deploy a national antimissile defense system as soon as technologically feasible.

• **2000.** Citing technical problems and diplomatic opposition, President Clinton announced that he would defer to his successor the decision on whether or not to deploy a national missile defense.

When Thad Cochran, R-Miss., introduced the bill early in 1999, the administration and Senate Democratic leaders reiterated their adamant opposition. They argued that Russia would interpret passage of the measure as a declaration of U.S. intent to proceed, regardless of whether changes to the treaty could be negotiated. Thus, they contended, the bill could make it harder to obtain Moscow's agreement to amend the ABM pact.

But the administration and its congressional allies soon discovered they might not have the votes to back up their position.

The previous year, forty-one Senate Democrats—enough to sustain a filibuster—had backed the White House position

and twice blocked action on the 1998 version of Cochran's bill. But the sense that any foreign threat was decades away had vanished. In July 1998 a bipartisan panel of experts led by former Ford administration Defense Secretary Donald H. Rumsfeld warned that North Korea and Iran could deploy missiles able to reach U.S. territory within five years—much sooner than U.S. officials had estimated. Six weeks later, North Korea had tried unsuccessfully to launch a satellite using a modified version of its Taepo-Dong missile, nearly powerful enough to carry a small warhead to Alaska or Hawaii. *(1998 action, p. 265)*

In January 1999 Clinton beefed up his antimissile defense program by including deployment funds in the Pentagon's long-range budget plans, for the first time. And at a Jan. 20 news conference, Defense Secretary William S. Cohen cited the Rumsfeld report and the North Korean launch as evidence that a threat to U.S. territory was practically at hand.

By early March several Senate Democrats had made it clear that merely stiff-arming the Cochran initiative for the sake of arms control negotiations with Russia was not their preferred approach. Because four of the Senate's forty-five Democrats already supported the bill, the defection of one more would give Cochran the sixty votes he would need to break a filibuster. But beyond that, White House officials and some of their key Senate allies were worried that if they simply continued their flat opposition to the legislation, they could not even muster the thirty-four Democrats they would need to sustain Clinton's threatened veto.

To stave off defeat, the White House and its allies embraced the two amendments, which were adopted by identical 99–0 votes on March 16. Cochran offered the amendment declaring that the antimissile program would be subject to the annual authorization and appropriations process. Mary Landrieu, D-La., sponsored the amendment stipulating that the United States continue to negotiate reductions in Russian nuclear forces.

HOUSE ACTION

The House Armed Services Committee reported its version (HR 4—H Rept 106-39, Pt. I) on March 2. HR 4 called for deployment of a nationwide antimissile defense system but set no date or particulars.

The full House took up the bill on March 18. The extent of Democratic support for a limited antimissile system became apparent when the House voted on a motion by Tom Allen, D-Maine, to recommit the bill to committee with instructions to amend it to endorse Clinton's policy of basing a deployment decision on several factors, including whether it jeopardized arms reduction efforts. The motion was rejected by a **key vote of 152–269 (R 2–212; D 150–56; I 0–1)**. The House then passed HR 4 by a vote of 317–105. *(1999 key votes, p. 899)*

FINAL ACTION

On May 18, the Senate passed HR 4, after substituting the language of S 257. The House approved that amended version of HR 4 on May 20 by a vote of 345–71, clearing the bill. President Clinton signed the bill on July 22.

The bill neither provided more money nor accelerated the timetable of Clinton's antimissile development program. But advocates insisted the legislation was significant because it repudiated Clinton's plan to defer until June 2000 a decision on whether to deploy the system under development.

2000 DEVELOPMENTS

But the debate was not over. Although Clinton had signed HR 4 into law, he worried about the international consequences of the law. Both Russia and China had strongly opposed even the most limited U.S. defense system as a potential threat to their own security. European leaders worried that by building a missile defense system, the United States would be retreating from the NATO alliance, protecting itself while leaving its friends vulnerable. Clinton had even met resistance from Britain, where the cabinet of Prime Minister Tony Blair was split on the issue—the defense ministry supported the concept of missile defense and the foreign ministry opposed it.

A classified U.S. intelligence report disclosed in August 2000 predicted that China would accelerate its nuclear weapons buildup if the United States deployed a national missile defense system. That could, in turn, speed up the nuclear arms race between India and Pakistan and solidify cooperation between potential U.S. foes who feared the new system.

Even if the diplomatic problems could be resolved, there were still technology setbacks to contend with. The Defense Department had theorized about deploying a national defense system in 2003 and then in 1999 pushed the target date back to 2005. Soon even the 2005 date was in doubt.

Citing technical problems and diplomatic opposition, Clinton announced on Sept. 1, 2000, that he would leave to his successor a decision on whether or not to deploy a national missile defense. After a series of failed tests and problems with developing a faster booster rocket, Clinton said further testing was needed before deployment.

Clinton's action drew a mixed—and predictable—reaction from Capitol Hill.

ANTIMISSILE FUNDING

Clinton in 1999 requested $3.3 billion for antimissile defense in his fiscal 2000 budget, but Congress opted for increased funding, authorizing $3.7 billion (S 1059—PL 106-65) and appropriating $3.6 billion (HR 2561—PL 106-79). Within these totals, $852 million was authorized and the requested $837 million appropriated for national missile defense. *(2000 defense authorization, p. 276; 2000 defense appropriations, p. 283)*

The following year Clinton requested $4.5 billion for ballistic missile defense in fiscal 2001. Congress authorized nearly $4.8 billion (HR 4205—PL 106-398), including nearly $1.9 billion for national missile defense—$135 million more than requested. Congress appropriated $4.8 billion (HR 4576—PL 106-259), including the same amount as autho-

rized for the national system. *(2001 defense authorization, p. 290; 2001 defense appropriations, p. 296)*

Terrorism Policy

Despite a widespread consensus that more needed to be done to fight terrorism, lawmakers in the 106th Congress were unable to pass even modest legislation. Both chambers approved bills (HR 4210, S 3205) in 2000, but neither measure went further. *(1998 action, p. 267)*

Republicans criticized the Clinton administration for not taking a more comprehensive approach to combating terrorism. They complained that the effort to fight terrorism was spread among too many federal agencies and that there was no one with authority to oversee the effort.

Attorney General Janet Reno in January 1999 had laid out in a report to Congress a wide-ranging plan for a coordinated response to a domestic terrorist attack that was well-received on Capitol Hill. But the Clinton administration generally was reluctant to encroach on the turf of agencies already dealing with terrorism. Although Clinton had appointed National Security Council official Richard A. Clarke in 1998 to coordinate federal efforts, Republicans said Clarke lacked the authority to tackle the terrorism issue. Moreover, he was not subject to Senate confirmation.

Two separate antiterrorism study panels released reports in December 2000 echoing some of the GOP complaints. A study released in June 2000 had stirred controversy with its recommendation that the Defense Department take the lead in responding to a major terrorist attack on U.S. soil.

RENO REPORT

On orders from Congress (HR 2267—PL 105-119), the Clinton administration developed a comprehensive antiterrorism plan that focused on how federal, state, and local officials should work together. The plan, prepared by the Justice Department and submitted to Congress on Jan. 7, 1999, attempted to address criticism from Capitol Hill that the administration had not adequately coordinated with local police, fire, and emergency workers as American cities prepared for the possibility of a terrorist attack.

The plan outlined a variety of methods for improving communication and intelligence-sharing among agencies as well as improving the training and equipping of those who would respond to chemical and biological attacks. The plan also called for building international cooperation to fight terrorism as well as promoting research into preventing terrorist attacks. Judd Gregg, R-N.H., chairman of the Senate Appropriations Subcommittee that funded the departments of Commerce, Justice, and State, praised Reno's report, saying it was well done and a positive step.

Among actions taken by various federal agencies was the Pentagon's designation of ten National Guard units around the country as emergency response teams to attacks involving weapons of mass destruction—nuclear bombs, poison gas, and biological toxins such as anthrax or smallpox. At the behest of Senate Armed Services Committee Chairman John W. Warner, R-Va., and other lawmakers, the Defense Department subsequently added seventeen more National Guard emergency response teams to the ten already designated.

NATIONAL COMMISSION REPORT

A ten-member National Commission on Terrorism—six appointed by Republican leaders and four appointed by Democrats—issued a report June 5, 2000, suggesting that the Defense Department take the lead in responding to especially severe terrorist attacks on U.S. soil—an idea that civil libertarians immediately condemned. The commission had been created by Congress in 1999 legislation (HR 4328—PL 105-277).

The commission urged the president to have his national security adviser work with the secretary of defense and attorney general to develop detailed contingency plans that would transfer lead authority from the FBI and the Federal Emergency Management Agency to the Pentagon before or during a catastrophic terrorist attack. But the American Civil Liberties Union insisted that soldiers had no place patrolling city streets. For more than a century, the federal Posse Comitatus Act had barred military involvement in civilian law enforcement.

The commission also recommended a national program to collect information electronically on foreign students attending U.S. colleges. The Immigration and Naturalization Service had had a similar pilot program since 1997, but commission members said it was limited to twenty colleges in the South.

The commission predicted that future terrorist attacks on U.S. soil with chemical, biological, or nuclear weapons were increasingly likely and that countering them "requires significantly stepped up U.S. efforts."

The report recommended that the CIA loosen restrictions on recruiting "unsavory" counterterrorist informants in other countries. The CIA had adopted the restrictions in 1995 in response to human rights abuses in Guatemala by informants. The commission also stressed the growing need for more funding for high-technology intelligence collection.

The commission agreed with some lawmakers that the White House and Congress needed to overhaul the system for reviewing and funding the dozens of counterterrorism programs run by federal agencies.

OTHER REPORTS

A commission established by Congress and chaired by Virginia Gov. James S. Gilmore III recommended in a Dec. 15, 2000, report that the White House create a national office to deter, prepare for, and respond to international and domestic terrorist attacks, including those with chemical, biological, and nuclear weapons. The Gilmore panel was made up of local and state government law enforcement and public health officials, as well as other experts. Its report called for better planning, training, and equipping of agencies that would respond to terrorist incidents.

The Center for Strategic and International Studies (CSIS), a Washington think tank, on Dec. 15 released a series of studies that also highlighted the need for a comprehensive "homeland defense" against domestic terrorist attacks. The CSIS effort was produced by four working groups, each consisting of federal, state, local, and private officials. An advisory group that included several members of Congress also provided input.

The CSIS groups proposed making the vice president responsible for creating a comprehensive antiterrorism plan and making the national coordinator a position subject to Senate confirmation. They also called for taking a variety of steps to protect computer networks against terrorist attacks.

CONGRESSIONAL RESPONSE

Lawmakers' concern over terrorism had been growing with every attack abroad and every warning at home. "There is not the slightest doubt that Osama bin Laden, his worldwide allies and his sympathizers are planning further attacks against us," Director of Central Intelligence George J. Tenet told the Senate Armed Services Committee on Feb. 2, 1999. *(Embassy attacks, p. 267)*

A year later Tenet told the Senate Intelligence Committee, "Although 1999 did not witness the dramatic terrorist attacks that punctuated 1998, our profile in the world—and thus our attraction as a terrorist target—will not diminish any time soon." In his Feb. 2, 2000, testimony he told the Intelligence panel that foreign users of nuclear, chemical, and biological weapons were becoming more deceptive, had easier access to "dual-use" technologies with both civilian and military applications, were buying outside expertise, and were taking advantage of rapidly accelerating technological progress.

Although Congress had paid increasing attention to the threat of terrorism, mainly by giving federal agencies more money, it had not passed any broad legislation.

Sen. Jon Kyl, R-Ariz., chairman of the Senate Judiciary Subcommittee on Technology, Terrorism and Government Information, introduced legislation (S 3205) in response to the June 2000 national commission report. His bill directed the president to take a variety of steps, including establishing an interagency task force to find ways to discourage fundraising by international terrorist groups. The bill directed the attorney general to review the legal authority of federal agencies to respond to terrorist attacks. It also called for establishing a long-term research and development program to devise technology that could deal with terrorist attacks.

S 3205, however, did not include any of the commission's more controversial recommendations, such as collecting information on foreign students or having the Defense Department lead the response to a severe terrorist attack on U.S. soil.

During debate on the bill, Kyl said the Oct. 14 attack on the USS *Cole* in Yemen "illustrates the continuing danger we face from terrorism and underscores the need for this legislation." The Senate passed S 3205 by voice vote Nov. 14, 2000, but the House took no action on the bill.

On July 25 the House had passed by voice vote a bill (HR 4210) to change the way the federal government coordinated its domestic antiterrorism programs. The administration strongly opposed the bill and was particularly concerned about dividing U.S. efforts at home and abroad to combat terrorism. The Senate took no action on the bill. (*Antiterrorism, p. 645*)

Test Ban Treaty

The Senate in 1999 soundly rejected the Comprehensive Test Ban Treaty (Treaty Doc 105-28). The treaty's defeat was a major blow to President Clinton, who had called it "the longest-sought, hardest-fought prize in the history of arms control." His administration had negotiated the final pact.

The treaty, which would expand an existing ban on atmospheric nuclear tests to include underground tests and those for peaceful purposes, was to go into effect on the approval of the forty-four nations with nuclear capability. At the time of the Senate vote, twenty-six had approved it.

Supporters hailed the treaty as the most effective means of halting the global arms race. But opponents, including all but four Senate Republicans, said the test ban treaty would be difficult to implement, would weaken U.S. defenses, and would give nations outside the pact an unfair nuclear advantage.

The treaty was defeated because most Republican senators, moderate and conservative alike, had serious doubts about it. But the political haggling that surrounded Senate consideration of the treaty—and ultimately sealed its fate—also reflected the deep animosity and mistrust conservative Republicans felt toward Clinton. Defeating the treaty gave them one of their few clear triumphs over the president in 1999.

BACKGROUND

President Clinton signed the treaty on Sept. 24, 1996. Agreement had come after four decades of intermittent efforts to negotiate such a ban. (*Congress and the Nation Vol. IX, p. 322*)

Considered by some the Holy Grail of arms control, it drew increased attention after the nuclear tests in India and Pakistan in May 1998. (*Economic sanctions, p. 199, p. 223*)

The treaty was intended to ban underground tests, using an international network of monitoring stations to verify compliance. It would allow tests of nuclear weapons components, including the high explosives used to trigger the weapons, as long as no radioactivity was released. It would also allow on-site inspections—on short notice, in some cases—where testing was suspected. (*Treaty provisions, box p. 311*)

As an alternative to explosive testing, the United States had developed an expensive and ambitious program called "science-based stockpile stewardship" that replaced large-scale tests with supercomputer simulations and high-powered lasers at the Department of Energy's nuclear weapons laboratories.

Proponents of the treaty emphasized the importance of establishing a strong legal framework to fight against proliferation and for the United States to show the world that it took seriously the prevention of nuclear tests.

But critics questioned the adequacy of U.S. monitoring capability and its alternatives to actual testing. They also contended that Clinton's desire to set an example for other countries was misguided in light of the fact that the United States, which had test-fired more nuclear weapons than any other country, had refrained from testing for the previous seven years.

SCHEDULING A VOTE

The treaty was submitted to the Senate on Sept. 22, 1997. But Foreign Relations Committee Chairman Jesse Helms refused to hold hearings until the administration submitted the 1997 Kyoto protocol on global warming and changes to the 1972 Anti-Ballistic Missile (ABM) Treaty. (*Kyoto protocol, p. 345; antimissile defenses, p. 306*)

Administration officials lobbied sporadically for the treaty after it was submitted. In the fall of 1999 they stepped up their efforts in advance of an Oct. 6 conference in Vienna of treaty signatories to determine what might be done to get nonratifying members to join.

But Senate Democrats were taken by surprise when Senate Majority Leader Trent Lott, R-Miss., announced Sept. 30 that he would schedule the treaty for a vote. Democrats rejected Lott's first offer to hold ten hours of debate beginning Oct. 6 but agreed on twenty-two hours of debate beginning Oct. 8. Meanwhile, Armed Services Committee Chairman John W. Warner, R-Va., who had announced his opposition to the treaty, agreed to hold three days of hearings. Helms scheduled a one-day hearing.

Democrats complained that the amount of time was inadequate but concluded that it might be their best chance of getting a vote during the 106th Congress. But they soon realized they were not close to the necessary sixty-seven votes to approve a resolution of ratification (if all senators were present and voting), having failed to dent an unyielding wall of Republican opposition.

A number of the Republicans that Democrats had counted on courting said flatly there was no way they could support the pact. Such "internationalist" Republicans as Warner, Pete V. Domenici of New Mexico, Richard G. Lugar of Indiana, and Ted Stevens of Alaska joined their more isolationist GOP colleagues in opposing the treaty because of serious doubts that it could be enforced or that it provided enough assurances for U.S. national security interests. In particular, some lawmakers worried about the Energy Department's alternatives to nuclear testing. Critics said stockpile stewardship remained unlikely to be fully operational for another decade or so.

TRYING TO STOP A VOTE

Faced with such a situation, a bipartisan group of senators began struggling to craft a graceful exit strategy. They said they feared the treaty's defeat would send an alarming

TREATY PROVISIONS

Nine years after the United States exploded its first atomic bomb in July 1945, efforts were under way to halt such testing. Proposals for an outright test ban had been under discussion since 1957, but not until 1994 were serious talks started on a Comprehensive Test Ban Treaty, which was finished and opened for signatures on Sept. 24, 1996.

Following were the main features:

• **All nuclear explosions banned.** Each nation that was a party to the treaty agreed not to conduct "any nuclear weapon test explosion or any other nuclear explosion," including those for peaceful purposes and those underground.

• **When treaty would take effect.** The treaty would take effect six months after it had been ratified by forty-four nations that had nuclear power and research reactors, including these nuclear weapon states and "threshold" states: the United States, Russia, Britain, France, China, India, Israel, and Pakistan.

• **Ratification.** A nation could not ratify the treaty with reservations.

• **Decision-making authority.** An Executive Council of fifty-one member nations, elected from geographic regions by all member nations and based in Vienna, would make most decisions.

• **Monitoring compliance.** Treaty compliance would be monitored by a network of fifty primary and 120 auxiliary seismological stations, eighty radionuclide stations and sixteen radionuclide laboratories that could sample radioactive particles in the atmosphere, and seventy-one listening stations that could pick up the sound of a nuclear explosion in the atmosphere or underwater. Data would be collected and analyzed by a data center.

• **Suspicious events.** Nations that were parties to the treaty would be encouraged to resolve possible instances of nuclear explosions among themselves. A nation that was asked to clarify a suspicious event had to do so within forty-eight hours.

• **Inspections.** If the circumstances of an "ambiguous" event could not be resolved, any party to the treaty could request an on-site inspection, which had to be approved by thirty members of the Executive Council. The council had to act on any request within four days and an inspection team had to arrive within six. Any drilling had to be approved by twenty-six council members.

• **Frivolous challenges.** A nation found to have submitted a frivolous or abusive inspection request could be fined or lose its power to request inspections.

• **Test notifications.** Each party to the treaty would notify the council's technical office of any chemical explosion equal to 300 tons or more of TNT.

• **Enforcement.** In cases of treaty violations, a conference of nations that were parties to the treaty could revoke a state's treaty rights, recommend sanctions to the other parties, or bring it to the attention of the United Nations.

---

and unwelcome signal to other nations—mainly India, Pakistan, and North Korea—that either had developed or were interested in developing nuclear weapons of their own.

Warner and Daniel Patrick Moynihan, D-N.Y., circulated a letter to Lott and Minority Leader Tom Daschle, D-S.D., urging a "statesmanlike initiative" to delay the vote until the 107th Congress. The letter was eventually signed by sixty-two senators—twenty-four Republicans and thirty-eight Democrats. While the letter was circulating, Daschle agreed in writing not to push for a vote until after a new president and Congress took office in 2001, "absent unforeseen changes in the international situation," such as renewed testing by nuclear-capable nations. He later agreed to change the language to "extraordinary circumstances."

Under Senate rules, however, Lott had to obtain the unanimous consent of all senators. And treaty critics such as Helms and Jon Kyl, R-Ariz., told him they wanted to see the pact voted down. Those critics, as well as Lott, had reservations with the vagueness of the "extraordinary circumstances" language. And so, on a strictly party-line vote of 55–45, the Senate on Oct. 13 agreed to a motion to return to consideration of the treaty.

That same day, by a **key vote of 48–51 (R 4–50; D 44–0; I 0–1),** the Senate rejected the resolution of ratification of the test ban treaty. Sixty-six votes had been needed to meet the required two-thirds majority of those present and voting for adoption of a resolution of ratification. Robert C. Byrd, D.-W.Va., voted "present," for the first time in more than forty years, citing procedural concerns. *(1999 key votes, p. 899)*

The results left some of the treaty's opponents jubilant, but the older GOP veterans were considerably more sober about the turn of events. An unusually subdued Stevens summed up his feelings just before he entered the chamber to cast his vote. "I'm sad," he said. "I'm sad."

The administration vowed that the treaty was not dead, but analysts and leadership aides in both parties predicted that it would not get another chance until a new president was sworn in. Democratic candidates former senator Bill Bradley and Vice President Al Gore supported the treaty; Texas Gov. George W. Bush, the Republican front-runner, opposed it.

Moderate opponents of the treaty agreed that if lawmakers were to be coaxed into revisiting the treaty, their concern over protecting the U.S. nuclear arsenal would have to be addressed.

CHAPTER 6

Transportation, Commerce, and Communications

Introduction   315

1997–1998 Chronology   318

1999–2000 Chronology   331

Transportation, Commerce, and Communications

The 105th and 106th Congresses worked on a variety of new issues prompted by the growth of the Internet and the digital economy. Measures to confer legality on electronic signatures and expand copyright protection for digital works were intended to set some ground rules for conduct in cyberspace without imposing burdensome new regulations on the fast-growing high-tech sector.

Republicans in control of the agenda had less success dealing with more traditional industries. Efforts to deregulate the electric utility market failed in both Congresses, and lawmakers also came up short in efforts to craft a national tobacco policy.

After pursuing an ideological agenda built around deregulation in the 104th Congress, GOP leaders took a more pragmatic course. Most legislative accomplishments came on narrowly focused bills that were carefully brought through the committee process and garnered bipartisan majorities. More ambitious efforts faltered due to partisan divisions and infighting within the increasingly fractious House Republican caucus.

TRANSPORTATION INFRASTRUCTURE

Authorizers and appropriators clashed over large spending programs on highways, mass transit, airports, and other infrastructure, as authorizers tried to direct money sequestered in trust funds for the purpose of deficit reduction on new capital spending.

Republicans, whose interest in the early 1990s was on alternatives to highways and building links between different modes of transportation, succeeded in shifting focus to huge increases in funding for both highways and mass transit. They also gave states and local governments more flexibility to use federal funds to reduce a backlog of repairs and needed projects.

House Transportation and Infrastructure Committee Chairman Bud Shuster, R-Pa., used budget surplus projections at the start of 1998 to win passage of a huge and controversial surface transportation reauthorization bill. The measure guaranteed that all revenues collected from the 18.3 cents-per-gallon federal gas tax, including the 4.3 cents-per-gallon share formerly devoted to deficit reduction, would be spent on transportation.

Shuster did not succeed in a related bit of budget politics that would have pushed the Highway Trust Fund "off budget." But the bill erected a "firewall," or guarantee, around most funding for highway and mass transit projects. The guarantee, designed to protect overall spending and specific projects, sparked a major turf war with appropriators, who complained it left little room for revisions or other projects.

Shuster was less successful in a similar effort in 2000 to guarantee spending on aviation programs. However, when Congress passed an FAA reauthorization that year, it provided that all of the receipts and interest in the Airport and Airway Trust Fund—projected to total $33 billion—would be spent on aviation programs, with a priority on capital accounts.

Congress took steps to restructure management of Amtrak, passing legislation in 1997 that freed up $2.3 billion for rail capital improvements and saved the ailing passenger railroad from bankruptcy. The bill gave managers more control over routes and personnel, eased worker protections, and capped liabilities from passenger lawsuits. It also set Amtrak on a glide path to eventual privatization.

Republican leaders showed a limited interest in safety issues, passing legislation directing tire manufacturers to give

REFERENCES

Discussion of transportation, commerce, and communications policy for the years 1945–1964 may be found in *Congress and the Nation Vol. I*, pp. 517–562, 1159–1185; for the years 1965–1968, *Congress and the Nation Vol. II*, pp. 227–251, 281–305, 779–823; for the years 1969–1972, *Congress and the Nation Vol. III*, pp. 147–187, 659–700; for the years 1973–1976, *Congress and the Nation Vol. IV*, pp. 146–147, 433–451, 505–555; for the years 1977–1980, *Congress and the Nation Vol. V*, pp. 291–362; for the years 1981–1984, *Congress and the Nation Vol. VI*, pp. 261–286, 289–329; for the years 1985–1988, *Congress and the Nation Vol. VII*, pp. 357–413; for the years 1989–1992, *Congress and the Nation Vol. VIII*, pp. 415–464; for the years 1993–1996, *Congress and the Nation Vol. IX*, pp. 327–398.

Outlays for Transportation

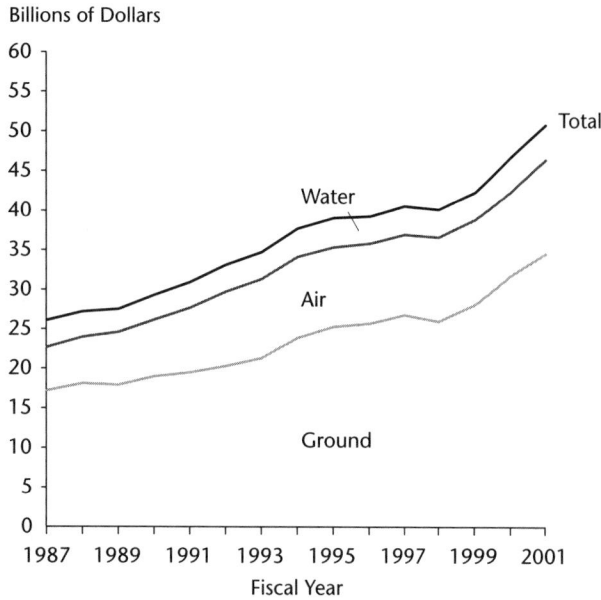

Billions of Dollars

NOTE: Data for 2001 are estimated.

SOURCE: Office of Management and Budget, *Historical Tables, Budget of the United States Government: Fiscal Year 2002* (Washington, D.C.: U.S. Government Printing Office, 2001), Table 3.2.

the government more data about possible defects and mandating crash tests for rollovers.

COMPETITIVENESS AND COMMERCE

Republicans continued their efforts to pare back the power of government and the courts, but the White House and congressional Democrats stymied the GOP's most ambitious proposals.

The latest in a series of GOP attempts to ease product-liability laws and raise the legal standard for plaintiffs to collect punitive damages was halted in the Senate in 1998. President Bill Clinton, however, signed a narrower measure making it more difficult to sue suppliers who provide raw materials for medical devices.

Efforts to pass legislation deregulating the electricity market—deemed a top priority at the beginning of the 105th Congress—failed in two consecutive Congresses, as lawmakers split over timetables and how to divide oversight between state and federal regulators. Reports of delays and mixed success in some states that adopted deregulation sank an effort that would have allowed power companies to sell to any customers, enabling consumers to select their electricity providers in the same way they choose long-distance phone carriers. Consumer groups and other opponents maintained deregulation would have mainly benefited big industrial power users, not average consumers. *(Details, p. 404)*

Congress also had high hopes for crafting a federal tobacco policy in 1998 but was unable to endorse a $368.5 billion settlement between cigarette makers and state attorneys general that required lawmakers' imprimatur to become binding. Members had hoped to direct money from the settlement toward efforts to reduce teen smoking and to pay smokers' health costs that had been shouldered by states. Failure to draft legislation also left the federal government with no oversight over the sale, distribution, and use of cigarettes and other tobacco products after the 4th U.S. Circuit Court of Appeals overturned a Clinton administration rule issued in 1996 that gave the Food and Drug Administration such power to regulate the products. The court said Congress had to confer the power on the FDA.

Lawmakers had success with some more narrowly tailored legislation. They passed a limited rollback of Major League Baseball's seventy-six-year-old antitrust exemption, giving big league ballplayers the same rights and protections enjoyed by other professional athletes. Lawmakers also overhauled the nation's patent system and approved federally subsidized loans for the steel, oil, and gas industries.

COMMUNICATIONS AND THE INTERNET

Mindful that information technology fueled the economic boom for much of the 1990s, Congress enacted a series of laws designed to encourage the growth of business on the Internet and establish basic rules for conduct in cyberspace. Throughout the deliberations, lawmakers tended to heed high-tech companies' calls for self-regulation whenever practical.

Lawmakers in 1998 placed a three-year moratorium on new taxes imposed on Internet access and commerce, over the objections of state and local officials, who charged it would usurp their taxing authorities. The moratorium—a priority of the high-tech industry—barred new access charges and fees for e-mail but did not apply to existing state sales taxes.

Congress in 1998 also expanded copyright protections for digital works, such as computer software and compact discs, and it banned the use of devices that circumvent technology designed to protect copyrighted works from theft. The effort addressed technology firms' concerns that the growth of the Internet increased the frequency with which copyrighted works could be pirated.

Another key piece of legislation, enacted in 2000, authorized the use of electronic signatures in Internet business deals. The bill gave transactions that were sealed electronically the same legal standing as those backed by paper records, despite concerns that it could compromise consumer protections and antifraud laws designed for a society based on paper records.

In a further bow to high-tech interests, Congress approved liability caps in connection with lawsuits over computer breakdowns associated with the so-called Year 2000, or Y2K, bug.

Congress was not able to address many issues related to Internet content, failing to pass any significant laws protecting the dissemination of personal information on the Internet. Efforts to ban gambling on the Internet also failed, though lawmakers passed narrow measures addressing pornography and liquor sales in cyberspace.

Congress addressed next-generation telecommunications services by authorizing a new round of electromagnetic spectrum auctions by Sept. 30, 2002, despite disagreements over how much the auctions would return to the Treasury. In addition, lawmakers cleared legislation in 1999 giving satellite television companies the right to deliver local broadcast signals in cities across the country, effectively putting them on even footing with cable television providers.

Congress also pressed a reluctant broadcast industry to change the voluntary ratings system in place for television programs and to give consumers more information about program content. Lawmakers also approved new federal loan guarantees to help satellite and cable systems beam local broadcast stations to viewers where over-the-air reception was poor.

Chronology of Action on Transportation, Commerce, and Communications

1997–1998

After completing much of the agenda that helped them win control of Congress in 1994, Republicans struggled to find a new direction. Lawmakers in 1997–1998 were less likely to stick to ideological purity and more willing to work steadily through the committee system to build bipartisan majority coalitions.

While this approach yielded legislative results, such as a $2.3 billion bailout of Amtrak and a three-year moratorium on state taxes on Internet commerce, it often broke down on more complicated, politically divisive issues. After Republicans in 1998 launched an impeachment inquiry based on allegations President Clinton lied about an illicit affair, leadership of both parties also seemed more interested in honing their election-year messages. *(Impeachment, p. 813)*

Perhaps the most important commerce issue on Congress's plate was the groundbreaking $368.5 billion agreement between tobacco companies and state attorneys general to combat teenage smoking. The failure of legislation to implement the settlement—which expanded far beyond the terms of the original deal—died in the Senate when GOP conservatives objected to its sharply higher cigarette taxes and new bureaucracies. In what would serve an apt metaphor for the entire year, the bill simply became too big. The demise of the tobacco bill was especially disappointing to Democrats and the Clinton administration, who were counting on money from new cigarette taxes to expand aid for child care and other programs.

Efforts to deregulate the electric utility industry and narrow the gap in competitive electricity rates between states also failed when House and Senate Republicans could not agree on the timetable and terms of a deregulatory plan. House lawmakers tended to favor broad deregulatory plans mandating open competition by a certain date while Senate Republicans advocated more incremental change.

In transportation, budget politics hampered efforts to reauthorize a wide-ranging surface transportation law and increase spending on roads, bridges, and highways. Im-

proved budget projections showing a surplus led lawmakers in 1998 to enact stopgap legislation to keep federal transportation money flowing to states while Congress continued work on a new six-year transportation bill.

The Amtrak bailout saved the struggling passenger railroad from bankruptcy while restructuring management and authorizing $5.2 billion in operating subsidies, capital improvements, and retirement funds. Only an extended round of negotiations between Democrats and Republicans over liability provisions saved the measure.

The high-tech community achieved considerable success, reflecting its growing political muscle. The Internet tax moratorium on online access or services represented a major industry victory over state and local leaders, who contended it would have a devastating effect on local tax collections. Congress also cleared legislation giving expanded copyright protection for intellectual property in digital form.

In telecommunications, Congress authorized the federal government to speed up its auctions of electromagnetic spectrum to raise revenues and balance the budget, despite widely varying estimates over how much the auctions actually would raise. Lawmakers also pressured television broadcasters to change the voluntary ratings system they had devised and provide more information about program content. Congress failed, however, to craft legislation that would have loosened Clinton administration controls on the export of technology that scrambles data or communications for privacy.

Surface Transportation Reauthorization

One of the first big tasks facing the 105th Congress was reauthorizing the nation's preeminent transportation law, the Intermodal Surface Transportation Efficiency Act of 1991, which was due to expire in September 1997. While the 1991 law emphasized support for alternatives to highways and building links between different modes of transportation, the new six-year, $217.9 billion reauthorization bill

(HR 2400—PL 105-178) included huge increases in funding for highways and mass transit. Lawmakers gave states and localities increased flexibility to use federal funds to help them reduce a backlog of repairs and priority projects. The law also provided support for innovative financing, in the form of loans and lines of credit, to encourage a mixture of public and private funding for big construction projects.

LEGISLATIVE ACTION

Early efforts in 1997 to reauthorize the act were hindered by budget politics, preventing lawmakers from passing a comprehensive law to keep funding for highways, bridges, and transit projects flowing to their states. In the House, Transportation and Infrastructure Committee Chairman Bud Shuster, R-Pa., unsuccessfully pushed a six-year, $218.3 billion proposal that would have shattered the spending limits established by the balanced-budget agreement. House Speaker Newt Gingrich, R-Ga., refused to bring the bill to the floor. Shuster narrowly failed in an effort to amend the fiscal 1998 budget resolution (H Con Res 84) to increase transportation spending sharply and cut other discretionary spending when his proposal was defeated on a **key vote of 214–216 (R 58–168; D 155–48; I 1–0).** The defeat prompted Shuster and his allies to delay further work on reauthorization until 1998, hoping that improved revenue projections would erase opposition to increased spending. *(1997 key votes, p. 865)*

Senate leaders on the Environment and Public Works and Banking, Housing and Urban Development Committees chose to stay within the framework of the budget deal, producing a six-year bill with $145 billion for highways and $35.7 billion for transit. The Senate bill reflected tough decisions on spending priorities that House lawmakers ignored, for example, shifting billions of dollars from northeastern states to southern and midwestern states that traditionally have paid more in federal gas taxes than they have received in transportation funding. However, it took months to assemble a large enough coalition to ensure passage. By the time the bill reached the Senate floor in October, the House had given up. Democrats also decided to use the bill as a vehicle for efforts to revamp the campaign finance system, assuring its demise. In place of a multiyear reauthorization, lawmakers Nov. 10 passed a $9.8 billion, short-term bill (S 1519—PL 105-130) that authorized the release of $8.1 billion in new transportation money and freed up $9.8 billion in reserves held by states—enough to get them comfortably through March. The House passed the short-term extension Nov. 12.

New federal budget projections showing a surplus greatly helped Shuster's cause when Congress reconvened in early 1998. Shuster found broad bipartisan support for his proposal to set the level of highway spending at the level of the prior year's gasoline tax receipts. Governors backed his efforts and urged quick action to avert a cutoff of federal funds.

With tacit support from GOP House leaders, Shuster's main opposition in 1998 came from Republican lawmakers who felt his spending bill went counter to the budget-balancing spirit of the House GOP's "Contract with America." Lindsey Graham, R-S.C., offered an amendment to strip $9 billion in special road and transit projects from the bill. Graham and his supporters objected to these "pork-barrel" earmarks. Graham's amendment, however, was easily defeated by a **key vote of 79–337 (R 67–152; D 12–184; I 0–1),** and Shuster's bill passed the House by a vote of 337–80 on April 1. *(1998 key votes, p. 883)*

In the Senate, Phil Gramm, R-Tex., and Robert C. Byrd, D-W.Va., led the battle to spend the 4.3-cent share of the gas tax once used for deficit reduction. Senators also approved $25.8 billion in additional highway spending, with most of the funding directed at projects in the Appalachian region, trade corridors near the Mexican and Canadian borders, and highways on public lands.

Under pressure to reach a deal after short-term funding expired at the end of April, House and Senate negotiators deleted a vital Senate provision that would withhold a share of federal funding from states that did not adopt a new lower blood-alcohol content threshold of 0.08 percent for drunken driving violations. President Clinton supported the drunken driving provision and criticized 1,850 highway projects worth $9.35 billion left in the compromise legislation. Despite the objections, Clinton said the bill did "a lot more good than harm, much more." The House and Senate each cleared the conference report (H Rept 105-550) on HR 2400 on May 22, and Clinton signed the legislation (PL 105-178) June 9.

MAJOR PROVISIONS

The law guaranteed that all revenues collected from the 18.3-cents-per-gallon gasoline tax, including the 4.3-cent share formerly used for deficit reduction, will be spent on transportation. So-called "donor states" that receive less than a dollar of federal funding for each dollar paid in federal gas taxes won a guarantee that 90.5 percent of their transportation funding allocations will be based on gas tax payments. The package also included funding for mass transit projects at the Salt Lake City Winter Olympics in 2002. A series of technical corrections added to the conference report on a bill (HR 2676—PL 105-206) to restructure the Internal Revenue Service restored several accidentally deleted measures to deter drunken driving, including $500 million in incentives for states that enact the new blood-alcohol standard of 0.08 percent.

Shuster failed in an effort to move four transportation trust funds dealing with mass transit, aviation, harbors, and inland waterways "off-budget"—meaning the government could not use the sizable cash balances in the funds to offset the deficit. The trust funds were supported by taxes on items such as fuel, tires, and cargo. Supporters, including powerful road-building lobbies, said it could potentially free up $3 billion or more per year for transportation improvements. The provision was opposed by both the Clinton administration and congressional appropriators, who typically spent less on

COMMERCE, TRANSPORTATION, SMALL BUSINESS LEADERSHIP

William M. Daley won easy Senate confirmation Jan. 30, 1997, to head the Commerce Department, although the 95–2 vote yielded the first "no" votes of any Clinton confirmation that year. The forty-eight-year-old Chicago lawyer succeeded Mickey Kantor, who took over Commerce after his predecessor, Ronald H. Brown, was killed in April 1996 while on a trade mission to the Balkans. The Commerce, Science and Transportation Committee had cleared Daley's nomination, 19–1, on Jan. 29.

Daley was a member of Chicago's prominent Democratic political family; his father, Richard J. Daley, dominated as mayor from 1955 to 1976, and his brother, Richard M. Daley, was elected mayor in 1989. In 1992 Daley served as Illinois chairman of Bill Clinton's presidential campaign. During Clinton's first administration, Daley served on the board of the Federal National Mortgage Association (Fannie Mae) and as special counsel on the North American Free Trade Agreement. In 1996 he managed the fund-raising for the 1996 Democratic National Convention in Chicago.

During his Jan. 22 confirmation hearing he dealt with Republican allegations that the Clinton administration had turned the Commerce Department into a Democratic political operation by declaring that he would eschew partisanship and keep the department free of political activity during his tenure. He specifically vowed to reduce the number of political appointees at the Commerce Department by 40 percent. Some conservative Republicans questioned whether the department should be eliminated altogether. While acknowledging that some changes needed to be made, Daley defended the department, saying it remained a vital advocate for U.S. businesses facing global competition. *(Background, cabinet profiles, p. 977)*

Rodney Slater won Senate confirmation to become transportation secretary Feb. 6, 1997, after breezing through the confirmation process. Slater was approved 98–0, succeeding Federico F. Peña, who became energy secretary in the second-term Clinton administration.

Slater was a longtime Clinton ally, having served as head of the Arkansas highway program when Clinton was governor. During Clinton's first administration, Slater headed the Federal Highway Administration. The Senate Commerce, Science and Transportation Committee unanimously recommended Slater's confirmation by voice vote on Feb. 5 after Slater won strong bipartisan praise at a Jan. 29 confirmation hearing. He pledged to make transportation safety his top priority. *(Background, cabinet profiles, p. 981)*

Investment banker and former television journalist Aida Alvarez won voice vote confirmation from the Senate Feb. 13, 1997, to head the Small Business Administration after winning approval, 18–0, from the Senate Small Business Committee the previous day. Alvarez previously was the first director of the Office of Federal Housing Enterprise Oversight.

During her confirmation hearings, Alvarez recalled her humble origins as a child in rural Puerto Rico before her family emigrated to New York City. She took her first job waiting tables in a small business—her family's restaurant. She told lawmakers that small business was the "incubator of America's entrepreneurial spirit."

---

transportation projects than Congress authorized, largely due to caps on discretionary spending. However, the bill established a "firewall," or guarantee, around most funding for highways and mass transit, assuring that overall funding and specific projects would be protected.

Amtrak

Legislation (S 738—PL 105-134) more than two years in the making to rescue Amtrak from the brink of bankruptcy cleared a last-minute obstacle before Congress adjourned for 1997 and was signed into law by President Clinton on Dec. 2. The legislation restructured the management of the nation's ailing passenger railroad and authorized $5.2 billion in operating subsidies, capital improvements, and retirement funds through fiscal 2002. Enactment was vital to Amtrak, which was scheduled to go to creditors in December for an extension of its $150 million line of credit after borrowing heavily to meet its payroll.

BACKGROUND

Amtrak, officially the National Railroad Passenger Corporation, was created by the Rail Passenger Service Act of 1970 to relieve privately owned railroads of their money-losing passenger lines. Early optimism faded as the venture proved no more profitable under government control with federal grants and loan guarantees than it had been in private hands. Congress added to Amtrak's problems by requiring service on unprofitable routes and by imposing labor rules that deterred layoffs and private contracting. Lawmakers in the 1980s also made deep cuts in capital grants, saddling the railroad with aging, expensive equipment and leaving it ill-prepared to compete with fare-cutting airlines and bus services.

Amtrak hit the wall in 1994 as its operating deficit approached $200 million and management announced plans to slash service. Management said its goal was to survive without operating subsidies by fiscal 2002, but that it would continue to rely on federal support for capital. After Republicans took control of Congress in 1995, some key GOP allies moved into important committee positions, easing the worries of some railroad supporters, who feared conservative Republicans' historic opposition to Amtrak subsidies. But by early 1997, the General Accounting Office reported Amtrak was sliding deeper into debt, losing $1.6 billion in 1995 and 1996, despite streamlining its operations and cutting routes. *(Congress and the Nation Vol. IX, p. 369)*

LEGISLATIVE ACTION

Legislation to restructure the management of the railroad passed the Senate Nov. 7, 1997, by voice vote after an extended round of negotiations between Democrats and Republicans over liability provisions. Republicans succeeded in limiting damages sought by those injured in Amtrak accidents and in making Amtrak absolve freight rail carriers on whose tracks it traveled from any liability in the event of a passenger rail accident.

The bill ran into trouble in the House when Transportation and Infrastructure Committee Chairman Bud Shuster, R-Pa., insisted on replacing Amtrak's board of directors. Shuster's version of the Amtrak bill had been defeated on the House floor Oct. 24 when an unusual coalition of Democrats, prounion Republicans, and deficit hawks teamed up to defeat crucial labor provisions that GOP leaders insisted remain in the bill.

To almost everyone's surprise, a deal was struck saving the bill on the final day of the first session. Under the legislation Amtrak's political board would be replaced by a more professional "reform board," as Shuster had insisted, but Republican leaders would not get to name four of the seven board members, as Shuster had proposed. The bill eliminated statutory restrictions that generally prohibited Amtrak from contracting out for work or services and eliminated some labor protections, including guaranteed severance benefits equal to a year of wages for every year worked, up to a maximum of six years' pay, for employees who lost their jobs because of rail service cutbacks. The bill also capped Amtrak's liability for rail accidents to a total of $200 million per accident for all claims made by passengers for economic, noneconomic and punitive damages. The cap did not apply to other parties harmed by an Amtrak accident.

Airline Ticket Taxes

The five-year balanced budget deal (HR 2014—PL 105-34) reached in 1997 between the Republican-controlled Congress and the Clinton administration settled a major battle between big airlines and their discount competitors over airline ticket taxes. The agreement increased airline ticket taxes from $30 billion to $79.7 billion over ten years and restructured the taxes in a way that split the difference between big carriers such as American and Delta—which lobbied vigorously for a new system of fees tied to the distance a passenger traveled—and discount airlines such as

Southwest—which wanted to continue the existing 10 percent tax on the price of an airline ticket. *(Tax bill, p. 90)*

The bill reauthorized the ticket excise tax for ten years, but at a gradually declining rate. Beginning in 1998, the excise tax would be supplemented by a per-passenger tax on each segment of a domestic flight that would increase gradually in subsequent years. In addition, the bill imposed a $12 tax on international arrivals and a separate $12 tax on departures. The new taxes replaced the existing $6 tax on departures. Republicans needed the revenue from airline taxes to offset the huge tax cuts contained in the tax-reconciliation bill.

FAA Reauthorization

A bill reauthorizing Federal Aviation Administration (FAA) research, engineering, and development programs (HR 1271—PL 105-155) came close to enactment at the end of 1997 and was signed into law Feb. 11, 1998. The legislation authorized $457 million for the programs through fiscal 1999 and established a new undergraduate research grants program. The programs—aimed at improving the safety, security, capacity, and productivity of the airways and air traffic control system—had been covered under an FAA reauthorization bill enacted in 1996 but had only been authorized for one year. The programs were generally conducted by FAA technical personnel and by colleges and universities. *(Congress and the Nation Vol. IX, p. 359)*

The bill urged the FAA to address the year 2000 computer problem, and it barred contractors from receiving FAA research grants if they received any other federal grants through a noncompetitive process.

Separate efforts to pass freestanding legislation reauthorizing FAA airport improvements grants fell apart late in 1998 because House and Senate negotiators were unable to agree on provisions to eliminate flight restrictions at several airports. Consequently, provisions were included in the 1998 omnibus appropriations law (HR 4328—PL 105-277) to fund the airport grants for the first six months of fiscal 1999, forcing Congress to revisit the issue. *(Omnibus bill, p. 62)*

The biggest issues centered on the length of the reauthorization and on efforts by Senate Commerce Committee Chairman John McCain, R-Ariz., to loosen Ronald Reagan Washington National Airport's "perimeter rule"—which limits flights to 1,250 miles—and to increase the number of landing and takeoff slots at National, O'Hare International Airport in Chicago, and John F. Kennedy and LaGuardia airports in New York.

Ocean Shipping

The Senate Commerce, Science and Transportation Committee unanimously approved a bill in 1997 that would revise shipping laws to allow companies greater flexibility in contracting for ocean shipping. The legislation would make changes to the Shipping Act of 1984, which prohibited confidential service contracts and required that all rates be made publicly available. Supporters of the changes said the existing law's disclosure requirement sometimes put companies at a competitive disadvantage because many foreign countries, such as Japan, let companies keep their rates and contracts confidential.

The bill proposed to eliminate requirements that carriers file rate increases or decreases with the Federal Maritime Commission, the independent agency that regulated domestic and international shipping in U.S. waters. The only demand for posting would be that it be easily accessible—say, by posting shipping rates on a company's Internet home page. The bill also would allow limited, confidential service contracting by shippers and common carriers, but shippers would have to stay within the bounds of antitrust law. The bill also would merge the Federal Maritime Commission with the Surface Transportation Board, which regulated ground transportation, to form a new agency to be called the Intermodal Transportation Board. The bill cleared the committee by a 20–0 vote May 1.

Product Liability

Supporters of legislation to overhaul the nation's laws governing faulty products got half a loaf from the 105th Congress. Although proponents of a broad overhaul crafted a compromise deal with the Clinton administration in 1997, they could not shepherd it through the Senate. As a consolation prize, President Clinton signed into law in August 1998 a smaller bill (HR 872—PL 105-230) that makes it more difficult to sue suppliers who provide raw materials for medical devices.

Biomedical companies had complained that they had trouble getting raw materials from suppliers wary of liability concerns, and the biomaterials legislation enjoyed the active or tacit support of many who opposed broader product liability overhaul.

The product liability fight was the latest chapter of a battle that dated back to the 1980s. Clinton vetoed a Republican product liability bill in 1996, although he promised to support "common sense" liability legislation. The Senate Commerce, Science and Transportation Committee approved a version of a broad overhaul in May 1997 on a party-line vote, in what was seen as merely a starting point for serious talks with the White House. Negotiations produced a less ambitious proposal that would have placed a $250,000 cap on punitive damages against small businesses, defined as those with fewer than twenty-five employees and less than $5 million in annual revenues. The 1996 bill, in contrast, would have covered big businesses, as well. *(Congress and the Nation Vol. IX, p. 376)*

Plaintiffs could only receive punitive damages if they showed "clear and convincing" evidence that a defendant acted with a "conscious, flagrant indifference" to the rights and safety of others. The deal also sought to place an eighteen-year limit on the filing of lawsuits relating to harm caused by goods used in the workplace.

Sen. John D. Rockefeller IV, D-W.Va., an important player in the negotiations, warned fellow Democrats that any changes could unravel the package and prompt a veto, but they insisted on their right to try to amend the bill, specifically to exempt gun manufacturers from the proposed protections.

A motion to invoke cloture on the bill failed in July 1998, with some Republican skeptics of product liability joining a united Democratic Caucus to oppose shutting off debate. With the broad bill effectively dead, Rockefeller and Slade Gorton, R-Wash., moved the biomaterials portion separately. Under the slimmed-down measure, civil action against a supplier must be dismissed if the material met the manufacturer's specifications and if the supplier did not make or market the final product. It also required plaintiffs to submit an affidavit stating that the alleged harm was caused by the raw material used in the device. Both the House and Senate quickly cleared the compromise by voice votes the evening of July 30.

Tobacco Settlement

The creation of a federal tobacco policy was supposed to be one of the main accomplishments of the 105th Congress, but it never happened. An ambitious bill that would have raised the price of cigarettes $1.10 per pack over five years and imposed penalties on tobacco companies if youth smoking reduction targets were not met died under its own weight in the Senate. House Republican leaders, meanwhile, could never agree on legislation.

The Senate bill (S 1415—S Rept 105-180) came to the floor in May 1998 with its fate uncertain. Senate Commerce, Science and Transportation Committee Chairman John McCain, R-Ariz., who had been charged with crafting a bill that could be a vehicle for further progress, believed with Senate Majority Leader Trent Lott, R-Miss., that a House-Senate conference would be the true birthplace of federal tobacco policy. To keep the ball rolling, McCain was given control of a bill over which many committees would normally have shared jurisdiction.

The bill appeared to gain momentum as it neared the floor, especially after the Senate Finance Committee echoed growing antitobacco sentiment and pressed to raise cigarette prices by $1.50 per pack over three years. But as McCain pleaded with colleagues not to upset his "carefully balanced package" with amendments from the right and left, opponents sought to drag out the debate. In the end, they succeeded in adding extraneous amendments offering tax breaks and increased funding for interdiction of illegal drugs. Supporters helped make the measure unpassable with tough amendments to lift all legal liability caps against tobacco companies.

With hundreds of amendments still pending, a closed Senate Republican conference June 17, 1998, led to two procedural votes that brought the bill down. In the House, Speaker Newt Gingrich, R-Ga., had a week earlier declared that he thought the House would never conference the McCain bill.

Instead, Reps. Deborah Pryce, R-Ohio, and Scott McInnis, R-Colo., released an "outline of principles" after the Senate bill died, promising a narrower bill that would create a model set of penalties to discourage youth smoking. Democrats were against such a modest approach, while Republicans were split about the political wisdom of doing little versus doing nothing. The Pryce-McInnis plan was never introduced.

BACKGROUND

The tobacco issue had come to Congress through the offices of state attorneys general and cigarette makers, who reached a $368.5 billion legal settlement in June 1997 that needed Congress's imprimatur to become binding. The settlement aimed to reduce teen smoking and to require tobacco companies to pay some of the smokers' health costs shouldered by the states in the past. Tobacco companies also agreed to conditional federal regulation of nicotine in their products. In exchange, all pending lawsuits and state lawsuits were to be dismissed. Future litigants would be prohibited from joining in class action suits, and individuals could not sue for punitive damages.

The tobacco industry portrayed the deal as a framework to reduce the nation's smoking habit and pay its share of the devastating consequences. Antismoking advocates said it did not contain enough penalties for the industry and fell short of protecting the public health. They maintained the industry was up to its old tricks, looking to mostly Republican allies in Congress for the best deal possible after securing a settlement that for the first time gave it the promise of legal immunity.

The tobacco companies wanted the deal approved as written almost immediately. Attorneys general of states suing the companies concurred, saying it was the best deal they could hope for and warning Congress against tampering with it. But lawmakers quickly declared they would not rubber stamp any legislation. President Clinton also weighed in, saying some of the provisions were not tough enough, such as limits to be placed on the Food and Drug Administration's ability to issue new tobacco regulations.

The federal government added another twist in November 1997, when it laid claim to half of the money the states recovered from tobacco companies to pay for the costs of treating Medicaid beneficiaries with smoking-related illnesses. The Health Care Financing Administration notified states that they were required under the Social Security Act to reimburse the government for its share of Medicaid expenses when damages were recovered. States insisted they should control the settlement money because they had fought the tobacco industry without help from Washington.

LEGISLATIVE ACTION

There were few major votes on the tobacco deal in 1997, although both the House and Senate held hearings, and leaders on both sides of the aisle created task forces to study the settlement. Momentum began building to toughen terms of the settlement after tobacco industry allies slipped a last-minute provision into the budget reconciliation bill (HR 2014—PL 105-34) stipulating that any money raised by a cigarette tax increase be applied toward the total amount the industry had agreed to pay in the settlement. The ploy, which would have shaved about $50 billion from cigarette-makers' liabilities over the expected twenty-five-year span of the settlement, backfired on the industry, with adversaries saying it was a backroom deal that symbolized Congress's continued coddling of big tobacco. Amid an uproar, the Senate and later the House repealed the measure. *(Reconciliation bill, p. 48)*

In the Senate McCain began 1998 by marking up a tough bill that would raise the price of cigarettes, restrict advertising of tobacco products in an effort to cut down on the 3,000 teenagers who start smoking each day, and cap liability claims against the industry at $6.5 billion a year. The bill would force tobacco companies to pay $10 billion up front and an additional $506 billion over the course of twenty-five years for a host of antismoking programs, legal damages, and advertising campaigns and health-care costs.

The industry found the terms too harsh and withdrew its support from the process, earning McCain a formidable enemy. Tobacco companies would spend upward of $40 million on issue ads against his legislation by the time the bill died.

With the Finance Committee signaling support, McCain brought to the Senate floor May 18 a manager's amendment that was an amalgam of the Commerce bill and Finance changes with input from the White House. Opponents sought to drag out the debate to build time for their case. With debate on the Senate floor entering its fourth week, and with myriad amendments pending, Majority Leader Trent Lott, R-Miss., convened a closed-door conference with three dozen Republicans on June 17, 1998. The GOP leaders decided to hold a cloture vote later in the day. The motion to invoke cloture fell three votes short of the 60 required on a **key vote of 57–42 (R 14–40; D 43–2)**. Following the cloture vote, 53 senators—seven shy of the 60 needed—voted to waive a budget point of order against the bill, which violated spending limits allowed for the Commerce Committee. The twin procedural actions killed the bill and led to political repercussions, with Democrats charging one reason Senate Republicans iced the bill was to spare their House colleagues a contentious vote. They argued GOP members in both chambers would be held accountable in the midterm elections. *(1998 key votes, p. 883)*

In an interesting postscript, the 4th U.S. Circuit Court of Appeals in August 1998 overturned the Clinton administration's ambitious 1996 rules giving the FDA the power to regulate the sale, distribution, and use of cigarettes and other tobacco products. The federal appeals court, located in the heart of tobacco country in Richmond, Virginia, in a 2–1 decision, ruled Congress never intended the FDA to regulate tobacco, and therefore did not equip it with the laws to do so. While Congress never explicitly prohibited the agency from regulating tobacco products, the court determined that the agency attempted to stretch the law beyond the scope intended by Congress. The decision validated arguments put forward by some Republicans, such as Sen. Bill Frist, R-Tenn., that tobacco products are unique and should be put in their own category in the law.

Baseball Antitrust Exemption

After a lengthy effort, Congress in 1998 cleared legislation partially lifting Major League Baseball's seventy-six-year-old antitrust exemption. President Clinton signed the bill into law in October (S 53—PL 105-297). The measure superseded a unanimous 1922 Supreme Court decision that baseball was a sport involving state exhibitions, rather than a business spawning interstate commerce within the definition of antitrust laws. *(Background, Congress and the Nation Vol. IX, p. 385)*

The exemption prevented big league ballplayers from having some of the rights and protections enjoyed by other professional athletes. In labor disputes, for example, players were unable to challenge owners' actions under antitrust laws. The lack of legal recourse contributed to the strike that ultimately led to cancellation of the 1994 World Series. The bill did not affect other vital aspects of professional baseball, such as franchise relocations, ties between major and minor leagues, and broadcasting rights.

Major league players and owners had concurred as part of a 1996 collective bargaining agreement to seek legislation providing a limited rollback of the antitrust exemption. A markup was scheduled and postponed several times in 1997 to give the owners and players a chance to agree on bill provisions. Although the two sides reached a compromise in June, the owners drew back, saying the draft bill did not specify clearly that minor leagues' antitrust exemption would remain intact. Senate Judiciary Committee Chairman Orrin G. Hatch, R-Utah, offered an amendment clarifying that the bill would not address the minor leagues' exemption. Although the amendment was adopted, the owners still did not support the bill, and it went no further in 1997.

Hatch and Judiciary Committee ranking Democrat Patrick J. Leahy of Vermont finally broke the impasse and announced an agreement with owners in late July 1998. The language again clarified that the bill would not apply to minor league teams, thus protecting the system under which major league clubs subsidize and transfer players among their farm teams, which represent a training and player selection system not found in most other professional sports.

The Senate passed the bill by voice vote July 30, a day after the agreement was struck, and the House cleared the bill by voice vote Oct. 30. Leahy said it would restore public confidence in the game that had lingered after cancellation of the 1994 World Series.

Patent Overhaul

The House voted in April 1997 on legislation (HR 400) to alter the way patents were granted and reviewed, but only after critics significantly scaled back a controversial provision that would have required the publication of all patent applications eighteen months after they were filed. Under existing law, patents remained confidential until they were granted. The Senate Judiciary Committee approved a companion bill (S 507), but it went no further in the session.

The House-passed bill exempted small businesses, independent inventors, and universities from the advance publication requirement. Critics, however, argued that allowing publication after eighteen months would give foreign companies and others the opportunity to steal the ideas of U.S. inventors and allow big businesses to prey on small companies and independent inventors.

Supporters of the provision said it was needed to bring intellectual property protections in the United States into line with those in the rest of the industrialized world. Other provisions in the House bill included converting the U.S. Patent and Trademark Office from a division of the Department of Commerce into a wholly owned government corporation. The office's managers would run its daily activities without the supervision of a government agency but would still be subject to policy direction by the secretary of commerce and the White House.

The patent office, which did not receive tax dollars, would be allowed to keep all of the money it collected through applications and user fees. Under existing law, some of the money was diverted to other government agencies. *(1999 action, p. 334)*

Small Business Programs Reauthorization

Congress cleared legislation in fall 1997 (S 1139—PL 105-135) reauthorizing a number of Small Business Administration (SBA) programs through fiscal 2000, including $12 billion in fiscal 1998 for the SBA's popular "7(a)" general business loan program. Other provisions established a loan program for former welfare recipients, provided incentives for small businesses to locate in low-income areas known as "HUBZones" (for historically underutilized business zones), and allowed the SBA to do criminal background checks on applicants for certain loan programs. President Clinton signed the bill into law on Dec. 2, 1997.

The Senate and House cleared their respective versions of the legislation without major controversy in June. The House added two significant provisions, allowing SBA to accept money from other federal agencies to provide additional grants to loan borrowers who were on welfare. The second provision would direct existing SBA aid programs to provide counseling to small businesses that had suffered economic damages from the North American Free Trade Agreement (NAFTA) or by the relocation of jobs overseas for any reason. Rather than hold a conference, the House and Senate held informal negotiations from August to November 1997, using the original text of the Senate bill as a starting point.

One important provision of the bill defined "bundling" of federal contracts, a practice of consolidating several smaller contracts into one large contract, and granted SBA greater authority to challenge such contract consolidations. Critics said the practice of bundling often precluded small businesses from bidding on government work because it made jobs too large for them to compete on.

Spectrum Auctions

The federal government in 1997 was authorized to speed up its auctions of electromagnetic spectrum as part of an effort to raise revenues and balance the budget. The Congressional Budget Office (CBO) estimated that the Treasury would net $21.4 billion over five years from the spectrum auction provisions, which were included in budget-reconciliation legislation (HR 2015—PL 105-33) signed in August 1997. *(Reconciliation bill, p. 48)*

Budget negotiators originally hoped the auctions would raise $26.3 billion. But members of the committees with jurisdiction—House Commerce and Senate Commerce, Science and Transportation—refused to include some controversial provisions that might have boosted the CBO estimate to that level. Rejected proposals included a White House plan to impose fees on spectrum users, which was staunchly opposed by broadcasters, and another provision to auction toll-free "vanity" telephone numbers. Lawmakers expressed doubts that the spectrum provisions would yield the expected revenues.

BACKGROUND

The Federal Communications Commission (FCC) in April 1997 adopted rules giving broadcasters an additional channel of spectrum to make the conversion from analog to more technologically advanced digital television. The agency set a target date of 2006, after which broadcasters would have to return their analog spectrum and begin broadcasting exclusively in digital form.

Critics unsuccessfully tried to forestall what they viewed as a giveaway of a valuable asset. Before leaving the Senate in 1996 to concentrate on his unsuccessful run for the presidency, Majority Leader Bob Dole, R-Kan., attempted to require broadcasters to pay for additional spectrum space to provide digital television, but his efforts were stymied by the National Association of Broadcasters and its allies in Congress. *(Congress and the Nation Vol. IX, p. 396)*

LEGISLATIVE ACTION

The House Commerce Committee narrowly approved its version of spectrum auction provisions in June 1997, with Republicans playing down concerns the auctions would raise anything near $26.3 billion in order to advance a big chunk of money for the spending-reconciliation bill then working its way through Congress.

The panel called on the FCC to find 100 megahertz of spectrum, including 45 megahertz to be used exclusively by the federal government, to auction by Sept. 30, 2002. Broadcasters would be required to return 78 megahertz of spectrum being used for analog broadcasts by the end of 2006.

The FCC would be required to begin auctioning the returned spectrum by July 1, 2001. The agency also would be required to extend the deadline in areas where more than 5 percent of households continued to rely exclusively on over-the-air television signals. Democrats argued this loophole would significantly reduce the dollar value of analog spectrum. Republicans later added a provision that required the FCC to void auctions if it determined aggregate proceeds would total less than two-thirds of the amount the CBO had estimated such auctions would generate.

As the bill headed to the House floor, the budget office dramatically changed the tone of the debate when it revised its estimate downward saying the auctions would generate $16.6 billion less than originally estimated—to only $9.7 billion over five years—for various reasons including the loophole for stations to retain their analog spectrum. The House further changed bill language that was passed as part of rules for floor debate on the broader bill. Among the changes was revising the wording so that the FCC was allowed, instead of required, to extend the spectrum giveback deadline.

The Senate passed its version of spectrum provisions in June 1997, after the Commerce, Science and Transportation Committee cleared auction proposals expected to raise $15.9 billion. The committee struck a provision opposed by broadcasters that would have authorized the FCC to impose fees on spectrum users. It also removed the language calling for the auction of toll-free vanity phone numbers. Senators also rejected a proposal to give the FCC more leeway in deciding when to conduct spectrum auctions by holding an auction when the agency determined it would yield maximum returns to the government.

The House-Senate conference reconciled the House and Senate versions and managed to get total revenue estimates up to $21.4 billion. Conferees added an accounting mechanism under which $3 billion was to be appropriated in fiscal 2001 for the Universal Service Fund, which subsidized local phone service. Because the fund is required to return an equal amount to the Treasury in 2002, the money could be counted as a revenue increase within the five-year period covered by the reconciliation bill.

MAJOR PROVISIONS

As enacted, the spectrum sales section in the 1997 reconciliation bill (HR 2015—PL 105-33) contained the following major provisions:

FCC Auction Authority

Extended the FCC's authority to use competitive bidding to assign licenses for the use of spectrum until Sept. 30, 2007. The agency's previous authority was set to expire Sept. 30, 1998.

The bill also expanded the FCC's auction authority, generally allowing it to use competitive bidding for all radio-based licenses for mutually exclusive rights to use a portion of the spectrum. Auctions could not be used for assigning public broadcasting licenses, providing additional spectrum to television stations to broadcast advanced digital signals or for public safety radio services.

Previously, the FCC could only use auctions to award spectrum to companies that resold communications services, such as paging or cellular telephone services, to subscribers.

Radio or television licenses that were being disputed prior to July 1, 1997, also were to be auctioned under the new legislation.

Auction of New Spectrum

Required the auction of a total of 120 megahertz of spectrum for commercial uses by the end of fiscal 2002: 45 megahertz that had been set aside for government use, an additional 55 megahertz to be located by the FCC, and 20 megahertz to be located by the secretary of commerce from spectrum that had been reserved for government use. Federal agencies could be reimbursed for the cost of relocating federal broadcast operations to another frequency to accommodate a private party's use of the spectrum.

Reclaiming Analog Spectrum

Required the FCC to reclaim by Dec. 31, 2006, spectrum that was being used by broadcasters to transmit analog television signals. The FCC had allocated broadcasters an additional channel of spectrum to allow them to transmit both analog and digital signals while they made the transition to digital.

Because of concern that some consumers might be left without free over-the-air television on Jan. 1, 2007, however, the bill required the FCC to grant broadcasters an extension under certain conditions, including:

• If one or more of the affiliates of the four largest networks in a market was not broadcasting in digital.

• If technology allowing analog television sets to receive digital signals was not generally available in a market.

• If at least 15 percent or more of television households in a market did not subscribe to a multichannel video programming distributor, such as cable television, that carried the digital signals of local broadcasters, or did not have at least one digital television set or at least one analog television set with a converter box allowing it to receive digital TV signals.

Auctioning Reclaimed Spectrum

Required the FCC to auction the reclaimed analog spectrum by the end of 2002. Critics cited the disparity between the deadlines for reclaiming and auctioning the spectrum as evidence that the spectrum provisions would not raise as much as estimated.

Duopoly and Cross-Ownership Waivers

Required the FCC to grant a waiver from its "duopoly" and "cross-ownership" rules in cities of more than 400,000 to allow newspapers and broadcasters to bid on the reclaimed analog spectrum.

The duopoly rule barred a broadcaster from owning more than one television station in the same market. The cross-ownership rules barred a newspaper from owning a television station in the same market in which it circulated or a television station from owning a newspaper in the same market in which it broadcast.

Spectrum for Public Safety Use

Reallocated 60 megahertz of spectrum being used for channels 60–69, which were adjacent to spectrum already being used for public safety purposes. The FCC, after consulting with the secretary of Commerce and the attorney general, was required to reallocate 24 megahertz of this amount for public safety services use. The rest, 36 megahertz, had to be auctioned for commercial use after Jan. 1, 2001.

The FCC was required to begin assigning public safety licenses by Sept. 30, 1998. Before granting the licenses, the FCC had to make five findings, including ensuring that spectrum was not immediately available on a frequency already allocated to public service and determining that granting the application was consistent with the public interest.

Universal Service Fund

Required an appropriation of $3 billion in 2001 to the universal service fund, which was established to ensure that affordable telecommunications services were available to all regions of the country.

The $3 billion was to then be repaid to the federal government from the universal service fund in 2002. To accommodate this, telecommunications carriers and providers would be directed in 2001 to defer $3 billion in payments to the universal service fund until 2002. The CBO estimated that this provision would have a neutral impact on the budget but would be counted as a net increase in revenues in 2002, the year the budget was supposed to be balanced.

Encryption Exports

Lawmakers in 1997 and 1998 failed to settle a long-running policy dispute over encryption—technology that scrambles data or communications for privacy. High-tech industry leaders complained existing export restrictions put them at a competitive disadvantage to foreign firms and could also enable the foreign companies that did not face the same restrictions to gain a toehold in the U.S. market. The Clinton administration, however, was reluctant to lift export controls because of concerns that increasing the availability of encryption software will hamper law enforcement and intelligence gathering.

In 1997 five House committees approved a bill (HR 695—H Rept 105-108) backed by industry leaders that would have allowed for the export of encryption products that are generally available overseas. However, Rules Committee Chairman Gerald B. H. Solomon, R-N.Y., insisted that any bill that went to the House floor include restrictions favored by the FBI and other law enforcement agencies. Because the bill's chief sponsors and industry officials opposed this version, the stalemate was not settled. A Senate version of the bill

(S 909) was approved by the Commerce, Science and Transportation Committee but went no further.

In 1998 the Clinton administration, sensitive that a hard-line stand would contradict its policy of touting increased high-tech exports to sustain U.S. prosperity, relaxed some export controls. The White House, for example, said in July it would allow U.S. companies to sell encryption products to banks and financial institutions in forty-five countries without previously proposed restrictions. However, industry officials, privacy advocates, and some lawmakers said they would continue to push for legislation that provided broader relief. *(1999 action, p. 336)*

Television Ratings

After months of mounting pressure by members of Congress and family advocacy groups, the broadcast industry agreed in July 1997 to change the voluntary television ratings system it had put in place at the beginning of the year to include more information about the content of programs.

The broadcasters' move came in response to complaints by lawmakers and advocacy groups that the industry's age-based system did not give viewers enough information about the content of programming. The industry's original system was based on guidelines used for movies, with ratings based on suitability for certain ages.

The roots of the dispute lay in the 1996 Telecommunications Act, which required new television sets to include a "V-chip" that would allow viewers to block objectionable programming. The device blocked programs based on their rating. Broadcast and cable companies were given until Feb. 8, 1997 to develop their own ratings system or defer to the Federal Communications Commission to develop guidelines. *(1996 act, Congress and the Nation Vol. IX, pp. 387, 397)*

Hoping to prod the industry to take greater action, the Senate Commerce, Science and Transportation Committee in May approved a bill (S 363—S Rept 105-89) that would give broadcasters a choice: adopt a content-based system or restrict violent programming to late-night hours. Lawmakers used the threat of legislation to prod the industry to act voluntarily. Finally in July, the industry agreed to make many of the changes called for by critics. The revised system added icons to signify sex, violence, coarse language, and suggestive dialogue to the original age-based rating system. The industry, in turn, secured a promise from lawmakers, including Senate Republican and Democratic leaders, that they would refrain for "several years" from pushing legislation that would change the ratings. Top House lawmakers gave similar assurances.

Internet Taxes

After months of negotiations, the high-tech industry scored a major victory in 1998 when the Senate cleared legislation placing a three-year moratorium on new taxes imposed on Internet access and commerce. During the required timeout period, a nineteen-member commission would study how taxes should be applied to the world of cyberspace. The measure was included in the fiscal 1999 omnibus spending bill (HR 4328—PL 105-277). *(Omnibus bill, p. 62)*

The moratorium legislation was first introduced in 1997 and drew harsh criticism from state and local government leaders, who asserted it would unfairly and unnecessarily preempt their taxing authority. Of particular concern were the potential effects the moratorium would have on sales taxes, which the National Governors' Association (NGA) said made up almost half of state revenues. But subsequent negotiations gave them enough concessions to withdraw their opposition.

BACKGROUND

Supporters of a moratorium warned that overzealous state and local officials in the nation's 30,000 taxing jurisdictions could obstruct the growth of the Internet by imposing new taxes. While acknowledging that there was no widespread effort to do this, they argued that the Internet would become an irresistible target.

Opponents such as the NGA and National League of Cities claimed the legislation would preempt state taxing authority. They were worried that a loophole used by mail-order companies would have a devastating effect on sales tax collections as shopping on the Internet becomes more popular. The Supreme Court had ruled that companies were not required to collect sales taxes from customers in states where the companies did not have a physical presence.

While House and Senate legislation proposed exempting sales, income, and other traditional taxes, they did not call for closing the out-of-state sales tax loophole.

LEGISLATIVE ACTION

The House was first out of the box when an early version of the bill cleared House Commerce and Judiciary subcommittees with jurisdiction over the Internet in October 1997. The bill sought to bar federal and state governments from implementing or enforcing taxes on Internet commerce indefinitely. The president would be required to seek agreements through various international trade organizations to make international activity on the Internet and interactive computer services tariff and taxation-free.

Changes were made at the full committee level by sponsor Rep. Christopher Cox, R-Calif., to address criticism from state and local leaders regarding their taxing authority. A substitute measure expanded the list of taxes that would be exempt from the moratorium, such as property taxes and levies paid by telecommunications vendors. It also limited the proposed moratorium to six years, instead of making it indefinite.

The Senate Commerce, Science and Transportation Committee approved its version of the legislation in November 1997, making many of the same changes Cox made in the House. However, action was deferred due to lingering concerns, such as the effect of the Internet on universal service, which sought to ensure that all Americans had access to affordable telephone service.

A revised bill emerged from the House Commerce Committee in May 1998, reflecting further negotiations between online industry representatives and state and local governments. The new bill imposed a three-year moratorium on taxing Internet access or online services. It also banned the Federal Communications Commission from regulating the charges subscribers pay for Internet access or online services. Another change was including a grandfather clause allowing states that were collecting Internet access taxes before Oct. 1, 1998, to continue doing so.

The House passed the revised bill in June, with the NGA offering a cautiously optimistic assessment. After a lengthy debate, the Senate passed its carefully crafted compromise in October 1998. Rather than go through further negotiations, the Senate then added the provision to the omnibus spending bill. *(2000 action, p. 335)*

Digital Copyright

Congress in 1998 cleared legislation (HR 2281—PL 105-304) updating protections for intellectual property in the digital age, marking the first significant updating of the nation's copyright laws in two decades. The legislation implemented two international treaties aimed at protecting legal protections for digital works, such as computer software and compact discs. It also gave Internet service providers limited liability protection for copyright infringement that takes place on their networks without their knowledge.

One important provision banned the manufacture, use, or sale of devices primarily designed to circumvent technology, such as encryption software, used to protect copyrighted works from theft. Librarians and educators expressed concern this would make it more difficult for people to access such works.

The legislation was introduced to update U.S. law in response to two World Intellectual Property Organization treaties signed in 1996 that established international recognition of copyrights for digitally produced goods, such as movies and software.

The growth of the Internet increased the frequency with which copyrighted works can be stolen. Moreover the digital format allowed thieves to send identical copies of software or music around the world with the click of a computer mouse, becoming de facto worldwide distributors.

The House Judiciary Committee spent much time debating the provision banning circumvention devices. Responding to concerns from librarians, lawmakers included a provision waiving fines established in the bill (H Rept 105-551, Pt. I) against nonprofit libraries, archives, and educational institutions for unintentionally violating the ban on circumventing technology. Meanwhile, online providers, telephone companies, libraries, universities, and copyright holders met for months with key lawmakers on the issue of limited liability protection.

The Senate Judiciary Committee further addressed the issue when it took up its version of the bill (S 2037—S Rept 105-190) in April, adding language sought by electronics manufacturers that clarified the manufacturers do not have to design their products to work with certain technological safeguards used by copyright holders to protect their works from infringers. The Senate passed its version in May. The House, after further negotiations, cleared its measure in August. The House-Senate conference removed a crucial sticking point by striking House-approved language, originally the subject of a separate bill, that would have provided legal protection for information collections such as computer databases.

The conference report (H Rept 105-796) was cleared by the Senate on Oct. 8, and by the House on Oct. 12. The bill was signed by President Clinton on Oct. 28. The legislation ensured that Americans will have "fair use" of copyrighted digital works, addressing concerns the bill could punish Americans who bypass technological protections for the purpose of using a product in a noninfringing way. Bill supporters, most notably Hollywood film studios that contributed more than $2.5 million in individual and political action committee donations to members of Congress in 1997–1998, said it brought them a step closer to using the Internet as a means of providing information and entertainment to consumers.

Internet Gambling

Efforts to curb Internet gambling died in 1998 after House and Senate negotiators could not reconcile their versions of legislation and add it to the year-end omnibus spending bill. The legislation would have made Internet gambling a crime punishable by up to four years in prison and $20,000 in fines, or the total amount of gambling proceeds. It also would have required Internet service providers to cut off service to gambling sites identified by authorities.

The Senate Judiciary Committee took the first step in trying to crack down on unregulated cyperspace gambling parlors in October 1997, approving a measure that would specifically prohibit gambling on the Internet. Existing law banned interstate gambling over telephone or other wire communications but did not specifically outlaw wagering on the Internet. Sponsor Sen. Jon Kyl, R-Ariz., said the legislation was needed to ensure that activity that was illegal in one forum is not allowed in another.

Most online gaming operations were, in fact, located outside of the United States and, thus, out of the reach of U.S. law, according to online industry representatives. The Senate measure attempted to address this with a provision that would allow state and federal officials with a court order to require an Internet service provider to block service to gambling sites.

The House Judiciary Committee took up the issue in 1998, with its crime subcommittee passing a version of the bill in September. The House bill would have directed Internet service providers to shut down gambling sites on their networks and prescribed fines of up to four years in prison for site operators. The Senate had added similar provisions in its fiscal 1999 Commerce-Justice-State appropriations bill in July. However, Kyl said the House measure was unacceptable because it contained too many loopholes, such as allowing parimutuel activities—for example horse racing—to be placed over the Internet as long as they were legal in the state or on the Native American reservation where the bet was being sent. The Senate measure only would allow bets to be placed on such races over closed-loop networks other than the Internet.

When an agreement could not be struck, the provisions were dropped when the Commerce-Justice-State bill was folded into the omnibus appropriations measure (HR 4328). *(1999 action, p. 337; omnibus bill, p. 62)*

Online Pornography

In a campaign against sin in cyberspace, lawmakers in 1998 agreed to crack down on Web sites that allow children to access pornography, and to increase penalties for sex offenders who use the Internet to distribute child pornography.

Over the objections of the Clinton administration, congressional leaders added the House-passed version of an antipornography bill (HR 3783) to the fiscal 1999 spending package (HR 4328—PL 105-277). The House passed the measure in October, while the Senate inserted a similar measure in its version of the fiscal 1999 Commerce-Justice-State spending bill.

Under the legislation, Web sites must require proof that Internet surfers are adults before providing access to material deemed "harmful to minors." Violators could face a $50,000 fine and six months in jail. The White House said it opposed the bill on the grounds that it preferred to promote the use of filtering software or other voluntary means to limit children's exposure to online smut. The Justice Department also questioned whether the legislation was constitutional.

Lawmakers also cleared a separate bill (HR 3494—PL 105-314) in October that targeted pedophiles who stalk children on the Internet. The bill prohibited knowingly transferring obscene material to a minor over the Internet or advertising information about a child to encourage or facilitate criminal sexual activity. The measure doubled from five to ten years the maximum prison sentence for enticing a minor to travel across state lines to engage in illegal sexual activity and increased from ten to fifteen years the maximum prison sentence for persuading a minor to engage in prostitution or a sexual act. The House initially passed the bill in June. The Senate passed a revised version in October, which the House accepted. The president signed the measure Oct. 30, 1998.

Satellite Fees/Cable TV Rates

Congress failed to pass legislation in 1998 that would have delayed increases in copyright rates for satellite retransmissions of superstation and distant network signals to home satellite television subscribers.

The bill (HR 2921) would have delayed until 2000 enforcement of a U.S. Copyright Office decision to raise those fees above the rates paid by cable television companies for the same transmissions. Proponents contended the increase makes it more difficult for satellite companies to compete with cable, and the delay would give Congress time to consider more equitable treatment. Opponents, especially the Motion Picture Association of America, said higher fees reflect the market value of those signals.

A revised version of the legislative language was incorporated in the Senate-passed Commerce-Justice-State appropriations bill but was not included in the final legislation. A delay in the satellite fee increase also was included in a broader bill (S 1720) approved by the Senate Judiciary Committee that also would have allowed satellite TV companies to retransmit local broadcast signals to subscribers. But supporters were unable to move the measure to the floor before adjournment. *(1999 action, p. 338)*

Cell Phone Fraud

Congress cleared legislation (S 493—PL 105-172) in 1998 making it a federal crime to use computer software to copy, or "clone," the electronic serial numbers of legal cellular phone users, then use the numbers to charge calls to the legal user's account.

Previously, prosecutors had to prove an "intent to defraud" in the use of such cloning devices, which they said was difficult unless an offender was caught in the act. The electronic serial numbers are transmitted to gain access to a telecommunications network. Thieves use scanners to pick up serial numbers, which can then be electronically copied into another cellular phone. Calls made from those doctored phones are then charged to the account of the phone from which the serial number was stolen.

The Senate first passed the anticloning bill in November 1997, in response to increasing reports of cell phone crime. In February 1998 the House passed its own version of the bill, proposing to ban the production, trafficking, and possession of "copycat" machines that allow thieves to clone cellular phones. Violators could face a fine and fifteen years in prison for a first offense. The legislation also allowed the government to seize property used to commit the crimes outlawed under the bill.

The Senate approved the House-amended version of the bill in April 1998, and President Clinton signed it April 24, 1998. The administration supported the bill, in part because of the property seizure provision the House added. The Senate never acted on a separate House-passed bill (HR 2369—H Rept 105-425) that would have made illegal the simple interception of cellular calls. The bill was a response to the 1996 interception of a cellular phone call between House Speaker Newt Gingrich, R-Ga., and members of the GOP leadership. Under existing law, the action was illegal only if a call is intentionally intercepted and disclosed.

'Slamming' Restrictions

Congress in 1998 sought to crack down on telecommunications companies that change a customer's long-distance service without permission, a practice known as "slamming." But the measure died in the final day of the session after getting entangled in an unrelated dispute in the Senate.

Backers of the legislation (HR 3888, S 1618) said slamming was a growing problem, generating more than 14,000 complaints to the Federal Communications Commission (FCC) in 1998. The House passed its version in October 1998, giving telecommunications vendors a choice: abide by voluntary antislamming rules that would be developed by the FCC, the industry, and consumer groups, or be subject to tougher FCC regulations. Some lawmakers worried the legislation would preempt tougher state laws and did not give states adequate authority to allow consumers to lock in their choice of a long-distance carrier. AT&T and some House members, however, objected that some companies might use lock-in language to freeze customers' choices and thwart competition.

One day before Congress adjourned, leaders of the Senate and House commerce committees announced an agreement on compromise language that would require the FCC to develop rules that would prevent companies from marketing freezes in an unfair or deceptive manner. However, Senate floor action on the legislation was blocked after Wendell H. Ford, D-Ky., tried to add an unrelated provision naming a federal courthouse after a Kentucky judge.

Year 2000 Computer Glitch

With the new century approaching, lawmakers in 1998 addressed growing concern that the federal government and key private industries might not be able to solve what was widely referred to as the Year 2000 computer problem. The problems stemmed from computer software written to assume the first two digits of a year are "19." If not corrected, policy makers said the glitch could cause computers to malfunction or crash on Jan. 1, 2000, with potential massive disruptions to government, commerce, and public utilities.

Congressional committees held numerous hearings to review public and private-sector efforts to address the problem. President Clinton in July announced a series of initiatives to address the problem, saying it could have disastrous consequences for government, banks, airlines, and other computer-dependent sectors. But Clinton's requests for emergency funding to speed Year 2000 preparations on federal computer systems ran into trouble when House Republican conservatives demanded that such funding be offset by spending cuts elsewhere. The lawmakers stripped emergency funds from the defense and Treasury-Postal appropriations bills, delaying approval of those and other funding measures.

Ultimately, Republican leaders and the White House negotiated the inclusion of $3.35 billion in emergency funding to fix government computers in the fiscal 1999 omnibus appropriations package (HR 4328—PL 105-277). Separately, Congress cleared legislation (S 2392—PL 105-271) in early October to encourage corporations to disclose information about their compliance efforts by limiting their liability for statements concerning such efforts. Companies had been reluctant to share information because of concerns that any disclosure they made could be used against them in court. *(Year 2000 liability, p. 336; omnibus bill, p. 62)*

The compromise version of the Senate disclosure bill barred, with a few exceptions, the use in court of a company's Year 2000 "readiness disclosure statement" to prove the accuracy of the company's assertions about how it dealt with the problem, except in cases where the court finds fraud. The measure also protected companies from liability for Year 2000 statements that are alleged to be false, misleading or inaccurate, unless it is proved that the company knowingly made false statements with the intent to deceive or mislead.

Congress also cleared legislation (HR 3116—PL 105-164) in late February and early March requiring federal banking agencies to offer suggestions to banks and other financial institutions on fixing their computers, and to monitor companies performing services for banks to ensure that they, too, addressed the problem.

1999–2000

Members of the 106th Congress continued to struggle to pass politically difficult measures dealing with commerce, communications, and transportation. For the second consecutive Congress, lawmakers failed to pass an electricity deregulation bill, or to draft new legislation to protect consumers' personal information from release on the Internet.

The House and Senate generally focused on narrowly tailored bills dealing with such topics as transportation safety and doing business in the digital age. One exception—a $40 billion, three-year reauthorization of the Federal Aviation Administration that guaranteed a spending boost for airport construction—was cleared only after a lengthy and tense fight over the federal aviation trust fund that mixed budget politics with transportation policy.

In transportation, lawmakers responded to public safety concerns arising from a huge recall of Firestone tires by requiring tiremakers to give federal regulators data on possible defects and by requiring the government to devise a crash test for auto rollovers. Congress also cleared legislation in response to critical government audits that established a new motor carrier administration to oversee truck and bus safety.

Lawmakers' attention to consumer issues in a presidential election cycle also was evidenced in telecommunications, where Congress cleared legislation that for the first time allowed satellite companies to deliver local broadcast stations in cities across the country, effectively matching those services offered by cable TV systems. The move was intended to place a check on the cable providers after federal cable rate regulation ended in 1999. Lawmakers also established a new $1.25 billion loan guarantee program to improve local broadcast reception in remote areas.

The high-tech industry continued to display influence, winning passage of contentious legislation authorizing the use of electronic signatures to close business transactions on the Internet. The industry also successfully lobbied for liability caps for businesses responsible for Year 2000, or Y2K, computer failures. High-tech business also won targeted legislation increasing statutory damages for copyright infringement in order to deter piracy of computer software.

Efforts to devise parameters for conduct for the Internet were decidedly mixed, as lawmakers tried to balance high-tech firms' calls for self-regulation with consumers' increasing desire for some basic protections. States won the right to halt interstate sales of alcohol via the Internet, but efforts to halt Internet gambling were defeated. Republicans and Democrats agreed to extend the moratorium on taxation of electronic commerce, but the effort stalled after governors insisted on the authority to collect sales taxes from online vendors.

Clashes between federal and state interests also dominated the debate over electricity deregulation, as House Republicans split on how to divide jurisdiction over deregulated markets. The Clinton administration and Democrats' insistence on requirements for the use of renewable energy further lessened chances for a resolution to the long-running issue.

If lawmakers had problems sorting out matters on Earth, they were more decisive in space matters. The House and Senate cleared a three-year NASA reauthorization in 2000, marking the first time in eight years the space agency had its own authorizing legislation. Lawmakers also passed a five-year extension of an arrangement in which the government shared the risk of commercial space launches with the aerospace industry.

FAA Reauthorization

Congress in spring 2000 cleared a three-year, $40 billion bill (HR 1000—PL 106-181) reauthorizing the Federal Aviation Administration (FAA) and guaranteeing huge spending increases for airport construction. The measure included a controversial provision ensuring that all revenue credited each year to the Airport and Airway Trust Fund will be taken "off-budget" and spent on aviation programs. The bill also allowed airports to increase the local fee on airline tickets and eased flight restrictions at some of the nation's most congested airports.

BACKGROUND

The aviation trust fund is a government bank account created in 1970 (PL 91-258) to help pay for the nation's airports and air transport system. It is financed mostly through a tax on domestic airline tickets and a separate flight segment tax. Other revenues come from taxes on aviation fuel, cargo, and international arrivals and departures

The growing balance in the trust fund at the time of the debate was due to several factors. Delays in modernizing the FAA's air traffic control computer system piled up money intended to pay for the project. Meanwhile, some funds could not be used to finance FAA operations due to restrictions transportation authorizing committees passed in the 1980s. The Congressional Budget Office estimated that the unobligated balance in the trust fund totaled $8.5 billion in fiscal 1999 and would grow to $45.6 billion in 2009.

LEGISLATIVE ACTION

House Transportation and Infrastructure Committee Chairman Bud Shuster, R-Pa., declared 1999 the year of aviation and put together an authorization bill that would triple airport construction grants and erect budgetary fences to lock in aviation spending levels. Shuster also added a provision to take the trust fund off-budget, meaning it would be exclusively dedicated to aviation capital projects and that any balance in the trust fund would not count toward the federal surplus or deficit.

But Shuster's Senate counterpart, Commerce, Science and Transportation Committee Chairman John McCain, R-Ariz., was more intent on trying to increase airline competition by relaxing restrictions on the number of flights allowed at four busy airports: Chicago's O'Hare International, New York's John F. Kennedy and LaGuardia, and Washington's Ronald Reagan National. McCain's bill was silent on the issue of taking the Airport and Airway Trust Fund off-budget, as Shuster proposed. McCain's Senate committee marked up its version of the bill in February 1999, but months of delay followed as some senators pressed objections to additional flights at the crowded airports.

The House Transportation and Infrastructure Committee approved Shuster's $89 billion proposal in March 1999. The legislation also included added flights at the four busy airports. The bill's off-budget treatment of the aviation trust fund drew fire from appropriators and fiscal conservatives.

Moving the fund off-budget shifted control to authorizers such as Shuster at the expense of appropriators, who bitterly opposed such changes and said it made balancing the budget more difficult. They also noted that general tax revenues already subsidize the aviation system.

With tensions mounting, Shuster in May convened an unusual, second markup of the bill, scaling the size of it to $16.5 billion and delaying the off-budget treatment of the trust fund to fiscal 2001, in order to conform with the fiscal 2000 budget resolution. While opponents again cried foul, Shuster pressed ahead.

During House floor debate on HR 1000, two powerful Republican appropriators, Appropriations Committee Chairman C. W. Bill Young, Fla., and Budget Committee Chairman John R. Kasich, Ohio, offered an amendment to remove the off-budget language from the reauthorization bill. The amendment was defeated in a **key vote of 179–248 (R 111–108; D 68–139; I 0–1)** on June 15, 1999. Later that day the House passed Shuster's measure on a roll-call vote of 316–110. *(1999 key votes, p. 899)*

McCain worked through the problems of senators who opposed added flights, and the Senate passed his version of the reauthorization (S 82—S Rept 106-9) on Oct. 5, 1999. Soon afterwards conferees began meeting to reconcile the significantly different versions of the bill. The major sticking point was the proposal by Shuster to make spending on aviation programs mandatory, effectively exempting it from the congressional appropriations process. Opponents, especially members of appropriations committees, argued such a spending guarantee would leave little money for other transportation needs. The conference dragged on for months as conferees were not able to narrow the gap on budget issues, as Shuster's insistence on spending guarantees drew the ire of budget hawks.

A six-month deadlock ended March 1, with an agreement brokered by Senate Majority Leader Trent Lott, R-Miss. All of the revenue and interest from the aviation trust fund would be appropriated for the next three years for aviation

programs—a projected total of $33 billion. Authorized spending for the airport improvement program would also increase from $1.9 billion in fiscal 2000 to $3.2 billion in 2001 and $3.4 billion by 2003. The deal also would increase the maximum passenger facility charge from $3 to $4.50 for each leg of travel. Airports can levy the charge for their own use. Airlines had opposed any increase in the fee. The measure also began to phase out restrictions on the number of flights at the New York and Chicago airports and allowed two dozen more flights per day at Reagan National.

Shuster had hoped to duplicate the success he had with the 1998 surface transportation bill, but he probably secured less than he expected. He was helped immeasurably by Lott, who was convinced that big spending increases were justified and who was eager to move the bill before budget season closed its window of opportunity.

The conference report on the bill passed the Senate on a roll-call vote of 82–17 on March 8, 2000. The House agreed to the conference report March 15, 2000, by a vote of 319–101. President Clinton signed the bill into law April 5, 2000.

Truck Safety

Congress in late 1999 cleared legislation (HR 3419—PL 106-159) creating a Federal Motor Carrier Administration to oversee truck and bus safety. The move stemmed from increased congressional concern over highway deaths in truck and bus accidents and reports from the Department of Transportation's inspector general that the department scaled back the enforcement activities of the Office of Motor Carriers even after the death toll was on the rise. The fiscal 2000 transportation appropriations bill cut off the budget of the motor carriers office unless it was moved out of the Federal Highway Administration.

Five House hearings on the issue led lawmakers to strip regulatory authority from the highway administration, which inherited many safety and regulatory functions of the Interstate Commerce Commission after Congress shut the agency down in 1995. Lawmakers and consumer advocates argued the safety mission had become buried in a bureaucracy that was primarily concerned with a $29 billion highway construction program. Critics also noted the Office of Motor Carriers often sided with the trucking industry.

Legislation by House Transportation and Infrastructure Committee Chairman Bud Shuster, R-Pa., would have created a motor carrier safety administration patterned on the Federal Aviation Administration to conduct compliance reviews of trucking companies and transfer money to states for roadside inspections. The bill passed the House in October.

Senate Commerce, Science and Transportation Committee Chairman John McCain, R-Ariz., pushed legislation that would have required a safety administration to implement all of the inspector general's recommendations for strengthening enforcement and overhauling data collection methods. In the final days of the session Shuster put together a new House bill combining elements of his and McCain's measures, informally worked out differences with Senate Commerce Committee members and quickly moved the measure through both houses. President Clinton signed it on Dec. 9.

Auto Safety

Riding a crest of consumer concern over a huge recall of Firestone tires, Congress in the fall of 2000 cleared legislation (HR 5164—PL 106-414) requiring manufacturers to give federal regulators a broad range of data on possible product defects and increased the penalties for those that withhold information. The bill also broke an impasse on whether the government should test and rate vehicles on rollover dangers, and it set the stage for revising federal tire standards for the first time since 1968. President Clinton signed the bill into law Nov. 1.

The legislative action began after Congress returned from its August recess following weeks of intense news coverage and public concern over the recall of 6.5 million tires made by Bridgestone/Firestone Inc. on sport utility vehicles. Tread separation was linked to accidents that claimed 101 lives, most when Ford Explorers rolled over. In several congressional hearings, executives from Bridgestone/Firestone and Ford Motor Co. acknowledged they had not told the government that some tires had been recalled overseas. The government, in turn, ignored tips from someone at State Farm Insurance Co. about a pattern of tire-related claims.

Senate Commerce, Science and Transportation Committee Chairman John McCain, R-Ariz., and House Commerce Committee Chairman W. J. "Billy" Tauzin, R-La., set out to try to close loopholes in federal regulations but wound up going much further, reaching a compromise on criminal penalties that had been anathema to industry.

McCain began the process with a hard-edged bill that the industry found totally unacceptable, warning that it would criminalize ordinary business decisions. McCain's efforts to bring the legislation to the Senate floor were blocked on several occasions by senators exercising anonymous "holds." The House bill mollified the industry with "safe harbor" language providing amnesty to employees who eventually admit to their criminal violations. With strong bipartisan backing and at least partial support from both business and consumer groups, the measure sailed easily through both chambers in October. The final bill included a provision requiring the government to devise a crash test for rollovers and offer the result to consumers. Before the Firestone recall, the auto industry had fought off rollover tests for years.

Steel, Oil, and Gas Subsidies

The domestic steel, oil, and gas industries got a boost from Congress in 1999 in the form of $1.5 billion in federally subsidized loans under a bill (HR 1664—PL 106-51) signed

---

FUEL EFFICIENCY STANDARDS

The ongoing tug-of-war between environmentalists and the automobile industry over fuel efficiency continued during President Bill Clinton's second term, producing an uneasy stalemate generally favorable to car manufacturers but keeping the issue on the public agenda.

Every year since Republicans took control of Congress in 1995, the House inserted a rider in the transportation appropriations bill to block the Transportation Department from developing new fuel standards, and the Senate always went along. The restriction was aggressively pushed by automakers and was endorsed, implicitly or sometimes explicitly, by labor unions affected by the economic health of the auto business.

But in 1999, a bipartisan group of senators, concerned about the rising number of fuel-hungry trucks, sport utility vehicles, and vans on the road, vowed to reverse the policy on environmental grounds. Backed by environmental advocacy groups, senators argued that more efficient cars and trucks would save consumers money while reducing pollution, global warming, and the U.S. trade deficit.

The effort to remove the House prohibition was made during consideration of the appropriation bill (HR 2084). Rather than a specific requirement, the amendment essentially expressed the sense of the Senate that the Department of Transportation should be allowed to study whether to raise the corporate average fuel economy (CAFE) standard for vehicles. The amendment also urged the Senate not to accept the House prohibition. But even the possibility of a study of new fuel-efficiency standards was too much for the auto industry and the Senate, which rejected the amendment on a **key vote of 40–55 (R 6–45; D 34–9; I 0–1)**. *(1999 key votes, p. 899)*

However, as part of the action on the transportation bill, the Senate insisted on the completion of study of the standards by the Transportation Department and the National Academy of Sciences, which was due in June 2001. The House went along with the Senate on the study.

---

by President Clinton in August. A simultaneous drive by the steel industry to impose import quotas on steel died in the Senate. *(Steel trade restrictions, p. 168)*

The legislation established a $1 billion loan guarantee program for qualified midsize steel companies hurt by "dumping" of below-cost foreign steel on the U.S. market. It also set up a $500 million fund for similar sized domestic oil and gas companies operating "stripper" wells, which had been hard hit by low oil prices. Authority to make loans under the program was to expire at the end of 2001. The guaranteed loans were to be repaid by the end of 2005 for steel companies and by the end of 2010 for oil and gas producers.

Bill champions initially folded the measure into the Senate-passed version of a supplemental spending bill for Central America and U.S. farmers, but it was stripped out, with conservative critics saying it was a well-intentioned but poorly designed special interest giveaway. Supporters made several changes, striking the emergency spending designation, shifting some of the loan risk back to the lenders and putting the chiefs of the Federal Reserve Board and the Securities and Exchange Commission on the loan funds' governing boards. The legislation authorized $270 million to cover loan defaults.

Patent Overhaul

Congress in November 1999 cleared legislation to overhaul the nation's patent system, including it in the omnibus spending bill (HR 3194—PL 106-113). The measure would allow publication of some patents within eighteen months of filing, cut some patent filing fees and restructure the U.S. Patent and Trademark Office. President Clinton signed the omnibus legislation Nov. 29, 1999. *(1997 action, p. 324; omnibus bill, p. 73)*

The requirement for publication of patent applications was a prime obstacle to passage of patent overhaul legislation in the 105th Congress. The key to compromise was a House agreement that would require publication within eighteen months only when inventors filed duplicate applications in the United States and another country that had similar requirements for publishing applications, such as Japan. The original bill would require publication of patents within eighteen months after applications were filed, a provision opponents said would infringe on the rights of inventors. The compromise effectively gave inventors the option of keeping applications secret by not filing them abroad.

Senators agreed on a compromise, similar to the House bill. House and Senate negotiators then put patent reform language in the conference report for a satellite television bill. The satellite language was later inserted in another bill (S 1948) which was, in turn, incorporated by reference in the omnibus. It included a House provision calling for a clear separation of the patent and trademark units of the Patent and Trademark Office. Manufacturers such as IBM Corp. and Dow Chemical Co. saw the patent overhaul measure as vital to speed up patent approvals and help U.S. businesses beat back foreign rivals in the race to get patent protection for new products, including computer chips and pharmaceuticals. Passage was assured when small inventors' concerns about publication of applications was addressed.

Copyright Infringement

The Senate in July 1999 cleared a bill (HR 3456—PL 106-160) to increase statutory damages for copyright infringe-

ment in order to deter piracy of computer software. President Clinton signed the measure on Dec. 9.

The bill provided statutory damages ranging from $750 to $30,000 for copyright infringement. The new minimum and maximum amounts would be approximately 50 percent higher than those in current law. Supporters said the measure was needed because copyright piracy of intellectual property had skyrocketed, made easier by the Internet and other advanced technologies. Software industry groups estimated that counterfeiting and piracy cost the affected copyright holders more than $11 billion in 1998.

Key lawmakers resolved differences between House and Senate versions of copyright infringement legislation. The key compromise was a deal on language calling for development of sentencing guidelines to enforce a 1997 law (HR 2265—PL 105-147) that prohibits software piracy. The bill had been delayed to allow time for the confirmation of new members of the U.S. Sentencing Commission, which develops sentencing guidelines for federal judges.

Telephone Excise Tax

One of congressional Republicans' last hopes for cutting taxes—legislation to repeal the 3 percent federal excise tax on telephones—died as the session came to a close in October 2000.

The tax, first enacted in 1898 to help finance the Spanish-American War, was widely regarded as archaic and regressive. The original 1 percent tax had been imposed on long-distance service at a time when telephones were a luxury. Congress repealed it in 1902 but brought it back to help pay for World War I. The tax was repealed again in 1924 but resurrected in 1932 during the Great Depression. In 1941 the tax was extended to general local service to help pay for World War II. The tax was increased to 3 percent in 1982 and made permanent in 1990 as part of efforts to balance the budget.

The House voted overwhelmingly, 420–2, on May 25, 2000, to approve legislation (HR 3916) that would phase out the levy over three years, at an estimated cost of $19.9 billion over five years. Both Democrats and Republicans said the tax was a burden on the poor that could widen the so-called "digital divide," limiting disadvantaged people's access to the Internet.

The Senate Finance Committee approved an amended version of the bill in June, proposing to repeal the tax in full on all phone bills after August 2000 at an estimated cost of $24.2 billion over five years. The White House was lukewarm to the idea, saying a repeal should not be put before other budget priorities, such as shoring up Medicare and Social Security. The administration also said it wanted to see the entire Republican tax package for the year before deciding whether to accept any one piece.

Uncertain about the fate of their other tax proposals, GOP leaders folded the three-year phase-out into the conference report on the fiscal 2001 Treasury-Postal Service and legislative branch appropriations bill. President Clinton vetoed that package Oct. 30.

Internet Taxes

Republicans and Democrats supported an extension of the moratorium on new Internet-specific taxes (PL 105-277) in 2000, but efforts to move legislation stalled after governors requested broader authority to collect current sales taxes from online vendors. The moratorium, created in 1998, was set to end in October 2001. The House, on a vote of 352–75, passed legislation (HR 3709) in May to provide a five-year extension, but the measure died in the Senate. *(1997–1998 action, p. 327)*

Extending the moratorium was a top goal of Internet-related business officials, who argued it would encourage the further growth of electronic commerce. The existing moratorium bars new access charges and e-mail tariffs but does not cover existing state sales taxes.

Initially, some lawmakers backed a plan to make the moratorium permanent. But governors urged Congress not to extend the moratorium unless it addressed an inequity between main street retailers, who must pay sales taxes, and online vendors, who often do not. Existing law allowed states to collect sales taxes only from businesses with a physical presence in their borders. Many governors asked lawmakers to endorse a plan to simplify state sales taxes and allow them to be collected from online vendors in other states.

Congress got less help than it had hoped from a nineteen-member advisory commission it created to study online taxation. The commission issued a report in April that called for a five-year extension of the moratorium, but the report was supported by only eleven members, two short of the two-thirds majority needed to make formal recommendations to Congress.

Despite the divided views of the panel, the House passed a five-year extension of the moratorium. Senate Commerce, Science and Transportation Committee Chairman John McCain, R-Ariz., introduced a similar bill, but it stalled in his committee when lawmakers split on whether to expand state sales tax collection powers. A compromise was elusive, as lawmakers were unable to cut a deal on language that would allow states to develop a national system for collecting state sales taxes.

Electronic Signatures

In June 2000 Congress cleared legislation (S 761—PL 106-229) authorizing the use of electronic signatures to close business transactions on the Internet. The final bill was a hard-fought bipartisan compromise and hailed by Republicans and Democrats as a milestone that would spur much wider use of the Internet while also protecting consumers from fraud.

The House and Senate produced significantly different versions of the bill in 1999, laying the foundation for a contentious conference in 2000. Conferees remained stalemated for weeks, largely over issues that went beyond the electronic signature provisions in both bills. The final bill conferred legal validity on electronic signatures, thus effectively superseding state laws that require written records to be kept.

The House bill (HR 1714) was a priority of the high-tech industry and would have authorized the use of electronic signatures and records in business transactions on the Internet. House Commerce Committee Chairman and bill sponsor Thomas J. Bliley, R-Va., said the measure constituted arguably the most important technology vote members would make. But Democrats and the Clinton administration opposed the House bill, saying it would allow businesses to run roughshod over important consumer protections, including requirements for written notice of such actions as foreclosure on a house or termination of electrical service. The House bill was passed on Nov. 9, 1999, in a roll-call vote of 356–66, after majority Republicans defeated a Democratic substitute that would have limited its scope.

In the Senate key lawmakers reached a compromise on legislation that the Democratic substitute offered in the House. The bill authorized the use of electronic signatures, ranging from passwords to signatures written on touch-sensitive computer screens, and established a national standard for using them in electronic commerce.

Negotiations pitted high-tech interests and financial service companies against consumer groups and state governors. The House bill, backed by a wide range of business groups, offered companies the option of providing loan terms and other consumer protection information electronically to consumers who preferred to receive it that way. It also sought to preempt existing laws requiring companies to keep original paper records of transactions. Financial service firms hoped that reducing paperwork could produce significant savings in handling and storage costs.

But consumer protection organizations and state officials backed the Senate measure, which would have given states considerable leeway to continue requiring paper records. Advocates said adopting the House language could lead to a rush to electronic commerce that could outstrip antifraud laws designed for a society based on paper records. Democrats additionally argued that many Americans were not familiar with the use of e-mail and might not be able to get important consumer information that is provided only over the Internet and not by regular mail.

A compromise finally was reached in June 2000, when Sen. Phil Gramm, R-Tex., a champion of financial service companies, agreed to concessions on consumer protections offered by Bliley to assuage key Democrats. The final language gave deals signed electronically the same legal standing as paper contracts. Consumers could open bank accounts, transfer money, and buy major items such as cars without having to sign any paperwork. However, the bill also required companies to verify that customers have the necessary technology to receive electronic records before they waive their right to receive paper copies. Customers must demonstrate they can open electronic files and can opt out of the agreement at any time. Some sensitive documents, such as wills, court orders, and eviction notices, would still be provided on paper. The bill also required that new regulations be developed to ensure that electronic data are stored in a way that prevents tampering.

The House approved the conference report in a **key vote of 426–4 (R 216–3; D 208–1; I 2–0)** on June 14. The Senate cleared the final agreement, 87–0, on June 16, and President Clinton signed the measure on June 30. *(2000 key votes, p. 915)*

Year 2000 Liability

Five months before the arrival of the new millennium, in July 1999, Congress cleared and President Clinton signed a law (HR 775—PL 106-37) designed to resolve lawsuits over potential computer breakdowns associated with the so-called Year 2000, or Y2K, problems. The high-tech industry argued liability caps in the law were essential to prevent companies from being crippled by lawsuits.

A wide range of businesses had expressed concern that they could be held liable for damages if they were unable to deliver products or services because of computer glitches on Jan. 1, 2000. The Y2K bug is the result of shortcomings in software that caused many computers to only recognize the last two digits of every year and assume the first two were "19." If the problem went uncorrected, those computers would mistakenly recognize the year 2000 as the year 1900. *(Year 2000 computer glitch, p. 330)*

Representatives of high-tech companies said during congressional hearings that many newer computer systems did not contain the Y2K flaw and would not malfunction. But they remained concerned that older computers and software would not operate properly, creating scenarios where grocers' cash register systems would not accept credit cards with expiration dates in 2000 or doctors' office management software would not make appointments beyond December 1999.

The legislation ran into opposition from trial lawyers and some consumer groups, who feared it would set a precedent for broader product liability reform. Opponents argued that liability limits would relieve pressure on companies to fix defective computers. Two House Republicans from Virginia, Thomas M. Davis III and Robert W. Goodlatte, helped shepherd the bill through the House in May over the trial lawyers' opposition. Senate passage came after two motions to invoke cloture failed in April and May, and Commerce Committee Chairman John McCain, R-Ariz., worked out a compromise with Democrats to drop liability protections for corporate officers and narrow a cap on damages so that it only applied to small businesses.

In conference, Republicans ended an impasse by agreeing with a Clinton administration demand to narrow federal jurisdiction for larger legal claims. The compromise required lawsuits seeking more than $10 million in damages to be filed in federal court. The House cleared the final version, 404–24, on July 1. That same day the Senate passed the measure by a vote of 81–18. The president signed the bill into law July 20.

The high-tech industry got much of what it wanted, however. The law applied to lawsuits in state or federal courts brought after Jan. 1, 1999, that allege actual or potential Y2K-related computer failures that occur or cause harm before 2003. It provides that defendants are liable only for their share of blame for any Y2K damage. That language was designed to prevent big companies from being held liable for the lion's share of damages in lawsuits. The law gave companies up to ninety days to fix problems before a lawsuit can be brought. Punitive damages were capped at $250,000 or three times the amount of compensatory damages, whichever is less, for companies with fewer than fifty employees or individuals with a net worth of $500,000 or less.

Encryption Exports

The White House in September 1999 announced it would relax its policy on restricting exports of strong technology to encode communications, in an effort to preempt congressional action. The move came as the House was preparing to pass legislation (HR 850) that would lift most export controls on encryption technology used to scramble telephone calls and online communications. The more liberal White House policy would not apply to exports to seven nations: Cuba, Iran, Iraq, Libya, North Korea, Sudan, and Syria.

Law enforcement officials, including the FBI, had complained the legislation could put strong encoding technology in the hands of criminals, making it harder to wiretap their telephone calls. But supporters argued the House bill would prevent illegal activities by setting penalties of up to five years in prison for using encryption to try to hide a crime.

Senate Commerce, Science and Transportation Committee Chairman John McCain, R-Ariz., proposed a compromise (S 798) that would have allowed the export of some stronger encryption products and permitted exports of other products if they were found by the Commerce Department to be generally available. Despite support for the two bills, some senior lawmakers in the House and Senate opposed the weakening of export controls. Congress decided to consider the White House plan before continuing work on the legislation.

Internet Domain Names

Congress late in 1999 moved to crack down on the practice of "cyber-squatting," the unauthorized use of trademark-protected names in Internet addresses. Language to extend protection of trademarks to such addresses was added to the conference report for the omnibus spending bill (HR 3194—PL 106-113), which President Clinton signed on Nov. 29.

Lawmakers from both parties sought to end the practice of individuals registering and using choice Internet addresses that featured trademark-protected names, such as Coca-Cola or Microsoft. The problem arose when companies tried to establish Internet addresses and discovered that others had already registered their trademarks as part of an Internet address. In some cases, investors marked up prices for these addresses and offered to sell them back to the trademark owners at inflated prices.

Senate language would allow trademark owners to collect civil damages of $1,000 to $100,000 for unauthorized use of their brand names in Internet addresses. In the House, lawmakers inserted provisions to cover unauthorized use of the names of famous persons and to prevent civil damages in cases of inadvertent use of trademarks.

The domain-name language was first added to the conference report on a satellite television bill, then later included in a new Senate bill that was added to the omnibus.

Internet Alcohol/Gambling

States got new power to halt interstate sales of alcohol via the Internet as part of an anticrime package (HR 3244—PL 106-386) enacted in October 2000. Attempts to ban gambling on the Internet, however, died in the House. *(1998 action, p. 328; crime package, p. 629)*

Liquor wholesalers successfully teamed up with proponents of restricting liquor sales to minors to pass the legislation giving states new power to limit Internet alcohol sales. The provision allowed state attorneys general to file federal suits for injunctive relief against alcohol distributors who sell directly to consumers in states where such sales are banned.

Supporters said the changes would help enforce the laws of at least nineteen states and, while no proof-of-age requirements are in place for Internet alcohol sales, would discourage liquor sales to minors. Opponents, particularly California wineries, argued Internet alcohol sales are important for smaller wineries and breweries that are unable to secure limited shelf space in liquor stores for their products. The provisions resembled a bill (HR 2031) passed by the House in 1999 and language in the Senate-passed version of a juvenile crime bill (HR 1501).

Attempts to outlaw Internet casinos gained momentum in late 1999 after the Senate resolved a dispute over online gambling operations owned by Native American tribes. Legislation (S 692) passed at the end of the session would permit tribes to collect bets from online gambling customers physically located on Native American reservations in states where games were allowed.

A House bill (HR 3125) did not include language on Native American tribes but mirrored the Senate measure by out-lawing gambling businesses from using the Internet to place or receive a bet. Both bills proposed penalties of up to four years in prison and up to a $20,000 fine. However, an unlikely alliance of the Clinton administration, state lottery advocates, and social conservatives teamed up to scuttle the legislative effort. Social conservatives and the White House opposed exemptions that would allow state-sanctioned, closed-circuit networks for dog, horse, and jai alai betting that bill sponsors included to mollify lawmakers from states such as Florida, where such betting is legal. State lottery interests, meanwhile, opposed the bill because it would ban lottery ticket sales to consumers in their homes via the Internet. In the end the House bill was defeated in July under suspension of the rules, a procedure requiring a two-thirds majority for passage and usually reserved for noncontroversial measures.

Internet Privacy

Despite pressure from consumer groups and the Clinton administration, lawmakers in 2000 were unable to craft legislation to protect consumers' personal information from release on the Internet.

Top lawmakers in both chambers tended to side with high-tech companies' demands for self-regulation. As a result, there was little movement on numerous proposals aimed at protecting an individual's right to prevent personal information from being distributed by off-line and Internet companies.

Lack of a consensus was evident on Oct. 2, 2000, when the House failed on a procedural vote, 250–146, to pass a bill (HR 4049) establishing a commission to study privacy issues. At the same time, Senate Judiciary Committee Chairman Orrin G. Hatch, R-Utah, agreed to pull provisions from a bill to combat electronic crime (S 2448) that would have required commercial web sites to post privacy policies.

Lawmakers also failed to make headway on a package of electronic surveillance and privacy measures backed by the White House that included safeguards for the release of personal medical and financial information (HR 4380). The Clinton-backed proposal was introduced amidst revelations that market research firm DoubleClick Inc. was doing in-depth profiling of Internet users based on their web surfing habits, and that the FBI was using the controversial Carnivore e-mail wiretap system.

One piece of privacy-related legislation that received serious consideration was a provision in the fiscal 2001 Commerce-Justice-State spending bill (HR 4942—PL 106-553) that would have barred acquisition of a person's Social Security number with the intent to do harm. The proposal was designed to keep Social Security numbers from being sold over the Internet, but critics said changes made during negotiations with financial service firms left loopholes that actually could weaken existing personal information protection. The provision was in the spending bill as cleared in October, but was removed during negotiations in December before the measure was sent to the president.

Satellite TV

Congress in November 1999 cleared legislation allowing satellite television companies to deliver local broadcast stations in cities across the country, effectively matching the services provided by rival cable television systems. President Clinton on Nov. 29 signed the bill, which was incorporated into the omnibus spending measure (HR 3194—PL 106-113).

Lawmakers worried the end of cable TV rate regulation on March 31 under the 1996 Telecommunications Act would lead to higher prices and wanted to enact legislation to help satellite services compete with cable. The centerpiece of their effort was a measure to permit satellite television companies for the first time to carry the same local broadcast signals that are routinely offered on the basic tiers of cable service. *(1998 action, p. 329)*

Supporters of the legislation in the House and Senate quickly agreed on key provisions to give satellite companies the new capabilities. But lawmakers disagreed over conditions for retransmission agreements and proposals by satellite providers to carry network affiliates nationally to some suburban customers.

In the House, lawmakers kept a ban enacted as part of legislation in the 100th Congress banning satellite delivery of broadcast signals from other cities to customers who already receive local stations via over-the-air antennas. The House measure instructed the Federal Communications Commission (FCC) to develop a new standard to determine whether viewers could qualify to receive stations from other cities.

In the Senate, Commerce, Science and Transportation Committee Chairman John McCain, R-Ariz., an ally of satellite TV interests, developed other proposals, such as giving satellite providers a temporary waiver to allow them to continue developing the same level of service they provided customers in July 1998, while conducting tests to determine whether they violated the ban on providing programming from other cities that competed with local stations.

House and Senate negotiators cleared the way for completing a conference report for the satellite TV bill (HR 1554) by reaching a compromise to let satellite TV providers carry local broadcast stations immediately, even before they begin negotiations on retransmission agreements with local station owners. The agreements would have to be signed within six months of enactment. The compromise bill also required satellite providers to carry all local stations—or none—in areas they serve by 2002. Lawmakers overcame the final obstacle to floor action by deleting a $1.25 billion loan guarantee program to improve television reception in rural areas. They added the remaining provisions to another bill (S 1948), which was then incorporated into the omnibus spending measure and cleared Nov. 19.

The bill also renewed licenses for satellite providers to carry copyright-protected broadcast programming. The copyright licenses would have expired on Dec. 31, without action by Congress. Other provisions dealing with a range of pending issues included a requirement that public broadcasting stations obtain the permission of donors before sharing their names with any third parties including marketing companies. The language barred federal funding for stations that share any donor lists with political parties and candidates. The bill language also authorized a new FCC license for low power television.

Rural TV Subsidy

Congress in 2000 agreed to create a loan guarantee program to help rural direct-broadcast satellite and cable television systems beam local broadcast stations to viewers who do not have access to local over-the-air television reception. The measure was enacted as part of the Commerce-Justice-State appropriations bill (HR 4942—PL 106-553).

Senate leaders during the 1999 appropriations process agreed to delete the loan guarantee program from a broader bill designed to allow satellite services to transmit local stations. Senate Banking, Housing and Urban Affairs Committee Chairman Phil Gramm, R-Tex., objected that the loan guarantee program had to be examined by his committee. The compromise stipulated that Congress begin debate on the program by March 30, 2000.

Proponents of loan guarantees argued they would ensure that rural residents could receive local broadcast signals. Residents in remote areas often cannot receive the broadcast signals of the major networks from the nearest metropolitan areas. Satellite providers and cable systems argued they do not have the money or the broadcast spectrum to expand their coverage to include these areas.

The Senate passed a bill (S 2097—S Rept 106-243) that sought to authorize a $1.25 billion loan program and guarantee up to 80 percent of each loan. The measure passed without a single nay vote, 97–0, on March 30, 2000. A similar House bill (HR 3615—H Rept 106-508, Pt. I) that passed in April, by a vote of 375–37, was a compromise between a $1 billion program with an 80 percent limit on guarantees passed by the Commerce Committee and a $1.25 billion program with guarantees of up to 100 percent approved by the Agriculture Committee. The bill called for the loans to be administered by the Rural Utilities Service, a division of the Department of Agriculture that oversees a $42 billion loan portfolio supporting rural telecommunications, electric, and water projects.

Lawmakers voiced some concern over two audits questioning the effectiveness of the Rural Utilities Service and over the bill's cost. The Congressional Budget Office estimated the bill would translate into a taxpayer subsidy of $350 million. After months of negotiations over the details, the House and Senate agreed to a $1.25 billion loan program and an 80 percent loan guarantee, with loans available to cable companies only for use in providing service to areas that currently are underserved.

CHAPTER 7

Environment and Energy

Introduction   341

1997–1998 Chronology   345

1999–2000 Chronology   372

Environment and Energy

With partisan tensions sharply dividing the Democratic White House and congressional GOP leaders, lawmakers made little headway on environmental and energy issues during Bill Clinton's second term. The 105th Congress could lay claim to just two significant environmental bills: implementing an international agreement to protect dolphins during tuna fishing operations and revamping management of the national wildlife refuge system. The 106th Congress produced just one major piece of legislation, a multibillion-dollar measure that aimed to restore the biologically diverse Florida Everglades.

On the energy front, Congress cleared a low-level nuclear waste measure in 1998 and partially revamped the embattled Department of Energy in 1999. Energy issues, a relatively low priority during much of the 1990s, generated sharp partisan debate when fuel prices began climbing in 2000.

Repeatedly clashing with each other and the Clinton administration, however, members of Congress found themselves unable to reach consensus on a far longer list of issues, including the superfund toxic waste cleanup program, Endangered Species Act, clean water act, grazing rights on western lands, government purchases of ecologically sensitive land, the disposal of high-level nuclear waste, and deregulation of the electricity markets. Many of those items had lingered on the congressional agenda for years, and there was no indication that Congress was making significant progress in resolving them.

Ominously, political leaders could not come to terms on environmentally pressing issues that scientists believed could ultimately sap the nation's economic vigor. At the top of the list, the threat of global warming captured the attention of world leaders in the 1990s. A somewhat reluctant President Clinton signed the 1997 Kyoto protocol on global warming, an international agreement that committed the United States to sharply cut emissions of carbon dioxide and other gases blamed for warming the earth's climate. The treaty, however, ran into such a storm of criticism on Capitol Hill that the White House never submitted it to the Senate for ratification.

With Republicans holding slender majorities in the House and Senate, business leaders and advocates of private property rights hoped to roll back environmental regulations that they blamed for stifling economic growth. But many Democrats, joined by a coalition of moderate Republicans from the Northeast, the Great Lakes, and Florida, parried attempts to relax requirements to clean up toxic waste, protect rare species, and limit logging in national forests. Even as conservatives fumed that environmental laws had grown too inflexible, they found themselves unable to revamp them.

In all, the 105th and 106th Congresses ranked as among the least productive on environmental issues since the 1960s or earlier. In addition, despite facing skyrocketing fuel costs in 2000, Congress failed to coalesce behind a national strategy to either boost production or encourage conservation.

With lawmakers at an impasse, the administration took a series of extraordinary steps to protect public lands and tighten air and water quality laws. Clinton dusted off the 1906 Antiquities Act to create more than a dozen national monuments, thereby forestalling efforts to mine or otherwise develop economically valuable land. He also barred the building of roads in almost sixty million acres of national forest land, and his administration rolled out stringent new air and water pollution regulations.

Such actions won strong kudos from the weakened environmental movement. Even though Republicans assailed Clinton for abusing his powers and putting rural economies at risk, they failed to muster the votes to block the White House initiatives.

REFERENCES

Discussion of environmental and energy policy for the years 1945–1964 may be found in *Congress and the Nation Vol. I*, pp. 771–1095; for the years 1965–1968, *Congress and the Nation Vol. II*, pp. 463–528; for the years 1969–1972, *Congress and the Nation Vol. III*, pp. 745–849; for the years 1973–1976, *Congress and the Nation Vol. IV*, pp. 201–320; for the years 1977–1980, *Congress and the Nation Vol. V*, pp. 451–530, 533–597; for the years 1981–1984, *Congress and the Nation Vol. VI*, pp. 333–400, 403–482; for the years 1985–1988, *Congress and the Nation Vol. VII*, pp. 417–495; for the years 1989–1992, *Congress and the Nation Vol. VIII*, pp. 467–532; for the years 1993–1996, *Congress and the Nation Vol. IX*, pp. 401–476.

Outlays for Natural Resources and Environment

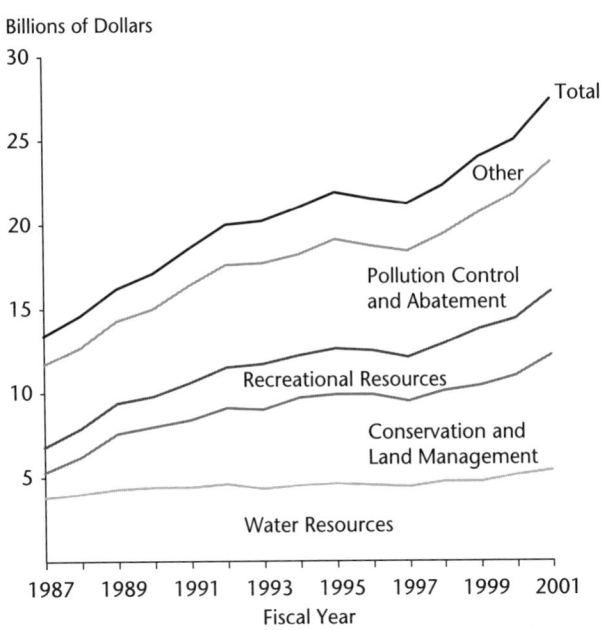

Billions of Dollars

NOTE: Data for 2001 are estimated.

SOURCE: Office of Management and Budget, *Historical Tables, Budget of the United States Government: Fiscal Year 2002* (Washington, D.C.: U.S. Government Printing Office, 2001), Table 3.2.

THE ENVIRONMENTAL MOVEMENT

The ambivalence over environmental regulation seemed to mark a return to an earlier era. Before the environmental movement began to gather strength in the 1960s, pollution had been widely tolerated as the price of progress, a necessary byproduct of the emergence of the United States as the world's economic and industrial giant.

But by the 1960s, worsening air pollution and the spread of industrial chemicals raised widespread public concerns about the environment. The mass media focused attention on smog-choked cities, coastal oil spills, and waste-clogged waterways, and dangerous use of pesticides and other chemicals. A number of scientific studies also warned of the potentially dire consequences of air, water, and soil contamination—both to the environment and to public health.

What had been mainly a localized, grassroots environmental movement became a large-scale national campaign. The perceived public demand for pollution cleanup and prevention elevated environmentalism to a bipartisan cause in Washington. Responding to the public clamor, President Richard Nixon vowed in his 1971 State of the Union address "to restore and enhance our natural environment," and the Democratic-controlled Congress lent overwhelming support for environmental initiatives. In such a climate, there was little resistance to enactment of the nation's fundamental environmental laws, including the National Environmental Policy Act of 1970, the Clean Air Act of 1970, a clean water rewrite in 1972, the Endangered Species Act of 1973, and the Safe Drinking Water Act of 1974.

The energy shortages of the 1970s also sparked a series of conservation acts. Lawmakers funded research to improve the use of existing fuels and promote the development of new sources of energy, in addition to imposing fuel efficiency standards on new cars.

Revelations of health-endangering industrial carelessness continued to drive the environmental agenda. The discovery of toxic chemical wastes buried at the Love Canal subdivision in Niagara Falls, N.Y., spurred the enactment in 1980 of the Comprehensive Environmental Response, Compensation, and Liability Act, better known as the superfund law. At the same time, Congress also pursued the protection of public lands—an effort that culminated with the 1980 Alaska National Interest Lands Conservation Act, which set aside more than 100 million acres of land.

Perhaps inevitably, the web of new laws sparked an antienvironmental reaction. As early as 1975 President Gerald R. Ford argued that expensive pollution controls contributed to both inflation and unemployment. In the late 1970s western conservatives, harboring a historic resentment over federal ownership of much of their region's land, sparked a "Sagebrush Rebellion" to demand greater access to public lands for natural resource development and livestock grazing.

Ronald Reagan, the Republican who capitalized on anti-Washington sentiment to win the presidency in 1980, sought to ease environmental laws. But his administration's controversial promotion of selling off public lands and slashing EPA's enforcement of regulations turned into great fund-raising tools for environmentalist groups, who succeeded in labeling his White House as extremist. By the end of his presidency, Reagan had signed bills to remove asbestos from public school buildings and increase funding for superfund cleanups.

Reagan's GOP successor, George Bush, campaigned in 1988 on a pledge to be the "environmental president." Although he frequently drew the ire of environmentalists over such issues as failing to protect endangered species, he signed a revision of the Clean Air Act in 1990 that clamped down on pollutants that could cause acid rain. He also signed the 1992 Energy Policy Act, which sough to boost alternative energy use and increase energy efficiency.

ANTIREGULATORY BACKLASH

By the early 1990s sharp partisan and regional divisions had fractured the formerly broad support for environmental laws. Manufacturers and other large businesses complained that federal regulators set overly costly, super-clean standards that were disproportionate to the environmental risks. Small business owners saw their livelihoods threatened by regulatory and paperwork burdens. State and local officials said their coffers were being depleted by unfounded mandates issued under federal environmental laws. Landowners worried that the Endangered Species Act and other laws unfairly prevented them from developing their properties.

In some respects, the environmental movement had become a victim of its own success. With air, water, and soil at least somewhat cleaner, and endangered species such as the bald eagle staging a comeback, public interest in environmental regulations began to wane. Some worried that the push to remove all residual pollutants had diverted resources from other pressing social problems.

Furthermore, maintaining public support for environmental regulation was easier when most of the direct impact was on industry smokestacks and water discharge pipes. As the environmental statutes succeeded in cleaning up many of these "point sources," lawmakers and regulators turned their attention to more widespread "non-point source" pollution, such as generalized water runoff from lawns, roadways, farm fields, and other surfaces. Efforts to reduce pollution from these sources affected individuals, farmers, and small business owners, some of whom rebelled against the imposition of costs or lifestyle restrictions threatened by new regulations.

But the most politically explosive element of the regulatory regime was its effect on private property use. Regulatory restrictions on land uses under such laws as the Endangered Species Act and the wetlands provisions of the clean water act spurred the rapid development of a "private property rights" movement. Private property rights advocates, who took their cause to courts as well as to Congress, wanted to ensure that landowners who lost their livelihoods or whose property values decreased because of federal regulations were compensated by the federal government.

When Clinton took office in 1993, he faced enormous resistance in the 103rd Congress to an ambitious but unfocused agenda of environmental regulations. Even though Democrats controlled the White House and both chambers of Congress for the first time since 1980, Democratic initiatives to toughen the clean water act, update superfund and other environmental statutes, and transform the EPA into a cabinet-level agency all foundered in the face of conservative resistance. Clinton drew fire from environmentalists and loggers alike when he proposed limits on logging in the Pacific Northwest to protect the endangered northern spotted owl. The new administration also was forced to backpedal on an ambitious effort to increase grazing fees on federal lands.

After capturing control of Congress in the 1994 elections, Republicans mounted a major effort to scale back environmental regulations. But GOP efforts to force federal agencies to justify new regulations, give states and localities more leeway in waiving certain environmental requirements, and boost the rights of private property owners sparked a dramatic political backlash. Skewered in the press for siding with polluters and criticized by some moderates within their own ranks, chastened Republican leaders abandoned their more ambitious environmental efforts. Instead, they settled for compromise bills to bolster pesticide regulations and reauthorize the Safe Drinking Water Act.

AN INCREMENTAL APPROACH

After failing to wrest the White House from Bill Clinton in 1996, Republicans in the 105th Congress returned warily to the fray. Rather than attempting to enact sweeping legislation to transform the nation's environmental policies, they focused on narrower bills and incremental changes.

Outlays for Energy

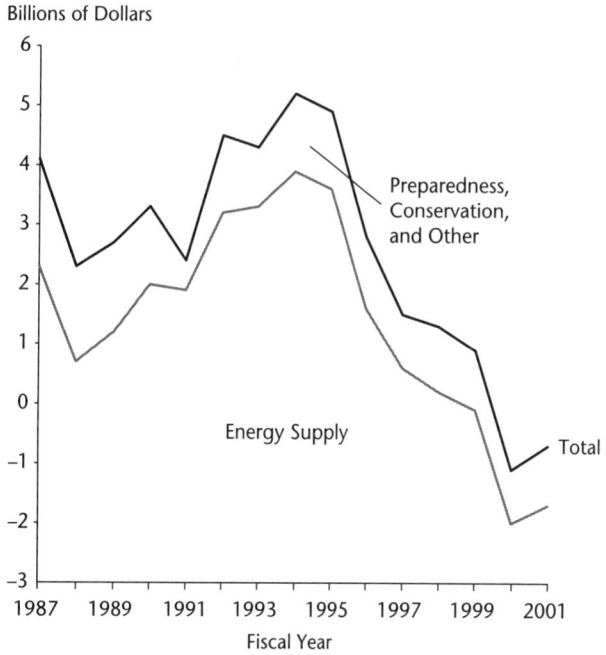

NOTE: Data for 2001 are estimated.

SOURCE: Office of Management and Budget, *Historical Tables, Budget of the United States Government: Fiscal Year 2002* (Washington, D.C.: U.S. Government Printing Office, 2001), Table 3.2.

Republicans who lived west of the Mississippi River used their newfound moderation to score some preliminary victories in the 105th Congress, especially in the House. They won votes in 1997 on such issues as:

• Giving property owners greater access to federal courts and new clout with local zoning boards.

• Revising grazing policy on federal lands, while agreeing to a modest increase in grazing fees.

• Curbing presidential authority, granted under the 1906 Antiquities Law, to set aside federal tracts vulnerable to environmental threats.

Western Republicans still continued to favor the rights of property owners, back commercial uses of public land, and champion such causes as federal funding for building logging roads in national forests. But they sought to portray their efforts as moderate and friendly to the environment, sloughing off the "extremist" label they had acquired in the 104th Congress. Tensions still ran high between eastern Republicans, who often voted against the westerners on environmental proposals, and the westerners, who resented them for it. But in some cases, the differences were overcome.

Despite such efforts at moderation, Republicans in the 105th Congress could not press home even incremental changes to such contentious programs as superfund. Attempts to make significant changes in environmental laws tended to provoke a presidential veto threat, while more moderate plans sparked the opposition of key conservatives. A rewrite of the Endangered Species Act drew opposition from both environmentalists and property rights advocates; a modest rewrite of grazing fees regulations won over eastern

Republicans but provoked White House opposition, and attempts to revamp superfund never made it to the House or Senate floor.

Efforts at compromise, however, did produce one significant domestic environmental achievement in the 105th Congress: revamping management of the National Wildlife Refuge System. Lawmakers also cleared a much-discussed bill to implement an international agreement aimed at protecting dolphins from being drowned inadvertently during tuna fishing expeditions.

If the 105th Congress saw relatively little progress on environmental issues, the 106th proved just as disappointing. House Resources Committee Chairman Don Young, R-Alaska, reached across the aisle in an ambitious effort to guarantee $3 billion annually in offshore drilling revenues for a host of federal and state conservation programs. The popular plan, a top priority for environmentalists and the administration, died because of opposition by property rights advocates and deficit hawks.

Lawmakers in the 106th Congress also failed to make headway on the usual lineup of hotly debated environmental issues. But with Republicans concerned about perceptions that they favored industry over the environment, GOP leaders in 2000 won passage of landmark legislation to restore the Florida Everglades. Congress also created two new national parks—the first since the Republican takeover in 1995.

ENERGY DEBATES

Energy issues commanded relatively little attention in the 105th Congress. In fact, boosting energy supplies was a secondary concern throughout much of the 1990s because of low fuel prices and relatively abundant supplies. Instead, lawmakers focused primarily on nuclear waste issues. As in previous years, they could not agree on creating a temporary repository for nuclear waste in Nevada, even though they worried that continuing to store the waste at nuclear power plants throughout the country could pose a safety hazard. A bipartisan majority did succeed in clearing a less-controversial measure establishing a three-state compact on the disposal of low-level waste in Texas.

By 2000 energy had emerged as a major political issue because of a series of oil and natural gas price spikes. Neither GOP proposals to increase supply nor Democratic plans to encourage conservation made their way through Congress. Lawmakers also found themselves divided over the highly contentious issue of deregulating the electricity market, although a House subcommittee succeeded in marking up a deregulatory plan.

The disposal of high-level nuclear waste continued to stymie policymakers. When Congress cleared a bill to create a short-term storage facility in Nevada, Clinton vetoed it—and supporters lacked the votes in Congress to override the veto.

One issue that did unite lawmakers was the need to boost security at the Department of Energy. When a series of security breaches spurred alarms that the department's weapons programs were vulnerable to espionage, Congress added provisions to the fiscal 2001 defense appropriations bill to create a separate security unit within the department.

CLINTON'S INITIATIVES

Much of the environmental skirmishing during the 105th and 106th Congresses focused on the administration's efforts to reduce emissions of greenhouse gas emissions, strengthen air and water pollution regulations, and protect public lands. Republicans turned repeatedly to the appropriations process to prevent the White House from following the Kyoto protocol in reducing U.S. emissions of carbon dioxide and other pollutants. Lawmakers from both parties also raised concerns about an aggressive plan unveiled by EPA administrator Carol Browner in 1997 to crack down on two air pollutants: ozone and particulate matter. Two years later, Browner set off another firestorm when she announced a plan to force states to cut down on non-point source pollution.

Clinton stirred even more controversy by repeatedly using his authority to create national monuments without congressional consent. He protected more than three million acres from drilling, logging, mining, grazing, and other potentially environmentally destructive activities. Such actions won strong praise from environmentalists who likened him to Theodore Roosevelt, but harsh criticism from conservatives who claimed he was usurping the democratic process. To the exasperation of Republicans, Clinton also unveiled rules late in his term to ban new logging roads in nearly sixty million acres of national forests despite warnings that such a prohibition could set back rural economies dependent on logging. With the Senate and the House closely divided between Republicans and Democrats, lawmakers found themselves hopelessly deadlocked over proposals to revamp existing laws or modify Clinton's actions.

In many ways, the congressional deadlock reflected public ambivalence over environmental protection. Although environmentalists pointed to polls showing support for such proposals as protecting more land from development, conservation appeared to have faded as a major priority among voters. Vice President Al Gore, a longtime environmentalist and the Democratic presidential nominee in 2000, downplayed environmental issues in his campaign—even though the Republican nominee, George W. Bush, appeared to be vulnerable to charges that he failed to crack down on polluters as governor of Texas.

Throughout the 105th and 106th Congresses, environmentalists repeatedly urged Congress and the White House to take strong action to reverse national—and even worldwide—ecological degradation. They pointed to scientific studies showing that pollution was causing a dangerous warming trend in the earth's climate, plant and animal species were disappearing at an alarming rate, as many as 40 percent of the nation's rivers and lakes were too polluted for swimming or fishing, nuclear waste was piling up at a dangerous rate, and increasingly congested highways posed a threat to air quality. But with the nation's air, water, and soil noticeably cleaner than in the early 1970s, such warnings failed to resonate with many in the public.

Chronology of Action on Environment and Energy

1997–1998

With the White House and Congress controlled by different parties, there was little expectation for sweeping environmental action when the 105th Congress began. Both President Clinton and GOP leaders were still licking their wounds from a series of stalemates during the past two Congresses. Clinton had failed to score major environmental victories in 1993 and 1994, when Democrats last enjoyed a congressional majority; conservative Republicans, in turn, got roughed up in 1995 and 1996 for trying to scale back clean water and other environmental regulations.

High on the agenda were changes to the Endangered Species Act and the superfund hazardous waste program—two controversial laws that were widely regarded as in need of some adjustments, if not a total overhaul. Lawmakers failed to revamp either law because of both regional and partisan divisions. Western Republicans, who regarded the Endangered Species Act as an infringement of private property rights, found their efforts frustrated by a bloc of northeastern and midwestern Republicans who took a more moderate approach to environmental issues. Rewriting the superfund law proved so divisive that lawmakers could not even come to terms on less controversial elements, such as cleaning up less hazardous sites known as brownfields.

Congress did somewhat better on secondary environmental issues. Despite divisions among environmentalists, Congress cleared legislation implementing an international agreement to protect dolphins from tuna fishing operations. It also revamped management of the National Wildlife Refuge System by establishing conservation as the primary goal of the system, and it established a tristate pact on low-level nuclear waste. However, lawmakers failed to come to terms with the administration on other long-simmering environmental disputes, such as grazing regulations on public lands.

Although scientists regarded global warming as one of the most troubling threats to the world's environment, Congress took little action on the issue. Senators of both parties criticized the Kyoto Protocol on global warming, an international agreement that required industrialized countries to reduce emissions of carbon dioxide and other pollutants blamed for warming the earth's atmosphere. The administration signed the deal, but it opted not to submit it to the Senate for ratification because of overwhelming opposition.

Lawmakers paid scant attention to conservation or other energy issues, in part because of the plentiful oil supplies during most of the 1990s. They also failed to come to terms on creating a temporary repository for high-level nuclear waste. However, they did clear a bill to create a three-state compact for low-level waste.

'Dolphin-Safe' Tuna

After nearly two years of trying, Congress in 1997 cleared legislation (HR 408—PL 105-42) in 1997 implementing a 1995 international pact aimed at protecting dolphins from potentially deadly tuna nets. The bill lifted an ongoing U.S. embargo on tuna from Mexico, Venezuela, and other Latin American countries that was originally imposed because those nations' fishing boats caught tuna using encircling nets that also snagged and killed dolphins.

The measure drew strong support from the White House, but it provoked the ire of many congressional Democrats and created an unusually deep division among environmental groups. Some activists hailed the international pact for its trendsetting emphasis on protecting the environment; others worried that it could weaken the dolphin-safe standard in the United States.

The bill sailed easily through the House before running into a threatened filibuster in the Senate by Barbara Boxer, D-Calif. With Boxer concerned that the United States was changing its legal definition of dolphin-safe tuna, both sides reached a compromise that delayed a label change for eighteen months and required a scientific study.

BACKGROUND

With Latin American nations pushing to open international markets, the dolphin-safe tuna bill was seen as a test of how the United States would balance its pursuit of free trade with environmental protections.

Before enactment of the measure, only tuna determined to be "dolphin safe" could be imported into the United States, and tuna could be labeled dolphin-safe only if it was caught using fishing methods that did not harm dolphins. The prohibition grew out of an effort to protect dolphins in the eastern tropical Pacific Ocean (5 million square miles stretching from southern California to Chile), where dolphins regularly swam above schools of large yellowfin tuna.

Since the late 1950s, commercial fishing fleets had deployed large purse seine nets around schools of dolphins to harvest the tuna swimming below. These nets encircled the fish and were then drawn shut, like a purse. During this process, dolphins often became trapped in the nets and drowned.

Concern over this killing led to enactment in 1972 of the Marine Mammal Protection Act (PL 92-522), which called for U.S. efforts to virtually eliminate the incidental killing of marine mammals during commercial fishing. In 1984 the law was amended to prohibit foreign nations from selling yellowfin tuna in U.S. markets if they did not have dolphin-protection programs similar to those in the United States.

Despite protests by Mexico, Congress went a step further in 1990, specifying that dolphin labels could not be used on eastern tropical Pacific tuna that were caught in conjunction with the use of purse seine nets, and prohibiting the import into the United States of tuna not considered dolphin-safe.

In 1992 nations that fished the eastern tropical Pacific agreed to use nets that would not ensnarl dolphins, to use a procedure that allowed the back edge of the net to sink below the surface so that dolphins could swim out, to use rafts and divers to help herd dolphins out of nets, to have in place international observers who would monitor fishing practices and dolphin mortalities, and to place restrictions on fishing vessels that exceeded annual dolphin mortality rates.

In the wake of this voluntary agreement, estimates of dolphin mortality in the eastern tropical Pacific declined from more than 100,000 in 1991 to 2,547 in 1996.

In 1995 the United States, several international environmental groups, and eleven other nations met in Panama to develop a binding international agreement under which the twelve signatory nations agreed to continue using the dolphin-protection fishing practices and to establish an annual limit of 5,000 dolphins that could be killed during such fishing. The United States agreed to lift its embargo on tuna imports and to modify the definition of dolphin-safe tuna to include tuna caught with purse seines in which no dolphin mortalities were observed.

In 1996 the House voted 316–108 to pass a bill that would have changed U.S. laws to comply with the Panama accord. However, the measure died in the Senate at the end of the 104th Congress under filibuster threats from Boxer and Joseph R. Biden Jr., D-Del., authors of the 1990 dolphin-safe label law. *(Congress and the Nation Vol. IX, p. 467)*

Supporters of the legislation, including Clinton, many Republicans in Congress, and some environmental groups, argued that the Panama Declaration was a model for reconciling the often competing pressures of global economics and environmental protection. But some environmentalists and congressional Democrats worried that the Panama agreement was the kind of sellout of U.S. environmental laws that they argued was becoming increasingly frequent as the Clinton administration bent over backward to accommodate trading partners.

"Mexico gets virtually everything it wants, and no one holds its feet to the fire on environmental issues," said House Minority Whip David Bonior of Michigan, the Democratic Party's leading opponent of the North American Free Trade Agreement (NAFTA). Other opponents included Defenders of Wildlife and the Humane Society of the United States, which argued that the measure would allow dolphins to be killed unnecessarily.

Among environmental groups, Greenpeace and the Center for Marine Conservation supported the measure. "What we want to do is end dolphin mortality," said Nina Young, a marine mammal scientist with the marine conservation center. "This is a model for what we want to do with all fishery trade agreements."

The House easily passed the bill on May 21 on a 262–166 vote that broke largely along party lines. The opposition was stronger than it had been the previous year.

HR 408, sponsored by Wayne T. Gilchrest, R-Md., began in the House Resources Subcommittee on Fisheries Conservation, Wildlife and Oceans, which approved it by voice vote April 10. The full committee gave its voice vote approval April 16. The House Ways and Means Committee, which had jurisdiction over the bill's trade-related provisions, approved the bill without amendment April 30 by a vote of 28–9 (H Rept 105-74, Pts. 1 and 2).

In addition to provisions endorsing the Panama agreement, the bill called for the Commerce Department to study the impact of encirclement techniques on dolphins in the eastern tropical Pacific, and it proposed to authorize $1 million for the study.

Leading the opposition to the bill was George Miller, D-Calif., the senior Democrat on the Resources Committee. He said the new dolphin-safe standard would be unenforceable, allowing needless dolphin deaths.

At the Resources subcommittee markup, Miller pushed a substitute amendment, rejected 4–7, that would have lifted the embargo only for dolphin-safe tuna and revised the existing standard to include a more stringent prohibition on activities such as chasing or seriously injuring dolphins.

On the House floor, the debate revolved largely around the issues of environmental protection and international trade. "If we really, truly believe in conservation and believe in saving the dolphins, this is a piece of legislation that must pass," said House Resources Committee Chairman Don Young, R-Alaska.

ENVIRONMENT, ENERGY LEADERSHIP

At the start of his second term President Bill Clinton asked Bruce Babbitt to remain as secretary of interior. Babbitt—a committed environmentalist as well as a member of one of Arizona's oldest ranching families—had served as governor of Arizona before joining the administration in 1993. Babbitt had been confirmed by voice vote of the Senate on Jan. 21, 1993. *(Background, cabinet profiles, p. 977)*

Another holdover from Clinton's first term, Carol M. Browner stayed on as administrator of the Environmental Protection Agency (EPA). Browner had served as Vice President Al Gore's legislative director for several years when he was in the Senate and as secretary of the Florida Department of Environmental Regulation. She had been confirmed by the Senate as EPA chief by voice vote on Jan. 21, 1993. *(Congress and the Nation Vol. IX, pp. 407, 1116)*

For secretary of energy, Clinton chose Federico F. Peña to replace retiring Hazel R. O'Leary. Peña, who had served as Denver mayor from 1983 to 1991, was secretary of transportation during Clinton's first term. Senate action on Peña's confirmation, however, was delayed for nearly three months in a political squabble. Senators did not object to Peña's qualifications for the post, despite his lack of background on energy issues. His abilities were proven, they said, during his four years as transportation secretary. But Senate Republicans tried to use Peña's confirmation to pressure the White House to drop a veto threat against a bill to establish a temporary nuclear waste repository in Nevada. *(Nuclear waste storage, p. 361).*

After the Republican attempt to budge Clinton on the issue failed, Peña's nomination was sent to the Senate floor. With only one senator, Rod Grams, R-Minn., voting against Peña to protest the White House's nuclear waste policies, Peña was confirmed by a 99–1 vote on March 12, 1997. *(Background, cabinet profiles, p. 979)*

In June 1998 Peña resigned his post to return to private life. Clinton tapped Bill Richardson, who had served as ambassador to the United Nations since 1997, to head the Energy Department. Before joining the administration, Richardson had served as a New Mexico representative for eight terms (1983–1997), rising to the leadership post of chief deputy whip.

Once again, however, the confirmation of Clinton's energy secretary got ensnared in nuclear waste politics. This time, Sen. Larry E. Craig, R-Idaho, threatened to delay a floor vote on Richardson's confirmation because of Craig's unhappiness with the administration's opposition to the nuclear waste repository. Pete V. Domenici, R-N.M., said Craig should not hold up Richardson's nomination. "I don't believe it's realistic or even fair to say that the nominee who's apparently following the policy direction of the president will be denied a position," Domenici said.

Craig relented after receiving assurances from the administration that the new energy secretary would have the authority to negotiate a solution to the problem of storing high-level nuclear waste generated by U.S. power plants.

The Senate by voice vote confirmed Richardson on July 31. Shortly afterwards Energy and Natural Resources Chairman Frank H. Murkowski, R-Alaska, asked President Clinton to delay the swearing-in so the committee could check out a newly published report that Richardson had misled the panel at his confirmation hearing about his dealings with White House intern Monica Lewinsky when he was U.N. ambassador. Richardson denied the allegation and a bipartisan Energy Committee staff report issued on Aug. 17 found "clear and convincing evidence corroborating the ambassador's testimony." Richardson was sworn in as energy secretary on Aug. 18, 1998. *(Background, cabinet profiles, p. 980)*

But foes said the bill would lead to the killing of more dolphins while doing little to protect other marine life. "Tuna would be labeled as dolphin-safe even if dolphins were chased, netted or harmed, seriously injured, or even killed, as long as the dead dolphins were not observed," said Frank Pallone Jr., D-N.J.

SENATE ACTION

The Senate Commerce, Science and Transportation Committee joined the fray on June 26, giving voice vote approval to a bill (S 39) similar to the House-passed measure. However, the Senate bill would authorize $8 million for research on the effect of encirclement fishing methods on dolphin safety, $7 million more than in the House bill.

Under an amendment offered by Olympia J. Snowe, R-Maine, and adopted by voice vote, the dolphin-safe label restrictions could apply not only to tuna from a catch that did not immediately kill dolphins but also seriously or mortally wounded them.

After weeks of behind-the-scenes maneuvering aimed at avoiding a filibuster by Boxer and others, the Senate passed a revised version of S 39 on July 30 by a vote of 99–0. Senators then took up the House version (HR 408), substituted the text of S 39, and passed it by voice vote. The House accepted the Senate changes and cleared HR 408 by voice vote July 31.

The breakthrough on the bill came July 25 when Snowe and others announced a compromise: the embargo would be lifted, but the easing of the definition of dolphin-safe tuna would be postponed for at least eighteen months. The deal also required a three-year study on the effects of "international encirclement on dolphins and dolphin populations."

MAJOR PROVISIONS

As signed into law Aug 15, the major provisions of HR 408:

• **Study.** The commerce secretary was required to conduct a three-year study of the effects in the eastern tropical Pacific Ocean of the use of encircling fishing nets, which captured tuna but also trap and kill dolphins swimming above tuna schools. The study, scheduled to begin Oct. 1, was to include an examination of stress that dolphins experienced when encircled.

Defining "dolphin-safe." The bill redefined the "dolphin-safe" label affixed to tuna cans. Previously, tuna was defined as dolphin-safe if it was caught without using encircling nets. The bill initially tightened the definition: encircling nets would not be used during the entire fishing trip. However, the definition could be loosened as early as March 1999, if the Commerce secretary made a preliminary finding, based on the study and "any other relevant information," that encircling nets did not have a "significant adverse impact on any depleted dolphin stock." Encircling nets would then be allowed as long as the tuna were caught without killing or seriously injuring dolphins. The definition could be revised again after July 1, 2001, based on the final outcome of the study.

• **Label.** Only one dolphin-safe label could be attached to each tuna can. The Commerce secretary was directed to develop an official dolphin-safe label, but tuna canners were free to use the label of their choice. The definition of any label had to be at least as strong as that embodied in the bill. It would be a violation of the Federal Trade Commission Act to use a label "to mislead or deceive consumers" about the protections for dolphins under the bill.

• **Limits.** As many as 5,000 dolphins could be killed each year in the eastern tropical Pacific Ocean, with the objective of entirely eliminating dolphin deaths through the setting of annual limits. An overall mortality limit was to be set through 2000 at between 0.1 percent and 0.2 percent of the estimated minimum dolphin populations. The level in 2001 was to drop to 0.1 percent. Rights to fish for tuna with dolphins swimming in close proximity would be suspended if the limits were breached.

• **Bycatch.** The secretary of state was directed to seek an international agreement for a program in the eastern tropical Pacific Ocean to reduce the incidental killing of sea turtles, sharks, and other species during tuna fishing. The bycatch reduction program was to include measures to release threatened and endangered species alive and minimize overall mortality.

National Wildlife Refuges

Overcoming past disputes between conservationists and recreational users, Congress in 1997 cleared legislation re-

vamping management of the National Wildlife Refuge System. The measure (HR 1420—105-57) officially established conservation as the basic mission of the system—the first time the refuges had been given a clearly defined legal purpose.

To the satisfaction of those who hunted and fished recreationally, the bill also recognized hunting and other recreation as a priority in the refuges whenever it was compatible with conservation. An earlier version, which would have put recreational activities on an equal footing with conservation efforts, drew a veto threat from the Clinton administration.

BACKGROUND

The National Wildlife Refuge System, which could be traced back to 1903, was a sprawling and diverse system covering ninety-two million acres and designed to protect plants and wildlife and provide recreation for millions of Americans. Run by the Interior Department's Fish and Wildlife Service, the system's 509 refuges were scattered across all fifty states and served a variety of users. The majority of acreage was in Alaska. But refuges were found amid the sprawl of West Coast subdivisions as well as in the isolation of Alaska's Arctic National Wildlife Refuge.

Some refuges offered isolation and sanctuary for threatened plants and animals, as well as a solitary experience for campers and backpackers. Others had become tourist meccas; Chincoteague National Wildlife Refuge off the Virginia coast, for example, got more than one million visitors each year.

The system—which was managed under the Refuge Recreation Act of 1962 and the 1966 National Wildlife Refuge System Administration Act—labored under funding constraints and a lack of management oversight. In particular, there was broad agreement that the system suffered from the lack of an explicit, singular mission. While existing federal law allowed uses "compatible" with the major purposes of the system, it did not state what those purposes were, nor did it define "compatible."

Attempts to clarify the law had bogged down in previous Congresses, stymied by disputes between conservationists, who wanted to ensure that the refuges focused on protecting plants and wildlife, and hunters and other recreational users, who wanted to protect their access to the refuges.

A House-passed bill that would have elevated the priority given to recreational activities was halted in 1996 by Senate opposition and a presidential veto threat. (*Congress and the Nation Vol. IX, p. 465*)

As the 105th Congress began, a rematch seemed in the offing. Young introduced a bill (HR 511) that would have established a list of six purposes for the refuge system, including conservation and compatible recreational uses, and permitted fishing and hunting on a refuge unless a specific finding was made to bar it.

In the face of administration opposition, the plan once again appeared headed for oblivion. But within two months of the contentious hearing, and after weeks of intense talks between the Clinton administration and key House Republicans and Democrats, negotiators produced a compromise bill that both sides seemed ready to support.

"HR 1420 addresses all of the concerns raised in my March 6, 1997, testimony," Babbitt wrote in a letter April 29, "while securing an appropriate role for America's sportsmen and women and fish and wildlife-dependent recreation generally in the refuge system."

Babbitt gave himself an escape clause, however: "Any substantive change would obligate the parties now supporting it to reevaluate their positions."

LEGISLATIVE ACTION

On April 30 the House Resources Committee approved the compromise bill by voice vote (H Rept 105-106). The measure had bipartisan support and provoked relatively little debate, a contrast to the panel's tradition of partisan fighting over management of federal lands.

Young gave it his support, as did Miller. Young said he believed the bill would achieve his goal of creating "a statutory shield to ensure that hunting and fishing . . . could continue within the system and to facilitate these traditional activities where compatible with conservation."

The bill also had the support of John D. Dingell of Michigan, the ranking Democrat on the Commerce Committee, author of the 1966 legislation, and a senior member of the influential Congressional Sportsmen's Caucus.

Environmental groups, however, had a mixed reaction, cheering some provisions that they had sought for years but taking issue with others. Groups were pleased that the bill would, for the first time, require conservation plans for each refuge, and that it called for the refuges to "ensure that the biological integrity, diversity, and environmental health of the system are maintained for the benefit of present and future generations of Americans."

"Frankly, we're still concerned the bill is skewed [away from conservation]," said Jim Waltman, director of refuges and wildlife for the Wilderness Society. "But it's moving substantially back in the right direction," compared with earlier Republican proposals.

At the markup, Miller, traditionally an ally of the environmentalists, played down such concerns.

The House gave the bill a ringing endorsement June 3, passing it, 407–1. Ron Paul, R-Texas, an advocate of limiting federal government activities, cast the lone "no" vote.

The Senate made only minor adjustments to HR 1420 before passing it by voice vote Sept. 10. Among the Senate changes were provisions to clarify that activities did not have to be wildlife-dependent to be considered compatible with the primary purpose of a refuge.

Also included by the Senate was a provision requiring the Interior Department to monitor the condition of fish, wildlife, and plants in the refuges.

The House accepted the Senate amendments and cleared the bill Sept. 23 by a vote of 419–1.

MAJOR PROVISIONS

As signed into law on Oct. 9, 1997, the major provisions of HR 511 were:

• **Mission.** The bill amended the 1966 National Wildlife Refuge System Administration Act to state that the mission of the National Wildlife Refuge System was to administer a national network of lands and waters for the conservation, management, and restoration of fish, wildlife, and plant resources and their habitats. The secretary of the interior was directed to monitor the status and trends of fish, wildlife, and plants in each refuge. The Interior Department could temporarily suspend any refuge activity when necessary to protect the health and safety of the public or any fish or wildlife population.

• **Recreation and other uses.** Wildlife-dependent recreation within the national wildlife refuge system was supported by the bill. Such recreation could involve hunting, fishing, wildlife observation and photography, or environmental education and interpretation. The Interior Department could work with state fish and wildlife agencies to manage refuge programs.

• **Compatible uses.** The measure established standards and procedures for Interior to follow when determining which activities should be considered compatible with the system's mission. The secretary of the interior was directed to issue final regulations to establish the process for determining a compatible use. The compatibility provisions did not apply to overflights above a refuge or to activities authorized, funded, or conducted by a federal agency that had primary jurisdiction over a refuge.

• **Conservation plans.** The Interior Department had to develop comprehensive conservation plans for each refuge except for those in Alaska. The plans should take into account fish and wildlife distribution and migration patterns, plant populations, archaeological and cultural values, habitat problems, and opportunities for compatible wildlife-dependent recreation. They had to be revised on a fifteen-year cycle.

Endangered Species

Lawmakers in the 105th Congress once again failed to reauthorize the controversial 1973 Endangered Species Act. Senate Republicans assembled a bill that won bipartisan approval in the Environment and Public Works Committee in 1997, but it lost momentum in the face of opposition from both environmentalists and property rights advocates. Neither the House nor Senate took up the measure, and lawmakers took no formal action on the law in 1998.

The Senate measure proposed a new process for recovering species and offered greater involvement to ranchers, property owners, and communities in federal decision-making. The bill had the support of industry groups, including timber companies, homebuilders, and ranchers, who saw it as a moderate but important step toward revamping what they considered an onerous law. Moderates in the Senate rallied behind it, but environmentalists warned that it could undermine a popular environmental law, and conservative senators wanted more protections for property owners.

BACKGROUND

Efforts by Congress to revise the 1973 Endangered Species Act (PL 93-205) had been bogged down for years by fierce disagreements over how to protect species without trampling on the rights of property owners.

The 1973 act made it illegal to kill, injure, trap, harass, or otherwise "take" any animal or plant that was deemed endangered or threatened. It also established a process for designating an endangered or threatened species, and required development of a plan for its recovery.

Although Congress passed the act with scant opposition, it soon developed into one of the nation's most controversial and far-ranging environmental laws. It drew numerous lawsuits by environmentalists seeking stronger enforcement and by businesses and property owners contending that the government was overstepping its bounds. The two sides were especially at odds over a provision barring the taking of a species, which the government used to prevent the property owners from destroying habitat for endangered species.

The Endangered Species Act spurred controversy for two reasons that were unforeseen in 1973. First, although it originally was conceived to protect such charismatic species as the gray whale, it eventually listed mostly obscure species of plants and animals like the kangaroo rat and the Delhi fly. Environmentalists said such species were vital to maintain ecosystems, but conservative critics said it was not worth slowing economic growth for such insignificant species.

Second, activists used the law as a tactic to stop development even when their primary interest was not saving a rare species. In the late 1970s, for example, residents along the Little Tennessee River went to court over the endangered snail darter in an effort to stop a $31 million dam that threatened their homes. As a result, the Endangered Species Act provoked an angry backlash among private property advocates.

Some also questioned the law's effectiveness. Supporters credited it with helping to spur the recovery of such keystone species as the bald eagle and the grizzly bear, while stabilizing the populations of many other animals and plants. Critics, however, pointed out that even though the law listed more than 1,000 species as endangered, no more than a handful had recovered to the point of no longer needing federal protection.

Revamping the law was a top priority for many westerners and some southerners, who argued that it imposed unjustified restrictions on land use while doing too little for the recovery of endangered plants and animals. Critics said the burdens of the law were so onerous that landowners sometimes preferred to destroy the habitat to get rid of any sign of threatened species on their land rather than allow federal regulators to put strict restrictions on the use of their property. On the other hand, environmentalists worried that the government was moving too slowly to list endangered species for protection.

The Endangered Species Act had last been reauthorized in 1988. The law expired in 1992, but it remained fully in effect because of annual appropriations bills. The government continued to enforce the act as well as consider the listing of new species.

The House Resources Committee approved a major overhaul of the act in 1995, but the bill stalled when moderate and conservative Republicans were unable to resolve differences over property rights and other issues. *(Congress and the Nation Vol. IX, p. 458)*

LEGISLATIVE ACTION

The Senate Environment and Public Works Committee on Sept. 30, 1997, approved a bill, 15–3, with few amendments (S Rept 105-128).

The bill (S 1180), which was supported by the Clinton administration as well as many Republican lawmakers, was the culmination of more than a year of painstaking work by Dirk Kempthorne, R-Idaho. The senator's goal was to do a better job of recovering species while cutting through the red tape that frustrated average citizens. It would have created greater flexibility and incentives for landowners to protect plants and animals on their own. Provisions included:

- **Habitat agreements.** Allowed private landowners to develop "habitat conservation plans" to protect a number of species in a single habitat. If the plan was approved by the Interior Department, the landowners would be guaranteed that they would not have to spend additional money or set aside more land.

- **'Safe harbor.'** Allowed landowners to enter into voluntary "safe harbor" agreements with the Interior Department. Landowners would agree to maintain, create, restore, or improve habitat in return for being exempted for additional liability under the act.

- **Recovery.** Required the federal government to issue final recovery plans within thirty months of placing a species on the endangered list. There was no such deadline under existing law.

- **Consultation.** Streamlined the consultation process under which federal agencies were required to consult with the U.S. Fish and Wildlife Service, which ran the program, to ensure that their actions did not harm threatened or endangered species or destroy critical habitat.

- **Listing.** Required certain minimum scientific evidence for listing a species as endangered, including specific threats to the species. The bill also included a procedure for delisting a species once its recovery goal has been reached.

At the Sept. 30 markup, Kempthorne—who chaired the committee's Drinking Water, Fisheries and Wildlife Subcommittee—and his core supporters lobbied hard to fend off conservative amendments that could jeopardize Democratic support. Committee member Craig Thomas, R-Wyo., said that while many westerners might not like the bill, they had to recognize that the political climate was unlikely to yield anything better. "You either take what you can get or get nothing at all," he said.

Kempthorne acknowledged the constraints at the markup. In what he said was a symbolic move, he proposed and then withdrew an amendment to provide compensation to landowners for federal decisions that affected property values. "It was just to demonstrate how strongly I feel," he said. "We need to keep showcasing the issue."

The other western Republicans on the panel showed similar restraint, in part out of deference to Kempthorne and the work he had put into the bill. Thomas, for example, withdrew an amendment popular in the West that would have given states greater control over water rights.

The committee approved a handful of amendments, including a proposal by Ron Wyden, D-Ore., adopted by voice vote, to allow states to establish conservation agreements to protect species and avoid their inclusion on the federal endangered list. It also gave voice vote approval to an amendment by James M. Inhofe, R-Okla., to temporarily suspend some federal oversight of species during an emergency repair of a pipeline or utility line.

After the markup, however, the bill lost momentum, and GOP leaders never brought it up on the floor. Environmentalists criticized it as overly generous to private property owners, developers, mining concerns, and timber companies. Some conservative Republicans, meanwhile, worried that the bill did not contain enough protections for property owners.

A more environmentally leaning House bill (HR 2351) by Rep. George Miller, D-Calif., included the public-private initiatives of S 1180 while giving the government more tools for protecting plants and animals. It included an assortment of tax incentives for landowners who agreed to protect threatened habitat. A controversial provision would have allowed citizens to sue if there was a violation of the conservation plan. The House did not take up HR 2351 because leaders could not bridge the gap between private property owners and environmentalists.

Earlier in 1997, western Republicans in the House had attempted to tackle the Endangered Species Act incrementally. HR 478 proposed to waive certain provisions of the act for flood-control projects. Western Republicans argued that the bill pitted safeguarding people over bugs and rodents. But the strategy did not work. Republican moderate Sherwood Boehlert of New York offered an amendment that all but gutted the measure. When Boehlert's amendment passed on May 7 in a **key vote of 227–196 (R 54–169; D 172–27; I 1–0),** supporters of HR 478 pulled the bill from the floor. The amendment vote revealed the rift between Republican conservatives and moderates over any major overhaul of the act. *(1997 key votes, p. 865; 1999 action, p. 385)*

Clean Air Act

Stringent new clean air regulations finalized by the Environmental Protection Agency (EPA) in 1997 divided Con-

gress along regional and ideological lines. Although opponents threatened to try to block the rules, they were unable to muster enough support in either chamber to pass a bill that could withstand a presidential veto. *(1999 action, p. 382)*

The regulations tightened existing environmental regulations for ozone, a main component of smog, and created a standard for tiny airborne particles of soot, known as particulate matter. EPA Administrator Carol M. Browner, who appeared several times before congressional panels during the year, said the rules were needed to protect asthmatics, children, and the elderly and were primarily aimed at utilities and smokestack industries.

But critics argued that the new standards were based on flimsy science and would impose millions of dollars in compliance costs with no appreciable benefit. Democrats from the Midwest and oil states joined the mainly Republican opposition because power plants and refineries in their states would suffer under the rules. However, many Republicans from states that were downwind from such facilities joined Democrats in support of the rules.

Opponents in the House introduced a bill (HR 1984) in June calling for a four-year moratorium on implementing the new rules and requiring more scientific studies. Sponsor Ron Klink, R-Pa., called it "an issue we will go to war on." Shortly before the August recess, House Commerce Committee Chairman Thomas J. Bliley Jr., R-Va., pledged to move forward on a bill—if it could win the two-thirds majority necessary to overturn a presidential veto. But it became evident that goal was out of reach, and the bill never moved in the House.

In the Senate, a moratorium bill had little chance. Environment and Public Works Committee Chairman John H. Chafee, R-R.I., did not support overturning the rules through legislation. He and other northeastern Republicans, whose states were downwind from polluting midwestern power plants, were strongly supportive of the EPA rules.

James M. Inhofe, R-Okla., said he would lead a bipartisan effort to block the EPA rules with legislation that mirrored the House bill. But Inhofe said he wanted the House to act first, which never happened.

Instead, Republicans used hearings to lambaste the rules and challenge their legality. Conservatives such as George W. Gekas, R-Pa., accused the EPA of failing to analyze the effect of rules on small businesses as required by the Regulatory Flexibility Act (PL 96-354); ignoring the requirement that federal agencies consult with small businesses under the Small Business Regulatory Enforcement Fairness Act (PL 104-121); and neglecting consideration of how the rules would affect state and local governments as required by the Unfunded Mandates Act (PL 104-4).

Browner countered that the Clean Air Act, amended in 1990 (PL 101-549), required the EPA to consider first and foremost the adequacy of existing standards to protect public health in proposing new rules. Based on 250 studies, Browner said, the EPA concluded that the previous standards were not sufficient to protect public health.

'Superfund' Overhaul

Partisan bickering over how far to go in rewriting the superfund hazardous waste law once again stymied efforts to overhaul the beleaguered cleanup program. Although Senate Republican leaders placed a rewrite on their top ten list of legislative priorities in 1997, the 105th Congress ended without a floor vote in either chamber. Bipartisan negotiations repeatedly broke down, and a Senate Republican measure won approval in the Environment and Public Works Committee in 1998 only after overcoming stiff Democratic resistance.

Among the perennial disagreements that kept lawmakers apart were differences over how to clean up sites, who should pay the tab, and how to remedy damage done by severely polluted sites to rivers, streams, and other natural resources. Perhaps the biggest bone of contention between Republicans and the administration was how far to go in scaling back existing retroactive liability provisions, which allowed the government to hold a company responsible for the costs of cleaning up toxic waste dumped before the superfund law was enacted in 1980.

BACKGROUND

Long accepted as the inevitable byproduct of industrial progress, toxic waste sites came to be seen as intolerable threats to public health in the 1970s. Among the high-profile environmental disasters that grabbed public attention was the 1977 discovery in Niagara Falls, N.Y., that the Love Canal residential subdivision had been built atop a former chemical dump. The public clamored for action.

In 1980 Congress responded by enacting the superfund law (PL 96-510), founded on the basic principle that those responsible for toxic-waste pollution, not the government, should pay for cleanup, even if they broke no environmental laws at the time of disposal.

The law created a trust fund, better known as the "superfund," fed by taxes on petroleum and hazardous chemicals, a broad-based environmental tax on large companies and annual appropriations. The EPA was charged with creating a priority list of contaminated sites around the country that were most in need of attention. The government was authorized to make a single individual or business pay to clean up a site, even if others contributed to the pollution.

However, the program quickly became entangled in a web of litigation. Polluters went to court to find other polluters, such as municipalities that hauled household garbage to toxic waste sites, to share the cleanup costs. Polluters also often sued their insurance companies when they balked at paying claims filed to recover cleanup costs. By 1997 the federal government had spent $17.9 billion on the program. In all, 504 of the nation's most dangerous toxic waste sites had been cleaned, but nearly 1,300 remained on the priority list.

The program had last been reauthorized in 1986 and extended through fiscal 1994 as part of the 1990 budget-reconciliation bill. The taxes that helped finance the cleanups were authorized through fiscal 1995. Both authorizations had expired.

According to the Congressional Budget Office, there was still enough money in the trust fund to pay for the program through 2000. The EPA estimated that by the end of fiscal 1997, the fund would have an unobligated balance of $2.5 billion. House Ways and Means Committee Chairman Bill Archer, R-Texas, said he would not agree to renew the taxes until the program had been revamped.

For nearly five years, Congress had been struggling over how to rewrite the superfund law. Despite bipartisan approval from five committees and the Clinton administration, overhaul legislation died in the final weeks of the 103rd Congress, the victim of divisions over proposed taxes, new cleanup standards, and wages paid by federal contractors. In the 104th Congress, the Republican majority pushed to repeal retroactive liability, but gave up in the face of strong opposition from most congressional Democrats and the Clinton administration. Republicans conceded that they could not find the money to pay for a full repeal. *(Congress and the Nation Vol. IX, pp. 410, 453)*

1997 LEGISLATIVE ACTION

Republicans contended that exempting some businesses from such costs would actually speed cleanups by clearing away much of the litigation that had bogged down the program. They also argued that it was unfair to punish a company later for something that was legal at the time. But the administration and its Democratic allies in Congress opposed broad liability repeal, saying it would "let polluters off the hook" and shift more of the cost to taxpayers.

Typical of the jockeying for position by both parties was a dispute over so-called brownfields—sites that were not hazardous enough to come under superfund but that had been certified by a state environmental agency as containing or potentially containing a hazardous substance. Although both parties embraced the concept of reducing potential financial liability for businesses willing to purchase the sites, Republicans were piqued when Democrats unveiled a brownfields bill at a 1997 press conference one day after formal bipartisan negotiations began on a broad superfund reform.

"This isn't a serious legislative effort. It's a photo op," scoffed House Commerce Committee Chairman Thomas J. Bliley Jr., R-Va. But House Minority Leader Richard A. Gephardt, D-Mo., said he would not allow Republicans to shift cleanup costs from polluters to taxpayers.

The Clinton administration wanted to reauthorize the superfund taxes, which raised about $1.7 billion a year. It also wanted to increase federal funding for the program from $1.4 billion in fiscal 1997 to $2.1 billion annually beginning in fiscal 1998 to clean up an additional 250 toxic waste sites over the following four years.

Some White House officials seemed to indicate support for a major overhaul of the superfund program, as well. But in a statement of principles for superfund reform released May 7, the administration emphasized that any legislative fix must be "narrowly targeted," and it strongly opposed GOP proposals to revise existing superfund liability standards. Administration officials touted what they said was improved management of the program, leaving the impression that they did not want a significant bill.

Senate Republicans scheduled a markup of legislation in September but backed off in the face of stiff Democratic opposition. The bill (S 8) proposed to eliminate an existing requirement that the EPA pursue cleanups that offered permanent remedies. Bill supporters said the requirement could add millions of dollars to the cost of a cleanup and that the EPA needed greater flexibility to balance costs against other factors such as human health protection and the long-term effectiveness of the treatment. But some Democrats and many environmentalists said the law already provided significant flexibility and worried that easing standards would lead to less thorough cleanups, putting communities at risk.

Another issue, which became prominent in 1997, was liability for damage to natural resources. S 8 proposed to limit the damages that could be recovered from a polluter, including some of the costs unrelated to site restoration. Businesses, municipalities, and others worried that they could be required to pay for both site cleanups and the costs for damage to nearby rivers and other natural resources. But senators from states where damaged natural resources were an issue, as well as administration officials, worried that the limits could stand in the way of cleanups.

Trying to force action, Senate Republicans broke off bipartisan negotiations in early summer and then set a firm date for the markup. "We decided months ago if we don't impose a deadline on ourselves, we're not going to get anywhere," said Sen. Robert C. Smith, R-N.H., a sponsor of the bill. But despite some concessions, the draft provoked strong opposition and a stern warning that a superfund bill without bipartisan support would be doomed. "It is a mistake to move ahead without Democratic support," said Senate Minority Leader Tom Daschle, D-S.D. "And it will not pass into law, I can assure you that."

At a Sept. 4 hearing, chastened Republicans announced they would delay the markup and resume negotiations.

At that hearing, EPA Administrator Carol M. Browner praised the latest draft of S 8 as a step forward. She backed provisions that would allow for more public participation, require that groundwater be cleaned up under the same standards as drinking water, and create a legal settlement process for businesses that contributed small amounts of waste.

But she objected to provisions that she said would not go far enough to clean up groundwater, allow states to assume more responsibility over the program but shut the public out of decision-making, and put too many limits on legal claims for damage to natural resources. In addition, she said S 8 would not provide sufficient cleanups for the most toxic waste sites.

Late in the session, Rep. Michael G. Oxley, R-Ohio, chairman of the House Commerce Subcommittee on Finance and Hazardous Materials, introduced a narrower superfund bill (HR 3000) cosponsored by a nearly equal number of Democrats and Republicans. The bill proposed to exempt from cleanup responsibility those whose waste "did not contribute significantly to the cleanup costs" as a priority site. It also proposed exemptions for those who generated or transported only municipal solid waste to the site.

Bliley endorsed the bill in November, but the measure failed to pick up the support of key Democrats, including John D. Dingell of Michigan, the senior Democrat on the Commerce Committee. In the absence of such backing, the measure never moved.

1998 LEGISLATIVE ACTION

Separate bills in the Senate and House made faint progress in the face of sharp partisan disagreements. Both the Senate Environment and Public Works Committee and the House Transportation and Infrastructure Subcommittee on Water Resources and Environment approved measures on split votes. Neither bill moved further.

In the House, Water Resources and Environment Subcommittee Chairman Sherwood Boehlert, R-N.Y., scheduled a March 4 markup of his superfund bill (HR 2727) in the belief that the timing and the politics were finally right to push the legislation forward.

He was wrong. After two hours of opening statements, no votes and unbending Democratic opposition to HR 2727, Boehlert abruptly adjourned the markup.

Instead of waging a partisan battle, he decided to delay the markup until March 10 to give all sides one last chance to resolve their differences. In explaining his reasoning, Boehlert said he was bowing to pressure from subcommittee members who were encouraged by the progress negotiators had made in other sessions.

The chairman did indeed drive his bill through the subcommittee on March 11, but the 18–12 vote gave little cheer to supporters of the measure. Only two Democrats voted for HR 2727, which was widely viewed as the most moderate of several superfund proposals put forth by Republicans.

The split vote essentially killed the plan because full committee chairman Bud Shuster, R-Pa., insisted on garnering bipartisan support before moving ahead. The outcome was all the more surprising because marathon negotiations between Boehlert and Democrats narrowed differences to the point where "our fingers were almost touching," Boehlert said.

Boehlert had hoped that his reputation as a proenvironment Republican and his warm relations with Democrats would bring all sides together and provide momentum for his bill. He spent weeks negotiating with Democrats and the EPA in the hope of putting together a package that could earn bipartisan support.

But Democrats, complaining that negotiations were cut short, offered no amendments aiming to try to change the bill in full committee. The administration also criticized the bill, which aimed to provide relief for small businesses and reauthorize superfund through 2002. Among the difficult issues left unresolved were the role that states should play in cleanups, how to correct damage to natural resources, and how to protect groundwater.

Attempting to lay claim to the issue, the Senate Environment and Public Works Committee finished work March 26 on its own measure to update superfund. But the 11–7, mostly party-line vote for S 8 scarcely provided the bill with any momentum.

Both congressional Democrats and the administration sharply objected to provisions in the bill, which called for $7.5 billion over five years to finance the program. Some of the most difficult issues centered on the roles to be played by states and the federal government. Republicans were determined to shift more power to states to decide how sites should be cleaned up, while Democrats believed the EPA should have the leading role.

Despite the overall failure, the committee agreed on some topics that only a year earlier seemed beyond reach. For example, they decided to protect small businesses with less than seventy-five employees or $3 million in annual revenues from shouldering excessive cleanup costs. They also agreed to provide money for the economic redevelopment of brownfields, which were industrial sites in cities that were not contaminated enough to be declared superfund sites but were too polluted to be used for any other purpose until cleaned.

In addition, the bill would have streamlined the process for determining the best method for cleaning up a site and set aside money to pay for cleaning up waste whose source could not be determined. (1999–2000 action, p. 396).

Global Warming

A landmark international treaty on global warming, negotiated in Kyoto at the end of 1997, sparked such furious opposition in Congress that President Clinton never submitted it to the Senate for ratification. Congressional critics of both parties denounced the Kyoto Protocol on global warming even before negotiators wrapped up their work on Dec. 11, 1997, and many conservatives in 1998 used spending bills to try to stop the administration from using any money to implement the agreement.

"The Kyoto deal is dead on arrival," declared Frank H. Murkowski, R-Alaska, chairman of the Senate Energy and Natural Resources Committee, at a Dec. 10, 1997, press conference.

Environmentalists viewed the Kyoto treaty as an important first step toward containing emissions of carbon dioxide and other pollutants that were blamed for changing the earth's climate. Many—including Clinton and some in Congress—viewed global warming as a critical problem that could ultimately affect food supplies and human health. Although the treaty fell short of environmental expectations, advocates nevertheless hailed Kyoto as a breakthrough be-

cause diverse nations often balked at complex conservation agreements.

However, U.S. lawmakers denounced the treaty because it would require the United States to reduce its greenhouse gas emissions to 7 percent below 1990 levels by 2012. They were angered that developing nations would not have to adhere to any firm limits.

In the months leading up to the Kyoto conference, it was clear that the linchpin for members of Congress was the participation of India, China, and other developing nations in cutting emission levels. In its only legislative action on the issue in 1997, the Senate fired a warning shot on July 25, 1997, voting 95–0 in favor of a nonbinding resolution (S Res 98) stating that the administration should sign such a deal only if it included commitments from developing countries.

But developing countries argued that because the United States and the other industrialized nations had produced the bulk of the pollution, they should take the first step toward cleaning it up. To a large degree, their argument carried the day in Kyoto.

By disregarding the Senate resolution and signing a treaty that exempted developing countries, Clinton left many on Capitol Hill feeling betrayed. In addition, senators were angered because the White House appeared to ignore an agreement made with the Senate before going to Kyoto that the target for reduction would be to 1990 levels, not the 7 percent below 1990 emissions as ultimately agreed to by U.S. negotiators.

As a result, few lawmakers evinced any support for the treaty. Republicans and business groups vowed to kill it. Even Democrats chose their words carefully. The General Accounting Office also warned in June 1998 that the administration's strategy for complying with the Kyoto agreement was adrift.

President Clinton signed the treaty late in 1998, but he did not submit it to the Senate for ratification because of overwhelming opposition. In an ominous development for environmentalists, other countries also refrained from ratifying the treaty.

BACKGROUND

As worldwide temperatures warmed late in the twentieth century, many scientists blamed the climate change on the buildup of "greenhouse gases" in the atmosphere. These gases, including carbon dioxide and methane, were wrapping the earth in a layer of insulation and heating the climate. Although the gases occurred naturally, they were also emitted by industrial activities that involved the burning of oil, coal, and natural gas.

Scientists debated the effect of the gases on global climate patterns, and some even questioned whether industrial activities could be linked to the warmer climate. However, the century-old theory that pollution caused high temperatures gained more credence throughout the 1990s as researchers found increased evidence of a warming climate. Environmentalists warned that higher temperatures worldwide could melt ice caps and raise worldwide sea levels, as well as cause severe drought, more intense storms and widespread diseases. According to the federal Energy Information Administration, the United States was producing 24 percent of carbon dioxide emissions, regarded as the chief culprit in global warming. U.S. emissions of carbon dioxide, already significantly above 1990 levels, were expected to grow by 34 percent above 1990 levels by 2010.

In advance of the Kyoto talks, the president on Oct. 22 proposed reducing so-called greenhouse gas emissions to 1990 levels sometime between 2008 and 2012. That drew considerable opposition, both from environmental groups who favored stricter limits and from business groups that were resisting tough restrictions.

Environmentalists joined forces with legislators from areas that could be affected by global warming, such as coastal communities and eastern states that were downwind from aging coal-fired power plants in the Midwest. Many international leaders also favored strong action on global warming, and European allies criticized Clinton for being too cautious on the issue.

But a well-financed coalition of automobile makers, coal-fired power plants, refineries, and other energy-dependent industries and their unions strongly opposed stringent new controls. They also could count on some powerful allies in Congress, including House and Senate GOP leaders, Democrats from coal-dependent states, and allies of unions, particularly the coal miners and automobile workers, who warned that the treaty might bring layoffs.

No technology existed to control carbon emissions. That meant the only way to reduce greenhouse gases was to burn less fuel or find alternative sources of energy. Industries warned that the federal government would be forced to place costly requirements on them to reduce emissions.

1997 LEGISLATIVE ACTION

The Senate resolution adopted in July was sponsored by Robert C. Byrd, D-W.Va. In pushing his measure, Byrd said developing countries should have to live by the same rules as everyone else. He noted that third world nations produced an abundance of greenhouse gases and might gain a competitive advantage if they did not have to impose costly pollution controls.

The resolution initially drew fire from environmental groups. They feared it was a thinly veiled attempt by Byrd, who was worried that emissions restrictions would hurt coal-producing states such as West Virginia, to undermine treaty negotiations.

Prior to the debate, treaty supporter John Kerry, D-Mass., expressed concern that the resolution might undercut the administration's negotiating position in Kyoto. But Kerry said on the floor that a closer reading of the resolution had convinced him that it would not tie the negotiators' hands.

1998 LEGISLATIVE ACTION

Although he elected not to submit the treaty to the Senate for ratification, Clinton pressed for a $6.3 billion package of tax credits and research into more energy-efficient products that was intended to reduce greenhouse gas emissions. The administration contended that the tax credits, combined with new energy-efficient products such as autos and building materials, would reduce demand for carbon-based fuels and electricity.

But the General Accounting Office (GAO) concluded that the White House had no hard data to support that assumption.

"The extent to which the $6.3 billion . . . proposal will help the United States meet the protocol's target for emission reduction is unclear," Victor S. Rezendes, GAO's director of energy, resource, and science issues, told the Senate Energy and Natural Resources Committee on June 4.

Although the White House pointed out that 1997 was the warmest year on record, capping an unusually warm century, many in the Senate had doubts about the scientific claims that industrial activity was creating climatic changes. They focused instead on the potential threat that the Kyoto Protocol posed to the nation's economy. "Let's make no mistake what we are talking about here," Murkowski said on June 4. "We are talking about profoundly altering the economic destiny of this country. We are talking about severe disruptions to the energy sector of our economy."

One analysis, by Wharton Econometric Forecasting Associates, an independent economic forecasting firm, concluded that the treaty would drive up the price of gasoline by 50 cents per gallon. Another study, by the Global Climate Coalition, a group of energy industries opposed to the treaty, said 3.2 million American jobs would be at risk if the treaty were signed. The White House offered its own analysis, which suggested a minimal economic impact, ranging between $70 and $110 for the average American household.

The conflicting scientific and economic projections, not to mention the politics, bred open suspicions among Republicans that the Clinton administration would bypass Congress and adopt parts of the treaty. In response, the Senate included in its version of the budget resolution (S Con Res 86) a recommendation that no federal money should be spent on the programs related to the Kyoto protocol—including Clinton's $6.3 billion initiative—until it was ratified by the Senate.

Republican appropriators piled on. In at least three spending bills, they sharply cut the administration's requests for climate change programs and inserted language aimed at curbing the EPA and other departments that dealt with climate change.

In the most contentious debate, House critics inserted sweeping language to restrict Environmental Protection Agency actions to promote the treaty in the fiscal 1999 spending bill for the departments of Veterans Affairs and Housing and Urban Development for fiscal 1999 (HR 4194—PL 105-276). But that language was narrowed in the House-Senate conference.

In the end, the administration got $1 billion in the conference report on the fiscal 1999 omnibus appropriations bill (HR 4328—PL 105-277) for climate change initiatives, with most of the money focused on research into alternative fuels and renewable energy. But that money also came with language limiting the administration's ability to promote the Kyoto accord.

Filming Fees at National Parks

The House passed legislation in 1998 that would allow national parks to collect fees for the commercial filming of national park lands or scenery for motion pictures, television programs, advertisements, or other commercial productions. The Senate, however, did not take up the measure.

The bill (HR 2993) would direct the interior secretary to develop a fee rate structure for all of the department's services and established a civil penalty of 200 percent of the fees assessed for violations. The fee-based permits would not apply to videotaping or photography connected with news coverage, educational projects, or artwork.

The House passed the measure by voice vote on Sept. 15.

Before 1948, filmmakers were required to pay fees when federal lands were used for film productions. But that year, the administration of Harry S. Truman ended fee collection for commercial productions in national parks and wildlife refuges. The parks and other public lands subsequently became popular sites for both movies and commercials.

The House Resources Committee approved the measure (H Rept 105-678) by voice vote on Aug. 5. It also gave voice vote approval to an amendment by bill sponsor Joel Hefley, R-Colo., that would ensure the film projects did not interfere with public use and subject violators to fines and prison sentences for up to six months. *(2000 action, p. 387)*

Fish and Wildlife Foundation

The House in 1998 unexpectedly rejected a bill that would have reauthorized the activities of the Fish and Wildlife Foundation for five years.

The bill (S 2095—S Rept 105-224) would authorize $30 million annually for the foundation, a nonprofit organization that Congress established in 1984 to research fish, wildlife, and plant conservation issues, as well as to conduct environmental education programs. It also would expand the foundation's governing board from fifteen to twenty-five members, which would include the heads of the National Oceanic and Atmospheric Administration and the Fish and Wildlife Service.

The Senate passed the seemingly noncontroversial measure by unanimous consent on Oct. 6. But the House on Oct. 12 rejected it on a 153–248 vote.

House Democrats and moderate Republicans voted against the legislation after they learned it had been altered to include provisions such as one that would have prevented the foundation from participating in wolf and grizzly bear reintroduction programs.

Energy Conservation

Congress in 1998 cleared two bills to reauthorize several energy conservation and export programs through 2002. Among the reauthorized programs was one that offered federal grants to states and local agencies to reduce the home energy costs of low-income families. The weatherization program was created as part of the Energy Conservation and Production Act of 1976 (PL 94-385).

The legislation also would reauthorize international export promotion programs for renewable energy technologies and energy-efficient products, and various programs to promote conservation in hospitals and schools.

Another provision would allow federal agencies to receive credit toward requirements regarding the use of alternative fuels if they use biodiesel fuel—a blend of diesel oil and renewable agricultural products, such as vegetable oils—that could be used in traditional diesel engines.

The House bill (HR 2472—PL 105-177) reauthorized for one year the Energy Policy and Conservation Act, thereby extending the authorization for the International Energy Program (IEP), a multinational agreement to develop and share information on energy markets and coordinate the international response to oil shortages.

The bill also extended certain programs such as the Strategic Petroleum Reserve, which was created in 1975 to reduce the impact of future oil import disruptions.

The Commerce Committee approved the measure Sept. 18, 1997, by voice vote, and the full House passed it (H Rept 105-275) Sept. 29 by a vote of 405–8. After the Senate passed an amended version of HR 2472 by unanimous consent on Feb. 12, 1998, the House cleared the measure by voice vote on May 19. President Clinton signed HR 2472 on June 1, 1998.

A similar Senate bill (S 417—PL 105-388), sponsored by Frank H. Murkowski, R-Alaska, proposed extending the same programs through Sept. 30, 2002. In addition, it included antitrust provisions aimed at allowing U.S. oil companies to participate in international energy programs. Ultimately, S 417 (S Rept 105-25) became the vehicle for other energy conservation programs. The measure passed the Senate by unanimous consent on June 27, 1997.

By voice vote, the House passed a related measure (HR 4017—H Rept 105-727) on Sept. 28, 1998. Then the House called up S 417, amended it with the text of the House-passed measure and passed the Senate bill by voice vote. The Senate passed the measure with an amendment by unanimous consent on Oct. 8, and the House cleared the measure by voice vote on Oct. 15. President Clinton signed S 417 on Nov. 13, 1998.

Grazing Fees

A bill aimed at addressing one of the most contentious regional land-use issues—the fee structure governing grazing on federal lands—won House passage and the approval of the Senate Energy and Natural Resources Committee, but it never made it to the Senate floor. Though a majority consensus on a modest rewrite of the fees developed in the House, the measure provoked a White House veto threat. The issue pitted environmentalists and deficit hawks, who asserted that the current fee structure amounted to a federal giveaway, against western conservatives, who fought to preserve low fees for ranchers.

BACKGROUND

Grazing fees, established by the Taylor Grazing Act of 1934, had long provoked controversy over the proper use of federal lands. Under a 1986 executive order by President Ronald Reagan, the fees averaged about $1.35 per animal month (a unit that measures the amount of acreage needed to feed a cow and her calf for a month). That was far lower than the approximately $10 per animal month fees on private lands, but ranchers defended the price discrepancy because they had to pay for improvements, such as fences and stock ponds, on public lands.

When Clinton took office in 1993, he pledged to overhaul grazing fees as part of a larger budget package. Even after he retreated in the face of stiff resistance by western senators, interior secretary Bruce Babbitt announced administrative steps to increase grazing fees gradually to $4.28 and impose tougher environmental standards. Western senators retaliated by maneuvering to block funding for the proposal, and a chastened Babbitt agreed to defer to Congress on the issue.

But Babbitt returned to the fray in 1995 by using his administrative authority to impose new regulations on the lands, which were overseen by the Bureau of Land Management. The new rules allowed the government to claim title to all land improvements and water developments that ranchers made on public lands, and they laid the groundwork for developing environmental plans to preserve rangeland ecosystems.

Congressional conservatives fired back with legislation that would have overturned the administration's rules, while imposing a modest increase of about 50 cents in grazing fees and giving ranchers more influence in federal decision-making about public rangelands. The bill passed the Senate and was approved, with slight modification, by a House committee in 1996. But it ran up against a veto threat and opposition in the House from a coalition of deficit hawks and environmentalists, and it died at the end of the 104th Congress. (*Congress and the Nation Vol. IX, p. 455*)

LEGISLATIVE ACTION

In contrast to 1996 attempts to advance a broad rewrite of rangeland management rules, House Agriculture Committee Chairman Bob Smith, R-Ore., crafted a narrow bill (HR 2493) and worked diligently to resolve differences with Sherwood Boehlert, R-N.Y., the House GOP's leading voice on environmental issues. As a result, proenvironment eastern Republicans, who otherwise might have sided with the Democrats against the bill, generally supported it. Only twenty-two Republicans voted against the bill in the House.

The cornerstone of the legislation was a new formula for calculating the fees for grazing on federal land. It would have increased the current fee from $1.35 to $1.84 per animal unit month. Though many fiscal conservatives and environmentalists favored much higher fees, Boehlert's support for the measure proved pivotal in the defeat of floor amendments to increase the fees sharply. Those votes were close, though: an effort by Bruce F. Vento, D-Minn., to force big livestock producers to pay higher fees failed narrowly, by a vote of 208–212.

The version of the bill approved by the Senate Energy and Natural Resources Committee was similar to the House measure but never made it to the floor for consideration. The White House stood firm with an adamant veto threat, criticizing the bill's complex grazing fee schedule and low return to the federal Treasury.

On a related issue, the final omnibus appropriations measure (HR 4328—PL 105-277) included a provision that allowed existing grazing permits on federal lands to be renewed without final completion of site-specific environmental reviews. Under the omnibus measure, roughly 5,000 permits set to expire in fiscal 1999 could be renewed while the site-specific reviews were still being processed.

The House Resources Committee approved HR 2493, 22–7, on Oct. 22, 1997, and the House approved the bill by 242–182 on Oct. 30. The Senate Energy and Natural Resources Committee approved the measure, 11–9, on July 28, 1998. The House adopted the conference report on the appropriations bill (H Rept 105-825) 333–95 on Oct. 20, and the Senate cleared the conference report by a vote of 65–29 on Oct. 21.

Great Lakes

Congress cleared legislation in 1998 to authorize $40 million through fiscal 2003 for wildlife, conservation, and other restoration projects in and around the Great Lakes.

The bill (HR 1481—PL 105-265) reauthorized and amended a 1990 law (PL 101-596) that sought to revitalize the five lakes and more than 10,000 miles of shoreline that constituted the largest system of surface freshwater in the world. It also implemented the recommendations of a 1995 Great Lakes resources study and created a committee to review restoration proposals.

The 1995 study found that the problems facing the Great Lakes region included chemical contamination, overexploitation of fish and wildlife resources, and the introduction of nonindigenous species. The bill required the Fish and Wildlife Service to annually request from states and Native American tribes restoration proposals for the region. It set up a committee, composed of representatives of all the affected states and tribes, to review the proposals.

The Fish and Wildlife Service then would select proposals to be funded under the bill. At least 25 percent of the cost of each project would have to be funded with nonfederal money.

The House Resources Committee approved the measure (H Rept 105-715) by voice vote on Aug. 5. The House passed it by voice vote on Sept. 23, and the Senate cleared it by unanimous consent on Oct. 2. Clinton signed it Oct. 19.

Hunting of Migratory Birds

The House and Senate in 1998 passed slightly differing versions of a bill that would have made it more difficult to prosecute individuals accused of hunting migratory birds that were baited illegally.

The measure (HR 2863—H Rept 105-542) would have amended the 1918 Migratory Bird Treaty Act—which implemented an international treaty governing the management of birds such as ducks and geese—to ease the liability standard for those accused of using feed, grain, or salt to lure birds within shooting range.

The law allowed the prosecution of hunters even if they were unaware they were hunting baited fowl. Baiting still would be prohibited under the bill. However, the bill would remove the strict liability interpretation of the original act and instead require the Fish and Wildlife Service to prove that a hunter "knows or reasonably should have known" that bait was present.

Penalties for violating the baiting rule would include seizure of guns, fines, or incarceration. If the facts showed that the hunter could not have known that bait was present, the court would not impose liability or assess penalties. Some critics said the bill would make charges of baiting almost impossible to prove.

The House Resources Committee approved the measure by voice vote on April 29, and the House passed it on Sept. 10 by a vote of 322–90. The Senate passed the bill by unanimous consent on Oct. 13 after amending it with minor changes. The House did not take up the amended measure.

National Park Operations

After years of delicate negotiation among congressional factions, Congress in 1998 cleared legislation to overhaul management practices and the bidding process for concession contracts in national parks.

The bill (S 1693—PL 105-391) established new criteria for adding land to the national park system; required five-year strategic and performance evaluations for individual parks; and mandated more budget analysis, audits, and improved training for park service employees.

It also changed the often-criticized system of awarding contracts for concessions in national parks by eliminating most preferential rights of renewal and creating a competitive bidding process. Some lawmakers had criticized that process as anticompetitive.

The measure extended through 2005 the pilot projects that allowed parks to charge admission and user fees. It established a "passport entrance system" that allowed visitors to buy a national parks passport and collectors' stamps.

The Senate on June 11 passed a somewhat broader version of the measure (S Rept 105-202) by unanimous consent. In addition to overhauling concessions policy, the Senate bill, sponsored by Craig Thomas, R-Wyo., would require filmmakers shooting in the park system to pay a portion of their commercial production budgets toward resource protection projects.

But the bill stirred considerable debate in the House Resources Committee. The National Parks and Public Lands Subcommittee approved S 1693 on a voice vote on June 23, but moved it to the full committee without a recommendation. Subcommittee chairman James V. Hansen, R-Utah, said major portions of the bill needed to be reworked.

The House Resources Committee approved the bill by voice vote on Aug. 5 after adopting several amendments. An amendment by Joel Hefley, R-Colo., struck the section in the bill allowing parks to impose fees on production companies that filmed movies, television shows, or commercials within their boundaries. Also approved by voice vote was an amendment offered by Bruce F. Vento, D-Minn., that would allow revenues generated from concession contracts to be returned to national parks without annual appropriations.

The panel's ranking Democrat, George Miller of California, complained that language that would allow concessionaires to include the cost of structural improvements in their bids for contract renewals would be anticompetitive. But a Miller amendment to strike the language failed, 20–21, despite support from several Republicans.

The House passed the bill by voice vote on Oct. 13, and the Senate cleared it by unanimous consent the next day.

MAJOR PROVISIONS

As signed into law on Nov. 13, 1998, the major provisions of S 1693 were:

• **Concessions contracts.** The National Park Service was directed to use concessions contracts, awarded through a competitive bid process, to authorize companies to provide accommodations and other services to park visitors. Before awarding a new contract, the agency had to solicit proposals publicly for the contract. The interior secretary, however, had the authority to award a temporary contract to avoid an interruption of services at a park unit. The bill required that Congress be notified of any proposed contract that was expected to last more than ten years or gross more than $5 million.

The park service generally was prohibited from providing preferential rights to concessions when renewing contracts or awarding new ones (although the bill included exceptions for certain contracts grossing less than $500,000 annually, and it also exempted certain guide and outfitter contracts).

- **Franchise fees.** The bill established criteria for determining franchise fees. It directed that 80 percent of the fees would be used at the park service unit at which they were collected; 20 percent would be used for activities throughout the park service.
- **Training.** A comprehensive training program would be developed for National Park Service employees. The interior secretary would also create a management development program to enable qualified employees to move into park management positions.
- **Five-year plans.** Each unit in the park service would prepare and make public a five-year strategic plan, as well as an annual performance plan.
- **Resource inventory and management.** The measure encouraged the National Park Service to enter into agreements with colleges and universities to research and provide information on park resources or on the larger regions that encompassed the parks. The interior secretary was to monitor the resources, establishing baseline information and providing information on long-term trends.
- **Additional park service areas.** The interior secretary was directed to submit to Congress a list of areas that should be studied for possible inclusion in the national park system. The studies, which could not be conducted without congressional authorization, would consider whether the area included nationally significant natural or cultural resources.
- **Advisory board.** The bill established a National Park Service Concessions Management Advisory Board to advise the Interior secretary and National Park Service on concession issues.
- **Transportation.** The park service was authorized to levy charges on visitors who used park transportation services. The funds that were collected had to be spent on transportation-related items within that park unit.
- **Passport program.** The interior secretary was directed to establish a national park passport program that would include a collectible stamp providing the holder with admission to all park units.

National Parks Projects

A sweeping parks and public lands bill studded with popular projects in thirty-six states, as well as numerous controversial provisions, was defeated soundly in the House two weeks before adjournment. However, many of the projects were resurrected in individual bills.

The omnibus legislation (HR 4570) consisted of nearly 100 bills rolled into one giant measure. It included dozens of relatively noncontroversial projects, such as authorization for the 6,000-mile cross-country American Discovery Trail, expansion of the Fort Davis National Historic Site in Texas, and permission for the government of India to build a memorial to Mohandas K. Gandhi in the District of Columbia. But environmentalists said those items did not outweigh various unpalatable provisions.

Most troublesome, they said, was language that would limit new wilderness areas, accelerate timber harvests on federal lands, and convey a road easement through a national forest in Alaska. The administration objected to those and more than two dozen other provisions in the bill and threatened a presidential veto.

Critics argued during debate that the bill was designed to surround unpalatable measures with popular ones. Minnesota Democrat Bruce F. Vento described the bill as stuffed with "rancid pork."

Sherwood Boehlert, R-N.Y., leader of proenvironment, moderate Republicans, derided the tactics, charging that sponsors decided to "hold perfectly good projects hostage in an attempt to jam through the Congress bad policies that don't have a prayer of passing independently."

But supporters, as well as the bill's sponsor, James V. Hansen, R-Utah, urged lawmakers to pass the bill because 90 percent of the items were noncontroversial. In an attempt to win over some support, Hansen offered a substitute that dropped and modified a handful of the bill's most controversial items.

The concessions, however, led a group of conservatives, led by Richard W. Pombo, R-Calif., to vote "no" because they felt Hansen had gone too far to placate the environmentalists.

In the end, the House voted down the bill, 123–302, on Oct. 7. Most Democrats and 107 Republicans voted against it.

But in the wake of the defeat, Hansen split off the noncontroversial items and moved them through the unanimous consent calendar or attached them to other legislation. Dozens of them became law in the frenzied last days of the 105th Congress.

Among the resuscitated provisions were those designating Little Rock's Central High School a National Historic Site, creating an Automobile Heritage Area in Michigan, establishing the Tuskegee Airmen National Historic Site in Alabama, and revising the boundary of the Abraham Lincoln Birthplace National Historic Site in Kentucky to include the former president's boyhood home.

Texas Low-Level Waste Site

Lawmakers in 1998 cleared a bill (HR 629—PL 105-236) to create a three-state compact for the disposal of low-level nuclear waste, ending a three-year legislative battle that culminated in opponents of the project accusing lawmakers of "environmental racism."

Under the compact, Texas would accept low-level waste from Vermont and Maine. Each state would pay $25 million toward development of the proposed site in Sierra Blanca, a remote area of western Texas near the Mexican border. Supporters had tried since 1995 to enact the compact.

While the measure was endorsed by the governors and state legislatures of the three states, it was vigorously opposed by some Texas lawmakers, reflecting strong local opposition to the compact. Resistance was particularly strong in Sierra Blanca, the town closest to the proposed site.

BACKGROUND

The Low Level Radioactive Waste Policy Act, enacted in 1980 (PL 96-573) and amended in 1985 (PL 99-240), made states responsible for disposing low-level radioactive waste generated within their borders. Examples of such waste included protective clothing worn by nuclear power workers, and radiological and other waste generated by hospitals. *(1980 law, Congress and the Nation Vol. V, p. 521; 1985 law, Congress and the Nation Vol. VII, p. 449)*

The act encouraged states to form regional waste disposal compacts in order to limit the number of disposal sites. Congress had consented to nine such interstate compacts involving forty-one states. States participating in a congressionally approved disposal compact could exclude from their disposal facilities any waste generated in states that were not members of that compact.

Despite bipartisan support, the proposed Texas compact had a difficult time in Congress. A nearly identical measure had breezed through the Commerce Committee in 1995 but was defeated on the House floor. *(Congress and the Nation Vol. IX, p. 469)*

The plan received mixed reviews, including an even split among the Texas delegation. Supporters of the bill asserted that Congress was simply fulfilling its role in approving a compact already agreed to among the states. Opponents contended that the proposed waste site—a ranch about fifteen miles from the Rio Grande, near the border town of Sierra Blanca—would violate accords with Mexico that prohibited environmental degradation within sixty miles of the U.S.-Mexico border.

Two west Texas House members, Democrat Silvestre Reyes and Republican Henry Bonilla, warned that the area's population, predominantly poor and Latino, felt betrayed.

1997 LEGISLATIVE ACTION

Those ill feelings became evident when the House Commerce Energy and Power Subcommittee held a hearing prior to approving the bill May 13. Texans squared off against Texans, with Bonilla and Reyes dueling with Republican Joe L. Barton and Democrat Gene Green, who supported the plan.

But the subcommittee shrugged off the opposition as a matter for Texans to resolve among themselves. Both Dan Schaefer, R-Colo., the subcommittee's chairman, and Ralph M. Hall of Texas, its ranking Democrat, noted that nowhere in the bill was Sierra Blanca designated as the site for the waste dump. That had been determined by Texas officials and endorsed by Republican Gov. George W. Bush and his predecessor, Democrat Ann W. Richards.

The full Commerce Committee gave voice vote approval to the bill on June 25 with little debate (H Rept 105-181).

Although the project drew opposition from the League of United Latin American Citizens as well as from environmental groups, the House passed the bill Oct. 7 by a vote of 309–107. During the floor debate, supporters of the bill, including many members of the Texas delegation, argued that Congress should give its consent to an agreement that had been reached by local officials.

But Bonilla and Reyes again argued against the bill. "Who would want radioactive waste shipped to their district?" Reyes asked. Reyes argued that the Sierra Blanca site was prone to earthquakes and said the compact would disproportionately affect Hispanics, who made up 75 percent of the population surrounding the site.

1998 LEGISLATIVE ACTION

Opponents of the measure found an ally in Sen. Paul Wellstone, D-Minn., who focused on civil rights issues. Wellstone argued that the Texas site was chosen because it was in a low-income and predominantly Hispanic area.

"This isn't just a Texas issue. This is a national civil rights issue," he said. "Every time they decide to put a nuclear waste site somewhere . . . it's always the path of least resistance."

But proponents of the compact countered that Congress was simply fulfilling its role in approving the legislation to give Texas, Maine, and Vermont the same waste disposal options practiced in forty-one other states.

Sen. Olympia J. Snowe, R-Maine, noted that the legislation did not endorse a particular location for the waste. The bill left the selection up to the state of Texas, which had been evaluating the Sierra Blanca site, she said.

When the Senate passed its version of the bill on April 1, Wellstone added an amendment allowing local residents to challenge the site if they believed they had been discriminated against on the basis of race, color, national origin, or income level. He added another amendment stipulating no states other than Texas, Maine, and Vermont could send waste to the site. Both amendments were passed by unanimous consent, as was the underlying bill. But conferees stripped the amendments from the bill.

In the House, some Texans objected to the conference report because additional states might be allowed to ship waste to their home state. "Our concern is that all fifty states would like to send their garbage to Texas," said Lloyd Doggett, D-Texas.

Other Texans supported the bill, saying it simply would allow the states to carry out a deal that had been negotiated by the three governors and approved by each state's legislature. Hall said that six of the eight commissioners who would govern the site under the bill would come from Texas and that lawmakers should trust them not to let the site become a dumping ground for the whole nation.

The House took up HR 629 on July 29, adopting a rule by a vote of 313–108 that prohibited opponents from altering the final version of the legislation. The House then voted, 305–117, to adopt the conference report.

In a last-ditch effort to stop the bill, Wellstone held up action on the measure prior to the summer recess in a bid to generate last-minute opposition. But supporters of the legislation, including some residents of Sierra Blanca, said the project would create much-needed jobs. The town was already home to a waste disposal site used by New York City for its treated sewage.

The Senate on Sept. 2 voted, 78–15, to adopt the conference report on HR 629 (H Rept 105-630). All the "no" votes were cast by Democrats. President Clinton signed the bill Sept. 20, 1998.

Nuclear Waste Storage

A proposal to open a temporary nuclear waste storage site 100 miles northwest of Las Vegas in the barren Nevada desert fell victim to continued opposition from the state's congressional delegation, as well as 1998 election-year political considerations.

The interim site, near Yucca Mountain, was a priority for nuclear power companies, which complained that waste was piling up at utility sites across the nation. Safety and environmental problems were expected to delay the opening of a permanent repository at Yucca Mountain until at least 2010.

In 1997 nuclear utilities scored a victory of sorts when both the House and Senate passed bills (HR 1270, S 104) to require the Department of Energy to build an interim storage site for spent fuel from commercial reactors. The House bill proposed a deadline of January 2002; the Senate opted for Nov. 30, 1999.

The plan was intended to sidestep the lengthy process of building a permanent dump at the mountain site—a battle that had entangled Congress for more than a decade. Utilities pressured Congress and the White House for quick action, saying they were running out of room in storage pools for spent nuclear fuel.

But Clinton administration officials remained resolute in their opposition to the supposedly temporary solution, which they feared could kill efforts to implement long-term underground waste disposal. They argued that a temporary location would bias scientific studies of the waste site and drain resources aimed at a permanent solution.

Nevada's congressional delegation was vehemently opposed to storing the waste in their state. The state's two Democratic senators, Harry Reid and Richard H. Bryan, warned they would use every tactic they could to slow or thwart final passage of a bill that their constituents detested. "It's Armageddon," Bryan warned, vowing to repeat his lengthy 1996 filibuster on similar legislation. (*Congress and the Nation Vol. IX, p. 473*)

Rep. John Ensign, R-Nev., was able to use a procedural move to insist that the Senate act on HR 1270, thereby exposing it to a filibuster. On June 2, 1998, the Senate came up 4 votes short of the 60 needed to shut off debate and move to a vote. The action followed a statement from House Speaker Newt Gingrich, R-Ga., that he did not expect to bring the bill before the House—a decision some Republicans complained was designed to boost Ensign in his challenge to incumbent Democratic Sen. Harry Reid. (*1999–2000 action, p. 407*)

BACKGROUND

The 1982 Nuclear Waste Policy Act (PL 97-425) established a national nuclear waste disposal system and gave the Energy Department until 1998 to open a permanent underground repository for high-level nuclear waste. The department was required to take possession of the waste by Jan. 31, 1998. To finance development of the facility, the law also established the Nuclear Waste Fund to collect fees from nuclear utilities. About $12 billion had been raised by the fund, about $5 billion of which had been spent on the program.

In 1987 Congress directed the department to limit its evaluation of potential nuclear waste repository sites to one location, an arid ridge called Yucca Mountain on Nevada's former nuclear weapons testing grounds, and to subject only that site to a series of intensive geological and hydrological studies. If the studies determined that the site was suitable, it would then be formally selected. The department expected to complete the initial viability assessment in 1998, but its target date for opening a permanent repository had been put off until 2010.

The 1987 law also directed the Energy Department to develop a temporary facility to store nuclear waste until a permanent site was ready. But attempts to place that site at Yucca Mountain had been unsuccessful. In the meantime, storage space for spent nuclear fuel was being exhausted at dozens of nuclear utilities.

1997 LEGISLATIVE ACTION

After weeks of delay, the Senate Energy and Natural Resources Committee approved its version of the bill on March 13 by a vote of 15–5 (S 104—S Rept 105-10). The committee-approved bill gave the president until Dec. 31, 1998, to halt construction at a temporary waste site at Yucca Mountain if he determined that the site was not viable for permanent storage. He then would have eighteen months to find an alternative location that Congress would have to approve within twenty-four months.

The major committee debate came when Jeff Bingaman, D-N.M., tried to address White House objections by introducing four broad amendments, all of which were defeated. Bingaman's proposals would have ratcheted up radiation safety standards; removed a provision to preempt all federal, state, and local laws that conflicted with the waste legislation; made it more difficult for Congress to use certain fees collected from utilities for purposes other than nuclear waste disposal; and mitigated financial claims against the federal government that could arise if the government missed the 1998 deadline for assuming control over utilities' nuclear waste.

Democrats complained that chairman Frank H. Murkowski, R-Alaska, gave little serious thought to Bingaman's proposals. "You want to drive this bill out of here, and we want to work it out before driving it out," said Democrat Wendell H. Ford of Kentucky.

After several days of debate, the Senate passed the bill April 15 in a **key vote of 65–34 (R 53–2; D 12–32).** But the Senate tally was still two votes shy of the margin needed to override Clinton's threatened veto. *(1997 key votes, p. 865)*

When the Senate began work on the bill April 9, Murkowski made several concessions aimed at swaying key Democratic votes. The changes, which surprised even the Democrats, included tightening environmental rules on the waste site, bolstering training provisions for transportation workers, and moving back the opening date for the repository from 1999, as originally proposed, until June 30, 2003.

But the modifications were not enough to attain the backing of the White House. Bill proponents also lost their chance to cross the veto-proof threshold when they came out against a key amendment by Bingaman, who was highly regarded by Democrats for his acumen on nuclear issues. Bingaman's amendment would have barred interim storage at the Nevada site if Energy Department scientists found Yucca Mountain to be unsuitable for permanent storage.

Murkowski said he was 90 percent sure Yucca would be suitable, but he refused to give in, saying the Bingaman amendment would invite the president to find the site wanting and do nothing. In the end, Murkowski's motion to table (kill) Bingaman's amendment passed, 59–39.

House action on the measure began in the Commerce Subcommittee on Energy and Power, which approved its version of the bill (HR 1270) on July 31 by a lopsided vote of 21–3, despite dogged efforts by Edward J. Markey, D-Mass., to derail the measure.

The draft bill mandated opening the temporary waste site by 2002. In a compromise with the nuclear power industry, the bill proposed setting up new formulas to allow the amount of money taken from ratepayers for the project to increase by as much as 50 percent in some years. In exchange, the utilities' payments would be lower in other years.

The draft bill also proposed limiting the capacity of the temporary site to 40,000 metric tons of waste, considerably less than the total amount of nuclear waste that was expected to be generated by the end of the next century. The limit was meant to ensure that the temporary site did not become the de facto permanent site. The bill also proposed to require the Energy Department to develop a nationwide rail and truck transportation system, including help for towns along the way to plan for potential emergencies; preempt environmental laws; and set a deadline of January 2010 to open a permanent repository at Yucca Mountain.

Markey, a longtime foe of the nuclear industry, began his battle against the bill with a series of amendments, all of which were defeated. He proposed to strike a clause forbidding the Environmental Protection Agency (EPA) from setting radiation protection standards for the project; strike proposed restrictions on an Energy Department environmental impact statement; reduce the size of the temporary site; eliminate caps on the amount of money that utilities would have to pay in a given year for site construction; and

ensure that the permanent waste site would be large enough to handle all the civilian and defense nuclear waste that the nation would generate.

The full Commerce Committee approved the bill on Sept. 18, 43–3, after shucking off more than a half-dozen Democratic amendments.

Energy and Power Subcommittee Chairman Dan Schaefer, R-Colo., tried to placate some Democratic concerns with a new version of the bill that allowed for a more diligent environmental review and gave a larger oversight role to the EPA. His substitute also included a provision specifically aimed at committee member Elizabeth Furse, D-Ore., to make it easier for shutdown reactors to get their waste included in the interim storage site. Oregon was home to such a reactor.

As he had done in the subcommittee, Markey peppered the proceedings with amendments, none of which came close to passage. Among other things, the amendments would have denied nuclear waste transport contractors immunity from civil liability in the event of an accident; potentially tightened a radiation-exposure standard; and barred selection of an interim storage site until the suitability of Yucca Mountain had been determined.

The House Resources Committee, which shared jurisdiction over the bill, voted Oct. 8 to report the measure unfavorably (H Rept 105-290, Pt. 2). The decision, approved by voice vote, meant the committee recommended that the House not pass the bill. That left it to the Rules Committee to choose between two competing versions of the legislation.

The unfavorable report by the Resources Committee, chaired by Don Young, R-Alaska, served notice that Nevada was not without allies. Nevada's Ensign called the bill a "war on the West," echoing a battle cry started in the 1980s, when Congress decided to build a repository in the remote West rather than on the East or West Coasts or in the Midwest, South, or Northeast, where much of the nation's nuclear power was generated.

As expected, the House Rules Committee made the Commerce Committee's version of the bill in order. After considering numerous amendments, the House passed the measure Oct. 30 by a vote of 307–120.

Nevada Republicans Ensign and Jim Gibbons led the floor fight against the bill. They complained that the Republican leadership did not allow consideration of enough key amendments, such as one that Dennis J. Kucinich, D-Ohio, had proposed which would have prohibited companies from transporting high-level radioactive waste through cities with more than 50,000 residents.

Markey tried to recommit the bill before final passage, with instructions to insert language to remove indemnification for nuclear waste transporters that were involved in accidents. The motion to recommit failed by a 142–283 vote.

1998 LEGISLATIVE ACTION

The Senate on June 2 fell four votes short of the 60 votes needed for cloture in order to move to a vote on HR 1270.

The 39–56 vote came after Senate Democrats complained that taking up the nuclear waste bill would interrupt debate on, and possibly kill, a comprehensive tobacco proposal (S 1415—S Rept 105-180) that was being debated.

The Senate's action also followed a statement from House Speaker Newt Gingrich, R-Ga., who said he did not expect to bring the nuclear waste bill before the House in 1998.

Gingrich said his decision was the result of "the crowded calendar and the strong opposition of some members." But some lawmakers also saw it as a nod to Rep. John Ensign, R-Nev., in his challenge to Democratic Sen. Harry Reid. Ensign startled many senators by announcing the Speaker's decision even before Gingrich did.

After the Senate vote, representatives of the nuclear power industry vowed to continue exploring ways to clear the bill by the end of the 105th Congress. But Senate Energy and Natural Resources Chairman Frank H. Murkowski, R-Alaska, said the bill was dead for the year.

"It looks like it's dead until Ensign's election comes up," Murkowski said. "It's a loss for the taxpayer, it's a loss for the industry and it's a loss for Congress, because it ain't going to go away."

Nevada senators Reid and Bryan declared victory. The Republicans, Reid said, were trying to drop tobacco and "trying to make nuclear waste the fall guy."

Senate Majority Leader Trent Lott, R-Miss., decided to scheduled the June 2 cloture vote during a break in the tobacco debate. Lott said June 1 that he had been told the nuclear waste bill had more than the 67 votes to override a presidential veto. The version the Senate passed in 1997 got 65 votes.

But some Democrats portrayed Lott's decision as a tactic to delay action on tobacco. Although the tobacco bill had bipartisan support, some Republicans objected to the comprehensive bill, which would have increased cigarette taxes and launched a campaign to cut teen smoking.

On the cloture vote, all 53 of the Republicans present supported limiting debate on the waste bill. They were joined by three of the 42 Democrats present: Carl Levin of Michigan, Ernest F. Hollings of South Carolina, and Charles S. Robb of Virginia.

Murkowski accused the other Democrats of uniting behind the bill to bolster Reid's chances. "It's crass politics to save Reid; that's what that caucus was all about," he said.

But among those who joined Reid and Bryan in opposing cloture was Bob Graham, D-Fla., a supporter of the storage proposal. Graham said before the vote that he was "unwilling to take the risk" of consuming floor time.

SUPREME COURT ACTION

Adding to the complexity of the issue, the Supreme Court on Nov. 30, 1998, let stand a ruling concerning the perplexing problem of finding a permanent, safe repository for thousands of tons of highly radioactive waste generated by the nuclear power industry. The justices, without comment, let stand an earlier ruling by a federal appeals court in a case, *Michigan v. Department of Energy,* that pitted nuclear power plant operators and states against the federal government.

Under a 1982 law (PL 97-425), the Energy Department was to provide a repository by Feb. 1, 1998, for the 40,000-plus tons of used reactor fuel stored at seventy-two nuclear power plants in thirty-four states.

When it became clear that the 1998 deadline would not be met, the Energy Department interpreted the 1982 law to mean that no government collection of nuclear waste need begin until a storage facility is completed. Challenging that interpretation in federal appeals court were states, state utility commissions, and reactor operators, who sought an order that the government begin collecting nuclear waste and escrow all fee payments due after the 1998 deadline.

In 1997 the U.S. Court of Appeals for the District of Columbia Circuit ruled that the government did not have to start its nuclear waste collection until it decided on a permanent repository. But it also ruled that the Energy Department could be sued for monetary damages by entities that had relied on the 1998 deadline. By late 1998, eleven utility companies had filed lawsuits in the Court of Federal Claims seeking damages ranging from $70 million to $1.5 billion.

Nutria Eradication Program

Congress in 1998 cleared legislation that aimed to eradicate nutria, a semiaquatic species of rodent blamed for damaging environmentally sensitive wetlands on Maryland's Eastern Shore.

The bill (HR 4337—PL 105-322) authorized $2.9 million over three years for the eradication program. The Interior Department would fund a pilot program to implement recommendations outlined in an April 1998 report issued by several state and federal agencies. Part of the program would involve trapping nutria in certain Maryland wildlife areas. Results from the pilot project would be shared with other regions and states, such as Louisiana, that have similar animal-control problems. The bill also specified that the federal government could pay for no more than 75 percent of the program.

Nutria were indigenous to Latin America and were introduced into Maryland in the 1940s for their durable fur. With no natural predators in North America, they multiplied rapidly and threatened to overwhelm native ecosystems. Over the past few years, it was estimated that 7,000 of the 17,000 total acres of marshland in Maryland's Blackwater National Wildlife Refuge was been lost because of the rodent's eating habits. The lost marshland endangered the habitats of waterfowl and fish, which in turn jeopardized the winter habitats of migratory birds.

The House Resources subcommittee on Fisheries Conservation, Wildlife and Oceans approved the measure by voice vote on Sept. 17. The House passed it by voice vote just eleven days later, and the Senate cleared it by unanimous consent on Oct. 9. President Clinton signed it Oct. 30, 1998.

Ocean Policy Panel

With concerns mounting about overfishing and other marine environmental threats, the House in 1998 passed legislation that would establish a sixteen-member bipartisan panel on ocean policy to make recommendations to Congress. But the Senate, which had passed a similar measure one year earlier, took no action on the House bill.

The bill (HR 3445—H Rept 105-718) would authorize $3 million over two years for the panel, which would study oceanic environments and review the policies and projects of the numerous agencies and departments with jurisdiction over nonmilitary oceanic policy and research. It would issue a biennial report outlining its recommendations to Congress beginning in 1999.

The measure would call on the commission to address seven specific issues: expansion of knowledge of the marine environment and ocean resources; responsible and economically beneficial use of ocean resources; prevention of marine pollution; protection of life and property against natural and man-made hazards; development and improvement of technology for use in ocean and coastal activities; consistency and cooperation between federal departments and agencies and state and local governments involved in ocean and coastal activities; and preservation of the U.S. role as a leader in ocean activities and cooperation by the United States with other nations and international organizations involved with ocean and coastal activities.

The panel would review the policies and projects of the numerous agencies and departments that have jurisdiction over nonmilitary oceanic policy and research, such as the National Oceanic and Atmospheric Administration, the U.S. Fish and Wildlife Service, and the Army Corps of Engineers.

The bill called for coastal states to be consulted during the report drafting. It also would require the panel to consider the impact of its recommendations on ocean-related industries and private property holders. The recommendations would have to be peer-reviewed.

Members of the panel would be appointed by the president and congressional leaders to recommend "responsible and economically beneficial use and stewardship" of ocean resources, including new technologies. The commission would release a biennial report outlining its recommendations, beginning in 1999.

"These matters are in urgent need of study" and of a comprehensive legislative policy approach, said bill sponsor Rep. Jim Saxton, R-N.J., who chaired the Resources subcommittee on Fisheries Conservation, Wildlife and Oceans.

Saxton's subcommittee approved the measure on April 23 by voice vote after Saxton quashed efforts by W. J. "Billy" Tauzin, R-La., to limit the bill's scope. Tauzin offered an amendment, which was rejected 12–24, to eliminate near-

shore estuaries from the commission's scope of inquiry. But ranking Democrat George Miller of California argued that estuaries were a part of the oceanic ecosystem and should be studied.

The Resources Committee approved the bill by voice vote on July 29. But, in a concession to chairman Don Young, R-Alaska, the amended legislation excluded Alaska from the study. Young said that, while he supported the bill and was "under great pressure" to get the bill out of committee, he had concerns about how it would affect his state.

The House passed the legislation on Sept. 15.

The Senate, which passed a similar bill (S 1213—S Rept 105-151) by unanimous consent in 1997, took no action on the House measure.

Salton Sea Rehabilitation

Congress in 1998 cleared legislation to authorize $350 million to rehabilitate California's Salton Sea as a tribute to the late Sonny Bono, R-Calif., and to name a wildlife refuge in his honor. Bono, a well-known singer before winning a seat in Congress, died in a skiing accident in January. He had led an effort to clean up the Salton Sea, which was also a wildlife habitat but had become degraded by increasingly high levels of salt in the water.

The bill (HR 3267—PL 105-372) would require the Interior Department to spend eighteen months studying rescue alternatives for the site, threatened in recent years by rising salt and pollution levels. It also renamed the refuge the "Sonny Bono Salton Sea National Wildlife Refuge."

The eighty-foot deep sea spanned 378 square miles and was originally created by accidental irrigation runoff in the early 1900s. Without tributaries or other outlets to cleanse its waters, salt and minerals have built up, causing water to evaporate rapidly and endangering wildlife. Salt levels were 25 percent higher than in the Pacific Ocean.

The House Resources Committee approved the measure (H Rept 105-621) by voice vote on May 21. However, California Democrats George Miller and Sam Farr raised concerns about water allocation issues and the bill's requirement that the $350 million in construction funds be earmarked from the Interior Department's land and water conservation fund. Both offered amendments, defeated by voice votes, that would have changed the funding arrangement.

The House on July 15 narrowly passed the bill on a 221–200 vote that veered closely along party lines. "We must act fast to save this great body of water," said Mary Bono, R-Calif., shortly before the House vote to approve the bill initially spearheaded by her late husband. "It's like an oasis in the middle of the desert, as Sonny used to say."

Under fire from Democrats and environmentalists, Republicans offered an amendment to ensure the cleanup would not be funded by the Interior Department's land and water conservation fund. While the amendment was adopted by voice vote, many Democrats were not appeased.

George Miller, D-Calif., unsuccessfully offered a substitute amendment that would have struck funding for the reclamation project and initiated a $30 million study to look into other ways to improve water quality. It also called for $5 million to study wildlife resources.

The amendment would guarantee "the money we spend will be spent in a scientifically sound fashion," said Miller.

The amendment was struck down by a vote of 202–218.

The Senate on Oct. 13 passed the measure with an amendment, and the House cleared it by voice vote on Oct. 21.

MAJOR PROVISIONS

As signed into law on Nov. 12, 1998, the major provisions of HR 3267:

• **Reclamation.** The interior secretary, by Jan. 1, 2000, would complete all feasibility studies and cost analyses into reclaiming the Salton Sea. The studies would include options for reducing and stabilizing the sea's salinity, stabilizing the surface elevation, restoring fish and wildlife resources, and enhancing the area's recreational use and economic development.

• **Colorado River.** The feasibility studies could not include any option that included the importation of any additional water from the Colorado River. The bill explicitly preserved all current rights and obligations regarding the use of Colorado River water.

• **New name.** The Salton Sea National Wildlife Refuge was renamed the Sonny Bono Salton Sea National Wildlife Refuge.

• **Alamo River and New River.** The interior secretary would construct river reclamation and wetlands projects to improve water quality in the Alamo and New Rivers in California by treating water in those rivers and irrigation drainage water that flowed into the rivers.

• **Appropriations.** The bill authorized $350 million for the reclamation project.

Uranium Cleanup

Congress in 1998 cleared legislation to earmark nearly $400 million for cleanup of depleted uranium that was stored at uranium enrichment plants near Portsmouth, Ohio, and Paducah, Kentucky.

The Energy Department's former uranium enrichment program, which produced the principal ingredient of the fuel used by nuclear power plants, was turned over to a federally owned U.S. Enrichment Corporation. In the final step in a privatization process, the corporation was to be sold to private investors through a stock offering.

The legislation (S 2316—PL 105-204), sponsored by Ohio and Kentucky lawmakers, would require the government to retain and reserve for plant cleanup the $385 million the uranium enrichment program had collected from customers for environmental restoration.

Sen. Mitch McConnell, R-Ky., the lead sponsor of the Senate version of the measure, said the administration's current plan was to allow the corporation to retain $50 million of the money for cleanup and put the remainder into the government's general fund.

Ohio and Kentucky lawmakers wanted the full amount to be used for a new facility that would convert the uranium hexafluoride, which was stored in thousands of aging canisters at the plants, to a more stable uranium oxide.

The Senate passed the bill by voice vote on July 16, and the House cleared it by voice vote on July 20. President Clinton signed it on July 21.

Vehicle Emissions

Amid concerns over Mexican-registered cars contributing to U.S. air pollution, Congress cleared a bill in 1998 to tighten air quality standards on the U.S.-Mexico border.

Rep. Brian P. Bilbray, R-Calif., the sponsor of the measure, said some U.S. citizens and legal migrant workers were registering their cars in Mexico to avoid U.S. emissions standards. As a result, an estimated 13 percent of the smog in Southern California was caused by cars that could not pass state emissions tests, he said.

The Environmental Protection Agency estimated that vehicle inspection and maintenance programs reduced pollution at a cost of $500 per ton, as opposed to $2,000 to $10,000 per ton for stationary sources.

The bill (HR 8—PL 105-286) would require U.S. customs officials to administer emissions tests to cars with Mexico registration. Noncomplying vehicles would be barred from entering the United States more than twice in a month in areas that did meet federal standards for ozone pollution as specified in the Clean Air Act. First-time violators would face up to $200 in fines and $400 for repeat offenses.

The General Accounting Office also would have to study whether the bill's provisions have an impact on air quality.

States bordering Canada would not be required to check for emissions compliance, but they could opt into the program.

The House passed the measure (H Rept 105-634) by voice vote on July 20. The Senate Environment and Public Works Committee approved it on Sept. 28 after strengthening language on inspections and fines. The Senate passed it by voice vote on Oct. 5, and the House cleared it on Oct. 7. The president signed it Oct. 27, 1998.

Antiquities Act

The House in 1997 passed legislation (HR 1127) aimed at curbing the authority of presidents to protect environmentally sensitive lands as national monuments. Western Republicans pressed for the bill in reaction to a 1996 decision by President Clinton to set aside 1.7 million acres in Utah as the Grand Staircase-Escalante National Monument. But the bill drew vigorous protests from environmental groups and an administration veto threat, and the Senate did not take it up.

BACKGROUND

The 1906 Antiquities Act gave the president authority to designate a national monument on federal land, thereby protecting natural or cultural resources. A powerful environmental tool, it had been invoked by thirteen presidents to designate more than 100 national monuments, including Muir Woods in California, Death Valley in Nevada and California, the Edison Lab in New Jersey, and Bryce Canyon in Utah. Many were later designated as national parks, historic sites, or historical parks.

Administration officials hailed the 1906 act as one of the most successful environmental laws of the century, and Interior Secretary Bruce Babbitt warned lawmakers that Clinton would veto any attempt to weaken it.

Bill sponsor James V. Hansen, R-Utah, agreed that the law had been a valuable asset in protecting environmentally sensitive lands. But he and other westerners said that Clinton, in issuing the Utah designation, had overstepped the bounds and focused on election-year politics rather than environmental preservation.

Clinton's Sept. 18, 1996, designation of Grand Staircase-Escalante won plaudits from environmental groups, which had made it one of their priorities during the 1996 presidential campaign. The designation, which protected a vast expanse of labyrinthine canyons and red rock cliffs, was issued after Congress reached an impasse on legislation to create a new Utah wilderness area. Much of the land that would have been protected by that effort was included in Grand Staircase-Escalante. (*Congress and the Nation Vol. IX, p. 464*)

But Hansen asserted that much of the monument was an unsightly landscape that included "one of the ugliest places in the state of Utah." At the same time, Hansen said, the designation locked up access to 200,000 acres of income-producing land set aside in trust for public education in the state and an energy reserve valued at more than $1 trillion. For the critics, the Clinton decision amounted to trampling on the rights of average citizens.

HOUSE ACTION

The House Resources Subcommittee on National Parks and Public Lands approved HR 1127 by voice vote May 8. The full Resources Committee approved it June 25, also by voice vote (H Rept 105-191). The House passed a significantly amended version on Oct. 7 by a vote of 229–197.

The subcommittee version would have amended the 1906 Antiquities Act to bar the president from designating more than 50,000 acres as a national monument without first getting authorization from Congress, as well as from the governor and legislature of the state in which the monument was to be established.

The full committee added language to limit the president to designating no more than one monument per state each year. The amendment, by Helen Chenoweth, R-Idaho, was adopted by voice vote. "This administration has demonstrated a very voracious attitude for the acquisition of land," said Chenoweth, who was a leading property rights advocate.

On the House floor, conservatives had to make concessions to party moderates to get the bill through. Sherwood Boehlert, R-N.Y., a leading voice on environmental concerns, objected to the requirement that the president get congressional approval for any designation greater than 50,000 acres. He said the proviso would allow designation to be blocked through congressional inaction.

Boehlert supported a substitute amendment, adopted 222–202, that contained language allowing the president to make a designation of any size without first securing congressional approval. For monuments larger than 50,000 acres, the designation would expire within two years unless Congress passed a joint resolution endorsing it.

Earlier, the House rejected, 201–224, a proposal by Bruce F. Vento, D-Minn., to drop the 50,000-acre restriction in the bill and instead establish a one-year delay from the time the president announced a monument designation to the date it would take effect. (*1999 action, p. 389.*)

Utah Wilderness

Congress in 1998 cleared legislation to resolve a dispute created by competing land management missions of the state of Utah and the National Park Service in regard to the new Grand Staircase-Escalante National Monument.

The state owned about 176,600 acres of land, as well as approximately 24,165 acres of mineral interests, within the boundaries of the national monument, which Clinton created in 1996. The lands were granted to the state by Congress in 1894, and were administered by the Utah School and Institutional Trust Lands Administration.

To prevent the state from mining and developing its school trust land to fund state education programs, the federal government struck a deal with Utah early in 1998 calling for a swap of lands and cash. The bill (HR 3830—PL 105-335) codified that deal.

Under the legislation, the federal government would acquire all state land within Utah's national parks, forests, monuments, and recreation areas, as well as all state land within the Navajo and Goshute reservations. The total transfer would involve 377,000 acres.

In return, Utah would receive $50 million in cash previously set aside by Congress under the Utah Schools and Lands Improvement Act of 1993 (PL 103-93). The state would also receive 160 million tons of coal, 139,000 acres of land and minerals, and $13 million from the sale of unleased coal.

The House passed the measure (H Rept 105-598) by voice vote on June 24. The Senate cleared it by voice vote on Oct. 9. President Clinton signed it Oct. 31, 1998.

Alaska Land Swaps

A bill (S 967—S Rept 105-119) to allow development and land swaps in Alaska was approved on Sept. 24, 1997 by the

Senate Energy and Natural Resources Committee, but lawmakers took no further action on it.

The measure, sponsored by Frank H. Murkowski, R-Alaska, was endorsed on a 12–8 vote. Most Democrats voted "no" to support the administration, which threatened to veto the bill because of environmental concerns.

The bill sought to amend land claims laws for Alaska to allow a land exchange with the Calista Native Regional Corporation in which the government would get about 225,000 acres of land within the Yukon Delta National Wildlife Refuge. It would also affect traditional fishing rights in Glacier Bay National Park. Other provisions sought to allow property owners to retain ownership of cabins on certain lands and permit continued helicopter use on designated land under regulation by the Interior secretary.

Minnesota Boundary Wilderness

House and Senate panels in 1997 approved versions of a bill to ease motorboat and truck restrictions in the Boundary Waters Canoe Area Wilderness in northern Minnesota, bringing cheers from recreational boaters and boos from environmental groups. Although lawmakers did not clear those measures, they added a controversial provision to an omnibus transportation bill (HR 2400—PL 105-178) that allowed trucks to portage boats in two areas in the wilderness.

Stretching nearly 150 miles along the U.S.-Canadian border from Voyageurs National Park to Lake Superior, the wilderness was a popular tourist destination, attracting about 200,000 visitors a year. Heavy use had led to a dispute in Minnesota over whether trucks and motorboats should be banned permanently.

The Senate Energy and Natural Resources Committee was the first to act, approving its version of the bill (S 783—S Rept 105-80) on an 11–9 party-line vote July 30. Sponsored by Rod Grams, R-Minn., the legislation proposed allowing trucks to transport boats over three portage routes connecting five lakes in the area. It also would have deleted a provision in the 1978 Boundary Waters Act (PL 95-495) that phased out motorboats on part of Sea Gull Lake, located within the wilderness.

Grams argued that expanded access would benefit senior citizens and northern Minnesota families. But echoing the concerns of environmental groups, Dale Bumpers of Arkansas, the ranking Democrat on the panel, said the bill could damage the land and disrupt the placid wilderness.

A House subcommittee on Oct. 7 approved a companion bill (HR 1739) sponsored by James L. Oberstar, R-Minn. The Resources Subcommittee on Forests and Forest Health approved the measure, 5–2, after rejecting six amendments by Bruce Vento, D-Minn., that would have sharply curtailed truck and motorboat access.

The Resources Committee approved the bill, 22–7, on Oct. 22. Most of Vento's attempts to pare back the bill failed again, but two were approved as part of a proposal offered by Helen Chenoweth, R-Idaho. Her amendment, adopted by

voice vote, clarified that the bill would apply only to portages opened in 1992. It also sought to bar federal subsidies for private portage services, and prohibit the use of commercial equipment on portages.

The issue returned in 1998, when Vento acceded to a controversial plan by Oberstar to allow trucks to transport boats in two portages in the wilderness, while banning motorboats on part of Sea Gull Lake and two other lakes. The provision was added rather abruptly to the Transportation Equity Act for the 21st Century, a massive highway funding bill that was signed by Clinton on June 9, 1998. But the president singled out the Boundary Waters provision for criticism.

Vento defended the deal, saying it was the best agreement that could be negotiated in an antienvironmental Congress and contending that it would put to rest controversy over the Boundary Waters. "With the antienvironmental climate in Congress, no wilderness, national park, forest, lake or stream is safe," he said.

Hells Canyon

Committees in both chambers approved legislation in 1997 to lift a restriction on jetboats using the Snake River inside the Hells Canyon National Recreation Area in Oregon and Idaho. Congress, however, took no further action on the issue.

Created by Congress in 1975, the recreation area featured the deepest river canyon in North America (more than 7,900 feet deep) that contained habitat for numerous species of fish and wildlife, as well as old homesteads, mining sites, and prehistoric pictographs and petroglyphs. Although much of the Hells Canyon National Recreation Area was designated as wilderness, the river itself was open to motorized craft. Commercial jet boats had been used on the river since the early 1960s.

With rafters and jetboat users facing off over use of the river, a Forest Service management plan barred jetboats from a twenty-one-mile segment of the river on eight three-day periods during the summer. The legislation would remove the restriction and allow jetboats to use the river at any time.

The Senate Energy and Natural Resources Committee approved the bill (S 360—S Rept 105-78) on July 30 by a vote of 11–9. Bill sponsor Larry E. Craig, R-Idaho, said the Forest Service restrictions threatened to "wipe out an entire industry. . . . I'm willing to limit jetboating, but I'm not willing to take them off the river."

Ron Wyden, D-Ore., disagreed, saying the restrictions were not putting jetboaters out of business and that limits were necessary to protect the river ecosystem as well as commercial operators who ran rafting trips on the river.

The House Resources Committee approved a companion bill (HR 838—H Rept 105-378) on July 16.

U.N. Lands Designation

The House passed legislation in 1997 to sharply curtail U.S. participation in a United Nations program to recognize and preserve environmentally sensitive international areas. But the bill, which faced a presidential veto threat, was never taken up in the Senate. *(1999 action, p. 401)*

Supporters portrayed the bill (HR 901) as an attempt to protect federally controlled property from international influence. They warned that U.S. citizens could lose some sovereignty over land that was designated by the United Nations Educational, Scientific and Cultural Organization (UNESCO) as World Heritage sites and biosphere reserves.

Under a 1972 treaty approved by the United States and more than 100 other countries, twenty-two sites in the United States, including Yellowstone National Park, had been designated as World Heritage sites; forty-seven sites had been selected for the biosphere program. The designations were aimed at enhancing international cooperation in scientific research and establishing international alliances to protect the world's most valued cultural and natural sites.

The bill proposed that congressional approval be required for any new biosphere reserve or heritage sites and that existing biosphere reserve designations be terminated by 2000 unless they were authorized by Congress. Supporters said the measure would protect domestic land use decisions from international interference. But opponents, including the Clinton administration, said it would undercut international research and recognition that had benefited many of the designated areas.

The House Resources Committee approved the bill June 25 by a vote of 25–9 (H Rept 105-245). The House passed it Oct. 8 by a vote of 236–191, but only after opponents won passage of an amendment that was designed to change the focus of the bill.

The amendment, by Democrats George Miller of California and Bruce F. Vento of Minnesota, would require congressional approval when a foreign company wanted to mine or otherwise commercially develop federally controlled lands. The House passed the amendment 242–182.

In handouts distributed to members on the floor, Vento portrayed the amendment as a move to stop foreign companies from picking up cheap leases to mineral rights and otherwise using public lands at taxpayer expense. He said the true agenda of bill sponsor Don Young, R-Alaska, was to ease the way for greater commercial development. Young denied this, saying Vento's amendment was a toothless tiger that did not change the intent of his bill.

Forest Health

Though an array of bills related to forest maintenance and management were introduced in the 105th Congress, the only significant forest health measures that survived were tucked deep within the catchall legislative spending package: HR 4328 (PL 105-277). One controversial provision contained language to launch a pilot program for selective logging in three national forests in California—Plumas, Lassen, and Tahoe—to help reduce the risk of catastrophic fires.

It would require the Forest Service to start a five-year trial management plan.

The omnibus package also terminated the contentious forest road construction program, or "purchaser road credits," which allowed timber companies to cut more trees to offset the cost of roads they build on public land.

A stand-alone bill (HR 2515) that would have created a forest service program intended to clear dead and dying trees and otherwise improve forest health made it to the House floor, but it was defeated, 181–201. Some Republicans said the bill would inhibit timber harvesting, while Democrats and other Republicans complained it would allow trees to be taken without restraint.

The most contentious debate involved the pilot logging program in California. The House on July 9, 1997, gave overwhelming support to a bill (HR 858) to create the pilot projects. The plan, opposed by some environmentalists, stalled in the Senate, but supporters added it to the omnibus spending bill at the end of the 105th Congress.

HR 858 directed forest managers to take certain steps, including thinning timber stands and building firebreaks. It was intended to implement a proposal by what was known as the Quincy Library Group—a group of environmentalists, timber industry officials, and northern California community representatives who met in Quincy, Calif., in 1993 to work out more effective ways to prevent forest wildfires.

Even though the House passed the measure by 429–1, partisan disputes dogged the measure for much of the first session. When the measure was before the House Resources Committee in May 1997, environmental groups and liberal Democrats such as George Miller of California urged that it be withdrawn or rejected. They said it did not effectively reflect the ideas and goals of the Quincy group and that the committee had not had time to assess all of the environmental implications.

The Resources Committee nevertheless approved the bill by voice vote May 21 (H Rept 105-136, Pt. 1).

In the opening hours of the House floor debate, Miller continued to lambaste the bill even after Resources Committee Chairman Don Young, R-Alaska, strengthened environmental provisions. Opponents flagged provisions on maintaining areas around streams and other waterways, known as riparian management, and on the degree of scientific justification needed for forest management decisions. They initially backed a Miller amendment to correct the problems.

But just as the House was poised to begin the major part of the debate on HR 858, Young announced a new compromise, supported by Miller and approved by voice vote as an amendment. The key provision, Miller said, was a more explicit statement that agencies carrying out the bill's provisions should comply with environmental laws.

The compromise also increased the time for assessing the environmental impact of the project and provided for an environmental impact study of the project as a whole.

But national environmental groups rallied against the plan, contending that it would have greatly increased logging in the three California national forests. Amid the controversy, Sen. Barbara Boxer, D-Calif., announced she would oppose the measure, even though she had previously supported it.

Boxer's decision stalled the measure in the Senate throughout much of 1998. But lawmakers added it to an end-of-session appropriations bill that a reluctant Clinton signed Oct. 21, 1998.

Debt Forgiveness

With both Republicans and Democrats concerned over the destruction of tropical rain forests, Congress in 1998 cleared legislation to give developing countries a financial incentive to preserve their forests. The measure would forgive debts that some developing nations owed the United States in exchange for those countries undertaking certain conservation measures.

Rep. Rob Portman, R-Ohio, said he sponsored the measure because of reports that the world had lost roughly half its tropical rain forests, with millions of additional acres destroyed each year for farms, houses and other types of development. Scientists credited the lush forests with stabilizing local soil and water conditions and helping to regulate the world's climate. In addition, researchers believed the many species in the rain forests represented a treasure of genetic information that could help spur medical breakthroughs.

The bill (HR 2870—PL 105-214) authorized $325 million over three years. It built upon an earlier initiative from the administration of George Bush that forgave debts of $675 million owed by seven Latin American nations; the nations then invested $154 million in tropical-forest protection programs.

The administration would negotiate how much the countries would have to devote to forest protection for the amount of debt forgiven. It called for a recipient country to establish a forest protection fund, from which competitive grants would go to local nongovernmental groups and environmental and conservation organizations.

Recipient countries would have to meet certain criteria, such as the presence of a democratically elected government that cooperated in drug control efforts. The country also could not support international terrorism or engage in human rights abuses.

The bill (H Rept 105-443) won voice vote approval in the House International Relations Committee on March 11. The House passed it on March 19 by a 356–61 vote. The Senate passed it by voice vote on July 14 after amending it by inserting the text of a nearly identical measure (S 1758) by Richard G. Lugar, R-Ind., and Joseph R. Biden Jr., D-Del. The House cleared the legislation by voice vote on July 15. Clinton signed it July 29, 1998.

African Elephant Conservation Act

Congress in 1998 cleared legislation to reauthorize an African elephant conservation program in cooperation with African nations. The bill (HR 39—PL 105-217) would provide $5 million annually for elephant protection projects through 2002.

The number of African elephants dropped from about 1.3 million in 1979 to 700,000 in 1987, prompting Congress to pass the African Elephant Conservation Act of 1988 (PL 100-478). The bill required the secretary of the interior to evaluate the effectiveness of elephant conservation programs of every ivory-producing nation. It authorized $5 million yearly to assist African nations and prohibited ivory imports from those countries unable to adequately protect their elephants from poaching.

As a major consumer of carved ivory, the United States was contributing indirectly to the slaughter of African elephants. President Bush in 1989 used his authority under the new law to ban the importation of all carved elephant ivory into the United States.

In its first decade, the African Elephant Conservation Fund paid for the development and implementation of elephant conservation programs, the purchase of antihunting equipment for wildlife rangers, the creation of a comprehensive reference library on the African elephant, and ambitious projects to relocate elephants from certain drought regions. Despite such efforts, the estimated number of African elephants declined to about 543,000 by 1996.

The House Resources Committee approved HR 39 by voice vote on April 16, 1997. The House passed the legislation (H Rept 105-59) by voice vote on April 23. The Senate Environment and Public Works Committee approved it without any amendments on May 21, 1998, and the Senate cleared it on July 23. President Clinton signed the bill on Aug. 5.

Fish and Wildlife Service Revenue

Congress in 1998 cleared legislation to allow the Fish and Wildlife Service to keep revenue generated from the sale of fish, wildlife, and plant parts seized by the agency.

In the course of enforcing wildlife laws, the agency obtained forfeited and abandoned items made from wildlife parts, such as boots, belts, and jackets made from skins or furs. Most of these items—about 450,000 out of a total of 500,000—were warehoused in the National Wildlife Property Repository in Commerce City, Colorado. The agency was allowed to sell the items, but it could keep the proceeds only if the items were forfeited. Revenues generated from the sales of abandoned items went to the general treasury.

The bill (S 2094—PL 105-328) would allow the Fish and Wildlife Service to keep the revenues, which would help it defray the costs for appraisals, auctions, and lending the items to scientific and cultural organizations. The Senate Environment and Public Works Committee estimated that the agency could raise more than $1 million by selling a backlog of 200,000 abandoned items, which would otherwise continue to decay in the repository.

The Environment and Public Works Committee approved the bill (S Rept 105-285) on July 22, and the Senate passed it by unanimous consent on Sept. 11. The House cleared it by voice vote on Oct. 9.

Underground Storage Tanks

Different bills that aimed to speed the cleanup of leaking underground storage tanks passed the House in 1997 and a Senate committee in 1998, but advanced no further.

The House on April 23, 1997, passed a bill (HR 688) that would have assured states of a set share of federal funding for underground storage tank cleanups. The bill, sponsored by Dan Schaefer, R-Colo., passed by voice vote with bipartisan support and relatively little debate.

HR 688 would have required that the Environmental Protection Agency (EPA) transfer to the states at least 85 percent of federal money appropriated to the agency each year from the Leaking Underground Storage Tank Trust Fund (LUST).

The EPA traditionally turned over roughly that percentage to the states for use in cleaning up petroleum and other hazardous liquids leaking from underground tanks at gasoline stations and other sites. But bill proponents said states needed additional assurances that the funds would be there. "The 85 percent provision helps satisfy us that the EPA will keep following good practices regardless of budget fluctuations," said Commerce Committee Chairman Thomas J. Bliley Jr., R-Va.

The bill also sought to give states more flexibility in determining how to spend the money, which totaled $60 million in fiscal 1997.

HR 688 began in the Commerce panel's Finance and Hazardous Materials Subcommittee, which approved it by voice vote March 20. The full Commerce Committee approved the measure without change by voice vote April 16 (H Rept 105-58, Pt. I).

In a hearing before the markup, the Clinton administration expressed qualms that the bill would let tank owners off the hook for pollution that they should be paying to clean up.

The Senate Environment and Public Works Committee approved, by voice vote, its version of the bill on Sept. 24, 1998. The Senate measure (S 555—S Rept 105-360) would require the EPA to transfer at least 80 percent of federal funds that normally go to LUST directly to the states.

The bill also would require states to set up cooperative agreements with the EPA to schedule allocations from the trust fund, require the EPA to distribute the money based upon the number of leaking tanks and the amount of state contributions to the fund, and call for the EPA to examine the problem of leaking storage tanks located on tribal lands.

LUST was created in 1986 to ensure a reliable stream of federal funding to clean up and contain toxic substances leaking from underground tanks. It was financed by a 0.1-cent-per-gallon gasoline tax that expired in December 1995; it had a balance of about $1 billion. Of the 1 million active

and regulated petroleum tanks, Schaefer said 33,345 leaking tanks were reported to the EPA for cleanup in 1996 alone.

American Heritage Rivers

An administration initiative to designate ten rivers of national significance ran into an unexpected maelstrom of opposition, but conservative lawmakers failed to cut off funding for it. The debate over the voluntary program exposed the emotional political divide over public lands issues.

Unveiled in Clinton's 1997 State-of-the-Union address, the American Heritage Rivers Initiative was designed as something of a beauty pageant for rivers, fostering homegrown efforts to restore and protect the environmental, economic, and cultural values of the selected rivers and riverfronts. The White House stressed that the voluntary program would not cost the federal government any money.

Nevertheless, western Republicans blasted the administration for trying to undercut state sovereignty and usurp private property rights and water rights. Rep. Helen Chenoweth, R-Idaho, denounced the program as "a bold and shocking attempt by the administration to usurp individual water rights, private property rights and state sovereignty."

Major waterways, including parts of the Rio Grande and Missouri Rivers, were removed from consideration at the insistence of area lawmakers. The objections were as diverse as the rivers themselves, ranging from constitutional concerns (federal funds might be used that were not explicitly authorized) to more general distrust of government.

On Oct. 22, 1997, the House Resources Committee, 15–8, approved a bill sponsored by Chenoweth (HR 1842—H Rept 105-781) to "terminate further development and implementation of the American Heritage Rivers Initiative." But the House never took it up. Chenoweth also filed an unsuccessful suit against the program in the U.S. District Court for the District of Columbia.

Administration officials were clearly taken aback at the vehemence of the criticism, but Clinton aides pointed out that the response in Congress was generally positive. They noted that many prominent eastern Republicans, such as senators Alfonse D'Amato of New York and Strom Thurmond of South Carolina, supported the initiative.

Despite the controversy, the administration received 126 nominations and in 1998 designated fourteen rivers (officials concluded that ten would not be enough). The designated rivers included the Connecticut, Detroit, Hudson, Potomac, Willamette, and parts of the Mississippi. Each river was assigned a "river navigator"—a federal employee whose role was to help riverside communities identify federal programs and grants.

Tennessee Valley Authority

House budget hawks mounted a vigorous attempt in 1997 and 1998 to wipe out the federal subsidy for the once-sacrosanct Tennessee Valley Authority (TVA). But TVA advocates on the Senate Appropriations Committee kept the subsidy alive.

BACKGROUND

Created in 1933 under emergency legislation enacted during the landmark first 100 days of President Franklin D. Roosevelt's administration, the TVA's origins were humble compared with its scope in 1997. The TVA had come to serve 7.3 million customers in seven southern states using forty-four power sources. Even at the start, however, the agency's size and influence were questioned by private utilities that saw a threat of competition. Private power companies twice took their case to the Supreme Court, but the justices upheld the TVA both times.

After building a series of hydroelectric dams, the TVA got another boost in 1959, when Congress allowed it to finance construction projects through revenue bonds. To appease private competitors, the same bill also restricted the areas into which the TVA could expand.

For decades, the TVA enjoyed favorable treatment from members of both parties whose districts were served by it. But after Republicans took control of the House in 1995 calling for budget cuts and a smaller federal role, the idea of privatizing the TVA began to catch on. Some House Republicans in 1995 and 1996 pressed for amendments that would have cut the TVA's ties to the federal government. But the attempts failed in the face of divided Republican support and overwhelming Democratic opposition.

LEGISLATIVE ACTION

The situation appeared to change in January 1997, when TVA chairman Craven Crowell announced that he favored doing away with the agency's federal subsidy. Crowell wanted to wait a year. But his controversial stance was virtually an invitation to Congress to cut the TVA's historic ties to the government.

The fiscal 1998 Energy and Water Appropriations bill (HR 2203—PL 105-62) provided $70 million for the giant federally owned utility, well short of the president's $106 million request. Moreover, an unyielding House contingent won explicit legislative language to ensure that the 1998 federal subsidy would be the last. The House had initially voted to zero out the agency in fiscal 1998, but it ran into opposition from the mostly Republican senators who represented the region, including Jeff Sessions and Richard C. Shelby of Alabama and Bill Frist and Fred Thompson of Tennessee.

One year later, the House appropriators appeared to carry the day. The fiscal 1999 Energy and Water Appropriations bill (HR 4060—PL 105-245) zeroed out funding for the agency.

But in an indication of the resilience of federal spending, Congress boosted energy and water funding with a second bill (HR 4328—PL 105-277) just two weeks after President Clinton signed the appropriations measure. HR 4328 provided the TVA with $50 million in funds.

1999–2000

Amid unusually fierce partisan divisions in the wake of the impeachment of President Bill Clinton, the Republican-controlled 106th Congress failed to make substantial headway on environmental issues. Lawmakers in 2000 passed one significant bill: a $7.8 billion federal-state project to restore Florida's Everglades. Members once again failed, however, to bridge their differences over such issues as protecting endangered species and cleaning up hazardous waste sites. Lawmakers also could not agree on a strategy to reduce the threat of global warming. Although Congress boosted annual funding for programs to buy and preserve land, a bipartisan effort to guarantee funding for such initiatives died at the end of the 106th Congress, in part because of opposition from property rights advocates.

Compared to past years, the environment appeared to recede as a major political issue. Republicans parried attacks from environmentalists by establishing two national parks in Colorado and endorsing such secondary initiatives as boosting programs to protect coastal water quality and banning the killing of sharks for their fins. Neither party focused on issues that had sparked political battles earlier in the decade, such as revising the clean water act. Vice President Al Gore, despite his environmental credentials, did not elevate environmental protection into a major issue during the 2000 campaign.

Instead, much of the action on Capitol Hill took the form of skirmishes over Clinton's environmental initiatives. The White House, frustrated by Congress's failure to tighten environmental laws, used its authority to issue new clean air and clean water regulations, halt road-building in large areas of national forests, and designate new national monuments. Conservatives warned that the president was abusing his power, but they failed to significantly scale back the president's actions.

For the first time since the early 1990s, energy also emerged as a major issue. Lawmakers proposed a variety of tactics to curb rising oil and natural gas prices, including increasing production and cutting the federal gas tax. None of these plans made their way into law, even though high heating bills and costly gasoline threatened to become a campaign issue. Congress also failed to establish a repository of high-level nuclear waste or to set up a system for deregulating electricity prices. But with the Clinton administration facing harsh criticism over security lapses at the Department of Energy, lawmakers cleared a plan to create a new unit within the department to upgrade security.

Florida Everglades, Water Projects

Environmentalists scored a major victory when legislation to restore Florida's Everglades made it through Congress just before Election Day. The measure authorized the first $1.4 billion of a thirty-five-year, $7.8 billion federal-state project that sought to restore the biologically diverse wetland and undo decades of degradation. The Everglades plan, which was characterized as the largest and most expensive ecosystem restoration project ever, sought to reverse the effects of a 1948 project of the U.S. Army Corps of Engineers designed to control flooding and supply water to South Florida.

Widespread bipartisan support for the Everglades restoration project, along with election-year pressures, kept the measure alive even as the water resources bill that it was attached to met with several near-death experiences.

BACKGROUND

One of the most ecologically important regions in the country, the vast subtropical Everglades contained four national parks, sixteen national wildlife refuges, and one national marine sanctuary. It was home to dozens of endangered species, as well as spectacular flocks of herons, egrets, and other wading birds. Known as the "river of grass," the expansive wetland once covered the southern half of Florida from Lake Okeechobee to Florida Bay. But it shrunk by almost half after 1948, when the Army Corps of Engineers built a vast network of canals and dikes to divert the natural water flow and clear the way for the construction of housing developments and sugar plantations.

The reengineering of the sprawling ecosystem had the unintended consequence of drying out large portions of the Everglades by flushing some 1.7 billion gallons of water a day into the Atlantic Ocean and the Gulf of Mexico. The remaining marshes were threatened by agricultural runoff that contained fertilizers and other damaging substances, the spread of nonnative species, and changes in water flow. Some scientists warned that the Everglades were dying. In addition, South Florida faced the prospect of water supply problems.

In 1994 Florida agreed to a landmark plan to try to restore the Everglades by creating filtering marshes to absorb phosphorus and other runoff from sugar fields. The plan ended a six-year lawsuit that the federal government brought against the state for failing to protect the Everglades. But it deferred cleanup standards and left other environmental issues unresolved.

Five years later, the Clinton administration negotiated an agreement with Florida officials, Native American tribal leaders, agricultural groups and environmentalists for an ambitious joint federal-state effort to restore the 2.4 million-acre ecosystem. It called for a thirty-five-year effort that would involve the construction of water projects to restore the original flow of the marshes. Any water captured through various restoration projects would go first to environmental uses, with the remaining water then distributed according to Florida's permit process. The agreement also provided for supplying water to agricultural and urban areas and threatened estuaries, improving water quality, and providing flood protection.

Sen. Robert C. Smith, R-N.H., the newly installed chairman of the Environment and Public Works Committee, made a visit to the Everglades in January 2000 and vowed to pursue legislation authorizing the agreement. "The Everglades are very special; it's a very environmentally sensitive region of the country, and it clearly is a treasure," he said.

SENATE COMMITTEE ACTION

The plan began its march through Congress on June 28, when the Senate Environment and Public Works Committee approved Smith's bill (S 2797) to begin a $7.8 billion restoration project. But proponents had to overcome objections over the plan's price tag.

The measure, approved 16–1, would authorize some $1.4 billion to begin ten specific projects, start six pilot projects, and conduct additional planning to replenish the vast South Florida ecosystem. Carefully crafted provisions governing the distribution of the water captured by the restoration projects were instrumental in building broad support among agricultural and environmental groups, state and federal officials, and Republicans and Democrats.

The bill would require the president and Florida's governor to make a binding agreement under which the state would reserve water captured by the various projects for the ecosystem before reallocating it for other uses. The army also would have to issue rules within two years—acceptable to both Florida's governor and the Interior Department—setting out the goals of the restoration plan and requiring all the projects to be in line with those goals.

After the committee's vote, Smith sought to boost the Everglades legislation's chances of swift Senate passage by offering it as an amendment to a popular water resources bill (S 2796) that would fund an array of flood control, navigation and water projects. His amendment was approved unanimously.

The bill contained a controversial provision that would require the federal government to pay half the operations and maintenance costs for the sweeping Army Corps of Engineers project, which was slated to last until 2036. However, in an attempt to control federal costs, it would prohibit projects from exceeding their authorizations by more than 20 percent, requiring that Congress authorize any future Everglades projects and mandating that House and Senate panels approve implementation reports before any of the ten authorized projects could receive funding.

Despite such conditions, James M. Inhofe, R-Okla.—who was the only panel member to vote against the legislation—and John W. Warner, R-Va., warned the plan could still commit the government to decades of out-of-control spending. In most water projects, the costs were covered by the states. "This project is going to be a giant sucking machine," Warner complained.

Warner offered an amendment that would have removed the cost-sharing provisions from the bill and retained provisions in the 1996 water resources law (PL 104-303) that require states to pay all operations and maintenance costs for corps projects. But the committee rejected it, 8–10. (*Congress and the Nation Vol. IX, p. 469*)

Supporters said the federal government's role in the initial damage, coupled with its interest in the entire ecosystem, justified its participation in the restoration. "The federal government was a willing partner. . . . They destroyed the Everglades ecosystem," Smith said. "We are now coming back to undo that damage."

The legislation also would settle the question of who decides how water recaptured by the project is distributed. The Clinton administration proposed in April that the federal government reallocate water with the state in a consultative role, while Smith's bill would require the secretary of the interior and Florida's governor to share responsibility for distribution.

The issue also concerned House lawmakers. "The question is, who gets what in terms of the water?" asked Bud Shuster, R-Pa., chairman of the Transportation and Infrastructure Committee, which had jurisdiction over water projects.

RELATED ACTION

The underlying water projects bill that Smith used as a vehicle for the Everglades authorized $7 billion for dozens of water projects and feasibility studies, from flood damage reduction in Chesterfield, Missouri, to fish and wildlife restoration in the Ohio River.

The 2000 Water Resources Development Act focused on controlling flooding, bulking up eroding beaches, deepening harbors, providing hurricane protection, and repairing the environment. Such bills were popular because the projects they would authorize reached across much of the country, generating jobs, helping commerce, and enhancing public safety.

The first water resources bill passed in 1986 (PL 99-662), ending a sixteen-year deadlock between Congress and the White House regarding authorization of public works. In addition to authorizing numerous projects, the 1986 law resolved long-standing disputes relating to cost sharing, user fees, and environmental requirements.

Prior to the deadlock, Congress had authorized major water bills about every two years between 1947 and 1970.

In the 106th Congress, lawmakers repeatedly found themselves mired in disputes over individual projects. The Everglades plan, in fact, was one of the less-controversial projects in the bill.

A major battle broke out over water usage in California, when Rep. John T. Doolittle, R-Calif., proposed diverting water from the Sacramento and American Rivers to his district. Even though the House passed the bill without Doolittle's provision, the lawmaker continued to press for his plan. But many in Congress said water distribution fell beyond the jurisdiction of the bill.

SENATE ACTION

Opponents took aim at the Everglades plan in S 2796 when it came to the Senate floor. Several senators took issue with the plan's cost-sharing element, which envisioned the federal government footing 50 percent of the bill for operations and maintenance.

However, the Senate on Sept. 21 roundly rejected, 24–71, an amendment by Warner that would have required Florida to pay all operations and maintenance costs during the Everglades restoration program.

Supporters of the federal commitment to the Everglades project acknowledged during the debate that much remained to be learned about how to handle the many needs of the troubled ecosystem. A provision in the bill known as "adaptive management" would provide for changes to be made to the restoration plan as the Army Corps of Engineers and the state of Florida learned which strategies worked and which needed modification.

The Senate on Sept. 25 overwhelmingly passed S 2796. But the elation that accompanied the 85–1 passage of the measure was tempered by uncertainty over the bill's murky future in the House, where lawmakers had reached an impasse in their efforts to craft similar legislation. The House bill (HR 4411) was hung up over a labor-related provision in the larger water projects bill—specifically, whether federal wage standards in the Davis-Bacon Act should be applied to some federal water projects.

The lone "no" vote in the Senate was cast by James M. Inhofe, R-Okla. "All of us support protecting the environment and preserving the Everglades," he said. "But this bill is not sound stewardship of federal policy and public resources. This is an open-ended commitment which will end up costing the taxpayers a tremendous amount of money."

HOUSE ACTION

With Florida representatives pressing hard for the Everglades restoration, the House on Oct. 19 passed S 2796 by a resounding vote of 394–14. The lopsided margin gave a big boost to the Everglades, but the underlying $6.9 billion water bill continued to face an uncertain future because of substantial differences between the House and Senate versions.

Conservatives complained that the House added numerous expensive projects designed to appeal to members, such as a $15 million navigation initiative in False Pass, Alaska. It also included $85 million for groundwater improvements in California's San Gabriel Basin and would allow the corps to participate in a massive California estuary rehabilitation project known as CALFED.

In addition, natural resources groups complained the House version added several provisions that could harm the environment, including language that they said would lead to an increase in dredging in the nation's harbors by contributing more federal money for such projects.

But with bipartisan support building behind the Everglades portion of the bill, environmentalists hoped that House Appropriations Committee Chairman C. W. Bill Young, R-Fla., could attach the Everglades language to a spending bill if the water resources measure got stuck in conference. Such major authorizing initiatives were rarely attached to annual appropriations bills. But Senate Majority Leader Trent Lott, R-Miss., gave the plan a boost on Oct. 25 when he said he would support such an unusual legislative maneuver.

CONFERENCE, FINAL ACTION

For several days in late October, the fate of the Everglades plan hung in the balance because of House and Senate differences over the larger water projects bill, known as the Water Resources Development Act (WRDA). The sticking point was a House provision that was intended to increase the Army Corps of Engineers' participation in the construction and maintenance of water treatment plants, water distribution systems, and sewer lines. Backed by Shuster, the powerful transportation chairman, it was known as the "environmental infrastructure" provision. Smith adamantly refused to include the language, saying the corps had enough work to do without adding more. However, he and House negotiators were in lockstep over the importance of the Everglades bill.

"I want to be very clear," Smith said. "If we cannot reach agreement on a WRDA bill, we should attach the Everglades to an appropriations bill. Put it right on that appropriations train. Couple it right up."

As it turned out, conferees salvaged both the Everglades and the larger WRDA measure by removing the controversial environmental infrastructure projects. With GOP leaders making an intense push to move the popular bill before Election Day, Young and Speaker J. Dennis Hastert, R-Ill., gave assurances to Shuster that more than $400 million in infrastructure projects would be added instead to the spending bill for Labor, Health and Human Services, and Education (HR 4577). Despite the popularity of the Everglades plan, Shuster had refused to move the water bill until a home was found for his projects.

The Senate passed the conference report on Oct. 31 by unanimous consent. The House cleared the measure, 312–2, on Nov. 3. Clinton signed the measure on Dec. 11.

Despite widespread bipartisan support for the measure, a few Democrats criticized the water resources bill for lacking a provision that would overhaul the corps.

"We should require the corps to be more aware of potential adverse consequences," said Rep. Robert A. Borski, D-Pa. "I plan to revisit this in the next Congress."

MAJOR PROVISIONS

As signed into law, the major Everglades provisions of S 2796 (PL 106-541):

• **Comprehensive Everglades Restoration Plan.** The plan aimed to restore the Everglades ecosystem and ensure an adequate water supply. Key goals included improving the timing and distribution of water flows and levels and restoring the connectivity of the system, which had been compartmentalized by the Army Corps of Engineers.

- **Project components.** The legislation called for sixty-eight projects that would be constructed over thirty-five years by the Army Corps of Engineers and the South Florida Water Management District. These projects would seek to stabilize the water levels of Lake Okeechobee; boost urban and agricultural water supply; ensure water flow to the Florida Bay, Biscayne Bay, and other coastal estuaries; and improve regional water quality conditions. The projects also sought to maintain existing levels of flood protection. They would eliminate damaging freshwater releases to the Caloosahatchee and St. Lucie estuaries. The first phase would include ten construction projects and six pilot projects. Later projects would be submitted to Congress for authorization biennially as part of larger water development bills.

- **Costs.** The plan would split the $7.8 billion cost of the projects evenly between Florida and the federal government. The average federal cost would be $200 million a year over the next twenty years, according to congressional estimates. Annual operation and maintenance costs, which were also split 50–50 between Florida and Washington, were estimated to be $172 million.

- **Water use agreement.** The federal government and the state of Florida would enter into an agreement to ensure that sufficient water generated by the projects would be available for the Everglades. According to an Army Corps of Engineers estimate, 80 percent of the water produced by the projects would have to be directed toward the Everglades in order to attain the goals of the restoration. The remaining 20 percent would be available for human use.

- **Water quality.** The secretary of the army, in concurrence with the secretary of the interior and Florida's governor, would promulgate regulations that took into account state water quality standards. The secretary would also ensure that all groundwater and surface water discharges from any project authorized in the bill met all applicable water quality standards and permitting requirements.

- **Adaptive assessment.** Officials overseeing the projects would have the authority to make modifications, based on new information or modeling.

- **Pilot projects.** The plan included six pilot projects at a cost of $69 million, which would be split evenly between the federal government and Florida. The pilot projects were designed to test restoration approaches. Most would be constructed within five years and then monitored by the Army Corps of Engineers for several additional years. Three of the projects involved aquifer storage and recovery, and they were designed to identify the most suitable sites for the aquifer storage and recovery wells, determine the water quality necessary for injections into the well, determine the water quality of the receiving aquifer, and provide information on the hydrogeological and geotechnical characteristics of the area. A fourth pilot project, called the Lake Belt In-Ground Reservoir Technology project, would store water in areas where lime rock mining had occurred to make sure that such mines retained water. A fifth project, the L-31 Seepage Management project, would investigate seepage management technologies and seek to determine the appropriate amount of wet season groundwater flow to return to Everglades National Park. A sixth project, the Wastewater Reuse Technology project, would address water quality issues associated with discharging treated wastewater into natural areas such as West Palm Beach's Catchment Area, Biscayne National Park, and the Bird Drive Basin.

- **Initial construction projects.** The legislation authorized ten initial projects, which were recommended by the Army Corps of Engineers and the South Florida Water Management District because of the potential to provide widespread improvements in water quantity, quality, and flow distribution. Before beginning construction, the secretary of the army was required to submit a project implementation report to the Senate Environment and Public Works Committee and the House Transportation and Infrastructure Committee. The committees would approve the reports before money could be appropriated for the work. If the cost of constructing the projects was to exceed 20 percent of the authorized amount (after accounting for inflation), the Army Corps of Engineers was required to obtain authorization from Congress for the additional amount. The ten projects consisted of three storage reservoirs to prevent damaging water releases while redirecting some water flows and meeting agricultural needs; a seepage management project; two impoundment and stormwater treatment areas; a combined reservoir and treatment facility; and three canal projects to enhance water flows.

- **Future projects.** Prior to the authorization of additional projects, the secretary of the army would complete additional studies and submit a project implementation report to Congress. The report would address such issues as cost-effectiveness, engineering feasibility, and potential environmental impacts.

- **Dispute resolution.** The Florida governor and the secretary of the army were directed to develop an agreement for resolving disputes between the Army Corps of Engineers and the South Florida Water Management District. The agreement was to be developed within 180 days of enactment of the legislation.

- **Independent review.** The secretary of the army, the secretary of the interior, and the state of Florida, in consultation with the South Florida Ecosystem Restoration Task Force, were directed to establish an independent scientific review panel. The panel would submit a biennial report for federal and state officials, including members of Congress, on the progress toward achieving the restoration of the Everglades.

Conservation and Reinvestment Act

A closely watched bipartisan measure that would have guaranteed about $3 billion annually in offshore drilling revenues to a host of federal and state conservation programs died at the close of the 106th Congress. Instead, environmentalists won a consolation prize of sorts as congressional appropriators and the White House worked out an end-of-session compromise on a smaller conservation measure subject to annual appropriations.

The Conservation and Reinvestment Act (CARA) aimed to provide steady, predictable funding for recreation and conservation programs by setting aside a portion of offshore oil and gas royalties exclusively for that purpose over fifteen years. It would include full funding of $900 million a year for the Land and Water Conservation Fund (PL 88-578), which was established in 1964 to pay for federal land purchases, as well as $1 billion annually for coastal states and $350 million for state wildlife programs.

The legislation grew out of an effort by officials and legislators from coastal states such as Louisiana and Alaska to capture some of the windfall from oil and gas drilling off their shores and "reinvest" it to mitigate the punishing effects of these activities on their coastlines. However, a small but powerful group of appropriators, joined by a determined bloc of western lawmakers, vowed to prevent the measure from coming to the Senate floor, even after the House passed the plan by an overwhelming margin.

President Clinton swore to make passage of CARA a priority in final budget negotiations. But resistance to making conservation funding an entitlement—which would have deprived appropriators of politically advantageous sway over where the money should be spent—proved too strong.

BACKGROUND

Congress created the Land and Water Conservation Fund in 1964, amid mounting concern over the need to preserve the nation's undeveloped lands. The goal was to funnel royalties from oil and gas drilling on federal lands into efforts to protect ecologically important places. To underscore its seriousness, Congress authorized that as much as $900 million a year be spent on land acquisition.

In addition to financing federal land purchases, the fund provided matching grants to state and local governments to obtain outdoor recreation areas. Over the years, the fund was instrumental in protecting popular recreation areas such as beaches and ecologically sensitive habitats such as wetlands. Many states ran similar programs with bond revenues to provide more open space to residents.

Unlike some trust funds, spending from the Land and Water Conservation Fund was determined each year by the appropriations process. As a result, the money was vulnerable to fiscal pressures. In the 1970s lawmakers gradually increased annual funding for land purchases to about $800 million. But concerns about the deficit and budget cuts during the 1980s and early 1990s drastically reduced the amount available, even though conservationists warned that the government should purchase additional land before it became prohibitively expensive. In fiscal 1999, Congress appropriated $328 million—a typical amount for the fund.

By the 106th Congress, with the deficit wiped out and voters openly worried about suburban sprawl and other land-use issues, many lawmakers wanted to boost the fund to provide more money for parks, recreation, and wildlife conservation. Conservatives from coastal states lent their support because they saw an opportunity to steer some of the royalties from offshore drilling to local communities. Under the original law, all the royalties were deposited into the federal Treasury.

As a result, the plan attracted backing from such ideological opposites as Rep. Don Young, a conservative Republican from Alaska who backed private property rights, and Rep. George Miller, a liberal Democrat from California who championed many of the environmental initiatives that Young resisted.

The Clinton administration went full bore as well. The administration in 1999 proposed an initiative that would have represented the largest one-year investment in lands conservation ever and set the wheels in motion for protecting more than five million acres involving seventeen national parks and monuments. The administration's fiscal 2000 budget, for example, proposed spending $36 million to acquire land bordering the Mojave National Preserve in California and $84 million for the Everglades National Park in Florida.

But in the effort to provide money for land conservation, urban parks, and outdoor recreation, the president and lawmakers discovered a confounding truth: it was not easy to pass legislation even when long-time adversaries supported it and billions of dollars were available to pay for a popular cause.

1999 LEGISLATIVE ACTION

Young and Miller negotiated for months before producing a bipartisan bill that won approval in the House Resources Committee. Despite opposition from some western conservatives, lawmakers planned to take up the bill on the House floor in 2000.

Members started turning their attention to the issue in February, when Young teamed up with John D. Dingell, D-Mich., on a bill (HR 701) to pump more money into the fund. "I anticipate that, in most years, over $1 billion will be available for the valuable conservation and recreation programs included in this bill," Young said. "I believe it's vital that Congress invest this revenue into lasting conservation efforts and fairly distribute funding to our coastal communities."

In the Senate, Frank Murkowski, R-Alaska, and Mary L. Landrieu, D-La., introduced a similar measure (S 25).

Although Young's bill would have guaranteed generous spending for fish and wildlife conservation, as well as about $100 million a year for urban parks, it drew criticism from the administration and environmentalists. The reason: Young's measure would have provided hundreds of millions of dollars a year for coastal states that had oil and gas production offshore. Many Democrats warned that tying funding to oil and gas royalties would encourage drilling and unravel a moratorium on new offshore drilling leases that had been in place for more than seventeen years.

Young also faced opposition on the right because property rights groups believed the government already owned more than enough land, especially in the West. Young sought to appease his conservative critics by stipulating that two-thirds of the money must be spent east of the Dakotas and that Congress must approve expenditures of more than $1 million. His bill also would have required that land be bought only from willing sellers and that the government could not condemn property.

Miller introduced a counterproposal (HR 798) that would have permanently funded the conservation fund without providing incentives for offshore drilling. The Miller plan, along with a similar Senate proposal (S 446) by Barbara Boxer, D-Calif., also would have provided more than $1 billion yearly for a variety of conservation and historic preservation programs. Environmentalists endorsed the proposal.

Joining the fray, the Clinton administration's budget request included $1.1 billion to "save and restore America's natural treasures."

After months of false starts, Young and Miller struck a compromise in November between their two plans. The combined bill (HR 701) would guarantee $900 million annually for the Land and Water Conservation Fund, as well as $125 million for urban parks and $150 million for conservation easements. It would disburse $1 billion a year to coastal states to offset the effects of offshore drilling. The amount a state would receive would be tied to how much oil and gas is drilled off its coast.

Funding for the bill would come from the proceeds of offshore oil and gas drilling. That revenue had averaged about $4 billion a year, mostly generated by wells in the Gulf of Mexico and off the California coast.

The plan continued to face criticism, however, from western Republicans and property rights advocates who did not want the government buying more land. In addition, House appropriators objected to having more than $3 billion taken from discretionary spending. Some environmental groups also opposed the bill because they said it would encourage additional offshore oil drilling and because the funding for the Land and Water Conservation Fund would still be subject to annual appropriations.

Despite the controversy, the House Resources Committee approved the measure, 37–12, on Nov. 10. The markup lasted four hours, with property rights advocates such as Helen Chenoweth, R-Idaho, criticizing the measure. "When did we conclude that the government can manage the land more responsibly and efficiently than the private property owner?" she asked.

Chenoweth made her displeasure known by filing thirty-nine amendments. Though she did not offer them all during the markup, she did present some amendments that Young clearly considered nuisances. Those included provisions to limit the government to purchases of less than 100 acres in Idaho; prohibit the introduction of grizzly bears in Idaho or Montana; and require state legislatures to approve the purchase of property within their borders.

Those amendments and all others except one minor one were defeated in committee by a solid block of Democrats, Young, and handful of moderate Republicans. Young said he decided to oppose all amendments because approving even one substantive amendment would upset the bill's delicate compromise.

2000 LEGISLATIVE ACTION

The Conservation and Reinvestment Act passed the House and won approval in the Senate Energy and Natural Resources Committee. But a determined band of western conservatives prevented the full Senate from taking it up.

As the measure picked up momentum during the 106th Congress, it became a top priority of the nation's governors, thousands of state legislators, and a slew of organizations from the Camp Fire Girls to the Wilderness Society. Within Congress, however, private property advocates branded it a massive federal land grab and warned that it would divert money from an estimated $5 billion maintenance backlog on federal lands, such as national parks and forests.

Early in the year, House appropriators and Budget Committee members attempted to bottle up HR 701 after it passed the Resources Committee because they were alarmed by the prospect of fencing off up to $3 billion each year that had been subject to annual appropriations. "I've got billions and billions of dollars of backlogged maintenance and they want to take away" several billion dollars, protested Rep. Ralph Regula, R-Ohio and chairman of the Interior Appropriations Subcommittee, on Feb. 29.

Members of the Budget Committee claimed partial jurisdiction and wanted several months to review the bill. The House Agriculture Committee also claimed partial jurisdiction.

But Young fought to bring the bill to the floor as soon as possible, knowing that any delay would reduce the chance for the bill's enactment in an election-shortened year. He scored a victory when House leaders worked out a deal giving the Agriculture Committee a crack at the bill until March 17 and the Budget Committee a shot until March 31. Those committees gave up their formal opposition.

The House on May 11 passed the measure, 315–102, after adding last-minute language on Social Security and Medicare. Under the measure, about $2.8 billion a year in royalties that the federal government received from oil and gas drilling on federal lands would be set aside annually for the next fifteen years to purchase environmentally sensitive land and other conservation programs. Those royalties would otherwise be deposited in the federal Treasury.

The bill would mandate $1 billion annually for a coastal conservation fund, $900 million for the Land and Water Conservation Fund, and $350 million for wildlife conservation and education programs. It would also provide annual payments of $575 million for everything from urban parks to Native American land restoration to historic preservation. "This is the largest environmental bill for the conservation of American resources in the past thirty-six years," Miller said.

The tensions over the bill played out in House debate. Young and Miller, along with Dingell and W. J. "Billy" Tauzin, R-La., who were also strong supporters of the bill, fended off all but a handful of amendments that were proposed on the House floor. Among those were efforts to provide additional protections for private landowners and limit the scope of the measure.

But bill sponsors were temporarily thrown for a loop when lawmakers, 216–208, narrowly approved an amendment setting spending guidelines. Offered by John Shadegg, R-Ariz., the amendment would prohibit the Treasury Department from transferring oil royalty revenue to the CARA fund unless certain conditions were met, including that Congress was on track to eliminate all publicly held debt by 2013, and that Congress could certify that Social Security and Medicare were not going to run a deficit in the next five years.

Rather than fight the Shadegg proposal, bill sponsors opted to hold a procedural vote to recommit the bill. That motion, approved 413–3, included language that would prohibit any funds to be spent under the bill if they would diminish benefit obligations to several trust funds, including those for federal disability insurance and supplementary medical insurance.

"We made a decision we would not accept any amendments. They were a threat to the bill," Young said. "After we had a good night's sleep . . . we decided [the Shadegg amendment] was probably better for the bill." As a result, the amendment stayed in the bill.

In a final effort to alter the bill, opponents offered a substitute amendment combining several private property and funding proposals. That amendment, sponsored by William M. "Mac" Thornberry, R-Texas, was rejected 126–291.

Despite the overwhelming House passage, the measure faced significant opposition in the Senate. The Senate version (S 2123) was cosponsored by Majority Leader Trent Lott, R-Miss., whose coastal state would reap major benefits. But western conservatives such as Larry E. Craig, an Idaho Republican, threatened a filibuster.

Roiling the waters, supporters said they were undercut by a series of Clinton land actions, including the creation of new national monuments that were off-limits to development and a federal order to bar roads in tens of millions of acres of federal forests.

Murkowski said he believed he could mollify western lawmakers with a provision that would guarantee no net loss of private land. To try to appease appropriators, he and the committee's ranking Democrat, Jeff Bingaman of New Mexico, worked out an unusual funding relationship. The plan was to create an entitlement for conservation and land preservation programs but allow it to be spent only after Congress voted to appropriate the $450 million authorized in the bill for federal land acquisition. The mechanism was designed to mollify critics who said an automatic appropriation would limit congressional oversight.

To benefit small states, the bill would change the funding formula for grants that had been used to build soccer fields and hiking trails. Sixty percent of the funds would be distributed equally among states, and the remaining 40 percent would be allocated based on population.

To safeguard private property rights, the Senate bill stated: "Nothing in the act creates any new authority for Federal agencies to apply regulations on privately owned land." It also said, "Nothing in the act shall authorize that private property be taken for public use without just compensation."

The state wildlife and conservation fund would receive $350 million. About $75 million would go toward repairing urban parks, with another $50 million going for maintenance. Historic preservation was funded at $150 million, and $50 million was also included to buy easements of land surrounding federal forests threatened with development.

Murkowski brought up the measure in his committee on July 19, but he faced a flurry of hostile amendments and procedural maneuvers. In particular, Majority Whip Don Nickles, R-Okla., delayed the markup for a week by objecting to the routine unanimous consent agreement needed to permit committees to conduct business for more than two hours once the Senate convened. Despite the obstacles, the Energy and Natural Resources Committee approved HR 701 by voice vote on July 25.

But in a sign of the battles to come, Nickles and other budget hardliners offered amendments—all rejected—to radically change the funding for the measure. The amendments included provisions that would have made the entire bill subject to annual appropriations and prevent the CARA funds from being spent until the maintenance backlog in national parks was eliminated.

Energy panel opponents also focused on the measure's land acquisition funding. Craig Thomas, R-Wyo., offered a "no net loss" amendment that would have required the federal government to sell a parcel of land of equal value if it wanted to buy more than 100 acres in a state where more than 25 percent of the land was federally owned. Nickles offered an amendment that would have eliminated Congress's ability to authorize federal land acquisitions unless the property owner was a "willing seller."

The committee rejected those amendments. But it adopted by voice vote an amendment by Conrad Burns, R-Mont., to require federal officials to consult with state authorities on which lands to purchase.

After the markup, Craig and other conservatives vowed to do everything possible to delay the bill. Lott said he was ready for a parliamentary war over the measure, but he also conceded that the Senate would be hard-pressed to find the time to do anything other than must-pass legislation, such as appropriations bills.

In the end, the fierce opposition of western conservatives carried the day. With the Senate unable to find the time to schedule such a controversial piece of legislation, CARA proponents instead settled for a six-year, $12 billion discretionary fund for public land programs that was created through the fiscal 2001 Interior appropriations bill.

Alaska Development

The sometimes conflicting demands of environmentalists who wanted to protect the Alaskan wilderness and Alaska natives who favored more development spurred several pieces of legislation.

In 1999 the House Resources Committee, frustrated by administration delays over allowing construction of a controversial one-lane access road through the nation's second-largest national forest, passed a bill to permit the construction to go forward. The administration subsequently granted a right-of-way easement for the road despite environmental concerns.

The bill (HR 2547—H Rept 106-451), approved by the Resources Committee on Sept. 22 by voice vote, would have granted the Chugach Alaska Corp. an easement to build a road through the Chugach National Forest. The road would have given the corporation, which represented native Alaskans living along the rim of Prince William Sound, access to a 73,000-acre tract of land granted to the organization in 1982.

Bill sponsor and committee chairman Don Young, R-Alaska, said the Clinton administration had dragged its feet on the issue, thwarting the natives' ability to develop their property. Environmentalists, however, worried that the road would cut through the Copper River delta, damaging salmon streams, harming waterfowl feeding areas, and opening the forest to clear-cutting and mining.

The administration objected to the bill's interference with ongoing negotiations between the U.S. Forest Service and the native Alaskans, especially a clause that would automatically grant the easement after one month following passage.

The committee had passed similar legislation during the 105th Congress but agreed to set it aside when President Clinton pledged to settle the issue by the end of 1998.

The Forest Service ultimately granted the right-of-way easement in 2000. Under its agreement with the tribe, the public could use the road for access to national forest lands, but not for entering tribal property.

The road would cross twenty-seven miles of Chugach National Forest lands, passing over more than 150 streams. Responding to environmental concerns, Forest Service officials insisted they would monitor construction closely to protect natural resources.

On another issue, Congress in 2000 cleared a measure (S 430—PL 106-283) to authorize a land exchange for the Kake Tribal Corp. in Alaska. The Kake Tribal Corp. had been awarded land in and around Kake in 1975 as part of a 1971 law enacted to settle aboriginal land claims of Alaska natives. The purpose of the law was to transfer lands from the natives to native regional corporations, which would secure the cultural and economic benefits of the land for their shareholders.

A portion of the land in Kake lay on a watershed. Because it was a source for local drinking water, villagers did not want the area logged. The aim of the land transfer was to give the corporation land in an area where logging did not pose problems. The measure included a provision that prohibited the Kake Tribal Corp. from exporting unprocessed logs from the land it acquired.

As introduced by Sen. Frank R. Murkowski, the measure provided for an equal value land exchange in which the tribal corporation would convey watershed lands to the Tongass National Forest in return for other lands. The Senate Energy and Natural Resources Committee approved the bill (S Rept 106-31) by voice vote on March 22, 1999, and the Senate passed it by voice vote on April 19.

The House Resources Committee approved the bill (H Rept 106-489) by voice vote on Nov. 3 after adopting a substitute amendment. Under the amendment, the tribal corporation would agree to convey 1,430 acres of its watershed property to the city of Kake, and retain ownership of the remaining 1,127 acres of its watershed land. A conservation easement on both the land that conveyed to the city and the land retained by the corporation would prohibit logging and protect the watershed.

The House passed the amended measure on May 22, and the Senate cleared it on Sept. 22. Clinton signed it Oct. 6, 2000.

Great Ape Protection

With populations of great apes in decline throughout the world, Congress in 2000 cleared legislation (HR 4320—PL 106-411) to bolster support for international conservation efforts to protect ape populations. The measure would authorize up to $5 million per year from fiscal 2001 through 2005 to fund projects that would preserve chimpanzees, gorillas, bonobos, gibbons, and orangutans, all of which had been listed as endangered species.

Great apes faced threats from habitat loss, hunters, and live capture. The consumption of ape meat was particularly concerning because it posed health risks to humans. (Medical researchers hypothesized that humans contracted AIDS and HIV after consuming ape meat.)

Even though great apes were stringently protected, scientists warned that some apes could disappear from equatorial jungles within a decade unless more innovative conservation policies were undertaken. Chimpanzee populations had plummeted by an estimated 95 percent in the twentieth century, and some subspecies of gorillas were believed to number only in the hundreds.

Saving the apes became a major environmental cause because the animals provided links to the evolutionary past of humans. Apes demonstrated qualities, such as the use of tools, problem-solving and communication, that humans used in more sophisticated ways to create societies. Moreover, scientists believed that studying apes could provide clues to curing tropical diseases such as AIDS and the ebola virus.

Under the bill, funds would be used to protect natural habitats for the animals, enforce species protection laws, establish animal sanctuaries, rehabilitate animals to the wild, and create community outreach programs. Conservationists viewed the $5 million as something of a down payment, warning that about $35 million or so annually would be needed to reverse the trade in bush meat.

The House Resources Subcommittee on Fisheries Conservation, Wildlife and Oceans gave voice vote approval to the measure (H Rept 106-792) on June 29 after amending it to add gibbons, which were lesser apes indigenous to Southeast Asia. The Resources Committee approved it without dissent on July 19, and the House passed it by voice vote on July 25. The Senate Environment and Public Works Committee approved it (S Rept 106-472) on Sept. 21, and the Senate cleared it by voice vote on Oct. 19. President Clinton signed the measure Oct. 20, 2000.

Coastal Water Quality Standards

In an effort to make beaches cleaner and safer, Congress in 2000 cleared legislation (HR 999—PL 106-284) to encourage states to establish water quality standards and monitoring programs for coastal recreational areas. The legislation aimed to prevent outbreaks of pathogens that could cause swimmers in popular recreation areas to experience ear and digestive tract ailments.

The legislation's passage came after the Natural Resources Defense Council reported that the number of beach closings and water pollution advisories had increased from 484 in 1988 to 6,260 in 1999. The group attributed the increase to the amount of sewage and polluted runoff that was released into public waters, as well as a rise in monitoring by some states.

Despite concerns about water pollution, supporters of the legislation warned that only about eight states had comprehensive monitoring programs for their coastal waters. Some states conducted little or no water quality monitoring.

The federal government lacked mandatory standards for testing and monitoring coastal recreational waters. Those eight states and federal agencies such as the Environmental Protection Agency (EPA), the National Oceanic and Atmospheric Administration, and the U.S. Geological Survey used varying methods and standards for testing water quality. Nor were there uniform requirements for notifying the public when water violates health standards.

As a result, states with strict monitoring programs issued a large percentage of the nation's pollution alerts. California lawmakers worried that their state could be perceived as highly polluted because it regularly tested its waters and issued thousands of alerts. The House version of the measure was sponsored by Republican Brian Bilbray of San Diego, a one-time lifeguard and avid surfer who appeared on Capitol Hill with his surfboard to promote the measure.

Under the legislation, states would have three and a half years to adopt water quality standards under the bill, and

they would be eligible to seek grants for between 50 percent and 100 percent of the costs of monitoring pollution. The state programs would have to meet criteria on the frequency and location of the monitoring. The EPA would conduct testing and notification in those states that failed to create their own programs.

The program would be authorized for $30 million for fiscal 2000 through 2004.

Originally, the bill would have required the nation's thirty coastal states (including Great Lakes states) to test their waters and notify the public if bacteria levels violated federal standards. But state officials complained that such a plan would amount to an unfunded federal mandate.

The bill (H Rept 106-98) won voice vote approval on April 15, 1999, in the House Transportation and Infrastructure Committee. The House passed it by voice vote on April 22 (Earth Day). The Senate Environment and Public Works Committee approved it by voice vote on April 13, 2000. The full Senate passed it with an amendment on Sept. 21, and the House cleared it on Sept. 26. The president signed it Sept. 28, 2000.

Beached Marine Mammals

Congress in 2000 cleared a measure (HR 2903—PL 106-555) to rehabilitate stranded marine mammals as part of a larger measure to reauthorize the Atlantic Striped Bass Conservation Act (PL 98-613) through fiscal 2003.

The bill would authorize $5 million each for fiscal years 2001 through 2003 to rehabilitate beached mammals. The funding would go to individuals or centers authorized under the Marine Mammals Protection Act (PL 103-238) to rescue stranded marine mammals for eventual release. There were about three dozen qualified centers in the United States.

Unlike existing law, which provided funding only for "unusual mortality events" associated with marine mammals, the measure would authorize grants of up to $100,000 to be used for the recovery and treatment of any marine mammals, the collection of health information on the animals, and general operation of the facilities.

The unrelated Atlantic Striped Bass Conservation Act, enacted in 1984, gave the secretary of commerce authority to declare a moratorium on striped bass fishing in any state that failed to reduce its annual catch of the species by 55 percent. Striped bass landings had dropped dramatically since 1960, and environmentalists blamed overfishing and water pollution. HR 2903 (H Rept 106) reauthorized the law through fiscal 2003 and directed the secretaries of interior and commerce to submit a report to Congress on methods to sustain the populations of the species.

Action on the issue began when the House Resources Subcommittee on Fisheries Conservation, Wildlife and Oceans gave voice vote approval to a marine mammal stranding bill (HR 1934—H Rept 106-242) on June 22, 1999. However, the ranking minority member, Eni F. H. Faleomavaega, D-Am. Samoa, expressed concern over the geographical distribution of funds. He said it was important to ensure that certain regions of the country did not receive more grant money simply because they had more rescue centers in place.

The Resources Committee approved the bill by voice vote on June 30, and the full House passed it by voice vote on Sept. 27. The language was then inserted into the striped bass conservation measure, which passed the House by voice vote on Oct. 31, 2000. The Senate cleared the measure on Dec. 8. Clinton signed it Dec. 15, 2000.

Bear Parts

The Senate in 2000 passed a measure to prohibit trading in bear organs and meat, but the House declined to take up the matter. As sponsored by Sen. Mitch McConnell, R-Ky., the bill (S 1109) would prohibit the importation of all bear viscera and products containing, or labeled as containing, bear viscera. It also prohibited interstate commerce of the organs or products.

Bill supporters warned that the use of bear organs and fluids in Asian medicines, shampoos, and cosmetics threatened the population of the animals. Bear parts were in such demand that a gall bladder could reportedly be sold for as much as $55,000 in South Korea and Taiwan. Bears were also hunted for their paws and meat. With bear populations in decline in Asia, environmentalists worried that hunters would begin to target them in North America.

The Senate Environment and Public Works Committee, 15–3, approved the bill (S Rept 106-484) on July 26. But Sen. Michael D. Crapo, R-Idaho, who voted against the measure, described it as an "unwarranted encroachment on state authority." He also contended that the trade in bear parts did not threaten bears in the United States.

The Senate passed the bill on Oct. 17 by voice vote.

Two New National Parks

In a victory for environmentalists, Congress elevated two national monuments to national parks. The parks, both in Colorado, were the first that the government established since the GOP takeover of Congress in 1995.

Congress in 1999 created Black Canyon of the Gunnison National Park, located about 250 miles southwest of Denver. The gorge, which had been designated a national monument by President Herbert Hoover, was known for its narrow canyon walls and spectacular 2,000-foot vertical drops to the Gunnison River. It was home to a variety of animals and was one of the last shelters left in Colorado for the endangered peregrine falcon.

The new park included the monument's 20,766 acres and an additional 4,460 acres from the Bureau of Land Management. The measure also set up a 57,725-acre national conservation area in nearby Gunnison Gorge.

The measure (S 323—PL 106-76) was introduced by Ben Nighthorse Campbell, R-Colo., who had been trying to attain national park status for the area for more than a decade. Through the years, he reduced the size of the proposed park in an attempt to win enactment of the bill.

At one point, the bill included a "wild and scenic" designation for part of the river, but after vigorous disputes with water rights interests that provision was removed. The Senate Energy and Natural Resources Committee added a provision designed to protect grazing rights within the area before approving the bill (S Rept 106-69) on May 19.

The Senate passed the bill by voice vote on July 1. The House Resources Committee approved it (H Rept 106-307) with an amendment on Sept. 8. The House passed it by voice vote on Sept. 27, and the Senate cleared it on Oct. 1.

The following year, Congress created the Great Sand Dunes National Park and Preserve near Alamosa, Colorado. The new national park featured stunning 700-foot high sand dunes—the highest in the nation—against a backdrop of snow-covered mountains.

The measure (S 2547—PL 106-530), by Sen. Wayne Allard, R-Colo., whipped through Congress in the final weeks of 2000. The Senate Energy and Natural Resources Committee approved it (S Rept 106-479) on Sept. 20; the Senate passed it by voice vote on Oct. 5, and the House cleared it, 366–34, on Oct. 25.

The legislation would elevate the 39,000-acre national monument into a national park, contingent upon the government purchase of the adjoining 100,000-acre Baca Ranch. In addition to the dunes, the land covered by the bill included meadows, alpine tundra, and the 14,165-foot Kit Carson Peak.

Despite the quick passage, western lawmakers split sharply over the bill. Rep. Scott McInnis, R-Colo., supported the measure and likened the dunes to such natural treasures as Yosemite Valley. But fellow Colorado Republican Joel Hefley called the dunes a "pile of sand" that did not warrant national park status. Hefley, chairman of the Resources Committee National Parks and Public Lands subcommittee, attempted to block the bill, but McInnis persuaded GOP leaders to circumvent the committee and bring it directly to the House floor.

California Water Project

A bill (HR 3077—H Rept 106-435) to allow nonfederal water to be transferred to farmers within the San Luis Unit of a California water project passed the House in 1999, but it died in the Senate.

Under a 1960 law that sought to ensure that the federal government was repaid for California's Central Valley Water Project (CVP), the state could not provide long-term water service to the San Luis Unit. The unit included the 600,000-acre Westlands Water District, which in 1999 was negotiating to purchase a large state water entitlement.

The CVP had faced water shortages for much of the past decade, and the legislation would clear the way for the area to receive California State Water Project resources.

The bill, sponsored by Rep. Cal Dooley, D-Calif., was approved by voice vote by the House Resources Committee on Oct. 27, 1999. The House passed it by voice vote on Nov. 8. The Senate Energy and Natural Resources Committee held hearings on the measure in 2000, but it took no further action.

Clean Air Act Rewrite

Congress took little action on the venerable Clean Air Act, despite rumblings by conservatives that stringent standards adopted by the Environmental Protection Agency (EPA) and the courts were threatening economic development. *(1997 action, p. 351)*

The only significant bill to receive a vote was a Senate measure (S 1053—S Rept 106-228) that aimed to reinstate transportation projects that were struck down in a court decision over the Clean Air Act. The bill won approval in the Environment and Public Works Committee, but it did not make it to the Senate floor.

The transportation controversy stemmed from provisions in the 1990 rewrite of the Clean Air Act that blocked federal funding for highway projects that did not conform to states' air quality plans. Those provisions sparked a court battle over whether the EPA had the right to grandfather previously approved transportation projects into new air quality plans, even in areas that failed to meet clean air requirements.

Environmentalists sued the EPA over its grandfather policy, scoring a pivotal victory when the U.S. Court of Appeals for the District of Columbia overturned the agency's rule on March 2, 1999. This effectively blocked dozens of new road projects in Atlanta, as well as in other fast-growing cities.

Transportation lobbyists looked to Congress for a legislative remedy, contending that the court decision tied the hands of local planning officials. But some Democratic lawmakers and environmentalists contended that the court ruling would have a positive effect, forcing metropolitan areas to revise construction plans that otherwise would have worsened sprawl and threatened open spaces.

On a party-line vote, 10–8, the Environment and Public Works Committee on Nov. 29, 1999, adopted a substitute amendment to S 1053, introduced by committee chairman John H. Chafee, R-R.I., and bill sponsor Christopher S. Bond, R-Mo. The amendment included a provision that would have reinstated the EPA regulation for only one year or until the EPA created new procedures for ensuring conformity in transportation plans.

Conservative lawmakers also criticized new EPA standards to reduce air pollution from cars. In the last two years of the Clinton administration, the EPA stiffened emissions requirements for sport utility vehicles and light trucks, and it sharply decreased allowable levels of sulfur in gasoline. "In their rush to issue new environmental regulations, I fear the administration is short-changing important considerations . . . in the proposed sulfur rule," said Sen. James M. Inhofe, R-Okla., chairman of the Senate Environment and Public Works Subcommittee on Clean Air, Wetlands, Private Property and Nuclear Safety. "The administration has also consistently failed to supply the Senate with important analysis and justifications for this proposal."

However, Congress did not pass legislation to curtail the regulations.

Clean Water Regulations

Conservative lawmakers clashed with the administration over the implementation of new clean water regulations, but they failed to win enactment of legislation that would have delayed the regulations for a year. Proposals that would have bolstered clean water programs also failed in the 106th Congress.

At the center of the debate were regulations proposed by the Environmental Protection Agency (EPA) that would require states within two years to identify bodies of water that were not in compliance. The approach, known in EPA parlance as "total maximum daily load," would then require states to calculate the total amount of pollution that would have to be eliminated in order to bring the water bodies within compliance of the law. The regulations would also require states to establish a timetable for accomplishing the work.

The EPA plan was driven by concerns that some 40 percent of the nation's waters were failing to meet the quality standards established by the clean water act (PL 92-500). That meant that 218 million Americans lived within ten miles of a polluted river, stream, or lake.

Announced by President Clinton in August 1999, the regulations were designed to address the largest and most difficult remaining source of water pollution—storm water runoff that, in regulatory language, was called "non-point" pollution.

More difficult than factory effluents to contain, runoff came from many places and at unpredictable times. Whenever it rained, runoff formed a toxic brew by stripping pesticides, chemicals, and assorted other pollutants from backyards, city streets, construction sites, farms, mines, logging operations, and any other exposed area. Most runoff found its way to streams, lakes, and rivers. The rest percolated to underground aquifers.

Environmental groups complained that the new EPA regulations were not tough enough, but agriculture and forestry groups said the rules would be far too costly and burdensome.

To prevent contaminated runoff from draining into streams, for instance, farmers might be required to plant buffer strips near streambeds or let productive land lie fallow. Farms that operated large feedlots could be required to install costly treatment plants to cleanse animal waste before it was released. Loggers could be required to walk away from valuable timber because felling the trees would allow unacceptable levels of silt and sediment to wash into streams.

"It would be a nightmare of regulations which would cause all kinds of problems," Sen. Robert C. Smith, R-N.H., chairman of the Environment and Public Works Committee, said on March 7, 2000. Like many critics, Smith took the view that current regulations were sufficient to address the problem if they were aggressively enforced.

EPA Administrator Carol M. Browner pointed out that states would be primarily responsible for monitoring and enforcing the regulations. The Environmental Protection Agency would get involved only if states were unable or unwilling to carry out the program.

The debate reached the boiling point when the EPA, racing to beat the signing of a congressionally mandated delay, issued the new regulations on July 11 despite fierce opposition from most Republicans and many farm state Democrats. The EPA action essentially negated a policy rider tacked onto the fiscal 2001 military construction appropriations bill (HR 4425—H Rept 106-614) that would have stopped it from spending funds to implement any new water quality rules during fiscal 2000 or fiscal 2001. Since the total maximum daily load rules were no longer "new water quality rules" by the time that Clinton signed the appropriations bill (PL 106-246) July 13, the rider did not apply to them.

Trying to strike back, the Senate Environment and Public Works Committee approved a bill (S 2417—S Rept 106-485) by voice vote on July 26 that would delay EPA implementation of more stringent water standards. Under the measure, sponsored by Michael D. Crapo, R-Idaho, the rules would be delayed for a year to allow the new standards to be studied. The studies would have to consider both the costs and the benefits of the rules.

Under the bipartisan proposal, funding for existing state clean water programs would be bolstered by $750 million annually for seven years. The Senate cleared the measure by unanimous consent on Oct. 10, but the House did not take it up.

Other clean water measures also failed to clear Congress.

One bill (HR 2328—H Rept 106-560) would have reauthorized the Clean Lakes Program, created under the Water Pollution Control Act of 1972. The measure would have funded the program at $50 million a year for fiscal years 2000 through 2005. It also would have authorized $25 million for a study of the impact of acid rain on lakes.

The Clean Lakes Program provided federal financial and technical assistance to states for improving the water quality of public lakes. The House, 420–5, passed the measure on April 12, 2000, but the Senate did not vote on it.

Another bill (HR 910—H Rept 545) would have established a fund to restore the San Gabriel groundwater basin in southern California and study groundwater contamination caused by perchlorates, which were chemicals used in rocket fuel that had been found in drinking water. It would have authorized $25 million annually for fiscal years 2000 through 2004. The House passed the measure by voice vote on March 28, 2000, but the Senate did not take it up.

Coastal Barrier Resources

Congress cleared a measure in 2000 to reauthorize the Coastal Barrier Resources Act at $2 million through 2004 and $3 million from 2004 to 2007.

The 1982 act was designed to counter storm damage and pollution and to discourage residential and commercial development in vulnerable coastal areas. It established the Coastal Barrier Resources System, encompassing 535 barrier islands and other coastal habitats and a total of 1.2 million miles of coastline. People who owned property within the system could not receive any federal development assistance—such as federal flood insurance—though they were not prohibited from using their own money for development. By creating such a system, Congress aimed to protect human safety, preserve fish and wildlife habitat, and reduce the amount of tax dollars that went to subsidize coastal properties.

The bill (S 1752—514) would allow the Interior Department to add coastal barrier lands to the system at the requests of private landowners, instead of relying exclusively on Congress to designate the units. It also would authorize $500,000 annually for a three-year pilot program to create digital versions of Interior's coastal barrier system maps, with the goal of integrating the coastal barrier system with other federal, state, and local planning efforts. Interior would be required to report to Congress within a year on savings achieved under the program by avoiding federal payments for disaster relief, flood insurance, roads, and water treatment facilities.

The Senate Environment and Public Works Committee approved the measure (S Rept 106-252) on Feb. 9. The Senate on Sept. 27 passed the bill by voice vote, along with an amendment to rename the Coastal Barrier Resources System after the late Sen. John H. Chafee, R-R.I., who served in the Senate from 1976 to 1999. The House cleared the measure on Oct. 24 by voice vote. Clinton signed it Nov. 13, 2000.

Coastal Zone Management Act

Congress failed to clear legislation to reauthorize the Coastal Zone Management Act (PL 92-583) because of clashes over private property rights and other issues.

Under the act, states received grants to develop and implement federally approved coastal management plans. Once in place, the state had the authority to monitor federal activities along the coast to ensure they were consistent with the management plans. The law empowered the states to try to stop activities that could damage the environment, such as offshore drilling for oil and gas.

The federal grants, which were based on a state's coastal population and shoreline miles, ranged from $500,000 to $2.15 million annually for each eligible state with an approved plan.

House efforts to reauthorize the law stalled when the bill (HR 2669) provoked a battle over private property rights. The House measure would have authorized $55 million in fiscal 2000 for developing state plans and an additional $30 million to create a new category of grants designed to increase local involvement in coastal management.

The House Resources Committee approved the bill (H Rept 106-485) by voice vote on Oct. 6, 1999, but not before voting 24–23 to adopt a private property amendment that drew sharp criticism from bill sponsor H. James Saxton, R-N.J. The amendment, sponsored by Richard W. Pombo, R-Calif., would restrict the use or "taking" of private land without just compensation to the owner.

Saxton worried that the provision would weaken the ability of states and localities to protect coastal zones. He had already reworked the legislation (formerly HR 1110) to drop language that would have required states to regulate where people could ride personal watercraft, better known by such brand names as Jet Skis. Although highly popular, personal watercraft drew criticism from environmentalists and some outdoor recreational users such as canoeists and windsurfers because they were noisy and polluting.

Another controversial issue that sparked debate was nonpoint pollution, which occurred when rainfall or melting snow flowed over the ground, carrying away pollutants before depositing them into rivers and lakes. On a 26–15 vote, the panel adopted a Republican-backed amendment to remove provisions dealing with non-point pollution, because they were deemed outside the committee's jurisdiction.

The House failed to take up the measure, or a related bill (S 1534—S Rept 106-412) that the Senate passed by unanimous consent on Sept. 28, 1999.

Controlling Bird Populations

Amid concerns about the skyrocketing population of double-crested cormorants, the House Resources Committee in 2000 approved a bill (HR 3118—H Rept 106-916) to allow hunters to shoot more of the birds. Congress did not take additional action on that measure, but it did add language to the fiscal 2001 agriculture appropriations bill directing the Department of Agriculture to intensify efforts to control cormorants and other fish-eating birds, such as pelicans.

On a related issue, Congress cleared legislation to relax hunting restrictions on fast-growing geese populations.

The increasing number of cormorants stirred concern in the Capitol because they targeted catfish, causing problems for both commercial catfish farmers in the Southeast and recreational fishermen. The aggressive cormorants also took the nests of other birds.

Under the Migratory Bird Treaty Act, cormorants could not be killed without the permission of the federal government, which was responsible for managing their populations. Cormorant populations declined sharply in the 1960s and early 1970s because of pesticides such as DDT, but they had since rebounded.

The Resources Committee Fisheries Conservation, Wildlife and Oceans Subcommittee approved HR 3118 by voice vote on July 20. The bill would allow an individual hunter to shoot up to ten birds each day during an established hunting season, which would correspond with the hunting season for other waterfowl.

But Del. Eni F. H. Faleomavaega, D-Am. Samoa, questioned how much good the bill would do. He said the Fish and Wildlife Service allowed the cormorant population to grow out of control despite ten years of warnings and wondered whether it would take advantage of this bill to solve the problem.

The Resources Committee approved the bill by voice vote on Sept. 20.

The agriculture spending bill (HR 4924—PL 106-553) directed the Animal and Plant Health Inspection Service to step up research and operations to control the birds. Environmentalists criticized the language, saying that the Fish and Wildlife Service was conducting a study into whether controls were necessary.

Taking aim at another species of bird, the House on Nov. 11, 1999 cleared a measure to relax hunting restrictions on the fast-growing population of midcontinent light geese. Lawmakers hoped that reducing the geese population would stop the birds from destroying their habitat in the Great Plains and the arctic.

The debate over controlling light geese, which included lesser snow geese and Ross's geese, was touched off by the explosive growth in the number of the birds. The U.S. Fish and Wildlife Service estimated that the geese population had skyrocketed from about 800,000 in 1969 to 5 million in the late 1990s and warned that the geese would destroy their habitat through overfeeding unless steps were taking to control the population. The birds nested in the spring in the Canadian Arctic and migrated south through Canada and the United States during the winter months.

The proposal split environmentalists and animal protection advocates, who were traditional allies. While groups such as the National Audubon Society supported the plan, the Humane Society vehemently opposed it. When the Fish and Wildlife Service issued rules on Feb. 16 to make it easier to hunt the geese, it was challenged in court by the Humane Society of the United States. The agency withdrew its proposal on June 17, electing to conduct an environmental impact study instead.

But Rep. H. James Saxton, R-N.J., introduced legislation (HR 2454—PL 106-108) to implement the agency's proposed regulations immediately. Tracking the agency's proposed regulation, his plan would allow the twenty-four states that are in the migratory path of the geese to extend the hunting season beyond its normal Sept. 1–March 10 boundary. Hunters could use recorded goose calls (which had been prohibited) and "unplug" their shotguns, taking more shots at once. The bill would sunset when the Fish and Wildlife Service completed its impact study and issued a new regulation by March 15, 2001.

The House Resources Committee approved the bill (H Rept 106-271) by voice vote on July 21. The House, under suspension of the rules, passed the bill by voice vote on Aug. 2. On Sept. 29, the Senate Environment and Public Works Committee attached to the end of the bill a measure (S 148) aimed at protecting the habitats of neotropical migratory birds. On Nov. 8, however, the Senate adopted an amendment to strip the neotropical migratory bird language from the bill because lawmakers feared it would prevent the original measure from passing. It then passed the measure by voice vote.

The House cleared the measure by voice vote on Nov. 10.

Restoring Watershed Dams

Congress in 2000 cleared an agriculture bill (HR 4788—PL 106-472) that, among other provisions, would restore aging watershed dams. The measure directed the Agriculture Department to contribute to local authorities up to 65 percent of the cost of rebuilding old watershed dams.

Senate Democrats initially expressed reservations about the provisions, questioning whether such dams should be rebuilt or scrapped. Dams were a significant environmental concern because of their effects on freshwater ecosystems. Accordingly, the Senate on Oct. 24 passed a related measure (S 1762—S Rept 106-408) requiring the USDA to give the same weight to requests to decommission dams as it gave to proposals to rebuild them.

Beginning in 1948, the government initiated several watershed programs in which the USDA served as a partner with states and local governments, providing cost-sharing for construction, site and geological surveys and engineering and design services. In turn, local governments and community organizations covered local construction costs, provided land easements and rights of way, managed the contracting process and maintained the completed facilities.

By 2000, more than 1,300 small flood control dams nationwide were within a decade or so of reaching the end of their fifty-year life expectancy. Many of them had endured so much wear and tear that local governments could not repair them without assistance, supporters of HR 4788 warned.

Under the bill, which amended the Watershed and Flood Prevention Act, the rehabilitation process would work the same way, with roughly 65 percent of costs covered by the USDA and 35 percent funded locally. The measure would require the USDA to rank and approve the rehabilitation requests—based on need and merit—and set aside $5 million in fiscal 2000 and 2001 to assess the overall rehabilitation needs of watershed projects nationwide.

The plan to restore the dams began moving in the House as HR 728. As approved by voice vote by the Transportation Committee (H Rept 106-484, Pt. 1) on Nov. 18, 1999, it would authorize $600 million over ten years for the Agriculture Department to provide funding to local governments and community organizations to rehabilitate dams. The measure next won voice vote approval on April 4, 2000 in the Agriculture Committee (H Rept 106-484, Pt. 2). Chairman Larry Combest, R-Texas, offered a substitute amendment, approved by voice vote, that would allow the USDA to turn down a funding request if it found that the dam had not been properly maintained.

The House included the measure in HR 4788, which it passed on Oct. 17, 2000. The Senate cleared the measure by voice vote on Oct. 24. Clinton signed the bill Nov. 9, 2000.

Endangered Species Act

Amid ongoing controversy over the 1973 Endangered Species Act (PL 93-205), lawmakers attempted to change key provisions of the powerful law in 1999 and 2000. But with Democrats and Republicans deeply divided over the issue, Congress failed again to advance any proposal.

The act, which expired in 1992 but remained fully in effect because of annual appropriations measures, sought to preserve threatened animals and plants by making sure their environment was protected. It prohibited actions that harmed or killed any listed species, or destroyed their habitat. More than most environmental laws, the Endangered Species Act drew fire from conservatives who viewed it as infringing on the rights of property owners. But environmentalists, worried about the loss of plant and animal species, battled to defend it. *(1997 action, p. 349)*

One bill (S 1100—S Rept 106-126), that won voice vote approval in the Senate Environment and Public Works Committee on June 29, 1999, would revise the process for designating a "critical habitat" under the Endangered Species Act.

Critical habitats were federally designated areas that were home to endangered species and require special management. Once an agency such as the Fish and Wildlife Service identified the critical habitat of a threatened species, it could restrict development in those areas.

Existing law required federal agencies to designate a critical habitat as soon as the species was declared endangered. But S 1100, introduced by committee chairman John H. Chafee, R-R.I., would allow federal agencies to move more slowly, designating critical habitat as part of the planning for the recovery of listed species.

Chafee warned that the time constraint for declaring critical habitat forced agencies to make their decisions without vital information, including the needs of the species and various economic assessments. Consequently, critical habitats were often not designated, which in turn often sparked lawsuits by environmental groups to force the government to make the designation.

Bill supporters acknowledged that the bill was only a small change within the broad scope of the Endangered Species Act, but they believed that this was the most effective way to bring about significant change. "We have attempted major ESA reform before and it didn't go anywhere," said Max Baucus, D-Mont. "This is a smaller slice and will allow us to make some progress."

Some environmentalists viewed critical habitat as an important mechanism to force the government to set aside land for rare species. Others, however, thought it mostly duplicated more important provisions of the Endangered Species Act. Amid the controversy, the Senate declined to take up Chafee's measure.

The following year, critics of the Endangered Species Act scored a temporary victory when the House Resources Committee approved two bills June 21 that would have overhauled the 1973 law. But Congress took no further action on the proposals.

The panel approved the first measure (HR 3160—H Rept 106-1013), which would make it more difficult to list new species as "endangered," by a 24–15 vote. The second bill (HR 1142—H Rept 106-1011), which would give landowners rights to government compensation if their property was inhabited by endangered species, was approved by a vote of 27–11.

Resources Committee Chairman Don Young, R-Alaska, who sponsored both bills, acknowledged in an interview that election-year pressures—which make it important for many westerners to vote for property rights measures to appeal to their constituents—played a role in his decision to bring the bills to a markup even though he conceded that only the compensation bill had any chance of progressing in 2000.

George Miller of California, ranking Democrat on the Resources panel, said Young's measures were a virtual repeal of the act that "would fundamentally undermine the premise of protecting endangered species in the United States."

HR 3160 would give states and private citizens a greater role in the process of listing plants and animals as threatened or endangered. It also would require petitions to list a species as threatened or endangered to be based on "peer-reviewed science."

The bill would require the petition to include evidence that the plant or animal was a distinct species and proof that its population was declining or had declined below normal historic fluctuations. Another provision would impose deadlines on federal agencies involved in the decision-making process. The bill also would require the removal of species from the endangered list that were no longer endangered or threatened.

Young's compensation measure specifically tied a species designation to "taking"—a legal process by which the federal government used private property for a public purpose. The bill would require the government to pay property owners if species protection measures interfered with their ability to use their land as they chose, reduced the value of any part of their property by 25 percent or more, or affected their water rights.

The House took no further action on either measure.

Estuary Restoration Program

Congress cleared legislation (S 835—PL 106-457) in 2000 to establish a national estuary restoration program. The bill authorized $275 million over five years in an attempt to restore more than one million acres of estuary habitat in ten years.

Estuaries were water inlets created at the meeting place of rivers and oceans. They tended to be highly biologically productive because of the mix of salt and freshwater ecosystems. But their fragile ecosystems were threatened by development that eliminated coastal habitat, as well as by polluted runoff that swept off farms and roads into waterways.

Lawmakers worried that the deterioration of estuaries could have serious economic consequences because of reduced fish and shellfish harvests. In the nation's largest estuary, the Chesapeake Bay, the oyster population had dropped dramatically in recent years.

The House Resources subcommittee on Fisheries Conservation, Wildlife and Oceans gave voice vote approval on Oct. 28, 1999, to a bill (HR 1775) that would authorize about $315 million over five years in matching grant funds for restoration projects sponsored by groups and state and local governments. To be eligible for the funding, local restoration groups would have to provide at least 35 percent of project costs, with the federal share accounting for no more than 65 percent.

The measure, sponsored by Wayne T. Gilchrest, R-Md., also would direct the Commerce Department's National Oceanic and Atmospheric Administration to maintain a database of information to track the success of the projects. It also would establish the Estuary Habitat Restoration Council to review projects and submit to Congress a strategy for restoring estuary habitats nationwide.

The House Transportation and Infrastructure Committee gave voice vote approval to the bill (H Rept 106-561, Pt. I) on April 4, 2000. The House Resources Committee approved the bill (H Rept 106-561, Pt. II) by voice vote on June 9 after amending it to authorize $153 million over three years for matching grants.

The House passed the bill by voice vote on Sept. 12.

A companion measure (S 835—S Rept 106-189) won voice vote approval in the Senate Environment and Public Works Committee on Sept. 29, 1999. The Senate version would authorize about $315 million. It also would establish a national council to oversee the projects and allocate funding, and it would direct the National Oceanic and Atmospheric Administration to maintain a database of monitoring information to track the success of the projects.

The Senate passed S 835 by voice vote on March 30.

Splitting the difference between the funding levels in the two bills, House and Senate conferees agreed to authorize $275 million over five years. The package also incorporated eight other water bills, including versions of legislation (HR 3039—H Rept 550) that would authorize $40 million annually through fiscal 2005 for continued restoration of the country's largest estuary, the Chesapeake Bay; a bill (HR 3313—H Rept 106-597) to reauthorize restoration efforts in the Long Island Sound; and a measure (HR 1106—H Rept 106-593) that would authorize a pilot program to award federal grants for so-called alternative water resource programs, designed to give areas with critical water needs an environmentally sustainable water supply through the conservation, management, reclamation or reuse of water, or by treating wastewater. Clinton signed the bill Nov. 7, 2000.

Filming Fees at National Parks

With many cash-strapped national parks unable to pay for maintenance costs, Congress in 2000 overturned a 1948 regulation that had prevented the National Park Service and Fish and Wildlife Service from collecting fees for films shot on many public lands. Under the legislation, which won the support of the Motion Picture Association of America, movie studios, television producers, and the recorders of soundtracks would have to pay a fee if they filmed in national parks, monuments, or wildlife refuges. The fees would vary, depending on how long a site was used, how many people were involved, and other factors. Television news productions and newsreels would be exempt.

Such fees had been collected by the government until 1948, when the Truman administration exempted producers of movies, print ads, and commercials from paying to film in national parks and wildlife refuges. Since then, national parks and other federal lands were integral parts of some highly popular movies, but collected no money from the movies' success.

Much of *Dances with Wolves* was staged at Badlands National Park in South Dakota; *Star Wars* used White Sands National Monument in New Mexico; and part of *Close Encounters of the Third Kind* was filmed at Devil's Tower National Monument in Wyoming. In addition, companies that produced fast food, cars, and other products flocked to public lands, such as Joshua Tree National Monument in California, to shoot commercials.

The House had passed similar legislation in 1998. But it died at the end of the 105th. *(1998 action, p. 356)*

The bill (HR 154—PL 106-206), by Rep. Joel Hefley, R-Colo., authorized the Interior Department to create a fee scale for using public lands for commercial purposes. It also required companies that produced commercial footage of national park scenery to first purchase a permit.

The bill would give the secretary of interior the authority to set fees, based on the number of people on site, the amount of equipment used during filming, and the duration of the shoot. In addition, the permit would have to generate enough revenue to compensate for all government costs associated with the project, including cleanup and restoration of a site. The Interior Department could prohibit filming if it would unreasonably disrupt park visitors or damage the park's environment.

Of the fees collected, 70 percent would remain in the park that was used for the shoot, and the other 30 percent would be distributed to other park units.

Hefley agreed to amend the bill to limit the definition of what constituted appropriate use of the land to activities that would neither damage the resources nor create a significant disruption for park visitors. The motion picture industry requested the change after raising concerns that, without narrow language, the secretary would have the authority to approve details of film production such as script material.

The House Resources Committee approved the bill (H Rept 106-75) by voice vote on March 3, 1999. The House passed the popular bipartisan measure on April 12 by voice vote. The bill then won voice vote approval by the Energy and Natural Resources Committee on May 19. The Senate passed the bill by voice vote on Nov. 19 after expanding the measure's jurisdiction to include all land administered by the Interior Department, as well as U.S. Forest Service lands administered by the Agriculture Department. The House cleared the amended bill by voice vote on May 22, 2000. President Clinton signed the measure on May 26.

National Forests

Amid western criticism of administration restrictions on logging, the House Resources Committee approved a bill (HR 1524) in 1999 that would require federal agencies to seek an expedited review for the authority to remove dead or dying trees from more than a dozen national forests. But the House did not take up the controversial plan.

Bill sponsor Helen Chenoweth, R-Idaho, said certain forests "are in a state of near collapse," and she contended that affected local communities needed a process to deal with the deteriorating forest conditions. She noted that the National Environmental Policy Act (PL 91-103) allowed the Council of Environmental Quality to grant expedited environmental reviews in cases deemed emergencies by federal agencies.

Her bill used as a precedent a 1998 decision by the Interior and Agriculture Departments to seek such a waiver after storms led to fire and insect infestation risks on federal lands in Texas.

The bill would have required the agencies to seek the expedited review to remove damaged trees on fourteen sites, including 100,000 acres of ice storm-damaged and beetle-infested lands in Washington and Idaho, as well as 50,000 acres of fire- and insect-damaged lands in Oregon's Malheur National Forest.

Democrats opposed the bill, noting that the Forest Service already had a process in place to handle forest emergencies. Panel ranking Democrat Adam Smith, D-Wash., said the bill "steps over local communities and the local Forest Service units" that could use the NEPA process if they decide the situation warrants emergency consideration.

The Resources Committee approved the bill (H Rept 106-1021) on a party-line vote, 21–8, on June 9.

The committee also approved another Chenoweth bill (HR 1523—H Rept 106-604, Pt. I) that would have required federal agencies to follow strict guidelines before permanently closing roads on federal lands. Chenoweth argued that action was necessary to make federal agencies more accountable to local communities, who were often "left in the dark" when decisions are made to close roads.

Under the measure, the Forest Service and the Bureau of Land Management would be required to publish the proposed closing in local newspapers before moving forward with a permanent road closing. After the announcement, the agencies would initiate a ninety-day public comment period.

Democrats said the bill would tie the hands of federal officials. The committee approved the measure, 22–16, on May 5, but Congress took no further action on it.

Subsistence Fishing

Congress cleared a measure in 2000 to require the Interior Department to allow subsistence fishing in Alaska's Glacier Bay National Park and give Alaska primary control of the fishery. In addition, the bill (S 501—PL 106-455) authorized up to $2 million each fiscal year to be paid to commercial fisheries harmed by restrictions in the area.

The issue stemmed from a 1997 National Park Service proposed rule that would have prohibited commercial and subsistence fishing in Glacier Bay. The fiscal 1999 Interior spending bill (PL 105-277) prevented the park service from enforcing the rules until commercial fishing and processing companies, environmental representatives and local officials agreed on fishing regulations in the bay.

"The Alaska natives have been using the bay for over 9,000 years and there have been no complaints of any species being over-harvested," said bill sponsor Frank H. Murkowski. "They are dependent on subsistence fishing for their lifestyle and livelihood."

The Senate Energy and Natural Resources Committee, which Murkowski chaired, approved the measure on a 13–7 vote on June 30, 1999. Murkowski had earlier tried to attach language to the midyear supplemental law (HR 1141—PL 106-31) but it was taken out in conference.

The Senate passed Murkowski's measure (S Rept 106-128) by unanimous consent on Nov. 19. The House cleared it on Oct. 23, 2000. The president signed it on Nov. 7.

National Marine Sanctuaries

Congress in 2000 cleared legislation to provide continued protection to national marine sanctuaries, authorizing a total of $180 million over five years.

Marine sanctuaries were established under the 1972 Marine Protection, Research and Sanctuaries Act to protect marine habitats and preserve cultural artifacts such as shipwrecks. The nation's twelve sanctuaries sought to balance conservation with recreational and commercial activities. Activities such as drilling, mining, and dredging were generally prohibited in the sanctuaries, as was dumping waste and salvaging artifacts. Shipping, commercial and sport fishing, boating, and scuba diving were generally allowed.

The Clinton administration sought to put a greater emphasis on marine conservation, in part because overfishing and pollution was taking a toll on fish populations.

The bill (S 1482—PL 106-513) would reauthorize the sanctuaries through fiscal 2005. It would authorize a total of $180 million, beginning with $32 million for fiscal 2001, increasing by $2 million annually to $40 million in fiscal 2005. It also would authorize $30 million over the period for construction projects, as well as scientific research and outreach programs at each sanctuary.

The House Resources Fisheries Conservation, Wildlife and Oceans Subcommittee gave voice-vote approval on May 27 to a measure (HR 1243) that would have matched the administration's authorization request of $29 million annually for five years.

The bill also would authorize $105 million over five years for the National Estuarine Reserve System, which studied coastal issues and habitats. Estuaries are areas where salty tides meet freshwater.

The House Resources Committee approved the bill (H Rept 106-224) by voice vote on June 9, and the House passed the measure on Sept. 21 by voice vote.

The Senate Commerce, Science, and Transportation Committee approved higher funding levels in S 1482 (S Rept 106-353) on July 21, 2000. The Senate passed it by unanimous consent on Oct. 17, and the House cleared it by voice vote on Oct. 24. President Clinton signed the measure Nov. 13, 2000.

Methane Research

Congress cleared legislation in 2000 to authorize $35.5 million over five years for federal research on methane as an energy source.

Methane hydrate was a stable, ice-like substance that occurred naturally in deep ocean sediments of the Arctic, the seabed adjacent to northern California, the Gulf of Mexico, and the eastern seaboard. The high percentage of methane in the crystals made it a nearly limitless source of energy in the form of natural gas, but only if it could be extracted safely.

An Energy Department official told the Energy and Science subcommittee of the House Science Committee in 1999 that the natural gas potential of hydrates was nearly 400 million trillion cubic feet—some 80,000 times the world's currently known natural gas reserves.

Sen. Daniel Akaka, D-Hawaii, who sponsored the Senate version of the bill, said: "As our nation's energy resources dwindle and our reliance on imported energy increases, we cannot afford to miss this important opportunity."

However, extraction was not commercially viable with existing technology. If the methane escaped its subterranean deposits, scientists warned that it had the potential to destabilize sea bottoms and cause devastating global climate shifts.

The legislation (HR 1753—PL 106-193) allowed the energy secretary to collaborate with universities and industry to research gas hydrate as an energy source and develop the technology necessary for effective and environmentally friendly development. It directed the Energy Department, the Naval Research Laboratory, and the U.S. Geological Survey to research the development of methane resources and determine safe ways to transport and store methane extracted from hydrates.

Both the House Science and House Resources committees approved the bill (H Rept 106-377, Pts. I and II) by voice vote in 1999. The House passed it by voice vote on Oct. 26; the Senate passed it with an amendment by unanimous consent on Nov. 19; the House passed it with another amendment on April 3, 2000; and the Senate cleared it by unanimous consent on April 13. Clinton signed it on May 2.

Migratory Birds

Congress cleared a measure in 2000 to authorize funding for projects designed to conserve the habitat of certain types of tropical migratory birds.

The bill (S 148—PL 106-247), sponsored by Michigan Republican Spencer Abraham, would authorize $8 million each fiscal year through 2003 for habitat conservation projects approved by the Interior Department. Modeled on similar habitat conservation programs for rhinoceroses and tigers, it would funnel the dollars into an account within the larger Treasury Department multinational species conservation fund.

The legislation was spurred by growing concern that habitat loss in both the United States and Latin American countries was taking its toll on songbirds and other species that migrated between North America and tropical regions. Supporters of the bill warned that ninety out of 500 species of migratory birds were listed as either threatened or endangered.

Congressional action on the issue started in 1999, with the House Resources Subcommittee on Fisheries Conservation, Wildlife and Oceans giving voice vote approval on March 11 to a bill (HR 39) to create an account to fund national and international projects to conserve the habitat of certain tropical migratory birds. The Resources Committee approved the bill (H Rept 106-80) by voice vote on April 12.

But action stalled temporarily in the House after private property rights advocates expressed concerns that the bill could impose burdensome regulations on property owners and localities. Conservatives such as Helen Chenoweth, R-Idaho, wanted project organizers to enter into written

agreements with property owners governing the use of the land.

The similar Senate measure (S 148—S Rept 106-36), was bolstered by the support of several influential lawmakers. The Senate passed the bill by unanimous consent on April 13. The House, 384–22, passed the measure with an amendment on June 26, 2000. The Senate cleared it by unanimous consent on June 29. The president signed it on July 20.

National Monuments

During the 106th Congress, President Clinton sparked heated controversy by repeatedly invoking the 1906 Antiquities Act to designate national monuments without congressional consent. His executive actions protected more than three million acres, mostly in western states, from drilling, logging, mining, grazing, and other potentially environmentally destructive activities.

Environmentalists applauded Clinton's actions, comparing them to the century-old conservation accomplishments of President Theodore Roosevelt. But western conservatives, who were previously angered by the president's 1996 creation of the Grand Staircase-Escalante National Monument in Utah, denounced Clinton for walling off economically valuable lands without soliciting the input of local residents. *(1997 action, p. 365.)*

"The president continues to usurp the power of state legislatures and local officials," Rep. George P. Radanovich, R-Calif., chairman of the Western Caucus, said in January 2000 after Clinton barred development on more than 1 million acres in Arizona and California from development. "This circumvention of power by the president must be stopped by Congress."

The 1906 Antiquities Act gave the president the power to protect federal lands by designating them monuments. The law had been used since 1906 by every president except Ronald Reagan, George Bush and Richard M. Nixon, and it generally provoked little controversy. But few presidents had turned to the law as aggressively as Clinton, who seemed determined to create an environmental legacy with or without the help of Congress.

Polls showed wide support for Clinton's actions, and the politically savvy president wasted few opportunities to stress the importance of preserving natural resources. "If there is one thing that unites our fractious, argumentative country . . . it is the love we have for our land," he said in early 2000. "The only thing we can add to it is our protection."

To curb the president's power, conservatives sought to pare back the Antiquities Act. But environmental groups and the administration pledged to battle any attempt to change it. Republicans, who had failed to clear legislation modifying the Antiquities Act in the 105th, conceded they lacked the votes to significantly alter the law.

In 1999 the House took a small step toward modifying the law by passing a bill (HR 1487—H Rept 106-252) that would have required the president to consult with the governor and congressional delegation of a state at least sixty days before declaring land a national monument. This largely symbolic legislation, sponsored by James V. Hansen, R-Utah, won voice vote approval in the House Resources Committee on June 30. The House passed it on Sept. 24 by an overwhelming margin, 408–2.

Hansen initially favored a more restrictive approach that would have required lengthy environmental studies. Even the weaker House-passed version drew a veto threat, however, with the White House complaining that it "would undermine the president's authority to move decisively to protect and preserve the nation's treasures for future generations."

The Senate Energy and Natural Resources Committee, 12–8, reluctantly approved the measure on Oct. 20. Only three Republicans, including chairman Frank R. Murkowski, R-Alaska, voted for the bill. But the Senate did not take it up on the floor, in large part because western Republicans thought it was not tough enough. "The House basically creates a process to inform the public," said Larry E. Craig, R-Idaho. "But it does not tie the hands of the president."

Instead, Craig's bill (S 729—S Rept 106-372) would have required lengthy environmental studies before land could be designated a monument. His plan also required congressional approval of any designation.

The Senate Energy and Natural Resources Committee approved S 729 on June 7, 2000. At the time, western conservatives were concerned that the Clinton administration was moving toward creating additional national monuments, protecting about 550,000 acres in Arizona, Colorado, Oregon, and Washington. Although the bill was approved by voice vote, ranking Democrat Jeff Bingaman of New Mexico expressed opposition to it for weakening the president's ability to preserve environmentally fragile areas. The bill never advanced to the Senate floor.

On April 5, 2000, the House Resources Committee, 20–12, approved a measure (HR 4021—H Rept 106-570) that could have interfered with President Clinton's ultimately successful effort to create a national monument near California's Sequoia National Park. Under the proposed legislation, the National Academy of Sciences' board on agriculture and natural resources would conduct a study and file a final report within two years. The president would be prohibited from proclaiming land within the Sequoia National Forest a national monument until at least ninety days after publication of the final report.

However, Democrats sharply criticized the bill for tying the president's hands until after the election. Congress took no further action on the measure.

However, in drafting the fiscal 2001 appropriations for the Department of the Interior, House Republicans led by Hansen, made one more attempt to curb Clinton's use of the Antiquities Act. GOP appropriators succeeded in inserting a policy rider to the bill that limited management funds for any monuments designated after 1999. On the floor Norm Dicks, D-Wash., drafted an amendment to strip the rider

from the bill. On June 15, 2000, right before Dicks's amendment was voted, Hansen offered an amendment to reinstate the restriction. Hansen's amendment in a **key vote of 187–234 (R 177–38; D 9–195; I 1–1)** was defeated, and Dicks's amendment was then adopted. *(2000 key votes, p. 915)*

Gasoline Additive MTBE

Legislation to ban the clean-burning gasoline additive methyl tertiary butyl ether (MTBE)—a suspected carcinogen that was found to be leaking from underground storage tanks in some thirty states—died at the end of the 106th Congress after lawmakers failed to forge a compromise that could satisfy both the agriculture and petroleum industries. Oil refiners criticized the bill as a "de facto ethanol mandate" that would exacerbate the problem of skyrocketing fuel prices. Agriculture groups and farm state lawmakers said the measure did not go far enough to ensure that air quality benefits would be maintained.

BACKGROUND

MTBE was added to gasoline in large quantities to satisfy a provision in the 1990 amendments to the Clean Air Act requiring that clean-burning, "reformulated" gasoline be used in the nine U.S. cities with the worst air pollution.

The compound helped reduce the amount of toxic materials spewed into the air by millions of pounds, according to the Environmental Protection Agency (EPA). But MTBE was also a suspected carcinogen that had leaked from underground storage tanks and polluted groundwater in almost every state. Ten years after the 1990 law, California had at least 10,000 contaminated sites, New York identified some 1,500 and New Jersey was coping with nearly 500 contaminated water supplies.

Compounding the problem, MTBE—which was used in more than 85 percent of all gasoline to comply with EPA regulations—dissolved in water, allowing it to travel very far and very fast. The chemical, even in very small amounts, could leave water tasting and smelling like turpentine.

In the 106th Congress, the American Lung Association and the Natural Resources Defense Council found themselves in an unusual coalition with the American Petroleum Institute, which was the lobbying arm of the major oil companies. Working with air quality regulators from eight northeastern states, the group called for repeal of the oxygen mandate in reformulated fuel but not an outright ban of MTBE. It also supported statutory language prohibiting any "backsliding" in air quality gains.

If the oxygenation standard were waived, the coalition believed that refiners could cut the use of MTBE by as much as 70 percent with no loss in air quality. Furthermore, it contended that reduced use of MTBE, coupled with more aggressive enforcement of existing standards for underground storage tanks, would largely address the water pollution problem.

The fight, however, was far from one-sided. Agricultural interests, particularly corn growers, agreed that MTBE should be phased out, but they wanted to preserve the 2 percent standard. Their goal was to replace MTBE with ethanol, a derivative of corn, to create reformulated gasoline. That would create a huge new market for corn growers struggling with low commodity prices. But refiners insisted that ethanol was more expensive and difficult to obtain than MTBE.

Taking the side of agriculture, the Clinton administration in March 2000 recommended replacing MTBE with a renewable fuel source, such as ethanol. EPA administrator Carol Browner said the agency was taking steps to eliminate MTBE from gasoline, but she urged Congress to act immediately because the regulatory process could take considerable time.

Some Republicans on Capitol Hill reacted coolly. "The issue of renewable fuels has nothing to do with eliminating MTBE from our drinking water, and I am not yet convinced that we should replace one mandate with another," said Sen. Robert C. Smith, R-N.H., chairman of the Environment and Public Works Committee.

But Smith, who wanted to eliminate MTBE from drinking water, said he would try to forge a compromise with the administration.

LEGISLATIVE ACTION

Lawmakers in 1999 introduced several measures designed to resolve the MTBE problem. Smith cosponsored legislation (S 1886) with James M. Inhofe, R-Okla., and Dianne Feinstein, D-Calif., that would have allowed states to waive the oxygen mandate. The bill drew attention because water sources in the California communities of Santa Monica, Sacramento, and Lake Tahoe were tainted by MTBE. Several House members also introduced MTBE measures.

Following the administration's proposal, Smith worked to bridge the gap between agricultural and petroleum interests. On July 27, 2000, he introduced a bill (S 2962) that would allow states to waive the oxygenate requirement but require them to live up to the toxic emission reductions they achieved under the mandate. To do so, states would rely in large part on the corn-based oxygenate ethanol, the only commercially developed MTBE alternative.

A provision in the bill that Smith called a "market-based incentive program"—included to appease oil interests that say a straight ethanol mandate would be too expensive—would establish a portion of the gasoline market to be comprised of "clean alternative fuels," which could include premium gasoline blends or fuel cell technology in addition to ethanol. The bill also would authorize $200 million to clean up MTBE contamination.

Despite the attempt at compromise, Smith's bill drew criticism from oil refiners who saw the bill as a "de facto ethanol mandate" that would exacerbate the problem of skyrocketing fuel prices by tying the hands of refiners already struggling to address shortages in supply.

Agriculture groups and farm state lawmakers—who estimated that an ethanol mandate could increase the demand for corn by 600 million bushels a year—also criticized the measure. In particular, they said the bill did not go far enough to ensure that air quality benefits were maintained without the oxygenate requirement.

With little time left on the legislative calendar, the Environment and Public Works Committee, 11–6, approved the controversial measure (S Rept 106-426) on Sept. 7. By voice votes, the panel rejected an amendment by Republican James M. Inhofe of Oklahoma to protect oil companies that manufactured or handled MTBE from liability for injury or damage associated with it, and an amendment by Kay Bailey Hutchison, R-Texas, to establish a federal fund for oil companies that invested in MTBE to modify or refit their facilities to accommodate substitutes.

While no amendments were adopted during the markup, opponents signaled plans to offer their own provisions should the bill reach the floor. Inhofe, for example, withdrew an amendment that would have required the EPA to study the effects of the bill's renewable fuels requirements on fuel supply, the economy, human health and the environment before allowing them to take effect. Christopher S. Bond, R-Mo., floated an amendment to ban MTBE but retain the oxygenate requirement.

After the markup, Smith acknowledged that his zeal for compromise may have led him too far in guaranteeing the use of ethanol. "I moved over toward ethanol further than I actually wanted to," he said.

The committee approval provided scant momentum to the plan. With only five weeks left in the legislative session, no House action on the subject and a sizable group of opponents, Smith said he would resurrect the issue in the 107th Congress.

Native Alaskan Lands

Congress cleared legislation (HR 3090—PL 106-194) in 2000 to allow native residents near Elim, Alaska, to reclaim 50,000 acres of land from the federal government.

In 1917 the federal government set aside 350,000 acres for indigenous inhabitants of Elim. But President Herbert Hoover in 1929 used an executive order to take 50,000 acres from the Elim reservation.

The legislation would allow the Elim Native Corp., representing about 300 native Alaskans living more than 100 miles southeast of Nome, to select up to 60,000 acres and file a selection application with the Bureau of Land Management. The corporation would be granted 50,000 of the selected 60,000 acres.

The selected parcel would have to be "reasonably intact, contiguous and in whole sections." The bill would require members of the Elim Native Corp. to put various parcels on a priority list.

The bill (H Rept 106-452) by Rep. Don Young, R-Alaska, was approved by voice vote in the Resources Committee on

Oct. 20, 1999. The House passed it by voice vote on Nov. 9. The Senate Energy and Resources Committee approved it by voice vote on Feb. 10, 2000, and the Senate cleared it by voice vote on April 13. Clinton signed it May 2, 2000.

Congress in 2000 also cleared legislation (S 430—PL 106-283) to authorize a land exchange for the Kake Tribal Corporation, which owned land on islands near Juneau that were part of the tribe's historic homelands.

While the tribe had logged much of the land to provide income for the corporation's members, further logging on portions would have harmed watersheds that provide the tribe's drinking water. Under the measure, the corporation would relinquish half of its watershed property to the city of Kake and place a conservation easement on the other half. In addition, the state would convey several pieces of nearby land that are not within the watershed to the corporation for development.

The Senate Energy and Natural Resources Committee approved the bill (S Rept 106-31) on March 22, 1999. The Senate passed it by unanimous consent on April 19. The House Resources Committee approved it with an amendment by voice vote on Jan. 27, 2000. The House passed it by voice vote on May 22, and the Senate cleared it by unanimous consent on Sept. 22. Clinton signed it Sept. 26, 2000.

Northern Spotted Owl

With lawmakers sharply divided over logging issues, a bill (HR 3089) to examine a Clinton administration policy on Northwest forests and its impact on the northern spotted owl won approval in 1999 from a House Resources subcommittee despite Democratic objections. However, Congress took no further action on the controversial measure.

Efforts to protect the northern spotted owl, which lived in old-growth forests in Washington, Oregon, and northern California, had touched off fiery battles between environmentalists and loggers since the Interior Department listed the bird as a threatened species in 1990.

Campaigning for president in 1992, Bill Clinton pledged to balance economic and environmental interests, and he strived to satisfy all sides in the dispute with his 1994 Northwest Forest Plan. Covering 24 million acres of public land, the plan sought to encourage sustainable forestry for timber-dependent counties while leaving enough undisturbed forest land for the northern spotted owl to survive. The president appeased neither side, but his plan survived lawsuits.

Amid continuing controversy over protecting the owl, Forests and Forest Health Subcommittee Chairwoman Helen Chenoweth, R-Idaho, introduced HR 3089 to direct the Interior and Agriculture departments to enter into a contract with the National Research Council of the National Academy of Sciences to study owl populations.

The study would include a determination of whether the conservation strategy under the plan was likely to help the owl's survival and an assessment of the scientific data concerning the owl.

The panel approved the bill 6–5 on Nov. 2, 1999. However, Democrats sharply criticized it. "The study is duplicative and an unnecessary expense," said the panel's ranking Democrat, Adam Smith, Wash. "There is already enough light being shed on the issue."

The bill was referred to the Agriculture Committee, which did not vote on it.

National Ocean Policies

Congress cleared legislation in 2000 to update the nation's coastal policies. Since the 1970 creation of the National Oceanic and Atmospheric Administration (NOAA), the country's population had shifted, with half of all Americans living in coastal areas. That number was expected to swell to 75 percent by 2025. The increasing threat to ocean and coastal resources—and confusing regulations—prompted lawmakers to create the first full-scale federal review of the nation's coastal policies in three decades.

Sponsored by Sen. Ernest Hollings, D-S.C., the bill (S 2327—PL 106-256) would establish a sixteen-member Commission on Ocean Policy to review existing policies and make recommendations to Congress on a new comprehensive plan. The measure would authorize $6 million for the commission through fiscal year 2004.

All commission meetings would be open to the public and at least six would be held in specific, geographically diverse coastal areas, including Alaska.

The commission would have eighteen months to prepare and submit a report to Congress and the president. Recommendations would have to provide more coherent and consistent regulation of ocean and coastal activities (including those in the Great Lakes), protecting life and property and conserving the underwater environment and fish populations.

The president would have 120 days after receiving the report to submit legislative proposals to Congress implementing the commission's recommendations.

The Senate Commerce, Science and Transportation Committee approved the measure (S Rept 106-301) without amendment on May 23, 2000. The Senate passed it by unanimous consent on June 26, and the House cleared it by voice vote on July 25. Clinton signed it Aug. 7, 2000.

Fish and Wildlife Spending

Congress in 2000 cleared legislation that would cap spending for some fish and wildlife programs that deal with land management.

The bill (HR 3671—PL 106-408) would restrict U.S. Fish and Wildlife Service spending on the administration of two programs that provide state grants for restoration and expansion of hunting and fishing areas. It would cap administrative spending for both the wildlife and sport fishing programs at $18 million in 2001 and 2002, and at $16 million in 2003. These rates would then be adjusted for inflation in 2004 and subsequent years.

During congressional oversight hearings in 1999, the General Accounting Office (GAO) estimated that as much as one-half of the money earmarked for administration of the funds had been misused. During one hearing, a GAO official said, "This is, if not the worst, one of the worst managed programs we have encountered."

The Fish and Wildlife programs that provide the grants to states were created under the Wildlife Restoration Act of 1937 and the Sport Fish Restoration Act of 1950. The 1937 law is commonly known as the Pittman-Robertson Act, and the 1950 law is known as the Dingell-Johnson Act.

Funding for both programs came from excise taxes on guns, ammunition, archery equipment, and fishing equipment. The programs provided grants to states for fish and wildlife conservation projects to improve and expand areas available for hunting and fishing.

Under existing law, the agency was allowed to keep 8 percent of wildlife funds and 6 percent of sport fish funds for program administration.

The bill also would set aside up to $6 million for grants that benefit states. It would authorize approximately $8 million annually for various hunting education and safety programs and reauthorize the National Fish & Wildlife Foundation through 2003, as well as establish a National Wildlife Refuge System Centennial Commission.

The House Resources Committee approved the bill (H Rept 106-554) on March 15 by a vote of 36–0. The House on April 5 passed the bill, 423–2, after amending it to address concerns by Democrats that the spending restrictions were too strict. The Senate Committee on Environment and Public Works approved the bill (S Rept 106-495) with an amendment on Sept. 28, and the Senate passed it by unanimous consent on Oct. 12. The House cleared it by voice vote on Oct. 18. Clinton signed the bill Nov. 1, 2000.

Coral Reef Protection

Spurred by scientific warnings about a massive die-off of the world's coral reefs, Congress considered a bill that would have bolstered protection for the environmentally diverse underwater habitats. Although lawmakers failed to clear the measure, President Clinton used the 1906 Antiquities Act to place much of the nation's coral reefs in nature preserves.

Coral reefs were sometimes likened to tropical rain forests because they were among the richest ecosystems on Earth, containing as much as 25 percent of all marine life. They also protected fragile shorelines by absorbing the force of ocean waves. But much of the world's reefs were being destroyed by pollution, overfishing, and a warming of ocean waters.

The bipartisan bill (HR 3919—H Rept 106-762) would have authorized the expenditure of $4 million between fiscal 2001 and 2004 by the Coral Reef Task Force to coordinate federal coral reef activities, establish a coral reef improvement strategy, and develop a comprehensive mapping, monitoring and assessment program.

The bill would also authorize $38 million over four years for 50 percent matching grants for coral reef mapping, monitoring, restoration, and law enforcement projects in communities, states and U.S. territories. Nonprofit groups and educational institutions would be eligible for grants.

The measure would designate the National Oceanic and Atmospheric Administration as the lead federal agency for reef conservation, and provide $18 million over four years for the agency's reef restoration, mapping, and monitoring.

The Resources subcommittee on Fisheries Conservation, Wildlife and Oceans passed the bill by voice vote on March 23, 2000, and the full committee passed it by voice vote on June 20. But the House did not take it up.

Using his executive authority in late 2000, Clinton created the nation's largest nature preserve, an underwater expanse off Hawaii that contained nearly 70 percent of U.S. coral reefs. The creation of the 84-million-acre Northwestern Hawaiian Island Coral Reef Reserve drew criticism from some in the Hawaiian fishing industry, but Clinton said the reefs must be preserved to support thousands of species of fish and other sea life, as well as generate revenues from fishing and tourism revenues. The following month, he protected additional reefs by creating another underwater national monument off the Virgin Islands.

Steller Sea Lions

High-level negotiations yielded an agreement in December 2000 to allow Alaskan pollock fishermen to continue casting their nets despite concerns that depleted fish stocks were depleting the populations of the already endangered Steller sea lion.

Senate Appropriations Chairman Ted Stevens, R-Alaska, held up the final fiscal 2001 spending conference report (HR 4577), because he opposed efforts to protect the sea lions' habitat by banning fishing off the Alaska coast. He won a partial victory with a provision to allow the winter fishing season to begin in January 2001. *(HR 4577, p. 81)*

The fall fishing season had been interrupted by a judge's ruling that blocked trawling in 156,000 square miles of ocean that was designated as critical sea lion habitat. The judge also ordered the National Marine Fisheries Service, a Commerce Department agency, to protect the sea lions.

Under the agreement, regulations that were in place before the judge's ruling would apply. However, the commerce secretary could issue new regulations before January 20. Those regulations could not reduce the amount of fish caught by more than 10 percent, even though scientists recommended that the catch be reduced by 40 percent to preserve the sea lions.

The agreement also included language to compensate fishermen for past losses resulting from restrictions. It earmarked $20 million for research and recovery of the Steller sea lion.

Stevens, however, hardly won a clear-cut victory over environmentalists. The administration, worried about creating a precedent that would have undermined the Endangered Species Act, refused to put the fishing restrictions under local control.

Pollock were the main food for the sea lions, and industrial fishing depleted the stock. Stevens blamed killer whales for the decreased population of Steller sea lions.

Las Cienegas National Conservation Area

Congress in 2000 cleared a bill (HR 2941—PL 106-538) to establish the Las Cienegas National Conservation Area in southern Arizona. The area comprised land in the Cienega Creek and Babocmari River watersheds in Pima, Santa Cruz, and Cochise Counties.

Supporters of the measure say it would provide for flexible and effective management of the watersheds, while not decreasing the percentage of private property in Arizona.

The bill would prohibit any land exchange involving the proposed conservation area that would reduce the state's tax base.

The vast majority of the proposed conservation area would be composed of land owned by the federal government or the state. The interior secretary would have to receive the state's consent before using eminent domain to acquire state land.

The bill would place limits on acquisition of private lands for the conservation area. The secretary would be allowed to accept donations of private lands, or exchange parcels of federally owned land for private lands. Purchases of private land would be permitted only if the owner had set up a conservation easement.

In the process of creating a management plan for the area, the Interior Department would have to consult with local and state officials. The plan would permit hunting in the conservation area at the discretion of the interior secretary and the Arizona Game and Fish Department.

The House Resources Committee gave voice vote approval to the bill (H Rept 106-934) on Sept. 20. The House passed it by voice vote on Oct. 5, and the Senate cleared it by unanimous consent on Oct. 27. The president signed it Dec. 6, 2000.

Route 66 Preservation

Congress cleared legislation in 1999 to authorize up to $10 million over nine years for a program to preserve the cultural heritage of the 2,200-mile-long federal highway known as Route 66.

Under the bill (HR 66—H Rept 106-45), the Interior Department would pay up to 50 percent of the costs to protect areas of the highway, as well as businesses and other buildings located along the historic road. States, municipalities, and nonprofit groups would provide the rest of the funding and would carry out the preservation projects.

Route 66, stretching from Chicago to Santa Monica, Calif., was memorialized in popular culture as America's "Main Street." The government designated it a federal highway in 1926, and it served as a primary route for hundreds of thousands of vehicles going across the country until the Interstate Highway System gradually replaced it. The road figured prominently in John Steinbeck's classic novel, "The Grapes of Wrath."

The House Resources Committee approved the bill (H Rept 106-137) by voice vote on May 13. The House passed it by voice vote on June 30, and the Senate cleared it by unanimous consent on July 27. Clinton signed it Aug. 10, 1999.

Roadless Areas

President Clinton's plan to ban new logging roads in nearly sixty million acres of national forest land received a strong scolding from conservative lawmakers, but Congress took no action to overturn the ban.

The 192-million-acre national forest system had long been the subject of a fierce policy dispute between environmentalists, who wanted to preserve them for wildlife habitat, watershed protection, and other ecological benefits, and loggers, who wanted to cut down trees for timber. Although the forests were originally established in the late nineteenth century to guarantee the nation an adequate supply of timber, more and more Americans were using them for recreation. Polls showed strong support for preserving the forests as wilderness. However, many westerners worried that the growing list of federal restrictions on forest activities was costing them jobs.

In the 1970s the U.S. Forest Service conducted two roadless area reviews, known as RARE I and RARE II, to inventory roadless areas of 5,000 acres or more. The Forest Service built roads in some of those areas; Congress designated others as wilderness which would remain untouched. But about sixty million acres of nonwilderness national forest lands remained undeveloped.

In October 1999 Clinton directed the Forest Service to draw up a rule to protect those remaining roadless areas. Predictably, the plan sparked mixed reviews. Environmentalists praised it for protecting pristine areas from timber and mining. But western lawmakers said it could hurt the federal timber program and rural economies by restricting access to lands needed by resource-dependent communities.

Republicans were particularly concerned over the Forest Service's rulemaking process. At a February 2000 hearing by a Senate Energy and Natural Resources subcommittee, Republican committee members said the administration deliberately circumvented open meetings laws and met secretly with environmental groups to develop its proposed policy.

Calling the policy a "fatally tainted rulemaking," Larry E. Craig, R-Idaho, the chairman of the Forests and Public Land Management subcommittee, said the process violated the Administrative Procedures Act and the Federal Advisory Committee Act.

Administration officials, including U.S. Forest Service chief Mike Dombeck, responded that the administration had held about 200 public meetings and made efforts to solicit public comments.

The dispute boiled over at the end of the 106th Congress, when the administration announced it would include parts of Alaska's Tongass National Forest in the ban. The Tongass, the largest national forest and a refuge for numerous rare species of plants and animals, was considered vital for lumber mills that helped sustain the economy of southeastern Alaska.

Powerful Alaskan lawmakers, who had fought tirelessly to exempt the Tongass from more federal regulations, conceded that there was no time left on the legislative calendar to fight the ban. But they pledged to overturn it in the 107th Congress. "What they're attempting to do is to terminate harvesting in the national forests," Senate Energy and Natural Resources Committee Chairman Frank H. Murkowski, R-Alaska, said in a Nov. 14 interview. "It's a failure to recognize that we have a different situation in our state."

Salmon Project

Trying to improve the survival rates of salmon in the Pacific Northwest, Congress cleared a measure (HR 1444—PL 106-502) to authorize $25 million each year for construction of fish screens, which would keep young salmon and other fish out of irrigation trenches. The screens would be installed throughout the Snake and Columbia river systems in Oregon, Washington, Montana, and Idaho. Participation in the program would be voluntary.

The Bureau of Reclamation and the Army Corps of Engineers operated fourteen large-scale water projects in the region, providing navigation assistance, flood control, crop irrigation, hydroelectric power, and recreation. But the water diversion necessary for those activities hindered salmon migration. The measure called on the U.S. Fish and Wildlife Service to develop and implement a program to use fish screens and passage devices where stream and river water was diverted.

Both environmentalists and northwestern fishing fleets had a strong interest in bolstering stocks of the economically important fish. With salmon stocks declining, the federal government in 1998 listed nine West Coast salmon populations as threatened or endangered under the Endangered Species Act.

The Fisheries Conservation, Wildlife and Oceans Subcommittee of the Resources Committee approved the measure (H Rept 106-454, Pt. I) by voice vote on June 22, 1999. The full committee approved it by voice vote on Aug. 4, and the House passed it by voice vote on Nov. 9.

In the Senate, where the bill (S Rept 106-239) sailed through the Environment and Public Works Committee on Feb. 10, 2000 and the full Senate on April 13, amendments were added to make projects in California ineligible and to require that the program be administered by the Interior Department's Bureau of Reclamation, rather than the Fish and Wildlife Service.

The House on Oct. 17 passed the bill by voice vote after adding an amendment to put the Fish and Wildlife Service back in charge of the program. The Senate cleared the bill by voice vote on Oct. 27. Clinton signed the bill on Nov. 13.

Other issues involving salmon also provoked congressional debate. The House Resources Committee on July 21, 1999, went on record to oppose a controversial plan to remove four dams on the Snake River in Washington state. The dams blocked salmon from returning to the sea after they were born and then going back up river to spawn. Artificial efforts, such as barging salmons across the dams, had limited success.

The resolution to keep the dams (H Con Res 63), sponsored by Republican Richard "Doc" Hastings of Washington and approved by voice vote, squared with the views of many western members who believed that removing the four relatively new dams would represent a setback for the local economy.

But environmentalists, backed by at least one independent study, argued that removing the dams was the only way to keep salmon from becoming extinct in the region. The four dams at the center of the debate were the Ice Harbor Dam, the Lower Monument Dam, the Little Goose Dam, and the Lower Granite Dam.

Shark Protection

Taking a step toward protecting dwindling numbers of sharks, Congress in 2000 cleared a bill (HR 5461—PL 106-557) that would ban the practice of cutting the fins off sharks caught in U.S. waters. The measure would make it illegal to catch sharks for the purpose of cutting off their fins or tails and throwing the maimed fish back in the ocean to die.

Shark populations were becoming decimated because of the increasing popularity in Asia of such culinary delicacies as shark fin soup. In 1991 2,289 sharks were killed for their fins, according to the National Marine Fisheries Service. By 1998 the number had increased to 60,857, sparking alarms among environmentalists.

Opponents said the practice was wasteful because it used a small percentage of the shark. The practice was also considered cruel, as sharks were sometimes finned while alive. They died afterward because they could not swim without their fins.

HR 5461 marked the fifth time in the 106th Congress that one chamber or the other passed a measure to prohibit killing sharks for their fins. The House adopted a resolution (H Con Res 189) condemning the practice by voice vote Nov. 1, 1999, but the Senate did not act. The House then voted, 390–1, for a bill (HR 3535—H Rept 106-650) to ban the practice, but the Senate again did not act.

In addition, the prohibition was contained in two other massive ocean and fisheries bills: HR 3417 and HR 5086. After the House passed HR 3417 (H Rept 106-569) on June 26, the Senate amended and passed the measure by unanimous consent Oct. 13. The House passed HR 5086 by voice vote Oct. 23. Neither chamber followed up on either bill.

Some of the proposals had sparked concerns among Democrats such as Rep. Neil Abercrombie of Hawaii, who said lawmakers should consider the impact on the fishing industry. Abercrombie said putting an end to hunting of sharks would require action in international waters. "We must deal with this comprehensively," he said.

With HR 5461, lawmakers in both chambers finally agreed on a ban. The legislation, sponsored by Rep. Randy Cunningham, R-Calif., was a broader version of previous bills. It would ban the practice in all U.S. waters, promote international talks to ban the practice worldwide, and authorize various studies on shark populations.

The House passed the measure by voice vote on Oct. 30, and the Senate cleared it by voice vote on Dec. 7. President Clinton signed it Dec. 31, 2000.

'Superfund' Overhaul

Congress again failed to overhaul the "superfund" program, despite widespread concerns about the costs and liability associated with the hazardous waste cleanups. In 1999 two House committees marked up competing versions of the bill. The following year, the House defeated legislation to protect small businesses from liability under the program. The Senate was unable to produce a superfund bill. However, lawmakers in 1999 added a provision exempting certain recycling businesses from superfund liability to the omnibus spending bill (HR 3194—PL 106-113). *(Superfund background, p. 352).*

1999 LEGISLATIVE ACTION

Action on superfund stalled after two House committees marked up competing versions of superfund legislation that drew criticism from environmentalists. Senate Majority Leader Trent Lott, R-Miss., succeeded in adding a superfund provision to an omnibus appropriations bill that exempted recycling companies from liability.

Lawmakers began the 106th Congress under no illusion that the superfund program would be easy to revamp. The 1980 toxic waste law (PL 96-510), formally known as the Comprehensive Environmental Response, Compensation, and Liability Act, had repeatedly sparked inconclusive legislative battles throughout the 1990s. In the 105th Congress, GOP leaders failed to bring superfund legislation to the floor even though revamping the program ranked as one of their top environmental priorities. *(1997–1998 action, p. 352)*

For year after year, lawmakers had locked horns over such issues as how to clean up sites, who should pay the tab, and how to remedy damage done by severely polluted sites to rivers, streams and other natural resources. Perhaps the biggest bone of contention between Republicans and the administration was how far to go in scaling back existing retroactive liability provisions, which allowed the govern-ment to hold a company responsible for the costs of cleaning up toxic waste dumped before the superfund law was enacted in 1980.

In early 1999 key House Republicans, such as House Commerce Committee Chairman Tom Bliley of Virginia and Finance and Hazardous Materials Subcommittee Chairman Michael G. Oxley of Ohio, began pushing for comprehensive superfund legislation. They wanted to base their plans on bills introduced in the previous two Congresses. However, neither the Clinton administration nor congressional Democrats evinced much support for such an overhaul.

Some Republicans called for more targeted adjustments. A proposal by Greg Ganske, R-Iowa, and James C. Greenwood, R-Pa., would have allowed states to take full responsibility for cleanups of industrial sites and would provide liability relief for those who purchased the land after it has been reclaimed.

"When you've got the votes, you move comprehensive reform," Ganske said. "When you don't, you look at fixing parts of it."

The administration supported targeted liability relief. But it raised questions about allowing states to take full responsibility, which would essentially prohibit the EPA from intervening once a state certified that a site was clean. Instead, it backed the EPA policy of giving states full cleanup authority through written agreements.

In May, House Transportation Water Resources and the Environment Subcommittee Chairman Sherwood Boehlert, R-N.Y., announced a "targeted, very specific" superfund measure (HR 1300). It would authorize a total of $1.5 billion through fiscal 2004 for the superfund program, including $25 million annually for state-run, voluntary cleanup programs that target the redevelopment of the so-called brownfields—the abandoned urban industrial sites that remain vacant because of toxic leftovers.

The taxes on chemical and petroleum manufacturers, which expired in 1995, would be reinstated. $300 million would be authorized annually for the cleanup of sites where the responsible party is either absent or defunct.

Small businesses, innocent landowners, prospective purchasers of contaminated property, and contiguous property owners would be shielded from liability under the bill. Cleanup costs for municipalities and landfill operators would be capped.

Boehlert's measure attracted more than two dozen Democratic cosponsors, ranging from the chair of the moderate Blue Dog Coalition, Robert E. "Bud" Cramer, Ala., to well-known environmentalists such as Peter A. DeFazio, Ore., and James P. Moran, Va. It also drew backing from the U.S. Conference of Mayors, organized labor groups and various realty and development organizations.

But many Democrats fell behind an alternative bill (HR 1750) by Commerce Committee ranking Democrat John D. Dingell of Michigan. Dingell's bill addressed only brownfields funding and a narrow package of liability exemptions.

In a tense hearing before Boehlert's panel on May 11, Environmental Protection Agency Administrator Carol M. Browner told Boehlert that his bill "fixes problems that perhaps don't exist and breaks things that are actually working." The measure exempted all parties that disposed of garbage at superfund sites, regardless of volume, and made changes in the law's groundwater provisions and responsible party allocation process—adjustments that Browner argued would balloon litigation, delay cleanups and pollute groundwater.

On June 10 the House Transportation Water Resources and Environment Subcommittee approved a compromise version of Boehlert's bill that would adjust portions of the nation's superfund toxic-waste cleanup program. Five Democrats joined Republicans to approve the bill 22–9.

The panel adopted several amendments addressing Browner's concerns, although the full committee's top Democrat, James L. Oberstar of Minnesota, said a number of issues required resolution before committee Democrats would support the bill.

The panel adopted, by voice vote, a Boehlert amendment striking controversial responsible-party allocation language. The amendment also would limit liability exemptions for large-volume paper recyclers and recyclers of any material containing PCB levels that exceed federal standards.

Another amendment, offered by Ellen O. Tauscher, D-Calif., and adopted by voice vote, would require that a neutral party determine the division of liability at superfund sites. Also adopted by voice vote was an amendment by Earl Blumenauer, D-Ore., clarifying that companies contributing large amounts of municipal solid waste to a superfund site would not receive the same liability protections as households that disposed of waste at the site.

With prospects for a superfund overhaul still deeply buried under partisan differences, business and industry critics of the current law got a small piece of good news in the Republican tax bill (HR 2488) that the Ways and Means Committee approved on July 14. A provision in the bill, pushed by Ways and Means Chairman Bill Archer, R-Texas, would prohibit reinstating a tax that lapsed in 1995 on companies whose products could create hazardous waste sites. The money was designated to pay for superfund cleanups.

If Archer's language were to become law, the superfund tax would be set aside for at least two years, yielding a savings of millions of dollars annually for the oil and chemical industries. To replace the lost money, Archer's proposal would consolidate trust funds that together amount to $1 billion. That money would double the account to clean up the nation's most dangerous hazardous waste sites and extend its life to 2003.

Under Archer's plan, the superfund trust fund would merge with another large fund created to pay for cleaning up leaking underground storage tanks that hold oil and other toxins. That fund had not been tapped as often as expected because states have similar trust funds that have paid for thousands of such cleanups.

But while some business lobbyists cheered the proposed end of the tax, they conceded that it would have almost no effect on the larger effort to pass a meaningful overhaul of the superfund program.

In the Senate, Environment and Public Works Chairman John H. Chafee, R-R.I., pursued legislation (S 1090) in July that focused on issues on which there was bipartisan consensus, including to clean up industrial brownfields and exempt small business from liability.

The measure, which was similar to Boehlert's, would authorize $100 million annually in grants to clean up brownfields and another $100 million annually to underwrite state-sponsored cleanups. It would exempt from liability small generators of only municipal waste as well as small businesses with fewer than 75 employees or $3 million in gross annual revenue.

But, despite weeks of closed-door meetings, he failed to bring the measure to markup. Republicans complained that it was not comprehensive enough, and Democrats voiced opposition to key provisions, such as decreased funding, a failure to overhaul the liability system and so-called "state finality" provisions that would greatly restrict the federal government from intervening in a state cleanup project.

On Aug. 5, however, the House Transportation and Infrastructure Committee overwhelmingly approved HR 1300 (H Rept 106-353, Pt. I) by a 69–2 vote. Largely tilted toward the priorities of businesses, the measure would:

• Provide $1.5 billion annually for superfund from fiscal 2000 through fiscal 2003, then decrease funding as the number of sites declined. The bill calls for $975 million in funding in fiscal 2007, the final year.

• Set aside $25 million annually to assist state-run, voluntary cleanups.

• Exempt from liability businesses with fewer than seventy-five employees and less than $3 million in revenues. The bill also would exempt municipal solid waste operators and those who contribute less than 200 pounds of waste to a superfund site.

• Streamline the regulatory process for redeveloping thousands of brownfields in cities where officials believe these prime locations could be cleaned up and redeveloped.

Those provisions won the support of influential business groups, including the National Association of Realtors, the American Insurance Association, the National Automobile Dealers Association, and the National Federation of Independent Business, which praised the bill for removing "innocent small businesses from superfund prosecution and [focusing] resources on actual cleanup, rather than costly litigation."

But legislators remained deeply divided over reinstating a superfund tax on industries. Moreover, the House bill would have to win approval from the ideologically divided Commerce Committee.

Environmental groups and the EPA lined up against the bill. Among its complaints, the EPA said the bill "does away with the critical principle of 'polluter pays at hundreds of toxic waste sites' and instead shifts the cost of cleanup to the ... taxpayer." Contradicting supporters of HR 1300, who insisted the bill would accelerate cleanups and bring fairness back to the program, the EPA charged that the bill "would delay cleanups, drive up their costs and bring lawyers and litigation back into the system."

Putting its own stamp on the issue, the House Commerce Finance and Hazardous Materials Subcommittee approved a superfund overhaul bill (HR 2580) on Sept. 29 on a 17–12 vote after nearly six hours of debate, in which votes on most amendments broke along party lines. Only one Democrat, Ralph M. Hall of Texas, voted for the final bill.

Subcommittee chairman Michael G. Oxley, R-Ohio, and bill sponsor James C. Greenwood, R-Pa., geared HR 2580 toward providing limited liability relief for small business, streamlining site cleanups by giving states and local governments more authority, and spurring redevelopment of urban brownfields.

The bill would exempt small businesses from having to pay a portion of the cleanup cost. This language was a major goal of small businesses and their powerful voice, the National Federation of Independent Business, which had long argued that regulators went after small businesses that contributed only a fraction of the contaminants and forced them to pay an excessive amount of the cleanup costs.

The bill would cap liability of municipal landfill owners on superfund's list of national priorities at 10 percent for small municipalities and 20 percent for larger municipalities. It also would allow states to keep a site off the list by obtaining an agreement from parties to conduct a voluntary cleanup.

A major difference between HR 2580 and Boehlert's bill was that HR 2580 made no mention of reinstating superfund taxes.

Democratic amendments to toughen cleanup standards and ensure a robust federal presence in the cleanups were all rejected on party-line votes. A substitute amendment by Edolphus Towns, D-N.Y., based on his bill (HR 1750) to limit superfund revisions to brownfields, was defeated, 12–15, also on a party-line vote.

Business interests, led by the U.S. Chamber of Commerce, immediately hailed the Commerce subcommittee's outcome, while environmental groups condemned it.

The battle resumed on Oct. 13, when the House Commerce Committee approved HR 2580 (H Rept 106-775, Pt. I) by a vote of 30–21. Just two Democrats—Ralph Hall of Texas and Bart Gordon of Tennessee—broke party lines to support the measure.

Several Democrats blasted provisions in the bill that provided exemptions from cleanup liability for buyers, sellers, innocent landowners, prospective purchasers, contiguous property owners, and small businesses from having to pay a portion of cleanup costs.

"This bill will let the polluter off the hook because of its excessive liability exemptions. We need to stick with the 'polluter pays' principle," said Frank Pallone Jr., D-N.J.

The administration hinted that the measure could face a veto if it ever reached the president's desk. In a letter to ranking committee Democrat John D. Dingell of Michigan, Browner said, "Given the significant progress we have been able to achieve in the superfund program over the past six years, the administration cannot support legislation that would undermine that progress and therefore must oppose HR 2580."

With two competing bills in play, the House took no further action on superfund legislation in 1999. Instead, a key superfund provision ended up in the massive omnibus appropriations measure. That provision, championed by Senate Majority Leader Trent Lott, R-Miss., and backed by environmentalists, would exempt certain recycling businesses from superfund liability.

Some lawmakers raised concerns that carving out an exemption for one industry could disadvantage other industries, although they did not go so far as to oppose the appropriations measure. "The rest that are left in the program will have their burden increased. It is not fair anyway you slice it," Boehlert said.

2000 LEGISLATIVE ACTION

Legislation to protect small businesses from liability for toxic waste cleanups under the superfund program was defeated in the House less than two weeks after it was introduced by Michael G. Oxley, R-Ohio, chairman of the House Commerce Subcommittee on Finance and Hazardous Materials. Congress failed to take other action on the controversial environmental program.

With action stalled on the two major superfund bills, lawmakers focused on a modest bill (HR 5175) by Oxley to exempt small businesses from cleanup costs if they dumped trash at a superfund site but contributed little or no hazardous waste to it. The bill was based on an agreement reached in 1999 between the EPA and the National Federation of Independent Business. It was designed to keep small businesses that dumped household trash from getting ensnared in superfund lawsuits, while preserving EPA's ability to enforce the law against polluters.

The measure would exempt any business with 100 or fewer employees and revenues of $3 million or less as long as they dumped less than 110 gallons or 200 pounds of hazardous waste. Companies that did not qualify for the exemption from the superfund law would still be eligible for an "expedited" settlement with the government if they only dumped "minimal" amounts of hazardous waste or cannot pay the cleanup costs.

To speed passage, House leaders decided that the bill should be considered under suspension of the rules, which limited debate and required a two-thirds majority for passage.

However, the House vote on Sept. 26 was 253–161—short of the required two-thirds majority. Supporters said the measure was necessary to spare small business owners from lawsuits, but critics called it special interest legislation that was being rushed through the process at the end of the legislative session.

Forest Revenues

Congress in 2000 cleared a bill (HR 2389—PL 106-393) to guarantee federal payments to rural communities that depended on forest revenues to help pay for their schools and roads. Lawmakers passed the measure after working out a compromise to alleviate environmental concerns that the legislation could encourage more logging.

BACKGROUND

For many rural communities, the U.S. Forest Service—which was exempt from local property taxes that traditionally funded school districts and local road projects—was the dominant landowner in the region. A revenue-sharing program was created in 1908 under which the Forest Service paid affected counties 25 percent of its receipts for national forest activities, primarily logging sales.

A similar revenue-sharing program established in 1937 mandated that the Bureau of Land Management (BLM) pay affected governments 50 percent of its receipts from activities on the land.

As environmental concerns in the 1990s slowed down logging sales, the corresponding drop in Forest Service and BLM revenues drastically reduced payments to some rural communities. An estimated 800 counties adjacent to National Forest Service lands were suffering from shrinking budgets, with federal payments to some of the counties dropping by as much as 90 percent, according to bill supporters.

The Clinton administration and environmentalists saw the funding crisis as an opportunity to overhaul the revenue-sharing program, putting an end to the link between logging receipts and school budgets. They worried that the program, as currently structured, provided counties with an economic incentive to destroy their natural resources. But environmentalists faced opposition from a powerful coalition of county, education, and timber interests.

Rural lawmakers were especially determined to preserve the traditional funding structure. "Children in forest counties deserve the same educational opportunities as those in the rest of America," said Rep. Nathan Deal, R-Ga.

The issue primarily affected western communities. In 1998 the Forest Service and BLM sent $273 million to 800 counties in 41 states to pay for roads and schools. More than 75 percent of the payments went to five states: Washington, Oregon, California, Idaho, and Montana.

1999 LEGISLATIVE ACTION

The House passed HR 2389 (H-Rept 106-392, Pt. I) by a vote of 274–153 on Nov. 3. But the administration sharply objected to an amendment that would require the Treasury Department to provide money to counties that were suffering from reduced forest revenues.

The measure, as approved by voice vote by the House Agriculture Committee on Sept. 23, would establish a five-year interim payment program aimed at lending stability to the payment compact. Counties would receive a payment equal to the average of the three highest timber payments they received between fiscal year 1985 and the date of the bill's enactment. Overall, the bill would roughly double the annual payments to counties from $200 million to $400 million.

The bill also established a Forest Counties Payment Committee that would be charged with developing a permanent solution to the revenue sharing.

By voice vote, the panel adopted an amendment to address administration concerns. It included language intended to safeguard against reckless logging by requiring the use of sustainable forest management techniques on federal lands.

The Congressional Budget Office estimated that the bill would increase direct federal spending in rural counties by $173 million in fiscal 2000.

An alternative plan, backed by Peter DeFazio, D-Ore., would have decoupled county and school funding from logging proceeds. But many lawmakers regarded the funding issue as primarily a rural concern, and DeFazio said he could round up only about twenty cosponsors.

The measure sparked controversy on the House floor after Robert W. Goodlatte, R-Va., added a substitute amendment that would require the Treasury Department to make up the difference if forest revenues were not sufficient to compensate county payments.

Goodlatte's language—added at the behest of Idaho Republican Sen. Larry Craig—would require that state and local governments receiving more than $100,000 under the bill use 20 percent of the safety net payments for "locally initiated projects," which could include logging. The other 80 percent would go toward the currently authorized uses, schools and road projects.

Opponents, who sought to steer 100 percent of the payments to their original use, worried that the set-aside could put public lands under the control of local officials. They also warned that it would keep counties in the untenable position of promoting tree-cutting to finance schools.

"Why do we have this silly policy of addicting schools to forest timber harvests?" asked Sam Farr, D-Calif. But lawmakers, 186–241, rejected an amendment by Mark Udall, D-Colo., that would have made the 20-percent set-aside optional.

In a statement, the administration warned that it would "strongly oppose" the bill because it "would continue to link timber sales to an annual federal payment to states."

2000 LEGISLATIVE ACTION

The Senate on Sept. 13 cleared a bill (S 1608) by voice vote that provided counties with general treasury funds based in part on past timber sales. The bill reflected a bipartisan compromise that did not directly link the payments to logging on federal lands.

In early 2000 Craig and Ron Wyden, D-Ore., cosponsored S 1608, and they agreed to a different funding formula than the House plan. Under their plan, counties would continue to receive money from timber receipts. However, the revenues would not be dependent on continued high levels of logging. Instead, the federal government would make up any shortfall if the timber revenues did not equal the average of the highest three timber payments over the last fourteen years.

The formula would more than double the annual payments to rural counties. The biggest beneficiaries would be Oregon counties, which would collect an extra $71.5 million yearly, and California, which would pick up an additional $35 million.

Between 80 percent and 85 percent of the funding to counties would be reserved for traditional county schools and services supported by federal revenues. The remaining revenues would be set aside for specific projects on federal lands agreed to by local counties and federal land agencies such as the BLM and the Forest Service.

The projects could include such activities as thinning trees, maintaining roads, and restoring wildlife habitat. Some environmentalists raised concerns about the provision, contending that the money could be used for environmentally harmful projects that were supported by local interests.

The Senate Energy and Natural Resources Committee passed S 1608 (S Rept 106-275) by voice vote on April 25. The Senate passed the bill by voice vote on Sept. 13 and met the House in an informal conference. The resulting bill, HR 2389, substantially reflected the Senate measure. The Senate passed the measure on Oct. 6 by voice vote, and the House cleared it by voice vote on Oct. 10. The president signed it Oct. 30, 2000.

MAJOR PROVISIONS

As signed into law, the major provisions of HR 2389:

• **Federal payments to states and counties.** Eligible states and counties, defined as areas that received timber-related and other revenue-sharing payments from the Forest Service and the BLM, would receive federal payments from fiscal 2001 to 2006. The secretary of the Treasury was directed to calculate those payments by averaging the safety net payments and the three highest annual payments during the fiscal 1986 through fiscal 1999 eligibility period. The law provided for annual adjustments.

• **County projects.** The bill authorized county projects for: search, rescue, and emergency services, including fire fighting; community service work camps; conservation and recreation easement purchases; forest related educational opportunities; fire prevention and county planning; and community forestry.

Low-Flow Toilets

A much-discussed initiative to repeal the federal law requiring low-flow toilets failed in the 106th Congress. The bill (HR 623) sought to reverse a provision in the 1992 Energy Policy and Conservation Act (PL 102-486) that introduced the 1.6-gallon-per-flush toilet into homes. The "low-flow" toilets replaced the familiar 3.5-gallon toilets in new construction and remodeling.

Supporters said smaller toilets lacked the proper flushing power and that the 1992 act was an example of the government interfering in matters that should be left to the states to regulate. But opponents said the 1992 law encouraged water conservation and relieved overloaded sewage treatment systems.

The seemingly innocuous issue stirred considerable debate on talk radio shows and other forums. Many residents, frustrated over the need to flush toilets twice, assailed the government's tendency to overregulate. Rep. Joe Knollenberg, R-Mich., brought up the issue with such regularity that he became dubbed the "prince of porcelain."

Despite Knollenberg's efforts, the House Commerce subcommittee on Water and Power rejected the bill, 12–13, on April 12, 2000.

National Discovery Trails

Legislation to designate a new coast-to-coast American Discovery Trail system won approval in a House subcommittee in 1999, but it stalled after private property advocates raised concerns about it.

The bill (HR 2339) would create a new category of trails, known as National Discovery Trails, to link 6,000 miles of already existing pathways into one network. The first of those trails, the American Discovery Trail, would run from Cape Henlopen State Park in Delaware to Point Reyes National Seashore near San Francisco.

The western portion of the trail would run through Berkeley and Sacramento, continuing into Lake Tahoe in the Sierra Nevada Mountains and Nevada's Pony Express Historic Trail and Great Basin National Park. The southern route would follow the tracks of early pioneers through the Midwest until it met the northern route in Cincinnati.

The trail was conceived in 1989 by editors of Backpacker magazine. Congress in 1992 passed legislation directing the National Park Service to study the route to determine whether it qualified for designation as part of the national trails system. The Park Service in 1995 concluded that the trail did not qualify, but it recommended creating a new category of long-distance trails.

Private property rights advocates raised concerns about the plan. When the House Resources subcommittee on National Parks and Public Lands took up HR 2339 on Aug. 5, Richard W. Pombo, R-Calif., attempted to offer an amendment that would have required local and state officials to keep hikers from trespassing on private land. But it was ruled out of order.

The subcommittee approved the measure, 7–5, but Congress took no further action on the bill.

U.N. Lands Designation

The House in 1999 passed a bill to give Congress veto power over designating U.S. lands for the United Nations (U.N.) international conservation programs, but the Senate took no action on the measure. *(1997 action, p. 367)*

The U.N. Educational, Scientific and Cultural Organization designated World Heritage sites to draw attention to the world's most valued natural and cultural places. The program, created under a 1972 treaty, provided funding to nations that requested help with protecting their sites; it also coordinated scientific research. About twenty sites had been designated in the United States, including Yellowstone National Park and the Statue of Liberty.

The bill (HR 883) would require congressional approval before any area within the United States was included in an international land reserve. In contrast, such land designations were left to the executive branch and the United Nations.

The measure would stop U.S. officials from designating sites as biosphere reserves under the Man and Biosphere program of the Biosphere reserves that already existed would be dissolved unless authorized by Congress by Dec. 31, 2000.

The bill also would set strict guidelines for the secretary of interior in nominating federal lands for inclusion in the World Heritage List, which were comprised of areas with international natural, cultural or historical significance. It would make inclusion contingent on congressional authorization.

Bill supporters said they were concerned that the U.N. program could enable international interests to override domestic land-use decisions. Since the international land designations often included a U.S. pledge to monitor adjacent areas, which could be privately held, GOP supporters of the bill said Congress should have a role in the process. "We have a constitutional duty to protect our sovereignty in every way we can," said Rep. Helen Chenoweth, R-Idaho.

But Democratic opponents countered that the legislation would undermine U.S. participation in important conservation programs.

The House Resources Committee, 26–14, approved the measure (H Rept 106-142) on May 5. The House passed it by voice vote on May 20 after adopting, 262–158, a Democratic amendment that would subject foreign acquisitions of U.S. land for commercial purposes to the same congressional approval requirements as the bill imposed on U.N. land conservation nominations.

Otay Mountain Wilderness

Congress in 1999 cleared a bill (HR 15—PL 106-145) to designate a portion of southern California's Otay Mountain region as a national wilderness area. Under the measure, approximately 18,500 acres in the region would receive the protected status, which effectively curtails road construction and commercial activities within the designated area. The region was home to a number of rare plant species.

Because the area abutted the Mexican border, the measure would allow some drug interdiction, border patrol, and wildfire management activities to continue in the region.

Rep. Brian P. Bilbray, R-Calif., the bill sponsor, said the rugged area would be better protected by law enforcement activities along the border because there would be fewer illegal trails and campfires.

The House Resources Committee on March 3 gave voice vote approval to the bill (H Rept 106-65), and the House passed it by voice vote on April 12. The Senate Energy and Natural Resources Committee approved it (S Rept 106-116) by voice vote on June 30. The Senate cleared it on Nov. 19.

Las Vegas Airport

Despite environmental concerns, Congress cleared legislation in 2000 to allow the sale of federal land for a new Las Vegas airport.

The bill (HR 1695—PL 106-362), by Jim Gibbons, R-Nev., would authorize the sale of federal land to Clark County, Nev., for a second airport to serve the fast-growing Las Vegas area. The measure would allow the county to buy 6,000 acres in the Ivanpah Valley, about thirty miles south of Las Vegas and near the California border. Bill supporters said Las Vegas's existing airport, the ninth busiest in the nation, could no longer handle the volume of travelers resulting from a tourism boom.

Many Democrats opposed the original measure because they said construction and flights near the Mojave National Preservation would disrupt the desert ecosystem and encourage suburban sprawl.

The House Resources Committee approved the bill (H Rept 106-471) by voice vote on Oct. 20, 1999, after adopting an amendment to guarantee an environmental study under the National Environmental Policy Act once the land was transferred to the county. But some Democrats pressed for a more rigorous standard.

To mollify environmental critics, the House adopted a floor amendment on March 9 to provide for an environmental impact statement after the land had been sold to the county, and allowed the Interior Department to take a leading role in the study. Under the amendment, adopted 417–3, the Interior Department, working with the Federal Aviation Administration, also would develop an airport management plan that would minimize the airport's impact on the desert habitat.

The language paved the way for the once-controversial bill to pass by 420–1. The Senate passed an amended version by unanimous consent on Oct. 5, and the House cleared it on Oct. 17. President Clinton signed the bill on Oct. 27.

Sequoia National Park

Congress in 2000 cleared legislation (HR 4020—PL 106-574) to add 1,540 acres to Sequoia National Park in California. Under the bill, the park boundaries would be expanded to include the 1,540-acre Dillonwood Grove, which bordered the southern boundary of the park.

The grove was the largest privately owned stand of giant sequoias in the nation. The measure was intended to adjust the park's boundaries to accommodate the Save-the-Redwoods League plan to purchase Dillonwood Grove for $10 million.

The League was seeking $5 million in federal funding and $5 million through private donations.

The House passed the bill by voice vote on Oct. 31, and the Senate cleared it by unanimous consent on Dec. 15. Clinton signed it Oct. 27, 2000.

Cat Island Refuge

Congress in 2000 cleared legislation (HR 3292—PL 106-369) to establish a 36,500-acre wildlife refuge on Louisiana's Cat Island. The area was considered a critical habitat for songbirds, wild turkeys, mink, and bobcats, and was also home to the nation's largest cypress tree.

Bill sponsor Richard H. Baker, R-La., said adding the island to the National Wildlife Refuge System would conserve wetlands, protect endangered species, and promote hunting and other recreation activities.

The area would be managed by the Interior Department, which would be required to acquire the island and adjacent water areas. The department either could accept the island as a donation or authorize its purchase.

HR 3292 authorized the interior secretary to spend however much was needed to purchase the island. It also authorized the expenditure of whatever sums were needed to develop, operate, and maintain the refuge.

The House Resources Committee approved the bill (H Rept 106-659) by voice vote on May 24, and the House passed it by voice vote on June 19. The Senate passed an amended version by unanimous consent on Oct. 5, and the House cleared it by voice vote on Oct. 12. President Clinton signed it Oct. 19, 2000.

Colorado River

Congress in 2000 cleared legislation to increase the authorization for desalinating the Colorado River.

The legislation (S 1211—PL 106-459) would authorize $175 million to extend the Colorado River Basin Salinity Control Act. The salinity control program identified the source of salt along the Colorado River and worked with state conservation programs to reduce the salt level.

The river provided significant amounts of drinking and irrigation water to the Southwest.

The Senate Energy and Natural Resources Committee approved the bill (S Rept 106-175) on Sept. 22, 1999. The Senate passed it by voice vote on Nov. 19. The House Resources Committee gave voice vote approval to the bill (H Rept 106-814) on May 24, 2000, and the House cleared it by voice vote on Oct. 23. The president signed the bill on Nov. 7.

San Rafael Swell

House and Senate committees approved measures to create a 2.8 million-acre "western legacy district" and national conservation area in Utah, but the proposal foundered because of differences between loggers, ranchers, local government officials, and environmental groups.

The San Rafael Swell featured rugged sandstone cliffs and canyons, and it attracted numerous outdoors enthusiasts. It included areas of largely untouched land that conservationists wanted to protect as wilderness. In addition, the land was once a hideout for Butch Cassidy and the Sundance Kid.

Residents of Emery County, where the swell was located, began working with federal land managers in 1995 to develop a management plan for the area. They proposed a 2.8 million-acre district that would grant varying levels of protection for the land. Environmentalists, however, worried that the plan tilted too far toward local ranchers and off-road vehicle enthusiasts.

The House Resources Committee on May 16 gave voice vote approval to a bill (HR 3605—H Rept 106-647) that was based on the Emery County plan. But in a sign of divisions over the measure, members rejected, 10–21, an amendment by Mark Udall, D-Colo., that would have designated slightly more than one million acres as wilderness study land.

As drafted by sponsor Christopher B. Cannon, R-Utah, the bill would include six wilderness study areas totaling 269,736 acres.

Udall said about one million acres should be designated wilderness area, which would prevent road building and the use of off-road vehicles on the land.

By designating the land as wilderness study areas, Congress would be able to designate it as wilderness area in the future, Udall said. Without the designation, he said the land would be used in a manner which would prevent it from qualifying as wilderness area in the future.

The Senate Energy and Natural Resources Committee approved a similar measure (S 2048—S Rept 106-401) on Sept. 7.

Lake Tahoe

Congress in 2000 cleared a bill to restore California's Lake Tahoe basin.

The bill (HR 3388—PL 106-506) directed the Agriculture Department to develop a list of environmental restoration projects for the area, and it authorized funding for their implementation.

Lawmakers were jolted into action by U.S. Forest Service studies showing that the lake's water clarity had declined from a visibility of 105 feet in 1967 to seventy feet in 1999, and roughly 40 percent of the trees in the basin were either dead or dying. The decline in water quality was attributed to erosion, agricultural runoff, and decreased wetlands.

Forest Service officials warned that the large number of dead trees could serve as fuel for a "catastrophic" fire. The federal government managed 77 percent of the land in the Lake Tahoe basin.

The bill authorized $20 million annually for ten years for the restoration projects. It also authorized $10 million annually in payments to local governments that participated in the programs.

The House Resources Committee marked up the bill (H Rept 106-833, Pt. I) on July 26. The House passed it by voice vote on Oct. 23, and the Senate passed it by unanimous consent on Oct. 27. The president signed the bill Oct. 24, 2000.

California Monument

Congress in 2000 cleared a bill (HR 3676—PL 106-351) to establish a 280,000-acre Santa Rosa and San Jacinto Mountains National Monument in southern California. The federal government already owned 152,000 acres of the land that was designated for the monument. HR 3766, sponsored by Mary Bono, R-Calif., directed the government to acquire the remaining 128,000 acres through purchases and swaps from willing sellers. Much of the land was owned by individuals and Native American tribes.

The national monument would be managed jointly by the interior and agriculture secretaries, but the bill authorized creation of a local advisory committee. The management plan would generally have to permit most of the currently authorized land uses, including recreational activities, hunting, trapping, fishing, and grazing.

The monument designation could not have any impact on nonfederal property rights. Also, the measure would prevent the federal government from creating buffer zones between the monument and adjacent private lands.

The House Resources Committee on June 20 gave voice vote approval to the bill (H Rept 106-750). The House passed it by voice vote on July 25, and the Senate cleared it by unanimous consent on Oct. 5. President Clinton signed it Sept. 26, 2000.

Oregon Land Exchanges

Despite a government audit questioning the benefit of land exchanges, Congress in 2000 cleared a bill (S 1629—PL 106-257) to authorize two land exchanges in Oregon.

Under the measure, the government would trade about 54,000 acres of federal land for nearly 50,000 acres held by private landowners, thereby consolidating patchwork parcels of federal and private land. The bill directed the Agriculture Department and Bureau of Land Management to exchange three parcels of land that covered 44,150 acres for three privately owned parcels that covered 50,484 acres.

Taking into consideration the difference in the total acreage, the bill required appraisals to ensure that the value of the land is equal.

All of the land was located in either the Central Oregon Resource Area or the Baker Resource Area. The land acquired by the federal government would be added to the Malheur, Wallowa-Whitman, and Umatilla national forests.

Sponsors of the two bills said the monument and land transfer would help preserve wildlife and result in recreational, scientific, and educational benefits.

But a July 13 report by the General Accounting Office concluded the federal government often did not benefit when it swapped federally owned land for privately held properties. The report revealed that the government failed to ensure the exchanged land was appropriately valued, or that land exchanges served the public interest.

The Senate Energy and Natural Resources Committee gave voice vote approval to the bill (S Rept 106-248) on Feb. 10, and the Senate passed it by unanimous consent on April 13. The House Resources Committee gave voice vote approval to the bill (H Rept 106-747) on May 24, and the House cleared it by voice vote on July 25. Clinton signed it Aug. 8, 2000.

Oregon Wilderness

Congress in 2000 cleared legislation (HR 4828—PL 106-399) designating six wilderness areas in the Steens Mountain area of Oregon.

The region, known for its mountain lakes and unique wildflowers, is home to golden eagles, antelope, and the world's only population of a small fish called a chub.

Under the measure, an advisory committee would manage the 500,000-acre Steens Mountain Cooperative Management and Protection Area. Within that area, 174,000 acres would be wilderness areas, and 100,000 acres of that would be nongrazing areas.

It also designated within the area three wild and scenic rivers and the first-ever redband trout reserve to improve stream health and fish habitat. It also provided for the acquisition of private land through exchange or purchase for inclusion in the wilderness areas and the protection area.

The House Resources Committee approved the bill (H Rept 106-929) by a vote of 24–5. The House passed it by voice vote on Oct 4, and the Senate cleared it by unanimous consent on Oct. 12. President Clinton signed it Oct 30, 2000.

Conservation Areas

Almost 200,000 acres of public land in Colorado and Utah were set aside for conservation under a bill that Congress cleared in 2000.

The bill (HR 4275—PL 106-353) preserved 120,000 acres in the two states to establish the Colorado Canyons National Conservation Area. Another 75,000 acres from the states would be used to create the Black Ridge Canyons Wilderness.

Within three years of enactment, the Interior Department would have to create a management plan to ensure the long-term protection of the areas.

Under the bill, the federal government could not authorize the development of new water projects within the designated areas. A ten-member council would also be created to advise on budgeting and management.

The House Resources Committee approved the plan by unanimous consent on July 19, and the House passed it by voice vote on July 25. The Senate Energy and Natural Resources Committee gave voice vote approval to the bill (S Rept 106-460) on Sept. 20. The Senate cleared it by unanimous consent on Oct. 5. Clinton signed it Oct. 24, 2000.

Electricity Deregulation

Supporters of legislation to deregulate the nation's electric utility industry achieved a significant milestone in 1999, when the House Commerce Energy and Power Subcommittee approved legislation designed to spur competition and consumer choice. But the bill (HR 2944) failed to bridge any of the differences that had stalled progress on past electricity deregulation measures, and Congress took no further action in the 106th.

BACKGROUND

The seed of the debate over deregulation was planted in 1992, with the enactment of a sweeping energy law (PL 102-486) in the closing days of the 102nd Congress. It set the stage for the current debate over nationalizing electricity restructuring when it allowed utilities and independent producers to compete in the wholesale power market by ensuring them access to one another's utility lines.

Since then, about twenty-four states and the District of Columbia moved to create retail competition for electricity, putting pressure on Congress and the administration to find a workable bill.

All players in the debate agreed on one threshold point. In order for robust, comprehensive, nationwide competition in the electric power market to get under way, Congress would have to make one sweeping deregulatory move: repeal the 1935 Public Utility Holding Company Act (PUHCA). The statute, enacted to prevent the nation's power supply from being held in only a few corporate hands, restricted the growth and business activities of the biggest, multistate corporate utilities, barring them from doing business outside their areas. While repeal would take away the monopolies the big utilities have in their geographic area, it would allow them to expand their reach, with the ensuing competition presumably lowering monthly utility bills for consumers.

Beyond that, the various factions were at odds over a broad range of issues. One key question was who should be responsible for oversight of the flow of electricity in a nationally restructured market: state legislators and utility commissioners, or the Federal Energy Regulatory Commission (FERC).

In Congress, supporters of a strong federal hand included Thomas J. Bliley Jr., R-Va., and key Democrats in the debate,

such as House Commerce's Edward J. Markey of Massachusetts and Jeff Bingaman of New Mexico, the ranking minority member on the Senate Energy panel. The associations representing investor-owned and municipal utilities, and the coalition of big-volume electrical consumers, all endorsed putting FERC in charge, believing they would benefit from the application of a uniform set of rules nationwide.

On the other side Joe L. Barton, R-Texas, chairman of the House Commerce Energy and Power Subcommittee, and Senate Energy Committee Chairman Frank H. Murkowski, R-Alaska, were the leading congressional proponents of giving the states most decision-making power. State governments were better equipped to deal with local conditions, they said, and restructuring should allow states to take innovative approaches rather than deal with a "one size fits all" framework set in Washington.

The rural cooperatives group was the lone utility trade association in this camp, although it was joined by the two shadow coalitions. The investor-owned companies participating in those coalitions concluded that they would get their best treatment from state legislators and public utility commissioners.

Associated issues were whether Congress should create "regional transmission organizations," or RTOs, to operate and maintain the infrastructure handling electricity transmission; whether utility participation should be compulsory or voluntary; and whether RTO oversight should be handled by the states or the federal government.

THE ADMINISTRATION'S PLAN

In an effort to get the debate moving on Capitol Hill, the Clinton administration in 1999 unveiled its plan for bringing competition to the nation's $215 billion electric utility market.

Unlike a 1998 administration initiative, the latest edition was warmly received on Capitol Hill. "This is an important step forward in moving toward a bipartisan electricity restructuring bill," said Rep. Steve Largent, R-Okla., who joined Energy Secretary Bill Richardson, Environmental Protection Agency Administrator Carol M. Browner and others at the April 15 news conference to present the proposal.

The administration's plan called for the advent of open competition among electricity suppliers nationwide by 2003. The proposal also contained a circuit breaker, allowing states to "opt out" if there was evidence competition would not yield savings for consumers.

In theory, retail restructuring would allow competition that would give homeowners choices among power sellers, driving down prices and making service more reliable. Richardson said the average family of four would save $232 a year in lower electric bills if the administration's plan were adopted.

The administration's plan would also:

• Give FERC new oversight powers to ensure that utilities promote competition.

• Establish a $3 billion "Public Benefits Fund" to support continued funding for low-income energy assistance, energy conservation, and other programs that promote development of clean and efficient technologies.

• Establish a grant program to ensure that people in remote and rural areas benefit from competition.

Despite the encouraging start, deregulation legislation clearly faced major hurdles. In addition to the technical and economic complexities of dismantling monopolies, there were regional and political differences that often were hard to reconcile.

For example, the administration's requirement that 7.5 percent of all electricity sold by 2010 come from "nonhydroelectric renewable resources" such as wind or solar energy, drew fire from such critics as Sen. Frank H. Murkowski, R-Alaska, who chaired the Energy and Natural Resources Committee.

While he supported some proposals, Murkowski said the new plan did not go far enough to allow real competition and expressed concern that "many of the provisions still involve more government manipulation and interference with the marketplace."

More criticism came from such disparate groups as the Sierra Club and the Edison Electric Institute, which represented big investor-owned utilities. The Sierra Club expressed "deep disappointment" with the plan because it did not contain "concrete goals for reducing global warming and air pollutants."

Thomas R. Kuhn, president of the Washington-based Edison Electric Institute, said there were some elements his group could support, but warned that: "In many respects, this bill amounts to reregulation and not deregulation."

1999 LEGISLATIVE ACTION

After a marathon markup, the Commerce Energy and Power Subcommittee on Oct. 27 approved a bill (HR 2944) by a vote of 17–11. But the measure failed to advance further because it was opposed by most Democrats on the panel, as well as by the administration and a web of consumer, environmental, and industry interests.

Subcommittee chairman Joe L. Barton, R-Texas, who sponsored the measure, had hoped to schedule the markup before the August recess. But he faced daunting challenges in bridging disparate interests and meeting such administration priorities as the 7.5 percent requirement for renewable energy.

Other sticking points revolved around such questions as how to ensure access to the electric transmission network for any company wanting to compete in a market. A single state could deny access if it was located between a state that generated electricity and a state that wanted to consume it.

In addition, there was the challenge of finding the right balance between a bill that was too limited to achieve real competition in the $215 billion electricity market, and one that was too loaded down with mandates and would not pass.

Writing a bill that only dismantled the Depression-era PUHCA, which restricted sixteen big utility companies from diversifying into new businesses, would be too modest a step for some lawmakers, even though it was a widely voiced goal of utilities.

Despite the hurdles, Barton elected to muscle HR 2944 through his subcommittee in October. "We created a cooperative, bipartisan atmosphere, and crafted the first major electricity restructuring bill to ever pass a . . . subcommittee. I am very proud of our work," Barton said.

But he faced withering criticism from panel Democrats such as Edward J. Markey of Massachusetts, who derided the plan as a "monopoly bill."

The lack of consensus was reflected in the fifty-one amendments that were filed before the markup. Many of those amendments were withdrawn, including one that would make sweeping changes in how utilities are regulated and another that would impose tougher environmental standards. The sponsors of those amendments, Markey and Frank Pallone Jr., D-N.J., said they would offer them when the full committee considered the bill, which was expected to occur in 2000.

Even Commerce Committee Chairman Bliley, who might have been expected to support his GOP colleague, expressed reservations, in part because the bill would give broad latitude to states to set the rules for a deregulated market. "I don't know if this bill strikes the right balance for consumers," Bliley said. "I believe we still have a long way to go."

Barton's bill was intended to promote competition by opening access to the transmission system, removing such barriers as the Public Utility Holding Company Act of 1935, which restricted big utilities from entering new markets. It also attempted to improve the reliability of the transmission system.

Those changes, however, would be largely orchestrated by the states. Barton's bill provided no significant new authority to FERC to oversee a more competitive marketplace. Nor did the bill include a "date certain" by which time states must move to open competition.

HR 2944 also would not require utilities to generate power from renewable sources, unlike the administration's approach.

The subcommittee adopted an amendment by Richard M. Burr, R-N.C., requiring FERC review of utility company mergers within 180 days. If FERC failed to act, the mergers would be automatically approved.

The subcommittee also adopted an amendment by Robert L. Ehrlich Jr., R-Md., giving precedence to state laws dealing with consumer protection, mergers and interconnecting power systems if the state laws are enacted within three years of HR 2944's enactment.

Those amendments did little, however, to address the larger disputes. Those included:

• How much authority FERC should have in overseeing a new electricity industry that spans state borders and is based on competition rather than monopolies.

• How to fold enormous federal government electric utilities, such as the Tennessee Valley Authority (TVA) and the Bonneville Power Administration, into the new market without trampling competing utilities that have not benefited from a federal subsidy. (Barton's bill would limit TVA's reach and its ability to compete outside its service area.)

• How to keep other large, well-financed utilities from snuffing out competitors.

• How to ensure the reliability of the transmission system in an era of competition.

The Senate did not take any formal action on the issue. Murkowski sponsored a deregulatory bill (S 1047) that broke with the administration on such issues as setting a renewable energy standard and creating a $3 billion "public benefits fund" to support continued funding for low-income energy assistance and energy conservation.

2000 LEGISLATIVE ACTION

Neither the House Commerce Committee nor the Senate Energy and Natural Resources Committee were able to cobble together a majority to mark up a deregulatory bill. However, the Senate on June 30 passed a far narrower measure by voice vote that would bolster the reliability of the national electric grid. The House did not take up the measure.

With some states facing the possibility of power shortages and summer blackouts, lawmakers found themselves under pressure early in the year to clear a deregulatory measure. In April a group called the Electricity Restructuring Stakeholders—representing consumers, electric generating companies, senior citizens, and others—released a set of goals for restructing legislation, including repeal of PUHCA and changes to a 1978 law (PL 95-617) that required state utility commissions and utilities to reform their electric rates and take other measures to even out daily electric consumption.

Energy Secretary Richardson acknowledged the stakeholder progress in an April 17 speech to the National Energy Marketers Association, and he urged Congress to pass an electric restructuring bill. "Our interstate electricity markets are in need of repair," he said, adding that transmission access and generation capacity were decreasing as demand for electricity grew. "If Congress fails to act—and act soon—on restructuring legislation, it will strangle the development of competitive electricity markets."

In the House, Bliley named a six-member task force on the issue and pressed to mark up HR 2944 as early as Memorial Day. Murkowski likewise vowed to try to move a bill through the Senate Energy committee.

Moving first, Murkowski's panel held two markups in May to try to hammer out a consensus on key components of a comprehensive bill by the chairman (S 2098). But the panel threw in the towel in June, giving its blessing instead to a fallback election-year measure designed only to bolster the reliability of the national electric grid.

Murkowski's bill would give the Nuclear Regulatory Commission the authority to determine if a utility had ade-

quate funds for nuclear decommissioning and to direct a utility to increase collections if necessary. Murkowski also suggested letting a utility apply to FERC for a "wires charge" on consumers to pay decommissioning costs.

Bingaman objected, saying such a charge ultimately would spread decommissioning costs to ratepayers in areas not served by the utility that needed the money for decommissioning. Those customers, Bingaman said, should not be forced to pay for cleaning up nuclear plants "that benefit them not one iota." Bingaman said he would offer an amendment striking that portion of the bill.

Murkowski said Bingaman's amendment would make states responsible for ensuring that utilities raised money for decommissioning, a task he said he doubted states would follow through on. "We need to enforce and have the assurance that we're going to have enough money for decommissioning," Murkowski said.

Murkowski and Bingaman spent several weeks in May and June trying to cut a deal to spur federal incentives to deregulate electricity—an idea that had foundered for four years amid intense lobbying from several quarters. But they could not agree on how much jurisdiction to give the FERC, how to prevent significant differences between wholesale and retail service, or whether to include federal requirements designed to increase the generation of electricity from renewable sources.

The narrower measure by Slade Gorton, R-Wash., that the committee ultimately adopted (S 2071—S Rept 106-324) would not repeal PUHCA. Instead, it would replace the North American Electric Reliability Council, a group in which utility participation was voluntary, with an Electric Reliability Organization, charged with setting reliability standards for utilities.

Any utility or power marketer that used the national network of interconnected power lines and generators to move electricity would be required to participate in the organization, which would fall under FERC jurisdiction. The organization would be allowed to set rules governing the emergency supply of power that was kept on the grid—which utilities may tap to cover peak needs—and could penalize those that did not donate their fair share or took from the reserve inappropriately.

The Senate passed the measure on June 30, but the House took no action on it.

Groups representing rural electric cooperatives, municipal utilities, and independent power producers all hailed the scaled-back bill. But the Electric Power Supply Association, which represented independent producers, said only comprehensive restructuring would create "an efficient, seamless and truly competitive nationwide marketplace for electricity."

The administration also expressed disappointment that the Senate was settling for a narrower bill.

In the House, Bliley postponed a Commerce Committee markup of HR 2944 in early July because he could not put together a consensus on deregulation. Bliley wanted to amend the bill to give much of the oversight of electric transmission in a deregulated era to FERC, stripping out Barton's language that gave principal oversight to the states.

Barton warned that members of his subcommittee would support him on the electric transmission issue, potentially costing Bliley as many as 29 votes on the 52-member committee. With the two men also differing on whether municipal utilities should continue to receive tax breaks for generation facilities they built, Bliley never held a markup, signaling the demise of the issue in the 106th Congress.

Although negotiations among senior lawmakers in both chambers failed to hatch a sweeping compromise, the areas of disagreement at least appeared to be narrowed, giving rise to some claims of optimism that 2001 would be the issue's year, no matter which party controlled the White House and the Capitol.

"There's a time when the process matures," said Rep. W. J. "Billy" Tauzin, R-La., during the summer of 2000. "That moment's close, and if this moment doesn't happen this year, it will happen early next year."

Nuclear Waste Storage

While awaiting the go-ahead for permanent storage of nuclear waste at Yucca Mountain in Nevada, Congress cleared legislation (S 1287) to facilitate short-term storage by the utilities that generate it. But President Clinton vetoed the bill and a Senate attempt to override the veto failed, leaving the issue of nuclear waste storage unresolved.

BACKGROUND

The issue of how to store at least 40,000 metric tons of nuclear waste that was piled up around the country affected almost every state. By 2015 the eighty-five U.S. reactors were expected to run out of storage space.

A 1982 law required the Energy Department to set up a permanent site by 1998 to house the nuclear waste, which would remain radioactive for 10,000 years.

In 1987 Congress designated Yucca Mountain as the likely permanent burial site for high-level nuclear waste from nuclear power plants in thirty-four states. But the project, which had been slowed by questions about safety and feasibility, was not expected to begin receiving waste before 2010. Since the Energy Department was unable to meet the law's 1998 deadline, it faced millions of dollars in liability as nuclear utilities scrambled for storage alternatives.

The issue had sparked fierce debates in Congress for years. Republicans tried repeatedly since 1995 to win enactment of legislation that would allow temporary storage above ground near Yucca Mountain, but they were thwarted by regional and partisan differences. *(1997–1998 action, p. 361)*

1999 LEGISLATIVE ACTION

The House Commerce Committee, 39–6, approved HR 45 (H Rept 106-155) on April 21. The Senate Energy and Natural Resources Committee, 14–6, approved an alternative measure, S 1287 (S Rept 106-98), on June 16. The Senate bill relied on a proposal by Energy Secretary Bill Richardson that would keep the waste where it was generated and hand the legal title and responsibility for managing it to the government. But it drew a White House veto threat because it would give authority for setting environmental standards at Yucca Mountain to the Nuclear Regulatory Commission, rather than the Environmental Protection Agency (EPA).

Fireworks over the issue began almost immediately in 1999. The administration, which favored the management of stockpiled nuclear waste at commercial plants, threatened to veto plans to build an interim repository. Undaunted, Republicans pressed on.

In March Senate Energy and Natural Resources Committee Chairman Frank H. Murkowski, R-Alaska, introduced a bill (S 608) to require the Energy Department to build an interim repository for the high-level nuclear waste by June 30, 2003, and a permanent waste site by Jan. 17, 2010. Dismissing the administration's position, he asked at a news conference: "Do we really want nuclear waste piling up at seventy-one sites around the nation rather than one?"

The House Commerce Energy and Power Subcommittee on April 14 unanimously approved a bill (HR 45) to establish a repository.

The measure would authorize the Energy Department to take responsibility for on-site storage of waste in return for an agreement by nuclear utilities to drop their multibillion-dollar lawsuits. It would also prevent utilities from initiating lawsuits against the department for failing to meet any new statutory deadlines.

"Congressional oversight, rather than utility litigation, will keep the department to its deadlines," said subcommittee chairman Joe L. Barton, R-Texas.

In an effort at compromise, Barton offered a substitute amendment, adopted by voice vote, that would move the $8 billion nuclear waste fund off-budget. This would free up additional funding for construction of both interim and permanent storage facilities at Yucca Mountain.

Barton's panel approved the measure 25–0, but the vote belied deep divisions over the bill. A number of Republicans voiced concern that the revised legislation would let the Energy Department off the hook too easily. Rep. Charlie Norwood, R-Ga., called the liability relief "political blackmail" and argued that utilities "would be held hostage for a facility they have already paid for."

The changes also failed to mollify the White House. Richardson sent a letter to Barton reiterating the administration's opposition to any legislation that created an interim storage site in Nevada before safety reviews were completed on the permanent site at Yucca Mountain.

The Commerce Committee approved the bill (H Rept 106-155, Pt. I) on April 21 by an overwhelming vote of 40–6. But House leaders refrained from further action on the measure while the Senate tried to find a compromise.

After months of negotiations, Murkowski in June acceded to the administration's position on where to store nuclear waste. Instead of shipping the waste to a temporary storage site in Nevada, the Energy panel chairman agreed to let the waste remain at nuclear reactors in thirty-four states.

The Energy and Natural Resources Committee on June 16 approved, 14–6, Murkowski's revised bill (S 1287—S Rept 106-98) authorizing the Department of Energy to take responsibility for the temporary on-site management of high-level nuclear waste. In return, the agency would negotiate agreements with utilities to drop lawsuits against the agency for missing the Jan. 31, 1998, statutory deadline to haul the waste from reactor sites.

However, the committee's ranking Democrat, Jeff Bingaman of New Mexico, objected to a provision giving the Nuclear Regulatory Commission, rather than the EPA, authority to set radiation standards at the permanent repository.

Under existing law, the EPA had the authority to promulgate radiation standards. Murkowski and other Republicans said they feared EPA's proposed standards would prove impossible to meet, effectively killing permanent storage at Yucca Mountain. Democrats responded that it would be improper to take the power from an agency that has wielded it for three decades.

Bingaman called the provision "a show stopper with this administration and with me." Richardson threatened a presidential veto if the EPA did not set radiation standards.

The panel rejected, 7–13, Bingaman's substitute amendment that would have created a cabinet-level commission to review the EPA standards.

A crowded end-of-session calendar and objections from Nevada senators prevented the Senate from debating nuclear waste storage legislation, but proponents said it would be among the first bills the Senate would consider in 2000. House members awaited the Senate's action before determining how to proceed.

2000 LEGISLATIVE ACTION

The Senate passed a heavily reworked version of S 1287 by a vote of 64–34 on Feb. 10. It would have allowed the EPA to establish radiation standards before June 1, 2001—but only after consulting with the National Academy of Sciences and the Nuclear Regulatory Commission.

The Senate passed the bill after months of intensive negotiations between Republicans and Democrats. In trying to find a compromise, Murkowski ended up alienating both the administration and key Democrats by deleting the provision, proposed by Richardson, that would have allowed the Energy Department to assume legal title and management responsibility for the waste generated by nuclear utilities.

Richardson suggested it as an alternative to temporarily storing waste above ground near Yucca Mountain—an approach that remained a central feature of the House bill.

Murkowski's final proposal instead called for giving the department authority to offer utilities a combination of money and storage casks for the spent fuel in the settlement negotiations over what to do with the waste.

By dropping Richardson's language, Murkowski sought to appease a handful of senators from northeastern states whose governors had come out against the so-called take title provision, saying it would remove Congress's incentive to find a permanent disposal site.

But Bingaman said Murkowski's move was "a major step backward" that could invite another veto. The New Mexico Democrat also complained that the storage deadlines and milestones included throughout the bill were unrealistic.

The Senate took action after intensive negotiations between Democrats and Republicans. In a significant concession, Murkowski agreed to allow the EPA to issue standards after consultations with other agencies.

But Bingaman pointed to other problems with the Senate committee-approved legislation. In particular, he cited language in the bill that would require the Energy Department to enter into contracts to store spent fuel for commercial utilities that run out of storage space. He also criticized the requirement that the EPA consult with other agencies before issuing radiation standards.

Murkowski and other supporters expressed dismay when the bill passed the Senate with three votes short of the 67 needed to override a promised presidential veto. Lawmakers conceded that the two chambers would have little chance to produce a conference report that would win Clinton's signature or become law over his veto.

"This bill is dead until we get a new administration," Murkowski told reporters after the vote.

The White House warned lawmakers that it objected to numerous provisions. "The legislation limits the ability of the Environmental Protection Agency to exercise its existing authority to fully protect public health and the environment," Clinton's chief of staff, John Podesta, wrote in a letter to House Minority Leader Richard A. Gephardt of Missouri. "S 1287 also contains unrealistic and unworkable milestones, insufficient funding mechanisms, unfunded new liabilities, and burdensome and unworkable transportation provisions that do not provide a commensurate improvement in safety."

The strong opposition and the promised presidential veto did not deter House action. Although many House Republicans preferred HR 45, GOP leaders decided to proceed with the Senate version in an attempt to avoid a filibuster threatened by Nevada's senators on any conference report to the legislation.

During the floor debate, several members criticized the bill's lack of regulations regarding the transportation of the waste to Nevada.

The bill puts "mobile Chernobyls" on the streets heading toward Nevada, said Edward J. Markey, D-Mass.

But supporters of the measure countered that the legislation was a needed solution to the nuclear waste storage problem faced by the nation. "It is time for us to settle this issue," said W. J. "Billy" Tauzin, R-La.

The House on March 22 cleared S 1287 by a 253–167 vote. Clinton vetoed the bill on April 25. Because supporters in both chambers were unable to secure a two-thirds majority for passage, it was clear that a veto would stand.

The Senate narrowly sustained the veto on May 2 by a **key vote of 64–35 (R 51–3; D 13–32).** Republicans gained a last-minute convert when Democrat John Edwards, N.C., voted to override. In a procedural move, Majority Leader Trent Lott, Miss., voted against the override, thereby giving him the authority to bring up the bill again in the unlikely event that senators changed their positions. *(2000 key votes, p. 915)*

Despite Edwards's defection, Democrats expressed few qualms before the vote. "We will always have thirty-four votes" to sustain the veto, Sen. Harry Reid insisted.

Strategic Petroleum Reserve

After failing several times to move a broader energy package in a year of rising fuel prices, Congress in 2000 sent President Clinton a bill (HR 2884—PL 106-469) to reauthorize the Strategic Petroleum Reserve and create a home heating oil reserve in the Northeast.

There was little controversy over the central element of the bill: reauthorizing for three years the Strategic Petroleum Reserve. The reserve, a network of oil reservoirs in salt caves along the Gulf Coast, was the nation's main insurance against oil supply and price disruptions. But the legislation was bogged down for months by a political dispute over whether Clinton should sell oil from the reserve and whether Congress should take other steps to address tight oil supplies.

The Senate passed a bill (S 1051—S Rept 106-103) by unanimous consent on Sept. 29, 1999, to reauthorize the reserve for four years. On the same day, the House Commerce Committee gave voice vote approval to HR 2884 (H Rept 106-359), which also reauthorized the reserve. By the time the House was ready to act on the issue, however, higher prices at the pump in an election year were touching off heated political exchanges over the nation's energy policy.

The authorization for the reserve expired March 31, 2000. Clinton, who claimed he still had the authority to swap small quantities of oil to deal with minor supply problems, blasted House Republicans for failing to take up reauthorization legislation. In a letter to House Speaker J. Dennis Hastert, R-Ill., the president warned that Congress "has failed to take one of the most critical steps necessary to maintain America's energy security."

Republicans accused Clinton of political posturing. They said he needed to take a firmer line with oil-exporting nations.

On April 12 the House, 416–8, passed an amended version of HR 2884, which would reauthorize the Energy Policy and Conservation Act through 2003 and reestablish the president's authority to tap the Strategic Petroleum Reserve. Northeastern Democratic members worked alongside Commerce Energy and Power Subcommittee Chairman Joe L. Barton, R-Texas, to tack on a key provision that would enable the creation of a home heating oil reserve in their home region.

As amended, the bill would reauthorize the refined product reserve and allow use of that reserve during a regional, as opposed to national, emergency.

With lawmakers continuing to move too slowly for the White House, Clinton issued an executive order on July 10 creating a two-million-barrel home heating oil stockpile in the Northeast. But he could not release the oil without authorizing legislation.

In September HR 2884 was blocked in the Senate by Barbara Boxer, D-Calif. She objected to a provision added by Energy and Natural Resources Committee Chairman Frank H. Murkowski, R-Alaska, that she warned could allow oil companies to avoid paying higher royalties for drilling on public lands. Murkowski relented and dropped his royalties provision.

But Murkowski added a requirement that the defense secretary must assess and report whether any future draw-down of oil from the petroleum reserve would harm national security. This stemmed in part from a controversial Clinton decision to swap some oil from the reserve. Republicans criticized the move and some even questioned its legality.

The Senate passed the bill with Murkowski's requirement by voice vote Oct. 19. The House cleared it Oct. 24. Clinton signed it Oct. 28, 2000.

Energy Supplies

In an effort to quell the rising price of gasoline and score election-year points with constituents complaining about price spikes, Republican lawmakers in 2000 crafted a far-ranging energy plan to increase supplies. But GOP lawmakers never coalesced behind such controversial plans as suspending the federal gasoline tax, and the plan died at the end of the 106th Congress.

After a month of negotiations, Senate Republicans unveiled a preliminary legislative package in March intended to spur domestic energy production through steps ranging from oil exploration in the Arctic National Wildlife Refuge to tax incentives for producers. Majority Leader Trent Lott of Mississippi praised the proposal (S 2557) developed by the Republican energy task force and panned the administration for not developing a coherent energy policy.

"We have a very serious problem facing our country in the future due to our dependence on foreign oil," Lott said. "I am not comfortable depending on foreign oil, OPEC oil, and oil from Iraq."

The package contained provisions to create a northeastern petroleum reserve that would be tapped when heating oil prices rise. It required a report on existing coal-fired plants and recommendations for a clean coal technology program. Also included were incentives for independent oil producers, and provisions to promote the use of natural gas, hydro-power, and solar energy.

The goal of the proposal was to decrease dependency on foreign oil from 55 percent to 50 percent by 2010.

But GOP divisions quickly emerged. Four out of ten members of the Republican-appointed energy task force opposed drilling in the Arctic refuge, but Frank H. Murkowski, R-Alaska, the task force chairman, nonetheless added the drilling language.

Democrats blasted the plan as dangerously weighted toward production and almost silent on consumption. "The demand for gas as a transportation fuel continues on a steep incline," said Sen. Jeff Bingaman, the ranking Democrat on the Energy and Natural Resources Committee. "If we're going to get a handle on this issue, we're going to have to deal with this at some stage."

Murkowski scratched out a temporary victory on April 6. On a 51–49 vote, the Senate agreed to leave in the budget an assumption that the Arctic refuge would be opened to drilling and provide $1.2 billion in revenue. But the deeply divided lawmakers did not return to the issue of the Arctic refuge in the 106th Congress.

Republicans also found themselves divided over the 18.4-cent-a-gallon gasoline tax. Even though Lott wanted to repeal 4.3 cents of the tax through the end of the year, he had to pull from the floor a gas tax repeal bill (S 2285) after failing to win a vote on April 11 to limit debate. The vote was 43–55—some 17 votes short of the 60 necessary.

With their major legislative initiatives blocked and gas prices peaking at more than $2 a gallon, congressional Republicans sought to focus attention on what they regarded as the Clinton administration's failed energy policy. Over the long term, the administration allowed America to become 55 percent dependent on foreign oil imports, which put U.S. consumers at the mercy of oil-exporting countries, Republicans charged. They noted that oil prices soared after the Arab-led cartel of oil-producing nations restricted its production over the past year.

In the short-term, the administration's reliance on Energy Secretary Bill Richardson's "energy diplomacy" also failed, Republicans argued. Production increased slightly in March after appeals to the Organization of Petroleum Exporting Countries (OPEC), but oil and gasoline prices shot up again—even higher than in the spring.

Republicans said the Clinton administration has fostered the greater dependence on imports by discouraging domestic oil production, because of environmental concerns or overregulation.

Democrats responded that Republicans had prevented the administration from using the single greatest energy conservation tool: an adjustment of the fuel economy standards that apply to automobile manufacturers. The standards had remained virtually unchanged since 1985. Since 1995, Congress had blocked the Transportation Department from even studying the issue.

Senators from both sides of the aisle asked how high gasoline prices had to go before the public demanded action on energy issues.

"The reality is we have not been able to develop the collective will to address the problem," Bingaman said.

Lott returned to the fray in September, making a series of motions to take up S 2557 on the Senate floor. But the bill, which had not been marked up, received a tepid reaction. Senators made a number of floor speeches about energy, but they never decided to proceed to the bill itself.

Democrats took advantage of the GOP divisions by going on the attack. "Our agenda for renewable energy and conservation and efficiency have been rejected by this Congress," said Vice President Al Gore, the Democratic presidential nominee.

Republicans responded that environmental concerns had trumped energy considerations. "The questions are never asked about what would be good for American energy policy," said Sen. Pete V. Domenici, R-N.M. "America's environmental laws are out of tune with America's energy needs."

Security at Energy Department

Security lapses at the Department of Energy became a monumental embarrassment for Energy Secretary Bill Richardson during the 106th Congress. As Richardson's star fell, Republicans and Democrats alike sharply criticized his department's security policies, and they created a new unit within Energy to bolster security as part of the fiscal 2000 defense appropriations bill (S 1059—PL 106-65).

More than a half-dozen congressional panels opened hearings into the security problems and the possibility that the administration allowed China to obtain sensitive technology. Although the theft of technology was believed to have occurred during the 1980s, it did not come to light until 1995, and the Energy Department did not take steps until early 1999 to remove a Los Alamos National Laboratory employee suspected of providing data to the Chinese. Republicans accused the administration of being too slow to act.

ADVISORY BOARD REPORT

Spurring lawmakers into action, the President's Foreign Intelligence Advisory Board, chaired by former Sen. Warren B. Rudman, R-N.H. (1980–1993), concluded in a June report that the Department of Energy (DOE) had "a cavalier attitude" about security and that "organizational disarray, managerial neglect and a culture of arrogance—both at DOE headquarters and the labs themselves—conspired to create an espionage scandal waiting to happen." The board proposed reorganizing the department's security functions.

Clinton had asked the commission to study DOE security in March in the wake of revelations that China apparently acquired highly classified nuclear weapons data.

The board proposed two options for improving security: creating an independent agency, similar to NASA and separate from the DOE, to oversee all weapons programs, or forming a semiautonomous agency to function as "a self-contained unit" within Energy. Contrary to the leanings of some Republicans, the board did not recommend that the Defense Department be given the responsibility for managing the nation's nuclear weapons stockpile.

Although the board generally praised recent efforts by Richardson to tighten security, it questioned whether those efforts would remain in place once Richardson left office.

Lawmakers in both parties predicted that the board's severe criticisms of security at the DOE would provide the momentum needed to restructure the agency.

The report "shows the callousness, the recklessness with which security was ignored at our nuclear labs," Senate Majority Leader Trent Lott told reporters. "Clearly we need reorganization in the department. There must be clear lines of authority."

Even before the board's report, three Republican senators—Jon Kyl of Arizona, Pete V. Domenici of New Mexico, and Frank H. Murkowski of Alaska—proposed restructuring the Energy Department by creating a Nuclear Security Administration within the department to handle all security issues. Under the proposal, the new agency would function as a separate "stovepipe" within the Energy Department, insulated from normal bureaucracy and procedures and accountable directly to the energy secretary.

The senators in May had wanted to attach the plan to the fiscal 2000 defense authorization bill (S 1059—S Rept 106-50), but they backed down in the face of opposition by Richardson. Spurred by the report, they said they would revive the plan.

"This [report] makes it inevitable. . . . I don't see how this can be resisted in Congress," Domenici told reporters.

LEGISLATIVE ACTION

Richardson strenuously opposed any bureaucratic changes, saying they would undermine the security reforms he had put in place. "To set up an agency, a new fiefdom, in the department of fiefdoms is not what I need," Richardson told the Senate Intelligence Committee in June. He also warned in a written statement that the shake-up would risk weakening the link "between national security and 'science at its best,' which has been the strength of our nuclear deterrent from its very inception."

Alarmed by the security lapses, lawmakers had already used several spending bills to remedy the problems. The Senate's fiscal 2000 appropriations bill for the departments of Commerce, Justice and State (S 1217—S Rept 106-76) called for sixty FBI agents to be reassigned "as soon as possible" to field offices in eight cities to augment counterintelligence efforts at the Energy Department's labs. And the Senate's fiscal 2000 energy and water appropriations bill (S 1168—S Rept 106-58) boosted funding for Energy's counterintelligence program.

In late June Richardson appeared to soften his resistance to a partial restructuring of his agency. At a rare joint meeting of the Senate Armed Services, Intelligence, Energy and Natural Resources, and Governmental Affairs committees on June 22, Richardson said he saw "a large patch of common ground" between his views and those of the advisory board. But he continued to object to specific language drafted by Republican senators, saying the provisions would undermine his authority.

Trying to bridge the gap, Republicans submitted a reworked draft amendment that included a number of changes aimed at clarifying the authority of the Energy secretary. But Richardson, as well as some Democrats, continued to raise concerns about the details, leading Kyl to predict that an agreement might not be reached before the intelligence bill went to the Senate floor.

In an escalation of the clash between the two sides, Domenici, Kyl, and Murkowski issued a harshly worded statement June 25 charging that their efforts were "being politicized and resisted by the Department of Energy at the expense of national security."

Ratcheting up the pressure on the administration, the House Appropriations Committee on July 20 approved a $20.2 billion energy and water appropriations bill that included a provision calling for withholding $1 billion from the Energy Department until Congress restructured the agency's national security programs.

Energy and Water Subcommittee Chairman Ron Packard, R-Calif., said he would push for an autonomous agency to oversee security, which would be structured similar to NASA and would report directly to the president. He said the only way to steer Congress in such a direction would be to withhold money from the DOE if necessary. His position contrasted with the GOP senators who pressed to create a semiautonomous agency within the DOE.

Ultimately, appropriators in August added language creating a semiautonomous agency within the DOE to the conference version of the fiscal 2000 defense spending bill (S 1059—H Rept 106-301).

Richardson initially said he would likely urge Clinton to veto the bill, warning that that conference agreement undermined the secretary's authority and "blurs the lines" of nuclear security, counterintelligence, environmental safety and health matters within DOE.

He also noted that his department had begun to change its nuclear oversight in the wake of allegations that former DOE scientist Wen Ho Lee provided sensitive nuclear information to China. The energy secretary cited polygraph tests, stiffer background checks on foreign visitors to the labs, a threefold increase in the number of counterintelligence employees, and upgraded cyber security as initial steps toward improving oversight of nuclear weapons information.

After weeks of criticizing the defense spending bill, Richardson relented on Sept. 26. The popular defense bill, which contained the largest military pay raise in eighteen years, had been adopted by overwhelming majorities in the House and Senate.

"I recognize the importance to the troops of the pay raise, readiness and retirement legislation," Richardson said in a prepared statement. He added that he would try to prevent the reorganization from causing disruptions within the department's current operations. President Clinton signed the measure Oct. 5, 1999.

Under the plan, the National Nuclear Security Administration would be headed by an undersecretary for nuclear security who would be subject to Senate confirmation. The new agency, which would come into existence on March 1, 2000, would be responsible for nuclear weapons development, defense activities to prevent the spread of nuclear weapons and the disposition of fissionable material.

ADMINISTRATION REACTION

When Clinton signed the spending bill creating the Nuclear Security Administration in October, he announced his intention to allow Richardson to head the new agency. That provoked a furious reaction from congressional Republicans, who vowed to reverse the decision.

"It is as if the president has exercised a line-item veto, signing the overall bill but denying effect to these provisions," said Governmental Affairs Chairman Fred Thompson, R-Tenn. "That approach is unconstitutional."

In the face of such criticism, the administration backed down. Richardson set up a search committee, led by former Deputy Energy Secretary Charles B. Curtis, to find an administrator of the nuclear security agency. But he angered Republicans by pursuing a policy that would allow department officials to hold their current positions as well as new ones within the nuclear weapons agency.

Richardson's plan, unveiled in early 2000, called for the Energy Department to operate with two undersecretaries—one to serve as administrator of the new agency and another to oversee energy, environmental, and science programs.

Some GOP lawmakers who helped write S 1059 complained that Richardson's blueprint for the agency calls for "dual-hatting" officials in several key positions, thus weakening the agency's independence.

But Richardson, who still enjoyed support from some key congressional Democrats, said at a January news conference that allowing the employees to oversee the new agency and retain their current jobs was "essential" for overall security operations to run smoothly. "It makes no sense for [the employees'] work to be duplicative," he said. "We don't have the budget to fully implement this new entity. We are going to continue this cross-cutting for the time being."

He scored political points with the announcement that highly regarded Air Force Gen. John A. Gordon would head the National Nuclear Security Administration.

In June, however, the tide shifted dramatically against Richardson. The much-publicized disappearance of two computer hard drives containing sensitive data at Los Alamos National Laboratory severely embarrassed the administration.

On June 16 the hard drives turned up in the same secured area from which they had vanished.

The debacle spurred lawmakers to add several DOE provisions to spending bills, even though Republicans conceded they were probably micromanaging the agency. "There is just a political desire for Congress to do something about this," said William M. "Mac" Thornberry, R-Texas, a member of the House Armed Services Committee.

The House on June 27 adopted an amendment, 239–187, to the fiscal 2001 energy and water development appropriations bill (HR 4733) to prohibit "dual-hatting." The Senate included similar language in its version of the fiscal 2001 defense authorization bill (S 2549), despite objections from Richardson.

House members also approved, by voice vote, an amendment to the energy and water bill by Jack Kingston, R-Ga., to cut off the salaries of Los Alamos officials with access to highly sensitive data who did not undergo the polygraph tests required of them under the fiscal 2000 defense authorization law (PL 106-65).

A General Accounting Office report released June 29 found that in addition to the Los Alamos incident, there were "significant continuing vulnerabilities" in the Energy Department's computer systems for unclassified civilian research.

Richardson, a Democrat who was a former House member from New Mexico (1983–1997) and former U.S. ambassador to the United Nations, had been mentioned as a possible running mate for Vice President Al Gore before the hard drives turned up missing. Many lawmakers and political observers agreed that the withering criticism of Richardson after the incident had likely eliminated him from consideration—and possibly even ended his political career.

Congressional Democrats joined Republicans in lambasting the beleaguered secretary. Sen. Robert C. Byrd, D-W.Va., gave the Energy secretary a remarkable tongue-lashing during a June 21 Senate Armed Services Committee hearing on the missing hard drives. Richardson appeared at the hearing after refusing an invitation to testify a week earlier before the Senate Intelligence Committee.

Byrd accused Richardson of "a contempt of Congress that borders on a supreme arrogance of this institution."

"I think it's a rather sad story that you had a bright and brilliant career," Byrd said coldly, "but you will never again receive the support of the Senate of the United States for any office to which you might be appointed. It's gone. You've squandered your treasure, and I'm sorry."

Senate sources said Byrd's frustration with Richardson stemmed not just from security at the nuclear labs or his refusal to cooperate with committees, but from the secretary's practice of negotiating with lawmakers by threatening to withhold money earmarked for projects in their states. Byrd was ranking Democrat on the Appropriations Committee.

Richardson answered Byrd's criticisms at the Armed Services hearing by saying he had wanted to have more information about the Los Alamos incident before appearing before senators. "I hope to earn Sen. Byrd's trust again," Richardson said.

Arctic National Wildlife Refuge

Wading into a divisive environmental issue, the Senate in 2000 signaled support for drilling for oil in Alaska's Arctic National Wildlife Refuge (ANWR).

The issue arose during debate over the fiscal 2001 budget resolution (S Con Res 101), which included a nonbinding provision that assumed $1.2 billion in anticipated revenue from oil and gas leases at the refuge. Environmentalists took aim at the language, and William V. Roth Jr., R-Del., proposed an amendment to delete it. His amendment was tabled (killed) by a 51–49 vote on April 6 after an intensive lobbying campaign.

Despite the vote, Congress took no further action on the drilling proposal in 2000. As a result, the pristine refuge remained off-limits to petroleum development.

Environmentalists and energy companies had battled ferociously over the Arctic refuge for the better part of two decades. One of the nation's most pristine ecosystems, the preserve was protected as part of the 1980 Alaska Public Lands Act (PL 96-487), which barred development in the refuge unless approved by Congress.

Alaska's powerful congressional delegation fought tirelessly to allow at least limited oil exploration in the refuge's 1.5 million-acre coastal plain, which sat atop an estimated 5.6 billion to 16 billion barrels of oil.

Supporters of opening the refuge believed that defeating the Roth amendment was crucial. "The time has come to debunk the myth that development and the environment are an either/or proposition," Alaska's Gov. Tony Knowles said April 5 during an appearance before the Senate Energy and Natural Resources Committee. "By doing development right, I know we can extract the potentially enormous oil and gas reserves under the Arctic refuge while protecting the important wildlife and environmental values there."

In making their appeal to open the refuge, supporters cited gasoline prices that continued to hover around $1.50 a gallon, the United States' growing dependence on foreign petroleum to fuel cars, and technological improvements that they say lessen the environmental threats posed by drilling.

"ANWR is a serious issue," said Senate Energy and Natural Resources Chairman Frank H. Murkowski, R-Alaska, in an April 5 floor speech. "It is so serious that I hope you will all remember that if [the Roth] amendment is adopted, I can assure every single member of this body, we will be well on our way to jeopardizing our national security by further increasing our dependence on imported oil."

Murkowski, like other supporters of tapping the refuge's oil reserves, pointed out that the United States imported more than 50 percent of its oil. During the oil crisis of 1973, the United States imported 36 percent, according to the Department of Energy.

The administration, however, was just as resolute in its opposition, dismissing suggestions that the oil was needed and could be extracted without harming the environment. President Clinton stated publicly that he would veto any legislation allowing the Arctic refuge to be opened to drilling.

Barbara Boxer, D-Calif., who joined Roth in cosponsoring the amendment that would have kept the refuge closed to commercial drilling, argued that the short-term benefits of oil extraction would not make up for the long-term damage to the environment. "The bottom line is, I think the public is really smart, and they are going to see that these high prices are being used as an excuse to destroy a wildlife refuge which they know has inherent value greater than whatever oil is produced," she said in an April 4 interview.

Roth appeared to be on the verge of victory until two Republicans, Gordon H. Smith of Oregon and Arlen Specter of Pennsylvania, switched their votes. Four Democrats also voted in favor of opening the wildlife refuge to drilling, while eight Republicans voted to keep it closed to commercial activity.

"When it became clear to me that a vote for this amendment would jeopardize funding for my budget priorities, such as prescription drug coverage, I felt it necessary to change my vote," Smith said.

Roth, who chaired the Finance Committee, used a completely different rationale for offering his amendment.

"My reason for offering this amendment is based on beauty, not on budgets," Roth said April 5 to open debate on the measure. "I do not want to see us make an irreparable mistake in one of America's remaining natural treasures. We can afford to forego this momentary revenue, but we can't afford not to protect this Arctic Eden."

While the narrow vote marked a significant victory for those who wanted to open the refuge, it did not move Congress to allow drilling. A Murkowski bill (S 2214) that would have allowed the drilling never advanced in the Energy and Natural Resources Committee.

Coal Leases

The maximum acreage of federal leases for coal a company could hold was increased under legislation cleared by the House in 2000. The bill (S 2300—PL 106-463) would increase the lease maximum by about 60 percent within one state and by 50 percent nationally. Under the bill, the individual limit would be raised from 46,080 acres to 75,000 acres in a single state, and from 100,000 acres to 150,000 nationwide.

Existing law limited the number of acres a person, association, corporation or any of their affiliates could hold under a federal coal lease or permit.

Supporters said the measure would provide for more efficient capital investments by coal operators, and would remove unintended incentives for coal companies to bypass coal on federal land.

The Senate Energy and Natural Resources Committee gave voice vote approval to the bill (S Rept 106-378) on July 13. The Senate passed the measure by voice vote on Oct. 5, and the House cleared it by voice vote on Oct. 23. The president signed it Nov. 7, 2000.

Economic Sanctions Against Oil Producers

Frustrated by rising oil prices, the House passed legislation (HR 3822) in 2000 that would authorize the president to impose multilateral sanctions against countries that fixed oil prices with the intent of injuring the U.S. economy. But the bill, which was not taken up by the Senate, was largely symbolic because the president already had the power to restrict foreign assistance and defense sales under laws such as the 1977 International Emergency Economic Powers Act (PL 95-223).

The International Relations Committee March 15 approved the measure (H Rept 106-528) by voice vote. Chairman Benjamin A. Gilman, R-N.Y., said Congress needed to weigh in on a 1999 decision by the Organization of Petroleum Exporting Countries (OPEC) to cut production by 4.3 million barrels a day to raise prices. As a result, the average price of oil rose from $11 to about $32 per barrel.

Gilman said his New York constituents, hit hard by extraordinarily high winter heating bills that winter, were bombarding his Washington office asking, "What are we doing about [the situation] in Congress?" Gilman said the bill would "galvanize the administration into action" and give U.S. negotiators "teeth" when urging oil-producing nations to boost production.

Doug Bereuter, R-Neb., dismissed the bill as largely meaningless. "This is much ado about nothing," he said.

"Let's admit we're making ourselves feel good, but that's really all it is."

The only real opposition to the bill came from Bill Delahunt, D-Mass., who said Congress should not move legislation before OPEC held a meeting on March 27. Energy Secretary Bill Richardson had predicted OPEC nations would decide to increase oil production at that time.

The House passed the bill on March 22 by a vote of 382–38, with one member voting "present."

During several hours of highly partisan debate, Democrats repeatedly blamed the Republican-controlled Congress for cutting funding for alternate energy and conservation programs. Republicans responded by blaming the Clinton administration for pursuing a weak foreign policy in the Middle East and thwarting domestic oil exploration.

The most substantive debate occurred prior to the House adopting, 222–200, a procedural motion on the rule governing floor debate on the bill. The rule allowed a substitute amendment by Pete Sessions, R-Texas, to be considered as the original text. The amendment stripped the International Relations Committee version of the bill of its core provision, which would have authorized the president to restrict foreign assistance and military sales to countries found to be manipulating oil prices to injure the U.S. economy.

That authority was provided under current law (PL 95-223), but GOP leaders objected, and the Rules Committee removed the sanctions provision.

An aide said Gilman voted for the rule out of deference to Republican leaders but was disappointed and frustrated about their mandate to strip the sanctions provision.

## CHAPTER 8

Agricultural Policy

Introduction   417

1997–1998 Chronology   419

1999–2000 Chronology   424

Agricultural Policy

In contrast to the robust economic growth sweeping most of the nation, rural America confronted hard times during the 105th and 106th Congresses. The number of U.S. farms declined, farm income went into a free fall, and access to critical foreign markets, particularly in Asia and Europe, remained an unrealized dream for many agricultural producers.

Lawmakers found themselves under increasing pressure to act. But lacking a clear consensus, Congress mostly responded in a way it had done in the past: by approving huge packages of emergency aid totaling more than $20 billion. Members had mixed success implementing policy changes many believed were necessary to make U.S. agriculture successful again.

Much of the congressional action during President Bill Clinton's second term stemmed from the sweeping rewrite in agriculture policy contained in the 1996 farm bill (PL 104-127), also known as the Freedom to Farm Act. The law was designed to wean farmers off the government controls and many of the subsidies that had long been the backbone of the agriculture economy. Although they had to give up their federal subsidies, farmers gained the freedom to plant what they wanted and an opportunity to exploit market demand.

To ease the transition, the 1996 law called for "market transition" payments averaging $5 billion a year between 1996 and 2002. The payments were popular because they were for fixed amounts, replacing old variable target price supports. Bad weather and plummeting commodity prices for such staples as wheat, corn, soybeans, and hogs, however, soon began to create a crisis atmosphere in farm country. The price for a bushel of wheat in 1999—about $2.50—was nearly half of what it was in 1996. To make matters worse, three years of remarkably good weather worldwide helped swamp global markets with bumper foreign crops, which were sold at cut-throat prices. The Asian recession of 1998 and 1999 further hammered U.S. agriculture's ability to find new overseas markets.

As these market difficulties unfolded, congressional Democrats blamed the 1996 law that removed the farm safety net just as the rural economy went into a deep economic slump. Republicans countered that U.S. agriculture was hit with unprecedented circumstances. Despite political differences, lawmakers responded by increasing the very federal pay-

ments that were supposed to fall under the 1996 act. In 1999 alone, Congress approved $9.3 billion in aid to distressed farmers via the fiscal 2000 agriculture appropriations act (PL 106-78) and the omnibus appropriations bill (PL 106-113). *(See farm income stabilization spending in figure on page 418.)*

While some suggested it was time to reopen the 1996 law, congressional leaders deferred, with many saying the free market approach still could work with adequate trade and access to foreign markets. Fiscal conservatives, meanwhile, criticized the continued funneling of money to farmers, saying agriculture should be treated more like other businesses, rising or failing with a farmer's entrepreneurial skills instead of relying on government controls.

In such an environment, it was often difficult to craft and pass significant legislation. One major development was passage of a 1998 bill reauthorizing mandatory crop insurance funding that also authorized spending on agricultural research and restored food stamp benefits to certain illegal immigrants. It was followed by 2000 legislation that encouraged farmers to purchase insurance by having the government pick up a greater share of the premiums.

Both bills reflected the Clinton administration and congressional Republicans' common belief that the federal crop insurance program—which allows farmers to buy protection

REFERENCES

Discussion of agricultural policy for the years 1945–1964 may be found in *Congress and the Nation Vol. I*, pp. 665–767; for the years 1965–1968, *Congress and the Nation Vol. II*, pp. 555–597; for the years 1969–1972, *Congress and the Nation Vol. III*, pp. 331–352; for the years 1973–1976, *Congress and the Nation Vol. IV*, pp. 717–740; for the years 1977–1980, *Congress and the Nation Vol. V*, pp. 365–395; for the years 1981–1984, *Congress and the Nation Vol. VI*, pp. 485–516; for the years 1985–1988, *Congress and the Nation Vol. VII*, pp. 499–539; for the years 1989–1992, *Congress and the Nation Vol. VIII*, pp. 535–557; for the years 1993–1996, *Congress and the Nation Vol. IX*, pp. 479–505.

Outlays for Agriculture

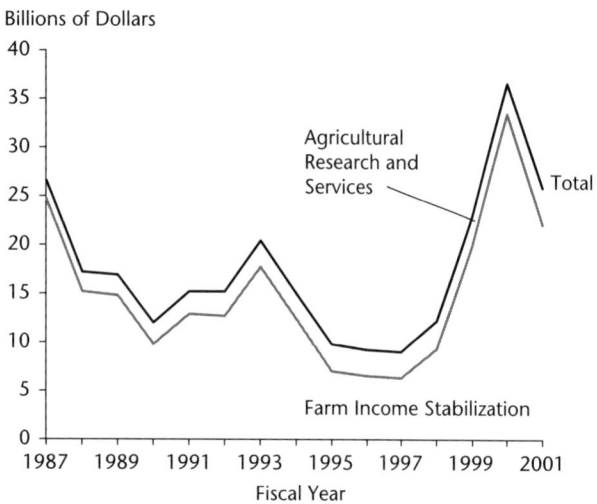

Billions of Dollars

NOTE: Data for 2001 are estimated.

SOURCE: Office of Management and Budget, *Historical Tables, Budget of the United States Government: Fiscal Year 2002* (Washington, D.C.: U.S. Government Printing Office, 2001), Table 3.2.

against crop losses—was the best tool farmers could use to get through difficult times. Many had been reluctant to buy insurance, believing the government regularly provided free insurance in the form of disaster payments. Though the 2000 bill was aimed at making farmers less dependent on emergency aid, lawmakers sent mixed signals, also using the measure to pay out $5.5 billion in supplemental fiscal 2000 payments to make up for low prices on wheat, cotton, corn, and other crops.

Congress also tackled the difficult issue of dairy price supports—largely a response by members from dairy states outside the Midwest to the Department of Agriculture's proposal to cut prices received by milk producers outside of Wisconsin and Minnesota. In the late 1990s dairy prices fell because of overproduction, in part linked to large farming operations in western states. The cuts in dairy price supports spawned intense regional battles in the House and Senate, as all sides tried to come to grips with an archaic pricing system. The system, designed to pay each farmer equally on per amount produced, also guarantees them a higher base price for fluid milk the farther it is produced from Eau Claire, Wisconsin—the historical heart of the milk industry. In the end, the majority voted to keep the status quo—much to the chagrin of lawmakers from the upper Midwest, who have seen dairy farms in their districts hammered by market conditions—and extend a compact among New England states that sets the price farmers are paid for milk above the federally mandated level.

Lawmakers attempted to open new doors to agricultural exports by overturning long-standing sanctions on sales of food to Cuba, Iran, Libya, North Korea, and Sudan. Farm groups rallied with Democrats long opposed to sanctions on humanitarian grounds to overcome opposition from those lawmakers opposed to warming relations with the nations, especially the communist regime of Cuban leader Fidel Castro.

Congress also revisited old debates over land stewardship. Two thorny issues to tackle were determining how much fragile farm land to take out of production at what price, and how much to charge ranchers for grazing livestock on federally owned land.

Chronology of Action on Agriculture

1997–1998

With some farmers and ranchers facing their first hard times since federal farm law was revamped in 1996, Congress and the White House competed to see who could be more generous to them. The farm lobby exploited public sentiment toward farmers, strategic alliances with other interest groups, and fairly intense political activity in anticipation of the 1998 midterm elections to keep agriculture a sympathetic concern in American politics.

Among other actions, Congress lifted sanctions that would have cut into foreign wheat sales and approved $1 billion of mandatory funding over five years for the federal crop insurance program to aid farmers hit hard by poor prices and bad weather. In addition, after President Clinton vetoed a fiscal 1999 agriculture spending bill because it did not contain sufficient aid for farmers and ranchers, lawmakers enacted "emergency" tax breaks for farmers that were not offset elsewhere in the budget.

The Clinton administration used farm legislation to reverse a major domestic policy by authorizing $818 million over five years in an agriculture research bill to restore food stamp benefits to some 250,000 legal immigrants who were removed from welfare rolls by the 1996 welfare overhaul. The bill was enacted thanks to a coalition of agriculture, nutrition, and immigration interest groups, who put aside past differences to rally wavering lawmakers over the objections of congressional Republican leaders, who resisted any changes to the welfare law.

The White House also nullified House action to remove environmentally fragile farm land from production by enrolling 16.1 million acres into the Conservation Reserve Program, which pays food producers to idle acreage. Other land management issues were left unsettled. The House attempted to raise the fees ranchers pay to graze livestock on public lands and enact a new statutory fee formula, but the Senate did not act.

Grazing Fees

The House in 1997 passed legislation to increase the fees ranchers pay to graze livestock on federal lands, but the Senate took no action on the bill (HR 2493).

The bill would have raised the fees for grazing cattle on government-owned land by an average of 15 percent over the following five years while reducing the grazing fee for sheep by about one-third. The measure was supported by livestock groups but opposed by the Clinton administration and environmental organizations, who expressed concern it would tip land-use decisions in favor of ranching interests.

BACKGROUND

Grazing fees have sparked seeming perennial squabbles between ranchers, who want to keep the fees down, and environmentalists, who assert that lower fees result in overgrazing and the deterioration of public lands through runoff pollution and excessive foraging. In the 1990s the environmentalists were joined by deficit hawks, who contended the fees constituted a huge government subsidy for ranching interests.

The issue sparked regional battles in the 104th Congress, as eastern lawmakers raised objections on environmental grounds to several grazing bills and succeeded in scuttling the legislative efforts. Westerners predicted the failure to enact legislation would spell doom for small family-owned ranches.

Under existing law, grazing fees were established by executive order and varied according to market conditions. The fees hinged on several factors, including cattle prices, private lease rates for grazing lands, and costs associated with beef production. Fees are measured in "animal unit months," or the amount of forage necessary to feed one cow, five sheep, or one horse for a month. The minimal fees for the 1996 and 1997 grazing seasons were $1.35 per animal unit month.

The House bill proposed a new, statutory fee formula largely based on the value of beef cattle as determined by the Department of Agriculture and the interest rate over the previous twelve months. The new formula did not include a floor, or minimum amount, below which fees could not fall. The effect would have been to increase the cattle grazing fee to $1.84 per animal unit month. The bill also proposed changes to existing grazing advisory panels established by Interior Secretary Bruce Babbitt to increase state and local

---

AGRICULTURE LEADERSHIP

When President Bill Clinton assembled his cabinet for his second term, Dan Glickman remained as secretary of agriculture. Glickman had served in the post for the last two years of Clinton's first term and was one of eight returning cabinet members in 1997. A nine-term Democratic representative from Kansas (1977–1995), Glickman had been confirmed as secretary of agriculture on March 30, 1995, by a 94–0 vote of the Senate.

Glickman succeeded Mike Espy, of Mississippi, who had resigned after being accused of improperly accepting gifts—allegations of which he was ultimately cleared in 1998. *(Cabinet profiles, p. 977; Espy investigation, Glickman background, Congress and the Nation Vol. IX, pp. 483, 943, 1109)*

---

participation. The Clinton administration made a push in 1993 to nearly triple grazing fees to $4.28 per animal unit month—a figure still well below many private fees—but the effort was snuffed out by fierce opposition from ranchers.

LEGISLATIVE ACTION

The House Agriculture Committee approved HR 2493 (H Rept 105-346, Pt. 1) in September by voice vote and with relatively little debate. Bill supporters hailed the measure for the way it would streamline the management of federal lands, adding it provided needed stability to ranching communities in the West. However, Babbitt immediately threatened to recommend a veto of the measure because he said the legislation would undermine the advisory councils by requiring that decisions be approved by a majority vote, instead of by consensus.

The House passed the measure on Oct. 30, 242–182, only after westerners brokered a compromise with leery eastern colleagues. To satisfy conservation-minded lawmakers, supporters dropped several provisions, including one giving ranchers greater influence over grazing policy developed by the advisory panels. House Speaker Newt Gingrich, R-Ga., personally appealed to both sides to reach a compromise, saying it could soothe bitter feelings about federal land management issues.

Fiscal conservatives and some environmentally conscious Republicans argued ranchers were supporting the measure only to stave off much larger hikes. During floor debate they unsuccessfully offered several amendments to raise fees further. Floor proposals included tying federal grazing fees to the often higher fee charged by the state in which the rancher was located or levying a 25 percent federal fee on top of the bill's grazing formula to make up the difference between federal and state rates. Another rejected amendment would have eliminated proposed reduced grazing fees for sheep and

goats. Defenders of the bill said it was a reasonable compromise, pointing out that the grazing industry was effectively supporting a 36 percent increase in its cost of doing business.

Dairy Recalls

The House in 1997 voted to reauthorize a program that helped dairy farmers recoup losses on recalled products but the Senate did not take up the measure (HR 1789).

The bill proposed reauthorizing the Dairy Indemnity Program through fiscal 2002. The program compensated farmers whose dairy products were pulled from the consumer market because of contamination from toxins, pesticides, chemicals, or other substances through no fault of the producer.

The program's fiscal 1997 budget had been depleted in February by a large-scale milk recall affecting thirty producers, and the Farm Service Agency additionally stopped accepting claim requests. Under the bill, funds appropriated in fiscal 1998 could be used to pay claims arising from the 1997 shortfall.

The House Agriculture Livestock, Dairy and Poultry Subcommittee approved the measure by voice vote in June, and the full committee approved it in September (H Rept 105-294). The House passed it by voice vote under suspension of the rules on Oct. 21, 1997.

Conservation Reserve Program

The Department of Agriculture announced in May 1997 that it would enroll 16.1 million acres into the federal Conservation Reserve Program, which pays farmers to remove environmentally fragile land from production. The decision nullified the impetus for a bill (HR 1342—H Rept 105–80) passed by the House in April that would have provided a one-year extension to certain farmers of winter crops whose contracts with the program were set to expire that year. A provision in the bill said it would be void if the Agriculture Department acted on the program's contract renewals.

The deal, brokered in part by Senate Agriculture Committee Chairman Richard G. Lugar, R-Ind., would pay farmers an average of $40 per acre to idle the land. Lugar's counterpart in the House, Bob Smith, R-Ore., however, said the administration's plan did not enroll enough land and was inadequate.

The House had passed HR 1342, 325–92, over the objections of some lawmakers who believed it would prevent the Agriculture Department from enrolling more environmentally important land in the program.

Sanctions

Senate Agriculture Committee Chairman Richard G. Lugar, R-Ind., also a senior Republican on the Foreign Relations Committee, waged an often lonely fight in 1998 to slow down the use of overseas economic sanctions by Congress and the executive branch. Lugar argued that, while some sanctions may have merit, their cumulative weight had potentially crippled American foreign policy and weighed heavily on farmers and other exporters. *(Economic sanctions, p. 199)*

Lugar introduced a bill (S 1413) that would have slowed the imposition of new sanctions by instituting a formal process under which lawmakers would have to weigh the costs and benefits of new restrictions on aid and trade. The arguments made little headway until India and Pakistan tested nuclear weapons in May, triggering automatic sanctions under the Arms Control Export Act, contained in the 1994 State Department authorization bill (PL 103-236). The sanctions hit Pakistan much harder than its larger, richer neighbor, India. U.S. farmers also were threatened when the Clinton administration decided the law's credit ban would prevent the United States from guaranteeing bank loans on exports of wheat and other crops to Pakistan.

With American wheat farmers about to be squeezed out of a major wheat auction, the Senate unanimously approved legislation (S 2282) allowing India and Pakistan to continue to use guaranteed loans to import U.S. food, fertilizer, and other agricultural commodities. But with farmers up in arms about the sanctions and other restrictions, Lugar sought to bring up his broader bill. In July Lugar introduced the language as an amendment to the fiscal 1999 agriculture appropriations bill (S 2159), trying to use the pressure of the farm lobby to make his case. But Lugar was opposed by Senate Foreign Relations Committee Chairman Jesse Helms, R-N.C., coauthor of a 1996 law (PL 104-114) that tightened the decades-old U.S. embargo on trade with Cuba, as well as other sanctions laws. Although a majority of Republican senators voted with him, Lugar's amendment was tabled (killed), by a **key vote of 53–46 (R 27–28; D 26–18).** *(1998 key votes, p. 883)*

Crop Insurance, Food Stamps

Congress passed and President Clinton signed legislation (S 1150—PL 105-185) in 1998 authorizing funding for research, extension, and education programs of the Department of Agriculture that provided mandatory crop insurance funding for the next five fiscal years and notably restored food stamp benefits to certain legal immigrants who were removed from welfare rolls by the 1996 welfare overhaul (PL 104-193).

The bill authorized $818 million over five years to restore food stamp benefits to 250,000 elderly and disabled legal immigrants, as well as children under eighteen, who already were in the country when the welfare law was signed in August 1996. The provision triggered furious debate as conservatives resisted any further rollback of the welfare law— one of the Republican Congress's signature social policy achievements. President Clinton in 1997 had forced Con-

gress to restore Supplemental Security Income and Medicaid benefits to the legal immigrants. He threatened to veto the agriculture bill unless restored funding for food stamps was included.

Support for the legislation hinged on a coalition of agriculture, nutrition, and immigrant groups who each had a strong interest in seeing provisions in the bill passed. Farm state lawmakers, for example, pushed for enactment of agriculture provisions that would provide $1 billion in mandatory funding over five years to pay the commissions of agents who sell federally subsidized crop insurance policies. Mandatory funding for the crop insurance program became a rallying cry for growers concerned that federal subsidies were in decline. Also included in the bill were $600 million in mandatory funding for competitive grants for agriculture research, a reauthorization of the administration's Fund for Rural America, and funding for a variety of new programs, such as a honey promotion system funded through assessments on honey producers. Administration opponents issued a rebuke to the president by later denying funding in fiscal 1999 for two administration priorities—the mandatory research program and the Fund for Rural America— through provisions in the omnibus appropriations bill (HR 4328—PL 105-277).

BACKGROUND

For decades, food and agriculture groups were linked by a fruitful, if sometimes awkward, political marriage of convenience. Farm state lawmakers expanded food stamps as part of broad crop subsidy measures. The nutrition aid attracted support from urban votes, helping ensure passage of farm bills even through the rural population was declining.

In the mid-1990s, however, the push to balance the federal budget squeezed the funding available to the House and Senate agriculture committees, which oversee both crop and nutrition programs. That funding pressure forced direct budget trade-offs between the interest groups and a gradual shift from cooperation to competition. For example, farm groups quietly lobbied to make deeper cuts in nutrition programs in order to protect funding for crop and environmental programs. Immigrant groups also entered the equation after the 1996 welfare overhaul, waging a battle to win some money for the 935,000 legal immigrants dropped from food stamp rolls. The Clinton administration became engaged on the issue and proposed reinstating the food stamp program for some legal immigrants.

About half of the savings derived from welfare overhaul came from food stamps, specifically a provision that cut $27 billion over six years—the largest dollar reduction in the program's history. Advocates for the poor said the cuts had the effect of leaving one sector of the population hungry while the economy boomed and many people went off welfare. However, Republicans said data did not point to higher-than-expected demand at food banks, adding they would seek to cut down on fraud and quality control problems in the food stamp program. The bulk of the program cuts came through accounting changes that limited inflationary adjustments and made other technical changes to the entitlement.

LEGISLATIVE ACTION

Congress in 1997 began debating legislation that would restore food stamps to 250,000 legal immigrants who were cut from federal benefit rolls. The House and Senate passed conflicting versions of a five-year reauthorization of an agriculture research and education bill. But Republican House members objected to provisions in the Senate bill (S 1150) that they said would create more than $1 billion of new mandatory spending. The objections prevented the legislation from going to conference during the first session.

Congress returned to the issue in spring 1998 when a House-Senate conference agreed to a compromise version of S 1150 providing $600 million in new, mandatory spending over five years to expand food safety, genetic engineering, and education programs; some $1 billion to pay agent commissions under the federal crop insurance program; and $100 million for rural development and research programs. Again, some House Republicans objected to creating mandatory spending for agricultural research at a time when federal funds were scarce. Meanwhile, the Clinton administration threatened to oppose the measure unless it restored aid to immigrants.

As the various sides in the debate dithered over the measure, the Senate in April complicated matters by approving a fiscal 1999 budget resolution (S Con Res 86) that would use the more than $1.7 billion earmarked for food stamps and agriculture programs to pay for increased highway spending. The move did not kill the food stamp measure outright but made it more politically difficult for farm state lawmakers to claim the funds needed to pay for it. Senate Majority Leader Trent Lott, R-Miss., who by all accounts had been working with the White House to move the bill, suggested the money could be better used for transportation needs.

The Senate May 12 approved the measure, 92–8, after food and farm groups worked together to round up more than seventy senators' signatures on a letter supporting the bill. The efforts were bolstered by White House support and a study by a Boston-based human rights group, Physicians for Human Rights, that found high levels of hunger among immigrants in three states.

Drama surrounding the bill intensified May 22, when House Republican leaders suffered a dramatic defeat when members of their party rebelled against an effort to strip the provision that would restore food stamps to the legal immigrants. After an emotional debate on the House floor, lawmakers defeated, by a **key vote of 120–289 (R 118–98; D 2–190; I 0–1)**, a rule for floor debate that would have allowed a point of order automatically stripping the immigrant aid. Republicans defected en masse out of concern both for the immigrants and a desire to preserve new agriculture money. Supporters noted the Clinton administration's threat to veto

any bill that did not include immigrant aid. The House passed the measure on June 4, 364–50, sending the legislation to the White House. *(1998 key votes, p. 883)*

KEY PROVISIONS

The bill provided $818 million over five years to restore food stamp benefits to elderly and disabled legal immigrants who were in the country when the welfare law was signed Aug. 22, 1996, as well as children under eighteen. Refugees and those granted political asylum would be allowed to receive food stamps for seven years, up from the current five.

The bill also provided $1 billion in mandatory crop insurance funding for five years. About half of the spending would be offset by cuts elsewhere in the crop insurance program. The money was needed to cover commissions of agents who sell federally subsidized crop insurance policies. The legislation also included $600 million in mandatory funding for competitive grants for agriculture research into areas such as food safety and crop yields and sets up new programs, including a honey promotion system.

Minority Farmers Legislation

Congress in 1998 included language in the omnibus spending package (HR 4328—PL 105-277) to waive the statute of limitations for claims by black and Hispanic farmers that they suffered racial discrimination between 1981 and 1996 in dealings with the Department of Agriculture. The language authorized farmers who were blocked by the statute of limitations either to take their complaints to a federal court or to resolve the complaint within the dispute resolution procedures at the Agriculture Department. At a National Association for the Advancement of Colored People convention July 15, Agriculture Secretary Dan Glickman repeated his apologies for instances of past department discrimination. The language was originally included in the fiscal 1999 agriculture appropriations bill (HR 4101), which was vetoed by President Clinton, then rolled into the omnibus spending package.

Farm Tax Breaks

Congress included language in the 1998 omnibus spending package (HR 4328—PL 105-277) that offered "emergency" tax aid to farmers that was not offset elsewhere in the budget and ate into the projected budget surplus. Republicans added the provisions after President Clinton vetoed a fiscal 1999 agriculture spending bill (HR 4101), saying it did not contain sufficient aid for farmers and ranchers devastated by weather, falling commodity prices, and exports. Clinton backed a Senate Democratic plan that would lift caps on marketing loan rates. Republicans preferred to boost aid through tax cuts.

The revised agriculture package would allow 100 percent deductibility of health insurance for independently owned businesses and the self-employed by 2003, up from 45 percent in 1998, at a cost of $880 million over five years. The package also would allow farmers and ranchers to average out their incomes over five-year periods for tax purposes, at a cost of $45 million over five years.

In addition, the bill included a "carryback" provision allowing farmers who suffer an operating loss in one year to receive a refund against taxes paid in an earlier, profitable year, at a cost of $81 million over five years. Farmers and ranchers would be offered $3.1 billion in direct payments. Another $875 million would be available to farmers, espe-

cially those in the Upper Plains, who have suffered multiyear losses.

Ranchers who require livestock feed assistance can tap a pool of $200 million available. The bill also offered $3 million in indemnity payments to compensate certain dairy farmers for losses. Ranchers won an additional victory with a one-year pilot program requiring meatpackers to post their prices, creating greater transparency in meat markets. Cattle ranchers had complained that meatpackers unfairly withhold price information in order to lowball them, but the meatpackers denied the charge.

1999–2000

The 106th Congress tackled two of the most contentious and complicated issues in agriculture—dairy pricing and crop insurance—in an effort to develop new approaches to address market problems.

The dairy issued pivoted around changes the Department of Agriculture proposed to the government's Great Depression–era regional price supports that would have cut prices received for milk by many farmers outside of the Upper Midwest. The action came as the $70 billion dairy industry struggled with falling prices for milk that were largely brought on by overproduction. Besides changing the existing system, the department would also have put an end to dairy compacts, which allow interstate commissions to raise the minimum price paid to dairy farmers above the federal level and can wall off states from the dairy products of other regions when certain price conditions prevail.

In a battle that pitted regions of the country against one another, Congress eventually decided to override the department's decision and maintain the status quo on pricing, as well as extend a Northeast Dairy Compact. The moves dealt twin blows to Wisconsin and Minnesota, the two largest dairy states in the Upper Midwest. Lawmakers from the states called off a filibuster only after receiving assurances that the issue would be revisited.

On crop insurance, lawmakers tried to encourage farmers to buy protection against crop losses by having the government subsidize a bigger share of the premium. Congress's readiness to bail out farmers suffering from hard times—there had been a dozen separate disaster bills since 1980—discouraged farmers from buying crop insurance because they were convinced the government would provide free insurance in the form of disaster payments.

There was widespread agreement among farm state lawmakers that the crop insurance program should be revamped to make it more attractive to farmers. In addition to raising the government's share of insurance premiums, lawmakers also threw in $7.1 billion of emergency spending, on top of $15 billion in aid enacted since fiscal 1999.

Congress in 2000 also took up the issue of food sanctions as farm state lawmakers teamed with Democrats to include language in the agriculture appropriations bill to lift prohibitions on the sale of food to five so-called "rogue" nations—Cuba, Iran, Libya, North Korea, and Sudan. Amid concerns the move would improve ties with the communist regime of Fidel Castro, lawmakers included language in the measure barring public or private financing of Cuban agricultural purchases.

Dairy Pricing

Congress in 1999 tackled the combustible issue of dairy pricing, clearing two provisions benefiting other regions of the country at the expense of the Upper Midwest. The measures, included in the omnibus fiscal 2000 appropriations package (HR 3194—PL 106-113), maintained existing milk pricing rules and extended the Northeast Dairy Compact. Frustrated midwestern lawmakers gave up end-of-session attempts to block the omnibus bill in exchange for a promise that Congress again would address the dairy issue in early 2000 (which it failed to do however). *(Omnibus appropriations bill, p. 73)*

LEGISLATIVE ACTION

Under the 1996 farm law (PL 104-127), Congress directed the Department of Agriculture to streamline the nation's complex system of regional dairy price supports. The so-called milk marketing orders date from the 1930s and ensure that all regions of the country have access to perishable dairy products. The system requires dairy processors within each marketing order, or region, to pay farmers a minimum price for milk. Currently, farmers are paid more for milk the farther they are located from Eau Claire, Wisconsin, the traditional center of the dairy industry. Bonuses given to farmers outside the Upper Midwest were intended to reflect different production and transportation costs. The Clinton administration's March 1999 proposed changes would have minimized those bonuses and had the effect of cutting prices that processors pay for fresh milk outside of Wisconsin and Minnesota.

The department proposed cutting the number of milk marketing orders from thirty-one to eleven regions—a move that aroused regional passions and led lawmakers from the South, Southwest, and Northeast to ready legislation to block the move before it was even formally announced. A bill (HR 1402) to override the Agriculture Department's decision and maintain the status quo for many states quickly attracted 138 cosponsors. The House Agriculture Committee cleared the bill, 32–15, June 30, adding amendments that would allow dairy farmers to sign forward pricing contracts with private entities for future delivery and that would overturn a new Agriculture Department formula for pricing milk used in cheese production.

Separately, the House Judiciary Committee took up legislation (HR 1604) to authorize two regional dairy compacts. A compact is quasi-public interstate commission that consists of farm, processor and consumer representatives, and state officials and sets the price farmers are paid for milk above the federally mandated level. The nation's only dairy compact, in the Northeast, was set to expire Oct. 1, 1999. HR 1604 would make the Northeast compact permanent and expand it into New York and the mid-Atlantic region. The bill also would authorize a new compact in the South. While the Judiciary Committee did not act on the bill, senators sought to include identical language in a fiscal 2000 agriculture spending bill (S 1233).

The House Sept. 22 passed HR 1402, 285–140—a margin apparently large enough to override an anticipated presidential veto. Lawmakers from New England and the South worked simultaneously to preserve the existing pricing system by attaching language similar to HR 1402 in the fiscal 2000 agriculture appropriations bill (HR 1906)—a move that complicated a House-Senate conference on the measure. House GOP leaders requested members to keep dairy provisions out of the conference report. But lawmakers from the East and Southeast continued to press for the language, saying the new Agriculture Department formula would drive thousands of dairy farmers out of business by shifting $200 million in revenues, all to benefit two states.

The matter came to a head in November, when HR 1402 and the separate regional dairy compact language were assembled as a bill (HR 3428) that was in turn incorporated into the catch-all appropriations legislation (HR 3194) for fiscal 2000. The Senate voted 74–24 to clear the bill Nov. 19, one day after the House voted 296–135 to adopt the conference report (H Rept 106-479).

Midwesterners delayed the final Senate vote for twenty-four hours, finally giving up a parliamentary war against the measure that accomplished little except exasperating the already frayed nerves of the chamber. The midwesterners officially lost the battle when the Senate voted 87–9 to invoke cloture, thereby limiting debate on the conference agreement. Majority Leader Trent Lott, R-Miss., said he opposed the dairy provisions but concluded they were necessary to get the omnibus appropriations package through the House. Language in the bill kept alive until Sept. 30, 2001, the Northeast Dairy Compact, despite criticism that it violates free-market principles and sets a bad precedent for other industries.

Crop Insurance

Congress in 2000 passed, and President Clinton signed, legislation (HR 2559—PL 106-224) that encouraged farmers to purchase crop insurance by having the government subsidize a greater share of the premium. The bill also included $7.1 billion in emergency spending for farmers hurt by low commodity prices—a sum that came on top of $15 billion in aid enacted since fiscal 1999.

The bill increased the government's share of insurance premiums to a range of 38 percent to 67 percent. The government previously paid 13 percent to 57 percent. The House had passed its version of the bill (H Rept 106-300, Pts. 1 and 2) in 1999.

Though the bill ostensibly was aimed at making farmers less dependent on emergency aid by making it easier to buy crop insurance, lawmakers also used the measure to pay out $5.5 billion in supplemental fiscal 2000 payments to make up for low market prices on crops such as wheat, cotton, and corn. Livestock also were covered for the first time. The remaining $1.6 billion, to be paid out in fiscal 2001, was tar-

geted at producers of specialty crops not covered by current programs. The bill also included $50 million in special interest provisions, including $14 million for a plant to make the gasoline additive ethanol in the home state of House Speaker J. Dennis Hastert, R-Ill., and special payments to tobacco growers hurt by declining sales.

BACKGROUND

The federal government entered the crop insurance business in 1938, but the federal program was relatively minor until Congress created a subsidy system in 1980. The last major revision of the crop insurance law took place in 1994 (PL 103-354).

Under the system, farmers purchase policies from private insurers and the government picks up a portion of the tab. For example, before the 2000 overhaul, the government paid 42 percent of the premium for crop insurance policies that had a 35 percent deductible; the farmer paid the rest. The bill increased the government's share to 60 percent. The government also reimbursed insurance companies for certain losses. The subsidies and administrative expenses cost the government approximately $1.5 billion per year at the time of the debate.

Major farm groups supported the overhaul, saying lower premiums would encourage more producers to participate. The groups were anxious because the $6 billion allocated in the fiscal 1999 budget agreement for crop insurance between 2001 and 2004 could have been taken away if Congress created a new budget blueprint for fiscal 2001. Groups such as the American Farm Bureau Federation believed the $6 billion could be a tempting target unless Congress quickly passed a crop insurance bill and took the issue off the table.

Farm organizations and the Clinton administration argued that increased participation in crop insurance programs would be one of the most effective ways of helping them avoid financial ruin caused by bad weather or lower prices. Farmers had balked at buying coverage because many believed the premiums were too expensive.

Sentiment toward crop insurance broke according to geographic lines, with lawmakers from the Great Plains—which suffer from a high rate of drought and severe weather—supporting increased subsidies, and those from the South and Northeast more wary. Farmers in those areas are more likely to grow such regional specialty crops as apples or cranberries, which are not covered by crop insurance. About sixty-five crops are eligible for coverage, and the bill included $55 million per year to develop new kinds of insurance plans, in an effort to win over senators and representatives from these areas.

Efforts to revamp the program appeared to be on the fast track in the House in mid-1999, with the House Agriculture Committee approving HR 2559, by voice vote, Aug. 3. The House followed, passing the measure by voice vote Sept. 29. However, the Senate did not act. Some farm state members, including Senate Agriculture Committee Chairman Richard G. Lugar, R-Ind., argued at least a portion of the bill's estimated $6 billion cost over four years should go toward helping farmers through other programs.

LEGISLATIVE ACTION

Momentum to pass a crop insurance bill resurfaced in March 2000, when a determined group of senators from the Great Plains led by Pat Roberts, R-Kan., and Bob Kerrey, D-Neb., pushed an unnumbered bill through the Senate Agriculture Committee March 2. In accepting the measure, the committee turned its back on a competing bill (S 1666) by Lugar. Instead of increasing the government's share of crop insurance premiums, Lugar's bill contained a broader risk-management initiative that provided direct payments to farmers who agreed to use any two of twelve risk-management practices each year. Among the choices were purchasing crop insurance at the current rate, diversifying crops to lessen chances that a failure of one crop would cause financial ruin, and attending a seminar on risk management. Faced with unyielding opposition, Lugar then unsuccessfully tried to mark up a hybrid bill that combined his language with the Roberts-Kerrey plan.

After sweetening the pot for northeastern farmers by $126 million, the Senate easily passed crop insurance legislation, 95–5, March 23. The added payments helped producers of specialty crops such as fruits, nuts, and nursery plants. The measure headed to a conference with the House that was largely free of snags. Congress May 25 cleared the legislation, with the House approving the measure by voice vote, and the Senate by a vote of 91–4. President Clinton signed the measure on June 22, 2000.

Agriculture Exports

Farm state Republicans joined with Democrats in 2000 to remove sanctions on food and medicine exports to Cuba, Iran, Libya, North Korea, and Sudan—in the process overriding cold war sanctions that had been placed on Cuba in 1962 by President John F. Kennedy. The action, carried out through language in the fiscal 2001 agriculture appropriations bill (HR 4461—PL 106-307), triggered fiery debate between farm interests seeking liberalized trade and lawmakers who staunchly oppose improving ties with the communist regime of Fidel Castro.

The move to lift medical and agricultural sanctions was played out during the dispute over repatriating seven-year-old Cuban shipwreck victim Elián González. Supporters of language drafted by Rep. George Nethercutt, R-Wash., said it would open commodity markets valued at $7 billion that were unnecessarily closed to American farmers. The five countries in question been branded "rogue nations" by the Department of State. However, debate quickly centered on Cuba and the pros and cons of dealing with the Castro regime, specifically whether allowing agriculture sales would free Castro from U.S. embargoes after nearly forty years. Lawmakers acknowledged the perils of dealing with trade and foreign policy through a spending bill but said it was vital to help farmers who had been hammered by low commodity prices at home. Most of the Democratic support came on humanitarian grounds. *(González, box, p. 225)*

Opposition chiefly came from House Republican leaders and Florida lawmakers representing Cuban expatriates. After months of negotiations, the sides compromised, allowing exports but barring public or private financing of Cuban agricultural purchases. The bill allowed third-party purchases, such as through a foreign bank, or barter arrangements if Cuban purchasers lacked hard currency. Final bill language, crafted by House Republicans, also codified travel restrictions, previously implemented by executive order, that prevent most Americans from visiting Cuba. Because the language was included in an annual spending bill, it amounted to a one-year travel ban that could be renewed or struck in the fiscal 2002 bill.

The issue of food sanctions also was the subject of House and Senate legislation in 1999. HR 17, passed by the House Agriculture Committee by voice vote Feb. 10, would require congressional approval of agricultural embargoes ordered by the president. Supporters said Congress should play an oversight role because American farmers were bearing a disproportionate share of the burden of U.S. foreign policy decisions. Under the bill, Congress would have 100 days to approve or disapprove of any farm export embargo. Embargoes approved by Congress would be limited to one year, and the president could end them sooner. The measure would not apply to agricultural products that were part of a total embargo on a particular country, such as Cuba. Companion legislation in the Senate (S 315) was not acted on.

CHAPTER 9

Health and Human Services

Introduction   429

Health   432

Human Services   486

Veterans Affairs   497

Health and Human Services

In many ways, health and human services were ground zero of the ideological battle between the Republican Congress and Democratic President Bill Clinton from 1997–2000. As a result, Congress considered many more bills than actually became law.

By far the most significant piece of health and human services legislation passed during Clinton's second term was the 1997 Balanced Budget Act. For quite literally a single moment during the term, Republicans and the president found it in their interest to compromise not just on balancing the federal budget but also on reshaping the financially ailing Medicare program. Also as part of that bill, Clinton was successful in convincing lawmakers to restore a portion of the cuts imposed in the 1996 welfare reform bill that he thought had gone too far. And he and a bipartisan group of senators and representatives also managed to enact, as part of what was supposed to be a bill cutting spending, a new program to help provide health insurance to up to half the nation's estimated ten million uninsured children.

In the end, it turned out Congress cut Medicare more deeply than was needed to achieve the projected savings, and lawmakers spent part of 1998, and much of 1999 and 2000, fighting over how and how much to "give back" to health care providers.

Congress in 1997 also overhauled the workings of the Food and Drug Administration, at the same time reauthorizing a popular program that employed "user fees" on drugmakers to help speed the approval of prescription drugs.

But those were the few points of agreement. On most other big-ticket issues, Congress and the president continued to disagree. President Clinton badly wanted Congress to enact a "patients' bill of rights" to protect consumers who belonged to managed health care plans; to expand coverage to uninsured adults, as well as children; and to add a prescription drug benefit to Medicare. Congress, however, could not agree on how those goals could be accomplished.

Conversely, Republican lawmakers wanted to further restrict abortion, block Oregon's first-in-the-nation assisted suicide law, and provide further modernizations to Medicare, but Clinton would not agree.

And both Clinton and the Congress wanted to address the problem of medical errors—which a federal study said were responsible for as many as 100,000 deaths annually—and the issue of privacy of medical records. But, again, no compromise could be found.

MEDICARE, MEDICAID

Medicare was a central point in the 1997 budget-balancing discussions for two reasons. First, it was, quite literally, where the money was. At a cost approaching $200 billion per year, Medicare accounted for some 12 percent of federal spending. And having more than doubled in cost since the 1980s, it was consuming an ever-growing share of federal resources. Federal costs for the joint federal-state Medicaid program were also growing rapidly—in large part because of techniques states were using to leverage more federal dollars.

The measure signed by the president in August 1997 was expected to slow Medicare spending by an estimated $112 billion over five years, and trim Medicaid spending by $7 billion over the same period. But for Medicare at least, for a variety of reasons, the cuts would go much deeper. Medicare spending increases slowed dramatically, with the program actually showing a drop in spending for fiscal year 1999. Analysts said the slowdown was due as much to the atmosphere created by dramatic new fraud-fighting efforts as to the payment reductions themselves.

REFERENCES

Discussion of health policy for the years 1945–1964 may be found in *Congress and the Nation Vol. I*, pp. 1122–1194; for the years 1965–1968, *Congress and the Nation Vol. II* pp. 665–707; for the years 1969–1972, *Congress and the Nation Vol. III*, pp. 551–580; for the years 1973–1976, *Congress and the Nation Vol. IV*, pp. 323–375; for the years 1977–1980, *Congress and the Nation Vol. V*, pp. 601–653; for the years 1981–1984, *Congress and the Nation Vol. VI*, pp. 521–556; for the years 1985–1988, *Congress and the Nation Vol. VII*, pp. 547–606; for the years 1989–1992, *Congress and the Nation Vol. VIII*, pp. 561–610; for the years 1993–1996, *Congress and the Nation Vol. IX*, pp. 513–569.

Mandatory Outlays for Medicaid and Medicare

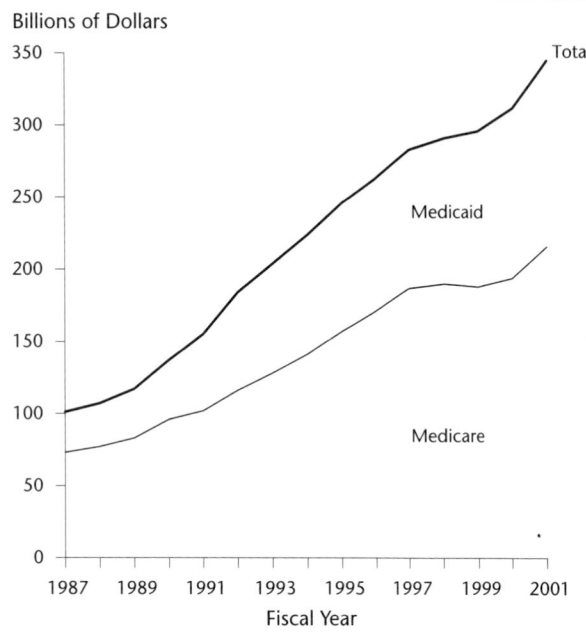

Billions of Dollars

NOTE: Data for 2001 are estimated.

SOURCE: Office of Management and Budget, *Historical Tables, Budget of the United States Government: Fiscal Year 2002* (Washington, D.C.: U.S. Government Printing Office, 2001), Table 8.5.

Secondly, the law reshaped Medicare in many ways, in anticipation of the flood of beneficiaries that would begin becoming eligible in the year 2010. The law ordered new reimbursement systems for home health agencies, nursing homes, and outpatient hospital care. It changed the system by which the program paid private managed care plans that participated in the program. And it sought to make more types of plans available to beneficiaries (previously, only health maintenance organizations, or HMOs, were available). It also sought to redistribute funding for those managed care plans to try to increase payments in rural areas where few plans had agreed to serve, and to decrease payments in urban areas, where analysts said Medicare was overpaying.

The changes, however, backfired. Instead of adding plans to the program, the number of available choices declined. The rural increases were not large enough to entice plans into areas where it remained difficult to find enough doctors and hospitals to create managed care networks, and the limits on payments to urban areas prompted plans there to either cut benefits and raise premiums for beneficiaries, or else drop out of Medicare altogether, which dozens of plans did, leaving 1.7 million beneficiaries seeking alternate arrangements over the ensuing three years.

With both displaced beneficiaries and providers complaining bitterly, Congress was forced to act. Lawmakers passed separate bills in 1998, 1999, and 2000 restoring a portion of the cuts.

Still unresolved at the end of Clinton's presidency, however, was the long-term financial viability of Medicare. The 1997 law created a bipartisan commission charged with coming up with alternatives for accommodating some 80 million baby-boomers. But Democrats and President Clinton found the commission's proposal to increase the program's reliance on private plans unacceptable. At the same time, Congress and the White House could not reach agreement on proposals to add outpatient prescription drug coverage to the program.

PATIENTS' BILL OF RIGHTS

Congress and the president were similarly unable to agree on ways to protect the rights of patients in managed care plans. By 1997 the managed care backlash among the public was in full force. During cost-cutting efforts of the late 1980s and early 1990s, millions of workers were encouraged and in some cases forced into plans that gave them many more rules and many fewer choices of providers. The media was full of "horror stories" about care delayed and denied with tragic consequences. And although much of the information was anecdotal and there was little evidence that the quality of care in managed care plans was declining, the public nevertheless demanded that elected officials deal with it.

Congress did try. The House passed a GOP-backed bill in 1998, which died in the Senate. Both the House and Senate passed bills in 1999, but they languished in conference and ultimately died. All of the bills would have guaranteed patients new rights to care, including the right to go to the nearest hospital emergency room if a "prudent layperson" would find that warranted, and the right to see specialists and to participate in clinical trials of new drugs or medical devices. But most at issue was the knotty question of lawsuits. A 1974 law, the Employee Retirement Income Security Act (ERISA), largely blocked lawsuits in state court for injuries arising from denied benefits; lawsuits in federal court were allowed, but injured parties could recover only the cost of the denied benefit, not damages for the consequences of the denial.

President Clinton, most congressional Democrats, and a significant minority of Republicans, led by a cadre of Republican physicians and other health professionals, wanted to eliminate the ERISA lawsuit "shield." They argued that no other industry was legally unaccountable for its actions. But the majority of Republicans, the insurance industry, and the business community argued that the bill would not only encourage frivolous lawsuits, it would boost the cost of insurance to the point that employers would stop providing coverage. Opponents also argued that the bill would expose employers themselves to lawsuits. In the end the lawsuit issue sank the measure.

ABORTION

Disagreement also continued to reign over the divisive abortion issue. Congress and Clinton maintained their standoff over legislation to ban a procedure called "partial birth" abortion. The 105th Congress cleared a bill but then failed to override the president's veto. And the 106th Congress never sent its bill to the president after the Supreme Court struck down a similar law in Nebraska.

Other abortion issues managed to divide not only Congress and the president but also the House and Senate. The more antiabortion House passed several bills that failed to clear the Senate, including one, the "Child Custody Protection Act," which would have made it a crime to take a minor across state lines for an abortion in contravention of the minor's home-state parental notification or consent law.

Abortion-related controversies also dogged annual spending bills. Riders that would have barred the Food and Drug Administration from approving the abortion pill RU486 and imposed parental notification requirements for teenagers seeking federally funded family planning services were dropped. But Congress did, in limited form, manage in 1999 to overcome President Clinton's resistance to the so-called "Mexico City" policy that barred U.S. aid to international family planning organizations that performed or advocated for legal abortion.

OTHER HEALTH LEGISLATION

Among other key health changes made during the 105th Congress was the enactment of a bill intended to streamline the approval of drugs and medical devices by the Food and Drug Administration. Responding to complaints from businesses regulated by the agency that it was too bureaucratic and cumbersome was a major GOP priority; Democrats went along when the bill was coupled with a popular renewal of a program that had speeded up drug approvals by imposing "user fees" on drugmakers.

At the urging of the White House, Congress also passed a bill to make it easier for those with disabilities who received federal benefits to return to work without losing their health insurance through Medicare or Medicaid. The president personally lobbied for the "Work Incentives Improvement Act," which had strong bipartisan backing.

Another bipartisan bill that became law was one to allow states to extend Medicaid coverage to women diagnosed with breast or cervical cancer through a federal screening program for the uninsured run by the Centers for Disease Control and Prevention.

HUMAN SERVICES AND WELFARE REFORM

On the human services front, Congress passed several bills restoring some of the cuts imposed in the 1996 welfare reform law. President Clinton signed that bill in August 1996 but warned at the time he would seek changes. Although the president did not object to the central change in the bill—turning the federal entitlement for welfare benefits into a time-limited state block grant, he did object to money-saving provisions that curtailed eligibility for legal immigrants for a wide array of health and social services. Bills passed by the 105th and 106th Congresses restored some of the eligibility for legal immigrants for Medicaid, Supplemental Security Income, and food stamp benefits.

Congress also passed bills to encourage the more speedy adoption of children in foster care. In 1996 a half million children were in foster care, including many who had been there two years or more. But only 27,000 of them were placed in permanent homes that year.

Congress also reauthorized the popular Women, Infants and Children (WIC) feeding program and added federal funding for after-school snacks for low-income teenagers. The bill was a sharp contrast to fights over nutrition program in the 104th Congress, when Republicans had been charged with trying to cut the school lunch program.

After several years of effort, Congress managed to reauthorize the popular Older Americans Act, which provided services ranging from legal aid to adult day care to "meals on wheels" for seniors.

VETERANS

The most significant bill addressing veterans issues was passed in 1999, when Congress voted to expand long-term health care services. The measure created a four-year plan to provide extended care services to veterans who needed it for a service-connected disability and to any veteran 70 percent disabled by a service-related injury. The bill also expanded noninstitutional care for all enrolled veterans and allowed the Department of Veterans Affairs (VA) to offset some costs by charging copayments for certain services.

In 2000 Congress voted to increase veterans education benefits and made it easier for veterans to file benefit claims.

Chronology of Action on Health

1997–1998

The first year of the 105th Congress marked a series of compromises on health issues that Congress and President Clinton had been unable to reach in the previous Congress—and would prove unable to match in the remaining three years of Clinton's presidency.

The crown jewel of cooperation was enactment of legislation to balance the federal budget—and make the most far-reaching changes to the Medicare program since its inception thirty-two years earlier. Many of the provisions had been included in legislation the Republican-led 104th Congress passed—and whose veto by Clinton helped prompt the federal government shutdown in 1995. But this time Republicans scaled back elements Democrats found most objectionable, and Democrats agreed to go along with provisions to encourage more private health plan participation in the program, in hopes of creating a viable, cost-controlling model for the future.

Medicare, Medicaid, Children's Insurance

Congress made sweeping changes to its principal federal health entitlement programs in 1997 and created a new initiative to broaden health insurance coverage for uninsured children. The legislation was the centerpiece of a massive, bipartisan budget-reconciliation bill President Clinton signed into law on Aug. 5 (HR 2015—PL 105-33). *(Budget-reconciliation bill, p. 50)*

When it passed, budget officials estimated the bill would trim Medicare spending by $112 billion over five years and reduce Medicaid spending by $7 billion. For a variety of reasons, however, Medicare spending fell much more dramatically over the next two years, and financially squeezed hospitals, nursing homes, home health agencies, managed care plans, and other providers were successful in convincing Congress in 1998, 1999, and 2000 to pass a series of measures to "give back" some of the cuts. *(1998 action, p. 443; 1999–2000 action, p. 461)*

The bill also created a $20 billion state grant program to help provide insurance to some 3.4 million children in families not poor enough to qualify for Medicaid but not wealthy enough to afford private coverage.

• **Medicare.** The Medicare changes were the most sweeping ever made to the thirty-two-year-old program, which provided health care to more than 38 million elderly and disabled Americans. In hopes of reducing federal spending, lawmakers broadened the types of private managed care plans from which Medicare beneficiaries could choose, allowing "preferred provider organizations" to join the more limited "health maintenance organizations" that had been previously available. In an effort to expand the number of managed care plans in Medicare, particularly in rural areas, the bill also allowed groups of doctors, hospitals, or other providers to create their own "provider-sponsored organizations," and allowed creation of "private fee-for-service" plans to assuage concerns of those who said the managed care plans would ration care too severely. However, payment changes made in an effort to keep spending down ended up reducing, rather than increasing, the number of managed care plans participating in the program.

The bill established a pilot program for medical savings accounts (MSAs), which allowed seniors to use tax-exempt accounts for qualified medical expenses, combined with high-deductible (up to $6,000) insurance policies. The program allowed up to 390,000 seniors to enroll, although no company had stepped forward to offer the accounts by the year 2001.

The bill established consumer protections for beneficiaries in Medicare managed care plans, including a requirement that plans provide coverage for hospital emergency department care if a "prudent layperson" would consider such care warranted. The measure also banned so-called gag clauses in managed care contracts that limited what doctors could tell patients about treatments or other physicians not covered by the patient's health plan.

• **Medicaid.** The cuts in Medicaid, the federal-state health program for the poor, were achieved primarily by reducing so-called disproportionate share payments, intended for hospitals that served large numbers of poor and uninsured patients.

State governors won wide latitude to place Medicaid patients in managed care plans, no longer needing a waiver from the federal government to do so. The measure also repealed a 1980 requirement that states pay "reasonable and adequate" rates to hospitals and nursing homes.

• **Children's health.** Congress also agreed to provide $20 billion over five years in grants to help states tackle the problem of children without health insurance. Through the State Children's Health Insurance Program, known as CHIP or S-CHIP, states could choose from several options, including expanding Medicaid or enrolling children in one of several "benchmark" plans. The initiative was financed partly by a 15-cents-per-pack increase in the federal cigarette tax.

The changes to Medicare and Medicaid and creation of CHIP were made in an unusual atmosphere of bipartisanship. The administration worked closely with congressional Republicans to broker the changes, particularly those made to Medicare. Both sides generally stuck to parameters established in the balanced-budget deal that Republicans and the White House had agreed to in May.

But although the final bill provided several short-term fixes to shore up the financially ailing Medicare program, lawmakers fell short of making the comprehensive adjustments needed to sustain Medicare's long-term financial health. The legislation did, however, create a bipartisan commission to make recommendations on how the Medicare program might handle the financial impact of the retirement of some 80 million baby-boomers beginning in the year 2010.

BACKGROUND

Despite partisan disagreements, the Medicare debate went far more smoothly than it had in 1995, when partisan bickering prevailed and President Clinton eventually vetoed the GOP package.

There were several differences in 1997. One was the size of the cuts. In 1995 Republicans sought to reduce the growth of federal spending on Medicare by $270 billion, compared with $115 billion in 1997. Both Clinton and GOP lawmakers also recognized the need to turn to Medicare for savings as part of an overall drive to get government spending under control and balance the federal budget.

Of immediate concern was improving the prospects of the Part A trust fund, which covered inpatient hospital care and was financed by a dedicated payroll tax. In 1995 the trust fund began to take in less money than it spent, and the fund's reserves were expected to run out by fiscal 2001. Clinton proposed extending the trust fund to 2007 by cutting provider payments and shifting about $50 billion in home health care costs from Part A to the program's outpatient Part B program, which was funded by a combination of beneficiary premiums and general tax revenues.

Despite the general bipartisan agreement, however, the House, Senate, and administration struggled to craft the health package. The White House generally preferred reducing payments to providers, while House Republicans wanted more of an emphasis on expanding private plan options. Senate Republicans, meanwhile, wanted even more sweeping changes, including proposals to raise from sixty-five to sixty-seven the eligibility age for Medicare, to match age increases for Social Security eligibility, and to institute, for the first time, a copayment for some home health services.

HOUSE ACTION

Two House committees—Ways and Means and Commerce—moved quickly to approve portions of the legislation. The two panels shared jurisdiction over Medicare; the Commerce Committee also oversaw Medicaid and the proposed new children's health insurance program.

The Ways and Means Health Subcommittee voted 13–0 on June 4 to approve the proposal offered by chairman William M. Thomas, R-Calif. The full Ways and Means Committee approved the same legislation on June 9 by a 36–3 vote.

In addition to seeking to trim Medicare spending by an estimated $102 billion and increase private plan options, Thomas's bill also sought to address criticism that Medicare had not focused enough on preventive care, by including expanded coverage for mammograms, Pap smears, and screening to detect prostate and colorectal cancer. To please doctors, it also included a provision to cap medical malpractice noneconomic damage awards at $250,000.

The MSA portion of the Thomas plan called for a pilot program in which up to 500,000 seniors would be allowed to put Medicare money into tax-exempt accounts that could be used to pay for qualifying "routine" medical expenses. Beneficiaries who chose the accounts would also be required to select a government-provided, high-deductible health insurance policy to cover catastrophic injuries or illnesses.

Democrats criticized the program, saying only the healthiest and wealthiest seniors would choose MSAs, while the ill and less affluent would remain in fee-for-service plans, whose costs would rise because of the loss of the lower-cost, healthy individuals. "This is the fastest and surest way to undermine the Medicare system and create new problems down the road for its financial solvency," said House Minority Leader Richard A. Gephardt, D-Mo.

Medicare beneficiaries were also asked to share in the cost of trimming the program. Under Thomas's plan, Part B premiums would rise to $67 monthly by 2002. But there would also be new protections for people who chose managed care. It proposed to outlaw "gag clauses" in contracts limiting the information doctors could share with patients about treatments or specialists not covered by the plan. The plan also included a requirement that health plans pay for care in a hospital emergency room if the patient had a condition a "prudent layperson" would consider an emergency.

Democrats tried, but largely failed, to amend the package during both subcommittee and full committee considera-

Outlays for Health

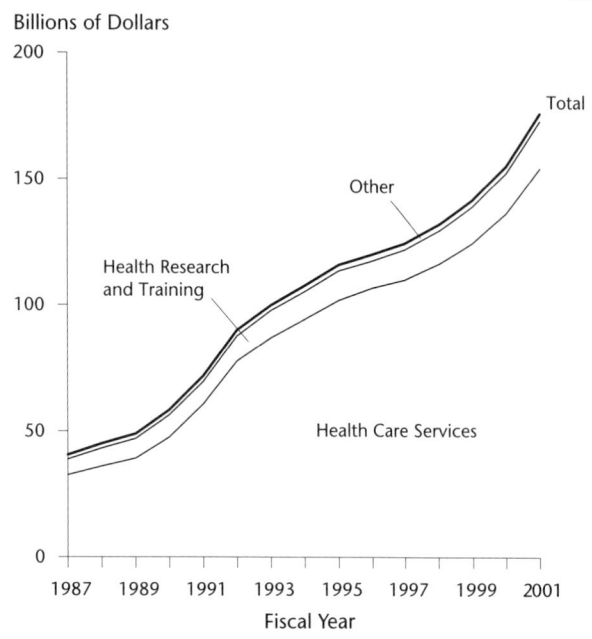

Billions of Dollars

NOTE: Data for 2001 are estimated.

SOURCE: Office of Management and Budget, *Historical Tables, Budget of the United States Government: Fiscal Year 2002* (Washington, D.C.: U.S. Government Printing Office, 2001), Table 3.2.

tion. Among provisions they wanted to strike or cut back were those on MSAs and medical malpractice.

Sounding a far less bipartisan tone, the Commerce Committee's Health and Environment Subcommittee approved its package of Medicare changes on June 10 by a vote of 15–11. The full Commerce Committee approved the proposals on June 12 on a 29–17 vote, with only two Democrats—John D. Dingell of Michigan and Ralph M. Hall of Texas—voting "yes." Democrats were just as unsuccessful as they had been in the Ways and Means Committee at stripping medical savings accounts and malpractice caps from the bill.

The Commerce package of Medicare changes resembled the package approved by Ways and Means in many ways. One important difference, however, was the way the Commerce plan proposed to pay managed care companies. It would take away, or "carve out," the portion of HMO reimbursements targeted to fund graduate medical education and help finance hospitals serving a disproportionate share of low-income and uninsured patients. The money—about $11 billion over five years—would instead be paid directly to the institutions that trained medical residents and provided charity care. The change came in response to complaints from academic medical centers that managed care plans failed to contract with them because their overhead costs were higher—a charge the managed care industry denied.

Commerce Committee Democrats and some Republicans also joined forces during the subcommittee markup to broaden the consumer protections in the legislation. Physi-

cians Tom Coburn, R-Okla., and Greg Ganske, R-Iowa, and dentist Charlie Norwood, R-Ga., fought to let physicians and patients, rather than managed care companies, have the final say on when patients should check out of the hospital. Democrats backed their efforts, and the subcommittee approved the amendment, 17–10.

The Commerce Committee also approved a Medicaid package, which proposed to reduce federal spending by $15.3 billion over five years, largely by reducing disproportionate share payments. The measure also proposed to make it easier for states to move Medicaid patients into managed care plans.

The Health and Environment Subcommittee approved the Medicaid package on June 10 by a vote of 16–12; the full committee sent it to the House floor by a 28–18 margin on June 12. Both approvals came over the objections of Democrats that the bill reneged on a promise made in the budget negotiations to use Medicaid to help low-income Medicare beneficiaries pay their required premiums. The budget agreement called for new spending of $1.5 billion over five years; the Commerce bill included only $500 million. An effort by Henry A. Waxman, D-Calif., to pay Medicare Part B premiums for seniors with incomes up to 150 percent of the federal poverty line (up from 120 percent in existing law), however, failed on a party-line vote of 19–25.

Another point of dispute between the White House and Democrats concerned the so-called Boren amendment. Named for former Sen. David L. Boren, D-Okla. (1979–1994), the amendment, originally adopted in 1980, required state Medicaid programs to pay "reasonable and adequate" rates to hospitals and nursing homes. The Commerce Committee proposed to repeal the requirement, with Republicans and President Clinton (a former governor) claiming it tied states' hands too tightly. On June 10, at the subcommittee markup, Waxman successfully led an effort to keep the requirement in place, adding it back to the bill on a vote of 15–13. It was subsequently dropped again at the full committee, however, on a vote of 28–19.

The committee voted 39–7 to approve a new $16 billion children's health insurance program.

The House acted quickly on the budget bill (HR 2015—H Rept 105-149), which was assembled from the provisions produced by Ways and Means, Commerce, and a number of other authorizing committees. The rule governing floor debate allowed no Democratic substitutes. The House passed the bill on June 25 on a 270–162 vote.

The rule on the bill had automatically made several changes, including:

• Adding $1 billion to the $500 million in the measure to help pay the Medicare premiums of low-income seniors.

• Stripping out provisions that would have allowed doctors and patients, rather than managed care companies, to decide when a patient would be discharged from the hospital. The Congressional Budget Office (CBO) had estimated that the provision, added by the Commerce Committee,

---

HEALTH LEADERSHIP

President Clinton's chosen leadership for health and human services was a tale of continuity and controversy during his eight years in office. Donna E. Shalala, the first woman to head a Big Ten school as chancellor of the University of Wisconsin at Madison, became Clinton's secretary of health and human services (HHS) in 1993 and remained with him until he left office in 2001, one of only four of the fourteen cabinet officers who stayed throughout his tenure. (Attorney General Janet Reno, Interior Secretary Bruce Babbitt, and Education Secretary Richard W. Riley were the others.)

Shalala was a surprise pick to head HHS. She was mentioned as a possible secretary of the Department of Education because of her involvement in higher education, and as secretary of the Department of Housing and Urban Development because she served as an assistant secretary under President Jimmy Carter. Shalala had little experience in health policy but had been involved in children's programs as chairman of the board of the Children's Defense Fund, a children's advocacy group, succeeding Hillary Rodham Clinton in that post. Shalala was generally well regarded during her eight years as secretary. *(Background, cabinet profiles, p. 977; Congress and the Nation Vol. IX, p. 515)*

Clinton was less successful in his choices for surgeon general of the United States. His first nomination, Dr. Joycelyn Elders, was approved by the Senate in 1993 but only after two months of acrimony. Her outspoken attitude on such matters as abortion and teenage sex got her labeled as a radical abortion rights proponent by foes who dubbed her the "condom queen." She was one of the most controversial nominees to survive Clinton's early confirmation fights. But Elders's views ultimately cost her the job of surgeon general when Clinton fired her on Dec. 9, 1994, after she made remarks on sex education with which the president disagreed. *(Congress and the Nation Vol. IX, p. 1118)*

Clinton had no better luck with his next nominee for surgeon general. The politics of abortion and the presidential race intertwined in 1995 to drag down the Feb. 2, 1995, nomination of Henry W. Foster Jr., a Nashville obstetrician/gynecologist, to succeed Elders. Foster's nomination faced opposition from antiabortion activists, as well as from several senators who were vying for the GOP presidential nomination and seeking the support of the party's conservative wing. *(Congress and the Nation Vol. IX, p. 1121)*

Clinton finally got the post filled on Feb. 10, 1998, when the Senate approved the nomination of Dr. David Satcher to be both surgeon general and assistant secretary of health in the Department of Health and Human Services. The vote was 63–35. Satcher's nomination was not without its own controversy, even though he was already serving in the administration, as head of the Centers for Disease Control and Prevention. Questions were raised about his participation in AIDS drug studies in Africa and his support for a procedure known by opponents of abortion as "partial-birth" abortion. *(Controversial nominations, p. 985)*

---

would boost federal Medicaid spending by $800 million over five years.

The House turned back a Democratic attempt to drop the children's health insurance block grant and instead expand the existing Medicaid program to supply additional coverage and permit states to establish their own programs to provide health coverage to uninsured children. The amendment, offered by Sherrod Brown, D-Ohio, was defeated on June 25 by a vote of 207–223.

SENATE ACTION

After nineteen hours spread over two days and consideration of more than sixty amendments, the Senate Finance Committee approved its package of changes on June 18 on a bipartisan vote of 20–0. Before its approval, members revised key elements of a medical savings account proposal included in the measure by chairman William V. Roth Jr., R-Del., and added a plan to link Medicare Part B deductibles to patients' incomes. The Medicaid and children's health insurance package received the same 20–0 backing.

The Medicare package—whose outlines closely tracked the House version—also included controversial provisions to increase Medicare's eligibility age from sixty-five to sixty-seven (tracking the previously approved increase for Social Security eligibility), as well as a new $5 per visit copayment for some Medicare home health services.

The committee adopted, 12–8, an amendment by John H. Chafee, R-R.I., and Robert Graham, D-Fla., that reduced the size of the proposed MSA demonstration program to 100,000 people from 500,000 in Roth's plan. Savings from the change were directed to other areas, including $300 million to cover copayments for mammograms to detect breast cancer and $400 million for a "telemedicine" project for rural areas.

The committee also accepted, 11–9, an amendment by John D. Rockefeller IV, D-W.Va., to lower the maximum deductibles allowed in the "catastrophic" insurance policies to accompany medical savings accounts, and to cap beneficiaries' out-of-pocket expenses. Both were significant departures from the House proposal.

In what had the potential to become the most significant change in Medicare since the program's inception, the Finance Committee also approved language linking some beneficiaries' insurance deductibles under Medicare Part B to their incomes. The amendment, sponsored by Chafee and Robert Kerrey, D-Neb., was approved 18–2 in a late-night vote on June 17, with Roth and Carol Moseley Braun, D-Ill., casting the dissenting votes. Under the amendment, the annual deductible of $100 for all enrollees would have risen to about $540 for people with adjusted gross incomes above $50,000 and couples with incomes above $75,000. The deductible would have climbed to a maximum of $2,160 for people with adjusted gross incomes above $100,000 and couples above $125,000.

Supporters of the amendment said it would represent a fairer way of financing Medicare, while opponents, mostly liberal Democrats, said it would undercut support for Medicare as a universal program. The White House complained that the amendment violated the budget agreement, while advocates for senior citizens said that particular program would be unworkable to administer.

Managed care companies were also unhappy with portions of the bill. Similar to the House Commerce Committee plan, the Finance Committee package proposed to "carve out" funds intended for graduate medical education and disproportionate care hospitals. In addition, the package included a "risk adjuster" that would pay plans less if they enrolled healthier individuals. Max Baucus, D-Mont., won voice vote approval to give new managed care plans a one-year reprieve from the risk-adjuster. The amendment was intended as an incentive to managed care providers to offer coverage in rural areas, where traditionally low payments had long deterred companies from setting up shop.

To further boost the appeal of managed care in rural areas, Charles E. Grassley, R-Iowa, won support of a plan to raise the $350 minimum payment per month per beneficiary for Medicare managed care providers to about $400. The amendment was approved 11–9.

Overall, however, the payment changes would hurt managed care plans, said Karen Ignagni, president of the American Association of Health Plans, the managed care industry's trade group. She said the plan "would hurt real people by increasing out-of-pocket expenses and significantly cutting the benefits of Medicare beneficiaries in HMOs." Such benefit reductions could include eliminating prescription drug and dental coverage, Ignagni said.

Similar to the initial House bill, the Senate Medicaid package included only $500 million to help low-income Medicare beneficiaries, prompting the same complaint from Clinton administration officials that the budget deal called for $1.5 billion.

As in the House, backers of a proposal to expand Medicaid rather than create a new block grant for children's health insurance were unable to change the measure in committee. The panel rejected, 9–11, a proposal by Senators Chafee and Rockefeller and backed by the Clinton administration that would have spent substantially more to expand the existing Medicaid program than on the new block grant program.

They were also unsuccessful in adding funds to the program—at least at first. Roth ruled out of order an amendment offered by Orrin G. Hatch, R-Utah, to boost funding by $20 billion by increasing the federal cigarette tax. But the day after the package was approved, the committee as part of a second reconciliation package (HR 2014) did agree to raise tobacco taxes, producing an additional $8 billion for the children's health program.

Donald L. Nickles, R-Okla., succeeded in adding "Hyde amendment"—named for Rep. Henry J. Hyde, R-Ill.—language barring use of federal children's health insurance funds for abortion, by a vote of 12–8. Similar language was included in the House bill.

Just as the Finance Committee took its time with the massive measure, the full Senate undertook an eight-hour voting marathon before passing its version of the bill (S 947) on June 25 by a vote of 73–27.

Among amendments adopted was one offered by Roth and Daniel Patrick Moynihan, D-N.Y., to require some higher-income Medicare beneficiaries to pay higher Medicare Part B premiums. The amendment, adopted by voice vote on June 24, replaced the Finance Committee provision that would have linked deductibles to income. Under existing law, beneficiaries paid premiums equal to 25 percent of the cost of the program. The amendment would have increased that share for individuals with adjusted gross incomes above $50,000 and couples above $75,000. Individuals with adjusted gross incomes above $100,000 and couples above $125,000 would have paid premiums equal to the full cost of the program. The amendment devoted the savings to boosting to $1.5 billion the amount in the bill to help low-income beneficiaries pay their premiums.

The full Senate also turned back several efforts on June 24 to strike the provisions that would have increased costs to beneficiaries. By a vote of 59–41, senators voted to table (kill) an amendment offered by Edward M. Kennedy, D-Mass., and Paul Wellstone, D-Minn., to eliminate the proposed $5 copayment for some home health services. Then the Senate voted 62–38 to bar an attempt by Kennedy to challenge the proposed increase in the eligibility age for Medicare. Lastly, the Senate by a **key vote of 70–30 (R 49–6; D 21–24),** tabled (killed) a Kennedy amendment to strike the provisions linking Part B premiums to incomes for better-off beneficiaries. *(1997 key votes, p. 865)*

In other action, the Senate:

• Adopted by voice vote an amendment by Jon L. Kyl, R-Ariz., to permit Medicare beneficiaries to "privately contract" with physicians to pay out-of-pocket for services not covered by Medicare in some cases.

• Rejected, 66–34, on a procedural motion an attempt by Barbara A. Mikulski, D-Md., to strike the section of the bill calling for repeal of the Boren amendment.

• Defeated, 39–61, a motion by Kerrey to strike the Hyde amendment antiabortion language from the children's health initiative.

• Adopted by voice vote a package of changes from Chafee and Rockefeller requiring states that expanded children's health coverage to ensure children's health benefits packages were equivalent to the services provided to children under the Federal Employees Health Benefits Program's standard Blue Cross/Blue Shield plan. The amendment also proposed to limit premiums, deductibles, and copayments for low-income families.

CONFERENCE, FINAL ACTION

After lengthy negotiations that dominated much of June and July, House and Senate conferees finally reached agreement on July 30 on the conference report to the budget-reconciliation bill (HR 2015—H Rept 105-217). The House acted first, voting 346–85 on July 30 to adopt the report. The Senate followed the next day, clearing the bill by a vote of 85–15.

In the end, conferees agreed to stave off Medicare's immediate problem—the expected depletion of the Part A trust fund by 2001—putting projected insolvency off until 2010 (originally projected as 2007). But they left unanswered the question of how to ensure Medicare's long-term financial health. Instead, Congress created a seventeen-member bipartisan commission to address Medicare's long-term structural and financial problems. The panel was to begin its deliberations in 1998. (*Medicare commission, p. 464*)

The three controversial Senate proposals—raising Medicare's eligibility age, relating income to Medicare premiums, and adding a copayment for some home health care—were dropped in the face of strong House opposition.

Medicare Changes

The bill postponed the Medicare Part A trust fund problems mainly by shifting home health care costs, the fastest growing element of Medicare spending, from Part A to Part B, the outpatient program financed by a combination of general revenues and beneficiary premiums. The shift increased Part B monthly premiums from $43.80 in 1997 to a projected $67 in 2002.

The conference report retained the original principles included in the House and Senate Medicare proposals. It gave seniors an expanded set of managed care choices that went beyond the standard HMO option already available to them. It broadened Medicare coverage to include preventive services, and it added medical savings accounts to the program, although in a more restricted way than Republicans wanted.

The bill also included two changes seniors' advocates feared would end up costing beneficiaries more. One change allowed seniors to choose an unrestricted fee-for-service plan that allowed them to select their own doctors. Such plans did not have to follow the Medicare fee schedule. Doctors and other providers could charge patients up to 115 percent of what their insurance plan paid.

The other change permitted private contracting—the ability of physicians to enter into private contracts with beneficiaries for services otherwise covered by Medicare. However, doctors who wanted to contract with patients privately had to agree to remain completely outside the Medicare program for at least two years.

Kyl, who added the original amendment allowing private contracting to the Senate bill, led a fight to delete the two-year ban, but senior groups including AARP charged that lifting the restrictions could lead to a two-tiered system of care for the elderly.

The final bill included the House version of the medical savings account plan, though the number of participants was reduced to 390,000. As in the House bill, annual deductibles as high as $6,000 were allowed for accompanying "catastrophic" insurance policies, and there was no cap on out-of-pocket expenses.

The bill increased Medicare spending by $4 billion over five years to provide a package of preventive care initiatives, including mammograms, Pap smears, screening for prostate and colorectal cancer, diabetes self-management, and the diagnosis of osteoporosis.

Protections for beneficiaries in managed care programs included a requirement that the plans provide coverage for hospital emergency department care if a "prudent layperson" would consider the symptoms to warrant such care. The measure also banned so-called gag clauses in managed care contracts that limited what doctors could tell patients about treatments or other physicians not covered by the patient's health plan.

Negotiators also agreed to permit Medicare beneficiaries who enrolled in managed care plans to continue to be able to leave those plans and return to traditional fee-for-service Medicare until the year 2002, when beneficiaries would be required to remain with a plan for a year at a time, a requirement known as "lock-in."

The final package included incentives to encourage managed care providers to set up business in rural areas, including a guaranteed minimum payment of $367 per month per beneficiary for the first year—up from as little as $223 per month in some counties. Another change called for a gradual blending of local and national reimbursement rates, which would have the effect of raising payments in lower-paid counties and holding rates down in higher-paid areas.

In addition to calling for creation of prospective payment, or fee schedule, systems for nursing homes, outpatient care, and home health care similar to the system already in place for hospitals, the bill also trimmed reimbursement for those providers as well as managed care plans. Conferees agreed to take money for teaching hospitals that had previously been included in payments to Medicare managed care companies and send those funds directly to the teaching institutions instead.

The agreement guaranteed managed care providers at least a 2 percent increase per year. It also included tough new measures to fight health fraud, which some studies in the 1990s suggested boosted health spending by as much as 10 percent. In a widely expected move, negotiators also dropped the House's controversial provision capping noneconomic damages in medical malpractice suits.

Medicaid Changes

Although the final package reduced Medicaid spending by reducing so-called disproportionate share payments, at the last minute $600 million was added back to aid states, including Texas and New York, with large numbers of low-income and uninsured residents. In an effort to appease lawmakers angry at the cuts, conferees decided that no state's reimbursement would be reduced more than 3.5 percentage points below its fiscal 1995 Medicaid funding.

Children's Health Insurance

Soon to be dubbed "CHIP" or "S-CHIP," the new state children's health insurance program was to provide $20 billion over five years in grants to states, which blended the House and Senate approaches. The program was expected to provide health care coverage for up to half the nation's estimated ten million uninsured children. To help pay for the program, the final bill incorporated the 15 cents-per-pack increase in the federal cigarette tax that had begun as part of the companion tax bill.

States could choose from several options, such as broadening their existing Medicaid coverage or enrolling uninsured children in private health plans. Benefits packages had to be equivalent to one of several benchmark plans, such as the standard Blue Cross/Blue Shield preferred provider option offered to federal workers. States also could develop their own plans as long as they were similar financially to a benchmark package and included a specific list of services. Existing children's health programs in New York, Pennsylvania, and Florida were "grandfathered" to be allowed to continue in their current form.

MAJOR PROVISIONS

As signed into law on Aug. 5, HR 2015 included major health-related provisions.

Medicare

The bill included some of the most significant alterations to Medicare, the federal health insurance program for the elderly and disabled, since the program was created in 1965. Among other things, the bill broadened the options available to seniors to include several managed care alternatives, such as preferred provider organizations (PPOs) and provider sponsored organizations (PSOs). It also allowed up to 390,000 seniors to open medical savings accounts that could be used for qualified medical expenses but had to be coupled with high-deductible health insurance plans to pay for catastrophic illnesses.

Legislators decided to leave to a commission some of the toughest decisions about Medicare: its long-term solvency, and whether to raise the eligibility age, require higher-income

beneficiaries to pay more for their care, and require a copayment on some home health care services.

Major Medicare provisions:

• **Expanded choices.** Permitted seniors to receive their health care from an expanded set of managed care options that went beyond the standard health maintenance organization (HMO) option that had been available to Medicare beneficiaries. An HMO provided health care in a geographic area with set benefits at a set fee. A primary care doctor often served as a "gatekeeper," controlling access to specialists and medical procedures.

The new "Medicare+Choice" options, as well as changes in payments to managed care providers, were expected to save $22.5 billion over five years. All Medicare+Choice enrollees would continue to pay monthly premiums ($43.50 in 1997) for Medicare Part B, which paid for doctor's visits and outpatient services, with additional out-of-pocket costs varying with the plan selected. Options included:

• **PPOs and PSOs.** Preferred provider organizations and provider-sponsored organizations could collect monthly premiums and small copayments from beneficiaries and would generally restrict enrollees to visiting doctors on a specific list.

A PSO, however, would not have a separate administrative entity. Doctors and hospitals would run the plans themselves. PSOs had to apply first to state authorities for licensing. If state officials failed to complete action on the license within ninety days, or if the application was improperly denied, the PSO could apply to the federal government for a waiver. A federal waiver would be good for thirty-six months and could not be renewed.

• **Medical savings accounts.** These plans, open to 390,000 people as a pilot program, allowed seniors to use special tax-exempt accounts for qualified medical expenses. Seniors who selected this option also had to purchase a high-deductible insurance policy (up to $6,000 deductible) to cover catastrophic illnesses.

They could spend some of the money in their accounts—up to 40 percent of the policy deductible—for purposes other than medical expenses, although such money would be included in taxable income. Seniors who withdrew more than 40 percent would face a 50 percent penalty tax. When an account holder died, the beneficiary could continue the account, but not add to it.

The demonstration program was scheduled to sunset on Dec. 31, 2002. Those with the accounts could keep them.

• **Private fee-for-service.** These private indemnity plans covered at least the same services as Medicare's fee-for-service program but did not have to abide by the same fee schedule. Premiums were not capped and doctors and other providers could charge patients up to 115 percent of what the indemnity plan paid providers. Backers of the provision said it would give Medicare beneficiaries more choice in providers.

- **Private contracting.** This option allowed physicians not in the Medicare program to enter into private contracts with beneficiaries for a particular service covered by Medicare. The doctors could charge the beneficiary more than what was allowed under Medicare's fee-for-service schedule. Physicians who participated in private contracting could not participate in the Medicare program for two years. To help protect beneficiaries, they were not allowed to enter into a contract when facing an emergency or urgent health problem. The contract the beneficiary signed had to state clearly that no Medicare claims would be submitted, nor would any supplementary insurance pick up part of the cost. The provision was effective on Jan. 1, 1998.

- **Payment rates.** Changed payment rates for providers in the Medicare+Choice program. Providers were previously paid under a system of county rates, a fixed monthly amount per beneficiary per county. Under the bill, providers were to be paid according to a system that more evenly blended local county rates with national rates over the five-year period.

Every health plan would be paid a minimum, or "floor," of $367 per month per beneficiary, starting in 1998. That amount was to be updated annually to reflect the growth in Medicare fee-for-service payments minus 0.8 percentage point in fiscal 1998 and minus 0.5 percentage point each year through fiscal 2002. Each plan would receive at least a 2 percent increase every year. Starting on Jan. 1, 2000, Medicare payments to managed care providers would reflect updated factors that affected health costs, such as demographics and patients' health history.

In a change from previous practice, payments for graduate medical education were to be "carved out" of payments to Medicare+Choice plans over the following five years. Instead, those payments would be distributed directly to teaching hospitals when they provided inpatient care to Medicare+Choice enrollees. The change was made, in part, to help teaching institutions compete for managed care patients.

- **Services covered.** Allowed managed care plans participating in Medicare to offer coverage beyond what Medicare's traditional fee-for-service plan covered. For example, they could cover prescription drugs. The plans also had to cover emergency medical treatment—including treatment for severe pain—that would be sought by a "prudent layperson," someone with an average knowledge of health or medicine. Seniors could not be rejected from managed care plans because of their health status.

- **Enrollment.** Generally required new or expanded options to be in place by Jan. 1, 1999. The secretary of the Department of Health and Human Services (HHS) was directed to conduct an education and publicity campaign in November 1998 to tell seniors about their new options in Medicare coverage and how to select them. A coordinated, open enrollment campaign was set to begin in November 1999, with health information fairs throughout the country scheduled for November of each year.

Health plans were required to disclose, in a clear, accurate, and standardized form, information such as the plan's service area, benefits offered, the number of providers participating in the plan, and out-of-network coverage provided.

- **Disenrollment.** Allowed seniors to change their Medicare options on a monthly basis through 2001. In 2002 seniors would be allowed to leave a managed care plan only during their first six months of enrollment. By 2003 that would drop to three months. Exceptions included first-time enrollees, who could leave any month during the first year, or seniors who moved out of a plan's service area.

- **50:50 rule.** Repealed as of Jan. 1, 1999, a regulation requiring that at least half of enrollees in Medicare HMOs be people who were not enrolled in Medicare or Medicaid. Until then, the HHS secretary had broad authority to waive the 50:50 rule.

- **Guaranteed Medigap renewal.** Assured that in the first year in which seniors left traditional fee-for-service plans, leaving behind their supplemental insurance known as Medigap, they could in most cases return to their same Medigap policy should they decide to drop out of a Medicare+Choice plan.

In other Medigap changes, the bill limited insurers' ability to exclude beneficiaries from coverage because of preexisting medical conditions if they enrolled during specific periods. It also permitted a new high-deductible option for Medigap insurance, with two new standard benefit plans that charged a $1,500 deductible before the policy began paying benefits.

- **Information on quality factors.** Required Medicare+Choice plans to give beneficiaries information about quality of care and specific procedures for grievances and appeals. The health plans also had to comply with specific quality assurance requirements, such as monitoring how the plans dealt with seniors suffering from acute and chronic conditions. The plans also had to disclose on request how they compensated participating physicians.

- **Antigag clause.** Prohibited Medicare+Choice plans from restricting communications between physicians (and other medical providers) and Medicare patients. Such restrictions, known as gag clauses, limited what doctors could discuss with their patients, stipulating that they could not discuss treatments or specialists not covered by the health plan. Conscience clauses exempted religious institutions and others with similar concerns from being forced to discuss treatments or services—such as abortion or family planning—that they found objectionable. Such concerns had to be made clear to beneficiaries at the time of enrollment.

Hospitals

The bill took steps to trim hospital costs that were expected to save $39.8 billion through fiscal 2002. They included changes in payment rates in Part A of Medicare, which covered hospital costs, and a widening of the prospective payment system, which governed Medicare reimbursements to most hospitals. Prospective payments were a fixed, predetermined amount paid according to the patient's diagnosis. The bill called for the prospective payment system to be broadened to outpatient, skilled nursing facilities, home health services, and rehabilitation hospitals. Hospital provisions in the bill included the following:

• **Payments update.** Kept prospective payments to hospitals flat for fiscal 1998. Payments over the following four years would be tied to the market basket index, which measured the costs of goods and services purchased by hospitals. The market basket was projected to rise by 3 percent in fiscal 1998, 3.5 percent in fiscal 1999–2001, and 3.4 percent in fiscal 2002.

Prospective payments would increase by the rise in the market basket index minus 1.9 percentage points in fiscal 1999; minus 1.8 percentage points in 2000; and minus 1.1 percentage points in fiscal 2001 and 2002.

Slightly higher payments would be given to certain hospitals, such as those that were dependent on Medicare for large amounts of revenue but did not receive "disproportionate share" payments. Such payments went to hospitals that served many of the poor and uninsured. In fiscal 1998, those hospitals would receive a payment equal to the update provided for all other hospitals plus 0.5 percentage point; it would be plus 0.3 percentage point in fiscal 1999.

• **Disproportionate share payments.** Reduced payment formula amounts for hospitals that served a disproportionate share of low-income patients by 1 percent in fiscal 1998; 2 percent in fiscal 1999; 3 percent in fiscal 2000; 4 percent in fiscal 2001; and 5 percent in fiscal 2002, with no reductions in fiscal 2003 and beyond.

Within a year of the bill's enactment, the HHS secretary was to submit a report to the House Ways and Means Committee and the Senate Finance Committee that included a formula for determining any additional disproportionate share payments to hospitals.

• **Graduate medical education payments.** Cut the indirect medical education (IME) adjustment that compensated teaching hospitals for higher costs involved in having residents treat patients and in treating patients who required special services available only in teaching hospitals.

Under prior law, the IME adjustment increased Medicare's hospital payments by about 7.7 percent for each 10 percent increase in a hospital's ratio of interns and residents to beds. The new adjustment reduced those reimbursement rates from 7.7 percent to 7 percent in fiscal 1998, 6.5 percent in fiscal 1999, 6.0 percent in fiscal 2000, and 5.5 percent in fiscal 2001 and subsequent years.

The bill also provided incentive payments to teaching hospitals to voluntarily reduce the number of medical residents in training.

• **Payment reductions to specialty hospitals.** Cut Medicare payments to five types of specialty hospitals and psychiatric and rehabilitation units in general hospitals that were exempt from the program's prospective payment system. Those facilities were to receive no update in fiscal 1998. For fiscal 1999–2002, updates would vary depending on several factors, including how much a hospital spent on each patient.

• **Capital payments.** Cut 17.8 percent from payments to hospitals covered by the prospective payment system for so-called inpatient capital, such as land and buildings, for fiscal 1998–2002. For hospitals not participating in the prospective payment system, the reduction would be 15 percent over five years.

• **New prospective payment systems.** Required the HHS secretary to establish prospective payment systems for psychiatric, rehabilitation, and long-term care hospitals and skilled nursing facilities, as well as psychiatric and rehabilitation units in general hospitals.

Physicians and Other Providers

The bill included savings of $33.6 billion over five years from reducing payments to providers. The bill:

• **Physician services.** Saved $5.3 billion over five years by reducing payments for physician services.

• **Physician practice expense.** Postponed until Jan. 1, 1999, implementation of regulations governing reimbursements for physician practice expenses, which included overhead costs. With a three-year phase-in, the new regulations would become fully effective on Jan. 1, 2002. The HHS secretary was required to report to Congress by March 1, 1998, on the data and methodology used in crafting the regulations.

• **Single conversion factor.** Established a single so-called conversion factor beginning in 1998 for Medicare reimbursements for physician services, replacing the existing three. Medicare's fee schedule assigned relative values to services reflecting three factors: a physician's time, skill, and intensity involved in performing the service; practice expenses; and malpractice costs. The schedule was also adjusted for geographic cost variations.

• **Durable medical equipment.** Eliminated scheduled payment increases for fiscal 1998 through fiscal 2002 for durable medical equipment such as wheelchairs. In addition, oxygen and oxygen equipment payments were to be cut 25 percent in fiscal 1998 and an additional 5 percent in 1999. The HHS secretary was required to overhaul reimbursement regulations governing durable medical equipment and oxygen. Payment increases for prosthetics and orthotics were limited to 1 percent a year for fiscal 1998–2002.

• **Chiropractic services.** Eliminated by Jan. 1, 2000, a requirement that Medicare recipients first receive an X-ray before seeking coverage for certain chiropractic services. In the past, Medicare did not pay for X-rays if they were performed or ordered by a chiropractor, forcing Medicare recipients to visit a doctor first. With that requirement removed, use of chiropractic services was expected to increase.

• **Ambulance services.** Maintained "reasonable cost and charge limits" for ambulance services through fiscal 1999, with annual increases equal to the Consumer Price Index minus 1 percentage point. A new payment schedule for ambulance services was to be negotiated by 2002.

- **Clinical laboratory services.** Froze fee schedule payments for clinical laboratory services from 1998 to 2002. Beginning in 1998, the cap on payment amounts was to fall to 74 percent of the median of all laboratory fee schedules nationwide.
- **Outpatient services.** Froze, then gradually reduced, the Medicare beneficiary's share of payments for outpatient services to lower the beneficiary's out-of-pocket expenses. Previously, beneficiaries paid 20 percent of what a hospital charged. Medicare paid 80 percent of the so-called reasonable and customary amount established by the government—often considerably less than what the hospital charged. In some cases, beneficiaries ended up paying much more than 20 percent of "reasonable and customary" amounts. The HHS secretary was directed to develop a prospective payment system for covered outpatient services.

Other Medicare Provisions

Other provisions in the bill:
- **Commission on the future.** Established a seventeen-member national bipartisan commission to report to Congress by March 1, 1999, on the long-term financial condition of Medicare. The panel was to identify problems that threatened the financial integrity of the Medicare Part A trust fund, which paid hospital costs, and to analyze potential solutions. The commission was required to report any findings that were approved by at least eleven commission members.
- **Commission on payments.** Created the Medicare Payment Advisory Commission to replace the Physician Payment Review Commission and the Prospective Payment Assessment Commission. The new commission was to advise Congress on Medicare payments.
- **Competitive bidding.** Required the HHS secretary to set up several competitive bidding demonstration projects that covered Part B items other than physician services. Under existing law, Medicare did not use competitive bidding to select providers. The HHS secretary was also directed to study coordinated care and case management for chronically ill seniors.
- **Fraud and abuse.** Strengthened civil and criminal penalties for Medicare fraud and abuse. Individuals convicted of three health-related crimes would be permanently excluded from the Medicare program. Those convicted of two health-related offenses would be excluded from federal health programs for ten years.

The HHS secretary could impose new civil penalties on people who contracted with an excluded provider.

Providers were required to provide surety bonds and certain identification numbers to HHS. Beneficiaries were allowed to request an itemized bill for Medicare services. Providers could seek written advisory opinions concerning whether certain physician self-referrals were prohibited under federal law.
- **Part B premiums.** Kept the monthly premiums that Medicare beneficiaries paid for Part B, which covered doctor's visits and other outpatient costs, at 25 percent of the cost of Part B. Premiums, $45.80 at the time, were slated to rise to $67 a month in fiscal 2002. Part of the increase was because of the transfer from Part A to Part B of home health benefits, whose costs were growing rapidly.
- **Home health transfer.** Gradually transferred from Part A to Part B the cost of home health visits that were not part of the first 100 visits following a beneficiary's stay in a hospital or skilled nursing facility. The transfer was to be phased in over six years, from 1998 through 2003. The increase in the Part B premium attributable to the transfer was to be phased in over seven years, beginning in 1998. The bill directed the HHS secretary to create a prospective payment system for home health agencies by Oct. 1, 1999.
- **Low-income beneficiaries.** Required the federal government, instead of states, to pay the costs associated with expanding Medicare Part B premium assistance for people with incomes at 120 percent of the federal poverty level to those at 135 percent, as well as the extra premium costs attributable to the home health transfer for people at between 135 percent and 175 percent of the poverty level. The $1.5 billion allocated applied to payments between January 1998 and December 2002.
- **Prevention initiatives.** Broadened standard Medicare coverage on Jan. 1, 1998, to include preventive services such as annual mammograms for women age forty and over, waiving the deductible, and pelvic exams and clinical breast examination every three years, with coverage authorized yearly for Pap smears and pelvic exams for women at high risk of developing cervical or vaginal cancer. Yearly coverage was also authorized for women of childbearing age who had had a positive test in any of the three preceding years.

The bill covered colorectal screening tests, diabetes screening tests, and diabetes outpatient self-management training services. As of Jan. 1, 2000, prostate cancer screening tests were to be covered for men age fifty or older. Bone mass measurement would be covered for high-risk patients, such as an estrogen-deficient woman at clinical risk for osteoporosis, as of July 1, 1998.
- **Rural initiatives.** Established a telemedicine program for patients in rural areas, with programs to be in operation by Jan. 1, 1999. Telemedicine programs allowed patients in rural areas to contact medical providers through telecommunications systems, such as televisions and computers, for diagnosis and treatment of some illnesses.

Medicaid

The changes in Medicaid, the federal-state health insurance program for the poor, gave states more flexibility to put enrollees in managed care. The bill also reduced so-called disproportionate share payments from the federal government that helped states care for the poor or uninsured.

Medicaid provisions in the bill:
- **Boren amendment.** Repealed the Boren amendment, which required state Medicaid programs to pay hospitals

and nursing homes "reasonable and adequate" rates to help the facilities cover operating costs. The amendment was named for its creator, former Oklahoma senator David Boren, who said it was needed to guard against state governments squeezing nursing home budgets, which could reduce the quality of care.

The amendment's repeal gave states more flexibility in setting provider payment levels, but it required them to do so through a public process. The bill required a study to determine how repeal of the Boren amendment affected patient access to hospitals, quality, and safety. The repeal applied to payment for items and services beginning Oct. 1, 1997.

• **Disproportionate share payments.** Reduced federal disproportionate share allotments to states by imposing freezes and making graduated proportional reductions. The legislation also placed additional caps on state disproportionate share allotments starting in fiscal 1998, with specified caps through fiscal 2002. For 2003 and beyond, allotments would be equal to the previous year's allotment plus the percentage change in the Consumer Price Index for medical services. They could not exceed 12 percent of a state's medical assistance expenditures.

• **Managed care.** Permitted governors to place Medicaid enrollees in managed care without first seeking a waiver from the federal government.

States were required to provide beneficiaries with at least two plans to choose from and to meet quality assurance standards established by the HHS secretary. States could establish a minimum enrollment period of up to one year. Plans had to cover emergency medical treatment, including severe pain. Covered services had to be specified to beneficiaries, with grievance procedures in place and penalties applied if a managed care firm did not provide required services.

Medicaid beneficiaries who were exempt from state requirements that they enroll in managed care included children with special needs and certain Medicare patients.

• **Cost-sharing.** Permitted deductibles, copayments, and other cost-sharing to be applied to Medicaid beneficiaries in managed care, but only to the same extent that states imposed cost-sharing on fee-for-service beneficiaries. Managed care providers could not withhold services even if a patient was unable to pay a cost-sharing amount. Eligible pregnant women and children under age nineteen were exempt from deductibles and cost-sharing.

A related provision gave states the option of not paying Medicare cost-sharing amounts to providers if they exceeded Medicaid reimbursement rates. Previously, states had been required to pay Medicare cost-sharing charges, which were higher than Medicaid's, for people who were beneficiaries under both Medicare and Medicaid, and for other low-income Medicare beneficiaries. The beneficiary would not be liable for payment to a managed care entity or other provider.

• **Antigag clause.** Prohibited managed care plans from restricting communications between Medicaid patients and their physicians or other medical providers. Such clauses limited what doctors could discuss with their patients, stipu-

lating they could not discuss treatments or specialists not covered by the health plan. Conscience clauses exempted religious institutions and others with similar concerns from being forced to discuss treatments or services—such as abortion or family planning—that they found objectionable.

• **Immigrants' eligibility.** Restored Medicaid eligibility for legal immigrants who entered the country by Aug. 22, 1996, and who were elderly or disabled and qualified for Supplemental Security Income (SSI) benefits, or who subsequently became disabled and then eligible for SSI.

The bill also gave states the option of guaranteeing that legal immigrant children under age nineteen who were determined to be eligible for Medicaid would continue to receive it for up to twelve months without a redetermination of eligibility. Also, states could extend Medicaid coverage to children on the basis of "presumptive" eligibility until a formal determination could be made.

• **Disabled children.** Required that states extend Medicaid coverage to disabled children who were no longer eligible for SSI disability payments under the 1996 welfare law (PL 104-193).

• **75/25 rule.** Repealed as of June 20, 1997, a rule that required at least 25 percent of enrollees in Medicaid managed care organizations to be beneficiaries who were not in Medicaid or Medicare.

• **Matching payments.** Permanently raised the matching rate—the federal share of a state's expenditures for Medicaid items and services—in several places. For example, the rate for the District of Columbia was raised from 50 percent to 70 percent. For Alaska, the federal matching rate was to increase from 50 percent to 59.8 percent over three years.

The bill also authorized $25 million a year for the following four years to reimburse the twelve states with the most legal immigrants to offset costs for emergency health services for them.

• **Disabled workers.** Permitted disabled SSI beneficiaries with incomes up to 250 percent of the federal poverty level to buy into the Medicaid program, with premiums based on a sliding scale.

• **PACE.** Permitted states to offer Programs of All-Inclusive Care for the Elderly (PACE) as an optional benefit, with states allowed to limit enrollment. PACE programs provided health and long-term care services to frail elderly people who might otherwise be institutionalized. Previously, PACE programs were limited and experimental.

• **Waste and fraud.** Created protections against Medicaid waste, fraud, and abuse, including requiring a surety bond of at least $50,000 for home health agencies and durable medical equipment suppliers. States could refuse to allow any person or entity convicted of a felony from serving as a Medicaid provider.

Children's Health

The bill provided $20 billion to expand children's health insurance coverage over five years, with the costs offset by an increase of 15 cents per pack in cigarette taxes. States were given broad flexibility in determining benefits packages. The children's health provisions:

• **Funding.** Guaranteed each state a fixed allotment based on a blend, over time, of its percentage of all children who were uninsured and its percentage of children who lived in families with incomes less than 200 percent of the poverty level. States were required to provide matching funds.

A state could participate in the program by selecting a capped block grant, expanding its Medicaid program above its existing state eligibility requirements for children's coverage or combining both approaches. Existing children's health programs in New York, Pennsylvania, and Florida could continue. States were eligible to receive federal grants as of Oct. 1, 1997.

• **Capped grants.** Required states to provide coverage equivalent to one of several benchmark packages: the federal employees Blue Cross/Blue Shield standard option coverage; any health benefits plan available to state employees; or the health maintenance organization in the state with the largest commercial enrollment.

The plans had to include, at a minimum, coverage of inpatient and outpatient hospital services, physician medical and surgical services, laboratory and X-ray services, and well-baby and well-child care, including immunizations and other services.

Additional benefits could include coverage of prescription drugs, mental health, and vision and hearing services, but coverage of these additional services had to have an actuarial value that was at least 75 percent of the value of coverage in a benchmark package. Only 10 percent of an allotment could be spent on items such as administrative costs and outreach activities. States also could seek a waiver from the HHS secretary to craft a package that departed from these requirements.

• **Medicaid expansion.** Permitted states to receive additional federal funds to expand Medicaid coverage of children beyond the Medicaid eligibility in their state as of March 31, 1997. The enhanced match would apply to costs for covering children in the expanded eligibility category until the allotment for the year was spent. After that, regular federal Medicaid matching rates would apply.

• **Expanded eligibility.** Broadened eligibility for Medicaid to permit states to serve children in families with incomes up to 200 percent of the federal poverty level, or up to 50 percentage points higher than its Medicaid eligibility level.

• **Cost-sharing.** Limited the amount of deductibles, co-insurance, or copayments that could be charged on children enrolled in programs financed with capped block grant funds. No cost-sharing could be imposed for well-baby and well-child care, including immunizations. Only "nominal" cost-sharing requirements could be levied against families whose income was at or below 150 percent of the poverty level. For families above that level, cost-sharing would be imposed on a sliding-scale basis. States could not count money raised through premiums or cost-sharing toward a matching funds requirement.

• **Abortion.** Mandated that the children's health initiative be governed by the so-called Hyde Amendment, named for its author, Rep. Henry J. Hyde, R-Ill. The amendment, a perennial appropriations rider, prohibited federal funding of abortions except in cases of rape or incest or to save the woman's life. But states could spend their own money to pay for abortions as long as the funds were not mingled with federal funds.

• **Diabetes grant program.** Created a $30 million a year grant program from fiscal 1998 through 2002 to support prevention and treatment services and research for type I diabetes in children. The legislation also established a separate grant program to support prevention, treatment, and research on diabetes in Native Americans, with $30 million a year for fiscal 1998 through 2002.

Medicare "Givebacks"

In what would prove to be the first of several rounds of "givebacks" of cuts that had been imposed on health care providers by the 1997 Balanced Budget Act (HR 2015—PL 105-33), Congress in 1998 as part of a year-end omnibus spending bill restored some $1.7 billion over five years to Medicare home health care providers. President Clinton signed the bill (HR 4328—PL 105-277) on Oct. 21.

The relief measure included both an immediate increase in Medicare payments to home health agencies and a one-year postponement of a 15 percent payment reduction that had been scheduled to take effect Oct. 1, 1999. Backers of the plan said that it would provide payment increases to 65 percent of home health providers, with none seeing a payment decrease.

Congress was moved to act when home health agencies complained that the interim payment system implemented as a placeholder while the Health Care Financing Administration tried to craft a new "prospective" payment system for home health care was not working, and payment cuts were threatening to bankrupt providers and leave beneficiaries with no way to obtain covered care.

Crafting the "fix" was not only complicated in and of itself, but Congress also had difficulty finding something to offset the new funding. Ultimately, the bill paid for the increases by lowering inflation adjustments for home health providers, and providing casino and lottery winners the option of taking their payments in a lump sum, thus increasing tax revenues for the federal government.

The home health problem was the first indication that the 1997 budget-balancing law cut payments to health care providers more deeply than Congress intended. Home health was a key target for lawmakers in the 1997 law—home health payments under Medicare had ballooned from $2.5 billion in fiscal 1989 to $18.1 billion in 1996. *(1997 Medicare legislation, p. 432)*

But the interim system devised by Medicare officials, based on 1994 payment levels, proved so stringent that by 1998, according to the National Association for Home Care,

8 percent of certified home health agencies had closed down or withdrawn from the system. Many other agencies that remained in the program stopped taking more complicated and expensive cases, leaving those most in need of care with the most difficulty finding it.

The House had passed its version of the home health care relief plan as a separate bill (HR 4567) Oct. 10 by a vote of 412–2. The House bill, which had been reported by the Ways and Means Committee (H Rept 105-773, Pt. I) on Oct. 5, called for $2 billion to be spent to increase payments to more than 70 percent of all home health agencies, with none seeing a decrease.

The Senate version, which never came to the floor for a separate vote, would have redistributed money within the current system, boosting payments to about 85 percent of the agencies but decreasing them for the rest. The Senate bill would have included a one-year delay in the 15 percent payment reduction scheduled to take effect Oct. 1, 1999, at a cost of approximately $1 billion. The House bill did not address that issue.

Food and Drug Administration Overhaul

Republicans realized a key piece of their agenda in 1997 with the enactment of legislation to overhaul and streamline the operations of the Food and Drug Administration (FDA). President Clinton signed the bill into law (S 830—PL 105-115) on Nov. 21, with a host of members looking on. With regulatory oversight of products accounting for one of every $4 spent in the U.S. marketplace, the FDA often spent years reviewing prescription drugs, medical devices, biologic products (such as blood and insulin), and foods. Republicans and some Democrats argued that the painstaking product studies had kept life-improving remedies from reaching the U.S. market as quickly as in other countries, causing hardship for consumers and threatening the economic viability of some of the nation's most successful companies.

Much of the legislation codified actions the agency had taken previously to speed drugs for life-threatening diseases to market and to make experimental drugs more available to patients with few or no other treatment options. The law also reauthorized the popular 1992 "Prescription Drug User Fee Act" (PL 102-571), known as PDUFA. That law, passed with the encouragement and cooperation of the drug industry, required drug companies to pay the FDA for the required reviews, but those funds went to hire additional reviewers, which in turn cut the review time in half. *(Congress and the Nation Vol. VIII, p. 603)*

Among the other key provisions of the law was an attempt to similarly speed up FDA review of medical devices by expanding a program to test whether outside "third parties" could safely review applications.

A similar but more strident bill introduced in the 104th Congress never made it further than committee consideration in either the House or Senate because of fights between Republicans who wanted more efforts to speed operations

and Democrats who were more concerned about maintaining safety. Republicans managed to avoid the same fate in the 105th Congress by tying the popular PDUFA reauthorization to the bill and by scaling back some of its more sweeping proposals. *(Congress and the Nation Vol. IX, p. 568)*

As signed into law, the bill's highlights included:

• **Prescription drugs.** Reauthorized the drug user fee act, increasing the fees and requiring FDA to try to speed the prereview, or development, stage for drugs, which typically was about seven years. The bill also made treatments not yet approved by FDA more available to patients with serious conditions. Previously, only patients with cancer or HIV/AIDS were eligible for such expedited help. And it established procedures to speed up review of drugs with the potential to help patients with conditions for which there were few existing treatments.

• **Medical devices.** Expanded a pilot program allowing outside groups, such as university laboratories, to evaluate medical devices submitted to the FDA for approval. Manufacturers would contract with FDA-accredited consultants to review some products that manufacturers said were "substantially equivalent" to ones already on the market, though the FDA would still make the final decisions. Risky medical products, such as those that are implanted, were exempt from such outside reviews. The bill required the FDA to focus on the intended use listed on manufacturers' labels when reviewing medical devices for which the manufacturers said a "substantial equivalent" already existed.

• **Food labeling.** Allowed food manufacturers to use health and nutrient claims made by the federal scientific agencies, such as the Centers for Disease Control and Prevention, on their packaging, unless the FDA objected.

• **Pediatric drugs.** Allowed drugmakers to gain an additional six months of patent life (known as "exclusivity") if they agreed to test drugs on children if requested to do so by the secretary of health and human services. The provision was set to sunset, or end, on Jan. 1, 2002.

BACKGROUND

The battle at its essence pitted patients and companies regulated by the FDA against consumer and some medical groups.

Republican deregulators in both chambers said Congress and the FDA had gone too far, that the process was interminable, and that patients were being made to suffer for FDA's foot-dragging. The FDA was required by statute to act within 180 days on applications to market most new drugs and devices. But that deadline was so rarely met that it had become almost irrelevant. In 1992, for example, the average approval time for a new drug was nineteen months. That dropped to fifteen months in 1996, largely because the user fee act allowed extra reviewers to be hired.

Even before drug manufacturers could apply for approval of a new product—starting the 180-day clock—they had to go through a much lengthier approval process that could last many years. It involved "preclinical testing" of the drug on animals, followed by three phases of clinical tests on humans. Manufacturers complained that after the FDA agreed to an approval process, the agency raised the bar, requiring more data or tests. As a result, Republicans said, it took an average of twelve years and $359 million to bring a new drug from the test tube to the patient. Critics said the FDA had moved beyond its role as consumer protector and instead acted as an abusive regulator that denied the public valuable, sometimes life-saving products.

But opponents of the bill, led by Edward M. Kennedy, D-Mass., warned that forcing the FDA to speed up its review of food and drug products would threaten public safety by putting potentially dangerous products on the market. They noted that although it took the FDA longer to approve products than many other nations' regulatory agencies, fewer products allowed on the market were found to be dangerous in the United States than in other nations.

In fact, the FDA—with help from Congress—had been speeding up approvals throughout the 1990s. A General Accounting Office study commissioned by Senate Labor and Human Resources Committee Chair Nancy Landon Kassebaum, R-Kan., found that review times declined 42 percent between 1987 and 1992. The FDA credited voluntary administrative changes for the decline.

By 1994 the agency was exceeding the requirements set by the 1992 user fee law. According to then-FDA Commissioner David Kessler, the law stipulated that by 1994 the agency review 55 percent of pending applications within a year of their submission; instead, FDA completed work on 96 percent of those applications. The agency also simplified the approval process for most biological products—such as vaccines and blood products—by eliminating the need to license the manufacturing facilities. And the agency cut the backlog of pending applications for medical devices, which included products ranging from tongue depressors to pacemakers.

Industry representatives said the changes cited by Kessler were welcome but inadequate. "The fact of the matter is they are way short of their statutory requirements for approvals," said Jeffrey J. Kimbell, executive director of the Medical Device Manufacturers Association.

When Republicans took control of Congress following the 1994 elections, FDA reform was high on their list of priorities. After hundreds of hours of hearings, however, action on their FDA bills stalled at the end of the 104th Congress. Members disagreed on the scope of the proposed changes, and the support of some industry groups waned.

At the start of the 105th Congress, the new chairman of the Senate Labor committee—James Jeffords, R-Vt.—tried a new tack. He suggested combining the FDA overhaul with the renewal of the popular user fee law, whose original five-year authorization was set to expire.

SENATE ACTION

The Senate Labor and Human Resources Committee approved Jeffords's bill (S 830) on June 18 by a vote of 14–4.

Half the panel's Democrats and all ten Republicans voted for it. The bill was reported (S Rept 105-43) on July 1.

The four Democrats who supported the bill—Christopher J. Dodd of Connecticut, Barbara A. Mikulski of Maryland, Paul Wellstone of Minnesota, and Patty Murray of Washington—also helped in the adoption of a handful of Republican amendments during the markup.

Kennedy, the committee's ranking Democrat, led the opposition, offering a glimpse of the problems that lay ahead for the bill. Although he said it was imperative to reauthorize the drug user fee law, which he had cosponsored, he said he would let that law die before accepting some of the bill's proposals. "Timely reauthorization is tremendously important, but it is not so important that Americans should accept the threats to public health included in this bill," he said.

The most contentious issue for the committee involved proposed changes in food labeling. The bill included a proposal to amend the 1990 Nutritional Labeling and Education Act (PL 101-535) to allow the use on food labels of health claims approved by "an authoritative scientific body of the United States government" other than the FDA—such as the Centers for Disease Control and Prevention or the National Academy of Sciences or its subdivisions. *(Congress and the Nation Vol. VIII, p. 585)*

Republicans complained that the FDA had dragged its feet in approving health claims. They cited a four-year lag from the time the Public Health Service announced the benefits of folic acid in preventing birth defects in 1992 and the time FDA approved the use of the information on food labels. But Kennedy complained that the bill—which would require the FDA to act within 120 days on such requests (up from ninety days in the original bill, thanks to committee approval of an amendment by Judd A. Gregg, R-N.H.)—would undermine the food labeling act and confuse consumers. The committee, however, rejected, 5–13, a Kennedy amendment to strike the provision.

Another Gregg amendment, to establish national uniformity for warning labels on nonprescription drugs and cosmetics, also touched off a lengthy and sometimes angry debate. Backers said standards were needed to prevent manufacturers from having to relabel products for sale in states with differing laws. Opponents said states should retain the right to provide warnings as they saw fit. The committee ultimately approved Gregg's uniformity amendment by a vote of 15–3.

Democrats also objected to a proposal in the bill to expand an FDA pilot program that farmed out reviews of low-risk medical devices such as surgical gloves or electronic thermometers. Under the bill, a manufacturer would notify the FDA that it wanted its product reviewed by an accredited outside expert. The FDA would select two organizations, and the manufacturer would contract with one for review of the device. The FDA would have the final say on the recommendations of the outside expert.

Democrats warned about potential conflicts of interest, including the possibility that outside experts would approve products in hopes of continuing a potentially lucrative business arrangement. But they were ultimately unsuccessful in amending the bill on that point. The committee rejected amendments that would have allowed the FDA to review the compensation agreements between the manufacturers and third parties and that would have exempted more sophisticated devices, such as heart valves and pacemakers, from outside review.

Despite the strong support for the bill in committee, Kennedy's concerns came back to haunt Republicans. It took two weeks of debate before the Senate passed the measure on Sept. 24 by a vote of 98–2. Kennedy and John F. "Jack" Reed, D-R.I., cast the lone nay votes.

The drawn-out debate surprised Republicans, who had spent months trying to negotiate with Kennedy and the Department of Health and Human Services (HHS), which also expressed concerns with the bill. Among the changes made in an attempt to assuage them was reserving to FDA alone the ability to review the most dangerous (called Class III) medical devices. But Kennedy and HHS Secretary Donna Shalala said the changes did not go far enough, and Shalala said she would recommend a veto unless the bill was changed.

The standardization of warning labels for cosmetics was the main sticking point. Kennedy said, among other things, that the FDA had neither the legal authority nor adequate staffing to accurately regulate cosmetics. Jeffords responded that many states did not efficiently regulate cosmetics, leaving many consumers unprotected. He also agreed to "grandfather in" existing state laws regarding the products. Kennedy, Gregg, and the Clinton administration finally forged an agreement under which states could continue to regulate cosmetics as they had been doing. But the FDA also could issue warning labels, and states could not issue their own labels in cases in which the FDA already had ruled on the need for labels.

Kennedy was less successful obtaining other changes in the bill. The Senate tabled (killed) an attempt by Kennedy and Reed to change the medical device language to allow the FDA to investigate whether a device manufacturer's claim that its product was "substantially equivalent" to a product already on the market was "false or misleading." The vote was 65–35.

The Senate also defeated, 40–59, an amendment by Richard J. Durbin, D-Ill., that would have imposed conflict of interest standards on the private parties chosen to evaluate medical devices. A second Durbin amendment, defeated 39–61, would have retained existing law requiring the FDA and medical device manufacturers to keep lists of patients who had devices implanted.

HOUSE ACTION

While the Senate was locked in debate over S 830, the House Commerce Committee's Health and Environment Subcommittee marked up three separate bills to revamp the FDA's prescription, medical device, and food safety oversight programs.

The full House Commerce Committee took up the three bills on Sept. 25 and 26, approving the drug and food labeling measure with little opposition the first day, but putting off the vote on the medical device bill until Sept. 26 to allow more time for a compromise.

The committee approved the user fee reauthorization (HR 1411) by a vote of 43–0, after adding an amendment by Frank Pallone Jr., D-N.J., requiring that the sole manufacturer of a life-sustaining, life-supporting, or preventive drug or vaccine notify the HHS secretary at least six months before it stopped making the product. HR 1411 was reported (H Rept 105-310) on Oct. 7.

The food-labeling bill (HR 2469) also won 43–0 approval. The measure proposed changing the way FDA evaluated health and nutrient claims on foods, allowing manufacturers to use health rulings by qualified scientific agencies other than the FDA on their labels. The bill included an eighteen-month deadline for FDA to act on proposed new labels. An amendment added during subcommittee consideration required the agency to act within sixty days of enactment on long-pending applications to use irradiation to kill foodborne pathogens in red meat. A change added by the full committee relieved manufacturers, in many cases, of the obligation to put packaging that came in contact with food through the same rigorous testing as food additives. HR 2469 was reported (H Rept 105-306) on Oct. 6.

After some negotiation, the panel approved the medical device bill (HR 1710) by voice vote on Sept. 26. The compromise worked out between bill sponsor Joe L. Barton, R-Texas, and Anna G. Eshoo, D-Calif., allowed the FDA to authorize reviewers to test devices for other purposes if they believed there was a reasonable chance the device would be used for a purpose other than the one listed on the label and that the nondisclosed purpose could cause harm. If the product was judged to be safe and equivalent to other products already on the market, the FDA could allow it to go to market while it was evaluating its safety for other uses. The Barton-Eshoo compromise won the approval of Kennedy and Reed, as well as of the FDA. HR 1710 was reported (H Rept 105-307) on Oct. 6.

With strong bipartisan support, the House took up a merged version of the FDA bills (HR 1411), on Oct. 7, passing it by voice vote.

The measure drew only faint criticism on the floor. Henry A. Waxman, D-Calif., reiterated concern first expressed in committee, about focusing FDA evaluations of medical devices on the manufacturer's intended use, predicting that "over the long run, we will regret that we have changed FDA law in this way." He nevertheless supported the compromise, as did the Clinton administration.

After passing HR 1411, the House inserted its text into S 830 and passed that bill by voice vote.

CONFERENCE, FINAL ACTION

Despite bipartisan predictions that resolving differences between the House and Senate bills would take little time, the conference report was not completed until Nov. 9 (H Rept 105-399).

Conservative Republicans, led by Sen. Daniel R. Coats, R-Ind., signaled that they preferred the Senate bill's controversial language on medical device reviews, the language Kennedy had fought against so vociferously. In a letter to conferees Nov. 4, Shalala reiterated that she would advise Clinton to veto the bill if it included the Senate medical device language instead of the compromise House provision.

In the end, conferees agreed to require FDA to base its evaluation on the manufacturer's intended use of the product but allowed FDA to require manufacturers to include warning labels on their products if the agency believed the device would be used in another way that could cause harm. Conferees also agreed to limit the types of medical devices that could be reviewed by third parties. In addition to banning outside review of the most dangerous, Class III devices, the bill also allowed FDA to restrict outside review of less risky, Class II devices (such as digital mammography machines) if the FDA needed clinical data to review them.

The Senate took up the conference report during a rare Sunday session Nov. 9 and adopted it by voice vote. The House cleared the bill later the same day, also by voice vote.

MAJOR PROVISIONS

As signed into law by President Clinton on Nov. 21, 1997, S 830 streamlined FDA procedures for regulating food, medical devices, and pharmaceuticals, and reauthorized the 1992 Prescription Drug User Fee Act.

Drug User Fees

Prescription drugs went through a mazelike approval process before they reached consumers. A handful of new over-the-counter drugs were also tested in this way.

When a company developed a new drug, it first conducted "preclinical testing" during which the compound was tested on animals to determine if it was safe to test on humans. If the animal tests were successful, the company developed a blueprint for clinical trials on humans, called a protocol.

The second stage was a preapproval process. With animal test results and its protocol in hand, the company contacted the FDA and filed an Investigational New Drug application. If the FDA accepted both the animal test results and the protocol, the company could begin a three-phase clinical-trial period.

During the first phase, the drug was tested on about twenty to eighty healthy volunteers to determine its safety, dosage range, and how it was absorbed, metabolized, distributed, and excreted by the body.

The second phase of the clinical trials was controlled, using about 100 to 300 volunteers afflicted with the disease targeted by the new drug, to test effectiveness and monitor side effects.

The third phase was similar but involved about 1,000 to 3,000 patients in clinics and hospitals. Doctors tried to verify effectiveness and track reactions to long-term use.

After the clinical trials were complete, the company compiled its data and presented its case to the FDA in a New Drug Application, asserting that the new product was safe and effective.

The final stage was the approval process. Although the FDA was required by law to review the application within six months, it typically took much longer. Under the 1992 law, the approval stage had decreased from an average of nineteen months to fifteen months. If the application was approved, the drug went to market and the FDA continued to monitor it.

Provisions of the new law:

• **Reauthorization.** Reauthorized the Prescription Drug User Fee Act of 1992 (PL 102-571), which expired on Oct. 1, 1997, through Oct. 1, 2002. Under the act, drug companies paid both annual fees and fees upon submission of drugs for review. The revenue was used to hire additional FDA staff.

• **New fees.** Increased user fees by about 21 percent. The 1992 law created three types of fees. Application fees were paid by most manufacturers submitting a drug or biological product, such as a vaccine, to the FDA for review. Establishment fees were paid annually by drug companies that manufactured at least one approved prescription drug but had an application pending for another drug or a supplemental use of the marketed drug. Product fees were paid annually by those with pending applications for drug approvals.

The bill increased the fee for new drug applications from $233,000 in fiscal 1997 to $250,704 in fiscal 1998 and ultimately to $258,451 in fiscal 2002. Annual establishment fees were about half that amount, while product fees were significantly less—$14,000 in fiscal 1997. The Congressional Budget Office estimated the fees would bring in $601 million over five years.

• **Trigger.** Left intact a "trigger" mechanism that suggested annual FDA appropriations levels. Recommended funding increases for the FDA would continue to be based on the lower of two inflation indicators: the Consumer Price Index or the growth in discretionary budget authority for domestic spending. The bill authorized $549 million in funding over five years.

• **Preapproval process.** Pledged, in exchange for the higher fees, a reduction in the time it took the FDA to get drugs through the preapproval process, or clinical trial phase. That process, the second of the three stages that drug companies went through when trying to move their products to market, had been taking about seven years.

Prescription Drugs

• **Pediatric studies.** Allowed the HHS secretary to ask drug companies to study how a specific product could be used to treat children. As a reward for completing the study within the secretary's time frame, the companies would be granted six additional months of patent protection. Extending patent terms benefited the company by delaying the marketing of generic replicas.

The provision addressed a question that had long plagued parents and doctors: How much of an adult medicine should be given to a child? Few companies studied the effects of their products on children, prompting many parents to mash pills or break them in half to give children an amount commensurate with their size.

Within 180 days of the law's enactment, the HHS secretary was required to develop a list of approved drugs on which additional pediatric information might be of benefit. To receive the patent extension, drug companies had to submit the product to the FDA for review by Jan. 1, 2002. The secretary could waive that deadline if the drug was on the market before enactment, if it was included in the priority list the secretary had developed, and if he or she felt it would be beneficial to have pediatric information about the drug. The secretary was required to report to Congress by Jan. 1, 2002, on the effect and adequacy of the provision.

The provision differed from a pending Clinton administration proposal to require drug manufacturers to test their products to determine proper doses for children; Clinton's plan did not include patent incentives.

• **'Fast-track' process.** Expanded the FDA's "fast-track" process to expedite reviews for all new drugs and biological products, including vaccines, intended to treat life-threatening or serious conditions. The FDA already had such policies, but they chiefly benefited AIDS and cancer patients. Manufacturers could apply to the HHS secretary to have their products considered for fast track.

The process aimed to allow certain drugs onto the market more quickly by allowing the HHS secretary to approve them if preliminary FDA assessments showed that they met certain goals (known as surrogate end points), such as reducing the amount of HIV virus in an AIDS patient's blood, but that further study was needed to determine the drug's ultimate effectiveness.

The FDA could require the manufacturer to conduct further studies and to submit proposed promotional material to the FDA at least thirty days before the material was disseminated. The agency could withdraw its approval of the product if follow-up tests indicated such action was warranted.

The HHS secretary was required to issue guidelines for the process within one year of the law's enactment and to disseminate information on the program to health care professionals and biomedical companies.

• **Clinical trials database.** Required the HHS secretary to work with the National Institutes of Health (NIH) to establish a data bank of information on clinical trials for drugs intended to treat serious or life-threatening diseases and conditions. The information was to be distributed to the public through a toll-free number and other venues.

The information provided would include a description of eligibility criteria for the trials, the trial sites, and contact information for those who wanted to enroll in the trials. If manufacturers consented, the database could also include information on the results of clinical trials.

The bill required the HHS secretary to submit within two years to the Senate Labor and Human Resources Committee and the House Commerce Committee a study on whether information about medical device trials should be included in the data bank. The FDA already ran a data bank on clinical trials relating to AIDS; the National Cancer Institute ran one relating to cancer.

• **Economic benefits.** Defined the detailed economic information that drugmakers and biological product manufacturers were allowed to share with managed care providers and others who selected drugs.

The bill required that the information made available be directly linked to the drug's main purpose. For instance, the maker of a drug used only to treat the symptoms of rheumatoid arthritis could not claim the prevention of deformities as part of the drug's economic benefits. Also, the information had to be based on "competent and reliable scientific evidence," but it no longer had to be substantiated by two adequate and well-controlled clinical trials.

The HHS secretary could request information on how the company devised the economic information.

The comptroller general of the United States, who heads the General Accounting Office, an investigative arm of Congress, was required to study the effects of this provision on health care delivery and consumers and to report to Congress no later than four years and six months after enactment.

• **Clinical investigations.** Allowed the HHS secretary to determine that a single "adequate and well-controlled" clinical trial could provide enough information for a specific new drug approval. Previous law required the FDA to base approval on "substantial evidence of effectiveness." Officials within the FDA had differed over whether that meant one trial or at least two. The new law specified that one investigation could be "substantial evidence."

The secretary was required to consult with the NIH and the drug industry to develop guidelines for including women and minorities in clinical trials.

• **Manufacturing changes.** Allowed the FDA to devise a list of minor manufacturing changes to already approved drugs, animal drugs, or biological products that did not require FDA approval. Manufacturers would have to prove that the changes did not alter the product's identity, strength, quality, purity, or potency.

For major changes, drug companies would only be able to market the newly made product after the FDA approved a supplemental drug application submitted by the company.

The FDA had allowed manufacturers to make some changes without approval, but the industry charged that the agency was not flexible enough. The law allowed more changes without FDA approval, but manufacturers were required to keep a record of changes and make it available to the FDA.

Previous regulations would stay in effect for two years or until the secretary promulgated new regulations.

• **Streamlining clinical research.** Reduced the amount of information the manufacturer was required to submit to the FDA before clinical trials could begin, allowing a trial to begin thirty days after the manufacturer submitted detailed plans and tabulations from past tests.

- **Streamlining data.** Required the HHS secretary, acting through the FDA commissioner, to compile within one year of bill enactment guidelines for when manufacturers could submit abbreviated information on clinical trials as they entered the FDA's final drug approval phase.

- **Regulatory changes.** Required the HHS secretary to issue guidelines advising FDA reviewers on the importance of "promptness, technical excellence, lack of bias and conflict of interest, and knowledge of regulatory and scientific standards" in their work.

Also, the secretary was required to meet with the maker of a drug or biological product with a pending application if the manufacturer made a "reasonable" request to discuss review of the product. Any agreement reached between the secretary and the company would have to be followed unless the manufacturer requested a change or the director of the reviewing division at the FDA certified that an essential element in determining the product's safety or efficacy was identified after testing began.

An identical procedure was established for the makers of generic drugs, which had to be found "bioequivalent" to a drug already on the market.

This section responded to industry complaints that different FDA reviewers requested varying amounts of information about products and that the review process was not uniform.

- **Scientific advisory panels.** Required the HHS secretary to create panels of experts or use existing ones to provide expertise regarding clinical trials and drug approvals. The bill changed the makeup of the panels, adding several new types of experts, including at least two people expert in the disease or condition for which the drug would be used. It set stricter statutory deadlines, including reviewing products within sixty days of when they were ready for consideration and giving the FDA ninety days after the panel's recommendation to announce the agency's decision.

- **Positron Emission Tomography.** Removed existing FDA requirements that makers of Positron Emission Tomography (PET), a class of short-lived drugs used to diagnose ailments such as cancer, submit applications to the FDA. Such drugs were usually mixed by pharmacists, who tradionally were regulated by states. The FDA had moved recently to regulate them.

Within two years of bill enactment, the HHS secretary had to establish procedures for approving PET products and outline good manufacturing processes for them. Drug manufacturers could not be required to file approval applications until at least two years after those guidelines were established.

- **Radiopharmaceuticals.** Required the HHS secretary to issue within 180 days of enactment regulations for the radiopharmaceutical industry. Final regulations had to be promulgated within eighteen months. Radiopharmaceuticals were drugs intended to diagnose or monitor a disease. They emitted nuclear particles or photons when they disintegrated.

- **Modernizing regulations.** Incorporated a Clinton administration initiative to require only one license for biological products and their manufacturing plants. Previously, each needed to be licensed separately. Biologicals were "live" products, such as vaccines, blood products, and viruses.

- **Small-scale manufacturing.** Allowed the FDA to approve new human or animal drugs made on a small-scale or pilot basis before the manufacturer upgraded to a larger facility. The policy had been in place for biological products for two years.

- **Insulin and antibiotics.** Allowed the makers of new insulin and antibiotics to claim the same extended patent protection that manufacturers of some other new drugs received. The manufacturer had to submit the new product for approval after bill enactment to qualify for the market exclusivity.

- **Labeling requirements.** Eliminated mandates that prescription drugs contain the following two statements: "Caution: Federal law prohibits dispensing without a prescription" and "Warning: May be habit forming." Henceforth, labels had to include "Rx only," unless manufacturers chose to add other warnings.

- **Pharmacy regulation.** Clarified the parameters under which "compounding" was legal and to be regulated by the states. Compounding was the practice of a licensed pharmacist or physician making a custom medicine for a patient based on a valid prescription.

However, pharmacies that compounded too many drugs that were essentially copies of a commercially available product or pharmacies that used ingredients that the FDA had pulled from the market because of safety concerns would be subject to federal regulation.

Advertising a compounded drug was prohibited under the bill, although pharmacists could advertise their ability to compound prescriptions. The measure required the FDA to consult with the U.S. Pharmacopoeia Convention and other groups to develop a list of bulk drug substances that could be used in compounding. The provision was effective one year after bill enactment.

- **Clinical pharmacology.** Authorized $3 million for each fiscal year through 2002 for the Clinical Pharmacology Training Program (PL 102-222). The program, which began in 1991, provided funding for colleges and universities that established pilot programs to train students in clinical pharmacology.

- **Sunscreens.** Required the secretary to issue regulations no later than eighteen months after bill enactment for over-the-counter products that prevented or treated sunburns. The FDA had been working on such regulations for years.

- **Postmarketing studies.** Mandated that drug manufacturers required by the FDA to conduct postmarketing studies of their product report annually to the agency on the status of those studies. The status would be printed each year in the Federal Register. The secretary was required to submit no later than Oct. 1, 2001, a report to the Senate Labor and

Human Resources Committee and the House Commerce Committee about manufacturers' compliance with the requirements and the FDA's response to any completed studies.

• **Notice of discontinuing a drug.** Required manufacturers who were the sole makers of drugs that were life-sustaining, life-supporting, or intended to prevent debilitating conditions to notify the HHS secretary at least six months before discontinuing production of the drug. The secretary could grant exceptions to the six-month period if manufacturers certified that they faced hardships in continuing production that long. Upon receiving notice, the secretary was required to distribute the information to appropriate physician and patient groups.

Medical Devices

Medical devices—ranging from simple items such as toothbrushes to more complex ones such as pacemakers and artificial heart valves—took one of two routes through the FDA approval process.

Devices employing breakthrough technologies went through the premarket approval process, which put them through a series of clinical trials to ensure that they were safe and effective for market use. The FDA approved about thirty products through this process in 1996.

Far more products—about 6,000—were approved by the generally less rigorous process known as the 510(k) process. Products eligible for this option were similar to products already on the market. To achieve FDA approval, the products had to be found to be "substantially equivalent" to a previous product.

The FDA classified medical devices into three categories based on their ability to cause harm. Class I devices, such as bandages, toothbrushes, and tongue depressors, faced less scrutiny than Class II devices—products such as hearing aids, catheters, and contact lenses. The most extensive FDA scrutiny was reserved for Class III devices—high-risk products such as artificial heart valves, heart-lung machines, and pacemakers.

Provisions of the FDA overhaul bill:

• **Manufacturing changes.** Required the secretary to establish no later than a year after bill enactment guidelines on changes manufacturers could make to devices in the clinical trial review phase without having to submit an additional application for approval. An additional application would not be required for insignificant alterations in the way the device was made or for modifications to clinical testing protocols that would not affect the validity of data or scientific outcome, or harm people taking part in the trials. Manufacturers would have to notify the FDA no later than five days after making the changes.

The provision required the HHS secretary to meet with the makers of Class III or implantable medical devices no later than thirty days after they requested a meeting to discuss clinical protocols for their product. Any agreement reached could not be changed unless the manufacturer

agreed to the change or the director of the office reviewing the device identified an additional "substantial scientific issue essential to determining the safety or effectiveness of the device involved."

• **Breakthrough devices.** Required the secretary to give priority to reviewing devices that were breakthrough technologies for which no approved alternative existed, which offered a significant advantage over existing alternatives or which would benefit patients.

• **Rare conditions.** Allowed the HHS secretary to permit doctors to use devices that had not yet been determined to be effective to treat small groups of patients for whom treatment was not generally available. The secretary had to rule within seventy-five days on an application to use the device.

Underlying law required that such devices only be used at facilities that had established committees to oversee clinical testing. The bill allowed physicians to use the device before gaining approval from an institutional review committee if the doctor believed waiting would cause the patient harm or death. The physician had to notify the committee afterward that the device was used.

• **Device standards.** Authorized the FDA to recognize all or part of the medical device performance standards developed by national or international standards-setting organizations, such as the American Association of Mechanical Instrumentation. This would allow manufacturers to declare conformity with outside groups' standards accepted by the FDA to fulfill all or part of premarket requirements. Bill sponsors believed this would speed review of new medical devices and allow manufacturers to comply with standards recognized in other countries.

• **Scope of review.** Required the HHS secretary to meet with device manufacturers to determine what type of scientific evidence would be necessary for the FDA to determine the effectiveness of a device that the manufacturer planned to submit later for premarket approval. No later than thirty days after the meeting, the secretary was required to send the manufacturer a document outlining the scientific evidence that would be required. The secretary was required to consider the "least burdensome" means of effectively evaluating the device.

The bill also required the secretary, when considering 510(k) devices, to only request information necessary to determine whether the product was substantially equivalent. That determination had to be based on the intended use as indicated on the proposed labeling submitted by the manufacturer. The secretary was required to take the "least burdensome" approach to determining whether it was equivalent.

However, if the director of the FDA unit that regulated devices determined there was a "reasonable likelihood" that the 510(k) device had other intended uses and that those uses could cause harm, the director could require the manufacturer to disclose such information to purchasers, through labels or other means. Those FDA powers would expire five years after bill enactment.

The secretary would permanently retain the power to take into account whether the originally proposed label was "false or misleading" and to keep the product off the market if he or she determined that the labeling was incorrect.

• **Changes to devices.** Maintained existing requirements that manufacturers of devices considered under the premarket approval process submit a supplemental application for the product to the FDA if they made changes that might affect its safety or efficacy.

If the changes only altered manufacturing practices, the company could submit a notice to the FDA detailing the changes. The product could be marketed thirty days after the secretary received the notice, unless the secretary requested additional information. If the secretary required the manufacturer to submit a supplemental application for product approval, the secretary had to complete the review within 135 days.

• **Repealing some reviews.** Exempted Class I medical devices from 510(k) reviews unless they were of "substantial importance" in preventing impairments or if the device posed a "potential unreasonable risk of illness or injury."

The secretary was required to publish, within sixty days of the law's enactment, a list of Class II devices that could be exempted from such review. After the list came out, the secretary could exempt additional Class II devices from review if manufacturers petitioned for it or the secretary otherwise determined a review was not needed. Products exempt from such reviews would still be subject to other FDA regulations, such as good manufacturing practice guidelines.

Because most medical devices were not entirely new products, they were categorized with similar products already on the market. For instance, a new bandage would be classified as a Class I device, similar to other bandages.

The provision also required that the secretary base a decision on classifying the 510(k) device only on information about whether it was "substantially equivalent" to a device already on the market. The secretary was prohibited from withholding a classification because of a manufacturer's previous failure to comply with unrelated provisions, including good manufacturing requirements.

• **Class III designation.** Allowed manufacturers of devices the FDA had classified as Class III, or the most risky, to appeal the decision. The FDA was required to rule on the appeal within sixty days. Under existing law, devices for which there was no substantially equivalent precedent were automatically classified as Class III.

• **Classification panels.** Allowed manufacturers to participate fully in panels convened to review classification of devices. They were to receive the same access to information, opportunity to submit data, and chance to participate in debate as the FDA.

• **Review details.** Clarified that the FDA had to review a 510(k) submission within ninety days—a time frame that was already part of the agency's guidelines. The provision also required the secretary to meet with manufacturers with device applications pending within 100 days of their request to discuss the status of the review. Before the meeting, the secretary had to provide in writing a list of any deficiencies in the application that the FDA had noticed.

• **Third-party review.** Expanded an FDA pilot program to require the secretary, no later than one year after enactment, to accredit consultants, such as university or private laboratories, to review 510(k) devices. After the reviewer submitted a written recommendation, the secretary would have thirty days to make a determination.

Certain devices were exempt from outside review: all Class III devices; Class II devices that were intended to be permanently implanted or life-sustaining or -supporting; or Class II devices which required clinical data. Exemptions based on clinical data had to be limited to 6 percent of the total number of 510(k) reports submitted to the FDA in that year.

Within 180 days of the law's enactment, the secretary was required to publish guidelines for reviewers. In addition to the technical requirements the secretary would propose, the bill specified that reviewers had to be independent of the government and of manufacturers, suppliers, and vendors of devices.

They were to be paid by the manufacturer submitting the application. The manufacturer could choose only consultants from the accredited list, though the FDA had to give the company at least two accredited choices. The secretary was required to oversee the private consultants and could withdraw their accreditation if they did not comply with health and safety laws or if they had a conflict of interest in considering the device.

This section expired five years after the secretary notified Congress that at least two consultants were accredited to review at least 60 percent of the 510(k) submissions or four years after the secretary notified Congress that he or she used third-party consultants in at least 35 percent of the reviews completed by the FDA.

The secretary was required to submit a report to the House Commerce Committee and the Senate Labor and Human Resources Committee no later than three years after enactment on whether outside consultants should be permitted to review Class II devices requiring clinical data.

The comptroller general was required to report to both committees, no later than five years after bill enactment, on the extent to which the FDA had implemented this section. At least six months before the section was to expire, the comptroller was to submit a report to the committees evaluating the program's role in helping HHS carry out its duties.

• **Postmarket surveillance.** Allowed the HHS secretary to reduce the number of Class II and III devices that manufacturers needed to track after they had been used or implanted in patients. The Safe Medical Devices Act of 1990 (PL 101-629) had required tracking every permanently implanted or life-sustaining device that could have serious adverse health effects had it failed. Tracking involved keeping a list of every patient in whom the device was implanted or on whom it had been used.

Postmarket surveillance involved follow-up studies of people involved in clinical trials of the product to ensure that the device was safe and effective for the long run. The secretary could require manufacturers to carry out such surveillance for as long as thirty-six months, unless the manufacturer agreed to do so for a longer period.

- **Distributors.** Reduced reporting requirements on distributors and some paperwork requirements for manufacturers.
- **Device data.** Allowed the secretary to use information from premarket approval reviews of a device to assist the FDA's review of subsequent devices for up to six years after the first device was approved.
- **Clinical investigations.** Clarified that one clinical trial could be sufficient to determine a device's efficacy. The FDA had debated how many were needed.

Food Labels and Claims

- **Nutrient and health claims.** Created an expedited rule-making procedure for nutrient and health claims that food manufacturers planned to include on their product's labeling. If manufacturers petitioned to use a claim and the FDA did not approve the use within 100 days, the application would be deemed denied unless the secretary and the manufacturer mutually agreed to give the FDA more time to consider it. If the FDA did not propose a regulation to authorize or deny a claim within ninety days of receiving it, it was deemed denied, unless there was mutual agreement to extend the time. The bill also required the secretary to complete final rule-making on a claim within eighteen months of proposing a regulation.
- **Expanding use of claims.** Allowed manufacturers to use on their food packaging authoritative statements published by scientific federal agencies, such as the Centers for Disease Control and Prevention (CDC) and the National Academy of Sciences.

The statements had to refer to "the relationship between a nutrient and a disease or health-related condition to which the claim refers." An example of such a statement was one the CDC issued in 1992 recommending that women of childbearing age consume 0.4 milligrams of folic acid per day to reduce the risk of birth defects. The FDA did not approve the use of such a claim on products containing folic acid until 1996.

Manufacturers intending to include health claims on their labels had to submit notice to the FDA at least 120 days before the product was marketed across state lines. Those intending to use nutrient claims, such as "contains only 5 grams of fat," were required to notify the FDA at least 120 days before the product was marketed. The FDA could block a proposed label.

- **Labeling requirements.** Allowed the secretary, when considering a nutrient claim on a product, to require that the manufacturer include labeling referring to the mandatory nutrition information elsewhere on the package. This would

be done if the food contained levels of a nutrient that would increase the risk of diet-related disease or conditions in the general public.

- **Irradiation.** Repealed requirements that packages of foods treated with irradiation—low doses of radiation that killed most pathogens—state so in type more prominent than the ingredients section. The bill also required that within sixty days of enactment the FDA rule on a New Jersey company's three-year-old petition to use irradiation to treat red meat. On Dec. 2, the FDA approved the petition.
- **Glass and ceramic ware.** Prevented the secretary from banning the use of lead- and cadmium-based enamel in the lip and rim area of glass and ceramic ware less than one year after it published its intention to do so. The secretary was also prohibited from banning it before Jan. 1, 2003, unless the use of such enamel as decoration in glass or ceramic ware not intended for children was determined to be unsafe. The FDA had authority over such products because they could be considered food additives.
- **Food contact surfaces.** Simplified the process for FDA approval of substances used in food preparation, packaging, transporting, and holding if appropriators provided $3 million for fiscal 2000 and following years, or the amount in the president's budget request, to meet the FDA's costs. Under existing law, the FDA had to subject "food contact surfaces," such as plastic packaging, to the same rigorous tests it used for food additives, such as dyes. Under the bill, the FDA would have 120 days to disapprove after a manufacturer notified the agency of its intent to use a "contact surface."

Other Provisions

- **Off-label uses.** Allowed drug and medical device manufacturers to distribute information to doctors, pharmacists, insurance officials, and state and federal officials on unapproved or unofficial uses for their FDA-approved products, if the information came from medical journals and textbooks. The FDA based its testing and approval primarily on the use for which the manufacturer intended to market the item, but many products were also used in other ways supported by new research. For example, most drugs used to treat cancer were approved for other uses.

Manufacturers planning to distribute information on such "off-label" uses had to agree to submit to the FDA a supplemental application on the additional proposed use. The FDA could require manufacturers to share contrary information or could prevent them from disseminating information on "off-label" uses if the secretary determined that the information did not comply with the law.

The changes were to take effect one year after enactment, or when the secretary issued final regulations on it. It would expire seven years after those regulations were promulgated or Sept. 30, 2006, whichever was later.

Before 1996, manufacturers were not supposed to circulate such information. The FDA had allowed limited circulation of some journal and textbook articles beginning in October 1996.

The bill also required several studies on off-label uses. The comptroller general was required to determine the section's effects on HHS resources, reporting results to the House Commerce Committee and the Senate Labor and Human Resources Committee no later than Jan. 1, 2002. The National Academy of Science's Institute of Medicine was required to study the effectiveness of the provision and the quality of information being disseminated, reporting to the two committees no later than Sept. 30, 2005.

- **Unapproved treatments.** Allowed a physician to use a drug or medical device not yet approved by the FDA to diagnose, monitor, or treat a serious disease or condition if there was no satisfactory alternative, if the FDA certified that there was sufficient evidence that the drug or device was safe and effective, if the FDA determined that use of the product would not interrupt ongoing testing, and if the manufacturer or clinical investigator told the FDA how the physician intended to use it.

The drug or medical device could be used to treat one patient or a group of patients. The FDA could immediately terminate the expanded access if the secretary determined that it no longer met the requirements. The FDA's previous policies to allow for expedited use of some drugs and devices benefited mostly cancer and AIDS patients.

- **Cosmetics and nonprescription drugs.** Allowed the FDA to create national standards, including warning label standards, for cosmetics and over-the-counter drugs, preempting state laws. But states could petition the FDA to continue using their own regulations, including warning labels, when their rules conflicted with the FDA's. In addition, states could continue requiring labels in cases in which the FDA had not acted. State regulations in place before Sept. 1, 1997, would stand, including California's Proposition 65, which required warning labels on products containing certain toxins. Previously, states had had almost exclusive regulation of cosmetics and over-the-counter drugs.

- **Expert review.** Allowed the HHS secretary to contract with outside experts to review part or all of an application or petition. The FDA would retain the right to make final decisions.

- **Supplemental reviews.** Required the HHS secretary no later than 180 days after bill enactment to publish standards to promptly review additional uses for drugs and biological products that the FDA had already approved.

- **Dispute resolution.** Required the HHS secretary to establish a procedure to allow manufacturers of drugs and medical devices to dispute scientific decisions in a product review.

- **Mission statement and reports.** Established a formal mission for the FDA stipulating that the agency aimed to "promote the public health by promptly and efficiently reviewing clinical research and taking appropriate action on the marketing of regulated products within a timely manner."

The bill also required the HHS secretary to develop a plan within one year to bring the FDA into compliance with bill provisions. The secretary had to report annually on the FDA's progress.

- **Tracking applications.** Required the HHS secretary to maintain information to monitor the progress of all applications and requests submitted to the FDA. Within one year of enactment, the secretary had to report to the House Commerce Committee and the Senate Labor and Human Resources Committee on the status of the system, its projected costs, and how it would deal with confidentiality concerns.

- **Training.** Required the FDA to provide scientific and specialized training for its employees and to provide fellowships and training to students. The latter provision also applied to other public health agencies.

- **Information on therapy.** Authorized $11 million through fiscal 2002 for a demonstration grant project to be run by the Agency for Health Care Policy and Research to study and increase awareness of new drugs, biological products, and medical devices and the risks of using them or using them in combination with another product.

- **Global agreements.** Required the HHS secretary, within 180 days of bill enactment, to release a strategy for implementing worldwide standards on good manufacturing practices for drugs, devices, and foods. The bill required the secretary to work with the Office of the U.S. Trade Representative on international biomedical and food issues. The secretary was not required to work on global agreements about dietary supplements.

- **Environmental impact.** Codified existing policy exempting manufacturers of certain categories of drugs and biological products from having to file environmental impact reports.

- **Mercury.** Required the HHS secretary within two years of enactment to compile a list and undertake a study of drugs and foods that contained intentionally introduced mercury compounds, and to issue regulations restricting the sale of products containing mercury, if the secretary found that they posed a human health risk. The secretary was required to study the health effects of using nasal sprays containing mercury.

- **Interagency cooperation.** Required the HHS secretary to foster collaboration among the FDA, the NIH, and other science-based federal agencies regarding emerging medical therapies and advances in nutrition and food science.

- **Classification of products.** Allowed manufacturers to petition the HHS secretary to determine within sixty days whether their product should be classified as a drug, a biologic, or a medical device. If the secretary failed to issue a decision in sixty days, the recommendation of the applicant would be accepted.

- **Foreign manufacturers.** Required foreign companies that made drugs or medical devices to register their U.S. agents with the HHS secretary. The secretary could contact foreign governments to determine whether the product met U.S. standards.

- **Interstate commerce.** Extended the FDA's jurisdiction over matters involving interstate commerce to include food, drugs, and cosmetics. Previously, it applied only to medical devices.

- **Disclaimers.** Specified that entities required to file reports about adverse reactions to a product were not necessarily admitting that the product malfunctioned. Such a disclaimer had already been in place for drug and medical device manufacturers. The bill extended it to the makers of foods, dietary supplements, and cosmetics.
- **Labeling.** Repealed a prohibition against using "FDA approved" on product labeling.
- **Tobacco.** Specified that nothing in the bill affected the secretary's authority to regulate tobacco products.

Patients' Rights

Congress in 1998 debated but failed to reach agreement on comprehensive legislation to give patients new rights to obtain services from their managed health care plans.

As part of a year-end budget bill in 1998 (HR 4238—PL 105-277), however, Congress did require that health plans pay for reconstructive breast surgery for women who had undergone mastectomies to treat breast cancer. The legislation was passed at the insistence of Sen. Alfonse M. D'Amato, R-N.Y., who was locked in a tough—and, ultimately, unsuccessful—reelection battle against Rep. Charles E. Schumer, D-N.Y. The measure did not include the other half of the bill D'Amato had been pushing for much of the year, which would have required plans to allow women undergoing mastectomies to have the procedure done as an inpatient if the woman and her doctor thought that appropriate.

The fight over whether to give patients more power to determine their own health care dated back at least to 1996, when Congress took its first tentative steps to address a growing consumer backlash against restrictive practices of managed care companies, particularly the practices of health maintenance organizations, or HMOs. Although dozens of bills had been introduced in the 104th Congress addressing individual managed care issues, two provisions were included in an unrelated fiscal 1997 spending bill for the Departments of Veterans Affairs and Housing and Urban Development (PL 104-204). One required that health plans cover at least forty-eight hours of hospitalization for mothers and newborns after a conventional delivery, and ninety-six hours in the hospital following a caesarean section. The other required that health plans that provided coverage for mental health care not impose lower annual or lifetime dollar limits for that care that were lower than for other medical or surgical benefits.

By 1997, it was clear that Congress wanted to pursue a more comprehensive approach, with lawmakers in both parties (many Republicans backing action were also health professionals) unveiling bills addressing a broad array of issues, from care in emergency rooms to the ability of women to see obstetricians or gynecologists without first having to get permission from their "primary care" doctor. The issue was spurred further by a commission appointed by President Clinton, which in November 1997 issued a proposed "Consumer Bill of Rights and Responsibilities." The commission was unable to reach a consensus on whether the new rights should be guaranteed by federal legislation.

But the single member of Congress most credited with putting the issue on lawmakers' agenda was second-term Rep. Charlie Norwood, R-Ga. A retired dentist, Norwood introduced the first version of his "Patient Access to Responsible Care Act," or PARCA, in 1995. In 1997 Norwood asked his friend and home-state colleague, Republican House Speaker Newt Gingrich, what it would take to get a floor vote on his bill. Gingrich—trying to brush Norwood off—said he would need to find a majority of the House, 218 members, to cosponsor the bill. That is exactly what Norwood did.

By early 1998 Republicans and business and insurance groups who opposed the bill realized they had a problem. As more and more consumers came forward with horror stories about medical care delayed or denied by managed care plans, more and more of their elected representatives vowed to pass legislation.

But opponents of the bill feared that new mandates on care would boost costs. Even worse, they said, were provisions in some of the bills that would eliminate the federal "shield" that protected health plans from most lawsuits for damages resulting from care denials. They said this would spawn billions of dollars worth of frivolous lawsuits and even prompt some employers to stop offering health insurance altogether.

With likely majorities supporting sweeping bills, Republican leaders in both the House and Senate appointed working groups to develop alternatives to the "patients' bill of rights" being pushed by Democrats, led by Rep. John D. Dingell Jr., D-Mich., in the House and Sen. Edward M. Kennedy, D-Mass., in the Senate—and endorsed by President Clinton.

Although both the House and Senate GOP groups produced bills, only the House bill, called the "Patient Protection Act" (HR 4250), ever made it to the floor.

The bill, put together with the aid of Norwood, included many of the protections originally included in PARCA, such as easier access to specialists and emergency care, as well as the right to have an outside "independent" review of health plan care denials. It also included GOP-backed health changes not directly related to managed care, such as a $250,000 cap on noneconomic damages in medical malpractice cases and various methods intended to expand health insurance by allowing small businesses to band together to buy coverage at lower rates.

But the measure was most notable for what it did not include—any new right for patients to sue their health plans. Under existing federal law, virtually anyone with employer-provided health insurance could sue if they were harmed by denial of care, but only in federal court and not for damages—they could recover only the cost of the denied care and, in some cases, attorney fees.

House Republicans, after much infighting, unveiled their bill on July 16 at a news conference held in the shadow of the emergency room of George Washington University Hospital. Rather than trying to push the measure through committee—where it would be subject to amendment by not only Democrats but by moderate Republicans—leaders instead opted to bring the bill straight to the floor, which they did on July 24.

The outcome was in doubt until the very end. Not only had a half dozen Republicans, led by Greg Ganske, R-Iowa, a plastic surgeon, joined Democrats in backing their bill, but Republicans were also stung by the endorsement of the Democrats' bill by the American Medical Association, a longtime GOP ally.

Republicans were also hurt by the Congressional Budget Office (CBO) estimate of the Democrats' bill, which said it would raise health insurance premiums by far less than business and insurance groups predicted. CBO said the bill, when fully phased in, would raise costs by about four percentage points, or about $2 per month. "Two dollars per month to guarantee that you get the care you need seems well worth the price," said Senate Minority Leader Thomas A. Daschle, D-S.D.

The GOP bill ultimately passed by a **key vote of 216–210 (R 213–12; D 3–197; I 0–1)**, after Republicans narrowly defeated the Democrats' patients' rights bill (HR 3605) by a vote of 212–217. News coverage of the measure, however, was nearly cancelled out by coverage of the Capitol shootings that resulted in the deaths of two Capitol police officers, which took place minutes after final passage. *(1998 key votes, p. 883)*

Meanwhile, Senate Republicans managed to hold off the debate entirely. Over the summer, Republican leaders offered Democrats a chance to debate the GOP bill, but with only a handful of amendments. Democrats refused, insisting on a broader debate. In October, as the session was winding down, Democrats ultimately tried to force to the floor the House-passed bill, in an effort to amend its proposal. But Republicans tabled (killed) a motion to bring up the measure on Oct. 9 by a vote of 50–47, effectively pushing the debate over to the next Congress. *(1999–2000 action, p. 466)*

Abortion

The battle between the pro–abortion-rights Clinton White House and a predominantly antiabortion Congress raged on in 1997 and 1998. And although few changes in policy were made, both sides said they scored points that would help them with voters later.

For the second Congress in a row, the top issue was a proposed ban on a procedure abortion opponents called "partial birth" abortion and abortion-rights backers called "intact dilation and extraction," or D&X. Congress cleared the bill for the second consecutive Congress in 1997, and President Clinton again vetoed it, citing the measure's lack of an exception allowing the procedure in cases in which the pregnant woman's health would be threatened. But leaders delayed an override vote until 1998 in hopes that moving the issue

closer to the 1998 elections might prompt enough senators to switch votes to enact the measure over the president's objections. That strategy ultimately proved unsuccessful; the Senate fell three votes short of the required two-thirds majority needed to override.

Abortion opponents also probed support on a new front—parental involvement in a minor's abortion decision. The House in 1998 approved a bill making it a crime to take a minor residing in a state with a parental involvement law to another state for an abortion. The measure, however, called the "Child Custody Protection Act," fell victim to a Senate filibuster and never reached the president's desk.

The House also approved, as a rider to the Agriculture Department spending bill for fiscal 1999, language that would have barred the Food and Drug Administration from approving the abortion pill RU486. The rider, however, was dropped in conference.

Abortion-rights advocates did win one battle—inserting into the fiscal 1999 spending bill for the Treasury Department and Postal Service language requiring that health plans serving federal workers include coverage of prescription contraceptives. Abortion opponents argued that some contraceptives act by causing abortions at the earliest possible moment, before a fertilized egg implants into a woman's uterus.

And the two sides continued the fight to a draw over whether or not to reinstitute the so-called Mexico City policy that barred U.S. funding for international family planning groups that performed or advocated for abortion, even if they used non-U.S. money. Although the policy, in effect from 1984 until Clinton took office in 1993, was not reinstated, funding for the international family planning program remained effectively frozen at the previous year's level as a result. *(1999–2000 action, p. 472)*

PARTIAL-BIRTH ABORTION

Although the two sides disagreed strongly over how many times the "partial-birth" procedure was used—estimates ranged from a few hundred to several thousand per year—no one ever suggested that the number was more than a tiny fraction of the million or so abortion procedures performed in the United States annually. Nevertheless, the issue dominated the abortion debate for more than four years—until the Supreme Court overturned a Nebraska law closely resembling the federal bill in June 2000. The Court found in a 5–4 decision that the law—as abortion-rights advocates and President Clinton had claimed all along—violated the landmark 1973 *Roe v. Wade* ruling legalizing abortion because it was too vague and because it lacked an exception allowing it to be used in cases threatening a woman's health as well as her life. *(Court decision, p. 717; 1999–2000 action, p. 473)*

The bill passed by the House in 1997 (HR 1122), similar to the one passed and vetoed in 1996, would have banned a procedure defined as one in which "the person performing the abortion partially vaginally delivers a living fetus before killing the fetus and completing delivery." The Senate version—the one ultimately sent to the president—included slightly different language aimed at broadening the bill's appeal. The final bill would have subjected anyone performing the procedure, except in cases in which the woman's life would be endangered if she were not to have it, to fines and up to two years in prison. Women undergoing the procedure would not have faced punishment under the bill. *(1996 action, Congress and the Nation Vol. IX, p. 563)*

Abortion opponents hoped focusing on what everyone agreed was a horrendous-sounding procedure would help draw attention to the brutality of abortion. Abortion-rights advocates were put on the defensive, and many of their allies in Congress switched sides to vote for the ban. Among the most prominent was Sen. Daniel Patrick Moynihan, D-N.Y., who likened the procedure to infanticide.

The House Judiciary Committee picked up in 1997 where it left off in 1996, approving a new version of the bill (HR 929) on March 12 by a party-line vote of 20–11. The bill was reported (H Rept 105-24) on March 14.

HR 929 was similar to the vetoed 1996 measure, but it specifically stated that the procedure could be performed to save a woman whose life was endangered by the pregnancy itself. It also contained provisions to prevent a prospective father who had abused or abandoned the woman from suing the person performing the abortion. The committee rejected several Democratic amendments that would have banned the procedure only after viability, and to add an exception allowing its use to protect the woman's health.

The House passed the bill on March 20 by a **key vote of 295–136 (R 218–8; D 77–127; I 0–1)**—well more than required for an override—after leaders chose to substitute for the committee's version of the measure a new bill (HR 1122) identical to the one vetoed in 1996. Antiabortion leaders thought the old bill had gained momentum, in part because of admissions by a prominent abortion-rights supporter, Ron Fitzsimmons of the National Abortion Federation, that he had lied the year before when he claimed the procedure was used only in rare circumstances. Indeed, three members switched their votes from the previous year to support the bill—Christopher Shays, R-Conn., Rodney Frelinghuysen, R-N.J., and Sue W. Kelly, R-N.Y. *(1997 key votes, p. 865)*

Also, because HR 1122 was identical to the version that had been introduced in the Senate (S 6), substituting it for the committee bill was expected to speed things up by eliminating the need for a House-Senate conference.

But that proved wrong, when the Senate altered the measure. After negotiations with the American Medical Association, which had never before endorsed an abortion-procedure ban, Senate sponsor Rick Santorum, R-Pa., made what both sides termed "cosmetic" changes to the bill that were nevertheless enough to win the backing of the most influential doctors' group on the eve of the Senate vote. Santorum's changes further clarified what the bill would ban as "deliberately and intentionally deliver[ing] into the vagina a living fetus, or a substantial portion thereof, for the purpose of

performing a procedure the physician knows will kill the fetus, and kills the fetus." AMA officials said that would effectively protect a common second-term abortion procedure called "dilation and evacuation," although other groups, including the American College of Obstetricians and Gynecologists, disagreed. ACOG continued to oppose the bill. Santorum also added language shielding physicians from prosecution if they used the procedure in an emergency to save a woman's life.

The Senate passed the revised version on May 20 by a **key vote of 64–36 (R 51–4; D 13–32).** That was ten votes more than the margin by which the bill passed originally in 1995 but still three short of the margin needed to override President Clinton's promised veto. Changing their votes to support the measure were Minority Leader Thomas A. Daschle, D-S.D., Robert C. Byrd, D-W.Va., and Ernest F. Hollings, D-S.C. Sens. Patrick J. Leahy, D-Vt., and Arlen Specter, R-Pa., also voted against the measure in 1995 but voted to override Clinton's veto in 1996. The remaining additional votes for the measure came from Republicans elected in 1996. *(1997 key votes, p. 865)*

Before passing the measure, the Senate turned back an attempt by Daschle to instead outlaw all abortions after a fetus was viable, except in cases where the woman's life was in danger or to prevent "grievous injury" to her physical health. But backers of the bill said the measure would not have banned many abortions, because the procedure in question was most frequently used prior to viability, and because, they said, a "health" exception could be so broadly interpreted as to allow virtually every case to fit within it. The amendment failed on May 15 by a vote of 36–64.

A similar amendment offered by California Democrats Barbara Boxer and Dianne Feinstein, which would have banned postviability abortions but with a still broader exception for a woman's health, failed that same day by a vote of 28–72.

The House easily accepted the Senate changes, clearing the revised bill 296–132 on Oct. 8. Clinton vetoed it on Oct. 10, saying he was objecting for the same reason he had in 1996—namely that the bill did not allow an exception for the health of the woman. The House voted to override the veto on July 23, 1998, by the identical margin by which it had cleared eight months earlier—296–132. That included the backing of Minority Leader Richard A. Gephardt, D-Mo.

But votes in the Senate had not changed, either, and on Sept. 18, a **key vote of 64–36 (R 51–4; D 13–32)**—the same tally as the previous year—left the measure short of the two-thirds needed to override. *(1998 key votes, p. 883)*

PARENTAL NOTIFICATION

The "Child Custody Protection Act," which passed the House but failed in the Senate in 1998, would have made it a crime for a person to accompany a minor across state lines for an abortion in contravention of the girl's home state parental involvement law. Violators could have been subject to fines of up to $100,000 and a year in prison. Critics of the measure pointed out that it even made it illegal for a parent to accompany the girl if the home state law required notification or consent of both parents (which several state laws did).

The measure was inspired by a case in Pennsylvania, where a woman named Rosa Hartford was convicted of violating that state's "Interference with Custody of a Minor Act" by taking her eighteen-year-old son's thirteen-year-old girlfriend across state lines to Binghamton, New York, for an abortion. Pennsylvania law required at least one parent's consent or a judge's permission for a minor to have an abortion; New York had no parental involvement law.

The measure was intended to be abortion opponents' follow-on to the "partial birth" abortion ban, because, similar to abortions performed late in pregnancy, parental involvement in a minor's abortion decisions had long been an area of overwhelming public support.

Proponents of the measure insisted that regulating interstate activities was the federal government's natural role and pointed to Yellow Pages ads for clinics proclaiming "no parental consent required" in states without parental involvement laws. They said parents had the right to counsel their children and that leaving them out of abortion decisions could endanger teenagers' health because they knew medical information about their children that would be important for doctors to know. Opponents said that the act, however, would endanger, not protect, minors facing unintended pregnancies. The bill, opponents complained, would force young women to travel alone to another state or go much farther away from home in their own state—causing unnecessary delays that increased the risks to their health.

In spite of strong opposition, however, the measure did enjoy significant support. Even President Clinton said he would sign it if "it is carefully targeted at punishing nonrelatives who transport minors across state lines for the purpose of avoiding parental involvement requirements."

The House Judiciary Committee approved the bill (HR 3682) on June 23, by a party-line vote of 17–10. The Subcommittee on the Constitution had approved the measure on June 11 by a vote of 7–2, also along party lines. The bill was reported (H Rept 105-605) on June 25.

Democrats tried repeatedly but failed to amend the bill in both subcommittee and full committee. Proposed amendments included ones to exempt ministers, rabbis, and other religious leaders, and to exempt family members. Bill sponsor Charles T. Canady, R-Fla., did, however, win voice vote approval of an amendment barring prosecution of a parent for taking a child across state lines for an abortion, even if both parents did not agree to the procedure.

The House passed the measure, 276–150, on July 15—eight votes short of the total needed to override a promised veto from President Clinton. The administration said the president could sign the bill if changes were made—but the House rejected the changes by adopting a rule, 247–173, barring amendments including those exempting grandparents

and shielding from liability those who provided information, counseling, referral, or medical services.

The Senate Judiciary Committee a day later approved, 10–6, and reported a substitute bill that conformed to the House-passed bill (S 1645—S Rept 105-268). As in the House, Senate committee members rejected Democrats' attempts to exempt family members from prosecution.

Plans to send the bill to Clinton for what abortion opponents hoped would prove an unpopular veto went awry, however, when Senate backers of the measure proved unable to break a filibuster as the session drew to a close. After the Senate failed to invoke cloture on S 1645 on Sept. 22 by a vote of 54–45—six short of the sixty needed—Republican leaders pulled the bill. Ironically, the measure got caught up in the ongoing fight over the "patients' bill of rights," which Democrats had wanted to add to S 1645 as an amendment. When it was clear that Republicans would block most amendments, Democrats, including some who supported the underlying bill, held together to block further debate. *(1999 action, p. 472)*

MEXICO CITY POLICY

The battle over whether to bar U.S. aid to international family planning organizations that used non-U.S. funds to perform or advocate for abortion rights continued unabated in 1997 and 1998. By the end of the 105th Congress, however, things were not much changed from the 104th.

From the moment Republicans took over Congress in 1995, reinstating the "Mexico City" policy, named for the United Nations conference where the policy was unveiled in 1984, was a top priority. President Clinton rescinded the policy, originally implemented by executive order by President Ronald Reagan, on his second full day in office in 1993.

But although the House had voted repeatedly for the policy, the Senate refused to go along. The standoff produced a complicated compromise at the end of 1996 to fund the foreign operations spending bill for fiscal 1997. Congress provided $385 million for the international family planning program, but none of the money would be available until July 1, 1997 (more than halfway through the year) and would then be "metered out" at a rate of 8 percent per month. The measure, however, also stipulated that the funds could be made available as early as March 1, 1997, if the president issued a finding that the lack of funding was having "a negative impact on the proper functions of the population planning program" and if both houses of Congress voted to concur with that finding. *(Congress and the Nation Vol. IX, p. 564)*

President Clinton issued the finding on Feb. 1, 1997, and, much to the surprise of advocates of the Mexico City policy, both the House and Senate voted to release the funds. The House on Feb. 13 voted 220–209 to approve the bill (H J Res 36) to release the funds, and the Senate followed suit on Feb. 25, clearing the resolution by a vote of 53–46. Clinton signed the measure into law on Feb. 28 (PL 105-3). *(Family planning funds, p. 194)*

The issue reemerged later in 1997, during work on the fiscal 1998 foreign operations bill (HR 2159). Again, the House voted to reinstate the policy; the Senate did not. In the end, House Republicans agreed to drop the language to reinstate the policy, and to maintain program funding at $385 million. But they made President Clinton pay a steep price—also dropped from the final measure were provisions the Clinton administration badly wanted to pay back dues to the United Nations and provide additional credit for the International Monetary Fund. Clinton signed the bill into law on Nov. 26 (PL 105-118). *(1998 foreign aid, p. 183; 1999 action, p. 473)*

Despite the vows of Mexico City policy proponents in Congress not to leave in 1998 without getting their policy reinstated, the final result was much the same. But this time there was a different twist. As approved by the House on Sept. 17, the foreign operations spending bill (HR 4569) would have permitted funding for the minority of groups that actually performed abortions, although in that case funding would have been reduced from $385 million to $356 million. The measure, however, would still have barred any organization receiving U.S. funds from advocating, lobbying, or in any way trying to influence the abortion laws of any country in which it operated. But the administration didn't bite at what was intended as a compromise. Ultimately included in a year-end omnibus bill (HR 4328—PL 105-277) the program again received $385 million, again "metered out" at 8 percent per month. And the administration did finally get its funding for the IMF. But no funds were paid back to the United Nations. Instead, the U.N. repayment plan was included in a separate State Department authorization (HR 1757), but Clinton vetoed that bill on Oct. 21 because it also included the Mexico City language. *(1999 foreign aid, p. 186; State Department authorization, p. 189)*

CONTRACEPTIVE COVERAGE

The lone legislative victory for abortion-rights backers in the 105th Congress came in the form of a requirement included in the fiscal 1999 omnibus spending bill (HR 4328—PL 105-277) that health plans that cover prescription drugs also cover prescription contraceptives. But it had not been easily achieved. The language had been added to the fiscal 1999 spending bill for the Department of Treasury, the Postal Service, and other government agencies (HR 4104) at the House Appropriations Committee markup by a vote of 28–26 on June 17. But abortion opponents—led by Christopher H. Smith, R-N.J.—initially struck the language on the floor, complaining that some forms of contraception actually induce abortion by blocking the ability of a fertilized egg to implant in a woman's uterus.

Democrats, however, outmaneuvered Smith and his allies, scoring a surprising victory when they came to the floor with a slightly reworded version of the language that had been added in committee by Nita M. Lowey, D-N.Y. The amendment would have barred federal funds from being used to renew contracts with health plans for federal workers that provided coverage for prescription drugs but not for contraceptives. It exempted five health plans with a religious orientation. The amendment was in line with House rules, which allowed for limitations on how money could be spent. It was adopted by a **key vote of 224–198 (R 48–177; D 175–21; I 1–0)** on July 16. *(1998 key votes, p. 883)*

Despite the loss, Smith was not ready to give up. He countered with an amendment seeking to bar the use of contraceptives that chemically induced abortion. But the House rejected that proposal, 198–222.

Although the House and Senate had approved identical language, Republican leaders decided to drop it after the conference report (H Rept 105-760) was initially blocked in the House on Oct. 1. That move helped the bill through the House on Oct. 7 but hurt it in the Senate, where amendment sponsor Harry Reid, D-Nev., blocked the bill.

The bill ultimately was rolled into the omnibus spending bill (HR 4328), with the contraceptive language restored, along with a conscience clause permitting religious-based health plans, as well as individual practitioners with moral or religious objections to some or all of the methods, to opt out.

HYDE AMENDMENT EXPANSION

In 1997 antiabortion forces decided it was time for an "update" of the language that for two decades had banned federal funding for most abortions except when the pregnancy endangered the pregnant woman's life. They thought the so-called "Hyde amendment," named for the House's leading abortion foe, Henry J. Hyde, R-Ill., needed to take into account the fact that a significant portion of Medicaid recipients—those most directly affected by the language—were being moved into managed care plans. Worried that plans could offer abortion services without technically running afoul of the funding ban, Hyde wrote language to add that no federal funds could be used to pay premiums for plans that provided abortions.

Abortion rights forces, however, complained that Hyde's language was so broad it could end up forcing managed care plans to drop abortion coverage for their non-Medicaid enrollees. Hyde and Lowey negotiated the issue for weeks, finally coming up with a compromise. The new language also refined the "life of the woman" exception, noting that abortions could be funded only if the endangerment was "a physical disorder, physical injury, or physical illness, including a life-endangering physical condition caused by or arising from the pregnancy itself."

The House added the expanded language during floor consideration of the fiscal 1998 spending bill for the Departments of Health and Human Services, Labor, and Education (HR 2264—PL 105-78), by a vote of 270–150 on Sept. 11. The Senate gave voice vote approval the same day to a similar amendment by John Ashcroft, R-Mo.

Abortion foes in 1997 also sought to write the Hyde language—which had to be repassed in each year's spending bill—into permanent law as part of the Balanced Budget Act (HR 2015—PL 105-33). But they had mixed success. That measure did permanently bar federal funding for abortion except in cases of rape or incest or to save the life of the woman through the newly created Children's Health Insurance Program. But other language that would have had the effect of making permanent the language that barred most abortions through the Medicaid program was dropped.

Hemophiliacs with HIV

Congress in 1998 approved legislation (HR 1023—PL 105-369) creating a $750 million trust fund to provide "compassionate payments" of $100,000 each to people with hemophilia who contracted HIV from contaminated blood products, or to the families of those who had already died of it.

Congress cleared the "Ricky Ray Hemophilia Relief Fund Act" on Oct. 21, 1998, after a protracted debate over whether the trust fund should compensate only those with hemophilia or all those who contracted the deadly virus from tainted blood. President Clinton signed the bill into law on Nov. 12.

The measure was the culmination of five years of lobbying by the hemophilia community, an estimated half of whose members became HIV-positive from using contaminated "clotting factor" before widespread testing for the virus was in use. Unlike the blood used in regular blood transfusions, the clotting factor was derived from thousands of donors, substantially increasing the risk of recipients' contracting HIV.

The bill was named for a Florida teenager who was the oldest of three hemophiliac brothers who contracted HIV and whose family was shunned by their community in the mid-1980s, before AIDS and its modes of transmission were well understood. Ricky Ray died in 1992, at age fifteen.

In 1997 manufacturers of the clotting factor reached a settlement with some 7,200 hemophiliacs or their survivors, agreeing to pay them $100,000 each to compensate for alleged delays in testing blood products. But because HIV-positive hemophiliacs were already spending $100,000 a year on clotting factor alone and up to $50,000 more on AIDS-related treatment, Congress decided to match the private settlement funds.

The House Judiciary Committee reported the bill (H Rept 105-465, Pt. I) on March 25, 1998, and the Ways and Means Committee reported it (H Rept 105-465, Pt. II) on May 7. The full House passed it by voice vote on May 19. The Senate Labor and Human Resources Committee reported it (no written report) on Oct. 7 and the Senate passed it by voice vote on Oct. 21.

Final action on the bill was delayed when several senators sought to expand the measure's reach to cover all those with transfusion-related AIDS. But that would have doubled the bill's cost, and the hemophilia community was ultimately successful in limiting the bill in order to get it passed.

The final bill authorized compensation for hemophiliacs who had been infected between July 1, 1982, and Dec. 31, 1987. The fund would expire after five years.

Assisted Suicide

President Clinton signed into law in 1997 a bill (HR 1003—PL 105-12) prohibiting the use of federal funds for physician-assisted suicide. But legislation (HR 4006; S 2151) penalizing medical professionals who helped patients commit suicide with controlled substances failed to reach the floor in either chamber the following year.

HR 1003 was one of the first bills of the 105th Congress to reach the president's desk. Clinton said he had no objection to the measure but considered it a reiteration of existing policy. At the time, no federal agency funded such suicides. But bill supporters said it was necessary to clarify the government's position, particularly if states started to legalize assisted suicide and judges ruled that it qualified for federal funding. Critics said the likelihood of a judge forcing the federal government to pay for suicides was at best remote. They said the legislation fixed a problem that did not exist (federal funding) and did not address a problem that did exist (suicide).

HR 1003 did not address ethical or legal issues surrounding acts by terminally ill patients to end their lives. It only barred the use of taxpayer dollars to subsidize or promote such acts. Specifically, it prohibited Medicare, Medicaid, and military and federal employee health plans from paying for doctors to help terminally ill patients end their lives. The bill did not affect a patient's right to reject or discontinue medical treatment, nor did it affect funding for treatment to alleviate pain or discomfort. States that legalized assisted suicide would be free to fund it or to allow patients to pay for it themselves. Doctors who assisted at a suicide would not be in jeopardy of losing Medicare, Medicaid, or other forms of federal reimbursement for other services performed. For these reasons, the bill's impact was expected to be limited.

At the time of HR 1003's passage, the Supreme Court was considering, in *Vacco v. Quill* and *Washington v. Glucksberg*, whether Americans had a right to assisted suicide. The Court ruled the week of June 23 that states could bar assisted suicide and that individuals did not have a constitutional right to end their lives.

Far more sweeping legislation to deter physician-assisted suicides was reported out of committee in both chambers in 1998, but the bills faced strong opposition from the medical community and neither advanced further. The bills would have required revocation of a doctor's right to prescribe controlled drugs if there was evidence that the physician dispensed or prescribed drugs to assist suicide. Medical professionals said the legislation would impede doctors' ability to control the pain of terminally ill patients. *(Other 1997–1998 action, p. 606; 1999 action, p. 477)*

Human Cloning

Alarmed by the announcement by a Chicago physicist that he planned to try to clone a human being, the Senate in 1998 rushed to the floor legislation to make such an attempt illegal. The legislation foundered, however, when lawmakers could not find a way to craft language that would make illegal attempts to produce the live birth of a cloned child but not block what scientists said could prove to be groundbreaking research.

At least some members of Congress had been trying to ban human cloning since the February 1997 announcement by scientists in Scotland that they had successfully cloned a sheep—Dolly—thus rendering the prospect of human cloning more than mere science fiction. On March 4, 1997, President Clinton issued a directive barring any federal agency from supporting, funding, or undertaking any research related to human cloning. The president also urged a private moratorium on research so "we can ensure that as we move forward on this issue, we weigh the concerns of faith and family and philosophy and values, not merely of science alone."

But when Richard Seed announced in January 1998 that he intended to try to clone a human, Congress jumped to act. The Senate in February brought to the floor—bypassing committee action—a version of legislation (S 1601) introduced the previous year by Christopher J. Bond, R-Mo., that had been rewritten with the input of Bill Frist, R-Tenn., the Senate's lone physician and a former researcher, and was formally sponsored by Senate Majority Leader Trent Lott, R-Miss. The GOP bill would have banned the use of "human somatic cell nuclear transfer," in which the nucleus of a woman's egg, which contains its DNA, is removed and then is replaced with the DNA of another human being. Supporters said Congress needed to act quickly. "No longer can we divorce science from ethical consideration," said Frist. "Science moves too fast today."

But some biotechnology organizations complained that the Republican bill would go further than intended, banning not only human cloning research but also other types of potentially breakthrough research into a wide array of diseases. Instead of the Bond-Frist bill, biotech firms rallied around a measure (S 1602) offered by Sens. Dianne Feinstein, D-Calif., and Edward M. Kennedy, D-Mass., that would have placed a ten-year moratorium on the implantation of embryos created using the nuclear transfer technique.

Right-to-life groups, however, decried the Feinstein-Kennedy bill. "Under the Feinstein-Kennedy approach," said the National Right to Life Committee, "it would be perfectly legal to create cloned human embryos and use them as subjects for harmful experimentation, so long as they are killed before being implanted into a woman's womb."

In the end, backers of biomedical research prevailed. After several days of debate, the Senate on Feb. 11 failed to break a filibuster on the GOP bill by a **key vote of 42–54 (R 42–12; D 0–42),** thus sending the measure to committee. No further action was taken in the 105th Congress. *(1998 key votes, p. 883)*

1999–2000

On health care, the 106th Congress in many ways continued the efforts of its predecessor. After having passed a major Medicare and Medicaid bill in 1997 that included significant payment reductions aimed at helping balance the federal budget, Congress in 1999 and 2000 passed separate measures to "give back" some of the cuts. Similar to the 105th Congress, the 106th Congress fought over a "patients' bill of rights" measure and was unable to reach agreement.

The 106th Congress proved unable to address other controversial health issues, including long-term Medicare reform, a Medicare drug benefit, and efforts to protect medical privacy and address the problem of medical errors. But lawmakers did manage to pass bills to help those with disabilities keep their health insurance if they returned to work, to help low-income women with breast and cervical cancer pay for their treatment, and to prepare for a potential bioterrorist attack.

Medicare "Givebacks"

Congress in 1999 and 2000 passed separate bills to restore to Medicare providers some of the cuts imposed by the 1997 Balanced Budget Act (PL 105-33) that proved deeper than intended. *(1997 Medicare legislation, p. 432)*

The 1999 bill (HR 3194—PL 106-113) restored an estimated $16 billion over five years to hospitals, nursing homes, rehabilitation therapists, managed care plans, home health agencies, and others. The 2000 measure (HR 4577—PL 106-554) increased payments to providers—including some who benefited from the previous year's bill—and made some expansions to the Medicaid program, at a projected cost of some $35 billion over five years.

The issue was not that the estimates made when the 1997 bill was passed were wrong, but rather that the health system entered an unexpected period of deflation that rendered the inflation-pegged increases smaller than expected. That, coupled with reduced private payments from managed care plans, had left many providers strapped and forced many home health agencies and nursing homes into bankruptcy.

In 1997, when the original Balanced Budget Act (BBA) was passed, the Congressional Budget Office estimated it would reduce Medicare spending by $112 billion between 1998 and 2002. By July 1999, that estimate had grown to $206 billion.

Providers were, not surprisingly, frantic at the turn of events. "Congress way overshot its savings goals—and it will hurt communities and patients unless some BBA adjustments are made," said Tom Scully, president of the Federation of American Hospital Systems, which represented for-profit hospitals, in July 1999.

Provider groups not only lobbied Congress furiously, but they also tried to get the public to help by launching millions of dollars worth of television and radio advertising accusing legislators of cutting Medicare funding so deeply that seniors were suffering.

But Medicare analysts repeatedly warned Congress not to go too far. "Providers' complaints notwithstanding, we have no evidence that wholesale changes in the BBA are either necessary or desirable," Murray Ross of the Medicare Payment Advisory Commission told the House Commerce Subcommittee on Health and Environment in September 1999.

The pressure from providers, however, in the end proved too much for their elected representatives to resist. "Hospitals, home health agencies, and nursing homes in our home districts are all saying they can't live within the cuts we made in 1997," said Anna G. Eshoo, D-Calif.

Agreed Benjamin L. Cardin, D-Md., "Hospitals and nursing homes were threatening to close. Those aren't idle threats. That gets people's attention."

1999 BILL

The House Ways and Means Health Subcommittee kicked off action on what was formally known as the "Balanced Budget Refinement Act," but which quickly became known as the "giveback" package, approving on Oct. 15, 1999, a bill (HR 3075) that would have restored about $9.4 billion in cuts over the next five years. The package assumed the Clinton administration would make administrative changes related to Medicare hospital outpatient payments that would result in an additional $5.6 billion over that same time period, for a total of about $15 billion in payment restorations. Financing for the package was to come from the non-Social Security surplus, said subcommittee chairman Bill Thomas, R-Calif. Although funds were tight, he said the GOP leadership had promised him about $600 million for fiscal 2000 for the initial down payment.

But Democrats were not convinced that the measure would not adversely affect Medicare's long-term financing—and continually cited a memorandum from the Health Care Financing Administration estimating that the measure would reduce the life of the Medicare Part A trust fund by a year. When the full Ways and Means Committee approved the package on Oct. 21, by a vote of 26–11, all but four Democrats voted against it. Subcommittee ranking Democrat Pete Stark Jr. of California offered an amendment that would have made administrative changes and other payment reductions to finance the proposal, but it failed on a party-line vote of 15–22. HR 3075 was reported (H Rept 106-436, Pt. I) on Nov. 2.

The Senate Finance Committee also weighed in on Oct. 21, approving a plan worth some $15.4 billion over five years drafted by committee chairman William V. Roth Jr., R-Del. Although the Senate markup was less divisive than the House action, Senate Democrats were also frustrated by their inability to finance the plan. Roth ruled that a financing package offered by Bob Graham, D-Fla., was out of order, and the committee upheld his ruling by a vote of 14–5. The bill (S 1788—S Rept 106-199) was reported on Oct. 26.

After Thomas struck a deal with the House Commerce Committee, which shared jurisdiction over Medicare, the House passed HR 3075 on Nov. 5 by a vote of 388–25. Commerce committee changes incorporated into the bill included more money for Medicaid and the Children's Health Insurance Program (CHIP).

The House bill was passed under a suspension of the House rules, which meant that a two-thirds vote was needed for passage and amendments from the floor were barred. That angered Democrats, who had wanted to offer several amendments, including one to provide about $2.7 billion more over five years to teaching and rural hospitals, nursing homes, and home health agencies. Democrats also wanted to offer an amendment they said could reduce drug prices for Medicare beneficiaries by as much as 40 percent. But Thomas called the measure a "very narrow, very shallow canoe that cannot support" the weighty issue of prescription drugs.

In the end, the full Senate did not act on S 1788. Instead, leaders of the House and Senate committees with jurisdiction over Medicare worked out a deal with the Clinton administration that was added to an omnibus appropriations bill (HR 3194). The House approved the conference report on the omnibus bill (H Rept 106-479), 296–135, on Nov. 18. The Senate cleared it the next day, 74–24, and President Clinton signed it on Nov. 29.

Major Provisions

Hospitals were the biggest winners in the final, $16 billion package, scoring payment increases of an estimated $7.2 billion over five years.

Managed care plans also did well. They got $1.9 billion in direct relief, largely the result of changes to the phase-in of a planned "risk-adjuster" that would reduce payments to plans that served healthier-than-average beneficiaries. But managed care payments would also rise—by about $2.9 billion—along with the increases for other providers, because the formula that determined managed care payments was tied to overall Medicare spending. Managed care plans were also excused from a requirement in the 1997 law that they underwrite the total costs of a new beneficiary education program.

Nursing homes were expected to receive $2.1 billion in increased payments; home health agencies and hospice providers, $1.3 billion; and dialysis and durable medical equipment providers, $300 million. Most of the funds for home health providers came from a one-year delay of a planned 15 percent payment reduction. It was the second consecutive year home health agencies got the cut postponed.

The bill included help for beneficiaries, as well. It authorized $200 million to increase Medicare payments for Pap smears to detect cervical cancer in women and to help pay for immunosuppressive drugs for organ transplant patients.

Funding for Medicaid was boosted by an estimated $700 million, with $200 million more to expand enrollment in the CHIP program.

A provision on hospital outpatient departments that at one point threatened to derail the entire measure was remedied on Nov. 15, with a letter from White House chief of staff John D. Podesta to House Speaker J. Dennis Hastert, R-Ill. Although both Congress and the administration acknowledged the change needed to correct a drafting error, fixing it without being "charged" a cost turned out to be trickier than expected. Podesta's letter said the administration would not count the cost of a legislative fix toward the bill's final price tag, nor would the White House "characterize such legislation as having an adverse effect . . . on the Social Security surplus."

President Clinton signed the measure, but he was not pleased with its final price tag. "It exceeds our preference," said White House health policy adviser Chris Jennings, particularly the amount provided to Medicare managed care plans.

2000 BILL

The ink was barely dry on the 1999 measure when health care providers started pleading with lawmakers for more money. "We appreciate the relief that Congress and the president provided last year," American Hospital Association President Dick Davidson told a rally in January. "But given the magnitude of the BBA, that can only be viewed as a first step. More relief is needed to help hospitals keep pace with the costs of caring for patients."

Managed care firms also said more was needed, particularly in light of a growing number of plans leaving the Medicare program—because, they said, reimbursements were growing too slowly to keep up with medical costs. "While the [1999] legislation was a step in the right direction, it provided only a small fraction of the resources that are needed to fully stabilize the program on a long-term basis," George Renaudin of the Ochsner Health Plan in Louisiana told the House Ways and Means Health Subcommittee in July 2000. Renaudin, on behalf of the American Association of Health Plans, said "Congress must provide $15 billion directly to Medicare+Choice plans over the next five years to stabilize the Medicare+Choice program on a long-term basis." The Medicare+Choice program was created by the 1997 balanced budget law to encourage more managed-care and other private insurers to offer coverage to Medicare beneficiaries. *(Medicare+Choice, p. 438)*

Again, Medicare analysts warned Congress not to be persuaded by the entreaties—and advertising campaigns—of providers. "There is no systematic evidence that access to care is being compromised," Medicare Payment Advisory Commission Chair Gail Wilensky told the House Ways and Means Committee in July 2000. William Scanlon of the General Accounting Office (GAO), an investigative arm of Congress, agreed. The changes made in 1999 addressed the immediate needs of home health and nursing home providers, he said, and despite the problems managed care plans were having with Medicare+Choice program payments, GAO analysis, he testified, had found that "Medicare managed care, although originally expected to achieve program savings, continues instead to add to program cost."

Still, as they had a year earlier, Congress and President Clinton responded to the complaints with more money.

As part of his proposed Medicare reform and prescription plan, Clinton in June proposed restoring some $21 billion worth of cuts to hospitals, nursing homes, home health agencies, and others.

This time it was the House Commerce Committee—which had not marked up a Medicare giveback bill the previous year—that acted first. With bipartisan support, the panel approved the "Beneficiary Improvement and Protection Act" on Sept. 26, 2000. The measure (HR 5291) would spend an estimated $18.2 billion over five years for managed care plans, home health providers, and kidney dialysis facilities. (The Commerce panel did not have jurisdiction over the hospital or nursing home portions of the program.) The Commerce bill also boosted available funding for states through the Medicaid and CHIP programs, and included direct beneficiary improvements such as lifting the cap on payments for immunosuppressive drugs, increasing coverage of screening colonoscopies, and waiving the twenty-four-month waiting period for Medicare for those disabled by amyotrophic lateral sclerosis, better known as Lou Gehrig's disease. HR 5291 was formally reported (H Rept 106-1019) on Oct. 30.

The Ways and Means Health Subcommittee unanimously approved on Oct. 3 an unnumbered bill giving back as much as $30 billion to Medicare. Similar to the Commerce Committee plan, the proposal included not just payment increases for providers but also improvements in benefits, including lower copayments for outpatient hospital care, unlimited coverage of immunosuppressive drugs for transplant patients, and glaucoma screenings.

As he had a year earlier, however, subcommittee chairman Thomas again fended off Democratic efforts to broaden the bill's reach. Republicans voted down Democrats' efforts to add their $40 billion prescription drug proposal to the bill. GOP lawmakers also defeated Democratic amendments to add other benefits, such as annual physicals and an expansion of coverage of the few prescription drugs Medicare did cover. "This is not the Queen Mary," said Thomas, picking up on his nautical analogy from the year before. "It's relatively more of a small rowboat."

Across the Capitol, Senate Finance Chairman Roth introduced a measure (S 3165) on Oct. 5 that would have cost an estimated $28 billion. But Democrats complained that they were not included in the deliberations over the bill—and criticized Roth for failing to mark it up in public session. "I've never seen such an aversion to voting," said Finance Committee member Graham. But Roth knew if he held a markup, Democrats would do what they tried at the Ways and Means

subcommittee markup—attempt to add a prescription drug benefit to the package. And unlike in the House, Roth was not sure he had the votes to defeat such an effort.

Republicans in the House and Senate subsequently gathered to try to forge a package out of the three committee plans, prompting complaints from congressional Democrats and from President Clinton. The president, in particular, was unhappy at the amount of the package being allocated to managed care plans—reportedly a third of the total. Those funds, he said in a letter to House Speaker Hastert Oct. 10, "are effectively diverting resources from critically important health care priorities" such as increased payments for hospitals and new benefits for patients.

By the following week, Democrats' dissatisfaction had risen to the level of a veto threat offered by Health and Human Services Secretary Donna Shalala and White House Budget Director Jacob Lew. "Should these untargeted, excessive and unaccountable HMO (health maintenance organization) payment increases crowd out critical beneficiary and health care provider policies, we would recommend that the president veto your legislation," they said in an Oct. 17 letter to Hastert.

Republicans unveiled their plan on Oct. 19. It proposed to spend $28.2 billion over five years, with managed care plans to receive $10.2 billion of the total. Hospitals would receive about $7.4 billion over five years, while a $5.7 billion beneficiary improvement package would pay for new preventive screenings for various cancers, as well as nutritional therapy for diabetes or kidney disease, and unlimited coverage of immunosuppressive drugs for organ transplant patients.

Ignoring the veto threats and complaints from congressional Democrats, House GOP leaders packaged the Medicare plan into a separate measure that included tax and pension provisions and an increase in the minimum wage. The House adopted the conference report on that bill (HR 2614—H Rept 106-1004) on Oct. 26, 237–174. At the last minute, House leaders also added to the package a controversial bill that would effectively overturn Oregon's first-in-the-nation physician assisted suicide law. (Tax bill, p. 117; assisted suicide, p. 477)

This time it was Clinton himself who threatened a veto. "If this current tax and Medicare/Medicaid package is presented to me in its current form, I will have no choice but to veto it," he wrote in a letter to GOP leaders the day of the vote.

The inclusion of the assisted suicide bill, the "Pain Relief Promotion Act," also drew a filibuster threat from Sen. Ron Wyden, D-Ore., who had been trying to fend off the measure for two years. "I'm ruling out no options," he said of his plans for the measure. "I'm going to make very sure the American people see that this legislation will hurt suffering patients and families in every community in the country."

An accounting change ultimately helped smooth the way for the negotiations. The Clinton administration had proposed closing a Medicaid loophole known as the "upper payment limit," which allowed states to pay county-owned health facilities Medicare rates, then reclaim some of the money for other purposes. Many states, however, protested, claiming they were depending on the funds to help underwrite care for low-income patients. Congress in the end decided to weaken the administration's proposal, saving the government less money. But because they were making a change that saved money, they were by budget rules allowed to count those savings toward the cost of the measure. On paper, that reduced the measure's cost from around $30 billion over five years to $10.9 billion, and the ten-year price tag from more than $80 billion to $4.2 billion.

A deal on the package was finally reached in December, after Congress returned for its lame-duck session. The compromise measure—costing an estimated $35 billion over five years—was included in a catch-all measure that also included four fiscal 2001 spending bills (HR 4577—PL 106-554). The House approved the conference report (H Rept 106-1033) on Dec. 15, by a vote of 292–60. The Senate cleared the bill by voice vote that same day, and the president signed it on Dec. 21. *(Omnibus bill, p. 81)*

Major Provisions

The giveback package was estimated to provide $14 billion to hospitals and $11 billion for managed care companies—still more than Clinton thought was warranted. It provided about $1.6 billion for nursing homes, and $1.7 billion for home health agencies, primarily by again—for the third year in a row—delaying their scheduled 15 percent payment cut.

The final package included the House-proposed benefit expansions, as well as the provision from the House Commerce Committee bill providing automatic Medicare eligibility for those disabled by Lou Gehrig's disease, at a total cost of about $7 billion.

To satisfy Clinton and Democrats, the package agreed to boost funding for Medicaid by approximately $700 million to extend benefits for an additional year for welfare recipients who enter the workforce. Republicans, however, refused to add a Democrat-backed proposal to make it easier for immigrants and disabled children to qualify for Medicaid.

Approximately $300 million was also added to make it easier for children to enroll in the CHIP program, and a formula was included to distribute some states' unused CHIP funds. Under the original 1997 law, funds unused at the end of fiscal 2000 were supposed to go to states that had used all their money, but states with unused allocations complained they would use the money if they got more time. The new formula divided the money between states that had and had not used their allocations.

Medicare Commission

A bipartisan commission created to settle a dispute over Medicare's long-term financing problems packed up shop in 1999 without recommending a plan to Congress. But the proposal favored by ten of the panel's seventeen members at its final meeting March 16 saw new life in legislation introduced later that year.

Congress created the National Bipartisan Commission on the Future of Medicare as part of the 1997 Balanced Budget Act (PL 105-33). Although that measure did shore up Medicare's troubled finances for the short-term, lawmakers did not address the financing problem facing the program when the 80 million-member "baby boom" generation started to become eligible for the program in the year 2010. *(1997 act, p. 50)*

Recognizing that long-term solutions were likely to be both painful and controversial, Congress required that in order to make a formal recommendation, the commission would have to gain support of a "supermajority" of eleven members for a particular plan.

The panel got off to a late start when Republicans and Democrats could not agree on a chairman. They ultimately settled on Sen. John B. Breaux, D-La., a moderate Democrat who had sided with Republicans in the past on Medicare issues and who was known for his dealmaking abilities. Breaux was appointed in January 1998—just fourteen months before the commission's deadline of March 1, 1999.

In exchange for allowing a Democrat to be appointed chairman (giving Democrats a 9–8 majority of the members), Democrats agreed to appoint as the panel's "administrative chairman" Rep. Bill Thomas, R-Calif., the chairman of the House Ways and Means Subcommittee on Health.

But many observers were already predicting the commission would end in deadlock, as House Speaker Newt Gingrich, R-Ga., made his four appointees promise not to support any proposal calling for tax increases.

Breaux made it clear from the start his support for a proposal based on the Federal Employee Health Benefits Plan, which allowed federal workers to choose from among a raft of private health plans. Breaux and Thomas presented what they called their "premium support" plan for Medicare that would have private plans compete on an equal footing with Medicare's traditional fee-for-service program in January 1999. The plan also proposed increasing Medicare's eligibility age from sixty-five to sixty-seven to match the planned increase in the eligibility age for Social Security that was scheduled to stretch over a number of years.

But the partisanship was already clear. Although the Breaux-Thomas proposal was clearly favored by Republicans on the panel, providing nine of the needed eleven votes, the remaining Democrats held out for the inclusion of a prescription drug benefit for Medicare. They also urged the commission to consider the proposal offered by President Clinton in his State of the Union Address to reserve 15 percent of the projected budget surplus to help keep Medicare financially solvent.

As the commission's termination deadline neared, with Sen. Robert Kerrey, D-Neb., siding with Breaux, the search for the pivotal eleventh vote centered on two Clinton administration appointees, former Clinton economic adviser Laura

D'Andrea Tyson and Brandeis University health policy professor Stuart H. Altman, who had worked on health issues during Clinton's transition in 1992 and previously had chaired Medicare's Prospective Payment Assessment Commission.

In the end, neither Tyson nor Altman, both of whom had expressed some interest in the premium support strategy, voted for the proposal. They said it did not do enough to shore up the program's finances and the proposed drug benefit did not aid enough beneficiaries.

Breaux, along with commission member Sen. Bill Frist, R-Tenn., subsequently introduced legislation based on the plan in November. That bill, however, while the basis for much discussion, failed to move in the 106th Congress.

Medicare Drug Benefit

Attempting to capitalize on one of the most popular political issues in years, Congress in 2000 sought to add a prescription drug benefit to the Medicare program. But although the House passed a bill (HR 4680) with almost exclusively Republican support, the Senate was unable to agree on an approach, and the issue was put off for another year.

Medicare's failure to cover the cost of most outpatient prescription drugs had long been a subject of some concern. (The program did pay for drugs administered in the hospital; a few, such as chemotherapy drugs, administered in doctors' offices; and immunosuppressive medications for those who had organ transplants.) Congress actually did add an outpatient drug benefit as part of the ill-fated 1988 "Medicare Catastrophic Coverage Act" (PL 100-360). But it was repealed along with the rest of that law after beneficiaries revolted over the fact that Congress expected them to pay the full cost of the new benefits. *(1988 law, Congress and the Nation Vol. VII, p. 561; repeal, Congress and the Nation Vol. VIII, p. 565)*

By the late 1990s, the issue was reaching critical mass politically. Thanks in large part to a 1992 law that speeded up the drug approval process, drugmakers were delivering to market a broad array of new medicines to treat ailments of particular concern to the elderly—arthritis, high blood pressure, high cholesterol, and diabetes, for example. At the same time, however, drug prices and drug spending were skyrocketing. Spending on prescription drugs grew by 18 percent in 1999 alone.

Most of the working-age population—at least the majority with health insurance coverage—was largely shielded from the worst of the increases. Some members of the Medicare population had drug coverage as well, either through a former employer, through a private Medicare HMO, through the Medicaid program for the poor, or through private supplemental "Medigap" insurance. But a third of all beneficiaries had no drug coverage, and were forced to pay drug costs that often left them choosing between their medicines and their meals, or their medicines and their utilities.

Even those with coverage were threatened. Faced with rising costs, many employers were scaling back their retiree plans; Medicare HMOs were likewise dropping or cutting back drug coverage or leaving the program entirely; and Medigap insurance that covered drugs often cost as much as or more than the benefit provided.

Since the collapse of the National Bipartisan Commission on the Future of Medicare in March 1999, congressional Republicans had insisted that Medicare not add a drug benefit until it was also reformed enough financially to withstand the onslaught of the "baby boom" generation that would begin becoming eligible in 2010. But Democrats objected to most of the Republican-backed reforms. They—and President Clinton—wanted a drug benefit first, and reform later. *(Medicare commission, p. 464)*

By the spring of 2000, House Republicans realized they had no choice but to act on a drug benefit alone. "If we don't pass something, [Democrats] will say we hate senior citizens and that we don't want them to have medication. I can hear it all now," said Rep. Charlie Norwood, R-Ga.

But although the House did pass a bill, the Senate had other ideas. The Senate Finance Committee held more than a dozen hearings on Medicare issues in 1999 and 2000. A series of closed-door meetings failed to produce a consensus, however, and time ultimately ran out on the effort.

LEGISLATIVE ACTION

The prescription drug debate officially kicked off when President Clinton called on Congress to enact a drug benefit in his 1999 State of the Union Address, and proposed using 15 percent of the budget surplus to that goal.

But the administration did not support a proposal backed by ten of the Medicare commission's seventeen members in March of that year because it would not have guaranteed coverage to all Medicare beneficiaries. Rather, the proposal put together by commission co-chairs Sen. John B. Breaux, D-La., and Rep. Bill Thomas, R-Calif., would have required beneficiaries to purchase private coverage in order to obtain drug benefits, or else purchase a "high option" plan from the government. Those with incomes under 135 percent of the poverty line ($10,658 for individuals; $13,334 for couples) would have received subsidies.

President Clinton proposed his Medicare reform plan in late June 1999. The president's proposal would have devoted $794 billion from the projected budget surplus to Medicare over the ensuing fifteen years, $108 billion more than Clinton proposed in January. Of that, $118 billion would have gone to the universal drug benefit to be added to Medicare. The plan proposed premiums of $24 per month to cover half the cost of the first $2,000 of prescription drugs each year. By 2008, when the plan was fully phased in, premiums of $44 per month would underwrite $5,000 worth of drugs. The proposal also included incentives for employers to maintain prescription drug coverage in retiree health plans.

In November 1999 Breaux, along with fellow commission member Sen. Bill Frist, R-Tenn., introduced as legislation a modified version of the commission's plan. The proposal built on the commission's "premium support" plan by establishing a "competitive premium system." Under the bill, private plans and traditional Medicare would both offer standard and high-option packages. High-option plans would be required to offer both prescription drug coverage worth at least $800 per year, as well as an annual "stop loss" for all out-of-pocket expenses over $2,000. Every beneficiary would receive at least a 25 percent subsidy for their prescription drug coverage, with low-income beneficiaries getting more help.

In the House, Thomas, who chaired the Ways and Means Subcommittee on Health, was trying to put together a bipartisan package based on the commission's plan. In the end, though, House Republicans decided to pursue a plan on their own. In January 2000, House Speaker J. Dennis Hastert, R-Ill., instructed GOP leaders of the Ways and Means and the Energy and Commerce Committees to come up with a drug bill.

Meanwhile, House and Senate Democrats and the Clinton administration were coming up with their own approach. They ultimately settled on a plan originally drafted by a group of moderates led by Sen. Bob Graham, D-Fla. That plan called for premiums to cover half the program's costs (estimated at between $35 and $40 per month). Beneficiaries would have half their drug costs covered for the first $3,500; 75 percent of the amount between $3,500 and $4,000; and all costs covered for amounts over $4,000 annually.

House Republicans finally unveiled their bill (HR 4680)—with two Democratic cosponsors—in late June. That proposal, under orders to spend no more than $40 billion over five years, was far less generous. It envisioned private companies creating "drug-only" insurance plans that the government would help beneficiaries purchase. For a premium of $40 per month, and after paying a $250 annual deductible, beneficiaries would receive coverage for half their drug costs up to $2,100 annually. There would be no coverage for expenses between $2,100 and $6,000, but those with expenses higher than $6,000 per year would have all their costs covered.

Although the plan envisioned federal "reinsurance" for the private plans, the insurance industry was skeptical. "Private drug-only coverage would have to clear insurmountable financial, regulatory, and administrative hurdles simply to get to market," said Chip Kahn, president of the Health Insurance Association of America. Even if plans did offer the policies, he said, "the likelihood that the people most likely to purchase this coverage will be the people anticipating the highest drug claims would make drug-only coverage virtually impossible for insurers to offer to seniors at an affordable premium."

Republicans proceeded regardless. The Ways and Means Committee approved the measure on June 21 by a party-line vote of 23–14 and reported it (H Rept 106-703) on June 27.

"Under our plan, all seniors will be given a choice of drug coverage options, an immediate 25 percent or greater discount off retail prices, a discounted premium, and the security of catastrophic coverage," said Ways and Means Chairman Bill Archer, R-Texas.

But Democrats said the benefit was hardly worth the money. "So for $7,050 in drug costs, the patient pays $6,000 and the plan $1,050," said Rep. Robert T. Matsui, D-Calif.

Republicans, however, defeated a Democratic alternative resembling the consensus Senate plan, 14–23. The Democratic proposal also included $21 billion in provider "givebacks," much of which would be enacted later in the session. *(Medicare "givebacks," p. 461)*

Although the House moved toward a showdown vote, it was the Senate that actually got a proposal to the floor first. Democrats tried to force their plan onto the fiscal 2001 appropriation for the departments of Labor, Health and Human Services, and Education (HR 4577). Senate Republicans turned back the effort by a vote of 44–53 on June 22. Senate Minority Leader Thomas A. Daschle, D-S.D., defended the surprise attack by saying that his Democratic colleagues felt strongly that "debate not be limited to what the House Republicans have offered."

The following week the House held its widely anticipated debate, but it was delayed by a walkout of House Democrats, angry that the Rules Committee did not grant them the right to offer their substitute amendment. Republicans said the Democratic amendment was "out of order" because it would have cost more than the $40 billion set aside by the fiscal 2001 budget resolution. The Democrats' walkout was followed by a series of delaying votes, including three separate roll calls on whether members should be allowed to use posters to accompany their spoken remarks.

Republicans said their plan would offer beneficiaries a choice. "It won't force seniors into a government-run plan that dictates what drugs seniors can and can't have," said Archer.

But Democrats said Republicans were less interested in helping Medicare beneficiaries and more interested in helping their political futures. "They are intent on passing anything called 'prescription coverage' in order to avoid the issue being raised in the fall elections," charged House Minority Leader Richard A. Gephardt, D-Mo.

The bill passed on June 28 by a near party-line **key vote of 217–214 (R 211–10; D 5–203; I 1–1)**. *(2000 key votes, p. 915)*

That turned out to be the high-water mark in the debate. Members of the Senate Finance Committee went behind closed doors in July and again in September in an effort to find common ground. But the effort was ultimately shelved in favor of a more achievable Medicare "giveback" bill.

Patients' Rights

The 106th Congress had no more luck than its predecessor clearing legislation to guarantee patients in managed health plans a series of rights to obtain care. The 106th Congress did get further than the 105th Congress, in which only the House passed a bill. In 1999 both the Senate and House passed bills. No compromise, however, emerged from a prolonged conference, and in the end the issue was again pushed off to the next Congress. *(1998 action, p. 454)*

The Senate, which failed to pass a bill in the 105th Congress, came out of the gate early in 1999. The Senate Health, Education, Labor and Pensions Committee was the only full committee in either chamber to move a measure through the committee process, with Republicans solidly backing a measure (S 326) that included some patient protections but no new right to sue health plans for damages—what would become the key sticking point in the debate. The full Senate passed another bill (S 1344) on July 15, after four days of bitter, partisan debate.

Although in 1998 the House passed a bill President Clinton threatened to veto, in 1999 it was the House bill the president—and most Democrats—supported. Rep. Charlie Norwood, R-Ga., a retired dentist, after experiencing nothing but frustration with his fellow Republicans, allied himself with House Energy and Commerce Committee ranking Democrat John D. Dingell Jr., D-Mich., who had been leading his party's patients' rights effort. Together, Norwood and Dingell created an unbeatable bloc for Republican leaders who opposed the measure's liability provisions that would set aside the federal law blocking most damage awards against health plans.

But although House leaders could not defeat what came to be known as the Dingell-Norwood bill, they were able to find other ways to thwart the bill. On the floor, they folded the patients' rights measure into a controversial package of health-related tax changes, then appointed to the House-Senate conference committee supporters of the tax measure who opposed the House-passed patients' rights bill. Norwood was, noticeably, left off the list of conferees.

Meanwhile, Senate Majority Whip Don Nickles, R-Okla., a close ally of business and insurance groups who opposed any patients' rights bill, chaired the conference. Although Nickles insisted he wanted to find a compromise, weeks of meetings ultimately proved fruitless.

LEGISLATIVE ACTION

The Senate Health, Education, Labor and Pensions Committee spent thirteen hours over two days, March 17 and 18, 1999, working on the issue before finally approving "The Patients' Bill of Rights Plus Act" (S 326) by a straight party-line vote of 10–8. During the grueling session, Democrats offered twenty-two amendments, of which twenty were defeated, nineteen on straight party-line votes.

One of the Democrats' biggest complaint with the GOP bill was the fact that most of its protections extended only to the estimated 48 million Americans in "self-insured" plans exempt from state regulation. An amendment to broaden the scope to cover everyone with private health insurance failed along party lines.

Democrats also opposed a GOP provision allowing patients to seek an external appeal if a plan denied care that was "medically necessary." Under the GOP bill, there was no set definition of "medical necessity"; that determination was left up to the outside reviewer, who was required to be a physician. Bill Frist, R-Tenn., the Senate's only physician, argued that a statutory definition would limit health plans' ability to

offer the most up-to-date care, and that continuing scientific advances required a flexible definition. Democrats, on the other hand, insisted that with no statutory definition, health plans would be able to arbitrarily set limits in their contracts and later contend that the treatment was never a covered benefit. "Without this protection, all the other safeguards are worthless," said Edward M. Kennedy of Massachusetts, the ranking Democrat on the committee.

But Republicans turned back efforts to set the definition, as well as amendments requiring broader coverage of emergency room care, freer access to specialists, minimum hospital stays for women undergoing mastectomies for breast cancer, and access to clinical trials for those with life-threatening conditions.

Republicans said they were pleased with their bill. "For the first time, millions and millions of people are going to have protections they didn't have before," said Health, Education, Labor and Pensions Committee Chairman James M. Jeffords, R-Vt. Democrats were less impressed, including President Clinton, who in a statement said the bill "falls far short of the legislation the American people deserve."

The debate on the Senate floor on July 14 picked up right where it had left off in the Senate committee, although, in a twist, Senate Majority Leader Trent Lott, R-Miss., opted to bring to the floor not the committee-approved bill, but rather, the Democrats' own measure, under a new number, S 1344. The move was apparently aimed at preventing Democrats from introducing numerous amendments that would have forced Republicans to cast politically unpopular votes against a variety of patient protection proposals. Under the agreement that got the measure to the floor, Lott was given the right to offer the final amendment, planned as the committee-approved bill, combined with some health-related tax provisions. (The tax provisions, including ones permitting more people to open "medical savings accounts," had been stalled in the Finance Committee, where the refusal of Sen. John H. Chafee, R-R.I., to support them had left Republicans lacking the votes to approve them.)

The GOP tactic to avoid delicate floor votes did not work, though, as Democrats turned the tables and offered as their substitute the GOP bill, which they then proceeded to seek to amend. The result was a convoluted process in which each side alternated offering amendments to the opposition's bill.

Some of the disputes appeared semantic in nature but were actually more substantive. For example, Democrats opposed a GOP amendment offered by Susan Collins, R-Maine, which would have allowed women to see obstetricians or gynecologists for routine care without prior authorization. Democrats noted that, unlike their bill, the amendment did not allow women "direct access" to their obstetricians or gynecologists if they had a specific problem.

Similarly, Democrats opposed the GOP provision purporting to make it easier for patients in managed care plans to use the nearest emergency room even if the hospital was not part of their plan, because although it would require plans to pay for care needed to stabilize a patient, it would not require coverage of any needed subsequent treatment.

Republicans prevailed on the key issues of scope and liability. By a vote of 48–52 on July 14, a Democratic amendment that would have broadened coverage under the GOP bill to all 161 million Americans with private insurance, failed, with Republicans John McCain, Ariz., Chafee, and Arlen Specter, Pa., joining with Democrats. On July 15 Republicans offered an amendment striking from the Democrats' bill language allowing patients to sue health plans for damages in cases in which denied care resulted in death or injury. Specter and Peter G. Fitzgerald of Illinois were the only Republicans to join Democrats in trying to fend off the amendment, but it was adopted 53–47.

Chafee and Fitzgerald were the only Republicans in the end to vote against the bill, which, similar to the earlier amendment, passed by a **key vote of 53–47 (R 52–2; D 0–45; I 1–0)** on July 15. *(1999 key votes, p. 899)*

HOUSE ACTION

Meanwhile, the House had been trying much of the year to deal with the issue. Speaker Hastert vowed in January that unlike in 1998, when the patients' rights bill was drafted by a task force behind closed doors and moved directly to the floor, the 1999 measure would move through committees of jurisdiction under "regular order."

That, however, was thwarted by the presence of Norwood and other health professionals on the two main committees, House Commerce and House Education and the Workforce. Their support for a stronger bill effectively gave Democrats working majorities on the issue.

Thus, although the Education and the Workforce Subcommittee on Employer/Employee Relations managed to mark up a package of eight separate bills on June 16, 1999, similar to the 1998 measure that passed the House, those measures (HR 2041-2047, and HR 2089) moved no further. That is because Norwood had vowed to try in the full committee to expand the bills to allow new rights to sue, among other things.

Norwood was also a factor in his other committee, Commerce, where chairman Thomas J. Bliley Jr., R-Va., appointed all three of his renegade health professionals—Norwood and physicians Greg Ganske, R-Iowa, and Tom Coburn, R-Okla.—to come up with a bill. They did produce a bill that Bliley was prepared to take to the committee, but GOP leaders could not sign off on the liability provisions, and the primary jurisdiction was taken from Commerce and given to Education and the Workforce, instead.

When negotiations between Bliley and Dingell reached an impasse at the end of July, a frustrated Norwood stepped in to deal with Democrats himself. On Aug. 5 Norwood turned the debate on its head when he, Dingell, Ganske, and nineteen GOP cosponsors—more than enough to pass the bill—announced their support for a measure that included right-to-sue provisions only slightly less sweeping than in the Democrats' original bill.

Meanwhile, Republican leaders ultimately rallied around a competing bill (HR 2824) that included a more limited right to sue that was put together by Coburn and fellow Commerce Committee member John Shadegg, R-Ariz., and promised a vote on the issue in September. It was the first time House GOP leaders supported any expansion in the right to sue, and they hoped the limited lawsuits in federal court would satisfy the Republicans who had endorsed the Norwood-Dingell bill (HR 2723).

In the end, the House was given three options on a patients' rights bill: Norwood/Dingell, with its broad new right to sue; Coburn/Shadegg, with its more limited new rights; and a revamped version of the Education and the Workforce package put together by subcommittee chairman John A. Boehner, R-Ohio. Boehner's bill (HR 2926), crafted to appeal to the more conservative elements of the party, included no new lawsuit provisions.

By late September it was clear that Norwood and Dingell were likely to prevail. So House leaders tried another tack—they tied the patients' rights issue to a series of health related tax changes that had broad Republican support—even from those who also supported a sweeping patients' rights bill.

On Oct. 6, the day before the House voted on patients' rights, it took up and passed, 227–205, the tax legislation (HR 2990) crafted by James M. Talent, R-Mo., and Shadegg. To the dismay of Democrats (only eleven of whom supported the measure), the rule governing floor debate decreed that whatever patients' rights bill passed the next day would be folded into the tax measure.

The tax bill would have allowed all taxpayers to establish "medical savings accounts," or MSAs, which were tax-exempt accounts that could be used to pay routine medical expenses and were combined with "catastrophic" insurance policies for major events. The bill also sought to speed up the phase-in of 100 percent tax deductibility for health insurance premiums paid by self-employed individuals, and allow, for the first time, deductibility of premiums for individuals who bought their own insurance but were not self-employed.

The package also would have allowed the establishment of "HealthMarts," regional alliances of employers, insurers, and health care providers who could band together to provide less expensive insurance products for small businesses. The bill allowed a second type of health insurance alliance known as "association health plans" that would let small businesses, church groups, or other organizations offer insurance.

Democrats—including President Clinton, who issued a veto threat—argued that the provisions would primarily help the healthy and wealthy and do very little for the uninsured. They also argued that the bill's GOP sponsors had not found ways to offset its estimated cost of approximately $48 billion over ten years.

But Republicans insisted that something needed to be done to help those without coverage, because the patients' rights bill, by definition, only helped those who were already insured. "This is the only bill that we're going to consider that does anything for the uninsured," said Talent.

MANAGED CARE BILLS COMPARED

Key differences between the House (HR 2990) and Senate (S 1344) managed care bills included the following:

- **Scope.** Although the House bill would have applied to all 161 million Americans in private insurance plans, some protections in the Senate plan would have applied only to the 48 million people in plans exempt from state regulations. Some provisions in the Senate bill would have covered 124 million Americans in employer-sponsored plans, while others would have affected everyone in a private plan.
- **Liability.** The House bill would have permitted patients to sue their health plans for damages in state courts. The Senate bill would not have. Both plans also called for large penalties against health plans that did not follow the decision of an external review panel. For example, the Senate bill would have allowed penalties up to $10,000 if a health plan ignored a reviewer's decision. The House bill had penalties as well, including a $1,000 fine per day if a plan did not abide by a reviewer's decision.
- **Purchasing groups.** The House bill would have allowed the creation of so-called HealthMarts and association health plans, which backers said would help consumers form purchasing groups that would make insurance more affordable. The Senate bill did not contain these provisions.

Both bills shared a series of tax provisions, such as allowing a 100 percent tax deduction for health care insurance premiums for the self-employed and for long-term care premiums. Both measures also would have expanded an existing pilot program for medical savings accounts, which were tax-exempt and were used to pay medical expenses. Democrats said they viewed many of the tax provisions as "poison pills" they wanted stripped from the legislation.

Although Republican leaders prevailed on HR 2990, the tax bill, Democrats prevailed on HR 2723, the patients' rights bill. On Oct. 7 the House first defeated, 145–284, Boehner's substitute, without any new right to sue. Then, despite furious lobbying by House GOP leaders, the Coburn-Shadegg amendment failed as well, by a vote of 193–238, with twenty-nine Republicans breaking ranks to vote against it. On final passage of HR 2723, sixty-eight Republicans joined all but two Democrats in voting for the measure, which passed by a **key vote of 275–151 (R 68–149; D 206–2; I 1–0).** *(1999 key votes, p. 899)*

HR 2990 and HR 2723 were then combined and sent to conference as one bill, HR 2990.

But it took Republican leaders a month to appoint conferees, and when they did, Democrats cried foul. Although

House rules dictated that a majority of conferees support the House position, House leaders used the vote on the tax measure into which the patients' rights bill was folded to determine support. Thus, of the thirteen House conferees, only one, Commerce Committee Health and the Environment Subcommittee Chairman Michael Bilirakis, R-Fla., voted for the Dingell-Norwood measure.

Conspicuously absent from the list was Norwood. Democrats actually offered him one of their conference slots, but he declined, telling colleagues it would be better "if I remain free to continue my outspokenness" on the issue.

Major Provisions of House Bill

As passed by the House, major provisions of HR 2723 would have:

- **Scope.** Covered all privately insured Americans, about 161 million people.
- **Liability.** Allowed patients who claimed that they had been physically or mentally injured when wrongly denied care by their health plans to sue in state court for damages. Plans that had complied with the decision of an independent, external reviewer would not be subject to punitive damages, and any state caps on damages would apply. Employers could not be sued unless they made a decision on a benefits claim.
- **Emergency care.** Required health plans that covered emergency room care to pay for it without prior approval if a "prudent layperson" would deem it necessary. The patient could seek care at any hospital. The care would include medical screenings as well as any treatment needed to stabilize the patient's health.
- **Gag rules.** Barred plans from restricting what a doctor could tell a patient about treatment options. Even if a treatment was not covered by a plan, medical professionals could not be prevented from discussing that option.
- **Internal appeals.** Required plans to respond within fourteen days (with a possible fourteen-day extension) to a patient's internal appeal of a denial of coverage, and within seventy-two hours in urgent cases. The reviewer would be chosen by the plan but could not have made the initial denial. If the decision involved medical judgment, the reviewer would have to be a doctor. Any patient whose internal review was rejected could appeal to an independent reviewer.
- **External appeals.** Allowed any patient whose internal appeal was rejected to appeal to an independent, external reviewer who would have to issue a binding, final decision within seventy-two hours in case of an emergency or twenty-one days otherwise. Penalties could include federal court action such as civil fines of up to $1,000 per day. Plan officials who repeatedly violated external review decisions could be fined up to $500,000.
- **Medical necessity.** Guaranteed that doctors, not health plan officials, determined what treatment was medically necessary. Patients could appeal a decision that found a treatment medically unnecessary or experimental.
- **Women's health.** Allowed women in plans that covered obstetrical and gynecological care to visit obstetricians or gy-

necologists without going through a "gatekeeper" primary care physician.

• **Access to specialists.** Required plans that covered specialty care to provide referrals for such care when needed, including treatment by out-of-network providers if no appropriate specialist was available in the network. Parents could designate pediatricians as primary care doctors for their children. Patients with ongoing special conditions would have continued access to their specialists for up to ninety days after a health plan dropped that specialist for reasons other than fraud or failure to meet quality standards. In cases such as pregnancy, scheduled surgery, or terminal illness, patients could see the doctor throughout the duration of the experience.

• **"Whistleblower" protections.** Protected medical professionals who reported any actions by a plan affecting quality of care for patients. No health plan could retaliate against a protected health care professional who disclosed health plan abuses to a regulatory agency or other oversight officials.

• **Choice of plans.** Permitted patients to choose a point-of-service option if their health plan did not offer access to nonnetwork providers. The patient could pay additional costs associated with this option.

CONFERENCE ACTION

With Nickles acting as chairman, the conference did not get underway until March, in part because of a case of pneumonia that sidelined Senator Kennedy for several weeks in February 2000. Staff members were able to work out some smaller issues—reaching agreement, for example, that patients should be able to designate pediatricians as their children's "primary care" physicians. But there was little movement on the three biggest issues—scope, liability, and whether plans or physicians should define "medical necessity."

Although a tentative agreement was reached on the issue of how an "external appeals" process should work for patients, the conference found no further common ground.

Finally, on June 8, the standoff moved to the Senate floor, where after a bitter, partisan debate, the Senate rejected Democrats' attempt to attach a version of the House patients' rights bill as an amendment to the fiscal 2001 defense authorization measure (S 2549). Four Republicans, Lincoln Chafee of Rhode Island (who succeeded his father, who died the previous autumn), Fitzgerald of Illinois, McCain of Arizona, and Specter of Pennsylvania joined Democrats on the 51–48 vote to table (kill) the amendment.

The final action on the issue came on June 29, when Democrats again tried to push the House bill through the Senate, this time as an amendment to the fiscal 2001 Labor-Health and Human Services-Education appropriation (HR 4577). Republicans were ready, and offered a new substitute that would have allowed limited lawsuits in cases in which a managed care company imposed "unreasonable delays" in providing care or if they failed to provide care ordered by an outside appeals panel.

The amendment, offered by Nickles, was adopted by a **key vote of 51–47 (R 51–4; D 0–43),** with the same four Republicans who voted with the Democrats three weeks earlier voting with them again. The Democrats' attempt to force the House bill through failed by an identical 47–51 vote. *(2000 key votes, p. 915)*

Disabled Workers' Insurance

At the repeated and personal urging of President Clinton, Congress in 1999 approved legislation (HR 1180—PL 106-170) that would allow adults with disabilities to return to work without jeopardizing their public health insurance coverage through Medicare or Medicaid. Clinton signed the "Work Incentives Improvement Act" on Dec. 17.

Despite strong bipartisan support in both the House and Senate (the measure received a total of twelve votes against it in four votes in both chambers), the measure had a harrowing trip to the president's desk. The bill's few opponents, including Senate Majority Leader Trent Lott, R-Miss., and Senate Majority Whip Don Nickles, R-Okla., said they did not like the precedent of allowing people who were by definition not poor to receive Medicaid benefits.

Sponsors of the measure, including William V. Roth Jr., R-Del., Daniel Patrick Moynihan, D-N.Y., James M. Jeffords, R-Vt., and Edward M. Kennedy, D-Mass., in the Senate, and Rick A. Lazio, R-N.Y., and Kenny Hulshof, R-Mo., in the House, also had difficulty finding ways to offset the bill's estimated five-year cost of $500 million.

The measure was designed to end the paradox in which those receiving benefits under the Social Security Disability Insurance (SSDI) or Supplemental Security Income (SSI) programs could not attempt to return to work without throwing their ability to obtain health insurance into considerable doubt. The bill also revamped vocational rehabilitation and employment services for those with disabilities.

LEGISLATIVE ACTION

Before most people had ever heard of it, President Clinton singled out the measure and urged Congress to pass it in his State of the Union address in 1999 and in the fiscal 2000 budget.

After testimony from former Senate Majority Leader Robert J. Dole, R-Kan. (House 1961–1969; Senate 1969–1996), who was disabled as a result of a World War II injury, the Senate Finance Committee approved the bill on March 4, with Lott and Nickles casting the lone "nay" votes.

The House Commerce Committee health subcommittee approved it on April 20, with the full committee following suit on May 19. The bill emerged from both markups with no amendments but also no financing mechanism. That outraged the chairman of the competing House Ways and Means Committee, which shared jurisdiction over Medicare with the Commerce panel. In a sharply worded letter to Commerce Chairman Thomas J. Bliley Jr., R-Va., Ways and Means Chairman Bill Archer, R-Texas, reminded his colleague that the committees shared responsibility for paying for the program as well as for passing it.

The Senate passed its version of the bill (S 331) on June 16, by a vote of 99–0, after still more delays, including one imposed by Phil Gramm, R-Texas, who objected to raising a tax on foreign business to offset the bill's costs. President Clinton traveled to the Senate to urge the chamber to act the day before passage.

The financing issue continued to plague the legislation into the fall. The House Ways and Means Committee approved HR 1180 on Oct. 14, by a vote of 33–1, but only after paring back the bill's benefits. Commerce Committee members, including bill sponsor Lazio, were outraged that Ways and Means made some of the bill's Medicaid demonstration programs optional, because Ways and Means did not have jurisdiction over that program.

The House passed the bill, 412–9, on Oct. 12, but the White House immediately signaled it preferred the Senate-passed version. Because it only extended Medicare coverage for a period of years, rather than permanently as the Senate bill did, the House measure "extends the status quo that requires people with a disability to choose between work and health care, albeit six years later," Health and Human Services Secretary Donna Shalala wrote in a letter to Ways and Means Chairman Archer.

It took more than another month for informal negotiations to agree on "offsets" for the measure, as well as a final shape. Republican bill sponsors complained that although the White House urged passage of the bill, administration officials were not helping find alternatives.

In the end the White House proposed funding the measure using, among other things, changes to the earned income tax credit. Clinton administration officials also persuaded the House to add back $100 million for the Medicaid demonstration projects, but Nickles—who was not a conferee—managed to get the Medicare benefits cut back.

The bill was then delayed further when Commerce Chairman Bliley inserted into the bill a ninety-day moratorium on controversial Clinton administration regulations governing the allocation of organs for transplant. *(Organ transplants, p. 475)*

An accord was finally reached just as Congress prepared to leave for the year. The House approved the final version of HR 1180, on a 418–2 vote, on Nov. 18; the Senate cleared it the following day, 95–1.

MAJOR PROVISIONS

As signed into law on Dec. 17, HR 1180 included the following major provisions:

Medicare

The bill allowed those receiving SSDI benefits to work an additional four and a half years without losing their eligibility for Medicare. Under previous law, SSDI recipients could work

for nine months in a five-year period without jeopardizing benefits. They could then work an additional thirty-nine months and keep Medicare. The law extended that to a total of eight and a half years.

Medicaid

Effective Oct. 1, 2000, the bill allowed states to offer Medicaid coverage to individuals with disabilities whose incomes would otherwise disqualify them from receiving SSI. States could also continue coverage to workers with disabilities whose medical conditions had improved. Individuals whose incomes rose could buy into Medicaid coverage under a sliding fee scale. Those with incomes above $75,000 a year would pay the full premium.

Other

The bill also included a pilot program, funded at $250 million over six years, that would let states provide Medicaid to individuals with degenerative conditions who did not yet meet the stringent definition of disability. The provision was intended to provide prescription drugs and other treatment early in the course of a disease to keep those individuals healthy and able to work for as long as possible.

The measure also created a "ticket to work" allowing individuals to purchase rehabilitation and job services through state agencies or private providers. To give individuals reassurance that working would not endanger their benefits, the bill provided that taking a job would not automatically trigger a review of their disability status.

The measure included a pilot program to test the impact of gradually reducing SSDI benefits by $1 for every $2 of earnings over a salary level set by the Social Security commissioner. Under previous law, workers faced a "cliff" that cut benefits off entirely if they earned more than $700 per month.

The bill was financed by altering payments for the federal school lunch program and changing earned-income tax credit rules relating to payments for low-income foster children.

Breast and Cervical Cancer

Legislation (HR 4386—PL 106-354) enacted in 2000 allowed states to extend Medicaid coverage to previously uninsured low-income women whose breast or cervical cancer was discovered through a federally funded screening program. Although the bill was hugely popular, its trip to the president's desk was marked by partisan politics. Indeed, Clinton signed the bill in private, presumably to avoid having to invite its original sponsor, Rep. Rick A. Lazio, R-N.Y., to the White House for a signing ceremony just weeks before Lazio would face off at the polls against First Lady Hillary Rodham Clinton for a Senate seat.

The measure was also slowed by a related fight waged almost single-handedly by Rep. Tom Coburn, R-Okla., to require warning labels on condoms about their inability to protect against the human papillomavirus (HPV)—a major cause of cervical cancer.

The bill allowed—but did not require—states to provide Medicaid coverage to women whose cancers were found after they were screened under a program created in 1990 and run by the Centers for Disease Control and Prevention (CDC). In its first decade, the program screened about 1.5 million women with incomes under 250 percent of the federal poverty level for two of the most detectable cancers. More than 9,000 were found to have cancer. But under the terms of the 1990 Breast and Cervical Cancer Mortality Prevention Act (PL 100-354), none of the funds for the program could be used to pay for treatment. That left the women—who were, by definition, uninsured—scrambling to find charity care, or to run up huge debts obtaining treatment. *(1990 law, Congress and the Nation Vol. VIII, p. 593)*

Disputes over the original bill (HR 1070) were clear during the House Commerce Subcommittee on Health and Environment markup. Coburn—a family practitioner who said he diagnosed HPV in women weekly when he was practicing medicine—withdrew his HPV amendments, but he made it clear he would pursue them before the full committee.

The full House Commerce Committee reported the bill (H Rept 106-486) on Nov. 22, 1999. Included were Coburn's amendments requiring condom warning labels and ordering the CDC to increase its surveillance of HPV and to develop prevention and education activities to reduce the spread of the disease.

The bill, however, languished in the Senate, in part because of the death of its lead sponsor, Sen. John H. Chafee, R-R.I.

In February 2000 President Clinton endorsed the measure, calling on Congress to pass the bill in a weekly radio address to the nation and including $220 million to pay for the program in his fiscal 2001 budget. That marked a shift in administration policy on the bill. Previously, officials at the Department of Health and Human Services had expressed private concerns about granting Medicaid eligibility on the basis of a specific disease. Republicans responded by setting aside $250 million in the fiscal 2001 budget resolution.

The House passed a new bill (HR 4386) on May 9, 421–1, under a fast-track procedure that barred amendments but required a two-thirds majority for passage. House leaders had replaced Lazio's bill with one sponsored by Sue Myrick, R-N.C., and Pat Danner, D-Mo., two of the chamber's breast cancer survivors. And it was not just the sponsors that changed. The bill no longer included an "enhanced match" that would make it attractive to states. As approved by the committee, HR 1070 would have had the federal government paying 75 percent of costs for the women, with states having to put up only 25 percent. But HR 4386 offered states only their regular Medicaid matching rate.

Lazio said the change was needed because the Congressional Budget Office estimated the bill would cost more than the $250 million set aside in the budget resolution. But Democratic sponsors of the bill cried foul. Noting that GOP leaders had made much of the timing of the vote, the week before Mother's Day, Anna G. Eshoo, D-Calif., said "we might as well have passed a resolution that said 'we're thinking of you on Mother's Day.' "

After breast cancer advocates flooded members with complaints—and after Democratic backers of the measure threatened to vote against it—leaders hastily restored the enhanced match and instead moved the start date of the program to 2001 to make up the funding shortfall.

Meanwhile, medical officials complained about Coburn's HPV language. The American College of Obstetricians and Gynecologists said the language was "not medically appropriate."

The Senate Finance Committee reported its version of the bill (S 662—S Rept 106-323) on June 27, 2000. That measure was slightly less generous. Rather than the 75–25 match in the House bill, the Senate bill would follow the match formula for the Children's Health Insurance Program, which provided states 15 percentage points more than their regular Medicaid match, for an average of about 68 percent federal funding. But unlike the House bill, which delayed the effective date to keep the measure within the funding limit, the Senate measure was set to take effect Oct. 1, 2000. The Senate finally passed HR 4386 without debate and by voice vote on Oct. 4, after breast cancer advocates again launched grassroots attacks.

The House agreed to the Senate version of the bill by voice vote on Oct. 12, clearing the measure for the president. House leaders were planning to send back another version of the bill including HPV language Coburn had worked out with the medical community, but the breast cancer community said it feared the Senate would again let the measure languish. House leaders ultimately promised an angry Coburn his HPV language would be included in another bill. (It was subsequently added to that year's appropriation for the Department of Health and Human Services.) Clinton signed HR 4386 on Oct. 24, 2000.

Abortion

The 106th Congress wrangled over various abortion issues, but the continuing standoff between a Congress opposed to abortion rights and a president supportive of them resulted in only marginal changes in law or policy. *(1997–1998 action, p. 455)*

The highest-profile fight, the third effort in as many Congresses to pass a law banning a specific abortion procedure known by opponents as "partial-birth" abortion, was effectively made moot by a June 2000 U.S. Supreme Court decision. The Court struck down a Nebraska law that closely resembled the one President Clinton had vetoed on three separate occasions. *(Partial-birth, p, 455; Court decision, p. 717)*

One policy that did change was the so-called Mexico City policy that barred U.S. funds from going to international family planning organizations that "perform or promote" abortion, even if they used non-U.S. funds. But although abortion opponents were successful in reinstituting the policy in 1999 for the first time since Clinton overturned it in 1993, in 2000 the policy was again reversed. (*Mexico City policy, this page*)

In most cases, however, the more strongly antiabortion House passed a variety of measures that were never taken up by the Senate, or, in the case of riders to spending bills, were dropped by conferees.

PARTIAL-BIRTH ABORTION

It was hardly a surprise when the Senate on Oct. 21, 1999, voted to approve the "Partial Birth Abortion Ban Act." Congress had considered such a measure each year since the Republicans took control in 1995. Twice a bill was sent to President Clinton; twice he vetoed the measure; twice the House voted to override the veto; and twice the Senate voted to sustain it. (*1997–1998 action, p. 455*)

No senator changed votes in 1999 from his or her previous position; the 63–34 margin for the measure (S 1692) reflected a pickup of one vote for bill supporters because of changes in membership resulting from the 1998 elections.

Bill supporters did, however, lose a key ally, when the American Medical Association (AMA) announced it would not support the measure—a reversal of its position from the previous Congress. "The current version . . . subjects physicians to criminal prosecution. For this reason we do not support the bill," said a statement from AMA trustee John C. Nelson. AMA officials had been criticized by outside auditors for their 1997 endorsement of the bill, which auditors said was made outside AMA policy-making procedures.

The bill was changed somewhat from earlier versions. Responding to charges that the definition of the procedure was too vague, sponsor Rick Santorum, R-Pa., won voice vote approval of an amendment changing the definition to when a person "vaginally delivers some portion of an intact living fetus until the fetus is partially outside the body of the mother" and then "performs the overt act that kills the fetus."

But more attention was paid to a nonbinding amendment offered by abortion-rights supporters Barbara Boxer, D-Calif., and Tom Harkin, D-Iowa. By a **key vote of 51–47 (R 8–44; D 43–2; I 0–1)**, senators approved an amendment stating that *Roe v. Wade,* the Supreme Court's 1973 decision establishing a constitutional right to abortion, was "appropriate" and should not be overturned. Sponsors said it marked the first time Congress had ever taken a vote on whether to endorse the historic ruling. (*1999 key votes, p. 899*)

Bypassing its Judiciary Committee, the House took up its version (HR 3660) on April 5, 2000, approving it by a vote of 287–141. That was down from the 296 votes the measure received in the House in the previous Congress, but still more than enough to override President Clinton's promised veto. The president had complained repeatedly that the bill was too vague and could be interpreted to cover other, more commonly used abortion procedures, and that it lacked an exception allowing it to be used to protect the health, not just the life, of the pregnant woman.

On May 25 the House approved S 1692 by voice vote, after inserting into it the text of HR 3660. But Congress took no further action on the measure, as the debate moved from the legislative to the judicial branch of the federal government. On June 28, in *Stenberg v. Carhart,* the Supreme Court ruled, 5–4, that Nebraska's "partial birth" law was unconstitutional because it was too vague and did not require a health exception, as earlier decisions required. That appeared to make it obvious that unless the makeup of the Court changed, the federal bill, if passed, would be similarly struck down.

Although backers of the bill said they could deal with the vagueness problem, the health exception remained a stumbling block. Abortion opponents had long maintained that health has been defined so broadly, to include mental distress, that a health exception rendered a ban meaningless. The Court, however, had been steadfast that such exceptions were required even in the final trimester of pregnancy.

Still, backers of the measure said they had been able to change the shape of the nation's abortion debate even if they were unsuccessful in changing the law. "It's opened [members'] eyes to the violence of abortion," said Rep. Christopher H. Smith, R-N.J., longtime head of the House Pro-Life Caucus. Once lawmakers hear the details of one procedure, Smith said, they wonder "how violent are the other methods?"

MEXICO CITY POLICY

In its fight over the "Mexico City policy" that forbade U.S. funds from going to international family planning organizations that used non-U.S. funds to "perform or promote" abortion, the 106th Congress took a complicated debate and made it even more complicated. Since taking control of Congress in 1995, abortion foes, particularly in the House, had vowed to reinstate the policy, which was in effect from 1984 until President Clinton repealed it in 1993 on his second full day in office.

In 1996, 1997, and 1998 Congress and Clinton effectively fought to a draw. Although the policy was not reimposed, funding for the international family planning program under the Agency for International Development was frozen, and funds "metered out" in monthly increments of 8 percent. Also in 1998 Republicans took a hostage, blocking payment of back U.N. dues unless Clinton would agree to accept Mexico City language. The president refused. (*1995–1996 action, Congress and the Nation Vol. IX, p. 231, p. 234; 1997–1998 action, p. 457; U.N. dues, p. 192*)

In 1999 the House approved two conflicting family planning provisions during debate on the fiscal 2000 foreign operations spending bill (HR 2606). On July 29 members approved, 228–200, an amendment offered by Rep. Smith of New Jersey that would have prohibited aid to international family planning groups that performed abortions—except when the life of the woman would have been endangered by the pregnancy or in cases of rape or incest. Smith's amendment also would have barred family planning groups from using non-U.S. funds to lobby to change abortion laws. (*2000 foreign aid, p. 210*)

But the House also approved, 221–208, an amendment by abortion-rights supporter Jim Greenwood, R-Pa., that would have prohibited the use of U.S. funds to promote abortion as a means of family planning or to lobby for or against abortion. The amendment would not have limited what groups could do with non-U.S. funds. Twenty-two House members voted for both the Smith and Greenwood amendments.

The Senate version of the bill was silent on the issue, but the Senate in the past had largely opposed the Mexico City language. That left the matter unresolved, again, in conference. And, after an unrelated veto of the first version of the bill, the Clinton administration reluctantly agreed to allow the policy to be imposed as part of a deal to get the U.N. back dues paid.

The compromise version, included in a catch-all year end spending bill (HR 3194—PL 106-113), carried the first ever codification of the Mexico City policy. It barred U.S. aid to groups that performed abortions—except in cases of rape, incest, or where the life of the woman was in danger—or lobby to change abortion laws or government policies in other countries. Clinton was permitted to waive the restrictions, but that would trigger a shift of $12.5 million of the program's $385 million to an account for child survival and disease prevention. (Clinton subsequently did waive the restrictions.)

Family planning advocates were angry, but more at Republicans than Clinton. They accused Republicans of blackmailing the president because if the U.N. back dues were not paid, the United States could have faced loss of its seat in the body's General Assembly. "This is not a compromise, it is capitulation," said Nancy Pelosi, D-Calif., ranking member of the foreign operations subcommittee. "But the Republicans gave President Clinton no choice."

The victory for abortion foes, however, proved short-lived. Clinton vowed not to let the language remain in the bill the following year, and, to an extent, he prevailed. The final language in the fiscal 2001 foreign operations spending bill (HR 4811—PL 106-429) increased funding for the international family planning program to $425 million and dropped the restrictions, although it delayed any spending of the money until the following Feb. 15. That allowed the next president to reimpose the restrictions, which George W. Bush subsequently did, eight years to the day after Clinton rescinded them. *(2001 foreign aid, p. 214)*

PARENTAL NOTIFICATION

For the second consecutive Congress, the House passed legislation making it a crime to take a minor across state lines for an abortion in contravention of the minor's home state parental involvement law. And for the second consecutive Congress, the Senate took no action on the bill. *(1998 action, p. 456)*

The measure was inspired by a case in Pennsylvania, where a woman named Rosa Hartford was convicted of violating that state's "Interference with Custody of a Minor Act" by taking her eighteen-year-old son's thirteen-year-old girl-

friend across state lines to Binghamton, New York, for an abortion. Pennsylvania law required at least one parent's consent or a judge's permission for a minor to have an abortion; New York had no parental involvement law.

Under the bill, violators would have been subject to fines of as much as $100,000 and a year in prison. The bill would have barred prosecution when the abortion was necessary to save the girl's life and would exempt the recipient of the abortion from liability. Supporters of the measure said it was needed to bolster state efforts to ensure that parents are involved in such momentous decisions made by their daughters. But opponents said that criminalizing abortion assistance could further endanger minors, who might try to travel across state lines on their own or who might wait longer to have an abortion, making the procedure more dangerous.

President Clinton also expressed concerns about the bill. He wanted changes to allow close relatives, such as grandparents, exempted from the bill's requirements.

The House Judiciary Committee approved the measure (HR 1218—H Rept 106-204) by a 16–13 party-line vote on June 23, 1999, and reported it on June 25. As it had the year before, the committee turned back several amendments by Democrats to exempt not only close relatives but also clergy and godparents from potential criminal penalties. The committee also turned back efforts to include exceptions for girls who were the victim of incest or whose health would be endangered by the pregnancy.

The House passed the bill on June 30, 270–159, sixteen votes shy of the two-thirds required to override the president's promised veto. The Senate never acted on its version of the bill (S 661).

Unborn Victims of Violence

The House in 1999 passed legislation that would, for the first time, establish legal rights for a fetus. The "Unborn Victims of Violence Act," passed on Sept. 30, would have established as a separate federal crime the killing or injuring of a child "in utero at the time the conduct takes place" during the commission of another federal crime, such as an assault on a federal employee, or a crime taking place in a national park, military base, or other federal facility. The Senate, however, never acted on the measure.

The House Judiciary Committee approved the bill (HR 2436—H Rept 106-332, Pt. I) on Sept. 14, by a party-line vote of 14–11 and reported it on Sept. 24. Supporters said it was needed for cases such as the 1995 bombing in Oklahoma City, which killed three pregnant women. Under the measure, the perpetrator could have been charged not only with the deaths of the women but of their unborn children. "This legislation is not about abortion, but rather holding criminals accountable for their actions," said bill sponsor Lindsey Graham, R-S.C.

But opponents said abortion was exactly what the bill was about—that establishing rights for a fetus was a first step toward outlawing abortion. Among those opponents was the Clinton administration, which said in a letter Sept. 9 that its identification of a fetus as a separate and distinct victim was "unprecedented as a matter of federal statute" and "unnecessary for legislation that would augment punishment of violence against pregnant women."

Debate on the House floor on Sept. 30 was much as it was at the Judiciary Committee. The House approved the bill by a **key vote of 254–172 (R 198–21; D 56–150; I 0–1),** well short of the two-thirds required to override the promised presidential veto. Members defeated a Zoe Lofgren, D-Calif., amendment to replace the bill with enhanced federal penalties against perpetrators of violent federal crimes against pregnant women that resulted in the injury or death of her fetus. The amendment, which was rejected 201–224, would not have recognized the offense against the fetus as a separate crime. Lofgren's proposal had been defeated during committee consideration as well. *(1999 key votes, p. 899)*

Organ Transplants

A two-year fight between the Department of Health and Human Services (HHS) and the contractor that operated the nation's transplant system culminated in 2000 in Congress finally allowing to take effect controversial HHS rules creating an organ distribution system based more on medical need and less on geography. Congress had acted on three separate bills to delay the regulations since 1998, and the House in 1999 passed a bill that would have cancelled the rules outright. In 2000, however, the two chambers failed to agree on legislation that would have reauthorized the nation's transplant programs and settled the dispute legislatively.

At issue was the way scarce organs were distributed for transplants. By 1997 the waiting list for organs had tripled since 1990. In 1997 20,045 patients received transplants, while 56,716 patients remained on waiting lists, and 4,316 patients died before receiving a needed organ.

The system in effect, operated by the Richmond, Va.-based United Network for Organ Sharing (UNOS), gave first priority for an available organ to patients locally, then regionally, then nationally. As a result, a patient with a lesser medical need might get an organ before a sicker person only slightly farther away.

That was unfair, said officials at HHS. With new technologies and an increased ability to move organs longer distances without jeopardizing their viability, the old system in which patients in some areas waited only days while those in others waited years no longer made sense. Its regulations ordered UNOS to come up with a new allocation system that would if not equalize waiting times in different parts of the country, at least significantly narrow the differences.

But UNOS disagreed with HHS's interpretation of the situation. It charged that the rules would result in a national waiting list in which patients too sick to benefit from an organ transplant would receive organs. It also said that basing

distribution on medical need rather than geography would channel most organs to the largest transplant centers with the sickest patients and longest lists. That, in turn, UNOS said, could force smaller centers to close and might deter people from becoming organ donors.

Congress got involved in the dispute more on a regional than a partisan basis. Lawmakers from states home to smaller centers sided with UNOS, as did House Energy and Commerce Chairman Thomas J. Bliley Jr., R-Va., whose district was home to UNOS headquarters. Meanwhile, lawmakers from areas with larger centers, notably Pennsylvania, home to the nation's largest transplant center at the University of Pittsburgh, sided with the Clinton administration.

In the end, Congress's only true expert on the subject, former heart-lung transplant surgeon Sen. Bill Frist, R-Tenn., tried to forge a compromise. But it was ultimately blocked by complaints from the Wisconsin delegation, which had been in the forefront of efforts to block the rules.

With no reauthorizing legislation and no further delays imposed by Congress, the disputed regulations finally took effect on March 16, 2000.

BACKGROUND

The fight began in earnest on April 2, 1998, when HHS published the first version of the rules. Congress reacted almost immediately. House Appropriations Chairman Bob Livingston, R-La., reflecting the desires of his state, which had a law requiring that organs harvested in the state first be offered to state residents, inserted language into the fiscal 1998 supplemental spending bill (HR 3579—PL 105-174), extending the rule's comment period from June 1 to Aug. 31, and delaying implementation from July 1 to "no earlier than Oct. 1."

Over that summer, the fight raged. In June HHS Secretary Donna Shalala traded jabs with UNOS officials at a joint hearing held by the Senate Labor and Human Resources Committee and the House Commerce health subcommittee. "I am personally and deeply saddened that UNOS has frightened patients and perhaps jeopardized organ donation in some areas of the country," she told the hearing, referring to UNOS's million-dollar lobbying campaign. UNOS President Dr. Lawrence Hunsicker repeated UNOS's assertions that the regulations would require a single, national list and that organs would be transplanted into patients too sick to benefit from them.

In August UNOS and HHS officials tried to work out a compromise, but the UNOS board rejected a settlement document after HHS refused to rewrite the rules. With no deal in sight, attention turned to the fiscal 1999 appropriation bill for the department, to which Livingston had already added language imposing a year-long moratorium on the rules. Livingston, however, had to contend in the Senate with the chairman of the Labor-HHS-Education Appropriations Subcommittee, Arlen Specter, R-Pa., who was "prepared to go to the mat" over keeping that language out, said an aide.

Meanwhile, the rules were blocked an additional two weeks beyond Oct. 1 by a federal judge in Baton Rouge in response to a lawsuit filed by the governor of Louisiana. The suit charged that the regulations violated the Louisiana law giving state residents first right to donated organs.

In the end the Labor-HHS portion of the omnibus spending bill (HR 4328—PL 105-277) included the year-long delay but also ordered UNOS to provide center-by-center statistics on survival rates, organ wastage, and waiting list information. The bill also called for the independent Institute of Medicine (IoM), an arm of the National Academy of Sciences, to report on existing organ distribution policies and the potential effect of the new rules.

1999 LEGISLATIVE ACTION

Both sides in the dispute claimed that the IoM report, released July 20, 1999, sided with them. UNOS noted the report found that the current system worked relatively well. HHS, on the other hand, noted that the report also found that larger organ-sharing regions "will result in more opportunities to transplant sicker patients without adversely affecting less sick patients" and that larger regions would not result in fewer organs being donated, closure of smaller centers, wasting organs on those unlikely to survive, or making organs less available to minorities and those in rural areas—all charges leveled by UNOS in its fight against the rules.

Although most of the legislative action had been at the appropriations level, the authorizers weighed in that fall. On Nov. 1, the House Energy and Commerce Committee reported legislation (HR 2418—H Rept 106-429) reauthorizing programs under the 1984 National Organ Transplant Act (PL 98-507) and stripping the department of much of its authority to oversee the activities of the contractor that ran the organ allocation program. Health and Environment Subcommittee Chairman Michael Bilirakis, R-Fla., sponsored the bill and full committee chairman Bliley cosponsored it. *(1984 act, Congress and the Nation Vol. VI, p. 549)*

The debate in committee was sharp—with opponents charging that UNOS was trying to thwart efforts to make the allocation process more fair to protect the economic interests of transplant centers that could lose patients if organs were given to the sickest, not just the nearest, patients. The Clinton administration also charged that the bill was unconstitutional because it "[gives] to a private organization regulatory authority unfettered by executive involvement," said a letter to the committee from the Justice Department.

Meanwhile, the House Appropriations Committee version of the fiscal 2000 Labor-HHS appropriations bill (HR 3037—H Rept 106-370) included another year-long delay.

On Oct. 18 HHS issued a revised version of its final rules, including language clarifying that organs should not be wasted by giving them to patients unlikely to live. But UNOS and its allies in Congress said the changes did not go far enough. The regulations were scheduled to take effect on Nov. 19.

On Nov. 10, however, after a late-night meeting in the Capitol, Shalala reached agreement with the chairmen of the Appropriations committees, Rep. Bill Young, R-Fla., and Sen. Ted Stevens, R-Alaska, to include in the year's omnibus spending bill (HR 3194—PL 106-113) language to delay the rules by an additional forty-two days—twenty-one days for an additional comment period and twenty-one more days for a review of those suggestions.

Opponents of the rules, including Senate Majority Leader Trent Lott, R-Miss., complained that the deal meant the rules would take effect before Congress returned to legislative business in 2000, and before it had a chance to complete action on a reauthorization bill.

Bliley stalled action on a bill he had been working on with Frist, chairman of the Senate Health, Education, Labor and Pensions Committee's Public Health Subcommittee, to reauthorize the Agency for Health Care Policy and Research, in an effort to get Frist to move an organ transplant bill before the end of the session. Frist, who had not yet taken sides in the organ allocation dispute, refused. "If [the rule] went in as it is now I don't think patients would be hurt," he said.

The fight between Bliley and Frist was ultimately made moot when, on Nov. 17, Lott and Senate Majority Whip Don Nickles, R-Okla., inserted into the conference version of the Work Incentives Improvement Act (HR 1180—PL 106-170)—a bill badly wanted by President Clinton—a rider that would block the rules from going into effect for ninety days, overriding the forty-two-day deal reached earlier. That bill, including the rider, passed the House on Nov. 18 by a vote of 418–2 and the Senate the next day by a vote of 95–1. Although White House officials accused leaders of "bad faith" in reneging on the earlier deal, Clinton ultimately signed the bill on Dec. 17, 1999. Leaders had carefully not sent the president the work incentives bill until he had signed the omnibus appropriation measure with its forty-two-day delay because the measure the president signed last prevailed as policy. *(Disabled workers insurance, p. 470)*

2000 LEGISLATIVE ACTION

Because Congress had not acted by the time the last legislative delay expired, the rules took effect as scheduled on March 16, 2000. But the fight was not over.

On April 4 the House passed HR 2418 by a vote of 275–147, after a nasty debate and over the veto threat of the president. Members defeated, 160–260, an amendment by Ray LaHood, R-Ill., that would have replaced the language overturning the regulations with a scheme along the lines of the contested regulations. And they approved, by voice vote, an amendment by Joe Scarborough, R-Fla., and Karen Thurman, D-Fla., nullifying the rules outright.

Lawmakers took turns accusing UNOS and HHS of attempting a power grab. "Unless we pass this bill, federal bureaucrats will be the masters of what happens to your body when you die," said Ernest Istook, R-Okla.

But others responded that UNOS was trying to protect its member transplant centers rather than patients at large. "This bill is founded on deceit, misrepresentation, and falsehood by a rather shoddy, shabby contractor who seeks an absolute monopoly over the handling of organs in this nation," said Energy and Commerce Committee ranking Democrat John D. Dingell Jr., Mich.

The Senate moved quickly thereafter. Frist, along with UNOS backers Jeff Sessions, R-Ala., and Tim Hutchinson, R-Ark., the next day unveiled what he called an effort to find a middle ground. He said his bill (S 2366), the "Organ Procurement and Transplantation Network Act of 2000," sought to "ensure that organ transplant policies are developed by the medical community while allowing for appropriate federal oversight of the organ transplant system." The bill called for creation of a board charged with setting transplant policies based on "sound medical principles and valid scientific data that balance the ethical goals of equity and utility in the establishment of organ transplant policy." Disputes would be settled by a separate, independent, scientific advisory board comprised of fifteen members—five each appointed by HHS, UNOS, and the Institute of Medicine.

Just hours before a scheduled markup on April 12, Frist reached agreement with Edward M. Kennedy, D-Mass., ranking Democrat on the Senate health panel as well as Frist's subcommittee, and Clinton administration officials on a compromise measure. The talks produced three major changes in S 2366. One was a list of criteria the transplant community would have to consider in developing an allocation system; the second would have allowed the HHS secretary to prod the policy-making board into action if it failed to address an issue; and the final one expanded the dispute-resolution board from fifteen to twenty-one members. The committee unanimously approved the measure that day and reported it the following day (no written report).

But it progressed no further. Wisconsin Democratic Sens. Herb Kohl and Russell Feingold refused to allow the bill to come to the floor, in deference to their governor, Republican Tommy G. Thompson, who had sued HHS to overturn the rules. Thompson charged that Shalala had exceeded her authority.

The fight was ultimately settled between HHS and UNOS in September, when UNOS signed a new contract to continue to run the program in which it essentially agreed to many of the provisions of the regulations.

Negotiations continued in Congress, however, because the overall transplant program remained unauthorized. In October negotiators gave up when the House and Senate proved unable to resolve the broader issues. "We would have liked to have had a bill," said HHS Assistant Secretary for Legislation Richard Tarplin, "but the contract goes a long way to ensure a fairer transplant system in the future."

Assisted Suicide

The House in 1999 passed legislation (HR 2660) that would have blocked Oregon's first-in-the-nation assisted suicide law, but for the second straight Congress, the measure failed to clear the Senate under a filibuster threat from Oregon Democratic Sen. Ron Wyden.

The bill's primary purpose was to overturn a 1998 ruling by Attorney General Janet Reno that Oregon's "Death with Dignity Act" did not violate the federal Controlled Substances Act. The Oregon law, approved by voters in that state in 1994 and again in 1997, permitted physicians to prescribe lethal doses of certain drugs to aid a suicide for certain terminally ill patients.

Reno's ruling itself overturned a 1997 ruling by the Drug Enforcement Administration, which found that the Oregon law did, in fact, violate the federal statute. DEA administrator Thomas Constantine wrote in a letter to House Judiciary Committee Chairman Henry J. Hyde, R-Ill., and Senate Judiciary Committee Chairman Orrin G. Hatch, R-Utah, that the federal law allowed physicians to prescribe drugs on the controlled substances list only for "legitimate medical purposes" and that assisted suicide or euthanasia was not a legitimate medical purpose.

Reno disagreed. "We have concluded that the [Controlled Substances Act] does not authorize DEA to prosecute, or to revoke the DEA registration of, a physician who has assisted in a suicide in compliance with Oregon law," she wrote in a letter to Wyden.

Hyde and Senate Majority Whip Don Nickles, R-Okla., set about to write the DEA interpretation into law, introducing the "Lethal Drug Abuse Prevention Act" only days after Reno's decision was made public. The bill barred physicians from prescribing controlled substances "with the purpose of causing, or assisting in causing, the suicide or euthanasia of any individual."

But although the legislation (HR 4006, S 2151) was reported by both the House and Senate Judiciary Committees in 1998, it never came up for a vote in either chamber. The House scheduled the bill several times in the autumn of 1998, but action was fought not only by Wyden, a self-professed opponent of the Oregon law who nevertheless objected to the bill on state's rights grounds, but also by the medical community, which said that allowing the DEA to pass judgment on physicians' prescribing habits would discourage them from prescribing strong painkillers for terminally ill patients, lest that be mistaken for an attempt to aid a suicide. *(1998 action, p. 606)*

Health Policy Research Agency

Congress in 1999 reauthorized, renamed, and redirected the Agency for Health Care Policy and Research (AHCPR), which had been created a decade earlier (PL 101-239) to study medical "outcomes" in an effort to help determine what kind of care worked best and was most cost-effective.

As signed by President Clinton on Dec. 6, 1999, the measure (S 580—PL 106-129) renewed the agency for four years under the new name of Agency for Healthcare Research and Quality (to be known as AHRQ, pronounced "arc"). The measure refocused the agency's mission toward helping private-sector efforts to measure and improve the quality of health care.

The measure also authorized, for the first time, a separate program to help underwrite the costs of training pediatricians and pediatric specialists in children's hospitals. Although the federal government had long underwritten a large portion of the nation's graduate medical education bill through the Medicare program, relatively few children's hospitals qualified for any of those funds because such a tiny portion of Medicare beneficiaries were children. The provision, which authorized a total of $280 million in fiscal 2000 and $285 million in fiscal 2001, was originally a separate bill introduced by Rep. Nancy L. Johnson, R-Conn.

The reauthorization legislation, said House Commerce Committee Chairman Thomas J. Bliley Jr., R-Va., "builds on the progress [AHCPR] had already made. It will enable us to benefit from our investment in biomedical research, to improve the health care delivery programs under our jurisdiction, and to build the science of quality measurement and improvement."

In its original form, one of AHCPR's roles had been to develop "clinical practice guidelines" to help educate health care professionals about the best ways to treat common ailments. Some of the guidelines, however, ruffled feathers. AHCPR's guideline questioning the value of surgery to treat chronic low back pain prompted outrage from back surgeons, who set out—and nearly succeeded—to strip the agency of its funding in the mid-1990s. The agency subsequently had its budget cut roughly in half, and soon got out of the business of publishing practice guidelines. The 1999 legislation eliminated that authority.

The Senate acted first on the measure, approving the text of S 580 as part of the "Patients' Bill of Rights" (S 1344) on July 15. Senators said the inclusion was meant to address the fact that the Democrats' version of that bill did not directly address quality issues.

The House went through a more standard process, starting at the Health and Environment Subcommittee of the Commerce Committee, which approved its version (HR 2506) on July 27. "The bill specifically prohibits the agency from mandating 'national standards of clinical practice or quality health care standards,'" said subcommittee chairman Michael Bilirakis, R-Fla. "Instead, it emphasizes the agency's nonregulatory role in building the science of health care quality," he said.

The full Commerce Committee reported HR 2506 (H Rept 106-305) on Sept. 8 and, following a brief debate, the House passed the measure by a vote of 417–7 on Sept. 28.

The amendment adding the children's graduate medical education provisions was adopted by voice vote. "Freestanding children's hospitals receive on average less than one-half of one percent of what other teaching facilities receive in federal [graduate medical education] funding," said Johnson. "This amendment merely establishes interim assistance to our children's hospitals to maintain their teaching

programs while Congress reforms the way we as a nation fund medical education."

With both houses having technically passed the bill, no formal conference was convened and members and staff worked out their relatively minor differences informally. The Senate passed a compromise version of S 580—including the children's hospital graduate medical education provisions—by voice vote on Nov. 3.

But its own House sponsor, Commerce Committee Chairman Bliley, blocked final approval of the compromise. Bliley held up scheduled House approval of the compromise in an effort to pressure the bill's Senate sponsor, Bill Frist, R-Tenn., on a separate issue. Bliley wanted badly before the end of the 1999 session for the Senate to pass legislation he had already pushed through the committee that would overturn controversial Clinton administration rules regarding the distribution of human organs for transplant. Frist, a transplant surgeon before being elected to the Senate in 1994, had not, at that point, taken a position on the transplant issue, although he would attempt to find a compromise in the year 2000. *(Organ transplants, p. 475)*

Although the bill would not have died if it was not passed by the end of the session in 1999, backers of the children's hospital program did have an imperative—appropriators had included $40 million in the final version of the fiscal 2000 spending bill for the Department of Health and Human Services, but with a stipulation that the funds could not be used unless the program was authorized.

Bliley ultimately backed off when Senate Republican leaders dealt with the organ transplant issue on another bill, and the House cleared S 580 by voice vote on Nov. 18.

Medical Errors

Congress reacted quickly to a report from the Institute of Medicine issued in November 1999 that found medical errors caused between 44,000 and 98,000 deaths annually. But although members vowed to act on the institute's recommendations and several bills were introduced, action stalled over the question of whether to require mandatory reporting of errors resulting in injury or death.

Congress did take one concrete step in 2000 to address the issue, adding language to the fiscal 2001 spending bill (HR 4577—PL 106-554) for the Department of Health and Human Services (HHS) authorizing creation of a Center for Patient Safety within the Agency for Healthcare Research and Quality (AHRQ) to act as a clearinghouse for studies into ways to prevent and address medical errors. The measure appropriated $50 million for the activities.

The report by a committee of the congressionally chartered Institute of Medicine was issued while Congress was in recess in 1999. But even before members returned, several vowed to act quickly and hearings were held.

Senate Health, Education, Labor and Pensions Committee ranking Democrat Edward M. Kennedy of Massachusetts, said within days he would introduce legislation to carry out the panel's recommendations, including creation of the patient safety center and establishment of a mandatory reporting system for serious or fatal errors and a voluntary reporting system for less serious incidents.

In mid-December 1999, a hearing of the Senate Appropriations subcommittee responsible for HHS's spending bill showed just how controversial efforts to address the problem would be. Members of the institute's panel said that reporting was key to reaching its goal of reducing errors by half over five years. "The public has a right to know about errors resulting in serious harm, and this information should be made available to the public with appropriate safeguards for protecting patient and provider confidentiality," testified panel member Mary Wakefield of George Mason University.

But the health care provider community insisted that reporting would do more harm than good. "We have to create an environment in which we learn from failure," testified Stanton Smullens on behalf of the American Hospital Association. "This cannot be achieved in an environment of punishment or fear of legal prosecution for doctors, nurses and other care givers who step forward after an unfortunate mistake is made."

In the end, efforts to produce a bipartisan bill bogged down. By June Democrats and Republicans on the Health, Education, Labor and Pensions Committee introduced separate measures. The Democratic bill, cosponsored by Kennedy and Christopher J. Dodd, D-Conn., would ultimately have called for mandatory reporting of errors, while the GOP measure, sponsored by committee chairman James M. Jeffords, R-Vt., and Public Health Subcommittee Chairman Bill Frist, R-Tenn., would have made reporting systems entirely voluntary.

Neither of the bills moved, nor did bipartisan measures sponsored by Labor-HHS Appropriations Subcommittee Chairman Arlen Specter, R-Pa., and ranking Democrat Tom Harkin of Iowa, nor by a group led by Senate Aging Committee Chairman Charles E. Grassley, R-Iowa, and Joseph I. Lieberman, D-Conn.

Medical Privacy

Congress in 2000 failed to pass legislation to ensure the confidentiality of medical records and instead let controversial rules issued by the Clinton administration take effect.

Congress had been grappling with the issue since 1996. It had failed to reach agreement on the best way to protect people's privacy while still ensuring the smooth operation of the health care system during consideration of the Health Insurance Portability and Accountability Act (HIPAA; PL 104-191), but instead Congress had set a deadline for itself. If it did not pass legislation on the subject by Aug. 21, 1999, then it ordered the administration to issue its own rules within six months.

Members did try to meet the deadline—the Senate Health, Education, Labor and Pensions Committee scheduled three separate markups on a bill in 1999. But each was cancelled, when it became clear that bipartisan consensus was unreach-

able, and that no bill could go forward without bipartisan support.

Most at issue was the degree to which health care providers and researchers should be able to use personal medical information. Privacy advocates wanted to require patients to give explicit permission each time their information was to be used. Health industry officials and, particularly, researchers said that would be both expensive and impractical, and that the quality of patient care could be compromised.

Privacy advocates, however, responded that care was already being compromised by patients who were not telling doctors important information for fear it could be disclosed, or by patients who were not seeking care for sensitive conditions such as mental ailments or sexually transmitted diseases.

Also at issue for lawmakers was the extent to which parents should have access to their children's medical records. Many states had individual laws protecting the privacy of teenagers to encourage them to seek needed care, particularly regarding reproductive health.

Following Congress's failure to meet the deadline, the Department of Health and Human Services issued its regulations on Oct. 29, 1999. The first-ever rules on medical privacy would guarantee patients access to their medical records and strictly limit who else could use that information. The rules also extended to the private sector existing privacy protections for federal researchers.

To the dismay of privacy advocates, it allowed health insurance companies to seek a one-time authorization for a broad array of activities under the heading "health plan operations." But advocates were cheered because, unlike a draft of the rules released in 1997, the regulation did include restrictions on access to identifiable medical information by law enforcement officials.

But both supporters and opponents continued to urge Congress to act. Industry officials wanted a national standard for privacy rules to prevent insurance companies and other interstate providers from having to abide by what they called "a patchwork" of state laws. Advocates—as well as the Clinton administration—also wanted Congress to create a "right of action" that would let individuals sue anyone who wrongly disclosed their information. Under the rules, violators could be punished only by fines.

Under the terms of HIPAA, the administration was also able to cover only a limited number of entities that handled sensitive medical information—health plans, health care clearinghouses, and health care providers who transmitted information in electronic form. And it could cover only information transmitted electronically, despite the fact that the majority of medical records continued to be kept on paper.

With both sides complaining about some aspects of the rules—40,000 separate sets of comments were filed—Congress continued to struggle with the issue in 2000. Although the comprehensive approach remained on hold, other attempts to address individual facets of the issue were made.

On July 20 the House Banking and Financial Services Committee reported a bill (HR 4585—H Rept 106-773, Pt. I) that would have required insurance companies and banks to get consumers' consent before sharing their medical records with affiliated companies and third parties. That bill would have allowed individuals to sue financial institutions for disclosing personal medical information without consent. The bill, however, was bottled up in the House Commerce Committee, which was also struggling with the broader bill.

The Senate that same day also addressed concerns about the use of medical records. By a **key vote of 58–40 (R 55–0; D 3–40)**, it adopted a James M. Jeffords, R-Vt., amendment to a Labor, Health and Human Services, and Education funding bill (HR 4577) prohibiting health insurers from discriminating against customers based on genetic information. *(2000 key votes, p. 915)*

Meanwhile, President Clinton issued the final version of the required medical privacy regulations on Dec. 20, 2000. The final rules included some significant changes from the version unveiled fourteen months earlier. The administration decided it had the authority, after all, to protect paper records as well as electronic ones. The new version barred employers from accessing medical records for any purpose not directly related to providing health care. In a bow to privacy advocates, the new rules also required patient consent even for routine use of medical information.

Industry officials were outraged. Although the Clinton administration estimated the rules would cost industry about $18 billion over five years, they insisted it would be much higher. The American Hospital Association said it would cost hospitals alone as much as $22 billion to make the changes the rules required. Industry vowed to seek to have the rules changed by the incoming Bush administration.

Physician Antitrust

At the behest of the nation's doctors, the House in 2000 passed legislation (HR 1304) that would have made it easier for health professionals to band together to negotiate with health insurance companies without running afoul of the nation's antitrust laws. But faced with strong opposition from both the insurance industry and the Clinton administration, the measure never came up for a vote in the Senate.

Physicians, led by the American Medical Association (AMA), said the bill was needed to allow doctors to deal on a more equal footing with rapidly consolidating health insurers, who were able to offer physicians "take it or leave it" deals that, they said, not only drove down their fees but compromised the quality of care they could deliver to their patients.

"While there have been positive changes in the health care delivery system over the past decade to provide health care in more economically efficient ways, the pendulum has swung too far," Dr. E. Ratcliffe Anderson, AMA executive vice president, told the House Judiciary Committee at a June 1999 hearing on the measure before the House Judiciary Committee. "Health plans now have a degree of leverage and influence over medical decision-making which is not offset by any countervailing force because of the antitrust limitations applied to physicians."

But antitrust officials said that relaxing those laws— which prevent physicians who are not employees from jointly negotiating—was not the answer to abuses by the health insurance industry. Rather, they said, the bill was aimed more at increasing doctors' incomes than helping patients. "The AMA could pull every single doctor together, or its local chapters, and go to each and every HMO or managed care program and say 'we will not work for you unless you pay us X.' That is unprecedented, irrational economic power," testified Justice Department antitrust head Joel Klein at that same hearing.

The bill, sponsored by Rep. Tom Campbell, R-Calif., a former head of the Federal Trade Commission's Bureau of Competition, created some surprising political alliances. Although the Clinton administration was working with the AMA and against the insurance industry to pass a "patients' bill of rights," it was working with the insurance industry and against the AMA on the antitrust bill.

LEGISLATIVE ACTION

The bill's trip was a complicated one. Because Campbell was running for the Senate, Republican leaders in the House wanted to help him. But with the insurance and business communities dead set against his bill, leaders were left in a tight spot.

Despite the misgivings, the House Judiciary Committee approved the bill by a lopsided vote of 26–2 on March 30, 2000, and reported it (H Rept 106-625) on May 18. Both the committee's chairman, Henry J. Hyde, R-Ill., and its ranking member, John Conyers Jr., D-Mich., supported it.

But the measure sustained a setback when the Congressional Budget Office estimated it could cost the government more than $6 billion over ten years because of higher physician fees, and increase the cost of private insurance by 2.6 percent.

Nevertheless, House leaders scheduled the measure for a vote to keep a promise House Speaker J. Dennis Hastert, R-Ill., made to Campbell. But just hours before the planned vote on May 25, the bill was pulled after the Rules Committee—controlled by the leadership—failed to reach agreement on the terms for the debate. Earlier the previous day, a majority of Republicans had voted in a closed caucus meeting to stop the bill from coming up, but the proposal did not receive the required two-thirds vote for approval.

Campbell was infuriated, accusing leaders of bowing to demands by rank-and-file Republicans that they not have to choose between their friends in the insurance community and their friends in the medical community. He said, "What members have told me individually, the most common expression was 'don't force me to choose between two potential contributors, insurance and medicine. As long as I don't have to vote on this bill, I have a chance of getting contributions from both.'"

Campbell finally got his debate—from 11 p.m. on June 29 until 2 the next morning. During that time, the House adopted an amendment by Tom Coburn, R-Okla., which would have barred discussion of abortion during collective bargaining negotiations. It was approved 213–202. Members, however, rejected other amendments intended to water down the bill, including one by Cass Ballenger, R-N.C., which would have barred discussions of fees. It failed 71–345.

The House on June 30 passed the bill 276–136, with two members voting present.

Public Health, Bioterrorism

The 106th Congress just before adjournment in 2000 packaged together a series of bills addressing public health needs, including a measure to authorize the nation's health agencies to protect against bioterrorism and other deadly health threats. President Clinton signed the "Public Health Improvement Act" (HR 2498—PL 106-505) into law on Nov. 13.

As enacted, the measure included the following bills:

• S 2731, the "Public Health Threats and Emergencies Act," which authorized $540 million to help both local and federal agencies better prepare to detect and respond to disease outbreaks. The bill called for coordination of efforts with the Department of Health and Human Services (HHS) and the Department of Defense to examine the nation's preparedness for a bioterrorist attack; to require HHS, the Federal Emergency Management Agency, and the attorney general to review the medical consequences of such an attack; and authorize health agencies to develop new vaccines for biological weapons. The measure also authorized $180 million for the Centers for Disease Control and Prevention (CDC) to modernize its laboratories. Finally, it called for a public information campaign for doctors and patients on the appropriate use of antibiotics and established a task force to coordinate federal efforts to fight antibiotic-resistant germs. The Senate Health, Education, Labor, and Pensions Committee reported the bill (S Rept 106-505) on Oct. 18, 2000.

• S 1813, the "Clinical Research Enhancement Act," which established clinical research fellowships to encourage more health professionals to pursue careers in research by helping pay off student loans and other educational expenses. The measure also authorized creation of "general clinical research centers" that would support clinical studies and career development in hospitals and academic medical centers. The Senate originally passed the bill by voice vote on Nov. 19, 1999.

• S 1268, the "Twenty-First Century Research Laboratories Act," which authorized grants for the construction or renovation of laboratory facilities and the purchase of new equipment for recipients of funding from the National Institutes of Health. The Senate passed the bill by voice vote on Nov. 19, 1999.

• HR 2498, originally the "Cardiac Arrest Survival Act," which required the secretary of health and human services to make recommendations about the placement of automated

electronic defibrillators (AEDs) in public places, and provided "good Samaritan" protection from lawsuits in most cases for those who use the devices to aid an apparent victim of cardiac arrest. The original version of HR 2498—before the other public health bills were attached to it—was reported (H Rept 106-634) by the House Commerce Committee on May 23, 2000, and was passed by the full House later that day by a 415–2 vote. The Senate had passed its version (S 1488) by voice vote on Nov. 19, 1999.

• S 2528, the "Rural Access to Emergency Devices Act," which authorized grants to help rural communities purchase AEDs. The Senate passed the bill on Oct. 10, 2000.

• HR 762, the "Lupus Research Act," which authorized grants for activities at the NIH related to lupus, an autoimmune disease with a survival rate of 80 to 90 percent. The grants would include research on the basic cause of the disease and an examination to determine reasons it disproportionately affects African American women, and to develop new tests and treatments. The measure also authorized grants to projects that provide services to lupus patients through local government agencies and nonprofit organizations. The House Commerce Committee reported the bill (H Rept 106-950) on Oct. 10, 2000, and the full House passed it later that day by a vote of 385–2.

• S 1243, the "Prostate Cancer Research and Protection Act," which expanded authority for research activities at the NIH and detection activities by the CDC. The Senate originally passed the bill by voice vote on Nov. 19, 1999.

• S 2625, the "Organ Procurement Organization Certification Act," which required the HHS Department to extend the recruitment period for organ procurement organizations from two to four years, improve performance standards for recertification, and establish an appeals process for organizations that are decertified. The Senate originally passed the bill by voice vote on June 7, 2000.

LEGISLATIVE ACTION

The Senate's version of the defibrillator legislation that would serve as the base for what members called the "minibus" measure, S 1488, originally passed the Senate on the last legislative day of 1999, Nov. 19. It called for a study of the appropriateness of placing automated defibrillators, which could be used by laypeople, in public places. It also provided protections from lawsuits for those using the devices in most situations.

But that "good Samaritan" language proved controversial in the House, and it took several months to work out a compromise. The House finally acted, passing its version of the measure, HR 2498, by a vote of 415–2 on May 23, 2000. The House bill provided protection from lawsuits unless the person using the device "engaged in gross negligence or willful or wanton misconduct."

In the process of working out the details on the bill, members and staffs of the Senate Health, Education, Labor, and Pensions Committee and House Energy and Commerce Committee decided to use it as a vehicle to pull several other non-controversial health measures, most of which had already passed in one chamber or the other.

The measure, however, was held up briefly when Energy and Commerce Chairman Thomas J. Bliley Jr., R-Va., threatened to add a very controversial bill to the measure—one opening up to the public the National Practitioner Data Bank, which collected raw data on malpractice settlements and disciplinary information taken against health care practitioners. Physician groups vehemently opposed making the information, used by hospitals and health plans in background checks, available to the general public. The American Medical Association accused Bliley of pushing the issue to punish the normally Republican-leaning organization for its support of the largely Democrat-backed "patients' bill of rights," a charge Bliley denied.

Bliley, who originally offered to keep the malpractice information confidential but make the disciplinary information public, subsequently backed down. The Senate passed the compromise bill by voice vote on Oct. 26, 2000. The House cleared it by a vote of 384–2 the following day.

Children's Health

President Clinton on Oct. 17, 2000, signed into law what began as a noncontroversial bill (HR 4365—PL 106-310) combining a series of measures affecting the health of children, and, after some controversy, grew to include other bills reauthorizing mental health and substance abuse programs, as well as day care programs.

As enacted, the bill included provisions to:

• Create a new, $50 million per year Pediatric Research Initiative within the National Institutes of Health. The measure also directed new research resources toward a variety of ailments, including unintentional injury, autism, Fragile X mental retardation syndrome, juvenile arthritis, diabetes, asthma, birth defects, hearing loss, epilepsy, maternal health, prenatal care, traumatic brain injury, poisoning, hepatitis C, and other conditions. The measure also created new protections for children in federally funded research projects, including new ways to determine acceptable levels of risk as well as obtain parental informed consent.

• Authorize $200 million in block grants to states to improve the quality of day care services.

• Reauthorize the Substance Abuse and Mental Health Services Administration, giving states new flexibility in using funds but requiring reports to track accountability. The bill authorized grants of $100 million to help cities fight youth violence and $50 million for research into psychiatric disorders among children who have witnessed violence. It authorized another $70 million for substance abuse programs, including those aimed at preventing the use of methamphetamines and the drug "Ecstacy"; $40 million to help offenders released from juvenile justice facilities; $25 million for programs to prevent underage drinking; and $75 million for suicide prevention.

The measure, backed by a variety of health groups, was nearly derailed at the start when the House Commerce Committee's Health and Environment Subcommittee had to cancel a planned markup in April 2000 after members threatened to make the measure a vehicle for a wide array of controversial riders.

"Democrats had arranged to turn the markup into a three-ring circus," said a spokesperson for committee chairman Thomas J. Bliley Jr., R-Va. "Election-year politics came ahead of children today."

But Democrats said it was Bliley who started the problem, by threatening to attach to the measure what turned out to be controversial language encouraging health clinic counselors to advise pregnant women that adoption is a viable alternative to abortion. When abortion-rights groups objected, Democrats threatened to add to the bill amendments regarding the treatment of children in managed care plans taken from the stalled "patients' bill of rights." *(Patients' rights, p. 466)*

Republicans also joined the free-for-all. Tom Coburn, R-Okla., prepared amendments to further regulate the distribution and sale of fetal tissue, and to block pending Food and Drug Administration (FDA) approval of the abortion drug RU486. At the same time, Greg Ganske, R-Iowa, was ready to offer an amendment giving FDA the authority to regulate tobacco products, noting that tobacco use "is a pediatric disease," because most smokers take up the habit before reaching adulthood.

The dispute was subsequently worked out—with none of the controversial amendments added and a deal on the adoption provision—and the measure went straight to the floor, where the House passed it on May 9 by a vote of 419–2.

But even that almost did not happen. At the last minute, antiabortion groups objected to the adoption language, because, they said, it appeared to codify controversial guidelines that required family planning clinic workers to advise women with unintentional pregnancies of all their options, including both adoption and abortion. Instead, language was substituted that authorized grants to adoption organizations to develop programs to train personnel in federally funded health clinics of all types to counsel women about adoption.

Senate action on the bill was far smoother. Bypassing formal action by the Senate Health, Education, Labor, and Pensions Committee, Public Health Subcommittee Chairman Bill Frist, R-Tenn., worked out compromise language on the measure with full committee ranking Democrat Edward M. Kennedy, D-Mass., and then with House sponsors before bringing the consensus measure to the Senate floor. It passed by voice vote on Sept. 22.

The senators added to the bill the texts of a substance abuse and mental health measure (S 976—S Rept 106-196) reported by the Senate Health, Education, Labor, and Pensions Committee on Oct. 19, 1999, and a day care bill (S 2236), in addition to the provisions on methamphetamines and Ecstacy.

The House cleared HR 4365 by a vote of 394–25 on Sept. 27.

AIDS Program

Ten years after Congress first addressed the AIDS epidemic in a comprehensive way, members in 2000 reauthorized the measure named for the Indiana teenager whose fight against not only the disease but the discrimination and stigma attached to it helped educate the nation. President Clinton signed the "Ryan White CARE Act Amendments" (S 2311—PL 106-345) on Oct. 20.

The measure attempted to refocus the programs it authorized away from treatment and toward prevention, including not only preventing infection but also preventing those living with HIV, AIDS' precursor ailment, from developing the full-blown illness. The House version of the measure attempted to shift the funding formulas away from areas with large numbers of cases of AIDS and toward areas with high numbers of HIV-positive individuals. That set up a fight with the Senate.

The Senate acted first, with the Health, Education, Labor, and Pensions Committee reporting the measure (S Rept 106-294) on May 15. The full Senate passed the measure without debate by voice vote on June 6.

The Senate bill reauthorized the law's treatment, prevention, and support programs for five years at a total of $9 billion. Both it and the House measure (HR 4807) sought to shift money toward areas with a high concentration of people with HIV, but the Senate bill did not go as far.

Most at issue was how much funding would be reduced for San Francisco, which at the start of the program in 1990 was by far the area hardest hit by the AIDS epidemic. The Senate bill, attempting to cushion the blow, would limit San Francisco's funding decreases to 2 percent per year, while the House version would reduce funding by 25 percent over five years. *(1990 law, Congress and the Nation Vol. VIII, p. 588)*

The House bill, reported by the Commerce Committee (H Rept 106-788) on July 25, also included two new programs not in the Senate bill—one providing funds for states operating partner-notification programs for those who test positive for HIV, and one to help fund programs to test newborns for HIV.

The House passed HR 4807 by voice vote just after midnight on July 26, although its sponsors, conservative Republican (and physician) Tom Coburn of Oklahoma, and liberal Democrat Henry A. Waxman of California (who helped draft the original law in 1990) complained about the late hour at which it was taken up. "I stand here embarrassed that we are not going to be able to have an opportunity to educate the American people about the needs that are addressed in this bill," said Coburn.

The bill also prompted complaints from members from areas around San Francisco, including Anna G. Eshoo, D-Calif., who vowed to try to change the formula to make it closer to the Senate-passed bill.

Informal negotiations ultimately split the difference—San Francisco would lose no more than 15 percent of its funding over the life of the measure. The final bill also included provisions on partner-notification and testing of newborns for HIV.

The House approved the compromise version of S 2311 411–0 on Oct. 5. The Senate cleared the measure by voice vote later that same day.

Drug "Reimportation"

Congress in 2000 passed legislation intended to loosen restrictions on the importation of U.S.-made drugs shipped to other countries, but Clinton administration Health and Human Services Secretary Donna Shalala declined to implement the new law, saying she could not certify, as the law required, that allowing the imports would both lower drug prices for U.S. consumers and continue to guarantee the safety of the nation's drug supply.

The legislation, appended to the fiscal 2001 spending bill for the Department of Agriculture (HR 4461—PL 106-387) passed the House and Senate in different forms. It was rewritten in conference by Republican leaders who wanted simultaneously to be seen as doing something to aid consumers, particularly Medicare beneficiaries, unable to afford their prescription drugs, while not reopening U.S. markets to the potential for counterfeit, expired, or misbranded drugs that had led to passage in 1988 of legislation (PL 100-293) that made "reimportation" illegal in the first place. *(Congress and the Nation Vol. VII, p. 601)*

The original sponsors of the reimportation efforts split over the final language, with some supporting it, but others saying it had been rendered meaningless. House Minority Leader Richard A. Gephardt, D-Mo., called it "a sham reimportation that isn't worth the government paper it's printed on."

Shalala ultimately agreed with Gephardt. On Dec. 27 she announced she would not implement the requirement and declined to spend the $23 million appropriated for the Food and Drug Administration (FDA) to regulate the new policy. "I feel compelled to inform you that the flaws and loopholes contained in the reimportation provision make it impossible for me to demonstrate that it is safe and cost effective," Shalala wrote in a letter to President Clinton.

LEGISLATIVE ACTION

The drug reimportation issue had been discussed for several months, a parallel effort to one to create a drug benefit for Medicare beneficiaries. Still, two votes on July 10, during House consideration of the Agriculture spending bill (which also included funding for the FDA), took opponents by surprise.

First the House voted, 363–12, for an amendment offered by Joseph Crowley, D-N.Y., to block the FDA from enforcing the 1988 reimportation ban. Later that evening, the House voted by a nearly identical 370–12 for a slightly more restrictive amendment offered by Tom Coburn, R-Okla. Coburn's amendment would have blocked the FDA from interfering with the importation of drugs approved in the United States that were made in an FDA-approved facility in the United States, Canada, or Mexico. The House passed the bill on July 11 by a 339–82 vote.

The drug industry immediately sprang into action in an effort to get the amendments struck from the bill. The 1988 law, said Judy Bello of the Pharmaceutical Research and Manufacturers of America (PhRMA), "was based on a two-year investigation of this issue, many days of hearings, and a thorough set of congressional findings" about the dangers of reimported drugs. Among the handful of members voting against the amendments was House Commerce Committee ranking Democrat John D. Dingell Jr., D-Mich., who, as chairman of the committee, led the investigation that resulted in the 1988 law.

The Senate passed HR 4461 by a vote of 79–13 on July 20. A day earlier the Senate had added, by a vote of 74–21, an amendment offered by Health, Education, Labor, and Pensions Committee Chairman James M. Jeffords, R-Vt., and Byron L. Dorgan, D-N.D., that included stringent safety provisions that won the grudging support of the Clinton administration, where FDA officials had earlier expressed serious doubts. A major change to win that support was the inclusion of $23 million in new funding to enforce the new law.

"Our amendment will allow pharmacists and wholesalers to import safe, U.S.-made, FDA-approved, lower-cost prescription drugs from other countries," said Jeffords. "We maintain the gold standard for safety in this country, but hope to rein in the platinum standard we have for prices."

But the Senate also added language that would, in the end, prove the measure's undoing. By a vote of 96–0, senators approved an amendment by Thad Cochran, R-Miss., stipulating that reimportation would only be allowed if the secretary of health and human services certified "that the implementation . . . will pose no risk to the public's health and safety, and result in a significant reduction in the cost of covered products to the American consumer."

As in the House, there were doubters in the Senate, including Senate Judiciary Committee Chairman Orrin G. Hatch, R-Utah. "A fake Rolex may be right two times a day, but a fake drug could kill you," he said.

The drug industry also stepped up its warnings after the Senate action, getting ten former FDA heads to write letters warning of the dangers of reimportation, and running full-page ads in major newspapers. One showed two identical-looking pills, under the headline "One of these pills is counterfeit. Can you guess which one?"

On Oct. 5 House and Senate negotiators reached an agreement on the reimportation amendment to the spending bill. The agreement allowed imports from seven major developed countries plus the European Union. The FDA would be allowed to add other nations. The language excluded imports of controlled substances and drugs donated to other countries for charitable purposes. The measure was also slated to expire after five years.

Backers of the original language said that the entire effort had been rendered ineffectual by the "sunset" after five years, plus conferees' refusal to add language requiring manufacturers to provide labeling to wholesalers or to bar manufacturers from imposing contract requirements on wholesalers that would prevent drugs from being sold in the United States at their lower, international prices.

After an unsuccessful attempt by House Democrats to substitute a Medicare prescription drug benefit plan for the drug-reimportation language, the House adopted the conference report (H Rept 106-948) on Oct. 11, by a 340–75 vote. The Senate cleared the bill on Oct. 18 by a vote of 86–8. Although President Clinton complained about the loopholes in the language, he signed the bill because of its other provisions on Oct. 28.

Minority Health

Congress in 2000 reauthorized programs aimed at improving the health of minority groups, with a new emphasis on addressing not only racial and ethnic but also geographic disparities in health care. President Clinton signed the "Minority Health and Health Disparities Research and Education Act" (S 1880—PL 106-525) on Nov. 22, 2000.

The bill created a National Center on Minority Health and Health Disparities within the National Institutes of Health, charged with backing research, education, and training efforts with the goal of uncovering and addressing the biomedical, behavioral, economic, institutional, and environmental factors that contribute to health disparities. The bill authorized $100 million for fiscal 2001, and "such sums as are necessary" for fiscal 2002 through 2005. The bill also authorized $50 million for the Agency for Healthcare Research and Quality to identify populations at risk and to engage in research to identify factors contributing to health disparities and ways to address them.

The measure also authorized grants to biomedical and behavioral research institutions to help encourage the training of researchers who are members of minority or "other health disparity" populations, as well as loan repayment programs for those who would become health disparity researchers.

The House acted first, with the Commerce Committee reporting a companion bill (HR 3250—H Rept 106-986) on Oct. 18, 2000. The Senate passed S 1880 by voice vote on Oct. 26.

House consideration of the final version of the bill, however, was delayed by accusations by some Republicans that it would create illegal quotas. An e-mail from the executive director of the House Conservative Action Team notified members that the bill "contains several racial set-asides and quotas for grant programs and loan repayment policies." The Justice Department, however, had previously notified House Commerce Chairman Thomas J. Bliley Jr., R-Va., that the new provisions drafted for the bill "do not impose racial classifications that would trigger strict scrutiny . . . and therefore are constitutional."

The House ultimately cleared the measure for the president on Oct. 31, by voice vote.

Nursing Home Evictions

Nursing homes would be prohibited from evicting patients whose care was paid for by the joint federal-state Medicaid program under legislation signed by President Clinton on March 25, 1999.

The measure (HR 540—PL 106-4) was prompted by a 1998 incident in which a Tampa, Fla., nursing home, owned by the Vencor Inc. chain, attempted to evict fifty-three Medicaid patients from the facility by telling families the move was a temporary one needed so the home could be remodeled. Medicaid, whose rates were set by states, had long paid nursing homes less than private payers.

The nursing home industry supported the bill, introduced by Rep. Jim Davis, D-Fla., in whose district the attempted eviction took place. Another Florida Democrat, Bob Graham, sponsored the Senate version. But industry officials complained that Congress needed to address the low Medicaid reimbursement levels that were prompting the eviction attempts in the first place.

As signed into law, the bill required that facilities that voluntarily dropped out of the Medicaid program continue to care for existing Medicaid patients and to meet current care standards. The bill also required those facilities to continue to care for existing private patients who subsequently exhausted their savings and qualified for Medicaid. An estimated half of all nursing home patients who entered paying their own way ultimately "spent down" to Medicaid eligibility levels.

New private-pay patients had to be notified in writing that the facility no longer participated in Medicaid and that they might have to move if they subsequently became eligible for Medicaid.

The House Commerce Committee reported HR 540 (H Rept 106-44) on March 8, 1999. The Senate Finance Committee reported its version (S 494—S Rept 106-13) on March 10.

The House passed the bill with no changes on March 10, by a vote of 398–12, under a fast-track procedure that barred amendments but required a two-thirds majority to pass. The Senate passed it by voice vote on March 15, clearing the measure for the president.

Chronology of Action on Human Services

1997–1998

Fresh off its landmark overhaul of the nation's half-century old welfare system, Congress in 1997 and 1998 backtracked somewhat. When President Clinton signed the bill in 1996, he said he supported elimination of the open-ended entitlement statutes of the former Aid to Families with Dependent Children program. But he was unhappy with some $23 billion in cuts the bill made to eligibility for legal immigrants for a variety of federal programs, calling them unnecessary.

The 105th Congress responded to the president's complaints—in part—restoring about $13 billion worth of the cuts as part of the massive 1997 budget-reconciliation package. In 1998 an unrelated agriculture research bill included about $800 million to restore food stamp benefits cut off for legal immigrants in the 1996 bill.

Congress also extended the Head Start program, along with energy assistance and Community Services Block Grant programs.

Welfare Law Revisions

President Clinton in 1997 succeeded in changing some elements of the 1996 welfare overhaul act that had drawn sharp criticism from social welfare groups and from the president himself. The changes were negotiated as part of the bipartisan 1997 balanced budget deal and enacted in the spending portion (HR 2015—PL 105-33) of the budget-reconciliation package.

A second, smaller package of revisions (HR 4558—PL 105-306, S 1150—PL 105-185) was enacted in 1998.

The changes did not affect the central features of the 1996 welfare overhaul law (PL 104-193), which ended the federal guarantee of cash welfare to all eligible low-income mothers and children, set limits on eligibility for welfare, and gave the states broad new authority over their welfare programs. It was the first time the federal government had transformed a major individual entitlement program into a block grant to the states. (*Welfare reform, Congress and the Nation Vol. IX, p. 578*)

Congress agreed in 1997 to restore about $13 billion that had been cut from welfare-related programs. Although Clinton did not get everything he wanted—he had no luck in restoring most of the cuts in eligibility or allotments for food stamps, for example—he was able to restore key benefits for legal immigrants, get more help for welfare recipients joining the labor force and provide some additional money for the food stamp program.

In fact, the $54.6 billion in savings attributed to the welfare bill when it passed in 1996 did not come from ending federal welfare benefits. About $23.3 billion came from scaling back food stamp benefits by cutting individual allotments and making other adjustments. The other major savings came from denying an array of federal benefits, including food stamps and Supplemental Security Income (SSI) payments, to most legal immigrants, including those who were already in the United States when the law was signed on Aug. 22, 1996. The benefits were to be cut off after one year, on Aug. 22, 1997.

Clinton had objected to the cuts in the food stamp program and to the denial of government services to legal immi-

REFERENCES

Discussion of human services policy for the years 1945–1964 may be found in *Congress and the Nation Vol. I*, pp. 1225–1331; for the years 1965–1968, *Congress and the Nation Vol. II*, pp. 745–778; for the years 1969–1972, *Congress and the Nation Vol. III*, pp. 605–633; for the years 1973–1976, *Congress and the Nation Vol. IV*, pp. 403–432; for the years 1977–1980, *Congress and the Nation Vol. V*, pp. 679–712; for the years 1981–1984, *Congress and the Nation Vol. VI*, pp. 581–612; for the years 1985–1988, *Congress and the Nation Vol. VII*, pp. 607–632; for the years 1989–1992, *Congress and the Nation Vol. VIII*, pp. 611–624; for the years 1993–1996, *Congress and the Nation Vol. IX*, pp. 571–596.

grants even as he signed the 1996 overhaul. He said those changes were irrelevant to the legislation's main goal of moving welfare recipients into the workforce. Clinton signed the bill despite a last-ditch appeal from liberals, but he registered his own objections and promised to seek changes. "I think it can be easily fixed," he said.

Fixing it proved harder than the president anticipated, largely because of the cost. It was for that reason that the changes were embedded in the wide-ranging budget deal that fulfilled the Republicans' goal of reducing taxes and producing a balanced budget by 2002, while containing enough additional cuts to offset the welfare modifications.

The following were among the main changes to the welfare law made in the 1997 budget-reconciliation bill.

• **Supplemental Security Income.** In the most protracted struggle, Clinton and other Democrats ensured that all legal immigrants who were receiving SSI and related Medicaid benefits on Aug. 22, 1996, the date the welfare overhaul was signed, would remain eligible for the programs. SSI provided cash assistance to low-income individuals who were aged or disabled. SSI recipients were automatically eligible for Medicaid health insurance coverage as well. In addition, legal immigrants who were in the country on that date and later became disabled would be eligible for SSI and Medicaid benefits. Without the change, all noncitizens would have been removed from the SSI rolls on Oct. 1, 1997.

• **Medicaid.** The bill assured that Medicaid coverage would continue for disabled children who lost SSI benefits because of changes in the welfare law that tightened the definition of childhood disability.

• **Welfare-to-work.** A $3 billion fund was created to help states move long-term welfare recipients into the workforce, targeted to areas with many such recipients and high poverty rates.

• **Food stamps.** The bill provided an additional $1.5 billion over five years for food stamps and for employment and training for people who might otherwise have lost their eligibility under the welfare overhaul law.

Democrats also blocked several Republican initiatives. Most notably, Clinton thwarted attempts by House Republicans to overturn a Labor Department directive that applied a wide variety of federal labor laws to welfare recipients who were required to work. Labor unions had strongly urged Clinton to buck Republicans on this issue.

The House GOP also tried and failed to add language that would have allowed states that supplemented their federal SSI payments to reduce their support below existing levels. And Democrats blocked an attempt by Republicans to allow private companies to run state Medicaid and food stamp programs.

Although Republicans initially resisted efforts to reopen the welfare law, saying it could end up being unraveled on many fronts, they were faced with some agitation from the nation's governors. The National Governors' Association

(NGA) generally supported the 1996 welfare reform law. However, governors in states most affected by immigration, including Republican George E. Pataki of New York, were becoming increasingly concerned about the prospect of having the states provide for immigrants who were denied federal aid.

But while congressional Republican leaders officially convinced the NGA to issue a policy saying the 1996 law need not be reopened, they were faced with support for changes from some GOP lawmakers from states with large immigrant populations. Sen. Alfonse M. D'Amato, R-N.Y., who had endorsed the welfare overhaul, heaped scorn on colleagues who resisted efforts to restore the benefits. "Let them try living with no money and being disabled," he said.

As part of the budget-balancing negotiations between the White House and Congress, Republicans ultimately agreed in the fiscal 1998 budget resolution (H Con Res 84) to restore some $14.2 billion worth of cuts. The deal was only a blueprint, however, and the welfare-to-work provisions fell under the jurisdiction of several committees, including Ways and Means, Education and Workforce, and Agriculture in the House, and Finance and Agriculture in the Senate. *(Budget resolution, p. 43; budget-reconciliation bill, p. 50)*

1997 LEGISLATIVE ACTION

The House Ways and Means Committee was the first to depart from the agreement. The package it approved on June 10 by a largely party-line vote of 21–18, proposed restoring SSI benefits to those legal immigrants who were receiving them when the welfare overhaul was enacted, whether they qualified because of disability or age. But legal immigrants who were in the country but not on the rolls on Aug. 22, 1996, would not be eligible—even if they later became disabled.

Republicans also included language—sharply criticized by Democrats—that would have allowed states to pay less than the minimum wage to welfare recipients who were required to work in government or nonprofit jobs as a condition of receiving their welfare benefits. Under the provision, states could have counted the recipients' welfare, food stamps, Medicaid, child care, and housing benefits as part of their compensation. The provision would effectively have reversed an administration directive that required states to pay the minimum wage to working welfare recipients.

The committee did, however, drop a provision added in subcommittee by Jim McCrery, R-La., that would have denied SSI benefits to immigrants whose sponsors made $40,000 or more annually. Although no sponsor had ever been required to support an immigrant for more than three or five years, the McCrery plan would have effectively required those sponsors making more than $40,000 to support people indefinitely.

The House Education and Workforce Committee approved its package on June 12 by a vote of 24–20. As in the Ways and Means bill, the Education and Workforce bill

Outlays for Income Security

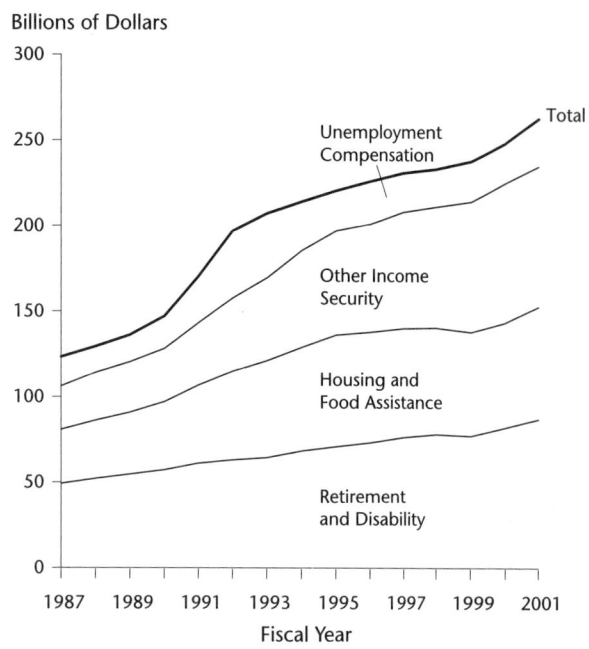

Billions of Dollars

NOTE: Data for 2001 are estimated.

SOURCE: Office of Management and Budget, *Historical Tables, Budget of the United States Government: Fiscal Year 2002* (Washington, D.C.: U.S. Government Printing Office, 2001), Table 3.2.

called for creation of a $3 billion fund to help welfare recipients make the transition to work, although the two proposals would have distributed the money differently.

Also like the Ways and Means bill, the committee package proposed to exempt "workfare" recipients from minimum wage requirements. And as happened during Ways and Means consideration, Democratic attempts to strike the provision failed.

The Senate Finance Committee approved its welfare-related provisions on June 18 by a vote of 20–0. Avoiding the partisanship that had accompanied the bill in the House, the committee bypassed one contentious topic and struck a compromise on another.

At the behest of chairman William V. Roth Jr., R-Del., the Finance panel took no position on whether to exempt workfare beneficiaries from minimum wage laws. The panel did approve by voice vote an amendment by Don Nickles, R-Okla., to clarify that welfare recipients could earn less than the minimum wage if they had been penalized by a state for not complying with the welfare law.

Roth also sought middle ground in the battle over which legal immigrants would regain access to SSI benefits. Similar to the House bill, Roth's plan would have allowed legal immigrants who were receiving SSI on Aug. 22, 1996, to remain eligible for the aid. But his measure also allowed for legal immigrants who were in the country at that time and later became disabled to qualify for the aid if they applied by Sept. 30, 1997.

The House and Senate Agriculture Committees endorsed a plan to allocate about $1.5 billion in new spending over five years for food stamps, employment, and training for people who might otherwise have lost their eligibility under the new welfare law. As in the budget agreement, the money was to go largely toward easing the effects of the 1996 welfare law on able-bodied, childless people who could not find jobs in time to comply with the law's new work requirements.

The Senate Agriculture Committee approved the provisions 16–1 on June 10. Jesse A. Helms, R-N.C., cast the lone "no" vote by proxy. The House Agriculture Committee approved virtually the same provisions by voice vote on June 12. The House Budget Committee reported HR 2015 (H Rept 105-149) on June 24.

Both chambers made changes to the welfare-related provisions during floor action. The House passed the bill on June 25 by a vote of 270–162; the Senate passed its version (S 947) by a vote of 73–27 the same day.

The most significant change was a Senate amendment by Frank R. Lautenberg, D-N.J., to make legal immigrants who were in the United States as of Aug. 22, 1996, eligible for SSI regardless of when they became disabled. The Senate adopted the change on June 25 by voice vote, bringing the bill into compliance with the budget agreement.

In the House, Republicans modified their minimum wage provisions slightly. As part of the leadership's rule governing floor debate on the bill, the provision was altered so that only cash welfare benefits and food stamps could be counted toward compensation.

Democrats ultimately prevailed on many of the welfare-related provisions in the bill. At Clinton's insistence, the final bill followed the Senate version, restoring SSI and Medicaid eligibility for legal immigrants on the rolls as of Aug. 22, 1996, as well as for those who were in the country on that date and later became disabled. Clinton had threatened to veto the entire budget reconciliation bill if the provision was not included. Democrats also prevailed on the minimum wage issue, dropping the proposal to allow states to pay lower wages to those in workfare jobs.

The House adopted the conference report (H Rept 105-217) on the reconciliation bill, 346–85, on July 30. The Senate cleared the bill, 85–15, on July 31, and Clinton signed it into law on Aug. 5.

MAJOR PROVISIONS

As enacted, major welfare provisions in HR 2015 included the following.

Food Stamps

Food stamp provisions in the bill included:

• **Exemptions from work requirement.** Allowed states to exempt from work requirements up to 15 percent of food stamp recipients who would otherwise be required to work. States that exempted more or less than 15 percent would have their allowable exemptions adjusted by the same amount the following year.

The 1996 welfare overhaul law (PL 104-193) required able-bodied food stamp recipients between the ages of eighteen and fifty who did not have dependents to work an average of at least twenty hours per week or to participate in a state-approved work, training or workfare program. Otherwise, they could receive no more than three months of food stamps out of every three years, plus an additional three months if they reestablished their food stamp eligibility through work or a work-related activity and then became unemployed.

• **Federal funding.** Increased federal funding for food stamp employment and training programs from the amounts established in the welfare law. The new amounts were $212 million in fiscal 1998, $215 million in fiscal 1999, $217 million in fiscal 2000, $219 million in fiscal 2001, and $165 million in fiscal 2002.

States had to use at least 80 percent of these funds to help food stamp recipients who were required to participate in the work-related activities.

To receive the new federal funds—beyond the amounts set in the welfare law—states had to spend at least as much on employment and training programs for food stamp recipients as they did in fiscal 1996.

• **Prisoners.** Required states to ensure that prisoners incarcerated for more than thirty days did not receive food stamps. However, the secretary of agriculture could decide that "extraordinary circumstances" prevented a state from complying. States were required to abide by this provision by Aug. 5, 1998, a year after the law's enactment. The agriculture secretary could grant states an extra year to comply.

Welfare-to-Work Grants

The legislation provided $3 billion to states and localities to support welfare-to-work efforts. The Department of Labor was responsible for administering the program. The welfare-to-work provisions:

• **Distribution of funds.** Made available $1.5 billion in fiscal 1998 and in fiscal 1999. Of that amount, 75 percent was to be distributed as formula grants to states, and 25 percent as competitive grants.

• **Set-asides.** Set aside some of the money as follows:

• **Work** 0.8 percent for evaluations of the welfare-to-work grant by the secretary of Health and Human Services. Of that amount, up to $6 million could be used to evaluate abstinence programs.

• **Native American tribes** 1 percent for Native American tribes that chose to run their own programs.

• **Bonuses** $100 million for performance bonuses (to be set aside from fiscal 1999 funding and paid to states in fiscal 2000).

• **Matching requirements.** Required states to spend 50 cents for every $1 in federal welfare-to-work funds they received. Native American tribes were not required to match their funds.

• **State spending.** Required states receiving the aid to meet the maintenance of effort requirements in the Temporary Assistance for Needy Families (TANF) block grant created by the 1996 welfare overhaul. That meant states had to spend at least 75 percent of the state funds they spent for welfare-related programs in fiscal 1994. States that did not place the required percentage of welfare recipients into the workforce had to spend 80 percent of their funds. (States were required to have a certain percentage of their welfare caseload participating in work activities, starting at 25 percent in fiscal 1997 and rising to 50 percent in fiscal 2002.)

• **State shares.** Apportioned the funds made available under the formula based on a state's pro rata share of the national poverty population and pro rata share of the national population receiving temporary assistance for needy families.

• **Distribution of funds within states.** Required that at least 85 percent of a state's formula grant be used in areas with high unemployment rates and high rates of people who had been on temporary assistance for at least thirty months.

• **Competitive grants.** Required the secretary of labor to award competitive grants to projects that would expand knowledge about moving people into the workforce. Eligible grant recipients included private industry councils, cities, or counties, or private entities that applied in conjunction with private industry councils, cities, or counties.

• **Use of funds.** Allowed funds to be used for such activities as community service and work experience programs; job creation through wage subsidies; on-the-job training, and contracts or vouchers for employment-related services. At least 70 percent of the funds had to be used to help people who met at least two of the following three criteria: they had not graduated from high school, they required treatment for substance abuse, and they had a poor work history.

In addition, recipients had to have received welfare payments for at least thirty months (not necessarily consecutively) or be within twelve months of reaching the state's time limit for benefits. States were permitted to assist recipients after they had reached the five-year time limit on welfare benefits.

• **Penalties.** Allowed states, notwithstanding minimum wage requirements, to penalize a family on welfare for not complying with the program's rules.

• **Worker protection.** Applied the following provisions to welfare-to-work participants, but not necessarily to other recipients of temporary assistance:

• **Nondisplacement.** They could not fill a position created by a layoff or fill a vacancy created when an employer fired a worker specifically to create an opening for a welfare-to-work participant. Nor could an employer reduce an employee's hours of work to accommodate a welfare-to-work participant. A work activity could not violate an existing contract for services or collective bargaining agreement.

• **Nondiscrimination.** A welfare-to-work participant could not be discriminated against because of gender, in addition to other antidiscrimination provisions included in TANF.

- **Health and safety.** Federal and state health and safety standards, including worker's compensation, applied to welfare-to-work participants.

- **Grievances.** States had to establish grievance procedures for complaints that a program violated worker protection requirements.

Temporary Assistance for Needy Families

The 1996 welfare overhaul created Temporary Assistance for Needy Families (TANF) to replace Title IV-A of the Social Security Act, which provided Aid to Families with Dependent Children (AFDC).

In doing so, the law ended the sixty-one-year-old federal guarantee of providing welfare checks to all eligible low-income mothers and children. In its place, federal funding was provided to states in predetermined lump sums, known as block grants, giving states almost complete control over eligibility and benefits. However, the law also imposed certain requirements on the states and on welfare recipients.

The TANF provisions in the budget bill:

- **Limit on funds transfer.** Clarified that states could transfer only up to 10 percent of their TANF funds to the social services block grant, which provided money to states for services such as child care.

- **Limit on education activities.** Allowed no more than 30 percent of a state's TANF participants who were counted toward the state's work requirement to fulfill that requirement by taking part in educational activities. However, in fiscal 1998 and 1999, an unlimited number of teen parents participating in educational activities could be counted as working. Beginning in fiscal 2000, teen parents would be included in the 30 percent cap.

- **Penalties for not working.** Made states that did not reduce TANF participants' benefits for every hour that they refused to work subject to reductions of 1 percent to 5 percent in the state's TANF grant.

States that failed to meet their work participation rates would lose 5 percent of their TANF grant for the first year of noncompliance, rising in subsequent years by 2 percentage points, for a maximum penalty of 21 percent. Previously, the Health and Human Services secretary had the option to penalize states up to 5 percent the first year, with up to 2 percent added in additional years. The secretary could reduce the penalty because of extraordinary circumstances, which had to be specified in writing and provided to Congress.

Supplemental Security Income (SSI)

The legislation included provisions that:

- **Redetermination.** Gave the Social Security Administration until February 1998 to determine whether children who were receiving SSI—which provided cash to the low-income aged and disabled—still qualified for the aid. The redeterminations were needed because the welfare law put in place a stricter definition of disability for children. The welfare law would have required the redeterminations to be finished by August 1997.

- **State supplements.** Increased the fees to states for having the federal government administer state supplementary SSI payments.

Aid to Legal Immigrants

- **Refugees and others.** Made refugees, those granted asylum, and aliens whose deportation had been withheld eligible for SSI and Medicaid for seven years after entering the United States. Cuban and Haitian entrants, as well as certain Amerasian immigrants, were also allowed to qualify for aid under these terms. The law previously granted them the aid for five years after arrival.

- **Eligibility for legal immigrants.** Allowed legal immigrants who were receiving SSI on Aug. 22, 1996—the day Clinton signed the welfare law—to continue to be eligible for SSI. This provision applied regardless of whether the immigrants were receiving the aid because they were aged or disabled. In addition, legal immigrants who were in the United States by Aug. 22, 1996, and subsequently became disabled, would be eligible for SSI. The welfare overhaul law would have ended SSI eligibility for legal immigrants.

- **Elderly immigrants.** Allowed legal immigrants who had been receiving SSI on the basis of applications filed before Jan. 1, 1979 (before the Social Security Administration tracked citizenship), to remain eligible for SSI.

1998 LEGISLATIVE ACTION

A 1998 bill (HR 4558—PL 105-306) continued Medicaid and SSI benefits for thousands of noncitizens whose immigration status was in doubt. A separate provision cleared that year as part of an agriculture research bill (S 1150—PL 105-185) restored food stamp eligibility to about 250,000 legal immigrants who were cut off by the welfare law. (*Agriculture bill, p. 421*)

The 1997 changes had allowed so-called nonqualified immigrants—those whose immigration status was in doubt—to continue to receive aid through Sept. 30, 1998, while the Social Security Administration reviewed cases filed to weed out illegal immigrants.

Based on file reviews and statistical sampling, the Social Security Administration reported to Congress that the vast majority of the 16,438 nonqualified immigrants who were on the rolls when the welfare bill was signed were either legal immigrants or had become citizens.

Rather than approve another short-term extension, the House passed HR 4558 by voice vote on Sept. 23, 1998, to make all immigrants in the nonqualified category permanently eligible for benefits. The Senate cleared the bill by voice vote on Oct. 8. Clinton signed it on Oct. 28.

The Clinton administration in a statement supporting the bill said it would "further the president's efforts to reverse unduly harsh benefit restrictions on legal immigrants that have nothing to do with moving people from welfare to work."

The measure also permanently extended a special program that helped individuals receiving federal unemployment aid to start their own businesses. The program allowed individuals who are self-employed to keep their income but still draw unemployment benefits.

The bill also clarified that the 1996 welfare law did not bar foreign nationals from getting or renewing professional licenses in the United States. And it clarified that children with life-threatening illnesses who received vacations or other gifts from nonprofit groups like the Make-a-Wish Foundation, would not lose their benefits.

Head Start

Congress in 1998 cleared a five-year reauthorization (S 2206—PL 105-285) of the 1965 Head Start preschool program for poor children, with lawmakers striving both to improve quality and to expand full-day, full-year child-care services for women moving from welfare to work. The bill also extended the Low-Income Home Energy Assistance Program (LIHEAP) and Community Services Block Grant.

Although Head Start had enjoyed bipartisan support in past years, it weathered a difficult passage in the House because of several controversial Republican provisions. After the Clinton administration condemned the version, House Education and the Workforce Committee Chairman Bill Goodling, R-Pa., resolved the dispute by bringing a substitute to the floor that did not include the disputed provisions. It passed easily.

The final act required that by 2003 a majority of Head Start instructors have an associate or bachelor's degree in early childhood education or a related field. It dedicated 60 percent of new funds in fiscal 1999 for quality improvements, such as better training. Under previous law, three-quarters of new funds went to expand enrollment and one-fourth to quality. The ratio would revert to 75–25 by 2003.

The law also increased funding for Early Head Start, which served infants and toddlers to age three, to 10 percent of the overall program. It allowed for-profit child care agencies to be designated as primary Head Start providers.

The legislation also extended LIHEAP for five years. Funding was unspecified for 2000–2001 and capped at $2 billion in 2002–2004. The Community Services Block Grant was extended for five years, with new authorization for family literacy, community policing, and youth development activities, as well as parenting and gang prevention programs. Faith-based organizations would be allowed to receive funding under the Community Services Block Grant program.

The legislation included a five-year pilot program of savings accounts where contributions by low-income individuals would be matched with private or public funds. The accounts could be used to begin a business, pay for school, or buy a house. Funding would be capped at $25 million a year.

BACKGROUND

Head Start was based on the premise that early intervention with disadvantaged children and their parents would improve their chances for academic success and family self-sufficiency. The program offered more than day care or most other preschool programs did. It included social services such as dental screening and mental health referrals, an education program, and it required considerable parental involvement.

When Head Start began in 1965, about 40 percent of American women were in the labor force. Because many states did not even have kindergarten programs, it stood alone on the frontier of early childhood development.

But by the late 1990s, times had changed. There had long been a recognition that Head Start, which was usually run as a half-day program that closed down in the summer, needed to become more responsive to a growing number of families in which both parents worked, as well as to single-parent households.

That did not mean lawmakers wanted to turn the program into glorified day care or even use Head Start funds for full-time services. Rather, the emphasis was to combine Head Start with existing child care and a growing host of state programs for families who worked, and to allow coordination of the expanding universe of early childhood efforts.

The push to provide comprehensive care took on new urgency in light of state and federal welfare laws that were moving people quickly into jobs. The 1996 welfare law (PL 104-193) required states to have 50 percent of welfare recipients working by 2002. As of 1997, nearly half the children in Head Start came from families on welfare. (*Welfare reform, Congress and the Nation Vol. IX, p. 578*)

The emphasis on full-time care was just one component of a wider plan to revamp Head Start. Lawmakers also wanted to improve the program's educational basis.

Despite tougher standards imposed by a 1994 reauthorization (PL 103-252)—including improved education and social services—and a push by the Department of Health and Human Services (HHS) to eliminate subpar programs, there was concern that the quality of services was far too uneven across the country. (*1994 reauthorization, Congress and the Nation Vol. IX, p. 573*)

There were also charges that Head Start, which cost about $5,000 annually per student, was too expensive compared with private preschools. Goodling wanted to aim the bulk of future funding increases at quality improvements such as better training for Head Start instructors—only half of whom had college degrees—rather than at program expansion.

In recent years, Congress and the White House had increased the program's funding, from $2.2 billion in fiscal 1992 to $4.4 billion in fiscal 1998. President Clinton's goal was to enroll one million children in Head Start by 2002 and double the Early Head Start program to 80,000 infants and toddlers.

HHS in 1997 focused millions of dollars on collaboration projects in which Head Start centers worked with state and local governments to provide expanded care. Of the roughly 37,000 additional children who entered the program in 1997, 30,000 received full-time care. Overall, about 10 percent of Head Start programs were full-time, though studies showed about 40 percent of its families needed full-time care.

According to the National Head Start Association, welfare changes increased the need for flexibility in the program's income standards. Head Start was aimed at the poorest of the poor, children under 100 percent of the national poverty line, which was an annual income of $16,450 for a family of four.

As parents moved from welfare into jobs, even at minimum wage, they could lose eligibility for Head Start. But as the working poor, those parents would still need the services and continuity the program provided. The Head Start association wanted to exempt 25 percent of children from income rules, up from 10 percent. The Clinton administration and Congress were leery, because the program served only 40 percent of eligible children.

SENATE ACTION

Senators coalesced easily around their version of the Head Start legislation (S 2206). The Senate Labor and Human Resources Committee on June 24, 1998, voted 18–0 to approve the bill to reauthorize the Head Start, Community Services Block Grant, and Low-Income Home Energy Assistance (LIHEAP) programs for five years. It also created a new pilot program to help the poor save for life's big purchases by allowing some low-income people to set up special savings accounts to save for college, a house, or business.

The measure doubled, to 10 percent, the amount of Head Start funds set aside annually for the part of the program that provided education, health, and other services to infants and toddlers. It also set tougher education and teacher training programs for the Head Start program and provided new incentives for Head Start centers to work with states and local agencies to provide full-day care for children. The bill allowed private for-profit organizations to receive Head Start grants. Christopher J. Dodd, D-Conn., offered an amendment, approved by voice vote, to ensure that a nonprofit group would be given priority over a business if both submitted applications of equivalent quality.

The Senate bill allowed religious-based organizations to receive federal funds to run programs under the Community Services Block Grant program. A similar provision in the 1996 welfare law had allowed faith-based groups to receive federal funds for welfare-to-work programs.

The committee reported S 2206 (S Rept 105-256) on July 21 and the full Senate passed the bill by voice vote on July 27.

HOUSE ACTION

A bitterly divided House Education and the Workforce Committee on July 29, 1998, approved legislation (HR 4241) to reauthorize the Head Start program for five years. Republicans adopted controversial amendments requiring poor women to cooperate in paternity establishment in order to receive aid and allowing a limited program of "parental certificates," or vouchers, that parents could use to pay for alternative child care programs.

Although Head Start had enjoyed strong bipartisan support since its creation in 1965, HR 4241 was approved by a mostly party-line vote of 23–18 with Democrats voting "no." Even before the committee adopted the disputed amendments, HHS Secretary Donna E. Shalala said the administration would "strongly oppose" the bill.

The administration objected to provisions increasing funding for Early Head Start more slowly than it wanted. Shalala also expressed opposition to the bill's requirement that funding increases for the next several years be targeted primarily at quality improvement, rather than increasing enrollment.

Angry about the amendments and a provision eliminating use of the federal prevailing wage law on Head Start construction, Democrats said they were forced into the unusual position of opposing legislation to extend and expand one of President Lyndon B. Johnson's war on poverty programs. Goodling defended the bill, which focused the bulk of new funding during the first two years of the five-year reauthorization on quality improvements, such as teacher training, rather than enrolling more children.

The committee-approved bill would have made it easier for states to provide full-day, full-year care to meet the needs of working women and those moving off welfare. It would have required half the Head Start teachers to have a degree in early childhood education by 2003, set new education standards to ensure that children were ready to learn reading when they left the program, mandated studies of effectiveness, and set aside funds for family literacy programs.

Goodling had delayed the markup for a week in an effort to work out a bipartisan compromise. He offered a substitute bill that did not include the paternity establishment or voucher provisions, both of which were in a draft developed by Frank Riggs, R-Calif., chairman of the Subcommittee on Early Childhood, Youth and Families. Goodling's substitute also eliminated a Riggs provision that would have allowed private, for-profit groups to compete for Head Start grants.

But the wheels came off during the markup, in part because of Democratic anger over a provision that would have eliminated the requirement that Head Start comply with the 1931 Davis-Bacon Act, which required federal construction contractors to pay workers the local prevailing wage. An amendment by Donald M. Payne, D-N.J., to reinstate Davis-Bacon failed 16–21.

The fight over Davis-Bacon poisoned the atmosphere, prompting Republicans to push other controversial proposals. Voting 22–17, the committee approved Riggs's plan for government-funded certificates that could be used to pay for alternative child care. The certificates could be used in cases where Head Start centers had been closed and a replacement had not been named. HHS said the provision was unneeded because it routinely named interim providers in such cases. Democrats worried it was a step toward broader vouchers for the program.

By 20–19, the panel approved another Riggs amendment, which mimicked a provision of the 1996 welfare law (PL 104-193) that would have required women to cooperate in establishing the paternity of their children.

HR 4241 was never formally reported out of committee. However, the House panel on Aug. 7 reported a separate measure (HR 4271—H Rept 105-686) extending the Community Services Block Grant Act for five years and LIHEAP for two years.

To avoid a potentially bitter battle with the Clinton administration and the Senate, Goodling guided the House toward an amended version of S 2206. The stripped-down bill, passed by the House 346–20 on Sept. 14, did not include the three controversial amendments approved by his committee relating to paternity establishment, vouchers, and Davis-Bacon prevailing wage requirements. Democrats who had voted against the measure when it was reported out of committee backed the leaner version on the floor.

CONFERENCE, FINAL ACTION

Although the House and Senate bills moved in the same general direction, conferees had to address some key differences.

The Senate measure, in line with Clinton administration priorities, directed most of the additional funding for Head Start toward increasing enrollment. Existing policy, which would have been continued under the Senate bill, was to use 75 percent of any new funding to increase enrollment. The House bill would have set aside 65 percent of new funds for quality improvements in fiscal 1999 and 2000, a number that would have decreased gradually through 2003, when 25 percent was to be directed to improving the quality of instruction.

To provide continuity, the House bill would have allowed providers to have up to 25 percent of total enrollment over the poverty level. The Senate bill continued the existing 10 percent exemption.

Both bills included incentives to providers to offer full-day, full-year services. The Senate bill would have let for-profit child care facilities be designated as primary Head Start grantees. The House would not have.

The Senate bill reauthorized LIHEAP for five years, while the House's had a two-year expansion.

Moving quickly, House and Senate negotiators agreed on Sept. 29 to a compromise that would temporarily shift new funds from expanding Head Start toward improving the program.

The compromise represented a victory for Goodling, who persuaded senators to accept his argument that Congress should emphasize quality over quantity. "We must ensure that all children enrolled in Head Start receive high-quality educational services before continuing with unchecked expansion of the program," Goodling argued, saying that some Head Start programs had become essentially "child care."

The compromise allowed 60 percent of new funds spent in fiscal 1999 to be used for quality improvements such as higher salaries and training, with 40 percent designated for expansion. It would eventually return funding to the existing ratio using the following formula: 50 percent quality, 50 percent quantity in 2000; 47.5 percent quality, 52.5 percent quantity in 2001; 35 percent quality, 65 percent quantity in 2002; and 25 percent quality, 75 percent quantity in 2003.

Conferees agreed to follow the Senate plan to allow funding levels to be set by annual appropriations bills rather than include a House limit on fiscal 1999 spending of $4.6 billion.

The final bill included a requirement to set aside at least $3 million for technical aid to Head Start providers that offered family literacy programs, which were designed to improve parents' reading skills. The House bill had included $5 million for 100 Head Start family literacy demonstration projects, while the Senate had no similar provision.

Also surviving was a House provision setting performance requirements for Head Start providers. The agreement would give the Education Department until July 1, 1999—rather than Jan. 1, as in the House bill—to come up with additional criteria for measuring performance.

House conferees went along with the Senate in allowing for-profit agencies to operate Head Start programs and to continuing to allow the health and human services secretary to limit to 10 percent the number of Head Start participants from households above the poverty level.

The Senate adopted the conference report on S 2206 (H Rept 105-788) by voice vote on Oct. 8, with the House following suit on Oct. 9. President Clinton signed the bill on Oct. 27.

Adoption of Foster Children

Legislation designed to hasten the adoption of children in foster care was enacted in 1997. The Adoption and Safe Families Act (HR 867—PL 105-89) changed existing law to give more emphasis to protecting children's safety and less to trying to reunite them with troubled families. It also gave states new financial incentives to find permanent adoptive parents for children in foster care.

President Clinton said the legislation was consistent with his goal, announced in December 1996, of doubling the number of foster children who were adopted or otherwise permanently placed in homes by 2002. There were 27,000 such placements in 1996. About a half million children were in foster care, including many who had been there for two years or more.

The legislation was a recognition of the unintended consequences of the 1980 Child Welfare Act (PL 96-272), which required that states make a "reasonable effort" to reunite a child's natural family before allowing the child to be permanently adopted. Those efforts had contributed to an increase in the amount of time children spent in foster care, as states tried, often in vain, to reunite their families. *(1980 law, Congress and the Nation Vol. V, p. 710)*

The final bill, worked out in informal negotiations with the Senate, gave states considerable leeway in determining what those efforts should be. It made the child's health and safety the paramount factors.

HR 867 had an effortless journey through the House. The Ways and Means Committee reported it on April 28 (H Rept

105-77). The House passed the bill, unchanged, on April 30 by a vote of 416–5.

After lingering for months, the legislation moved swiftly at the end of the session. The Senate gave voice vote approval on Nov. 8 both to HR 867 and to an amendment by Larry E. Craig, R-Idaho, and John H. Chafee, R-R.I., that contained revisions to the House-passed version. Among the changes, the Senate amendment tightened requirements on screening foster and permanent adoptive parents, and added language to aid out-of-state adoptions. The Senate also attached a section reauthorizing the Family Preservation Act, originally included in the 1993 budget-reconciliation law (PL 103-66). *(1993 law, Congress and the Nation Vol. IX, p. 574)*

Members worked out the relatively minor differences between the two versions of the bill in the waning days of the session without formally convening a conference committee. The House then approved a resolution (H Res 327) agreeing to the compromise version of HR 867 by a vote of 406–7 on Nov. 13. The Senate accepted this latest version by voice vote later that day, clearing HR 867 for Clinton. The president signed it on Nov. 19.

MAJOR PROVISIONS

As enacted, the bill included the following major provisions:

• **State flexibility.** The legislation specified that states were not required to try to reunite a family if a court determined that the child had been subjected to "aggravated circumstances," such as abandonment, torture, chronic abuse, and sexual abuse or when the parent had killed or assaulted another child.

• **Hastening adoption proceedings.** States were required to terminate parental rights and begin adoption proceedings once a child had been in foster care for fifteen out of the preceding twenty-two months. The bill also required states to hold earlier and more frequent hearings to track children after they enter the foster care system. The child was entitled to a hearing within twelve months, reduced from eighteen months under previous law.

• **Criminal records check.** States were required to run criminal records checks on any prospective foster or adoptive parents. An application would be denied in the case of a felony conviction for child abuse or neglect, spousal abuse, crimes against children, or violent crimes. States could opt out of this provision but only by action of the governor or state legislature.

• **Health insurance for special needs children.** States were also required to provide health insurance for adopted children with special needs or disabilities in cases where the state determined the child would not have been adopted without medical assistance.

• **Financial incentives to states.** The legislation gave states a financial incentive to get children out of foster care. A state would receive $4,000 for each adoption of a foster child that exceeded its previous annual level. For children with disabilities, the figure would rise to $6,000. Total federal

incentive payments were authorized at $20 million a year for five years beginning in fiscal 1999. The funding was in addition to existing federal payments to states for placing children in foster care. The Congressional Budget Office estimated that the legislation would cost nothing—because the federal government would spend less on foster care.

• **Out-of-state adoptions.** The bill sought to encourage adoptions by prohibiting states from postponing or denying a suitable out-of-state adoption in order to find an in-state placement.

• **Safe families program.** In a section added by the Senate, the bill reauthorized and revised a program designed to keep troubled families together and give early help to children at risk of being put in foster care. The family preservation program was renamed the "Promoting Safe and Stable Families" program. The program's mission was revised so that it could also be used to promote adoptions and to help reunify families for up to fifteen months after a child was removed from the home. The program was authorized at $875 million over three years.

WIC, Child Nutrition

Congress in 1998 voted to expand and reauthorize for five years the school lunch and Woman, Infants, and Children (WIC) programs, as well as other food programs (HR 3874—PL 105-336). The bipartisan action on the measure marked a sharp turnaround from 1995, when Republicans unsuccessfully sought to convert the popular school lunch program into a block grant.

The WIC program provided food vouchers and nutrition and health services to low-income, pregnant woman and to children up to age five. As signed into law, HR 3874 authorized a new program pushed by the Clinton administration to provide after-school snacks to teenagers in low-income areas—previously, the federal government provided subsidies for snacks only for children up to age twelve. The new program would pay for children up to age eighteen who participated in school-based activities or programs run by community groups such as the Boys Club. The aid to community groups would be targeted to low-income areas. Teenagers in more affluent areas could qualify for school-sponsored programs.

The measure also authorized a three-year study of the potential benefits of offering free school breakfasts to all public school children. Some states and school districts had begun to experiment with their own funds with programs providing universal free breakfasts, citing studies indicating that such programs can have a positive impact on discipline, health, and academic performance. But opponents said most students eat breakfast at home and called the plan a middle-class subsidy. HR 3874 also reauthorized the summer meals program for children from low-income families.

The bill set tougher penalties for those who defrauded the WIC program. Grocers convicted of trafficking in WIC food vouchers, or who sold guns or drugs in exchange for vouchers, would be disqualified. And it increased penalties for fraud.

Stung by the public relations backlash to their failed school lunch plan in 1995, House Republicans did not unveil their bill until they reached accord with Democrats. That accord came in the shape of a 36–1 approval of the bill, crafted primarily by Rep. Michael N. Castle, R-Del., by the House Education and Workforce Committee on June 4, 1998. The panel reported HR 3874 (H Rept 105-633) on July 20. *(1995 action, Congress and the Nation Vol. IX, p. 579)*

The Senate Agriculture, Nutrition, and Forestry Committee approved its bill (S 2286), 17–0, on June 25. The bill was reported (S Rept 105-243) on July 10.

The House approved the bill on July 20 by a vote of 383–1, and the Senate passed it by voice vote on Sept. 17, after substituting the text of S 2286.

During the brief House-Senate conference, negotiators dropped a Senate provision that would have required, rather than allowed, the study on universal school breakfasts.

The Senate adopted the conference report on the bill (H Rept 105-786) on Oct. 7 and the House cleared it by a vote of 422–1 on Oct. 9. President Clinton signed the bill on Oct. 31.

Child Support Enforcement

The 105th Congress in 1998 followed its predecessors in clearing bills aimed at helping ensure that absent parents make court-ordered child support payments. The first bill (HR 3130—PL 105-200) reduced federal penalties on states that failed to meet a federal deadline for computerizing their child-support enforcement systems. *(1993 action, Congress and the Nation Vol. IX, p. 576)*

The bipartisan measure was intended to fix a problem arising from the 1988 Family Support Act (PL 100-485), which set an Oct. 1, 1995, deadline for states to implement automated data processing systems to aid in child-support enforcement. The federal government agreed to pay 90 percent of administrative costs for creating the systems.

Most states missed the deadline, however, so Congress in 1995 extended it to Oct. 1, 1997 (PL 104-35). Still, sixteen states and jurisdictions could not meet that deadline, either.

Under the 1988 law, a state that missed the deadline faced the loss of all federal child-support payments and its Temporary Assistance for Needy Families welfare block grants. California, for example, stood to lose more than $4 billion, while Michigan faced the loss of more than $880 million if the law was not changed. Lawmakers said penalties of that magnitude would jeopardize the very low-income families the 1988 law was intended to help.

HR 3130 created an alternative penalty system that was far less draconian, but still imposed significant fines for states behind schedule. The new law provided graduated penalties depending on how late a state was in complying. The measure also replaced the existing child-support incentive program with a system rewarding states for efficient and effective performance in five areas of child-support enforcement.

The House Ways and Means Committee reported the bill (H Rept 105-422) on Feb. 27, 1998, and the full House passed it on March 5 by a vote of 414–1. The Senate passed its version by voice vote on April 2. The bills differed primarily in the size of the potential penalties. A compromise was worked out informally that would penalize states up to 30 percent after five years. The House approved the compromise measure by voice vote on June 25 and the Senate cleared it, also by voice vote, the next day. President Clinton signed it on July 16.

The second bill (HR 3811—PL 105-187) created two new felony offenses for parents who willfully neglected making child-support payments. This was over and above existing federal penalties for first offenses of up to six months in prison and a $5,000 fine. Federal law applied when the "deadbeat" parent and child lived in different states.

Under the legislation, sponsored by House Judiciary Committee Chairman Henry J. Hyde, R-Ill., offenders who owed more than $10,000 in child support to children in another state could be jailed for up to two years. The same penalty applied to those who crossed state lines to avoid child-support obligations.

The House passed HR 3811 on May 12, 1998, by a vote of 402–16. The Senate cleared it by voice vote on June 5, and President Clinton signed it on June 24.

Inmate Benefits Restriction

Under a provision of the 1997 budget-reconciliation act (HR 2015—PL 105-33), enacted on Aug. 5, states were required to verify that prisoners were not receiving food stamps or being counted as part of a household that received them.

The legislation required states to set up systems, or use the Social Security Administration system, to gather the information. The requirement was to take effect one year after the bill was enacted, although the secretary of agriculture was given authority to extend that if "extraordinary circumstances" made it impractical for a state to obtain such information. *(Budget-reconciliation act, p. 50)*

1999–2000

Following the major changes to the welfare system in 1996 and 1997, the 106th Congress was relatively inactive in the human services realm. Congress did, after a squabble, manage to reauthorize the popular Older Americans Act.

Older Americans Act

After a five-year struggle, Congress in 2000 finally managed to reauthorize popular programs that provided nutrition, home help, legal aid, and employment counseling to the nation's senior citizens. President Clinton signed the five-year reauthorization of the Older Americans Act (HR 782—PL 106-501) on Nov. 13.

The measure, originally passed as part of the 1965 War on Poverty (PL 89-73), authorized such programs as Meals on Wheels, senior centers, and transportation, job placement, and legal services for the elderly.

But despite its popularity, the measure was hung up in the GOP-controlled Congress, largely over a seniors' jobs program, which placed people age fifty-five and older in part-time, community service jobs. The program was the target of many conservative Republicans who viewed it as an inefficient handout to liberal groups. The jobs program had been run for decades by ten nonprofit organizations, including affiliates of the AARP and National Council of Senior Citizens. Republicans also tangled with Democrats and senior groups over efforts to turn the Meals on Wheels program into a state block grant.

The House Education and Workforce Committee approved HR 782 by voice vote on Sept. 15, 1999, and reported it (H Rept 106-343) on Sept. 28. The measure would have provided for a new $125 million-per-year family caregiver program. But it also would have revamped the controversial jobs program. Under the existing program, 78 percent of the job funds went to community organizations and 22 percent to states. The bill approved by the committee would have gradually changed that formula to a 55–45 split.

Labor Secretary Alexis Herman, in a Sept. 15 letter to lawmakers, said the cuts in the employment program were "unacceptable" and would "significantly diminish" its effectiveness. More than 120 members signed a separate letter opposing the changes.

The measure languished for the rest of the year, and the Senate Health, Education, Labor and Pensions Committee did not act until the following summer, when, on July 21, 2000, it approved its own, compromise bill (S 1536) by voice vote. The panel reported it (S Rept 106-399) on Sept. 7.

The Senate bill included a "hold harmless" provision to guarantee that each state and advocacy group receive at least as much funding as they needed to continue their fiscal 2000 level of operations. If appropriators provided more money than needed to maintain those efforts, additional funds would be split between the seniors' groups and the states: The groups would get 25 percent and the states 75 percent.

Any funds beyond $35 million would be divided equally. That formula won the blessing of nearly all Senate committee members and thirty major advocacy groups.

The bill also allowed states to impose cost-sharing requirements on seniors for such things as respite care and home care services, although other services, such as ombudsman services and legal aid, were exempted from the cost-sharing charges. The charges were to be based on beneficiaries' income in order to protect low-income seniors.

The House and Senate worked out a compromise similar to the Senate bill, making a conference unnecessary. The House incorporated the language into HR 782, which it passed by a vote of 405–2 on Oct. 25. The full Senate ratified the compromise in a 94–0 vote on Oct. 26, clearing the measure for the president.

Post-Foster Care Aid

Congress in 1999 passed legislation to double federal aid to adolescents forced out of foster care at age eighteen. President Clinton signed the bill (HR 3443—PL 106-169) on Dec. 14.

The legislation authorized expanded aid for education, counseling, and other services to youths up to age twenty-one; allowed states to extend Medicaid health coverage to teenagers moving off foster care; and allowed foster children to accumulate up to $10,000 in assets, up from $1,000.

In addition to raising funding for the Independent Living Program, which helped foster care children make the transition to living on their own, from $70 million to $140 million per year, the measure also renamed the program in honor of the late Sen. John H. Chafee, R-R.I., who helped create it.

The measure was an attempt to address what many lawmakers said was a major shortcoming in the nation's foster care system: thousands of youths were discharged from foster care each year even though they were not prepared to become self-sufficient. Sponsors said that rates of homelessness, unemployment, and unplanned pregnancy were especially high among these youth. Lawmakers had originally wanted to require states to make extended Medicaid health coverage mandatory but could not find a way to pay for it. The bill was ultimately financed partially by altering a federal child support program.

The House Ways and Means Subcommittee on Human Resources approved an earlier measure (HR 1802) by voice vote on May 20. The full Ways and Means Committee approved that bill, also by voice vote, on May 26 and reported it (H Rept 106-182) on June 10. The House passed the bill 380–6 on June 25, after it was made a priority by House Majority Whip Tom DeLay, R-Texas, himself a foster parent of two.

A House-Senate compromise version of HR 1802 was subsequently incorporated into HR 3443, which the House passed by voice vote on Nov. 18. The Senate passed an amended version of HR 1802 by voice vote on Nov. 19 and later that day cleared HR 3443 by voice vote.

Chronology of Action on Veterans Affairs

1997–1998

The 105th Congress continued its attention to mysterious illnesses suffered by veterans of the Persian Gulf War in legislation passed in 1997 and 1998. Lawmakers also made several minor changes to veterans programs, including new provisions to deal with sexual harassment complaints and making it easier for veterans to appeal disability rulings.

Omnibus Veterans Bill

President Clinton on Nov. 21, 1997, signed into law a measure (S 714—PL 105-114) that reauthorized and modified several veterans programs. Among its provisions, the bill changed the way the Department of Veterans Affairs (VA) handled sexual harassment and other discrimination claims and directed the department to create a project targeting the health care needs of veterans of the 1991 Persian Gulf War. Other provisions extended and streamlined laws under which the VA provided care to homeless veterans and veterans who suffered from chronic mental illness.

• **Sexual harassment.** The measure incorporated provisions, though in watered-down form, of a previously passed House bill (HR 1703) dealing with sexual harassment and other discrimination claims. Originally, the House bill would have required the department to hire employment law experts with no direct ties to the VA to investigate complaints. It also would have required that final rulings in discrimination cases be made by an independent administrative law judge rather than by a VA employee. HR 1703 had been reported (H Rept 105-292) in that form by the House Veterans' Affairs Committee on Oct. 2, 1997. The House passed the bill by voice vote on Oct. 6.

But at the request of the VA, the legislation was changed before it was added to S 714. The final version still required the VA to establish new employment complaint resolution procedures, but the bill no longer required that the matter be handled completely independent of the department. As enacted, it required the VA to establish a quasi-independent Office of Employment Discrimination Complaint Adjudication and contract with a private entity to assess the VA's handling of such complaints.

• **Gulf War veterans.** The omnibus bill also included a House-passed measure (HR 2206) authorizing $5 million to establish a pilot project at ten VA hospitals to serve veterans of the Persian Gulf War who suffered from undiagnosed illnesses. The program, to begin on July 1, 1998, was subject to annual appropriations. The hospitals were required to test new approaches to treating Gulf War illnesses and improve existing treatments to help veterans cope. The VA supported the initiative, though some officials claimed it might be unnecessary because Persian Gulf War veterans already were being treated within accepted medical standards.

The section of the bill also rewrote existing law to make all veterans who served in the Gulf War eligible for immediate VA care. Previously, services were offered only to veterans whose illnesses could be linked to exposure to toxic or hazardous compounds. The VA supported the change. *(1994 action, Congress and the Nation Vol. IX, p. 597)*

The House Veterans' Affairs Committee reported HR 2206 (H Rept 105-293) on Oct. 2, 1997, and the measure passed the House on Oct. 6 by voice vote.

Some lawmakers also had contemplated liberalizing the rules governing disability compensation payments for Gulf War veterans with undiagnosed illnesses, such as chronic fatigue, skin rashes, and joint aches. Veterans had been eligible

REFERENCES

Discussion of veterans programs for the years 1945–1964 may be found in *Congress and the Nation Vol. I*, pp. 1335–1373; for the years 1965–1968, *Congress and the Nation Vol. II*, pp. 453–460; for the years 1969–1972, *Congress and the Nation Vol. III*, pp. 537–548; for the years 1973–1976, *Congress and the Nation Vol. IV*, pp. 158–181; for the years 1977–1980, *Congress and the Nation Vol. V*, pp. 177–191; for the years 1981–1984, *Congress and the Nation Vol. VI*, pp. 613–625; for the years 1985–1988, *Congress and the Nation Vol. VII*, pp. 633–644; for the years 1989–1992, *Congress and the Nation Vol. VIII*, pp. 625–637; for the years 1993–1996, *Congress and the Nation Vol. IX*, pp. 597–603.

Outlays for Veterans Benefits and Services

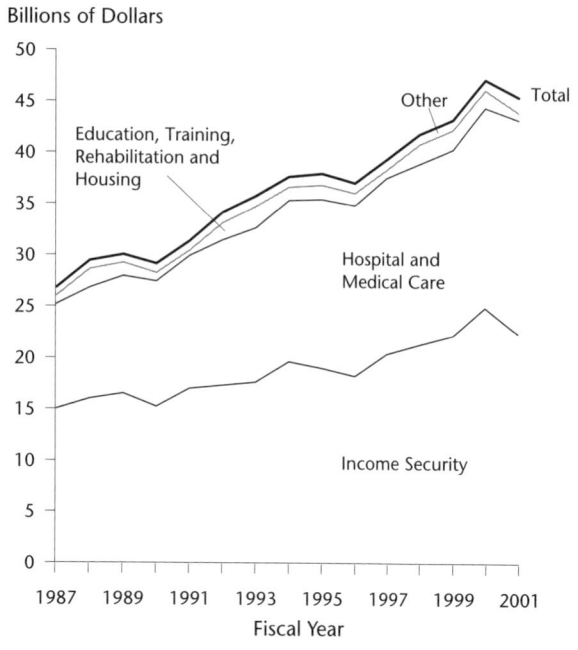

Billions of Dollars

NOTE: Data for 2001 are estimated.

SOURCE: Office of Management and Budget, *Historical Tables, Budget of the United States Government: Fiscal Year 2002* (Washington, D.C.: U.S. Government Printing Office, 2001), Table 3.2.

for disability benefits for such undiagnosed illnesses, but only if they proved that their symptoms had appeared within two years of their return from the 1991 war.

Veterans' advocates, including lawmakers from both parties, said the two-year window had allowed the VA to deny benefits to a majority of Gulf War veterans who had filed claims. They said many veterans became ill after the deadline.

But Clinton headed off possible action by Congress, announcing on March 7 that the administration would issue new rules to expand from two years to ten years the window of opportunity for veterans to file disability claims.

LEGISLATIVE ACTION

The Senate Veterans' Affairs Committee reported the original version of S 714 (S Rept 105-123), without the sexual harassment or Gulf War provisions, on Oct. 30. The Senate passed the bill by voice vote on Nov. 5.

On Nov. 9, the House passed the bill by voice vote, but only after adding provisions from several other bills, including the sexual harassment and VA provisions. The changes had been worked out in advance by the House and Senate Veterans' Affairs panels.

The Senate concurred in the House changes by voice vote on Nov. 10, clearing the measure for the president.

Veterans COLAs

Disabled veterans and their survivors received cost-of-living adjustments (COLAs) in their benefits under bills en-

acted in 1997 and 1998. Payments to disabled veterans were not automatically indexed to inflation and, therefore, required annual action by Congress and the president.

The 1997 bill (HR 2367—PL 105-98) set the increase to take place on Dec. 1, 1997, at 2.1 percent. Amounts were rounded down to the nearest dollar in compliance with the 1997 balanced-budget package (HR 2015—PL 105-33), saving roughly $391 million over five years. Payments from 1998 through 2002 could not exceed adjustments made for Social Security recipients.

In 1997 it was estimated that the cost-of-living increase affected roughly 2.2 million veterans with service-connected injuries. It also increased dependency and indemnity compensation paid to about 300,000 survivors of veterans who had died from service-connected injuries.

The House Veterans' Affairs Committee reported HR 2367 (H Rept 105-320) on Oct. 9. The House passed the measure on Oct. 31 and the Senate cleared it on Nov. 5, both by voice votes. It was signed into law on Nov. 19. *(1999–2000 action, p. 503)*

The 1998 bill (HR 4110—PL 105-368) authorizing the COLA increase was a catch-all measure that covered a variety of veterans benefits. A 1.3 percent COLA increase went into effect on Dec. 1, 1998. *(Veterans benefits, p. 500)*

Loss of Burial Rights

Veterans convicted of capital crimes became ineligible for burial with military honors under a bill signed into law on Nov. 21, 1997 (S 923—PL 105-116). The bill prohibited the "performance of military honors upon death" for veterans who had been sentenced to death or life imprisonment for a federal capital crime, or sentenced to death or life imprisonment without parole for a state capital crime. Previously, veterans remained eligible for military burial and other benefits even if they had committed offenses such as murder that were punishable by death under federal law. The 1997 legislation was prompted by the conviction of Army veteran Timothy McVeigh in the April 1995 bombing of a federal building in Oklahoma City that killed 168 people.

The final bill was considerably narrower than the one passed by the Senate on June 18, 1997, by a vote of 98–0. That initial version, sponsored by Arlen Specter, R-Pa., and Robert G. Torricelli, D-N.J., would have denied all veterans benefits, not just burial rights, to persons convicted of federal capital offenses. A veteran who committed such an offense would have forfeited all benefits, including aid for education, employment, disability, and dependents. The bill would not have applied to veterans whose capital crimes were committed under state law.

The measure was then sent to the House, where the Veterans' Affairs Committee revised it to apply only to military burials. Veterans groups had complained that the original Senate version would have unfairly penalized the families of such veterans. The committee reported the revised bill (H Rept 105-319) on Oct. 9, after debating a move to expand its scope to cover those convicted of crimes in state court. Spencer Bachus, R-Ala., offered the amendment, arguing that only a small percentage of capital cases were tried in federal court. But the VA said including state crimes would make the provision difficult to administer. Bachus eventually withdrew his amendment after committee chairman Bob Stump, R-Ariz., assured him that his concerns would be considered before House floor debate.

The House passed S 923 by voice vote on Oct. 31 after adopting a substitute amendment that denied military burials to veterans convicted of murder in state capital cases, as well as those convicted of federal capital crimes. The Senate cleared the bill by voice vote on Nov. 10.

Disability Appeals

It became easier for veterans to appeal rulings on disability benefits under a bill signed into law on Nov. 21, 1997 (HR 1090—PL 105-111). Previous law gave the Department of Veterans Affairs (VA) discretion to review only those appeals it found to have merit. HR 1090 required the department to review any appeal claiming that the VA had made "clear and unmistakable errors," so long as the appeal was properly filed.

The VA opposed the bill, arguing that it would add to an already lengthy backlog of cases and could potentially reopen cases dating back to the 1930s. Veterans' advocates countered that no veteran should be denied benefits because of a VA error.

The House Veterans' Affairs Committee reported the bill (H Rept 105-52) on April 14 and the House passed it by voice vote on April 16. The Senate cleared the bill by voice vote on Nov. 10; its Veterans' Affairs Committee had approved a similar measure (S 464—S Rept 105-157) on Oct. 7 and reported it on Nov. 13.

Cost-Saving Programs

Under the budget-reconciliation bill signed by President Clinton on Aug. 5, 1997 (HR 2015—PL 105-33), the Department of Veterans Affairs (VA) gained the authority to keep the money it received from private insurance companies for treating veterans. The VA had been trying for years to gain this authority instead of having the money go into the general Treasury.

If the change had been made outside the budget-reconciliation process, lawmakers would have had to offset the cost to the Treasury—approximately $600 million annually—by cutting other veterans programs. Adding it to reconciliation allowed greater flexibility to finding offsets.

The health insurance payments, along with other provisions in PL 105-33 that extended cost-saving programs already in place, would reduce mandatory veterans spending by about $2.7 billion over five years.

The Senate Veterans' Affairs Committee approved the provisions, 11–0, on June 12. The House Veterans' Affairs panel approved a nearly identical plan the same day, 18–4.

VETERANS LEADERSHIP

Two heads of the Department of Veterans Affairs served under President Bill Clinton during his two terms in office. The first was Jesse Brown, confirmed in 1993. Brown had been a lobbyist for disabled veterans and a Purple Heart recipient who had lost partial use of his right arm as a Marine in Vietnam. *(Congress and the Nation Vol. IX, p. 599)*

Brown resigned in July 1997 and was replaced by Togo D. West Jr., who was confirmed by the Senate by voice vote on April 28, 1998. West's nomination was approved by the Senate Veterans' Affairs Committee on April 22. *(Background, cabinet profiles, p. 977)*

An attorney and former member of the U.S. Army Field Artillery Corps, West also served as general counsel for the Navy and later held that same position for the Department of Defense. He had also been a lobbyist for the defense contractor Northrop Grumman Corp. West served in the Clinton administration as secretary of the Army from 1993 to 1998. On Jan. 2, 1998, he became acting Veterans Affairs secretary.

West's confirmation had been delayed when questions were raised about problems in the Army that had occurred during his tenure as secretary. Some veterans organizations also had expressed reservations about the nomination, citing West's lack of experience in areas such as veterans benefits. West said he would work to forge a relationship with veterans groups and with Congress to "seek and do what is right for our veterans."

As enacted, veterans provisions of PL 105-33:

• **Loan guarantees.** Extended VA authority to guarantee, on the secondary market, loans that the VA had made to purchasers of its property. This authority was extended through Dec. 31, 2002.

• **Mortgage fees.** Extended through Oct. 1, 2002, fees on VA-guaranteed, insured, or direct home loans. For first-time loans, the fee ranged from 0.5 percent to 2 percent, depending on the amount of the down payment and whether the veteran was on active duty or in the reserves. Veterans paid 3 percent in fees for all subsequent loans except those in which they had made down payments of more than 5 percent.

• **Decisions on foreclosed properties.** Extended through Oct. 1, 2002, the VA's authority to use a "no-bid" procedure to determine whether it should purchase foreclosed properties it had guaranteed and resell them, or pay the guaranteed amount to the holder of the loan.

• **Income verification.** Extended through Sept. 30, 2002, the VA's access to financial records at the Department of Health and Human Services, Social Security Administration, and Internal Revenue Service to determine eligibility for needs-based pensions and health care services.

• **Pension limits.** Extended through Sept. 30, 2002, limits on the amount of VA pensions that could be paid to veterans or spouses who were eligible for Medicaid, lived in nursing homes that received Medicaid payments, and had no dependents. As under existing law, which was set to expire on Sept. 30, 1998, such veterans and spouses were limited to $90 in pensions per month.

• **Veterans copayments.** Extended through Sept. 30, 2002, existing laws that required veterans with higher incomes to pay for a portion of their medical and nursing home care. Also, veterans without service-connected disabilities or low incomes were required to pay $2 for each thirty-day prescription provided on an outpatient basis.

• **Cost recovery.** Extended through Oct. 1, 2002, the VA's ability to collect reimbursement from health insurance companies and other third-party payers for VA treatment of veterans with conditions not related to their service.

• **New fund.** Established a Medical Care Collections Fund, which began receiving payments on Sept. 30, to replace the Medical-Care Cost Recovery Fund. The new fund provided a more reliable stream of funding to the VA, because the Treasury Department was required to subsidize it if receipts did not meet Congressional Budget Office projections in fiscal 1998, 1999, and 2000. If income was at least $25 million less than projected in those years, the Treasury Department would be required to deposit the estimated shortfall in the account. If additional receipts came in, the VA would be required to use them to repay the Treasury.

• **Inflation adjustments.** Stipulated that increases in disability and survivors benefits could not exceed the rate of growth in Social Security payments from 1998 through 2002. Any increase in benefits was to be rounded to the next lowest dollar figure.

• **Fees on foreclosed properties.** Increased from 1 percent to 2.25 percent the loan fee that borrowers had to pay if they purchased, through a VA loan, a property that the VA had repossessed.

• **Recovery of loan losses.** Eliminated requirements that the VA obtain consent from veterans or surviving spouses who were defaulting on a VA loan before it attempted to mitigate its losses by reducing other federal payments or benefits to them, such as federal salaries or tax refunds. The bill eliminated provisions that required courts to determine whether a veteran or surviving spouse was liable for the loan. Instead, the VA had to notify the veteran or surviving spouse by certified mail and give him or her a chance to request that the VA secretary waive the debt.

Veterans Benefits

Congress pulled together several major pieces of veterans-benefits legislation into one bill (HR 4110—PL 105-368) at the end of the 105th Congress. The final bill authorized the 1999 cost-of-living adjustment (COLA) for disabled veterans and their survivors, expanded research into Persian Gulf War illnesses, and increased certain education and housing benefits.

The measure also made incremental changes to medical and compensation policies. Sponsors won the support of veterans groups mainly because of the COLA, which was scheduled to take effect on Dec. 1. *(Veterans COLAs, p. 498)*

To counter charges that the Department of Veterans Affairs (VA) was unresponsive to Gulf War veterans complaining of mysterious illnesses, the bill allowed the VA to continue to treat those veterans with undiagnosed illnesses through 2001, and the veterans' immediate family members would be entitled to treatment for related problems through 1999. The National Academy of Sciences was directed to review scientific evidence to determine whether unusual ailments could be traced to exposures in the Gulf War.

Certain veterans were to receive greater benefits under the bill; for example, it increased the special monthly pension given to Medal of Honor recipients from $400 to $600 and allowed terminally ill veterans to collect their death benefits on an advance basis.

Under the bill, the VA could guarantee loans for facilities that provided multifamily transitional housing for homeless veterans. National Guard and Reserve members would be allowed to continue receiving guaranteed home loans through Sept. 30, 2003.

The bill created more flexible payment options for veterans attending college under the Montgomery G.I. bill and expanded the number of former service members eligible for the G.I. bill by allowing credits for certain life experiences. The World War II–era "G.I. Bill of Rights" had been revived by 1984 legislation (PL 98-525) after lapsing in 1976 with the end of the draft. Rep. G. V. "Sonny" Montgomery, D-Miss. (1964–1997), had led the move to resurrect the program. *(G.I. bill, Congress and the Nation Vol. VI, p. 621)*

The bill also included construction authorizations for veterans facilities and made changes in veterans cemetery funding formulas.

The House Veterans' Affairs Committee reported HR 4110 (H Rept 105-627) on July 15, 1998, and the House passed it by voice vote on Aug. 3. The Senate Veterans' Affairs Committee reported its version (S 2273—S Rept 105-341) on Sept. 21 and then passed HR 4110 by voice vote on Sept. 30, after substituting the text of its bill. On Oct. 10 the House, 423–0, adopted a resolution (H Res 592) agreeing to the Senate amendment with an amendment. The Senate agreed, clearing the bill by voice vote on Oct. 21. President Clinton signed it into law on Nov. 11.

Job Preference

Congress in 1998 cleared legislation (S 1021—PL 105-339) that refined hiring and job retention practices for veterans in the federal workforce. The bill created a more uniform procedure than previously existed for veterans to use if they believe that their job preference rights had been violated.

The system included review in the Labor Department and the Merit System Protection Board and eventually the court system if a veteran wanted to pursue a claim beyond administrative remedies.

S 1021 also extended or broadened preference rights coverage to certain agencies and parts of the legislative and executive branches. This included the General Accounting Office and generally nonpolicy and nonpolitical offices in Congress and the executive office of the president as well as certain areas of the federal judiciary.

The Veterans Preference Act dated from 1944 to help wartime and disabled veterans return to civilian life. The law provided a "preference" in hiring decisions for jobs in the federal government and generally applied to disabled veterans and those who served in military campaigns during specified time periods. It gave these persons an advantage in getting a government job over nonveterans and other veterans who were not in the preference class. The law also provided extra protection for these workers during periods of downsizing in the government. Preference eligible veterans were believed to be about twice as large in the federal workforce as in civilian jobs. Federal job figures also showed that federal employees who were not preference eligible were about four times as likely to lose their jobs in so-called "reduction-in-force" actions.

S 1021 was reported by the Senate Veterans' Affairs Committee on Sept. 21, 1998 (S Rept 105-340) and passed by the Senate on Oct. 5. It was passed by the House on Oct. 8 under suspension of the rules and signed into law by President Clinton on Oct. 31. The House in 1997 had passed a similar but broader bill (HR 240) in 1997.

1999–2000

The 106th Congress made few major policy changes to veterans programs, instead passing bills both in 1999 and 2000 making small changes. Among them were increases for educational assistance and attempts to streamline the Department of Veterans Affair's health care system. Lawmakers also passed a bill to make it easier for veterans to make claims for benefits.

Long-Term Health Care

Congress in 1999 passed legislation that would expand the availability of long-term health care services to veterans. The bill, signed by President Clinton on Nov. 30 (HR 2116—PL 106-117), created a four-year plan requiring the Department of Veterans Affairs (VA) to provide extended care services to veterans needing it for a service-connected disability and to any veteran at least 70 percent disabled by service-related injuries. The bill also expanded noninstitutional care for all enrolled veterans and allowed the VA to offset some costs by setting copayments on certain services.

Previously, the VA was permitted to provide institutional care to any enrolled veteran but was not required to do so. The four-year limit on the program was included to address concerns by some lawmakers that creating more VA health programs could squeeze the agency's budget to the extent that some veterans might be forced out of the VA health system. Congress was to review the plan after three years to determine before the program expired whether it should be eliminated, expanded, or left as it was.

Other provisions of the bill lifted a six-month limit on VA adult day-care, increased mental health services, and started a pilot program for contracting for assisted living services. The bill also authorized $57.5 million for fiscal 2000 and 2001 for construction and $2.2 million for leasing VA medical facilities. The measure also provided coverage for uninsured veterans who needed emergency care but did not have access to a VA facility.

The House Veterans' Affairs Committee reported the bill (H Rept 106-237) on July 16. The House passed the measure, 369–46, on Sept. 21. The Senate amended and passed the bill on Nov. 5 by voice vote. During a brief conference, House members dropped some controversial provisions, including one that would have further restricted eligibility for burial in Arlington National Cemetery. The House approved the conference report on the measure (H Rept 106-470) by voice vote on Nov. 16. The Senate followed suit on Nov. 19.

Appeals Aid

President Clinton on Nov. 9, 2000, signed into law a bill (HR 4864—PL 106-475) to make it easier for veterans to file claims with the Department of Veterans Affairs (VA).

The bill required the VA to be more specific when dealing with claimants whose applications were incomplete, by informing them of the specific medical or lay evidence still required, as well as which of that evidence the veteran was expected to obtain and which the department would seek. The bill also required the VA to "make reasonable efforts to assist in obtaining evidence necessary to substantiate a claimant's eligibility for a benefit," and to inform the veteran when such records could not be obtained.

For claims regarding disability compensation, the measure required the VA to obtain the veteran's service medical records, and, if the veteran provided adequate information, to obtain other relevant service records, and to provide a medical examination if warranted. The department would pay for the retrieval of records.

Rep. Bob Stump, R-Ariz., the bill's sponsor and chairman of the House Veterans' Affairs Committee, said the bill would clarify the department's duty to help claimants and "restore the balance in the VA claims system." The measure reversed a July 1999 decision by the Court of Appeals for Veterans Claims that the VA may only help veterans obtain records relevant to filing a benefit claim if it could be proved that the claim was "well grounded."

The House Veterans' Affairs Committee reported the measure (H Rept 106-781) on July 24, 2000, and the House passed it 414–0 the following day. Similar legislation (S 1810—S Rept 106-397) had been reported by the Senate Veterans' Affairs Committee on Sept. 6 and was passed by voice vote of the full Senate on Sept. 21. The Senate next passed a slightly amended version of HR 4864 by voice vote on Sept. 25. The House agreed to the Senate changes and cleared the measure by voice vote on Oct. 17.

Health, Education Benefits

President Clinton signed into law on Nov. 1, 2000, a bill (S 1402—PL 106-419) to increase veterans education benefits under the Montgomery G.I. bill, improve certain health benefits, and boost pay for Department of Veterans Affairs (VA) nurses and dentists.

The legislation, a compromise that incorporated provisions from several veterans bills, increased education assistance under the G.I. bill from $552 per month to $650 per month for three years of service. It guaranteed VA nurses the same annual pay increase that federal employees received, increased pay for dentists, and allowed VA hospitals to hire physician assistants. The measure also authorized the VA to provide temporary lodging for veterans getting treatment or other services, and expanded health benefits to a number of specific groups.

As passed by a voice vote of the Senate on July 26, 1999, S 1402 focused on veterans education benefits. The Senate Veterans' Affairs Committee had reported the bill (S Rept 106-114) on July 20. The House passed S 1402 on May 23, 2000, by a vote of 417–0, after substituting its own veterans education bill (HR 4268). HR 4268 had been reported (H Rept 106-628) by the House Veterans' Affairs Committee on May 19.

On Sept. 21, 2000, each chamber passed a version of veterans health care legislation. The House bill (HR 5109) had been reported (H Rept 106-863) by the Veterans' Affairs panel on Sept. 18 and passed by a 411–0 vote of the full House. It contained a controversial provision by Dave Weldon, R-Fla., which would have allowed veterans to receive health care funded by the Department of Veterans Affairs at non-VA hospitals. The Senate legislation (S 1810—S Rept 106-397), reported by the Veterans' Affairs Committee on Sept. 6, 2000, and passed by a voice vote of the full Senate on Sept. 21, had no comparable language.

The pilot program was supported by some of the largest veterans associations, including the American Legion and the Veterans of Foreign Wars. Other veterans groups, however, including the Disabled American Veterans and the Paralyzed Veterans of America, lobbied against it, arguing that it would begin a process that would eventually close the VA health care system by making it more convenient for veterans to seek care at local hospitals. *(1996 action, Congress and the Nation Vol. IX, p. 601)*

Working behind the scenes, House and Senate negotiators blended the bills into a single package, dropping Weldon's pilot program. The Senate passed the compromise on Oct. 12 as a substitute to S 1402 and the House cleared it on Oct. 17, both by voice votes.

Veterans COLAs

Cost-of-living adjustments (COLAs) in the benefits of disabled veterans and their survivors were enacted in 1999 and 2000, as part of broader veterans bills (HR 2280—PL 106-118 and HR 4850—PL 106-413).

The measures authorized COLA increases that would match those of Social Security beneficiaries, in keeping with a requirement of the 1997 Balanced Budget Act (HR 2015—PL 105-33). That amounted to a COLA increase of 2.4 percent as of Dec. 1, 1999, and 3.5 percent as of Dec. 1, 2000. *(1997– 1998 action, p. 498)*

HR 2280 (H Rept 106-202) was reported by the House Veterans' Affairs Committee on June 25, 1999, and passed by the full House, 424–0, on June 29. The Senate Veterans' Affairs Committee reported its version (S 1393—S Rept 106-108) on July 19. The full Senate passed an amended version of HR 2280 on July 26, the House amended it further on Nov. 9, and the Senate cleared the bill on Nov. 19, all by voice votes. President Clinton signed it into law on Nov. 30.

HR 4850 was reported (H Rept 106-783) by the House Veterans' Affairs Committee on July 24, 2000, and was passed by voice vote of the House the next day. By voice votes, the Senate passed an amended version on Oct. 12 and the House agreed to the Senate changes by voice vote on Oct. 17, clearing the bill for the president. Clinton signed it on Nov. 1.

## CHAPTER 10

Education Policy

Introduction 507

1997–1998 Chronology 509

1999–2000 Chronology 531

Education Policy

Education issues provoked such sharp partisan fighting during President Bill Clinton's second term that lawmakers, for the first time in thirty-five years, failed to reauthorize the Elementary and Secondary Education Act (ESEA), which was the main source of federal aid to private schools. Members regularly found themselves at odds over such issues as whether to give parents tax breaks for sending their children to private schools and the extent to which states, rather than the federal government, should determine education priorities.

Although education was hardly the bipartisan issue it had been in earlier years, Republicans and Democrats were able to brush aside their differences on a number of secondary bills. Despite the charged partisan environment and the impeachment of President Clinton, lawmakers succeeded in reauthorizing the Higher Education Act and establishing an "ed-flex" program to give local school systems greater control over federal dollars.

Education had become a top voter concern by the late 1990s, in part because there were few economic problems or overseas threats to dominate the country's attention. Yet the federal government had limited control over public schools, providing only about seven cents of every education dollar.

Accountability emerged as the buzzword for Republicans and Democrats (as well as the 2000 presidential nominees, Vice President Al Gore and Texas Gov. George W. Bush). Politicians wanted to ensure that schools and teachers who did their jobs were rewarded and those who failed were sanctioned.

For Republicans, this meant giving to local school officials more flexibility over the spending of federal dollars. But President Clinton and many Democrats wanted to increase the federal role in education by requiring teacher certifications, comprehensive disciplinary policies, and annual report cards on performance, as well as spending more money for teacher salaries and school construction.

MAJOR BATTLES

The two parties clashed most dramatically over education during the 106th Congress, when Congress set about to reauthorize ESEA. Republicans attempted to use the reauthorization to revamp federal education policies. Their plans included allowing officials to convert most federal categorical aid into block grants, creating a "Straight A's" pilot program giving ten states unprecedented flexibility to spend federal education funds, and setting up a limited program of school vouchers. GOP leaders even ventured into such controversial areas as proposing to ban the Department of Education from funding classes about the prevention of hate crimes.

Clinton, in contrast, wanted to tighten federal control over education standards. Democrats in Congress also battled vigorously to increase funding for school construction, reduce class size, and improve teacher training, among other priorities.

Inevitably, the contentious fight stalled the ESEA reauthorization. Breaking with precedent, House leaders in 1999 elected to break up ESEA into seven smaller pieces, while the Senate in 2000 tried to move ESEA as one massive bill. Three less controversial elements eventually were enacted, but the central portions of the law—including the massive Title I program, which provided billions of dollars for low-income students—were left for the 107th Congress to sort out.

Education Savings Accounts proved to be another top GOP priority that set off repeated debates. Republicans in the 105th Congress overcame strenuous Democratic objections and cleared legislation that would have created tax-preferred savings accounts for elementary and secondary ed-

REFERENCES

Discussion of education policy for the years 1945–1964 may be found in *Congress and the Nation Vol. I*, pp. 1195–1215; for the years 1965–1968, *Congress and the Nation Vol. II*, pp. 709–733; for the years 1969–1972, *Congress and the Nation Vol. III*, pp. 581–604; for the years 1973–1976, *Congress and the Nation Vol. IV*, pp. 377–402; for the years 1977–1980, *Congress and the Nation Vol. V*, pp. 655–677; for the years 1981–1984, *Congress and the Nation Vol. VI*, pp. 555–580; for the years 1985–1988, *Congress and the Nation Vol. VII*, pp. 647–663; for the years 1989–1992, *Congress and the Nation Vol. VIII*, pp. 641–660; for the years 1993–1996, *Congress and the Nation Vol. IX*, pp. 607–634.

Outlays for Education

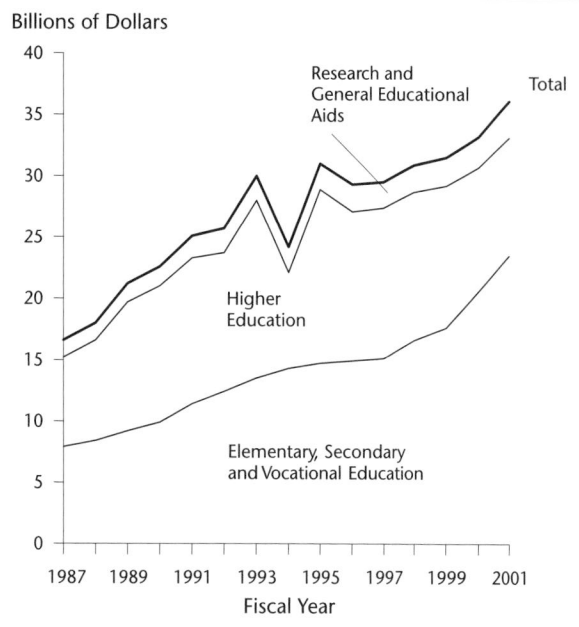

NOTE: Data for 2001 are estimated.

SOURCE: Office of Management and Budget, *Historical Tables, Budget of the United States Government: Fiscal Year 2002* (Washington, D.C.: U.S. Government Printing Office, 2001), Table 3.2

ucation expenses, including private school tuition. But President Clinton vetoed it.

These so-called education IRAs were a top conservative priority. Supporters said the measure would help out middle-class parents by allowing them to set aside $2,000 in special savings accounts and withdraw the principal and interest tax-free. Sen. Paul Coverdell, R-Ga., who sponsored the plan, said the expanded education accounts could make "millions of families better positioned to make the best education choices for their children."

Democrats, however, assailed the proposal as tilted toward affluent Americans who could afford to set aside thousands of dollars a year. The president agreed and vetoed the bill in 1998, contending it would "weaken public education and shortchange our children."

Republicans turned again to the issue of education IRAs in the 106th Congress. The Senate passed a bill (S 1134) that would allow families to set aside up to $2,000 per child annually in tax-free accounts. But in the House, a similar bill was blocked on the floor when a band of GOP moderates threw their weight behind a plan to set up a tax credit to help spur school construction.

On another politically charged issue, Republicans and Democrats deadlocked in the 105th Congress over an attempt by House conservatives to revamp federally supported bilingual education. The legislation sought to turn over the funding authority for bilingual and immigrant education programs to the states. Supporters wanted to allow states and localities more latitude to try alternatives such as English immersion.

Under the legislation, some 90 percent of bilingual education grants would be used for English-language programs.

Opponents decried the measure's potential effects, saying that it would handicap the efforts of children who were trying to learn English. Although the House passed the plan in 1998, momentum stalled in the face of sharp criticism from the Clinton administration and a lack of commitment from Senate Republicans.

BIPARTISAN VICTORIES

Despite such clashes, Congress cleared a number of significant education bills with bipartisan support. The 105th Congress passed a five-year reauthorization of the Higher Education Act of 1965 that expanded federal assistance to college students. GOP support for the measure was a major reversal from 1995 Republican proposals to cut student loan subsidies.

The legislation reduced interest rates on federally backed student loans, created a new grant program that awarded $300 million annually for teacher training and recruitment, and even included a White House program to provide $200 million to prepare low-income middle school students for college. Perhaps most significantly, it featured a compromise—forged by Reps. Howard P. "Buck" McKeon, R-Calif., and Dale Kildee, D-Mich.—to change the formula for calculating interest rates on student loans. The administration backed the bill somewhat grudgingly, contending the new formula was overly generous to banks, but bankers contended that student loans would have become unprofitable without the change.

After years of battling over the issue, Congress in 1998 also cleared legislation to overhaul and extend federal vocational education programs. In addition, lawmakers reauthorized the main federal education program for disabled students—the Individuals with Disabilities Education Act, known as IDEA.

Although the 106th Congress was somewhat less productive because of the ESEA deadlock, members nevertheless scratched out agreements on several prominent measures. Most notably, Congress cleared legislation in 1999 giving local school systems greater autonomy in how they used federal education money. The bill, modeled on a twelve-state pilot program, gave states the power to approve waivers from many federal regulations at the local level. Most Democrats supported the bill and Clinton signed it, although some liberals worried that it could undercut programs designed to assist low-income students.

Much of the action on education issues took place in budget and appropriations bills. The 1997 budget-reconciliation legislation contained a $35 billion package of tax breaks for higher education. These included child tax credits, HOPE college tax credits, and lifetime learning credits. Appropriations bills also served as the battlegrounds over some of Clinton's key education initiatives, such as his plan to promote voluntary national testing of fourth-graders in reading and eighth-graders in math.

Chronology of Action on Education

1997–1998

The 105th Congress completed action on several significant education initiatives, including the reauthorization of the 1965 Higher Education Act, an overhaul of federal vocational education programs, and the reauthorization of the twenty-two-year-old Individuals with Disabilities Education Act (IDEA). As part of the 1997 budget-reconciliation package, lawmakers also cleared a package of tax breaks for higher education. In addition, lawmakers agreed to a bipartisan initiative to expand federal aid for private schools.

Conservatives, however, failed to move several of their top priorities. A measure to grant tax breaks for elementary and secondary education expenses, including private school tuition, ran into a presidential veto, and a plan to overhaul bilingual education programs foundered in the face of White House resistance. Similarly, Republicans failed to win broad backing for plans to consolidate federal education programs into block grants and provide private school vouchers for low-income D.C. students. Clinton, for his part, could not win over conservatives for his plan to institute national voluntary math testing.

Higher Education

Congress in 1998 cleared a five-year reauthorization of the Higher Education Act of 1965, expanding federal assistance to college students, a sharp reversal from 1995 Republican proposals to cut student loan subsidies. *(1995 action, Congress and the Nation Vol. IX, p. 631)*

The bipartisan measure (HR 6—PL 105-244) reduced interest rates on federally backed student loans, created a grant program for teacher training and recruitment, and funded a White House program to help low-income middle school students prepare for college. It also created an organization within the Education Department to oversee performance-based student lending, increased the maximum authorized Pell Grant for low-income students, forgave up to $5,000 in loans to students who taught for five years in underserved areas, and required loan guaranty agencies to return $250 million in reserves to the government.

BACKGROUND

Congress passed the Higher Education Act (PL 89-329) in 1965 to set up federal student aid programs that were intended to expand access to postsecondary education. The higher education law, last reauthorized in 1992, governed tens of billions of dollars in loans, grants, and work-study funds. However, rapidly increasing tuition costs sparked concerns that many Americans could not afford to send their children to college. Officials were also concerned about the number of student loan defaults. *(1965 law, Congress and the Nation Vol. II, p. 716)*

Republicans and Democrats in the 105th Congress worked closely to develop the bill. The biggest hurdle was a threat by commercial bankers to pull out of college lending unless Congress altered a long-planned change in the formula for calculating interest rates on student loans. Bankers contended the formula, set in the 1993 budget-reconciliation act (PL 103-66), would make such lending unprofitable. *(1993 action, Congress and the Nation Vol. IX, p. 625)*

The formula, which was to take effect on July 1, 1998, for the first time would peg interest rates to long-term Treasury bonds, rather than the ninety-one-day short-term notes that had been used. However, unexpected declines in long-term bond yields over the preceding five years meant the planned formula would cut rates considerably more than anticipated. Banks said that in addition to being unprofitable, the formula created unpredictability because banks would have to pay higher short-term interest rates to attract capital but would be forced to lend at long-term rates that were often lower.

The White House on Feb. 25 unveiled a Treasury Department study that said banks made too much under the current formula but would earn too little under the July 1 change. Vice President Al Gore proposed a compromise that would continue to peg interest rates to ninety-one-day Treasury bills but would add a smaller 2.3 percent when a loan was in repayment and 1.7 percent while a student was in school. Lenders said that plan was too draconian.

Determined to avert a disruption in lending, Rep. Howard P. "Buck" McKeon, R-Calif., and Rep. Dale Kildee,

D-Mich., worked out a compromise. Under their two-tiered rate plan, students would pay 1.7 percent above the ninety-one-day Treasury bill rate while in school and 2.3 percent above it afterward. Bankers would receive a second, slightly higher rate, which would be 2.2 percent higher than the short-term note while a student was in school and 2.8 percent higher while in repayment. The federal government would provide millions of dollars in subsidies to banks to guarantee that rate of return.

The White House supported the student loan interest rate but complained that the formula was far too generous to banks.

HOUSE COMMITTEE ACTION

The House Committee on Education and the Workforce took up HR 6 in March 1998. The measure reflected an attempt to split the difference between students and banks on the politically sensitive issue of where to set interest rates on federally backed college loans.

HR 6 sought to respond to threats by commercial lenders, who provided 70 percent of student loans, that they would drop out of the federally guaranteed lending program unless Congress reworked a scheduled July 1 change in the formula for setting interest rates. But student groups and college officials, citing rising tuition costs, made the interest rate reduction a top priority, putting lawmakers in a tough spot.

The committee bill was an effort to satisfy both sides. It would give students interest rate relief but provide $300 million a year or more in special federal payments to banks.

After working for months to come up with a bipartisan solution on interest rates, McKeon and Kildee struck a compromise that used the student loan interest rate formula in the White House plan, but it also created a second, slightly higher, interest rate for banks. Under the committee bill, as with the White House proposal, students in academic year 1998–1999 would pay an estimated 7.43 percent interest rate during repayment, down from the current 8.23 percent. Banks would get a 7.93 percent interest rate, slightly higher than students would pay. The separate bank formula would cost the federal government from $1.2 billion to $3.8 billion over five years, depending on what methodology Congress ultimately adopted, according to the Congressional Budget Office.

Although it gained broad support with lawmakers and student groups, lenders were unhappy, maintaining it would not provide banks with a high enough return. Education Secretary Richard W. Riley criticized the legislation, saying the new subsidy to lenders was unwarranted.

Some Democrats were skeptical about the deal but did not make a major push to change it. "Not all of us are convinced the compromise is totally justified," said Robert E. Andrews, D-N.J., who offered an unsuccessful amendment to reduce by 1 percentage point the 4 percent origination fee students pay when taking out loans. The White House plan also included the origination fee cut.

EDUCATION LEADERSHIP

Former South Carolina governor Richard W. Riley served as secretary of education throughout the Clinton presidency, the longest tenure of anybody in that position. He was confirmed by voice vote on Jan. 21, 1993, two days after the Senate Labor and Human Resources Committee had given voice vote approval to his nomination, and he remained secretary until Clinton's second term ended in 2001. He generally avoided the controversy that dogged some of Clinton's other top aides.

Riley's appointment drew high praise from the education community. Similar to Clinton, Riley was seen as at the vanguard of the education reform movement at the state level, where he had successfully implemented a school improvement plan by slightly raising sales taxes. His South Carolina reform plan had included initiatives to emphasize preschools, improve teacher training and workplace conditions, and improve testing and student performance.

Andrews and the Clinton administration also objected to a provision of HR 6 that would eliminate a requirement in current law that Sallie Mae and other guaranty agencies act as lenders of last resort in case of a breakdown in the commercial market. Adding to the uncertainty, given the tight budget situation, Democrats in Congress and the administration did not know where they would find the money to pay for the measure.

Other provisions of the bill were somewhat less controversial. The legislation sought to dramatically increase the maximum allowable Pell grant for disadvantaged students from the existing $3,000 to $5,300 in 2003–2004. The measure called on colleges to take cost-cutting steps. It also would create a "performance-based" organization within the Department of Education, with a chief operating officer to oversee student financial aid programs and simplify the process of applying for federal loans and grants.

The committee by voice vote adopted an amendment sponsored by Lindsey Graham, R-S.C., and Kildee to partially forgive student loans for teachers who worked for at least three years in high-poverty public and private schools.

It also approved an amendment by Mark Souder, R-Ind., that would bar student aid to anyone convicted of a drug charge. Students could lose eligibility for at least a year, and possibly longer, depending on the severity of the crime.

Democrats, led by Kildee, offered a White House-backed proposal that would create four new teacher training programs, including partnerships between colleges and local education agencies and a new effort to recruit teachers to work in high-poverty urban and rural areas. The amendment failed, 18–19.

In an effort to respond to concerns about the quality of teachers, as well as a shortage of instructors in low-income urban and rural areas, HR 6 included a plan by committee chairman Bill Goodling, R-Pa., to create new, competitive block grants that states could use to beef up teacher certification requirements. The plan was an alternative to Clinton's well-publicized call to hire 100,000 new teachers.

By voice vote, the panel defeated an amendment by Bill Barrett, R-Neb., to eliminate the Goodling teacher training block grant in the bill. The Goodling plan, which included some elements developed by committee Democrats, would provide $18.5 million annually in block grants that states could use to toughen certification requirements to ensure that teachers are knowledgeable in their subject areas, revamp college teacher preparation programs, create or expand efforts to provide alternative routes to certification, and develop initiatives to more quickly remove incompetent or unqualified teachers from classrooms.

In a compromise that defused a dispute between the black and Hispanic caucuses, the panel by voice vote approved an amendment to move language governing aid to Hispanic-serving institutions from Title III of the act to a separate part of the law. Rubin Hinojosa, D-Texas, had wanted to create a new section under Title III—which covered financial support to historically black colleges and universities—to recognize the growing needs of Hispanic students. Members of the black caucus had worried that the change could, among other things, increase competition for federal funds. William L. Clay, D-Mo., offered the compromise amendment.

The committee adopted an amendment by Chaka Fattah, D-Pa., to implement a White House initiative promoting partnerships between colleges and middle and junior high schools in poor areas to provide counseling, tutoring, and other services.

On March 19 the House Committee on Education and the Workforce approved HR 6 (H Rept 105-481) by a vote of 38–3.

HOUSE FLOOR ACTION

When HR 6 reached the House floor, members considered dozens of amendments, including a controversial plan by Frank Riggs, R-Calif., to end admissions preferences based on race, sex, ethnicity, color, or national origin. The amendment, modeled on California's 1996 Proposition 209, would apply to public colleges and universities that received federal funds under the bill.

Although intended to make affirmative action a defining issue between the two parties, the amendment and other Republican proposals instead served to expose internal splits within the GOP. The House defeated the Riggs amendment by a 171–249 vote, despite what Riggs said were pledges from the Republican leadership to help pass it. Fifty-five Republicans voted no, including J. C. Watts of Oklahoma, the lone black Republican in the House. Watts joined John Lewis, D-Ga., a former civil rights leader, on a letter to colleagues urging opposition.

The House also grappled with the issue of wrestling, specifically a provision that would require colleges to report if they expected to drop any sports programs in the next four years. The provision was championed by J. Dennis Hastert, R-Ill., a former wrestler and coach frustrated that schools had been dropping less glamorous sports such as wrestling to save money. But the House voted 292–129 to adopt an amendment by Tim Roemer, D-Ind., to delete it.

The wrestling debate brought out the tensions arising from Title IX of the 1972 Education Amendments (PL 92-318) that required schools to provide women with equal access to sports programs. Critics said the law forced schools to cut funds for some men's programs.

The House passed three amendments to HR 6:

• By voice vote, an amendment by Mark Foley, R-Fla., to allow schools to disclose disciplinary records of students who commit violent crimes.

• By 220–187, an amendment by Jim McGovern, D-Mass., to increase Pell Grants to students who graduated in the top 10 percent of their high school class.

• By 393–28, an amendment by George Miller, D-Calif., expressing the sense of Congress that colleges adopt merchandise licensing codes to ensure goods are not made in sweatshops.

Overshadowing everything else in the bill, however, was the controversy over interest rates. The administration contended that the interest rate plan would enable banks to reap excessive profits and force Congress to cut education and other domestic programs to pay for it.

Congress had tried unsuccessfully to add the interest rate provisions to another bill, a supplemental spending measure that lawmakers cleared April 30 and was signed into law May 1 (PL 105-174). But that effort was stymied by White House veto threats and the need to come up with about $1 billion in offsetting costs.

Although lenders also did not like all the provisions in HR 6, they shifted from trying to alter it to asking Congress to pass it before the long-planned interest rate formula took effect on July 1. The House passed HR 6 by a lopsided 414–4 vote on May 6 despite the strong White House opposition to the interest rate provisions. Given the broad support for the bill, lawmakers said they were increasingly confident that President Clinton would not veto it over the interest rate issue alone.

SENATE ACTION

Before the Senate could act, and with commercial banks threatening to drop out of the student loan business, Congress bought a little time by adding a provision to the new highway law (HR 2400—PL 105-178) to help bankers. The provision discarded the contested formula and instead implemented the proposed two-pronged interest rate plan temporarily from July 1 to Sept. 30.

On July 9 the Senate debated its version of the higher education legislation (S 1882). Both S 1882 and HR 6 would reduce interest rates on student loans while providing new subsidies to banks as an incentive to stay in the college lending market. In the 1998–1999 academic year, both bills would set an interest rate on student loans pegged to short-term Treasury bills, expected to be about 7.43 percent. With the bank subsidy factored in, banks would receive about 7.93 percent.

Edward M. Kennedy, Mass., the bill manager for the Democrats, endorsed many parts of the measure even while labeling the subsidy to banks a "sweetheart deal" that could cost taxpayers between $1 billion and $3 billion over five years. Kennedy offered an amendment, backed by the White House, that would set up a pilot program to auction the right to make student loans, letting the market—not the government—set the interest rates. But the amendment was defeated, 39–58.

Labor and Human Resources Chairman James M. Jeffords, R-Vt., said the federal government would guarantee nearly 90 million student loans, totaling $383.5 billion, during the next decade. The Senate version also would increase the maximum Pell grant for disadvantaged students from the current $3,000 to $5,000 in the 1999–2000 academic year, and by an additional $200 each year thereafter. Over the next five years, more than 25.4 million Pell Grants will be issued, Jeffords said.

The Senate measure would trade off current teacher-training programs in exchange for $300 million in competitive block grants that states could use to revamp teacher training. The bill included an incentive for teachers to work in distressed areas, forgiving as much as $10,000 in student debt for those who do.

By 55–43, the Senate approved an amendment by Paul Wellstone, D-Minn., to give states the option of allowing welfare recipients to enroll in vocational or postsecondary education for two years, without losing monthly benefits. It also would exempt teen parents from the 30 percent requirement on the number of welfare recipients in each state who must be involved in some new welfare-to-work activities. The new welfare law (PL 104-193), which required states to have 50 percent of their caseload working by 2002, allowed one year of vocational training as a permissible work activity.

By voice vote, senators approved an amendment by Bob Graham, D-Fla., that would make it easier for veterans who receive federal education benefits under the Montgomery GI bill to qualify for other federal college aid.

After an all-day debate on July 9, the Senate then inserted the text of S 1882 into HR 6 and passed the House bill by a resounding vote of 96–1. The sole dissenter was Jesse Helms, R-N.C.

CONFERENCE, FINAL ACTION

House and Senate negotiators on Sept. 25 reached agreement on nearly all elements of HR 6. The final version would cut interest rates on federal college loans to the lowest level in nearly twenty years, expand grants to low-income students, and create a new teacher training program.

Education Secretary Richard W. Riley said in a statement he supported the deal despite disappointment that it provided new subsidies to bankers. As it had been since lawmakers started work on the bill the previous year, the issue of where to set interest rates on student loans was the major dispute. Under the conference report, the temporary fix in the transportation bill (PL 105-178) would be extended until 2003. The Clinton administration initially had opposed the interest rate formula, arguing that it was too generous to banks.

A big sticking point for lawmakers was finding the hundreds of millions of dollars needed to pay for the bank subsidies. After months of negotiations, the conferees agreed to fund the measure by preventing students from discharging student loan debt if they declared bankruptcy. They also hoped to wring some savings out of federal mortgage guarantee programs. The agreement would require federal student loan guaranty agencies to return $250 million in outstanding reserve funds to the federal government, set up a federal student loan reserve fund, and reduce guaranty agencies' share of collections on loan defaults.

Lawmakers also had to deal with an unexpected controversy when the Education Department announced that it would apply the lower student interest rate not only to new college loans, but also to students who consolidated direct and guaranteed loans into one package for easier repayment. In effect, that announcement allowed students to refinance outstanding loans at a lower rate of interest.

Commercial lenders complained the move gave the Education Department, which directly competes with them through its direct loan program, an unfair advantage. The conferees settled the issue by only allowing the Education Department to offer the lower rate on consolidated loans until Feb. 1, 1999.

The House passed the conference report by voice vote Sept. 28. The Senate cleared it, 96–0, on Sept. 29. President Clinton signed the bill into law on Oct. 27, 1998.

MAJOR PROVISIONS

The following are highlights of HR 6 (PL 105-244):

• **Interest rates.** The measure created a two-tiered system providing one interest rate for students and a second, slightly higher rate for banks. Though banks would receive hundreds of millions of dollars in special interest subsidies, the new rate would be lower than under previous law.

The rates, based on short-term Treasury bonds, would vary annually. Based on July 1, 1998, data, students in the 1998–1999 academic year would receive a 7.46 percent interest rate during repayment. Banks would get an estimated 7.96 percent rate. Earlier in 1998 those rates were 8.23 percent.

• **New grant programs.** The bill created three new grant programs, authorized at a total of $300 million in fiscal 1999, to help states improve teacher training and performance and recruit qualified teachers. The funding could be used for such initiatives as upgrading teacher certification programs or providing merit pay to excellent teachers.

• **Loans for teachers.** In an effort to address shortages of teachers in rural and low-income urban areas, the measure would forgive up to $5,000 of college loans, and in some instances more, for newly graduated teachers who stay in the profession for at least five years.

• **"GEAR UP."** Blending suggestions from the White House and House- and Senate-passed measures, the bill established a "GEAR UP" program of expanded outreach to low-income youths in middle school. The initiative, authorized at $200 million in fiscal 1999, was designed to increase the number of poor students who attended college.

• **Pell Grants.** The agreement would gradually increase the maximum authorized Pell Grant for low-income college students to $5,800 in academic year 2003–2004, up from the current appropriated level of $3,000. It would expand eligibility of Pell Grants to postgraduate teaching programs and set up a discretionary program of financial awards, equal to a student's Pell Grant, to college freshmen and sophomores who graduated in the top 10 percent of their high school class.

• **Work study.** The authorization for college work study was increased to $1 billion in fiscal 1999, up from the fiscal 1998 appropriated level of $830 million.

• **Performance-based organization.** The bill set up a performance-based organization in the Education Department to improve oversight of federal student aid. The federal government provided more than $48 billion in grants, loans, and federal work study funding in fiscal 1998.

• **Alcohol abuse.** Responding to violence on some U.S. campuses that tried to crack down on drinking, HR 6 created a program to combat college alcohol abuse. It provided grants to help low-income students with child care and to combat violent crime against women on college campuses.

Vocational Education

After years of battling over the issue, Congress finally cleared legislation in 1998 to overhaul and extend federal vocational education programs. The measure (HR 1853—PL 105-332) reduced the amount of money states had to spend to help women reenter the workforce, directed more aid to local schools, and created a reserve fund that rural areas could tap into for training.

The Senate originally passed its version of the vocational education bill as part of a larger bill (HR 1385) to overhaul a host of federal job training programs. The House approved vocational education as a stand-alone measure.

Lawmakers in the end chose to clear a freestanding bill. The agreement was reached in part because of objections from conservative groups, which worried that including vocational education in a broader job training initiative could be seen as an effort to direct some high school students toward the workplace, rather than to college. The vocational education community also wanted its own bill.

The measure increased to 85 percent from 75 percent the amount of federal funds allocated to local schools and organizations. It set aside 10 percent of that allocation to create a fund to aid rural areas, regions with a large percentage or number of vocational students, or areas that could be affected by formula changes in the bill.

The measure ended a requirement that states allocate 10.5 percent of funding to assist pregnant women, single parents, and homemakers seeking to reenter the workforce and to fund gender equity programs designed to increase the number of men or women in professions where they are underrepresented.

States instead would be required to spend from $60,000 to $150,000 on activities to help individuals move into nontraditional occupations. The bill encouraged school districts to form partnerships with community colleges, technical schools, and private businesses to improve training.

HOUSE COMMITTEE ACTION

The House Education and the Workforce Subcommittee on Early Childhood, Youth and Families took up HR 1853 before Republicans and Democrats could agree on a bipartisan approach to revising the main federal vocational and technical education program. Members from both parties said they hoped to reach a deal before the measure went to the House floor.

In the meantime, Democrats complained that Republicans were rewriting the program to help suburban and rural schools at the expense of urban ones. Republicans responded that they were willing to compromise on many issues, but that Democrats had adopted a take-it-or-leave-it attitude and refused to budge.

The bill would reauthorize and revise the Carl D. Perkins Vocational and Applied Technology Education Act of 1990 (PL 101-392). Authorization for the program had expired, though Congress continued to appropriate funds. It received $1.1 billion in fiscal 1997. The legislation would authorize $1.3 billion in fiscal 1998 and unspecified sums through fiscal 2002.

The bill would change both the formula used to distribute federal money to the states and the formula that guides how states allocate their funds to schools. The proposed change in the federal formula would give more money to states based on their population between ages fifteen and twenty-four, the general target group for vocational and technical education programs. Under the bill, 50 percent of the funds to the states would be based on each state's population between ages fifteen and nineteen, and 50 percent on the population between ages twenty and twenty-four. The state per capita income would have a bearing on the calculation.

That change was less contentious than the proposed overhaul in how states distribute the funds. Under existing law, 70 percent of the state distribution was based on the number of children in the Title I remedial education program for low-income students, 20 percent on the number enrolled in education programs for disabled students, and 10 percent on the general school enrollment. The bill would change the formula beginning in fiscal 1999, so that half the money would be distributed based on each state's population between ages fifteen and nineteen, and half on the number of those children in that age group living in poverty.

States would also have to send 90 percent of the federal money they received to schools, compared with 75 percent under current law. The remaining 8 percent would be for state activities, with 2 percent for administrative costs.

Forcing states to distribute a higher percentage of their federal funds to schools was a favorite theme of committee chairman Bill Goodling, R-Pa. "If we are going to see true change occur in vocational-technical education, it is going to come from the local level, and that is where our money should be," he said.

Rural schools could benefit from two provisions. One would enable states to set aside 10 percent of their grant for rural districts. The other would lower the minimum grant for secondary and postsecondary programs, enabling more small schools to qualify.

Rep. Matthew G. Martinez of California, ranking Democrat on the Early Childhood, Youth and Families Subcommittee, said the measure would mainly benefit districts that are represented by the Republicans. He said the legislation was "a clear winner for Republicans and a clear loser for most Democrats."

Republicans said that virtually every congressional district represented by committee members would gain under the legislation. But Democrats countered that in some cases that was true only because states would be forced to send a greater percentage of aid to localities—possibly jeopardizing state administrative abilities.

The full committee approved by voice vote an amendment by Goodling that substituted for the subcommittee bill, making mostly minor changes. The committee rejected several Democratic amendments, including those by:

• Martinez, to base some of the state distribution formula on current law and some on a ratio of 60 percent for poverty rates and 40 percent for population. It lost, 16–22.

• Martinez, to substitute a Democratic proposal that would, among other things, change the GOP state distribution formula. It lost, 18–19.

• Donald M. Payne, D-N.J., to strike the allowable 10 percent set aside for rural areas. It lost, 16–20.

• Carolyn McCarthy, D-N.Y., to lower the minimum grant for secondary schools from $15,000 to $10,000, instead of the bill's proposed $7,500. The amendment failed by voice vote.

The House Education and the Workforce Subcommittee on Early Childhood, Youth and Families approved HR 1853 by voice vote on June 12, 1997. The full committee approved the bill (H Rept 105-177) June 25 by a party-line vote of 20–18.

HOUSE FLOOR ACTION

Although the committee had achieved bipartisan consensus on the new formula for distributing vocational money to the states, HR 1853 faced other challenges when the measure came to the House floor July 17.

Patsy T. Mink, D-Hawaii, several other Democratic women, and Constance A. Morella, R-Md., doggedly pushed an amendment to require localities with training programs for displaced homemakers, single parents, and pregnant women to continue funding them at current levels. The chamber defeated the amendment 207–214, reaffirming its vote several minutes later when it defeated, 207–220, a Democratic attempt sponsored by Mink to send the bill back to the Education and the Workforce Committee with instructions to attach the Mink language to it.

Democrats said the Mink amendment would guarantee existing services to the women. The underlying bill would abolish laws requiring states to set aside 10.5 percent of their funding to ensure that women have equal access to job training and to run special programs to train displaced homemakers, single parents, and single, pregnant women for jobs. Delegate Eleanor Holmes Norton, D-D.C., said it was in the government's interest to train these women. "These are the women most likely to cost the government the most," she said.

But education chairman Bill Goodling, R-Pa., and other panel Republicans said the amendment would interfere with the bill's effort to give states and local governments wider latitude in spending their education money. "It is not a welfare program. It is an education bill," Goodling said.

The House also defeated, 189–230, an amendment by Joseph P. Kennedy II, D-Mass., to allow school districts to hire employees to coordinate vocational programs with the needs of local employers. Goodling said the bill would already allow such hiring, without specifically mentioning workforce coordinators. He said such specifics could have cost the bill votes.

The House passed HR 1853 overwhelmingly, 414–12, on July 22. Overall, HR 1853 would authorize $1.3 billion in fiscal 1998 and unspecified sums through fiscal 2002 for secondary and postsecondary school programs.

SENATE, FINAL ACTION

The Senate first took up vocational education by including the issue in a larger bill (HR 1385) that it passed, 91–7, on May 5, 1998. But on June 12 it passed HR 1853 as a standalone vocational education bill by voice vote and without debate.

The Senate version incorporated a substitute amendment by James M. Jeffords, R-Vt., that contained many of the same authorizations as the House but did not include a specific authorized funding level.

The House and Senate reached consensus on a freestanding vocational bill after a protracted dispute about how much money to set aside for training and outreach programs designed to help displaced homemakers. The conference report (H Rept 105-800) eliminated the current 10.5 percent set-aside and staff position. States instead would be required to spend from $60,000 to $150,000 on activities to help individuals move into nontraditional occupations.

The bill would also increase to 85 percent from 75 percent the amount of overall vocational education funds allocated to local schools and organizations. It would also set aside 10 percent of that allocation to create a new fund that would aid rural areas, regions with a large percentage or number of vocational students, or areas that may have been negatively affected by formula changes in the bill.

It would encourage school districts to form partnerships with community colleges, technical schools, and private businesses to improve training. The legislation did not set specific authorization funding levels for vocational education programs, which were currently funded at about $1 billion.

The Senate approved the measure by voice vote Oct. 8, and the House followed suit early on Oct. 9. President Clinton signed the bill on Oct. 31, 1998.

IDEA Reauthorization

A bill to reauthorize and revise the main federal education program for disabled students became law in 1997 (HR 5— PL 105-17), after backers crafted a compromise. An earlier attempt to reauthorize the twenty-two-year-old Individuals with Disabilities Education Act (IDEA) died in the 104th Congress after it became caught up in disputes over controversial GOP proposals to rewrite the law's federal funding formula and give states more leeway to discipline disabled students. (*1996 action, Congress and the Nation Vol. IX, p. 630*)

To head off a repeat of that experience, key members of the House Education and the Workforce Committee and Senate Labor and Human Resources Committee adopted a consensus measure that had been worked out in closed-door negotiations by committee staffers, Education Department officials, and interest groups.

The final bill gave states slightly more flexibility to discipline disabled students, although states still could not cut off educational services to them. The funding formula continued to stress the number of disabled students in a state, although a portion of it could reflect the state's overall number of school age children and its poverty rates.

BACKGROUND

First enacted in 1975 as the Education for All Handicapped Children Act (PL 94-142), IDEA guaranteed the right of disabled children to a free education and required that disabled students be in "the least restrictive environment." Unlike most civil rights legislation, IDEA also provided some federal funds to help carry out its mandates. Advocates for the disabled were proud of the program—which benefited an estimated 5.4 million children nationwide—and cautious about making substantive changes.

But educators as well as some lawmakers, Republicans in particular, had seized on the need to reauthorize parts of the program as a chance to make sweeping changes. They were particularly interested in giving local school districts more flexibility to reduce costs and to discipline unruly disabled students.

In 1996 the House passed an IDEA reauthorization bill that would distribute funds based mainly on a state's school-age population, rather than the number of disabled children. Also, in cases where misconduct was unrelated to a student's disability, the bill would allow schools to apply the same disciplinary procedures to disabled students as to others, including expulsion without services.

Though the 1996 bill incorporated many suggestions made by a broad coalition representing disabled children and the general education community, advocates for disabled children still harbored reservations. Although the House passed the bill by voice vote, Democrats cautioned they would seek changes in conference.

The Senate Labor and Human Resources Committee approved a somewhat narrower bill in 1996 that said that if misconduct was not related to a student's disability, schools could employ the same disciplinary procedures they used for other students, including expulsion. But unless weapons or drugs were involved, the school would still be required to provide educational services.

Some GOP conservatives thought the Senate bill did not go far enough on discipline or in helping schools reduce the costs of special education. Republican leaders had little interest in a protracted debate, and the bill never came to the floor.

COMMITTEE ACTION

As the 105th Congress began, two committee chairmen— James M. Jeffords, R-Vt., of the Senate Labor and Human Resources Committee and Bill Goodling, R-Pa., of the House Education and the Workforce Committee—introduced bills (S 717, HR 5) that were virtually identical to those considered the year before. However, at the urging of top Republican leaders, Goodling and Jeffords agreed to put their proposals aside and let staff members try to devise a bill with more universal appeal.

Beginning in February, a group of congressional educational aides and officials from the Education Department quietly searched for a consensus. The negotiations were led by David Hoppe, the chief of staff to Senate Majority Leader Trent Lott, R-Miss., and the father of a child with Down's syndrome. The negotiators also worked closely with advocates for the disabled and for the public schools.

On May 7 the House Committee on Education and the Workforce and the Senate Labor and Human Resources Committee took up virtually identical versions of the resulting bill and approved them by voice vote. HR 5 (H Rept 105-95) was cleared by the House committee, while S 717 (S Rept 105-17) was the companion bill in the Senate.

The bills would give states slightly more flexibility to discipline disabled students, although most of the protections in current law would be retained. For example, a disabled student could be removed from the regular classroom for up to forty-five days for misconduct involving illegal drugs, whereas that option under existing law was restricted to guns. The bill also would allow a disabled student's disciplinary record to accompany the student to a new school. States could not cut off educational services to disabled students in extreme cases, as had been proposed in 1996. The Clinton administration and congressional leaders touted the speedy action as a triumph of bipartisanship.

SENATE ACTION

In the Senate Jeffords urged his colleagues not to offer amendments that could undo the compromise. But not all senators agreed. Robert C. Smith, R-N.H., said in a May 13 floor speech that he objected to bringing up HR 5 as a "locked-up agreement" with amendments discouraged.

Jeffords fought to turn back three amendments. The closest call came when thirty-seven Republicans and eleven Democrats voted for an amendment that would gut the bill's delicately balanced provision on how much leeway to give school officials to discipline disabled students. The amendment, offered by Slade Gorton, R-Wash., would leave it up to each state or local school district to set its own discipline rules for disabled children. It was tabled (killed), 51–48.

Gorton and other critics argued that though the bill offered local officials more flexibility to punish disabled children than did existing law, it would still leave a "double standard" for disabled pupils versus other children and could lead to dangerous situations. Jeffords did not want to allow states and school districts to set their own policies. "This would create chaos," he said.

The second amendment, offered by Smith, would require a court, when ordering a school district to pay attorney's fees incurred by parents involved in IDEA disputes, to consider the impact such awards would have on the education of all children in the district. Smith and others argued that school districts spend too much money settling disputes between school districts and parents of disabled children. The Senate voted to table (kill) Smith's amendment, 68–31.

Sen. Judd Gregg, R-N.H., offered, then withdrew, an amendment to add language to the bill to increase federal contributions to IDEA funding over seven years. The bill did not set authorization levels for federal contributions, leaving the issue to appropriators. Gregg and other lawmakers complained that Congress did not live up to the pledge made when the law was created to provide 40 percent of its funding. The $4 billion appropriated in fiscal 1997 paid for less than 9 percent of the program.

The Senate cleared the bill May 14 by a vote of 98–1. The House had passed the bill the previous day by an overwhelming vote of 420–3 after taking it up under expedited procedures that precluded amendments. President Clinton signed HR 5 on June 4, 1997.

MAJOR PROVISIONS

The following are the major provisions of HR 5:
- **Discipline.** The bill allowed schools to discipline disruptive disabled students for behavior not related to their disability in the same manner as they disciplined children without disabilities. Schools could automatically remove a disabled child from the regular classroom for up to forty-five days for bringing a weapon or illegal drugs to school. Prior law allowed a forty-five-day removal from the classroom, but only for bringing a gun to school; otherwise, a school could not suspend, expel, or change the placement of a disabled student for more than ten days without the parents' consent or a court order.

The bill also allowed hearing officers rather than a court to determine whether disabled students could be moved to prevent them from endangering themselves or others. States were permitted to require that a disabled student's disciplinary record accompany the student to a new school. As under previous law, states could not end educational services to disabled students, even in extreme cases.
- **Funding formulas.** The measure retained existing funding formulas—which allocated federal money according to the number of disabled children in a school district—until appropriations reached $4.9 billion. (The fiscal 1997 appropriation was $4 billion.) Funds appropriated beyond $4.9 billion were to be allocated under a new formula based on a combination of school-age population (85 percent) and district poverty rates (15 percent).

Previously, funds had been distributed solely on the basis of the number of disabled children. Critics argued that this encouraged states to "overidentify" children as disabled in order to collect more money.

No state could receive less money under the new formula than it received the year the formula took effect.
- **Local contribution.** The bill required local school districts to contribute at least as much funding to the program as they had the previous year, until appropriations reached $4.1 billion. After that, school districts could use up to 20 percent of the increase in federal funding to supplant local money.
- **Attorneys' fees.** HR 5 no longer required school districts to pay the fees of attorneys who represented the parents of disabled students in meetings that involved the student's individualized education plan, unless the meetings were under a court or administrative order.

Bilingual Education

A 1998 attempt by House conservatives to revamp federally supported bilingual education was first weakened and then dropped.

BACKGROUND

The House took up the issue at a time of growing dissatisfaction over bilingual education. California voters on June 2, 1998, strongly approved Proposition 227, a plan to dismantle that state's thirty-year-old bilingual education program and replace it with a system that favored English-only instruction. Some other states and school districts were beginning to move away from bilingual education, in which students received instruction in both their native language and English.

The goal of bilingual education was to help students who were not proficient in English learn the language while keeping pace with their peers in other subjects. The federal government had helped fund bilingual education programs since 1968. The Supreme Court, ruling in the 1974 case *Lau v. Nichols*, ordered states to provide assistance to students who did not speak English. But critics charged that bilingual instruction had instead held too many students back and prevented them from becoming fluent in English.

As the number of immigrant children in American schools increased, the issue became more heated. By the late 1990s school districts were struggling to educate an estimated 3.2 million students who were not proficient in English. Nearly 73 percent of these were Hispanic; other major groups were Vietnamese, Hmong, Cantonese, and Cambodian. The vast majority of students with limited English attended schools in low-income areas.

Some 1.3 million students were in state and local bilingual programs, according to the Department of Education. California had about half of all students whose first language was not English. Of those, only 30 percent were in bilingual education programs, in large part because of a shortage of qualified instructors. The federal government in fiscal 1998 provided $354 million for bilingual and immigrant education including program development, grants to expand existing programs and grants to support bilingual education.

President Clinton and Education Secretary Richard W. Riley publicly opposed the California initiative and called for a series of changes to improve bilingual instruction. The administration wanted states to move children out of bilingual programs in three years and to double the funding to train teachers in bilingual and other English instruction.

The emerging debate had the potential to pit Republicans in Congress against Hispanics, a growing voting bloc that GOP leaders repeatedly said they wanted to court. Opponents of bilingual education often link such programs to the stubbornly high Hispanic dropout rate. Nearly one-third of Hispanics dropped out of school, a higher rate than any other segment of the U.S. population.

Congress had waded into the issue of language instruction a few other times during the 105th Congress. Lawmakers had proposed making English the official language of the United States. The Senate also passed legislation, sponsored by Sen. Slade Gorton, R-Wash., to turn a host of federal education programs, including bilingual education, into broad block grants. And House Appropriations Committee Chairman Robert L. Livingston, R-La., proposed cutting bilingual education funding to offset spending in a fiscal 1998 supplemental spending bill. None of those plans, however, made their way into law.

HOUSE COMMITTEE ACTION

The Early Childhood, Youth and Families Subcommittee of the House Education and the Workforce Committee on May 21 approved a GOP plan, HR 3892, by a vote of 10–5, that would turn federal bilingual education aid into block grants. HR 3892 would create state block grants and require that programs using federal funds under the bill be designed to move students, in two years, to a classroom where instruction was not tailored to those learning English. None of the funds could be used to teach a child who had been in a bilingual program for three years.

The bill would void consent decrees between the federal government and hundreds of state and school district programs governing bilingual instruction. It would change the name of the Education Department's Office of Bilingual Education and Minority Languages Affairs to the Office of English Language Acquisition. Parents would have to sign permission forms before their children could be placed in English instruction programs, and schools would be required to let parents remove their children from bilingual programs.

Opponents of bilingual education argued that too few children moved out of classes taught in two languages, leaving them unprepared for higher education or the workplace. They said it was to blame in part for the high Hispanic dropout rate. "These children are very much at risk of being left behind . . . and becoming the future have-nots of tomorrow," said Frank Riggs, R-Calif., subcommittee chairman and author of the bill.

Opponents of the measure said it would gut bilingual education programs, arguing that current law already provided states with flexibility to experiment with different approaches. "I am an [English] immersion product. Fifty percent of students who started with me . . . failed by the time they were in ninth or tenth grade," said Matthew G. Martinez, D-Calif.

The Clinton administration did not like the legislation, but it had not issued a formal veto threat. Lawmakers expressed mixed feelings about the issue during the debate. Riggs volunteered that he considered his state's ballot measure "draconian" and pointed out that state Attorney General Dan Lungren, the GOP nominee for governor, opposed it.

During debate, the committee made few changes to the measure. It approved a modified amendment by Carlos Romero-Barcelo, Puerto Rico's Democratic delegate, to soften language that originally said it was "imperative" for every person in the United States to learn English.

Martinez said at the markup that it was unfair to draw a direct connection between bilingual education and the high Hispanic dropout rate. He noted that most students in his state did not receive such bilingual education. Instead, Martinez said, opposition to bilingual education was based in part on "emotion and the unwillingness of most Americans to pay for instruction in two languages."

Many Republicans, however, said that instead of rapidly moving students into regular classes, bilingual education instead trapped too many students for years in separate programs. They pointed to the academic success of many Vietnamese immigrants to make the case that Spanish-speaking students could make rapid gains without bilingual programs.

"We're refusing to give these people an opportunity," said Cass Ballenger, R-N.C., who voted for the bill. He said employers in his region of the country had difficulty hiring Hispanics for good, higher-wage jobs because too few spoke English.

The full Education and the Workforce Committee approved the plan June 4 by a 22–17 vote that broke along party lines.

HOUSE FLOOR ACTION

The contentious debate over the best way to teach students who were not proficient in English continued when HR 3892 reached the House floor. Some Democrats blasted the bill as an anti-immigrant move that would undermine civil rights protections for non-English speakers. "This bill punishes children with limited English skills by imposing rigid time lines that are inconsistent with current research about how children learn a second language," said Nancy Pelosi, D-Calif.

But supporters said the education system had an obligation to teach English to immigrant children. "We are consigning whole generations of young people to failure by passing them through twelve years of public education without giving them a proper understanding of English," Riggs said.

The House adopted, 230–184, an amendment to stipulate that school districts could receive a subgrant under the bill only if they were not in violation of any state law regarding bilingual education. The amendment was aimed in part to prevent California school districts that were not implementing Proposition 227 from receiving money under the bill.

But members rejected, 205–208, a Democratic attempt to alter the amendment to allow school districts to receive subgrants under the bill if they were in compliance with federal law.

The House narrowly passed the bill on Sept. 10 on a 230–184 vote. All but ten Republicans voted for the bill and only fourteen Democrats voted for the measure. After House passage, however, prospects for HR 3892 withered in the face of sharp criticism from the Clinton administration and a lack of support from Senate Republicans, who did not take the bill up. Trying to salvage their plan, House Republicans mounted a late-session effort to have a limited demonstration project authorized as one of the myriad riders to the omnibus appropriations measure (HR 4328—PL 105-277). When that idea was blocked by the White House, conservatives considered requiring a study of the efficacy of existing language-transition programs—but administration officials balked again and the plan went nowhere.

Education Savings Accounts

President Clinton in 1998 vetoed a bill (HR 2646) that would have created tax-preferred savings accounts for elementary and secondary education expenses, including private school tuition. He sent the bill back to Congress saying it would "weaken public education and shortchange our children."

Republicans charged that the White House had caved in to pressure from teachers' unions that opposed the bill, and that the measure would have given a helping hand to middle-class parents who could withdraw the principal and interest tax-free from the special savings accounts for education-related expenses, including private school tuition, tutoring, home computers, and transportation costs. Sen. Paul Coverdell, R-Ga., a leading sponsor of the plan and GOP point man on education, said the expanded education accounts could make "millions of families better positioned to make the best education choices for their children."

Democrats, however, assailed the bill as tilted toward affluent Americans who can afford to set aside thousands of dollars a year.

HOUSE ACTION

The House bill (HR 2646—H Rept 105-332), sponsored by Ways and Means Chairman Bill Archer, R-Texas, was narrowly approved 19–17 by the committee. It proposed to allow parents to invest up to $2,500 a year in special accounts and use the principal and interest tax free for education-related expenses. The accounts would be structured somewhat like Individual Retirement Accounts (IRAs). The Joint Tax Committee estimated that more than fourteen million households would take advantage of the accounts, with benefits going mostly to families earning $50,000 to $75,000 a year.

The measure would cost an estimated $2.6 billion over five years, after which the $2,500 limit would drop to $500 annually. This money would be offset by tightening rules under which employers could deduct the cost of vacation and severance pay.

HR 2646 would have built on a provision in the tax portion of the balanced-budget reconciliation package (HR 2014—PL 105-34) that allows parents to put away money for higher education expenses in so-called education savings accounts similar to Individual Retirement Accounts.

GOP leaders and social conservative organizations, such as the Christian Coalition, said the proposal would help families put a stronger emphasis on education. But Democrats said few parents could afford to set aside such a large amount of money, and warned that many of the benefits would go to wealthy parents who sent their children to private schools.

On the House floor underlying the partisan debate were greatly conflicting estimates of who would benefit from the tax break. Bill supporters, citing estimates by the Joint Committee on Taxation, said 70 percent of the savings would go to families earning $75,000 or less. Individuals with adjusted gross annual incomes of more than $110,000 would not be eligible for the accounts.

But the Treasury Department released an estimate that the wealthiest 20 percent of families would get nearly 70 percent of the benefits. Lower-income residents would receive only a marginal tax benefit—as little as $1 a year—because they did not pay much in taxes anyway, administration officials said.

President Clinton, who threatened to veto a similar provision in the budget-reconciliation bill until Republicans dropped it, appeared to be just as opposed to the latest version. "The senior staff, including myself, would advise him to veto it," said Education Secretary Richard W. Riley, one day before the House voted on the measure.

After rejecting, 199–224, a Democratic substitute by Charles B. Rangel, D-N.Y., that would enable schools to raise more money for construction and other needs with bonds, the House passed the measure, 230–198, on Oct. 23, 1997.

SENATE ACTION

Senate Republicans immediately took up the House bill the following week and hoped to pass it quickly. But Senate Democrats objected on procedural grounds. Because there had been no Senate hearing held on the bill, Democrats would be barred from amending it to the full extent possible. A GOP attempt to invoke cloture, thereby limiting debate on the bill, failed Oct. 31, 1997, on a **key vote of 56–41 (R 54–1; D 2–40)**. Republicans tried again on Nov. 4 to invoke cloture, but still came up short, 56–44. *(1997 key votes, p. 865)*

In 1998 the Senate took up a similar bill (S 1133), which would allow family members, charitable groups, or private donors to contribute up to $2,000 a year per child in special accounts for private school tuition, tutoring, transportation costs, home computers, or other education expenses. Contributions could generally be made until a student turned eighteen. Interest on the accounts would accrue tax-free, and any unused savings could be rolled over into the next year and eventually be used for college expenses.

The accounts would begin to phase out for individuals with annual adjusted gross incomes of $95,000 ($150,000 for couples) and would be eliminated for those at $110,000 a year ($160,000 for couples).

In an attempt to attract Democratic votes, Republicans added provisions during Finance Committee consideration that would make prepaid college tuition plans completely tax deductible and extend a tax deduction for employee education. The bill represented an effort by Republicans to appeal to middle-class voters and to move beyond the party's more narrow emphasis on federally funded vouchers for private school education. But Senate Minority Leader Tom Daschle, D-S.D., contended that the tax breaks in the bill would be of minimal benefit to average families and to children in public school. "This is about $7 worth of help for public schools," Daschle said, saying it was enough for "some Elmer's glue, a couple of pencils."

The debate gave voters, who listed education as one of their top issues, a clear election-year choice: a Republican agenda providing states greater control over federal education spending versus Democratic efforts to increase assistance from Washington. Clinton continued to vow to veto the bill, calling it bad education and bad tax policy.

But Republicans argued that it was Democrats who were the enemies of public schools, defenders of an education bu-reaucracy that had produced falling test scores and rising public dissatisfaction. Coverdell, the chief sponsor of the measure, warned the president to reconsider before he "cast his lot with the status quo and becomes another obstructionist."

As the Senate debated the bill, Clinton, Daschle, and other Democratic opponents said the savings account plan would divert money from public schools. Supporters said it would spur much-needed savings. They argued that unlike previous Republican proposals for private education federal vouchers, the bill would also aid children in public schools.

Early in the debate, lobbyists and lawmakers predicted the measure could pass with more than 60 votes. That changed after April 22 when the Senate, on a largely party-line vote of 50–49, approved an amendment by Slade Gorton, R-Wash., that could turn $10.3 billion in annual elementary and secondary programs, including aid to the disadvantaged and bilingual education, into broad block grants.

The Senate had approved a similar plan the previous year as part of the fiscal 1998 appropriations bill funding the departments of Labor, Health and Human Services, and Education, but dropped it in conference. Programs covered by the amendment included Title I aid to disadvantaged students, bilingual education, Clinton's Goals 2000 education improvement program, technology grants, and aid to drug-free schools. States could continue funding under current rules, create state-wide block grants, or channel aid directly to local school districts.

The Senate also approved 52–47 an amendment by John Ashcroft, R-Mo., to bar the Clinton administration from proceeding with plans for voluntary national exams to assess fourth-graders in reading and eighth-graders in math, unless specifically authorized by Congress.

After the amendments passed, some Democrats who had planned to vote for the bill changed their minds, including Joseph R. Biden Jr. of Delaware. He contended the value of the savings accounts paled when compared with the changes under Gorton's amendment. Though Senate Majority Leader Trent Lott, R-Miss., and Coverdell supported the two contentious amendments, they also made a series of efforts to attract Democratic support.

Finance Committee Chairman William V. Roth Jr., R-Del., sponsored a floor amendment that would add $58 million in tax credits over five years to leverage up to $3 billion in school construction bonds. This caused some Republicans to complain that most of the provisions in the underlying bill were put in at the behest of Democrats.

The Senate also:

• Approved, 74–26, an amendment by Jeff Bingaman, D-N.M., to create a national program to try to reduce the high school dropout rate. The plan included an initial authorization of $150 million for teacher training, curriculum improvement, and other changes.

• Tabled (killed), 56–41, a substitute bill by Edward M. Kennedy, D-Mass., that would replace the savings account provisions with a plan to provide federal student loan forgiveness to teachers who served in schools with a high number of poor students. The amendment was designed to fulfill President Clinton's earlier pledge to hire 100,000 new teachers.

- Tabled (killed), 56–42, a substitute by Carol Moseley-Braun, D-Ill., that would provide tax credits to leverage $22 billion in local bonds for school construction and renovation. This was also a White House priority.
- Approved, 63–35, an amendment by Connie Mack, R-Fla., and Alfonse M. D'Amato, R-N.Y., to provide incentive payments to states that carried out teacher testing and merit pay.
- Defeated, 46–54, an amendment by Daniel R. Coats, R-Ind., that would provide a 110 percent tax deduction for donations to scholarship programs for low-income children. The cost would be offset by eliminating the federal deductibility of gambling losses. The gaming industry lobbied against the plan.
- Passed, 69–29, an amendment by Kay Bailey Hutchison, R-Texas, to allow use of federal funds for same-sex classrooms or schools.

After weeks of bickering, the Senate passed HR 2646 on April 23, 1998, by a vote of 56–43. The vote came after senators substituted language from their own version (S 1133) into the House measure. Five Democrats voted for the measure, including Robert G. Torricelli of New Jersey, a main cosponsor of the bill.

After the vote, Torricelli and the other four Democrats who voted "aye" sent a letter to Lott warning that unless the Gorton and Ashcroft amendments were dropped in conference, "unfortunately our support and bipartisan cooperation . . . cannot be counted on."

CONFERENCE, FINAL ACTION

House and Senate negotiators on June 10 unveiled a compromise on HR 2646. To attract support from Democrats, the conferees dropped the controversial Senate-passed provisions that would bar Clinton from implementing his proposed voluntary national math and reading tests and also would turn more than half the Education Department's elementary and secondary programs into block grants.

The conference report would allow families, charitable groups, or private donors to contribute a combined total of $2,000 a year to the savings accounts. The House bill originally set a ceiling of $2,500. The contributions would be in after-tax dollars. Earnings would accrue tax-free as long as they were spent on approved uses such as elementary or secondary private school tuition, tutoring or home computers. Individuals with annual adjusted gross incomes of up to $110,000 ($160,000 for couples) could contribute.

The bill also would create a program to train teachers in reading instruction methods, including use of phonics. The bill would make state prepaid college tuition plans completely tax-free and, starting in 2006, allow private colleges to offer prepaid tuition plans.

It would expand the current $5,250 tax exclusion for employer-paid tuition assistance from June 1, 2000, through Dec. 31, 2002. Conferees dropped a Senate amendment that would provide $58 million in tax credits over five years to leverage up to $3 billion in school construction bonds.

Clinton did not move from his threat to veto the legislation, however, contending the savings accounts still would give a tax break to the middle class and divert money from public schools. The White House countered by emphasizing its own education agenda that focused on renovating public schools and reducing class size.

The House passed the conference report on HR 2646 (H Rept 105-577) on June 18, well short of the two-thirds vote needed to override the promised presidential veto. Twelve Democrats voted for the measure, while ten Republicans voted against it. Before final passage, the House defeated, 196–225, a motion by Rangel to send the bill back to a House-Senate conference committee and replace it with a Democratic proposal to create tax-free bonds for public school construction and renovation.

The Senate cleared the measure by a **key vote of 59–36 (R 51–2; D 8–34)** on June 24. Eight Democrats supported the bill while two Republicans voted nay. As with the House vote, senators in support of the bill fell short of the number needed to override a White House veto. *(1998 key votes, p. 883)*

As expected, Clinton vetoed it July 21. In his veto message Clinton said the measure would have weakened public education. The way to improve education, he said, was to "increase standards, accountability and choice within the public schools." House Republican leaders protested the veto, but they did not attempt to override it. *(2000 action, p. 544)*

Budget Reconciliation

A $35 billion package of tax breaks for higher education was enacted as part of budget-reconciliation legislation signed by President Clinton on Aug. 5, 1997 (HR 2014—PL 105-34). The spending portion of the reconciliation package (HR 2015—PL 105-33) also contained a small number of education provisions, reducing spending by $1.76 billion over five years. *(Reconciliation bill, p. 90)*

The education tax incentives, including credits and penalty-free withdrawals from individual retirement accounts (IRAs), were a high priority for Clinton, who made them a condition for agreeing to the twin bills that made up the massive reconciliation legislation.

Republican leaders had agreed in May to include "roughly" $35 billion over five years in tax breaks to help middle-income families pay postsecondary education costs. But the nature and exact amount of the cuts remained a hot topic through the summer as the White House and Congress negotiated the terms of the tax- and spending-cut bills that made up the reconciliation package.

In the end, although Republicans shaped some of the details, Clinton met his goal with a five-year set of education tax breaks that totaled $35 billion. The House and Senate versions of the bill had called for $31 billion and $33 billion, respectively. The final bill also leaned heavily toward tax credits, favored by Clinton, rather than IRAs, which Democrats said would be used mainly by better-off taxpayers.

BACKGROUND

In his Feb. 4 State of the Union address, Clinton outlined a series of tax breaks as part of a broader plan to boost higher education. On June 30, as the tax-reconciliation bill moved to the conference stage, he released a revised tax cut plan that added a so-called Kidsave IRA.

Clinton aimed his education cuts almost entirely at middle- and lower-income taxpayers while focusing on credits and deductions to offset the cost of tuition. The president's main proposals were:

- **HOPE credit.** A "HOPE Scholarship" tax credit of $1,500 per student for two years, with the second year contingent on the student earning a B average. Clinton wanted the credit limited to families with gross adjusted incomes of up to $80,000 a year and phased out for those earning more than $100,000.
- **Deductions.** A tax deduction of up to $5,000, rising eventually to $10,000, to offset the cost of postsecondary education and training. The deduction, which was not tied to an IRA, was to be available for families with adjusted gross incomes of less than $80,000, phasing out for those earning up to $100,000.
- **IRAs.** Penalty-free IRA withdrawals for postsecondary education for families with adjusted gross incomes of up to $100,000.
- **Kidsave.** Families receiving the new $500-per-child tax credit being created under the bill could put the funds into a so-called Kidsave account, along with $500 of their own money. The interest and principal could be withdrawn tax-free if the money was used for the child's education, the purchase of the child's first house, or the taxpayer's retirement.

Clinton wanted to make the child credit partially refundable, meaning that families too poor to owe taxes could receive some or all of the money as a check.

In contrast to Clinton's emphasis on credits and deductions, Republicans proposed devoting nearly one-third of the education tax cuts to IRAs. Democrats argued that lower-income taxpayers typically did not have enough money to save in an IRA. The House and Senate passed somewhat different versions of the GOP education tax plan.

HOUSE ACTION

The House version of the tax bill, written in the Ways and Means Committee, included $31 billion in education tax breaks. The panel approved the overall proposal June 13 on a straight party-line vote of 22–16. The full House passed the tax bill (HR 2014—H Rept 105-148) June 26 by a 253–179 vote.

The House bill included the nonrefundable HOPE credit of up to $1,500 per student for tuition and books in each of the first two years of college. The income thresholds were the same as in Clinton's plan.

As an alternative, under the House plan, parents could deduct up to $10,000 per year for each student from a new education investment account, similar to an IRA, or from a qualified prepaid tuition program, as long as the money was used to pay for undergraduate education. Eligible expenses would include tuition, room and board.

Under the House bill, parents could put up to $5,000 a year per student into such an investment account, with a lifetime limit of $50,000 for each student. In addition, money could be withdrawn from a traditional IRA without penalty if it was used for higher education expenses, including tuition, books, room and board.

The House bill also included a small, nonrefundable credit of up to $150 for extra costs, such as tutoring, for elementary and secondary school children.

SENATE ACTION

The Senate tax-reconciliation provisions—drawn up by the Finance Committee and modified on the Senate floor—called for $33 billion in education incentives over five years. The Finance Committee approved the bill (S 949—S Rept 105-33) by a bipartisan vote of 18–2 on June 19. The full Senate passed HR 2014, 80–18, on June 27 after substituting the text of S 949.

The Senate plan contained incentives similar to those in the House bill, including an almost identical HOPE credit. The Senate measure also offered a tax break for money withdrawn from a special education savings account or a prepaid tuition program for education expenses. But instead of allowing a $10,000 per year deduction, the Senate opted to make the withdrawals tax free. The money could be used for undergraduate or graduate student expenses, including tuition, books, room, and board.

Under the Senate bill, taxpayers could contribute up to $2,000 per year for each student, plus money from the child tax credit, into the new education IRA. (The Senate bill would have required taxpayers receiving the separate child credit to put a like amount into an education IRA.)

During floor action, the Senate agreed to a controversial amendment by Paul Coverdell, R-Ga., that would have allowed tax-free withdrawals from an education IRA to pay tuition for elementary and secondary students at parochial and private schools. The amendment was adopted June 27 by a vote of 58–42.

FINAL ACTION

On July 19, as Republicans met among themselves to work out a joint House-Senate proposal on the overall tax bill to take to the White House, Clinton sent a letter to Senate Majority Leader Trent Lott, R-Miss., laying out his tax priorities. High among them, he wanted most of the GOP education proposals replaced with his own, which were targeted more at middle- and lower-income families.

Also, at the last minute, the administration threatened to veto the entire bill over Coverdell's amendment. GOP leaders said they were not willing to abandon it unless Clinton put the veto threat in writing—which he did in a brief letter saying he "would veto any tax package that would undermine public education by providing tax benefits for private and parochial school expenses."

Republican negotiators, intent on avoiding a showdown with the White House, abandoned the provision—at the same time lambasting the president. House Speaker Newt Gingrich, R-Ga., said Clinton once again had "chosen to place the interests of the powerful teachers' union bosses over those of America's schoolchildren."

The conference report on the budget-reconciliation bill (HR 2014) with its package of tax breaks for higher education passed the House by a vote of 389–43 on July 31. The Senate passed the measure, 92–8, the same day. President Clinton signed it into law on Aug. 5, 1997.

MAJOR PROVISIONS

In HR 2014 the $35 billion package of tax breaks for higher education included the following:

Child Credit

Families with children under age seventeen could take a $400-per-child tax credit starting in 1998, rising to $500 per child in 1999. Grandparents could claim the credit if they claimed the child as a dependent on their tax form.

The tax credit began to phase out for single taxpayers with adjusted gross annual incomes of more than $75,000 and for couples with incomes of more than $110,000. The maximum child credit available to the taxpayer ($500 times the number of qualifying children) was reduced by $50 for each $1,000 that the taxpayer's adjusted gross income exceeded the threshold amounts. The more children a family had, the higher the income level at which the tax credit phased out entirely. For instance, a couple with an income of $150,000 and five qualifying children would still be eligible for a $500 credit.

Low-income families that were eligible for the earned-income tax credit (generally those with incomes of $30,000 a year or less) could take the child credit before they figured their earned-income credit. If the child credit exceeded a tax-payer's regular tax liability, the taxpayer was required to calculate whether the tax liability plus the employee share of federal payroll taxes exceeded the earned-income credit. If so, the new law provided that the amount by which the child credit exceeded the amount calculated above was refundable to the taxpayer. This applied only to taxpayers with three or more children.

Effective date: Jan. 1, 1998. Estimated cost: $85 billion over five years; $183.4 billion over ten years.

Education Incentives

• **HOPE college tax credit.** Taxpayers could receive a nonrefundable credit of up to $1,500 per student for each of the first two years of college. The credit could be applied to 100 percent of the first $1,000 of tuition and fees, and 50 percent of the next $1,000 in costs. The credit could not be claimed against the purchase of books or the cost of student

activities. The credit would be indexed for inflation starting in 2002.

A single taxpayer would be eligible for the full credit if his or her adjusted gross annual income was less than $40,000; the ceiling for joint filers was $80,000. The first taxable year in which the income limits would be adjusted for inflation was 2001.

• **Lifetime learning credit.** For the second two years of college, or for graduate and postgraduate education and thereafter, a lifetime tax credit was available equal to 20 percent of up to $5,000 in tuition and related school expenses; after 2002, the credit would be equal to 20 percent of up to $10,000. Taxpayers would be eligible for the full credit if their adjusted gross annual incomes were less than $40,000 for single filers and $80,000 for joint filers. The first taxable year in which the income limits could be increased to reflect inflation was 2001.

Effective date for both the HOPE credit and the lifetime learning credit: Dec. 31, 1997. Estimated cost of both: $31.6 billion over five years and $76 billion over ten years.

• **Education savings accounts.** Modeled on individual retirement accounts (IRAs), these accounts allowed taxpayers to make nondeductible contributions of up to $500 per year for each child under age eighteen. The principal and interest could be withdrawn tax-free at any time to help pay for a child's college or graduate education. Virtually all taxpayers—except those with incomes in the top 3 percent or so—were eligible to make use of the accounts. The adjusted gross annual income limit for single filers was $95,000; for joint filers, $150,000.

Any balance remaining in an education account at the time a beneficiary reached thirty years old had to be distributed, and the earnings portion of such a distribution would be subject to tax and to an additional 10 percent penalty.

Effective date: Dec. 31, 1997. Estimated cost: $3.9 billion over five years and $14.2 billion over ten years.

Each year, for each student, the taxpayer could choose either the HOPE credit, the lifetime learning credit, or a tax-free distribution from an education savings account.

• **Penalty-free IRA withdrawals.** Penalty-free withdrawals could be made from all IRAs for undergraduate, postsecondary vocational, and graduate education expenses.

Effective date: Dec. 31, 1997. Estimated cost: $812 million over five years and $1.7 billion over ten years.

• **Student loan interest deduction.** A deduction of up to $1,000 was permitted for interest payments on student loans starting in 1998, rising to $2,500 in 2001. The deduction was available to individual taxpayers with adjusted gross annual incomes of up to $40,000 and couples with incomes of up to $60,000. Income ranges would increase for inflation after 2002. (This provision largely reversed a provision of the 1986 tax act, which disallowed the deduction of personal interest, including student loan interest.)

Effective date: Dec. 31, 1997. Estimated cost: $690 million over five years and $2.4 billion over ten years.

• **Deduction for state-sponsored tuition programs.** Deductions for state-sponsored prepaid tuition programs and other state savings programs were expanded to include the costs of room and board in addition to tuition.

Effective date: Dec. 31, 1997. Estimated cost: $533 million over five years and $1.5 billion over ten years.

• **Exemption for employer-provided educational assistance.** The law extended through May 31, 2000, the exemption from taxation of employer-provided educational assistance for undergraduates. The exclusion had previously applied to graduate as well as undergraduate education, but the 1996 small business tax bill (PL 104-188) limited the exemption to undergraduate courses beginning after June 30, 1996.

Estimated cost: $1.2 billion over five years.

• **Tax credit for qualified zone academy bonds.** The bill made it easier for public schools in impoverished neighborhoods to form partnerships with corporations to provide job training. The school districts could borrow money and pay only 50 percent of the present value of the loan—half the total interest payments due over the term of the loan, plus the principal. The government would pay the lender, such as a bank or insurance company, the other 50 percent.

Corporations would have to make an investment in the school worth at least 10 percent of the value of the bond. All investments had to be in schools in designated "enterprise zones," or in areas where at least 35 percent of the students qualified for the school lunch program. Up to $400 million of "qualified zone academy bonds" could be issued in 1998 and $400 million in 1999. The bonds could be issued by a state or a local unit of government.

Effective date: Dec. 31, 1997. Estimated cost: $172 million over five years and $408 million over ten years.

• **Deduction for corporate contributions of computer technology.** Companies became eligible for an income tax deduction when they contributed new or unused computers, computer printers and computer technology such as software to educational organizations with students in kindergarten through twelfth grade. The provision was effective from Jan. 1, 1998, until Jan. 1, 2001.

Estimated cost: $225 million over five years.

• **Repeal of limit on bonds issued by nonprofits.** Nonprofit entities—those organized under section 501(c)(3) of the tax code—were allowed to issue an unlimited amount of tax-exempt bonds. Interest paid on the bonds was not subject to federal tax.

The provision reversed a policy in place since the 1986 tax act, which placed a $150 million cap on the amount of tax-exempt debt that each nonprofit entity could issue. However, any bonds above the prior cap could only be issued for new projects, not to help finance existing projects. The provision was expected to be used primarily by universities and nursing homes.

Effective date: Aug. 5, 1997. Estimated cost: $315 million over five years and $962 million over ten years.

• **Cancellation of certain student loans.** Under existing law, the forgiveness of indebtedness with respect to student loans did not count as gross income when the student agreed to work in certain professions. The new law expanded the exemption to include student loans that were forgiven by tax-exempt charitable organizations and foundations.

Estimated cost: Negligible.

• **Bonds for public school construction.** Government units (such as a school district) that were classified as "small issuers" of tax-exempt bonds because their issues were worth $5 million or less could issue an additional $5 million in bonds to finance public school capital expenditures. These bonds were not subject to the rebate-on-earnings requirement that governed larger issues. That meant the issuer could sell the bonds months before the building project got under way and invest the bond proceeds until needed without having to rebate the earnings to the federal government. Larger issuers had to rebate the earnings.

Effective date: Dec. 31, 1997. Estimated cost: $36 million over five years and $199 million over ten years.

Spending Cuts

The budget-reconciliation package also included $1.76 billion of education spending cuts over five years. Mostly, it reduced funding for administrative functions and required student loan agencies to transfer much of their reserve funds to the federal treasury. The bill authorized the following items.

• **Return of reserve funds.** Required agencies that guaranteed student loans to return $1 billion in reserve funds to the federal Treasury by Sept. 1, 2002. GOP aides said this represented about half the agencies' reserves. Most agencies were required to return the money in five equal annual installments. The measure also reduced mandatory administrative accounts for both the direct student loan and guaranteed student loan programs.

• **Repeal of institution payments.** Eliminated the $10 payment per loan that the federal government gave to institutions that made direct student loans.

• **Extension of student aid programs.** Extended student loan programs through 2006, including guaranteed student loans and loan consolidation programs.

• **Repeal of vocational education act.** Repealed a 1917 law known as the Smith-Hughes Vocational Education Act, which authorized grants to states to provide vocational education. That mandate had been usurped in 1963 by the Perkins Vocational Act. Funding for the Smith-Hughes Act was redirected to the Perkins program, long the main grant provider to states.

National Testing

Republicans in both 1997 and 1998 blocked President Clinton's plans to promote voluntary national testing of fourth-graders in reading and eighth-graders in math. In both cases, the battle was fought primarily on appropriations bills.

1997 LEGISLATIVE ACTION

Clinton proposed annual voluntary national reading and math tests in his Feb. 4 State of the Union address as part of his "national crusade" for education. "Good tests will show us who needs help, what changes in teaching to make, and which schools need to improve," he said.

But the proposal sparked criticism from the right, which warned that such comprehensive national tests could lead to the imposition of a federal curriculum. Those on the left feared that students in inner-city schools would be the most likely to test badly. Ideology aside, lawmakers expressed growing dissatisfaction with the administration having almost unfettered control over developing the tests.

Even proponents of national testing raised concerns about Clinton's handling of the issue. The administration initially drew flak for insisting that it could develop the tests without congressional approval and for giving the project to the Education Department instead of an independent entity.

Among the critics of the initial plan were several prominent proponents of national testing who otherwise might have helped build public support for it. They included Chester E. Finn Jr., assistant education secretary under President Ronald Reagan, and Diane Ravitch, assistant education secretary under George Bush. Ravitch, a senior fellow at the Brookings Institution, called the administration's action "clumsy and ham-handed and political." Finn, a senior fellow at the Hudson Institute, described it as "arrogant and stupid."

Education Secretary Richard W. Riley responded by drawing up legislation that would give an existing bipartisan organization, the National Assessment Governing Board, the authority to develop the tests. "I am convinced that a strong and early focus on reading will go a long way to reducing special education and remedial costs, reducing truancy, and keeping more young people from dropping out of school," Riley told a House subcommittee April 29.

The tests, which the Education Department said would cost about $32 million to develop, would first be available in the spring of 1999. They would consist of an annual reading test in the fourth grade and a math test in the eighth grade.

They would be based on two national tests—the National Assessment of Educational Progress and the Third International Mathematics and Science Study. In those tests, however, only a random sample of students is tested, and no student is tested on all items. The new tests would allow evaluation of individual students, as well as school districts and states.

Rep. Bill Goodling, R-Pa., was skeptical of the idea. As chairman of the Education and the Workforce Committee, he had focused much of his attention on limiting the federal role in education. "We already have plenty of testing," Goodling said in announcing his opposition to the administration's plans. "Why have another measurement instrument to tell us what we already know?" he asked, saying he would rather send the money directly to classrooms.

By the time Riley sent his proposed legislation to Congress on Sept. 3, momentum seemed to have stalled. Only seven states and about fifteen large city school districts said they would administer them.

The issue provoked sharp debate in September, when the House blocked federal funds from being used to develop the tests by adding a provision to the fiscal 1998 spending bill (HR 2264) for the departments of Labor, Health and Human Services (HHS), and Education. The amendment, by Goodling, passed by a 295–125 vote. It was supported not only by virtually every Republican, but also by most members of the black and Hispanic caucuses. Many of them complained that the tests would stigmatize students in low-income neighborhoods.

The House language provoked a strong reaction from Clinton, who said: "The House vote is unacceptable, and it will not stand."

The Senate in contrast approved a compromise, worked out with the administration, to permit the tests to be developed under the aegis of the National Assessment Governing Board, an independent entity. The compromise also would prohibit any trial runs of the tests during the fiscal year that ends Sept. 30, 1998. The agreement directed the National Academy of Sciences to study the tests while they were being developed. The academy also would examine whether existing commercially available tests and state tests could be correlated and used as a substitute for a new national test.

The deal set the stage for further congressional consideration of the issue in 1998. It also essentially postponed White House plans to fully administer the tests in the spring of 1999.

1998 LEGISLATIVE ACTION

The House weighed in on the issue of national testing early in the session. The Education and Workforce Committee approved a bill (HR 2846—H Rept 105-409) by a vote of 23–16 to bar the administration from developing or implementing national math and reading tests until specifically authorized by Congress. The House passed the measure on Feb. 5 by a vote of 242–174.

Clinton angered Republicans by saying in his State of the Union address Jan. 27 that states would soon have the option of using nationalized tests. The lawmakers also pointed to Education Department data suggesting trial tests would begin in the fall.

Goodling said HR 2846 was necessary because the Clinton administration, by planning field testing when the fiscal year ended Sept. 30, was not living up to the spirit of the 1997 agreement. "Once again Congress has spoken on federal testing and said there should be no new federal tests unless authorized," he said.

The Senate never took up the measure. However, lawmakers added a policy rider to the fiscal 1999 omnibus appropriations bill (HR 4328—PL 105-277) stopping the tests for another year. The provision barred use of federal funds for pilot testing, field testing or distribution of national tests, unless Congress enacted an authorization beforehand.

The National Assessment Governing Board (NAGB) and the National Academy of Sciences (NAS) also were ordered to report to Congress on certain testing issues.

By Sept. 30, 1999, the NAGB had to describe the purpose and intended uses of any federally sponsored national tests, define "voluntary" as it applied to administration of any test, and describe achievement levels and reporting methods to be used in grading any national test.

The NAGB also had to react to an NAS report that suggested there were flaws in the achievement levels for the current National Assessment of Educational Progress tests, on which the proposed national tests were to be based. By Sept. 30, the NAS also was required to report on the technical feasibility and reliability of including test items from those or other existing tests in state and district assessments for the purpose of providing a common measuring stick.

The House adopted the conference report on HR 4328 (H Rept 105-825) by a vote of 333–95 on Oct. 20. The Senate cleared the bill, 65–29, on Oct. 21, and Clinton signed it the same day.

Charter Schools

In a bipartisan move to encourage innovation in public schools, President Clinton in 1998 signed legislation (HR 2616—PL 105-278) to expand federal aid to so-called charter schools, authorizing up to $100 million for fiscal year 1999, with unspecified sums allowed through 2003.

Charter schools were publicly funded but operated free from many state regulations if school officials met certain performance criteria. Both Clinton and congressional Republicans supported the experimental schools, viewing them as a way to test innovative teaching and organizational plans and to offer families a broader choice within the context of public education.

But charter schools had been criticized by some educators who warned they were not a panacea for the problems besetting education and were sometimes poorly run. Parents, community activists, teachers, or private companies could set up schools under a special charter, depending on state law. Clinton set a goal of 3,000 operating charter schools by 2002, up from 1,000 in 1998.

HOUSE ACTION

By a vote of 24–8, the House Committee on Education and the Workforce approved legislation on Oct. 9, 1997, to boost federal funding for charter schools. The House, 367–57, passed the measure Nov. 7. The legislation (HR 2616—H Rept 105-321) would authorize $100 million in fiscal 1998. Appropriators provided $80 million, up from the $51 million in fiscal 1997.

The measure would channel money for charter schools above $51 million to states that met the following conditions: they gave charter schools a high degree of autonomy over their budgets; they increased the number of charter schools; and they conducted reviews to determine whether charter schools were meeting or exceeding academic requirements and goals.

The House defeated, 164–260, an amendment by John F. Tierney, D-Mass., that would delete the provisions to send funding above $51 million to states that meet the conditions.

An amendment approved by voice vote would require local school districts that apply for charter schools to outline how they would comply with the Individuals with Disabilities Education Act (IDEA), which guaranteed a free, appropriate education to all students with disabilities.

SENATE ACTION

The Senate Labor and Human Resources Committee took up S 1380, its version of similar legislation. Sponsored by Sen. Daniel R. Coats, R-Ind., S 1380 would direct the secretary of education to ensure that charter schools were treated equitably under federal public education programs including Title I, which provided aid to disadvantaged students, and the Individuals with Disabilities Education Act. It would let schools receive startup funding under current federal Title VI education grants.

The bill would give funding priority to states that met certain criteria, including holding schools accountable for meeting education standards, requiring schools to participate in testing programs and evaluating charter schools every five years. "By challenging the status quo, these innovative new programs are helping to reinvent public schools as we know them," Coats said in a statement.

The Senate Labor and Human Resources Committee by voice vote July 29, 1998, approved S 1380 (S Rept 105-301). The full Senate then set aside that bill, passing a slightly amended version of HR 2616 on Oct. 8 by unanimous consent. In its final version, the bill authorized unspecified sums for fiscal years 2000 through 2003.

Once appropriations exceeded $51 million, the bill would target a larger share of funding to states that gave charter schools a high degree of autonomy, increase the number of charter schools and conduct reviews to determine whether charter schools are meeting academic requirements and goals.

For fiscal 2002 and 2003, the Education Department would distribute all appropriations, not just funds in excess of $51 million, to states meeting those criteria.

The measure required the department to reserve the greater of 5 percent or $5 million of the total funds appropriated, up to a maximum of $8 million, to inform charter schools of federal funds available to them and federal programs in which they may participate; to ensure completion of a four-year study of charter schools that began in 1995; and to underwrite other evaluations of the impact of charter schools, including an analysis of student attendance at charter schools reported on the basis of race, age, disability, gender, limited English proficiency, and previous enrollment in public school.

FINAL ACTION

On Oct. 10 the House agreed to the Senate amendments under suspension of the rules, clearing the bill, 369–50. President Clinton singed the measure into law on Oct. 22, 1998.

Student Loans

Legislation aimed at making it easier for students to consolidate their loans was enacted as part of the fiscal 1998 appropriations bill (HR 2264—PL 105-78) for the departments of Labor, Health and Human Services (HHS) and Education. The proposal had advanced in separate bills in both chambers in 1997 before being rolled into the spending measure in conference.

Many students received loans from several sources and later combined them to obtain more favorable financing terms or simplify their payments. Previously, however, students with direct loans from the government were not permitted to consolidate their loans through private lenders under the guaranteed student loan program. The bill allowed them to do so, and to retain the favorable interest rate subsidy they got through the direct loan program.

The measure was a response to the Department of Education's difficulty in consolidating direct loans. The department's contractor had announced that it had a backlog of more than 80,000 borrowers trying to refinance multiple student loans into a single direct loan from the federal government. The department blamed computer programs and said the backlog would be eliminated by Dec. 1, 1997. However, Republicans remained skeptical.

BACKGROUND

Under the traditional student loan program, created in 1965, the federal government guaranteed student loans issued by private banks or other financial institutions. If a student defaulted, the loan was paid off by a state guarantee agency, which was eventually reimbursed by the federal government.

Under the direct loan program, created in 1993 as part of that year's budget-reconciliation law (PL 103-66), students could apply for loans directly to the government through their schools, bypassing the banks altogether. Students dealt with one entity for the life of their loan and had several repayment options, including one that tied payments to their income. *(1993 action, Congress and the Nation Vol. IX, p. 625)*

Borrowers who had taken out both guaranteed and direct student loans could combine their debts only by going to the government and obtaining a direct consolidated student loan. They could not combine both types of loans into a new guaranteed loan from a private lender.

Supporters argued that the direct loan program would lower interest rates for students and save the government money by cutting federal subsidies to banks. The direct student loan rate generally was capped at 8.25 percent.

Republicans doubted from the outset whether the government could handle student loans more efficiently than the guaranteed student loan market, and they seized on the Education Department's problems with consolidating loans as proof of the program's overall shortcomings.

LEGISLATIVE ACTION

The consolidation plan began in the House as a separate bill (HR 2535), introduced Sept. 24, 1997, by California Republican Howard P. "Buck" McKeon. Moving with uncommon speed, the House Education and the Workforce Committee approved the measure Oct. 1 by an unanimous vote of 43–0 (H Rept 105-322).

William L. Clay, the committee's ranking Democrat, objected to plans to pay the $25 million cost of the legislation out of the Education Department's administrative budget. He also said it was unclear whether private lenders would refinance any of the direct loans.

Robert D. Andrews, D-N.J., defended the direct loan program, noting that it had provided aid to 2.1 million students in the 1996–1997 academic year and was expected to benefit 2.8 million students in 1997–1998.

McKeon said the legislation was not a prelude to a GOP attempt to abolish the direct loan program. "I don't like it," he said. "But I'm a realist. There's no way to kill direct loans. The president would veto it if we had the votes."

McKeon and Dale E. Kildee of Michigan, the subcommittee's ranking Democrat, both said after the markup that under a truce reached earlier in the year, they had agreed that they would not try to eliminate either the direct loan or the guaranteed loan program.

The committee approved by voice vote an amendment by McKeon to clarify that the measure would cover all applications received after it was enacted. The panel also gave voice vote approval to an amendment by Clay and Kildee to ensure that those who received the new HOPE Scholarship would not have their Pell grants or other student financial aid reduced as a consequence.

The House passed the bill by voice vote Oct. 21 despite administration objections. The White House released a statement the day of the vote saying it opposed the legislation because it would not help those who could not get or did not want a guaranteed student loan and the $25 million to help pay for the legislation would come out of the Education Department's administrative budget for student loans. However, Clinton did not raise the veto threat.

The Senate Labor and Human Resources Committee gave voice vote approval to a companion bill Oct. 22 (S 1294—S Rept 105-122). But the panel's ranking Democrat, Edward M. Kennedy of Massachusetts, signaled that he would try to change the bill. "It makes no sense to solve the consolidation problem by weakening the department's ability" to process loans, he said.

The student loan consolidation plan was never sent to the White House as a separate bill. It became one of many provisions added to the fiscal 1998 Labor, Health and Human Services (HHS) and Education appropriations bill during conference deliberations. The House passed the conference report, 352–65, on Nov. 7. The Senate passed in 91–4 on Nov. 8. President Clinton signed the bill (HR 2264—PL 105-78) into law Nov. 13.

Block Grants

Saying that local school officials needed to be liberated from rigid federal rules, House Republicans in 1998 won passage of a controversial measure that would consolidate thirty-one federal education programs into broad grants to states and localities. But the bill (HR 3248) died at the end of the session in the face of opposition from most Democrats and a veto threat from President Clinton.

The U.S. Chamber of Commerce and Family Research Council, a conservative family values group, were among the organizations supporting the legislation, sponsored by Joseph R. Pitts, R-Pa. It was opposed by a host of education organizations, which charged that the bill would gut federal education aid, including some of Clinton's top priorities such as the Goals 2000 program to help schools improve academic standards. (Goals 2000, Congress and the Nation Vol. IX, p. 620)

HOUSE ACTION

The debate in the House was part of a long-running, partisan sparring in Congress over the proper approach on education. Republicans generally favored loosening federal restrictions and giving local schools more control. Democrats, led by Clinton, called for greater federal involvement.

HR 3248 would roll thirty-one federal education programs into a $2.74 billion annual grant to states. Programs that would be eliminated included Clinton's Goals 2000, grants for teacher training and professional development, school-to-work aid, math and science funding, and assistance for instruction of gifted and talented children as well as homeless students.

The block grant money would be distributed through a formula that would allocate half the funds based on a state's population of five- to seven-year-olds and half based on its overall level of low-income students. Governors, legislatures, and local school districts would then decide how to divide the money, with the proviso that 95 percent of overall funding would have to flow to the classroom. Local districts could continue to use the money for activities previously funded under the categorical programs, and no state would get less money than it currently receives.

Republicans said only 65 percent of federal funds under the existing system reached the classroom. They said eliminating bureaucracy would free hundreds of millions of dollars for classroom use. Democrats cited competing studies showing about 90 percent of federal education dollars reached

classrooms and said there would be little accountability in the block grants.

The House Education and the Workforce Committee on June 24 narrowly approved HR 3248 (H Rept 106-710), 19–18, despite a letter that Secretary of Education Richard W. Riley sent to the committee warning of a presidential veto. "The issue here is not about who controls public education; we all agree that the responsibility rests at the local and state levels," Riley wrote. "At stake, rather, is whether the federal government will maintain its long-standing, bipartisan commitment to helping local communities strengthen accountability."

Proponents, such as committee chairman Bill Goodling, R-Pa., said the plan would increase the amount of funding that states would receive, with each state getting an additional $1.6 million to $89 million, based on the formula. An amendment, offered by Michael N. Castle, R-Del., and adopted by voice vote, would authorize funding to stabilize the plan for the next five years, with adjustments for inflation. Fiscal 2003 spending would be set at $3 billion.

Republicans said their aim was to return control to local communities who can respond better to specific needs in their areas. Goodling argued that current programs were not working and represented less than one-fifth of the federal spending on elementary and secondary education. Democrats maintained that the legislation would greatly diminish oversight of the federal contribution to the country's educational programs.

The House passed the bill, 212–198, on Sept. 18. It rejected a Democratic substitute, 190–215, that would reduce average class size to eighteen in first through third grades and called for hiring 100,000 more teachers by 2005. The bill did not advance beyond the House as the Senate never considered the plan.

Ed-Flex

The Senate Labor and Human Resources Committee approved legislation in 1998 to allow local school districts in all fifty states and the District of Columbia to waive federal education regulations they found burdensome. But lawmakers took no further action on the measure.

The bill (S 2213—S Rept 105-327), which the committee approved July 30 by a 17–1 vote, would expand a twelve-state pilot program known as "ed-flex" to all school districts, enabling them to waive federal requirements that they believed impeded their ability to improve schools. Sponsor Bill Frist, R-Tenn., said states could allocate federal funds more efficiently when they were "free from the unnecessary burden of Washington regulation."

Under existing law, states needed permission from the secretary of education to waive regulations if, for example, they wanted to use money earmarked for classroom renovations. Under the ed-flex program, states could waive the regulations themselves, as long as their students continued to meet a number of performance standards. Rules that involved health, safety, or civil rights could not be waived.

Frist said the Clinton administration and the National Governors Association supported the measure. But some committee Democrats expressed concern about expanding the program without first getting results from the pilot project. To that end, Jack Reed, D-R.I., offered an amendment to delay the expansion until the education secretary was able to complete a comprehensive report on the outcome of the pilot program. It was rejected on a 7–10, party-line vote.

Democrats also attempted to capitalize on the bill's broad support by offering several unrelated education amendments. Christopher J. Dodd, D-Conn., offered two: an amendment that would authorize $1 billion for after-school child care projects, defeated 8–10 along party lines; and another that would authorize $240 million over three years for a truancy prevention program, defeated on 9–9 vote.

Frist opposed the Democratic amendments, saying their generous funding allocations would doom the bill's chances on the floor. Paul Wellstone, D-Minn., cast the sole vote against the bill. *(1999 action, p. 539)*

Education Vouchers

Republican lawmakers during the 105th Congress failed in two attempts to pass legislation dealing with education vouchers. School vouchers were funded by the federal government to assist families in sending their children to private schools, particularly at the elementary and secondary level. In 1997 GOP legislation to use federal Title VI money to provide private school vouchers failed in the House. In 1998 a GOP bill to provide education vouchers to help poor children in Washington, D.C., attend private schools was stopped by the president's veto.

Republicans had made private school vouchers a major plank of their education platform, arguing that too many low-income children were trapped in substandard schools. GOP leaders from House Speaker Newt Gingrich, Ga., on down, attempted to use the issue to reach out to minority voters. They pointed to polls showing rising support for vouchers among African American voters.

PRIVATE SCHOOL VOUCHERS

In 1997 the House rejected a GOP proposal to provide private school vouchers—known as HELP (Helping Empower Low-Income Parents) scholarships—to low-income families that wanted to send their children to private school.

HR 2746 would allow states to use money from Title VI of the Elementary and Secondary Education Act to provide scholarships to low-income families to send their children to private schools, including religious schools. The bill would allow states to reserve up to 25 percent of their Title VI funds for public and private school choice programs authorized by state law. States and local school districts received $310 million in Title VI money in fiscal 1997.

The bill was sponsored by Frank Riggs, R-Calif, chairman of the House Education and Workforce Committee, and had the strong backing of Speaker Gingrich and other GOP leaders. Riggs and the bill supporters, however, bypassed committee action on the bill, apparently out of concern that they lacked the votes for approval in the Education and Workforce Committee.

On the House floor Democrats were united in their opposition to the legislation. They portrayed the bill as a GOP attempt at shifting badly needed federal funds away from public schools. Matthew G. Martinez of California, ranking Democrat on the Early Childhood subcommittee, described it as "the extreme right's modern version of white flight from our cities. Just like we abandoned the poor parts of our cities . . . this bill will leave our public schools in ruin in search of a panacea for just a few."

The GOP rebuttal was just as fervid. "The only people in America without choice are the poorest children in the poorest neighborhoods who are trapped by the bureaucracies and the unions and exploited against their will," said Gingrich. Riggs, Gingrich, Majority Leader Dick Armey, R-Texas, and other Republicans argued that it was vital to assist low-income school children to find alternatives to poorly performing public schools.

HR 2746 clearly revealed the sharp division between the two parties over school vouchers. With teacher unions and organized labor—major backers of Democratic candidates—working aggressively against the legislation, the Democrats, however, were able to keep all of their troops in line. In the four roll-call votes on the bill on Nov. 4, the Democratic opposition was nearly 100 percent. In the major vote on the bill the House rejected HR 2746 by a **key vote of 191–228 (R 187–35; D 4–192; I 0–1)**. *(1997 key votes, p. 865)*

Had the Republicans been able to unite their party as solidly as the Democrats had, the bill would have passed. But thirty-five Republicans, many of them moderates, voted against it. Marge Roukema, R-N.J., was one of the defectors. "Ultimately," she said, "these vouchers will result in gutting the public school system" by shifting money from public schools to private schools.

DC VOUCHERS

Republicans in 1997 first began making political hay of problems in the District of Columbia's public schools when about 78,000 District students found themselves at home for three weeks past the Sept. 2 scheduled opening because schools were in disrepair. Gingrich renewed GOP calls for a voucher program that would help poor D.C. students escape substandard educations by attending private schools. In a meeting with D.C. schools chief Julius W. Becton Jr., the Speaker said he felt "very strongly that parents ought to have the right to choose."

Republicans, however, backed off a controversial plan to attach a private school vouchers provision to the 1998 D.C. appropriations bill. As one of its final acts in the last hours of the first session of the 105th Congress, the Senate spun off the measure from the fiscal 1998 District of Columbia appropriations bill (HR 2607—PL 105-100). President Clinton had threatened to veto the spending bill because of the school voucher provision.

The Senate passed the separate measure (S 1502) on Nov. 9, 1997, by unanimous consent without considering the bill in committee. The bill would authorize $45 million through fiscal 2002 to provide up to 2,000 low-income D.C. students with an annual scholarship of $3,200, to be used for tuition at any area public or private school. It also would provide $500 scholarships to pay tutoring costs for students staying in D.C. schools. The program would be run by a private, nonprofit scholarship corporation directed by a seven-member board. The president would choose six of the members, with the seventh selected by the District's mayor.

The House took up S 1502 in 1998 and cleared it on April 30, on a mostly party-line, 214–206 vote. The plan had become a rallying cry for House GOP leaders, who said that Congress should give low-income parents options to remove their children from failing public schools.

But as the House neared passage of the measure, Education Secretary Richard W. Riley complained that the bill would provide eight times as much federal money to students attending private schools as was now spent, on average, for those in public schools. Riley also protested that schools receiving the vouchers would not have to comply with federal civil rights laws.

Del. Eleanor Holmes Norton, D-D.C., said Republicans merely were trying to allow private and religious schools to gain a "foothold" into the federal Treasury. Most Democrats, the White House and some Republicans also asserted the bill would take needed resources from the public schools, where most city children would remain.

Clinton vetoed the bill on May 20. In his veto message, the president said the bill would have drawn resources from a majority of the District's public school students and would not have provided sufficient accountability for how the money would be used. "Although I appreciate the interest of the Congress in the educational needs of the children in our nation's capital, this bill is fundamentally misguided and a disservice to those children," Clinton said.

Gingrich criticized the veto, arguing that "President Clinton is keeping the children of our nation's capital literally trapped in failing schools where they can't learn." But GOP leaders, conceding they lacked support, made no attempt to override the veto.

Literacy

The House and Senate passed slightly different versions of a bill (HR 2614) to improve children's literacy. However, the session ended before they could negotiate their differences.

The impetus for the legislation was President Clinton's proposed "America Reads" program. Whereas Clinton pro-

posed training volunteer tutors for the task, including those in his National Service program, HR 2614 would authorize most of the money to train teachers to help students read and combat illiteracy.

Action on the bill began in 1997, with the House Education and the Workforce Committee giving it voice vote approval Oct. 22 (H Rept 105-348). The House passed it by voice vote Nov. 8.

The House version would authorize $260 million annually for three years beginning in fiscal 1998 for the program, which aimed to have all children reading by the end of third grade.

The legislation would authorize the Education Department to make grants to state reading and literacy partnerships. These partnerships would consist of the governor and chief state school officer, the chairmen and ranking members of state legislative committees with jurisdiction over education, and a representative of a school district with at least one school in the Title I school improvement program for disadvantaged students. The partnerships would make subgrants for reading improvement assistance to school districts that have more than one school in the Title I program.

Partnerships also would make tutorial assistance subgrants to school districts that had at least one school in a low-income area that has been designated a federal empowerment zone or enterprise community. Parents who had children with reading difficulties could use this money to get a tutor from a list of providers approved by the school.

The bill would set aside $10 million for the Even Start family literacy program, to plan statewide initiatives.

The Senate Labor and Human Resources Committee May 13 approved HR 2614 by an 18–0 vote. On voice votes, the committee approved a block of amendments by chairman James M. Jeffords, R-Vt. The amendments would require that the state grants be competitive and targeted to high-poverty school districts, ensure that literacy efforts find the best methods for reading instruction, mandate annual progress reports from state agencies receiving grants, and require consultations between the Education Department and literacy councils.

Another amendment approved by voice vote, by Judd Gregg, R-N.H., would force higher appropriations for education for the disabled. The amendment would require that those programs receive $500 million more than the previous year's allocation before literacy funds could be disbursed.

The Senate Oct. 6 passed the measure by voice vote. It would authorize $260 million in both fiscal 1999 and 2000 to attack illiteracy by beefing up teacher training and improving instructional materials.

Republican aides, however, cautioned that the House might not move on the Senate-passed bill until it received assurances that a ban on Clinton's proposed national math and reading tests would be included in an omnibus spending bill. In a further complication, the fiscal 1998 Labor, Health and Human Services and Education appropriation (PL 105-78) set aside $210 million for literacy efforts, contingent on passage of authorizing legislation by July 1, 1998.

Because lawmakers did not meet the deadline, House and Senate appropriators took action to reallocate the $210 million in fiscal 1999 funds that were earmarked for literacy.

School Resources Officers

Lawmakers in 1998 easily cleared a bill (S 2235—PL 105-302) that built on a school-based partnership grant program administered by the Justice Department's Office of Community Oriented Policing Services. Grants were given to encourage the use of school resources officers.

The legislation required school resources officers to be career law enforcement officers directed by their agencies to collaborate with schools in educating students about crime and violence prevention. Resources officers would be encouraged to focus on gangs and drug-related activities, as well as to educate potential school-age victims in crime prevention and personal safety.

The bill "will be an important step in our efforts to end crime in our nation's schools," said Sen. Ben Nighthorse Campbell, R-Colo., who sponsored the measure.

The Senate passed S 2235 by unanimous consent Oct. 7. The House cleared it by voice vote just two days later. President Clinton signed the bill Oct. 27.

1999–2000

Debate over education programs in the 106th Congress was dominated by the battle over reauthorizing the Elementary and Secondary Education Act (ESEA). The House began moving the reauthorization in seven separate bills in 1999; the Senate waited until 2000 to take up a single massive bill. In both cases, the outcome proved to be fierce partisan battles over GOP plans to give the states far more flexibility over federal education funds. The House managed to pass six of its seven bills, but several of them ran into ferocious Democratic objections and White House veto threats. The Senate bill (S 2) survived a contentious committee markup before running into an onslaught of amendments—including an amendment on the ever-controversial issue of gun control. Senate Majority Leader Trent Lott, R-Miss., elected to pull the bill from the floor.

Lawmakers nevertheless managed to clear three elements of ESEA: an "ed-flex" measure granting states more flexibility over spending for federal education programs, a reauthorization of the Even Start program on literacy, and a plan endorsing impact aid for school districts that had small tax bases because of a large federal presence in their localities. Congress also cleared several relatively minor bills, including measures that would provide tuition breaks for District of Columbia high school graduates, crack down on financial aid scams, and establish a new national award for arts education.

Elementary and Secondary Education Act

For the first time in the thirty-five-year history of the Elementary and Secondary Education Act, Congress failed to reauthorize the sweeping law. Instead, lawmakers ended up funding ESEA programs for an additional year in the omnibus spending package, which included the fiscal 2001 Labor, Health and Human Services, and Education appropriations bill (HR 4577—PL 106-554). The task of giving the programs a longer lease on life, and possibly restructuring them along the way, was left for the 107th Congress.

In the House, the legislation was broken into seven bills aimed at reauthorizing and revising separate titles of the 1965 law. The strategy allowed Republicans to respond to the public clamor for improvements in school quality and enabled them to point to specific votes on education. Four passed the House in 1999, including a so-called "ed-flex" proposal. The other three bills passed by the House in 1999 were HR 1995, a bill to combine teacher training and President Clinton's plan to hire 100,000 new teachers; HR 2, which would rewrite the Title I program; and HR 2300, which would set up a ten-state pilot program allowing officials to convert most federal categorical aid into block grants. *(Ed-flex, p. 539)*

The 1999 House-passed bills incorporated a two-track strategy. Although HR 2 would tighten federal control over the $8 billion-a-year Title I program, the teacher training bill

and the ten-state pilot program would give states more flexibility. The White House supported HR 2 but threatened to veto the other two bills.

The House passed two more ESEA bills in 2000 that sparked little controversy and made their way into law after being attached to other pieces of legislation. The final ESEA bill, which would have allowed school districts to shift federal funds between programs, was passed by the House Education and the Workforce Committee but proved so controversial that GOP leaders never brought it up on the floor.

The Senate, after only taking up the ed-flex measure separately in 1999, decided instead to wait to move a single massive ESEA bill in 2000—largely because its floor rules and procedures differed markedly from those of the House. Otherwise, without the discipline of a Rules Committee, the Senate might find itself having the same debate repeatedly over each piece of the reauthorization. The Senate ESEA bill won committee approval but was pulled from the Senate floor in the face of numerous amendments and a flap over gun control.

The debate over ESEA took place against a backdrop of strong public interest in education. Polls consistently showed that voters rated education as their top concern, and both parties put the issue high on their agendas.

BACKGROUND

First authorized in 1965 as part of President Lyndon B. Johnson's War on Poverty, the Elementary and Secondary Education Act (PL 89-10) was the main source of federal aid to public schools. The law provided for Title I grants for remedial education for disadvantaged children, bilingual education, Drug Free Schools grants to prevent and treat alcohol and drug abuse, and the Eisenhower grants to improve the teaching of math and science.

The primary intent was to give extra help to poor children to bring them up to par with their classmates. A secondary goal was to help any educationally disadvantaged child who was doing poorly in class and on standardized tests, regardless of family income. The law had last been reauthorized in 1994 (PL 103-382).

In the 106th Congress, both parties shared the common goals of improving teacher quality and strengthening state and local standards. But they differed over the central question of who was better suited to close the "achievement gap" between low-income and minority students and their peers—the federal government or states and school districts.

Majority Leader Trent Lott, R-Miss., and other Republicans said the gap was growing, proof that ESEA had not worked and a powerful argument for letting states and school districts take charge. Democrats contended that the gap instead was shrinking, proof that the federal programs have made a difference.

The truth was more complicated, according to education analysts. The gap narrowed substantially in the 1970s and 1980s, they generally agreed, but progress stopped around 1988. Some studies suggest that disadvantaged students' test scores had risen since then, although other research indicate they had dropped. The somewhat technical question of how to measure the progress made by disadvantaged students was critical to the debate over whether ESEA programs such as Title I, which spent about $8 billion a year on programs for low-income students, were working.

The Department of Education reported that disadvantaged students' scores on the National Assessment of Educational Progress (NAEP), the test that many education experts consider the "nation's report card," had gone up in recent years. But the conservative-leaning Heritage Foundation warned that some states exempted more special-education students from the test in 1998 than they did in 1994, possibly contributing to the rise in average test scores.

Lawmakers also debated over the issue of accountability—requiring schools that receive Title I funds to prove their programs were effective. In 1994, when Congress last reauthorized ESEA (PL 103-382), it required states to establish content and student performance standards for schools receiving Title I funds by the 2000–2001 school year. States were also supposed to set up systems for measuring how much their students have learned. Poorly performing schools and districts that did not show enough progress, as measured by tests, could face overhauls. *(1994 action, Congress and the Nation Vol. IX, p. 609)*

As of the 106th Congress, however, the accountability standards had yet to be fully implemented. According to the Senate Health, Education, Labor and Pensions Committee, forty-eight states developed content standards and twenty-five had performance standards in place, but none had finished their systems for measuring student progress. And a 1999 Department of Education report concluded that many states still asked students to demonstrate only a basic level of competence, not a "proficient level of performance." Democrats and Republicans alike said the 1994 changes should be expanded to penalize schools that do not measure up.

CLINTON'S PLAN

President Clinton on May 19, 1999, asked Congress to increase the federal role in nearly every aspect of public education, from teacher certification to school discipline, saying that taxpayers could no longer afford to subsidize failing schools. "It took 100 years for laws mandating universal education to spread from a few states to every state. That pace of change might have been all right in the nineteenth century—it won't do in the twenty-first," the president said during a White House event to unveil his proposal for rewriting ESEA.

Although many of Clinton's proposals had been previewed in his Jan. 19 State of the Union address, the announcement set off a firestorm of criticism. Conservatives and top Republicans decried the plan as a massive federal in-

trusion in education. House Education and the Workforce Committee Chairman Bill Goodling, R-Pa., said the White House proposals "trample on our nation's long and proven traditions of local control of education."

At the other end of the spectrum, some liberal lawmakers and advocates complained that Clinton's plan was not as tough as it looked. They said it gave states too much time to phase in changes, such as ending the use of teachers' aides or unqualified instructors in the Title I program.

Clinton's proposal represented a broad expansion of the federal role and would tie federal aid to several requirements. It would:

• Require that new teachers paid through Title I funds or in Title I schools be fully certified and that all newly hired secondary school teachers be certified in their subject. It would limit the use by July 2002 of Title I teacher aides.

• Require states within four years to ensure that at least 95 percent of its teachers were fully qualified or moving toward certification.

• Require districts to intervene with schools that do not show academic improvement over a two-year period. The act would set aside more money to turn around low-performing schools.

• Give states four years to end the policy of "social promotion," whereby students are advanced to the next grade even though they are not academically ready.

• Require schools to implement comprehensive discipline policies and direct Safe and Drug Free Schools program funds to high-risk schools and require more competition for grants.

• Fold Goals 2000 and teacher training aid into a new program to improve curricula and professional development.

• Require school, state, and district annual report cards including information on student achievement, teacher qualifications, class size, and school safety.

• Continue Clinton's proposal to hire 100,000 new teachers and reduce average class size to eighteen in the early grades.

• Expand programs to provide technology and technology training.

TEACHER TRAINING (HR 1995)

The first ESEA bill considered in 1999 (HR 1995—H Rept 106-232, Pt. I) would establish a new teacher training and classroom reduction block grant. House Republicans had unveiled the plan at a May 27 press conference. They said they tried to develop a middle-ground measure that could draw Democratic support, but no Democrats endorsed the bill, which was cosponsored by House Speaker J. Dennis Hastert, R-Ill., and Majority Leader Dick Armey, R-Texas.

The focus on block grants and local control contrasted sharply with Clinton's ESEA proposal.

House Committee Action

Although Democrats were virulently opposed to the $10 billion legislation—which they argued would gut Clinton's long-standing plan to hire 100,000 new teachers nationally within seven years—debate in the House Education and the Workforce Committee on the measure was somewhat staid.

As modified by a substitute amendment offered by committee chairman Bill Goodling, R-Pa., the bill would authorize $2 billion per year over five years for programs aimed at reducing class sizes and improving teacher performance. States would administer the grants to local school districts, which would decide how best to use the money to improve student achievement.

Although Republicans said the bill would require schools to use some of the grant money to reduce class sizes, it would allow state departments of education to waive that requirement if local schools could demonstrate that other uses for the funds, such as hiring more special education teachers, would benefit students more.

Rep. Matthew G. Martinez, D-Calif., unsuccessfully offered an amendment that would establish two funding streams, keeping money to reduce class sizes separate from money to improve continuing teacher improvement.

Despite the partisan stances, members were not far apart on the legislation—with the main dividing line the new-teacher money. Republicans said the legislation gave schools the leeway they needed to determine how best to improve education, either by hiring more teachers to reduce class size or by improving the classroom skills of their current teachers. One provision would allow teachers to receive grants for certain professional development programs.

Democrats argued that the legislation would undermine an agreement reached in 1998 in the omnibus spending bill (PL 105-227) that reserved $1.2 billion for the hiring of 100,000 new teachers over seven years. Democrats also worried that the GOP proposal did not mandate hiring qualified teachers, instead relying on the term "certified teachers."

Members of both parties had lamented the high number of teachers who taught subjects for which they did not have a college degree or much educational background. The Republican proposal would require schools to spend at least as much money on math and science training for teachers as they planned to in the current fiscal year, unless they were granted waivers from their states.

The Education and the Workforce Committee June 30 voted 27–19 for HR 1995, with Democrats Tim Roemer, Ind., and Rush D. Holt, N.J., crossing party lines.

House Floor Action

The House on July 20 passed HR 1995 by a vote of 239–185, acting despite a veto threat from Clinton, who said the bill undercut his plan to hire 100,000 teachers and reduce class size. Some twenty-four Democrats split with the White House and supported the legislation to fold a trio of education programs into broad grants.

Supporters said it would give needed flexibility to school districts, some of which had already met Clinton's goal of reducing average class size to eighteen in the first through third grades. Opponents argued that the proposed $2 billion an-nual grant was so vague that there was no guarantee that any money would be spent on new teachers.

Although the Democratic support was not strong enough to ensure the two-thirds vote needed to override a veto, it was greater than the GOP, or the administration, had expected. Among those supporting the measure was Democrat George Miller of California, a leading liberal on education issues. He argued that provisions in the bill to improve teacher quality were more important than focusing solely on reducing class size, which he says can lead to hiring unqualified teachers.

The House-passed legislation would consolidate the three programs into annual grants to states and school districts. They were the $335 million Eisenhower Professional Development program for teacher training, Clinton's $491 million Goals 2000 grants for improving education quality, and the 100,000-teacher proposal.

Localities would have to spend some of the funds to hire new teachers. That provision could be waived, however, if it would result in hiring underqualified teachers or would have a negative effect on student achievement. The grants could also be used for training and other purposes, including merit pay, hiring special education instructors, and revamping tenure.

Before approving the bill, the House, 424–1, adopted a bipartisan manager's amendment offered by Goodling. The amendment, worked out with Miller and other Democrats, imposed tougher requirements on states than the original bill. It would require states to ensure that all teachers were fully qualified by the beginning of 2004 and mandate that local school districts report on efforts to raise the performance of poor and disadvantaged students. It also would ensure that no school district would receive less money than it received in fiscal 1999 under existing programs.

On the other side of the aisle, the Democrats were eager to get a separate vote on President Clinton's plan to hire 100,000 new teachers. Matthew G. Martinez, D-Calif., offered a substitute amendment that would provide separate authorization for the teacher program, while providing $1.5 billion annually for an initiative aimed at reducing class size. It would also direct $500 million to special education training and target more overall funding to low-income areas. The Martinez amendment was defeated by a **key vote of 207–217 (R 3–215; D 203–2; I 1–0).** *(1999 key votes, p. 899)*

The House also:

• Defeated, 181–242, an amendment by Patsy T. Mink, D-Hawaii, to allow grants for teachers who take sabbatical leave.

• Adopted, by voice vote, an amendment by Michael N. Castle, R-Del., to increase teacher technology training.

• Passed, by voice vote, an amendment by Dennis J. Kucinich, D-Ohio, and Robert E. Andrews, D-N.J., to set up a national clearinghouse for entrepeneurship education.

• Passed, by voice vote, an amendment by Tim Roemer, D-Ind., to create a competitive program to recruit math and science teachers.

The Senate did not take up HR 1995.

TITLE I (HR 2)

The House in 1999 also passed ESEA legislation reauthorizing Title I, a federal grant program for poor and disadvantaged children. Despite partisan clashes, most Democrats ended up supporting the bill.

House Committee Action

The House Education and the Workforce Committee Oct. 13 approved legislation (HR 2—H Rept 106) to reauthorize Title I and lower the threshold for determining whether the money could be spent schoolwide or had to be targeted at individual students.

The bill, touted as a bipartisan compromise, was approved by the committee on a 42–6 vote with a few changes. Members had offered nearly fifty amendments over four days of consideration.

The measure would authorize $8.35 billion for the Title I Local Educational Agency Grants in fiscal 2000, plus more for related programs for native, rural, homeless, and other special students, for a total of about $9.33 billion a year for five years.

Title I grants were allotted to states based on their population of poor children. Schools in which half the population was below the poverty level could use the federal funds with state and local money to increase student achievement schoolwide. Under the current law schools with a population below the 50 percent threshold had to target the federal funds at individual students, generally by pulling them out of regular classes or providing additional instruction beyond school hours.

As introduced by committee chairman Bill Goodling, R-Pa., the bill would make the threshold 40 percent. The committee then voted 24–21 to bump the level back to 50 percent. Supporting that proposal were several conservative Republicans unhappy with the overall bill and with the closed-door negotiations between Goodling and ranking Democrat William L. Clay, Mo. However, the committee later reversed itself, voting 26–21 along party lines to drop the threshold down to 40 percent, as proposed in the original bill.

Also adopted was an amendment affecting a key provision in the bill. As drafted, the bill would require states to reserve 25 percent of new Title I money to reward schools and teachers that improve student performance. Bob Schaffer, R-Colo., unsuccessfully offered two amendments that would kill the reward program or make it optional. Finally, Schaffer was able to convince his party on the last day of the markup to increase the set-aside to 30 percent but make it optional. The amendment was adopted, 23–20.

Another Schaffer amendment, adopted 28–21, would require public schools to ensure that educational services or benefits provided by Title I funds were nonideological, neutral, and secular, the same restrictions placed on private schools. David Wu, D-Ore., voted with Republicans.

Another amendment, adopted 27–22, would kill a $20 million program for Native Hawaiians. Sponsor John A. Boehner, R-Ohio, said the program, which provided additional money beyond Title I grants, was unnecessary because a private trust with assets of at least $10 billion was designed to help those children. The $20 million should be spent on other programs without a wealthy benefactor, he argued.

Patsy T. Mink, D-Hawaii, said the amendment was unfair because it targeted one Native American program for elimination and because Hawaii had suffered at the hands of the United States.

House Floor Action

Despite lingering disagreements about how many strings should be attached to Title I funds, the reauthorization of the grant program at a level $1.5 billion higher than in the original bill—to $9.8 billion in fiscal 2000—received wide bipartisan support in the full House.

As approved in committee, the bill would require states to report Title I student and program results; allow students to transfer their Title I funds to another public school in the same district if their home school is failing; require students in U.S. schools for three years to be tested in reading and language arts in English; freeze the number of teacher aides that can be hired; and increase the standards for hiring classroom aides.

During House floor debate, the House adopted, by voice vote, a manager's amendment offered by Goodling that made minor changes to the bill and included bilingual education provisions left out of the original measure but drafted in a last-minute compromise with Democrats.

A bipartisan amendment by Tim Roemer, D-Ind., and Jack Quinn, R-N.Y., to boost the funding level passed, 243–181.

An amendment by Schaffer that would require school districts to allow children who had been victims of violent crimes or were in unsafe schools to transfer to any public school in their state chosen by their parents also passed by voice vote.

The House passed HR 2 on Oct. 21 by a vote of 358–67. Again, the Senate took no action on HR 2.

STRAIGHT A's (HR 2300)

The third piece of ESEA that the House passed in 1999 was a controversial measure, known as "Straight A's," to create a pilot program giving ten states unprecedented flexibility to spend federal education funds.

The measure was a centerpiece of the GOP educational agenda. But pressure from moderates forced House leaders to reshape the flexibility bill. Instead of creating an option for all fifty states to receive federal education money as block grants in exchange for pledges to improve student achievement, they agreed to limit the experiment to ten states.

Leaders narrowly avoided alienating the conservative faction, who were convinced in the end that the bill moved in the right direction even if it did not go far enough. Mark

Souder, R-Ind., supported the bill although he said it had been changed from "Straight A's Academic Achievement for All" to "a B, an A and an F—Better Alternatives for a Few."

Republicans touted the proposal as a bold initiative to counter thirty years of unproductive federal educational involvement. But Democrats said the bill lacked accountability and would result in less federal money being used to help those students who need the most assistance. The White House threatened a veto, arguing the bill would "undermine the federal government's commitment" to improve education.

The Education and the Workforce Committee approved the bill (HR 2300—H Rept 106-386) 26–19 on Oct. 13. As passed by committee, states would have the option of entering the program or continuing to receive funds through current federal programs and guidelines. Participating states would have to establish a statewide accountability system, install content and performance standards, and provide detailed information on how poor and disadvantaged students are performing.

States that did not reach goals as agreed with the Education Department within five years would not be able to participate in the program. The bill would not affect how much federal funding each state receives, nor would states be able to violate civil rights laws or use federal money to reduce the local tax burden.

But GOP moderates, led by Michael N. Castle, R-Del., prevailed upon the Rules Committee to greatly scale back the measure to make it a demonstration program for a limited number of states. Castle's language influenced key moderate GOP support for the bill, which was opposed by all the mainstream education groups but advocated passionately by conservative organizations.

The full House passed it 213–208 on Oct. 21. The close House vote resulted from a handful of moderates joining Democrats in opposition to the bill. Only nine Republicans opposed the measure, while five conservative Democrats crossed party lines to support it. The Senate did not take up the bill.

EVEN START (HR 3222)/IMPACT AID (HR 3616)

The House Education and the Workforce Committee started work in 2000 on two relatively noncontroversial bills, approving both of them by voice vote on Feb. 16, 2000. Unlike other pieces of ESEA, both the plans ultimately became law, although as part of other bills.

One bill (HR 3222—H Rept 106-503) would reauthorize the Even Start program on literacy, which Goodling wrote. The other bill (HR 3616—H Rept 106-504) would endorse impact aid for school districts that had small tax bases because of a large federal presence in their localities.

Even Start, which provided federal funding to help children and adults learn to read, grew out of a program Goodling initiated when he was a school superintendent in

Pennsylvania. As approved by the committee, the bill would increase the program's funding from $118 million to $500 million. It would authorize grants to states for programs that help adults and their children learn how to read.

Although committee members from both parties directed glowing compliments to Goodling, approval of the literacy bill was not without pointed debate. As Goodling had predicted earlier in the week, some members were concerned about a provision that would allow faith-based groups to run literacy programs.

The provision was strengthened by an amendment offered by Mark Souder, R-Ind., and adopted by voice vote, that would allow religious and faith-based organizations to receive funds through state subgrants to administer programs. The amendment had language that would bar such groups from preaching, recruiting, or otherwise trying to force their religion on the students.

Supporters of the provision said some people were connected to the community through their churches and might be unaware of education programs to help them learn to read, while others might be more comfortable learning from church members.

Robert C. Scott, D-Va., offered several amendments related to the Souder provision that would emphasize a separation between church and state. One would prohibit any faith-based group that received federal money, albeit indirectly from the state, to discriminate in hiring. Another would hold such religious groups to all federal civil rights law from which they might otherwise be exempt. Both were rejected.

The committee did accept one Scott amendment that would consider all groups administering the programs to have accepted federal aid and money, a designation that in turn could lead to stricter imposition of federal laws.

The other bill, HR 3616, would reauthorize a federal program that made payments to local school districts that did not have a large tax base because of a significant presence of federal property. Most school districts were funded through property taxes, which the federal government did not pay.

Payments to districts under the impact aid program were based on several formulas, depending on the circumstances of the students. For example, districts could qualify for payments based on the number of children who lived in town but had parents who worked for a federal office or were civilian Defense employees. Districts also might be eligible for aid based on the number of students who live on military bases or Indian reservations but attend local schools.

In addition, some districts were unable to secure bonding for capital projects because of their small tax base. The bill would allow schools to apply for impact aid for construction projects, with priority given to districts facing facility emergencies.

The bill would authorize $910.5 million for fiscal 2001, the same level as fiscal 2000. The House passed HR 3616 by voice vote May 15. It passed HR 3222 by voice vote Sept. 12.

Both bills became law, albeit by somewhat indirect routes. HR 3222 was added as a rider to the year-end omnibus spending package (HR 4577—PL 106-554). HR 3616 was signed into law as part of the fiscal 2001 defense authorization bill (HR 4205—PL 106-398).

SHIFTING FEDERAL FUNDS (HR 4141)

After a grueling and often bitter five-day markup, the House Education and the Workforce Committee April 13 approved the last of the House ESEA bills on a 25–21 vote. The bill, which would allow school districts to shift federal funds between programs, proved so controversial that GOP leaders never brought it up on the floor.

This final bill (HR 4141—H Rept 106-608), which would allow school districts to shift federal funds among programs, turned out to be the most difficult piece of the House ESEA reauthorization effort. Republicans rejected one Democratic attempt after another to restore existing education programs or create new ones. On the final vote, all Republicans present except Ron Paul of Texas supported the measure, and all Democrats present voted against it.

By the time the markup was over, the committee had plowed through sixty-eight amendments, mostly Democratic measures that were killed off on party-line votes. Republicans said they produced a measure that would end the status quo of piling on one federal program after another; Democrats said they simply caved in to the demands of their most hard-line conservative backers.

"I have never seen anything like this in my thirty-two years in Congress," William L. Clay, D-Mo., the ranking Democrat on the committee, said in an April 13 interview. "If they want to lose the majority in the House of Representatives, let them go to the floor with this piece of junk and see how the American people respond."

Goodling said the measure provided a needed challenge to the status quo—a long history of federal programs that he said have failed children because there was no evidence they have improved academic achievement or accomplished their other goals.

The centerpiece of HR 4141 was a GOP-crafted provision that would let local school districts shift funds from one program to another—transferring money between teacher training, technology, substance abuse, and other areas—to meet their needs.

The legislation would address other Republican priorities by consolidating eight education technology programs into one, $731 million block grant. It also would combine the Safe and Drug-Free Schools program and the 21st Century Community Learning Centers initiative for after-school programs. Republicans said that would be more efficient because 75 percent of the funds requested in 1997 for after-school programs went to antidrug efforts, anyway.

Republicans stuck together on those themes, but the markup also showed how divided they had become on the issue of school vouchers—or anything resembling them. An amendment by Peter Hoekstra, R-Mich., that would let states use federal funds for public and private school choice programs was defeated, 22–23, when four moderate Republicans joined with the Democrats to kill the measure.

Hoekstra said his amendment was not a voucher proposal, because it did not involve a fixed amount of money. He called it a "scholarship" that would be considered aid to the student, not the school. But Clay and other Democrats said anything that took federal money from public schools and gave it to private or parochial schools would hurt public education.

HR 4141 would continue the GOP theme of flexibility for states and school districts. It also strayed into such social issues as hate crimes and religious freedom—issues Goodling felt he had to include to win the support of conservative Republicans, but at the cost of even more bruising attacks from Democrats.

For example, the bill would eliminate the Department of Education's authority to fund classes that taught the prevention of hate crimes. Robert C. Scott, D-Va., tried to restore those programs, but his amendment failed, 23–24.

The hate crimes language sparked some of the most bitter debate of the markup. Donald M. Payne, D-N.J., said schools should reach out to children to end the nation's "climate of intolerance." But Goodling countered that the bill "shouldn't be fostering any political correctness issues."

Scott also tried unsuccessfully to apply the employment discrimination protections of the Civil Rights Act of 1964 to religious organizations that received Safe and Drug-Free Schools funds; his amendment failed, 18–28. Clay later accused Republicans of allowing religious discrimination in hiring, but Souder said the amendment would force religious organizations to change their character.

Even though moderate Republicans ultimately supported the bill, some of the social issues made them nervous. Castle, who voted for the Scott amendment to restore the hate crimes program, said in an April 11 interview that the GOP's hate crimes language and other provisions were needed to bring conservatives on board, though admitting that "any one of them could screw the bill up" when it got to the House floor.

Goodling did take the steam out of one Democratic issue by accepting two relatively mild gun control amendments: a measure by Carolyn McCarthy of New York that would allow school districts to promote child safety locks on guns, and another McCarthy amendment that would require the National Center for Education Statistics to collect data on the common characteristics of school shootings. Both were approved by voice vote.

The Democrats lost a series of battles to preserve existing programs that they believed were working. A McCarthy amendment to preserve the 21st Century Community Learning Centers program was defeated, 21–25, and an attempt by Ron Kind of Wisconsin to restore the Technology Literacy Challenge Fund to help schools work computer technology into their classes was defeated, 21–27.

Democrats also lost whenever they tried to add new programs. An amendment by Lynn Woolsey of California to create a $50 million "Go Girl" program, which would support efforts to draw more girls into math and science classes, was rejected, 21–22. And an effort by Patsy Mink of Hawaii to authorize $14 billion over five years to help schools hire 100,000 new counselors was defeated, 20–25.

The full House or Senate did not take up the bill.

ESEA REAUTHORIZATION IN THE SENATE (S 2)

In 2000 the a Senate committee managed to approve a massive ESEA bill (S 2—S Rept 106-261) after a heated partisan debate. But the bill was pulled from the Senate floor in May in the face of unyielding Democratic opposition, a presidential veto threat, and the prospect of a contentious gun control amendment.

Senate Committee Action

Unlike the House attempt to spin off sections of ESEA in bite-size pieces, the bill introduced in the Senate Health, Education, Labor and Pensions Committee was a comprehensive reauthorization and overhaul of ESEA. Committee chairman James M. Jeffords, R-Vt., opened debate on the Senate bill March 1, offering a draft that would authorize roughly $19.7 billion a year for the myriad programs in the ESEA, including Title I, bilingual education, and safe and drug-free schools. It also included the Impact Aid program for local districts that were burdened by having nontaxable federal installations within their boundaries.

Jeffords's draft moved existing teacher development programs and Clinton's plan to hire 100,000 teachers into a new $2 billion annual block grant for teacher training. Similar to the Title I bill that the House passed in 1999 (HR 2), it would require tougher state standards to ensure that students served by Title I were showing academic improvement.

Democrats roundly rejected Jeffords's proposal, particularly the block grant portion, as giving a blank check to state governors. Criticism also came from the right, as some of Jeffords's fellow Republicans argued that his plan did not deviate enough from thirty-five years of federal intervention.

Most of the GOP complaints were directed at Title I, which provided funds to schools specifically to raise the academic performance of disadvantaged students. At the markup, Jeffords, who was more moderate than his fellow committee Republicans, voted "present" on two successful amendments by Judd Gregg, R-N.H., that would rewrite the Title I program.

The first Gregg amendment, adopted by the committee, 9–8, would turn some Title I funds into vouchers that could be used to purchase educational services from private or religious schools. It would establish a fifteen-state pilot program under which governors could elect to receive nearly all federal education funding, including parts of Title I, as a block grant.

The other amendment adopted by the committee was based on one of the GOP leadership's primary education priorities, the so-called Straight A's bill. It would let states roll Title I and most other federal programs into block grants. In exchange for the greater flexibility, states would have to enter a five-year agreement with the Department of Education that would include student performance goals. States would have to establish, and show progress in reaching, student performance standards or risk losing their flexibility.

That language went further than the House-passed version of Straight A's legislation (HR 2300) that would allow ten states to participate in a similar block grant pilot.

Gregg shepherded two other major amendments through the panel. One would allow ten states to turn Title I into a "portable" program. Under his plan, pupils from low-income families who received Title I funds would receive a voucher instead. The funds would move with the students if they transferred to another public school and could be used to purchase services from private schools. That passed 9–8.

A second amendment approved by voice vote would allow students in Title I schools classified as failing to transfer to other public schools. More than 7,000 schools receiving Title I funds had been classified as failing. If a school did not improve its performance after four years, the district would have to pay the transportation costs to move students to another school.

The committee also adopted by voice vote an amendment by Bill Frist, R-Tenn., that would allow schools with 40 percent of students in poverty to set up schoolwide Title I programs, down from the current 50 percent threshold.

Republicans based many of their arguments for change on the belief that the ESEA had been a massive failure. States and local school districts were better positioned than Washington to determine their own needs and priorities, they said.

Democrats countered that states could use their own funds to make the kinds of improvements Republicans claimed were priorities. Federal money accounted for 7 percent of education, and states and local governments provided the remaining 93 percent. Democrats also said the federal government did a far better job than states of directing aid to low-income students.

At the markup, Democrats offered dozens of amendments, including an effort by Edward M. Kennedy of Massachusetts, the committee's ranking Democrat, to specify that the $2 billion teacher training block grant in the bill would have to be spent in specific areas.

Patty Murray, D-Wash., proposed an amendment that would authorize $1.75 billion for the third year of Clinton's seven-year plan to hire 100,000 new teachers and reduce average class size to eighteen in early grades. Similar to the Kennedy amendment, Murray's proposal was rejected on party lines.

Republicans, outnumbering Democrats 10–8 on the committee, voted cohesively throughout most deliberations. Five GOP members joined Democrats, however, to soundly reject an amendment offered by Jeff Sessions, R-Ala., that would prohibit the Department of Education from using funds to develop publications on hate crimes. Sessions said hate crimes were too difficult to define.

All Republicans joined Democrats to raise the authorization for Title I in fiscal 2001 to $15 billion from the $10 billion Jeffords had suggested. The Clinton administration's fiscal 2001 budget called for $8.4 billion for Title I. Funding would be determined by a separate appropriations bill.

The committee also:

• Adopted by voice vote an amendment by Barbara A. Mikulski, D-Md., that would establish as a national goal having all students computer literate by the eighth grade.

• Adopted, 9–8, a Sessions amendment that would incorporate several provisions from a juvenile justice bill (S 254), such as violence-prevention programs and the transfer of records of expelled students to new schools.

• Rejected, 8–10, an amendment by Tom Harkin, D-Iowa, that would authorize $1.3 billion for school construction grants and loans.

• Rejected, 8–10, an amendment by Jack Reed, D-R.I., that would dedicate funding for school library collections.

• Rejected, 8–10, a Reed amendment that would require states to publish names of schools that were considered failing.

On March 9, 2000, the committee approved S 2 on a 10–8 party-line vote. But the bill continued to generate a firestorm of criticism from the administration and Senate Democrats. Education Secretary Richard W. Riley promised that Clinton would veto the bill. Senate Democrats, who were unsuccessful in adding amendments in committee, vowed an all-out battle on the chamber floor. "They turned their backs on the progress that has been made in setting and implementing high standards for all children," said Kennedy.

Republicans countered that Democratic efforts to maintain tight federal regulations would stymie state attempts to improve academic performance. They pointed out that the test scores of low-income children had improved little in the thirty-five years since the ESEA became law, despite federal spending to the tune of $185 billion.

Senate Floor Action

Senate GOP leaders pulled S 2 from the floor May 9, conceding the measure was so controversial it might never come to a final vote. Senate Majority Leader Trent Lott, R-Miss., said the bill could move on and off the floor as other appropriations bills were debated. But Democrats said that strategy was mostly a dodge to avoid a gun control amendment that Frank R. Lautenberg, D-N.J., wanted to offer.

The action capped a week in which the Senate inched along in a partisan and largely repetitive debate on the ESEA bill, consuming hours of debate and voting on only a handful of amendments before Lott shelved it.

The one factor that had come to overshadow the entire education debate, even more than the ideological differences over who could do the best job fixing the schools, was the stalemate over the shifting politics of gun control.

For nearly a year, the juvenile crime bill (S 254), which passed the Senate in May 2000 with several far-reaching gun provisions, had been stuck in a conference committee with a House measure that did not include the gun restrictions (HR 1501). The conferees had met only once, and Democrats such as Lautenberg, the author of the Senate provision that would require background checks for everyone who bought firearms at gun shows, had been looking for ways to get the gun measures out of limbo. *(Juvenile crime bill, p. 633)*

Democrats thought they would have their chance with the education bill the week of May 8, and they wanted to squeeze in a gun control amendment before the May 14 "Million Mom March" on the National Mall, a gathering designed to step up the pressure for Congress to pass new gun control laws. When Lott pulled the education bill off the floor May 9, that chance disappeared.

The amendment Lautenberg wanted to offer would include gun show background checks and all of the other gun measures in the Senate juvenile justice bill, including a ban on importing high-capacity ammunition clips and a requirement that all handguns be sold with child safety trigger locks or safety storage boxes.

To avoid a repeat of the juvenile justice showdown in 1999, when the gun show provision squeaked through in a tie vote that was broken by Gore, Lott would have to file a cloture motion to cut off debate and round up 60 votes to approve it. But he lacked the votes.

Lott's other problem, even if he could find a way to hold off the gun amendment, was that Democrats and Republicans kept lining up with new education amendments to offer, and each one consumed hours and hours of debate time on the floor. Democrats wanted to offer amendments that would add targeted funds for school construction and teacher training. Republicans had their own priorities, including an amendment Jeff Sessions, R-Ala., wanted to offer that would allow teachers to discipline special education students in the same ways that other children were punished for violent or disruptive behavior.

Moreover, the White House issued its most detailed veto threat to date on May 1, saying the bill would weaken accountability for schools that receive federal funds and hurt programs to address national education priorities by turning them into "unfocused block grants."

On May 9, Lott suggested an on-again, off-again scenario in which the Senate could set aside ESEA every time an appropriations bill became available, pass the appropriations bill, return to the education bill, then set it aside again when the next spending bill was ready for floor action.

The "dual track" strategy, as Lott called it, was not unusual in the Senate, where the must-pass appropriations bills have the highest priority and often bump other bills off the agenda. But with all the amendments the Senate still had to plow through, such a strategy was likely to force the education debate to drag on for weeks—if it did not simply fade away.

Before the bill was set aside, the Senate on May 9 rejected, 13–84, a substitute by Sen. Joseph I. Lieberman, D-Conn., and other centrist Democrats that would have moved toward the Republican proposals by condensing the more than fifty ESEA programs into five grants aimed at achieving general goals.

The proposal drew praise from some Republicans, but no GOP votes. Republicans said it did not offer as much flexibility as their bill would give to states and local school districts. Democratic critics said it would dilute the effectiveness of such important programs as after-school initiatives and the Safe and Drug-Free Schools program by folding them into grants.

The Senate did adopt, 97–0, a Lott-Gregg amendment that would establish what they called a "Teachers Bill of Rights"—liability protections for teachers who take "reasonable actions" to discipline unruly students. The measure would limit the noneconomic damages teachers would have to pay in any lawsuit and would shield them from punitive damages unless they showed a "conscious, flagrant indifference" to the student's rights or safety.

One of the most significant votes on S 2 came when the Senate defeated a Democratic substitute May 3, on a party-line vote of 45–54. The Democrats' proposal would replace the Republican rewrite of ESEA with a collection of programs that reflected their own priorities: school construction, class-size reduction, after-school programs, and funds to help schools recruit and train teachers. All of those elements were expected to return as individual Democratic amendments.

The Senate on May 4 defeated, 44–53, one of the Democrats' main amendments, a proposal by Patty Murray of Washington that would authorize funds for the remaining five years of President Clinton's program to provide funds to hire 100,000 new teachers.

In other ESEA amendment votes, the Senate:

• Adopted, 54–42, an amendment by Spencer Abraham, R-Mich., and Connie Mack, R-Fla., that would let states use federal funds under Title II of ESEA to test teachers on the subjects they teach and give merit pay increases to the best instructors.

• Rejected, 43–54, a second-degree amendment by Kennedy that would eliminate the teacher testing language and allowed merit pay for all teachers in schools that improved student achievement, rather than just individual teachers.

• Adopted, 98–0, an amendment by Slade Gorton, R-Wash., intended to ensure that the bill did not create a new right to use federal funds for school vouchers. Democrats charged that a proposed demonstration program allowing parents to use federal funds for private educational services would open the door to vouchers for private schools, ultimately draining funds from the public schools.

Ed-Flex

Congress in 1999 enacted legislation to give local school systems greater autonomy in how they use federal education money. Debate on the measure was often rancorous, and it exemplified how both parties wanted to seize the education debate. *(1998 action, p. 527)*

The bill (HR 800—PL 106-25), modeled on a twelve-state pilot program, gave states the power to approve waivers from federal regulations at the local level. Some regulations, such as those concerning health, safety, and civil rights, could not be waived.

In the Senate, Republicans stymied Democratic attempts to use the bill as a vehicle for many of President Clinton's education priorities, including more money for after-school programs and dropout prevention, and an end to promoting students not academically ready to advance. Republicans also pushed, but later backed away from, an amendment that would allow schools to use $1.2 billion designated for class-size reduction for educating disabled children instead. The money was in the fiscal 1999 omnibus spending law (PL 105-277).

On the House side, Democrats tried to reduce waivers for Title I programs, which they worried would be diluted by the legislation, and pushed for tighter accountability measures.

BACKGROUND

Although the Elementary and Secondary Education Act of 1965 (PL 89-10) and other federal statutes had given governors some latitude in developing curricula, myriad federal regulations were seen by the states as impediments for reform efforts.

The Education Flexibility Partnership Demonstration Act (PL 103-227), in effect since 1994, allowed state educational agencies to waive certain state and federal requirements, but it had been limited to twelve states. Expansion of the waiver authority nationwide would allow states to experiment with alternative approaches to education.

Early in 1999, Senators Bill Frist, R-Tenn., and Ron Wyden, D-Ore., introduced legislation to allow states to seek a waiver of federal regulations governing how schools can spend federal education money in designing curricula. In the House, Michael N. Castle, R-Del., and Tim Roemer, D-Ind., sponsored a similar bill.

Both parties were responding to public opinion polls showing that education was a top priority for voters. During the winter meeting of the National Governors' Association (NGA) in Washington on Feb. 20–23, state executives, members of Congress and Clinton sparred over the best strategy for improving schools.

Clinton wanted Congress to toughen the 1965 law to require that states adopt performance incentives, including ending "social promotion," by which students were advanced to the next grade even though they were not academically ready.

Governors from both parties, however, supported the ed-flex bill, which was a top priority of governors. The administration supported the bill but wanted it to be considered as part of the education act reauthorization.

The waiver authority under both existing law and the legislation would apply to the $8 billion-a-year Title I program of aid to disadvantaged students and to the Title II Eisenhower Professional Development Program, which funded teacher training. It would also cover vocational and adult education and aid to immigrant children.

States would have to waive their own regulations to receive federal relief. The flexibility would not apply to health, safety, or civil rights rules.

Some states, such as Texas, had used the waiver authority to revamp teacher training. Studies by the Congressional Research Service and General Accounting Office (GAO) found that most waivers were designed to either allow schools in danger of losing Title I funds to continue receiving aid or to let schools with a relatively low population of Title I students implement schoolwide education improvement programs, rather than target aid more narrowly.

Under existing law, 50 percent of students had to receive free or reduced-price federal lunches in order for an institution to qualify for a schoolwide program.

The Education Trust, which worked to improve achievement of poor students, said in a Feb. 24 letter to the House Education and the Workforce Committee that the ed-flex legislation would "dilute and redirect federal funds in ways that would ultimately hurt, rather than help, our nation's most vulnerable students."

At a Feb. 25 hearing before the House Education and the Workforce Subcommittee on Early Childhood, Youth and Families, GAO officials expressed concerns about the bill. In return for flexibility, the current program and proposed law required states to demonstrate that their new approaches were effective. Carlotta C. Joyner, GAO director of education and employment issues, said the requirements were not specific enough.

COMMITTEE ACTION

The Senate's ed-flex legislation (S 280) was approved by the Health, Education, Labor and Pensions Committee Jan. 28 by a 10–0 vote. But none of the committee's eight Democrats was present for the vote.

Congressional aides said it was not an organized boycott as Democrats generally supported the substance of the measure. There was grumbling, however, about the decision to schedule the markup right on the heels of the unsuccessful Democratic motion to dismiss the impeachment trial of President Clinton. *(Clinton impeachment, p. 813).*

A similar bill passed the committee the previous year. Republicans endorsed the measure as a first step toward giving states greater autonomy on education spending. "[The bill] doesn't go anywhere near as far as some of us would like, but it's a step in the right direction," said Judd Gregg, R-N.H.

The House Education and the Workforce Committee approved its version (HR 800) by a vote of 33–9 on March 3. The House bill (H Rept 106-43) won committee approval after a vote that ruled out of order an amendment by David Wu, D-Ore., to add Clinton's teacher plan. Opposition to the overall bill came from Democrats who said expanding the waiver authority could undermine Title I. Committee chairman Bill Goodling, R-Pa., said the pilot program had allowed some states to make major gains.

The panel defeated an amendment by George Miller, D-Calif., and Dale E. Kildee, D-Mich., to require states seeking waivers to submit detailed plans. It voted to end waivers if student performance declined two years in a row.

SENATE FLOOR ACTION

Senate GOP leaders had hoped to quickly pass S 280 in early March. But Republicans faced a barrage of Democratic amendments calculated to force votes on President Clinton's education initiatives, such as his proposal to hire 100,000 new teachers over seven years to reduce class size.

Democrats viewed S 280 as a launching pad for a broader debate over Clinton's education agenda. Sen. Patty Murray, D-Wash., said the ed-flex legislation was a "small, tiny baby step" that Democrats planned to turn into a "large step" to improve schools.

The controversy highlighted the importance that both parties attached to the education issue. Despite the sparring over amendments, the underlying ed-flex legislation was relatively noncontroversial.

On largely party-line votes, the Senate on March 11 effectively killed Democratic amendments that would authorize $11.4 billion over six years for Clinton's plan to hire 100,000 teachers and reduce class size, expand after-school aid, increase dropout prevention assistance, and end social promotion, in which students were advanced to the next grade even though they were not academically ready. The major Democratic amendment, offered by Patty Murray, D-Wash., to implement Clinton's class-size plan was tabled (killed) in a **key vote of 55–44 (R 55–0; D 0–44).** *(1999 key votes, p. 899)*

Further, the Senate, by a vote of 60–39, passed an amendment by Majority Leader Trent Lott, R-Miss., that would give states the option of using the $1.2 billion in the omnibus spending law to fund education programs for the disabled rather than hiring new teachers. Although Clinton previously endorsed the legislation, both he and Senate Democrats raised concerns about the Lott amendment.

The ed-flex debate was a clear sign of the deep divisions between Democrats, who want to expand the federal role in education, and Republicans, who had proposed more funding but fewer federal strings. Despite the overcharged rhetoric from both sides, ed-flex sponsors conceded that the bill would likely have only a minimal impact on national education policy.

The legislation would apply to about $11 billion in annual elementary and secondary education funding, including the $8 billion Title I program of aid to the disadvantaged, teacher training funds, vocational education, technology assistance, and immigrant education.

The already contentious debate was further complicated by a March 3 Supreme Court decision that expanded disabled individuals' right to a free public education. The ruling gave new impetus to long-standing Republican efforts to increase federal aid under disability laws and set off a new round of political jockeying.

After Democrat Jeff Bingaman of New Mexico on March 4 offered an amendment to provide $150 million to establish a drop-out prevention program, James M. Jeffords, R-Vt., chairman of the Health, Education, Labor and Pensions Committee, offered a substitute to instead direct the aid to education of the disabled. The Senate adopted the Jeffords amendment, 100–0.

A 1975 law (PL 94-142) guaranteed disabled individuals a free, appropriate education. That requirement had imposed enormous costs on public schools.

The Supreme Court appeared to expand the scope of the law, ruling that schools must provide intensive medical care for disabled children. Specifically, the Court ruled that a school district in Iowa must provide all-day nursing care to a quadriplegic boy. When the 1975 law was passed, it was expected that the federal government would cover 40 percent of the costs. Despite recent increases pushed by the GOP, Congress had appropriated only about 10 percent.

In other action the Senate:

• By a 59–40 vote, tabled (killed) an amendment by Dianne Feinstein, D-Calif., that would authorize $500 million in annual grants in fiscal 2000–2004 for remedial education programs and early intervention. To receive funding, states would have to adopt policies ending social promotion. The amendment would also require schools to issue detailed report cards on student achievement, class size, and other quality indicators.

• By a 55–44 vote, tabled an amendment by Barbara Boxer, D-Calif., that would increase funding for an existing network of after-school programs to $600 million a year.

• By a 55–44 vote, tabled an amendment by New Mexico Democrat Jeff Bingaman that would authorize $150 million a year for programs aimed at reducing drop-out rates in middle school and high school. The program would include a national clearinghouse on effective prevention programs.

• By a 57–42 vote, tabled an amendment by Paul Wellstone, D-Minn., that would impose tighter state accountability standards for waivers of vocational education and Title I regulations.

Despite the fierce partisan jockeying, the Senate passed S 280 by an overwhelming 98–1 on March 11. The lone senator to vote against final passage was Wellstone.

HOUSE FLOOR ACTION

The partisan divisions were not confined to the Senate. The House operated under a rule for debate that prevented Rep. William L. Clay, D-Mo., and Rep. David Wu, D-Ore.,

from offering an amendment to add the 100,000-teacher authorization. Other Democratic amendments that would require states to meet tougher standards for student performance in order to receive waivers were also defeated.

The House by a 196–228 vote on March 10 defeated an amendment by George Miller, D-Calif., and Dale E. Kildee, D-Mich., that would require states to set specific goals for reducing achievement gaps between disadvantaged students and their peers and to have a detailed plan to assess performance. The amendment was based on Texas policies.

On March 11, the House also defeated, 195–223, an amendment by Rep. Robert C. Scott, D-Va., and Rep. Donald M. Payne, D-N.J., that would bar waivers for schoolwide Title I programs unless at least 35 percent of students were in poverty. Under current law, schools must have 50 percent of students in poverty to run schoolwide programs.

The Congressional Black Caucus in a March 11 statement said the bill would dilute the Title I program. "The bill is being pushed at stampede speed for seemingly little reason other than the desire to establish a legislative precedent for block grants," said Rep. James E. Clyburn, D-S.C., chairman of the caucus.

In response to the complaints, House and Senate sponsors added more detailed requirements to the bill, such as a House provision ending waivers if student performance declined two years in a row. Some Democrats wanted to go further.

Most of the opposition in the House came from members of the Congressional Black Caucus and other Democrats who were concerned that the bill could undermine federal programs for disadvantaged students. Yet when it came to the final vote, the House bill (HR 800), as with the Senate version, passed by a huge margin, 330–90.

FINAL ACTION

Temporarily papering over sharp partisan differences about how to improve the nation's schools, the conferees reached agreement in mid-April only after Senate Republicans gave up on efforts to loosen provisions in the fiscal 1999 omnibus spending law that allocated $1.2 billion for Clinton's plan to reduce average class size.

In an April 13 letter to conferees, Education Secretary Richard W. Riley said such language, included in the amendment that Lott had added to the Senate version, would undermine Clinton's teacher plan. He promised to recommend that the White House veto the measure unless it was removed.

Although more than thirty senators signed a letter supporting the amendment, thirty-five Senate Democrats in a competing letter promised to vote against the final bill if the provision remained.

Eager to strike a deal, House Republicans gave the Senate little support. "I agree philosophically with the language. . . . I don't think this is the place to do it," said House Education and the Workforce Committee Chairman Bill Goodling, R-Pa.

In a concession to Jeffords, the conferees agreed to add language that would make it slightly easier for schools that had already reduced class size to use their share of the $1.2 billion for teacher training and other purposes.

The omnibus spending bill already provided such authority, but Jeffords said the procedures in the law were too cumbersome to be of much use to small, rural schools in his state.

The compromise bill tightened accountability standards to ensure that states receiving waivers actually improve student achievement. It included an amendment by Wellstone that would prohibit waivers of the requirement that states first allocate Title I aid to schools with more than 75 percent of children in poverty.

Despite the partisan rhetoric over the bill, debate was muted when lawmakers took final action. On April 21 the House adopted the compromise ed-flex conference report (H Rept 106-100), 368–57. Opposition came from Democrats who worried that it could undercut programs designed to assist low-income students. The Senate cleared the measure the same day, 98–1, with Wellstone voting no.

MAJOR PROVISIONS

The following are major provisions of HR 800.

Authority

The law gave the education secretary authority to implement a nationwide program under which state educational agencies could receive waivers of federal rules relating to a list of federal programs, including Title I aid to the disadvantaged, teacher training, or vocational aid for any local educational agency or school within the state.

To be named an eligible "ed-flex" state, state officials must have developed and implemented educational content and student performance standards and aligned tests as required by the 1994 reauthorization of the Elementary and Secondary Education Act (PL 103-382).

States that did not have the standards and assessments in place would still be eligible if they had developed and implemented content standards and pilot tests or other methods for measuring student performance and made substantial progress, as determined by the secretary of education, in developing final standards and assessments and producing school profiles.

States also had to have a procedure in place to hold districts and schools accountable for meeting educational goals outlined in their waiver applications and for taking corrective action in case schools did not meet the higher standards. As a third condition for receiving a waiver of federal regulations, states would have to agree to waive state statutory or regulatory requirements relating to education.

State Application

States that wanted to receive waivers had to submit a formal application to the secretary of education. The application must describe the process the state education agency would use to evaluate requests from local districts or schools

requesting waivers, give a detailed description of state rules to be waived, and clearly describe the objectives of the waiver.

In addition, the application must include a description of how the increased flexibility will complement the state's overall education improvement plan, or, if the state did not have such a plan, how the waiver would mesh with education improvement requirements of the Elementary and Secondary Education Act.

States must describe how they would evaluate the performance of students and local education agencies affected by the waivers and how they would provide for public comment on their proposed plan.

Federal Approval of State Plans

The secretary of education would approve a state plan only if he or she determined that it would provide substantial promise of assisting the state, local districts, and schools in carrying out educational improvements. The secretary would consider whether the state met eligibility requirements, whether the plan was comprehensive and ensured accountability, whether the state goals were clear, and the significance of state laws and regulations to be waived.

Local Applications

Each district or school seeking a waiver would submit an application to the state educational agency. The application would list the affected federal programs and regulations and laws to be waived; describe the overall purpose of waivers; and describe specific, measurable education goals for each district or school.

States would not be able to approve the waivers unless the district or school developed a local improvement plan, the waiver would assist the district or school in meeting its educational goals, and the state was satisfied that the underlying purposes of the laws being waived would continue to be met.

State Termination

States would annually review district or schoolwide waivers. States would terminate waivers if school performance had been inadequate or a school's academic performance had decreased for two consecutive years—unless the state determined that the decline was due to "exceptional and uncontrollable circumstances."

Oversight

Each state must submit an annual report to the secretary of education describing its oversight and the schools receiving waivers. Not less than two years after the date that a state is designated an "ed-flex partnership state" it must include, as part of its annual report, data outlining how waivers have contributed to state goals for improving education.

Required data would include information on the total number of state and federal waivers granted; the effect of waivers on state education improvement plans and student performance; the relationship of the waivers to the performance of students and schools; and an assurance that the data reported are reliable, complete, and accurate.

Not later than two years after enactment and annually thereafter, the secretary of education must submit a report to Congress and the public that summarizes state reports and describes the impact of the act on state initiatives and student performance.

Authority to Issue Waivers

The ed-flex authorization ran from fiscal 1999 through fiscal 2004. In general, the secretary of education could not grant a state authority to issue waivers for longer than five years. The secretary could make exceptions if the state authority had been effective in helping to carry out education improvement plans such as proposals to revamp curriculum and testing, met accountability standards or had improved student performance.

Performance Review

Three years after a state was designated an ed-flex state, the secretary of education must review the performance of the state educational agency in granting waivers. The secretary must terminate a state's authority to grant waivers if it was determined, after notice and an opportunity for a hearing, that the state education agency had failed to adequately implement the law.

When deciding whether to extend a state's waiver authority, the secretary of education must review the progress of the state toward achieving student progress and determining that local districts or schools covered by waivers have moved toward the specific goals outlined in their applications.

Public Notice

Each state and school district seeking waiver authority must provide public notice of the proposal, including a description of the proposed waiver and specific expectations for improved student performance. The notice was to be posted in a "widely read or distributed" medium. Parents, educators, and community members had to have an opportunity to comment. Comments would be submitted to the education secretary as part of state waiver applications.

Education Programs Affected

The ed-flex law applied to the following programs:

• Title I of the Elementary and Secondary Education Act of 1965, which provided compensatory education for low-income and disadvantaged students; the Even Start literacy program; migrant education; and neglected, delinquent, and at-risk youth programs.

• Part B of Title II of the Elementary and Secondary Education Act of 1965, the Eisenhower Professional Development Program of teacher training.

• Subpart 2 of Part A of Title III of the Elementary and Secondary Education Act of 1965 (other than section 3136),

which applied to most education technology assistance programs.

• Title IV of the Elementary and Secondary Education Act of 1965, the Safe and Drug Free Schools and Communities Program.

• Title VI of the Elementary and Secondary Education Act of 1965, Innovative Education Program Strategies.

• Part C of Title VII of the Elementary and Secondary Education Act of 1965, Emergency Immigrant Education.

• The Carl D. Perkins Vocational and Technical Education Act of 1998.

Waivers Not Authorized

The secretary of education and states could not waive statutory or regulatory requirements relating to the following:

• State maintenance of effort regarding funding.

• Comparability of services to all students.

• Equitable participation of students and professional staff in private schools.

• Parental participation and involvement.

• Distribution of funds to states or to local education agencies.

• The requirement to first serve schools under the Title I program where more than 75 percent of students are in poverty. However, the law allowed schools that might not otherwise qualify for Title I to seek program waivers to participate if the percentage of low-income children in the attendance area or school seeking a waiver was not less than 10 percentage points below the lowest percentage of such children for any school or attendance area that met Title I requirements.

• Use of federal funds to supplement, not supplant, non-federal funds.

• Applicable civil rights statutes.

The law allowed for exceptions if the secretary of education was satisfied that the underlying purposes of the program for which a waiver was granted continue to be met.

Existing Ed-Flex States

In general, the law would not apply to states already operating under the ed-flex pilot program. Exceptions included a provision that allowed states to expand existing waivers to include programs under technology assistance programs that provide funding for computers and training in computer technology. States would come under the new law once existing waivers expire.

Further, a notice describing the secretary of education's initial decision to authorize state educational agencies to issue waivers under the pilot program was to be published in the *Federal Register*. The notice was to be distributed to states, educators, advocacy groups and the general public.

Related Provisions

• **Class size reduction.** The act amended a provision of the fiscal 1999 omnibus spending bill (PL 105-277) that provided $1.2 billion to states as a down payment on President

Clinton's long-term plan to hire 100,000 teachers and reduce average class size to eighteen students in the early grades. The ed-flex legislation allowed school districts that had already met the class size goal to use their funds, instead, for professional development programs without having to form a consortium. The original omnibus law required schools that wanted to use the funds for teacher training to band with other, similar school districts to spend the money. That was because the amount of money provided to some districts was so small it would not otherwise be efficient to spend the funds. Lawmakers in rural areas complained, however, that the provision was so cumbersome that schools were unable to use the funds at all.

• **Education of the disabled.** The legislation clarified a provision of the Individuals with Disabilities Education Act (PL 105-17) to make it clear that school officials may discipline disabled students who either carry or possess a weapon at a school, on school premises or at a school function. The provision was an effort to clarify what lawmakers criticized as vague draft regulations.

Education Savings Accounts

The Senate in 2000 passed a bill (S 1134) that would allow families to set aside up to $2,000 per child annually in tax-free accounts for a broad range of education expenses. It also would make permanent a tax exemption for employee-provided education assistance. A similar bill (HR 7) won committee approval in the House, but floor action was blocked by a dispute over a school construction amendment.

The attempt to expand so-called Education IRAs was a priority of Republican leaders. Both the House and Senate versions of the legislation would raise the annual limit on the amount that could be contributed to such an account to $2,000 per child, up from $500 under existing law. In addition, the funds could have been used for prekindergarten through twelfth-grade education expenses, including private school tuition. Existing law restricted the accounts to higher education expenses.

President Clinton vetoed a similar bill in 1998 and threatened to do the same to S 1134. He and other Democratic critics argued that expanding the accounts would do little to benefit low- and middle-income families. They also said use of the accounts should be more limited. Republicans argued that the accounts would encourage personal savings and that no money would be diverted from public schools. *(1998 action, p. 518)*

SENATE COMMITTEE ACTION

The Senate Finance Committee on May 19, 1999, approved S 1134 (S Rept 106-54) on a roll-call vote of 11–5 (the vote was 12–8 including proxies, which the committee did not count in official tallies).

Although the vote broke down mainly across party lines, the measure drew support from three panel Democrats: John

B. Breaux of Louisiana, Bob Graham of Florida, and Bob Kerrey of Nebraska (Kerrey voted for it by proxy). Republicans John H. Chafee of Rhode Island and James M. Jeffords of Vermont voted against it.

As in the 105th Congress, the plan would expand so-called Individual Retirement Accounts for education, or "education IRAs," to cover primary and secondary school expenses, including private school tuition. Under existing law, single tax filers with annual adjusted gross incomes of less than $95,000 and joint filers with less than $150,000 could set aside $500 annually in an education IRA exclusively to pay for the higher-education expenses of a designated beneficiary. Single filers making less than $110,000 and joint filers making less than $160,000 could also qualify, though their contribution amount was more limited. When using that money for education, both the principal and interest could be used tax-free.

The bill would increase the amount taxpayers could save to $2,000 a year from 2000 through 2003 and would allow parents to use the money for tuition, fees, books, home computers, after-school programs, room and board, and other costs related to secondary and primary education.

The Joint Tax Committee estimated that the bill would cost $7.6 billion from fiscal 2000 to 2009, beginning with $331 million in fiscal 2000. The bill contained ten proposed offsets, including a change in accounting methods for some taxpayers.

To garner more support from the administration and Democrats, sponsors made several changes. Unlike the previous year's measure, the bill did not include provisions encouraging states to test teachers or institute a merit pay system. And it included a proposal from President Clinton's fiscal 2000 budget request to remove a sixty-month limit on the deductibility of student loan interest and a Graham plan to liberalize tax-exempt financing rules for public school construction.

The bill also included a provision by Jeff Sessions, R-Ala., that would make distributions from prepaid tuition tax-free whether they were made to state plans, some of which were currently tax-free, or to private plans. The measure would also extend until June 30, 2004, a tax provision that allowed employers to deduct the costs of graduate or undergraduate education provided to employees. The previous year's measure contained similar provisions.

During the markup, conservative Republicans and liberal Democrats argued emotionally over both the bill and an amendment by Charles S. Robb, D-Va., and Kent Conrad, D-N.D., to strike the bill's savings account centerpiece and use the funding to provide tax credits to purchasers of school construction bonds. The proposal, similar to a plan touted by Clinton, would have generated about $25 billion to build and modernize school buildings.

The amendment drew fire from conservatives, such as Majority Whip Don Nickles, R-Okla., and Phil Gramm, R-Texas. Gramm said Robb and Conrad's proposal highlighted the differences between the two parties, with Republicans opting to "try to empower working families" and Democrats favoring money for "bricks and mortar." Robb agreed that the amendment exposed the differences, saying Democrats wanted to "help the most students who are most likely to need assistance," instead of helping parents send their children to private schools.

The amendment was defeated, 8–12, with Graham and all Republicans voting against it.

SENATE FLOOR ACTION

After turning back a series of Democratic amendments, the Senate on March 2, 2000, passed S 1134. But the 61–37 vote was short of the two-thirds margin needed to override President Clinton's threatened veto.

In a Feb. 24 statement, the Office of Management and Budget said the bill's tax benefits were too heavily weighted toward affluent families and would do little to help lower-income and middle-class parents. Still, nine Democrats voted for the measure, sponsored by Paul Coverdell, R-Ga., and Robert G. Torricelli, D-N.J.

On March 2, the Senate adopted, 59–40, a substitute amendment by Finance Committee Chairman William V. Roth Jr., R-Del., that would make the accounts permanent by deleting a provision that would end them after 2003. It eliminated an estimated $5.5 billion worth of revenue-raising provisions that had been designed to help cover the ten-year cost of the measure. Roth said the bill should be funded out of the federal budget surplus.

Another provision in his substitute would make permanent an exclusion from taxable income for employer-provided educational assistance for undergraduate education and extended the provision to graduate studies.

The Senate also adopted a Republican amendment, 54–43, that would allow at least partial eligibility for the program for married couples with combined income of up to $220,000, double the amount for a single parent. The amendment was sponsored by Orrin G. Hatch, R-Utah, and Connie Mack, R-Fla.

The Senate adopted other key changes, including a proposal by Richard J. Durbin, D-Ill., to authorize $7 million for fiscal 2001 and more for succeeding years for violence prevention programs in elementary and secondary schools. The proposal, adopted 91–7, was spurred by the Feb. 29 shooting of a first-grader by her six-year-old classmate in a school near Flint, Mich.

The Senate also adopted:

• By voice vote, a bipartisan amendment that would set aside money, starting with $25 million in 2001, to provide incentives for those switching careers to go into teaching. Clinton had sought funding for that purpose in his budget proposal. The measure would award grants to colleges and universities that train midcareer professionals as teachers. In return for this training, new teachers would agree to work for three years in low-income schools.

• By voice vote, an amendment by Kay Bailey Hutchison, R-Texas, that would provide incentives for military retirees to go into teaching. Small stipends would be available for those who decide to teach in schools of high need.

• By 96–2, a bipartisan amendment to extend from two years to three the age of computers that companies could donate to schools for a tax deduction.

• By 98–0, an amendment by Susan Collins, R-Maine, to let teachers deduct the cost of school supplies and related expenses from their taxes. The National Education Association estimated that teachers spent an average of $408 of their own money on supplies each year.

• By 89–9, an amendment by Paul Wellstone, D-Minn., to require the Department of Health and Human Services' secretary to report on the severity of child poverty in the United States. It would detail changes in child poverty since the 1996 welfare overhaul law (PL 104-193).

However, the Senate rejected, 25–73, a Democratic amendment that would create $5.5 billion in offsets—different from the original bill—to pay for Roth's amendment.

The Senate also rejected Democratic amendments by:

• Edward M. Kennedy of Massachusetts, 39–60, to provide $1.2 billion over five years for teacher training, mentoring, and recruitment programs.

• Kennedy and New Mexico's Jeff Bingaman, 41–57, to take funds that would be used for the savings accounts and increase funding for federal Pell grants by $250 million.

• Christopher J. Dodd of Connecticut, to allocate the estimated $1.2 billion cost of the savings accounts over five years to education for the disabled. The amendment was halted on a 54–44 vote, failing to win the 60 votes necessary to overcome a budget rule that prevented its consideration.

• Dianne Feinstein of California, 30–68, that would threaten states with losing federal education money if they did not have policies directing school jurisdictions to end "social promotion" for students who are not qualified for the next grade.

• Paul Wellstone of Minnesota, 29–69, to Feinstein's amendment that would exempt any child that was not provided an "adequate opportunity" to learn by the state or local school agency.

• Barbara Boxer of California, 49–49, to express the sense of the Senate that before April 20, 2000—the one-year anniversary of shootings in Littleton, Colo.—Congress would implement policies reducing the risk of gun violence in schools.

Although most of the debate focused on the education savings accounts which would sunset by 2003, senators ignored the more expensive provision of the bill: tax breaks for business.

At a cost of $2.6 billion, this provision would continue to give employers a tax exemption for their contributions to undergraduate courses for their employees, and it would add graduate courses to the exemption. The tax break would expire June 30, 2004.

The bill would also make tax-free the money parents contribute to certain prepaid college tuition programs. Many private colleges and forty-three states instituted prepaid tuition programs to help parents prepare for the rising costs of higher education. Currently, the prepaid tuition programs are tax deferred. The provision would cost $959 million over ten years.

HOUSE COMMITTEE ACTION

On March 22, the House Ways and Means Committee approved its version of Education IRA legislation, HR 7, on a mostly party-line vote of 21–16. The lone GOP defector was Nancy L. Johnson of Connecticut.

The House did not take up the bill because moderate Republicans insisted instead on using the money for school construction. The bill (H Rept 106-546), which carried a ten-year price tag of $11.6 billion, would provide more generous deductions for student loan interest payments, offer tax incentives for school modernization and construction, and permit private colleges to offer tax-exempt prepaid tuition plans.

Johnson teamed with Charles B. Rangel, D-N.Y., on an unsuccessful amendment that would kill the education savings account expansion and replace it with a school modernization proposal that was backed by the White House. The Johnson-Rangel proposal would set up a tax credit to pay the interest on $24.8 billion in school modernization bonds. That would help states and school districts "do what they really want to do," said Rangel, while education savings accounts would just be "tax gimmicks."

The proposal would help states and school districts offer $22 billion in bonds, with 60 percent going to states and 40 percent going to the school districts with the highest number of low-income students. The rest of the federal aid would go to Bureau of Indian Affairs schools and an expansion of the Qualified Zone Academy Bond program, which helped schools in low-income neighborhoods. The amendment was defeated by voice vote.

But one week later, a group of moderate Republicans threw their weight behind the school construction initiative. Led by Johnson, the group of about a dozen GOP members demanded a floor vote on the plan. With virtually all House Democrats in their camp, the moderates appeared to have enough votes to win on a planned motion to recommit the savings account bill to the Ways and Means Committee. The situation threatened to turn into a political nightmare for GOP leaders as the education agenda shifted from their priorities to President Clinton's—thanks to Johnson and the other moderates.

The House deadlock may have looked like a clear-cut disagreement between savings account supporters on one side and school construction advocates on the other, but the reality was more complicated.

There were moderate Republicans who, like most Democrats, were uneasy with the idea that parents could use tax-free savings to send their kids to private schools. "I fail to see how denying resources to public schools improves public education," said Sherwood Boehlert, R-N.Y.

And then there were Republicans such as Fred Upton, R-Mich., who liked both the education savings accounts and the school modernization bill. "I'd rather make it an add-on," Upton said of the school bond legislation, rather than a replacement for savings accounts.

Some Democrats might have crossed over and voted for savings accounts, as they did in the Senate. The problem for GOP leaders was that they could not count on those Democrats to vote against a motion to recommit.

Rather than face defeat on the floor, Republican leaders postponed debate indefinitely.

Financial Aid

Lawmakers in 2000 easily cleared legislation (S 1455—PL 106-420) that targeted individuals and companies that purported to help students obtain financial aid for a fee but instead provided misleading or false information.

In 1996 the Federal Trade Commission (FTC) initiated "Project Scholarscam," a joint law enforcement and consumer education campaign. But despite the efforts of the FTC, colleges, universities, and nongovernmental organizations to make consumers more aware of scholarship fraud, a significant amount of fraudulent activity continued to occur. S 1455 sought to augment the 1996 program.

The measure directed the U.S. Sentencing Commission to establish penalties for offenses involving fraud or misrepresentation in connection with student scholarships, grants or loans. It would require the Justice and Education Departments and the FTC to submit a joint annual report to Congress on college scholarship fraud that occurred during the previous year.

It also would require the Education Department and the FTC to establish a scholarship fraud awareness Web site that would feature examples of common fraudulent schemes, a list of companies and people who have been convicted of scholarship fraud, a message-board, a reporting system, and Internet links. The department would be required to submit an annual report detailing the extent of college loan fraud from the previous year.

The Senate Judiciary Committee approved the measure on Oct. 28, 1999, without a written report. The Senate passed it by unanimous consent Nov. 4. The House cleared it by voice vote on Sept. 25, 2000. The president signed it Nov. 1, 2000.

National Award for Arts Education

Lawmakers in 2000 cleared a measure to help establish a new national award for arts education. The bill (S 2789—PL 106-533) amended the Congressional Award Act to establish a nine-member Congressional Recognition for the Excellence in Arts Education Awards Board, appointed by congressional leaders, as well as a fifteen-member advisory board, consisting of artistic and educational professionals, appointed to assist and advise the congressional board.

Both boards would be responsible for administering annual awards to elementary and secondary schools demonstrating excellence in arts education. The bill established a trust fund to carry out the provisions under the measure and authorized the board to accept nongovernmental donations. No federal funds were authorized under the measure.

"This bill sends a clear message of support and appreciation to those teachers in our schools who dedicate their lives to the teaching of music, art, theater and dance; and to those school administrators who support comprehensive arts programs," said Sen. Thad Cochran, R-Miss., who sponsored the measure.

In addition to deciding who would receive the awards, the congressional and citizen boards would determine how best to reward the recipients. The legislation established a trust fund for the awards but did not authorize any appropriations.

The bill, which did not go through committee, was passed by the Senate on Oct. 27 by unanimous consent. The House cleared it by voice vote on Oct. 31. President Clinton signed it Nov. 22, 2000.

Sex Offenders on Campus

Colleges and universities receiving federal funds would have to publish the names of students convicted of violent sex crimes, under a bill the House passed by voice vote on June 12, 2000. The Senate did not act on it.

The measure (HR 4504) would be an extension of Megan's Law (PL 104-145), which required state and local police to release information about violent sexual predators. Supporters said many universities did not provide the information to students or parents.

The bill also would make mostly technical changes to the Higher Education Act, last amended in 1998 (PL 105-244). Those would include programs to encourage new students to enroll in higher education programs, and a requirement that schools notify parents about their policies on investigation and notification when a student is reported missing. *(Higher Education Act, p. 509)*

In addition, HR 4504 would clarify repayment terms for student loans and mandate notification to parents and students about the status of fire alarms and sprinklers in dormitories.

Although the House Education and the Workforce Committee on May 25 agreed by voice vote to amend the higher education measure with the sexual offender language, some Democrats on the committee had concerns about the provision. "Pretty soon we'll have people wearing buttons. How far do we go?" asked Donald M. Payne, D-N.J. "I'm as concerned as anyone else about sexual predators, but I think we're taking this Megan's Law too far."

But Matt Salmon, R-Ariz., who sponsored the amendment, dismissed arguments that the law identified and stigmatized specific criminals.

Democrats also sought to strike bill language concerning how students convicted of some drug crimes would lose eligibility for federal funds. The bill would clarify the law that students convicted of drug possession or distribution would lose federal eligibility for a year, unless they enter a treatment program and pass chemical tests. Repeat offenders would lose all eligibility after a third violation. A Democratic amendment to strike the provision was rejected 16–30.

The committee adopted an amendment that would allow public defenders and prosecutors who make less than $30,000 in adjusted annual income to be eligible for the same student loan forgiveness programs established for police officers and prison guards. Then it approved the bill by voice vote (H Rept 106-665).

Historic Buildings

The House in 2000 passed legislation (HR 4503) to preserve historic buildings at seven traditionally women's colleges, but the Senate did not act on the measure. The seven institutions were: Mississippi University for Women, Columbus; University of Montevallo, Montevallo, Ala.; Georgia College and State University, Milledgeville; Winthrop University in Rock Hill, S.C.; University of North Carolina at Greensboro; Texas Women's University, Denton; and University of Science and Arts of Oklahoma, Chickasha.

The institutions were created as industrial schools for women in 1884 after women began pressing for the same sort of educational opportunities that were available for men through government-funded agricultural and mechanical colleges. The institutions remained open and were currently providing coed education in liberal arts.

HR 4503 would authorize up to $14 million from the National Historic Preservation Fund to be distributed equally among the institutions. State and local governments would have to match 50 percent of the funds.

The House Resources Committee approved the bill by voice vote Sept. 20 (H Rept 106-915). The House passed it by voice vote Oct. 3.

Tuition for D.C. Students

District of Columbia high school graduates would get help paying tuition at state colleges in Maryland and Virginia under legislation (HR 974—PL 106-98) cleared by Congress in 1999.

The bill established a grant program to allow D.C. students to pay in-state tuition rates at Maryland and Virginia state colleges and universities. It authorized $12 million in fiscal 2000 to cover the difference between in-state and out-of-state tuition and "such sums as are necessary" to run the program through the next five fiscal years.

District students were eligible for up to $10,000 a year, paid directly to the school, or a total of $50,000. Students also were eligible to receive up to $2,500 in grants to attend private schools in neighboring counties or to attend historically black private schools in Maryland and Virginia.

The far more expansive version of HR 974 began moving on April 15, when the House Government Reform Subcommittee on the District of Columbia gave it voice vote approval. The original bill would allow high school graduates from the District of Columbia to attend public colleges or universities anywhere in the country at in-state tuition rates.

Graduating seniors who had lived in the District for at least a year would be allotted up to $10,000 to offset the difference between the tuition normally charged for an out-of-state student at a state school and that charged a resident of the state. The Washington city government would pay the funds, which would come from the federal government and private donations, directly to the school.

Supporters of the legislation described it as part of the subcommittee's effort to offer incentives for individuals to remain residents of the District.

The panel approved by voice vote a substitute amendment by chairman Thomas M. Davis III, R-Va., the sponsor of the bill. That amendment would provide qualified applicants with up to $3,000 a year in federal funds to pay tuition at private colleges and universities in the District of Columbia, Maryland, or Virginia.

"The same choices and opportunities simply do not exist for students and parents here as exist elsewhere. This has too often led to an out-migration of population in order to take advantage of the educational opportunities all other Americans enjoy as residents of a particular state," said Davis.

On May 19 the full Government Reform panel gave voice vote approval to the measure (H Rept 106-158, Pt. I). The House passed it by voice vote May 24.

The Senate on Oct. 19 passed a narrower version of the bill by unanimous consent. The Senate version would allow the District to provide up to $10,000 per year, and up to $50,000 over the course of a student's college career, to each eligible student who attends a public college in Maryland or Virginia. Students also could receive up to $2,500 per year toward private school tuition, with up to $12,500 total, for colleges in the District of Columbia and several surrounding counties.

The District city government office would award scholarships to each qualified graduate submitting an application who meets certain eligibility requirements, such as residency in the District during the year before college, and university attendance within three years of receiving a high school diploma.

The bill authorized a total cost of $17 million. It would only apply to students graduating high school after Jan. 1, 1999.

The House cleared the bill, with the Senate changes, on Nov. 1 by voice vote. President Clinton signed the measure on Nov. 12, 1999.

Department of Education Audit

The House in 2000 responded to a series of hearings into the Department of Education's ability to do basic bookkeeping by overwhelmingly passing a bill calling for a fraud audit of the department. The Senate took no action on the measure.

The bill (HR 4079), sponsored by Peter Hoekstra, R-Mich., chairman of the House Education and the Workforce Subcommittee on Oversight and Investigations, would require the General Accounting Office to audit any Department of Education accounts it considered susceptible to waste, fraud, and abuse.

The Education and the Workforce Committee approved it by voice vote May 25 (H Rept 106-666). The House passed it by a vote of 380–19 on June 13.

In a statement, Hoekstra, who held hearings on the issue in December and March, said the audit was needed to make the department more accountable and put an end to repeated breakdowns in its management practices. Hoekstra said the department had failed its last two annual audits and was plagued by fraud and abuse. He said the department sent out $175 million in duplicate checks to contractors and grant recipients earlier in 2000. He also claimed that more than $300,000 in equipment was stolen and the agency bilked out of $600,000 in overtime pay over the past three years.

In response, Erica Lepping, a department spokesperson, noted that all departments were already audited by inspectors general and said the Education Department inspector general was "well-suited to continue in [that] role at no additional cost to the taxpayers." She said all the money paid out in duplicate checks had been recovered and the department official alleged to be responsible for the thefts was being prosecuted. The audits, she said, did not find any evidence of fraud and abuse.

The Senate Health, Education, Labor, and Pensions Committee gave voice vote approval to a similar bill (S 2829—S Rept 106-448) Oct. 2. But the full Senate did not act on it.

National Academy

The House Early Childhood, Youth and Families Subcommittee of the House Education and the Workforce Committee in 2000 approved legislation to let the Department of Education oversee a new agency that would conduct educational research and improve teaching techniques. The bill (HR 4875) passed the subcommittee on a voice vote July 26. Lawmakers took no further action on the measure.

Republicans originally wanted to establish the agency—the National Academy for Education Research, Statistics, Evaluation and Information—outside the Department of Education. They amended the bill after Democrats complained the academy could not effectively monitor some education-related programs if it operated outside the education department.

Subcommittee chairman Michael N. Castle, R-Del., agreed that, even inside the Education Department, the academy would operate with greater independence than the individual department offices whose functions the academy would inherit. "There must be change," Castle said. "Precisely how we're going to do that may vary." He added that the reorganization would improve the quality and objectivity of the government's education research.

The academy would be run by a director appointed by the president and confirmed by the Senate. Under a Castle amendment approved by the subcommittee, the secretary of education would delegate research and related activities to the new director.

The academy would oversee three national centers for education research, program evaluation and development, and educational statistics, as well as a national education library.

The legislation would authorize $368.6 million a year for the academy from fiscal 2002 through 2006. It also would give the National Assessment Governing Board more authority in putting together the National Assessment of Educational Progress, also known as the Nation's Report Card.

Students Abroad

The House in 2000 passed a measure to provide some college students with additional financial aid to help pay for overseas study programs. The bill (HR 4528) would authorize $1.5 million annually. Under the program, the State Department would provide grants of up to $5,000 to U.S. students who had been accepted for an academic year of study at an overseas college or university.

The grants, to be named for International Relations Committee Chairman Benjamin A. Gilman, R-N.Y., would be available only to students in good academic standing and already receiving federal financial aid.

The International Affairs Committee approved the bill by voice vote June 29 without a written report, and the House passed it by voice vote July 11. The Senate did not take action on it.

CHAPTER 11

Housing and Urban Aid

Introduction   553

1997–1998 Chronology   555

1999–2000 Chronology   564

Housing and Urban Aid

Public housing, a New Deal program created by the U.S. Housing Act of 1937, was envisioned to operate much similar to welfare, as a temporary home for those who found themselves briefly out of work. But in the decades since the law's enactment, public housing increasingly became a permanent warehouse for the poor, many of whom lacked the training or skills needed to hold a job. Most public housing was located in inner cities or rural areas, both of which lacked job opportunities.

The impetus for revamping the housing system began building as housing authorities increasingly found themselves with growing federal mandates and shrinking operating funds. Since the 1970s, the federal government required that locally run public housing authorities, generally made up of community officials appointed by the city council, reserve public housing for their poorest areas, charge rents no greater than 30 percent of income (which meant those with no income paid no rent), and replace each housing unit they demolished.

During the 1970s and 1980s, federal housing policy was an ideological battleground between congressional Democrats who wanted the government to provide more low-income housing and Republicans who wanted to get government out of the housing business. Democrats focused on tying the hands of federal bureaucrats, who, under President Ronald Reagan, had permitted housing authorities to tear down public housing units without any plans for replacing them. But the resulting restrictions, coupled with a lack of funds, often meant that dilapidated projects were kept in place.

HOUSING REFORM

When Democrats controlled Congress, subsidies to housing authorities increased or held steady, in part because most Democrats believed in paying the cost to ensure public housing went to the poorest people. The political dynamics changed drastically when Democrats, with encouragement from the Clinton administration, joined Republicans in embracing legislation to give state and local officials more control over housing programs. The Republican takeover of Congress in 1995 pushed congressional thinking even further. Republicans included the Department of Housing and Urban Development (HUD) among the federal agencies they hoped to eliminate. Such efforts never got off the ground, in large part because of the Clinton administration's willingness to remake the troubled department as well as the moderate Republicans' unwillingness to eliminate a department that oversaw 1.25 million housing units that provided homes to about three million people. Nevertheless, Republicans, who saw HUD as wasteful, were determined to make changes. One of the GOP Congress's first fiscal acts was to rescind $6.5 billion in housing funds to pay for California disaster relief and other emergencies.

Moderate Republicans and Democrats who supported public housing felt that, with the loss of funds, already stringent federal housing guidelines would be a noose around housing authorities' necks. These lawmakers moved to reform the guidelines. Changes enacted in the 104th Congress aimed to enable housing authorities to generate more cash from nonfederal sources, such as their tenants. For example, a 1996 appropriations measure required housing authorities to charge minimum rents of $25 to $50 per month, even for residents with no income. Another provision, also enacted in the stopgap spending bill (PL 104-99), waived federal rules that required local authorities to give priority to applicants in the worst financial conditions. But the changes, renewed

REFERENCES

Discussion of housing and urban aid action for the years 1945–1964 may be found in *Congress and the Nation Vol. I*, pp. 459–515; for the years 1965–1968, *Congress and the Nation Vol. II*, pp. 183–226; for the years 1969–1972, *Congress and the Nation Vol. III*, pp. 635–657; for the years 1973–1976, *Congress and the Nation Vol. IV*, pp. 471–502; for the years 1977–1980, *Congress and the Nation Vol. V*, pp. 429–448; for the years 1981–1984, *Congress and the Nation Vol. VI*, pp. 629–639; for the years 1985–1988, *Congress and the Nation Vol. VII*, pp. 667–684; for the years 1989–1992, *Congress and the Nation Vol. VIII*, pp. 663–700; for the years 1993–1996, *Congress and the Nation Vol. IX*, pp. 637–650.

Outlays for Community and Regional Development

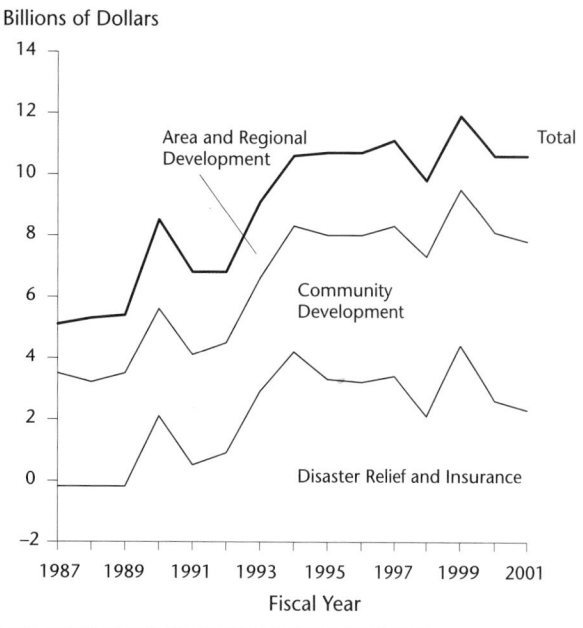

Billions of Dollars

Area and Regional Development

Total

Community Development

Disaster Relief and Insurance

Fiscal Year

NOTE: Data for 2001 are estimated.

SOURCE: Office of Management and Budget, *Historical Tables, Budget of the United States Government: Fiscal Year 2002* (Washington, D.C.: U.S. Government Printing Office, 2001), Table 3.2.

in subsequent annual appropriations bills, suspended requirements only one year at a time. Some housing authorities, fearing a political turnover or change of heart, stuck to their old rules and saw their financial situations worsen. Even the housing authorities who made the changes still felt extremely strapped for cash, largely because of reduced federal subsidies.

Furthermore, HUD secretary Henry G. Cisneros and his successor, Andrew M. Cuomo, proposed drastic staffing cuts and organizational changes to the department. They also recognized that if housing programs were to survive in increasingly tight budget years, they would have to have more flexible rules; many Republicans in Congress agreed. Key GOP committee chairmen—Rep. Rick A. Lazio of New York

and Sen. Connie Mack of Florida, who chaired the House and Senate Banking subcommittees responsible for housing, introduced bills to loosen many requirements on housing authorities in an effort to improve the cash flow of housing projects.

The story of public housing reform had long been one of apathy, missed opportunities, and territorialism. Compromise was elusive in part because some members staked out territory mainly to prevent others from gaining a political foothold in the overhaul legislation. Some interest groups were not enthusiastic about change, preferring the ineffective system they knew to the one they did not. Other issues, such as how far to go in revamping the housing system, also continued to divide lawmakers and lobbyists.

To be sure, Congress managed to reach beyond the authorizers to modernize housing laws, particularly laws on subsidized housing, through the appropriations process. Where appropriators did not act, HUD stepped in. Both worked to give local housing authorities more control over the tenants they choose, the rents they charge, and the units they demolish. But the failure to pass an overhaul measure had political and practical ramifications.

OVERHAUL AGREEMENT

The Republican-led Congress was criticized for missing an opportunity to fulfill what GOP leaders once described as the second step—after the 1996 welfare reform effort—in transforming the nation's social policy by transferring power to states and localities. Congress's failure to act also kept in limbo those who provided and lived in the nation's publicly funded housing units. Public housing authorities, continually strapped for money, found it more and more difficult to plan ahead. Residents faced the same problem: one-third of welfare recipients lived in public housing, and under the welfare law, most were required to get jobs.

Finally, a three-year logjam was broken in 1998, when proponents of overhauling the nation's public housing program shepherded legislation through Congress and onto the president's desk for his signature. The new law gave local housing authorities greater flexibility to choose tenants, set rents, and make funding decisions.

Chronology of Action on Housing and Urban Aid

1997–1998

Public Housing

Congress in 1998 replaced existing public housing and low-income rental assistance programs with block grants to local housing authorities, which gained greater latitude in using the funds for locally tailored housing programs. The action came when public housing overhaul legislation (HR 2) was attached to the fiscal 1999 appropriations bill (HR 4194—PL 105-276) for the departments of Veterans Affairs (VA) and Housing and Urban Development (HUD).

1997 LEGISLATIVE ACTION

For the second time in as many years, Republican plans to overhaul New Deal-era housing laws stalled in 1997 as the House and Senate failed to agree on how far to go in rewriting public and subsidized housing programs. *(1995–1996 action, Congress and the Nation Vol. IX, p. 645)*

House Committee Action

The House Banking and Financial Services Committee approved HR 2 by 28–19, largely along party lines, on April 23, 1997. The measure was formally reported (H Rept 105-76) on April 25. A supplemental report (H Rept 105-76, Pt. II) was filed on April 29. Republicans praised HR 2 as a blueprint for moving people off government dependency and into self-sufficiency. Democrats said the bill was too prescriptive and would fail to protect those with extremely low incomes. Some predicted that, if enacted, the measure would lead to increased homelessness nationwide.

The committee-approved measure would repeal the U.S. Housing Act of 1937, deregulate public housing and rental assistance programs, and increase community control over such programs. The bill included provisions to:

• Shift more control and decision-making responsibilities from the federal government to local housing authori-

ties, and allow housing authorities to create alternative programs to complement existing initiatives.

• Revise the so-called Brooke Amendment (named after former senator Edward W. Brooke, R-Mass., 1967–1979), which limited rent for public housing tenants to 30 percent of their adjusted income. Under that system, the rent automatically increased when the tenant earned more money, providing a disincentive to work. The bill would allow local housing agencies to offer tenants a choice between paying 30 percent of their income in rent as they did under existing law or paying a presumably lower flat rent that they could negotiate with the housing authority.

• Require that unemployed, able-bodied public housing tenants who were not on welfare perform eight hours a month of community service. Welfare recipients were already subject to work requirements.

• Require the federal government to move quickly to assume control of dysfunctional housing authorities by direct takeover or by placing such agencies in receivership.

Existing law required that about 75 percent of tenants in public housing projects earn no more than 30 percent of the median income in their local area. The vast majority of such tenants were unemployed and received public assistance such as welfare or Social Security disability benefits. The bill proposed to alter the ratio by requiring that 65 percent of new tenants be from the so-called working poor—those who held jobs but lived at or below the poverty line. The remaining 35 percent of new residents would be those earning no more than 30 percent of the median income.

Republicans contended that increasing the percentage of working poor residents in public housing through such income mixing or "income targeting" would improve the culture in troubled housing projects and ultimately reduce incidents of crime and the presence of gangs and drugs. But Democrats said such income mixing would pit poor people against each other. Joseph P. Kennedy II, D-Mass., tried unsuccessfully to amend the income targeting provisions. He proposed that at least 40 percent of new public housing tenants have incomes at 30 percent or less of an area's median income and that no less than 90 percent of new residents have incomes at or below 60 percent of the median income. He proposal was defeated 25–26.

Committee Amendments

The committee defeated a number of other amendments aimed at softening what Democrats saw as harsh treatment of tenants under the bill. The panel April 16 rejected:

• An amendment by Jesse L. Jackson Jr., D-Ill., 19–26, to remove the proposed community service requirements.

• A Jackson amendment, 14–26, to delete language allowing public housing tenants to be evicted if they failed to comply with community service requirements.

• A Jackson proposal, 17–23, to define the bill's work, job training, and educational requirements as an unfunded federal mandate and to require the government to pay for it.

• An amendment by Melvin Watt, D-N.C., 15–27, to remove the community service requirements.

• An amendment by Barney Frank, D-Mass., 13–24, to make the work, job training, and educational requirements optional and to place them under the purview of local housing authorities.

• An amendment by Maxine Waters, D-Calif., and Carolyn Cheeks Kilpatrick, D-Mich., 17–24, to retain existing law permitting tenants suspected of noncriminal infractions to appear before housing review boards made up of their peers before being evicted from housing projects.

• An amendment by Nydia M. Velázquez, D-N.Y., 16–22, to set minimum rents at public housing projects at zero to $25 a month instead of the $25 to $50 a month in the bill. The amendment also would allow "hardship cases"—those who could not afford to pay any rent—to be determined by HUD, not by local housing authorities.

• A Waters proposal, 19–20, to require that when new housing units were constructed on land previously owned or occupied by a public housing authority, at least one-third of the units be reserved for low-income families.

The committee April 16 did adopt by voice vote a Waters amendment to require housing authorities to collect demographic data about poor people—those whose incomes did not exceed 30 percent of the median—who failed to receive housing assistance.

The panel considered a slew of other amendments April 23. It acted to:

• Defeat, 19–29, a Kennedy amendment to eliminate the new Home Rule Flexibility Grant proposal. Under the initiative, localities would apply for federal block grants to be drawn from the housing dollars allocated to a community. With HUD's approval, such money could be used to develop housing initiatives that could compete with or complement

existing programs. Republicans said this would foster cooperation between local governments and housing authorities.

• Reject, 14–27, an amendment by Luis V. Gutierrez, D-Ill., to delete language authorizing HUD to increase income eligibility levels to allow more communities—in some cases, better-off communities—to receive money under the Community Development Block Grant program and the HOME initiative. The block grant provided funds to localities for affordable housing and urban renewal. HOME provided funds to encourage home ownership in low-income areas.

• Reject, 19–26, an amendment by Bruce F. Vento, D-Minn., to eliminate a provision to permit HUD to impose sanctions on dysfunctional housing authorities by withholding Community Development Block Grant money.

• Reject, by voice vote, a Vento amendment to replace the proposed public housing accreditation board, which would approve the operations of local housing agencies, with a less powerful performance evaluation board to assist HUD in monitoring local housing authorities.

• Approve, by voice vote, a Vento amendment to extend the Community Partnership Against Crime program from one year to five years, ending in fiscal 2002. The program provided funds to housing authorities to pay for security measures such as fences, security guards, and increased police presence.

• Approve, by voice vote, an amendment by House Banking and Financial Services Subcommittee on Housing and Community Development Chairman Rick A. Lazio, R-N.Y., Kennedy, House Banking Committee Chairman Jim Leach, R-Iowa, and ranking committee Democrat Henry B. Gonzalez of Texas to authorize HUD to retain unspent funds from the Section 8 subsidized housing program to pay for Section 8 contracts or renewals. Under existing law, such contracts could be reallocated for other purposes.

• Approve, by voice vote, an amendment by Michael N. Castle, R-Del., to give housing authorities access to state and local registries of sex offenders. Such lists could be used to screen adult applicants for public housing assistance.

- Approve, by voice vote, a Watt amendment to stipulate that HUD would not establish national occupancy standards for public housing.

House Floor Action

As House debate opened on HR 2, the Clinton administration offered its assessment, saying it supported many of the bill's objectives and provisions as well as the "determination to enact long overdue program reforms." But it added that unless several provisions were amended, it would oppose the legislation. Specifically, the White House opposed the income-eligibility level, instead favoring the existing requirement that 75 percent of public housing residents earn 30 percent or less of an area's median income. The administration also said the minimum rent for public housing and subsidized rental units should be $25 per month, not the bill's range of $25 to $50 per month. The White House also opposed the creation of a Housing Evaluation and Accreditation Board.

During floor debate, Democrats took particular exception to the proposed community service requirements. Watt raised a question as to whether consideration of the bill could be blocked on the basis that the community service provisions would impose an unfunded mandate on the localities that had to administer them. The House voted 237–183 on May 1 to consider the bill. Also on May 1, the House rejected a Jackson amendment, 160–251, to eliminate a provision requiring housing authorities to evict tenants who failed to meet the community service requirement; a Jackson amendment, 181–216, to exempt from the community service requirement single parents, grandparents, or spouses who were the primary caregivers for children ages six or younger; and an amendment by Dave Weldon, R-Fla., 153–252, to exempt 20 percent of the people that would have been exempted under the Jackson amendment.

Watt offered an amendment, rejected 140–286 on May 6, to require that public housing residents who participated in the community service program be paid at least the prevailing minimum wage. Democrats argued that requiring people to work without pay was equivalent to involuntary servitude, which was outlawed by the Thirteenth Amendment. A Frank amendment, defeated 168–253 on May 6, would have made the community service requirement optional. The amendment also would have made optional a requirement that certain tenants sign agreements with their housing authorities establishing a target date for moving out of public housing.

By voice vote, the House adopted a Lazio amendment to prohibit anyone classified as a "sexually violent predator" from receiving public housing assistance; an amendment by Sheila Jackson-Lee, D-Texas, to encourage, but not require, contractors working in public housing projects to employ residents of such communities in some capacity; and a Kennedy amendment to increase from $2.5 billion to $3.7 billion the measure's annual authorization for capital grants

and from $2.9 billion to $3.2 billion the bill's fiscal 1998 authorization for operating grants.

Kennedy tried unsuccessfully to require that owners of public rental units perform the same eight hours a month of community service that the bill expected of tenants. The House rejected his amendment, 87–341, on May 13.

In other action the same day, the House:

- Approved, by voice vote, an amendment by Edolphus Towns, D-N.Y., to require HUD to include in its performance standards for a housing authority whether it had identified and tried to eradicate pest problems, such as cockroach infestations.

- Rejected, 162–260, a Kennedy amendment to require that 75 percent of housing vouchers be given to families with incomes below 30 percent of the area's median income.

- Rejected, 153–270, a Kennedy amendment to strike a provision allowing low-income housing programs developed and administered by local governments to be eligible for federal public housing funds.

- Rejected, 200–228, a Vento amendment to strike provisions to create a Housing Evaluation and Accreditation Board to evaluate the performance of local housing authorities.

- Rejected, 145–282, an amendment by Danny K. Davis, D-Ill., to allow HUD, when it took over or replaced the management of a troubled public housing authority, to exempt tenants and families that received rental assistance from the community service work requirements.

Kennedy offered a substitute amendment that, like the bill, would consolidate public housing programs into two block grants and require local housing authorities to submit a management plan to HUD. Unlike the bill, however, the Kennedy amendment would reserve 75 percent of tenant housing vouchers for families with incomes below 30 percent of the area's median income and would deny vouchers to those earning more than 50 percent of an area's median income. The amendment would establish minimum rents of zero to $25 a month, compared with $25 to $50 in the bill, with exemptions for legal immigrants who lost their welfare benefits. Local housing authorities would be allowed to adopt any minimum rent within the acceptable range. The House rejected the Kennedy substitute amendment, 163–261, on May 14 and then rejected by voice vote a Kennedy effort to send the bill back to committee.

The full House passed HR 2 on May 14 on a **key vote of 293–132 (R 222–1; D 71–130; I 0–1)**. *(1997 key votes, p. 865)*

Senate Action

In contrast with House consideration of HR 2, the Senate Banking, Housing, and Urban Affairs Committee marked up its version of the bill (S 462) quickly and quietly. The measure was approved, 18–0, on May 8 and formally reported (S Rept 105-21) on May 23. Republicans said the legislation would dramatically improve the operation of local housing authorities while increasing the livability of many housing projects. Democrats said that although the bill would do much to improve public housing, many aspects of the existing program worked well.

Like HR 2, S 462 would grant more control to local housing authorities and require more community involvement by housing residents. It included a requirement that able-bodied adults residing in public housing perform at least eight hours of community service a month; residents could also fulfill the requirement by taking literacy or job training courses. Despite their similarities, the Senate bill was much less sweeping. For example, it proposed to amend, not repeal, the 1937 U.S. Housing Act, and it did not call for the same rent flexibility as HR 2.

The committee adopted, by voice vote, an amendment by Jack Reed, D-R.I., to allow local authorities to reduce rents for tenants whose welfare benefits were cut as a result of the 1996 welfare overhaul law (PL 104-193). The panel rejected, by voice vote, an amendment by Robert F. Bennett, R-Utah, to strike language requiring that public housing agencies permit tenants to own pets. Federal laws permitted pets under certain circumstances. *(Welfare reform, Congress and the Nation Vol. IX, p. 578)*

The Senate did not take up S 462 until Sept. 26, when it passed the measure by voice vote with little fanfare or discussion. In the interim, Housing Opportunity and Community Development Subcommittee Chairman Connie Mack, R-Fla., and his staff worked with Democrats to fashion a bill that senators could easily accept. Mack and his staff were also distracted by an ongoing disagreement with Leach and Lazio over whether to include a fix for the Section 8 subsidized housing program in the fiscal 1998 appropriations bill to fund HUD, veterans programs, and independent agencies. *(HUD cost reductions, p. 562)*

Among the most controversial issues was the proposal to give public housing authorities more incentives to attract the working poor to public housing, thereby creating a greater mix of incomes in public and subsidized housing. According to the Senate Banking Committee, under the existing system, the average public housing resident made less than 20 percent of median area income. Democrats argued that increasing rents and loosening other requirements would prompt local authorities to evict their poorest residents and replace them with tenants who could pay more. Mack agreed to compromise, increasing the percentage of housing vouchers the bill would set aside for those with very low incomes under the Section 8 program.

Under the agreement, which the Senate adopted as part of a manager's amendment to the bill, housing authorities would have to distribute no less than 65 percent of the vouchers—up from 50 percent in the original bill—to the very poor. Mack also agreed to add a requirement that at least 90 percent of the vouchers would go to people who earned less than 60 percent of an area's median income. Remaining vouchers could go to people who made 80 percent or less. The bill's income requirements for public and Section 8 subsidized housing were also changed. At least 40 per-

cent of units would have to be occupied by the very poor. At least 70 percent—down from 75 percent—would have to be occupied by those who made no more than 60 percent of the median income, and the remainder could go to those who made no more than 80 percent.

1998 LEGISLATIVE ACTION

Despite a desire by some congressional leaders to show-case housing reform as the second step—after welfare reform—toward revamping the social safety net, efforts to work out the differences among proposals to overhaul public housing had failed over the years. While in 1998 the legislation appeared to be headed for the same fate, the House revived the issue when on July 17 it attached its version of the housing bill (HR 2) to the fiscal 1999 VA-HUD appropriations bill (HR 4194) by a **key vote of 230–181 (R 215–4; D 15–176; I 0–1)**. *(1998 key votes, p. 883)*

That action rejuvenated talks between the two chambers of Congress and the administration, which eventually led to an agreement. Some staff members involved in negotiations and lobbyists following the process said that although HUD secretary Andrew M. Cuomo and Lazio deserved credit for their ideas and commitment, the responsibility for holding the bill together went largely to two senators who stayed in the background—Mack and Banking Committee ranking Democrat Paul S. Sarbanes of Maryland. Mack and Sarbanes met on several occasions over the summer whenever it appeared that talks on the housing bill were collapsing. Time and again, each would agree to keep the process going: Mack would talk to Lazio and Sarbanes to Cuomo.

A major issue that held up Democratic and administration support for the plan was their desire to provide 100,000 more Section 8 vouchers to help low-income people pay their rents in private apartments. Everyone at the table agreed that more vouchers were needed, but authorizers could not make that commitment. That was up to the appropriators, who would have to find $500 million to pay for the new vouchers. Appropriators finally came up with half that much, providing 50,000 new permanent vouchers and agreeing to drop a controversial provision to impose a three-month holdover period between the time that a previous tenant returned a voucher and a new tenant could receive it.

Among the last items to be settled were issues brought up by Cuomo and Lazio. Cuomo wanted to move Operation Safe Home, a public housing anticrime initiative, from the jurisdiction of HUD's inspector general to HUD or the Justice Department. Lazio wanted to force HUD to raise income standards for the Community Development Block Grant program, often used to spruce up low-income neighborhoods, and the HOME program, which helped low-income people buy their own homes. The inspector general provision was not included in the bill. The bill did contain language that would require HUD within ninety days to set new income limits for Community Development Block Grant and HOME eligibility in at least ten geographic areas.

VA-HUD Spending Bill

In several respects, the housing provisions in the final VA-HUD spending bill were an amalgam of the House, Senate, and administration proposals. Both Democrats and Republicans believed that housing authorities and their tenants would be better off if public housing no longer served as a warehouse for the poorest of the poor. All sides agreed that a certain number of higher-income, working tenants should be allowed into public or subsidized housing. But they disagreed on how much should be reserved for the very poor, who at that time occupied most of that housing. The final measure would require housing authorities to reserve at least 40 percent of public housing for the very poor—those making 30 percent or less of an area's median income. That provision was similar to one in the Senate version of the bill (S 462). Regarding Section 8 vouchers, the final legislation would require that 75 percent be reserved for those making less than 30 percent of the median income. That was from the administration proposal. However, the final bill also would allow public housing authorities that gave more than 75 percent of their vouchers to the very poor to bring in an additional 10 percent of higher-income tenants into public housing—raising the maximum percentage of higher-income tenants from 60 percent to 70 percent. This clause, known as "fungibility," would apply to housing authorities located in census tracts identified as poverty-stricken. The provision came from the House bill.

In addition to allowing a greater mix of incomes in public housing, the bill aimed to increase the earning potential of those in public housing. About 20 percent of public housing residents nationwide also received welfare, and they would be required to follow the welfare overhaul law's work requirements. Others would have to perform community service, a requirement that sponsors hoped would give them job skills. The elderly and disabled—who made up about 40 percent of public housing residents—and those already working would be exempt from service requirements. By increasing tenants' income, the bill aimed to increase the income of housing authorities, which were so strapped for cash that routine maintenance went undone. The bill would allow housing authorities to take out mortgages on their buildings and otherwise contract with private or government entities to generate funds to build housing projects or rehabilitate existing ones.

Final Action

The House passed the VA-HUD spending bill (HR 4194—H Rept 105-610) on July 29 by 259–164. The Senate passed the bill by voice vote July 30. The House agreed to the conference report (H Rept 105-769) by 409–14 on Oct. 6; the Senate followed suit, 96–1, on Oct. 8. The president signed the bill into law on Oct. 21.

MAJOR PROVISIONS

As enacted, the spending bill for veterans, housing, and science programs (HR 4194—PL 105-276) included the following housing-related provisions.

Local Housing Authorities

The bill required local housing authorities designated by the Department of Housing and Urban Development (HUD) as "troubled" to submit plans outlining specific goals for improving their projects and services. If the housing authority failed to meet those goals, HUD would be required to take over the authority or to seek appointment of a receiver.

The measure required HUD to study the effectiveness of its current housing authority evaluations, as well as alternative methods of evaluating performance. This study must evaluate the merit of establishing an independent accreditation organization to assist or replace HUD's role in assessing housing authorities.

Public Housing Block Grants

The bill converted federal funding for public housing into two block grants—one for capital improvements and the other for operating costs. The measure authorized and appropriated $3 billion for public housing capital grants in fiscal 1999 and unspecified funds through fiscal 2003. For operating grants, the legislation authorized $2.9 billion and appropriated $2.8 billion in fiscal 1999 and unspecified sums through fiscal 2003.

Changes in Rent

Under existing law, the rent of public housing tenants and families receiving Section 8 assistance to live in private apartments was limited to 30 percent of adjusted income under the so-called Brooke amendment. The Brooke amendment acted as both a ceiling and floor for rents, so that the rent of most tenants was effectively set at 30 percent of income and a tenant's rent automatically increased as earnings increased—which did not encourage tenants to find work. In addition, because tenants were not subject to minimum rents and some renters had little or no income, some paid no rent.

The bill changed the system by:

• Restoring the Brooke amendment to its original intent, so that it acted only as a rent ceiling—allowing housing authorities to set rents at lower levels. Under the measure, a family's rent would be limited to no more than 30 percent of adjusted income, 10 percent of monthly income, or that portion of a welfare payment designated as housing assistance. Adjusted income is annual income minus exclusions allowed by HUD, such as medical expenses and child support payments.

• Allowing public housing tenants an alternative in calculating rents, giving them a choice between having their rent based on their income (limited to 30 percent of income) or set at a flat rate determined by the housing authority, based on the rental value of the housing. Such flat-rate rents could be either higher or lower than the rent level based on income, depending on the rental value of the unit. Tenants who chose such flat-rate rents would be permitted to switch back to income-based rents if they experienced financial hardship.

Minimum Rents

The bill generally required local housing authorities to establish minimum rents for public housing and rental vouchers—with such minimum rents not to exceed $50 a month. Housing authorities would be allowed to grant hardship exemptions from minimum rent requirements.

Occupancy Changes

The legislation eliminated federal occupancy preference rules and left it to local authorities to develop, based on local housing needs and priorities, their own guidelines for choosing tenants. These rules determined who could be granted public housing or housing subsidy assistance and their priority in receiving such assistance.

The measure also aimed to promote a greater mix of incomes in public and assisted housing. As under existing law, public housing assistance generally could be provided only to families making less than 80 percent of an area's median income. To ensure that housing authorities did not try to serve just the higher-income families in this low-income population, the bill required that at least 40 percent of public housing units available each year be reserved for families with incomes no higher than 30 percent of the area median income. At least 75 percent of the vouchers made available each year would have to be reserved for families with incomes at or below 30 percent of the median.

The measure included a "fungibility" provision that allowed housing authorities to reserve a lower portion (down to 30 percent of available units) of public housing units for the very poor if more than 75 percent of vouchers were provided for such poor families. The measure also included provisions to ensure that local housing authorities did not concentrate low-income families in certain housing projects.

Under existing law, 75 percent to 85 percent of public housing units must be provided to tenants with incomes at or below 50 percent of the area median, and all vouchers were reserved for such families.

Community Work Requirements

The bill required adult residents of public and assisted housing to contribute eight hours a month of service within their community or to participate in an economic self-sufficiency program for eight hours a month. People who failed to do such community service work would have their lease terminated when it came up for annual review. Working adults, senior citizens, disabled people, and those in school or work training would be exempt from this requirement, as would people who were complying with work or training requirements under the 1996 welfare overhaul law (PL 104-193).

Other Occupancy Standards

The bill allowed local housing authorities to deny public housing or rental assistance to a person who was abusing drugs or alcohol, or whose history of drug and alcohol abuse provided reasonable cause for the authority to believe that the person could interfere with the health, safety, or right to peaceful surroundings of other residents. It also prohibited anyone classified as a "sexually violent predator" from receiving public housing assistance.

Leases for public housing and assisted housing would be modified to allow for the eviction of tenants who used illegal drugs, whose abusive use of alcohol interfered with the rights of other residents, or who engaged in certain criminal activities. Tenants who were evicted because of drug-related crimes would be prohibited from receiving federal housing assistance for three years.

Home Rule Flexible Grants

The bill established a four-year demonstration program under which local governments, if approved by HUD, could develop their own flexible low-income housing programs—generally receiving all the public housing and assisted housing funding that would otherwise be provided to the local housing authority.

Under the legislation, only 100 local jurisdictions could participate in the program, which also would be limited to jurisdictions where local housing authorities scored in the lowest 40 percent nationwide in performance. No jurisdiction with a housing authority deemed to be a "high-performing" authority could participate. Of the 100, the measure further provided that no more than fifty-five authorities participating in the demonstration could be "troubled" (as designated by HUD), and no more than forty-five could be "non-troubled."

Disposal of Obsolete Housing

The bill eliminated requirements that housing authorities replace, on a one-for-one basis, every unit of public housing the housing authority disposed of or demolished. It established the conditions under which housing authorities could demolish housing, requiring that it be obsolete, either in condition, location, or other factors, and that rehabilitating it would not be cost effective.

The measure also reauthorized through fiscal 2002 the HOPE VI program, which helped local authorities demolish dilapidated public housing units and replace many of them.

Section 8 Rental Assistance

The legislation consolidated into a new block grant program the existing programs through which tenant-based rental assistance was provided through Section 8 certificates and vouchers. The measure authorized unspecified sums in fiscal 2000 and fiscal 2001 to fund 100,000 new "incremental" vouchers each year. They would provide housing assistance to an additional 100,000 families each year. HUD already provided 1.4 million vouchers. The bill would add another 50,000 vouchers in fiscal 1999.

Resident Management Activities

The bill authorized public housing residents to form resident councils to consider issues affecting public housing developments and to consult with the local housing authorities. Residents also would be authorized to create resident management corporations that could contract with a local housing authority to manage one or more public housing developments. The measure allowed HUD, if requested by residents under certain circumstances, to transfer management of a public housing development or portion of one to an independent management entity.

Reverse Mortgages

The measure authorized HUD to issue rules that would prohibit organizations from charging excessive fees for advising senior citizens on the availability of HUD-insured so-called reverse mortgages, as well as rules to prohibit lenders from dealing with organizations that charge such excessive fees. It also would expand and permanently authorize HUD's reverse mortgages program, called Home Equity Conversion Mortgages, which allowed cash-strapped senior citizens to borrow against the equity in their homes for everyday expenses without having to make monthly interest or principal payments. The loan was repaid when the home was sold. The number of reverse mortgages would expand from 50,000 to 150,000.

(On Sept. 16, 1997, the House had voted 422–1 under suspension of the rules to pass S 562, to authorize HUD to issue rules to prevent the charging of excessive fees for advising senior citizens seeking to obtain reverse mortgages. The Senate had passed the measure by voice vote April 25.)

Other Provisions

The bill also:

• Prohibited HUD from establishing national occupancy standards, such as those established by some states to specify the maximum number of people who could live in a housing unit.

• Required local housing authorities to inspect annually each public housing development and privately owned voucher-subsidized unit to ensure that such units were safe and clean.

• Permitted housing authorities to remove a dilapidated or otherwise distressed public housing development, or a portion of one, from the available public housing stock and provide housing vouchers to affected persons.

• Allowed residents of public housing to own one or more "common household pets," subject to "reasonable" requirements of the local housing authority and local laws or ordinances.

• Allowed housing authorities to establish programs under which public housing residents, and families that were eligible for public housing, could purchase units of public housing or other low-income housing owned by the local housing authority.

• Reauthorized the National Flood Insurance program through fiscal year 2001. The program provided government-subsidized flood insurance to those who lived in flood-prone areas.

Homeless Programs

On March 3, 1998, the House passed, by a 386–23 vote under suspension of the rules, legislation (HR 217) that sought to merge seven federal programs for the homeless into block grants. States, localities, territorial governments, and other groups who served the homeless would be encouraged to use the grants to devise long-term solutions to homelessness, particularly by building permanent housing instead of shelters. Other federal departments would be urged to assume the cost of support services for the homeless, such as drug treatment or mental health counseling.

Funding for homeless assistance programs had declined 25 percent since 1995. HR 217 aimed to reshape the shrinking pie by sending money directly to those providing services. Rep. Rick A. Lazio, R-N.Y., bill sponsor and chairman of the House Banking and Financial Services Subcommittee on Housing and Community Development, wanted to direct Department of Housing and Urban Development (HUD) money at brick-and-mortar projects as well as to limit what providers could spend on emergency shelters and social services. Under HR 217, such services were to be identified and funded by a new Interagency Council on the Homeless to include representatives from HUD and the departments of Health and Human Services, Labor, Education, Veterans Affairs, and Agriculture. The council could issue its own block grants to local providers, if it used available funds in existing programs.

Lazio said the approach was groundbreaking, but Democratic critics said it probably would not work. Others argued that bill sponsors were focusing too blindly on their goal of constructing more permanent housing, at the cost of other services.

The House Banking and Financial Services Committee approved HR 217 by voice vote Nov. 5, 1997, with broad support from committee Democrats. The bill was reported (H Rept 105-407) on Dec. 19, 1997, and a supplemental report (H Rept 105-407, Pt. II) was filed on March 3, 1998. The committee approved, 35–5, a Lazio substitute amendment to authorize $1 billion annually for homeless programs through fiscal 2002. The five Republicans voting against the amendment believed the authorization level was too high. Earlier the committee had defeated, 10–26, a Jim Ryun, R-Kan., amendment to cut the annual authorization to $850 million. The committee also rejected, 14–18, an amendment by Bernard Sanders, I-Vt., to increase the authorization to $1.6 billion.

Sanders, Donald Manzullo, R-Ill., and Jesse L. Jackson Jr., D-Ill., won voice vote approval for an amendment intended to reduce the emphasis on permanent housing. It removed a provision that would have barred providers from using more than 15 percent of their block grant on emergency shelters. The committee also accepted an amendment by Jackson, Sanders, Luis V. Gutierrez, D-Ill., and Lucille Roybal-Allard, D-Calif., to increase from 30 percent to 35 percent the portion of block grants that providers could spend on support services, such as drug treatment, without matching each federal dollar. The panel adopted an amendment by Bruce F. Vento, D-Minn., to allow those providing rooms for the homeless to continue to operate as part of the Section 8 subsidized housing program. This would allow contracts with such facilities to be renewed in coming years.

HR 217 was received in the Senate and referred to the Banking, Housing, and Urban Affairs Committee. But the measure did not advance farther during the 105th Congress.

HUD Cost Reductions

Congress as part of the 1997 budget-reconciliation package (HR 2015—PL 105-33) made permanent three changes in housing law that had been reducing costs at the Department of Housing and Urban Development (HUD) since they were enacted in 1996. The provisions, initially enacted as part of the fiscal 1996 appropriations bill (PL 104-134) for HUD and the Department of Veterans Affairs, were projected to save $1.8 billion over five years. *(Reconciliation, p. 48)*

• First, HR 2015 eliminated a HUD program that provided up to three years of foreclosure relief for borrowers who had defaulted on their federal home mortgages but who showed some potential for resuming payments. Lawmakers said the federal losses from this program were too great.

To minimize the losses but still provide some foreclosure relief, the bill allowed the Federal Housing Administration (FHA) and HUD to grant up to twelve months of relief from mortgage payments. In exchange for the government assuming the cost of those payments, lenders would be required to alter the terms of the loan, at least on a short-term basis, to make it easier for the borrower to pay.

• Second, HR 2015 prohibited annual market-based increases in the federal subsidies paid to owners of Section 8 housing units if the rents the owners were charging exceeded HUD's fair market rent for that housing area. Under the Section 8 program, low-income tenants paid a certain percentage of their income in rent, and the federal government made up the difference through subsidies to the property owner. Before enactment of this provision, owners of subsidized units received annual subsidy increases to keep up with any increases in local rents and to account for maintenance costs of vacated apartments.

Under the bill, rent increases had to reflect actual increases in operating costs, not inflation in the housing market. Landlords could increase rents only if they demonstrated that the increases would not make the unit's rent higher than the rent for a similar unsubsidized unit. Owners of new or recently renovated units could adjust rents for inflation only if their units did not exceed the fair market rents for their area. These changes were effective in fiscal 1999.

• Third, HR 2015 reduced annual subsidy increases by 1 percentage point for owners of Section 8 properties that had no tenant turnover since the last annual increase. However,

the annual adjustment factor, the formula on which the federal government based rent increases, could not be reduced to less than 1 percent, so landlords could increase rents at least that much. The changes were effective in fiscal 1999.

LEGISLATIVE ACTION

The House Banking and Financial Services Committee on June 11, 1997, approved a five-year, $1.8 billion package of housing-related savings. The Senate Banking, Housing, and Urban Affairs Committee on June 18 voted 18–0 in favor of a set of proposals projected to save $2 billion over five years. Both committees got much of their savings from the proposed reductions in Section 8 rental housing subsidies. Both also included the limits on FHA foreclosure relief.

However, the Senate committee added so-called mark-to-market provisions for Section 8 housing. The plan was projected to reduce the costs of renewing expiring Section 8 contracts by $500 million in fiscal 1998. Crafted by Housing Opportunity and Community Development Subcommittee Chairman Connie Mack, R-Fla., the mark-to-market proposal called for subsidized Section 8 rent to be reduced to comparable rates in an area for nonsubsidized housing or to 90 percent of fair market rents if comparable properties did not exist. Comparable rates would be the rents charged in the neighborhood; fair market rents would be the average for a specific area. State and local housing finance agencies, not HUD, would restructure the contracts. The proposal also called for restructuring Section 8 mortgage debt insured by the FHA to reduce the number of expected defaults. When the House and Senate conferees on the housing section of the reconciliation measure met, they were unable to reach agreement on the mark-to-market provisions, which were dropped at the insistence of the House Banking Committee members.

Subsequently, at the request of the Senate Banking Committee, Senate appropriators agreed to include the Mack proposal in their version of the VA-HUD appropriations bill (S 1034). House appropriators did not include it in their version, and when the measure when to conference, the provision became one of the chief stumbling blocks. The dispute was not among the appropriators, but between House and Senate authorizers. House Banking Committee Chairman Jim Leach, R-Iowa, and Rick A. Lazio, R-N.Y., chairman of the panel's Housing and Community Opportunity Subcommittee, opposed putting the provision in the spending bill. They disagreed with some of the details, and they feared such a move would reduce momentum to enact a big public housing overhaul bill (HR 2). *(Public housing, p. 555)*

House Speaker Newt Gingrich, R-Ga., and the appropriators eventually brokered a compromise that maintained the bulk of Mack's proposal but added a few House ideas for implementing the changes. Under the final agreement, HUD was allowed to restructure the FHA-insured mortgages of multifamily properties where above-market-rate Section 8 rental assistance contracts were used, with the aim of cutting the federal subsidy costs, reducing the likelihood of FHA loan defaults, and ensuring the continued use of such properties for low-income housing.

Mortgage Insurance

A measure (S 318—PL 105-216) designed to lessen the financial burden of home ownership by making it easier to cancel mortgage insurance was enacted in July 1998.

BACKGROUND

Lenders often require potential homeowners to purchase private mortgage insurance if they cannot make a 20 percent down payment on the purchase price of the house. Premiums generally cost between $20 and $200 a month. The insurance guarantees that the lender, or subsequent purchasers of the mortgage, would be paid if the homeowner defaulted. But many homeowners, including Rep. James V. Hansen, R-Utah, who sponsored HR 607, complained that they could not cancel the insurance policy once their equity in the home reached 20 percent. Consumer advocates said that about a fifth of all homeowners continued to pay the monthly mortgage insurance premiums even after they had built up significant equity in their homes and could no longer reasonably be considered a risk to lenders. The insurance industry said only about 5 percent of homeowners paid the premiums unnecessarily. The insurance industry claimed it supported the legislation in principle but said it placed too much additional regulation on the mortgage industry.

LEGISLATIVE ACTION

The House Banking and Financial Services Committee reported a companion version to S 318 (HR 607—H Rept 105-55) on April 16, 1997. The full House passed the bill 421–7 under suspension of the rules April 16. The Senate passed an amended HR 607 on Nov. 13 by voice vote.

The Senate Banking, Housing, and Urban Affairs Committee reported S 318 (S Rept 105-129) on Oct. 31, 1997. The Senate passed the bill by voice vote Nov. 9. The House passed an amended S 318 by voice vote under suspension of the rules July 14, 1998. The Senate agreed to the House amendments with amendments on July 15. The House accepted the Senate changes the next day, completing congressional action. President Clinton signed the measure into law on July 29, 1998.

MAJOR PROVISIONS

The bill required lenders and insurance companies to notify homeowners about the process for canceling their mortgage insurance policies. Once home equity reaches 20 percent, homeowners could petition to cancel the policy. The bill required insurance companies to automatically cancel the policy for most conventional mortgages if the home-owner's equity reaches 22 percent. Homeowners with high-risk mortgages generally could not cancel the insurance until midway through their loan—after fifteen years, for example, on a thirty-year mortgage.

One compromise enacted with the bill effectively allowed eight states (California, Connecticut, Maryland, Massachusetts, Minnesota, Missouri, New York, and Texas) to keep their stronger mortgage insurance laws.

The measure also abolished the Thrift Depositor Protection Oversight Board and transferred its remaining responsibilities to the Treasury Department. The board monitored the Resolution Trust Corporation (RTC), which was created in 1989 (PL 101-73) to manage the savings and loan bailout. The RTC had completed its work, and the Treasury Department had asked that it be dissolved. The board's remaining responsibilities included overseeing the payoff of $30 billion worth of bonds issued from 1989 to 1991. *(1989 law, Congress and the Nation Vol. VIII, p. 117)*

Home Ownership

The House by voice vote under suspension of the rules Oct. 13, 1998, passed a bill (HR 3899) that aimed to increase the number of people who own homes by providing more government help for home purchases and lessening regulatory burdens on builders. The measure faced no vocal opposition from House members or the Department of Housing and Urban Development (HUD), but several senators had concerns, and the Senate never took it up.

One of the bill's most contentious provisions would create a twenty-five-member committee to propose new standards for manufactured housing, in consultation with HUD. The makers of mobile homes had long tried to budge HUD from twenty-year-old standards that manufacturers believed were obsolete. The issue was controversial because manufacturers and others in the mobile home industry would have ten seats on the committee, a number some consumer groups feared would give makers and sellers too much control. Other seats would go to mobile home owners, consumer groups, local inspection officials, and other experts.

The bill would make several Federal Housing Administration (FHA) changes. It would allow HUD to increase the limits on the worth of mortgages the FHA could insure in some areas adjacent to higher-cost cities and suburbs. It would allow HUD to increase the number of adjustable rate mortgages it insured by up to 40 percent of the previous year's number. And it would require the General Accounting Office to study the effects of requiring inspections on all FHA homes before purchase.

HR 3899 also would require all federal regulations to include a "housing impact analysis" to ensure that the proposal would not make housing less affordable. *(2000 action, p. 565)*

1999–2000

Community Development

Congress included a package of antipoverty initiatives in a fiscal 2001 omnibus spending bill (HR 4577—PL 106-554), signed into law on Dec. 21, 2000.

BACKGROUND

President Clinton and House Speaker J. Dennis Hastert, R-Ill., announced in November 1999 that they intended to merge the administration's New Markets initiative (HR 2848), which included a tax credit and other incentives to attract capital to low-income areas, with a House Republican proposal called the American Community Renewal Act (HR 815), which would give tax and regulatory relief to economically distressed areas and help poor families set up subsidized savings accounts. The deal was stymied for months, however, as lawmakers discovered problems with reconciling not only different legislative provisions but also different philosophies of how best to help the poor. Republicans saw the Clinton-Hastert drive as a chance to get capital gains tax and regulatory relief and bolster the use of faith-based organizations, to help the poor help themselves. Democrats traditionally opposed those approaches and moved more in the direction of subsidies for private investment—an approach that to some Republicans smacked of central government planning.

HOUSE COMMITTEE ACTION

The House Banking and Financial Services Committee on April 12, 2000, approved, 33–14, a key piece of the administration plan that would encourage large business developments in low-income communities. According to Chairman Jim Leach, R-Iowa, because both Clinton and Hastert wanted the legislation (HR 2764—H Rept 106-638), the panel acted on it to "get as much consensus as possible" and fill in the details in case a broader agreement could be reached. However, Rep. Paul D. Ryan, R-Wis., tried to derail the bill with a substitute that called for the General Accounting Office to study the best ways of helping low-income communities. Ryan said the administration proposal would get the federal government involved in picking "winners and losers." Ryan's substitute failed 15–31.

Some committee Republicans were concerned that businesses would not use the federal aid for the right purposes and were wary of putting the Department of Housing and Urban Development (HUD) in charge of issuing loan guarantees to help companies with their investments. To address those issues, a manager's amendment, approved by voice vote, gave Republicans a number of concessions. Annual audits would be held of each company and HUD would have to report to Congress every year on the companies' activities. In addition, the HUD inspector general would keep a close

watch on the program. As an added safety measure, the committee adopted 24–23 an amendment by Richard H. Baker, R-La., to end the program five years after the first company was licensed.

ADMINISTRATION'S DEAL

Clinton and Hastert announced agreement May 23 on a community development package. They decided not to split the difference between their ideas but to splice them together and then throw in something for everybody to brag about. Clinton got most of the main pieces of his New Markets proposal, including the centerpiece—a tax credit that would lure private investors to economically deprived neighborhoods by giving them credit for more than 30 percent of their investment. He also won a commitment from Republicans to support the New Markets venture capital program, which would provide loans and technical assistance grants to help small businesses get started in low-income areas.

The House Small Business Committee moved quickly on the venture capital firms legislation (HR 4530—H Rept 106-785), approving the bill by voice vote May 25. Republicans, meanwhile, won a big concession from Clinton: support for a capital gains tax exclusion to lure private investors into "renewal communities"—low-income neighborhoods that would offer tax and regulatory relief to attract new businesses. Clinton also agreed to allow faith-based organizations to receive federal funds to provide substance abuse treatment services.

The deal also struck a compromise between the empowerment zones favored by Clinton, which gave tax breaks and performance-based grants and loans to businesses that located in impoverished neighborhoods, and the GOP proposal for renewable communities. Clinton won nine new empowerment zones and extended the life of the thirty-one existing ones. In return, Republicans won forty renewal communities. One key area where Clinton and Hastert could not reach agreement involved competing proposals for subsidized savings accounts for poor people.

HOUSE ACTION

The House on July 25 overwhelmingly passed an economic development bill, the Community Renewal and New Markets Act (HR 4923). To get the bill to the floor, House GOP leaders bypassed the Ways and Means Committee, where Chairman Bill Archer, R-Texas, was holding out for a no-amendment pledge from Democrats. They took the package to the floor under a suspension of the rules, which protected it from amendment but required a two-thirds majority for passage. The measure passed on a **key vote of 394–27 (R 214–1; D 179–25; I 1–1).** *(2000 key votes, p. 915)*

The House-passed bill included provisions of HR 4530 and HR 2764, as well as tax-related language that Archer had been unable to move through his committee. In addition to providing for the forty empowerment zones and forty renewal communities, HR 4923 attempted to tackle the shortage of affordable housing by allowing states to issue more tax credits to property owners who rent to low-income people. It would also require HUD to give its vacant, substandard single-family properties to local governments or nonprofit organizations.

At the time of the House action, the only issue that seemed able to derail the bill was a provision to subsidize faith-based drug and alcohol treatment programs. Opponents said the provision could lead to taxpayer-subsidized employment discrimination because faith-based groups do not have to comply with federal antidiscrimination laws.

SENATE ACTION

The economic development package swelled in size and cost as senators clamored to attach seventy-two amendments, mostly tax breaks and pet projects that had little to do with the legislation's original goal of helping poor people. Senate Finance Committee Chairman William V. Roth Jr., R-Del., gave up trying to mark up the measure and announced on Sept. 28 that he would simply introduce a new bill to take into negotiations with the House.

The Roth proposal (S 3152) would extend the life of the thirty-one existing empowerment zones but would not create nine new ones. Furthermore, it would create thirty renewal communities, not the forty called for in the House-passed legislation. The antipoverty efforts were only some of the tax provisions in Roth's package. Provisions also called for $2.4 billion worth of tax breaks for farmers, $1.5 billion in energy tax breaks, and $1.8 billion in conservation proposals, including an expanded tax credit for electricity produced by biomass or poultry waste facilities.

Majority Leader Trent Lott, R-Miss., filed amendments to repeal the "marriage penalty" and estate taxes, which Clinton had vetoed as stand-alone bills. Charles E. Grassley, R-Iowa, wanted to attach a bill (S 2274), cosponsored by Edward M. Kennedy, D-Mass., to let states allow the parents of children with disabilities to buy Medicaid coverage.

The biggest problem with the legislation proved not to be the added proposals, but the fact that the Senate was never involved in the negotiations that led to the original Clinton-Hastert deal—and therefore never had a stake in ensuring the package became law.

FINAL ACTION

After the antipoverty package managed to survive its brush with death by amendment in the Senate, Republican leaders wrapped the community renewal bill into a broader tax relief package (HR 2614), which the president threatened to veto. The rescue came during postelection budget talks, as Clinton asked Republicans to add the community renewal package to an omnibus spending package (HR 4577). The provisions would cost $25.2 billion over ten years, according to the Joint Committee on Taxation.

In its final form, the community renewal section more closely resembled the House bill than the Senate version. In one major departure from the Senate bill, Republicans dropped a plan for individual development accounts—special matched savings accounts that would help low-income workers save enough money to buy a home, go to college, or start a business by giving banks tax credits to match their contributions. The provision, sponsored by Sen. Rick Santorum, R-Pa., ran into opposition from Archer, who opposed adding new credits to the tax code. Clinton signed the omnibus bill in December 2000, a month before he left office.

MAJOR PROVISIONS

The following are highlights of the community renewal section of HR 4577:

• **Empowerment zones and renewal communities.** The law extended the life of the existing thirty-one empowerment zones, created nine new empowerment zones, and established forty new renewal communities. Empowerment zones provide wage credits and other tax incentives to lure businesses; renewal communities were similar, except that they would also provide regulatory relief by requiring state and local governments to cut rules and red tape. In addition, business owners would pay no capital gains taxes on the sale of businesses or assets held for more than five years.

• **New Markets tax credit.** This Clinton proposal hoped to lure investors to low-income areas by letting them claim up to $15 billion of investments over seven years for investing in community development entities.

• **Low-income housing tax credit.** More of a credit would be issued to property owners who rent to low-income people by raising the per capita state limits from $1.25 to $1.75 by 2002.

• **Private activity bond volume caps.** The law would help state and local governments issue more private activity bonds, the interest on which was exempt from federal income taxes, by raising the limits to $75 for each state resident or $225 million in 2002, whichever was greater. The bonds could be used for such infrastructure projects as low-income housing and small manufacturing facilities.

• **Charitable choice.** Sponsored by House GOP Conference Chairman J. C. Watts Jr., R-Okla., this provision would allow faith-based substance abuse treatment programs to receive federal funds. Watts and other supporters said the provision was needed to bolster religion-based drug treatment programs, which they said could be more effective than conventional initiatives.

Home Ownership

Concerned that the thriving economy was making housing too expensive for poor and moderate-income families, lawmakers in 2000 cleared legislation (HR 5640—PL 106-569) designed to make home ownership easier. The bill also included a revised system for regulating manufactured housing. *(1998 action, p. 563)*

SENATE ACTION

The Senate Banking, Housing, and Urban Affairs Committee approved by voice vote March 8, 2000, and formally reported April 13 legislation (S 1452—S Rept 106-274) to change the way government set regulations for manufactured housing—prefabricated and mobile homes. S 1452, sponsored by Richard C. Shelby, R-Ala., and John D. Rockefeller IV, D-W.Va., would create a twenty-six-member independent panel to recommend safety regulations for building, operating, and installing manufactured houses. The provisions would become federal regulation unless the Department of Housing and Urban Development (HUD) rejected them within one year. The measure would allow HUD to impose small fees on home manufacturers to cover safety inspection costs and pay the panel's expenses. Since federal safety regulation of manufactured homes was first enacted in 1974 (PL 93-383), the department's staff to assess and modify the rules had been cut to eight from 34. *(1974 law, Congress and the Nation Vol. IV, p. 477)*

The full Senate passed S 1452 by voice vote May 4.

HOUSE ACTION

The House Banking and Financial Services Committee approved by voice vote March 14, 2000, a bill (HR 1776) designed to ease barriers to home ownership. HR 1776 was formally reported (H Rept 106-553) on May 29; a supplemental report was filed (H Rept 106-553, Pt. II) on April 5. The bill incorporated many proposals left out of the 1998 public housing law (PL 105-276). *(Public housing, p. 555)*

The committee-approved measure would encourage municipalities to reduce regulatory barriers to the purchase of affordable housing by low-income residents. It would raise the income ceiling for people who want to borrow from loan pools—money people may borrow for home purchases—funded through the HOME Investment Partnerships Program, which helped residents refurbish dilapidated housing, and Community Development Block Grants, often used to revitalize economically distressed areas. The measure would allow cities to use Community Development Block Grants and HOME grants to help teachers, police officers, firefighters, and sanitation workers with closing costs, down payments, counseling, and subsidized mortgage rates on homes inside their city's limits. HR 1776 would create a test program under which families with disabled members could use their Section 8 rental vouchers for house down payments. The bill would reauthorize both community development grants and HOME through fiscal 2005. In fiscal 2001 the authorized limits would be $4.8 billion for Community Development Block Grants and $1.7 billion for HOME.

The House committee rejected two amendments offered by Barney Frank, D-Mass. The first, defeated 19–23, would let states inspect prefabricated homes as they were being manufactured, in addition to at their point of sale. The second, defeated 11–28, would give consumers greater access to information about manufactured housing defects. The committee by voice vote approved an amendment by Dave Weldon, R-Fla., to require municipal workers qualifying for the new type of assistance to pay back what they borrowed in full if they sold their home within seven years—and to limit their aid to a single year; an amendment by Michael E. Capuano, D-Mass., to create a down payment assistance program under HOME and the community development program for buyers of two- and three-family homes; and an amendment by Jan Schakowsky, D-Ill., to strike language that would make it more difficult for disabled home buyers under the pilot program to requalify for Section 8 rental subsidies after a default.

The full House passed HR 1776 by 417–8 on April 6. The bill would allow disabled recipients of the Section 8 rent-subsidy program to use their vouchers for down payments on homes. It also would expand the use of so-called reverse mortgages to let senior citizens include long-term health care expenses in the cost of buying a home. A consensus committee, with representation balanced among consumers, government officials, and industry experts, would be established and would advise HUD on safety standards and regulations for manufactured housing. In addition, HR 1776 would reauthorize two HUD programs through fiscal 2005, allocating up to $4.9 billion for the Community Development Block Grant program in fiscal 2001 and $1.65 billion for the HOME program.

One of the more controversial amendments added to the bill was a $35 million allocation of Community Development Block Grant money for a convocation and community center for Youngstown, Ohio, the home of Democratic representative James A. Traficant Jr. With both parties fighting for majority control of the House in the November 2000 elections, Traficant had begun hinting that he might vote with Republicans in selecting a Speaker when the 107th Congress convened in 2001. The House approved the Ohio grant on a raucous, 225–201 roll-call vote April 6.

A provision added during House Banking Subcommittee on Housing and Community Opportunity consideration by Capuano would allow teachers and "uniformed municipal employees" such as police officers and firefighters earning less than 150 percent of the area median income to buy homes through the Community Development Block Grant and HOME programs. That income cutoff was subsequently revised to 115 percent, with the proviso that the HUD secretary could designate "high cost" areas to use the 150 percent income limit. A group of Democratic representatives from poor urban districts sought to keep income guidelines at 80 percent. However, the House rejected the amendment by Maxine Waters, D-Calif., by a 60–367 vote on April 6.

A more controversial amendment by Mark Souder, R-Ind., would make religious organizations eligible to compete for Community Development Block Grant money. Chet Edwards, D-Texas, argued that Souder's language contradicted legal precedents restricting the flow of public money to religious organizations. The amendment was adopted, 299–124 on April 6, after Souder modified it on the House floor to prevent organizations from discriminating against participants who did not belong to that denomination or did not practice a religion.

The House approved by voice vote an amendment by Christopher Shays, R-Conn., Jerrold Nadler, D-N.Y., Constance A. Morella, R-Md., and Joseph Crowley, D-N.Y., to increase the funding authorization level for Housing Opportunities for Persons With AIDS (HOPWA) from $260 million to $275 million for fiscal 2001.

The House on Oct. 24 by voice vote under suspension of the rules passed S 1452, after amending the legislation with parts of seven other housing and banking bills, including several sections of HR 1776. However, the measure stalled in the Senate, where Republicans said it went too far and Democrats attempted to attach to it provisions that could find no other legislative vehicle.

FINAL ACTION

Although S 1452 was dead for the remainder of the 106th Congress, lawmakers quickly found a new vehicle to promote home ownership. The House on Dec. 5, 2000, by voice vote under suspension of the rules, passed HR 5640, which sought to promote home ownership among elderly, disabled, and low-income Americans. The Senate passed the bill by voice vote Dec. 7, and President Bill Clinton signed the measure Dec. 27.

HR 5640 created several new programs and changed housing laws to make it easier for low-income people to purchase homes. Section 8 federal rental subsidies could be used to make a down payment. Provisions in the House-passed S 1452 that would allow police officers to buy homes in high-crime areas with no down payment and would allow public employees to purchase homes in low-income neighborhoods with a down payment of 1 percent were dropped from HR 5640.

The bill authorized $15 million annually through fiscal 2005 to help local governments lower regulatory barriers to the development of affordable housing. It clarified a 1998 law (PL 105-216) ensuring the right of homeowners, even those with adjustable-rate mortgages, to cancel their private mortgage insurance once they have enough equity in their property, usually 20 percent. *(Mortgage insurance, p. 563)*

HR 5640 would make Federal Housing Administration reverse mortgages more affordable for seniors who use the money for long-term health care insurance. Such mortgages generally allow seniors to borrow against the equity in their home for living expenses, with the loans repaid from the proceeds when the house was sold. Mortgage insurance premiums would be waived for those using funds for long-term care insurance. The bill contained no new housing production program. Negotiations between appropriators and the Clinton administration on the fiscal 2001 Veterans Affairs and HUD appropriations bill (HR 4635) nearly added a one-year housing production program using $1 billion of unspent Section 8 money, but it was eliminated after some senators objected.

Affordable Housing for Elderly, Disabled

The House of Representatives on Sept. 27, 1999, under suspension of the rules, passed a bill (HR 202) by a near-unanimous 405–5 vote to preserve existing affordable housing for the elderly and disabled. Many provisions of HR 202 were subsequently included in the fiscal 2000 appropriations bill (HR 2684—PL 106-74) for the departments of Veterans Affairs (VA) and Housing and Urban Development (HUD). The VA-HUD provisions aimed to keep residents of federally assisted housing from being forced out of their homes if landlords gave up federal housing contracts. The provisions also expanded housing and housing services for the elderly and disabled.

Since the mid-1970s, the federal government expanded its Section 8 rental subsidy program to make more housing available for low-income residents, including senior citizens. Many of these housing units were taken off Section 8 rolls as twenty-year contracts offered through the program expired or as owners paid off federally insured mortgages. Such "opt out" moves by landlords allowed them to rent apartments at fair market value, in effect pushing rents out of reach of low-income tenants. The House Banking and Financial Services Committee estimated that contracts covering one million Section 8 units nationwide would expire by 2004, with half of those in jeopardy of being lost through owner opt-outs.

The parts of HR 202 included in the VA-HUD spending bill (HR 2684) would keep current residents of federally assisted housing from losing their homes by offering "enhanced" vouchers with higher subsidies, allowing tenants to remain in their homes if landlords opted out of Section 8 or paid off Federal Housing Administration mortgages. The bill also allowed funds to be used to convert housing projects for the elderly into assisted-living facilities where residents could continue to live when they were no longer entirely independent.

President Clinton signed HR 2684 (PL 106-74) into law on Oct. 20, 1999.

## CHAPTER 12

Labor and Pension Policy

Introduction   571

1997–1998 Chronology   573

1999–2000 Chronology   579

Labor and Pension Policy

In January 1997, when President Bill Clinton took the oath of office for his second term, the United States was in the middle of unprecedented economic growth. The economy had been expanding steadily—in the 2 to 3 percent range—since the end of the mild recession of 1990–1991. But in the later half of the decade, annual increases in the gross domestic product averaged more than 4 percent, an unprecedented sustained growth rate for a highly developed economy like the United States.

Also during Clinton's second term, unemployment rates dipped to new lows, dropping from roughly 5 percent to below 4 percent in 2000. This sustained low unemployment rate was also unprecedented and produced a labor shortage in many sectors of the economy.

With high growth and low unemployment, many Americans felt more secure about their future. This confidence was bolstered by a booming stock market, in which more and more average Americans were investing and in many cases reaping huge rewards.

Amid this prosperity, organized union membership continued to fall, reflecting the ongoing decline in high-paying, blue-collar jobs, especially in the manufacturing sector. The decline also represented an increase in service-oriented employment, most notably in the high-tech, information sector, where unions held little sway. In 1995 union membership stood at 14.9 percent of the working population. By 2000 that figure had fallen to 13.5 percent.

LABOR AND PENSION LEGISLATION

Although President Clinton's first term began with a burst of optimism for unions and their supporters, the four years from 1993 to 1996 were ultimately disappointing ones for organized labor. Not only did Congress come under the control of Republicans after the 1994 midterm elections, but Clinton himself proved to be—in the eyes of many labor supporters—a less than staunch supporter of labor's goals than had been anticipated. The president was accused of neglecting priorities, such as striker replacement, while fighting for proposals that unions opposed, such as the North American Free Trade Agreement. Still, Clinton's first term produced some victories for labor—in particular passage of the Family Leave Act in 1992 and a 90-cent-an-hour increase in the minimum wage in 1996.

During Clinton's second term the situation changed dramatically. The White House almost completely stopped pushing issues important to organized labor. Instead, both Democrats and Republicans made small gestures towards unions and their supporters and contented themselves with scoring the occasional political point.

The Republicans, who retained control of Congress during the entire four years of Clinton's second term, felt as though they had been taken advantage of by the president in the budget battles of 1995 and were rarely in a mood to cooperate with the White House. Meanwhile, the president and his Democratic allies on Capitol Hill focused on other issues that they could use to campaign against the GOP in the elections of 1998 and 2000.

PARTISAN GRIDLOCK

In the areas of labor and pension policy, little was accomplished. The only major piece of labor legislation enacted

REFERENCES

Discussion of labor and pension policy for the years 1945–1964 may be found in *Congress and the Nation Vol. I,* pp. 565–657, 1220–1272, 1289–1320; for the years 1965–1968, *Congress and the Nation Vol. II,* pp. 601–622, 734–743, 745–778; for the years 1969–1972, *Congress and the Nation Vol. III,* pp. 605–621, 703–742; for the years 1973–1976, *Congress and the Nation Vol. IV,* pp. 403–432, 681–713; for the years 1977–1980, *Congress and the Nation Vol. V,* pp. 231–251, 399–425; for the years 1981–1984, *Congress and the Nation Vol. VI,* pp. 643–672; for the years 1985–1988, *Congress and the Nation Vol. VII,* pp. 687–709; for the years 1989–1992, *Congress and the Nation Vol. VIII,* pp. 703–738; for the years 1993–1996, *Congress and the Nation Vol. IX,* pp. 653–675.

Outlays for Social Security

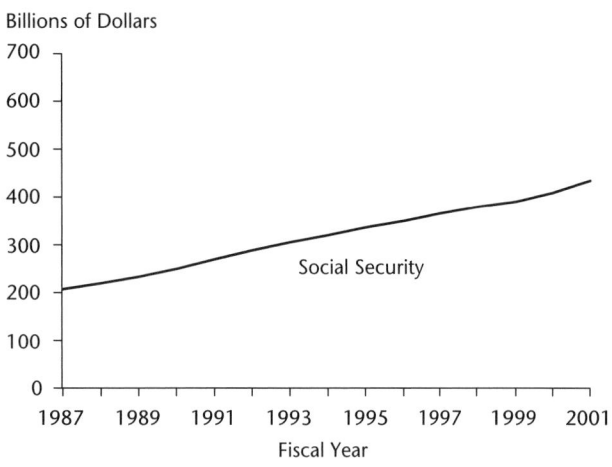

Billions of Dollars

NOTE: Data for 2001 are estimated.

SOURCE: Office of Management and Budget, *Historical Tables, Budget of the United States Government: Fiscal Year 2002* (Washington, D.C.: U.S. Government Printing Office, 2001), Table 3.2.

during this time was a 1998 overhaul of the myriad federal job training programs, which long enjoyed bipartisan support. Congress also approved a number of small labor-related bills, including minor changes in the Occupational Safety and Health Act and a measure easing employers' ability to give stock options to hourly workers.

A number of other proposals seemed likely to become law but got caught in the political bickering and bad feeling that permeated the president's second term. The most important of these measures was a one-dollar increase in the minimum wage, which was slated to be added to an end-of-year tax package in 2000 but died (along with the tax proposals) in election-year partisan controversy.

Republicans tried to push through a number of measures vigorously opposed by organized labor, Clinton, and most congressional Democrats. Some of these bills, including measures aimed at allowing employees greater flexibility in taking comp time and a ban on union "salting," passed the House only to stall in the Senate, where the minority Democrats had more power to hold up legislation.

Congress also grappled with a number of pension-related proposals during this time including, in 1999 and 2000, significant legislation that would allow workers to set aside more money in their company pension plans and to transfer those assets when they change jobs. But that measure became part of the same last-minute tax package that included the minimum wage and thus died in the last days of the 106th Congress.

In spite of considerable rhetoric, neither the executive branch nor Congress seriously considered changes to the nation's Social Security system, which was of intense interest as baby-boomers headed in huge numbers toward retirement. Long-term projections for the Social Security trust fund indicated that the existing financial underpinnings could come apart, without more funds or fewer benefits, as the boomer generation retired. Congress did, however, repeal the unpopular Social Security "earnings test," which economists, many seniors, and an increasing number of employers contended discouraged a large and able portion of the workforce who were over age sixty-five from seeking even part-time employment. Lawmakers also significantly trimmed spending on Social Security's sibling Medicare health program during the 105th Congress, but then they changed their minds and took back some of those cuts in the 106th Congress. *(Medicare, pp. 432, 461)*

Chronology of Action on Labor and Pension Policy

1997–1998

The 105th Congress saw enactment of the only major labor-related bill in Clinton's entire second term—legislation that overhauled the entire federal job training system. The measure won enough support to become law because Republicans and Democrats agreed that the existing system was a mess and needed to be consolidated.

But the job training victory was the exception, not the rule. Four GOP-supported labor measures all failed to pass because of strong Democratic opposition. The most important of these bills, a measure aimed at allowing hourly employees the option of taking comp time instead of overtime, was bitterly opposed by Democrats.

Another far-reaching measure that stalled because of Democratic opposition was a 1997 bill that would have dramatically overhauled the Occupational Safety and Health Administration (OSHA) by shifting the agency's focus from enforcement to cooperation with employers. The less controversial parts of the OSHA overhaul became law the following year, as one of a number of small work-safety bills cleared by Congress in 1998.

Democrats also worked to kill a measure to allow employers to reject "salts" or job applicants who are working for unions and have applied for work with an eye toward organizing a company's employees. While not defending the practice, labor supporters on Capitol Hill feared that the measure could be used by companies to discriminate against legitimate job applicants who also happened to be active union members.

Job Training Overhaul

In response to criticism that federal job training and placement programs were antiquated and redundant, Congress on July 31, 1998, cleared legislation (HR 1385—PL 105-220) that overhauled the system, giving individuals and states new power to design new programs tailored to their specific needs.

The bill consolidated more than sixty federal job training and related programs into three block grants that states would administer. The legislation also gave workers vouchers that allowed them to "buy" the type of job training they needed. The measure also aimed to build more flexibility and accountability into the system.

The original Senate bill (S 1186), introduced by Mike DeWine, R-Ohio, had also included federal secondary and postsecondary vocational education programs as well. The House opted to pass separate bills on job training (HR 1385) and vocational education (HR 1853). Because of pressure from a variety of sources, including conservative groups and those who lobby for vocational education funding, the vocational provisions were stripped from the final version. Congress later approved and sent to the White House a freestanding vocational education bill (PL 105-332.) *(Vocational education, p. 513)*

BACKGROUND

For years, there was broad agreement that the federal job training system needed significant change. A 1995 study by the General Accounting Office found that the federal government funded a confusing web of 163 different programs scattered across fifteen separate agencies.

As a result, coordination between these various programs and entities was often poor or nonexistent, leading to redundancies and a waste of resources. Coordination with employers also was often poor, leading the government to train people for jobs that were in short supply or unavailable.

At the same time, the nation had a large labor shortage. In particular, high-technology companies were hard-pressed to find qualified workers and often resorted to importing employees from overseas.

Much of the blame for this situation rested with Congress. Beginning in the late 1960s, legislators gradually added new programs to meet specific vocational needs, often with little regard for how these additions fit into the federal job training system.

A well-functioning federal job training system, however, is important for the nation's economy. The Labor Department alone—which administers many of the programs— spent about $6 billion annually on training and placing workers. The year the bill cleared Congress, the department enrolled about one million adults and more than 700,000 young people in some sort of job training program.

In 1996 Republicans had tried to push through Congress legislation that consolidated even more programs than HR 1385 did into one large block grant only to see the measure stall that summer from lack of Democratic and White House support. Liberals opposed the sweeping nature of the bill and feared that states would ultimately get shortchanged as they tried to finance a wide range of programs with one lump sum of money. *(Congress and the Nation Vol. IX, p. 669)*

HOUSE ACTION

The House Education and Workforce Subcommittee on Postsecondary Education, Training and Life-Long Learning on April 24, 1997, approved HR 1385 (H Rept 105-93) by voice vote. On April 30, the measure, which was sponsored by Howard P. "Buck" McKeon, R-Calif., also earned the voice vote approval of the full Education and Workforce Committee.

During full committee markup, the panel approved an amendment that gave state legislatures final authority over how to spend the block grant money. Originally, the measure gave this authority to state governors.

The panel also approved an amendment to make displaced homemakers—such as widows or divorced women who need to find work—eligible for job training.

During both markups, Democrats expressed qualified support for the bill, which they said was a big improvement over legislation that had passed the House in 1996. The administration also expressed support for the measure.

The bill's strong bipartisan backing was evident on May 16 when the measure was passed by the full House by a vote of 343–60. The primary opposition to the bill came from a group of conservative Republicans who said the legislation might create a system that intruded too deeply into people's personal lives.

With this criticism in mind, the House gave voice vote approval to an amendment by Lindsey Graham, R-S.C., stipulating that parents and their children who were schooled at home would not be required to participate in any of the bill's programs.

SENATE ACTION

In the Senate, a measure (S 1186—S Rept 105-109) that combined most of the provisions of HR 1385 as well as the House's separate vocational education bill was given voice vote approval by the Labor and Human Resources Committee on Sept. 24. The bill was sponsored by a bipartisan group of senators headed up by DeWine and the panel's ranking member, Edward M. Kennedy, D-Mass.

At markup, committee chairman Jim Jeffords, R-Vt., warned that combining the two House bills would slow enactment. Jeffords argued that quick passage of the measure was crucial in light of the passage of welfare reform in 1996. *(Congress and the Nation Vol. IX, p. 571)* "Welfare reform has no hope of success unless individuals have the appropriate education and training to compete in the workforce," he said.

In spite of Jeffords's sense of urgency and warning about combining the two House bills, the Senate did not take up the measure for almost eight months. When it did on May 5, it passed it overwhelmingly 97–7.

In passing HR 1385, however, the Senate had first substituted in the entire text of S 1186, including the provisions regarding vocational education. The inclusion of the vocational education section presented a problem, as conservative groups such as the Family Research Council and Phyllis Schlafly's Eagle Forum opposed putting all of the programs together. These critics argued that combining vocational education for young people and job training for adults would unfairly steer students into training for menial work and away from college.

At conference committee in July, senators agreed to drop the vocational education provisions and proceed with them as a separate bill, as was done in the House. The resulting conference report (H Rept 105-659) passed the Senate by unanimous consent on July 30 and the House by voice vote on July 31. President Clinton signed HR 1385 into law on Aug. 7.

MAJOR PROVISIONS

As signed into law, HR 1385:

• Consolidated sixty federal programs into three block grants that states will administer. These block grants were for:

  • **Job training.** An Adult Employment and Training Opportunities Grant for disadvantaged adults and dislocated workers who were chronically unemployed or who had lost their jobs as a result of economic shifts or corporate downsizing.

  • **At-risk youths.** A Disadvantaged Youth Employment and Training Opportunities Grant for at-risk, low-income teenagers and young adults, including high school dropouts.

  • **Adult literacy.** An Adult Education and Literacy Grant to assist low-income people to obtain the skills necessary to become employed, particularly those attempting to make the transition from public assistance to the workforce.

• Provided individuals with vouchers that they can use to "purchase" the training programs of their choice.

• Required job training institutions to provide a public assessment of their success, giving information on how many students graduate, how many find work, and how much these graduates earn.

- Gave state and local governments greater discretion in designing their training systems.

- Encouraged state and local governments to create one-stop customer service centers that could provide prospective workers with everything they needed, from job training to placement. At the time of the bill's enactment, one thousand such centers were already in operation around the country.

- Required the creation of Workforce Development Boards at the local level. These boards, made up of business leaders, local education officials, community activists, and others would be charged with submitting a workplace development plan for an area.

Employers and "Salting"

Legislation that would permit employers to refuse to hire "salts"—union organizers or supporters who seek a job with a nonunion employer in order to organize the workers from within—failed to become law even though it had passed the House and had the support of a majority of senators.

The bills (HR 3246, S 1981) were strongly opposed by congressional Democrats and their allies in the organized labor movement. As a result, Republican supporters were unable to muster the 60 votes needed in the Senate to cut off debate and bring the measure to a final vote. It also faced a veto threat from the White House.

BACKGROUND

Unions have long engaged in a practice known as "salting," in which organizers apply for jobs at nonunion plants hoping to work from the inside to push fellow workers to sign union cards. The House and Senate bills aimed to end salting by allowing employers to refuse to hire job applicants whose "primary purpose" was not to actually work at the company.

Businesses and their Republican allies in Congress have long been irked by the practice. They argued that job applicants should be willing to work for the employer, and that their purpose in signing up for a job should not be to organize a union. Representative Sam Johnson, R-Texas, compared "salting" to a form of economic warfare that is used "to sabotage the company and drive them out of business."

But labor leaders and most Democrats countered that if "salting" were banned, employers could use union ties to discriminate against workers, regardless of their intended purpose. In particular, they argued that such a ban would open the door for employers to make intrusive inquiries into job applicants' backgrounds and lead to the blacklisting of job applicants who are union sympathizers.

In addition, they said, the practice was perfectly legal according to a 1995 Supreme Court ruling, *National Labor Relations Board v. Town and Country Electric Inc.* That Court decision said a worker may be considered an "employee"

LABOR LEADERSHIP

The Senate confirmed Alexis Herman as secretary of labor on April 30, 1997, on a bipartisan vote of 85–13. Herman, the first African American to serve in the post, faced opposition from some Senate Republicans because of allegations that she engaged in improper fund-raising activities while in her previous job as director of the White House Office of Public Liaison. In an effort to mollify Republicans over the Herman nomination, President Bill Clinton agreed to forgo a planned executive order giving priority to unionized companies in federal contract bids. Clinton's gesture helped weaken GOP opposition, ensuring Herman's confirmation.

Before serving at the public liaison office, Herman was chief of staff at the Democratic National Committee. She also founded and ran an employment consulting firm and worked at the Department of Labor from 1977 to 1981. (*Background, cabinet profiles, p. 980*)

---

under federal labor laws even if he or she is being paid by the union to organize fellow workers.

LEGISLATIVE ACTION

In the House the legislation won the approval of the Education and Workforce Committee on March 11, 1998. The bill (HR 3246—H Rept 105-453) was approved by a straight party-line vote of 23–18, with all Democrats opposed.

The bill was passed by the full House on March 26 by a narrow vote of 202–200. Supporters of the measure were aided by the fact that at the time of the vote, seventeen House Democrats were traveling with President Clinton in Africa.

Debate on the House floor was heated, with both sides claiming that their position was fair and just. Republicans argued that the bill would help protect small businesses from union intimidation. "The issue [with] salting [is that] you go into a small business and try to destroy it," said Randy "Duke" Cunningham, R-Calif.

Democrats countered that it was unions and workers, not businesses that needed help. They said unions are on the decline and often face a hostile reception by most employers and that organizing workers was more difficult than ever.

In September Senate Republicans tried to bring up a companion measure (S 1981) for a vote on the floor. But Senate rules stood in their way, as Democrats were able to muster enough support to prevent the GOP from obtaining the 60 votes needed to end debate and vote on the bill. The Sept. 14 vote to invoke cloture failed by a vote of 52–42, with one Republican, Ben Nighthorse Campbell of Colorado, voting with the Democrats.

A few days earlier, on Sept. 11, the bill suffered another blow when President Clinton formally announced his intention to veto it, claiming that the legislation would "seriously erode fundamental . . . protections of workers' rights to organize by allowing businesses" to refuse to hire union organizers.

Compensatory Time

During the 105th Congress Republicans failed to pass an important item on their labor agenda—flexibility for employers to offer workers a choice between compensatory time off and overtime pay. Although a House measure (HR 1) passed that body in March 1997, Senate Democrats blocked similar legislation (S 4) in June.

Many thought the issue would resurface in 1998, but the bill never came up to debate in the Senate because of strong opposition from congressional Democrats and the White House, who were convinced that it would force employees to take compensatory time off instead of receiving overtime pay.

BACKGROUND

Over the strong objections of organized labor and many Democrats, the House had passed a comp time bill in July 1996. But across the Capitol, where the minority had more clout, Senate Democrats blocked an attempt by GOP Majority Leader Trent Lott, R-Miss., to bring a similar bill up for consideration. *(Congress and the Nation Vol. IX, p. 671).*

The crux of the dispute was whether the bill would lead employers to coerce workers into accepting compensatory time instead of the usual time-and-a-half pay for work beyond forty hours a week. Republicans said the bill would let workers determine whether to accept time or pay; Democrats said it did not have enough protections against subtle coercion by employers.

Under the 1938 Fair Labor Standards Act, employers are required to compensate most work beyond a forty-hour week at a rate of one-and-a-half times a worker's hourly wage. In 1985 the law was amended to allow federal, state, and local government employees to be compensated with time off instead of overtime wages. Employees who were considered professionals were exempt from federal wage-and-hour laws.

In 1997 new bills were introduced in both houses of Congress. The House version (HR 1) would allow employers to give private-sector employees the option of being paid at one-and-a-half times their hourly rate for hours worked beyond the traditional forty-hour week, or taking compensatory time off figured at the same rate.

A companion measure in the Senate (S 4) was similar to HR 1 with one exception: It proposed replacing the forty-hour week with an eighty-hour two-week period for purposes of calculating overtime. Hence, employees could work more than forty hours one week and not gain overtime or comp time so long as they worked a corresponding number of hours less the next week.

HOUSE ACTION

HR 1 began in the House Education and the Workforce Committee, which approved it, 23–17, on March 5 in a vote that fell largely along party lines (H Rept 105-21). The bill was sponsored by Cass Ballenger, R-N.C.

The committee rejected nine Democratic amendments; most of them aimed at protecting low-income workers from being coerced into accepting one type of compensation over another.

On March 19, HR 1 passed the House by a vote of 222–210, once again largely along party lines. During more than five hours of floor debate, Republicans argued that the bill would give working families more opportunities to attend to personal affairs or spend time with their school-age children. "For some families, time is as important as money," said Deborah Pryce, R-Ohio.

But Democrats argued that attempts to amend the Fair Labor Standards Act would put workers at a serious disadvantage. They feared workers could be pressured into accepting one form of compensation over another and might be subject to discrimination or harassment for not complying with employers' wishes.

During debate, members approved a number of amendments including one offered by Bill Goodling, R-Pa., that would have required employees to have worked a minimum of 1000 hours during the last twelve months to be eligible for comp time. The amendment was approved by a lopsided vote of 408–19.

In addition, the House approved, 390–36, an amendment offered by Allen Boyd, D-Fla., that would have sunset the law five years after enactment, allowing sufficient time to determine how well it worked.

The House also rejected a number of amendments, including one offered by George Miller, D-Calif., that would have prohibited employers from directly or indirectly soliciting employees to take comp time instead of overtime pay. Miller's amendment failed by a vote of 193–237.

SENATE ACTION

On March 18, the day before House passage of HR 1, the Senate Labor and Human Resources Committee approved its own comp time bill (S 4—S Rept 105-11) by a strict party-line vote of 10–8.

In committee, Democrats made the same arguments against the measure as had their counterparts in the House, worrying about employers coercing their workers into taking one form of overtime, particularly comp time, over another. "The employers supporting this bill want to pay their workers less," said the panel's ranking member, Edward M. Kennedy, D-Mass. "This is the real story."

But Republicans noted that the system had worked well for more than ten years in the public sector. "This has not been a problem" in the public sector, said Mike DeWine, R-Ohio. "It's voluntary. The employee doesn't have to enter this."

The panel approved 10–8 an amendment by DeWine clarifying that employee acceptance of comp time would be voluntary and permissible only after mutual agreement by workers and employers.

The committee also rejected a number of Democratic amendments, all by party-line votes of 8–10. Among the proposed changes was an amendment offered by Kennedy that would have prohibited employers from discriminating against workers or forcing them to accept one form of compensation over another.

The bill reached the Senate floor a few months later, but stalled as Democrats blocked a number of attempts to limit debate and bring the measure to a vote. The first attempt to invoke cloture—on May 15—failed by a **key vote of 53–47 (R 53–2; D 0–45)**. A three-fifths majority (60 votes) is required to limit debate and bring the measure to a vote. *(1997 key votes, p. 865)*

A second and final attempt to invoke cloture occurred a few weeks later on June 4 and also failed. This time, supporters could only muster 51 votes to opponents' 47. Three Republicans who were up for reelection in 1998—Ben Nighthorse Campbell of Colorado, Alfonse M. D'Amato of New York, and Arlen Specter of Pennsylvania—voted against cloture.

After the June 4 vote, Republican leaders gave up trying to invoke cloture and contented themselves with the prospect of using the issue against the Democrats in the following year's congressional elections.

Work Safety Bills

Efforts by Congress to overhaul the workings of the Occupational Safety and Health Administration (OSHA) stalled in 1997 because of fierce opposition from congressional Democrats and the White House. But three narrowly tailored OSHA-related bills were enacted in 1998.

On Oct. 22, 1997, the Senate Labor and Human Resources Committee approved legislation (S 1237—S Rept 105-159) aimed at reining in OSHA—an agency that business groups and congressional conservatives had long targeted as too confrontational toward employers, but that labor groups and Democrats regard as essential to ensuring worker safety. The bill was approved by a strict party-line vote of 10–8.

The bill and a companion measure in the House (HR 2579) would have shifted OSHA's focus from enforcing workplace health and safety laws to helping employers fix problems, often without fining companies for infractions. It proposed giving employers several other options, including using private and state consultants, in determining whether they met OSHA requirements.

The bills—the brainchild of Rep. Michael Enzi, R-Wyo.—tried to address GOP concerns that the agency acted as an enforcer instead of a teacher. The measures included provisions to limit the types of safety violations that triggered citations and to allow employers two years of freedom from citations and fines if private consultants certified that their workplace met OSHA standards.

Although Democrats supported parts of the legislation, they opposed the incentives Republicans wanted to give employers for hiring such consultants. Sen. Jack Reed, D-R.I., said that two years of protection from civil OSHA penalties just for hiring an outside consultant would allow employers to "write a check and buy themselves two years of immunity."

Enzi said that he would try to work out differences between Republicans and Democrats, but the gap was too wide. After winning narrow approval in the Labor Committee, S 1237 was pushed to the back burner. Meanwhile, HR 2579 was never even taken up by a House committee.

Instead, in 1998, both parties focused on quickly clearing the following three more narrowly tailored workplace safety bills that could attract bipartisan support.

• The first (HR 2864—PL 105-197) bill authorized an existing program that allowed state officials to offer advice to employers on improving worker safety without fear of federal penalties.

OSHA had long worked with states—under the authority granted it in the Occupational Safety and Health Act of 1970 (PL 91-596)—to provide workplace consultants to businesses on how to meet OSHA standards. The bill formally authorized the program and provided that if a state consultant found a possible violation of federal worker safety laws, the employer would not suffer federal penalties if he or she quickly fixed the problem.

The House passed the measure, sponsored by Cass Ballenger, R-N.C., on March 17, and the Senate cleared it June 24—both on voice votes. President Clinton signed it July 16.

• A second measure (HR 2877—PL 105-198), also sponsored by Ballenger, barred OSHA from including any references in the job performance reviews of its inspectors to the number of citations or enforcement actions they had issued.

While the Clinton administration opposed using citations in performance reviews, Ballenger said he had heard that the agency had wrongly encouraged OSHA inspectors to take a harder line with employers by including the number of citations in annual job performance reviews. Proponents of the bill said such a policy had forced inspectors to operate under a de facto quota system.

The House passed HR 2877 on March 17 by voice vote; the Senate cleared the measure on June 24, also by voice vote. Clinton signed the bill on July 16.

• A third bill (S 2112—PL 105-241) allowed the full enforcement of OSHA regulations in U.S. Postal Service facilities and offices. OSHA standards already applied to the Postal Service, but the Labor Department and many state agencies lacked authority to issue citations to the agency, making the regulations difficult to enforce.

TEAMSTERS PROBE

Republicans in 1997 once again turned a spotlight on the 1.4 million-member International Brotherhood of Teamsters, but the GOP focus was no longer on the union's Mafia ties, as it had been in the 1980s. Instead, GOP members took a close look at a recent union election and the role of the federal government in that process.

At issue was the December 1996 Teamsters leadership election, which was court-monitored, federally funded under a consent decree, and subsequently invalidated because of funding irregularities involving the reelection campaign of Ron Carey, who had beaten James P. Hoffa, son of the legendary Teamsters leader. The federal government had spent $17.6 million to oversee the election yet had been unable to keep it free from fraud. On Aug. 17, 1997, a federal court invalidated the election and ordered a rerun in light of evidence that Carey had funneled illegal contributions into his campaign. In addition, evidence was presented showing that the Carey campaign had approached the Democratic National Committee in an effort to use it as a conduit for additional campaign funds that Carey could not take legally. Carey was

prohibited from running again, and Hoffa was subsequently elected Teamster's president.

For the rerun election, Congress barred the use of federal funds. The language was included in the spending bills for the departments of Labor, Health and Human Services (HHS), and Education (PL 105-78), signed by President Clinton on Nov. 13, 1997, and for the departments of Commerce, Justice, and State (PL 105-119), signed on Nov. 26.

One month earlier in October, Republicans on the House Education and the Workforce Subcommittee on Oversight and Investigations had started hearings on the Teamsters' election and the role of money and politics in unions in general. The House panel eventually issued a report in February 1999 that criticized Carey and other Teamsters leaders with nearly bankrupting the union—due partly to the union's effort to financially support Democratic candidates for Congress. Congressional Democrats, while condemning the Teamsters for the botched election, criticized Republicans for taking things too far. They argued that the GOP was looking for ways to retaliate against unions for their aggressive and well-financed attacks on Republican candidates during the 1996 elections.

In addition to facilitating enforcement, the measure prohibited the Postal Service from citing the cost of OSHA compliance as a factor in deciding whether to close or consolidate post offices, restrict or eliminate any service, or raise postal rates. It also required the Postal Service to consider the effect of any closings or consolidations on the community, employees, and economic savings.

The Senate passed the bill by voice vote on July 31; the House cleared it Sept. 14, also by voice vote. Clinton signed it Sept. 28.

Workplace Teams

A Republican effort to allow businesses to set up groups of workers and managers to address workplace issues stalled in the Senate in spring 1997 under vociferous opposition from Democrats and the White House. The so-called TEAM Act (S 295—S Rept 105-12) had proposed amending the 1935 Labor Relations Act to allow the formation of worker-management groups to address such as issues as productivity, quality control, and workplace safety.

Republicans said the changes would promote innovation and give U.S. employers an edge in the global marketplace. "Rather than look backwards at the workplace of the 1930s, we should look forward to the twenty-first century," said Labor panel chairman James M. Jeffords, R-Vt. "The law needs to be fixed."

But Democrats said the bill would undermine the rights of workers to unionize and bargain collectively. President Clinton, who had vetoed a similar bill in 1996, threatened to do the same to S 295. (*Congress and the Nation Vol. IX, p. 673*)

The Senate Labor and Human Resources Committee approved S 295 on March 5 by a party-line vote of 10–8. The panel rejected a number of Democratic amendments including one offered by ranking Democratic member Edward M. Kennedy of Massachusetts that would protect workers who participated in workplace teams from losing their right to unionize. Kennedy contended that workers could be deemed supervisors or managers as a result of their involvement in a worker-management group. The proposal was rejected 8–10.

1999–2000

The 106th Congress produced little labor-related legislation. Congress did approve legislation that made it easier for employers to give hourly workers stock options. It also repealed the unpopular limit on the amount of income that persons over sixty-five could earn if they did not want to lose some or all Social Security benefits. Seniors, and many employers looking for workers, said this was an outdated provision from New Deal days that discouraged retired persons from remaining part of the workforce.

A one-dollar increase in the minimum wage was considered but not approved even though leaders of both parties supported the idea. The increase became entangled in a controversial GOP tax cut package that died in the waning days before the 2000 election.

Another significant measure—legislation that would have allowed workers to contribute more to tax-free pension plans—also fell victim to the fight over taxes at the end of 2000. Like the minimum wage increase, the pension overhaul enjoyed bipartisan support.

Congress also tried to shore up the sagging railroad worker pension system with legislation that would allow pension managers to invest employee contributions in stocks and bonds. But Senate Republicans worried about its consequences for the fiscal 2001 budget.

Minimum Wage

Efforts to raise the minimum wage by one dollar stalled in Congress, even though both chambers passed versions of an increase. There were a number of obstacles to enactment, including differences in the House and Senate bills over how to phase in the wage boost. But the legislation also was caught up in a procedural thicket for much of 2000, with the Senate version attached to a bankruptcy law overhaul bill (S 625) and the House language part of a number of different tax cut bills.

The Senate finally disentangled the minimum wage and bankruptcy measures, clearing the bankruptcy bill but setting the minimum wage provisions aside. Meanwhile, the House passed a wage increase as part of a large tax cut, but the proposal died in the Senate in the face of a presidential veto.

BACKGROUND

Congress first established a nationwide uniform minimum wage—25 cents an hour—in the Fair Labor Standards Act of 1938 (PL 75-718). Since then, Congress has raised the minimum wage periodically.

Increasing the wage has traditionally been popular and usually attracts broad support on Capitol Hill. Labor groups and others often claim that the minimum wage is too low and it does not provide enough income for someone to support a family. But business groups and some Republicans

counter that raising the minimum wage too much or too frequently produces layoffs as employers are forced to cut workers in an effort to meet higher payroll costs.

This clash of ideologies was in evidence when the minimum wage was last raised in 1996. That year, Democrats did not control either house of Congress, but they did have the moral high ground since, at $4.15 per hour, the minimum wage was nearing a forty-year low in inflation-adjusted dollars. *(Congress and the Nation Vol. IX, p. 666)*

In 1996 President Clinton and congressional Democrats used the minimum wage issue to bludgeon Republicans in the court of public opinion, depicting opponents of the measure as unfair to the working poor and generous to wealthy business interests. GOP leaders in Congress, who had vowed not to allow a vote on a minimum wage bill, increasingly found themselves on the defensive.

Eventually, the Democratic public relations campaign forced the defection of about two dozen Republican moderates in the House and weakened the GOP leadership's resolve to keep the issue off the floor. As a result, legislation (PL 104-188) raising the minimum wage to $5.15 an hour over two years was eventually brought to the House and Senate floor, where it passed easily.

LEGISLATIVE ACTION

In an effort to avoid appearing as obstructionists, as the Democrats had portrayed them successfully in 1996, Republican leaders in the House put their weight behind legislation (HR 3081) that would raise the minimum wage from $5.15 to $6.15 over three years. The measure, sponsored by Rep. Rick Lazio, R-N.Y., also would cut taxes for a variety of businesses and individuals by more than $30 billion over five years.

But as Congress moved into the fall of 1999, the plan showed its weakness. Some moderate Republicans—who had defected in the 1996 showdown—were leaning toward voting for a Democratic bill that would raise the minimum wage by one dollar over two years without tax cuts. Meanwhile, conservative Democrats, usually reliable for the GOP on business issues, had different opinions on how to increase the wage.

In early November Senate leaders from both parties came to an agreement to allow a floor vote on competing minimum wage and tax cut provisions. The Republican version would raise the wage by one dollar over three years and include $18.4 billion in business tax breaks over five years. A Democratic alternative would raise the wage by one dollar over two years and contain $11.5 billion in tax breaks over five years.

On Nov. 9, the first official votes on the issue occurred in both the House and Senate. On that day the House Ways and Means Committee approved HR 3081 (H Rept 106-467, Pt. 1) by a vote of 23–14. During the markup the panel rejected, 12–23, an amendment offered by Charles Rangel, D-N.Y., that would raise the business meal deduction from 50 to 65 percent and allow employers a $2,000-per-child deduction for educating and training employees' children.

In the Senate the competing Democratic and Republican provisions were offered as amendments to a bankruptcy overhaul bill (S 625—S Rept 106-49) then on the floor. The Democratic amendment—offered by Edward M. Kennedy of Massachusetts—was tabled by a vote of 50–48. Four Republicans—Lincoln Chafee of Rhode Island, James Jeffords of Vermont, Olympia J. Snowe of Maine, and Arlen Specter of Pennsylvania—voted with the Democrats and against tabling the amendment.

The Republican proposal was then brought up and approved by a vote of 55–45.

But the Senate did not finish consideration of S 625 before adjourning for 1999. The measure, substituted into a House-passed bankruptcy bill (HR 833), did not leave the Senate until Feb. 2, 2000, when it was passed by a vote of 83–14. During the interim, the Senate had dramatically increased the package's tax cuts, reaching a total of $103 billion over ten years.

During the next six months Senate Majority Leader Trent Lott, R-Miss., worked to disentangle the minimum wage, bankruptcy, and tax cut provisions in order to move them through the Senate as separate bills. The tax provisions were an obstacle to clearing the other parts of the bill because they originated in the Senate and could have been subject to an objection in the House as they violated its constitutional prerogative to act first on revenue proposals. Also, Democratic opposition to the three-year phase in of the minimum wage imperiled the bankruptcy bill.

But Lott ran into opposition on a whole host of issues, including disagreements about bankruptcy provisions. The minimum wage legislation stalled in the Senate and did not come up for a vote in 2000.

Meanwhile on March 9, 2000, the House took up HR 3846—its version of the minimum wage increase. A critical moment came when forty-two Republicans joined 203 Democrats in a **key vote of 246–179 (R 42–173; D 203–5; I 1–1)** to adopt an amendment by James A. Traficant Jr., D-Ohio, that would raise the minimum wage by one dollar over two years—as Democrats had requested. The amendment showed the strength of support for the wage boost in the House among moderates within the Republican ranks. The House went on to pass HR 3846 by a vote of 282–143. *(2000 key votes, p. 915)*

That same day, the text of HR 3846 was, by previous agreement, automatically appended to the House's original minimum wage and tax bill, HR 3081, which then passed 257–169. HR 3081 also contained much expanded tax breaks for businesses, totaling $122.7 billion over ten years. However, Congress did not complete action on the tax cut.

In late August President Clinton and House Speaker J. Dennis Hastert, R-Ill., agreed in principle on a plan to provide the minimum wage increase over two years and $76 billion in tax breaks for businesses over the next ten years.

But congressional Democrats still worried about the size of the tax breaks for businesses. In addition, they opposed a provision in the wage increase that excluded telemarketers from the increase since their employees make the bulk of their salary on commission.

In September Republican congressional leaders—smarting from presidential vetoes of bills repealing the marriage and estate taxes—began an effort to cobble together a new bill including those tax provisions. Into this catchall, the leaders added the dollar increase in the minimum wage, many of the original business tax reductions, as well as an increase in the amount workers could contribute to tax-deferred retirement accounts and provisions to allow the self-employed to deduct 100 percent of their health insurance costs. The package would have cut taxes $270 billion over ten years.

On Oct. 26 the House passed HR 2614 (H Rept 106-1004) containing these measures by a vote of 237–174. The measure attracted the support of thirty-three mostly centrist House Democrats. But Senate Democrats and the White House bitterly opposed the bill, and the president threatened to veto it.

With just days remaining before the 2000 elections on Nov. 7, many conservative Republicans in both chambers were in no mood this late in the session to find a compromise that Democrats and the White House could support. Instead, they preferred to pin their hopes on the election of George W. Bush as president and the passage of a much more sweeping tax package in the 107th Congress.

Railroad Retirement

The House passed legislation (HR 4844) aimed at bolstering the long-term solvency of federally guaranteed pensions for nearly one million railroad workers, retirees, and their families. The legislation represented a long-running effort by railroad workers and companies to revamp the industry's ailing pension system.

But the measure died in the Senate in late 2000 because of opposition by fiscally conservative Republicans who worried about its potential impact on the fiscal 2001 budget.

BACKGROUND

After many railroads went bankrupt during the Great Depression of the 1930s, the government assumed responsibility for workers' pensions. Under that federal system—still in place in 2000—railroad companies and their employees paid a special payroll tax to finance these pensions. The tax was separate from the one that financed Social Security, for which rail workers do not qualify.

But the railroad pension system was facing long-term insolvency problems, with a $40 billion shortfall in potential benefit payments to all workers who had yet to retire and their survivors.

The measure aimed to address this potential trouble by transferring the $15 billion held by the U.S. Treasury for railroad retirees to a new board that would invest the money in stocks and bonds in the hope of getting a much higher return. The backers of the bill believed that profits from this type of investment could also reduce the percentage that the railroad companies have to pay into the pension system for each covered worker—dropping from 16.1 percent of a worker's annual compensation to as low as 13.1 percent. The bill also would reduce the vesting requirement for a rail worker from ten to five years on the job.

This proposal was agreed to by the railroads and rail unions, which had worked for years to hammer out a compromise. Both said that they were confident the move would boost workers' retirement security.

LEGISLATIVE ACTION

The House Transportation and Infrastructure Committee approved the measure (H Rept 106-777, Pt. 1) by voice vote on July 19, 2000. Members of the committee refrained from offering amendments because they did not want to jeopardize a deal that was the result of years of talks between the parties.

But when the House Ways and Means Committee took up the bill on July 25, the panel added a provision repealing the 4.3 cents-per-gallon tax on diesel fuel paid by freight railroads and inland barges. The committee then approved the bill (H Rept 106-777, Pt. 2) by voice vote.

Transportation and Infrastructure Committee Chairman Bud Shuster, R-Pa., urged Ways and Means Chairman Bill Archer, R-Texas, to remove the diesel tax repeal, fearing that the pension bill could become a vehicle for other tax provisions. At the urging of the House GOP leadership, Archer complied and the full House passed HR 4844 on Sept. 7 by an overwhelming vote of 391–25.

But the bill ran into trouble among Republicans in the Senate, even though it was given voice vote approval by the Finance Committee on Sept. 28. GOP lawmakers had promised to use no more than ten percent—about $28 billion in fiscal 2001—of the budget surplus for discretionary spending. As a matter of congressional scorekeeping, transferring funds from the Treasury Department to the new rail board—as required in HR 4844—would count as $15 billion in lost revenue in fiscal 2001.

As a result, powerful Republicans, such as Majority Whip Don Nickles of Oklahoma and Phil Gramm of Texas, came out against the measure in its existing form. This opposition, coming so late in the session, killed all chances for enactment in 2000.

Stock Options

The Senate on April 12, 2000, cleared a widely supported bill (S 2323) aimed at allowing companies to offer stock options to their rank-and-file employees, without also having to increase overtime pay—a move intended to increase the availability of such benefits to hourly workers. The Senate vote was 95–0.

The House, a month later on May 3, 2000, passed the measure, again with full bipartisan backing, 421–0. Because of its popularity, the bill was not taken up by committees in either chamber and was moved quickly to the House and Senate floors for votes. President Clinton signed the bill (PL 106-202) on May 18.

The measure, sponsored by Sen. Mitch McConnell, R-Ky., amended the Fair Labor Standards Act of 1938 to exclude stock options, stock appreciation rights, and stock purchase programs from employees' regular pay rates, which are used to calculate overtime pay.

Historically, companies provided stocks or other equity-based benefits mainly to upper management, but not to hourly employees. In recent years this has changed, as more companies, especially technology firms, have offered such options to hourly workers.

An advisory opinion issued by the Labor Department in February 1999, however, appeared likely to dampen that trend. The Labor Department said that, under the Fair Labor Standards Act, employers are required to include profits from the exercise of stock options in determining hourly workers' "regular rate of pay." This pay rate, according to the 1938 law, then determines the amount employees are then paid for overtime. Companies must pay hourly employees overtime of at least one-and-a-half times their hourly rate of pay after they work more than forty hours a week.

In response to the 1999 ruling, a bipartisan group of senators held negotiations with the Labor Department to determine what changes would be needed to prevent the likelihood that employers would stop offering stock or equity benefits to employees out of fear that profits would boost hourly rates and overtime pay in the process. The talks yielded a deal that produced the bill.

Pension Changes

On July 19, 2000, the House, by an overwhelming vote of 401–25, passed legislation that would allow workers to set aside more money in their company pension plans and to transfer those assets when they change jobs. But instead of moving forward as a freestanding bill, the language in the measure became part of the end-of-the-year tax package, which died in the last days of the 106th Congress because of opposition by the Clinton administration.

The measure (HR 1102) would increase the annual contribution limit to a tax-free individual retirement account (IRA) from $2,000 to $5,000 by 2003 with an increase in the limit of at least $500 a year after that. The change would apply to both Roth IRAs, in which contributions are taxed but withdrawals are generally tax-free, and traditional IRAs, in which taxes are deferred until funds are withdrawn.

SOCIAL SECURITY REFORM PROPOSALS GENERATE LITTLE AGREEMENT

In his 1998 State of the Union address, President Clinton made Social Security the centerpiece of his domestic policy agenda when he urged lawmakers to "save Social Security first." His high-profile call for action dramatized an issue long studied (and worried over) by policy wonks and politicians alike. But Clinton's charge to Congress went nowhere, victim to fundamental differences between the political parties and an unresolved public debate about the basic purpose of Social Security.

The Social Security system dated from the New Deal programs enacted in the 1930s during the presidency of Franklin D. Roosevelt. It was designed to provide financial security for Americans in old age to prevent the ravages of poverty that had become so evident during the Great Depression of that decade. It was constructed as an income transfer program in which the earnings of working individuals would be taxed to pay the benefits of their older generations in retirement. Throughout most of its history, the system worked as planned, with plenty of workers to support the still small community of senior citizens.

Although the system remained financially sound when Clinton made his comments, the actuarial projections into the twenty-first century were gloomy. These projections showed looming financial problems as the post–World War II baby boom generation retired, life expectancy continued to increase, and fewer workers remained in the economy to pay benefits of their elders.

Although Social Security at the turn of the century was running a trust fund surplus, projections indicated that by 2032 the fund could be bankrupt when benefits paid to retirees exceed revenues the system collected. Most lawmakers and policy analysts—but not all—accepted this view and agreed that changes would be needed. At that point, however, agreement ended. Instead, members of Congress, Washington think tanks, academics, and others proposed various remedies for overhauling the sixty-three-year-old retirement program. Suggestions ranged from minor adjustments to the system, such as gradually raising workers' payroll taxes, cutting benefits, or preserving the surplus in a "lockbox," to the following major structural changes.

Raising the Retirement Age

Although the retirement age had been raised since Social Security's inception in 1935, some advocates argued for additional increases to reduce the strain on Social Security. For example, a bipartisan plan from the National Commission on Retirement Policy suggested increasing the early retirement age from sixty-two to sixty-five by 2017 and the normal retirement age from sixty-five to seventy by 2029. (Under law in effect in 2000, an individual can take early retirement at age sixty-two but with reduced benefit payments.) Supporters of this proposal noted that if the retirement age increased to seventy, Social Security could pay recipients later and, presumably, for a shorter time, thereby building up Social Security's reserves. Opponents argued that allowing workers to stay on the job longer could force older workers to labor in pain or with debilitating conditions. Some might then have to apply for disability benefits, increasing the cost to the government. They also argued that this trend could prevent younger workers from moving up the career ladder as quickly, creating job frustrations among this group.

The bill also would increase the annual limit on contributions to tax-deferred 401(k) pension plans, from $10,000 to $15,000 by 2005. In addition, the measure would make it easier for workers to take their pension benefits with them when changing jobs and would allow workers to become vested in their pension plans in three years, rather than the current five. HR 1102 would cost the Treasury an estimated $52.2 billion in lost revenue during its first decade.

The House Education and the Workforce Committee approved the bill (H Rept 106-753), which was sponsored by Reps. Rob Portman, R-Ohio, and Benjamin L. Cardin, D-Md., by voice vote on July 14, 1999. Just one day shy of a year later, on July 13, 2000, the House Ways and Means Committee approved a similar measure (HR 4843—H Rept 106-753) by a vote of 27–9. The following week, the full House took up the issue, passing the text of HR 1102, the original bill.

The measure then moved to the Senate, where the Finance Committee approved it 16–0 on Sept. 7. The panel's marked-up version included provisions not contained in the House-passed bill. Most notably, the bill provided $8.3 billion in tax credits for lower-income individuals who contributed to an IRA or other retirement plan and $5.4 billion in tax credits for small businesses that established retirement accounts for one hundred or more workers. The panel also adopted by voice vote an amendment, offered by Sen. Daniel Patrick Moynihan, D-N.Y., creating a Roth 401(k), which would have worked the same way as a Roth IRA does.

By the time the Senate began working on HR 1102, in early September, GOP leaders thought it might be a vehicle for a catch-all tax package. Instead, though, the text of HR 1102 as well as other tax-related provisions were added to HR 2614, a relatively obscure small business bill that passed the House on Oct. 26. HR 2614 ultimately stalled because of a failure on the part of Republican leaders to come to an agreement with the White House and congressional Democrats. *(Tax bill, p. 117)*

"Privatizing" the System

The most significant debate swirled around this approach. A growing number of policy makers embraced the idea of "privatizing" the system, or shifting some payroll taxes to private retirement accounts that would be invested in the stock market. The existing Social Security payroll tax was 12.4 percent (with 6.2 percent each paid by workers and employers). Various proposals suggested diverting anywhere from 2 percent to two-thirds of this tax into personal investment savings accounts.

Generally favored by Republicans and fellow conservatives, as well as enthusiastically endorsed by Wall Street investment brokers, and heralded by George W. Bush during the 2000 presidential campaign, this plan promised to earn workers higher rates of return than possible under the current system and to raise money to finance Social Security without raising taxes. The presumed higher rate of return from private accounts would be offset in reduced guaranteed monthly Social Security payments.

Skeptics insisted that the stock market was too volatile a place to entrust the retirement welfare of any generation, and could threaten the system's pledge to guarantee the elderly well-defined benefits. They also raised concerns about the expense of establishing and administering private accounts.

Although not always well articulated, at the heart of this argument was the unresolved public debate about whether Social Security was a fundamental social contract between generations, as well as a system to at least modestly redistribute income among Americans, or was and should be seen as simply a mechanism for individuals, acting on their own, to increase their wealth and look after their own needs as best their abilities allowed.

Another dimension of this aspect of the debate involved the social safety net that undergirds the system. Critics of privatizing feared that some workers would make unwise investment decisions that would lead to impoverished old age. They argued that traditional Social Security guaranteed at least a minimal monthly income.

Direct Federal Investment

Similar to privatization, this reform plan proposed diverting part of Social Security taxes to the financial markets, allowing the government to place Social Security trust funds in common stocks instead of in low-yielding government bonds. In his 1999 State of the Union address, President Clinton outlined a proposal that called for the government to directly invest about 15 percent of the trust fund in the stock market in an effort to realize higher financial returns.

Many Democrats argued that this proposal, or variations of it, could boost the system's investment returns while preserving the core elements of the government's social safety net. However, critics were skeptical about the government's ability to make the right investment decisions and worried about whether this approach would give Washington too much influence on private capital markets. Conservatives were horrified at the thought of politicians having a major say in the way funds were invested on Wall Street, fearing that elected officials would try to steer the money toward favored political goals.

Social Security Earnings Limit

Congress in 2000 cleared legislation that removed the limit on how much outside income retirees age sixty-five through sixty-nine could earn and still collect full Social Security benefits. The president signed the bill (HR 5—PL 106-182) on April 7.

The Social Security "earnings test" was created during the Depression in an effort to discourage senior citizens from holding onto their jobs during a period of high unemployment. It reduced benefits by $1 for every $3 earned for Social Security beneficiaries up to age sixty-nine up to an annual limit ($17,000 in 2000).

Those who lost benefits in this way received higher monthly checks later on to compensate for the loss. There were no earnings tests for recipients age seventy and older. According to the Social Security Administration, 800,000 people were affected by the earnings limit in 1999.

The bill repealed the test for people above the age required to collect full Social Security retirement benefits, which was gradually increasing from sixty-five to sixty-seven. It did not repeal the earnings test for retirees age sixty-two through sixty-four nor for individuals receiving Social Security disability benefits.

Enactment of the earnings repeal was the end result of twenty-seven months of discussion on overhauling Social Security, which was unprepared financially to withstand the impending eligibility of the huge baby boom generation. Still, despite several attempts by the White House and various members of Congress to revamp the Social Security system, the politically popular earnings test was the only Social Security bill enacted in the 106th Congress.

Bipartisan enthusiasm for the legislation was made easier by the endorsement of the AARP, voiced at a hearing of the House Ways and Means Social Security Subcommittee on Feb. 15, 2000. "Given the increased longevity and generally improved health of many retirees, the prospect of an aging society, and a slower-growing workforce, it is critical that we find ways to better tap the valuable and underutilized skills of older workers," said AARP board member Jane Baumgarten.

The following day, the subcommittee approved the measure by voice vote, after only ten minutes of cursory debate. The full Ways and Means Committee approved it Feb. 29, also by voice vote. The panel reported it (H Rept 106-507) March 1, and the full House passed it that same day by a vote of 422–0.

The Senate likewise managed to resist adding what could have proved divisive amendments to the bill. It approved the measure by a vote of 100–0 on March 22, with one technical correction added by Senate Finance Committee Chairman William V. Roth Jr., R-Del., which kept sixty-four-year-olds from hitting a lower income limit than they would have under the existing law.

The House ratified the change, clearing the measure March 28 by a vote of 419–0.

Ergonomics Standards

Republican efforts to stop proposed new ergonomics regulations on repetitive tasks from taking effect stalled at the very end of the 106th Congress. But the newly elected 107th Congress overturned the rules.

Since the early 1990s, the Occupational Safety and Health Administration (OSHA) had been at work on regulations to limit injuries or disabilities from performing repetitive tasks. The proposed rules would require that 1.6 million employers set up programs to limit the repetitive motion injuries of about 27 million workers—from airport cargo handlers to automobile assembly-line workers, and from grocery checkout clerks to textile mill weavers. Another 300,000 businesses each year would have to act the first time any worker suffered a job-related repetitive stress disorder that required medical treatment, reassignment to light duty, or time off.

Business groups vigorously opposed the OSHA rules, arguing that their vagueness and breadth would tremendously drive up the price of compliance, costing companies up to $80 billion a year and leading to reduced competitiveness and even lay-offs. OSHA and labor unions, however, claimed that the rules were flexible enough not to be disruptive or expensive and would only cost employers $4.2 billion annually. In addition, they claimed, the new regulations would actually save companies money by reducing injuries and, hence, lost productivity.

As the Jan. 16, 2001, deadline for the new rules to take effect approached, key congressional Republicans and Democrats met with White House staff to hammer out a deal. On Oct. 30, 2000, the negotiators announced that they had worked out an agreement that would be added to the fiscal 2001 appropriations bill (HR 4577) for the departments of Labor, Health and Human Services, and Education. Under the deal, OSHA would be allowed to issue its final rule on schedule, but the new president would have the option until June 1, 2001, of stopping the regulations from taking effect.

By the end of the day, however, Republican leaders were repudiating the deal, arguing that the legislative language—drafted by President Clinton's Office of Management and Budget—did not clearly give the new president the authority he would need to stop the regulations. Democrats countered that the draft language was fine and that the GOP was simply looking for an excuse to scuttle the agreement because business groups were still not happy with it. Regardless, the language was removed from HR 4577 and the regulations went into effect unencumbered by congressional conditions.

But the GOP strategy paid off. On March 7, 2001, the new 107th Congress cleared a measure (SJ 6—PL 107-5) that entirely overturned the OSHA regulations less than two months after they had taken effect. Republicans used an untested legislative tool, known as the Congressional Review Act (PL 104-121), which allows lawmakers to erase rules with simple majority votes in both chambers.

Amish Work Exception

On March 2, 1999, the House passed legislation that would allow Amish youth to work in sawmills and other woodworking settings, exempting them from Labor Department rules designed to protect children. But the measure (HR 221—H Rept 106-31) died after stalling in the Senate.

The bill aimed to help preserve Amish religious traditions that call for youngsters to work in apprenticeship settings after they finish eighth grade, which is the end of schooling for Amish youth.

The measure, sponsored by Rep. Joseph R. Pitts, R-Pa., was given voice vote approval by the House Committee on Education and the Workforce on Feb. 10. The House also approved the bill by voice vote.

Federal child-protection laws prohibit those under sixteen from working in manufacturing operations, such as sawmills, and those under eighteen from working in other hazardous occupations, even for tasks that do not require mechanical equipment. Amish businesses, which by tradition employ boys in their early teens, have been fined thousands of dollars for violating these rules.

Under the bill, Amish teens would be able to work in limited woodworking settings and still would be prohibited from directly operating mechanical equipment.

Supporters argued that the measure balanced the conflict between the need to protect the young and preserve the Amish way of life. But opponents in the Senate and elsewhere worried that allowing teenagers to work in potentially dangerous settings could lead to tragic accidents. Others argued that exempting one religious group from a law might be unconstitutional.

"Salting" Revisited

In 1999 House Republicans tried to resurrect their legislation to ban union "salting," but the attempt proved short-lived because of fierce Democratic opposition. Salting is a practice in which union organizers apply for jobs at non-union plants in hopes of working from inside to push fellow workers to sign union cards.

Legislation that would permit employers to refuse to hire "salts" passed the House in 1997 but failed to pass in the Senate in the face of strong Democratic opposition. *("Salting" ban, p. 575)* A similar bill (HR 1441), introduced by House Education and the Workforce Committee Chairman Bill Goodling, R-Pa., did not advance nearly so far. Goodling's committee approved the bill on July 29 by a vote of 21–18.

Democrats did not defend the practice, but they argued that a "salting" ban would lead to discrimination against legitimate applicants who had been active union members. This opposition, as well as a threatened presidential veto, led bill supporters to abandon their efforts to pass the measure.

Attorney's Fees

Legislation (HR 1987—H Rept 106-385) that would have awarded attorney's fees and court costs to some companies that prevailed in government-instigated labor proceedings was approved 24–19 by the House Education and the Workforce Committee on July 29, 1999.

House Republican leaders had planned to bring the bill to the floor in early 2000, but they pulled it after learning that labor lobbyists had blocked the support of the twenty to twenty-five Democrats that the Republicans needed to pass the measure.

Under the bill, small companies that prevailed in suits filed by the National Labor Relations Board (NLRB) or the Occupational Safety and Health Administration (OSHA) would be reimbursed. Only firms with fewer than one hundred employees would be eligible to recover costs.

House Republicans said that the bill was necessary because the agencies sometimes unfairly and aggressively pursued companies, forcing them to pay high attorney's fees to defend themselves. The measure aimed to make the NLRB and OSHA less "trigger happy." But Democrats countered that the bill would simply make these agencies more reluctant to enforce the law, hurting workers and unions.

CHAPTER 13

Law and Justice

Introduction 589

Law and Law Enforcement 593

The Supreme Court 684

Law and Law Enforcement

During the second administration of President Bill Clinton, lawmakers engaged in fierce partisan battles over such issues as gun control and juvenile crime. GOP leaders, rather than the White House, largely set the law enforcement agenda, but they generally failed to win a consensus on major initiatives. Republicans and Democrats also wrangled over judicial appointments, leaving numerous judgeships vacant. A frustrated Clinton suggested that GOP leaders were targeting minority and women appointees.

Against the backdrop of unusually strained partisan relations and the 1998 impeachment of the president, lawmakers deadlocked over a number of emotional issues, ranging from requiring background checks of purchases at gun shows to banning flag desecration. In addition to traditional divides over toughening punishments for criminals, many of the battles spilled over into social areas, such as whether to accord legal protection to a fetus and to rein in a judiciary that conservatives viewed as overly activist.

But Congress did manage to clear two significant bipartisan measures in 2000: an election-year crime bill and a measure curbing the government's ability to seize the assets of suspected criminals. Both measures, significantly modified during negotiations, cleared in their final form with little dissent.

Lawmakers also kept themselves busy on immigration matters. In both the 105th and the 106th Congresses, they sided with high-tech companies by expanding the number of visas that could be issued to overseas workers in the high-tech industry, and they softened some of the requirements of the 1996 immigration bill.

Many issues, predictably, pitted liberals against conservatives. Gun control initiatives, for example, stalled because GOP leaders refused to assent to the regulations promoted by liberal Democrats and administration officials. But when it came to matters involving the power of law enforcement agencies to investigate U.S. citizens, the most conservative and liberal members of Congress often found common ground, forming an unusual alliance to curb the reach of federal agents.

JUVENILES AND GUNS

Few issues roiled Congress more than plans to reduce the juvenile crime rate. Despite widespread public concern over violent acts committed by teenagers, lawmakers could not come to terms over the question of whether juveniles should be tried as adults. Conservatives—and, to a lesser degree, the White House—favored a get-tough approach on young criminals, including longer sentences. Many Democrats, however, wanted to emphasize prevention programs.

The politically sensitive issue of gun control became inextricably tangled in the debate, as Democrats attempted to use juvenile justice legislation to advance gun control aims. Despite strong public support for tougher restrictions on gun ownership, Congress failed to enact even modest gun control provisions—much to the exasperation of Clinton.

After deadlocking over a juvenile justice measure in the 105th, lawmakers appeared to be nearing a deal on the issue early in 1999. To pick up support of key Democrats, Republicans dropped provisions that violent teens be tried in adult courts. Instead, negotiators struck a bipartisan deal to give crime-fighting grants to the states, allowing them to decide how best to combat youth crime.

The deal unraveled on April 20, when two heavily armed teenagers went on a rampage in their Littleton, Colo., high school, killing a total of fifteen people, including themselves. Anger over the worst school shooting in the nation's history spurred demands for tougher gun control measures. Lawmakers, facing a new type of youth violence, found them-

REFERENCES

Discussion of law enforcement policy for the years 1945–1964 may be found in *Congress and the Nation Vol. I*, pp. 1671–1676; for the years 1965–1968, *Congress and the Nation Vol. II*, pp. 309–334; for the years 1969–1972, *Congress and the Nation Vol. III*, pp. 255–286; for the years 1973–1976, *Congress and the Nation Vol. IV*, pp. 559–618; for the years 1977–1980, *Congress and the Nation Vol. V*, pp. 715–753; for the years 1981–1984, *Congress and the Nation Vol. VI*, pp. 675–709; for the years 1985–1988, *Congress and the Nation Vol. VII*, pp. 713–784; for the years 1989–1992, *Congress and the Nation Vol. VIII*, pp. 741–799; for the years 1993–1996, *Congress and the Nation Vol. IX*, pp. 679–758.

selves deeply divided over the approach that Washington should take.

Senators plunged into the issue in May, debating a controversial measure that would allow prosecutors to try the most violent of youth offenders as adults. The bill also would authorize $5 billion in grants to states, with an emphasis on enforcement over prevention. During a chaotic, two-week debate, GOP leaders initially fended off a series of gun control amendments. But with moderate Republicans wavering and the public clamoring for action on firearms, the Senate unexpectedly adopted a series of gun control amendments that would require child-safety trigger locks on handguns and mandate that individuals who purchased firearms at gun shows undergo background checks.

Elated gun control advocates then turned to the House. But GOP leaders in that chamber skillfully separated the divisive issue of gun control from the more politically appealing issue of juvenile justice. As a result, the House first passed a juvenile justice bill that would create a number of mandatory minimum sentences then defeated a heavily amended gun control measure that was criticized as too weak by many on the left and overly burdensome by many on the right.

For the rest of the 106th Congress, lawmakers could not agree on whether to accept the gun control provisions in the Senate bill or keep them out, as the House had done. Had it not been for the issue of guns, conference negotiators said they probably could have resolved the differences between the House and Senate juvenile justice bills in short order, producing a youth crime bill for a nation severely shaken by a series of school shootings. Instead, negotiations collapsed, leaving gun control as an election issue in 2000.

BIPARTISAN SUCCESSES

Despite the partisan differences that hampered numerous initiatives, Congress did produce an election-year crime bill in 2000, which proved to be an assortment of sometimes unrelated law enforcement initiatives. It also cleared legislation to curb the government's ability to seize private assets—a top priority of House Judiciary Chairman Henry Hyde, R-Ill.

The most prominent provisions of the omnibus crime bill were a reauthorization of the Violence Against Women Act and a new effort to combat international slavery and sex trafficking. In addition, the legislation contained pieces of three other bills that punished states that prematurely released certain violent criminals, cracked down on the sale of alcohol over the Internet, and aided victims of international terrorism.

Lawmakers first began addressing the issue of sexual trafficking in 1999. Rep. Christopher H. Smith, R-N.J., introduced a measure to set up a new State Department office to help the victims of sexual trafficking and impose stronger penalties on sex traffickers. Smith reported that at least one million women and children each year were taken across international borders by force or fraud for prostitution or sexual slavery, with about 50,000 of the victims crossing U.S.

Outlays for Law Enforcement

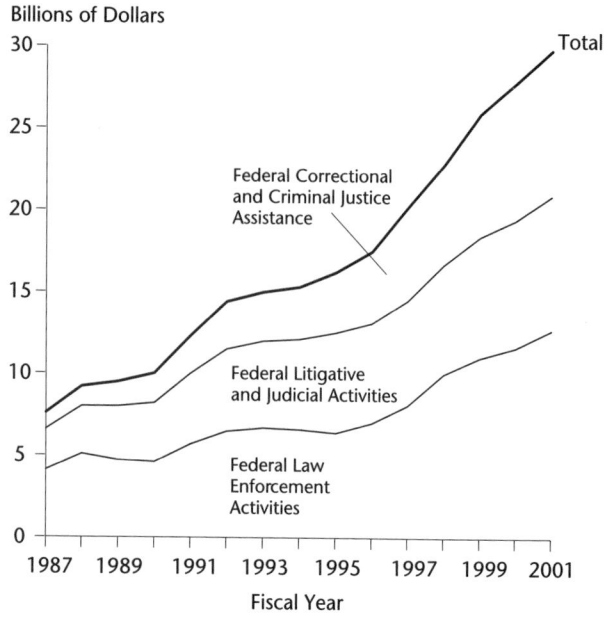

NOTE: Data for 2001 are estimated.

SOURCE: Office of Management and Budget, *Historical Tables, Budget of the United States Government: Fiscal Year 2002* (Washington, D.C.: U.S. Government Printing Office, 2001), Table 3.2.

borders annually. The measure would also create a new "T" visa category for trafficking victims.

Legislation to reauthorize federal grant programs under the 1994 Violence Against Women Act began moving through the House in May 2000. However, the Supreme Court that month ruled that parts of the act were unconstitutional. The justices held that Congress had exceeded its authority in a section of the law that allowed women who were victims of gender-motivated violence, such as rape, to sue their attackers in federal court. Although lawmakers such as Sen. Joseph R. Biden Jr., D-Del., a prime sponsor of the 1994 act, fumed over the ruling, they concluded there was little they could do about it.

Late in 2000, lawmakers packaged the Violence Against Women Act reauthorization and sexual trafficking measures with three other crime-related bills. By far the most controversial was a provision that required states that prematurely released convicted murderers, rapists, or child molesters from prison to pay the cost of apprehending, prosecuting, and jailing them if the offenders later committed the same crime in another state. That measure, dubbed "Aimee's Law" after a twenty-two-year-old woman who was raped and murdered in Philadelphia by a convicted killer released from a Nevada prison, drew fire as an unconstitutional infringement of states' rights. Nevertheless, Congress easily cleared the crime package.

Hyde had been working on the civil assets bill since 1993. He was concerned that law enforcement abused its authority to seize property, and that too few protections existed for innocent property owners. The civil assets bill was supported by an unlikely alliance of liberals and conservatives seeking to bolster the rights of private citizens. But law enforcement agencies, including the Justice Department, contended that asset seizure served as a formidable deterrent to criminal activity.

After the House passed a sweeping version of the bill in 1999, Hyde, Senate Judiciary Committee Chairman Orrin Hatch, R-Utah, and Attorney General Janet Reno fleshed out a compromise. The resulting legislation would require the government to prove by a "preponderance of the evidence" that an asset had been used in a crime before it could seize it. The original Hyde measure would have required the government to meet a higher standard. The bill contained additional protection for property owners, but it also allowed a judge to levy a fine against a property owner whose case was found to be without merit.

SOCIAL ISSUES

As in previous years, social conservatives failed to advance two high-profile constitutional amendments that would have barred the physical desecration of the U.S. flag and expanded the right of religious expression. In both the 105th and 106th Congresses, the House passed the flag desecration measure by more than the two-thirds majority required for constitutional amendments. But the Senate did not take up the popular measure in the 105th Congress, and it fell four votes short of a two-thirds majority in 2000.

Amid controversy over school prayer, the religious expression amendment garnered a majority of votes in the House in 1998, but it fell well short of the two-thirds necessary for approval. Lawmakers did not return to the issue in the 106th Congress. However, Congress in 2000 cleared a narrowly tailored religious expression bill that would make it harder for local governments to enforce zoning or other land-use regulations against religious groups. The measure was a response to a 1997 Supreme Court ruling that struck down a 1993 law in which Congress had said local governments could not limit religious expression without a compelling reason, even as part of a broader aim.

Lawmakers also rejected a constitutional amendment to ensure the rights of crime victims, although the opposition did not break down along partisan lines. The initiative made it through the Senate Judiciary Committee in the 106th Congress, but sponsors pulled it from the Senate floor because they lacked support. The measure was not taken up in the House. Members on both sides of the aisle expressed concerns about changing the Constitution with such a lengthy amendment, and some suggested that a statute be passed instead.

While they failed to win support for other initiatives, social conservatives scored a symbolic victory in 1999. The House passed a bill that for the first time would recognize the fetus as an entity distinct from the pregnant woman. Although sponsors characterized the bill as a crime-fighting measure, it was drafted with the aid of antiabortion groups. Many on the left viewed it as a backdoor attempt to undermine abortion rights. Clinton threatened to veto the measure, and the Senate never took it up.

IMMIGRATION

High-technology companies demonstrated their clout when they successfully lobbied Congress in 1998, and again in 2000, to increase the number of "H-1B" visas, thereby allowing more highly skilled foreign workers into the country on a temporary basis. The visas were a top priority for the booming high-tech industry, which warned about shortages of skilled workers in high-tech fields.

To some degree, the issue cut across party lines. Many Democrats, along with House Judiciary Immigration Chairman Lamar Smith, R-Texas, wanted to impose strict standards on high-tech companies to ensure they gave preference to U.S. workers before turning to holders of H-1B visas. But some Democrats who represented high-tech areas, such as Sen. Dianne Feinstein of California, voted even for versions of the bill that lacked stringent labor protections.

In the 105th Congress, Congress passed a compromise version that included limited labor protection, although not to the degree to mollify some Democrats. Sen. Tom Harkin, D-Iowa, nearly derailed the plan at the end of the session when he raised an objection to passing it by voice vote. Lawmakers passed a subsequent bill increasing the number of H-1B visas in 2000 after settling labor and unrelated immigration issues.

Republicans in the 105th Congress backed away somewhat from several of the stringent provisions they had supported in the 1996 immigration bill. They agreed to restore certain welfare benefits to legal immigrants who were already in the United States when the 1996 welfare overhaul law (PL 104-193) was enacted, and they also eased provisions allowing refugees from certain countries to apply for permanent residence.

OTHER ISSUES

Republicans retreated from some of their most conservative initiatives during Clinton's second administration, in part because of concerns (especially among moderates) that tacking to the right could alienate voters. Conservatives, for example, wanted to scale back affirmative action programs. But the House Judiciary Committee in 1997 rejected a measure that would have banned racial and gender preferences in federal contracting. The bill exposed divisions in GOP ranks, with some Republicans worried that their party was in danger of alienating nonwhite citizens.

Similarly, House Republicans were forced to back down from an ambitious attempt to rein in the judicial branch. Many conservatives criticized the "activist" tendency of liberal judges to legislate from the bench instead of adhering strictly to the law. Accordingly, the GOP advanced a House measure in the 105th that would have restricted such controversial judicial practices as ordering the early release of prisoners and requiring local governments to raise taxes. On the floor, however, conservatives were obliged to remove some of the bill's most sweeping and controversial provisions.

Although they continued to investigate administration actions (most notably, of course, by impeaching Clinton), Republican lawmakers in the 106th eased up on some of their attacks. When Attorney General Reno favored sending back a six-year-old Cuban refugee to his father, some outraged conservatives attempted to circumvent her by granting citizenship to the boy, Elián González. But they failed to muster a congressional majority because a number of conservatives (many of whom had children of their own) took the position that a child should be with his immediate family. And, after the Immigration and Naturalization Service forcibly removed Elián from his temporary Miami guardians to reunite him with his father, GOP leaders found little support for holding investigations into the matter. *(Impeachment, p. 813; Elián González controversy, box, p. 225)*

Instead, conservatives directed much of their fire at Clinton's appointments. While the Senate rejected just one judicial nominee (Ronnie White, who was defeated on a party-line vote in 1999), GOP leaders stalled consideration of numerous other judges, arguing that Clinton was trying to stack the federal judiciary with liberals who would try to impose their own political philosophy from the bench. One 1996 nominee to the Ninth Circuit Court of Appeals, Richard A. Paez, did not win confirmation until 2000—a record delay for a federal nominee. Republicans also repeatedly blocked confirmation of Bill Lann Lee to be assistant attorney general for civil rights; Clinton eventually used his power of recess appointments to name Lee to the post.

Chronology of Action on Law Enforcement

1997–1998

Amid mounting partisan divisions over alleged misbehavior by President Clinton that culminated in the impeachment of Clinton at the end of the 105th Congress, lawmakers could find little common ground on law enforcement issues. Ambitious plans to overhaul juvenile justice laws and allow certain juveniles to be tried as adults were advanced in both chambers, but lawmakers could not agree on the extent to emphasize punishment as opposed to prevention. Further roiling the waters, Democrats tried to add a provision to the Senate bill requiring safety locks on handguns, a proposal fiercely resisted by conservatives.

Lawmakers similarly deadlocked over bills to strengthen state registration programs for convicted sex offenders, stiffen penalties for the use and trafficking of the drug methamphetamine, and overhaul the White House Office of National Drug Control Policy. The House passed the first Justice reauthorization measure in nearly two decades, but the Senate did not take it up. However, lawmakers cleared a number of modest law enforcement measures, such as cracking down on identity theft and authorizing various antidrug programs.

On social issues, conservatives took up legislation to prevent assisted suicide and to amend the Constitution to ban flag desecration and strengthen the right of religious expression, such as praying in school. These initiatives were turned back. Conservatives also failed to enact measures to rein in "activist" judges and scale back the reach of affirmative action programs, partly because of divisions in GOP ranks.

The issue of immigration, although occasionally bringing the parties together, also proved divisive. Lawmakers battled throughout 1998 over one of the top priorities of the high-technology industry: increasing the number of H-1B visas to allow more skilled foreign workers into the United States. They cleared a plan to temporarily increase the number of visas, but only after adding it to an omnibus spending package.

Presidential appointees sparked especially heated debates. Clinton's nomination of Bill Lann Lee to be assistant attorney general for civil rights failed to make it to the Senate floor for a vote, causing the president to use his authority to install Lee in the post on an acting basis. The Senate moved so slowly to confirm some of Clinton's judicial nominees that Chief Justice William Rehnquist in 1998 issued a rare warning to Congress, urging it to move with more dispatch.

Juvenile Crime

Lawmakers in the 105th Congress advanced separate measures aimed at reducing the juvenile crime rate, but they could not clear the plans. The centerpiece of both the most comprehensive House bill (HR 3) and Senate bill (S 10) was a $500 million-per-year grant program for states that agreed to try violent teens as if they were adults. The Senate bill included a provision reauthorizing crime prevention programs. The House split this into a separate bill (HR 1818).

The principal area of partisan dispute centered on whether juveniles should be tried as adults and, if so, which juveniles should be so tried and who in the judicial system should decide.

Republicans argued that juvenile justice systems across the country were failing to hold violent offenders accountable for their wrongdoing. Conservative lawmakers argued that juveniles who commit serious crimes should expect to be tried and punished as adults. Bill supporters also argued that the surge in the youth population expected shortly after the turn of the century could produce gang violence on an unprecedented scale if steps were not taken quickly.

Democrats were split on the issue of trying youths as adults. Some moderates were willing to do so in the case of unusually dangerous criminals. But liberals argued that the best way to reduce juvenile crime was through prevention programs. They said trying juveniles as adults would foreclose any chance of reforming young people before they became lifelong criminals.

President Clinton produced a plan of his own that combined get-tough policies with money for prevention programs. To the dismay of many liberal Democrats, the administration used the plan as the basis for negotiations with House Republicans aimed at producing a compromise that could win the support of moderate Democrats. Clinton pressed Republicans to add several of his provisions to their legislation, including stepped-up prosecution of gun-related crimes, a requirement that handguns be sold with childproof gun locks, and more money for prevention programs.

The House was able to pass both HR 3 and HR 1818 in 1997, but the Senate bill never made it to the floor. Liberals objected to its overall approach and conservatives saw it as allowing the government to clamp down on gun sales. The Gun Owners of America opposed a provision allowing the federal government to use the Racketeer Influenced and Corrupt Organizations (RICO) statute to prosecute gangs. The group said it could be used to prosecute gun dealers.

With the Senate bill stalled, the House late in 1998 added the provisions of HR 3 to a bill (S 2073) that had already passed the Senate reauthorizing the National Center for Missing and Exploited Children. The move provided the chance for the House juvenile justice bill to go to conference with the Senate never having taken action on its version. But time ran out before a conference.

BACKGROUND

Juvenile crime, especially when it included violence, had become a hot issue for lawmakers in both parties. Although violent crime arrest rates for youths aged ten to seventeen had dropped 2.9 percent in 1995, they remained nearly 70 percent higher than in 1985. Arrests of juveniles accused of murder rose 96 percent over the same time period. In contrast, violent crime arrest rates for adults had risen only slightly in the previous decade and murder arrest rates had fallen.

Teenagers accounted for the largest portion of all violent crime in the country, and those aged seventeen to nineteen were the most violent of all age groups. More murder and robbery was committed by eighteen-year-old males than by any other group, and more than one-third of all murders were committed by offenders under age twenty-one.

The vast majority of juvenile offenses were handled by state authorities. Only 10 percent of violent juvenile offenders—those convicted of murder, rape, robbery and assault—received any secure confinement in the states. According to the Justice Department, 43 percent of juveniles in state institutions had more than five prior arrests, and 20 percent had been arrested more than ten times.

The question of what the federal government could do to deal with the stubbornly high rates of juvenile crime posed several key challenges for bill sponsors. First, they needed to overcome deep partisan differences. Second, they had to prevent the debate from turning into one on gun control, the death penalty or other hot-button issues.

More broadly, lawmakers faced the question of whether the federal government should or could play an effective role in fighting juvenile crime, which in most cases involved local statutes and prosecution.

Fewer than 200 juveniles were prosecuted in federal courts annually; the vast majority were tried in state courts. Congress was limited primarily to improving federal en-

LAW LEADERSHIP

For his second term President Bill Clinton held over his entire law enforcement leadership team. Janet Reno, the first woman in U.S. history to serve as attorney general, continued to head the Justice Department. Before entering the Clinton administration, Reno had spent fifteen years as the top prosecutor in crime-ridden Dade County, Florida. (*Background, Congress and the Nation Vol. IX, p. 1110*)

Clinton's first director of the Federal Bureau of Investigation (FBI), Louis J. Freeh, also continued to run the FBI for the next four years. Freeh previously had served as a federal judge, a federal prosecutor, and former FBI agent. (*Background, Congress and the Nation Vol. IX, p. 1116*)

Gen. Barry McCaffrey, Clinton's director of the Office of National Drug Control Policy, or "drug czar," was another holdover from the first term, although he had only been in the post since January 1996. McCaffrey was the former top officer of the U.S. military's Southern Command. Lee P. Brown had served as Clinton's first drug czar from 1993 to 1996.

forcement, authorizing funds to localities and placing conditions on those funds. Moreover, some critics contended that the problem of juvenile crime went well beyond the limits of federal authority to an inability or unwillingness at all levels of government to face a systemic problem that could get worse as the teenage population grew.

HOUSE AND SENATE BILLS

The House bill (HR 3), sponsored by Bill McCollum, R-Fla., essentially tracked a bill that Republicans had pushed in the 104th Congress. That bill had come under vociferous attack from Democrats and never made it out of the Judiciary Committee despite a markup that spanned four days. This time, however, GOP leaders put the issue near the top of their agenda. (*Congress and the Nation Vol. IX, p. 740*)

HR 3 was designed to work in tandem with a smaller funding bill (HR 1818) that proposed to combine several juvenile crime prevention programs into block grants to the states. That bill passed the House in July.

HR 3 called for providing $1.5 billion over three years in grants to states that agreed to try violent juvenile offenders age fifteen and over as adults. The states would have to develop a graduated system of penalties that ensured a sanction for every delinquent or criminal act and escalated the sanction with each more serious crime.

State and local authorities would be required to collect fingerprints and criminal records of juvenile offenders, and make them available to law enforcement agencies and school officials. Under existing law, these records, if collected at all, remained sealed until the offender's eighteenth birthday, when they were expunged.

The bill also proposed what backers said was a model federal system of juvenile justice. For the few federal crimes involving juveniles—perhaps including crimes against federal property, Native American reservations, or those involving interstate travel—the bill would make it easier for federal authorities to prosecute and try as adults juveniles aged fourteen years and older who committed violent federal crimes or federal drug-trafficking offenses. With the approval of the attorney general, teenagers thirteen years old who broke such laws could be prosecuted as adults. Existing law allowed youths aged fifteen and older to be tried as adults.

The Senate bill (S 10), sponsored by Judiciary Committee Chairman Orrin Hatch, R-Utah, was more sweeping than the two House bills combined. Like HR 3, it included provisions to require the federal government and urge the states to try the most violent juveniles in adult court. It called for $500 million a year in incentive grants to the states over five years, for a total of $2.5 billion.

Like HR 1818, the Senate bill authorized funding for juvenile crime prevention programs. It would combine several programs—such as boot camps, treatment for abused and neglected children and gang-prevention programs in schools—into a single Juvenile Delinquency Prevention Block Grant Program, giving states and localities wide leeway to decide how to spend the money. And it would allocate $100 million to create additional Boys and Girls Clubs of America.

CLINTON'S PROPOSAL

The Clinton administration, which made reducing crime by minors a high priority, spent the three-month interregnum between the 104th and 105th Congresses devising legislation from scratch.

The Justice Department held brainstorming sessions with participants ranging from the Office of Juvenile Justice and Delinquency Prevention, to the Immigration and Naturalization Service and the U.S. Marshals Office, among others. The brainstormers threw out some ideas as unworkable in order to limit the bill's scope to juvenile issues. The final product (HR 810) was introduced in late February by Rep. Charles E. Schumer, D-N.Y.

The administration's bill was much less stern than HR 3 on the issue of trying juveniles as adults. It proposed allowing, but not requiring, federal prosecutors to do so. It also called for giving federal judges considerable discretion to throw a case back into the juvenile system—an important selling point in getting Democrats to support the measure.

In another key difference with the GOP plans, Clinton sought to combine punishment with prevention. His proposal would give money to schools and communities to develop antitruancy programs and after-school programs to keep juveniles occupied when they might otherwise commit crimes.

Otherwise, much of HR 810 resembled a Republican bill. It had a long section on new penalties for gang, gun, and drug crimes. It proposed expanding the use of the Racketeer Influenced and Corrupt Organizations (RICO) statute in prosecuting gangs, which would allow prosecutors to go after more perpetrators by charging them with conspiracy to commit crimes.

Other provisions included increased penalties for firearms-related conspiracies and for discharging a firearm during a crime, a requirement that safety locks be sold on all firearms in an effort to prevent accidental shootings by children and requirements for how gun merchants stored their merchandise.

HOUSE COMMITTEE ACTION

The House Judiciary Committee approved HR 3 (H Rept 105-86) on April 29, after two long and contentious markup sessions in which Republicans turned back numerous Democratic amendments. The final 15–9 vote fell along party lines with the exception of Schumer, the ranking Democrat on the crime subcommittee, who supported the bill.

Behind-the-scenes negotiations between Republicans, the White House, and moderate Democrats such as Schumer left many of the committee's traditional liberals openly frustrated. "The administration is wrong," entreated Maxine Waters, D-Calif. "Please don't listen to what they say."

During the initial markup session April 24, Democrats sought to delay the bill with a series of amendments, and Melvin Watt, D-N.C., ordered that the entire thirty-six-page bill be read aloud. Democrats argued vehemently that the bill was unnecessarily harsh and counterproductive, contending that trying juveniles as adults would not necessarily reduce crime. But McCollum responded that his approach was needed to fix a juvenile justice system that simply did not work in many states.

Republicans defeated, 10–11, a Schumer amendment to fund juvenile correctional facilities, additional prosecutors, after-school programs and youth violence courts for young offenders. They also defeated, 7–17, a substitute by John Conyers Jr., D-Mich., that would prohibit people who committed violent crimes as juveniles from owning a gun, establish special sentences for drug dealers, set up drug treatment programs for incarcerated juveniles, and support a host of crime prevention programs.

In the second markup session on April 29, Republicans again held together, turning away a dozen Democratic amendments. Two amendments by Watt, both defeated on votes of 9–16, would delete the provision allowing thirteen-year-olds to be tried as adults and would allow judges (rather than prosecutors) to decide on a case-by-case basis whether to try juveniles as adults. The panel also rejected, 11–14, an amendment by Waters that would prohibit adult prosecution of juveniles for conspiracy under certain federal drug laws.

But the panel did give voice vote approval to three relatively minor Democratic amendments, such as a proposal by Zoe Lofgren, D-Calif., to allow states to use the block grants to hire additional juvenile judges, probation officers, and court-appointed defenders, as well as to provide pretrial services for juveniles. McCollum also made some changes to accommodate administration requests, including language clarifying that juveniles, even if tried as adults, would be housed with other juveniles, and restricting the applications of mandatory minimum sentences to older and more violent juveniles.

In a sign of conflicts to come, however, the committee did not include the administration's proposal that safety locks be sold with each gun. (Schumer tried to amend such a provision onto the bill during the markup, but his language was ruled nongermane.) The administration also objected to a lack of funding in the bill for crime prevention, such as after-school programs and antitruancy efforts.

HOUSE FLOOR ACTION

Despite talk of a grand compromise that would win the support of moderate Democrats, the House passed HR 3 on May 8 by a largely party-line vote of 286–132. The bill looked much the same as it had when it left the committee.

McCollum had anticipated adding much of Clinton's juvenile crime bill to HR 3 in a manager's amendment that was to include new penalties for gun, gang, and drug crimes, in addition to other provisions. But McCollum backed off out of concern that liberal Democrats would try to recommit the bill, sending it back to committee with instructions to add the safety lock language. Democrats could not do that as long as the underlying bill had no gun provisions.

McCollum also said the administration had been unwilling to close a deal, perhaps in hopes of gaining more leverage later.

With the collapse of the negotiations, Democratic lawmakers rallied against the bill. Schumer, who had supported the measure in committee, voted against it on the floor. Clinton formally opposed HR 3, though both sides held out the hope of future accommodation.

The House rejected, 200–224, a Democratic alternative assembled by some of the younger and more liberal members of the party. It focused heavily on crime prevention, with 60 percent of its $1.5 billion in grants targeted to programs such as education, drug treatment, and after-school activities. Several other Democratic amendments went down as well, including:

• An attempt to delete language requiring that juveniles convicted of conspiracy to commit drug crimes be tried as adults, by a vote of 100–320.

• An amendment to delete the provision allowing thirteen-year-olds in some instances to be tried as adults, 129–288.

• An amendment to prevent grants from being used for prison construction, 101–321.

• A plan to allow half the bill's funding to be spent on prevention programs, 191–227.

Much of the House debate focused on whether the measure amounted to undue meddling by Washington in an area some felt was best left to states and localities.

Democrats pointed out that most states would have to change their laws to qualify for grants under the bill. McCollum responded that that was the purpose of the legislation.

"The fact that we don't have a lot of states that already qualify is no reason to vote against this bill," he said. "In fact it is the essence of why to vote for it."

SENATE COMMITTEE ACTION

After eight sessions spanning almost two months, the Senate Judiciary Committee concluded work on its juvenile crime bill July 24, approving the broad measure by a 12–6 vote (S 10—S Rept 105-108).

Work on the bill was delayed repeatedly for lack of a quorum. To end the seemingly interminable markup, several senators from both parties finally agreed to withhold further amendments until the bill reached the floor.

At the committee's opening session June 12, the bill came under attack from several fronts. Joseph R. Biden Jr., D-Del., said it lacked sufficient funding for prevention programs and was overly harsh on those teens who were not beyond rehabilitation. Arlen Specter, R-Pa., questioned the wisdom of telling states they should try violent youths as adults and Fred Thompson, R-Tenn., said the bill might constitute federal intrusion into criminal justice areas best left to states.

By the time the markup resumed one month later, chairman Orrin Hatch, R-Utah, had modified his bill to address some Democratic concerns. For example, he removed a provision that would allow juveniles convicted as adults of capital offenses to be subject to the death penalty.

The committee agreed by voice vote July 11 to add language by John Ashcroft, R-Mo., to increase penalties for drug traffickers who distributed drugs to minors or used minors to commit drug-related crimes.

After one of the more contentious debates, Republicans defeated, 8–9, an attempt to add a gun lock provision to the bill. The amendment, by Herb Kohl, D-Wis., would require firearms dealers to sell safety locks with each handgun. Democrats argued that it was sensible consumer product safety legislation directed at children, likening it to childproof caps on dangerous medicines.

But Hatch said that forcing dealers to sell one lock with each pistol made no sense. He offered an alternative, adopted 10–7, to require all dealers to have gun locks or other safety devices available for sale, and to allow federal crime-fighting funds to be used to train private citizens in gun safety.

The committee defeated several Democratic amendments, including attempts to give state courts the right of first refusal over nonviolent juvenile cases before a federal court could take the cases (defeated 7–9), allow a juvenile being tried as a nonviolent adult offender in federal court to petition to be transferred to a juvenile court (6–10), make it more difficult for the federal government to assert jurisdiction in minor crimes committed by juveniles (7–8), make it more difficult for juveniles to waive their right to counsel in judicial proceedings (6–10), and place new safety requirements on how gun dealers stored their firearms (6–12).

But the committee approved by voice vote an amendment by Biden that incorporated some of Clinton's proposals for enhanced federal penalties for gun crimes, such as selling a weapon with the knowledge that it would be used in a violent drug-trafficking crime. It also gave voice vote approval to an amendment by Charles E. Grassley, R-Iowa, to require that juveniles convicted of sex crimes be tested for sexually transmitted diseases.

1998 LEGISLATIVE ACTION

The Senate bill never made it to the floor. Liberals objected to its overall approach and conservatives worried that it gave the government an opportunity to clamp down on gun sales.

With the Senate bill stalled, the House late in the year added the provisions of HR 3 to a bill (S 2073) that had already passed the Senate reauthorizing the National Center for Missing and Exploited Children. The move provided the chance for the House juvenile justice bill to go to conference with the Senate never having taken action on its version. Time ran out before a conference.

Throughout the year, the juvenile justice measures drew attack from an unusual grouping of interest groups. The Gun Owners of America opposed a provision allowing the federal government to use the Racketeer Influenced and Corrupt Organizations (RICO) statute to prosecute gangs. The group said it could be used to prosecute gun dealers.

From a more liberal perspective, the Children's Defense Fund warned that the plan could hurt children, especially minorities. "S 10 encourages states and federal prosecutors to try children as young as fourteen in adult courts," the group said on its Web site. "Black children are 50 percent more likely than white children to be transferred to adult courts."

Although the National Association of Criminal Defense Lawyers and the National District Attorneys Association were natural enemies, the presidents of those groups joined with an American Bar Association official to attack the juvenile justice bill. Members of the organizations were concerned about the legislation's federalization of crimes traditionally handled by the states and mandates placed on states hoping to receive the new federal funds. In a similar vein, the National Governors' Association objected to the bill's record-keeping requirements.

As a result, the legislation's once-bright prospects dimmed dramatically. Even some supporters acknowledged that the bill would not win Senate passage without major changes.

Trying to jump-start the debate, the House on Sept. 15 voted, 280–126, to send to the Senate a bill that consolidated a number of juvenile crime proposals included in HR 3 and HR 1818. The underlying bill (S 2973) that drew the juvenile crime measures was a five-year authorization of $10 million a year for the National Center for Missing and Exploited Children.

McCollum said packaging the bills was intended to induce the Senate to take up all of the proposals, including the contentious provisions contained in HR 3. But Democrats opposed to HR 3 protested what they called "holding hostage" the popular measure to reauthorize the center for missing children with the provisions of HR 3. The contentious provisions taken from HR 3 would allow prosecutors to decide when juveniles aged fourteen and older should be tried as adults in federal court for violent or drug crimes.

"The combining of these bills is a Republican ploy to force members who already opposed HR 3 to vote for it now," William L. Clay, D-Mo., said during the debate.

Gun Penalties

Lawmakers in the 105th Congress took little action to advance measures favored by gun control advocates, such as a requirement that gun locks be sold with new guns. However, Congress in 1998 did clear a measure (S 191—PL 105-386) to stiffen penalties against individuals who possessed a gun while committing a crime.

MANDATORY SENTENCES

The main purpose of S 191 was to clarify for the courts what Congress meant in a 1988 law (PL 100-649) when it created penalties for using a gun in committing a crime. The Supreme Court ruled in 1995, in *Bailey v. United States,* that the criminal had to discharge or brandish the weapon for federally enhanced or minimum penalties to kick in. Some believed that interpretation was too narrow.

Lawmakers first took up the issue in the House. A bill (HR 424) by Sue Myrick, R-N.C., stated that the criminal merely had to possess a gun in order to face enhanced penalties. The measure also would expand existing mandatory minimum sentences for gun crimes. Possession of a gun during commission of a violent or drug-trafficking crime would add ten years to the offender's sentence for the underlying crime. Brandishing the weapon during a crime would yield an additional fifteen years. Firing it would add twenty years.

Bill McCollum, R-Fla., said the bill aimed to send the message that Congress was serious about gun crimes. "If you use a gun in the commission of a crime, you will get the book thrown at you," he said. Democrats charged that Congress should not be in the business of micromanaging criminal justice procedures.

Rep. Bill Delahunt, D-Mass., said the types of mandated sentences in HR 424 would encroach on the mission of the U.S. Sentencing Commission, which was created to take politics out of sentencing. "We are legislatively beating ourselves on the chest," Delahunt said. "It just doesn't make sense."

HR 424 won voice vote approval in the Judiciary Committee's crime subcommittee July 16. The Judiciary Committee approved it, 17–8, on Sept. 9 (H Rept 105-344), and the House passed it Feb. 24, 1998, by a vote of 350–59.

Under the Senate version, S 191, those possessing a gun during the commission of a crime would face a mandatory minimum sentence of five years in prison. A person who discharged a firearm during a violent or drug-related crime would receive at least ten years behind bars; a repeat offender would face a minimum term of twenty-five years in prison. The bill sought to impose harsher penalties on those who use sawed-off shotguns and other higher powered weapons, as well as devices such as "silencers."

The Senate Judiciary Committee approved it by voice vote Nov. 6, 1997, without a written report. The Senate passed it by unanimous consent Nov. 13. The House by voice vote passed S 191 Oct. 9, 1998, with an amendment, and the Senate cleared it by unanimous consent Oct. 15. President Clinton signed the bill into law on Nov. 13, 1998.

Safety Locks

On another gun issue, Democrats put much of their energy into requiring safety locks on handguns. Clinton ordered that all federal law enforcement officers carry guns that come with safety locks, and he called for legislation to require locks on guns sold to the general public to make it harder for children to use the weapons.

For proponents of gun safety locks, the issue was as simple as child-proof aspirin bottles. "If we require safety caps on medicine to protect kids, we should clearly require safety locks on guns," said Sen. Christopher J. Dodd, D-Conn.

But opponents said safety training was a more effective method to prevent accidents than gun locks. They also said the locks could be dangerous. Placing a trigger lock on a loaded firearm could cause the gun to accidentally discharge, and using safety locks on an unloaded gun would create extra steps and delays for someone who needed to use a gun quickly against an assailant.

The issue came up in both the fiscal 1999 Commerce-Justice-State funding bill (S 2260) and a bill to rein in juvenile crime (S 10), but Democrats were short of votes in both instances. During debate on S 10, for example, the Senate Judiciary Committee defeated an amendment that would require gun dealers to sell gun locks with each handgun by a 9–10 vote. Instead, the committee approved, 10–7, a substitute by Chairman Orrin G. Hatch, R-Utah, that would require only that gun dealers have such gun locks for sale.

Conservatives also scored a victory with the fiscal 1999 omnibus spending bill (HR 4328—PL 105-277). It contained a provision prohibiting the FBI from funding its new national gun registry by fees collected from gun purchasers. The FBI had planned to levy user fees to finance its new criminal background database to allow licensed gun dealers to determine if a customer would be disqualified from purchasing a handgun.

Armored Car Employees

The Senate in 1998 cleared legislation to make it easier for employees of armored car companies to carry their guns into other states by easing the process for obtaining required gun permits. The measure (HR 624—PL 105-287) required all states to recognize the weapons permits issued by other states. It also required local officials to conduct criminal background checks when initial weapons licenses were granted.

Typical armored car shipments ranged in value from $100,000 to $40 million, making them lucrative targets for thieves. The FBI investigated sixty-eight attempted robberies of armored vehicles during fiscal 1995 and another thirty attempted robberies in the first six months of calendar year 1996—and the robbery attempts were becoming increasingly violent.

To assist the approximately 3,000 armored car crew members who traveled interstate, Congress in 1993 enacted legislation (PL 103-55) to eliminate the need for guards to obtain gun permits in every state they passed through, provided that their home states met certain standards. To qualify, a state had to check the guard's arrest record annually and certify that he or she underwent gun safety training every year.

Nevertheless, lawmakers said the provisions of HR 624 were needed because it still was sometimes time-consuming and difficult for guards to obtain all the needed permits, particularly because of the different requirements in various states. Among the problems that had come to light since 1993: some states required a private security officer's license in addition to a weapons license and most states had instituted two-year renewal cycles for weapons permits, making it difficult for them to meet the law's annual requirements.

An identical bill to HR 624 passed the House in the 104th Congress but was not taken up by the Senate. Rep. W. J. "Billy" Tauzin, R-La., said the bill received bipartisan support in 1996 until it was "hijacked" by other top-priority bills that surfaced toward the end of the 104th Congress.

The House Commerce Committee approved HR 624 (H Rept 105-6) by voice vote on Feb. 13, 1997. The House passed it, 416–0, on Feb. 26. The Senate Commerce Committee approved it by voice vote on Nov. 4 (S Rept 105-297), and the Senate cleared it by unanimous consent the following year on Oct. 9, 1998. Clinton signed the bill on Oct. 20, 1998.

Concealed Weapons

Legislation to allow citizens with concealed-weapons permits to carry their handguns into some other states won approval in the House Judiciary Committee in 1998. But the House did not take it up.

The bill (HR 218—H Rept 105-819), approved by voice vote on Aug. 5, would allow active-duty and retired law enforcement officers, as well as citizens with concealed carry permits, to travel to another state with a firearm if the second state granted similar permits to all of its own qualified residents. Alternatively, the second state could choose to accept other states' permits. The system would be overseen by the attorney general, who would divide states into two classes based on their gun laws.

Supporters said the bill's national standard would mark an advance over the complex patchwork of federal, state, and local laws regarding concealed firearms. They also cited studies indicating that laws permitting citizens to carry concealed firearms can deter crime. "This Congress has the unique opportunity to reaffirm the right of people to defend themselves," said Steve Chabot, R-Ohio.

The bill as introduced would allow only qualified current or former law enforcement officers to carry concealed handguns. Democrats supported that approach in the Crime subcommittee, which approved the measure by voice vote on June 19. But they strongly objected when the panel broadened the bill to cover anyone with a concealed-weapons permit in his or her state.

They contended that HR 218 would conflict with state concealed weapons laws, create enforcement problems, and lead to an increase in firearm accidents and crimes.

Background Checks

A bill to set up an expedited procedure for checking the criminal backgrounds of private security officers easily passed the House in 1997, but the Senate did not take it up. The measure (HR 103) by Rep. Bob Barr, R-Ga., would require associations of employers of security officers to submit fingerprints to the Justice Department for criminal background checks. Although many states already conducted such background checks, they usually checked only the officers' fingerprints against those in that state, bill supporters said.

Two years after enactment of the legislation, the attorney general would have to report to the House and Senate Judiciary Committees on the number of background checks made by the new association, as well as the disposition of those checks.

The Justice Department, in a letter to lawmakers, warned it had "serious concerns" about increasing the federal role in background checks. Supporters of the measure noted that the growing numbers of private security officers were estimated to outnumber sworn law enforcement officers by a ratio of three-to-one by 2000. State laws requiring background checks of these officers were inconsistent, and the few states that required national criminal history checks warned that it could take several months to gather all the necessary information.

As a result, convicted criminals occasionally landed jobs as private security officers. In a particularly infamous incident, a former security guard was convicted of raping fifteen women in Los Angeles in 1994.

The House Judiciary crime subcommittee approved HR 103 by voice vote on June 12. The full committee gave voice vote approval to the measure (H Rept 105-161, Pt. I) on June 18. The House passed it under suspension of the rules on July 28.

Bounty Hunters

The House Judiciary Committee in 1998 narrowly defeated a bill (HR 3168) that would make bail bondsmen and bounty hunters liable for using excessive force or abusing pursued suspects who have jumped bail. Republicans concerned with states' rights and Democrats wary of the measure's civil rights implications banded together to kill the bill on an 11–12 vote on May 6.

Rep. Asa Hutchinson, R-Ark., sponsored the measure because of concerns that legitimate or rogue bounty hunters could break into the homes of potential criminals in pursuit of bond-jumpers even though their actions could injure innocent citizens. In a much-publicized incident in September 1997, five men claiming to be bounty hunters forced their way into an Arizona residence and killed a young couple.

The bill was rejected after the committee voted, 12–9, to significantly narrow its scope, making only the bounty hunters—not the bail bondsmen who hired them—liable for civil rights violations. McCollum offered the amendment, arguing that the original measure would create unnecessary federal regulations for an industry that was best overseen by the states.

Democrats were initially concerned the bill would hold bail agents responsible for actions beyond their control, such as when rogue bounty hunters took it upon themselves to hunt down bail jumpers. However, Robert C. Scott, D-Va., argued the McCollum amendment would grant bail agents "total immunity" instead of clarifying the situations in which they would be liable.

Bulletproof Vests

Congress in 1998 cleared legislation to authorize $25 million in matching-fund block grants to furnish police with bulletproof vests. Under the bill (S 1605—PL 105-154), local law enforcement agencies would supply at least 50 percent of the cost of the equipment. At least half of the money allocated in any given fiscal year must be awarded to cities or Native American reservations with populations of less than 100,000 people.

The Justice Department estimated that about 150,000 law enforcement officers nationwide did not have access to the vests, which cost about $500 each.

Colorado Republican Ben Nighthorse Campbell, a former deputy sheriff, sponsored the measure. "While we know that there is no way to end the risks inherent to a career in law enforcement, we must do everything possible to ensure that officers who put their lives on the line every day also put on a vest," he said on the Senate floor. "Body armor is one of the most important pieces of equipment an officer can have and often means the difference between life and death."

As originally introduced, the legislation would provide 50-50 matching grants to state and local law enforcement agencies and Native American tribes to assist in purchasing bulletproof vests and body armor. The matching requirement could be waived for those jurisdictions that cannot afford it.

The Senate Judiciary Committee gave voice vote approval to the measure on Feb. 26 without a written report. The Senate passed it on March 11 by unanimous consent.

House lawmakers advanced a similar bill, HR 2829. The House Judiciary Subcommittee on Crime approved its measure on May 7 by voice vote after adopting a substitute amendment by Bill McCollum, R-Fla. McCollum's substitute, prompted by concerns raised by the National League of Cities, would give preference to jurisdictions that did not receive existing block grants under a local law enforcement program.

The amendment also granted preference to localities with populations below 100,000; average or above-average violent crime rates; local policies requiring officers to wear vests; and greater-than-average need for additional vests.

Subcommittee member Bob Barr, R-Ga., asked the panel to add a provision to the substitute restoring the original bill's ban on the use of the federal grants to purchase bullet-proof vests made by federal prisoners. Barr dropped his request after McCollum promised to introduce separate legislation within a few months to overhaul the federal prison system's production of commercial goods.

HR 2829 went directly to the House floor, where it was passed on May 12 on a 412–4 vote. The House then called up S 1605 and amended it by inserting the text of its legislation in a procedural move aimed at speeding final action.

The Senate cleared the measure by voice vote on May 15, on a day when thousands of police officers and survivors of officers killed in the line of duty gathered for a rally outside the Capitol. President Clinton signed the measure on June 16, 1998. *(2000 action, p. 645)*

HIV Testing

The House in 1998 cleared legislation that allowed HIV testing of federal prison inmates who were considered to be at risk of having the virus that causes AIDS. The measure (HR 2070—PL 105-370), which was the last bill to clear the 105th Congress, allowed a federal prison to conduct tests if there was a "well-founded reason to believe" that the inmate was at risk, or that the inmate's bodily fluids came into contact with prison employees or visitors who requested that a test be conducted.

Federal prisons were required to offer health care, counseling, and support services for those found to have the virus. The bill stipulated that test results were to be considered inadmissible in any federal or state civil or criminal case. The Bureau of Prisons would conduct the testing, and the results would be confidential.

Supporters said the legislation was needed because a corrections officer who came into contact with the blood of an inmate had the right to know that inmate's HIV status. If the inmate had HIV, the corrections officer could opt to take drugs immediately that would prevent the transmission of the virus.

The Judiciary Committee approved the legislation (H Rept 105-665) July 21. But members scaled the bill back from its original version, which called for mandatory testing of prisoners for tuberculosis and hepatitis B and C, as well as HIV. The bill was rewritten to limit the testing strictly to HIV after officials at the Bureau of Prisons said the more extensive testing was unnecessary.

However, the amended version directed the attorney general to develop model guidelines for states to follow to prevent, detect and treat infectious diseases in correctional facilities.

The House passed the measure by voice vote Aug. 3. The Senate Oct. 20 passed it by unanimous consent, but only after adopting a substitute amendment by unanimous consent that would allow tests to be conducted on inmates incarcerated for longer than six months.

The House without objection cleared the bill with the Senate language Oct. 21. President Clinton signed the bill on Nov. 12, 1998. *(2000 action, p. 644)*

Identity Theft

Congress easily cleared legislation in 1998 making it illegal to knowingly transfer or use someone else's personal identifying information, such as a Social Security number, with the intent of committing a crime. The problem, known as identity theft, was a growing side effect of the information age. Thieves could use the information to obtain credit cards, get bank loans, or commit other crimes. Such actions cost credit card companies alone hundreds of millions of dollars annually, while leaving some victims unable to obtain a job or qualify for a mortgage because they were identified as having a bad credit history or even a criminal record.

Under the bill (HR 4151—PL 105-318), violators faced enhanced penalties of as much as twenty years in prison and a fine for certain offenses such as using the information in the commission of a violent crime. Other less serious crimes carried a fifteen-year penalty or less.

Identity theft victims were also entitled to restitution for losses and costs they incurred. In addition, the bill required the Federal Trade Commission (FTC) to track consumer identity theft complaints and provide information to victims on how to clear up problems caused by the crime.

Previously, federal law criminalized the fraudulent possession, transfer, and production of identity documents, but it required law enforcement officials to catch the culprit in possession of those documents.

Lawmakers began taking formal action on the issue on July 9, when the Senate Judiciary Committee gave voice vote approval to an identity theft measure (S 512—S Rept 105-274). The measure imposed enhanced penalties on those who used another person's identifying information, provided restitution for victims needing to clear their credit histories, directed the U.S. Sentencing Commission to review federal sentencing guidelines regarding such crimes, and directed the FTC to track identity thefts and help the victims.

The Senate passed the bill by unanimous consent July 30.

In the House, Rep. John Shadegg, R-Ariz., had introduced a similar measure, HR 4151, on June 25, but the Judiciary Committee had not taken it up. House lawmakers inserted the text of S 512 into HR 4151 and passed it by voice vote

Oct. 7. The Senate cleared it by voice vote Oct. 14. President Clinton signed the measure into law on Oct. 30, 1998.

Witness Intimidation

The House in 1998 passed a measure intended to reduce gang-related intimidation of witnesses in criminal cases, but the Senate did not take it up. The bill (HR 2181) would make it a federal offense to travel across state or foreign borders with the intent of influencing the testimony of a witness in a state criminal proceeding by bribery, force, or threat. It also would establish tougher penalties for obstruction of justice offenses involving victims, witnesses, and informants.

Supporters said the legislation was needed because key witnesses often refused to testify in drug- and gang-related cases for fear of retaliation. They said the problem was growing, and it was undermining both public confidence in law enforcement agencies and the ability of police to secure the cooperation of communities.

"Violent street gangs are intimidating and retaliating against witnesses that have the courage to testify against them," said bill sponsor Bill McCollum, R-Fla.

The bill called for fines and up to twenty years in prison for violators. It also would allow the death penalty if a violator killed a witness—a provision that drew the opposition of many Democrats, who otherwise generally supported the bill.

The House Judiciary Committee approved the bill, 20–4, on July 23 (H Rept 105-258). The committee rejected, 7–17, an amendment by Jerrold Nadler, D-N.Y., that would eliminate the death penalty provision. "Any time there's a crime bill, it's boiler-plate language," Nadler said. "Throw them some red meat."

Melvin Watt, D-N.C., also said the death penalty was applied in a racist manner, and the committee's ranking Democrat, John Conyers Jr., Mich., urged committee chairman Henry J. Hyde, R-Ill., to hold a meeting on the topic, which Hyde agreed to do. The panel nevertheless insisted on keeping the provision in the bill.

The bill won House passage Feb. 25, 1998, by a vote of 366–49 amid continuing debate over its death penalty provision. Conyers said he was concerned that the attachment of the death penalty to another crime would make the application of capital punishment more "capricious." A Conyers amendment to substitute a life sentence if a judge doubted a defendant's guilt was defeated, 113–300.

Crimes Against the Disabled

The House in 1998 cleared legislation to require a federal survey to measure the extent of crimes against people with developmental disabilities. The bill (S 1976—PL 105-301) directed the attorney general to conduct a study of the nature and extent of crimes against disabled people and how the Jus-

tice Department handled such cases. The department then would recommend steps that states should take to establish a centralized computer database of such crimes. In addition, questions related to crimes against disabled people had to be added to the National Crime Victims Survey.

Sen. Mike DeWine, R-Ohio, who sponsored the measure, said research in other countries showed that people with developmental disabilities were at a four to ten times higher risk of being victimized than those without disabilities. Studies in Canada, Britain, and Australia also indicated that few of the crimes against people with developmental disabilities were reported, and that justice officials were reluctant to rely on the testimony of a disabled person.

Nevertheless, the United States had conducted virtually no research into the issue, DeWine warned. "What we're trying to do with this legislation is to raise considerably the national profile of this issue among research agencies and the academic community, and to continue to define and develop solutions to this problem," he said. The Senate Judiciary Committee approved the measure without a written report on June 25. The Senate passed it by unanimous consent on July 13, and the House cleared it by voice vote on Oct. 7. President Clinton signed the bill on Oct. 27, 1998.

Methamphetamine

Separate proposals in 1998 to stiffen penalties for the drug methamphetamine won House passage and the approval of the Senate Judiciary Committee. But the lawmakers failed to clear either measure in the 105th Congress.

House lawmakers tackled a bill (HR 3898) that would lower the threshold to trigger mandatory minimum sentences for use and trafficking in methamphetamine. It would align the penalties for the drug, also known as "crank," with those for crack cocaine. Trafficking in 5 grams would carry a five-year minimum jail term, and distributing 50 grams would bring a mandatory ten-year sentence.

The measure also would lower the threshold for imposing mandatory penalties involving smaller amounts of the drug. Under existing law, the penalty for the manufacture, distribution or possession of 10 grams of the drug was five to forty years in prison, or no less than twenty years and a fine up to $2 million if use of the drug caused death or serious injury. The bill lowered the threshold for imposing those penalties from 10 grams to 5 grams.

Another provision would require the U.S. Sentencing Commission to study the penalties for selling methamphetamine, compared with other drugs.

Supporters warned that methamphetamine use had spread east from California and the Southwest, threatening to cause the same type of devastation as cocaine had caused in the 1980s. Since 1991, methamphetamine deaths had more than doubled and clandestine methamphetamine labs had now been reported in every state.

Some Democrats, however, raised concerns about the bill's mandatory minimum sentences. Rep. William D. Delahunt, D-Mass., a former prosecutor, said the Sentencing Commission should have the flexibility to establish sentences for the drug, taking into account differing circumstances, such as the amount of the drug in possession.

The Judiciary Committee approved HR 3898 (H Rept 105-711, Pt. I) July 21 by a 21–6 vote. The House passed it by voice vote on Sept. 15.

The Senate Judiciary Committee Oct. 8 approved a similar bill (S 2024) on a 12–3 vote without issuing a written report. Like HR 3898, the Senate legislation would impose minimum mandatory penalties similar to those imposed in connection with crack cocaine crimes.

Bill sponsor John Ashcroft, R-Missouri, said the distribution and increased use of methamphetamine, especially among teenagers, had "wreaked havoc" on U.S. cities. He said the current penalties for possession and distribution of the drug fell short of creating an adequate deterrent to its use. Democrats Patrick J. Leahy, Vt., Edward M. Kennedy, Mass., and Russell D. Feingold, Wis., voted against the bill. They warned it would worsen overcrowding at federal prisons and do little to address the underlying drug problem itself. The Justice Department and the Drug Enforcement Administration indicated their support for the measure. But the full Senate did not take it up.

Drug Prevention and Treatment

The House passed legislation in 1998 to authorize numerous drug prevention and treatment programs, from workplace interdiction to television commercials. Although the Senate did not take up the bill, many of the provisions were added to the fiscal 1999 transportation appropriations bill.

The authorizing measure (HR 4550), sponsored by Rob Portman, R-Ohio, would authorize $195 million annually through 2002 for an antidrug media blitz. Also in the bill was $10 million for a Small Business Administration program to provide grants to nonprofit groups that help businesses implement drug-free workplace programs, $50 million over two years for drug treatment for prison inmates and another $10 million annually through fiscal 2001 for programs designed to help parents keep their children off drugs.

The bill also would require the National Highway Traffic Safety Administration to establish a demonstration program under which several states would provide voluntary drug testing for all teenagers who apply for driver's licenses.

Democrats supported the bill, but some, including John D. Dingell, Mich., and Frank Pallone Jr., N.J., said many of the programs it authorized already were operating and that the move was a Republican election-year ploy. Democrats also complained that the bill came directly to the floor without going through the normal committee process.

The House passed the measure 396–9, on Sept. 16 after adopting a substitute amendment by voice vote to alter parts of the bill. The most significant change deleted a provision that aimed to encourage drug companies to develop new antiaddiction medications by extending a company's exclusive right to market certain other drugs.

On a 123–281 vote, the House rejected an amendment offered by Gene Taylor, D-Miss., that would require all new federal employees to take drug tests.

Several of the initiatives in HR 4550 surfaced in the annual transportation spending bill (HR 4328—PL 105-277). The spending measure funded an antidrug media campaign, a substance-abuse program for inmates, and an antidrug program in public schools. It also stiffened trafficking penalties for methamphetamine.

Antidrug Grants

The Senate in 1997 cleared legislation (HR 956—PL 105-20) transferring $10 million of the $16 billion federal drug control budget during fiscal 1998 for small grants to community-based groups that establish effective plans to stem drug use.

The measure authorized $143.5 million over five years for the grants from the Office of National Drug Control Policy. Community groups could receive up to $100,000, but they had to match the federal grants with their own money.

The bill authorized increasing amounts for the program until fiscal 2002. It established the Advisory Commission on Drug-Free Communities to advise the Office of National Drug Control Policy. The commission's authority would terminate at the end of fiscal 2002.

Bill supporters in both parties said local groups were better situated to fight drug use in their communities than the federal government. "This legislation recognizes that the very serious and growing drug problem in this country is not going to be solved here in Washington, but is going to be solved at the local level, in our communities and neighborhoods," said Rep. Rob Portman, R-Ohio.

The House Government Reform and Oversight Committee on May 16 gave voice vote approval to the bill (H Rept 105-105, Pt. I), and the House passed it by 420–1 on May 22.

The Senate Judiciary Committee had passed a similar measure (S 536) by voice vote on May 8. But the Senate took up HR 956 instead, clearing it by unanimous consent on June 18. The president signed the bill on June 27, 1997.

Office of National Drug Control Policy

Despite opposition from Democrats, the House in 1997 passed a bill to overhaul the White House office that coordinates the federal fight against illegal drugs. But the measure never made it to the Senate floor.

The Office of National Drug Control Policy had been created in 1988 to coordinate government efforts to stem growing use of illegal drugs. But amid concerns that the nation needed to do far more to curb illegal drug use, Republicans insisted that the office should be held to strict standards.

The bill (HR 2610), sponsored by Rep. J. Dennis Hastert, R-Ill., would set specific goals for reducing drug consumption. It would require that by the end of 2001, drug usage drop from 6.1 percent of the population to 3 percent. The availability of cocaine, heroin, marijuana, and methamphetamines would have to be cut by 80 percent. The street purity levels of these drugs would have to be cut by 60 percent. Drug-related crime would have to go down 50 percent.

The two-year reauthorization of the agency would also expand the duties of its director, known as the drug czar. It would require the director to submit a report each year detailing all funds spent on drug control efforts. The director also would be required to oppose the legalization of marijuana and a number of other drugs. The measure would prohibit funds from being spent for a study on the legalization of such drugs.

Republicans said the bill would hold the director responsible for reducing drug use. "We want to win the fight against drugs, and we have to take extraordinary efforts to get it done," Hastert said.

Democrats and the White House argued that the legislation would put unrealistic expectations on the office, apparently to set up the administration for political failure. After the agency failed to meet these goals, they predicted, Republicans would surely attack the administration. Democrats also complained the bill set four-year goals, but only authorized the agency for half of that time.

"Judging by its major provisions, the bill appears designed to achieve political advantage in the 1998 and 2000 election," said Rep. Thomas M. Barrett, D-Wis.

The Clinton administration criticized several elements in the bill. The targets could not be met in the allotted time, a White House statement said, because they did not take into account budget constraints, time needed to train personnel, and the lag time between changes in attitudes about drugs and changes in behavior. The administration faulted the bill for reauthorizing the office for only two years, rather than the twelve years it was pushing for, and called reporting requirements overly burdensome.

Republicans, however, maintained that the bill gave the agency sufficient resources while requiring a level of accountability to help reduce illegal drug use. Despite such controversies, the House Government Reform and Oversight Committee gave voice vote approval to the bill on Oct. 7, without issuing a written report. The House passed HR 2610 by voice vote on Oct. 21.

The measure was approved without debate by the Senate Judiciary Committee on a voice vote on Nov. 6. But it failed to advance further.

Prison Labor

A House Judiciary subcommittee in 1997 approved a measure (HR 926) that would permit federal prison inmates to work for state and local governments, but lawmakers did not take further action on the plan.

The bill would allow the Bureau of Prisons to authorize federal inmates to work for state and local governments and nonprofit agencies, either free of charge or at minimal cost. It aimed to create work for able-bodied inmates who were not needed for jobs in the prison facility.

HR 926 would protect the jobs and benefits of the regular employees of the organizations receiving the help from inmates, according to Chairman Bill McCollum, R-Fla., chairman of the Crime Subcommittee. The subcommittee approved the bill March 6 by voice vote.

Sex Offenders

The House passed a bill (HR 1683) in 1997 aimed at strengthening state registration programs for convicted sex offenders and closing several loopholes in existing law. The Senate did not vote on the House measure or a related bill (S 767).

Under the bill, sex offenders convicted in military and federal courts would be required to register under existing state programs. In an effort to track offenders who crossed state borders, the bill would require them to register in the state where they lived and any state where they were employed or enrolled as a student.

"Some child sex offenders are slipping through the cracks," said the bill's sponsor, Bill McCollum, R-Fla. "It is well-recognized that sexual predators are remarkably clever and persistently transient. These offenders are not confined within state lines, and neither should be our efforts to keep track of them."

BACKGROUND

Legislation requiring states to set up registries of sex offenders was first enacted as part of the 1994 omnibus crime law (PL 103-322). The 1994 law required states to register the names, addresses, and other pertinent information on anyone being released from prison who had kidnapped or sexually molested a child, or who had committed sexually violent crimes. Local law enforcement officials were authorized to release information to the public if it was considered necessary for public safety. (Congress and the Nation Vol. IX, p. 683)

The states were given until September 1997 to establish a registration system using guidelines drawn up by the Justice Department. Those that did not would lose 10 percent of their federal crime-fighting funds available under the so-called Byrne grant program.

Two laws enacted in 1996 expanded the sexual offender registration provisions. The first law (PL 104-145) required state and local law enforcement agencies to make public "relevant information" about the release and whereabouts of sexual offenders who were required to register under the 1994 act. It mandated that local communities be notified when sex offenders moved into their neighborhoods. The law was known as Megan's Law, after seven-year-old Megan Kanka of Hamilton, N.J., who was raped and murdered in 1994 by a twice-convicted sex offender who lived across the street from her home. The second 1996 law (PL 104-236) required the

FBI to keep a national database of sexual offenders registered on state lists to enable law enforcement officers to track them across state lines. Sex offenders were required to verify their addresses regularly by returning cards with fingerprints to the FBI. *(Congress and the Nation Vol. IX, p. 738)*

By May 1996, all fifty states and the District of Columbia had some sort of registration system in place, and at least forty had some form of notification program to inform residents when sex offenders moved into their neighborhoods. By 1997, however, most states still had not complied with all the technicalities of the law.

McCollum's bill proposed to give states two additional years to comply, and to allow states more time to implement what the report accompanying the bill described as "ideas that may not have come from Congress but may be equally effective or even more effective in keeping track of sex offenders."

1997 LEGISLATIVE ACTION

HR 1683 began in the Judiciary Subcommittee on Crime, chaired by McCollum, which approved the measure by voice vote June 12, 1997. The full Judiciary Committee followed suit Sept. 9, also by voice vote (H Rept 105-256).

While the bill appeared relatively noncontroversial, Charles E. Schumer of New York and other Democrats raised a potential problem with the registries. Schumer said five states that had antisodomy laws—Arizona, Mississippi, Kansas, Louisiana, and South Carolina—had indicated that they would put consenting adults convicted of sodomy on state sex offender registries.

Schumer proposed cutting federal Byrne grants by 10 percent to any state that put such consenting adults in the registries, but the committee defeated the amendment, 12–19, in a party-line vote. Schumer argued that any state that published names of people who engaged in consensual sex acts was perverting the purpose of the legislation. McCollum countered that nothing in the original legislation authorized the names of nonviolent sex offenders to be placed in the registries. He also said the federal government should not pass judgment on state laws. The House passed the bill under suspension of the rules Sept. 23 by a vote of 415–2.

Cemetery Vandalism

The Senate in 1997 cleared legislation (S 813—PL 105-101) that created a new federal crime of vandalism and theft at a national cemetery. The measure established enhanced penalties, including prison sentences of up to fifteen years, for those accused of stealing property at national cemeteries operated by the Department of Veterans Affairs, the Department of Defense, and the Department of Interior. The penalties for vandalism and theft were made consistent with similar crimes against other types of federal property. The measure also established penalties for attempted vandalism and theft.

Supporters said the legislation was a necessary response to cases of criminal activity in national cemeteries. In 1997,

for example, vandals spray-painted racial epithets and obscenities on graves and monuments in the National Memorial Cemetery of the Pacific in Hawaii, and thieves made off with grave markers at the Riverside National Cemetery in California in 1996.

The House Judiciary Committee marked up a companion measure (HR 1532—H Rept 105-142) by voice vote on June 18. The House passed it under suspension of the rules on June 23.

The Senate Judiciary Committee gave voice vote approval to S 813 on Oct. 23 without issuing a written report. The Senate passed the measure on Nov. 4 by unanimous consent, and the House cleared it under suspension of the rules on Nov. 8. Clinton signed the bill into law on Nov. 19, 1998.

Civil Forfeiture

After six years of negotiations with the Justice Department and interest groups, the House Judiciary Committee in 1997 approved a bill that would make it more difficult for the government to seize assets as part of federal prosecutions. But the measure never reached the House floor. The measure (HR 1965) would make it more difficult for the government to seize assets—such as boats, planes, real estate, and currency—used in crimes such as drug smuggling. The changes would principally affect civil forfeiture proceedings, although language was added to apply the new law to certain criminal cases such as money-laundering.

The bill's main effect would make the government's job of justifying a seizure more difficult. The burden of proof would be placed squarely on the government, instead of on the individual. The government would have to show by "a preponderance of the evidence" that the asset was used in association with a crime.

Such a change in the nation's forfeiture laws had been a longtime goal of Judiciary Chairman Henry Hyde, R-Ill., who said it was unfair that people were required to prove their assets were not used in a crime, rather than for the government to prove that they were. The Justice Department had been equally adamant that revising the law could undermine its prosecutorial abilities.

HR 1965 would provide several protections to people at risk of having their assets seized. It would create an automatic "innocent owner" defense for those who took reasonable measures to make sure their property was not used illegally. It would provide for counsel for the indigent and would allow return of assets in cases of economic hardship.

But the Justice Department won a number of exemptions and softening provisions. Originally prosecutors would have been required to show "clear and convincing evidence" that the asset was used in a crime—a higher judicial standard than the "preponderance" language that was agreed to. And the department also gained some provisions expanding its powers in criminal forfeiture cases.

Although the Judiciary Committee approved HR 1965 on June 20 by a lopsided vote of 26–1 (Bob Barr, R-Ga., dissented), some members and groups expressed concerns about the compromise. The Justice Department changes caused the National Association of Criminal Defense Lawyers to turn against the bill, calling it "worse than no reform at all." Its reservations were shared by a number of committee members, among them Barr and Robert C. Scott, D-Va.

After the markup Hyde said he would try to devise a manager's amendment for floor action. "We're still trying to keep this agreement viable," he said. "It is a balance of a lot of delicate positions."

Antiterrorism

The Senate in 1998 passed legislation to strengthen and expand U.S. laws used to combat international terrorism. But the measure died in the House at the end of the session. (1995–1996 action, Congress and the Nation Vol. IX, p. 727)

The bill (S 2536) reflected months of negotiations among members of the Senate Judiciary Committee and several executive agencies, including the Justice Department, the Treasury Department, and the Customs Service. The bill originally was to be much wider in scope, but it was narrowed significantly to increase its chances for consideration on the floor.

The bill would grant the FBI broader powers to investigate crimes committed against U.S. citizens abroad and the actions of foreign terrorist groups. The Coast Guard would gain expanded authority to board marine vessels believed to be smuggling drugs or other contraband. In addition, the Immigration and Naturalization Service could deport individuals who had fled to the United States to escape prosecution for terrorist acts in other countries.

The measure also would expand the wiretap authority of federal law enforcement agencies to cover computer fraud and hacking. Several recent break-ins at government and private computer networks had led members of Congress to demand that law enforcement do more about the problem.

The Judiciary Committee approved the bill by voice vote on Oct. 1 without a written report. The Senate passed the measure by unanimous consent on Oct. 15. (2000 action, p. 645)

Money Laundering

Congress in 1998 cleared a measure (HR 1756—PL 105-310) that created a national strategy to combat money laundering and provided assistance to areas besieged by drug traffickers and others who launder illegally gained funds through local institutions. But lawmakers failed to clear two related bills (HR 4005 and HR 3745) that also sought to combat money laundering.

HR 1756, sponsored by Rep. Nydia M. Velazquez, D-N.Y., gave most of the power to create a national antilaundering strategy to the Treasury Department but required consultation with the attorney general. Velazquez, who represented parts of Brooklyn and Queens, said in a floor speech Oct. 5 that money laundering "seems like something from a spy novel. To the families and the communities that I represent, these criminal enterprises are a reality."

Her bill authorized grants to prosecutors and state and local law enforcement agencies in areas the department identified as high-risk for money laundering. It also authorized $50 million over five years for the effort.

The House Banking and Financial Services Committee approved HR 1756 (H Rept 105-608, Pt. I) June 11 by voice vote. The House passed it by voice vote on Oct. 5.

The Senate passed it by unanimous consent on Oct. 15 after clarifying the definition of money laundering so that it applied to state and local government statutes regarding the movement of illicit cash. The House cleared the measure Oct. 16 by voice vote. President Clinton signed the bill on Oct. 30, 1998.

Lawmakers, however, failed to clear HR 4005, which aimed to help law enforcement agencies track down drug traffickers and others who launder an estimated $500 million through the U.S. financial system each year.

Among other things, HR 4005 would require financial institutions to maintain all accounts with the account holder's name and number in tandem at all times. It also would require the Treasury Department, within four months of the bill's enactment, to issue "know your customer" regulations for financial institutions.

Other provisions would change reporting requirements for suspicious activity to expedite such information to law enforcement and financial regulatory agencies. For example, the measure sought to protect accountants who reported suspicious transactions and provided liability protection to financial institutions that disclosed suspicious actions by former workers when they used the institution as an employment reference.

The bill won voice vote approval in the House Banking and Financial Services Committee June 11 (H Rept 105-611, Pt. I). The House passed it by voice vote Oct. 5. The Senate took no action on the measure.

A third bill, HR 3745, would grant greater powers to combat money laundering. The House Judiciary Crime Subcommittee approved the measure by voice vote June 5, but no further action was taken on it.

Panel chairman Bill McCollum, R-Fla., said federal antilaundering laws, last revised in 1986, were insufficient to deal with the increasingly sophisticated methods that criminal organizations used to mask illegal transactions. More than $500 billion—nearly 2 percent of the global domestic product—was laundered worldwide each year, he said.

The legislation would broaden the powers of federal courts to freeze or demand the forfeiture of civil assets involved in money laundering. It also would expand the federal government's ability to prosecute money launderers who fled the country or who committed the majority of their financial crimes abroad.

Assisted Suicide

An attempt by social conservatives to deter physicians from helping patients use prescription drugs to commit suicide faltered late in the 105th Congress. The legislation arose from the Justice Department's reaction to an Oregon law that legalized assisted suicide under certain guidelines. In a 1997 letter, Drug Enforcement Administrator Thomas A. Constantine agreed with congressional conservatives that prescribing a regulated drug for the purposes of assisting a patient who wanted to commit suicide was not a "legitimate medical purpose," as the 1970 Controlled Substances Act required. Attorney General Janet Reno overturned Constantine's interpretation.

Conservatives in both chambers in 1998 attempted to advance bills that would override Reno. However, support fractured when doctors and other health professionals protested the legislation's potentially chilling effect on pain treatment for terminally ill patients. Late in the session, Senate Assistant Majority Leader Don Nickles, R-Okla., tried to codify the Constantine letter through a rider to the omnibus appropriations act (HR 4328—PL 105-277), but he retreated in the face of objections.

Conservatives did win at least a symbolic victory in 1997, however, when Clinton signed into law on April 30 a bill (HR 1003—PL 105-12) to prohibit the use of federal funds for doctor-assisted suicides.

The bill had no immediate impact because no federal funds currently were spent on physician-assisted suicides. Supporters of the measure, however, said it was necessary to prevent such spending in the future. Two months later, the Supreme Court ruled that there was no constitutional right to assisted suicide.

1997 LEGISLATIVE ACTION

The knotty issue of assisted suicide drew the attention of lawmakers from the onset of the 105th Congress, with Sens. Byron L. Dorgan, D-N.D., and John Ashcroft, R-Mo., announcing in January 1997 that they would introduce a bill to prohibit the use of federal funds for physician-assisted suicides.

Both senators stressed that the bill would not address the complex question of whether assisted suicide should be legalized, an issue they said should be decided by states and the courts. Their plan was in response to statements by Oregon officials raising the prospect of using Medicaid money to fund assisted suicide. Ashcroft said the measure would affirm a "cultural understanding that most Americans embrace" that federal tax dollars should not be used to fund euthanasia.

The two senators had introduced a similar measure (S 2108) in the 104th Congress. It garnered seventeen cosponsors, but the Senate took no action on it.

The House moved first. On March 13, the Commerce panel's Health and Environment Subcommittee gave voice vote approval to a measure (HR 1003) that would prohibit Medicare, Medicaid, and military and federal employee health plans from subsidizing or promoting assisted suicides for terminally ill patients.

Some Democrats called the bill redundant because assisted suicide was illegal in most states. But sponsor Ralph M. Hall, D-Texas, called it "proactive," saying he wanted to make sure that taxpayers would not pay for suicides if the Supreme Court ruled that assisted suicides are constitutional.

The Commerce Committee approved the bill (HR 1003—H Rept 105-46, Pt. I), 45–2, on March 20. The House passed the bill on April 10 by a 398–16 vote. Only a smattering of members, all Democrats, opposed the bill, saying it was unnecessary because the federal government does not fund assisted suicides and has no plans to do so.

Jim McDermott, D-Wash., a psychiatrist, called the measure "very simple-minded," and he criticized it for not defining what constituted assisted suicide. But Commerce Committee Chairman Thomas J. Bliley Jr., R-Va., said the bill "in no way interferes with a patient's right to discontinue medical treatment" but rather ensures that "no taxpayer dollars will be used to end the life of an American patient."

The Senate cleared the measure, 99–0, on April 16.

1998 LEGISLATIVE ACTION

Lawmakers in 1998 took on the much more contentious question of whether to ban assisted suicides altogether. Both the House and Senate Judiciary Committees approved measures to stop assisted suicide. But neither bill advanced to the floor because of widespread opposition from the medical community.

On July 22, the House Judiciary Constitution Subcommittee gave narrow approval, 6–5, to a bill to penalize doctors who prescribe drugs to help patients commit suicide.

Judiciary Chairman Henry J. Hyde, R-Ill., said his bill (HR 4006) was designed to reverse a recent decision by Attorney General Janet Reno on the issue. Reno had overruled a decision by the Drug Enforcement Administration (DEA) to prohibit doctors from dispensing drugs for assisted suicides, contending that the ban exceeded the agency's authority. Hyde said he wanted to reverse Reno's decision because it made doctors "social engineers with a license to kill."

HR 4006 would require the revocation of the federal prescription-writing license of a doctor who "intentionally dispensed or distributed a controlled substance with a purpose of causing, or assisting in causing, the suicide or euthanasia of any individual." The bill would exempt doctors whose patients accidentally die from drugs prescribed to relieve pain.

John Conyers Jr., D-Mich., said he opposed the bill because it would preempt state laws: "We are thwarting debate by imposing a single, Republican, Washington-knows-best solution."

By voice vote, the panel adopted an amendment by Charles T. Canady, R-Fla., that would require the government to prove through "clear and convincing evidence" that drugs were for anything other than pain management.

The Judiciary Committee on Aug. 4 approved HR 4006 by voice vote (H Rept 105-683, Pt. I).

Although no committee member voted against the bill, Democrats warned it could deter doctors from providing essential pain-killing drugs. Organizations such as the American Medical Association opposed the bill, saying doctors might be forced to justify their prescriptions for legitimate pain-alleviating drugs. Hyde said he trusted that doctors would not refrain from prescribing painkillers to people in severe pain.

Democrats' attempts to soften the bill failed. The panel defeated, 8–14, an amendment that would exempt doctors in states with laws similar to Oregon's. Another amendment, defeated 6–14, would protect doctors from federal civil or criminal penalties.

But a powerful coalition of health-care professionals, pharmacists, and medical patients suffering severe pain ratcheted up their lobbying efforts in mid-August, calling on Congress to hold off on passing HR 4006 and a related Senate bill, S 2151. The coalition argued that the measures would deter doctors from prescribing needed medication to block the pain experienced by terminally ill patients.

"The perverse effect of this bill, and we really do believe this, is that it would increase suffering," said Samira Beckwith, the chair of the legislative committee of the National Hospice Organization.

Many in the health care community, including the American Medical Association, opposed assisted suicide, but said the pending legislation was not the proper response. The bill "has a noble intent," said Pamela Bennett, president of the American Society of Pain Management Nurses.

However, she and others warned that doctors might so fear a DEA investigation that they would not prescribe medication, creating a situation that could increase the likelihood of suicide. The medical community's opposition forced Senate opponents of assisted suicide to backpedal somewhat.

On Sept. 24, Senate Judiciary Committee Chairman Orrin Hatch, R-Utah, conceded that S 2151 would not come up for a full Senate vote before adjournment. Nevertheless, he persuaded his committee to approve a substitute of the bill on a vote of 11–6. "Getting it out today at least creates a massive debate that may help us get to the bottom of this," Hatch said at the markup.

The substitute bill would require the Justice Department to revoke or deny a doctor's federal prescription-writing license if "clear and convincing" evidence proved he or she intentionally dispensed a controlled substance for a patient to commit suicide.

But some senators raised concerns about the impact the measure would have on pain management for terminally ill patients. Several Republicans joined ranking Democrat Patrick J. Leahy, Vt., as he contended that doctors already underprescribed pain medication and would avoid prescribing drugs out of fear of losing their licenses.

In an effort to address criticism by doctors, Hatch added a requirement that before the department could initiate an investigation, the attorney general would determine that the medical professional dispensed a drug that caused a person's death, and that the professional did not prescribe the drug as medically needed. Hatch's substitute also would clarify that other medical professionals, such as pharmacists, could face penalties under the bill. Neither of those provisions were in the House bill.

The substitute bill would allow an accused medical professional to request a nonbinding review by a newly created Medical Advisory Board on Pain Relief. The board would be composed of pain control experts chosen by the secretary of Health and Human Services and the attorney general. The board's recommendations would be considered by the attorney general in determining whether to revoke or deny a professional's registration.

With House leaders lacking the votes to pass HR 4006, and S 2151 facing the threat of a filibuster, Assistant Majority Leader Don Nickles, R-Okla., stepped into the breach in early October. He said he planned to add a one-sentence amendment into the omnibus appropriations bill that would ban assisted suicide from being defined as a "legitimate medical practice."

The amendment could effectively prohibit doctors from prescribing controlled substances for assisted suicide. But after Ron Wyden, D-Ore., voiced objections on the Senate floor, Nickles said he would hold off on action for the year. *(1999–2000 action, p. 658)*

Arbitration

Lawmakers in 1997 easily cleared legislation (S 996—PL 105-53) to permanently authorize an arbitration program in federal district courts. Congress first began experimenting with pretrial arbitration in 1988 when it set up an arbitration pilot program at twenty of the nation's ninety-four federal court districts. Some fifteen days after the pilot program expired in 1993, lawmakers renewed the program for one year. They cleared a three-year reauthorization in 1994.

Sen. Charles Grassley, R-Iowa, introduced S 996 in 1997 to continue the program permanently. He praised arbitration for alleviating overcrowded dockets in the courts and for providing a less costly process than litigation to settle disputes. "This will not only lessen the burden on the judicial branch, but also enable people who feel they have been wronged to get a decision without waiting months for the usual verdict and without spending tons of money on attorney's fees," he said in a floor speech introducing the bill.

The Senate Judiciary Committee discharged S 996 on July 31, and the Senate passed it by unanimous consent the same day. Senators added an amendment to make permanent a temporary requirement under the 1990 Civil Justice Reform Act for the semiannual publication of each federal judge's motions that had been pending for more than six months, as well as lists of delays in bench trials and other cases.

The House on Sept. 23 passed the measure, 421–0, after adding an amendment extending temporary judgeships. The Senate cleared the bill on Sept. 30. Clinton signed the bill on Oct. 6.

Bankruptcy Judges

With federal courts facing a growing caseload of bankruptcy filings, the House in 1997 passed legislation to authorize additional bankruptcy judgeships. The Senate took no action on the measure.

The bill (HR 1596), by Rep. George W. Gekas, R-Pa., would have added seven permanent bankruptcy judgeships and eleven temporary positions. A similar bill won House Judiciary Committee approval in the 104th Congress but never made it to the House floor.

Supporters of the bill said the new judgeships were necessary to keep pace with the increasing rate of bankruptcy filings, which ballooned from 971,000 in 1992, the last time extra judges were added, to 1.2 million in 1996.

"We are getting a deluge of cases, and we are getting more and more complex issues that require quality time by a judge to hear, consider and hopefully rule correctly," Judge Frank Koger, speaking on behalf of the National Conference of Bankruptcy Judges, told lawmakers.

Judiciary Chairman Henry J. Hyde, R-Ill., attributed the increased caseload in part to a large number of new start-up businesses. Personal filings due to excessive credit card debt also were blamed.

During debate on the House floor, Frank R. Wolf, R-Va., suggested another cause. He cited a private study that concluded that legalized gambling could be "the single fastest-growing driver of bankruptcy," with gambling losses blamed for up to 10 percent of personal filings.

Under HR 1596, seven of the eighteen judgeships would be permanent. Four of those would go to the central district of California, while Maryland, New Jersey, and the western district of Tennessee would receive one each.

Eleven judgeships would be temporary, with appointments lasting at least five years. They would go to districts in California, Florida, Maryland, Michigan, Mississippi, New York, Pennsylvania, and Virginia. Also, an existing temporary judgeship in Delaware would be extended at least through 2003.

The Judiciary panel's Commercial and Administrative Law Subcommittee gave voice vote approval to the measure on June 19, with Gekas calling it a high priority. The full committee approved the bill (H Rept 105-208) on July 16. The House passed the bill under suspension of the rules on July 28.

Traffic Stops

Amid concerns that law enforcement officials were targeting minority drivers, the House in 1998 passed legislation that would ask the Justice Department to conduct a study of who got stopped for routine violations, and why.

Judiciary Committee ranking Democrat John Conyers, Jr., Mich., who introduced the bill (HR 118), said a disproportionate number of those pulled over were African Americans, whose only crime was "driving while black." Conyers, who was one of the more prominent black lawmakers in the House, said "very few of us" who had been stopped by police had not believed that the purpose was "simple racial harassment." Statistics showed that while blacks made up 14 percent of the population, they accounted for 72 percent of all drivers pulled over in routine traffic stops.

The Justice Department would be required to report its findings to Congress within two years of enactment of the bill.

The Judiciary Committee March 4 approved the measure by voice vote (H Rept 105-435). But Republicans successfully added a provision to prevent the Justice Department report from being used in discrimination lawsuits. Despite the party-line, 19–13 vote on the amendment, Democrats continued to support the bill. The House passed it by voice vote March 24.

Civil Rights Commission

The House in 1998 passed a bill to reauthorize the U.S. Commission on Civil Rights through fiscal 2001 and make a number of administrative changes to the agency. But the measure was not taken up in the Senate.

Originally established by the Civil Rights Act of 1957, the commission was an independent fact-finding executive branch agency. The eight-member body was charged with investigating claims of discrimination, appraising the impact of federal laws on equal protection, and preparing public service announcements and advertising campaigns to discourage discrimination. Although initially designed as a temporary agency, the commission was reauthorized numerous times by Congress. The most recent reauthorization, contained in the Civil Rights Commission Amendments Act of 1994 (PL 103-419), expired in 1996.

The 1998 bill (HR 3117) would limit the commission's staff director to a four-year term of office and require commissioners to review the staff director's performance every year. It would also reduce the term of membership for future commissioners from six years to five years.

The commission would be required to put in place a number of administrative changes, including preparing an annual financial statement for audit by an independent external auditor and implementing certain General Accounting Office structural regulations. It would also have to operate under the Freedom of Information Act and prepare a number of reports on such subjects as the enforcement of the Americans with Disabilities Act of 1990.

The House Judiciary Committee approved the legislation (H Rept 105-439) by voice vote on March 4. The House passed it by voice vote on March 18.

Victims' Rights

Advocates of a constitutional amendment to bolster the rights of crime victims succeeded in ushering their measure through the Senate Judiciary Committee in 1998. But the proposed amendment failed to advance further.

The measure (S J Res 44) would guarantee that victims of violent crimes be given the chance to attend all proceedings related to their case and speak at sentencing and parole hearings. This would greatly change court proceedings. In order to avoid the potential for tainted testimony, witnesses, including victims, often were not allowed to attend trials and other legal proceedings in their entirety.

The proposed amendment would give victims the same right as government investigators to attend a trial in which they are scheduled to testify. The victims also would be entitled to restitution by the convicted, and they would be notified if the convicted person was released or escaped from prison.

Judges would have to consider victims' needs when scheduling trials and to consider a victim's safety when deciding whether to allow conditional releases such as bail, parole or probation. Across the country, twenty-nine states had enacted similar measures as constitutional amendments and a number of others had victims' rights statutes on the books.

However, opponents warned that this provision could create political pressure to incorporate a victim's wishes in a prosecutor's strategy and possibly hinder flexibility in trying the case.

Leading the battle for the amendment were Sens. Jon Kyl, R-Ariz., and Dianne Feinstein, D-Calif. Kyl had introduced a similar bill (S J Res 52) in April 1996, but it did not get out of the Judiciary Committee. "Our intent here is to rebalance the scales of justice so that no longer will victims of crimes be victimized twice, first by the criminal, then by the justice system," Kyl said.

He noted that the Constitution, in the Fourth, Fifth, and Fourteenth Amendments, specifically listed fifteen rights guaranteed to defendants, but that no such protections were guaranteed for victims. "If we can amend the Constitution to provide the rights to defendants, why can't we amend the Constitution to protect the rights of victims?" Kyl asked.

The amendment won the support of the Clinton administration. Attorney General Janet Reno, echoing other supporters of the measure, said a constitutional amendment was necessary to put the rights of victims on equal footing with the rights of defendants.

"Unless the Constitution is amended to ensure basic rights to crime victims, we will never correct the existing imbalance in this country between defendants' irreducible constitutional rights and the current haphazard patchwork of victims' rights," she said.

But some lawmakers, including such Judiciary Committee liberal stalwarts as Patrick J. Leahy, D-Vt., and Edward M. Kennedy, D-Mass., said they were opposed to amending the Constitution to achieve goals they said could be reached through simple legislation. "These are all matters that can pass easily," Leahy said.

Fred Thompson, R-Tenn., an ex-prosecutor, contended that the measure infringed on states' rights and the rights of the accused. He warned it could lead to even more litigation. "It is going to be very, very disruptive in ways we are not aware of," he said.

The proposed amendment drew support from many victims' rights groups, but the National Victims Center opposed it, saying it did not go far enough.

The Judiciary Committee on July 7 approved S J Res 44 (S Rept 105-409) by a vote of 11–6. But supporters conceded that they were about 15 to 20 votes short of the two-thirds majority needed for passage. *(2000 action, p. 668)*

Victim Impact Statements

Moving with unusual alacrity, Congress in 1997 cleared legislation to prevent federal judges from excluding from courtrooms those crime victims who intended only to make victim impact statements during the sentencing portions of trials. The bill (HR 924—PL 105-6) allowed victims of the Oklahoma City bombing and their families to attend the trials of Timothy McVeigh and Terry Nichols, the two men charged in the case.

The action clarified a 1994 law (PL 103-322) that was designed to grant a victim the right to make a statement to the court at the time of sentencing. Such victim impact testimony was seen as important for the court to understand the effect of the crime on the victim or the victim's family.

Left unresolved by the 1994 law was a victim's right to attend a trial. Federal evidentiary rules allowed a judge to exclude a witness from portions of a trial if the judge believed the proceedings could influence the witness's later testimony. Some judges were using the evidentiary rules to exclude victims and their family members who planned to make statements from attending the sentencing phase of a criminal trial.

The issue gained urgency when both a lower court judge and the 10th Circuit Court of Appeals ruled that the trial judge in the Oklahoma City case could exclude from the entire trial witnesses who would testify only in the sentencing phase.

Almost two dozen state attorneys general appealed to Congress for swift action to overturn the court rulings and allow surviving family members to attend the trials. McVeigh's trial, which had been moved to the U.S. District Court in Denver, was scheduled to get under way March 31.

"This new interpretation of federal law, if left uncorrected, will deprive numerous family members of victims the chance to observe the trial and learn the facts surrounding the bombing," the attorneys general told Congress.

HR 924 still allowed a judge to exclude crime victims from courtrooms if they intend to testify during the fact-finding portion of a trial.

The House Judiciary Committee approved the measure (H Rept 105-28) on March 12 by voice vote. The House passed it, 418–9, on March 18, and the Senate cleared it by unanimous consent on the next day. President Clinton signed the bill into law on March 19, 1997.

Flag Protection

Lawmakers again fell short of mustering the supermajorities needed for a proposed constitutional amendment intended to prevent the physical desecration of the U.S. flag. The House passed the measure (H J Res 54) by a bipartisan vote of 310–114 on June 12, 1997. But the amendment won approval in the Senate Judiciary Committee by only a narrow 10–7 margin, and the full Senate did not take it up.

BACKGROUND

The effort in the 105th Congress marked the third time lawmakers had pushed a resolution to protect the flag since the U.S. Supreme Court struck down state and federal flag desecration statutes in 1989 and 1990. In both cases, the Court held that flag desecration was a form of political expression protected under the First Amendment.

The first attempt came in 1990, when the House fell 34 votes short of the required two-thirds majority. In 1995 the House easily passed the resolution, but a companion measure failed in the Senate, 63–36—four votes shy of the two-thirds mark. *(Congress and the Nation Vol. IX, p. 754; Congress and the Nation Vol. VIII, p. 836)*

The proposal that passed the House in 1995 would have given Congress and the states the constitutional authority to pass laws banning flag desecration. Some opponents argued that would create a hodgepodge of different laws in the states. H J Res 54 proposed giving that authority only to Congress, a change that sponsor Gerald B. H. Solomon, R-N.Y., accepted in hopes of picking up additional support. The amendment read simply: "The Congress shall have power to prohibit the physical desecration of the flag of the United States."

Supporters contended that the flag amendment was necessary to prevent people from defiling a sacred symbol of American democracy and patriotism. "There still are some standards that ought to be maintained," said House Judiciary Committee Chairman Henry J. Hyde, R-Ill.

Opponents maintained that it was impossible to force people to be patriotic, and that prohibiting desecration of the flag would violate the constitutionally protected right to free speech. "What's more important to me than even the flag is the Constitution of the United States," said Rep. Melvin Watt, D-N.C.

As required by the Constitution, the amendment had to garner a two-thirds majority in each chamber to be sent to the states for ratification. Ratification by three-fourths (thirty-eight) of the state legislatures was required for the amendment to take effect. H J Res 54 provided seven years for the states to act. The president played no constitutional role in the consideration of a constitutional amendment, but the White House opposed this one.

HOUSE COMMITTEE ACTION

The House Judiciary Subcommittee on the Constitution approved H J Res 54 by voice vote May 8, though most, if not all, panel Democrats could be heard voting "no."

At the markup, Hyde argued that those who would burn a U.S. flag deserved no more protection than those who would vandalize a synagogue or tip over tombstones. "I would say it's a hate crime," he said.

The full Judiciary Committee approved the resolution May 14 by a vote of 20–9 (H Rept 105-121). Critics argued that flag desecration was a form of free speech, but Hyde said that banning flag desecration was an acceptable limit on that freedom.

Some Democrats also argued that the resolution was not specific enough in defining a flag or desecration. "Any criminal statute enacted under this amendment will be inherently . . . unworkable," said Robert C. Scott, D-Va. "Wearing a flag tie will be an offense punishable by jail time."

Zoe Lofgren, D-Calif., offered an amendment to replace the resolution with a requirement that all U.S. flags be made of flameproof material. She then withdrew it, saying she only wanted to point out alternative measures that would be "less intrusive to the constitutional scheme and constitutional rights."

Two Democrats, Steven R. Rothman of New Jersey and Robert Wexler of Florida, supported the resolution, saying it was worth limiting a form of expression to protect the symbol of the nation.

HOUSE FLOOR ACTION

The House adopted the resolution June 12 by a vote of 310–114—27 more than the necessary two-thirds. Republicans backed the measure by an overwhelming majority, 210–13, while Democrats were evenly split—100 yeas and 100 nays.

Solomon said he and his Senate counterpart, Orrin G. Hatch, R-Utah, would step up their efforts to gain support from a handful of senators who could change the outcome in that chamber.

Most Republicans and many Democrats spoke for the measure, saying it would fulfill the public's wish to protect the flag. Some liberal Democrats and a handful of Republicans opposed it on the grounds that it would violate the First Amendment right of free speech.

"Too many brave Americans have marched behind it," Hyde said of the flag. "Too many have come home in a box covered by a flag. Too many parents and widows have clutched that flag to their hearts as the last remembrance of their beloved one, to treat that flag with anything less than reverence and respect."

But David E. Skaggs, D-Colo., said "Respect cannot be mandated." He added that supporters, "In their understandable passion to protect the flag . . . ask us to undermine the Bill of Rights."

The wishes of the nation's veterans factored heavily in the debate. As about thirty members of the American Legion watched from the gallery, Solomon's staff carted out two stacks of signatures on a petition asking Congress to protect the flag. Most of the three million signatures came from veterans and religious groups.

SENATE ACTION

Despite the overwhelming bipartisan approval in the House, the full Senate did not vote on the amendment. On June 24 a divided Senate Judiciary Committee reported its version (S J Res 40), as well as the House plan. From the beginning, the Senate was viewed as the real battleground because it voted down the 1995 proposal. Proponents in 1997 conceded they were still about three votes short in the Senate, but hoped to make up that ground.

In 1998 Senate GOP leaders indicated that they wanted to begin debating the measure in June. With one eye on the polls (which showed that as many as 81 percent of Americans supported the plan) and another on the election-year calendar, Majority Leader Trent Lott, R-Miss., wanted to take action before the Fourth of July recess.

Beginning on Memorial Day weekend, the American Legion and other advocates launched a grassroots lobbying push for its adoption. Marty Justis, executive director of the Citizens Flag Alliance, said the Indianapolis-based group was using a Web site to encourage people to fly their flags in a show of support. "There is a massive grassroots effort getting underway," he said. But the matter crept almost silently through the Senate.

The Judiciary Committee June 24 approved two amendments that were virtually identical but for minor differences in their enacting clauses. Both H J Res 54 and S J Res 40 were approved, 10–7, with California Democrat Dianne Feinstein joining nine Republicans. Arlen Specter, R-Pa., was absent because of recent heart surgery.

Judiciary Committee Chairman Orrin G. Hatch, R-Utah, argued that an amendment was necessary because of Supreme Court rulings in 1989 and 1990 protecting flag desecration as a form of free speech. Opponents of the measure, such as Joseph R. Biden Jr., D-Del., said it is impossible to legislate patriotic values.

The committee adoption garnered almost no attention, with supporters still appearing to lack three votes on the floor. Democrats Carol Moseley-Braun of Illinois and Byron L. Dorgan of North Dakota were targeted as potential support-

ers, as was Republican Robert F. Bennett of Utah. All three were up for reelection in 1998. Kent Conrad, D-N.D., and Joseph I. Lieberman, D-Conn., were also on the target list.

With the Senate taking no action during the summer, supporters in September prepared a last-minute grassroots lobbying and advertising campaign in hopes of mustering the elusive few votes needed to reach the two-thirds majority needed in the Senate. They thought it would be difficult for senators to oppose the popular measure just before Election Day.

"We have 60 absolute cosponsors and a number of others have said they'll vote for it," Hatch said. But the needed support failed to materialize, and Senate leaders never called for a formal vote.

Religious Expression

A proposed constitutional amendment that would expand and clarify rights of religious expression gained a majority of votes in the House in 1998 but fell well short of the two-thirds necessary for approval.

The amendment (H J Res 78) would guarantee the right to pray and to recognize religious beliefs on public property—including schools—and would prohibit the federal government or any state from establishing an official religion. It was sponsored by Rep. Ernest Istook, R-Okla., and backed by the Christian Coalition, which had been pushing for a floor vote on the popular conservative measure since the summer of 1996.

The vote on the resolution marked the ninth time the House had voted on a constitutional amendment since the GOP took over in 1995. None of the proposals had come close to being sent to the states, of which three-fourths, or thirty-eight, would need to endorse any change for it to be added to the Constitution.

BACKGROUND

The proposal, called the "religious liberties" amendment by its sponsors, was an expansion of the school prayer amendments that Congress began considering in 1996. Those measures focused on allowing prayer in the public schools. The 1997 version covered school prayer and other forms of religious expression on public property, such as placing a Nativity scene in front of a town hall. (*Congress and the Nation Vol. IX, p. 750*)

The most controversial element was a provision stating that the government could not deny "equal access to a benefit on account of religion." The benefits clause could allow for school voucher programs that provided tuition money for parents to use for private or parochial schooling. The constitutionality of such programs had not yet been resolved by the Supreme Court. Depending on interpretation, the clause might even require government financing of religious schools. Supporters, however, said it would require government support of religious schools only if the government supported nonreligious private schools.

The resolution effectively sought to make a change to the First Amendment, which banned laws that prohibited "the free exercise of religion," while also banning laws that provided for the "establishment of religion." Supporters said it was needed not because the First Amendment's wording on religion was flawed, but because courts had misinterpreted it. "This amendment is the only way we can end thirty years of court decisions that turned First Amendment rights upside-down," Istook said. He said court decisions "have aided a systematic campaign to strip religious symbols, references and heritage from public view."

The amendment was supported by House Speaker Newt Gingrich, R-Ga., but it faced long odds. It appeared to lack the necessary two-thirds majority in the House, and the Senate had no plans to take it up.

An alliance of about fifty national religious, educational, and civil liberties groups, called the Coalition to Preserve Religious Liberty, announced it would lobby aggressively against the amendment. Opponents said they feared the amendment would marginalize religious minorities, fatten ministry coffers with public money and potentially lead to cities restricted to members of one religion.

1998 LEGISLATIVE ACTION

The House Judiciary Committee's Constitution Subcommittee Oct. 28, 1998, approved the proposed amendment on an 8–4 party-line vote.

Judiciary Committee Chairman Henry J. Hyde, R-Ill., said H J Res 78 was needed because of "judicial amendments to the Constitution"—court rulings that he said went beyond the intended meaning of the Constitution.

Opponents of the resolution, which would amend the Bill of Rights for the first time, said the Founding Fathers' language was clearer than anything the Judiciary Committee might come up with. And if the problem was court interpretation, they added, why assume the courts would do any better with the new language? "The more words we give to the Supreme Court to interpret, the more interpreting they are going to do," said Rep. Melvin Watt, D-N.C. Hyde conceded he did not have a good answer for Watt. He said he had "just hope."

The amendment, which had been revised many times over the past two years, was again changed at the markup. The version adopted was an amendment in the nature of a substitute offered by Rep. Asa Hutchinson, R-Ark. His version stipulated that states, as well as the federal government, could not establish an official religion, and that no government could "prescribe" school prayer. The original language would not allow government officials to "initiate" school prayer.

The language read in part: "To secure the people's right to acknowledge God according to the dictates of conscience: Neither the United States nor any State shall establish any official religion, but the people's right to pray and to recognize their religious beliefs, heritage, or traditions on public property, including schools, shall not be infringed. Neither the United States nor any State shall require any person to join in prayer or other religious activity, prescribe school prayers, discriminate against religion, or deny equal access to a benefit on account of religion."

Democrats sought to water down or eliminate the language that would expand rights to religious expression. Watt offered an amendment, defeated by voice vote, to add a clause deleting all portions of the First Amendment dealing with religion. He said the new language would clash with the old. Rep. Robert C. Scott, D-Va., offered an amendment, defeated by voice vote, saying that any religious institution that received a government "benefit" would have to follow civil rights laws. Religious institutions were otherwise exempt.

After knocking down a number of Democratic amendments, Republicans on the House Judiciary Committee approved H J Res 78 March 4, 1998, by a 16–11 party-line vote. The House effectively killed the measure June 4 on a 224–203 vote—61 votes short of the required two-thirds majority.

The Judiciary Committee approved the plan only after Democrats forced unsuccessful votes on seven amendments, including one that would replace the wording of the resolution with the exact wording of a religious freedom provision included in the First Amendment.

For more than two hours, members of the two parties offered contrary but passionate arguments, each claiming their goal was to attain more freedom for Americans. While Democrats said the measure would result in state-sponsored religion, Republicans argued it would reverse public policy that had arisen from numerous misguided court decisions.

Charles T. Canady, R-Fla., said the resolution was needed because public officials had grown increasingly hostile toward religious expression. To make his case, Canady pointed to stories of students ordered not to read bibles on school buses and workers punished for their religious activities.

Democrats, however, said many of the cases outlined by Canady and other Republicans were already protected activities, even on public property. Instead of a constitutional amendment, they argued that more public education on the law was needed. Moreover, they contended, the resolution conflicted with the First Amendment.

Although the votes fell along party lines, some Republicans voiced concern about altering the Constitution. "I like what is already in the Constitution," said Steve Buyer, R-Ind., who nevertheless supported the measure.

Among the amendments shot down by the committee were measures that would prohibit school prayer and remove the word "God" from the resolution.

The House tally mostly followed party lines. Just 27 Republicans voted "no" and just 28 Democrats voted "yes." Support for the measure was short of the level enjoyed by a similar proposal in 1971; even with the Democrats in control, it came within 28 votes of the two-thirds majority required.

The Senate had no plans to take up the amendment. The last time it voted on a religious expression amendment, thirteen years before, the proposal came up 11 votes short of the required two-thirds majority. *(1999–2000 action, p. 660)*

Justice Department Reauthorization

The House in 1998 passed the first authorization of the Justice Department in nearly two decades. But the plan sparked little discussion on the House floor, and the full Senate did not take it up. The bill (HR 3303—H Rept 105-526) served as a notice from Judiciary Committee Chairman Henry J. Hyde, R-Ill., that he intended to push the reauthorization issue in future years. Since 1979, the last time an authorization was passed, Justice Department policy had been set by legislative language added to appropriations bills. HR 3303 was Hyde's attempt to wrest control back to the Judiciary Committee and to signal his interest in greater scrutiny of department activities.

The department's budget had doubled during the Clinton administration as the president and Congress poured money into crime fighting and border control programs. The authorization bill would provide nearly $15.5 billion for fiscal 1999 (closely following the administration's budget request) and provide 5 percent increases in the two subsequent years.

Despite the department's request for a five-year authorization, Hyde insisted on a three-year plan. He said lawmakers could not accurately project the department's financial needs beyond 2001.

HR 3303 would reauthorize several programs due to expire at the end of the year. The programs included border patrol, vehicle theft prevention, rural domestic violence, antiterrorism, and deportation proceeding initiatives. Permanent authorizing authority would be granted for normal governmental tasks such as buying automobiles.

The measure would repeal the open-ended authorizations of the National Institute of Corrections and the U.S. Marshals Service, placing them more in line with the rest of the department.

The House Judiciary Committee approved the measure by voice vote on April 29 after Hyde agreed to change the bill to elicit as little controversy as possible. The one mildly controversial element—a provision requiring the department to move 200 lawyers from the Washington, D.C., headquarters to field offices around the country—was made discretionary under an amendment by Rep. John Conyers Jr., D-Mich., the committee's ranking member. The amendment was approved by voice vote.

The panel approved a number of other noncontroversial amendments by voice vote, including one by Rep. Bill McCollum, R-Fla., clarifying that the Secret Service—and not the FBI—had the authority to protect the president. Another one by Rep. Ed Bryant, R-Tenn., would upgrade INS offices in Charlotte, N.C., Memphis and Nashville, Tenn., and San Jose, Calif.

The House passed the measure by voice vote on June 22.

The Senate Judiciary Committee approved a substitute of HR 3303 by voice vote on Sept. 17. The committee removed one notable provision that would change requirements while extending the grandfather dates for an FBI wiretapping capability program. The FBI had protested that the provision would be difficult to implement.

Kennedy Assassination

Congress in 1997 voted to extend for one year the authorization for the federal board assigned with reviewing whether to release to the public various documents related to the assassination of President John F. Kennedy. The bill (HR 1553—PL 105-25) authorized $1.6 million in fiscal 1998 for the Assassination Records Review Board to finish reviewing government records. Without the extension, funding for the board was due to expire at the end of September.

The panel was created in the wake of public outcry following director Oliver Stone's 1992 film, "JFK," which specifically criticized the federal government for failing to release many records associated with the assassination. The five-member board had transferred more than 14,000 previously secret documents to the Kennedy collection at the National Archives since June 1995.

The House Government Reform and Oversight Committee approved the measure (H Rept 105-138, Pt. I) on June 11 by voice vote. The House passed it by voice vote on June 23, and the Senate cleared it on June 25 by unanimous consent. President Clinton signed the measure into law on July 3, 1997.

Assaults on Federal Judges

The Senate in 1997 passed legislation to increase penalties for threatening or assaulting federal judges or law enforcement officials. The bill (S 1189), seeking to protect federal officials from the people they arrest and convict, would increase the maximum prison term to twenty years for any convict who used a gun to assault a federal law enforcement official, including a judge. The courts could impose an extra ten-year sentence on an individual who threatened a judge or law enforcement officer, or their family, by phone.

The measure also directed the U.S. Sentencing Commission to amend federal sentencing guidelines to provide appropriate sentences for those who assaulted or threatened federal judges or other law enforcement officials. Sen. Gordon Smith, R-Oregon, introduced the measure partly because an Oregon judge had faced repeated threats from a man he had sent to prison. Lawmakers cited additional instances of judges facing threats from people they had sentenced.

The Judiciary Committee approved the measure on Oct. 9 without a written report. The Senate passed it by unanimous consent on Nov. 9. The House did not take up the bill.

Dispute Resolution

Congress in 1998 approved legislation to try to discourage unnecessary litigation and reduce judicial caseloads. The measure (HR 3528—PL 105-315) directed each U.S. District Court to devise and implement a dispute resolution program or to examine and improve an existing program. Most of the ninety-four federal District Courts already had established such programs. Courts would require litigants in civil cases to at least consider using various alternatives to resolve disagreements. Supporters of the bill said it would address the growing concern about high caseloads, while offering litigants a relatively inexpensive way to settle disputes.

The House Judiciary Committee approved the measure (H Rept 105-487) March 24 by voice vote after accepting a Democratic amendment to prohibit parties in lawsuits from being placed in alternative resolution involuntarily. The amendment, passed by voice vote, also weakened language allowing those who declined to participate to be financially penalized. The House on April 21 passed the measure by a 405–2 vote. The Senate passed a slightly amended version on Oct. 7 by unanimous consent, and the House cleared it by voice vote on Oct. 10. President Clinton signed the bill on Oct. 30.

U.S. Marshals

The attorney general would gain the authority to name U.S. marshals without going through the nomination and confirmation process, under a bill that the House passed in 1997. But the Senate Judiciary Committee approved a far different version, and the issue never came to the Senate floor. U.S. marshals were appointed to four-year terms by the president and confirmed by the Senate. Critics complained that these presidential appointees often lacked the law enforcement background needed for the job. Bill sponsor Bill McCollum, R-Fla., said the U.S. Marshal Service had to create unnecessary middle management positions to compensate for this lack of experience.

The House version (H Rept 105-27), which won voice vote approval in the Judiciary Committee on March 12 and passed the floor by voice vote on March 18, would transfer the appointment power to the attorney general. The substitute version approved March 26 by the Senate Judiciary Committee only slightly resembled its House counterpart. It would keep the appointment power with the president, but it would establish new criteria for selection of U.S. marshals. Candidates would be required to be U.S. citizens, undergo a Justice Department background investigation, submit to a medical evaluation and one or more drug tests, pass a firearms proficiency test, hold a bachelor's degree, have not less than ten years of professional law enforcement experience—including five years of management experience—and demonstrate several qualities deemed necessary to fulfilling the demands of a U.S. marshal's position.

Although they approved the plan by voice vote, several senators worried that the criteria in the bill (which did not include a written report) were too specific and could narrow the pool of potential applicants considerably. Chairman Orrin G. Hatch, R-Utah, said he would work to resolve those concerns before the bill came to the floor. But the Senate took no further action.

Medals of Valor

The House in 1998 passed legislation to establish a medal of valor that would be awarded each year for public safety of-

ficers who "act with extraordinary valor above and beyond the call of duty." Under the bill (HR 4090), the president would award the medal, on behalf of Congress, to a public safety officer who is recognized by the attorney general and a special review board. Congressional leaders and the president would appoint the eleven-member review board to select candidates based on applications to the Justice Department.

Panel members would have to be public safety experts and the bill would direct the Justice Department to establish the specific criteria for the medal.

The House Judiciary Committee July 16 gave voice vote approval to the measure (H Rept 105-667). The House passed it by voice vote Sept. 9. The Senate did not take it up.

Off-Duty Officers

Federal law enforcement officers who responded to crimes while off duty or outside of their normal jurisdictions would be shielded from liability under a bill (S 1031) the Senate Judiciary Committee approved in 1998. Sponsor Charles E. Grassley, R-Iowa, said the measure was needed to prevent officers from being sued when they respond to a crime while off duty, and to allow them to use their health benefits if they are injured doing so.

The legislation would protect off-duty Secret Service agents or members of the Drug Enforcement Agency, for example, from liability for assistance they offered "outside the scope of their employment"—intervening in a convenience store robbery, for instance. The shield would apply only if the officer acted to protect someone from a violent crime or to prevent the escape of a suspect. The bill would not prevent injured parties from suing or collecting damages if they could prove an officer acted unreasonably, Grassley said.

The panel approved the measure July 30 by voice vote. The Senate did not take it up.

Slain Officers

Congress in 1998 cleared a pair of bills to help the families of law enforcement officers killed or disabled in the line of duty. One of the bills (HR 3565—PL 105-180) targeted at least $150,000 toward programs to assist families of slain police officers.

Under current law, the Bureau of Justice Assistance (BJA) received a mandatory appropriation to pay death benefits to the families of public safety officers killed in the line of duty. Up to $150,000 of those funds each year could be used by the BJA to support and counsel the families of slain officers. HR 3565 required the BJA to spend at least that amount.

The House Judiciary Committee gave voice vote approval to the measure April 1 (H Rept 105-486). The House passed it under suspension of the rules by a vote of 403–8 April 21. The Senate cleared it by unanimous consent May 15. The president signed the measure on June 16, 1998.

The second bill (S 1525—PL 105-390) expanded a program that provided financial aid for higher education to the dependents of public safety officers who were killed or permanently disabled in the line of duty. The bill made the federal grants available to spouses, sons and daughters of all public safety officers. The current law allowed grants only to dependents of federal peace officers.

As much as $4,485 a year would be authorized for each dependent to attend a four-year university—the same amount of educational assistance provided to dependents of slain or disabled veterans and federal law enforcement officers.

The Senate Judiciary Committee approved it by voice vote May 7 without a written report. The Senate passed it May 18 by unanimous consent. The House amended it Oct. 10 by inserting the text of a similar bill, HR 3046, then passed it by voice vote. The Senate cleared the measure Oct. 15 by unanimous consent. Clinton signed the bill on Nov. 13. *(2000 action, p. 651)*

Volunteers

Volunteers gained new legal protections under a bill signed into law in 1997 (S 543—PL 105-19). The bill shielded volunteers from personal civil liability for harm caused while they were acting on behalf of a nonprofit organization, as long as they were not guilty of negligence, or willful, malicious, or criminal conduct. Even in cases where they could be held liable, they would be partially protected.

Volunteers could only be forced to pay noneconomic penalties—for such things as causing mental anguish or pain and suffering—in proportion to their level of responsibility. This was aimed at preventing litigants from seeking out the wealthiest person with some level of liability, such as a nonprofit organization board member, and forcing that person to pay the entire penalty. The practice could still be used to impose economic penalties such as for hospital costs or lost work.

Supporters said the measure would protect volunteers from "frivolous lawsuits" that could discourage them from volunteering.

LEGISLATIVE ACTION

The first action on S 543 occurred on the Senate floor, where the measure passed May 1, 99–1. Fred Thompson, R-Tenn., cast the lone dissenting vote, saying the issue was better addressed at the state level.

Democrats had temporarily delayed the floor action to protest the fact that the bill had not gone through the usual committee process, as well as to demonstrate their unhappiness over a separate GOP delay in taking up the nomination of Alexis Herman to be Labor secretary.

Republicans tried twice and failed to cut off debate and proceed to the bill. The first attempt, which was also the year's first cloture showdown, failed April 29 by a vote of 53–46, seven votes shy of the 60 votes needed to cut off debate. The second attempt failed April 30, 55–44.

Herman was confirmed shortly after the second cloture vote, and Democrats allowed S 543 to come to the floor. But they raised concerns that the bill could provide unintended protections to hate groups such as the Ku Klux Klan and to volunteers who abused children. Senators approved by voice vote an amendment to ensure that the bill's protections would not extend to members of hate groups.

Another amendment approved by voice vote would allow states to opt out of the federal law if they determined their own laws were adequate to protect volunteers from frivolous lawsuits.

Less than two weeks after the Senate passage, a similar bill began moving in the House. The House Judiciary Committee approved the measure (H 911—H Rept 105-101, Pt. I) May 13 by a vote of 20–7. The panel first adopted by voice vote a substitute amendment by Bob Inglis, R-S.C., aimed at bringing the House bill more in line with Senate provisions regarding the ability of states to opt out.

The original House bill would increase block grants for social services if states without laws shielding volunteers from liability adopted such statutes. Inglis's substitute did not include that provision, and an amendment by John Conyers Jr., D-Mich., to restore the incentives was rejected, 5–21.

The House passed HR 911 on May 21 by a vote of 390–35, then passed S 543 by voice vote, amended to reflect the House version. Later that day, the Senate cleared the House version by voice vote. President Clinton signed the bill on June 18, 1997.

Affirmative Action

Although conservative Republicans wanted to launch a major offensive against affirmative action programs in the 105th Congress, they found that their party's support for the issue was not as strong as they thought. A bill (HR 1909) to ban racial and gender preferences in federal contracting was tabled (killed) by the House Judiciary Committee in 1997 on a 17–9 vote. A similar Senate measure (S 950) never received action.

HR 1909, sponsored by Charles T. Canady, R-Fla., exposed rifts in the ranks of the GOP. Some Republicans worried that their party was in danger of alienating nonwhite citizens, which was unwise politically and philosophically. "As the party of Lincoln, we need to stand up against discrimination," said Rep. Steve Buyer, R-Ind.

The debate over the measure seemed to be part of a wider effort to package conservative social policy issues in a more saleable form. Several Republicans, including both supporters and opponents of Canady's bill, said that affirmative action initiatives needed to be sharpened, narrowed, or otherwise modified to prevent attracting such virulent opposition. Others said affirmative action legislation should be paired with an alternative to affirmative action—aid to inner cities, for example—to demonstrate that the party was not antiminority.

If Republicans were divided on the matter, Democrats and their supporters were not—and they made clear that they would make a lot of noise. On Nov. 7 so many representatives of civil rights organizations showed up at the House Judiciary Committee room that they blocked most entrances.

Former presidential candidate Jesse Jackson arrived and led the group in a prayer. But at other times the gathering looked more like a pep rally than a prayer vigil. When Chairman Henry J. Hyde, R-Ill., announced the outcome and gaveled the meeting to an end, the room filled with cheers.

At the markup, four Republicans crossed over to vote with thirteen committee Democrats to kill HR 1909. The four were Buyer, Elton Gallegly of California, George W. Gekas of Pennsylvania, and Ed Pease of Indiana.

The crowd may have prevented some members from getting into the room to vote. Several Democrats initially voted "pass" to give colleagues more time to get in. When they were in the room, they voted "aye."

Most Democrats made it through the throngs. Seven Republicans did not show up. A party caucus occurred at the same time, and Canady said some members had not rushed from that meeting fast enough. Others may have avoided weighing in on the controversial matter.

The debate over affirmative action spilled over to Clinton's controversial nomination of Bill Lann Lee to be the Justice Department's chief enforcer of affirmative action programs. On the same day that the House Judiciary Committee took up HR 1909, conservatives on the Senate Judiciary Committee sought to block Lee's nomination. In the end, the Senate never voted on the nominee, and Clinton used his executive powers to install him in the Justice post. *(Lee nomination, p. 624)*

The issue of affirmative action also rose again in 1998 during debate on the reauthorization of the Higher Education Act. An amendment by Frank Riggs, R-Calif., that sought to end affirmative action at public colleges and universities was defeated in a **key vote of 171–249 (R 166–55; D 5–193; I 0–1)** *(1998 key votes, p. 883; Riggs amendment, p. 511)*

Supreme Court Volunteers

A measure to allow volunteers to give tours of the Supreme Court building was cleared by lawmakers in 1998. Senate Judiciary Committee Chairman Orrin G. Hatch, R-Utah, who sponsored the bill (S 2143—PL 105-233) said it would help the court deal with the millions of visitors it received each year without added cost to the taxpayers. The legislation made a technical change to federal law, allowing the chief justice to use volunteers in the court's public and visitor programs. The tours would be conducted by members of the Supreme Court Historical Society.

S 2143 protected Supreme Court employees from pay reductions or layoffs caused by the influx of volunteer labor. Hatch noted that volunteers had been conducting tours in the Capitol since the 104th Congress. As a result, the volume of Capitol tours had increased by 25 percent.

The Senate Judiciary Committee approved the measure by voice vote July 9 without issuing a written report. The Senate passed it by unanimous consent July 16, and the

House cleared it by voice vote Aug. 3. Clinton signed the bill on Aug. 13, 1998.

High-Tech Visas

At the beginning of 1998, high-tech companies hurting for technology-trained workers launched a lobbying campaign in favor of legislation to increase the number of temporary visas issued to highly skilled foreigners. The negotiations took all year and at one point appeared as if they would come to naught. But a provision temporarily increasing the number of "H-1B" visas from 65,000 to 115,000 was included in the omnibus spending package (HR 4328—PL 105-277) passed at the end of the 105th Congress. *(2000 action, p. 670)*

BACKGROUND

Concern on Capitol Hill grew rapidly about reported shortages of skilled workers in computer-related fields. With the economy booming and unemployment low, companies were scrambling to find the talent necessary to keep on innovating while also solving the massive computer problems associated with the year 2000.

As recently as 1997, few lawmakers had even heard of H-1B visas, which permitted employers to bring in workers from overseas if they declared a need for skills unavailable in the domestic workforce. But the 1998 allotment of 65,000 visas for computer engineers, programmers, university researchers, and a variety of other workers—including fashion models—was fully committed by May 9. After a massive lobbying campaign by the technology sector, Congress put an increase in those visas on a fast track.

Senate Commerce Committee Chairman John McCain, R-Ariz., said the number of visas for skilled workers was "the first issue raised" when he met with Intel Corp. chairman Andy Grove in early 1998.

Backers of the plan noted that the limit of 65,000 H-1B visas had already been reached for the fiscal year. Some major telecommunications companies were at a disadvantage by not being allowed to hire more specialists, many of whom were young computer engineers who studied at U.S. universities and were seeking to remain in the country. Majority Leader Trent Lott, Miss., said the measure was "needed for our economy."

But opponents warned the program was rife with abuse and was not sufficiently targeted. The Labor Department estimated that only 40 percent of the H-1B visas in the past went to people with computer-related skills.

Both the Senate and House measures would increase the number of visas to 95,000 or higher. Such increases were a major goal of companies such as Microsoft and Intel. But the House measure drew fire from the high-tech industry because it would impose restrictions on recruitment and layoff procedures in an effort to protect domestic workers. The

Clinton administration also raised concerns about some provisions, warning that the easing of the labor market might lead companies to favor foreign workers at the expense of domestic workers.

SENATE ACTION

The Senate Judiciary Committee on April 2 approved a bill (S 1723) by a vote of 12–6 increasing the number of temporary visas issued to highly skilled foreign workers. Sponsored by Spencer Abraham, R-Mich., who chaired the Senate Judiciary Immigration Subcommittee, the bill would increase the number from 65,000 to approximately 95,000. The total could go higher, because the bill also allowed unused visas in other categories to be transferred to the H-1B program.

Although Democrats at the Judiciary Committee markup wanted to protect domestic workers, their opposition to the bill was muted. Rather than attack Abraham's plan, Democrats chose to press their own version of an H-1B expansion. A substitute offered by Dianne Feinstein, D-Calif., and Edward M. Kennedy, D-Mass., would increase the number of visas to 90,000 but limit them to three years, as opposed to the six years allowed under Abraham's bill. It would make a number of other changes, including requiring companies to attest that they had not laid off anyone to make room for the foreign worker.

The Kennedy-Feinstein amendment failed 8–10 along party lines, as did a narrower Feinstein amendment addressing only the duration of the visas. With her amendments defeated, Feinstein—along with Democrat Herb Kohl of Wisconsin—joined the panel's Republicans in voting for S 1723.

The full Senate took up the bill in the face of opposition from the Clinton administration and some Democrats. The White House threatened a veto, arguing the bill did not contain enough protections for U.S. workers who might be fired or turned away to make room for foreigners.

Despite such warnings, the Senate tabled, 60–38, an amendment by Kennedy that would prohibit companies from hiring foreign workers under the H-1B program if they have laid off similar domestic workers within six months prior to applying for an H-1B worker.

Kennedy said companies would rather hire foreign "computer programmers and make them work longer hours at less pay." But opponents of Kennedy's amendment said the bill included sufficient sanctions for companies that hired foreign workers with the intent of replacing U.S. workers.

Members tabled, 59–39, another Democratic amendment that would require high-technology companies to try to recruit U.S. workers before turning to foreign workers. Many Republicans opposed that, saying it would place more federal regulatory hurdles on the high-technology industry.

The Senate also tabled, 74–24, an amendment by Dale Bumpers, D-Ark., that would eliminate a small visa program that provided residency status to some wealthy foreigners who invest in U.S. enterprises. Bumpers said some foreign investors were using a loophole to gain visas and in some cases full citizenship from the temporary visa program by providing only a portion of the minimum required investment in U.S. companies. But opponents said the investors provided U.S. jobs and rejected Bumpers's claim that the program was being abused to the degree that it should be eliminated.

The Senate on May 18 passed the measure on a **key vote of 78–20 (R 51–2; D 27–18)**. *(1998 key votes, p. 883)*

HOUSE COMMITTEE ACTION

Plotting a course protective of U.S. workers, the House Judiciary Immigration Subcommittee on April 30 gave voice vote approval to a bill (HR 3736) to boost the number of H-1B visas. The Judiciary Committee approved it, 20–4, on May 20. The subcommittee's approval belied the controversy that surrounded the measure, sponsored by subcommittee chairman Lamar Smith, R-Texas.

After heavily lobbying for a big increase in such H-1B visas, business groups turned against the Smith bill once they saw the fine print. As high-tech lobbyists had hoped, the measure would increase the number of H-1B visas that could be awarded, from 65,000 in 1998 to 95,000 in 1999, and ultimately as high as 115,000.

But Smith included in his measure provisions that business groups detested. Employers would have to go through a much more lengthy process than under current law to get approval to bring in a high-tech worker in the H-1B program. And they would have a hard time participating in the program if they laid off any American workers.

The provisions appeared to be a last-minute addition. They were not mentioned in early fact sheets Smith put out on what would be in the bill. They appeared to be related to another controversial provision that the chairman threatened to include: language that would give preference to high school-educated immigrants trying to enter this country via a family sponsorship.

Business groups vehemently opposed that provision, not wanting to appear to be adding staff to their companies at the expense of someone seeking to be reunited with his or her family. The last-minute moves to add the worker furlough and visa approval provisions were in retaliation for business opposition to Smith's high school graduate language, one Republican aide said. Despite the controversial provisions, Democrats and Republicans agreed to withhold a long list of proposed amendments until the bill reached full committee.

In the full committee markup, an effort by Rep. James A. Rogan, R-Calif., to remove the labor provisions was defeated, 7–21, with the panel's more senior Republicans joining all Democrats in voting no. Rogan and his supporters argued the provisions would greatly increase the Labor Department's regulation of American businesses.

Although industry officials contended they would rather have no bill at all than one with the labor provisions, they did not try to block the measure. Instead, they held out hope that the labor provisions might be softened or even eliminated by the House leadership before the bill went to the floor. "It is not in the leadership's interest to bring up a bill that doesn't have the business community's support," said Randy Johnson, vice president of labor policy for the U.S. Chamber of Commerce. "We are their base."

Pushing for the House bill but opposing the Senate-passed version were powerful labor organizations, including the AFL-CIO, United Auto Workers, and several health workers' unions.

FURTHER NEGOTIATIONS

After weeks of negotiations, key lawmakers in late July reached a tentative deal on proposals to increase the number of highly skilled immigrants admitted to the country. "This agreement is a major breakthrough, and I expect both chambers to pass it before the August recess," declared Abraham.

The compromise language kept the basic outline of the two requirements contained in an earlier House draft that had labor support, but it scaled back both considerably. Under the agreement, companies sponsoring H-1B immigrants would have to attest that they tried and failed to find U.S. workers for the jobs in question, and that they had not laid off U.S. workers to make room for lower-paid immigrants. But those requirements would apply only to companies of at least fifty-one people whose workforce was composed of at least 15 percent H-1B workers.

None of the nation's major high-tech firms would be affected by such a deal. Instead, the provision was aimed at "job shop" companies that imported workers, then distributed them to other firms. The Labor Department would not be involved in the process, as it would be under Smith's bill. Instead, enforcement would shift to a three-member arbitration panel selected by the parties. And the layoff provision would be greatly diluted. Companies could be barred from the visa program only if they had laid off someone with almost exactly the same job expertise as the person brought in. The Smith plan was far less specific.

With companies warning of worker shortages, House leaders scheduled floor action for the new bill (HR 3736) July 31. But they pulled the bill after the administration issued a veto threat. Action on the legislation was also blocked in the Senate, where Democrats objected to Majority Leader Trent Lott's request for passage of the bill by unanimous consent.

The administration objected to the compromise on the same grounds that it opposed the version of S 1723 passed by the Senate on May 18: that it would not provide enough protection for American workers competing with the H-1B hires.

In September administration officials sat down with House staffers to work out other differences over the measure, attempting to wade through a fifteen-point list of changes the administration requested when it issued a veto threat. While calling for more protections for American workers, White House officials said they were willing to work on a compromise that could increase the number of visas somewhat in 1999.

HOUSE FLOOR ACTION

After months of negotiations, the House on Sept. 25 passed a compromise version of HR 3736 by a **key vote of 288–133 (R 189–34; D 99–98; I 0–1).** The Senate appeared poised to clear the measure, but it failed to take it up because of a singular objection. *(1998 key votes, p. 883)*

The measure embodied a compromise that had been worked out the previous evening between the administration and Abraham. It would boost the number of temporary H-1B visas available each year to 115,000 in 1999 and in 2000, and 107,500 in 2001. Thereafter, the limit would return to 65,000.

Companies that drew 15 percent or more of their workforce from H-1B visa holders would have to attest they have not laid off Americans from those jobs, and all employers would face stiff penalties and exclusion from the visa program if they violated rules against layoffs of Americans.

Among its other provisions, the measure would assess a $500 fee on employers for every visa application and renewal, raising about $75 million a year for college scholarships and job training for low-income students pursuing math, engineering or computer sciences training.

The bill's proponents dismissed critics' claims that the legislation would cost U.S. jobs. "Skilled people create jobs, they don't take jobs away," said David Dreier, R-Calif. "This is a very good compromise worked out by all parties."

Many of the Democrats who opposed the compromise complained that they had not been in on the negotiating and had not had adequate time to review the new version, which they believed still would not do enough to protect American workers. In fact, the measure was toggled on and off the House schedule several times before GOP leaders concluded it had the votes to pass.

Before the final vote, the House rejected, 177–242, a substitute offered by Melvin Watt, D-N.C., that contained the labor provisions that had been in the earlier version approved by the Judiciary Committee.

SENATE ACTION

Although the bill appeared destined for Senate passage, Tom Harkin, D-Iowa, effectively killed it Oct. 9 when he objected to an effort to pass the bill by voice vote. Although supporters considered the measure (HR 3736) vital to the high-technology industry, Harkin said there was no shortage of available domestic high-technology workers. "The programming shortage never materialized," Harkin said. "And we don't need to pass this now. . . . We can always come back if there is a shortage."

To get around Harkin, backers of the H-1B visa expansion added the provision to the omnibus spending package (HR 4328). The House adopted the conference report (H

Rept 105-825) on HR 4328, 333–95, on Oct. 20, and the Senate cleared it, 65–29, on Oct. 21. President Clinton signed the omnibus bill the same day.

The final version increased the number of H-1B visas to 115,000 in 1999 and 2000, then dropped them to 107,500 in 2001. Thereafter, the number of visas would fall back to 65,000. The plan included the House-passed requirements on businesses, but applied them only to a small class of employers that heavily depended on the H-1B program.

Citizenship for Children Born Abroad

Lawmakers in 1997 cleared a measure (S 670—PL 105-38) clarifying citizenship procedures for children born abroad to U.S. parents. The bill restored a correction made in 1994, and inadvertently repealed under the 1996 Immigration Overhaul Law (PL 104-208).

Under S 670, children born abroad to U.S. parents were guaranteed citizenship if at least one of the child's parents had lived in the United States for at least five years before the child's birth. Without the change, some children born in 1987 might be eligible for citizenship while a sibling born in 1985 might not be, according to bill sponsor Spencer Abraham, R-Mich.

The measure won voice vote approval May 8 in the Senate Judiciary Committee. The Senate passed it by unanimous consent May 14, and the House cleared it by voice vote July 28. Clinton signed it Aug. 8.

Lawmakers in 1998 also cleared a measure (S 1198—PL 105-54) to waive processing fees for visas for certain nonimmigrants. The measure aimed to help those nonimmigrants engaged in a limited number of charitable activities, including health or nursing care, or providing food or housing for the needy.

The Senate passed it by unanimous consent Sept. 18. The House passed it by voice vote with an amendment Oct. 1, and the Senate cleared it by unanimous consent Oct. 1. Clinton signed it Oct. 6.

Immigration

Republicans in the 105th Congress backed away from several of the tough immigration policies they had enacted the previous year. In August 1997 they agreed to restore certain welfare benefits to legal immigrants who were already in the United States when the 1996 welfare overhaul law (PL 104-193) was enacted—a move made to avert a political backlash in states with large immigrant populations such as California and Florida. The change was included in the spending portion of the budget reconciliation package (PL 105-33) signed Aug. 5. (*Congress and the Nation Vol. IX, p. 590–591; 511, 578, 681, 717*)

Then, facing a late September deadline, lawmakers were faced with two problems stemming from the 1996 immigration law (PL 104-208) aimed at clamping down on illegal immigrants. The first problem was the imminent deportation of some 280,000 refugees from three Central American nations; the second involved a "Catch-22" situation created by the 1996 law for hundreds of thousands of illegal immigrants who were working toward permanent resident visas.

CENTRAL AMERICAN REFUGEES

The 1996 immigration law made most of the 280,000 Salvadoran, Guatemalan, and Nicaraguan refugees who had come to the United States in the 1980s subject to deportation. Under the earlier law, they were exempt from deportation if they stayed in the United States for seven years and showed that the deportation would cause hardship to a family member legally in the United States, such as a child born here. The 1996 law stopped the clock for most refugees and required them to have been in the country for ten years to be exempt from deportation.

Rep. Lamar Smith, R-Texas, an author of the language making the Central Americans deportable, argued that, with the civil wars over and elected governments in power, refugees from these three countries should be required to return home. But the governments of Nicaragua, El Salvador, and Guatemala argued strenuously that their fragile economies could not handle so massive a repatriation. Clinton, deluged by their appeals when he toured Mexico and Costa Rica during the spring, said in July he would do as much as he could through executive action.

Some elements of the 1996 law could be altered only through legislation, however. For example, the law said that under no circumstances were more than 4,000 people per year to be exempt from deportation proceedings.

Rep. Lincoln Diaz-Balart, R-Fla., and Sen. Connie Mack, R-Fla., introduced legislation (HR 2302, S 1076) to remove that cap and exempt about half the Central American refugees from the new law. Working in the Senate with Edward M. Kennedy, D-Mass., and Bob Graham, D-Fla., they successfully attached an amendment to the DC appropriations bill (S 1156) on Oct. 8 by a vote of 99–1. Robert C. Byrd cast the lone "no" vote to protest the fact that the amendment was unrelated to the underlying spending bill. However, Sen. Carol Moseley-Braun, D-Ill., held up further action on the bill while she demanded similar protection for more than 10,000 Haitians who had entered the country by the early 1990s.

With the Senate version of the D.C. bill stalled, Republican leaders put together a revised appropriations bill that finally cleared Nov. 13, the last day of the session, and was signed into law Nov. 19 (PL 105-100). The cleared immigration provisions did not provide any protection for Haitians, but the administration assuaged members of the Black Caucus with an assurance that it would not deport the Haitians until Congress had a chance to act on their fate.

Under the bill, refugees from Nicaragua and Cuba who entered the United States before Dec. 1, 1995, were eligible to apply for permanent residence if they did so before April 1,

2000. In addition, certain refugees from Guatemala, El Salvador, the former Soviet republics, and former eastern bloc countries who sought asylum before 1990, could have their cases reviewed under the rules in place before the 1996 immigration law was enacted.

245(i) PROVISION

The second issue involved the pending expiration of a 1994 provision affecting illegal immigrants who were working toward obtaining legal status. The provision—known as 245(i) after a section of the 1994 State Department spending bill (PL 103-317)—allowed them to get permanent resident visas in the United States after paying a $1,000 fine, rather than first returning to their country.

The provision was due to expire Sept. 30, after which the permanent visas would only be issued by U.S. embassies and consulates overseas. That created a dilemma for hundreds of thousands of immigrants. Under the 1996 immigration law, illegal aliens who left the United States after Sept. 27 could not come back for three years. After April 1, they would be barred for ten years. The 245(i) issue was fought out on the fiscal 1996 appropriations bill for the departments of Commerce, Justice and State.

Lawmakers who wanted to stay tough on illegal aliens, such as Smith and Elton Gallegly, R-Calif., led the opposition. Smith, in a letter to the Rules Committee, argued that Section 245(i) "rewards those who have jumped the line by entering the U.S. illegally or overstaying a visa." But supporters of the extension argued that forcing so many people to leave the United States—or go underground—would have an adverse effect on immigrant communities and on businesses that relied on immigrants.

Others noted that the State Department was not prepared to go back to screening permanent visa applications at its overseas missions. And fiscal politics also played a role, since the $1,000 charged to process a visa application under 245(i) was expected to bring in more than $200 million in 1997.

The Senate version of the Commerce, Justice, State spending bill (S 1022), passed July 29, included a provision to extend the 245(i) program permanently. By contrast, the slow-moving House version (HR 2267) was silent on the issue.

The House did not pass the bill until Sept. 30, which was both the end of the fiscal year and the expiration date for section 245(i). To keep agencies operating, lawmakers passed a series of stopgap appropriations bills that also kept the 245(i) program alive—first until Nov. 7 and then until Nov. 14.

Pro-immigration forces won a significant victory Oct. 29 when the House took a nonbinding, but highly revealing, vote on the issue. Dana Rohrabacher, R-Calif., moved to instruct conferees on the Commerce, Justice, State bill to terminate the 245(i) program. The motion was rejected, 153–268, virtually ensuring that the conference report would include an extension.

Under the compromise ultimately contained in the conference report (H Rept 105-405), most future permanent visas would be issued only in an immigrant's home country.

But anyone in the United States who submitted an application by Jan. 14, 1998, would be allowed to get one here.

The language included two exceptions for immigrants seeking permanent status through an employer. They did not need a pending green card application by Jan. 14, but just a pending application for Labor Department certification that they possessed a job skill in high demand. Also, any skilled immigrant who fell into the status of an illegal alien for less than six months while waiting for paperwork could get a permanent visa in the United States.

The Senate adopted the conference report Nov. 13, and the House cleared it late the same day. The bill (PL 105-119) was signed into law by Clinton on Nov. 26.

Illegal Immigrants

Congress in 1997 cleared legislation (HR 1493—PL 105-141) to establish pilot programs in local prisons aimed at identifying illegal immigrants before they were arraigned. Under the measure, the Justice Department was required to assign at least one Immigration and Naturalization Service (INS) employee to each jail in each town, city or county participating in the program.

Such an approach differed from the INS's Institutional Hearing Program, under which INS employees at state and federal prisons sought to identify illegal immigrants who had already been convicted. Under HR 1493, the INS would identify even those illegal immigrants who were never convicted of the offenses for which they were most recently arrested.

Supporters pointed to a 1995 study by police in Anaheim, Calif., which found that 36 percent of people who were booked at the city detention facility were suspected of being illegal immigrants.

The House Judiciary Committee approved the measure (HR 105-338) by voice vote Sept. 9. The House Nov. 4 passed it, 410–2, and the Senate cleared it by unanimous consent Nov. 13. President Clinton signed HR 1493 on Dec. 5, 1997.

Judicial Activism

With conservatives bristling over federal judges who they said were setting policy from the bench, the House passed a far-ranging bill in 1998 to rein in such controversial judicial practices as ordering the early release of prisoners and requiring local governments to raise taxes.

But Democrats warned that the measure would undermine the independence of the judicial branch, and House Republicans were forced to strip away some of the most controversial provisions. The Senate—which exercised considerable influence over the judiciary through its constitutional mandate to confirm federal judges—never considered the measure.

BACKGROUND

For many years, conservative lawmakers had railed against "judicial activism"—the perceived practice of some judges to impose their own views in the courtroom instead of following a strict interpretation of the law. Such criticism appeared to grow in the late 1990s. House Majority Whip Tom DeLay, R-Texas, called for widespread impeachments, and individual members launched rhetorical broadsides: "There is no doubt in my mind that there is a special place in hell for a number of federal court judges. . . ." Rep. Jack Kingston, R-Ga., declared in a 1998 floor speech on school prayer. Starting when the Democrats controlled Capitol Hill, but picking up considerably under Republican rule, Congress increasingly tried to tell the courts what they could and could not rule on.

The 1996 immigration bill (PL 104-208), for instance, contained a section saying certain deportation orders issued by the Justice Department were "not reviewable in a court of law." A similar provision, included in a portion of the 1996 omnibus spending bill, was designed to limit prison inmates' ability to file grievance cases in federal courts (PL 103-134). Another measure (PL 104-132) would significantly limit the ability of prisoners to use habeas corpus appeals to federal judges to question the constitutionality of their convictions. (*Congress and the Nation Vol. IX, pp. 717, 727, 731, 733*)

Not surprisingly, such limitations enraged civil rights groups, which said Congress was imposing its ideology on the courts by preventing them from ruling on certain issues. "When Congress selectively removes particular issues, then it is in effect prescribing the outcome," said Nadine Strossen, national president of the American Civil Liberties Union.

Some analysts warned that the attacks on the judiciary threaten its very independence and ultimately could upset the system of checks and balances envisioned by the Founding Fathers. "The erosion of the independence of the judiciary is not something absolutely dramatic," said Sheldon Goldman, a political scientist at the University of Massachusetts. "It's an incremental thing. It's a cancer on the American constitutional framework. Someday we may wake up to find a very different United States."

But courts' harshest critics, including DeLay and Sen. John Ashcroft, R-Mo., saw some sitting judges as arrogant, unresponsive to the public and prone to "activist" rulings that overstepped their constitutional role of applying, rather than creating, the law. "There is an activist judge behind each of most of the perverse failures of today's justice system," DeLay said in a floor speech April 23. "When judges legislate, they usurp the power of Congress. When judges stray beyond the Constitution, they usurp the power of the people."

One of the most often-cited examples was Missouri District Court Judge Russell Clark, who forced $1.8 billion in tax increases in Kansas City to fund court-ordered improvements to inner-city schools. Other judges struck down public referendums that won popular majorities, such as a California vote to limit affirmative action (Proposition 209) and a 1992 Colorado proposition to limit civil rights protections for homosexuals. Judges who appeared to be soft on crime were highly unpopular with conservatives, as were those who impose a rigid church-state separation.

DeLay argued that such rulings indicated the judicial branch had exceeded its authority. "The system of checks and balances so carefully crafted is in serious disrepair and has been for years," he said.

Constitutionally shut out of the process of confirming judges, the House tried to put its imprint on the federal judiciary through legislation. Conservatives coalesced behind HR 1252—a broad measure that, in its original form, would greatly diminish the power of judges.

HOUSE COMMITTEE ACTION

The Judiciary Committee's Courts and Intellectual Property Subcommittee approved HR 1252, 8–7, on June 11, 1997. The full panel on March 24, 1998, gave voice vote approval to the measure (H Rept 105-478). Among other things, the bill would make it more difficult for judges to order tax increases to remedy problems such as a substandard school or an environmental hazard. It would also require that appeals of public referendums be heard by three-judge panels and give litigants in the twenty-one largest judicial districts the right to reject the first judge assigned to their case.

The measure included some controversial provisions not connected with the overall theme of restraining activism. Judges' pay would no longer be linked to that of members of Congress, allowing them to get an automatic cost of living increase even if lawmakers blocked the increase for themselves.

Democrats scored a major victory in the subcommittee, watering down the section dealing with tax increases. As originally written, the bill would ban any judicial remedies with even an indirect effect of forcing any government entity to raise taxes. This meant that a judge could not compel a state to clean up a polluted site, force a city to improve its schools, or take any other action that might prompt a tax increase.

An amendment by Bill Delahunt, D-Mass., changed the provision to ban only the explicit increase of taxes by a judge, already banned by the Supreme Court ruling in *Missouri v. Jenkins*. Delahunt's amendment was first defeated, 5–7. But he then combined it into a second amendment which further weakened the portion restricting tax increases. Then the amendment was approved on a voice vote.

In the full committee, Charles T. Canady, R-Fla., called the measure "balanced and sensible." He said there were numerous examples of judges acting as "quasi-lawmakers" or making up legal doctrine with no constitutional basis.

Democrats argued that the legislation was little more than an attempt to bully judges into making rulings more in line with Republicans' conservative political goals. It would harm judicial independence without necessarily stopping judges from making unpopular rulings, said Barney Frank, D-Mass. "It would do nothing in most cases to prevent the type of decisions we do not like," he said.

The minority offered four amendments that were defeated largely along party lines. The amendment that triggered the most debate would limit the sealing of evidence in cases that were settled out of court. Democrats said material that would alert the public of a danger should not be sealed, while Republicans argued that the amendment would reduce out-of-court settlements. The amendment failed on a 6–16 vote.

Howard L. Berman, D-Calif., offered an amendment striking the three-judge requirement for public referendums, arguing that it was an inefficient use of scarce judicial resources. Republicans countered that the practice was currently mandated for hearing cases brought under voting rights laws. The amendment was rejected, 10–14.

The one amendment that was approved with bipartisan support was offered by Steve Chabot, R-Ohio, to allow television cameras in district courtrooms if the judge permitted it. The underlying bill allowed this for appellate courts, where there were no witnesses, just legal discussions between lawyers and judges. Chabot's amendment extending coverage to trial courts was approved, 12–6.

What appeared a united Republican front during most of the committee consideration, however, belied reservations some Republicans had about the bill. A number opposed the pay raise provision, a priority of Chairman Henry J. Hyde, R-Ill. The most vocal critic of this provision, F. James Sensenbrenner Jr., R-Wis., was so angered that he declined to show up for any portion of the committee's consideration of the bill.

HOUSE FLOOR ACTION

On an anticlimactic voice vote, the House on April 23 passed HR 1252. The measure won easy passage only after some of its most sweeping and contentious provisions were removed. The amended measure still would deny federal judges the power to order prisoner releases to deal with overcrowding. It would attempt to limit their ability to block executions by granting death-row habeas corpus appeals. And it would require appeals of ballot initiatives to be heard by three-judge panels, rather than by a single judge. Conservatives also took heart in the fact that the bill no longer delinked judges' pay from lawmakers' pay.

But the two most controversial items—preventing judges from forcing tax increases and giving parties in civil lawsuits the right to reject the first judge assigned to their case—were stripped from the bill. The authors of these provisions either lost floor votes or foresaw they would if they had pressed their case.

"I caved," said Canady with a shrug and a smile, after he accepted an amendment by James E. Rogan, R-Calif., striking his provision allowing parties to reject their first judge. Rogan won over a number of fellow Republicans by arguing the Canady language would encourage litigants to shop around for a judge they deemed favorable to their cause.

Donald Manzullo, R-Ill., sponsor of the tax-increase prohibition, removed the section after it was amended to his dislike. By a 230–181 vote, the House adopted an amendment by Bill Delahunt, D-Mass., considerably narrowing the Manzullo provision. Delahunt's language said that judges could still issue stiff penalties against localities that would force them to raise taxes. They just could not "expressly direct" them to raise taxes.

With the two most significant items gone, and with the bill facing an uphill battle in the Senate and a veto threat from President Clinton, Republicans chose to declare victory and move on. "We brought this to the floor to begin the national debate," Manzullo said. "It was a great debate."

Aside from the stripping of the tax and judicial-assignment provisions, several major changes were made to the bill during floor consideration. The provision delinking federal judges' pay from that of members of Congress was stripped from the bill through a parliamentary maneuver. A number of Republicans either thought it was inappropriate for judges to make more than members of Congress or wanted to use the salary issue to stress that they are unhappy with the performance of the federal bench.

A second significant change was made in an amendment by DeLay barring federal judges from forcing state prisons to release prisoners to handle overcrowding. That measure was adopted, 367–52.

A third change was made by a voice vote on an amendment by Jerrold Nadler, D-N.Y. The underlying bill would permit cameras in federal district and appellate courts at the discretion of the presiding judge. The Nadler amendment would allow witnesses in district courts to have their audio and video signals scrambled.

Judicial Nominations

Senate Republicans and Democrats locked horns throughout the 105th Congress over the pace of confirming President Clinton's judicial nominees. The partisan battles reached such a pitch that Chief Justice William Rehnquist issued a rare warning to Congress in 1998, urging that more judges be confirmed.

BACKGROUND

Since Republicans took control of the Senate in 1995, they had been under pressure from conservative groups to vet Clinton's judicial nominees carefully. That pressure intensified after Clinton won reelection in 1996. Conservatives objected to what they viewed as "judicial activism"—the tendency, they said, of some judges to legislate from the bench instead of following existing law. In 1998 the House passed a measure to curb judicial activism (HR 1252), but the Senate did not take it up. *(Judicial activism, p. 620)*

The fight over who gets to serve in the judiciary normally was of interest only inside the Beltway. Occasionally, however, it flared up into a confrontation that enabled interest groups to focus national attention on the process.

Controversial Supreme Court nominees often triggered this. Robert Bork's unsuccessful bid in 1987 and Clarence Thomas's successful one in 1991 generated intense scrutiny. Occasionally, the same happened with groups of lower court judges, if one party charged the other with trying to pack the bench with extremists. When Democrats took the Senate in 1987, they attacked President Ronald Reagan's picks with renewed vigor. Bork was their main quarry, but in 1988 they also stopped two lower court nominees.

A year after recapturing the Senate in 1995, Republicans began a concerted campaign to challenge Clinton's judicial nominees. Although they had not rejected a single nominee, scores of the nominations were put in a deep freeze. For example, William A. Fletcher, a University of California law professor, was appointed to fill a Ninth Circuit appellate judgeship in April 1995. Ann L. Aiken, an Oregon state judge, was nominated for a district judgeship in November 1995. Neither had been confirmed as of the beginning of the 105th Congress.

These types of delays, Democrats said, added a new element to judicial politics. When Democrats ran the Senate, their style was to pick out a few nominees and reject them very publicly while letting the vast majority through.

Democrats cited the number of judges confirmed during the past three presidential election years. In 1988 a Democratic Senate confirmed forty-one of Reagan's nominees. In 1992 it confirmed sixty-six of President George Bush's nominees. In contrast, in 1996, when the tables were turned, only twenty of President Clinton's judges were approved by a Republican Senate. (Three of these, including the only appellate judge in the group, were spillovers approved in January.)

Robert A. Katzmann, visiting fellow at the Brookings Institution, said another new development was senators' interest in blocking appointments to district judgeships, the lowest rung on the federal ladder.

Traditionally, district judgeships had been viewed as patronage jobs senators could use to enhance their power and prestige in their home state. Politics was limited to horse-trading, in which senators would round up support for their recommendations by agreeing to support other senators' picks. Although some influential Republican senators were still able to succeed at this in the 105th Congress, many district judge nominees were being held up by interparty politics.

Much of the change could be attributed to interest groups. The main pressure brought to bear on senators was coming from Thomas L. Jipping and Paul M. Weyrich. Jipping was head of the Judicial Selection Monitoring Project. Weyrich was head of its parent organization, the Free Congress Research and Education Foundation, a conservative fundraising, direct-mail, and television broadcasting organization. The foundation mounted a broad-based attack in the Senate by forming coalitions with other conservative groups and stirring up interest in judicial politics outside the Beltway.

One nominee whose confirmation was placed in doubt because of the Free Congress Foundation was Michael D. Schattman, a longtime Texas state judge Clinton nominated for a place on the federal bench. He had been backed by his state's Republican Senators, Phil Gramm and Kay Bailey Hutchison. But after the foundation targeted him because of his links to the Democratic Party, both senators dropped their support.

The foundation's list of objectionable nominees was long and deep. It charged several with being too liberal. Hawaii district court nominee Susan Oki Mollway, for instance, was opposed because she was a board member of the state's

American Civil Liberties Union, which supported legalizing same-sex marriage.

Jipping's group did not get everything it wanted. It failed to strip confirmation powers from Judiciary Committee Chairman Orrin G. Hatch, R-Utah, whose conservative credentials in judicial matters were often questioned by Jipping and others on the right.

But Jipping's group succeeded in winning converts among GOP senators. Three Republicans considering presidential bids, Phil Gramm of Texas, John Ashcroft of Missouri, and Robert C. Smith of New Hampshire, made judicial politics an important part of their early strategy.

The battle over judgeships represented the broadest front in a war over Clinton nominees. Republicans showed an increasing willingness to challenge Clinton's choices government-wide, blocking the nomination of former Massachusetts Gov. William F. Weld, a Republican, to be ambassador to Mexico, and Bill Lann Lee to be assistant attorney general for civil rights. *(Lee nomination, p. 624)*

The most troublesome result of the judicial stalemate, judges warned, was the growing backlog of cases, which forced them to make difficult choices in which cases get heard. In many instances, important civil cases could be delayed for years because of the constitutional right to speedy trials in criminal cases.

But a few judges said the vacancies were having little impact on the court system. For example, Reagan appointee J. Harvie Wilkinson III, chief judge of the 4th Circuit, based in Richmond, Virginia, argued in late 1997 that, although some areas may be short of judges, overall there were enough judges.

He noted that Congress in 1984 created eighty-five new judgeships (PL 98-353), sixty-one at the district level and twenty-four on the appellate bench. Six years later, Congress added eighty-five more (PL 101-650). As a result, the current federal judiciary, even with eighty-one openings, was bigger than a completely staffed judiciary in 1990, Wilkinson pointed out.

SENATE ACTION

Senate tensions over confirming nominees flared at the first Senate Judiciary Committee meeting of the 105th Congress, which took place on Jan. 23, 1997. The panel's new ranking Democrat, Patrick J. Leahy of Vermont, challenged Chairman Orrin G. Hatch, R-Utah, to quickly move the twenty-one nominations Clinton had submitted, many of them the same people he nominated in the 104th Congress.

Leahy complained that eighty-four federal judgeships were vacant and that some courts were in emergency need of new judges. Hatch retorted that Clinton had not been "treated in a slouchy way" considering that he was able to put 202 judges on the federal bench in his first term, compared with 194 for President Bush and 164 in President Reagan's first term. He also said that the vacancy rate of about 10 percent—there were 846 authorized slots in the federal judiciary—was not unusual.

Roiling the waters, Senate Republicans on April 29, formally affirmed their right to scrutinize and criticize President Clinton's judicial selections, but they declined to grant themselves sweeping new powers to influence the process for choosing nominees.

The Senate Republican Conference, the caucus of all fifty-five GOP senators, voted by secret ballot to adopt an internal task force's list of recommendations—including one that requires all of Clinton's nominees to go through a "prenomination consultation" between Republicans and the administration. The task force of GOP senators called for separate floor votes on each nomination and excluding the American Bar Association from its traditional role in assessing judicial candidates as qualified or unqualified.

However, signaling an interest in compromise, the Republicans voted down a proposal by Gramm on appointees to appeals courts. Gramm's plan would require Judiciary Committee Republicans to kill a nomination if a majority of GOP senators from the states covered by a circuit objected to the appointee.

Senators also voted down a proposal by Slade Gorton, Wash., that called for Republicans to go on the record as saying the Constitution gives their party the right to be "a major participant" in appointing judges. Gorton's proposal would require the administration to get advance approval of nominees from Senate Republicans representing the states included in that circuit.

Democrats renewed their criticism of GOP tactics in September, after Weld withdrew his nomination to be ambassador to Mexico. They held a news conference to point out that fifteen federal trial and appeals court judges had been confirmed during the 105th Congress, but that ninety-seven vacancies remained.

The growing number of judicial vacancies was having a serious impact on the courts, the Democrats said. Minority Leader Tom Daschle, D-S.D., said that some GOP senators, whom he declined to name, had told him privately that the lack of progress was intended to "send a message to activist judges."

But Majority Leader Trent Lott, Miss., said that the federal judges added to the bench by Clinton were "some of the most unpopular people in America" because "judicial activism is a big problem." Lott said the GOP's slow pace on confirmations would likely continue as a result.

The administration weighed in with pointed criticisms of the Republican inaction on nominees, both in public remarks and private conversations. When Lott started the end-of-the-session telephone conversation with Clinton by saying he had "good news," the president could not pass up the chance at a little gentle ribbing and responded with a grin: "You confirmed all my judges."

REHNQUIST WEIGHS IN

Rehnquist put fellow conservatives on the defensive Jan. 1, 1998, when he used his annual report on the state of the judiciary to deliver tough criticism of Congress. The nation's top judge warned that the high level of vacancies could not continue without "eroding the quality of justice" on the federal bench. In his report, Rehnquist noted that the number of cases in federal courts continued to climb in 1997, due partly to laws passed by Congress expanding their jurisdiction, while at the same time nearly one in ten federal judgeships remained vacant.

While suggesting that the White House could have acted more quickly to nominate judges, Rehnquist emphasized the Senate's sluggish pace. "The Senate is surely under no obligation to confirm any particular nominee, but after the necessary time for inquiry it should vote him up or vote him down. In the latter case, the president can then send up another nominee," Rehnquist said.

The Republican-run Senate confirmed thirty-six judges in 1997, up from the seventeen approved in 1996, but well below other years. In 1992, when Republican George Bush was president and Democrats controlled the Senate, sixty-six nominees were approved.

The White House quickly seized on the Rehnquist report, calling on lawmakers to get moving. But Republicans refused to yield. Hatch promptly defended the Senate and asserted that the White House bore much of the blame for the situation. In a statement Jan. 2, he said Republicans could not solve the problem of an increasing caseload without assistance from Clinton on legislation to rein in lawsuits. "The Senate cannot confirm judges that the President does not nominate nor can the Congress implement litigation reform the president opposes," Hatch said.

He also challenged some of Rehnquist's complaints about overload, saying there were more judges at present on the federal bench than during the Reagan and Bush administrations. Charting his course for the coming year, Hatch pledged at the end of January that his committee would not expedite confirmation of administration nominees. "The Judiciary Committee [will not], under my stewardship," he said, "push nominees through just for the sake of filling vacancies."

Lee Nomination

Despite furious lobbying by both supporters and critics, Clinton's 1997 nomination of Bill Lann Lee to become assistant attorney general for civil rights never came to a vote in the Senate. Instead, the president announced on Dec. 15 that he would make Lee acting assistant attorney general for civil rights.

BACKGROUND

When Clinton nominated Lee July 21, the president presented Republicans with a difficult decision. If they opposed Lee for supporting affirmative action programs, they risked political fallout by blocking a highly regarded Asian American lawyer. But if they backed him, they risked a backlash from conservative supporters.

The resulting struggle escalated into one of the biggest battles over a Clinton nominee in the 105th Congress. It became the focal point of a larger debate between congressional Republicans and Democrats over what was right and wrong with affirmative action programs, which aimed to give women and minorities a boost in employment, college admissions, and government contracting.

Clinton turned to Lee to replace Deval L. Patrick, who resigned earlier in the year. Lee, the western regional counsel for the NAACP Legal Defense and Educational Fund, had been an active opponent of California's Proposition 209 to outlaw preferences intended to remedy discrimination. Conservative groups wanted to make his nomination a Senate referendum on the California initiative, which passed in 1996. (The Supreme Court in November declined to hear a challenge to Proposition 209's constitutionality.)

But Lee posed a problem for moderate Republicans who wanted to maintain support among Asian American voters. His background was impressive. He was the son of a Chinese immigrant who owned a laundry shop in Harlem. He went to Yale University and Columbia Law School before becoming a civil rights lawyer. His decision to go into civil rights was heavily influenced by the experiences of his father, who was denied housing and employment opportunities even after serving in the U.S. Army in World War II.

At Lee's confirmation hearing Oct. 22, Republicans on the Senate Judiciary Committee alternated between questioning him and apologizing for having to do so. "I like you very much personally, there is no doubt of that," said Chairman Orrin G. Hatch, R-Utah. "But you're going to have to answer some of these questions."

Democrats sought to portray Lee as a pragmatist who favored settling cases out of court and making reasonable accommodations to his adversaries. Conservative groups tried to portray Lee as a liberal ideologue wedded to views of affirmative action that were increasingly being struck down by courts.

But Lee's testimony was of little help to either his supporters or detractors. He declined to give substantive answers to questions about his views on busing and on what he believed his role in the administration would be on Proposition 209. He cited several reasons for deflecting questions: some issues, he said, might come before him in his capacity as assistant attorney general; others would be better addressed to people higher in the administration.

Republicans would later say they were not comfortable with some answers Lee gave at his hearing. His testimony, under hostile questioning, was cautious and technical. When Mike DeWine, R-Ohio, asked what he would say to parents concerned about busing, Lee gave a legalistic answer. When asked if his question was answered, DeWine said, "With all due respect, it is not."

Following Lee's testimony, Republicans brought in two minority witnesses who opposed him, and Democrats produced two white witnesses who supported him. The Republican witnesses were Gerald A. Reynolds, president of the Center for New Black Leadership, a conservative African American organization, and Susan Au Allen, president of the U.S. Pan Asian Chamber of Commerce. Reynolds said Lee's opposition to Proposition 209 was undemocratic. Allen said Lee was ideologically predisposed to quotas.

The Democratic witnesses were Andrew C. Patterson, an attorney for several companies that Lee sued for sex or race discrimination, and Barbara Towers, a self-described conservative Republican and California homeowner whom Lee represented in a class action suit. Both said they had firsthand knowledge that Lee was pragmatic and easy to work with. Patterson said Lee never insisted on quotas, was always willing to negotiate, and, in one case, dropped a suit when the preliminary "discovery" process led to a new understanding of the company's promotion policy.

COMMITTEE DEADLOCK

The Senate Judiciary Committee failed to vote on the nomination. Democrats blocked action throughout November because they could not round up the votes needed on committee for Lee's approval. The nomination clearly was in trouble beginning Nov. 4, when Hatch announced his opposition.

In a speech on the Senate floor, Hatch said he could not support Lee because of the nominee's advocacy of affirmative action preferences. "Unfortunately, much of Mr. Lee's work has been devoted to preserving constitutionally suspect race-conscious public policies that ultimately sort and divide citizens by race," the senator declared.

Hatch praised the career of the civil rights lawyer—who would become the highest ranking Asian American ever at Justice—but questioned his "commitment to serve every citizen of this nation in equal measure."

Minority Leader Tom Daschle, S.D., said Hatch's announcement "does a disservice to civil rights." He said the chairman's declaration of opposition did not necessarily kill the nomination, but Majority Whip Don Nickles, Okla., predicted it was doomed.

Turning up the heat, the administration argued that rejecting Lee would set an unfortunate precedent: nominees to an administration post usually were not rejected for agreeing with the president instead of the Senate majority party. "The Constitution's framers simply did not envision a process where the Senate would only confirm nominees who denounced the views of the president who nominates them," Attorney General Janet Reno said.

Judiciary Committee Democrats staved off the inevitable on Nov. 6, insisting on putting off the vote for a week after a sharp, two-hour committee debate. They lacked confidence that enough Republicans would join them to favorably recommend Lee's nomination to the full Senate, and they wanted more time to press wavering Republicans.

The Republican on the committee who appeared to be most likely to vote for Lee was Arlen Specter, R-Pa. If he were the only one, the vote would be tied. Hatch said he opposed sending a nomination to the floor without a clear majority. Democrats countered that they did so when they were in the majority—including on the controversial nomination of Clarence Thomas to the Supreme Court.

Other committee Republicans who were courted were Spencer Abraham of Michigan and Fred Thompson of Tennessee. Strom Thurmond of South Carolina had written a letter supporting Lee but was firmly in the opposition camp by Nov. 6.

During the Nov. 6 debate, Hatch said he was moved by Lee's rise from poverty. But he said the nominee's advocacy of preference programs indicates he would not be a "balanced" assistant attorney general for civil rights. Hatch and other Republicans cited Lee's opposition to California's Proposition 209. They also criticized Lee for failing to rule out future challenges to similar measures, if he were confirmed.

Democrats maintained Lee would simply uphold President Clinton's views on affirmative action. By blocking him from assuming the office, Republicans were insisting that Clinton appoint someone who supports the GOP's more conservative views, said Dianne Feinstein, D-Calif. Robert G. Torricelli, D-N.J., said killing Lee's nomination would send "a terrible message" to Asian Americans.

Although the debate was sometimes emotional, both sides tried to see that it never got personal. Republicans praised Lee's career as an "advocate" and Democrats moved swiftly to crush charges that Hatch's position was racially motivated.

One week later, having failed to pick up the necessary Republican votes, Democrats on the Judiciary Committee blocked a formal vote on the nominee. Hatch promptly said he would send the nomination back to the White House, telling Clinton that the committee was hopelessly deadlocked over Lee.

At the committee session, Hatch succeeded in obtaining a 10–8 vote on a motion to "proceed to vote" on the nomination. But under committee rules, that motion required the support of at least one member of the minority party to prevail. All eight committee Democrats voted "no." The meeting was adjourned.

Sen. Arlen Specter of Pennsylvania, the only Judiciary Committee Republican who appeared ready to vote for Lee, said, "If this matter went to the full Senate, there would be quite a few Republicans voting for Mr. Lee, and it wouldn't even be a close vote." Hatch immediately disagreed. "What would happen on the floor of the Senate, nobody knows," he said.

CLINTON'S DILEMMA

The lack of Senate action left Clinton with several options, including sending Lee's name back to the Senate or appointing him during the congressional recess, a move that would allow Lee to stay on board through the end of 1998.

Sen. Carol Moseley-Braun, D-Ill., and Rep. Patsy T. Mink, D-Hawaii, were among the Democrats openly urging Clinton to make the appointment. Similar sentiments were ex-

pressed by outsiders. Thomas E. Mann, director of governmental studies at the Brookings Institution, said a recess appointment could both shore up Clinton's support among liberals and retaliate against Republicans for holding up his judicial nominees.

But Clinton appeared loath to pick a fight with a Senate that could retaliate. Recess appointments had traditionally been limited to noncontroversial nominees. If the president decided to use the recess appointment in Lee's case, his decision would escalate the ongoing confrontation over nominees, and Republicans would likely charge him with violating the spirit of the constitutional provision allowing such appointments. Complicating the matter for Clinton was the end-of-session passage of a little-noticed resolution (S J Res 39) that delayed the opening of the second session of the 105th Congress until Jan. 27.

Recess appointments fell into two categories: those that occurred between sessions, and those that occurred during recesses in the middle of session. The former lasted until the end of the upcoming session. The latter lasted until the end of the session after the one in which the appointment was made. Consequently, if Clinton appointed Lee before Congress came back, Lee could serve only until fall 1998. But if he waited until the first recess of the second session, Lee could serve until fall 1999.

Recess appointments were provided for in Article II, Section 2 of the Constitution. It was a remnant of the days when members of Congress could be out of touch from Washington for months, traveling to and from their states and districts by horseback. Presidents were reluctant to use this appointment power for all but routine nominations. With the powers over the budget and the confirmation process, Congress had plenty of opportunities to retaliate if it felt its prerogative was being undermined. Of the thirty-seven people Clinton had appointed so far using this method, none had created an uproar. The highest ranking was Mickey Kantor, who was appointed Commerce secretary after Ronald H. Brown died in a plane crash in 1996.

Hatch noted that Democrats blocked two Republican nominees to the civil rights post—Bill Lucas in 1989 and William Bradford Reynolds in 1985—when the Senate was under Democratic control, and neither was given a recess appointment. Instead new nominations were submitted that were acceptable to all, Hatch said. Hatch also said a recess appointment would be a "serious mistake." Firing back, White House spokesman Michael McCurry said a recess appointment was under consideration.

"Orrin Hatch has gone too far in insisting that his personal political philosophy ought to prevail over the president who was elected by the American people," McCurry said. "I think the Republicans ought to think about what they're doing to themselves when they insist on their very narrow, hard conservative point of view as being the only legitimate view on the subject of civil rights. . . . They alienate a large number of Americans from very diverse backgrounds."

THE WHITE HOUSE ACTS

In a display of political skill, Clinton bypassed the Senate roadblock on Dec. 15 by naming Lee acting head of the Justice Department's civil rights division. Republicans promptly warned that they would keep close watch over Lee's conduct in office, but overall their response was remarkably muted.

Clinton, who announced his decision at a White House ceremony, said he concluded that putting Lee into the civil rights post on an acting basis was the best way to get him on the job quickly and the best way to win his eventual Senate confirmation. "I was elected president," Clinton said. "I didn't make any secret of my position on affirmative action. . . . We can never be in a position of saying that a president shouldn't have someone in office who agrees with him."

Hatch conceded that Clinton's move was "technically permissible," and he was pleased that Clinton made Lee "acting" assistant attorney general rather than giving him a recess appointment. But the senator vowed: "Mr. Lee will be among the most congressionally scrutinized bureaucrats in history." In brief remarks, Lee paid tribute to his immigrant parents and promised to enforce federal civil rights laws. "Without proper enforcement, these laws are merely empty promises," he said.

For Lee, the appointment as an "acting" meant he would have less prestige but more time in office. There were no tenure limits on an acting appointment. Clinton, furthermore, had not given up on Senate confirmation. Under terms of the Vacancies Act (PL 89-554), which covered acting positions, Clinton apparently had to formally nominate Lee for a non-acting position within 120 days. If Lee was rejected by the full Senate, he would have to leave his post within 120 days of the vote. But if the Senate simply failed to act, Lee could stay on.

Clinton nominated Lee again in early 1998, but the Senate took no action. On Aug. 3, 2000, the president announced the recess appointment of Lee as the assistant attorney general for civil rights, thereby finally removing the word "acting" from his title.

Fletcher Nomination

After a delay of more than three years and a pair of unusual political maneuvers, the Senate in 1998 voted 57–41 to confirm the nomination of William A. Fletcher to be a judge on the Ninth U.S. Circuit Court of Appeals. Fletcher, a law professor at the University of California at Berkeley who was nominated for the judgeship in 1995, drew fire from conservatives who criticized him as another liberal judge on the activist Ninth Circuit court. John Ashcroft, R-Mo., leader of the cadre that sought to block consideration of Fletcher's nomination, said the Ninth Circuit—which served nine western states, Guam and the Northern Mariana Islands—was the "epicenter of judicial activism in this country."

The nomination was among the hardest fought of the 105th Congress. To get Fletcher to the bench, Clinton and congressional Democrats had to swallow hard and agree to GOP terms on two other matters.

A PAIR OF DEALS

First, the Clinton administration made a deal with Sen. Slade Gorton, R-Wash., to nominate Barbara Durham, a conservative Republican who was chief judge of the Washington State Supreme Court, to the Ninth Circuit in exchange for Fletcher's confirmation. For the president to essentially cede his constitutional prerogative to nominate a federal appeals court judge to a senator was highly unusual.

(Gorton, however, had been involved in such horse trading before. In 1986 the senator cut a deal with President Reagan over Daniel Manion, an Indiana lawyer whom Reagan had named to the 7th U.S. Circuit Court of Appeals. His last-minute switch, which assured Manion's confirmation by a one-vote margin, came after Reagan agreed to press action on William Dwyer, a Seattle lawyer Gorton favored for a Washington state district court judgeship.)

Senate Democrats subsequently agreed to a GOP-backed antinepotism measure, S 1892. The measure (PL 105-300) cleared both chambers by voice vote, even though some Democrats warned it was unconstitutional.

After the Durham agreement, Judiciary Chairman Orrin Hatch, R-Utah, pressed for a committee vote in early May and indicated that he could support the nominee. Nevertheless, he served notice through a spokesperson that he did not feel bound by the Durham deal. "This has been held up for far too long," the chairman said. While Fletcher was liberal, the traditionally conservative Hatch said, he "appears to be about as apolitical a person as you can find."

With one of the committee's ten Republicans objecting anonymously to a vote, the committee on May 7 decided to delay action on Fletcher. At the same time, Hatch delayed marking up S 1892 amid signs that the bill had also become linked to the Fletcher-Durham swap. S 1892 would prohibit the appointment of close relatives to the same federal court. The bill would apply to first cousins and closer relatives. Betty Binns Fletcher, the mother of professor Fletcher, had served since 1979 on the Ninth Circuit. But at age seventy-five she had already served notice that she would be taking semi-retirement, known as senior status, if her son was confirmed. The bill would not affect the Fletchers in any event; it would apply only to nominations made after it became law.

Bill sponsor Sen. Jon Kyl, R-Ariz., introduced the legislation to clarify the intent of a little-known antinepotism law that had been on the books since 1922. He said the possibility of a mother-son team in the circuit courts was not a good idea. But opponents said the restriction was unconstitutional. The legislation would not apply to the Supreme Court, but it would affect all other federal court nominations, including district courts of single judicial districts or appeals courts of single circuits.

1998 LEGISLATIVE ACTION

The Judiciary Committee approved the Fletcher nomination on May 21 by a 12–6 vote. All eight Democrats were joined by four Republicans in favor: Hatch; Jon Kyl, Ariz.; Arlen Specter, Pa.; and Fred Thompson, Tenn. No mention was made of the unusual deal under which Clinton promised to nominate Durham.

The endorsement came after Republicans complained that the Ninth Circuit was too liberal and that "a tougher standard must be applied to bring this court back to the mainstream," as Mike DeWine, R-Ohio, put it.

Opponents said that the Ninth Circuit's high rate of reversal called for a more conservative judge to balance other liberal judges, such as Fletcher's mother. The nominee, a friend of Clinton's, had said that he was more conservative than his mother, although he was left-leaning on many issues.

Dianne Feinstein, D-Calif., criticized some senators' assumptions that he would be as liberal as his mother. "This is a man who has greatness in him, whether you agree with him or not," said Feinstein. "And to vote against him because you don't like his mother's votes? That seems to me very hard."

Hatch supported the nomination despite his concern about the Ninth Circuit's liberal rulings. "This court is out of the mainstream," he said. "It's terrible, it's embarrassing, but I just can't translate that into voting against" Fletcher.

At the same markup, the committee also backed S 1892 on a 10–7 vote. It did not issue a written report on the measure.

On Oct. 6, Senate Democrats allowed S 1892 to pass by a simple voice vote. Patrick Leahy, D-Vt., the ranking Democrat on the Judiciary Committee, opposed the bill. But he agreed not to object to it in exchange for a vote on the Fletcher confirmation. The House cleared S 1892 (PL 105-300) on Oct. 7 by voice vote. One day later, a deeply divided Senate, 57–41, confirmed the Fletcher nomination.

1999–2000

Despite ongoing partisan tensions, Congress succeeded in clearing two significant law enforcement bills in the 106th Congress. Lawmakers assembled a far-ranging crime bill in 2000 that reauthorized the Violence Against Women Act and attempted to curb sex trafficking, among other provisions. House Judiciary Chairman Henry Hyde, R-Ill., also finally succeeded in his longtime battle to curb one of the most powerful tools in the arsenal of law enforcement agencies: the ability to seize private property allegedly linked to a crime.

But lawmakers failed to find common ground on the pressing issue of juvenile justice. The shocking 1999 school shooting in Littleton, Colo., that left fifteen dead sparked a national debate on violent youth offenders and their access to guns. Conservatives wanted to impose tougher sentences on young offenders, including trying some as adults; liberals favored prevention programs and stricter gun control measures. Although both chambers passed different versions of juvenile justice legislation, conferees were unable to bridge the gap between the measures. The biggest sticking point proved to be whether to require background checks on purchases at gun shows and enact other gun control provisions.

Social conservatives, as in the 105th Congress, continued to fall short of such goals as winning passage of a constitutional amendment to ban flag desecration. Liberals also failed to win passage of one of their high priorities: expanding federal hate crimes law to include sexual orientation, gender, and disability.

On immigration matters, Congress at the behest of the high-technology industry once again cleared legislation to increase the number of H-1B visas, thereby allowing more skilled foreigners into the country. But lawmakers could not agree on a measure to allow more farmworkers into the country.

Apart from gun control, few issues sparked fiercer partisan battles than Clinton's judicial appointments. The Senate in 1999 rejected a judicial nominee for the first time in twelve years when, on a party-line vote, it turned down the nomination of Ronnie White to be a U.S. District Court judge in eastern Missouri. The following year, senators approved two controversial nominees, one of whom—Richard A. Paez—had waited longer than any nominee in history for his confirmation. But Democrats continued to assail Republicans for refusing to act on numerous other nominees.

Crime Bill

A popular election-year anticrime package assembled late in 2000 (HR 3244—PL 106-386) reauthorized the Violence Against Women Act and launched a new effort to combat international slavery and sex trafficking.

The legislation bundled a series of five bills into the conference report on HR 3244 (H Rept 106-939). In addition to the Violence Against Women Act (HR 1248) and the underlying sex trafficking act (HR 3244), the package included a bill on sexual predators (HR 894), tighter limits on the sale of alcohol over the Internet (HR 2031), and a measure to aid victims of international terrorism (HR 3485). *(Internet alcohol sales, p. 337)*

SEXUAL TRAFFICKING

Lawmakers began taking action on the issue of sexual trafficking in 1999, when the House International Relations Subcommittee on International Operations and Human Rights gave voice vote approval to an antitrafficking measure Aug. 4.

According to bill sponsor Christopher H. Smith, R-N.J., at least one million women and children each year were taken across international borders by force or fraud for prostitution or sexual slavery. A State Department report stated that there were about 100,000 incidents annually in Russia alone. About 50,000 such victims crossed U.S. borders each year, Smith said, and were sold into prostitution or slave labor for an average of $24,000.

The measure (HR 1356) would set up a new State Department office to monitor the problem and offer counseling and treatment for victims. It would authorize $20 million per year in fiscal 2000 and 2001, split between programs administered by the new office to aid sexual trafficking victims in the United States and programs in other countries.

The measure also would impose stronger penalties on any sex traffickers—inside or outside the United States—found guilty of kidnapping, slavery, false imprisonment, assault, battery, pandering, fraud, and extortion. And it would withhold nonhumanitarian assistance to countries that failed not meet minimal standards for combating sexual trafficking.

At the request of ranking Democrat Cynthia A. McKinney, Ga., the panel gave voice vote approval to a Smith amendment that would place the office under the jurisdiction of State's Department of Human Rights and Labor.

While supporting the measure, McKinney warned that it continued a trend of creating many subgroups within the State Department to monitor human rights violations overseas. She also said she would work to combine Smith's proposals with a bill (HR 1238) by Louise M. Slaughter, D-N.Y., that aimed to combat the sale of women and children into domestic servitude and sweatshop labor. "We ought to look for a way to deal with all of these conditions at once," she said.

The House International Relations Committee Nov. 9 gave voice vote approval to a revamped antitrafficking measure (HR 3244—H Rept 106-487, Pt. I). Smith fashioned the latest proposal in order to incorporate language from Slaughter's bill that include trafficking for slavery or peonage through fraud or coercion.

The new measure would authorize $32 million in fiscal 2000 and $63 million in fiscal 2001 for the State Department and other agencies to monitor the problem, to offer counseling and treatment for victims and to work with foreign governments and independent organizations to combat the practice.

The bill would create an interagency task force within the State Department to report on which countries support, allow, or promote human trafficking and require the president to withhold all nonhumanitarian assistance from such countries.

The administration opposed this requirement, but Smith stressed at the markup that trade would not be prohibited and that the president still could waive the sanctions for reasons of national security or overall national interest.

The bill would double, from ten to twenty years, the maximum prison sentence for perpetrators of human trafficking and add the possibility of life imprisonment for involvement in kidnapping, aggravated sexual abuse, or an attempt to kill.

Wading into the issue, the House Judiciary Immigration Subcommittee gave voice vote approval to a pared-down version of HR 3244 on March 8, 2000. Chairman Lamar Smith, R-Texas, had jurisdiction over certain provisions relating to visas, and he narrowed the scope of the measure.

The version of the bill approved by the International Relations Committee would create a new "T" visa category for all victims of trafficking who cooperated with law enforcement and who would face a "significant possibility of persecution" if returned to their country of origin. This was a lower standard than current immigration law for battered spouses, which required "well-founded fear of persecution." The bill also would allow the victim's immediate family to receive "T" visas, and all could become permanent U.S. residents in three years.

Smith was concerned that this could result in an eruption of visa applications by "hundreds of thousands of people claiming to be trafficking victims and their family members, which could open the door to a significant number of fraudulent claims and lead to a massive amnesty for illegal aliens."

He introduced an amendment, adopted by voice vote, that would narrow the visa provisions to apply only to children sixteen years old or younger, without extending them to family members. Supporters of the original version worried that the changes essentially gutted the bill.

But when the full Judiciary Committee took up the measure April 4, Smith and Charles T. Canady, R-Fla., offered an amendment that would make anyone who was a victim of sex trafficking or involuntary servitude and who was afraid of retribution eligible for the visa. The amendment was adopted by voice vote.

Before approving the bill by voice vote, the committee rejected, 14–16, an amendment by ranking Democrat John Conyers Jr. of Michigan that would allow the attorney general to lift the cap on T visas for humanitarian reasons. The committee also rejected, 14–16, an amendment by Sheila Jackson-Lee, D-Texas, that would make it easier for victims' families to come to the United States.

The House passed the measure by voice vote May 9 with supporters urging swift final action on the measure. "We cannot wait one more day to begin saving these millions of women and children who are forced every day to submit to the most atrocious offenses against their persons and against their dignity as human beings," said bill sponsor Christopher H. Smith, R-N.J.

The Senate amended the measure, then passed it by voice vote July 27. The Senate bill would create an interagency task force, headed by the secretary of state, to coordinate antitrafficking efforts. The task force also would assess domestic and international progress on trafficking prevention, protection and assistance to trafficking victims, as well as the prosecution of traffickers.

VIOLENCE AGAINST WOMEN

Lawmakers next turned to the issue of violence against women in 2000, when the House Judiciary Subcommittee on Crime May 11 gave voice vote approval to a measure (HR 1248) to reauthorize federal grant programs under the 1994 Violence Against Women Act. Just four days after the markup, however, the Supreme Court ruled that parts of the 1994 act were unconstitutional.

The Violence Against Women Act was a part of the 1994 omnibus anticrime bill (PL 103-322). Although many of its provisions were designed to make permanent changes to law, the grant programs were due expire at the end of 2000 if they were not reauthorized.

HR 2448, sponsored by Constance A. Morella, R-Md., would authorize $185 million for each of fiscal years 2001 through 2003 and $195 million in fiscal 2004 and 2005 for the law enforcement and prosecution grant program. It also would authorize $1 billion over five years for family violence prevention programs.

Morella said the law had made a "tremendous difference" for abused women and children. She said a hotline for domestic violence, created by the 1994 law, received some 13,000 calls a month and could answer callers' questions in dozens of different languages.

The subcommittee approved, by voice vote, an amendment by Anthony Weiner, D-N.Y., and Steve Chabot, R-Ohio, that would allow funds in the bill to be used to ensure that hospitals had nurses on staff at all times who had specialized training in the treatment of evidence from rape and other sexual assaults.

On May 15, the legal landscape changed dramatically when the Supreme Court, ruling 5–4 in *United States v. Morrison*, held that Congress had exceeded its authority in a section of the law that allowed women who were victims of gender-motivated violence, such as rape, to sue their attackers in federal court. The Court said the law intruded on states' power to regulate crime. (*Morrison decision, p. 719*)

Other provisions of the law (PL 103-322), including the grant programs in HR 2448, were not affected by the Court's ruling. (*Congress and the Nation Vol. IX, pp. 683, 684, 697*)

Lawmakers blasted the ruling, but most said they recognized that the broadly written decision precluded them from redrafting the provision to pass muster. Sen. Joseph R. Biden Jr., D-Del., a prime sponsor of the 1994 act, said he could not figure out a way to rewrite the law to allow rape victims to circumvent the ruling. Asked by the Associated Press if there were any changes that could be made to make federal rape lawsuits legal, he replied: "Yes, two new justices."

Broadening the scope of HR 1248, the House Judiciary Committee voted June 21 to create a legal assistance program for female victims of violence to help them obtain protective orders and other help. The committee approved the program by voice vote as an amendment to HR 1248. It then approved the bill by voice vote June 27 (H Rept 106-891, Pt. I).

The legal aid amendment, offered by Asa Hutchinson, R-Ark., would authorize $225 million over five years. The money, to be given as grants to nonprofits and other groups, could be used to help women obtain protective orders or deal with immigration or housing problems. The funds could not be used to help a woman obtain an abortion. The committee rejected attempts by Democrats to delete or narrow this restriction.

The committee rejected, 8–13, an amendment by ranking Democrat John Conyers Jr., Mich., that would require that states pass laws allowing victims of gender-motivated violence to sue for damages in state courts in order to get federal funds. His amendment was an attempt to get around *United States v. Morrison.*

Conyers said it was one way of "fixing" the law to meet the Supreme Court decision, which held that state courts were the proper forum for the suits. Bill McCollum, R-Fla., chairman of the Crime Subcommittee, said he agreed with the intent of the proposal but was concerned that it conditioned too many of the grants on the change in state law.

The committee did adopt, by voice vote, an amendment by Tammy Baldwin, D-Wis., that would authorize grants specifically targeted at providing help to disabled women who were the victims of violence. The amendment would authorize $10 million a year for five years for such grants.

The committee also approved by voice vote a McCollum amendment to establish a $30 million, two-year pilot program aimed at protecting children during visits with a parent who has been accused of domestic violence.

Democrats tried to restore changes that had been made to the bill in subcommittee. An amendment that would restore dating violence to the definition of domestic violence was defeated 11–14. Another amendment, defeated 11–16, would add sexual orientation, religion, and alien status to "underserved populations" that were targeted to receive more funds under the bill.

McCollum had removed both provisions from the bill during subcommittee. In his manager's amendment, adopted at the full committee by voice vote, he added dating violence to the victim services and law enforcement training portions of the bill, but Democrats complained that the move was not enough.

Overall, the bill would authorize more than $3 billion over five years, more than double the funding level of the preceding five years. The grant money would be divided among law enforcement, prosecutors, victim services, and court grants. Nine months into each fiscal year, unused money from other areas would be transferred to victim services programs.

States would be allowed to use the grants to improve their reporting of domestic violence records to the National Instant Criminal Background Check System, which was designed to keep guns out of the hands of those who were not allowed to own them.

The House overwhelmingly passed the measure, 415–3, on Sept. 26. Clinton urged the bill's passage, which was seen to have major political significance in the upcoming elections.

The Senate Judiciary Committee June 29 approved a companion measure (S 2787), but the Senate took no further action on that bill. A key difference between the House and Senate versions was that S 2787 contained a provision making it easier for battered immigrant women to report abuse without fear of deportation.

FINAL ACTION

Seeking to pass a broad anticrime package just weeks before Election Day, the judiciary committees in late September combined the violence against women and sexual trafficking measures with three other bills. The conference report to HR 3244 (H Rept 106-939) included "Aimee's Law," which addressed sexual predators; a ban on the sale of alcohol over the Internet; and a measure to aid victims of terrorism.

The alcohol sales provisions would grant state attorneys general authority to use federal courts to make other states enforce their own laws on Internet alcohol sales when the alcohol is shipped across state lines. That language was similar to House-passed legislation (HR 2031), and to provisions in the Senate's version of the juvenile justice bill (HR 1501).

Many states limited or banned direct shipment of alcohol across their borders, forcing alcohol producers to go through wholesalers. The proposal aimed to crack down on small alcohol producers who violated these laws by shipping directly to consumers, primarily through the Internet.

The House Judiciary Committee had approved HR 2031 (H Rept 106-265) by voice vote on July 20, 1999, and the House passed it Aug. 3 by a vote of 310–112. Lawmakers from wine-producing regions had opposed HR 2031, which was seen as giving an advantage to liquor wholesalers in a tug of war with small wineries and breweries that wanted to sell their products directly to consumers.

In addition, the conference report included controversial language similar to a bill (HR 894) passed by the House by voice vote July 11 without any committee action. Under the bill's provisions, any state that prematurely released convicted murderers, rapists, or child molesters from prison would be required to pay the cost of apprehending, prosecuting, and jailing them if they later committed the same crime in another state. The measure was dubbed "Aimee's Law" after a twenty-two-year-old woman who was raped and murdered in Philadelphia by a convicted killer released from a Nevada prison.

Sen. Fred Thompson, R-Tenn., objected to the provision, arguing that it usurped states' rights to establish their own sentencing guidelines and parole systems. He also said the proposal contained procedural complications that would make it difficult to enforce.

His attempt to strike the provision from the conference report failed, 90–5. But he and other critics of the measure warned that the legislation would be struck down in court.

Finally, the conference agreement included provisions from a bill (HR 3495) to allow victims of terrorism, or their families in the United States, to recover judgments against countries listed by the State Department as sponsors of terrorism.

In the 1996 antiterrorism law (PL 104-132), Congress gave American citizens or their families killed or injured by state-sponsored terrorism the ability to sue the government they believe responsible for damages. Since then, a variety of cases had been brought against the governments of Iran and Cuba. Although the victims had won judgments in court, they had not been able to collect because any assets those countries had in the United States were controlled or frozen by the federal government. Under the legislation, federal courts could allow damages to terrorist victims and their families, using the frozen assets of countries suspected of supporting terrorism.

While voting for the conference report, several Democrats said they were troubled at how the seemingly disparate measures were bundled together—especially inclusion of the ban on Internet sales of alcohol. "It doesn't belong in this package," said Zoe Lofgren, D-Calif.

The House passed the conference report 371–1 on Oct. 6, and the Senate cleared it, 95–0, on Oct. 11. President Clinton signed the bill into law on Oct. 28.

MAJOR PROVISIONS

Key provisions of the anticrime bill (HR 3244—PL 106-386) included the following:

• **Violence against women.** The bill authorized nearly $3.3 billion for a variety of grant programs that were designed to address domestic violence and other crimes directed largely at women. It authorized $185 million a year for five years for a state grant program designed to coordinate the work of victim advocates, police, and prosecutors in the fight against domestic violence. It also authorized $175 million a year through fiscal 2005 for grants to communities to support shelters for battered women and children. Several grant programs to aid victims of child abuse were authorized at more than $15 million annually.

The bill also made several changes to the underlying act, making it easier for women to get enforcement of protective orders, even when the order was issued in a state different from the one where it would be enforced.

In addition, it made it easier for battered immigrant women to call police and get help from government agencies without fear of deportation. The bill also authorized new programs designed to reach out to older women and women with disabilities who are the victims of violence.

The bill required states to honor one another's court orders on child support and child custody, as well. It also broadened the definition of stalking to include "cyber-stalking," harassment done through e-mail or other electronic means.

The bill broadened the circumstances for using some of the grant money, allowing it to be used for crimes such as date rape as well as domestic violence.

Several new grant programs were also authorized. They included a $40 million annual program to provide legal assistance to battered women, and a $25 million, one-year, transitional housing assistance program for women seeking to reestablish their lives after leaving a shelter.

• **Sex trafficking.** The bill created a new federal crime for trafficking in persons. Although the current law already prohibited slavery and the sale of persons into slavery, the legislation extended that prohibition to a variety of activities that made up "trafficking." Those included the forced transportation of persons across a country's borders or coercing or threatening others into service.

The bill authorized nearly $94.5 million over two years to combat trafficking and aid its victims. The bill doubled to twenty years imprisonment the punishment for selling someone into slavery, as well as for other similar crimes.

It also created a new, nonimmigrant, "T" visa for up to 5,000 victims of trafficking per year. To be eligible for the visa, victims had to show they would suffer extreme hardship involving unusual or severe harm. If the victims could meet certain criteria, they could be eligible to adjust their status and apply for permanent residency several years after receiving the "T" visa.

The bill also required the president, in some limited circumstances, to withhold nonhumanitarian foreign aid to any country that was the origin of much of the human trafficking, and which the State Department decided had not met minimum standards for combating the trafficking. But it also contained several waivers of this provision, including a waiver the president could exercise for national security reasons.

• **Aimee's law.** The most controversial addition to the package was Aimee's law, named after Aimee Willard, a twenty-two-year-old student at George Mason University in Virginia, who was raped and killed in 1996 by a convicted murderer who had served twelve years of a life sentence before being released from jail in Nevada.

Under the bill, states that did not ensure that murderers, rapists, or others convicted of "dangerous sexual offenses" served stiff sentences could find their federal crime-fighting grants cut if a criminal committed an offense in another state after being released. States would be penalized if the criminal did not serve at least 85 percent of the sentence, or if the average sentence for the crime in the state was below the national average. The federal funds instead would go to reimburse the second state for the cost of catching, prosecuting, and incarcerating the criminal.

The provisions of the bill were retroactive and applied to any criminals a state had ever released, if they committed another crime. However, critics warned that would run afoul of the prohibition in the Constitution on retroactive punishment.

• **Liquor and terrorism.** The bill allowed state attorneys general to go to federal court for an injunction to stop the shipments, if they had good reason to believe their state laws were being violated. But the new law allowed only injunctive relief—and the traditional threat of court sanction for violating the injunction. It did not provide for penalties, either civil or criminal, or allow the awarding of attorneys' fees.

The measure also included language that was designed to give the president greater authority to help victims of state-sponsored terrorism collect on court-won judgments against the sponsoring government. The bill allowed the president to review each case independently and decide whether to pay the court judgments out of the blocked assets. And the language of the report made it clear that Congress intended for the president to do so unless he believed it would hurt national security.

Juvenile Justice

Amid growing concerns about school violence, both the House and Senate in 1999 passed measures to crack down on juvenile crime. But lawmakers were unable to bridge the differences between the two versions, in large part because they could not agree on gun control provisions.

BACKGROUND

Lawmakers who had failed to clear juvenile justice legislation in the 105th Congress returned to the fray in April 1999, jolted by a murderous rampage at Columbine High School in Littleton, Colo. On April 20, two seniors killed twelve students and a teacher before taking their own lives, shocking the nation and propelling the issue of teen violence to center stage in Washington *(1997–1998 action, p. 593)*

Until the Littleton events, the juvenile crime bill was relatively free of discord. Language that gun rights groups had objected to in 1998 had been abandoned. And although Democrats were still grumbling about some of the bill's crime-fighting provisions, enough other changes had been made that the bill's sponsors saw themselves as picking up more than enough Democratic support to pass.

In the 105th Congress, House Judiciary Crime Subcommittee Chairman Bill McCollum, R-Fla., had insisted on provisions tying the funding to requirements that violent teens be tried in adult courts, that states keep extensive records on youth crime and that judges be allowed to take action against parents for the behavior of their children. The House passed the bill but the full Senate never took it up. By dropping those mandates in 1999, McCollum won key Democratic backers.

McCollum and Bobby C. Scott, D-Va., produced a bill with a novel approach: give states a total of $1.5 billion over three years and let them decide how best to combat youth crime. With one fell swoop they had taken politics, and the presumption that Washington knew best, out of crime policy.

But the Littleton shootings, which left fifteen dead, caused a thorough reevaluation. The bill was taken off the fast track and expanded from a twenty-page consensus document to an omnibus package of controversial provisions.

Furthermore, the juvenile crime measures became entangled in a volatile debate over gun control. Anger after the worst school shooting in American history spurred victories for gun control legislation in several statehouses, and gun control advocates in the capital pressed for national measures. They wanted to penalize gun dealers for selling to minors, hold gun owners responsible if their guns were used by a minor to commit a crime, and require a number of safety features on guns, including trigger locks. The powerful National Rifle Association opposed such measures.

Even setting aside the gun debate, lawmakers of both parties were quick to admit they had limited expectations for juvenile justice legislation and its impact on the kind of violence visited on Columbine High School. "You're not going to change the culture with a series of amendments, or a series of bills," said Judd Gregg, R-N.H.

The legislation seemed to be based on the understanding that youths could be divided neatly into groups: serious and dangerous criminals, who would be dealt with harshly; teens who had run afoul of the law and could be encouraged to straighten up; and teens at risk of becoming criminals if not provided with something approaching a structured and nurturing environment.

But with Eric Harris and Dylan Klebold, the two perpetrators at Columbine, authorities said they had a case of teens progressing, in a single year, from law-abiding youths to petty thieves to mass murderers. "It's an irrational, suicidal attack we have here," McCollum said. "It may well be that no amount of law will be effective."

HOUSE COMMITTEE ACTION

With school shootings in Littleton, Colo., weighing heavily on their minds, members of two House subcommittees approved bills April 22 intended to boost local efforts to deter and combat youth crimes.

By voice vote, the House Judiciary Crime Subcommittee approved a measure (HR 1501) that would authorize $1.5 billion in anticrime funding over three years to states and local governments. The bill would focus funding on prevention efforts and programs for first-time, nonviolent juvenile offenders. States receiving funds would have to implement graduated sanctions for young first-time offenders proportional to the offense committed. Such sanctions could include counseling, restitution, community service, fines, supervised probation, or confinement.

Bill supporters said states used the bulk of their resources on violent juvenile offenders. Other offenders received little or no attention, and penalties were often not effective, they warned. The bill would allow grant recipients to "opt out" of graduated sanctions but would also require an annual written report detailing the reasons for their decision.

Funds also could be used for construction or expansion of justice and detention facilities; establishment of juvenile gun court and drug court programs; hiring of additional prosecutors, judges, and probation officers; mental health intervention and counseling programs; and the establishment of accountability programs to reduce juvenile recidivism.

Members frequently mentioned the Colorado school shooting during their deliberations. "The 'tough-on-crime' approach will not work when administered alone," said Bobby C. Scott, D-Va. The Littleton suspects, he noted, "killed themselves. Even the toughest penalty—the death penalty—would not have deterred them."

Meanwhile, the House Education and the Workforce Subcommittee on Early Childhood, Youth and Families gave voice vote approval to a bill (HR 1150) to reauthorize the Juvenile Justice and Delinquency Prevention Act. Under the bill, states would receive funds to support local efforts to reduce juvenile crime through an existing formula grant program and through a new prevention block grant.

The bill outlined four core areas upon which localities should concentrate. Children arrested for purely juvenile offenses, such as running away from home or truancy, should be placed in shelters or centers and not detention facilities; juveniles should be separated from adults in other institutions; juveniles should be removed from jails and adult facilities; and the overrepresentation of minorities in the juvenile justice system should be addressed.

States would continue to receive at least 50 percent of their formula grant funding whether or not they complied with the core requirements. They would get 12.5 percent of the remaining allocation for each core requirement with which they could demonstrate compliance.

The bill also would consolidate funds for discretionary programs such as boot camps, mentoring programs, state challenge activities, and other community-based programs into a flexible Juvenile Delinquency Prevention Block Grant program. Funding for the bill, which was not specified, would be authorized for fiscal 2000 through 2003.

Lawmakers took no further action on HR 1150, as the juvenile justice debate focused on HR 1501 and the Senate version, S 254.

SENATE ACTION

The debate over juvenile justice shifted to the Senate, which became a battleground for much of May over the contentious issue of gun control. After a dramatic tie-breaking vote by Vice President Al Gore handed a signature victory to gun control forces, the Senate adopted its juvenile justice measure (S 254) on a 72–25 vote May 21.

For most of the 105th Congress, legislation designed to prevent and punish juvenile crime had languished in the Senate. After surviving a bruising markup, the bill sat untouched for eighteen months because of opposition on both the political left, which found the bill too hard on teenage offenders, and the political right, which was afraid the measure's antigang provisions could be used to prosecute gun dealers or that the bill would become the vehicle for new federal gun lock requirements.

But in the wake of the carnage at Columbine High School, the Senate's approach was radically different. A revised juvenile crime bill (S 254) was brought to the floor in May without so much as a hearing, let alone a committee markup. Few senators had even been briefed on the bill until the weeks leading up to floor action.

And advocates of the rights of gun owners—who were fearful in 1998 that they might lose a vote on whether to require that trigger locks be sold with all handguns—suddenly had a host of other amendments to look out for.

But adoption of any of the gun amendments threatened to change the political dynamics on final passage. Some Republicans, who would otherwise embrace a bill to get tough on juvenile crime, could spur legislation with gun control provisions; some Democrats, who would otherwise reject the bill as too draconian for children, could endorse it if it embodied gun curbs.

The underlying bill, sponsored by Judiciary Committee Chairman Orrin G. Hatch, R-Utah, was far from the bipartisan juvenile crime bill (HR 1501) approved without opposition in the House Judiciary Crime Subcommittee.

The aim of the Senate bill was to prevent and punish youth crime at both the state and federal levels. Under the plan, federal prosecutors would be allowed to try the most violent of youth offenders as adults. This was opposed by children's rights advocates, who said that if anyone decided to try a child as an adult it should be the judge, not the prosecutor.

The bill would authorize $5 billion in grants to states in the next five years, with fewer strings attached than under the 1997 bill. The only requirements would be that states draft policies laying out a system of graduated sanctions, addressing drug testing, and outlining victims' rights. In return, they could use the money for both crime prevention and enforcement. At least half the money would be earmarked for enforcement. Some Democrats argued that too little would be guaranteed for prevention.

In other departures from the previous version of the bill, states would not be required to try teens fourteen years or older as adults and would not be required to keep elaborate records and share them with other states, although 7.5 percent of the money in S 254 was designated for voluntary record keeping.

At the request of small towns, which cited budget constraints, the bill would relax current requirements for segregating youth and adult prisoners to allow some contact, although they would still be housed separately. That language was opposed by children's rights groups.

The Senate began its debate May 12, with Minority Leader Tom Daschle, S.D., announcing a package of amendments backed by Democratic leaders that would address violence prevention, school safety, and better law enforcement.

Seeking to avoid partisan deadlocks that doomed past juvenile justice bills, Orrin G. Hatch, R-Utah, Joseph R. Biden Jr., D-Del., and Jeff Sessions, R-Ala., announced a compromise that they hoped would increase Democratic support by adding funds for drug treatment and school counseling programs. The compromise would dedicate nearly half the $1 billion per year cost of the entire bill to prevention programs.

But the bill quickly ran into a firestorm over gun control. The Senate Republican leadership introduced an amendment to close a loophole that allowed individuals to buy firearms at gun shows without background checks, but Democrats contended the provision would create new loopholes.

Buffeted by political crosscurrents, the Senate voted 51–47 to table (kill) a proposal May 12 that would have required background checks for all sales at gun shows, then two days later adopted a GOP-drafted amendment, 48–47, that purported to do just that but was criticized by Democrats as creating a loophole for pawnshops to avoid checks. With the help of Gore's vote, gun control supporters scored a major victory the following week, as the Senate adopted on a **key vote of 51–50 (R 6–49; D 44–1)**, an amendment by Frank R. Lautenberg, D-N.J., that would require mandatory background checks for all transactions at gun shows and for anyone who redeemed a gun at a pawn shop. *(1999 key votes, p. 899)*

In a reversal from 1998, the Senate also adopted, 78–20, a bipartisan amendment to S 254 to require child safety trigger locks or a safety storage box to accompany each sale of a handgun.

Republicans made two significant concessions without any prodding from Democrats. The first was language in the underlying bill sometimes called "juvenile Brady," referring to the Brady Act curbs on handguns. Existing law prohibited felons from ever owning a firearm. The provision would extend that ban to juveniles who were convicted of a violent crime but were not felons because they were not adjudicated in adult courts.

Republicans also offered an amendment, sponsored by John Ashcroft of Missouri, that would close a loophole allowing juveniles to privately purchase semi-automatic assault weapons. The language, however, would exempt the children of farmers and ranchers, and people who needed the firearms for their work.

While some senators focused on the gun lobby with their amendments, others took aim at Hollywood for producing movies, music, video games, and other products that glorify violence. Democrats tended to blame youth violence on the availability of firearms; Republicans wanted to look harder at deeper causes, which they saw as breakdowns in cultural norms and morality brought about in part by the mass media.

The Senate voted 60–39 to kill an amendment by Ernest F. Hollings, D-S.C., that would subject broadcasters to civil liabilities if they distributed "violent video programming" by wire, microwave, or satellite during hours when children were a "substantial portion" of the likely audience.

However, the Senate adopted language, 66–34, by Mitch McConnell, R-Ky., to require federal agencies that granted permits for filming movies or television programs on federal property to consider whether the production "glorifies or endorses wanton and gratuitous violence." It exempted news and public service productions.

Late in the debate, senators accepted by voice vote a "manager's amendment" that included at least forty-eight proposals from thirty senators. It "removes a lot of obstacles toward passage," said Democrat Patrick J. Leahy of Vermont, adding he was particularly pleased with the youth crime prevention provisions added to the underlying bill.

The Senate also passed:

• A Hatch amendment, 100–0, to encourage Internet service providers to give parents software that could block access to objectionable material.

• A bipartisan amendment, 85–13, to increase penalties for gang members who committed federal crimes and impose a three-year mandatory minimum sentence for knowingly transferring firearms to juveniles for use in violent crimes or drug offenses. The amendment also would establish penalties for teaching, including over the Internet, how to make or use a bomb with knowledge that the information will be used to commit a federal crime. It would increase penalties for using body armor when committing a federal crime.

• An amendment, 85–13, to allow prayers and memorial services to be held at public schools when students have been slain on campus. The measure authorized the attorney general to defend school districts sued on constitutional grounds for conducting such services.

• An amendment by Robert C. Byrd, D-W.Va., 80–17, to allow state attorneys general to seek federal injunctions to stop commercial out-of-state shipments of alcohol to minors. Senators then adopted, by voice vote, an amendment by Dianne Feinstein, D-Calif., to require companies to label clearly packages that contain alcohol.

• An amendment by Rick Santorum, R-Pa., 81–17, to encourage states to keep murderers and some sex-crime offenders in prison by making states pay for prosecuting criminals they released who subsequently committed repeat offenses in other states.

• A wide-ranging GOP amendment, by voice vote, to allow schools to use federal funds for metal detectors and safety equipment and allow school disciplinary records to follow a student from school to school.

But the Senate tabled (killed) a number of amendments, including:

• A Democratic initiative, 53–47, that called for $600 million in block grants for after-school programs.

• A proposal, 61–38, by Paul Wellstone, D-Minn., to authorize the hiring of 141,000 new school counselors, psychologists, and social workers.

• An amendment, 52–48, by Wellstone and Edward M. Kennedy, D-Mass., to require states to evaluate whether a disproportionate number of minority children are incarcerated. This would continue an existing program which the underlying bill sought to change.

• An amendment, 73–26, by Ashcroft that encouraged states to prosecute as adults any juvenile as young as fourteen who used, carried, or possessed a firearm to commit murder, robbery, assault, rape, or a serious drug offense.

• An amendment, 55–44, by Wellstone to allow the bill's block grants to be used for children who witnessed domestic violence.

At the last minute, Tom Harkin, D-Iowa, filibustered a Republican amendment that would allow special education students to be expelled if they brought a weapon or bomb to school. The Senate adopted the amendment, 74–25, but it also accepted an alternative by voice vote as a concession to Harkin. The differences between the two amendments were to be hashed out in conference.

HOUSE FLOOR ACTION

The House passed a greatly amended version of HR 1501 on June 17 by a vote of 287–139 after separating the issue from gun control by placing gun provisions in a separate bill. The bill moved directly to the floor from the House Judiciary Crime Subcommittee.

As passed, the bill would impose new mandatory minimum sentences on youths who commit crimes with guns. It also would authorize $1.5 billion over three years for grants to states seeking to improve their juvenile justice systems, allowing states to obtain the funds only if they adopted a policy of meeting every juvenile crime or misdemeanor with a sanction.

The guts of the juvenile crime provisions were not in the bill as it came to the floor. The language the House started with merely called for a $1.5 billion authorization to states for combating teen crime.

By far the most significant amendment adopted was an omnibus juvenile crime package, sponsored by McCollum, that would create a number of mandatory minimum sentences and allow juveniles to be tried as adults in federal court. It was approved 249–181.

The amendment was, in effect, the underlying bill. Thirty-eight of the forty-four amendments offered were amendments to the McCollum amendment. McCollum's proposal spawned a classic split, with conservatives and some moderates accepting the "get-tough" approach while traditional liberals attacked it as counterproductive and inhumane.

McCollum said the juvenile justice system in America simply had not caught up with the fact that many teens were exceptionally violent and dangerous people. Democrats

countered that treating teens as adult criminals would only ensure that they continued to behave violently into their adulthood. "Lock up a 13-year-old with a murderer, a rapist, and a robber, and guess what he'll want to be when he grows up?" said Melvin Watt, D-N.C.

The vote represented a complete reversal from the approach pursued earlier the same year and a return to the approach used in the 105th Congress, when the House passed a tough juvenile crime bill only to see it stall in the Senate.

But the Columbine shooting caused an outpouring of ideas and plans to address the social decline thought to be behind it. In fact, as the debate continued, it became a forum for members' frustrations and aspirations about contemporary society and its governance.

Running through the debate were two contradictory themes: that the federal government could not possibly have much effect on the forces that would create a Littleton-like shooting, and that it should try to do just about anything it can think of.

Because gun control advocates seized immediately on the issue after the shooting, Republican members felt they needed to come up with alternatives to gun control, said James C. Greenwood, R-Pa. "The Congress would have done a lot better had it not waded into a lot of these gun and culture issues," he said. "I think things went downhill when Republicans perceived Democrats were trying to win points on guns. That's when we came up with this 'best defense is an offense' strategy."

The result was a far-ranging debate that touched on guns, religion and the media.

By 248–180, the House approved an amendment that would allow states to display the Ten Commandments in schools and other public buildings. "It is one step that states can take to promote morality and work toward an end of children killing children," said sponsor Robert B. Aderholt, R-Ala. But Democrats attacked the amendment as a violation of the separation of church and state.

The House narrowly rejected, 210–216, an amendment offered by Mark Souder, R-Ind., that would prohibit the Office of Juvenile Justice and Delinquency Prevention from producing literature or curriculum that "undermines or denigrates" the religious beliefs of any program authorized under the bill.

Members adopted, by voice vote, an amendment that would condemn the entertainment industry for pointless displays of brutality in movies, on television, and in video games. They also adopted, 417–9, an amendment that would require the surgeon general to report on the crisis of violence in the United States, including the media's positive and negative effects on culture.

But in a closely watched vote, the House rejected an amendment by House Judiciary Committee Chairman Henry J. Hyde, R-Ill., that called for five-year prison terms for selling or lending violent or sexually explicit material to juveniles. The amendment split the GOP ranks, pitting social conservatives against business interests, and was defeated in a **key vote of 146–282 (R 127–92; D 19–189; I 0–1).** *(1999 key votes, p. 899)*

By voice vote, the House adopted amendments to allow juvenile delinquency grants to be used to install metal detectors in schools, and to make it illegal to sell or give a gun to a juvenile if the transferor had reason to believe the weapon would be used in a school zone.

The House also adopted amendments by:

• Tom DeLay, R-Texas, to limit federal judges' ability to order the release of inmates on the grounds of prison crowding, by a vote of 296–133.

• Matt Salmon, R-Ariz., to penalize states whose convicts committed crimes in other states after release, by a vote of 412–15. The cost of incarcerating the criminal in the second state would be docked from the first state's federal crime assistance fund and transferred to the second.

• Charlie Norwood, R-Ga., to allow schools to discipline children with mental or physical disabilities the same way that other children were disciplined if they came to school with a weapon or illegal drugs, by a vote of 300–128.

• Souder, to ensure that religious organizations could not be discriminated against when they sought government grants to provide juvenile services, by a vote of 346–83.

The House defeated, 161–266, an amendment by Zach Wamp, R-Tenn., to create a uniform system of ratings covering television, music videos and other forms of entertainment.

CONFERENCE

Lawmakers were unable to reconcile the two versions of the legislation, in large part because of differences over gun control. Conferees began work Aug. 5 with a meeting that was limited to opening statements. The top Republican conferees announced agreement on two things: some gun control proposals would be in the final bill, and the deal would not be done quickly. "There is pressure to do it before school opens, but the complexity and volatility of these issues doesn't lend itself to rapid resolution," warned House Judiciary Chairman Hyde.

By far the most contentious issues were the gun control measures in S 254, especially a requirement that sales at gun shows be subject to background checks, a ban on the importation of large-capacity ammunition magazines, and a requirement that gun locks or storage devices be sold with handguns.

Not only did the House measure lack gun control language, but a House bill with modest gun restrictions (HR 2122) was defeated when it was opposed by both gun rights defenders who said it went too far, and gun control stalwarts who said it would weaken current gun laws.

Hyde and Hatch indicated that the Senate gun show language, as written, could not pass the House. Neither gave any indication how much it would have to be altered to get a majority. But both said dropping all gun provisions was not an option.

Sen. Charles E. Schumer, D-N.Y., said Aug. 3 that he would help mount a filibuster if the conference report contained much less than the Senate gun show language. President Clinton threatened a veto if he concluded that the final bill could weaken current gun laws.

The House voted 305–84 on July 30 for a nonbinding motion to instruct conferees to include unspecified gun show language in the final bill.

Even routine procedural steps proved difficult. Sen. Robert C. Smith, R-N.H., a staunch supporter of gun rights, tried to mount a filibuster on the question of whether to insert the text of S 254 into HR 1501 in order to clear the way for conferees to negotiate. He backed down after the Senate passed a cloture vote by a lopsided margin of 77–22.

Although conferees focused their attention on gun issues, many outside groups scrutinized the hundreds of other provisions in the bill aimed at curbing juvenile violence. The Children's Defense Fund and the Children's Welfare League of America assailed "draconian" provisions that would allow those as young as thirteen to be held in adult prisons, require regular federal trials—rather than juvenile delinquency proceedings—for those as young as fourteen who committed violent felonies or drug crimes, impose tougher mandatory sentences on juveniles, and allow their crime records to go to schools and colleges.

House and Senate leaders struggled to find common ground on the gun provisions, believing that the underlying bills could then easily be negotiated. But in November, top GOP senators conceded that HR 1501 was dead for the year. And with elections looming, conferees never met formally in 2000.

Instead, lawmakers moved some of its provisions into omnibus crime legislation, such as punishing states that did not give murderers, rapists, and child molesters lengthy prison sentences and regulating the sale of alcohol on the Internet and creating new federal judgeships.

Gun Control

A series of deadly shootings in 1999 sparked impassioned gun control debates in both chambers. But despite efforts by congressional Democrats and the Clinton administration to toughen restrictions on firearms, lawmakers failed to clear any gun control legislation.

The Senate in 1999 added a limited gun control package to juvenile justice legislation, with Vice President Al Gore casting the tie-breaking vote on a pivotal amendment. The measure would have required background checks on purchases at gun shows, banned ammunition clips holding more than ten rounds, and prohibited anyone convicted of a violent offense while a teenager from ever being allowed to own a gun. The House that year rejected a separate gun control bill (HR 2122), and passed its version of the juvenile justice bill (HR 1501) without gun control language.

Largely as a result of the impasse over gun control, conferees did not even meet in 2000 on the juvenile justice measure, which died at session's end. The House did pass a bill (HR 4051) in April, designed to encourage states to toughen their enforcement of gun laws, but the measure was never considered in the Senate.

Also in April, the House voted overwhelmingly to instruct conferees on the juvenile justice bill to accept a package of gun control provisions that was included in the Senate version of HR 1501. In May the Senate adopted a sense-of-the-Senate amendment offered by Minority Leader Tom Daschle, D-S.D., to express support for the juvenile justice bill and the Senate's gun provisions.

BACKGROUND

When two heavily armed seniors at Columbine High School in Littleton, Colo., killed a dozen schoolmates, a teacher and then themselves in a rampage April 20 that stunned the nation, gun control advocates kicked off a renewed campaign to keep guns out of the hands of children.

A group led by Rep. Carolyn McCarthy, D-N.Y., and Sen. Edward M. Kennedy, D-Mass., vowed to push for enactment that year of legislation (HR 1342, S 735) designed to make it harder for children to get and use guns. Similar legislation failed to advance in the previous Congress. Kennedy said he would seize any opportunity to press the legislation in the Senate. "We cannot wait for the next tragedy before we act," he said.

The most controversial piece of the Kennedy-McCarthy legislation would set a one-year prison sentence for parents whose children used the adults' weapons in the commission of a crime or even brandish it "in a public place."

President Clinton weighed in April 27 with a proposal embodying much of the McCarthy-Kennedy bill but with the addition of several provisions. The president's package would limit citizens to one handgun purchase a month; raise the legal age for buying a gun to twenty-one from eighteen; ban imports of high-capacity ammunition clips; institute a background check for explosives; and reinstate the federal waiting period for handgun purchases, which lapsed in November.

Clinton predicted that his proposals would face staunch opposition from the NRA but would amount to no more than short delays and minor inconvenience for law-abiding gun owners. "It's going to be a hassle for them. It's worth it . . . People's lives are at stake here," the president said. Subsequent shootings, including one that left eight students wounded at a high school in Atlanta, lent more urgency to the debate.

Lawmakers on both sides of the gun debate had basically fought to a draw in Congress over the past several years. In general, Republicans sided with the powerful National Rifle Association (NRA) in opposing new gun restrictions, while Democrats pressed for gun control.

Despite the Republican takeover of Congress in 1995, the NRA and other pro–gun rights groups had not made the gains they were hoping for. In fact, they had had to spend a significant amount of time and effort playing defense against the Clinton administration and Democrats, particularly in the Senate.

Though pro–gun rights forces succeeded in deleting key provisions from the 1996 antiterrorism law (PL 104-132), they were not able to kill a provision Sen. Frank R. Lautenberg, D-N.J., quietly inserted in the fiscal 1997 omnibus spending bill (PL 104-208) that prohibited anyone convicted of a domestic violence misdemeanor from owning a gun. And though they won a 1996 vote in the House to repeal the 1993 assault weapons ban (PL 103-322), pro–gun rights forces were unable to get the Senate to take up the measure.

In the 105th Congress, McCarthy wrote an amendment requiring that trigger locks be sold with each gun. Ultimately, Republicans blocked legislation that would create new sanctions for those who use guns in their crimes, worried in part that they could not stop McCarthy's gun locks amendment.

After Columbine, however, the political calculus tilted toward the gun control forces, at least temporarily. Senate Majority Leader Trent Lott, R-Miss., who in 1998 had promised the annual convention of the NRA that he would oppose any more gun control measures, signaled after the high school massacre that he was rethinking his position. "There are some things we can do, hopefully, to keep guns out of the hands of kids," Lott told reporters April 27. "Hopefully, we can limit, you know, their access to assault weapons. We can have trigger devices for safety in the home."

Even NRA Executive Vice President Wayne LaPierre, appearing on CBS's "Face the Nation" on April 25, took the tack of openly advocating one federal gun control measure: closing a loophole that allows violent juveniles to purchase firearms when they become adults.

Congress issued its first official response April 27 to the Colorado shooting and bombing spree. By voice vote the House adopted a resolution (H Con Res 92) expressing condolences to the victims' families. The Senate adopted the measure 99–0.

In deliberating what to do after that, Congress had much experience to draw on. There was a long history at the Capitol of producing legislation in response to high-profile crimes. The assassinations of Sen. Robert F. Kennedy, D-N.Y. (1965–1968), and the Rev. Dr. Martin Luther King Jr. spurred enactment of two laws (PL 90-351, PL 90-618) designed to limit interstate sales of weapons and ammunition.

A year after the bombing of a federal building in Oklahoma City, Congress produced a law (PL 104-132) designed to enhance the fight against terrorism and increase the application of the death penalty. But it did little to address the circumstances of the case. Its terrorism provisions were focused on the threat from international syndicates, not the type of disgruntled citizens who were convicted. And its capital punishment provision was a limit on death-row appeals, which conservatives had supported for years.

Two laws had been so closely identified with a particular crime that they were named for the victims. The handgun-waiting-period law that Clinton wanted to revive (PL 103-159) was named for James S. Brady, the White House press secretary paralyzed during a 1981 assassination attempt on President Ronald Reagan. And the law requiring states to notify communities if a sexual offender has moved into their midst (PL 104-145) was named after seven-year-old Megan Kanka, who was raped and murdered by a repeat offender.

Such laws prompted some observers to take a cynical view of Congress's crime-fighting strategy. John Velleco, chief spokesperson for the Gun Owners of America, a staunchly anti–gun control group, said each crime, particularly those involving shootings, seemed to spawn new legislation. "There's a shooting, a law passes. There's another shooting. There's another law," Velleco said in an April 29 interview. "The one thing that doesn't change is that we have shootings. What does change is we have more laws."

Gun control advocates such as McCarthy chafed at such statements. But she and her colleagues were also quick to concede that their measures were only a partial solution and did not address the root causes of crime. And when Clinton unveiled his gun package, he spent as much time talking about mental health issues and the violent nature of American culture as he did about the specifics of his package.

SENATE ACTION

With the help of a tie-breaking vote by Gore, the Senate in May adopted a series of amendments to a juvenile crime bill (S 254) that toughened restrictions on firearms. The gun control votes came during two weeks of often-chaotic debate in which Senate Republicans passed, and then retreated from, weaker versions of gun control amendments.

After settling the gun issues, the chamber, by a vote of 73–25, passed S 254, which also included an amendment that would allow the immediate expulsion of any special education student who brought a weapon or bomb to school.

When the Senate began its debate on the juvenile justice bill May 12, Republicans were expected to ward off Democratic gun control initiatives with amendments developed by the GOP's Youth Violence Task Force. These amendments included spending $50 million to hire more federal prosecutors to prosecute gun crimes; increasing penalties for firearms offenses for juveniles; establishing a special optional license for nondealers who wished to sell firearms at gun shows; and restricting youth access to semiautomatic assault weapons.

But in a remarkable series of votes, GOP leaders lost control over the issue. Two weeks of debate over S 254 started with a May 12 show of strength by the NRA, as the Senate voted 51–47 to table (and thus kill) an amendment by Frank R. Lautenberg, D-N.J., to require background checks for all purchases at gun shows. Democrats had thought this to be one of their more popular gun-control proposals.

Instead, the Senate approved by a 53–45 vote an amendment offered by Larry E. Craig, R-Idaho, a member of the NRA board and a staunch foe of controls. It would allow, but not require, private gun sellers to use a national database to check the background of purchasers at gun shows. It would offer civil liability protection to those sellers.

Scarcely had the votes been taken before a handful of Republicans began expressing misgivings. Gordon H. Smith, R-Ore., grew increasingly dismayed as he read through the text of what he had voted for. He said he had been given the impression that the Craig alternative would not be purely voluntary. By the following morning, he and a host of senators were hopping mad.

The consequences of the first votes became apparent when they were featured in newspapers the morning of May 13. Clinton and Attorney General Janet Reno used unusually sharp language in their public statements. "For the life of me I can't figure out how they did it, or why they passed up this chance to save lives," Clinton said at the White House. "There is simply no excuse for letting criminals get arms at gun shows they can't get at gun stores."

Within a few hours, Craig had been forced by restive colleagues to draft new language to make the background checks mandatory. But Democrats attacked this new language with undiminished ardor, saying it was full of loopholes and concessions to gun dealers.

The amendment passed by only the slimmest of margins, 48–47. Seven Republicans refused to support the Craig proposal, either because they were staunch gun control foes who thought it went too far, or because they had voted for the Lautenberg proposal and felt this one did not go far enough.

Both the Lautenberg and Craig proposals targeted gun show transactions that did not go through licensed dealers—roughly 40 percent, according to Craig. These transactions were conducted by private vendors and gun hobbyists who were not subject to the background check provisions of the 1993 Brady law.

The Lautenberg proposal would require these private vendors to take their customers to a licensed dealer at the show and ask him or her to run the background check using a nationwide computer database. The proposal also would require all gun show organizers and promoters to register their guns with the Treasury Department at least thirty days before the show and pay a registration fee to be set by the department.

The Craig counterproposal would allow unlicensed vendors to avail themselves of licensed dealers to do the background check. Alternatively, it would allow an unlicensed vendor to go to a "special registrant"—a person who was not licensed but who would be specifically authorized to do background checks.

The language would create something called a "special licensee," a new type of licensed federal dealer who operated primarily or solely at gun shows. Whether or not these special licensees would be required to do background checks was the matter of some debate.

Further aggravating Democrats were several extra concessions given to the NRA. Anyone at a show who conducted a check or sold a firearm for which a check had been made would be granted immunity from civil prosecution. Pawnbrokers would be exempt from conducting background checks when selling a gun back to the person who pawned it. And information gathered in a background check, which included sensitive personal information such as criminal records, mental health histories and military service records, would be destroyed immediately following the transaction unless it revealed a reason to prohibit the sale.

With the Craig language under fire, Republicans found themselves in headlong retreat by May 21. Hours after a shooting at a high school outside Atlanta that left eight people wounded, the Senate adopted, 51–50, a Lautenberg amendment to require mandatory background checks for all transactions at gun shows and for anyone who redeems a gun at a pawn shop.

Lautenberg was able to pick up the two Democrats who were absent for the vote on the earlier version of his amendment, and also Democrat Max Cleland of Georgia, who won some modified language, including a narrower definition of what was a "gun show." In the end, Sen. Max Baucus of Montana was the only Democrat to vote against Lautenberg; six Republicans voted for the amendment.

During the debate over S 254, Democrats also prevailed in a surprise voice vote adoption of an amendment, offered by Dianne Feinstein, D-Calif., to ban imports of high-capacity ammunition clips. Senators first defeated, 39–59, a motion to table the provision. Twenty Republicans crossed party lines to support Feinstein, while four Democrats voted against her.

The 1994 Brady Law banned certain ammunition clips but grandfathered existing ones. Because enforcement had been virtually impossible on imports, foreign countries had been able to export the banned ammunition magazines, Feinstein said. The Feinstein amendment was adopted only after she dropped strict language prohibiting juveniles from buying or possessing semiautomatic assault weapons.

In another watershed for gun control supporters, the Senate adopted 78–20, a bipartisan amendment to S 254 to require child safety trigger locks or a safety storage box to accompany each sale of a handgun. The provision's bipartisan support, including thirty-four Republicans, contrasted with a 61–39 vote just one year earlier to table a similar measure. Only three Republicans voted for the measure then.

During the chaotic, highly partisan gun control debate, Republicans argued that Democrats were trouncing on the constitutional right to carry a gun. They also argued that the Clinton administration was not enforcing laws currently on the books. Craig, an NRA board member, said that Democrats believed "the Second Amendment is a loophole."

The victory was particularly sweet for Democrats, who fought tooth and nail to first get the issue to the floor and keep it under consideration, despite threats by Senate Majority Leader Trent Lott, Miss., to pull the bill. "We are all just elated over this victory. This is a turning point in our country," Gore said.

HOUSE ACTION

Unlikely alliances and political gamesmanship in the House conspired on June 18 to bring to defeat a volatile Re-

publican gun control bill (HR 2122). Squeezed between anti-gun control conservatives, and liberals and moderates who said the bill was unacceptably weak, the House legislation failed on a **key vote of 147–280 (R 137–82; D 10–197; I 0–1).** (1999 key votes, p. 899)

In the weeks after the Colorado high school shootings, House Republicans vowed not to react to emotion and pass new gun controls, as they saw the Senate scrambling to do under the whip hand of the Democrats. Instead, Majority Leader Dick Armey, R-Texas, told reporters May 18 that the House would hold "fresh new hearings, recognizing the broad breadth of all the influences that might impact these young people."

But the May 20 shootings outside Atlanta gave fresh impetus to gun control forces. The news came just as House Republicans were plotting strategy to deflect a Democratic gun control amendment at an appropriations markup that same morning. By day's end, House Republicans had canceled the markup and offered to broaden their juvenile justice bill (HR 1501) and make it a vehicle for gun control amendments, with floor debate the week of June 14.

GOP leaders were forced to undergo a reluctant metamorphosis on the issue. "Clearly, we need to tighten current laws to make it more difficult for kids to get guns," said House Speaker J. Dennis Hastert, R-Ill., in a brief floor speech May 20.

Five days later, in one of the most remarkable political adjustments of recent congressional vintage, Hastert announced that Republicans would move a gun control measure. The political dynamics were shifting so dramatically that even Bob Barr, R-Ga., an NRA board member who led past fights against gun restrictions, said that requiring background checks at gun shows was "a good idea in need of some work."

But Hastert faced resistance from powerful Republicans who objected to any gun control measures and Democrats who insisted on far stricter provisions than Hastert envisioned. By early June, Hastert found himself in exactly the position he hoped not to be in: struggling with both a lack of consensus among his fellow Republicans and rancorous opposition from a solid majority of Democrats.

Both Armey and Majority Whip Tom DeLay, R-Texas, served notice that they were disavowing the Speaker's positions supporting several gun control measures, including mandatory background checks for buyers at gun shows and mandatory sales of safety devices with every handgun.

Democrats focused their anger on gun language drafted by Judiciary Chairman Henry Hyde, R-Ill., and Bill McCollum, R-Fla., that they said was a pale and inadequate imitation of the Senate's.

High on their list of complaints was the provision on gun locks, under which the "safety device" that must be sold with each handgun could be any piece that was already part of the weapon but that—once removed—would render the gun inoperable. Democrats said that would put almost every gun now manufactured in compliance, because it could be disarmed by partial disassembly.

They also said the much narrower definitions of gun shows would allow sales without background checks any time fewer than ten vendors assembled, no matter how many guns were sold.

In one important respect, however, the Hyde-McCollum package went well beyond what was in the Senate bill and adopted a key tenet of the gun control package that Clinton unveiled after the Littleton shootings. It would subject adults to criminal culpability, and as long as three years in prison, if their firearms fell into the hands of a young person who used them to kill or injure someone.

The bulk of the Republican language was contained in legislation (HR 2037) that Hyde and McCollum introduced June 8. The GOP plan was to take it up on the floor without going through committee.

The package included several provisions that conservatives advocated as essential to fighting crime by young people, including a new set of mandatory minimum sentences—ten years for discharging a firearm at a school, life if someone is killed in a school shooting, for example—and allowing teens to be tried as adults in federal court. The Democrats opposed much of this, and their ire at similar provisions thwarted a juvenile crime package in the 105th Congress.

Torn by a myriad of competing interests within their ranks, GOP leaders announced on June 14 that they would take up the gun provisions (HR 2122) separately from other juvenile crime measures. Democrats reacted with outrage, arguing that segregating gun measures from the rest of the juvenile crime provisions—many of which enjoyed wide bipartisan support—was a poorly disguised way to defeat gun control legislation in the House. They also took aim at what they described as a convoluted procedure that bypassed the Judiciary panel and left the minority in the dark until the last moment about what legislative vehicle would be used for the debate.

Bowing to Democratic pressure, Hastert agreed to allow the minority party to offer a substitute amendment to HR 2122. The amendment, by Judiciary ranking Democrat John Conyers Jr., Mich., would replicate gun provisions in the Senate-passed juvenile crime bill (S 254), including required child safety devices on handguns and a ban on imports of large capacity ammunition clips. It also would require background checks of people seeking to buy firearms at gun shows and would give law enforcement officers three business days to complete the checks if a standard instant check did not go through.

But the Democrats faced divisions in their ranks. Gun control opponent John D. Dingell, D-Mich., won the right to offer an amendment that would weaken the Senate gun show provision by allowing law enforcement only twenty-four hours for background checks, instead of the three business days provided in existing law.

When the House began debating HR 2122 June 17, the Dingell language was adopted by anti–gun control Democrats and Republicans on a 218–211 vote. The next day, the House turned back the Conyers language, 184–242. The House also defeated an amendment by McCarthy, 193–235, that would strengthen gun regulations.

The deeply divided chamber also approved amendments adding modest gun control measures that would prohibit juveniles under eighteen from possessing semiautomatic assault weapons and would require a secure gun storage or safety device to be sold with every handgun.

Then it rejected the underlying bill by a wide margin, with Democrats saying it would water down current gun regulations and some Republicans complaining it went too far. Only ten Democrats joined 137 Republicans in support of the bill. Eighty-two Republicans, 197 Democrats, and the House's lone independent voted "no."

A disappointed Clinton said after the House votes: "One more time, the Congress of the United States . . . said, 'We don't care what's necessary to protect our children. We can't possibly bear to make anyone in the NRA mad.' "

But Hastert, who had promised that the GOP leadership would work to "expedite" a gun control bill, blamed the setback on Democrats "who put partisanship over progress." And DeLay said that "the bill had four of five things they [Democrats] wanted [and] still was not good enough for them. So it's quite obvious to me that they're just interested in politics."

FINAL DEBATES

The defeat of HR 2122 shifted the tide, and gun control advocates were unable to regain their earlier momentum in the 106th Congress despite sporadic negotiations over gun provisions in the juvenile justice package.

In September Hyde proposed providing twenty-four hours to complete an FBI computer background check on gun purchases, and adding three business days for a more thorough investigation if the computer check raised any red flags. Democrats reacted coolly to that and subsequent Hyde proposals, warning that anything less than the Senate provision could be riddled with loopholes.

Clouding the issue, the House on Sept. 23 and 24 voted on a series of different nonbinding motions to instruct conferees on the juvenile justice bills. Two measures sponsored by gun control advocates easily passed, but broad support was given to a measure sponsored by gun control opponents.

The first motion, introduced by gun control advocate Rep. Zoe Lofgren, D-Calif., passed 305–117. It called on conferees to support language that did not weaken current gun control laws, closed "loopholes" that allowed criminals to obtain guns and strengthened enforcement of current laws against criminals who used guns.

A second Lofgren motion, passed 241–167, instructed conferees to include language that would require unlicensed gun dealers at gun shows to conduct background checks, ban juvenile possession of assault weapons, require child safety locks to be sold with handguns, and prohibit juvenile felons from ever buying guns.

But opponents of strict gun control measures offered their motion to instruct conferees to reject all Senate provisions that "impose unconstitutional restrictions on the Second Amendment rights of individuals" to keep and bear arms. That motion, by California Republican John T. Doolittle, passed, 337–73.

Searching for a consensus within GOP ranks, Republican leaders met Oct. 14 and agreed only that any compromise would need the support of enough Democrats to offset the cadre of GOP lawmakers who would vote against any gun controls.

Hyde said that he thought common ground could still be found on Senate provisions to ban imports of high-capacity ammunition clips, require safety locks on all guns sold, and prohibit juveniles convicted of serious crimes from ever owning a gun. But the gun show language was a "very tough, difficult issue," he conceded, because "there are many special interest groups that have a vital interest in what we're doing."

With Congress deadlocked, attention turned to the issue of lawsuits against gun companies. Some thirty cities and localities, beginning with New Orleans in late 1998, had filed a combined total of twenty lawsuits against dozens of gun manufacturers and distributors, seeking hundreds of millions of dollars in damages that they charged were the result of violence attributable to the gun industry's negligence and malfeasance.

But the localities were concerned that the gun industry would use the shield of bankruptcy laws to protect itself from any damages owed as a result of the lawsuits. An effort by Sen. Carl Levin, D-Mich., to close that road to the gun industry was defeated Feb. 2, 2000. The Senate voted, 29–68, against a Levin amendment to the bankruptcy overhaul bill (S 625) that would prohibit gun manufacturers and dealers from discharging debts arising from the lawsuits through bankruptcy proceedings.

In early March Clinton urged key Republican lawmakers to work out gun legislation that he could sign into law by April 20, the anniversary of the shooting at Columbine High School. But after a White House meeting, Senate Judiciary Committee Chairman Orrin G. Hatch, R-Utah, said he made no promise to Clinton that he would call a conference with the House on the long-stalled juvenile justice bill, telling reporters he was concerned that "instead of compromise it might help polarize it more." He said he preferred to continue informal negotiations.

Lawmakers on both sides blamed the stalled conference on politics. Democrats fingered the powerful gun lobby, while Republicans said Democrats wanted the bill to fail because they did not want to give the Republican-controlled Congress an election year boost.

Despite calls for more comprehensive legislation, the House on April 11 passed, 358–60, legislation instituting nationwide a program dubbed Project Exile that would require mandatory sentences for convictions involving firearms. The legislation did not go through committee.

The measure (HR 4051), already used by some local governments, would authorize $100 million in incentive block grants over five years to states that require mandatory mini-

mum sentences of five years without parole for anyone who uses or carries a firearm during any violent or drug trafficking crime. The sentencing also would apply to felons convicted of violent crimes who later are caught with a gun. The Senate did not take up the bill.

On the same day it passed HR 4051, the House also endorsed, 406–22, a nonbinding motion by Democrats to instruct conferees on the moribund House-Senate juvenile justice bill to meet and send the bill back to the House with additional gun law enforcement and safety provisions.

But conferees did not meet, leaving the bill and its gun control provisions to languish.

Hate Crimes

Senators in 1999 and again in 2000 attempted unsuccessfully to expand federal hate crimes law to include sexual orientation, gender, and disability. Their efforts in 1999 focused on attaching the hate crimes language to the fiscal 2000 Commerce-Justice-State appropriations bill, but those provisions were abandoned in conference. The following year, the Senate amended the defense authorization bill to include a hate crimes provision, but conferees ultimately dropped the provision from the final version of the bill.

Hate crimes were defined under a 1968 law (PL 90-284) as those motivated by the race, color, religion, or national origin of the victim. The federal government was allowed to intervene and prosecute such crimes only if they occurred on federal property or during specific protected activities, such as voting.

Despite opposition from conservatives, momentum for tougher hate crimes action grew during 1999 following a spate of vicious attacks on minorities and homosexuals. A twenty-one-year-old gay man, Matthew Shepard, was beaten to death in Laramie, Wyo., in a case that garnered national media attention. Over the Fourth of July weekend in 1999, white supremacist Benjamin Nathaniel Smith went on a shooting spree that targeted minorities and Jews in Illinois and Indiana.

1999 LEGISLATIVE ACTION

Lawmakers in both parties urged the enactment of hate crimes legislation. Sen. Edward M. Kennedy, D-Mass., and Rep. John Conyers Jr., D-Mich., proposed identical bills (S 622, HR 1082) to expand the definition to include gender, sexual orientation, and disability. The plans also would allow federal prosecution of any hate crime linked to interstate commerce.

Three GOP lawmakers were outspoken in their support of hate crimes legislation: Sen. Gordon H. Smith of Oregon, Sen. James M. Jeffords of Vermont, and Rep. Mark Foley of Florida. Asked why GOP leaders opposed the initiative, Smith said at a Nov. 8 news conference: "It's because it has to do with the issue of homosexuality. Many people are uncomfortable with that."

But Republican leaders in the House and Senate said all violent crimes were egregious and that special federal categories should not be created for some of them. Others objected particularly to making crimes motivated by gender bias federal hate crimes, contending that that could federalize all rape cases. Some GOP leaders supported alternative approaches. Senate Judiciary Committee Chairman Orrin G. Hatch, R-Utah, proposed creating a $5 million federal grant to help states prosecute hate crimes.

On July 22, supporters of hate crimes legislation won a temporary victory when the Senate by voice vote amended its fiscal 2000 Commerce-Justice-State appropriations bill (S 1217) to federalize crimes motivated by the dislike of gays or the disabled, or by gender bias. The amendment, by Kennedy, also expanded federal jurisdiction over hate crimes and created new grants for states to prosecute such cases.

The Senate on the same day also added Hatch's language to the bill by voice vote. "We'll do our best to have a meeting of the minds," in conference, Hatch said. But the House version of the appropriations bill did not contain hate crimes language, and conferees ultimately dropped the Senate amendments. Key GOP senators said they opposed the language all along but allowed it to be added to the bill to speed its passage.

When President Clinton vetoed a later version of the appropriations bill (HR 2670), he lamented that the hate crimes proposals had been dropped, although he signaled that their revival was not essential to a year-ending budget agreement.

Despite the obstacles, several senior members of both chambers and both parties pressed to revive at least some of the language at the end of the session. Staff aides to Hatch and Kennedy tried to devise a compromise the week of Nov. 8 that could be slipped into an appropriations bill at the last minute. They did not succeed. "I'd like to do something," Hatch said Nov. 10. "But getting something done in that area is very hard."

2000 LEGISLATIVE ACTION

The Senate on June 20 adopted a hate crimes amendment June 20 to the fiscal 2001 defense authorization bill (S 2549) by the surprising **key vote of 57–42 (R 13–41; D 44–1)**. Although the House voted on Sept. 13 to instruct House conferees on the defense bill to accept the Senate language, conferees ultimately dropped it after a lengthy standoff. *(2000 key votes, p. 915)*

Democrats pulled out all the stops on the hate crimes amendment to the defense authorization bill, calling in Vice President Al Gore to preside over the Senate in case of a tie vote. But Gore's vote was unnecessary because thirteen Republicans joined forty-four Democrats to pass the measure. One Democrat, Robert C. Byrd, W.Va., voted against the proposal.

Besides adding to categories considered hate crimes—acts motivated by racial, religious or ethnic bias already are covered—the amendment would expand the federal government's jurisdiction to prosecute such crimes. "Crimes based upon hatred and bigotry wound not only the individual, but they also wound and scar an entire community," said amendment sponsor Edward M. Kennedy, D-Mass. But Republicans argued that there was no need for the amendment because hate crimes were not going unpunished.

Although many Republicans were uncomfortable with the amendment, few except Hatch spoke against it. Republican Policy Committee Chairman Larry E. Craig of Idaho said many senators decided not to voice their objections because of the issue's sensitivity. "I think all of us are extremely concerned that we don't appear to be racist or prejudiced, because none of us are," he said.

Senate Majority Leader Trent Lott, R-Miss., ducked several questions about why he opposed the amendment, finally saying: "I would prefer we not rush in here and start taking over state functions." Republicans, as well as Byrd, also warned the provision was unconstitutional.

The current federal hate crime law, passed in 1968, allowed federal prosecution of crimes that are based on the victim's race, color, religion, or national origin. But the federal government could get involved only if the act occurred while the victim was on federal property or engaged in one of six federally protected activities, such as voting.

Kennedy's plan would broaden federal jurisdiction to cover most existing hate crimes by stipulating that the Thirteenth Amendment, which eliminated slavery, allowed the federal government to protect people from such crimes. The measure also would create a federal hate crime for acts of violence based on prejudice toward the victim's gender, sexual orientation, or disability. It based that federal right on the Constitution's commerce clause, which allowed Congress to regulate interstate commerce.

However, the Supreme Court ruled in May in *United States v. Morrison* that there must be a substantial economic interest at stake for Congress to rely on commerce clause authority. Amendment supporters argued that because the provision would require that a link to interstate commerce be established for each case, it would pass constitutional muster. *(Morrison decision, p. 719)*

Civil rights groups—especially gay rights groups—cheered the outcome of the June 20 vote, but the provision's fate was unclear. The House did not include a hate crimes provision in its version of the defense authorization bill (HR 4205), meaning that the fight over hate crimes would once again take place in a conference committee.

Supporters of hate crimes legislation won a symbolic victory Sept. 13 when the House passed a motion to instruct conferees of the fiscal 2001 defense authorization bill to include Senate-passed hate crimes language in the final version of the bill. The motion, which passed on a 232–192 vote, was nonbinding. But supporters of hate crimes legislation believed it would send a powerful message to conferees and force all House members to go on record on the controversial issue.

Many Republicans who supported the motion were in tight reelection races or swing districts. But GOP leaders continued to oppose the hate crimes language. "I expect we'll drop that," said House Majority Leader Dick Armey who, similar to other top GOP leaders, argued that the measure was not needed because all crimes were hate crimes.

The issue was a double-edged sword for some lawmakers. Although gay rights groups, growing in political clout, strongly supported it, conservative organizations were adamantly opposed. "We are issuing a warning to those who voted for this legislation: we will notify our 43,000 churches about your vote today, and Christians will remember this on Election Day," said Andrea Lafferty, executive director of the Traditional Values Coalition in a Sept. 12 statement.

President Clinton made enactment of the hate crimes bill a top priority in the final days of his term. The same day the House voted to support the amendment, Clinton announced a new report showing that the frequency of hate crimes could be seriously underreported. "I don't think any of us believe we can ever root it out just by punishing people," Clinton said. "The most important thing is that we do have the tools we need to take a strong stand before these things spread even wider."

But the effort to pass a hate crimes measure failed Oct. 5 when, after a lengthy standoff, conferees on the fiscal 2001 defense authorization bill (HR 4205) dropped the provision from the final version of their bill. Clinton vowed to continue fighting for the measure. But once it was stripped from the defense authorization bill, supporters could not find another suitable vehicle.

HIV Testing

Sexual assault victims would be able to find out the HIV status of their alleged assailants under a measure the House passed overwhelmingly in 2000. But the measure died in the Senate. The bill (HR 3088) was designed to persuade states to pass laws requiring HIV testing for someone who has been indicted on rape charges if the victim requested it—even before a criminal trial took place. It would withhold 10 percent of a state's Byrne crime-fighting block grant money if that state failed to pass a testing law, redistributing that money among states that did have such laws. *(1998 action, p. 600)*

The test would be required if the attack led to a risk of HIV infection, but victims also could force the accused to submit to being tested simply by requesting it. Sponsor Dave Weldon, R-Fla., said the early testing was necessary because medical studies showed that if anti-HIV drugs were administered within forty-eight hours of exposure, an HIV infection could be prevented. "It is literally a matter of life and death," he said.

Only a few states allowed release of HIV information on a suspect before a conviction, and some did not release HIV information even after a conviction. Weldon said the measure would prevent accused sex offenders from benefiting from withholding information by refusing to submit to testing until

they get lighter sentences. The legislation also would allow positive test results to be considered at the suspect's trial.

HR 3088 went directly to the floor of the House, which passed it Oct. 2 on a 380–19 vote. Despite the wide margin, some Democrats expressed concerns about the effect of the bill on those who had been accused but were innocent.

Robert C. Scott, D-Va., warned that there was no way to protect the confidentiality of the test results because the bill would require that the information be given to the victim, the victim's attorney, the defense attorney, the prosecuting attorney, and the presiding judge. Scott said he thought mandatory testing should come after a higher burden of proof was met, such as after a probable cause hearing. But Weldon said that would take too long because anti-HIV drugs had to be administered promptly.

Alternative Sentencing

The House and Senate in 2000 passed slightly differing versions of a bill (HR 4493) intended to encourage drug treatment as an alternative to prison for certain offenders. But the 106th Congress ended before they could resolve the differences.

As passed by the House, the measure would allow the Justice Department to provide grants to state or local prosecutors to develop, implement, or expand drug treatment alternative programs. It would authorize $485 million over the following five years for grants that would facilitate eligible offenders undergoing drug treatment as an alternative to prison. The bill specified that the federal share of a grant could not exceed 75 percent of the cost of the program. It also would mandate that grants must be used to supplement, rather than supplant, nonfederal funds that would otherwise be available for activities funded by the bill.

Under the measure, each eligible offender who participated in the program would be placed with a licensed, long-term, drug-free residential substance abuse treatment provider as an alternative to incarceration. If an offender did not successfully complete treatment, he or she would then serve time in prison.

The bill, which was not considered in committee, passed the House by voice vote on Oct. 17. The Senate Dec. 6 passed the bill by unanimous consent, but only after adopting a substitute amendment by Orrin G. Hatch, R-Utah, to make the project a pilot, or temporary program. It also would grant judges the authority to waive existing sentencing laws to implement the program by sentencing misdemeanor offenders to treatment and probation.

Counterfeit Badges

Lawmakers in 2000 cleared a measure (HR 4827—PL 106-547) intended to crack down on the use of counterfeit police badges in the commission of a crime by making it a federal offense to enter federal facilities or secure airport areas under false pretenses. The law made it illegal to misuse or sell authentic and counterfeit law enforcement badges. Some Democrats argued that it would criminalize some novelty items, but bill sponsor Steve Horn, R-Calif., said fake badges were especially dangerous when used to commit crimes under the guise of law enforcement.

The impetus for the bill was a General Accounting Office probe in which investigators used false identification to enter secure airport areas and government offices.

The House Judiciary Committee approved the bill by voice vote on July 20 (H Rept 106-913). The House passed it by voice vote Oct. 2, and the Senate cleared it by unanimous consent Dec. 6. President Clinton signed the bill into law on Dec. 8, 2000.

Body Armor

The Senate passed a bill late in 2000 to increase penalties for wearing body armor while committing a crime. But the measure died in the House at the end of the session. Supporters of the bill (S 783) said the incidence of criminal suspects wearing body armor was increasing and more police officers were being killed.

The bill also would bar offenders with prior violent convictions from buying, using, or possessing body armor. And it would allow federal law enforcement agencies to donate surplus body armor directly to local police.

Bill sponsor Dianne Feinstein, D-Calif., said "body armor in the possession of a criminal is an offensive weapon." She said the goal of the bill was to decrease use of body armor by criminals, while ensuring police officers had adequate access to it.

The Senate Judiciary Committee, which approved the bill by voice vote July 27 without a written report, adopted a substitute clarifying that the government could not be held liable for defects in donated vests. Bill language also was changed to make that provision correspond to the equivalent provision in the juvenile justice bill (S 254, HR 1501) that was stalled in conference. The Senate passed S 783 by unanimous consent Oct. 25.

Bulletproof Vests

Lawmakers in 2000 cleared legislation (S 2413—PL 106-517) to increase the federal share of the cost of providing bulletproof vests for some community police departments. The measure increased federal matching grants to 50 percent of the cost of bulletproof vests in certain communities, directing more of the money to smaller jurisdictions. It redefined "armor vest" to include body armor that has been tested through the voluntary compliance testing program and found to meet or exceed federal requirements. It also authorized $50 million a year for the grant program from fiscal 2002 through 2004. *(1998 action, p. 599)*

The Senate Judiciary Committee approved S 2413 June 29 without a written report, and the Senate passed it Oct. 10 by unanimous consent. The House, which had passed a similar measure (HR 4033—H Rept 106-776) on July 26 by a vote of 413–3, cleared S 2413 without objection Oct. 25. The president signed the bill on Nov. 6, 2000.

Stalking

The House in 1999 passed legislation (HR 1869—H Rept 106-455) designed to assist federal law enforcement in prosecuting stalkers by expanding the definition of stalking to include the use of the telephone, mail or the Internet. But the Senate did not take action on the bill.

The measure also would require a judge to issue a protective order for the stalking victim after the stalker was convicted, and it would allow the court to immediately detain someone accused of stalking while the trial was pending—something victims' advocates had long desired.

Under current law (PL 104-201), stalking was a federal offense only when a stalker crossed state lines intending to injure or harass a person. Because that definition required the physical presence of the stalker, offenses that involved threatening letters, phone calls, or e-mails were not covered under the federal statute.

HR 1869 was prompted specifically by the increasing frequency and seriousness of so-called "cyberstalking," which was detailed in a Justice Department report that found in 1999 that the new offense had potentially affected tens or even hundreds of thousands of victims in the United States.

The House Judiciary Crime Subcommittee gave voice vote approval to the plan on Oct. 7. The Judiciary Committee approved it by voice vote Nov. 2 after adopting a substitute that would no longer expand the definition of stalking to include generally threatening behavior. It would instead retain the current, narrow legal language of "the demonstration of specific threats."

Bill McCollum, R-Fla., offered the substitute to address constitutional concerns he had about the underlying measure. The Justice Department and Democrats had similar concerns.

The House passed HR 1869 Nov. 10 by voice vote.

Antiterrorism

The House in 2000 passed a bill that would combine the efforts of 100 federal terrorism response teams, but the Senate did not act on it. The bill (HR 4210) would establish a presidential office headed by a director who would establish a national domestic terrorism preparedness plan, as well as coordinate funding for, and execution of, federal antiterrorism programs. It would authorize $9 million for the Office of Terrorism Preparedness for fiscal 2001, as well as necessary funding through 2005. *(1998 action, p. 605)*

Supporters worried that programs meant to fight terrorism had mushroomed into uncoordinated, fragmented, and often duplicate operations at a number of federal agencies and that many of them did not address the needs of state and local authorities. At the time, more than forty federal departments and agencies had established terrorism preparedness programs and more than 100 federal terrorism response teams had been created. The Federal Bureau of Investigation had a dormant National Domestic Preparedness Office since 1998 that had not been given necessary congressional authority to operate.

The House Transportation and Infrastructure Subcommittee on Oversight, Investigations and Emergency Management approved HR 4210 by voice vote on May 25. The full committee approved it by voice vote June 21 (H Rept 106-731). The House passed it by voice vote July 25.

Unidentified Persons

The House in 1999 overwhelmingly passed legislation to authorize $6 million over three years in grants to help states improve the reporting of unidentified persons. The Senate did not take up the measure. Bill sponsor Rick A. Lazio, R-N.Y., called the measure (HR 1915) "Jennifer's Law," after a twenty-one-year-old Long Island woman who disappeared in California in 1993.

The bill would authorize $2 million for fiscal 2000, 2001, and 2002. To qualify for the grants, states would have to require local law enforcement agencies to enter information on all unidentified persons—including those suffering with memory loss and the deceased—into the Unidentified Persons File of the FBI's National Crime Information Center. Under existing law, local agencies only had to enter information on missing persons to the Missing Person File. Cross-referencing the lists was impossible without complete information. "Coordination of these files could close thousands of missing persons cases," Lazio said. "The issue is not negligence, but inadequate funding." The bill, which advanced directly to the House floor without Judiciary Committee action, was passed on June 7 by a vote of 370–4.

War Criminals

A House Judiciary subcommittee in late 2000 approved a bill by voice vote to keep war criminals out of the country after members worked out an agreement designed to satisfy human rights activists. Lawmakers took no further action on it. The legislation (HR 5285) would bar prospective immigrants who participated in war crimes, genocide, or religious persecution from entering the United States. Lawmakers were spurred to action by news reports of accused war criminals living in the United States, including a former military leader in Haiti who allegedly supervised the torture and killing of thousands of Haitians before moving to New York.

Before the Oct. 3 markup, activists protested the last-minute bill, saying some of its provisions would conflict with human rights treaties the United States had signed that held war criminals and abusers accountable for their crimes.

House Judiciary Subcommittee on Immigration and Claims Chairman Lamar Smith, R-Texas, worked out a compromise with ranking member Sheila Jackson-Lee, D-Texas, to take care of those concerns and to garner bipartisan support. The changes to the legislation included provisions stating that a would-be immigrant must have "knowingly and intentionally" participated in abuse in order to be targeted as a human rights violator, and that suspected violators could ask a judge to review their cases.

Wiretapping

Suspected child-sex offenders would be subject to wiretapping by police and federal agents under a bill that the House passed at the end of the 106th Congress. The Senate did not take action on it. The bill (HR 3484) extended police wiretap authority to conversations involving suspects who police believed were sending or receiving child pornography or transporting children for sexual purposes. Under existing law, police were not allowed to wiretap suspected sexual predators who enticed children to cross state lines or entered the United States from another country.

Members of the Judiciary Committee agreed to the measure (H Rept 106-920) by voice vote on Sept. 20, 2000, despite concerns by some Democrats that the bill was too broad and could infringe on privacy rights. "Wiretaps are now becoming routine instead of a last resort," said Robert C. Scott, D-Va. "They should be used only to hold criminals responsible for serious crimes."

The House passed the measure by voice vote Oct. 3.

Child Abuse Programs

With little dissent, the House in 2000 cleared legislation intended to increase resources for child abuse victims and abuse prevention programs. Lawmakers said the bill (HR 764—PL 106-177) would increase prevention and treatment programs with no cost to taxpayers because $10 million from the federal Crime Victims' Fund would be reserved for grants to child abuse programs. The fund was supplied through fines and forfeited assets and bail bonds.

As amended by the Senate in late 1999, one section of the bill also authorized $2 million a year for fiscal 2000 through 2002 for state grants to develop information-sharing and reporting programs among states for identifying deceased persons, as in cases when a local government may discover a body and not be aware the victim was reported missing in another state.

States participating in the program would report every unidentified body to a National Crime Information Center. The state also would keep a file documenting dental information, DNA records, X-rays, and fingerprints. The language of the section, known as Jennifer's Law, was based on legislation (HR 1915) the House passed 370–4, on June 7, 1999, named for a twenty-one-year-old New York woman who moved to California in 1993 and disappeared.

HR 764 also allowed increased grants funding for abuse programs, to $20 million, if the victims' fund exceeded the fiscal 1998 deposits level of $363 million. The measure also expanded a federal grant program to allow state and local officials to use more money for child abuse prevention efforts.

The accelerated funding would help train people who work with abused children, supporters said. "They're undertrained, they're overworked, they're burned out," said Stephanie Tubbs Jones, D-Ohio.

Another provision allowed grant money to be used specifically to form cooperative programs between law enforcement and media organizations to better apprehend criminals. The bill also provided grants to expand a program designed to improve criminal justice record keeping. The program gave police officers, child protective services employees, and child welfare workers access to legal records, including criminal conviction information and protective orders based on domestic or child abuse.

The bill, introduced by Deborah Pryce, R-Ohio, won voice vote approval from the House Judiciary Committee on Sept. 28, 1999 (H Rept 106-360). The House passed it, 425–2, on Oct. 5. The Senate passed the bill by voice vote on Nov. 19, after inserting its own language (S 1750). The House cleared it on Feb. 1 by a vote of 410–2. President Clinton signed the measure on March 10.

Child Molesters

The House passed a bill (HR 4047) by voice vote in 2000 that would automatically sentence second-time child molesters to life in prison. The bill would apply to second-time federal offenders unless the death sentence was imposed.

"This bill is not about rehabilitation, openly admitted," said Mark Green, R-Wis., the measure's sponsor. "This bill is not even about deterrence. It is about removing bad people from society." Wisconsin had an identical law, which Green helped draft in 1997.

Some studies showed that child molesters were four times more likely than other violent criminals to commit more crimes. An Emory University study revealed 453 sex offenders who admitted molesting a total of more than 67,000 children in their lifetimes.

The measure would apply to second convictions for aggravated sexual abuse, sexual abuse of a minor, sexual abuse resulting in death, selling or buying of children, and transporting a minor in interstate or foreign commerce for illegal sexual purposes.

Green's legislation originally appeared in the bill (HR 1501) to overhaul the juvenile justice system. But that bill had become mired in conference. HR 4047, which was not considered as a standalone bill in committee, was passed by the House July 25.

Government Seizure of Civil Assets

President Clinton and members of Congress agreed in the 106th Congress to rein in one of the most powerful tools in law enforcement's arsenal: the ability to seize private property allegedly linked to a crime. The bill (HR 1658—PL 106-185) made a variety of changes to seizure laws, with the aim of making it more difficult for the government to seize some property, while granting more authority to seize assets once criminal charges have been proved.

The bill shifted the burden of proof to the government, which would have to prove property was used in the commission of a crime before seizing it. Previously, the burden was on the property owner to show that the property was not used in a crime. The bill also repealed a portion of forfeiture law that had required those seeking to reclaim their property to post a bond. At the same time, it gave law enforcement greater ability to seize property once a person is convicted.

BACKGROUND

The legislation represented the culmination of years of effort, especially by House Judiciary Committee Chairman Henry J. Hyde, R-Ill., who introduced his first overhaul of civil asset forfeiture laws in 1993. Hyde and others were concerned that law enforcement abused its authority to seize property, and that too few protections existed for innocent property owners. In fact, the chairman wrote a 1995 book about civil forfeitures after studying cases of innocent people who had their property taken by the federal government because of vague suspicions that the assets were criminally tainted.

Forfeiture rules dated back to English admiralty law involving seizure of smugglers' cargoes. In recent years they had been used more aggressively by prosecutors as part of the war on drugs. Under existing law, the government needed only to show "probable cause," the lowest standard of proof, to take property with a suspected crime connection, regardless of whether the owner was criminally involved. The burden of proof was on the owner to establish that it was not subject to forfeiture.

Hyde said the existing rules were abused by the government, which collected millions of dollars each year from the sale of properties. Proponents complained that innocent parties or their heirs often had to undergo great expense to recover property seized without even an arrest or a hearing.

Often cited was the example of the Red Carpet Motel in Houston, which was seized by the government in 1998 because the owners had not done enough to stop drug activity in some of the rooms. The property was returned to the owners after several months of expensive legal wrangling.

Hyde pushed a bill through his committee in 1997. But the bill died when Hyde failed to broker a compromise with the Justice Department, which viewed forfeitures as a key weapon in its war on drugs.

In the 106th Congress—Hyde's last as chairman—he returned to his original approach to force the government to show "by clear and convincing evidence" that confiscated property was tied to illegal misuse. The 1997 bill would have set a lower standard, requiring a "preponderance of the evidence."

Within his committee, whose sharp partisan divide was highlighted by the question of President Clinton's impeachment in 1998, the bill was carried by an odd coalition that included ranking Democrat John Conyers Jr. of Michigan, conservative Republican Bob Barr of Georgia, and liberal Democrat Barney Frank of Massachusetts.

Hyde drew support from oddly divergent groups representing lawyers, real estate agents, bankers, the American Civil Liberties Union, and the National Rifle Association. But the measure drew fire from powerful law enforcement groups, including the International Association of Chiefs of Police, which argued that it would hinder drug interdiction efforts such as seizing cash profits at airports and on highways.

HOUSE ACTION

The Judiciary Committee approved the measure (H Rept—106-192) on June 15, 1999, by a vote of 27–3. Casting the "no" votes in committee were Republicans Asa Hutchinson, Ark., and Ed Bryant, Tenn.—both former federal prosecutors—as well as Democrat Anthony Weiner, N.Y.

HR 1658 would give the government the burden of proving in court that a civil asset forfeiture was warranted. Owners would get more time to challenge seizures and could sue the government for taking the assets, with a heavy burden placed on the government to prove the forfeiture was warranted.

The legislation also would allow judges to release seized assets while forfeiture cases were being decided, if the forfeit caused the owner substantial hardship, and award interest to owners who were successful in winning their money back. It would help owners seeking to contest civil asset seizures by allowing judges to appoint counsel for them if they cannot afford a lawyer and eliminating the requirement that they post a 10 percent bond.

Chairman Henry J. Hyde, R-Ill., the bill's sponsor, conceded that asset seizure was a formidable deterrent to criminal activity, but he contended it had become "all too apparent in recent years that sometimes these laws are being used in terribly unjust ways, depriving innocent citizens of their property without basic due process."

Hutchinson agreed some changes were needed, but he voiced "grave reservations" about the bill. In particular, he said the legal standards imposed on the government would exceed the norm for other civil cases. He said the bill's requirement that free legal counsel be provided to indigents contesting asset seizures could inadvertently aid frivolous claims. Overall, Hutchinson said the bill "tilts too far against law enforcement in favor of criminal elements."

The Justice Department opposed the measure on similar grounds. On the House floor, Hutchinson, Weiner, and John E. Sweeney, R-N.Y., offered a substitute amendment that would reduce the government's burden of proof and make it more difficult for owners of seized property to take advantage of the bill's protections. It was rejected, 155–268. The House then passed HR 1658, 375–48, on June 24.

After the House vote, Hyde said his next step was to find a proponent in the Senate who could champion the civil asset forfeiture issue as consistently and tirelessly as he had for the past several years. Kissing a sheet of paper that displayed the lopsided vote on passage, Hyde said, "I've got to find a senator who's comfortable with it, who's excited about it and who will push it."

SENATE ACTION

Throughout months of negotiations from late 1999 into 2000, members of the Senate Judiciary Committee tried to find a compromise version of HR 1658 that would protect civil rights while preserving the ability of federal law enforcement to seize private property allegedly used in a criminal enterprise.

Senate Judiciary Chairman Orrin G. Hatch, R-Utah, and ranking Democrat Patrick Leahy, Vt., crafted a bill (S 1931) they had hoped would serve as a compromise between Hyde's measure and a much narrower proposal by Senate Judiciary members Jeff Sessions, R-Ala., and Charles E. Schumer, D-N.Y.

All three proposals would change the burden of proof in forfeiture cases to require that the government prove the property targeted for seizure was connected to a crime. In addition, all would establish a uniform "innocent owners" defense to protect the property of spouses and children or buyers who proved they were not aware of illegal activity.

But the bills set up differing standards that the government must meet to seize property, and they also took differing approaches on whether and when to allow court-appointed counsels for aggrieved property owners.

On March 22, 2000, Hyde, Hatch, Attorney General Janet Reno and others finalized the compromise that had been months in the making. "We had huge differences at the beginning," said Charles E. Schumer, D-N.Y., a key negotiator. "But we really balanced them and came to the middle. I think everyone walks away pretty happy."

One day later, the Senate Judiciary Committee approved the amended version of HR 1658 by voice vote.

The revamped bill would shift the burden to the government to prove by "preponderance of the evidence" that an asset had been used in a crime. The original Hyde bill would have required the government to meet an even more difficult "clear and convincing evidence" threshold.

The bill also would eliminate a requirement that the person trying to retrieve property post a "cost bond," usually 10 percent of the value of the asset. The owner must post the bond in cash at the start of a legal challenge, which the government said would deter frivolous cases.

But Hyde and others successfully argued that it made the process far too burdensome on property owners. Instead, to prevent bad-faith attempts to regain property, the bill would permit a judge to levy a fine on someone whose claim was found to be without merit.

Hyde's most controversial provision would provide legal representation to all property owners who could not afford to hire a lawyer. The final version allowed appointment of a lawyer only if a person was being prosecuted criminally and had already qualified for a court-appointed attorney or in cases in which an indigent person's primary residence had been seized.

The bill also would provide an "innocent owner" defense to allow certain people, such as a child or a spouse, whose property was used in a crime to regain it if they can show that they did not know about the crime or that when they found out about it, they did all they could to prevent it.

The bill would expand the Justice Department's ability to use criminal forfeiture, in which the department first proved that a crime occurred then seized the property.

It included a provision by Sen. Jeff Sessions, R-Ala., that would allow a judge to dismiss a complaint if the property owner was a fugitive outside the country and refused to come back for fear of arrest. It also would make it easier for other countries to seize assets in the United States in connection with civil cases in that country.

After the Senate passed the once-contentious measure by voice vote, the House cleared it by voice vote on April 11. President Clinton signed it on April 25, 2000.

MAJOR PROVISIONS

Key provisions of HR 1658, most of which took effect 120 days after enactment:

- **Burden of proof.** The bill switched the burden of proof from the owner to the government. It required the government to show, by a "preponderance of the evidence," that the asset was used in a crime. Existing law required the owner to prove that the asset was not used in a crime.

- **Cost bond.** The bill repealed a law requiring the property owner to post a cost bond before challenging the government's seizure. Cost bonds were set at 10 percent of the value of the asset or $5,000, whichever was less, with a minimum of $250. Instead, the bill allowed a judge to fine a property owner for filing a frivolous complaint, using the same calculations previously used to determine the amount of the cost bond. Property owners found to have filed three frivolous complaints while in prison were prohibited from filing further complaints unless they could show "extraordinary and exceptional circumstances."

- **Attorney fees and representation.** The bill required the government to reimburse the property owner for "reasonable" attorney fees in cases in which the owner substantially prevailed in a challenge to a seizure. Before the bill's passage, few property owners were repaid for their legal costs. The bill required the appointment of counsel by the Legal Services Corporation for a property owner whose home was subject to forfeiture and who could not afford an attorney. It also required appointment of counsel for indigents already represented in a criminal case.

- **Innocent owners.** The measure established a uniform, innocent-owner defense in civil asset forfeiture cases for people who could show, by a preponderance of the evidence, that they were not connected to a crime. To be considered innocent, an owner either could not have known the illegal activity was occurring or, once aware of it, would have done "all that reasonably could be expected" to stop the use of the property. Owners had to show that they notified law enforcement about the situation and tried to take back the asset in question. These requirements would be waived if the owner reasonably believed that meeting them would subject someone to physical harm. Owners who bought tainted property had to show they did not know it was connected to a crime.

- **Release of property.** The bill required the government to release property to the owner pending a decision on the seizure if the owner had strong community ties and could show that government possession of the asset would cause "substantial hardship." Examples of hardship included leaving someone homeless or making it difficult for a person to run a business. The owner had to show that the asset was unlikely to be disposed of or destroyed while out of government custody.

- **Damage claims.** The measure allowed property owners who prevailed in a forfeiture case to recoup some costs for damages to their assets incurred while the government held them. Under current law, the government was immune from liability for damages.

- **Criminal assets.** The bill expanded federal agents' ability to seize assets after the owner was convicted of a crime. It broadened criminal forfeiture laws to mirror civil forfeiture laws.

- **Statute of limitations.** The bill gave the government more time to lay claims against assets. Under the current law, claims had to be made within five years of the date of the crime. The bill set the limit at five years or two years after the discovery that the asset was used in the crime, whichever was later.

- **Foreign enforcement.** The bill made it easier for foreign governments that had signed agreements with the United States to get help from a U.S. court in enforcing an asset forfeiture decision. The court could decline to enforce the judgment if it found that the process in the other country was unfair to the property owner.

- **Fugitive forfeiture.** The bill allowed a judge to deny a claim by a property owner if the owner left the country to avoid arrest and refused to return, unless the owner was in custody elsewhere.

- **Banking records.** The bill allowed a judge to sanction a property owner, up to dismissing a claim, if the owner refused to supply foreign banking records that could be material to the case.

- **Civil restraining orders.** The bill allowed the government to take steps, such as appointing a conservator, to protect property it had decided to seize if there was a substantial probability that the government would win the case and that the asset would be destroyed before being turned over.

- **Reports.** The bill required the attorney general to send Congress an annual report on assets the government seized during the year, broken down by state and other parameters.

Concealed Weapons

A House Judiciary subcommittee in 1999 approved a bill (HR 218) that would exempt current and former law enforcement officers from state laws that prohibit the carrying of concealed firearms across state lines. But lawmakers took no further action on the measure.

Most states allowed off-duty officers to carry concealed weapons. However, such permission was usually not extended to law enforcement personnel while they were on vacation. HR 218 would grant vacationing officers the option to carry concealed weapons—provided they were authorized to carry firearms in the line of duty, were not under any disciplinary actions, did not retire because of a mental disability, and were carrying proper identification cards issued by a law enforcement agency.

The bill would not supersede any state laws that permit private individuals or state and local government from restricting the possession of concealed firearms on their property.

The bill language was originally included in a controversial gun show measure (HR 2122) that was rejected by the full House in June. The Crime Subcommittee gave voice vote approval to HR 218 July 1.

Police Athletic League Chapters

Lawmakers in 2000 cleared legislation (HR 3235—PL 106-367) that awarded $16 million in grants to help local communities establish their own chapters of a Police Athletic League (PAL). Founded by New York City police officers in 1914, PAL offered athletic programs to lure teens away from criminal activity and to increase trust between teenagers and police, especially in urban and high-crime areas. Since its founding, it had grown into one of the country's largest crime-prevention programs, with 320 local chapters serving more than 3,000 communities. The PAL chapters, staffed by off-duty police officers, received most of their funding from private sources.

The bill won voice vote approval in the House Judiciary Subcommittee on Crime on July 20 and the full committee on July 25 (H Rept 106-859). The House passed it by voice vote on Oct. 2; the Senate cleared it by unanimous consent on Oct. 13. The president signed it into law on Oct. 27.

Overseas Crimes

Lawmakers in 2000 cleared a measure (S 768—PL 106-523) intended to close a loophole that allowed American citizens who committed crimes overseas to escape U.S. prosecution. The bill allowed civilians connected with the armed forces to be prosecuted under federal criminal or military law. Prosecution of suspects would be at the discretion of the host nation. If such a crime were committed in the United States and punishable by more than a year's imprisonment,

the overseas offender would be subject to prosecution by a military court, if the military chose to act, or to federal criminal prosecution.

The Senate Judiciary Committee approved its version of S 768 by voice vote June 24, 1999 without a written report. The Senate passed it by unanimous consent July 1. On June 27, 2000, the House Judiciary Committee gave voice vote approval to a similar measure (HR 3380—H Rept 106-778, Pt. I). The House inserted the text of HR 3380 into S 768 on July 25 and then passed the measure by voice vote. On Oct. 26 the Senate by unanimous consent agreed to the House language, clearing the bill for the president's signature on Nov. 22, 2000.

Law Enforcement Animals

Lawmakers in 2000 cleared legislation (HR 1791—PL 106-254) to establish penalties for harming law enforcement animals. Under existing law, law enforcement animals such as dogs and horses were treated as "federal property," so penalties for harming them were similar to those for misdemeanors. HR 1791 established fines and prison sentences of up to one year for willfully harming, attempting, or conspiring to harm a police animal. If the offense disabled, disfigured, or caused the animal's death, the crime could bring up to a ten-year prison term.

The House Judiciary Crime Subcommittee approved the bill by voice vote on July 1, 1999. The full committee gave voice vote approval Sept. 22 (H Rept 106-372). During the full committee proceedings, Robert C. Scott, D-Va., offered a group of minor amendments—adopted by unanimous consent—clarifying that the bill did not apply to people who acted in self-defense or harmed an animal by accident, and that the ten-year maximum penalty could only apply to those who caused "permanent" disability or disfigurement, "serious bodily injury" or death to the animal. The bill would establish prison sentences of up to ten years for harming, seriously injuring or killing the animals. The House passed the measure by voice vote Oct. 12. The Senate cleared it the following year on July 19, 2000, by unanimous consent. The president signed the bill on Aug. 2, 2000.

Animal Cruelty

Lawmakers in 1999 cleared legislation to make it a federal crime to sell, or create with the intent of selling, videotaped depictions of animal cruelty. The bill (HR 1887—PL 106-152) was drafted to respond to the production—described in graphic detail by bill supporters—of videos showing women torturing small animals such as rodents and even small cats, dogs, and monkeys by slowly crushing them with their stiletto heels.

"I don't believe in my time in Congress that I've ever seen anything quite like this," House Judiciary Crime Subcommittee Chairman Bill McCollum, R-Fla., said, referring to tapes he viewed during a hearing on the "foot fetish" videos, which he called "repulsive." Bill sponsor Elton Gallegly, R-Calif., said that the videos sold for anywhere from $30 to $100 to "sick individuals who enjoy this foot fetish."

Gallegly was alerted to the issue by the Ventura County District Attorney's Office and the Doris Day Animal League. The D.A.'s office said it had had substantial difficulty prosecuting such crimes because no faces were shown in the videos and most state laws applied only to the person who harmed the animal, not the producer or distributor of a video.

The resulting bill was an attempt to rectify this by focusing on the commercial aspect of the animal cruelty. Under the measure, it would be a federal crime to sell a depiction of animal cruelty, or to create or possess it with the intention of selling it. People convicted of such actions would face fines and up to five years in prison.

The House Judiciary Crime Subcommittee approved the measure, 8–2, on Oct. 7. In response to concerns on both sides of the aisle over regulating free speech, subcommittee chairman McCollum offered an amendment, adopted by voice vote, that would exempt from the bill any depictions of animal cruelty that had serious religious, political, scientific, educational, journalistic, historic, or artistic value. This would include educational videos of bullfights or elephant poachers.

The House Judiciary Committee approved the measure, 22–4, on Oct. 13 (H Rept 106-397). The House passed HR 1887 on Oct. 19 by a vote of 372–42 after an unusually graphic, even nauseating debate about the videos. McCollum characterized the measure as "a necessary complement to state animal cruelty laws."

A diverse coalition of Democrats and Republicans opposed the measure on First Amendment grounds, saying it would violate constitutional free speech and insert the federal government into an area where it did not belong. "Communication through film is speech," said Robert C. Scott, D-Va., the ranking member on the crime subcommittee. He compared the animal torture tapes to closed circuit television recordings of robberies or other crimes routinely shown on programs such as "COPS" and "America's Most Wanted."

The Senate cleared HR 1887 on Nov. 19 by unanimous consent. Clinton signed the bill on Dec. 9, 1999.

Secret Service

Lawmakers in 2000 cleared legislation that expanded the Secret Service's authority to investigate threats against major public figures and help organize security arrangements at large public gatherings. The measure (HR 3048—PL 106-544) allowed the Secret Service to investigate threats against all current and former presidents, vice presidents and their immediate families, and major party candidates for the two offices and their families. It also authorized the Secret Service to protect visiting foreign dignitaries.

The Secret Service, a division of the Treasury Department, had been protecting the president since the assassination of President William McKinley in 1901. Under existing law, the service could only investigate threats against people it is protecting. If a candidate declined protection, the service was prohibited from investigating threats against the candidate.

Also, a 1994 law (PL 103-329) limited Secret Service protection of former presidents and vice presidents to ten years after they left office. That limit would take effect for people elected in 2000 and thereafter.

HR 3048 allowed the Secret Service to plan for security at large gatherings of "national significance," according to Rep. Bill McCollum, R-Fla., the bill sponsor. Under the current law, the service was only allowed to participate if someone it was protecting was attending the event.

The bill also allowed the agency under certain circumstances to obtain an administrative subpoena—one issued by police rather than a court—to get documents and other materials at times when a court was not available, such as on a weekend or holiday.

The House Judiciary Crime Subcommittee gave voice vote approval to the measure March 16. It approved by voice vote an amendment by McCollum that circumscribed the use of administrative subpoenas and stripped from the bill provisions that made it easier for federal agencies to seize property used in making a threat.

The Judiciary Committee gave voice vote approval May 24 (H Rept 106-669), and the House passed it by June 26. The Senate passed an amended version Oct. 13. After the House by voice vote agreed to some amendments and rejected others, senators receded from some of the contentious amendments, clearing the bill by unanimous consent Dec. 6. President Clinton signed it on Dec. 19, 2000.

College Aid for Slain Officers' Families

Congress in 2000 cleared legislation that expanded a program providing college aid to family members of slain police officers. A program established in 1992 awarded college scholarships of $485 per month for up to forty-five months to spouses and children of officers killed in the line of duty after that year. *(1998 action, p. 614)*

The bill (S 1638—PL 106-276) made eligibility retroactive to families of officers killed since 1978, allowing an additional 4,100 families to participate. Under the expansion, family members could be reimbursed for college costs incurred in the 1980s and 1990s.

The program, which initially applied only to children or spouses of slain or severely wounded federal officers, was extended to state and local officers' families under a 1998 law (PL 105-390). It also included police, firefighters, and corrections officers.

"The least we can do is help their families get the type of education they might not otherwise be able to afford," said Rep. Asa Hutchinson, R-Ark.

The Senate Judiciary Committee approved the bill without a written report on Feb. 10, and the Senate passed it by unanimous consent on May 15. The House cleared it by voice vote on Sept. 19. The president signed it on Oct. 2, 2000.

Racial Profiling

A bill (HR 1443) aimed at measuring the prevalence of racial profiling by police won voice vote approval from the House Judiciary Committee on March 13, 2000, but lawmakers took no further action on it.

In profiling, police officers targeted suspects based on how closely those suspect matched an image of what some would think was a typical criminal. The profile often included racial or ethnic characteristics—prompting some African Americans to observe that their offense appeared to be "driving while black."

Most police organizations denied that their officers practiced racial profiling, but abundant anecdotal evidence convinced others that the practice was widespread. The American Civil Liberties Union monitored the practice for years, and it established a nationwide campaign to eradicate it.

Dozens of city police forces had begun collecting data on their traffic stops, including police in San Francisco, Houston, and Ann Arbor, Mich. Several local studies showed that minorities were stopped in a disproportionate percentage of incidents. For example, a state study of traffic stops along the New Jersey Turnpike found that the majority of car searches were of vehicles belonging to black or Hispanic drivers, though such drivers made up a minority of all drivers on the turnpike. In 1999 the state of New Jersey reached an agreement with the Justice Department to hire an independent monitor to help put a stop to racial profiling.

HR 1443 (H Rept 106-517) would authorize a study by the attorney general on the use of racial profiling in police decisions to stop motorists. It called on the Justice Department to collect data on the circumstances of traffic stops in a nationwide sample of jurisdictions and report back to Congress within two years. "Race-based traffic stops turn driving into one of the most dangerous and risk-taking activities for people of color," said bill sponsor John Conyers Jr. of Michigan.

The Clinton administration strongly supported the bill, as did House Judiciary Chairman Henry J. Hyde, R-Ill. In 1999 President Clinton required all federal law enforcement agencies to start keeping track of their stops and searches. The House passed similar legislation in the 105th Congress, but the Senate never acted on it.

Railroad Officers

The House in 1999 cleared legislation (S 1235—PL 106-110) by voice vote that enabled law officers who worked for railroads to receive training at the FBI academy in Quantico,

Va. The academy was generally reserved for federal, state, and local law enforcement officers. However, bill supporters said railroad police were encountering the kinds of criminal activity—apprehending illegal aliens and drug smugglers, investigations concerning sabotage—as most other law enforcement personnel and they would benefit from the special FBI training.

Under the bill, the officers who enrolled in FBI training were required to pay for their own room, board, and transportation or have such costs covered by their employers.

The Senate Judiciary Committee approved the bill by voice vote on Oct. 21 without a written report. The Senate passed it by unanimous consent on Oct. 26, and the House cleared it by voice vote on Nov. 17. Clinton signed it on Nov. 24.

Federal Prison Industries

A bill (HR 2558) that would expand market opportunities for the government-owned Federal Prison Industries Inc., known as UNICOR, won voice vote in the House Judiciary Crime Subcommittee in 1999. But it failed to advance further.

Congress created UNICOR in 1934 to help federal inmates gain job skills they could use once they were released. The program generated $534.4 million in net sales in fiscal 1998, most of which was funneled back into the program.

State and federal studies consistently indicated that inmates who worked in a prison industries program were significantly less likely to be rearrested than those who did not.

But bill sponsor Bill McCollum, R-Fla., and other supporters of the bill contended that UNICOR needed increased competition and market opportunities to create enough jobs to satisfy the inmate population, expected to more than double in the next ten years. According to McCollum, there were enough jobs to allow only 20 percent of federal inmates to participate in the program. Most were on long waiting lists.

Business groups and organized labor had long opposed the program, viewing it as unfair competition to private industry. UNICOR paid inmates between 23 cents and $1.15 per hour, far less than the federal minimum wage of $5.15. Furthermore, UNICOR enjoyed preferential status in the sale of goods to federal agencies.

The bill would eliminate that preferential status by phasing out the "federal source provision," which mandated that federal agencies must order from prison industries instead of private industries in most cases.

However, at the same time, the bill would allow inmate-made goods to be sold on the open market, which was prohibited under existing law. To satisfy competition concerns of labor unions, the bill would require that inmates be paid the minimum wage in contract situations.

Both McCollum's bill and a similar measure, introduced by Peter Hoekstra, R-Mich., would eliminate the federal source provision. But Hoekstra and his allies vehemently opposed allowing the prison industries to sell their goods on the open market.

The crime subcommittee approved HR 2558 Sept. 23. By voice vote the panel adopted en bloc amendments that would make a series of clarifications and incorporate some minor provisions of Hoekstra's bill, including requiring UNICOR to perform its contractual obligations with the government the same as everyone else, make sure inmates did not have access to citizen information, use 20 percent of its annual profits for inmate vocational training and report annually to Congress.

Prisoner Deaths

States seeking federal prison money were held more accountable for prisoners who died in custody through legislation (HR 1800—PL 106-297) cleared by Congress in 2000. In order for states to receive federal grants for prisons, states were required to follow Justice Department guidelines when they collected data on the deaths of those who died while in police custody.

States were required to report quarterly on deaths that occurred while an individual was locked up, was headed to a state or local jail or prison, or was otherwise under the control of law enforcement. The information included the name, gender, ethnicity, and age of the person who died; the time and location of death; and the circumstances surrounding the death.

According to bill supporters, an estimated 1,000 people each year died under questionable circumstances while in police custody or in jail. "I've always been concerned that there was no national system for accounting for deaths in law enforcement custody," said Robert C. Scott, D-Va. "We don't know whether there is any pattern or practice related to such deaths."

The bill, which did not go through committee, was passed by the House by voice vote July 24. The Senate cleared it by unanimous consent Oct. 3. The president signed the bill on Oct. 13.

Prisoner Health Care

Lawmakers in 2000 cleared a measure (S 704—PL 106-294) that required federal prisoners to pay for their health care. Bill sponsor Jon Kyl, R-Ariz., said during a floor speech that prisoner copayment programs would "reduce the overutilization of health care services without denying necessary care to the indigent." More than half of all state prisons had similar programs, he said.

The bill allowed the Federal Bureau of Prisons to establish fees of at least $1 for each doctor visit initiated by the prisoner. Prisoners could not be denied medical care on financial grounds, and no fees would be imposed if prison officials sent an inmate for medical treatment. Certain types of services, such as preventive health care, prenatal care and emer-

gency services, were excluded from the fees. If the prisoner's sentence included restitution, the fees would be given to the victims.

The Senate Judiciary Committee approved S 704 by voice vote on April 29, 1999, without a written report. The Senate passed it by unanimous consent May 27.

House members advanced a similar bill (HR 1349) to direct the federal Bureau of Prisons to establish fees for each doctor visit initiated by a prisoner. As in the Senate version, an inmate could not be refused care if he or she lacked money. The fees would go to victim restitution, the federal Crime Victims' Fund, or to offset prison administrative expenses.

The House Judiciary Crime Subcommittee approved the bill by voice vote on March 16, 2000. Chairman Bill McCollum, R-Fla., offered an amendment adopted by voice vote that would lower the minimum fee from $2 to $1, and clarify that there would be no fee for certain treatment, including prenatal care and diagnosis or treatment of chronic infectious diseases.

The panel turned back several attempts by ranking Democrat Bobby C. Scott, Va., to weaken the bill, including one amendment that would allow the fee only if the inmate was found to have "no reasonable basis" for requesting the doctor's visit. "If the point is to discourage bogus health care visits, then we shouldn't discourage valid health care visits," he said.

Scott warned that the bill threatened to diminish the quality of prisoners' health care, which was "notoriously inadequate already" and could increase the number of untreated cases of AIDS. The panel gave voice vote approval to a Scott amendment that would require reports on the cost of assessing fees on inmates and the state of inmate health.

The House Judiciary Committee approved the bill by voice vote July 19 (H Rept 106-851). The House passed it by voice vote Sept. 19, then inserted the provisions of HR 1349 into S 704. The Senate cleared the amended version of S 704 Sept. 28. Clinton signed it on Oct. 12.

Transport of Prisoners

Lawmakers in 2000 cleared legislation that created standards for transporting dangerous criminals between prisons across state lines. Supporters of the bill (S 1898—PL 106-560) said it stemmed from concerns about prisoners being transported by private companies, pointing out that twenty-one prisoners convicted of violent crimes had escaped while being moved by private companies in the past three years.

Under the bill, the Justice Department would create standards that private companies must meet to qualify to transport criminals convicted of violent crimes. The standards would include requiring inmates to wear bright, distinctive clothing and certain types of handcuffs and shackles.

The bill also required employees who transported violent felons to be trained in using restraints, weapons, CPR, searches, maps, and defensive driving. Prospective employees convicted of domestic violence or a felony would not qualify for such positions.

The Senate Judiciary Committee approved S 1898 Sept. 28 without a written report. The Senate passed it by unanimous consent Oct. 25, and the House cleared it by voice vote Dec. 7.

President Clinton signed the bill on Dec. 21.

Law Enforcement Grants

The House in late 2000 passed a measure (HR 4999) that supporters said would increase the flexibility for local governments' use of federal funds for law enforcement. The measure died in the Senate.

The plan would authorize $10 billion, or $2 billion a year, over five years to local law enforcement agencies in the form of block grants. The grants could be used for a variety of programs intended to reduce crime and improve public safety, including hiring officers; paying overtime; buying equipment; enhancing security measures in and around schools or other public areas considered to be high risk; establishing drug courts; forming community task forces; and creating prevention programs for juveniles. No more than 3 percent of the funds could be used by the Justice Department to study the program's effectiveness and efficiency. The program was created as an alternative to the Clinton administration's Community Oriented Policing Services (COPS) program.

The House passed a bill during the 104th Congress to authorize the program, but the Senate did not act on it. HR 4999, which was not considered by committee, won House passage on a voice vote Sept. 19. Once again the Senate failed to act on it.

Date Rape Drugs

A bill to toughen penalties for illegal possession of so-called date-rape drugs became law in 2000. The legislation (HR 2130—PL 106-172) made it illegal—and more difficult—to possess gamma hydroxybutyric acid or GHB. Relatively easy to make, the behavioral depressant and hypnotic substance was often slipped into a victim's drink, making the person more susceptible to attack. Several such victims died after unknowingly ingesting the drug.

The bill directed the Justice Department to classify GHB as a Schedule I drug under the Controlled Substances Act, increasing criminal penalties for illicit manufacture, possession, and distribution. An exception was made for use in clinical studies of sleep disorders. In addition, the bill classified a solvent used to make the drug, Gamma Butyrolactone, as a List I chemical. Such designation made the chemical susceptible to increased regulation. By classifying the drugs, the bill made defendants subject to mandatory minimum sentences similar to those for possession of marijuana, cocaine, and heroin.

The bill also allowed the attorney general to fund research to develop new toxicology tests to assist law enforcement efforts in detecting GHB in the bloodstream. Further, the bill directed the secretary of Health and Human Services to order a study on the rate of GHB abuse and use as a date-rape drug and to develop a public awareness campaign about the drug, its uses, and effects.

Taken in excessive amounts or combined with alcohol, the drugs could reduce respiration and heartbeat to dangerously low levels, resulting in seizures, coma, or death.

Rep. Michael Bilirakis, R-Fla., said abuse of these drugs had increased substantially in recent years. He cited a Drug Enforcement Agency (DEA) study that documented more than 4,000 overdoses and law enforcement encounters with GHB, and thirty-two GHB-related deaths.

Supporters of the bill, dubbed the Hillory J. Farias and Samantha Reid Date-Rape Drug Prohibition Act after two teens who died after unknowingly ingesting the drug, said the measure was necessary to stave off more rapes and deaths. Some seventeen sexual assaults had been tied directly to the use of the chemical, known colloquially as "liquid ecstasy."

"Without this bill, illicit use of GHB would increase drastically," said Rep. Sheila Jackson-Lee, D-Texas. "It's being made in bathtubs. It's being made on the Internet."

In 1996 Congress enacted a law (PL 104-305) that tightened regulation of the date-rape drug flunitrazepam, known commercially as Rohypnol. The law, however, did not reclassify the drug from its Schedule IV category to the Schedule I category. *(Congress and the Nation Vol. IX, p. 740)*

By voice vote, the House Commerce Health and Environment Subcommittee approved the bill July 27, 1999. Members adopted a substitute amendment by voice vote that would allow continued research use of GHB as a treatment for narcolepsy patients. The Commerce Committee approved it Aug. 5 (H Rept 106-340, Pt. I). The House passed it 423–1 on Oct. 12.

The Senate on Nov. 19 passed the bill by unanimous consent after substituting the language of a similar measure, S 1561. The Senate version did not include House language that would place less stringent restrictions on the animal tranquilizer Ketamine.

The House cleared the measure, 339–2, on Jan. 31, 2000. President Clinton signed the bill on Feb. 18.

DNA Evidence

At the end of the 106th Congress lawmakers cleared legislation to authorize $170 million to help state authorities catch up on the analysis and logging of DNA evidence. The bill (HR 4640—PL 106-546) also required that federal inmates convicted of violent or sexual crimes supply DNA samples to the FBI's nationwide database of DNA materials. The database was designed to help match DNA evidence from crime scenes to samples taken from convicts.

The testing of DNA evidence had matured in recent years. The tests could detect unique genetic information from even small amounts of residue, such as hair or skin particles. That information could provide a high degree of certainty in establishing the guilt or innocence of a suspect.

Testing could be complicated and expensive. According to the Justice Department, about 69 percent of publicly operated crime labs across the country, including the FBI's lab, had a backlog of DNA evidence waiting for analysis.

HR 4640 authorized $170 million over four years for grants to states, of which $45 million would be aimed at collecting DNA samples from convicts and getting them into the database. The remaining $125 million was authorized to speed the processing of DNA samples from crime scenes, and to upgrade DNA labs.

Lawmakers largely avoided a larger debate on DNA testing in death penalty cases. The bill did not include money to perform DNA testing requested by prisoners seeking to prove their claims of having been wrongfully convicted, although it did include language encouraging states to offer DNA testing to some prisoners. This had become a particularly high-profile issue in death penalty convictions at a time when some eighty-seven people on death rows had been shown to be innocent, and a significant portion of those cases was determined by DNA evidence.

Many advocates of DNA testing focused on its value in proving the guilt or innocence of people already convicted of crimes. Prisoners did not routinely have access to DNA testing, which largely was performed at the discretion of the prosecutor and judge in a particular case. Sen. Patrick J. Leahy, D-Vt., introduced legislation (S 2073) designed to guarantee access for those facing execution.

The cause was strengthened by a recent federal district court ruling in Alexandria, Va., that gave prisoners the right to go to federal court to request DNA testing. The bill passed by the House did not address this issue but would require that DNA samples from prisoners whose convictions have been overturned be removed from the national database.

HOUSE ACTION

By voice votes, the House Judiciary Crime Subcommittee approved the bill June 15, and the full Judiciary Committee approved the measure July 26 (H Rept 106-900, Pt. I).

The Judiciary Committee acted after adopting by voice vote a substitute amendment by sponsor Bill McCollum, R-Fla., to include burglary in the list of covered crimes. "Half of all child molesters also commit burglaries," McCollum said.

McCollum's substitute also increased the bill's funding from $50 million to $170 million, and it split the grants into two accounts, one for analyzing DNA samples taken from convicted criminals and one to increase the capacity of state laboratories to analyze DNA samples. Under the bill, all samples would be included in the FBI's Combined DNA Index System, a comprehensive data base of DNA from criminals.

McCollum said the bill was needed to eliminate a backlog of hundreds of thousands of DNA samples now awaiting analysis in state labs. He said about 69 percent of forensic crime labs across the country had a backlog.

The committee accepted by voice vote an amendment by Robert C. Scott, D-Va., that would allow the District of Columbia to determine which offenses under its jurisdiction would trigger DNA sampling.

Scott offered an amendment that would require states that receive funding to test the DNA of convicted criminals if it could prove their innocence and if the people did not have access to DNA testing at the time of the conviction. McCollum said he supported the purpose of the amendment but feared that the language could delay states from receiving money needed to eliminate DNA backlogs.

Scott withdrew his amendment after McCollum said he would pursue the use of DNA testing to prove people's innocence in separate legislation. The committee also accepted by voice vote an amendment by Bob Barr, R-Ga., that would limit the use of the DNA samples to law enforcement matters.

The full House passed HR 4640 by voice vote Oct. 2.

SENATE ACTION

The Senate passed a slightly different version of the bill Dec. 6 by unanimous consent. The chamber adopted, by voice vote, an amendment by Leahy designed to encourage states to offer DNA testing to inmates who were convicted of a crime before the technology behind DNA testing had matured enough to provide conclusive evidence in their cases.

Leahy's amendment said it was the sense of Congress that receipt of the new grant money from the federal government should be conditioned on a state's agreement to provide post-conviction DNA testing to prisoners. The amendment also said Congress should work with the states to improve the level of legal representation provided to defendants in capital cases.

The House cleared the amended version by voice vote on Dec. 7. President Clinton signed the measure on Dec. 19.

Access to Electronic Information

Attempting to guarantee the privacy of citizens, the House Judiciary panel late in 2000 approved a measure limiting law enforcement's access to electronic information in criminal investigations. But with the session winding down and the White House warning that the bill could impede law enforcement efforts, supporters failed to move the measure to the House floor.

The bill (HR 5018) sought to address concerns about inconsistencies and contradictions in current statutes that provided authority for law enforcement officers to obtain private information. Federal officials had to meet a relatively low evidentiary threshold to get e-mail address information, for example, but faced a higher standard to listen in on voice communications.

The bill would raise the burden of proof for eavesdropping on most communications and would make it tougher for the government to track an individual using his or her cell phone. Instead of merely certifying that requested information would be relevant, the bill would require that law enforcement officers prove that "specific and articulable facts reasonably indicate that a crime has been, is being or will be committed and information likely to be obtained . . . is relevant to the investigation of that crime."

Constitution Subcommittee Chairman Charles T. Canady, R-Fla., said the bill would "provide a measure of needed protection of privacy rights."

The subcommittee approved HR 5018 by voice vote Sept. 14. Canady acknowledged that the bill did not include provisions sought by the Clinton administration to redefine and clarify some areas of criminal law to reflect new kinds of cyber-crimes, such as the intentional use of viruses to disrupt business. The chairman said those kinds of issues were not under his panel's jurisdiction but fell under the purview of the crime subcommittee.

At the subcommittee markup, Bob Barr, R-Ga., won voice vote approval of an amendment that would require police and federal agents to get a warrant before tracing the location of a cell phone. Under the amendment, an officer would have to prove probable cause that a crime has been or will be committed. The restriction would not apply in emergencies, such as when a cell-phone user had been kidnapped.

Barr also offered an amendment to extend the amount of time law enforcement would have to get a warrant to tap into stored electronic information. Under existing law, police had to obtain a warrant for information stored 180 days or less. Barr wanted to increase that time period to one year, but he withdrew his amendment after Canady objected.

On Sept. 26 the Judiciary Committee emphatically approved the bill, 20–1. The lone dissenter, Anthony Weiner, D-N.Y., said he agreed with the administration that the measure would hamper crime-fighting efforts.

The panel gave voice vote approval to a manager's amendment by Canady. Originally, Canady's amendment would allow prosecutors to continue using opened e-mails that people store on the Internet, no matter how the e-mails were obtained. But the panel voted, 9–7, to nullify that provision and bar police from using stored e-mail in court if they obtained it illegally.

The Judiciary Committee also adopted a Democratic amendment that would require police to get a warrant to obtain stored e-mails. Under current law, police needed only an administrative subpoena. "I have an expectation that the e-mails I save on my Yahoo account . . . are private," said Zoe Lofgren, D-Calif.

Another amendment the committee adopted would require police to get a warrant to obtain unopened e-mails that were stored on the Internet for up to one year. The committee also adopted an amendment by ranking Democrat John

Conyers Jr., Mich., that would make it illegal to deface or destroy a Web site, even if the damage amounts to less than $5,000.

Committee members defeated attempts to expand provisions relating to law enforcement's reporting requirements, as well as proposals that police be required to notify anyone whose e-mails they have been monitoring once the monitoring order expires.

Crimes Against Judges

The Senate in 2000 passed a bill that would impose harsher criminal penalties for harming or threatening a federal judge or law enforcement officer. The House, however, did not take it up.

Under the legislation (S 113), the penalties also would apply to threats made or harm to family members of judges or federal agents. The maximum prison sentence for assaulting or obstructing a federal law enforcement officer would increase from three years to eight years. Brandishing a weapon at the same time would be punishable by a new maximum sentence of twenty years, up from ten years.

The bill also would impose a ten-year maximum term for sending threatening mail to a federal law enforcement official, including a U.S. judge. The Judiciary Committee approved the measure July 27 by voice vote. The Senate passed it by unanimous consent Sept. 28.

Mental Health Courts

Congress in 2000 cleared legislation that sought to address the special circumstances of prison inmates who were mentally ill. The bill (S 1865—PL 106-515) set up a four-year pilot program to help states and municipalities develop twenty-five "Mental Health Courts."

A 1999 Justice Department survey found that 16 percent of inmates in state prisons and local jails were mentally ill. Sponsor Sen. Mike DeWine, R-Ohio, and others contended that a mental health court system would be a less expensive and more effective way to treat mentally ill inmates than incarceration.

The mental health courts would hear only cases alleging nonviolent offenses by mentally ill or retarded defendants. The courts would offer alternative sentencing, including life-skills programs. DeWine's staff said about twelve states, including Ohio, operated similar programs that helped the mentally ill while saving money and easing jail overcrowding.

The Senate Judiciary Committee approved the bill by voice vote on July 27. The Senate passed it by unanimous consent on Sept. 26, and the House cleared it by voice vote on Oct. 24. The president signed the bill on Nov. 13.

Missing Adults

Lawmakers in 2000 cleared legislation to authorize $1 million annual grants to help law enforcement find missing adults. The bill (HR 2780—PL 106-468), known as Kristen's Act, was named after Kristen Modafferi, a college student from North Carolina who disappeared a few weeks after her eighteenth birthday.

Under the bill, grants went to public agencies or nonprofit organizations and could be used to maintain a national database to track missing adults who were in danger because of their age, diminished mental capacity, or the possibility of foul play. The grant money also could be used to help police maintain statistical information on adults reported as missing and provide information and referrals to families of missing adults.

The House passed the measure by voice vote Oct. 19. The Senate cleared it by unanimous consent on Oct. 26. Clinton signed the measure on Oct. 28.

National Center for Missing and Exploited Children

Lawmakers in 1999 cleared legislation (S 249—PL 106-71) to authorize $10 million a year for five years to help operate the National Center for Missing and Exploited Children.

Based in Arlington, Va., the center was a private, nonprofit corporation that ran a twenty-four-hour, toll-free hotline where callers could report information about missing children or receive help in locating them. It also ran a "CyberTipline" that allowed Web users to report online child exploitation, including material directed at minors and the transmission of electronic "kiddie porn," over the Internet.

The center, created in 1984, also trained law enforcement, juvenile justice and health care professionals in investigative techniques concerning child sexual exploitation and missing child cases.

Although the center was not a government entity, it raised private funds to match congressional appropriations and collected private in-kind support, such as technology donated by the computer industry that could age the photographs of long-term missing children.

S 249 also reauthorized the Runaway and Homeless Youth Act, which helped public and private nonprofit groups establish and operate local aid centers.

The Senate Judiciary Committee approved the measure on March 4, and the Senate passed it by unanimous consent April 19. The House passed an amended version May 25 by a vote of 414–1. The Senate cleared the bill Sept. 28 by unanimous consent. The president signed it on Oct. 12.

False IDs

Lawmakers in 2000 cleared legislation (S 2924—PL 106-578) that aimed to pull the plug on Web sites that sold tools for making false identification. Sponsor Susan Collins, R-Maine, said some Web sites offered templates and other tools that made it easy to create fake documents—from a driver's license to a diploma. The tools could be used to steal another person's identity or commit financial fraud.

"Anyone with a computer and a credit card can obtain, almost instantly, a seemingly genuine Social Security card printed with the name and number of their choosing," James G. Huse, Inspector General of the Social Security Administration, told a Senate panel in May.

S 2924 would broaden existing law to criminalize making, selling or distributing false documents or computer files or templates used to make them. Offering those products on the Internet also would be a crime. The bill would direct the attorney general and the secretary of the Treasury to establish a commission to crack down on false IDs.

The Senate Judiciary Committee gave voice vote approval to the measure on Sept. 28 without a written report. The Senate passed it by unanimous consent on Oct. 31. The House passed it with an amendment by voice vote on Dec. 15, and the Senate cleared it the same day. Clinton signed the bill on Dec. 28.

Forensics

Lawmakers in 2000 cleared legislation (S 3045—PL 106-561) that authorized the attorney general to make block grants to states to improve forensic science services provided by state and local crime labs. The bill authorized $512 million in grants over six years. Funds were directed to states and cities based in part on their population and on crime statistics.

The measure, sponsored by Jeff Sessions, R-Ala., was based on legislation (S 1196) sponsored by the late Sen. Paul Coverdell, R-Ga. The Senate passed the bill by unanimous consent Oct. 26. The House cleared it by voice vote Dec. 7. President Clinton signed it on Dec. 21.

Federal Protective Service

The House in 2000 passed legislation that would allow officers of the Federal Protective Service (FPS) to function as full-fledged police officers. The FPS was the law enforcement branch of the General Services Administration. It provided security for federal buildings run by the GSA. The bill (HR 809) would give FPS officers the right to carry firearms, conduct investigations, petition courts for arrest and search warrants, and coordinate activities with other law enforcement agencies. It also would allow FPS officers to use their expanded authority off federal property if other law enforcement officials agreed.

Under the measure, the pay for FPS officers would be boosted, putting it on par with other federal law enforcement agencies. Also, security guards hired under contract to protect federal buildings would undergo background checks. The measure would increase the maximum penalty for violations on federal property and mandate that the FPS be staffed with at least 730 full-time officers, up from 668.

The bill stemmed partially from a report on the 1995 bombing of the Alfred P. Murrah Federal Building in Oklahoma City in which 168 people were killed. The report identified weaknesses in security at federal buildings.

The bill won voice vote approval from the House Transportation Subcommittee on Economic Development, Public Buildings, Hazardous Materials and Pipeline Transportation Nov. 9, 1999. The Transportation Committee approved it by voice vote March 16, 2000 (H Rept 106-676, Pt. I).

The House passed it by voice vote June 27. The Senate did not vote on the measure.

Assisted Suicide

An effort to make the use of federally controlled drugs in physician-assisted suicide illegal failed in the 106th Congress when supporters could not muster enough support to overcome a filibuster in the Senate. *(1997–1998 action, p. 606)*

The House in 1999 passed a bill (HR 2260) that would bar doctors from helping patients kill themselves with prescription drugs but would permit them to prescribe controlled substances to alleviate pain. The Senate Judiciary Committee approved a slightly different version in April 2000. But Democrat Ron Wyden, Oregon's senior senator, vowed to filibuster the bill.

The bill was a top priority for Senate Assistant Majority Leader Don Nickles, R-Okla., and he won inclusion of the Senate version in the conference report on a year-end, catch-all tax bill (HR 2614). The tax bill conference report was adopted by the House on Oct. 26, but when it reached the Senate floor, Wyden began his threatened filibuster. In the end, GOP leaders decided to abandon the tax bill (which also faced a veto threat), and with it the assisted suicide measure.

BACKGROUND

The issue of assisted suicide drew the attention of policy-makers after Oregon voters in 1994 approved a referendum authorizing doctors to prescribe drugs to help terminally ill people end their lives. After a court challenge ended and the law took effect in 1997, the federal Drug Enforcement Administration (DEA) prohibited doctors from dispensing drugs for suicides, declaring that was not a "legitimate medical purpose." When Attorney General Janet Reno said she would not enforce the DEA ruling, the GOP drafted legislation designed to countermand her.

Nickles and House Judiciary Committee Chairman Henry Hyde, R-Ill., pushed legislation in the 105th Congress to deter doctors from assisting in suicides. But the plan faltered when medical professionals protested that the bill would also deter doctors from prescribing pain-relief medication for the terminally ill.

To overcome that opposition, their revamped legislation in the 106th Congress would make it legal for doctors to prescribe federally controlled substances to treat the pain and suffering of their dying patients, even if such drugs "increased the risk of death." The bill would also authorize an increase of $5 million for federal programs to promote "pal-liative care," or vigorous pain management for terminally ill patients.

The bill was technically an amendment to the 1970 law (PL 91-513) that regulated the use of narcotics. As such, opponents said, enactment would give DEA agents the job of deciding whether a doctor's intent in writing prescriptions was to hasten a patient's death or ease suffering.

The bill said the attorney general "shall give no force and effect" to any state law permitting assisted suicide or euthanasia. Opponents said that would in effect overturn the Oregon law, which allowed lethal prescriptions to be issued to the terminally ill after they consulted with physicians and if they administered the drugs themselves. The state said that 15 people took their lives with lethal medication last year.

Republicans said enacting the bill would help the dying by encouraging doctors to use aggressive pain treatment. The measure won the backing of two key groups that opposed the previous version, the American Medical Association (AMA) and the National Hospice Organization. The bill "strikes a fair balance of opposing assisted suicide while reaffirming physicians' ability to aggressively manage patients' pain and discomfort," the AMA said Sept. 14. But several state medical associations opposed various forms of the bill.

HOUSE COMMITTEE ACTION

The House Judiciary Subcommittee on the Constitution approved HR 2260 on July 20, 1999, by voice vote. After a long partisan markup that lasted for several days, the full committee approved the bill (H Rept 106-378) on Sept. 14 by a party-line vote of 16–8.

The measure would amend the 1970 Controlled Substances Act to clarify that the dispensing of strong pain-relieving drugs would be prohibited for physician-assisted suicide. But the bill also contained a universally backed proposal to promote palliative care and authorized $5 million for training programs that would focus on pain management and the laws on controlled substances.

Constitution Subcommittee Chairman Charles T. Canady, R-Fla., said the bill focused attention on the country's "underutilization of palliative care." The failure of states to expressly permit pain management that unintentionally may hasten death had generated a reluctance to aggressively manage pain, leaving people "suffering needlessly," Canady said. Some Democrats, however, argued that Congress should not be interfering with state laws.

An amendment that would strip the bill of its language affecting Oregon, offered by the subcommittee's ranking Democrat, Melvin Watt, N.C., failed by voice vote.

In the full committee, Democrats united in opposition to the bill, even as all the panel's Republicans rallied behind it. Democrats said the bill would disregard the wishes of the people of Oregon and undermine physicians' decisions to prescribe pain medication. Republicans countered that the bill had a purpose worthy of federal action. "It will help protect vulnerable people in this country from the misuse of controlled substances," Canady said.

The panel's ranking Democrat, John Conyers Jr. of Michigan, offered an amendment to require that a doctor's intent to kill a patient with drugs be established "beyond a reasonable doubt" for a criminal conviction and that "clear and convincing evidence" be shown in a civil proceeding. Republicans argued that because the bill did not create any new criminal liability for doctors, the amendment was not needed, and it was defeated 9–15 along party lines.

On a 10–16 party-line vote, Conyers was defeated when he offered an amendment to allow doctors to argue as an "affirmative defense" that they used controlled substances with the sole intent of alleviating pain. Republicans called the amendment "nonsensical" because the bill would allow doctors to use drugs to alleviate pain even if it increased the risk of death.

Sheila Jackson-Lee, D-Texas, proposed an amendment that would grandfather the Oregon assisted-suicide measure under the federal law. It was rejected, 9–14. "We come in with this Big Brother attitude that we should overcome the Oregon law," Jackson-Lee said. "I believe what we will do is increase suicide. . . . [Patients] will use their own means."

HOUSE FLOOR ACTION

On the House floor, opponents failed to win support for several amendments that would weaken the bill. An amendment that would exempt Oregon from the measure failed, 160–268. Lawmakers also voted 188–239 to reject a substitute measure that would be limited to the promotion of palliative care.

The public appeared to want doctors to have leeway to help their patients die. In a Gallup Poll in March, 61 percent said they support allowing doctors "to assist the patient to commit suicide."

Nevertheless, sponsors of HR 2260 said public sentiment must come second. "Facilitating the intentional killing of a human life is the opposite of healing," said Judiciary Committee Chairman Henry J. Hyde, R-Ill. "There is a sanctity of life that must be respected and defended."

Opponents, including some Republicans, complained that the bill's move to preempt state law undermined the GOP boast that it was the party of states' rights and the diminution of federal power. These opponents, led by the delegation from Oregon, took solace in the fact that the vote in the House suggested that support was not great enough to overcome a veto by President Clinton, even though the White House had not yet weighed in on the measure.

While the Justice Department "strongly opposes" doctor-assisted suicide, it said in a letter to the House Judiciary Committee on Oct. 19 that provisions in the bill that would have the effect of overturning Oregon's law were "heavy-handed" and "intrusive." "We were disappointed in the vote, and we will be working in the Senate to see what can be done," Attorney General Janet Reno told reporters Oct. 28.

The full House passed the measure Oct. 27 on a **key vote of 271–156 (R 200–20; D 71–135; I 0–1).** *(1999 key votes, p. 899)*

SENATE ACTION

After weeks of delay, the Senate Judiciary Committee on April 27, 2000, approved an amended version of HR 2260 on a largely party-line vote of 10–8. Although the measure was a top priority of Nickles, he was unable to advance it to the Senate floor because of determined opposition from Wyden.

The committee adopted by voice vote a substitute version of the bill written by chairman Orrin Hatch, R-Utah, in which he tried to alleviate the major concern of health care groups—that the bill would have a chilling effect on doctors prescribing pain relief for the terminally ill.

Hatch said the amended version would create a "safe haven" for doctors who prescribed drugs that unintentionally caused a patient's death when they were intended to relieve intense pain.

All committee Democrats except Joseph R. Biden Jr. of Delaware voted against the bill. All committee Republicans except Arlen Specter of Pennsylvania voted for it.

The bill would not strike down the Oregon law, but it would prohibit doctors from using controlled substances for assisted suicide, thus making it nearly impossible for Oregon doctors to assist in suicides in what they would call a humane fashion.

Hatch's substitute also would raise the bar for the attorney general to prove that a doctor had intended to aid in a suicide, requiring "clear and convincing" evidence rather than the lower "preponderance of the evidence" standard. Hatch said his substitute stated that a doctor could knowingly prescribe a dose of medication for pain that may lead to death, as long as the doctor's intent is not to kill the patient.

The bill would authorize unspecified grants to schools, hospices and other groups to provide training and education on pain management.

Wyden forced the committee to delay consideration of the bill for several weeks, and he vowed to prevent the Senate from passing it. "If nothing else, this vote should give the Senate leadership an unmistakable sign that walking all over Oregon will be no stroll in the park," he warned.

For the rest of 2000, Wyden and Nickles engaged in a series of battles over the measure. When Wyden kept it off the floor by putting a "hold" on it, Nickles retaliated with a hold on legislation (S 1608) cosponsored by Wyden that would provide federal payments to rural communities to make up for declining logging revenue from nearby national forests. That measure was vital to Oregon.

In September Wyden struck a deal with Nickles: he agreed to lift his hold on HR 2260 after the timber bill was considered on the floor. But Wyden said he still intended to filibuster the bill and force a cloture vote, tying up precious floor time at the end of session that Majority Leader Trent Lott, R-Miss., could not afford.

Nickles then tried to add an assisted suicide measure to a tax bill (HR 2614). But with congressional Democrats and the White House opposing the rider, and Wyden filibustering that bill as well, Nickles had to yield.

Religious Expression

Crafting a compromise on a delicate matter, lawmakers in 2000 cleared a narrowly tailored bill on religious expression that made it harder for local governments to enforce zoning or other land-use regulations against religious groups. The measure (S 2869—PL 106-274) also eased obstacles to prisoners in state-run institutions who wanted to practice their faith. *(1998 action, p. 611)*

Indicative of its bipartisan support, the bill was introduced by Senate Judiciary Committee Chairman Orrin G. Hatch, R-Utah, with veteran liberal Sen. Edward M. Kennedy, D-Mass., as a cosponsor.

BACKGROUND

The bill was an unexpectedly quick resolution to a thorny issue that could be traced back to a 1990 Supreme Court ruling in the case of *Employment Division v. Smith.* Justices agreed that local governments could pass laws that interfered with religious expression so long as that was not the statute's principal intent. A county, for instance, could ban wine at communion as part of an ordinance making the entire county dry.

That ruling so shocked lawmakers at both ends of the political spectrum that in 1993 Congress enacted the Religious Freedom Restoration Act (PL 103-141), which said local governments would need a compelling interest in limiting religious expression, even as part of a broader aim. *(Congress and the Nation Vol. IX, p. 709)*

Four years later, that law was struck down by the Supreme Court in *City of Boerne v. Flores.* In their decision, the justices agreed that Congress could not make such an edict to states.

S 2869 was far more limited than the 1993 law. It focused on land-use disputes such as zoning issues. Its central provisions required that when land use regulations imposed a significant burden on a religious institution, the government must show that its rules served a compelling state interest and were the least restrictive means of doing so. It also required that those institutionalized in a state facility be allowed to practice their faith, unless the government could show it had a compelling interest in blocking such activity.

The bill applied to any program or activity that receives federal money.

1999 LEGISLATIVE ACTION

Action on the issue began in the House in 1999, when the Judiciary Constitution Subcommittee gave voice vote approval May 26 to a bill (HR 1691) that would require state and local governments to meet a number of legal criteria before they could force individuals and organizations to comply with laws that might infringe on the practice of their religious beliefs. The Judiciary Committee approved the measure by voice vote June 23, and the House passed it, 306–118, July 15.

Bill sponsor and subcommittee chairman Charles T. Canady, R-Fla., said HR 1691 was constitutional because it applied only to activities with a clear federal jurisdiction, such as interstate commerce or the practices of local governmental entities that received federal funding.

Under the bill, local governments would be prohibited from "substantially burdening a person's religious exercise" unless they could prove a "compelling governmental interest" to do so. The measure specifically addressed the application of local land use ordinances, stipulating that religious institutions must be treated "in equal terms" with nonreligious institutions when being subjected to such rules.

Some Democrats raised concerns that the bill might give religious organizations license to subvert federal civil rights protections or inadvertently allow nonreligious corporations to avoid complying with certain laws.

New York Democrat Jerrold Nadler offered an amendment that would define exactly who would be allowed to raise a claim under the act, and exempt its application in discrimination cases. That proposal was rejected on a voice vote.

Also rejected by voice vote was an amendment by Melvin Watt, D-N.C., that would require only that the government make "fair and reasonable accommodation of the special requirements of persons acting pursuant to their religious beliefs." The Judiciary Committee approved HR 1691 (H Rept 106-219) by voice vote June 23.

Canady said the legislation was needed to remedy a "pervasive pattern of discrimination and abusive treatment suffered by religious individuals and organizations." He cited cases in which church renovations were blocked by local zoning boards and in which Roman Catholic prisoners were warned that what they said in the confessional could be reported to police.

Several Democrats expressed concern that the bill would be held unconstitutional because it singled out religious practices for special consideration, and at times, exemption from local laws. Also of concern to Democrats was how the bill would impact the enforcement of civil rights laws. "It wasn't long ago that religion was used to justify all kinds of abominable views like slavery and segregation," said Barney Frank, D-Mass.

The measure also drew opposition from the National League of Cities. It warned that the bill would establish "a class of landowners and business operators that are given the right to ignore . . . valid municipal regulation simply because they profess a religious belief."

Nadler offered an amendment to limit the bill's protections to single-family homeowners, the smallest businesses and organizations that met specific religious criteria, but it was defeated on a voice vote.

Several Judiciary Committee Democrats, concerned that the bill's reach would not go far enough to protect the civil rights of minorities, lobbied for a substitute amendment drafted by Nadler that would prevent a business or large property owner from using the expanded rights included in the bill to discriminate against the disabled, homosexuals, or any other minority under the guise of religious belief. It was rejected, 190–234.

2000 LEGISLATIVE ACTION

Lawmakers elected to scale back their approach after HR 1691 drew protests from a wide range of groups who argued that the bill could offer a religious expression shield to conduct ranging from discriminatory apartment leasing to child abuse. Instead, Hatch and Kennedy sponsored a more narrowly crafted measure, S 2869, that offered protection to religious groups only in land-use disputes such as zoning issues.

That change hastened its voyage through Congress. No committee marked up the bill, which was passed by the Senate by unanimous consent July 27 and cleared by the House by voice vote later the same day.

Because the bill was so narrowly focused, the Leadership Conference on Civil Rights, which had opposed previous versions, endorsed it—as did lawmakers across the political spectrum. "Our goal in passing this legislation is to reach a reasonable and constitutionally sound balance between respecting the compelling interests of government and protecting the ability of people to freely exercise their religion," Kennedy said in a statement issued the day the bill cleared.

Still, not everyone supported the effort, and it remained to be seen whether the courts would allow Congress to assert this authority. A coalition of state and local municipal groups opposed the measure, arguing it would essentially exempt religious organizations from critical local land regulation.

In one sense, S 2869 was an attempt by Congress to reassert its authority on constitutional rights. The bill would require that when land use regulations imposed a significant burden on a religious institution the government must show that its rules served a compelling state interest and were the least restrictive means of doing so.

The bill also would require all governments to allow those who were institutionalized in a state facility to practice their faith, unless the government could show it had a compelling interest in blocking such activity. That standard would apply to prisons, state hospitals, nursing homes, and similar institutions.

In addition to narrowing the bill's focus, drafters of the current measure aimed to get around the 1997 Supreme Court ruling by tying the new law's authority to federal purse strings. The bill would apply to any organization that received federal money, including the vast majority of state and local prisons that get federal construction and maintenance funds.

The bill also would apply when a conflict over religious practices was in any way linked to interstate commerce. Bill sponsors said that because construction materials were shipped between states, the measure would cover the construction or renovation of buildings owned by religious organizations.

Finally, the bill would apply when a government had formal or informal procedures by which it made individual assessments of the proposed use of property, a description that would fit most local zoning plans.

The Senate passed the bill by voice vote on July 27; the House cleared it later the same day; and President Clinton signed it on Sept. 22.

Fetal Rights

The House in 1999 passed a bill that for the first time would recognize the fetus as an entity distinct from the pregnant woman, although by a margin insufficient to override a veto threatened by President Clinton. The Senate did not vote on its own version of the measure.

BACKGROUND

The bill (HR 2436) would mark the first time in federal law that a fetus from the time of conception would be recognized as a person with rights separate and distinct from the woman carrying it. The bill would make it a separate crime to harm or kill "any member of the species homo sapiens, at any stage of development, who is carried in the womb" while committing a federal crime.

Sponsors described their proposal principally as a crime-fighting bill. But it was drafted with the help of antiabortion groups, which said they would welcome the codification of their belief that a fetus had distinct rights. Abortion rights groups said the bill would undermine the Supreme Court's 1973 ruling in *Roe v. Wade,* which legalized abortion after concluding "the unborn have never been recognized in the law as persons in the whole sense."

Although social conservative lawmakers had attempted in other ways to scale back the scope of legalized abortions, most notably by targeting an abortion procedure that opponents called "partial birth," they had failed to muster the votes needed to override threatened and actual presidential vetoes. HR 2436 represented a different tactic, in that it sought to bolster rights for the unborn instead of restricting abortions.

The bill would make it a separate federal crime to harm a fetus while committing any of 68 existing federal offenses or a crime under military law, regardless of whether the assailant knew the woman was pregnant or intended fetal harm. Doctors who performed consensual abortions would be exempt from prosecution, as would women whose actions harmed the fetuses they carry.

Because its provisions would apply only to federal crimes, the bill would cover attacks against pregnant women in national parks or on military bases, as well as against government workers. Because most states had some form of "fetal protection" statute, none of which had been struck down by the Supreme Court, sponsors said their bill could "exist in harmony" with the acceptance of abortion rights.

Abortion rights advocates strenuously disagreed. They said the existing state laws were limiting the reach of the constitutional right granted twenty-six years ago, and that the bill before the House would go much further. The National Abortion Federation cited a 1984 South Carolina statute that considered killing a fetus after viability as homicide, which the group says opened the door to a 1997 state law that allowed a pregnant woman to be punished for any behavior that could endanger her fetus.

Despite the exceptions in HR 2436 for abortions, most Democrats and prochoice lawmakers pounced on the bill as an insidious measure that would erode *Roe* abortion rights guarantees.

The Senate version of HR 2436 (S 1673) by Michael DeWine, R-Ohio, was the subject of Judiciary Committee hearings in 2000. But senators did not take a vote on the measure.

HOUSE ACTION

At the Judiciary Committee markup, bill sponsor Lindsey Graham, R-S.C., defended his highly contentious bill. Graham argued that "protecting the unborn is not a novel idea," and pointed to numerous state laws that penalized harm to an unborn child without violating *Roe v. Wade.* He said federal law was needed to ensure that criminals paid fully for both harm to mothers and harm to fetuses.

Committee chairman Henry Hyde, R-Ill., weighed in with his GOP colleagues, saying, "a pregnant woman is two special persons. She is carrying a tiny member of the human family. Those who deny that are in my humble opinion clinically primitive." Hyde went on to argue that numerous advances in science had proven that "it is not randomly multiplying cells, it is not a tumor, it is a human child."

Democrats countered that Hyde's statements further proved the bill's true intent was not to protect women but rather to make a political statement that attached "personhood" to a fetus. Zoe Lofgren, D-Calif., introduced an amendment that would establish sentencing enhancements instead of separate counts of murder in such instances. But it was defeated, 8–20. The House Judiciary Committee approved HR 2436 on a 14–11 vote (H Rept 106-332, Pt. I) on Sept. 14.

The debate on the potential effect of the bill on abortion rights was no less contentious in the full House. "Let's confess that we're taking another few little baby steps forward to eat away at the fundamental premises of *Roe v. Wade,*" said John Conyers Jr., Mich., ranking Democrat on the House Judiciary Committee. But supporters defended the measure as a way of defending "unborn victims" from violent acts, thus filling a loophole they said existed in federal law.

Many House Democrats, as well as the White House—which issued a veto threat on the bill—said that instead of focusing on the fetus, Congress should focus on protecting mothers by reauthorizing the Violence Against Women Act.

An amendment by Lofgren that would enhance sentences for a federal crime during which a fetus was harmed or killed but stopped short of creating a new federal crime against the fetus failed narrowly, 201–224. The proposal would stiffen sentences for federal crimes against pregnant women, calling for up to life imprisonment if a fetus was killed during the attack.

But bill supporters rejected the notion that an injured or killed fetus should be considered only an added burden to the harmed mother, rather than a victim in and of itself.

The House passed the bill Sept. 30 in a 254–172 vote. Despite House passage, supporters conceded they lacked the necessary 290 votes—or two-thirds of the House—to override a presidential veto. Abortion opponents instead turned their attention to two other bills: HR 1218, which would make it a crime to help a girl cross state lines for an abortion in order to evade her state's parental consent laws, and S 928, which would outlaw "partial-birth" abortion.

Independent Counsel Law

The independent counsel law lapsed June 30, 1999, when the more recent version (PL 103-270) expired without Congress taking any steps to reauthorize it. Attorney General Janet Reno then issued guidelines for how she would name special prosecutors to probe alleged executive branch malfeasance.

A grandfather clause in the law allowed the five independent counsels still in office to keep working. Advocates of independent counsels said they hope the current "cooling off" period would build support for reviving the debate. The law that expired in 1999 took effect in 1994, eighteen months after the previous version had lapsed. (*Congress and the Nation, Vol. IX, p. 705*)

BACKGROUND

Before there was an independent counsel law, executive branch scandals generally were addressed by special prosecutors hired from outside the Justice Department and given objectives by the attorney general. Until Watergate, the belief was that public pressure—exerted by Congress or through the media—guaranteed fairness. That belief dissipated quickly after the "Saturday Night Massacre," during which President Richard M. Nixon ordered the firing of Archibald Cox, the special prosecutor who was investigating the Watergate scandal.

That Nixon gained no lasting peace from that action—public outrage prompted him to pick Leon Jaworski to complete the job—was not seen by Congress as evidence that the system of reliance on public pressure had worked, but that it almost failed. In response, Congress passed the first independent counsel law in 1978.

The initial law, and the three subsequent reauthorizations, all were premised on the belief that an administration could not be trusted to investigate itself. So, to minimize Justice Department discretion, each law set a mechanism under which appointment of counsels was automatic under certain circumstances. The initial version of the law was used just twice, and the initial reauthorization (PL 97-409) occurred with minimal fanfare.

It was in the Reagan administration that the law began to attract serious opposition, as a string of officials—including three Cabinet secretaries—became targets with the help of vigorous public pressure applied by congressional Democrats. Despite growing controversy over the law, Reagan in 1987 signed a reauthorization at a time when the Iran-contra scandal was in full bloom.

Five years later, Republican resolve against the measure was strong enough to kill it. Had a reauthorization come to a vote, sponsors asserted, it would have passed. But Bob Dole, R-Kan. (1969–1996), then the Senate minority leader, bottled the measure up in the waning days of the 102nd Congress. When Clinton was elected the next month, Republican opposition soon began to fade.

What distinguished the mood of 1999 from that of 1992 was that, by then, both Democrats and Republicans had been bloodied by independent counsels. Until Clinton's election, the statute had been written mostly by Democratic Congresses and used mostly against Republican administrations, in a type of a political corollary to Mark Twain's adage that "nothing so needs reforming as other people's habits."

But during the Clinton administration the Democrats' handiwork was turned against them, culminating in a presidential impeachment that grew out of Independent Counsel Kenneth Starr's scrutiny of a sexual affair that had not even begun when he was named to investigate a completely different matter. *(Impeachment, p. 813)*

1999 DEBATE

In hearings in the aftermath of President Clinton's acquittal in his impeachment trial, most witnesses argued against reviving the law because they disagreed with its basic premise— that the independent counsel must be almost entirely free of oversight to avoid the possible conflicts of interest that gave rise to the position's creation after Watergate. The Justice Department and Kenneth W. Starr, the independent counsel who investigated the president, agreed that such a level of independence was unnecessary and created the potential for abuse.

Among those urging Congress to let the independent counsel law die was Reno, who had requested more independent counsels than any other attorney general. "We at the department have come to believe that the act's goals have not been well-served by the act itself—and that we could do better without a statute," she told the Senate Governmental Affairs Committee on March 17.

The statute had almost no support outside Congress. Groups that once championed it, such as Common Cause, had turned against it.

Nevertheless, some on Capitol Hill wanted to retain the law, albeit with major revisions. Senate Governmental Affairs Chairman Fred Thompson, R-Tenn., told Reno he was reluctant—given her decision not to appoint an independent counsel to investigate the financing of President Clinton's 1996 reelection campaign—to leave the decision on how to investigate high officials entirely to her, or to her successors. "When the attorney general says, 'Give me even more discretion' . . . that causes me some concern," Thompson said.

Four senators offered a bill (S 1297) that would retain the expired law's procedure by which federal judges name independent counsels at the attorney general's request, although with tight new restrictions: The counsels could not expand their jurisdiction beyond their original scope, would generally have two years to finish their inquiries and would need to hew to federal prosecutorial procedures. Another bill (S 1427) would allow the Justice Department to appoint a special counsel only with congressional approval.

One House bill (HR 117) would limit the scope of independent counsel probes and subject them to more congressional financial oversight. Another (HR 2083) would reaffirm the attorney general's power to name special counsels.

A bipartisan commission recommended May 18 that the independent counsel law should be replaced by enhanced procedures allowing the attorney general to name special prosecutors to investigate allegations of criminal activity by top government officials. The panel, convened by the Brookings Institution and the American Enterprise Institute, was chaired by the two previous Senate majority leaders: Dole, who opposed the current law, and George J. Mitchell, D-Maine (1980–1995), who supported it.

The panel concluded that Congress should enact legislation requiring the attorney general to set rules on the conduct of special prosecutors, whose jurisdictions should be clearly defined at the outset of each inquiry. Prosecutors should be named when a Justice Department inquiry would pose a conflict of interest, the panel said, and after two years and each year after that, the attorney general should be required to decide if the prosecutors' work should be terminated.

But instead of revamping the law, Congress ultimately took no action to stop it from expiring. As a result, the Justice Department unveiled a plan, backed by Thompson, to return the power to investigate high-ranking officials to special prosecutors appointed by the attorney general.

Secret Evidence

The House Judiciary Committee in 2000 approved a bipartisan measure that would make it harder for the Immigration and Naturalization Service (INS) to use secret evidence to deport immigrants or to deny them asylum. But lawmakers took no further action on the bill.

With terrorist threats on the rise, the INS had joined other agencies in efforts to locate and deport potential terrorists in the country. Under existing law, the INS could use undisclosed, classified evidence to deport immigrants suspected of being terrorists or deny them benefits, permanent residency, or citizenship. That included evidence from undercover or other sources that agents felt would be dangerous to release.

But Judiciary Committee members on both sides of the aisle argued that withholding evidence from immigrants was fundamentally unfair. The panel approved an amended version of the bill (HR 2121—H Rept 106-981) by voice vote on Sept. 26.

The original bill, by Democratic whip David Bonior of Michigan, would prohibit the INS from using secret evidence against immigrants. The panel on Sept. 26 voted 26–2 to approve a bipartisan substitute that would submit the evidence to a district judge for review. The judge could delete all or some of the evidence, reporting whatever evidence remained to the immigrant facing INS action and to the immigration judge handling the case.

Anthony Weiner, D-N.Y., warned that the bill would allow more terrorists to get into and remain in the country. "While we may be troubled by a few cases, let's not lose sight of the many cases where we have prevented someone from coming here as a terrorist," he said. Weiner and Asa Hutchinson, R-Ark., voted against the substitute.

Italian Americans

Lawmakers in 2000 overwhelmingly cleared legislation (HR 2442—PL 106-451) that for the first time recognized the restrictions placed on Americans of Italian origin during World War II. The bill gave the Justice Department one year to study and report to Congress on the treatment received by Italian Americans during the war.

According to bill sponsor Rick Lazio, R-N.Y., more than 10,000 families were forced from their homes and another 52,000 were subjected to strict curfews. The treatment of Italian Americans during the war was less familiar to most Americans, he said, than U.S. actions against those of Japanese ancestry.

The bill expressed the sense of Congress that the story should be told and called on the president to acknowledge the government's role in restricting the rights of Italian-Americans.

The House passed HR 2442 by voice vote on Nov. 10, 1999. The Senate Judiciary Committee approved a slightly amended version by voice vote on Sept. 28, 2000, without a written report. The Senate passed it by unanimous consent on Oct. 19, although Sen. Russell Feingold said he would have preferred that the bill also recognize the mistreatment of other Americans during World War II, including those of German descent and refugees who had fled Europe.

The House cleared the amended version of HR 2442 by voice vote Oct. 24. President Clinton signed it into law on Nov. 7.

Asbestos Compensation

A hotly contested bill that would federalize the compensation process for people exposed to asbestos was narrowly approved by the House Judiciary Committee in 2000. But lawmakers took no further action on it or on a companion Senate bill (S 758).

With billions of settlement dollars at stake, neither side in the asbestos fight pulled punches during two weeks of Judiciary Committee consideration in March. Bill supporters, led by chairman Henry J. Hyde, R-Ill., argued that trial lawyers were flooding the courts with claims for people who were not really sick, making it harder for those who had become ill from asbestos to get compensation. Opponents of the bill called it a gift to asbestos companies, which spent millions lobbying for its passage.

The bill (HR 1283), sponsored by Hyde, would federalize thousands of asbestos lawsuits filed against manufacturers and builders during the preceding thirty years. It would require anyone who sought compensation from an asbestos company to first obtain a certificate from a new federal agency verifying that they suffered from one of a specific set of illnesses outlined in the bill.

The issue took on political overtones after a series of articles in the *Seattle Post-Intelligencer* detailed the suffering of people in the small mining town of Libby, Mont., population 2,700, where at least 192 people had died of asbestos-related illnesses and some 375 were sick. Sen. Conrad Burns, R-Mont., a cosponsor of the Senate bill, dropped his support after the Libby exposé. Despite the Judiciary Committee approval, House GOP leaders chose not to bring the bill to the floor and force their members to cast what could have been politically dangerous votes.

BACKGROUND

Asbestos was a fibrous mineral that had been used in insulation and other products for nearly a century. It was a popular choice in shipyards, buildings, and mines because it was nearly indestructible. But that virtue made asbestos a killer. The fibers, once inhaled, lodged in the lungs and scarred them, leading to several severe illnesses.

The most virulent was malignant mesothelioma, a cancer of the lining of the lung or abdomen. Doctors said almost all cases of the disease were caused by asbestos. Rep. Bruce F. Vento, D-Minn., announced Feb. 2 that he was retiring from Congress at the end of the session because he was suffering from the disease.

The fibers also caused asbestosis, a severe scarring of the lungs, and were suspects in diseases such as lung cancer and cancer of the larynx and stomach. About 9,600 people had died from asbestosis since 1986.

Millions of workers had been exposed to asbestos over the years, resulting in decades of litigation with more to come: it could take up to forty years for an illness to appear. There had been about 300,000 settlements, with 200,000 cases pending, industry officials said at a hearing in 1999. Trial lawyers said both figures were too low.

A key dispute between the lawyers and the companies revolved around people who had been exposed to asbestos and showed signs of lung damage but had not yet developed any impairment. Lawyers argued that the impairment was a sign of impending disease and that victims had to sue to avoid statutes of limitations and to get restitution while the companies could still pay.

Asbestos companies and bill sponsors said that by winning awards for people who were not yet sick, lawyers were taking money away from those already suffering. They added that many people exposed to asbestos never developed a serious ailment.

Despite the acrimony, the two sides nearly reached a deal in 1997. Some asbestos companies established a fund of more than $1 billion to pay claimants and settle thousands of lawsuits. But in 1997 the Supreme Court, in *Amchem Products Inc. v. Windsor,* threw out the settlement on a technicality. In that case and in a 1999 case, *Ortiz v. Fibreboard,* the Court called on Congress to craft a national solution. The "elephantine mass of asbestos cases . . . defies customary judicial administration and calls for national legislation," Associate Justice David H. Souter wrote for the majority.

After the Amchem settlement fell apart, the industry looked to Washington for help. GAF Corp., based in Wayne, N.J., and other major asbestos companies spent millions of dollars lobbying Congress. At first, the campaign seemed to work. Hyde got seventy-seven cosponsors, including House Majority Leader Dick Armey, R-Texas, and Majority Whip Tom DeLay, R-Texas, and a companion bill by Sen. John Ashcroft, R-Mo., won the support of Senate Majority Leader Trent Lott, R-Miss., and Majority Whip Don Nickles, R-Okla., as well as several influential Democrats.

But wrenching stories in the *Seattle Post-Intelligencer,* beginning in late 1999, appeared to push the bill off the fast track. The stories detailed suffering in Libby, Mont., a small town of 2,700 in the northwest corner of the state, where hundreds of people had died or were sick. It turned out that as part of operations at a mine three miles east of town, workers had dug up tremolite asbestos, a particularly hazardous form of the mineral. The mine closed in 1990, but with the potential forty-year latency period, the people of Libby could feel repercussions in 2030.

HOUSE COMMITTEE ACTION

Hyde's original bill, introduced in 1999, met with strong opposition from trial lawyers, labor unions, and consumer groups, who argued that it cut the risk for asbestos companies while making it more difficult for asbestos victims to make their case. On Feb. 14, 2000, Hyde brought before the House Judiciary Committee a substitute, which supporters said answered many of those criticisms. The bill included major changes but did not win over its critics.

The revised bill would create a large government clearinghouse, the Office of Asbestos Compensation, within the Justice Department. Its leader would be appointed by the president for a ten-year term, subject to Senate confirmation.

The office would be a required stop for anyone seeking restitution for an asbestos-related ailment. It would issue a certificate to claimants who proved they had an ailment, verifying that the person was suffering from specific diseases related to asbestos exposure. Claimants could not proceed without the certificate.

The revised bill included specific medical criteria for granting a certificate, and it would limit claims by those not yet impaired to reimbursement of up to 80 percent for testing.

Once they got a certificate, claimants could choose between filing a lawsuit in state or federal court, or going through a settlement process created under the bill.

The bill would set deadlines that seek to speed up the process. It also addressed a concern of many asbestos victims: it would prohibit any state's statute of limitations from applying to asbestos-related diseases, because of the long latency period. It also would retain joint and several liability for asbestos companies, the legal doctrine that held that all defendants in a suit were liable for all damages awarded.

The legislation set off a contentious debate stretching over two weeks. Bill supporters—mostly asbestos companies—argued that people who had become sick from exposure to asbestos were being held hostage by trial lawyers who improperly solicited cases and filed fraudulent claims. But the AFL-CIO and the Association of Trial Lawyers of America worked overtime to defeat the measure, which they said would protect large, unscrupulous companies while taking away the legal rights of many victims.

The congressional debate broke down largely along party lines, with Republicans supporting efforts to consolidate asbestos litigation and most Democrats opposed. Democrats were confident that President Clinton would react as he had to other attempts to rewrite civil litigation laws—with a veto threat.

To pick up support, Hyde began working with Judiciary Committee Democrat Barney Frank, Mass., in a bid to strike a compromise that could sway some Democrats. A deeply divided Judiciary Committee approved a substitute version of HR 1283 (H Rept 106-782) on March 16 by a vote of 18–15.

As approved by the committee, the bill would require people who claimed they were harmed by exposure to asbestos to obtain a certificate from a new federal agency, the Office of Asbestos Compensation, proving that they were impaired.

Without the certificate, which would be given only to those who met strict medical criteria specified in the bill, claimants could not recover damages from asbestos companies. Those who obtained certificates could choose to pursue their case in state or federal court or through a federally negotiated settlement process.

COMMITTEE AMENDMENTS

Democrats initially threatened to bog down the markup by offering as many as 100 amendments, but they changed tactics and settled for offering amendments to the provisions they found most troubling. The committee considered thirteen amendments and approved four.

Although the final vote for the bill was 18–15, the true margin was one vote. At the last minute, when the tally was 17–16, Robert C. Scott, D-Va., changed his vote to "yea" as a parliamentary maneuver aimed at forcing a second vote on the bill. Weiner and Maxine Waters, D-Calif., were absent at the time, and Democrats hoped if they could delay the proceedings long enough for one of them to get to the markup, they could defeat the bill.

But Republicans rallied and tabled, or killed, Scott's motion for a second vote, 17–16.

During the markup, the committee rejected a series of amendments offered by Democrats that would strip the bill's medical provisions, delay its effective date, and make the new procedures voluntary.

The medical criteria provoked the strongest debate. Members agreed by voice vote to an amendment by Hyde, Scott, and ranking Democrat John Conyers Jr. of Michigan that would make it clear that race would play no part in the medical evaluation.

In a markup session March 9, Conyers had said the bill referred to medical studies saying that African Americans have lower lung capacity than whites, something Conyers said could make it harder for blacks to prove they were hurt by asbestos.

But agreement ended when the discussion turned to the section of the bill on medical qualifications. The legislation includes more than five pages of detailed medical provisions and definitions to be used to determine whether someone is eligible for compensation.

For example, the bill said someone "whose chest X-ray shows either small irregular opacities of ILO Grade 1/0 or bilateral pleural thickening of ILO Grade b/2" would be eligible to be reimbursed for medical tests.

Members defeated, 10–10, an amendment by Scott that sought to delete the medical standards and leave the determination of those standards to the attorney general and the National Institute for Occupational Safety and Health, a division of the Centers for Disease Control and Prevention.

"I am not trained to do this kind of assessment," said Melvin Watt, D-N.C., noting that one group told him the provisions were fair and another said they were not. "I have, as a member of Congress, not one iota of ability to tell me which group is telling me the truth."

Hyde said the medical criteria were drawn from a large-scale settlement in Louisiana and were the "most favorable known criteria for asbestos victims." He said Congress had a responsibility to set up a fair system, including medical criteria.

The committee also rejected, 12–17, an amendment by Scott that sought to delay the bill's effective date until the new asbestos office was up and running with appropriated funds; rejected, 11–18, an amendment by Conyers that would make the new process voluntary; and approved by voice vote an amendment by Weiner that aimed to ensure taxpayers were not left paying for the claims of asbestos victims.

The original bill would have allowed the administrator for the compensation program to collect funds from asbestos companies to pay for the program's administrative costs.

Weiner's amendment would broaden that authority to allow the administrator to devise a plan to obtain payment for all costs from the asbestos companies. His amendment clarified that the administrator would have the authority to take the companies to federal court to get the money.

The committee first adopted, then rejected, an amendment by Ed Pease, R-Ind., to allow states to pass legislation to exempt claims within a state from the federal process. The committee initially voted 15–14 for the amendment, which Hyde said would "gut" the bill. Then Christopher B. Cannon, R-Utah, switched his vote and the amendment was defeated, 14–15.

The committee approved by voice vote an amendment by Asa Hutchinson, R-Ark., that would protect existing large settlements from the new process. In recent years there had been several large-scale settlements between asbestos companies and plaintiffs, including payouts over several years.

Throughout the debate, bill supporters, including Hyde and a coalition of asbestos companies, argued that thousands of pending asbestos lawsuits were overwhelming the courts. They also said that awards were going to people who had been exposed to asbestos but were not yet sick, which could take money away from those who are ill now. "You've got to get the people who have been impaired to the front of the line," Hyde said. "We cannot allow the system to remain clogged."

The mostly Democratic opponents responded that the bill would provide unwarranted protection to companies that manufactured or distributed asbestos, many of which knowingly exposed workers to the deadly substance. They also said the bill would exclude from compensation thousands of people who have been hurt by asbestos. "These companies face enormous liability because they ought to," said Anthony Weiner, D-N.Y., whose grandfather suffered from asbestos-related diseases after working in the Brooklyn Naval Yard. "They've done harm to people."

Two Republicans—Joe Scarborough of Florida and Lindsey Graham of South Carolina—voted against the bill. Scarborough said he "didn't think it was an especially bright bill for the Republicans to support."

Flag Desecration

Supporters of a constitutional amendment that would give Congress the authority to ban desecration of the American flag again failed to muster the required support. The House passed the measure in 1999, but the Senate in 2000 fell four votes short of the required two-thirds majority.

Congress has been debating the antidesecration issue for a decade, since the Supreme Court ruled in 1989 that flag burning was a form of political expression protected by the First Amendment. "It seems difficult to believe that protection of our flag—with its deep historical roots—somehow violated the Constitution all along. I sincerely doubt that the framers intended the First Amendment of the Constitution to prevent Congress from protecting the flag of the nation for which they shed their blood," said amendment supporter Sen. John Ashcroft, R-Mo.

But critics of the resolution disagreed. Sen. Russell D. Feingold, D-Wis., contended that the amendment "will abridge the most precious and most important freedom that our country stands for—the freedom of speech," as well as "create one more source of division."

In a report prepared for Sen. John H. Chafee, R-R.I., the Congressional Research Service found forty-three reported incidents of flag desecration in the United States from 1995 through 1998—not only protest burnings but also acts of vandalism, disorderly conduct by drunken teenagers, and the case of a boy who used a flag to wipe oil from his car's dipstick.

Presidents played no formal role in amending the Constitution, but President Clinton reiterated his opposition to the flag proposal. "Efforts to limit the First Amendment to make a narrow exception for flag desecration are misguided," presidential spokesperson Joe Lockhart said after the House vote.

The 1999 House passage marked the third time that House members rallied behind such an amendment. But the high-water mark in the Senate was in 1995, a 63–33 tally that left the proposal four votes short of being sent to the states for ratification. (Congress and the Nation Vol. IX, p. 754)

In the 105th Congress, the Senate never took up the issue.

HOUSE ACTION

By a 7–4 party-line vote, the House Judiciary Subcommittee on the Constitution, on April 14, 1999, approved a resolution (H J Res 33) that would propose a constitutional amendment to allow Congress to prohibit desecration of the American flag. The Judiciary Committee gave voice vote approval to the measure May 26 (H Rept 106-191), and the House overwhelmingly passed it June 24, 305–124—19 votes more than the two-thirds majority required to advance a constitutional change.

The Judiciary Committee debate highlighted the ideological divide on whether the flag should be singled out for the permanent and weighty protection promised by a constitutional amendment. Supporters of the plan, including most Republicans and some Democrats, contended the flag was synonymous with the nation itself and therefore its destruction would be, in effect, an act against the state. But opponents raised concerns that any prohibition against flag desecration would violate the free speech protections afforded by the First Amendment.

"Through this amendment you are elevating a symbol of freedom over freedom itself," said the panel's top Democrat, John Conyers Jr., Mich., who argued the strength of a democracy was evident in how well it tolerated the dissemination of unpopular ideas.

Melvin Watt, D-N.C., echoed these concerns and offered an amendment that would add language specifying the reso-

lution should be "not inconsistent" with the First Amendment. The panel rejected that proposal on a 7–17 vote.

The 305 votes for the measure on the House floor represented a slight retreat from earlier votes. Similar measures had garnered 310 votes in 1997, and 312 votes two years before that.

Lawmakers tried to shed the fierce partisan pall that had hung over past flag burning debates, as Republicans took the rare step of allowing Democrats to offer a substitute proposal. That amendment, by Watt, would allow the freedom of speech guarantees in the First Amendment to supercede the flag desecration ban. It was defeated, 115–310.

Amendment opponents cited a 1989 Supreme Court ruling in Texas v. Johnson, which found that flag burning was an act of expression protected by the First Amendment. Gary L. Ackerman, D-N.Y., appeared on the House floor wearing an American flag tie and argued against the measure. "Even a despicable low-life malcontent has the right to disagree, and he has the right to disagree in an obnoxious fashion," he said. "Real patriots choose freedom over symbolism."

Many Republicans said the flag held special meaning to the country and its citizens. Flag burning "is a form of expression, like obscenity, that is not protected by the First Amendment," said Charles T. Canady, R-Fla., chairman of the House Judiciary Subcommittee on the Constitution. Canady said forty-nine states—all but Vermont—had passed resolutions calling for Congress to approve a flag protection amendment.

SENATE ACTION

The Senate Judiciary Subcommittee on the Constitution, Federalism and Property approved legislation (S J Res 14) by a party-line vote of 5–3 that proposed a constitutional amendment granting Congress the power to prohibit desecration of the flag of the United States. The measure, approved April 21, 1999, was identical to H J Res 33.

The Senate Judiciary Committee approved the measure, 11–7, on April 29 (S Rept 106-246). After a yearlong interlude during which supporters trolled unsuccessfully for more votes, the Senate defeated the measure, 63–37, on March 29, 2000. "The flag is, in effect, a monument," said Dianne Feinstein, D-Calif., the only committee Democrat who supported the measure. "We're not talking about free speech, we're talking about conduct."

But ranking committee Democrat Patrick J. Leahy of Vermont said the one-sentence amendment—"The Congress shall have power to prohibit the physical desecration of the flag of the United States"—would be the "first-ever cutback on American civil liberties" enshrined in the Constitution.

Vote counts after the markup suggested that S J Res 14 had sixty-five Senate supporters, two short of the two-thirds majority required for passage.

Supporters hoped to win votes from North Dakota Democrats Kent Conrad and Byron L. Dorgan, who both voted "no" on the last Senate ballot in 1995. The Citizens' Flag Alliance Inc., a coalition supported by the American Legion, organized a campaign of newspaper and television advertising in North Dakota, featuring the entertainers Pat Boone and Wayne Newton, designed to press those senators into voting for the amendment after all.

Conrad and Dorgan both said earlier in the year that they were reconsidering their past opposition to the amendment. But they announced April 30 that instead of voting for the amendment this year they would promote a bill (S 931) to outlaw some flag desecration because they believed it could withstand constitutional scrutiny.

Supporters lost more ground in March 2000, when Sen. Robert C. Byrd, D-W.Va., announced that he had decided to oppose S J Res 14. In 1995, the last time the Senate took up the measure, Byrd voted for the proposed amendment to the Constitution.

Byrd said he was concerned that the proposed amendment could infringe on the constitutional guarantee of free speech. "The flag symbolizes the nation. The flag symbolizes its history. The flag is a symbol we all love," he said. "But the Constitution is far more. The Constitution is not a symbol. It is a thing itself and must be protected."

Despite certain defeat, GOP leaders elected to take up the resolution during the week of March 27, 2000. Floor debate centered on whether burning or defacing a flag should be considered a crime or a form of protected speech.

Before the final vote March 29, senators rejected 36–64 a legislative alternative to the flag amendment. Offered by Mitch McConnell, R-Ky., it would make it a crime to steal or destroy a U.S. flag.

The Senate also rejected an amendment by Ernest F. Hollings, D-S.C., to give Congress the power to regulate campaign finance spending. Senators voted 67–33 on a motion to table, or kill, the Hollings amendment.

Hollings had hoped to take the steam out of campaign finance overhaul opponents who said laws restricting donations to candidates infringe on the First Amendment because the allocation of money amounts to political speech. He questioned the sincerity of lawmakers who vote for campaign finance overhaul but were unwilling to back his measure.

On the final, 63–37 vote, a dozen Senate Democrats supported the amendment, and four Republicans voted against it. Supporters lost the backing of Byrd and Richard H. Bryan, D-Nev.

The March 29 vote ended the effort to pass the amendment in the 106th Congress, but supporters said the issue would not go away. "This is going to pass. Whether it does today or tomorrow or next year, it's going to pass," said Judiciary Committee Chairman Orrin G. Hatch, R-Utah, sponsor of S J Res 14.

Victims' Rights

The Senate in 2000 shelved a proposed constitutional amendment that would guarantee nine specific rights to crime victims. The House version of the amendment never made it out of subcommittee. *(1998 action, p. 609)*

The provisions, identical in both the House and Senate resolutions (S J Res 3, H J Res 64), included among other guarantees the right of crime victims to attend, speak at, and be notified of important proceedings during the trial of the accused. The Senate debate on April 25 to 27 represented the furthest that sponsors Jon Kyl, R-Ariz., and Dianne Feinstein, D-Calif., had been able to advance their proposed constitutional amendment since they began their joint effort in 1996.

Their inability to garner the two-thirds majority required to approve such an amendment was due primarily to members' wariness of altering the Constitution and concern about vagueness in some of the proposed language.

According to the Senate Judiciary Committee, thirty-two states had adopted some version of a victims' rights amendment to their constitutions. Dozens of groups lobbied for the constitutional amendment, including Mothers Against Drunk Driving, the National Governors' Association, and the National Center for Missing and Exploited Children.

But the amendment also picked up some high-profile detractors, such as conservative columnist George Will. The Judicial Conference, the administrative organ of the federal judicial system, also opposed the amendment and urged Congress to pass a statute instead.

1999 LEGISLATIVE ACTION

The Senate Judiciary Constitution Subcommittee approved S J Res 3 by a 4–3 party-line vote on May 26, 1999. The full committee approved it, 12–6, on Sept. 30.

The measure would establish the right of victims to be notified of, and participate in, public hearings related to the trial, parole, or escape of their attackers. It also would stipulate that the trial of the accused be free from unreasonable delay, and the safety of the victim be considered when the offender is released from custody. However, state legislatures could create certain exceptions to these rights if they found a "compelling interest" to do so.

By a vote of 7–0, panel members adopted an amendment to the resolution offered by chairman John Ashcroft, R-Mo., that would give victims the additional right to be notified of, and participate in, pardons or commutations of their attackers' sentences.

Panel Democrats objected to the resolution, instead favoring a statutory approach to addressing victims' rights. Ranking Democrat Russell D. Feingold, Wis., called the resolution a "blunt instrument" that would needlessly alter the Constitution over an issue that states already were able to address. But Ashcroft said such statutory rights were "of little help when they conflict with the constitutional rights of the accused."

The panel also defeated, 3–4, a Feingold amendment that would add language to ensure that nothing in the measure would interfere with the constitutional rights of the accused. A similar amendment by Feingold was defeated in the full committee, 5–11.

Complicating the outlook for the legislation, the previously supportive Justice Department reversed its position because of a provision in the Ashcroft amendment that would give crime victims the right to be notified of any state or federal grant of clemency. The provision touched on a matter that polarized Congress in the late summer: President Clinton's offer of clemency to sixteen Puerto Rican independence activists and his claim of executive privilege in declining to detail his rationale. Ashcroft added the language before the Puerto Rico imbroglio began.

Although Clinton did not have veto power over a constitutional amendment (which required the support of two-thirds of each congressional chamber and ratification by three-quarters of state legislatures), his wishes could sway Democrats.

2000 LEGISLATIVE ACTION

The Senate invoked cloture on a motion to proceed to the proposal, 82–12, on April 25, 2000. But the unwieldy and frequently changing nature of S J Res 3, combined with members' general reluctance to amend the Constitution, left supporters far short of the two-thirds majority needed for approval of such an amendment. As a result, supporters pulled the plug on the measure April 27. Many Democrats and some Republicans said they would rather protect victims through passage of a law, turning to a constitutional amendment only if the law proved inadequate.

The process on the Senate floor also made many members uncomfortable. Kyl said his proposal had gone through sixty-three drafts in four years and that negotiations with the White House were ongoing. "The fact that so many changes were made over the years indicates to me that the subject matter would be better dealt with by legislation than by a federal constitutional amendment," said Robert C. Byrd, D-W. Va.

Adding to that problem was what critics said was the bulky nature of the proposal—composing more than two pages of text, compared with the leaner, less specific language of other constitutional amendments.

The nine specific rights for victims of violent crimes that would be added to the Constitution under the Senate resolution were the following:
- To be notified of proceedings in the case.
- To attend important proceedings, such as a trial or plea bargain.
- To be heard at five points in the process: at plea bargain, bail or release hearings, sentencing, parole hearings, and pardon or commutation decisions.
- To be notified of a proposed pardon and to be heard on the proposal.
- To be notified of escape or release.
- To be considered in decisions regarding delay of trial.
- To be allowed to recover restitution for the crime.
- To have their safety considered.
- To be notified of these rights.

Kyl announced April 27 that resolution sponsors had decided to pull the measure without an up-or-down vote. "We recognize that to proceed would result in a vote that would

not be successful," he said. But he added: "That merely means a timeout in our efforts to secure passage of this constitutional amendment." The House Judiciary Constitution Subcommittee held hearings Feb. 10 on its version (H J Res 64) but took no further action.

Federal Court System

Lawmakers in 2000 cleared a bill (S 2915—PL 106-518) that made mostly minor housekeeping changes to the federal court system, which were requested by the U.S. Judicial Conference. A broader bill (HR 1752) that the House passed died in the Senate.

S 2915 expanded the authority of U.S. magistrate judges by allowing them to issue contempt of court orders. It also increased the amount of money public defenders could spend before asking a judge to approve funds. The change was designed to give judges more time to spend on other issues.

The Senate Judiciary Committee approved the bill without a written report on Sept. 28, and the Senate passed it on Oct. 19 by unanimous consent. The House passed it with amendments by voice vote on Oct. 25, and the Senate cleared it on Oct. 27. President Clinton signed in on Nov. 13.

The broader House bill would allow federal judges to carry concealed weapons in any state, regardless of that state's laws. It also would allow television cameras in federal courtrooms. The House Judiciary Courts and Intellectual Property Subcommittee approved HR 1752 by voice vote on July 15, 1999, and the full committee approved it by voice vote on July 27 (H Rept 106-312). The House passed it by voice vote on May 22, 2000.

Transferee Courts

The House and Senate in 1999 passed separate versions of a bill (HR 2112) that would overturn a 1998 Supreme Court decision and allow continued operations of "transferee courts" that supporters credited with improving the responsiveness and efficiency of federal courts.

Transferee courts helped consolidate lawsuits that shared common questions of fact that were filed in more than one federal judicial district. Typically, the panels handled cases stemming from plane crashes, train wrecks, or other cases in which the plaintiffs came from many different states.

Originally, panels would adjudicate pretrial matters before sending the cases back to the districts in which they were originally filed for trial. More recently, however, transferee courts managed to retain jurisdiction over many of the cases by invoking a general rule permitting district courts to transfer a civil action to any other district or division where it may have been brought. Essentially, a transferee court assigned itself the case.

Supporters, including the Administrative Office of the U.S. Court System, said the system worked well because the transferee court usually was versed in the facts and law of consolidated litigation and was the one court that could compel all parties to settle when appropriate. But in a 1998 decision, known as the *Lexecon* case, the Supreme Court ruled that current law explicitly requires that the transferee court remand all cases for trial back to the district in which they were filed.

The House Judiciary Courts and Intellectual Property Subcommittee approved HR 2112 by voice vote July 15, and the full committee gave voice vote approval to the measure July 27 (H Rept 106-276). The House on Sept. 13 passed the measure by voice vote.

The Senate passed HR 2112 by unanimous consent Oct. 27 after substituting the text of its similar bill (S 1748). Lawmakers from the two chambers failed to reconcile the differences.

H-1B Visas

After an intense push from the business community, Congress in 2000 agreed to dramatically increase the number of nonimmigrant visas available for highly skilled workers. The measure (S 2045—PL 106-313) authorized 195,000 H-1B visas each year for fiscal years 2001, 2002, and 2003. Congress also cleared a second, smaller bill (HR 5362—PL 106-311) to raise the fee paid by businesses for such visas to $1,000. (*Visas, p. 672*)

BACKGROUND

Getting Congress to increase the number of H-1B visas was one of the high-tech community's top priorities for the year. Many of the top math, science, and computer graduates recruited out of college by high-tech companies were foreign nationals, but federal immigration policy limited the pool of potential employees.

Under a 1998 law (PL 105-277), H-1B visas had increased from 65,000 annually to 115,000 in fiscal 2000. But the level was slated to drop back to 107,500 in fiscal 2001 and 65,000 after that. Moreover, heavy demand for tech workers in the roaring economy had consumed the 2000 allotment of H-1B visas by March. (*1998 action, p. 616*)

The visas allowed individuals to come to the United States for three years and could be renewed once, for an additional three years. The H-1B was the only nonimmigrant visa that allowed an alien to apply for permanent residency.

Action began early in the year, with a bipartisan group of senators in February introducing an industry-backed measure that would raise the cap on the number of temporary visas to 195,000. The bill also would potentially free up an additional 20,000 H-1B visas by exempting from the caps foreigners who were employed by U.S. universities or research organizations, or those who earned a graduate-level degree from a U.S. university in the prior six months. These people still would be included in the H-1B visa program and subject to the six-year limitation, but they would not be counted in the caps.

Judiciary Committee Chairman Orrin G. Hatch, R-Utah, a primary sponsor of the bill, was anxious to move quickly

on the measure, which aimed to issue six-year visas to more than 200,000 skilled foreign workers each year. "It could go through tomorrow and it wouldn't be soon enough," he said.

But critics called the measure a "quick fix" that would threaten American jobs. "[The bill] would give away our best-paying jobs to nationals from other countries," said Dan Stein, executive director of the Federation for American Immigration Reform, a conservative group which generally opposes increased immigration proposals.

A competing Senate bill, introduced by Charles S. Robb, D-Va., was more attractive to some Democrats. That bill (S 1645) would establish a pilot program allowing certain high-tech students, who had completed a master's or doctorate degree from an American university, to stay in the United States for five additional years. Rep. Zoe Lofgren, D-Calif., introduced a similar bill (HR 2687) in the House.

Wading into the debate, Lamar Smith of Texas, chairman of the House Judiciary Subcommittee on Immigration and Claims, introduced a bill (HR 3814) on March 1 that would authorize fewer additional H-1B visas than the industry requested, increasing the number of visas for highly skilled workers from 115,000 to 160,000 for fiscal 2000.

Smith called his approach "a reasonable and measured response to the concerns of the high-tech industry." His bill would permit the increase in visas only after the administration showed that it was enforcing provisions in the 1998 immigration law (PL 105-277) aimed at preventing companies from abusing the program at the expense of U.S. workers.

Smith's bill would require employers to show that they had hired more full-time U.S. workers than in the previous year and had increased both the average and total wages paid to U.S. workers. Those conditions aimed to answer critics of the H-1B program who argued that the influx of foreign workers kept high-tech wages artificially low.

But with industry saying the cap was too tight, Smith in April introduced a far different version (HR 4227) that would lift the cap on H-1B visas for three years, allowing as many as are necessary to be issued. Still, the new bill contained worker protection provisions that industry leaders feared they could not meet.

SENATE COMMITTEE ACTION

The Senate Judiciary Committee approved the Hatch bill (S 2045—S Rept 106-260) March 9 by a vote of 16–2. The measure would allow 195,000 H-1B visas to be issued each year for the following three years. It also would exempt from the cap foreigners employed by universities or governmental or nonprofit research organizations, potentially allowing entry for an additional 20,000 foreign workers.

But many members were concerned that the bill did not adequately protect and promote American workers and students. The panel defeated, 8–10, a substitute by Edward M. Kennedy, D-Mass., that would make a more modest increase in the number of visas—to 145,000 per year through fiscal 2002—and would increase the current $500 visa fee paid by businesses to between $1,000 and $3,000. The majority of that money would go to U.S. worker training and the rest to high-tech college scholarships and computers for low-income areas. Kennedy also wanted to tighten requirements for companies that participate in the visa program to protect U.S. workers.

Hatch, Dianne Feinstein, D-Calif., and others said protections were already in place and stricter ones were unnecessary. They also objected to the increased visa fees, saying that the high-tech industry already poured billions into training and scholarships.

However, the panel did adopt, 12–6, an amendment by Feinstein that would reallocate the distribution of visa fee revenues, directing more money to computer training programs for elementary and secondary schools and low-income scholarships.

HOUSE COMMITTEE ACTION

The House Judiciary Immigration and Claims Subcommittee gave voice vote approval to the second Smith bill, HR 4227, on April 12. The full committee approved it, 18–11, on May 17 (H Rept 106-692). The bill would lift the cap on H-1B visas for three years, allowing as many as were necessary to be issued. It also contained requirements designed to ensure that foreign workers would not take the place of American workers.

Critics warned that the bill's stringent worker requirements could never be met in time to address what they call a serious and immediate job shortage in the high-tech industry. In order to qualify for an H-1B, a company would have to show that compared with the previous year, it increased the number of American workers employed, and increased both the total compensation and average compensation paid to American employees.

H-1B visas would be available only if the job paid $40,000 a year or more and foreign workers were employed in full-time positions. Government and research positions would be exempt.

For the cap to be lifted in the second and third year of the bill, the Clinton administration would have to implement provisions from the 1998 law (PL 105-277), which raised the number of H-1B visas for three years. Those provisions required that companies where H-1B employees make up 15 percent or more of the work force advertise for American workers and not lay any of them off.

According to Smith, the Clinton administration had not issued regulations to implement those requirements. "Simply having an uncapped program, which is impossible for the employer to use, is giving the employer nothing," Howard L. Berman, D-Calif., said at the subcommittee markup.

Smith remained unconvinced that more foreign workers were needed. "Today there is still no objective, credible study that documents a shortage of American high-tech workers," he said.

In the subcommittee, Zoe Lofgren, D-Calif., offered then withdrew a substitute amendment that included the language of a bill (HR 3983) she cosponsored with Rules Com-

mittee Chairman David Dreier, R-Calif., that would raise the cap to 200,000 for three years. Lofgren's substitute would add several new provisions, including a Clinton administration proposal that would offer legal residency to more than 500,000 illegal immigrants, mostly Central Americans and Haitians, who were left out of the sweeping federal amnesty program of 1986. More than one-third of them are believed to live in southern California.

Ranking subcommittee Democrat Sheila Jackson-Lee, Texas, also introduced and withdrew a substitute that would raise the cap to 225,000 for three years without conditions, increase the visa fees that companies must pay, and redistribute the money to a variety of educational, training, and scholarship programs.

The subcommittee approved by voice vote an amendment by Elton Gallegly, R-Calif., that would require all H-1B recipients entering the program as physical therapists to hold a master's degree, rather than the current requirement of a bachelor's degree. This would dramatically reduce the numbers of foreigners entering the program as physical therapists, because most countries did not have master's programs for physical therapists.

In the full committee, Smith and Jackson-Lee, D-Texas, offered an amendment, approved 24–7, which drastically eased the worker requirements. Among other things, the amendment would eliminate the requirement that H-1B employers increase the number of American workers before receiving new visas. In addition, it would ease requirements that academic degrees held by H-1B workers be verified and their names posted on the Internet. However, it would continue to require the administration to implement certain antifraud regulations passed in 1998, but would not tie this to the granting of visas. The amendment also would require new studies on how H-1B employers are treating incumbent U.S. workers and recruiting minorities.

Three Republicans voted against the amendment, including Spencer Bachus, Ala., who said easing the requirements for companies would hurt American workers.

Most Democrats voted for the amendment, but many preferred a substitute version crafted by Lofgren and Dreier. That amendment, offered but ruled nongermane, would increase the visa cap to 200,000 each year for three years, institute few requirements for companies, provide education and training programs for U.S. students and workers, improve the INS's handling of visa applications, and address several related immigration issues.

The committee adopted, 15–13, an amendment by chairman Henry J. Hyde, R-Ill., that would exempt elementary and secondary schools from having to pay a minimum salary of $40,000 for H-1B workers. Hyde said lawmakers should "think of the students first" and fill vacancies in the math and science field any way possible—including recruiting teachers from other countries.

Democrats fought to include provisions to expedite the immigration process for a certain group of immigrants who entered the country in the 1980s from Guatemala, El Salvador, and Honduras. They said the INS had subjected these immigrants to more stringent immigration requirements than other groups.

Ranking Democrat John Conyers Jr., Mich., offered an amendment that would make these groups part of the H-1B program, allowing them to stay in the United States an additional six years. But the amendment was ruled nongermane.

SENATE FLOOR ACTION

Hatch's hopes for quick action on the bill were dashed as Democrats waged procedural battles throughout the summer in order to offer amendments related to revisions of immigration laws, as well as education and training. The Democrats, who supported the increase in H-1B visas, contended that training and education programs should be bolstered to ensure that Americans would be able to fill the jobs in the future. But the larger debate turned to a proposal by President Clinton that would grant amnesty to thousands of illegal immigrants and relief to some Central American and Haitian immigrants.

When Majority Leader Trent Lott, R-Miss., sought to pass the bill by unanimous consent in early July, Democrats seeking to amend the bill objected. The bill finally came to the floor in September with members of both parties agreeing that the measure needed to be passed. But senators remained at odds over Democratic immigration amendments.

Republicans proceeded carefully, using complicated parliamentary tools to protect their members from difficult votes on immigration issues that Democrats sought to attach to the measure. In a sign of the partisan differences, the Senate voted 43–55 along party lines against a motion to consider a Democratic immigration amendment that would grant amnesty to immigrants who have lived in the United States since 1986, even if they arrived illegally.

After Democrats changed their target and tried to attach immigration provisions to the already troubled fiscal 2001 appropriations bill for the departments of Commerce, Justice, State and the federal judiciary (HR 4690), the Senate finally passed S 2045 by a lopsided 96–1 vote on Oct. 3, 2000. The lone dissenter was Ernest F. Hollings, D-S.C.

HOUSE FLOOR ACTION

Just hours after the Senate action, House GOP leaders called up the measure under suspension of the rules, a procedure that barred amendments and required a two-thirds majority vote for passage. Although several House members grumbled about the fast-track procedure, and about the failure of the bill to do more to help U.S. workers, no one called for a roll-call vote.

House GOP leaders decided to act swiftly to clear the Senate-passed bill in part because Hatch warned pointedly that there was no time for a conference if the House passed its own version of the legislation. The basic problem for House leaders was a split within GOP ranks. HR 4227, which had won approval from the House Judiciary Committee, was

denounced by industry groups because of its strict labor provisions.

In the end, House leaders simply rolled over Smith. He put up only a mild protest on the floor. "We need to protect American workers from being undercut," he said. "We need to recognize the opposition of the American people to the H-1B visa increase." The House cleared the bill by voice vote, avoiding a contentious debate over immigration. President Clinton signed the measure on Oct. 17, 2000.

Democrats and Republicans alike described the visa program as a stopgap measure until more American workers could be trained to fill technology jobs. Under the bill, more than half of the money collected from a $500 fee for each work visa would be used to provide American workers with technical skills training. Smaller portions of the fee would fund scholarships for low-income students, and grants for math, science, and technology education programs.

Visa Fees

The Senate in 2000 cleared legislation (HR 5362—PL 106-311) that increased the fee paid by companies that used certain high-tech workers. The workers entered the United States under a visa program to help technology companies fill a burgeoning number of openings. The new law doubled the fee to $1,000 per worker. Money from the fee would be used for a variety of worker training and education programs. The Senate's action closely followed passage of another bill (S 2045—PL 106-313) that would increase the number of visas that can be issued. The House cleared that legislation on Oct. 3. HR 5362, which did not go through committee, passed by the House by voice vote on Oct. 6. The Senate cleared it by unanimous consent on Oct. 10. The president signed the two bills together on Oct. 17.

Immigration Relief

Pro-immigration groups, with the aid of Democrats and the Clinton administration, managed to win approval of a small portion of their plan to provide immigration relief for several specific groups in the 106th Congress.

Included in the end-of-session omnibus bill in 2000 (HR 4577—PL 106-554) were provisions that made it easier for some illegal immigrants who felt they were unfairly denied a chance to apply for amnesty under the 1986 immigration overhaul (PL 99-603) to have their claims reviewed. It opened a four-month window for those who came to the country legally but whose visas had expired and who were waiting for their residency to be decided, to finish the process in the United States.

But the bill did not provide the large-scale amnesty for illegal immigrants the Clinton administration and Democrats had sought, nor did it provide relief for some illegal aliens from Central America who were hoping to be able to stay in the country as legal residents. In addition, Republicans failed to streamline the H-2A program to help farmers hire more migrant workers.

The immigration issue first arose as Congress considered increasing the number of temporary H-1B visas that allow highly skilled foreign workers to come to the United States. Immigration groups argued that if Congress was going to help the better-off group of would-be immigrants, it should also address some imbalances in other immigration programs.

In the Senate, Democrats tried to attach their broad immigration proposal to the H-1B bill (S 2045), but Senate Majority Leader Trent Lott, R-Miss., structured the debate to preclude their amendment. Democrats tried, but failed, to overcome that roadblock. They then turned to another must-pass piece of legislation, the fiscal 2001 appropriations bill for the departments of Commerce, Justice, State, and the federal judiciary (HR 4942). With Democrats assuring Clinton they had the votes to sustain him, the White House said flatly that the president would veto the spending bill if it did not contain the immigration provisions.

The GOP leadership cleared the appropriations bill without the provisions, then held it, promising to attach whatever the two sides negotiated to the later omnibus bill.

During negotiations in December, Sen. Orrin Hatch, R-Utah, proposed creating a temporary visa for foreign-born family members of permanent resident aliens and U.S. citizens. The visa would let the family members stay in the United States while their residency applications were being processed.

That plan seemed to move closer to the White House immigration proposal, which would restore a provision to make it easier for some immigrants—those whose visas have expired or who are in the country illegally for other reasons—to stay in the United States as long as a residency application is pending.

Also, instead of granting amnesty to all illegal immigrants who were unfairly denied amnesty by the Immigration and Naturalization Service (INS) under the 1986 immigration overhaul, Hatch's proposal would allow plaintiffs in two massive class action lawsuits against the INS to apply for amnesty.

Throughout negotiations, the major stumbling block to an immigration agreement remained a provision that would make it easier for some Central Americans, Haitians, and Liberians to gain permanent residency.

Republicans said broadly granting amnesty to illegal immigrants would be unfair to immigrants who waited years to come to the United States legally. Hatch said the administration's amnesty proposal—known as NACARA parity, for Nicaraguan and Cuban Adjustment and Relief Act—was unacceptable to Republicans.

In the end, White House officials and Republican leaders drafted an immigration agreement that omitted both the amnesty measures demanded by the administration and changes to the migrant farmworker program that Republicans sought. But it did allow many immigrant families to remain together in the United States as they wait for permanent residency.

Congressional members of the Hispanic Caucus railed against White House officials for dropping their insistence that the immigration package include broad amnesty for certain illegal aliens.

Nevertheless, the agreement was added to HR 4577, which was passed by both chambers Dec. 15 without any dissenting votes. President Clinton signed the bill on Dec. 21, 2000.

Orphaned Immigrant Siblings

Lawmakers in 1999 cleared a measure (HR 2886—PL 106-139) to make it easier for orphaned immigrant siblings to stay together. Existing law prevented foreign children who are sixteen years or older, and had been adopted by U.S. families, from qualifying as immediate relatives of the adopting family, making it difficult for American families to keep orphaned siblings. The measure specifically allowed an adoptive child age sixteen or seventeen at the time immigration papers were filed to qualify as an immediate relative child if the adoptive U.S. family already had taken in a younger sibling of the applicant.

The House Judiciary Immigration and Claims Subcommittee gave voice vote approval to the measure on Sept. 30, and the full committee gave voice vote approval on Oct. 5 (H Rept 106-383). The House passed it, 404–0, Oct. 18. The Senate cleared it on Nov. 19. Clinton signed the bill on Dec. 7.

Farmworker Visas

Lawmakers in 2000 failed to clear legislation designed to remedy a shortage of agricultural workers, although GOP leaders tried into December to win the backing of the administration and congressional Democrats. At the heart of the issue was a federal program, known as H-2A, that let Mexican and other foreign farmworkers into the United States on temporary visas to help farmers bring in their crops.

Farmers said the program had overwhelmed them with paperwork and unfair wage requirements while doing almost nothing to expand the pool of legal farmworkers. As a result, they said they have come to depend more and more on illegal farm help. Some 52 percent of the farmworkers who responded to a March 2000 National Agricultural Workers Survey admitted they were illegal aliens.

The shortage of farm labor led to expensive crop losses and even forced some farmers out of business, according to agricultural spokespeople. Their proposed solution would overhaul the H-2A visa program to ease wage requirements and make it easier for farmers to recruit domestic and foreign farm labor.

But a coalition of groups representing farmworkers said such changes would leave H-2A farmworkers worse off and would make it almost impossible for them to win permanent resident status. The groups, including the Farmworker Justice Fund, the AFL-CIO, and Hispanic and religious groups said growers instead should raise wages to attract more domestic workers and give green cards to undocumented agricultural workers from Mexico.

Seeking to help the farmers, House Republicans drafted a bill (HR 4548) to create a three-year pilot program that would aim to reduce paperwork for farmers and make it easier for immigrant farmworkers to find jobs legally in the United States. Farmers would no longer have to provide their workers—including American workers—with benefits such as housing. The workers, however, would earn more money.

But Democrats worried that the measure would worsen working conditions for immigrant farm laborers. And they said the bill would draw so many farmworkers into the streamlined agricultural program that newly arrived immigrant workers would find demand for farm labor had already been met. Those workers would remain in the country to work illegally in other employment, the bill's critics said.

HOUSE COMMITTEE ACTION

Despite such concerns, HR 4548 won voice vote approval July 27 from the Judiciary Immigration and Claims Subcommittee. The measure survived a lengthy full committee markup, winning approval by a 16–11 vote on Sept. 20 (H Rept 106-982, Pt. I).

The subcommittee approved several amendments by voice vote, including one that would require seasonal workers to leave the United States for two months after their one-year visas expire. That drew protests from committee members who worried the amendment would encourage foreign farmworkers to flee into other sectors of the U.S. economy rather than leave the country. Under another amendment, the identification cards issued to immigrant workers would be more difficult to tamper with.

Several Democratic amendments were defeated, including one by Sheila Jackson-Lee that would require farmers to provide housing for workers if local housing was not available. It fell 5–7.

Howard L. Berman, D-Calif., offered an amendment that would require farmers to confirm that all their employees—immigrant and American workers—had received the new, tamper-resistant worker cards. His proposal failed on a 6–5 vote.

At the full Judiciary Committee markup, lawmakers haggled at length over proposed changes to the housing requirement. They voted 17–14 along party lines to accept a change that would allow farmers to pay their workers a housing stipend—in lieu of providing housing for them—with a state governor's certification that adequate housing existed.

The bill's housing-related changes were a deal-breaker for Judiciary Committee Chairman Henry Hyde, R-Ill., who voted against the bill despite the leadership's support for the measure. "The bill is unfair to workers," Hyde said.

Committee members also voted 24–5 to adopt an amendment by Bob Barr, R-Ga., stripping the bill of a provision designed to make it easier for farmworkers to reenter the country after being kicked out as illegals. And the panel defeated a bid by Berman to limit the H-2A visa program to 100,000 visas per year.

LAST-MINUTE NEGOTIATIONS

With little time left on the congressional calendar, leaders struggled to hammer out a compromise. One tentative plan would allow farmers to fill out a simple, one-page application certifying they met the H-2A program's criteria, and the application would be processed almost immediately. The agreement also would allow farmworkers in the United States illegally to receive permanent residency—a provision designed to gain key Democratic support.

Under such an agreement, farmworker wages under the H-2A program would be frozen for four years. During that time, two studies—one by an independent commission and one by the General Accounting Office—would examine the effectiveness of different wage rates. But such an arrangement faced the potential of opposition from conservative Republicans who did not like the amnesty provision and from liberal Democrats who did not want to ease the requirements on farmers.

Although GOP leaders made enough concessions to win the backing of at least some Democrats—and possibly the White House—they were unable to add the plan to an omnibus spending bill (HR 4577—PL 106-554) that Congress cleared Dec. 15. The H-2A measure appeared to fail because of a combination of factors, including disagreements over other immigration issues (such as the administration's plan to grant amnesty to illegal aliens) and a potential filibuster from opponents such as Sen. Phil Gramm, R-Texas.

Nurses' Visas

Nurses from outside the United States would be able to work in some needy urban and rural U.S. hospitals over the next four years under legislation (HR 441—PL 106-95) that lawmakers cleared in 1999. Supporters said the program would help a number of hospitals that could not attract enough health care providers because they were located in the inner city or in remote rural areas. The bill allowed up to 500 nurses a year for the next four years to apply for temporary visas to work in designated U.S. health care facilities.

The bill also contained a number of safeguards to prevent American nurses from losing their jobs or suffering pay cuts due to the possible influx of foreign workers. Hospitals, for example, would have to show they made serious efforts to fill nursing positions with domestic applicants before they were allowed to participate in the program.

The House Judiciary Subcommittee on Immigration and Claims approved HR 441 by voice vote March 18, and the full committee approved it by voice vote March 24 (H Rept

106-135). The House passed it on May 24. The Senate Judiciary Committee approved it on June 24; the Senate passed an amended version by unanimous consent on Oct. 22, and the House cleared it on Nov. 2. Clinton signed the bill into law on Nov. 12, 1999.

Religious Worker Visas

Lawmakers in 2000 cleared legislation (HR 4068—PL 106-409) to reauthorize a religious worker visa program set to expire Sept. 30. The law extended the current program for three years without making any changes. Workers who participated in the popular program included nuns, religious brothers, cantors, pastoral service workers, missionaries, and religious broadcasters.

The program covered two groups: workers eligible to apply for permanent resident status in the United States after three years, and workers who had to return home after five years.

The bill, which did not go through committee, was passed by voice vote by the House on Sept. 19. The Senate cleared it by unanimous consent on Oct. 19. President Clinton signed it on Nov. 1.

Fraud Against the Elderly

Congress late in 2000 cleared legislation (S 3164—PL 106-534) to reduce the number of elderly victims of fraud each year through education efforts. The bill authorized $1 million a year for five years to support a program initiated by the National Sheriffs Association, International Association of Chiefs of Police, and the AARP to reduce crimes against the elderly.

The legislation required the Department of Health and Human Services to develop education programs to inform seniors of the prevalence of telemarketing and sweepstakes fraud; the dangers of providing bank account, credit card, or other financial or personal information over the telephone to unsolicited callers; methods of reporting suspected attempts at or acts of fraud; and consumer-protection rights under federal law. Backers of the legislation said seniors are defrauded by telemarketers of as much as $14.8 billion annually. The elderly also often fall victim to sweepstakes frauds.

The Senate passed the bill on Oct. 24, and the House passed it by voice vote under suspension of the rules on Oct. 30. The president signed the measure on Nov. 22, 2000.

Alien Smugglers

The House in 2000 passed legislation imposing harsh mandatory minimum sentences on those who were paid to smuggle illegal aliens into the country. But the Senate did not take up the measure.

Backers of the bill (HR 238) warned that smuggling had become a lucrative business that often resulted in the mis-

treatment or death of the illegal aliens. Judiciary Committee members recounted stories of aliens smuggled in shipping cargo containers, left in the desert to die, or forced into slave labor or prostitution to repay debts to their smugglers.

James E. Rogan, R-Calif., said that on a recent visit to the U.S.-Mexican border, he learned that illegal immigrants were slain by smugglers—known as "coyotes"—on almost a daily basis.

Under the measure, smugglers who were paid to bring in aliens would face a mandatory minimum sentence of two years for bringing aliens into the country, five to twenty-five years if the smuggling resulted in serious injury to aliens, and at least twenty years if death resulted. These mandatory minimums would double with a second conviction. Federal prosecutors could seek an additional five-year sentence if the smugglers were armed.

Democrats attacked the new mandatory minimums that the bill would create, saying they would be unfair and ineffective. During Judiciary Committee consideration, Maxine Waters, D-Calif., said mandatory minimums were "crippling the prison system" by forcing more taxpayer dollars to be designated to build new prisons and by imprisoning drug users and others "who should be in treatment."

Nevertheless, the bill won voice vote approval in the House Judiciary Immigration Subcommittee March 9. The Judiciary Committee approved the measure (H Rept 106-850) by voice vote July 25 after adopting a pair of Democratic amendments.

An amendment by Zoe Lofgren, D-Calif., adopted by voice vote, clarified that all offenses covered by the bill would be for financial profit. Lofgren said those who harbored aliens for reasons other than financial profit could face penalties under current law, but should not be subject to mandatory minimums. The bill already contained an exception for harboring immediate family members.

The Judiciary Committee also adopted an amendment by Sheila Jackson-Lee, D-Texas, that sought to ensure that anyone who provided emergency assistance to an illegal alien in a life-threatening situation would not face penalties.

Robert C. Scott, D-Va., tried unsuccessfully to strike the mandatory minimums in the bill and instead allow the U.S. Sentencing Commission to evaluate the situation and decide if increases were necessary. But Rogan countered: "It's the prerogative of Congress, and not a commission, to decide what is appropriate."

The House passed the measure by voice vote Oct. 3.

Border Controls

Resolving a fight that spanned years on how to tighten controls at U.S. borders, lawmakers in 2000 cleared legislation to set up computerized tracking of entry and exit data from all U.S. land, sea, and air ports of entry. The bill (HR 4489—PL 106-215) sought to ease the 1996 immigration law (PL 104-208) that required such a system. The immigration law had been the source of complaints from U.S. businesses and Canadian interests fearful that new border checks would stall traffic and hurt commerce.

HR 4489 reflected an agreement between the chairmen of the House and Senate Judiciary Immigration subcommittees, Rep. Lamar Smith, R-Texas, and Sen. Spencer Abraham, R-Mich. Abraham had introduced an identical bill (S 2599).

The negotiations included an array of business and government groups from both the United States and Canada. The compromise sought to balance beefed-up border security with the need to speed the flow of legal border traffic. Abraham believed the bill would appease those concerned with the original law, which required the Immigration and Naturalization Service to document the entry and departure of every alien beginning in September 1998. Congress later changed the deadline to March 30, 2001.

The legislation called for a system that would feed into a centralized database all entry and exit information that was already collected. No additional documentation would be required. Bill sponsors said the database would aid in detection of terrorists and assist the apprehension of those who overstay temporary visas.

The legislation set a Dec. 31, 2003, deadline for implementation in airports and seaports. The fifty most popular land entry points would be added to the system by Dec. 31, 2004, with remaining ports of entry functional in 2005.

The bill also required the Justice Department to establish a task force to recommend how to improve traffic flow at airports, seaports, and land border points of entry. The department was required to submit a report on the recommendations by Dec. 31, 2002.

The 1996 immigration law had been designed to tighten security and collect information, but there was widespread disagreement over whether it would require additional documentation and consequently slow down legal traffic to and from Canada. Most Canadians did not need visas, passports, or border crossing cards to travel into the United States, and vice versa. Neither did certain foreign business personnel.

Canadian officials, members of Congress from border states, and the business community warned that the requirement in the immigration law would produce endless delays in traffic and trade across the border, severely damaging relations with the single biggest trading partner of the United States and prompting retaliatory measures from Canada.

Once Smith and Abraham reached their compromise, the bill moved through Congress on a fast track without going through committees. HR 4489, introduced on May 18, won House passage by voice vote on May 23 and was cleared by the Senate by unanimous consent on May 25. The president signed it on June 15.

Citizenship for the Disabled

Moved by the plight of some disabled applicants for U.S. citizenship, lawmakers in 2000 eased a requirement that had proved an insurmountable barrier to naturalization. The bill (S 2812—PL 106-448) gave the attorney general the authority to grant citizenship to mentally disabled applicants who could not understand the oath of renunciation and allegiance.

Under existing law, the attorney general could waive the requirement that applicants pass English and civics tests. For adults, however, there was no such flexibility in the mandate that people seeking citizenship renounce allegiance to any other country and pledge their allegiance to the United States.

Bill sponsor Orrin Hatch, R-Utah, said the "discriminatory" lack of waiver was preventing about 1,100 people with severe disabilities from becoming citizens.

The plight of Gustavo Galvez Letona, whose parents and siblings were naturalized citizens, convinced Hatch to introduce the bill. The twenty-seven-year old Guatemala native suffered from Downs Syndrome and was not able to understand the oath, causing the U.S. government to deny his citizenship application.

S 2812, which would not relax other citizenship rules regarding moral character and residency, built on previous efforts by Congress to clear roadblocks for people with disabilities. In the 1990s Congress gave the attorney general waiver powers for the civics and English tests and addressed the problems of people who had trouble making their way to certain ceremonies.

The Senate Judiciary Committee approved the measure July 20, and the Senate passed it the next day by unanimous consent. The House on Oct. 10 passed it by voice vote after inserting the text of a similar bill, HR 4838, that had been introduced by Ileana Ros-Lehtinen, R-Fla. The Senate cleared the measure on Oct. 19 by unanimous consent. Clinton signed the bill on Nov. 6.

Deportations

The House in 2000 voted to reverse part of a 1996 law that required automatic deportation of legal immigrants who committed certain crimes, even if they had not been sentenced to prison. The bill was not addressed in the Senate. Supporters said the bill (HR 5062) would reverse a wrong that fell on some immigrants as a result of two 1996 laws that barred them from application for permission to remain in the United States.

The Anti-terrorism and Effective Death Penalty Act and the Illegal Immigration Reform and Immigration Responsibility Act both prohibited the applications of certain immigrants. Immigrants who committed aggravated felonies—and the 1996 laws broadened the definition of such crimes—could no longer apply to stop their deportation, nor could immigrants who committed such offenses prior to the 1996 laws. In addition, immigrants could lose their "continuous residence" status by committing a felony, even if the resident had lived in the United States for years after the offense occurred.

HR 5062 would reverse some of those changes by allowing persons who committed certain aggravated felonies prior to 1996, excluding rape or sexual abuse of a minor, to apply for "cancellation of removal." Legal permanent residents who were deported for such offenses could reopen their removal proceedings.

In addition, immigrants who committed offenses before 1996 would no longer lose their continuous residence status as a result. Under the bill, those residents already deported because of retroactive application of the 1996 legislation could reopen their deportation proceedings to apply for cancellation of removal.

Bob Filner, D-Calif., said the bill had to be passed because the 1996 laws were "denying people their most basic rights." The bill, which went directly to the floor, was passed by the House by voice vote on Sept. 19.

Visa Reauthorization

Lawmakers in 2000 cleared legislation to permanently authorize a program that allowed some visitors, mainly from industrialized Western countries, to enter the United States for up to ninety days without a visa. The bill (HR 3767—PL 106-396), backed by the travel industry, required participating countries to create and use a machine-readable passport to improve security and facilitate processing procedures. It also encouraged the development of better techniques and programs designed to track those who overstay their visas and become illegal aliens.

The program that HR 3767 permanently authorized had been created as a pilot program in the 1986 immigration overhaul (PL 99-603), and it had been extended several times since then. It permitted people from twenty-nine select countries to come to the United States for travel or business without obtaining a visa. Countries on the list, such as Germany, Japan, and the United Kingdom, had to reciprocate by allowing Americans to visit their countries without visas.

According to the Immigration and Naturalization Service, seventeen million people used the program in 1998. The program was due to expire April 30.

Under existing law, the attorney general decided which countries were included, using information provided by the State Department. A country qualified if no more than 3 percent of those seeking a visa were rejected each year.

HR 3767 required foreigners coming to the United States under the program to have a machine-readable passport, which allowed U.S. Customs agents to process visitors without physically entering information into the system. Most U.S. passports already were machine-readable. The measure also required foreigners traveling to the United States under the program to be matched against an electronic database to determine whether they were eligible to come into the United States.

Before a country could become eligible for the program, the attorney general was required to consult with the secretary of state and report to the House and Senate Judiciary committees on the effect of the country's waiver on U.S. law enforcement and national security. The attorney general, in consultation with the secretary of state, also had to reevaluate countries already in the program every five years to determine whether travelers from that country pose a problem for law enforcement or national security.

A country's participation in the program could be terminated in the case of an emergency in that country, such as a war or the overthrow of a democratically elected government.

HR 3767 required the Immigration and Naturalization Service to set up an automated system for monitoring the entry and exit of foreigners who arrived by sea or air to determine how many stayed beyond the ninety-day limit. That information would be used to determine whether residents of a particular country were abusing the program.

The House Judiciary Committee approved HR 3767 April 4 by voice vote (H Rept 106-564). Democrats, who noted that none of the countries on the approved list were from Africa or the Caribbean, offered an amendment—rejected 9–13—that would authorize a study to determine whether race played a role in determination of the rates of visa refusals.

The committee did approve, by voice vote, an amendment by ranking Democrat John Conyers Jr., Mich., that prohibited the inclusion of visas that were refused for reasons of race, sex, sexual orientation, or disability in the overall calculation of refusal rates. The committee also approved, by voice vote, an amendment by Sheila Jackson-Lee, D-Texas, designed to ensure that people were not deported in the event they were in the United States and their country is removed from the program.

The House passed HR 3767 by voice vote on April 11. The Senate passed the measure by unanimous consent Oct. 3. As amended by a previous unanimous consent decree, the Senate version waived the visa requirement for companies that flew workers in on corporate aircraft.

Senate Democrats reluctantly accepted an amendment offered by Jesse Helms, R-N.C., that established, in certain cases, that no courts would have jurisdiction to review visa refusals based on sex, race, or disability.

The House cleared the measure by voice vote on Oct. 10. President Clinton signed the bill into law on Oct. 30.

Judicial Nominations

Amid mounting tensions between the Clinton administration and Senate GOP leaders over the pace of filling judicial vacancies, the Senate in 1999 rejected the nomination of a Missouri judge, Ronnie L. White, to a seat on the U.S. District Court—the first rejection of a judicial nominee in twelve years. The defeat of the black jurist on a party-line vote infuriated Democrats and threatened to torpedo the nomination process for the rest of the Clinton presidency.

The following year, however, the Senate confirmed two long-stalled judicial nominees: Richard A. Paez and Marsha

Berzon both won confirmation to the Ninth U.S. Circuit Court of Appeals. Paez, who drew fire from Senate conservatives, had been nominated in 1996. He waited longer than any nominee in history for his confirmation.

In all, the Senate confirmed thirty-nine federal judges in 2000, bringing the total for the 106th Congress to seventy-three. A total of 377 judges were confirmed during the eight years of the Clinton administration; forty nominations were left pending at the end of the session.

Democrats were deeply frustrated that more Clinton appointees were not considered, and Senate Minority Leader Tom Daschle, D-S.D., complained bitterly about the process. But Republicans protested that Clinton's nominees were too liberal, and independent analysts said Clinton moved more slowly than other recent presidents in making nominations.

Liberals, for their part, worried about Clinton's willingness to cut deals with Republicans and appoint such avowed conservatives as Ted Stewart, chief of staff to Gov. Michael O. Leavitt of Utah. Clinton, under intense pressure by Hatch, nominated Stewart for a district court seat in 1999.

Democrats and many in the judiciary system—including Chief Justice William H. Rehnquist—bemoaned the slow pace of confirmations of judicial nominees, which they warned impeded the workings of the court system. To ease the problem, the courts often relied on retired, or "senior," judges to assist with the caseloads. *(1997–1998 action, p. 622)*

THE REJECTION OF WHITE

The Senate on Oct. 5, 1999, turned down Clinton's nomination of White to be a U.S. District Court judge in eastern Missouri. The 45–54 party-line vote opened a heated debate about racial diversity in the judiciary. It also marked the first time the full Senate had rejected a judicial nomination since Robert H. Bork's bid for a seat on the Supreme Court was defeated a dozen years before.

The last time the Senate thwarted any presidential nominee was four years earlier, when Clinton's nomination of Henry W. Foster Jr. to be surgeon general was derailed after senators twice voted against stopping a promised filibuster.

Republicans attacked White, who was Missouri's first African American state supreme court justice, for his reluctance to impose the death penalty and for alleged judicial activism. "During his tenure, he has far more frequently dissented in capital cases than any other judge," said John Ashcroft, R-Mo., who led the fight against White. Despite publicly supporting White in the past, Missouri's other Republican senator, Christopher S. Bond, voted against the nominee.

White served in the Missouri legislature, the Office of the City Council for the city of St. Louis, and as a judge in the Court of Appeals for the Eastern District of Missouri before his appointment to the state high court. Clinton nominated White to the District Court in June 1997. Although the Senate Judiciary Committee recommended his nomination, the Senate did not act on the nomination during the 105th Congress, effectively killing it. Clinton nominated White again in January 1999, and the Judiciary panel again recommended him.

To protest Senate delays in taking up White and other nominees, Democrats in late September held a Republican-backed nominee hostage from floor consideration. Ted Stewart, a longtime GOP operative and close friend of Judiciary Committee Chairman Orrin G. Hatch, R-Utah, was nominated for a District Court seat on July 27. He was approved by the Judiciary Committee three days later. On Sept. 21 Democrats defeated a cloture motion to bring Stewart's nomination to a floor vote.

Hatch attacked the cloture defeat as unprecedented and a dangerous move that could permanently taint the judicial process. On Oct. 1 Democrats agreed to allow the Stewart vote in exchange for floor consideration of several other nominees, including White. But Ashcroft took to the floor Oct. 4 to attack White's dissents in death penalty cases and cited opposition to his nomination from several Missouri law enforcement organizations.

The party-line rejection "was a calculated political maneuver" and "yet another troubling example of the way the radical right is attempting to politicize the judiciary," said Daschle. Democrats also warned that, in a Republican-led Senate, minorities and women had a tougher time being confirmed. "I am hoping . . . the United States has not reverted to a time in its history when there was a color test on nominations," Patrick J. Leahy of Vermont, the top Democrat on the Judiciary Committee, said after White's defeat.

But Majority Leader Trent Lott, Miss., defended the Senate's record in confirming minorities and women. "I am sure that the United States Senate would never use any basis for a vote, anything other than the qualifications of a nominee," Lott said, adding that of the previous nineteen confirmed nominees, four had been women, four Hispanic, and one African American.

Fanning the flames, Clinton on Oct. 6 accused Senate Republicans of discriminating against minorities. "The Republican-controlled Senate is adding credence to the perceptions that they treat minority and women judicial nominees unfairly and unequally," the president said. Republicans, in turn, accused Clinton of intentionally nominating unqualified minorities and women to the bench in hopes of painting the GOP as bigoted.

A study by the bipartisan group Citizens for Independent Courts pointed blame at both sides. The study showed that the Senate in recent years had in fact been slower to confirm women and minorities. According to the Sept. 22 report, the GOP Senate took an average of thirty-three days longer to confirm female than male nominees in the 104th Congress, and an average of sixty-five days longer to confirm women in the 105th Congress. The study also showed that the Senate took an average of sixty days longer to act on minority nominees than whites.

But the study also levied blame against Clinton for delays in filling judicial vacancies. It found that Clinton had taken longer to nominate judges to fill vacancies than any of his predecessors since Carter. "It's silly for the Congress and the president to be pointing fingers at each other for this judicial crisis—and it is a crisis—when neither has performed well in this area on behalf of the American people," said former Rep. Mickey Edwards, R-Okla. (1977–1993), cochairman of the group.

CONTINUING FRICTION

Trying to smooth the way for more votes on nominees, Lott and Daschle agreed in November to move forward with votes on Paez and Berzon to serve on the Ninth U.S. Circuit Court of Appeals. Paez was first nominated in 1996 and Berzon in 1998. Many Republicans opposed both nominees, calling them too liberal, and "holds" imposed by GOP conservatives had kept them from a floor vote.

Democrats wrung a public promise from Lott that he would proceed to consideration of the two nominations by March 15. In return, they removed holds on a nominee backed by Lott: Glenn McCullough, mayor of Tupelo, Miss., for a seat on the Tennessee Valley Authority board.

But the ongoing partisan friction erupted again into full-scale battle at the end of 1999. Sen. James M. Inhofe, R-Okla., vowed on Dec. 23 to block confirmation votes on all judicial nominations until the end of Clinton's term. He said the president had broken an agreement on the use of recess appointments, which allowed recipients to serve until the end of the 106th Congress without requiring Senate confirmation.

Inhofe's decision was sparked by the president's December recess appointment of Sarah Fox to the National Labor Relations Board. The appointment, Inhofe asserted, violated an agreement that the full Senate would be informed of any planned recess appointments shortly before the chamber adjourned for the year.

"The president is going to have a problem confirming judges [in 2000], and it is a problem of his own making," Inhofe said. He and seventeen other Republican senators sent a letter to the White House in January announcing their intentions to block votes on judges.

White House officials maintained that the December recess appointment did not violate the agreement, as they told Lott of their plans to appoint Fox before doing so. Lott, in a decisive show of his power, announced in February that he would not allow Inhofe to maintain a blanket "hold" on the nominees. He also bluntly warned that he would not take kindly to threatened filibusters on judicial nominations. Such talkathons, generally off limits in the past, would set a precedent that could haunt Republicans when one of their own was in the White House, the majority leader warned.

Although Lott made it clear that he had no personal desire to allow Clinton to make more appointments, he said he would honor his promise to bring up Paez and Berzon for a vote by March 15. Democrats had cited the long delays on Paez, first nominated in 1996, and Berzon, nominated in 1998, as evidence of GOP bias against minority and female appointees.

PAEZ AND BERZON

The Senate cleared away one of its most contentious judicial issues March 9 when it voted to give California U.S. District Court Judge Paez and labor lawyer Berzon lifetime appointments to the Ninth U.S. Circuit Court of Appeals.

Democrats and Republicans had battled over the two nominations for much of the past year. But in the end a group of mostly moderate GOP senators, joined with all of the chamber's Democrats, rejected their party leaders and gave Paez and Berzon the necessary support.

Although conservative social groups and business organizations rallied against him, Paez was confirmed by a 59–39 vote. Berzon also attracted opposition but less so than Paez, possibly because she lacked a judicial record for critics to scour. After waiting two years, she was confirmed by a vote of 64–34.

Relieved that the long battle was over, Senate Democrats hugged each other as the voting came to a close. "I'm glad the Senate has done the right thing," Leahy said.

Democrats from Clinton on down had repeatedly cited Paez, who was Hispanic, and Berzon as examples of the GOP's alleged unfair treatment of minority and female nominees. To make the point, Vice President Al Gore began a press conference after the vote by saying, in Spanish, "Friends, today we've finally achieved justice."

Republicans angrily denied the charge, saying the problem with Paez and Berzon was their liberal activism—a trait they said was shared by judges on the Ninth Circuit.

Although Lott voted against the nominees, he took steps to block procedural tactics by other opponents of the nominees. First, he discouraged a filibuster by conservative Republican Robert C. Smith, N.H., who emerged as the fiercest critic of Paez, Berzon and the Ninth Circuit. Then, after announcing his opposition to the nominees, Lott said he would not support a motion to indefinitely postpone a vote on Paez's nomination.

Jeff Sessions, R-Ala., pushed for a postponement so the Senate could look into Paez's handling of the criminal fraud case against Democratic fund-raiser John Huang. Paez had sentenced Huang to one year of probation following a guilty plea the previous August. Lott agreed that "there's something not right about that. It doesn't pass the smell test." But he opposed the motion to postpone the confirmation vote, which fell on a 31–67 vote.

The March 9 debate spanned five hours, allowing Smith and other Republicans to criticize statements made by Paez, as well as rulings he had made as a municipal and District Court judge during the past eighteen years. In one case, Paez declined to dismiss a lawsuit against a U.S. oil company being sued for alleged human rights abuses in Burma, where it was building a pipeline, which led the U.S. Chamber of Commerce to lobby against his confirmation.

Democratic supporters said Paez had also ruled in favor of tobacco companies and foreign car manufacturers and argued that no particular ruling should be used to judge his record. Supporters successfully painted the two nominees as moderates rather than political activists.

Berzon's critics focused on her legal work on behalf of labor unions. They contended that Berzon's appointment to the Ninth Circuit would continue the panel's leftward drift. "This is a renegade circuit out of the mainstream of American jurisprudence," said Smith, adding the circuit had "an abysmal record" of being overturned by the Supreme Court. He and other senators called for an overhaul of the circuit, which served about fifty million people.

Recess Appointments

The long-running Senate battle over Clinton's nominations erupted in new hostilities toward the end of the 106th Congress after the president announced seventeen recess appointments in August, including that of Bill Lann Lee to be assistant attorney general for civil rights. In so doing, Clinton basically tossed salt on an old wound.

A number of Senate Republican conservatives had angrily protested Clinton's use of his recess appointment power in the past two years, and Lee was often at the center of their fury. Clinton first nominated the soft-spoken son of a Chinese immigrant in 1997, but conservatives blocked Senate action on his nomination. They objected to his support for affirmative action, portraying him as a liberal ideologue.

With the nomination stalled, Clinton had made Lee acting head of the civil rights division. With the recess appointment, he made the appointment official for the remainder of his presidency. *(Lee nomination, p. 624)*

Historically used when the Senate was unavailable to consider an important nomination, recess appointments had increasingly become a method of skirting unpopular nominations past an unsympathetic Senate. The Clinton administration and Senate Republicans had already tussled several times over such appointments, much as President Reagan and the Democratic Senate did in the mid-1980s.

On Sept. 11 Inhofe announced he would place holds on any judicial nominations the Senate received from the White House through the end of the session. The appointments were an "arrogant defiance of the Senate's prerogative of advise and consent for confirmation purposes," Inhofe said.

Nevertheless, the Senate on Oct. 3 approved four U.S. District Court nominees—three from Arizona and one from Illinois—without any dissenting votes. The debate centered on the GOP leadership's handling of many other stalled nominations.

Members from both parties trotted out charts and numbers to bolster their arguments, with Republicans noting that

Clinton had successfully nominated 377 judicial nominees in eight years, second only to President Ronald Reagan; Democrats countered that Congress approved nearly seventy nominees in the last year of President George Bush, compared with fewer than forty approved in Clinton's last year.

Waco Investigation

Lawmakers in 1999 briefly returned to the issue of the 1993 federal siege and subsequent raid of the Branch Davidian compound in Waco, Texas. But an independent commission headed by former Sen. John C. Danforth of Missouri (1976–1995) flatly concluded in 2000 that the government was innocent of wrongdoing.

The renewed controversy was touched off Aug. 25, 1999, when FBI officials first acknowledged that agents had launched potentially flammable tear gas canisters at a concrete outpost adjacent to the cult's compound on April 19, 1993. The FBI had spent the previous six years denying that it had taken any action that could have started the fire that day, including the use of such pyrotechnic canisters.

The ramshackle compound on the Texas prairie burned April 19, 1993, when, after a fifty-one-day standoff, FBI agents attempted to force cult members out by using armored vehicles to pump tear gas into the buildings. Fires broke out in several spots and quickly engulfed the structures. They left as many as eighty people dead inside the compound, of whom perhaps two dozen were children. Only a few Davidians escaped. Autopsies found that some sect members died from the effects of the fire, others from gunshot wounds. Cult leader David Koresh was among those who died. The FBI launched its tear gas canisters several hours before the conflagration erupted.

Congress, which had held hearings on the issue in 1995, promptly promised to revive its inquiry into the siege. In addition, Attorney General Janet Reno said she would name a person who was free of "conflicts of interest and will be well-received" to lead an independent investigation into why it took the FBI six years to acknowledge its use of the canisters.

The raid occurred six weeks after Reno took over the Justice Department and had bedeviled her ever since. As the last witness before the House inquiry, she said she alone made the decision to try to force Koresh and his followers from the compound, and that it "will live with me for the rest of my life."

Reno's appointment of Danforth in September to head the inquiry won praise from lawmakers. But Republican leaders still said they would proceed with their investigation, despite Democratic criticism of overlapping probes. "We're all investigated out," conceded Senate Majority Whip Don Nickles, R-Okla. "We've got burnout. But we have a responsibility."

Since winning control of Congress in the 1994 elections, the GOP had pressed a series of investigations of the Clinton administration, on topics ranging from the firing of workers in the White House travel office in 1993 to allegations of illegal campaign fundraising during the 1996 presidential race to the impeachment of the president in 1998. None of them had been noted for bipartisanship.

Both Nickles and Senate Majority Leader Trent Lott, R-Miss., called for Reno's resignation. Tensions between GOP leaders and the White House worsened after the Clinton administration missed a House Government Reform Committee deadline Sept. 17 to hand over documents on the deadly Waco siege.

In late September Senate Republican leaders announced the creation of a special task force to investigate alleged wrongdoing in the Justice Department in three areas: Waco, the investigation of espionage at U.S. nuclear laboratories, and improper campaign fundraising by the Clinton administration. The task force was to be chaired by Sen. Arlen Specter, R-Pa.

But Senate Judiciary Chairman Orrin Hatch, R-Utah, said he did not think a task force was the best way to proceed with an investigation. "I would have preferred they do this through one of the subcommittees," a clearly irritated Hatch said.

Partisan bickering erupted almost immediately. Democrats refused to appoint any members to the task force, saying the Judiciary Committee or one of its subcommittees should instead conduct the investigation. When Specter requested that Attorney General Janet Reno be subpoenaed, the Judiciary Committee's top Democrat, Patrick J. Leahy of Vermont, vehemently objected to the request.

Bowing to the inevitable, top Senate Republicans in October agreed to disband the special task force they created less than a month before. Instead, in a victory for Hatch, Specter agreed to conduct the investigation through the Judiciary Subcommittee on Administrative Oversight and the Courts. But even that investigation ran into partisan squabbling.

The issue of Waco finally appeared to be resolved when Danforth announced on July 21, 2000, that he had concluded "with 100 percent certainty" that federal officials were innocent of wrongdoing in the 1993 conflagration. Danforth declared that government agents did not start the fire and did not shoot at the Davidians. He also said the government did not improperly enlist the military in its operation and did not engage in a major cover-up.

But Danforth said that some employees of the Justice Department, including some lawyers, hid the fact that FBI agents on the scene had fired pyrotechnic devices—exploding tear gas canisters—near the compound during the siege.

Those devices were fired hours before the blaze and had nothing to do with it, Danforth concluded. But the "failure to disclose that information, more than anything else, is responsible for the loss of the public faith in the government's actions at Waco, and it led directly to this investigation," his report stated.

It was the second time in a week that federal agents had been exonerated in Waco. On July 14, a five-member jury decided in a civil trial that the government was not negligent in its handling of the siege.

Clemency for FALN Members

President Clinton's controversial grant of clemency to sixteen members of a Puerto Rican terrorist group in 1999 sparked withering criticism and a flurry of hearings on Capitol Hill, with both chambers passing resolutions of opposition. In addition, the Senate Judiciary Committee approved a bill (S 2042) to make changes in the clemency process.

The controversy marked one of the sharpest partisan clashes between the White House and congressional Republicans since the House voted to impeach Clinton in 1998.

BACKGROUND

On Aug. 12 Clinton offered to release eleven FALN members if they agreed to renounce violence, to reduce the sentences of two other members, and to eliminate fines on three more. The FALN, a group seeking independence for Puerto Rico, made 130 bomb attacks on political and military targets in the United States between 1974 and 1983, authorities had said.

Outraged Republicans promptly said Congress should weigh in on the matter. "I have grave concerns about granting clemency to known terrorists," House Majority Leader Dick Armey said in a written statement. "An important question needs to be answered: Was the clemency process used for political purposes?"

Some charged that Clinton made the offer to attract the Hispanic vote to Hillary Rodham Clinton's New York bid for the Senate. At least some in the Puerto Rican community embraced the move, however. Rep. Nydia M. Velazquez, D-N.Y., hailed the clemency offer when it was announced, calling it a "great day for the Puerto Rican community."

CONGRESSIONAL RESOLUTIONS

Both chambers passed separate resolutions opposing Clinton's action. However, lawmakers failed to clear either version. With 71 House Democrats and the lone Independent, Bernard Sanders, Vt., voting "present," the House on Sept. 9, 1999, passed a Republican-backed resolution (H Con Res 180) opposing the clemency offer.

The vote was 311–41. All 41 "no" votes were cast by Democrats, while 218 Republicans and 93 Democrats supported the measure. Most House Democrats had earlier opposed consideration of the resolution by voting against the rule to bring the measure to the floor.

The House had no place voting on a clemency issue, said Minority Leader Richard A. Gephardt, Mo., who voted present. "This is not our responsibility," he told reporters before the House vote. "Congress does not grant clemency." Democrats also accused Republicans of playing politics with the issue.

But Republicans said it would be irresponsible for Congress not to take a position. "If we want to speak for the law-abiding citizens, we should keep these people behind bars where they belong," said sponsor Vito J. Fossella, R-N.Y. Congress's four Puerto Rican members, including nonvoting Puerto Rico Del. Carlos A. Romero-Barcelo, supported Clinton's offer.

In the Senate Democrats blocked consideration of a strongly worded joint resolution (S J Res 33) deploring the president's actions. But after GOP leaders softened the language, the Senate passed the resolution Sept. 14 on an overwhelming 95–2 vote.

S J Res 33 resolved "that making concessions to terrorists is deplorable and that President Clinton should not have granted clemency to the FALN terrorists."

The initial version, blocked by Democrats, stated: "President Clinton should not have granted clemency to the FALN terrorists and that in doing so he has made deplorable concessions to terrorists, undermined national security and emboldened domestic and international terrorists."

Republicans agreed to the changes to win bipartisan support. "We gave some ground so [Democrats] can say they participated" in drafting the resolution, said Paul Coverdell, Ga., a key sponsor.

Neither chamber took up the other's legislation, meaning that neither resolution was cleared for the White House.

COMMITTEE HEARINGS

The clemency offer also provoked hearings by the House Government Reform Committee and the Senate Judiciary Committee, with GOP lawmakers issuing subpoenas demanding information and testimony about the issue. In response, Clinton invoked executive privilege over much of the subpoenaed information regarding his decision-making process.

After Attorney General Janet Reno prohibited Assistant FBI Director Neil Gallagher from offering a formal statement to the Government Reform Committee in September, chairman Dan Burton said he would issue a subpoena for Gallagher's opening statement. He added: "I have run out of words to describe my frustration with the political games played by Janet Reno and this Justice Department."

But Clinton sent a letter to the panel's ranking Democrat, Henry A. Waxman, Calif., defending the privilege claim. The president stated: "Political consideration played no role" in the clemency process, and the decision was based on careful consideration of each prisoner's case.

Clinton said he asked a number of questions before allowing the process to move forward, including "whether the prisoners' sentences were unduly severe" for the crimes committed, and "whether their continuing incarceration served any meaningful purpose."

Burton contended that the letter still did not give the reasons behind the decision. A bulwark defense used by those who supported clemency was that none of the sixteen was convicted of violent crimes. Burton and other committee members said the reason that many of the prisoners were not convicted of murders or direct acts of violence was because they were stopped by law enforcement before the planned acts occurred.

Furthermore, panel members and witnesses said reports indicated that some of the prisoners released might still intend to participate in FALN activities. Victims of FALN violence said that they were never notified of the prisoners' impending release or consulted by the administration in the clemency process.

Republicans on the Senate Judiciary Committee were equally critical. In October chairman Orrin G. Hatch, R-Utah, said that after reviewing documents provided by Justice, the committee had concluded the president's reasons for granting clemency "do not survive scrutiny"; the Justice Department "did not follow its own rules" for the clemency process and modified its original recommendation; and the department acknowledged that releasing the prisoners could increase the risk of domestic terrorism.

Justifying his decision, Clinton argued that by current standards, the sentences were excessive for the crimes committed. However, Hatch cited an Oct. 19 analysis by the U.S. Sentencing Commission that concluded the FALN defendants convicted of seditious conspiracy would receive "at least thirty years to life" if tried today. Justice officials responded that the analysis was inconclusive.

2000 LEGISLATIVE ACTION

Lawmakers took action on one bill related to the clemency controversy. That measure (S 2042—S Rept 106-231) won voice vote approval from the Senate Judiciary Committee on Feb. 24, 2000, but it did not advance any further.

The legislation would require the Justice Department's pardon attorney to seek information from police and notify victims whenever the president considered an executive grant of clemency and sought advice from Justice. Victims could offer their opinions at any time, and all information would be offered to the president.

Hatch, the bill's sponsor, said its aims are simple: "To make sure future presidents will have available to them relevant facts when weighing decisions involving executive clemency, and to notify victims of important events in the process." The Justice Department and panel Democrats strongly opposed the bill, saying it would unconstitutionally infringe on the president's exclusive right to grant clemency.

The bill would require the pardon attorney to notify victims of any Justice decision to investigate a potential grant of clemency, the attorney general's recommendation and the president's ultimate decision. Law enforcement agencies would be questioned about the decision's likely effect and whether the potential clemency recipient posed a danger, had expressed remorse, or had useful information on open investigations.

The Justice Department expressed its objections in a letter to Hatch and ranking Democrat Patrick J. Leahy of Vermont. Assistant Attorney General Robert Raben said the Supreme Court "has repeatedly affirmed that the President's pardon power must be left unfettered and is not subject to congressional encroachment."

Supporters argued that the bill was valid because it would apply only to the Justice Department and not to the president. "The president will still be able to grant clemency with or without considering whatever information and counsel he or she chooses," Hatch said.

Raben argued, however, that the bill would "require the Attorney General to take various steps designed to ensure that the President is aware of views that Congress believes the President should consider. . . . But it is up to the President, not Congress, to determine what information the Attorney General should gather."

To address some of these issues, the panel adopted a Hatch amendment by voice vote to impose the requirements on the pardon attorney instead of the attorney general, as in the original bill. But that failed to appease the administration.

Supreme Court

The Supreme Court remained on a predominantly conservative course in the last half of the 1990s but confounded easy categorization by producing some notable liberal rulings as well. The Court was closely split between a conservative majority led by Chief Justice William H. Rehnquist and a bloc of four moderate-to-liberal justices that included President Clinton's two appointees, Ruth Bader Ginsburg and Stephen G. Breyer.

All of the justices, however, seemed to share an expansive view of the Court's institutional authority. The result was an increasing assertiveness reflected in decisions striking down federal statutes at a record pace and running roughshod over other institutions of government, including the presidency itself.

The conservative majority flexed its muscles most dramatically in a 5–4 decision in December 2000 that cinched the presidential election for Republican George W. Bush over Democrat Al Gore. The ruling blocked a recount sought by Gore in an effort to overcome Bush's narrow lead in Florida, where the state's twenty-five electoral votes would provide the margin of victory for either candidate. *(Florida election cases, box, p. 26)*

In less extraordinary cases, the Court's conservative majority held together to produce rulings favoring the states in power disputes with the federal government. The conservative justices also provided the critical votes to ease restrictions on government aid to parochial schools. The Court generally spurned efforts to expand civil rights remedies or protections for criminal suspects and defendants—often in 5–4 splits along ideological lines.

Liberals, however, counted some significant victories, including closely divided decisions in 2000 rebuffing efforts to ban so-called "partial birth abortions" and blocking organized prayers at public high school football games. In these and several other significant rulings, the liberal justices forged majorities by picking up one or both of the Court's centrist conservatives, Sandra Day O'Connor or Anthony M. Kennedy.

The conservative-liberal dichotomy was somewhat blurred in free-speech cases, a particularly active area in which the Court occasionally proved receptive to constitutional claims. Liberal justices, joined by some conservatives, voted to strike down government regulations of sexual speech. In the most significant of those decisions, the Court in 1997 struck down, 7–2, a federal law aimed at limiting youngsters' access to sexual material on the Internet. On the other hand, liberals supported and conservatives opposed government regulation of campaign finance. In the key decision, the Court in 2000 upheld, 5–4, state limits on campaign contributions.

Congress often found itself put down by its supposedly coequal branch of government. The Court ruled eighteen federal statutes unconstitutional during the four-year period; only thirteen such decisions were handed down during Rehnquist's first ten terms as chief justice. But the Court also proved to be no respecter of presidential prerogatives. In a unanimous decision, the Court in 1997 refused to protect President Bill Clinton from a federal court suit charging that he sexually harassed an Arkansas state employee while he was governor.

The Court's membership remained unchanged through Clinton's second term, depriving him of a third chance to soften its conservative edge. By 2000 the justices had served together for six terms—the longest stretch without a vacancy since 1811–1823. Speculation about possible retirements focused on the three oldest justices: John Paul Stevens, who turned eighty in 2000; Rehnquist, who was seventy-six; and O'Connor, who was seventy. All three appeared in good

REFERENCES

Discussion of the Supreme Court for the years 1945–1964 may be found in *Congress and the Nation Vol. I*, pp. 1441–1454; for the years 1965–1968, *Congress and the Nation Vol. II*, pp. 335–340; for the years 1969–1972, *Congress and the Nation Vol. III*, pp. 289–327; for the years 1973–1976, *Congress and the Nation Vol. IV*, pp. 619–659; for the years 1977–1980, *Congress and the Nation Vol. V*, pp. 755–791; for the years 1981–1984, *Congress and the Nation Vol. VI*, pp. 711–768; for the years 1985–1988, *Congress and the Nation Vol. VII*, pp. 785–840; for the years 1989–1992, *Congress and the Nation Vol. VIII*, pp. 801–851; for the years 1993–1996, *Congress and the Nation Vol. IX*, pp. 759–799.

health, however, and showed no inclination to retire. Ginsburg was diagnosed with colon cancer in summer 1999; she successfully underwent surgery in September and six months of chemotherapy from January to June 2000 without missing a single Court session.

Statistically, the Court's output continued to be lower than in previous decades. The number of signed decisions rose to ninety-one in the 1997–1998 term, but fell in the next two terms. The seventy-four decisions in the 1999–2000 term represented the lowest number since the 1953–1954 term when the Court issued sixty-five decisions. Meanwhile, the Court's docket continued to increase to a new record: 8,445 cases in the 1999–2000 term.

FEDERALISM

Under Rehnquist's leadership, the Court continued to build on what was likely to be his major historical legacy: new doctrines to limit the powers of the federal government in the interest of protecting state sovereignty.

The Court struck down two popular federal laws on the ground that Congress had exceeded its power to enlist state governments in enforcing federal regulations or to regulate interstate commerce or protect individual rights. It acted in four cases to bar private damage suits against state governments for violating federal laws. And it ruled that Congress went too far when it tried to give churches and religious groups special exemptions from state and local laws.

Most of the cases were decided 5–4, reflecting the Court's ideological split. The conservative justices said they were safeguarding the constitutional scheme of dual sovereignty between the federal and state governments. Liberal justices accused the majority of distorting precedent and depriving the federal government of power to deal with national issues.

In the first of the cases, the Court in 1997 invalidated a 1993 law—the Brady Handgun Violence Protection Act—that required state or local law enforcement officials to conduct background checks on prospective gun purchasers. "The Federal government may not compel the States to implement, by legislation or executive action, federal regulatory programs," Rehnquist wrote. In dissent, Stevens said that history and precedent supported Congress's power to "impose affirmative obligations on executive and judicial officers of state and local governments."

Three years later, the Court struck down part of a 1994 law—the Violence Against Women Act—that gave victims of "gender-motivated" violence a right to sue their attackers for damages in federal court. Again writing for the majority, Rehnquist said Congress had no authority to regulate "non-economic, violent conduct based solely on its aggregate effect on interstate commerce." He also rejected arguments that the law was justified by Congress's power to enforce individual rights under the Fourteenth Amendment; that amendment, he said, applied only to state action, not individual conduct.

Four rulings limited private suits against state governments. These decisions built on a 1996 opinion interpreting the Eleventh Amendment to bar Congress's power to authorize suits against states in federal court under its power to regulate interstate commerce. In 1999 the Court extended that ruling in two ways. First, it held, 5–4, that the Eleventh Amendment also barred private damage suits in state courts for violations of federal law. The decision threw out a suit by prison guards in Maine to collect back pay owed them for violations of federal wage and hour laws governing overtime work. Second, the Court set a difficult standard for Congress to use the Fourteenth Amendment to authorize damage suits against states. In companion decisions, the Court threw out suits charging the state of Florida with patent infringement and trademark violations against a private bank in connection with a state-operated college savings plan. By 5–4 votes, the Court said that Congress had to identify a "pattern of constitutional violations" to permit private damage suits under the Fourteenth Amendment and that any remedy could not be "out of proportion" to the states' behavior.

One year later, the Court further strengthened the states' immunity from suits by barring federal court actions for violations of the federal Age Discrimination in Employment Act. Once again by a 5–4 vote, the Court—in an opinion by O'Connor—held that Congress had failed to establish "a pattern of age discrimination by the States, much less any discrimination that rose to the level of a constitutional violation." Dissenting justices sharply challenged the entire line of cases. "There is not a word in the text of the Constitution," Stevens wrote, "supporting the Court's conclusion that the judge-made doctrine of sovereign immunity limits Congress' power to authorize private parties . . . to enforce federal laws against the States."

In one other ruling, the Court in 1997 protected the states as well as its own power in striking down a law—the Religious Freedom Restoration Act—aimed at limiting state and local laws affecting religious organizations. The city of Boerne, Texas, challenged the law when a local church invoked it to try to override the city's historic preservation act. By a 6–3 vote, the Court ruled the law unconstitutional because it intruded on state and local government prerogatives and also because it sought to override an earlier Court decision limiting churches' exemption from generally applicable laws.

The Court's solicitude for states was also seen in a nearly unanimous decision in 2000 that blocked private suits against states under the federal False Claims Act. The 8–1 ruling was based on statutory rather than constitutional grounds. In the same year, the Court cited the states' traditional police powers in a unanimous decision that somewhat narrowed a federal law prohibiting arson or bombing of property by excluding from federal jurisdiction crimes against personal residences.

In one exception to the pro–states' rights trend, however, the Court in 2000 upheld a federal law that prohibited states from selling driver license lists to private entities such as insurance companies. The Court unanimously held that the

BUSH V. GORE

A bitterly divided Supreme Court settled the 2000 presidential election in favor of Republican George W. Bush by cutting off a vote recount sought by his Democratic opponent, Vice President Al Gore. The justices divided along ideological lines in the 5–4 decision, *Bush v. Gore,* that brought the election to a dramatic end five weeks after the Nov. 7 balloting. The Dec. 12 ruling safeguarded Bush's narrow popular vote margin in Florida and assured him the state's 25 electoral votes, which he needed to win the White House. The final electoral college vote was 271 for Bush and 266 for Gore. (One elector in the District of Columbia refused to cast a ballot.)

The Court's conservative majority ruled that a manual recount ordered by the Florida Supreme Court violated the equal protection clause because of the lack of uniform standards for retallying ballots. In dissent, liberal justices criticized the majority for second-guessing the Florida court and for refusing to give it time to fashion a proper recount.

The late-night decision provoked harsh criticism in Democratic circles and from many legal experts. But Gore ended his tenacious postelection battle the next day. "While I strongly disagree with the Court's decision, I accept it," Gore said in the televised address Dec. 13. Bush, who had matched Gore's tenacity in resisting a recount, claimed his victory immediately afterward without mentioning the Court fight.

Closeness of Vote in Florida

The legal battle drew the Supreme Court into largely uncharted waters of state and federal election law in the context of one of the closest presidential elections in U.S. history. Gore ended election night with a narrow popular vote lead nationwide and an apparent lead in electoral votes—267 to 246—with one state, Florida, too close to call.

Bush led in Florida by 1,784 votes, but state law mandated a recount because of the slim margin. The initial recount completed by week's ended left Bush in the lead by 327 votes. Gore then invoked another provision of state law to demand manual recounts in four counties (Broward, Miami-Dade, Volusia, and Palm Beach), but the state's top election official—Secretary of State Katherine Harris, a Republican—announced she would not accept returns submitted after the normal seven-day deadline set by state law.

Bush Appeals to Supreme Court

Gore contested Harris's refusal to extend the deadline in state court. The Florida Supreme Court unanimously ordered Harris to accept any returns submitted by Nov. 26. Bush then asked the U.S. Supreme Court to override the state high court.

The justices surprised many observers by agreeing to hear Bush's plea on Nov. 24 and scheduled arguments for Dec. 1. In the meantime, Harris had accepted some but not all of the new tabulations and certified Bush as the winner by 537 votes. But Gore's decision to file an "election contest" under another provision of Florida law meant that the legal battle continued.

In Washington, the Court made the unprecedented decision to allow an audio recording of the Dec. 1 arguments in *Bush v. Palm Beach Canvassing Board* to be broadcast immediately afterward.

Bush's lawyer, Theodore Olson, told the justices that the Florida court infringed the state legislature's authority under the U.S. Constitution to determine the method of choosing presidential electors. Olson said the recount also ran afoul of a federal law aimed at safeguarding a state's selection of electors if chosen by methods fixed prior to election day. Gore's

---

Driver Privacy Protection Act of 1994 did not intrude on state sovereignty.

The Court's decisions on federal preemption of state laws provided an occasional counterpoint to the general trend in favor of the states. In three rulings in 2000, the Court held that federal laws overrode state statutes or state court actions. Unanimously, the Court struck down a Massachusetts law imposing economic sanctions on the Asian nation of Myanmar (Burma) because the act went beyond penalties Congress had imposed. In a second decision, the Court, 5–4, barred states from allowing suits against automobile manufacturers for failure to install airbags before they were required by federal law. Finally, by a 7–2 vote the Court blocked states from imposing their own safety standards in suits against railroads for improper or inadequate warning signs at highway crossings.

INDIVIDUAL RIGHTS

The Court's individual rights decisions covered a wide range of issues, with no strong overall trend. It strengthened

protections against sexual harassment in the workplace, but not in schools. It construed the federal disability rights law broadly in two cases, narrowly in a third. It rejected broad remedies in minority voting rights cases but backed welfare recipients' right to equal treatment when moving to a new state. Finally, in two unrelated privacy cases, the Court refused to recognize a right to physician-assisted suicide but struck down a state law banning a certain type of late-term abortion, the so-called "partial birth abortion."

The ruling in the abortion procedure case struck down a Nebraska law that was comparable to statutes enacted by thirty-one states. The laws sought to ban abortion procedures done by dilation and extraction. The Court in 2000 struck down the law by a 5–4 vote. O'Connor joined the four liberal justices in voting against the statutes. For the majority, Breyer said that the law was unconstitutional because it could be construed to ban more common abortion procedures and because it failed to include a constitutionally required exception permitting the surgery if necessary to protect the health

lawyer, Harvard law professor Laurence Tribe, countered by arguing that the state court's decision was a routine exercise of statutory construction. The Court's ruling three days later dealt Gore a setback. In an unsigned, unanimous opinion, the justices sent the case back to the Florida high court because there was "considerable uncertainty" about the basis for its decision.

The case returned to the Court a second time after the Florida justices on Dec. 8 ordered a statewide recount—overturning a lower court judge who had found Gore's evidence for a recount too weak. Bush's lawyers immediately appealed to the U.S. Supreme Court and asked the justices to block any recount, pending arguments. In a dramatic Saturday afternoon action on Dec. 9, the Court agreed, by a 5–4 vote.

In a new round of arguments on Dec. 11—again broadcast immediately afterward—Olson and Gore's new lawyer, David Boies, disagreed over the Florida court's authority to order a recount and over the procedures for the new tally. Olson contended the state justices had failed to set a uniform standard for county election officials to use in counting disputed ballots. Boies contended the court had simply allowed local officials to use a criterion—"intent of the voter"—set out in state election law.

The Court Rules for Bush

The Court's ruling, issued shortly before 10 o'clock the next night, cleared the way for Bush to claim the White House by blocking any further recounts. Without ruling on the Florida Supreme Court's authority to prescribe the recount, the Court pronounced the standards and procedures wanting: "The recount mechanisms . . . do not satisfy the minimum requirement for non-arbitrary treatment of voters necessary to secure the fundamental right." The intent-of-the-voter test was "unobjectionable as an abstract proposition," the Court's opinion said, but more specific standards were "practicable and, we conclude, necessary."

The five-justice majority included Chief Justice William H. Rehnquist and Justices Sandra Day O'Connor, Antonin Scalia, Anthony M. Kennedy, and Clarence Thomas. Although the majority opinion was unsigned, later information indicated it was written mainly by Kennedy with help from O'Connor. In a concurring opinion, Rehnquist, joined by Scalia and Thomas, said they also believed the Florida court's decision infringed on the state legislature's authority to control selection of electors.

Two of the four dissenting justices, David H. Souter and Stephen G. Breyer, agreed that the recount procedures violated the equal protection clause, but said they would have given the Florida court time to fix the problem. The other dissenters, John Paul Stevens and Ruth Bader Ginsburg, rejected the equal protection claim and Bush's other arguments for blocking the recount. *(Court decision, appendix, p. 1046)*

In a postscript to the recount dispute, a consortium of media organizations in November 2001 announced the findings of its unofficial study of nearly 200,000 disputed presidential ballots across Florida. The study found that had Gore gotten a manual recount of just the four counties that he was seeking, he still would have lost the election to Bush in all likelihood. However, the same study found that had Gore pressed for a statewide recount of all uncounted ballots, it was likely Gore would have won Florida, and hence the presidency, by a slim margin.

of the woman. Thomas led the four dissenters in a sharply written opinion that termed the ruling "indefensible."

The assisted-suicide issue reached the Court in challenges to similar state laws in New York and Washington that prohibited physicians from helping a terminally ill patient end his or her life. Federal appeals courts had issued separate rulings that the laws interfered with patients' equal protection or due process rights. The Court in 1997 unanimously overturned the appeals courts' decisions. In the main opinion, Rehnquist said the government has "important and legitimate interests" in banning assisted suicide. In a concurring opinion, however, O'Connor—joined by Ginsburg and Breyer—said the ruling would allow physicians to prescribe pain-killing medications even if they knew the drugs could hasten the patient's death.

The Court's rulings on sexual harassment in the workplace came in three unrelated cases in 1998. In two of them, female employees claimed that male supervisors made improper advances but made no complaints about the alleged behavior until after leaving the jobs. The employers—a private company and a municipal government—argued that they could not be liable for individual supervisors' conduct and that the women in any event had suffered no financial harm.

In companion 7–2 decisions, the Court rejected both defenses. An employer could be liable for sexual harassment even if the employee suffered no tangible consequences, the Court held. And an employer was subject to indirect or vicarious liability for improper sexual conduct by a supervisor unless the employer took reasonable steps to prevent the conduct. Dissenters Thomas and Scalia argued that an employer should be liable only if he or she knew or should have known of the conduct.

In a third decision, the Court unanimously held that sexual harassment law covers improper conduct by someone of the same sex. The ruling reinstated a suit by an oil-rig worker who claimed male employees taunted him—inaccurately—for being gay.

The Court in the same year, however, limited the ability of students to recover for sexual harassment by a teacher. By a

5–4 vote, the Court ruled that a school district could be held liable only if a ranking official knew of the improper conduct or was "deliberately indifferent" to it. A year later, however, the Court said school districts could be liable for sexual harassment by one student against another if the conduct was severe and officials did nothing to stop it.

In a 1999 case the Court refused to set a special standard for punitive damages in federal job discrimination suits. But it said employers could avoid punitive damages if they proved they had made good-faith efforts to comply with the law. The Court that year also ruled that the Equal Employment Opportunity Commission could award compensatory or punitive damages to federal employees.

The Court narrowed the scope of the Americans with Disabilities Act (ADA) in 1999 by ruling that it did not prohibit discrimination against employees with "correctable" impairments, such as nearsightedness or high blood pressure. One year before, however, the Court had ruled that a person with the AIDS-causing virus HIV could use the law to sue a dentist who refused to treat her.

In a different context, the Court in 1999 ruled that the ADA prohibits state governments from unnecessarily segregating mentally ill patients in "unnecessary isolation." By a 6–3 vote, the Court ruled that someone with a mental illness is entitled to placement in a community setting if the placement is medically appropriate and within the available mental health treatment resources.

In a significant minority voting rights case, the Court in 2000 ruled, 5–4, that state and local governments do not have to obtain prior approval for election law changes unless they leave minority voters worse off than before. Instead, the Court said, minority voters had to prove intentional discrimination to block such changes. The Court also continued its series of rulings limiting racial redistricting by upholding a Georgia plan that created one but not a second district with a majority black population.

The welfare rights case stemmed from a California law that limited new residents to the benefits provided by the state they had moved from. The Court in 1999 ruled, 7–2, that the law violated the rarely cited provision of the Fourteenth Amendment that prohibits states from abridging the "privileges and immunities of citizens of the United States."

In another novel case, the Court in 2000 declined to back "grandparents' rights" over parents' rights in a child visitation dispute. The decision overturned a Washington state judge's order granting visitation rights to the grandparents of two young girls over the mother's objections.

FIRST AMENDMENT

The Court's First Amendment rulings alternated between striking down or upholding government regulation of speech. Conservative and liberal justices often switched sides from their customary stance toward expanding or restricting constitutional rights. Kennedy proved to be one of the most consistent supporters of First Amendment claims, while Breyer tended more often to uphold government restrictions on speech. In church-state issues, the Court's rulings allowing expanded government aid to parochial schools cheered religious advocacy groups while raising concerns among organizations favoring stricter separation of church and state.

In the most significant of the free speech rulings, the Court in 1997 struck down a 1996 law—the Communications Decency Act—that made it a crime to transmit "patently offensive" sexual material over the Internet in a way that would be accessible to minors. The American Civil Liberties Union challenged the law, contending that it would restrict speech for adults.

In a forceful opinion by Stevens, the Court agreed. The act, he wrote, "effectively suppresses a large amount of speech that adults have a constitutional right to receive and to address to one another." Stevens concluded by warning that government regulation was likely to stunt the growth of the Internet. Six justices joined his opinion; two others—Rehnquist and O'Connor—agreed the law was unconstitutional but suggested a narrower statute might be upheld.

The Court in 2000 struck down a second federal law aimed at regulating sexual material on a mass medium—in this instance, cable television. The act required cable television channels either to scramble sexually explicit programming or to limit the material to late night and early morning hours. By a 5–4 vote, the Court said Congress had failed to show a need for the law. Kennedy wrote for the majority; Breyer led the dissenters.

On another sex-related issue, the Court in the same year upheld the right of cities and states to ban nude dancing. Despite the impact on free expression, the Court said such laws were justified as efforts to regulate public health and safety problems associated with adult entertainment.

Other free speech disputes arose in an assortment of settings ranging from campaign finance laws to cable television, from antiabortion protests to Boy Scout membership policies. The rulings followed no consistent patterns.

In the campaign finance case, the Court upheld, 6–3, the right of states to set limits on campaign contributions to candidates for state offices. Justice David H. Souter wrote the majority opinion, which reaffirmed the controversial 1976 decision *Buckley v. Valeo* that struck down limits on campaign spending but allowed restrictions on contributions. Echoing the earlier decision, Souter said contribution limits were justified to prevent corruption or the appearance of corruption; Thomas led three dissenters who said the earlier ruling should be overruled and, in any event, not extended.

The Court in 2000 struck down a state "blanket primary" law allowing voters to vote for candidates from different parties for different offices in nomination elections. By a 7–2 vote, the Court said the California law interfered with political parties' freedom of association. The year before the Court struck down major parts of a Colorado law regulating circulation of initiative petitions. The invalidated provisions—requiring circulators to identify themselves and disclose any amounts they had been paid—unjustifiably inhibited the initiative process, Ginsburg explained for the majority.

THE COURT OF 1997–2000

The members of the U.S. Supreme Court in 1997–2000 were:

• Chief Justice William H. Rehnquist, born in 1924, appointed to the Court by President Nixon in 1971; promoted to chief justice by President Reagan in 1986.

• Justice John Paul Stevens, born in 1920, appointed by President Ford in 1975.

• Justice Sandra Day O'Connor, born in 1930, appointed by President Reagan in 1981.

• Justice Antonin Scalia, born in 1936, appointed by President Reagan in 1986.

• Justice Anthony M. Kennedy, born in 1936, appointed by President Reagan in 1987.

• Justice David H. Souter, born in 1939, appointed by President Bush in 1990.

• Justice Clarence Thomas, born in 1948, appointed by President Bush in 1991.

• Justice Ruth Bader Ginsburg, born in 1933, appointed by President Clinton in 1993.

• Justice Stephen G. Breyer, born in 1938, appointed by President Clinton in 1994.

In a major regulatory dispute between broadcasters and cable operators, the Court in 1997 upheld a federal law requiring cable systems to carry the signals of local broadcast stations. The 5–4 ruling said that the so-called "must carry" law served an important government interest in "preserving a multiplicity of broadcasters." In a unanimous decision, however, the Court applied its commercial speech doctrines in 1999 to strike down a federal ban on broadcast advertising of casino gambling.

Some disputes seemed to pit competing constitutional claims against each other. The Court in 2000 upheld, 6–3, a state law limiting leafleting or so-called "sidewalk counseling" by antiabortion protesters outside clinics where abortions were performed; Stevens based the decision in part on patients' right to be left alone. For the dissenters, Scalia said the law interfered with protesters' free speech rights and mocked what he called the "unheard of 'right to be left alone' on the public streets." In another clash between competing First Amendment interests, the Court in 2000 said state universities can impose a mandatory fee to support political and ideological groups even if a student objects to some of the organizations receiving funds.

The Court also issued an important freedom of association ruling in a closely watched case challenging the Boy Scouts' policy of excluding homosexuals as adult leaders. By a 5–4 vote along conservative-liberal lines, the Court in 2000 held that the Scouts' First Amendment rights took precedence over a New Jersey state law prohibiting discrimination on the basis of sexual orientation.

In church-state cases, the Court twice ruled that general aid programs benefiting parochial schools did not necessarily violate the constitutional prohibition against the establishment of religion. In the first case, the Court in 1997 ruled, 5–4, that public school teachers could provide remedial educational services to disadvantaged students at church-affiliated schools. The decision overturned a contrary ruling twelve years earlier that had forced New York City to set up mobile classrooms adjacent to parochial schools to provide the services. Then in 2000 the Court ruled, 6–3, that governments could lend computers and other instructional equipment to religious schools. That ruling also overturned an earlier decision.

In the same year, however, the Court strengthened its prohibition against organized prayer at public high schools. By a 6–3 vote, the Court rejected a Texas school district's policy of allowing a student-elected speaker to deliver a prayer at the start of high school football games. The policy, Stevens wrote for the majority, "has the purpose and creates the perception of encouraging the delivery of prayer at a series of important school events."

CRIMINAL LAW

The Court's criminal law decisions continued to favor police and prosecutors against suspects, defendants, or prisoners most of the time, but with some notable exceptions. In the most important, the Court in 2000 forcefully reaffirmed the Miranda rule on police interrogation—invalidating a federal law aimed at overturning the once-controversial decision. The Court also for the first time struck down a forfeiture provision as an excessive fine under the Eighth Amendment. And it produced a mixed bag of Fourth Amendment decisions that included some limiting police search and seizure powers.

The Miranda rule case involved a law Congress passed in 1968, just two years after the Court's decision that required police to inform suspects of their rights before interrogation while in custody. The law provided that any "voluntary" confession would be admissible in federal court. Most legal experts thought the law unconstitutional, and the Justice Department generally had refrained from using it. But the federal appeals court in Virginia cited the law in 1999 in deciding to admit a challenged confession in a bank robbery case.

The Court appointed a University of Utah law professor, Paul Cassell, to defend the law when the Justice Department refused. By a 7–2 vote, the Court ruled the law unconstitutional in a decision written by Chief Justice Rehnquist, who had often voted in the past to narrow applications of the Miranda rule and who had voiced doubts about its constitutional status. In this decision, however, Rehnquist said that *Miranda* established "a constitutional rule" that Congress "may not legislatively supersede." He also said that the warnings had become "embedded in police practice." Only the Court's two most conservative justices—Antonin Scalia and Clarence Thomas—dissented.

In another prodefendant decision, the Court in 1998 ruled that the federal government had violated the Eighth Amendment's prohibition against excessive fines by confiscating some $350,000 from a defendant in a currency violation case. The ruling followed two decisions in 1993 that established the principle that forfeitures were subject to the Eighth Amendment but set no guidelines. In the new case, the Court voted 5–4 that the confiscation of the cash for violating the $10,000 limit on taking currency out of the country was "grossly disproportional to the gravity of the offense." Thomas, a strong critic of forfeiture provisions, led the four liberal justices in forming the majority, in opposition to his usual conservative allies.

The Court also made it harder for prosecutors to obtain longer sentences in so-called "hate crime" cases. A New Jersey law—comparable to laws in other states—provided for enhanced penalties for certain offenses if they were based on race, ethnicity, religion, gender, or sexual orientation. By a 5–4 vote, the Court in 2000 held that defendants were entitled to a jury trial and to proof beyond a reasonable doubt of the alleged motivation if that raised the sentence beyond the normal statutory maximum. Scalia and Thomas—strong proponents of jury trial rights—joined three liberals to form the majority.

On the other hand, the Court gave states leeway to use civil commitment procedures to keep sexual offenders off the streets after the expiration of their sentences. The 5–4 ruling upheld the application of a Kansas law that allowed a violent sexual offender to be committed to a mental hospital after his criminal sentence if he or she suffered from "a mental abnormality or disorder" and was "likely to engage" in similar acts in the future. The conservative majority rejected arguments that the law violated due process or amounted to retroactive punishment.

In its most important search and seizure case for the period, the Court in 1999 struck down a Chicago antiloitering ordinance aimed at preventing gangs from congregating on public streets. In a splintered 6–3 decision, the Court said the 1992 ordinance gave police too much discretion to arrest people for disobeying an order to disperse. In another significant limit on police power in 1999, the Court unanimously said that police cannot automatically conduct a full search of an automobile after stopping the driver for a routine traffic violation.

In other Fourth Amendment cases, however, the Court gave police broader discretion in automobile searches—for example, in a 1997 ruling allowing police to order a passenger as well as a driver out of a vehicle after a traffic stop. The Court in 1998 allowed the use of illegally obtained evidence in parole revocation hearings. Four rulings in 1999 rebuffed state appellate courts for expanding Fourth Amendment restrictions on police beyond the Court's own rulings. And in 2000 the Court ruled that police may have sufficient grounds to stop and a frisk a suspect who runs away upon seeing the officer. On the other hand, the Court in the same year turned

U.S. Supreme Court Caseload

	1996–1997	1997–1998	1998–1999	1999–2000
Number of cases on docket	7,602	7,692	8,083	8,445
Cases decided summarily	81	50	55	50
Cases argued and decided	92	97	94	87
Cases disposed of by signed opinions	87	93	84	79
Number of signed opinions	80	91	75	74

SOURCE: Harold W. Stanley and Richard G. Niemi, *Vital Statistics on American Politics, 2001–2002* (Washington, D.C.: CQ Press, 2001), 282–283.

aside an effort to allow a "stop-and-frisk" based on an anonymous tip that the suspect was carrying a firearm.

The Court began grappling with a host of issues posed by a new law—the Antiterrorism and Effective Death Penalty Act of 1996—aimed at making it harder for state prison inmates to use federal habeas corpus petitions to challenge their convictions or sentences. One of the most important provisions barred federal judges from granting an inmate's habeas corpus petition unless a state court decision was "contrary to" or "an unreasonable application" of a Supreme Court precedent. In its first interpretation of that provision, the Court in 2000 somewhat softened a federal appeals court's stringent construction of the law and granted a Virginia death row inmate a chance to win a new trial based on a claim of ineffective assistance of counsel. The Court also somewhat softened the impact of the law in two unrelated rulings in 1998. The Court continued to strictly regulate habeas corpus petitions in other areas, however. In two rulings in 1997, for example, it refused to let state inmates use Supreme Court decisions announcing new criminal procedure protections to retroactively invalidate convictions obtained under previous rules.

MISCELLANEOUS ISSUES

The Court several times found itself policing the separation of powers between the three branches of the federal government. In the most significant of the rulings, the Court refused to give President Bill Clinton protection from a federal court civil suit for alleged conduct before he took office. The Court also limited presidential power by striking down a law—the Line Item Veto Act—that would have given the president power to excise individual spending items from omnibus congressional appropriations bills.

The Clinton administration suffered losses in two other politically charged disputes. The Court refused to allow the Census Bureau to use so-called "statistical sampling" to determine population counts to be used in apportioning seats in the House of Representatives. The justices also denied the Food and Drug Administration (FDA) authority to regulate tobacco products.

Separation of Powers

The ruling subjecting Clinton to civil suit while in office stemmed from a federal civil rights suit charging that he made a sexual advance against an Arkansas state employee, Paula Jones, while serving as governor. The Court previously had ruled that presidents enjoy absolute immunity from private suit for official conduct while in office, but had not decided whether the immunity extended to actions before taking office. In Jones's suit, a lower court decided that pretrial discovery should be stayed until after Clinton left office, but the federal appeals court in St. Louis rejected any delay in the proceedings.

In a unanimous decision, the Court in 1997 held that the president has no "categorical immunity" in civil lawsuits involving conduct unrelated to his office. Writing for eight justices, Stevens said that Jones had "a right to an orderly disposition of her claims." He rejected the possibility that the proceedings would create an "unacceptable burden" on the president. In a separate concurrence, Breyer agreed that the president was not entitled to "automatic temporary immunity" but cautioned that federal judges should not "interfere with the President's discharge of his public duties."

The ruling played an important part in the events that eventually resulted in Clinton's impeachment by the House of Representatives for allegedly lying to a federal grand jury and obstructing justice. Once discovery resumed, Jones's attorneys questioned Clinton about his relationship with a White House intern, Monica Lewinsky. Later, Independent Counsel Kenneth Starr also questioned Clinton about Lewinsky in testimony for a federal grand jury. Starr referred the matter to the House, which voted to impeach Clinton in December 1998. The Senate acquitted Clinton on Feb. 12, 1999, after a trial that spanned five weeks and that was presided over—as specified by the Constitution—by Chief Justice Rehnquist.

In the other major separation-of-powers ruling, the Court threw out a law passed by a budget-minded, Republican-controlled Congress to let the president veto individual spending items in appropriations bills. Presidents of both parties had long sought such powers, but the Court in 1998 held, 6–3, that the law violated the constitutional scheme for enacting legislation. For the majority, Stevens said that the Constitution does not give the president "the unilateral power to change the text of duly enacted statutes."

Census

The ruling on the census rejected a plan to use statistical techniques to try to correct for an anticipated undercount of minorities in the constitutionally required population tally used every ten years to allocate seats in the House of Representatives among the states. The Census Bureau said the technique was statistically valid, but Republicans questioned the methodology and Democrats' motivation in supporting it.

In a 5–4 decision, the Court in 1999 held that the proposed method violated a provision of the 1976 Census Act that permitted sampling "except for the determination of population for apportionment purposes." O'Connor wrote the majority opinion; the four conservative justices who joined her opinion also wrote separately to say that they believed sampling would also violate the Constitution. The four liberal justices pointed to a different statutory section as giving the Census Bureau broad discretion to use statistical sampling.

Tobacco Regulation

The Court's decision denying the FDA power to regulate tobacco products struck down an initiative pushed by the agency's commissioner, David Kessler, and personally endorsed by Clinton. The FDA found a statutory basis for a series of marketing and advertising restrictions by classifying nicotine as a drug and cigarettes and smokeless tobacco as "drug delivery devices." Tobacco companies challenged the regulations on statutory and First Amendment grounds.

The justices split along conservative-liberal lines in the 5–4 decision in 2000 striking down the regulations. For the majority, O'Connor said that Congress had not given the FDA any authority to regulate tobacco products. The Court did not rule on the First Amendment issues.

Property Rights

The Court displayed sensitivity to property rights in several decisions. In one ruling, the Court in 1998 struck down a federal law that required companies that had once been in the coal business to pay lifetime health benefits for retired miners and their families. Four justices found the law violated the Takings Clause because of what O'Connor called the "disproportionate and severely retroactive" financial burden on the companies; Kennedy, who provided the fifth vote against the law, said it violated due process.

In another case, the Court in 1998 allowed a Texas lawyer to proceed with a Takings Clause challenge to a legal-aid financing system adopted in all other states and the District of Columbia. The so-called "Interest on Lawyer Trust Accounts" plans established by courts or state bars pooled interest from client funds held in trust accounts and funneled the money to organizations providing legal assistance to the poor.

By a 5–4 vote, the Court agreed with the Texas lawyer's claim that the interest was "property" subject to the Takings Clause and sent the case back to lower courts for further proceedings.

Environmental Law

In an important environmental ruling, the Court in 2000 upheld the power of courts to fine polluters in private citizen suits. The 7–2 ruling reinstated a $405,000 fine against a company for toxic discharges into a waterway. The decision rejected the company's claims that only the government could seek civil penalties or that the fine should be lifted because it had eliminated the alleged violations while the case was pending.

Supreme Court Decisions
November 1996–June 2000

Business Law

ANTITRUST

State Oil Company v. Khan (522 U.S. 3), decided by a 9–0 vote, Nov. 4, 1997; O'Connor wrote the opinion.

A manufacturer or supplier may set a maximum price to be charged by dealers without necessarily violating federal antitrust law. The decision overruled a twenty-nine-year-old precedent, *Albrecht v. Herald Co.* (1968), that such agreements were per se illegal. Instead, the Court held that maximum price agreements between suppliers and dealers—vertical as opposed to horizontal price-fixing—were subject to the so-called rule of reason: illegal only if they actually resulted in reduced competition.

Nynex Corp. v. Discon, Inc. (525 U.S. 128), decided by a 9–0 vote, Dec. 14, 1998; Breyer wrote the opinion.

The automatic antitrust rule against group boycotts does not apply to an individual buyer's decision to purchase goods or services from one seller instead of from another.

BANKING

Atherton v. Federal Deposit Insurance Corporation (519 U.S. 213), decided by a 9–0 vote, Jan. 14, 1997; Breyer wrote the opinion.

Federal law sets an intermediate standard of gross negligence for imposing liability in suits against directors or officers of federally chartered banks, but states can adopt a lower standard of simple negligence. The ruling—a partial setback for government regulators—held that federally chartered banks were not subject to a federal common law standard.

National Credit Union Administration v. First National Bank & Trust Co. (522 U.S. 479), decided by a 5–4 vote, Feb. 25, 1998; Thomas wrote the opinion; O'Connor, Stevens, Souter, and Breyer dissented.

In a victory for the banking industry, the Court blocked federally chartered credit unions from expanding to include members from different employers.

Beach v. Ocwen Federal Bank (523 U.S. 410), decided by a 9–0 vote, April 21, 1998; Souter wrote the opinion.

The Court set a three-year time limit on a homeowner's ability to use the federal Truth in Lending Act to rescind a mortgage for a bank's failure to disclose financing charges accurately.

BANKRUPTCY

Associates Commercial Corp. v. Rash (520 U.S. 953), decided by an 8–1 vote, June 16, 1997; Ginsburg wrote the opinion; Stevens dissented.

A debtor in a bankruptcy reorganization who chooses, over a creditor's objections, to keep rather than surrender property that serves as collateral on a loan must pay the creditor the replacement value of the property. The ruling—a victory for creditors—settled a conflict between federal courts of appeals over what valuation method should be used in a so-called cramdown procedure in a bankruptcy reorganization. The procedure allows a debtor, as part of a court-approved reorganization, to retain property over the objections of a secured creditor who has a lien on the property. But the debtor—who "crams the plan down the creditor's throat"—must agree to pay the creditor the value of the property. Some courts ruled that the value of the property was the debtor's cost to replace it; others ruled the value was the lower amount that the creditor could recoup in a foreclosure sale. The Court held that the Bankruptcy Code called for the replacement-value standard.

Fidelity Financial Services, Inc. v. Fink (522 U.S. 211), decided by a 9–0 vote, Jan. 13, 1998; Souter wrote the opinion.

In a setback for lenders, the Court strictly interpreted the twenty-day deadline for lenders to file liens on a borrower's property in order to have a preferential right to repayment in a federal bankruptcy proceeding.

Kawaauhau v. Geiger (523 U.S. 57), decided by a 9–0 vote, March 3, 1998; Ginsburg wrote the opinion.

Federal bankruptcy law allows someone to wipe out a debt for a medical malpractice judgment. The ruling resolved a conflict between federal courts of appeals on how to interpret a Bankruptcy Code provision that barred a debtor from discharging any debt "for willful and malicious injury." The Court ruled that the statutory exception did not apply to medical negligence.

Cohen v. De La Cruz (523 U.S. 213), decided by a 9–0 vote, March 24, 1998; O'Connor wrote the opinion.

Federal bankruptcy law does not protect someone from being required to pay a court judgment for fraud.

Bank of America National Trust and Savings Association v. 203 North LaSalle Street Partnership (526 U.S. 434), decided by an 8–1 vote, May 3, 1999; Souter wrote the opinion; Stevens dissented.

Partners or stockholders in a business in a bankruptcy proceeding cannot acquire an equity interest in the reorganized concern by investing new money without safeguards to ensure the fairness of the transaction. The ruling bolstered creditors' rights but failed to completely resolve whether the so-called old equity holders can emerge as owners after reorganization by contributing money or labor.

Hartford Underwriters Insurance Co. v. Union Planters Bank, N.A. (530 U.S. 1), decided by a 9–0 vote, May 30, 2000; Scalia wrote the opinion.

Unsecured creditors cannot seek payment of a claim against a bankrupt estate by using a Bankruptcy Code provision that allows the trustee to recover administrative costs before secured creditors are paid. The Court held that only the bankruptcy trustee could invoke a provision of the Bankruptcy Code—section 506(c)—that allows the trustee to recover administrative expenses.

Raleigh v. Illinois Department of Revenue (530 U.S. 15), decided by a 9–0 vote, May 30, 2000; Souter wrote the opinion.

The Court eased the burden on local or state taxing authorities to collect unpaid taxes in bankruptcy proceedings. The Court held that state law governs the burden of proof on tax claims in federal bankruptcy proceedings.

COPYRIGHT

Quality King Distributors, Inc. v. L'anza Research International, Inc. (523 U.S. 135), decided by a 9–0 vote, March 9, 1998; Stevens wrote the opinion.

The Court rejected an effort to use federal copyright law to control so-called gray market imports of goods manufactured in the United States, sold abroad, and then brought back into the U.S. for resale. In a victory for discount retailers, the Court unanimously held that the infringement claim was barred by the "first sale doctrine," which generally prevents a copyright holder from controlling distribution of a particular copy after selling it.

Feltner v. Columbia Pictures Television, Inc. (523 U.S. 340), decided by a 9–0 vote, March 31, 1998; Thomas wrote the opinion.

A jury trial is constitutionally required in a copyright infringement suit brought under a provision for specified "statutory damages" if either party requests one. The Court held that a provision added to the Copyright Act in 1976, section 504(c), did not provide for a jury trial, but the Seventh Amendment required one.

INTERNATIONAL TRADE

United States v. Haggar Apparel Co. (526 U.S. 380), decided by 9–0 and 7–2 votes, April 21, 1999; Kennedy wrote the opinion; Stevens and Ginsburg dissented in part.

The government won a partial and possibly determinative victory in its effort to deny a major clothing manufacturer a tariff exemption on pants that are permapressed in Mexico. The dispute involved a tariff provision that allows an exemption from duties for products made from components manufactured in the United States but assembled abroad. The exemption applied if the foreign operations included assembly or "operations incidental to the assembly process." The ruling sent the case back to the trade tribunal for reconsideration.

MARITIME LAW

Saratoga Fishing Co. v. J. M. Martinac & Co. (520 U.S. 875), decided by a 6–3 vote, June 2, 1997; Breyer wrote the opinion; Scalia, O'Connor, and Thomas dissented.

Boat manufacturers may be held liable in product-defect suits for damage to property or equipment added by someone who bought the vessel and then resold it to a second purchaser. The liability-expanding rule said that barring recovery from the manufacturer for damage to added equipment would reduce the incentive to produce safe products.

PATENTS

Warner-Jenkinson Co., Inc. v. Hilton Davis Chemical Co. (520 U.S. 17), decided by a 9–0 vote, March 3, 1997; Thomas wrote the opinion.

The Court reaffirmed but narrowed somewhat a judicially created doctrine that protects patent holders against inventors who develop products or processes that are similar but not identical. The decision rejected arguments that Congress implicitly repealed the so-called doctrine of equivalents when it revised the federal Patent Act in 1952. The doctrine allows a patent holder to win an infringement claim even if a rival product or process is not identical as long as there is "equivalence" between its elements and the elements of the patented invention.

The Court noted that the doctrine should not be applied so broadly as to weaken the rule that patents generally are confined to their explicit terms. The justices declined to rule on whether the doctrine can be applied only by a judge, not by a jury.

Pfaff v. Wells Electronics, Inc. (525 U.S. 55), decided by a 9–0 vote, Nov. 10, 1998; Stevens wrote the opinion.

The statutory prohibition against patenting an invention that has been on sale for more than a year applies even if the inventor did not complete a working prototype before offering the device for sale. The Patent Act provides that no one is entitled to patent an "invention" that has been "on sale" more than one year before filing a patent application. The Court wrote that the Patent Act's "on-sale bar" applies if the product "is the subject of a commercial offer for sale" and is "ready for patenting" more than one year before the application for a patent is filed.

Dickinson, Acting Commissioner of Patents and Trademarks v. Zurko (527 U.S. 150), decided by a 6–3 vote, June 10, 1999; Breyer wrote the opinion; Rehnquist, Kennedy, and Ginsburg dissented.

The federal appeals court that hears patent cases was told to give greater deference to rulings by the Patent and Trademark Office. The ruling changed a long-established policy of somewhat stricter judicial review of decisions by the patent office.

SHAREHOLDER SUITS

California Public Employees' Retirement System v. Felzen (525 U.S. 315), affirmed by an equally divided Court, Jan. 20, 1999; *per curiam* (unsigned) opinion; O'Connor did not participate.

The Court upheld, on a tie vote, a lower court decision that limited legal challenges to settlements of shareholder suits against officers or directors of corporations for financial misconduct. The deadlock left unresolved an important procedural issue involving so-called derivative suits—actions by shareholders seeking to recover, on behalf of a corporation, moneys lost because of financial misconduct by officers or directors of the company. The often lucrative litigation goes by the name *derivative suits* because the shareholders' rights are said to "derive" from the corporation's.

The Court does not announce individual votes in tie cases, but questioning during the argument indicated the justices were divided along expected ideological lines, with conservatives inclined to bar the appeal and more liberal justices inclined to permit it.

TAXATION

United States v. Jose (519 U.S. 54), decided by a 9–0 vote, Dec. 2, 1996; *per curiam* (unsigned) opinion.

The government can immediately appeal a federal court order limiting the enforcement of an Internal Revenue Service (IRS) summons issued in a tax investigation. The decision allowed the IRS to contest a federal judge's order that the agency's civil investigation branch give a taxpayer five days' notice before transferring any records to the agency's branch for criminal investigations.

O'Gilvie v. United States (519 U.S. 79), decided by a 6–3 vote, Dec. 10, 1996; Breyer wrote the opinion; Scalia, O'Connor, and Thomas dissented.

People who receive punitive damages in lawsuits must pay federal income taxes on them. The ruling backed the government's interpretation of a federal tax code provision that allows taxpayers to avoid taxation on "any damages received . . . on account of personal injuries or sickness." The Court ruled that punitive damages do not qualify for the exclusion because they are not received "on account of" personal injuries, but "on account of a defendant's reprehensible conduct and the jury's need to punish and deter it."

United States v. Brockamp (519 U.S. 347), decided by a 9–0 vote, Feb. 18, 1997; Breyer wrote the opinion.

A taxpayer's mental disability cannot, under existing law, excuse a late filing for a refund of overpaid taxes. The Court held that the equitable tolling doctrine, which allows a court to extend statutory time limits for equitable reasons, cannot be used to extend the time limit for seeking a tax refund.

Commissioner of Internal Revenue v. Estate of Hubert (520 U.S. 93), decided by a 7–2 vote, March 18, 1997; Kennedy wrote the plurality opinion; Scalia and Breyer dissented.

The Court allowed the administrator of a nearly $30 million estate to avoid taxes on income generated by the legacy that was used to pay expenses of administering the estate. The ruling rejected the position of the Internal Revenue Service (IRS) on a recurrent issue in wrapping up estates. The federal estate tax allows a deduction for amounts passed to a spouse or charity. Generally, the deduction must be reduced—and the taxable amounts increased—by the value of assets used to pay for wrapping up the estate. The IRS contended that no deduction could be claimed for income generated during administration by assets being passed to a spouse or a charity.

United States v. United States Shoe Corp. (523 U.S. 360), decided by a 9–0 vote, March 31, 1998; Ginsburg wrote the opinion.

The Court exempted exporters from the Harbor Maintenance Tax Act of 1986, which had been enacted to pay for maintaining and developing harbors, saying the levy violated the constitutional prohibition on taxing exports. The Court also held that the levy violated the Export Clause, rejecting the government's argument that it amounted to a user fee.

Atlantic Mutual Insurance Co. v. Commissioner of Internal Revenue (523 U.S. 382), decided by a 9–0 vote, April 21, 1998; Scalia wrote the opinion.

The Court sided with the Internal Revenue Service in narrowing the ability of property and casualty insurers to avoid the effect of the Tax Reform Act of 1986 provision limiting the deductibility of funds set aside for unpaid claims. The act provided that insurers could not deduct the full amount of claims reserves for a given year but had to discount the amount over time. A transition provision softened the law's impact for the first year, but insurers were still barred from "reserve strengthening"—taking a full deduction for net additions to reserves during the year.

United States v. Estate of Romani (523 U.S. 517), decided by a 9–0 vote, April 29, 1998; Stevens wrote the opinion.

The Court limited the federal government's ability to go ahead of other creditors in collecting debts from the estate of someone who has died. The ruling resolved a seeming conflict between a 200-year-old law, known as the "priority statute," which gave the government priority in collecting debts from a decedent's estate, and a more recent law, the Tax Lien Act of 1966, which set specific conditions for the government to follow in imposing a lien—legal notice of a debt—on property for the collection of unpaid taxes. The Court held that the Tax Lien Act took precedence over the priority statute.

Drye v. United States (528 U.S. 49), decided by a 9–0 vote, Dec. 7, 1999; Ginsburg wrote the opinion.

Persons eligible to inherit money or property cannot circumvent a federal tax lien on the value of the estate by disclaiming their right to the inheritance.

Baral v. United States (528 U.S. 431), decided by a 9–0 vote, Feb. 22, 2000; Thomas wrote the opinion.

The three-year period established by the federal tax code for seeking a refund begins on the normal due date for the taxpayer's return, not when the return is actually filed. The Court held that federal income taxes are considered to have been paid on the due date regardless when the return was actually filed.

TRADEMARKS

Wal-Mart Stores, Inc. v. Samara Brothers, Inc. (529 U.S. 205), decided by a 9–0 vote, March 22, 2000; Scalia wrote the opinion.

The design of a product is not ordinarily distinctive enough to qualify for trademark protection.

Courts and Procedure

APPEALS

Caterpillar Inc. v. Lewis (519 U.S. 61), decided by a 9–0 vote, Dec. 10, 1996; Ginsburg wrote the opinion.

A Kentucky construction worker lost a bid to get a new trial in state court despite a federal judge's erroneous interim ruling that this personal injury suit belonged in federal court because of diversity of citizenship.

M.L.B. v. S.L.J. (519 U.S. 79), decided by a 6–3 vote, Dec. 16, 1996; Ginsburg wrote the opinion; Thomas, Rehnquist, and Scalia dissented.

States cannot prevent someone from appealing a parental termination order solely because of inability to pay for a transcript of the proceeding. The Court said that denying such an appeal solely because of indigency violated rights to due process and equal protection.

Weisgram v. Marley Co. (528 U.S. 440), decided by a 9–0 vote, Feb. 22, 2000; Ginsburg wrote the opinion.

A federal appeals court may set aside a jury verdict and enter a judgment in favor of the losing party if it rules expert testimony was improperly admitted at trial.

ARBITRATION

Cortez Byrd Chips, Inc. v. Bill Harbert Construction Co. (529 U.S. 193), decided by a 9–0 vote, March 21, 2000; Souter wrote the opinion.

The Court gave parties to an arbitration wide discretion as to where to file a court action to enforce, modify, or set aside the arbitrator's award. The Court held that the Federal Arbitration Act allowed an action to confirm, modify, or vacate an arbitration to be filed in any court where venue would be proper under general federal law.

ATTORNEY FEES

Martin, Director, Michigan Department of Corrections v. Hadix (527 U.S. 343), decided by a 7–2 vote, June 21, 1999; O'Connor wrote the opinion; Ginsburg and Stevens dissented in part.

Limits on attorney's fees in prison condition lawsuits in federal courts imposed by the Prison Litigation Reform Act of 1995, signed into law on April 26, 1996, apply to any work by lawyers performed in pending cases after the date of enactment.

ATTORNEYS

Swidler & Berlin v. United States (524 U.S. 399), decided by a 6–3 vote, June 25, 1998; Rehnquist wrote the opinion; O'Connor, Scalia, and Thomas dissented.

The attorney-client privilege ordinarily survives the death of the client and protects a lawyer from being compelled to disclose a client's confidences in response to a grand jury subpoena. The ruling rejected an effort by Independent Counsel Kenneth Starr to subpoena notes taken by attorney James Hamilton of a conversation Hamilton had with then–White House deputy counsel Vincent Foster nine days before Foster's suicide in July 1993. Starr sought the notes for his investigation of possible obstruction of justice or other offenses in connection with the dismissal of employees in the White House Travel Office in May 1993.

Conn v. Gabbert (526 U.S. 286), decided by a 9–0 vote, April 5, 1999; Rehnquist wrote the opinion.

Law enforcement officers did not violate a criminal defense lawyer's civil rights when they searched him in a manner that interfered with his consultation with a client testifying before a grand jury.

Cunningham v. Hamilton County, Ohio (527 U.S. 198), decided by a 9–0 vote, June 14, 1999; Thomas wrote the opinion.

An attorney ordinarily cannot appeal a judge's decision to impose sanctions for misconduct during a lawsuit while the case is still going on.

CLASS ACTIONS

Amchem Products, Inc. v. Windsor (521 U.S. 591), decided by a 6–2 vote, June 25, 1997; Ginsburg wrote the opinion; Breyer and Stevens dissented in part; O'Connor did not participate.

The Court refused to revive a $1.3 billion class-action settlement for hundreds of thousands of asbestos-exposure claims, saying that the proposed class was too big and the issues too disparate to permit class action treatment.

Ortiz v. Fibreboard Corp. (527 U.S. 815), decided by a 7–2 vote, June 23, 1999; Souter wrote the opinion; Breyer and Stevens dissented.

Federal courts cannot approve mandatory class settlements in mass tort cases unless the money available for compensation is definitely fixed and potential conflicts of interest between classes of claimants are addressed.

Free v. Abbott Laboratories, Inc. (529 U.S. 333), affirmed on a 4–4 vote, April 3, 2000; *per curiam* opinion; O'Connor did not participate.

The Court upheld on a tie vote a federal appeals court decision making it easier for defendants in certain class action suits to have the cases tried in federal courts. The 4–4 vote left the appeals court decision standing but established no precedent on the issue. The Court does not announce how the justices vote in deadlocked cases. O'Connor recused herself because she owned a small amount of stock in one of the companies named as defendants.

EVIDENCE

General Electric Co. v. Joiner (522 U.S. 156), decided by 9–0 and 8–1 votes, Dec. 15, 1997; Rehnquist wrote the opinion; Stevens dissented in part.

In a setback for plaintiffs' group, federal trial judges were given strengthened authority to rule on the admissibility of scientific evidence.

EXPERT TESTIMONY

Kumho Tire Co., Ltd. v. Carmichael (526 U.S. 137), decided by 9–0 and 8–1 votes, March 23, 1999; Breyer wrote the opinion; Stevens dissented in part.

Trial judges have broad discretion to apply a test developed for determining the admissibility of scientific testimony to any expert evidence based on technical or other specialized knowledge. The ruling—a victory for business and insurance groups—stemmed from an effort by plaintiffs in an automobile accident case to introduce testimony by ev-

idence from a supposed tire expert blaming the mishap on a defective tire. The trial judge ruled the testimony inadmissible, citing standards for reliability established by the Court's 1993 decision, *Daubert v. Merrell Dow Pharmaceuticals, Inc.*, which required judges to exercise a "gatekeeping" function regarding scientific testimony and listed four criteria to consider in determining reliability: the testability of a scientific method, peer review, potential rate of error, and general rate of acceptance within the scientific community.

FALSE CLAIMS

Hughes Aircraft Co. v. United States ex rel. Schumer (525 U.S. 432), decided by a 9–0 vote, June 16, 1997; Thomas wrote the opinion.

The Court refused to give retroactive effect to a law easing the rules for so-called *qui tam* actions—suits brought by a private individual to recover money from someone who submitted a false claim to the government. The ruling limited the effect of a 1986 law designed to make it easier for "whistleblowers" to use the rarely invoked procedure, which allows a private party to sue on behalf of the government and to share in any recovery. Previously, the law barred a *qui tam* action if the government had any prior information or evidence about the claim; the 1986 amendment allowed a *qui tam* claim as long as the government had not publicly disclosed any information in its possession.

FEDERAL COURTS

City of Chicago v. International College of Surgeons (522 U.S. 156), decided by a 7–2 vote, Dec. 15, 1997; O'Connor wrote the opinion; Ginsburg and Stevens dissented.

Federal courts can exercise jurisdiction over state court appeals from local administrative agencies if the case also raises federal law claims. The Court added, however, that a district court could decline to hear such cases on several grounds—for example, if the state law issues were "novel" or "complex" or the state law claim "substantially predominates" over the federal claim.

Rivet v. Regions Bank of Louisiana (522 U.S. 470), decided by a 9–0 vote, Feb. 24, 1998; Ginsburg wrote the opinion.

A defendant in a state court suit cannot remove a case to federal court by claiming that the suit is barred by an earlier judgment in a federal case.

Lexecon Inc. v. Milberg Weiss Bershad Hynes & Lerach (523 U.S. 26), decided by a 9–0 vote, March 3, 1998; Souter wrote the opinion.

The Court made it harder to consolidate related cases for trial in a single federal court. The ruling upset a common practice for handling so-called multidistrict lawsuits in federal courts. A federal statute allows a special panel, the Judicial Panel on Multidistrict Litigation, to combine pretrial proceedings in such cases. Over the years, judges handling such pretrial proceedings also began to assign to themselves the trial of such cases. Reversing this long-standing practice, the Court said the statute on multidistrict litigation requires the judge handling pretrial proceedings to return the case to the district where it was filed.

Wisconsin Department of Corrections v. Schacht (524 U.S. 381), decided by a 9–0 vote, June 22, 1998; Breyer wrote the opinion.

In a complex ruling, the Court held that a federal court can hear part of a case that has been removed from state court even if it cannot hear other claims because of the Eleventh Amendment's prohibition of suits against states in federal court.

INJUNCTIONS

Grupo Mexicano de Desarrollo, S. A. v. Alliance Bond Fund, Inc. (527 U.S. 308), decided by a 5–4 vote, June 17, 1999; Scalia wrote the opinion; Ginsburg, Stevens, Souter, and Breyer dissented.

Federal courts have no power in a suit for money damages to block the defendant from transferring assets before a judgment. The sharply divided ruling represented a setback for creditors.

JUDGMENTS

Nelson v. Adams USA, Inc. (529 U.S. 460), decided by a 9–0 vote, April 25, 2000; Ginsburg wrote the opinion.

A court cannot add a party to a lawsuit after judgment and simultaneously make him subject to the judgment without giving him an opportunity to contest liability. The Court held that the procedure violated due process rights set out in the Federal Rules of Civil Procedure.

JURY TRIALS

Hetzel v. Prince William County, Virginia (523 U.S. 208), decided by a 9–0 vote, March 23, 1998; *per curiam* (unsigned) opinion.

Federal courts are barred by the Seventh Amendment's jury trial guarantee from reducing a jury's damage award without offering the plaintiff the option of a new trial.

QUIET TITLE ACTIONS

United States v. Beggerly (524 U.S. 38), decided by a 9–0 vote, June 8, 1998; Rehnquist wrote the opinion.

A Mississippi family failed in its effort to use belatedly discovered historical evidence to reopen a property ownership dispute with the federal government over land on a barrier island off the state's coast.

REMOVAL

Murphy Brothers, Inc. v. Michetti Pipe Stringing, Inc. (526 U.S. 344), decided by a 6–3 vote, April 5, 1999; Ginsburg wrote the opinion; Rehnquist, Scalia, and Thomas dissented.

The thirty-day time period for a defendant to file a motion to move a case from state to federal court starts only after official service of the complaint or summons, not after informal notice of the suit.

El Paso Natural Gas Co. v. Neztsosie (526 U.S. 473), decided by a 9–0 vote, May 3, 1999; Souter wrote the opinion.

Two energy companies won a procedural victory in their effort to avoid a trial in Native American courts in a suit by Native American plaintiffs for alleged radiation-exposure injuries from uranium mining. The ruling said that a lower federal court, rather than a Navajo tribal court, should decide where the suit by three members of the Navajo tribe was to be tried. The Court held that the 1988 amendment to the Price-Anderson Act, which generally limits liability of nuclear power companies resulting from "a nuclear incident," required federal courts rather than tribal courts to rule on its application to the suits.

Ruhrgas AG v. Marathon Oil Company (526 U.S. 574), decided by a 9–0 vote, May 17, 1999; Ginsburg wrote the opinion.

Federal courts considering cases removed from state courts have leeway in deciding which of two jurisdictional issues—jurisdiction over the defendant or over the subject of the lawsuit—to rule on first.

STATE COURTS

Baker v. General Motors Corp. (522 U.S. 222), decided by a 9–0 vote, Jan. 13, 1998; Ginsburg wrote the opinion.

A state court cannot enter an injunction preventing a person from testifying in a proceeding involving different parties in a court in another state. The ruling cleared the way for a former General Motors engineer to testify in a product liability suit brought against the carmaker by the family of a Missouri woman killed in a 1990 auto crash while driving a GM-made pickup truck. GM had previously obtained an injunction from a Michigan state court prohibiting the engineer from testifying against the company in any civil suits.

Criminal Law and Procedure

APPEALS

Johnson v. United States (529 U.S. 694), decided by a 9–0 vote, May 12, 1997; Rehnquist wrote the opinion.

A Florida woman convicted of perjury before a federal grand jury during a drug investigation failed to win a new trial despite a jury instruction that was held after trial to be erroneous.

Martinez v. Court of Appeal of California, Fourth Appellate District (528 U.S. 152), decided by a 9–0 vote, Jan. 12, 2000; Stevens wrote the opinion.

Criminal defendants have no federal constitutional right to represent themselves in appealing their convictions. The ruling barred an effort by a self-taught paralegal, Salvador

---

DUE PROCESS, EQUAL PROTECTION

... Nor shall any state deprive any person of life, liberty, or property, without due process of law; nor deny to any person within its jurisdiction the equal protection of the laws.

Fourteenth Amendment, U.S. Constitution

Martinez, to represent himself in appealing his embezzlement conviction. Martinez had argued that the Supreme Court's 1975 decision, *Faretta v. California,* which guaranteed a defendant the right to represent himself at trial, should be extended to appeals.

Smith, Warden v. Robbins (528 U.S. 259), decided by a 5–4 vote, Jan. 19, 2000; Thomas wrote the opinion; Souter, Stevens, Ginsburg, and Breyer dissented.

A lawyer for an indigent criminal defendant does not have to file a full appellate brief or try to identify potentially valid grounds for attacking a conviction if he believes the appeal is frivolous. The ruling rejected a federal habeas corpus petition by a convicted murderer, who claimed that a California procedure for indigent appeals conflicted with the requirements set out in 1967 by the Supreme Court in *Anders v. California.*

Ohler v. United States (529 U.S. 753), decided by a 5–4 vote, May 22, 2000; Rehnquist wrote the opinion; Souter, Stevens, Ginsburg, and Breyer dissented.

A defendant cannot appeal a judge's pretrial ruling to allow evidence of a prior criminal conviction if the defendant takes the stand and acknowledges the conviction herself in her direct testimony.

CAPITAL PUNISHMENT

Greene v. Georgia (519 U.S. 145), decided by a 9–0 vote, Dec. 16, 1996; *per curiam* (unsigned) opinion.

State appellate courts need not defer to trial judges' rulings on disqualifying potential jurors in capital punishment cases. The Court summarily ruled that the Georgia Supreme Court misapplied a 1985 decision, *Wainwright v. Witt,* in rejecting a death row inmate's claim that a trial judge improperly excused five potential jurors for expressing reservations about capital punishment. The Court said the 1985 ruling concerned federal judges' power in habeas corpus cases and did not require state appellate courts to adopt the same limitation in reviewing state cases.

Buchanan v. Angelone, Director, Virginia Department of Corrections (522 U.S. 269), decided by a 6–3 vote, Jan. 21,

1998; Rehnquist wrote the opinion; Breyer, Stevens, and Ginsburg dissented.

A defendant in a capital murder case has no constitutional right to have the jury instructed that it must consider mitigating evidence against imposing a death sentence.

Ohio Adult Parole Authority v. Woodard (523 U.S. 272), decided by an 8–1 vote, March 25, 1998; Rehnquist wrote the main opinion; O'Connor wrote a concurring opinion; Stevens dissented in part.

The Court rejected a constitutional challenge to Ohio's executive clemency procedures for death penalty cases, but a majority of the justices said due process may set some limits on the practice. The ruling rejected a claim by an Ohio inmate, Eugene Woodard, that the state's executive clemency procedure violated his rights under the Fifth Amendment's privilege against self-incrimination and the Fourteenth Amendment's Due Process Clause. The Court unanimously rejected Woodard's Fifth Amendment claim and voted 8–1 to reject his due process argument.

Hopkins, Warden v. Reeves (524 U.S. 88), decided by an 8–1 vote, June 8, 1998; Thomas wrote the opinion; Stevens dissented.

States have no constitutional responsibility to allow judges or juries in capital murder cases to consider lesser degrees of homicide, such as manslaughter.

Jones v. United States (527 U.S. 373), decided by a 5–4 vote, June 21, 1999; Thomas wrote the opinion; Ginsburg, Stevens, Souter, and Breyer dissented.

In the first case involving the comprehensive Federal Death Penalty Act of 1994, the Court ruled that juries in federal death penalty cases need not be told that in the event of a deadlock the judge will sentence the defendant either to death or to life imprisonment without possibility of parole.

Weeks v. Angelone, Director, Virginia Department of Corrections (528 U.S. 225), decided by a 5–4 vote, Jan. 19, 2000; Rehnquist wrote the opinion; Stevens, Souter, Ginsburg, and Breyer dissented.

The Court rejected a Virginia death row inmate's argument that the trial judge had failed to give the jury clear instructions on how to choose between imposing the death penalty and life imprisonment.

Ramdass v. Angelone, Director, Virginia Department of Corrections (530 U.S. 156), decided by a 5–4 vote, June 12, 2000; Kennedy wrote the plurality opinion; O'Connor concurred in the judgment; Stevens, Souter, Ginsburg, and Breyer dissented.

The Court somewhat limited the due process requirement that jurors in capital cases be told of a defendant's ineligibility for parole if the prosecution cites future dangerousness to justify a death sentence.

CONFRONTATION

Lilly v. Virginia (527 U.S. 116), decided by a 9–0 vote, June 10, 1999; Stevens wrote the main opinion; Scalia and Thomas wrote partial concurring opinions; Rehnquist wrote an opinion concurring in the judgment.

A Virginia death row inmate won a round in his effort to overturn his murder conviction because of the use of a statement by an accomplice who refused to testify at trial.

CONTEMPT OF COURT

Pounders, Judge, Superior Court of California, Los Angeles County v. Watson (521 U.S. 982), decided by a 7–2 vote, June 27, 1997; *per curiam* (unsigned) opinion; Stevens and Breyer dissented.

The Court summarily upheld a summary contempt of court citation against a Los Angeles defense attorney for violating a judge's instruction not to comment on the sentence her client faced if convicted. Ruling on the case without oral argument, the Court held that a "pattern of repeated violations" is not required for a judge to summarily impose a contempt of court citation.

CRIMINAL OFFENSES

United States v. Wells (519 U.S. 482), decided by an 8–1 vote, Feb. 26, 1997; Souter wrote the opinion; Stevens dissented.

The Court eased the requirements for a conviction under a federal law that prohibits making false statements to a federally insured bank. The Court held that the statute does not require prosecutors to prove that a false statement was a "material" factor in inducing a bank to make a loan.

United States v. Lanier (520 U.S. 259), decided by a 9–0 vote, March 31, 1997; Souter wrote the opinion.

The Court revived the federal prosecution of a former Tennessee judge for allegedly violating constitutional rights of five women by sexually assaulting them in his chambers. The ruling reversed a decision by the Sixth U.S. Circuit Court of Appeals to set aside the 1992 conviction of the former judge, David Lanier, who had been found guilty of sexually assaulting five women on seven separate occasions. The unanimous but limited ruling returned the case to the appeals court for reevaluation.

United States v. O'Hagan (521 U.S. 642), decided by 6–3, 7–2, and 9–0 votes, June 25, 1997; Ginsburg wrote the opinion; Thomas, Rehnquist, and Scalia dissented in part.

Federal securities law prohibits someone from using inside information to trade in a company's stock even if the individual does not work for the company or owe it any legal duty. The ruling upheld the convictions of a Minneapolis lawyer, James O'Hagan, who made $3.4 million in profits by trading in securities of a company that was being taken over by another company that his law firm briefly represented.

O'Hagan was convicted of securities fraud, fraudulent trading in connection with a tender offer, and mail fraud, but the Eighth U.S. Circuit Court of Appeals reversed all the convictions. The Court reinstated the convictions in a critical victory for the government's expansive theories of insider trading liability.

Bates v. United States (522 U.S. 23), decided by a 9–0 vote, Nov. 4, 1997; Ginsburg wrote the opinion.

The crime of willful misapplication of federally insured student loan funds does not require proof of an intent to defraud the federal government or the private lender that made the loans. The Court held that it was unnecessary to prove a fraudulent intent in a prosecution for misapplying the federally guaranteed loan funds.

Salinas v. United States (522 U.S. 52), decided by a 9–0 vote, Dec. 2, 1997; Kennedy wrote the opinion.

The federal bribery statute applies to bribes paid to officials of any state or local agency receiving federal funds, even if the payments do not involve federal funds. In a second holding, the Court eased the requirements for a conspiracy conviction under the federal racketeering law.

Brogan v. United States (522 U.S. 398), decided by a 7–2 vote, Jan. 26, 1998; Scalia wrote the opinion; Stevens and Breyer dissented.

Someone can be prosecuted under the federal false-statements law for a false denial of guilt. The ruling rejected the so-called exculpatory no doctrine recognized by several federal appeals courts that barred a separate prosecution of someone for falsely denying to investigators an accusation of a crime. The Court held that the federal statute did not permit any exception for an initial denial of guilt.

Lewis v. United States (531 U.S. 438), decided by an 8–1 vote, March 9, 1998; Breyer wrote the opinion; Kennedy dissented.

The federal murder statute, rather than state law, applies to homicides committed on military bases or other federal enclaves. The ruling involved application of the Assimilative Crimes Act, a federal law dating to the 1820s aimed at filling in gaps in the federal criminal code. The act provides that under certain conditions state criminal laws can be "assimilated" into federal law and made applicable to federal enclaves located within the state. The Court used the case to set out a general approach to deciding when state laws are assimilated into federal law under the act.

Muscarello v. United States (524 U.S. 125), decided by a 5–4 vote, June 8, 1998; Breyer wrote the opinion; Ginsburg, Rehnquist, Scalia, and Souter dissented.

The Court broadly applied a federal firearms provision imposing a mandatory five-year sentence to someone who "carries" a weapon during a drug trafficking crime. The

Court held that the provision applies to a defendant who carries a weapon in the trunk or locked glove compartment of a car while driving to commit a drug trafficking offense.

Bryan v. United States (524 U.S. 184), decided by a 6–3 vote, June 15, 1998; Stevens wrote the opinion; Scalia, Rehnquist, and Ginsburg dissented.

The Court eased the prosecution's burden for convicting someone of violating the federal law against dealing in firearms without a federal license. The Court held that defendants can be convicted of "willfully" violating the law even if they do not know about the provision as long as they are aware that their conduct is unlawful in some other respect.

Caron v. United States (524 U.S. 308), decided by a 6–3 vote, June 22, 1998; Kennedy wrote the opinion; Thomas, Scalia, and Souter dissented.

Someone can be subject to a federal law prohibiting repeat offenders from possessing firearms even if state law permits them to own the weapons in question. The ruling involved a federal law that prohibited someone convicted of a serious crime from possessing any firearm and imposed a longer term on someone with three prior violent felonies who violated the provision. The Court adopted the interpretation that the federal law applied as long as an ex-offender was subject to some state law firearms restrictions.

Holloway v. United States (526 U.S. 1), decided by a 7–2 vote, March 2, 1999; Stevens wrote the opinion; Scalia and Thomas dissented.

The Court made it easier to obtain convictions under a newly enacted federal carjacking law by softening the requirement for proving an intent to kill or injure the victim. The ruling interpreted a 1994 amendment to the anticarjacking law passed two years earlier that defined the offense to be taking a motor vehicle "by force or intimidation . . . with the intent to cause death or serious bodily harm." The Court agreed that "conditional intent" to kill or harm the victim satisfies the requirement for a conviction under the law.

Jones v. United States (529 U.S. 848), decided by a 5–4 vote, March 24, 1999; Souter wrote the opinion; Kennedy, Rehnquist, O'Connor, and Breyer dissented.

The Court made it harder to impose long prison sentences under a recently enacted federal carjacking law in a closely divided decision that could affect penalty enhancements under other criminal statutes.

United States v. Sun-Diamond Growers of California (526 U.S. 398), decided by a 9–0 vote, April 27, 1999; Scalia wrote the opinion.

A conviction under the federal illegal gratuity statute requires the prosecution to prove a connection between a gift to a federal official and a specific act motivating the gift. The ruling set aside the 1996 conviction of Sun-Diamond

Growers of California for giving Agriculture Secretary Michael Espy about $5,900 in gifts, including tickets to tennis matches, luggage, and other presents. An independent counsel prosecuted the trade association under a federal law that makes it illegal to give a federal official "anything of value . . . for or because of any official act performed or to be performed by such public official. . . ." Sun-Diamond argued successfully to the federal appeals court in Washington that the statute required the prosecution to show a link between the gift and a specific official action. The Court upheld the appeals court's decision overturning the conviction.

Espy was also prosecuted under the statute, but was acquitted by a federal jury in Washington in December 1998.

Fischer v. United States (529 U.S. 667), decided by a 7–2 vote, May 15, 2000; Kennedy wrote the opinion; Thomas and Scalia dissented.

The federal bribery statute can be used to prosecute someone for defrauding a hospital that receives reimbursements from the federal Medicare program.

Jones v. United States (529 U.S. 848), decided by a 9–0 vote, May 22, 2000; Ginsburg wrote the opinion.

A federal law prohibiting arson or bombing of property used in interstate commerce does not cover arson of an owner-occupied private residence. The Court ruled the law applied only to arson of property actively used for commercial purposes.

Castillo v. United States (530 U.S. 120), decided by a 9–0 vote, June 5, 2000; Breyer wrote the opinion.

The Court made it harder for federal prosecutors to use a provision in a firearms statute that imposes a mandatory, thirty-year prison sentence for using a machine gun while committing a violent crime.

Carter v. United States (530 U.S. 255), decided by a 5–4 vote, June 12, 2000; Thomas wrote the opinion; Ginsburg, Stevens, Souter, and Breyer dissented.

A person charged under the major federal bank robbery statute is not entitled to ask the jury to consider a bank larceny charge as a lesser offense.

DETAINERS

New York v. Hill (528 U.S. 110), decided by a 9–0 vote, Jan. 11, 2000; Scalia wrote the opinion.

A defense lawyer can waive or give up a defendant's right to a speedy trial under a provision of the Interstate Agreement on Detainers, which governs the transfer of a prisoner from one state to another.

DISCOVERY

Strickler v. Greene, Warden (527 U.S. 263), decided by a 7–2 vote, June 17, 1999; Stevens wrote the opinion; Souter and Kennedy dissented.

A Virginia death row inmate failed to set aside his murder conviction or death sentence despite the prosecution's failure to turn over potentially useful evidence for his defense.

DOUBLE JEOPARDY

Hudson v. United States (522 U.S. 93), decided by 9–0 and 5–4 votes, Dec. 10, 1997; Rehnquist wrote the opinion; Stevens, Souter, Ginsburg, and Breyer concurred in the result but not the legal holding.

The imposition of civil penalties ordinarily does not prevent the government from prosecuting someone for the same conduct unless the legislature intended the civil enforcement scheme to be punitive.

Monge v. California (524 U.S. 721), decided by a 5–4 vote, June 26, 1998; O'Connor wrote the opinion; Scalia, Stevens, Souter, and Ginsburg dissented.

The Double Jeopardy Clause does not prevent the prosecution from having a second chance to prove a defendant's prior criminal record for purposes of enhancing a sentence for a new offense. The ruling eased the use of so-called three-strikes laws enacted in California and other states that provided for substantially increased sentences for defendants with two or more prior convictions. The Court held that the Double Jeopardy Clause did not bar a retrial on a prior conviction allegation in noncapital sentencing proceedings.

DRUG OFFENSES

Richardson v. United States (526 U.S. 813), decided by a 6–3 vote, June 1, 1999; Breyer wrote the opinion; Kennedy, O'Connor, and Ginsburg dissented.

The Court made it harder to convict a federal defendant under a "drug kingpin" statute by requiring jurors to agree unanimously on each of three offenses needed to trigger the law.

EVIDENCE

Old Chief v. United States (519 U.S. 172), decided by a 5–4 vote, Jan. 7, 1997; Souter wrote the opinion; O'Connor, Rehnquist, Scalia, and Thomas dissented.

Defendants charged under a law prohibiting possession of a firearm by a felon may prevent the government from offering specific evidence about their previous offense by stipulating to their prior conviction.

Gray v. Maryland (523 U.S. 206), decided by a 5–4 vote, March 9, 1998; Breyer wrote the opinion; Scalia, Rehnquist, Kennedy, and Thomas dissented.

The Court made it harder for the prosecution to use a confession by one defendant that also implicates a codefendant being tried at the same time. The ruling tightened a restriction first established in a 1968 case, *Bruton v. United States*, which prohibited the use of a confession by one defendant as evidence against the other.

United States v. Scheffer (523 U.S. 296), decided by an 8–1 vote, March 31, 1998; Thomas wrote the main opinion; Kennedy wrote a concurring opinion; Stevens dissented.

The Court held that an accused has no constitutional right to present evidence of a lie detector test, even though a majority of the justices said they opposed a complete ban on polygraph evidence. The ruling reinstated a per se exclusion on the use of polygraph evidence in military courts, Military Rule of Evidence 707, adopted in 1991. The Court rejected the argument that the Sixth Amendment entitles a defendant to present lie detector evidence at trial.

EX POST FACTO LAWS

Carmell v. Texas (529 U.S. 513), decided by a 5–4 vote, May 1, 2000; Stevens wrote the opinion; Ginsburg, Rehnquist, O'Connor, and Kennedy dissented.

The Court reversed some of a Texas man's child abuse convictions because prosecutors used a state law aimed at easing prosecution of sex crimes that was passed after some of his offenses. The Court said use of the law violated the Ex Post Facto Clause.

EXTRADITION

New Mexico ex rel. Ortiz v. Reed (524 U.S. 151), decided by a 9–0 vote, June 8, 1998; *per curiam* (unsigned) opinion.

The Court reinforced states' obligation in extradition proceedings to return a fugitive to another state without considering any legal issues besides the procedural formalities of the request. The decision required New Mexico authorities to return a prominent Native American–rights activist, Timothy Reed, to Ohio to face a parole violation charge. In an unsigned decision issued without hearing oral argument, the Court said Reed's claims could be considered only in Ohio, the "demanding state," not in "the asylum state," New Mexico.

FORFEITURES

United States v. Bajakajian (524 U.S. 321), decided by a 5–4 vote, June 22, 1998; Thomas wrote the opinion; Kennedy, Rehnquist, O'Connor, and Scalia dissented.

The Court, citing the Eighth Amendment's Excessive Fines Clause, struck down as "grossly disproportional" the government's attempt to seize $357,144 from a California man for failing to report the currency as he was leaving the United States.

GUILTY PLEAS

United States v. Hyde (520 U.S. 670), decided by a 9–0 vote, May 27, 1997; Rehnquist wrote the opinion.

A defendant has no absolute right to withdraw a guilty plea after a judge has accepted the plea but before the judge approves a plea agreement between the defense and prosecution.

Bousley v. United States (523 U.S. 614), decided by a 7–2 vote, May 18, 1998; Rehnquist wrote the opinion; Scalia and Thomas dissented.

A defendant may bring a belated challenge to a guilty plea by showing that he is probably innocent of the charge.

HABEAS CORPUS

California v. Roy (519 U.S. 2), decided by a 9–0 vote, Nov. 4, 1996; *per curiam* (unsigned) opinion.

Federal courts hearing habeas corpus challenges by state inmates should apply a relaxed standard in determining whether an error at trial is "harmless" and does not require a new trial.

Lambrix v. Singletary, Secretary, Florida Department of Corrections (520 U.S. 518), decided by a 5–4 vote, May 12, 1997; Scalia wrote the opinion; Stevens, O'Connor, Ginsburg, and Breyer dissented.

The Court said the 1992 decision in *Espinosa v. Florida*, which held that a defective jury instruction taints a judge's decision to impose the death penalty in states where the judge is required to give great weight to the jury's recommendation, could not be applied retroactively in federal habeas corpus cases.

Bracy v. Gramley, Warden (520 U.S. 899), decided by a 9–0 vote, June 9, 1997; Rehnquist wrote the opinion.

A convicted triple murderer, William Bracy, was given a chance to prove that he should have a new trial because of alleged bias by the corrupt judge who presided over his trial. The Court held that Bracy had made a sufficient factual showing to establish "good cause" for discovery as required by federal rules governing habeas corpus cases.

O'Dell v. Netherland, Warden (521 U.S. 151), decided by a 5–4 vote, June 19, 1997; Thomas wrote the opinion; Stevens, Souter, Ginsburg, and Breyer dissented.

The Court limited the ability of death row inmates to invalidate their sentences through federal habeas corpus petitions by invoking the decision in *Simmons v. South Carolina*, which required judges in some capital cases to tell jurors about the option of sentencing a defendant to life imprisonment without possibility of parole.

Lindh v. Murphy, Warden (521 U.S. 320), decided by a 5–4 vote, June 23, 1997; Souter wrote the opinion; Rehnquist, Scalia, Kennedy, and Thomas dissented.

Newly enacted provisions limiting state inmates' ability to challenge their convictions in federal court do not apply to cases pending when the law went into effect. The ruling limited the scope of the Antiterrorism and Effective Death Penalty Act of 1996, which contained a variety of new restrictions on federal habeas corpus petitions in capital and noncapital cases.

Trest v. Cain, Warden (522 U.S. 87), decided by a 9–0 vote, Dec. 9, 1997; Breyer wrote the opinion.

A federal appeals court is not required to raise on its own the question whether a state inmate's habeas corpus petition should be barred for failing to properly challenge his conviction in state court. In a brief and unanimous opinion, the Court rejected the appeals court's conclusion that it was required to raise the issue, but the Court declined to decide whether the appeals court had discretion to raise the issue on its own.

Spencer v. Kemna, Superintendent, Western Missouri Correctional Center (523 U.S. 1), decided by an 8–1 vote, March 3, 1998; Scalia wrote the opinion; Stevens dissented.

Former inmates cannot use federal habeas corpus to challenge a parole revocation after the expiration of their sentence.

Calderon, Warden v. Thompson (523 U.S. 538), decided by a 5–4 vote, April 29, 1998; Kennedy wrote the opinion; Souter, Stevens, Ginsburg, and Breyer dissented.

A federal appeals court was sharply rebuked for its last-minute change of mind to grant a new trial to a California death row inmate convicted of a rape-murder fifteen years earlier.

Stewart, Director, Arizona Department of Correction v. Martinez-Villareal (523 U.S. 637), decided by a 7–2 vote, May 18, 1998; Rehnquist wrote the opinion; Scalia and Thomas dissented.

The Court somewhat eased the effect of a recently enacted law aimed at limiting the ability of state prison inmates to file repeated habeas corpus petitions in federal court. The ruling allowed an Arizona death row inmate, Ramon Martinez-Villareal, to proceed with a federal habeas corpus petition seeking to block his execution on grounds of mental incompetency. The state had sought to bar consideration of the claim by invoking a provision of the 1996 Antiterrorism and Effective Death Penalty Act that barred state inmates from filing a "second or successive habeas corpus application" except under limited circumstances. The Court held that Martinez-Villareal's return to federal court with the mental incompetency issue did not amount to a "second or successive" application under the 1996 law.

Calderon, Warden v. Ashmus (523 U.S. 740), decided by a 9–0 vote, May 26, 1998; Rehnquist wrote the opinion.

The Court blocked a class action suit by California death row inmates seeking an early determination whether the state met the requirements of a new law for expedited procedures in federal habeas corpus cases. The ruling involved the habeas corpus revisions in the 1996 Antiterrorism and Effective Death Penalty Act, which established a number of restrictions on the ability of inmates to file habeas corpus challenges in death penalty cases, including a short, 180-day deadline for filing a petition and a limit on amending a petition after the state has filed an answer. A state could invoke the restrictions only if it met certain standards for providing legal representation for death row inmates.

Hohn v. United States (524 U.S. 236), decided by a 5–4 vote, June 15, 1998; Kennedy wrote the opinion; Scalia, Rehnquist, O'Connor, and Thomas dissented.

The Court reduced the impact of a recently enacted habeas corpus law aimed at making it harder for prison inmates to appeal a federal judge's refusal to overturn their convictions or sentences. The Court held that it has the power to review an action by a federal appeals judge or court denying an inmate a "certificate of appealability" needed to appeal the lower court judge's ruling. The requirement was one of many provisions that Congress included in the 1996 Antiterrorism and Effective Death Penalty Act in an effort to reduce prisoners' ability to use habeas corpus to challenge convictions or sentences.

Calderon, Warden v. Coleman (525 U.S. 141), decided by a 5–4 vote, Dec. 14, 1998; *per curiam* (unsigned) opinion; Stevens, Souter, Ginsburg, and Breyer dissented.

The Court overturned a decision requiring resentencing in an old murder case because the federal appeals court did not properly consider the effect of a constitutional defect at trial. The unsigned ruling—issued without hearing oral argument—ordered a new hearing in a federal habeas corpus case brought by a California death row inmate, Russell Coleman, who sought to overturn his 1981 death sentence because of a jury instruction, held improper under state law, regarding the governor's power to commute prison sentences. The Court said the appeals court had not properly applied its most recent precedent limiting habeas corpus relief in cases of so-called harmless error.

Peguero v. United States (526 U.S. 32), decided by a 9–0 vote, March 2, 1999; Kennedy wrote the opinion.

A federal judge's failure to inform a defendant of the right to appeal a sentence is no basis for setting aside the sentence if the defendant knows of his right anyway.

O'Sullivan v. Boerckel (526 U.S. 838), decided by a 6–3 vote, June 7, 1999; O'Connor wrote the opinion; Stevens, Ginsburg, and Breyer dissented.

State inmates ordinarily cannot raise a claim in a federal habeas corpus petition unless the issue has been presented to the state's highest court—even if the tribunal exercises limited review in criminal appeals. The ruling tightened the so-called exhaustion requirement in habeas corpus cases.

Fiore v. White, Warden (531 U.S. 225), decided by a 9–0 vote, Nov. 30, 1999; Breyer wrote the opinion.

In a rarely used, interim procedure, the Court asked Pennsylvania's highest court to resolve a state law question needed to decide a Pennsylvania man's federal habeas corpus claim that he had been improperly convicted of operating a hazardous waste facility without a permit.

Williams v. Taylor, Warden (Michael Williams) (529 U.S. 362), decided by a 9–0 vote, April 18, 2000; Kennedy wrote the opinion.

A Virginia death row inmate was given a chance to show juror misconduct in his murder trial as the Court gave a relaxed interpretation to the Antiterrorism and Effective Death Penalty Act, which was aimed at restricting federal habeas corpus hearings.

Williams v. Taylor, Warden (Terry Williams) (529 U.S. 420), decided by 6–3 and 5–4 votes, April 18, 2000; Stevens wrote the main opinion; O'Connor wrote an opinion for the Court on one legal issue; Stevens, Souter, Ginsburg, and Breyer disagreed with the Court's ruling on that issue; Rehnquist, Scalia, and Thomas dissented in part.

Federal courts cannot grant a state inmate's habeas corpus petition unless a state court decision was contrary to clearly established Supreme Court precedent or was an objectively unreasonable application of Supreme Court precedent to the facts of the case. The ruling, interpreting a newly enacted provision of federal habeas corpus law, made it somewhat more difficult for state inmates to challenge their convictions in federal courts.

Edwards, Warden v. Carpenter (529 U.S. 446), decided by a 9–0 vote, April 25, 2000; Scalia wrote the opinion.

A state prisoner in a federal habeas corpus case ordinarily cannot use a claim of inadequate legal representation that was filed too late in state courts to excuse a failure to raise other claims.

Slack v. McDaniel, Warden (529 U.S. 473), decided by a 7–2 vote, April 26, 2000; Kennedy wrote the opinion; Scalia and Thomas dissented.

In a complex ruling, the Court ruled that a state prisoner is ordinarily not barred from filing a second federal habeas corpus petition if his first petition is dismissed on procedural grounds so that he can return to state courts to raise his claims.

HARMLESS ERROR

Neder v. United States (527 U.S. 1), decided by a 6–3 vote, June 10, 1999; Rehnquist wrote the opinion; Scalia, Souter, and Ginsburg dissented.

A Florida man failed to overturn a real estate fraud conviction because the judge failed to instruct the jury about one element of the offense: the "materiality" of false statements used to carry out the scheme. The Court unanimously held that materiality is an element of federal fraud offenses but voted 6–3 that a harmless error analysis could be applied to uphold the conviction of Ellis E. Neder Jr. for federal mail, wire, and bank fraud and filing a false income tax return in connection with a multimillion-dollar series of real estate schemes in the 1980s.

JURY SELECTION

Campbell v. Louisiana (523 U.S. 392), decided by a 7–2 vote, April 21, 1998; Kennedy wrote the opinion; Thomas and Scalia dissented in part.

The Court held that a white criminal defendant may challenge his second-degree murder conviction, for the killing of another white man, on grounds that blacks were discriminated against in the selection of grand jurors. The defendant, Terry Campbell, introduced evidence that no black had served as foreperson of the Evangeline Parish grand jury over a seventeen-year period, from Jan. 1976 to August 1993, even though blacks comprised about 20 percent of the parish's population. The Court ruled that Campbell had so-called third-party standing to assert what it called "the well-established equal protection rights of black persons not to be excluded from grand jury service on the basis of their race."

United States v. Martinez-Salazar (528 U.S. 304), decided by a 9–0 vote, Jan. 19, 2000; Ginsburg wrote the opinion.

The Court ruled that defendants' constitutional rights are not violated when they choose to use a peremptory challenge to remove a juror who should have been removed for cause.

LOITERING

City of Chicago v. Morales (527 U.S. 41), decided by a 6–3 vote, June 10, 1999; Stevens wrote the main opinion; O'Connor, Kennedy, and Breyer wrote concurring opinions; Thomas, Rehnquist, and Scalia dissented.

A local ordinance aimed at preventing loitering by gang members was struck down because it gave police too much discretion to arrest people for disobeying an order to get off the public streets. The splintered ruling invalidated a 1992 Chicago criminal ordinance that authorized police to tell someone loitering on the streets with someone suspected of being a criminal gang member to disperse and to arrest anyone who refused.

PAROLE AND PROBATION

Pennsylvania Board of Probation and Parole v. Scott (524 U.S. 357), decided by a 5–4 vote, June 22, 1998; Thomas wrote the opinion; Souter, Stevens, Ginsburg, and Breyer dissented.

In some circumstances, illegally obtained evidence may be introduced against a parolee at a parole revocation hearing. The ruling rejected an extension of the exclusionary rule barring use of illegally obtained evidence to such hearings.

United States v. Johnson (529 U.S. 53), decided by a 9–0 vote, March 1, 2000; Kennedy wrote the opinion.

A federal inmate is not entitled to a reduction of a period of supervised release for time served in prison under a sentence later ruled invalid. The Court held that the federal statute governing supervised release allowed the period to begin only after an inmate was actually released from prison.

Garner, Former Chairman of the State Board of Pardons and Paroles of Georgia v. Jones (529 U.S. 244), decided by a 6–3 vote, March 28, 2000; Kennedy wrote the opinion; Souter, Stevens, and Ginsburg dissented.

The Court turned aside a Georgia inmate's constitutional challenge to a parole board's retroactive application of a new policy that changed from three years to eight the time period for making a new parole application after an inmate was denied parole.

PRISONS AND JAILS

Lynce v. Mathis, Superintendent, Tomoka Correctional Institution (519 U.S. 433), decided by a 9–0 vote, Feb. 19, 1997; Stevens wrote the opinion.

A Florida law retroactively canceling early release credits awarded inmates to alleviate prison overcrowding violated the Constitution's Ex Post Facto Clause, which prohibits some governmental actions that have retroactive effects.

Young v. Harper (520 U.S. 143), decided by a 9–0 vote, March 18, 1997; Thomas wrote the opinion.

An Oklahoma inmate released under a "preparole" program aimed at relieving prison overcrowding had a due process right to a hearing before being reincarcerated. The decision upheld an appeals court ruling granting a habeas corpus petition filed by inmate Ernest Harper, who had been released under the overcrowding relief plan in 1990 after serving fifteen years of a life sentence for two murders. Harper claimed that the state violated his due process rights by reincarcerating him without a hearing five months after the governor denied his application for normal parole. The Court said Harper's case was governed by the Court's 1972 decision, *Morrissey v. Brewer*, requiring a hearing in parole matters.

Miller, Superintendent, Pendleton Correctional Facility v. French (530 U.S. 327), decided by a 5–4 vote, June 19, 2000; O'Connor wrote the opinion; Souter and Ginsburg dissented in part; Breyer and Stevens dissented.

The Court upheld the "automatic stay" provision of the Prison Litigation Reform Act of 1995, which limits federal judges' power to continue enforcement of court-ordered remedies in suits over prison conditions. The law established stricter standards to be met before federal judges could order relief in inmates' suits over prison conditions and allowed state or local prison officials to move to modify or terminate any existing injunction.

RIGHT TO COUNSEL

Roe, Warden v. Flores-Ortega (528 U.S. 470), decided by a 6–3 vote, Feb. 23, 2000; O'Connor wrote the opinion; Souter, Stevens, and Ginsburg dissented.

The Court adopted a case-by-case approach to evaluate whether a court-appointed lawyer's failure to file an appeal for an indigent defendant violated the defendant's right to effective assistance of counsel.

SEARCH AND SEIZURE

Ohio v. Robinette (519 U.S. 33), decided by an 8–1 vote, Nov. 18, 1996; Rehnquist wrote the opinion; Stevens dissented in part.

The Fourth Amendment does not require police in a routine traffic stop to tell motorists they are free to go before asking permission to search their vehicle. The decision set aside a ruling by the Ohio Supreme Court that relied on both the state and federal constitutions in imposing the so-called first-tell-then-ask rule.

Maryland v. Wilson (519 U.S. 408), decided by a 7–2 vote, Feb. 19, 1997; Rehnquist wrote the opinion; Stevens and Kennedy dissented.

When making a traffic stop, police may order a passenger as well as the driver to get out of the car pending completion of the stop. The decision extended the Court's 1977 ruling, *Pennsylvania v. Mimms,* that allowed police to order a driver out of an automobile in order to protect the officer's safety.

Richards v. Wisconsin (526 U.S. 813), decided by a 9–0 vote, April 28, 1997; Stevens wrote the opinion.

The Court refused to allow a blanket exception for drug cases to its general rule requiring police to knock and announce their identity before executing a search warrant at a residence. The ruling said the Wisconsin Supreme Court was wrong to carve out a broad exception to *Wilson v. Arkansas,* the Court's 1995 decision limiting no-knock searches. The Court nonetheless upheld the conviction challenged in the case, holding that police had adequate grounds for their unannounced entry into a motel.

United States v. Ramirez (523 U.S. 65), decided by a 9–0 vote, March 4, 1998; Rehnquist wrote the opinion.

Police executing a no-knock search warrant, with a "reasonable suspicion" that knocking and announcing would be futile or dangerous, do not need special justification if they damage or destroy property while entering the premises.

SEARCH AND SEIZURE

The right of the people to be secure in their person, houses, papers and effects, against unreasonable searches and seizures, shall not be violated, and no warrants shall issue but upon probable cause, supported by oath or affirmation and particularly describing the place to be searched, and the persons or things to be seized.

Fourth Amendment, U.S. Constitution

Minnesota v. Carter (525 U.S. 83), decided by 6–3 and 5–4 votes, Dec. 1, 1998; Rehnquist wrote the opinion; Breyer concurred in the judgment but disagreed with the legal holding; Ginsburg, Stevens, and Souter dissented.

Someone in a private premises for business purposes on a short-term basis has no standing to object to a police search of the location. The ruling narrowed a prior decision, *Minnesota v. Olson* (1980), that allowed an overnight house guest to contest a search.

Knowles v. Iowa (525 U.S. 83), decided by a 9–0 vote, Dec. 8, 1998; Rehnquist wrote the opinion.

Police officers cannot automatically conduct a full search of an automobile after stopping the driver for a traffic citation. The ruling reversed the marijuana conviction of an Iowa man, Patrick Knowles, stemming from a search of his car after he was stopped for speeding. An Iowa law—unique among the states—gave police authority to search a car after making a traffic stop even if the driver was not placed under arrest. The Court ruled that the search violated the Fourth Amendment's prohibition against unreasonable searches.

City of West Covina v. Perkins (525 U.S. 234), decided by a 9–0 vote, Jan. 13, 1999; Kennedy wrote the opinion.

Police are not constitutionally required to tell someone whose property has been seized during a search what procedures to use to try to reclaim the items.

Wyoming v. Houghton (526 U.S. 295), decided by a 6–3 vote, April 5, 1999; Scalia wrote the opinion; Stevens, Souter, and Ginsburg dissented.

Police who have probable cause to believe a driver is carrying illegal drugs or other contraband can search a passenger's belongings even if the passenger is not suspected of wrongdoing. The Court held that police in such cases may "inspect" a passenger's belongings that are "capable of concealing the object of the search." The ruling significantly expanded police discretion in automobile searches.

Florida v. White (526 U.S. 559), decided by a 7–2 vote, May 17, 1999; Thomas wrote the opinion; Stevens and Ginsburg dissented.

Police do not need a search warrant to seize an automobile that is subject to forfeiture because it has been used in illegal activity such as drug trafficking. The Court ruled that the Fourth Amendment does not require police to obtain a warrant "before seizing an automobile from a public place when they have probable cause to believe that it is forfeitable contraband."

Maryland v. Dyson (527 U.S. 465), decided by a 9–0 vote, June 21, 1999; *per curiam* (unsigned) opinion.

Police do not need to show special urgency before searching an automobile, as long as they have probable cause to believe that the car contains contraband, such as illegal drugs.

Flippo v. West Virginia (528 U.S. 11), decided by a 9–0 vote, Oct. 18, 1999; *per curiam* (unsigned) opinion.

Police ordinarily need a warrant to search a crime scene unless some other exception to the requirement applies.

Illinois v. Wardlow (528 U.S. 119), decided by a 5–4 vote, Jan. 12, 2000; Rehnquist wrote the opinion; Stevens, Souter, Ginsburg, and Breyer dissented as to the result.

Police may have sufficient cause to stop and frisk suspects if they run away upon seeing the officer. The ruling reinstated a firearms possession conviction against an Illinois man, Sam Wardlow, who was apprehended by police on a Chicago street after running away at the approach of a drug-patrol team.

Florida v. J. L. (529 U.S. 266), decided by a 9–0 vote, March 28, 2000; Ginsburg wrote the opinion.

Police have no automatic right to stop and frisk people after receiving an anonymous tip that they are carrying a firearm. The ruling upheld the Florida Supreme Court's decision that Miami-Dade County police officers violated an African American teenager's Fourth Amendment rights when they frisked him after receiving an anonymous telephone tip. The Court refused to create a "firearm exception" to the normal rules limiting the use of anonymous tips to justify a police stop or search, but the opinion was limited by saying that it did not bar public safety officials from using anonymous tips to justify frisks in airports or schools.

Bond v. United States (529 U.S. 266), decided by a 7–2 vote, April 17, 2000; Rehnquist wrote the opinion; Breyer and Scalia dissented.

Police may not physically manipulate a bus passenger's carry-on luggage to try to determine its contents without a warrant or other legal justification. The ruling overturned the drug convictions of a bus passenger, Steven Bond, stemming from a search of a canvas carry-on bag by a U.S. Border Patrol agent. The Court held that the agent's action constituted an

unreasonable search under the Fourth Amendment because it violated Bond's "reasonable expectation of privacy."

SELF-INCRIMINATION

United States v. Balsys (524 U.S. 666), decided by a 7–2 vote, June 25, 1998; Souter wrote the opinion; Breyer and Ginsburg dissented.

The Fifth Amendment's privilege against self-incrimination does not protect people from being compelled to give testimony in a civil proceeding that might subject them to criminal prosecution in another country. The ruling rejected an effort by a suspected Nazi war criminal, Aloyzas Balsys, to avoid giving a deposition in an investigation that could have led to his deportation to his native Latvia or some other country.

Mitchell v. United States (526 U.S. 314), decided by a 5–4 vote, April 5, 1999; Kennedy wrote the opinion; Scalia, Rehnquist, O'Connor, and Thomas dissented.

A judge may not use a defendant's refusal to testify at a sentencing hearing to draw conclusions about the facts of the offense.

United States v. Hubbell (530 U.S. 27), decided by an 8–1 vote, June 5, 2000; Stevens wrote the opinion; Rehnquist dissented.

The Court threw out the tax conviction of Webster Hubbell, a former high-ranking Clinton administration official, by ruling that Independent Counsel Kenneth Starr violated Hubbell's privilege against self-incrimination and broke an immunity agreement when he used the defendant's subpoenaed business records to build a prosecution.

Dickerson v. United States (530 U.S. 428), decided by a 7–2 vote, June 26, 2000; Rehnquist wrote the opinion; Scalia and Thomas dissented.

The Court invalidated a law Congress passed aimed at overturning the *Miranda* decision requiring police to warn suspects of their rights to remain silent and to be represented by a lawyer before conducting interrogation. The ruling—a decisive defeat for conservative critics of the famous 1966 decision—reversed an appeals court decision upholding the 1968 law—section 3501 of the U.S. criminal code, Title 18—which provided that any confession "voluntarily given" would be admissible in criminal prosecutions in federal court.

SENTENCING

United States v. Watts (519 U.S. 148), decided by a 7–2 vote, Jan. 6, 1997; *per curiam* (unsigned) opinion; Stevens and Kennedy dissented.

A federal judge, in sentencing a defendant, may consider charges of which the defendant has been acquitted if the prosecution proves the defendant probably committed the offenses. The ruling, issued without hearing argument, reversed decisions by separate appellate panels that said judges could not consider offenses that juries had rejected by returning acquittals on those counts. The Court said the "blanket prohibition" imposed by the appellate rulings ignored "the broad discretion" allowed to sentencing courts in considering information about a defendant and the lower standard of proof for the prosecution in introducing such information.

United States v. Gonzales (520 U.S. 1), decided by a 7–2 vote, March 3, 1997; O'Connor wrote the opinion; Stevens and Breyer dissented.

The mandatory five-year federal sentence for using a gun in connection with a drug-related crime must be served after rather than at the same time as any state prison term.

United States v. LaBonte (520 U.S. 751), decided by a 6–3 vote, May 27, 1997; Thomas wrote the opinion; Breyer, Stevens, and Ginsburg dissented.

The Court required the federal Sentencing Commission to increase the maximum possible sentences for repeat drug or violent crime offenders. The ruling backed the government's plea to throw out a commission guideline that prescribed sentences based on the penalties for the underlying offenses without regard to sentence enhancements provided for repeat offenders. The Court held that the guideline was inconsistent with "the plain and unambiguous language" of the sentencing law.

Almendarez-Torres v. United States (523 U.S. 224), decided by a 5–4 vote, March 24, 1998; Breyer wrote the opinion; Scalia, Stevens, Souter, and Ginsburg dissented.

The Court eased the burden on federal prosecutors to seek heightened prison sentences for aliens who return to the United States after having been deported because of criminal convictions.

Edwards v. United States (523 U.S. 511), decided by a 9–0 vote, April 28, 1998; Breyer wrote the opinion.

The Court, interpreting the federal Sentencing Guidelines, strengthened the power of federal judges to determine sentences in cocaine trafficking cases.

Johnson v. United States (529 U.S. 694), decided by an 8–1 vote, May 15, 2000; Souter wrote the opinion; Scalia dissented.

Federal judges can impose a second term of supervised release on a defendant after revoking the defendant's freedom and ordering him to prison for violating the conditions of the release.

Apprendi v. New Jersey (530 U.S. 466), decided by a 5–4 vote, June 26, 2000; Stevens wrote the opinion; O'Connor, Rehnquist, Kennedy, and Breyer dissented.

A defendant is entitled to a jury trial and to proof beyond a reasonable doubt of any fact other than a prior criminal conviction that may be used to increase a sentence beyond the statutory maximum. The ruling invalidated provisions of New Jersey's "hate crime" law, which provided for enhanced sentences for any offense committed "with a purpose to intimidate an individual or group of individuals because of race, color, gender, handicap, religion, sexual orientation or ethnicity." The law gave the responsibility for imposing the sentence to a judge rather than to a jury, and finding was to be based on a preponderance of the evidence rather than the beyond-a-reasonable-doubt standard required for a criminal conviction. In an unexpectedly broad decision, the Court held that the law violated the Due Process Clause by bypassing the jury and lowering the standard of proof.

SEXUAL OFFENDERS

Kansas v. Hendricks (521 U.S. 346), decided by a 5–4 vote, June 23, 1997; Thomas wrote the opinion; Breyer, Stevens, Souter, and Ginsburg dissented.

States can confine violent sexual predators in mental institutions after they complete their prison sentences without violating their rights. The ruling upheld a 1994 Kansas law establishing a civil commitment procedure for anyone who had been convicted of or charged with a sexually violent offense and who suffers from "a mental abnormality or personality disorder" that makes the person "likely to engage" in similar acts in the future.

TRIALS

Portuondo, Superintendent, Fishkill Correctional Facility v. Agard (529 U.S. 61), decided by a 7–2 vote, March 6, 2000; Scalia wrote the opinion; Ginsburg and Souter dissented.

A prosecutor does not violate defendants' rights by suggesting that defendants who testify might tailor their testimony based on having heard the previous witnesses.

VENUE

United States v. Cabrales (524 U.S. 1), decided by a 9–0 vote, June 1, 1998; Ginsburg wrote the opinion.

A defendant cannot be prosecuted for money laundering in one state if it took place entirely in another state.

United States v. Rodriguez-Moreno (526 U.S. 275), decided by a 7–2 vote, March 30, 1999; Thomas wrote the opinion; Scalia and Stevens dissented.

Anyone who uses a gun while committing a violent crime across state lines can be prosecuted for a federal firearms provision in any state where the crime occurred, even if they did not use the gun in that state.

Election Law

BALLOT ACCESS

Timmons, Acting Director, Ramsey County Department of Property Records and Revenue v. Twin Cities Area New Party (520 U.S. 351), decided by a 6–3 vote, April 28, 1997; Rehnquist wrote the opinion; Stevens, Souter, and Ginsburg dissented.

States may enact laws prohibiting candidates from being listed on the ballot by more than one political party. The ruling rejected a First Amendment challenge by a minor party regarding the infringement of the right of political association with respect to a Minnesota law that is comparable to so-called antifusion statutes enacted in about forty states.

CAMPAIGN FINANCE

Nixon, Attorney General of Missouri v. Shrink Missouri Government PAC (528 U.S. 377), decided by a 6–3 vote, Jan. 24, 2000; Souter wrote the opinion; Thomas, Scalia, and Kennedy dissented.

States can limit contributions to political candidates by individuals or political committees, to as low as $250 for some races, without violating the First Amendment's protections for freedom of speech or association. The ruling rejected a constitutional challenge to a 1994 Missouri law limiting the amounts that individuals or political action committees could donate to candidates for state offices. A lower federal court upheld the statute on the strength of the Supreme Court's 1976 decision, *Buckley v. Valeo,* upholding individual campaign contribution limits of $1,000 in congressional races. The Court upheld the law, rejecting calls from the three dissenters to overrule *Buckley.*

CONGRESSIONAL ELECTIONS

Foster, Governor of Louisiana v. Love (522 U.S. 67), decided by a 9–0 vote, Dec. 2, 1997; Souter wrote the opinion.

The Court struck down Louisiana's "open primary" system that allowed members of Congress to be elected in balloting among candidates of all parties conducted before the general election in November. The Louisiana system, unique among the states, provided for the election of any congressional candidate who received a majority of the votes cast in a so-called open primary in October or a runoff in November between the top two candidates if no one received a majority. Four one-time congressional candidates challenged the procedure as a violation of federal law, which established the Tuesday after the first Monday in November in even-numbered years as the date for congressional elections. The state argued that the system, established in 1975, fell within the federal law provision giving states discretion to control the "manner" of electing members of Congress.

FEDERAL ELECTION COMMISSION

Federal Election Commission v. Akins (524 U.S. 11), decided by a 6–3 vote, June 1, 1998; Breyer wrote the opinion; Scalia, O'Connor, and Thomas dissented.

Voters have legal standing to sue the Federal Election Commission for failing to bring an action to enforce political contribution and expenditure reporting requirements. The ruling was a significant procedural victory for a group of voters seeking to compel the American Israel Public Affairs

Committee (AIPAC) to disclose how much money it contributes to political candidates. The plaintiffs claimed that AIPAC was a "political committee" under the Federal Election Campaign Act and subject to the act's requirement to disclose spending aimed at influencing a federal election. The Court sent the case back to the FEC to reconsider the issue whether AIPAC's expenditures amounted to communications with members that did not have to be disclosed under the law.

INITIATIVES

Buckley, Secretary of State of Colorado v. American Constitutional Law Foundation, Inc. (525 U.S. 182), decided by 9–0 and 6–3 votes, Jan. 12, 1999; Ginsburg wrote the opinion; O'Connor and Breyer dissented in part; Rehnquist dissented.

The Court struck down the registered voter and financial disclosure provisions of a Colorado law imposing requirements on people who circulate petitions for ballot initiatives, saying they imposed unjustifiable restrictions on constitutionally protected political speech. The invalidated provisions required petition circulators to be registered voters, to wear identification badges while gathering signatures, and to disclose any amounts they were paid. The justices struck down the registered voter and financial disclosure provisions and unanimously agreed that the registered voter requirement was unconstitutional.

PRIMARY ELECTIONS

California Democratic Party v. Jones, Secretary of State of California (530 U.S. 567), decided by a 7–2 vote, June 26, 2000; Scalia wrote the opinion; Stevens and Ginsburg dissented.

The Court ruled that state "blanket primary" laws allowing voters to choose freely among candidates for separate offices regardless of party affiliation violates a political party's First Amendment freedom of association. The ruling invalidated a primary system adopted by California voters in a 1996 initiative and also followed in Alaska and Washington.

REAPPORTIONMENT
AND REDISTRICTING

Abrams v. Johnson (521 U.S. 74), decided by a 5–4 vote, June 19, 1997; Kennedy wrote the opinion; Breyer, Stevens, Souter, and Ginsburg dissented.

The Court upheld a lower court's decision to adopt a congressional redistricting plan for Georgia that created only one majority-black district. The ruling was the Court's second decision on redistricting plans adopted after Georgia gained a congressional seat as a result of the 1990 census. In the first ruling, *Miller v. Johnson* (1995), the Court struck down a plan with three majority-black districts. After the Georgia legislature could not agree on a new plan, the three-judge federal district court drew its own map with one majority-black district. By the same 5–4 vote as in its first ruling in the case, the Court upheld the court-drawn redistricting.

Lawyer v. Department of Justice (521 U.S. 567), decided by a 5–4 vote, June 25, 1997; Souter wrote the opinion; Scalia, O'Connor, Kennedy, and Thomas dissented.

The Court upheld a lower federal court's decision to approve a redrawn Florida legislative district without first ruling the original districting plan unconstitutional or allowing the legislature itself to revise the plan.

Hunt, Governor of North Carolina v. Cromartie (526 U.S. 541), decided by a 9–0 vote, May 17, 1999; Thomas wrote the opinion; Stevens, Souter, Ginsburg, and Breyer concurred separately.

A federal court must hold a trial in a suit challenging a redistricting plan as a racial gerrymander when the state's motivation for the plan is in dispute. The ruling—the Court's third in the dispute—sent back to a three-judge federal court a challenge to a North Carolina congressional redistricting plan adopted in 1997. The Court said the lower court should have held a full trial because of the dispute over the motivation for the plan.

TERRITORIES

Gutierrez v. Ada (528 U.S. 250), decided by a 9–0 vote, Jan. 19, 2000; Souter wrote the opinion.

Guam's governing law does not require a runoff election for governor or lieutenant governor if the leading candidate fails to receive an absolute majority of all ballots cast in the election. The ruling upheld the results of a closely contested race for governor of the island territory in 1998.

VOTING RIGHTS

Lopez v. Monterey County, California (519 U.S. 9), decided by a 9–0 vote, Nov. 6, 1996; O'Connor wrote the opinion.

A federal court may not order a change in voting procedure in a jurisdiction covered by the Voting Rights Act's requirement to preclear such changes with either the Justice Department or the federal district court in Washington. The ruling reversed a decision by a federal court to put into effect for a 1995 election a racially drawn districting plan for municipal courts in Monterey County, California. The county crafted the plan as an interim solution to a suit by Latino residents. The Court ruled that the lower court was wrong to circumvent the preclearance provision, but left unsettled the underlying issues in the case: whether the court consolidation did violate the Voting Rights Act and, if so, whether the county's decision to create Latino majorities in three of four judicial districts was consistent with the Court's recent rulings limiting the use of race in drawing district lines.

Young v. Fordice, Governor of Mississippi (520 U.S. 273), decided by a 9–0 vote, March 31, 1997; Breyer wrote the opinion.

Mississippi was required under the Voting Rights Act to obtain prior approval for its decision to adopt a simplified voting registration system for federal elections but not for state and local balloting.

Reno, Attorney General v. Bossier Parish School Board (528 U.S. 320), decided by a 7–2 vote, May 12, 1997; O'Connor wrote the opinion; Stevens and Souter dissented in part.

The Court limited the impact of the federal Voting Rights Act provision requiring localities with a history of discrimination to obtain prior approval before making any change in voting practices or procedures. The Court said the Justice Department could not withhold approval solely because an election law change diluted minority voting strength as long as minority voters were not worse off than before, with no "retrogressive" effect.

Foreman v. Dallas County, Texas (521 U.S. 979), decided by a 9–0 vote, June 27, 1997; *per curiam* (unsigned) opinion.

The Court summarily ordered additional proceedings to determine whether Dallas County should have sought Justice Department approval under the Voting Rights Act to change its method of appointing election precinct judges. The decision set aside a ruling by a three-judge court that the Voting Rights Act's preclearance requirement did not apply to a move by the County Commission in 1996 to appoint only Republicans as election judges. The decision returned the case for further evidence on the method of appointing judges as of 1972, when Texas became subject to the Voting Rights Act.

City of Monroe v. United States (522 U.S. 34), decided by a 7–2 vote, Nov. 17, 1997; *per curiam* (unsigned) opinion; Souter and Breyer dissented.

Without hearing argument, the Court agreed that the city of Monroe, Georgia, was allowed to use a majority voting system for local elections even though it did not obtain specific approval under the Voting Rights Act to change from a plurality system.

Texas v. United States (523 U.S. 296), decided by a 9–0 vote, March 31, 1998; Scalia wrote the opinion.

In a brief opinion, the Court declined to decide whether the Voting Rights Act limits the ability of Texas officials to use a state law permitting the displacement of elected local school boards in certain circumstances.

Lopez v. Monterey County (525 U.S. 266), decided by an 8–1 vote, Jan. 20, 1999; O'Connor wrote the opinion; Thomas dissented.

A county subject to the Voting Rights Act's preclearance requirement must obtain advance approval for a change in election procedures even if it results from a state law that does not have to be precleared. The decision was the Court's second ruling in the case. In 1996 the Court overturned the district court's decision to put into effect a judicial districting plan that had not been submitted for preclearance.

Rice v. Cayetano, Governor of Hawaii (528 U.S. 495), decided by a 7–2 vote, Feb. 23, 2000; Kennedy wrote the opinion; Stevens and Ginsburg dissented.

A Hawaii law that allowed only people of native Hawaiian ancestry to vote for members of a state agency in charge of programs aimed at benefiting native Hawaiians was struck down as unconstitutional racial discrimination. The Court ruled the voting scheme violated the Fifteenth Amendment.

VOTING RIGHTS ACT

Reno, Attorney General v. Bossier Parish School Board (528 U.S. 320), decided by a 5–4 vote, Jan. 24, 2000; Scalia wrote the opinion; Souter, Stevens, Ginsburg, and Breyer dissented.

In a setback for civil rights organizations, the Court ruled that governments covered by the Voting Rights Act's preclearance requirement can obtain federal approval for election law changes as long as the revisions do not leave minority voters worse off than before. In an initial ruling, *Reno v. Bossier Parish School Board (1997)*, the Court said the Justice Department could not withhold approval solely because an election law change diluted minority voting strength.

Environmental Law

ENDANGERED SPECIES

Bennett v. Spear (520 U.S. 154), decided by a 9–0 vote, March 19, 1997; Scalia wrote the opinion.

The Endangered Species Act allows any person, not just environmentalists, to go to court to challenge regulatory actions not only for underenforcement of the law but also for overenforcement.

FINES

Friends of the Earth, Inc. v. Laidlaw Environmental Services (TOC), Inc. (528 U.S. 167), decided by a 7–2 vote, Jan. 12, 2000; Ginsburg wrote the opinion; Scalia and Thomas dissented.

Courts can fine polluters in citizen suits brought under the federal Clean Water Act and can enforce those fines even if the company eliminates any violations while the case is proceeding.

NATIONAL FORESTS

Ohio Forestry Association, Inc. v. Sierra Club (523 U.S. 726), decided by a 9–0 vote, May 18, 1998; Breyer wrote the opinion.

The Court rejected as premature an environmental organization's legal challenge to a National Forest Service management plan for the Wayne National Forest in southern Ohio.

"RIGHT TO KNOW" LAWS

Steel Co. v. Citizens for a Better Environment (523 U.S. 83), decided by 9–0 and 6–3 votes, March 4, 1998; Scalia wrote the opinion; Stevens, Souter, and Ginsburg agreed with the outcome but disagreed with the legal holding.

The Court left unresolved the issue of whether businesses can be sued by private citizens for past violations of a federal law requiring public disclosure of the use of toxic chemicals. Instead, the Court used the case to narrow the doctrine of legal standing in cases where plaintiffs are not seeking damages or future injunctive relief.

TOXIC WASTE

United States v. Bestfoods (524 U.S. 51), decided by a 9–0 vote, June 8, 1998; Souter wrote the opinion.

A corporation can be held liable for the costs of cleaning up toxic wastes at a subsidiary's plant if the parent company participated in and controlled the plant's operations. The ruling was a partial setback for the government in enforcing the 1980 federal "Superfund" law—formally called the Comprehensive Environmental Response, Compensation, and Liability Act.

Family Law

CHILD SUPPORT ENFORCEMENT

Blessing, Director, Arizona Department of Economic Security v. Freestone (520 U.S. 329), decided by a 9–0 vote, April 21, 1997; O'Connor wrote the opinion.

The Court barred a broad class-action suit aimed at forcing Arizona to improve its compliance with a federal child-support enforcement law, but it returned the case to lower federal courts to consider the validity of more limited claims. The Court held that Title IV-D of the Social Security Act does not give individuals a federal right to force a state to substantially comply with its provisions.

VISITATION

Troxel v. Granville (530 U.S. 57), decided by a 6–3 vote, June 5, 2000; O'Connor wrote the main opinion; Stevens, Scalia, and Kennedy dissented.

The Court ruled that a Washington state judge went too far in applying a state law to grant visitation rights to the grandparents of two young girls over the mother's objections, but it skirted the major constitutional question of whether nonparental visitation statutes always violate parents' due process rights.

Federal Government

CENSUS

Department of Commerce v. United States House of Representatives (525 U.S. 316), decided by a 5–4 vote, Jan. 25, 1999; O'Connor wrote the opinion; Stevens, Souter, Ginsburg, and Breyer dissented.

In a politically charged ruling, the Court ruled that the Census Bureau may not use statistical sampling to determine population counts to be used in apportioning seats in the

House of Representatives among the states. However, the ruling allowed the use of adjusted population figures for other purposes, including legislative and congressional redistricting and allocation of federal aid to state and local governments. The ruling represented a victory for Republican opponents of the Clinton administration's plan to use statistical sampling techniques in an effort to achieve a more accurate count in the 2000 census.

FEDERAL EMPLOYEES

LaChance, Acting Director, Office of Personnel Management v. Erickson (522 U.S. 262), decided by a 9–0 vote, Jan. 21, 1998; Rehnquist wrote the opinion.

Federal employees can be disciplined for lying to agency investigators about allegations of employment-related misconduct. The ruling came in six consolidated cases involving federal employees who were punished for various instances of misconduct and for making false statements during the investigations.

FEDERAL REGULATION

Dunn v. Commodity Futures Trading Commission (519 U.S. 465), decided by a 9–0 vote, Feb. 25, 1997; Stevens wrote the opinion.

The Commodity Futures Trading Commission has no authority to regulate over-the-counter trading in options to buy or sell foreign currency.

Glickman, Secretary of Agriculture v. Wileman Brothers & Elliott, Inc. (521 U.S. 457), decided by a 5–4 vote, June 25, 1997; Stevens wrote the opinion; Souter, Rehnquist, Scalia, and Thomas dissented.

The federal government can require agricultural producers to pay the costs of industry-wide generic advertising programs without violating the First Amendment's protections for freedom of speech.

Printz, Sheriff/Coroner, Ravalli County, Montana v. United States (521 U.S. 898), decided by a 5–4 vote, June 27, 1997; Scalia wrote the opinion; Stevens, Souter, Ginsburg, and Breyer dissented.

The federal government cannot require state or local law enforcement officials to conduct background checks on prospective gun purchasers. The ruling—an important victory for states' rights advocates and gun control opponents—struck down a provision of the Brady Handgun Violence Prevention Act establishing a five-day waiting period to purchase a handgun and, pending completion of a nationwide "instant-check system," required local law enforcement officers to determine the prospective gun purchaser's eligibility to own the weapon. The Court ruled that the background-check requirement exceeded federal powers.

Regions Hospital v. Shalala, Secretary of Health and Human Services (522 U.S. 448), decided by a 6–3 vote, Feb. 24, 1998; Ginsburg wrote the opinion; Scalia, O'Connor, and Thomas dissented.

The Court upheld a federal regulation aimed at limiting Medicare and Medicaid reimbursements to hospitals for the costs of training medical residents.

American Telephone & Telegraph Co. v. Central Office Telephone, Inc. (524 U.S. 214), decided by a 7–1 vote, June 15, 1998; Scalia wrote the opinion; Stevens dissented; O'Connor did not participate.

Customers cannot sue federally regulated telephone companies for breach of contract in state court for failing to provide services as specified in rate tariffs filed with the Federal Communications Commission.

Roberts v. Galen of Virginia, Inc. (525 U.S. 249), decided by a 9–0 vote, Jan. 13, 1999; *per curiam* (unsigned) opinion.

The Court eased the burden for recovering damages from hospitals for violating a federal law restricting the transfer of emergency patients to other facilities. In a brief opinion, the Court said that plaintiffs do not need to show a hospital acted with an improper motive in transferring an emergency patient. The law, aimed at preventing the "dumping" of patients with potentially high medical costs and limited or no insurance, requires hospitals to provide "such treatment as may be required to stabilize" an emergency medical condition before transferring the patient.

AT&T Corp. v. Iowa Utilities Board (525 U.S. 366), decided by votes of 8–0, 7–1, and 5–3, Jan. 25, 1999; Scalia wrote the opinion; Souter dissented from one part of the ruling; Thomas, Rehnquist, and Breyer dissented from another, broader part; O'Connor did not participate.

The Federal Communications Commission has authority under the Telecommunications Act of 1996 to regulate the price and other conditions for new telephone companies to gain access to local telephone networks.

O'Connor did not participate in the case because of a financial conflict.

Your Home Visiting Nurse Services, Inc. v. Shalala, Secretary of Health and Human Services (525 U.S. 449), decided by a 9–0 vote, Feb. 23, 1999; Scalia wrote the opinion.

The Court limited the ability of health care providers to contest an insurance company's refusal to reconsider the amount of money the provider receives as reimbursement under the Medicare program. The case involved a Medicare regulation that gave health care providers three years to ask an insurance company to reconsider a reimbursement decision.

California Dental Association v. Federal Trade Commission (526 U.S. 756), decided by 9–0 and 5–4 votes, May 24, 1999; Souter wrote the opinion; Breyer, Stevens, Kennedy, and Ginsburg dissented in part.

The Court upheld the jurisdiction of the Federal Trade Commission (FTC) over nonprofit professional associations but said a federal appeals court acted too quickly in sustaining the FTC's challenge to advertising restrictions adopted by a state dental association.

Reno, Attorney General v. Condon, Attorney General of South Carolina (528 U.S. 141), decided by a 9–0 vote, Jan. 12, 2000; Rehnquist wrote the opinion.

The federal government can prohibit state governments from selling personal information obtained in issuing driver's licenses. The ruling upheld the constitutionality of a 1994 law, the Driver's Privacy Protection Act, challenged by a number of states on federalism grounds.

Shalala, Secretary of Health and Human Services v. Illinois Council on Long Term Care, Inc. (529 U.S. 1), decided by a 5–4 vote, Feb. 29, 2000; Breyer wrote the opinion; Thomas, Stevens, Scalia, and Kennedy dissented.

Nursing homes seeking to challenge Medicare regulations must do so through administrative enforcement proceedings at the Department of Health and Human Services, not in federal court.

United States v. Locke, Governor of Washington (529 U.S. 89), decided by a 9–0 vote, March 6, 2000; Kennedy wrote the opinion.

Federal laws and regulations generally preempt state regulation of oil tankers. The ruling invalidated four oil tanker regulations and cast doubt on other restrictions that were part of a stringent regulatory scheme adopted by the state of Washington following the *Exxon Valdez* oil spill off the coast of Alaska in 1989.

Food and Drug Administration v. Brown & Williamson Tobacco Corp. (529 U.S. 120), decided by a 5–4 vote, March 21, 2000; O'Connor wrote the opinion; Breyer, Stevens, Souter, and Ginsburg dissented.

The Food and Drug Administration has no authority under its statutory charter to regulate cigarettes or other tobacco products. The ruling represented a major victory for the tobacco industry against a Clinton administration initiative to impose advertising and marketing restrictions on manufacturers and retailers of cigarettes and smokeless tobacco.

Norfolk Southern Railway Co. v. Shanklin (529 U.S. 334), decided by a 7–2 vote, April 17, 2000; O'Connor wrote the opinion; Ginsburg and Stevens dissented.

Federal law prevents states from applying their own standards in personal injury suits based on allegedly inadequate warnings at railway crossings if federal funds were used in installing the safety devices.

Public Lands Council v. Babbitt, Secretary of Interior (529 U.S. 728), decided by a 9–0 vote, May 15, 2000; Breyer wrote the opinion.

The Court upheld three revised Interior Department regulations issued in 1995 under the Taylor Grazing Act, which governs livestock grazing on public lands. Ranchers argued that the regulations undermined their livelihood and infringed on rights protected under a 1934 federal law. The Court held that the regulatory changes did not exceed the interior secretary's authority under the grazing law.

Geier v. American Honda Motor Company, Inc. (529 U.S. 861), decided by a 5–4 vote, May 22, 2000; Breyer wrote the opinion; Stevens, Souter, Thomas, and Ginsburg dissented.

In a closely watched business dispute, the Court ruled that a federal regulation aimed at encouraging but not requiring airbags protected automobile manufacturers from damage suits by consumers injured in crashes involving cars that were not equipped with the devices.

Crosby, Secretary of Finance and Administration of Massachusetts v. National Foreign Trade Council (530 U.S. 363), decided by a 9–0 vote, June 19, 2000; Souter wrote the opinion.

The Court struck down a Massachusetts law imposing economic sanctions on companies doing business in Myanmar (formerly Burma), saying the act was preempted by a less stringent federal measure aimed at penalizing the country's dictatorial government.

FREEDOM OF INFORMATION

Bibles, Director, Oregon Bureau of Land Management v. Oregon Natural Desert Association (519 U.S. 355), decided by a 9–0 vote, Feb. 18, 1997; *per curiam* (unsigned) opinion.

The federal Bureau of Land Management (BLM) did not have to comply with a conservation group's Freedom of Information Act request to turn over its mailing list of people who receive BLM information and publications.

GOVERNMENT CONTRACTS

Department of the Army v. Blue Fox, Inc. (525 U.S. 255), decided by a 9–0 vote, Jan. 20, 1999; Rehnquist wrote the opinion.

The Court refused to soften a long-standing rule that creditors cannot enforce liens on property of the federal government. The Court held the suit amounted to an action for money damages that was barred by principles of sovereign immunity.

Mobil Oil Exploration and Producing Southeast, Inc. v. United States (530 U.S. 604), decided by an 8–1 vote, June 26, 2000; Breyer wrote the opinion; Stevens dissented.

The Court ordered the government to repay two oil companies $156 million for reneging on contracts for crude oil and natural gas leases off the North Carolina coast.

MILITARY AFFAIRS

Edmond v. United States (520 U.S. 651), decided by a 9–0 vote, May 19, 1997; Scalia wrote the opinion.

The Court rejected a challenge to the method of appointment of civilian judges on the Coast Guard Court of Criminal Appeals. The ruling came in six consolidated cases challenging the appointment of the civilian judges on the appellate tribunal by the secretary of transportation rather than by the president. The Court said the appellate judges were "inferior officers" under the Constitution and Congress could give the power to appoint them to the head of a department instead of the president.

Clinton, President of the United States v. Goldsmith (526 U.S. 529), decided by a 9–0 vote, May 17, 1999; Souter wrote the opinion.

The Court limited the authority of the Court of Appeals for the Armed Forces, the highest military court, while sidestepping a constitutional challenge to a law giving the president power to dismiss a service member following a court-martial conviction.

NATIVE AMERICANS

Babbitt, Secretary of the Interior v. Youpee (519 U.S. 234), decided by an 8–1 vote, Jan. 21, 1997; Ginsburg wrote the opinion; Stevens dissented.

The Court struck down the Indian Land Consolidation Act (1983), which prohibited Native Americans who own small parcels of land within reservations from passing down the property to their heirs. The ruling struck down a second attempt by Congress to reduce the fractionation of lands on reservations.

Strate, Associate Tribal Judge, Tribal Court of the Three Affiliated Tribes of the Fort Berthold Indian Reservation v. A-1 Contractors (520 U.S. 438), decided by a 9–0 vote, April 28, 1997; Ginsburg wrote the opinion.

Tribal courts ordinarily do not have jurisdiction over civil suits involving nontribe members arising from automobile accidents on state highways that cross Native American reservations.

South Dakota v. Yankton Sioux Tribe (522 U.S. 329), decided by a 9–0 vote, Jan. 26, 1998; O'Connor wrote the opinion.

Resolving a dispute over state versus federal authority of a municipal landfill site, the Court ruled that an 1894 law had taken out of tribal control most of the Yankton Sioux Indian reservation.

Alaska v. Native Village of Venetie Tribal Government (522 U.S. 520), decided by a 9–0 vote, Feb. 25, 1998; Thomas wrote the opinion.

Native Alaskans failed in an effort to establish sovereign "Indian country" status for a 1.8-million-acre swath of land surrounding two villages north of the Arctic Circle. The Court held that the villages and surrounding areas were not Native American country.

Montana v. Crow Tribe of Indians (523 U.S. 696), decided by 9–0 and 7–2 votes, May 18, 1998; Ginsburg wrote the opinion; Souter and O'Connor dissented in part.

The Court rejected the Crow tribe's effort to recover about $58 million that a mining company paid in coal severance taxes under a Montana levy that was later invalidated as an intrusion on the tribe's powers.

Kiowa Tribe of Oklahoma v. Manufacturing Technologies, Inc. (523 U.S. 751), decided by a 6–3 vote, May 26, 1998; Kennedy wrote the opinion; Stevens, Thomas, and Ginsburg dissented.

The Court reaffirmed the rule of tribal immunity barring suits against Native American tribes in state courts but appeared to invite Congress to consider limiting the doctrine.

Cass County, Minnesota v. Leech Lake Band of Chippewa Indians (524 U.S. 103), decided by a 9–0 vote, June 8, 1998; Thomas wrote the opinion.

The Court strictly enforced procedures for exempting lands owned by Native American tribes from state or local property taxation. The ruling involved the common situation of property once part of an Indian reservation that was allotted to Native Americans for private ownership or sold to non-Native Americans and later repurchased by a tribe. Although Native American reservations are exempt from state and local property taxes, the Court said this property was subject to local taxation.

Amoco Production Co. v. Southern Ute Indian Tribe (526 U.S. 865), decided by a 7–1 vote, June 7, 1999; Kennedy wrote the opinion; Ginsburg dissented; Breyer did not participate.

Federal laws reserving ownership of coal on formerly public lands for the government did not apply to methane gas buried within coalbeds. Instead, the now valuable energy source belongs to private owners, the Court ruled.

Minnesota v. Mille Lacs Band of Chippewa Indians (526 U.S. 172), decided by a 5–4 vote, March 24, 1999; O'Connor wrote the opinion; Rehnquist, Scalia, Kennedy, and Thomas dissented.

The Court upheld the right of Chippewa Indians to hunt and fish free of state game regulation on thirteen million acres of public land in central Minnesota. The ruling came in a closely watched case that pitted eight Chippewa bands, supported by the federal government, against the state of Minnesota and a number of local governments and private property owners. In an exhaustive historical reconstruction, the Court concluded that President Zachary Taylor had no authority under an 1837 treaty with the United States to issue a presidential order removing the Chippewas from parts of the Minnesota territory and that the revocation of hunting and fishing rights in the order was also void. The Court went on to say that neither an 1855 treaty nor the act of Congress admitting Minnesota expressly terminated the Chippewas' hunting and fishing rights.

SEPARATION OF POWERS

Clinton v. Jones (520 U.S. 681), decided by a 9–0 vote, May 27, 1997; Stevens wrote the opinion.

The president is not entitled to an automatic stay during his term in office of proceedings in a civil lawsuit relating to private, unofficial conduct that occurred before his election. The Court held that the separation of powers doctrine gives the president no "categorical immunity" in civil lawsuits involving conduct unrelated to his office.

Raines, Director, Office of Management and Budget v. Byrd (521 U.S. 811), decided by a 7–2 vote, June 26, 1997; Rehnquist wrote the opinion; Stevens and Breyer dissented.

The Court dismissed a lawsuit by members of Congress challenging the Line Item Veto Act and sharply curtailed the ability of lawmakers to bring similar constitutional suits in the future. The ruling—the Court's first direct holding on the issue of "legislative standing"—left unsettled the constitutionality of the 1996 act allowing the president to "cancel" individual spending items or limited tax breaks after signing a bill into law.

Clinton, President of the United States v. City of New York (524 U.S. 417), decided by a 6–3 vote, June 25, 1998; Stevens wrote the opinion; Scalia, O'Connor, and Breyer dissented.

The Line Item Veto Act's provision giving the president the power to cancel individual items in spending or certain tax laws violates the procedures for enacting laws in the Constitution's Presentment Clause. The ruling upheld separate challenges filed by groups affected by President Bill Clinton's use of the 1996 law in August 1997.

SOCIAL SECURITY

Forney v. Apfel, Commissioner of Social Security (524 U.S. 266), decided by a 9–0 vote, June 15, 1998; Breyer wrote the opinion.

Someone contesting a denial of Social Security disability benefits may immediately appeal a federal judge's order returning the case to an administrative law judge for further proceedings.

Sims v. Apfel, Commissioner of Social Security (530 U.S. 103), decided by a 5–4 vote, June 5, 2000; Thomas wrote the main opinion; O'Connor concurred in part; Breyer, Rehnquist, Scalia, and Kennedy dissented.

The Court made it easier for people who have been denied Social Security disability benefits to contest the decision in federal court. The Court held that Social Security applicants can raise issues in a federal court suit even if they did not raise them in an administrative appeal.

First Amendment

CHURCH AND STATE

Agostini v. Felton (521 U.S. 203), decided by a 5–4 vote, June 23, 1997; O'Connor wrote the opinion; Souter, Stevens, Ginsburg, and Breyer dissented.

Public school teachers can provide remedial educational services to disadvantaged students at church-affiliated schools without violating the constitutional prohibition against governmental establishment of religion. The decision, in a New York City case, overturned a twelve-year-old precedent in the face of a significant procedural obstacle. The Court in 1985 voted 5–4 in *Aguilar v. Felton* to bar the use of federal funds to pay public school teachers for providing remedial services at parochial schools. In this ruling, the Court held that the city could use federal funds to provide services on a neutral basis to disadvantaged children on the premises of parochial schools under safeguards to prevent improper aid to religion.

City of Boerne v. Flores, Archbishop of San Antonio (521 U.S. 507), decided by a 6–3 vote, June 25, 1997; Kennedy wrote the opinion; O'Connor, Souter, and Breyer dissented.

Congress exceeded its power in passing a law, the Religious Freedom Restoration Act, that sharply restricted the power of states to enforce laws that have an incidental effect on religious practices. The 1993 law provided that a state could not enforce a law that burdened religious practices unless the measure had a "compelling governmental interest" and was "the least restrictive means" of furthering that interest. Congress passed the law after the Court in a 1990 decision, *Employment Div., Dept. of Human Resources of Oregon v. Smith,* set a more lax standard for judging laws that burdened religious practices. The Court struck down the statute, saying the law sought to broadly override state and local laws by attempting to make "a substantive change in constitutional protections" as determined by the Court.

Santa Fe Independent School District v. Doe (530 U.S. 290), decided by a 6–3 vote, June 19, 2000; Stevens wrote the opinion; Rehnquist, Scalia, and Thomas dissented.

The Court strengthened its restrictions on school-sponsored religious observances by barring a Texas school district's policy permitting an elected student-speaker to deliver an invocation before high school football games. The Court held that a student-led, student-initiated prayer at public high school football games violates the Establishment Clause.

Mitchell v. Helms (530 U.S. 793), decided by a 6–3 vote, June 28, 2000; Thomas wrote the main opinion; O'Connor and Breyer concurred in the judgment; Souter, Stevens, and Ginsburg dissented.

Governments can lend computers and other instructional equipment to religious and other private schools without violating the constitutional prohibition against establishment of religion. The ruling—in a fractured decision with no majority opinion—turned aside an Establishment Clause challenge to the operation of the federal government's so-called Chapter 2 program. Under the program, the federal government provided funds via state education agencies to local school systems, which in turn bought instructional materials and equipment to be lent to public or private secondary and elementary schools.

COMMERCIAL SPEECH

Greater New Orleans Broadcasting Association, Inc. v. United States (527 U.S. 173), decided by a 9–0 vote, June 14, 1999; Stevens wrote the opinion.

The Court struck down a federal ban on broadcast advertising of casino gambling, saying the law was not well tailored to promote the interests advanced by the government to justify the restriction. The ruling invalidated a law that, as originally enacted in 1934, prohibited radio or television stations from broadcasting any advertisements for lotteries or other games of chance.

Los Angeles Police Department v. United Reporting Publishing Corp. (528 U.S. 32), decided by a 7–2 vote, Dec. 7, 1999; Rehnquist wrote the opinion; Stevens and Kennedy dissented.

The Court turned aside a First Amendment challenge to a California law that limited access to information about arrestees to anyone requesting the data for commercial purposes. The narrow ruling sent back to lower federal courts a suit brought by a company that wanted to collect names and addresses of arrestees for sale to attorneys, insurance companies, driving schools, and drug and alcohol counselors, who could then use the lists to solicit clients or customers. The Court ruled that the company could not bring a facial challenge to the law because the statute did not directly infringe on the company's own free speech rights. The opinion left unanswered whether a so-called applied challenge to the law could be brought by someone who had a direct interest in using the address information for commercial purposes.

FREEDOM OF ASSOCIATION

Boy Scouts of America v. Dale (530 U.S. 640), decided by a 5–4 vote, June 28, 2000; Rehnquist wrote the opinion; Stevens, Souter, Ginsburg, and Breyer dissented.

The Boy Scouts may continue to enforce a policy prohibiting avowed homosexuals from serving as adult Scout leaders despite a state law prohibiting discrimination in public accommodations on the basis of sexual orientation. The ruling barred a complaint brought under a New Jersey antidiscrimination law by a former Boy Scout assistant scoutmaster, after his local Scout council revoked his membership because of his homosexuality. The Court held that application of the state's antidiscrimination law would violate the Boy Scouts' "freedom of expressive association."

FREEDOM OF SPEECH

Reno, Attorney General v. American Civil Liberties Union (521 U.S. 844), decided by 9–0 and 7–2 votes, June 26, 1997; Stevens wrote the opinion; O'Connor and Rehnquist dissented in part.

A new federal law aimed at limiting access by minors to sexually oriented material on the Internet violated the First Amendment by suppressing constitutionally protected speech for adults. The ruling struck down the Communications Decency Act, enacted as part of a broad telecommunications law rewrite in 1996. The law made it a crime to knowingly transmit an obscene or indecent message or image to a minor.

National Endowment for the Arts v. Finley (524 U.S. 569), decided by an 8–1 vote, June 25, 1998; O'Connor wrote the opinion; Souter dissented.

The National Endowment for the Arts (NEA) may consider "general standards of decency" in awarding grants to artists without violating the First Amendment's protections for freedom of speech. The ruling upheld but significantly softened a restriction passed by Congress in 1990 after controversies had arisen over the use of some NEA grants for works criticized as sexually indecent or sacrilegious.

Board of Regents, University of Wisconsin System v. Southworth (529 U.S. 217), decided by a 9–0 vote, March 22, 2000; Kennedy wrote the opinion.

Public universities can impose mandatory student activity fees to support political and ideological groups as long as the funds are distributed in a viewpoint-neutral manner.

City of Erie v. Pap's A. M. (529 U.S. 277), decided by a 6–3 vote, March 29, 2000; O'Connor wrote the main opinion; Scalia and Thomas concurred in the judgment; Souter dissented in part; Stevens and Ginsburg dissented.

Cities and states can ban nude dancing. The ruling revived an ordinance enacted by Erie, Pennsylvania, in 1994 after the opening of a bar in the city's downtown area featuring nude female dancers. The Court had upheld a similar ordinance in a fractured decision in 1991, *Barnes v. Glen Theatre, Inc.* In a decision slightly less fractured than its previous ruling, the Court ruled that the ordinance did not violate the First Amendment because it was subject to a lesser "intermediate scrutiny" test used to judge laws that are not aimed at regulating the content of speech.

Hill v. Colorado (530 U.S. 640), decided by a 6–3 vote, June 28, 2000; Stevens wrote the opinion; Scalia, Kennedy, and Thomas dissented.

The Court upheld a Colorado law that limited leafleting or so-called sidewalk counseling at abortion clinics or other health care facilities except with a person's consent or at a distance of at least eight feet. The ruling—a setback for antiabortion protesters—rejected a First Amendment challenge to the Colorado statute, passed in 1993, which made it a misdemeanor for any person within 100 feet of a health care facility's entrance to "knowingly approach" within eight feet of another person, without that person's consent.

PUBLIC TELEVISION

Arkansas Educational Television Commission v. Forbes (523 U.S. 666), decided by a 6–3 vote, May 18, 1998; Kennedy wrote the opinion; Stevens, Ginsburg, and Breyer dissented.

Government-owned public television stations have discretion to exclude minor candidates from campaign debates if the decisions are reasonable and not based on the candidates' views.

TELECOMMUNICATIONS

Turner Broadcasting System, Inc. v. Federal Communications Commission (520 U.S. 180), decided by a 5–4 vote, March 31, 1997; Kennedy wrote the opinion; O'Connor, Scalia, Thomas, and Ginsburg dissented.

The federal law requiring cable television systems to carry the signals of local broadcast stations does not violate the First Amendment. The ruling upholding the so-called must-carry provisions of a 1992 cable television law was a victory for broadcasters and a setback for cable operators and programmers, who challenged the law as an unconstitutional infringement on their editorial freedom.

United States v. Playboy Entertainment Group, Inc. (529 U.S. 803), decided by a 5–4 vote, May 22, 2000; Kennedy wrote the opinion; Breyer, Rehnquist, O'Connor, and Scalia dissented.

The Court struck down on First Amendment grounds a federal law requiring cable channels primarily devoted to sexually explicit programming either to fully scramble their programs or to limit the material to late night and early morning hours. The ruling invalidated a provision of the Telecommunications Act of 1996—section 505—ostensibly aimed at preventing children from inadvertently being exposed to so-called signal bleed from cable sex channels.

Immigration Law

CITIZENSHIP

Miller v. Albright, Secretary of State (523 U.S. 420), decided by a 6–3 vote, April 22, 1998; Stevens wrote the main opinion; O'Connor and Scalia wrote opinions concurring in the judgment, each on different grounds; Ginsburg, Souter, and Breyer dissented.

The Court left on the books a law setting different citizenship requirements for an illegitimate child born abroad depending on whether the mother or father is a U.S. citizen. But a majority of the justices cast doubt that the provision would be upheld if challenged in a different case.

DEPORTATION

Immigration and Naturalization Service v. Yueh-Shaio Yang (519 U.S. 26), decided by a 9–0 vote, Nov. 13, 1996; Scalia wrote the opinion.

Immigration authorities have discretion to use an immigrant's fraud in entering the United States as grounds for deporting the immigrant, despite a general policy of disregarding such conduct in deportation hearings.

Reno, Attorney General v. American-Arab Anti-Discrimination Committee (525 U.S. 471), decided by 8–1 and 6–3 votes, Feb. 24, 1999; Scalia wrote the opinion; Breyer and Ginsburg did not join part of the ruling; Souter dissented.

Illegal aliens cannot challenge the government's effort to deport them on grounds that they are being singled out because of their political views, in violation of the First Amendment. The ruling also allowed retroactive application of a new law restricting judicial review of deportation cases. The Court ruled that the jurisdiction limitation provision allowed aliens to challenge deportations only after the issuance of a final order and that the provision applied retroactively.

Immigration and Naturalization Service v. Aguirre-Aguirre (526 U.S. 415), decided by a 9–0 vote, May 3, 1999; Kennedy wrote the opinion.

The Court strengthened immigration authorities' discretion to deport aliens who committed serious nonpolitical crimes outside the United States even if they face persecution if returned to their native country.

Individual Rights

ABORTION

Schenck v. Pro-Choice Network of Western New York (519 U.S. 357), decided by 6–3 and 8–1 votes, Feb. 19, 1997; Rehnquist wrote the opinion; Scalia, Kennedy, and Thomas dissented in part; Breyer dissented in part.

The Court upheld a federal judge's injunction ordering antiabortion demonstrators to stay at least fifteen feet away from entrances to abortion clinics, but it struck down part of the order establishing a "floating buffer zone" around patients and clinic staff as they approached or left the clinics. The defendants had asked the Court to review the ruling, contending that it went beyond the restrictions on antiabortion demonstrations permitted under the Court's 1994 ruling in a similar case, *Madsen v. Women's Health Center, Inc.* Applying the *Madsen* ruling, the Court said the floating buffer zones were improper, but, by contrast, a fixed buffer zone was "necessary to ensure that people and vehicles trying to enter or exit the clinic property or clinic parking lots can do so."

Lambert, Gallatin County Attorney v. Wicklund (520 U.S. 292), decided by a 9–0 vote, March 31, 1997; *per curiam* (unsigned) opinion.

The Court reinstituted Montana's parental notice abortion law, saying that a federal appeals court misapplied prior rulings in striking down the statute. The Montana law prohibited physicians from performing abortions on a minor unless one or both parents were notified at least forty-eight hours in advance, but allowed a court to waive the requirement if notification was "not in the best interests" of the minor.

Mazurek, Attorney General of Montana v. Armstrong (520 U.S. 968), decided by a 6–3 vote, June 19, 1997; *per curiam* (unsigned) opinion; Stevens, Ginsburg, and Breyer dissented.

The Court allowed Montana to enforce a state law requiring abortions to be performed only by a licensed physician. The summary ruling—issued without hearing argument—overturned a ruling by the Ninth U.S. Circuit Court of Appeals that had enjoined enforcement of the 1995 law. The unsigned opinion pointed to a number of rulings, including the 1992 decision in *Planned Parenthood of Southeastern Pa. v. Casey*, as upholding the right of states to adopt physician-only abortion statutes.

Stenberg, Attorney General of Nebraska v. Carhart (530 U.S. 914), decided by a 5–4 vote, June 28, 2000; Breyer wrote the opinion; Thomas, Rehnquist, Scalia, and Kennedy dissented.

The Court invalidated a Nebraska law that sought to ban so-called partial-birth abortions. It said the statute imposed an undue burden on a woman's right to abortion and failed to include an exception for the health of the mother. The ruling was a defeat for antiabortion groups, which had won enactment of similar laws by overwhelming legislative majorities in thirty-one states. The Court also held the law unconstitutional, saying that it contradicted holdings in two previous abortion rights decisions: the "undue burden"

standard announced in *Planned Parenthood of Southeastern Pa. v. Casey* (1992) and the "health exception" requirement contained in *Roe v. Wade* (1973) and reaffirmed in *Casey*.

AFFIRMATIVE ACTION

Texas v. Lesage (528 U.S. 18), decided by a 9–0 vote, Nov. 29, 1999; *per curiam* (unsigned) opinion.

State college or university applicants who claim reverse discrimination because of a race-conscious admissions process cannot recover damages without showing that they would have been admitted to the school or program but for the racial preference.

Adarand Constructors, Inc. v. Slater, Secretary of Transportation (528 U.S. 216), decided by a 9–0 vote, Jan. 12, 2000; *per curiam* (unsigned) opinion.

The Court revived a white contractor's challenge to a minority preference program for federal Department of Transportation (DOT) road contracts. The ruling sent back to lower federal courts a reverse-discrimination case brought by the owner of Adarand Constructors, Inc., after he lost out to a minority contractor for a DOT contract despite having submitted a lower bid. In an initial ruling, the Court in 1995 ruled that federal minority preference programs must meet the strictest constitutional standard—strict scrutiny—and sent the case to lower federal courts to apply that standard (*Adarand Constructors, Inc. v. Peña*).

AGE DISCRIMINATION

Oubre v. Entergy Operations, Inc. (522 U.S. 422), decided by a 6–3 vote, Jan. 26, 1998; Kennedy wrote the opinion; Thomas, Rehnquist, and Scalia dissented.

The Court, strictly interpreting the federal Age Discrimination in Employment Act, made it harder for employers to enforce provisions in severance agreements with older workers giving up their right to sue for age discrimination.

Reeves v. Sanderson Plumbing Products, Inc. (530 U.S. 133), decided by a 9–0 vote, June 12, 2000; O'Connor wrote the opinion.

In an important victory for plaintiffs likely to be applied to all federal job discrimination suits, the Court ruled that workers in federal age discrimination suits do not have to produce direct evidence that an employer fired or demoted them because of age if they cast doubt on the employer's claimed explanation for the action.

ASSISTED SUICIDE

Washington v. Glucksberg (521 U.S. 702), decided by a 9–0 vote, June 26, 1997; Rehnquist wrote the opinion.

Vacco, Attorney General of New York v. Quill (521 U.S. 793), decided by a 9–0 vote, June 26, 1997; Rehnquist wrote the opinion.

State laws prohibiting physicians from assisting a terminally ill patient to commit suicide do not violate the patients' or the physicians' rights to due process or equal protection of the laws. The unanimous decisions in two separate cases rejected rulings by federal appeals courts that barred the enforcement of laws banning physician-assisted suicide for the terminally ill. The Court ruled that both laws were constitutional.

DAMAGE SUITS

Board of County Commissioners of Bryan County, Oklahoma v. Brown (520 U.S. 397), decided by a 5–4 vote, April 28, 1997; O'Connor wrote the opinion; Souter, Stevens, Ginsburg, and Breyer dissented.

The Court made it harder for victims of police brutality to recover damages in federal civil rights suits from municipal governments for inadequately screening or training law enforcement officers.

Edwards v. Balisok (520 U.S. 641), decided by a 9–0 vote, May 19, 1997; Scalia wrote the opinion.

The Court barred a Washington state prison inmate's effort to use a federal civil rights suit to obtain damages for what he claimed was a wrongful disciplinary decision to take away thirty days of "good-time credit." The ruling relied on a 1994 precedent that limited prison inmates' use of so-called section 1983 suits—named after the section of the U.S. code in which the provision appears. The Court extended the earlier ruling and barred the inmate's plea for damages.

McMillian v. Monroe County, Alabama (520 U.S. 781), decided by a 5–4 vote, June 2, 1997; Rehnquist wrote the opinion; Ginsburg, Stevens, Souter, and Breyer dissented.

In a setback for civil rights groups, the Court ruled that Alabama sheriffs are state rather than county policymakers for purposes of determining their liability in federal court suits for violating an individual's constitutional rights.

Johnson v. Fankell (520 U.S. 911), decided by a 9–0 vote, June 9, 1997; Stevens wrote the opinion.

Public officials named as defendants in a federal civil rights suit filed in state court have no federal right to a preliminary appeal from a ruling denying qualified immunity.

Richardson v. McKnight (521 U.S. 399), decided by a 5–4 vote, June 23, 1997; Breyer wrote the opinion; Scalia, Rehnquist, Kennedy, and Thomas dissented.

Private prison guards do not have special legal protection from federal civil rights suits brought by inmates for alleged excessive use of force or other mistreatment. The Court refused to grant the private guards the same "qualified immunity" accorded to prison guards at state-run facilities.

Jefferson v. City of Tarrant, Alabama (522 U.S. 75), decided by an 8–1 vote, Dec. 9, 1997; Ginsburg wrote the opinion; Stevens dissented.

The Court declined to decide whether damages in a suit for federal civil rights violations are limited by a state law that bars compensatory damages in wrongful-death suits. The ruling sent back to Alabama state courts a suit by the survivors of an African American woman who blamed her death in a house fire on racial discrimination by the city's fire department in failing to respond promptly to the fire.

Kalina v. Fletcher (522 U.S. 118), decided by a 9–0 vote, Dec. 10, 1997; Stevens wrote the opinion.

Prosecutors are not entitled to absolute immunity and may be held liable in a federal civil rights suit for making false statements of fact in an affidavit supporting an application for an arrest warrant. The ruling seemed likely to have limited impact because federal prosecutors and most state prosecutors typically do not personally attest to facts used in obtaining an arrest warrant.

Bogan v. Scott-Harris (523 U.S. 44), decided by a 9–0 vote, March 3, 1998; Thomas wrote the opinion.

Local lawmakers are entitled to absolute immunity from liability in federal civil rights suits. The ruling extended the doctrine of immunity from just members of Congress and state legislators.

Crawford-El v. Britton (523 U.S. 574), decided by a 5–4 vote, May 4, 1998; Stevens wrote the opinion; Rehnquist, O'Connor, Scalia, and Thomas dissented.

The Court rejected a heightened standard of proof for plaintiffs claiming that state or local officials violated their civil rights by retaliating against them for exercising their freedom of speech.

County of Sacramento v. Lewis (523 U.S. 833), decided by a 9–0 vote, May 26, 1998; Souter wrote the opinion.

Police officers cannot be held liable for injuries or deaths resulting from automobile chases unless they intend to hurt the suspects being pursued. The Court held that officers could not be liable unless their conduct met a higher, so-called shocks the conscience test and that only an intentional action would satisfy that standard.

Gebser v. Lago Vista Independent School District (524 U.S. 274), decided by a 5–4 vote, June 22, 1998; O'Connor wrote the opinion; Stevens, Souter, Ginsburg, and Breyer dissented.

A school district cannot be ordered to pay damages under Title IX of the Education Amendments of 1972 for sexual harassment of a student by a teacher unless a ranking official knows of and is "deliberately indifferent" to the conduct.

Haddle v. Garrison (525 U.S. 121), decided by a 9–0 vote, Dec. 14, 1998; Rehnquist wrote the opinion.

Persons fired from a job in retaliation for agreeing to testify in a federal criminal investigation may recover damages from those responsible for their termination under a provision of federal civil rights law, 42 U.S.C. section 1985(2), which allows suits if someone is "injured in his property or person" in retaliation for testifying in a federal court proceeding.

National Collegiate Athletic Association v. Smith (525 U.S. 459), decided by a 9–0 vote, Feb. 23, 1999; Ginsburg wrote the opinion.

The Court turned aside an effort to apply Title IX of the Education Amendments of 1972—the federal law prohibiting sex discrimination by educational institutions receiving federal assistance—to the National Collegiate Athletic Association (NCAA). But the ruling allowed a former women's college volleyball player and the federal government a second chance to argue in lower federal courts for rulings on whether Title IX applied either because the NCAA directly received federal funds for a youth sports program it administered or because it exercised "controlling authority" over federally funded programs at colleges and universities.

Davis v. Monroe County Board of Education (526 U.S. 629), decided by a 5–4 vote, May 24, 1999; O'Connor wrote the opinion; Kennedy, Rehnquist, Scalia, and Thomas dissented.

In a suit brought under Title IX of the Education Amendments of 1972, which prohibits discrimination on account of sex by school districts receiving federal financial assistance, the Court ruled that a school district that receives federal aid may be required to pay damages to a student for severe sexual harassment by another student. The school district may be held liable if it knows of the sexual harassment and is deliberately indifferent to preventing it and if the behavior deprives the victim of access to educational opportunities or benefits provided by the school.

Wilson v. Layne, Deputy United States Marshal (526 U.S. 603), decided by 9–0 and 8–1 votes, May 24, 1999; Rehnquist wrote the opinion; Stevens dissented in part.

Police violate the Fourth Amendment and may be held liable for damages by inviting news media representatives to accompany them when executing a warrant inside a private home. The ruling limited the common but sometimes controversial practice of "media ride-alongs," but it said the officers involved in a 1992 incident in Maryland were entitled to a defense of "qualified immunity" to avoid liability because the law was not settled at that time. The Court also issued an unsigned opinion the same day on a similar case, *Hanlon v. Berger.*

Hanlon v. Berger (526 U.S. 808), decided by 9–0 and 8–1 votes, May 24, 1999; *per curiam* (unsigned) opinion; Stevens dissented in part.

In a ruling issued the same day as a similar case, *Wilson v. Layne,* federal officers were given a second chance to avoid liability for inviting a television news crew to accompany them on a raid of the grounds and outbuildings of a Montana ranch. The Court sent the Montana case back to lower federal courts to determine whether the law was any clearer in 1993, when this raid occurred, than in 1992, when the *Wilson* incident took place. The ruling also appeared to leave open the question whether it would make any difference that the Cable News Network crew did not go inside the home.

Village of Willowbrook v. Olech (528 U.S. 562), decided by a 9–0 vote, Feb. 23, 2000; *per curiam* (unsigned) opinion.

Someone who was not a member of a racial or ethnic minority or other specially protected class—a so-called class of one—can bring suit against the government for intentional and arbitrary discrimination under the Fourteenth Amendment's Equal Protection Clause.

United States v. Morrison (529 U.S. 598), decided by a 5–4 vote, May 15, 2000; Rehnquist wrote the opinion; Souter, Stevens, Ginsburg, and Breyer dissented.

The Court ruled unconstitutional a recently enacted federal law giving victims of gender-motivated violence the right to sue their attackers in federal court for compensatory and punitive damages. The ruling—another in a series of Rehnquist Court decisions citing principles of federalism to limit Congress's powers—struck down the civil damage remedy provision of the 1994 Violence Against Women Act. The Court held the law could not be sustained under either the Commerce Clause or the Fourteenth Amendment.

DISABILITY RIGHTS

Pennsylvania Department of Corrections v. Yeskey (524 U.S. 206), decided by a 9–0 vote, June 15, 1998; Scalia wrote the opinion.

The federal Americans with Disabilities Act (ADA) prohibits state prisons from discriminating against persons with disabilities in determining eligibility for programs or services.

Bragdon v. Abbott (524 U.S. 624), decided by a 5–4 vote, June 25, 1998; Kennedy wrote the opinion; Rehnquist, O'Connor, Scalia, and Thomas dissented.

In an important victory for AIDS organizations and disability rights groups, the Court ruled that Persons with HIV, the virus that causes AIDS, are protected by the Americans with Disabilities Act from discrimination in employment, housing, or public accommodations even if they have no outward symptoms of the disease. The ruling also returned the case to a lower court for further proceedings, where Randon Bragdon, a Maine dentist, was given another opportunity to prove that he did not violate the ADA in refusing to treat an HIV-positive woman in his dental office.

Cedar Rapids Community School District v. Garret F. (526 U.S. 66), decided by a 7–2 vote, March 3, 1999; Stevens wrote the opinion; Thomas and Kennedy dissented.

In a significant victory for disability rights advocates and a setback for local school districts, the Court ruled that public schools receiving federal aid for educating children with disabilities may be required to provide students with continuous nursing services if necessary for them to attend school.

Cleveland v. Policy Management Systems Corp. (526 U.S. 795), decided by a 9–0 vote, May 24, 1999; Breyer wrote the opinion.

Someone who applies for or receives benefits under the Social Security Disability Insurance program may also be able to sue an employer over alleged discrimination under the federal Americans with Disabilities Act.

Albertson's, Inc. v. Kirkingburg (527 U.S. 555), decided by a 9–0 vote, June 22, 1999; Souter wrote the opinion.

Following a decision the same day in *Sutton v. United Air Lines, Inc.*, regarding corrective measures for disabilities, the Court ruled that an employer can ordinarily require job applicants with physical impairments to meet standards of federal safety regulations without violating the federal Americans with Disabilities Act.

Sutton v. United Air Lines, Inc. (527 U.S. 471), decided by a 7–2 vote, June 22, 1999; O'Connor wrote the opinion; Stevens and Breyer dissented.

In an important victory for employers, the Court rejected a discrimination claim and ruled that individuals are not disabled under the federal Americans with Disabilities Act if corrective measures, such as eyeglasses, mitigate impairment so that they are not "substantially limited" in a major life activity.

Murphy v. United Parcel Service, Inc. (527 U.S. 516), decided by a 7–2 vote, June 22, 1999; O'Connor wrote the opinion; Stevens and Breyer dissented.

The Court rejected a discrimination claim under the Americans with Disabilities Act brought by a Kansas man fired from a job as a mechanic because of correctable high blood pressure. The Court applied its decision the same day in a comparable case, *Sutton v. United Air Lines, Inc.*, to reject the mechanic's claim. O'Connor said that the determination of a disability under the ADA should take into account any measures to correct or mitigate a physical or mental impairment. Stevens and Breyer dissented, as they did in *Sutton.*

Olmstead, Commissioner, Georgia Department of Human Resources v. L. C. (527 U.S. 581), decided by a 6–3 vote, June 22, 1999; Ginsburg wrote the main opinion; Thomas, Rehnquist, and Scalia dissented.

Someone with a mental disability may be entitled to be placed in a community setting rather than an institution if the placement is medically appropriate and can be accommodated within the available mental health treatment resources. The ruling—a partial victory for disability rights'

advocates—sent back for further consideration a suit initiated by two mental health patients in Georgia to win placements in community treatment centers. They claimed the state discriminated against them under the federal Americans with Disabilities Act by keeping them in institutions.

DRUG TESTING

Chandler v. Miller, Governor of Georgia (520 U.S. 305), decided by an 8–1 vote, April 15, 1997; Ginsburg wrote the opinion; Rehnquist dissented.

A Georgia law requiring drug testing for candidates for major state offices was held unconstitutional as an unreasonable search under the Fourth Amendment. The 1990 law—the only one of its kind among the states—required candidates for governor and other executive offices, state legislator, and state court judgeships to submit to a urinalysis drug test sometime prior to thirty days before an election. The Court ruled that the state had not presented sufficient grounds for an exception to the normal rule against suspicionless searches.

JOB DISCRIMINATION

Walters v. Metropolitan Educational Enterprises, Inc. (519 U.S. 202), decided by a 9–0 vote, Jan. 14, 1997; Scalia wrote the opinion.

The Court slightly eased the test used to determine whether small businesses have enough employees to be covered by the Civil Rights Act of 1964, the federal antijob discrimination law. Title VII of the ACT applies to any employer that "has fifteen or more employees for each working day in each of twenty or more calendar weeks in the current or preceding calendar year." The Court adopted what it called the "payroll method" for counting number of employees: "whether the employer has an employment relationship with the individual on the day in question."

Robinson v. Shell Oil Co. (519 U.S. 337), decided by a 9–0 vote, Feb. 18, 1997; Thomas wrote the opinion.

Federal civil rights law prohibits employers from giving an unfavorable job reference about a former employee in retaliation for filing a job discrimination complaint.

Oncale v. Sundowner Offshore Services, Inc. (523 U.S. 75), decided by a 9–0 vote, March 4, 1998; Scalia wrote the opinion.

In a victory for gay rights groups, the Court ruled that federal civil rights law prohibits sexual harassment in the workplace by someone of the same sex.

Burlington Industries, Inc. v. Ellerth (524 U.S. 742), decided by a 7–2 vote, June 26, 1998; Kennedy wrote the opinion; Thomas and Scalia dissented.

An employer may be liable for sexual harassment of an employee by a supervisor even if the employee suffers no tangible consequences. The employer can avoid liability, however, by proving that it took reasonable steps to prevent the conduct and that the employee failed to take reasonable steps to prevent or avoid harm. The ruling—and the companion decision *Faragher v. City of Boca Raton* issued the same day—sought to clarify the rules for holding employers responsible for sexual harassment by supervisors. The Court ruled that the case should be returned to the lower court for trial.

Faragher v. City of Boca Raton (524 U.S. 775), decided by a 7–2 vote, June 26, 1998; Souter wrote the opinion; Thomas and Scalia dissented.

An employer is liable for sexual harassment of an employee by a supervisor if the conduct results in any tangible employment action, including discharge, demotion, or undesirable reassignment. The ruling—and a companion decision issued the same day, *Burlington Industries, Inc. v. Ellerth*—was aimed at setting clear guidelines for employer responsibility for sexual harassment by supervisors.

West, Secretary of Veterans Affairs v. Gibson (527 U.S. 212), decided by a 5–4 vote, June 14, 1999; Breyer wrote the opinion; Kennedy, Rehnquist, Scalia, and Thomas dissented.

The Equal Employment Opportunity Commission can award compensatory damages as well as back pay and reinstatement in job discrimination claims by federal government employees. The ruling broadened the application of the federal job discrimination law known as Title VII (1991), which allowed courts to award compensatory damages.

Kolstad v. American Dental Association (527 U.S. 526), decided by 7–2 and 5–4 votes, June 22, 1999; O'Connor wrote the opinion; Rehnquist and Thomas dissented from one part of the decision; Stevens, Souter, Ginsburg, and Breyer dissented from another part.

Employers can be ordered to pay punitive damages for intentional or reckless job discrimination but not for actions by a manager that are contrary to the employer's "good faith efforts" to prevent discrimination. The ruling was a mixed result for civil rights advocates and employers alike in interpreting the Civil Rights Act of 1991, which broadened damage remedies for plaintiffs in employment discrimination cases.

OFFICIAL ENGLISH

Arizonans for Official English v. Arizona (520 U.S. 43), decided by a 9–0 vote, March 3, 1997; Ginsburg wrote the opinion.

The Court sidestepped a ruling on a free speech challenge to a state ballot initiative requiring all governmental actions to be conducted in English. The decision ordered the dismissal of a suit by a former Arizona state employee seeking to invalidate the "official English" initiative narrowly approved by the state's voters in 1988. The suit was dismissed as moot because the plaintiff no longer worked for the government.

WELFARE

Saenz, Director, California Department of Social Services v. Roe (526 U.S. 489), decided by a 7–2 vote, May 17, 1999; Stevens wrote the opinion; Rehnquist and Thomas dissented.

States cannot establish separate welfare benefits for newly arrived residents based on the benefit levels of the state where they previously lived. The ruling—based on the rarely used Privileges and Immunities Clause of the Fourteenth Amendment—invalidated a 1992 California law that limited welfare benefits for people who moved there from another state to the amounts provided by the other state.

Labor Law

AGENCY SHOP FEES

Air Line Pilots Association v. Miller (523 U.S. 866), decided by a 7–2 vote, May 26, 1998; Ginsburg wrote the opinion; Breyer and Stevens dissented.

Nonunion members who object to the amount they are required to pay the union for collective bargaining purposes can go directly to federal court without being forced to take their dispute to arbitration.

ARBITRATION

Wright v. Universal Maritime Service Corp. (525 U.S. 70), decided by a 9–0 vote, Nov. 16, 1998; Scalia wrote the opinion.

Employers cannot use a collective bargaining agreement to force employees to arbitrate complaints about job discrimination unless the contract includes an explicit waiver of the right to sue in federal court.

FEDERAL EMPLOYEES

National Federation of Federal Employees, Local 1309 v. Department of Interior (526 U.S. 86), decided by a 5–4 vote, March 3, 1999; Breyer wrote the opinion; O'Connor, Rehnquist, Scalia, and Thomas dissented.

Federal agencies may be required to negotiate with labor unions during the term of a collective bargaining agreement.

National Aeronautics and Space Administration v. Federal Labor Relations Authority (527 U.S. 229), decided by a 5–4 vote, June 17, 1999; Stevens wrote the opinion; Thomas, Rehnquist, O'Connor, and Scalia dissented.

Federal employees are entitled to have a union representative present and allowed to participate in interviews by investigators from the inspector general's office of the agency they work for.

LABOR-MANAGEMENT RELATIONS

Allentown Mack Sales and Service, Inc. v. National Labor Relations Board (522 U.S. 359), decided by separate 5–4 votes, Jan. 26, 1998; Scalia wrote the opinion; Rehnquist,

O'Connor, Kennedy, and Thomas dissented in part; Breyer, Stevens, Souter, and Ginsburg dissented in part.

The Court upheld but weakened a National Labor Relations Board policy limiting the ability of employers to poll workers to determine whether a union has lost majority support.

OVERTIME

Auer v. Robbins (519 U.S. 452), decided by a 9–0 vote, Feb. 19, 1997; Scalia wrote the opinion.

Public employees can be treated as salaried workers and denied overtime pay as long as they are not normally subjected to pay deductions for disciplinary reasons.

PENSIONS AND BENEFITS

Inter-Modal Rail Employees Association v. Atchison, Topeka & Santa Fe Railway Co. (520 U.S. 510), decided by a 9–0 vote, May 12, 1997; O'Connor wrote the opinion.

The Employee Retirement Income Security Act (ERISA), the federal pension security law, prohibits an employer from firing a worker for the purpose of taking away health or welfare benefits.

Boggs v. Boggs (520 U.S. 833), decided by 7–2 and 5–4 votes, June 2, 1997; Kennedy wrote the opinion; Breyer and O'Connor dissented, joined in part by Rehnquist and Ginsburg.

The federal pension protection law—ERISA—overrides state community property law so as to prevent a spouse from controlling the disposition of proceeds of a pension plan or other retirement benefits.

Bay Area Laundry and Dry Cleaning Pension Trust Fund v. Ferbar Corporation of California, Inc. (522 U.S. 192), decided by a 9–0 vote, Dec. 15, 1997; Ginsburg wrote the opinion.

The Court adopted an expansive time limit for industry-wide pension plans to sue an employer for failing to make mandatory payments after withdrawing from the plan. The Court held that a suit by the trustees of a pension plan may be brought within six years after an employer fails to make any monthly installment required under the federal law governing industry-wide pension plans. The decision settled a conflict between federal courts of appeals on what statute of limitations should be applied under the Multiemployer Pension Plan Amendments Act of 1980.

Geissal v. Moore Medical Corp. (524 U.S. 74), decided by a 9–0 vote, June 8, 1998; Souter wrote the opinion.

Employers must offer former workers the chance to pay for continuation of their health insurance coverage, even if they are also covered by their spouses' health plans. The ruling settled a conflict among federal appeals courts on the interpretation of a provision of the Consolidated Omnibus Budget Reconciliation Act of 1985, known as COBRA.

Eastern Enterprises v. Apfel, Commissioner of Social Security (524 U.S. 498), decided by a 5–4 vote, June 25, 1998; O'Connor wrote the plurality opinion; Breyer, Stevens, Souter, and Ginsburg dissented.

The Court ruled unconstitutional a federal law requiring companies that had once been in the coal business to pay for lifetime health benefits for retired miners and families of miners who had worked for them decades earlier. The decision struck down part of a 1992 law, the Coal Industry Retiree Health Benefit Act, aimed at guaranteeing the solvency of an industry-wide health benefits fund.

Hughes Aircraft Co. v. Jacobson (525 U.S. 432), decided by a 9–0 vote, Jan. 25, 1999; Thomas wrote the opinion.

Employers with pension plans providing fixed benefits to retirees can use any surpluses in those plans for purposes other than increasing benefits or reducing contributions from participants in the plan. The Court ruled the retirees had no legal claim under the Employee Retirement Income Security Act to block the changes.

UNUM Life Insurance Co. of America v. Ward (526 U.S. 358), decided by a 9–0 vote, April 20, 1999; Ginsburg wrote the opinion.

A state law allowing late-filed claims for insurance benefits is not preempted by the federal law governing pensions and health benefits provided by employers. The Court ruled that the California notice-prejudice rule was not preempted by the Employee Retirement Income Security Act.

Harris Trust and Savings Bank v. Salomon Smith Barney Inc. (530 U.S. 238), decided by a 9–0 vote, June 12, 2000; Thomas wrote the opinion.

The Court expanded the types of businesses subject to suit under ERISA, the federal pension protection law, for entering into self-interested transactions with pension or employee benefit funds.

Pegram v. Herdrich (530 U.S. 211), decided by a 9–0 vote, June 12, 2000; Souter wrote the opinion.

In a closely watched case, the Court ruled that patients covered by employer-provided health insurance plans cannot use the federal law regulating employee benefit plans to sue health maintenance organizations or their physicians for making treatment decisions in order to hold down costs.

PREVAILING WAGE LAWS

California Division of Labor Standards Enforcement v. Dillingham Construction, N.A., Inc. (519 U.S. 316), decided by a 9–0 vote, Feb. 18, 1997; Thomas wrote the opinion.

State prevailing wage laws are not preempted by the federal law governing employee benefit plans. The decision marked another effort by the Court to define the extent that the federal Employee Retirement Income Security Act overrides state laws affecting employee benefits.

PUBLIC EMPLOYEES

Gilbert, President, East Stroudsburg University v. Homar (520 U.S. 924), decided by a 9–0 vote, June 9, 1997; Scalia wrote the opinion.

A public employee arrested for a crime has no constitutional right under the Due Process Clause to a hearing before being suspended without pay.

Central State University v. American Association of University Professors, Central State University Chapter (526 U.S. 124), decided by an 8–1 vote, March 22, 1999; *per curiam* (unsigned) opinion; Stevens dissented.

In an unsigned decision issued without hearing argument, the Court said a state law barring collective bargaining over teaching workload policies for professors at public colleges and universities does not violate the Equal Protection Clause of the U.S. Constitution. The dispute involved an Ohio law, enacted in 1993, aimed at reversing a decline in the amount of time public university professors devoted to teaching.

Christensen v. Harris County (529 U.S. 576), decided by a 6–3 vote, May 1, 2000; Thomas wrote the opinion; Stevens, Ginsburg, and Breyer dissented.

State and local governments can require public employees to take compensatory time off for having worked overtime. The ruling backed state and local governments' interpretation of a 1985 law that created an exception to the general time-and-a-half overtime pay provisions of the federal Fair Labor Standards Act.

REMEDIES

Metro-North Commuter Railroad Co. v. Buckley (521 U.S. 424), decided by 9–0 and 7–2 votes, June 23, 1997; Breyer wrote the opinion; Ginsburg and Stevens dissented in part.

Railway workers cannot recover damages under the Federal Employees' Liability Act, a 1907 law that provides tort remedies for railway employees for workplace injuries, for emotional distress resulting from exposure to toxic substances such as asbestos if they show no physical symptoms of disease. The ruling also tentatively rejected a railway worker's suit requesting a lump-sum recovery of medical monitoring resulting from exposure to asbestos.

Textron Lycoming Reciprocating Engine Division, AVCO Corp. v. United Automobile, Aerospace and Agricultural Implement Workers of America (523 U.S. 653), decided by a 9–0 vote, May 18, 1998; Scalia wrote the opinion.

A labor union was blocked from using section 301(a) of the Labor Management Relations Act, a federal law allowing suits for violation of collective bargaining agreements, to win damages for a contract that it claimed resulted from fraud by the employer.

UNIONS

Marquez v. Screen Actors Guild, Inc. (525 U.S. 33), decided by a 9–0 vote, Nov. 3, 1998; O'Connor wrote the opinion.

Unions do not have to specify in contracts with employers that members do not have to pay fees and dues for union activities outside collective bargaining. The Court ruled that a union is not required under the National Labor Relations Act to include the limitation on mandatory fees in a contract with employers.

WORKERS' COMPENSATION

Ingalls Shipbuilding, Inc. v. Director, Office of Workers' Compensation Programs, Department of Labor (519 U.S. 248), decided by 9–0 and 7–2 votes, Feb. 18, 1997; O'Connor wrote the opinion; Scalia and Thomas dissented in part.

The Court allowed the surviving spouse of a shipyard worker who died from workplace exposure to asbestos to seek workers' compensation benefits despite a settlement her husband reached with the asbestos manufacturer and suppliers before his death. The somewhat complex ruling rejected an argument by the shipbuilding company that the widow had forfeited her right to the statutory death benefits by failing to obtain its approval to the settlements. The law requires a person "entitled to compensation" to obtain the employer's written approval of any settlement with third parties. The Court said that the requirement did not apply to the woman because she was not "entitled to compensation" while her husband was still alive.

Harbor Tug & Barge Co. v. Papai (520 U.S. 548), decided by a 6–3 vote, May 12, 1997; Kennedy wrote the opinion; Stevens, Ginsburg, and Breyer dissented.

The Court made it harder for some harbor workers to take advantage of the federal law governing injuries to seamen instead of the less generous law governing injuries to longshore workers. The Court held that harbor workers who take short-term assignments on a number of boats with different owners ordinarily do not qualify as seamen under the federal Jones Act, which allows an injured seaman to sue in court for open-ended damages. Longshore workers, by contrast, receive scheduled compensation for injuries under a different federal law, the Longshore and Harbor Workers' Compensation Act.

Metropolitan Stevedore Co. v. Rambo (521 U.S. 121), decided by a 6–3 vote, June 19, 1997; Souter wrote the opinion; O'Connor, Scalia, and Thomas dissented.

A longshore worker can receive nominal compensation for a workplace injury that has the potential for affecting future earnings even if it does not hurt his earning capacity at present. The ruling favored a California man, John Rambo, who suffered a partial permanent disability as a result of an injury to his leg and back while doing longshore work for Metropolitan Stevedore Co. After being awarded benefits under the federal Longshore and Harbor Workers' Compensation Act, he got a new job as a crane operator, earning considerably more than in his previous work. The Court held that Rambo was still entitled to nominal compensation because his injury could affect his earnings in the future.

American Manufacturers Mutual Insurance Co. v. Sullivan (526 U.S. 40), decided by an 8–1 vote, March 3, 1999; Rehnquist wrote the opinion; Stevens dissented in part.

States and private insurers can delay paying workers' compensation benefits pending a review of medical claims without violating workers' rights. The ruling—an important victory for health insurers—turned back a labor-backed challenge to a claims review procedure the state of Pennsylvania adopted to try to contain medical benefits under its worker compensation system. The scheme, adopted in 1993, allowed insurers to dispute a medical claim by demanding a "utilization review" and to withhold payment of the claim during the thirty-day period for the review. The Court held that the private insurers were not "state actors" subject to the Due Process Clause and that the withholding of payment of medical claims did not infringe on the workers' property rights.

Property Law

INTEREST ON LAWYERS' TRUST ACCOUNTS

Phillips v. Washington Legal Foundation (525 U.S. 156), decided by a 5–4 vote, June 15, 1998; Rehnquist wrote the opinion; Breyer, Stevens, Souter, and Ginsburg dissented.

Interest earned on client funds held in trust accounts set up by state bars to generate funds for legal aid for the poor is the client's property for purposes of the Takings Clause. The ruling cast doubt on the constitutionality of legal aid funding programs operating in all fifty states and the District of Columbia. The so-called IOLTA programs—an acronym for "Interest on Lawyers' Trust Accounts"—pooled nominal funds held by lawyers for clients and funneled the interest from the accounts to legal aid organizations. The Fifth U.S. Circuit Court of Appeals, ruling on an unconstitutional takings claim brought by the conservative Washington Legal Foundation on behalf of a Texas client, held that the interest belonged to the client but did not determine whether there had been a taking. In a closely divided decision, the Court held that the interest was the client's property and sent the case back to the appeals court for further proceedings.

LAND USE REGULATION

Suitum v. Tahoe Regional Planning Agency (520 U.S. 725), decided by a 9–0 vote, May 27, 1997; Souter wrote the opinion.

A California woman won the right to a trial of her suit for compensation because of a regulatory scheme that barred her from building on a Lake Tahoe-area lot. The ruling—a victory for property rights groups—overturned decisions by two lower federal courts that had blocked Bernadine Suitum from an immediate trial of her suit against the bistate Tahoe Regional Planning Agency. The agency's plan for limiting development around Lake Tahoe compensated landowners by allotting "transferable development rights" that they could sell to other property owners in the area. Suitum filed a federal court suit claiming the regulations deprived her of all valuable use of her property. Two lower federal courts said the case was not "ripe"—ready for trial—because Suitum had not first tried to sell the development rights allotted to her. The Court disagreed and said the agency's determination that Suitum could not build on her lot was a "final action" for purposes of satisfying the ripeness doctrine and said the agency had "no discretion to exercise" over her right to use the land or to obtain development rights.

REGULATORY TAKINGS

City of Monterey v. Del Monte Dunes at Monterey, Ltd. (526 U.S. 687), decided by a 5–4 vote, May 24, 1999; Kennedy wrote the main opinion; Scalia concurred separately; Souter, O'Connor, Ginsburg, and Breyer dissented.

Property owners have a right to a jury trial in federal court in regulatory takings cases brought against state or local governments under the federal civil rights law. The ruling—an important victory for property rights advocates—upheld a $1.45 million jury award won by a developer against the city of Monterey, California, for blocking a planned oceanfront residential development over a five-year period in the 1980s. The city cited a number of land-use and environmental issues, including the Endangered Species Act, in denying the construction permit. But the developer, Del Monte Dunes, argued the city's action was arbitrary and filed suit under the federal civil rights law known as section 1983 for alleged violations of its property, due process, and equal protection rights. The Court ruled that the Seventh Amendment's guarantee of a jury trial for suits "at common law" did apply to so-called regulatory takings suits because the developer had been denied any opportunity for compensation in state courts.

States

BOUNDARY DISPUTES

United States v. Alaska (521 U.S. 1), decided by 9–0 and 6–3 votes, June 19, 1997; O'Connor wrote the opinion; Thomas, Rehnquist, and Scalia dissented in part.

The Court sided with the United States and against Alaska in an eighteen-year dispute over ownership of oil- and natural gas-rich submerged lands off the state's Arctic coast. In 1979 the federal government filed an original claim with the Court seeking to establish title to the lands in order to sell mineral leases for lands in the Beaufort Sea, off the state's northeastern coast. Alaska filed a counterclaim for title to submerged coastal lands within the National Petroleum Reserve in the northwestern part of the state and the Arctic National Wildlife Refuge in the northeast. A "special master" appointed by the Court to hold hearings and make recommendations ruled in favor of the United States on most of the issues but found that Alaska owned the coastal lands within the wildlife refuge. The Court ruled that the federal government had retained ownership of submerged lands off the petroleum reserve's coast at the time of Alaskan statehood in 1957 and also retained ownership of lands off the coast of the wildlife refuge because the U.S. Fish and Wildlife Service had a pending application to create a federal refuge as of 1957. The Court limited the state's ownership of lands off the coast of barrier islands to a three-mile belt from each individual island.

The ruling meant that the federal government would get some $1 billion in mineral lease payments held in escrow during the dispute. The ruling also cheered environmentalists, who believed the federal government would do a better job than the state protecting the environmentally fragile areas off the wildlife refuge coast.

New Jersey v. New York (523 U.S. 767), decided by a 6–3 vote, May 26, 1998; Souter wrote the opinion; Scalia, Stevens, and Thomas dissented.

The Court awarded sovereignty over most of Ellis Island, the historic gateway to the United States for 12 million immigrants between 1890 and 1954, to New Jersey, not New York. The ruling, settling a border dispute that dated to the 1600s, gave New Jersey authority over about 24.5 acres of filled land added to the island by the federal government beginning in the 1880s. New York retained authority under an 1834 compact between the two states over the island's original three acres. The island—entirely owned by the federal government since 1800—lies in New York Harbor, about 1,300 feet from Jersey City, New Jersey, and one mile from the southern tip of Manhattan.

IMMUNITY

Regents of the University of California v. Doe (519 U.S. 425), decided by a 9–0 vote, Feb. 19, 1997; Stevens wrote the opinion.

An arm of state government is immune from suit in federal court even if the federal government has agreed by contract to indemnify it for any judgment. The decision barred a federal court suit by a New York scientist who said the federally funded Lawrence Livermore National Laboratory at the University of California in Berkeley broke an agreement to hire him. The Court said the indemnification provision had no effect on the state's immunity.

Idaho v. Coeur d'Alene Tribe of Idaho (521 U.S. 261), decided by a 5–4 vote, June 23, 1997; Kennedy wrote the main

opinion; O'Connor wrote a concurring opinion; Souter, Stevens, Ginsburg, and Breyer dissented.

The Court rejected on state immunity grounds a Native American tribe's effort to bring a federal court suit to settle a property dispute between the tribe and the state of Idaho. The ruling stemmed from a suit against Idaho officials by the Coeur d'Alene Tribe over ownership of the submerged lands below Lake Coeur d'Alene, which lies to the north of the most populated part of the tribe's reservation. The tribe claimed ownership based on executive orders and congressional action dating to 1873, but the state disputed the claim. The tribe claimed the suit was authorized under the Court's 1908 decision, *Ex parte Young,* which allows federal court suits against state officials for an injunction against future violations of federally protected rights. The Court rejected the suit but stopped short of a substantial narrowing of the important doctrine permitting federal court actions against state officials.

California v. Deep Sea Research, Inc. (523 U.S. 491), decided by a 9–0 vote, April 22, 1998; O'Connor wrote the opinion.

Federal courts have jurisdiction to rule on a state's claim to own a sunken ship despite the general rule barring suits against states in federal courts. The ruling allowed a treasure-hunting concern, Deep Sea Research, Inc., to proceed with a federal court suit seeking to establish its right to the *S.S. Brother Jonathan,* which sank off the coast of California in 1865 while carrying an estimated $2 million in gold bars and an army payroll of $250,000. After the treasure hunters located the shipwreck, the state of California claimed title under federal and state statutes. The state argued the suit belonged in state courts because of the Eleventh Amendment, which bars most suits against states in federal court. The Court agreed that federal courts could rule on the so-called *in rem* action—a suit to determine ownership of property—because the state did not have possession of the ship. The decision returned the case to lower federal courts to rule on other issues.

Alden v. Maine (527 U.S. 706), decided by a 5–4 vote, June 23, 1999; Kennedy wrote the opinion; Souter, Stevens, Ginsburg, and Breyer dissented.

The Court sharply limited the power of Congress to authorize private citizen suits to enforce federal laws against state governments in state courts. The ruling—the most important of three major states' rights decisions on the last day of the Court's term (see also *College Savings Bank v. Florida Prepaid Postsecondary Education Expense Board* and *Florida Prepaid Postsecondary Education Expense Board v. College Savings Bank*)—barred a back pay suit by a group of probation officers against the state of Maine for alleged violations of the federal Fair Labor Standards Act. The suit was originally filed in federal court, but was dismissed following the

Supreme Court's 1996 decision, *Seminole Tribe of Florida v. Florida,* which barred most private damage suits against states in federal court. When the officers refiled the suit in Maine courts, the state moved to dismiss the action on grounds of state sovereign immunity. In an exhaustively argued decision, the Court ruled that Congress has only limited power to override a state's sovereign immunity from suits in its own courts.

College Savings Bank v. Florida Prepaid Postsecondary Education Expense Board (527 U.S. 666), decided by a 5–4 vote, June 23, 1999; Scalia wrote the opinion; Breyer, Stevens, Souter, and Ginsburg dissented.

The Court invalidated an effort by Congress to subject states to federal court suits for trademark violations or false advertising. The decision also overturned a thirty-five-year-old precedent that made it easier to sue states in federal court when they engage in commercial activities. The ruling—one of three major states' rights decisions on the final day of the Court's term (see also *Alden v. Maine* and *Florida Prepaid Postsecondary Education Expense Board v. College Savings Bank*)—barred a false advertising suit brought by the New Jersey-based College Savings Bank in federal court against a Florida state agency, the Florida Prepaid Postsecondary Education Expense Board. The bank marketed certificates of deposit designed to cover future costs of college tuition. The bank alleged that Florida Prepaid made false claims about a competing product that the state agency sold to Florida residents. To bring the suit, the bank invoked a 1992 law, the Trademark Remedy Clarification Act, which provided for states to be sued in federal court for false advertising. Florida argued that the law was unconstitutional under the Eleventh Amendment, and that under the Court's 1964 decision, *Parden v. Terminal R. Co. of Ala. Docks Dept.,* the state had waived its sovereign immunity by engaging in commercial activity. The Court ruled that the trademark law was unconstitutional in providing for federal court suits against states and that the state could not be subjected to federal court suit merely because it had engaged in commercial activity.

Florida Prepaid Postsecondary Education Expense Board v. College Savings Bank (527 U.S. 627), decided by a 5–4 vote, June 23, 1999; Rehnquist wrote the opinion; Stevens, Souter, Ginsburg, and Breyer dissented.

The Court struck down on state sovereign immunity grounds a federal statute providing that states could be sued in federal courts for patent infringements. The ruling—one of three major states' rights decisions on the final day of the Court's term (see also *Alden v. Maine* and *College Savings Bank v. Florida Prepaid Postsecondary Education Expense Board*)—barred a patent infringement suit brought by the College Savings Bank in federal court against the Florida Prepaid Postsecondary Education Expense Board. The bank marketed certificates of deposit designed to cover future costs of college tuition. It claimed that Florida Prepaid infringed its patented financing methodology when the agency began sell-

ing a similar product to Florida residents. Florida moved to dismiss the suit on grounds of sovereign immunity under the Eleventh Amendment. A lower federal court and the U.S. Court of Appeals for the Federal Circuit ruled that Congress had authority under the Fourteenth Amendment when it provided in the Patent Remedy Act of 1992 that states are subject to suit in federal court for patent infringement. The Court held that the patent law could not be justified under Congress's powers to enact remedial legislation protecting constitutional rights under the Fourteenth Amendment.

Kimel v. Florida Board of Regents (528 U.S. 62), decided by a 5–4 vote, Jan. 11, 2000; O'Connor wrote the opinion; Stevens, Souter, Ginsburg, and Breyer dissented.

Congress has no power to authorize state government employees to sue states for violating the federal law against age discrimination. The ruling—in a trio of consolidated suits brought by employees of state universities in Alabama and Florida and a Florida prison guard—invalidated as unconstitutional parts of 1974 amendments to the Age Discrimination in Employment Act. The amendments extended the 1967 law to state and local government employees and appeared to authorize them to sue to enforce the law. State governments challenged the provision, saying it violated the Eleventh Amendment's guarantee of sovereign immunity for the states against private damage suits. The Court ruled that Congress had no power under the Fourteenth Amendment's enforcement provision to authorize private age discrimination suits against state governments. The ruling did not nullify the substantive provisions of the law as applied to state governments.

Vermont Agency of Natural Resources v. United States ex rel. Stevens (529 U.S. 765), decided by a 7–2 vote, May 22, 2000; Scalia wrote the opinion; Stevens and Souter dissented.

States cannot be sued by private individuals under the federal False Claims Act, a Civil War–era statute that permits suits to recover money for false or fraudulent claims against the federal government. The ruling barred a suit initiated by Jonathan Stevens against his former employer, the Vermont Agency of Natural Resources, for allegedly overstating the amount of staff time devoted to a federally funded program in order to increase federal aid to the state for the program. Stevens brought the suit—a so-called *qui tam* action—in the name of the United States with himself listed as a "relator." The False Claims Act, originally enacted in 1863 and significantly amended in 1986, authorized the procedure and provided that a private citizen could be awarded a portion of any funds recovered for the federal government through such a suit. The state sought to dismiss the suit on the grounds that a private citizen had no standing to bring such a suit and that the state could not be sued under the law. The Court ruled on the narrowest ground presented that the law did not include states within the definition of "persons" subject to suit under the act. The ruling added that the text of the 1863 law, along with a provision in the 1986 amendments for triple punitive damages in suits under the act and other features of the amended law, indicated that Congress did not intend to provide for private suits against states.

TAXATION

General Motors Corp. v. Tracy, Tax Commissioner of Ohio (519 U.S. 278), decided by an 8–1 vote, Feb. 18, 1997; Souter wrote the opinion; Stevens dissented.

States may impose a sales tax on unregulated out-of-state natural gas producers and marketers even if regulated natural gas utilities within the state are exempt from the levy. The ruling rejected an argument by General Motors Corp. that the Ohio tax scheme—a product of the partial deregulation of the natural gas market—amounted to unconstitutional discrimination against interstate commerce.

Camps Newfound/Owatonna, Inc. v. Town of Harrison (520 U.S. 564), decided by a 5–4 vote, May 19, 1997; Stevens wrote the opinion; Scalia, Rehnquist, Thomas, and Ginsburg dissented.

States cannot deny a tax exemption to a nonprofit organization solely because it primarily serves people from outside the state. The ruling struck down a Maine law that provided a property tax exemption for charitable organizations only if most of their clients were state residents. The Court ruled the measure unconstitutional under the so-called Dormant Commerce Clause, a court-made doctrine that limits the ability of states to impose economic burdens on businesses engaged in interstate commerce.

Arkansas v. Farm Credit Services of Central Arkansas (520 U.S. 821), decided by a 9–0 vote, June 2, 1997; Kennedy wrote the opinion.

Farm credit associations established under federal law cannot use a federal court suit to contest imposition of a state tax. The ruling dismissed on jurisdictional grounds a suit brought by four production credit associations (PCAs) in Arkansas seeking to win a broad exemption from state property and income taxes. The Court ruled that the suit did not belong in federal court because of the Tax Injunction Act, which generally bars federal court suits seeking to block state taxes.

De Buono, New York Commissioner of Health v. NYSA-ILA Medical and Clinical Services Fund (520 U.S. 806), decided by a 7–2 vote, June 2, 1997; Stevens wrote the opinion; Scalia and Thomas dissented on jurisdictional grounds.

The federal law regulating employee benefit plans does not prevent states from taxing hospitals or clinics owned by benefit plans. The ruling rejected an effort by a longshore workers' benefits plan, which owned two medical clinics in New York, to escape a state tax on health care facilities.

Lunding v. New York Tax Appeals Tribunal (522 U.S. 287), decided by a 6–3 vote, Jan. 21, 1998; O'Connor wrote the opinion; Ginsburg, Rehnquist, and Kennedy dissented.

States cannot deny to nonresidents a tax deduction for alimony payments that is allowed to resident taxpayers. The Court found unconstitutional a New York state law, enacted in 1987 to reverse a ruling three years earlier by the state's highest court, that barred nonresidents from taking a deduction on their state income tax for alimony payments even though residents could.

Newsweek, Inc. v. Florida Department of Revenue (522 U.S. 442), decided by a 9–0 vote, Feb. 23, 1998; *per curiam* (unsigned) opinion.

The Court broadened the right of taxpayers to receive a refund for payments made under a tax later ruled invalid. The ruling backed an effort by *Newsweek* magazine to recover a refund for sales taxes paid under a Florida law that was held unconstitutional in 1990 because it exempted newspapers but not magazines. Florida tax authorities refused the refund, saying *Newsweek* should have contested the tax before paying it. The Court held that Florida had violated the magazine's due process rights because the state had previously interpreted its law to allow postpayment refunds.

Arizona Department of Revenue v. Blaze Construction Co., Inc. (526 U.S. 32), decided by a 9–0 vote, March 2, 1999; Thomas wrote the opinion.

States may impose nondiscriminatory taxes on contractors hired by the federal government to do work on Native American reservations. The ruling allowed the state of Arizona to collect a gross receipts tax from a construction company for road construction and repair work performed on Native American reservations in the state. The Arizona Court of Appeals had barred the levy, saying federal law preempted imposition of the tax. The Court upheld the tax, in line with a 1982 decision, *United States v. New Mexico,* permitting state taxation of federal contractors.

South Central Bell Telephone Co. v. Alabama (526 U.S. 160), decided by a 9–0 vote, March 23, 1999; Breyer wrote the opinion.

An Alabama tax scheme that resulted in higher levies on out-of-state corporations than on Alabama companies was struck down as an unconstitutional discrimination against interstate commerce. Alabama corporations were subject to a franchise tax equal to 1 percent of the so-called par value of the firm's stock—an amount determined by the corporation itself and usually below the company's actual capitalized value. An out-of-state corporation, on the other hand, had to pay 0.3 percent of the actual value of its capital within the state. South Central Bell Telephone Co. challenged the scheme in state court, saying that it resulted in substantially higher levies on out-of-state corporations. The Court held that the tax "facially discriminates against interstate commerce" without justification.

Jefferson County, Alabama v. Acker, Senior Judge, United States District Court, Northern District of Alabama (527 U.S.

423), decided by a 5–4 vote on a procedural issue and a 7–2 vote on the merits, June 21, 1999; Ginsburg wrote the opinion; Scalia, Rehnquist, Souter, and Thomas dissented on the procedural issue; Breyer and O'Connor dissented on the merits.

The Court upheld application of an Alabama county's "occupational tax" on federal judges. The ruling stemmed from a suit by Jefferson County (Birmingham), Alabama, to enforce provisions of an occupational tax enacted in 1987 against two federal judges with offices in the county. The judges argued—and the Eleventh U.S. Circuit Court of Appeals agreed—that the tax amounted to a licensing scheme that would violate the so-called intergovernmental tax immunity doctrine, which sets limits on the ability of the federal or a state government to tax the operations of the other. The Court held that the tax did not violate the intergovernmental tax immunity doctrine, which had been limited by the Court and then by Congress in the late 1930s to permit the state to impose a nondiscriminatory income tax on federal employees and the federal government to impose a similar levy on state employees.

The ruling on the merits came after the Court ruled on a preliminary issue: whether the federal judges had properly removed the tax collection case from state to federal court. Five justices—Ginsburg, Stevens, O'Connor, Kennedy, and Breyer—said yes; the other four—Scalia, Rehnquist, Souter, and Thomas—said no.

Hunt-Wesson, Inc. v. Franchise Tax Board of California (528 U.S. 458), decided by a 9–0 vote, Feb. 22, 2000; Breyer wrote the opinion.

The Court ruled unconstitutional a California tax provision that limited the interest deduction that out-of-state corporations could take on the basis of the income generated by operations outside the state. The ruling came in a suit challenging a provision that allowed an out-of-state corporation to take an interest deduction only to the extent that the amount exceeded out-of-state income arising from unrelated business activity. The suit argued that the limit amounted to a levy on income with no "nexus" or connection to the state—so-called nonunitary income—that California was constitutionally barred from taxing. The Court said the tax provision violated the Constitution's Commerce and Due Process Clauses. The ruling seemed likely to have limited effect, as California's provision was unique among state and federal jurisdictions.

WATER RIGHTS

Arizona v. California (531 U.S. 1), decided by a 6–3 vote, June 19, 2000; Ginsburg wrote the opinion; Rehnquist, O'Connor, and Thomas dissented.

The Court rejected an effort by Arizona and California and two local water districts to bar the Quechan Indian tribe from claiming water rights in the long-running litigation over allocating water from the Colorado River. The ruling stemmed from a case brought under the Court's "original" jurisdiction in 1963 that allocated the waters of the Colorado River between seven western states. One unsettled question was a claim by the Quechan Indian tribe to about 78,000 acre-feet of water per year—a relatively small amount—located in an area straddling the river along the Arizona-California border. The states and two local water districts in California argued that the tribe's claim—supported by the Clinton administration—was barred either by the 1963 ruling or by a 1983 consent decree in which the government paid the tribe $15 million to settle a dispute over ownership of 250,000 acres of the reservation. The Court held that neither the tribe nor the government had forfeited its right to litigate the claim, that the tribe's water rights had not been decided in the 1963 ruling, and that the 1983 decree also failed to resolve the issue because it was "ambiguous" as to the tribe's ownership of the disputed lands.

Torts

AIRLINE CRASHES

Dooley v. Korean Air Lines Co., Ltd. (524 U.S. 116), decided by a 9–0 vote, June 8, 1998; Thomas wrote the opinion.

The federal law governing deaths on the high seas does not allow an air crash victim's survivors to recover damages for their pain and suffering before death. The ruling rejected claims by relatives of some of the victims of Korean Air Lines Flight 007, which was shot down over the Sea of Japan in 1983. The Court ruled that the federal Death on the High Seas Act did not permit recovery for so-called predeath pain and suffering. The federal law provided the "exclusive recovery" for deaths on the high seas and limited recovery to "the pecuniary losses suffered by surviving relatives." The Court had ruled two years earlier, in another case arising from the same crash, that the law also did not allow survivors to recover for loss of companionship.

RACKETEERING

Klehr v. A.O. Smith Corp. (521 U.S. 179), decided by a 9–0 vote, June 19, 1997; Breyer wrote the opinion.

The Court rejected an expansive ruling for setting the deadline for bringing a suit under the Racketeer Influenced and Corrupt Organizations (RICO) Act, but the decision failed to resolve a conflict among lower courts on three other possible methods of deciding when a plaintiff must file such a suit. The Court agreed to review the case to try to settle a conflict between four different approaches for deciding what date to use to determine whether a RICO suit was filed within the four-year statute of limitations. The Court rejected the broadest of the four rulings on the issue: a rule adopted by the Third Circuit that allowed a plaintiff to bring suit within four years after "the last predicate act" that was part of the alleged pattern of racketeering, but the Court said this case did not require the Court to settle which of three other rules should be adopted.

Humana Inc. v. Forsyth (525 U.S. 299), decided by a 9–0 vote, Jan. 20, 1999; Ginsburg wrote the opinion.

Insurance companies can be sued for fraud under the federal antiracketeering law despite a separate federal law that generally protects states' authority to regulate insurers. The ruling allowed Nevada policyholders of the Humana health insurance company to proceed with a class action suit under the Racketeer Influenced and Corrupt Organizations Act, which provides triple damages for a pattern of fraudulent conduct. Humana's customers charged that the insurer violated the law by negotiating deep discounts with hospitals but failing to pass on the savings to policyholders in the form of reduced copayments. Humana argued the suit was barred by the McCarran-Ferguson Act, which protects state regulation of insurance from any general federal law that would "invalidate, impair, or supersede" the state law. The Court allowed the suit to proceed and said the McCarran-Ferguson Act did not block the suit because RICO "appears to complement" remedies under Nevada state law.

Rotella v. Wood (528 U.S. 549), decided by a 9–0 vote, Feb. 23, 2000; Souter wrote the opinion.

The Court rejected an expansive rule for calculating the four-year time period for plaintiffs to bring a civil damage suit under the federal Racketeer Influenced and Corrupt Organizations Act. The ruling barred a suit brought in 1997 by a Texas man, Mark Rotella, against doctors at a private psychiatric hospital where he had been treated for depression from 1985 to 1986. Rotella claimed that the doctors violated the racketeering law by conspiring to keep him in the hospital solely for financial reasons. The hospital argued the suit was barred by the four-year statute of limitations for RICO suits. Rotella contended that the time period did not begin to run until 1994, when he learned that the hospital's parent company had pleaded guilty to fraud charges. Rotella cited that conduct as the "pattern of racketeering" required for his RICO claim. The Court held that the time period ended in 1990, rejecting the broader "injury and pattern discovery rule" Rotella advocated.

Beck v. Prupis (529 U.S. 494), decided by a 7–2 vote, April 26, 2000; Thomas wrote the opinion; Stevens and Souter dissented.

A whistleblower fired from his job ordinarily cannot use a wrongful termination claim as a basis for a federal antiracketeering suit against his employer. The ruling rejected a triple-damage suit under the federal Racketeer Influenced and Corrupt Organizations Act filed by a Florida man, Robert Beck, against officers and directors of his former company, Southeastern Insurance Group. Beck claimed that he was fired after reporting various allegations of financial fraud and that the firing was part of a conspiracy in furtherance of a "pattern of racketeering activity" as defined by the law. The Court held that the firing could not provide the basis for a civil RICO claim unless it was itself an act of racketeering.

WARSAW CONVENTION

El Al Israel Airlines, Ltd. v. Tsui Yuan Tseng (525 U.S. 155), decided by an 8–1 vote, Jan. 12, 1999; Ginsburg wrote the opinion; Stevens dissented.

The Court blocked an effort to use state tort remedies to get around limits on lawsuits by international air travel passengers contained in the treaty known as the Warsaw Convention. The ruling barred a suit by a New York woman, Tsui Yuan Tseng, stemming from a security search before boarding an El Al Israel Airlines flight at Kennedy International Airport in 1993. Tseng filed suit for assault and false imprisonment against the airline in New York state court; she claimed emotional distress but no bodily injury. After removing the case to federal court, El Al argued that the 1929 Warsaw Convention—which governs liability for international air transportation—allowed recovery in an airline "accident" only for "bodily injury." The Court said the Warsaw Convention precludes use of state law to recover damages if a claim does not satisfy the treaty's requirements for liability. The Court based the ruling on an interpretation of the treaty's original language, but noted that a new provision, ratified by the U.S. Senate in September 1998, explicitly added such a restriction.

## CHAPTER 14

General Government

Introduction	733
1997–1998 Chronology	736
1999–2000 Chronology	748

General Government

The allocation of money was a matter of dispute on two major general government issues during the 105th and 106th Congresses: the 2000 census and National Aeronautics and Space Administration (NASA) funding.

DECENNIAL CENSUS

In 1792 George Washington issued the first presidential veto in history because he disagreed with the way Congress decided to apportion itself based on the 1790 census. According to the General Accounting Office (GAO), that experience set the stage for the next two centuries. "Ever since George Washington questioned the results of the first census in [1792], the accuracy of any given census has been in question," said a GAO report issued in May 1998. "The questions have always been legitimate: The census has never counted 100 percent of those it should, in part, because American sensibilities would probably not tolerate more foolproof census-taking methods."

Experts said that ways existed to ensure a better count using traditional practices, but Americans, not to mention Congress, would never accept the conditions that would have to be imposed. For example, the census could be made more precise if people were required to register with the government. Or, the country could follow the example set by Turkey, where a fourteen-hour mandatory curfew was imposed in December 1997 so census canvassers could easily count people.

Doubts and disputes about the census have surfaced with regularity every ten years, with much of the attention focused on the size of the undercount. As the GAO report also stated: "The debates over the years about methods of apportionment focused on mathematics, but the crux of the matter was political power." The pressure became acute in 1911, when Congress set the number of representatives at 435. After that action, a gain of representation in any one state came only at the loss of representation in another. Concerns about the accuracy of the census crystallized in 1941, when the number of men turning out for the wartime draft was considerably higher than the number anticipated by the 1940 census.

There have been more recent controversies, too. Several states and cities sued the federal government in 1991, when Commerce Secretary Robert A. Mosbacher refused a Census Bureau request to adjust the 1990 census to compensate for an undercount. The Supreme Court ruled in 1996, in *Wisconsin v. City of New York,* that the federal government has no constitutional duty to correct an acknowledged undercount.

The fights over the census, said historian Margo J. Anderson of the University of Wisconsin at Milwaukee, "are structural to the process. The decision over how to count can be dressed up as science over politics, but the bottom line is, one side usually ends up with the advantage." Census results helped determine how billions of federal dollars were distributed annually through numerous grant programs, including Medicaid and educational assistance to poor children. And, most important for the political landscape, the results formed the basis for redrawing boundary lines for congressional districts as well as those for state legislatures.

House Democrats and Republicans engaged in a protracted argument over how the 2000 decennial census would be conducted. Democrats believed a more accurate count would help them because minorities, who tended to vote for Democrats, were the most-often-missed group. As a result, they supported the use of statistical sampling to augment the traditional head count. Republicans, recognizing that Democrats likely would gain an advantage by a more accurate count, charged that a census with sampling would be flawed. They maintained that the Constitution provided only for an

REFERENCES

Discussion of general government action for the years 1945–1964 may be found in *Congress and the Nation Vol. I,* pp. 1455–1516; for the years 1965–1968, *Congress and the Nation Vol. II,* pp. 655–660; for the years 1969–1972, *Congress and the Nation Vol. III,* pp. 435–468; for the years 1973–1976, *Congress and the Nation Vol. IV,* pp. 795–826; for the years 1977–1980, *Congress and the Nation Vol. V,* pp. 817–870; for the years 1981–1984, *Congress and the Nation Vol. VI,* pp. 771–793; for the years 1985–1988, *Congress and the Nation Vol. VII,* pp. 843–867; for the years 1989–1992, *Congress and the Nation Vol. VIII,* pp. 855–909; for the years 1993–1996, *Congress and the Nation Vol. IX,* pp. 803–858.

Outlays for Science, Space, and General Government

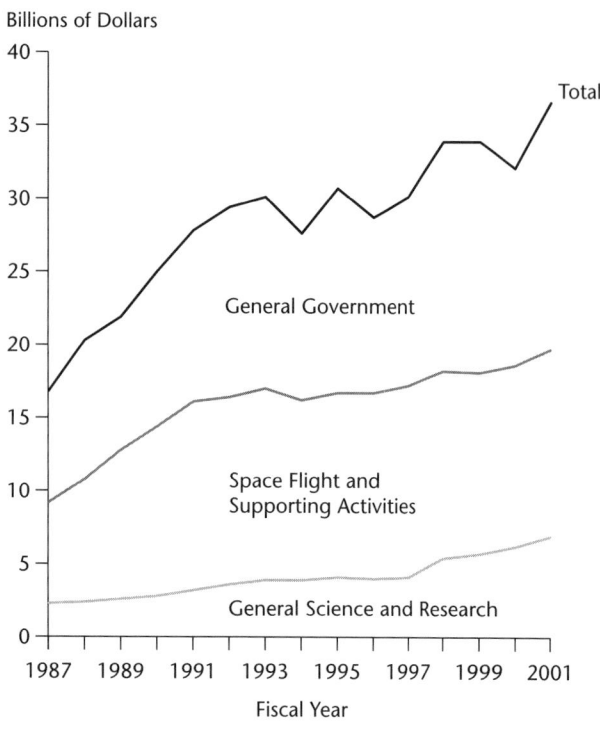

Billions of Dollars

NOTE: Data for 2001 are estimated.

SOURCE: Office of Management and Budget, *Historical Tables, Budget of the United States Government: Fiscal Year 2002* (Washington, D.C.: U.S. Government Printing Office, 2001), Table 3.2.

enumeration; that is, the census must be based on a physical counting of the population and not statistical extrapolation. Republicans also argued that the numbers derived from sampling could be manipulated.

In the end, the U.S. Supreme Court ruled in 1999 that a population count using sampling could not be used to apportion congressional seats among the states. However, it left the door open to using a statistically adjusted count for deciding how House seats within states are determined and where federal funds would be allocated.

NASA WOES

NASA was once among the best public relations tools of the federal government. Its missions, particularly the manned flights to the moon, brought pride to Americans and their government. In time, however, as missions became more routine, mishaps occurred, and budget deficits soared, lawmakers on Capitol Hill looked to NASA to do some belt-tightening. Frustrated by the agency's practice of describing only the first- and second-year costs of new projects, members in a 1991 law required NASA to estimate the full cost of projects when submitting annual budget requests. Typically, once projects got off the ground, costs ballooned and Congress was left with the choice of spending much more money than planned or killing projects in progress.

For most of the 1990s, NASA officials stoically accepted declining budgets as they sought to transform the agency from what critics in the 1980s described as a bloated bureaucracy into what NASA administrator Daniel S. Goldin came to hail as a "faster, better, cheaper" example of government. By the late 1990s, however, some members of Congress wondered if NASA had become a victim of its own success. On the one hand, the agency had faithfully demonstrated that it could do more with less. On the other hand, it began to suffer from seemingly pervasive problems.

The idea behind the "faster, better, cheaper" philosophy was for NASA to concentrate on small-scale missions that could be conducted with proven technologies and fewer staff. NASA traditionally had run big missions that could cost upwards of a billion dollars and took years to complete. By scaling down, the reasoning went, NASA could, for example, field more missions more frequently because of the savings in cost and time. This played out, for example, with record numbers of space shuttle launches in the 1990s. The Mars Pathfinder was another success story for NASA. The project took three years and $250 million, and the Pathfinder landed on Mars in July 1997.

However, the tight schedules and cost cutting came at the price of increased risk—and highly public mission failures. For example, NASA in 1997 lost the Lewis Spacecraft Mission, which was to measure changes in the Earth's land surfaces using advanced science instruments and spacecraft technologies. The Mars Climate Orbiter Mission, which was to "orbit Mars as the first interplanetary weather satellite and provide a communications relay for the Mars Polar Lander," was lost in 1999. NASA ran into production problems with the X-33 prototype reusable space launch vehicle, which was intended to drastically reduce space transportation costs. Lawmakers also publicly castigated NASA for relying on Russia to build a critical space station module. While members overcame persistent opposition to the project as a whole, they were disturbed by the cost overruns and time delays.

NASA also experienced more insidious problems. The GAO in 1999 found that 135 of 155 NASA computer systems did not meet all of the space agency's requirements for risk assessment and that NASA had not conducted an agency-wide review of its security since 1991. Furthermore, Goldin acknowledged that NASA, in some cases, suffered from a lack of communication in its ranks and that turnover and budget cuts had left the agency with an insufficient number of senior scientists and engineers at a time when it was flying more missions. Meanwhile, despite the emphasis on "faster, better, cheaper," some scientific objectives could be reached only by the old-fashioned kind of NASA missions; that is, large-scale and long term.

In 1999 the House Veterans Affairs-Housing and Urban Development Appropriations Subcommittee proposed a 10 percent cut in funding for NASA. In response, Goldin warned: "The ultimate effect could be the loss of critical, long-term scientific and technological investment not only for space science, but also for the nation's national security and economic well-being." In particular, Goldin said that the proposed cuts could force the closure of between one and three unspecified NASA space centers, as well as "significant" layoffs. He also said the reductions would force him to furlough all agency employees for three weeks. House Science Committee chairman F. James Sensenbrenner Jr., R-Wis., took issue with such dire forecasts. Noting that NASA had not criticized past budget projections that called for giving the agency even less than the subcommittee recommended, Sensenbrenner said Goldin's statements were "disingenuous at best and purposely inflammatory at worst."

Goldin was criticized for not objecting more strenuously to previous efforts to downsize his agency, a situation that some lawmakers attributed to President Bill Clinton's lack of leadership on space. The situation with the president, lawmakers said, was offset by NASA's presence in many members' districts across the country, including such politically powerful states as Florida and Texas. In the past, the agency also drew support from House Speaker Newt Gingrich, R-Ga., a space enthusiast. In the end, lobbying on behalf of NASA helped restore funding for the agency. However, the glitches continued to cause friction between NASA and the congressional committees that oversaw the agency, which translated into battles over funding.

Chronology of Action on General Government

1997–1998

2000 Census

Upon adjournment of the 105th Congress, a standoff was ongoing over how the 2000 census would be conducted. At issue was the legality of using statistical sampling to augment the traditional head count. Billions of federal dollars would be allocated and the boundaries of House districts for the 2002 elections and beyond would be based on the 2000 population data. Supporters argued that sampling would correct a persistent undercount of low-income and minority Americans. *(1999–2000 action, p. 748)*

As the 2000 census approached, criticism spilled beyond questions of how the count would be conducted to the motives of key officials to charges of racism from both sides. The struggle for advantage played out in full fury in the House, where Democrats supported the sampling proposal as the best way to count every American. Embarrassed by missing an estimated four million people in the 1990 census, the Census Bureau recommended that statistical sampling be used in 2000 to ensure a more accurate count. Under the bureau's proposal, at least 90 percent of the people in every census tract (a geographic area) would be physically counted. Sampling would then be used to fill in the statistical holes. Census officials insisted that sampling was a valid approach that would yield a more accurate census at a lower cost. The method proposed by the Census Bureau was deemed scientifically valid by the National Academy of Sciences, the General Accounting Office, and the Commerce Department's inspector general. Republicans, however, claimed the technique was unconstitutional and open to political manipulation. Republicans also opposed sampling because counting more low-income and minority Americans was viewed as helpful to Democrats.

House Republicans, led by Speaker Newt Gingrich of Georgia, filed a lawsuit in U.S. District Court in Washington, D.C., claiming that sampling was illegal because the Constitution requires an "actual enumeration" every ten years. A three-judge panel ruled Aug. 25, 1998, that existing law barred use of the sampling method. However, the panel avoided the question of whether sampling violated the constitutional requirement for an "actual enumeration" of the population. The Supreme Court was expected to rule on the case in 1999. A second lawsuit was filed with a special three-judge federal panel in U.S. District Court in Alexandria, Va., on behalf of several plaintiffs led by Matthew Galvin, president of the Southeastern Legal Foundation of Atlanta. *(Sampling ruling, box, p. 748)*

The battle over the census helped delay passage of disaster relief in 1997. President Clinton June 9, 1997, vetoed HR 1469, a supplemental appropriations bill, in part because of a provision blocking the use of sampling techniques during the 2000 census. Sampling was just one of a number of controversial policy issues that Republicans had attached to HR 1469 despite repeated White House warnings that they would draw a veto. Battered by the national media, losing in the polls as flood victims remained desperate for federal help, and fighting among themselves, Republican leaders decided to cut their losses and send Clinton a clean bill (HR 1871). Clinton signed HR 1871, which did not contain the prohibition against sampling, into law (PL 105-18) June 12. *(Disaster aid, p. 58)*

The House Appropriations Committee July 15, 1998, approved HR 4276 (H Rept 105-636), the fiscal 1999 appropriations bill for the Commerce, State, and Justice Departments and the federal judiciary. Hoping to avoid a showdown during consideration of the legislation, Alan B. Mollohan, D-W.Va., offered an amendment to provide full funding for the census, allowing the Census Bureau to prepare for a count that uses sampling as well as one that uses a traditional head count. It was rejected on a 22–31 party-line vote. The committee-approved bill provided $956 million for conducting the 2000 census, half of which could not be spent unless Congress and the president agreed by March 31, 1999, in separate authorization legislation whether to allow the use of statistical sampling. President Clinton threatened to veto the spending bill, signaling his desire to resolve the sampling issue in the fall. The House passed HR 4276 on Aug. 6 by 225–203. The House had rejected, 201–227, on Aug. 5 a

Mollohan amendment to strike language restricting funding for the 2000 census.

In an ironic twist, Clinton pushed to make the entire bill's funding—not just the Census Bureau's—contingent upon an agreement on the census method. Administration officials argued that just holding up the census funding would not put enough pressure on lawmakers and the president to reach an agreement. The Commerce, State, and Justice spending bill signed into law Oct. 21 (HR 4328—PL 105-277) cut off all funding—a total of $33.7 billion—on June 15, 1999, unless a separate authorization bill specifying whether sampling would be used was enacted.

The 2000 count was officially set to begin April 1, 2000.

Federal Rulemaking

A bill (S 981—S Rept 105-188) aimed at refining the process used by federal agencies to write regulations was reported from the Senate Governmental Affairs Committee on May 11, 1998.

Bill sponsors—committee chairman Fred Thompson, R-Tenn., and senior committee member Carl Levin, D-Mich.—hoped the modest regulatory overhaul bill would avoid the pitfalls that killed more sweeping proposals in the 104th Congress. S 981 proposed that agencies be required to conduct a peer-reviewed, cost-benefit analysis before issuing any rule that would have an impact on the economy of $100 million or more a year. The agencies would have to assess whether the benefits of the rule justified its cost and whether the choice of regulatory action was more cost-effective and would provide greater benefits than other options. In addition, risk assessments would be required for proposed federal standards affecting health, safety, and the environment.

Supporters said the bill would not change existing rules or establish a standard for agencies to meet, unlike a bill that senators filibustered in 1995. While agencies would be required to analyze prospective rules, they could go ahead with a rule that was not found to be cost-effective as long as they explained their reasons for doing so. *(1995 action, Congress and the Nation Vol. IX, p. 845)*

Property Rights

The House in 1997 passed legislation (HR 1534) designed to give property owners greater access to federal courts and greater clout with local zoning boards. A Senate committee reported the bill, which saw no further action.

HR 1534 sought to give landowners and business developers a new legal tool to challenge local zoning laws that prevented them from developing their property. Such laws qualified as "takings" under the Fifth Amendment, which prohibits the federal government from taking property without compensating the property owner. Under existing law, takings claims were handled primarily by local administrative review panels and state courts. If they did reach the fed-

eral courts, bill supporters said, it was only after many years. Under HR 1534, landowners would be able to go straight to federal court after an appeal to a local administrative board had been denied.

Democratic opponents maintained that the legislation contradicted much of what the GOP had said about handing federal powers back to states and local government. They also noted that Republicans were generally critical of what they saw as federal courts usurping powers from elected officials. Yet, in this case, the GOP wanted to hand the same courts broad new powers at the expense of local government in the name of helping landowners.

One of developers' biggest complaints about existing law was that it required them to exhaust appeals to planning agency decisions in state courts and be denied compensation before a federal court would hear a Fifth Amendment takings claim. Bill proponents said the process could stretch on for years, forcing average homeowners and developers into legal limbo. It also offered no incentive for planning boards to act expeditiously on building requests. Boards could keep developers at bay by turning down proposals and asking for endless revisions to building plans, proponents argued.

Under HR 1534, property owners would have the option of taking their case directly to a federal court after filing at least two appeals to a planning board decision. At least one of the appeals would have to be to an elected body, such as a city council, if available in the locality. Other appeals could be filed to the planning board or other agency with jurisdiction over planning decisions.

The narrow focus of HR 1534 reflected lessons learned by western lawmakers and other property rights activists in the 104th Congress, when attempts to enact more sweeping legislation met with defeat. Those bills were aimed at compensating owners for government actions that diminished property values. Property rights advocates argued in 1995 and 1996 that federal regulators were flouting the Fifth Amendment when they imposed money-losing restrictions on property owners but offered no compensation to make up for the losses. But environmentalists prevailed in the 104th Congress using the counterargument that requiring greater compensation would tie agencies in knots. Also, many fiscal conservatives worried the approach would bankrupt agencies with costly compensation claims. *(Background, Congress and the Nation Vol. IX, p. 843)*

The House Judiciary Subcommittee on Courts and Intellectual Property approved HR 1534 on Sept. 30, 1997, by 7–4. The full Judiciary Committee approved the bill Oct. 7 by 18–10. The bill was reported (H Rept 105-323) on Oct. 21. The House passed the measure Oct. 22 by a **key vote of 248–178 (R 193–30; D 55–147; I 0–1).** *(1997 key votes, p. 865)*

The House floor debate brought out long-festering tensions between western and eastern Republicans. The westerners had long been frustrated with their eastern colleagues who often allied themselves with environmental groups to defeat legislation important to western constituents. On HR 1534, westerners were not about to brook opposition. They issued a blunt warning: pass HR 1534 or the westerners would work to defeat a bill (HR 2247) to reauthorize Amtrak, the national passenger railroad network. The Amtrak bill was a priority for many easterners, whose constituents rode the rails every day.

Some moderate Republicans, including Sherwood Boehlert of New York, argued that HR 1534 would intrude into local land use planning and would benefit developers at the expense of average citizens. Boehlert tried to delete the provisions that would allow landowners to appeal local land-use decisions in the federal courts, while retaining expedited federal court consideration in land-use disputes that involved the federal government. The amendment was rejected Oct. 22, 178–242.

The Senate Judiciary Committee reported an amended HR 1534 (S Rept 105-242) on Feb. 26, 1998.

Paul Coverdell, R-Ga., introduced similar legislation (S 1204) in the Senate. It included a provision from a separate bill (HR 992—H Rept 105-424) passed 230–180 by the House March 12, 1998, aimed at giving landowners greater leeway in suing the federal government for takings. Under S 1204, such suits could be heard either in the U.S. District Court or in the U.S. Court of Federal Claims. Key Democrats objected to the measure, saying it would upset the delicate balance between developers and average citizens.

NEA Funding

The much-maligned National Endowment for the Arts (NEA) managed to survive in 1997–1998. *(1999–2000 action, p. 750)*

NEA opponents argued that federal arts funding was an unnecessary subsidy for private-sector activities and that the money often went to arts projects of questionable taste and dubious artistic merit. They also noted that the House leadership had promised to zero out the agency by fiscal 1998. NEA proponents countered that the agency provided much-needed seed money for cash-strapped arts organizations, particularly in small towns across America. They also asserted that although the agency made some mistakes, its overall mission was sound.

1997 LEGISLATIVE ACTION

During consideration of the fiscal 1998 Interior spending bill (HR 2107—PL 105-83), the House Appropriations Interior Subcommittee included $10 million for NEA, down from $99.5 million in fiscal 1997. Chairman Ralph Regula, R-Ohio, agreed to drop language calling for the agency's elimination, but that move was largely moot, given that the $10 million was intended to cover shutdown costs and could be used for little else. The panel rejected, 5–6, a Sidney R. Yates, D-Ill., amendment to restore funding for the agency to $99.5 million.

In the full committee, Yates again offered his amendment to restore funding to the fiscal 1997 level. It was rejected 28–31, largely along party lines.

NEA FUNDING RULING

The U.S. Supreme Court on June 25, 1998, ruled 8–1 to uphold a controversial 1990 law that required the National Endowment for the Arts (NEA) to consider decency standards in awarding grants to artists.

Justice Sandra Day O'Connor, who wrote the majority opinion in *National Endowment for the Arts v. Finley*, emphasized the limited force of the decency clause compared with other legislative proposals Congress rejected. The provision "imposes no categorical requirement," she said, "in sharp contrast to congressional efforts to prohibit the funding of certain classes of speech." The decency clause was subject to so many different interpretations, O'Connor said, that it could not "in practice . . . effectively preclude or punish the expression of particular views." On that basis, she concluded, there was no "realistic danger that [the clause] will compromise First Amendment values."

The majority opinion also rejected the argument that the decency clause was unconstitutionally vague. The provision, O'Connor said, "merely adds some imprecise considerations to an already subjective process." *(Supreme Court case, p. 715)*

During House floor consideration of HR 2107, a nearly unified Democratic Party and a band of Republicans, most of them northeastern moderates, demanded an up-or-down vote on the NEA. But the GOP leadership balked, instead crafting a rule guaranteed to block such an amendment to the bill. The rule effectively barred the NEA funding on the grounds that the agency's authorization had expired.

Twenty-eight Republicans signed a June 26 letter to Speaker Newt Gingrich, R-Ga., calling for continued NEA funding. Behind the scenes, some conservatives acknowledged that they did not have the votes and would lose the vote unless something was done. Vernon J. Ehlers, R-Mich., then offered a proposal to terminate the NEA but provide $80 million directly to the states in arts and education grants. The leadership wrote the rule in a way that ensured floor consideration of the Ehlers amendment. Democrats charged that Republican leaders had embraced the Ehlers amendment purely as a political cover to attract moderate and conservative support for the rule.

The House adopted the rule (H Res 181) on July 10 on a **key vote of 217–216 (R 212–15; D 5–200; I 0–1).** The next day, the House rejected the Ehlers amendment, 155–271. Philip M. Crane, R-Ill., then raised a point of order striking even the $10 million in shutdown costs for the NEA included in the bill. *(1997 key votes, p. 865)*

Opposition to the NEA was not nearly as wide or as deep in the Senate as compared with the House. In the end the

Senate's action on the NEA language in HR 2107 solidified the endowment's standing and sent a clear message to the House. The Senate rejected 23–77 on Sept. 17 an amendment offered by Jesse Helms, R-N.C., and John Ashcroft, R-Mo., to eliminate the agency and all federal funding outright. An amendment by Tim Hutchinson, R-Ark., to eliminate the NEA but send arts funding to the states in lump sum payments based on a per capita formula was defeated, 36–63 on Sept. 17. Each state would have received at least a $500,000 basic grant. The Senate rejected, 26–73 on Sept. 17, an amendment offered by Spencer Abraham, R-Mich., to phase out NEA funding over three years and privatize the agency. On Sept. 18, an amendment by Kay Bailey Hutchison, R-Texas, to retain the agency but send 75 percent of the money to the states in lump sum payments, reserve 5 percent for administrative costs, and spend the remainder on national grants to major ballet, opera, and other arts groups, was defeated on a **key vote of 39–61 (R 39–16; D 0–45).** *(1997 key votes, p. 865)*

The NEA survived the House-Senate conference on HR 2107 intact. Lawmakers provided the arts agency with $98 million, slightly less than the $100 million included in the Senate version, but a far cry from the zero funding in the House bill. At Regula's urging, however, the conference agreed to a number of new conditions, including:

• An increase in the amount of money that would be sent directly to the states from 35 percent to 40 percent.

• A 15 percent flexible cap on the amount of money that could be sent to any one state. A number of senators objected that, under the existing system, a handful of states received the bulk of the money. New York, for example, received about 20 percent.

• No limits on money for touring theatre, ballet, and opera companies and other arts groups with a national focus.

Appropriators also agreed to provisions aimed at ensuring that education was a focus of grants and allowing NEA to raise money privately. President Clinton signed the final bill into law (PL 105-83) on Nov. 14.

1998 LEGISLATIVE ACTION

Under an agreement with the House leadership, Interior Appropriations Subcommittee Chairman Regula deleted all funding for the NEA in the fiscal 1999 Interior funding bill (HR 4193) but said the issue would be revisited by the full House. The Appropriations Committee, in a surprising move that set the stage for a showdown on the House floor, voted 31–27 to restore $98 million in funding for the NEA. Meanwhile, the Senate Appropriations Committee included $100 million for NEA in its version of the Interior spending measure (S 2237).

During House floor consideration of HR 4193, Regula structured a deal approved by Republican leaders in which the rule that would allow funding for the agency would be deleted on a point of order and then immediately restored. Despite complaints by Democrats, such as David R. Obey of

Wisconsin, who called the rule "a Mickey Mouse procedure," the plan unfolded as intended: $98 million in funding for the agency was deleted on a technical point of order. The entire amount was then restored by an amendment offered by Nancy L. Johnson, R-Conn., on a 253–173 vote July 21.

Fiscal 1999 NEA funding of $98 million was provided in the omnibus appropriations bill (HR 4328—PL 105-277) signed by President Clinton on Oct. 21.

Government Documents

The Senate Rules and Administration Committee on Oct. 16, 1998, reported a bill (S 2288—S Rept 105-413) to overhaul the way the federal government prints and disseminates information. The legislation was designed to centralize printing decisions in the Government Printing Office (GPO) and to push the GPO into adopting new technologies to make government publications more easily available. It also called for agencies, courts, and other government entities to make documents available to the GPO for posting on the Internet.

The fundamental purpose of S 2288 was to address a constitutional problem stemming from the 1983 U.S. Supreme Court decision in *Chadha v. Immigration and Naturalization Service* that barred Congress from exercising legislative vetoes of executive branch action. In the wake of that decision, the Justice Department had said the Joint Committee on Printing, a congressional panel that serves as the GPO's de facto board of directors, violated the court ruling because it effectively had the power to veto executive branch printing decisions. *(1983 ruling, Congress and the Nation Vol. VI, p. 833)*

Critics complained that the bill would gum up a system that was improving. Representatives from the information technology and printing industries protested that the legislation would change too many of the government's procurement rules and enlarge the GPO bureaucracy. Some Republican members also said the bill was at odds with efforts to privatize some government functions. Supporters said the measure would make for more efficient operations, knit together a fractured system that made it difficult to ensure that all government documents were collected and disseminated, and provide agencies with flexibility for meeting their printing needs or contracting their own service if certain requirements were fulfilled.

Federal–D.C. Ties

The federal government in 1997 forged a new relationship with the nation's capital. Lawmakers included plans to take over a host of costly District of Columbia services in the budget reconciliation package (HR 2015—PL 105-33) and a companion tax bill (HR 2014—PL 105-34). *(D.C. provisions in reconciliation, p. 54; and in tax bill, p. 99)*

The blueprint for the "D.C. rescue plan" came in President Clinton's fiscal 1998 budget request. White House budget director Franklin D. Raines, a one-time D.C. financial adviser, determined that the District needed an entity to act as its "state government" by taking greater responsibility for Medicaid health insurance, criminal justice, and other programs. In exchange for this new financial arrangement, the federal government could discontinue its annual payment to the city and demand changes in city ordinances.

The House Government Reform and Oversight Committee District of Columbia Subcommittee pared back the plan June 19 and added language to provide a $140 million federal payment to the city in fiscal 1998.

Congressional leaders agreed to form several discussion groups on different provisions relating to the District, such as management initiatives and the debt provisions. Sen. Connie Mack, R-Fla., was appointed to oversee the efforts. But lawmakers made little headway in three weeks of discussions, and a proposal by Senate D.C. Appropriations Subcommittee Chairman Lauch Faircloth, R-N.C., to install a city manager to run the District government threatened to derail the whole plan. The District's Democratic House delegate Eleanor Holmes Norton, who had earned bipartisan respect on city issues, fought that proposal.

Other issues also needed to be resolved. Virginia lawmakers demanded that the District's much maligned Lorton prison in northern Virginia be closed, while Sam Brownback, R-Kan., chairman of the D.C. subcommittee of the Senate Governmental Affairs Committee, insisted that the District contract out its prison operations to the private sector. Brownback and Norton joined to push her plan to cut federal taxes in the city.

At that point, House Speaker Newt Gingrich, R-Ga., Senate Majority Leader Trent Lott, R-Miss., and Clinton administration officials stepped in to work out the details. The package, which came together in the last hours of the budget negotiations, provided unprecedented federal aid for the city. It also stripped power, however, from the District's elected government, including controversial mayor Marion S. Barry Jr., and gave the financial control board, created by Congress and President Clinton in 1995 to oversee the city's finances, wide latitude to reorganize the city's troubled bureaucracy. The mayor and the city council would have to give up power over nine major city departments. The control board would approve nominees to run the departments, and only the board could fire them. Consultants would be hired to recommend and implement changes to departments. Barry charged that Republicans were trying to "recolorize" the District by undoing the home rule system in effect since 1973. But others said Barry prompted the takeover by failing to cooperate with the control board until he clearly had no other option. (*D.C. control board, Congress and the Nation Vol. IX, p. 854*)

Under HR 2015 and HR 2014, the federal government would:

• Resume responsibility after eighteen years for a fund that provided pensions to city police officers, firefighters,

and teachers. The fund's liabilities exceeded available resources by nearly $5 billion.

• Pay 70 percent of the cost of the District's Medicaid program, up from 50 percent.

• Provide a $190 million federal payment in fiscal 1998. Such payments were not guaranteed in future years.

• Lend the city up to $300 million for a ten-year period.

• Transfer prison administration to the Federal Bureau of Prisons, with the Lorton facility to close by 2002. Half the prison population would have to be sent to privately run facilities. A seven-member board headed by a Justice Department designee would recommend changes to the District's sentencing guidelines.

• Provide a $5,000 tax credit for single first-time homebuyers with adjusted gross income of less than $70,000 and joint filers with adjusted gross incomes of less than $110,000.

• Include much of the city in a new enterprise zone. Employers who moved into the zone would be eligible for a 20 percent wage credit. Capital gains on sales of business property in such neighborhoods were reduced to zero.

The fiscal 1998 District of Columbia appropriations bill (HR 2607—PL 105-100) provided a total of $855 million in federal funds for the District, $136 million more than in fiscal 1997 and $78 million more than Clinton requested. Of the total, only $190 million went directly to the city. The remaining $665 million went to the agencies and trustees charged with assuming responsibility for courts, prisons, and other city services. The House Appropriations Committee reported HR 2607 (H Rept 105-298) on Oct. 6, 1997. The House passed the bill Oct. 9 by 203–202. The Senate passed an amended version Nov. 9 by voice vote. The measure cleared conference Nov. 13. The president signed it Nov. 19.

Puerto Rico Status

The House in 1998 passed a bill (HR 856) requiring a plebiscite in Puerto Rico through which the island's residents would vote on their political destiny. A companion Senate bill (S 472) never made it to committee markup. (*1996 action, Congress and the Nation Vol. IX, p. 854*)

Puerto Rico was ceded to the United States by Spain under the treaty ending the Spanish-American War in 1898. In 1952 it became a U.S. commonwealth, meaning its residents have some, but not all, the rights of U.S. citizens. Puerto Ricans are subject to the military draft but cannot vote in federal elections. They do not pay federal taxes if they live on the island. In a 1993 plebiscite, 48.4 percent voted for an enhanced commonwealth; 46.2 percent, statehood; and 4.4 percent, independence. Two House committees in 1996 reported legislation regarding Puerto Rico's status. (*1996 action, Congress and the Nation Vol. IX, p. 854*)

The House Resources Committee May 21, 1997, approved HR 856 by 43–1. The bill was formally reported (H Rept 105-131, Pt. I) on June 12. It would require a referendum by Dec. 31, 1998, in which Puerto Ricans could vote to continue their commonwealth relationship with the United States, support independence, or seek statehood. A vote for statehood would require the president to submit legislation to Congress that would allow for a transition plan spanning no more than ten years. If voters chose independence, a constitutional convention would be held on the island. If the commonwealth status prevailed, a new referendum would be held every ten years.

The committee rejected 10–32 a George Miller, D-Calif., amendment to broaden the definition of commonwealth status to allow greater Puerto Rican autonomy. Miller said HR 856 did not fairly represent the views of the island's Commonwealth Party leaders. But Puerto Rico's House delegate, Democrat Carlos Romero-Barceló, said Miller's amendment was misleading, proposing benefits from commonwealth status that Congress would never enact as law. W. J. "Billy" Tauzin, R-La., underscored the point, calling Miller's definition of commonwealth too generous. Tauzin interpreted Miller's amendment as specifying that federal benefits to residents of Puerto Rico would have to be comparable to those received by other Americans, although Puerto Ricans did not face tax obligations equal to those of other Americans.

After more than ten hours of debate, the House on a dramatic 209–208 vote passed HR 856 on March 4, 1998. The bill ran into opposition both from advocates of the island's commonwealth status—who said the bill was stacked in favor of statehood—and from Republicans who feared Puerto Rican statehood would boost the number of Democrats in Congress.

The House rejected, 13–406, a Luis V. Gutierrez, D-Ill., amendment to keep Spanish as the official language of Puerto Rico. Lawmakers adopted, 238–182, an amendment by Dan Burton, R-Ind., saying that if Puerto Rico becomes a state, it would have to follow whatever official language policy applies to the rest of the country. The House adopted 265–153 a Gerald B. H. Solomon, R-N.Y., amendment to make English the official language of the United States, including Puerto Rico if it chose statehood. Attachment of the language amendment had threatened to kill the bill in the House and prompted veto threats from the White House. Opponents argued that such a requirement would have been opposed by the framers of the Constitution, who designated neither an official religion nor an official language. The House also defeated a Jose E. Serrano, D-N.Y., amendment, 57–356, to allow Puerto Ricans who were born on the island but live in the U.S. mainland to vote in the referendum. An amendment by Bob Barr, R-Ga., to require a three-quarters supermajority vote before Puerto Rico could become a state was rejected 131–282.

The Senate did not take up the issue of the Puerto Rico plebiscite. However, it did Sept. 17 by voice vote adopt a nonbinding resolution (S Res 279) expressing support for the citizens of Puerto Rico and their decision to hold a Dec. 13, 1998, referendum on their political status.

Reagan National Airport

President Clinton on Feb. 6, 1998, signed into law a bill (S 1575—PL 105-154) changing the name of the Washington National Airport to the Ronald Reagan Washington National Airport. Reagan was the fortieth U.S. president, a Republican who served from 1981 to 1989.

The Reagan Legacy Project of the Americans for Tax Reform, a conservative group, launched the airport campaign in 1997 as part of a wider effort to put Reagan's name on buildings and his face on Mount Rushmore. Some Democrats offered to name practically anything else for Reagan except the airport, suggesting the Pentagon or Dulles International Airport. Others suggested Reagan had been honored enough with a new Washington office complex and a new Nimitz-class aircraft carrier, both of which carried his name. Some Democrats also objected to naming the airport, which lawmakers of both parties used, for a GOP hero. Furthermore, the 10,500-member National Air Traffic Controllers Association joined Democrats in criticizing Reagan for firing 11,000 air-traffic controllers during a 1981 strike. Randy Schwitz, the association's executive vice president, said he would prefer to have a "hot poker in the eye" than an airport named for Reagan.

Democrats thwarted a Senate floor vote Jan. 29, 1998, on an airport-renaming bill (S 1297). Sponsor Paul Coverdell, R-Ga., accused Democrats of trying to "exact a quid pro quo" for the Reagan tribute. Coverdell referred to the Democrats' action as "a cynical attack . . . launched against a great national leader." Senate Minority Leader Tom Daschle, D-S.D., replied that Democrats would not agree to a GOP plan to permit only one amendment, which would revise the name to Ronald Reagan National Airport from Ronald Reagan Washington National Airport. That is, they were critical of ending the identification of the airport with the nation's first president, George Washington, who lived nearby at Mount Vernon, Virginia.

The Senate Feb. 4 passed S 1575 by 76–22. The House Transportation and Infrastructure Committee on Jan. 27, 1998, voted 39–28 along party lines to approve a companion measure (HR 2625). The committee rejected 28–38 an amendment by Gene Taylor, D-Miss., to require private interests to pay half the expense of the renaming. The committee also rejected, 30–37, an amendment by Peter A. DeFazio, D-Ore., to require the airport authority's approval of the change. The bill was formally reported (H Rept 105-408) on Jan. 29. The House approved HR 2625 on Feb. 4, 240–186, and then passed S 1575 by voice vote the next day.

In floor debate in both chambers, Democrats raised the issue of names for other buildings. In the Senate, Harry Reid, D-Nev., proposed an amendment to remove J. Edgar Hoover's name from the headquarters of the Federal Bureau of Investigation. Reid said, "J. Edgar Hoover stands for what is bad about this country. This small man violated the rights of hundreds, if not thousands, of people, famous and not so famous." Orrin G. Hatch, R-Utah, opposed the amendment, saying that Hoover had many accomplishments and that many FBI agents would be offended by such a change. The Senate Feb. 4 voted 62–36 to table (kill) the amendment.

In the House, Minority Leader Richard A. Gephardt, D-Mo., tried unsuccessfully to broker a compromise on the airport bill that would have permitted consideration of legislation (HR 1383) to name the Justice Department after Robert F. Kennedy, the former attorney general and senator from New York. Congress had considered renaming the Justice building for Kennedy for years. (President George W. Bush by executive order bestowed that honor on Kennedy in 2001).

The biggest challenge to the airport measure came in the House, where Republicans Thomas M. Davis III of Virginia and Constance A. Morella of Maryland joined Democrats James P. Moran of Virginia and Peter A. DeFazio of Oregon in sponsoring an amendment to require approval of the local Metropolitan Washington Airports Authority. Backers of the amendment argued that the bill would preempt local decision making, which Reagan championed. The House narrowly, 206–215, rejected the amendment Feb. 4. A last attempt to derail the bill failed Feb. 4, when the House voted 186–237 against a James L. Oberstar, D-Minn., motion to name one of the airport's terminals for Reagan instead.

NASA Authorization

Congress in 1997 and 1998 was unable to complete action on National Aeronautics and Space Administration (NASA) authorization legislation. Amidst rising criticism, the international space station project moved forward. (*Space station, p. 743*)

The House Science Committee by voice vote April 16, 1997, approved HR 1275, authorizing fiscal 1998 and 1999 funding for NASA. The measure was formally reported (H Rept 105-65) on April 21.

Unlike in recent years, the committee spent little time debating the controversial Mission to Planet Earth program, which consisted of a series of satellites monitoring the Earth's environment. Republicans, who opposed the program, agreed to the $1.4 billion requested in each of fiscal years 1998 and 1999. The committee adopted an amendment, sponsored by Space and Aeronautics Subcommittee Chairman Dana Rohrabacher, R-Calif., to remove a provision that would require NASA to use $200 million from an existing reserve fund to help pay part of the program's budget.

The full House passed HR 1275 by voice vote April 24. Earlier the same day, the House had rejected, 186–226, an amendment by Sheila Jackson-Lee, D-Texas, to increase funding under NASA's minority research and education program for universities and colleges that had large minority enrollments.

The Senate Commerce, Science, and Transportation Committee by voice vote March 12, 1998, approved S 1250, which

---

GLENN IN SPACE

Hundreds of thousands of spectators, including President Bill Clinton and First Lady Hillary Rodham Clinton, and a worldwide television audience of millions watched Oct. 29, 1998, as Sen. John Glenn, D-Ohio, the first American to orbit the Earth in 1962, became the oldest person ever sent into space. Glenn, serving as second payload specialist, was aboard the space shuttle *Discovery*, which was launched from the Kennedy Space Center in Florida. Glenn conducted ten experiments aboard the shuttle, which returned to Earth Nov. 7.

A unique blend of science, symbolism, and spectacle, Glenn's mission touched a latent chord in the nation. It focused a torrent of attention on an earlier age when the activities of the National Aeronautics and Space Administration (NASA) could unite and enthrall the country like no other government agency. The "Glennmania" raised hopes among NASA officials and lawmakers that at least some of the interest would rub off on the space agency as it moved beyond the shuttle into other projects, such as the international space station. (*Space station, p. 743*)

Glenn was selected for the mission in January 1998, after spending two years lobbying NASA officials to allow him to help research the similarities between aging and space flight. In addition to providing regular blood and urine samples for analysis, Glenn spent his time in space sleeping with electrodes attached to his scalp and swallowing a pill with a radio transmitter to monitor his temperature and circadian rhythms.

NASA had decided in late summer to remove Glenn from a major experiment in which he was to have taken the drug melatonin. Glenn was dropped because he did not meet the Food and Drug Administration's criteria for the experiment. The decision renewed criticism that the senator's trip was more a public relations stunt than a scientific mission.

---

would authorize $13.63 billion for fiscal 1998, $13.46 billion for fiscal 1999, and $13.68 billion for fiscal 2000 for NASA. The bill (S Rept 105-195) was formally reported on May 22.

HR 2158 (PL 105-65), the fiscal 1998 Veterans Affairs-Housing and Urban Development (VA-HUD) appropriations bill, provided $13.6 billion for NASA. The amount included $5.5 billion for NASA's human space flight activities.

On Nov. 1, 1997, President Clinton used his line-item veto authority to eliminate $10 million set aside to fund telescopes in Arizona and Chile as part of NASA's Origins project, which used ground- and space-based telescopes to search for planets capable of supporting life. Clinton said that the two telescopes would not add to NASA's knowledge and that the Arizona telescope, located at the University of Arizona, would duplicate work already being done at the NASA-funded Keck Observatory in Mauna Kea, Hawaii. After the Supreme Court ruled in June 1998 that the president's new line-item veto powers were unconstitutional, however, the Office of Management and Budget announced that all funding that had been vetoed using the voided 1996 law would be restored.

HR 4194 (PL 105-276), the fiscal 1999 VA-HUD appropriations legislation, provided $13.7 billion for NASA.

Space Station

The space station was a joint venture among the United States, Russia, Canada, Brazil, and a number of European countries. As the showcase project of the National Aeronautics and Space Administration (NASA), the space station would be the most complex structure ever planned for launch into orbit. Supporters said it would advance scientific understanding, space exploration, and international cooperation. *(1995 action, Congress and the Nation Vol. IX, p. 851)*

In 1993 the Clinton administration estimated that the project would cost $17.4 billion through assembly. But that amount began rising after Russia signed on as a partner the following year—a move that administration officials said would reduce costs and speed up construction because Russia was the only other country with a manned space program. NASA officials announced April 9, 1997, that they were delaying the start of construction of the space station—from November 1997 to no later than October 1998—because of Russia's inability to deliver on time the service module, which would house astronauts and keep the station from falling out of orbit. The Russian fiscal problems came in addition to a variety of other administrative difficulties. The situation led NASA to institute management controls on the station's prime contractor, Boeing. NASA did not award the company a bonus in 1997 because of problems with program planning, cost estimation, and hardware manufacturing.

COMMITTEE ACTION

During 1997 consideration of HR 1275, a NASA authorization bill, House Science Committee members expressed their frustration with the agency's handling of the international space station project. Committee chairman F. James Sensenbrenner Jr., R-Wis., a space station supporter, criticized the Clinton administration for not heeding his warnings about making the Russians such a major partner in the project. He and the committee's ranking Democrat, George E. Brown Jr. of California, offered an amendment, adopted 25–0, to force the administration to develop guidelines to govern future relations with Russia on the space station. NASA would be barred from giving Russia any funds to help it pay for its portion of the program, and the NASA administrator would have to report to Congress every month on Russia's progress on the project.

The committee rejected, 2–16, an amendment by Tim Roemer, D-Ind., to remove the Russians from participation in the project. The committee also soundly rejected amendments by Roemer to kill the space station and to reduce funding for the project by $75 million. On April 24, 1997, the full House rejected, 112–305, a Roemer amendment to HR 1275 to terminate the space station program. *(NASA authorization, p. 742)*

Senate Commerce, Science, and Transportation Committee Chairman John McCain, R-Ariz., in 1997 called on NASA to adopt a price cap on the space station and warned that he would try to impose one if the agency could not keep its costs under control. Because of the cost problems, NASA had to transfer funds within its budget to keep the space station going. In 1997 it was forced to use $200 million in space shuttle reserve funds, although Congress refused to let NASA transfer another $200 million from other internal accounts.

The fiscal 1998 Veterans Affairs-Housing and Urban Development appropriations bill (HR 2158—PL 105-65) provided $2.4 billion for continued development of the space station. However, only $1.5 billion of the space station funds would be available before March 31, 1998; the remainder would be released once NASA provided a detailed report on the project's outlook and potential effect on other NASA programs.

The Senate Commerce, Science, and Transportation Committee, during 1998 consideration of S 1250, a NASA authorization bill, gave voice vote approval to a McCain amendment to limit NASA space station costs to $21.9 billion through the assembly process. NASA estimated its share of the costs through assembly at around $21 billion; an independent appraisal to determine the true cost, which the agency requested, was pending. McCain said the cap was intended to signal that lawmakers would no longer tolerate the schedule slippages and cost overruns that plagued the project. The amendment also would limit the U.S. share of transportation costs to assemble the complex to $17.7 billion.

In April 1998 a panel of military and civilian space experts, picked by NASA to audit the space station project, concluded that the total cost through assembly of the station could be $24 billion. The task force also determined that the station could take as much as three years longer to build than expected—December 2006, not December 2003. The panel, headed by aerospace consultant Jay W. Chabrow, estimated NASA would need an extra $130 million to $250 million a year over the next seven years to cover the expected increased costs.

FLOOR ACTION

Critics of the space station pointed to the report as further evidence that the project should be killed. Although they came within one vote of doing so in 1993, they failed to come close in either chamber since then—including in the 105th Congress. The Senate on July 7, 1998, rejected 33–66, an amendment by Dale Bumpers, D-Ark., on S 2168, a fiscal 1999 VA-HUD funding bill, to eliminate the measure's $2.3 billion appropriation for the space station and provide $850 million to terminate the program. The House on July 29, 1998, rejected 109–323 a Roemer amendment to HR 4194, a fiscal 1999 VA-HUD appropriations bill, to cut NASA funding by $1.6 billion and terminate the international space station. *(1993 action, Congress and the Nation Vol. IX, pp. 825, 851)*

A NASA report to Vice President Al Gore in July 1998 said Russia's space program had received only $20 million of the $340 million needed for the space station in 1998. At a House Science Committee hearing Aug. 5, 1998, members of both parties excoriated the Clinton administration for its willingness to keep Russia as a partner in the space station and its refusal to come up with a plan to solve the station's funding problems. Russia's economic crisis had left its space agency desperately strapped for cash.

NASA administrator Daniel S. Goldin warned the House Science Committee Oct. 7, 1998, that unless extra funding was provided over the next few years to help keep the space station on track, the project probably should be abandoned. NASA's budget had been flat, as the Clinton administration chose to concentrate on priorities other than space. The fiscal 1999 Veterans Affairs-Housing and Urban Development appropriations bill (HR 4194—PL 105-276) included $2.27 billion for the space station, the amount President Clinton had sought.

In a move to keep the project on schedule, conferees on the VA-HUD appropriations bill added language calling for NASA to study alternatives to contracting with Russia's government for space station parts and services. Some station supporters advocated bypassing the Russian government and dealing directly with its private space contractors. But some experts contended that Russia's problems were so formidable that it would be dangerous to continue to rely on that nation's help in building the station. Russian space historian and author James Oberg told House Science Committee members that Russia's inability to fulfill its commitments was not because of temporary conditions that would easily disappear. He also accused NASA of overlooking evidence of corruption in the Russian space program.

House and Senate appropriators agreed Oct. 15, 1998, to let NASA transfer $60 million within its budget to keep the space station on schedule after the space agency submitted a plan for how it expected to minimize Russia's future involvement in the project. The money would come from reducing the agency's obligations within its fiscal 1998 budget for station development and operations.

Committee aides said the appropriators agreed to the transfer of funds after the agency provided details on how it was working to lessen its dependence on Russia. The aides said NASA also promised to include a definitive schedule for reducing Russia's involvement on building the station in submitting its fiscal 2000 budget request in 1999. NASA officials had warned that they might need to spend as much as

$660 million to buy Russian space vehicles to support the station over the next few years, as well as an additional $600 million to develop new U.S. hardware to reduce reliance on Russia.

Private Shuttles

Congress in 1998 cleared legislation (HR 1702—PL 105-303) to allow the federal government to license private space shuttles.

Lawmakers, worried by the number of U.S. companies launching satellites overseas, where costs were lower and red tape less prevalent, became increasingly eager to aid the domestic launch industry. HR 1702 contained a regulatory framework to give the Federal Aviation Administration authority to issue licenses for private reusable launch vehicles. Supporters hoped such vehicles, when developed, could significantly bring down the cost of sending satellites and other commercial payloads into orbit. Under current law, companies were not permitted to hold such licenses. In essence, they could fly launch vehicles into space but could not return them to Earth.

HR 1702 also called for the Defense Department to conduct a comprehensive study of the nation's launch infrastructure. Many observers said the technology at U.S. launch sites was outdated. To ensure President Clinton's support, Republicans removed language from the bill dealing with requirements for obtaining a license to own and operate a remote-sensing satellite, which could be run by remote control from Earth. State Department officials had raised questions about remote-sensing and did not want the process to compromise national security.

The House Science Committee approved the bill by voice vote June 18, 1997, and formally reported it (H Rept 105-347) Oct. 24. The House passed HR 1702 by voice vote under suspension of the rules Nov. 4. The Senate Commerce, Science, and Transportation Committee reported the bill (S Rept 105-198) on June 2, 1998. The Senate passed an amended HR 1702 on July 30 by voice vote. The measure cleared Oct. 8, completing congressional action. Clinton signed the bill Oct. 28.

NSF Authorization

President Clinton on July 29, 1998, signed a bill into law (HR 1273—PL 105-207) that authorized $3.5 billion in fiscal 1998, $3.8 billion in fiscal 1999, and $3.9 billion for fiscal 2000 for the National Science Foundation (NSF).

The House Science Committee reported the measure (H Rept 105-63) on April 21, 1997. During floor debate, the House adopted by voice vote an amendment by Tom Coburn, R-Okla., to prohibit the agency from providing money for the Man and Biosphere Program, a U.N.-sponsored environmental preservation program. Helen Chenoweth, R-Idaho, contended that the program would give "the international community an open invitation to interfere in domestic land use decisions." George E. Brown Jr. of California, ranking Democrat on the committee, disputed this notion, saying, "There is nothing here which provides the U.N. any authority whatsoever over any territory of the United States." The House passed HR 1273 by voice vote April 24.

The Senate Labor and Human Resources Committee reported a companion measure (S 1046—S Rept 105-110) on Oct. 15. The full Senate passed an amended version of HR 1273 by 99–0 on May 12, 1998. The House cleared the measure July 14.

The fiscal 1999 Veterans Affairs-Housing and Urban Development appropriations bill (HR 4194—PL 105-276) provided $3.7 billion for the foundation.

NIST Reauthorization

President Clinton on Oct. 30, 1998, signed a bill (HR 1274—PL 105-309) reauthorizing the Commerce Department's National Institute of Standards and Technology (NIST). The measure reduced funding for the agency's Advanced Technology Program, which provided grants to assist industries in developing cutting-edge technologies.

HR 1274 authorized $609 million in fiscal 1998 for NIST, of which $185 million was earmarked for the Advanced Technology Program—$90 million less than the administration requested for fiscal 1998 and $40 million less than was appropriated for fiscal 1997. The 1996 omnibus science authorization measure had included no funding for the program. While the program was a high priority for the Clinton administration, conservative Republicans attacked it as a form of corporate welfare. *(1996 action, Congress and the Nation Vol. IX, p. 851)*

The House Science Committee approved HR 1274 by voice vote April 16, 1997. The committee had rejected 19–20 an amendment offered by Debbie Stabenow, D-Mich., to bring funding for the program up to the fiscal 1997 level. She called the program "extremely beneficial" in bringing public and private sectors together to fund projects that might not otherwise be pursued. The bill was formally reported (H Rept 105-64) on April 21. The full House passed the measure by voice vote April 24. The Senate passed an amended version by voice vote Oct. 9, 1998. The bill cleared Oct. 13.

The fiscal 1999 omnibus spending law (HR 4328—PL 105-277) provided $647 million for NIST.

NOAA Reauthorization

Two House committees in 1997 knocked heads over a two-year reauthorization bill (HR 1278) for several National Oceanic and Atmospheric Administration (NOAA) activities, including atmospheric, weather, and satellite programs; oceanographic and marine research; and hydrographic and coastal assessment and monitoring.

The House Science Committee by voice vote April 16, 1997, approved a version of the bill that recommended $1.45 billion for the programs in fiscal 1998. It included an increase of $26.8 million over fiscal 1997 levels for the National Weather Service. HR 1278 (H Rept 105-66, Pt. I) was formally reported by the House Science Committee April 22.

The House Resources Committee approved its version June 11, also by voice vote. The measure would authorize $1.2 billion for the programs in fiscal 1998. The panel stripped out about 10 percent of the funding approved by the Science Committee, money directed toward programs that Resources Committee Chairman Don Young, R-Alaska, argued fell solely within his panel's jurisdiction. Among the programs chopped from the bill were navigation services provided by the National Ocean Service and coastal and ocean assessments. The committee also removed a Science panel provision to eliminate NOAA's corps of commissioned officers. The Resources Committee adopted by voice vote an amendment by Ken Calvert, R-Calif., to cut NOAA administration funding by 5 percent, to $18.2 million in fiscal 1998, and 5 percent more to $17.3 million in fiscal 1999.

House Resources formally reported the bill (H Rept 105-66, Pt. II) on June 20.

The fiscal 1998 funding bill for the Departments of Commerce, Justice, and State and the federal judiciary (HR 2267—PL 105-119) provided $2 billion for NOAA; the fiscal 1999 omnibus appropriations measure (HR 4328—PL 105-277), $2.2 billion.

Human Cloning

The Senate Feb. 11, 1998, blocked floor debate on a bill (S 1601) to ban human cloning. The bill died upon adjournment of the 105th Congress.

S 1601 would ban a process known as somatic cell nuclear transfer to create a human embryo. Somatic cell nuclear transfer involves replacing the nucleus of an egg cell with the nucleus of some other cell—an adult cell that would not multiply if left in its original state. Scientists have found that the remaining part of the egg cell could somehow "reprogram" the new nucleus, causing it to multiply. In theory, this organism could be implanted into a womb and allowed to develop into a human being.

Bill supporters considered that organism an embryo, worthy of the same protection abortion opponents would accord to embryos conceived through fertilization. Groups that funded medical research did not share that view. They saw the organism as a growing mass of cells that could generate certain types of cells to treat specific diseases. A leukemia patient, for instance, could receive bone marrow generated in a lab. A heart patient could receive new cells instead of an entire transplant. Burn victims could get new skin cells. Because the new cells would genetically match the patient's, rejection of the transplanted tissue would not be a problem.

The measure was blocked in the Senate when Dianne Feinstein, D-Calif., objected to bringing it up. On a **key vote of 42–54 (R 42–12; D 0–42)** the cloture motion to overcome her objection was 18 votes short of the needed 60. Champions of S 1601, such as Christopher S. Bond, R-Mo., and Bill Frist, R-Tenn., said the vote was the result of misinformation spread by rogue scientists and special interest groups. Opponents, such as the American Heart Association and the Cystic Fibrosis Foundation, said the measure could cut off entire avenues of research into cloning of individual cells to treat cancer, heart disease, and other maladies. Although a consensus emerged that creating a carbon copy of any living or dead person is morally repugnant, the vote indicated that the Senate had serious reservations about the broadness of the legislation. The outcome also suggested that opponents could have difficulty putting cloning into the context of the abortion debate. *(1998 key votes, p. 883)*

Next Generation Internet

Congress in 1998 cleared legislation (HR 3332) to authorize funding for research and development of a faster and more sophisticated Internet.

HR 3332 authorized $67 million for fiscal 1999 and $75 million for fiscal 2000 to be spread among the Energy Department, National Aeronautics and Space Administration, National Institutes of Health, National Institute of Standards and Technology, and National Science Foundation (NSF). The NSF was slated to get the biggest chunk of money—$50 million over the two years.

The Internet, which originated as a computer network linking the Defense Department with research universities, has evolved into a popular medium for communication and commerce. By the late 1990s, more than 100 million people worldwide used the international computer network.

The Senate Commerce, Science, and Transportation Committee reported a companion measure (S 1609—S Rept 105-173) on April 2, 1998, and the full Senate passed the bill by voice vote June 26. The House passed HR 3332 by voice vote under suspension of the rules Sept. 14. The Senate passed the bill Oct. 8 by voice vote, completing congressional action. President Clinton signed the measure (PL 105-305) on Oct. 28.

Energy Research and Development

A turf fight broke out in 1997 between the House Science and House Commerce Committees over a bill (HR 1277) to reauthorize civilian research and development (R&D) activities at the Department of Energy.

The Science Committee April 16 gave voice vote approval to HR 1277, recommending $4.6 billion in fiscal 1998, about $200 million less than the Clinton administration request. The bill was formally reported (H Rept 105-67, Pt. I) on April 22.

INTERNET ADDRESSES RULING

In an order filed Aug. 28, 1998, but not announced until the week of Aug. 31, U.S. District Judge Thomas F. Hogan dismissed a lawsuit seeking recovery of money collected for registering Internet addresses that end with such suffixes as "com" or "org" used by businesses, individuals, and organizations. The lawsuit was filed by a group of individuals and companies that registered Internet addresses.

Since 1995 Network Solutions Inc., which contracts with the National Science Foundation (NSF) to coordinate the registration of Internet addresses, had been collecting $100 per site from those seeking to register an Internet address for two years. Of this amount, $70 went to Network Solutions and $30 went to the NSF's Internet Intellectual Infrastructure Fund, which was established to preserve and enhance the Internet. The plaintiffs in the suit argued that the $30 collected for the Internet fund was an illegal tax.

Hogan initially agreed in April 1998 that the $30 fee was illegal because Congress had not ratified it. In response, lawmakers added a provision to the fiscal 1998 supplemental appropriations bill (HR 3579—PL 105-174) to retroactively legalize the $30 fee. The legislation also directed that the $60 million that had been collected for the fund be used for the Next Generation Internet. *(Next Generation Internet, this page)*

Hogan thus reversed himself and ruled against the plaintiffs.

The committee unanimously adopted an amendment, offered by Energy and Environment Subcommittee Chairman Ken Calvert, R-Calif., to delete language that would cut funding for renewable energy and energy efficiency programs. The bill included a provision to prohibit the department from using $50 million for a "clean coal" plant in China.

The panel revived its debate over the controversial superconducting supercollider project, the $11 billion giant atom smasher that was being built in Texas when its funding was killed by Congress in 1993. The debate came over the U.S. share of funding for the Large Hadron Collider in Switzerland, a high-energy physics project similar to, though on a much smaller scale than, the superconducting supercollider. Joe L. Barton, R-Texas, tried to eliminate funding for the Large Hadron Collider, which amounted to $35 million for fiscal 1998. He said that, while he was not opposed to the collider, he was concerned about providing funding for a non-U.S. project without having adequate knowledge of how it would be managed and without sufficient guarantees that U.S. scientists would have equal access and partnership in the project. Sherwood Boehlert, R-N.Y., who supported the project, countered that it was important for those who had argued in favor of saving the supercollider on the merits of the scientific benefits to support the collider in Switzerland. The committee rejected the Barton amendment, 12–20. However, it retained language to prohibit funding for the project unless the energy secretary reported on the impact that funding the project would have on U.S. high-energy and nuclear physics facilities.

The Commerce Committee approved a pared-back $3.7 billion version of HR 1277 by voice vote June 4. The bill was formally reported (H Rept 105-67, Pt. II) on June 9.

The Commerce Committee excluded about $924 million in projects that were approved by the Science Committee. The Commerce panel objected that many projects in the Science panel's version—including isotope manufacturing, safety oversight, environmental cleanup, and uranium production—had little to do with scientific research and fell within Commerce's vast jurisdiction. In one area of agreement, however, both committees rejected funding for the White House's high-profile $300 million Next Generation Internet program. *(Next Generation Internet, p. 746)*

EPA Research

Two committees—House Science and House Commerce—locked horns in 1997 over a bill (HR 1276) to authorize research, development, and demonstration activities at the Environmental Protection Agency (EPA).

The Science Committee by voice vote April 16 approved a $640 million bill. The measure was formally reported (H Rept 105-99, Pt. I) on May 16.

The Commerce Committee approved a revised version by voice vote June 25, after cutting $208 million. Commerce members said the Science Committee had no jurisdiction over several items in the original bill. The committee by voice vote adopted a Michael G. Oxley, R-Ohio, amendment that deleted $115 million for drinking water and air pollution research by EPA's Office of Research and Development and $82 million for the Office of Air and Radiation. HR 1276 (H Rept 105-99, Pt. II) was formally reported from Commerce on June 26.

Federal Invention Licensing

The House on July 14, 1998, suspended the rules and by voice vote passed HR 2544, making it easier for federal agencies to license inventions created in federal laboratories. The House Science Committee approved the bill May 13 and formally reported it (H Rept 105-620, Pt. I) on July 14.

HR 2544, as passed by the House, would simplify requirements imposed on the approximately 700 government-owned and -operated labs seeking to license inventions. The bill would give lab officials the option of either licensing inventions by themselves under an existing regulatory framework used for licensing university-operated federal laboratory patents or incorporating existing patented inventions into a cooperative research and development agreement with business.

Technology subcommittee chairwoman and bill sponsor Constance A. Morella, R-Md., said such an approach would give agencies two new tools for commercializing federally owned technologies while continuing Congress's efforts to promote the transfer of technology from federal labs to the private sector and state and local governments.

1999–2000

2000 Census

The House in 1999 passed a bill (HR 472) to allow local officials to verify head counts in the 2000 census before the numbers were made official. The measure was part of a broader fight between congressional Republicans and the Democratic White House over whether the Census Bureau could use a method called statistical sampling to adjust census figures to correct for undercounts, which typically occurred among racial minorities, immigrants, and the poor living in cities or remote rural areas. The administration threatened a veto of the legislation, but the Senate never considered the bill and it died upon adjournment.

Republicans said HR 472 would increase the accuracy of the population figures gathered by enumerators. But Democrats and administration officials asserted that GOP leaders did not want minorities to be counted and that allowing local reviews after the census would reduce the accuracy of the count by eating into the time allotted for sampling.

Soon after the U.S. Supreme Court handed down its equivocal Jan. 25, 1999, decision about the methodology that could be used to conduct the 2000 census, congressional Democrats and the Clinton administration began talking about conducting one census that would produce two population counts. Under this plan, the population figures used to allocate the 435 House seats among states would be derived the traditional way—with mail-in questionnaires sent to every household and census takers knocking on the doors of millions of homes from which no form was received. But political redistricting and the allocation of federal funds would be based on numbers derived with the help of statistical sampling. The Census Bureau would use traditional methods to obtain information on about 90 percent of the homes in each of the nation's neighborhoods, or census tracts, then could conduct a detailed examination of the demographics of 750,000 randomly selected homes nationwide to project the remaining population. *(Sampling ruling, box, this page)*

With the backing of the House Republican leadership, House Government Reform Subcommittee on the Census Chairman Dan Miller, R-Fla., a bitter opponent of the Clinton administration plan to use sampling, on Jan. 27 unveiled a legislative package of four bills that he said would foster more accurate census numbers. The subcommittee approved the bills March 11. HR 1010, approved by voice vote, would quadruple the bureau's budget for fiscal 2000 to $400 million to pay for an advertising campaign aimed at educating people about the importance of filling out and returning their census forms. HR 928, approved 5–2, would require the bureau to mail a second round of census forms to those who did not return the original. HR 929, approved 6–4, would require census forms to be printed in more than 30 languages. HR 1009, approved by voice vote, would establish a $26 million matching grant program for localities to conduct out-reach efforts. Democrats opposed all but HR 1010, which they unsuccessfully tried to amend to target funding to communities that traditionally had been undercounted.

The House Government Reform Committee formally reported HR 472 (H Rept 106-71) on March 19; HR 928 (H Rept 106-88) and HR 1009 (H Rept 106-89) on April 13; HR 929 (H Rept 106-96) and HR 1010 (H Rept 106-97) on April 19; and HR 683 (H Rept 106-104) on April 26. HR 472 would give local communities the right to challenge census results before they became final and to force the Census Bureau to recount areas. HR 683, which the committee approved 31–1, would allow welfare recipients to continue receiving benefits while working as paid census enumerators.

The House on a party-line 223–206 vote on April 14 passed HR 472. None of the other census-related bills received further congressional action.

As part of the omnibus fiscal 1999 spending law (PL 105-277) enacted in 1998, funding for the Departments of Com-

---

SAMPLING RULING

The U.S. Supreme Court, in a 5–4 ruling issued Jan. 25, 1999, held that the Census Bureau may not employ statistical sampling if the results were to be used to apportion congressional seats among the states. Sampling would attempt to correct undercounts in the census. *(Supreme Court case, p. 710)*

Republicans were pleased by the Court's upholding of the party's argument against statistically adjusting the national head count. However, the GOP conceded that its victory was only partial and was narrowly focused. Democrats seized on a section of the ruling in *Department of Commerce v. United States House of Representatives* that suggested sampling could—or even must—be used in 2000 to generate the population figures that would be needed for all other endeavors besides reapportionment of House seats among the states for the next decade. Principal among these would be the redistricting of House seats within states, the redrawing of all other political boundaries, and the allocation of billions in federal funds a year among the states, counties, and cities.

Justice Sandra Day O'Connor, in the majority opinion, did not specify whether sampling was unconstitutional. Instead, she decided the case by declaring that amendments to the Census Act added in 1976 (PL 94-521) forbade "the use of sampling in calculating the population for the purpose of apportionment." But the same law, she wrote, "required" that sampling be used for other purposes if the Census Bureau and the secretary of commerce deemed it "feasible." *(1976 law, Congress and the Nation Vol. IV, p. 825)*

merce, Justice, and State and the federal judiciary would have been cut off as of June 15, 1999, if no agreement on sampling had been reached by then. The cutoff was lifted as part of the fiscal 1999 supplemental spending bill (HR 1141) signed into law May 21, 1999 (PL 106-31). *(1997–1998 action, p. 736)*

Federal Regulations Review

The Truth in Regulating Act (S 1198—PL 106-312), signed into law Oct. 17, 2000, would establish a pilot program requiring the General Accounting Office (GAO)—when asked to do so by the House or Senate or by a committee chairman or ranking member—to review federal rules and regulations that have a potential economic impact of $100 million or more. S 1198 would authorize $5.2 million annually from fiscal 2001 to fiscal 2003.

The bill required the GAO to review an agency's analysis of the potential costs, benefits, alternatives, regulatory impact, and other effects of a proposed rule. The GAO would not do any analysis of its own. The purpose was to provide lawmakers with timely information so that they could weigh in effectively while a rule was being formulated and was in the public comment period.

The Senate Governmental Affairs Committee reported S 1198 (S Rept 106-225) on Dec. 7, 1999. The Senate passed the bill by voice vote May 9, 2000. The House passed a companion measure (HR 4924) by voice vote under suspension of the rules July 25. The House by voice vote passed S 1198 under suspension of the rules Oct. 3. President Clinton signed it Oct. 17.

Rules Impact Analyses

The House in 1999 passed legislation (HR 1074) to require government agencies to detail the costs and benefits of proposed federal rules.

The House Government Reform Subcommittee on National Economic Growth, Natural Resources, and Regulatory Affairs by voice vote April 20 approved HR 1074, which would direct the White House's Office of Management and Budget (OMB) to submit an annual account of the costs and benefits that federal regulations would have for different agencies and programs. The report would detail the regulatory impact of federal rules on small business, local and state governments, consumer prices, and economic growth, among other criteria. Under the bill, two or more nongovernmental organizations with experience in reviewing the effects of government regulations would examine the OMB reports.

The subcommittee approved a substitute amendment by chairman David M. McIntosh, R-Ind., to eliminate some of the required impact analyses, such as reports on the effects on productivity and the way products are distributed. The panel also adopted an amendment by ranking Democrat Dennis J. Kucinich of Ohio to require OMB to study the impact of regulations on public health and safety, the environment, and consumer protection. The subcommittee rejected a Kucinich amendment to prevent OMB from spending more than $1 million a year on impact analyses and to clarify that agencies would not be required to generate new data or conduct new analyses.

The full committee approved HR 1074 on May 19 and formally reported it (H Rept 106-168) on June 7. Under the measure, which passed the House 254–157 on July 26, OMB would be required to estimate the costs and benefits of all federal regulatory programs, including paperwork requirements. The president would submit the report to Congress along with the annual budget. The House-passed bill would require OMB to provide cost-benefit estimates in a number of formats: across all agencies, by agency and program, and by "major" rule—those that generate costs of $100 million or more. The OMB report also would analyze the impact of federal rules and paperwork on federal, state, and local governments; the private sector; small business; wages; consumer prices; economic growth; public health and safety; and the environment. Before the report was submitted to Congress, OMB would be required to consult with the Congressional Budget Office, submit the information to peer review, and allow sixty days for public review and comment. The results would be included in the report. OMB would be given nine months to issue guidelines to standardize cost-benefit measurements across federal agencies.

Republicans successfully fought off a Democratic attempt to cap the annual cost of the proposed agency assessment at $1 million and to sunset the program after four years. The amendment, by Joseph M. Hoeffel, D-Pa., also would require OMB to report on the degree to which regulatory costs imposed on corporations were offset by government subsidies, including grants, preferential tax treatment, and federally funded research. It was rejected 192–217 on July 26.

Supporters argued that the bill, dubbed the Regulatory Right-to-Know Act, was necessary to fulfill the government's obligation to inform the public about the magnitude and impact of federal regulations. The Clinton administration and most Democrats opposed the bill, saying it would place an undue burden on OMB, requiring information that was not being generated by the agencies. They also argued that it would force federal agencies to place cost considerations above hard-to-quantify benefits such as environmental protection or lives saved.

The Senate took no action on a companion measure (S 59). The Senate Governmental Affairs Committee July 20, 1999, reported S 746 (S Rept 106-110), to provide for analysis of major rules, to promote the public's right to know the costs and benefits of major rules, and to increase the accountability of quality of government.

Federal Subcontractors

President Clinton on Aug. 17, 1999, signed into law a bill (HR 1219—PL 106-49) to protect federal subcontractors when a federal contractor goes into default or files for bankruptcy.

Under existing law, all federal contractors were required to provide a payment bond to all subcontractors who supply labor or material. The bonds, meant to protect against default or bankruptcy by the contractor, were limited to $2.5 million, regardless of the size of the contract.

HR 1219 would instead require general contractors to obtain payment bonds equal to the total value of the contract. The contracting officer would be allowed to release contractors from that requirement if they determined the amount was impractical. The bill also would prohibit subcontractors from waiving the right to sue on the payment bond until after the work was completed.

The House Government Reform Committee reported HR 1219 (H Rept 106-277, Pt. I) on July 30, 1999. The House passed the bill by 416–0 under suspension of the rules Aug. 2. The Senate passed the measure by voice vote Aug. 5, completing congressional action.

Ethics Office Reauthorization

Both the House and Senate in 1999 passed legislation to reauthorize the Office of Government Ethics, which set and enforced rules for executive branch workers to use in avoiding conflicts of interest. *(1994 action, Congress and the Nation Vol. IX, p. 820)*

The House Government Reform Committee reported HR 2904 (H Rept 106-433, Pt. I) on Nov. 2, 1999. The full House passed the bill 386–1 under suspension of the rules Nov. 8. The House-passed measure would expand the definition of a "special government employee" to include any paid or unpaid adviser who gave "regular advice, counsel or recommendations" to the president, vice president, or other federal workers. Under the bill, any such person would be required to abide by the same financial disclosure and conflict-of-interest reporting requirements and regulations as other federal workers.

According to the committee report, the change was drafted after congressional investigations of alleged misconduct at the White House Travel Office found "certain advisers to the president used their position . . . to promote their own business interests by encouraging the firing of" seven employees in the office in 1993. At the time, Republicans alleged that Harry Thomason, the television producer who was serving as one of President Clinton's advisers, pressed for the internal investigation that led to the firings because he had a stake in an airline charter company. In the debate over HR 2904, Rep. John M. McHugh, R-N.Y., cited Thomason and presidential strategists Paul Begala and Dick Morris as examples of advisers who were highly influential in the White House, yet were exempt from sufficient ethical reporting requirements. Henry A. Waxman, D-Calif., opposed the measure during committee markup, arguing that the change would tie the hands of agencies that regularly call on outside experts for advice. However, he did not fight the bill on the floor. *(Travel office, Congress and the Nation Vol. IX, p. 944)*

No similar provision was in the Senate companion measure (S 1503), which passed by voice vote Nov. 19. A spokesperson for the Senate Governmental Affairs Committee, which drafted S 1503 and reported it (S Rept 106-216) on Nov. 5, said Democratic senators were at least initially unwilling to accept the House provision.

NEA Funding

The National Endowment for the Arts (NEA), long a target for elimination among some conservative Republicans, did not have to fight so hard for its existence in 1999–2000 as it had in the past. *(1997–1998 action, p. 738)*

1999 LEGISLATIVE ACTION

The Senate Appropriations Committee allocated $99 million for the NEA in its version of the fiscal 2000 Interior appropriations bill (S 1292). The House Appropriations Committee bill (HR 2466) kept funding for the endowment at the fiscal 1999 level—$98 million, and the full House accepted the committee's recommendation. The Senate took up HR 2466 and agreed 80–16 on Aug. 5 to a Slade Gorton, R-Wash., motion to table (kill) an amendment offered by Robert C. Smith, I-N.H., to eliminate funding for the agency. The Senate on Sept. 14 approved a group of amendments, including one that added $4 million for the NEA, for a budgeting total of $103 million for the agency.

House-Senate conferees on HR 2466 agreed to freeze fiscal 2000 funding for NEA at the 1999 level. The Clinton administration had asked for $150 million. The conference agreement brought scorn from Democrats and the White House. Provisions for Interior spending were provided in the fiscal 2000 omnibus funding bill (HR 3194—PL 106-113). The appropriation for the NEA was $98 million.

2000 LEGISLATIVE ACTION

The House Appropriations Committee proposed keeping NEA funding for fiscal 2000 at $98 million in the annual Interior spending bill (HR 4578). Norm Dicks, D-Wash., offered an amendment in committee to set funding for NEA at $125 million. It was rejected 25–33, along party lines. Also rejected, 27–31, was a Dicks amendment to give the agency $115.3 million.

In a particularly bitter defeat for Democrats, the House on June 16 rejected 184–188 a Dicks motion to recommit the bill to the committee with instructions to increase the provision for NEA funding by $15 million as well as boost humanities spending. Arts supporters argued that the NEA, which had implemented congressionally mandated policy changes and had a new, popular leader in chairman William J. Ivey, deserved a break. Louise M. Slaughter, D-N.Y., offered an amendment—adopted in a nail-biting 207–204 vote on June 15 with the support of twenty-five Republicans—to defer an additional $22 million in funding for the Energy Department's Clean Coal Technology program. Before Slaughter had a chance to propose setting the money aside for an arts and humanities funding increase, George Nethercutt, R-Wash., offered an amendment to assign the $22 million to another underfunded, and more popular, program: the Indian Health Service. Democrats cried foul, accusing Republicans of manipulating the process to pose an impossible choice between Native American health and support for the arts. Republicans argued that their move to divert money to the Indian Health Service was simply a question of priorities. In the end, Democrats allowed the Indian Health Service amendment, which was adopted by voice vote.

The Senate Appropriations Committee provided $105 million for NEA in HR 4578. On the Senate floor, members rejected, 27–73 on July 12, an amendment by James M. Inhofe, R-Okla., to reallocate $7.4 million designated for the NEA to diabetes treatment, prevention, and research within the Indian Health Service. The final measure, signed by the president on Oct. 11 (PL 106-291), provided $105 million for NEA, with $7 million earmarked for educational and outreach programs for underserved areas.

Presidential Pay Raise

The fiscal 2000 appropriations bill (HR 2490) for the Treasury Department, Postal Service, and general government agencies, signed into law (PL 106-58) on Sept. 29, 1999, doubled the pay of the president—bringing it to $400,000 a year. The Constitution prohibits raising the pay of the current occupant of the office, so the pay raise took effect with the inauguration of the next president in January 2001.

The president's annual salary had been frozen at $200,000 since 1969. At that time, the salaries of the vice president and the chief justice of the United States—$62,500 each—amounted to 31 percent of the president's salary. As of 1999, those two officials were paid $175,400, or 88 percent of the president's salary. Depending on inflation, the salary of the vice president, which had increased automatically since Congress passed the 1975 Executive Salary Cost of Living Adjustment Act (PL 94-82), could eventually overtake the president's salary if it were not increased. *(1975 law, Congress and the Nation Vol. IV, p. 813)*

Also at issue was the pay of members of Congress, which in time could be greater than that of the president's. A 1989 law (PL 101-194) allowed members an annual cost-of-living adjustment unless they actively blocked it. As of 1999, members made $136,700 per year. The leadership was more generously compensated: Speaker of the House, $175,400; majority and minority leader of both chambers, $151,800. Advocates of an increase in presidential pay said that the president's low salary was holding down the pay of other federal officials and would start driving well-qualified people from public service. Opponents of the pay increase accused Congress of conspiring to raise the presidential salary just to ease the "compression" that could hold down congressional and judicial salaries. *(1989 law, Congress and the Nation Vol. VIII, p. 965)*

Presidential Commemoratives

The 106th Congress cleared several pieces of legislation honoring former Republican presidents.

On July 27, 2000, President Clinton signed a measure (HR 3591—PL 106-251) providing for the awarding of a Congressional Gold Medal to Ronald Reagan and his wife, Nancy. The House passed HR 3591 by 350–8 under suspension of the rules April 3, 2000. The Senate passed the bill by voice vote July 13. Congress in 1998 renamed Washington's National Airport to honor Reagan, who served from 1981 to 1989. *(Reagan National Airport, p. 741)*

A measure (S 1652—PL 106-92) to rename the Old Executive Office Building after Dwight D. Eisenhower passed the Senate by voice vote Oct. 19; the House followed suit Oct. 26. Clinton signed the bill on Nov. 9, 1999. President Eisenhower held office from 1953 to 1961.

A commission to plan festivities in honor of the bicentennial of Abraham Lincoln's birth in 2009 was established in HR 1451. The House passed the bill 411–2 under suspension of the rules Oct. 4, 1999. The Senate passed an amended version by voice vote Nov. 19. The House cleared the bill 385–9 under suspension of the rules Feb. 8, 2000. The president signed HR 1451 (PL 106-173) on Feb. 25. Lincoln served as president from 1861 to 1865.

Charity Postal Stamps

Congress in 2000 cleared legislation (HR 4437—PL 106-253) to allow the U.S. Postal Service to design and sell so-called semipostals, which highlight a specific cause or charity. Part of the proceeds from the stamps, which would be limited to a 25 percent premium over regular postage rates, go to the designated causes.

The bill would also reauthorize a breast cancer stamp through July 2002. That semipostal raised $15 million for research. Other causes that could benefit from special semipostals are prostate cancer, domestic violence programs, and railroad crossing safety.

The House Government Reform Committee reported HR 4437 (H Rept 106-734) on July 17, 2000. The House passed the measure the same day by voice vote under suspension of the rules. The Senate passed HR 4437 by voice vote July 26, completing congressional action. The president signed the bill on July 28.

Martin Luther King Jr. Legacy

Two bills aimed at preserving the legacy of civil rights leader the Rev. Dr. Martin Luther King Jr. were cleared by the 106th Congress.

President Clinton on Oct. 25, 1999, signed legislation (S 322—PL 106-80) adding the Jan. 17 Martin Luther King Jr. federal holiday to the list of days on which the American flag should be especially displayed. The 1983 law (PL 98-144) that created the King holiday did not include the "flag code." *(1983 law, Congress and the Nation Vol. VI, p. 786)*

The Senate passed S 322 by voice vote June 14, 1999. The House followed suit Oct. 12, clearing the measure.

The president on Oct. 27, 2000, signed HR 2879 (PL 106-365), which provided for the installation of a plaque in the area of the Lincoln Memorial to commemorate the King speech known as the "I Have a Dream" speech. King had delivered it Aug. 28, 1963.

The House Resources Committee reported the bill (H Rept 106-448) on Nov. 4, 1999. The House passed it by voice vote under suspension of the rules Nov. 9. The Senate Energy and Natural Resources Committee reported the measure (S Rept 106-334) on July 10, 2000. The Senate amended the bill to provide the interior secretary with discretion in the placement of the plaque and then passed it by voice vote Oct. 5. The House-passed version stipulated that the plaque was to be placed on the steps where King had delivered the speech. The House accepted the Senate changes by voice vote under suspension of the rules Oct. 10.

Congress failed to complete action on S 1791, authorizing the Library of Congress to purchase the slain civil rights leader's personal papers from the King family. The Senate passed the bill by voice vote Oct. 29, 1999, but it stalled in the House, in part because of the estimated cost of $20 million.

NASA Authorization

For the first time since 1992, Congress in 2000 cleared a National Aeronautics and Space Administration (NASA) authorization bill (HR 1654—PL 106-391). The three-year, $42.4 billion measure included a curb on space station costs. *(1992 action, Congress and the Nation Vol. VIII, p. 898; space station, p. 753)*

The Senate Commerce, Science, and Transportation Committee on May 5, 1999, by voice vote approved S 342, to reauthorize the space agency at $13.4 billion in fiscal year 2000, $13.8 billion in fiscal 2001, and $13.9 billion in fiscal 2002. The committee by voice vote adopted an amendment, offered by Conrad Burns, R-Mont., and John D. Rockefeller IV, D-W.Va., to increase funding for the Experimental Program to Stimulate Competitive Research by $45 million over three years. The program provides grants to academic centers for scientific research projects in rural states. The committee also adopted by voice vote an amendment offered by Majority Leader Trent Lott, R-Miss., to add over three years $95 million for space shuttle safety and performance upgrades, $92.7 million for academic programs, and $580 million for planning of future shuttle launches.

S 342, sponsored by Science, Technology, and Space Subcommittee Chairman Bill Frist, R-Tenn., was formally reported (S Rept 106-77) on June 16.

The House Science Committee approved HR 1654 by 27–13 on May 13, 1999. The measure, sponsored by Space and Aeronautics Subcommittee Chairman Dana Rohrabacher,

R-Calif., would fund NASA at $13.6 billion in fiscal 2000, $13.7 billion in fiscal 2001, and $13.8 billion in fiscal 2002.

The panel voted along party-lines, 21–18, to terminate the $75 million Triana project and transfer the funding to other space research programs. The project, proposed by Vice President Al Gore and named for the sailor aboard Christopher Columbus's ship who first saw the New World in 1492, called for sending a camera-equipped satellite into orbit in 2000 that could transmit a color image of the entire sunlit side of Earth to the Internet. NASA had selected the Scripps Institution of Oceanography to undertake the mission after the vice president suggested it in 1998. NASA officials maintained that the project would help scientists better understand global climate patterns and the degree to which the sun's energy is absorbed in the atmosphere. But committee members Dave Weldon, R-Fla., and George Nethercutt, R-Wash., who offered the amendment to terminate Triana, argued that the project was never subject to advance review and that NASA had better ways to spend its money. Some Democrats accused GOP members of wanting only to score political points against Gore, who at the time was the Democratic front-runner to succeed Clinton as president.

HR 1654 was formally reported (H Rept 106-145) on May 18. The full House passed the measure, 259–168, the next day. The House adopted, 225–203, an amendment, offered by Anthony Weiner, D-N.Y., to add an average of $10 million over 2000–2002 for aircraft noise reduction research. Republican critics of the amendment noted that NASA already added $25.3 million to the original $46 million dedicated for noise reduction research over 2000–2002 and that it would be fiscally irresponsible to spend any more. Weiner and other Democrats argued that more research needed to be done to make airports quieter in light of action pending on HR 1000, legislation to reauthorize the Federal Aviation Administration (FAA). *(FAA reauthorization, p. 331)*

The House-passed bill also included funds to continue the agency's ongoing work on advanced space transportation technologies. House Science Committee Chairman F. James Sensenbrenner Jr., R-Wis., pointed to a string of six military and commercial launch failures. President Clinton on May 19 directed Defense Secretary William S. Cohen to provide a report on why the space launches failed.

The Senate passed an amended HR 1654 by voice vote Nov. 5. Conferees spent months in on-and-off talks to solve lingering differences in the House- and Senate-passed legislation. The House voted 399–17 on Sept. 14, 2000, to adopt the conference report on HR 1654 (H Rept 106-843), which called for spending $42.4 billion over three years. Republican conferees agreed to drop a provision in the House bill that would have blocked funding for the Triana project. The final bill contained language modeled on a provision in the fiscal 2000 defense authorization law (S 1059—PL 106-65) stipulating that any joint venture between NASA and the People's Republic of China not indirectly help Chinese efforts to develop new commercial launch vehicles or ballistic missile capabilities. The bill also included Senate language prohibiting "obtrusive space advertising" that could be viewed by the naked eye. The prohibition did not apply to such advertising practices as placing logos on commercial space launch vehicles and satellites. The Senate agreed to the conference report by voice vote Oct. 13, completing congressional action. The president signed the measure (PL 106-391) on Oct. 30. *(Fiscal 2000 defense authorization, p. 276)*

Congress appropriated $13.7 billion for NASA in the fiscal 2000 Veterans Affairs-Housing and Urban Development (VA-HUD) funding bill (HR 2684—PL 106-74). Conferees on HR 2684 (H Rept 106-379) approved an amendment by House Majority Whip Tom DeLay, R-Texas, to suspend until 2001 the launch of the Triana satellite. The measure would allow time for the National Academy of Sciences to conduct a study on the scientific value of the project. Conferees also added a controversial provision to create a demonstration program that would allow NASA to make deals with companies to launch commercial projects such as zero-gravity biological research and production of educational videos. NASA would be able to charge the companies fees and to retain some of the funds for investment in other commercial projects. Congress appropriated $14.3 billion for NASA in the fiscal 2001 VA-HUD spending legislation (HR 4635—PL 106-377).

Space Station

As part of the National Aeronautics and Space Administration (NASA) authorization bill (HR 1654—PL 106-391), Congress in 2000 capped international space station development costs at $25 billion over three years. The space station, an orbiting laboratory and living quarters roughly the size of two football fields, had been plagued by schedule delays and cost overruns. *(1997–1998 action, p. 743)*

COMMITTEE ACTION

The Senate Commerce, Science, and Transportation Committee in S 342 (S Rept 106-77) limited space station costs to $21.9 billion through the assembly phase. It also limited space shuttle launch costs in connection with the station's assembly to $17.7 billion. Science, Technology, and Space Subcommittee Chairman Bill Frist, R-Tenn., noted at an April 29, 1999, hearing that the estimated price for the station's assembly had grown from $17.4 billion in 1997 to as much as $26 billion. The nearly $9 billion difference, he said, was about equal to the original total estimate for the station in 1984.

NASA officials expressed reservations about a price cap, emphasizing that the project was a research program and that anticipating future expenses was difficult. Frist, however, said the legislation gave NASA flexibility. S 342 would allow the cap to increase to reflect any costs attributed to inflation or to new technologies that would either improve safety or reduce station costs once assembly was complete.

Many of the space station's problems were attributed to Russia's inability to deliver crucial components on time be-

cause of its ongoing financial crisis. The situation led NASA to develop backup contingency plans to reduce its primary partner's role. Some lawmakers wanted Russia's involvement to be greatly reduced, perhaps to subcontractor status. Problems with the station also stemmed from cost overruns by Boeing, the project's prime contractor.

The House Science Committee did not include a price cap for the space station in HR 1654. House members joined senators in criticizing the schedule delays and cost overruns, but they heeded NASA's assertion that a price cap could hurt its flexibility in building the station. However, the House bill prohibited NASA from spending money on an inflatable module called TransHub as a home for astronauts on the space station. NASA was testing the module as an alternative to the planned aluminum quarters. Republicans said they included the prohibition language because they feared TransHub would lead to a redesign of the space station.

FLOOR/FINAL ACTION

During House floor consideration of the NASA authorization measure, Tim Roemer, D-Ind., on May 19 offered three unsuccessful amendments related to the space station. The first, rejected 114–315, would have imposed a price cap on the project of $21.9 billion through assembly and capped space shuttle costs in connection with assembly at $17.7 billion. The second, defeated 114–313, would have removed Russia as a primary partner in the station. The third, which lost 92–337, would have terminated the space station project.

A key point of contention during the House-Senate conference on HR 1654 was the cost and scope of the international space station. Sensenbrenner, chairman of the conference, and Senate Commerce Committee Chairman John McCain, R-Ariz., also a conferee, supported the project but were concerned about Russia's failure to deliver the service module as well as about NASA's management of program costs. The two lawmakers asked the General Accounting Office (GAO) on June 21, 2000, to investigate development of a U.S. module designed as a backup to the Russian unit. The U.S. module, which consisted of a propulsion segment and short-term crew quarters, had encountered design difficulties and could have been as much as $200 million over budget. The Russian module consisted of a propulsion unit and permanent crew quarters. Sensenbrenner and McCain contended that U.S. dependence on Russian performance in the space station program had cost taxpayers an estimated $5 billion and delayed the program by three years.

Republican conferees wanted language in the authorization bill instructing NASA to recover $1.3 billion from Russia in goods and services the space agency had to purchase because of the production delays. The GOP lawmakers also insisted on capping space station costs at $25 billion, which they said would ensure that NASA did not overspend to complete the project. They also wanted to keep a restriction in the House-passed bill to prevent spending money on the TransHub. House Democrats, while echoing concerns about

Russian involvement in the program, wanted to allow spending exemptions to improve space shuttle safety and reliability. They also wanted language in the bill that would allow NASA to cooperate on a commercially developed TransHub module.

The final bill capped development costs for the station at $25 billion and limited the amount of money that could be spent flying the space shuttle on assembly missions to $17.7 billion, or $380 million per launch. It established contingency funds of $5 billion for the space shuttle and $3.5 billion for the shuttle to address "any urgent situation" on the station that could endanger the crew. The measure also contained language instructing NASA to obtain assurances from Russia that it placed completion of the station ahead of keeping its own *Mir* space station in orbit. The provision reflected congressional frustration with Russia's decision in 2000 to divert three spacecraft intended for the international station to *Mir*. In addition, the bill barred any federal money from being used to buy or design the TransHub module. However, it allowed NASA to lease a privately developed TransHub. Conferees gave NASA until April 2, 2001, to assess its options.

During consideration of the fiscal 2000 Veterans Affairs-Housing and Urban Development (VA-HUD) appropriations bill (HR 2684—PL 106-74), the House rejected 121–298 on Sept. 8, 1999, an amendment offered by Roemer and Mark Sanford, R-S.C., to kill the space station project by eliminating $2 billion in funding and allocating it to veterans' medical care, housing, and other NASA programs. The House also defeated, 185–235 on Sept. 8, an amendment by James E. Rogan, R-Calif., to provide $95 million for space science research and technology programs by taking money from discretionary and other funds for the Environmental Protection Agency. During House floor consideration of the fiscal 2001 VA-HUD spending measure (HR 4635—PL 106-377), members rejected 98–325 on June 21, 2000, a Roemer amendment to take $1.8 billion designated for the international space station, spend $1 billion on other programs in the bill, and dedicate the rest of the money to debt reduction. The House also rejected, 138–286 on June 21, an amendment by Jerrold Nadler, D-N.Y., to take $344 million from the space station and use it to pay for 60,000 additional Section 8 rental vouchers.

Space Launches

Congress in 1999 and in 2000 extended the government-industry arrangement for sharing the risk of space launches.

The risk-sharing arrangement, known as indemnification, was one of the aerospace industry's top legislative priorities. Enacted in 1984 (PL 98-575), the law required launch companies to insure each commercial launch privately for up to $500 million, with the government covering liability claims beyond that. Without the law, which was set to expire Dec. 31, 1999, U.S. launch providers said they could not buy insurance at rates that would allow them to compete with foreign companies. *(1984 law, Congress and the Nation Vol. VI, p. 789)*

The Senate Commerce, Science, and Transportation Committee on June 23, 1999, approved and on Aug. 4 formally reported a bill (S 832—S Rept 106-135) to limit for ten years the amount of liability insurance coverage needed by commercial launch companies. Ernest F. Hollings of South Carolina, the committee's ranking Democrat, criticized the program as "a ten-year subsidy of the richest industry there is." He offered an amendment to limit the extension of indemnification to three years, but he withdrew it after committee chairman John McCain, R-Ariz., promised to seek a compromise of between three and ten years.

The House by voice vote under suspension of the rules Oct. 4 passed HR 2607 (no written report), to authorize $31.4 million in fiscal years 1999–2002 for the Office of Commercial Space Transportation at the Department of Transportation and $1.7 million in fiscal years 2000–2002 for the new Office of Space Commercialization at the Department of Commerce. The transportation secretary would be required to give Congress a long-term report on risk sharing, aimed at ensuring future U.S. competitiveness in the international launch market.

With action incomplete on S 832 and HR 2607, Congress included a one-year extension of the risk-sharing arrangement in the fiscal 2000 appropriations bill for the departments of Veterans Affairs and Housing and Urban Development (HR 2684—PL 106-74), which Clinton signed on Oct. 20.

The Senate by voice vote passed an amended version of HR 2607 on Oct. 13, 2000. The House agreed to the Senate changes by voice vote under suspension of the rules Oct. 17. The bill, signed into law (PL 106-405) on Nov. 1, extended indemnification through the end of 2004.

Energy Research and Development

The House in 1999 passed a bill (HR 1655) to authorize $8 billion for research and development (R&D) projects at the Department of Energy—$3.9 billion in fiscal 2000 and $4.1 billion in fiscal 2001.

HR 1655, approved by voice vote Sept. 15, covered civilian research projects in areas such as energy supply, high-energy physics, fossil energy research, and energy conservation. It provided $100 million for the construction of the controversial Spallation Neutron Source in Tennessee, intended to produce neutrons for use in scientific research. Funding would be withheld, however, if the department did not abide by a list of requirements, such as providing Congress with a baseline cost and reports on each stage of construction.

The House Science Committee had approved HR 1655 (H Rept 106-243) on July 20 and formally reported it the same day.

## CHAPTER 15

Inside Congress

Introduction	757
Members and Procedures	759
Election Issues	776
Pay and Benefits	791

Inside Congress

Much about congressional affairs in the mid-to-late 1990s centered around one person: Speaker Newt Gingrich, R-Ga., an ingenious and charismatic but extraordinarily controversial leader who guided the House GOP out of minority oblivion and then nearly lost his party's majority just a few years later.

Gingrich had built a strong following within his party for being instrumental in ushering in, as a result of the 1994 elections, a new era of Republican control of the House for the first time in forty years. However, Gingrich was dogged throughout his tenure as Speaker with persistent, nagging doubts about his ability to lead. The increasingly discontented GOP rank and file felt he had a tendency to become disengaged, his divisiveness and bombast alienated many mainstream voters, and he was unable to form a large and stable coalition to get policy enacted. The self-styled revolutionary, who sought to elevate the Speaker to the level of the president, was forced from his leadership post after four years. Gingrich's influence, in a certain way, was still evident when House Republicans chose his successor. They looked for a leader who would not follow his confrontational style but instead would focus on behind-the-scenes consensus building. They wanted someone who would represent a new beginning, in essence the opposite of Gingrich.

GINGRICH'S WOES

The 105th Congress opened in January 1997 with Gingrich in the midst of an all-out struggle to retain the Speakership. The biennial election for House officers at the start of each new Congress—usually a prefabricated event that affirmed the majority party's choice for Speaker—had become an intrigue-filled drama. A few weeks earlier, Gingrich, who had been mired in an ethics probe, admitted breaking House rules. A loosely aligned group of Republicans, disillusioned with Gingrich, was engaged in a silent revolt, refusing to proclaim publicly their support of him for Speaker.

Their votes were pivotal. The Speaker was chosen by a majority of lawmakers present and voting, and Republicans held a relatively slim 227–207 majority in the House, with one independent lawmaker. With all the Democrats and the one independent expected to vote for Minority Leader Richard A. Gephardt, D-Mo., just twenty Republicans voting

"present" instead of casting votes for Gingrich would tip the contest: Gephardt would win the Speakership on a 208–207 vote, a disastrous scenario for Republicans.

The rebels hoped Gingrich would bow out before that happened, allowing some other prominent Republican leader to take over. The Speaker's conservative allies outside the House deserted him, calling on him to step aside until all the questions about his ethics could be aired. They worried that Gingrich's weakness would make it impossible for the GOP to compete effectively with Democratic president Bill Clinton for control of the policy agenda, jeopardizing the strides the Republicans felt they had made during the 104th Congress.

But the Speaker hunkered down for a fight, bringing to bear all the resources of the presiding officer of the House, and turning up the heat on wavering members. One of the strongest arguments to retain Gingrich was the absence of a clear successor. On Jan. 7, joyless House Republicans reelected their Speaker, 216–205, over Gephardt—just three more votes needed to attain a majority of those present and voting. Six Republicans voted "present," and four voted for various other Republicans. Turmoil for House Republicans, brought on by Gingrich, did not end there. Two weeks later, almost all Republicans, along with almost all Democrats, voted to reprimand and fine Gingrich for his ethics viola-

REFERENCES

Discussion of congressional affairs for the years 1945–1964 may be found in *Congress and the Nation Vol. I,* pp. 1407–1431; for the years 1965–1968, *Congress and the Nation Vol. II,* pp. 893–924; for the years 1969–1972, *Congress and the Nation Vol. III,* pp. 353–433; for the years 1973–1976, *Congress and the Nation Vol. IV,* pp. 743–794; for the years 1977–1980, *Congress and the Nation Vol. V,* pp. 873–953; for the years 1981–1984, *Congress and the Nation Vol. VI,* pp. 797–840; for the years 1985–1988, *Congress and the Nation Vol. VII,* pp. 871–910; for the years 1989–1992, *Congress and the Nation Vol. VIII,* pp. 913–988; for the years 1993–1996, *Congress and the Nation Vol. IX,* pp. 861–925.

tions. Gingrich became the first sitting Speaker in history to be thus punished.

During the next few months Gingrich proved unable to overcome a lingering backlash from the ethics case and the rank and file's misgivings about his erratic leadership. A mostly conservative group of junior members viewed Gingrich as too conciliatory toward moderates and the Democratically controlled White House. Furthermore, among other things, Gingrich was hurt by his perceived arrogance. He traveled extensively to give speeches, taking him far away from the daily concerns of members. While his missions often involved raising money for the party and for lawmakers' reelection campaigns, they were also designed to improve his standing in public opinion polls in advance of a possible campaign for president in 2000. Gingrich also was prone to unilateral decisions that took even some of his top lieutenants by surprise. In some cases, his on-the-spot proclamations undermined weeks or months of painstaking strategy.

Unhappiness with the Speaker culminated in July 1997 with an ill-conceived coup attempt plotted by a band of disgruntled House Republicans with behind-the-scenes encouragement from some of the leaders serving under Gingrich. The Speaker survived the ouster, which collapsed before it even got under way. But his hold on power was severely weakened, and Republicans for the first time began talking seriously about eventually finding a replacement for him.

The near-rebellion forced Gingrich to reevaluate his own operation and the way he had redesigned the Speaker's role for himself. He began to stick closer to the House and involve himself in the day-to-day concerns of fellow Republicans, giving up some of his self-assigned duties as party visionary. However, as the year drew to a close, Gingrich's once formidable leadership team was unable to rebuild their close bonds. The members began to operate independently of one another, each concerned with his standing in the GOP Conference and his future in leadership.

While Gingrich weathered the reprimand and the attempted coup, he was felled by the results of the 1998 midterm elections. The Republicans lost a net five House seats, giving them the thinnest margin a majority had held in forty-six years. It was only the second time since the Civil War that the party not in control of the White House lost seats in the midterm elections. Many Republicans blamed the party's obsession with Clinton and his possible impeachment for their electoral setback. Other criticisms, depending on one's ideology, included the leadership's inability to develop and communicate a broad message, its unwillingness to stick to a conservative agenda, and the lack of legislative accomplishments. Three days after the election, Gingrich announced that he would not seek another term as Speaker and that he intended to resign from the House. (He resigned Jan. 3, 1999.) Gingrich's decision to step down from his leadership post came just hours after he drew a challenge from a candidate with the stature and connections to beat him—Appropriations Committee chairman Robert L. Livingston, R-La.

GINGRICH'S SUCCESSOR

Livingston was nominated Speaker when the Republicans caucused in mid-November 1998. A month later, amidst the Republicans' push for Clinton's impeachment for alleged wrongdoings stemming from an extramarital dalliance, Livingston confessed publicly that he had "on occasion" engaged in adulterous affairs. The online version of *Roll Call* had disclosed the affairs. Some House conservatives were disturbed by Livingston's indiscretions and his failure to mention them before being nominated Speaker.

On Dec. 19, Livingston strode to the well of the House. He made the case for and against Clinton and then, addressing the president, said, "You, sir, may resign your post." Democrats erupted; a few shouted, "You resign! You resign!" Livingston continued, "I can only challenge you in such fashion if I am willing to heed my own words. I was prepared to lead our narrow majority as Speaker, and I believe I had it in me to do a fine job. But I cannot do that job or be the kind of leader I would like under current circumstances. So I must set the example that I hope President Clinton will follow. I will not stand for Speaker of the House." He went on to say that he would leave the House. Livingston, as Speaker-designate, had promised to restore civility to a chamber where partisan tensions had boiled over. In the end, Democrats were most adamant that he reconsider his decision to resign. "Bob Livingston is a worthy and good and honorable man," said Minority Leader Gephardt. "I believe his decision to retire is a terrible capitulation to the negative forces that are consuming our political system and our country."

House Republicans subsequently rallied behind J. Dennis Hastert, an affable and respected Illinois Republican known for his relaxed style, low profile, and solidly conservative record. During his first two years as Speaker, Hastert relied on the skills he honed as chief deputy whip to build a loyal following among his Republican colleagues. He earned high praise within the GOP for his personal style as a good listener and consensus builder, but he frequently moved forward independently and ultimately stuck to conservative ideals.

Although Hastert's election as Speaker was aimed at healing a House divided by bitter partisanship over Clinton's impeachment, members on both sides of the aisle said political rancor remained as high as ever. The poor relationship between Hastert and Gephardt did not help the parties cooperate. The two rarely met and had a dislike for each other that extended beyond politics. Hastert in 2000 campaigned for Gephardt's Republican challenger—a move Congress-watchers said was a blatant departure from traditional leadership decorum.

Apart from Hastert's legislative abilities, Democrats and Republicans agreed that Hastert accomplished the first task given to him as Speaker: changing the political face of congressional Republicans. After Gingrich—whose low public opinion ratings were blamed in part for GOP losses in 1998—House Republicans wanted a leader who would not spark the public's wrath. While Hastert avoided the deadly public opinion numbers suffered by Gingrich, Hastert was unable to score high approval ratings, at least in part because the public did not know who he was.

Chronology of Action on Congress: Members and Procedures

1997–1998

The House made history in 1997 when, for the first time, it reprimanded and fined the sitting Speaker—Newt Gingrich, R-Ga. Gingrich broke House rules by failing to obtain proper legal advice when he used a network of tax-exempt foundations to raise money for televised town hall meetings and college courses and by giving false information to the House Committee on Standards of Official Conduct. The bad news for Gingrich was not over, as he faced an attempted coup by dissatisfied members of the GOP rank and file six months after the reprimand.

Numerous other members in 1997–1998 were investigated for alleged ethical misconduct, including House Majority Whip Tom DeLay, R-Texas.

In other action, a group of young conservatives, using a strategy aimed at embarrassing the House leadership, held up adoption of a resolution providing funding for House committees. The House also installed changes in its ethics process and brought into line with the Senate restrictions on the outside income of physician members.

Organization: 105th Congress

Republicans continued to hold the majority in the Senate and House that they had won in the 1994 elections. Leadership changes on both sides of the aisle in both chambers of Congress were minimal.

The House voted along party lines to adopt a few rules changes.

SENATE

Most Republican and Democratic leaders in the 105th Congress retained their posts from the 104th Congress.

Majority Leadership

Senate Republicans chose their leaders Dec. 3, 1996. The nearly all-southern makeup of the GOP leadership reflected the party's strength in the South and mirrored the leadership lineup in the House.

Majority Leader Trent Lott of Mississippi and Majority Whip Don Nickles of Oklahoma were both reelected. Neither faced opposition. The only contested race was for secretary of the Republican Conference, which pitted first-term Paul Coverdell of Georgia against Conrad Burns of Montana. The post opened up when Conference chairman Thad Cochran of Mississippi decided to step down and Connie Mack of Florida, who had been serving as secretary, was chosen to succeed him. Coverdell easily defeated Burns, 41–14. Strom Thurmond of South Carolina remained as president pro tempore of the Senate.

Minority Leadership

Senate Democrats made no changes in their top leadership spots. On Dec. 3, 1996, Tom Daschle of South Dakota was reelected minority leader; Wendell H. Ford of Kentucky, minority whip; and Barbara A. Mikulski of Maryland, Democratic Conference secretary. All were unopposed.

Committees

Ted Stevens of Alaska took over the helm at the Appropriations Committee, succeeding Mark O. Hatfield, who retired from the Senate. Stevens left the chairmanship of the Governmental Affairs Committee, which was filled by Fred Thompson of Tennessee. John McCain of Arizona became chairman of the Commerce, Science and Transportation Committee, a post that had been held by Larry Pressler of South Dakota, who was an unsuccessful candidate for reelection in 1996. Ben Nighthorse Campbell of Colorado succeeded McCain as chairman of the Indian Affairs Committee. Upon the retirement from the Senate of Nancy Landon Kassebaum of Kansas, James M. Jeffords of Vermont became Labor and Human Resources Committee chairman. Robert C. Smith of New Hampshire took over the chairmanship of the Select Ethics Committee from Mitch McConnell of Kentucky. McConnell became chairman of the National Republican Senatorial Campaign Committee. Richard C. Shelby of Alabama succeeded Arlen Specter of Pennsylvania as head of Select Intelligence. Specter became chairman of the Veterans' Affairs Committee. He succeeded Alan K. Simpson of Wyoming, who retired from the Senate. Charles E. Grassley of Iowa became chairman of the Special Aging Committee, succeeding William S. Cohen of Maine. Cohen did not run for reelection in 1996; he became defense secretary in 1997.

Tom Harkin of Iowa succeeded Patrick J. Leahy of Vermont as ranking Democrat of the Agriculture, Nutrition and Forestry Committee. Leahy became ranking member on the Judiciary Committee, succeeding Joseph R. Biden Jr. of Delaware. Biden became ranking member of Foreign Relations, succeeding Claiborne Pell of Rhode Island, who retired from the Senate. Carl Levin of Michigan became top Democrat on Arms Services, replacing Sam Nunn of Georgia, who did not run for reelection to the Senate in 1996. Dale Bumpers of Arkansas gave up his ranking member position on the Small Business Committee and assumed that post on the Energy and Natural Resources Committee. He was succeeded by John Kerry of Massachusetts on Small Business and replaced J. Bennett Johnston of Louisiana on Energy and Natural Resources. Johnston did not run for reelection in 1996. Harry Reid of Nevada succeeded Byron L. Dorgan of North Dakota as vice chairman of the Select Ethics Committee. John B. Breaux of Louisiana succeeded David Pryor of Arkansas, who retired from the Senate, as ranking member of the Special Aging Committee.

HOUSE

The roster of Republican and Democratic leaders remained largely unchanged from the preceding Congress.

Majority Leadership

The House GOP caucused Nov. 20, 1996, and agreed to return the controversial Newt Gingrich, R-Ga., as Speaker. Although, by the time the 105th Congress convened, Gingrich had admitted violating House rules, House Republicans on Jan. 7, 1997, reelected their Speaker on a **key vote of 216–205 (R 216–0; D 0–204; I 0–1).** *(1997 key votes, p. 865)*

Reelected at the party caucus without opposition were Dick Armey of Texas as majority leader; Tom DeLay of Texas as majority whip; John A. Boehner of Ohio as Republican Conference chairman; and Christopher Cox of California as Policy Committee chairman. John Linder of Georgia was elected chairman of the National Republican Congressional Committee; Bill Paxon of New York had held that post in the 104th Congress.

Minority Leadership

Democrats on Nov. 18, 1996, reelected their top leaders, all of whom ran unopposed. Richard A. Gephardt of Missouri remained minority leader; David E. Bonior of Michigan,

minority whip; Vic Fazio of California, Democratic Caucus chairman; and Barbara B. Kennelly of Connecticut, Democratic Caucus vice chair. While the Republican leadership had a southern tilt, the Democratic roster reflected the party's political strength in the Northeast, Midwest, and West.

Committees

Bob Smith of Oregon succeeded Pat Roberts of Kansas as chairman of the Agriculture Committee. Roberts had been elected to the Senate. Dan Burton of Indiana became chairman of Government Reform and Oversight, succeeding William F. Clinger of Pennsylvania, who retired from Congress. F. James Sensenbrenner Jr. of Wisconsin became Science Committee chairman. Robert S. Walker of Pennsylvania, who had held the post, did not run for reelection in 1996. Porter J. Goss of Florida succeeded Larry Combest of Texas as chairman of the Select Intelligence Committee. James M. Talent of Missouri became Small Business Committee chairman. He succeeded Jan Meyers of Kansas, who retired from the House. James V. Hansen of Utah succeeded Nancy L. Johnson of Connecticut as the head of Standards of Official Conduct.

Charles W. Stenholm of Texas succeeded E. "Kika" de la Garza, also of Texas, as ranking member of the Agriculture Committee. De la Garza retired from Congress. John M. Spratt Jr. of South Carolina took over the top Democratic spot on the Budget Committee from Martin Olav Sabo of Minnesota. Henry A. Waxman of California succeeded Cardiss Collins of Illinois as ranking member on the Government Reform and Oversight Committee. Collins did not run for reelection in 1996. Vic Fazio of California was succeeded by Sam Gejdenson of Connecticut as ranking member of House Oversight. Howard R. Berman of California succeeded Jim McDermott of Washington as ranking member of the Standards of Official Conduct Committee. Lane Evans of Illinois succeeded G. V. "Sonny" Montgomery of Mississippi, who retired from Congress, as ranking Democrat on Veterans' Affairs. Charles B. Rangel of New York became ranking member of the Ways and Means Committee, succeeding Sam M. Gibbons of Florida. Gibbons retired from the House.

Rules

The House Jan. 7, 1997, on a party-line vote of 226–202 approved a package of new rules to govern the chamber for the 105th Congress. In large part, the rules changes were technical.

Lawmakers offered only limited debate on the package, concentrating on one element relating to a completion date for the ethics investigation of Speaker Newt Gingrich. The ethics provision cleared the way for the members of the Committee on Standards of Official Conduct to continue serving on the panel until Jan. 21 to complete work on the Gingrich case. Most of the committee members had wanted to rotate off the panel when their terms expired at the start of the 105th Congress. *(Gingrich reprimand, p. 761)*

The most controversial change required nongovernmental agencies that testified before House committees to provide a list of the federal grants and contracts they had received in the previous three years. The change was a response to GOP concerns that nonprofit organizations that received federal funds had been improperly active in elections.

Another adopted rule directed the Speaker and minority leader to draw up a drug-testing policy for members and staff that was at least as strong as that which governed executive branch agencies. The Republicans also moved to repeal a rule that prohibited committees from working in the afternoon while the House was conducting business. Republicans discovered in the 104th Congress that committees could not complete their markups in the morning hours and had to go to the full House to get the rule waived. The package also allowed committees to have a contingency fund for "unanticipated committee expenses."

Clarifying an existing rule, the package specified that any legislation to increase income tax rates would require a two-thirds majority vote of the House for approval. In 1996 Democrats had tried to apply the rule to all tax rate increases, not just to income taxes. Another rule banned members from distributing campaign contributions on the House floor. The package also renamed the Committee on Economic and Educational Opportunities as the Committee on Education and the Workforce.

The House in September 1997 would adopt new rules aimed at making the ethics process more timely and bipartisan. *(House ethics overhaul, p. 766)*

Gingrich Reprimand

Newt Gingrich, R-Ga., on Jan. 21, 1997, became the first sitting Speaker to be reprimanded by his peers for violations of House ethics rules. He also was required to pay an unprecedented $300,000 fine.

On Dec. 21, 1996, Gingrich, in a kind of plea-bargaining arrangement with the House Committee on Standards of Official Conduct, acknowledged that he had failed to properly manage the financing of his political activities through charitable foundations. He also conceded a more serious offense—giving the committee misleading information in the course of its investigation. In formal terms, Gingrich admitted that he violated a House rule requiring that members act in a way that "shall reflect creditably on the House of Representatives." For two years Gingrich made repeated denials of wrongdoing. He long claimed that the case was a partisan vendetta by Democrats.

The ethics charges grew out of a series of televised town hall meetings and college classes, called Renewing American Civilization, that Gingrich created and taught between 1993 and 1995. They were financed through donations solicited by tax-exempt groups, which allowed supporters to make undisclosed contributions and to claim tax write-offs as well—two benefits not available to them under election laws, which required full disclosure and provided no such tax write-offs. *(Gingrich case, Congress and the Nation Vol. IX, p. 898)*

While Gingrich maintained that the course was nonpartisan and thus eligible for tax-exempt support, an ethics investigatory subcommittee found that it was probably tied to party politics and to Gingrich's quest to lead a Republican takeover of Congress. Gingrich did not admit to improperly using tax-exempt groups for partisan politics, but he instead acknowledged a lesser crime of failing to seek legal advice in his use of foundations to finance the course and town hall meetings. He also acknowledged submitting misleading information to the panel about the course. However, he publicly blamed his attorney for the mistake and said he was unaware at the time that the attorney was conveying bad information to the ethics committee.

In a related incident in late December 1996, ethics committee ranking member Jim McDermott, D-Wash., was accused by Republicans of leaking to the press a clandestinely tape recorded conversation among Gingrich and his allies, who were talking about ways to control damage and salvage his Speakership. A lawsuit would be brought against McDermott. *(McDermott probe, p. 765)*

The ethics committee held a televised hearing Jan. 17, 1997, in which James M. Cole, the panel's special counsel, outlined his findings. Cole said that Gingrich had lied to the ethics subcommittee investigating the political connections of the tax-exempt networks that funded Gingrich's course. He said the financing arrangements violated federal tax law. Cole's report said Gingrich had engaged in a pattern of "disregard and lack of respect for the standards of conduct." It contradicted the Speaker's contention that he decided to teach the course and some televised workshops to spread his ideas and inadvertently brushed up against the tax code along the way.

Cole and the investigatory subcommittee recommended that Gingrich be reprimanded and fined $300,000 to offset the cost of the investigation, particularly those portions devoted to discerning the truth from the Speaker's misleading submissions. The full committee voted 7–1 on Jan. 17 to accept the subcommittee's recommendation, and it also released Cole's report.

The House Jan. 21 accepted the committee's recommendation, reprimanding the Speaker and imposing a $300,000 fine, on a **key vote of 395–28 (R 196–26; D 198–2; I 1–0).** During the debate, Gingrich stayed out of public view, sequestered in his second-floor suite at the Capitol. For all the partisan rancor the case aroused, the vote was uneventful. Republicans were resigned to casting the first vote in history to reprimand a sitting Speaker. Democrats were purposely quiet, a strategy designed to focus public attention on Gingrich's punishment, not on their reaction. The effect of the reprimand was to severely weaken Gingrich's hold on power. *(1997 key votes, p. 865; Gingrich attempted coup, box, p. 762)*

With the GOP leadership under intense pressure to respond to the controversy and the bad press it was causing the party, Majority Leader Dick Armey, R-Texas, appointed

ATTEMPTED COUP TO REMOVE GINGRICH

Discontent with Newt Gingrich, R-Ga., particularly in the aftermath of his becoming in January 1997 the first sitting House Speaker to be reprimanded, grew among the rank and file and infected the upper reaches of the Republican leadership. Doubts about his ability to lead culminated in a coup attempt, which ultimately failed. *(Gingrich reprimand, p. 761)*

Background

While Gingrich traveled extensively, giving speeches to raise money for the party and to improve his standing with the public, he delegated much of the responsibility for the day-to-day running of the House to Majority Leader Dick Armey, R-Texas. However, at times, Gingrich would jump back into his Speaker's role, attempting to resolve differences between warring factions in the Republican Conference, doing political combat with the White House, or setting the Republican message of the week. His on-again, off-again management style as well as his penchant for acting unilaterally began to cause problems with Armey and the other GOP leaders.

In early 1997 Gingrich, along with Senate majority leader Trent Lott, R-Miss., and the Republican chairmen of the House and Senate Budget committees, began to make significant progress in negotiating a balanced-budget deal with President Bill Clinton. With his reelection out of the way, Clinton conceded the need for deeper cuts in Medicare spending and signaled newfound flexibility on tax cuts. Extracting a big win from Clinton was perhaps Gingrich's best chance to reassure conservatives who were increasingly suspect of his leadership. A show of force on tax cuts could also insulate him from criticism from the right when he would have to make compromises on the spending side of the budget.

However, in mid-March, Gingrich inflamed core GOP conservatives, including Armey, by announcing in the press that House Republicans would agree to postpone their tax cut proposals temporarily to achieve a budget agreement with Clinton. Without tax cuts on the table, Gingrich reasoned, Clinton would have no excuse to back out of a budget deal. Later, Congress could present him with the tax cut package, perhaps in 1998 when the midterm elections would make it difficult for the president to say no. The logic did not fly with conservatives, who interpreted Gingrich's remarks as a retreat from a core GOP commitment. In a highly public split with Gingrich, Armey declared he would never support a budget deal without tax cuts.

Restless junior conservatives in the conference grew openly defiant. On March 20, eleven of them forced the defeat of a leadership-backed rule on the floor, embarrassing Gingrich. The rule governed floor debate on a resolution (H Res 91) to increase funding for standing committees, a betrayal, the rebels charged, of the institutional reforms they had ushered in two years earlier. *(House committee funding, p. 767)*

Behind the scenes, a loosely aligned group of a dozen to 20 lawmakers began meeting in secret to discuss what to do about—in their opinion—the party's increasingly ineffectual leadership. Although cloakroom talk of replacing Gingrich as Speaker grew steadily, Republicans remained undecided over who might replace him.

Ironically, even as reservations about Gingrich spread, he was able to lead Republicans to their crowning achievement—a deal with Clinton to balance the budget in five years. The budget resolution was adopted in May. Gingrich was not able to savor the victory for long, however. Problems with his stewardship of the House suddenly grew acute during work

---

James V. Hansen, R-Utah, as ethics chair, replacing Nancy L. Johnson, R-Conn., who had openly warred with ranking member McDermott. Armey and Minority Leader Richard A. Gephardt, D-Mo., subsequently agreed to disband the rest of the committee temporarily to foster a cessation of hostilities between the two parties. The two appointed a task force to come up with ways to make the panel more immune to partisan bickering. *(House ethics overhaul, p. 766)*

To pay the fine, Gingrich on April 17 announced an unusual arrangement in which he would borrow the money from former Senate majority leader and 1996 GOP presidential candidate Bob Dole of Kansas. Under the terms agreed to by the two men, Gingrich would not have to pay any of the principal or the 10 percent interest on the loan until 2005, after he no longer could serve as Speaker. The deal kicked up

a new round of criticism about Gingrich's judgment. Some Republicans thought Gingrich gave the appearance of accepting a special deal from Dole, who had gone to work for a major lobbying and law firm with dozens of clients interested in legislative outcomes on Capitol Hill. Ethics committee chairman Hansen and ranking member Howard L. Berman, D-Calif., refused to approve the deal. Gingrich worked out a modified arrangement in which he agreed to pay half the fine out of his own pocket and borrow the rest from Dole under more conventional terms. The loan was to be secured by a life insurance policy, Gingrich's house in Georgia, and other of the Speaker's assets. On Sept. 14, 1998, however, Gingrich announced that he would not need a loan from Dole. As a result, the ethics committee released Dole from restrictions that kept him from registering as a lobbyist or contacting

on a supplemental appropriations bill to provide relief for flood-ravaged states in the Midwest and Upper Plains.

Armey and other GOP leaders had adopted a strategy of attaching to such legislation items they hoped Clinton could be forced to accept; they did not think he would veto a popular bill. The most controversial riders were a provision that would effectively avert any further government shutdowns such as the ones that had hurt Republicans in 1995–1996 and a provision that would regulate how the 2000 census would be conducted. The strategy failed miserably. Clinton vetoed the bill over the add-ons, and public attention was focused on television images of flood victims suffering while politicians in Washington squabbled. As in the government shutdowns, the public blamed the GOP, not Clinton.

At that point, Gingrich stepped into the crisis and, without consulting Armey or the other leaders, swiftly replaced the earlier strategy. He and Lott ordered the bill stripped of extraneous provisions. Although the House passed the bill, all of Gingrich's top lieutenants—Armey, Majority Whip Tom DeLay, R-Texas, and GOP Conference Chairman John A. Boehner, R-Ohio—snubbed him by voting against it. The events sparked a crisis in leadership. Armey refused to defend the Speaker and, along with DeLay and Boehner, began meeting secretly with the rebellious Republicans to hear their complaints about Gingrich.

The Coup

The breakdown of the leadership, which had mostly unfolded behind closed doors, came into public view with revelations in July that the leaders and some of the rebels had secretly discussed ways of ousting Gingrich. The coup never got off the ground, hampered by the continuing problem of deciding on a suitable successor.

The chain of events began July 10, when Armey, DeLay, Boehner, and former National Republican Congressional Committee chairman Bill Paxon, R-N.Y., who held an informal post as chairman of the leadership meetings, started to engage in a series of late-night meetings. At one of those sessions, Armey expressed frustration with Gingrich and said he was tired of taking the political heat for what he viewed as the Speaker's repeated blunders. The men decided that DeLay would meet with the rebels to find out whether they were serious about ousting Gingrich. The leaders later claimed they were simply trying to find out what the rebels were up to and to intervene if necessary. But many of the junior lawmakers reported that DeLay urged them to move ahead with a parliamentary maneuver called a motion to vacate the chair, which, on a simple majority, could be used to oust the Speaker. It was also revealed that Armey, DeLay, and Paxon discussed succession scenarios but could not agree on whose name would be put forward. If Republicans were unable to agree among themselves on a successor, the Democrats might be able to elect Minority Leader Richard A. Gephardt, D-Mo., as Speaker.

The plotting ended the next morning when Armey told the others he would no longer take part and informed Gingrich of the previous night's discussions. The following days were tumultuous. Gingrich demanded and received Paxon's resignation from his appointive post, but Gingrich did not move against the other three, who were all elected to their positions by the Republican Conference. Despite their reservations about Gingrich, many Republicans felt their Speaker had been betrayed.

In an extraordinary closed-door gathering on July 23, lawmakers compelled Armey, DeLay, and Boehner to stand and describe their roles in the ouster talks. For the most part, the leaders blamed the bungled coup on fatigue, frustration, and a series of miscues in which they inadvertently sent signals of readiness to the rebels.

Gingrich on behalf of any clients with his Washington, D.C. law firm.

As of May 1998, Gingrich was refusing to pay off his legal bills from the ethics probe. Records showed that Gingrich owed $196,022 to his former attorney, Jan Baran. Sources said Gingrich's actions reflected his contention that Baran, not he, was responsible for misleading the ethics committee. Gingrich, who had paid Baran's firm about $700,000 before the dispute, regularly reported the unpaid portion to the Federal Election Commission—with a footnote that it "does not constitute an admission of liability."

On Oct. 10, 1998, the ethics committee unanimously decided to drop the final ethics charges against Gingrich, even though the panel found that he had repeatedly violated House Rule 45, which prohibits outside consultants from conducting House duties. A letter from Hansen and Berman said that political consultant Jeffrey Eisenbach helped develop the 1990–1991 GOP legislative agenda at Gingrich's request. The work occurred while Gingrich was minority whip and Eisenbach was a paid consultant to GOPAC, a political action committee Gingrich headed until 1995. Hansen and Berman also said that Gingrich had received "letters of admonition" regarding more recent Rule 45 violations during Gingrich's tenure as Speaker in 1995 and 1996. It referred to work done for Gingrich by Joseph Gaylord, a political consultant, and Donald Jones, a telecommunications entrepreneur. But because the violations occurred "so long ago" and because there was no evidence that such violations persisted, the committee dropped the complaint. It also dropped charges that GOPAC had improperly subsidized his 1990 campaign and that he had personally benefited from its support. A case against GOPAC brought by the Federal Election Commission had been dismissed by a U.S. District Court.

Ethics Probes

In addition to House Speaker Newt Gingrich, R-Ga., a number of other members of Congress ran into ethics difficulties in the 105th Congress. (*Gingrich reprimand, p. 761*)

REP. TOM DELAY

In a Nov. 7, 1997, letter, the House Committee on Standards of Official Conduct said that it "found no basis for launching an investigation" of influence-peddling by Majority Whip Tom DeLay, R-Texas, and that his contacts with lobbyist brother Randy DeLay's clients either predated his brother's hiring or could be considered normal constituent service. The committee also dismissed an allegation that DeLay might have linked favors to campaign contributions.

As part of its complaint, the Congressional Accountability Project cited a 1995 *Washington Post* story that described how DeLay checked the frequency and amount of campaign contributions from lobbyists when they visited his office, leaving the impression that they should give to GOP candidates. The group, which was affiliated with consumer activist Ralph Nader, filed the complaint in September 1996. The committee noted that DeLay's written response to the committee "did not contain a denial that the event mentioned in the newspaper story occurred." The panel also appeared to caution DeLay about his fund-raising. The letter noted that fund-raising was illegal in the Capitol or congressional office buildings and added: "Rep. DeLay was advised that it is particularly important that a member not make statements that create the impression that the member would consider an individual's requests for access or for official action based on such campaign contributions."

Among other things, the complaint also alleged that DeLay worked to round up congressional support for a letter to Commerce Secretary Ronald H. Brown and U.S. Trade Representative Mickey Kantor urging them to support Cemex, a Mexican cement-making company that was embroiled in a trade dispute with the United States and a foreign company represented by Randy DeLay. (*1999–2000 action, p. 770*)

REP. JAY C. KIM

After four years of protesting his innocence, Rep. Jay C. Kim, R-Calif., and his wife, June, pleaded guilty Aug. 11, 1997, in Los Angeles federal court to ten counts stemming from receipt of more than $230,000 in illegal campaign contributions. On March 9, 1998, Kim was sentenced to two months of home detention, one year of probation, 200 hours of community service, and a $5,000 fine.

Kim's attorneys asked U.S. District Judge Richard A. Paez March 25 to postpone Kim's period of home detention until after California's June 2 primary. The lawyers argued that the

---

ROTA SENTENCED

Former House postmaster Robert V. Rota was sentenced Feb. 20, 1997, to four months in prison for his role in the House Post Office scandal. Rota had pleaded guilty to misdemeanor charges of supplying Reps. Dan Rostenkowski, D-Ill. (1959–1995), and Joe Kolter, D-Pa. (1983–1993), with cash in exchange for government-purchased stamps. U.S. District Court Judge Norma Holloway Johnson of Washington, D.C., also ordered Rota to pay a $2,000 fine and to pay Congress $5,000 in restitution for his role in the scam.

Rota denied the existence of a cash-for-stamps scheme in 1980 and persuaded Post Office employees to lie to investigators. The allegations resurfaced in 1991, and Rota again lied. However, another Post Office employee told the truth to the new investigators. Rota subsequently was indicted and reached a plea bargain. Despite Rota's cooperation with federal investigators, Johnson rejected probation and accepted the prosecutor's argument that Rota should be punished more harshly. (*House Post Office, Congress and the Nation Vol. VIII, p. 939; Congress and the Nation Vol. IX, p. 867*)

---

timing of the sentence would have an "unduly harsh impact" on Kim's bid for a fourth term. Federal prosecutors moved to block the request, saying that Kim should serve his sentence immediately and not be treated differently from other convicted defendants.

In a written order, Paez denied Kim's request and added a surprise clarification to the original sentence. Paez said he wanted Kim to perform his congressional duties in Washington, so he ordered the lawmaker to remain in the nation's capital for the two-month period, even when Congress was not in session. He also restricted Kim's travel to Washington and northern Virginia, where Kim had a second home. His movement would be tracked by an electronic monitoring device, a first for a sitting member of Congress.

An attempt by Kim to cut short his probation was rejected Oct. 8 by a federal judge. Kim wanted to be allowed to move to South Korea to host a television talk show.

On Oct. 9 the House Committee on Standards of Official Conduct announced that Kim had violated federal campaign laws and House rules in at least six instances. However, the panel said it would take no action against Kim because he was defeated in the June GOP primary. (*Kim case, Congress and the Nation Vol. IX, p. 904*)

On behalf of his campaign committee, Kim pleaded guilty to five felony counts. The committee faced potential fines of as much as $2.5 million; Kim, however, would not be personally liable. Kim did plead guilty to three misdemeanor charges for which he was personally culpable: that he knowingly accepted a $50,000 campaign contribution from a Taiwanese national and laundered it through his personal bank account; that he accepted an illegal $12,000 corporate contribution from Nikko Enterprises Inc.; and that he directed his firm, JayKim Engineers Inc., to give more than $83,000 in illegal corporate contributions to his campaign.

Kim's wife pleaded guilty to two charges that stemmed from her acceptance of more than $19,000 in illegal corporate campaign contributions. The bulk of that amount, $14,000, had been laundered through an electronics firm owned by Kim campaign treasurer Seokuk Ma. Ma was convicted in April 1997 of having accepted and concealed at least $23,000 in illegal contributions and was sentenced to five years' probation and fined $12,000.

According to the plea agreement with federal prosecutors, the Kims faced up to six months in jail and fines totaling $635,000. Because the charges against Kim were misdemeanors, he was not covered by a House Republican Conference rule that would have stripped him of his subcommittee chairmanship for a felony conviction. Kim chaired the Transportation and Infrastructure Subcommittee on Public Buildings and Economic Development.

REP. JIM MCDERMOTT

U.S. District Judge Thomas F. Hogan on July 28, 1998, dismissed a lawsuit by Rep. John A. Boehner, R-Ohio, against Rep. Jim McDermott, D-Wash., for disclosing a taped cell phone conversation concerning the ethics investigation of House Speaker Newt Gingrich, R-Ga. Hogan ruled McDermott's First Amendment rights were paramount in the case. He said McDermott had obtained the tape legally and had a constitutional right to disclose its content. He did, however, chastise McDermott, noting that he was serving on the House Committee on Standards of Official Conduct at the time of the incident. The lawsuit subsequently was reinstated by a federal appeals court. *(Gingrich reprimand, p. 761; 1999–2000 action, p. 774)*

On Dec. 21, 1996, Boehner, head of the House GOP Conference, was driving in Florida, talking to other Republican leaders on a cell phone about the predicament facing Gingrich. That same day, Gingrich admitted that he had violated House rules by failing to properly manage the financing of his political activities through tax-exempt foundations and by giving the House ethics committee inaccurate information about the matter. The call was intercepted by a Florida couple listening to their police scanner. They said they taped the call because they thought it had historic value. The contents of the tape subsequently showed up in the *New York Times* and the *Atlanta Journal-Constitution.* Democrats immediately charged that the tape showed that Gingrich had violated an agreement not to rally opposition to the ethics committee decision to reprimand him.

The lawsuit was filed under the Electronic Communications Privacy Act. In early 1997 Boehner won permission from the House ethics committee and the Federal Election Commission to use campaign funds to pay for the lawsuit.

On April 25, 1997, the Florida couple pleaded guilty to eavesdropping and were each fined $500. In a plea agreement,

the couple also agreed to cooperate with the prosecution investigation. *(Eavesdropping legislation, p. 655)*

REP. BUD SHUSTER

The House Committee on Standards of Official Conduct June 10, 1998, announced that it was curtailing its investigation of Bud Shuster, R-Pa., to steer clear of an ongoing Justice Department criminal probe. The ethics committee had launched its investigation Nov. 14, 1997, in response to a request made by the Congressional Accountability Project, a Ralph Nader-affiliated group, which alleged that Shuster had accepted improper favors from Ann Eppard, a former top aide who had become a lobbyist. *(Shuster case, Congress and the Nation Vol. IX, p. 905; 1999–2000 action, p. 771)*

Shuster was chairman of the House Transportation and Infrastructure Committee.

REP. CORRINE BROWN

The House Committee on Standards of Official Conduct in 1998 questioned Rep. Corrine Brown, D-Fla., about several ethical issues raised by newspaper stories. The fact-finding involved, but apparently was not limited to, a $10,000 check that she received from an embattled Baptist leader and a luxury car worth nearly $50,000 that her daughter received from an aide to a West African businessman whom the lawmaker tried to keep out of prison. *(1999–2000 action, p. 773)*

REP. DAN BURTON

The Justice Department, which was conducting an investigation into possible illegal fund-raising practices during the 1996 election, issued Republican representative Dan Burton's campaign committee in Indiana a subpoena July 11, 1997, for financial records. The *Washington Post* on March 19, 1997, had reported on a memo by a lobbyist for the Pakistani government of Prime Minister Benazir Bhutto, Mark A. Siegel, which said that he had been "shaken down" for a $5,000 contribution to Burton's campaign. A Burton aide stated that the representative had asked Siegel to raise $5,000 from Pakistani Americans and that Burton had mentioned Siegel's failure to do so to the ambassador for the Bhutto government. The aide, however, disputed many of the claims made in Siegel's memo.

Burton served on the House International Relations Committee and had a particular interest in U.S.-Pakistani relations. As chairman of the House Government Reform and Oversight Committee, he was leading an investigation into the Democrats' 1996 fund-raising. *(Campaign finance probes, box, p. 778)*

REP. EARL F. HILLIARD

The House Committee on Standards of Official Conduct on Nov. 9, 1997, dismissed a complaint that Rep. Earl F. Hilliard, D-Ala., traveled to Libya in August 1997 without required State Department permission. The United States considered Libya a terrorist state, and travel or business dealings there needed government approval. The ethics committee found no evidence that Hilliard had violated U.S. sanctions against Libya. Republican representatives Bob Barr of Georgia and Spencer Bachus of Alabama brought the complaint against Hilliard.

FORMER MEMBERS

Wes Cooley

Former representative Wes Cooley, R-Ore. (1995–1997), was found guilty March 18, 1997, of lying about his military record in official state voters' pamphlets. He was sentenced the same day to two years' probation and ordered to perform 100 hours of community service and pay $7,110 in fines and prosecution costs.

Cooley did not challenge facts presented by state prosecutors. He was indicted in December 1996 for claiming in 1994 primary and general election pamphlets that he had been a member of the Army Special Forces in Korea. Prosecutors said they could prove that Cooley was in the United States during the Korean War. (*Cooley case, Congress and the Nation Vol. IX, p. 904*)

Federal officials also investigated allegations that Cooley and his wife lied about their marital status so she could continue to collect widow's benefits from her first husband through the Department of Veterans Affairs.

Mary Rose Oakar

Former representative Mary Rose Oakar, D-Ohio (1977–1993), pleaded guilty Sept. 30, 1997, to a misdemeanor conspiracy charge and a misdemeanor campaign finance violation. She was sentenced Jan. 21, 1998, to two years' probation, fined $32,000, and ordered to perform 200 hours of community service. (*Oakar case, Congress and the Nation Vol. IX, p. 907*)

Oakar lost her 1992 reelection bid amid accusations that she had abused the House bank by writing 213 checks she could not cover. Subsequent scrutiny of her 1992 campaign accounts by federal investigators revealed that she had shifted $16,000 in campaign contributions from her House bank account to her campaign using false names to evade individual contribution limits. Oakar admitted the shift as well as admitted giving false information to the Federal Election Commission. (*House bank, Congress and the Nation Vol. VIII, p. 929; Congress and the Nation Vol. IX, p. 877*)

Barbara-Rose Collins

The House Committee on Standards of Official Conduct Jan. 2, 1997, announced that former representative Barbara-Rose Collins, D-Mich. (1991–1997), improperly used congressional staff members to do personal chores or campaign work and misused official, campaign, and scholarship funds in violation of law and House rules. (*Collins case, Congress and the Nation Vol. IX, p. 904*)

The panel said Collins improperly directed congressional staff members to clean her house and arrange campaign

fund-raising events on office time. Evidence also showed that she used House office funds for campaign purposes.

House Ethics Overhaul

The House Sept. 18, 1997, adopted 258–154 a new set of rules for its ethics process (H Res 168). Overall, however, the House maintained the existing bifurcated system, in which an investigatory subcommittee reviewed a complaint and then made recommendations to an adjudicatory subcommittee that took over the trial-like phase of the process. The system, established in a 1989 law (PL 101-194), had been in place since 1991. (*Ethics process, Congress and the Nation Vol. VIII, p. 920*)

House majority leader Dick Armey, R-Texas, and Minority Leader Richard A. Gephardt, D-Mo., on Feb. 12, 1997, jointly announced the creation of a ten-member ethics task force, evenly divided between the two parties, to begin a review of the ethics process. A two-month moratorium was imposed on the filing of new ethics cases. The impetus for the House to revamp its self-policing process was the highly partisan atmosphere surrounding the ethics investigation of House Speaker Newt Gingrich, R-Ga., and the near-breakdown of the Committee on Standards of Official Conduct (ethics committee) that resulted. (*Gingrich reprimand, p. 761*)

The new rules were based largely on the task force's recommendations, issued in a report June 18. The task force had voted to approve the report 8–1 the day before. The House made two major changes to the package put forward by the task force and defeated a third.

In the most controversial change adopted by the House, the new rules barred nonmembers from filing complaints with the ethics committee. In place of the task force recommendation that outside groups be allowed to file complaints if they had "personal knowledge of a transgression," the House approved, 228–193 on Sept. 18, the outside filing ban sponsored by John P. Murtha, D-Pa. He and other advocates argued that members needed to be protected from frivolous ethics complaints, especially from their political foes during reelection campaigns. Under the approved change, outsiders were required to find a lawmaker to sponsor the complaint, which meant they had to find a member willing to risk political controversy and potential career hardship by bringing a formal complaint against colleagues including a House leader or an influential committee chairman.

A second amendment, sponsored by Jim Bunning, R-Ky., and approved by the House 221–194 on Sept. 18, required a majority vote of the full committee to expand the scope of a subcommittee investigation when additional information was uncovered. The task force had recommended that the investigative subcommittee that handled the initial steps of a case have the power to expand the scope. The intent was to safeguard the subcommittee's autonomy.

The House rejected, 181–236 on Sept. 18, a W. J. "Billy" Tauzin, R-La., amendment to require that complaints against members be dismissed if the committee deadlocked for six months over the issue of whether to open an investigation. Supporters of the amendment argued that lawmakers needed protection from election-year opponents who filed baseless ethics complaints with the intent of having them linger long enough to do political damage. But critics said the amendment would encourage stalemate by giving committee members favoring dismissal an incentive to dig in and wait for the clock to run out. The task force position prevailed: If the committee were deadlocked, it would notify the target of the investigation of the delay but would not automatically dismiss the case.

The rules changes adopted by the House also included the following:

• Set a time limit of forty-five days during which the committee was required to either dismiss a complaint, resolve it with a letter to the lawmaker, or establish a subcommittee to open an investigation. If the committee failed to act within forty-five calendar days—or five legislative days, whichever was longer—a complaint would automatically go to the investigation stage. The panel could extend the review period for an additional forty-five calendar days.

• Formation of a twenty-member pool, ten members from each party who were not on the ethics committee, to serve on the panel's investigatory subcommittees. This was designed to relieve the time demands of serving on the committee, a common complaint of past members, and to increase understanding of the difficulty of handling ethics complaints.

• Creation of a permanent, nonpartisan ethics committee staff.

• Reduction of the term on ethics from six to four years, with the chairman and ranking member permitted to stay longer.

• Establishment of enhanced powers for the chairman and ranking member, who were empowered to refer a complaint to an investigative subcommittee on their own. Under previous rules, only a vote of the full committee could kick off an investigation. The ranking member also was given greater power to place items on the committee's agenda.

• Creation of strict new standards of confidentiality that would require committee members to take nondisclosure oaths, close almost all investigative deliberation to the public, restrict the release of evidence, and hide roll-call votes unless the committee voted to divulge them.

House Committee Funding

The House May 1, 1997, approved a resolution (H Res 129) authorizing $149.9 million for eighteen committees for the remainder of the 105th Congress. A group of angry GOP fiscal conservatives had blocked an earlier version of the measure (H Res 91).

The eleven restless junior Republicans grew openly defiant of the leadership, joining with Democrats to defeat the rule (H Res 101—H Rept 105-33) for floor debate on H Res 91 (H Rept 105-30) by 210–213 on March 20, 1997. The resolution would have increased committee funding by 14 percent over the previous year, which the GOP rebels charged was a betrayal of the institutional reforms implemented in 1995. The bigger budgets were pushed by the GOP leadership as a means of strengthening House committees' ability to oversee federal programs and agencies. Increased oversight was part of a leadership strategy to build a case for additional cuts in what Republicans considered wasteful or unproductive programs.

After the vote, Speaker Newt Gingrich, R-Ga., further enraged conservatives by making the defectors stand and explain their votes to their colleagues in a closed-door meeting of House Republicans. Following that confrontation, the leadership won approval, 213–179 on March 21, of H Res 91. The resolution authorized temporary funding at current levels from April 1 to May 2, 1997. It also provided $20 million for the Government Reform and Oversight Committee, part of which was earmarked for a high-priority investigation of White House fund-raising practices, and a $7.9 million reserve fund for committees. The rule (H Res 105—H Rept 105-41) laying out floor consideration of the resolution was approved earlier the same day, 218–179.

The Oversight Committee April 24 by voice approved H Res 129, which authorized funding for the rest of the Congress. The resolution was formally reported (H Rept 105-79) on April 28. On the House floor, only one of the eleven defectors—Mark W. Neumann of Wisconsin—voted against the revised measure. The May 1 vote was 262–157.

Adding together the reserve fund, the separate funding for the Government Reform and Oversight Committee, and the funds provided in H Res 129, the total was $177.8 million—only about $550,000 less than the funding level that had sparked the rebels' mutiny.

Physicians' Outside Income

The House Committee on Standards of Official Conduct on Feb. 25, 1998, said that House members who were physicians, like those who practiced law or other professions, would no longer be able to make a profit treating patients.

The ruling was intended to clarify the application of the 1989 congressional pay raise bill (HR 101-194), which imposed restrictions on outside income earned by members and senior staff. The ethics panel had previously ruled that the restrictions applied to lawyers and real estate and insurance agents, but it had been less clear about other professions, including physicians. *(Pay raise bill, Congress and the Nation Vol. VIII, p. 965)*

The panel ruled that allowing members who were physicians to make money on their continued outside employment violated the law's prohibition on collecting income for work in which there is a "fiduciary relationship," defined as "an obligation to act in another person's best interests . . . or a relationship of trust in which one relies on the integrity, fidelity and judgment of another." Doctors, the ruling said, had such a relationship with their patients. The Senate and executive branch included doctors under their outside income rules. The House ruling does allow physicians to collect fees that cover their expenses, such as malpractice insurance and maintaining an office.

The 1989 ethics law also prohibited members from affiliating with a firm that provided services involving a fiduciary relationship or allowing their name to be used by such a firm. The House ruling did not address those prohibitions as they related to doctors.

Chief Administrative Officer

The House by voice vote July 31, 1997, approved H Res 207, naming James M. "Jay" Eagen III as the new chief administrative officer of the House, responsible for overseeing some 1,000 employees and the finances of the House's administrative offices. Eagen was staff director of the House Education and the Workforce Committee.

A four-member bipartisan task force recommended Eagen after a five-month search to replace Scot M. Faulkner, who was forced to resign in November 1996 after a rocky two-year tenure, which included an investigation launched by the House inspector general. Democrats on the House Oversight Committee called on Chairman Bill Thomas, R-Calif., to release the inspector general's report on Faulkner and to hold hearings on his alleged mismanagement and abuse of authority. A draft report of the inspector general's findings stated that Faulkner exhibited "poor judgment, mismanagement, abuse of authority and gross disregard for established policies and procedures." Faulkner said the report was false.

The position of chief administrative officer, replacing the director of nonlegislative services, was created in 1995.

1999–2000

Disaffected Republicans forced Newt Gingrich, R-Ga., from the Speakership, a post he held for four years and with which he had been rewarded after helping to engineer the GOP takeover of the House in the 1994 elections. After a false start, when Robert L. Livingston, R-La., emerged as the likely successor to Gingrich, J. Dennis Hastert, R-Ill., was voted the new Speaker at the start of the 106th Congress.

As in every Congress, a number of members faced allegations of wrongdoing. The Senate adopted a new process for conducting ethics investigations. And the House, for the first time, installed a Roman Catholic as House chaplain.

Organization: 106th Congress

Republicans held on to their majority status in both houses of Congress. The relative calm in the Senate Republican leadership was offset by dramatic events that unfolded in the House Republican leadership. The man who was instrumental in the 1994 GOP takeover of Congress after four decades as the minority did not run for reelection as Speaker. The Democrats, meanwhile, unanimously reelected their top leader in the Senate and House.

The House adopted several rules changes, the most notable of which relaxed restrictions on the acceptance of gifts.

SENATE

The status quo was largely maintained in the Senate Republican and Democratic leadership.

Majority Leadership

Republicans picked their leaders Dec. 1, 1998. Trent Lott of Mississippi was reelected majority leader; Don Nickles of Oklahoma, majority whip. Also reelected was Connie Mack of Florida as Republican Conference chairman and Paul Coverdell of Georgia as Republican Conference secretary. North Carolina senator Strom Thurmond remained as president pro tempore.

Minority Leadership

On Dec. 1, 1998, Democrats by acclamation reelected Tom Daschle of South Dakota as minority leader. Harry Reid of Nevada ran unopposed for minority whip. Barbara A. Mikulski of Maryland remained as Democratic Conference secretary.

Committees

John Warner of Virginia succeeded Strom Thurmond of South Carolina as chairman of the Armed Services Committee. Warner was succeeded by Mitch McConnell of Kentucky as chairman of the Rules and Administration Committee. Phil Gramm of Texas succeeded Alfonse M. D'Amato of New York as Banking, Housing and Urban Affairs Committee chairman. D'Amato lost his Senate reelection bid.

Jeff Bingaman of New Mexico became ranking member of the Energy and Natural Resources Committee, succeeding Dale Bumpers of Arkansas, who retired from the Senate. Joseph I. Lieberman of Connecticut succeeded John Glenn of Ohio as ranking member of Governmental Affairs. Glenn did not run for reelection in 1998. Christopher J. Dodd of Connecticut became ranking member of Rules and Administration, succeeding Wendell H. Ford of Kentucky, who retired from the Senate.

HOUSE

The biggest shakeup in the House organization took place at the highest echelon of the GOP leadership, as members got a new Speaker. The Democrats hung on to their top leaders and made some changes further down the leadership ladder.

Majority Leadership

In party leadership elections Nov. 18, 1998, Republicans opted to entrust their fragile majority to Robert L. Livingston of Louisiana, who forced out Newt Gingrich of Georgia, as Speaker. (However, Livingston on Dec. 19 announced that he would not run for Speaker and would resign from the House. J. Dennis Hastert of Illinois was elected Speaker 220–205 on Jan. 6, 1999.) *(Background, p. 757)*

It took Dick Armey of Texas three ballots to beat back Steve Largent of Oklahoma and Jennifer Dunn of Washington for the majority leader post. On the first ballot, Armey got 100 votes; Largent, 58; Dunn, 45; and Hastert, 18. On the second ballot, Armey got 99 votes; Largent, 73; and Dunn, 49. On the final ballot, Armey received 127 to Largent's 95. The third-ranking House Republican, Tom DeLay of Texas, was unopposed for another term as majority whip. But the party's yearning for a new, softer image cost John A. Boehner of Ohio his leadership post. He was upended by J. C. Watts of Oklahoma for chairmanship of the GOP Conference by a vote of 121–93. The winds of change also removed John Linder of Georgia as chairman of the National Republican Congressional Committee. He lost to Thomas M. Davis III of Virginia, 77 to 130. Christopher Cox of California was reelected chairman of the Policy Committee.

Minority Leadership

Richard A. Gephardt of Missouri was unanimously reelected as minority leader by the Democrats. David E. Bonior of Michigan ran unopposed and was reelected as minority whip. Vic Fazio of California, who retired from the House, was succeeded by Martin Frost of Texas as Democratic Caucus chairman. Frost beat out Rosa DeLauro of Connecticut for the post, 108–97. Two ballots were necessary

---

HOUSE AUDIT

On Sept. 24, 1999, Speaker J. Dennis Hastert, R-Ill., and Administration Committee Chairman Bill Thomas, R-Calif., released the results of a PricewaterhouseCoopers audit for 1998 that contained an "unqualified opinion" of the House's bookkeeping, the auditing equivalent of a clean bill of health. The auditors found "no instances of non-compliance" with laws and regulations. The results stood in sharp contrast to the first outside, professional audit of the House, undertaken in 1995. (*Earlier audit, Congress and the Nation Vol. IX, p. 889*)

The results of the audit meant that the accounting firm was able to verify that the chamber's books balance, with money clearly tracked from one account to the next and with a system of accountability for financial decisions. The report listed five remaining internal control weaknesses, including an obsolete payroll system, poor control over computers and data, and poor tracking of food and services.

---

to fill the vacant Democratic Caucus vice chairman slot. On the first ballot, Robert Menendez of New Jersey received 92 votes; Cal Dooley of California, 65; and Albert R. Wynn of Maryland, 50. On the second ballot, Menendez defeated Dooley, 124–81. Barbara B. Kennelly of Connecticut, who had held the post, retired at the end of the 105th Congress.

Committees

Larry Combest of Texas succeeded Bob Smith of Oregon as chairman of the Agriculture Committee. Smith did not run for reelection in 1998. C. W. Bill Young of Florida took over the helm at Appropriations from Robert L. Livingston of Louisiana. Before the 106th Congress convened, Livingston announced his intention to resign his seat. David Dreier of California succeeded Gerald B. H. Solomon of New York as chairman of the Rules Committee. Solomon retired from the House. Lamar Smith of Texas succeeded James V. Hansen of Utah as head of the Standards of Official Conduct Committee.

Ike Skelton of Missouri became ranking member of the Armed Services Committee. In the 105th Congress the ranking member of the committee, which was called National Security, was Ronald V. Dellums of California. John J. LaFalce of New York succeeded Henry B. Gonzalez of Texas as ranking member of the Banking and Financial Services Committee. Gonzalez did not run for reelection in 1998. Nydia M. Valázquez of New York succeeded LaFalce as ranking member of the Small Business Committee. Steny H. Hoyer of Maryland became ranking member of the House Administration Committee. In the 105th Congress the ranking member of the committee, which was called House Oversight, was Sam Gejdenson of Connecticut. Gejdenson became ranking

member of International Relations, succeeding Lee H. Hamilton of Indiana, who retired from Congress. Julian C. Dixon of California succeeded Norm Dicks of Washington as ranking member of Select Intelligence.

Rules

By voice vote Jan. 6, 1999, the House adopted a resolution (H Res 9) that changed the nearly outright ban on representatives accepting gifts from anyone other than a family member or personal friend. The rule changes thus matched the House gift restrictions to those of the Senate.

As adopted by the House, lawmakers and aides may take noncash gifts worth less than $50, but presents from any one source may not have a combined value above $100 a year. Unchanged was the rule that allowed private organizations to pay the travel expenses of lawmakers and aides for speeches, meetings, or fact-finding trips related to their states.

By 217–204 on Jan. 6, the House adopted a measure (H Res 5) making the rest of the GOP rules changes. They included allowing committees to add a sixth subcommittee if one deals with oversight; permitting certain House employees to receive honoraria; extending the life of the Government Reform Committee's Census Subcommittee and the select committee on technology transfers to China; and allowing the Budget Committee chairman to establish multiyear spending allocations as if Congress had enacted a fiscal 1999 budget resolution.

The GOP rules changes also renamed three committees. Government Reform and Oversight became Government Reform; House Oversight reclaimed its former name of House Administration; and National Security reverted to its longtime name of Armed Services. Furthermore, absent members no longer could stipulate how they would have voted by arranging to be "paired" with an absentee on the opposite side of the issue. Such pairs were announced by the clerk of the House and noted in the *Congressional Record*.

The House rejected a Democratic move to rewrite the rules to, among other things, guarantee that the minority receive more seats on House committees.

Ethics Probes

Numerous members of the 106th Congress were investigated for alleged ethical misconduct.

SEN. BEN NIGHTHORSE CAMPBELL

The Senate Select Committee on Ethics on Nov. 5, 1999, notified the Citizens Progressive Alliance that it had dismissed the group's complaint against Ben Nighthorse Campbell, R-Colo., on technical grounds. It nonetheless criticized Campbell for creating the appearance of a conflict of interest by sponsoring a bill (S 2142) that would have benefited him and his wife financially.

The legislation would have transferred the federally owned Vallecito Reservoir and Dam to the privately owned

Pine River Irrigation District. The Campbells owned 110 of 18,000 shares in the district. Campbell's original bill put a $492,000 price on the Vallecito complex. But when the Senate passed it by voice vote Oct. 7, 1998, there was no money involved. The House never acted on the bill.

Senate rules prohibit a senator from sponsoring or aiding legislation whose principal purpose was to benefit that senator, his or her immediate family, or a "limited class" of people. Although there were only 1,100 landowners potentially affected by Campbell's bill, they could not be considered a "limited class," the committee's letter to the citizens' group said.

SEN. MAX BAUCUS

Christine M. Niedermeier, former chief of staff to Sen. Max Baucus, D-Mont., on Oct. 18, 2000, filed a lawsuit claiming employment discrimination. In the complaint, Niedermeier alleged that Baucus had retaliated against her by thwarting her efforts to find a job since she had filed a sexual harassment complaint. The suit sought $300,000 in damages because Niedermeier's "personal life, her financial security and her professional career have been devastated."

Niedermeier's original complaint, released Sept. 23, 1999, and filed with the congressional Office of Compliance, alleged that the senator had engaged in a "continuous course of conduct of sexual harassment" and had fired her when she complained. However, Niedermeier declined to follow up her complaint, lodged under the Congressional Accountability Act (PL 104-1), with a lawsuit. (*Workplace compliance law, Congress and the Nation Vol. IX, p. 890*)

Baucus said he had not harassed Niedermeier "in any way" and had dismissed her "because she abused my staff, abused my constituents, and abused other people she dealt with on the job." Baucus's spokesperson called Niedermeier's charge that Baucus and his staff had sought to "blackball" her efforts to find a job "completely and absolutely 100 percent false."

SEN. JOHN MCCAIN

The National Smokers Alliance on June 22, 1999, filed a complaint with the Senate Ethics Committee against Sen. John McCain, R-Ariz., alleging misuse of the franking privilege. McCain, who unsuccessfully sought the 2000 Republican presidential nomination, allegedly sent a letter to GOP voters in a number of early-primary states regarding antitobacco legislation (S 1415) that he had sponsored. The alliance worked against restrictions on smoking in public places.

McCain's office said the letter was a response to queries sent to the senator.

REP. BUD SHUSTER

The House Committee on Standards of Official Conduct Oct. 4, 2000, concluded a three-year investigation of Bud Shuster, R-Pa., with a formal letter of reproval saying that the representative had "engaged in serious official misconduct" and "committed substantial violations" of House rules. The panel also faulted Shuster for improperly accepting gifts and for spending campaign contributions on travel and meals at fancy restaurants. The rebuke was approved unanimously by the committee and did not require action by the full House.

The panel launched its probe in November 1997 in response to a complaint filed by the Congressional Accountability Project. The original complaint focused on Shuster's relationship with Ann Eppard, who served as Shuster's chief of staff for twenty-two years and later became a transportation lobbyist representing clients with business before the House Transportation and Infrastructure Committee, which Shuster chaired. House rules prohibit staff members from lobbying their former bosses for one year after leaving.

During the course of the investigation, the committee issued more than 150 subpoenas, interviewed approximately seventy-five people, and deposed thirty-three witnesses. It eventually expanded its probe into Shuster's campaign committee. The ethics panel ruled that Shuster violated House rules by:

- "Engaging in a pattern and practice" of contact with Eppard in an official capacity during the twelve months following her resignation from his office. Shuster's interaction with Eppard "created the appearance that your official decisions might have been improperly affected," the committee said.

- Accepting lodging for himself and his family during a trip to Puerto Rico. "The American people should not be made to question whether, through gifts or favors, the public interest has been subordinated to those with business before the House," the panel said.

- Accepting scheduling and advisory services from Eppard on official matters for eighteen months after she left Shuster's office.

- Allowing congressional employees to work for Shuster's political campaign committee while in his congressional office "to the apparent detriment of the time they were required to spend" on congressional business.

- Spending hundreds of thousands of dollars in campaign contributions between 1993 and 1998 that "may not have been attributable to bona fide campaign or political purposes." The panel said Shuster could not prove the expenses were campaign-related.

In accepting the committee's decision, Shuster admitted that his actions created "the appearance of impropriety," and he waived the right to separate hearings on the charges and the penalty. But in an Oct. 5 speech on the House floor after the committee released its findings, Shuster defended his behavior and said he accepted the negotiated settlement to "stop the hemorrhaging of legal fees" and to "put this behind us."

Shuster submitted a thirty-page response to the committee's findings, describing the settlement as a "negotiated armistice" and called the letter of reproval "overkill for the charge of causing misguided public perceptions . . . contrary to the objective truth." Shuster said he "complied with the law, and with his understanding of what was right." He also said "there is not a single instance" when he "took legislative action to benefit private interests instead of the public good." The committee attacked Shuster's declarations of innocence, saying his written response was "rife with patently inaccurate and misleading statements." The panel said it was "disturbed not only by the content of your response but by its tone. It is one of blame-shifting about and trivialization of misconduct to which you have admitted and which this Committee does not and can not characterize as *de minimis* or technical, either in whole or in part."

The ethics committee had suspended its investigation in 1998 while the Justice Department conducted a criminal probe of related allegations. Eppard on April 9, 1998, was indicted along with transportation lobbyist Vernon A. Clark by a federal grand jury in Boston on seven counts of public corruption. Included were felony charges that Eppard accepted $230,000 in illegal gratuities from Clark in exchange for assisting two of Clark's clients in their effort to stop federal eminent domain proceedings against property that was to be used in the "Big Dig," a massive road and tunnel project in Boston. It was widely reported that the grand jury was also looking at whether Shuster helped property owners get better deals for land required for the road project in return for campaign donations.

Federal prosecutors ended their investigation Nov. 1, 1996, when Eppard pleaded guilty to a single federal misdemeanor charge that she took $15,000 in cash and a $30,000 interest-free loan from Clark as compensation for helping two of Clark's clients while she was a congressional employee. She was fined $5,000. The prospect that Eppard could be convicted on more serious charges faded after the Supreme Court in April 1999 raised the standard for proving a crime had been committed when a gratuity was given to a public official. Clark pleaded guilty to a misdemeanor for giving Eppard the illegal payments and to a second charge of filing false tax statements with the Internal Revenue Service. He was fined $10,000. *(Gratuities law ruling, box, p. 792)*

After the Eppard case ended, House ethics committee investigators decided they needed to review Shuster's 1995 and 1996 calendars to complete their probe. On Feb. 17, 2000, the panel sent Shuster a letter requesting unredacted copies of the two calendars. (Shuster previously had sent the committee the calendars after redacting portions. His attorneys claimed the redacted sections were protected from committee inspection because they dealt with national security concerns, personal issues, or attorney-client privilege.) Shuster's lawyers advised him not to comply with the request unless he was given "act of production immunity."

The ethics committee unanimously agreed to provide the requested immunity on March 15, and on March 17 the U.S. District Court for the District of Columbia granted the request. According to the committee, the Justice Department did not object. The "act of production immunity" is limited to evidence prosecutors could not have found without the redacted portions of the calendars, a distinction that leaves open the potential for criminal prosecution if evidence of wrongdoing found in the calendar can also be found elsewhere, experts said.

Shuster's case was believed to be the first time a sitting member of Congress received immunity from the ethics committee. Despite its precedent-setting nature, the limited type of immunity granted and the apparent lack of significant information the evidence provided could make the immunity of little practical consequence. (The findings in the committee's report were backed by 125 citations to documentary evidence collected during the investigation, but the calendars accounted for only five of those citations. Three of the five related to the committee finding that was of no legal consequence at all—that Shuster "created the appearance that your official decisions might have been improperly affected.") Furthermore, as of the end of 2000, it remained unclear whether federal prosecutors, who previously declined to prosecute Shuster, would attempt to pursue criminal charges.

Legal experts said that of the five violations of House rules outlined by the ethics committee, three also might be considered violations of federal law. But the calendars provided only a small portion of the evidence against Shuster in one of those three and none in the other two. The calendars figured most prominently in the panel's finding that Shuster engaged in significant contact with Eppard after she left his staff. Shuster could face criminal charges that through this contact he aided or abetted Eppard. In addition, the panel charged, "While under your supervision and control, employees of your congressional office performed services for your campaign in your congressional office." According to one ethics source, that could lead to a criminal charge that Shuster "misused" money appropriated to his congressional office. The committee also found that Shuster violated House gift rules by accepting a trip to Puerto Rico for him and his family from a lobbyist. A legal expert said the trip could be grounds for a criminal charge of accepting a bribe if it were determined that Shuster helped those who paid for the trip, although the committee offered no such conclusion. The calendars were not cited in either of the use of office staff for campaign purposes or the Puerto Rico trip.

The calendars were cited by the committee to criticize Shuster for allowing Eppard to act as a member of his staff after she had resigned. But legal experts said such activity would not be the basis for criminal charges.

Shuster, citing health reasons, resigned his seat on Feb. 2, 2001. His son, Bill Shuster, R-Pa., was elected May 15, 2001, to succeed him.

REP. EARL F. HILLIARD

The House Committee on Standards of Official Conduct announced Sept. 23, 1999, that it was opening an investigation into the use of campaign funds since 1992 by Rep. Earl F. Hilliard, D-Ala., and some investments that he had failed to list in his annual House financial disclosure reports.

The probe was in response to questions raised by *The Hill*, a weekly newspaper, which reported in 1997 that Hilliard's campaign committee paid more than $100,000 to companies and nonprofit organizations linked to Hilliard, many of which shared the address of his campaign headquarters in Birmingham. Federal election law permits campaigns to contract with companies owned by the candidate, so long as the goods or services relate to campaign activities and are sold at market value. *The Hill* suggested that some of the Hilliard campaign's money might have been used for non-campaign purposes. *(Hilliard 1997–1998 investigation, p. 765)*

An investigative subcommittee of the ethics panel was to look at the occupancy of office space in Birmingham by Hilliard's campaign from 1992 to 1998, including money spent for rent and utilities; several loans made by the campaign committee; and Hilliard's compliance with financial disclosure requirements regarding his ownership of Hilliards & Co. Inc. and Birmingham Greater Golf Associates Inc. A Hilliard spokeswoman said that the campaign made loans to several people who worked for it but that there was nothing amiss about them. She said one loan was repaid but two were not. And she said Hilliard did not initially disclose his interest in the two companies because they had neither assets nor value. He later amended his reports to mention both concerns.

REP. CORRINE BROWN

The House ethics committee Sept. 20, 2000, wrapped up its investigation of Corrine Brown, D-Fla., saying it could not find sufficient evidence to prove improper conduct but concluding that her dealings with wealthy west African businessman Fountanga Dit Babani Sissoko "raised concerns" and "demonstrated, at the least, poor judgment." *(1997–1998 action, p. 765)*

The committee launched its probe on June 9, 1999, after the *St. Petersburg Times* reported that Sissoko provided Brown free lodging in his luxury Miami condominium and that Sissoko's chief financial officer gave Brown's daughter a $50,000 Lexus automobile. The newspaper reported that the automobile was given to Brown's daughter just weeks after the lawmaker aggressively lobbied the Clinton administration to have Sissoko released from a U.S. prison where he was serving time in a bribery case.

In a written statement, the committee said the dearth of evidence against Brown "was due in large part to the fact that key witnesses who had actual knowledge of the events . . . were beyond the reach of the committee's subpoena power and could not be compelled to give testimony." (Sissoko and his financial officer were in Africa, where they were not subject to U.S. subpoenas.) The statement added that the committee believed Brown's "actions and associations . . . created substantial concerns regarding both the appearance of impropriety and the reputation of the House of Representatives." Brown denied any wrongdoing.

REP. TOM DELAY

In a May 1999 letter, the House Committee on Standards of Official Conduct took Majority Whip Tom DeLay, R-Texas, to task for threatening to punish the Electronic Industries Alliance for hiring as its president former representative Dave McCurdy (D-Okla., 1981–1995). The committee cited House rules that prohibited lawmakers from using their offices to take punitive action for partisan reasons.

House leaders, including DeLay, had postponed for one day a vote on an international treaty, which was opposed by some members of the alliance, to show displeasure with the selection of McCurdy for a job they felt should go to a Republican. The committee did not explain why it singled out DeLay. He might have been targeted because of his reputation for using bare-knuckled tactics to persuade Washington business interests not only to support Republicans but also to withhold money and support from Democrats.

The panel on May 11 also issued an advisory opinion to all members addressing the matter. It said that members and staff "are prohibited from taking or withholding any official action on the basis of the partisan affiliation of the campaign contributors or support of the involved individuals. House members and staff are likewise prohibited from threatening punitive action on the basis of such considerations."

DeLay in 1999 was called to account for testimony he gave under oath while defending himself in a civil lawsuit. The suit was brought by Robert Blankenship, a former business partner who accused DeLay of fraud in the operations of Albo Pest Control Co., which they had co-owned. In a 1994 deposition, DeLay testified that he was not chairman of the firm and had not held that title for two or three years. But on his annual financial disclosure reports to the House from 1991 through 1994, he said he was the concern's chairman. After being pressed by Blankenship's lawyer, DeLay said he was unsure whether he had ever formally resigned as chairman.

According to copies of his deposition, DeLay also testified that he had no other income aside from his congressional salary and some stock in Exxon. But on his disclosure reports, he said his income from Albo was between $5,000 and $15,000 in both 1992 and 1993.

In a private meeting of House deputy whips March 3, 1999, DeLay said the allegations were part of a plot by his political enemies to discredit him. In a public statement March 4, DeLay said that during his deposition he could not remember what position he held at Albo.

The suit, heard in state court in Texas, was settled in 1995. The terms were sealed by mutual agreement.

On May 3, 2000, the Democratic Congressional Campaign Committee (DCCC) filed a civil suit accusing DeLay of establishing a web of nonprofit organizations to evade federal disclosure laws and extorting campaign contributions from lobbyists. The DCCC suit, filed under the Racketeer Influenced and Corrupt Organizations Act (PL 91-452), alleged that DeLay funneled money through three nonprofit groups—the U.S. Family Network, the Republican Majority Issues Committee, and Americans for Economic Growth—to avoid scrutiny. DeLay denied the charges. *(1997–1998 action, p. 764)*

REP. JIM MCDERMOTT

The U.S. Circuit Court of Appeals for the District of Columbia Sept. 24, 1999, voted 2–1 to reinstate a lawsuit in which Rep. John A. Boehner, R-Ohio, alleged that his right to privacy was violated when Rep. Jim McDermott, D-Wash., disclosed a 1996 telephone conversation among GOP leaders, an alleged violation of federal laws. A trial judge had said that McDermott had a First Amendment right to release the tape, which pertained to an ethics investigation of House Speaker Newt Gingrich, R-Ga. The circuit court said McDermott's actions were not a form of speech and thus were not protected. *(1997–1998 action, p. 765; Gingrich reprimand, p. 761)*

REP. JAMES A. TRAFICANT JR.

In December 1999 the U.S. Attorney's Office from the Northern District of Ohio issued three subpoenas to the House's general counsel asking for phone records, payroll records, and rental documents for the office of Rep. James A. Traficant Jr., D-Ohio. Several boxes of documents were handed over to investigators Jan. 6, 2000.

The subpoenas were part of a long-running probe into organized crime in Youngstown, Ohio, which was in Traficant's district. The investigation had resulted in dozens of convictions, including one against Traficant's former district director, Charles O'Nesti. O'Nesti, who had worked with Traficant since he first came to Congress in 1985, pleaded guilty in March 1998 to perjury and racketeering charges.

Traficant denied any knowledge of wrongdoing by O'Nesti and any illegal activity of his own. On Jan. 28, 2000, Traficant issued a biting statement attacking the Justice Department and charging that the investigation might be motivated by revenge. (In 1982, while he was serving as the Mahoning County sheriff, Traficant was indicted for taking bribes from organized crime bosses. Acting as his own attorney, he defended himself and was acquitted.)

REP. BOB BARR

The Federal Election Commission (FEC) on Aug. 27, 1999, announced that Rep. Bob Barr, R-Ga., was fined $28,055 for campaign finance violations during his 1994 and 1996 reelection campaigns.

An FEC audit found that Barr's campaign committee accepted contributions in excess of the federal limit and failed to list the names of contributors who gave at least $200 cash. The 1994 campaign understated receipts and expenditures on one report, and his 1996 campaign did not file the special reports disclosing big donations just before election day.

FORMER MEMBERS

Newt Gingrich

It was announced on Feb. 3, 1999, that the Internal Revenue Service (IRS) had cleared organizations affiliated with Rep. Newt Gingrich, R-Ga. (1979–1999) that were alleged to have circumvented tax law to broadcast a politically oriented college course in the early 1990s.

Before he was elected Speaker in 1995, Gingrich used tax-exempt groups to finance the course—called Renewing American Civilization—raising questions about whether the groups violated their tax-exempt status by engaging in partisan politics. The House Committee on Standards of Official Conduct deferred on that issue to the IRS in 1997 without a conclusion. But in an agreement with the panel, Gingrich admitted he lied to the committee during its probe and that he failed to seek good legal advice when he used the foundations as part of an overarching GOP strategy to gain control of the House. *(Gingrich reprimand, p. 761)*

The IRS, in notices to three of the tax-exempt organizations (the Washington-based think tank Progress and Freedom Foundation and two Georgia schools—Kennesaw State College and Reinhardt College), concluded that the content of the course was educational and "never favored or opposed a candidate for public office." James M. Cole, special counsel in the Gingrich ethics probe, said he still believed the course was designed to boost Gingrich's efforts to elect more Republicans to public office. And, he said, "when you look at what the ethics committee found and what Mr. Gingrich himself agreed was misconduct, nothing in the IRS opinion affects that."

Senate Ethics Process

The Senate by voice vote Nov. 5, 1999, adopted a resolution (S Res 222) to streamline its process for investigating allegations of misconduct by senators. The most important change limited the ranges of punishment that could be imposed on a senator. In descending order of severity, they were: expulsion, censure, referral to a party conference for possible loss of seniority or a position of responsibility, and a fine or restitution.

The committee could issue a letter of admonishment, though the new rule made it clear that the Senate did not consider this a form of discipline. The panel would no longer use the terms "denouncement" or "condemnation," which the Senate historian's office long considered to be the same as censure.

In cases in which a majority of the Ethics Committee did not believe action by the full Senate was warranted, the panel could reprimand a senator, even without the senator's consent. Under the old rules, the senator had to agree to be reprimanded.

The new rules also simplified the investigative process. The chairman and ranking minority member of the panel would direct a preliminary inquiry in all cases. If they found "substantial credible evidence" of wrongdoing, the panel would open a more thorough "adjudicative review" to take evidence and propose a punishment, and an outside counsel would generally be hired.

The rules retained the right of people or groups outside the Senate to file ethical complaints.

House Chaplain

Speaker J. Dennis Hastert, R-Ill., on March 23, 2000, appointed the Rev. Daniel P. Coughlin, a vicar with the Archdiocese of Chicago, as House chaplain. Coughlin became the first Roman Catholic to serve as chaplain in the history of the House. The chaplain, a little-known House official whose confirmation was usually routine, opened the House's daily sessions with a prayer and counseled members and their families.

James D. Ford, a Lutheran who held the job since 1979, announced in early 1999 that he planned to resign in 2000. In May 1999 Hastert and Minority Leader Richard A. Gephardt, R-Mo., appointed an eighteen-member search committee, evenly split between Democrats and Republicans. In the fall, committee members interviewed numerous applicants and eventually voted on six finalists, choosing their top three. The Rev. Timothy O'Brien, a Roman Catholic priest, received the greatest support (14 votes), followed by the Rev. Bob Dvorak, regional director of the Evangelical Covenant Church, who received the second highest number of votes, followed by the Rev. Charles Parker Wright, a Presbyterian.

The committee did not rank the candidates when it forwarded their names to Hastert, Gephardt, and Majority Leader Dick Armey, R-Texas. However, Democratic members of the selection committee said that the leaders were aware of the overwhelming support for O'Brien. In November GOP leaders selected Wright. Democrats promptly accused the Republican leaders of anti-Catholic bias. GOP leaders said merit—not religion—was the ultimate factor in selecting Wright over O'Brien. They charged that Democrats had turned the issue into a partisan witch-hunt.

Republicans were reluctant to schedule a floor vote to confirm Wright, fearing it would provide Democrats a platform to launch political attacks against them. A spokesperson for Armey said a vote would not be held until Democrats invited Wright to speak at their weekly party caucus. But Gephardt refused to invite Wright, saying the selection process was unfair and a meeting with Wright would do little to quell Democrats' concerns.

Coughlin was first interviewed for the position in mid-March 2000 and met Hastert for the first time March 20. The announcement of Coughlin's appointment came one day after Wright withdrew his name from consideration. Coughlin's selection did not need a floor vote, because Hastert appointed him under a House rule that allowed him to fill a chaplain vacancy unilaterally until the end of the year. Ford officially resigned March 23. The full House would have to vote on Coughlin when it convened a new session in 2001.

Immediately after Hastert appointed Coughlin, Democrats introduced a resolution (H Res 447) to revamp how the position was filled. The proposal, by Earl Pomeroy, D-N.D., and Cal Dooley, D-Calif., would require the Speaker, minority leader, and majority leader to approve the chaplain unanimously. The House took no action on the measure.

POGO Contempt of Congress

The House Resources Committee July 19, 2000, approved a contempt of Congress resolution (H Res 657) citing Project on Government Oversight (POGO) officials for refusing to cooperate with the panel's probe into the group's ties with government officials. Lacking sufficient support, committee Republicans pulled the measure from floor consideration Oct. 27.

POGO's troubles dated to 1998, when the group made payments of $383,600 to Interior Department employee Robert A. Berman and to retired Energy Department employee Robert A. Speir after receiving $1.2 million in a whistleblower suit against Mobil Oil. The company settled with the Justice Department for $45 million in a case involving royalty underpayments.

Passage of a contempt citation would send the charges to the U.S. attorney, who would convene a grand jury to decide whether to seek an indictment.

Chronology of Action on Congress: Election Issues

1997–1998

The unprecedented levels of campaign spending during the 1996 election cycle, as well as allegations of fund-raising abuses, gave hope to campaign finance reform advocates in 1997–1998 that Congress would pass a sweeping overhaul of the existing campaign finance system. However, partisan debate halted campaign finance legislation. Partisanship also tainted investigations by the Senate and House into 1996 fund-raising practices.

Support for term limits for members of Congress—a key plank in the House Republicans' agenda-setting 1995 "Contract with America"—had been waning. A proposed constitutional amendment failed in the House to garner the two-thirds majority vote it needed to pass.

Campaign Finance

The House Aug. 6, 1998, by 252–179 passed a campaign finance reform bill (HR 2183). The measure died upon adjournment. The 106th Congress also failed to enact a broad overhaul of the campaign finance system. *(1999–2000 action, p. 788)*

The legislation would ban national parties from receiving or spending soft money, the unlimited and largely unregulated donations to political parties. State and local parties would no longer be able to use soft money for federal election activity. And new restrictions would be placed on campaign-related expenditures by third-party groups.

BACKGROUND

The House and Senate struggled since 1980 to overhaul the campaign finance system put in place after the Watergate scandal in 1974 (PL 93-433). Both chambers passed versions of a campaign finance bill in 1993, but the Democratic majority allowed it to languish until the final days of the 103rd Congress, when Senate Republicans used a filibuster to block a conference with the House. GOP and Democratic leaders—including President Bill Clinton and House Speaker Newt Gingrich, R-Ga.—repeatedly promised action on campaign finance reform in 1995 but made little effort to deliver, leaving it to rank-and-file members to push the issue. House and Senate committees took no action, but House Republicans appointed a task force to study the matter. In 1996 a bipartisan bill that included voluntary spending limits and a ban on contributions by political action committees (PACs) was stopped by a filibuster in the Senate, while the House defeated both a GOP bill to impose new contribution limits and a Democratic alternative. *(Earlier action, Congress and the Nation Vol. IV, p. 991; Congress and the Nation Vol. V, pp. 943, 947; Congress and the Nation Vol. VII, pp. 892, 894; Congress and the Nation Vol. VIII, pp. 951, 959; Congress and the Nation Vol. IX, pp. 909, 914)*

Investigations in both chambers in 1997 revealed campaign finance abuses by both parties as well as the ineffectiveness of the existing restrictions. The parties' unprecedented use in the 1996 election cycle of more than $263 million in largely unregulated donations from corporations, unions, and wealthy individuals made soft money the leading issue in the ensuing debate. Soft money was supposed to be used for party-building efforts such as get-out-the-vote and voter registration drives, but it was often spent on thinly veiled campaign activities. The U.S. Supreme Court opened the door for the broader use of soft money with a June 1996 ruling in *Colorado Republican Federal Campaign Committee v. Federal Election Commission* that parties could spend an unlimited amount to promote their positions on issues as long as they did not coordinate that activity directly with candidates. *(Campaign finance probes, box, p. 778; court ruling, Congress and the Nation Vol. IX, pp. 782, 915)*

1997 ACTION

The Senate Rules and Administration Committee, which has jurisdiction over campaign finance, did not act on campaign finance legislation in 1997. However, the Senate Governmental Affairs Committee, chaired by Fred Thompson, R-Tenn., held a series of hearings between July and October that established the parties' pursuit and use of soft money as the leading campaign finance issue. In an effort to build pressure on his colleagues to take up campaign reform legislation, Thompson abruptly shifted the course of the hearings in late September away from specific abuses to what was wrong with the existing system and how to fix it. The panel heard repeated calls for banning soft money.

Majority Leader Trent Lott, R-Miss., who strongly opposed the leading campaign finance bill (S 25) sponsored by John McCain, R-Ariz., and Russell D. Feingold, D-Wis., kept the measure off the floor for most of the year. During the fall, however, supporters used threats and delaying tactics to force Lott to bring up the bill.

To maximize GOP support for the bill, McCain and Feingold decided to scale it back. Three key elements were central to the revised bill. First, it proposed to ban contributions of soft money. Second, it would require labor unions to notify nonunion members that they could seek refunds of dues used to make political contributions. Third, it attempted to place some conditions on the use of so-called issue advocacy television commercials. Because the ads ostensibly focused on issues, they were not covered by federal election laws, even though they often implicitly supported individual candidates. The bill addressed this complex issue by proposing to modify the statutory definition of what was termed "express advocacy," drawing what McCain said would be a "bright line" between expenditures on ads promoting issues and those promoting candidates.

S 25 also included provisions to require more public disclosure of contributions and expenditures and to impose tougher penalties on violators. And it proposed to bar political parties from making "coordinated expenditures" in behalf of Senate candidates who did not agree to limit their personal spending on their campaigns to $50,000 per election. Dropped from the original bill were provisions that would impose lower limits on PAC contributions, provide bargain-rate television time for candidates who accepted voluntary spending limits, and set voluntary campaign spending limits to restrict both total spending by a campaign and personal spending by a candidate.

An initial deal in mid-September to bring up the bill collapsed amid angry charges by Minority Leader Tom Daschle, D-S.D., that Republicans were trying to blindside Democrats. After Clinton upped the ante Sept. 23, threatening to call Congress into special session if leaders adjourned without allowing a vote, Lott agreed to bring up the bill. But Lott was able to use his power as majority leader to erect a formidable series of procedural roadblocks. He opened a debate on the bill Sept. 26, after springing the news on McCain just the day before. Then, on Sept. 29, Lott changed the dynamics by offering an amendment that would force unions to seek prior consent from workers before using their dues to make political donations or conduct political education campaigns. The effect would be to force unions to scale back their political activities dramatically. The amendment, dubbed the "Paycheck Protection Act" by Republicans, offered Lott an opportunity to pursue two key political objec-

tives: targeting political activity by labor unions, which had donated millions of dollars to Democratic congressional campaigns in 1996, and, presuming the amendment was adopted, forcing Democrats to scuttle McCain-Feingold instead of seeing the restriction enacted.

Lott used his power to block any changes to his amendment by "filling up the amendment tree," a time-honored procedure under which Senate leaders foreclosed all the procedural possibilities for amendments with slightly different versions of their own proposal. Precluded from amending Lott's amendment, McCain and Feingold needed 50 votes to table (kill) it, assuming that Vice President Al Gore would cast the fifty-first and deciding vote. But Democrats had just 49 presumably solid votes, which left them with few options other than to filibuster.

Republicans Olympia J. Snowe of Maine and James M. Jeffords of Vermont tried unsuccessfully to broker a compromise that would expand Lott's union proposal to cover advocacy groups such as the National Rifle Association and the Sierra Club. Daschle told Snowe that Democrats would not agree to support the deal.

The struggle came down to a pair of procedural votes on Oct. 7. The first was a motion to invoke cloture on Lott's union dues amendment, thereby limiting debate and allowing an up-or-down roll-call vote. In the 52–48 tally, Republicans fell eight votes short of the 60 they needed to stop a Democratic filibuster. The second vote was on limiting debate on the underlying bill. This time, Democrats fell seven votes short of the 60 needed for cloture. The **key vote was 53–47 (R 8–47; D 45–0).** Daschle forced more votes during the next two days, with the same results. On Oct. 8, the Senate rejected a motion to invoke cloture on the bill, 58–47. On Oct. 9, it rejected by a 52–47 vote another cloture motion on the bill, and by a 51–48 vote a cloture motion on an amendment to require labor organizations, banks, or corporations to secure voluntary authorization from their members before using any membership dues, initiation fees, or other payments to fund political activities. *(1997 key votes, p. 865)*

The October showdown did not end the Senate's campaign finance debate. Democrats renewed their pressure on Lott to set a date for considering S 25 early in 1998 under procedures that would assure an up-or-down vote. The Democrats filibustered a massive six-year transportation bill, defeating four attempts to invoke cloture and prompting Lott to abandon the bill until the following year. Democrats also threatened to block all other legislation except appropriations bills. On Oct. 30, under a carefully crafted agreement, Lott promised to bring campaign finance legislation back to the Senate floor no later than March 6, 1998. *(Transportation bill, p. 318)*

The House Government Reform and Oversight Committee, while faltering in its efforts to mount hearings parallel to the Senate Governmental Affairs Committee's probe, heard testimony from lawmakers on campaign finance overhaul proposals. Chairman Bill Thomas, R-Calif., said he wanted to wait until 1998 for legislative action and suggested that

SENATE AND HOUSE CAMPAIGN FINANCE PROBES: COST MUCH BUT PRODUCED LITTLE

Senate and House Republicans opened investigations in 1997 excited about the prospect of showcasing what they saw as egregious abuses of campaign finance laws by Democrats during the 1996 elections. Many instances of fund-raising excesses were found, but no smoking gun emerged.

Senate Investigation

The Senate Governmental Affairs Committee, chaired by Fred Thompson, R-Tenn., held thirty-two hearings between July and October 1997 into the fund-raising charges. Committee Republican and Democratic senators on March 5, 1998, issued separate reports. The majority report blamed President Bill Clinton, his allies, and the Democratic National Committee (DNC) for widespread fund-raising abuses. The majority report did not propose any legislative fixes to the current fund-raising system. Its key recommendation was that an independent counsel be appointed to conduct a full-blown criminal probe. The Democratic report condemned questionable practices on both sides, including access-peddling, acceptance of foreign contributions, and the use of outside groups and nonprofit organizations to wage what in effect were attack campaigns against political enemies.

Following are some of the key developments from the Senate hearings:

• **John Huang.** Republicans attempted to portray John Huang as a man who used his fund-raising prowess to burrow his way into the federal government in a post at the Commerce Department, from which, they charged, he could have sent sensitive U.S. intelligence data back to his former employers at the Lippo Group, the Indonesian conglomerate with intimate ties to the Chinese government. Democrats countered that Huang was nothing more than a careless fund-raiser who cut corners and often disregarded even the most basic fund-raising rules in his quest to bring Asian Americans to the forefront of U.S. politics. Half of the $3.4 million he raised in 1996 was returned as improper. Democrats scoffed at the espionage charges, insisting that the evidence showed no proof that Huang was a spy.

Republicans also moved to link Huang and the Democrats to illegal foreign funds. Republicans produced a copy of a cancelled check for a $50,000 donation to the DNC in 1992 made by a California-based subsidiary of the Lippo Group that Huang ran. Documents showed that one week after pledging the money, Huang asked his superiors in Indonesia for reimbursement. Federal law permitted political parties to accept contributions from U.S. subsidiaries of foreign corporations, but the money had to be earned on U.S. soil. The DNC returned the $50,000.

• **Charlie Yah din Trie.** Charlie Yah din Trie was a one-time Chinese restaurant owner from Little Rock, Ark., and friend of then-governor Clinton. Lured by the impression that Trie had access to the president, foreign individuals and companies pumped $1.4 million into Trie's bank account. Trie's chief benefactor was Ng Lap Seng, a business associate from Macao, a Portuguese territory near Hong Kong. The hearings showed that Trie used $905,000 from Ng to make donations to the DNC and fuel several business ventures. Trie gave $200,000 to the DNC. The money was also used to reimburse individuals for donations they made at a February 1996 fund-raiser. Making a political contribution in the name of another person was against federal law, as were donations from foreign sources. The DNC returned all of the money donated by Trie as well as $425,000 he raised from others.

Investigators also questioned how Trie raised money for the Presidential Legal Expense Trust, a private fund set up to help the Clintons pay their mounting legal bills. Trie tried on three occasions to give a total of $789,000 to the trust. Most of the money was contributed by hundreds of members of a Taiwan-based Buddhist sect called the Suma Ching Hai Meditation Association. Even though the trust returned the money almost as soon as Trie turned it in, Republicans contended that a White House conspiracy existed to keep the donations secret until after the 1996 election.

• **Haley Barbour.** The hearings offered Democrats few chances to showcase alleged GOP fund-raising abuses, but they got an opportunity to question former Republican National Committee (RNC) Chairman Haley Barbour about his alleged solicitation of foreign money for an RNC think tank called the National Policy Forum (NPF). Barbour created the NPF as a policy-generating arm of the RNC, but by the spring of 1994 it owed the RNC $2.5 million—money the RNC badly needed to bankroll the upcoming congressional elections. To get the money, the NPF turned to wealthy Hong Kong business owner Ambrous Tung Young. The patriarch of Young Brothers Development Co., a multibillion-dollar Asian building and aviation firm, Young agreed to guarantee a $2.1 million loan to the forum. Democrats charged that Barbour, in effect, knowingly solicited foreign money for GOP activities by funneling it through the NPF, which was seeking tax-exempt status and could legally accept such donations when the party could not. Barbour denied all allegations.

• **Vice President Al Gore.** GOP members presented evidence that they said showed Al Gore knew or should have known that a controversial April 1996 luncheon at a Buddhist temple near Los Angeles was actually a political fund-raiser. Gore had consistently denied he knew it was a fund-raiser. Three Buddhist nuns testified that the temple illegally reimbursed its members for $65,000 in political contributions after the luncheon. One nun said she destroyed documents when the controversy over the event first surfaced in the fall of 1996; another nun said she altered checks to protect Gore and the temple. There was no evidence that Gore knew anything about the donation scheme at the temple.

The panel also pursued the question of telephone calls Gore made from his vice-presidential office to solicit campaign donations. Republicans said he knowingly skirted the law when he contacted forty-six donors from his White House office. Five of the contributions Gore raised—a total of $100,000—were kept in the party's hard money account, according to DNC officials. No one disputed that Gore made the calls. What critics disputed was what he knew when he made the calls. Was he raising hard money in possible violation of the law or was he raising unregulated, and possibly legal, soft money? The statute prohibited anyone from asking for or receiving a political contribution "in any room or building occupied in the discharge of official duties." But interpretations of what that meant varied widely.

• **Roger Tamraz.** Sheila Heslin, a former National Security Council official, testified that officials from the CIA, the Department of Energy, and the DNC pressured her to drop her objections to granting White House access to Roger Tamraz, an international oil financier she had determined was "shady and untrustworthy." Heslin said she was told that Tamraz had given the Democrats at least $200,000 and would give double that again if he could meet the president and discuss his proposal for building an oil pipeline across the Caspian Sea. The fact that Tamraz did get access to Clinton and assistance from senior administration officials struck Republicans as evidence that the administration was auctioning off policy decisions. Democrats countered that Tamraz never got administration approval for the pipeline project.

• **Interior Secretary Bruce Babbitt.** Republicans suggested that a group of impoverished Chippewa tribes in Wisconsin was denied permission by the Interior Department to open a casino at an abandoned dog track in Hudson, Wis., because of improper pressure from former White House deputy chief of staff Harold M. Ickes in behalf of a rival group of wealthy tribes that eventually donated at least $300,000 to the Democratic Party. Interior secretary Bruce Babbitt hotly denied the contention, saying that the decision to deny the license was made by an eighteen-year veteran of the department because local officials opposed the casino.

House Investigation

When the Senate investigation was winding down, the House Government Reform and Oversight Committee was just getting revved up. The general public apathy over the Senate hearings caused some House Republicans to wonder whether it was worthwhile to start a new round in the House. Nevertheless, the House probe continued throughout the 105th and 106th Congresses.

Committee chairman Dan Burton, R-Ind., became a lightning rod of controversy for his handling of the probe. Many charged that the open-ended and increasingly costly investigation did not turn up anything new. Burton focused almost exclusively on Democratic fund-raising, and he did not hide his dislike for President Clinton. For example, in an April 16, 1998, interview with the *Indianapolis Star/News*, Burton described Clinton as "a scumbag" and said, "That's why I'm after him."

Burton came under additional fire in May 1998 after he released transcripts of tape recordings of jailhouse conversations of Clinton's one-time close friend Webster L. Hubbell, a former associate attorney general who was convicted of overcharging his clients while a partner at the Rose Law Firm in Arkansas. The transcripts, however, were heavily edited to leave the impression that First Lady Hillary Rodham Clinton, who also had been a partner at the Rose Law Firm, may have known about the kind of client billing fraud that landed Hubbell in jail. Democrats forced a floor vote May 14 on H Res 431, criticizing Burton for his handling of the campaign finance probe. The House voted 223–196, largely along party lines, to table (kill) the measure.

The majority's interim report cited "the unprecedented lack of cooperation of witnesses" that hampered the committee's probe into the funneling of "foreign money" into Democratic campaigns. It was highly critical of the Justice Department for refusing to grant immunity to certain witnesses and of Attorney General Janet Reno for failing to appoint an independent counsel.

The minority's interim report called the investigation "the most partisan, inept, abusive, and wasteful congressional investigation since the McCarthy hearings in the 1950s." According to statistics released by the minority, as of Jan. 19, 2001, Burton had issued 935 subpoenas (923 of which concerned allegations involving Democrats) and 514 formal document and information requests (505 of which concerned Democratic fund-raising). All sixty-nine witnesses who testified before the committee did so about Democratic fund-raising practices. Of the 162 people deposed in the 105th Congress, 160 were asked about Democratic fund-raising. The committee immunized thirteen witnesses, all whom provided testimony about Democratic fund-raising. The cost of the House investigation was estimated to exceed $8 million, making it the most expensive congressional investigation in history.

FEC ISSUE ADS RULING

On Dec. 10, 1998, the Federal Election Commission (FEC) upheld the use of political issue advertising. The FEC's commissioners—three Democrats and three Republicans—unanimously turned down recommendations by their auditors that the presidential campaigns of Democrat Bill Clinton and Republican Bob Dole return more than $24 million they received in public funding in the 1996 election.

Auditors charged that the two campaigns illegally coordinated with the Democratic National Committee and the Republican National Committee to spend millions on issue ads that benefited the parties' respective candidates. The auditors said the ads contained a clear "electioneering message" and should count against the spending limits to which the campaigns agreed to receive public money. The campaigns argued that the ads fell outside federal regulation because they did not explicitly call for the election of a candidate but instead praised or attacked candidates' stances.

Congress move in small, unified steps. During hearings that grew testy, Democrats accused Republican leaders of blocking campaign finance legislation to protect a GOP fund-raising advantage.

House Democrats began gathering signatures for a discharge petition to force floor action on campaign finance legislation, but the full House took no action on overhaul proposals. GOP leaders agreed to permit votes in February or March on unspecified proposals aimed at addressing various concerns, including foreign contributions and the violation of presidential campaign spending limits.

1998 ACTION

On Feb. 26, 1998, for the second time in five months, S 25 fell victim to a Republican-led filibuster in the Senate. The **key vote of 51–48 (R 7–48; D 44–0)** fell nine votes short of the 60 needed to invoke cloture and thus limit debate. Snowe and Jeffords had offered an amendment to modify the bill's controversial provision on issue ads and to bar unions and corporations from funding politically oriented ads thirty days before a primary election or sixty days before a general election. A Mitch McConnell, R-Ky., motion to table (kill) the amendment was rejected 47–50 on Feb. 25. The Senate subsequently adopted the amendment by voice vote. The Senate then rejected a McConnell motion to table the modified bill, 48–50 on Feb. 25. A motion to invoke cloture on a Lott proposal to impose curbs on political activity by unions was rejected 45–54 on Feb. 26. (*1998 key votes, p. 883*)

The House Government Reform and Oversight Committee approved HR 3485 on a 5–3, party-line vote March 18 and formally reported the measure (H Rept 105-457, Pt. I) March 23. Committee Democrats accused Republicans of

including provisions in the bill that would clearly harm Democratic constituencies and of throwing in language intended to prevent the bill from picking up widespread support. Unions, a political ally of the Democrats, would be required to get prior written permission from every member before using their dues for political purposes. The bill also would allow citizenship verification programs that Democrats said were anti-Hispanic.

The bill also gave some Republicans heartburn by seeking to ban national political parties from receiving soft money. In another controversial move, the measure would regulate political advertisements by third-party groups in the final three months before an election. Both provisions were criticized by Republicans and some conservative groups as unacceptable attacks on free speech.

Other provisions would ban contributions by noncitizens, tighten reporting requirements, allow national parties to exceed contribution limits when a candidate faced a wealthy, self-financed opponent, and increase the contribution limits imposed on individuals. Democrats jumped on the latter provision in an attempt to paint Republicans as the party of the rich. The bill would double the amount of money individuals could give to a particular candidate for federal office (from $1,000 per election to $2,000). Total contributions by an individual to federal candidates and political parties would be capped at $75,000 a year.

The House March 30 rejected HR 3581 under suspension of the rules by an overwhelming 74–337. The legislation had been approved by committee in the preliminary form of HR 3485. HR 3581's fate seemed less important to the GOP hierarchy than having prevented HR 3526, a bipartisan rewrite of campaign finance legislation sponsored by Christopher Shays, R-Conn., and Martin T. Meehan, D-Mass., from coming to the floor. That leadership strategy provoked complaints from Republicans who had pushed for the bipartisan legislation and anger from Democrats.

The House March 30 also considered three other campaign finance bills offered by House Oversight Committee chairman Thomas. The House agreed to suspend the rules and pass HR 34, to prohibit noncitizens from contributing to federal campaigns, 369–43. The House also agreed to suspend the rules and pass HR 3582, to strengthen reporting requirements for campaign contributions and expand the type of information that must be reported, 405–6. A motion to suspend the rules and pass HR 2608, to prohibit labor unions or corporations from making campaign contributions on behalf of union members or stockholders without their approval, was rejected 166–246.

Speaker Gingrich agreed April 22 to bring campaign finance reform legislation to the floor in May after a small but growing group of Republicans joined with Democrats in support of a discharge petition. If the requisite 218 signatures were gathered, the GOP leaders would lose control of the floor and backers would be allowed to debate a variety of campaign finance bills on their own terms. But while Democrats and some Republicans hailed the decision to schedule a debate, no consensus emerged on which overhaul proposal the House ought to pass. Any change in campaign finance laws would threaten the way both parties raised and spent money for elections.

Gingrich plucked HR 2183, as developed by a bipartisan group of freshmen led by Asa Hutchinson, R-Ark., and Tom Allen, D-Maine, from obscurity and made it the starting point for floor debate, not the better-known Shays-Meehan measure (HR 3526). That forced self-styled reformers to spend time arguing about which of their proposals was best instead of moving ahead as a united front.

Both Shays-Meehan and the freshman bill would ban national parties from soliciting, receiving, and spending soft money. They would also prohibit federal candidates and officials from raising soft money for federal elections beyond their own. But while Shays-Meehan would ban state and local parties from using soft money for federal election activities, the freshman bill contained no such restrictions, though it would bar state parties from transferring soft money to parties in other states. Shays-Meehan backers contended that this amounted to a huge loophole in the freshman bill that would allow state parties to use soft money to influence federal elections. Big contributors of soft money could give their funds directly to state parties instead of using national parties as a conduit. On the flip side, critics of Shays-Meehan said that the bill went too far. For instance, they charged that it would block a state party's ability to run get-out-the-vote efforts for its gubernatorial candidate if the election coincided with the congressional election.

Another major point of contention between the two bills was the rapidly growing phenomenon of issue advocacy ads. These advertisements often implicitly support the candidates of one political party. But because they nominally focus on an issue, campaign laws do not apply. As long as the ads do not expressly urge people to vote for or against a candidate, the groups paying for them could avoid disclosure or reporting requirements. Shays-Meehan would expand the definition of ads covered by federal election laws to include those that have "no reasonable meaning" other than to advocate the election or defeat of a candidate. The definition would specifically include any ad broadcast within sixty days of an election that mentions a congressional candidate. Numerous legal scholars were convinced that such a provision would not pass constitutional muster.

The House reopened the debate on campaign finance legislation May 21. The rule made HR 2183, the freshman bill, the starting point for debate and permitted eleven substitute amendments to be considered, all of which would replace the underlying bill. Whichever got the most votes (and at least a majority) would prevail. The rule also permitted each of the substitute amendments to be further amended, and it allowed a constitutional amendment to be offered as well.

A three-hour debate took place June 10 on a constitutional amendment (H J Res 119) opposed by the member who offered it (Majority Whip Tom DeLay, R-Texas) and by the vast majority of the House. The measure would allow Congress and the states to go beyond court-set limits on the government's right to regulate campaign spending. DeLay said he offered the amendment to show that "we have to manipulate and shred the First Amendment to the Constitution" to pave the way for the restrictive campaign finance overhaul bills offered by reformers. The amendment was rejected June 11 by 29–345, far short of the two-thirds needed for adoption.

The House voted 221–189 on June 18 to approve a second rule, crafted by GOP leaders, governing floor debate. The new rule would allow at least 258 more amendments to the broader substitute proposals.

The first test to the Shays-Meehan proposal came June 19, with a potentially crippling amendment offered by Thomas to negate the entire act if any part of it were struck down by the courts. The amendment played to the members' fears that the courts might strike down the proposal's tough limits on third-party issue ads while leaving the ban on soft money intact. Some members said that that would effectively limit political party spending while not restricting third-party groups. The 155–254 vote rejecting the Thomas amendment demonstrated the bipartisan support of Shays-Meehan. Also on June 19 the House voted 325–78 to add to Shays-Meehan a plan to create an independent commission to recommend changes in campaign laws. Two days earlier, the House had rejected 156–201 a proposal by Rick White, R-Wash., to create such a commission, which would have reported its findings by spring 1999. That amendment would have been a substitute for Shays-Meehan and represented a traditional way for members to defer difficult decisions.

The House July 20 voted on nine amendments to the Shays-Meehan bill, dispensing with less than one-fifth of the fifty-five amendments originally made to the proposal. (That number did drop, however, as some lawmakers withdrew their amendments or as separate initiatives were combined.) The biggest test to HR 3526 among the nine amendments came in the form of a proposal by Bill Paxon, R-N.Y., that would require labor unions to report in detail their expenditures on political activities. Democrats and prolabor Republicans joined forces to defeat the amendment, 150–248. DeLay offered an amendment that tweaked Vice President Al Gore, whose legalistic defense of the fund-raising calls he made from his office was that there was "no controlling legal authority" barring such fund-raising. DeLay's amendment, asserting that such a controlling legal authority did exist, was adopted 360–36. A Roger Wicker, R-Mass., amendment to prohibit use of White House facilities in exchange for campaign donations was adopted 391–4. A Cliff Stearns, R-Fla., amendment to prohibit donations from resident aliens and other noncitizens to state and local elections, as well as political parties, was adopted 267–131. Charles W. "Chip" Pickering Jr., R-Miss., offered an amendment, adopted 344–56, to prohibit "willful blindness" as a defense against a charge of violating the ban on accepting campaign contributions from foreign nationals. An amendment, by Scott McInnis, R-Colo., to prohibit anyone from soliciting or accepting campaign contributions in exchange for access to the White House, vice president's residence, or the planes or helicopters on which the president and vice president traveled, was adopted 391–9. A Joel Hefley, R-Colo., amendment to require political parties to reimburse the Air Force for the costs of using *Air Force One* if the president, vice president, or any Cabinet secretary used the aircraft for travel that included a political fund-raising event was adopted 222–177. The House adopted, 284–114, an amendment offered by Anne M. Northup, R-Ky., to prohibit "walking around money" to candidates to be taken from campaign funds.

By wide margins July 30–31, Shays-Meehan supporters defeated fifteen amendments that likely would have killed the overhaul bill if adopted. An amendment, offered by Robert W. Goodlatte, R-Va., and rejected 165–260 on July 30, was aimed at rolling back provisions in the so-called "motor voter" act (PL 103-31) that made it easier for people to register to vote. The amendment would require proof of citizenship and Social Security numbers to register and would allow states to require photo identification when voters went to the polls. A Wicker amendment to allow states to require voters to produce valid photo identification at their ballot stations in order to vote was rejected 192–231 on July 30. An amendment by Ken Calvert, R-Calif., which would require candidates to raise at least 50 percent of their campaign contributions from within their home districts, was defeated 147–278 on July 30. A Dana Rohrabacher, R-Calif., amendment to allow a candidate whose opponent spends more than $1,000 in personal funds to accept contributions from any legal source up to the same amount of personal funds spent in the campaign was defeated 155–272 on July 30. An amendment by Ron Paul, R-Texas, rejected 62–363 on July 30, would alter certain petition signature requirements to try to widen participation by third parties in national elections. Another Paul amendment, defeated 88–337 on July 30, would require recipients of federal matching campaign funds to agree not to participate in debates in which every other candidate for that office who either qualified for federal funds or was on the ballot in a minimum of forty states was not invited. Majority Whip Tom DeLay, R-Texas, offered an amendment to remove certain restrictions on issue ads by creating an exemption for any communication dealing with any issue that may be the subject of a vote. It was rejected 185–241 on July 30. An amendment by John E. Peterson, R-Pa., rejected 165–260 on July 30, would require the establishment of a voluntary pilot program to help state and local officials determine voter eligibility by testing citizenship. The House rejected 142–261 on July 31 an amendment by Bob Barr, R-Ga., to prohibit states from providing voters with voting materials in any language other than English. An amendment, offered by David M. McIntosh, R-Ind., to clarify that contact between a federal officeholder and interest groups regarding pending legislation or an officeholder's position on legislation was not considered a coordinated campaign contribution, was defeated 195–218 on July 31. Also on July 31, the House rejected 117–294 an amendment by Steve Horn, R-Calif., to allow candidates to use the lowest available postage rates of seven cents

for up to two campaign mailings per household within the district they seek to represent. (Current law allows a 14-cent rate for candidates.) An amendment by E. Clay Shaw Jr., R-Fla., to require candidates to raise 50 percent of contributions from inside their own state was rejected 160–253 on July 31. An amendment offered by Edward Whitfield, R-Ky., to raise the individual contribution limit to candidates from $1,000 to $3,000 was rejected July 31 by 102–315. Another Whitfield amendment, to remove the bill's expanded version of the definition of express advocacy and maintain current law, was rejected 173–238 on July 31. The House also defeated, 134–276 on July 31, an amendment by Paul English, R-Pa., to prohibit bundling of campaign contributions for distribution to candidates or political parties. *(Motor voter, Congress and the Nation Vol. IX, p. 807)*

Not all amendments were rejected on the House floor July 30–31. Members 343–84 on July 30 adopted an amendment by Linda Smith, R-Wash., to clarify that only voter guides clearly advocating the election or defeat of a candidate were required to be disclosed to the Federal Election Commission (FEC). An amendment by Marcy Kaptur, D-Ohio, was adopted 341–74 on July 31. It would establish a clearinghouse of political activities within the FEC. A Stearns amendment to allow permanent legal residents who served in the military to make political contributions was adopted 385–29 on July 31. Another Stearns amendment, adopted 368–44 on July 31, would prohibit presidential and vice-presidential candidates from receiving public funding from the federal Presidential Election Campaign Fund unless the candidates certified that they would not solicit soft money donations.

A crowning moment for the supporters of Shays-Meehan came Aug. 3, when the House voted 237–186 for their substitute amendment. The relatively strong vote in favor of HR 3526 prompted the authors of several other substitute amendments to withdraw their measures. One who persisted was John T. Doolittle, R-Calif. His amendment, to abolish limits on campaign contributions and rely instead on quicker and fuller public disclosure, failed 131–299 in the session that began Aug. 5. The final hurdle was a substitute amendment by Hutchinson and Allen, the freshman bill, which was also the base bill. GOP leaders toyed with embracing the measure to get the 238 votes needed to topple Shays-Meehan. That prompted Shays-Meehan supporters to elaborately praise the freshmen for their efforts but urge the bill's defeat. The freshman measure was rejected 147–222 on Aug. 6, with sixty-one members voting "present."

The House Aug. 6 on a **key vote of 252–179 (R 61–164; D 190–15; I 1–0)** passed HR 2183, which had been amended largely along the lines of Shays-Meehan. *(1998 key votes, p. 883)*

As passed, HR 2183 would:

• Ban national parties from soliciting, receiving, or spending soft money, which was supposed to be used solely for party-building activities and not to promote individual candidates.

• Prohibit state parties and local parties from using soft money for federal election activity.

• Increase the limits on how much individuals could give to parties.

• Expand full federal disclosure, contribution limits, and other regulations to advertising that could be more broadly defined as advocating a candidate and to paid broadcasts that cited a candidate within sixty days of an election.

• Tighten the definition of what expenditures by individuals and groups constituted coordination and cooperation with a campaign; increase the frequency of disclosure of large amounts of money spent in independent campaigns close to an election.

• Ban parties from making coordinated expenditures for House candidates who exceeded a $50,000 voluntary limit on using their personal or family funds.

• Permit the Federal Election Commission to conduct random campaign audits within twelve months after an election and give the agency more leeway to initiate enforcement.

The Senate Sept. 10 failed to cut off debate on campaign finance legislation by a vote of 52–48, eight votes shy of the 60 needed to invoke cloture. McCain and Feingold had offered the language of S 25 as an amendment to the Senate interior appropriations bill (S 2237). The Senate took no further action on the issue in the 106th Congress.

Term Limitations

A constitutional amendment (H J Res 2) to limit the number of terms a member of Congress could serve failed in 1997 to muster the necessary two-thirds majority in the House. The Senate never considered the amendment. *(Earlier action, Congress and the Nation Vol. IX, p. 917; related action, box, this page)*

H J Res 2 would have limited House and Senate service to twelve years, not counting time already served in Congress. Rep. Bill McCollum, R-Fla., the key proponent of the main term limits measure in the House, had difficulty building a consensus for his proposal, which was criticized both by those who opposed term limits and by those who felt twelve years was too long, particularly for House members. Had H J Res 2 passed both chambers, three-quarters of the states, or thirty-eight, would have had to ratify the measure within seven years for it to take effect.

Consideration of H J Res 2 by the House Judiciary Committee was fraught with gamesmanship. Chairman Henry J. Hyde, R-Ill., began the markup by announcing that he was unalterably opposed to term limits but would vote to send the measure to the floor. He later spoke in favor of an amendment to make the proposal retroactive—and then voted against it. Rep. Barney Frank, D-Mass., expressed deep philosophical problems with limiting terms and then offered the two most restrictive amendments. One would have limited House and Senate members to six years; the other would have made the limits retroactive. Both were rejected 12–16. Two African American Democrats from the South, Robert C. Scott of Virginia and Sheila Jackson-Lee of Texas, took up the cause

---

CALIFORNIA TERM LIMITS

A three-judge panel of the Ninth U.S. Circuit Court of Appeals on Oct. 7, 1997, struck down a California law limiting members of the state assembly to three two-year terms and state senators to two four-year terms.

The California Supreme Court in 1991 reviewed the statute, which had resulted from a successful ballot initiative in 1990. The court interpreted the limits as referring not to consecutive terms but as being effective for the span of a person's life. That finding led to a challenge filed by several legislators and an April 24, 1997, federal district court ruling that the lifetime ban violated legislators' First Amendment and Fourteenth Amendment rights of voting, expression, and association. However, the Oct. 7 decision did not strike down the lifetime limits. The panel, by 2–1, ruled only that the law was invalid because voters in 1990 had not been adequately informed that the limits amounted to a lifetime ban. *(California law, Congress and the Nation Vol. VIII, pp. 958, 963)*

---

of states' rights. The Scott amendment, rejected 13–15, would have allowed states to set limits more restrictive than the twelve-year national standard. The Jackson-Lee amendment, rejected 7–12, would have left the matter to the states. Jackson-Lee said her amendment was difficult for her "inasmuch as I suffered under states' rights as an African American," but she was offering it in the spirit of comity, to help capture the essence of what Republicans wanted. McCollum said "good government" would not be served by allowing states discretion to set terms. He argued that a national guidepost was necessary for term limits to be effective, otherwise Congress would be governed by a "crazy quilt" of varying standards.

The Judiciary panel rejected, 4–24, a Bob Inglis, R-S.C., amendment to set term limits at six years for House members and twelve years for senators, but not retroactively. It also rejected, 3–25, an Asa Hutchinson, R-Ark., amendment that would have made those limits retroactive. The committee rejected, 11–19, a proposal by Jerrold Nadler, D-N.Y., to ban more than twelve consecutive years in office, not twelve years total.

The House Judiciary Committee Feb. 4 voted 19–12, largely along party lines, to send H J Res 2 to the House floor without recommendation. The measure was formally reported (H Rept 105-2) on Feb. 6.

The House Feb. 12 rejected eleven versions of the term limits amendment; only the main proposal attained a simple majority of 217–211, 69 votes short of the two-thirds needed.

The floor debate was heavily influenced by the so-called scarlet letter strategy of U.S. Term Limits, a Washington, D.C.-based group that served as a national clearinghouse for the term limits movement. The group in 1996 won approval in nine states of initiatives that threatened members who failed to vote for a specific term limits proposal approved by their own state to have a statement next to their name on the next ballot that read: "Disregarded voter instructions on term limits." The strategy backfired on the House floor during consideration of H J Res 2, however, because it splintered the vote and prevented members from supporting any single proposal.

Seven of the eleven versions reflected efforts to comply with individual state initiatives. The measures failed as follows: Arkansas, 85–341; Colorado, 87–339; Idaho, 85–339; Missouri, 72–353; Nebraska, 83–342; Nevada, 85–339; and South Dakota, 83–342. All seven would have restricted House members to six years and senators to twelve years. All but one were identical except for technicalities as minor as punctuation. The Missouri version contained a clause allowing states to shorten or lengthen the terms. Some delegations appeared to have more leeway than others. The Nebraska secretary of state, for instance, told members of Nebraska's delegation that they could vote for the other six-year/twelve-year plans. But members from Arkansas and Colorado received stern warnings not to vote for any other proposal.

Members also debated an alternative offered by Tillie Fowler, R-Fla., which would set House limits at eight consecutive years and Senate limits at twelve. Billed as a compromise between those who insisted on six years in the House and those who favored twelve, the amendment was rejected 91–335. A Scott proposal to set the limits at twelve years for both chambers, but giving states the option to draft limits, was rejected 97–329. A Joe L. Barton, R-Texas, and John D. Dingell, D-Mich., alternative to make the McCollum proposal retroactive to time served at the time of state ratification of the amendment was rejected 152–274.

Landrieu Election

The Senate Rules and Administration Committee on Oct. 1, 1997, voted 16–0 to end its investigation into charges that voter fraud tainted the outcome of the 1996 Louisiana Senate election, concluding that no evidence existed of widespread malfeasance to warrant unseating Democratic senator Mary L. Landrieu. On Nov. 5, 1996, Landrieu defeated Republican state representative Louis "Woody" Jenkins by 5,788 votes out of 1.7 million cast. GOP governor Mike Foster certified Landrieu as the winner on Nov. 20, 1996.

Jenkins, who had the strong backing of conservatives and the Republican right, leveled no specific charges at Landrieu but alleged that systematic illegality propelled his opponent to victory. Jenkins initially pursued a challenge of the election results in the Louisiana courts but abandoned that effort for lack of time and chose redress in the Senate, which is the final arbiter of its membership.

Hired by the Rules and Administration Committee in December 1996, Republican William B. Canfield III and Democrat Robert F. Bauer examined more than 8,000 pages of material submitted to the panel by Jenkins. On April 8, 1997, Canfield and Bauer reported to the committee that a limited investigation of Jenkins's charges of vote buying, multiple voting, and fraudulent voter registration were disturbing enough to examine whether "vote-by-vote, 5,788 or more illegal, fraudulent or stolen votes" were cast for Landrieu. They stressed that the evidence Jenkins provided indicated a need for a limited probe. In particular, they cited affidavits signed and sworn by Jenkins's campaign workers who said they interviewed individuals who might have participated in voter fraud or witnessed it. "Affidavits based on hearsay [and in many cases double or triple hearsay] alone are not sufficiently reliable and credible to merit a full investigation," the counsels said. They sought authority to conduct a four-week, limited investigation, and they stressed the need for Jenkins to provide the names of those interviewed. The GOP candidate withheld the names, contending that disclosing their identity would pose a threat to their safety. Canfield and Bauer recommended dismissal of four other charges related to transporting voters, campaign finance violations, voting machine malfunctions, and election commissioner malfeasance.

The Rules and Administration Committee on a 9–7 party-line vote April 17 rejected the lawyers' recommendation and opened a broad-scale investigation. The committee also approved the appointment of a new investigative team, headed by prominent Republicans from committee GOP chairman John W. Warner's home state of Virginia. Democrats saw the majority's push for an aggressive investigation as a move driven by the Republican leadership, particularly Senate majority leader Trent Lott of Mississippi. They reacted with surprise and vitriol to Warner's decision to carry out the leader's wishes.

On May 1 committee Republicans and Democrats reached an uneasy truce on the protocol for the investigation. The probe would be a forty-five-day, $250,000 investigation employing outside counsels, FBI agents, and detailees from the General Accounting Office (GAO). Subpoena and deposition power was limited to members of the committee, not staff or counsels—a key concession extracted by Democrats.

Democrats on June 25 withdrew their cooperation from the inquiry, saying the probe had exceeded its deadline and its budget. Furthermore, investigators found that convicted felon Thomas "Papa Bear" Miller, working as a political operative for Jenkins, had paid individuals to fabricate stories of voter fraud. FBI agents found that two witnesses said they had been paid to lie about selling their votes. Two other witnesses gave contradictory accounts in several interviews with agents. Two GAO investigators found that Jenkins's claims of illegal, phantom votes were completely without foundation. Republicans subsequently joined Democrats in asking the Justice Department to investigate tales of witness intimidation and witness tampering uncovered during the probe.

With the probe in limbo, Senate minority leader Tom Daschle, D-S.D., threatened a legislative slowdown to force resolution of the matter and hinted that Democratic senators might resort to describing the sordid details of the case on the Senate floor. Lott said it was the Democrats' refusal to cooperate that prevented the investigation from wrapping up. Democrats and Republicans did agree that, to date, the investigation had produced no evidence of fraud to warrant unseating Landrieu and ordering a new election. But the two sides were deeply divided over the scope and cost of the probe, and the timetable and means for concluding it.

Democrats wanted the investigation to end July 31, the day the contract expired on the office space committee investigators had leased in the Hale Boggs Federal Building in New Orleans. They argued that there was a dearth of evidence to support Jenkins's charges. However, after talks between Democrats and Republicans collapsed and a free-agent effort by Sen. John B. Breaux, D-La., was rejected by his party, Republicans on July 31 voted 9–7 along party lines to revive the investigation with no deadlines, six FBI agents, and outside counsels who would be paid from the GOP share of $450,000 that had been earmarked for campaign finance hearings. (In the absence of a bipartisan request, the Justice Department was unwilling to provide FBI agents.) The committee also granted Warner the authority to subpoena "any individual, organization, corporation, or other entity who has or is believed to have, documents or other information related to the investigation." Warner could act without the consent of the minority.

Warner issued twenty-six subpoenas in August, including ones to New Orleans Democratic mayor Marc Morial's political organization Louisiana Independent Federation of Electors (LIFE); Carl Mullican Communications, an advertising company that worked for LIFE; and Harrah's Entertainment, one of several casino operators interested in a gambling measure on the November 1996 ballot. Warner also appealed to Attorney General Janet Reno and FBI director Louis J. Freeh to reverse Justice Department policy of assigning FBI agents to committees only in response to bipartisan requests. Warner traveled to New Orleans on Aug. 13–14 to question city officials and review documents.

When the Senate returned in September from its August recess, Democrats held true to their threat and disrupted Senate business in an attempt to force Republicans to end the investigation. Daschle said the selective disruption, which included barring committees from meeting for more than two hours after the opening of the floor session, was a prudent step. An angry Lott recessed the Senate to allow the committees to convene. Late in September, while Republicans and Democrats indicated that the probe was coming to an end, Warner dispatched the committee's general counsel and a team of former FBI agents to New Orleans to continue the investigation.

On Oct. 1 the committee met briefly behind closed doors and then opened the session as they voted unanimously to end the investigation. In a final action, the committee decided against reimbursing either Landrieu or Jenkins for their legal fees, as lawmakers were leery of encouraging a losing candidate to challenge an election knowing the taxpayers would eventually foot the bill.

Sanchez Election

By 378–33, the House on Feb. 12, 1998, adopted H Res 355, ending its investigation of Democratic representative Loretta Sanchez's upset defeat of Republican representative Robert K. Dornan in California's 46th District in 1996. Dornan, a fiery conservative, had served eighteen years in the House before his defeat. He claimed Sanchez unseated him by 984 votes because of a rash of illegal voting by noncitizens. Sanchez, who was Hispanic, contended Dornan's charges were racially motivated.

House Oversight Committee chairman Bill Thomas, R-Calif., in 1997 appointed a three-member task force—Republicans Vernon J. Ehlers of Michigan and Bob Ney of Ohio and Democrat Steny H. Hoyer of Maryland—to conduct the investigation. The panel subpoenaed and collected hundreds of documents, including files from Hispanic citizens groups, voter rolls from the Orange County, Calif., registrar, and databases from the Immigration and Naturalization Service to determine whether people who were not yet U.S. citizens cast votes in the election.

The investigation focused on Hermandad Mexicana Nacional, a group that helped register Hispanic voters in California in 1996. The task force found evidence of 748 illegal votes by noncitizens. Although that was not enough to negate Sanchez's victory, Republicans said the results showed that Dornan's challenge was not frivolous and that the GOP was not unfairly targeting Hispanics. Democrats disputed the task force's findings about election fraud and said Republicans were trying to intimidate Hispanic voters.

The House by 289–65 on Sept. 18, 1997, adopted a resolution (H Res 233) that barred Dornan from the House floor or surrounding areas until the contested election was resolved. That action came after Dornan, using his privilege as a former member to visit the House floor, got into a nasty confrontation with Robert Menendez, D-N.J., about the probe.

The task force on Oct. 24, 1997, voted 2–1 (with Hoyer dissenting) to ask the California secretary of state for help in the investigation. Meanwhile, Democrats introduced a slew of privileged resolutions to halt the probe, charging it targeted Hispanic voters. While none of the resolutions succeeded, Democrats did grind action on the floor to a halt several times. The House on Oct. 23 rejected 204–222 a privileged resolution (H Res 276) offered by Minority Leader Richard A. Gephardt, D-Mo., calling for an end to the investigation by Oct. 29, 1997.

Before ending the probe by adopting H Res 355, which was based on a recommendation by the task force, the House defeated a Hoyer motion, 194–215 on Feb. 12, 1998, to return the resolution to the House Oversight Committee and strip most of its findings and conclusions.

In a Nov. 3, 1998, rematch, Sanchez beat Dornan by more than 12,000 votes.

1999–2000

Congress in 2000 passed, and the president signed, the first change in federal election law in two decades. The legislation cracked down on "527" political action committees (PACs), which were not required to fully disclose their donors and expenditures. Campaign finance reform advocates took the more targeted approach in going after the 527 PACs because they were unable to gain support for a broad overhaul of the nation's campaign finance system.

'527' PACs

President Clinton July 1, 2000, signed into law a bill (HR 4762—PL 106-230) to close the tax loophole on so-called 527 political action committees (PACs). The 106th Congress, however, was unable to clear a sweeping campaign finance reform measure. *(Campaign finance reform, p. 788)*

The secret fund-raising groups, organized under Section 527 of the tax code, were formed to influence elections. Individuals, corporations, and unions could donate unlimited amounts of money to these organizations. The groups did not have to disclose their donors or expenditures to the Federal Election Commission as long as they did not expressly advocate the election or defeat of specific candidates. They generally were involved in issue advocacy. Section 527 was written in 1975 after the Watergate scandal to set tax rules for political groups.

As enacted, HR 4762 required 527 groups that raised at least $25,000 to:

• Disclose their existence to the Internal Revenue Service (IRS) and file publicly available tax returns. Disclosure included the group's name and address, e-mail address, purpose, and names and addresses of officers and highly paid employees. A list of 527s would be posted on the Internet and be available through the IRS.

• File reports specifying annual expenditures of more than $500 to any individual, including the person's name, address, and occupation. The IRS would be required to make the reports available to the public.

• Disclose the names and addresses of those who contributed more than $200 a year.

LEGISLATIVE ACTION

Sen. John McCain, R-Ariz., Congress's leading proponent of campaign finance reform, in 2000 decided to take a more focused approach and pushed for narrow legislative action that would crack down on 527 PACs. McCain had been the target of such a group, Republicans for Clean Air, which ran more than $2 million in television ads attacking the senator shortly before the March primaries in his race for the 2000 GOP presidential nomination against Texas governor George W. Bush.

McCain, along with Sens. Russell D. Feingold, D-Wis., and Joseph I. Lieberman, D-Conn., on June 8 offered an amendment to the defense authorization bill (S 2549) requiring full disclosure of 527 groups. The Senate adopted the amendment by voice vote after it rejected on a **key vote of 42–57 (R 41–14; D 1–43)** a point of order that would have blocked the vote. *(2000 key votes, p. 915)*

S 2742, sponsored by Gordon H. Smith, R-Ore., with the blessing of GOP leaders such as Majority Leader Trent Lott of Mississippi, appeared to be an effort to wrest control of the debate from McCain and his allies. The bill covered trade and business associations and unions, including Democratic-tilting groups such as the Association of Trial Lawyers of America. But it would not apply to nonprofit civic and social welfare groups, such as the National Right to Life Committee and the National Rifle Association (NRA).

McCain cautiously embraced the measure even though it contained elements that he regarded as "poison pills," such as a requirement that unions and business trade associations disclose spending not just on advertising but also on grass-roots political and lobbying efforts. McCain also criticized a provision that would invalidate the entire measure if any piece of it were declared unconstitutional. The effect of such a "nonseverability" clause would be to invalidate disclosure requirements on 527s, which would be constitutional, if greater disclosure requirements on other groups were found to be unconstitutional. Among the main legal issues was whether requiring groups to list donors of political money would violate a 1958 Supreme Court decision in *NAACP v. Alabama.* The justices held that private organizations cannot be forced to divulge their membership. Another was whether it would violate the 1976 decision in *Buckley v. Valeo* that said the government cannot require disclosure of issue advocacy activities, including election-related activities that do not expressly call for the defeat or election of a particular candidate.

Mitch McConnell, R-Ky., the leading Senate opponent of campaign finance reform, canceled a June 14 Rules and Administration Committee markup of S 1816, which was sponsored by Chuck Hagel, R-Neb. The bill would increase limits on hard money contributions to candidates from $1,000 per election to $3,000 and would limit soft money giving to national party committees. McConnell said he called off the markup because he did not want to force panel Republicans, whose roster was dominated by senior senators, to sit through a lengthy markup. The bill, which was opposed by McCain and his allies, was unlikely to make it to the floor in any event.

After a brief, heated exchange on the floor June 9, the House defeated a procedural motion on an estate tax bill (HR 8) that would force a vote on a proposal by Lloyd Doggett, D-Texas, to require all political organizations to disclose their contributors. The 202–216 tally was largely partisan. The GOP leadership, however, agreed to allow a disclosure proposal to be brought to the floor before the July 4 recess, bowing to pressure from overhaul advocates in their own ranks.

The House Ways and Means Committee June 22 in a 23–14 party-line vote approved HR 4717, sponsored by moderate Amo Houghton, R-N.Y., chairman of the Ways and Means Subcommittee on Oversight, but believed to be heavily influenced by House GOP whip Tom DeLay of Texas. What started as an attempt to force 527 PACs to disclose their political activities and funding sources was broadened to apply to the politicking of virtually all tax-exempt organizations, including labor unions, trade associations, and issue-oriented nonprofits such as the NRA and the Sierra Club.

Democrats on the often-partisan panel protested that the bill was drafted so broadly that it would apply to nonpolitical activities by nonprofits and would almost certainly be declared unconstitutional by the Supreme Court, which had held that groups that do not specifically call for a vote for or against a candidate do not have to reveal their activities or who paid for them. This standard left room for issue advocacy ads financed by soft money contributions to support or attack candidates.

HR 4717 was sweeping in scope. It would require any tax-exempt group that spent $10,000 or more per year on political activity to disclose to the IRS any actions that seek to influence the selection or election of any federal, state, or local public official. The names of those who contributed $1,000 or more per year to the organization would also have to be disclosed. Only veterans' groups would be exempt. In addition, the groups would have to disclose all mass media communications—including mailings, ads, phone banks, and e-mail alerts—that mentioned any federal officeholder or candidate. Democrats complained that this requirement would cover many nonpolitical activities by nonprofits, which would then have to disclose many of their members.

A Democratic alternative, offered in committee by 527 critic Lloyd Doggett of Texas, also had potential constitutional problems. The plan, based on a proposal by House campaign finance overhaul advocates Michael N. Castle, R-Del., Christopher Shays, R-Conn., and Martin T. Meehan, D-Mass., combined a 527 disclosure requirement with a provision to require virtually all groups or individuals who ran political ads within ninety days of a federal general election to disclose their spending and the names of anyone who gave more than $1,000 for such electioneering. The plan, defeated on a 14–23 party-line vote, mirrored elements of a proposal by Sens. Olympia J. Snowe, R-Maine, and James M. Jeffords, R-Vt., that the Senate narrowly endorsed in 1998. *(Campaign finance, 1997–1998 action, p. 776)*

A federal appeals court ruling in *Vermont Right to Life Committee, Inc. v. Sorrell,* issued a week before the markup, held that the Snowe-Jeffords approach endorsed by Democrats and some GOP moderates was "unconstitutional on its face" because it would apply to issue-related speech specifically protected under the *Buckley v. Valeo* decision. Compounding the constitutional questions surrounding efforts to require disclosure of those who finance political ads is the fact that lawyers advising 527s and other politically active nonprofits could probably find ways to avert any new disclosure requirements passed by Congress. For example, a 527 nonprofit could be converted into a for-profit shell corporation devoted to the same political purposes.

When the week of June 26 began, House GOP leaders stood behind the Ways and Means-approved HR 4717. That bill, however, immediately came under withering fire from nonprofit groups across the political spectrum. Opponents argued that the measure would deprive their members of their rights to free association and to participate in legislative and political advocacy without having to name their members and subject them to possible harassment from the government or their rivals. Opponents also said that the bill was drafted so broadly that even routine grassroots advocacy would trigger reporting requirements.

House GOP leaders had promised to bring a proposal to the floor for a vote before the July 4 recess. As time passed, the question became how to fulfill that promise. Moderates saw a plot aimed at ensuring failure. The Houghton bill, which almost certainly would not garner a majority, was first tentatively slated for consideration under House rules that require a two-thirds vote for passage. Castle and Shays protested and sought the chance to offer a bipartisan alternative. Efforts to produce such an alternative failed, however, and might have been defeated anyway. Speaker J. Dennis Hastert, R-Ill., wanted the issue out of his hair, so GOP leaders turned to what they knew would pass—a straightforward 527 disclosure bill.

The House, in the session that began June 27, voted to suspend the rules and pass HR 4762 on a **key vote of 385–39 (R 178–39; D 205–0; I 2–0).** The Senate followed suit June 29, clearing the measure by a 92–6 vote. The bill required that any 527 group that raised at least $25,000 annually report to the IRS each donor of $200 or more and any spending of more than $500. *(2000 key votes, p. 915)*

LAWSUIT

The National Federation of Republican Assemblies filed suit Aug. 21, 2000, with a U.S. district court in Alabama saying the new 527 disclosure law violated the First Amendment right of free speech and the Tenth Amendment guarantee of states' rights.

"It gives the IRS absolute power to regulate political activities, organizations and clubs around the country—even those already controlled by local and state campaign finance law," said Steve Frank, president of the foundation. "There is essentially no limit to the IRS' power to demand that organizations surrender their internal records to the federal government."

MINORITY DISTRICTS RULING

The Supreme Court's unanimous decision in *Hunt v. Cromartie* on May 17, 1999, made it more difficult for lower federal courts to invalidate districts when they suspect race was the major factor in setting the boundaries. Conscious consideration of race was not automatically unconstitutional, if the state's primary motivation was potentially political rather than racial.

The decision could influence redistricting disputes nationwide after the 2000 census. "A jurisdiction may engage in constitutional political gerrymandering, even if doing so happens that the most loyal Democrats happen to be black Democrats and even if the state were conscious of that fact," Justice Clarence Thomas wrote for the Court. "Evidence that blacks constitute even a supermajority in one congressional district while amounting to less than a plurality in a neighboring district will not, by itself, suffice to prove that a jurisdiction was motivated by race in drawing its district lines when the evidence also shows a high correlation between race and party preference." *(Court decision, p. 709)*

The ruling overturned the conclusion of a panel of three federal judges that North Carolina's 12th Congressional District was unlawfully drawn by the state general assembly in 1997. The judges made the ruling without holding a trial, at which the state was expected to present evidence that its motive was political, not racial. The justices said the state should have been allowed to make the case and sent the case back to the three-judge panel.

Campaign Finance

For the second year in a row, the House in 1999 passed legislation (HR 417) to revamp the laws governing the financing of presidential and congressional campaigns. The measure died upon adjournment. *(1997–1998 action, p. 776)*

HOUSE ACTION

The House Rules Committee Aug. 6, 1999, approved procedures for floor debate over HR 417, the campaign finance bill sponsored by Christopher Shays, R-Conn., and Martin T. Meehan, D-Mass. The plan (H Res 283), adopted by the full House Sept. 14 by voice vote, set the stage for a vote on HR 417—but only if the House first rejected three alternatives.

The biggest potential threat to the bill came from a substitute amendment that House Administration Committee chairman Bill Thomas, R-Calif., was allowed to offer. That measure (HR 2668) would tighten disclosure requirements, streamline operations at the Federal Election Commission, and crack down on political donations by foreigners. Thomas's bill was relatively noncontroversial, and many of its provisions appeared to have broad support. Under the

rule, adoption of the Thomas amendment would make it the base bill, wiping out the Shays-Meehan legislation.

The rule also provided for votes on two other alternatives: one (HR 1867), by Asa Hutchinson, R-Ark., was less aggressive than Shays-Meehan in restricting soft money; the other (HR 1922), by John T. Doolittle, R-Calif., would eliminate limits on the size of campaign donations and mandate faster and more complete disclosure of contributions.

Thomas's committee marked up all four bills Aug. 2 and formally reported them Aug. 5: HR 417 (H Rept 106-297, Pt. I); HR 2668 (H Rept 106-295); HR 1867 (H Rept 106-294); HR 1922 (H Rept 106-296, Pt. I).

Democrats claimed that GOP leaders stacked the deck in trying to squash tough campaign finance legislation. Some were worried that the rule allowed votes on ten other amendments aside from the three alternatives, only one by a Democrat. Some were "poison pills" designed to splinter support for Shays-Meehan.

Supporters of HR 417 rallied behind the theme that the electoral system had been seized by out-of-control special interests. They emphasized that it would be to the long-term benefit of both parties to reorder the balance of power. Opponents countered that the bill was unconstitutional because it would limit the ability of citizen groups to communicate with the public about upcoming congressional action.

HR 417 overcame a series of legislative hurdles—amendments and substitutes opposed by Shays and Meehan—erected by GOP leaders as part of their effort to fracture the coalition behind the bill to defeat it. All six amendments labeled "poison pills" by Shays and Meehan were rejected Sept. 14. The amendment offered by Edward Whitfield, R-Ky., to increase the limit on individual campaign contributions per election from $1,000 to $3,000, was rejected 127–300. John T. Doolittle, R-Calif., offered two amendments. One, defeated 123–302, would increase the aggregate annual individual contribution level from $30,000 to $75,000. The other, rejected 189–238, would exempt voter guides from the bill's issue advocacy regulations. The House rejected 179–248 an amendment by Ken Calvert, R-Calif., to require that candidates running for the House or Senate collect at least 50 percent of their total contributions from people living within their states, unless their opponent used more than $250,000 in personal funds. Majority Whip Tom DeLay, R-Texas, offered an amendment to exempt Internet communication from all regulations under the measure. It was defeated 160–268. An amendment by Thomas W. Ewing, R-Ill., to revise the bill to state that if any provision of the legislation were held unconstitutional, then the entire act would be considered revoked was rejected 167–259.

Three amendments were adopted Sept. 14, one of which appeared to be a clear swipe by Republicans at the expected Democratic Senate candidacy in New York of First Lady Hillary Rodham Clinton. It would require candidates for federal office who were not federal officeholders to repay the government for the use of any federal property for transportation associated with a campaign. The amendment, sponsored by John E. Sweeney, R-N.Y., was adopted 261–167. By voice vote, the House adopted a provision clarifying the right of American Samoans to make campaign donations. And, by 242–181, the House added language offered by Doug Bereuter, R-Neb., to strengthen the ban on gifts by noncitizens.

Shays and Meehan perceived as the greatest threat a substitute that Bill Thomas, R-Calif., designed to be "purposefully modest" in a bid to gain widespread support. Its central provisions were tighter requirements for finance reports to the Federal Election Commission and a crackdown on political donations by foreigners. While similar provisions were in the Shays-Meehan bill, adoption of Thomas's package would have taken the more sweeping bill off the table under the rules for debate arranged by GOP leaders. It was rejected, 173–256, on Sept. 14.

A substitute by Doolittle that would repeal all donation limits and end presidential campaign public financing was defeated Sept. 14, 117–306. In addition, a substitute by Hutchinson, proposing lesser curbs on soft money and issue advocacy, was rejected 99–327 on Sept. 14.

The House Sept. 14 passed HR 417 on a **key vote of 252–177 (R 54–164; D 197–13; I 1–0)**. *(1999 key votes, p. 899)*

The legislation would:

• Ban national party committees from soliciting, receiving, or spending soft money donations. These were the currently unlimited and unregulated contributions from unions, corporations, and wealthy people that were supposed to be used solely for party-building activities and not to promote individual candidates. It would also prohibit state parties and local parties from using soft money for any federal election activity, including voter registration drives within four months of a federal election.

• Increase, to $30,000 from $25,000, the aggregate annual limit on an individual's contributions. It would double, to $10,000, the annual limit on an individual's gifts to state party committees. It would require unions to notify dues-paying nonmembers that they could disallow political use of their fees.

• Prohibit donations by foreign nationals and set procedures for expulsion of House members who accepted such contributions.

• Broaden the definition of "express advocacy" advertising to include those ads that "can have no other reasonable meaning" other than to advocate a candidate's election or defeat, and to paid broadcasts that cite a candidate by name within sixty days of an election. It would require that express advocacy advertising be financed with contributions subject to federal limits and disclosures.

• Tighten the definition of what expenditures by individuals and groups constitute coordination and cooperation with a campaign. It would increase the frequency of disclosure of large amounts of money spent in independent campaigns close to an election.

• Ban political parties from making coordinated expenditures for House candidates who exceeded a $50,000 voluntary limit on using their personal or family funds.

• Permit the Federal Election Commission to conduct random audits within a year of an election and give the agency more leeway to initiate enforcement. It would require all campaign committees to file electronically and the FEC to post those reports on the Internet within a day of receipt. It would lower the threshold for contributor name and address disclosure to $50, from $200. It would require nonreligious groups spending more than $50,000 a year to sway federal elections to file monthly FEC reports.

• Enhance curbs on the use of federal property for fund-raising. It would prohibit franked mass mailings within 180 days of a general election. It would restrict use of the White House and *Air Force One* for fund-raising and require those who did not hold federal office to reimburse the government for the use of any government vehicle for campaign purposes.

SENATE ACTION

John McCain, R-Ariz., and Russell D. Feingold, D-Wis., the leading Senate proponents of limiting the influence of money in politics, decided to push a narrow bill (S 1593) to focus on ending unregulated and unlimited donations to the political parties—that is, soft money. By putting aside their aspiration to more closely regulate issue advocacy advertising by third parties, McCain and Feingold hoped to dilute Republican objections to revamping the federal campaign finance system at least enough to pick up the needed votes to overcome a filibuster. Opponents' chief argument against past campaign bills was that their restrictions on issue advocacy advertising would unconstitutionally limit the types of political speech that the First Amendment protects.

The Senate debate opened in earnest Oct. 14, 1999, when Mitch McConnell, R-Ky., and Robert F. Bennett, R-Utah, launched an extraordinarily pointed and personal attack on McCain, who was seeking the 2000 GOP presidential nomination. McConnell and Bennett claimed that in attacking the current fund-raising system McCain had impugned their integrity. At issue was the central theme of McCain's campaign—namely, that Washington had been corrupted by the rapidly rising wave of special interest cash. But McConnell and Bennett contended that McCain, in stump speeches and on his campaign Web site, had gone too far in drawing a cause-and-effect relationship between the proliferation of soft money to political parties and lawmakers' support for pork barrel spending. Bennett's ire was raised because a $2.2 million sewer project to help ready Salt Lake City for the 2002 Winter Olympic Games was identified by McCain as part of the "pork stew that is choking the American people." McCain responded that his charge of corruption was not aimed at Bennett or any other lawmaker. "I'm trying to change a system that corrupts us all," he said.

That contretemps proved to be a prelude to the procedural maneuvering that followed. McConnell appeared to

VOTER GUIDES RULING

On Aug. 2, 1999, U.S. District Judge Joyce Hens Green of Washington, D.C., rejected most of the claims in a lawsuit that accused the Christian Coalition of violating election law by coordinating its voter guides with Republican candidates. The suit was brought by the Federal Election Commission (FEC) in 1996 after complaints by Democratic Party organizations. The decision could clear the way for further growth of issue advertising, which is paid for by advocacy groups, sometimes with and sometimes without coordination of the candidates they supported.

Green ruled that most of the coalition's contact with GOP candidates amounted to constitutionally protected free speech that did not violate federal election law, which barred all corporations from engaging in partisan activity in concert with campaigns and parties. The FEC alleged that by discussing its plans for publishing voter guides, the coalition had made an estimated $1.3 million in-kind contribution to 1992 campaigns, most to the unsuccessful reelection effort of President George Bush.

Green, however, did find evidence of improper coordination by the group with the 1994 campaigns of Rep. Newt Gingrich, R-Ga., and Oliver L. North, the GOP nominee against Sen. Charles S. Robb, R-Va. The coalition faced a civil penalty for those violations.

---

blindside the proponents by proposing the seemingly innocuous requirement that senators report "credible information" of corruption to the Ethics Committee. The amendment, an obvious jab at McCain, was adopted by voice vote on Oct. 14. Only later did most senators realize that, because it would change Senate rules, the new language raised the number of votes needed to overcome a filibuster of the underlying bill to 67 from 60. McConnell subsequently promised, however, not to force McCain and Feingold to come up with the seven extra votes.

Minority Leader Tom Daschle, D-S.D., then proposed the text of the House-passed bill as a substitute amendment. And Minority Whip Harry Reid, D-Nev., offered an amendment that contained the text of McCain and Feingold's modified bill, minus McConnell's rules change. The net effect was to set up a head-to-head matchup between those competing versions. Furthermore, the gambit enabled the Democrats to gain control over the floor from McConnell and the Republicans and also seemed to foreclose any immediate chances for a freewheeling amendment process. All along, McCain and

Feingold had been open to seeing their streamlined bill reconfigured on the floor, perhaps significantly. Proponents of the bill felt whipsawed by both sides.

The Senate voted Oct. 14 by 77–20 to adopt a McCain amendment to speed up the disclosures of contributions to the Federal Election Commission and require national political parties to report to the election agency any transfer of funds to state or local parties.

In reaction to the procedural maneuverings, McCain tried to force action Oct. 18, with an unusual attempt to table, and thereby kill, the amendment that contained the soft money ban. By moving to shelve his own proposal, McCain wanted to end the confusion over his bill and force a "defining vote on whether or not we want to ban soft money." His maneuver came to naught, however. McConnell and the opponents of soft money, confident that they had the votes to sustain their filibuster, concluded that there was no danger in allowing the amendment to stay alive another day. As a result, McCain and McConnell were on the same side as the Senate voted 1–92 to reject the tabling motion.

The new plan picked up the votes of three GOP senators, but that gain was nearly offset by the defections of two other Republicans, who supported the broader McCain-Feingold legislation. Senators on a **key vote of 53–47 (R 8–46; D 45–0; I 0–1)** on Oct. 19 voted on a motion to limit debate on an amendment embodying a soft money ban, falling seven short of the 60 votes needed to invoke cloture. They earlier had voted 52–48 to limit debate on language copying HR 417—again an outright majority but still shy of the required votes to halt a filibuster. *(1999 key votes, p. 899)*

Both the Democrats and McCain felt cheated by the debate. Under an informal agreement reached in July, Majority Leader Trent Lott, R-Miss., had promised to allow five days of debate on the McCain-Feingold bill. He lived up to the letter of that agreement, if not its spirit: The bill was put before the Senate on Oct. 13 and was the pending business for debate for at least part of the next four days that the Senate was in session. But the debate was brief and perfunctory. After the cloture votes, when Lott announced he was ready to move on, Democrats and McCain registered strong objections. "This hasn't been a debate, this has been an exercise in futility," Daschle said Oct. 19. "The majority leader is acting extremely irresponsibly in pulling this bill."

Democratic objections grew louder when Lott moved to end debate and bring up legislation (S 1692) to outlaw "partial birth" abortions. But traditionally such votes became a test of loyalty to the majority leader. Most Republicans had no intention of rolling Lott, and the motion to take up the abortion bill was agreed to, with the effect that the campaign finance bill had lost its place in the Senate's legislative pecking order.

Chronology of Action on Congress: Pay and Benefits

1997–1998

Shrugging off a spate of critical news stories, lawmakers in 1997 allowed the first pay raise for members of Congress in five years. A number of younger members, many of whom came into office promising to eliminate congressional perks and privileges, staunchly opposed the pay raise. But leaders from both parties worked quietly behind the scenes to squelch opposition before it could gain momentum. The leadership was bolstered by polls showing a reversal in the downward slide in public opinion about Congress and by the overwhelming majority of members who wanted the raise.

Members forwent the cost-of-living adjustment in 1998, an election year.

Congressional Pay

Congress in 1997 allowed lawmakers' yearly $133,600 salary to increase by 2.3 percent, to $136,700, effective Jan. 1, 1998. In 1998, however, members rejected the automatic annual pay increase that would have gone into effect the next year.

In 1989 Congress attempted to take the politics out of the pay raise issue with bipartisan legislation (PL 101-194) that provided members with a big boost in pay in return for giving up lucrative speaking fees. The legislation also allowed for a yearly cost-of-living adjustment (COLA) thereafter. However, the arrangement fell apart beginning in 1993, when members started approving amendments to the annual Treasury-Postal Service appropriations bill to block the COLA. *(1989 law, Congress and the Nation Vol. VIII, p. 965; congressional pay history, table, p. 794)*

1997 LEGISLATIVE ACTION

The hope of reviving the annual COLA for members in 1997 began with a group of rank-and-file lawmakers in both parties who were active in the campaign to return institutional civility to Congress. It was among the issues that the group believed could improve the quality of life for members, many of whom were juggling two residences—one in their district and one in Washington, D.C. Speaker Newt Gingrich, R-Ga., and Minority Leader Richard A. Gephardt, D-Mo., on July 9 met with Majority Leader Dick Armey, R-Texas, and the party whips—Tom DeLay, R-Texas, and David E. Bonior, D-Mich.—to discuss the possibility of a members' pay raise. The leaders agreed to poll members of their respective caucuses to test whether a détente on the politically explosive issue was possible. If lawmakers on both sides could be persuaded to refrain from offering amendments to kill the COLA, the increase would go through automatically. Some members in both chambers, however, believed Congress should continue the salary freeze until it erased the federal deficit.

Unable for political reasons to launch a frontal assault against a COLA amendment, the House and Senate took different tacks. House leaders decided to sit on the Treasury-Postal Service bill (HR 2378) and refused to field questions about the pay raise issue. They blamed their lack of action on a scheduling conflict. Meanwhile, both parties were informally whipping the issue in the House to test support for a rule that would bar a pay raise amendment. On July 17, the Senate agreed by voice vote to add language eliminating the COLA to its version of the Treasury-Postal Service bill (S 1023). The amendment was offered by Sam Brownback, R-Kan. It also adopted, by voice vote, an amendment by Orrin G. Hatch, R-Utah, to ensure that federal judges, whose salaries were tied to those of lawmakers, would receive the COLA. The Senate passed S 1023 on July 22 by 99–0.

House leaders brought HR 2378 to the floor on Sept. 17 without warning and without sending it through the Rules Committee, where opponents typically introduced their COLA-blocking amendment. Caught off guard, opponents led by Linda Smith, R-Wash., had too little time to organize an effort on the floor. The bill passed, 231–192, without pay freeze language.

GRATUITIES LAW RULING

The Supreme Court on April 27, 1999, ruled unanimously in *U.S. v. Sun Diamond Growers of California* that simply presenting a gift to a public official was not a crime. To break the law, a gift-giver's generosity must be tied to some specific action taken by the official who received the present. The ruling would make it more difficult for government officials, including members of Congress, to be prosecuted for taking gifts.

The concept of illegal gratuities was added to the federal books by a 1962 law (PL 87-849) designed to create a new crime for accepting things of value that did not rise to the level of an outright bribe. While bribe-taking by a federal official was punishable by fifteen years in prison, the maximum sentence for accepting an illegal gratuity was only two years. The quid pro quo between the payment and the action by a public official, the defining feature of bribery, was somewhat more nebulous in the illegal gratuities law, which barred the giving of gifts to an official "for or because of any official act performed or to be performed by such public official." The Court in its ruling said that if Congress had wanted to enact a broad prohibition on gifts, it could have done so. It also said that a narrow interpretation of the 1962 law was more compatible with the fact that the statute was just one strand of an intricate rule of regulation and laws governing government ethics.

Although members of Congress are also governed by their own ethics rules, which normally kept them within the confines of the gratuities law, examples exist of members who have been prosecuted. The law was used to bring an indictment against Rep. Joseph M. McDade, R-Pa. (1963–1999), even before the House Committee on Standards of Official Conduct had finished reviewing his case. McDade was acquitted after a lengthy and costly trial. *(McDade case, Congress and the Nation Vol. IX, pp. 875, 902)*

Sun Diamond was convicted of providing former agriculture secretary Mike Espy with $5,900 worth of tennis tickets, luggage, and other gifts. The U.S. Court of Appeals for the District of Columbia overturned the conviction on the grounds that the independent counsel did not prove that Espy did anything in return for the gifts.

By the following week, Smith, along with other Republicans, a few Democrats, and several national organizations—ranging from consumer activist Ralph Nader's Congressional Accountability Project to conservative commentator Paul M. Weyrich's Coalitions for America—argued that Congress did not deserve a pay raise until the federal budget was balanced. Some objected less to the COLA than to the leadership's deft maneuvering to avoid a vote. The Smith forces threatened to raise the COLA issue on other spending bills, including the Commerce, Justice, State bill (HR 2267). On Sept. 24, as that bill was heading to the floor, DeLay brokered a compromise with Smith, J. D. Hayworth, R-Ariz., and David M. McIntosh, R-Ind. The leadership agreed to hold a roll-call vote on a procedural motion on the Treasury-Postal Service bill as the House prepared to send it to conference. If the motion, called "ordering the previous question," was agreed to, Smith would be barred under House rules from amending the bill with a COLA block. If it failed, she could offer her amendment. The motion prevailed Sept. 24 on a **key vote of 229–199 (R 114–110; D 115–88; I 0–1).** Gingrich, who worked behind the scenes to negotiate a bipartisan agreement in favor of the pay raise, cast one of the early votes in favor of the motion. (The House Speaker rarely votes.) *(1997 key votes, p. 865)*

House and Senate conferees agreed Sept. 29 to a final version of HR 2378 (H Rept 105-284) that dropped the Senate pay freeze provision. That left the bill silent on the issue, permitting the scheduled pay increase to take effect in fiscal 1998. The change translated to an extra $3,073 per year for lawmakers, which was rounded to $3,100. The House approved the conference report Sept. 30 by 220–207. The Senate cleared the bill Oct. 1, 55–45. The bill was signed into law (PL 105-61) on Oct. 10, 1997.

1998 LEGISLATIVE ACTION

The fiscal 1999 Treasury-Postal Service appropriations bill (HR 4104), which included a provision blocking the COLA to members of Congress, federal judges, and high-level executive branch officials, was rolled into an end-of-session omnibus spending bill (HR 4328) signed into law (PL 105-277) on Oct. 21, 1998.

Instead of waging a losing battle for a congressional pay raise in an election year, the members of the House Appropriations Committee Treasury, Postal Service, and General Government Subcommittee reluctantly gave voice vote approval June 11 during markup of the annual spending bill to a bipartisan amendment, offered by Chairman Jim Kolbe, R-Ariz., and ranking Democrat Steny H. Hoyer of Maryland, to freeze the automatic cost-of-living increase for fiscal 1999. Otherwise, Kolbe conceded, rank-and-file members were sure to prevail on a pay-freeze amendment sometime later in the process.

GOP leaders tried to bring HR 4104 to the floor June 25 but were caught off guard when conservative Republicans joined with Democrats to reject the rule (H Res 485), 125–291. Republicans voted against the rule because it would have protected a provision on contraceptives for federal employees from being removed on a point of order. Democrats objected because the rule would have eliminated emergency funding to help federal agencies deal with year 2000 computer problems.

House leaders returned with a second rule, which protected only the bill's language that would bar an otherwise automatic cost-of-living increase for members of Congress. It aimed to bring conservatives back on board by leaving the contraception language open to deletion. Republicans also tried to pressure Democrats into voting for the rule by claiming a vote against it was a vote in support of a congressional pay raise. The rule (H Res 498) was adopted 218–201 on July 15. The next day, still angered by GOP efforts to turn the debate on the rule into a vote on the pay raise, W. G. "Bill" Hefner, D-N.C., offered an amendment to remove the provision to freeze the cost-of-living increase. His amendment was defeated 79–342.

The Senate version of the spending measure (S 2312) also contained language that would freeze the COLA for members of Congress for fiscal 1999. Herb Kohl of Wisconsin, top Democrat on the Treasury-Postal Service Appropriations Subcommittee, said he was concerned because the language differed slightly from the House provision, making the item open for debate in a House-Senate conference. After initially dismissing such concerns, Chairman Ted Stevens, R-Alaska, decided to change the provision to make it identical to the House's language.

1999–2000

Lawmakers in 1999 and even in election year 2000 quietly allowed their salaries to be boosted by a cost-of-living increase.

Congressional Pay

Members of Congress receive an automatic increase in their annual salary unless they vote to block it. Traditionally, the spending bill for the Treasury Department, Postal Service, and general government agencies has been used as the vehicle to do so. However, in both 1999 and 2000, Congress did not include a provision in the annual appropriations measure to halt the pay hike.

The fiscal 2000 spending bill (HR 2490—PL 106-58) was silent on congressional pay, thus allowing the automatic increase to take effect. Members' $136,700 salary thus went up by $4,600.

With almost no debate, House members sidestepped an opportunity to block a pay raise for themselves during consideration of HR 2490. They voted 276–147 on July 15, 1999, on a procedural motion that prevented the measure from being offered.

The fiscal 2001 Treasury-Postal Service appropriations measure (HR 4577—PL 106-554), signed into law on Dec. 21, 2000, also lacked language to stop the annual cost-of-living adjustment. As a result, lawmakers' annual salary rose from $141,300 to $145,100.

A firm opponent of the cost-of-living pay raise, Rep. Bob Schaffer, R-Colo., took an unusual route to fight it during the 106th Congress. Schaffer brought suit in federal court seeking to block the annual practice. Schaffer's lawyers told the court that the representative's "personal, political and professional reputation has been threatened to be damaged as a direct result of his receipt of the unconstitutional" increases. An unsympathetic appeals court dismissed the suit in the spring of 2001, noting that Schaffer has gotten more popular since his first election in 1996, winning his latest contest in 2000 with more than 80 percent of the vote. In October 2001 the U.S. Supreme Court refused to consider reinstating Schaffer's lawsuit.

Congressional Pay History

Year	Salary
1789–1795	$6 per diem
1795–1796	$6 per diem (House)
	$7 per diem (Senate)
1796–1815	$6 per diem
1815–1817	$1,500 per year
1817–1855	$8 per diem
1855–1865	$3,000 per year
1865–1871	$5,000 per year
1871–1874	$7,500 per year
1874–1907	$5,000 per year
1907–1925	$7,500 per year
1925–1932	$10,000 per year
1932–1933	$9,000 per year
1933–1934	$8,500 per year
February–July 1934	$9,000 per year
July 1934–1935	$9,500 per year
1935–1947	$10,000 per year
1947–1955	$12,500 per year
1955–1965	$22,500 per year
1965–1969	$30,000 per year
1969–1975	$42,500 per year
1975–1977	$44,600 per year
1977–1979	$57,500 per year
1979–1982	$60,662.50 per year
1982–1983	$69,800 per year (House)
1983–1984	$69,800 per year (Senate)
1984	$72,600 per year
1985–1986	$75,100 per year
January–February 1987	$77,400 per year
March 1987–1990	$89,500 per year
1990	$96,600 per year (House)
	$98,400 per year (Senate)
January–August 1991	$125,100 per year (House)
	$101,900 per year (Senate)
August–December 1991	$125,100 per year
1992–1993	$129,500 per year
1993–1997	$133,600 per year
1998–1999	$136,700 per year
2000	$141,300 per year
2001	$145,100 per year

NOTE: Salary increases are generally rounded to the nearest $100. The 1979 increase was not rounded because of specific language in the enacting legislation. The top six leaders in Congress—the Speaker of the House, the Senate president pro tempore, and the majority and minority leaders of both chambers—received additional pay. Highest paid was the Speaker.

SOURCES: Congressional Research Service; House sergeant-at-arms; Senate Disbursing Office.

## CHAPTER 16

The Clinton Presidency

Clinton's Second Term   797

Clinton Impeachment   813

The Presidency: Bill Clinton's Second Term

Less than an hour after witnessing the inauguration of his successor on Jan. 20, 2001, Bill Clinton appeared before a cheering crowd of political supporters and officials from his administration. "We did a lot of good," he said with a reassuring nod of his head, briefly summarizing what he, and his administration, had accomplished during the previous eight years.

Clinton's many detractors disputed that assessment. They insisted that any good that came during the Clinton years—especially the unprecedented degree of economic growth that started just before he took office and ended just after he left—occurred despite, not because of, his efforts. Even many supporters acknowledged disappointments with the Clinton presidency. They spoke of missed opportunities, of misused political talent, and most important of betrayal by a man who allowed personal indiscretions to sap his initiative and mar his achievements.

With the possible exception of Franklin D. Roosevelt, Clinton was the most complex American political leader of the twentieth century. He was the first Democratic president since Roosevelt to win reelection and, similar to Roosevelt, he had a magical ability to confound and infuriate his political opponents. Clinton mastered public relations as had no modern president except Ronald Reagan, but he also mastered the details of public policy as few presidents ever have. Clinton could move the nation with stirring words at times of crisis or trauma, but he could also annoy and even disgust the nation with his immature personal behavior. No president of recent times reveled in the powers and responsibilities of the office as did Bill Clinton, but no modern president, other than Richard M. Nixon, so harmed and debased the office. Throughout it all Clinton had an unusually complex relationship with the American people, who somehow seemed able to distinguish his personal failings from his presidency.

More than any of his accomplishments or failures on domestic and foreign policy, Clinton likely will be remembered in history as only the second president to be impeached by the House and then acquitted by the Senate. A full year of Clinton's second term, from January 1998 until February 1999, was dominated by a national furor over the president's relationship with a White House intern, Monica Lewinsky,

and his clumsy efforts to deny it. Although Clinton never faced a serious danger of being removed from office, the impeachment crisis deprived him of moral and political authority and worsened the already poisonous political climate in Washington. *(Impeachment, p. 813)*

Clinton's list of major legislative achievements was remarkably short for a president who served two full terms. The president's record on Capitol Hill is perhaps best remembered for two events of his first term: the failure of a health care plan and the passage of welfare reform written by Republicans, for his impeachment by the House and acquittal by the Senate during his second term, and for his successful deficit reduction efforts in both terms. But with little public attention, Clinton was able to win incremental victories on several significant domestic programs, including expanded aid to education, tax incentives for low-wage workers, and health coverage for children of poor families. Significantly, Clinton stymied large parts of the Republican agenda, as expressed in the 1994 "Contract with America," that called for turning many of the federal government's responsibilities over to state and local governments. *(Clinton's first term, Congress and the Nation, Vol. IX, p. 929)*

To accomplish these victories, Clinton positioned himself as a centrist defender of the national interest against conservative Republican overreach. He practiced what came to be called the politics of "triangulation," distancing himself not only from the strident conservatism of the Republican Congress but also from many traditional liberal tenets of the Democratic Party. A similar strategy of appealing to swing voters in the middle of the political spectrum while still supporting the previous Democratic focus on the poor and the working class—particularly organized labor—and other identifiable groups propelled him into the White House in 1992 and kept him there in 1996.

Clinton's personal political success did not translate into success for his party, however. He entered office with Democrats in charge of both houses of Congress and occupying a majority of the fifty governorships. Republicans won control of Congress in the 1994 elections, a victory that was widely interpreted as a rebuke to Clinton for his first two years in office, although its roots stretched back further into the long Democratic dominance of Congress. During the rest of the

1990s Republicans retained control of Congress and captured a majority of the governorships. Clinton's ultimate political failure was his inability to pass the presidency to his designated successor, Vice President Al Gore, who narrowly lost to George W. Bush in the 2000 elections. If Gore failed to make a compelling argument for putting him in the White House, he also suffered from "Clinton fatigue," a weariness with the president's foibles and a readiness to try something new. (2000 presidential elections, p. 20)

The Economy

Clinton benefited throughout his presidency from a strong and growing economy. As he left office in January 2001, he could claim to have presided over the longest economic expansion in the nation's history. During his eight years as president, 22 million new jobs were created, unemployment fell to its lowest rate in thirty years, the child poverty rate fell to its lowest levels in twenty years, and wages were rising at all income levels for the first time in history. Although economists and others debated whether this new prosperity was attributable to the Clinton administration, many credited the president with taking necessary steps in Washington to bring the ballooning federal budget under control.

Throughout his presidency, Clinton had a strong economic team, respected on Wall Street, but also a solid personal grasp of economic issues that linked lower deficits to declining interest rates and economic growth. He had promised during his 1992 campaign to cut the deficit, which was approaching $300 billion, in half. In 1993 he pushed through Congress a package of tax increases and spending constraints that allowed him to keep that promise, even though it contributed to the remarkable elections in 1994 that produced the first Republican-controlled Congress since 1953–1954 when Dwight D. Eisenhower was in the White House.

Two years later Republicans suffered their own political consequences when they tried to force on the president a budget making deep cuts in both taxes and spending. Clinton did commit to the principle of balancing the budget, however, and in 1997 he and congressional leaders agreed to a plan to end the deficit within five years. The expanding economy made even that long a projection appear unduly pessimistic. In fiscal 1998 the government ran a budget surplus for the first time since 1969. In fiscal 2000 the budget surplus reached an estimated $236 billion, and Clinton was offering a new goal: paying off the $3.4 trillion national debt by 2012.

Domestic Policies

After the 1994 failure of his complex plan for a national health insurance system, Clinton generally settled for an incremental approach to dealing with most domestic policy questions. The one major exception was the welfare system, which he had promised to end "as we know it." In 1996 Clinton accepted a Republican-written plan to replace the federal welfare program with block grants to the states. In other areas, during both terms, Clinton settled for the expansion of existing programs or for modest new programs. He became increasingly adept at using his veto power, and often simply the threat of a veto, to pressure the Republican-led Congress into accepting many of his domestic priorities. Clinton also used the veto to block some Republican initiatives and implemented some of his policies through executive orders that did not require congressional action.

Many of Clinton's most important domestic initiatives were intended to provide new or additional federal help for low- and moderate-income Americans. Clinton did not frame these initiatives in terms of an all-encompassing "Great Society" program—as had Lyndon B. Johnson (1963–1969) three decades earlier. But the combined effect of Clinton's efforts, as approved by Congress, was to add tens of billions of dollars in federal spending to benefit the bottom half of Americans who, combined, earned less than 20 percent of the national income.

One of the best examples of Clinton's priorities was the earned income tax credit, a previously existing program that could add a dollar or two to the effective hourly wages of low-income workers. Clinton won a major increase for the program as part of his budget-reduction program enacted by Congress in 1993 over strong Republican opposition. He added more money for the program at other points in his presidency, and defended it against attacks by Republicans, who said the program was open to abuse. In 1998, according to administration calculations, the tax credit lifted 4.3 million Americans above the income-poverty level. By 2000 the tax credit provided about $30 billion in benefits for low-income Americans, more than had been spent on the old federal welfare program.

As a son of the South from Arkansas who counted many blacks as close personal friends throughout his life, Clinton enjoyed excellent relations with black Americans. In 1997 he sought to use his empathy with blacks to start a national discussion of ways to bridge the racial divide in America. His "race initiative" resulted in several institutional changes in the federal government but failed to provoke a widespread reexamination of the nation's race problems.

Clinton promoted education as a major theme in his 1996 campaign for reelection, and he substantially increased federal funding for education at all levels, in some cases over Republican opposition but in others with GOP support. During Clinton's tenure funding was doubled for the Head Start program, which had broad political support in Washington; by 2001 the program served an estimated 935,000 children. Clinton also proposed, and generally got congressional support for, federal funding enabling local school districts to pay for emergency school repairs and to hire additional teachers to reduce class sizes.

Two significant trends in the nation's education system gathered strength during the 1990s, both with important encouragement and budgetary support from the Clinton administration. One was the development of "charter schools," a concept of publicly funded institutions that had much greater freedom to try new approaches than did traditional public schools. In 1993, according to the Clinton White House, the nation had only one charter school; by the 2000–2001 school year there were more than 2,000. Another trend was the increasing use of standardized testing to judge the performance of schools, as well as the children attending them. Although Clinton's efforts to establish national competency standards failed early in his first term, by 2000, nearly every state had adopted uniform standards in core curriculum subjects, and some were awarding high school diplomas only to those who had passed certain achievement tests.

Aid to low- and moderate-income college students was another Clinton priority that won broad support in Congress. According to White House figures, federal aid to college students doubled to nearly $60 billion annually during Clinton's tenure. That figure included increased student grants and loans, which reached 59 percent of the nation's college students as of 1999, compared to 43 percent in 1992.

Largely because of economic growth, crime dropped sharply during the Clinton years. The overall crime rate fell to the lowest point in nearly three decades in 2000, as did the rates for violent crime and homicide. Tough new policies at the federal, state, and local levels also helped reduce the crime rate in schools and the rate of teenage drug use.

Clinton did not set out to be an "environmental" president but during the course of his eight years in office he took numerous actions that enabled him to claim an environmental record as strong as any president in history. He used his veto power to block Republican efforts in Congress to weaken the Clean Water Act and the Endangered Species Act and to open the Arctic National Wildlife Reserve in Alaska to oil exploration. Clinton approved new federal standards intended to reduce pollution from automobiles and diesel trucks, and his administration substantially increased the number of toxic waste sites cleaned under the superfund program. Beginning in 1996, when he created the mammoth Grand Staircase-Escalante National Monument in southern Utah, Clinton joined Theodore Roosevelt and Jimmy Carter in the class of presidents who protected enormous areas of land from commercial exploitation. Clinton created eleven new national monuments and expanded two others, setting aside a total of more than 4.6 million acres. He also supported the creation of five new national parks. Near the end of his presidency Clinton issued rules intended to prohibit the construction of roads in about 60 million acres of national forest land (nearly all of it in the West), thus preserving that land from logging, mining, and other commercial activities. That step followed the longest, and most complex rulemaking process in government history.

Clinton had a mixed record on what arguably was the most important environmental issue at the end of the century: global warming. Under the guidance of Vice President Gore, an ardent environmentalist, Clinton embraced the argument that the burning of fossil fuels was the primary cause of a trend toward higher temperatures during the twentieth century. Most scientists agreed that global warming eventually would cause major changes in climate worldwide, including more severe floods and droughts. The Clinton administration devoted more than $13 billion to scientific research on climate change, and it boosted funding on programs to develop energy-efficient technologies. Clinton also sent Gore to a 1997 international conference in Kyoto, Japan, where diplomats negotiated a treaty requiring the industrialized nations to reduce their emissions of the so-called "greenhouse" gases that cause global warming. But Clinton made no attempt to overcome strong congressional opposition to that treaty, and he did little to prepare the American people for the lifestyle changes that might be necessary to reduce the use of fossil fuels.

Presidential Nominations

The Senate approved the vast majority of Clinton's nominations for major administration posts, during both his first and second terms, but after the Republican takeover of Congress in the 1994 elections the Senate delayed or killed several dozen of the president's appointees to federal judgeships. Clinton's cabinet reflected the diversity of the American people more than that of any previous president; among other firsts, he appointed the first female attorney general (Janet Reno), the first female secretary of state (Madeleine K. Albright) and the first Asian American cabinet member (Commerce Secretary Norman Minetta).

Only one of Clinton's second-term nominees for a cabinet-level post failed: The 1997 appointment of Clinton's former national security advisor, Anthony C. Lake, to be director of the Central Intelligence Agency (CIA). Lake's nomination was caught up in a partisan dispute over alleged improprieties in Democratic Party fund-raising for the 1996 elections cycle, and he asked that his nomination be withdrawn. The Senate then readily approved Clinton's nomination of George Tenet to the CIA post; Tenet was a former staff member of the Senate Intelligence Committee.

Alexis Herman, a former White House aide, had to wait six months between late 1996 and early 1997 before the Senate would approve her nomination to be secretary of labor. Herman, the first black nominated for the post, at first faced questions from Republican senators about her involvement in White House fund-raising for the 1996 election. She had been director of the White House Office of Public Liaison during Clinton's first term. Herman's nomination later became embroiled in a dispute between Republicans and the White House over Clinton's plans to issue an executive order urging federal agencies to give priority to unionized companies on government construction projects. Once that dispute was settled with a compromise, Herman's nomination cleared the Senate on April 30, 1997, on a bipartisan vote of 85–13.

Two other nominations caused considerable controversy in 1997. The first was the appointment of former Massachusetts governor William F. Weld, a Republican, as ambassador to Mexico. Weld had resigned his governorship to accept the appointment but then faced unrelenting opposition from Jesse Helms, R-N.C., the chairman of the Foreign Relations Committee. Helms charged that Weld was "unqualified" for the Mexico post because of his positions on narcotics issues, including his support for the medical use of marijuana. Weld undermined his chances for confirmation by directly attacking Helms for using "ideological extortion." After Helms refused for several months even to hold a committee hearing on the nomination, Weld withdrew his name on Sept. 15, 1997.

A few weeks after Weld withdrew, the Senate Judiciary Committee blocked approval of Bill Lann Lee as assistant attorney general for civil rights. Lee, who had been a lawyer for the NAACP Legal Defense and Education Fund, came under attack from Republicans who disagreed with his support for affirmative action programs. The committee on Nov. 13 deadlocked, 9–9, on a vote to report Lee's nomination to the full Senate; because a majority vote was needed to send the nomination to the floor, the tie vote effectively blocked Lee's chances of being confirmed. The vote was along party lines except for Arlen Specter, R-Pa., who supported Lee. Clinton on Dec. 15 named Lee as "acting" assistant attorney general, a move that put Lee into the post without having to face a formal confirmation by the Senate. Lee remained in that capacity for the remainder of Clinton's second term.

The full Senate formally rejected only one nominee during Clinton's second term: Ronnie L. White, nominated for a federal district court judgeship in St. Louis. Clinton nominated White, who was the first black justice on the Missouri Supreme Court, for the federal bench in June 1997. The Judiciary Committee delayed action on the nomination for nearly a year, but then approved it in May 1998. White's nomination encountered further delays and was not scheduled for a vote in the full Senate until the fall of 1999. By that time, White had come under attack from Republicans, most notably John Ashcroft, of Missouri, who speculated that White would be too much of an "activist" on the federal bench. Pressed by Democrats for a vote on the nomination, the Senate finally acted on Oct. 5, 1999, rejecting White 45–54, along party lines. White was the first nominee for a federal judgeship to be rejected by the Senate since 1987, when President Ronald Reagan's nomination of Robert H. Bork to be a justice of the Supreme Court was defeated.

The Senate in March 2000 approved two of the longest-pending nominations for the federal bench: those of Richard A. Paez and Marcia L. Berzon to seats on the 9th Circuit Court of Appeals. Paez, a federal district court judge in California, had been nominated in January 1996, but one or more unidentified Republican senators held up action on his nomination for four years. Berzon, an attorney in San Francisco, had been nominated in 1998. Republicans complained that both Paez and Berzon were too liberal. Democrats said that Republicans were merely opposed to the nominations of women and members of racial minorities.

The Senate approved 377 of Clinton's nominations for the federal bench: 203 during his first term and 174 during his second term. At the end of Clinton's tenure sixty-three federal judgeships were vacant, forty at the district court level and twenty-three at the appellate court level. Clinton had nominated candidates for thirty-eight of those vacancies; all were still pending in the Senate at the end of 2000, but only four of those nominees had received a hearing in the Judiciary Committee.

Foreign Policy

As with most other aspects of his second term, Clinton's record on foreign policy was a mixture of solid accomplishment, disappointing failures, and missed opportunities. Many critics blamed the president for failing to articulate and then follow a coherent plan for U.S. foreign policy at the outset of the post–cold war era. Others argued that any uncertainties in the president's approach merely reflected the ambiguous position of the world's sole remaining superpower, which was confronted by numerous miniconflicts around the world rather than one overriding challenge from a rival superpower.

If there was a single broad theme to Clinton's foreign policy, it was the promotion of U.S. economic interests in the world through the process that came to be known as "globalization." With deep conviction, Clinton preached the virtues of free trade and open markets to audiences both at home and abroad. He argued that every country, rich or poor, benefited from increased exchanges of goods, services, and ideas. Largely at his urging, U.S. diplomats and representatives of international financial institutions pressed other countries to reduce their tariffs, minimize government control of their economies, and open their markets to foreign trade and investment.

In his second term, Clinton's most notable success on the globalization front came with an agreement normalizing trade relations between the United States and China. Completed in 1999 after several years of on-and-off negotiations, the agreement was intended to pave the way for China's entry into the World Trade Organization (WTO), a relatively new agency that policed compliance with the rules of trade. Clinton argued that getting China into the WTO would help ensure that the world's most populous nation stayed on a path of converting its economy from communism to capitalism. Moreover, he said, the growth of economic freedoms in China inevitably would lead to popular demands for political freedoms.

Clinton had influential domestic support for his position, primarily from the U.S. business community that saw China as a gigantic potential market for American goods and services. Labor unions and environmental groups opposed the China trade accord, however, arguing that Beijing systematically flouted international standards on worker rights and environmental protection. China would use the trade agreement to flood the U.S. market with cheap goods, using trade to bolster a repressive regime, the opponents argued.

A high-stakes political battle in Washington over the issue ended in May 2000 when the House solidly approved the trade agreement. The Senate followed suit four months later. Despite Washington's approval of the agreement, it was clear that some elements of the Chinese leadership remained fearful of the effects on that country of expanded world trade. Chinese foot-dragging on negotiating follow-up agreements with the WTO delayed its entry into that body for more than a year.

The Clinton administration also negotiated a trade agreement with Vietnam, another Asian communist country that was attempting to open its economy while maintaining a closed political system. The United States and Vietnam normalized their diplomatic relations during Clinton's first term and then began negotiating an agreement normalizing their trade relations. The two sides reached an agreement in 1999, but Vietnamese leaders delayed a final signing until July 2000. Clinton visited Vietnam in November 2000, two months before leaving office. He was the first U.S. president to visit any part of that country since the Vietnam War in the 1960s and 1970s. Clinton used the opportunity to argue forcefully for political, as well as economic, reforms in Vietnam.

Clinton's unabashed promotion of globalization suffered some rocky moments, especially in 1997–1998 when the collapse of Thailand's currency led to a broad financial crisis in East Asia that damaged economies as far away as South America and Russia. The crisis was directly related to globalization because it began when foreign investors lost confidence in Thailand's economy and sold their holdings in the local currency, and the Thai government nearly bankrupted itself trying to support the currency. Investors began pulling their money out of other East Asian countries, setting off a chain reaction that caused deep recessions in Thailand, the Philippines, Indonesia, and South Korea, and even battering the economies of such financial powerhouses as Hong Kong and Singapore. Suddenly worried about all "emerging market" economies, investors also pulled back from Argentina, Brazil, Russia, and several other countries. With U.S. support, the International Monetary Fund (IMF) pumped billions of dollars into the East Asian economies to try to stem the crisis. But the IMF demanded austerity measures that resulted in millions more people being thrown out of work and thousands of businesses being forced to close. The long-term impact of the crisis was most severe in Indonesia, where public protests in 1998 toppled the dictatorship of President Suharto and led to a period of political instability that lasted for more than three years.

When it reached Russia in August 1998, the financial crisis had the effect of damaging an economic transformation that already was troubled despite large infusions of aid from the United States, the IMF, and other sources. Since the collapse of the Soviet Union at the end of 1991, Russia had been dismantling the economic and political machinery of the Soviet communist state as it moved toward capitalism and democracy. A handful of entrepreneurs and former communist officials accumulated vast fortunes while millions of Russians lost their jobs when inefficient state-owned industries were closed. The sudden withdrawal of billions of dollars in foreign investment in the summer of 1998 compounded Russia's economic turmoil and weakened public support for President Boris Yeltsin, who had led the reform efforts. A year later, at the end of 1999, Yeltsin stepped aside for a hand-picked successor, Vladimir Putin, a previously obscure government official and former counterintelligence agent. Putin promised to stay the course of reform, but several autocratic-style actions after he won the presidency in his own right in 2000 raised questions about his commitment to democracy. The Clinton administration gently urged Putin to continue reforms but found that its influence on domestic events in Russia was limited.

Clinton had reason to believe that he could have more influence in the Middle East, where the United States was a major source of financial aid and the ultimate security guarantor for several countries. The revival after 1991 of peace talks between Israel and some of its Arab neighbors led to agreements between 1993 and 1995 that offered some hope for a lasting settlement of the major conflicts in the region. The central conflict was between Israel and the nearly 8 million Palestinian Arabs who had been displaced since Israel's creation in 1948. Israel and the Palestine Liberation Organization (PLO) recognized each other in 1993 and entered into a series of U.S.-led negotiations intended to give the Palestinians some control over territories that Israel had occupied since the 1967 Arab-Israel War. But progress was slow because of lingering mistrust between the two sides. Clinton and his aides intervened repeatedly to keep the talks on track, most importantly in 1998 when he summoned the Israeli and Palestinian leaders to a conference center outside Washington for intense negotiations that succeeded in papering over some of the continuing differences.

With his own time in office running out, Clinton decided in 2000 on another round of personal diplomacy patterned after the 1978 summit meeting at Camp David, the presidential retreat in Maryland, that had produced a landmark peace agreement between Israel and Egypt. Clinton believed he had a good chance of success because Israel had elected a new prime minister, Ehud Barak, who seemed to have an intense interest in making peace with his country's former enemies. For days on end, Clinton, Barak, and Palestinian leader Yasser Arafat met at Camp David in an attempt to resolve issues that divided the Israelis and the Palestinians. Barak ultimately made a proposal that was substantially more conciliatory than any previous Israeli proposal, but it failed to sway Arafat.

The central disputes revolved around who would control portions of Jerusalem considered vital by both Jews and Muslims, and how many, if any, Palestinian refugees in neighboring Arab countries could return to Israel. The Camp David talks collapsed at the end of July 2000, with Clinton appearing to lay most of the blame on Arafat. Subsequent attempts to get the negotiations restarted made progress, but failed, as well.

Violence broke out between Israelis and Palestinians at the end of September 2000 and quickly escalated into a cycle of provocation and retaliation that killed hundreds of people, most of them Palestinians. Between late December 2000 and early January 2001, as the violence intensified and with his own presidency about to end, Clinton made another last-minute effort to get a peace agreement. But the violence had hardened positions on both sides, and a lame-duck president found his once-vaunted persuasive abilities diminished. The violence continued well into 2001, and Clinton's successor, George W. Bush, took a more cautious, hands-off approach in the early months of his administration.

Clinton's personal leadership played an important role in the most important expansion in several decades of the NATO alliance. After the collapse of communism in eastern Europe in 1989–1990, several former communist countries expressed interest in joining NATO, a step they seemed to view as ratifying their new independence from Moscow's control. NATO in 1997 invited three countries to apply for membership—the Czech Republic, Hungary, and Poland—and Clinton embarked on an aggressive campaign to win support for the move. His biggest challenge came from Russia, which feared a move by the Western alliance so close to its borders. To calm those fears, Clinton in 1998 persuaded Moscow to accept a document called the "Founding Act," under which NATO pledged not to station nuclear weapons within the territory of the three new members. Also in 1998, Clinton won Senate approval for required changes to the NATO treaty, despite broad opposition from those who feared that the United States would shoulder most of the costs of NATO expansion and others who worried about unduly provoking Russia. The Czech Republic, Hungary, and Poland were then admitted into NATO in 1999.

During Clinton's first term, ethnic conflicts in the former Yugoslavia had been a constant source of frustration for the United States. Clinton's predecessor, George Bush, essentially took a hands-off posture toward Yugoslavia when it began disintegrating in 1991–1992. By the time Clinton entered office in 1993, wars were under way in Bosnia, where ethnic Croats, Muslims, and Serbs were battling one an-

other, and in Croatia, where the majority Croats and the minority Serbs also were in conflict. Both conflicts lasted until 1995. The Bosnia war ended after a U.S.-brokered peace agreement ratified a de facto split of the republic into two sectors, one controlled by ethnic Serbs and the other by ethnic Croats and Muslims. The war in Croatia ended after the Croatian majority succeeded in expelling most ethnic Serbs from the republic.

During Clinton's second term, the principal tasks of Western powers, including the United States, were to maintain the peace and promote economic and political progress in Bosnia, encourage Croatia to move away from the extreme nationalism that had characterized its government, and pressure the Yugoslav government in Belgrade to refrain from further provocative acts, such as its backing for Serbian nationalist forces in Bosnia and Croatia. All these tasks proved difficult and demonstrated the limits to the influence of Western financial aid and diplomatic pressure. Bosnia and Croatia stayed at peace, but Bosnia remained an ethnic tinderbox where each step toward reestablishing a civil society seemed to be matched by a step backward. The death of Croatia's hard-line nationalist leader, Franjo Tudjman, in late 1999 finally created a political opening in that country. Moderate leaders took power in Croatia the following year.

In 1998 a new conflict arose in the most dangerous place in all the Balkans: Kosovo, a province of Serbia where 90 percent of the people were ethnic Albania Muslims and the remainder were ethnic Serbs, who held most of the economic and political power. As the site of an epic battle in 1389 between the Serbs and the Turkish Ottoman empire, Kosovo has great emotional significance for Serbs. The province also borders on Macedonia, another former Yugoslav republic divided along ethnic lines. For years, Western diplomats had worried that an ethnic conflict would break out in Kosovo and then spill over into Macedonia, prompting one or more neighboring countries to intervene in a broader war.

Kosovar Albanian guerrillas launched attacks against Serbian security forces early in 1998. The Serbs reacted with predictable harshness, burning Albanian farms and villages and forcing tens of thousands of people to flee their homes. U.S. and European diplomats intervened to try to stop the fighting, but with no long-term success. In a last-ditch attempt to head off a major war, the Clinton administration sponsored a major peace conference on Kosovo in February 1999. The Kosovar Albanians accepted a U.S.-written political settlement giving them a bigger role in Kosovo's government, but leaders in Belgrade refused. On March 24, 1999, Clinton announced that NATO forces, led by the United States, had launched bomb and missile attacks against military targets in Yugoslavia with the aim of forcing the country's security forces to pull out of Kosovo.

As the bombing got under way, the Yugoslav military stepped up its attacks on Kosovar Albanians forcing more than one million of them to flee into Albania, Macedonia, and other countries. The bombing lasted for seventy-eight days and was the biggest U.S. military operation since the Persian Gulf War of 1991. Ultimately, Yugoslav leader Slobodan Milosevic agreed to withdraw his troops and police from Kosovo. The Albanian refugees returned to a province that had been devastated by more than a year of war; as they streamed back, thousands of ethnic Serbs left their homes in Kosovo and moved across the provincial border into Serbia proper. NATO established a 50,000-strong peacekeeping force, and the United Nations took over the role of providing a civil government in the province. That arrangement left unresolved the fundamental question of Kosovo's legal status. Kosovo technically remained a province of Serbia, and Western powers (including the United States) were reluctant to allow yet another independent nation in the former Yugoslavia. But for all practical purposes Kosovo became a de facto independent state heavily dependent on NATO for security, on the United States and Western Europe for financial aid, and on the United Nations for political administration.

Clinton undertook several other significant foreign policy initiatives in his second term with mixed success. In 1998 and 2000 he made important visits to Africa that improved U.S. relations with several countries, including Nigeria. The Clinton administration in late 2000 negotiated an end to a long-running dispute with Congress concerning U.S. dues to the United Nations. And in 2000 Clinton made some progress in neutralizing a potential threat by the communist government of North Korea, which Washington had long accused of developing long-range ballistic missiles. With U.S. encouragement, North Korean leader Kim il-Jong and South Korean president Kim Dae Jung met in June 2000 and pledged better relations; among other things, Kim il-Jong reportedly accepted the continued presence of more than 35,000 U.S. troops in South Korea. Four months later, Secretary of State Madeleine K. Albright traveled to Pyongyang and secured a promise from Kim il-Jong to continue, indefinitely, a 1999 moratorium on missile tests. Albright's visit also was supposed to set the stage for a possible visit by Clinton to North Vietnam, the first ever by a U.S. president, but Clinton instead devoted much of his remaining months in office to his failed attempt to negotiate a final peace between Israel and the Palestinians.

Aside from the stalled Middle East peace initiative, perhaps Clinton's greatest foreign policy frustration during his second term involved an old U.S. nemesis, Iraqi leader Saddam Hussein. In the six years after the Persian Gulf war in 1991, teams of weapons inspectors from the United Nations had succeeded in locating and destroying much, but not all, of Iraq's reported arsenal of ballistic missiles and biological and chemical weapons, as well as its program to develop nuclear weapons. Progress on the weapons inspections was slow, however, and generally came only after the United States and Great Britain used military force to convince Saddam to comply. All progress ended in December 1998, however, when the Iraqi government blocked a key round of weapons inspections and Clinton responded by ordering missile and bombing attacks on Iraqi military targets. Subsequent negotiations aimed at resuming the weapons inspections failed during 1999 and 2000; in the meantime, intelligence analysts said Iraq undoubtedly was attempting to rebuild its capability to produce weapons of mass destruction.

The confrontation over UN weapons inspections was followed by growing international unease about the humanitarian situation in Iraq. During the 1990s, tens of thousands of Iraqi citizens had died from malnutrition and disease resulting from the country's postwar economic collapse. The Iraqi government claimed that all the deaths were caused by economic sanctions imposed by the United Nations Security Council after the Gulf War. The Clinton administration blamed Saddam for the deaths, saying that he had spent millions of dollars in oil revenues rebuilding his military while his citizens starved. International negotiations on the sanctions issue failed to result in any agreement by the end of 2000.

Clinton's second term coincided with an upsurge in anti-American terrorism, most of it apparently originating among radical Islamic groups angered by U.S. policies in the Middle East. In August 1998 terrorists exploded simultaneous truck bombs outside the U.S. embassies in Nairobi, Kenya, and Dar es Salaam, Tanzania, killing more than 250 people (most of them local citizens) and wounding thousands of others. Clinton said the bombings had been ordered by Osama bin Laden, a wealthy Saudi Arabian living in Afghanistan, where he headed a terrorist network known as Al Qaeda. The president ordered an attack against bin Laden's camps, but the bombing apparently caused no lasting damage to bin Laden's operations. In late 1999 and early 2000 law enforcement officials in the United States, Jordan, and other countries blocked attacks against U.S. targets, including Los Angeles International Airport, apparently planned for the period of the "Millennium" celebrations at the beginning of 2000. Then in October 2000, the destroyer USS *Cole* was bombed while docked in Yemen; seventeen sailors died in the attack. Administration officials blamed the attack on bin Laden's network.

Clinton generally was able to win congressional support for his foreign policies, although he often had to engage in substantial horse-trading and compromising. He suffered one major setback in 1999, when the Senate rejected the Comprehensive Nuclear Test Ban Treaty, a United Nations–sponsored accord aimed at halting all nuclear tests worldwide. Republican opponents argued that other nations' compliance with the treaty could not be verified, and they managed to defeat the treaty when supporters pushed for a vote on it. The treaty was the most important international agreement rejected by the Senate since the Treaty of Versailles, which ended World War I and established the League of Nations, failed in the early 1920s.

Scandals and Pardons

From nearly the beginning of his second term, when the Supreme Court ruled that a sitting president was vulnerable to civil suit for alleged actions committed before entering office, until the last hours of his term, when Clinton agreed to a plea bargain to avoid indictment for perjury after he left office, the president was distracted by legal suits and investigations. Chief among these was the investigation into Clinton's relationship with a White House intern and his subsequent impeachment. Most of the inquiries stemmed from allegations about his personal behavior rather than his conduct as president. Nonetheless, they embroiled Clinton, Congress, and the American public in an ongoing soap opera that many commentators and citizens alike said undermined the dignity of the office.

The circumstances that led to the impeachment proceedings in 1998 and 1999 grew out of two separate investigations. The first involved the president's personal financial involvement in a failed Arkansas land deal, known as Whitewater, which was eventually expanded to include the firing of White House travel office employees, the White House request for FBI background files on former Republican administration officials, and the president's relationship with White House intern Monica Lewinsky. The second involved a sexual harassment suit brought by a former Arkansas state employee named Paula Corbin Jones. In addition, questions were repeatedly raised about the White House's campaign funding-raising practices.

WRAPPING UP A FAR-REACHING INQUIRY

The Whitewater inquiry arose during the 1992 presidential campaign with allegations that Clinton and his wife Hillary Rodham Clinton had received preferential treatment for their 1978 investment in a real estate development deal because he was governor of Arkansas. Hillary Clinton also came under suspicion for her possible role, while she was an Arkansas attorney, of working to prop up a failing savings and loan association, Madison Guaranty, which was used to keep the troubled land development project going. Madison Guaranty was owned by James B. McDougal, who together with his wife, Susan, were investors with the Clintons in the Whitewater deal. The failure of Madison Guaranty eventually cost taxpayers $73 million. (*First term scandals, Congress and the Nation Vol. IX, p. 942*)

Once Clinton was in office, congressional pressure built on Attorney General Janet Reno to name an independent counsel to investigate the charges. The investigation's first special prosecutor, Robert B. Fiske, began work in January 1994. In August 1994, Fiske was replaced by Kenneth W. Starr, who expanded the investigation to cover the FBI files and the travel office firings. Starr became involved in the Lewinsky case late in 1997 and early 1998 when his office was given evidence that Clinton had asked her to lie about their

relationship in a deposition she was asked to give in the sexual harassment case brought against the president by Paula Corbin Jones. In his deposition in that case and in public statements, Clinton denied that he had had a sexual relationship with Lewinsky or that he had asked her to lie about it. Starr's investigation of the Lewinsky case led directly to the president's impeachment in December 1998 and his acquittal on charges of perjury and obstruction of justice in February 1999. (*Impeachment, p. 813*)

In October 1999 Starr resigned, turning the investigation over to Robert W. Ray, who was to conclude the investigation. The Whitewater investigation drew to a formal close on Sept. 20, 2000, when Ray announced that the evidence gathered was insufficient to being criminal charges against either the president or his wife. The related investigations into the travel office firings and the confidential FBI files had been closed earlier in the year.

Although the Whitewater investigation was finished, Ray's wording did not specifically exonerate the Clintons. He would say only that "the evidence was insufficient to prove to a jury beyond a reasonable doubt" that either the president or the first lady had committed a crime. For Hillary Clinton, who was running for the U.S. Senate in New York, Ray's announcement was a two-edged sword, lifting the threat of indictment while also reminding voters that she was under investigation. (*Clinton Senate race, box, p. 806*)

The timing of Ray's announcement was also an unwelcome event for Vice President Al Gore, who had struggled throughout his presidential campaign to disassociate himself from President Clinton's personal scandals, in particular the conduct that gave rise to his impeachment. The low point for Gore may have come on Aug. 17, 2000, when news that a grand jury was considering indicting Clinton for perjury was leaked to the press just hours before Gore was scheduled to make his speech accepting the Democratic presidential nomination. (*Gore candidacy, p. 21*)

Although the Whitewater investigations were concluded, Ray said that a federal grand jury might indict Clinton for perjury in the Lewinsky matter once the president left office. On Jan. 19, 2001, the president's last full day in office, the White House and Ray announced separately that an immunity deal had been reached. In exchange for being immune to indictment in connection with the Lewinsky affair, Clinton agreed to make a public statement saying that he had lied under oath and accepted the suspension of his Arkansas attorney's license for five years.

That agreement brought to a conclusion the investigations that were nearly as controversial in their own right as the public revelations about the president's affair and subsequent cover-up. The Clintons and their supporters said that the special prosecutor's office was allied with conservative interests who wanted to drive the president out of office. Starr's long pursuit of Clinton led to growing public and congressional dissatisfaction with the law that authorized the

SCANDALS AND CHARGES ENGULFED CLINTON

President Clinton's final years in office were framed largely by a number of loosely interrelated scandals and charges of impropriety.

Whitewater

In his Sept. 20, 2000, announcement, independent counsel Robert W. Ray said his office determined that "the evidence was insufficient" to prove beyond a reasonable doubt that either President Bill Clinton or first lady Hillary Rodham Clinton "knowingly participated in," knew of, or tried to cover up any criminal conduct involving Madison Guaranty Savings and Loan, the Whitewater Development Corporation, a land development project, or Capital Management Services (CMS), an investment firm that had dealings with Madison Guaranty. Madison owner James B. McDougal and his wife Susan and Jim Guy Tucker, who succeeded Clinton as governor of Arkansas, were convicted of fraud in the case in 1996.

The statement said that the independent counsel had specifically investigated whether Clinton had knowingly given false testimony when he said that he had never received a loan from Madison Guaranty; that he did not know about a $300,000 loan from CMS to Susan McDougal, $50,000 of which was used to benefit Whitewater; and that he did not know how Madison Guaranty had come to retain the services of the Rose Law Firm, where Hillary Clinton was a partner. Ray's office also investigated whether Hillary Clinton had lied about the relationship between the savings and loan and her law firm and about her work for Madison Guaranty. Ray also said that the circumstances surrounding her delay in turning her billing records over to investigators "could not be established."

Confidential FBI Files

The first report Ray filed, on March 16, 2000, exonerated the White House of criminal wrongdoing in connection with several hundred confidential FBI files found in the White House. Ray's office concluded that the files were inadvertently collected when a midlevel security officer requisitioned them from the FBI using an outdated list compiled by the Secret Service of people who had passes to the White House. Among the mistakenly collected files were those of several prominent Republicans, including Brent Scowcroft, who was President George Bush's national security adviser, and Marlin Fitzwater, who had served as press secretary to Presidents Bush and Ronald Reagan. The report also cleared Bernard W. Nussbaum, Clinton's first White House counsel, of allegations that he had lied in sworn testimony to a congressional committee.

In a statement, Ray said: "In the FBI files matter, the independent counsel determined there was no evidence that any senior White House official, or first lady Hillary Rodham Clinton, was involved" in seeking the confidential reports.

Travel Office Firings

The report on the travel office firings was filed June 23, 2000, and made public Oct. 19, just three weeks before the November elections, in which Hillary Clinton was running for a U.S. Senate seat from New York. The case involved charges that the first lady had lied or obstructed justice to cover up her role in the May 1993 firing of seven employees of the White House Travel Office. At the time the White House said evidence of financial mismanagement had been found in the office, but when the employees were replaced with Clinton friends and relatives, congressional Republicans accused the Clintons of cronyism.

Ray concluded that the fired employees were all political employees who could be fired without cause and that the concerns about financial irregularities were legitimate. But he said that the first lady had made "factually false" statements when she said in a sworn deposition that she had played no role in the firings. In fact, Ray said, evidence showed that she had had eight separate conversations with three White House aides about the matter, although he was unable to show that Hillary Clinton had "knowingly intended to influence the Travel Office [firing] decision or was aware that she had such influence at this early stage of the Administration."

In a written response to Ray's findings, Mrs. Clinton's attorney, David E. Kendall, said characterizing the first lady's statements as factually false was "highly unfair and misleading." In June and again in October, Mrs. Clinton said that "after all these years and millions of dollars," she was just glad the investigation was over. On Nov. 7, Clinton won her Senate election, becoming the first first lady to win elected office.

Office of Independent Counsel. Partly as a result Congress did not renew the law when it expired on June 30, 1999.

The investigation was also expensive. The Office of Independent Counsel had spent at least $56 million on the Whitewater investigations. The Clintons themselves incurred more than $11 million in legal fees.

JONES HARASSMENT SUIT

Paula Corbin Jones, a former state employee in Arkansas, filed suit against President Clinton in 1994 charging that he had sexually harassed her when he was governor of Arkansas. Jones claimed that Clinton had sent a state trooper to

HILLARY CLINTON: FROM FIRST LADY TO U.S. SENATOR

Overcoming widespread concerns about her character, integrity, and intentions, Hillary Rodham Clinton became the only first lady ever to win election to public office. Clinton soundly defeated Republican Rep. Rick A. Lazio on Nov. 7, 2000, to win the New York Senate seat being vacated by retiring Democrat Daniel Patrick Moynihan. Clinton won the race with 55 percent of the vote to Lazio's 43 percent, a notable feat for someone who had never before held public office, who had not lived in the state when she began her campaign, and who evoked nearly as much controversy as her husband, President Bill Clinton.

No other first lady had ever run for public office. The only former first lady to hold an official government position was Eleanor Roosevelt, who was named as a delegate to the new United Nations in 1946, where she was instrumental in writing the Universal Declaration of Human Rights. Clinton was also the first woman to be independently elected to statewide office in New York.

Clinton denied widespread rumors that she was using the New York Senate seat simply as a platform to run for president in 2004. In her first news conference after the election, Clinton said she was "going to serve my six years as the junior senator from New York."

Decision to Run

Not since Eleanor Roosevelt had a first lady been as controversial as Hillary Clinton. Both first ladies were interested in public affairs, strong-willed, highly opinionated, and outspoken—traits that did not always fit well with the traditional role of supportive wife and hostess played by most other first ladies. Both women were also political liberals, a fact that exacerbated tensions with at least some conservatives who thought the first ladies were overstepping their bounds.

A lawyer by profession, who practiced in Little Rock, Clinton came to Washington expecting to play a key policy role in her husband's administration. But her first effort, as head of the President's Task Force on National Health Care Reform, was a disaster, and she was assigned a large share of

the blame for mishandling the health care reform that contributed to the Republican takeover of Congress in 1995. At about the same time, an independent counsel began a criminal investigation into the Clintons' roles in a failed Arkansas land deal, and the first lady also came under investigation for her role in the firing of White House travel employees. When the president's affair with White House intern Monica Lewinsky first came to light in January 1998, Hillary Clinton was initially vilified for covering up for him. Then, when it became apparent that he had deceived her as well, she became an object of public pity as well as criticism from those who said she was staying in her marriage only to hold on to political power.

Although Clinton had been mentioned as a possible New York Senate candidate since Moynihan announced that he would not seek reelection, she made few public statements on the matter until July 1999, when she traveled throughout the state on a "listening tour." Her candidacy seemed assured when it was announced in September 1999 that the Clintons had bought a house in the wealthy New York City suburb of Chappaqua in Westchester County. But Clinton did not formally announce her candidacy until February 2000. "I may be new to your neighborhood," she said, "but I'm not new to your concerns."

The Campaign

Clinton began her campaign expecting to be in a tight race with Republican Rudolph W. Guiliani, the combative mayor of New York City and former prosecutor who had a love-hate relationship with the voters. On May 19 Guiliani abruptly withdrew from the race to grapple with prostate cancer. The New York GOP quickly turned to Lazio, a member of the U.S. House from Long Island, to replace Guiliani.

As Guiliani had, Lazio tried to capitalize on those aspects of the first lady's career that roused the most negative feelings among the voters. He continually questioned her trustworthiness, scoffed at her stated concern for the people of New York, and hammered away at her lack of experience. Clinton

---

invite her to Clinton's hotel room, where he asked her for sex. Clinton denied the charge.

In December 1994 a federal court granted a stay in the Jones matter, accepting the White House contention that the president should not be subject to civil suits while in office. That ruling was appealed and the U.S. Supreme Court decided in May 1997 that a sitting president was not excused from facing lawsuits over issues unrelated to his official duties. It was in the course of subsequent preparations in this

case that both Monica Lewinsky and Clinton were deposed, giving the testimony that would lead to the president's impeachment.

On April 1, 1998, the federal district judge hearing the case in Arkansas dismissed the suit, ruling that there were "no genuine issues for trial." In November 1998 Clinton agreed to pay Jones $850,000 in return for her pledge not to appeal the dismissal. In April 1999, just two months after his acquittal by the Senate, the federal district judge in the Jones

tried to identify Lazio with the conservative policies of Newt Gingrich, the former Republican House Speaker whose unrelenting pursuit of driving President Clinton out of the White House backfired, causing him to resign his seat in office. She also noted that she had been fighting for education and health issues for years and that she had played a key role behind the scenes in the passage of several progressive programs, including the provision of health insurance coverage for poor children.

The turning point in the campaign may well have been the nationally televised debate on Sept. 13, in which Lazio went on the attack, describing Clinton as "beyond shameless" and asking her to sign a pledge, which he thrust in front of her, not to use unregulated "soft money" during the campaign. During that same debate, the moderator caught Clinton by surprise when he asked her if she regretted "misleading the American people" when she denied that her husband had had a relationship with Lewinsky. "Obviously, I didn't mislead anyone," Clinton replied, with her head bowed. "I didn't know the truth."

Shortly after the debate, state polls began to show a decided upswing in support for Clinton among women, who found Lazio's debate performance overbearing and rude. Lazio's campaign also made several other tactical errors. The most damaging may have been a telephone campaign organized by the state Republican chairman to attempt to link Clinton to the terrorist attack on the USS *Cole* in Yemen. The "link" was a campaign donation from a Muslim group that Clinton had received and later returned. Lazio did not denounce the telephone campaign for nearly four days.

On election day, Clinton was helped not only by Lazio's inept campaign but also by Vice President Al Gore's large margin in the state over Republican George W. Bush, an increase in the number of registered Democratic voters in the state, and a well-organized get-out-the-vote drive by labor unions. But it was Clinton's campaigning in upstate New York—virtually everything outside metropolitan New York City—that tipped the state in her favor. Generally Republicans need to carry upstate New York by 10 percentage points

to compensate for the heavy Democratic majority in New York City. On Nov. 7, Lazio's margin in upstate was only 3 percentage points. In her victory speech Clinton promised that her first bill would be a package of measures to help the upstate economy and similarly afflicted areas elsewhere in the country by improving the technological infrastructure and high-tech work skills.

The race was the most expensive in the state's history. Together the three campaigns spent more then $83 million, much of it raised from contributions outside the state. Clinton raised much of her money among the entertainment and celebrity crowd that had supported her husband throughout his presidency, while Guiliani and Lazio appealed to contributors who wanted to see both Clintons out of office and out of Washington. In one fund-raising letter, Lazio said he could sum up in six words why people should support his candidacy: "I'm running against Hillary Rodham Clinton."

Clinton ran into a similar cold reception as she prepared to enter what has been called "the world's most exclusive club." Shortly after the election, Senate Republican Leader Trent Lott, Miss., said, "I tell you one thing, when this Hillary gets to the Senate, if she does—maybe lightning will strike and she won't—she will be one of 100 and we won't let her forget it." Clinton herself seemed sensitive to the fact that her celebrity status might not count for much in her new career. "You have to be willing to work hard to learn the ropes and the rules, build relationships with people, all of which I intend to do," she said.

Even before she was sworn in, Clinton sparked yet another controversy when she signed a deal with Simon & Schuster on Dec. 15, 2000, that would give her an $8 million advance for a memoir about her years in the White House. Republicans and others questioned the propriety of the advance, which was one of the largest in history. After the 1994 elections, persistent questioning by Democrats about the ethics of the deal forced Gingrich to forgo a $4.5 million advance for a book contract he had signed. Under Senate rules, book advances were permissible so long as they were "usual and customary."

case held Clinton in contempt of court for providing false evidence in his deposition in that case; Clinton had testified that he did not have sexual relations with Lewinsky. Clinton eventually paid a fine of $89,483.

CAMPAIGN FINANCING PRACTICES

Republican allegations of improper or even illegal campaign finance practices during the 1996 election campaign dogged Clinton and Vice President Gore for much of their

second term. Specifically, Republicans and others alleged that:

- The White House improperly held "coffees" with the president and arranged overnight stays and attendance at other White House events in exchange for political donations.
- The Democratic Party accepted campaign contributions from foreign nationals in violation of U.S. law. The do-

nations were said to be an attempt by the Chinese government to influence the 1996 elections and U.S. policy.

• Vice President Al Gore made fund-raising telephone calls from his White House office in violation of an 1883 law prohibiting political fund-raising on federal property. Gore was also damaged by first denying and then admitting that he had known that an event he had attended at a Buddhist temple in California was in fact a party fund-raiser.

Many Democratic activities that brought criticism were also standard procedure for Republicans over the years. Campaign contributors were routinely hosted at the White House and given special favors by presidents of both parties. Members of Congress from both parties routinely solicited contributions from lobbyists and others seeking to influence federal policy.

The Clinton administration was vulnerable to criticism, however, because the Democratic Party appeared to be so desperate for campaign funds that it failed to exercise caution in soliciting contributions. The *Washington Post,* summarizing Senate hearings on the matter in 1997, said the Clinton administration had been shown to be "a modern model of campaign excesses."

That vulnerability gave rise to GOP hopes that they might be able to uncover extensive wrongdoing by the Democrats, possibly even enough to force Clinton from office. House Speaker Newt Gingrich said in March 1997 that investigations by two congressional committees would show that Democrats had engaged in conspiracies "even bigger than Watergate." The probes did turn up embarrassing information about the Democrats but nothing that could lead to criminal indictments.

Republicans and others kept constant pressure on Attorney General Janet Reno to name an independent counsel to investigate the White House fund-raising practices. On three separate occasions, Reno announced that internal Justice Department investigations had not found sufficient evidence to warrant such an appointment. Reno's first refusal came in December 1997, when she said a thorough Justice Department investigation had failed to turn up evidence that the president and vice president had violated the 1883 law barring campaign solicitations on federal property. In issuing her refusal, Reno overrode the objections of FBI director Louis J. Freeh, who had recommended the appointment.

In 1998 Reno reopened Justice Department investigations into two specific inquiries that had been subjects of inquiries in 1997: whether Gore had lied in testimony about telephone calls he had made soliciting donations and whether Clinton and his aides had evaded campaign finance laws by using state Democratic committees to pay for television ads supporting the presidential ticket. On Nov. 24, Reno announced that she had determined there were "no reasonable grounds" to believe that Gore had lied in his testimony. And on Dec. 7 she said she had found no evidence of "criminal intent" on the part of the president or his aides to violate federal campaign spending laws.

In 2000 Reno again refused for the third time to appoint a special prosecutor to look into the allegations against Gore. Although Gore escaped any legal complications stemming from his actions, the allegations themselves may have contributed to his failure to succeed Clinton to the presidency. Throughout his long political career, Gore had a reputation for rectitude that was the envy of many politicians; his involvement in questionable fund-raising schemes marked the first time he had ever been challenged on legal or ethical grounds. In the 2000 campaign in which Gore struggled to define himself, the allegations fed into questions about Gore's personality and character.

PARDONS

Clinton touched off another brouhaha during his final hours in office, when he issued presidential pardons to 140 people, including fugitive financier Mark Rich and his partner Pincus Green. Rich and Green had been fugitives since September 1983, when they were indicted on fifty-one charges, including tax evasion, racketeering, and mail fraud. They moved to Switzerland before the indictment and renounced their American citizenship to fight extradition.

The pardon was controversial in and of itself, but the controversy was exacerbated when questions were brought up about whether Clinton's decision had been influenced by numerous political donations made by Rich's former wife. According to the Federal Election Commission, Denise Rich gave at least $361,500 in "soft money" to various Democratic campaign committees, and $24,000 to individual candidates and committees, including a $2,000 donation (the maximum amount permitted) to Hillary Clinton's New York Senate campaign. According to press reports, Rich also donated at least $450,000 to Clinton's presidential library fund (information about donations to that fund was not made public).

Committees in both chambers of Congress held hearings on the matter early in 2001, but no further action was expected. Legislators acknowledged that even if Rich's pardon had been "bought," there was little Congress could do to punish the now-former president Clinton.

Since 1792, when President George Washington issued the first one, thousands of people have been granted presidential pardons; only a few were contentious. Perhaps the most famous was President Gerald R. Ford's 1974 pardon of Richard M. Nixon just one month after Nixon's resignation over the Watergate scandal. The furor was so intense that Ford asked to testify before the House Judiciary Committee to explain himself. President George Bush, in his final days in office, pardoned six members of the Reagan administration for their parts in the Iran-contra affair. *(Ford pardon, Congress and the Nation, Vol. IV, p. 949)*

Among those Clinton pardoned were John Deutsch, former director of central intelligence, who had been punished for storing government secrets on his home computer; Henry G. Cisneros, former secretary of housing and urban development, who had pleaded guilty to lying to the FBI to cover up an extramarital affair; Patricia Hearst Shaw, the newspaper heiress, who had been convicted of participating in a 1974 bank robbery mounted by the members of the Symbionese Liberation Army that had kidnapped her; and Clinton's half-brother Roger Clinton, who had pleaded guilty in 1985 to charges of distributing cocaine. Clinton also pardoned Susan McDougal, one of the partners in the failed Whitewater development scheme, who had been convicted of bank fraud, but he declined to pardon Webster Hubbell, a former law partner of Mrs. Clinton's, and a former associate attorney general, who had been jailed for financial violations involving his former law firm clients.

Relationship with Congress

President Clinton's relationship with Congress in his second term was about what might be expected for a Democratic president who had survived impeachment and trial proceedings at the hands of the Republican-dominated Congress: The drawn-out impeachment fight shattered Clinton's already tenuous relationships with top GOP leaders and contributed to an extraordinarily partisan and polarized climate in Congress. Overall, little legislation of significance was enacted in Clinton's second term.

Even without the impeachment battle, Clinton would have had trouble pushing an ambitious agenda through the closely divided Congress. In the House Republicans held only a thin margin, and on close votes GOP leaders had to walk a fine line to avoid potentially fatal defections among their members. Republicans held fifty-five seats in the Senate, a healthy majority, but not enough to cut off filibusters or other delaying tactics if all the Democrats held together. Moreover, House and Senate Republicans often disagreed with each other, making it difficult for Republicans to present a united front. The victims of these disagreements were often compromise, bipartisanship, and civility.

Throughout his second term, Clinton had little success in advancing his priorities. The successes he did have came largely through his adroit use of his veto threat to negotiate more spending for education, health care, and other Democratic priorities than the Republicans wanted. Other successes came in blocking Republicans from enacting key elements of their agenda, notably a tax cut of $100 billion or more. Clinton used executive branch agencies to issue myriad orders and regulations that did not require congressional action—and that might have been blocked had congressional action been required. Those included directives setting time limits on how long managed care plans could take to render decisions on medical claims, imposing new workplace safety rules, and placing roadless areas of national forests off limits to development. *(Use of veto, box, p. 810)*

Once its limitations are taken into account, Congressional Quarterly's annual presidential success study—the percentage of the time that members vote in accord with the president's position—generally supports this picture of a president and Congress engaged in four years of skirmishes in which tactical maneuvering, rather than grand strategic plans, carried the day. In 1997 President Clinton prevailed on 53.6 percent of the roll call votes on which he staked out a clear position. The president achieved important victories when Republicans agreed to a compromise plan to eliminate the budget deficit within five years and reduce taxes at the same time and when the Senate approved a treaty outlawing chemical weapons. But Congress refused to give him "fast track" trade negotiating authority, new funding for the United Nations and the International Monetary Fund, or campaign finance reform.

In 1998—the year in which the House impeached Clinton on two of four charges—Clinton's success score was 50.6 percent. Almost none of the priorities that Clinton set at the beginning of the year became law, and few of them even got a floor vote. Tobacco regulation, campaign finance overhaul, "fast track" trade authority, and a "bill of rights" for patients in managed health care plans all fell far short of enactment. At the same time, Clinton occasionally snatched victory from the jaws of defeat. For example, he lost a series of House appropriations floor votes, but then recovered most of those losses when eight of the measures were folded into a massive omnibus bill at the end of the session. The resulting package (PL 105-277) funded several Democratic priorities, including increased spending for teachers, while excluding most of the conservative policy "riders" added in the House.

In the wake of his Senate impeachment trial, Clinton and the Republican-led Congress found little room for compromise in 1999. For the most part, they did not even try. In this atmosphere, Clinton's ability to persuade Congress fell to near record lows. None of the major initiatives outlined in his State of the Union address—overhauling Social Security and Medicare, raising the minimum wage, or tightening regulation of health maintenance organizations—became law; few ever came up for a vote. On those issues that did prompt votes, Clinton fared poorly, scoring a 37.8 percent overall success rate, the second-lowest score since CQ began evaluating presidential success in 1953. Clinton also held the lowest-ever score, 36.2 percent; it came in 1995, when the Republicans had just taken control of Congress for the first time in forty years.

Many legislators said partisanship in Congress was the worst they had ever seen. In the Senate GOP leaders frequently used procedural tactics to deny Democrats opportunities to offer amendments to bills. Democrats responded with filibusters to force Republicans to give them votes on Democratic priorities such as regulating HMOs and lifting the minimum wage. In the House legislators attributed Clinton's failure to win more votes in the narrowly divided House to J. Dennis Hastert, R-Ill., who succeeded the fiery

CLINTON VETOES: NEW USES FOR AN OLD WEAPON

Two years into his presidency, Bill Clinton lost control of the legislative agenda when in 1994 jubilant Republicans took control of both chambers of Congress for the first time in forty years. Led by House Speaker Newt Gingrich, R-Ga., the GOP set out to overturn decades of Democratic social welfare programs.

But by the end of 1995, Clinton had turned the tables, regaining the initiative by finding a new use for an old weapon: the presidential veto.

Although Republicans retained control of Congress for the rest of Clinton's presidency, Clinton was never again without power to shape the legislative agenda. Together with his highly skilled use of presidential publicity advantages, Clinton made vetoes and veto threats a powerful tool not only to ward off assaults on his agenda but to advance his priority programs.

A prime example was Clinton's drive to hire 100,000 teachers to reduce class size. Although Republicans never agreed to authorize the initiative, Clinton used veto threats to win $4.1 billion for the program over three years.

George C. Edwards, a professor of political science at Texas A&M University, called Clinton's use of the veto "nearly unprecedented." Typically, Edwards said, presidents vetoed bills to prevent enactment of programs they dislike—the creation of a new entitlement, for example. In contrast, Clinton's most successful use of the veto power was not to block legislation—although he did halt most GOP efforts to cut taxes and shrink domestic programs—but to win increased spending for his own domestic priorities.

Altogether Clinton vetoed just 37 bills, an annual average of 4.6 a year—less than any president since Warren G. Harding. During his first two years in office, while Democrats controlled Congress, Clinton did not veto a single bill. According to Robert J. Spitzer, a political science professor at the State University of New York at Cortland, that was the longest stretch without a veto since 1850, when Millard Fillmore was president.

The Turning Point

The turning point came during 1995 and 1996, when Republicans, led by Gingrich, sought to enact a host of social policy objectives as riders on appropriations bills despite the president's objections. Clinton had already vetoed three bills in 1995 when the first showdown came on a stopgap spending measure needed to keep the government running while negotiations continued on nine of the thirteen regular fiscal 1996 spending bills.

Rather than drop the provisions that Clinton opposed, the Republicans dared the president to veto the legislation and shut the government down. They gambled that Clinton would back down or, barring that, take the blame from an angry public. Either way, they expected to win.

As promised, Clinton vetoed the bill on Nov. 13, along with a separate, short-term measure to extend the Treasury Department's borrowing authority. On Nov. 14, much of the federal government shut down. Polls that week indicated that two-thirds of Americans blamed the Republicans. Clinton went on to veto the GOP reconciliation bill and three more appropriations bills before exhausted Republicans conceded in 1996, only to suffer losses in the 1996 general elections that were widely attributed to their handling of the crisis. (*Congress and the Nation Vol. IX, pp. 71–73*)

Appropriating by Veto

The experience haunted Republicans through the rest of Clinton's presidency. Year after year they pushed conservative priorities in the annual appropriations process, only to eventually relent to avoid blame for another government shutdown. The mere threat of a veto—usually in the form of a Statement of Administration Policy, or SAP, issued by the Office of Management and Budget and detailing White House objections—was often enough to win crucial changes in spending bills.

In 1998, for example, Republicans agreed to a $500 billion year-end appropriations package for fiscal 1999, substantially over budget guidelines. Although it included substantial increases for GOP priorities, Clinton won major victories despite being weakened by scandal and impeachment hearings. The bill provided $3 billion more for Labor, Health and Human Services, and Education than Clinton had originally requested. The president won a $1.2 billion down payment on his plan to hire 100,000 teachers, as well as the full $18 billion he had requested for the International Monetary Fund.

In 1999 Clinton vetoed four appropriations bills and threatened to veto one other. In the end he won more than $5 billion in year-end additions included in the fiscal 2000 omnibus spending bill.

In 2000 Clinton vetoed two fiscal 2001 appropriations bills—energy and water and a combined bill covering the Treasury Department, Postal Service, and the legislative branch. A veto threat also stopped Congress from sending a cleared Commerce-Justice-State appropriations bill to the White House. When the negotiations were finally concluded, Republicans had agreed to add an extra $10 billion to the president's original request, which they had initially sought to slash. The Department of Education, which the GOP had targeted for elimination in 1994, received its biggest spending increase since its creation in 1979.

Clinton's use of the veto and his success in dictating fiscal and legislative policy infuriated Republicans. "When the president gets to the point that he can either accept or veto a bill, he becomes as powerful . . . as two-thirds of us, because if he does not agree with something that we have done, it takes two-thirds of us to override that veto," House Appropriations Committee Chairman C. W. "Bill" Young, R-Fla., said on the House floor.

Speaking on the Senate floor, Republican Senator Arlen Specter of Pennsylvania characterized the period since the government shutdown as "a dictatorial system of the president saying what is acceptable, and the Congress being held hostage in effect, concerned about being blamed for shutting down the government." (*Clinton vetoes 1993–1996, Congress and the Nation Vol. IX, p. 1122; 1997–2000, Appendix, p. 994*)

Early Use of the Veto

Rarely had the veto been used as Clinton used it. In the early years of the republic, presidents vetoed bills infrequently, usually to block legislation they believed was unconstitutional. Between 1789 and 1828, only ten bills were vetoed, none overridden.

In the nineteenth century, the veto was used mainly by presidents who saw themselves as bulwarks against congressional supremacy or who faced active opposition from their own parties. Andrew Jackson, who saw himself as a man of the people standing against the establishment-controlled legislature, was the first to use the veto as a tool to attack Congress.

Several modern presidents used their veto power more often, primarily to prevent spending they opposed, to stop congressional forays into foreign policy and other areas of executive authority, or to block social policy legislation.

Gerald R. Ford relied on the veto more frequently than any other president since President Dwight D. Eisenhower, vetoing sixty-six bills in his short presidency (August 1974– January 1977). Ford's vetoes were regarded as a sign of his weakness in the office. His lack of an electoral mandate and the cloud that surrounded his presidency after he pardoned his predecessor, Richard M. Nixon, handicapped him in promoting a legislative agenda of his own. With Democrats pushing an agenda he opposed, he had little alternative.

Strong presidents also have used the veto pen, but they, too, were mainly trying to stop legislation they opposed. Franklin D. Roosevelt was the first president to veto major tax legislation and to use the threat of the veto to control the legislative agenda.

Although vetoes occurred most often under divided government, that did not necessarily result in veto overrides, which require a two-thirds majority in both chambers. George Bush, who faced a Democratic Congress, had only one veto out of forty-four overridden in his four years from 1989 to 1993. Clinton, who faced a majority of Republicans in both chambers from 1995 on, was overridden only twice.

Historically, overrides were infrequent—only 106 of 2,551 vetoes issued between 1789 and 2000 were overridden.

In the period after World War II, President Harry S. Truman—locked in partisan struggle with the Republican-controlled 80th Congress—vetoed far more bills than any of the presidents who followed him. This table lists the vetoes and veto overrides of all presidents from Truman to Clinton.

President (Congresses)	Regular Vetoes	Pocket Vetoes	Total Vetoes	Vetoes Overriden
Harry S. Truman (79th–82nd)	180	70	250	12
Dwight D. Eisenhower (83rd–86th)	73	108	181	2
John F. Kennedy (87th–88th)	12	9	21	—
Lyndon B. Johnson (88th–90th)	16	14	30	—
Richard M. Nixon (91st–93rd)	26	17	43	7
Gerald R. Ford (93rd–94th)	48	18	66	12
Jimmy Carter (95th–96th)	13	18	31	2
Ronald Reagan (97th–100th)	39	39	78	9
George Bush[1] (101st–102nd)	29	15	44	1
Bill Clinton (103rd–106th)	37	1	38	2

1. President Bush attempted to pocket veto two bills during intrasession recess periods. Congress considered the two bills enacted into law because of the president's failure to return the legislation. The bills are not counted as pocket vetoes in this table.

SOURCE: Congressional Research Service

Line-Item Veto

Clinton's presidency also marked the beginning and the end of the so-called line-item veto. Long sought by presidents of both parties, the line-item veto—actually an enhanced rescission power over tax and spending bills—was enacted in 1996 (PL 104-130) and took effect in 1997. Clinton used the line-item veto to delete items in eleven bills.

Although Congress had enthusiastically passed the bill, members objected when Clinton began using it, leading to one of the two veto overrides of his presidency. In 1998 the Supreme Court struck down the Line Item Veto Act, ruling that it was unconstitutional because it allowed the president to rewrite bills he had already signed. (*Line item veto, p. 64*)

Newt Gingrich as Speaker. Hastert inspired remarkable loyalty among his members.

By Clinton's last year in office, any pretense of trying to work together had faded. Clinton's presidential success rating shot up to 55.1 percent, primarily because the Senate confirmed a large number of nominations by roll call vote. The Republican leaders in Congress—especially in the Senate—were in no mood to hand Clinton victories that would make him look better in the history books. Nor were they interested in promoting the fortunes of Vice President Gore or of Democratic congressional candidates in the 2000 elections. Congressional Democrats, for their part, refused to take any action that might give the Republicans an edge at the polls. The result was legislative stalemate.

The one saving grace for Clinton in 2000, as in every year since the 1995–1996 government shutdown in a standoff with congressional Republicans, was his skillful use of veto threats to maximize his bargaining leverage, enabling him to salvage some real successes out of the appropriations process. In 2000 he persuaded Republicans to accept a 17 percent increase in education spending for fiscal 2001, by far the largest increase in the history of the Department of Education. But this achievement paled in comparison to the weighty list of proposals he offered in his State of the Union address, including prescription drug coverage for seniors, new rules for managed care plans, new health coverage for low-income parents as well as their children, gun control, expansion of the earned income tax credit, and Senate approval of the Comprehensive Test Ban Treaty.

Clinton Impeachment

Whatever his legislative and foreign policy legacy, it is safe to say that Bill Clinton will be remembered most as the president who was impeached on and acquitted of charges that he committed perjury and obstructed justice in an effort to cover up an affair with a young White House intern, Monica Lewinsky. Clinton was never in any real danger of being removed from office, and his job ratings with the public remained high. But the historical record will forever record the president's adamant denials of wrongdoing followed by his abject apologies and finally, on his last full day in office, his admission that he had indeed lied under oath.

For more than a year the U.S. government, the national media, and the American public were caught up in the unfolding drama as Kenneth W. Starr, the independent counsel investigating unrelated allegations of presidential misconduct, and Republicans in Congress and their supporters outside attempted to remove the president from office. In the end they failed, and numerous observers believed they may have lost as much as the president.

Republicans, who insisted on pressing ahead with the impeachment proceedings—despite clear indications that a majority of the public opposed impeachment and Clinton's removal from the White House—lost five seats in the House in the 1998 elections, narrowing their margin to just six seats. As a result of those losses and growing GOP dissatisfaction with his strident leadership, House Speaker Newt Gingrich, R-Ga., one of Clinton's most aggressive foes, resigned from the House only days after the election. Six weeks later, in one of the more dramatic moments in the impeachment saga, Gingrich's successor also resigned, leaving House Republicans in disarray for some months. *(Gingrich's successor, p. 758)*

With less fanfare Congress in 1999 allowed the law under which Starr's investigation was authorized to lapse. The Office of Independent Counsel had been controversial since it was enacted in the wake of the Watergate scandal that forced President Richard M. Nixon from office in 1974. But never did an independent counsel investigation cause as much controversy as Starr's five-year investigation of President Clinton, characterized by the president and his supporters as nothing more than a nasty partisan vendetta aimed at driving Clinton out of office.

More indirectly, Clinton's conduct may have adversely affected the fortunes of his vice president and heir apparent, Al Gore. Commentators noted many reasons to explain Gore's failure to win an electoral college majority in the 2000 presidential race even though he won the popular vote, including his own flawed campaign. But high on almost every list was residual public distaste for the Clinton scandals, and especially the president's personal conduct, that were paraded through the months of the impeachment proceedings. *(2000 presidential elections, p. 21)*

Less clear was the lasting effect, if any, that the president's conduct would have on the presidency itself. Only once before in U.S. history had a president been impeached. That occurred on Feb. 24, 1868, when the House voted to impeach President Andrew Johnson in a dispute rooted in disagreements over post–Civil War Reconstruction. Johnson was subsequently acquitted by a single vote in a Senate trial. *(Johnson impeachment, box, p. 814)*

Unfolding of a Scandal

Starr had been investigating Clinton and his wife, Hillary Rodham Clinton, since August 1994 in connection with their involvement in a complicated Arkansas land deal known as Whitewater. A former U.S. solicitor general, with close ties to conservative Republicans known to despise the president, Starr soon expanded his operations to look into several events: the abrupt firing of White House travel office personnel in 1993; the subsequent suicide of Vincent W. Foster Jr., a close friend of the first family and a White House aide who played a role in the firings; and administration requests in 1993 and 1994 for hundreds of confidential FBI files, including those of former Republican White House officials. *(Whitewater investigations, p. 805; Congress and the Nation Vol. IX, pp. 938, 942)*

SEXUAL HARASSMENT SUIT

Clinton was also the defendant in a sexual harassment suit brought against him in February 1994 by Paula Corbin Jones. Jones had accused the president of requesting oral sex from her in a Little Rock hotel room when he was governor of Arkansas and she was a minor state functionary. Clinton's attorneys had fought off the case until May 1997, when the

JOHNSON IMPEACHMENT

Andrew Johnson, the only other president to be impeached, was thrust into the presidency after the assassination of Abraham Lincoln in April 1865. Johnson, a Democrat who served Tennessee as a state senator, U.S. representative, governor, and U.S. senator, was the only southerner to remain in the Senate when the southern states seceded from the Union in 1861. In 1862, after Union forces had captured much of Tennessee, Lincoln appointed Johnson military governor of the state. At Johnson's urging, Tennessee became the only seceding state to outlaw slavery before the 1863 Emancipation Proclamation. Johnson's loyalty to the Union was rewarded with a vice-presidential nomination in 1864. (The Republican Party briefly became the Union Party in 1864 to include southerners loyal to the Union.) Lincoln and Johnson defeated the regular Democratic ticket handily.

Johnson served as vice president only six weeks before Lincoln died on April 15 from a gunshot inflicted by assassin John Wilkes Booth. An outsider without allies or connections in the Republican Party, the new president faced the problem of reconstructing a broken South, which had surrendered six days before. Johnson tried to implement Lincoln's lenient Reconstruction program, but he was blocked by "Radical" Republicans in Congress who were intent upon punishing the region and limiting the influence of white southerners in national politics. Johnson successfully vetoed several harsh Reconstruction bills early in his presidency, but in the 1866 congressional elections the Radical Republicans gained firm control of Congress, and the scene was set for repeated legislative battles.

Johnson survived the first attempt to impeach him, when the House on Dec. 6, 1867, overwhelmingly defeated an impeachment resolution charging him with usurpation of power and corrupt use of the appointment, pardon, and veto powers. Most members saw these charges as political grievances instead of illegal acts. But Radical Republicans did not have long to wait before they tried again.

On Dec. 12, 1867, Johnson suspended Secretary of War Edwin M. Stanton, a close ally of the more extreme Radical Republicans. Johnson had long wanted to get rid of Stanton, but his efforts to persuade Stanton to resign were to no avail. In January 1868 the Senate refused to approve Stanton's suspension. Under the terms of the Tenure of Office Act, which Republicans had passed in early 1867 over Johnson's veto, the Senate's failure to approve Stanton's suspension had the effect of reinstating him. Apparently flushed by his victory on the earlier impeachment effort, Johnson decided to force the issue, citing his constitutional power and authority to dismiss Stanton outright on Feb. 21.

The dismissal enraged Congress, driving conservative Republicans into alliance with the Radical Republicans. An impeachment resolution was reported out of committee on Feb. 22, and two days later the House voted to impeach Johnson on a party-line vote of 126–47. A week later the House approved eleven articles of impeachment. Eight concerned Johnson's removal of Stanton; the others alleged violation of another law and seditious libel against Congress.

The Senate trial opened March 30, 1868. During the weeks of argument and testimony, Johnson's lawyers insisted that the Tenure of Office Act was unconstitutional, that in any event it did not apply to Johnson in this case because Lincoln had appointed Stanton, and that Stanton had not actually been removed from office because he remained physically barricaded in his office at the War Department.

At the same time, some conservative Republicans were beginning to have second thoughts. Their main concern was fiery Benjamin Wade of Ohio (1851–1869), one of the most radical of the Radical Republicans. Under the succession law then in effect, Wade, the president pro tempore of the Senate, was the next in line for the presidency.

The Senate on May 16 took a test vote on a general catch-all article of impeachment, one that House managers thought most likely to produce a vote for conviction. With 36 votes needed for conviction, the final count was 35, guilty, to 19, not guilty. Ten days later Johnson was acquitted on two more charges by identical 35–19 votes. The Senate abandoned the remaining articles and adjourned, abruptly ending the trial. President Johnson had been acquitted of impeachment charges by a single vote.

Supreme Court ruled that a sitting president was not immune to a civil suit for a personal action alleged to have occurred before he took office. Hoping to show at the trial, scheduled for May 1998, that Clinton's alleged conduct with Jones was part of an established pattern of sexual harassment, Jones's attorneys compiled a list of women whose names had been linked publicly and privately with Clinton's over the years. One name on that list was Monica Lewinsky.

Arguing that she had no information relevant to the Jones case, Lewinsky filed a sworn affidavit on Jan. 7, 1998, in which she denied ever having sexual relations with Clinton. Lewinsky, however, had told several friends about an affair with the president, which began in November 1995, when she was twenty-two and working in the White House legislative affairs office, and continued sporadically through 1996 and early 1997. One of her confidants was Linda R. Tripp, a former White House employee whom Lewinsky had met at the Pentagon, where they both worked for a period. Unbeknownst to Lewinsky, Tripp had taped several of the conversations in which Lewinsky described her sexual relations with Clinton and said that Clinton had urged her to lie about their affair. Lewinsky was recorded urging Tripp, herself a witness in the Jones case, to lie to the court about her knowledge of Lewinsky's affair with the president.

The two investigations were linked, according to Starr, when Tripp turned the tapes over to the independent counsel's office on Jan. 12, 1998. She subsequently agreed to wear a "body wire" recorder at a Jan. 16 meeting she arranged with Lewinsky at a suburban Virginia hotel. With FBI agents monitoring the conversation, Tripp got Lewinsky once again to say that the president had urged her to lie about their relationship and again asked Tripp to lie about it.

Later the same day, prosecutors from Starr's office confronted Lewinsky with the tapes and sought her cooperation in their investigation of the president. Starr also used the tapes to persuade Attorney General Janet Reno to recommend to the three-judge "special division" that oversaw the jurisdiction of independent counsels that Starr be permitted to investigate the Lewinsky affair. That permission was granted.

Unaware that Starr had confronted Lewinsky, President Clinton in a sworn deposition on Jan. 17 told Jones's attorneys that he had never had sexual relations with Lewinsky—a denial that he repeated publicly after the *Washington Post* broke the news of the alleged affair and the possible perjury on Jan. 21. On Jan. 26, the day before he was scheduled to give the annual State of the Union address, Clinton looked directly into the television cameras, wagged his finger, and said, "I want to say one thing to the American people. I want you to listen to me. I'm going to say this again. I did not have sexual relations with that woman, Miss Lewinsky. I never told anyone to lie. Not a single time. Never. These allegations are false. And I need to go back to work for the American people."

At the same time, Clinton and the White House mounted a counterattack on Starr. Hillary Clinton scathingly referred to Starr as a "politically motivated prosecutor" allied with "right-wing opponents of my husband" to try to drive the president from office. "It's obvious, I think, to the American people," Clinton said at an April 30 news conference, that the Starr investigation "has been a hard, well-financed, vigorous effort over a long period of time" to discredit the president by any means available. Others said Starr began investigating the president's sex life only because he was unable to develop any damaging evidence against Clinton in the Whitewater case—the original reason for his appointment. For the remainder of the year, the White House and Starr each accused the other of unethical conduct, illegal leaks to news organizations, and other underhanded behavior.

Throughout the spring and summer, Starr called a steady stream of White House aides and Lewinsky friends before a federal grand jury in Washington, issuing a series of subpoenas for those who refused to testify voluntarily. Several White House efforts to block Starr from taking testimony from key officials failed when federal courts rejected claims of execu-

Although ultimately acquitted, President Bill Clinton's legacy in the White House may always be overshadowed by his impeachment ordeal during his second term. *Source: Scott J. Ferrell, Congressional Quarterly*

tive privilege and attorney-client privilege. A unique assertion that secret service agents guarding the president enjoyed a "protective function privilege" that allowed them to refuse to testify about the president's movements also failed.

The one case the president did win was the Jones sexual harassment case. On April 1, Susan Webber Wright, the U.S. federal judge in Arkansas hearing the case, threw out the suit, ruling that there were "no genuine issues for trial." (In November Clinton agreed to settle the case, giving Jones $850,000 in return for her pledge not to appeal the dismissal.)

By mid-July, the only two people who had not appeared before Starr's grand jury were Lewinsky and Clinton. Starr subpoenaed Clinton on July 17; it was the first time a sitting president had been subpoenaed to appear before a federal grand jury. Clinton's lawyers immediately began to stall for time, but on July 29 Clinton agreed to testify voluntarily. His decision came a day after Starr and Lewinsky concluded months of negotiations on a deal giving her immunity in return for her grand jury testimony.

Starr withdrew his subpoena of Clinton, thus averting any potential clash over whether a sitting president could be forced to testify. (In another unprecedented move, Clinton also agreed to a blood test, which was used to determine that his DNA matched that of stains on a blue dress that Lewinsky wore at one of their encounters.) Appearing before the grand jury on Aug. 6, Lewinsky acknowledged that she and the president had had a sexual relationship but insisted that he had never told her to lie about it.

CLINTON'S GRAND JURY TESTIMONY

Clinton's turn before the grand jury came Aug. 17, when he testified from the White House through a remote television arrangement. Previous presidents had given sworn testimony in legal proceedings but Clinton was the first to give evidence to a grand jury investigating alleged criminal conduct of the president himself. Under the unique arrangement, Clinton was questioned for four hours by attorneys from the independent counsel's office, including Starr, Robert Bittman, and Solomon L. Wisenberg, in the White House Map Room. The president's private attorney David E. Kendall was also present. The questions and the president's answers were transmitted through closed circuit television to a nearby federal courthouse, where the grand jurors watched on two large television screens. Jurors could also call in with questions that were then relayed to the president.

Although Clinton's testimony was given in private, as are all grand jury proceedings, the House Judiciary Committee, on a party-line vote, released videotapes of that testimony on Sept. 21, which were immediately aired on all major television networks. As he had in his deposition in the Jones case, Clinton gave narrow, literal, and legalistic answers to most of the questions. He began with a prepared statement in which he acknowledged "inappropriate intimate contact" with Lewinsky but said it "did not constitute sexual relations as I understood that term to be defined" at his January deposition. He refused to provide any specific details about the intimate contact, and he avoided directly answering many questions. "It depends on what the meaning of the word 'is' means," he said in response to a question about his January denial that he was having an affair with Lewinsky. "If 'is' means 'is and never has been,' that's one thing. If it means, 'there is none,' that was a completely true statement." Perhaps this statement, reminiscent of Clinton's 1992 campaign statement that he had not inhaled when he experimented with marijuana in his youth, more than any other from Clinton convinced viewers that the president was attempting to paper over the obvious.

After giving his grand jury testimony on Aug. 17, Clinton appeared on national television that evening and admitted to the American people that he had misled them. "I did have a relationship with Miss Lewinsky that was not appropriate. In fact it was wrong," the president said. But he denied that he had done anything illegal, and he lashed out at Starr for pursuing a politically motivated investigation into what were essentially private matters. "Even presidents have private lives," Clinton said. "It is time to stop the pursuit of personal destruction and the prying into private lives and get on with our national lives." It was a challenge that went unheeded.

Starr Report

Any hope in the White House that a confrontation with Congress over Clinton's misconduct could be avoided was dashed on Sept. 9, when Starr delivered a report to Congress containing what he described as "substantial and credible evidence" that the president had committed impeachable offenses in his effort to cover up his relationship with Lewinsky. The eleven charges Starr outlined included perjury, obstruction of justice, witness tampering, and abuse of power. Nearly overshadowing these charges, however, were Starr's graphic and detailed descriptions of the sexual encounters between Clinton and Lewinsky. The explicit descriptions, which read more like a bad pulp novel than a somber legal document, were regrettable but necessary, Starr said, to show that the president had lied under oath when he said that he had never had sexual relations with Lewinsky.

Because the House had not expected Starr's report for several more weeks, the unannounced arrival on Capitol Hill of the 445-page report and thirty-six boxes of grand jury material caught legislators off guard. "Nobody knows what to do. We've never done this before," an aide to House Minority Leader Richard A. Gephardt, D-Mo., said.

Although Democratic and Republican leaders had pledged to consider any charges Starr might level in a spirit of bipartisanship, that resolve evaporated in the debate over when and how to release the report. Republican leaders announced Sept. 10 that they would release the report and post it on the Internet simultaneously the next day, before anyone in Congress had had an opportunity to read it.

Democrats argued that the president's attorneys should be given at least forty-eight hours to review the report before it was made public. "The House of Representatives is not the U.S. Postal Service," said John Conyers Jr., the ranking Democrat on the House Judiciary Committee. "We are not a delivery system for Kenneth W. Starr. . . . We cannot, we ought not, we should not release anything to anybody unless we know what it is we are releasing."

Only a handful of legislators followed Conyers's lead. With a large majority concurring with Judiciary Committee Chairman Henry J. Hyde that "it is important that the American people learn the facts," the House in a **key vote, 363–63 (R 224–0; D 138–63; I 1–0),** on the morning of Sept. 11 approved release of the report immediately. *(1998 key votes p. 883)*

GROUNDS FOR IMPEACHMENT

In the report, or referral, as it was formally called, the independent counsel listed eleven "possible grounds for impeachment," which the White House rebutted point for point in a document released Sept. 12. The referral leveled charges against Clinton in four areas.

Perjury

The referral said that Clinton had lied numerous times, both in his civil deposition in the Jones sexual harassment case and in his Aug. 17 grand jury testimony, about the nature of his relationship with Lewinsky and efforts to conceal it. In his deposition Clinton denied that he had had a sexual relationship with Lewinsky. In his grand jury testimony,

On Sept. 9, 1998, the independent counsel's office delivered to Congress thirty-six boxes of grand jury material—dramatically transferred here by Capitol police—concerning possible impeachable conduct of the president. *Source: Scott J. Ferrell, Congressional Quarterly*

Clinton said that his statements, while misleading, were accurate and that he had not engaged in sex with Lewinsky as defined by Jones's lawyers. To show that Clinton had lied, the report detailed several encounters between Clinton and Lewinsky from Nov. 15, 1995, to Dec. 28, 1997.

According to Lewinsky's testimony, the two never had sexual intercourse, but she had performed oral sex on the president nine times, and he had touched her breasts and genitals during some of these encounters. Although a narrow, literal interpretation of the definition used by the Jones lawyers might not cover oral sex, Clinton's fondling of Lewinsky clearly fell within the scope of the definition, the referral said. The report further charged that Clinton was untruthful during his deposition when he said he could not recall whether he had ever been alone with Lewinsky or had exchanged gifts with her.

Obstruction of Justice

The referral said Clinton and Lewinsky had an understanding that they would deny their relationship and that she would lie under oath in the Jones case. Lewinsky originally signed an affidavit denying her affair with Clinton but changed her story after she received a grant of immunity from Starr. According to the report, Clinton and Lewinsky also had agreed to conceal gifts they had given each other instead of turning them over to lawyers in the Jones suit. Although testimony on the matter conflicted, Starr said it was possible that Clinton had asked his personal secretary, Betty Currie, to retrieve gifts he had given to Lewinsky and to hide those gifts, which had been subpoenaed by Jones's attorneys. The "reasonable inference" from the evidence, the Starr report said, was that Clinton "orchestrated or approved the concealment of gifts."

The referral further said that Clinton attempted to impede investigators by helping Lewinsky find a job in New York at a time when she would have been a witness harmful to him if she had testified in the Jones cases. Starr also said Clinton had not told the truth about discussions with his friend Vernon E. Jordan Jr., who tried to help Lewinsky find a job in New York.

Witness Tampering

The report charged that Clinton had improperly tampered with a potential witness by attempting to influence Currie's testimony before the grand jury. Starr also said Clinton deliberately lied to key staff members, knowing that they would repeat those falsehoods in their subsequent grand jury testimony.

Abuse of Constitutional Authority

In a catch-all charge, Starr said that since Clinton's deposition in the Jones case on Jan. 17, his actions in the Lewinsky matter were inconsistent with his constitutional duty to faithfully execute the laws. Specifically, Starr said, the president had promised to cooperate with the investigation and then refused six invitations to testify voluntarily; he deliberately misled his senior aides, his cabinet, and the American people about the affair; and he asserted executive privilege "all as part of an effort to hinder, impede and deflect a possible inquiry by the Congress of the United States."

WHITE HOUSE REBUTTAL

In a rebuttal, Clinton's attorneys declared that as a matter of law, Clinton had not done any of the things of which he was accused. On the perjury charges, they said that Starr had to show that Clinton not only was wrong about his interpretation of sex as defined by Jones's attorneys at his deposition, but that he knew he was wrong and intentionally lied. All the independent counsel had shown, they said, was that Clinton gave "narrow answers to ambiguous questions."

The rebuttal said that Clinton had acknowledged in his deposition that he and Lewinsky exchanged gifts and denied that the president had ever taken steps to conceal the gifts. Clinton's attorneys said it was Lewinsky, not the president, who had asked Currie to retrieve the gifts. Nor did Clinton ever try to get Lewinsky a job in order to influence her testimony. Clinton's attorneys quoted the Starr report in which it acknowledged that there was "no evidence" of any "arrangement . . . explicitly spelled out."

Clinton's attorneys were blistering in their remarks castigating Starr's motives. "Any fair reader of the Referral," they wrote, "will easily discern that many of the lurid allegations . . . have no justification at all, even in terms of any [Office of Independent Counsel (OIC)] legal theory. . . . They are simply part of a hit-and-run smear campaign and their inclusion says volumes about the OIC's tactics and objectives. . . ."

The president's conduct was wrong, the rebuttal said, and his efforts to keep his illicit affair from becoming public, while understandable, were also wrong. But, the attorneys said, the president's actions did not rise to the level of high crimes and misdemeanors required for impeachment. The report was "at bottom overreaching in an extravagant effort to find a case where there is none."

REACTION TO THE REPORT

Reaction to the report was immediate. By late afternoon, people across the country were reading the Starr report, which was posted on the Internet at the same time it became available to House members. Portions of it were being read on radio and television. Some broadcasts warned that the material was unsuitable for children and might be offensive to some adults. Some television reporters were visibly embarrassed by the explicit sexual descriptions that they were reporting. People expressed a range of emotions, from embarrassment to outrage, and Clinton's personal ratings, which had fallen considerably after his Aug. 17 address to the nation admitting the relationship, fell even further in the days following release of the Starr report.

On Capitol Hill, legislators in both parties expressed outrage, shock, and deep disappointment with the president's behavior as described in the report. The two Democratic leaders of Congress, House Minority Leader Gephardt and Senate Minority Leader Tom Daschle, D-S.D., asked Congress to move quickly to determine whether and how to punish Clinton. Some legislators had already begun to explore the possibility of censuring and perhaps fining the president for his misconduct.

In Pursuit of Impeachment

Republican leaders, however, were eager to press ahead with a full-scale impeachment inquiry that examined not only Clinton's conduct with Lewinsky, but also several other allegations against the president. Clinton had long been a focus of political animosity from many Republican legislators, particularly House members, who resented Clinton for managing to co-opt or block much of the "Contract with America" that the GOP had promised to pass after it gained control of Congress in 1994. Republicans were also frustrated that Clinton managed to pin the blame on them for forcing a shutdown of most of the government in late 1995.

Moreover, some Republicans had not forgiven the Democrats for mounting a lengthy investigation of Ronald Reagan and several White House aides for their actions in the Iran-contra scandal in the 1980s. Many conservative Republicans also remained bitter with the Democrats for defeating the nominations of several Republicans for cabinet positions or court appointments. Prominent among these were former solicitor general Robert H. Bork, a conservative appeals court judge whose nomination for a seat on the Supreme Court was rejected in 1987, and former Sen. John Tower of Texas, whose nomination to be secretary of defense was defeated in 1989. Allegations of drinking and womanizing figured prominently in the Tower defeat. *(Bork nomination, Congress and the Nation Vol. VII, p. 786; Tower nomination, Congress and the Nation Vol. VIII, p. 339)*

Even before the formal debate on impeachment opened, the partisan gulf on the issue was evident. Behind closed doors and by a party-line vote, the House Judiciary Committee voted on Sept. 21 to release the tapes of Clinton's Aug. 17 grand jury testimony and some 2,800 pages of printed material. Describing the meeting as "vigorously partisan," Chairman Henry Hyde, R-Ill., said "there was a general view among Democrats not to reveal anything, and a general view among Republicans to reveal as much as possible."

If the Republicans had hoped to embarrass Clinton further with the videotapes, the move backfired. Polls taken the day after the tapes were released showed that although a majority of those surveyed believed that Clinton had lied under oath, the president's job rating had gone up six to nine points since the tapes were aired. Moreover, according to a *New York Times*/CBS News Poll conducted Sept. 22–23, 65 percent of those surveyed did not want Congress to hold impeachment hearings; 78 percent said Starr's investigation was not worth the time and money. Hyde himself also experienced embarrassment after *Salon,* an online Internet magazine, published a story revealing that he, as a married man, had had an affair many years earlier with a married woman.

The Judiciary Committee began its formal public deliberations on impeachment on Oct. 8, after several days of behind-the-scenes debates about procedure. A round of opening statements from each of the panel's twenty-one Republicans and sixteen Democrats laid out the arguments for and against impeachment that would be heard repeatedly in the following months. Republicans argued that Clinton had committed perjury and obstructed justice in dereliction of his duty as president to take care that the laws be faithfully executed. Clinton's alleged lies under oath constituted "an assault on the rule of the law" that threatened "our system of government," Hyde argued. Democrats countered that Clinton's actions to cover up his affairs were the natural reactions of a man trying to avoid personal and public embarrassment and that they did not rise to the level of impeachable "high crimes and misdemeanors." Conyers summarized the Democrats' argument: "Under our constitutional system of government, if the president misbehaves in a way that does not impact on his official duties, the remedy still lies in the voting booth and not in a legislative takeover of the executive branch."

By straight party-line votes, the committee then rejected two Democratic resolutions that sought to limit the time and scope of the inquiry and adopted the open-ended plan proposed by Republicans. Modeled on the plan the committee used in the Watergate impeachment inquiry, the resolution set no limits on the scope of the inquiry or on the time for its completion. Hyde and Conyers were authorized jointly to subpoena witnesses and material. Matters on which the two could not agree would be submitted to the full committee for decision. The Democratic alternatives would have limited the scope of the inquiry only to the Lewinsky matter and ended the inquiry by Nov. 25.

Following a curiously undramatic debate given the historic nature of the vote, the full House, by a vote of 258–176 on Oct. 8, adopted House Resolution 581, directing the Judiciary Committee to open the impeachment inquiry. Thirty-one Democrats joined all the Republicans in support of the resolution. A Democratic resolution to limit the scope and length of the inquiry was defeated by a vote of 198–236. The Judiciary Committee immediately put the inquiry on a back burner as Congress rushed to complete work on an omnibus appropriations bill before going home to campaign for the 1998 off-year November elections.

POSTELECTION DELIBERATIONS

When the committee returned to Washington after the elections, the situation had changed dramatically. Instead of the twenty House seats they had hoped to gain, Republicans lost five seats, giving the GOP only a six-vote margin in the 106th Congress. Speaker Newt Gingrich, who had been credited with helping Republicans win control of the House in 1994, was now being blamed for taking positions unpopular with voters, including pursuing impeachment of the president, a path that opinion polls consistently showed the public opposed. Rather than face a certain challenge to his leadership from within the party, Gingrich announced that he was resigning his Speakership and leaving the House.

With leadership of the party uncertain, Judiciary Committee Republicans found themselves between the proverbial rock and a hard place. Support from rank-and-file Republicans for a full-blown investigation was dwindling not only because of the public opposition, but because it was not clear that the committee could finish its work before the end of the year. Republicans wanted to avoid a House vote on impeachment in the 106th Congress, where their reduced numbers would work to Clinton's advantage. But committee Republicans could not simply drop the matter, partly because many of them sincerely believed that Clinton's actions amounted to impeachable offenses and partly because of pressure from staunchly conservative Republicans both in and out of Congress who would not be content until Clinton was removed from office.

The Judiciary Committee seemed unfocused, even somewhat erratic, as committee Republicans struggled with these competing pressures. Apparently trying to avoid a soap opera atmosphere, the committee sought no testimony from Lewinsky and others with firsthand information of the events. At the same time, however, it voted to extend its inquiry into campaign finance issues and other sexual misconduct allegations against Clinton. Although it voted to subpoena witnesses in these side inquiries, the committee then never called them. The inquiry's public hearings ranged from thoughtful, if somewhat tangential, discourses by judges and scholars on the definition of impeachable offenses to testimony from two convicted perjurers whose cases involved deceptions related to sex.

The one major witness the committee did hear was Starr, who appeared for twelve hours on Nov. 19 to lay out his case against the president in person. The president's attorneys were allowed to present witnesses during two days in early December. These witnesses included prosecutors, defense attorneys, constitutional scholars, and three former members of the Judiciary Committee who had voted to impeach President Nixon in 1974.

Independent Counsel Kenneth W. Starr (standing lower left) takes oath before testifying before the House Judiciary Committee on Nov. 19, 1998. *Source: Scott J. Ferrell, Congressional Quarterly*

Perhaps the most significant event in the committee's deliberations, and certainly the most damaging to Clinton, was the president's response to a series of eighty-one questions posed by the committee. Clinton's responses, carefully phrased in the same legalese that marked his grand jury testimony, disappointed many legislators, including moderates, who wanted the president to admit openly that he had lied under oath—regardless of how his enemies might use such an admission or whether it would place him in greater jeopardy of criminal charges after he left the White House.

The inquiry wound to its end when the Judiciary Committee on Dec. 11 and 12 approved four articles of impeachment against Clinton, charging him with two counts of perjury, obstruction of justice, and abuse of power *(Articles of Impeachment, box, p. 821; full text, Appendix, p. 1020).*

In a move reflecting their animosity toward Clinton, Republicans included language in each of the articles that would bar Clinton from ever again holding a federal elected or appointed office. Only one Republican broke ranks to vote with the Democrats on one article of impeachment. Rep. Lindsay Graham of South Carolina said he gave Clinton "the benefit of the legal doubt" on one of the two articles charging Clinton with perjury.

On Dec. 12 the committee also voted down a resolution offered by the Democrats that would have censured Clinton for "making false statements." It also said that by his conduct Clinton had "violated the trust of the people, lessened their esteem for the office of the President, and dishonored the presidency." All twenty-one Republicans and one Democrat, Robert C. Scott of Virginia, voted against censure.

That vote may have scotched any chance Clinton had to escape impeachment. Shortly after the committee vote, Robert L. Livingston, R-La., the chairman of the House Appropriations Committee whom Republicans had chosen to succeed Gingrich as Speaker in January 1999, announced that a censure resolution would not be permitted on the floor. Soon many of the Republicans who had been known to favor censure began to announce that they would vote to impeach.

Republican leaders in the House (and during the subsequent trial, the Senate) objected to a censure resolution on two principal grounds. First, they argued that the Constitution did not provide for a congressional censure of the president. Unpleasant and tortuous as it might be, impeachment was the only route constitutionally open to Congress in cases of extreme presidential misbehavior, they said. Second, and perhaps more important in political terms, Republican leaders viewed censure as providing political "cover" for members who did not want to vote to remove the president in the face of public opposition.

ARTICLES OF IMPEACHMENT CONSIDERED BY THE HOUSE

Following are summaries of the four articles of impeachment (H Res 611) against President Bill Clinton as recommended by the House Judiciary Committee, followed by the Dec. 19, 1998, votes by the House. *(Full text, p. 1020)*

Article I: Perjury Before the Grand Jury

In its report (H Rept 105-830), the committee concluded Clinton lied on Aug. 17, 1998, in his federal grand jury testimony about "the nature and details of his relationship" with former White House intern Monica Lewinsky; about his testimony in a Jan. 17, 1998, deposition in a sexual-harassment suit filed by former Arkansas state employee Paula Corbin Jones; about statements he allowed his lawyer to make; and about "his corrupt efforts to influence the testimony of witnesses and to impede the discovery of evidence." Although he acknowledged an "improper relationship," Clinton resorted to "legal hairsplitting . . . to bypass the requirement of telling the complete truth."

The House adopted the article on a 228–206 vote.

Article II: Perjury in His Deposition

The committee concluded that Clinton lied to Jones's lawyers during his Jan. 17, 1998, deposition in the sexual-harassment suit about his relationship with Lewinsky, about gifts he had given her, and about efforts to conceal the relationship, including help given to Lewinsky in her pursuit of a job in New York.

The House rejected the article on a 205–229 vote.

Article III: Obstruction of Justice

The committee found that Clinton, "using the powers of his high office," engaged in a plan "to delay, impede, cover up and conceal" his involvement with Lewinsky and subsequent lies. The scheme included encouraging Lewinsky to file a false affidavit in the Jones case and making misleading statements to secretary Betty Currie when he knew she was likely to be a witness in the case.

The House adopted the article on a 221–212 vote.

Article IV: Abuse of Power

The committee said Clinton continued "a pattern of deceit and obstruction of duly authorized investigations" in his answers to eighty-one "requests for admission" that were submitted to him by the panel. "Several" of the president's answers "are clearly perjurious, false and misleading," the report says. It also accused Clinton of lying about his infidelities in six public statements, and of lying to cabinet members and White House aides "knowing that they would repeat his false statements to the American public." His deceptions "caused millions of tax dollars to be spent by not only the Office of the Independent Counsel [Kenneth W. Starr] in its duly authorized investigation, but also by White House lawyers, communications employees and other government employees, who were utilized to help perpetuate the president's lies and defend him."

The House rejected the article on a 148–285 vote.

VOTE TO IMPEACH

A week later, on Dec. 19, as U.S. planes bombed Iraq in retaliation for Iraqi President Saddam Hussein's refusal to cooperate with United Nations weapons inspectors, the House of Representatives voted to impeach Clinton on charges of perjury and obstruction of justice. As television networks preempted Saturday morning cartoons and switched between showing the debate on the House floor and bombs falling on Baghdad, representatives adopted two articles of impeachment against Clinton, largely along party lines.

Clinton's decision to launch air strikes against Iraq starting on Dec. 16, the night before the impeachment debate was scheduled to begin, drew harsh remarks in both the House and Senate, further poisoning the already acrid partisan atmosphere on Capitol Hill. "Never underestimate a desperate president," warned House Rules Committee Chairman Gerald B. H. Solomon of New York. Senate Majority Leader Trent Lott, R-Miss., said that the timing of the strikes as well as the policy underlying them were both "subject to question." House leaders nonetheless did not want to appear to

be undercutting the military and so postponed the impeachment debate for one day. *(Air strikes, box, p. 822)*

The impeachment debate was nearly upstaged by another dramatic political development. On Dec. 19, just hours before the scheduled votes on impeachment, Livingston announced that he was resigning from the House in response to his own sex scandal—an admission that he had had extramarital affairs. Livingston called on the president to follow his example and resign. But at a South Lawn solidarity gathering with several dozen Democratic House members immediately following the impeachment votes, Clinton said that he had "accepted responsibility" for his actions and vowed to serve out his term. *(Livingston resignation, p. 769)*

Formal debate on the articles of impeachment began on the House floor at 9 a.m., Dec. 18, with Ray LaHood, R-Ill., respected by members of both parties for his fairness, wielding the gavel. A Democratic motion to adjourn, offered to protest the Republican leadership's decision to proceed with the impeachment votes while air strikes against Iraq were continuing, was easily turned aside. A nearly full House then sat quietly as the clerk read the four articles of impeachment.

WARY GOP LEADERS CRITICIZE IRAQ BOMBING

On the evening before the House of Representatives was scheduled to begin debating for only the second time in the nation's history whether to impeach a president for "high crimes and misdemeanors," that president, Bill Clinton, ordered a major bombing campaign against military targets in Iraq. The Clinton administration was frustrated by Iraqi president Saddam Hussein's repeated blocking of inspections by United Nations personnel assigned to locate and destroy Iraq's weapons of mass inspections. Nonetheless, Clinton's decision to launch the biggest military attack on Iraq since the Persian Gulf War in 1991 drew accusations from angry Republicans that the president was using the military action to delay or escape impeachment.

The bombing, which began on the evening of Dec. 16, lasted four days and was focused on wiping out Iraq's nuclear, chemical, and biological weapons programs. Although the House was scheduled to begin debate on four articles of impeachment against Clinton on Dec. 17, Republican leaders reluctantly decided to delay that debate by one day. "It's obvious they're trying to do everything they can to postpone the vote in order to get as much leverage as they can," said Gerald B. H. Solomon, R-N.Y., chairman of the House Rules Committee.

Perhaps the strongest criticism came from Senate Majority Leader Trent Lott, R-Miss., who issued a statement saying: "I cannot support this military action in the Persian Gulf at this time. Both the timing and the policy are subject to question." Lott and most other Republicans modified their criticism when senior military officials briefed them on the reasons for the attack.

The bombing raids lasted four days, with television newscasts often splitting their screens to show the debate on the House floor next to flares and explosions in the nighttime sky over Baghdad. Clinton announced on Dec. 19—the same day the House voted two articles of impeachment against him—that the military operation "is now complete." U.S. and British warplanes later resumed low-level attacks on Iraqi installations that lasted into 1999. *(Iraq policy, p. 196)*

Judiciary Committee members began the debate with short statements summarizing the charges against the president. The speech by James E. Rogan, R-Calif., was typical. "The president was obliged, under his sacred oath, to faithfully execute our nation's laws," he said. "Yet he repeatedly perjured himself and obstructed justice."

The mood on the House floor darkened Dec. 19, after Livingston announced that he would not serve as Speaker and would resign from Congress. Democrats and Republicans alike seemed stunned. Several Democrats asked Livingston to reconsider, saying that his decision to resign was as misguided as the impeachment effort. "It is a surrender to a developing sexual McCarthyism," said Jerrold Nadler, D-N.Y., a member of the Judiciary Committee. In an emotional speech that drew a standing ovation, Democratic Minority Leader Richard A. Gephardt of Missouri asked for an end to the "fratricide" that "dominates our public debate. . . . America is held hostage with tactics of smear and fear. Let all of us here today say no to resignation, no to impeachment, no to hatred, no to intolerance of each other, and no to vicious self-righteousness."

The voting then began. Republicans first won a procedural vote that prevented the Democrats from offering a censure resolution. The vote was 230–204. Democrats responded with a brief, staged walkout in protest. When they returned, each of the four articles of impeachment contained in House Resolution 611 was called for a vote.

By a **key vote of 228–206 (R 223–5; D 5–200; I 0–1),** with five Republicans and five Democrats crossing party lines, the House adopted the first article, which accused Clinton of having committed perjury in his Aug. 17 grand jury testimony. This article had always been considered the most likely to succeed, legislators said, because Clinton's testimony was clearly material to Starr's investigation. *(1998 key votes, p. 883)*

By a vote of 205–229, the House rejected the second article, which charged the president with committing perjury in his deposition in the sexual harassment suit brought by Paula Corbin Jones. It was this deposition that was the basis for the president's later grand jury testimony, and many observers noted the irony of dismissing perjury charges connected to his deposition while pressing them in his grand jury testimony. On this article, twenty-eight Republicans and five Democrats broke ranks with their party.

By a vote 221–212, the House adopted the third article, which charged Clinton with obstruction of justice for his efforts to find Lewinsky a job, possibly in return for her silence, and his alleged witness tampering involving his personal secretary, Betty Currie. Five Democrats voted for this article, twelve Republicans voted against it.

By a vote of 148–285, the House rejected the fourth article, which accused the president of abuse of power. Among other things this article charged Clinton with "a pattern of deceit and obstruction" in providing misleading statements to the questions posed by the Judiciary Committee. Only one Democrat voted for this article, while eighty-one Republicans voted against it.

After voting on the impeachment articles, the House authorized the appointment of thirteen Republican members of the Judiciary Committee to prosecute the case in the Senate. (Democrats had refused to serve as managers, in large part to highlight the essentially partisan nature of the House case against Clinton.) The "managers," as they were called,

House Judiciary Chairman Henry Hyde (right) leads the procession of the thirteen House trial managers to the Senate to read the two impeachment articles against President Bill Clinton on Dec. 19, 1998. *Source: Douglas Graham, Congressional Quarterly*

then walked across the Capitol, where chairman Hyde presented a leather-bound book containing the two approved articles of impeachment to the secretary of the Senate.

At roughly the same time, several dozen loyal House Democrats arrived at the White House for a show of solidarity with President Clinton. Accompanied by his wife and Vice President Al Gore, Clinton appeared somber but determined. "I will continue to do the work of the American people," the president vowed. "It's what I've tried to do for six years. It's what I intend to do for two more until the last hour of the last day of my term."

Senate Trial

As the Senate convened in January 1999 for the first session of the 106th Congress, its first order of business was to deal with the two articles of impeachment that had been voted by the full House three weeks earlier. With a majority of the public opposed to impeachment, let alone conviction of the president, and with the Senate closely divided, with fifty-five Republicans and forty-five Democrats, there was never any serious prospect that Republican senators would muster the two-thirds vote needed to remove Clinton from office. Despite the public's clear disgust with Clinton's personal behavior, the president continued to enjoy extraordinarily high popularity ratings in the polls, while Clinton's Republican accusers suffered a comparable level of public

disapproval. In that political atmosphere, the Senate trial became an exercise in damage control for Republicans in the Senate, with members of both parties eager to be seen as handling the case expeditiously but with dignity.

The Senate formally opened the Clinton trial on Jan. 7, with William H. Rehnquist, Chief Justice of the United States presiding, as mandated by the Constitution. The next day all 100 senators met privately in the Old Senate Chamber in the Capitol for an extraordinary "bipartisan caucus" that produced a general agreement on the conduct of the trial. The overwhelming majority of senators appeared to want the trial to be as short as possible but long enough to assure the public that the Senate had taken its constitutional responsibilities seriously.

Despite occasional efforts by both sides to portray the trial as a bipartisan, or even nonpartisan, affair, partisan politics played a major role in the Senate deliberations as they had in the House impeachment proceedings. Three crucial votes in late January demonstrated the deep divide between the parties. Two of those votes came on Jan. 27. First the Senate rejected in a **key vote of 44–56 (R 0–55; D 44–1)**, a motion by senior Democrat Robert C. Byrd of West Virginia to dismiss the charges against Clinton. Then the Senate voted, 56–44, to subpoena Lewinsky and two other witnesses for closed-door depositions. In both votes, Russell D. Feingold of Wisconsin was the only Democrat to break ranks and vote with the Republican majority. The next day, in a vote strictly

A rare sight in the Senate: the impeachment trial of a president. Here on Jan. 7, 1999, the one hundred members of the body take an oath of impartiality at the start of President Bill Clinton's trial. *Source: U.S. Senate*

along party lines, the Senate adopted a Republican plan for the closing stages of the trial. Even though the Democrats were on the losing side in all three votes, the tallies demonstrated clearly that there would not be sixty-seven votes in the Senate to convict Clinton on either impeachment charge. *(1999 key votes p. 899)*

As the trial progressed, the major procedural issues involved the number of witnesses the House managers could call and the format of their testimony. The managers wanted the right to call several dozen witnesses to bolster their case, most of whom had not testified during the House Judiciary Committee hearings in the fall of 1998. Senate Democrats, and even many Republicans, objected to the House maneuver, saying it would delay the trial unnecessarily and arguing that the place for detailed testimony and cross-examination of witnesses was during the House hearings, not the Senate trial.

The key step in the witness issue came on Feb. 4, when senators voted 70–30 not to require Lewinsky to testify in person before the full Senate. Instead, the Senate approved a procedure under which videotaped testimony Lewinsky had given House managers on Feb. 1 would be available for either side during the presentation of arguments in the Senate. Senators agreed to a similar procedure for the videotaped testimony of two other witnesses: Vernon Jordan, the Washington lawyer whom Republicans suspected of trying to silence Lewinsky by finding a job for her in New York City; and Sidney Blumenthal, a Clinton aide deeply involved in the White House public relations offensive against the Republicans.

HOUSE CASE AGAINST CLINTON

Led by Judiciary Committee Chairman Hyde, the thirteen House managers began presenting their case against Clinton on Jan. 14. Each of the managers made one or more presentations highlighting specific parts of the impeachment articles. Perhaps because the outcome was a foregone conclusion, the House managers devoted much of their effort to a public campaign countering Clinton's defense and attacking the Senate trial procedures. Hyde and other managers held numerous press conferences just outside the Senate chamber, to the annoyance of many senators. Hyde on Jan. 22 acknowledged the uneasy relationship between the House managers and the senators, telling them: "I know, oh, do I know, what an annoyance we are in the bosom of this great body. But we're a constitutional annoyance, and I remind you of that fact."

In their presentations, some of the managers engaged in florid denunciations of the president's actions during the Lewinsky affair. Hyde in particular used numerous quotations from Shakespeare, along with allusions to historical events such as the signing of the Magna Carta, the American Revolution, and the Civil War. "This case is a test of where what the Founding Fathers described as 'sacred trust' still has meaning in our time, 222 years after those two words, 'sacred honor,' were inscribed in our country's birth certificate, our national charter of freedom, our Declaration of Independence," Hyde said during a Jan. 16 summary of the managers' initial presentation.

Other House managers gave detailed analysis of how the charges contained in the two impeachment articles constituted impeachable offenses. Several senators later said the most compelling presentations were made by Rep. Asa Hutchinson, an Arkansas Republican whose brother, Tim, was a senator. Rep. Hutchinson used detailed charts attempting to demonstrate that Clinton had obstructed justice through such actions as orchestrating efforts to find a job for Lewinsky in New York City.

For many senators and other observers, the strongest argument made by the House managers was that Clinton should be made to face the consequences of his actions, even if he was president. Several House managers noted that the Senate had repeatedly removed federal judges from office for offenses bearing some similarity to the president's, and that military officers had suffered serious penalties for lying about adulterous relationships. Rep. F. James Sensenbrenner Jr., R-Wis., summarized that argument in his closing arguments to the Senate: "To keep a president in office, whose gross misconduct and criminal actions are a well-established fact, will weaken the authority of the presidency, undermine the rule of law, and cheapen those words which have made America different from most other nations . . . 'equal justice under the law.' "

One of the highlights of the House case came Feb. 6, when prosecutors showed senators a videotape of Lewinsky's testimony, contrasting the former White House intern with videotape of Clinton's denials of a sexual relationship between the two of them. It was the first time the public had a chance to hear Lewinsky speak directly about her relationship with the president. Contradicting several media reports shortly after the scandal emerged early in 1998, Lewinsky said Clinton had never asked her to lie about their relationship. However, she said she had known she would deny involvement with the president because "it was part of the pattern of the relationship."

CLINTON'S DEFENSE

The president's defenders opened their case Jan. 19, accusing the Republican House managers of constructing a flimsy case against the president. Led by White House Counsel Charles F. C. Ruff, the president's lawyers responded to the charges contained in the two impeachment articles point by point, at several stages ridiculing the allegations as lacking any basis in fact. At one point, Ruff summarized a key part of the Republican case as consisting of "sealing wax and strings and spiders' webs."

From the outset, Clinton's lawyers opted for a strategy of acknowledging that the president's behavior with Lewinsky had been inexcusable and wrong. The lawyers also admitted that Clinton had misled the public about the relationship and had been "evasive" and "misleading" in his grand jury testimony, But, the lawyers insisted, the president had not committed perjury and had not obstructed justice—as the impeachment articles alleged—and therefore should not be removed from office. The House charges against Clinton were "frivolous" and not worthy of the impeachment stan-

Portions of the videotaped deposition of former White House intern Monica Lewinsky were shown during the 1999 impeachment trial of President Bill Clinton. *Source: Reuters*

dard envisioned by the Constitution, said White House lawyer Gregory B. Craig. "If you convict and remove President Clinton on the basis of these allegations, no president of the United States will ever be safe from impeachment again."

One of the key elements of the obstruction-of-justice charge was that Clinton had conspired with Lewinsky to hide numerous gifts that the two had exchanged during their relationship. The House managers repeatedly drew attention to a meeting between the two on Dec. 28, 1997, during which Lewinsky asked Clinton if she should hide or return the gifts he had given her. In a presentation to the Senate, Cheryl D. Mills, an assistant White House counsel, derided the House managers' focus on the gift issue and in particular the Dec. 28 meeting between Clinton and Lewinsky. Noting that Clinton gave Lewinsky more gifts at that meeting, Mills asked: "Why would the president give Ms. Lewinsky gifts if he wanted her to give them right back?" Mills said this was one of several examples of where the House case against Clinton could not withstand the presence of "stubborn facts."

The president's lawyers also sought to focus attention on the actions of those who had investigated Clinton, primarily Starr and the House Republicans. In the midst of the trial, Starr's office handed the White House a political bonus by leaking word to the *New York Times* that Starr was consider-

As mandated by the Constitution, Chief Justice William H. Rehnquist presided over the president's impeachment trial in the Senate. *Source: Reuters*

ing seeking an indictment against Clinton after he left office. The newspaper's report, on Jan. 31, set off a flurry of charges and countercharges about Starr's handling of his investigation, in particular his apparent use of news leaks to try to shape public opinion. All this played into the hands of the president's defenders.

To cap the defense of the president, the White House turned Jan. 21 to one of the most eloquent speakers from the ranks of the Senate itself: Dale Bumpers, an Arkansas Democrat who had retired from the Senate just a few weeks earlier. A longtime friend of the president, Bumpers nevertheless described Clinton's conduct as "indefensible, outrageous, unforgivable, shameless." Even so, Bumpers said, it would be folly for the Senate to remove Clinton from office. "If you vote to convict, in my opinion, you're going to be creating more havoc than he could ever possibly create," he told his former colleagues. "After all, he's only got two years left."

VOTES TO ACQUIT

Senators voted Feb. 9 to conduct their final deliberations in private. After three days of closed-door speeches to each other—speeches that many senators later delivered in public news conferences—senators opened the doors to their chamber for a public reckoning on Feb. 12. "Senators, how say you? Is the respondent, William Jefferson Clinton, guilty or not guilty?" Chief Justice Rehnquist asked. One by one senators stood at their desks as their names were called

and responded "guilty" or "not guilty" to the two articles of impeachment.

On article one, accusing Clinton of perjury, the Senate voted forty-five in favor of conviction, fifty-five against, far short of the two-thirds vote necessary for conviction. Ten Republicans joined all forty-five Democrats in voting "not guilty." All ten were moderate or liberal Republicans who said they strongly disapproved of Clinton's behavior but did not believe his denials in the Lewinsky case amounted to a perjury offense for which he should be removed from office.

On article two, accusing Clinton of obstruction of justice, House managers were unable to obtain a simple majority. On a **key vote, the Senate split 50–50 (R 50–5; D 0–45),** with five Republicans joining all the Democrats in voting "not guilty." *(1999 key votes p. 899)*

Following the vote, Rehnquist praised the Senate for its deliberations, even while confessing his bewilderment at the procedural differences between the Supreme Court and the Senate—institutions separated by one street and some 200 years of established practice. The Senate, in turn, passed a resolution thanking Rehnquist for his work as its temporary president.

After the Senate votes, Clinton made his most direct apology yet for his actions. "I want to say again to the American people how profoundly sorry I am for what I said and did to trigger these events and the great burden they have imposed on the Congress and on the American people," he said in a televised address from the Rose Garden at the White House. "Now, I ask all Americans, and I hope all Americans here in Washington and throughout our land, will rededicate ourselves to the work of serving our nation and building our future together."

One piece of business remained. In the final days of the Senate trial, Democrats Joseph I. Lieberman of Connecticut and Dianne Feinstein of California, along with Republican Robert F. Bennett of Utah, developed a draft bipartisan resolution denouncing Clinton's "shameless, reckless and indefensible" behavior in the Lewinsky affair. Moments after Rehnquist gaveled the impeachment trial to a close, Feinstein rose to ask permission to offer that censure resolution. The Senate blocked her move by a vote of 43–56, effectively killing any prospect for censure.

Postimpeachment Developments

The not guilty verdict in the Senate trial did not end Clinton's legal troubles. Two months later, on April 12, Judge Wright, the U.S. District Court judge in Arkansas who had been overseeing the Jones case, held Clinton in contempt of court for providing false evidence in his Jan. 17, 1998, deposition in that case.

Judge Wright, who had studied law with Clinton in Arkansas, said in her finding: "The record demonstrates by clear and convincing evidence that the president responded to plaintiff's [Jones's attorneys'] questions by giving false, misleading, and evasive answers that were designed to obstruct the judicial process." Judge Wright ordered Clinton to pay "any reasonable expenses" incurred by Jones as a result of his testimony. Jones's lawyers sought $496,000 from the president, but Judge Wright on July 29 reduced the payments to $89,483, which Clinton later paid.

In September 2000, the six-year-long investigation into the failed Arkansas land deal known as Whitewater came to a formal close, when Independent Counsel Robert W. Ray announced that the evidence gathered was insufficient to bring criminal charges against either President Clinton or his wife, Hillary Rodham Clinton. (Ray had replaced Starr after Starr's resignation on Oct. 18, 1999.) Earlier in the year, Ray had also closed related investigations into allegations of misconduct in connection with the firing of several White House travel office employees and acquisition by the Clinton White House of confidential FBI files. (*Whitewater investigations, box, p. 805*)

Still pending, however, was a grand jury investigation into whether President Clinton had lied under oath to cover up his relationship with Lewinsky. Ray said he still might indict the president for perjury or obstruction of justice after he left the White House on Jan. 20, 2001.

On Jan. 19, 2001, Clinton's last full day as president, the White House announced that Clinton had agreed to a settlement with Ray. In return for avoiding the possibility of indictment, Clinton admitted that he had given false testimony under oath and agreed to give up his right to practice law for five years. Clinton also agreed to pay a fine of $25,000 to the Arkansas Committee on Professional Conduct, which had been considering whether to disbar him from the practice of law. And he promised not to seek reimbursement for legal fees in connection with the Starr investigation, something he would have been entitled to do under the independent counsel law if he had been investigated but not indicted. (Clinton's legal fees were at least $11 million.)

The agreement—in essence a plea bargain—had been under negotiation for several weeks. From the outset, Ray reportedly insisted upon two conditions for any deal: the president would have to accept some sort of sanction for his conduct, and he would have to make a public statement acknowledging more than he had in the past. The two sides quickly agreed that the suspension of Clinton's law license would suffice as the sanction. But they spent several weeks debating the content of the public statement.

In his statement released Jan. 19, Clinton said that in his Jan. 17, 1998, deposition in the Jones case, he "tried to walk a fine line between acting lawfully and testifying falsely, but I now recognize that I did not fully accomplish this goal and certain of my responses to questions about Ms. Lewinsky were false."

Clinton's attorney David Kendall said in a statement that the president was glad to have "closure" in the matter. As the *New York Times* noted in an editorial, Ray achieved his goal of "vindicating the principle that 'no person is above the law, not even the president of the United States.'"

On March 6, 2002, Ray said his office decided to close the long-running investigation even though it had sufficient evidence to prosecute Clinton for violating federal criminal laws. Ray said the decision was influenced by the agreement announced Jan. 19, 2001, with Clinton. In a press release, Ray cited other factors in the case including the sizeable penalties Clinton paid and "the substantial public condemnation . . . arising from his impeachment."

The press release also noted that the independent counsel's office had spent approximately $70 million in the probe including direct costs of $48,149,096.

Appendix

Glossary of Congressional Terms 831

The Legislative Process in Brief 857

Key Votes, 1997–2000 863

Congress and Its Members 933

The Presidency 975

Selected Texts 997

Political Charts 1057

Public Laws 1097

Glossary of Congressional Terms

AA—*(See Administrative Assistant.)*

Absence of a Quorum—Absence of the required number of members to conduct business in a house or a committee. When a quorum call or roll-call vote in a house establishes that a quorum is not present, no debate or other business is permitted except a motion to adjourn or motions to request or compel the attendance of absent members, if necessary by arresting them.

Absolute Majority—A vote requiring approval by a majority of all members of a house rather than a majority of members present and voting. Also referred to as constitutional majority.

Account—Organizational units used in the federal budget primarily for recording spending and revenue transactions.

Act—(1) A bill passed in identical form by both houses of Congress and signed into law by the president or enacted over the president's veto. A bill also becomes an act without the president's signature if he does not return it to Congress within ten days (Sundays excepted) and if Congress has not adjourned within that period. (2) Also, the technical term for a bill passed by at least one house and engrossed.

Ad Hoc Select Committee—A temporary committee formed for a special purpose or to deal with a specific subject. Conference committees are ad hoc joint committees. A House rule adopted in 1975 authorizes the Speaker to refer measures to special ad hoc committees, appointed by the Speaker with the approval of the House.

Adjourn—A motion to adjourn is a formal motion to end a day's session or meeting of a house or a committee. A motion to adjourn usually has no conditions attached to it, but it sometimes may specify the day or time for reconvening or make reconvening subject to the call of the chamber's presiding officer or the committee's chairman. In both houses, a motion to adjourn is of the highest privilege, takes precedence over all other motions, is not debatable, and must be put to an immediate vote. Adjournment of a house ends its legislative day. For this reason, the House or Senate sometimes adjourns for only one minute, or some other very brief period of time, during the course of a day's session. The House does not permit a motion to adjourn after it has resolved into Committee of the Whole or when the previous question has been ordered on a measure to final passage without an intervening motion.

Adjourn for More Than Three Days—Under Article I, Section 5 of the Constitution, neither house may adjourn for more than three days without the approval of the other. The necessary approval is given in a concurrent resolution to which both houses have agreed.

Adjournment *Sine Die*—Final adjournment of an annual or two-year session of Congress; literally, adjournment without a day. The two houses must agree to a privileged concurrent resolution for such an adjournment. A *sine die* adjournment precludes Congress from meeting again until the next constitutionally fixed date of a session (Jan. 3 of the following year) unless Congress determines otherwise by law or the president calls it into special session. Article II, Section 3

of the Constitution authorizes the president to adjourn both houses until such time as the president thinks proper when the two houses cannot agree to a time of adjournment. No president, however, has ever exercised this authority.

Adjournment to a Day (and Time) Certain—An adjournment that fixes the next date and time of meeting for one or both houses. It does not end an annual session of Congress.

Administration Bill—A bill drafted in the executive office of the president or in an executive department or agency to implement part of the president's program. An administration bill is introduced in Congress by a member who supports it or as a courtesy to the administration.

Administrative Assistant (AA)—The title usually given to a member's chief aide, political advisor, and head of office staff. The administrative assistant often represents the member at meetings with visitors or officials when the member is unable (or unwilling) to attend.

Adoption—The usual parliamentary term for approval of a conference report. It is also commonly applied to amendments.

Advance Appropriation—In an appropriation act for a particular fiscal year, an appropriation that does not become available for spending or obligation until a subsequent fiscal year. The amount of the advance appropriation is counted as part of the budget for the fiscal year in which it becomes available for obligation.

Advance Funding—A mechanism whereby statutory language may allow budget authority for a fiscal year to be increased, and obligations to be incurred, with an offsetting decrease in the budget authority available in the succeeding fiscal year. If not used, the budget authority remains available for obligation in the succeeding fiscal year. Advance funding is sometimes used to provide contingency funding of a few benefit programs.

Adverse Report—A committee report recommending against approval of a measure or some other matter. Committees usually pigeonhole measures they oppose instead of reporting them adversely, but they may be required to report them by a statutory rule or an instruction from their parent body.

Advice and Consent—The Senate's constitutional role in consenting to or rejecting the president's nominations to executive branch and judicial offices and treaties with other nations. Confirmation of nominees requires a simple majority vote of senators present and voting. Treaties must be approved by a two-thirds majority of those present and voting.

Aisle—The center aisle of each chamber. When facing the presiding officer, Republicans usually sit to the right of the aisle, Democrats to the left. When members speak of "my side of the aisle" or "this side," they are referring to their party.

Amendment—A formal proposal to alter the text of a bill, resolution, amendment, motion, treaty, or some other text. Technically, it is a motion. An amendment may strike out (eliminate) part of a text, insert new text, or strike out and insert—that is, replace all or part of the text with new text. The texts of amendments considered on the floor are printed in full in the *Congressional Record*.

Amendment in the Nature of a Substitute—Usually, an amendment to replace the entire text of a measure. It strikes out everything after the enacting clause and inserts a version that may be somewhat, substantially, or entirely different. When a committee adopts extensive amendments to a measure, it often incorporates them into such an amendment. Occasionally, the term is applied to an amendment that replaces a major portion of a measure's text.

Amendment Tree—A diagram showing the number and types of amendments that the rules and practices of a house permit to be offered to a measure before any of the amendments is voted on. It shows the relationship of one amendment to the others, and it may also indicate the degree of each amendment, whether it is a perfecting or substitute amendment, the order in which amendments may be offered, and the order in which they are put to a vote. The same type of diagram can be used to display an actual amendment situation.

Annual Authorization—Legislation that authorizes appropriations for a single fiscal year and usually for a specific amount. Under the rules of the authorization-appropriation process, an annually authorized agency or program must be reauthorized each year if it is to receive appropriations for that year. Sometimes Congress fails to enact the reauthorization but nevertheless provides appropriations to continue the program, circumventing the rules by one means or another.

Appeal—A member's formal challenge of a ruling or decision by the presiding officer. On appeal, a house or a committee may overturn the ruling by majority vote. The right of appeal ensures the body against arbitrary control by the chair. Appeals are rarely made in the House and are even more rarely successful. Rulings are more frequently appealed in the Senate and occasionally overturned, in part because its presiding officer is not the majority party's leader, as in the House.

Apportionment—The action, after each decennial census, of allocating the number of members in the House of Representatives to each state. By law, the total number of House members (not counting delegates and a resident commissioner) is fixed at 435. The number allotted to each state is based approximately on its proportion of the nation's total population. Because the Constitution guarantees each state one representative no matter how small its population, exact proportional distribution is virtually impossible. The mathematical formula currently used to determine the apportionment is called the Method of Equal Proportions. *(See Method of Equal Proportions.)*

Appropriated Entitlement—An entitlement program, such as veterans' pensions, that is funded through annual appropriations rather than by a permanent appropriation. Because such an entitlement law requires the government to provide eligible recipients the benefits to which they are entitled, whatever the cost, Congress must appropriate the necessary funds.

Appropriation—(1) Legislative language that permits a federal agency to incur obligations and make payments from the Treasury for specified purposes, usually during a specified period of time. (2) The specific amount of money made available by such language. The Constitution prohibits payments from the Treasury except "in Consequence of Appropriations made by Law." With some exceptions, the rules of both houses forbid consideration of appropriations for purposes that are unauthorized in law or of appropriation amounts larger than those authorized in law. The House of Representatives claims the exclusive right to originate appropriation bills—a claim the Senate denies in theory but accepts in practice.

At-Large—Elected by and representing an entire state instead of a district within a state. The term usually refers to a representative rather than to a senator. *(See Apportionment; Congressional District; Redistricting.)*

August Adjournment—A congressional adjournment during the month of August in odd-numbered years, required by the Legislative Reorganization Act of 1970. The law instructs the two houses to adjourn for a period of at least thirty days before the second day after Labor Day, unless Congress provides otherwise or if, on July 31, a state of war exists by congressional declaration.

Authorization—(1) A statutory provision that establishes or continues a federal agency, activity, or program for a fixed or indefinite period of time. It may also establish policies and restrictions and deal with organizational and administrative matters. (2) A statutory provision, as described in (1), may also, explicitly or implicitly, authorize congressional action to provide appropriations for an agency, activity, or program. The appropriations may be authorized for one year, several years, or an indefinite period of time, and the authorization may be for a specific amount of money or an indefinite amount ("such sums as may be necessary"). Authorizations of specific amounts are construed as ceilings on the amounts that subsequently may be appropriated in an appropriation bill, but not as minimums; either house may appropriate lesser amounts or nothing at all.

Authorization-Appropriation Process—The two-stage procedural system that the rules of each house require for establishing and funding federal agencies and programs: first, enactment of authorizing legislation that creates or continues an agency or program; second, enactment of appropriations legislation that provides funds for the authorized agency or program.

Automatic Roll Call—Under a House rule, the automatic ordering of the yeas and nays when a quorum is not present on a voice or division vote and a member objects to the vote on that ground. It is not permitted in the Committee of the Whole.

Backdoor Spending Authority—Authority to incur obligations that evades the normal congressional appropriations process because it is provided in legislation other than appropriation acts. The most common forms are borrowing authority, contract authority, and entitlement authority.

Baseline—A projection of the levels of federal spending, revenues, and the resulting budgetary surpluses or deficits for the upcoming and subsequent fiscal years, taking into account laws enacted to date and assuming no new policy decisions. It provides a benchmark for measuring the budgetary effects of proposed changes in federal revenues or spending, assuming certain economic conditions.

Bells—A system of electric signals and lights that informs members of activities in each chamber. The type of activity taking place is indicated by the number of signals and the interval between them. When the signals are sounded, a corresponding number of lights are lit around the perimeter of many clocks in House or Senate offices.

Bicameral—Consisting of two houses or chambers. Congress is a bicameral legislature whose two houses have an equal role in enacting legislation. In most other national bicameral legislatures, one house is significantly more powerful than the other.

Bigger Bite Amendment—An amendment that substantively changes a portion of a text including language that had previously been amended. Normally, language that has been amended may not be amended again. However, a part of a sentence that has been changed by amendment, for example, may be changed again by an amendment that amends a "bigger bite" of the text—that is, by an amendment that also substantively changes the unamended parts of the sentence or the entire section or title in which the previously amended language appears. The biggest possible bite is an amendment in the nature of a substitute that amends the entire text of a measure. Once adopted, therefore, such an amendment ends the amending process.

Bill—The term for the chief vehicle Congress uses for enacting laws. Bills that originate in the House of Representatives are designated as HR, those in the Senate as S, followed by a number assigned in the order in which they are introduced during a two-year Congress. A bill becomes a law if passed in identical language by both houses and signed by the president, or passed over the president's veto, or if the president fails to sign it within ten days after receiving it while Congress is in session.

Bill of Attainder—An act of a legislature finding a person guilty of treason or a felony. The Constitution prohibits the passage of such a bill by the U.S. Congress or any state legislature.

Bills and Resolutions Introduced—Members formally present measures to their respective houses by delivering them to a clerk in the chamber when their house is in session. Both houses permit any number of members to join in introducing a bill or resolution. The first member listed on the measure is the sponsor; the other members listed are its cosponsors.

Bills and Resolutions Referred—After a bill or resolution is introduced, it is normally sent to one or more committees that have jurisdiction over its subject, as defined by House and Senate rules and precedents. A Senate measure is usually referred to the committee with jurisdiction over the predominant subject of its text, but it may be sent to two or more committees by unanimous consent or on a motion offered jointly by the majority and minority leaders. In the House, a rule requires the Speaker to refer a measure to the committee that has primary jurisdiction. The Speaker is also authorized to refer measures sequentially to additional committees and to impose time limits on such referrals.

Bipartisan Committee—A committee with an equal number of members from each political party. The House Committee on Standards of Official Conduct and the Senate Select Committee on Ethics are the only bipartisan, permanent full committees.

Borrowing Authority—Statutory authority permitting a federal agency, such as the Export-Import Bank, to borrow money from the public or the Treasury to finance its operations. It is a form of backdoor spending. To bring such spending under the control of the congressional appropriation process, the Congressional Budget Act requires that new borrowing authority shall be effective only to the extent and in such amounts as are provided in appropriations acts.

Budget—A detailed statement of actual or anticipated revenues and expenditures during an accounting period. For the national government, the period is the federal fiscal year (Oct. 1 to Sept. 30). The budget usually refers to the president's budget submission to Congress early each calendar year. The president's budget estimates federal government income and spending for the upcoming fiscal year and contains detailed recommendations for appropriation, revenue, and other legislation. Congress is not required to accept or even vote directly on the president's proposals, and it often revises the president's budget extensively. *(See Fiscal Year.)*

Budget Act—Common name for the Congressional Budget and Impoundment Control Act of 1974, which established the basic procedures of the current congressional budget process; created the House and Senate Budget Committees; and enacted procedures for reconciliation, deferrals, and rescissions. *(See Budget Process; Deferral; Impoundment; Reconciliation; Rescission. See also Gramm-Rudman-Hollings Act of 1985.)*

Budget and Accounting Act of 1921—The law that, for the first time, authorized the president to submit to Congress an annual budget for the entire federal government. Before passage of the act, most federal agencies sent their budget requests to the appropriate congressional committees without review by the president.

Budget Authority—Generally, the amount of money that may be spent or obligated by a government agency or for a government program or activity. Technically, it is statutory authority to enter into obligations that normally result in outlays. The main forms of budget authority are appropriations, borrowing authority, and contract authority. It also includes authority to obligate and expend the proceeds of offsetting receipts and collections. Congress may make budget authority available for only one year, several years, or an indefinite period, and it may specify definite or indefinite amounts.

Budget Enforcement Act of 1990—An act that revised the sequestration process established by the Gramm-Rudman-Hollings Act of 1985, replaced the earlier act's fixed deficit targets with adjustable ones, established discretionary spending limits for fiscal years 1991 through 1995, instituted pay-as-you-go rules to enforce deficit neutrality on revenue and mandatory spending legislation, and reformed the budget and accounting rules for federal credit activities. Unlike the Gramm-Rudman-Hollings Act, the 1990 act emphasized restraints on legislated changes in taxes and spending instead of fixed deficit limits.

Budget Enforcement Act of 1997—An act that revised and updated the provisions of the Budget Enforcement Act of 1990, including by extending the discretionary spending caps and pay-as-you-go rules through 2002.

Budget Process—(1) In Congress, the procedural system it uses (a) to approve an annual concurrent resolution on the budget that sets goals for aggregate and functional categories of federal expenditures, revenues, and the surplus or deficit for an upcoming fiscal year; and (b) to implement those goals in spending, revenue, and, if necessary, reconciliation and debt-limit legislation. (2) In the executive branch, the process of formulating the president's annual budget, submitting it to Congress, defending it before congressional committees, implementing subsequent budget-related legislation, impounding or sequestering expenditures as permitted by law, auditing and evaluating programs, and compiling final budget data. The Budget and Accounting Act of 1921 and the Congressional Budget and Impoundment Control Act of 1974 established the basic elements of the current budget process. Major revisions were enacted in the Gramm-Rudman-Hollings Act of 1985 and the Budget Enforcement Act of 1990.

Budget Resolution—A concurrent resolution in which Congress establishes or revises its version of the federal budget's broad financial features for the upcoming fiscal year and several additional fiscal years. Like other concurrent resolutions, it does not have the force of law, but it provides the framework within which Congress subsequently considers revenue, spending, and other budget-implementing legislation. The framework consists of two basic elements: (1) aggregate budget amounts (total revenues, new budget authority, outlays, loan obligations and loan guarantee commitments, deficit or surplus, and debt limit); and (2) subdivisions of the relevant aggregate amounts among the functional categories of the budget. Although it does not allocate funds to specific programs or accounts, the budget committees' reports accompanying the resolution often discuss the major program assumptions underlying its functional amounts. Unlike those amounts, however, the assumptions are not binding on Congress.

By Request—A designation indicating that a member has introduced a measure on behalf of the president, an executive agency, or a private individual or organization. Members often introduce such measures as a courtesy because neither the president nor any person other than a member of Congress can do so. The term, which appears next to the sponsor's name, implies that the member who introduced the measure does not necessarily endorse it. A House rule dealing with by-request introductions dates from 1888, but the practice goes back to the earliest history of Congress.

Byrd Rule—The popular name of an amendment to the Congressional Budget Act that bars the inclusion of extraneous matter in any reconciliation legislation considered in the Senate. The ban is enforced by points of order that the presiding officer sustains. The provision defines different categories of extraneous matter, but it also permits certain exceptions. Its chief sponsor was Sen. Robert C. Byrd, D-W.Va.

Calendar—A list of measures or other matters (most of them favorably reported by committees) that are eligible for floor consideration. The House has five calendars; the Senate has two. A place on a calendar does not guarantee consideration. Each house decides which measures and matters it will take up, when, and in what order, in accordance with its rules and practices.

Calendar Wednesday—A House procedure that on Wednesdays permits its committees to bring up for floor consideration nonprivileged measures they have reported. The procedure is so cumbersome and susceptible to dilatory tactics, however, that it is rarely used.

Call Up—To bring a measure or report to the floor for immediate consideration.

Casework—Assistance to constituents who seek assistance in dealing with federal and local government agencies. Constituent service is a high priority in most members' offices.

Caucus—(1) A common term for the official organization of each party in each house. (2) The official title of the organization of House Democrats. House and Senate Republicans and Senate Democrats call their organizations "conferences." (3) A term for an informal group of members who share legislative interests, such as the Black Caucus, Hispanic Caucus, and Children's Caucus.

Censure—The strongest formal condemnation of a member for misconduct short of expulsion. A house usually adopts a resolution of censure to express its condemnation, after which the presiding officer reads its rebuke aloud to the member in the presence of his or her colleagues.

Chairman—The presiding officer of a committee, a subcommittee, or a task force. At meetings, the chairman preserves order, enforces the rules, recognizes members to speak or offer motions, and puts questions to a vote. The chairman of a committee or subcommittee usually appoints its staff and sets its agenda, subject to the panel's veto.

Chamber—The Capitol room in which a house of Congress normally holds its sessions. The chamber of the House of Representatives, officially called the Hall of the House, is considerably larger than that of the Senate because it must accommodate 435 representatives, four delegates, and one resident commissioner. Unlike the Senate chamber, members have no desks or assigned seats. In both chambers, the floor slopes downward to the well in front of the presiding officer's raised desk. A chamber is often referred to as "the floor," as when members are said to be on or going to the floor. Those expressions usually imply that the member's house is in session.

Christmas Tree Bill—Jargon for a bill adorned with amendments, many of them unrelated to the bill's subject, that provide benefits for interest groups, specific states, congressional districts, companies, and individuals.

Classes of Senators—A class consists of the thirty-three or thirty-four senators elected to a six-year term in the same general election. Because the terms of approximately one-third of the senators expire every two years, there are three classes.

Clean Bill—After a House committee extensively amends a bill, it often assembles its amendments and what is left of the bill into a new measure that one or more of its members introduces as a "clean bill." The revised measure is assigned a new number.

Clerk of the House—An officer of the House of Representatives responsible principally for administrative support of the legislative process in the House. The clerk is invariably the candidate of the majority party.

Cloakrooms—Two rooms with access to the rear of each chamber's floor, one for each party's members, where members may confer privately, sit quietly, or have a snack. The presiding officer sometimes urges members who are conversing too loudly on the floor to retire to their cloakrooms.

Closed Hearing—A hearing closed to the public and the media. A House committee may close a hearing only if it determines that disclosure of the testimony to be taken would endanger national security, violate any law, or tend to defame, degrade, or incriminate any person. The Senate has a similar rule. Both houses require roll-call votes in open session to close a hearing.

Closed Rule—A special rule reported from the House Rules Committee that prohibits amendments to a measure or that only permits amendments offered by the reporting committee.

Cloture—A Senate procedure that limits further consideration of a pending proposal to thirty hours in order to end a filibuster. Sixteen senators must first sign and submit a cloture motion to the presiding officer. One hour after the Senate meets on the second calendar day thereafter, the chair puts the motion to a yea-and-nay vote following a live quorum call. If three-fifths of all senators (sixty if there are no vacancies) vote for the motion, the Senate must take final action on the cloture proposal by the end of the thirty hours of consideration and may consider no other business until it takes that action. Cloture on a proposal to amend the Senate's standing rules requires approval by two-thirds of the senators present and voting.

Code of Official Conduct—A House rule that bans certain actions by House members, officers, and employees; requires them to conduct themselves in ways that "reflect creditably" on the House; and orders them to adhere to the spirit and the letter of House rules and those of its committees. The code's provisions govern the receipt of outside compensation, gifts, and honoraria, and the use of campaign funds; prohibit members from using their clerk-hire allowance to pay anyone who does not perform duties commensurate with that pay; forbids discrimination in members' hiring or treatment of employees on the grounds of race, color, religion, sex, handicap, age, or national origin; orders members convicted of a crime who might be punished by imprisonment of two or more years not to participate in committee business or vote on the floor until exonerated or reelected; and restricts employees' contact with federal agencies on matters in which they have a significant financial interest. The Senate's rules contain some similar prohibitions.

College of Cardinals—A popular term for the subcommittee chairmen of the appropriations committees, reflecting their influence over appropriation measures. The chairmen of the full appropriations committees are sometimes referred to as popes.

Comity—The practice of maintaining mutual courtesy and civility between the two houses in their dealings with each other and in members' speeches on the floor. Although the practice is largely governed by long-established customs, a House rule explicitly cautions its members not to characterize any Senate action or inaction, refer to individual senators except under certain circumstances, or quote from Senate proceedings except to make legislative history on a measure. The Senate has no rule on the subject but references to the House have been held out of order on several occasions. Generally the houses do not interfere with each other's appropriations although minor conflicts sometimes occur. A refusal to receive a message from the other house has also been held to violate the practice of comity.

Committee—A panel of members elected or appointed to perform some service or function for its parent body. Congress has four types of committees: standing, special or select, joint, and, in the House, a Committee of the Whole. Committees conduct investigations, make studies, issue reports and recommendations, and, in the case of standing committees, review and prepare measures on their assigned subjects for action by their respective houses. Most committees divide their work among several subcommittees. With rare exceptions, the majority party in a house holds a majority of the seats on its committees, and their chairmen are also from that party.

Committee Jurisdiction—The legislative subjects and other functions assigned to a committee by rule, precedent, resolution, or statute. A committee's title usually indicates the general scope of its jurisdiction but often fails to mention other significant subjects assigned to it.

Committee of the Whole—Common name of the Committee of the Whole House on the State of the Union, a committee consisting of all members of the House of Representatives. Measures from the union calendar must be considered in the Committee of the Whole before the House officially completes action on them; the committee often considers other major bills as well. A quorum of the committee is 100, and it meets in the House chamber under a chairman appointed by the Speaker. Procedures in the Committee of the Whole expedite consideration of legislation because of its smaller quorum requirement, its ban on certain motions, and its five-minute rule for debate on amendments. Those procedures usually permit more members to offer amendments and participate in the debate on a measure than is normally possible. The Senate no longer uses a Committee of the Whole.

Committee Ratios—The ratios of majority to minority party members on committees. By custom, the ratios of most committees reflect party strength in their respective houses as closely as possible.

Committee Report on a Measure—A document submitted by a committee to report a measure to its parent chamber. Customarily, the report explains the measure's purpose, describes provisions and any amendments recommended by the committee, and presents arguments for its approval.

Committee Veto—A procedure that requires an executive department or agency to submit certain proposed policies, programs, or action to designated committees for review before implementing them. Before 1983, when the Supreme Court declared that a legislative veto was unconstitutional, these provisions permitted committees to veto the proposals. Committees no longer conduct this type of policy review, and the term is now something of a misnomer. Nevertheless, agencies usually take the pragmatic approach of trying to reach a consensus with the committees before carrying out their proposals, especially when an appropriations committee is involved.

Concur—To agree to an amendment of the other house, either by adopting a motion to concur in that amendment or a motion to concur with an amendment to that amendment. After both houses have agreed to the same version of an amendment, neither house may amend it further, nor may any subsequent conference change it or delete it from the measure. Concurrence by one house in all amendments of the other house completes action on the measure; no vote is then necessary on the measure as a whole because both houses previously passed it.

Concurrent Resolution—A resolution that requires approval by both houses but does not need the president's signature and therefore cannot have the force of law. Concurrent resolutions deal with the prerogatives or internal affairs of Congress as a whole. Designated H. Con. Res. in the House and S. Con. Res. in the Senate, they are numbered consecutively in each house in their order of introduction during a two-year Congress.

Conferees—A common title for managers, the members from each house appointed to a conference committee. The Senate usually authorizes its presiding officer to appoint its conferees. The Speaker appoints House conferees, and under a rule adopted in 1993, can remove conferees "at any time after an original appointment" and also appoint additional conferees at any time. Conferees are expected to support the positions of their houses despite their personal views, but in practice this is not always the case. The party ratios of conferees generally reflect the ratios in their houses. Each house may appoint as many conferees as it pleases. House conferees often outnumber their Senate colleagues; however, each house has only one vote in a conference, so the size of its delegation is immaterial.

Conference—(1) A formal meeting or series of meetings between members representing each house to reconcile House and Senate differences on a measure (occasionally several measures). Because one house cannot require the other to agree to its proposals, the conference usually reaches agreement by compromise. When a conference completes action on a measure, or as much action as appears possible, it sends its recommendations to both houses in the form of a conference report, accompanied by an explanatory statement. (2) The official title of the organization of all Democrats or Republicans in the Senate and of all Republicans in the House of Representatives. *(See Party Caucus.)*

Conference Committee—A temporary joint committee formed for the purpose of resolving differences between the houses on a measure. Major and controversial legislation usually requires conference committee action. Voting in a conference committee is not by individuals but within the House and Senate delegations. Consequently, a conference committee report requires the support of a majority of the conferees from each house. Both houses require that conference committees open their meetings to the public. The Senate's rule permits the committee to close its meetings if a majority of conferees in each delegation agree by a roll-call vote. The House rule permits closed meetings only if the House authorizes them to do so on a roll-call vote. Otherwise, there are no congressional rules governing the organization of, or procedure in, a conference committee. The committee chooses its chairman, but on measures that go to conference annually, such as general appropriation bills, the chairmanship traditionally rotates between the houses.

Conference Report—A document submitted to both houses that contains a conference committee's agreements for resolving their differences on a measure. It must be signed by a majority of the conferees from each house separately and must be accompanied by an explanatory statement. Both houses prohibit amendments to a conference report and require it to be accepted or rejected in its entirety.

Congress—(1) The national legislature of the United States, consisting of the House of Representatives and the Senate. (2) The national legislature in office during a two-year period. Congresses are numbered sequentially; thus, the 1st Congress of 1789–1791 and the 106th Congress of 1999–2001. Before 1935, the two-year period began on the first Monday in December of odd-numbered years. Since then it has extended from January of an odd-numbered year through noon on Jan. 3 of the next odd-numbered year. A Congress usually holds two annual sessions, but some have had three sessions and the 67th Congress had four. When a Congress expires, measures die if they have not yet been enacted.

Congressional Accountability Act of 1995 (CAA)—An act applying eleven labor, workplace, and civil rights laws to the legislative branch and establishing procedures and remedies for legislative branch employees with grievances in violation of these laws. The following laws are covered by the CAA: the Fair Labor Standards Act of 1938; Title VII of the Civil Rights Act of 1964; Americans with Disabilities Act of 1990; Age Discrimination in Employment Act of 1967; Family and Medical Leave Act of 1993; Occupational Safety and Health Act of 1970; Chapter 71 of Title 5, *U.S. Code* (relating to federal service labor-management relations); Employee Polygraph Protection Act of 1988; Worker Adjustment and Retraining Notification Act; Rehabilitation Act of 1973; and Chapter 43 of Title 38, *U.S. Code* (relating to veterans' employment and reemployment).

Congressional Budget and Impoundment Control Act of 1974—The law that established the basic elements of the congressional budget process, the House and Senate Budget Committees, the Congressional Budget Office, and the procedures for congressional review of impoundments in the form of rescissions and deferrals proposed by the president. The budget process consists of procedures for coordinating congressional revenue and spending decisions made in separate tax, appropriations, and legislative measures. The impoundment provisions were intended to give Congress greater control over executive branch actions that delay or prevent the spending of funds provided by Congress.

Congressional Budget Office (CBO)—A congressional support agency created by the Congressional Budget and Impoundment Control Act of 1974 to provide nonpartisan budgetary information and analysis to Congress and its committees. CBO acts as a scorekeeper when Congress is voting on the federal budget, tracking bills to ensure they comply with overall budget goals. The agency also estimates what proposed legislation would cost over a five-year period. CBO works most closely with the House and Senate Budget Committees.

Congressional Directory—The official who's who of Congress, usually published during the first session of a two-year Congress.

Congressional District—The geographical area represented by a single member of the House of Representatives. For states with only one representative, the entire state is a congressional district. As of 2001 seven states had only one representative each: Alaska, Delaware, Montana, North Dakota, South Dakota, Vermont and Wyoming.

Congressional Record—The daily, printed, and substantially verbatim account of proceedings in both the House and Senate chambers. Extraneous materials submitted by members appear in a section titled "Extensions of Remarks." A "Daily Digest" appendix contains highlights of the day's floor and committee action plus a list of committee meetings and floor agendas for the next day's session.

Although the official reporters of each house take down every word spoken during the proceedings, members are permitted to edit and "revise and extend" their remarks before they are printed. In the Senate section, all speeches, articles, and other material submitted by senators but not actually spoken or read on the floor are set off by large black dots, called bullets. However, bullets do not appear when a senator reads part of a speech and inserts the rest. In the House section, undelivered speeches and materials are printed in a distinctive typeface. The term "permanent *Record*" refers to the bound volumes of the daily *Records* of an entire session of Congress.

Congressional Research Service (CRS)—Established in 1917, a department of the Library of Congress whose staff provide nonpartisan, objective analysis, and information on virtually any subject to committees, members, and staff of Congress. Originally the Legislative Reference Service, it is the oldest congressional support agency.

Congressional Support Agencies—A term often applied to three agencies in the legislative branch that provide nonpartisan information and analysis to committees and members of Congress: the Congressional Budget Office, the Congressional Research Service of the Library of Congress, and the General Accounting Office. A fourth support agency, the Office of Technology Assessment, formerly provided such support but was abolished in the 104th Congress.

Congressional Terms of Office—A term normally begins on Jan. 3 of the year following a general election and runs two years for representatives and six years for senators. A representative chosen in a special election to fill a vacancy is sworn in for the remainder of the predecessor's term. An individual appointed to fill a Senate vacancy usually serves until the next general election or until the end of the predecessor's term, whichever comes first. Some states, however, require their governors to call a special election to fill a Senate vacancy shortly after an appointment has been made.

Constitutional Rules—Constitutional provisions that prescribe procedures for Congress. In addition to certain types of votes required in particular situations, these provisions include the following: (1) the House chooses its Speaker, the Senate its president pro tempore, and both houses their officers; (2) each house requires a majority quorum to conduct business; (3) less than a majority may adjourn from day to day and compel the attendance of absent members; (4) neither house may adjourn for more than three days without the consent of the other; (5) each house must keep a journal; (6) the yeas and nays are ordered when supported by one-fifth of the members present; (7) all revenue-raising bills must originate in the House, but the Senate may propose amendments to them. The Constitution also sets out the procedure in the House for electing a president, the procedure in the Senate for electing a vice president, the procedure for filling a vacancy in the office of vice president, and the procedure for overriding a presidential veto.

Constitutional Votes—Constitutional provisions that require certain votes or voting methods in specific situations. They include (1) the yeas and nays at the desire of one-fifth of the members present; (2) a two-thirds vote by the yeas and nays to override a veto; (3) a two-thirds vote by one house to expel one of its members and by both houses to propose a constitutional amendment; (4) a two-thirds vote of senators present to convict someone whom the House has impeached and to consent to ratification of treaties; (5) a two-thirds vote in each house to remove political disabilities from persons who have engaged in insurrection or rebellion or given aid or comfort to the enemies of the United States; (6) a majority vote in each house to fill a vacancy in the office of vice president; (7) a majority vote of all states to elect a president in the House of Representatives when no candidate receives a majority of the electoral votes; (8) a majority vote of all senators when the Senate elects a vice president

under the same circumstances; and (9) the casting vote of the vice president in case of tie votes in the Senate.

Contempt of Congress—Willful obstruction of the proper functions of Congress. Most frequently, it is a refusal to obey a subpoena to appear and testify before a committee or to produce documents demanded by it. Such obstruction is a misdemeanor and persons cited for contempt are subject to prosecution in federal courts. A house cites an individual for contempt by agreeing to a privileged resolution to that effect reported by a committee. The presiding officer then refers the matter to a U.S. attorney for prosecution.

Continuing Body—A characterization of the Senate on the theory that it continues from Congress to Congress and has existed continuously since it first convened in 1789. The rationale for the theory is that under the system of staggered six-year terms for senators, the terms of only about one-third of them expire after each Congress and, therefore, a quorum of the Senate is always in office. Consequently, under this theory, the Senate, unlike the House, does not have to adopt its rules at the beginning of each Congress because those rules continue from one Congress to the next. This makes it extremely difficult for the Senate to change its rules against the opposition of a determined minority because those rules require a two-thirds vote of the senators present and voting to invoke cloture on a proposed rules change.

Continuing Resolution (CR)—A joint resolution that provides funds to continue the operation of federal agencies and programs at the beginning of a new fiscal year if their annual appropriation bills have not yet been enacted; also called continuing appropriations. Continuing resolutions are enacted shortly before or after the new fiscal year begins and usually make funds available for a specified period. Additional resolutions are often needed after the first expires. Some continuing resolutions have provided appropriations for an entire fiscal year. Continuing resolutions for specific periods customarily fix a rate at which agencies may incur obligations based either on the previous year's appropriations, the president's budget request, or the amount as specified in the agency's regular annual appropriation bill if that bill has already been passed by one or both houses. In the House, continuing resolutions are privileged after Sept. 15.

Contract Authority—Statutory authority permitting an agency to enter into contracts or incur other obligations even though it has not received an appropriation to pay for them. Congress must eventually fund them because the government is legally liable for such payments. The Congressional Budget Act of 1974 requires that new contract authority may not be used unless provided for in advance by an appropriation act, but it permits a few exceptions.

Correcting Recorded Votes—The rules of both houses prohibit members from changing their votes after a vote result has been announced. Nevertheless, the Senate permits its members to withdraw or change their votes, by unanimous consent, immediately after the announcement. In rare instances, senators have been granted unanimous consent to change their votes several days or weeks after the announcement. Votes tallied by the electronic voting system in the House may not be changed. But when a vote actually given is not recorded during an oral call of the roll, a member may demand a correction as a matter of right. On all other alleged errors in a recorded vote, the Speaker determines whether the circumstances justify a change. Occasionally, members merely announce that they were incorrectly recorded; announcements can occur hours, days, or even months after the vote and appear in the *Congressional Record*.

Cosponsor—A member who has joined one or more other members to sponsor a measure.

Credit Authority—Authority granted to an agency to incur direct loan obligations or to make loan guarantee commitments. The Congressional Budget Act of 1974 bans congressional consideration of credit authority legislation unless the extent of that authority is made subject to provisions in appropriation acts.

C-SPAN—Cable-Satellite Public Affairs Network, which provides live, gavel-to-gavel coverage of Senate floor proceedings on one cable television channel and coverage of House floor proceedings on another channel. C-SPAN also televises important committee hearings in both houses. Each house also transmits its televised proceedings directly to congressional offices.

Current Services Estimates—Executive branch estimates of the anticipated costs of federal programs and operations for the next and future fiscal years at existing levels of service and assuming no new initiatives or changes in existing law. The president submits these estimates to Congress with the annual budget and includes an explanation of the underlying economic and policy assumptions on which they are based, such as anticipated rates of inflation, real economic growth, and unemployment, plus program caseloads and pay increases.

Custody of the Papers—Possession of an engrossed measure and certain related basic documents that the two houses produce as they try to resolve their differences over the measure.

Dance of the Swans and the Ducks—A whimsical description of the gestures some members use in connection with a request for a recorded vote, especially in the House. When members want their colleagues to stand in support of the request, they move their hands and arms in a gentle upward motion resembling the beginning flight of a graceful swan. When they want their colleagues to remain seated to avoid such a vote, they move their hands and arms in a vigorous downward motion resembling a diving duck.

Dean—Within a state's delegation in the House of Representatives, the member with the longest continuous service.

Debate—In congressional parlance, speeches delivered during consideration of a measure, motion, or other matter, as distinguished from speeches in other parliamentary situations, such as one-minute and special order speeches when no business is pending. Virtually all debate in the House of Representatives is under some kind of time limitation. Most debate in the Senate is unlimited; that is, a senator, once recognized, may speak for as long as he or she chooses, unless the Senate invokes cloture.

Debt Limit—The maximum amount of outstanding federal public debt permitted by law. The limit (or ceiling) covers virtually all debt incurred by the government except agency debt. Each congressional budget resolution sets forth the new debt limit that may be required under its provisions.

Deferral—An impoundment of funds for a specific period of time that may not extend beyond the fiscal year in which it is pro-

posed. Under the Impoundment Control Act of 1974, the president must notify Congress that he is deferring the spending or obligation of funds provided by law for a project or activity. Congress can disapprove the deferral by legislation.

Deficit—The amount by which the government's outlays exceed its budget receipts for a given fiscal year. Both the president's budget and the annual congressional budget resolution provide estimates of the deficit or surplus for the upcoming and several future fiscal years.

Degrees of Amendment—Designations that indicate the relationships of amendments to the text of a measure and to each other. In general, an amendment offered directly to the text of a measure is an amendment in the first degree, and an amendment to that amendment is an amendment in the second degree. Both houses normally prohibit amendments in the third degree—that is, an amendment to an amendment to an amendment.

Delegate—A nonvoting member of the House of Representatives elected to a two-year term from the District of Columbia, the territory of Guam, the territory of the Virgin Islands, or the territory of American Samoa. By law, delegates may not vote in the full House but they may participate in debate, offer motions (except to reconsider), and serve and vote on standing and select committees. On their committees, delegates possess the same powers and privileges as other members and the Speaker may appoint them to appropriate conference committees and select committees.

Denounce—A formal action that condemns a member for misbehavior; considered by some experts to be equivalent to censure. *(See Censure.)*

Dilatory Tactics—Procedural actions intended to delay or prevent action by a house or a committee. They include, among others, offering numerous motions, demanding quorum calls and recorded votes at every opportunity, making numerous points of order and parliamentary inquiries, and speaking as long as the applicable rules permit. The Senate rules permit a battery of dilatory tactics, especially lengthy speeches, except under cloture. In the House, possible dilatory tactics are more limited. Speeches are always subject to time limits and debate-ending motions. Moreover, a House rule instructs the Speaker not to entertain dilatory motions and lets the Speaker decide whether a motion is dilatory. However, the Speaker may not override the constitutional right of a member to demand the yeas and nays, and in practice usually waits for a point of order before exercising that authority. *(See Cloture.)*

Discharge a Committee—Remove a measure from a committee to which it has been referred in order to make it available for floor consideration. Noncontroversial measures are often discharged by unanimous consent. However, because congressional committees have no obligation to report measures referred to them, each house has procedures to extract controversial measures from recalcitrant committees. Six discharge procedures are available in the House of Representatives. The Senate uses a motion to discharge, which is usually converted into a discharge resolution.

District Office—Representatives maintain one or more offices in their districts for the purpose of assisting and communicating with constituents. The costs of maintaining these offices are paid from members' official allowances. Senators can use the official expense allowance to rent offices in their home state, subject to a funding formula based on their state's population and other factors.

District Work Period—The House term for a scheduled congressional recess during which members may visit their districts and conduct constituency business.

Division Vote—A vote in which the chair first counts those in favor of a proposition and then those opposed to it, with no record made of how each member votes. In the Senate, the chair may count raised hands or ask senators to stand, whereas the House requires members to stand; hence, often called a standing vote. Committees in both houses ordinarily use a show of hands. A division usually occurs after a voice vote and may be demanded by any member or ordered by the chair if there is any doubt about the outcome of the voice vote. The demand for a division can also come before a voice vote. In the Senate, the demand must come before the result of a voice vote is announced. It may be made after a voice vote announcement in the House, but only if no intervening business has transpired and only if the member was standing and seeking recognition at the time of the announcement. A demand for the yeas and nays or, in the House, for a recorded vote, takes precedence over a division vote.

Doorkeeper of the House—A former officer of the House of Representatives who was responsible for enforcing the rules prohibiting unauthorized persons from entering the chamber when the House is in session. The doorkeeper was usually the candidate of the majority party. In 1995 the office was abolished and its functions transferred to the sergeant at arms.

Effective Dates—Provisions of an act that specify when the entire act or individual provisions in it become effective as law. Most acts become effective on the date of enactment, but it is sometimes necessary or prudent to delay the effective dates of some provisions.

Electronic Voting—Since 1973 the House has used an electronic voting system to record the yeas and nays and to conduct recorded votes. Members vote by inserting their voting cards in one of the boxes at several locations in the chamber. They are given at least fifteen minutes to vote. When several votes occur immediately after each other, the Speaker may reduce the voting time to five minutes on the second and subsequent votes. The Speaker may allow additional time on each vote but may also close a vote at any time after the minimum time has expired. Members can change their votes at any time before the Speaker announces the result. The House also uses the electronic system for quorum calls. While a vote is in progress, a large panel above the Speaker's desk displays how each member has voted. Smaller panels on either side of the chamber display running totals of the votes and the time remaining. The Senate does not have electronic voting.

Enacting Clause—The opening language of each bill, beginning "Be it enacted by the Senate and House of Representatives of the United States of America in Congress assembled . . ." This language gives legal force to measures approved by Congress and signed by the president or enacted over the president's veto. A successful motion to strike it from a bill kills the entire measure.

Engrossed Bill—The official copy of a bill or joint resolution as passed by one chamber, including the text as amended by floor action, and certified by the clerk of the House or the secretary of the Senate (as appropriate). Amendments by one house to a measure or

amendments of the other also are engrossed. House engrossed documents are printed on blue paper; the Senate's are printed on white paper.

Enrolled Bill—The final official copy of a bill or joint resolution passed in identical form by both houses. An enrolled bill is printed on parchment. After it is certified by the chief officer of the house in which it originated and signed by the House Speaker and the Senate president pro tempore, the measure is sent to the White House for the president's signature.

Entitlement Program—A federal program under which individuals, businesses, or units of government that meet the requirements or qualifications established by law are entitled to receive certain payments if they seek such payments. Major examples include Social Security, Medicare, Medicaid, unemployment insurance, and military and federal civilian pensions. Congress cannot control their expenditures by refusing to appropriate the sums necessary to fund them because the government is legally obligated to pay eligible recipients the amounts to which the law entitles them.

Equality of the Houses—A component of the Constitution's emphasis on checks and balances under which each house is given essentially equal status in the enactment of legislation and in the relations and negotiations between the two houses. Although the House of Representatives initiates revenue and appropriation measures, the Senate has the right to amend them. Either house may initiate any other type of legislation, and neither can force the other to agree to, or even act on, its measures. Moreover, each house has a potential veto over the other because legislation requires agreement by both. Similarly, in a conference to resolve their differences on a measure, each house casts one vote, as determined by a majority of its conferees. In most other national bicameral legislatures, the powers of one house are markedly greater than those of the other.

Ethics Rules—Several rules or standing orders in each house that mandate certain standards of conduct for members and congressional employees in finance, employment, franking, and other areas. The Senate Permanent Select Committee on Ethics and the House Committee on Standards of Official Conduct investigate alleged violations of conduct and recommend appropriate actions to their respective houses.

Exclusive Committee—(1) Under the rules of the Republican Conference and House Democratic Caucus, a standing committee whose members usually cannot serve on any other standing committee. As of 2000 the Appropriations, Energy and Commerce (beginning in the 105th Congress), Ways and Means, and Rules Committees were designated as exclusive committees. (2) Under the rules of the two party conferences in the Senate, a standing committee whose members may not simultaneously serve on any other exclusive committee.

Executive Calendar—The Senate's calendar for committee reports on its executive business, namely treaties and nominations. The calendar numbers indicate the order in which items were referred to the calendar but have no bearing on when or if the Senate will consider them. The Senate, by motion or unanimous consent, resolves itself into executive session to consider them.

Executive Document—A document, usually a treaty, sent by the president to the Senate for approval. It is referred to a committee in the same manner as other measures. Resolutions to ratify treaties have their own "treaty document" numbers. For example, the first treaty submitted in the 106th Congress would be "Treaty Doc 106-1."

Executive Order—A unilateral proclamation by the president that has a policy-making or legislative impact. Members of Congress have challenged some executive orders on the grounds that they usurped the authority of the legislative branch. Although the Supreme Court has ruled that a particular order exceeded the president's authority, it has upheld others as falling within the president's general constitutional powers.

Executive Privilege—The assertion that presidents have the right to withhold certain information from Congress. Presidents have based their claim on (1) the constitutional separation of powers; (2) the need for secrecy in military and diplomatic affairs; (3) the need to protect individuals from unfavorable publicity; (4) the need to safeguard the confidential exchange of ideas in the executive branch; and (5) the need to protect individuals who provide confidential advice to the president.

Executive Session—(1) A Senate meeting devoted to the consideration of treaties or nominations. Normally, the Senate meets in legislative session; it resolves itself into executive session, by motion or by unanimous consent, to deal with its executive business. It also keeps a separate *Journal* for executive sessions. Executive sessions are usually open to the public, but the Senate may choose to close them.

Expulsion—A member's removal from office by a two-thirds vote of his or her house; the supermajority is required by the Constitution. It is the most severe and most rarely used sanction a house can invoke against a member. Although the Constitution provides no explicit grounds for expulsion, the courts have ruled that it may be applied only for misconduct during a member's term of office, not for conduct before the member's election. Generally, neither house will consider expulsion of a member convicted of a crime until the judicial processes have been exhausted. At that stage, members sometimes resign rather than face expulsion. In 1977 the House adopted a rule urging members convicted of certain crimes to voluntarily abstain from voting or participating in other legislative business.

Extensions of Remarks—An appendix to the daily *Congressional Record* that consists primarily of miscellaneous extraneous material submitted by members. It often includes members' statements not delivered on the floor, newspaper articles and editorials, praise for a member's constituents, and noteworthy letters received by a member, among other material. Representatives supply the bulk of this material; senators submit very little. "Extensions of Remarks" pages are separately numbered, and each number is preceded by the letter "E." Materials may be placed in the Extensions of Remarks section only by unanimous consent. Usually, one member of each party makes the request each day on behalf of his or her party colleagues after the House has completed its legislative business of the day.

Federal Debt—The total amount of monies borrowed and not yet repaid by the federal government. Federal debt consists of public debt and agency debt. Public debt is the portion of the federal debt borrowed by the Treasury or the Federal Financing Bank directly from the public or from another federal fund or account. For example, the Treasury regularly borrows money from the Social Security trust fund. Public debt accounts for about 99 percent of the federal debt. Agency debt refers to the debt incurred by federal agencies such as the Export-Import Bank but excluding the Treasury and the Federal Financing Bank, which are authorized by law to borrow funds from the public or from another government fund or account.

Filibuster—The use of obstructive and time-consuming parliamentary tactics by one member or a minority of members to delay, modify, or defeat proposed legislation or rules changes. Filibusters are also sometimes used to delay urgently needed measures to force the body to accept other legislation. The Senate's rules permitting unlimited debate and the extraordinary majority it requires to impose cloture make filibustering particularly effective in that chamber. Under the stricter rules of the House, filibusters in that body are short-lived and therefore ineffective and rarely attempted.

Fiscal Year—The federal government's annual accounting period. It begins Oct. 1 and ends on the following Sept. 30. A fiscal year is designated by the calendar year in which it ends and is often referred to as FY. Thus, fiscal year 1998 began Oct. 1, 1997, ended Sept. 30, 1998, and is called FY98. In theory, Congress is supposed to complete action on all budgetary measures applying to a fiscal year before that year begins. It rarely does so.

Five-Minute Rule—A House rule that limits debate on an amendment offered in Committee of the Whole to five minutes for its sponsor and five minutes for an opponent. In practice, the committee routinely permits longer debate by two devices: the offering of pro forma amendments, each debatable for five minutes, and unanimous consent for a member to speak longer than five minutes. Consequently, debate on an amendment sometimes continues for hours. At any time after the first ten minutes, however, the committee may shut off debate immediately or by a specified time, either by unanimous consent or by majority vote on a nondebatable motion. The motion, which dates from 1847, is also used in the House as in Committee of the Whole, where debate also may be shut off by a motion for the previous question.

Floor—The ground level of the House or Senate chamber where members sit and the houses conduct their business. When members are attending a meeting of their house they are said to be on the floor. Floor action refers to the procedural actions taken during floor consideration such as deciding on motions, taking up measures, amending them, and voting.

Floor Manager—A majority party member responsible for guiding a measure through its floor consideration in a house and for devising the political and procedural strategies that might be required to get it passed. The presiding officer gives the floor manager priority recognition to debate, offer amendments, oppose amendments, and make crucial procedural motions.

Frank—Informally, members' legal right to send official mail postage free under their signatures; often called the franking privilege. Technically, it is the autographic or facsimile signature used on envelopes instead of stamps that permits members and certain congressional officers to send their official mail free of charge. The franking privilege has been authorized by law since the first Congress, except for a few months in 1873. Congress reimburses the U.S. Postal Service for the franked mail it handles.

Function or Functional Category—A broad category of national need and spending of budgetary significance. A category provides an accounting method for allocating and keeping track of budgetary resources and expenditures for that function because it includes all budget accounts related to the function's subject or purpose such as agriculture, administration of justice, commerce and housing and energy. Functions do not necessarily correspond with appropriations acts or with the budgets of individual agencies. As of 2000 there were twenty functional categories, each divided into a number of subfunctions.

Gag Rule—A pejorative term for any type of special rule reported by the House Rules Committee that proposes to prohibit amendments to a measure or only permits amendments offered by the reporting committee.

Galleries—The balconies overlooking each chamber from which the public, news media, staff, and others may observe floor proceedings.

General Accounting Office (GAO)—A congressional support agency, often referred to as the investigative arm of Congress. It evaluates and audits federal agencies and programs in the United States and abroad on its initiative or at the request of congressional committees or members.

General Appropriation Bill—A term applied to each of the thirteen annual bills that provide funds for most federal agencies and programs and also to the supplemental appropriation bills that contain appropriations for more than one agency or program.

Germaneness—The requirement that an amendment be closely related—in terms of subject or purpose, for example—to the text it proposes to amend. A House rule requires that all amendments be germane. In the Senate, only amendments offered to general appropriation bills and budget measures or proposed under cloture must be germane. Germaneness rules can be waived by suspension of the rules in both houses, by unanimous consent agreements in the Senate, and by special rules from the Rules Committee in the House. Moreover, presiding officers usually do not enforce germaneness rules on their own initiative; therefore, a nongermane amendment can be adopted if no member raises a point of order against it. Under cloture in the Senate, however, the chair may take the initiative to rule amendments out of order as not being germane, without a point of order being made. All House debate must be germane except during general debate in the Committee of the Whole, but special rules invariably require that such debate be "confined to the bill." The Senate requires germane debate only during the first three hours of each daily session. Under the precedents of both houses, an amendment can be relevant but not necessarily germane. A crucial factor in determining germaneness in the House is how the subject of a measure or matter is defined. For example, the subject of a measure authorizing construction of a naval vessel is defined as being the construction of a single vessel; therefore, an amendment to authorize an additional vessel is not germane.

Gerrymandering—The manipulation of legislative district boundaries to benefit a particular party, politician, or minority group. The term originated in 1812 when the Massachusetts legislature redrew the lines of state legislative districts to favor the party of Gov. Elbridge Gerry, and some critics said one district looked like a salamander. *(See also Congressional District; Redistricting.)*

Gramm-Rudman-Hollings Act of 1985—Common name for the Balanced Budget and Emergency Deficit Control Act of 1985, which established new budget procedures intended to balance the federal budget by fiscal year 1991. (The timetable subsequently was extended and then deleted.) The act's chief sponsors were senators Phil Gramm (R-Texas), Warren Rudman (R-N.H.), and Ernest Hollings (D-S.C.).

Grandfather Clause—A provision in a measure, law, or rule that exempts an individual, entity, or a defined category of individuals or entities from complying with a new policy or restriction. For example, a bill that would raise taxes on persons who reach the age of sixty-five after a certain date inherently grandfathers out those who are sixty-five before that date. Similarly, a Senate rule limiting senators to two major committee assignments also grandfathers some senators who were sitting on a third major committee before a specified date.

Grants-in-Aid—Payments by the federal government to state and local governments to help provide for assistance programs or public services.

Hearing—Committee or subcommittee meetings to receive testimony on proposed legislation during investigations or for oversight purposes. Relatively few bills are important enough to justify formal hearings. Witnesses often include experts, government officials, spokespersons for interested groups, officials of the General Accounting Office, and members of Congress.

Hold—A senator's request that his or her party leaders delay floor consideration of certain legislation or presidential nominations. The majority leader usually honors a hold for a reasonable period of time, especially if its purpose is to assure the senator that the matter will not be called up during his or her absence or to give the senator time to gather necessary information.

Hold (or Have) the Floor—A member's right to speak without interruption, unless he or she violates a rule, after recognition by the presiding officer. At the member's discretion, he or she may yield to another member for a question in the Senate or for a question or statement in the House, but may reclaim the floor at any time.

Hold-Harmless Clause—In legislation providing a new formula for allocating federal funds, a clause to ensure that recipients of those funds do not receive less in a future year than they did in the current year if the new formula would result in a reduction for them. Similar to a grandfather clause, it has been used most frequently to soften the impact of sudden reductions in federal grants. *(See Grandfather Clause.)*

Hopper—A box on the clerk's desk in the House chamber into which members deposit bills and resolutions to introduce them. In House jargon, to drop a bill in the hopper is to introduce it.

Hour Rule—A House rule that permits members, when recognized, to hold the floor in debate for no more than one hour each. The majority party member customarily yields one-half the time to a minority member. Although the hour rule applies to general debate in Committee of the Whole as well as in the House, special rules routinely vary the length of time for such debate and its control to fit the circumstances of particular measures.

House as in Committee of the Whole—A hybrid combination of procedures from the general rules of the House and from the rules of the Committee of the Whole, sometimes used to expedite consideration of a measure on the floor.

House Calendar—The calendar reserved for all public bills and resolutions that do not raise revenue or directly or indirectly appropriate money or property when they are favorably reported by House committees.

House Manual—A commonly used title for the handbook of the rules of the House of Representatives, published in each Congress. Its official title is *Constitution, Jefferson's Manual, and Rules of the House of Representatives.*

House of Representatives—The house of Congress in which states are represented roughly in proportion to their populations, but every state is guaranteed at least one representative. By law, the number of voting representatives is fixed at 435. Four delegates and one resident commissioner also serve in the House; they may vote in their committees but not on the House floor. Although the House and Senate have equal legislative power, the Constitution gives the House sole authority to originate revenue measures. The House also claims the right to originate appropriation measures, a claim the Senate disputes in theory but concedes in practice. The House has the sole power to impeach, and it elects the president when no candidate has received a majority of the electoral votes. It is sometimes referred to as the lower body.

Immunity—(1) Members' constitutional protection from lawsuits and arrest in connection with their legislative duties. They may not be tried for libel or slander for anything they say on the floor of a house or in committee. Nor may they be arrested while attending sessions of their houses or when traveling to or from sessions of Congress, except when charged with treason, a felony, or a breach of the peace. (2) In the case of a witness before a committee, a grant of protection from prosecution based on that person's testimony to the committee. It is used to compel witnesses to testify who would otherwise refuse to do so on the constitutional ground of possible self-incrimination. Under such a grant, none of a witness's testimony may be used against him or her in a court proceeding except in a prosecution for perjury or for giving a false statement to Congress. *(See also Contempt of Congress.)*

Impeachment—The first step to remove the president, vice president, or other federal civil officers from office and to disqualify them from any future federal office "of honor, Trust or Profit." An impeachment is a formal charge of treason, bribery, or "other high Crimes and Misdemeanors." The House has the sole power of impeachment and the Senate the sole power of trying the charges and convicting. The House impeaches by a simple majority vote; conviction requires a two-thirds vote of all senators present.

Impeachment Trial, Removal, and Disqualification—The Senate conducts an impeachment trial under a separate set of twenty-six rules that appears in the *Senate Manual.* Under the Constitution, the chief justice of the United States presides over trials of the president, but the vice president, the president pro tempore, or any other senator may preside over the impeachment trial of another official.

The Constitution requires senators to take an oath for an impeachment trial. During the trial, senators may not engage in colloquies or participate in arguments, but they may submit questions in writing to House managers or defense counsel. After the trial concludes, the Senate votes separately on each article of impeachment without debate unless the Senate orders the doors closed for private discussions. During deliberations senators may speak no more than once on a question, not for more than ten minutes on an interlocutory question and not more than fifteen minutes on the final question. These rules may be set aside by unanimous consent or suspended on motion by a two-thirds vote.

The Senate's impeachment trial of President Clinton in 1999 was only the second such trial involving a president. It continued for five weeks, with the Senate voting not to convict on the two impeachment articles.

Senate impeachment rules allow the Senate, at its own discretion, to name a committee to hear evidence and conduct the trial, with all senators thereafter voting on the charges. The impeachment trials of three federal judges were conducted this way, and the Supreme Court upheld the validity of these rules in *Nixon v. United States,* 506 U.S. 224, 1993.

An official convicted on impeachment charges is removed from office immediately. However, the convicted official is not barred from holding a federal office in the future unless the Senate, after its conviction vote, also approves a resolution disqualifying the convicted official from future office. For example, federal judge Alcee L. Hastings was impeached and convicted in 1989, but the Senate did not vote to bar him from office in the future. In 1992 Hastings was elected to the House of Representatives, and no challenge was raised against seating him when he took the oath of office in 1993.

Impoundment—An executive branch action or inaction that delays or withholds the expenditure or obligation of budget authority provided by law. The Impoundment Control Act of 1974 classifies impoundments as either deferrals or rescissions, requires the president to notify Congress about all such actions, and gives Congress authority to approve or reject them.

Inspector General (IG) in the House of Representatives—A position established with the passage of the House Administrative Reform Resolution of 1992. The duties of the office have been revised several times and are now contained in House Rule II. The inspector general (IG), who is subject to the policy direction and oversight of the Committee on House Administration, is appointed for a Congress jointly by the Speaker and the majority and minority leaders of the House. The IG communicates the results of audits to the House officers or officials who were the subjects of the audits and suggests appropriate corrective measures. The IG submits a report of each audit to the Speaker, the majority and minority leaders, and the chairman and ranking minority member of the House Administration Committee; notifies these five members in the case of any financial irregularity discovered; and reports to the Committee on Standards of Official Conduct on possible violations of House rules or any applicable law by any House member, officer, or employee. The IG's office also has certain duties to audit various financial operations of the House that had previously been performed by the General Accounting Office.

Instruct Conferees—A formal action by a house urging its conferees to uphold a particular position on a measure in conference. The instruction may be to insist on certain provisions in the measure as passed by that house or to accept a provision in the version passed by the other house. Instructions to conferees are not binding because the primary responsibility of conferees is to reach agreement on a measure and neither House can compel the other to accept particular provisions or positions.

Investigative Power—The authority of Congress and its committees to pursue investigations, upheld by the Supreme Court but limited to matters related to, and in furtherance of, a legitimate task of the Congress. Standing committees in both houses are permanently authorized to investigate matters within their jurisdictions. Major investigations are sometimes conducted by temporary select, special, or joint committees established by resolutions for that purpose.

Some rules of the House provide certain safeguards for witnesses and others during investigative hearings. These permit counsel to accompany witnesses, require that each witness receive a copy of the committee's rules, and order the committee to go into closed session if it believes the testimony to be heard might defame, degrade, or incriminate any person. The committee may subsequently decide to hear such testimony in open session. The Senate has no rules of this kind.

Item Veto—Item veto authority, which is available to most state governors, allows governors to eliminate or reduce items in legislative measures presented for their signature without vetoing the entire measure, and sign the rest into law. A similar authority was briefly granted to the U.S. president under the Line Item Veto Act of 1996. According to the majority opinion of the Supreme Court in its 1998 decision overturning that law, a constitutional amendment would be necessary to give the president such item veto authority.

Jefferson's Manual—Short title of *Jefferson's Manual of Parliamentary Practice,* prepared by Thomas Jefferson for his guidance when he was president of the Senate from 1797 to 1801. Although it reflects English parliamentary practice in his day, many procedures in both houses of Congress are still rooted in its basic precepts. Under a House rule adopted in 1837, the manual's provisions govern House procedures when applicable and when they are not inconsistent with its standing rules and orders. The Senate, however, has never officially acknowledged it as a direct authority for its legislative procedure.

Johnson Rule—A policy instituted in 1953 under which all Democratic senators are assigned to one major committee before any Democrat is assigned to two. The Johnson Rule is named after its author, Sen. Lyndon B. Johnson, D-Texas, then the Senate's Democratic leader. Senate Republicans adopted a similar policy soon thereafter.

Joint Committee—A committee composed of members selected from each house. The functions of most joint committees involve investigation, research, or oversight of agencies closely related to Congress. Permanent joint committees, created by statute, are sometimes called standing joint committees. Once quite numerous, only four joint committees remained as of 2002: Joint Economic, Joint Taxation, Joint Library, and Joint Printing. None has authority to report legislation.

Joint Resolution—A legislative measure that Congress uses for purposes other than general legislation. Similar to a bill, it has the force of law when passed by both houses and either approved by the president or passed over the president's veto. Unlike a bill, a joint resolution enacted into law is not called an act; it retains its original title. Most often, joint resolutions deal with such relatively limited matters as the correction of errors in existing law, continuing appropriations, a single appropriation, or the establishment of permanent joint committees. Unlike bills, however, joint resolutions also are used to propose constitutional amendments; these do not require the president's signature and become effective only when ratified by three-fourths of the states. The House designates joint resolutions as H.J. Res., the

Senate as S.J. Res. Each house numbers its joint resolutions consecutively in the order of introduction during a two-year Congress.

Joint Session—Informally, any combined meeting of the Senate and the House. Technically, a joint session is a combined meeting to count the electoral votes for president and vice president or to hear a presidential address, such as the State of the Union message; any other formal combined gathering of both houses is a joint meeting. Joint sessions are authorized by concurrent resolutions and are held in the House chamber, because of its larger seating capacity. Although the president of the Senate and the Speaker sit side by side at the Speaker's desk during combined meetings, the former presides over the electoral count and the latter presides on all other occasions and introduces the president or other guest speaker. The president and other guests may address a joint session or meeting only by invitation.

Joint Sponsorship—Two or more members sponsoring the same measure.

Journal—The official record of House or Senate actions, including every motion offered, every vote cast, amendments agreed to, quorum calls, and so forth. Unlike the *Congressional Record,* it does not provide reports of speeches, debates, statements, and the like. The Constitution requires each house to maintain a *Journal* and to publish it periodically.

Junket—A member's trip at government expense, especially abroad, ostensibly on official business but, it is often alleged, for pleasure.

Killer Amendment—An amendment that, if agreed to, might lead to the defeat of the measure it amends, either in the house in which the amendment is offered or at some later stage of the legislative process. Members sometimes deliberately offer or vote for such an amendment in the expectation that it will undermine support for the measure in Congress or increase the likelihood that the president will veto it.

King of the Mountain (or Hill) Rule—*(See Queen of the Hill Rule.)*

LA—*(See Legislative Assistant.)*

Lame Duck—Jargon for a member who has not been reelected, or did not seek reelection, and is serving the balance of his or her term.

Lame Duck Session—A session of a Congress held after the election for the succeeding Congress, so-called after the lame duck members still serving.

Last Train Out—Colloquial name for last must-pass bill of a session of Congress.

Law—An act of Congress that has been signed by the president, passed over the president's veto, or allowed to become law without the president's signature.

Lay on the Table—A motion to dispose of a pending proposition immediately, finally, and adversely; that is, to kill it without a direct vote on its substance. Often simply called a motion to table, it is not debatable and is adopted by majority vote or without objection. It is a highly privileged motion, taking precedence over all others except the motion to adjourn in the House and all but three additional motions in the Senate. It can kill a bill or resolution, an amendment, another motion, an appeal, or virtually any other matter.

Tabling an amendment also tables the measure to which the amendment is pending in the House, but not in the Senate. The House does not allow the motion against the motion to recommit, in Committee of the Whole, and in some other situations. In the Senate it is the only permissible motion that immediately ends debate on a proposition, but only to kill it.

(The) Leadership—Usually, a reference to the majority and minority leaders of the Senate or to the Speaker and minority leader of the House. The term sometimes includes the majority leader in the House and the majority and minority whips in each house and, at other times, other party officials as well.

Legislation—(1) A synonym for legislative measures: bills and joint resolutions. (2) Provisions in such measures or in substantive amendments offered to them. (3) In some contexts, provisions that change existing substantive or authorizing law, rather than provisions that make appropriations.

Legislation on an Appropriation Bill—A common reference to provisions changing existing law that appear in, or are offered as amendments to, a general appropriation bill. A House rule prohibits the inclusion of such provisions in general appropriation bills unless they retrench expenditures. An analogous Senate rule permits points of order against amendments to a general appropriation bill that propose general legislation.

Legislative Assistant (LA)—A member's staff person responsible for monitoring and preparing legislation on particular subjects and for advising the member on them; commonly referred to as an LA.

Legislative Day—The day that begins when a house meets after an adjournment and ends when it next adjourns. Because the House of Representatives normally adjourns at the end of a daily session, its legislative and calendar days usually coincide. The Senate, however, frequently recesses at the end of a daily session, and its legislative day may extend over several calendar days, weeks, or months. Among other uses, this technicality permits the Senate to save time by circumventing its morning hour, a procedure required at the beginning of every legislative day.

Legislative History—(1) A chronological list of actions taken on a measure during its progress through the legislative process. (2) The official documents relating to a measure, the entries in the *Journals* of the two houses on that measure, and the *Congressional Record* text of its consideration in both houses. The documents include all committee reports and the conference report and joint explanatory statement, if any. Courts and affected federal agencies study a measure's legislative history for congressional intent about its purpose and interpretation.

Legislative Process—(1) Narrowly, the stages in the enactment of a law from introduction to final disposition. An introduced measure that becomes law typically travels through reference to committee; committee and subcommittee consideration; report to the chamber; floor consideration; amendment; passage; engrossment; messaging to the other house; similar steps in that house, including floor amendment of the measure; return of the measure to the first house; consid-

eration of amendments between the houses or a conference to resolve their differences; approval of the conference report by both houses; enrollment; approval by the president or override of the president's veto; and deposit with the Archivist of the United States. (2) Broadly, the political, lobbying, and other factors that affect or influence the process of enacting laws.

Legislative Veto—A procedure, declared unconstitutional in 1983, that allowed Congress or one of its houses to nullify certain actions of the president, executive branch agencies, or independent agencies. Sometimes called congressional vetoes or congressional disapprovals. Following the Supreme Court's 1983 decision, Congress amended several legislative veto statutes to require enactment of joint resolutions, which are subject to presidential veto, for nullifying executive branch actions.

Limitation on a General Appropriation Bill—Language that prohibits expenditures for part of an authorized purpose from funds provided in a general appropriation bill. Precedents require that the language be phrased in the negative: that none of the funds provided in a pending appropriation bill shall be used for a specified authorized activity. Limitations in general appropriation bills are permitted on the grounds that Congress can refuse to fund authorized programs and, therefore, can refuse to fund any part of them as long as the prohibition does not change existing law. House precedents have established that a limitation does not change existing law if it does not impose additional duties or burdens on executive branch officials, interfere with their discretionary authority, or require them to make judgments or determinations not required by existing law. The proliferation of limitation amendments in the 1970s and early 1980s prompted the House to adopt a rule in 1983 making it more difficult for members to offer them. The rule bans such amendments during the reading of an appropriation bill for amendments, unless they are specifically authorized in existing law. Other limitations may be offered after the reading, but the Committee of the Whole can foreclose them by adopting a motion to rise and report the bill back to the House. In 1995 the rule was amended to allow the motion to rise and report to be made only by the majority leader or his or her designee. The House Appropriations Committee, however, can include limitation provisions in the bills it reports.

Line Item—An amount in an appropriation measure. It can refer to a single appropriation account or to separate amounts within the account. In the congressional budget process, the term usually refers to assumptions about the funding of particular programs or accounts that underlie the broad functional amounts in a budget resolution. These assumptions are discussed in the reports accompanying each resolution and are not binding.

Line-Item Veto—*(See Item Veto.)*

Line Item Veto Act of 1996—A law, in effect only from January 1997 until June 1998, that granted the president authority intended to be functionally equivalent to an item veto, by amending the Impoundment Control Act of 1974 to incorporate an approach known as enhanced rescission. Key provisions established a new procedure that permitted the president to cancel amounts of new discretionary appropriations (budget authority), new items of direct spending (entitlements), or certain limited tax benefits. It also required the president to notify Congress of the cancellation in a special message within five calendar days after signing the measure. The cancellation would become permanent unless legislation disapproving it was enacted within thirty days. On June 25, 1998, in *Clinton v. City of New York* the Supreme Court held the Line Item Veto Act unconstitutional, on the grounds that its cancellation provisions violated the presentment clause in Article I, clause 7, of the Constitution.

Live Pair—A voluntary and informal agreement between two members on opposite sides of an issue, one of whom is absent for a recorded vote, under which the member who is present withholds or withdraws his or her vote to offset the failure to vote by the member who is absent. Usually the member in attendance announces that he or she has a live pair, states how each would have voted, and votes "present." In the House, under a rules change enacted in the 106th Congress, a live pair is only permitted on the rare occasions when electronic voting is not used.

Live Quorum—In the Senate, a quorum call to which senators are expected to respond. Senators usually suggest the absence of a quorum, not to force a quorum to appear, but to provide a pause in the proceedings during which senators can engage in private discussions or wait for a senator to come to the floor. A senator desiring a live quorum usually announces his or her intention, giving fair warning that there will be an objection to any unanimous consent request that the quorum call be dispensed with before it is completed.

Loan Guarantee—A statutory commitment by the federal government to pay part or all of a loan's principal and interest to a lender or the holder of a security in case the borrower defaults.

Lobby—To try to persuade members of Congress to propose, pass, modify, or defeat proposed legislation or to change or repeal existing laws. Lobbyists attempt to promote their preferences or those of a group, organization, or industry. Originally the term referred to persons frequenting the lobbies or corridors of legislative chambers in order to speak to lawmakers. In a general sense, lobbying includes not only direct contact with members but also indirect attempts to influence them, such as writing to them or persuading others to write or visit them, attempting to mold public opinion toward a desired legislative goal by various means, and contributing or arranging for contributions to members' election campaigns. The right to lobby stems from the First Amendment to the Constitution, which bans laws that abridge the right of the people to petition the government for a redress of grievances.

Lobbying Disclosure Act of 1995—The principal statute requiring disclosure of—and also, to a degree, circumscribing—the activities of lobbyists. In general, it requires lobbyists who spend more than 20 percent of their time on lobbying activities to register and make semiannual reports of their activities to the clerk of the House and the secretary of the Senate, although the law provides for a number of exemptions. Among the statute's prohibitions, lobbyists are not allowed to make contributions to the legal defense fund of a member or high government official or to reimburse for official travel. Civil penalties for failure to comply may include fines of up to $50,000. The act does not include grassroots lobbying in its definition of lobbying activities.

The act amends several other lobby laws, notably the Foreign Agents Registration Act (FARA), so that lobbyists can submit a single filing. Since the measure was enacted, the number of lobby registrations has risen from about 12,000 to more than 20,000. In 1998 expenditures on federal lobbying, as disclosed under the Lobbying Disclosure Act, totaled $1.42 billion. The 1995 act supersedes the 1946 Federal Regulation of Lobbying Act, which was repealed in Section 11 of the 1995 Act.

Logrolling—Jargon for a legislative tactic or bargaining strategy in which members try to build support for their legislation by promising to support legislation desired by other members or by accepting amendments they hope will induce their colleagues to vote for their bill.

Lower Body—A way to refer to the House of Representatives, which is considered pejorative by House members.

Mace—The symbol of the office of the House sergeant at arms. Under the direction of the Speaker, the sergeant at arms is responsible for preserving order on the House floor by holding up the mace in front of an unruly member, or by carrying the mace up and down the aisles to quell boisterous behavior. When the House is in session, the mace sits on a pedestal at the Speaker's right; when the House is in Committee of the Whole, it is moved to a lower pedestal. The mace is forty-six inches high and consists of thirteen ebony rods bound in silver and topped by a silver globe with a silver eagle, wings outstretched, perched on it.

Majority Leader—The majority party's chief floor spokesperson, elected by that party's caucus—sometimes called floor leader. In the Senate, the majority leader also develops the party's political and procedural strategy, usually in collaboration with other party officials and committee chairmen. The majority leader negotiates the Senate's agenda and committee ratios with the minority leader and usually calls up measures for floor action. The chamber traditionally concedes to the majority leader the right to determine the days on which it will meet and the hours at which it will convene and adjourn. In the House, the majority leader is the Speaker's deputy and heir apparent and helps plan the floor agenda and the party's legislative strategy and often speaks for the party leadership in debate.

Managers—(1) The official title of members appointed to a conference committee, commonly called conferees. The ranking majority and minority managers for each house also manage floor consideration of the committee's conference report. (2) The members who manage the initial floor consideration of a measure. (3) The official title of House members appointed to present impeachment articles to the Senate and to act as prosecutors on behalf of the House during the Senate trial of the impeached person.

Mandatory Appropriations—Amounts that Congress must appropriate annually because it has no discretion over them unless it first amends existing substantive law. Certain entitlement programs, for example, require annual appropriations.

Markup—A meeting or series of meetings by a committee or subcommittee during which members mark up a measure by offering, debating, and voting on amendments to it.

Means-Tested Programs—Programs that provide benefits or services to low-income individuals who meet a test of need. Most are entitlement programs, such as Medicaid, food stamps, and Supplementary Security Income. A few—for example, subsidized housing and various social services—are funded through discretionary appropriations.

Members' Allowances—Official expenses that are paid for or for which members are reimbursed by their houses. Among these are the costs of office space in congressional buildings and in their home states or districts; office equipment and supplies; postage-free mailings (the franking privilege); a set number of trips to and from home states or districts, as well as travel elsewhere on official business; telephone and other telecommunications services; and staff salaries.

Member's Staff—The personal staff to which a member is entitled. The House sets a maximum number of staff and a monetary allowance for each member. The Senate does not set a maximum staff level, but it does set a monetary allowance for each member. In each house, the staff allowance is included with office expenses allowances and official mail allowances in a consolidated allowance. Representatives and senators can spend as much money in their consolidated allowances for staff, office expenses, or official mail, as long as they do not exceed the monetary value of the three allowances combined. This provides members with flexibility in operating their offices.

Method of Equal Proportions—The mathematical formula used since 1950 to determine how the 435 seats in the House of Representatives should be distributed among the fifty states in the apportionment following each decennial census. It minimizes as much as possible the proportional difference between the average district population in any two states. Because the Constitution guarantees each state at least one representative, fifty seats are automatically apportioned. The formula calculates priority numbers for each state, assigns the first of the 385 remaining seats to the state with the highest priority number, the second to the state with the next highest number, and so on until all seats are distributed. *(See Apportionment.)*

Midterm Election—The general election for members of Congress that occurs in November of the second year in a presidential term.

Minority Leader—The minority party's leader and chief floor spokesman, elected by the party caucus; sometimes called minority floor leader. With the assistance of other party officials and the ranking minority members of committees, the minority leader devises the party's political and procedural strategy.

Minority Staff—Employees who assist the minority party members of a committee. Most committees hire separate majority and minority party staffs but they also may hire nonpartisan staff. Senate rules state that a committee's staff must reflect the relative number of its majority and minority party committee members, and the rules guarantee the minority at least one-third of the funds available for hiring partisan staff. In the House, each committee is authorized thirty professional staff, and the minority members of most committees may select up to ten of these staff (subject to full committee approval). Under House rules, the minority party is to be "treated fairly" in the apportionment of additional staff resources. Each House committee determines the portion of its additional staff it allocates to the minority; some committees allocate one-third; and others allot less.

Modified Rule—A special rule from the House Rules Committee that permits only certain amendments to be offered to a measure during its floor consideration or that bans certain specified amendments or amendments on certain subjects.

Morning Business—In the Senate, routine business that is to be transacted at the beginning of the morning hour. The business consists, first, of laying before the Senate, and referring to committees, matters such as messages from the president and the House, federal agency reports, and unreferred petitions, memorials, bills, and joint resolutions. Next, senators may present additional petitions and memorials. Then committees may present their reports, after which senators may introduce bills and resolutions. Finally, resolutions coming over from a previous day are taken up for consideration. In practice, the Senate adopts standing orders that permit senators to introduce measures and file reports at any time, but only if there has been a morning business period on that day. Because the Senate often remains in the same legislative day for several days, weeks, or months at a time, it orders a morning business period almost every calendar day for the convenience of senators who wish to introduce measures or make reports.

Morning Hour—A two-hour period at the beginning of a new legislative day during which the Senate is supposed to conduct routine business, call the calendar on Mondays, and deal with other matters described in a Senate rule. In practice, the morning hour very rarely, if ever, occurs, in part because the Senate frequently recesses, rather than adjourns, at the end of a daily session. Therefore the rule does not apply when the senate next meets. The Senate's rules reserve the first hour of the morning for morning business. After the completion of morning business, or at the end of the first hour, the rules permit a motion to proceed to the consideration of a measure on the calendar out of its regular order (except on Mondays). Because that normally debatable motion is not debatable if offered during the morning hour, the majority leader may, but rarely does, use this procedure in anticipating a filibuster on the motion to proceed. If the Senate agrees to the motion, it can consider the measure until the end of the morning hour, and if there is no unfinished business from the previous day it can continue considering it after the morning hour. But if there is unfinished business, a motion to continue consideration is necessary, and that motion is debatable.

Motion—A formal proposal for a procedural action, such as to consider, to amend, to lay on the table, to reconsider, to recess, or to adjourn. It has been estimated that at least eighty-five motions are possible under various circumstances in the House of Representatives, somewhat fewer in the Senate. Not all motions are created equal; some are privileged or preferential and enjoy priority over others. Some motions are debatable, amendable, or divisible, while others are not.

Multiple and Sequential Referrals—The practice of referring a measure to two or more committees for concurrent consideration (multiple referral) or successively to several committees in sequence (sequential referral). A measure may also be divided into several parts, with each referred to a different committee or to several committees sequentially (split referral). In theory this gives all committees that have jurisdiction over parts of a measure the opportunity to consider and report on them.

Before 1975, House precedents banned such referrals. A 1975 rule required the Speaker to make concurrent and sequential referrals "to the maximum extent feasible." On sequential referrals, the Speaker could set deadlines for reporting the measure. The Speaker ruled that this provision authorized him to discharge a committee from further consideration of a measure and place it on the appropriate calendar of the House if the committee fails to meet the Speaker's deadline. The Speaker also used combinations of concurrent and sequential referrals. In 1995 joint referrals were prohibited. Now each measure is referred to a primary committee and also may be referred, either concurrently or sequentially, to one or more other committees, but usually only for consideration of portions of the measure that fall within the jurisdiction of each of those other committees.

In the Senate, before 1977 concurrent and sequential referrals were permitted only by unanimous consent. In that year, a rule authorized a privileged motion for such a referral if offered jointly by the majority and minority leaders. Debate on the motion and all amendments to it is limited to two hours. The motion may set deadlines for reporting and provide for discharging the committees involved if they fail to meet the deadlines. To date, this procedure has never been invoked; multiple referrals in the Senate continue to be made by unanimous consent.

Multiyear Appropriation—An appropriation that remains available for spending or obligation for more than one fiscal year; the exact period of time is specified in the act making the appropriation.

Multiyear Authorization—(1) Legislation that authorizes the existence or continuation of an agency, program, or activity for more than one fiscal year. (2) Legislation that authorizes appropriations for an agency, program, or activity for more than one fiscal year.

Nomination—A proposed presidential appointment to a federal office submitted to the Senate for confirmation. Approval is by majority vote. The Constitution explicitly requires confirmation for ambassadors, consuls, "public Ministers" (department heads), and Supreme Court justices. By law, other federal judges, all military promotions of officers, and many high-level civilian officials must be confirmed.

Oath of Office—Upon taking office, members of Congress must swear or affirm that they will "support and defend the Constitution . . . against all enemies, foreign and domestic," that they will "bear true faith and allegiance" to the Constitution, that they take the obligation "freely, without any mental reservation or purpose of evasion," and that they will "well and faithfully discharge the duties" of their office. The oath is required by the Constitution, and the wording is prescribed by a statute. All House members must take the oath at the beginning of each new Congress. Usually, the member with the longest continuous service in the House swears in the Speaker, who then swears in the other members. The president of the Senate or a surrogate administers the oath to newly elected or reelected senators.

Obligation—A binding agreement by a government agency to pay for goods, products, services, studies, and the like, either immediately or in the future. When an agency enters into such an agreement, it incurs an obligation. As the agency makes the required payments, it liquidates the obligation. Appropriation laws usually make funds available for obligation for one or more fiscal years but do not require agencies to spend their funds during those specific years. The actual outlays can occur years after the appropriation is obligated, as with a contract for construction of a submarine that may provide for payment to be made when it is delivered in the future. Such obligated funds are often said to be "in the pipeline." Under these circumstances, an agency's outlays in a particular year can come from appropriations obligated in previous years as well as from its current-year appropriation. Consequently, the money Congress appropriates for a fiscal year does not equal the total amount of appropriated money the government will actually spend in that year.

Off-Budget Entities—Specific federal entities whose budget authority, outlays, and receipts are excluded by law from the calculation of budget totals, although they are part of government spending and income. As of early 2001, these included the Social Security trust funds (Federal Old-Age and Survivors Insurance Fund and the Federal Disability Insurance Trust Fund) and the Postal Service. Government-sponsored enterprises are also excluded from the budget because they are considered private rather than public organizations.

Office of Management and Budget (OMB)—A unit in the Executive Office of the President, reconstituted in 1970 from the former Bureau of the Budget. The Office of Management and Budget (OMB) assists the president in preparing the budget and in formulating the government's fiscal program. The OMB also plays a central role in supervising and controlling implementation of the budget, pursuant to provisions in appropriations laws, the Budget Enforcement Act, and other statutes. In addition to these budgetary functions, the OMB has various management duties, including those performed through its three statutory offices: Federal Financial Management, Federal Procurement Policy, and Information and Regulatory Affairs.

Officers of Congress—The Constitution refers to the Speaker of the House and the president of the Senate as officers and declares that each house "shall chuse" its "other Officers," but it does not name them or indicate how they should be selected. A House rule refers to its clerk, sergeant at arms, and chaplain as officers. Officers are not named in the Senate's rules, but *Riddick's Senate Procedure* lists the president pro tempore, secretary of the Senate, sergeant at arms, chaplain, and the secretaries for the majority and minority parties as officers. A few appointed officials are sometimes referred to as officers, including the parliamentarians and the legislative counsels. The House elects its officers by resolution at the beginning of each Congress. The Senate also elects its officers, but once elected Senate officers serve from Congress to Congress until their successors are chosen.

Omnibus Bill—A measure that combines the provisions of several disparate subjects into a single and often lengthy bill.

One-Minute Speeches—Addresses by House members that can be on any subject but are limited to one minute. They are usually permitted at the beginning of a daily session after the chaplain's prayer, the pledge of allegiance, and approval of the *Journal.* They are a customary practice, not a right granted by rule. Consequently, recognition for one-minute speeches requires unanimous consent and is entirely within the Speaker's discretion. The Speaker sometimes refuses to permit them when the House has a heavy legislative schedule or limits or postpones them until a later time of the day.

Open Rule—A special rule from the House Rules Committee that permits members to offer as many floor amendments as they wish as long as the amendments are germane and do not violate other House rules.

Order of Business (House)—The sequence of events prescribed by a House rule during the meeting of the House on a new legislative day that is supposed to take place, also called the general order of business. The sequence consists of (1) the chaplain's prayer; (2) reading and approval of the *Journal;* (3) the pledge of allegiance; (4) correction of the reference of public bills to committee; (5) disposal of business on the Speaker's table; (6) unfinished business; (7) the morning hour call of committees and consideration of their bills; (8) motions to go into Committee of the Whole; and (9) orders of the day. In practice, the House never fully complies with this rule. Instead, the items of business that follow the pledge of allegiance are supplanted by any special orders of business that are in order on that day (for example, conference reports; the corrections, discharge, or private calendars; or motions to suspend the rules) and by other privileged business (for example, general appropriation bills and special rules) or measures made in order by special rules or unanimous consent. The regular order of business is also modified by unanimous consent practices and orders that govern recognition for one-minute speeches (which date from 1937) and for morning-hour debates, begun in 1994. By this combination of an order of business with privileged interruptions, the House gives precedence to certain categories of important legislation, brings to the floor other major legislation from its calendars in any order it chooses, and provides expeditious processing for minor and noncontroversial measures.

Order of Business (Senate)—The sequence of events at the beginning of a new legislative day, as prescribed by Senate rules and standing orders. The sequence consists of (1) the chaplain's prayer; (2) the pledge of allegiance; (3) the designation of a temporary presiding officer if any; (4) *Journal* reading and approval; (5) recognition of the majority and minority leaders or their designees under the standing order; (6) morning business in the morning hour; (7) call of the calendar during the morning hour (largely obsolete); and (8) unfinished business from the previous session day.

Organization of Congress—The actions each house takes at the beginning of a Congress that are necessary to its operations. These include swearing in newly elected members, notifying the president that a quorum of each house is present, making committee assignments, and fixing the hour for daily meetings. Because the House of Representatives is not a continuing body, it must also elect its Speaker and other officers and adopt its rules.

Original Bill—(1) A measure drafted by a committee and introduced by its chairman or another designated member when the committee reports the measure to its house. Unlike a clean bill, it is not referred back to the committee after introduction. The Senate permits all its legislative committees to report original bills. In the House, this authority is referred to in the rules as the "right to report at any time," and five committees (Appropriations, Budget, House Administration, Rules, and Standards of Official Conduct) have such authority under circumstances specified in House Rule XIII, clause 5.

(2) In the House, special rules reported by the Rules Committee often propose that an amendment in the nature of a substitute be considered as an original bill for purposes of amendment, meaning that the substitute, as with a bill, may be amended in two degrees. Without that requirement, the substitute may only be amended in one further degree. In the Senate, an amendment in the nature of a substitute automatically is open to two degrees of amendment, as is the original text of the bill, if the substitute is offered when no other amendment is pending.

Original Jurisdiction—The authority of certain committees to originate a measure and report it to the chamber. For example, general appropriation bills reported by the House Appropriations Committee are original bills, and special rules reported by the House Rules Committee are original resolutions.

Other Body—A commonly used reference to a house by a member of the other house. Congressional comity discourages members from directly naming the other house during debate.

Outlays—Amounts of government spending. They consist of payments, usually by check or in cash, to liquidate obligations incurred in prior fiscal years as well as in the current year, including the net lending of funds under budget authority. In federal budget accounting, net outlays are calculated by subtracting the amounts of refunds and various kinds of reimbursements to the government from actual spending.

Override a Veto—Congressional enactment of a measure over the president's veto. A veto override requires a recorded two-thirds vote of those voting in each house, a quorum being present. Because the president must return the vetoed measure to its house of origin, that house votes first, but neither house is required to attempt an override, whether immediately or at all. If an override attempt fails in the house of origin, the veto stands and the measure dies.

Oversight—Congressional review of the way in which federal agencies implement laws to ensure that they are carrying out the intent of Congress and to inquire into the efficiency of the implementation and the effectiveness of the law. The Legislative Reorganization Act of 1946 defined oversight as the function of exercising continuous watchfulness over the execution of the laws by the executive branch.

Oxford-Style Debate—The House held three Oxford-style debates in 1994, modeled after the famous debating format favored by the Oxford Union in Great Britain. Neither chamber has held Oxford-style debates since then. The Oxford-style debates aired nationally over C-SPAN television and National Public Radio. The organized event featured eight participants divided evenly into two teams, one team representing the Democrats (then holding the majority in the chamber) and the other the Republicans. Both teams argued a single question chosen well ahead of the event. A moderator regulated the debate, and began it by stating the resolution at issue. The order of the speakers alternated by team, with a debater for the affirmative speaking first and a debater for the opposing team offering a rebuttal. The rest of the speakers alternated in kind until all gained the chance to speak.

Parliamentarian—The official advisor to the presiding officer in each house on questions of procedure. The parliamentarian and his or her assistants also answer procedural questions from members and congressional staff, refer measures to committees on behalf of the presiding officer, and maintain compilations of the precedents. The House parliamentarian revises the House Manual at the beginning of every Congress and usually reviews special rules before the Rules Committee reports them to the House. Either a parliamentarian or an assistant is always present and near the podium during sessions of each house.

Party Caucus—Generic term for each party's official organization in each house. Only House Democrats officially call their organization a caucus. House and Senate Republicans and Senate Democrats call their organizations conferences. The party caucuses elect their leaders, approve committee assignments and chairmanships (or ranking minority members, if the party is in the minority), establish party committees and study groups, and discuss party and legislative policies. On rare occasions, they have stripped members of committee seniority or expelled them from the caucus for party disloyalty.

Pay-as-You-Go (PAYGO)—A provision first instituted under the Budget Enforcement Act of 1990 that applies to legislation enacted before Oct. 1, 2002. It requires that the cumulative effect of legislation concerning either revenues or direct spending should not result in a net negative impact on the budget. If legislation does provide for an increase in spending or decrease in revenues, that effect is supposed to be offset by legislated spending reductions or revenue increases. If Congress fails to enact the appropriate offsets, the act requires presidential sequestration of sufficient offsetting amounts in specific direct spending accounts. Congress and the president can circumvent this requirement if both agree that an emergency requires a particular action or if a law is enacted declaring that deteriorated economic circumstances make it necessary to suspend the requirement.

Permanent Appropriation—An appropriation that remains continuously available, without current action or renewal by Congress, under the terms of a previously enacted authorization or appropriation law. One such appropriation provides for payment of interest on the public debt and another the salaries of members of Congress.

Permanent Authorization—An authorization without a time limit. It usually does not specify any limit on the funds that may be appropriated for the agency, program, or activity that it authorizes, leaving such amounts to the discretion of the appropriations committees and the two houses.

Permanent Staff—Term used formerly for committee staff authorized by law, who were funded through a permanent authorization and also called statutory staff. Most committees were authorized thirty permanent staff members. Most committees also were permitted additional staff, often called investigative staff, who were authorized by annual or biennial funding resolutions. The Senate eliminated the primary distinction between statutory and investigative staff in 1981. The House eliminated the distinction in 1995 by requiring that funding resolutions authorize money to hire both types of staff.

Personally Obnoxious (or Objectionable)—A characterization a senator sometimes applies to a president's nominee for a federal office in that senator's state to justify his or her opposition to the nomination.

Pocket Veto—The indirect veto of a bill as a result of the president withholding approval of it until after Congress has adjourned *sine die*. A bill the president does not sign but does not formally veto while Congress is in session automatically becomes a law ten days (excluding Sundays) after it is received. But if Congress adjourns its annual session during that ten-day period the measure dies even if the president does not formally veto it.

Point of Order—A parliamentary term used in committee and on the floor to object to an alleged violation of a rule and to demand that the chair enforce the rule. The point of order immediately halts the proceedings until the chair decides whether the contention is valid.

Pork or Pork Barrel Legislation—Pejorative terms for federal appropriations, bills, or policies that provide funds to benefit a legislator's district or state, with the implication that the legislator presses for enactment of such benefits to ingratiate himself or herself with constituents rather than on the basis of an impartial, objective assessment of need or merit. The terms are often applied to such benefits as new parks, post offices, dams, canals, bridges, roads, water projects, sewage treatment plants, and public works of any kind, as well as demonstration projects, research grants, and relocation of government facilities. Funds released by the president for various kinds of benefits or government contracts approved by him allegedly for political purposes are also sometimes referred to as pork.

Postcloture Filibuster—A filibuster conducted after the Senate invokes cloture. It employs an array of procedural tactics rather than lengthy speeches to delay final action. The Senate curtailed the postcloture filibuster's effectiveness by closing a variety of loopholes in the cloture rule in 1979 and 1986.

Power of the Purse—A reference to the constitutional power Congress has over legislation to raise revenue and appropriate monies from the Treasury. Article I, Section 8 states that Congress "shall have Power To lay and collect Taxes, Duties, Imposts and Excises, [and] to pay the Debts." Section 9 declares: "No Money shall be drawn from the Treasury, but in Consequence of Appropriations made by Law."

Preamble—Introductory language describing the reasons for and intent of a measure, sometimes called a whereas clause. It occasionally appears in joint, concurrent, and simple resolutions but rarely in bills.

Precedent—A previous ruling on a parliamentary matter or a long-standing practice or custom of a house. Precedents serve to control arbitrary rulings and serve as the common law of a house.

President of the Senate—One constitutional role of the vice president is serving as the presiding officer of the Senate, or president of the Senate. The Constitution permits the vice president to cast a vote in the Senate only to break a tie, but the vice president is not required to do so.

President Pro Tempore—Under the Constitution, an officer elected by the Senate to preside over it during the absence of the vice president of the United States. Often referred to as the "pro tem," this senator is usually a member of the majority party with the longest continuous service in the chamber and also, by virtue of seniority, a committee chairman. When attending to committee and other duties the president pro tempore appoints other senators to preside.

Presiding Officer—In a formal meeting, the individual authorized to maintain order and decorum, recognize members to speak or offer motions, and apply and interpret the chamber's rules, precedents, and practices. The Speaker of the House and the president of the Senate are the chief presiding officers in their respective houses.

Previous Question—A nondebatable motion which, when agreed to by majority vote, usually cuts off further debate, prevents the offering of additional amendments, and brings the pending matter to an immediate vote. It is a major debate-limiting device in the House; it is not permitted in Committee of the Whole in the House or in the Senate.

Private Bill—A bill that applies to one or more specified persons, corporations, institutions, or other entities, usually to grant relief when no other legal remedy is available to them. Many private bills deal with claims against the federal government, immigration and naturalization cases, and land titles.

Private Calendar—Commonly used title for a calendar in the House reserved for private bills and resolutions favorably reported by committees. The private calendar is officially called the Calendar of the Committee of the Whole House.

Private Law—A private bill enacted into law. Private laws are numbered in the same fashion as public laws.

Privilege—An attribute of a motion, measure, report, question, or proposition that gives it priority status for consideration. Privileged motions and motions to bring up privileged questions are not debatable.

Privilege of the Floor—In addition to the members of a house, certain individuals are admitted to its floor while it is in session. The rules of the two houses differ somewhat but both extend the privilege to the president and vice president, Supreme Court justices, cabinet members, state governors, former members of that house, members of the other house, certain officers and officials of Congress, certain staff of that house in the discharge of official duties, and the chamber's former parliamentarians. They also allow access to a limited number of committee and members' staff when their presence is necessary.

Pro Forma Amendment—In the House, an amendment that ostensibly proposes to change a measure or another amendment by moving "to strike the last word" or "to strike the requisite number of words." A member offers it not to make any actual change in the measure or amendment but only to obtain time for debate.

Pro Tem—A common reference to the president pro tempore of the Senate or, occasionally, to a Speaker pro tempore. *(See President Pro Tempore; Speaker Pro Tempore.)*

Procedures—The methods of conducting business in a deliberative body. The procedures of each house are governed first by applicable provisions of the Constitution, and then by its standing rules and orders, precedents, traditional practices, and any statutory rules that apply to it. The authority of the houses to adopt rules in addition to those specified in the Constitution is derived from Article I, Section 5, clause 2, of the Constitution, which states: "Each House may determine the Rules of its Proceedings. . . ." By rule, the House of Representatives also follows the procedures in *Jefferson's Manual* that are not inconsistent with its standing rules and orders. Many Senate procedures also conform with Jefferson's provisions, but by practice rather than by rule. At the beginning of each Congress, the House uses procedures in general parliamentary law until it adopts its standing rules.

Proxy Voting—The practice of permitting a member to cast the vote of an absent colleague in addition to his or her own vote. Proxy voting is prohibited on the floors of the House and Senate, but the Senate permits its committees to authorize proxy voting, and most do. In 1995, House rules were changed to prohibit proxy voting in committee.

Public Bill—A bill dealing with general legislative matters having national applicability or applying to the federal government or to a class of persons, groups, or organizations.

Public Debt—Federal government debt incurred by the Treasury or the Federal Financing Bank by the sale of securities to the public or borrowings from a federal fund or account.

Public Law—A public bill or joint resolution enacted into law. It is cited by the letters "PL" followed by a hyphenated number. The digits before the hyphen indicate the number of the Congress in which it was enacted; the digits after the hyphen indicate its position in the numerical sequence of public measures that became law during that Congress. For example, the Budget Enforcement Act of 1990 became PL 101-508 because it was the 508th measure in that sequence for the 101st Congress. *(See also Private Law.)*

Qualification (of Members)—The Constitution requires members of the House of Representatives to be twenty-five years of age at the time their terms begin. They must have been citizens of the United States for seven years before that date and, when elected, must be "Inhabitant[s]" of the state from which they were elected. There is no constitutional requirement that they reside in the districts they represent. Senators are required to be thirty years of age at the time their terms begin. They must have been citizens of the United States for nine years before that date and, when elected, must be "Inhabitant[s]" of the states in which they were elected. The "Inhabitant" qualification is broadly interpreted, and in modern times a candidate's declaration of state residence has generally been accepted as meeting the constitutional requirement.

Queen of the Hill Rule—A special rule from the House Rules Committee that permits votes on a series of amendments, especially complete substitutes for a measure, in a specified order, but directs that the amendment receiving the greatest number of votes shall be the winning one. This kind of rule permits the House to vote directly on a variety of alternatives to a measure. In doing so, it sets aside the precedent that once an amendment has been adopted, no further amendments may be offered to the text it has amended. Under an earlier practice, the Rules Committee reported "king of the hill" rules under which there also could be votes on a series of amendments, again in a specified order. If more than one of the amendments was adopted under this kind of rule, it was the last amendment to receive a majority vote that was considered as having been finally adopted, whether or not it had received the greatest number of votes.

Quorum—The minimum number of members required to be present for the transaction of business. Under the Constitution, a quorum in each house is a majority of its members: 218 in the House and 51 in the Senate when there are no vacancies. By House rule, a quorum in Committee of the Whole is 100. In practice, both houses usually assume a quorum is present even if it is not, unless a member makes a point of no quorum in the House or suggests the absence of a quorum in the Senate. Consequently, each house transacts much of its business, and even passes bills, when only a few members are present. For House and Senate committees, chamber rules allow a minimum quorum of one-third of a committee's members to conduct most types of business.

Quorum Call—A procedure for determining whether a quorum is present in a chamber. In the Senate, a clerk calls the roll (roster) of senators. The House usually employs its electronic voting system.

Ramseyer Rule—A House rule that requires a committee's report on a bill or joint resolution to show the changes the measure, and any committee amendments to it, would make in existing law. The rule requires the report to present the text of any statutory provision that would be repealed and a comparative print showing, through typographical devices such as stricken-through type or italics, other changes that would be made in existing law. The rule, adopted in 1929, is named after its sponsor, Rep. Christian W. Ramseyer, R-Iowa. The Senate's analogous rule is called the Cordon Rule.

Rank or Ranking—A member's position on the list of his or her party's members on a committee or subcommittee. When first assigned to a committee, a member is usually placed at the bottom of the list, then moves up as those above leave the committee. On subcommittees, however, a member's rank may not have anything to do with the length of his or her service on it.

Ranking Member—(1) Most often a reference to the minority member with the highest ranking on a committee or subcommittee. (2) A reference to the majority member next in rank to the chairman or to the highest ranking majority member present at a committee or subcommittee meeting.

Ratification—(1) The president's formal act of promulgating a treaty after the Senate has approved it. The resolution of ratification agreed to by the Senate is the procedural vehicle by which the Senate gives its consent to ratification. (2) A state legislature's act in approving a proposed constitutional amendment. Such an amendment becomes effective when ratified by three-fourths of the states.

Reapportionment—*(See Apportionment.)*

Recess—(1) A temporary interruption or suspension of a meeting of a chamber or committee. Unlike an adjournment, a recess does not end a legislative day. Because the Senate often recesses from one calendar day to another, its legislative day may extend over several calendar days, weeks, or even months. (2) A period of adjournment for more than three days to a day certain, especially over a holiday or in August during odd-numbered years.

Recess Appointment—A presidential appointment to a vacant federal position made after the Senate has adjourned *sine die* or has adjourned or recessed for more than thirty days. If the president submits the recess appointee's nomination during the next session of the Senate, that individual can continue to serve until the end of the session even though the Senate might have rejected the nomination. When appointed to a vacancy that existed thirty days before the end of the last Senate session, a recess appointee is not paid until confirmed.

Recommit—To send a measure back to the committee that reported it; sometimes called a straight motion to recommit to distinguish it from a motion to recommit with instructions. A successful motion to recommit kills the measure unless it is accompanied by instructions.

Recommit a Conference Report—To return a conference report to the conference committee for renegotiation of some or all of its agreements. A motion to recommit may be offered with or without instructions.

Recommit with Instructions—To send a measure back to a committee with instructions to take some action on it. Invariably in the House and often in the Senate, when the motion recommits to a standing committee, the instructions require the committee to report the measure "forthwith" with specified amendments.

Reconciliation—A procedure for changing existing revenue and spending laws to bring total federal revenues and spending within the limits established in a budget resolution. Congress has applied reconciliation chiefly to revenues and mandatory spending programs, es-

pecially entitlements. Discretionary spending is controlled through annual appropriation bills.

Recorded Vote—(1) Generally, any vote in which members are recorded by name for or against a measure; also called a record vote or roll-call vote. The only recorded vote in the Senate is a vote by the yeas and nays and is commonly called a roll-call vote. (2) Technically, a recorded vote is one demanded in the House of Representatives and supported by at least one-fifth of a quorum (forty-four members) in the House sitting as the House or at least twenty-five members in Committee of the Whole.

Recorded Vote by Clerks—A voting procedure in the House where members pass through the appropriate "aye" or "no" aisle in the chamber and cast their votes by depositing a signed green (yea) or red (no) card in a ballot box. These votes are tabulated by clerks and reported to the chair. The electronic voting system is much more convenient and has largely supplanted this procedure. *(See Committee of the Whole; Recorded Vote; Teller Vote.)*

Redistricting—The redrawing of congressional district boundaries within a state after a decennial census. Redistricting may be required to equalize district populations or to accommodate an increase or decrease in the number of a state's House seats that might have resulted from the decennial apportionment. The state governments determine the district lines. *(See Apportionment; Congressional District; Gerrymandering.)*

Referral—The assignment of a measure to committee for consideration. Under a House rule, the Speaker can refuse to refer a measure if the Speaker believes it is "of an obscene or insulting character."

Report—(1) As a verb, a committee is said to report when it submits a measure or other document to its parent chamber. (2) A clerk is said to report when he or she reads a measure's title, text, or the text of an amendment to the body at the direction of the chair. (3) As a noun, a committee document that accompanies a reported measure. It describes the measure, the committee's views on it, its costs, and the changes it proposes to make in existing law; it also includes certain impact statements. (4) A committee document submitted to its parent chamber that describes the results of an investigation or other study or provides information it is required to provide by rule or law.

Representative—An elected and duly sworn member of the House of Representatives who is entitled to vote in the chamber. The Constitution requires that a representative be at least twenty-five years old, a citizen of the United States for at least seven years, and an inhabitant of the state from which he or she is elected. Customarily, the member resides in the district he or she represents. Representatives are elected in even-numbered years to two-year terms that begin the following January.

Reprimand—A formal condemnation of a member for misbehavior, considered a milder reproof than censure. The House of Representatives first used it in 1976. The Senate first used it in 1991. *(See also Censure; Code of Official Conduct; Denounce; Ethics Rules; Expulsion; Seniority Loss.)*

Rescission—A provision of law that repeals previously enacted budget authority in whole or in part. Under the Impoundment Control Act of 1974, the president can impound such funds by sending a message to Congress requesting one or more rescissions and the reasons for doing so. If Congress does not pass a rescission bill for the programs requested by the president within forty-five days of continuous session after receiving the message, the president must make the funds available for obligation and expenditure. If the president does not, the comptroller general of the United States is authorized to bring suit to compel the release of those funds. A rescission bill may rescind all, part, or none of an amount proposed by the president, and may rescind funds the president has not impounded.

Reserving the Right to Object—Members' declaration that at some indefinite future time they may object to a unanimous consent request. It is an attempt to circumvent the requirement that members may prevent such an action only by objecting immediately after it is proposed.

Resident Commissioner from Puerto Rico—A nonvoting member of the House of Representatives, elected to a four-year term. The resident commissioner has the same status and privileges as delegates. Like the delegates, the resident commissioner may not vote in the House or Committee of the Whole.

Resolution—(1) A simple resolution; that is, a nonlegislative measure effective only in the house in which it is proposed and not requiring concurrence by the other chamber or approval by the president. Simple resolutions are designated H. Res. in the House and S. Res. in the Senate. Simple resolutions express nonbinding opinions on policies or issues or deal with the internal affairs or prerogatives of a house. (2) Any type of resolution: simple, concurrent, or joint. (*See Concurrent Resolution; Joint Resolution.*)

Resolution of Inquiry—A resolution usually simple rather than concurrent calling on the president or the head of an executive agency to provide specific information or papers to one or both houses.

Resolution of Ratification—The Senate vehicle for agreeing to a treaty. The constitutionally mandated vote of two-thirds of the senators present and voting applies to the adoption of this resolution. However, it may also contain amendments, reservations, declarations, or understandings that the Senate had previously added to it by majority vote.

Revenue Legislation—Measures that levy new taxes or tariffs or change existing ones. Under Article I, Section 7, clause 1 of the Constitution, the House of Representatives originates federal revenue measures, but the Senate can propose amendments to them. The House Ways and Means Committee and the Senate Finance Committee have jurisdiction over such measures, with a few minor exceptions.

Revise and Extend One's Remarks—A unanimous consent request to publish in the *Congressional Record* a statement a member did not deliver on the floor, a longer statement than the one made on the floor, or miscellaneous extraneous material.

Revolving Fund—A trust fund or account whose income remains available to finance its continuing operations without any fiscal year limitation.

Rider—Congressional slang for an amendment unrelated or extraneous to the subject matter of the measure to which it is attached. Riders often contain proposals that are less likely to become law on their own merits as separate bills, either because of opposition in the

committee of jurisdiction, resistance in the other house, or the probability of a presidential veto. Riders are more common in the Senate.

Roll Call—A call of the roll to determine whether a quorum is present, to establish a quorum, or to vote on a question. Usually, the House uses its electronic voting system for a roll call. The Senate does not have an electronic voting system; its roll is always called by a clerk.

Rule—(1) A permanent regulation that a house adopts to govern its conduct of business, its procedures, its internal organization, behavior of its members, regulation of its facilities, duties of an officer, or some other subject it chooses to govern in that form. (2) In the House, a privileged simple resolution reported by the Rules Committee that provides methods and conditions for floor consideration of a measure or, rarely, several measures.

Rule Twenty-Two—A common reference to the Senate's cloture rule. (*See Cloture*)

Second-Degree Amendment—An amendment to an amendment in the first degree. It is usually a perfecting amendment.

Secretary of the Senate—The chief financial, administrative, and legislative officer of the Senate. Elected by resolution or order of the Senate, the secretary is invariably the candidate of the majority party and usually chosen by the majority leader. In the absence of the vice president and pending the election of a president pro tempore, the secretary presides over the Senate. The secretary is subject to policy direction and oversight by the Senate Committee on Rules and Administration. The secretary manages a wide range of functions that support the administrative operations of the Senate as an organization as well as those functions necessary to its legislative process, including record keeping, document management, certifications, housekeeping services, administration of oaths, and lobbyist registrations. The secretary is responsible for accounting for all funds appropriated to the Senate and conducts audits of Senate financial activities. On a semiannual basis the secretary issues the Report of the Secretary of the Senate, a compilation of Senate expenditures.

Section—A subdivision of a bill or statute. By law, a section must be numbered and, as nearly as possible, contain "a single proposition of enactment."

Select or Special Committee—A committee established by a resolution in either house for a special purpose and, usually, for a limited time. Most select and special committees are assigned specific investigations or studies but are not authorized to report measures to their chambers. However, both houses have created several permanent select and special committees and have given legislative reporting authority to a few of them: the Ethics Committee in the Senate and the Intelligence Committees in both houses. There is no substantive difference between a select and a special committee; they are so called depending simply on whether the resolution creating the committee calls it one or the other.

Senate—The house of Congress in which each state is represented by two senators; each senator has one vote. Article V of the Constitution declares that "No State, without its Consent, shall be deprived of its equal Suffrage in the Senate." The Constitution also gives the Senate equal legislative power with the House of Representatives. Although the Senate is prohibited from originating revenue measures, and as a matter of practice it does not originate appropriation measures, it can amend both. Only the Senate can give or withhold consent to treaties and nominations from the president. It also acts as a court to try impeachments by the House and elects the vice president when no candidate receives a majority of the electoral votes. It is often referred to as "the upper body," but not by members of the House.

Senate Manual—The handbook of the Senate's standing rules and orders and the laws and other regulations that apply to the Senate, usually published once each Congress.

Senator—A duly sworn elected or appointed member of the Senate. The Constitution requires that a senator be at least thirty years old, a citizen of the United States for at least nine years, and an inhabitant of the state from which he or she is elected. Senators are usually elected in even-numbered years to six-year terms that begin the following January. When a vacancy occurs before the end of a term, the state governor can appoint a replacement to fill the position until a successor is chosen at the state's next general election or, if specified under state law, the next feasible date for such an election, to serve the remainder of the term. Until the Seventeenth Amendment was ratified in 1913, senators were chosen by their state legislatures.

Senatorial Courtesy—The Senate's practice of declining to confirm a presidential nominee for an office in the state of a senator of the president's party unless that senator approves.

Seniority—The priority, precedence, or status accorded members according to the length of their continuous service in a house or on a committee.

Seniority Loss—A type of punishment that reduces a member's seniority on his or her committees, including the loss of chairmanships. Party caucuses in both houses have occasionally imposed such punishment on their members, for example, for publicly supporting candidates of the other party.

Seniority Rule—The customary practice, rather than a rule, of assigning the chairmanship of a committee to the majority party member who has served on the committee for the longest continuous period of time.

Seniority System—A collection of long-standing customary practices under which members with longer continuous service than their colleagues in their house or on their committees receive various kinds of preferential treatment. Although some of the practices are no longer as rigidly observed as in the past, they still pervade the organization and procedures of Congress.

Sequestration—A procedure for canceling budgetary resources—that is, money available for obligation or spending—to enforce budget limitations established in law. Sequestered funds are no longer available for obligation or expenditure.

Sergeant at Arms—The officer in each house responsible for maintaining order, security, and decorum in its wing of the Capitol, including the chamber and its galleries. Although elected by their respective houses, both sergeants at arms are invariably the candidates of the majority party.

Session—(1) The annual series of meetings of a Congress. Under the Constitution, Congress must assemble at least once a year at noon on Jan. 3 unless it appoints a different day by law. (2) The special

meetings of Congress or of one house convened by the president, called a special session. (3) A house is said to be in session during the period of a day when it is meeting.

Severability (or Separability) Clause—Language stating that if any particular provisions of a measure are declared invalid by the courts the remaining provisions shall remain in effect.

Sine Die—Without fixing a day for a future meeting. An adjournment *sine die* signifies the end of an annual or special session of Congress.

Slip Law—The first official publication of a measure that has become law. It is published separately in unbound, single-sheet form or pamphlet form. A slip law usually is available two or three days after the date of the law's enactment.

Speaker—The presiding officer of the House of Representatives and the leader of its majority party. The Speaker is selected by the majority party and formally elected by the House at the beginning of each Congress. Although the Constitution does not require the Speaker to be a member of the House, in fact, all Speakers have been members.

Speaker Pro Tempore—A member of the House who is designated as the temporary presiding officer by the Speaker or elected by the House to that position during the Speaker's absence.

Speaker's Vote—The Speaker is not required to vote, and the Speaker's name is not called on a roll-call vote unless so requested. Usually, the Speaker votes either to create a tie vote, and thereby defeat a proposal, or to break a tie in favor of a proposal. Occasionally, the Speaker also votes to emphasize the importance of a matter.

Special Session—A session of Congress convened by the president, under his constitutional authority, after Congress has adjourned *sine die* at the end of a regular session. (*See Adjournment Sine Die; Session.*)

Spending Authority—The technical term for backdoor spending. The Congressional Budget Act of 1974 defines it as borrowing authority, contract authority, and entitlement authority for which appropriation acts do not provide budget authority in advance. Under the Budget Act, legislation that provides new spending authority may not be considered unless it provides that the authority shall be effective only to the extent or in such amounts as provided in an appropriation act.

Spending Cap—The statutory limit for a fiscal year on the amount of new budget authority and outlays allowed for discretionary spending. The Budget Enforcement Act of 1997 requires a sequester if the cap is exceeded.

Split Referral—A measure divided into two or more parts, with each part referred to a different committee.

Sponsor—The principal proponent and introducer of a measure or an amendment.

Staff Director—The most frequently used title for the head of staff of a committee or subcommittee. On some committees, that person is called chief of staff, clerk, chief clerk, chief counsel, general counsel, or executive director. The head of a committee's minority staff is usually called minority staff director.

Standing Committee—A permanent committee established by a House or Senate standing rule or standing order. The rule also describes the subject areas on which the committee may report bills and resolutions and conduct oversight. Most introduced measures must be referred to one or more standing committees according to their jurisdictions.

Standing Order—A continuing regulation or directive that has the force and effect of a rule, but is not incorporated into the standing rules. The Senate's numerous standing orders, like its standing rules, continue from Congress to Congress unless changed or the order states otherwise. The House uses relatively few standing orders, and those it adopts expire at the end of a session of Congress.

Standing Rules—The rules of the Senate that continue from one Congress to the next and the rules of the House of Representatives that it adopts at the beginning of each new Congress.

Standing Vote—An alternative and informal term for a division vote, during which members in favor of a proposal and then members opposed stand and are counted by the chair.

Star Print—A reprint of a bill, resolution, amendment, or committee report correcting technical or substantive errors in a previous printing; so called because of the small black star that appears on the front page or cover.

State of the Union Message—A presidential message to Congress under the constitutional directive that the president shall "from time to time give to the Congress Information of the State of the Union, and recommend to their Consideration such Measures as he shall judge necessary and expedient." Customarily, the president sends an annual State of the Union message to Congress, usually late in January.

Statutes at Large—A chronological arrangement of the laws enacted in each session of Congress. Though indexed, the laws are not arranged by subject matter nor is there an indication of how they affect or change previously enacted laws. The volumes are numbered by Congress, and the laws are cited by their volume and page number. The Gramm-Rudman-Hollings Act, for example, appears as 99 Stat. 1037.

Straw Vote Prohibition—Under a House precedent, a member who has the floor during debate may not conduct a straw vote or otherwise ask for a show of support for a proposition. Only the chair may put a question to a vote.

Strike from the *Record*—Expunge objectionable remarks from the *Congressional Record,* after a member's words have been taken down on a point of order.

Subcommittee—A panel of committee members assigned a portion of the committee's jurisdiction or other functions. On legislative committees, subcommittees hold hearings, mark up legislation, and report measures to their full committee for further action; they cannot report directly to the chamber. A subcommittee's party composition usually reflects the ratio on its parent committee.

Subpoena Power—The authority granted to committees by the rules of their respective houses to issue legal orders requiring individuals to appear and testify, or to produce documents pertinent to the

committee's functions, or both. Persons who do not comply with subpoenas can be cited for contempt of Congress and prosecuted.

Subsidy—Generally, a payment or benefit made by the federal government for which no current repayment is required. Subsidy payments may be designed to support the conduct of an economic enterprise or activity, such as ship operations, or to support certain market prices, as in the case of farm subsidies.

Sunset Legislation—A term sometimes applied to laws authorizing the existence of agencies or programs that expire annually or at the end of some other specified period of time. One of the purposes of setting specific expiration dates for agencies and programs is to encourage the committees with jurisdiction over them to determine whether they should be continued or terminated.

Sunshine Rules—Rules requiring open committee hearings and business meetings, including markup sessions, in both houses, and also open conference committee meetings. However, all may be closed under certain circumstances and using certain procedures required by the rules.

Supermajority—A term sometimes used for a vote on a matter that requires approval by more than a simple majority of those members present and voting; also referred to as extraordinary majority.

Supplemental Appropriation Bill—A measure providing appropriations for use in the current fiscal year, in addition to those already provided in annual general appropriation bills. Supplemental appropriations are often for unforeseen emergencies.

Suspension of the Rules (House)—An expeditious procedure for passing relatively noncontroversial or emergency measures by a two-thirds vote of those members voting, a quorum being present.

Suspension of the Rules (Senate)—A procedure to set aside one or more of the Senate's rules; it is used infrequently, and then most often to suspend the rule banning legislative amendments to appropriation bills.

Task Force—A title sometimes given to a panel of members assigned to a special project, study, or investigation. Ordinarily, these groups do not have authority to report measures to their respective houses.

Tax Expenditure—Loosely, a tax exemption or advantage, sometimes called an incentive or loophole; technically, a loss of governmental tax revenue attributable to some provision of federal tax laws that allows a special exclusion, exemption, or deduction from gross income or that provides a special credit, preferential tax rate, or deferral of tax liability.

Televised Proceedings—Television and radio coverage of the floor proceedings of the House of Representatives has been available since 1979 and of the Senate since 1986. They are broadcast over a coaxial cable system to all congressional offices and to some congressional agencies on channels reserved for that purpose. Coverage is also available free of charge to commercial and public television and radio broadcasters. The Cable-Satellite Public Affairs Network (C-SPAN) carries gavel-to-gavel coverage of both houses.

Teller Vote—A voting procedure, formerly used in the House, in which members cast their votes by passing through the center aisle to be counted, but not recorded by name, by a member from each party appointed by the chair. The House deleted the procedure from its rules in 1993, but during floor discussion of the deletion a leading member stated that a teller vote would still be available in the event of a breakdown of the electronic voting system.

Third-Degree Amendment—An amendment to a second-degree amendment. Both houses prohibit such amendments.

Third Reading—A required reading to a chamber of a bill or joint resolution by title only before the vote on passage. In modern practice, it has merely become a pro forma step.

Three-Day Rule—(1) In the House, a measure cannot be considered until the third calendar day on which the committee report has been available. (2) In the House, a conference report cannot be considered until the third calendar day on which its text has been available in the *Congressional Record*. (3) In the House, a general appropriation bill cannot be considered until the third calendar day on which printed hearings on the bill have been available. (4) In the Senate, when a committee votes to report a measure, a committee member is entitled to three calendar days within which to submit separate views for inclusion in the committee report. (In House committees, a member is entitled to two calendar days for this purpose, after the day on which the committee votes to report.) (5) In both houses, a majority of a committee's members may call a special meeting of the committee if its chairman fails to do so within three calendar days after three or more of the members, acting jointly, formally request such a meeting.

In calculating such periods, the House omits holiday and weekend days on which it does not meet. The Senate makes no such exclusion.

Tie Vote—When the votes for and against a proposition are equal, it loses. The president of the Senate may cast a vote only to break a tie. Because the Speaker is invariably a member of the House, the Speaker is entitled to vote but usually does not. The Speaker may choose to do so to break, or create, a tie vote.

Title—(1) A major subdivision of a bill or act, designated by a roman numeral and usually containing legislative provisions on the same general subject. Titles are sometimes divided into subtitles as well as sections. (2) The official name of a bill or act, also called a caption or long title. (3) Some bills also have short titles that appear in the sentence immediately following the enacting clause. (4) Popular titles are the unofficial names given to some bills or acts by common usage. For example, the Balanced Budget and Emergency Deficit Control Act of 1985 (short title) is almost invariably referred to as Gramm-Rudman (popular title). In other cases, significant legislation is popularly referred to by its title number (see definition (1) above). For example, the federal legislation that requires equality of funding for women's and men's sports in educational institutions that receive federal funds is popularly called Title IX.

Track System—An occasional Senate practice that expedites legislation by dividing a day's session into two or more specific time periods, commonly called tracks, each reserved for consideration of a different measure.

Transfer Payment—A federal government payment to which individuals or organizations are entitled under law and for which no goods or services are required in return. Payments include welfare and Social Security benefits, unemployment insurance, government pensions, and veterans benefits.

Treaty—A formal document containing an agreement between two or more sovereign nations. The Constitution authorizes the president to make treaties, but the president must submit them to the Senate for its approval by a two-thirds vote of the senators present. Under the Senate's rules, that vote actually occurs on a resolution of ratification. Although the Constitution does not give the House a direct role in approving treaties, that body has sometimes insisted that a revenue treaty is an invasion of its prerogatives. In any case, the House may significantly affect the application of a treaty by its equal role in enacting legislation to implement the treaty.

Trust Funds—Special accounts in the Treasury that receive earmarked taxes or other kinds of revenue collections, such as user fees, and from which payments are made for special purposes or to recipients who meet the requirements of the trust funds as established by law. Of the more than 150 federal government trust funds, several finance major entitlement programs, such as Social Security, Medicare, and retired federal employees' pensions. Others fund infrastructure construction and improvements, such as highways and airports.

Unanimous Consent—Without an objection by any member. A unanimous consent request asks permission, explicitly or implicitly, to set aside one or more rules. Both houses and their committees frequently use such requests to expedite their proceedings.

Uncontrollable Expenditures—A frequently used term for federal expenditures that are mandatory under existing law and therefore cannot be controlled by the president or Congress without a change in the existing law. Uncontrollable expenditures include spending required under entitlement programs and also fixed costs, such as interest on the public debt and outlays to pay for prior-year obligations. In recent years, uncontrollables have accounted for approximately three-quarters of federal spending in each fiscal year.

Unfunded Mandate—Generally, any provision in federal law or regulation that imposes a duty or obligation on a state or local government or private sector entity without providing the necessary funds to comply. The Unfunded Mandates Reform Act of 1995 amended the Congressional Budget Act of 1974 to provide a mechanism for the control of new unfunded mandates.

Union Calendar—A calendar of the House of Representatives for bills and resolutions favorably reported by committees that raise revenue or directly or indirectly appropriate money or property. In addition to appropriation bills, measures that authorize expenditures are also placed on this calendar. The calendar's full title is the Calendar of the Committee of the Whole House on the State of the Union.

Upper Body—A common reference to the Senate, but not used by members of the House.

U.S. Code—Popular title for the *United States Code: Containing the General and Permanent Laws of the United States in Force on. . . .* It is a consolidation and partial codification of the general and permanent laws of the United States arranged by subject under 50 titles. The first six titles deal with general or political subjects, the other forty-four with subjects ranging from agriculture to war, alphabetically arranged. A supplement is published after each session of Congress, and the entire Code is revised every six years.

User Fee—A fee charged to users of goods or services provided by the federal government. When Congress levies or authorizes such fees, it determines whether the revenues should go into the general collections of the Treasury or be available for expenditure by the agency that provides the goods or services.

Veto—The president's disapproval of a legislative measure passed by Congress. The president returns the measure to the house in which it originated without his signature but with a veto message stating his objections to it. When Congress is in session, the president must veto a bill within ten days, excluding Sundays, after the president has received it; otherwise it becomes law without his signature. The ten-day clock begins to run at midnight following his receipt of the bill. *(See also Committee Veto; Item Veto; Line Item Veto Act of 1996; Override a Veto; Pocket Veto.)*

Voice Vote—A method of voting in which members who favor a question answer aye in chorus, after which those opposed answer no in chorus, and the chair decides which position prevails.

Voting—Members vote in three ways on the floor: (1) by shouting "aye" or "no" on voice votes; (2) by standing for or against on division votes; and (3) on recorded votes (including the yeas and nays), by answering "aye" or "no" when their names are called or, in the House, by recording their votes through the electronic voting system.

War Powers Resolution of 1973—An act that requires the president "in every possible instance" to consult Congress before committing U.S. forces to ongoing or imminent hostilities. If the president commits them to a combat situation without congressional consultation, the president must notify Congress within forty-eight hours. Unless Congress declares war or otherwise authorizes the operation to continue, the forces must be withdrawn within sixty or ninety days, depending on certain conditions. No president has ever acknowledged the constitutionality of the resolution.

Well—The sunken, level, open space between members' seats and the podium at the front of each chamber. House members usually address their chamber from their party's lectern in the well on its side of the aisle. Senators usually speak at their assigned desks.

Whip—The majority or minority party member in each house who acts as assistant leader, helps plan and marshal support for party strategies, encourages party discipline, and advises his or her leader on how colleagues intend to vote on the floor. In the Senate, the Republican whip's official title is assistant leader.

Yeas and Nays—A vote in which members usually respond "aye" or "no" (despite the official title of the vote) on a question when their names are called in alphabetical order. The Constitution requires the yeas and nays when a demand for it is supported by one-fifth of the members present, and it also requires an automatic yea-and-nay vote on overriding a veto. Senate precedents require the support of at least one-fifth of a quorum, a minimum of eleven members with the present membership of 100.

The Legislative Process in Brief

Note: *Parliamentary terms used below are defined in the glossary.*

INTRODUCTION OF BILLS

A House member (including the resident commissioner of Puerto Rico and nonvoting delegates of the District of Columbia, Guam, the Virgin Islands, and American Samoa) may introduce any one of several types of bills and resolutions by handing it to the clerk of the House or placing it in a box called the hopper. A senator first gains recognition of the presiding officer to announce the introduction of a bill.

As the usual next step in either the House or Senate, the bill is numbered, referred to the appropriate committee, labeled with the sponsor's name, and sent to the Government Printing Office so that copies can be made for subsequent study and action. House and Senate bills may be jointly sponsored and carry several senators' names. A bill written in the executive branch and proposed as an administration measure usually is introduced by the chairman of the congressional committee that has jurisdiction, as a courtesy to the White House.

Bills—Prefixed with HR in the House, S in the Senate, followed by a number. Used as the form for most legislation, whether general or special, public or private.

Joint Resolutions—Designated H J Res or S J Res. Subject to the same procedure as bills, with the exception of a joint resolution proposing an amendment to the Constitution. The latter must be approved by two-thirds of both houses and is then sent directly to the administrator of general services for submission to the states for ratification instead of being presented to the president for his approval.

Concurrent Resolutions—Designated H Con Res or S Con Res. Used for matters affecting the operations of both houses. These resolutions do not become law.

Resolutions—Designated H Res or S Res. Used for a matter concerning the operation of either house alone and adopted only by the chamber in which it originates.

COMMITTEE ACTION

With few exceptions, bills are referred to the appropriate standing committees. The job of referral formally is the responsibility of the Speaker of the House and the presiding officer of the Senate, but this task usually is carried out on their behalf by the parliamentarians of the House and Senate. Precedent, statute, and the jurisdictional mandates of the committees as set forth in the rules of the House and Senate determine which committees receive what kinds of bills. Bills are technically considered "read for the first time" when referred to House committees.

When a bill reaches a committee it is placed on the committee's calendar. Failure of a committee to act on a bill is equivalent to killing it and most fall by the legislative roadside. The measure can be withdrawn from the committee's purview only by a discharge petition signed by a majority of the House membership on House bills, or by adoption of a special resolution in the Senate. Discharge attempts rarely succeed and the Senate procedure has not been used for decades.

The first committee action taken on a bill usually is a request for comment on it by interested agencies of the government. The committee chairman may assign the bill to a subcommittee for study and hearings, or it may be considered by the full committee. Hearings may be public, closed (executive session), or both. A subcommittee, after considering a bill, reports to the full committee its recommendations for action and any proposed amendments.

The full committee then votes on its recommendation to the House or Senate. This procedure is called "ordering a bill reported." Occasionally a committee may order a bill reported unfavorably; most of the time a report, submitted by the chairman of the committee to the House or Senate, calls for favorable action on the measure since the committee can effectively "kill" a bill by simply failing to take any action.

After the bill is reported, the committee chairman instructs the staff to prepare a written report. The report describes the purposes and scope of the bill, explains the committee revisions, notes proposed changes in existing law, and, usually, includes the views of the executive branch agencies consulted. Often committee members opposing a measure issue dissenting minority statements that are included in the report.

Usually, the committee "marks up" or proposes amendments to the bill. If the amendments are substantial and the measure is complicated, the committee may order a "clean bill" introduced, which will embody the proposed amendments. The original bill then is put aside and the clean bill, with a new number, is reported to the floor.

The chamber must approve, alter, or reject the committee amendments before the bill itself can be put to a vote.

FLOOR ACTION

After a bill is reported back to the house where it originated, it is placed on the calendar.

There are five legislative calendars in the House, issued in one cumulative calendar titled *Calendars of the United States House of Representatives and History of Legislation.* The House calendars are:

The Union Calendar to which are referred bills raising revenues, general appropriations bills, and any measures directly or indirectly appropriating money or property. It is the Calendar of the Committee of the Whole House on the State of the Union.

The House Calendar to which are referred bills of public character not raising revenue or appropriating money.

The Corrections Calendar to which are referred bills to repeal rules and regulations deemed excessive or unnecessary when the Corrections Calendar is called the second and fourth Tuesday of each month. (Instituted in the 104th Congress to replace the seldom-used Consent Calendar.) A three-fifths majority is required for passage.

The Private Calendar to which are referred bills for relief in the nature of claims against the United States or private immigration bills that are passed without debate when the Private Calendar is called the first and third Tuesdays of each month.

The Discharge Calendar to which are referred motions to discharge committees when the necessary signatures are signed to a discharge petition.

There is only one legislative calendar in the Senate and one "executive calendar" for treaties and nominations submitted to the Senate.

Debate

A bill is brought to debate by varying procedures. In the Senate the majority leader, in consultation with the minority leader and others, schedules the bills that will be taken up for debate. If it is urgent or important it can be taken up in the Senate either by unanimous consent or by a majority vote.

In the House, precedence is granted if a special rule is obtained from the Rules Committee. A request for a special rule usually is made by the chairman of the committee that favorably reported the bill. The request is considered by the Rules Committee in the same fashion that other committees consider legislative measures. The committee proposes a resolution providing for immediate consideration of the bill. The Rules Committee reports the resolution to the House where it is debated and voted on in the same fashion as regular bills.

The resolutions providing special rules are important because they specify how long the bill may be debated and whether it may be amended from the floor. If floor amendments are banned, the bill is considered under a "closed rule."

When a bill is debated under an "open rule," amendments may be offered from the floor. Committee amendments always are taken up first but may be changed, as may all amendments up to the second degree; that is, an amendment to an amendment to an amendment is not in order.

Duration of debate in the House depends on whether the bill is under discussion by the House proper or before the House when it is sitting as the Committee of the Whole House on the State of the Union. In the former, the amount of time for debate allocated with an hour for each member if the measure is under consideration without a rule. In the Committee of the Whole the amount of time agreed on for general debate is equally divided between proponents and opponents. At the end of general discussion, the bill is often read section by section for amendment. Debate on an amendment is limited to five minutes for each side; this is called the "five-minute rule." In practice, amendments regularly are debated more than ten minutes, with members gaining the floor by offering pro forma amendments or obtaining unanimous consent to speak longer than five minutes.

Senate debate usually is unlimited. It can be halted only by unanimous consent or by "cloture," which requires a three-fifths majority of the entire Senate except for proposed changes in the Senate rules. The latter requires a two-thirds vote.

The House considers almost all important bills within a parliamentary framework known as the Committee of the Whole. It is not a committee as the word usually is understood; it is the full House meeting under another name for the purpose of speeding action on legislation. Technically, the House sits as the Committee of the Whole when it considers any tax measure or bill dealing with public appropriations. Upon adoption of a special rule, the Speaker declares the House resolved into the Committee of the Whole and appoints a member of the majority party to serve as the chairman. The rules of the House permit the Committee of the Whole to meet when a quorum of 100 members is present on the floor and to amend and act on bills. When the Committee of the Whole has acted, it "rises," the Speaker returns as the presiding officer of the House and the member appointed chairman of the Committee of the Whole reports the action of the committee and its recommendations. The Committee of the Whole cannot pass a bill; instead it reports the measure to the full House with whatever changes it has approved. The full House then may pass or reject the bill—or, on occasion, recommit the bill to committee. Amendments adopted in the Committee of the Whole may be put to a second vote in the full House.

Votes

Voting on bills may occur repeatedly before they are finally approved or rejected. The House votes on the rule for the bill and on various amendments to the bill. Voting on amendments often is a more illuminating test of a bill's support than is the final tally. Sometimes members approve final passage of bills after vigorously supporting amendments that, if adopted, would have scuttled the legislation.

The Senate has three different methods of voting: an untabulated voice vote, a standing vote (called a division), and a recorded roll call to which members answer "yea" or "nay" when their names are called. The House also employs voice and standing votes, but since January 1973 yeas and nays have been recorded by an electronic voting device, eliminating the need for time-consuming roll calls.

After amendments to a bill have been voted upon, a vote may be taken on a motion to recommit the bill to committee. If carried, this vote is usually a death blow to the bill. If the motion is unsuccessful, the bill then is "read for the third time." After the third reading a vote on passage is taken. The final vote may be followed by a motion to reconsider, and this motion may be followed by a move to lay the motion on the table. Usually, those voting for the bill's passage vote for the tabling motion, thus safeguarding the final passage action. With that, the bill has been formally passed by the chamber.

ACTION IN SECOND CHAMBER

After a bill is passed it is sent to the other chamber. This body may then take one of several steps. It may pass the bill as is—accepting the other chamber's language. It may send the bill to committee for scrutiny or alteration, or reject the entire bill, advising the other house of its actions. Or it simply may ignore the bill submitted while it continues work on its own version of the proposed legislation. Frequently, one chamber may approve a version of a bill that is greatly at variance with the version already passed by the other house, and then substitute its contents for the language of the other, retaining only the latter's bill number.

Often the second chamber makes only minor changes. If these are readily agreed to by the other house, the bill then is routed to the president. However, if the opposite chamber significantly alters the bill submitted to it, the measure usually is "sent to conference." The chamber that has possession of the "papers" (engrossed bill, engrossed amendments, messages of transmittal) requests a conference and the other chamber may agree to it. If the second chamber does not agree, the bill dies.

CONFERENCE ACTION

A conference works out conflicting House and Senate versions of a legislative bill. The conferees usually are senior members from the committees that managed the legislation who are appointed by the presiding officers of the two houses. Under this arrangement the conferees of one house have the duty of trying to maintain their chamber's position in the face of amending actions by the conferees (also referred to as "managers") of the other house.

The number of conferees from each chamber may vary, the range usually being from seven to nine members in each group, depending on the length or complexity of the bill involved. But a majority vote controls the action of each group so that a large representation does not give one chamber a voting advantage over the other chamber's conferees.

Theoretically, conferees are not allowed to write new legislation in reconciling the two versions before them, but this curb sometimes is bypassed. Many bills have been put into acceptable compromise form only after new language was provided by the conferees. Frequently the ironing out of difficulties takes days or even weeks.

How a Bill Becomes Law

This graphic shows the most typical way in which proposed legislation is enacted into law. There are more complicated, as well as simpler, routes, and most bills never become law. The process is illustrated with two hypothetical bills, House bill No. 1 (HR 1) and Senate bill No. 2 (S 2). Bills must be passed by both houses in identical form before they can be sent to the president. The path of HR 1 is traced by a black line, that of S 2 by a gray line. In practice, most bills begin as similar proposals in both houses.

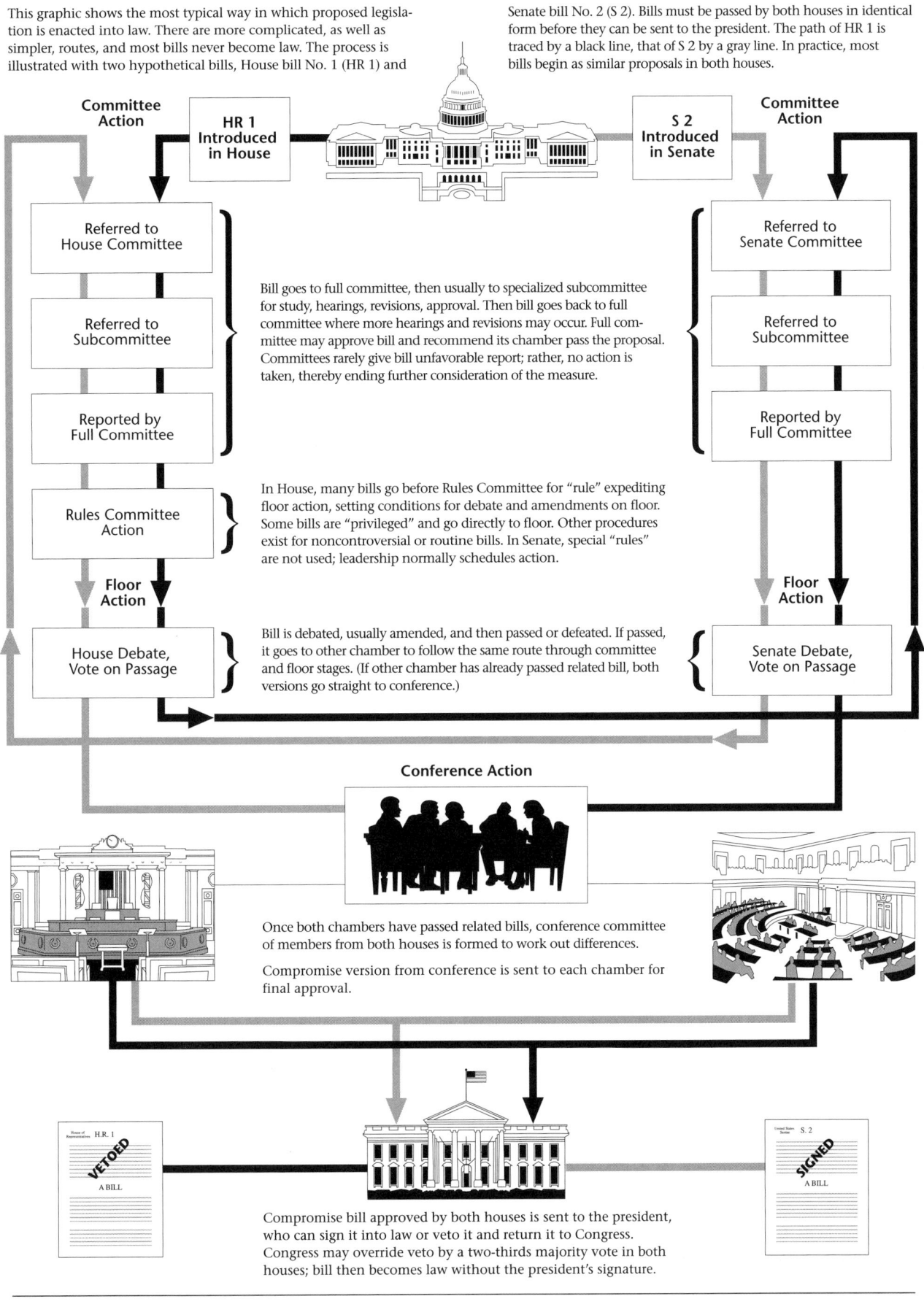

Committee Action

HR 1 Introduced in House

S 2 Introduced in Senate

Committee Action

Referred to House Committee

Referred to Subcommittee

Reported by Full Committee

Referred to Senate Committee

Referred to Subcommittee

Reported by Full Committee

Bill goes to full committee, then usually to specialized subcommittee for study, hearings, revisions, approval. Then bill goes back to full committee where more hearings and revisions may occur. Full committee may approve bill and recommend its chamber pass the proposal. Committees rarely give bill unfavorable report; rather, no action is taken, thereby ending further consideration of the measure.

Rules Committee Action

In House, many bills go before Rules Committee for "rule" expediting floor action, setting conditions for debate and amendments on floor. Some bills are "privileged" and go directly to floor. Other procedures exist for noncontroversial or routine bills. In Senate, special "rules" are not used; leadership normally schedules action.

Floor Action

Floor Action

House Debate, Vote on Passage

Senate Debate, Vote on Passage

Bill is debated, usually amended, and then passed or defeated. If passed, it goes to other chamber to follow the same route through committee and floor stages. (If other chamber has already passed related bill, both versions go straight to conference.)

Conference Action

Once both chambers have passed related bills, conference committee of members from both houses is formed to work out differences.

Compromise version from conference is sent to each chamber for final approval.

Compromise bill approved by both houses is sent to the president, who can sign it into law or veto it and return it to Congress. Congress may override veto by a two-thirds majority vote in both houses; bill then becomes law without the president's signature.

Examples of Legislative Documents

Conferences on involved, complex, and controversial bills sometimes are particularly drawn out.

As a conference proceeds, conferees reconcile differences between the versions, but generally they grant concessions only insofar as they remain sure that the chamber they represent will accept the compromises. Occasionally, uncertainty over how either house will react, or the positive refusal of a chamber to back down on a disputed amendment, results in an impasse, and the bills die in conference even though each was approved by its sponsoring chamber.

When the conferees have reached agreement, they prepare a conference report embodying their recommendations (compromises) and a joint explanatory statement. The report, in document form, must be submitted to each house. The conference report must be approved by each house. Consequently, approval of the report is approval of the compromise bill. In the order of voting on conference reports, the chamber that asked for a conference yields to the other chamber the opportunity to vote first.

FINAL ACTION

After a bill has been passed by both the House and Senate in identical form, all of the original papers are sent to the enrolling clerk of the chamber in which the bill originated. He then prepares an enrolled bill, which is printed on parchment paper.

When this bill has been certified as correct by the secretary of the Senate or the clerk of the House, depending on which chamber originated the bill, it is signed first (no matter whether it originated in the Senate or House) by the Speaker of the House and then by the president of the Senate. It is next sent to the White House to await action.

If the president approves the bill, he signs it, dates it, and usually writes the word "approved" on the document. If he does not sign it within ten days (Sundays excepted) and Congress is in session, the bill becomes law without his signature.

If Congress adjourns *sine die* at the end of the second session the president can pocket veto a bill and it dies without Congress having the opportunity to override.

A president vetoes a bill by refusing to sign it and, before the ten-day period expires, returning it to Congress with a message stating his reasons. The message is sent to the chamber that originated the bill. If no action is taken on the message, the bill dies. Congress, however, can attempt to override the president's veto and enact the bill, "the objections of the president to the contrary notwithstanding." Overriding a veto requires a two-thirds vote of those present in each chamber, who must number a quorum and vote by roll call.

If the president's veto is overridden by a two-thirds vote in both houses, the bill becomes law. Otherwise it is dead.

When bills are passed finally and signed, or passed over a veto, they are given law numbers in numerical order as they become law. There are two series of numbers, one for public and one for private laws, starting at the number "1" for each two-year term of Congress. They are then identified by law number and by Congress—for example, Private Law 10, 105th Congress; Public Law 33, 106th Congress (or PL 106-33).

Key Votes

1997 Key Votes	865
1998 Key Votes	883
1999 Key Votes	899
2000 Key Votes	915

Congressional Quarterly each year selects a series of key votes on major issues. An issue is judged by the extent it represents one or more of the following:

- A matter of major controversy.
- A test of presidential or political power.
- A decision of potentially great impact on the nation and lives of Americans.

For each series of related votes on an issue only one key vote is usually chosen. This vote is the roll call in the House or Senate that in the opinion of Congressional Quarterly was the most important in determining the outcome.

Senate

1. BALANCED-BUDGET AMENDMENT

Senate Democrats in 1995 again blocked an important proposal on the Republican agenda: a constitutional amendment to require a balanced federal budget (S J Res 1). During the 1995 debate, then-Majority Leader Bob Dole, R-Kan., delayed the vote as he tried to win over a wavering Democrat. In the end he did not and had to accept defeat on a 65–35 vote; 67 votes were required to approve a constitutional amendment.

Republicans entered the 1997 debate with high hopes. If every veteran of the 1995 vote remained consistent, and if every freshman elected in 1996 kept a campaign promise to support the amendment it would be approved with 68 votes. Fewer votes were considered uncertain than in 1995 when a half-dozen Democrats who had previously backed the amendment switched their votes. The positions of Senate veterans were well established after three years of debating and voting on the issue. Consequently, the outcome depended on the votes of four freshman Democrats: Robert G. Torricelli of New Jersey and Tim Johnson of South Dakota, both of whom had voted for the amendment as members of the House; and Max Cleland of Georgia and Mary L. Landrieu of Louisiana, who had supported it in their campaigns.

Majority Leader Trent Lott, R-Miss., and his floor lieutenants had limited influence on the four Democrats, none of whom were prepared to commit early. From the beginning, the four freshmen held private meetings to share thoughts about such a critical issue arising at the outset of Senate careers. Minority Leader Tom Daschle, D-S.D., held a series of one-on-one meetings with the newcomers, counseled them to avoid making any hasty decisions, and gently cajoled them to change their minds. Robert C. Byrd, D-W.Va., and Daniel Patrick Moynihan, D-N.Y.—veteran opponents of the amendment—also sought out the freshmen to make their case. By all accounts, Daschle was masterly in arguing his case with a light but determined hand. "He wasn't pushy at all," said Torricelli. "He asked me only to consider the consequences of being the deciding vote to amend the Constitution."

Cleland was first to commit when on Feb. 14 he said he would vote for the amendment. But Johnson announced on Feb. 20 he would switch and vote against it. That left the fate of the amendment with Torricelli and Landrieu. If either switched, the amendment would die. Advertising campaigns, both pro and con, went on the air in selected states but, as before, they appeared to have no impact on the outcome.

After weeks of wavering, Landrieu announced Feb. 25 that she would vote for the amendment. She acknowledged that had it not been for her campaign promise, she would have opposed it. That left it to Torricelli to be the deciding vote. On Feb. 26 he declared: "All doubts concerning amendments to the Constitution must be settled in leaving the genius of the Founding Fathers undisturbed."

The vote had been drained of suspense by the time it was taken on March 4. The only ripple of excitement came as the count, with time running down, stalled briefly at 66–33, a potentially winning two-thirds tally. But then Bob Kerrey, D-Neb., came into the chamber, voted "no," and the amendment died, 66–34: R 55–0; D 11–34 (ND 6–31, SD 5–3). (Vote, p. 876)

2. YUCCA MOUNTAIN

In a victory for the nuclear power industry, the Senate April 15 passed a bill (S 104) to create a temporary nuclear waste storage site in the Nevada desert. The bill received two more votes than had similar legislation passed by the Senate in 1996 but remained two votes short of the two-thirds needed to override a veto, which was promised by President Clinton. The vote was 65–34: R 53–2; D 12–32 (ND 8–28, SD 4–4). (Vote, p. 876)

President Clinton vowed a veto until a study was completed on the viability of Yucca Mountain to be the home of a permanent repository. The study was slated to be finished in 1998.

The bill would have required the temporary waste site to open in 2003. Frank H. Murkowski, R-Alaska, chairman of the Senate Energy and Natural Resources Committee, tried to attract support by adding a provision giving the president until March 1, 1999, to halt construction of the temporary storage site if he found that permanent storage was not viable at Yucca Mountain. The president and Congress would then have two years to approve an alternate site; if they failed, construction would begin automatically in Nevada.

Nuclear utilities argued the bill was needed to allow removal of the growing inventory of nuclear waste stored in thirty-five states. A 1982 law required the federal government to dispose of civilian nuclear waste starting Jan. 31, 1998.

Despite the deadline, the bill was opposed by thirty-two Democrats and two Republicans—Ben Nighthorse Campbell of Colorado and Daniel R. Coats of Indiana. Opponents were led by Nevada's two Democratic senators, Harry Reid and Richard H. Bryan.

Supporters would have had a veto-proof margin if not for "no" votes cast by first-year Democrats Richard J. Durbin of Illinois and Mary L. Landrieu of Louisiana. Their Democratic predecessors, Paul Simon of Illinois and J. Bennett Johnston of Louisiana, backed the temporary storage site in 1996. Durbin cited concerns about nuclear waste transportation and environmental protection; Landrieu expressed sympathy for nuclear utilities but cited concern about unfinished plans for permanent storage. Backers of the bill also picked up two votes they did not have in 1996. Environment and Public Works Committee Chairman John H. Chafee, R-R.I., switched his vote to "yes," citing improved environmental provisions in the 1997 bill. Ron Wyden, D-Ore., also switched from a "no" vote on the 1996 bill to a "yes" on S 104.

3. CHEMICAL WEAPONS TREATY

The most vigorous attack on President Clinton's national security policy during the year was defeated in April when the Senate approved a treaty banning chemical weapons after rejecting several amendments to weaken the pact. However, Clinton won only after making significant concessions to leading Republicans on other foreign policy matters.

At issue was the Chemical Weapons Convention, signed shortly before President George Bush left office in January 1993. The treaty banned the development, production, storage, use, sale, or purchase of chemical weapons. Negotiated by the Bush and Reagan administrations with the cooperation of major chemical manufacturing firms, the treaty was supported not only by most Democrats but also by many prominent members of the GOP foreign policy establishment. Nevertheless, conservatives had held up ratification in 1996, saying the treaty would be ineffective in halting the spread of chemical weapons and would lull the country into a false sense of security. Critics also said the treaty's far-reaching system of international inspections was a threat to U.S. sovereignty and to U.S. companies' competitive secrets.

In January 1997 Clinton and his top aides began vigorous lobbying for Senate approval by April 29, the date on which it was to take effect. Treaty supporters contended that public abhorrence of chemical weapons would provide the leverage needed to secure the necessary two-thirds majority if a Senate vote could be held. Ultimately, Clinton got that vote but he had to trade for it with Majority Leader Trent Lott, R-Miss., and Foreign Relations Committee Chairman Jesse Helms, R-N.C., who opposed the treaty and had the power to keep it bottled up in his committee.

Helms was mollified partly by the administration's acceptance of a raft of proposed amendments to the resolution of approval (S Res 75). One of these required the treaty's international inspection teams to obtain a criminal search warrant from a U.S. judge if they wanted to inspect an American company's facility without its consent. Helms also was persuaded by the administration's agreement to his long-standing goal of streamlining the foreign policy bureaucracy by consolidating the United States Information Agency, the Arms Control and Disarmament Agency, and parts of the Agency for International Development into the State Department.

At Lott's insistence, the administration also agreed that modifications to existing arms control treaties, which were being negotiated with Russia, would be sent to the Senate as formal amendments to those treaties, requiring a two-thirds majority vote. This was advantageous to conservatives who were particularly opposed to proposed changes in the 1972 treaty limiting antiballistic missile (ABM) defenses.

However, the Senate did reject five other proposed changes, dubbed "killer amendments" by the administration. Although Lott supported all of them, he announced that he would support the treaty, albeit unenthusiastically. The Senate approved the resolution April 24 by a vote of 74–26: R 29–26; D 45–0 (ND 37–0, SD 8–0). *(Vote, p. 876)*

4. COMPENSATORY TIME OFF

Less than a year after Senate Democrats blocked consideration of a key component in the GOP's labor agenda, Republican leaders made another attempt to pass legislation (S 4, HR 1) to allow employees to take compensatory time off instead of receive overtime pay, as required under existing federal law.

The House had passed a version of the plan in July 1996 and again on March 19, 1997, and Senate leaders wanted to see if support had increased in their chamber. Fifteen new members—nine Republicans and six Democrats—had joined the Senate. Mike DeWine, R-Ohio, acting on behalf of Republican bill sponsors, agreed to changes that might attract uncertain senators, including a provision to honor collective bargaining contracts.

The bill proposed to amend the 1938 Fair Labor Standards Act to allow private-sector hourly workers to take compensatory time in lieu of overtime pay and to work schedules other than the traditional forty-hour week. DeWine agreed to clarify that seasonal and temporary workers could not be offered the compensatory time option unless they worked at least 1,250 hours for an employer in a year. Republicans said the measure would give workers who earned an hourly wage the same opportunities to take time off that salaried workers had. But Democrats reiterated their charges that the bill would allow

employers, not employees, to choose how workers would be compensated for extra work. They also objected to undoing the forty-hour work week, which they considered a sacred element of labor law. The bill allowed for an eighty-hour, two-week work period in which employees could, for example, work fifty hours one week and thirty the next with no extra pay.

Democrats' arguments were backed by a veto threat from President Clinton and strong labor union opposition to the bill, reflecting the deep political chasm that existed between the two parties on labor issues. With the Democratic Party highly indebted to unions and Republicans indebted to the business community, the comptime bill was a measure on which neither party could afford to compromise.

Republicans on May 15 tried block a Democratic filibuster but the motion to invoke cloture failed 53–47: R 53–2; D 0–45 (ND 0–37, SD 0–8). A three-fifths majority, or sixty votes, was needed. The Democrats were joined by two Republicans facing 1998 reelection contests in strong union states: Alfonse M. D'Amato of New York and Arlen Specter of Pennsylvania. After a brief cooling-off period, Republicans made another attempt, also unsuccessful, to move the bill. A June 4 cloture vote failed 51–47. Another Republican, Ben Nighthorse Campbell of Colorado, joined D'Amato and Specter. *(Vote, p. 876)*

5. ABORTION PROCEDURE BAN

Both parties expected a close margin May 20 when the Senate voted to ban a controversial procedure that opponents termed "partial birth" abortion. The Senate had passed a similar bill in December 1995 by a vote of 54–44, well short of the 67 votes needed to override a presidential veto. The shortfall only increased in September 1997, when the Senate sustained President Clinton's veto, 57–41.

However, the political environment surrounding the debate differed substantially by 1997. New concerns had arisen about how often the practice, carried out in the second or third trimester of pregnancy, was performed. Some newly elected Republicans brought additional support for banning the practice. And the American Medical Association announced it would support the ban, a move that prompted some senators to switch their votes and support the bill.

Bill supporters, mostly Republicans, argued that the type of abortion described in the legislation was a violent and unnecessary procedure that should be outlawed. Opponents countered that the measure was too narrowly drawn and that women would be in jeopardy unless an exception were permitted to prevent serious injury to a woman's physical health.

The House already had passed the ban with a solid veto-proof majority. In the Senate Rick Santorum, R-Pa., the bill's sponsor, made what he termed "technical" changes to broaden support for the measure. Alterations included clarifying the definition of the procedure and reiterating that doctors would be shielded from criminal penalties if a life-threatening medical emergency forced them to use the procedure.

When the final count was taken May 20, supporters were still 3 votes short of the 67 needed for a veto override. However, their margin of victory had increased since December 1995. The vote was 64–36: R 51–4; D 13–32 (ND 9–28, SD 4–4). Several Democrats, including Minority Leader Tom Daschle of South Dakota, Robert C. Byrd of West Virginia, and Ernest F. Hollings of South Carolina, switched their votes to support the ban. Adding to the drama was a floor speech by Daschle, who had tried unsuccessfully to alter the bill. Daschle, a Roman Catholic, challenged church officials—including those in his home state—for criticizing his attempts to find a middle ground on the issue. "Their harsh rhetoric and vitriolic characterizations . . . proved to be a consequential impediment to the decision I have made today," he said. "It was most instructive." *(Vote, p. 876)*

6. BUDGET RESOLUTION

After bitter budget conflicts between Congress and President Clinton in 1995 and 1996, the Senate welcomed the opportunity in 1997 to produce a bipartisan budget agreement. Budget Committee Chairman Pete V. Domenici, R-N.M., was the chief player in early-stage talks with White House officials. A veteran of every major budget battle since becoming committee chairman in 1981, Domenici saw at the beginning of the year conditions that could lead to agreement for the first balanced budget in almost thirty years.

The 1997 agreement was helped by the unpopularity of budget deals earlier in the decade. In addition, the size of the deficit was shrinking in the years leading to 1997 as robust economic conditions brought more tax receipts to the government. Congressional Budget Office estimates of the 2002 deficit had shrunk from $349 billion in 1995 to $188 billion when the 1997 negotiations began in earnest.

Domenici, Budget Committee Staff Director G. William Hoagland, White House budget chief Franklin D. Raines, and top administration lobbyist John L. Hilley began back-channel talks that produced the outline of a deal and built up the more trusting atmosphere that was required to reach agreement.

Domenici held off writing the budget resolution until congressional Republicans and the White House had struck a deal, which traded long-term savings from Medicare and other programs for tax cuts and some short-term spending increases. Finally, on May 15, the agreement was ready and Domenici moved swiftly to translate it into a budget resolution (H Con Res 84) and get it through the Senate. The measure came to the floor with a series of proposed amendments that allowed members to point out what they considered to be flaws in the agreement.

It fell to Majority Leader Trent Lott, R-Miss., to sell the agreement to fellow conservatives. Some conservatives such as Phil Gramm, R-Texas, protested that the middle-of-the-road deal represented an abdication of core GOP values but almost everybody else found the opportunity to vote for a balanced budget and the first major tax cut since the beginning of Ronald Reagan's presidency in 1981 too alluring to pass up.

Despite potentially damaging amendments to shift additional funding to highway projects (killed, 51–49) and raise cigarette taxes to finance a children's health care initiative (killed 55–45), the budget resolution passed unscathed. The Senate adopted the measure May 23 by a vote of 78–22: R 41–14; D 37–8 (ND 31–6, SD 6–2). The bipartisanship witnessed during the debate on the budget resolution carried over into the crafting of the reconciliation bills required to implement the policy changes dictated by H Con Res 84. Despite extensive wrangling between the White House and Republicans, mostly over taxes, the mutual interest in enacting the budget deal kept Domenici and his House counterpart, John R. Kasich, R-Ohio, confident the deal would hold. *(Vote, p. 876)*

7. MEDICARE MEANS TESTING

In a move to restructure Medicare, the federal health insurance program for the elderly and disabled, the Senate proposed requiring that some wealthier beneficiaries pay higher premiums for visits to their doctors. Under existing law, beneficiaries paid 25 percent of the costs of Medicare Part B, which covered doctors' visits and other outpatient services. But in provisions written by the Finance Committee, the spending-cut portion of the Senate's reconciliation pack-

age (S 947) sought to introduce so-called means testing. The Senate bill proposed requiring individuals with at least $50,000 in adjusted gross annual incomes and couples with at least $75,000 to pay a larger share of their premiums. People with adjusted gross incomes of at least $100,000 and couples with incomes of at least $125,000 would pay the whole Part B premium.

Senate Budget Committee Chairman Pete V. Domenici, R-N.M., said linking premiums to income would raise about $4 billion and affect about 5 percent of Medicare's more than 38 million elderly and disabled beneficiaries. Supporters, who included both Democrats and Republicans, argued the change was fair because all taxpayers should not have to subsidize bills for wealthier seniors. But opponents, such as Edward M. Kennedy, D-Mass., said that requiring some seniors to pay more of their Part B premiums would be the first step toward making Medicare a welfare program rather than a federal entitlement program.

Kennedy fought to amend the means-testing provision. He tried to delay its onset by two years, having it begin in 2000 rather than 1998, but that proposal failed, 37–63. Kennedy did win a battle to make sure all senators had to abide by means testing. His amendment to require senators who earned more than $100,000 per year—as all of them did—to pay the full Part B premium, should the means-testing provision become law, passed by voice vote. But Kennedy failed to remove means testing from the bill. His amendment to do so was tabled (killed) on June 24 on a vote of 70–30: R 49–6; D 21–24 (ND 15–22, SD 6–2). *(Vote, p. 876)*

The Senate's landmark vote to include means testing had little staying power, however. The idea did not have wide bipartisan support in the House and was not included in the budget deal (H Con Res 84) that Republicans, Democrats, and the White House had agreed to in May. That fact brought opposition from the White House, although President Clinton had included means testing in his failed 1993 health care overhaul plan. Opposition also came from the AARP, a powerful lobbying group for senior citizens. Those concerns, plus a shortage of House members to back the proposal, forced means testing out of the final package adopted by Senate and House conferees. Instead, the spending cut bill (PL 105-33) created a bipartisan commission to review Medicare's long-term solvency.

8. ARTS FUNDING

The Senate once again demonstrated its strong support for the National Endowment for the Arts (NEA), defeating efforts to abolish or revamp federal funding for the arts. The issue developed when the House, in its version of the fiscal 1998 Interior appropriations bill (HR 2107), attempted to eliminate the agency. House conservatives had won a promise from the GOP leadership to try to kill the NEA, and the leadership lobbied hard for the no-funding position.

For the better part of the summer, senators and aides tried without success to find a compromise. Instead, the Senate version of HR 2107 was met with a host of NEA proposals, ranging from the outright elimination of federal arts funding to privatizing the NEA or restricting its funding options. A moderate attempt to revise the agency was made by Kay Bailey Hutchison, R-Texas, who spoke for a small band of senators who supported federal arts funding but backed changes in the agency. An important grievance was that the NEA directed too much money to a handful of states, such as New York, depriving others of needed resources. Another frequent complaint was that too much money went to administrative costs in Washington. These senators sought ways to put more money in the hands of state and local arts organizations, without increasing the overall funding ceiling for the agency.

Hutchison's amendment proposed to retain the agency while requiring it to send 75 percent of its funding directly to the states in lump sum payments. Of the remainder, 5 percent would be spent for administrative costs, and the rest on national grants to major ballet, opera, and other arts groups. Hutchison also proposed limiting the amount of money that could go to an individual state to 6.6 percent. She hoped her proposal would attract other moderates who supported the agency. Instead, the Senate defeated her proposal on Sept. 18 by a large margin, 39–61: R 39–16; 0–45 (ND 0–37, SD 0–8). Other amendments to change NEA practices also were defeated. As a result House conservatives had to retreat from their efforts to end the agency completely. The final bill included $98 million for the NEA, roughly equal to the Senate level. *(Vote, p. 876)*

9. CAMPAIGN FINANCE

Growing controversy over campaign finance practices in the 1996 elections prompted a broad Senate investigation, a spate of other congressional probes, and a steady stream of newspaper stories documenting fund-raising law abuses. But the furor did not lead to legislation revamping the political fund-raising system.

A pair of senators from opposite parties, Arizona Republican John McCain and Wisconsin Democrat Russell D. Feingold, sponsored a bill (S 25) aimed at closing what they said were two of the biggest fund-raising loopholes. The bill sought to eliminate "soft money"—unregulated donations to parties rather than candidates—and to place limits on independent, issue-oriented television advertisements that implicitly promoted candidates. McCain and Feingold hoped that voter anger over fund-raising scandals would overcome determined opposition led by Senate Majority Leader Trent Lott, R-Miss., and Mitch McConnell, R-Ky. Although polls showed that a majority of Americans were dissatisfied with the existing system, polls also showed that voters, cynical about the political system, did not expect Washington to change the rules.

Lott and McConnell said that the real problem lay with President Clinton and other Democrats who, they contended, were willing to ignore existing laws to finance their 1996 campaign. Not only were new laws not needed, they said, but the McCain-Feingold legislation would trample on constitutionally protected freedom of political speech.

As a vote approached in early October, it became clear that McCain and Feingold needed 60 votes to break an expected GOP-led filibuster. With commitments of support from all 45 Senate Democrats and 4 Republicans—McCain, Susan Collins of Maine, Fred Thompson of Tennessee, and Arlen Specter of Pennsylvania—they needed 11 more votes, all of which would have to come from Republicans.

The two senators went on radio talk shows, cable news shows, and network political chat shows to make the case for change in the campaign finance system. In an effort to widen support, McCain and Feingold scaled back their bill by dropping a controversial provision to provide free television time to candidates who voluntarily agreed to spending limits.

But the effort fell short, as Lott, McConnell, and allies successfully filibustered the bill. On Oct. 7 the Senate rejected a motion to invoke cloture and limit debate on the bill. The vote was 53–47: R 8–47; D 45–0 (ND 37–0, SD 8–0). A vote of three-fifths of the Senate (60 votes) was required to invoke cloture. McCain and Feingold had not picked up support over their earlier effort to pass the legislation. In June 1996 the Senate defeated a cloture motion on a more sweeping version of the McCain-Feingold bill on a 54–46 vote, with one more senator voting to end the filibuster than in 1997. Eight Republicans voted for cloture then, too; the key difference was that there were

two more Democrats in the Senate at the time, one of whom voted for cloture and one against. *(Vote, p. 876)*

10. LINE-ITEM VETO

The Senate promptly and pointedly expressed its disapproval of President Clinton's use of a newly acquired line-item veto authority. Three and a half weeks after Clinton first struck projects from an appropriations bill, better than two-thirds of the Senate voted to overturn his decision. Led by Appropriations Chairman Ted Stevens, R-Alaska, senators on Oct. 30 rejected Clinton's decision to veto 38 military construction projects, totaling $287 million. Clinton had signed the military construction bill (HR 2016—PL 105-45) on Sept. 30. The congressional reaction prompted Clinton to reassess his line-item veto strategy. He would not again try to excise as many projects from a single bill. Much of the floor debate on the disapproval bill (S 1292) centered on the question of how Clinton selected the items to veto, with a number of senators taking time to extol the virtues of canceled projects in their home states. With passage clear, the one contentious question was whether supporters of the line-item veto (PL 104-130), which Congress had granted to the president in 1996, were obliged to accept his decisions as falling within the intent of the new law. "What credibility can supporters of the line-item veto authority have if we disapprove vetoes on the first appropriations bill right out of the gate?" Charles S. Robb, D-Va., asked. But supporters of the disapproval bill argued that it was in keeping with the spirit of the line-item veto law. "I think this is exactly how the process is supposed to work," said Kay Bailey Hutchison, R-Texas. "Congress did not take away its right to disagree with the president."

The disapproval bill passed 69–30: R 42–12; D 27–18 (ND 24–13, SD 3–5). That gave sponsors a three-vote cushion over the two-thirds majority they would need to overcome Clinton's veto. *(Vote, p. 876)*

Although House appropriators initially signaled their disinterest in challenging the president, hinting they might instead try to restore the military construction funding through a supplemental appropriations bill, the Senate vote emboldened the House to pass a slightly different version of the disapproval bill (HR 2631), which the Senate then accepted. Although Clinton vetoed that bill Nov. 13, the veto-proof margins mustered in both chambers made it clear that he would ultimately be overridden. The HR 2631 veto was overridden in early 1998.

11. EDUCATION SAVINGS ACCOUNTS

Senate Democrats on Oct. 31 blocked a top Republican education priority: a bill to establish tax-free education savings accounts that could be used to defray private or public school costs. A GOP effort to invoke cloture, thereby limiting debate on the bill, failed by four votes. Republicans originally tried to include a similar provision in the tax portion of the balanced-budget reconciliation package (HR 2014—PL 105-34). But they withdrew it at the last moment when President Clinton, fearing that the measure would harm public schools, threatened to veto the whole tax bill if it were included. Republicans criticized Clinton for yielding to opposition from teachers' unions and vowed to pass the measure over Clinton's objections. Under subsequent legislation (HR 2646), sponsored by House Ways and Means Committee Chairman Bill Archer, R-Texas, parents would have been able to invest up to $2,500 a year in special accounts and use the principal and interest tax-free for education-related expenses. The accounts were to be structured somewhat like Individual Retirement Accounts. The legislation advanced through Ways and Means and the House in October on closely contested votes. Senate supporters hoped to move it swiftly to Clinton's desk.

Democrats initially opposed the cloture motion as part of their protest over a stalled bill (S 25) on campaign finance revisions. But even when senators agreed Oct. 30 on how to consider the campaign finance bill, Democrats still objected to the education measure on procedural grounds that no Senate hearings were held on it and Democrats would be barred from offering a full range of amendments.

Paul Coverdell, R-Ga., chief Senate sponsor of the legislation, had hoped to attract bipartisan support but only two Democrats voted for cloture: Robert G. Torricelli of New Jersey and Joseph I. Lieberman of Connecticut. On the other side, John H. Chafee of Rhode Island broke ranks with Republicans and voted against cloture. The cloture motion fell 4 votes short of the 60 needed to move the bill toward passage: 56–41: R 54–1; D 2–40 (ND 2–32, SD 0–8). Coverdell tried again to invoke cloture Nov. 4 but still fell 4 votes short, 56–44. *(Vote, p. 876)*

12. 'FAST-TRACK' TRADE AUTHORITY

With time running out on the congressional session, President Clinton made a determined bid to regain "fast-track" authority to negotiate and get expedited review of trade agreements. When it appeared he was badly behind in the House, he turned to the Senate. The Senate historically had favored free trade, and there was no doubt that that chamber could muster the majority required to pass the bill (S 1269). The only question was whether there would be enough votes to beat a promised filibuster by opponents such as Democrats Byron L. Dorgan of North Dakota and Ernest F. Hollings of South Carolina.

Under the Constitution, trade bills were required to originate in the House because they affected tariff revenues. But Senate Majority Leader Trent Lott, R-Miss., began the floor debate at the administration's request. The idea was that a big show of Senate support would give momentum to the troubled House effort. The Finance Committee quickly approved the bill as expected, Oct. 1, and Lott predicted from the outset that the votes were there to reach the 60-vote mark required to beat a filibuster. Dorgan, the most active of the opponents, cast the debate as a referendum on trade pacts such as the 1993 North American Free Trade Agreement (NAFTA). Dorgan criticized NAFTA for turning a $2 billion trade surplus with Mexico into a $16 billion deficit, and for accompanying job losses in certain manufacturing sectors. Supporters countered that fast track was merely a procedural device and that any trade pact negotiated under fast-track rules could be rejected by Congress.

As Lott predicted, the Senate on Nov. 4 acted to invoke cloture on the motion to proceed to the bill by a unexpectedly big vote of 69–31: R 43–12; D 26–19 (ND 20–17, SD 6–2). After invoking cloture, the Senate the next day approved the motion to proceed by a 68–31 vote. The Senate then turned to other business in the end-of-session crunch and the bill was put aside pending a vote in the House. But most House Democrats were dismissive of Clinton's request and not swayed by the large Senate margin favoring fast track. Republican leaders did not take up the legislation. *(Vote, p. 876)*

House

1. ELECTION OF SPEAKER

In a remarkable twist of history, Newt Gingrich, the upstart Georgian who led Republicans to a majority in Congress in 1995, found himself on the brink of ruin at the start of the 105th Congress. Two

years earlier he had been the undisputed leader of the Republican Party and one of the country's most important politicians. But a series of tactical missteps in his first two years in power, some of them highly embarrassing for his party, coupled with doubts raised about his personal conduct by a House ethics investigation, led to a make-or-break vote for the Speaker on Jan. 7. What should have been a routine exercise—the ratification of the majority party's nominee for Speaker—instead turned into an intrigue-filled squeaker.

Although Gingrich still commanded the support of a large share of House Republicans, losses in the November 1996 election had so narrowed the GOP advantage that he could withstand few defections. Republicans held only a 227–207 edge over the Democrats. If all the Democrats and the House's one independent voted for Minority Leader Richard A. Gephardt, D-Mo., and twenty Republicans voted "present" or for someone other than Gingrich, Gephardt would have become Speaker.

Some lawmakers, such as New York GOP Reps. Peter T. King and Michael P. Forbes, aired their doubts publicly, attracting the attention of the national media. But the biggest threat to Gingrich was a silent revolt among a loosely aligned group of disgruntled Republicans who held out as undecided votes, hoping to force him to step down. The rebels had grown disillusioned with Gingrich, convinced that his usefulness as chief party visionary no longer made up for his low public approval ratings, frequent gaffes, and often unpredictable leadership style. The unresolved issues of the ethics case only exacerbated their concerns.

Gingrich on Dec. 21, 1996, had admitted after two years of denials that he had failed to properly manage the financing of his political activities through charitable foundations. Gingrich also conceded that he gave the committee misleading information during the investigation. But the panel had not issued its final report or recommended a punishment and would not do so until after the Speaker's election, leaving lawmakers partly uninformed as they prepared to vote.

Gingrich, long a scrappy political fighter, refused to capitulate. He instead brought all the considerable resources of his office to bear. He and his five top allies and their staffs worked telephones and fax machines throughout the Christmas season, waging a one-on-one campaign to put down the rebellion. Gingrich was aided by the heavy hitters of the House GOP: Majority Leader Dick Armey and Whip Tom DeLay, both of Texas; Conference Chairman John A. Boehner of Ohio; National Republican Congressional Committee Chairman John Linder, a home-state ally from Georgia; and Bill Paxon of New York, the chairman of the Speaker's planning group.

The uncertainty lasted right up to the day of the vote. When the time came, five Republicans voted "present" rather than back Gingrich, and four more voted for other, undeclared candidates of their choosing. Two voted for Jim Leach, R-Iowa; one for former House Minority Leader Robert H. Michel, R-Ill. (1957–1995); and one for former Rep. Robert S. Walker, R-Pa. (1977–1997).

Gingrich only narrowly prevailed with 216 votes to 205 votes for Gephardt, who, as expected, captured all of the Democratic votes: R 216–0; D 0–204 (ND 0–150, SD 0–54); I 0–1. *(Vote, p. 878)*

2. REPRIMAND OF SPEAKER

After the controversy over electing a Speaker, House Republicans were further embarrassed Jan. 21 when they cast an historic vote to punish for rules violations the person they had just elected to the post: Newt Gingrich, R-Ga. The overwhelming vote marked the first time a sitting Speaker had been sanctioned formally.

Gingrich was reprimanded for bringing discredit on the House with his ethical misconduct. He was also fined $300,000 for the costs to the House of sorting out his misleading statements to the ethics committee. With five members voting present, the vote was 395–28: R 196–26; D 198–2 (ND 147–0, SD 51–2); I 1–0. *(Vote, p. 878)*

In what some observers saw as a plea bargain with the Committee on Standards of Official Conduct, the formal name of the ethics committee, Gingrich escaped the most serious charge: that he knowingly used charitable foundations to finance his political activities in the early 1990s, when he was planning the Republican takeover of Congress. But he admitted that he failed to seek proper legal advice in using the tax-exempt groups for political ends.

In a more damaging admission, the Speaker also acknowledged misleading the committee during its probe, though he blamed his lawyer for submitting conflicting and false statements to investigators.

The Speaker's admissions, coming after two years of consistent denials of wrongdoing, created turmoil in Republican ranks. Many were stunned when the ethics committee, including its GOP members, recommended a harsh penalty and an unprecedented $300,000 fine. Some who had been lobbied hard to cast votes for Gingrich for Speaker felt deceived when they saw the report by the panel and its special counsel, James M. Cole.

Although Republicans did not welcome reprimanding their Speaker, which would reflect poorly on the entire party, most felt they could not contest the findings of the independent counsel and the bipartisan ethics committee. Only 26 Republicans voted against the sanctions. Many of those who did so said they either did not want to set a precedent for fining members such extraordinary amounts or that they believed that the fine was simply too harsh a penalty. Two Southern Democrats also voted against sanctions: Gene Taylor of Mississippi and Earl F. Hilliard of Alabama.

The ethics issue reverberated through the year and was one of the events that presaged a midsummer attempt by a group of disgruntled Republicans along with some of Gingrich's allies to oust the Speaker.

Gingrich, once considered one of the country's most influential politicians, was, after the vote, a diminished figure, no longer able to dictate the national agenda. At the same time, President Clinton, fresh from winning reelection, was making a political comeback.

3. ABORTION PROCEDURE BAN

Opponents of a second- and third-trimester abortion procedure found support from an unlikely source in their battle to enact legislation banning the practice. Ron Fitzsimmons, executive director of the National Coalition of Abortion Providers, admitted in interviews that the procedure opponents called "partial-birth" abortion was performed more frequently than he had acknowledged in 1996, when Congress passed and President Clinton vetoed a similar measure. A significant part of abortion-rights advocates' defense of the procedure had rested on the assumption that it was rarely done. The revelation gave abortion foes renewed zeal in their bid to enact HR 1122, which called for fines and up to two years in jail for physicians who performed such abortions.

Attempts by abortion-rights supporters to broaden the legislation to allow an exception to protect a woman's health were rejected. Under the bill, the procedure would be allowed only if needed to save the woman's life. The final was unsurprising with the chamber overwhelmingly supporting the ban by more than the two-thirds majority needed to override a presidential veto. The vote on passage was 295–136: R 218–8; D 77–127 (ND 51–99, SD 26–28); I 0–1. Three members switched their votes from "no" in 1996 to "yes" in 1997. They were: Christopher Shays, R-Conn.; Rodney Frelinghuysen, R-N.J.; and Sue W. Kelly, R-N.Y. Peter J. Visclosky, D-Ind., also changed his vote to "yes," but he had changed his mind earlier,

voting Sept. 19, 1996, to override Clinton's veto. Martin Frost, D-Texas, switched his vote to oppose the bill. *(Vote, p. 878)*

4. ENDANGERED SPECIES ACT

After a number of defeats on environmental issues in the 104th Congress, western Republicans in the House pledged in the 105th to keep their bills narrowly focused and easy to explain. Gone from their must-do list were comprehensive bills to rewrite the 1973 Endangered Species Act, overhaul federal grazing policy, or push a major rewrite of federal regulations.

The new incrementalism embraced by the westerners got its first big test in early May on a bill (HR 478) to waive the Endangered Species Act for flood-control projects. Westerners believed that they could win by portraying their bill as a targeted attempt to protect people from rising flood waters. They sought support by casting the bill as a choice between protecting people or safeguarding bugs and rodents under the species law. But the strategy did not work. The House May 7 amended the bill so much that supporters pulled it from the floor. The vote on the amendment, offered by Sherwood Boehlert, R-N.Y., was 227–196: R 54–169; D 172–27 (ND 137–9, SD 35–18); I 1–0. *(Vote, p. 878)*

The vote worsened relations between many westerners and Boehlert, a moderate who often allied himself with environmental groups. Westerners charged that Boehlert and many of the moderate eastern House Republicans had failed them on an issue of great importance to their constituents, and vowed retaliation. They also were displeased with the GOP leadership, which did little to bolster the prospects for the flood-control bill.

Determined to aggressively advance their interests, and to demand leadership support, westerners were ready by the fall to push through the House bills revising federal grazing policy, property rights, and other statutes affecting western lands. This time, they got leadership backing. On a bill (HR 2493) to alter federal grazing policy House Speaker Newt Gingrich, R-Ga., was actively involved to broker a compromise.

5. HOUSING OVERHAUL

Unable in 1996 to get a consensus with the Senate to overhaul the public housing system, House Republicans hoped to get an early start on a nearly identical plan in 1997. In late April, they resurrected legislation (HR 2) that proposed sweeping changes in the nation's public and subsidized housing laws. The bill aimed to give local authorities more leeway over eligibility and rents, and to generate a steadier cash flow for housing projects.

The House floor action on the measure recalled the debate on welfare overhaul legislation (PL 104-193) in the 104th Congress: many members from both parties agreed that the system in question was broken but they differed over how far to go to fix it. The housing measure, similar to the welfare bill, proposed changing decades of social policy, sending block grants and authority for public and subsidized housing to local boards. To GOP leaders, it represented the next step in their plans to remake the nation's social programs. They emphasized the high priority they placed on the legislation by making it the second House bill introduced in the 105th Congress. The bill included repeal of the 1937 law that set up the public housing system, prompting liberal Democrats to fear the legislation and other proposed changes would cut the social safety net for the nation's poorest people.

Unlike the tightly controlled consideration of the welfare measure, however, leaders allowed nearly unlimited debate on the housing bill under an "open rule" for floor consideration that allowed any member to offer a germane amendment. Debate spanned seven days over three weeks.

The most vociferous arguments centered on a provision that would open public housing to the working poor. Democrats charged that Republicans were seeking to throw out the poorest tenants to make way for those who could afford to pay more. "It will fix public housing all right," said Joseph P. Kennedy II, D-Mass., ranking member on the Housing Subcommittee of the Banking and Financial Services Committee. "It fixes this problem by simply eliminating the poor from eligibility for this program."

But Republicans said that change, along with others, was needed to diversify public housing's clientele and to ensure that local authorities had the flexibility to make public housing a good place to live. Liberal Democrats also strongly objected to a provision to require able-bodied, unemployed tenants to perform eight hours of community service a month in exchange for their apartments. They said it was unfair because other recipients of federal aid were not required to perform similar service. Republicans said it was a small price to pay for housing.

Despite the objections from liberals, however, more than a third of the House Democrats joined all but one Republican in voting for the bill May 14. These Democrats were mostly white conservatives and moderates from the South, the West and rural areas, who believed that more local flexibility might improve housing programs. The final tally was 293–132: R 222–1; D 71–130 (ND 43–104, SD 28–26); I 0–1. *(Vote, p. 878)*

6. HIGHWAY FUNDING

One of the closest votes of the year occurred over the on-going battle between competing values that many members of Congress preferred not to confront: spending money on local benefits (in this case highway and related construction) or limiting benefits to a member's constituency in the interests of a larger goal (in this case, balancing the federal budget). It took a strenuous effort by the House leadership and the Clinton administration to block Congress's natural instinct to expand spending that benefits almost every member.

House Transportation and Infrastructure Committee Chairman Bud Shuster, R-Pa., proposed an amendment to the fiscal 1998 budget resolution (H Con Res 84) to increase transportation spending under the just-completed balanced-budget deal by $12 billion over five years. Shuster proposed to offset fully the increase with a 0.39 percent across-the-board reduction in other discretionary accounts, coupled with a comparable scaling back of proposed tax cuts. In the early morning hours of May 21 Shuster lost by just 2 votes, a margin that demonstrated vividly Congress's ambivalence between national goals, even when backed by party leadership, and local interests that can have a direct impact on a member's ability to get reelected.

Shuster and his committee colleagues had complained that the balanced-budget deal did not allow adequate funding for the nation's highways, roads, bridges, and transit systems. Although GOP leaders hailed the era of balanced budgets and fiscal restraint, Shuster was firing off a memo declaring, "The numbers . . . are unacceptable." Under pressure, congressional budget writers agreed during the week of May 12 to provide an additional $1 billion for transportation, raising highway spending levels under the budget deal to about $22 billion by 2002, compared with the 1997 level of $20 billion. But that still was nowhere near the $32 billion Shuster was demanding.

Shuster's showdown with the leadership put the GOP rank and file in a difficult position. About 400 members had already come to

the powerful chairman to request tens of billions of dollars for district projects. Even if, as Shuster insisted, there were no overt threats that requests would be denied if they failed to support the amendment, members perceived a threat.

At the same time, GOP leaders said Shuster's amendment would upset the delicate balance reached in the May budget deal, skew funding away from Republican priorities, and possibly bring down what many Republicans had come to Washington to produce: a balanced budget. The amendment would have reduced defense spending over five years by $6 billion, domestic programs by $5 billion, and the proposed tax cut by about $1 billion.

Belatedly realizing the amendment's appeal, House Speaker Newt Gingrich, R-Ga., and the Clinton administration launched a frantic counteroffensive May 20, warning that Shuster's plan could open the floodgates for every chairman to request more money. The leadership called a closed-door conference at 10 p.m., at which Gingrich and Budget Committee Chairman John R. Kasich, R-Ohio, urged members to stand by the budget accord. The late-night effort succeeded but barely. During the tense 3 a.m. vote, which seesawed back and forth, Gingrich fanned out to marshal support. The leadership held the vote open as they twisted just enough arms to defeat Shuster. The final vote was 214–216: R 58–168; D 155–48 (ND 118–32, SD 37–16); I 1–0. *(Vote, p. 878)*

7. BUDGET RESOLUTION

After the standoffs that led to government shutdowns in 1995 and 1996, it was difficult to imagine congressional Republicans and President Clinton agreeing on a new budget. But they did in a deal that proved relatively palatable to the overwhelming majority of the House. A thriving economy that brought unexpected tax revenues made the task much easier and certainly more rewarding. The federal deficit could be eliminated even while taxes were being cut and spending boosted in certain areas. The result was a balanced budget that was seemingly pain-free.

Also providing motivation to both sides was the 1996 election, which returned the incumbent president to office while retaining congressional control by the opposition party. It was seen as clear voter direction to work together.

Adoption of the budget resolution (H Con Res 84) was the first of many important junctures as Congress and the White House fleshed out the framework of the May 2 agreement. Later would come passage of the twin tax and spending cut bills (PL 105-34, PL 105-33) that traded long-term cuts in programs such as Medicare for GOP-inspired tax cuts and new spending for several Clinton priorities.

Despite having to compromise with the opposition most, Republicans embraced the deal, which met at least two of the chief criteria of the vetoed 1995 Republican budget: balance by 2002 and a sizable net tax cut, though only one-third the size of their earlier budget.

The budget resolution also had sweeping support among Democrats, though liberals and House Democratic Leader Richard A. Gephardt of Missouri attacked the deal as favoring the wealthy with tax cuts while cutting programs aimed at helping low-income families and the working poor.

For most Democrats the prospect of voting for a balanced budget was too appealing to give up. Indeed, prevailing sentiment among both Republicans and Democrats was to embrace the budget as the best either side could get in a time of divided government. Also contributing to the big vote on final passage was the fact that the resolution served as a blueprint and did not contain the actual policy changes that would come later. The House adopted the resolution May 21 by a vote of 333–99: R 201–26; D 132–72 (ND 90–60, SD 42–12); I 0–1. *(Vote, p. 878)*

8. BOSNIA DEADLINE

The House in June narrowly rejected a proposal to force the withdrawal of U.S. troops from Bosnia by the end of 1997. The vote highlighted both congressional opposition to the deployment and the difficulty critics faced in trying to overcome President Clinton's determination to pursue the Bosnia undertaking.

The House had opposed sending U.S. forces to Bosnia since late 1995 when Clinton promised up to 20,000 troops to help enforce a peace agreement ending that country's brutal civil war. Even before the start of the November 1995 negotiations in Dayton, Ohio, that ultimately produced the agreement, the House adopted, by a 3–1 margin, a nonbinding resolution repudiating Clinton's troop pledge. Once the Dayton agreement was signed efforts in the Senate to block deployment of U.S. troops collapsed. Clinton had committed the country's credibility to the deal, which was to be guaranteed for one year by a NATO-led force of 60,000 troops, including the Americans. Even then, however, the House came within a few votes of passing a bill that would have denied funds for the mission.

On Nov. 15, 1996, a week after he was reelected, Clinton announced that a smaller U.S. force would remain in Bosnia through June 1998, eighteen months after the Dec. 31, 1996, deadline he had promised a year earlier. The first congressional challenge to this policy change came in June 1997 when the House took up the annual defense authorization bill. Critics argued that the combat readiness of U.S. forces was being sapped to pay for the Bosnia operation, which was estimated to cost $7.3 billion through the end of fiscal 1997. Some opponents argued that the task of the peacekeeping force was hopeless because there was no chance of recreating the multiethnic Bosnian state envisaged by the Dayton agreement. Others argued for withdrawal of U.S. forces as a way to force European governments to shoulder the burden of keeping the peace with U.S. communications and intelligence support. The Clinton administration, backed by many House Democrats, warned that a U.S. pullout from Bosnia would undermine the tenuous peace that had been established because the other major participants in the peacekeeping force had made it clear their forces would leave if the Americans did.

In an effort to finesse that argument, Steve Buyer, R-Ind., offered an amendment to the fiscal 1998 defense authorization bill (HR 1119) requiring a pullout by June 30, 1998. Although that was the date Clinton himself had set for the end of the deployment, it was widely believed that the administration would break that deadline, just as it had broken its first one.

Van Hilleary, R-Tenn., and other Clinton opponents wanted a chance to go further, repudiating Clinton's policy outright. On June 24, Hilleary offered an amendment to force withdrawal of the troops by Dec. 31, 1997. It was rejected June 24 by a vote of 196–231: R 174–49; D 21–182 (ND 15–133, SD 6–49); I 1–0. The House subsequently adopted Buyer's provision, 278–148. A similar provision was included in the companion defense appropriations bill for fiscal 1998 (HR 2266). *(Vote, p. 878)*

The administration threatened to veto both the authorization and appropriations bills if they included a June 1998 deadline. Ultimately, both bills were enacted with provisions stipulating that Clinton could keep forces in Bosnia beyond the deadline if he first reported to Congress on the strategic rationale for his decision, along with estimates of the size, duration, cost, mission and exit strategy of the extended deployment.

9. ARTS FUNDING

Conservative House Republicans pressed aggressively to eliminate appropriations for the National Endowment for the Arts (NEA), arguing that the federal government had no role to play in arts funding and charging that the NEA funded lewd, pornographic, and objectionable art. NEA supporters argued that the endowment provided crucial seed money to struggling arts organizations. Although NEA opponents succeeded in the House, the final legislation kept the agency's funding largely intact.

The Republican House leadership, generally sympathetic to the conservative's view, arranged to have the $13 billion fiscal 1998 Interior appropriations bill (HR 2107) that was sent to the House floor include no funding for the agency. The leadership then set the ground rules for debate in such a way that precluded a clear vote on the merits of funding. As a result, the key House vote on this issue technically was on the procedures under which the bill was to be considered.

A nearly unified Democratic Party and a group of Republicans, most of them northeastern moderates, wanted an up-or-down vote on the agency. Supporters believed the leadership realized it did not have the votes to sustain the zero funding position and thus had to resort to procedural devices to prevail.

But the GOP leadership refused. House Majority Whip Tom DeLay, R-Texas, even made clear he considered the vote a crucial test of loyalty and lobbied hard to get Republicans to support the procedural rule. In the days leading up to the vote, DeLay stepped up the arm-twisting. The outcome remained in doubt until the very end when John M. McHugh, R-N.Y., in the closing minutes and only after the urgent pleas of the leadership, cast the final vote backing the leadership. Just five Democrats voted for the rule and 15 Republicans broke ranks to oppose it. The July 10 tally was 217–216: R 212–15; D 5–200 (ND 2–148, SD 3–52); I 0–1. *(Vote, p. 878)*

A number of NEA supporters came to the leadership's side. Sherwood Boehlert, R-N.Y., supported funding for the agency but said he voted for the rule "for the leadership." Boehlert and other NEA supporters figured they could show their loyalty to the leadership and still win on NEA because the Senate appeared likely to restore funding. In fact, the final bill included $98 million for the agency, just below the level included in the Senate version of the bill.

10. INTERNATIONAL FAMILY PLANNING

Seeking a compromise to prevent another protracted dispute over abortion and foreign aid programs, House Democrats and moderate Republicans proposed allowing overseas family planning groups to remain eligible for U.S. funds under some conditions, even if they performed abortions.

But their bipartisan amendment to the fiscal 1998 foreign operations spending bill (HR 2159) faltered in the face of continued support for a ban on aid to international family planning groups that used even their own money to subsidize abortions. The outcome assured a drawn-out fight with the Senate and the Clinton administration over the appropriations bill.

In his first week in office in January 1993, President Clinton rescinded the long-standing GOP policy barring funds for international groups that practiced or advocated abortion. It was one of several actions that Clinton, a supporter of abortion rights, took to reverse rules created during the Reagan and Bush eras. Several Republicans in Congress sought to overturn Clinton's move legislatively, by attaching restrictive abortion provisions to essential spending bills. With the GOP takeover of the House in 1994, Christopher H. Smith, R-N.J., succeeded in attaching an amendment reinstituting the prohibition on family planning funds to the House version of the foreign operations spending bill.

In the final hours of each congressional session after that House, Senate, and State Department negotiators had been forced to come up with a compromise acceptable to the Senate, whose legislation did not include the restrictions, and the White House, which threatened a veto if the language was included.

The compromise on family planning in the fiscal 1997 version of the foreign operations bill permitted distribution of U.S. aid to international groups on July 1, 1998. Earlier distribution on March 1, 1998, was permitted but only if both chambers passed a resolution by Feb. 28, 1998, agreeing to the early payment. Democratic leaders and the State Department won that battle by portraying the vote as an effort to promote family planning, not abortion, and warning that without the funds, family planning in third world countries would be devastated.

But Smith was not deterred. During the summer, he vexed negotiators on a separate, fiscal 1998 State Department authorization bill (HR 1757) by attaching a version of the family planning amendment. In September he turned his attention to the fiscal 1998 foreign operations spending bill.

The first hurdle was securing enough votes to defeat a bipartisan substitute offered by Nancy Pelosi, D-Calif.; Benjamin A. Gilman, R-N.Y.; and James C. Greenwood, R-Pa. Their amendment allowed U.S. aid to continue for organizations that did not promote abortion as a method of family planning. If those groups did provide abortions, they would have had to pay for those procedures from their own funds. Smith criticized the substitute as purposely vague and argued that only his proposal addressed the problems with the White House policy. Greenwood countered that adopting the Smith amendment would lead to an intractable controversy and delay adjournment yet again.

The House rejected the Pelosi-Gilman-Greenwood substitute on Sept. 4 by a narrow margin, 210–218: R 38–185; D 171–33 (ND 125–26, SD 46–7); I 1–0. The House then easily adopted Smith's amendment banning the funds. Months later, in the final days of the session, House and Senate leaders and the administration produced a compromise that pleased neither side. Family planning groups received the same amount for fiscal 1998 as they had in fiscal 1997, $385 million, but with no restrictions. *(Vote, p. 878)*

11. CONGRESSIONAL PAY RAISE

More than most bills, a pay raise for members of Congress required creative legislating. GOP House leaders proved their mettle by finessing a 2.3 percent pay increase through to passage, with thankful rank-and-file lawmakers suffering only a brief drubbing by hometown editorial writers.

Under a 1989 law, members of Congress were entitled to an automatic cost of living adjustment (COLA), which was intended to take the politics out of annual pay raise debates. But each year since fiscal 1993, someone had introduced an amendment blocking the raise. The amendments were usually offered on the annual appropriations bill for the Treasury Department, Postal Service, and other government operations. The amendment always passed, with lawmakers fearful of the political repercussions of voting against it.

This time, however, House leaders outwitted the perennial pay raise opponents. First, they brought the Treasury funding bill (HR 2378) to the floor Sept. 17 without warning and without sending it through the Rules Committee, where opponents typically introduced their amendment. Blindsided, the opposition had too little time to organize an effort on the floor, and the bill passed 231–192.

But the key vote came a week later. Now organized and fully aware that the leaders were angling to allow the raise to go through, opponents led by Linda Smith, R-Wash., insisted on an up-or-down vote on the issue. The leadership at first balked but then agreed to hold a roll call vote on a procedural motion on the Treasury funding bill as the House prepared to send it to conference, where differing House and Senate versions of the bill had yet to be resolved. If the technical motion, called "ordering the previous question," passed, Smith under House rules would be barred from amending the bill with a COLA block. But if it failed, she could offer her amendment.

The motion prevailed, 229–199: R 114–110; D 115–88 (ND 88–62, SD 27–26); I 0–1. Smith was unable to offer her amendment. The leaders in effect had given lawmakers a way to vote themselves a pay raise without appearing to do so. Those who voted for the motion could claim they were simply voting on a technical motion dealing with instructions to conferees, not a pay raise. The vote offered members crucial cover, a plausible way of obscuring their actual position on the issue. *(Vote, p. 878)*

The House vote was an important internal political victory for Speaker Newt Gingrich, R-Ga., and his leadership team. Mindful of their obligations to the rank-and-file members who elected them, they had managed to give lawmakers something they wanted with a minimal amount of political pain.

With the way prepared by the House, the Senate on Oct. 1 followed by approving the conference report on the Treasury bill without a ban on the pay raise. The raise boosted lawmakers' $133,600 annual salary to $136,700. Action on the raise was followed by a spate of negative news stories and condemnations in newspaper editorials. Some of the sharpest criticism was of the purposefully cunning way House leaders handled the matter, and of the absence of a clear up-or-down vote. But the uproar was short-lived.

12. PRIVATE PROPERTY RIGHTS

In 1997, the nation's home builders brought their considerable influence in Congress to bear on legislation providing new rights to property owners. Republicans had long favored such legislation, and the House GOP had included a bill to expand the rights of private property owners in its list of priorities for the 104th Congress. But their earlier effort fell short, attacked by a coalition of Democrats, environmentalists, and some local elected officials, as well as moderate Republicans, as an attempt to gut key environmental laws. The bills that failed in the 104th Congress, including one sponsored by then-Senate Majority Leader Bob Dole, R-Kan., were aimed at compensating owners for government actions that diminished property values. Sponsors argued that federal regulators were imposing money-losing restrictions on property owners but offering no compensation. They said this flouted the Fifth Amendment to the Constitution, which barred the government from "taking" property without just compensation. But environmentalists prevailed with the counterargument that requiring greater compensation would create significant bureaucratic delays. Fiscal conservatives were concerned about the cost of payments under this approach.

In 1997 the 190,000-member National Association of Home Builders and their congressional allies decided on a different approach. They focused on a plan (HR 1534) to give property owners more power to get their proposals addressed by local zoning boards. Republicans put the bill on the fast track in the fall, and it sailed easily through the House. The Oct. 22 vote was 248–178: R 193–30; D 55–147 (ND 25–124, SD 30–23); I 0–1. The outcome was largely the result of a high-profile lobbying campaign by the home builders, who mobilized support with many allies. They also benefited by selling the bill as a narrow procedural change. Under existing law, developers first had to exhaust appeals to planning agency decisions in state courts and be denied compensation before a federal court would hear a Fifth Amendment takings claim. The process could stretch for years. To address the situation, HR 1534 offered property owners the option of taking their case directly to a federal court after filing at least two appeals to a planning board decision. (Vote, p. 878)

Still, many in the opposition said the home builders had used their influence to pressure members into supporting a bill that few of them understood. Opponents said the bill would disrupt local zoning matters and give developers broad new powers to get zoning changes. Environmental groups said they would highlight the vote during the 1998 midterm elections.

13. PRIVATE SCHOOL VOUCHERS

The House rejected a key element of the Republican education agenda Nov. 4 by defeating a bill (HR 2746) that would have enabled low-income families to use federal money to send their children to private schools. Republicans pushed the proposal at least partly to distinguish their views on education from Democrats. They framed it as a way to enhance parental choices, especially among low-income families who were unable to flee poor-performing inner-city schools.

Republicans initially hoped to rally a broad coalition behind the bill, which called for the creation of Helping Empower Low-Income Parents (HELP) scholarships. They touted support from Rep. Floyd H. Flake, D-N.Y., an African American minister, plus the strong backing of Speaker Newt Gingrich, R-Ga., and Majority Leader Dick Armey, R-Texas.

The legislation, sponsored by Frank Riggs, R-Calif., proposed allowing states to use money from Title VI of the Elementary and Secondary Education Act to help low-income families send their children to private schools, including religious schools. Under existing law, states and local school districts used Title VI money—$310 million in fiscal 1997—for various public school programs. Under the bill, they could reserve up to 25 percent of their Title VI funds for public and private school choice programs authorized by state law.

But there were limits to the bill's appeal. In fact, the leadership bypassed committee action on the bill, apparently out of concern that it lacked the votes for approval in the Education and the Workforce Committee. Republicans tried to cast the issue as a matter of choice, saying that students from poor families ought to have access to the same education opportunities as those enjoyed by the well-to-do.

Democrats derided the legislation as an attempt to drain funds from public schools and said it would help relatively few low-income students. William L. Clay of Missouri, the Education committee's ranking Democrat, said the bill "sends a clear and chilling signal that the Republicans have declared war on public education." The administration warned that a veto was likely.

In the end, however, it was the opposition of 35 Republicans, many of them moderates, that caused the bill's defeat. One of them, Marge Roukema, R-N.J., said, "Ultimately, these vouchers will result in gutting the public school system" by shifting money from public schools to private schools. The vote was 191–228: R 187–35; D 4–192 (ND 2–140, SD 2–52); I 0–1. (Vote, p. 878)

14. CARIBBEAN TRADE

Legislation that sponsors viewed as a noncontroversial offer of equity to 26 small and friendly nations in the Caribbean turned into a showdown over U.S. trade policy. The unexpected result: House defeat of a bill (HR 2644) aimed at expanding trade preferences for key products from those countries. The vote on Nov. 4 was 182–234: R 136–83; D 46–150 (ND 32–111, SD 14–39); I 0–1. (Vote, p. 878)

Part of the opposition was the result of frustration over the mixed results of the 1993 North American Free Trade Agreement (NAFTA). Part of it was parochial concern on the part of members with industries in their districts that competed with plants in the Caribbean. But a major part of the opposition was an effort by Democrats to send a signal to President Clinton as he pressed his bid to win "fast-track" trade negotiating authority.

Supporters of the bill argued that the twenty-six nations—which had been given special status under President Ronald Reagan's 1983 economic-development program known as the Caribbean Basin Initiative (PL 98-67)—had suffered since the passage of NAFTA, because Mexican exports were given even greater benefits. The bill had been around since 1995, and the Ways and Means Committee had voted in June to make it a provision of the tax bill (HR 2014) that was moving as part of the budget reconciliation package. No controversy emerged until conference, when it was dropped at the insistence of the Senate because no committee in that chamber had considered it.

House Ways and Means Chairman Bill Archer, R-Texas, introduced the bill again Oct. 9, and it was approved by the committee by voice vote the same day. Supporters did not expect the bill to draw the opposition it did when it reached the floor Nov. 4. Some opponents argued that imports from the Caribbean countries had grown, not shrunk, since the passage of NAFTA and outpaced imports from Mexico in many sectors. Others argued that the expanded Caribbean benefits did not have as many safeguards attached as NAFTA did.

But the strongest objections came from lawmakers representing states that were home to textile industries. The imports that would have become eligible for duty-free treatment included textiles as well as finished apparel, footwear, handbags, and luggage. "HR 2644 will have a greater impact on the U.S. apparel industry and U.S. apparel workers than NAFTA ever had," warned John M. Spratt Jr., D-S.C.

15. IRS OVERHAUL

Even the most fervent supporters of overhauling the management of the Internal Revenue Service (IRS) were shocked at how swiftly the latest attack in the antitax movement took hold. By the time the vote was called, the outcome was certain. The political controversy around the IRS and its alleged abuse of taxpayers had rolled over any opposition in its path.

Congressional efforts to revamp the IRS began in June in the driest, most conventional of ways, with a sober, 190-page report issued by a bipartisan commission chaired by Sen. Bob Kerrey, D-Neb., and Rep. Rob Portman, R-Ohio. But by Nov. 5, when the House voted on an IRS restructuring bill (HR 2676), the issue had exploded. Senate Finance Committee hearings into alleged IRS abuses in September had struck a nerve nationwide. Indeed, pollsters were hearing that the IRS was one of the very few issues out of Congress that resonated with voters.

When it came time to vote on a broad package to restructure IRS management, provide new rights for taxpayers and curb additions to the tax code, almost no one on Capitol Hill wanted to be seen defending the tax collector. The tally was 426–4: R 225–0; D 200–4 (ND 146–4, SD 54–0); I 1–0. (Vote, p. 878)

The only "no" votes came from Democrat Steny H. Hoyer of Maryland, who had numerous federal employees in his suburban

Washington district, and three Ways and Means Committee Democrats: Jim McDermott of Washington and Robert T. Matsui and Pete Stark, both of California.

The administration and key House Democrats had initially opposed legislation unveiled by Kerrey and Portman to implement their commission's recommendations. They said the bills would give the private sector too much influence over the tax code, open the IRS to conflicts of interest and compromise the executive branch's authority on tax policy.

Ways and Means Committee Chairman Bill Archer, R-Texas, later added a provision shifting the burden of proof for malfeasance from the taxpayer to the IRS in tax court proceedings, a move decried by some accountants as an invitation for tax cheating and a prescription for a more intrusive IRS.

But voter sentiment was clearly against the Democrats. By the time the revised IRS bill reached the Ways and Means Committee, ranking Democrat Charles B. Rangel of New York and Minority Leader Richard A. Gephardt, D-Mo., had signed on. In an extraordinary bit of political theater, Treasury Secretary Robert E. Rubin was dispatched Oct. 21 to Capitol Hill to renounce his once-vociferous opposition, explain that he had won significant changes to the bill, and declare his support.

1. S J Res 1. Balanced-Budget Constitutional Amendment/Passage. Passage of the joint resolution to propose a constitutional amendment to balance the budget by the year 2002 or two years after ratification by three-fourths of the states, whichever is later. Rejected 66–34: R 55–0; D 11–34 (ND 6–31, SD 5–3), March 4, 1997. A two-thirds majority vote of those present and voting (67 in this case) is required to pass a joint resolution proposing an amendment to the Constitution. A "nay" was a vote in support of the president's position.

2. S 104. Interim Nuclear Waste Repository/Passage. Passage of the bill to establish an interim high-level nuclear waste repository at Yucca Mountain, Nev. The bill gives the president until March 1, 1999, to halt construction at the temporary waste site if it is deemed unsuitable as a permanent repository. The president would then have eighteen months to choose an alternate site, which Congress would have two years to approve. If an alternate is not agreed upon, construction would automatically begin at the Nevada site. Passed 65–34: R 53–2; D 12–32 (ND 8–28, SD 4–4), April 15, 1997. A "nay" was a vote in support of the president's position.

3. S Res 75. Chemical Weapons Treaty/Adoption. Adoption of the resolution of ratification of the treaty to prohibit development, production, acquisition, stockpiling, transfer, or use of chemical weapons. Adopted 74–26: R 29–26; D 45–0 (ND 37–0, SD 8–0), April 24, 1997. A two-thirds majority of those present and voting (67 in this case) is required for adoption of resolutions of ratification. A "yea" was a vote in support of the president's position.

4. S 4. Compensatory Time, Flexible Credit/Cloture. Motion to invoke cloture (thus limiting debate) on the bill to amend the 1938 Fair Labor Standards Act to allow private-sector employees to choose compensatory time off or flexible hour programs instead of overtime pay. Motion rejected 53–47: R 53–2; D 0–45 (ND 0–37, SD 0–8), May 15, 1997. Three-fifths of the total Senate (60) is required to invoke cloture.

5. HR 1122. Abortion Procedure Ban/Passage. Passage of the bill to impose penalties on doctors who perform certain abortion procedures, in which the person performing the abortion partially delivers the fetus before completing the abortion. An exception would be granted if the procedure was necessary to save the life of the woman. The bill was amended to clarify the definition of the procedure and to allow an accused doctor a hearing before a state medical board before trial. Passed 64–36: R 51–4; D 13–32 (ND 9–28, SD 4–4), May 20, 1997. A "nay" was a vote in support of the president's position.

6. H Con Res 84. Fiscal 1998 Budget Resolution/Adoption. Adoption of the concurrent resolution to adopt a five-year budget plan that would balance the budget by 2002 by cutting projected spending by approximately $320 billion and cutting taxes by a net $85 billion. Projected spending cuts would include reductions of $115 billion in Medicare, $13.6 billion in Medicaid, and $138 billion in discretionary spending. The resolution sets binding levels for the fiscal year ending Sept. 30, 1998: budget authority, $1,702.0 billion; outlays, $1,692.3 billion; revenues, $1,601.8 billion; deficit, $90.5 billion. Adopted 78–22: R 41–14; D 37–8 (ND 31–6, SD 6–2), May 23, 1997. (Before passage the Senate struck all after the enacting clause and inserted the text of S Con Res 27 as amended.) A "yea" was a vote in support of the president's position.

7. S 947. Fiscal 1998 Budget Reconciliation—Spending/Medicare Means Testing. Roth, R-Del., motion to table (kill) the Kennedy, D-Mass., amendment to strike the section that introduces a means-based formula to determine insurance premiums under Medicare Part B. Motion agreed to 70–30: R 49–6; D 21–24 (ND 15–22, SD 6–2), June 24, 1997.

8. HR 2107. Fiscal 1998 Interior Appropriations/NEA Funding. Hutchison, R-Texas, amendment to establish a $100 million state block grant program for the arts. The National Endowment for the Arts would be allowed to earmark 25 percent of the funds for major arts organizations. Rejected 39–61: R 39–16; D 0–45 (ND 0–37, SD 0–8), Sept. 18, 1997. A "nay" was a vote in support of the president's position.

9. S 25. Campaign Finance Overhaul/Cloture. Motion to invoke cloture (thus limiting debate) on the bill to revise financing of federal political campaigns. Motion rejected 53–47: R 8–47; D 45–0 (ND 37–0, SD 8–0), Oct. 7, 1997. Three-fifths of the total Senate (60) is required to invoke cloture. A "yea" was a vote in support of the president's position.

10. S 1292. Line-Item Veto Disapproval/Passage. Passage of the bill to disapprove President Clinton's line-item vetoes of thirty-six projects, totaling $287 million, in the fiscal 1998 military construction appropriations bill (HR 2016—PL 105-45). Passed 69–30: R 42–12; D 27–18 (ND 24–13, SD 3–5), Oct. 30, 1997. A "nay" was a vote in support of the president's position.

11. HR 2646. Education Savings Accounts/Cloture. Motion to invoke cloture (thus limiting debate) on the bill allowing parents to invest up to $2,500 annually in savings accounts designated for education-related expenses. Withdrawals of both principal and interest from such accounts could be made without incurring tax liability. Motion rejected 56–41: R 54–1; D 2–40 (ND 2–32, SD 0–8), Oct. 31, 1997. Three-fifths of the total Senate (60) is required to invoke cloture.

12. S 1269. Fast Track/Cloture. Motion to invoke cloture (thus limiting debate) on the motion to proceed to the bill allowing the president to submit bills implementing trade pacts to Congress under expedited review procedures requiring up-or-down votes without amendments. Motion agreed to 69–31: R 43–12; D 26–19 (ND 20–17, SD 6–2), Nov. 4, 1997. Three-fifths of the total Senate (60) is required to invoke cloture.

KEY

		Democrats	*Republicans*	
Y	Voted for ("yea")		–	Announced against
N	Voted against ("nay")		P	Voted "present"
+	Announced for		C	Voted "present" to avoid possible conflict of interest
#	Paired for		?	Did not vote or otherwise make a position known
X	Paired against			

ND Northern Democrats
SD Southern Democrats
Southern states – Ala., Ark., Fla., Ga., Ky., La., Miss., N.C., Okla., S.C., Tenn., Texas, Va.

Senate Key Votes	1	2	3	4	5	6	7	8	9	10	11	12
ALABAMA												
Sessions	Y	Y	N	Y	Y	Y	Y	Y	N	N	Y	Y
Shelby	Y	Y	N	Y	Y	Y	Y	Y	N	Y	Y	N
ALASKA												
Murkowski	Y	Y	Y	Y	Y	Y	Y	Y	N	Y	Y	Y
Stevens	Y	Y	Y	Y	Y	Y	Y	N	N	Y	Y	N
ARIZONA												
Kyl	Y	Y	N	Y	Y	N	Y	Y	N	N	Y	Y
McCain	Y	Y	Y	Y	Y	Y	N	Y	Y	N	Y	Y
ARKANSAS												
Hutchinson	Y	Y	N	Y	Y	Y	Y	Y	Y	N	Y	Y
Bumpers	N	N	Y	N	N	N	Y	N	Y	N	N	Y
CALIFORNIA												
Boxer	N	N	Y	N	N	Y	N	N	Y	Y	N	N
Feinstein	N	N	Y	N	N	Y	Y	N	Y	Y	N	N
COLORADO												
Allard	Y	Y	Y	Y	Y	N	Y	Y	N	Y	Y	Y
Campbell	Y	N	N	Y	Y	Y	Y	N	N	Y	Y	N
CONNECTICUT												
Dodd	N	N	Y	N	N	Y	Y	N	Y	N	N	Y
Lieberman	N	N	Y	N	N	Y	Y	N	Y	N	Y	Y
DELAWARE												
Roth	Y	Y	Y	Y	Y	Y	Y	N	Y	Y	Y	Y
Biden	Y	N	Y	N	Y	Y	N	N	Y	Y	N	Y
FLORIDA												
Mack	Y	Y	N	Y	Y	Y	Y	Y	N	Y	Y	Y
Graham	Y	Y	Y	N	N	N	Y	N	Y	Y	Y	Y
GEORGIA												
Coverdell	Y	Y	N	Y	Y	Y	N	Y	N	Y	Y	Y
Cleland	Y	Y	Y	N	N	N	N	N	Y	Y	N	Y
HAWAII												
Akaka	N	N	Y	N	N	Y	N	N	Y	Y	N	Y
Inouye	N	N	Y	N	N	Y	N	N	Y	Y	N	Y
IDAHO												
Craig	Y	Y	N	Y	Y	Y	Y	Y	N	Y	Y	Y
Kempthorne	Y	Y	N	Y	Y	Y	Y	Y	N	Y	Y	Y
ILLINOIS												
Durbin	N	N	Y	N	N	Y	N	N	Y	N	N	N
Moseley-Braun	Y	Y	Y	N	N	Y	N	N	Y	Y	N	N
INDIANA												
Coats	Y	N	Y	Y	Y	N	Y	Y	N	?	Y	Y
Lugar	Y	Y	Y	Y	Y	Y	Y	Y	N	Y	Y	Y
IOWA												
Grassley	Y	Y	N	Y	Y	Y	Y	Y	N	N	Y	Y
Harkin	Y	Y	Y	N	N	Y	Y	N	Y	Y	N	N
KANSAS												
Brownback	Y	Y	N	Y	Y	Y	Y	Y	N	Y	Y	Y
Roberts	Y	Y	Y	Y	Y	Y	Y	Y	N	Y	Y	Y
KENTUCKY												
McConnell	Y	Y	Y	Y	Y	Y	Y	Y	N	Y	Y	Y
Ford	N	N	Y	N	Y	Y	N	N	Y	Y	N	N
LOUISIANA												
Breaux	Y	N	Y	N	Y	Y	Y	N	Y	N	N	Y
Landrieu	Y	N	Y	N	Y	Y	Y	N	Y	N	N	Y
MAINE												
Collins	Y	Y	Y	Y	N	Y	Y	N	Y	Y	Y	Y
Snowe	Y	Y	Y	Y	N	Y	N	N	Y	Y	Y	N
MARYLAND												
Mikulski	N	N	Y	N	N	Y	N	N	Y	Y	N	N
Sarbanes	N	N	Y	N	N	N	N	N	Y	Y	N	N
MASSACHUSETTS												
Kennedy	N	N	Y	N	N	N	N	N	Y	Y	N	N
Kerry	N	N	Y	N	N	N	Y	N	Y	N	N	Y
MICHIGAN												
Abraham	Y	Y	Y	Y	Y	Y	N	Y	N	Y	Y	Y
Levin	N	Y	Y	N	N	Y	Y	N	Y	Y	N	N
MINNESOTA												
Grams	Y	Y	N	Y	Y	N	Y	Y	N	N	Y	Y
Wellstone	N	N	Y	N	N	N	N	N	Y	N	-	N
MISSISSIPPI												
Cochran	Y	Y	Y	Y	Y	Y	Y	N	N	Y	Y	Y
Lott	Y	Y	Y	Y	Y	Y	Y	Y	N	Y	Y	Y
MISSOURI												
Ashcroft	Y	Y	N	Y	Y	N	Y	Y	N	N	Y	Y
Bond	Y	Y	N	Y	Y	Y	Y	Y	N	Y	Y	Y
MONTANA												
Burns	Y	Y	N	Y	Y	Y	Y	Y	N	Y	Y	N
Baucus	Y	N	Y	N	N	Y	Y	N	Y	Y	-	Y
NEBRASKA												
Hagel	Y	Y	Y	Y	Y	Y	Y	Y	N	Y	Y	Y
Kerrey	N	N	Y	N	N	Y	Y	N	Y	N	N	Y
NEVADA												
Bryan	Y	N	Y	N	N	Y	Y	N	Y	N	N	Y
Reid	N	N	Y	N	Y	Y	N	N	Y	Y	N	N
NEW HAMPSHIRE												
Gregg	Y	Y	Y	Y	Y	Y	Y	N	Y	Y	Y	Y
Smith	Y	Y	N	Y	Y	N	Y	Y	N	Y	Y	N
NEW JERSEY												
Lautenberg	N	N	N	N	N	Y	N	N	Y	Y	N	Y
Torricelli	N	N	Y	N	N	Y	N	N	Y	Y	N	N
NEW MEXICO												
Domenici	Y	Y	Y	Y	Y	Y	Y	N	Y	Y	Y	Y
Bingaman	N	N	Y	N	N	Y	Y	N	Y	Y	N	Y
NEW YORK												
D'Amato	Y	Y	Y	N	Y	Y	N	N	N	Y	Y	Y
Moynihan	N	N	Y	N	Y	Y	Y	N	Y	Y	N	Y
NORTH CAROLINA												
Faircloth	Y	Y	N	Y	Y	N	Y	Y	N	Y	Y	N
Helms	Y	Y	N	Y	Y	N	Y	Y	N	Y	Y	Y
NORTH DAKOTA												
Conrad	N	N	Y	N	N	Y	N	N	Y	N	N	N
Dorgan	N	N	Y	N	N	Y	N	N	Y	Y	N	N
OHIO												
DeWine	Y	Y	Y	Y	Y	Y	Y	N	Y	Y	Y	Y
Glenn	N	N	Y	N	N	Y	Y	N	Y	Y	N	Y
OKLAHOMA												
Inhofe	Y	Y	N	Y	Y	N	Y	Y	N	Y	Y	N
Nickles	Y	Y	N	Y	Y	Y	Y	Y	N	N	Y	Y
OREGON												
Smith	Y	Y	Y	Y	Y	Y	Y	N	Y	Y	Y	Y
Wyden	N	Y	Y	N	N	Y	N	N	Y	N	N	Y
PENNSYLVANIA												
Santorum	Y	Y	Y	Y	Y	Y	Y	Y	N	Y	Y	N
Specter	Y	Y	Y	N	Y	N	N	N	Y	Y	Y	N
RHODE ISLAND												
Chafee	Y	Y	Y	Y	N	Y	Y	N	Y	Y	N	Y
Reed	N	N	Y	N	N	N	N	N	Y	Y	N	N
SOUTH CAROLINA												
Thurmond	Y	Y	N	Y	Y	Y	Y	Y	N	N	Y	N
Hollings	N	Y	Y	N	Y	N	Y	N	Y	N	N	N
SOUTH DAKOTA												
Daschle	N	N	Y	N	N	Y	N	N	Y	N	N	Y
Johnson	N	Y	Y	N	Y	Y	N	N	Y	N	N	Y
TENNESSEE												
Frist	Y	Y	Y	Y	Y	Y	Y	N	Y	Y	Y	Y
Thompson	Y	Y	N	Y	Y	N	Y	Y	Y	Y	Y	Y
TEXAS												
Gramm	Y	Y	N	Y	Y	N	Y	Y	N	N	Y	Y
Hutchison	Y	Y	N	Y	Y	Y	Y	Y	N	Y	Y	Y
UTAH												
Bennett	Y	Y	N	Y	Y	Y	Y	N	Y	Y	Y	Y
Hatch	Y	Y	Y	Y	Y	Y	Y	N	Y	Y	Y	Y
VERMONT												
Jeffords	Y	Y	Y	Y	N	Y	Y	N	Y	Y	Y	Y
Leahy	N	Y	Y	N	Y	Y	N	N	Y	Y	N	Y
VIRGINIA												
Warner	Y	Y	Y	Y	Y	Y	Y	N	N	Y	Y	Y
Robb	Y	Y	Y	N	N	Y	Y	N	Y	N	N	Y
WASHINGTON												
Gorton	Y	Y	Y	Y	Y	Y	Y	N	Y	Y	Y	Y
Murray	N	Y	Y	N	N	Y	N	N	Y	Y	N	Y
WEST VIRGINIA												
Byrd	N	N	Y	N	Y	Y	N	N	Y	Y	N	N
Rockefeller	N	?	Y	N	N	Y	N	N	Y	Y	?	Y
WISCONSIN												
Feingold	N	N	Y	N	N	Y	Y	N	Y	N	N	N
Kohl	Y	Y	Y	N	N	Y	Y	N	Y	N	N	Y
WYOMING												
Enzi	Y	Y	Y	Y	Y	N	Y	Y	N	Y	Y	N
Thomas	Y	Y	Y	Y	Y	N	Y	Y	N	N	Y	Y

1. Election of the Speaker. Nomination of Newt Gingrich, R-Ga., and Richard A. Gephardt, D-Mo., for Speaker of the House of Representatives for the 105th Congress. Gingrich elected 216–205, with four Republican votes cast for others: R 216–0; D 0–204 (ND 0–150, SD 0–54); I 0–1, Jan. 7, 1997. A "Y" on the chart represents a vote for Gingrich; an "N" represents a vote for Gephardt, except where footnoted.

2. H Res 31. Reprimand of Rep. Newt Gingrich/Adoption. Adoption of the resolution to adopt the Jan. 17, 1997, report of the ethics committee recommending that Speaker Newt Gingrich, R-Ga., be reprimanded and that he pay $300,000 to the House. Adopted 395–28: R 196–26; D 198–2 (ND 147–0, SD 51–2); I 1–0, Jan. 21, 1997.

3. HR 1122. Abortion Procedure Ban/Passage. Passage of the bill to impose penalties on doctors who perform certain abortion procedures, in which the person performing the abortion partially delivers the fetus before completing the abortion. An exception would be granted if the procedure was necessary to save the life of the woman. Passed 295–136: R 218–8; D 77–127 (ND 51–99, SD 26–28); I 0–1, March 20, 1997. A "nay" was a vote in support of the president's position.

4. HR 478. Endangered Species Act Flood Waivers/Project Exemption Limitation. Boehlert, R-N.Y., substitute amendment to provide waivers of the Endangered Species Act consultation regulations for repair or replacement of flood control facilities in counties declared federal disaster areas through 1998 and waive the requirements for any project to repair a flood control facility that presents a substantial threat to human lives and property. Adopted 227–196: R 54–169; D 172–27 (ND 137–9, SD 35–18); I 1–0, May 7, 1997.

5. HR 2. Public Housing System Overhaul/Passage. Passage of the bill to replace federal low-income housing programs with block grants to local authorities, eliminate most federal regulations affecting low-income housing assistance, and change tenant income, employment, and eligibility requirements. Passed 293–132: R 222–1; D 71–130 (ND 43–104, SD 28–26); I 0–1, May 14, 1997. A "nay" was a vote in support of the president's position.

6. H Con Res 84. Fiscal 1998 Budget Resolution/Shuster Substitute. Shuster, R-Pa., substitute amendment to balance the budget by 2002 by increasing outlays for federal highway and mass transit programs to $137 billion, offset by an across-the-board reduction of 0.39 percent in discretionary spending and tax cuts to be phased in over four years, beginning in fiscal 1999. Rejected 214–216: R 58–168; D 155–48 (ND 118–32, SD 37–16); I 1–0, May 21, 1997 (in the session that began and the *Congressional Record* dated May 20). A "nay" was a vote in support of the president's position.

7. H Con Res 84. Fiscal 1998 Budget Resolution/Adoption. Adoption of the concurrent resolution to adopt a five-year budget plan that would balance the budget by 2002 by cutting projected spending by approximately $280 billion and cutting taxes by $85 billion, for a net deficit reduction of $204.3 billion. Projected spending cuts would include reductions of $115 billion in Medicare, $13.6 billion in Medicaid, and approximately $140 billion in discretionary spending. The resolution sets binding levels for the fiscal year ending Sept. 30, 1998: budget authority, $1,702.2 billion; outlays, $1,692.2 billion; revenues, $1,601.8 billion; deficit, $90.4 billion. Adopted 333–99: R 201–26; D 132–72 (ND 90–60, SD 42–12); I 0–1, May 21, 1997 (in the session that began and the *Congressional Record* dated May 20). A "yea" was a vote in support of the president's position.

8. HR 1119. Fiscal 1998 Defense Authorization/Bosnia Troop Withdrawal Substitute. Hilleary, R-Tenn., substitute amendment to the Buyer, R-Ind., amendment to prohibit the obligation of funds for ground deployment of U.S. troops in Bosnia after Dec. 31, 1997, unless the president submits a report to Congress requesting an extension of funding. The Hilleary amendment would require the extension to be approved by a joint resolution of Congress and would permit deployment for an additional 180 days or until June 30, 1998. Rejected 196–231: R 174–49; D 21–182 (ND 15–133, SD 6–49); I 1–0, June 24, 1997. A "nay" was a vote in support of the president's position.

9. HR 2107. Fiscal 1998 Interior Appropriations/Rule. Adoption of the rule (H Res 181) to provide for House floor consideration of the bill to provide $13 billion in new budget authority for the Department of the Interior and related agencies for fiscal 1998. The rule did not waive a point of order against the $10 million of funding in the bill for the National Endowment for

the Arts because its authorization had expired. Adopted 217–216: R 212–15; D 5–200 (ND 2–148, SD 3–52); I 0–1, July 10, 1997.

10. HR 2159. Fiscal 1998 Foreign Operations Appropriations/Overseas Abortion Funding. Gilman, R-N.Y., amendment to the Smith, R-N.J., amendment to allow organizations that do not promote abortion as a method of family planning but use their own funds to perform abortions to remain eligible for international family planning funding. The amendment also would prohibit funding for lobbying for or against abortion, and for the U.N. Population Fund unless the president certifies that the organization has ceased all activity in China. Rejected 210–218: R 38–185; D 171–33 (ND 125–26, SD 46–7); I 1–0, Sept. 4, 1997.

11. HR 2378. Fiscal 1998 Treasury-Postal Service Appropriations/Previous Question. Hoyer, D-Md., motion to order the previous question (thus ending debate and the possibility of amendment) on the Hoyer motion to instruct conferees to increase funding for the Exploited Child Unit of the National Center for Missing and Exploited Children. A "nay" vote would have allowed Smith, R-Wash., to offer an amendment to block a cost of living adjustment for members of Congress. Motion agreed to 229–199: R 114–110; D 115–88 (ND 88–62, SD 27–26); I 0–1, Sept. 24, 1997.

12. HR 1534. Private Property Rights/Passage. Passage of the bill to establish guidelines for allowing private property owners to appeal local, state, and federal land use decisions in federal courts. The bill would require federal courts to consider all cases qualifying as "takings" under the Fifth Amendment to the Constitution. Passed 248–178: R 193–30; D 55–147 (ND 25–124, SD 30–23); I 0–1, Oct. 22, 1997. A "nay" was a vote in support of the president's position.

13. HR 2746. Private School Vouchers/Passage. Passage of the bill to authorize states to use certain federal elementary and secondary education funds to provide scholarships to low-income families to send their children to public, private, or religious schools. Rejected 191–228: R 187–35; D 4–192 (ND 2–140, SD 2–52); I 0–1, Nov. 4, 1997. A "nay" was a vote in support of the president's position.

14. HR 2644. Caribbean and Central American Trade/Passage. Crane, R-Ill., motion to suspend the rules and pass the bill to provide Caribbean and Central American countries duty-free trade benefits on certain products similar to those accorded to Mexico under the North American Free Trade Agreement. Motion rejected 182–234: R 136–83; D 46–150 (ND 32–111, SD 14–39); I 0–1, Nov. 4, 1997.

15. HR 2676. Internal Revenue Service Overhaul/Passage. Passage of the bill to restructure the management of the Internal Revenue Service by establishing an oversight board to oversee the agency's operations. The bill would shift the burden of proof from the taxpayer to the IRS in cases before the U.S. Tax Court. Passed 426–4: R 225–0; D 200–4 (ND 146–4, SD 54–0); I 1–0, Nov. 5, 1997. A "yea" was a vote in support of the president's position.

KEY

	Democrats	*Republicans*	Independent
Y	Voted for ("yea")		— Announced against
N	Voted against ("nay")		P Voted "present"
+	Announced for		C Voted "present" to avoid possible conflict of interest
#	Paired for		? Did not vote or otherwise make a position known
X	Paired against		

ND Northern Democrats
SD Southern Democrats
Southern states – Ala., Ark., Fla., Ga., Ky., La., Miss., N.C., Okla., S.C., Tenn., Texas, Va.

House Key Votes	1	2	3	4	5	6	7	8	9	10	11	12	13	14	15
ALABAMA															
1 Callahan	Y	N	N	N	Y	N	Y	N	N	N	Y	Y	Y	Y	Y
2 Everett	Y	Y	Y	N	Y	N	Y	Y	Y	N	N	Y	Y	N	Y
3 Riley	Y	Y	Y	N	Y	N	Y	Y	Y	N	N	Y	#	#	+
4 Aderholt	Y	Y	Y	N	Y	N	Y	Y	Y	N	N	Y	Y	N	Y
5 Cramer	N	Y	N	N	Y	Y	Y	N	N	Y	N	Y	N	N	Y
6 Bachus	Y	Y	Y	N	Y	Y	Y	Y	Y	N	Y	Y	Y	Y	Y
7 Hilliard	N	N	N	Y	N	Y	N	N	N	Y	Y	Y	N	N	Y
ALASKA															
AL *Young*	Y	N	Y	N	Y	Y	Y	Y	Y	N	Y	Y	Y	N	Y
ARIZONA															
1 *Salmon*	Y	Y	Y	N	Y	N	Y	N	Y	N	N	Y	Y	Y	Y
2 Pastor	Y	Y	N	Y	N	Y	Y	N	N	Y	N	N	N	Y	Y
3 *Stump*	Y	N	Y	N	Y	N	Y	Y	Y	N	N	Y	Y	N	Y
4 *Shadegg*	Y	Y	Y	N	Y	N	N	Y	Y	N	N	Y	Y	N	Y
5 *Kolbe*	Y	?	N	N	Y	N	Y	N	Y	Y	Y	Y	Y	Y	Y
6 *Hayworth*	Y	Y	Y	N	Y	N	Y	Y	Y	N	N	Y	Y	Y	Y
ARKANSAS															
1 Berry	N	Y	N	N	Y	Y	Y	Y	N	Y	N	Y	N	Y	Y
2 Snyder	N	Y	N	Y	Y	N	Y	N	N	Y	N	N	N	N	Y
3 *Hutchinson*	Y	Y	Y	N	Y	Y	Y	Y	Y	N	N	Y	N	N	Y
4 *Dickey*	Y	Y	Y	N	Y	Y	Y	Y	Y	N	Y	Y	Y	N	Y
CALIFORNIA															
1 *Riggs*	Y	Y	Y	N	Y	Y	Y	Y	Y	N	N	Y	Y	N	Y
2 *Herger*	Y	N	Y	N	Y	N	Y	Y	Y	N	N	Y	Y	Y	Y
3 Fazio	N	Y	N	Y	N	N	Y	N	N	Y	Y	Y	N	Y	Y
4 *Doolittle*	Y	N	Y	N	Y	N	Y	Y	Y	N	N	Y	Y	N	Y
5 Matsui	N	Y	N	Y	Y	Y	Y	N	N	Y	N	Y	N	N	N
6 Woolsey	N	Y	N	Y	N	Y	Y	N	N	Y	N	N	N	N	Y
7 Miller	N	Y	N	Y	Y	Y	N	N	N	Y	N	Y	N	N	Y
8 Pelosi	N	Y	N	Y	Y	Y	N	N	N	Y	Y	N	N	Y	Y
9 Dellums	N	Y	N	Y	Y	Y	N	N	N	Y	N	Y	N	N	Y
10 Tauscher	N	Y	N	Y	Y	Y	Y	N	N	Y	N	N	N	N	Y
11 *Pombo*	Y	Y	N	N	Y	N	N	Y	Y	N	Y	Y	Y	N	Y
12 Lantos	N	Y	N	Y	N	Y	Y	N	N	Y	Y	?	N	N	Y
13 Stark	N	Y	N	Y	N	Y	N	N	N	Y	Y	N	N	N	N
14 Eshoo	N	Y	N	Y	N	Y	Y	N	N	Y	N	N	N	N	Y
15 *Campbell*[1]	N	Y	N	N	Y	Y	Y	Y	Y	Y	Y	N	Y	Y	Y
16 Lofgren	N	Y	N	Y	N	Y	Y	N	N	Y	N	N	N	N	Y
17 Farr	N	Y	N	Y	N	Y	Y	N	N	Y	N	N	N	N	Y
18 Condit	N	Y	N	Y	N	Y	Y	Y	N	Y	Y	Y	N	N	Y
19 *Radanovich*	Y	Y	Y	N	Y	N	Y	Y	Y	N	N	Y	Y	N	Y
20 Dooley	N	Y	N	Y	Y	N	Y	N	N	Y	Y	Y	N	Y	Y
21 *Thomas*	Y	Y	Y	N	Y	N	Y	Y	Y	Y	Y	Y	Y	Y	Y
22 Capps[2]	N	Y	N	Y	Y	Y	Y	N	N	Y	N	N			
23 *Gallegly*	Y	Y	Y	N	Y	Y	Y	Y	Y	N	Y	Y	Y	N	Y
24 Sherman	N	Y	N	Y	N	Y	Y	N	N	Y	N	N	N	N	Y
25 *McKeon*	Y	N	Y	N	Y	N	Y	Y	Y	N	N	Y	Y	Y	Y
26 Berman	N	Y	N	Y	N	N	N	N	N	Y	Y	N	N	N	Y
27 *Rogan*	Y	Y	Y	N	Y	N	Y	Y	Y	N	N	Y	Y	N	Y
28 *Dreier*	Y	Y	Y	N	Y	N	Y	Y	Y	N	N	Y	Y	N	Y
29 Waxman	N	Y	N	Y	N	N	N	N	N	Y	Y	N	N	N	Y
30 Becerra	N	Y	N	+	N	Y	N	N	N	Y	N	N	N	N	Y
31 Martinez	N	Y	N	Y	N	Y	Y	N	N	Y	N	N	N	N	Y
32 Dixon	N	Y	N	Y	N	Y	N	N	N	Y	N	N	N	N	Y
33 Roybal-Allard	N	Y	N	Y	N	Y	N	N	N	Y	N	N	N	N	Y
34 Torres	N	Y	N	Y	N	Y	Y	?	N	Y	N	N	N	N	Y
35 Waters	N	P	N	Y	N	Y	N	N	N	Y	N	N	N	N	Y
36 Harman	N	Y	N	Y	N	N	Y	N	N	Y	Y	Y	N	Y	Y
37 Millender-McD.	N	Y	N	Y	N	Y	N	N	N	Y	N	N	N	N	Y
38 *Horn*	Y	Y	Y	N	Y	Y	Y	Y	Y	N	N	Y	N	Y	Y
39 *Royce*	Y	Y	Y	N	Y	N	Y	Y	Y	N	N	Y	Y	Y	Y
40 *Lewis*	Y	N	Y	N	Y	Y	Y	Y	Y	N	N	Y	Y	Y	Y
41 *Kim*	Y	Y	Y	N	Y	N	Y	Y	Y	N	N	Y	Y	N	Y
42 Brown	N	Y	N	Y	N	Y	N	N	N	Y	N	N	N	N	Y
43 *Calvert*	Y	Y	Y	N	Y	N	Y	Y	Y	N	N	Y	Y	N	Y
44 *Bono*	Y	Y	Y	N	Y	N	Y	Y	Y	N	N	Y	Y	N	Y
45 *Rohrabacher*	Y	Y	Y	N	Y	N	N	Y	Y	N	N	Y	Y	N	Y

House Key Votes	1	2	3	4	5	6	7	8	9	10	11	12	13	14	15
46 Sanchez	N	Y	N	Y	Y	Y	Y	N	N	Y	N	N	N	Y	Y
47 *Cox*	Y	Y	Y	N	Y	N	N	?	N	N	Y	Y	Y	Y	Y
48 *Packard*	Y	N	Y	N	Y	N	Y	Y	Y	N	N	Y	Y	Y	Y
49 *Bilbray*	Y	Y	Y	N	Y	N	Y	Y	Y	N	Y	Y	Y	Y	Y
50 Filner	N	Y	N	#	N	Y	N	N	N	Y	N	N	Y	Y	Y
51 *Cunningham*	Y	Y	Y	N	Y	N	Y	Y	Y	N	Y	Y	Y	Y	Y
52 *Hunter*	Y	N	Y	N	Y	N	N	N	Y	N	?	Y	Y	N	Y
COLORADO															
1 DeGette	N	Y	N	Y	Y	N	N	N	N	Y	N	Y	N	N	Y
2 Skaggs	N	Y	N	Y	Y	N	Y	N	N	Y	Y	N	N	Y	Y
3 *McInnis*	Y	Y	Y	N	Y	N	Y	Y	Y	N	N	Y	Y	N	Y
4 *Schaffer*	Y	Y	Y	N	Y	N	Y	Y	Y	N	N	Y	Y	N	Y
5 *Hefley*	Y	Y	Y	N	Y	N	Y	Y	Y	N	N	Y	Y	N	Y
6 *Schaefer*	Y	Y	Y	N	Y	N	Y	Y	Y	N	N	Y	Y	N	Y
CONNECTICUT															
1 Kennelly	N	Y	N	Y	N	Y	Y	N	N	Y	N	N	N	Y	Y
2 Gejdenson	N	Y	N	Y	N	Y	Y	N	N	Y	N	N	N	N	Y
3 DeLauro	N	Y	N	Y	N	Y	Y	N	N	Y	N	N	N	N	Y
4 *Shays*	Y	Y	Y	Y	Y	N	Y	Y	Y	Y	N	Y	N	Y	Y
5 Maloney	N	Y	Y	Y	N	Y	Y	N	N	Y	N	N	N	Y	Y
6 *Johnson*	Y	Y	N	Y	Y	N	Y	Y	Y	Y	N	Y	N	Y	Y
DELAWARE															
AL *Castle*	Y	Y	Y	Y	Y	N	Y	N	N	Y	N	Y	N	Y	Y
FLORIDA															
1 *Scarborough*	Y	Y	Y	N	Y	N	N	Y	Y	N	Y	Y	Y	N	Y
2 Boyd	N	Y	N	N	Y	Y	Y	N	N	Y	N	Y	N	N	Y
3 Brown	N	Y	N	Y	N	Y	N	N	N	Y	N	N	N	N	Y
4 *Fowler*	Y	Y	Y	N	Y	N	Y	Y	Y	N	N	Y	Y	Y	Y
5 Thurman	N	Y	N	Y	N	N	Y	N	N	Y	N	Y	N	N	Y
6 *Stearns*	Y	Y	Y	N	Y	N	Y	Y	Y	N	N	Y	Y	N	Y
7 *Mica*	Y	N	Y	N	Y	Y	Y	Y	Y	N	N	Y	Y	Y	Y
8 *McCollum*	Y	Y	Y	N	Y	N	Y	Y	Y	N	N	Y	Y	Y	Y
9 *Bilirakis*	Y	Y	Y	N	Y	N	Y	Y	Y	N	N	Y	Y	N	Y
10 *Young*	Y	Y	Y	N	Y	N	Y	Y	Y	N	N	Y	Y	Y	Y
11 Davis	N	Y	Y	Y	N	Y	Y	N	N	Y	N	N	N	Y	Y
12 *Canady*	Y	Y	Y	N	Y	N	Y	Y	Y	N	N	Y	Y	N	Y
13 *Miller*	Y	Y	Y	N	Y	N	Y	Y	Y	N	N	Y	Y	Y	Y
14 *Goss*	Y	Y	Y	N	Y	N	Y	Y	Y	N	N	Y	Y	Y	Y
15 *Weldon*	Y	Y	Y	N	Y	N	N	+	Y	N	N	Y	Y	Y	Y
16 *Foley*	Y	Y	Y	X	N	Y	Y	Y	Y	Y	Y	Y	Y	Y	Y
17 Meek	N	Y	N	Y	N	Y	N	N	N	Y	N	N	N	N	Y
18 *Ros-Lehtinen*	Y	Y	Y	Y	N	Y	Y	Y	N	Y	N	Y	Y	Y	Y
19 Wexler	N	Y	N	Y	Y	Y	Y	N	N	Y	N	Y	N	Y	Y
20 Deutsch	N	Y	N	Y	Y	Y	Y	N	N	Y	N	Y	N	Y	Y
21 *Diaz-Balart*	Y	Y	Y	Y	N	Y	Y	Y	N	Y	N	Y	Y	Y	Y
22 *Shaw*	Y	Y	Y	N	Y	N	Y	Y	Y	N	Y	Y	Y	Y	Y
23 Hastings	N	P	N	Y	N	Y	N	N	N	Y	?	N	N	N	Y
GEORGIA															
1 *Kingston*	Y	Y	Y	N	Y	N	Y	Y	Y	N	Y	Y	Y	N	Y
2 Bishop	N	Y	N	N	N	Y	Y	N	N	Y	Y	Y	Y	N	Y
3 *Collins*	Y	Y	Y	N	Y	N	Y	Y	Y	N	Y	Y	Y	N	Y
4 McKinney	N	Y	N	?	N	Y	N	N	N	Y	N	Y	N	N	Y
5 Lewis	N	Y	N	Y	N	Y	N	N	N	Y	N	Y	N	N	Y
6 *Gingrich*[3]		Y			N	Y	Y		Y		Y	Y	Y		Y
7 *Barr*	Y	N	Y	N	Y	N	Y	Y	Y	N	Y	Y	Y	N	Y
8 *Chambliss*	Y	Y	Y	N	Y	N	Y	Y	Y	N	N	?	Y	N	Y
9 *Deal*	Y	Y	Y	N	Y	N	Y	Y	Y	N	N	Y	Y	N	Y
10 *Norwood*	Y	Y	Y	N	Y	N	Y	Y	Y	N	N	Y	Y	N	Y
11 *Linder*	Y	Y	Y	N	Y	N	Y	Y	Y	N	N	Y	Y	N	Y
HAWAII															
1 Abercrombie	N	P	N	Y	N	Y	N	Y	N	Y	N	N	N	N	Y
2 Mink	N	Y	N	Y	N	Y	N	Y	N	Y	N	N	N	N	Y
IDAHO															
1 *Chenoweth*	Y	Y	Y	N	Y	N	N	Y	Y	N	N	Y	Y	N	Y
2 *Crapo*	Y	Y	Y	N	Y	N	N	Y	N	N	Y	Y	Y	N	Y
ILLINOIS															
1 Rush	N	Y	N	Y	Y	N	N	N	N	Y	N	N	N	N	Y
2 Jackson	N	Y	N	Y	N	Y	N	N	N	Y	N	N	N	N	Y
3 Lipinski	N	Y	N	Y	Y	N	Y	N	N	Y	N	Y	N	N	Y
4 Gutierrez	N	Y	N	Y	N	Y	Y	N	N	Y	N	N	N	N	Y
5 Blagojevich	N	Y	N	Y	N	Y	Y	N	N	Y	N	N	N	N	Y
6 *Hyde*	Y	Y	Y	N	Y	N	Y	Y	Y	N	N	Y	Y	N	Y
7 Davis	N	Y	N	Y	N	Y	N	N	N	Y	N	N	N	N	Y
8 *Crane*	Y	Y	Y	N	Y	N	Y	Y	Y	N	N	Y	Y	N	Y
9 Yates	N	Y	N	Y	N	?	X	?	N	Y	N	N	N	N	Y
10 *Porter*	Y	Y	Y	Y	Y	N	Y	N	Y	Y	N	Y	N	X	Y
11 *Weller*	Y	Y	Y	N	Y	N	Y	Y	Y	N	N	Y	Y	Y	Y
12 Costello	N	Y	N	Y	Y	N	Y	N	N	Y	N	Y	N	N	Y
13 *Fawell*	Y	Y	Y	Y	Y	N	Y	Y	Y	Y	N	Y	N	?	Y
14 *Hastert*	Y	Y	Y	N	Y	N	Y	Y	Y	N	N	Y	Y	Y	Y

House Key Votes	1	2	3	4	5	6	7	8	9	10	11	12	13	14	15
15 *Ewing*	Y	Y	Y	N	Y	N	Y	Y	Y	N	Y	N	Y	Y	Y
16 *Manzullo*	Y	Y	Y	N	Y	Y	Y	Y	Y	N	N	Y	Y	Y	Y
17 Evans	N	Y	Y	Y	N	N	N	Y	N	Y	N	N	N	N	Y
18 *LaHood*	Y	Y	Y	Y	Y	Y	Y	Y	Y	N	Y	N	N	Y	Y
19 Poshard	N	Y	Y	Y	N	Y	Y	N	N	N	N	N	N	N	Y
20 *Shimkus*	Y	Y	Y	N	Y	N	Y	Y	Y	N	N	Y	Y	Y	Y
INDIANA															
1 Visclosky	N	Y	Y	Y	Y	Y	Y	N	N	Y	N	N	N	N	Y
2 *McIntosh*	Y	Y	Y	N	Y	N	N	Y	Y	N	N	?	Y	Y	Y
3 Roemer	N	Y	Y	Y	Y	Y	Y	N	N	N	N	Y	N	Y	Y
4 *Souder*	Y	Y	Y	N	Y	N	Y	Y	Y	N	N	Y	Y	N	Y
5 *Buyer*	Y	N	Y	Y	Y	Y	Y	N	Y	N	Y	Y	Y	Y	Y
6 *Burton*	Y	N	Y	N	Y	N	Y	Y	Y	N	Y	Y	Y	Y	Y
7 *Pease*	Y	Y	Y	N	Y	Y	Y	Y	Y	N	N	Y	Y	Y	Y
8 *Hostettler*	P	Y	Y	N	Y	Y	Y	N	Y	N	N	Y	Y	Y	Y
9 Hamilton	N	Y	Y	Y	Y	Y	Y	N	N	Y	N	Y	N	Y	Y
10 Carson	?	?	N	Y	Y	Y	Y	N	N	Y	N	N	N	N	Y
IOWA															
1 *Leach*[4]	N	Y	Y	N	Y	N	Y	N	Y	N	Y	N	N	Y	Y
2 *Nussle*	Y	Y	Y	N	Y	N	Y	Y	Y	N	N	Y	Y	Y	Y
3 Boswell	N	Y	Y	N	N	Y	Y	N	N	N	N	Y	N	N	Y
4 *Ganske*	Y	Y	Y	N	Y	N	N	Y	Y	N	Y	N	Y	Y	Y
5 *Latham*	Y	Y	Y	N	Y	N	Y	Y	Y	N	Y	Y	Y	Y	Y
KANSAS															
1 *Moran*	Y	Y	Y	N	N	Y	Y	Y	Y	N	N	Y	N	N	Y
2 *Ryun*	Y	Y	Y	N	Y	N	Y	Y	Y	N	N	Y	Y	Y	Y
3 *Snowbarger*	Y	Y	Y	N	Y	N	Y	Y	Y	N	N	Y	Y	Y	Y
4 *Tiahrt*	Y	Y	Y	N	Y	N	Y	Y	Y	N	N	Y	Y	N	Y
KENTUCKY															
1 *Whitfield*	Y	Y	Y	N	Y	N	Y	Y	Y	N	N	Y	Y	N	Y
2 *Lewis*	Y	Y	Y	N	Y	N	Y	Y	Y	N	N	Y	Y	N	Y
3 *Northup*	Y	Y	Y	N	Y	Y	Y	Y	Y	N	N	Y	Y	Y	Y
4 *Bunning*	Y	Y	Y	N	Y	N	Y	Y	Y	N	N	Y	Y	Y	Y
5 *Rogers*	Y	Y	Y	N	Y	N	Y	Y	Y	N	Y	Y	Y	Y	Y
6 Baesler	N	Y	Y	N	Y	N	Y	N	Y	N	Y	N	N	N	Y
LOUISIANA															
1 *Livingston*	Y	N	Y	N	Y	N	Y	N	Y	N	Y	N	Y	Y	Y
2 Jefferson	N	Y	Y	N	N	?	?	N	N	Y	Y	Y	N	Y	Y
3 *Tauzin*	Y	+	Y	N	Y	N	Y	Y	Y	N	N	Y	Y	Y	Y
4 *McCrery*	Y	Y	Y	N	Y	N	Y	Y	Y	N	N	Y	Y	Y	Y
5 *Cooksey*	Y	Y	Y	N	Y	Y	Y	Y	Y	N	N	Y	Y	X	Y
6 *Baker*	Y	Y	Y	N	Y	Y	Y	Y	Y	N	N	Y	Y	Y	Y
7 John	N	Y	Y	N	Y	Y	Y	Y	N	N	N	Y	Y	N	Y
MAINE															
1 Allen	N	Y	N	Y	Y	Y	N	N	N	Y	N	N	N	N	Y
2 Baldacci	N	Y	N	Y	Y	N	N	N	N	Y	N	Y	N	N	Y
MARYLAND															
1 *Gilchrest*	Y	Y	Y	Y	Y	Y	Y	Y	Y	Y	Y	N	Y	Y	Y
2 *Ehrlich*	Y	Y	Y	N	Y	N	Y	Y	Y	Y	Y	Y	Y	Y	Y
3 Cardin	N	Y	Y	Y	N	N	Y	N	N	Y	Y	N	N	N	Y
4 Wynn	N	Y	N	Y	N	Y	Y	N	N	Y	Y	N	N	Y	Y
5 Hoyer	N	Y	N	Y	N	Y	Y	N	N	Y	Y	Y	N	Y	N
6 *Bartlett*	Y	N	Y	N	Y	N	Y	Y	Y	N	N	Y	Y	Y	Y
7 Cummings	N	Y	N	Y	N	Y	Y	N	N	Y	Y	N	N	Y	Y
8 *Morella*	P	Y	N	Y	Y	Y	Y	N	N	Y	Y	N	N	Y	Y
MASSACHUSETTS															
1 Olver	N	Y	Y	Y	N	Y	N	N	N	Y	Y	N	N	N	Y
2 Neal	N	Y	Y	Y	N	Y	Y	N	N	Y	Y	N	N	N	Y
3 McGovern	N	Y	Y	Y	N	Y	Y	N	N	Y	Y	N	N	N	Y
4 Frank	N	Y	Y	Y	N	Y	Y	N	N	Y	Y	N	N	N	Y
5 Meehan	N	Y	Y	Y	N	Y	Y	N	N	Y	Y	N	N	N	Y
6 Tierney	N	Y	Y	Y	N	Y	Y	N	N	Y	Y	N	N	N	Y
7 Markey	N	Y	Y	Y	N	Y	Y	N	N	Y	Y	N	N	N	Y
8 Kennedy	N	Y	Y	Y	N	Y	N	N	N	Y	Y	N	N	N	Y
9 Moakley	N	Y	Y	Y	N	Y	N	N	N	Y	Y	N	N	N	Y
10 Delahunt	N	Y	N	+	N	Y	N	N	N	Y	Y	N	N	N	Y
MICHIGAN															
1 Stupak	N	Y	Y	Y	N	Y	Y	N	N	N	Y	N	N	N	Y
2 *Hoekstra*	Y	Y	Y	N	Y	N	Y	Y	Y	N	Y	Y	Y	Y	Y
3 *Ehlers*	Y	Y	Y	Y	Y	Y	Y	N	Y	N	Y	N	Y	Y	Y
4 *Camp*	Y	Y	Y	Y	Y	Y	Y	N	Y	N	Y	Y	Y	Y	Y
5 Barcia	N	Y	Y	Y	Y	Y	Y	N	N	N	Y	N	N	N	Y
6 *Upton*	Y	Y	Y	Y	Y	Y	Y	N	N	N	Y	Y	Y	Y	Y
7 *Smith*	Y	Y	Y	Y	Y	N	Y	N	N	N	N	Y	Y	Y	Y
8 Stabenow	N	Y	N	Y	Y	Y	N	N	N	Y	Y	N	N	N	Y
9 Kildee	N	Y	N	Y	Y	Y	N	N	N	N	N	N	N	N	Y
10 Bonior	N	Y	N	Y	Y	Y	N	N	N	Y	Y	N	N	N	Y
11 *Knollenberg*	Y	Y	Y	N	Y	N	Y	Y	Y	N	Y	Y	Y	Y	Y
12 Levin	N	Y	N	Y	N	Y	Y	N	N	Y	Y	N	N	N	Y
13 Rivers	N	Y	N	Y	Y	Y	N	N	N	Y	N	N	N	N	Y

House Key Votes	1	2	3	4	5	6	7	8	9	10	11	12	13	14	15
14 Conyers	N	P	N	Y	N	N	N	N	N	Y	Y	N	N	N	Y
15 Kilpatrick	N	Y	N	Y	N	N	Y	N	N	Y	Y	N	N	N	Y
16 Dingell	N	Y	Y	Y	N	Y	Y	N	N	Y	Y	N	N	N	Y
MINNESOTA															
1 *Gutknecht*	Y	Y	Y	N	Y	Y	Y	Y	Y	N	N	Y	N	N	Y
2 Minge	N	Y	Y	Y	Y	N	Y	N	N	Y	N	N	N	Y	Y
3 *Ramstad*	Y	Y	Y	Y	Y	N	Y	Y	Y	N	N	Y	N	Y	Y
4 Vento	N	Y	N	Y	N	Y	Y	N	N	Y	N	N	N	N	Y
5 Sabo	N	Y	N	Y	N	Y	Y	N	N	Y	N	N	N	N	Y
6 Luther	N	Y	N	Y	Y	Y	Y	N	N	Y	N	N	N	N	Y
7 Peterson	N	Y	N	Y	N	Y	Y	N	N	N	N	N	N	Y	Y
8 Oberstar	N	Y	Y	Y	N	Y	N	N	N	N	Y	N	N	N	Y
MISSISSIPPI															
1 *Wicker*	Y	N	Y	N	Y	N	Y	N	Y	N	Y	Y	Y	Y	Y
2 Thompson	N	Y	N	Y	N	Y	N	N	N	Y	Y	Y	N	Y	Y
3 *Pickering*	Y	Y	Y	N	Y	N	Y	Y	Y	N	Y	Y	Y	Y	Y
4 *Parker*	Y	Y	Y	N	Y	N	Y	Y	Y	N	Y	Y	Y	Y	Y
5 Taylor	N	N	Y	N	Y	N	Y	N	N	N	N	Y	N	N	Y
MISSOURI															
1 Clay	N	Y	N	?	N	Y	N	N	N	Y	Y	N	N	N	Y
2 *Talent*	Y	Y	Y	N	Y	N	Y	Y	Y	N	N	Y	Y	Y	Y
3 Gephardt	P	Y	Y	Y	N	Y	N	N	N	Y	N	N	N	N	Y
4 Skelton	N	Y	Y	N	?	N	Y	N	N	N	N	N	N	N	Y
5 McCarthy	N	Y	Y	Y	Y	Y	Y	N	N	Y	N	N	N	N	Y
6 Danner	N	Y	Y	N	Y	Y	Y	Y	N	Y	N	N	N	N	Y
7 *Blunt*	Y	Y	Y	N	Y	N	Y	Y	Y	N	N	Y	Y	Y	Y
8 *Emerson*	Y	Y	Y	N	Y	N	Y	Y	Y	N	N	Y	Y	Y	Y
9 *Hulshof*	Y	Y	Y	N	Y	N	Y	Y	Y	N	N	Y	Y	Y	Y
MONTANA															
AL *Hill*	Y	Y	Y	N	Y	N	Y	N	Y	N	N	Y	Y	Y	Y
NEBRASKA															
1 *Bereuter*	Y	Y	Y	N	Y	N	Y	Y	Y	N	N	N	N	N	Y
2 *Christensen*	Y	Y	Y	N	Y	N	Y	Y	Y	N	N	N	Y	Y	Y
3 *Barrett*	Y	Y	Y	N	Y	N	Y	Y	Y	N	N	Y	N	Y	Y
NEVADA															
1 *Ensign*	Y	Y	Y	N	Y	+	Y	Y	Y	N	N	Y	Y	N	Y
2 *Gibbons*	Y	Y	Y	N	Y	N	Y	Y	Y	N	N	Y	Y	N	Y
NEW HAMPSHIRE															
1 *Sununu*	Y	Y	Y	Y	Y	N	Y	Y	Y	N	N	Y	Y	Y	Y
2 *Bass*	Y	Y	Y	Y	Y	Y	Y	Y	Y	Y	N	Y	Y	Y	Y
NEW JERSEY															
1 Andrews	N	Y	N	?	?	Y	N	Y	N	Y	N	N	N	N	Y
2 *LoBiondo*	Y	Y	Y	Y	Y	Y	Y	Y	N	Y	N	N	N	N	Y
3 *Saxton*	Y	Y	Y	Y	Y	Y	Y	N	N	Y	N	N	N	N	Y
4 *Smith*	Y	Y	Y	Y	Y	Y	Y	N	N	Y	N	N	N	N	Y
5 *Roukema*	Y	Y	Y	Y	N	Y	Y	N	N	Y	N	N	N	N	Y
6 Pallone	N	Y	N	Y	N	Y	Y	N	N	Y	N	N	N	N	Y
7 *Franks*	Y	Y	Y	Y	Y	Y	Y	N	N	Y	N	N	N	N	Y
8 Pascrell	N	Y	Y	Y	Y	Y	Y	N	N	Y	N	N	N	N	Y
9 Rothman	N	Y	N	Y	N	Y	Y	N	N	Y	N	N	N	N	Y
10 Payne	N	Y	N	Y	N	Y	N	N	N	Y	Y	N	N	?	?	Y
11 *Frelinghuysen*	Y	Y	Y	Y	Y	Y	Y	N	Y	Y	N	N	N	N	Y
12 *Pappas*	Y	Y	Y	Y	N	Y	Y	N	N	Y	N	N	Y	Y	Y
13 Menendez	N	Y	N	Y	N	Y	Y	N	N	Y	Y	N	?	?	Y
NEW MEXICO															
1 *Schiff*	Y	Y	Y	?	?	?	#	?	?	?	?	?	?	?	?
2 *Skeen*	Y	Y	Y	N	Y	N	Y	N	Y	Y	Y	Y	Y	Y	Y
3 *Redmond*[5]				N	Y	N	Y	N	Y	N	N	Y	Y	Y	Y
NEW YORK															
1 *Forbes*[6]	N	Y	Y	Y	Y	Y	Y	Y	N	N	N	N	Y	N	Y
2 *Lazio*	Y	Y	Y	Y	Y	N	Y	N	N	Y	Y	N	Y	Y	Y
3 *King*	Y	N	Y	N	Y	Y	N	N	Y	Y	N	N	Y	Y	Y
4 McCarthy	N	Y	N	Y	Y	Y	Y	N	N	Y	N	N	N	N	Y
5 Ackerman	N	Y	N	Y	Y	Y	Y	N	N	Y	Y	N	?	?	Y
6 Flake	N	Y	N	Y	?	Y	Y	N	N	Y	Y	N	N	N	Y
7 Manton	N	Y	N	Y	Y	Y	Y	N	N	Y	N	N	N	N	Y
8 Nadler	N	Y	N	Y	N	Y	Y	N	N	Y	N	N	N	N	Y
9 Schumer	N	Y	N	Y	N	Y	Y	?	N	Y	Y	N	N	N	Y
10 Towns	N	Y	N	Y	N	Y	Y	N	N	Y	Y	N	?	Y	Y
11 Owens	N	Y	N	Y	N	Y	N	N	N	Y	Y	N	N	N	Y

[1] On key vote 1, voted for Rep. Jim Leach, R–Iowa.

[2] Walter Capps, D–Calif., died Oct. 28.

[3] Newt Gingrich, R–Ga., as Speaker of the House, voted at his discretion.

[4] On key vote 1, voted for Rep. Robert H. Michel, R–Ill. (1957–1995).

[5] Bill Richardson, D–N.M., resigned Feb. 13. He was eligible to vote on key votes 1 and 2. Bill Redmond, R–N.M,. was sworn in May 20. He was eligible to vote on key votes 6–15.

[6] On key vote 1, voted for Rep. Jim Leach, R–Iowa.

KEY

	Democrats	*Republicans*	**Independent**

Y Voted for ("yea")
N Voted against ("nay")
+ Announced for
\# Paired for
X Paired against

– Announced against
P Voted "present"
C Voted "present" to avoid possible conflict of interest
? Did not vote or otherwise make a position known

ND Northern Democrats
SD Southern Democrats
Southern states – Ala., Ark., Fla., Ga., Ky., La., Miss., N.C., Okla., S.C., Tenn., Texas, Va.

House Key Votes	1	2	3	4	5	6	7	8	9	10	11	12	13	14	15
12 Velazquez	N	Y	N	Y	N	Y	N	N	N	Y	Y	N	N	N	Y
13 Molinari[7]	Y	Y	Y	N	Y	Y	Y								
Fossella															Y
14 Maloney	N	Y	N	Y	N	Y	Y	N	N	Y	Y	N	N	N	Y
15 Rangel	N	Y	N	Y	N	Y	N	N	N	Y	Y	N	N	Y	Y
16 Serrano	N	Y	N	Y	N	Y	N	Y	N	Y	Y	N	N	N	Y
17 Engel	N	Y	N	Y	N	Y	N	N	N	Y	Y	N	N	N	Y
18 Lowey	N	Y	N	Y	Y	Y	N	N	N	Y	Y	N	N	Y	Y
19 Kelly	Y	Y	Y	Y	Y	Y	Y	Y	N	Y	N	N	Y	Y	Y
20 Gilman	Y	Y	N	Y	Y	N	Y	N	Y	Y	Y	N	N	Y	Y
21 McNulty	N	Y	Y	Y	N	N	N	N	N	Y	Y	N	?	?	Y
22 Solomon	Y	N	Y	N	Y	N	Y	Y	Y	N	Y	Y	Y	N	Y
23 Boehlert	Y	Y	N	Y	Y	Y	Y	N	Y	Y	Y	N	N	N	Y
24 McHugh	Y	Y	Y	N	Y	N	Y	N	Y	N	Y	N	N	N	Y
25 Walsh	Y	Y	Y	Y	Y	N	Y	Y	Y	N	N	N	Y	N	Y
26 Hinchey	N	Y	N	Y	N	Y	N	N	N	Y	Y	N	N	N	Y
27 Paxon	Y	Y	Y	N	Y	N	Y	Y	Y	N	Y	Y	Y	Y	Y
28 Slaughter	N	Y	N	Y	N	Y	N	N	-	Y	N	N	-	-	Y
29 LaFalce	N	Y	Y	Y	N	Y	Y	N	N	Y	Y	N	N	N	Y
30 Quinn	Y	Y	Y	Y	Y	Y	N	N	N	N	Y	Y	N	N	Y
31 Houghton	Y	Y	Y	Y	Y	Y	Y	N	N	Y	Y	Y	N	Y	Y
NORTH CAROLINA															
1 Clayton	N	Y	N	Y	Y	Y	N	N	N	Y	N	N	N	N	Y
2 Etheridge	N	Y	Y	Y	N	Y	Y	N	N	Y	N	Y	N	N	Y
3 *Jones*	Y	Y	Y	N	Y	N	Y	Y	N	N	N	Y	Y	Y	Y
4 Price	N	Y	N	Y	N	Y	Y	N	N	Y	N	N	N	N	Y
5 *Burr*	Y	Y	Y	N	Y	N	Y	Y	Y	N	N	Y	N	Y	Y
6 *Coble*	Y	Y	Y	N	Y	N	Y	Y	Y	N	Y	Y	Y	Y	Y
7 McIntyre	N	Y	Y	Y	Y	Y	Y	N	N	Y	N	N	N	N	Y
8 Hefner	N	Y	Y	Y	?	Y	Y	N	N	Y	Y	N	N	N	Y
9 *Myrick*	Y	N	Y	N	Y	N	Y	Y	Y	N	N	Y	Y	N	Y
10 *Ballenger*	Y	Y	Y	N	Y	N	Y	Y	Y	N	Y	Y	Y	Y	Y
11 *Taylor*	Y	N	Y	N	Y	N	Y	Y	Y	N	Y	Y	Y	Y	Y
12 Watt	N	Y	N	Y	N	Y	N	N	N	Y	Y	N	N	N	Y
NORTH DAKOTA															
AL Pomeroy	N	Y	Y	N	Y	N	Y	N	N	Y	N	N	N	N	Y
OHIO															
1 *Chabot*	Y	Y	Y	N	Y	N	Y	Y	Y	N	N	Y	Y	Y	Y
2 *Portman*	Y	Y	Y	N	Y	N	Y	Y	Y	N	N	N	Y	Y	Y
3 Hall	N	Y	Y	Y	Y	N	Y	N	N	Y	N	N	N	Y	Y
4 *Oxley*	Y	Y	+	N	Y	N	Y	N	Y	N	Y	Y	Y	Y	Y
5 *Gillmor*	Y	Y	Y	Y	Y	N	Y	N	Y	N	N	Y	Y	Y	Y
6 Strickland	N	Y	Y	Y	Y	Y	N	N	N	Y	N	?	N	N	Y
7 *Hobson*	Y	Y	Y	Y	N	Y	Y	Y	Y	Y	Y	Y	Y	Y	Y
8 *Boehner*	Y	Y	Y	Y	N	Y	Y	Y	Y	N	Y	N	Y	N	Y
9 Kaptur	N	Y	?	Y	Y	Y	N	N	N	N	N	N	N'	N	Y
10 Kucinich	N	Y	Y	Y	N	N	N	N	N	N	N	N	N	N	Y
11 Stokes	N	Y	N	Y	Y	Y	N	N	N	Y	Y	N	N	N	Y
12 *Kasich*	Y	Y	Y	N	+	N	Y	Y	Y	N	Y	N	Y	N	Y
13 Brown	N	Y	N	Y	N	Y	N	N	N	Y	Y	N	N	N	Y
14 Sawyer	N	Y	N	Y	N	Y	Y	N	N	Y	Y	N	N	N	Y
15 *Pryce*	Y	Y	Y	N	Y	N	Y	Y	Y	+	Y	Y	Y	Y	Y
16 *Regula*	Y	Y	Y	N	Y	N	Y	N	Y	Y	Y	Y	Y	Y	Y
17 Traficant	N	Y	Y	Y	N	Y	N	Y	N	Y	N	N	N	Y	Y
18 *Ney*	Y	Y	Y	N	Y	N	Y	N	Y	N	Y	Y	N	Y	Y
19 *LaTourette*	Y	Y	Y	Y	Y	Y	Y	Y	Y	N	Y	Y	Y	Y	Y
OKLAHOMA															
1 *Largent*	Y	Y	Y	N	Y	N	N	N	Y	N	N	Y	Y	Y	Y
2 *Coburn*	Y	N	Y	N	Y	N	N	N	N	N	N	Y	?	?	Y
3 *Watkins*	Y	Y	Y	N	?	N	Y	Y	Y	N	N	Y	Y	N	Y
4 *Watts*	Y	+	Y	N	Y	N	Y	Y	Y	N	N	Y	Y	N	Y
5 *Istook*	Y	Y	Y	N	Y	N	Y	N	N	N	N	Y	Y	N	Y
6 *Lucas*	Y	Y	Y	N	Y	N	Y	N	N	N	N	Y	N	Y	Y
OREGON															
1 Furse	N	Y	N	Y	Y	Y	Y	N	N	Y	Y	N	N	N	Y
2 *Smith*	Y	Y	N	N	Y	N	Y	Y	N	N	Y	Y	Y	N	Y
3 Blumenauer	N	Y	N	Y	N	Y	N	N	N	Y	Y	N	N	N	Y

House Key Votes	1	2	3	4	5	6	7	8	9	10	11	12	13	14	15
4 DeFazio	N	Y	N	Y	N	Y	N	Y	N	Y	N	N	N	N	Y
5 Hooley	N	Y	N	Y	Y	Y	Y	N	N	Y	N	N	N	N	Y
PENNSYLVANIA															
1 Foglietta	N	Y	Y	Y	N	N	N	N	N	Y	?	N	?	?	Y
2 Fattah	N	Y	N	Y	N	Y	Y	N	N	Y	Y	N	N	Y	Y
3 Borski	N	Y	Y	Y	N	Y	N	N	N	N	Y	N	N	N	Y
4 Klink	N	Y	Y	Y	Y	Y	N	N	N	N	Y	N	N	N	Y
5 *Peterson*	Y	Y	Y	N	Y	Y	Y	Y	Y	N	N	Y	Y	N	Y
6 Holden	N	Y	Y	N	Y	Y	Y	N	N	N	N	Y	?	N	Y
7 *Weldon*	Y	Y	Y	Y	Y	Y	Y	N	Y	N	Y	Y	Y	N	Y
8 *Greenwood*	Y	Y	N	Y	Y	Y	Y	Y	Y	Y	Y	N	Y	Y	Y
9 *Shuster*	Y	Y	Y	N	Y	N	Y	N	Y	N	Y	Y	Y	N	Y
10 *McDade*	Y	Y	Y	Y	Y	Y	Y	Y	Y	N	Y	Y	N	N	Y
11 Kanjorski	N	Y	Y	Y	Y	N	N	N	N	Y	N	N	N	N	Y
12 Murtha	N	Y	Y	Y	Y	N	Y	N	N	N	N	Y	N	N	Y
13 *Fox*	Y	Y	Y	Y	Y	Y	Y	N	N	Y	Y	N	N	Y	Y
14 Coyne	N	Y	N	Y	N	Y	N	N	N	Y	Y	N	N	N	Y
15 McHale	N	Y	Y	Y	Y	Y	Y	N	N	Y	N	N	N	N	Y
16 *Pitts*	Y	Y	Y	N	Y	N	Y	Y	Y	N	N	Y	Y	Y	Y
17 *Gekas*	Y	Y	Y	N	Y	N	Y	Y	Y	N	N	Y	Y	N	Y
18 Doyle	N	Y	Y	Y	Y	Y	N	N	N	Y	N	N	N	N	Y
19 *Goodling*	Y	Y	Y	N	Y	N	Y	Y	N	N	N	Y	Y	N	Y
20 Mascara	N	Y	Y	Y	Y	Y	N	N	N	Y	N	N	N	N	Y
21 *English*	Y	Y	Y	Y	Y	Y	Y	Y	Y	N	N	Y	Y	Y	Y
RHODE ISLAND															
1 Kennedy	N	Y	Y	Y	N	N	N	N	N	Y	N	N	N	N	Y
2 Weygand	N	Y	Y	Y	N	N	N	N	N	N	N	N	N	N	Y
SOUTH CAROLINA															
1 *Sanford*	Y	Y	Y	Y	Y	N	N	Y	Y	N	N	N	Y	Y	Y
2 *Spence*	Y	Y	Y	N	Y	N	Y	Y	Y	N	Y	Y	Y	N	Y
3 *Graham*	Y	Y	Y	N	Y	N	Y	Y	Y	N	N	Y	Y	N	Y
4 *Inglis*	Y	Y	Y	N	Y	N	Y	Y	Y	N	N	Y	Y	N	Y
5 Spratt	N	Y	Y	Y	N	Y	Y	N	N	Y	Y	N	N	N	Y
6 *Clyburn*	N	Y	N	Y	N	Y	N	N	N	Y	Y	N	N	N	Y
SOUTH DAKOTA															
AL *Thune*	Y	Y	Y	N	Y	Y	Y	Y	Y	N	N	N	N	Y	Y
TENNESSEE															
1 *Jenkins*	Y	Y	Y	N	Y	N	Y	Y	Y	N	N	Y	Y	N	Y
2 *Duncan*	Y	Y	Y	N	Y	N	Y	Y	Y	N	N	Y	Y	N	Y
3 *Wamp*	Y	Y	Y	N	Y	N	Y	Y	Y	N	N	Y	Y	N	Y
4 *Hilleary*	Y	Y	Y	N	Y	N	Y	Y	Y	N	N	Y	Y	N	Y
5 Clement	N	Y	Y	Y	N	Y	Y	N	N	Y	Y	N	N	N	Y
6 Gordon	N	Y	Y	Y	N	Y	Y	N	N	Y	N	N	N	N	Y
7 *Bryant*	Y	Y	Y	N	Y	N	Y	+	Y	N	N	Y	N	N	Y
8 Tanner	Y	Y	Y	Y	Y	Y	Y	N	N	Y	N	N	N	Y	Y
9 Ford	N	Y	N	Y	Y	Y	N	N	N	Y	N	N	N	N	Y
TEXAS															
1 Sandlin	N	Y	Y	N	Y	Y	Y	N	N	Y	N	N	N	N	Y
2 Turner	N	Y	Y	N	Y	Y	Y	N	N	Y	N	N	N	N	Y
3 *Johnson, Sam*	+	N	Y	N	Y	N	Y	Y	Y	N	N	Y	Y	Y	Y
4 Hall	N	Y	Y	N	Y	N	Y	N	N	Y	N	N	N	N	Y
5 *Sessions*	Y	N	Y	N	Y	N	Y	Y	Y	N	N	Y	Y	Y	Y
6 *Barton*	Y	N	Y	?	Y	N	Y	Y	Y	N	N	Y	Y	Y	Y
7 *Archer*	Y	Y	Y	N	Y	N	Y	Y	Y	N	N	Y	Y	N	Y
8 *Brady*	Y	Y	Y	N	Y	N	Y	Y	Y	N	N	Y	Y	N	Y
9 Lampson	N	Y	Y	Y	Y	Y	Y	N	N	Y	N	N	N	N	Y
10 Doggett	N	Y	Y	Y	N	Y	N	N	N	Y	N	N	N	N	Y
11 Edwards	N	Y	Y	N	Y	Y	Y	N	N	Y	Y	N	N	?	Y
12 *Granger*	Y	?	Y	N	Y	N	Y	Y	Y	N	N	Y	Y	Y	Y
13 *Thornberry*	Y	Y	Y	N	Y	N	Y	Y	Y	N	N	Y	Y	Y	Y
14 *Paul*	Y	Y	N	N	N	N	Y	N	N	N	N	Y	N	N	Y
15 Hinojosa	N	Y	Y	Y	N	Y	Y	N	N	Y	N	N	N	N	Y
16 Reyes	N	Y	Y	?	Y	Y	Y	N	N	Y	N	N	N	N	Y
17 Stenholm	N	Y	Y	Y	Y	Y	Y	N	N	Y	N	N	N	N	Y
18 Jackson-Lee	N	Y	N	Y	Y	Y	N	N	N	Y	Y	-	N	N	Y
19 *Combest*	Y	Y	Y	N	Y	N	Y	Y	Y	N	N	Y	Y	Y	Y
20 Gonzalez	N	Y	Y	Y	N	Y	N	N	N	?	?	?	?	?	?
21 *Smith*	Y	N	Y	N	Y	N	Y	Y	Y	N	N	Y	Y	N	Y
22 *DeLay*	Y	N	Y	N	Y	N	Y	Y	Y	N	N	Y	Y	Y	Y
23 *Bonilla*	Y	Y	Y	N	Y	N	Y	Y	Y	N	?	Y	Y	N	Y
24 Frost	N	Y	Y	N	Y	Y	Y	N	N	Y	N	N	N	N	Y
25 Bentsen	N	Y	Y	N	Y	Y	Y	N	N	Y	N	N	N	N	Y
26 *Armey*	Y	Y	Y	N	Y	N	Y	Y	Y	N	N	Y	Y	Y	Y
27 Ortiz	N	Y	Y	N	Y	N	Y	N	N	Y	N	N	N	N	Y
28 Rodriguez[8]		N	N	N	Y	Y	Y	N	N	N	Y	N	N	N	N	Y
29 Green	N	Y	N	Y	Y	Y	N	N	N	Y	Y	N	N	N	Y
30 Johnson, E.B.	N	Y	N	Y	Y	Y	N	N	N	Y	Y	N	N	N	Y
UTAH															
1 *Hansen*	Y	Y	Y	N	Y	N	Y	Y	N	N	Y	Y	Y	N	Y
2 *Cook*	Y	Y	Y	N	Y	Y	Y	Y	N	N	N	Y	Y	N	Y

KEY

	Democrats	*Republicans*	**Independent**
Y	Voted for ("yea")		
N	Voted against ("nay")	–	Announced against
+	Announced for	P	Voted "present"
#	Paired for	C	Voted "present" to avoid possible conflict of interest
X	Paired against	?	Did not vote or otherwise make a position known

ND   Northern Democrats
SD   Southern Democrats
Southern states – Ala., Ark., Fla., Ga., Ky., La., Miss., N.C., Okla., S.C., Tenn., Texas, Va.

House Key Votes	1	2	3	4	5	6	7	8	9	10	11	12	13	14	15
3 *Cannon*	Y	Y	Y	N	Y	N	Y	Y	Y	N	N	Y	N	Y	Y
VERMONT															
AL *Sanders*	N	Y	N	Y	N	Y	N	Y	N	Y	N	N	N	N	Y
VIRGINIA															
1 *Bateman*	Y	Y	Y	N	Y	N	Y	N	Y	N	Y	Y	Y	Y	Y
2 Pickett	N	Y	N	N	Y	N	Y	N	Y	Y	Y	Y	N	Y	Y
3 Scott	N	Y	N	Y	N	Y	N	N	N	Y	Y	Y	N	N	Y
4 Sisisky	N	Y	N	N	Y	N	Y	N	N	Y	Y	Y	N	N	Y
5 Goode	N	Y	Y	N	Y	Y	Y	Y	N	N	N	Y	N	N	Y
6 *Goodlatte*	Y	Y	Y	N	Y	N	Y	Y	Y	N	Y	Y	N	Y	Y
7 *Bliley*	Y	Y	Y	N	Y	N	Y	N	Y	N	Y	Y	Y	Y	Y
8 Moran	N	Y	Y	Y	Y	N	Y	N	N	Y	Y	N	N	Y	Y
9 Boucher	N	Y	N	Y	N	?	N	N	N	?	Y	N	N	N	Y
10 *Wolf*	P	Y	Y	Y	Y	N	Y	N	Y	N	Y	Y	Y	N	Y
11 *Davis*	Y	Y	Y	Y	Y	Y	Y	N	Y	Y	Y	Y	N	Y	Y
WASHINGTON															
1 White	Y	Y	Y	Y	N	Y	N	Y	N	Y	N	Y	Y	Y	Y
2 *Metcalf*	Y	Y	Y	Y	Y	Y	Y	Y	Y	N	N	Y	Y	N	Y

House Key Votes	1	2	3	4	5	6	7	8	9	10	11	12	13	14	15
3 *Smith, Linda*[9]	N	Y	Y	Y	Y	Y	Y	Y	Y	N	N	Y	Y	N	Y
4 *Hastings*	Y	Y	Y	N	Y	N	Y	Y	Y	N	Y	Y	Y	Y	Y
5 *Nethercutt*	Y	Y	Y	N	Y	N	Y	Y	Y	N	N	Y	Y	Y	Y
6 Dicks	N	Y	N	Y	Y	N	Y	N	N	Y	Y	N	Y	N	Y
7 McDermott	N	P	N	Y	Y	Y	N	N	N	Y	Y	N	N	Y	N
8 *Dunn*	Y	Y	Y	N	Y	N	Y	Y	Y	Y	Y	Y	Y	Y	Y
9 Smith, Adam	N	Y	N	Y	Y	N	Y	N	N	Y	N	N	N	N	Y
WEST VIRGINIA															
1 Mollohan	N	Y	Y	Y	N	N	N	N	N	Y	Y	N	N	N	Y
2 Wise	N	Y	N	Y	Y	Y	Y	N	N	Y	N	N	N	?	Y
3 Rahall	N	Y	Y	Y	N	Y	N	N	N	Y	N	N	N	N	Y
WISCONSIN															
1 *Neumann*	P	Y	Y	Y	Y	N	Y	Y	Y	-	N	Y	Y	N	Y
2 *Klug*	P	Y	Y	Y	N	N	N	Y	Y	Y	Y	N	N	Y	Y
3 Kind	N	Y	Y	Y	Y	Y	N	N	Y	Y	N	N	N	N	Y
4 Kleczka	N	Y	Y	Y	-	Y	Y	N	N	Y	Y	N	N	N	Y
5 Barrett	N	Y	Y	Y	N	N	Y	N	N	Y	N	N	N	N	Y
6 *Petri*	Y	Y	Y	Y	Y	Y	Y	Y	Y	N	N	Y	Y	Y	Y
7 Obey	N	Y	Y	Y	N	N	N	N	N	Y	Y	N	N	N	Y
8 Johnson	N	Y	Y	Y	N	Y	Y	N	N	Y	N	N	N	N	Y
9 *Sensenbrenner*	Y	Y	Y	Y	N	Y	Y	Y	Y	N	N	Y	Y	Y	Y
WYOMING															
AL *Cubin*	Y	Y	Y	N	Y	N	N	Y	Y	N	N	?	?	?	?

[7] Susan Molinari, R–N.Y., resigned Aug. 1. She was eligible to vote on key votes 1–9. Vito J. Fossella, R–N.Y., was sworn in Nov. 5. He was eligible to vote on key vote 15.

[8] Frank Tejeda, D–Texas, died on Jan. 30. He was eligible to vote on key votes 1 and 2. Ciro D. Rodriguez, D–Texas, was sworn in April 17. He was eligible for key votes 4–15.

[9] On key vote 1, voted for Rep. Robert S. Walker, R–Pa. (1977–1997).

Senate

1. CLONING BAN

After scientists in Scotland announced in 1997 that they had cloned a sheep, which they named Dolly, legislation to ban human cloning became a more urgent political issue in Congress. For much of 1997 and early 1998, a broad anticloning ban won increasing Senate support amid indications it might pass. But a decision Feb. 11 to block debate on the bill (S 1601) reflected the aggressive case made by medical research groups and biotech companies, even while controversy over Dolly continued.

The decision not to invoke cloture on a filibuster also showed that the cloning issue would not be fought along the same divisions as abortion. Antiabortion forces wanted to have some products of genetic manipulation defined as human life even though scientists disagreed. They lost when not only Democrats but also abortion opponents such as Sens. Connie Mack, R-Fla., and Strom Thurmond, R-S.C., sided with researchers. They cited their experiences with serious diseases in concluding that medical knowledge might be gained in many areas that could not be readily classified in a simple debate over cloning.

Consideration of the legislation was blocked when the necessary 60 votes could not be obtained to invoke cloture on a motion to proceed to consideration of the bill. The votes was 42–54: R 42–12; D 0–42 (ND 0–34, SD 0–8). *(Vote, p. 892)*

Although there was widespread agreement that human cloning would be morally repugnant, medical groups and many senators contended that the measure, sponsored by Republicans Bill Frist of Tennessee and Christopher S. Bond of Missouri, was too broad and could interfere with research. They argued, for example, that reproducing human cells to replace burned skin could be halted as would an experimental process to have animals produce human antibodies.

The measure would have banned a process known as somatic cell nuclear transfer for the purposes of creating a human embryo. The process involves replacing the nucleus of an egg cell with the nucleus of some other cell—an adult cell that would not multiply if left in its original state. Scientists have found that the remaining portion of the cell can somehow "reprogram" the new nucleus into multiplying.

Bond and Frist argued that this new cell could be considered an embryo worthy of the same protection as an embryo created through sexual intercourse. They were backed by the National Right to Life Committee and other antiabortion groups. Scientific groups said the language was too broad.

2. CAMPAIGN FINANCE

In October 1997 Senate Democrats sought to force Majority Leader Trent Lott, R-Miss., to schedule a vote on a campaign finance bill that most Republicans opposed. Democrats threatened to bring the Senate to a halt in the session's closing days unless a vote occurred. Although Lott agreed to permit a debate in early 1998 he knew that supporters did not have enough votes to halt a filibuster against the legislation sponsored by John McCain, R-Ariz., and Russell D. Feingold, D-Wis. Lott led the filibuster, joined by Mitch McConnell, R-Ky., the Senate's arch-foe of campaign reform. Even before the debate, McCain acknowledged that his side did not have the

necessary 60 votes needed to break a filibuster. But reform advocates hoped to do better than they had in October 1997, when they got 52 votes. But they fared essentially just the same. On the key vote, which occurred Feb. 26, the Senate voted not to end the filibuster, 51–48: R 7–48; D 44–0 (ND 36–0, SD 8–0). Tom Harkin, D-Iowa, a supporter of McCain-Feingold, was absent. *(Vote, p. 892)*

The vote came on an amendment to a GOP bill (S 1663) that would have limited the use of union dues for political activity. The amendment, proposed by McCain and Feingold, was a modified version of their campaign finance bill (S 25).

The decisive factor was the willingness of GOP senators who faced reelection in 1998—as Alfonse M. D'Amato of New York, Christopher S. Bond of Missouri, and Sam Brownback of Kansas—to back Lott and McConnell. McConnell said that the forty-eight Republicans who opposed the bill the previous autumn remained opposed.

The McCain-Feingold bill banned "soft money," unregulated donations to political parties by unions, corporations, and wealthy individuals. It also imposed new restrictions on issue-oriented television ads run by interest groups. The legislation picked up support in 1997 as Congress investigated fundraising excesses in the 1996 presidential campaign. But opponents argued that the measure infringed on constitutionally protected political speech. Politically, many Republicans feared that it would diminish their substantial fundraising advantage over Democrats.

Although the finance bill was blocked, Lott's bill on union dues also was defeated. The Senate could not end a Democratic filibuster on that proposal, 45–54.

3. IMF FUNDING

The Senate's overwhelming early vote—84–16 on March 26—to appropriate $17.9 billion for the International Monetary Fund (IMF) set the tone for months of maneuvering between protrade business interests and an unusual array of environmentalists, free-trade conservatives, and others opposed to the funding.

Early in 1998, President Clinton requested the appropriation as part of an emergency supplemental bill (PL 105-174) to help IMF reserves, which had been drawn down by loans to economically troubled Asian nations. Clinton said the money was necessary to stabilize economies across much of the world. Many members of Congress, but not House leaders, agreed. Majority Leader Dick Armey, R-Texas, denounced the IMF for interfering with free markets, while liberal critics blamed the organization for contributing to deteriorating labor and environmental conditions overseas.

The House Appropriations Committee March 24 split IMF funding from the main supplemental bill (HR 3579). The Senate historically gave strong support to trade and international commerce measures. If the IMF appropriation was to be approved, it needed a strong Senate vote. But Senate appropriators did not help as expected. The Senate Appropriations Committee approved the funding but attached such contentious provisions that it was unclear whether the 182-nation organization would be able to comply. For example, the committee insisted that the IMF make loans only to countries that honored certain trade agreements.

When the supplemental bill (S 1768) went to the floor, Mitch McConnell, R-Ky., proposed an amendment to ease the IMF conditions. It would require that the United States and its major "G-7" industrial partners agree to push for such IMF measures as requiring borrowing countries to abide by international trade agreements.

McConnell's conditions fell far short of the demands of IMF critics. Conservatives such as Connie Mack, R-Fla., and Spencer Abraham, R-Mich., assailed the IMF for pressuring governments to raise taxes, devalue currencies, and delay regulatory changes, and said the organization would have to be completely revamped before getting their support. Among liberals, Democrats such as Paul Wellstone, D-Minn., criticized the international organization for promoting austerity policies that reduced the standard of living in recipient countries.

But funding supporters such as Chuck Hagel, R-Neb., and Patrick J. Leahy, D-Vt., eventually prevailed by contending that the funding was needed to restore confidence in the global economy. The Senate passed the amendment on March 26 by a vote of 84–16: R 41–14; D 43–2 (ND 35–2, SD 8–0). The overwhelming vote gave considerable momentum to the administration's funding request. Still skeptical, House leaders refused to include the funding in the supplemental bill. Instead, the IMF issue lingered all year, as appropriators wrestled with the issue in the fiscal 1999 foreign operations spending bill. But with the resounding Senate vote echoing throughout the negotiations, Congress finally cleared the IMF funding in the final days of the session. *(Vote, p. 892)*

4. NATO EXPANSION

The Senate endorsed admitting Poland, Hungary, and the Czech Republic to NATO on April 30 but first, by a large margin, warned that the alliance should not rush to invite additional former Soviet satellites to join. Expansion of the alliance was never in doubt by the time it reached the Senate floor in the spring. It was backed by President Clinton and most Republican and Democratic congressional leaders. The Clinton administration also orchestrated support from labor, veterans, and ethnic groups with ties to the three countries.

Opponents of expansion were politically diverse. Some conservatives contended that expanding the alliance would overextend U.S. overseas commitments. Some liberals argued that Polish, Hungarian, and Czech efforts to meld their armed forces into NATO would distract them from needed economic reforms. Several foreign policy experts worried that adding the three countries to NATO would exacerbate relations with Russia but their claims were hurt by Moscow's acquiescence in the changes.

It was clear that the protocol amending the treaty to add the three new countries, which was before the Senate, (Treaty Doc 105-36) would be supported by considerably more than the required two-thirds majority of the chamber when debate began in late April. Critics by then had shifted their focus to delaying invitations to other countries, at least for a few years. The leading candidates for a second round of expansion were Romania and Slovenia. But nine other countries also had applied for NATO membership, including the three Baltic republics: Estonia, Latvia, and Lithuania.

The Baltic states posed a particularly awkward problem for NATO. Each had made progress in establishing democratic institutions and free-market economies, prerequisites of membership. But each would be difficult to defend because they are small and adjacent to Russia. Moreover, the Soviet Union had annexed all three in 1940. Although the United States never recognized the annexation, it was widely believed that Russia would object strenuously to NATO membership for countries it deemed former Soviet republics.

The test came on an amendment to the treaty protocol offered by John W. Warner of Virginia, the second-ranking Republican on the Senate Armed Services Committee. Warner's proposal in effect prevented additional invitations for three years after the first group. The amendment was rejected, 41–59: R 24–31; D 17–28 (ND 15–22, SD 2–6). But 41 votes was 1 more than the one-third that would be needed to block admission of a second group of countries, if they were invited too quickly. The Senate approved the treaty amendment, 80–19. *(Vote, p. 892)*

5. SKILLED WORKER VISAS

In 1996 Congress substantially restricted immigration policy, cutting off welfare benefits to legal immigrants and approving tough new provisions on illegal immigration. The Senate's May 18 vote to expand the so-called H-1B visa program was evidence that important changes had occurred in two years. The vote was 78–20: R 51–2; D 27–18 (ND 20–17, SD 7–1). *(Vote, p. 892)*

The H-1B program is for skilled immigrants. Most go to work in the computer business but substantial numbers fill medium-skilled jobs as medical technicians, physical therapists, even fashion models. Unlike lesser-skilled immigrants, H-1B recipients had business lobbies, particularly Silicon Valley, arguing their case. But as immigrants they touch a nerve among groups and individuals that believe the country already has too many persons from other countries. Groups such as the Federation for American Immigration Reform argued that the program is a way for companies to import cheap labor instead of hiring equally skilled American workers. Labor unions said the program is a ruse for depressing wages.

The vote by such a large margin helped push an H-1B expansion to enactment. A similar bill encountered some trouble in the House but was eventually included in an omnibus spending package passed at year's end.

The Senate bill, increasing the annual allotment of H-1B visas from 65,000 to 115,000, sailed through both the Judiciary Committee and full Senate. Only two Republicans, and fewer than half the Democrats, voted against it.

The vote was a significant victory for high-technology companies, which were new to Washington lobbying. Many companies that pushed for the H-1B expansion were small businesses just a few years ago but by 1998 were corporate giants including Sun Microsystems Inc., Intel Corp., and Microsoft Corp. Their lobbying and political contributions grew more slowly than their profits, however. Many of these companies' leaders and employees were wary of Washington and politics; they saw it necessary to open government relations offices only in the late 1990s. The H-1B debate was their first industry-wide cooperative effort. At the beginning of 1998, few members outside of those who represent high-tech states had given much thought to the issue. But by spring the high-tech lobby had put it on senators' agendas. They argued that they could not continue to grow swiftly unless they could hire more skilled workers. They implicitly threatened to take jobs overseas if overseas workers could not be brought here.

6. TOBACCO LEGISLATION

The Senate in 1998 was not able to bring to a vote far-reaching legislation on tobacco. The bill (S 1415) would have raised fees on cigarettes by $1.10 per pack over five years, given the federal government's broad control over the distribution and marketing of tobacco products, and restricted tobacco advertising. The proposal required the industry to pay $516 billion over 25 years for antismoking, education, and research programs.

The creation of a federal tobacco policy had seemed almost a foregone conclusion at earlier stages of the legislative process. But as the bill bogged down in the Senate and both its friends and enemies loaded it with costly dollar amendments, the momentum for tobacco controls lost momentum. A motion to invoke cloture on a filibuster undertaken by opponents of the bill fell 3 votes short of the 60 required, 57–42: R 14–40; D 43–2 (ND 37–0, SD 6–2). *(Vote, p. 892)*

The tobacco industry had spent more than $40 million on ads that attacked S 1415, and a similar amount on lobbying against S 1415.

7. EDUCATION SAVINGS ACCOUNTS

Trying to assuage public concern about the quality of American education, congressional Republicans pushed legislation (HR 2646) allowing families to contribute up to $2,000 per child per year in special savings accounts for private school tuition, tutoring, computer equipment, and other education expenses. The legislation passed the House in 1997 by a comfortable margin, 230–198.

Despite veto threats by the Clinton administration and a determined effort by Senate Minority Leader Tom Daschle, D-S.D., to persuade Democrats not to vote for the legislation, the Senate approved the final version of the legislation in June when it adopted the conference report on the legislation by a key vote of 59–36: R 51–2; D 8–34 (ND 6–28, SD 2–6). *(Vote, p. 892)*

The vote indicated a willingness among some Democrats to act independently of the White House and search for new ways to give parents more control over their children's education. But it also showed the two parties were still far from consensus, a fact that the White House exploited later in the year when Clinton got Republicans to add $1.2 billion to an omnibus spending bill as a beginning on his plan to fund hiring of 100,000 new teachers.

The savings account bill, sponsored by Paul Coverdell, R-Ga., was designed to move Republicans beyond their narrow emphasis on federally funded vouchers for private schools. Republicans hoped the bill would appeal to Democrats because parents, rather than the government, could choose how to manage the accounts. A Democrat, Robert G. Torricelli, N.J., was a chief cosponsor of the bill. The middle ground turned out to be elusive. The Clinton administration charged that the legislation would mainly benefit upper-income taxpayers. Democrats used debate on the Coverdell bill to force votes on Clinton's proposals to hire teachers and allow local governments to issue $22 billion in federally backed bonds for school construction. Both those initiatives were defeated. The Senate then went on to pass the bill and send it to conference to resolve differences with the House version.

House-Senate conferees dropped a number of controversial amendments added during Senate debate. The final bill retained some bipartisan sweeteners attached in the Senate, including making prepaid college tuition completely tax free. The conference report passed the House easily, 225–197. As promised, Clinton vetoed the legislation. Republicans did not even attempt an override.

8. SAME-SEX TRAINING

Hoping to capitalize on support from a national commission, social conservatives tried to force the Army, Navy, and Air Force to follow the Marine Corps' example and segregate male and female recruits during training. But the effort, made through amendments to the fiscal 1999 defense authorization bill (HR 3616), was rejected by the Senate.

The key vote came in June when the Senate rejected an amendment by Robert C. Byrd, D-W. Va., that would have barred the services from putting male and female recruits in the same small unit, or housing them in the same building. The vote was 39–53: R 31–21; D 8–32 (ND 5–27, SD 3–5). *(Vote, p. 892)*

The underlying issue, a battle more than two decades old, was the proper role of women in the armed forces. Starting in 1975, when an amendment to the fiscal 1976 defense bill required the admission of women to the national military academies, Congress and successive administrations had eliminated or scaled back rules intended to keep women out of jobs involving any risk of combat. Women's rights groups and female officers vigorously promoted these changes, contending that excluding women from combat jobs—the most prestigious in the services—effectively barred them from rising to the highest ranks. Social conservatives, however, argued that allowing women into more jobs had undermined combat readiness by lowering standards for physical strength and creating sexual tensions in small units.

The long-running debate gained new prominence in 1996 following allegations of sexual abuse by drill sergeants at some Army training bases. Although the incidents occurred at advanced training facilities, conservatives seized on them to push for legislation that would require the services to organize new recruits in separate units and to house men and women in separate barracks. Efforts to pass such a bill came to nothing in 1997, partly because those who challenged mixed-gender training did not want to appear to be condoning the abusive behavior.

But in December 1997, a special commission created by Defense Secretary William S. Cohen and chaired by former Kansas Republican Sen. Nancy Kassebaum Baker (1978–1997), recommended separate housing and training units for male and female recruits. The change, Baker said, would reduce distractions for recruits and drill instructors. The Army, Navy, and Air Force vigorously objected, arguing that training men and women together helped acclimate them to working in mixed-gender teams.

Cohen adopted several other recommendations by the Baker panel aimed at making basic training more rigorous and improving the quality of the sergeants and petty officers who supervise recruits. But he allowed the services to continue mixing men and women in the same small units and allowed them to be housed in the same barracks, with physical barriers and supervision.

9. ECONOMIC SANCTIONS

For months, Richard G. Lugar of Indiana, a senior Republican on the Senate Foreign Relations Committee, had been waging an often lonely and seemingly hopeless fight to slow down the use of overseas economic sanctions by Congress and the executive branch. Despite the cost of sanctions to U.S. businesses and the restrictions they imposed on the administration's diplomatic flexibility, many lawmakers believed sanctions were an effective and relatively painless way of exerting influence over other nations and the conduct of U.S. foreign policy.

Lugar and influential Reps. Lee H. Hamilton, D-Ind., and Philip M. Crane, R-Ill., believed otherwise, arguing that although some sanctions might have merit, their cumulative weight had partially crippled American foreign policy, harmed U.S. exporters, and had little substantive effect on the behavior of foreign countries. The three were supported by USAEngage, an influential coalition of businesses that had joined together expressly to overturn sanctions that critics contended cost the U.S. economy as much as $20 billion a year.

Lugar introduced a bill (S 1413) that would have slowed down the imposition of new sanctions by instituting a formal process under which lawmakers would have to weigh the costs and benefits of new restrictions on aid and trade. The bill also would have put a two-year limit on any sanctions unless Congress renewed them. But their arguments made little headway until India and Pakistan tested nuclear weapons in May. The tests triggered automatic sanctions under the Arms Export Control Act, contained in the 1994 State Department authorization bill. That law, originally sponsored by Sen. John Glenn, D-Ohio, cuts off nonhumanitarian aid, bars the export of defense material and certain other technology, and halts U.S. credit and loan guarantees to nonnuclear nations that detonate nuclear weapons. It does not permit a presidential waiver.

The sanctions hit Pakistan, a poorer, smaller country, much harder than they hit India. U.S. farmers also were threatened when the Clinton administration decided that the law's credit ban would prevent the United States from guaranteeing bank loans on exports of wheat and other crops to Pakistan. With U.S. wheat farmers about to be squeezed out of a major wheat auction, the Senate unanimously approved legislation (S 2282) allowing India and Pakistan to continue to use guaranteed loans to import American food, fertilizer, and other agricultural commodities. Congress later allowed Clinton to waive sanctions against the two South Asian countries for a year.

But with farmers up in arms about the sanctions and other restrictions on trade, Lugar saw an opportunity to advance his broader bill. On July 15 he introduced it as an amendment to the agriculture appropriations bill (S 2159). Lugar tried to use the pressure of the farm lobby to make his case, noting that the measure was backed by the American Farm Bureau Federation. Lugar was opposed by Senate Foreign Relations Committee Chairman Jesse Helms, R-N.C., the coauthor of a 1996 law that tightened the decades-old U.S. embargo on trade with Cuba, as well as other sanctions laws.

Although a majority of GOP senators voted with him, Lugar's amendment was tabled (killed), 53–46: R 27–28; D 26–18 (ND 22–14, SD 4–4). *(Vote, p. 892)*

10. "PARTIAL BIRTH" ABORTION

A Senate vote toward the end of the 105th Congress showed that little had changed in the ongoing struggle over abortion. For months leading up to the vote, abortion opponents had hoped to gain support to override President Clinton's veto of legislation (HR 1122) to ban a procedure they referred to as "partial birth" abortion.

Despite their efforts the vote to override, taken in September, was the same as in May 1997, when an override action fell 3 votes short of the two-thirds majority—67—needed. The outcome indicated that in a year when both sides had hoped to capitalize on the twenty-fifth anniversary of the Supreme Court's affirmation of the right to an abortion, neither side had gained an advantage. The 1998 override vote was 64–36: R 51–4; D 13–32 (ND 9–28, SD 4–4). The House voted, 296–132, on July 23 to override the veto. *(Vote, p. 892)*

Clinton vetoed the bill on Oct. 10, 1997, because he said it did not provide exceptions to permit the procedure when necessary to protect a woman's health. Under the legislation, doctors who performed the abortion procedure were subject to two years in prison and fines and lawsuits for civil damages. The measure would have exempted the woman from criminal penalties.

11. OMNIBUS APPROPRIATIONS

Senate leaders wanted to avoid a recorded vote on the $500 billion-plus omnibus spending bill for fiscal 1999. Most senators had already left for home as congressional leaders and the White House worked out a deal. But the end product—which broke through the 1997 balanced-budget agreement—doled out hundreds of hometown projects and served as the engine to drive unrelated bills into law. In that context, it was considered too important to pass without putting members on record. The vote occurred on adoption of the conference report on the bill Oct. 21 by a vote of 65–29: R 33–20; D 32–9 (ND 26–9, SD 6–0). *(Vote, p. 892)*

For fiscal conservatives, the Senate's final vote of the 105th Congress was a dismaying retreat from fiscal discipline, as President Clinton and congressional Democrats obtained billions of dollars in late-stage concessions from Republicans eager to go home and campaign. Democrats enjoyed the opportunity to trumpet their education priorities and cast the Clinton administration in a favorable light.

The bill (HR 4328—PL 105-277) combined eight of the thirteen annual spending bills. It contained $21 billion in "emergency" spending that was not subject to budget "caps" set in place under the 1997 balanced-budget law. Some of this emergency spending, such as financing for a peacekeeping mission in Bosnia and year 2000 computer fixes, had already been passed by the Senate.

House

1. LINE-ITEM VETOES

Congress experimented briefly in the late 1990s with the line-item veto, a power long sought by presidents and by conservatives looking for ways to restrain federal government spending. It was a brief experiment because the Supreme Court in 1998 declared the law unconstitutional. But before that happened President Clinton and Congress used the procedures set out in the line-item veto law. Although the dollar amounts at issue were relatively modest in relation to the full federal budget, the specific items that the president sought to kill demonstrated the eternal struggle between the prerogatives of Congress, and the political interests of members seeking federal spending to benefit their districts and states, and the power of the executive charged with overseeing use of scarce tax resources.

The 1996 line-item veto law (PL 104-130) contained a complicated mechanism for permitting the president to eliminate individual projects from spending bills that he otherwise had little choice but to sign. Under the law the president's line-item vetoes would automatically take effect unless Congress passed a bill to void them. The president could then veto that "disapproval" bill, which would require a two-thirds vote to overturn.

At issue in 1998 was the military construction spending bill (PL 105-45), the first appropriations bill to be presented to a president with line-item veto authority. Clinton in 1997 had vetoed $287 million in projects contained in the bill, in the process angering both Republicans and Democrats in Congress. Most of the thirty-eight vetoed projects were included in the Pentagon's long-term plans, though none were included in Clinton's fiscal 1998 budget. The White House later admitted that Clinton vetoed some projects based on faulty information about them, which added momentum to the drive to roll back the vetoes.

Once the veto was made, the House and Senate quickly passed the disapproval bill (HR 2631) in November 1997 and Clinton promptly vetoed it. In February 1998 the House overrode Clinton's veto 347–69: R 197–23; D 149–46 (ND 100–41, SD 49–5); I 1–0. The Senate cleared the bill Feb. 25 in a 78–20 vote. *(Vote, p. 894)*

The successful override came as a constitutional challenge to the 1996 law was poised to erase Clinton's 1997 vetoes anyway. The Supreme Court struck down the law in a 6–3 ruling in June.

2. TRANSPORTATION PROJECTS

House Transportation and Infrastructure Committee Chairman Bud Shuster, R-Pa., renowned for his enthusiasm for highway construction funding, had in 1997 suffered an embarrassing, and for him unusual, defeat by the group of members seeking to impose more discipline on congressional spending habits.

On April 1, 1998, he got his chance to reverse that defeat. He cleared the way for passage of the $219 billion House version of the six-year surface transportation reauthorization bill (HR 2400) by defeating a campaign led by Lindsey Graham, R-S.C., to strip members' designated projects, known as earmarks, from the bill. Graham's amendment would have deleted $9 billion in road projects and erased money for specified transit and bus projects. Shuster not only won, but he won by an overwhelming margin. Graham's amendment was defeated 79–337: R 67–152; D 12–184 (ND 6–137, SD 6–47); I 0–1. Similar to the line-item veto key vote (see above), the action on Graham's amendment reflected the powerful instincts of political reality that control the actions of most members who think they must bring home local benefits to constituents in order to win reelection. *(Vote, p. 894)*

In May 1997 the House defeated by a 2-vote margin Shuster's proposal to pare tax cuts and reduce discretionary spending across the board in order to raise transportation spending by $12 billion over five years. In the ensuing stalemate Congress passed a temporary extension of funding. For Graham and many other members of the GOP class of 1994, the vote was a clash between old-fashioned "pork barrel" politics and the budget-balancing spirit of the House GOP's "Contract With America."

Shuster prevailed against less senior rivals with the help of economic projections showing a likely budget surplus. His bill called for a 40 percent increase in spending and required unspecified offsets because it exceeded the budget caps set in the balanced-budget deal by about $20 billion. Shuster said the spending would create new jobs and economic growth. And he offered a tempting sweetener: a project selection process that guaranteed each member a shot at earmarking $15 million in highway funds.

At a GOP Conference meeting before the vote, Shuster was tacitly supported by House leaders, who hoped projects would help win elections. But House Budget Committee Chairman John R. Kasich, R-Ohio, spoke in opposition, arguing that the bill spent too much money. On the floor, Kasich offered an amendment to cut the federal gasoline tax from 18.3 cents to 7.4 cents a gallon over four years; it was defeated. But the most intense battle was fought over the Graham amendment. Shuster said the alternative to projects was to give money to states, and, he argued, "It is not reasonable to believe somehow there is a nonpolitical, pure process back in the statehouses, as compared to the decisions made here." He suggested that Graham's opposition was "mystifying" because Graham had requested project funding in a letter. Graham replied that he had decided to reject the $15 million for his district. He said the bill made a "sham" of the balanced-budget agreement. Bob Inglis, R-S.C., summed up the feelings of many: "This is probably the most embarrassing night that I have ever spent in this Congress. We came here to change things, and we are not. We are participating in the big old trough that has characterized this place in the past."

3. AFFIRMATIVE ACTION

The Republican Party had long been deeply divided about federal requirements over race- or sex-based preferences in education and hiring. In presidential and congressional elections the GOP remained divided over its historic commitment to racial equality, reflected in modern times through support for civil rights laws, and its more recent vehement objection to special treatment to benefit women and minorities, generally reflecting the views of its dominant conservative wing.

The issue came up again in 1998 when the House GOP leadership decided to support an amendment to the Higher Education Act reauthorization (HR 6) by Frank Riggs of California to eliminate affirmative action at public colleges and universities. The Riggs amendment, modeled after California's 1996 Proposition 209, would have ended admissions preferences based on race, sex, ethnicity, or national origin. Rather than serving to make affirmative action a defining issue between the Republican and Democratic parties, however, the amendment exposed internal fissures within the GOP. It was rejected by a vote of 171–249: R 166–55; D 5–193 (ND 2–143, SD 3–50); I 0–1. *(Vote, p. 894)*

House Republican leaders voted for the Riggs proposal but in a move that contributed significantly to its defeat, J. C. Watts of Oklahoma, the House's only African American Republican, joined John Lewis, D-Ga., a noted civil rights leader, in a letter to colleagues urging them to vote against the amendment. The House on April 1 defeated a similar amendment by Marge Roukema, R-N.J., to the surface transportation reauthorization bill (HR 2400) that would have softened requirements that the Transportation Department use female- or minority-owned businesses for 10 percent of construction projects.

4. BANKING

With the securities and insurance industries lobbying Congress to again consider overhauling Depression-era financial services laws, House Republican leaders launched an intense effort in May to pass a bill allowing cross-ownership of banks, brokerages, and insurance firms. This time, the changes were approved by the House but by a single vote.

Speaker Newt Gingrich, R-Ga., and GOP Conference Chairman John A. Boehner of Ohio, the House leaders most active in crafting the bill (HR 10), knew that without their pressure, the measure would not succeed against strong opposition from all but the largest banks. That opposition had contributed to a hasty decision to pull the bill from floor consideration in late March after it became clear that the legislation, then attached to a credit union expansion measure (HR 1151), would not pass. History was also against them: the House had never passed a bill to tear down the 1933 Glass-Steagall Act and subsequent laws aimed at keeping securities and insurance separate from banking.

Because the House had not considered a measure similar to HR 10 since 1991 and had never passed one, many members found themselves faced with a complex bill they did not fully understand. In addition, many banks lobbied vigorously against the measure and the Clinton administration expressed concern about core provisions.

The House vote was a classic example of a cliff-hanger, a rare event in the chamber where most issues are decided by comfortable margins. As the voting began May 13, Republican leaders appeared uncertain of the final outcome. With the regular fifteen-minute voting period coming to a close, a defeat seemed imminent, as "nays" outnumbered "yeas." But with the deficit reaching more than a dozen votes, Gingrich emerged and began methodically working the GOP side of the chamber, persuading members one by one to support the measure. After talking to Gingrich, several Republicans went to the well to cast a "yea" vote or to change their vote from "nay" to "yea."

Among the last to switch were four Florida Republicans—Michael Bilirakis, Dan Miller, Cliff Stearns, and Dave Weldon—leading to speculation that Gingrich had promised benefits for the Sunshine State. But members and lobbyists said the four did not appear to receive any special guarantees. Their conversions brought the "yeas" and "nays" to a tie, until Connecticut Democrat Jim Maloney switched his vote from "yea" to "nay."

Then Gingrich called on Education Committee Chairman Bill Goodling, R-Pa., a moderate facing a tight election, to cast the deciding vote. Goodling had stood near the well for several minutes holding both a red "nay" card and a green "yea" card. He cast the deciding "yea" vote. The vote was 214–213: R 153–73; D 61–139 (ND 47–100, SD 14–39); I 0–1. *(Vote, p. 894)*

Opponents were not impressed at the 1-vote victory, saying the bill was as good as dead because Senate Banking Committee Chairman Alfonse D'Amato, R-N.Y., had pledged to bring it up only if it received broad bipartisan support in the House. But supporters said the vote was historic. Given the House's history of refusing to even bring such bills to the floor, "a one-vote victory looks like a landslide," Boehner said.

Despite skepticism that the vote would spur Senate action on the bill, D'Amato, facing a tough reelection battle he would eventually lose, moved the measure through his committee. It eventually died on the Senate floor, as conservatives Phil Gramm, R-Texas, and Richard C. Shelby, R-Ala., held it up, demanding changes to community investment provisions. Although that killed the legislation for the 105th Congress, the 106th Congress did pass a far-reaching financial services reform bill that President Clinton signed into law.

5. FOOD STAMPS FOR LEGAL IMMIGRANTS

Even before he signed a broad welfare overhaul in August 1996, President Clinton warned that he would seek to reverse provisions of the measure that eliminated federal benefits to legal immigrants. In 1997 Congress restored disability aid to legal immigrants. In 1998 Republicans and the White House sparred over Clinton's request to reinstate food stamps. The White House insisted that legislation (S 1150) to create new mandatory spending programs for agriculture research also include funding to restore nutrition aid to many of the 935,000 legal immigrants dropped from the food stamp rolls under the welfare law.

The White House and Democrats chose the research bill as their vehicle in part because the agriculture program was to be funded by reducing federal payments to states to administer the food stamp program. The initial Senate version of the bill focused on agriculture research. After Democrats and the White House weighed in, House and Senate negotiators worked out a conference report that included $818 million over five years to restore food stamps to elderly and disabled legal immigrants who were in the country when the welfare law was signed, as well as children under age eighteen.

Overall, the legislation would restore benefits to an estimated 250,000 legal immigrants as well as substantial spending for agriculture research programs and mandatory crop insurance funding over five years. In the Senate, Phil Gramm, R-Texas, held up the consideration of the measure for weeks. When it finally got to the Senate floor on May 12, the bill passed by a vote of 92–8.

In the House, a determined group of conservatives, led by Majority Leader Dick Armey, R-Texas, opposed restoration of food stamp benefits. Despite a deteriorating farm economy, some lawmakers also opposed the agriculture spending. When the bill came to the House floor on May 22, Republican leaders brought it up under a rule that would have automatically stripped the food stamp provisions. Nearly 100 Republicans voted against the rule, which was defeated in a key vote of 120–289: R 118–98; D 2–190 (ND 1–140, SD 1–50); I 0–1. *(Vote, p. 894)*

The defeat of the rule marked a turning point. With the House at an impasse, farm-state lawmakers were forced to go home for the Memorial Day recess without the promised agriculture and food stamp legislation. Under pressure from their rank and file, House GOP leaders were forced to stage a quick political turnabout. The House took up the bill again June 4 under a rule that protected the immigrant provisions. The conference report passed, 364–50, with Armey among those voting yea.

In the weeks that followed, Republicans also backed off their opposition to expanding aid to farmers affected by drought and falling prices. Congress ultimately approved a fiscal 1998 omnibus spending bill that included nearly $6 billion in emergency agriculture aid.

6. CONTRACEPTIVE COVERAGE

For years, abortion-rights supporters pushed unsuccessfully to require health plans that cover prescription drugs to also cover contraceptives. Rep. Nita M. Lowey, D-N.Y., won a partial victory on that issue as part of the House debate over legislation (HR 4104) to fund the Treasury Department, Postal Service, and general government spending for fiscal 1999.

After several attempts, Lowey won House acceptance of an amendment requiring health care plans for federal workers to provide coverage for contraceptives if they also cover other prescription drugs. The vote was strongly backed by Democrats, as expected, but also drew more Republican support than predicted in light of the party's position on the issue. The vote, which provided lawmakers with one of the year's few floor votes on the politically sensitive topic, was 224–198: R 48–177; D 175–21 (ND 130–17, SD 45–4); I 1–0. *(Vote, p. 894)*

Before that victory, however, Lowey had to fend off attacks from several abortion-rights opponents. The original Lowey contraceptive language was struck from the bill on a point of order because it was substantive legislation connected to an appropriations bill, which violates House rules. But Democrats, led by Lowey, outmaneuvered opponents when they returned to the floor with a slightly reworded version of the amendment. The new language barred federal funds from being used to renew contracts with health care plans for federal employees that provide coverage for prescription drugs but do not include coverage for contraceptives. That new language made the amendment in line with House rules, which allow for limitations on how money is spent. Lowey also added language to exempt five health care plans with a religious orientation that opposed her amendment.

7. PUBLIC HOUSING OVERHAUL

Twice in two years the House and Senate passed measures to overhaul the nation's public housing system as part of the GOP's effort to remake government social programs. In 1998 Republican leaders allowed House Banking and Financial Services Committee Chairman Jim Leach, R-Iowa, and Rick A. Lazio, R-N.Y., chairman of the committee's housing panel, to attach their bill (HR 2) to the fiscal 1999 spending measure for housing, veterans, and science programs, in order to make their case on the House floor. Leach and Lazio believed that attaching the measure to the spending bill would assist talks with Senate counterparts, who had somewhat different ideas about the legislation, and provide an extra incentive for another principal, Housing and Urban Development (HUD) Secretary Andrew M. Cuomo, to negotiate.

But the amendment was not without detractors. Both the chairman and ranking Democrat on the VA-HUD appropriations subcommittee vociferously opposed joining the bills, saying that attaching the 400-page bill made a mockery of House rules prohibiting authorization provisions on spending legislation. Not all Banking panel members wanted to combine the housing measure and spending bill. The panel's ranking Democrat, John J. LaFalce of New York, and top Housing Subcommittee Democrat Joseph P. Kennedy II of Massachusetts argued that Lazio and Leach should consent to convene a separate conference on HR 2 and the Senate housing overhaul measure (S 462).

Nonetheless, the House voted to attach HR 2 to the spending measure. The key vote was 230–181: R 215–4; D 15–176 (ND 8–136, SD 7–40); I 0–1. *(Vote, p. 894)*

As Leach and Lazio had predicted, pressure to complete work on the spending bill eventually forced a compromise. The final version was more moderate than the House bill, reserving more of public and subsidized housing for those with the lowest incomes, but it contained elements of the House and Senate bills and the administration's proposals.

8. MANAGED CARE REGULATIONS

Trying to wrest momentum from Democrats on the politically potent controversy of regulating managed health care was no easy task for the GOP in 1998, especially for House Republicans eager for a way to limit their exposure on the issue before the fall elections.

The solution came in a package developed by a House Republican task force that produced a bill (HR 4250) allowing GOP members to say they supported a managed care overhaul. But it split the House, mostly along party lines, and provided a glimpse of members' positions on one of the most controversial issues of the year. The White House threatened a veto but the legislation never got through Congress.

The task force, led by J. Dennis Hastert, R-Ill., who was later to become House Speaker, included many of the patient protections that both sides of the managed care debate had endorsed, such as giving broader rights to emergency-room care and allowing patients to appeal coverage decisions to an outside panel. The GOP bill did not, however, allow consumers in managed care plans that are exempt from state regulation to sue their health plans under state laws, a key element of a competing Democratic bill.

GOP leaders, noting that many chairmen of committees with jurisdiction for health care were on the task force, which had met in secret, said public hearings demanded by Democrats were unnecessary. The Clinton administration said the legislation was flawed. The Office of Management and Budget said the bill would cover too few people, provide too few patient protections, and "contains unnecessary and irrelevant provisions that undermine the chances for a bipartisan agreement on a patients' bill of rights."

Despite such objections, the bill passed July 24. The key vote was 216–210: R 213–12; D 3–197 (ND 2–147, SD 1–50); I 0–1. *(Vote, p. 894)*

Shortly before that vote the House rejected a Democratic alternative by a vote of 212–217. Supporters of the Democratic bill, including the American Medical Association and a host of provider and consumer groups, said it gave patients broader rights than the GOP plan, such as the ability to sue their plans for damages. Republicans criticized the Democratic plan as a costly creation to benefit trial lawyers, who were major contributors of Democratic campaign funds.

9. CAMPAIGN FINANCE OVERHAUL

A House vote on Aug. 6 to overhaul campaign finance laws marked the first time in six years that either chamber had acted to rewrite the laws. Although the effort died in the Senate, the House's action raised the prospect that Congress was inching closer to its first significant revision of campaign finance laws in nearly twenty years.

The leading proposal to overhaul the campaign finance laws was a bipartisan measure (HR 3526) sponsored by Christopher Shays, R-Conn., and Martin T. Meehan, D-Mass. It was based on a similar Senate plan (S 25) by John McCain, R-Ariz., and Russell D. Feingold, D-Wis. After much debate the Shays-Meehan bill passed on a key vote of 252–179: R 61–164; D 190–15 (ND 142–9, SD 48–6); I 1–0. *(Vote, p. 894)*

But passage came only after an arduous process. Its advocates endured numerous attempts by GOP leaders over several months to block or delay approval.

The legislation banned national parties from receiving or spending "soft money"—unlimited and largely unregulated donations to political parties. It also set new restrictions on campaign-related expenditures by third-party groups.

GOP leaders initially blocked the Shays-Meehan measure from coming to the House floor in March. That action only encouraged the bill's supporters to embrace a procedural device that would have let them debate a variety of campaign finance bills on their own terms.

GOP leaders finally relented to an open debate on the issue in May. But they made the bill open to dozens of amendments, then forced it to compete with ten other substitute amendments to the underlying bill. Whichever of the substitute amendments got the most votes, at least a majority, would prevail.

A significant victory for supporters of Shays-Meehan came in August when the House voted for their substitute amendment, 237–186. Fifty-one Republicans voted for the measure, outweighing the eleven Democrats who voted against it.

The relatively strong vote prompted the authors of several other substitute amendments to withdraw their measures. The final hurdle was a substitute amendment by Asa Hutchinson, R-Ark., and Tom Allen, D-Maine, based on the so-called freshman bill that took a less aggressive stance against soft money and issue advocacy advertising. GOP leaders considered embracing the freshman proposal to get the 238 votes needed to stop Shays-Meehan. Supporters of Shays-Meehan praised the freshmen for their efforts but urged defeat of that plan. The freshman measure ultimately failed, 147–222, with sixty-one members voting "present."

In spite of the advance made by campaign finance reform advocates, the legislation never made it to passage in either of the Congresses during President Clinton's second term.

10. RELEASE OF STARR REPORT

Undoubtedly the most controversial and politically divisive event of Bill Clinton's second term was the effort by House Republicans to impeach the president and see him removed from office. A central event in this drama occurred in September 1998 when an independent counsel, Kenneth W. Starr, investigating charges against the president, sent a report to the House suggesting that Clinton be impeached. Two days later, the House voted to release the report to the public. The report, sensational and in many places strikingly descriptive and even lurid about alleged sexual conduct by the president, provoked an enormous controversy.

The report gave Starr's version of Clinton's affair with former White House intern Monica Lewinsky and subsequent events. Clinton's representatives cautioned that it should be viewed as a one-sided document but the vote on the resolution to release the report

(H Res 525) showed that Republicans, in their effort to remove Clinton, were willing to accept Starr's allegations and move forward on impeachment charges despite a clear absence of public support. The resolution was adopted by a vote of 363–63: R 224–0; D 138–63 (ND 102–46, SD 36–17); I 1–0. (Vote, p. 894)

However, rather than reading the salacious details of the Starr report as evidence of Clinton's immorality and lack of respect for laws, much of the public was repulsed by the fact that these details were released, polls showed. The vote also represented the last time GOP efforts to investigate Clinton were able to pick up Democratic support.

No one in Congress had read the report before it was released, and many were appalled when they learned of its explicit descriptions of Clinton's liaisons with Lewinsky. The report was posted on the Internet and became the subject of voluminous media coverage. Although the report was harshly criticized and even lampooned as x-rated, Starr and his prosecutors insisted the details were necessary to document Clinton's lies and efforts to get others to lie.

Supporting material, including a videotape of Clinton's Aug. 17 testimony before a grand jury, was released in subsequent weeks, after having been screened, and to some extent redacted, by committee members. When the dust cleared, the public clearly remained opposed to impeachment and vehemently objected to being subjected to all of the details of the relationship.

The fact that most Democrats joined in the vote was lost on the public. The most vocal Democrats were those on the Judiciary Committee who voted against the release, on the grounds it violated due process and basic fairness. Those Democrats who voted for the release generally declined to defend their vote and in some cases expressed remorse.

The vote to release was a turning point in the Republican impeachment effort, one that Democrats say vividly demonstrated how out of step the GOP was with popular sentiment. And within days bipartisan cooperation on impeachment began eroding. By the time a vote authorizing an impeachment inquiry was taken in October the two parties had separated completely.

11. SKILLED WORKER VISAS

The House in 1998 remained a major stumbling block for legislation designed to increase the number of skilled temporary workers allowed to immigrate to the United States. Although a bill (S 1723) increasing the number of so-called H-1B visas went through the Senate without difficulty, an unlikely coalition of labor-backed Democrats and Republican immigration opponents held up the House bill (HR 3736) for most of the year. But behind-the-scenes negotiating helped get the measure enacted. The major turning point was House passage of the legislation in September by a key vote of 288–133: R 189–34; D 99–98 (ND 66–76; SD 33–22); I 0–1. (Vote, p. 894)

The vote represented a big success for a new lobby: the high-tech industry. It also represented a major departure from the anti-immigration policies pushed by the House in 1996. Since that year, Congress had voted to restore welfare benefits to legal immigrants, loosen requirements on immigrants waiting for permanent visas, and give partial or complete amnesty to a category of Central American refugees who came to America to escape civil wars in the 1980s. The vote to expand the number of skilled immigrant visas was more than merely a retreat from previous policies. It was an affirmative decision to expand immigration, at least for skilled workers. The legislation increased the number of H-1B visas allotted each year from 65,000 to as many as 115,000.

The vote was not the last chapter in the year's debate. With the House acting so late, a handful of senators was able to block action on

a conference report. In the end, the measure was added to an omnibus spending package passed at the end of the year. But the House vote was clearly the highest hurdle in a difficult year.

12. OMNIBUS APPROPRIATIONS

Republican leaders portrayed the massive, year-end omnibus spending bill as a victory for their party and an inevitable result of divided government but many in the rank and file saw it as an embarrassing retreat from GOP principles. For Democrats, the vote—and behind-the-scenes negotiations that led up to it—provided a rejuvenating breather that allowed them to change the subject from impeachment of President Clinton to their election-year agenda, especially education.

The vote capped a year of gridlock on the budget after President Clinton and congressional Republicans spent months talking past each other and trying to use the budget to score political points, mostly in vain. Action on most of the thirteen annual appropriations bills for fiscal 1999—the approximately one-third of the budget upon which Congress and the president must agree each year—slid past deadline, and eight of the measures were lumped together into an omnibus creation (HR 4328—PL 105-277) that broke through budget targets set only a year earlier. The eight bills had been slowed by numerous disagreements among Republicans, and between them and the White House.

Despite the impeachment inquiry hanging over his head, Clinton entered the talks with a strong hand. Ever since Republicans took the political blame for partial government shutdowns in 1995–1996 and for a vetoed 1997 flood aid bill, Clinton had used veto threats to extract concessions from them on spending bills. Negotiations started in early October but moved slowly, allowing Democrats advantage as the elections approached. Democrats took delight in having a forum for their election year agenda.

In the negotiations Clinton won a $1.2 billion down payment on his initiative to subsidize the hiring of 100,000 new teachers, obtained his full $17.9 billion request for the International Monetary Fund, and received many "emergency" spending items, including financing for the Bosnia peacekeeping mission and $5.9 billion in farm disaster aid.

Republican conservatives were appalled. "At a time when we are dealing with a weakened president . . . you would think that our leadership, who professed to be conservatives leading this revolution, could stand tough within that budget cap and stay true to the commitment that we . . . came here for in 1994," said Jon Christensen, R-Neb.

Despite grumbling from junior GOP conservatives, the bill passed later in October by a vote of 333–95: R 162–64; D 170–31 (ND 120–26, SD 50–5); I 1–0. (Vote, p. 894)

13. IMPEACHMENT

By the time the House was ready to vote Dec. 19 to make Bill Clinton only the second president ever to be impeached, the environment had become surreal in Washington. On the eve of the scheduled vote, Clinton had ordered a military strike against Iraq. That postponed debate for a day, enough time for Speaker-designate Robert L. Livingston, R-La., to publicly acknowledge that he, like Clinton, had been unfaithful to his wife. When debate finally began Dec. 18 on the four articles of impeachment, nerves were raw. The articles, approved Dec. 11 and 12 by the House Judiciary Committee along party lines, accused the president of two counts of perjury, one count of obstruction of justice, and one count of abuse of power.

Through it all, Democrats complained that the votes should be delayed until hostilities with Iraq ended. Their anger was increased by

Republicans' move to block consideration of a censure resolution. "To be spending the time of this House to smear our commander in chief when brave men and women are risking their lives for their country shocks the conscience," John Conyers Jr. of Michigan, the Judiciary Committee's ranking Democrat, said on the floor.

Then came a dramatic announcement from Livingston that he would not serve as Speaker and would leave Congress—setting an example for Clinton to follow, he said.

"Infidelity—adultery—is not a public act, it's a private act, and the government, the Congress, has no business intruding into private acts," Judiciary Chairman Henry J. Hyde, R-Ill., said in closing debate. "But it is our business, it is our duty to observe, to characterize public acts by public officials. . . . And when you have a serial violator of the oath who is the chief law enforcement officer of the country—who appoints the judges and the Supreme Court, the attorney general—we have a problem."

The House adopted the first article, which accused Clinton of lying to a grand jury about his affair with Monica Lewinsky, by a vote of 228–206: R 223–5; D 5–200 (ND 1–149, SD 4–51); I 0–1. A second count, accusing Clinton of obstructing justice, was also adopted, 221–212. The two other recommended articles were rejected. These actions sent the matter to the Senate for trial in 1999, as provided by the Constitution. *(Vote, p. 894)*

1. S 1601. Human Cloning Ban. Motion to invoke cloture (thus limiting debate) on the motion to proceed to the bill banning creation of a human embryo through cloning. Motion rejected 42–54: R 42–12; D 0–42 (ND 0–34, SD 0–8), Feb. 11, 1998. Three-fifths of the total Senate (60) is required to invoke cloture.

2. S 1663. Campaign Finance Overhaul. Motion to invoke cloture (thus limiting debate) on the McCain, R-Ariz., substitute amendment that would revise financing of federal political campaigns. Motion rejected 51–48: R 7–48; D 44–0 (ND 36–0, SD 8–0), Feb. 26, 1998. Three-fifths of the total Senate (60) is required to invoke cloture.

3. S 1768. IMF Funding. McConnell, R-Ky., amendment to provide $17.9 billion for the International Monetary Fund, including $3.4 billion for a new program aimed at preventing global financial crises and $14.5 billion for the U.S. "quota" to the international agency. The amendment would prohibit release of the quota funds unless the IMF agrees to certain conditions, including restricting aid to nations that do not conform to trade agreements. Adopted 84–16: R 41–14; D 43–2 (ND 35–2, SD 8–0), March 26, 1998.

4. S 1768. NATO Expansion. Warner, R-Va., amendment to add language to the resolution of ratification that would require the president to certify to Congress that the United States would not support any further NATO expansion for three years from the date Poland, Hungary, and the Czech Republic join the alliance. Rejected 41–59: R 24–31; D 17–28 (ND 15–22, SD 2–6), April 30, 1998. A "nay" was a vote in support of the president's position.

5. S 1723. Skilled Worker Visas. Passage of the bill to increase the number of so-called H-1B visas, which allow highly skilled immigrants to work in the United States for six years, from the current cap of 65,000 per year to 95,000 for the remainder of fiscal 1998. The measure also would increase the cap on the visas to 105,000 for fiscal 1999 and 115,000 for the following three fiscal years, but it would sunset the cap to its original level at the end of fiscal 2002. The bill also would increase the authorization for certain educational grants, authorize funding for an Internet job bank and authorize funding to provide training opportunities in information technology. Passed 78–20: R 51–2; D 27–18 (ND 20–17, SD 7–1), May 18, 1998. A "nay" was a vote in support of the president's position.

6. S 1415. Tobacco Restrictions. Motion to invoke cloture (thus limiting debate) on the modified Senate Commerce, Science and Transportation Committee substitute amendment to the bill to increase tobacco restrictions. The substitute would require the tobacco industry to pay $516 billion over twenty-five years for antismoking, education, and research programs; raise taxes on cigarettes by $1.10 per pack over five years; and impose penalties on the tobacco industry if youth smoking does not decrease by 60 percent over ten years. Motion rejected 57–42: R 14–40; D 43–2 (ND 37–0, SD 6–2), June 17, 1998. Three-fifths of the total Senate (60) is required to invoke cloture. A "yea" was a vote in support of the president's position.

7. HR 2646. Education Savings Accounts. Adoption of the conference report on the bill to allow individuals to contribute up to $2,000 a year of after-tax funds in tax-sheltered savings accounts that may be used to pay for educational expenses. Adopted (thus cleared for the president) 59–36: R 51–2; D 8–34 (ND 6–28, SD 2–6), June 24, 1998. A "nay" was a vote in support of the president's position.

8. S 2057. Same-Sex Military Training. Byrd, D-W.Va., amendment to the Gramm, R-Texas, amendment. The Byrd amendment would prohibit the armed forces from housing male and female recruits in the same barracks and would prohibit them from conducting gender-integrated basic training. The Gramm amendment would remove restrictions on recipients of Naval Reserve Officers' Training Corps scholarships. Rejected 39–53: R 31–21; D 8–32 (ND 5–27, SD 3–5), June 25, 1998. (Subsequently, the Gramm amendment was adopted by voice vote.) A "nay" was a vote in support of the president's position.

9. S 2159. Economic Sanctions. Stevens, R-Alaska, motion to table (kill) the Lugar, R-Ind., amendment that would revise the process the president and Congress use to impose unilateral economic sanctions by establishing guidelines for future sanctions and setting up procedures for consideration and implementation of sanctions proposals. The amendment would prohibit the president from implementing any unilateral economic sanction without forty-five days' notice, and it would express the sense of Congress that all future unilateral sanctions end within two years of their enactment unless extended by law. Motion agreed to 53–46: R 27–28; D 26–18 (ND 22–14, SD 4–4), July 15, 1998.

10. HR 1122. "Partial-Birth" Abortion. Passage, over President Clinton's veto on Oct. 10, 1997, of the bill to ban a certain late-term abortion procedure, in which the physician partially delivers the fetus before completing the abortion. Anyone convicted of performing such an abortion would be subject to a fine and up to two years in prison. Rejected 64–36: R 51–4; D 13–32 (ND 9–28, SD 4–4), Sept. 18, 1998. A two-thirds majority of those present and voting (67 in this case) of both houses is required to override a veto. A "nay" was a vote in support of the president's position.

11. HR 4328. Fiscal 1999 Omnibus Appropriations. Adoption of the conference report on the bill to provide almost $500 billion in new budget authority for those cabinet departments and federal agencies whose fiscal 1999 appropriations bills were never enacted. The measure incorporates eight previously separate appropriations bills: Labor-HHS-Education, Interior, Treasury-Postal, Foreign Operations, Commerce-Justice-State, District of Columbia, Agriculture, and Transportation. In addition, the bill provides $20.8 billion in "emergency" supplemental spending, including $6.8 billion for military spending ($1.9 billion of it for Bosnia operations), $5.9 billion for relief to farmers, $2.4 billion for antiterrorism programs, $3.35 billion to address Year 2000 computer problems, and $1.55 billion for disaster relief from Hurricane Georges. The measure also contains language to extend expiring tax provisions (at a cost of $9.7 billion over nine years). Adopted (thus cleared for the president) 65–29: R 33–20; D 32–9 (ND 26–9, SD 6–0), Oct. 21, 1998. A "yea" was a vote in support of the president's position.

KEY

	Democrats	*Republicans*
Y	Voted for ("yea")	– Announced against
N	Voted against ("nay")	P Voted "present"
+	Announced for	C Voted "present" to avoid possible conflict of interest
#	Paired for	? Did not vote or otherwise make a position known
X	Paired against	

ND Northern Democrats
SD Southern Democrats
Southern states – Ala., Ark., Fla., Ga., Ky., La., Miss., N.C., Okla., S.C., Tenn., Texas, Va.

Senate Key Votes	1	2	3	4	5	6	7	8	9	10	11
ALABAMA											
Sessions	Y	N	N	Y	Y	N	Y	Y	N	Y	N
Shelby	Y	N	Y	Y	Y	N	Y	Y	Y	Y	Y
ALASKA											
Murkowski	Y	N	Y	N	Y	N	Y	Y	N	Y	?
Stevens	Y	N	Y	Y	Y	N	Y	Y	Y	Y	Y
ARIZONA											
Kyl	Y	N	N	N	Y	N	Y	Y	Y	Y	Y
McCain	Y	Y	Y	N	Y	Y	Y	N	Y	Y	N
ARKANSAS											
Hutchinson	Y	N	Y	Y	N	N	Y	?	Y	Y	Y
Bumpers	N	Y	Y	Y	N	Y	N	Y	N	N	?
CALIFORNIA											
Boxer	N	Y	Y	N	Y	Y	N	N	Y	N	Y
Feinstein	N	Y	Y	Y	Y	Y	Y	N	N	N	Y
COLORADO											
Allard	Y	N	N	N	Y	N	Y	N	N	Y	N
Campbell	N	N	N	Y	Y	N	Y	Y	Y	Y	Y
CONNECTICUT											
Dodd	N	Y	Y	N	Y	Y	N	N	N	N	Y
Lieberman	N	Y	Y	N	Y	Y	Y	N	N	N	Y
DELAWARE											
Roth	N	N	Y	N	Y	Y	Y	?	N	Y	Y
Biden	N	Y	Y	N	N	Y	Y	N	N	Y	Y
FLORIDA											
Mack	N	N	N	N	Y	N	Y	N	Y	Y	Y
Graham	N	Y	Y	N	Y	Y	N	N	N	N	Y
GEORGIA											
Coverdell	Y	N	N	N	Y	N	Y	Y	Y	Y	Y
Cleland	N	Y	Y	N	Y	Y	Y	N	N	N	Y
HAWAII											
Akaka	N	Y	Y	N	N	Y	?	?	Y	N	Y
Inouye	N	Y	Y	N	Y	Y	N	Y	Y	N	?
IDAHO											
Craig	Y	N	Y	Y	Y	N	Y	Y	N	Y	Y
Kempthorne	Y	N	Y	Y	Y	N	Y	N	N	Y	Y
ILLINOIS											
Durbin	N	Y	Y	N	N	Y	N	N	N	N	Y
Moseley-Braun	N	Y	Y	N	N	Y	N	N	N	N	Y
INDIANA											
Coats	Y	N	Y	N	Y	N	Y	Y	N	Y	N
Lugar	N	N	Y	N	Y	N	Y	N	N	Y	N
IOWA											
Grassley	Y	N	Y	N	Y	Y	Y	Y	Y	Y	N
Harkin	N	?	Y	Y	N	Y	N	N	Y	N	Y
KANSAS											
Brownback	Y	N	Y	N	Y	N	Y	Y	N	Y	Y
Roberts	Y	N	Y	Y	Y	N	Y	Y	N	Y	Y
KENTUCKY											
McConnell	Y	N	Y	N	Y	N	Y	Y	Y	Y	Y
Ford	N	Y	Y	N	Y	N	N	Y	Y	Y	Y
LOUISIANA											
Breaux	N	Y	Y	N	Y	Y	Y	N	Y	Y	Y
Landrieu	N	Y	Y	N	Y	Y	N	N	N	Y	Y
MAINE											
Collins	N	Y	Y	N	Y	Y	Y	N	Y	N	N
Snowe	N	Y	Y	Y	Y	Y	Y	N	Y	N	N
MARYLAND											
Mikulski	N	Y	Y	N	N	Y	N	N	Y	N	Y
Sarbanes	N	Y	Y	N	N	Y	N	N	Y	N	Y
MASSACHUSETTS											
Kennedy	N	Y	Y	N	N	Y	N	N	N	N	Y
Kerry	N	Y	Y	N	N	Y	N	N	Y	N	Y
MICHIGAN											
Abraham	Y	N	N	N	Y	N	Y	Y	Y	Y	Y
Levin	?	Y	Y	N	N	Y	N	N	Y	N	N
MINNESOTA											
Grams	Y	N	Y	N	Y	N	Y	Y	N	Y	N
Wellstone	N	Y	N	Y	N	Y	N	N	N	N	N
MISSISSIPPI											
Cochran	Y	N	Y	N	Y	N	Y	N	N	Y	Y
Lott	Y	N	Y	N	Y	N	Y	Y	Y	Y	Y
MISSOURI											
Ashcroft	Y	N	N	Y	Y	N	Y	Y	Y	Y	N
Bond	Y	N	Y	Y	Y	N	Y	N	N	Y	Y

Senate Key Votes	1	2	3	4	5	6	7	8	9	10	11
MONTANA											
Burns	Y	N	Y	Y	Y	N	Y	Y	N	Y	Y
Baucus	N	Y	Y	N	Y	Y	?	?	N	N	N
NEBRASKA											
Hagel	Y	N	Y	N	Y	N	Y	N	N	Y	Y
Kerrey	N	Y	Y	N	Y	Y	N	N	N	N	N
NEVADA											
Bryan	-	Y	Y	N	Y	Y	N	N	Y	N	Y
Reid	?	Y	Y	Y	Y	Y	N	N	Y	Y	N
NEW HAMPSHIRE											
Gregg	Y	N	Y	N	Y	Y	Y	Y	N	Y	Y
Smith	Y	N	N	Y	Y	N	Y	Y	Y	Y	N
NEW JERSEY											
Lautenberg	N	Y	Y	N	Y	Y	N	N	Y	N	Y
Torricelli	N	Y	Y	Y	N	Y	Y	Y	Y	N	Y
NEW MEXICO											
Domenici	Y	N	Y	N	Y	N	+	N	N	Y	Y
Bingaman	N	Y	Y	Y	Y	Y	N	N	Y	N	Y
NEW YORK											
D'Amato	Y	N	Y	N	?	Y	Y	N	Y	Y	Y
Moynihan	N	Y	Y	Y	N	Y	N	Y	N	Y	N
NORTH CAROLINA											
Faircloth	Y	N	N	Y	?	N	Y	Y	Y	Y	Y
Helms	Y	N	N	Y	Y	N	Y	Y	Y	Y	?
NORTH DAKOTA											
Conrad	N	Y	Y	N	Y	Y	N	Y	N	Y	Y
Dorgan	N	Y	Y	N	Y	Y	N	N	N	Y	Y
OHIO											
DeWine	Y	N	Y	N	Y	N	Y	Y	Y	Y	Y
Glenn	N	Y	Y	N	N	Y	N	?	?	N	?
OKLAHOMA											
Inhofe	Y	N	N	Y	Y	N	Y	Y	Y	Y	N
Nickles	Y	N	N	Y	Y	N	Y	Y	Y	Y	N
OREGON											
Smith	N	N	Y	N	Y	Y	Y	N	N	Y	Y
Wyden	N	Y	Y	Y	Y	Y	N	-	Y	N	Y
PENNSYLVANIA											
Santorum	Y	N	Y	N	Y	N	Y	Y	N	Y	N
Specter	N	Y	Y	Y	Y	?	?	?	Y	Y	N
RHODE ISLAND											
Chafee	N	Y	Y	Y	Y	Y	N	N	N	N	Y
Reed	N	Y	Y	Y	Y	Y	N	N	Y	N	Y
SOUTH CAROLINA											
Thurmond	N	N	Y	Y	Y	N	Y	Y	Y	Y	Y
Hollings	N	Y	Y	Y	Y	Y	N	Y	Y	Y	?
SOUTH DAKOTA											
Daschle	N	Y	Y	N	Y	Y	N	N	N	Y	Y
Johnson	N	Y	Y	N	Y	Y	N	N	N	Y	Y
TENNESSEE											
Frist	Y	N	Y	N	Y	Y	Y	Y	N	Y	Y
Thompson	Y	Y	N	N	Y	N	Y	N	Y	Y	Y
TEXAS											
Gramm	Y	N	Y	N	Y	N	Y	Y	N	Y	N
Hutchison	Y	N	Y	Y	Y	N	Y	N	N	Y	Y
UTAH											
Bennett	N	N	Y	N	Y	Y	Y	Y	Y	Y	Y
Hatch	Y	N	Y	N	Y	Y	Y	Y	Y	Y	Y
VERMONT											
Jeffords	N	Y	Y	Y	Y	Y	N	N	N	N	Y
Leahy	N	Y	Y	Y	Y	Y	N	N	Y	Y	Y
VIRGINIA											
Warner	?	N	Y	Y	Y	N	Y	N	N	N	Y
Robb	N	Y	Y	N	Y	N	N	N	N	N	Y
WASHINGTON											
Gorton	Y	N	Y	N	Y	N	Y	Y	N	Y	Y
Murray	N	Y	Y	Y	Y	Y	N	N	Y	N	Y
WEST VIRGINIA											
Byrd	N	Y	Y	Y	Y	Y	Y	Y	N	Y	N
Rockefeller	N	Y	Y	N	N	Y	?	?	N	N	Y
WISCONSIN											
Feingold	N	Y	N	N	N	Y	N	Y	N	N	N
Kohl	N	Y	Y	Y	Y	Y	Y	N	Y	N	N
WYOMING											
Enzi	Y	N	Y	Y	Y	N	Y	Y	N	Y	N
Thomas	Y	N	Y	N	N	N	Y	Y	N	Y	N

1. HR 2631. Line-Item Vetoes. Passage, over President Clinton's veto on Nov. 13, 1997, of the bill to disapprove Clinton's line-item vetoes of thirty-eight projects, totaling $287 million, in the fiscal 1998 military construction appropriations bill (HR 2016—PL 105–45). Passed 347–69: R 197–23; D 149–46 (ND 100–41, SD 49–5); I 1–0, Feb. 5, 1998. A two-thirds majority of those present and voting (277 in this case) of both chambers is required to override a veto. A "nay" was a vote in support of the president's position.

2. HR 2400. Special Transportation Projects. Graham, R-S.C., amendment to strike provisions that provide funds for specified projects, including about $9 billion for highway projects, and other funding for specified transit and bus projects. Rejected 79–337: R 67–152; D 12–184 (ND 6–137, SD 6–47); I 0–1, April 1, 1998.

3. HR 6. Affirmative Action. Riggs, R-Calif., amendment to prohibit any public institution of higher education that participates in any Higher Education Act program from discriminating against, or granting preferential treatment to, any person or group in admissions based in whole or in part on race, sex, color, ethnicity, or national origin. Rejected 171–249: R 166–55; D 5–193 (ND 2–143, SD 3–50); I 0–1, May 6, 1998. A "nay" was a vote in support of the president's position.

4. HR 10. Financial Services Overhaul. Passage of the bill to eliminate current Glass-Steagall Act and Bank Holding Company Act barriers against affiliations between banking, securities, insurance, and other firms. Passed 214–213: R 153–73; D 61–139 (ND 47–100, SD 14–39); I 0–1, May 13, 1998. A "nay" was a vote in support of the president's position.

5. S 1150. Food Stamps for Legal Immigrants. Adoption of the rule (H Res 446) to dispose of the conference report on the bill to reauthorize agricultural research and education programs through fiscal 2002. The rule would have allowed a point of order to strike $818 million in funding in the conference report to restore food stamps to 250,000 legal immigrants. Rejected 120–289: R 118–98; D 2–190 (ND 1–140, SD 1–50); I 0–1, May 22, 1998.

6. HR 4104. Contraceptive Coverage. Lowey, D-N.Y., amendment to prohibit the Office of Personnel Management from accepting a contract that provides coverage for prescription drugs unless the plan also provides equivalent coverage for prescription contraception drugs. Adopted 224–198: R 48–177; D 175–21 (ND 130–17, SD 45–4); I 1–0, July 16, 1998.

7. HR 4194. Public Housing Overhaul. Lazio, R-N.Y., amendment to overhaul public housing management and allow increased local control over rents and occupancy standards. Adopted 230–181: R 215–4; D 15–176 (ND 8–136, SD 7–40); I 0–1, July 17, 1998.

8. HR 4250. Managed Care Regulations. Passage of the bill to revise managed care and medical insurance regulations. The bill would provide a range of patient protections, create a two-step appeals process for challenging a health plan administrator's decisions, and expand the availability of medical savings accounts. Passed 216–210: R 213–12; D 3–197 (ND 2–147, SD 1–50); I 0–1, July 24, 1998. A "nay" was a vote in support of the president's position.

9. HR 2183. Campaign Finance Overhaul. Passage of the bill to ban soft money contributions for federal elections, expand regulations on advertising that advocates a candidate, and tighten the definition of what constitutes coordination with a federal candidate. The text of the bill was the Shays-Meehan substitute adopted by the House on Aug. 3. Passed 252–179: R 61–164; D 190–15 (ND 142–9, SD 48–6); I 1–0, Aug. 6, 1998.

10. H Res 525. Release of Starr Report. Adoption of the resolution to provide for the release and distribution of the report from Independent Counsel Kenneth W. Starr regarding allegations of criminal offenses and other misconduct by President Clinton. Under the resolution, the Judiciary Committee would review the materials to determine whether they contain grounds for impeachment. It also required the committee to immediately release the initial 445-page report, and release other documents to the public on Sept. 28 unless the committee voted not to release certain materials. Adopted 363–63: R 224–0; D 138–63 (ND 102–46, SD 36–17); I 1–0, Sept. 11, 1998.

11. HR 3736. Skilled Worker Visas. Passage of the bill to increase the number of six-year H-1B skill- and profession-based visas for foreign workers from 65,000 to 115,000 in fiscal 1999 and 2000 and 107,500 in fiscal 2001. The bill also would require some employers using H-1B workers to prove they have tried to recruit qualified U.S. workers and have not laid off U.S. workers. Passed 288–133: R 189–34; D 99–98 (ND 66–76, SD 33–22); I 0–1, Sept. 24, 1998. A "nay" was a vote in support of the president's position.

12. HR 4328. Fiscal 1999 Omnibus Appropriations. Adoption of the conference report on the bill to provide almost $500 billion in new budget authority for those cabinet departments and federal agencies whose fiscal 1999 appropriations bills were never enacted. The measure incorporates eight previously separate appropriations bills: Labor-HHS-Education, Interior, Treasury-Postal, Foreign Operations, Commerce-Justice-State, District of Columbia, Agriculture, and Transportation. In addition, the bill provides $20.8 billion in "emergency" supplemental spending, including $6.8 billion for military spending ($1.9 billion of it for Bosnia operations), $5.9 billion for relief to farmers, $2.4 billion for antiterrorism programs, $3.35 billion to address Year 2000 computer problems, and $1.55 billion for disaster relief from Hurricane Georges. The measure also contains language to extend expiring tax provisions (at a cost of $9.7 billion over nine years), increase the number of H-1B visas for high-tech foreign workers, impose a three-year moratorium on new taxes on Internet access, implement the Chemical Weapons Convention, and extend for six months Chapter 12 of the bankruptcy code, which is designed to help struggling farmers. Adopted 333–95: R 162–64; D 170–31 (ND 120–26, SD 50–5); I 1–0, Oct. 20, 1998. (HR 4328 was originally the fiscal 1999 Transportation appropriations bill.) A "yea" was a vote in support of the president's position.

13. H Res 611. Impeachment of President Clinton/Article I—Grand Jury Perjury. Adoption of Article I of the resolution, which would impeach President Clinton for "perjurious, false and misleading testimony" during his Aug. 17, 1998, federal grand jury testimony about his relationship with former White House intern Monica Lewinsky, his prior testimony in the Paula Jones sexual harassment lawsuit, and his attempts to influence others' testimony in both. Adopted 228–206: R 223–5; D 5–200 (ND 1–149, SD 4–51); I 0–1, Dec. 19, 1998. A "nay" was a vote in support of the president's position.

KEY

	Democrats	*Republicans*	**Independent**

Y Voted for ("yea")
N Voted against ("nay")
+ Announced for
# Paired for
X Paired against

– Announced against
P Voted "present"
C Voted "present" to avoid possible conflict of interest
? Did not vote or otherwise make a position known

ND Northern Democrats
SD Southern Democrats
Southern states – Ala., Ark., Fla., Ga., Ky., La., Miss., N.C., Okla., S.C., Tenn., Texas, Va.

House Key Votes	1	2	3	4	5	6	7	8	9	10	11	12	13
ALABAMA													
1 *Callahan*	Y	N	Y	N	N	N	?	Y	Y	Y	Y	Y	Y
2 *Everett*	Y	N	Y	N	N	N	Y	Y	N	Y	Y	Y	Y
3 *Riley*	Y	N	Y	N	N	N	Y	Y	N	Y	Y	Y	Y
4 *Aderholt*	Y	N	Y	N	N	N	Y	Y	N	Y	Y	Y	Y
5 Cramer	Y	N	N	Y	N	Y	N	N	Y	Y	Y	Y	N
6 *Bachus*	Y	N	Y	N	N	N	Y	Y	N	Y	N	N	Y
7 Hilliard	Y	N	N	N	N	Y	N	N	Y	N	N	Y	N
ALASKA													
AL *Young*	Y	N	N	N	N	N	Y	Y	N	?	N	Y	Y
ARIZONA													
1 *Salmon*	N	Y	Y	Y	Y	N	Y	Y	N	Y	Y	N	Y
2 Pastor	Y	N	N	N	N	Y	N	N	Y	Y	Y	Y	N
3 *Stump*	Y	Y	Y	Y	N	N	Y	Y	N	Y	N	N	Y
4 *Shadegg*	Y	Y	Y	Y	Y	N	Y	Y	N	Y	Y	Y	Y
5 *Kolbe*	Y	Y	Y	Y	Y	Y	Y	Y	N	Y	Y	Y	Y
6 *Hayworth*	Y	Y	Y	Y	N	N	Y	Y	N	Y	Y	Y	Y
ARKANSAS													
1 Berry	Y	N	N	N	N	Y	N	N	Y	Y	N	Y	N
2 Snyder	Y	N	N	N	N	Y	?	N	Y	Y	Y	Y	N
3 *Hutchinson*	Y	N	Y	N	N	N	Y	Y	N	Y	N	Y	Y
4 Dickey	N	N	N	N	N	N	Y	Y	N	Y	Y	Y	Y
CALIFORNIA													
1 *Riggs*	Y	N	Y	Y	?	Y	Y	Y	Y	Y	N	N	Y
2 *Herger*	?	N	Y	Y	N	N	Y	Y	N	Y	Y	Y	Y
3 Fazio	Y	N	N	Y	N	Y	N	N	Y	Y	Y	?	N
4 *Doolittle*	Y	N	Y	Y	Y	N	+	Y	N	Y	Y	Y	Y
5 Matsui	Y	N	N	N	N	Y	N	N	Y	Y	Y	Y	N
6 Woolsey	Y	N	N	N	N	Y	N	N	Y	N	Y	Y	N
7 Miller	Y	N	N	N	?	Y	N	N	Y	N	Y	N	?
8 Pelosi	Y	N	N	N	N	Y	N	N	Y	N	N	Y	N
9 Lee[1]			N	N	N	Y	N	N	Y	N	N	N	N
10 Tauscher	Y	N	N	Y	N	Y	N	N	Y	Y	Y	Y	N
11 Pombo	Y	N	Y	N	Y	N	Y	Y	N	Y	Y	N	Y
12 Lantos	Y	N	N	N	N	Y	N	N	Y	Y	Y	Y	N
13 Stark	N	N	N	N	?	Y	N	N	Y	N	N	?	N
14 Eshoo	?	N	N	N	N	Y	N	N	Y	Y	Y	Y	N
15 *Campbell*	Y	Y	Y	Y	Y	Y	Y	Y	N	Y	Y	N	Y
16 Lofgren	N	P	N	N	N	Y	N	N	Y	N	Y	Y	N
17 Farr	Y	N	N	N	N	Y	N	N	Y	Y	Y	Y	N
18 Condit	Y	Y	N	N	N	Y	N	N	Y	N	N	N	N
19 *Radanovich*	Y	N	?	Y	Y	N	Y	Y	N	Y	Y	Y	Y
20 Dooley	N	N	N	Y	N	Y	N	N	Y	Y	N	Y	N
21 *Thomas*	Y	Y	Y	Y	Y	Y	Y	Y	N	Y	Y	Y	Y
22 Capps, L.[2]		N	N	N	N	Y	N	N	Y	Y	Y	Y	N
23 *Gallegly*	Y	N	Y	Y	Y	Y	Y	Y	N	Y	Y	N	Y
24 Sherman	N	N	N	N	N	Y	N	N	Y	Y	Y	Y	N
25 *McKeon*	+	N	Y	N	N	N	Y	Y	N	Y	Y	Y	Y
26 Berman	Y	N	N	N	N	Y	N	N	Y	Y	Y	Y	N
27 *Rogan*	Y	Y	Y	Y	N	N	Y	Y	N	Y	Y	Y	Y
28 *Dreier*	Y	Y	Y	Y	Y	N	Y	Y	N	Y	Y	Y	Y
29 Waxman	N	N	N	N	N	Y	N	N	Y	Y	Y	Y	N
30 Becerra	+	N	N	N	N	Y	N	N	Y	N	Y	Y	N
31 Martinez	N	N	N	N	N	Y	N	N	Y	N	N	Y	N
32 Dixon	Y	N	N	N	N	Y	N	N	Y	N	N	Y	N
33 Roybal-Allard	Y	N	N	N	N	+	–	N	Y	N	N	Y	N
34 Torres	Y	?	N	N	?	Y	N	N	Y	N	?	?	N
35 Waters	Y	?	N	N	N	Y	N	N	Y	N	?	Y	N
36 Harman	N	N	N	?	?	Y	?	N	Y	Y	Y	Y	N
37 Millender-McD.	Y	N	N	N	N	Y	–	N	Y	Y	Y	Y	N
38 *Horn*	Y	N	Y	N	Y	Y	Y	Y	N	Y	N	Y	Y
39 *Royce*	N	?	Y	Y	Y	N	Y	Y	N	Y	N	N	Y
40 *Lewis*	Y	N	Y	N	N	N	Y	Y	N	Y	Y	Y	Y
41 *Kim*	Y	N	Y	Y	N	N	Y	Y	N	Y	Y	Y	Y
42 Brown	Y	N	N	N	N	Y	N	N	Y	N	N	Y	N
43 *Calvert*	Y	N	Y	Y	N	N	Y	Y	N	Y	Y	Y	Y
44 Bono, M.[3]			Y	Y	Y	N	Y	Y	N	Y	Y	Y	Y

House Key Votes	1	2	3	4	5	6	7	8	9	10	11	12	13
45 *Rohrabacher*	N	Y	Y	Y	Y	N	Y	Y	N	Y	N	N	Y
46 Sanchez	N	N	N	N	N	Y	N	N	Y	Y	+	Y	N
47 *Cox*	Y	Y	Y	Y	Y	N	Y	Y	N	Y	Y	Y	Y
48 *Packard*	Y	N	Y	Y	Y	N	Y	Y	Y	Y	Y	Y	Y
49 *Bilbray*	Y	N	Y	N	Y	N	Y	Y	N	Y	Y	N	Y
50 Filner	N	N	N	N	N	#	–	N	Y	N	N	N	N
51 *Cunningham*	Y	N	Y	Y	Y	N	Y	Y	?	Y	Y	Y	Y
52 *Hunter*	Y	Y	Y	N	Y	N	Y	Y	N	Y	N	N	Y
COLORADO													
1 DeGette	N	N	N	Y	N	Y	N	N	Y	Y	N	N	N
2 Skaggs	N	Y	–	–	–	Y	N	N	Y	N	Y	N	N
3 *McInnis*	Y	N	Y	N	Y	N	Y	Y	N	Y	Y	Y	Y
4 *Schaffer*	Y	Y	Y	N	Y	N	Y	Y	N	Y	N	N	Y
5 *Hefley*	Y	N	Y	N	Y	N	Y	Y	N	Y	N	N	Y
6 *Schaefer*	Y	N	?	Y	Y	N	Y	Y	N	Y	?	Y	Y
CONNECTICUT													
1 *Kennelly*	Y	N	N	Y	N	?	?	N	Y	Y	?	Y	N
2 Gejdenson	Y	N	N	Y	N	Y	N	N	Y	Y	N	Y	N
3 DeLauro	Y	N	N	Y	N	Y	N	N	Y	Y	N	Y	N
4 *Shays*	N	Y	N	Y	N	Y	Y	Y	N	Y	Y	N	N
5 Maloney	Y	N	N	N	N	Y	N	N	Y	Y	N	Y	N
6 *Johnson*	Y	N	N	Y	N	Y	Y	Y	Y	Y	Y	Y	Y
DELAWARE													
AL *Castle*	Y	Y	N	Y	N	Y	Y	Y	Y	Y	Y	N	Y
FLORIDA													
1 *Scarborough*	Y	Y	Y	N	Y	N	Y	Y	N	?	Y	N	Y
2 Boyd	Y	N	N	N	N	Y	N	N	Y	Y	Y	N	N
3 Brown	Y	N	N	N	N	Y	N	N	Y	N	N	Y	N
4 *Fowler*	Y	N	Y	Y	Y	Y	Y	Y	N	Y	Y	Y	Y
5 Thurman	Y	N	N	N	N	Y	N	N	Y	Y	N	N	N
6 *Stearns*	Y	N	Y	Y	N	N	Y	Y	N	Y	Y	N	Y
7 *Mica*	Y	N	Y	Y	Y	N	+	Y	N	Y	Y	N	Y
8 *McCollum*	Y	Y	Y	N	Y	N	Y	Y	N	Y	N	Y	Y
9 *Bilirakis*	Y	N	Y	Y	Y	N	Y	Y	N	Y	Y	Y	Y
10 *Young*	Y	Y	Y	Y	Y	N	Y	?	N	Y	Y	Y	Y
11 Davis	N	N	N	N	N	Y	N	N	Y	N	Y	N	N
12 *Canady*	Y	N	Y	N	Y	N	Y	Y	N	Y	Y	Y	Y
13 *Miller*	N	Y	Y	Y	Y	N	Y	Y	N	Y	N	N	Y
14 *Goss*	Y	Y	Y	Y	Y	N	Y	Y	N	Y	Y	+	Y
15 *Weldon*	Y	Y	Y	N	N	N	Y	Y	N	Y	Y	N	Y
16 *Foley*	Y	Y	Y	?	Y	Y	Y	Y	Y	Y	Y	Y	Y
17 Meek	N	N	N	N	N	Y	N	N	Y	N	N	Y	N
18 *Ros-Lehtinen*	Y	?	N	Y	Y	Y	Y	Y	Y	Y	Y	Y	Y
19 Wexler	N	Y	N	N	N	Y	N	N	Y	N	N	Y	N
20 Deutsch	N	Y	N	N	?	Y	N	N	Y	Y	N	Y	N
21 *Diaz-Balart*	Y	N	N	Y	Y	Y	Y	Y	N	Y	Y	Y	Y
22 *Shaw*	Y	N	Y	Y	Y	Y	Y	Y	N	Y	Y	Y	Y
23 Hastings	Y	N	?	N	N	Y	N	N	Y	N	N	Y	N
GEORGIA													
1 *Kingston*	Y	Y	Y	Y	Y	N	Y	Y	N	Y	N	N	Y
2 Bishop	Y	N	N	Y	N	Y	N	N	Y	Y	N	N	Y
3 *Collins*	Y	N	Y	Y	Y	N	Y	Y	N	Y	N	N	Y
4 *McKinney*	N	N	N	N	N	Y	N	N	Y	N	N	N	N
5 Lewis	Y	Y	N	N	N	?	?	N	Y	N	N	N	N
6 *Gingrich*[4]			Y		Y				Y		Y	Y	Y	Y
7 *Barr*	Y	Y	Y	Y	N	N	Y	Y	N	Y	N	N	Y
8 *Chambliss*	Y	N	Y	N	N	N	Y	Y	N	Y	Y	Y	Y
9 *Deal*	Y	Y	Y	Y	N	N	Y	Y	N	Y	N	N	Y
10 *Norwood*	Y	N	Y	N	Y	N	Y	Y	N	Y	Y	Y	Y
11 *Linder*	Y	N	Y	Y	Y	N	Y	?	N	Y	Y	Y	Y
HAWAII													
1 Abercrombie	Y	N	N	N	N	Y	N	N	N	N	N	Y	N
2 Mink	Y	N	N	N	N	Y	N	N	N	N	N	Y	N
IDAHO													
1 *Chenoweth*	Y	N	N	N	N	N	Y	N	N	Y	N	Y	Y
2 *Crapo*	Y	N	Y	Y	N	N	Y	Y	N	Y	Y	Y	Y
ILLINOIS													
1 Rush	Y	N	N	N	N	Y	N	N	Y	N	N	Y	N
2 Jackson	Y	N	N	N	N	Y	N	N	Y	N	N	Y	N
3 Lipinski	Y	N	N	N	N	N	N	N	Y	N	N	Y	N
4 Gutierrez	N	N	N	N	N	Y	N	N	Y	Y	Y	Y	N
5 Blagojevich	Y	N	N	N	N	Y	N	N	Y	Y	Y	Y	N

[1] Barbara Lee, D-Calif., was sworn in April 21, replacing Ronald V. Dellums, D-Calif., who resigned Feb. 6.

[2] Lois Capps, D-Calif., was sworn in March 17, replacing Walter Capps, D-Calif., who died Oct. 28, 1997.

[3] Mary Bono, R-Calif., was sworn in April 21, replacing Sonny Bono, R-Calif., who died Jan. 5.

[4] Newt Gingrich, R-Ga., as Speaker of the House, voted at his discretion.

KEY

	Democrats	*Republicans*	**Independent**

Y Voted for ("yea")
N Voted against ("nay")
+ Announced for
# Paired for
X Paired against

– Announced against
P Voted "present"
C Voted "present" to avoid possible conflict of interest
? Did not vote or otherwise make a position known

ND Northern Democrats
SD Southern Democrats
Southern states – Ala., Ark., Fla., Ga., Ky., La., Miss., N.C., Okla., S.C., Tenn., Texas, Va.

House Key Votes	1	2	3	4	5	6	7	8	9	10	11	12	13
6 Hyde	Y	Y	Y	Y	N	N	N	Y	Y	Y	Y	N	Y
7 Davis	Y	N	N	N	N	Y	N	N	N	N	N	Y	N
8 Crane	Y	N	Y	Y	Y	N	Y	Y	Y	Y	Y	Y	Y
9 Yates	N	?	?	?	N	Y	N	?	Y	N	?	N	N
10 Porter	+	Y	Y	Y	N	Y	Y	Y	Y	Y	Y	Y	Y
11 Weller	Y	N	Y	Y	N	N	Y	Y	N	Y	Y	Y	Y
12 Costello	Y	N	N	N	N	N	N	N	Y	Y	N	N	N
13 Fawell	Y	N	Y	Y	Y	Y	Y	Y	N	Y	Y	Y	Y
14 Hastert	Y	N	Y	Y	Y	Y	Y	Y	N	Y	Y	Y	Y
15 Ewing	N	N	Y	N	N	N	Y	Y	N	Y	Y	Y	Y
16 Manzullo	Y	N	Y	N	N	Y	Y	Y	N	Y	Y	N	Y
17 Evans	Y	N	N	N	N	N	Y	N	N	Y	N	Y	N
18 LaHood	Y	N	N	N	N	N	Y	N	Y	Y	Y	N	Y
19 Poshard	Y	N	N	N	N	Y	N	N	Y	?	?	?	N
20 Shimkus	Y	N	Y	Y	N	N	Y	N	Y	Y	Y	Y	Y
INDIANA													
1 Visclosky	Y	N	N	N	N	Y	N	N	Y	Y	N	Y	N
2 McIntosh	Y	?	Y	Y	Y	N	Y	Y	N	Y	Y	N	Y
3 Roemer	Y	N	N	N	N	N	N	N	Y	Y	Y	Y	N
4 Souder	Y	Y	N	Y	N	N	Y	Y	N	Y	Y	Y	N
5 Buyer	Y	N	N	Y	Y	N	Y	Y	N	Y	Y	Y	Y
6 Burton	+	N	Y	Y	N	N	Y	Y	N	Y	+	Y	Y
7 Pease	Y	N	Y	Y	N	N	Y	Y	N	Y	Y	Y	Y
8 Hostettler	Y	N	Y	Y	Y	N	Y	Y	N	Y	N	N	Y
9 Hamilton	Y	N	N	N	N	Y	N	N	Y	Y	Y	Y	N
10 Carson	N	N	-	N	N	Y	N	N	Y	N	N	Y	N
IOWA													
1 Leach	N	Y	N	Y	N	N	Y	Y	Y	Y	Y	Y	Y
2 Nussle	N	N	N	N	N	N	Y	Y	N	Y	Y	Y	Y
3 Boswell	N	N	N	N	N	Y	N	N	Y	Y	Y	Y	N
4 Ganske	N	N	Y	Y	N	Y	Y	N	Y	Y	Y	Y	Y
5 Latham	Y	N	Y	Y	N	N	Y	Y	N	Y	Y	Y	Y
KANSAS													
1 Moran	Y	N	N	N	N	N	Y	Y	N	Y	Y	Y	Y
2 Ryun	Y	N	Y	N	N	N	Y	Y	N	Y	Y	Y	Y
3 Snowbarger	Y	N	Y	N	Y	N	Y	Y	N	Y	Y	Y	Y
4 Tiahrt	Y	N	Y	N	Y	N	Y	Y	N	Y	Y	Y	Y
KENTUCKY													
1 Whitfield	Y	N	Y	Y	Y	N	Y	Y	N	Y	N	Y	Y
2 Lewis	Y	N	Y	N	N	Y	Y	Y	N	Y	Y	Y	Y
3 Northup	Y	N	Y	Y	N	N	Y	Y	N	Y	Y	Y	Y
4 Bunning	Y	N	Y	Y	N	N	Y	Y	N	Y	Y	Y	Y
5 Rogers	Y	N	Y	N	Y	N	Y	Y	N	Y	Y	Y	Y
6 Baesler	Y	N	N	N	N	Y	Y	N	Y	Y	N	Y	N
LOUISIANA													
1 Livingston	Y	N	Y	Y	N	N	?	Y	N	Y	Y	Y	Y
2 Jefferson	Y	?	N	N	N	Y	?	N	Y	N	N	Y	N
3 Tauzin	Y	N	Y	Y	Y	N	Y	Y	N	Y	Y	Y	Y
4 McCrery	Y	P	Y	Y	Y	N	Y	Y	N	Y	Y	Y	Y
5 Cooksey	Y	N	Y	Y	N	N	Y	Y	N	Y	Y	Y	Y
6 Baker	Y	N	Y	Y	N	N	Y	Y	N	Y	Y	Y	Y
7 John	Y	N	N	Y	N	N	?	?	?	Y	Y	Y	N
MAINE													
1 Allen	Y	N	N	N	N	Y	N	N	Y	Y	Y	Y	N
2 Baldacci	Y	N	N	N	N	Y	N	N	Y	Y	Y	Y	N
MARYLAND													
1 Gilchrest	Y	N	N	Y	N	Y	Y	Y	Y	Y	Y	Y	Y
2 Ehrlich	Y	Y	Y	Y	Y	Y	Y	Y	N	Y	Y	Y	Y
3 Cardin	Y	N	N	N	N	Y	N	N	Y	Y	Y	N	Y
4 Wynn	?	N	N	N	N	Y	N	N	Y	Y	N	Y	N
5 Hoyer	Y	N	N	N	N	Y	N	N	Y	Y	Y	Y	N
6 Bartlett	Y	N	Y	Y	Y	Y	Y	Y	N	Y	Y	N	Y
7 Cummings	Y	N	N	N	N	Y	N	N	Y	N	N	Y	N
8 Morella	Y	Y	N	Y	N	Y	N	Y	N	Y	Y	Y	N
MASSACHUSETTS													
1 Olver	Y	N	N	N	N	N	N	N	Y	Y	N	Y	N
2 Neal	Y	N	N	Y	N	Y	N	N	Y	N	Y	Y	N

House Key Votes	1	2	3	4	5	6	7	8	9	10	11	12	13
3 McGovern	Y	N	N	Y	N	N	N	N	Y	Y	Y	Y	N
4 Frank	N	N	N	N	N	Y	N	N	Y	N	Y	Y	N
5 Meehan	N	N	N	N	N	Y	N	N	Y	N	Y	?	N
6 Tierney	Y	N	N	N	N	Y	N	N	Y	Y	Y	Y	N
7 Markey	N	N	N	Y	N	Y	N	?	Y	N	Y	Y	N
8 Kennedy	Y	N	N	N	N	Y	N	N	Y	N	Y	Y	N
9 Moakley	Y	N	N	N	N	Y	?	N	Y	Y	N	Y	N
10 Delahunt	Y	N	N	Y	N	Y	N	N	Y	N	Y	Y	N
MICHIGAN													
1 Stupak	N	N	N	Y	N	N	N	N	N	Y	N	N	N
2 Hoekstra	Y	Y	Y	Y	Y	N	Y	Y	N	Y	Y	N	Y
3 Ehlers	Y	N	N	Y	N	N	Y	N	N	Y	Y	N	Y
4 Camp	Y	N	Y	N	N	N	Y	Y	N	Y	Y	Y	Y
5 Barcia	Y	N	N	Y	N	N	N	N	Y	?	N	Y	N
6 Upton	N	N	N	Y	N	N	Y	Y	Y	Y	Y	N	Y
7 Smith	N	N	Y	Y	N	N	Y	Y	Y	Y	N	N	Y
8 Stabenow	Y	N	N	N	N	Y	N	N	Y	Y	Y	Y	N
9 Kildee	Y	N	N	N	N	N	N	N	Y	Y	Y	Y	N
10 Bonior	Y	N	N	N	N	Y	N	N	Y	N	Y	Y	N
11 Knollenberg	Y	N	Y	Y	Y	N	Y	Y	N	Y	Y	Y	Y
12 Levin	Y	N	N	N	N	Y	N	N	Y	Y	Y	Y	N
13 Rivers	N	N	N	N	N	Y	N	N	Y	Y	N	N	N
14 Conyers	N	N	N	N	?	Y	N	N	Y	N	Y	N	N
15 Kilpatrick	Y	N	N	N	N	Y	N	N	Y	N	N	N	N
16 Dingell	Y	N	N	Y	N	Y	N	N	Y	N	Y	Y	N
MINNESOTA													
1 Gutknecht	Y	Y	Y	N	N	N	Y	Y	N	Y	Y	Y	Y
2 Minge	N	Y	N	N	N	N	Y	N	N	Y	Y	Y	N
3 Ramstad	N	N	N	N	N	Y	Y	Y	Y	Y	Y	Y	Y
4 Vento	N	N	N	N	N	Y	N	N	Y	Y	Y	Y	N
5 Sabo	Y	N	N	N	N	Y	N	N	Y	Y	Y	Y	N
6 Luther	N	N	N	N	N	Y	Y	N	Y	Y	Y	N	N
7 Peterson	Y	N	N	N	N	N	N	N	Y	Y	N	Y	N
8 Oberstar	Y	N	N	N	N	Y	N	N	Y	Y	Y	Y	N
MISSISSIPPI													
1 Wicker	Y	N	Y	N	?	N	Y	Y	N	Y	Y	Y	Y
2 Thompson	Y	N	N	N	N	Y	N	N	Y	N	N	N	N
3 Pickering	Y	Y	Y	N	N	Y	Y	Y	N	Y	Y	Y	Y
4 Parker	Y	Y	Y	Y	?	?	?	Y	Y	Y	Y	Y	Y
5 Taylor	Y	N	N	N	N	N	N	Y	N	Y	Y	N	Y
MISSOURI													
1 Clay	Y	N	N	N	N	Y	N	N	Y	N	N	Y	N
2 Talent	Y	N	Y	Y	N	N	Y	Y	N	Y	Y	Y	Y
3 Gephardt	Y	N	N	N	N	N	N	N	Y	Y	Y	Y	N
4 Skelton	Y	N	N	N	N	N	Y	N	Y	Y	Y	Y	N
5 McCarthy	Y	N	N	N	N	Y	N	N	Y	Y	Y	Y	N
6 Danner	Y	N	N	N	N	Y	Y	Y	N	Y	Y	Y	N
7 Blunt	Y	Y	Y	N	Y	N	Y	Y	N	Y	N	Y	Y
8 Emerson	Y	N	Y	Y	N	Y	N	Y	N	Y	Y	Y	Y
9 Hulshof	Y	N	Y	N	Y	N	Y	Y	Y	Y	Y	Y	Y
MONTANA													
AL Hill	Y	Y	Y	Y	N	?	?	Y	N	Y	Y	Y	Y
NEBRASKA													
1 Bereuter	Y	N	Y	N	N	N	Y	Y	Y	Y	Y	Y	Y
2 Christensen	Y	Y	?	N	N	N	Y	Y	N	Y	Y	Y	Y
3 Barrett	Y	N	N	N	N	N	Y	Y	Y	Y	Y	Y	Y
NEVADA													
1 Ensign	N	N	N	Y	Y	Y	Y	Y	N	Y	Y	N	Y
2 Gibbons	Y	N	N	Y	Y	Y	Y	Y	N	Y	Y	Y	Y
NEW HAMPSHIRE													
1 Sununu	Y	N	Y	Y	Y	N	Y	Y	N	Y	Y	Y	Y
2 Bass	Y	N	Y	Y	Y	Y	Y	Y	Y	Y	Y	Y	Y
NEW JERSEY													
1 Andrews	N	N	N	Y	N	Y	N	N	Y	Y	N	Y	N
2 LoBiondo	Y	N	Y	Y	N	N	Y	N	Y	Y	N	Y	Y
3 Saxton	Y	N	N	Y	N	N	Y	Y	Y	Y	Y	Y	Y
4 Smith	Y	N	Y	Y	N	Y	Y	N	Y	Y	Y	Y	Y
5 Roukema	Y	N	Y	Y	Y	Y	Y	N	Y	Y	N	Y	Y
6 Pallone	Y	N	N	Y	N	Y	N	N	Y	Y	Y	Y	N
7 Franks	N	N	N	Y	N	Y	Y	Y	Y	Y	N	Y	Y
8 Pascrell	Y	N	N	N	N	Y	N	N	Y	Y	N	Y	N
9 Rothman	N	N	N	N	N	Y	N	N	Y	Y	Y	Y	N
10 Payne	N	?	N	N	N	Y	N	N	Y	N	N	N	N
11 Frelinghuysen	Y	Y	Y	Y	Y	Y	Y	Y	N	Y	Y	Y	Y
12 Pappas	Y	N	Y	Y	Y	Y	Y	Y	N	Y	Y	Y	Y
13 Menendez	Y	N	N	N	N	Y	N	N	Y	Y	N	Y	N
NEW MEXICO													
1 Wilson [5]							Y	Y	Y	Y	Y	N	Y
2 Skeen	Y	N	N	N	N	N	Y	Y	N	Y	Y	Y	Y
3 Redmond	Y	N	N	N	N	N	Y	Y	N	Y	Y	Y	Y

House Key Votes	1	2	3	4	5	6	7	8	9	10	11	12	13
NEW YORK													
1 Forbes	Y	N	N	Y	N	N	Y	N	Y	Y	Y	Y	Y
2 Lazio	Y	N	N	Y	N	Y	Y	Y	Y	Y	Y	Y	Y
3 King	Y	N	N	Y	?	N	Y	Y	N	Y	Y	N	N
4 McCarthy	Y	N	N	Y	N	Y	N	N	Y	Y	Y	Y	N
5 Ackerman	N	N	N	Y	N	Y	N	N	Y	N	Y	Y	N
6 Meeks[6]		N	N	Y	?	Y	N	N	Y	N	N	Y	N
7 Manton	Y	N	N	Y	N	Y	N	N	Y	Y	?	Y	N
8 Nadler	Y	N	N	Y	N	Y	N	N	Y	N	Y	Y	N
9 Schumer	Y	N	N	Y	N	Y	N	N	Y	Y	Y	Y	N
10 Towns	N	N	N	Y	?	Y	N	N	Y	N	N	Y	N
11 Owens	N	N	N	N	N	Y	N	N	Y	N	N	Y	N
12 Velázquez	Y	N	N	N	N	Y	N	N	Y	N	N	Y	N
13 Fossella	Y	N	Y	Y	N	N	Y	Y	N	Y	Y	Y	Y
14 Maloney	Y	N	N	Y	N	Y	N	N	Y	Y	Y	Y	N
15 Rangel	N	?	N	Y	N	Y	N	N	Y	N	Y	Y	N
16 Serrano	Y	N	N	N	N	Y	N	N	Y	N	N	Y	N
17 Engel	N	N	N	Y	N	Y	N	N	Y	N	N	Y	N
18 Lowey	Y	N	N	Y	N	Y	N	N	Y	Y	Y	Y	N
19 Kelly	Y	N	N	Y	N	Y	Y	Y	Y	Y	Y	Y	Y
20 Gilman	Y	N	N	Y	N	Y	Y	Y	Y	Y	Y	Y	Y
21 McNulty	Y	N	?	Y	N	?	?	N	Y	Y	Y	Y	N
22 Solomon	Y	N	Y	Y	Y	N	Y	Y	N	Y	N	Y	Y
23 Boehlert	Y	N	N	Y	N	Y	Y	Y	Y	Y	Y	Y	Y
24 McHugh	Y	N	Y	N	N	N	N	Y	Y	Y	Y	Y	Y
25 Walsh	Y	N	N	Y	N	Y	N	Y	Y	Y	Y	Y	Y
26 Hinchey	Y	N	N	N	N	Y	N	N	Y	N	N	Y	N
27 Paxon	Y	N	Y	Y	Y	N	Y	Y	N	Y	Y	Y	Y
28 Slaughter	Y	N	N	N	N	Y	N	N	Y	Y	Y	Y	N
29 LaFalce	Y	N	N	N	N	N	N	N	Y	Y	Y	Y	N
30 Quinn	Y	N	N	Y	-	N	Y	Y	Y	Y	Y	Y	Y
31 Houghton	Y	N	N	Y	Y	Y	Y	Y	Y	Y	Y	Y	N
NORTH CAROLINA													
1 Clayton	Y	N	N	N	N	?	N	N	Y	N	Y	Y	N
2 Etheridge	Y	N	N	N	N	Y	N	N	Y	Y	Y	Y	N
3 Jones	Y	Y	Y	N	Y	N	Y	Y	N	Y	Y	N	Y
4 Price	Y	N	N	Y	N	Y	N	N	Y	Y	Y	Y	N
5 Burr	Y	Y	N	N	N	Y	Y	Y	Y	Y	Y	Y	Y
6 Coble	Y	N	Y	Y	Y	N	Y	Y	N	Y	Y	N	Y
7 McIntyre	Y	N	N	N	N	Y	N	N	Y	Y	Y	Y	N
8 Hefner	Y	N	N	?	N	Y	N	N	Y	N	Y	Y	N
9 Myrick	Y	Y	N	Y	Y	N	Y	Y	N	Y	Y	Y	Y
10 Ballenger	Y	Y	Y	Y	Y	N	Y	Y	N	Y	Y	N	Y
11 Taylor	Y	Y	Y	Y	?	N	Y	Y	N	Y	Y	Y	Y
12 Watt	Y	N	N	N	N	N	N	N	Y	N	Y	Y	N
NORTH DAKOTA													
AL Pomeroy	Y	Y	N	Y	N	Y	N	N	Y	Y	Y	Y	N
OHIO													
1 Chabot	N	Y	Y	Y	N	Y	Y	Y	N	Y	Y	N	Y
2 Portman	Y	N	Y	Y	Y	N	Y	Y	N	Y	Y	N	Y
3 Hall	+	N	N	Y	N	N	N	N	Y	Y	Y	Y	N
4 Oxley	Y	N	Y	Y	N	Y	Y	Y	Y	Y	Y	Y	Y
5 Gillmor	Y	N	Y	Y	N	Y	Y	Y	Y	Y	Y	Y	Y
6 Strickland	N	N	N	N	N	Y	N	N	Y	Y	N	Y	N
7 Hobson	Y	N	N	Y	Y	Y	Y	Y	Y	Y	Y	Y	Y
8 Boehner	Y	Y	Y	Y	Y	N	Y	Y	N	Y	Y	Y	Y
9 Kaptur	Y	N	N	N	N	Y	N	N	Y	Y	N	N	N
10 Kucinich	Y	N	N	N	N	Y	N	N	Y	N	N	Y	N
11 Stokes	Y	N	N	N	N	Y	N	N	Y	N	N	Y	N
12 Kasich	Y	Y	N	Y	N	Y	Y	Y	N	Y	Y	Y	Y
13 Brown	N	N	N	Y	N	Y	N	N	Y	Y	Y	Y	N
14 Sawyer	Y	N	N	Y	N	Y	N	N	Y	Y	Y	Y	N
15 Pryce	Y	N	N	Y	N	Y	Y	Y	N	+	+	+	Y
16 Regula	Y	N	N	Y	N	Y	Y	Y	Y	Y	Y	Y	Y
17 Traficant	Y	N	N	Y	N	Y	Y	Y	Y	Y	N	Y	Y
18 Ney	Y	N	N	Y	N	N	Y	Y	Y	Y	N	Y	Y
19 LaTourette	Y	N	N	Y	N	N	Y	Y	Y	Y	Y	Y	Y
OKLAHOMA													
1 Largent	Y	Y	N	N	Y	N	Y	Y	Y	Y	Y	N	Y
2 Coburn	Y	Y	Y	N	Y	N	Y	Y	Y	Y	Y	Y	Y
3 Watkins	Y	Y	N	N	N	N	Y	Y	Y	Y	Y	Y	Y
4 Watts	Y	Y	N	N	N	N	Y	Y	Y	Y	Y	N	Y
5 Istook	Y	Y	N	N	N	N	Y	Y	Y	Y	Y	N	Y
6 Lucas	Y	Y	N	N	N	N	Y	Y	Y	Y	Y	Y	Y
OREGON													
1 Furse	?	N	N	N	?	Y	N	N	Y	?	Y	Y	N
2 Smith	Y	N	Y	N	P	N	Y	Y	Y	Y	Y	Y	Y
3 Blumenauer	Y	N	N	N	N	Y	N	N	Y	Y	Y	Y	N
4 DeFazio	N	N	N	N	?	Y	N	N	Y	Y	N	Y	N
5 Hooley	Y	N	N	N	N	Y	N	N	Y	Y	Y	Y	N
PENNSYLVANIA													
1 Brady[7]				N	Y		N	N	Y	N	N	Y	N
2 Fattah	Y	N	N	N	N	Y	N	N	Y	N	N	Y	N

House Key Votes	1	2	3	4	5	6	7	8	9	10	11	12	13
3 Borski	Y	N	N	N	N	Y	N	N	Y	Y	N	Y	N
4 Klink	?	N	N	N	N	N	Y	N	Y	Y	N	N	N
5 Peterson	Y	N	Y	N	N	N	Y	N	Y	Y	Y	Y	Y
6 Holden	Y	N	N	Y	N	N	N	N	Y	Y	N	N	N
7 Weldon	Y	N	N	Y	N	N	Y	N	Y	Y	Y	Y	Y
8 Greenwood	N	N	Y	Y	Y	Y	Y	Y	Y	Y	Y	Y	Y
9 Shuster	Y	N	?	N	Y	N	Y	Y	Y	Y	Y	Y	Y
10 McDade	Y	N	N	Y	N	N	Y	Y	Y	Y	Y	Y	Y
11 Kanjorski	N	N	N	N	N	Y	N	N	Y	Y	N	N	N
12 Murtha	Y	N	N	N	N	Y	N	N	Y	Y	?	Y	N
13 Fox	Y	N	N	Y	N	Y	Y	Y	Y	Y	Y	Y	Y
14 Coyne	Y	N	N	N	N	Y	N	N	Y	Y	Y	Y	N
15 McHale	Y	N	N	N	N	N	N	N	Y	Y	Y	Y	Y
16 Pitts	Y	N	Y	Y	Y	N	Y	N	Y	Y	Y	Y	Y
17 Gekas	Y	N	Y	Y	Y	N	Y	Y	Y	Y	Y	Y	Y
18 Doyle	Y	N	?	Y	N	N	N	N	Y	Y	Y	Y	N
19 Goodling	Y	N	Y	Y	Y	N	Y	Y	N	Y	N	Y	Y
20 Mascara	Y	N	N	N	N	Y	N	N	Y	Y	Y	Y	N
21 English	Y	N	N	Y	Y	N	Y	Y	Y	Y	Y	Y	Y
RHODE ISLAND													
1 Kennedy	Y	N	N	N	N	Y	N	N	Y	N	Y	Y	N
2 Weygand	Y	N	N	N	N	Y	N	N	Y	Y	Y	Y	N
SOUTH CAROLINA													
1 Sanford	N	N	Y	Y	N	Y	N	N	Y	Y	Y	N	Y
2 Spence	Y	N	Y	Y	Y	N	Y	Y	N	N	Y	Y	Y
3 Graham	Y	Y	Y	N	N	Y	Y	Y	Y	Y	Y	Y	Y
4 Inglis	Y	Y	Y	Y	Y	N	Y	Y	?	Y	N	Y	Y
5 Spratt	Y	N	N	N	N	Y	N	N	Y	Y	Y	Y	N
6 Clyburn	Y	N	N	N	N	Y	N	N	Y	Y	Y	Y	N
SOUTH DAKOTA													
AL Thune	Y	N	Y	N	N	N	Y	Y	Y	Y	Y	Y	Y
TENNESSEE													
1 Jenkins	Y	N	Y	N	Y	N	Y	Y	N	+	Y	Y	Y
2 Duncan	N	N	Y	N	Y	N	Y	Y	Y	Y	N	N	Y
3 Wamp	Y	Y	Y	Y	Y	N	Y	Y	Y	Y	N	N	Y
4 Hilleary	Y	Y	Y	Y	Y	N	Y	Y	N	Y	N	Y	Y
5 Clement	Y	N	N	N	N	Y	N	N	Y	Y	Y	Y	N
6 Gordon	Y	N	N	Y	N	Y	N	N	Y	Y	Y	Y	N
7 Bryant	Y	N	Y	Y	Y	N	Y	Y	Y	Y	Y	Y	Y
8 Tanner	Y	N	N	Y	N	Y	?	N	Y	Y	Y	Y	N
9 Ford	Y	N	N	Y	N	+	-	-	Y	N	Y	Y	N
TEXAS													
1 Sandlin	Y	N	N	N	N	Y	N	N	Y	Y	N	Y	N
2 Turner	Y	N	N	N	N	Y	N	N	Y	Y	Y	Y	N
3 Johnson, Sam	Y	Y	Y	N	?	Y	Y	Y	N	Y	Y	N	Y
4 Hall	Y	Y	Y	N	N	N	Y	Y	Y	Y	Y	Y	Y
5 Sessions	Y	Y	Y	N	Y	N	Y	Y	N	Y	Y	Y	Y
6 Barton	Y	Y	Y	N	Y	N	?	Y	N	Y	Y	Y	Y
7 Archer	Y	Y	Y	Y	Y	N	Y	Y	N	Y	Y	Y	Y
8 Brady	Y	Y	Y	N	Y	N	Y	Y	N	+	N	Y	Y
9 Lampson	Y	N	N	N	N	Y	N	N	Y	Y	Y	Y	N
10 Doggett	N	N	N	N	N	Y	N	N	Y	Y	Y	Y	N
11 Edwards	Y	Y	N	N	N	Y	N	N	Y	Y	Y	Y	N
12 Granger	Y	N	N	N	N	Y	Y	N	Y	Y	Y	Y	Y
13 Thornberry	Y	Y	Y	Y	Y	N	Y	Y	N	Y	Y	N	Y
14 Paul	Y	N	Y	N	N	N	N	N	N	N	Y	N	N
15 Hinojosa	Y	N	N	N	N	Y	N	N	Y	Y	Y	Y	N
16 Reyes	Y	N	N	?	N	Y	N	N	Y	Y	Y	Y	N
17 Stenholm	Y	Y	N	N	N	Y	N	N	Y	Y	Y	Y	N
18 Jackson-Lee	Y	N	N	N	N	Y	N	N	Y	Y	Y	Y	N
19 Combest	Y	Y	Y	N	N	N	Y	N	Y	Y	Y	Y	Y
20 Gonzalez	?	?	?	?	?	?	?	?	?	?	N	Y	N
21 Smith	Y	N	Y	N	N	N	Y	Y	N	Y	Y	Y	Y
22 DeLay	Y	N	Y	Y	Y	N	Y	Y	N	Y	Y	Y	Y
23 Bonilla	Y	Y	N	N	N	N	Y	N	Y	Y	Y	Y	Y
24 Frost	Y	N	N	Y	N	Y	N	N	Y	Y	Y	Y	N
25 Bentsen	Y	N	N	N	N	Y	N	N	Y	Y	Y	Y	N
26 Armey	?	N	Y	Y	N	N	Y	N	Y	Y	Y	Y	Y
27 Ortiz	Y	N	N	N	N	X	-	N	Y	Y	Y	Y	N
28 Rodriguez	Y	N	N	N	N	Y	N	?	N	Y	Y	Y	N
29 Green	Y	N	N	N	?	Y	N	N	Y	Y	N	Y	N
30 Johnson, E.B.	Y	N	N	N	N	Y	N	N	Y	-	Y	Y	N

[5] Heather Wilson, R-N.M., was sworn in June 25, replacing Stephen H. Schiff, R-N.M., who died March 25.

[6] Gregory W. Meeks, D-N.Y., was sworn in Feb. 5, replacing Floyd H. Flake, D-N.Y., who resigned Nov. 15, 1997.

[7] Robert A. Brady, D-Pa., was sworn in May 21, replacing Thomas M. Foglietta, D-Pa., who resigned Nov. 11, 1997.

KEY

	Democrats	*Republicans*	**Independent**
Y	Voted for ("yea")		– Announced against
N	Voted against ("nay")		P Voted "present"
+	Announced for		C Voted "present" to avoid
#	Paired for		possible conflict of interest
X	Paired against		? Did not vote or otherwise
			make a position known

ND   Northern Democrats
SD   Southern Democrats
Southern states – Ala., Ark., Fla., Ga., Ky., La., Miss., N.C., Okla., S.C., Tenn., Texas, Va.

House Key Votes	1	2	3	4	5	6	7	8	9	10	11	12	13
UTAH													
1 *Hansen*	Y	N		Y	N	N	Y	Y	N	Y	Y	?	Y
2 *Cook*	Y	N	Y	Y	N	Y	Y	Y	Y	Y	Y	Y	Y
3 *Cannon*	Y	?	Y	N	Y	N	Y	Y	N	Y	Y	Y	Y
VERMONT													
AL **Sanders**	Y	N	N	N	N	Y	N	N	Y	Y	N	Y	N
VIRGINIA													
1 *Bateman*	Y	N	+	+	–	N	Y	Y	N	Y	Y	Y	Y
2 Pickett	Y	N	N	N	N	Y	N	N	Y	Y	Y	Y	N
3 Scott	Y	N	N	N	N	Y	N	N	N	N	Y	Y	N
4 Sisisky	Y	N	N	N	N	Y	N	N	Y	Y	Y	Y	N
5 Goode	Y	N	N	N	Y	N	Y	Y	N	Y	N	N	Y
6 *Goodlatte*	Y	N	Y	Y	Y	N	Y	Y	N	Y	Y	Y	Y
7 *Bliley*	Y	N	Y	Y	Y	N	Y	Y	N	Y	Y	Y	Y
8 Moran	Y	N	N	Y	N	Y	N	N	Y	N	Y	Y	N

House Key Votes	1	2	3	4	5	6	7	8	9	10	11	12	13
9 Boucher	Y	N	N	N	N	Y	N	N	Y	Y	N	Y	N
10 *Wolf*	Y	Y	N	Y	N	N	Y	Y	N	Y	Y	N	Y
11 *Davis*	Y	N	N	N	N	Y	Y	Y	N	Y	Y	Y	Y
WASHINGTON													
1 *White*	Y	Y	N	Y	Y	N	Y	Y	Y	Y	Y	N	Y
2 *Metcalf*	Y	N	Y	Y	Y	N	Y	Y	Y	Y	N	Y	Y
3 *Smith, Linda*	Y	N	Y	Y	N	N	Y	Y	Y	Y	Y	N	Y
4 *Hastings*	Y	N	Y	Y	Y	N	Y	Y	N	Y	Y	Y	Y
5 *Nethercutt*	Y	Y	Y	Y	N	Y	N	Y	N	Y	Y	Y	Y
6 Dicks	Y	N	N	Y	N	Y	N	N	Y	Y	Y	Y	N
7 McDermott	N	N	N	N	N	Y	N	N	Y	N	Y	N	N
8 *Dunn*	Y	N	Y	Y	Y	Y	?	Y	N	Y	Y	Y	Y
9 Smith, Adam	Y	N	N	N	N	Y	N	N	Y	Y	Y	N	N
WEST VIRGINIA													
1 Mollohan	Y	N	N	Y	N	N	N	N	N	N	N	?	N
2 Wise	Y	N	N	Y	N	Y	N	N	Y	Y	N	Y	N
3 Rahall	Y	N	N	Y	N	N	N	N	N	Y	N	Y	N
WISCONSIN													
1 *Neumann*	N	Y	?	Y	Y	N	Y	Y	N	Y	Y	N	Y
2 *Klug*	N	?	N	Y	Y	Y	Y	?	Y	Y	Y	N	Y
3 Kind	N	N	N	N	N	Y	N	N	Y	Y	Y	N	N
4 Kleczka	Y	N	N	N	N	Y	N	N	Y	Y	N	N	N
5 Barrett	N	Y	N	N	N	Y	N	N	N	Y	Y	N	N
6 *Petri*	N	N	Y	N	Y	N	Y	Y	Y	Y	Y	N	N
7 Obey	Y	N	N	N	N	Y	N	N	Y	Y	N	Y	N
8 Johnson	N	N	N	N	N	Y	N	N	Y	Y	Y	N	N
9 *Sensenbrenner*	N	Y	Y	Y	Y	N	Y	Y	N	Y	Y	N	Y
WYOMING													
AL *Cubin*	Y	Y	Y	Y	Y	N	Y	Y	N	Y	Y	Y	Y

Senate

1. IMPEACHMENT: MOTION TO DISMISS

The Constitution stipulates that a two-thirds Senate majority is required to remove a president from office. Even as President Clinton's trial was convened as the first order of business for the 106th Congress, it was widely assumed that fewer than sixty-seven senators would vote for either of the articles of impeachment the House had adopted a month earlier.

The first evidence to support that assumption came on Jan. 22, the ninth day of the trial, when Robert C. Byrd, D-W.Va., announced that he would lead the effort to dismiss both charges and adjourn the trial. The president was charged with committing perjury in testimony to a federal grand jury about his relationship with Monica Lewinsky while she was a White House intern, and with leading a campaign to cover up the affair. Even if true, Byrd said, those offenses did not constitute grounds for removal.

Such a motion had been expected but the fact that Byrd had offered it was a clear indication that the thirteen Republican House "managers" of the impeachment charges were making no headway in their effort to build a bipartisan majority for conviction. As one of the harshest Democratic critics of the president's behavior during the previous year, and as someone legendary for both guarding senatorial prerogative and promoting propriety in public life, Byrd was central to the prosecution strategy. Were he to announce for conviction, the managers believed, other Democrats would be sure to follow.

Instead, the opposite occurred. In the bellwether vote of the trial, on Jan. 27 Byrd's motion was defeated, 44–56: R 0–55; D 44–1 (ND 36–1, SD 8–0). Although the vote kept the proceedings alive, it also signaled, in the words of Sen. Richard C. Shelby, R-Ala., that "you've read the end of the book, unless something drastic happens, which none of us foresee." That is because every Democrat except Russell D. Feingold of Wisconsin voted to dismiss the case before any witnesses had been deposed, let alone heard from. At least one-quarter of them, or eleven Democratic senators, would have had to reverse position for there to have been a chance of conviction. *(Vote, p. 908)*

The proceedings continued on for two more weeks. But the atmosphere was palpably different, with many who wanted Clinton out of the White House clearly against dragging out the trial any longer. The House prosecutors harbored a faint hope that one dramatic moment—Lewinsky giving sworn testimony against the president from the well of the Senate—could galvanize senatorial sentiment against Clinton. But on Feb. 4 that hope was dashed when twenty-five GOP senators joined all forty-five Democrats to defeat a motion to send her a subpoena. Instead, she was only heard on snippets of deposition videotape played near the trial's end on television monitors.

2. IMPEACHMENT: ACQUITTAL

Historic by its very occurrence—the first impeachment trial of an elected president and the only such trial since Andrew Johnson's 131 years earlier—the Senate proceedings of 1999 nonetheless ended not with a bang but a whimper. Acquittal was universally expected by the time Chief Justice William H. Rehnquist posed the final question of the trial on Feb. 12: "Senators, how say you? Is the respondent, William Jefferson Clinton, guilty or not guilty?"

From early on, it was clear that a Senate majority agreed with the president's lawyers, who argued that although Clinton's testimony before a federal grand jury about his relationship with White House intern Monica Lewinsky was evasive, it did not cross the high legal threshold to constitute perjury, as Article I alleged. All forty-five Democrats and ten Republicans, seven of them former prosecutors, formed the majority that rejected the charge.

That left the only real suspense for the last vote of the trial, on Article II, which alleged that the president obstructed justice, primarily by encouraging Lewinsky to file a false affidavit in a sexual harassment lawsuit against Clinton filed by an Arkansas woman.

The thirteen GOP prosecutors, or "managers," who had drafted the articles and won their endorsement by the House at the end of 1998, were hoping to spare themselves a measure of embarrassment by persuading at least a simple majority of senators to vote to convict the president on this charge. But even that symbolic victory narrowly eluded them. The vote was a 50–50 tie: R 50–5; D 0–45 (ND 0–37, SD 0–8). *(Vote, p. 908)*

Because a two-thirds majority was required for conviction, the prosecutors were 17 votes short. Put another way, the prosecutors obtained the support of only three of every four senators they needed.

The vote also reflected what many predicted would happen once a political entity such as the Senate was converted to a court. Democrats were united and were joined by a small but pivotal group of GOP moderates. In addition, the five Republicans who voted to acquit on Article II all represented states Clinton carried both in 1992 and 1996.

That there was a vote was something of a victory for Clinton's harshest critics. From the night of the 1998 election, when Democrats unexpectedly gained five House seats, pundits, congressional scholars, and many in Congress assumed that the House's GOP leaders were sufficiently chastened that they would settle on a way to stop the process before impeachment. That did not happen. Although the House prosecutors believed they were not allowed to present on the comprehensive case that the situation demanded, they at least were able to make their arguments to the Senate and the nation. And they were able to hear the verdict rendered in an official—albeit disappointing to them—climax.

3. EDUCATION

If voters were consistent about any one issue in polls taken during Clinton's years in office, it was education and, more specifically, their desire to see Congress enact policies to improve the quality of instruction in public schools.

President Clinton and Democrats seized on the issue with a broad-based program that included funding for school construction and renovation, better after-school programs, aid to turn around failing public schools, and a seven-year plan to help local districts hire 100,000 new teachers and reduce class size in the early grades.

Republicans at first resisted Clinton's calls for more federal activism. After a bitter debate, however, they provided the first $1.2 billion installment of his 100,000-teacher plan in the fiscal 1999 omnibus spending bill.

The GOP in 1999 took a more activist approach on education with an agenda designed to define the differences between the two parties as an issue of control, not money. Republicans argued that states and local schools, not the federal government, should decide spending priorities.

Democrats, arguing that states in the past have done a poor job of directing aid to low-income students, wanted the federal government to direct how funds are spent. The split came into focus in March when the Senate took up the "ed-flex" bill (S 280), designed to allow states to waive federal regulations in order to carry out school improvement programs. Although most Democrats supported the ed-flex legislation, they used it as the vehicle for highlighting Clinton's education priorities, especially his class-size reduction plan.

Sen. Patty Murray, D-Wash., announced she would offer an amendment to the bill that would authorize $11.4 billion over six years to carry out Clinton's program. Republicans fought back during the debate, with Majority Leader Trent Lott, R-Miss., offering an amendment to instead let local schools redirect the $1.2 billion already appropriated for Clinton's plan to other programs, including special education for the disabled. The GOP had provided major funding increases for special education programs during the previous several years.

Murray's amendment was tabled (killed) by the Senate on a 55–44 party-line vote: R 55–0; D 0–44 (ND 0–36, SD 0–8). But the vote was not the final word. The 100,000-teacher issue resurfaced in November as part of the debate on the fiscal 2000 Labor, Health and Human Services and Education spending bill. After intense negotiations, Congress and the White House worked out a deal to provide an additional $1.3 billion for the second year of the plan, while giving states more flexibility to use the money for teacher training and other purposes. *(Vote, p. 908)*

4. GUN CONTROL

For sheer drama, no vote the Senate took in 1999 could match the May cliffhanger on an amendment to the juvenile justice bill (S 254) by Frank R. Lautenberg, D-N.J. It was adopted by 1 vote—only the fourth ballot cast by Al Gore during his vice presidency—reversing the outcome on a similar amendment eight days before. The tally was 51–50: R 6–49; D 44–1 (ND 36–1, SD 8–0), with Gore voting "yea." *(Vote, p. 908)*

Gun control advocates claimed the amendment's adoption as their most significant achievement since Republicans regained control of the Senate in 1995. It set a requirement that all sales at almost all gun shows be subject to criminal background checks. The current allowed required only those prospective buyers who were doing business with federally licensed dealers to be subject to such a requirement. Momentum allowing such a vote was created by the April 20 shooting at Columbine High School in Littleton, Colo., which left fifteen people dead and put great pressure on Congress to address the relative ease with which children, convicted felons, and others may obtain firearms.

The vice president touted the importance of his role following that event while GOP leaders said Gore would regret the vote if he won the Democratic presidential nomination and had to explain it in several key states in the fall campaign. But, either way, Gore would have been unable to make his entry on to the scene had it not been for some intense backroom arm-twisting. In May a virtually identical version of the measure was tabled, or killed, when it obtained only 47 votes, with two sympathetic senators absent.

Needing 1 vote to set up a tie, Democrats focused on the two in their caucus who had voted to table Lautenberg's first proposal. They found their convert in Max Cleland of Georgia, who was offered some modest changes in the language and some heavy persuasion. His switch was made easier when, on the morning of the second vote, a fifteen-year-old walked into a high school near Atlanta and shot six classmates.

The vote vindicated the Democratic tactic of limiting their gun control proposals to a few for which there was broad public support. They did not, for instance, put forward a Clinton administration proposal to limit purchasers to one gun a month. Ultimately, all their proposals were adopted, with Lautenberg's the marquee item.

5. KOSOVO

The quarter-century duel between Congress and the White House over a president's unilateral right to commit U.S. military forces to battle was played out again in the Senate in May. As on several other occasions since Congress enacted the 1973 War Powers Resolution over President Richard Nixon's veto, most members declined to challenge the president's insistence that his constitutional power as commander in chief gives him the right to deploy forces without congressional approval.

This time, the test came on an amendment to the fiscal 2000 defense authorization bill by Arlen Specter, R-Pa., to bar the deployment of U.S. ground troops in the Serbian province of Kosovo unless Congress authorized it in advance. The amendment would not have affected the U.S.-led NATO air campaign against Yugoslavia, which began in March with the aim of halting the repression of ethnic Albanians. Nor would Specter's amendment have applied to the deployment of U.S. ground troops in Kosovo to enforce any peacekeeping agreement that might be negotiated.

From the outset of the bombing campaign, Clinton had insisted that he had no intention of committing ground forces to combat in Kosovo and that he would consult with Congress before making such a move. Indeed, he stressed his aversion to sending in ground troops to the point that some members of Congress and foreign policy experts warned that he was squandering the leverage that even an unspoken threat of a NATO ground invasion might have on Yugoslav President Slobodan Milosevic.

But Specter insisted that Congress could ensure its rightful role in such a portentous decision only by writing the requirement into law. His argument rested on the same facts of political life that the 1973 legislation was intended to circumvent: Once U.S. troops are committed members of Congress are loath to force a withdrawal that might expose the troops to enemy attack.

Specter insisted that Clinton might be able to persuade him to vote to authorize a ground invasion of Kosovo. But opponents contended that the amendment would bolster Milosevic's determination to wait out the NATO air attacks by reassuring him he need not fear ground troops. The amendment was tabled, and thus killed, by a vote of 52–48: R 17–38; D 35–10 (ND 29–8, SD 6–2). *(Vote, p. 908)*

6. MANAGED CARE

It may have been the most convoluted and politically tortuous Senate debate of the legislative year. The delicate politics of managed care were apparent as the Senate took up the issue in July. Majority Leader Trent Lott, R-Miss., introduced language from the Democrats' "patients' bill of rights" (S 6) as the underlying bill for debate. It was given a new number (S 1344). The Democratic language was used to prevent Democrats from offering a long series of amendments on the floor that would force Republicans to cast politically unpopular votes against a variety of patient protections, such as expanding the number of patients who would be guaranteed certain coverage and allowing patients to sue if they were harmed by the decisions of their health plans.

In turn, Democrats introduced the GOP managed care bill as a substitute, so that they could introduce their list of managed care provisions as secondary amendments. Both bills were then debated at the same time, with alternating amendments being offered to each—allowing ample opportunity for political gamesmanship. "The debate that's going on now is one of the most partisan and the most vacuous, the most devoid of effort to try to reach a solution that I've heard in a long time—and that's saying something," grumbled Max Baucus, D-Mont.

Throughout the debate, Republicans repeatedly offered amendments similar to ones offered by Democrats and defeated along party lines just hours earlier. Democrats charged—and several Republicans privately agreed—that the maneuver was aimed at allowing the GOP to claim victory for enacting certain patient protections. But Republican amendments generally offered more limited government oversight to a fewer number of patients—in keeping with the GOP philosophy of less government regulation. As their final amendment, Republicans offered a package that combined all the GOP-backed patient protections with a variety of tax incentives aimed at making health insurance more affordable. Democrats charged that the provisions would only help the rich and hurt the poor.

In an attempt to bridge the partisan divide, a bipartisan group of lawmakers, led by the late John H. Chafee, R-R.I., offered a compromise that would have taken provisions from both sides. But those efforts proved futile.

After four days of partisan debate and procedural contortion, the Republican package passed, 53–47: R 52–2; D 0–45 (ND 0–37, SD 0–8); I 1–0. *(Vote, p. 908)*

7. TAX CUTS

Senate Republicans had long been more cautious than their House counterparts about passing a huge tax cut. In 1998, for instance, they managed to whittle the House's $80.1 billion proposal down to $9.2 billion. But in 1999, with a projected budget surplus of $1 trillion over ten years, the Senate agreed to consider a major package.

After the Budget Committee reserved nearly $800 billion for a tax cut, Finance Committee Chairman William V. Roth Jr., R-Del., unveiled a $792 billion measure (S 1429). The bill would have cut the lowest income tax rate bracket from 15 to 14 percent, eased the so-called marriage penalty, and made changes to pension and retirement laws to give more favorable tax rates to those who saved.

Roth had always worked well with panel Democrats, but he focused this time on ensuring that the bill would appeal to both moderate and conservative Republicans. Meanwhile, President Clinton threatened consistently to veto the bill and its House counterpart (HR 2488), and most Senate Democrats backed the president.

The polarizing situation led to parliamentary maneuvers when the Senate took up the bill in July. First, Republicans had to contend with the so-called Byrd rule, which requires a supermajority of 60 votes to pass measures that are not offset by spending cuts or revenue increases. The Senate bill was not paid for beyond the first ten years, so when the Senate did not waive the Byrd rule the bill's provisions were set to expire Sept. 30, 2009. The vote was 51–48. Party leaders, particularly Minority Leader Tom Daschle, D-S.D., worked hard to keep their troops in line. Daschle succeeded, but three Republicans—Arlen Specter of Pennsylvania and Susan Collins and Olympia J. Snowe, both of Maine—voted no with the Democrats.

Meanwhile, moderates of both parties led by John B. Breaux, D-La., began formulating a $500 billion tax measure that they said was a workable, responsible compromise between the main GOP measure and Democrats' $290 billion proposal. It appeared for a time that the moderate measure might get enough support to challenge the bills but Daschle and Majority Leader Trent Lott, R-Miss., began peeling supporters off the effort. By the time the Senate was ready to vote on the Republican bill, moderates withdrew their plan, all

the while charging that partisanship should not keep Congress from agreeing to a tax bill.

The Senate passed S 1429 at the end of July 57–43: R 52–2; D 4–41 (ND 2–35, SD 2–6); I 1–0. Only two Republicans—Specter and George V. Voinovich of Ohio—voted against it, while four Democrats—Breaux, Bob Kerrey of Nebraska, Mary L. Landrieu of Louisiana, and Robert G. Torricelli of New Jersey—voted for it. *(Vote, p. 908)*

8. CUBA SANCTIONS

For years, a powerful lobbying group, the Cuban American National Foundation, played an important key role in maintaining a tough U.S. policy toward Cuba. Not only had the group helped sustain political support for maintaining the nearly forty-year trade embargo on Fidel Castro's Cuba, it directed considerable financial resources toward further hardening that embargo after the end of the cold war, when Cuba lost the support of its Soviet Union patron.

In 1992 the foundation rallied behind legislation by then-Rep. Robert G. Torricelli, D-N.J., by 1999 a senator, to tighten the Cuba embargo and strengthen opposition to Castro's rule. In 1996 the foundation helped push through a bill by Senate Foreign Relations Committee Chairman Jesse Helms, R-N.C., and Rep. Dan Burton, R-Ind., to write the embargo into permanent law. That meant it would be up to Congress rather than the White House to decide if and when to lift the restrictions on Cuba.

Support for the embargo remained strong in 1999 in the Cuban-American communities of Miami and New Jersey. But the end of the cold war and the 1997 death of the foundation's charismatic leader, Jorge Mas Canosa, weakened its influence in Washington, and encouraged business and farm interests eager to ease the embargo.

In January President Clinton, influenced by Pope John Paul II's 1998 visit to the island, took several small steps to increase contacts with Cuba. Clinton's decision to ease restrictions on travel, mail, and financial transfers won support from key lawmakers in both parties. But the clearest illustration of changing congressional sentiment came in August during debate on the fiscal 2000 agriculture appropriations bill when the Senate refused to table (kill) an amendment by John Ashcroft, R-Mo., to allow the export of food and medicine to Cuba. The vote on Helms's motion to table was 28–70: R 17–36; D 10–34 (ND 8–28, SD 2–6); I 1–0. *(Vote, p. 908)*

The Ashcroft amendment was aimed at broadening a law enacted in 1998 banning trade sanctions on food and medicine, except for countries—such as Cuba—on the State Department's list of terrorist states. At the time, an amendment to keep the sanctions in place on such states, including Cuba, was backed by sixty-seven senators including Ashcroft. In 1999 only twenty-eight senators supported a continued embargo on food and medicine to Cuba. The provision was ultimately pulled out of the agriculture spending bill in conference at the insistence of Cuban-American members of the House.

9. CAFE STANDARDS

Even the possibility of a study of new fuel-efficiency standards for cars and light trucks was too much for the auto industry to take. Pressure from the industry wilted an effort to lift a ban on the Clinton administration launching the study. Automakers came out in force to lobby the vote, which occurred on a sense of the Senate amendment to the fiscal 2000 transportation spending bill.

Each year since Republicans took control of Congress in 1995 the House inserted a rider in the transportation bill to block the Transportation Department from developing new fuel standards and the Senate went along. But in 1999 a bipartisan group of senators—concerned about the rising number of fuel-hungry trucks, sport utility vehicles (SUVs), and vans on the road—vowed to reverse the policy on environmental grounds. The debate reprised themes brought up in the 1970s, when the corporate average fuel economy (CAFE) standards were introduced—environmental and economic costs weighed against safety factors and consumer preferences.

Slade Gorton, R-Wash., Dianne Feinstein, D-Calif., and Richard H. Bryan, D-Nev., wrote President Clinton in March: "The freeze rider denies the purchasers of SUVs and other light trucks the benefits of existing fuel-saving technologies." The letter was signed by twenty-seven Democrats and four Republicans.

Gorton, Feinstein, and Bryan argued on the floor that more efficient cars and trucks would save consumers money while reducing pollution, global warming, and the U.S. trade deficit. They said their language stopped short of advocating new fuel standards, which would come about only after the Transportation Department was allowed to review current data. Groups such as the Union of Concerned Scientists, the Sierra Club, and the League of Conservation Voters published pamphlets and other material outlining technology already employed on popular cars that could help manufacturers meet more stringent standards.

But opponents, led by Spencer Abraham, R-Mich., and Carl Levin, D-Mich., said the amendment would lead inexorably to a fuel standard increase and that would force manufacturers to market smaller, lighter cars that are not as safe or as popular. Abraham cited National Academy of Sciences findings that current fuel-efficiency standards had contributed to thousands of deaths because the victims were driving in lighter vehicles.

Gorton's amendment, which would have allowed the Transportation Department to study changing the CAFE standards and would have encouraged the Senate to reject the House rider, failed 40–55: R 6–45; D 34–9 (ND 29–7, SD 5–2); I 0–1. *(Vote, p. 908)*

10. NUCLEAR TEST BAN TREATY

The Senate's rejection in October of a treaty to ban nuclear weapons testing was one of President Clinton's most embarrassing foreign policy defeats, as well as one of the clearest triumphs of conservative Republicans over his administration.

The Comprehensive Test Ban Treaty (Treaty Doc 105-28) became entangled in a series of partisan political skirmishes that left it with support from just four GOP senators. Administration officials had lobbied sporadically for the treaty since Clinton submitted it for ratification in September 1997. But Senate Democratic proponents intensified their efforts in the weeks leading up to an Oct. 6 conference in Vienna of treaty signatories. After learning of Democratic tactics to force consideration of the treaty, Majority Leader Trent Lott, R-Miss.—a staunch opponent of the test ban—abruptly agreed to schedule twenty-two hours of debate and a vote. Lott's move startled treaty advocates, who had hoped for more time to build political support for the measure.

Once debate began, it became clear that supporters would fall far short of the 67 votes needed for ratification. The administration had failed to win over some of the Senate's influential internationalist Republicans, including Armed Services Committee Chairman John W. Warner, R-Va., and Richard G. Lugar, R-Ind. Warner led a group of lawmakers seeking to delay the vote. He and Democrat Daniel Patrick Moynihan of New York circulated a letter urging that the issue be postponed until the 107th Congress. The letter was signed by sixty-two senators—twenty-four Republicans and thirty-eight Democrats. But the rules of the Senate, as well as pressure to support the Republican leadership, helped give the treaty's critics the upper hand. Several Republicans objected to a unanimous consent agreement, proposed by Minority Leader Tom Daschle, D-S.D., to shelve the vote. A proce-

dural motion by Lott to turn from other legislation back to the treaty passed on a 55–45 party-line vote.

The treaty was then rejected 48–51: R 4–50; D 44–0 (ND 36–0, SD 8–0); I 0–1. *(Vote, p. 908)*

11. CAMPAIGN FINANCE

If there was one constant in the story of campaign finance legislation it was the role played by Mitch McConnell of Kentucky in leading Senate Republicans against such measures. He mounted his first successful filibuster in the 100th Congress; by his count, his most recent effort, in October, was the twentieth time that he has marshaled most of his GOP colleagues to stop such a bill. In order to prevail this year, McConnell had to triumph over a strategy advanced by John McCain, R-Ariz., and Russell D. Feingold, D-Wis., who led the effort to limit the influence of money in politics.

Convinced that their comprehensive proposal could not overcome a McConnell filibuster, they wrote a narrower measure (S 1593). Its central element was a ban on "soft money," the unlimited and unregulated donations from unions, corporations, and wealthy people that were the fastest-growing source of cash to the Republican and Democratic committees that underwrite presidential and congressional campaigns. If they could win 60 votes for this narrow approach, they reasoned, they stood a chance of reassembling their original proposal—or perhaps finding a new bipartisan consensus—through the amendment process. Ultimately, McCain and Feingold sought to win passage of a bill, like the measure (HR 417) the House passed, that would not only ban soft money but would also regulate "issue advocacy" advertising, the campaigns paid for by third parties that promote a candidacy without ever explicitly urging a vote for or against anyone.

After a round of parliamentary maneuvering, in which proponents and opponents in both parties sought to frame the debate to their liking, the key vote came on in Oct. 19. It was on a motion to invoke cloture on an amendment by the Democratic leadership that essentially restated the text of the underlying bill. The vote was 53–47: R 8–46; D 45–0 (ND 37–0, SD 8–0); I 0–1, seven short of the number needed to bring debate to a close. The ballot showed the quicksand through which McCain and Feingold continue to labor. On the one hand, they won a net of one more ally than their previous best showing. And they did so with the help of three Republicans who had voted with McConnell in the past: Sam Brownback of Kansas, Tim Hutchinson of Arkansas, and William V. Roth Jr. of Delaware. But they also lost the votes of two Republicans who were on record as supporting a sweeping approach: Arlen Specter of Pennsylvania and John H. Chafee of Rhode Island. Their strategy also failed to win over several other Republicans who, the sponsors hoped, would see the narrow bill as a vehicle for testing the Senate's sentiment for other approaches. *(Vote, p. 908)*

12. ABORTION

Legislation to ban a procedure that opponents call "partial birth" abortion turned up in Congress every year since Republicans took over in 1995, although the bill never became law because proponents were unable to muster the two-thirds vote necessary to override President Clinton's veto. In that sense, the 1999 debate was no exception, as the Senate vote by less than the two-thirds majority needed for a veto override: 63–34.

The key vote on the bill (S 1692), however, came on what was essentially an effort by two Democratic senators to make a point. During the debate, Tom Harkin of Iowa and Barbara Boxer of California offered a nonbinding amendment to express the sense of Congress that the Supreme Court's 1973 *Roe v. Wade* decision that found that women have the right to abortion was "an appropriate decision" that "secures an important constitutional right" and "should not be overturned." Boxer and Harkin said they offered the amendment in hopes of "smoking out" those Republicans who argued that the "partial birth" ban had nothing to do with the broader issue of abortion rights.

"This is the first time that I know of that we have had the opportunity to vote up or down on whether or not we believe that *Roe v. Wade* should stand and should not be overturned, and that it is, indeed, a good decision," Harkin said.

After a Republican move to table the amendment failed, the amendment was adopted, 51–47: R 8–44; D 43–2 (ND 36–1, SD 7–1); I 0–1. Abortion-rights supporters expressed shock and dismay at their narrow victory, in which only one more senator than an outright majority took their side. They said the tally showed that antiabortion forces wield growing power in Congress and were within striking distance of pushing far more sweeping abortion bills through the Senate. And they said the tally demonstrated that Congress is out of step with the American people, citing polls showing that a solid majority believe abortion should remain legal. *(Vote, p. 908)*

Opponents of abortion rights said the vote revealed less than enthusiastic support for abortion on demand.

13. FINANCIAL SERVICES

Lawmakers agreed for years that the United States needed to repeal decades-old laws restricting cross-ownership among the banking, securities, and insurance industries. Supporters said it would help businesses compete globally and provide consumers with one-stop shopping for financial services. But partisan fights, along with battles among the industries over details, had made consensus in the Senate elusive.

Early in the year it looked as if 1999 would be no different. The new Banking Committee chairman was Phil Gramm, R-Texas, a key player in preventing a financial services overhaul from getting a floor vote in 1998. He was known for partisanship, and indeed, partisanship prevailed in May when the Senate passed an overhaul bill (S 900), 54–44, with only one Democrat, Ernest F. Hollings of South Carolina, on board.

Gramm plowed over Democratic opposition in committee and on the floor by insisting on inclusion of controversial changes to the 1977 Community Reinvestment Act (PL 95-128), an antiredlining measure aimed at forcing banks to make loans in low-income neighborhoods. Gramm insisted on including a provision to exempt small, rural banks from the act, drawing sharp objections from Democrats and a veto threat from the White House.

In the House-Senate conference, Gramm continued to make waves, saying he was willing to pass a partisan bill and dare the White House to veto it. But behind closed doors, Gramm was less unyielding. He fought for days with Democrats and the White House but never walked away from the table. Negotiators say each time a deal was on the verge of collapse, industry representatives stepped up pressure on Gramm, the White House, and others to keep working.

Gramm eventually agreed to drop the reinvestment law exemption for small rural banks but he won a provision to ease the law's regulatory requirements for most small banks. He also was able to include a "sunshine provision" to require disclosure of deals in which a bank offers grants or loans to a community group in exchange for the group's support of the bank's reinvestment activities.

After the protracted conference, the Senate voted overwhelmingly in early November to adopt the conference report on S 900. The vote was 90–8: R 52–1; D 38–7 (ND 30–7, SD 8–0). The House cleared the bill the same day, and President Clinton signed it the following week. *(Vote, p. 908)*

House

1. STEEL RESTRICTIONS

In the six years since passage of the North American Free Trade Agreement, debate over its impact on the nation's economy continued between free-trade advocates and supporters of protection for U.S. businesses. That debate sharpened in early 1999, when the steel industry found itself in a two-year slump. Prices for most steel products dropped sharply; several steel manufacturers filed for bankruptcy, and at least 10,000 of the nation's 170,000 steelworkers were laid off. Steelmakers and their workers blamed the troubles on a 33 percent increase in the volume of steel imported into the United States, much of it from Japan, Brazil, and Russia.

Lawmakers cheered President Clinton when he said in his January State of the Union address that if Japan did not reverse the surge of steel imports "America will respond." Members of the Congressional Steel Caucus went a step further. They introduced a bill (HR 975), sponsored by Peter J. Visclosky, D-Ind., to allow the president to limit steel imports for three years through quotas, tariffs, or other measures. The limits would have kept steel imports at their average monthly level as calculated between August 1994 and July 1997.

Treasury Secretary Robert E. Rubin warned that such a bill would run "a very real risk of triggering protectionist interests around the world." Federal Reserve Chairman Alan Greenspan warned that a "drift toward protectionist policies, which are always difficult to reverse, is a much greater threat than is generally understood." And Rep. Philip M. Crane, R-Ill., chairman of the Ways and Means Subcommittee on Trade, announced a series of hearings to counter what he called "protectionist temptations" in Congress. Free-traders called for the United States to stick to the same laws it expected other countries to live by.

With such opposition, it was unlikely that the Steel Caucus—supported by organized labor—would see its legislation enacted. But its vocal anti-import stance showed the public's discomfort over free trade and underscored how difficult it would be for the president and GOP leaders to enact major trade legislation.

In the end, the margin of victory for protectionism was so wide that even bill supporters were surprised. The House passed HR 975 in on March by a vote of 289–141: R 91–128; D 197–13 (ND 146–9, SD 51–4); I 1–0. Republicans split between those defending home-state industries and free-traders who felt they had done enough for steel manufacturers by approving $1 billion in loan guarantees for the industry. The steel import bill died in the Senate in June when a motion to invoke cloture failed, 42–57. *(Vote, p. 910)*

2. MISSILE DEFENSE

The push for a small-scale national antimissile defense gained momentum in 1998 when North Korea tested a rocket with nearly enough range to strike Alaska or Hawaii, when India and Pakistan tested nuclear weapons, and when a commission chaired by former Defense Secretary Donald H. Rumsfeld warned that a missile threat to U.S. territory could materialize within five years—much sooner than the Clinton administration had projected.

In February the administration included deployment funding for a national missile defense in its long-range budget plans for the first time. Defense Secretary William S. Cohen said the threat of a limited missile attack clearly warranted deployment, but he and other officials reiterated the administration's position that a decision also should be based on the technical success of the antimissile system, its projected cost, and its impact on arms reduction efforts. The administration emphasized the last point particularly, because any nationwide defense would require amending the 1972 Anti-Ballistic Missile (ABM) Treaty, a step Russia opposed.

To challenge the administration's conditional commitment to deployment, Curt Weldon, R-Pa., introduced a one-sentence bill (HR 4) declaring it to be national policy to deploy a national missile defense. John M. Spratt Jr., D-S.C., cosponsored the bill, arguing that it was vague enough that it did not threaten the ABM Treaty. However, the White House opposed the bill as an attack on the pact.

The GOP-led campaign for a limited nationwide antimissile defense system received a symbolic lift in March from a House vote that showed growing Democratic support for the idea. The vote, which came on a procedural motion, amounted to a test of President Clinton's policy of delaying a decision on deploying the antimissile system until the summer of 2000 and basing the decision on many factors, including whether a deployment would undercut talks with Russia.

More than a quarter of the Democrats who voted on the motion joined all but two voting Republicans to reject Clinton's position, thus backing an immediate and unconditional endorsement of an antimissile deployment. The key vote was on a motion by Tom Allen, D-Maine, to recommit the bill to committee with instructions that it be amended to endorse Clinton's policy of basing a deployment decision on several factors, including any possibly adverse impact on arms reduction negotiations. The motion was rejected 152–269: R 2–212; D 150–56 (ND 125–28, SD 25–28); I 0–1. The Weldon bill then was passed, 317–105, with Democrats splitting 103–102 in favor of the measure. *(Vote, p. 910)*

3. KOSOVO AIR ATTACKS

In the weeks before and during the NATO bombing campaign against Yugoslavia, intended to end the oppression of ethnic Albanians in the province of Kosovo, the House took a series of votes relating to the issue without defining a clear policy.

The most conspicuous of the lot occurred in late April when twenty-six Democrats joined all but thirty-one voting Republicans—led by Majority Whip Tom DeLay, R-Texas—in a tie vote that defeated a resolution (S Con Res 21) to authorize the air operations that had been under way for five weeks. The vote was symbolic because the House was moving swiftly toward passing a supplemental spending bill to pay for the Kosovo campaign. But it underscored the House GOP's contempt for Clinton, whom they had voted to impeach four months earlier, and their mistrust of his stewardship of U.S. armed forces.

GOP disdain for Clinton's handling of defense issues, rooted in his avoidance of the draft and his 1993 effort to allow openly gay persons to serve in the armed forces, came to focus on his commitment of troops to peacekeeping and humanitarian missions rather than training for war. In late 1995 Clinton overrode those objections and deployed U.S. troops as the backbone of a NATO-led peacekeeping force in Bosnia. But congressional critics were further outraged when the administration's promise to end that mission in a year was brushed aside only a few days after the 1996 election.

Against that backdrop, when Yugoslavia's ethnic Serb majority began brutalizing Kosovo's Albanians late in 1998, congressional sentiment about a U.S. response was chaotically divided. Once military operations against the Serbs began on March 24, the prevailing sentiment among GOP leaders seemed to be that Congress should avoid any votes that would require members either to endorse what they saw as Clinton's flawed leadership or to vote against the U.S. involvement and thus strengthen the hand of Yugoslav President Slobodan Milosevic.

But Republican Tom Campbell of California invoked provisions of the 1973 War Powers Resolution (PL 93-148) to force the House to vote on a declaration of war against Yugoslavia and a resolution ordering the withdrawal of U.S. forces from the conflict. Though both were defeated, Democrats insisted that the House vote on the Senate-passed resolution authorizing the air war. Speaker J. Dennis Hastert, R-Ill., supported the resolution but declined to lobby Republicans on it, calling it a vote of conscience. But DeLay strenuously opposed the measure, urging members not to "take ownership" of an "incompetent" administration's policy. The resolution was rejected on a tie vote of 213–213: R 31–187; D 181–26 (ND 131–21, SD 50–5); I 1–0. *(Vote, p. 910)*

4. AIRPORT TRUST FUND USE

For the second year in a row, House Transportation and Infrastructure Committee Chairman Bud Shuster, R-Pa., confronted a coalition of powerful fiscal conservatives intent on stopping his plans for transportation spending. In a June showdown on the House floor, Shuster again won big.

In the 1998 surface transportation law Shuster won a guarantee that gasoline tax revenues would be reserved for highway and transit spending. He beat Republican deficit hawks who argued that the six-year measure short-circuited the appropriations process and was full of pork-barrel spending.

In 1999 Shuster targeted the Airport and Airway Trust Fund, financed primarily by airline ticket taxes. The fund was intended for aviation spending but Shuster said that in practice appropriators underfunded aviation and spent part of the money on other purposes. With his five-year, $59.3 billion proposal (HR 1000), Shuster proposed taking the trust fund "off budget," keeping the money only for aviation projects.

Shuster built support for his bill by talking about the need to keep up with skyrocketing air passenger traffic. He argued that current spending levels would leave aviation wanting while unspent trust fund balances would grow to tens of billions of dollars. And he produced a chart showing how much every airport in the country would benefit from the tripling of the basic federal construction grant.

But Appropriations Committee Chairman C. W. Bill Young, R-Fla., and Budget Committee Chairman John R. Kasich, R-Ohio, said Shuster's bill would erode the checks and balances built into the federal budget process. Further, Young said Shuster's bill would authorize $14.3 billion in spending above the level set in the fiscal 2000 budget resolution (H Con Res 68).

Young and Kasich were backed by two other powerful lawmakers, Ways and Means panel Chairman Bill Archer, R-Texas, and Majority Whip Tom DeLay, R-Texas, on an amendment to remove the off-budget language from the bill. A bloc of fiscal conservatives, led by Tom Coburn, R-Okla., and Lindsey Graham, R-S.C., also backed the effort, as did Appropriations panel Democrats.

In the end, Shuster's opponents were overmatched by lawmakers eager to bring home the benefits of the bill. Airport construction projects have an impact on every congressional district, and added capacity can promote airline competition and lower ticket prices. The Young-Kasich amendment was defeated 179–248: R 111–108; D 68–139 (ND 49–106, SD 19–33); I 0–1. But the House decision did little to influence the Senate, whose version of the bill did not include Shuster's plan. A conference on the bill broke down for the year late in 1999. *(Vote, p. 910)*

5. MEDIA SEX AND VIOLENCE

Days after a shooting rampage left fifteen people dead at a Colorado high school, gun control advocates were on the offensive, hoping that public dismay could be leveraged into tighter restrictions on firearms. Cultural conservatives had a similar strategy—that the carnage would build support for proposals to address the "root causes" of youth violence. They pointed to what they perceive to be declining social values and the pernicious effects of sex and violence in the mass media.

Their most ambitious aspiration was adoption of an amendment that House Judiciary Committee Chairman Henry J. Hyde, R-Ill., offered to a bill (HR 1501) designed principally to crack down on juvenile criminals. It called for five-year prison terms for selling or lending to minors a wide array of violent or sexually explicit material. In doing so, it attempted to create a new legal definition of violence that could be constitutionally restricted, much the way obscenity has been since a 1973 Supreme Court ruling.

With intense media attention in the days before the vote in mid-June, Hyde's proposal appeared poised to pass. But furious lobbying by an array of interests across the ideological spectrum caused support to implode. The vote to defeat the amendment was a lopsided 146–282: R 127–92; D 19–189 (ND 10–143, SD 9–46); I 0–1. *(Vote, p. 910)*

Hollywood's lobbyists alone probably did not have sufficient clout to stop the proposal. But on this vote they were allied not only with civil libertarians but with many business groups including bookstore owners, movie rental outlets, and video game arcades. The U.S. Chamber of Commerce, which had increased its lobbying staff to have a bigger impact on legislation, got onto their side as well.

On a vote that pitted two key GOP constituencies against each other, business won. Social conservatives—who have had far less legislative success than they had expected since the Republicans took over Congress in 1995—were dealt another setback. The outcome also suggested how much more lobbying clout is still wielded by established retailers. Three years earlier the House agreed to enact an overhaul of telecommunications law with similar penalties for disseminating certain sexually explicit material to minors over the Internet. It was struck down the next year by the Supreme Court. Hyde attributed his defeat in part to posturing by colleagues who, he said, wanted to be perceived as equally fervent defenders of the First Amendment and the Second Amendment, the latter of which is raised as the main rationale for opposing gun control.

6. GUN CONTROL

Gun control advocates once again experienced bitter defeat in 1999 when the House rejected gun control legislation (HR 2122) in June, only two months after a massacre at Columbine High School in Littleton, Colo., and a May vote in the Senate to require background checks of would-be buyers at gun shows. But in the end the measure was defeated by an unusual coalition: defenders of the Second Amendment, who rejected any new gun restrictions, and proponents of gun control, who said that a "poison pill" was dropped in to make the measure weaker than current law. The vote halted the momentum toward increased gun restrictions that had been building since the April shootings in Colorado.

The House bill would have required gun show checks, too, but with a twenty-four-hour time limit—down from three business days under current law, which covered fewer gun show transactions. On one-quarter of checks, a national computer database provided incomplete records, forcing law enforcement officers to telephone courthouses and state records offices. A one-day limit would do little good, Clinton administration officials argued, because most gun shows are on weekends when government offices are closed.

Majority Whip Tom DeLay, R-Texas, arranged a series of votes on different versions of the gun control proposals so that some lawmakers could vote "yes" on some without crossing the National Rifle Association (NRA). Language by Carolyn McCarthy, D-N.Y., that was similar to the Senate gun show provision was defeated, 193–235. It lost out to the amendment that limited the background check, which was offered—at DeLay's request—by John D. Dingell, D-Mich. That prevented President Clinton or Democratic leaders from getting much partisan mileage out of the issue.

With the Dingell provision added, 218–211, the bill became so onerous to gun control advocates that they deserted it in droves. Gun control foes, meanwhile, were never comfortable with some of the other provisions in the bill, including a requirement that gun locks be sold with all handguns.

On the key vote in June the legislation was defeated 147–280: R 137–82; D 10–197 (ND 6–146, SD 4–51); I 0–1. *(Vote, p. 910)*

7. FINANCIAL SERVICES

Efforts to rewrite laws governing banks, brokerages, and insurers foundered repeatedly for decades, usually before a bill even reached a floor vote in either chamber. Thus when the House passed a financial services overhaul for the first time ever in 1998, GOP Conference Chairman John A. Boehner of Ohio quipped that the bill's one-vote margin of victory "looks like a landslide."

Still, GOP leaders had to twist arms and wring out last-minute vote switches on the floor to overcome Democratic opposition. And the measure died in the 105th Congress, as it had many times before. In 1999 things changed. The financial sectors toned down their long-running squabbles over details of the legislation, which sought to remove barriers between the banking, securities, and insurance industries. As veteran banking lobbyist Kenneth A. Guenther of the Independent Community Bankers of America noted, almost everyone involved was "just sick and tired of this, and they want it off their backs."

In July the House passed a financial services overhaul bill (HR 10) by a wide margin, suggesting that the measure's time had come. Bipartisan support for the legislation had been painstakingly nurtured by House Banking and Financial Services Committee Chairman Jim Leach, R-Iowa. Under House rules, Leach has to leave the banking chairmanship at the end of the 106th Congress, and after years of effort he wanted to pass an overhaul before surrendering the gavel. The vote was 343–86: R 205–16; D 138–69 (ND 95–58, SD 43–11); I 0–1. After the vote, House members from both parties smiled broadly and crossed the center aisle of the floor to shake hands. *(Vote, p. 910)*

The House vote gave the bill momentum. After traveling a tougher, more partisan road in the Senate it eventually was passed and sent to the president who signed it into law.

8. EDUCATION

As the House began the difficult task of reauthorizing the 1965 Elementary and Secondary Education Act (ESEA), the main law governing federal aid to public schools, President Clinton's seven-year plan to hire 100,000 teachers became central to the debate.

The act, rewritten every five years, historically was a lightning rod for controversial issues from private school vouchers to prayer in the classroom. The same was true in 1999 with the two parties sparring over Clinton's efforts to use the ESEA as a vehicle for authorizing his teacher hiring plan, designed to reduce class sizes in grades one through three.

The House addressed the issue in July when it took up a bill (HR 1995) to create a new education block grant, including the current Eisenhower teacher training program, Clinton's 100,000-teacher plan and the administration's Goals 2000 program of grants to help states improve educational quality. The bill also set standards to ensure that teachers are qualified in the subject area for which they are hired.

House Education and the Workforce Committee Chairman Bill Goodling, R-Pa., decided to rewrite the ESEA as a series of smaller bills, rather than one enormous measure. The teacher training package was the first to reach the floor.

Some Democrats, such as George Miller of California, supported the block grant plan. Miller believed that Congress should provide local districts with flexibility to use the money for either training or hiring new teachers.

White House officials, worried that other Democrats would follow Miller's lead, met with committee members before the floor vote and urged them to remain united behind Clinton's class-size reduction proposal. Clinton threatened to veto the Goodling bill on the grounds that it was too open-ended and provided no assurances that schools would use any of the $2 billion authorized under the block grant each year to hire new teachers.

Eager to get a vote on the teacher-hiring plan, Matthew G. Martinez, D-Calif., offered a substitute to increase funding for professional development while providing a separate authorization for the 100,000-teacher program. The amendment authorized $1.5 billion for class-size reduction in fiscal 2000, increasing to $3 billion in fiscal 2005.

The Martinez amendment died on a 207–217: R 3–215; D 203–2 (ND 151–0, SD 52–2); I 1–0. (Vote, p. 910)

The 100,000-teacher proposal resurfaced in November, when Congress provided $1.3 billion for it in the fiscal 2000 Labor, Health and Human Services and Education appropriations measure.

9. TAX CUTS

Republican leaders faced a difficult decision early in 1999. They could attempt to unite their often fractious party around the traditional GOP magnet of massive tax cuts. Or they could pursue a deal with President Clinton that would probably get them a tax cut albeit less than they wanted. They took the former route. Budget writers reserved about $800 billion of the projected surplus over the next ten years for tax-cutters.

The House Ways and Means Committee used that opportunity to forge an $864 billion tax cut package in July. The bill (HR 2488) included something for every Republican. Among its many provisions were several that conservatives had long waited to consider: a 10 percent across-the-board cut in income tax rates, a phase out of the estate tax, and a reduction in the capital gains tax rate.

The bill achieved one leadership goal—defining differences between the parties. Democrats, even moderates often attracted to tax cuts, vilified the bill as a sop to the rich, and the president repeatedly threatened to veto it.

But as GOP leaders attempted to move the bill, about twenty moderate Republicans said the measure did not contain what they wanted most—an assurance that tax cuts would not defer paying down the national debt.

With the bill scheduled to come to the House floor in mid-July, Republican leaders met with the moderates to win support for their plan. And Speaker J. Dennis Hastert, R-Ill., who often refrained from pressuring members on votes, staked his leadership on moving the bill. Hastert met with wavering members and eventually persuaded Ways and Means Chairman Bill Archer, R-Texas, to accept a provision that conditioned the portion of the 10 percent across-the-board cut scheduled to take place in 2004 on a reduction in the interest accrued on the national debt. That change, and Archer's decision to trim the bill to the Senate's proposed total tax cut of $792 billion, swayed most moderates back in the leaders' direction.

When the bill came to the floor the vote was 223–208: R 217–4; D 6–203 (ND 2–152, SD 4–51); I 0–1. Only four moderate Republicans—Michael N. Castle of Delaware, Greg Ganske of Iowa, Constance A. Morella of Maryland, and Jack Quinn of New York—voted against it. Democrats also stayed largely united, with only six moderates voting for the measure. On the day of the vote, Hastert said he had asked Republicans to vote for the bill because it was important "for us being able to move forward" as a party. (Vote, p. 910)

10. CAMPAIGN FINANCE

It took six years for those who advocate a revamped system of federal campaign finance to push legislation through the House. But having finally accomplished that goal in the 105th Congress, they were able to replicate it with remarkable exactitude fourteen months later.

The key vote in September was House passage of legislation (HR 417) by Christopher Shays, R-Conn., and Martin T. Meehan, D-Mass. The vote was 252–177: R 54–164; D 197–13 (ND 148–8, SD 49–5); I 1–0. The measure contained two principal provisions. It barred the political party committees that underwrite presidential, House, and Senate campaigns from taking or spending "soft money," the term for the unlimited and unregulated donations from corporations, unions, and wealthy individuals that are the fastest-growing source of campaign financing. It also tightened federal regulation of "express advocacy" advertising, in which third-party groups try to sway voters without explicitly calling for a vote for or against anyone. (Vote, p. 910)

Shays and Meehan won an identical number of votes for similar legislation in 1998, showing that another round of congressional campaigns fueled by soft money and supplemented by advocate advertising had not changed the chamber's sentiment in favor of limiting either practice. In 1999, as the year before, 58 percent of the House voted for the bill, and both times the measure obtained a comfortable thirty-four votes beyond a majority. The second time around, 24 percent of Republicans defied their leadership and supported the bill.

To win, Shays and Meehan again had to navigate their legislation through a parliamentary obstacle course set up by GOP leaders, in 1999 by defeating six amendments they called "poison pills" as well as three alternative campaign finance packages. But there were two small salves for the bill's opponents. The 1999 measure received seven fewer GOP votes than a year earlier and only two of the nineteen first-term GOP members voted for it. Shays said that, unlike freshmen of the 105th Congress who pushed their own campaign finance bill, these newcomers were against changing a system from which many have already reaped big donations. Four lawmakers voted "yes" in 1999 after voting "no" in 1998; three switched to "no" in 1999 from "yes" in 1998.

Still, the vote gave Shays and Meehan what they had said all year they desired: a solid House endorsement of their proposals early enough in the 106th Congress to raise the profile of the issue in the Senate and thereby make it more difficult for vulnerable GOP incumbents there to support a filibuster against the proposals by Shays and Meehan's allies, John McCain, R-Ariz., and Russell D. Feingold, D-Wis. But a month after House passage senators rejected attempts to limit debate on both a sweeping and a more narrow bill by McCain and Feingold.

11. FETAL PROTECTION

House Republicans opened a new venue for the abortion debate in 1999, pushing to passage legislation that, for the first time, recognized the fetus under federal law as an entity distinct from the pregnant woman. Although sponsors of the bill (HR 2436) acknowledged that the National Right to Life Committee had helped draft the language, they said that the measure's purpose was not to restrict abortions. Instead, they said, it was designed to create a new way to punish criminals.

The measure made it a federal offense to harm an "unborn child" while committing any of sixty-eight existing federal offenses or a crime under military law, regardless of whether the accused intended that harm or even knew the woman was pregnant. Those performing or undergoing an abortion would be explicitly exempt from prosecution.

Still, opponents argued that a vote for the bill was a vote to create a legal rationale for undermining the right to an abortion found by the Supreme Court in its 1973 *Roe v. Wade* decision, which was based in part on the conclusion that "the unborn have never been recognized in the law as persons in the whole sense." The bill defined "unborn child" as a "member of the species homo sapiens, at any stage of development, who is carried in the womb." Abortion-rights advocates said that language could be cited in litigation to support the argument that federal law is that life begins at conception.

In explaining the rationale for the bill, sponsors cited the 1995 bombing of an Oklahoma City federal building. Under the bill, the bombers could have been charged not only with killing the three pregnant women inside but also in the deaths of their fetuses. "A pregnant woman is two special persons, said Henry J. Hyde, R-Ill. "She is carrying a tiny member of the human family."

Opponents proposed an alternative that would have stiffened federal penalties for attacks on pregnant women that resulted in harm to the fetus but would not have recognized the offense as a separate crime. Sponsors of the bill argued that without creating a separate protection for the fetus, criminals would get away with murder. The amendment was defeated, 201–224.

On the key vote, the House overwhelmingly passed the bill in September but the majority was sufficient to override a veto promised by President Clinton. The vote was 254–172: R 198–21; D 56–150 (ND 40–113, SD 16–37); I 0–1. In announcing its opposition, the Justice Department said the bill may be unconstitutional and that its identification of a fetus as a separate and distinct victim is both "unprecedented" and "unwise to the extent that it may be perceived as gratuitously plunging the federal government into one of the most—if not the most—difficult and complex issues of religious and scientific consideration." *(Vote, p. 910)*

12. MANAGED CARE

After promising for months to take up legislation to expand protections for 161 million Americans enrolled in private health insurance plans, the House GOP leadership in October finally agreed to bring the issue to a vote. It was a rare instance in which floor consideration of high-profile legislation was unscripted in advance by the leadership.

House Speaker J. Dennis Hastert, R-Ill., had been looking for an alternative to a measure sponsored by Charlie Norwood, R-Ga., and John D. Dingell, D-Mich. Right up until October, the Speaker's scheduled date for consideration, however, none of the alternatives proposed generated enough enthusiasm to overcome the popularity of the Norwood-Dingell bill. The GOP leadership opposed that measure, mostly because it would allow people to sue their health plans for damages in state courts.

The debate started in early October with consideration of a Republican package of tax provisions (HR 2990) designed to ensure access to health insurance. That bill passed along party lines, 227–205.

The following day, the House took up a series of patient protection measures under a rule that made the Norwood-Dingell legislation the base bill. If any of the substitutes won a majority, debate would end and the passed bill would be combined with the tax measure and sent to a conference committee as one bill (HR 2990).

President Clinton and some Democrats had accused the Republican leadership of using the combined-bill rule as a "poison pill" strategy. Democrats, they said, would not want to vote for any managed care bill that would then be combined with a tax package they opposed. It did not turn out that way. When the votes were tallied, three alternatives were defeated, and Norwood-Dingell prevailed. The substitute to receive the most votes, a bill sponsored by Republicans Porter J. Goss of Florida, Tom Coburn of Oklahoma, and John Shadegg of Arizona, was defeated 193–238. Some backers of the alternative blamed Hastert because he did not endorse the bill until the day the House voted on the measure.

While passage of the Norwood-Dingell bill was predicted, no one could have guessed the margin: sixty-eight Republicans bucked their leadership position to vote for the bill. The passage vote was 275–151: R 68–149; D 206–2 (ND 153–1, SD 53–1); I 1–0. *(Vote, p. 910)*

13. ASSISTED SUICIDE

A debate in fall 1999 on outlawing doctor-assisted suicide forced House Republicans to choose between two fundamental tenets of their party: federal intrusion into state matters should be limited, and the sanctity of human life should be preserved.

In this case, the GOP overwhelmingly sided with groups such as the National Right to Life Committee that supported legislation (HR 2260) to effectively overturn a 1997 Oregon law that resulted from a referendum. The only state statute of its kind, it authorized physicians to prescribe drugs to help terminally ill people end their lives.

When the House passed the bill in late October only a score of Republicans opposed it, while 90 percent of the House's GOP members supported it. The vote was 271–156: R 200–20; D 71–135 (ND 48–104, SD 23–31); I 0–1. *(Vote, p. 910)*

The solid majority also suggested the power of the American Medical Association (AMA), which endorsed the measure. Opposition by the doctors' lobby to a similar bill prompted sponsors to shelve the proposal in the 105th Congress.

Several Democratic lawmakers who opposed the bill this year said they were doing so in a bid to defend both state and individual rights. "This is a patients' rights measure—it was so voted by the people," Barney Frank, D-Mass., said of the Oregon law. "Are the patients in control of their own lives or is the federal government going to step in?"

The bill said the attorney general "shall give no force and effect" to any state law permitting assisted suicide. Supporters said helping the sick is a cause worthy of federal action. "It will help protect vulnerable people," said Charles T. Canady, R-Fla. "Facilitating the intentional killing of a human life is the opposite of healing," said Henry J. Hyde, R-Ill. The bill allowed doctors to prescribe controlled substances to alleviate pain, even if that "may increase the risk of death," and would authorize $5 million annually to promote education and training in pain management for the dying. These "palliative care" provisions helped win over the AMA, and the House defeated amendments that would have essentially limited the legislation to those sections.

1. Impeachment of President Clinton/Motion to Dismiss. Byrd, D-W.Va., motion to dismiss impeachment proceedings against President Clinton. Motion rejected 44–56: R 0–55; D 44–1 (ND 36–1, SD 8–0), Jan. 27, 1999.

2. Impeachment of President Clinton/Article II—Obstruction of Justice. Conviction on Article II, which would find President Clinton guilty of obstruction of justice, concealing evidence, and delaying proceedings in the Paula Jones federal sexual harassment civil lawsuit. Acquitted 50–50: R 50–5; D 0–45 (ND 0–37, SD 0–8), Feb. 12, 1999. A two-thirds majority of those present and voting (67 in this case) is required to convict the president and remove him from office. A "nay" was a vote in support of the president's position.

3. S 280. Educational Flexibility/New Teachers. Jeffords, R-Vt., motion to table (kill) the Murray, D-Wash., amendment. The Murray amendment would authorize $11.4 billion over six years to fund President Clinton's proposal to hire 100,000 new teachers to reduce class size. Motion agreed to 55–44: R 55–0; D 0–44 (ND 0–36, SD 0–8), March 11, 1999. A "nay" was a vote in support of the president's position.

4. S 254. Juvenile Crime/Gun Show Checks. Lautenberg, D-N.J., amendment to require criminal background checks on all gun sales at gun shows, bar nonfederal licensees from transferring a firearm to a buyer at gun shows, and direct the U.S. attorney general to destroy background records within ninety days for purchasers who can legally purchase a firearm. Adopted 51–50: R 6–49; D 44–1 (ND 36–1, SD 8–0), with Vice President Gore casting a "yea" vote, May 20, 1999. A "yea" was a vote in support of the president's position.

5. S 1059. Fiscal 2000 Defense Authorization/Ground Troops in Kosovo. Warner, R-Va., motion to table (kill) the Specter, R-Pa., amendment that would bar the use of Defense Department funds for deployment of U.S. ground troops in Yugoslavia, except for peacekeeping personnel, unless Congress declares war or enacts a joint resolution authorizing the use of military force. Motion agreed to 52–48: R 17–38; D 35–10 (ND 29–8, SD 6–2), May 25, 1999. A "yea" was a vote in support of the president's position.

6. S 1344. Managed Care Revisions/Passage. Passage of the bill to provide federal protections, such as access to emergency care, continuing care and approved clinical cancer trials, primarily for those in self-insured health plans. The bill also would create internal and external appeals processes, bar denials based on predictive genetic data, allow self-employed individuals to deduct the full cost of health insurance premiums, and expand access to medical savings accounts. Passed 53–47: R 52–2; D 0–45 (ND 0–37, SD 0–8); I 1–0, July 15, 1999. (Before passage, the Senate adopted a Lott, R-Miss., substitute amendment by voice vote.) A "nay" was a vote in support of the president's position.

7. S 1429. Tax Package/Passage. Passage of the bill to reduce federal taxes by $792 billion over ten years. The measure would reduce the lowest income tax bracket from 15 percent to 14 percent beginning in 2001, increase the maximum income levels for the lowest bracket, allow couples to calculate their taxes as individuals on the same form, reduce estate and gift taxes, increase the annual amount transferable to an Individual Retirement Account, and extend the research and development tax credit. Passed 57–43: R 52–2; D 4–41 (ND 2–35, SD 2–6); I 1–0, July 30, 1999. A "nay" was a vote in support of the president's position.

8. S 1233. Fiscal 2000 Agriculture Appropriations/Unilateral Food and Medicine Sanctions. Helms, R-N.C., motion to table (kill) the Ashcroft, R-Mo., amendment to the Daschle, D-S.D., amendment. The Ashcroft amendment would end U.S. unilateral sanctions on agricultural and medicinal goods and bar the president from imposing such sanctions against a country without congressional approval, with certain exceptions. Motion rejected 28–70: R 17–36; D 10–34 (ND 8–28, SD 2–6); I 1–0, Aug. 3, 1999. (Subsequently, the Ashcroft amendment was adopted by voice vote.)

9. HR 2084. Fiscal 2000 Transportation Appropriations/Fuel Efficiency Standards. Gorton, R-Wash., amendment to express the sense of the Senate that the Department of Transportation should be allowed to study whether to raise the corporate average fuel economy (CAFE) standard for vehicles. It also would urge the Senate not to accept House-passed language that would prohibit an increase in CAFE standards. Rejected 40–55: R 6–45; D 34–9 (ND 29–7, SD 5–2); I 0–1, Sept. 15, 1999.

10. Nuclear Test Ban Treaty/Adoption. Adoption of the resolution to ratify the Comprehensive Nuclear Test Ban Treaty (Treaty Doc 105-28), which would ban nuclear weapons testing six months after the pact is ratified by the forty-four nations that have either nuclear power plants or nuclear research reactors. Rejected 48–51: R 4–50; D 44–0 (ND 36–0, SD 8–0); I 0–1, Oct. 13, 1999. A two-thirds majority of those present and voting (66 in this case) is required for adoption of resolutions of ratification. A "yea" was a vote in support of the president's position.

11. S 1593. Campaign Finance Revisions/Soft Money Donations and Union Dues/Cloture. Motion to invoke cloture (thus limiting debate) on the Reid, D-Nev., amendment to the Daschle, D-S.D., substitute amendment. The Reid amendment would prohibit national party committees from collecting "soft money" donations, which currently were unlimited and unregulated, and labor unions would have to notify dues-paying nonmembers of any portion of their dues used for political purposes. It included the previously adopted McCain, R-Ariz., amendment on disclosure requirements. Motion rejected 53–47: R 8–46; D 45–0 (ND 37–0, SD 8–0); I 0–1, Oct. 19, 1999. Three-fifths of the total Senate (60) is required to invoke cloture.

12. S 1692. Abortion Procedure Ban/*Roe v. Wade*. Harkin, D-Iowa, amendment to the Boxer, D-Calif., amendment. The Harkin amendment would express the sense of Congress that the Supreme Court's 1973 *Roe v. Wade* decision was appropriate, secures an important constitutional right, and should not be overturned. The Boxer amendment would express the sense of Congress that lawmakers must protect a woman's life and health in any reproductive health legislation Congress passes. Adopted 51–47: R 8–44; D 43–2 (ND 36–1, SD 7–1); I 0–1, Oct. 21, 1999. (Subsequently, the Boxer amendment as amended was adopted by voice vote.)

13. S 900. Financial Services Overhaul/Conference Report. Adoption of the conference report on the bill to eliminate current barriers erected by the 1933 Glass-Steagall Act and other laws that impede affiliations between banking, securities, insurance and other firms. Adopted (thus sent to the House) 90–8: R 52–1; D 38–7 (ND 30–7, SD 8–0), Nov. 4, 1999.

KEY			
	Democrats	*Republicans*	
Y	Voted for ("yea")	–	Announced against
N	Voted against ("nay")	P	Voted "present"
+	Announced for	C	Voted "present" to avoid possible conflict of interest
#	Paired for	?	Did not vote or otherwise make a position known
X	Paired against		

ND Northern Democrats
SD Southern Democrats
Southern states – Ala., Ark., Fla., Ga., Ky., La., Miss., N.C., Okla., S.C., Tenn., Texas, Va.

Senate Key Votes	1	2	3	4	5	6	7	8	9	10	11	12	13
ALABAMA													
Sessions	N	Y	Y	N	Y	Y	Y	N	N	N	N	N	Y
Shelby	N	Y	Y	N	Y	Y	Y	N	N	N	N	N	N
ALASKA													
Murkowski	N	Y	Y	N	N	Y	Y	Y	N	N	N	N	Y
Stevens	N	Y	Y	N	N	Y	Y	Y	N	N	N	Y	Y
ARIZONA													
Kyl	N	Y	Y	N	N	Y	Y	Y	N	N	N	N	Y
McCain	N	Y	Y	N	Y	Y	Y	Y	?	N	Y	?	?
ARKANSAS													
Hutchinson	N	Y	Y	N	N	Y	Y	N	N	N	Y	N	Y
Lincoln	Y	N	N	Y	Y	N	N	N	N	Y	Y	Y	Y
CALIFORNIA													
Boxer	Y	N	N	Y	Y	N	N	N	N	Y	Y	Y	N
Feinstein	Y	N	N	Y	Y	N	N	N	Y	Y	Y	Y	Y
COLORADO													
Allard	N	Y	Y	N	N	Y	Y	N	N	N	N	N	Y
Campbell	N	Y	Y	N	N	Y	Y	N	N	N	N	Y	Y
CONNECTICUT													
Dodd	Y	N	N	Y	Y	N	N	N	N	Y	Y	Y	Y
Lieberman	Y	N	N	Y	Y	N	N	Y	Y	Y	Y	Y	Y
DELAWARE													
Roth	N	Y	Y	N	Y	Y	Y	N	N	N	Y	N	Y
Biden	Y	N	N	Y	Y	N	N	N	N	Y	Y	Y	Y
FLORIDA													
Mack	N	Y	Y	N	Y	Y	Y	Y	N	N	N	N	Y
Graham	Y	N	N	Y	Y	N	N	N	Y	Y	Y	Y	Y
GEORGIA													
Coverdell	N	Y	Y	N	N	Y	Y	Y	N	N	N	N	Y
Cleland	Y	N	N	Y	N	N	N	N	N	Y	Y	Y	Y
HAWAII													
Akaka	Y	N	N	Y	Y	N	N	N	N	Y	Y	Y	Y
Inouye	Y	N	N	Y	Y	N	N	N	Y	Y	Y	Y	Y
IDAHO													
Craig	N	Y	Y	N	N	Y	Y	N	N	N	N	N	Y
Crapo	N	Y	Y	N	N	Y	Y	N	N	N	N	N	Y
ILLINOIS													
Fitzgerald	N	Y	Y	Y	N	N	Y	N	N	N	N	N	C
Durbin	Y	N	N	Y	N	N	N	N	Y	Y	Y	Y	Y
INDIANA													
Lugar	N	Y	Y	Y	Y	Y	Y	N	N	N	N	N	Y
Bayh	Y	N	N	Y	Y	N	N	N	N	Y	Y	Y	Y
IOWA													
Grassley	N	Y	Y	N	N	Y	Y	N	N	N	N	N	Y
Harkin	Y	N	N	Y	Y	N	N	N	Y	Y	Y	Y	N
KANSAS													
Brownback	N	Y	Y	N	N	Y	Y	N	N	N	Y	N	Y
Roberts	N	Y	Y	N	N	Y	Y	N	N	N	N	N	Y
KENTUCKY													
Bunning	N	Y	Y	N	N	Y	Y	Y	N	N	N	N	Y
McConnell	N	Y	Y	N	Y	Y	Y	Y	N	N	N	N	Y
LOUISIANA													
Breaux	Y	N	N	Y	Y	N	Y	N	?	Y	Y	N	Y
Landrieu	Y	N	N	Y	Y	N	Y	N	N	Y	Y	Y	Y
MAINE													
Collins	N	N	Y	N	N	Y	Y	N	Y	N	Y	Y	Y
Snowe	N	N	Y	N	N	Y	Y	Y	Y	N	Y	Y	Y
MARYLAND													
Mikulski	Y	N	N	Y	Y	N	N	N	N	Y	Y	Y	N
Sarbanes	Y	N	N	Y	Y	N	N	Y	Y	Y	Y	Y	Y
MASSACHUSETTS													
Kennedy	Y	N	N	Y	Y	N	N	?	Y	Y	Y	Y	Y
Kerry	Y	N	N	Y	Y	N	N	N	Y	Y	Y	Y	Y
MICHIGAN													
Abraham	N	Y	Y	N	N	Y	Y	N	N	N	N	N	Y
Levin	Y	N	N	Y	Y	N	N	N	N	Y	Y	Y	Y
MINNESOTA													
Grams	N	Y	Y	N	N	Y	Y	N	N	N	N	N	Y
Wellstone	Y	N	N	Y	Y	N	N	N	Y	Y	Y	Y	N
MISSISSIPPI													
Cochran	N	Y	Y	N	Y	Y	Y	N	N	N	N	N	Y
Lott	N	Y	Y	N	Y	Y	Y	Y	N	N	N	N	Y
MISSOURI													
Ashcroft	N	Y	Y	N	N	Y	Y	N	N	N	N	N	Y
Bond	N	Y	Y	N	N	Y	Y	N	N	N	N	N	Y
MONTANA													
Burns	N	Y	Y	N	Y	Y	Y	N	N	N	N	N	Y
Baucus	Y	N	N	N	Y	N	N	N	Y	Y	Y	Y	Y

Senate Key Votes	1	2	3	4	5	6	7	8	9	10	11	12	13
NEBRASKA													
Hagel	N	Y	Y	N	Y	Y	Y	N	N	N	N	N	Y
Kerrey	Y	N	N	Y	Y	N	Y	N	Y	Y	Y	Y	Y
NEVADA													
Bryan	Y	N	N	Y	Y	N	N	Y	Y	Y	Y	Y	N
Reid	Y	N	N	Y	Y	N	N	Y	Y	Y	Y	N	Y
NEW HAMPSHIRE													
Gregg	N	Y	Y	N	N	Y	Y	Y	Y	N	N	?	Y
Smith[1]	N	Y	Y	N	N	Y	Y	Y	N	N	N	N	Y
NEW JERSEY													
Lautenberg	Y	N	N	Y	Y	N	N	Y	Y	Y	Y	Y	Y
Torricelli	Y	N	N	Y	N	N	Y	Y	Y	Y	Y	Y	Y
NEW MEXICO													
Domenici	N	Y	Y	N	N	Y	Y	?	N	N	N	N	Y
Bingaman	Y	N	N	Y	Y	N	N	N	Y	Y	Y	Y	Y
NEW YORK													
Moynihan	Y	N	N	Y	Y	N	N	N	N	Y	Y	Y	Y
Schumer	Y	N	N	Y	Y	N	N	N	N	Y	Y	Y	Y
NORTH CAROLINA													
Helms	N	Y	Y	N	Y	Y	Y	N	N	N	N	N	Y
Edwards	Y	N	N	Y	Y	N	N	N	N	Y	Y	Y	Y
NORTH DAKOTA													
Conrad	Y	N	N	Y	N	N	N	N	N	Y	Y	Y	Y
Dorgan	Y	N	N	Y	N	N	N	N	Y	Y	Y	Y	N
OHIO													
DeWine	N	Y	Y	Y	Y	N	Y	Y	Y	N	N	N	Y
Voinovich	N	Y	Y	Y	Y	N	Y	Y	N	N	N	N	Y
OKLAHOMA													
Inhofe	N	Y	Y	N	N	Y	Y	N	N	N	N	N	Y
Nickles	N	Y	Y	N	N	Y	Y	N	N	N	N	N	Y
OREGON													
Smith	N	Y	Y	N	Y	Y	Y	Y	N	N	N	N	Y
Wyden	Y	N	N	Y	Y	N	N	N	Y	Y	Y	Y	Y
PENNSYLVANIA													
Santorum	N	Y	Y	N	N	Y	Y	Y	N	N	N	N	Y
Specter	N	N	Y	N	N	Y	Y	N	N	Y	N	Y	Y
RHODE ISLAND													
Chafee[2]	N	N	Y	Y	Y	N	Y	N	#	Y	N	Y	Y
Reed	Y	N	N	Y	Y	N	N	N	Y	Y	Y	Y	Y
SOUTH CAROLINA													
Thurmond	N	Y	Y	N	N	Y	Y	Y	N	N	N	N	Y
Hollings	Y	N	N	Y	N	N	N	N	N	Y	Y	Y	Y
SOUTH DAKOTA													
Daschle	Y	N	N	Y	Y	N	N	N	?	Y	Y	Y	Y
Johnson	Y	N	N	Y	Y	N	N	N	Y	Y	Y	Y	Y
TENNESSEE													
Frist	N	Y	Y	N	N	Y	Y	N	N	N	N	N	Y
Thompson	N	Y	Y	N	N	Y	Y	Y	N	N	Y	N	Y
TEXAS													
Gramm	N	Y	Y	N	N	Y	Y	Y	N	N	N	N	Y
Hutchison	N	Y	Y	N	N	Y	Y	Y	N	N	N	N	Y
UTAH													
Bennett	N	Y	Y	N	N	Y	Y	Y	N	N	N	N	Y
Hatch	N	Y	Y	N	Y	Y	Y	Y	N	N	N	N	Y
VERMONT													
Jeffords	N	N	Y	N	N	Y	Y	N	Y	N	Y	Y	Y
Leahy	Y	N	N	Y	Y	N	N	N	N	Y	Y	Y	Y
VIRGINIA													
Warner	N	Y	Y	Y	Y	Y	Y	N	X	N	N	N	Y
Robb	Y	N	N	Y	N	N	N	Y	N	Y	Y	Y	Y
WASHINGTON													
Gorton	N	Y	Y	N	N	Y	Y	Y	N	N	N	N	Y
Murray	Y	N	?	Y	Y	N	N	N	Y	Y	Y	Y	Y
WEST VIRGINIA													
Byrd	Y	N	N	Y	N	N	N	N	N	P	Y	Y	Y
Rockefeller	Y	N	N	Y	Y	N	N	N	Y	Y	Y	Y	Y
WISCONSIN													
Feingold	N	N	N	Y	Y	N	N	Y	N	Y	Y	Y	N
Kohl	Y	N	N	Y	Y	N	N	Y	N	Y	Y	Y	Y
WYOMING													
Enzi	N	Y	Y	N	N	Y	Y	N	N	N	N	N	Y
Thomas	N	Y	Y	N	N	Y	Y	N	N	N	N	N	Y

[1] Robert C. Smith, N.H., switched his party affiliation from Republican to Independent on July 13. He switched back to Republican on Nov. 1.

[2] John H. Chafee, R-R.I., died Oct. 24, 1999. Lincoln Chafee, R-R.I., was sworn in on Nov. 4, 1999.

1. HR 975. Steel Imports/Passage. Passage of the bill to direct the president, within sixty days of enactment, to take necessary steps—including imposing quotas, tariff surcharges, or negotiated enforceable voluntary export restraints—to ensure that the volume of steel products imported into the United States (based on tonnage) during any month does not exceed the average of monthly import volumes during the three years preceding July 1997. Passed 289–141: R 91–128; D 197–13 (ND 146–9, SD 51–4); I 1–0, March 17, 1999. A "nay" was a vote in support of the president's position.

2. HR 4. Anti-Missile Defense/Recommit. Allen, D-Maine, motion to recommit the bill to the Armed Services Committee with instructions to report it back with an amendment that it is the policy of the United States to deploy a missile defense system that is demonstrated to be effective, does not diminish overall national security by jeopardizing other efforts to reduce threats to the United States, is affordable, and does not compromise U.S. ability to provide for other military priorities. Motion rejected 152–269: R 2–212; D 150–56 (ND 125–28, SD 25–28); I 0–1, March 18, 1999.

3. S Con Res 21. Kosovo Conflict—Air Operation/Adoption. Adoption of the concurrent resolution to authorize military air operations and missile strikes against Yugoslavia. Rejected 213–213: R 31–187; D 181–26 (ND 131–21, SD 50–5); I 1–0, April 28, 1999. A "yea" was a vote in support of the president's position.

4. HR 1000. FAA Reauthorization/Off-Budget Funds. Young, R-Fla., amendment to strike the provisions of the bill that would take the Airport and Airway Trust Fund off budget and thereby permit all aviation tax revenue to be spent on aviation programs, exempt from budgetary restrictions but still subject to annual appropriations. Rejected 179–248: R 111–108; D 68–139 (ND 49–106, SD 19–33); I 0–1, June 15, 1999.

5. HR 1501. Juvenile Justice/Media Violence. Hyde, R-Ill., amendment to prohibit the sale, loan, or exhibition to juveniles of any material that contains sexual or violent depictions or detailed verbal descriptions, including any picture, drawing, sculpture, video game, motion picture, book, magazine, or sound recording. Offenders could face fines and up to five years in prison for a first offense and ten years for a second offense. Rejected 146–282: R 127–92; D 19–189 (ND 10–143, SD 9–46); I 0–1, June 16, 1999.

6. HR 2122. Gun Shows/Passage. Passage of the bill to require background checks for purchasers at gun shows, defined as any event with ten or more vendors and where fifty or more guns are offered for sale; background checks would have to be completed in twenty-four hours; gun show organizers would be required to destroy background records of those who pass background checks. Rejected 147–280: R 137–82; D 10–197 (ND 6–146, SD 4–51); I 0–1, June 18, 1999.

7. HR 10. Financial Services Overhaul/Passage. Passage of the bill to eliminate barriers against cross-ownership among banks, securities firms, insurance companies, and other firms. The bill would prohibit banks from selling private customer financial information to telemarketing firms and allow customers to "opt out" of having information shared with other companies; allow mutual insurance companies to move their businesses to a different state when reorganizing into a stock company; and bar financial companies from conditioning the sale of products on the purchase of other financial products. Passed 343–86: R 205–16; D 138–69 (ND 95–58, SD 43–11); I 0–1, July 1, 1999.

8. HR 1995. New Teachers and Training Programs/Funding Increases. Martinez, D-Calif., substitute amendment to increase funding for professional development and class-size reduction activities, with a separate authorization for the class-size reduction program. The amendment would authorize $1.5 billion in fiscal 2000 for the class-size reduction program, increasing to $3 billion by fiscal 2005; it would authorize $1.5 billion for teachers' professional development, increasing to $3 billion by fiscal 2004. Rejected 207–217: R 3–215; D 203–2 (ND 151–0, SD 52–2); I 1–0, July 20, 1999. A "yea" was a vote in support of the president's position.

9. HR 2488. Tax Cut Package/Passage. Passage of the bill to reduce federal taxes by $792 billion over ten years. The bill would reduce individual income tax rates by 10 percent over ten years, contingent on annual progress in reducing interest on the nation's debt. It would increase the standard deduction for married couples to double that for singles; cut the capital gains tax rate to 15 percent for individuals and to 30 percent for corporations; phase out estate and gift taxes by 2009; accelerate the phase-in of a 100 percent deduction for health insurance premiums for the self-employed, and allow taxpayers to deduct health care and long-term care insurance if employers pay 50 percent or less of the premium; increase the annual contribution limit for Education Savings Accounts from $500 to $2,000 and permit tax-free withdrawals to pay for public and private elementary and secondary tuition and expenses. Passed 223–208: R 217–4; D 6–203 (ND 2–152, SD 4–51); I 0–1, July 22, 1999. A "nay" was a vote in support of the president's position.

10. HR 417. Campaign Finance Overhaul/Passage. Passage of the bill to ban all contributions of soft money—money used for party-building activities as opposed to supporting a specific candidate—and impose restrictions on issue advocacy communications. The bill would raise the individual aggregate contribution limit from $25,000 to $30,000 per year and raise the limit on individual contributions to state political parties from $5,000 to $10,000. House candidates who receive coordinated party contributions could not spend more than $50,000 in personal funds. Labor unions would have to notify dues-paying nonmembers of any portion of their dues used for political purposes. Passed 252–177: R 54–164; D 197–13 (ND 148–8, SD 49–5); I 1–0, Sept. 14, 1999. A "yea" was a vote in support of the president's position.

11. HR 2436. Criminal Penalties for Harming a Fetus/Passage. Passage of the bill to make it a criminal offense to injure or kill a fetus during the commission of a violent crime, regardless of the perpetrator's knowledge of the pregnancy or intent to harm the fetus. The bill states that its provisions should not be interpreted to apply to consensual abortion or to a woman's actions with respect to her pregnancy. Passed 254–172: R 198–21; D 56–150 (ND 40–113, SD 16–37); I 0–1, Sept. 30, 1999. A "nay" was a vote in support of the president's position.

12. HR 2723. Managed Care Patient Protection/Passage. Passage of the bill to require health plans to cover emergency care when a "prudent layperson" could reasonably believe such care was required. Health plans would have to allow direct access to gynecological and pediatric care. The bill would establish an internal and external appeals process to review denial of care. Patients or their estates would have the right to sue their health plan in state courts when they believe plan decisions result in injury or death of patients. Passed 275–151: R 68–149; D 206–2 (ND 153–1, SD 53–1); I 1–0, Oct. 7, 1999. A "yea" was a vote in support of the president's position.

13. HR 2260. Physician-Assisted Suicide/Passage. Passage of the bill to allow doctors to use controlled substances aggressively to alleviate pain, while barring them from using such drugs for the purpose of assisted suicide. The measure would supersede state law, effectively overturning an Oregon law that allows lethal prescriptions to be issued to the terminally ill, and preventing such laws from going into effect in other states. Passed 271–156: R 200–20; D 71–135 (ND 48–104, SD 23–31); I 0–1, Oct. 27, 1999.

<table>
<tr><td colspan="2">KEY</td></tr>
</table>

KEY

	Democrats	*Republicans*	**Independent**
Y	Voted for ("yea")		– Announced against
N	Voted against ("nay")		P Voted "present"
+	Announced for		C Voted "present" to avoid
#	Paired for		possible conflict of interest
X	Paired against		? Did not vote or otherwise
			make a position known

ND Northern Democrats
SD Southern Democrats
Southern states – Ala., Ark., Fla., Ga., Ky., La., Miss., N.C., Okla., S.C., Tenn., Texas, Va.

House Key Votes	1	2	3	4	5	6	7	8	9	10	11	12	13
ALABAMA													
1 *Callahan*	Y	N	Y	Y	Y	N	Y	N	Y	N	Y	Y	Y
2 *Everett*	Y	N	N	Y	Y	N	Y	N	Y	N	Y	N	Y
3 *Riley*	Y	N	Y	Y	Y	N	Y	N	Y	N	Y	N	Y
4 *Aderholt*	Y	N	?	Y	Y	N	Y	N	Y	N	Y	N	Y
5 Cramer	Y	N	Y	Y	N	N	Y	Y	N	Y	Y	Y	Y
6 *Bachus*	Y	N	N	N	Y	N	Y	N	Y	Y	Y	Y	Y
7 Hilliard	Y	Y	Y	N	N	N	N	Y	N	Y	N	Y	N
ALASKA													
AL *Young*	Y	N	N	N	N	N	Y	N	Y	N	Y	N	Y
ARIZONA													
1 *Salmon*	N	N	N	Y	N	?	Y	N	Y	N	Y	N	Y
2 *Pastor*	Y	Y	Y	Y	N	N	Y	Y	N	Y	N	Y	N
3 *Stump*	N	N	N	Y	Y	N	Y	N	Y	N	Y	N	Y
4 *Shadegg*	N	N	N	Y	Y	N	Y	N	Y	N	Y	N	Y
5 *Kolbe*	N	N	Y	Y	N	Y	Y	N	Y	N	N	N	N
6 *Hayworth*	N	N	N	Y	N	N	Y	N	Y	N	Y	N	Y
ARKANSAS													
1 Berry	Y	Y	Y	N	N	N	Y	Y	N	Y	Y	Y	Y
2 Snyder	Y	Y	Y	Y	N	N	Y	Y	N	Y	N	Y	Y
3 *Hutchinson*	N	N	N	N	N	Y	Y	N	Y	N	Y	N	Y
4 Dickey	Y	N	N	Y	N	N	Y	N	Y	N	Y	N	Y
CALIFORNIA													
1 Thompson	Y	Y	Y	N	N	N	Y	Y	N	Y	N	Y	N
2 *Herger*	N	N	N	Y	N	N	Y	N	Y	N	Y	N	Y
3 *Ose*	N	N	N	Y	N	N	Y	N	Y	N	Y	N	Y
4 *Doolittle*	N	?	N	N	N	N	Y	N	Y	N	Y	N	Y
5 Matsui	Y	Y	Y	N	N	N	Y	Y	N	Y	N	Y	N
6 Woolsey	Y	Y	Y	N	N	N	N	Y	N	Y	N	Y	N
7 Miller, George	Y	Y	Y	N	N	N	Y	Y	N	Y	N	Y	N
8 Pelosi	Y	Y	Y	N	N	N	?	Y	N	Y	N	Y	N
9 Lee	Y	N	N	N	N	N	N	Y	N	Y	N	Y	N
10 Tauscher	Y	N	Y	N	N	N	Y	Y	N	Y	N	Y	N
11 Pombo	Y	N	N	N	N	N	Y	N	Y	N	Y	N	Y
12 Lantos	Y	Y	Y	N	N	N	N	Y	N	Y	N	Y	N
13 Stark	Y	+	N	N	N	N	N	?	N	Y	N	Y	N
14 Eshoo	N	N	Y	Y	N	N	N	Y	N	Y	N	Y	N
15 *Campbell*	N	N	N	N	N	N	N	Y	N	Y	N	Y	N
16 Lofgren	N	Y	Y	N	N	N	N	Y	N	Y	N	Y	N
17 Farr	Y	Y	Y	Y	N	N	N	Y	N	Y	N	Y	N
18 Condit	Y	N	N	Y	N	N	Y	Y	N	Y	N	Y	N
19 *Radanovich*	N	N	N	N	Y	N	Y	N	Y	N	Y	N	Y
20 Dooley	N	Y	Y	N	N	N	Y	Y	N	Y	N	Y	N
21 *Thomas*	N	N	N	Y	?	?	Y	N	Y	N	Y	N	Y
22 Capps	Y	Y	Y	N	N	N	N	Y	N	Y	N	Y	N
23 *Gallegly*	Y	Y	Y	N	Y	Y	N	Y	N	Y	Y	Y	Y
24 Sherman	Y	Y	Y	N	N	N	N	Y	N	Y	N	Y	N
25 *McKeon*	N	-	N	Y	Y	Y	Y	N	Y	N	Y	N	Y
26 Berman	N	Y	Y	Y	N	?	Y	Y	N	Y	N	Y	N
27 *Rogan*	Y	N	N	Y	Y	Y	Y	N	Y	N	Y	N	Y
28 *Dreier*	N	N	N	Y	Y	N	Y	N	Y	N	Y	N	Y
29 Waxman	Y	Y	Y	Y	N	N	N	Y	N	Y	N	Y	N
30 Becerra	Y	Y	Y	Y	N	N	Y	Y	N	Y	N	Y	N
31 Martinez	Y	Y	Y	N	N	N	Y	Y	N	Y	N	Y	N
32 Dixon	Y	Y	Y	Y	N	N	Y	Y	N	Y	N	Y	N
33 Roybal-Allard	Y	Y	Y	Y	N	N	Y	Y	N	Y	N	Y	N
34 Napolitano	Y	Y	Y	N	N	N	Y	Y	N	Y	N	Y	N
35 Waters	Y	Y	Y	N	N	N	N	Y	N	Y	N	Y	N
36 *Kuykendall*	N	N	N	N	Y	N	Y	N	Y	N	Y	N	Y
37 Millender-McD.	Y	Y	Y	N	N	N	Y	Y	N	Y	N	Y	N
38 Horn	Y	N	N	Y	Y	Y	Y	N	Y	N	Y	N	Y
39 *Royce*	N	N	N	Y	Y	N	Y	N	Y	N	Y	N	Y
40 *Lewis*	N	N	N	Y	N	?	Y	N	Y	N	Y	N	Y
41 *Miller*	N	N	N	N	Y	N	Y	N	Y	N	Y	N	Y
42 Brown[1]	Y	Y	Y	?	?	?	?						
43 *Calvert*	N	N	N	Y	Y	N	Y	N	Y	N	Y	N	Y
44 *Bono*	N	N	N	N	N	Y	Y	N	Y	N	Y	N	Y

House Key Votes	1	2	3	4	5	6	7	8	9	10	11	12	13
45 *Rohrabacher*	N	N	N	Y	N	Y	Y	N	Y	N	Y	N	N
46 Sanchez	Y	Y	Y	N	N	N	Y	Y	N	Y	N	Y	N
47 *Cox*	N	N	N	Y	N	Y	Y	N	Y	N	Y	N	Y
48 *Packard*	N	N	N	Y	Y	Y	Y	N	Y	N	Y	N	Y
49 *Bilbray*	N	N	N	N	Y	N	Y	Y	Y	Y	Y	Y	Y
50 Filner	Y	Y	Y	N	N	N	N	Y	N	Y	N	Y	N
51 *Cunningham*	N	N	N	Y	Y	Y	Y	N	Y	N	Y	N	Y
52 *Hunter*	Y	N	Y	Y	Y	Y	Y	N	Y	N	Y	Y	Y
COLORADO													
1 DeGette	Y	Y	N	N	N	N	N	Y	N	Y	Y	Y	N
2 Udall	Y	Y	Y	N	N	N	Y	Y	N	Y	N	Y	N
3 *McInnis*	Y	N	N	Y	N	N	Y	N	Y	N	Y	N	Y
4 *Schaffer*	N	N	N	Y	N	N	Y	N	Y	N	Y	N	Y
5 *Hefley*	Y	N	N	Y	N	N	N	N	Y	N	Y	N	Y
6 *Tancredo*	N	N	N	Y	N	N	Y	N	Y	N	Y	N	Y
CONNECTICUT													
1 Larson	Y	N	N	N	N	N	Y	Y	N	Y	N	Y	N
2 Gejdenson	Y	Y	Y	N	N	N	Y	Y	N	Y	N	Y	N
3 DeLauro	Y	Y	Y	Y	N	N	N	Y	N	Y	N	Y	N
4 *Shays*	N	N	N	Y	N	Y	Y	Y	N	Y	N	Y	N
5 Maloney	Y	N	Y	N	N	N	Y	Y	N	Y	N	Y	N
6 *Johnson*	N	N	N	Y	Y	N	Y	N	Y	N	Y	N	N
DELAWARE													
AL *Castle*	N	N	Y	N	N	N	Y	N	Y	Y	Y	Y	N
FLORIDA													
1 *Scarborough*	N	N	N	Y	N	N	Y	N	Y	N	?	?	?
2 Boyd	Y	N	Y	Y	N	N	Y	Y	N	Y	N	Y	N
3 Brown	Y	Y	Y	N	N	N	Y	Y	N	Y	N	Y	N
4 *Fowler*	N	N	N	N	N	Y	Y	N	Y	N	Y	N	Y
5 Thurman	Y	Y	Y	N	N	N	N	Y	N	Y	N	Y	N
6 *Stearns*	Y	N	N	Y	Y	Y	Y	N	Y	N	Y	N	Y
7 *Mica*	Y	N	N	N	N	N	Y	N	Y	N	Y	N	Y
8 *McCollum*	Y	N	N	N	Y	Y	Y	N	Y	N	Y	N	Y
9 *Bilirakis*	Y	N	N	Y	Y	Y	Y	N	Y	Y	Y	Y	Y
10 *Young*	Y	N	N	Y	Y	Y	Y	N	?	Y	Y	Y	Y
11 Davis	Y	N	N	Y	N	N	Y	Y	N	Y	N	Y	N
12 *Canady*	Y	N	N	Y	Y	N	Y	N	Y	N	Y	N	Y
13 *Miller*	N	N	N	Y	Y	N	Y	N	Y	N	Y	N	Y
14 *Goss*	N	N	N	Y	N	N	Y	N	Y	N	Y	N	Y
15 *Weldon*	N	N	N	N	Y	N	Y	N	Y	N	Y	N	Y
16 *Foley*	N	N	N	Y	Y	N	Y	N	Y	N	Y	N	Y
17 Meek	Y	Y	Y	N	N	N	N	Y	N	Y	N	Y	N
18 *Ros-Lehtinen*	Y	N	N	N	N	N	Y	N	Y	?	Y	Y	Y
19 Wexler	Y	N	Y	N	N	N	Y	Y	N	Y	N	Y	N
20 Deutsch	Y	N	Y	N	N	N	Y	Y	N	Y	N	Y	N
21 *Diaz-Balart*	Y	N	N	N	N	N	Y	N	Y	N	Y	N	Y
22 *Shaw*	N	N	N	Y	Y	N	Y	N	Y	?	Y	N	Y
23 Hastings	Y	Y	Y	N	N	N	Y	Y	N	?	N	Y	N
GEORGIA													
1 *Kingston*	N	N	N	Y	N	N	Y	N	Y	?	Y	N	Y
2 Bishop	Y	N	Y	Y	N	N	Y	Y	N	Y	N	Y	Y
3 *Collins*	Y	N	N	Y	N	N	Y	N	Y	Y	Y	N	Y
4 McKinney	Y	Y	Y	N	N	N	N	Y	N	Y	N	Y	N
5 Lewis	Y	Y	Y	?	N	N	N	?	N	Y	N	Y	N
6 *Isakson*	N	N	Y	Y	Y	N	Y	N	Y	N	Y	N	Y
7 *Barr*	Y	N	N	Y	N	N	Y	N	Y	Y	Y	N	Y
8 *Chambliss*	N	N	N	Y	N	N	Y	N	Y	N	Y	N	Y
9 *Deal*	N	N	N	N	N	N	Y	N	Y	N	Y	N	Y
10 *Norwood*	N	N	N	Y	N	N	Y	N	Y	N	Y	N	Y
11 *Linder*	N	N	N	N	N	N	Y	N	Y	N	Y	N	Y
HAWAII													
1 Abercrombie	Y	Y	N	N	N	N	N	Y	N	Y	N	Y	N
2 Mink	Y	Y	N	N	N	N	N	Y	N	N	N	N	N
IDAHO													
1 *Chenoweth-Hage*	N	N	N	N	N	N	N	N	Y	N	+	N	Y
2 *Simpson*	N	N	N	N	Y	Y	Y	N	Y	N	Y	N	Y
ILLINOIS													
1 Rush	Y	Y	Y	N	N	N	Y	Y	N	Y	N	Y	?
2 Jackson	Y	Y	N	Y	N	N	N	Y	N	Y	N	Y	N
3 Lipinski	Y	N	N	N	Y	Y	?	Y	N	Y	N	Y	N
4 Gutierrez	Y	Y	Y	N	N	N	Y	Y	N	Y	N	Y	N
5 Blagojevich	Y	Y	?	N	N	N	Y	Y	N	Y	N	Y	N
6 *Hyde*	N	N	Y	Y	Y	N	Y	N	Y	N	Y	N	Y
7 Davis	Y	Y	Y	N	?	N	Y	Y	N	Y	N	Y	N
8 *Crane*	N	N	N	N	N	N	Y	N	Y	N	Y	N	Y
9 Schakowsky	Y	N	N	N	N	N	N	Y	N	Y	N	Y	Y
10 *Porter*	N	N	N	Y	N	N	Y	N	Y	Y	Y	N	N
11 *Weller*	Y	N	N	Y	Y	N	Y	N	Y	N	Y	N	Y
12 Costello	Y	Y	Y	N	N	N	Y	Y	N	Y	N	Y	Y
13 *Biggert*	N	N	N	Y	N	Y	Y	N	Y	N	N	N	N

[1] George E. Brown Jr., D-Calif., died July 15.

KEY

	Democrats		*Republicans*		**Independent**
Y	Voted for ("yea")			−	Announced against
N	Voted against ("nay")			P	Voted "present"
+	Announced for			C	Voted "present" to avoid
#	Paired for				possible conflict of interest
X	Paired against			?	Did not vote or otherwise
					make a position known

ND   Northern Democrats
SD   Southern Democrats
Southern states – Ala., Ark., Fla., Ga., Ky., La., Miss., N.C., Okla., S.C., Tenn., Texas, Va.

House Key Votes	1	2	3	4	5	6	7	8	9	10	11	12	13
14 *Hastert*			Y		Y	Y	Y		Y	N		N	
15 Ewing	Y	N	N	N	Y	Y	Y	N	Y	N	Y	N	Y
16 *Manzullo*	N	N	N	N	N	Y	Y	N	Y	N	Y	N	Y
17 Evans	Y	Y	Y	N	N	N	N	Y	N	Y	Y	Y	N
18 *LaHood*	N	N	N	N	Y	Y	N	N	Y	N	Y	N	Y
19 Phelps	Y	N	Y	N	N	Y	N	Y	N	Y	Y	Y	Y
20 *Shimkus*	Y	N	N	N	Y	N	Y	N	Y	Y	Y	N	Y
INDIANA													
1 Visclosky	Y	N	N	Y	N	N	Y	Y	N	Y	N	Y	Y
2 *McIntosh*	Y	N	N	Y	Y	N	Y	N	N	Y	N	N	Y
3 Roemer	Y	N	Y	Y	N	N	Y	Y	N	Y	Y	Y	Y
4 *Souder*	Y	N	N	N	Y	N	Y	N	N	Y	N	N	Y
5 *Buyer*	Y	?	N	N	Y	N	Y	N	N	Y	N	N	Y
6 *Burton*	Y	−	N	N	N	Y	Y	N	N	Y	N	N	Y
7 *Pease*	Y	N	N	N	N	N	Y	N	N	Y	N	N	Y
8 *Hostettler*	Y	N	N	?	Y	N	Y	N	N	Y	N	N	Y
9 Hill	Y	Y	Y	N	N	N	Y	Y	N	Y	Y	Y	Y
10 Carson	Y	Y	Y	N	N	N	Y	Y	N	Y	N	Y	N
IOWA													
1 *Leach*	N	N	N	N	N	N	Y	N	Y	Y	Y	Y	Y
2 *Nussle*	Y	N	N	N	N	Y	Y	N	Y	N	Y	N	Y
3 Boswell	Y	N	Y	N	N	N	Y	Y	N	Y	Y	Y	Y
4 *Ganske*	Y	N	N	N	N	N	Y	N	Y	Y	Y	Y	Y
5 *Latham*	N	N	N	Y	N	Y	Y	N	Y	N	Y	N	Y
KANSAS													
1 *Moran*	N	N	N	N	N	N	N	N	Y	N	Y	Y	Y
2 *Ryun*	N	N	N	Y	Y	N	Y	N	Y	N	Y	N	Y
3 Moore	Y	N	Y	N	N	N	Y	Y	N	Y	N	Y	Y
4 *Tiahrt*	N	N	N	Y	Y	N	Y	N	Y	N	Y	N	Y
KENTUCKY													
1 *Whitfield*	Y	N	N	N	Y	N	Y	N	N	Y	N	N	Y
2 *Lewis*	Y	N	N	N	Y	N	Y	N	Y	Y	N	N	Y
3 *Northup*	N	N	N	N	N	Y	Y	N	Y	N	Y	N	Y
4 Lucas	Y	N	Y	N	Y	N	Y	Y	N	Y	Y	Y	Y
5 *Rogers*	Y	N	N	Y	Y	Y	Y	N	N	Y	N	N	Y
6 *Fletcher*	N	N	N	N	N	Y	Y	N	Y	N	Y	N	Y
LOUISIANA													
1 *Vitter*[2]				N	Y	N	Y	N	Y	N	Y	Y	Y	Y
2 Jefferson	Y	Y	Y	?	N	N	Y	Y	N	Y	?	Y	Y
3 *Tauzin*	N	N	?	N	N	Y	N	Y	N	Y	N	N	Y
4 *McCrery*	N	N	N	Y	Y	N	Y	N	N	Y	N	N	Y
5 *Cooksey*	N	Y	N	N	N	N	Y	N	N	Y	N	N	N
6 *Baker*	N	N	N	N	Y	N	Y	N	N	Y	N	N	Y
7 John	N	N	Y	N	N	N	Y	Y	N	Y	N	Y	Y
MAINE													
1 Allen	Y	Y	Y	N	N	N	Y	Y	N	Y	N	Y	N
2 Baldacci	Y	Y	Y	N	N	N	Y	Y	N	Y	N	Y	Y
MARYLAND													
1 *Gilchrest*	Y	N	Y	N	Y	Y	Y	N	Y	Y	Y	Y	N
2 *Ehrlich*	Y	N	Y	Y	N	Y	Y	N	Y	N	N	N	N
3 Cardin	Y	Y	Y	Y	N	N	Y	N	Y	N	N	Y	N
4 Wynn	Y	Y	+	N	N	N	Y	Y	N	Y	N	Y	Y
5 Hoyer	Y	N	Y	Y	N	N	Y	Y	N	Y	N	Y	Y
6 *Bartlett*	Y	N	N	N	Y	Y	N	Y	N	Y	N	N	Y
7 Cummings	Y	Y	Y	N	N	N	Y	Y	N	Y	N	Y	N
8 *Morella*	N	Y	Y	Y	N	N	Y	Y	N	Y	N	Y	N
MASSACHUSETTS													
1 Olver	Y	Y	Y	N	N	N	N	N	Y	Y	N	Y	N
2 Neal	Y	Y	Y	N	N	N	Y	Y	N	Y	Y	Y	Y
3 McGovern	Y	Y	Y	N	N	N	Y	Y	N	Y	N	Y	N
4 Frank	Y	Y	Y	N	N	N	Y	Y	N	Y	N	Y	N
5 Meehan	Y	Y	Y	N	N	N	Y	Y	N	Y	N	Y	N
6 Tierney	Y	Y	Y	N	N	N	Y	Y	N	Y	N	Y	N
7 Markey	Y	Y	Y	N	N	N	Y	Y	N	Y	N	Y	N
8 Capuano	Y	Y	Y	N	N	N	Y	Y	N	Y	N	Y	N
9 Moakley	Y	Y	Y	N	N	N	Y	Y	N	Y	Y	Y	Y
10 Delahunt	Y	Y	Y	N	N	N	N	Y	N	Y	N	Y	?

House Key Votes	1	2	3	4	5	6	7	8	9	10	11	12	13
MICHIGAN													
1 Stupak	Y	?	Y	N	N	N	N	Y	N	N	Y	Y	Y
2 *Hoekstra*	N	N	N	Y	N	Y	N	Y	N	N	Y	N	Y
3 *Ehlers*	N	N	N	N	N	Y	Y	N	Y	N	Y	N	Y
4 *Camp*	N	N	N	N	N	Y	Y	N	Y	N	Y	N	Y
5 Barcia	Y	N	Y	N	N	N	Y	Y	N	N	Y	Y	Y
6 *Upton*	N	N	N	N	Y	N	Y	N	Y	N	Y	N	Y
7 *Smith*	N	N	N	Y	Y	Y	Y	N	Y	Y	N	N	Y
8 Stabenow	Y	Y	Y	N	N	N	Y	Y	N	Y	N	Y	N
9 Kildee	Y	Y	Y	N	N	N	Y	Y	N	Y	Y	Y	Y
10 Bonior	Y	Y	Y	N	N	N	Y	Y	N	Y	Y	Y	Y
11 *Knollenberg*	N	N	N	Y	N	Y	Y	N	Y	N	N	N	Y
12 Levin	N	Y	Y	Y	N	N	Y	Y	N	Y	N	Y	Y
13 Rivers	Y	Y	N	N	N	N	Y	N	N	Y	N	Y	Y
14 Conyers	Y	Y	Y	N	N	N	Y	N	N	Y	N	Y	Y
15 Kilpatrick	Y	Y	Y	N	N	N	Y	Y	N	Y	Y	Y	Y
16 Dingell	Y	Y	Y	N	N	N	N	Y	N	Y	Y	Y	N
MINNESOTA													
1 *Gutknecht*	Y	N	N	N	Y	Y	Y	N	Y	N	N	Y	Y
2 Minge	Y	Y	Y	Y	N	−	Y	Y	N	Y	Y	Y	N
3 *Ramstad*	N	N	N	Y	N	Y	Y	N	Y	Y	Y	Y	Y
4 Vento	+	Y	Y	N	N	N	Y	N	Y	Y	N	Y	N
5 Sabo	Y	Y	Y	N	N	N	Y	Y	N	Y	N	+	N
6 Luther	Y	Y	Y	N	N	N	N	Y	N	Y	Y	Y	Y
7 Peterson	Y	N	Y	N	N	N	Y	Y	N	N	Y	N	Y
8 Oberstar	Y	Y	Y	N	N	N	Y	Y	N	Y	Y	Y	Y
MISSISSIPPI													
1 *Wicker*	N	N	N	Y	Y	Y	Y	N	Y	N	N	N	Y
2 Thompson	Y	Y	Y	Y	N	N	Y	Y	N	Y	N	Y	Y
3 *Pickering*	N	N	N	Y	Y	Y	Y	N	Y	N	Y	N	Y
4 Shows	Y	N	Y	N	Y	N	Y	Y	N	Y	Y	Y	Y
5 Taylor	Y	N	N	N	Y	N	Y	N	Y	Y	Y	Y	Y
MISSOURI													
1 *Clay*	Y	Y	Y	N	N	N	N	N	Y	Y	N	Y	Y
2 *Talent*	N	N	N	N	Y	Y	Y	N	Y	N	Y	N	Y
3 Gephardt	Y	Y	Y	N	N	N	Y	Y	N	Y	N	Y	N
4 Skelton	Y	Y	Y	Y	N	Y	Y	N	N	Y	Y	Y	Y
5 McCarthy	Y	+	Y	N	N	N	Y	Y	N	Y	N	Y	Y
6 Danner	Y	N	N	N	N	N	Y	Y	N	Y	Y	Y	Y
7 *Blunt*	N	N	N	Y	Y	Y	Y	N	Y	N	N	N	Y
8 *Emerson*	Y	N	N	Y	N	Y	Y	N	N	Y	N	N	Y
9 *Hulshof*	N	N	N	Y	N	N	Y	N	Y	N	Y	−	Y
MONTANA													
AL *Hill*	N	N	N	N	Y	N	Y	N	Y	Y	Y	N	Y
NEBRASKA													
1 *Bereuter*	N	N	N	N	Y	N	Y	N	Y	Y	Y	N	Y
2 *Terry*	N	N	N	N	N	Y	Y	N	Y	N	Y	Y	Y
3 *Barrett*	N	N	N	Y	N	N	Y	N	Y	Y	Y	N	Y
NEVADA													
1 *Berkley*	Y	Y	Y	N	N	N	Y	N	Y	Y	N	Y	N
2 *Gibbons*	Y	N	N	Y	N	N	Y	N	Y	N	Y	Y	Y
NEW HAMPSHIRE													
1 *Sununu*	N	N	N	Y	N	Y	N	N	Y	N	Y	N	Y
2 *Bass*	N	N	N	N	Y	N	Y	N	Y	Y	N	N	N
NEW JERSEY													
1 Andrews	Y	N	N	N	N	Y	Y	N	N	Y	N	Y	N
2 *LoBiondo*	Y	N	N	N	Y	Y	Y	N	Y	Y	Y	Y	N
3 *Saxton*	N	N	N	N	Y	Y	Y	N	Y	N	Y	Y	N
4 *Smith*	N	N	N	N	Y	N	Y	N	Y	N	Y	Y	N
5 *Roukema*	Y	N	N	Y	N	N	Y	N	Y	N	Y	Y	N
6 Pallone	Y	Y	Y	N	N	N	Y	N	Y	N	N	Y	Y
7 *Franks*	Y	N	Y	N	N	N	Y	N	Y	Y	Y	Y	Y
8 Pascrell	Y	N	Y	N	N	−	Y	N	N	Y	N	N	Y
9 Rothman	Y	Y	Y	N	N	N	Y	N	N	Y	N	Y	Y
10 Payne	Y	Y	Y	N	N	N	N	N	Y	N	N	Y	Y
11 *Frelinghuysen*	N	N	N	Y	Y	N	Y	N	N	Y	N	N	Y
12 Holt	Y	Y	Y	N	N	N	Y	N	N	Y	N	Y	Y
13 Menendez	Y	Y	Y	N	N	N	Y	N	N	Y	N	Y	Y
NEW MEXICO													
1 *Wilson*	N	N	N	N	N	N	Y	N	Y	N	Y	Y	Y
2 *Skeen*	Y	N	N	Y	N	Y	Y	N	Y	N	Y	N	Y
3 Udall	Y	Y	Y	N	N	N	Y	N	Y	N	N	Y	N
NEW YORK													
1 *Forbes*[3]	Y	N	Y	N	N	N	Y	N	N	Y	Y	Y	Y
2 *Lazio*	Y	N	Y	N	Y	Y	Y	N	Y	N	Y	Y	N
3 *King*	Y	N	N	N	Y	N	Y	N	N	Y	Y	Y	Y
4 McCarthy	Y	N	N	N	N	N	Y	N	N	Y	N	Y	N
5 Ackerman	Y	Y	Y	N	N	N	Y	N	N	Y	N	Y	N
6 Meeks	Y	Y	Y	N	N	N	Y	N	N	Y	?	Y	N
7 Crowley	Y	Y	Y	N	N	N	Y	N	N	Y	Y	Y	N

House Key Votes	1	2	3	4	5	6	7	8	9	10	11	12	13
8 Nadler	Y	Y	Y	N	N	N	N	Y	N	Y	N	Y	N
9 Weiner	Y	Y	Y	N	?	N	Y	Y	N	Y	N	Y	N
10 Towns	Y	Y	N	N	N	N	Y	Y	N	Y	N	Y	N
11 Owens	Y	Y	Y	N	N	N	Y	Y	N	Y	N	Y	N
12 Velázquez	Y	Y	Y	N	N	N	Y	Y	N	Y	N	Y	N
13 Fossella	N	N	N	Y	N	Y	+	N	Y	N	Y	N	Y
14 Maloney	Y	Y	Y	N	N	N	Y	Y	N	Y	N	Y	N
15 Rangel	Y	Y	Y	N	N	N	Y	Y	N	Y	N	Y	N
16 Serrano	Y	Y	N	Y	N	N	N	Y	N	Y	N	Y	N
17 Engel	Y	Y	Y	N	N	N	Y	Y	N	Y	N	Y	N
18 Lowey	Y	Y	Y	N	N	N	Y	Y	N	Y	N	Y	N
19 Kelly	Y	N	Y	N	Y	Y	Y	N	Y	Y	N	Y	Y
20 Gilman	Y	Y	Y	N	N	N	Y	N	Y	Y	N	Y	Y
21 McNulty	Y	Y	Y	N	N	N	Y	Y	N	Y	Y	Y	Y
22 Sweeney	Y	N	N	N	Y	Y	Y	N	Y	Y	N	Y	Y
23 Boehlert	Y	N	Y	N	Y	N	Y	N	Y	Y	N	Y	Y
24 McHugh	Y	N	Y	N	Y	Y	Y	Y	Y	Y	Y	Y	Y
25 Walsh	Y	N	Y	Y	Y	Y	Y	N	Y	Y	Y	Y	Y
26 Hinchey	Y	Y	Y	Y	N	N	N	?	N	Y	N	Y	N
27 Reynolds	N	N	N	N	Y	Y	Y	N	Y	Y	Y	Y	Y
28 Slaughter	Y	N	+	N	N	N	Y	Y	N	Y	N	Y	N
29 LaFalce	Y	Y	Y	Y	N	N	Y	Y	N	Y	Y	Y	N
30 Quinn	Y	N	N	Y	Y	N	Y	N	Y	Y	Y	Y	Y
31 Houghton	N	N	Y	?	?	Y	Y	N	Y	Y	N	N	Y
NORTH CAROLINA													
1 Clayton	Y	Y	Y	Y	N	N	Y	Y	N	Y	N	Y	N
2 Etheridge	Y	N	Y	Y	N	N	Y	Y	N	Y	N	Y	Y
3 Jones	Y	N	N	Y	Y	N	Y	N	Y	N	Y	Y	Y
4 Price	Y	Y	Y	Y	N	N	Y	Y	N	Y	N	Y	Y
5 Burr	N	N	N	Y	N	N	Y	N	Y	N	Y	N	Y
6 Coble	Y	N	N	N	N	Y	Y	N	Y	N	Y	Y	Y
7 McIntyre	Y	N	N	Y	N	N	Y	Y	N	Y	Y	Y	Y
8 Hayes	Y	N	Y	Y	N	N	Y	Y	N	Y	N	Y	Y
9 Myrick	+	-	N	Y	N	Y	Y	N	Y	N	Y	N	Y
10 Ballenger	N	N	N	Y	N	Y	Y	N	Y	N	Y	N	Y
11 Taylor	N	N	N	Y	Y	Y	Y	N	Y	N	Y	N	Y
12 Watt	Y	Y	Y	Y	N	N	Y	Y	N	Y	N	Y	N
NORTH DAKOTA													
AL Pomeroy	Y	Y	Y	N	N	N	Y	Y	N	Y	Y	Y	Y
OHIO													
1 Chabot	N	N	N	N	Y	N	Y	N	Y	N	Y	N	Y
2 Portman	N	N	N	Y	Y	Y	Y	Y	N	N	Y	-	Y
3 Hall	Y	Y	Y	Y	Y	N	Y	Y	Y	Y	Y	Y	Y
4 Oxley	N	N	Y	Y	Y	Y	Y	N	Y	N	Y	N	Y
5 Gillmor	Y	N	N	N	Y	Y	Y	N	Y	N	Y	N	Y
6 Strickland	Y	Y	Y	N	N	N	Y	Y	N	Y	N	Y	N
7 Hobson	Y	N	N	Y	Y	Y	Y	N	Y	N	Y	N	Y
8 Boehner	N	?	N	Y	N	Y	Y	N	Y	N	Y	N	Y
9 Kaptur	Y	Y	Y	Y	N	N	N	Y	N	Y	Y	?	N
10 Kucinich	Y	N	Y	N	N	N	Y	Y	N	Y	N	Y	N
11 Jones	Y	Y	Y	N	N	N	Y	Y	N	Y	N	Y	N
12 Kasich	Y	N	N	Y	?	Y	Y	N	Y	N	Y	N	N
13 Brown	Y	Y	Y	Y	N	N	N	Y	N	Y	N	Y	N
14 Sawyer	Y	Y	Y	Y	N	N	Y	Y	N	Y	N	Y	N
15 Pryce	N	N	N	?	N	Y	Y	N	Y	?	Y	N	Y
16 Regula	Y	N	N	Y	Y	Y	Y	N	Y	Y	Y	Y	Y
17 Traficant	Y	Y	Y	N	N	N	Y	Y	N	Y	N	Y	Y
18 Ney	Y	N	N	N	N	N	Y	N	Y	N	Y	N	Y
19 LaTourette	Y	N	N	N	N	Y	Y	N	Y	Y	Y	Y	Y
OKLAHOMA													
1 Largent	Y	N	N	N	Y	Y	Y	N	Y	N	Y	N	Y
2 Coburn	Y	-	N	Y	Y	N	N	N	Y	N	Y	Y	Y
3 Watkins	N	N	N	Y	Y	Y	Y	N	Y	N	Y	N	Y
4 Watts	N	N	N	Y	Y	Y	Y	N	Y	N	Y	N	Y
5 Istook	N	N	N	Y	Y	N	Y	N	Y	N	Y	N	Y
6 Lucas	N	N	N	Y	Y	N	Y	N	Y	N	Y	N	Y
OREGON													
1 Wu	Y	Y	Y	Y	N	N	Y	Y	N	Y	?	Y	N
2 Walden	N	N	N	N	Y	Y	Y	N	Y	N	Y	N	N
3 Blumenauer	Y	Y	Y	N	N	N	Y	Y	N	Y	N	Y	N
4 DeFazio	Y	Y	N	N	N	N	N	Y	N	Y	N	Y	N
5 Hooley	Y	Y	Y	N	N	N	Y	Y	N	Y	-	Y	N
PENNSYLVANIA													
1 Brady	Y	Y	Y	N	N	N	N	Y	N	Y	N	Y	Y
2 Fattah	Y	Y	Y	N	N	N	N	Y	N	Y	N	Y	N
3 Borski	Y	Y	Y	N	N	N	Y	Y	N	Y	N	Y	Y
4 Klink	Y	N	Y	N	N	N	Y	Y	N	Y	Y	Y	Y
5 Peterson	Y	N	N	N	Y	N	Y	N	?	?	N	Y	Y
6 Holden	Y	N	N	N	N	N	Y	N	?	Y	Y	Y	Y
7 Weldon	Y	N	N	N	Y	Y	Y	N	Y	Y	Y	Y	Y
8 Greenwood	Y	N	Y	N	Y	Y	Y	N	Y	Y	N	Y	Y

House Key Votes	1	2	3	4	5	6	7	8	9	10	11	12	13
9 Shuster	Y	N	?	N	Y	Y	Y	N	Y	N	Y	?	N
10 Sherwood	Y	N	N	N	Y	Y	Y	N	Y	N	Y	Y	Y
11 Kanjorski	Y	Y	Y	N	N	N	Y	Y	N	Y	Y	Y	Y
12 Murtha	Y	N	Y	N	N	N	Y	Y	N	Y	Y	Y	Y
13 Hoeffel	Y	Y	Y	Y	N	N	Y	Y	N	Y	N	Y	Y
14 Coyne	Y	Y	Y	N	N	N	N	Y	N	Y	N	Y	N
15 Toomey	Y	N	N	Y	N	Y	Y	N	Y	N	Y	N	Y
16 Pitts	?	N	N	Y	Y	Y	Y	N	Y	N	Y	N	Y
17 Gekas	Y	N	N	N	N	N	Y	N	Y	Y	N	Y	Y
18 Doyle	Y	N	Y	N	N	N	Y	Y	N	Y	N	Y	Y
19 Goodling	Y	N	N	N	Y	Y	Y	N	Y	N	Y	N	Y
20 Mascara	Y	N	Y	N	N	N	Y	Y	N	Y	Y	Y	+
21 English	Y	N	N	N	Y	Y	Y	?	Y	Y	N	Y	Y
RHODE ISLAND													
1 Kennedy	Y	Y	Y	N	N	N	Y	+	-	Y	N	Y	?
2 Weygand	Y	Y	Y	Y	N	N	Y	Y	N	Y	Y	Y	Y
SOUTH CAROLINA													
1 Sanford	N	N	N	N	N	N	Y	N	Y	Y	Y	N	N
2 Spence	N	N	N	Y	Y	Y	Y	N	Y	N	Y	Y	Y
3 Graham	Y	N	N	Y	Y	Y	Y	N	Y	Y	Y	Y	Y
4 DeMint	N	N	N	Y	Y	Y	Y	N	Y	Y	Y	N	Y
5 Spratt	Y	P	Y	Y	N	N	Y	N	Y	Y	Y	Y	Y
6 Clyburn	Y	?	Y	Y	N	N	Y	N	Y	N	Y	+	N
SOUTH DAKOTA													
AL Thune	N	N	N	N	N	N	Y	N	Y	N	Y	N	Y
TENNESSEE													
1 Jenkins	Y	N	N	N	Y	N	Y	N	Y	Y	Y	Y	Y
2 Duncan	Y	N	N	Y	Y	Y	Y	N	Y	Y	Y	Y	Y
3 Wamp	Y	N	N	Y	N	N	Y	N	Y	Y	Y	Y	Y
4 Hilleary	Y	N	N	Y	Y	Y	Y	N	Y	N	Y	N	Y
5 Clement	Y	N	Y	Y	N	Y	Y	Y	N	Y	Y	Y	Y
6 Gordon	Y	N	N	Y	N	N	Y	Y	N	Y	Y	Y	Y
7 Bryant	Y	N	N	Y	Y	Y	Y	N	Y	N	Y	N	Y
8 Tanner	Y	N	Y	N	Y	Y	Y	N	Y	Y	Y	Y	N
9 Ford	Y	Y	Y	N	N	N	Y	N	Y	Y	-	Y	N
TEXAS													
1 Sandlin	Y	Y	Y	N	N	N	Y	Y	N	Y	N	Y	N
2 Turner	Y	N	N	Y	Y	N	N	Y	N	Y	Y	Y	Y
3 Johnson, Sam	N	N	N	Y	Y	N	Y	N	Y	N	Y	N	Y
4 Hall	N	N	N	Y	Y	N	Y	N	Y	Y	Y	Y	Y
5 Sessions	N	N	N	Y	Y	Y	Y	N	Y	N	Y	N	Y
6 Barton	N	N	N	Y	Y	N	Y	N	Y	N	Y	N	Y
7 Archer	N	N	N	Y	Y	Y	?	N	Y	N	Y	N	Y
8 Brady	N	N	N	Y	Y	Y	Y	N	Y	N	Y	N	Y
9 Lampson	Y	Y	Y	N	N	N	Y	Y	N	Y	N	Y	Y
10 Doggett	Y	Y	Y	N	N	N	Y	Y	N	Y	N	Y	N
11 Edwards	Y	Y	Y	N	N	N	Y	Y	N	Y	N	Y	Y
12 Granger	N	N	N	Y	Y	Y	Y	N	Y	N	Y	?	Y
13 Thornberry	N	N	N	Y	Y	N	Y	N	Y	N	Y	N	Y
14 Paul	N	N	N	Y	N	N	Y	N	Y	N	N	N	Y
15 Hinojosa	Y	Y	Y	N	N	N	Y	Y	N	Y	N	Y	-
16 Reyes	Y	N	Y	N	N	N	Y	Y	N	Y	N	Y	Y
17 Stenholm	Y	N	Y	Y	N	N	Y	Y	N	Y	Y	Y	Y
18 Jackson-Lee	Y	Y	Y	N	N	N	Y	Y	N	Y	N	Y	Y
19 Combest	N	N	N	Y	Y	Y	Y	N	Y	N	Y	N	Y
20 Gonzalez	Y	Y	Y	N	N	N	Y	Y	N	Y	N	Y	N
21 Smith	N	N	N	Y	Y	Y	Y	N	Y	N	Y	N	Y
22 DeLay	N	N	N	Y	Y	N	Y	N	Y	N	Y	N	Y
23 Bonilla	N	N	N	Y	N	?	N	N	Y	N	Y	N	Y
24 Frost	Y	Y	Y	N	N	N	Y	Y	N	Y	N	Y	N
25 Bentsen	Y	Y	Y	N	N	N	Y	Y	N	Y	N	Y	Y
26 Armey	N	N	N	Y	Y	Y	Y	N	Y	N	Y	N	Y
27 Ortiz	Y	N	Y	N	N	N	Y	Y	N	Y	Y	Y	Y
28 Rodriguez	Y	Y	Y	N	N	N	Y	Y	N	Y	Y	Y	N
29 Green	Y	N	N	N	N	N	+	Y	N	Y	N	Y	Y
30 Johnson, E.B.	Y	Y	Y	N	N	N	Y	Y	N	Y	N	Y	N
UTAH													
1 Hansen	Y	N	?	N	Y	Y	Y	N	Y	N	Y	N	Y
2 Cook	Y	N	N	N	Y	Y	Y	N	Y	Y	Y	Y	Y
3 Cannon	Y	N	N	N	N	Y	Y	N	Y	N	Y	Y	Y
VERMONT													
AL **Sanders**	Y	N	Y	N	N	N	N	Y	N	Y	N	Y	N
VIRGINIA													
1 Bateman	N	N	N	N	N	N	Y	N	Y	N	Y	N	Y
2 Pickett	Y	N	Y	N	N	N	Y	Y	N	Y	N	Y	N
3 Scott	Y	N	Y	N	N	N	Y	Y	N	N	N	Y	N

[2] David Vitter, R-La., was sworn in June 8, replacing Robert L. Livingston, R-La., who resigned effective Feb. 28, 1999.

[3] Michael P. Forbes, N.Y., switched from the Republican Party to the Democratic Party on July 17.

KEY

	Democrats	*Republicans*	**Independent**
Y	Voted for ("yea")	–	Announced against
N	Voted against ("nay")	P	Voted "present"
+	Announced for	C	Voted "present" to avoid possible conflict of interest
#	Paired for	?	Did not vote or otherwise make a position known
X	Paired against		

ND Northern Democrats
SD Southern Democrats
Southern states – Ala., Ark., Fla., Ga., Ky., La., Miss., N.C., Okla., S.C., Tenn., Texas, Va.

House Key Votes	1	2	3	4	5	6	7	8	9	10	11	12	13
4 Sisisky	Y	N	Y	N	N	Y	Y	Y	Y	Y	N	Y	Y
5 Goode	Y	N	N	N	Y	N	Y	N	Y	N	Y	N	Y
6 *Goodlatte*	N	N	N	Y	Y	Y	Y	N	Y	N	Y	N	Y
7 *Bliley*	N	N	Y	Y	Y	Y	Y	N	Y	N	Y	N	Y
8 Moran	N	N	Y	Y	N	N	Y	Y	N	Y	N	Y	N
9 Boucher	Y	N	Y	?	N	N	Y	Y	N	Y	N	Y	N
10 *Wolf*	N	N	Y	Y	Y	Y	Y	N	Y	Y	Y	Y	Y
11 *Davis*	N	N	Y	N	N	Y	Y	N	Y	N	Y	Y	Y
WASHINGTON													
1 Inslee	Y	Y	N	N	N	N	N	Y	N	Y	N	Y	N

House Key Votes	1	2	3	4	5	6	7	8	9	10	11	12	13
2 *Metcalf*	Y	N	N	N	Y	N	Y	N	Y	Y	Y	N	N
3 *Baird*	Y	Y	Y	N	N	N	Y	Y	N	Y	N	Y	N
4 *Hastings*	N	N	N	N	N	N	Y	N	Y	N	Y	N	Y
5 *Nethercutt*	N	N	N	Y	N	N	Y	N	Y	N	Y	N	Y
6 Dicks	N	Y	Y	N	N	N	Y	Y	N	Y	N	Y	N
7 McDermott	N	Y	Y	N	N	N	N	+	-	Y	N	Y	N
8 *Dunn*	N	N	N	Y	N	Y	Y	N	Y	N	Y	N	Y
9 Smith	N	N	Y	Y	N	Y	Y	Y	N	Y	N	Y	N
WEST VIRGINIA													
1 Mollohan	Y	N	?	Y	Y	N	Y	Y	N	N	Y	Y	Y
2 Wise	Y	N	Y	N	Y	Y	Y	Y	N	Y	N	Y	Y
3 Rahall	Y	Y	Y	N	N	Y	Y	Y	N	N	Y	Y	Y
WISCONSIN													
1 *Ryan*	Y	N	N	Y	N	Y	Y	N	Y	N	Y	N	Y
2 Baldwin	Y	Y	N	Y	N	N	N	Y	N	Y	N	Y	N
3 Kind	N	Y	Y	Y	N	N	Y	Y	N	Y	N	Y	N
4 Kleczka	Y	Y	N	N	N	N	N	Y	N	Y	Y	Y	Y
5 Barrett	Y	Y	Y	Y	N	N	N	Y	N	Y	N	Y	N
6 *Petri*	Y	N	N	N	N	Y	Y	N	Y	Y	Y	N	Y
7 Obey	Y	Y	Y	Y	N	N	N	Y	N	Y	N	Y	N
8 *Green*	N	N	N	Y	N	Y	Y	N	Y	N	Y	N	Y
9 *Sensenbrenner*	N	N	N	Y	N	Y	Y	N	Y	N	Y	N	Y
WYOMING													
AL *Cubin*	N	N	N	N	Y	N	Y	N	Y	N	Y	Y	Y

Senate

1. FISCAL 2001 BUDGET RESOLUTION

A contentious fight among Senate Republicans in the spring over how much to spend in fiscal 2001 offered a preview of the budget-related turmoil within the party that would last through much of the year. Conservatives pressed for tight spending restraints, while centrists with an eye on the upcoming elections argued for spending levels high enough to boost funding for popular social programs.

The more tightfisted Senate Republicans won initially but their victory turned out to be short-lived. The intraparty squabbling, in the end, did little to restrain fiscal 2001 spending.

A defining moment came in April when the Senate voted to adopt the conference report on a budget resolution (H Con Res 290) that would limit discretionary budget authority to $600.3 billion—less than an inflationary increase and about $25 billion less than President Clinton requested. The budget resolution also called for $150 billion in tax cuts during the next five years, and perhaps more depending on changes in Congressional Budget Office surplus projections. The vote was 50–48: R 50–4; D 0–44 (ND 0–36, SD 0–8). Three Republican fiscal moderates—Arlen Specter of Pennsylvania, Lincoln Chafee of Rhode Island, and James M. Jeffords of Vermont—voted against the budget deal, as did John McCain of Arizona, who said it called for excessive tax cuts that could jeopardize debt reduction efforts. Chafee also complained about the lack of emphasis on debt reduction. *(Vote, p. 926)*

Democrats warned that the GOP was setting itself up for another end-of-session controversy in which Congress would be unable to pass several appropriations bills because of the tight budget constraints.

GOP moderates also worried that the budget resolution was unrealistic but they had been forced to give ground to fiscal conservatives in the party just to get the budget to the Senate floor for a vote. A band of four Republicans on the Senate Budget Committee, led by Phil Gramm of Texas, had threatened to sink the budget unless GOP leaders agreed to a tight spending limit. Gramm and his allies prevailed and the budget emerged from committee on a party-line vote with a spending limit of $596.5 billion. The total was plumped on the Senate floor with an additional $4.1 billion for defense spending. The budget resolution emerged from conference at $600.3 billion.

The House adopted the budget resolution on a near party-line vote; the Senate vote cleared it later the same day. It was the second straight year Congress met the April 15 deadline for settling on a budget, and GOP leaders hoped it would give them a running start on the difficult task ahead of clearing spending bills.

But as appropriators had warned, party leaders would quickly find themselves wedged between fiscal conservatives, who insisted at least initially on living within the budget, and President Clinton, who said he would refuse to sign bills that did not fund his priorities. The result was that by mid-September, GOP leaders had tacitly abandoned the limits of the budget resolution. They capitulated to most of Clinton's spending demands, and in some cases Republicans endorsed even more spending than Clinton requested, as special projects were heaped on to several spending bills.

2. NUCLEAR WASTE DISPOSAL

Legislation that would decide where the nation stores its most lethal nuclear waste fell victim to much of the same political squabbling in 2000 that has doomed previous attempts to resolve the issue.

Yucca Mountain in the remote Nevada desert was under study as the permanent disposal site, but it was not expected to be ready until 2010 at the earliest. That meant spent fuel was piling up at commercial nuclear power plants in thirty-four states. Until 1999 Republicans had concentrated on legislation that would store the fuel temporarily at an above-ground site near Yucca Mountain, but the bills had been blocked or threatened by a presidential veto.

In an attempt to reach a compromise with nuclear utilities that were running out of storage space, Energy Secretary Bill Richardson in 1999 proposed that the Energy Department assume legal title and management of the waste, instead of sending it to Nevada. The Senate Energy and Natural Resources Committee backed the idea, incorporating it into a bill (S 1287) it approved in June 1999.

Governors of several northeastern states, however, complained that such a provision would remove Congress's incentive to develop a permanent site. Frank H. Murkowski, R-Alaska, chairman of the Senate Energy and Natural Resources Committee, sought to placate those critics by calling for the Energy Department to offer utilities a combination of money and storage casks.

However, Murkowski ended up alienating the Clinton administration and key Democrats who backed the original proposal. Murkowski also angered the White House by including language that would have allowed the Environmental Protection Agency to establish radiation standards for the permanent site at Yucca Mountain only after consulting with the National Academy of Sciences and the Nuclear Regulatory Commission. Democrats complained that the storage deadlines and milestones included throughout the bill were unrealistic.

The Senate in early February passed the reworked storage bill, 64–34—three votes short of the two-thirds majority required to overturn a veto. Six weeks later the House voted to clear the bill, 253–167—twenty-seven votes short of a two-thirds majority. President Clinton vetoed the bill, calling it "a step backward" in developing a permanent waste storage solution. The veto prompted Murkowski and other supporters to scramble to find senators who would support an override.

In the end, however, backers of the bill came up short, thanks to a lobbying effort against the measure led by Nevada Democratic Sens. Richard H. Bryan and Harry Reid. The Senate in May failed to override the veto on a vote of 64–35: R 51–3; D 13–32 (ND 5–32, SD 8–0). The margin was actually two votes: Senate Majority Leader Trent Lott, R-Miss., switched his vote from "yes" to "no" in a procedural move that allowed him to call for another vote in the future. Lott promised to bring up the bill again if proponents could collect more support. However, another opportunity never arose on the Senate calendar, and supporters turned their sights toward reviving the storage issue under a new presidential administration. *(Vote, p. 926)*

3. KOSOVO DEPLOYMENT

Republican-led opponents of the deployment of U.S. troops on peacekeeping missions in the former Yugoslavia went one more round with President Clinton in May. They ran into the same unmovable obstacles they encountered every time they forced a vote since the troops went to Bosnia in late 1995.

In 2000 the test came on a provision in the fiscal 2001 military construction appropriations bill (S 2521) to require Clinton to withdraw by July 1, 2001, the 5,900 U.S. troops then serving as part of a NATO-led peacekeeping force in the Serbian province of Kosovo unless Congress authorized their continued deployment.

The language, cosponsored by Armed Services Committee Chairman John W. Warner, R-Va., and senior Appropriations Committee Democrat Robert C. Byrd of West Virginia, had been approved by the Appropriations panel, 23–3.

Contending that Clinton had given U.S. forces too little money and too many missions, most congressional Republicans—including even some committed internationalists like Warner—opposed committing U.S. ground forces to Balkan peacekeeping for fear of overstressing both the troops and their equipment.

For Byrd and some others, the fight was one more skirmish in the quarter-century conflict over the assertion by presidents of a unilateral right to commit military forces abroad without congressional sanction.

Clinton's Senate opponents had not won even one of their several legislative challenges to the deployments in Bosnia and Kosovo. Each time, Clinton had been backed by a Democratic-led majority, some of whom supported the Balkan mission on its merits, some of whom were loath to take action that might endanger U.S. forces already deployed, and some of whom simply feared undermining U.S. diplomatic clout by what would be a futile effort to reverse a presidential *fait accompli.*

Indeed, the critics had never come close to forcing a U.S. troop withdrawal. They fell short of even a simple majority in the Senate let alone the two-thirds majority they would need to override a Clinton veto of any binding language that would force a pullout.

When the full Senate took up the Warner-Byrd language, the administration weighed in as usual: a veto threat by Clinton, extensive lobbying by administration officials—and the presence of Vice President Al Gore in the chair in case his tie-breaking vote was needed. Ultimately, all but seven Democrats aligned with the president.

However, a new element was thrown into the mix by Texas Gov. George W. Bush, who at the time was the all-but-certain Republican presidential nominee. Just as every president of both parties has done since Congress tried to assert a role in deployment decisions by passing the 1973 War Powers Resolution, Bush came down squarely in favor of presidential prerogative, announcing his opposition to the Warner-Byrd language.

The key vote came on a motion by senior Armed Services Committee Democrat Carl Levin of Michigan to delete the provision from the military construction bill. The motion was agreed to, and the language was dropped, by a vote of 53–47: R 15–40; D 38–7 (ND 32–5, SD 6–2). Warner later claimed that the key to his defeat was Bush's intervention, pointing to the fifteen Republicans who voted to drop the restrictive language. *(Vote, p. 926)*

4. CAMPAIGN FINANCE

For years, Congress tried—and failed—to pass a broad overhaul of the nation's campaign finance system. But in June a leader in those efforts, Sen. John McCain, R-Ariz., shifted tactics and successfully pushed through a narrowly written bill that opened to public review an area of private political spending.

It was the first change in federal election law in two decades. The new law required so-called 527 organizations to publicly disclose their fund-raising and spending activities. The groups were named after the section of the tax code that previously exempted them from public disclosure so long as they did not expressly call for the election or defeat of specific candidates.

For years opponents of curbing campaign spending said the best way to improve the system was to require greater disclosure. McCain, who had been the target of attack ads by a secretly funded 527 group while he sought the GOP presidential nomination, saw an opening to do what the foes of campaign finance overhaul had long advocated. He took his rivals at their word and introduced the legislation along with Sens. Russell D. Feingold, D-Wis., and Joseph I. Lieberman, D-Conn.

McCain and his colleagues decided to offer the language as an amendment to an unrelated Defense Department authorization bill (S 2549). Majority Leader Trent Lott, R-Miss., agreed to allow the amendment, believing he had the votes to defeat it.

Lott and Armed Services Committee Chairman John W. Warner, R-Va., warned that the McCain amendment would mean the death of the underlying defense bill because it would be rejected by the House for violating the constitutional requirement that changes in tax law must originate in the House.

Debate on the amendment was replete with contradiction. Lawmakers who a year before attached an $18.4 billion tax cut for small business to the Senate bankruptcy bill as part of a proposal to raise the minimum wage, now fretted about whether McCain's amendment would, as Warner put it, "torpedo" the Pentagon bill and "send it to the bottom of the sea."

Lott and others also attacked McCain's proposal as unfairly narrow, arguing that it did not apply to campaign spending by labor unions and other Democratic-leaning political groups. McCain countered that 527s are used by both sides, noting the Sierra Club as a prime example of a left-leaning group that used the law to obscure its activities.

The decisive vote was not on the amendment itself but on a point of order motion by Warner on the constitutional issue he had raised. Warner's motion was soundly rejected, 42–57: R 41–14; D 1–43 (ND 1–35, SD 0–8). Election-year politics played into the vote. Of the thirteen Republicans who sided with McCain, eight were up for reelection that November. After defeating Warner's motion, the Senate passed McCain's amendment by voice vote. *(Vote, p. 926)*

The Senate vote broke the bottleneck of political maneuvering that for so long had blocked congressional efforts to change campaign financing. Within one month of the Senate's action, the House approved similar language (HR 4762). President Clinton signed it into law in July.

5. HATE CRIMES

Although expanding the federal definition of a hate crime to include offenses against gays and the disabled has been a top goal of civil rights groups and the Clinton administration, the issue had never been debated by the Senate. In 1999 the Senate attached a hate crimes provision to a fiscal 2000 spending bill by voice vote with no debate, but it was quickly dropped during conference on the measure.

In 2000 the chief sponsor of the provision, Edward M. Kennedy, D-Mass., changed his target. Instead of going after a spending bill, Kennedy offered his amendment during floor consideration of the fiscal 2001 defense authorization bill (S 2549). As a member of the Senate Armed Services Committee, Kennedy was sure to be on the conference committee where he could fight to preserve the provision.

Criminal acts motivated by racial, religious, or ethnic bias already were considered hate crimes under federal law. Kennedy's amendment added those in which victims were chosen because of sexual orientation, gender, or disability. In addition to expanding the definition, the measure also made it easier for the federal government to prosecute hate crimes. Under existing law the government could prosecute only if the crime took place on federal property or if it occurred during one of six very specific protected activities, such as voting. The Kennedy amendment allowed the federal government to get involved in most prosecutions of hate crimes.

Kennedy offered his amendment in June, and, despite the controversial nature of the language, there was little debate. Although many spoke in favor of it, few voiced opposition. GOP Policy Committee Chairman Larry E. Craig, R-Idaho, said after the June vote that members were concerned about how their opposition would be interpreted. "I think all of us are extremely concerned that we don't appear to be racist or prejudiced, because none of us are," he said.

Fearing a tie, Democrats called Vice President Al Gore back from the campaign trail to be on hand in case his vote was needed. But Gore was not needed because the first-ever recorded vote by the Senate on the volatile question passed by the surprisingly large margin of 57–42: R 13–41; D 44–1 (ND 36–1, SD 8–0). The thirteen Republicans who voted for the measure ranged from moderates such as Vermont's James M. Jeffords to conservatives such as Alaska's Ted Stevens. The one Democratic opponent, Robert C. Byrd of West Virginia, argued that the provision was unconstitutional. *(Vote, p. 926)*

Hate crimes became one of the most difficult issues to be decided by the House-Senate negotiators on the defense authorization bill. During the lengthy conference the strong Senate vote helped House supporters of the amendment pass a nonbinding motion instructing conferees to accept the Kennedy amendment. It passed, 232–192 in mid-September. Despite the strong votes and Kennedy's presence on the conference committee, the Republican leadership worked hard to strip the proposal from the defense bill. In October conferees announced it had been dropped from the final version.

6. COLOMBIA DRUG-FIGHTING AID

With strong support from President Clinton and House Speaker J. Dennis Hastert, R-Ill., Congress in 2000 made a major new foreign policy commitment by approving $1.3 billion in emergency spending to fight drug trafficking in South America, mainly in Colombia. Efforts to reduce the funding in the Senate version of the fiscal 2001 foreign operations bill or redirect it to other programs were overwhelmingly defeated, as only a small band of liberals and a few budget conservatives opposed the massive aid program. Some critics said the Colombia military and police were repressive while others worried that the cost to the United States would only escalate.

On the most explicit vote taken on the issue, an amendment by Slade Gorton, R-Wash., to cut the emergency counternarcotics spending from $934 million to $200 million was rejected, 19–79: R 13–41; D 6–38 (ND 6–30, SD 0–8). *(Vote, p. 926)*

The bipartisan push by Hastert and Clinton cemented support among centrists in both parties. The two leaders had expressed deep concern about the fate of Colombian President Andres Pastrana's government, which was under siege from leftist guerrillas and rightwing paramilitaries who profit from and protect drug traffickers. Hastert is the leader of a group of Republicans who had pushed for more aid to Colombia for four years before they were successful.

Supporters of the aid package also managed to mute some of the opposition from liberals by making the aid contingent on the president's certification that Colombia had met a number of human rights conditions. The president could waive the requirement in the interest of national security.

Pastrana and some of his top officials also became regular visitors to Capitol Hill, lobbying lawmakers on behalf of the aid package, a cornerstone of what Pastrana called "Plan Colombia," a multiyear effort to restore security, eliminate drug trafficking, and spur economic development in the Andean nation.

Opponents of the aid package, such as Sen. Patrick J. Leahy of Vermont, ranking Democrat on the Foreign Operations Appropriations Subcommittee, made clear that the Senate votes were only the first skirmish in an extended battle over the funds. Even the most optimistic forecasts were that Pastrana's government would need the aid for at least five years.

7. GENETIC INFORMATION PRIVACY

Just three days after two teams of scientists announced that they had decoded most of the human genome—mankind's genetic blueprint—the Senate debated an amendment by James M. Jeffords, R-Vt., to the fiscal 2001 Labor-HHS-Education spending bill (HR 4577) that prohibited health insurers from using genetic information to deny coverage or raise premiums.

The debate reflected a growing debate about the boundaries of genetic discrimination. Although deciphering the human genome was widely hailed as a landmark development that could lead to cures for many diseases, it also has raised questions about whether patients' health information could be used to single out individuals prone to certain medical conditions. An individual's genetic profile not only yields clues about current afflictions but may reveal whether a person or his or her offspring is more prone to certain cancers or other gene-based diseases.

The Senate's response reflected a cautious approach to potential problems. Just before the June vote on Jeffords's amendment, senators rejected, 44–54, an amendment by Minority Leader Tom Daschle, D-S.D., that prohibited employers from using genetic information to discriminate in hiring practices or promotions. The provision, which was defeated largely along party lines, also would have prevented insurers from tying coverage or premiums to genetic tests and from requiring genetic tests as a condition of coverage. Daschle's amendment also would have allowed an individual to take genetic discrimination claims to court.

Republicans argued that the 1990 Americans with Disabilities Act already prevented workplace discrimination based on one's genetic profile and said Daschle's measure would prompt a flood of lawsuits. Democrats responded there was ample evidence that genetic discrimination exists, pointing to the case of a North Carolina woman who claimed she lost her job at an insurance company after officials there learned she had tested positive for a potentially fatal amino acid deficiency.

The amendment by Jeffords, chairman of the Senate Health, Education, Labor and Pensions Committee, was similar to language in a Senate-passed bill (S 1344) to regulate the managed care industry that had stalled in conference negotiations. Jeffords said that with the fate of the managed care legislation in doubt, it was important to attach the language to another vehicle. The Jeffords amendment was adopted 58–40: R 55–0; D 3–40 (ND 3–32, SD 0–8). *(Vote, p. 926)*

8. MANAGED CARE REGULATION

As House and Senate negotiators stumbled in their efforts to strike a deal on managed care legislation (HR 2990), Democrats and Republicans in both chambers grew weary of the talks. Senate Democrats took their frustration a step further in June, forcing floor showdowns to embarrass Republicans who had blocked action on the politically volatile patients' rights issue. Edward M. Kennedy, D-Mass., tried unsuccessfully to attach the House-passed managed care bill— stripped of several provisions that Democrats disliked—to the fiscal

2001 Defense appropriations bill (S 2549). After that attempt, Majority Whip Don Nickles, R-Okla., said Kennedy's effort "certainly didn't help the cause of getting a good bipartisan bill."

Later that month Senate Democrats were at it again, this time trying to amend the fiscal 2001 Labor, Health and Human Services, and Education appropriations bill (HR 4577). Byron L. Dorgan, D-N.D., offered an amendment to require any managed care bill passed by Congress to cover all 193 million Americans who have private health insurance. Nickles and other Senate Republicans had said for months that any federal legislation should not interfere with state laws governing health benefits, while Democrats felt that any health care law coming from Washington had to apply to every state. Dorgan's amendment was rejected, 47–51, but it sparked a strategic move from Senate Republicans, who battled back with a proposal of their own.

Nickles offered an amendment that would permit patients, under limited circumstances, to sue health insurance plans for damages if they denied or delayed needed medical care. The GOP proposal broke new ground by endorsing a limited right to sue managed care plans for damages, something Senate Republicans had resisted fiercely when the Senate passed its first managed care bill in July 1999.

Lawsuits would be allowed under two conditions: unreasonable delays in medical care and a failure to cover treatment that an independent physician determined the plan should cover. Although patients could not win punitive damages, they could recover unlimited economic damages and up to $350,000 for noneconomic damages such as pain and suffering. Democrats wanted no caps on noneconomic damages and wanted the lawsuits to be handled in state courts, not federal courts. Nickles's amendment passed, 51–47: R 51–4; D 0–43 (ND 0–35, SD 0–8). *(Vote, p. 926)*

Although the vote marked a turning point in the debate, it was not enough to revive the stalled managed care talks, which concluded with no consensus package.

9. MISSILE DEFENSE

Though many Democrats remained skeptical of a nationwide missile defense system that the Clinton administration was developing, their opposition was muted until a test failure in July galvanized them to try to slow the program down.

The administration's program was intended to deploy by 2005 a defense that could shoot down a handful of missiles that might be launched at U.S. territory by regimes in North Korea or the Middle East. Republicans, who favored developing a more robust shield, attacked the Clinton program as inadequate and complained that its military capability was artificially constrained to live within limits set by the 1972 treaty limiting antiballistic missile (ABM) weapons.

On the other hand, many Democrats worried that even Clinton's limited antimissile program would violate the ABM Treaty and thus spark a nuclear arms race around the globe. However, many of these critics were loath to challenge the program head-on, especially since 1998 when North Korea tested a long-range ballistic missile.

Early in 2000 the liberal skeptics were heartened when Massachusetts Institute of Technology professor Theodore A. Postol and others launched a vigorous attack on the technical effectiveness of the current antimissile program. Even a minor adversary could flummox the system by using decoys and other relatively simple countermeasures, Postol argued.

Then in July a test was aborted by failure of a normally reliable booster rocket that was unrelated to the sophisticated "kill vehicle," designed to home in on an attacking warhead, which Postol had criticized. Nevertheless, the incident unleashed pent-up criticism of the antimissile program—particularly of its accelerated timetable.

The vehicle was an amendment by Richard J. Durbin, D-Ill., to the annual defense authorization bill (HR 4205) that would have required more extensive tests of the system against various types of decoys and other possible countermeasures. The amendment was tabled, or killed, by a vote of 52–48: R 52–3; D 0–45 (ND 0–37, SD 0–8). Three Republican centrists crossed party lines: Olympia J. Snowe and Susan Collins from Maine, and Vermont's James M. Jeffords. In September Clinton cited the July test failure in announcing that he was deferring to his successor a decision about whether to deploy the antimissile defense. *(Vote, p. 926)*

10. MARRIAGE PENALTY

Usually Congress considers tax provisions en masse. Leaders believe that a big package creates its own momentum and hides in its girth controversial tax fixes for specific individuals or interest groups. That pattern changed with Republicans in charge of Congress and the White House controlled by a Democrat. Republican majorities in both chambers would pass the large bill but President Clinton would always argue that the bills were too large even though he supported some provisions. Clinton said vetoing them was necessary to prevent growth of the national debt.

As the second session of the 106th Congress began, Speaker J. Dennis Hastert, R-Ill., sought a new strategy. With input from former Minority Leader Robert H. Michel, R-Ill. (1957–1995), Hastert devised a plan to move a host of smaller tax bills. That would accomplish two goals: giving members a chance for favorable publicity when their tax bills came to the floor and creating a campaign issue if Clinton vetoed a bill.

House Republicans knew that the first test of Hastert's strategy would come not at the White House but in the Senate. For several years, that chamber's Republicans had refused to go along with House tax plans, saying they were either too expensive or not well conceived. Although many Democrats welcomed certain tax proposals, it was unclear how many would go against their party's leaders.

The first stand-alone measure the House passed—a bill (HR 6) to cut taxes for married couples—was the one on which the Senate's intentions became clear. The House passed it easily in February but Senate Majority Leader Trent Lott, R-Miss., could not move his chamber's more generous version (HR 4810) until July, when it had been given protection from endless amendment and debate under the fiscal 2001 budget resolution (H Con Res 290). In the meantime, the House had passed it again.

After the Senate cleared it, Republicans quickly worked out their differences in an attempt to put the bill on Clinton's desk by the GOP presidential nominating convention, which began in late July. Conferees removed some of the most expensive Senate provisions, settling on a $90 billion tax cut over the next five years. They then pushed it to the Senate floor, setting up a political fight over a bill that had once held the promise of bipartisan compromise.

Republicans and Democrats had both long agreed that the tax code should be fairer for married couples, who often pay more in income taxes than they would if they had remained single individuals. Democrats generally insisted the fixes should go to the 24.8 million couples who suffered the penalty. Republicans said the 21 million couples who were not penalized, mostly single-income households, also should receive tax relief.

When Clinton said early in the year that he would not approve tax cuts before Social Security and Medicare were shored up, House Republicans moved their tax bill without Democratic input. Later, Clinton offered to sign a $250 billion-version of the "marriage penalty" bill, if Republicans approved his similarly priced measure to cover prescription drugs for the elderly. Republicans quickly rejected such a trade-off.

In the days before the vote, Minority Leader Tom Daschle, D-S.D., and Treasury Secretary Lawrence H. Summers worked mightily to make a case against the bill. Daschle and House Minority Leader Richard A. Gephardt, D-Mo., held news conferences charging that Republicans were up to "the same old tricks" when Summers released data showing that the bill's benefits were heavily weighted toward the richest families.

Republicans said Democrats were not for tax cuts at all. "The day of reckoning is here," Lott said July 18. "Do you actually want to eliminate the marriage penalty . . . or not?"

In the end, seven Senate Democrats voted for the conference report, as fifty-one of their House counterparts had. That was enough for the measure to pass but 6 votes short of the super-majority needed to override a veto. That tally was 60–34; R 53–1; D 7–33 (ND 5–27, SD 2–6). The outcome indicated that Hastert's individual tax bills might move through Congress but would not become law. Clinton vetoed the bill in August and the House failed in September to override his decision. *(Vote, p. 926)*

11. CHINA'S NUCLEAR THREAT

The Senate's resounding rejection of a proposal aimed at stemming China's nuclear proliferation showed the difficulty U.S. officials faced in addressing national security concerns while promoting commerce with the world's most populous nation.

Senior Republican lawmakers condemned the Clinton administration for conducting U.S.-China relations under a so-called strategic partnership—a policy of openness they say did not regard Beijing with enough wariness as a potential security threat. At the same time, though, GOP leaders heeded warnings from the party's business allies not to stir up anti-China sentiment.

The conflicts between the two competing interests came to a head in 2000 on a bill (HR 4444) that granted permanent normal trade relations to China. The House passed the trade measure in May after a hard-fought battle but supporters expected it to coast through the Senate. However, Sens. Fred Thompson, R-Tenn., and Robert G. Torricelli, D-N.J., argued that the national security concerns with China deserved to be debated on par with trade. They introduced a bill (S 2645) that would have required the president to punish the Chinese government or individual Chinese companies if they were found to be supplying weapons of mass destruction or components to other nations.

With the backing of Majority Leader Trent Lott, R-Miss., Thompson sought to offer his proposal as an amendment to the fiscal 2001 intelligence authorization bill (S 2507). The Senate, however, ground to a halt in July in an impasse over judicial nominees and several Democratic legislative priorities. The delays and procedural wrangling prompted an exasperated Thompson to seek to attach his proposal to the China trade bill after lawmakers returned from the August recess.

Supporters of the trade measure—including the Clinton administration and numerous industry groups—were anxious to keep the proliferation proposal at bay because approval of the amendment would have required the return of the trade bill to the House. They successfully lobbied Republicans who endorsed Thompson's measure not to jeopardize relations with China by adopting any amendments to the trade bill.

In the end, Thompson's amendment was tabled, or killed, 65–32: R 30–23; D 35–9 (ND 27–8, SD 8–1). The thirty Republicans who joined thirty-five Democrats in rejecting the measure included several of the Senate's most influential GOP voices on international matters: Richard G. Lugar of Indiana, John W. Warner of Virginia, and Chuck Hagel of Nebraska. *(Vote, p. 926)*

Thompson and Torricelli acknowledged that their proposal faced an uphill struggle in the context of the China trade bill but they vowed to continue to pursue the proliferation issue.

12. "MINI-OMNIBUS"

Republican prospects for finishing the fiscal 2001 appropriations process before the November election were dealt a major setback when the Senate took the unusual step of rejecting the conference report on a combined legislative branch and Treasury-Postal spending bill. The tactic of using the conference report on one spending bill to carry a second, unfinished measure was conceived in late summer. With only two fiscal 2001 appropriations bills cleared and the August recess and the two national political conventions looming, the leadership crafted its own $30.4 billion version of the Treasury-Postal bill—combining elements of the House-passed version with a version approved by the Senate Appropriations Committee—and inserted it into the conference report on the legislative branch spending measure. Also included was a proposal to repeal the 3 percent federal telephone excise tax, at an estimated cost of more than $19.9 billion over five years.

GOP leaders hoped to avert a lengthy and politically difficult debate over the Treasury bill on the Senate floor, where fights were expected both on House-passed provisions to broaden contacts with Cuba and on likely Democratic gun control amendments. Because it was a conference report, the combined measure was not subject to amendment.

Initial reaction in the House to the hastily assembled package was not encouraging. Democrats lambasted its secret overnight drafting; conservatives were unhappy with spending levels. Concluding they did not have the votes, GOP leaders pulled the package. When members returned after the recess, House leaders and other key supporters managed to rally enough support to win adoption of the conference report on a 212–209 vote in mid-September.

But the combination of anger over the way the measure was brought to the Senate floor and complaints from all sides over spending—Democrats said it was too little; conservatives said it was too much—produced a dramatic showdown a few days later. The Senate rejected the conference report by an overwhelming vote of 28–69: R 28–26; D 0–43 (ND 0–34, SD 0–9). *(Vote, p. 926)*

Angry that GOP leaders had never brought a stand-alone Treasury-Postal bill to the floor, Democrats united in voting against the measure. There was also bipartisan concern that, in an election year, the leadership had not allowed for a vote to add language to the bill blocking an automatic annual pay increase for members of Congress.

To quell the opposition, GOP leaders subsequently cut a deal with the White House to provide $348 million in additional funding for the IRS and antiterrorism programs in the Transportation spending bill. The Transportation bill also included language to nullify a provision in the Treasury conference report that would have erased a temporary increase in pension payments by lawmakers under the 1997 balanced-budget law. The Senate cleared the Treasury-Postal conference report, 58–37, in October.

But Republican prospects for moving the spending bills did not recover. Indeed, the Treasury-Postal-legislative branch package fell victim to the prolonged disarray. President Clinton vetoed it at the end of October, saying he could not sign a bill for the legislative branch when "the business of the American people remains unfinished."

The Treasury-Postal bill was resolved as part of the final budget negotiations in the lame-duck session.

House

1. MINIMUM WAGE

From early in the 106th Congress, Republican leaders had tried to block, or at least blunt, calls from Democrats including President Clinton for an increase in the minimum wage. They hoped to avoid the kind of defeat they suffered in 1996, when moderate Republicans joined with Democrats to pass a wage increase over the vociferous opposition of GOP leaders.

This time, the leadership sought to preempt the Democrats with a proposal to stretch a $1 increase to $6.15 an hour, over three years—Democrats wanted a two-year increase—and pair it with tax cuts to mollify business owners, as they had in 1996.

Though Democrats acknowledged they would have to allow some form of tax relief as the cost of a minimum wage increase, they held firm on their two-year time frame. In February Senate Democrats tried but failed to remove a three-year minimum wage amendment added in late 1999 to a rewrite of personal bankruptcy law and replace it with a two-year phase-in. That appeared to kill efforts to get a two-year increase included in a bill in 2000.

But in March, facing a threatened Clinton veto of any minimum-wage increase longer than two years, the House broke with its Republican leadership to adopt an amendment to a business tax-relief package offered by James A. Traficant Jr., D-Ohio, that raised the minimum wage by $1 over two years. The vote was 246–179: R 42–173; D 203–5 (ND 155–0, SD 48–5); I 1–1. The vote demonstrated the strength of support among moderate Republicans and all but the most conservative Democrats for a two-year increase, settling the question for the 106th Congress. Republicans also gained support for combining the increase with business tax relief, a fallback position for business owners opposed to an increase in the minimum wage. While the 106th Congress adjourned without clearing a minimum wage increase, the vote did encourage Congress and the White House to make several attempts over the rest of the year to combine the two-year phase-in that Clinton wanted with the business tax relief sought by Republicans. (Vote, p. 928)

2. KOSOVO DEPLOYMENT

Opponents of deploying U.S. ground troops in the former Yugoslavia won an impressive—though largely symbolic—victory in May by tapping into the widespread suspicion that other NATO allies were shirking their fair share of the peacekeeping burden. Critics of the dispatch of U.S. troops to Bosnia in 1995 and to Kosovo in 1999 contend that President Clinton was undermining U.S. military power by giving the forces too few resources and too many jobs peripheral to basic national interests. But for at least two decades before this issue arose, the demand for more equitable "burden sharing" by wealthy European allies—that is, higher European defense budgets to allow a lower Pentagon budget—had rallied some liberal Democrats and GOP conservatives alike.

Because the most immediate threat posed by the Yugoslavia conflict was that it would exacerbate ethnic tensions in neighboring countries, critics touted it as a prime opportunity for the European NATO members to take a larger role, particularly by relieving U.S. ground troops from the dangerous business of policing.

In March House Budget Committee Chairman John R. Kasich, R-Ohio, a leading opponent of the Balkan deployments, offered an amendment to the supplemental appropriations bill for fiscal 2000 that would have withheld half the $2.1 billion included in the bill for the Kosovo operation until the Europeans took on a larger role in the mission. The amendment was rejected, 200–219, with many mem-

bers objecting that it would have tied the president's hands in case of a crisis.

When the House took up the annual defense authorization bill several weeks later, Kasich refined his proposal to give the president more flexibility. This time, the amendment would require the president to withdraw U.S. ground troops from Kosovo unless he could certify to Congress by April 1, 2001, that European countries had actually delivered certain percentages of the police manpower and financial aid they had already pledged for the province's reconstruction. The president could waive this rule for up to six months in case of a military crisis, or if Congress approved a longer deployment.

Supporters of the deployment argued that Europeans already had taken on most of the heavy lifting, providing about 80 percent of the peacekeeping troops in Kosovo. But an overwhelming majority of Republicans joined by nearly one-third of the Democrats backed the amendment, 264–153: R 195–18; D 67–135 (ND 49–100, SD 18–35); I 2–0. Kasich's supporters fell 14 votes shy of the two-thirds majority they would have needed to override a certain Clinton veto but they never faced that test. The provision was not included in the final version on the bill that emerged from a Senate-House conference. (Vote, p. 928)

3. MILITARY RETIREES HEALTH CARE

A long-running debate over the adequacy of health care for military retirees was resolved in 2000 when Congress approved a sweeping expansion of medical benefits that was expected to cost $60 billion over ten years.

The House vote in May was interpreted as an extremely important development: Congress's first open break from its self-imposed budget limits as a result of burgeoning budget surpluses produced by a booming economy.

The issue was welcomed in both parties. Republicans argued that the complaints of military retirees were proving to be a detriment to the armed services, especially in recruitment and retention. At least some liberal Democrats backed the move in hopes that it would help create momentum for their effort to greatly expand the medical care entitlement currently available to all citizens over the age of sixty-five.

Specifically at issue was the retirees' contention that they had been promised free, lifetime medical care for themselves and their dependents if they served on active duty for at least twenty years. The government's legal obligation to the retirees was much narrower than that but for decades most retirees could easily obtain free health care either from military hospitals, which they could use on a space-available basis, or from private health-care providers who would accept reimbursement from a Pentagon-run insurance program. However, once they turned sixty-five retirees were to rely on Medicare.

Retirees had complained for years about being forced to turn to Medicare and about limitations in the Pentagon-run insurance program. But the complaints became more insistent in the mid-1990s. As many military bases were closed, access to military hospitals became more difficult, even as health costs were rising and the number of Medicare-eligible retirees and dependents was growing to a current total of nearly 1.4 million. In response, Congress created in 1997 several pilot programs to test alternative medical benefits for retirees.

President Clinton's fiscal 2001 defense budget requested $80 million to fix certain problems in the existing program but the administration turned down the Joint Chiefs' proposals to offer retirees cut-price, mail-order pharmacy service and "medi-gap" insurance to cover the difference between their expenses and what Medicare would pay.

The House Armed Services Committee added to the annual defense authorization bill provisions that would expand the mail-order pharmacy benefit. When the bill came to the House floor, committee member Gene Taylor, D-Miss., offered an amendment that would have transformed one of the pilot programs into a new benefit available to all retirees under which Medicare would reimburse the military for their medical care.

Warning that this approach was untested and would cost too much, House Armed Services military personnel subcommittee Chairman Steve Buyer, R-Ind., offered an alternative amendment to expand the pilot program and extended it through 2003. But Buyer's proposal was rejected, 95–323, after which the House passed Taylor's amendment by 406–10: R 207–9; D 197–1 (ND 145–1, SD 52–0); I 2–0. The conference report on the defense bill, approved in October, included even more generous health care entitlements for retirees. (Vote, p. 928)

4. CHINA'S TRADE STATUS

Every year since Chinese leaders sent tanks to quell student rebellions in Tiananmen Square in 1989, China's trade status with the United States had caused vigorous debates in Congress. Each year, the president would certify that China had met the conditions for maintaining a normal trade relationship with the United States. Under a provision of the 1974 Trade Act (known as the Jackson-Vanik amendment after its sponsors) communist nations must allow free immigration in order for their imports to win the same beneficial tariffs that the goods of other nations receive. After the president's annual certification, a member of Congress would challenge his decision and accuse the United States of forsaking human rights to make a buck. Efforts to overturn the certification inevitably failed, as the majority determined that isolation would not change China's policies.

With such a controversial history, it was unsurprising that the most contentious vote of the 106th Congress would be the Clinton administration's bid to exempt China from the annual review and grant it permanent normal trading status. The House, where trade expansion often divided both parties, became the main battleground. The more reliably protrade Senate was a lesser hurdle.

The 2000 action began in November 1999 when U.S. and Chinese officials concluded thirteen years of negotiations with a sweeping trade agreement. It provided unprecedented U.S. access to the more than one billion consumers of China, requiring the Asian nation to change hundreds of laws and practices. The United States was required only to make China a permanent normal trading partner. In addition, that move would put the U.S. imprimatur on China's bid to join the World Trade Organization (WTO).

But it also made life difficult for many members of Congress, particularly House Democrats who looked forward to their best chance in six years to retake the chamber and did not want to risk offending their allies in organized labor that vociferously opposed the bill.

As a result, President Clinton approached the issue gingerly. He did not release details of the agreement or send draft legislation to the Hill until March, several weeks after many Republicans worried publicly that Clinton would not engage in the debate to the extent necessary to ensure passage. They brought up his failure in 1997 and 1998 to win fast-track trading authority from Congress as proof that he was not sufficiently committed to expanding world trade. But Clinton had his own agenda. He had shepherded the North American Free Trade Agreement (NAFTA) and the General Agreement on Tariffs and Trade through skeptical Congresses in 1993 and 1994. Success on the China bill, which would allow the president to grant permanent trade status when China joined the WTO, would cap his achievements as a president who had greatly expanded international commerce.

Through weekly meetings with wavering members at the White House, frequent calls to the Capitol, and the appointment of NAFTA

veteran William M. Daley to head his lobbying efforts, Clinton showed he would actively pursue approval. Meanwhile, Clinton's usual union and environmental allies were preparing to fight the measure. They were joined by human rights organizations and groups focused on preventing abortions, which generally appealed to more conservative members. The nation's largest businesses, particularly those in the high-technology, agricultural, and manufacturing sectors, lined up on the other side. They provided millions of dollars for lobbying and advertising campaigns in favor of the bill. The target for both groups was a group of wavering members, which dwindled from almost a third of the House when the issue was first discussed to less than a dozen by the time the vote came in late May.

Opponents of the measure, led by Minority Whip David E. Bonior, D-Mich., held news conferences to hail members they had persuaded to vote against the bill. Minority Leader Richard A. Gephardt, D-Mo., opposed the bill but refrained from lobbying against it in deference to his caucus' mixed feelings. The administration's point man—inveterate protrader Robert T. Matsui, D-Calif.—and Majority Whip Tom DeLay, R-Texas, joined forces to round up votes for the bill. Well known for his intense dislike of Clinton, DeLay's involvement in whipping for the president's priority was key to keeping partisan tensions at a minimum during the critical final days of debate. And proponents' ability to win endorsement from some high-ranking Democrats, led by Charles B. Rangel of New York, helped sway some new members as well.

Despite the pressure, a number of undecided members still worried that they were giving China, a country with a history of human rights violations and saber rattling, a blank check by agreeing to the bill.

Two members—Sander M. Levin, D-Mich., and Doug Bereuter, R-Neb.—provided cover to some wavering members. They wrote an amendment to create a commission whose members, chosen by Congress and the administration, would monitor China's compliance with the November trade pact and its activity on human and labor rights, and to forward legislation to Congress if the need arose. Although opponents decried it as a "fig leaf," many wavering members said it gave them some peace of mind, and leaders eventually agreed to attach it to the measure.

When the vote finally came the House passed it by a margin of more than thirty votes, roughly the number of members who said they were swayed by the Levin-Bereuter amendment. The tally was 237–197: R 164–57; D 73–138 (ND 43–114, SD 30–24); I 0–2. The Senate approved the measure without difficulty four months later. (Vote, p. 928)

5. ESTATE TAX

With many Americans' stock portfolios becoming more and more valuable, the business groups pushing to repeal taxes on estates, gifts, and trust funds found their idea being well received in unexpected quarters. The main proponents of the bill were the small business, manufacturing, and farm groups that had pushed a repeal since Republicans took control of Congress in 1995. They were joined by a host of other groups, including several minority chambers of commerce, who believed that the estate tax was stemming the creation of wealth in black and Hispanic communities. That prompted some of the more liberal House Democrats to sign on to the measure.

The bill (HR 8), sponsored by Jennifer Dunn, R-Wash., and John Tanner, D-Tenn., had been long praised by Republicans and farm-district Democrats. In 2000 liberal Neil Abercrombie, D-Hawaii, frequently called for its passage at press events, and a number of other liberal members, including Eva Clayton, D-N.C., and Nydia M. Velázquez, D-N.Y., joined the cause.

As a result, Republican leaders expected a strong Democratic vote when they brought the bill to the floor in June. It was one of a host of stand-alone tax measures Speaker J. Dennis Hastert, R-Ill., presented as an alternative to the usual omnibus tax package that President Clinton had consistently vetoed.

Some Democratic leaders worked to head off "yes" votes from their party mates by proposing an alternative that would substantially cut tax rates on estates, gifts, and trust funds and would exempt more small farms and businesses from the estate tax altogether. The proposal, sponsored by Charles B. Rangel, D-N.Y., Charles W. Stenholm, D-Texas, and Benjamin L. Cardin, D-Md., won strong support but less than repeal itself.

The June vote on HR 8 was 279–136: R 213–0; D 65–135 (ND 43–104, SD 22–31); I 1–1. *(Vote, p. 928)*

It gave the measure life in the Senate where leaders had suggested they were not interested in taking up a stand-alone repeal bill. The measure cleared Congress in July, the eve of the party conventions, but President Clinton vetoed it in August, saying its $104 billion cost over ten years was too much. The House subsequently failed to override his decision.

6. ELECTRONIC SIGNATURES

It seemed a simple task at the start of the 106th Congress: establish a federal standard for sealing contracts on the Internet. The legislation would lay groundwork for use of binding electronic signatures, such as a scrawled moniker on a touch-sensitive computer screen, or bits of computer code that identify a buyer and seller.

Complications set in soon after high-tech companies began their effort to move the legislation, aimed at speeding up the growth of electronic commerce. A potential major obstacle emerged when the financial services industry insisted that the bill be used as a vehicle for new standards that would allow them to meet record retention requirements with computer records instead of paper. The industry also sought language that would allow customers over the Internet to fill out applications and receive disclosures that are required by law before they can open an account, get a loan, and conduct other financial transactions online.

For some Democrats, the paperwork elimination effort smacked of an attempt to skirt laws meant to ensure that consumers get important information from businesses in writing, including recall notices and foreclosure warnings.

Jay Inslee, D-Wash., resolved some of the consumer protection concerns with compromise language endorsed by a coalition of New Democrats in the House that required companies to get affirmative consent of consumers to receive records by e-mail instead of printed copies. The amendment was adopted 418–2 in November and the House passed the measure (HR 1714) overwhelmingly, 356–66. The Senate passed its own narrower version of the legislation (S 761) by voice vote soon after. It would have allowed the use of electronic signatures without addressing the issue of expanding use of electronic records.

In a conference committee of Senate and House negotiators, strong objections by the White House and consumer groups threatened to scuttle broader House language supported by industry. The administration and key lawmakers including Reps. John D. Dingell, D-Mich., and Edward J. Markey, D-Mass., and Sen. Patrick J. Leahy, D-Vt., insisted on language that would ensure consumers were given a chance to demonstrate they could receive important records electronically before they gave consent to receive them in lieu of paper records.

Commerce Committee Chairman Thomas J. Bliley Jr., R-Va., worked out a compromise requiring companies to confirm that customers could receive copies of disclosures and other information by e-mail before they gave formal consent to receive them in lieu of paper copies. The deal allowed for companies to meet record retention requirements with computer files in lieu of paper copies starting March 1, 2001, and required state and federal agencies to complete any new electronic record-keeping standards by June 1. In a colloquy on the floor with Markey, Bliley said companies could fulfill their consent obligation by sending a sample message to a consumer in an e-mail attachment. The recipient would then send an e-mail to the company stating he had received, opened, and read the attachment. The conversation helped clear the way for the compromise to become law.

The House voted to approve the conference report, 426–4: R 216–3; D 208–1 (ND 155–0, SD 53–1); I 2–0. The Senate cleared 87–0. *(Vote, p. 928)*

7. NATIONAL MONUMENTS

The long-running battle between the Clinton administration and Republicans over federal land management policy intensified during the 106th Congress, as western lawmakers attempted to halt President Clinton's actions protecting millions of acres by declaring them national monuments. The failed GOP efforts to block funding for the management of new monuments designated in the last months of Clinton's tenure highlighted the deep divide over the government's role in local land-use decisions that has been part of the issue ever since development began in western areas of the nation.

As Republicans sat down to craft the fiscal 2001 spending bill to fund the Department of the Interior, Rep. James V. Hansen, R-Utah, pressed appropriators to include language limiting funds to manage monuments designated after 1999. Hansen had objected vigorously in 1996 when Clinton declared nearly 1.7 million acres of southern Utah as the Grand Staircase Escalante National Monument—halting virtually all commercial development of that land—and tried unsuccessfully to change the 1906 Antiquities Act, which allows presidents to take such action.

In the months leading up to consideration of the Interior bill, Clinton created four national monuments totaling more than 1.4 million acres—including an area on the north rim of the Grand Canyon, a site in Arizona containing prehistoric ruins, the 840-mile-long California coast, and sequoia groves in California's Sierra Nevada. He also expanded the Pinnacles National Monument south of San Jose, Calif.

Heeding the pleas of Hansen and other western Republicans—who characterized the designations as federal land grabs that took decisions out of the hands of local authorities—appropriators ignored a veto threat and included a policy "rider" in the Interior measure to deny funds for the management of these areas.

As the Interior measure headed to the floor, Clinton created another four national monuments totaling 540,000 acres and Norm Dicks of Washington, the ranking Democrat on the House Appropriations Interior Subcommittee, drafted an amendment to strip the monuments funding rider from the spending legislation. Dicks and other Democrats argued that the GOP provision would interfere with a presidential prerogative and force federal land agencies to abandon management of existing monuments.

Dicks's amendment was adopted, but only after westerners tried a last-ditch attempt to stop Clinton from following through with his land initiatives, which they said were purely political. Right before the vote on Dicks's provision, Hansen offered an amendment that would have reinstated the restriction on monuments funding. It was rejected 187–234: R 177–38; D 9–195 (ND 4–148, SD 5–47); I 1–1. Following the vote, Clinton continued to exercise his power to declare monuments. He designated eleven monuments covering 4.6 million acres by the end of 2000 and repeatedly boasted—to Republicans' consternation—that he "protected more land as national monuments in the lower forty-eight states than any president in history." *(Vote, p. 928)*

8. CAMPAIGN FINANCE

House approval in late June of the first change in federal election law in two decades came only after a surprising victory for Senate overhaul advocates less than a month earlier.

Following the Senate's passage of legislation to stiffen campaign finance disclosure laws, Republican moderates on the House side increased pressure on their leadership to take up similar legislation. Realizing they were outnumbered, GOP leaders—who generally opposed any changes to the nation's campaign finance system—agreed to move forward.

But the leaders decided to craft their own legislation rather than simply take up what the Senate had passed as an amendment to the defense authorization bill. House leaders appointed moderate GOP Rep. Amo Houghton of New York to lead the effort, but many charged that Majority Whip Tom DeLay, R-Texas—a strong opponent of changing finance laws—played a major role in drafting the bill (HR 4717).

The House legislation was much broader than the Senate language, which simply called for so-called 527 organizations to publicly disclose to the Internal Revenue Service their political fund-raising and spending activities. The groups were named after the section of the tax code that exempted them from public disclosure requirements as long as they did not expressly call for the election or defeat of specific candidates.

The House bill included disclosure requirements for 527 groups, similar to the Senate language, but it expanded those rules to cover a huge number of other politically potent tax-exempt groups. The bill immediately came under withering attack from nonprofit groups across the political spectrum, including the National Rifle Association and Democratic-friendly unions. The groups argued that the bill would prevent them from participating in even routine grassroots advocacy without having to name their members and subject them to possible harassment from the government or their rivals. Opponents of the House bill also charged that it was drafted so broadly it would be declared unconstitutional for its infringement on the right of free association. Many charged that GOP leaders intentionally made the bill overly broad in hopes that it would crumble under its own weight.

It quickly became obvious the bill was doomed to failure on the House floor. But House leaders had promised overhaul-minded Republicans a vote on campaign finance, and Speaker J. Dennis Hastert, R-Ill., wanted the issue out of his hair in a tough election year. So GOP leaders turned to what they knew could pass: the straightforward 527 disclosure bill (HR 4762).

On the key vote, the House overwhelmingly passed the legislation 385–39: R 178–39; D 205–0 (ND 151–0, SD 54–0); I 2–0. Less than thirty-six hours later, the Senate, which had begun the process by approving the 527 language as an amendment offered by Sen. John McCain, R-Ariz., voted 92–6 to clear the House's free-standing bill. President Clinton signed it into law in July. *(Vote, p. 928)*

9. PRESCRIPTION DRUGS

Developing and passing legislation to give senior citizens drug coverage became, in the words of one GOP pollster, a "political imperative" for Republicans. Removing the issue from the fall election campaigns was a top priority for House Speaker J. Dennis Hastert, R-Ill., and he looked to House Ways and Means Health Subcommittee Chairman Bill Thomas, R-Calif., to take the reins.

Thomas developed a package that looked to the private sector to develop drug-only policies that seniors could purchase. The additional coverage would be optional under Medicare, the federal health insurance program for nearly 40 million elderly and disabled Americans.

Coverage would begin in fiscal 2003. The government would provide subsidies to help low-income seniors afford monthly premiums and deductibles and pay all medication costs for seniors whose annual drug bills were $6,000 or higher. Seniors would have at least two different options for their coverage. If private insurers did not offer coverage in a particular area, the government would.

The same week the House GOP unveiled its prescription drug plan, the White House held three events to blast it. President Clinton labeled the proposal a "trickle-down scheme that would provide a subsidy for insurers and not a single dollar of direct premium assistance for middle-class seniors." House Democrats offered similar assessments. Charles B. Rangel, D-N.Y., the ranking Democrat on Ways and Means, said the proposal was "not a true Medicare prescription drug benefit." Senate Republicans, preferring to wait until they could tackle a comprehensive Medicare overhaul, did little to support their House counterparts' plan.

Insurers, usually a strong GOP ally, balked at the proposal, fearing they could not make a profit by selling such policies. They felt that seniors with the highest drug costs would be most likely to purchase coverage. And with drug prices almost certain to rise, insurers feared lawmakers would pressure them not to raise premiums.

But Thomas said that if the plan became law, plenty of insurers would offer coverage to seniors. "When you tell somebody you don't need them and, in fact, it's going to succeed without them, you'll be amazed at how some people will come around the back door and want to be part of it," he told reporters.

Thomas tried to sell the proposal as a bipartisan measure, but it garnered just 5 Democratic votes when it squeaked through the House 217–214: R 211–10; D 5–203 (ND 4–150, SD 1–53); I 1–1. Although the bill went nowhere after the floor vote—Senate Republicans never acted on either the House bill or a package of their own—the measure did give House Republicans cover in the fall elections and put them on record as favoring prescription drugs for Medicare recipients. *(Vote, p. 928)*

10. DEBT RELIEF

A coalition that included religious leaders, President Clinton, lawmakers from both parties, and even rock star Bono of the Irish group U2 set about in 2000 trying to persuade Congress that the United States should contribute to an international debt relief fund for the world's poorest countries. Supporters said these countries, most of them in sub-Saharan Africa, needed help paying off debts to international financial institutions, such as the World Bank and International Monetary Fund (IMF). The burden of debt payments is so great, they said, that the countries have precious little money left over for social programs such as health and education.

The coalition's backing put the issue on the congressional agenda. But they had not succeeded in getting most of the money they had sought until the fiscal 2001 foreign operations appropriations bill (HR 4811) was taken up by the House. Clinton had asked for $435 million in cash and permission for the IMF to revalue its gold reserves so it could provide as much as $1 billion in additional debt relief.

In the House, Foreign Operations Appropriations Subcommittee Chairman Sonny Callahan, R-Ala., and House Majority Leader Dick Armey, R-Texas, had blocked most of the funds, saying the promise of aid should be used to force changes in the way the financial institutions do business and as a bargaining chip in end-of-session budget negotiations with the White House. Callahan's Senate counterpart, Mitch McConnell, R-Ky., and Senate Banking Committee Chairman Phil Gramm, R-Texas, had agreed to hold up substantial debt relief in that chamber.

The showdown between the groups came on an amendment by Rep. Maxine Waters, D-Calif., to the foreign operations bill to increase funds for debt relief by $156 million, with offsetting cuts in other areas, essentially giving Clinton what he had asked for. The amendment was adopted 216–211: R 26–194; D 189–16 (ND 142–9, SD 47–7); I 1–1. *(Vote, p. 928)*

Waters triumphed only after an extended tug-of-war between party leaders. With Waters and her supporters—including twenty-six Republicans—leading in the vote tally, GOP leaders held the vote open for an extra quarter-hour, as Majority Whip Tom DeLay of Texas urged wavering members such as Ernie Fletcher of Kentucky and Tom Coburn and Steve Largent of Oklahoma to oppose the amendment as part of his overall budget strategy. Just as DeLay appeared on the verge of victory by 1 vote, Democrats surprised him when they managed to get several of their own members to drop their "no" votes, convincing them that their support would both allow a breakthrough on debt relief and permit those funds that Waters cut (such as military aid to the Middle East) to be restored in a future House-Senate conference.

Their confidence proved well-founded. The final version of the foreign aid bill restored Waters's cuts and included the debt relief the coalition had favored: $435 million in cash and permission for the IMF to revalue its gold reserves in order to provide another $800 million.

11. COMMUNITY DEVELOPMENT

When the House Republican leadership decided to bring the Community Renewal and New Markets Act (HR 4923) straight to the floor, it was acknowledging that the political stakes on the bill were so high that the regular committee process could not be allowed to derail it. The antipoverty bill was the result of months of negotiations between President Clinton and Speaker J. Dennis Hastert, R-Ill. That history alone gave the bill special status—the backing of a Democratic president and a Republican Speaker is not to be taken lightly.

It was also one of the rare occasions when top Republicans and Democrats saw eye-to-eye on social policy, an area that traditionally has been a philosophical chasm between the two parties. By limiting the bill to tax incentives, regulatory relief, and economic development, the package struck a nonthreatening balance that avoided both new government programs and all-out deregulation—the approaches that had gotten Democrats and Republicans in trouble in the past.

Most of the provisions were tax-related, which put them under the jurisdiction of the Ways and Means Committee, but its key members had trouble translating the broad Clinton-Hastert agreement, announced in May, into detailed legislation.

By the end of July, the committee still had not scheduled a markup, as Chairman Bill Archer, R-Texas, and ranking Democrat Charles B. Rangel of New York found themselves disagreeing on everything from how quickly to expand the availability of the low-income housing tax credit to which provisions should count as Republican spending and which ones should count as Democratic

spending. In addition, Archer wanted a no-amendment pledge from Democrats, which Rangel was unwilling and unable to provide.

Other issues also surfaced as potential threats to the bill's passage. A key concession to Republicans was the inclusion of a "charitable choice" provision that would allow faith-based substance abuse treatment programs to receive federal funds. Robert C. Scott, D-Va., argued that the provision could lead to federally subsidized "religious bigotry" because the organizations running such programs could refuse to hire people who disagreed with their religious beliefs.

To steer past that and other obstacles and get the legislation through the House before the August recess, GOP leaders decided to finish writing the bill themselves and bring it straight to the floor under suspension of the rules, which limits debate, prohibits amendments and requires a two-thirds vote to pass. The gambit worked. Despite their concerns, few members were willing to vote against an antipoverty package with as much political momentum as this one. In late July the legislation passed the House 394–27: R 214–1; D 179–25 (ND 130–23, SD 49–2); I 1–1. *(Vote, p. 928)*

12. RESERVING THE SURPLUS

Using a proposal touted as a debt-reduction measure, Republican leaders got themselves out of a midyear appropriations jam and signaled their intention to break their own budget caps by about $27 billion. The problem the GOP was trying to solve with the debt-reduction plan began in the spring, when conservatives in both chambers successfully pushed for the adoption of a budget resolution that held discretionary spending to less than an inflationary increase.

Appropriators from both parties warned that the spending limit was too tight, and they turned out to be right. It became clear relatively early in the appropriations process that Congress would have to ignore the budget resolution's spending limits for there to be any hope of passing bills that President Clinton would sign. But by midyear, fiscally conservative Republicans were already nervous about the budget-breaking spending totals that were working their way through the appropriations process, and they were threatening to vote against appropriations bills that were too heavily funded.

In response, GOP leaders in September rolled out a so-called "90–10" debt reduction plan, which specified that 90 percent of the cumulative fiscal 2001 surplus would go to paying down the $3.1 trillion publicly held debt. The remaining 10 percent—about $28 billion based on the most recent fiscal 2001 surplus projections available at the time—could be used for a combination of tax cuts and spending increases, and party leaders said they likely would split it evenly between the two priorities.

Although Republican leaders trumpeted the debt reduction aspect of their plan, it actually amounted to a blueprint for a big increase in fiscal 2001 spending. In drafting their 90–10 plan, the GOP used an inflationary increase in the budget as its baseline. This assumption by itself amounted to an abandonment of the spending limit in the budget resolution. The plan used a Congressional Budget Office projection showing that discretionary spending would have to grow from $608 billion to $638 billion in outlays to keep pace with inflation. With an additional $14 billion on top of that, the 90–10 proposal's called-for spending would total about $652 billion—$27 billion more in outlays than allowed under the budget resolution.

Democrats said the GOP plan was a meaningless gimmick. Surplus funds are automatically used to pay down the public debt, they argued, so the way to reduce the debt was simply to not spend the money. Still, Democrats endorsed the measure, saying it amounted to a symbolic repudiation of the Republicans' own large tax cuts proposed earlier in the year, since there would be insufficient room for them under the 90–10 plan. Democrats also complained that the plan would be in effect only for fiscal 2001, leaving the door open to big, surplus-gobbling tax cuts in subsequent years if Texas Gov. George W. Bush were elected president.

The House had already voted three times previously on similar GOP debt "lockbox" measures but the 90–10 plan was unique in terms of its political ramifications. It was aimed in large part at the GOP's rank and file, particularly its most fiscally conservative members, who were beginning to squirm as appropriations bills with budget-breaking totals worked their way toward the House floor.

As part of their overall strategy, GOP leaders said they also would attach debt-reduction riders to the remaining appropriations bills, thereby setting aside specific amounts of surplus funds for debt relief with each corresponding spending bill approved. The strategy worked. Conservative Republicans liked the 90–10 plan and the debt-reduction riders. The 90–10 plan passed overwhelmingly—twice. The first measure (HR 5173) passed, 381–3: R 191–0; D 188–3 (ND 139–3, SD 49–0); I 2–0. The second measure (HR 5203), which also included a package of expanded tax breaks for retirement savings, passed, 401–20, the next day. *(Vote, p. 928)*

Senate Republicans endorsed the 90–10 idea but never moved companion legislation. GOP senators said they viewed the plan as a guide for the coming spate of deal-cutting rather than as a legislative vehicle. Although the proposal never neared the status of law, the House vote was the first clear acknowledgment of Congress's intention to abandon the budget resolution. And it cleared the way for approval of several subsequent spending bills. In the following six weeks the House passed eight of the thirteen appropriations bills.

Although policy fights and presidential politics would eventually stall the appropriations process again later in the year, the fight over how much to spend was largely over. The vote for the 90–10 plan gave appropriators all the room they needed to meet Clinton's requested fiscal 2001 spending levels, if not his priorities. It also gave GOP leaders support from GOP rank and file, who previously had threatened to walk away from any abandonment of the budget resolution.

1. H Con Res 290. Fiscal 2001 Budget Resolution/Conference Report. Adoption of the conference report on the fiscal 2001 concurrent resolution on the budget. The resolution called for cutting taxes by $150 billion over five years and created a "reserve fund" of $25 billion that could also be used for tax cuts. It also would establish a $40 billion reserve fund for Medicare overhaul and to provide prescription drug coverage for seniors. The plan called for $600.3 billion in discretionary spending and allowed for $310.8 billion in defense appropriations. Adopted 50–48: R 50–4; D 0–44 (ND 0–36, SD 0–8), April 13, 2000.

2. S 1287. Nuclear Waste Storage/Veto Override. Passage, over President Clinton's April 25, 2000, veto, of the bill that would provide for the completion of siting and licensing activities for a permanent nuclear waste repository at Yucca Mountain, Nev., and establish a timetable for the development of the proposed site. Rejected 64–35: R 51–3; D 13–32 (ND 5–32, SD 8–0), May 2, 2000. A two-thirds majority of those present and voting (66 in this case) of both houses is required to override a veto. A "nay" was a vote in support of the president's position.

3. S 2521. Fiscal 2001 Military Construction Appropriations/U.S. Troops in Kosovo. Levin, D-Mich., amendment that would strike the provision that would terminate funding for continued deployment of U.S. ground troops in Kosovo after July 1, 2001, unless Congress authorizes the deployment. The provision also would state that not more than 75 percent of the fiscal 2000 supplemental spending for Kosovo could be obligated until the president certifies that European allies are paying 33 percent of reconstruction assistance, 75 percent of humanitarian assistance, 75 percent of general administrative costs, and 75 percent of the civilian police force. Adopted 53–47: R 15–40; D 38–7 (ND 32–5, SD 6–2), May 18, 2000. A "yea" was a vote in support of the president's position.

4. S 2549. Fiscal 2001 Defense Authorization/Campaign Finance Disclosures. Warner, R-Va., point of order that the McCain, R-Ariz., amendment to the Smith, R-N.H., amendment was out of order because of the constitutional requirement that revenue provisions originate in the House. The McCain amendment would require section 527 organizations to disclose their existence to the IRS, file publicly available tax returns with the IRS, and make public reports specifying annual expenditures of more than $500 and identify those who contribute more than $200 annually to the organization. The Smith amendment would prohibit granting Defense Department security clearances to certain employees or contractors. Rejected 42–57: R 41–14; D 1–43 (ND 1–35, SD 0–8), June 8, 2000. Subsequently, the McCain amendment was adopted by voice vote.

5. S 2549. Fiscal 2001 Defense Authorization/Hate Crimes. Kennedy, D-Mass., amendment that would broaden hate crimes to include crimes related to gender, sexual orientation, and disability and would make it easier for the federal government to get involved in the investigation and prosecution of hate crimes. It would authorize $5 million per year for fiscal 2001–02 to assist states and local authorities in investigating and prosecuting hate crimes. Adopted 57–42: R 13–41; D 44–1 (ND 36–1, SD 8–0), June 20, 2000. A "yea" was a vote in support of the president's position.

6. S 2522. Fiscal 2001 Foreign Operations/Counternarcotics Funding Reduction. Gorton, R-Wash., amendment that would reduce the $934 million for South American and Caribbean counternarcotics activities to approximately $200 million. Rejected 19–79: R 13–41; D 6–38 (ND 6–30, SD 0–8), June 21, 2000. A "nay" was a vote in support of the president's position.

7. HR 4577. Fiscal 2001 Labor-HHS-Education Appropriations/Genetic Discrimination. Jeffords, R-Vt., amendment that would prohibit health insurers from using predictive genetic information to discriminate in the health care system. It also would prohibit insurance companies from raising rates or denying patients health coverage based on the results of genetic tests. Adopted 58–40: R 55–0; D 3–40 (ND 3–32, SD 0–8), June 29, 2000.

8. HR 4577. Fiscal 2001 Labor-HHS-Education Appropriations/Managed Care. Nickles, R-Okla., amendment that would provide federal protections, such as access to emergency care, internal and external appeals, specialists, and out-of-network doctors, primarily for the 56 million Americans in self-insured health plans. It also would prohibit denials based on predictive genetic information for patients in self-insured and employer plans, and allow patients to sue in federal court for harm caused by the failure to comply with the external medical review or harm caused because of delay in providing care. Adopted 51–47: R 51–4; D 0–43 (ND 0–35, SD 0–8), June 29, 2000.

9. S 2549. Fiscal 2001 Defense Authorization/Missile Defense System Testing. Cochran, R-Miss., motion to table (kill) the Durbin, D-Ill., amendment that would require the Pentagon to test the national missile defense system against reasonable decoys and countermeasures that the system could encounter in a launch, and establish an independent panel to review the testing. Motion agreed to 52–48: R 52–3; D 0–45 (ND 0–37, SD 0–8), July 13, 2000.

10. HR 4810. Alleviate "Marriage Penalty" Tax/Conference Report. Adoption of the conference report on the bill that would reduce taxes for married couples by approximately $89.8 billion over five years. The measure would increase the standard deduction claimed by married couples to twice the amount claimed by single taxpayers. The upper boundary of the 15 percent tax bracket would gradually increase to twice the limit for singles. The measure also would allow couples to earn an additional $2,000 before being disqualified from receiving the earned income tax credit. The bill would also allow couples to use certain tax credits without paying the alternative minimum tax. Adopted (thus cleared for the president) 60–34: R 53–1; D 7–33 (ND 5–27, SD 2–6), July 21, 2000. A "nay" was a vote in support of the president's position.

11. HR 4444. China Trade/Nonproliferation of Weapons. Roth, R-Del., motion to table (kill) the Thompson, R-Tenn., amendment that would provide for sanctions against China and other countries for selling illicit weapons of mass destruction. The proposal would establish an annual review process and require the president to impose nontrade related sanctions on individuals, companies, and groups found to be spreading weapons of mass destruction. The president also would be authorized to impose additional sanctions on key supplier countries. Motion agreed to 65–32: R 30–23; D 35–9 (ND 27–8, SD 8–1), Sept. 13, 2000.

12. HR 4516. Fiscal 2001 Legislative Branch, Treasury-Postal Service Appropriations/Conference Report. Adoption of the conference report on the bill that would appropriate $2.5 billion in fiscal 2001 for the legislative branch; appropriate $30.4 billion for the Treasury Department, Postal Service, executive office of the president, and certain independent agencies; and repeal the 3 percent federal excise tax on telecommunications services by the end of 2002. Rejected 28–69: R 28–26; D 0–43 (ND 0–34, SD 0–9), Sept. 20, 2000.

---

[1] Sen. Paul Coverdell, R-Ga., died July 18, 2000. The last vote for which he was eligible was 215. He was replaced by Democrat Zell Miller, who was sworn in July 27. The first vote for which Miller was eligible was 229.

KEY			
		Democrats	*Republicans*
Y	Voted for ("yea")		– Announced against
N	Voted against ("nay")		P Voted "present"
+	Announced for		C Voted "present" to avoid possible conflict of interest
#	Paired for		? Did not vote or otherwise
X	Paired against		make a position known

ND Northern Democrats
SD Southern Democrats
Southern states – Ala., Ark., Fla., Ga., Ky., La., Miss., N.C., Okla., S.C., Tenn., Texas, Va.

Senate Key Votes	1	2	3	4	5	6	7	8	9	10	11	12
ALABAMA												
Shelby	Y	Y	N	Y	N	N	Y	Y	Y	Y	N	Y
Sessions	Y	Y	N	Y	N	N	Y	Y	Y	Y	N	N
ALASKA												
Stevens	Y	Y	N	Y	Y	N	Y	Y	Y	Y	Y	N
Murkowski	Y	Y	N	Y	N	N	Y	Y	Y	Y	Y	Y
ARIZONA												
McCain	N	Y	Y	N	N	N	Y	N	Y	Y	N	N
Kyl	Y	Y	N	Y	N	N	Y	Y	Y	Y	N	Y
ARKANSAS												
Hutchinson	Y	Y	Y	N	Y	Y	Y	Y	Y	Y	N	Y
Lincoln	N	Y	Y	N	Y	N	N	N	N	N	Y	N
CALIFORNIA												
Feinstein	N	N	Y	N	Y	N	Y	N	N	Y	Y	?
Boxer	N	N	Y	N	Y	Y	N	N	N	?	Y	N
COLORADO												
Campbell	Y	N	N	Y	N	N	Y	Y	Y	Y	Y	Y
Allard	Y	Y	N	Y	N	Y	Y	Y	Y	Y	Y	Y
CONNECTICUT												
Dodd	N	N	Y	N	Y	N	N	N	N	N	Y	N
Lieberman	N	N	Y	N	Y	N	Y	N	N	N	?	?
DELAWARE												
Roth	?	?	Y	Y	Y	N	Y	Y	Y	Y	Y	N
Biden	N	N	Y	N	Y	N	N	N	N	Y	Y	N
FLORIDA												
Graham	N	Y	Y	N	Y	N	N	N	N	N	Y	N
Mack	Y	Y	Y	Y	Y	N	Y	Y	Y	Y	Y	Y
GEORGIA												
Coverdell[1]	Y	Y	N	Y	N	N	Y	Y	Y		Y	N
Cleland	N	Y	N	N	Y	N	N	N	N	Y	Y	N
HAWAII												
Inouye	N	N	N	N	Y	?	?	?	N	?	Y	N
Akaka	N	N	Y	N	Y	N	N	N	N	N	?	?
IDAHO												
Craig	Y	Y	N	Y	N	Y	Y	Y	Y	Y	Y	Y
Crapo	Y	Y	N	Y	N	Y	Y	Y	Y	Y	Y	Y
ILLINOIS												
Durbin	N	N	Y	N	Y	N	N	N	N	N	Y	N
Fitzgerald	Y	Y	N	Y	N	N	Y	N	Y	Y	Y	N
INDIANA												
Lugar	Y	Y	N	N	Y	N	Y	Y	Y	Y	Y	Y
Bayh	N	N	Y	N	Y	N	N	N	N	N	Y	N
IOWA												
Grassley	Y	Y	N	Y	N	N	Y	Y	Y	Y	Y	Y
Harkin	N	N	Y	N	Y	Y	N	N	N	N	Y	N
KANSAS												
Brownback	Y	Y	N	Y	N	N	Y	Y	Y	Y	Y	N
Roberts	Y	Y	N	Y	N	N	Y	Y	Y	Y	Y	N
KENTUCKY												
McConnell	Y	Y	N	Y	N	N	Y	Y	Y	Y	N	Y
Bunning	Y	Y	N	Y	N	N	Y	Y	Y	Y	N	N
LOUISIANA												
Breaux	N	Y	Y	N	Y	N	N	N	N	N	Y	N
Landrieu	N	Y	N	N	Y	N	N	N	N	Y	Y	N
MAINE												
Snowe	Y	Y	N	N	Y	N	Y	N	N	Y	N	N
Collins	Y	Y	N	N	Y	Y	Y	Y	N	Y	N	N
MARYLAND												
Sarbanes	N	N	Y	N	Y	N	N	N	N	N	N	N
Mikulski	N	N	Y	N	Y	Y	N	N	N	N	N	N
MASSACHUSETTS												
Kennedy	N	N	Y	N	Y	N	N	N	N	N	Y	N
Kerry	N	N	Y	N	Y	N	N	N	N	?	Y	N
MICHIGAN												
Levin	N	Y	Y	N	Y	N	N	N	N	N	Y	N
Abraham	Y	Y	Y	N	N	N	Y	Y	Y	Y	N	N
MINNESOTA												
Wellstone	N	N	N	N	Y	N	N	N	N	N	N	N
Grams	Y	Y	N	Y	N	Y	Y	Y	Y	Y	Y	N
MISSISSIPPI												
Cochran	Y	Y	Y	Y	N	N	Y	Y	Y	Y	Y	Y
Lott	Y	N	N	Y	N	N	Y	Y	Y	Y	N	Y
MISSOURI												
Bond	Y	Y	N	Y	N	N	Y	Y	Y	Y	Y	Y
Ashcroft	Y	Y	N	Y	N	N	Y	Y	Y	Y	N	N

Senate Key Votes	1	2	3	4	5	6	7	8	9	10	11	12
MONTANA												
Baucus	N	N	Y	N	Y	N	N	N	N	N	Y	N
Burns	Y	Y	N	Y	N	N	Y	Y	Y	Y	Y	N
NEBRASKA												
Kerrey	N	N	Y	N	Y	N	N	N	N	?	Y	N
Hagel	Y	Y	Y	N	N	N	Y	Y	Y	Y	Y	Y
NEVADA												
Reid	N	N	Y	N	Y	N	N	N	N	N	Y	N
Bryan	N	N	Y	N	Y	N	N	N	N	N	Y	N
NEW HAMPSHIRE												
Smith	Y	Y	N	Y	N	N	Y	Y	Y	Y	N	N
Gregg	Y	Y	N	Y	N	Y	Y	Y	Y	Y	N	Y
NEW JERSEY												
Lautenberg	N	N	Y	N	Y	N	N	N	N	N	Y	N
Torricelli	N	N	N	N	Y	N	N	N	N	N	Y	N
NEW MEXICO												
Domenici	Y	Y	N	Y	N	?	Y	Y	Y	Y	Y	Y
Bingaman	N	N	Y	N	Y	N	N	N	N	N	Y	N
NEW YORK												
Moynihan	?	N	Y	N	Y	N	N	N	N	N	Y	N
Schumer	N	N	Y	N	Y	N	N	N	N	N	Y	N
NORTH CAROLINA												
Helms	Y	Y	N	Y	N	N	Y	Y	Y	Y	N	N
Edwards	N	Y	Y	N	Y	N	N	N	N	N	Y	N
NORTH DAKOTA												
Conrad	N	N	Y	?	Y	N	N	N	N	N	N	N
Dorgan	N	N	Y	N	Y	N	N	N	N	N	Y	N
OHIO												
DeWine	Y	Y	Y	N	Y	N	Y	Y	Y	N	N	N
Voinovich	Y	Y	Y	Y	Y	N	Y	Y	Y	N	N	N
OKLAHOMA												
Nickles	Y	Y	N	Y	N	N	Y	Y	Y	Y	Y	Y
Inhofe	Y	Y	N	Y	?	N	Y	Y	Y	Y	N	Y
OREGON												
Wyden	N	N	Y	N	Y	N	N	N	N	N	Y	N
Smith	Y	Y	Y	N	Y	N	Y	Y	Y	Y	Y	Y
PENNSYLVANIA												
Specter	N	Y	N	N	Y	Y	Y	Y	N	Y	N	Y
Santorum	Y	Y	N	Y	N	N	Y	Y	Y	Y	N	N
RHODE ISLAND												
Reed	N	N	Y	N	Y	N	N	N	N	N	Y	N
Chafee, L.	N	N	Y	N	Y	N	Y	N	Y	Y	Y	N
SOUTH CAROLINA												
Thurmond	Y	Y	N	Y	N	N	Y	Y	Y	Y	N	Y
Hollings	N	Y	N	N	Y	N	N	N	N	N	N	N
SOUTH DAKOTA												
Daschle	N	N	Y	N	Y	N	N	N	N	N	Y	N
Johnson	N	N	Y	N	Y	N	N	N	N	N	Y	N
TENNESSEE												
Thompson	Y	Y	Y	N	N	N	Y	Y	Y	Y	N	N
Frist	Y	Y	Y	Y	N	N	Y	Y	Y	Y	N	N
TEXAS												
Gramm	Y	Y	N	N	N	Y	Y	Y	Y	Y	N	N
Hutchison	Y	Y	N	N	N	N	Y	Y	Y	Y	N	N
UTAH												
Hatch	Y	Y	Y	Y	N	N	Y	Y	Y	Y	Y	N
Bennett	Y	Y	N	Y	N	N	Y	Y	Y	Y	Y	Y
VERMONT												
Leahy	N	Y	N	N	Y	Y	?	?	N	N	Y	N
Jeffords	N	Y	N	N	Y	N	Y	Y	Y	Y	Y	N
VIRGINIA												
Warner	Y	Y	N	N	N	N	Y	Y	Y	Y	Y	N
Robb	N	Y	Y	N	Y	N	N	N	N	N	Y	N
WASHINGTON												
Gorton	Y	Y	N	Y	N	Y	Y	Y	Y	Y	?	Y
Murray	N	Y	Y	N	Y	Y	N	N	N	?	Y	N
WEST VIRGINIA												
Byrd	N	N	Y	N	Y	N	N	N	N	Y	N	N
Rockefeller	N	N	Y	N	Y	N	N	N	N	N	Y	N
WISCONSIN												
Kohl	N	Y	N	N	Y	Y	N	N	N	Y	N	N
Feingold	N	N	N	N	Y	N	N	N	N	N	N	N
WYOMING												
Thomas	Y	Y	N	Y	N	Y	Y	Y	Y	Y	Y	Y
Enzi	Y	Y	N	Y	N	Y	Y	Y	Y	Y	Y	Y

1. HR 3846. Minimum Wage/Two-Year Increase. Traficant, D-Ohio, amendment that would increase the minimum wage by $1 over two years. Adopted 246–179: R 42–173; D 203–5 (ND 155–0, SD 48–5); I 1–1, March 9, 2000. A "yea" was a vote in support of the president's position.

2. HR 4205. Fiscal 2001 Defense Authorization/Kosovo Operations. Kasich, R-Ohio, amendment that would withhold the bill's funding authorization for Kosovo operations, unless extenuating circumstances arise, until the president certifies that European nations are meeting specific burden-sharing targets by April 1, 2001. Kosovo funds could be used only for withdrawing U.S. ground forces from Kosovo if the president failed to provide such certification. Adopted 264–153: R 195–18; D 67–135 (ND 49–100, SD 18–35); I 2–0, May 17, 2000. A "nay" was a vote in support of the president's position.

3. HR 4205. Fiscal 2001 Defense Authorization/Retiree Health Care. Taylor, D-Miss., amendment that would expand and make permanent the Defense Department Medicare subvention demonstration program. The program would be available to all Medicare-eligible military retirees and their dependents by Jan. 1, 2006. Adopted 406–10: R 207–9; D 197–1 (ND 145–1, SD 52–0); I 2–0, May 18, 2000.

4. HR 4444. China Trade/Passage. Passage of the bill that would make normal trade relations with the People's Republic of China permanent. The bill includes provisions to protect U.S. businesses and workers from import surges; establish a commission to monitor human rights, labor standards, and religious freedom in China; require the administration to report annually on China's compliance with trade agreements; and express the sense of Congress that Taiwan should be admitted to the World Trade Organization. The measure would also authorize $99 million for Radio Free Asia and the Voice of America to expand broadcasts to China and neighboring countries. Passed 237–197: R 164–57; D 73–138 (ND 43–114, SD 30–24); I 0–2, May 24, 2000. A "yea" was a vote in support of the president's position.

5. HR 8. Estate Tax Repeal/Passage. Passage of the bill that would amend the Internal Revenue Code of 1986 to phase out the estate and gift taxes, repealing them entirely by 2010. Passed 279–136: R 213–0; D 65–135 (ND 43–104, SD 22–31); I 1–1, June 9, 2000. A "nay" was a vote in support of the president's position.

6. S 761. Electronic Signatures/Conference Report. Adoption of the conference report on the bill to promote electronic commerce and establish a minimum federal standard for the use and recognition of electronic signatures. The bill would ensure that electronic signatures are given the same legal validity and enforceability as written ones. Consumers would have to consent to the use of electronic records and be provided with information on how to access those records. Adopted (thus sent to the Senate) 426–4: R 216–3; D 208–1 (ND 155–0, SD 53–1); I 2–0, June 14, 2000.

7. HR 4578. Fiscal 2001 Interior Appropriations/National Monuments. Hansen, R-Utah, amendment to the Dicks, D-Wash., amendment that would reinstate the bill's provision that would prohibit the Interior Department from using funds to design, plan, or manage federal lands as national monuments that have been designated since 1999 under the Antiquities Act. Rejected 187–234: R 177–38; D 9–195 (ND 4–148, SD 5–47); I 1–1, June 15, 2000. A "nay" was a vote in support of the president's position.

8. HR 4762. Campaign Finance Disclosure/Passage. Houghton, R-N.Y., motion to suspend the rules and pass the bill that would amend the tax code to require groups organized under section 527 of the code to disclose contribution and expenditure information to the Treasury Department. Motion agreed to 385–39: R 178–39; D 205–0 (ND 151–0, SD 54–0); I 2–0, June 28, 2000. A two-thirds majority of those present and voting (283 in this case) is required for passage under suspension of the rules.

9. HR 4680. Prescription Drugs/Passage. Passage of the bill that would provide prescription drug coverage for Medicare beneficiaries and establish the Medicare Benefits Administration within the Department of Health and Human Services to administer the program. The benefit would be provided by private insurers with a choice between at least two plans. Passed 217–214: R 211–10; D 5–203 (ND 4–150, SD 1–53); I 1–1, June 28, 2000. A "nay" was a vote in support of the president's position.

10. HR 4811. Fiscal 2001 Foreign Operations Appropriations/Debt Relief. Waters, D-Calif., amendment that would increase funding for the Highly Indebted Poor Countries Trust Fund by $156 million and offset it with cuts to various other programs. The fund was created to help debtor countries write off most of the money owed to multilateral agencies. Adopted 216–211: R 26–194; D 189–16 (ND 142–9, SD 47–7); I 1–1, July 13, 2000.

11. HR 4923. Community Renewal Program/Passage. English, R-Pa., motion to suspend the rules and pass the bill that would provide tax credits and economic incentives to encourage investment and job creation in economically depressed urban and rural communities. It would authorize President Clinton's "New Markets Initiative," and designate nine new "empowerment zones" and forty new "renewal communities." Motion agreed to 394–27: R 214–1; D 179–25 (ND 130–23, SD 49–2); I 1–1, July 25, 2000. A two-thirds majority of those present and voting (281 in this case) is required for passage under suspension of the rules. A "yea" was a vote in support of the president's position.

12. HR 5173. Debt Reduction/Passage. Herger, R-Calif., motion to suspend the rules and pass the bill that would require all Social Security and Medicare surpluses to be used for debt reduction, pending enactment of legislation to overhaul those programs. In fiscal 2001, $42 billion of the non-Social Security and non-Medicare surplus would have to be used for debt reduction. Motion agreed to 381–3: R 191–0; D 188–3 (ND 139–3, SD 49–0); I 2–0, Sept. 18, 2000. A two-thirds majority of those present and voting (256 in this case) is required for passage under suspension of the rules.

KEY

	Democrats	*Republicans*	**Independent**

Y Voted for ("yea")
N Voted against ("nay")
+ Announced for
# Paired for
X Paired against

– Announced against
P Voted "present"
C Voted "present" to avoid possible conflict of interest
? Did not vote or otherwise make a position known

ND Northern Democrats
SD Southern Democrats
Southern states – Ala., Ark., Fla., Ga., Ky., La., Miss., N.C., Okla., S.C., Tenn., Texas, Va.

House Key Votes	1	2	3	4	5	6	7	8	9	10	11	12
ALABAMA												
1 *Callahan*	N	N	Y	Y	Y	Y	Y	Y	Y	N	Y	Y
2 *Everett*	N	Y	Y	Y	Y	Y	Y	Y	Y	N	Y	Y
3 *Riley*	N	Y	Y	N	Y	Y	Y	Y	Y	N	Y	Y
4 *Aderholt*	Y	Y	Y	N	Y	Y	Y	Y	Y	Y	Y	Y
5 Cramer	Y	N	Y	Y	Y	Y	N	Y	N	N	Y	Y
6 *Bachus*	N	Y	Y	Y	Y	Y	Y	Y	Y	Y	Y	Y
7 Hilliard	Y	N	Y	N	N	Y	N	Y	N	Y	Y	Y
ALASKA												
AL *Young*	Y	Y	Y	N	Y	Y	Y	?	Y	N	Y	Y
ARIZONA												
1 *Salmon*	N	Y	?	Y	Y	Y	Y	Y	Y	N	Y	Y
2 Pastor	Y	N	Y	N	N	Y	N	Y	N	Y	Y	Y
3 *Stump*	N	N	N	Y	Y	N	Y	N	Y	N	Y	Y
4 *Shadegg*	N	Y	+	Y	Y	Y	Y	Y	Y	N	Y	Y
5 *Kolbe*	N	N	Y	Y	Y	Y	Y	Y	Y	N	Y	Y
6 *Hayworth*	N	Y	Y	N	Y	Y	Y	N	Y	N	Y	Y
ARKANSAS												
1 Berry	Y	Y	Y	Y	Y	Y	N	Y	N	Y	Y	Y
2 Snyder	Y	N	Y	Y	N	Y	N	Y	N	Y	Y	Y
3 *Hutchinson*	N	Y	Y	Y	Y	Y	Y	Y	Y	N	Y	Y
4 *Dickey*	N	Y	Y	Y	Y	Y	Y	N	Y	N	Y	Y
CALIFORNIA												
1 Thompson	Y	Y	Y	Y	Y	Y	N	Y	N	Y	Y	Y
2 *Herger*	N	?	Y	Y	Y	Y	Y	N	Y	N	Y	Y
3 *Ose*	N	Y	Y	Y	Y	Y	Y	Y	Y	N	Y	Y
4 *Doolittle*	N	Y	Y	Y	Y	Y	Y	Y	Y	N	Y	Y
5 Matsui	Y	N	Y	Y	Y	Y	N	Y	N	Y	Y	Y
6 Woolsey	Y	Y	+	N	N	Y	N	Y	N	Y	Y	Y
7 Miller, George	Y	Y	Y	N	Y	Y	N	Y	N	Y	N	Y
8 Pelosi	Y	Y	Y	N	Y	Y	N	Y	N	Y	N	?
9 Lee	Y	Y	Y	N	Y	Y	N	Y	N	Y	Y	Y
10 Tauscher	Y	N	Y	Y	Y	Y	N	Y	N	Y	Y	Y
11 *Pombo*	N	Y	Y	N	Y	Y	Y	N	Y	N	Y	Y
12 Lantos	Y	N	Y	N	Y	Y	N	Y	N	Y	Y	Y
13 Stark	Y	Y	N	N	N	Y	N	Y	N	Y	N	?
14 Eshoo	Y	Y	Y	Y	Y	Y	N	Y	N	Y	Y	Y
15 *Campbell*	N	?	?	Y	Y	Y	?	Y	Y	Y	Y	?
16 Lofgren	Y	Y	Y	Y	Y	Y	?	Y	N	Y	Y	Y
17 Farr	Y	Y	Y	N	Y	Y	N	Y	N	Y	Y	Y
18 Condit	Y	Y	Y	N	Y	Y	N	Y	N	N	Y	Y
19 *Radanovich*	N	Y	Y	Y	Y	Y	Y	N	Y	N	Y	Y
20 Dooley	Y	N	Y	Y	Y	Y	Y	Y	N	Y	Y	?
21 *Thomas*	N	Y	N	Y	Y	Y	Y	Y	Y	N	Y	Y
22 Capps	Y	N	Y	Y	Y	Y	N	Y	N	Y	Y	Y
23 *Gallegly*	N	Y	Y	Y	Y	Y	Y	Y	Y	N	Y	Y
24 Sherman	Y	Y	Y	N	Y	Y	N	Y	N	Y	N	Y
25 *McKeon*	N	Y	Y	Y	Y	Y	Y	Y	Y	N	Y	Y
26 Berman	Y	N	Y	N	Y	Y	N	Y	N	Y	Y	Y
27 *Rogan*	N	Y	Y	Y	Y	Y	Y	Y	Y	N	Y	?
28 *Dreier*	N	Y	Y	Y	Y	Y	Y	Y	Y	N	Y	Y
29 Waxman	Y	N	Y	N	Y	Y	N	Y	N	Y	N	?
30 Becerra	Y	Y	Y	Y	N	Y	?	Y	N	Y	Y	Y
31 Martinez[1]	Y	Y	Y	Y	Y	Y	Y	?	Y	N	Y	Y
32 Dixon	Y	N	Y	N	Y	Y	N	Y	N	Y	Y	Y
33 Roybal-Allard	Y	N	Y	N	Y	Y	N	Y	N	Y	Y	Y
34 Napolitano	Y	N	Y	N	Y	Y	N	Y	N	Y	Y	Y
35 Waters	Y	N	?	N	Y	Y	N	?	N	Y	Y	Y
36 *Kuykendall*	N	Y	Y	Y	Y	Y	Y	Y	Y	Y	Y	Y
37 Millender-McD.	Y	Y	Y	N	Y	Y	N	Y	N	Y	Y	Y
38 *Horn*	Y	Y	Y	N	Y	Y	N	Y	Y	Y	Y	Y
39 *Royce*	N	Y	Y	Y	Y	Y	Y	Y	Y	N	Y	Y
40 *Lewis*	N	N	Y	Y	Y	Y	Y	N	Y	N	Y	?
41 *Miller, Gary*	N	Y	Y	Y	Y	Y	Y	Y	Y	N	Y	Y
42 Baca	Y	N	Y	N	Y	Y	N	Y	N	Y	Y	Y
43 *Calvert*	N	Y	Y	Y	Y	Y	Y	Y	Y	N	Y	Y
44 *Bono*	N	Y	Y	Y	Y	Y	Y	Y	Y	N	Y	Y

House Key Votes	1	2	3	4	5	6	7	8	9	10	11	12
45 *Rohrabacher*	N	Y	Y	N	Y	Y	Y	Y	Y	N	Y	Y
46 Sanchez	Y	N	Y	N	Y	Y	N	Y	Y	Y	Y	Y
47 *Cox*	N	Y	Y	Y	Y	Y	Y	Y	Y	N	Y	Y
48 *Packard*	N	Y	N	Y	?	Y	Y	Y	Y	N	Y	Y
49 *Bilbray*	Y	Y	Y	Y	Y	Y	N	Y	Y	N	Y	Y
50 Filner	Y	N	Y	N	N	Y	N	Y	-	Y	N	Y
51 *Cunningham*	N	Y	Y	Y	?	Y	Y	Y	Y	N	Y	Y
52 *Hunter*	N	N	Y	N	Y	Y	Y	Y	Y	N	Y	Y
COLORADO												
1 DeGette	Y	N	Y	Y	N	Y	N	Y	N	Y	Y	Y
2 Udall	Y	Y	Y	N	Y	Y	N	Y	N	Y	Y	Y
3 *McInnis*	N	Y	Y	Y	Y	Y	N	Y	Y	Y	Y	Y
4 *Schaffer*	?	Y	Y	Y	Y	Y	Y	?	N	Y	Y	Y
5 *Hefley*	N	Y	Y	N	Y	Y	Y	N	Y	N	Y	Y
6 *Tancredo*	N	Y	Y	N	Y	Y	Y	N	Y	N	Y	Y
CONNECTICUT												
1 Larson	Y	N	Y	N	N	Y	N	Y	N	Y	Y	Y
2 Gejdenson	Y	N	Y	N	N	Y	N	Y	N	Y	N	Y
3 DeLauro	Y	N	Y	N	N	Y	N	Y	N	Y	Y	Y
4 *Shays*	Y	Y	N	Y	Y	Y	Y	Y	Y	Y	Y	Y
5 Maloney	Y	N	Y	N	Y	Y	N	Y	N	Y	Y	Y
6 *Johnson*	Y	Y	Y	Y	Y	Y	Y	Y	Y	N	Y	Y
DELAWARE												
AL *Castle*	Y	Y	Y	Y	Y	Y	N	Y	Y	Y	Y	Y
FLORIDA												
1 *Scarborough*	?	Y	Y	?	Y	Y	N	Y	Y	N	Y	Y
2 Boyd	N	Y	Y	Y	Y	Y	N	Y	N	N	Y	Y
3 Brown	Y	Y	Y	N	N	Y	N	Y	N	Y	Y	Y
4 *Fowler*	N	Y	Y	Y	Y	Y	Y	Y	Y	N	Y	Y
5 Thurman	Y	Y	Y	Y	Y	Y	N	Y	N	Y	Y	?
6 *Stearns*	N	Y	Y	N	Y	Y	Y	Y	Y	N	Y	Y
7 *Mica*	N	Y	Y	N	Y	Y	Y	N	Y	N	Y	Y
8 *McCollum*	-	Y	Y	Y	Y	Y	?	Y	Y	N	?	?
9 *Bilirakis*	N	Y	Y	Y	Y	Y	Y	Y	Y	N	Y	Y
10 *Young*	Y	Y	Y	Y	Y	Y	?	Y	Y	N	Y	Y
11 Davis	Y	N	Y	Y	Y	Y	N	Y	N	Y	Y	Y
12 *Canady*	N	Y	Y	Y	Y	Y	Y	N	Y	N	Y	Y
13 *Miller*	N	Y	Y	Y	Y	Y	Y	Y	Y	N	Y	Y
14 *Goss*	N	Y	Y	Y	Y	Y	Y	Y	Y	N	Y	Y
15 *Weldon*	N	Y	Y	N	Y	Y	Y	Y	Y	N	Y	Y
16 *Foley*	N	Y	Y	Y	Y	Y	N	Y	Y	N	Y	Y
17 Meek	Y	Y	Y	N	Y	Y	N	Y	N	Y	Y	Y
18 *Ros-Lehtinen*	Y	Y	Y	N	Y	Y	Y	Y	Y	N	+	Y
19 Wexler	Y	N	Y	N	Y	Y	N	Y	N	Y	Y	Y
20 Deutsch	Y	Y	Y	N	Y	Y	N	Y	N	Y	Y	Y
21 *Diaz-Balart*	Y	N	Y	N	Y	Y	Y	Y	Y	Y	Y	Y
22 *Shaw*	N	Y	Y	Y	Y	Y	Y	Y	Y	N	Y	Y
23 Hastings	Y	N	Y	N	Y	Y	N	Y	N	Y	N	Y
GEORGIA												
1 *Kingston*	N	Y	Y	N	Y	Y	Y	N	Y	N	Y	?
2 Bishop	Y	Y	Y	Y	Y	Y	N	Y	N	Y	Y	Y
3 *Collins*	N	Y	Y	Y	Y	Y	Y	Y	Y	N	Y	Y
4 McKinney	Y	?	Y	N	Y	Y	N	Y	N	Y	Y	?
5 Lewis	Y	N	?	N	N	Y	N	Y	N	Y	Y	?
6 *Isakson*	N	Y	Y	Y	Y	Y	Y	Y	Y	N	Y	Y
7 *Barr*	N	Y	Y	N	Y	Y	Y	N	Y	N	Y	Y
8 *Chambliss*	N	Y	Y	Y	Y	Y	Y	Y	Y	N	Y	Y
9 *Deal*	N	Y	Y	N	Y	Y	Y	Y	Y	N	Y	Y
10 *Norwood*	N	Y	Y	N	Y	Y	?	Y	Y	N	Y	?
11 *Linder*	N	Y	Y	N	Y	Y	Y	Y	Y	N	Y	Y
HAWAII												
1 Abercrombie	Y	N	Y	N	Y	Y	N	Y	N	Y	Y	Y
2 Mink	Y	Y	Y	N	Y	Y	N	Y	N	Y	Y	Y
IDAHO												
1 *Chenoweth-Hage*	N	Y	Y	Y	Y	N	Y	Y	N	-	Y	+
2 *Simpson*	N	Y	Y	Y	Y	Y	Y	Y	Y	N	Y	Y
ILLINOIS												
1 Rush	Y	N	Y	N	Y	Y	N	N	Y	Y	Y	Y
2 Jackson	Y	Y	Y	N	N	Y	N	Y	N	Y	Y	Y
3 Lipinski	Y	Y	?	Y	Y	Y	N	Y	N	Y	N	Y
4 Gutierrez	Y	Y	Y	N	Y	Y	N	Y	N	Y	N	Y
5 Blagojevich	Y	Y	Y	N	N	Y	N	Y	N	Y	N	Y
6 *Hyde*	Y	Y	Y	Y	Y	Y	Y	Y	Y	N	Y	Y
7 Davis	Y	Y	Y	N	N	Y	N	Y	N	Y	Y	Y
8 *Crane*	N	Y	Y	Y	Y	Y	Y	Y	N	Y	Y	?
9 Schakowsky	Y	Y	Y	N	N	Y	N	Y	N	Y	N	Y
10 *Porter*	N	N	Y	Y	Y	Y	N	Y	Y	Y	Y	Y
11 *Weller*	Y	Y	Y	Y	Y	Y	N	Y	Y	N	Y	Y
12 Costello	Y	Y	Y	N	Y	Y	N	Y	N	Y	Y	Y

[1] Rep. Matthew G. Martinez of California switched parties from Democrat to Republican on July 26, 2000. The first vote he cast as a Republican was vote 439.

KEY

	Democrats	*Republicans*	Independent
Y	Voted for ("yea")		– Announced against
N	Voted against ("nay")		P Voted "present"
+	Announced for		C Voted "present" to avoid possible conflict of interest
#	Paired for		? Did not vote or otherwise make a position known
X	Paired against		

ND Northern Democrats
SD Southern Democrats
Southern states – Ala., Ark., Fla., Ga., Ky., La., Miss., N.C., Okla., S.C., Tenn., Texas, Va.

House Key Votes	1	2	3	4	5	6	7	8	9	10	11	12
13 Biggert	N	Y	Y	Y	Y	Y	N	Y	Y	N	Y	Y
14 Hastert[2]				Y	Y			Y	Y	N	Y	Y
15 Ewing	N	Y	Y	Y	Y	Y	Y	Y	Y	N	?	Y
16 Manzullo	N	Y	Y	Y	Y	Y	Y	N	Y	N	Y	Y
17 Evans	Y	Y	Y	N	N	Y	N	Y	N	Y	Y	Y
18 LaHood	Y	Y	Y	Y	Y	Y	Y	Y	Y	N	Y	Y
19 Phelps	Y	Y	Y	N	Y	Y	N	Y	N	Y	Y	Y
20 Shimkus	Y	Y	Y	Y	Y	Y	Y	Y	Y	N	Y	Y
INDIANA												
1 Visclosky	Y	N	Y	N	N	Y	N	Y	N	Y	N	Y
2 McIntosh	N	?	Y	Y	Y	Y	Y	?	Y	?	?	?
3 Roemer	Y	Y	Y	Y	Y	Y	N	Y	N	N	Y	Y
4 Souder	N	Y	Y	N	Y	Y	Y	N	Y	N	Y	Y
5 Buyer	N	Y	N	N	Y	Y	Y	Y	Y	N	Y	Y
6 Burton	N	Y	Y	N	Y	Y	Y	N	Y	N	Y	Y
7 Pease	N	Y	Y	N	Y	Y	Y	Y	Y	N	Y	Y
8 Hostettler	N	Y	Y	N	Y	Y	Y	N	N	N	Y	Y
9 Hill	Y	N	Y	Y	N	Y	N	N	Y	N	Y	Y
10 Carson	Y	Y	Y	N	N	Y	N	Y	N	Y	Y	Y
IOWA												
1 Leach	Y	Y	Y	Y	Y	Y	N	Y	Y	Y	Y	Y
2 Nussle	N	Y	Y	Y	Y	Y	Y	Y	Y	Y	Y	Y
3 Boswell	Y	Y	Y	Y	Y	Y	N	Y	Y	Y	Y	Y
4 Ganske	Y	Y	Y	Y	Y	Y	N	Y	Y	Y	Y	Y
5 Latham	N	Y	Y	Y	Y	Y	Y	Y	Y	Y	Y	Y
KANSAS												
1 Moran	N	Y	Y	Y	Y	Y	Y	Y	Y	N	Y	Y
2 Ryun	N	Y	Y	Y	Y	Y	Y	N	Y	N	Y	Y
3 Moore	Y	Y	Y	Y	Y	Y	N	N	Y	Y	Y	Y
4 Tiahrt	N	Y	Y	Y	Y	Y	Y	N	Y	N	Y	Y
KENTUCKY												
1 Whitfield	N	Y	Y	Y	+	Y	Y	Y	Y	N	Y	Y
2 Lewis	N	Y	Y	Y	Y	Y	Y	Y	Y	N	Y	Y
3 Northup	N	Y	Y	Y	Y	Y	Y	+	Y	N	Y	Y
4 Lucas	N	N	Y	Y	Y	Y	N	Y	N	Y	Y	Y
5 Rogers	N	Y	Y	N	Y	Y	Y	Y	Y	N	Y	Y
6 Fletcher	N	Y	Y	Y	Y	Y	Y	Y	Y	N	Y	Y
LOUISIANA												
1 Vitter	N	Y	Y	Y	Y	Y	Y	Y	Y	N	Y	Y
2 Jefferson	Y	N	Y	Y	Y	Y	N	Y	N	Y	Y	Y
3 Tauzin	N	Y	Y	Y	C	Y	Y	Y	Y	N	Y	Y
4 McCrery	N	Y	Y	Y	Y	Y	Y	Y	Y	N	Y	Y
5 Cooksey	?	Y	Y	Y	Y	Y	Y	N	Y	N	Y	Y
6 Baker	N	Y	Y	Y	Y	Y	Y	Y	Y	N	Y	Y
7 John	Y	N	Y	Y	Y	Y	N	Y	N	Y	Y	Y
MAINE												
1 Allen	Y	N	Y	Y	N	Y	N	Y	N	Y	Y	Y
2 Baldacci	Y	-	Y	N	N	Y	N	Y	N	Y	Y	Y
MARYLAND												
1 Gilchrest	Y	Y	Y	Y	Y	Y	N	Y	Y	Y	Y	Y
2 Ehrlich	N	Y	Y	N	Y	Y	Y	Y	Y	N	Y	?
3 Cardin	Y	N	Y	Y	N	Y	N	Y	Y	Y	Y	Y
4 Wynn	Y	N	Y	N	Y	Y	N	Y	N	Y	Y	Y
5 Hoyer	Y	N	Y	Y	N	Y	N	Y	N	Y	Y	Y
6 Bartlett	N	Y	Y	N	Y	Y	Y	Y	Y	N	Y	Y
7 Cummings	Y	N	Y	N	N	Y	N	Y	N	+	Y	Y
8 Morella	Y	Y	Y	Y	Y	Y	N	Y	N	Y	Y	Y
MASSACHUSETTS												
1 Olver	Y	N	Y	N	N	Y	N	Y	N	Y	N	Y
2 Neal	Y	Y	Y	N	N	Y	N	Y	N	Y	Y	?
3 McGovern	Y	N	Y	N	N	Y	N	Y	N	Y	Y	Y
4 Frank	Y	Y	Y	N	N	Y	N	Y	N	Y	N	Y
5 Meehan	Y	Y	?	N	N	Y	N	Y	N	Y	Y	Y
6 Tierney	Y	Y	Y	N	N	Y	N	Y	N	Y	Y	Y
7 Markey	Y	N	Y	N	?	Y	N	?	?	Y	Y	Y
8 Capuano	Y	N	Y	N	N	Y	N	Y	N	Y	Y	Y

House Key Votes	1	2	3	4	5	6	7	8	9	10	11	12
9 Moakley	Y	Y	Y	N	N	Y	N	Y	N	Y	Y	?
10 Delahunt	Y	Y	Y	N	Y	Y	N	Y	N	Y	Y	Y
MICHIGAN												
1 Stupak	Y	?	?	N	N	Y	N	Y	N	Y	Y	Y
2 Hoekstra	N	Y	Y	N	Y	Y	N	Y	Y	N	Y	Y
3 Ehlers	Y	Y	Y	Y	Y	Y	Y	Y	Y	Y	Y	Y
4 Camp	N	Y	Y	Y	Y	Y	Y	Y	Y	N	Y	Y
5 Barcia	Y	Y	Y	N	Y	Y	N	N	Y	Y	Y	Y
6 Upton	Y	Y	Y	Y	Y	Y	N	N	Y	N	Y	Y
7 Smith	N	Y	Y	Y	?	Y	Y	Y	Y	N	Y	Y
8 Stabenow	Y	N	Y	N	N	Y	N	Y	N	Y	Y	Y
9 Kildee	Y	N	Y	N	N	Y	N	Y	N	Y	Y	Y
10 Bonior	Y	N	Y	N	N	Y	N	Y	N	Y	Y	Y
11 Knollenberg	N	N	Y	Y	Y	Y	Y	Y	Y	N	Y	Y
12 Levin	Y	N	Y	Y	N	Y	N	Y	N	Y	Y	Y
13 Rivers	Y	Y	Y	N	N	Y	N	Y	N	Y	Y	Y
14 Conyers	Y	N	Y	N	-	Y	N	Y	N	Y	N	Y
15 Kilpatrick	Y	N	Y	N	N	Y	N	Y	N	Y	Y	Y
16 Dingell	Y	N	Y	N	N	Y	N	Y	N	Y	Y	Y
MINNESOTA												
1 Gutknecht	N	Y	Y	Y	Y	Y	Y	Y	Y	N	Y	Y
2 Minge	Y	Y	Y	Y	N	Y	N	Y	N	Y	Y	Y
3 Ramstad	N	Y	Y	Y	Y	Y	N	Y	Y	Y	Y	Y
4 Vento	?	N	?	N	?	?	?	?	?	?	?	?
5 Sabo	Y	N	Y	N	N	Y	N	Y	N	Y	Y	Y
6 Luther	Y	Y	Y	N	N	Y	N	Y	N	Y	Y	Y
7 Peterson	Y	Y	Y	Y	Y	Y	Y	Y	Y	Y	Y	Y
8 Oberstar	Y	N	Y	N	N	Y	N	+	N	Y	Y	+
MISSISSIPPI												
1 Wicker	N	Y	Y	Y	Y	Y	Y	Y	Y	N	Y	Y
2 Thompson	Y	N	Y	N	N	Y	N	Y	N	Y	Y	Y
3 Pickering	N	Y	Y	Y	Y	Y	Y	Y	Y	N	Y	Y
4 Shows	Y	Y	Y	N	Y	Y	?	Y	N	Y	Y	Y
5 Taylor	Y	N	Y	N	N	N	N	Y	N	N	Y	Y
MISSOURI												
1 Clay	Y	N	Y	N	?	Y	N	Y	N	?	Y	?
2 Talent	N	Y	Y	Y	Y	Y	Y	Y	Y	N	Y	?
3 Gephardt	Y	N	Y	N	N	Y	N	Y	N	Y	Y	Y
4 Skelton	Y	N	Y	Y	Y	Y	N	Y	N	Y	Y	Y
5 McCarthy	Y	N	Y	N	N	Y	N	#	N	Y	Y	Y
6 Danner	Y	Y	Y	N	?	?	?	Y	Y	N	?	Y
7 Blunt	N	Y	Y	Y	Y	Y	Y	Y	Y	N	Y	?
8 Emerson	N	Y	Y	Y	Y	Y	Y	Y	Y	N	Y	+
9 Hulshof	N	Y	Y	Y	Y	Y	Y	Y	Y	N	Y	Y
MONTANA												
AL Hill	N	Y	Y	Y	Y	Y	Y	Y	Y	N	Y	Y
NEBRASKA												
1 Bereuter	N	Y	Y	Y	Y	Y	Y	Y	Y	N	Y	Y
2 Terry	N	Y	Y	Y	Y	Y	Y	Y	Y	N	Y	Y
3 Barrett	N	Y	Y	Y	Y	Y	Y	Y	Y	N	Y	Y
NEVADA												
1 Berkley	Y	N	Y	N	Y	Y	N	Y	N	Y	Y	Y
2 Gibbons	Y	Y	Y	N	Y	Y	Y	Y	Y	N	Y	Y
NEW HAMPSHIRE												
1 Sununu	N	Y	Y	Y	Y	Y	Y	Y	Y	N	Y	Y
2 Bass	N	Y	Y	Y	Y	Y	N	Y	Y	N	Y	Y
NEW JERSEY												
1 Andrews	Y	N	Y	N	Y	Y	N	Y	Y	Y	Y	Y
2 LoBiondo	Y	Y	Y	N	Y	Y	N	Y	Y	N	Y	Y
3 Saxton	Y	Y	Y	N	Y	Y	N	Y	Y	N	Y	?
4 Smith	Y	Y	Y	N	Y	Y	N	Y	Y	Y	Y	Y
5 Roukema	N	Y	Y	Y	Y	Y	N	Y	Y	N	Y	Y
6 Pallone	Y	N	Y	N	N	Y	N	Y	Y	Y	Y	Y
7 Franks	Y	Y	?	Y	Y	Y	?	Y	Y	N	Y	?
8 Pascrell	Y	N	Y	N	N	Y	N	Y	Y	Y	Y	?
9 Rothman	Y	N	Y	N	N	Y	N	Y	Y	Y	Y	Y
10 Payne	Y	N	Y	N	N	Y	N	Y	N	Y	N	Y
11 Frelinghuysen	Y	Y	Y	Y	Y	Y	N	Y	Y	N	Y	Y
12 Holt	Y	N	Y	N	N	Y	N	Y	Y	Y	Y	Y
13 Menendez	Y	N	Y	N	N	Y	N	Y	Y	Y	?	Y
NEW MEXICO												
1 Wilson	Y	Y	Y	Y	Y	Y	Y	Y	Y	N	Y	Y
2 Skeen	N	Y	Y	Y	Y	Y	Y	Y	Y	N	Y	Y
3 Udall	Y	?	?	N	N	Y	N	Y	N	Y	Y	Y
NEW YORK												
1 Forbes	Y	N	Y	N	Y	Y	N	Y	N	?	Y	Y
2 Lazio	Y	Y	Y	Y	?	Y	N	Y	N	N	Y	?
3 King	Y	N	Y	N	Y	Y	N	Y	N	N	Y	Y
4 McCarthy	Y	N	Y	N	Y	Y	N	Y	N	Y	Y	Y

House Key Votes	1	2	3	4	5	6	7	8	9	10	11	12
5 Ackerman	Y	N	?	Y	N	Y	N	N	N	Y	N	Y
6 Meeks	Y	N	Y	Y	N	Y	N	N	N	Y	Y	Y
7 Crowley	Y	-	Y	N	N	Y	N	Y	N	Y	Y	Y
8 Nadler	Y	N	Y	N	N	Y	N	Y	N	Y	Y	N
9 Weiner	Y	N	Y	Y	N	Y	N	Y	N	Y	Y	Y
10 Towns	Y	N	?	N	N	Y	N	Y	N	Y	Y	Y
11 Owens	Y	N	Y	N	N	Y	N	Y	N	Y	Y	?
12 Velázquez	Y	N	Y	N	Y	Y	N	Y	N	Y	Y	Y
13 *Fossella*	N	N	Y	Y	Y	Y	Y	Y	Y	N	Y	Y
14 Maloney	Y	N	Y	Y	N	Y	N	Y	N	Y	Y	Y
15 Rangel	Y	N	?	Y	N	Y	N	Y	N	Y	Y	Y
16 Serrano	Y	N	Y	Y	N	Y	N	Y	N	Y	Y	Y
17 Engel	Y	N	Y	N	N	Y	N	Y	N	Y	Y	Y
18 Lowey	Y	N	Y	Y	N	Y	N	Y	N	Y	Y	Y
19 *Kelly*	N	N	Y	Y	Y	Y	N	Y	Y	Y	Y	Y
20 *Gilman*	Y	N	Y	N	?	Y	N	Y	Y	N	?	Y
21 McNulty	Y	N	Y	Y	N	Y	N	Y	N	?	Y	Y
22 *Sweeney*	N	Y	Y	Y	Y	Y	Y	Y	Y	N	Y	?
23 *Boehlert*	Y	N	Y	Y	Y	Y	N	Y	Y	Y	Y	Y
24 *McHugh*	Y	Y	Y	Y	Y	Y	Y	Y	Y	N	Y	Y
25 *Walsh*	Y	Y	Y	Y	Y	Y	N	Y	Y	N	Y	?
26 Hinchey	Y	N	Y	N	N	Y	N	Y	N	Y	Y	?
27 *Reynolds*	N	Y	Y	Y	Y	Y	N	Y	Y	N	Y	Y
28 Slaughter	Y	N	Y	N	N	Y	N	Y	N	Y	Y	Y
29 LaFalce	Y	?	Y	Y	N	Y	N	Y	N	Y	Y	Y
30 *Quinn*	Y	Y	?	N	Y	Y	N	Y	Y	N	Y	Y
31 *Houghton*	Y	N	N	Y	Y	Y	N	Y	Y	N	Y	Y

NORTH CAROLINA

House Key Votes	1	2	3	4	5	6	7	8	9	10	11	12
1 Clayton	Y	Y	Y	Y	Y	Y	N	Y	Y	Y	Y	Y
2 Etheridge	Y	N	Y	Y	Y	Y	N	Y	N	Y	Y	Y
3 *Jones*	N	Y	Y	N	Y	Y	Y	Y	Y	N	Y	+
4 Price	Y	N	Y	N	N	Y	N	Y	N	Y	Y	Y
5 *Burr*	N	Y	Y	N	Y	Y	Y	Y	Y	N	Y	Y
6 *Coble*	N	Y	Y	N	Y	Y	Y	Y	Y	N	Y	Y
7 McIntyre	Y	N	Y	N	Y	Y	N	Y	N	N	Y	Y
8 *Hayes*	N	Y	Y	Y	Y	Y	Y	Y	Y	N	Y	Y
9 *Myrick*	N	Y	Y	Y	Y	Y	Y	N	Y	N	Y	Y
10 *Ballenger*	N	+	Y	Y	Y	Y	Y	Y	Y	N	Y	Y
11 *Taylor*	N	Y	Y	N	Y	Y	Y	Y	Y	N	Y	+
12 Watt	Y	Y	Y	N	?	Y	N	Y	N	Y	Y	Y

NORTH DAKOTA

House Key Votes	1	2	3	4	5	6	7	8	9	10	11	12
AL Pomeroy	Y	N	Y	Y	N	Y	N	Y	N	Y	Y	Y

OHIO

House Key Votes	1	2	3	4	5	6	7	8	9	10	11	12
1 *Chabot*	N	Y	Y	Y	Y	Y	Y	Y	Y	N	Y	Y
2 *Portman*	N	Y	Y	Y	Y	Y	Y	Y	Y	N	Y	Y
3 Hall	Y	?	Y	N	N	Y	N	Y	N	Y	Y	Y
4 *Oxley*	N	Y	Y	Y	Y	Y	Y	N	Y	N	Y	?
5 *Gillmor*	N	Y	Y	Y	?	Y	Y	Y	Y	N	Y	Y
6 Strickland	Y	N	Y	N	N	Y	N	Y	N	Y	Y	Y
7 *Hobson*	N	N	Y	Y	Y	Y	N	Y	Y	N	Y	Y
8 *Boehner*	N	Y	Y	Y	?	Y	Y	Y	Y	N	Y	Y
9 Kaptur	Y	N	Y	N	N	Y	N	Y	N	Y	Y	Y
10 Kucinich	Y	Y	Y	N	N	Y	N	Y	N	Y	Y	Y
11 Jones	Y	N	Y	N	N	Y	?	Y	N	Y	Y	Y
12 *Kasich*	N	Y	Y	Y	Y	Y	N	Y	Y	Y	Y	?
13 Brown	Y	Y	Y	N	N	Y	N	Y	N	Y	Y	Y
14 Sawyer	Y	N	Y	N	N	Y	N	Y	N	Y	Y	Y
15 *Pryce*	N	Y	Y	Y	Y	Y	Y	Y	Y	N	Y	?
16 *Regula*	N	Y	Y	Y	Y	Y	Y	Y	Y	N	Y	Y
17 Traficant	Y	Y	Y	N	Y	Y	Y	Y	Y	Y	Y	Y
18 *Ney*	Y	Y	Y	N	Y	Y	Y	Y	Y	N	Y	Y
19 *LaTourette*	N	Y	Y	Y	Y	Y	Y	Y	Y	Y	Y	Y

OKLAHOMA

House Key Votes	1	2	3	4	5	6	7	8	9	10	11	12
1 *Largent*	N	?	Y	Y	Y	Y	Y	Y	Y	N	Y	Y
2 *Coburn*	N	?	Y	Y	Y	Y	Y	N	N	N	Y	Y
3 *Watkins*	N	Y	Y	Y	Y	Y	Y	Y	Y	N	Y	Y
4 *Watts*	N	Y	Y	Y	Y	Y	Y	Y	Y	N	Y	Y
5 *Istook*	N	Y	Y	Y	+	Y	Y	Y	Y	N	Y	Y
6 *Lucas*	N	Y	Y	Y	Y	Y	Y	Y	Y	N	Y	Y

OREGON

House Key Votes	1	2	3	4	5	6	7	8	9	10	11	12
1 Wu	Y	Y	Y	N	N	Y	N	Y	N	Y	Y	Y
2 *Walden*	N	Y	Y	Y	Y	Y	Y	Y	Y	N	Y	Y
3 Blumenauer	Y	N	Y	Y	?	Y	N	Y	N	Y	Y	Y
4 DeFazio	Y	Y	Y	N	N	Y	N	Y	N	Y	Y	Y
5 Hooley	Y	Y	Y	Y	Y	Y	N	Y	Y	N	Y	Y

PENNSYLVANIA

House Key Votes	1	2	3	4	5	6	7	8	9	10	11	12
1 Brady	Y	N	Y	N	N	Y	N	Y	N	Y	Y	Y
2 Fattah	Y	N	Y	N	N	Y	N	Y	N	Y	Y	?
3 Borski	Y	N	Y	N	N	Y	N	Y	N	Y	Y	Y
4 Klink	Y	N	Y	N	?	Y	N	Y	N	Y	Y	?
5 *Peterson*	N	Y	Y	Y	Y	Y	Y	Y	N	Y	Y	Y
6 Holden	Y	N	Y	N	N	Y	N	Y	N	Y	Y	Y
7 *Weldon*	Y	Y	Y	Y	Y	Y	N	Y	Y	N	Y	Y

House Key Votes	1	2	3	4	5	6	7	8	9	10	11	12
8 *Greenwood*	Y	Y	Y	Y	Y	Y	?	Y	Y	N	Y	Y
9 *Shuster*	N	Y	Y	Y	Y	Y	Y	Y	Y	N	Y	Y
10 *Sherwood*	Y	Y	Y	Y	Y	Y	Y	Y	Y	N	Y	Y
11 Kanjorski	Y	N	Y	N	N	Y	N	Y	N	Y	Y	Y
12 Murtha	Y	N	?	N	N	Y	N	Y	N	Y	Y	Y
13 Hoeffel	Y	N	Y	N	N	Y	N	Y	N	Y	Y	Y
14 Coyne	Y	N	Y	N	N	Y	N	Y	N	Y	Y	Y
15 *Toomey*	N	Y	Y	Y	Y	Y	Y	Y	Y	N	Y	Y
16 *Pitts*	N	Y	Y	Y	Y	Y	Y	N	Y	N	Y	Y
17 *Gekas*	N	Y	Y	Y	Y	Y	Y	Y	Y	N	Y	Y
18 Doyle	Y	+	Y	N	N	Y	N	Y	N	Y	Y	Y
19 *Goodling*	N	Y	Y	N	Y	Y	Y	Y	Y	N	Y	Y
20 Mascara	Y	N	Y	N	N	Y	N	Y	N	Y	Y	Y
21 *English*	Y	Y	Y	Y	Y	Y	N	Y	Y	Y	Y	Y

RHODE ISLAND

House Key Votes	1	2	3	4	5	6	7	8	9	10	11	12
1 Kennedy	Y	N	Y	N	N	Y	N	Y	N	Y	Y	Y
2 Weygand	Y	N	Y	N	N	Y	N	Y	N	Y	Y	Y

SOUTH CAROLINA

House Key Votes	1	2	3	4	5	6	7	8	9	10	11	12
1 *Sanford*	N	?	N	Y	Y	Y	Y	Y	Y	N	Y	Y
2 *Spence*	?	Y	Y	N	Y	Y	Y	Y	Y	N	Y	Y
3 *Graham*	N	Y	Y	N	Y	Y	Y	Y	Y	N	Y	Y
4 *DeMint*	N	Y	Y	Y	Y	Y	Y	Y	Y	N	Y	Y
5 Spratt	Y	N	Y	N	N	Y	N	Y	N	Y	Y	Y
6 Clyburn	Y	N	Y	N	N	Y	N	Y	N	Y	Y	Y

SOUTH DAKOTA

House Key Votes	1	2	3	4	5	6	7	8	9	10	11	12
AL *Thune*	Y	Y	Y	Y	Y	Y	Y	Y	Y	N	Y	Y

TENNESSEE

House Key Votes	1	2	3	4	5	6	7	8	9	10	11	12
1 *Jenkins*	N	Y	Y	Y	Y	Y	Y	N	Y	N	+	Y
2 *Duncan*	N	Y	Y	N	Y	Y	Y	Y	Y	N	Y	Y
3 *Wamp*	N	?	Y	N	Y	Y	Y	Y	Y	N	Y	Y
4 *Hilleary*	N	Y	Y	N	Y	Y	Y	Y	Y	N	Y	+
5 Clement	Y	N	Y	N	N	Y	N	Y	N	Y	Y	Y
6 Gordon	Y	Y	Y	N	N	Y	N	Y	N	Y	?	?
7 *Bryant*	N	Y	Y	Y	Y	Y	Y	Y	Y	N	Y	Y
8 Tanner	Y	Y	Y	N	N	Y	N	Y	N	Y	Y	Y
9 Ford	Y	Y	?	Y	Y	Y	N	Y	N	Y	Y	Y

TEXAS

House Key Votes	1	2	3	4	5	6	7	8	9	10	11	12
1 Sandlin	Y	N	Y	Y	N	Y	N	Y	N	Y	Y	Y
2 Turner	Y	N	Y	Y	N	Y	N	Y	N	Y	Y	Y
3 *Johnson, Sam*	N	Y	Y	Y	N	Y	N	Y	Y	N	Y	?
4 Hall	N	Y	Y	Y	Y	Y	Y	Y	Y	N	Y	Y
5 *Sessions*	N	Y	Y	Y	Y	Y	Y	Y	Y	N	Y	Y
6 *Barton*	N	Y	Y	N	Y	Y	Y	N	Y	N	?	Y
7 *Archer*	N	Y	N	Y	Y	Y	Y	Y	Y	N	Y	Y
8 *Brady*	N	Y	Y	Y	Y	Y	Y	Y	Y	N	Y	Y
9 Lampson	Y	N	Y	N	Y	Y	N	Y	N	Y	?	Y
10 *Doggett*	Y	Y	Y	N	N	Y	N	Y	N	Y	Y	Y
11 Edwards	Y	N	Y	Y	N	Y	N	Y	N	Y	?	Y
12 *Granger*	?	Y	Y	Y	Y	Y	Y	Y	Y	N	Y	Y
13 *Thornberry*	N	Y	Y	N	Y	Y	Y	Y	Y	N	Y	Y
14 *Paul*	N	Y	N	N	Y	N	Y	N	Y	N	N	Y
15 Hinojosa	Y	N	Y	Y	Y	Y	?	Y	N	Y	Y	Y
16 Reyes	Y	N	Y	N	N	Y	N	Y	N	Y	Y	Y
17 Stenholm	N	Y	Y	Y	N	Y	N	Y	N	Y	Y	Y
18 Jackson-Lee	Y	N	Y	N	N	Y	N	Y	N	Y	Y	Y
19 *Combest*	N	Y	Y	Y	Y	Y	Y	Y	Y	N	Y	Y
20 Gonzalez	Y	N	Y	N	N	Y	N	Y	N	Y	Y	Y
21 *Smith*	N	Y	Y	Y	Y	Y	Y	Y	Y	N	Y	Y
22 *DeLay*	N	Y	Y	Y	Y	Y	Y	Y	Y	N	Y	Y
23 *Bonilla*	N	Y	Y	N	Y	Y	Y	Y	Y	N	Y	Y
24 Frost	Y	N	Y	N	N	Y	N	Y	N	Y	Y	?
25 Bentsen	Y	N	Y	N	N	Y	N	Y	N	Y	Y	Y
26 *Armey*	N	Y	Y	Y	Y	Y	Y	Y	Y	N	Y	Y
27 *Ortiz*	Y	N	Y	N	N	Y	N	Y	N	Y	Y	Y
28 *Rodriguez*	Y	Y	Y	N	N	Y	N	Y	N	Y	Y	Y
29 Green	Y	Y	Y	N	N	Y	N	Y	N	Y	Y	Y
30 Johnson, E. B.	?	N	Y	Y	N	Y	N	Y	N	Y	Y	Y

UTAH

House Key Votes	1	2	3	4	5	6	7	8	9	10	11	12
1 *Hansen*	N	Y	Y	Y	Y	Y	Y	Y	Y	N	Y	Y
2 *Cook*	N	Y	Y	N	Y	?	Y	?	?	N	Y	?
3 *Cannon*	N	Y	Y	Y	Y	Y	Y	Y	Y	N	Y	Y

VERMONT

House Key Votes	1	2	3	4	5	6	7	8	9	10	11	12
AL **Sanders**	Y	Y	Y	N	N	Y				Y	N	Y

VIRGINIA

House Key Votes	1	2	3	4	5	6	7	8	9	10	11	12
1 *Bateman*[3]	N	Y	Y	Y	Y	Y	Y	N	Y	N	Y	
2 Pickett	N	N	Y	N	Y	Y	Y	N	Y	N	Y	Y

[2] The Speaker votes only at his discretion, usually to break a tie or to emphasize the importance of a matter.

[3] Rep. Herbert H. Bateman, R-Va., died on Sept. 11, 2000. The last vote for which he was eligible was 459.

<table>
<tr><td colspan="6" align="center">KEY</td></tr>
<tr><td></td><td>Democrats</td><td>Republicans</td><td>Independent</td></tr>
</table>

Y	Voted for ("yea")		–	Announced against
N	Voted against ("nay")		P	Voted "present"
+	Announced for		C	Voted "present" to avoid possible conflict of interest
#	Paired for			
X	Paired against		?	Did not vote or otherwise make a position known

ND Northern Democrats
SD Southern Democrats
Southern states – Ala., Ark., Fla., Ga., Ky., La., Miss., N.C., Okla., S.C., Tenn., Texas, Va.

House Key Votes	1	2	3	4	5	6	7	8	9	10	11	12
3 Scott	Y	N	Y	N	N	Y	N	Y	N	Y	N	Y
4 Sisisky	Y	N	Y	N	Y	Y	Y	Y	N	Y	Y	Y
5 **Goode**	N	Y	Y	N	Y	Y	Y	Y	Y	N	Y	Y
6 *Goodlatte*	N	Y	Y	Y	Y	Y	Y	Y	Y	N	Y	Y
7 *Bliley*	N	N	Y	Y	Y	Y	Y	Y	Y	N	Y	Y
8 Moran	Y	N	Y	Y	Y	Y	N	Y	N	Y	Y	Y
9 Boucher	Y	Y	Y	N	Y	Y	N	Y	N	Y	Y	?
10 *Wolf*	N	N	Y	N	Y	Y	Y	Y	Y	Y	Y	Y
11 *Davis, T.*	N	Y	Y	Y	Y	Y	N	Y	Y	N	Y	Y

House Key Votes	1	2	3	4	5	6	7	8	9	10	11	12
WASHINGTON												
1 Inslee	Y	Y	Y	Y	Y	Y	N	Y	N	Y	Y	Y
2 *Metcalf*	Y	Y	Y	N	Y	Y	Y	Y	Y	N	Y	Y
3 Baird	Y	N	Y	Y	Y	Y	N	Y	N	Y	Y	Y
4 *Hastings*	N	Y	Y	Y	Y	Y	Y	Y	Y	N	Y	?
5 *Nethercutt*	N	Y	Y	Y	Y	Y	Y	Y	Y	N	Y	?
6 Dicks	Y	N	Y	Y	N	Y	N	Y	N	N	Y	Y
7 McDermott	Y	N	Y	Y	–	Y	N	Y	N	Y	N	Y
8 *Dunn*	N	Y	Y	Y	Y	Y	Y	Y	Y	N	Y	?
9 Smith	+	N	Y	Y	+	Y	N	Y	N	?	?	Y
WEST VIRGINIA												
1 Mollohan	Y	N	Y	N	Y	Y	N	Y	N	Y	Y	N
2 Wise	Y	–	Y	N	Y	Y	N	Y	N	Y	Y	?
3 Rahall	Y	N	Y	N	Y	Y	N	Y	N	Y	Y	Y
WISCONSIN												
1 *Ryan*	N	Y	Y	Y	Y	Y	Y	Y	Y	N	Y	Y
2 Baldwin	Y	Y	Y	N	N	Y	N	Y	N	Y	N	Y
3 Kind	Y	N	Y	Y	?	Y	N	Y	N	Y	Y	Y
4 Kleczka	Y	Y	Y	N	N	Y	N	Y	N	Y	Y	Y
5 Barrett	Y	Y	Y	N	N	Y	N	Y	N	Y	Y	Y
6 *Petri*	N	Y	Y	Y	Y	Y	N	Y	Y	N	Y	Y
7 Obey	Y	N	Y	N	N	Y	N	Y	N	Y	Y	Y
8 *Green*	N	Y	Y	Y	Y	Y	Y	Y	Y	N	Y	Y
9 *Sensenbrenner*	N	Y	N	N	Y	?	Y	Y	Y	Y	Y	Y
WYOMING												
AL *Cubin*	N	Y	Y	Y	Y	Y	Y	Y	Y	Y	Y	?

Congress and Its Members

Senate Membership in the
105th Congress 935

House Membership in
the 105th Congress 936

Membership Changes, 105th and
106th Congresses 938

Senate Membership in the
106th Congress 939

House Membership in the
106th Congress 940

Members of Congress, 1997–2001 942

Congressional Committees,
105th and 106th Congresses 951

Postelection Sessions 965

Senate Cloture Votes, 1917–2000 967

House Discharge Petitions
Since 1931 972

Congressional Apportionment,
1789–2000 973

Senate Membership in the 105th Congress

Lineup as of Jan. 4, 1997: Republicans 55, Democrats 45

Alabama
Jeff Sessions (R)
Richard C. Shelby (R)

Alaska
Ted Stevens (R)
Frank H. Murkowski (R)

Arizona
John McCain (R)
Jon Kyl (R)

Arkansas
Dale Bumpers (D)
Tim Hutchinson (R)

California
Dianne Feinstein (D)
Barbara Boxer (D)

Colorado
Wayne Allard (R)
Ben Nighthorse Campbell (R)

Connecticut
Christopher J. Dodd (D)
Joseph I. Lieberman (D)

Delaware
William V. Roth Jr. (R)
Joseph R. Biden Jr. (D)

Florida
Bob Graham (D)
Connie Mack (R)

Georgia
Max Cleland (D)
Paul Coverdell (R)

Hawaii
Daniel K. Inouye (D)
Daniel K. Akaka (D)

Idaho
Larry E. Craig (R)
Dirk Kempthorne (R)

Illinois
Richard J. Durbin (D)
Carol Moseley-Braun (D)

Indiana
Richard G. Lugar (R)
Daniel R. Coats (R)

Iowa
Charles E. Grassley (R)
Tom Harkin (D)

Kansas
Pat Roberts (R)
Sam Brownback (R)

Kentucky
Wendell H. Ford (D)
Mitch McConnell (R)

Louisiana
Mary L. Landrieu (D)
John B. Breaux (D)

Maine
Susan Collins (R)
Olympia J. Snowe (R)

Maryland
Paul S. Sarbanes (D)
Barbara A. Mikulski (D)

Massachusetts
Edward M. Kennedy (D)
John F. Kerry (D)

Michigan
Carl Levin (D)
Spencer Abraham (R)

Minnesota
Paul D. Wellstone (D)
Rod Grams (R)

Mississippi
Thad Cochran (R)
Trent Lott (R)

Missouri
Christopher S. Bond (R)
John Ashcroft (R)

Montana
Max Baucus (D)
Conrad Burns (R)

Nebraska
Chuck Hagel (R)
Bob Kerrey (D)

Nevada
Harry Reid (D)
Richard H. Bryan (D)

New Hampshire
Robert C. Smith (R)
Judd Gregg (R)

New Jersey
Robert G. Torricelli (D)
Frank R. Lautenberg (D)

New Mexico
Pete V. Domenici (R)
Jeff Bingaman (D)

New York
Daniel Patrick Moynihan (D)
Alfonse M. D'Amato (R)

North Carolina
Jesse Helms (R)
Lauch Faircloth (R)

North Dakota
Kent Conrad (D)
Byron L. Dorgan (D)

Ohio
John Glenn (D)
Mike DeWine (R)

Oklahoma
Don Nickles (R)
James M. Inhofe (R)

Oregon
Gordon H. Smith (R)
Ron Wyden (D)

Pennsylvania
Arlen Specter (R)
Rick Santorum (R)

Rhode Island
Jack Reed (D)
John H. Chafee (R)

South Carolina
Strom Thurmond (R)
Ernest F. Hollings (D)

South Dakota
Tim Johnson (D)
Tom Daschle (D)

Tennessee
Fred Thompson (R)
Bill Frist (R)

Texas
Phil Gramm (R)
Kay Bailey Hutchison (R)

Utah
Orrin G. Hatch (R)
Robert F. Bennett (R)

Vermont
Patrick J. Leahy (D)
James M. Jeffords (R)

Virginia
John W. Warner (R)
Charles S. Robb (D)

Washington
Slade Gorton (R)
Patty Murray (D)

West Virginia
Robert C. Byrd (D)
John D. Rockefeller IV (D)

Wisconsin
Herb Kohl (D)
Russell D. Feingold (D)

Wyoming
Michael B. Enzi (R)
Craig Thomas (R)

House Membership in the 105th Congress

Lineup as of Jan. 4, 1997: Republicans 227, Democrats 207, Independent 1

Alabama
1. Sonny Callahan (R)
2. Terry Everett (R)
3. Bob Riley (R)
4. Robert B. Aderholt (R)
5. Robert E. "Bud" Cramer (D)
6. Spencer Bachus (R)
7. Earl F. Hilliard (D)

Alaska
AL Don Young (R)

Arizona
1. Matt Salmon (R)
2. Ed Pastor (D)
3. Bob Stump (R)
4. John Shadegg (R)
5. Jim Kolbe (R)
6. J. D. Hayworth (R)

Arkansas
1. Marion Berry (D)
2. Vic Snyder (D)
3. Asa Hutchinson (R)
4. Jay Dickey (R)

California
1. Frank Riggs (R)
2. Wally Herger (R)
3. Vic Fazio (D)
4. John T. Doolittle (R)
5. Robert T. Matsui (D)
6. Lynn Woolsey (D)
7. George Miller (D)
8. Nancy Pelosi (D)
9. Ronald V. Dellums (D)
      (resigned Feb. 6, 1998)
      Barbara Lee (D)
      (sworn in April 21, 1998)
10. Ellen O. Tauscher (D)
11. Richard W. Pombo (R)
12. Tom Lantos (D)
13. Fortney "Pete" Stark (D)
14. Anna G. Eshoo (D)
15. Tom Campbell (R)
16. Zoe Lofgren (D)
17. Sam Farr (D)
18. Gary A. Condit (D)
19. George P. Radanovich (R)
20. Cal Dooley (D)
21. Bill Thomas (R)
22. Walter H. Capps (D)
      (died Oct. 28, 1997)
      Lois D. Capps (D)
      (sworn in March 17, 1998)
23. Elton Gallegly (R)
24. Brad Sherman (D)
25. Howard P. "Buck" McKeon (R)
26. Howard L. Berman (D)
27. James E. Rogan (R)
28. David Dreier (R)
29. Henry A. Waxman (D)
30. Xavier Becerra (D)
31. Matthew G. Martinez (D)
32. Julian C. Dixon (D)
33. Lucille Roybal-Allard (D)
34. Esteban E. Torres (D)
35. Maxine Waters (D)
36. Jane Harman (D)
37. Juanita Millender-
      McDonald (D)
38. Steve Horn (R)
39. Ed Royce (R)
40. Jerry Lewis (R)
41. Jay C. Kim (R)
42. George E. Brown Jr. (D)
43. Ken Calvert (R)
44. Sonny Bono (R)
      (died Jan. 5, 1998)
      Mary Bono (R)
      (sworn in April 21, 1998)
45. Dana Rohrabacher (R)
46. Loretta Sanchez (D)
47. Christopher Cox (R)
48. Ron Packard (R)
49. Brian P. Bilbray (R)
50. Bob Filner (D)
51. Randy "Duke" Cunningham
      (R)
52. Duncan L. Hunter (R)

Colorado
1. Diana DeGette (D)
2. David E. Skaggs (D)
3. Scott McInnis (R)
4. Bob Schaffer (R)
5. Joel Hefley (R)
6. Daniel L. Schaefer (R)

Connecticut
1. Barbara B. Kennelly (D)
2. Sam Gejdenson (D)
3. Rosa DeLauro (D)
4. Christopher Shays (R)
5. James H. Maloney (D)
6. Nancy L. Johnson (R)

Delaware
AL Michael N. Castle (R)

Florida
1. Joe Scarborough (R)
2. Allen Boyd (D)
3. Corrine Brown (D)
4. Tillie Fowler (R)
5. Karen L. Thurman (D)
6. Clifford B. Stearns (R)
7. John L. Mica (R)
8. Bill McCollum (R)
9. Michael Bilirakis (R)
10. C. W. Bill Young (R)
11. Jim Davis (D)
12. Charles T. Canady (R)
13. Dan Miller (R)
14. Porter J. Goss (R)
15. Dave Weldon (R)
16. Mark Foley (R)
17. Carrie P. Meek (D)
18. Ileana Ros-Lehtinen (R)
19. Robert Wexler (D)
20. Peter Deutsch (D)
21. Lincoln Diaz-Balart (R)
22. E. Clay Shaw Jr. (R)
23. Alcee L. Hastings (D)

Georgia
1. Jack Kingston (R)
2. Sanford D. Bishop Jr. (D)
3. Mac Collins (R)
4. Cynthia A. McKinney (D)
5. John Lewis (D)
6. Newt Gingrich (R)
7. Bob Barr (R)
8. Saxby Chambliss (R)
9. Nathan Deal (R)
10. Charlie Norwood (R)
11. John Linder (R)

Hawaii
1. Neil Abercrombie (D)
2. Patsy T. Mink (D)

Idaho
1. Helen Chenoweth (R)
2. Michael D. Crapo (R)

Illinois
1. Bobby L. Rush (D)
2. Jesse L. Jackson Jr. (D)
3. William O. Lipinski (D)
4. Luis V. Gutierrez (D)
5. Rod R. Blagojevich (D)
6. Henry J. Hyde (R)
7. Danny K. Davis (D)
8. Philip M. Crane (R)
9. Sidney R. Yates (D)
10. John Edward Porter (R)
11. Gerald C. "Jerry" Weller (R)
12. Jerry F. Costello (D)
13. Harris W. Fawell (R)
14. J. Dennis Hastert (R)
15. Thomas W. Ewing (R)
16. Donald Manzullo (R)
17. Lane Evans (D)
18. Ray LaHood (R)
19. Glenn Poshard (D)
20. John M. Shimkus (R)

Indiana
1. Peter J. Visclosky (D)
2. David M. McIntosh (R)
3. Tim Roemer (D)
4. Mark E. Souder (R)
5. Steve Buyer (R)
6. Dan Burton (R)
7. Edward A. Pease (R)
8. John Hostettler (R)
9. Lee H. Hamilton (D)
10. Julia M. Carson (D)

Iowa
1. Jim Leach (R)
2. Jim Nussle (R)
3. Leonard L. Boswell (D)
4. Greg Ganske (R)
5. Tom Latham (R)

Kansas
1. Jerry Moran (R)
2. Jim Ryun (R)
3. Vince Snowbarger (R)
4. Todd Tiahrt (R)

Kentucky
1. Edward Whitfield (R)
2. Ron Lewis (R)
3. Anne M. Northrup (R)
4. Jim Bunning (R)
5. Harold Rogers (R)
6. Scotty Baesler (D)

Louisiana
1. Robert L. Livingston (R)
2. William J. Jefferson (D)
3. W. J. "Billy" Tauzin (R)
4. Jim McCrery (R)
5. John Cooksey (R)
6. Richard H. Baker (R)
7. Chris John (D)

Maine
1. Thomas H. Allen (D)
2. John Baldacci (D)

Maryland
1. Wayne T. Gilchrest (R)
2. Robert L. Ehrlich Jr. (R)
3. Benjamin L. Cardin (D)
4. Albert R. Wynn (D)
5. Steny H. Hoyer (D)
6. Roscoe G. Bartlett (R)
7. Elijah E. Cummings (D)
8. Constance A. Morella (R)

Massachusetts
1. John W. Olver (D)
2. Richard E. Neal (D)
3. James McGovern (D)
4. Barney Frank (D)
5. Martin T. Meehan (D)
6. John F. Tierney (D)
7. Edward J. Markey (D)
8. Joseph P. Kennedy II (D)
9. Joe Moakley (D)
10. William Delahunt (D)

Michigan
1. Bart Stupak (D)
2. Peter Hoekstra (R)
3. Vernon J. Ehlers (R)
4. Dave Camp (R)
5. James A. Barcia (D)
6. Fred Upton (R)
7. Nick Smith (R)
8. Debbie Stabenow (D)
9. Dale E. Kildee (D)
10. David E. Bonior (D)
11. Joe Knollenberg (R)
12. Sander M. Levin (D)
13. Lynn Rivers (D)
14. John Conyers Jr. (D)
15. Carolyn Cheeks Kilpatrick (D)
16. John D. Dingell (D)

Minnesota
1. Gil Gutknecht (R)
2. David Minge (D)
3. Jim Ramstad (R)
4. Bruce F. Vento (D)
5. Martin Olav Sabo (D)
6. William P. "Bill" Luther (D)
7. Collin C. Peterson (D)
8. James L. Oberstar (D)

Mississippi
1. Roger Wicker (R)
2. Bennie Thompson (D)
3. Charles W. "Chip" Pickering
      (R)
4. Mike Parker (R)
5. Gene Taylor (D)

Missouri
1. William L. Clay (D)
2. James M. Talent (R)
3. Richard A. Gephardt (D)

936

4. Ike Skelton (D)
5. Karen McCarthy (D)
6. Pat Danner (D)
7. Roy Blunt (R)
8. Jo Ann Emerson (R)
9. Kenny Hulshof (R)

Montana
AL Rick Hill (R)

Nebraska
1. Doug Bereuter (R)
2. Jon Christensen (R)
3. Bill Barrett (R)

Nevada
1. John Ensign (R)
2. Jim Gibbons (R)

New Hampshire
1. John E. Sununu (R)
2. Charles Bass (R)

New Jersey
1. Robert E. Andrews (D)
2. Frank A. LoBiondo (R)
3. H. James Saxton (R)
4. Christopher H. Smith (R)
5. Marge Roukema (R)
6. Frank Pallone Jr. (D)
7. Bob Franks (R)
8. Bill Pascrell Jr. (D)
9. Steven R. Rothman (D)
10. Donald M. Payne (D)
11. Rodney Frelinghuysen (R)
12. Michael Pappas (R)
13. Robert Menendez (D)

New Mexico
1. Steven H. Schiff (R)
       (died March 25, 1998)
   Heather Wilson (R)
       (sworn in June 25, 1998)
2. Joseph R. Skeen (R)
3. Bill Richardson (D)
       (resigned Feb. 13, 1997)
   Bill Redmond (D)
       (sworn in May 20, 1997)

New York
1. Michael P. Forbes (R)
2. Rick A. Lazio (R)
3. Peter T. King (R)
4. Carolyn McCarthy (D)
5. Gary L. Ackerman (D)
6. Floyd H. Flake (D)
       (resigned Nov. 15, 1997)
   Gregory W. Meeks (D)
       (sworn in Feb. 5, 1998)
7. Thomas J. Manton (D)
8. Jerrold Nadler (D)
9. Charles E. Schumer (D)
10. Edolphus Towns (D)
11. Major R. Owens (D)
12. Nydia M. Velazquez (D)
13. Susan Molinari (R)
       (resigned Aug. 1, 1997)
   Vito J. Fossella (R)
       (sworn in Nov. 5, 1997)
14. Carolyn B. Maloney (D)

15. Charles B. Rangel (D)
16. Jose E. Serrano (D)
17. Eliot L. Engel (D)
18. Nita M. Lowey (D)
19. Sue W. Kelly (R)
20. Benjamin A. Gilman (R)
21. Michael R. McNulty (D)
22. Gerald B. H. Solomon (R)
23. Sherwood Boehlert (R)
24. John M. McHugh (R)
25. James T. Walsh (R)
26. Maurice D. Hinchey (D)
27. Bill Paxon (R)
28. Louise M. Slaughter (D)
29. John J. LaFalce (D)
30. Jack Quinn (R)
31. Amory Houghton (R)

North Carolina
1. Eva Clayton (D)
2. Bob Etheridge (D)
3. Walter B. Jones Jr. (R)
4. David E. Price (D)
5. Richard M. Burr (R)
6. Howard Coble (R)
7. Mike McIntyre (D)
8. W. G. "Bill" Hefner (D)
9. Sue Myrick (R)
10. Cass Ballenger (R)
11. Charles H. Taylor (R)
12. Melvin Watt (D)

North Dakota
AL Earl Pomeroy (D)

Ohio
1. Steve Chabot (R)
2. Rob Portman (R)
3. Tony P. Hall (D)
4. Michael G. Oxley (R)
5. Paul E. Gillmor (R)
6. Ted Strickland (D)
7. David L. Hobson (R)
8. John A. Boehner (R)
9. Marcy Kaptur (D)
10. Dennis J. Kucinich (D)
11. Louis Stokes (D)
12. John R. Kasich (R)
13. Sherrod Brown (D)
14. Thomas C. Sawyer (D)
15. Deborah Pryce (R)
16. Ralph Regula (R)
17. James A. Traficant Jr. (D)
18. Bob Ney (R)
19. Steven C. LaTourette (R)

Oklahoma
1. Steve Largent (R)
2. Tom Coburn (R)
3. Wes Watkins (R)
4. J. C. Watts (R)
5. Ernest Jim Istook Jr. (R)
6. Frank D. Lucas (R)

Oregon
1. Elizabeth Furse (D)
2. Robert F. Smith (R)
3. Earl Blumenauer (D)
4. Peter A. DeFazio (D)
5. Darlene Hooley (D)

Pennsylvania
1. Thomas M. Foglietta (D)
       (resigned Nov. 12, 1997)
   Robert A. Brady (D)
       (sworn in May 21, 1998)
2. Chaka Fattah (D)
3. Robert A. Borski (D)
4. Ron Klink (D)
5. John E. Peterson (R)
6. Tim Holden (D)
7. Curt Weldon (R)
8. James C. Greenwood (R)
9. E. G. "Bud" Shuster (R)
10. Joseph M. McDade (R)
11. Paul E. Kanjorski (D)
12. John P. Murtha (D)
13. Jon D. Fox (R)
14. William J. Coyne (D)
15. Paul McHale (D)
16. Joseph R. Pitts (R)
17. George W. Gekas (R)
18. Mike Doyle (D)
19. William F. Goodling (R)
20. Frank R. Mascara (D)
21. Phil English (R)

Rhode Island
1. Patrick J. Kennedy (D)
2. Robert A. Weygand (D)

South Carolina
1. Mark Sanford (R)
2. Floyd D. Spence (R)
3. Lindsey Graham (R)
4. Robert D. Inglis (R)
5. John M. Spratt Jr. (D)
6. James E. Clyburn (D)

South Dakota
AL John Thune (R)

Tennessee
1. William L. Jenkins (R)
2. John J. "Jimmy" Duncan Jr. (R)
3. Zach Wamp (R)
4. Van Hilleary (R)
5. Bob Clement (D)
6. Bart Gordon (D)
7. Ed Bryant (R)
8. John Tanner (D)
9. Harold E. Ford Jr. (D)

Texas
1. Max Sandlin (D)
2. James Turner (D)
3. Sam Johnson (R)
4. Ralph M. Hall (D)
5. Pete Sessions (R)
6. Joe L. Barton (R)
7. W. R. "Bill" Archer (R)
8. Kevin Brady (R)
9. Nick Lampson (D)
10. Lloyd Doggett (D)
11. Chet Edwards (D)
12. Kay Granger (R)
13. William M. "Mac" Thornberry (R)
14. Ron Paul (R)
15. Rubén Hinojosa (D)

16. Silvestre Reyes (D)
17. Charles W. Stenholm (D)
18. Sheila Jackson-Lee (D)
19. Larry Combest (R)
20. Henry B. Gonzalez (D)
21. Lamar Smith (R)
22. Tom DeLay (R)
23. Henry Bonilla (R)
24. Martin Frost (D)
25. Ken Bentsen (D)
26. Dick Armey (R)
27. Solomon P. Ortiz (D)
28. Frank Tejeda (D)
       (died Jan. 30, 1997)
   Ciro D. Rodriguez (D)
       (sworn in April 17, 1997)
29. Gene Green (D)
30. Eddie Bernice Johnson (D)

Utah
1. James V. Hansen (R)
2. Merrill Cook (R)
3. Christopher B. Cannon (R)

Vermont
AL Bernard Sanders (I)

Virginia
1. Herbert H. Bateman (R)
2. Owen B. Pickett (D)
3. Robert C. Scott (D)
4. Norman Sisisky (D)
5. Virgil H. Goode Jr. (D)
6. Robert W. Goodlatte (R)
7. Thomas J. Bliley Jr. (R)
8. James P. Moran (D)
9. Rick C. Boucher (D)
10. Frank R. Wolf (R)
11. Thomas M. Davis III (R)

Washington
1. Rick White (R)
2. Jack Metcalf (R)
3. Linda Smith (R)
4. Richard "Doc" Hastings (R)
5. George Nethercutt (R)
6. Norm Dicks (D)
7. Jim McDermott (D)
8. Jennifer Dunn (R)
9. Adam Smith (D)

West Virginia
1. Alan B. Mollohan (D)
2. Robert E. Wise (D)
3. Nick J. Rahall II (D)

Wisconsin
1. Mark W. Neumann (R)
2. Scott L. Klug (R)
3. Ron Kind (D)
4. Gerald D. Kleczka (D)
5. Thomas M. Barrett (D)
6. Thomas E. Petri (R)
7. David R. Obey (D)
8. Jay Johnson (D)
9. F. James Sensenbrenner Jr. (R)

Wyoming
AL Barbara Cubin (R)

NOTE: Members of the 105th Congress also included delegates Eni F. H. Faleomavaega, D-American Samoa; Donna Christian-Green, D-Virgin Islands; Eleanor Holmes Norton, D-District of Columbia; Robert Underwood, D-Guam; and resident commissioner Carlos Romero-Barcelo, D-Puerto Rico.

Membership Changes, 105th and 106th Congresses

105th Congress

Member/Party	Died	Resigned	Switched party	Successor/Party	Elected	Sworn in
Senate						
None						
House						
Frank Tejeda, D-Texas	1/30/97			Ciro D. Rodriguez, D[1]	4/12/97	4/17/97
Bill Richardson, D-N.M.[2]		2/13/97		Bill Redmond, R	5/13/97	5/20/97
Susan Molinari, R-N.Y.[3]		8/1/97		Vito J. Fossella, R	11/4/97	11/5/97
Walter Capps. D-Calif.	10/28/97			Lois Capps, D[4]	3/10/98	3/17/98
Thomas M. Foglietta, D-Pa.[5]		11/12/97		Robert A. Brady, D	5/19/98	5/21/98
Floyd H. Flake, D-N.Y.[6]		11/15/97		Gregory W. Meeks, D	2/3/98	2/5/98
Sonny Bono, R-Calif.	1/5/98			Mary Bono, R[7]	4/7/98	4/21/98
Ronald V. Dellums, D-Calif.		2/6/98		Barbara Lee, D[8]	4/7/98	4/21/98
Steven H. Schiff, R-N.M.	3/25/98			Heather Wilson, R[9]	6/23/98	6/25/98
Newt Gingrich, R-Ga.[10]		1/3/99		Johnny Isakson, R	2/23/99	2/25/99

106th Congress

Member/Party	Died	Resigned	Switched party	Successor/Party	Elected	Sworn in
Senate						
Robert C. Smith, R-N.H.			I, 7/13/99[11]			
John Chafee, R-R.I.	10/24/99			Lincoln Chafee, R[12]	11/2/99	11/4/99
Paul Coverdell, R-Ga.	7/18/00			Zell Miller, D[13]	7/24/00	7/27/00
House						
Bob Livingston, R-La.		2/28/99[14]		David Vitter, R	5/29/99	6/8/99
George E. Brown, D-Calif.	7/15/99			Joe Baca, D	11/16/99	11/18/99
Michael Forbes, R-N.Y.			D, 7/17/99			
Virgil H. Goode, D-Va.			I, 1/24/00[15]			
Matthew G. Martinez, D-Calif.			R, 7/26/00			
Julian C. Dixon, D-Calif.	12/8/00			Diane E. Watson, D	6/5/01	6/7/01

1. Rodriguez was elected to fill out the remaining term in the 105th Congress.
2. Richardson resigned to become U.S. representative to the United Nations. Redmond was elected to fill out the remaining term in the 105th Congress.
3. Molinari resigned to join CBS News as an on-air personality. Fossella was elected to fill out the remaining term in the 105th Congress.
4. Lois Capps, Walter Capps's widow, was elected to fill out the remaining term in the 105th Congress.
5. Foglietta resigned to become U.S. ambassador to Italy. Brady was elected to fill out the remaining term in the 105th Congress.
6. Flake resigned to focus on his ministry. Meeks was elected to fill out the remaining term in the 105th Congress.
7. Mary Bono, Sonny Bono's widow, was elected to fill out the remaining term in the 105th Congress.
8. Lee was elected to fill out the remaining term in the 105th Congress.
9. Wilson was elected to fill out the remaining term in the 105th Congress.
10. House Speaker Gingrich announced late in 1998 that he would resign his seat in Congress, even though he won reelection in November 1998. He resigned on Jan. 3, 1999, as the 105th Congress ended; he was not sworn in for the 106th Congress. Isakson was elected to fill the term for the 106th Congress.
11. Smith returned to the Republican Party on Nov. 1, 1999.
12. Lincoln Chafee, son of John Chafee, was appointed to fill the remainder of the term of his father, which was to end in January 2001. Lincoln Chafee was elected to a six-year term in November 2000.
13. Former Georgia governor Zell Miller was appointed to fill the vacancy. In November 2000 he was elected to the remaining four years of Coverdell's term.
14. Livingston was the would-be successor to Newt Gingrich as House Speaker after Gingrich announced in late 1998 he would resign from the House. However, Livingston himself resigned after admitting to martial infidelity during the House debate on the impeachment of President Clinton in December 1998.
15. Goode announced he would seek reelection in 2000 as an Independent.

Senate Membership in the 106th Congress

Lineup as of Jan. 4, 1999: Republicans 55, Democrats 45

Alabama
Jeff Sessions (R)
Richard C. Shelby (R)

Alaska
Ted Stevens (R)
Frank H. Murkowski (R)

Arizona
John McCain (R)
Jon Kyl (R)

Arkansas
Blanche Lincoln (D)
Tim Hutchinson (R)

California
Dianne Feinstein (D)
Barbara Boxer (D)

Colorado
Wayne Allard (R)
Ben Nighthorse Campbell (R)

Connecticut
Christopher J. Dodd (D)
Joseph I. Lieberman (D)

Delaware
William V. Roth Jr. (R)
Joseph R. Biden Jr. (D)

Florida
Bob Graham (D)
Connie Mack (R)

Georgia
Max Cleland (D)
Paul Coverdell (R)
(died July 18, 2000)
Zell Miller (D)
(sworn in July 27, 2000)

Hawaii
Daniel K. Inouye (D)
Daniel K. Akaka (D)

Idaho
Larry E. Craig (R)
Michael D. Crapo (R)

Illinois
Richard J. Durbin (D)
Peter G. Fitzgerald (R)

Indiana
Richard G. Lugar (R)
Evan Bayh (D)

Iowa
Charles E. Grassley (R)
Tom Harkin (D)

Kansas
Pat Roberts (R)
Sam Brownback (R)

Kentucky
Jim Bunning (R)
Mitch McConnell (R)

Louisiana
Mary L. Landrieu (D)
John B. Breaux (D)

Maine
Susan Collins (R)
Olympia J. Snowe (R)

Maryland
Paul S. Sarbanes (D)
Barbara A. Mikulski (D)

Massachusetts
Edward M. Kennedy (D)
John F. Kerry (D)

Michigan
Carl Levin (D)
Spencer Abraham (R)

Minnesota
Paul D. Wellstone (D)
Rod Grams (R)

Mississippi
Thad Cochran (R)
Trent Lott (R)

Missouri
Christopher S. Bond (R)
John Ashcroft (R)

Montana
Max Baucus (D)
Conrad Burns (R)

Nebraska
Chuck Hagel (R)
Bob Kerrey (D)

Nevada
Harry Reid (D)
Richard H. Bryan (D)

New Hampshire
Robert C. Smith (R)[1]
Judd Gregg (R)

New Jersey
Robert G. Torricelli (D)
Frank R. Lautenberg (D)

New Mexico
Pete V. Domenici (R)
Jeff Bingaman (D)

New York
Daniel Patrick Moynihan (D)
Charles E. Schumer (D)

North Carolina
Jesse Helms (R)
John Edwards (D)

North Dakota
Kent Conrad (D)
Byron L. Dorgan (D)

Ohio
George Voinovich (R)
Mike DeWine (R)

Oklahoma
Don Nickles (R)
James M. Inhofe (R)

Oregon
Gordon H. Smith (R)
Ron Wyden (D)

Pennsylvania
Arlen Specter (R)
Rick Santorum (R)

Rhode Island
Jack Reed (D)
John H. Chafee (R)
(died Oct. 24, 1999)
Lincoln Chafee (R), son of John
H. Chafee
(sworn in Nov. 4, 1999)

South Carolina
Strom Thurmond (R)
Ernest F. Hollings (D)

South Dakota
Tim Johnson (D)
Tom Daschle (D)

Tennessee
Fred Thompson (R)
Bill Frist (R)

Texas
Phil Gramm (R)
Kay Bailey Hutchison (R)

Utah
Orrin G. Hatch (R)
Robert F. Bennett (R)

Vermont
Patrick J. Leahy (D)
James M. Jeffords (R)

Virginia
John W. Warner (R)
Charles S. Robb (D)

Washington
Slade Gorton (R)
Patty Murray (D)

West Virginia
Robert C. Byrd (D)
John D. Rockefeller IV (D)

Wisconsin
Herb Kohl (D)
Russell D. Feingold (D)

Wyoming
Michael B. Enzi (R)
Craig Thomas (R)

1. Robert C. Smith switched from Republican to Independent on July 13, 1999. Smith returned to the Republican Party on Nov. 1, 1999.

House Membership in the 106th Congress

Lineup as of Jan. 4, 1999: Republicans 223, Democrats 211, Independent 1

Alabama
1. Sonny Callahan (R)
2. Terry Everett (R)
3. Bob Riley (R)
4. Robert B. Aderholt (R)
5. Robert E. "Bud" Cramer (D)
6. Spencer Bachus (R)
7. Earl F. Hilliard (D)

Alaska
AL Don Young (R)

Arizona
1. Matt Salmon (R)
2. Ed Pastor (D)
3. Bob Stump (R)
4. John Shadegg (R)
5. Jim Kolbe (R)
6. J. D. Hayworth (R)

Arkansas
1. Marion Berry (D)
2. Vic Snyder (D)
3. Asa Hutchinson (R)
4. Jay Dickey (R)

California
1. Mike Thompson (D)
2. Wally Herger (R)
3. Doug Ose (R)
4. John T. Doolittle (R)
5. Robert T. Matsui (D)
6. Lynn Woolsey (D)
7. George Miller (D)
8. Nancy Pelosi (D)
9. Barbara Lee (D)
10. Ellen O. Tauscher (D)
11. Richard W. Pombo (R)
12. Tom Lantos (D)
13. Fortney "Pete" Stark (D)
14. Anna G. Eshoo (D)
15. Tom Campbell (R)
16. Zoe Lofgren (D)
17. Sam Farr (D)
18. Gary A. Condit (D)
19. George P. Radanovich (R)
20. Cal Dooley (D)
21. William Thomas (R)
22. Lois D. Capps (D)
23. Elton Gallegly (R)
24. Brad Sherman (D)
25. Howard P. "Buck" McKeon (R)
26. Howard L. Berman (D)
27. James E. Rogan (R)
28. David Dreier (R)
29. Henry A. Waxman (D)
30. Xavier Becerra (D)
31. Matthew G. Martinez (D)[1]
32. Julian C. Dixon (D)
        (died Dec. 8, 2000)
33. Lucille Roybal-Allard (D)
34. Grace Flores Napolitano (D)
35. Maxine Waters (D)
36. Steven Kuykendall (R)
37. Juanita Millender-McDonald (D)
38. Steve Horn (R)
39. Ed Royce (R)
40. Jerry Lewis (R)
41. Gary Miller (R)
42. George E. Brown Jr. (D)
        (died July 15, 1999)
    Joe Baca (D)
        (sworn in Nov. 18, 1999)
43. Ken Calvert (R)
44. Mary Bono (R)
45. Dana Rohrabacher (R)
46. Loretta Sanchez (D)
47. Christopher Cox (R)
48. Ron Packard (R)
49. Brian P. Bilbray (R)
50. Bob Filner (D)
51. Randy "Duke" Cunningham (R)
52. Duncan L. Hunter (R)

Colorado
1. Diana DeGette (D)
2. Mark Udall (D)
3. Scott McInnis (R)
4. Bob Schaffer (R)
5. Joel Hefley (R)
6. Tom Tancredo (R)

Connecticut
1. John B. Larson (D)
2. Sam Gejdenson (D)
3. Rosa DeLauro (D)
4. Christopher Shays (R)
5. James H. Maloney (D)
6. Nancy L. Johnson (R)

Delaware
AL Michael N. Castle (R)

Florida
1. Joe Scarborough (R)
2. Allen Boyd (D)
3. Corrine Brown (D)
4. Tillie Fowler (R)
5. Karen L. Thurman (D)
6. Clifford B. Stearns (R)
7. John L. Mica (R)
8. Bill McCollum (R)
9. Michael Bilirakis (R)
10. C. W. Bill Young (R)
11. Jim Davis (D)
12. Charles T. Canady (R)
13. Dan Miller (R)
14. Porter J. Goss (R)
15. Dave Weldon (R)
16. Mark Foley (R)
17. Carrie P. Meek (D)
18. Ileana Ros-Lehtinen (R)
19. Robert Wexler (D)
20. Peter Deutsch (D)
21. Lincoln Diaz-Balart (R)
22. E. Clay Shaw Jr. (R)
23. Alcee L. Hastings (D)

Georgia
1. Jack Kingston (R)
2. Sanford D. Bishop Jr. (D)
3. Mac Collins (R)
4. Cynthia A. McKinney (D)
5. John Lewis (D)
6. Newt Gingrich (R)
        (resigned Jan. 3, 1999)
    Johnny Isakson (R)
        (sworn in Feb. 25, 1999)
7. Bob Barr (R)
8. Saxby Chambliss (R)
9. Nathan Deal (R)
10. Charlie Norwood (R)
11. John Linder (R)

Hawaii
1. Neil Abercrombie (D)
2. Patsy T. Mink (D)

Idaho
1. Helen Chenoweth (R)
2. Mike Simpson (R)

Illinois
1. Bobby L. Rush (D)
2. Jesse L. Jackson Jr. (D)
3. William O. Lipinski (D)
4. Luis V. Gutierrez (D)
5. Rod R. Blagojevich (D)
6. Henry J. Hyde (R)
7. Danny K. Davis (D)
8. Philip M. Crane (R)
9. Janice D. "Jan" Schakowsky (D)
10. John Edward Porter (R)
11. Gerald C. "Jerry" Weller (R)
12. Jerry F. Costello (D)
13. Judy Biggert (R)
14. J. Dennis Hastert (R)
15. Thomas W. Ewing (R)
16. Donald Manzullo (R)
17. Lane Evans (D)
18. Ray LaHood (R)
19. David D. Phelps (D)
20. John M. Shimkus (R)

Indiana
1. Peter J. Visclosky (D)
2. David M. McIntosh (R)
3. Tim Roemer (D)
4. Mark E. Souder (R)
5. Steve Buyer (R)
6. Dan Burton (R)
7. Edward A. Pease (R)
8. John Hostettler (R)
9. Baron Hill (D)
10. Julia M. Carson (D)

Iowa
1. Jim Leach (R)
2. Jim Nussle (R)
3. Leonard L. Boswell (D)
4. Greg Ganske (R)
5. Tom Latham (R)

Kansas
1. Jerry Moran (R)
2. Jim Ryun (R)
3. Dennis Moore (D)
4. Todd Tiahrt (R)

Kentucky
1. Edward Whitfield (R)
2. Ron Lewis (R)
3. Anne M. Northrup (R)
4. Ken Lucas (D)
5. Harold Rogers (R)
6. Ernest Fletcher (R)

Louisiana
1. Robert L. Livingston (R)
        (resigned Feb. 28, 1999)
    David Vitter (R)
        (sworn in June 8, 1999)
2. William J. Jefferson (D)
3. W. J. "Billy" Tauzin (R)
4. Jim McCrery (R)
5. John Cooksey (R)
6. Richard H. Baker (R)
7. Chris John (D)

Maine
1. Thomas H. Allen (D)
2. John Baldacci (D)

Maryland
1. Wayne T. Gilchrest (R)
2. Robert L. Ehrlich Jr. (R)
3. Benjamin L. Cardin (D)
4. Albert R. Wynn (D)
5. Steny H. Hoyer (D)
6. Roscoe G. Bartlett (R)
7. Elijah E. Cummings (D)
8. Constance A. Morella (R)

Massachusetts
1. John W. Olver (D)
2. Richard E. Neal (D)
3. James McGovern (D)
4. Barney Frank (D)
5. Martin T. Meehan (D)
6. John F. Tierney (D)
7. Edward J. Markey (D)
8. Michael Capuano (D)
9. Joe Moakley (D)
10. William Delahunt (D)

Michigan
1. Bart Stupak (D)
2. Peter Hoekstra (R)
3. Vernon J. Ehlers (R)
4. Dave Camp (R)
5. James A. Barcia (D)
6. Fred Upton (R)
7. Nick Smith (R)
8. Debbie Stabenow (D)
9. Dale E. Kildee (D)
10. David E. Bonior (D)
11. Joe Knollenberg (R)
12. Sander M. Levin (D)
13. Lynn Rivers (D)
14. John Conyers Jr. (D)
15. Carolyn Cheeks Kilpatrick (D)
16. John D. Dingell (D)

Minnesota
1. Gil Gutknecht (R)
2. David Minge (D)
3. Jim Ramstad (R)
4. Bruce F. Vento (D)
5. Martin Olav Sabo (D)
6. William P. "Bill" Luther (D)

7. Collin C. Peterson (D)
8. James L. Oberstar (D)

Mississippi
1. Roger Wicker (R)
2. Bennie Thompson (D)
3. Charles W. "Chip" Pickering (R)
4. Ronnie Shows (D)
5. Gene Taylor (D)

Missouri
1. William L. Clay (D)
2. James M. Talent (R)
3. Richard A. Gephardt (D)
4. Ike Skelton (D)
5. Karen McCarthy (D)
6. Pat Danner (D)
7. Roy Blunt (R)
8. Jo Ann Emerson (R)
9. Kenny Hulshof (R)

Montana
AL Rick Hill (R)

Nebraska
1. Doug Bereuter (R)
2. Lee Terry (R)
3. Bill Barrett (R)

Nevada
1. Shelley Berkley (D)
2. Jim Gibbons (R)

New Hampshire
1. John E. Sununu (R)
2. Charles Bass (R)

New Jersey
1. Robert E. Andrews (D)
2. Frank A. LoBiondo (R)
3. H. James Saxton (R)
4. Christopher H. Smith (R)
5. Marge Roukema (R)
6. Frank Pallone Jr. (D)
7. Bob Franks (R)
8. Bill Pascrell Jr. (D)
9. Steven R. Rothman (D)
10. Donald M. Payne (D)
11. Rodney Frelinghuysen (R)
12. Rush Holt (D)
13. Robert Menendez (D)

New Mexico
1. Heather Wilson (R)
2. Joseph R. Skeen (R)
3. Tom Udall (D)

New York
1. Michael P. Forbes (R)[2]
2. Rick A. Lazio (R)
3. Peter T. King (R)
4. Carolyn McCarthy (D)
5. Gary L. Ackerman (D)
6. Gregory W. Meeks (D)
7. Joseph Crowley (D)
8. Jerrold Nadler (D)
9. Anthony Weiner (D)
10. Edolphus Towns (D)
11. Major R. Owens (D)

12. Nydia M. Velazquez (D)
13. Vito J. Fossella (R)
14. Carolyn B. Maloney (D)
15. Charles B. Rangel (D)
16. Jose E. Serrano (D)
17. Eliot L. Engel (D)
18. Nita M. Lowey (D)
19. Sue W. Kelly (R)
20. Benjamin A. Gilman (R)
21. Michael R. McNulty (D)
22. John E. Sweeney (R)
23. Sherwood Boehlert (R)
24. John M. McHugh (R)
25. James T. Walsh (R)
26. Maurice D. Hinchey (D)
27. Thomas M. Reynolds (R)
28. Louise M. Slaughter (D)
29. John J. LaFalce (D)
30. Jack Quinn (R)
31. Amory Houghton (R)

North Carolina
1. Eva Clayton (D)
2. Bob Etheridge (D)
3. Walter B. Jones Jr. (R)
4. David E. Price (D)
5. Richard M. Burr (R)
6. Howard Coble (R)
7. Mike McIntyre (D)
8. Robin Hayes (R)
9. Sue Myrick (R)
10. Cass Ballenger (R)
11. Charles H. Taylor (R)
12. Melvin Watt (D)

North Dakota
AL Earl Pomeroy (D)

Ohio
1. Steve Chabot (R)
2. Rob Portman (R)
3. Tony P. Hall (D)
4. Michael G. Oxley (R)
5. Paul E. Gillmor (R)
6. Ted Strickland (D)
7. David L. Hobson (R)
8. John A. Boehner (R)
9. Marcy Kaptur (D)
10. Dennis J. Kucinich (D)
11. Stephanie Tubbs Jones (D)
12. John R. Kasich (R)
13. Sherrod Brown (D)
14. Thomas C. Sawyer (D)
15. Deborah Pryce (R)
16. Ralph Regula (R)
17. James A. Traficant Jr. (D)
18. Bob Ney (R)
19. Steven C. LaTourette (R)

Oklahoma
1. Steve Largent (R)
2. Tom Coburn (R)
3. Wes Watkins (R)
4. J. C. Watts (R)
5. Ernest Jim Istook Jr. (R)
6. Frank D. Lucas (R)

Oregon
1. David Wu (R)

2. Greg Walden (R)
3. Earl Blumenauer (D)
4. Peter A. DeFazio (D)
5. Darlene Hooley (D)

Pennsylvania
1. Robert A. Brady (D)
2. Chaka Fattah (D)
3. Robert A. Borski (D)
4. Ron Klink (D)
5. John E. Peterson (R)
6. Tim Holden (D)
7. Curt Weldon (R)
8. James C. Greenwood (R)
9. E. G. "Bud" Shuster (R)
10. Don Sherwood (R)
11. Paul E. Kanjorski (D)
12. John P. Murtha (D)
13. Joseph M. Hoeffel III (D)
14. William J. Coyne (D)
15. Pat Toomey (R)
16. Joseph R. Pitts (R)
17. George W. Gekas (R)
18. Mike Doyle (D)
19. William F. Goodling (R)
20. Frank R. Mascara (D)
21. Phil English (R)

Rhode Island
1. Patrick J. Kennedy (D)
2. Robert A. Weygand (D)

South Carolina
1. Mark Sanford (R)
2. Floyd D. Spence (R)
3. Lindsey Graham (R)
4. Jim DeMint (R)
5. John M. Spratt Jr. (D)
6. James E. Clyburn (D)

South Dakota
AL John Thune (R)

Tennessee
1. William L. Jenkins (R)
2. John J. "Jimmy" Duncan Jr. (R)
3. Zach Wamp (R)
4. Van Hilleary (R)
5. Bob Clement (D)
6. Bart Gordon (D)
7. Ed Bryant (R)
8. John Tanner (D)
9. Harold E. Ford Jr. (D)

Texas
1. Max Sandlin (D)
2. James Turner (D)
3. Sam Johnson (R)
4. Ralph M. Hall (D)
5. Pete Sessions (R)
6. Joe L. Barton (R)
7. W. R. "Bill" Archer (R)
8. Kevin Brady (R)
9. Nick Lampson (D)
10. Lloyd Doggett (D)
11. Chet Edwards (D)
12. Kay Granger (R)
13. William M. "Mac" Thornberry (R)

14. Ron Paul (R)
15. Rubén Hinojosa (D)
16. Silvestre Reyes (D)
17. Charles W. Stenholm (D)
18. Sheila Jackson-Lee (D)
19. Larry Combest (R)
20. Charlie Gonzalez (D)
21. Lamar Smith (R)
22. Tom DeLay (R)
23. Henry Bonilla (R)
24. Martin Frost (D)
25. Ken Bentsen (D)
26. Dick Armey (R)
27. Solomon P. Ortiz (D)
28. Ciro D. Rodriguez (D)
29. Gene Green (D)
30. Eddie Bernice Johnson (D)

Utah
1. James V. Hansen (R)
2. Merrill Cook (R)
3. Christopher B. Cannon (R)

Vermont
AL Bernard Sanders (I)

Virginia
1. Herbert H. Bateman (R)
2. Owen B. Pickett (D)
3. Robert C. Scott (D)
4. Norman Sisisky (D)
5. Virgil H. Goode Jr. (D)[3]
6. Robert W. Goodlatte (R)
7. Thomas J. Bliley Jr. (R)
8. James P. Moran (D)
9. Rick C. Boucher (D)
10. Frank R. Wolf (R)
11. Thomas M. Davis III (R)

Washington
1. Jay Inslee (D)
2. Jack Metcalf (R)
3. Brian Baird (D)
4. Richard "Doc" Hastings (R)
5. George Nethercutt (R)
6. Norm Dicks (D)
7. Jim McDermott (D)
8. Jennifer Dunn (R)
9. Adam Smith (D)

West Virginia
1. Alan B. Mollohan (D)
2. Robert E. Wise (D)
3. Nick J. Rahall II (D)

Wisconsin
1. Paul Ryan (R)
2. Tammy Baldwin (D)
3. Ron Kind (D)
4. Gerald D. Kleczka (D)
5. Thomas M. Barrett (D)
6. Thomas E. Petri (R)
7. David R. Obey (D)
8. Mark Green (R)
9. F. James Sensenbrenner Jr. (R)

Wyoming
AL Barbara Cubin (R)

NOTES: Members of the 106th Congress also included delegates Eni F. H. Faleomavaega, D-American Samoa; Donna M. C. Christensen, D-Virgin Islands; Eleanor Holmes Norton, D-District of Columbia; Robert A. Underwood, D-Guam; and resident commissioner Carlos A. Romero-Barcelo, D-Puerto Rico.

1. Martinez switched from the Democrat to Republican on July 26, 2000. Martinez had lost his bid for renomination in California's March 7 Democratic primary.
2. Forbes switched from Republican to Democrat on July 17, 1999.
3. Goode, a Democrat, announced Jan. 24, 2000, that he would seek reelection as an Independent.

Members of Congress, 1997–2001

The names in this list include, alphabetically, all senators, representatives, resident commissioners, and territorial delegates who served in the 105th and 106th Congresses—from Jan. 3, 1997 to Jan. 3, 2001.

The material is organized as follows: name; relationship to other members and presidents and vice presidents; party, state (of service); date of birth; date of death (if applicable); congressional service; service as president, vice president, member of the cabinet or Supreme Court, governor, Speaker of the House, president pro tempore of the Senate, majority leader, minority leader, and chair of the Democratic or Republican National Committees.

If the member changed parties during his or her congressional service, the party designation appearing after the member's name is that which applied at the end of such service and further information is included in the entry. Where the service date is left open, the member continued to service in the 107th Congress (as of Jan. 4, 2001).

Dates of service are inclusive, starting in year of service and ending when service ends. Under the Constitution, terms of service since 1934 have been from Jan. 3 to Jan. 3. In actual practice, members have been sworn in on other dates at the beginning of a Congress. The exact date is shown (where available) if a member began or ended his or her service in midterm.

The major sources for the following list were Congressional Quarterly's *Biographical Directory of the American Congress 1774–1996; America Votes* series; *CQ Almanac; American Political Leaders 1789–2000; CQ Weekly* and CQ's online database.

In the list, D stands for Democrat; R, Republican; and I, Independent.

A

Abercrombie, Neil (D-Hawaii) June 26, 1938– ; House Sept. 23, 1986–1987, 1991– .

Abraham, Spencer (R-Mich.) June 12, 1952– ; Senate 1995–2001.

Ackerman, Gary L. (D-N.Y.) Nov. 19, 1942– ; House March 1, 1983– .

Aderholt, Robert B. (R-Ala.) July 22, 1965– ; House 1997– .

Akaka, Daniel K. (D-Hawaii) Sept. 11, 1924– ; House 1977–May 16, 1990; Senate May 16, 1990– .

Allard, Wayne (R-Colo.) Dec. 2, 1943– ; House 1991–1997; Senate 1997– .

Allen, Thomas H. (D-Maine) April 18, 1945– ; House 1997– .

Andrews, Robert E. (D-N.J.) Aug. 4, 1957– ; House 1990– .

Archer, Bill (R-Texas) March 22, 1928– ; House 1971–2001.

Armey, Dick (R-Texas) July 7, 1940– ; House 1985– ; House majority leader 1995– .

Ashcroft, John (R-Mo.) May 9, 1942– ; Senate 1995–2001.

B

Baca, Joe (D-Calif) Jan. 23, 1947– ; House Nov. 18, 1999– .

Bachus, Spencer (R-Ala.) Dec. 28, 1947– ; House 1993– .

Baesler, Scotty (D-Ky.) July 9, 1941– ; House 1993–1999.

Baird, Brian (D-Wash.) March 7, 1956– ; House 1999– .

Baker, Richard H. (R-La.) May 22, 1948– ; House 1987– .

Baldacci, John (D-Maine) Jan. 30, 1955– ; House 1995– .

Baldwin, Tammy (D-Wis.) Feb. 11, 1962– ; House 1999– .

Ballenger, Cass (great-great grandson of Lewis Cass) (R-N.C.) Dec. 6, 1926– ; House 1987– .

Barcia, James A. (D-Mich.) Feb. 25, 1952– ; House 1993– .

Barr, Bob (R-Ga.) Nov. 5, 1948– ; House 1995– .

Barrett, Bill (R-Neb.) Feb. 9, 1929– ; House 1991–2001.

Barrett, Thomas M. (D-Wis.) Dec. 8, 1953– ; House 1993– .

Bartlett, Roscoe G. (R-Md.) June 3, 1926– ; House 1993– .

Barton, Joe L. (R-Texas) Sept. 15, 1949– ; House 1985– .

Bass, Charles (son of Perkins Bass) (R-N.H.) Jan. 8, 1952– ; House 1995– .

Bateman, Herbert H. (R-Va.) Aug. 7, 1928–Sept. 11, 2000; House 1983–2000.

Baucus, Max (D-Mont.) Dec. 11, 1941– ; House 1975–Dec. 14, 1978; Senate Dec. 15, 1978– .

Bayh, Evan (son of Birch Evan Bayh) (D-Ind.) Dec. 26, 1955– ; Senate 1999– ; Gov. 1989–1997.

Becerra, Xavier (D-Calif.) Jan. 26, 1958– ; House 1993– .

Bennett, Robert F. (R-Utah) Sept. 18, 1933– ; Senate 1993– .

Bentsen, Ken (nephew of Lloyd Bentsen) (D-Texas) June 3, 1959– ; House 1995– .

Bereuter, Doug (R-Neb.) Oct. 6, 1939– ; House 1979– .

Berkley, Shelley (D-Nev.) Jan. 21, 1951– ; House 1999– .

Berman, Howard L. (D-Calif.) April 15, 1941– ; House 1983– .

Berry, Marion (D-Ark.) Aug. 27, 1942– ; House 1997– .

Biden, Joseph R. Jr. (D-Del.) Nov. 20, 1942– ; Senate 1973– .

Biggert, Judy (R-Ill.) Aug. 15, 1937– ; House 1999– .

Bilbray, Brian P. (nephew of James Bilbray) (R-Calif.) Jan. 28, 1951– ; House 1995–2001.

Bilirakis, Michael (R-Fla.) July 16, 1930– ; House 1983– .

Bingaman, Jeff (D-N.M.) Oct. 3, 1943– ; Senate 1983– .

Bishop, Sanford D. Jr. (D-Ga.) Feb. 4, 1947– ; House 1993– .

Blagojevich, Rod R. (D-Ill.) Dec. 10, 1956– ; House 1997– .

Bliley, Thomas J. Jr. (R-Va.) Jan. 28, 1932– ; House 1981–2001.

Blumenauer, Earl (D-Ore.) Aug. 16, 1949– ; House May 30, 1996– .

Blunt, Roy (R-Mo.) Jan. 10, 1950– ; House 1997– .

Boehlert, Sherwood (R-N.Y.) Sept. 28, 1936– ; House 1983– .

Boehner, John A. (R-Ohio) Nov. 17, 1949– ; House 1991– .

Bond, Christopher S. (R-Mo.) March 6, 1939– ; Senate 1987– .

Bonilla, Henry (R-Texas) Jan. 2, 1954– ; House 1993– .

Bonior, David E. (D-Mich.) June 6, 1945– ; House 1977– .

Bono, Mary (wife of Sonny Bono) (R-Calif.) Oct. 24, 1961– ; House April 21, 1998– .

Bono, Sonny (husband of Mary Bono) (R-Calif.) Feb. 16, 1935–Jan. 5, 1998; House 1995–Jan. 5, 1998.

Borski, Robert A. (D-Pa.) Oct. 20, 1948– ; House 1983– .

Boswell, Leonard L. (D-Iowa) Jan. 10, 1934– ; House 1997– .

Boucher, Rick (D-Va.) Aug. 1, 1946– ; House 1983– .

Boxer, Barbara (D-Calif.) Nov. 11, 1940– ; House 1983–1993; Senate 1993– .

Boyd, Allen (D-Fla.) June 6, 1945– ; House 1997– .

Brady, Kevin (R-Texas) April 11, 1955– ; House 1997– .

Brady, Robert A. (D-Pa.) April 7, 1945– ; House May 21, 1998– .

Breaux, John B. (D-La.) March 1, 1944– ; House Sept. 30, 1972–1987; Senate 1987– .

Brown, Corrine (D-Fla.) Nov. 11, 1946– ; House 1993– .

Brown, George E. Jr. (D-Calif.) March 6, 1920– July 15, 1999; House 1963–1971, 1973–July 15, 1999.

Brownback, Sam (R-Kan.) Sept. 12, 1956– ; House 1995–Nov. 6, 1996; Senate Nov. 27, 1996– .

Bryan, Richard H. (D-Nev.) July 16, 1937– ; Senate 1989–2001; Gov. 1983–1989.

Bryant, Ed (R-Tenn.) Sept. 7, 1948– ; House 1995– .

Bumpers, Dale (D-Ark.) Aug. 12, 1925– ; Senate 1975–1999.

Bunning, Jim (R-Ky.) Oct. 23, 1931– ; House 1987–1999; Senate 1999– .

Burns, Conrad (R-Mont.) Jan. 25, 1935– ; Senate 1989– .

Burr, Richard M. (R-N.C.) Nov. 30, 1955– ; House 1995– .

Burton, Dan (R-Ind.) June 21, 1938– ; House 1983– .

Buyer, Steve (R-Ind.) Nov. 26, 1958– ; House 1993– ; Gov. 1971–1975.

Byrd, Robert C. (D-W.Va.) Nov. 20, 1917– ; House 1953–1959; Senate 1959– ; Senate minority leader, 1981–1987; Senate majority leader 1977–1981, 1987–1989; Pres. pro tempore 1989–1995.

C

Callahan, Sonny (R-Ala.) Sept. 11, 1932– ; House 1985– .

Calvert, Ken (R-Calif.) June 8, 1953– ; House 1993– .

Camp, Dave (R-Mich.) July 9, 1953– ; House 1991– .

Campbell, Ben Nighthorse (R-Colo.) April 13, 1933– ; House 1987–1993; Senate 1993– (1987–March 3, 1995, Democrat).

Campbell, Tom (R-Calif.) Aug. 14, 1952– ; House 1989–1993; Dec. 15, 1995–2001.

Canady, Charles T. (R-Fla.) June 22, 1954– ; House 1993–2001.

Cannon, Christopher B. (R-Utah) Oct. 20, 1950– ; House 1997– .

Capps, Lois D. (wife of Walter Capps) (D-Calif.) Jan. 10, 1938– ; House March 17, 1998– .

Capps, Walter (husband of Lois D. Capps) (D-Calif.) May 5, 1934–Oct. 28, 1997; House 1997–Oct. 28, 1997.

Capuano, Michael E. (D-Mass.) Jan. 9, 1952– ; House 1999– .

Cardin, Benjamin L. (D-Md.) Oct. 5, 1943– ; House 1987– .

Carson, Julia M. (D-Ind.) July 8, 1938– ; House 1997– .

Castle, Michael N. (R-Del.) July 2, 1939– ; House 1993– .

Chabot, Steve (R-Ohio) Jan. 22, 1953– ; House 1995– .

Chafee, John H. (father of Lincoln Chafee) (R-R.I.) Oct. 22, 1922–Oct. 24, 1999; Senate 1976–Oct. 24, 1999; Gov. 1963–1969.

Chafee, Lincoln (son of John H. Chafee) (R-R.I.) March 26, 1953– ; Senate Nov. 4, 1999– .

Chambliss, Saxby (R-Ga.) Nov. 10, 1943– ; House 1995– .

Chenoweth, Helen (R-Idaho) Jan. 27, 1938– ; House 1995–2001.

Christensen, Donna M. C. (D-Virgin Is.) Sept. 19, 1945– ; House (delegate) 1997– .

Christensen, Jon (R-Neb.) Feb. 20, 1963– ; House 1995–1999.

Clay, William L. (D-Mo.) April 30, 1931– ; House 1969–2001.

Clayton, Eva (D-N.C.) Sept. 16, 1934– ; House Nov. 4, 1992– .

Cleland, Max (D-Ga.) Aug. 24, 1942– ; Senate 1997– .

Clement, Bob (D-Tenn.) Sept. 23, 1943– ; House 1988– .

Clyburn, James E. (D-S.C.) July 21, 1940– ; House 1993– .

Coats, Daniel R. (R-Ind.) May 16, 1943– ; House 1981–Jan. 1, 1989; Senate 1989–1999.

Coble, Howard (R-N.C.) March 18, 1931– ; House 1985– .

Coburn, Tom (R-Okla.) March 14, 1948– ; House 1995–2001.

Cochran, Thad (R-Miss.) Dec. 7, 1937– ; House 1973–Dec. 26, 1978; Senate Dec. 27, 1978– .

Collins, Mac (R-Ga.) Oct. 15, 1944– ; House 1993– .

Collins, Susan (R-Maine) Dec. 7, 1952– ; Senate 1997– .

Combest, Larry (R-Texas) March 20, 1945– ; House 1985– .

Condit, Gary A. (D-Calif.) April 21, 1948– ; House Sept. 20, 1989– .

Conrad, Kent (D-N.D.) March 12, 1948– ; Senate 1987–Dec. 14, 1992, Dec. 14, 1992– (Conrad resigned his Senate seat on Dec. 14, 1992, after having won a special election to North Dakota's other Senate seat).

Conyers, John Jr. (D-Mich.) May 16, 1929– ; House 1965– .

Cook, Merrill (R-Utah) May 6, 1946– ; House 1997–2001.

Cooksey, John (R-La.) Aug. 20, 1941– ; House 1997– .

Costello, Jerry F. (D-Ill.) Sept. 25, 1949– ; House Aug. 11, 1988– .

Coverdell, Paul (R-Ga.) Jan. 20, 1939–July 18, 2000 ; Senate 1993–July 18, 2000.

Cox, Christopher (R-Calif.) Oct. 16, 1952– ; House 1989– .

Coyne, William J. (D-Pa.) Aug. 24, 1936– ; House 1981– .

Craig, Larry E. (R-Idaho) July 20, 1945– ; House 1981–1991; Senate 1991– .

Cramer, Robert E. "Bud" (D-Ala.) Aug. 22, 1947– ; House 1991– .

Crane, Philip M. (brother of Daniel Bever Crane) (R-Ill.) Nov. 3, 1930– ; House 1969– .

Crapo, Michael D. (R-Idaho) May 20, 1951– ; House 1993–1999; Senate 1999– .

Crowley, Joseph (D-N.Y.) March 16, 1962– ; House 1999– .

Cubin, Barbara (R-Wyo.) Nov. 30, 1946– ; House 1995– .

Cummings, Elijah E. (D-Md.) Jan. 18, 1951– ; House April 25, 1996– .

Cunningham, Randy "Duke" (R-Calif.) Dec. 8, 1941– ; House 1991– .

D

D'Amato, Alfonse M. (R-N.Y.) Aug. 1, 1937– ; Senate 1981–1999.

Danner, Pat (D-Mo.) Jan. 13, 1934– ; House 1993–2001.

Daschle, Tom (D-S.D.) Dec. 9, 1947– ; House 1979–1987; Senate 1987– ; Senate minority leader 1995– .

Davis, Danny K. (D-Ill.) Sept. 6, 1941– ; House 1997– .

Davis, Jim (D-Fla.) Oct. 11, 1957– ; House 1997– .

Davis, Thomas M. III (R-Va.) Jan. 5, 1949– ; House 1995– .

Deal, Nathan (R-Ga.) Aug. 25, 1942– ; House 1993– (1993–April 10, 1995, Democrat).

DeFazio, Peter A. (D-Ore.) May 27, 1947– ; House 1987– .

DeGette, Diana (D-Colo.) July 29, 1957– ; House 1997– .

Delahunt, William (D-Mass.) July 18, 1941– ; House 1997– .

DeLauro, Rosa (D-Conn.) March 2, 1943– ; House 1991– .

DeLay, Tom (R-Texas) April 8, 1947– ; House 1985– .

Dellums, Ronald V. (D-Calif.) Nov. 24, 1935– ; House 1971–Feb. 6, 1998.

DeMint, Jim (R-S.C.) Sept. 2, 1951– ; House 1999– .

Derrick, Butler (D-S.C.) Sept. 30, 1936– ; House 1975– .

Deutsch, Peter (D-Fla.) April 1, 1957– ; House 1993– .

DeWine, Mike (R-Ohio) Jan. 5, 1947– ; House 1983–1991; Senate 1995– .

Diaz-Balart, Lincoln (R-Fla.) Aug. 13, 1954– ; House 1993– .

Dickey, Jay (R-Ark.) Dec. 14, 1939– ; House 1993–2001.

Dicks, Norm (D-Wash.) Dec. 16, 1940– ; House 1977– .

Dingell, John D. (son of John David Dingell) (D-Mich.) July 8, 1926– ; House Dec. 13, 1955– .

Dixon, Julian C. (D-Calif.) Aug. 8, 1934–Dec. 8, 2000 ; House 1979–Dec. 8, 2000.

Dodd, Christopher J. (son of Thomas Joseph Dodd) (D-Conn.) May 27, 1944– ; House 1975–1981; Senate 1981– .

Doggett, Lloyd (D-Texas) Oct. 6, 1946– ; House 1995– .

Domenici, Pete V. (R-N.M.) May 7, 1932– ; Senate 1973– .

Dooley, Cal (D-Calif.) Jan. 11, 1954– ; House 1991– .

Doolittle, John T. (R-Calif.) Oct. 30, 1950– ; House 1991– .

Dorgan, Byron L. (D-N.D.) May 14, 1942– ; House 1981–Dec. 14, 1992; Senate Dec. 15, 1992– .

Doyle, Mike (D-Pa.) Aug. 5, 1953– ; House 1995– .

Dreier, David (R-Calif.) July 5, 1952– ; House 1981– .

Duncan, John J. "Jimmy" Jr. (son of John J. Duncan) (R-Tenn.) July 21, 1947– ; House 1988– .

Dunn, Jennifer (R-Wash.) July 29, 1941– ; House 1993– .

Durbin, Richard J. (D-Ill.) Nov. 21, 1944– ; House 1983–1997; Senate 1997– .

E

Edwards, Chet (D-Texas) Nov. 24, 1951– ; House 1991– .

Edwards, John (D-N.C.) June 10, 1953– ; Senate 1999– .

Ehlers, Vernon J. (R-Mich.) Feb. 6, 1934– ; House Jan. 25, 1994– .

Ehrlich, Robert Jr. (R-Md.) Nov. 25, 1957– ; House 1995– .

Emerson, Jo Ann (R-Mo.) Sept. 16, 1950– ; House Nov. 5, 1996– (Emerson was elected as an Independent in a special election following the death of her husband, Bill Emerson, because the filing date had passed; she switched to Republican upon entering Congress).

Engel, Eliot L. (D-N.Y.) Feb. 18, 1947– ; House 1989– .

English, Phil (R-Pa.) June 20, 1956– ; House 1995– .

Ensign, John (R-Nev.) March 25, 1958– ; House 1995–1999.

Enzi, Michael B. (R-Wyo.) Feb. 1, 1944– ; Senate 1997– .

Eshoo, Anna G. (D-Calif.) Dec. 13, 1942– ; House 1993– .

Etheridge, Bob (D-N.C.) Aug. 7, 1941– ; House 1997– .

Evans, Lane (D-Ill.) Aug. 4, 1951– ; House 1983– .

Everett, Terry (R-Ala.) Feb. 15, 1937– ; House 1993– .

Ewing, Thomas W. (R-Ill.) Sept. 19, 1935– ; House July 10, 1991–2001.

F

Faircloth, Lauch (R-N.C.) Jan. 14, 1928– ; Senate 1993–1999.

Faleomavaega, Eni F. H. (D-Am. Samoa) Aug. 15, 1943– ; House (delegate) 1989– .

Farr, Sam (D-Calif.) July 4, 1941– ; House June 16, 1993– .

Fattah, Chaka (D-Pa.) Nov. 21, 1956– ; House 1995– .

Fawell, Harris W. (R-Ill.) March 25, 1929– ; House 1985–1999.

Fazio, Vic (D-Calif.) Oct. 11, 1942– ; House 1979–1999.

Feingold, Russell D. (D-Wis.) March 2, 1953– ; Senate 1993– .

Feinstein, Dianne (D-Calif.) June 22, 1933– ; Senate Nov. 10, 1992– .

Filner, Bob (D-Calif.) Sept. 4, 1942– ; House 1993– .

Fitzgerald, Peter G. (R-Ill.) Oct. 20, 1960– ; Senate 1999– .

Flake, Floyd H. (D-N.Y.) Jan. 30, 1945– ; House 1987–Nov. 15, 1997.

Fletcher, Ernest (R-Ky.) Nov. 12, 1952– ; House 1999– .

Foglietta, Thomas M. (D-Pa.) Dec. 3, 1928– ; House 1981–Nov. 12, 1997. (1981–1982, Independent).

Foley, Mark (R-Fla.) Sept. 8, 1954– ; House 1995– .

Forbes, Michael P. (D-N.Y.) July 16, 1952– ; House 1995–2001 (1995–July 2000, Republican).

Ford, Harold E. Jr. (D-Tenn.) May 11, 1970– ; House 1997– .

Ford, Wendell H. (D-Ky.) Sept. 8, 1924– ; Senate Dec. 28, 1974–1999; Gov. 1971–1974.

Fossella, Vito J. (R-N.Y.) March 9, 1965– ; House Nov. 5, 1997– .

Fowler, Tillie (R-Fla.) Dec. 23, 1942– ; House 1993–2001.

Fox, Jon D. (R-Pa.) April 22, 1947– ; House 1995–1999.

Frank, Barney (D-Mass.) March 31, 1940– ; House 1981– .

Franks, Bob (R-N.J.) Sept. 21, 1951– ; House 1993–2001.

Frelinghuysen, Rodney (son of Peter Hood Ballentine Frelinghuysen) (R-N.J.) April 29, 1946– ; House 1995– .

Frist, Bill (R-Tenn.) Feb. 22, 1952– ; Senate 1995– .

Frost, Martin (D-Texas) Jan. 1, 1942– ; House 1979– .

Furse, Elizabeth (D-Ore.) Oct. 13, 1936– ; House 1993–1999.

G

Gallegly, Elton (R-Calif.) March 7, 1944– ; House 1987– .

Ganske, Greg (R-Iowa) March 31, 1949– ; House 1995– .

Gejdenson, Sam (D-Conn.) May 20, 1948– ; House 1981–2001.

Gekas, George W. (R-Pa.) April 14, 1930– ; House 1983– .

Gephardt, Richard A. (D-Mo.) Jan. 31, 1941– ; House 1977– ; House majority leader June 14, 1989–1995; House minority leader 1995– .

Gibbons, Jim (R-Nev.) Dec. 16, 1944– ; House 1997– .

Gilchrest, Wayne T. (R-Md.) April 15, 1946– ; House 1991– .

Gillmor, Paul E. (R-Ohio) Feb. 1, 1939– ; House 1989– .

Gilman, Benjamin A. (R-N.Y.) Dec. 6, 1922– ; House 1973– .

Gingrich, Newt (R-Ga.) June 17, 1943– ; House 1979–Jan. 3, 1999 ; Speaker 1995–1999.

Glenn, John (D-Ohio) July 18, 1921– ; Senate 1974–1999.

Gonzalez, Charlie (son of Henry B. Gonzalez) (D-Texas) May 5, 1945– ; House 1999– .

Gonzalez, Henry B. (father of Charlie Gonzalez) (D-Texas) May 3, 1916–Nov. 28, 2000; House 1961–1999.

Goode, Virgil H. Jr. (I-Va.) Oct. 17, 1946– ; House 1997– (1997–Jan. 24, 2000, Democrat).

Goodlatte, Robert W. (R-Va.) Sept. 22, 1952– ; House 1993– .

Goodling, William F. (son of George Atlee Goodling) (R-Pa.) Dec. 5, 1927– ; House 1975–2001.

Gordon, Bart (D-Tenn.) Jan. 24, 1949– ; House 1985– .

Gorton, Slade (R-Wash.) Jan. 8, 1928– ; Senate 1989–2001.

Goss, Porter J. (R-Fla.) Nov. 26, 1938– ; House 1989– .

Graham, Bob (D-Fla.) Nov. 9, 1936– ; Senate 1987– .

Graham, Lindsey (R-S.C.) July 9, 1955– ; House 1995– .

Gramm, Phil (R-Texas) July 8, 1942– ; House 1979–Jan. 5, 1983, Feb. 22, 1983–1985 (1979–Jan. 5, 1983, Democrat); Senate 1985– .

Grams, Rod (R-Minn.) Feb. 4, 1948– ; House 1993–1995; Senate 1995–2001.

Granger, Kay (R-Texas) Jan. 18, 1943– ; House 1997– .

Grassley, Charles E. (R-Iowa) Sept. 17, 1933– ; House 1975–1981; Senate 1981– .

Green, Gene (D-Texas) Oct. 17, 1947– ; House 1993– .

Green, Mark (R-Wis.) June 1, 1960– ; House 1999– .

Greenwood, James C. (R-Pa.) May 4, 1951– ; House 1993– .

Gregg, Judd (R-N.H.) Feb. 14, 1947– ; Senate 1993– .

Gutierrez, Luis V. (D-Ill.) Dec. 10, 1954– ; House 1993– .

Gutknecht, Gil (R-Minn.) March 20, 1951– ; House 1995– .

H

Hagel, Chuck (R-Neb.) Oct. 4, 1946– ; Senate 1997– .

Hall, Ralph M. (D-Texas) May 3, 1923– ; House 1981– .

Hall, Tony P. (D-Ohio) Jan. 16, 1942– ; House 1979– .

Hamilton, Lee H. (D-Ind.) April 20, 1931– ; House 1965–1999.

Hansen, James V. (R-Utah) Aug. 14, 1932– ; House 1981– .

Harkin, Tom (D-Iowa) Nov. 19, 1939– ; House 1975–1985; Senate 1985– .

Harman, Jane (D-Calif.) June 28, 1945– ; House 1993–1999.

Hastert, J. Dennis (R-Ill.) Jan. 2, 1942– ; House 1987– ; Speaker 1999– .

Hastings, Alcee L. (D-Fla.) Sept. 5, 1936– ; House 1993– .

Hastings, Richard "Doc" (R-Wash.) Feb. 7, 1941– ; House 1995– .

Hatch, Orrin G. (R-Utah) March 22, 1934– ; Senate 1977– .

Hayes, Robin (R-N.C.) Aug. 14, 1945– ; House 1999– .

Hayworth, J. D. (R-Ariz.) July 12, 1958– ; House 1995– .

Hefley, Joel (R-Colo.) April 18, 1935– ; House 1987– .

Hefner, W. G. "Bill" (D-N.C.) April 11, 1930– ; House 1975–1999.

Helms, Jesse (R-N.C.) Oct. 18, 1921– ; Senate 1973– .

Herger, Wally (R-Calif.) May 20, 1945– ; House 1987– .

Hill, Baron P. (D-Ind.) June 23, 1953– ; House 1999– .

Hill, Rick (R-Mont.) Dec. 30, 1946– ; House 1997–2001.

Hilleary, Van (R-Tenn.) June 20, 1959– ; House 1995– .

Hilliard, Earl F. (D-Ala.) April 9, 1942– ; House 1993– .

Hinchey, Maurice D. (D-N.Y.) Oct. 27, 1938– ; House 1993– .

Hinojosa, Rubén (D-Texas) Aug. 20, 1940– ; House 1997– .

Hobson, David L. (R-Ohio) Oct. 17, 1936– ; House 1991– .

Hoeffel, Joseph M. (D-Pa.) Sept. 3, 1950– ; House 1999– .

Hoekstra, Peter (R-Mich.) Oct. 30, 1953– ; House 1993– .

Holden, Tim (D-Pa.) March 5, 1957– ; House 1993– .

Hollings, Ernest F. (D-S.C.) Jan. 1, 1922– ; Senate Nov. 9, 1966– ; Gov. 1959–1963.

Holt, Rush D. (D-N.J.) Oct. 15, 1948– ; House 1999– .

Hooley, Darlene (D-Ore.) April 4, 1939– ; House 1997– .

Horn, Steve (R-Calif.) May 31, 1931– ; House 1993– .

Hostettler, John (R-Ind.) July 19, 1961– ; House 1995– .

Houghton, Amo (grandson of Alanson Bigelow Houghton) (R-N.Y.) Aug. 7, 1926– ; House 1987– .

Hoyer, Steny H. (D-Md.) June 14, 1939– ; House June 3, 1981– .

Hulshof, Kenny (R-Mo.) May 22, 1958– ; House 1997– .

Hunter, Duncan (R-Calif.) May 31, 1948– ; House 1981– .

Hutchinson, Asa (R-Ark.) Dec. 3, 1950– ; House 1997– .

Hutchinson, Tim (R-Ark.) Aug. 11, 1949– ; House 1993–1997; Senate 1997– .

Hutchison, Kay Bailey (R-Texas) July 22, 1943– ; Senate June 14, 1993– .

Hyde, Henry J. (R-Ill.) April 18, 1924– ; House 1975– .

I

Inglis, Robert D. (R-S.C.) Oct. 11, 1959– ; House 1993–1999.

Inhofe, James M. (R-Okla.) Nov. 17, 1934– ; House 1987–Nov. 15, 1994; Senate Nov. 17, 1994– .

Inouye, Daniel K. (D-Hawaii) Sept. 7, 1924– ; House Aug. 21, 1959–1963; Senate 1963– .

Inslee, Jay (D-Wash.) Feb. 9, 1951– ; House 1993–1995; 1999– .

Isakson, Johnny (R-Ga.) Dec. 28, 1944– ; House Feb. 25, 1999– .

Istook, Ernest (R-Okla.) Feb. 11, 1950– ; House 1993– .

J

Jackson, Jesse L. Jr. (D-Ill.) March 11, 1965– ; House Dec. 14, 1995– .

Jackson-Lee, Sheila (D-Texas) Jan. 12, 1950– ; House 1995– .

Jefferson, William J. (D-La.) March 14, 1947– ; House 1991– .

Jeffords, James M. (R-Vt.) May 11, 1934– ; House 1975–1989; Senate 1989– .

Jenkins, William L. (R-Tenn.) Nov. 29, 1936– ; House 1997– .

John, Chris (D-La.) Jan. 5, 1960– ; House 1997– .

Johnson, Eddie Bernice (D-Texas) Dec. 3, 1935– ; House 1993– .

Johnson, Jay (D-Wis.) Sept. 30, 1943– ; House 1997–1999.

Johnson, Nancy L. (R-Conn.) Jan. 5, 1935– ; House 1983– .

Johnson, Sam (R-Texas) Oct. 11, 1930– ; House May 22, 1991– .

Johnson, Tim (D-S.D.) Dec. 28, 1946– ; House 1987–1997; Senate 1997– .

Jones, Stephanie Tubbs (D-Ohio) Sept. 10, 1949– ; House 1999– .

Jones, Walter B. Jr. (son of Walter Beaman Jones) (R-N.C.) Feb. 10, 1943– ; House 1995– .

K

Kanjorski, Paul E. (D-Pa.) April 2, 1937– ; House 1985– .

Kaptur, Marcy (D-Ohio) June 17, 1946– ; House 1983– .

Kasich, John R. (R-Ohio) May 13, 1952– ; House 1983–2001.

Kelly, Sue W. (R-N.Y.) Sept. 26, 1936– ; House 1995– .

Kempthorne, Dirk (R-Idaho) Oct. 29, 1951– ; Senate 1993–1999; Gov. 1999– .

Kennedy, Edward M. (father of Patrick J. Kennedy, brother of John Fitzgerald Kennedy and Robert Francis Kennedy, grandson of John Francis Fitzgerald, uncle of Joseph P. Kennedy II) (D-Mass.) Feb. 22, 1932– ; Senate Nov. 7, 1962– .

Kennedy, Joseph P. II (son of Robert Francis Kennedy, nephew of Edward M. Kennedy and John Fitzgerald Kennedy, cousin of Patrick J. Kennedy, great grandson of John Francis Fitzgerald) (D-Mass.) Sept. 24, 1952– ; House 1987–1999.

Kennedy, Patrick J. (son of Edward M. Kennedy, nephew of John Fitzgerald Kennedy and Robert Francis Kennedy, cousin of Joseph P. Kennedy II, great grandson of John Francis Fitzgerald) (D-R.I.) July 14, 1967– ; House 1995– .

Kennelly, Barbara B. (D-Conn.) July 10, 1936– ; House Jan. 25, 1982–1999.

Kerrey, Bob (D-Neb.) Aug. 27, 1943– ; Senate 1989–2001; Gov. 1983–1989.

Kerry, John (D-Mass.) Dec. 11, 1943– ; Senate 1985– .

Kildee, Dale E. (D-Mich.) Sept. 16, 1929– ; House 1977– .

Kilpatrick, Carolyn Cheeks (D-Mich.) June 25, 1945– ; House 1997– .

Kim, Jay C. (R-Calif.) March 27, 1939– ; House 1993–1999.

Kind, Ron (D-Wis.) March 16, 1963– ; House 1997– .

King, Peter T. (R-N.Y.) April 5, 1944– ; House 1993– .

Kingston, Jack (R-Ga.) April 24, 1955– ; House 1993– .

Kleczka, Gerald D. (D-Wis.) Nov. 26, 1943– ; House April 10, 1984– .

Klink, Ron (D-Pa.) Sept. 23, 1951– ; House 1993–2001.

Klug, Scott L. (R-Wis.) Jan. 16, 1953– ; House 1991–1999.

Knollenberg, Joe (R-Mich.) Nov. 28, 1933– ; House 1993– .

Kohl, Herb (D-Wis.) Feb. 7, 1935– ; Senate 1989– .

Kolbe, Jim (R-Ariz.) June 28, 1942– ; House 1985– .

Kucinich, Dennis J. (D-Ohio) Oct. 8, 1946– ; House 1997– .

Kuykendall, Steven T. (R-Calif.) Jan. 27, 1947– ; House 1999–2001.

Kyl, Jon (son of John Henry Kyl) (R-Ariz.) April 25, 1942– ; House 1987–1995; Senate 1995– .

L

LaFalce, John J. (D-N.Y.) Oct. 6, 1939– ; House 1975– .

LaHood, Ray (R-Ill.) Dec. 6, 1945– ; House 1995– .

Lampson, Nick (D-Texas) Feb. 14, 1945– ; House 1997– .

Landrieu, Mary L. (D-La.) Nov. 23, 1955– ; Senate 1997– .

Lantos, Tom (father-in-law of Dick Swett) (D-Calif.) Feb. 1, 1928– ; House 1981– .

Largent, Steve (R-Okla.) Sept. 28, 1955– ; House Nov. 29, 1994– .

Larson, John B. (D-Conn.) July 22, 1948– ; House 1999– .

Latham, Tom (R-Iowa) July 14, 1948– ; House 1995– .

LaTourette, Steven C. (R-Ohio) July 22, 1954– ; House 1995– .

Lautenberg, Frank R. (D-N.J.) Jan. 23, 1924– ; Senate Dec. 27, 1982–2001.

Lazio, Rick A. (R-N.Y.) March 13, 1958– ; House 1993–2001.

Leach, Jim (R-Iowa) Oct. 15, 1942– ; House 1977– .

Leahy, Patrick J. (D-Vt.) March 31, 1940– ; Senate 1975– .

Lee, Barbara (D-Calif.) July 16, 1946– ; House April 21, 1998– .

Levin, Carl (brother of Sander M. Levin) (D-Mich.) June 28, 1934– ; Senate 1979– .

Levin, Sander M. (brother of Carl Levin) (D-Mich.) Sept. 6, 1931– ; House 1983– .

Lewis, Jerry (R-Calif.) Oct. 21, 1934– ; House 1979– .

Lewis, John (D-Ga.) Feb. 21, 1940– ; House 1987– .

Lewis, Ron (R-Ky.) Sept. 14, 1946– ; House May 26, 1994– .

Lieberman, Joseph I. (D-Conn.) Feb. 24, 1942– ; Senate 1989– .

Lincoln, Blanche Lambert (D-Ark.) Sept. 30, 1960– ; House 1993–1997; Senate 1999– .

Linder, John (R-Ga.) Sept. 9, 1942– ; House 1993– .

Lipinski, William O. (D-Ill.) Dec. 22, 1937– ; House 1983– .

Livingston, Robert L. (R-La.) April 30, 1943– ; House Sept. 7, 1977–Feb. 22, 1999.

LoBiondo, Frank A. (R-N.J.) May 12, 1946– ; House 1995– .

Lofgren, Zoe (D-Calif.) Dec. 21, 1947– ; House 1995– .

Lott, Trent (R-Miss.) Oct. 9, 1941– ; House 1973–1989; Senate 1989– ; Senate majority leader June 12, 1996– .

Lowey, Nita M. (D-N.Y.) July 5, 1937– ; House 1989– .

Lucas, Frank D. (R-Okla.) Jan. 6, 1960– ; House May 17, 1994– .

Lucas, Ken (D-Ky.) Aug. 22, 1933– ; House 1999– .

Lugar, Richard G. (R-Ind.) April 4, 1932– ; Senate 1977– .

Luther, William P. "Bill" (D-Minn.) June 27, 1945– ; House 1995– .

M

Mack, Connie (R-Fla.) Oct. 29, 1940– ; House 1983–1989; Senate 1989–2001.

Maloney, Carolyn B. (D-N.Y.) Feb. 19, 1948– ; House 1993– .

Maloney, James H. (D-Conn.) Sept. 17, 1948– ; House– .

Manton, Thomas J. (D-N.Y.) Nov. 3, 1932– ; House 1985–1999.

Manzullo, Donald (R-Ill.) March 24, 1944– ; House 1993– .

Markey, Edward J. (D-Mass.) July 11, 1946– ; House Nov. 2, 1976– .

Martinez, Matthew G. (R-Calif.) Feb. 14, 1929– ; House July 15, 1982–2001 (1982–March 2000, Democrat).

Mascara, Frank R. (D-Pa.) Jan. 19, 1930– ; House 1995– .

Matsui, Robert T. (D-Calif.) Sept. 17, 1941– ; House 1979– .

McCain, John (R-Ariz.) Aug. 29, 1936– ; House 1983–1987; Senate 1987– .

McCarthy, Carolyn (D-N.Y.) Jan. 5, 1944– ; House 1997– .

McCarthy, Karen (D-Mo.) March 18, 1947– ; House 1995– .

McCollum, Bill (R-Fla.) July 12, 1944– ; House 1981–2001.

McConnell, Mitch (R-Ky.) Feb. 20, 1942– ; Senate 1985– .

McCrery, Jim (R-La.) Sept. 18, 1949– ; House 1988– .

McDade, Joseph M. (R-Pa.) Sept. 29, 1931– ; House 1963–1999.

McDermott, Jim (D-Wash.) Dec. 28, 1936– ; House 1989– .

McGovern, James (D-Mass.) Nov. 20, 1959– ; House 1997– .

McHale, Paul (D-Pa.) July 26, 1950– ; House 1993–1999.

McHugh, John M. (R-N.Y.) Sept. 29, 1948– ; House 1993– .

McInnis, Scott (R-Colo.) May 9, 1953– ; House 1993– .

McIntosh, David M. (R-Ind.) June 8, 1958– ; House 1995–2001.

McIntyre, Mike (D-N.C.) Aug. 6, 1956– ; House 1997– .

McKeon, Howard P. "Buck" (R-Calif.) Sept. 9, 1939– ; House 1993– .

McKinney, Cynthia A. (D-Ga.) March 17, 1955– ; House 1993– .

McNulty, Michael R. (D-N.Y.) Sept. 16, 1947– ; House 1989– .

Meehan, Martin T. (D-Mass.) Dec. 30, 1956– ; House 1993– .

Meek, Carrie P. (D-Fla.) April 29, 1926– ; House 1993– .

Meeks, Gregory W. (D-N.Y.) Sept. 25, 1953– ; House Feb. 5, 1998– .

Menendez, Robert (D-N.J.) Jan. 1, 1954– ; House 1993– .

Metcalf, Jack (R-Wash.) Nov. 30, 1927– ; House 1995–2001.

Mica, John L. (R-Fla.) Jan. 27, 1943– ; House 1993– .

Mikulski, Barbara A. (D-Md.) July 20, 1936– ; House 1977–1987; Senate 1987– .

Millender-McDonald, Juanita (D-Calif.) Sept. 7, 1938– ; House April 16, 1996– .

Miller, Dan (R-Fla.) May 30, 1942– ; House 1993– .

Miller, Gary (R-Calif.) Oct. 16, 1948– ; House 1999– .

Miller, George (D-Calif.) May 17, 1945– ; House 1975– .

Miller, Zell (D-Ga.) Feb. 24, 1932– ; Senate July 27, 2000– ; Gov. 1991–1999.

Minge, David (D-Minn.) March 19, 1942– ; House 1993–2001.

Mink, Patsy T. (D-Hawaii) Dec. 6, 1927– ; House 1965–1977, Sept. 27, 1990– .

Moakley, Joe (D-Mass.) April 27, 1927–May 28, 2001; House 1973–May 28, 2001 (elected as an Independent Democrat; changed affiliation to Democrat Jan. 2, 1973).

Molinari, Susan (daughter of Guy V. Molinari, wife of Bill Paxon) (R-N.Y.) March 27, 1958– ; House March 27, 1990–Aug. 1, 1997.

Mollohan, Alan B. (son of Robert Homer Mollohan) (D-W.Va.) May 14, 1943– ; House 1983– .

Moore, Dennis (D-Kan.) Nov. 8, 1945– ; House 1999– .

Moran, James P. (D-Va.) May 16, 1945– ; House 1991– .

Moran, Jerry (R-Kan.) May 29, 1954– ; House 1997– .

Morella, Constance A. (R-Md.) Feb. 12, 1931– ; House 1987– .

Moseley-Braun, Carol (D-Ill.) Aug. 16, 1947– ; Senate 1993–1999.

Moynihan, Daniel Patrick (D-N.Y.) March 16, 1927– ; Senate 1977–2001.

Murkowski, Frank H. (R-Alaska) March 28, 1933– ; Senate 1981– .

Murray, Patty (D-Wash.) Oct. 11, 1950– ; Senate 1993– .

Murtha, John P. (D-Pa.) June 17, 1932– ; House Feb. 5, 1974– .

Myrick, Sue (R-N.C.) Aug. 1, 1941– ; House 1995– .

N

Nadler, Jerrold (D-N.Y.) June 13, 1947– ; House Nov. 4, 1992– .

Napolitano, Grace Flores (D-Calif.) Dec. 4, 1936– ; House 1999– .

Neal, Richard E. (D-Mass.) Feb. 14, 1949– ; House 1989– .

Nethercutt, George (R-Wash.) Oct. 7, 1944– ; House 1995– .

Neumann, Mark W. (R-Wis.) Feb. 27, 1954– ; House 1995–1999.

Ney, Bob (R-Ohio) July 5, 1954– ; House 1995– .

Nickles, Don (R-Okla.) Dec. 6, 1948– ; Senate 1981– .

Northup, Anne M. (R-Ky.) July 22, 1948– ; House 1997– .

Norton, Eleanor Holmes (D-D.C.) June 13, 1937– ; House (delegate) 1991– .

Norwood, Charlie (R-Ga.) July 27, 1941– ; House 1995– .

Nussle, Jim (R-Iowa) June 27, 1960– ; House 1991– .

O

Oberstar, James L. (D-Minn.) Sept. 10, 1934– ; House 1975– .

Obey, David R. (D-Wis.) Oct. 3, 1938– ; House April 1, 1969– .

Olver, John W. (D-Mass.) Sept. 3, 1936– ; House June 18, 1991– .

Ortiz, Solomon P. (D-Texas) June 3, 1937– ; House 1983– .

Ose, Doug (R-Calif.) June 27, 1955– ; House 1999– .

Owens, Major R. (D-N.Y.) June 28, 1936– ; House 1983– .

Oxley, Michael G. (R-Ohio) Feb. 11, 1944– ; House June 25, 1981– .

P

Packard, Ron (R-Calif.) Jan. 19, 1931– ; House 1983–2001.

Pallone, Frank Jr. (D-N.J.) Oct. 30, 1951– ; House Nov. 8, 1988– .

Pappas, Michael (R-N.J.) Dec. 29, 1960– ; House 1997–1999.

Parker, Mike (R-Miss.) Oct. 31, 1949– ; House 1989–1999 (1993–Nov. 10, 1995, Democrat).

Pascrell, Bill Jr. (D-N.J.) Jan. 25, 1937– ; House 1997– .

Pastor, Ed (D-Ariz.) June 28, 1943– ; House Oct. 3, 1991– .

Paul, Ron (R-Texas) Aug. 20, 1935– ; House 1976–1977; 1979–1985; 1997– .

Paxon, Bill (husband of Susan Molinari, son-in-law of Guy Molinari) (R-N.Y.) April 29, 1954– ; House 1989–1999.

Payne, Donald M. (D-N.J.) July 16, 1934– ; House 1989– .

Pease, Edward A. (R-Ind.) May 22, 1951– ; House 1997–2001.

Pelosi, Nancy (daughter of Thomas D'Allesandro Jr.) (D-Calif.) March 26, 1940– ; House June 9, 1987– .

Peterson, Collin C. (D-Minn.) June 29, 1944– ; House 1991– .

Peterson, John E. (R-Pa.) Dec. 25, 1938– ; House 1997– .

Petri, Thomas E. (R-Wis.) May 28, 1940– ; House April 3, 1979– .

Phelps, David D. (D-Ill.) Oct. 26, 1947– ; House 1999– .

Pickering, Charles W. (R-Miss.) Aug. 10, 1963– ; House 1997– .

Pickett, Owen B. (D-Va.) Aug. 31, 1930– ; House 1987–2001.

Pitts, Joseph R. (R-Pa.) Oct. 10, 1939– ; House 1997– .

Pombo, Richard W. (R-Calif.) Jan. 8, 1961– ; House 1993– .

Pomeroy, Earl (D-N.D.) Sept. 2, 1952– ; House 1993– .

Porter, John Edward (R-Ill.) June 1, 1935– ; House Jan. 22, 1980–2001.

Portman, Rob (R-Ohio) Dec. 19, 1955– ; House May 5, 1993– .

Poshard, Glenn (D-Ill.) Oct. 30, 1945– ; House 1989–1999.

Price, David E. (D-N.C.) Aug. 17, 1940– ; House 1987–1995, 1997– .

Pryce, Deborah (R-Ohio) July 29, 1951– ; House 1993– .

Q

Quinn, Jack (R-N.Y.) April 13, 1951– ; House 1993– .

R

Radanovich, George P. (R-Calif.) June 20, 1955– ; House 1995– .

Rahall, Nick J. II (D-W.Va.) May 20, 1949– ; House 1977– .

Ramstad, Jim (R-Minn.) May 6, 1946– ; House 1991– .

Rangel, Charles B. (D-N.Y.) June 11, 1930– ; House 1971– .

Redmond, Bill (R-N.M.) Jan. 28, 1955– ; House May 20, 1997–1999.

Reed, Jack (D-R.I.) Nov. 12, 1949– ; House 1991–1997; Senate 1997– .

Regula, Ralph (R-Ohio) Dec. 3, 1924– ; House 1973– .

Reid, Harry (D-Nev.) Dec. 2, 1939– ; House 1983–1987; Senate 1987– .

Reyes, Silvestre (D-Texas) Nov. 10, 1944– ; House 1997– .

Reynolds, Thomas M. (R-N.Y.) Sept. 3, 1950– ; House 1999– .

Richardson, Bill (D-N.M.) Nov. 15, 1947– ; House 1983–Feb. 13, 1997; secretary of energy, 1998–2001.

Riggs, Frank (R-Calif.) Sept. 5, 1950– ; House 1995–1999.

Riley, Bob (R-Ala.) Oct. 3, 1944– ; House 1997– .

Rivers, Lynn (D-Mich.) Dec. 19, 1956– ; House 1995– .

Robb, Charles S. (son-in-law of Lyndon Johnson) (D-Va.) June 26, 1939– ; Senate 1989–2001; Gov. 1982–1986.

Roberts, Pat (R-Kan.) April 20, 1936– ; House 1981–1997; Senate 1997– .

Rockefeller, John D. IV (nephew of Nelson Aldrich Rockefeller and great grandson of Nelson Aldrich) (D-W.Va.) June 18, 1937– ; Senate Jan. 15, 1985– ; Gov. 1977–1985.

Rodriguez, Ciro D. (D-Texas) Dec. 9, 1946– ; House April 17, 1997– .

Roemer, Tim (son-in-law of J. Bennett Johnston) (D-Ind.) Oct. 30, 1956– ; House 1991– .

Rogan, James E. (R-Calif.) Aug. 21, 1957– ; House 1997–2001.

Rogers, Harold (R-Ky.) Dec. 31, 1937– ; House 1981– .

Rohrabacher, Dana (R-Calif.) June 21, 1947– ; House 1989– .

Romero-Barceló, Carlos A. (D-P.R.) Sept. 4, 1932– ; House (resident commissioner) 1993–2001.

Ros-Lehtinen, Ileana (R-Fla.) July 15, 1952– ; House 1989– .

Roth, William V. Jr. (R-Del.) July 22, 1921– ; House 1967–Dec. 31, 1970; Senate Jan. 1, 1971–2001.

Rothman, Steven R. (D-N.J.) Oct. 14, 1952– ; House 1997– .

Roukema, Marge (R-N.J.) Sept. 19, 1929– ; House 1981– .

Roybal-Allard, Lucille (D-Calif.) June 12, 1941– ; House 1993– .

Royce, Ed (R-Calif.) Oct. 12, 1951– ; House 1993– .

Rush, Bobby L. (D-Ill.) Nov. 23, 1946– ; House 1993– .

Ryan, Paul D. (R-Wis.) Jan. 29, 1970– ; House 1999– .

Ryun, Jim (R-Kan.) April 29, 1947– ; House Nov. 27, 1996– .

S

Sabo, Martin Olav (D-Minn.) Feb. 28, 1938– ; House 1979– .

Salmon, Matt (R-Ariz.) Jan. 21, 1958–; House 1995–2001.

Sanchez, Loretta (D-Calif.) Jan. 7, 1960– ; House 1997– .

Sanders, Bernard (I-Vt.) Sept. 8, 1941– ; House 1991– .

Sandlin, Max (D-Texas) Sept. 29, 1952– ; House 1997– .

Sanford, Mark (R-S.C.) May 28, 1960– ; House 1995–2001.

Santorum, Rick (R-Pa.) May 10, 1958– ; House 1991–1995; Senate 1995– .

Sarbanes, Paul S. (D-Md.) Feb. 3, 1933– ; House 1971–1977; Senate 1977– .

Sawyer, Thomas C. (D-Ohio) Aug. 15, 1945– ; House 1987– .

Saxton, H. James (R-N.J.) Jan. 22, 1943– ; House 1984– .

Scarborough, Joe (R-Fla.) April 9, 1963– ; House 1995– .

Schaefer, Daniel (R-Colo.) Jan. 25, 1936– ; House April 7, 1983–1999.

Schaffer, Bob (R-Colo.) July 24, 1962– ; House 1997– .

Schakowsky, Janice "Jan" (D-Ill.) May 26, 1944– ; House 1999– .

Schiff, Steven H. (R-N.M.) March 18, 1947–March 25, 1998; House 1989–March 25, 1998.

Schumer, Charles E. (D-N.Y.) Nov. 23, 1950– ; House 1981–1999; Senate 1999– .

Scott, Robert C. (D-Va.) April 30, 1947– ; House 1993– .

Sensenbrenner, F. James Jr. (R-Wis.) June 14, 1943– ; House 1979– .

Serrano, Jose E. (D-N.Y.) Oct. 24, 1943– ; House March 28, 1990– .

Sessions, Jeff (R-Ala.) Dec. 24, 1946– ; Senate 1997– .

Sessions, Pete (R-Texas) March 22, 1955– ; House 1997– .

Shadegg, John (R-Ariz.) Oct. 22, 1949– ; House 1995– .

Shaw, E. Clay Jr. (R-Fla.) April 19, 1939– ; House 1981– .

Shays, Christopher (R-Conn.) Oct. 18, 1945– ; House Sept. 9, 1987– .

Shelby, Richard C. (R-Ala.) May 6, 1934– ; House 1979–1987; Senate 1987– (1979–Nov. 19, 1994, Democrat).

Sherman, Brad (D-Calif.) Oct. 24, 1954– ; House 1997– .

Sherwood, Donald L. (R-Pa.) March 5, 1941– ; House 1999– .

Shimkus, John M. (R-Ill.) Feb. 21, 1958– ; House 1997– .

Shows, Ronnie (D-Miss.) Jan. 26, 1947– ; House 1999– .

Shuster, "Bud" (R-Pa.) Jan. 23, 1932– ; House 1973– .

Simpson, Mike (R-Idaho) Sept. 8, 1950– ; House 1999– .

Sisisky, Norman (D-Va.) June 9, 1927– ; House 1983– .

Skaggs, David E. (D-Colo.) Feb. 22, 1943– ; House 1987–1999.

Skeen, Joseph R. (R-N.M.) June 30, 1927– ; House 1981– .

Skelton, Ike (D-Mo.) Dec. 20, 1931– ; House 1977– .

Slaughter, Louise M. (D-N.Y.) Aug. 14, 1929– ; House 1987– .

Smith, Adam (D-Wash.) June 15, 1965– ; House 1997– .

Smith, Christopher H. (R-N.J.) March 4, 1953– ; House 1981– .

Smith, Gordon H. (R-Ore.) May 25, 1952– ; Senate 1997– .

Smith, Lamar (R-Texas) Nov. 19, 1947– ; House 1987– .

Smith, Nick (R-Mich.) Nov. 5, 1934– ; House 1993– .

Smith, Robert C. (R-N.H.) March 30, 1941– ; House 1985–Dec. 7, 1990; Senate Dec. 7, 1990– .

Smith, Robert F. (R-Ore.) June 16, 1931– ; House 1983–1995, 1997–1999.

Snowbarger, Vince (R-Kan.) Sept. 16, 1949– ; House 1997–1999.

Snowe, Olympia J. (wife of John R. McKernan Jr.) (R-Maine) Feb. 21, 1947– ; House 1979–1995; Senate 1995– .

Snyder, Vic (D-Ark.) Sept. 27, 1947– ; House 1997– .

Solomon, Gerald B. H. (R-N.Y.) Aug. 14, 1930– ; House 1979–1999.

Souder, Mark (R-Ind.) July 18, 1950– ; House 1995– .

Specter, Arlen (R-Pa.) Feb. 12, 1930– ; Senate 1981– .

Spence, Floyd D. (R-S.C.) April 9, 1928– ; House 1971– .

Spratt, John M. Jr. (D-S.C.) Nov. 1, 1942– ; House 1983– .

Stabenow, Debbie (D-Mich.) April 29, 1950– ; House 1997–2001.

Stark, Fortney "Pete" (D-Calif.) Nov. 11, 1931– ; House 1973– .

Stearns, Cliff (R-Fla.) April 16, 1941– ; House 1989– .

Stenholm, Charles W. (D-Texas) Oct. 26, 1938– ; House 1979– .

Stevens, Ted (R-Alaska) Nov. 18, 1923– ; Senate Dec. 24, 1968– .

Stokes, Louis (D-Ohio) Feb. 23, 1925– ; House 1969–1999.

Strickland, Ted (D-Ohio) Aug. 4, 1941– ; House 1993–1995, 1997– .

Stump, Bob (R-Ariz.) April 4, 1927– ; House 1977– (1977–June 11, 1982, Democrat).

Stupak, Bart (D-Mich.) Feb. 29, 1952– ; House 1993– .

Sununu, John E. (R-N.H.) Sept. 10, 1964– ; House 1997– .

Sweeney, John E. (R-N.Y.) Aug. 9, 1955– ; House 1999– .

T

Talent, James M. (R-Mo.) Oct. 18, 1956– ; House 1993–2001.

Tancredo, Tom (R-Colo.) Dec. 20, 1945– ; House 1999– .

Tanner, John (D-Tenn.) Sept. 22, 1944– ; House 1989– .

Tauscher, Ellen O. (D-Calif.) Nov. 15, 1951– ; House 1997– .

Tauzin, W. J. "Billy" (R-La.) June 14, 1943– ; House May 17, 1980– (1980–Aug. 6, 1995, Democrat).

Taylor, Charles H. (R-N.C.) Jan. 23, 1941– ; House 1991– .

Taylor, Gene (D-Miss.) Sept. 17, 1953– ; House Oct. 24, 1989– .

Tejeda, Frank (D-Texas) Oct. 2, 1945–Jan. 30, 1997; House 1993–Jan. 30, 1997.

Terry, Lee (R-Neb.) Jan. 29, 1962– ; House 1999– .

Thomas, Craig (R-Wyo.) Feb. 17, 1933– ; House May 2, 1989–1995; Senate 1995– .

Thomas, William (R-Calif.) Dec. 6, 1941– ; House 1979– .

Thompson, Bennie (D-Miss.) Jan. 28, 1948– ; House April 20, 1993– .

Thompson, Fred (R-Tenn.) Aug. 19, 1942– ; Senate Dec. 9, 1994– .

Thompson, Mike (D-Calif.) Jan. 24, 1951– ; House 1999– .

Thornberry, William M. "Mac" (R-Texas) July 15, 1958– ; House 1995– .

Thune, John (R-S.D.) Jan. 7, 1961– ; House 1997– .

Thurman, Karen L. (D-Fla.) Jan. 12, 1951– ; House 1993– .

Thurmond, Strom (R-S.C.) Dec. 5, 1902– ; Senate Dec. 24, 1954–April 4, 1956, Nov. 1956– (1947–Sept. 16, 1964, Democrat); Gov. 1947–1951; Pres. pro tempore 1981–1987, 1995–2001.

Tiahrt, Todd (R-Kan.) June 15, 1951– ; House 1995– .

Tierney, John F. (D-Mass.) Sept. 18, 1951– ; House 1997– .

Toomey, Patrick J. (R-Pa.) Nov. 17, 1961– ; House 1999– .

Torres, Esteban E. (D-Calif.) Jan. 27, 1930– ; House 1983–1999.

Torricelli, Robert G. (D-N.J.) Aug. 26, 1951– ; House 1983–1997; Senate 1997– .

Towns, Edolphus (D-N.Y.) July 21, 1934– ; House 1983– .

Traficant, James A. Jr. (D-Ohio) May 8, 1941– ; House 1985– .

Turner, James (D-Texas) Feb. 6, 1946– ; House 1997– .

U

Udall, Mark (son of Morris K. Udall, cousin of Tom Udall) (D-Colo.) July 18, 1950– ; House 1999– .

Udall, Tom (son of Steward Udall, cousin of Mark Udall) (D-N.M.) May 18, 1948– ; House 1999– .

Underwood, Robert A. (D-Guam) July 13, 1948– ; House (delegate) 1993– .

Upton, Fred (R-Mich.) April 23, 1953– ; House 1987– .

V

Velázquez, Nydia M. (D-N.Y.) March 22, 1953– ; House 1993– .

Vento, Bruce F. (D-Minn.) Oct. 7, 1940–Oct. 10, 2000; House 1977–Oct. 10, 2000.

Visclosky, Peter J. (D-Ind.) Aug. 13, 1949– ; House 1985– .

Vitter, David (R-La.) May 3, 1961– ; House June 8, 1999– .

Voinovich, George V. (R-Ohio) July 15, 1936– ; Senate 1999– ; Gov. 1991–1998.

W

Walden, Greg (R-Ore.) Jan. 10, 1957– ; House 1999– .

Walsh, James T. (R-N.Y.) June 19, 1947– ; House 1989– .

Wamp, Zach (R-Tenn.) Oct. 28, 1957– ; House 1995– .

Warner, John W. (R-Va.) Feb. 18, 1927– ; Senate Jan. 2, 1979– .

Waters, Maxine (D-Calif.) Aug. 15, 1938– ; House 1991– .

Watkins, Wes (R-Okla.) Dec. 15, 1938– ; House 1997– .

Watt, Melvin (D-N.C.) Aug. 26, 1945– ; House 1993– .

Watts, J. C. Jr. (R-Okla.) Nov. 18, 1957– ; House 1995– .

Waxman, Henry A. (D-Calif.) Sept. 12, 1939– ; House 1975– .

Weiner, Anthony D. (D-N.Y.) Sept. 4, 1964– ; House 1999– .

Weldon, Curt (R-Pa.) July 22, 1947– ; House 1987– .

Weldon, Dave (R-Fla.) Aug. 31, 1953– ; House 1995– .

Weller, Jerry C. (R-Ill.) July 7, 1957– ; House 1995– .

Wellstone, Paul (D-Minn.) July 21, 1944– ; Senate 1991– .

Wexler, Robert (D-Fla.) Jan. 2, 1961– ; House 1997– .

Weygand, Robert A. (D-R.I.) May 19, 1948– ; House 1997–2001.

White, Rick (R-Wash.) Nov. 6, 1953– ; House 1995–1999.

Whitfield, Edward (R-Ky.) May 25, 1943– ; House 1995– .

Wicker, Roger (R-Miss.) July 5, 1951– ; House 1995– .

Wilson, Heather A. (R-N.M.) Dec. 30, 1960– ; House June 25, 1998– .

Wise, Robert (D-W.Va.) Jan. 6, 1948– ; House 1983–2001; Gov. 2001– .

Wolf, Frank R. (R-Va.) Jan. 30, 1939– ; House 1981– .

Woolsey, Lynn (D-Calif.) Nov. 3, 1937– ; House 1993– .

Wu, David (R-Ore.) April 8, 1955– ; House 1999– .

Wyden, Ron (D-Ore.) May 3, 1949– ; House 1981–Feb. 5, 1996; Senate Feb. 6, 1996– .

Wynn, Albert R. (D-Md.) Sept. 10, 1951– ; House 1993– .

Y

Yates, Sidney R. (D-Ill.) Aug. 27, 1909– ; House 1949–1963, 1965–1999.

Young, C. W. Bill (R-Fla.) Dec. 16, 1930– ; House 1971– .

Young, Don (R-Alaska) June 9, 1933– ; House March 6, 1973– .

Congressional Committees, 105th and 106th Congresses

Following is a list of congressional committees and subcommittees as of the start of the 105th and 106th Congresses. Committee jurisdictions, party ratios, committee chairmen and the dates of their service in that capacity, ranking minority members (in italics), and subcommittee chairmen are included. Political and joint committees also are listed.

In both the 105th and 106th Congresses the Senate and House committees and subcommittee chairmen are Republicans and ranking minority members are Democrats.

Party ratios for House committees do not include delegates or the resident commissioner.

Senate Committees

AGRICULTURE, NUTRITION AND FORESTRY

Agriculture in general; animal industry and diseases; crop insurance and soil conservation; farm credit and farm security; food from fresh waters; food stamp programs; forestry in general; home economics; human nutrition; inspection of livestock, meat, and agricultural products; pests and pesticides; plant industry, soils, and agricultural engineering; rural development, rural electrification, and watersheds; school nutrition programs.

R 10–D 8 *(105th Congress)*

Richard G. Lugar, Ind.
Tom Harkin, Iowa

Forestry, Conservation and Rural Revitalization—Rick Santorum, Pa.
Marketing, Inspection and Product Promotion—Paul Coverdell, Ga.
Production and Price Competitiveness—Thad Cochran, Miss.
Research, Nutrition and General Legislation—Mitch McConnell, Ky.

R 10–D 8 *(106th Congress)*

Richard G. Lugar, Ind.
Tom Harkin, Iowa

Forestry, Conservation and Rural Revitalization—Larry E. Craig, Idaho
Marketing, Inspection and Product Promotion—Paul Coverdell, Ga.
Production and Price Competitiveness—Pat Roberts, Kan.
Research, Nutrition and General Legislation—Peter G. Fitzgerald, Ill.

APPROPRIATIONS

Appropriation of revenue; rescission of appropriations; new spending authority under the Congressional Budget Act.

R 15–D 13 *(105th Congress)*

Ted Stevens, Alaska
Robert C. Byrd, W.Va.

Agriculture, Rural Development and Related Agencies—Thad Cochran, Miss.
Commerce, Justice, State and Judiciary—Judd Gregg, N.H.
Defense—Ted Stevens, Alaska
District of Columbia—Lauch Faircloth, N.C.
Energy and Water Development—Pete V. Domenici, N.M.
Foreign Operations—Mitch McConnell, Ky.
Interior—Slade Gorton, Wash.
Labor, Health and Human Services and Education—Arlen Specter, Pa.
Legislative Branch—Robert F. Bennett, Utah
Military Construction—Conrad Burns, Mont.
Transportation—Richard C. Shelby, Ala.
Treasury and General Government—Ben Nighthorse Campbell, Colo.
VA, HUD and Independent Agencies—Christopher S. Bond, Mo.

R 15–D 13 *(106th Congress)*

Ted Stevens, Alaska
Robert C. Byrd, W.Va.

Agriculture, Rural Development and Related Agencies—Thad Cochran, Miss.
Commerce, Justice, State and Judiciary—Judd Gregg, N.H.
Defense—Ted Stevens, Alaska
District of Columbia—Kay Bailey Hutchison, Texas
Energy and Water Development—Pete V. Domenici, N.M.
Foreign Operations—Mitch McConnell, Ky.
Interior—Slade Gorton, Wash.
Labor, Health and Human Services and Education—Arlen Specter, Pa.
Legislative Branch—Robert F. Bennett, Utah
Military Construction—Conrad Burns, Mont.
Transportation—Richard C. Shelby, Ala.
Treasury and General Government—Ben Nighthorse Campbell, Colo.
VA, HUD and Independent Agencies—Christopher S. Bond, Mo.

ARMED SERVICES

Defense and defense policy generally; aeronautical and space activities peculiar to or primarily associated with the development of weapons systems or military operations; maintenance and operation of the Panama Canal, including the Canal Zone; military research and development; national security aspects of nuclear energy; naval petroleum reserves (except Alaska); armed forces generally; Selective Service System; strategic and critical materials.

R 10–D 8 (105th Congress)

Strom Thurmond, S.C.
Carl Levin, Mich.

Acquisition and Technology—Rick Santorum, Pa.
Airland Forces—Daniel R. Coats, Ind.
Personnel—Dirk Kempthorne, Idaho
Readiness—James M. Inhofe, Okla.
Seapower—John W. Warner, Va.
Strategic Forces—Robert C. Smith, N.H.

R 11–D 9 (106th Congress)

John W. Warner, Va.
Carl Levin, Mich.

Airland Forces—Rick Santorum, Pa.
Emerging Threats and Capabilities—Pat Roberts, Kan.
Personnel—Wayne Allard, Colo.
Readiness and Management Support—James M. Inhofe, Okla.
Seapower—Olympia J. Snowe, Maine
Strategic Forces—Robert C. Smith, N.H.

BANKING, HOUSING AND URBAN AFFAIRS

Banks, banking, and financial institutions; price controls; deposit insurance; economic stabilization and growth; defense production; export and foreign trade promotion; export controls; federal monetary policy, including Federal Reserve System; financial aid to commerce and industry; issuance and redemption of notes; money and credit, including currency and coinage; nursing home construction; public and private housing, including veterans' housing; renegotiation of government contracts; urban development and mass transit; international economic policy.

R 10–D 8 (105th Congress)

Alfonse M. D'Amato, N.Y.
Paul S. Sarbanes, Md.

Financial Institutions and Regulatory Relief—Lauch Faircloth, N.C.
Financial Services and Technology—Robert F. Bennett, Utah
Housing Opportunity and Community Development—Connie Mack, Fla.
International Finance—Rod Grams, Minn.
Securities—Phil Gramm, Texas

R 11–D 9 (106th Congress)

Phil Gramm, Texas
Paul S. Sarbanes, Md.

Economic Policy—Connie Mack, Fla.
Financial Institutions—Robert F. Bennett, Utah

Housing and Transportation—Wayne Allard, Colo.
International Trade and Finance—Michael B. Enzi, Wyo.
Securities—Rod Grams, Minn.

BUDGET

Federal budget generally; concurrent budget resolutions; Congressional Budget Office.

R 12–D 10 (105th Congress)

Pete V. Domenici, N.M.
Frank R. Lautenberg, N.J.

R 12–D 10 (106th Congress)

Pete V. Domenici, N.M.
Frank R. Lautenberg, N.J.

No standing subcommittees.

COMMERCE, SCIENCE AND TRANSPORTATION

Interstate commerce and transportation generally; Coast Guard; coastal zone management; communications; highway safety; inland waterways, except construction; marine fisheries; Merchant Marine and navigation; nonmilitary aeronautical and space sciences; oceans, weather, and atmospheric activities; interoceanic canals generally; regulation of consumer products and services; science, engineering, and technology research, development and policy; sports; standards and measurement; transportation and commerce aspects of outer continental shelf lands.

R 11–D 9 (105th Congress)

John McCain, Ariz.
Ernest F. Hollings, S.C.

Aviation—Slade Gorton, Wash.
Communications—Conrad Burns, Mont.
Consumer Affairs, Foreign Commerce and Tourism—John Ashcroft, Mo.
Manufacturing and Competitiveness—Spencer Abraham, Mich.
Oceans and Fisheries—Olympia J. Snowe, Maine
Science, Technology and Space—Bill Frist, Tenn.
Surface Transportation and Merchant Marine—Kay Bailey Hutchison, Texas

R 11–D 9 (106th Congress)

John McCain, Ariz.
Ernest F. Hollings, S.C.

Aviation—Slade Gorton, Wash.
Communications—Conrad Burns, Mont.
Consumer Affairs, Foreign Commerce and Tourism—John Ashcroft, Mo.
Manufacturing and Competitiveness—Spencer Abraham, Mich.
Oceans and Fisheries—Olympia J. Snowe, Maine

Science, Technology and Space—Bill Frist, Tenn.
Surface Transportation and Merchant Marine—Kay Bailey Hutchison, Texas

ENERGY AND NATURAL RESOURCES

Energy policy, regulation, conservation, research, and development; coal; energy-related aspects of deep-water ports; hydroelectric power, irrigation, and reclamation; mines, mining, and minerals generally; national parks, recreation areas, wilderness areas, wild and scenic rivers, historic sites, military parks, and battlefields; naval petroleum reserves in Alaska; nonmilitary development of nuclear energy; oil and gas production and distribution; public lands and forests; solar energy systems; territorial possessions of the United States.

R 11–D 9 *(105th Congress)*

Frank H. Murkowski, Alaska
Dale Bumpers, Ark.

Energy Research, Development, Production and Regulation—Don Nickles, Okla.
Forests and Public Land Management—Larry E. Craig, Idaho
National Parks, Historic Preservation and Recreation—Craig Thomas, Wyo.
Water and Power—Jon Kyl, Ariz.

R 11–D 9 *(106th Congress)*

Frank H. Murkowski, Alaska
Jeff Bingaman, N.M.

Energy Research, Development, Production and Regulation—Don Nickles, Okla.
Forests and Public Land Management—Larry E. Craig, Idaho
National Parks, Historic Preservation and Recreation—Craig Thomas, Wyo.
Water and Power—Gordon H. Smith, Ore.

ENVIRONMENT AND PUBLIC WORKS

Environmental policy, research, and development; air, water, and noise pollution; construction and maintenance of highways; environmental aspects of outer continental shelf lands; environmental effects of toxic substances other than pesticides; fisheries and wildlife; flood control and improvements of rivers and harbors; nonmilitary environmental regulation and control of nuclear energy; ocean dumping; public buildings and grounds; public works, bridges, and dams; regional economic development; solid waste disposal and recycling; water resources.

R 10–D 8 *(105th Congress)*

John H. Chafee, R.I.
Max Baucus, Mont.

Clean Air, Wetlands, Private Property and Nuclear Safety—James M. Inhofe, Okla.
Drinking Water, Fisheries and Wildlife—Dirk Kempthorne, Idaho

Superfund, Waste Control and Risk Assessment—Robert C. Smith, N.H.
Transportation and Infrastructure—John W. Warner, Va.

R 10–D 8 *(106th Congress)*

John H. Chafee, R.I.
Max Baucus, Mont.

Clean Air, Wetlands, Private Property and Nuclear Safety—James M. Inhofe, Okla.
Fisheries, Wildlife and Drinking Water—Michael D. Crapo, Idaho
Superfund, Waste Control and Risk Assessment—Robert C. Smith, N.H.
Transportation and Infrastructure—George V. Voinovich, Ohio

FINANCE

Revenue measures generally; taxes; tariffs and import quotas; reciprocal trade agreements; customs; revenue sharing; federal debt limit; Social Security; health programs financed by taxes or trust funds.

R 11–D 9 *(105th Congress)*

William V. Roth Jr., Del.
Daniel Patrick Moynihan, N.Y.

Health Care—Phil Gramm, Texas
International Trade—Charles E. Grassley, Iowa
Long-Term Growth, Debt and Deficit Reduction—Connie Mack, Fla.
Social Security and Family Policy—John H. Chafee, R.I.
Taxation and IRS Oversight—Don Nickles, Okla.

R 11–D 9 *(106th Congress)*

William V. Roth Jr., Del.
Daniel Patrick Moynihan, N.Y.

Health Care—John H. Chafee, R.I.
International Trade—Charles E. Grassley, Iowa
Long-Term Growth and Debt Reduction—Frank H. Murkowski, Alaska
Social Security and Family Policy—Don Nickles, Okla.
Taxation and IRS Oversight—Orrin G. Hatch, Utah

FOREIGN RELATIONS

Relations of the United States with foreign nations generally; treaties; foreign economic, military, technical, and humanitarian assistance; foreign loans; diplomatic service; International Red Cross; international aspects of nuclear energy; International Monetary Fund; intervention abroad and declarations of war; foreign trade; national security; oceans and international environmental and scientific affairs; protection of U.S. citizens abroad; United Nations; World Bank and other development assistance organizations.

R 10–D 8 (*105th Congress*)

Jesse Helms, N.C.
Joseph R. Biden Jr., Del.

African Affairs—John Ashcroft, Mo.
East Asian and Pacific Affairs—Craig Thomas, Wyo.
European Affairs—Gordon H. Smith, Ore.
International Economic Policy, Export and Trade Promotion—Chuck Hagel, Neb.
International Operations—Rod Grams, Minn.
Near Eastern and South Asian Affairs—Sam Brownback, Kan.
Western Hemisphere, Peace Corps, Narcotics and Terrorism—Paul Coverdell, Ga.

R 10–D 8 (*106th Congress*)

Jesse Helms, N.C.
Joseph R. Biden Jr., Del.

African Affairs—Bill Frist, Tenn.
East Asian and Pacific Affairs—Craig Thomas, Wyo.
European Affairs—Gordon H. Smith, Ore.
International Economic Policy, Export and Trade Promotion—Chuck Hagel, Neb.
International Operations—Rod Grams, Minn.
Near Eastern and South Asian Affairs—Sam Brownback, Kan.
Western Hemisphere, Peace Corps, Narcotics and Terrorism—Paul Coverdell, Ga.

GOVERNMENTAL AFFAIRS

Archives of the United States; budget and accounting measures; census and statistics; federal civil service; congressional organization; intergovernmental relations; government information; District of Columbia; organization and management of nuclear export policy; executive branch organization and reorganization; Postal Service; efficiency, economy, and effectiveness of government.

R 9–D 7 (*105th Congress*)

Fred Thompson, Tenn.
John Glenn, Ohio

International Security, Proliferation and Federal Services—Thad Cochran, Miss.
Investigations—Susan Collins, Maine
Oversight of Government Management, Restructuring and the District of Columbia—Sam Brownback, Kan.

R 9–D 7 (*106th Congress*)

Fred Thompson, Tenn.
Joseph I. Lieberman, Conn.

International Security, Proliferation and Federal Services—Thad Cochran, Miss.
Investigations—Susan Collins, Maine
Oversight of Government Management, Restructuring and the District of Columbia—George V. Voinovich, Ohio

HEALTH, EDUCATION, LABOR AND PENSIONS[1]

Education, labor, health, and public welfare in general; aging; arts and humanities; biomedical research and development; child labor; convict labor; domestic activities of the Red Cross; equal employment opportunity; disabled people; labor standards and statistics; mediation and arbitration of labor disputes; occupational safety and health; private pensions; public health; railway labor and retirement; regulation of foreign laborers; student loans; wages and hours; agricultural colleges; Gallaudet University; Howard University; St. Elizabeth's Hospital in Washington, D.C.

R 10–D 8 (*106th Congress*)

James M. Jeffords, Vt.
Edward M. Kennedy, Mass.

Aging—Mike DeWine, Ohio
Children and Families—Judd Gregg, N.H.
Employment, Safety and Training—Michael B. Enzi, Wyo.
Public Health—Bill Frist, Tenn.

INDIAN AFFAIRS

Problems and opportunities of Native Americans, including Native American land management and trust responsibilities, education, health, special services, loan programs, and claims against the United States.

R 8–D 6 (*105th Congress*)

Ben Nighthorse Campbell, Colo.
Daniel K. Inouye, Hawaii

R 8–D 6 (*106th Congress*)

Ben Nighthorse Campbell, Colo.
Daniel K. Inouye, Hawaii

No standing subcommittees.

JUDICIARY

Civil and criminal judicial proceedings in general; penitentiaries; bankruptcy, mutiny, espionage, and counterfeiting; civil liberties; constitutional amendments; apportionment of representatives; government information; immigration and naturalization; interstate compacts in general; claims against the United States; patents, copyrights, and trademarks; monopolies and unlawful restraints of trade; holidays and celebrations.

R 10–D 8 (*105th Congress*)

Orrin G. Hatch, Utah
Patrick J. Leahy, Vt.

Administrative Oversight and the Courts—Charles E. Grassley, Iowa
Antitrust, Business Rights and Competition—Mike DeWine, Ohio

Constitution, Federalism and Property Rights—John Ashcroft, Mo.

Immigration—Spencer Abraham, Mich.

Technology, Terrorism and Government Information—Jon Kyl, Ariz.

Youth Violence—Jeff Sessions, Ala.

R 10–D 8 *(106th Congress)*

Orrin G. Hatch, Utah

Patrick J. Leahy, Vt.

Administrative Oversight and the Courts—Charles E. Grassley, Iowa

Antitrust, Business Rights and Competition—Mike DeWine, Ohio

Constitution, Federalism and Property Rights—John Ashcroft, Mo.

Criminal Justice Oversight—Strom Thurmond, S.C.

Immigration—Spencer Abraham, Mich.

Technology, Terrorism and Government Information—Jon Kyl, Ariz.

Youth Violence—Jeff Sessions, Ala.

LABOR AND HUMAN RESOURCES[2]

Education, labor, health, and public welfare in general; aging; arts and humanities; biomedical research and development; child labor; convict labor; domestic activities of the Red Cross; equal employment opportunity; disabled people; labor standards and statistics; mediation and arbitration of labor disputes; occupational safety and health; private pensions; public health; railway labor and retirement; regulation of foreign laborers; student loans; wages and hours; agricultural colleges; Gallaudet University; Howard University; St. Elizabeth's Hospital in Washington, D.C.

R 10–D 8 *(105th Congress)*

James M. Jeffords, Vt.

Edward M. Kennedy, Mass.

Aging—Judd Gregg, N.H.

Children and Families—Daniel R. Coats, Ind.

Employment and Training—Mike DeWine, Ohio

Public Health and Safety—Bill Frist, Tenn.

RULES AND ADMINISTRATION

Senate administration in general; corrupt practices; qualifications of senators; contested elections; federal elections in general; Government Printing Office; *Congressional Record*; meetings of Congress and attendance of members; presidential succession; the Capitol, congressional office buildings, the Library of Congress, the Smithsonian Institution, and the Botanic Garden.

R 9–D 7 *(105th Congress)*

John W. Warner, Va.

Wendell H. Ford, Ky.

R 9–D 7 *(106th Congress)*

Mitch McConnell, Ky.

Christopher J. Dodd, Conn.

No standing subcommittees.

SELECT ETHICS

Studies and investigates standards and conduct of Senate members and employees and may recommend remedial action.

R 3–D 3 *(105th Congress)*

Robert C. Smith, N.H.

Harry Reid, Nev. (vice chairman)

R 3–D 3 *(106th Congress)*

Robert C. Smith, N.H.

Harry Reid, Nev. (vice chairman)

No standing subcommittees.

SELECT INTELLIGENCE

Legislative and budgetary authority over the Central Intelligence Agency, the Defense Intelligence Agency, the National Security Agency, and intelligence activities of the Federal Bureau of Investigation and other components of the federal intelligence community.

R 10–D 9 *(105th Congress)*

Richard C. Shelby, Ala.

Bob Kerrey, Neb.

R 9–D 8 *(106th Congress)*

Richard C. Shelby, Ala.

Bob Kerrey, Neb.

No standing subcommittees.

SMALL BUSINESS

Problems of small business; Small Business Administration.

R 10–D 8 *(105th Congress)*

Christopher S. Bond, Mo.

John Kerry, Mass.

R 10–D 8 *(106th Congress)*

Christopher S. Bond, Mo.

John Kerry, Mass.

No standing subcommittees.

SPECIAL AGING

Problems and opportunities of older people including health, income, employment, housing, and care and assistance. Reports findings and makes recommendations to the Senate, but cannot report legislation.

R 10–D 8 *(105th Congress)*

Charles E. Grassley, Iowa
John B. Breaux, La.

R 11–D 9 *(106th Congress)*

Charles E. Grassley, Iowa
John B. Breaux, La.

No standing subcommittees.

VETERANS' AFFAIRS

Veterans' measures in general; compensation; life insurance issued by the government on account of service in the armed forces; national cemeteries; pensions; readjustment benefits; veterans' hospitals, medical care and treatment; vocational rehabilitation and education.

R 7–D 5 *(105th Congress)*

Arlen Specter, Pa.
John D. Rockefeller IV, W.Va.

R 7–D 5 *(106th Congress)*

Arlen Specter, Pa.
John D. Rockefeller IV, W.Va.

No standing subcommittees.

SPECIAL COMMITTEE ON THE YEAR 2000 TECHNOLOGY PROBLEM[3]

Study the impact of the year 2000 technology problem on the executive and judicial branches of the federal government, state governments, and private-sector operations in the United States and abroad; make such findings of fact as are warranted and appropriate; and make such recommendations, including recommendations for new legislation and amendments to existing laws and any administrative or other actions, as the special committee may determine to be necessary or desirable. No proposed legislation shall be referred to the special committee, and the committee shall not have power to report by bill, or otherwise have legislative jurisdiction.

R 4–D 3 *(106th Congress)*

Robert F. Bennett, Utah
Christopher J. Dodd, Conn.

POLITICAL COMMITTEES

Democratic Policy Committee (an arm of the Democratic Caucus that advises on legislative priorities)—Tom Daschle, S.D., chairman (105th and 106th Congresses)

Democratic Senatorial Campaign Committee (campaign support committee for Democratic senatorial candidates)—Bob Kerrey, Neb., chairman (105th Congress); Robert G. Torricelli, N.J., chairman (106th Congress)

Democratic Steering and Coordination Committee (makes Democratic committee assignments)—John Kerry, Mass., chairman (105th and 106th Congresses)

Democratic Technology and Communications Committee (seeks to improve communications with the public about the Democratic Party and its policies)—John D. Rockefeller IV, W.Va., chairman (105th and 106th Congresses)

National Republican Senatorial Committee (campaign support committee for Republican senatorial candidates)—Mitch McConnell, Ky., chairman (105th and 106th Congresses)

Republican Committee on Committees (makes Republican committee assignments)—Slade Gorton, Wash., chairman (105th and 106th Congresses)

Republican Policy Committee (advises on party action and policy)—Larry E. Craig, Idaho, chairman (105th and 106th Congresses)

House Committees

AGRICULTURE

Agriculture generally; forestry in general, and forest reserves other than those created from the public domain; adulteration of seeds, insect pests, and protection of birds and animals in forest reserves; agricultural and industrial chemistry; agricultural colleges and experiment stations; agricultural economics and research; agricultural education extension services; agricultural production and marketing and stabilization of prices of agricultural products, and commodities (not including distribution outside the United States); animal industry and diseases of animals; commodities exchanges; crop insurance and soil conservation; dairy industry; entomology and plant quarantine; extension of farm credit and farm security; inspection of livestock, poultry, meat products, seafood and seafood products; human nutrition and home economics; plant industry, soils, and agricultural engineering; rural electrification; rural development; water conservation related to activities of the Department of Agriculture.

R 27–D 23 *(105th Congress)*

Bob Smith, Ore.
Charles W. Stenholm, Texas

Department Operations, Nutrition and Foreign Agriculture—Robert W. Goodlatte, Va.
Forestry, Resource Conservation and Research—Larry Combest, Texas
General Farm Commodities—Bill Barrett, Neb.
Livestock, Dairy and Poultry—Richard W. Pombo, Calif.
Risk Management and Specialty Crops—Thomas W. Ewing, Ill.

R 27–D 24 *(106th Congress)*

Larry Combest, Texas
Charles W. Stenholm, Texas

Department Operations, Oversight, Nutrition and Forestry—Robert W. Goodlatte, Va.

General Farm Commodities, Resource Conservation and Credit—Bill Barrett, Neb.

Livestock and Horticulture—Richard W. Pombo, Calif.

Risk Management, Research and Specialty Crops—Thomas W. Ewing, Ill.

APPROPRIATIONS

Appropriation of the revenue for the support of the government; rescissions of appropriations contained in appropriation acts; transfers of unexpended balances; new spending authority under the Congressional Budget Act.

R 34–D 26 *(105th Congress)*

Robert L. Livingston, La.
David R. Obey, Wis.

Agriculture, Rural Development, FDA and Related Agencies—Joe Skeen, N.M.

Commerce, Justice, State and Judiciary—Harold Rogers, Ky.

District of Columbia—Charles H. Taylor, N.C.

Energy and Water Development—Joseph M. McDade, Pa.

Foreign Operations, Export Financing and Related Programs—Sonny Callahan, Ala.

Interior—Ralph Regula, Ohio

Labor, Health and Human Services and Education—John Edward Porter, Ill.

Legislative—James T. Walsh, N.Y.

Military Construction—Ron Packard, Calif.

National Security—C. W. Bill Young, Fla.

Transportation—Frank R. Wolf, Va.

Treasury, Postal Service and General Government—Jim Kolbe, Ariz.

Veterans Affairs, Housing and Urban Development and Independent Agencies—Jerry Lewis, Calif.

R 34–D 27 *106th Congress*

C. W. Bill Young, Fla.
David R. Obey, Wis.

Agriculture, Rural Development, FDA and Related Agencies—Joe Skeen, N.M.

Commerce, Justice, State and Judiciary—Harold Rogers, Ky.

Defense—Jerry Lewis, Calif.

District of Columbia—Ernest Istook, Okla.

Energy and Water Development—Ron Packard, Calif.

Foreign Operations, Export Financing and Related Programs—Sonny Callahan, Ala.

Interior—Ralph Regula, Ohio

Labor, Health and Human Services and Education—John Edward Porter, Ill.

Legislative Branch—Charles H. Taylor, N.C.

Military Construction—David L. Hobson, Ohio

Transportation—Frank R. Wolf, Va.

Treasury, Postal Service and General Government—Jim Kolbe, Ariz.

Veterans Affairs, Housing and Urban Development and Independent Agencies—James T. Walsh, N.Y.

ARMED SERVICES[4]

Ammunition depots; forts; arsenals; Army, Navy, and Air Force reservations and establishments; common defense generally; conservation, development, and use of naval petroleum and oil shale reserves; Department of Defense generally, including the Departments of the Army, Navy, and Air Force generally; interoceanic canals generally; including measures relating to the maintenance, operation, and administration of interoceanic canals; Merchant Marine Academy, and state maritime academies; military applications of nuclear energy; tactical intelligence and intelligence related activities of the Department of Defense; national security aspects of merchant marine, including financial assistance for the construction and operation of vessels, the maintenance of the U.S. shipbuilding and ship repair industrial base, cabotage, cargo preference, and merchant marine officers and seamen as these matters relate to the national security; pay, promotion, retirement, and other benefits and privileges of members of the armed forces; scientific research and development in support of the armed services; selective service; size and composition of the Army, Navy, Marine Corps, and Air Force; soldiers' and sailors' homes; strategic and critical materials necessary for the common defense.

R 32–D 28 *(106th Congress)*

Floyd D. Spence, S.C.
Ike Skelton, Mo.

Merchant Marine—Herbert H. Bateman, Va.

Military Installations and Facilities—Joel Hefley, Colo.

Military Personnel—Steve Buyer, Ind.

Military Procurement—Duncan Hunter, Calif.

Military Readiness—Herbert H. Bateman, Va.

Military Research and Development—Curt Weldon, Pa.

Morale, Welfare and Recreation—John M. McHugh, N.Y.

BANKING AND FINANCIAL SERVICES

Banks and banking, including deposit insurance and federal monetary policy; bank capital markets activities generally; depository institution securities activities generally, including the activities of any affiliates, except for functional regulation under applicable securities laws not involving safety and soundness; economic stabilization, defense production, renegotiation, and control of the price of commodities, rents, and services; financial aid to commerce and industry (other than transportation); international finance; international financial and monetary organizations; money and credit, including currency and the issuance of notes and redemption thereof; gold and silver, including the coinage thereof; valuation and revaluation of the dollar; public and private housing; urban development.

R 30–D 25–I 1 *(105th Congress)*

Jim Leach, Iowa
Henry B. Gonzalez, Texas

Capital Markets, Securities and Government-Sponsored Enterprises—Richard H. Baker, La.

Domestic and International Monetary Policy—Michael N. Castle, Del.

Financial Institutions and Consumer Credit—Marge Roukema, N.J.

General Oversight and Investigations—Spencer Bachus, Ala.

Housing and Community Opportunity—Rick A. Lazio, N.Y.

R 32–D 27–I 1 *(106th Congress)*

Jim Leach, Iowa

John J. LaFalce, N.Y.

Capital Markets, Securities and Government-Sponsored Enterprises—Richard H. Baker, La.

Domestic and International Monetary Policy—Spencer Bachus, Ala.

Financial Institutions and Consumer Credit—Marge Roukema, N.J.

General Oversight and Investigations—Peter T. King, N.Y.

Housing and Community Opportunity—Rick A. Lazio, N.Y.

BUDGET

Congressional budget process generally; concurrent budget resolutions; measures relating to special controls over the federal budget; Congressional Budget Office.

R 24–D 19 *(105th Congress)*

John R. Kasich, Ohio

John M. Spratt Jr., S.C.

R 24–D 19 *(106th Congress)*

John R. Kasich, Ohio

John M. Spratt Jr., S.C.

No standing subcommittees.

CHINA INVESTIGATION[5]

Conduct a full and complete inquiry regarding the following matters and report such findings and recommendations, including those concerning the amendment of existing law or the enactment of new law, to the House as it considers appropriate: (1) The transfer of technology, information, advice, goods, or services that may have contributed to the enhancement of the accuracy, reliability, or capability of nuclear-armed intercontinental ballistic missiles or other weapons of the People's Republic of China, or that may have contributed to the enhancement of the intelligence capabilities of the People's Republic of China. (2) The transfer of technology, information, advice, goods, or services that may have contributed to the manufacture of weapons of mass destruction, missiles or other weapons or armaments by the People's Republic of China. (3) The effect of any transfer or enhancement referred to in paragraphs 1 or 2 on regional security and the national security of the United States. (4) The conduct of the executive branch of the United States government with respect to the transfers or enhancements referred to in paragraphs 1 or 2, and the effect of that conduct on regional security and the national security

of the United States. (5) The conduct of defense contractors, weapons manufactures, satellite manufacturers, and other private or government-owned commercial firms with respect to the transfers or enhancements referred to in paragraphs 1 or 2. (7) Any effort by the government of the People's Republic of China or any other person or entity to influence any of the foregoing matters through political contributions, commercial arrangements, or bribery, influence-peddling, or other illegal activities. (8) Decision-making within the executive branch of the United States government with respect to any of the foregoing matters. (9) Any effort to conceal or withhold information or documents relevant to any of the foregoing matters or to obstruct justice, or to obstruct the work of the Select Committee or any other committee of the House of Representatives in connection with those matters. (10) All matters relating directly or indirectly to any of the foregoing matters.

R 5–D 4 *(106th Congress)*

Christopher Cox, Calif.

Norm Dicks, Wash.

COMMERCE

Interstate and foreign commerce generally; biomedical research and development; consumer affairs and consumer protection; health and health facilities, except health care supported by payroll deductions; interstate energy compacts; measures relating to the exploration, production, storage, supply, marketing, pricing, and regulation of energy resources, including all fossil fuels, solar energy, and other unconventional or renewable energy resources; measures relating to the conservation of energy resources; measures relating to energy information generally; measures relating to (1) the generation and marketing of power (except by federally chartered or federal regional power marketing authorities), (2) the reliability and interstate transmission of, and ratemaking for, all power, and (3) the siting of generation facilities, except the installation of interconnections between government water power projects; measures relating to general management of the Department of Energy, and the management and all functions of the Federal Energy Regulatory Commission; national energy policy generally; public health and quarantine; regulation of the domestic nuclear energy industry, including regulation of research and development reactors and nuclear regulatory research; regulation of interstate and foreign communications; securities and exchanges; travel and tourism; nuclear and other energy, and nonmilitary nuclear energy and research and development including the disposal of nuclear waste.

R 28–D 23 *(105th Congress)*

Thomas J. Bliley Jr., Va.

John D. Dingell, Mich.

Energy and Power—Dan Schaefer, Colo.

Finance and Hazardous Materials—Michael G. Oxley, Ohio

Health and Environment—Michael Bilirakis, Fla.

Oversight and Investigations—Joe L. Barton, Texas

Telecommunications, Trade and Consumer Protection—W. J. "Billy" Tauzin, La.

R 29–D 24 *(106th Congress)*

Thomas J. Bliley Jr., Va.
John D. Dingell, Mich.

Energy and Power—Joe L. Barton, Texas
Finance and Hazardous Materials—Michael G. Oxley, Ohio
Health and Environment—Michael Bilirakis, Fla.
Oversight and Investigations—Fred Upton, Mich.
Telecommunications, Trade and Consumer Protection—W. J. "Billy" Tauzin, La.

EDUCATION AND THE WORKFORCE

Measures relating to education or labor generally; child labor; Columbia Institution for the Deaf, Dumb and Blind; Howard University; Freedmen's Hospital; convict labor and the entry of goods made by convicts into interstate commerce; food programs for children in schools; labor standards and statistics; mediation and arbitration of labor disputes; regulation or prevention of importation of foreign laborers under contract; U.S. Employees' Compensation Commission; vocational rehabilitation; wages and hours of labor; welfare of miners; work incentive programs.

R 25–D 20 *(105th Congress)*

Bill Goodling, Pa.
William L. Clay, Mo.

Early Childhood, Youth and Families—Frank Riggs, Calif.
Employer-Employee Relations—Harris W. Fawell, Ill.
Oversight and Investigations—Peter Hoekstra, Mich.
Postsecondary Education, Training and Life-Long Learning—Howard P. "Buck" McKeon, Calif.
Workforce Protections—Cass Ballenger, N.C.

R 27–D 22 *(106th Congress)*

Bill Goodling, Pa.
William L. Clay, Mo.

Early Childhood, Youth and Families—Michael N. Castle, Del.
Employer-Employee Relations—John A. Boehner, Ohio
Oversight and Investigations—Peter Hoekstra, Mich.
Postsecondary Education, Training and Life-Long Learning—Howard P. "Buck" McKeon, Calif.
Workforce Protections—Cass Ballenger, N.C.

GOVERNMENT REFORM AND OVERSIGHT

Civil service, including intergovernmental personnel; the status of officers and employees of the United States, including their compensation, classification, and retirement; measures relating to the municipal affairs of the District of Columbia in general, other than appropriations; federal paperwork reduction; budget and accounting measures, generally; holidays and celebrations; overall economy, efficiency, and management of government operations and activities, including federal procurement; National Archives; population and demography generally, including the census; Postal Service generally, including the transportation of mail; public information and records; relationship of the federal government to the states and municipalities generally; reorganizations in the executive branch of the government.

R 24–D 19–I 1 *(105th Congress)*

Dan Burton, Ind.
Henry A. Waxman, Calif.

Civil Service—John L. Mica, Fla.
District of Columbia—Thomas M. Davis III, Va.
Government Management, Information and Technology—Steve Horn, Calif.
Human Resources—Christopher Shays, Conn.
National Economic Growth, Natural Resources and Regulatory Affairs—David M. McIntosh, Ind.
National Security, International Affairs and Criminal Justice—Dennis Hastert, Ill.
Postal Service—John M. McHugh, N.Y.

R 24–D 19–I 1 *(106th Congress)*

Dan Burton, Ind.
Henry A. Waxman, Calif.

Civil Service—Joe Scarborough, Fla.
Criminal Justice, Drug Policy and Human Resources—John L. Mica, Fla.
District of Columbia—Thomas M. Davis III, Va.
Government Management, Information and Technology—Steve Horn, Calif.
National Economic Growth, Natural Resources and Regulatory Affairs—David M. McIntosh, Ind.
National Security, Veterans Affairs and International Relations—Christopher Shays, Conn.
Postal Service—John M. McHugh, N.Y.

HOUSE OVERSIGHT

Accounts of the House generally; assignment of office space for members and committees; disposition of useless executive papers; matters relating to the election of the president, vice president, or members of Congress; corrupt practices; contested elections; credentials and qualifications; federal elections generally; appropriations from accounts for committee salaries and expenses (except for the Committee on Appropriations), House Information Systems, and allowances and expenses of members, House officers, and administrative offices of the House; auditing and settling of all such accounts; expenditure of such accounts; employment of persons by the House, including clerks for members and committees, and reporters of debates; Library of Congress and the House Library; statuary and pictures; acceptance or purchase of works of art for the Capitol; the Botanic Garden; management of the Library of Congress; purchase of books and manuscripts; Smithsonian Institution and the incorporation of similar institutions; Franking Commission; printing and correction of the *Congressional Record*; services to the House, including the House restaurant, parking facilities, and administration of the House office buildings and of the House wing of the Capitol; travel of members of the House; raising, reporting, and use of campaign contributions for candidates for office of representative in the House of Representatives, of delegate, and of resident commissioner to the United States from Puerto Rico; compensation, retirement and other benefits of the members, officers, and employees of the Congress.

R 6–D 3 *(105th Congress)*

Bill Thomas, Calif.
Sam Gejdenson, Conn.

R 6–D 3 *(106th Congress)*

Bill Thomas, Calif.
Steny H. Hoyer, Md.

No standing subcommittees.

INTERNATIONAL RELATIONS

Relations of the United States with foreign nations generally; acquisition of land and buildings for embassies and legations in foreign countries; establishment of boundary lines between the United States and foreign nations; export controls, including nonproliferation of nuclear technology and nuclear hardware; foreign loans; international commodity agreements (other than those involving sugar), including all agreements for cooperation in the export of nuclear technology and nuclear hardware; international conferences and congresses; international education; intervention abroad and declarations of war; measures relating to the diplomatic service; measures to foster commercial intercourse with foreign nations and to safeguard American business interests abroad; measures relating to international economic policy; neutrality; protection of American citizens abroad and expatriation; American National Red Cross; trading with the enemy; U.N. organizations.

R 26–D 22 *(105th Congress)*

Benjamin A. Gilman, N.Y.
Lee H. Hamilton, Ind.

Africa—Ed Royce, Calif.
Asia and the Pacific—Doug Bereuter, Neb.
International Economic Policy and Trade—Ileana Ros-Lehtinen, Fla.
International Operations and Human Rights—Christopher H. Smith, N.J.
Western Hemisphere—Elton Gallegly, Calif.

R 26–D 23 *(106th Congress)*

Benjamin A. Gilman, N.Y.
Sam Gejdenson, Conn.

Africa—Ed Royce, Calif.
Asia and the Pacific—Doug Bereuter, Neb.
International Economic Policy and Trade—Ileana Ros-Lehtinen, Fla.
International Operations and Human Rights—Christopher H. Smith, N.J.
Western Hemisphere—Elton Gallegly, Calif.

JUDICIARY

The judiciary and judicial proceedings, civil and criminal; administrative practice and procedure; apportionment of representatives; bankruptcy, mutiny, espionage, and counterfeiting; civil liberties; constitutional amendments; federal courts and judges, and local courts in the territories and possessions; immigration and naturalization; interstate compacts, generally; measures relating to claims against the United States; meetings of Congress, attendance of members and their acceptance of incompatible offices; national penitentiaries; patents, the Patent Office, copyrights, and trademarks; presidential succession; protection of trade and commerce against unlawful restraints and monopolies; revision and codification of the Statutes of the United States; state and territorial boundaries; subversive activities affecting the internal security of the United States.

R 20–D 15 *(105th Congress)*

Henry J. Hyde, Ill.
John Conyers Jr., Mich.

Commercial and Administrative Law—George W. Gekas, Pa.
Constitution—Charles T. Canady, Fla.
Courts and Intellectual Property—Howard Coble, N.C.
Crime—Bill McCollum, Fla.
Immigration and Claims—Lamar Smith, Texas

R 21–D 16 *(106th Congress)*

Henry J. Hyde, Ill.
John Conyers Jr., Mich.

Commercial and Administrative Law—George W. Gekas, Pa.
Constitution—Charles T. Canady, Fla.
Courts and Intellectual Property—Howard Coble, N.C.
Crime—Bill McCollum, Fla.
Immigration and Claims—Lamar Smith, Texas

NATIONAL SECURITY[6]

Common defense generally; Department of Defense generally, including the Departments of the Army, Navy, and Air Force generally; ammunition depots; forts; arsenals; Army, Navy, and Air Force reservations and establishments; conservation, development, and use of naval petroleum and oil shale reserves; interoceanic canals generally, including measures relating to the maintenance, operation, and administration of interoceanic canals; Merchant Marine Academy, and State Maritime Academies; military applications of nuclear energy; tactical intelligence and intelligence related activities of the Department of the Defense; national security aspects of merchant marine, including financial assistance for the construction and operation of vessels, the maintenance of the U.S. shipbuilding and ship repair industrial base, cabotage, cargo preference, and merchant marine officers and seamen as these matters relate to the national security; pay, promotion, retirement, and other benefits and privileges of members of the armed forces; scientific research and development in support of the armed services; selective service; size and composition of the Army, Navy, Marine Corps, and Air Force; soldiers' and sailors' homes; strategic and critical materials necessary for the common defense.

R 30–D 25 *(105th Congress)*

Floyd D. Spence, S.C.
Ike Skelton, Mo.

Merchant Marine—Herbert H. Bateman, Va.
Military Installations and Facilities—Joel Hefley, Colo.
Military Personnel—Steve Buyer, Ind.
Military Procurement—Duncan Hunter, Calif.
Military Readiness—Herbert H. Bateman, Va.
Military Research and Development—Curt Weldon, Pa.
Morale, Welfare and Recreation—John M. McHugh, N.Y.

RESOURCES

Public lands generally, including entry, easements, and grazing; mining interests generally; fisheries and wildlife, including research, restoration, refuges, and conservation; forest reserves and national parks created from the public domain; forfeiture of land grants and alien ownership, including alien ownership of mineral lands; Geological Survey; international fishing agreements; interstate compacts relating to apportionment of waters for irrigation purposes; irrigation and reclamation, including water supply for reclamation projects, and easements of public lands for irrigation projects, and acquisition of private lands when necessary to complete irrigation projects; measures relating to the care and management of Indians, including the care and allotment of Native American lands and general and special measures relating to claims which are paid out of Native American funds; measures relating generally to the insular possessions of the United States, except those affecting the revenue and appropriations; military parks and battlefields, national cemeteries administered by the secretary of the interior, parks within the District of Columbia, and the erection of monuments to the memory of individuals; mineral land laws and claims and entries thereunder; mineral resources of the public lands; mining schools and experimental stations; marine affairs (including coastal zone management), except for measures relating to oil and other pollution of navigable waters; oceanography; petroleum conservation on the public lands and conservation of the radium supply in the United States; preservation of prehistoric ruins and objects of interest on the public domain; relations of the United States with the Native Americans and the Native American tribes; Trans-Alaska Oil Pipeline (except ratemaking).

R 27–D 23 *(105th Congress)*

Don Young, Alaska
George Miller, Calif.

Energy and Mineral Resources—Barbara Cubin, Wyo.
Fisheries, Conservation, Wildlife and Oceans—H. James Saxton, N.J.
Forests and Forest Health—Helen Chenoweth, Idaho
National Parks and Public Lands—James V. Hansen, Utah
Water and Power—John T. Doolittle, Calif.

R 28–D 24 *(106th Congress)*

Don Young, Alaska
George Miller, Calif.

Energy and Mineral Resources—Barbara Cubin, Wyo.
Fisheries Conservation, Wildlife and Oceans—H. James Saxton, N.J.
Forests and Forest Health—Helen Chenoweth, Idaho
National Parks and Public Lands—James V. Hansen, Utah
Water and Power—John T. Doolittle, Calif.

RULES

Rules and joint rules (other than rules or joint rules relating to the Code of Official Conduct), and order of business of the House; recesses and final adjournments of Congress.

R 9–D 4 *(105th Congress)*

Gerald B. H. Solomon, N.Y.
Joe Moakley, Mass.

Legislative and Budget Process—Porter J. Goss, Fla.
Rules and Organization of the House—David Dreier, Calif.

R 9–D 4 *(106th Congress)*

David Dreier, Calif.
Joe Moakley, Mass.

Legislative and Budget Process—Porter J. Goss, Fla.
Rules and Organization of the House—John Linder, Ga.

SCIENCE

All energy research, development, and demonstration, and projects thereof, and all federally owned or operated nonmilitary energy laboratories; astronautical research and development, including resources, personnel, equipment, and facilities; civil aviation research and development; environmental research and development; marine research; measures relating to the commercial application of energy technology; National Institute of Standards and Technology, standardization of weights and measures and the metric system; National Aeronautics and Space Administration; National Space Council; National Science Foundation; National Weather Service; outer space, including exploration and control thereof; science scholarships; scientific research, development, and demonstration, and projects thereof.

R 25–D 21 *(105th Congress)*

F. James Sensenbrenner Jr., Wis.
George E. Brown Jr., Calif.

Basic Research—Steven H. Schiff, N.M.
Energy and Environment—Ken Calvert, Calif.
Space and Aeronautics—Dana Rohrabacher, Calif.
Technology—Constance A. Morella, Md.

R 25–D 22 *(106th Congress)*

F. James Sensenbrenner Jr., Wis.
Ralph M. Hall, Texas

Basic Research—Nick Smith, Mich.
Energy and Environment—Ken Calvert, Calif.
Space and Aeronautics—Dana Rohrabacher, Calif.
Technology—Constance A. Morella, Md.

SELECT INTELLIGENCE

Legislative and budgetary authority over the National Security Agency and the director of central intelligence, the Defense Intelligence Agency, the National Security Agency, intelligence activities of the Federal Bureau of Investigation and other components of the federal intelligence community.

R 9–D 7 *(105th Congress)*

Porter J. Goss, Fla.
Norm Dicks, Wash.

Human Intelligence, Analysis and Counterintelligence—Bill McCollum, Fla.
Technical and Tactical Intelligence—Jerry Lewis, Calif.

R 9–D 7 *(106th Congress)*

Porter J. Goss, Fla.
Julian C. Dixon, Calif.

Human Intelligence, Analysis and Counterintelligence—Bill McCollum, Fla.
Technical and Tactical Intelligence—Michael N. Castle, Del.

SMALL BUSINESS

Assistance to and protection of small business, including financial aid, regulatory flexibility, and paperwork reduction; participation of small business enterprises in federal procurement and government contracts.

R 19–D 16 *(105th Congress)*

James M. Talent, Mo.
John J. LaFalce, N.Y.

Empowerment—Mark Souder, Ind.
Government Programs and Oversight—Roscoe G. Bartlett, Md.
Regulatory Reform and Paperwork Reduction—Sue W. Kelly, N.Y.
Tax, Finance and Exports—Donald Manzullo, Ill.

R 19–D 17 *(106th Congress)*

James M. Talent, Mo.
Nydia M. Velazquez, N.Y.

Empowerment—Joseph R. Pitts, Pa.
Government Programs and Oversight—Roscoe G. Bartlett, Md.
Regulatory Reform and Paperwork Reduction—Sue W. Kelly, N.Y.
Rural Enterprises, Business Opportunity and Special Small Business Problems—Frank A. LoBiondo, N.J.

Tax, Finance and Exports—Donald Manzullo, Ill.

STANDARDS OF OFFICIAL CONDUCT

Measures relating to the Code of Official Conduct.

R 5–D 5 *(105th Congress)*

James V. Hansen, Utah
Howard L. Berman, Calif.

Bud Shuster Inquiry—Joel Hefley, Colo.

R 5–D 5 *(106th Congress)*

Lamar Smith, Texas
Howard L. Berman, Calif.

Bud Shuster Inquiry—Joel Hefley, Colo.

TRANSPORTATION AND INFRASTRUCTURE

Transportation, including civil aviation, railroads, water transportation, transportation safety (except automobile safety), transportation infrastructure, transportation labor, and railroad retirement and unemployment (except revenue measures); water power; the Coast Guard; federal management of emergencies and natural disasters; flood control and improvement of waterways; inspection of merchant marine vessels; navigation and related laws; rules and international arrangements to prevent collisions at sea; measures, other than appropriations, that relate to construction, maintenance and safety of roads; buildings and grounds of the Botanic Gardens, the Library of Congress and the Smithsonian Institution and other government buildings within the District of Columbia; post offices, customhouses, Federal courthouses, and merchant marine, except for national security aspects; pollution of navigable waters; and bridges and dams and related transportation regulatory agencies.

R 40–D 33 *(105th Congress)*

Bud Shuster, Pa.
James L. Oberstar, Minn.

Aviation—John J. "Jimmy" Duncan Jr., Tenn.
Coast Guard and Maritime Transportation—Wayne T. Gilchrest, Md.
Public Buildings and Economic Development—Jay C. Kim, Calif.
Railroads—Susan Molinari, N.Y.
Surface Transportation—Tom Petri, Wis.
Water Resources and Environment—Sherwood Boehlert, N.Y.

R 41–D 34 *(106th Congress)*

Bud Shuster, Pa.
James L. Oberstar, Minn.

Aviation—John J. "Jimmy" Duncan Jr., Tenn.
Coast Guard and Maritime Transportation—Wayne T. Gilchrest, Md.

Economic Development, Public Buildings, Hazardous Materials and Pipeline Transportation—Bob Franks, N.J.
Ground Transportation—Tom Petri, Wis.
Oversight, Investigations and Emergency Management—Tillie Fowler, Fla.
Water Resources and Environment—Sherwood Boehlert, N.Y.

VETERANS' AFFAIRS

Veterans' measures generally; cemeteries of the United States in which veterans of any war or conflict are or may be buried, whether in the United States or abroad, except cemeteries administered by the secretary of the Interior; compensation, vocational rehabilitation, and education of veterans; life insurance issued by the government on account of service in the armed forces; pensions of all the wars of the United States, readjustment of service personnel to civil life; soldiers' and sailors, civil relief; veterans' hospitals, medical care, and treatment of veterans.

R 16–D 13 *(105th Congress)*

Bob Stump, Ariz.
Lane Evans, Ill.

Benefits—Jack Quinn, N.Y.
Health—Cliff Stearns, Fla.
Oversight and Investigations—Terry Everett, Ala.

R 17–D 14 *(106th Congress)*

Bob Stump, Ariz.
Lane Evans, Ill.

Benefits—Jack Quinn, N.Y.
Health—Cliff Stearns, Fla.
Oversight and Investigations—Terry Everett, Ala.

WAYS AND MEANS

Revenue measures generally; reciprocal trade agreements; customs, collection districts, and ports of entry and delivery; revenue measures relating to the insular possessions; bonded debt of the United States; deposit of public moneys; transportation of dutiable goods; tax-exempt foundations and charitable trusts; national Social Security, except (1) health care and facilities programs that are supported from general revenues as opposed to payroll deductions and (2) work incentive programs.

R 23–D 16 *(105th Congress)*

Bill Archer, Texas
Charles B. Rangel, N.Y.

Health—Bill Thomas, Calif.
Human Resources—E. Clay Shaw Jr., Fla.
Oversight—Nancy L. Johnson, Conn.
Social Security—Jim Bunning, Ky.
Trade—Philip M. Crane, Ill.

R 23–D 16 *(106th Congress)*

Bill Archer, Texas
Charles B. Rangel, N.Y.

Health—Bill Thomas, Calif.
Human Resources—Nancy L. Johnson, Conn.
Oversight—Amo Houghton, N.Y.
Social Security—E. Clay Shaw Jr., Fla.
Trade—Philip M. Crane, Ill.

POLITICAL COMMITTEES

Democratic Congressional Campaign Committee (provides campaign support for Democratic House candidates)—Martin Frost, Texas, chairman (105th Congress); Patrick J. Kennedy, R.I., chairman (106th Congress)

Democratic Policy Committee (studies and proposes legislation and makes public Democratic policy positions)—Richard A. Gephardt, Mo., chairman (105th and 106th Congresses)

Democratic Steering Committee (makes Democratic committee assignments)—Richard A. Gephardt, Mo., cochairman; Steny H. Hoyer, Md., cochairman (105th and 106th Congresses)

National Republican Congressional Committee (provides campaign support for Republican House candidates)—John Linder, Ga., chairman (105th Congress); Thomas M. Davis III, Va., chairman (106th Congress)

Republican Policy Committee (advises on party action and policy)—Christopher Cox, Calif., chairman (105th and 106th Congresses)

Republican Steering Committee (makes Republican committee assignments)—Newt Gingrich, Ga., chairman (105th Congress); J. Dennis Hastert, Ill., chairman (106th Congress)

Joint Committees

Joint committees are set up to examine specific questions and are established by public law. Membership is drawn from both chambers and both parties. When a senator serves as chairman, the vice chairman usually is a representative, and vice versa. The chairmanship traditionally rotates from one chamber to the other at the beginning of each Congress (except for the Committee on Taxation chairmanship, which rotates at the start of each session).

ECONOMIC

Studies and investigates all recommendations in the president's annual *Economic Report to Congress.* Reports findings and recommendations to the House and Senate.

Sen. Connie Mack, R-Fla., chairman (105th Congress)
Rep. H. James Saxton, R-N.J., vice chairman (105th Congress)
Sen. Connie Mack, R-Fla., chairman (106th Congress)
Rep. H. James Saxton, R-N.J., vice chairman (106th Congress)

No standing subcommittees.

LIBRARY

Management and expansion of the Library of Congress; receipt of gifts for the benefit of the library; development and maintenance of the Botanic Garden; placement of statues and other works of art in the Capitol.

Sen. John W. Warner, R-Va., chairman (105th Congress)
Rep. Bill Thomas, R-Calif., vice chairman (105th Congress)
Sen. Ted Stevens, R-Alaska, chairman (106th Congress)
Rep. Bill Thomas, R-Calif., vice chairman (106th Congress)

No standing subcommittees.

PRINTING

Probes inefficiency and waste in the printing, binding and distribution of federal government publications. Oversees arrangement and style of the *Congressional Record.*

John W. Warner, R-Va., chairman (105th Congress)
Rep. Bill Thomas, R-Calif., vice chairman (105th Congress)
Rep. Bill Thomas, R-Calif., chairman (106th Congress)
Sen. Mitch McConnell, R-Ky., vice chairman (106th Congress)

No standing subcommittees.

TAXATION

Operation, effects, and administration of the federal system of internal revenue taxes; measures and methods for simplification of taxes.

Sen. William V. Roth Jr., R-Del., chairman (105th Congress)
Rep. Bill Archer, R-Texas, vice chairman (105th Congress)
Rep. Bill Archer, R-Texas, chairman (106th Congress)
Sen. William V. Roth Jr., R-Del, vice chairman (106th Congress)

No standing subcommittees.

---

1. Reorganized from Labor and Human Resources in the 105th Congress.
2. Reorganized as Health, Education, Labor and Pensions in the 106th Congress.
3. Did not exist in the 105th Congress.
4. Reorganized from National Security in the 105th Congress.
5. Did not exist in the 105th Congress.
6. Reorganized as Armed Services in the 106th Congress.

Postelection Sessions

Congress held ten postelection sessions between 1945 and the end of 2000.

1948. The 1948 postelection session of the 80th Congress lasted only two hours. Both chambers swore in new members, approved several minor resolutions, and received last-minute reports from committees.

In addition to final floor action, several committees resumed work. The most active was the House Un-American Activities Committee, which continued its investigation of alleged communist espionage in the federal government.

1950. After the 1950 elections, President Harry S. Truman sent a "must" agenda to the lame-duck session of the 81st Congress. The president's list included supplemental defense appropriations, an excess profits tax, aid to Yugoslavia, a three-month extension of federal rent controls, and statehood for Hawaii and Alaska. During a marathon session that lasted until only a few hours before its successor took over, the 81st Congress acted on all of the president's legislative items except the statehood bills, which were blocked by a Senate filibuster.

1954. Only one chamber of the 83rd Congress convened after the 1954 elections. The Senate returned Nov. 8 to hold what has been called a "censure session," a continuing investigation into the conduct of Sen. Joseph R. McCarthy, R-Wis. (1947–1957). By a 67–22 roll call, the Senate Dec. 2 voted to "condemn" McCarthy for his behavior.

In other postelection floor action, the Senate passed a series of miscellaneous and administrative resolutions and swore in new members.

1970. President Richard Nixon criticized the lame-duck Congress as one that had "seemingly lost the capacity to decide and the will to act." Filibusters and intense controversy contributed to inaction on the president's request for trade legislation and welfare reform.

Congress nevertheless claimed some substantive results during the session, which ended Jan. 2, 1971. Several major appropriations bills were cleared for presidential signature. Congress also approved foreign aid to Cambodia, provided interim funding for the supersonic transport (SST) plane, and repealed the Tonkin Gulf Resolution that had been used as a basis for American military involvement in Vietnam.

1974. In a session that ran from Nov. 18 to Dec. 20, 1974, the 93rd Congress cleared several important bills for presidential signature, including a mass transit bill, a Labor-Health, Education and Welfare appropriations bill, and a foreign assistance package. A House-Senate conference committee reached agreement on a major strip-mining bill, but President Gerald R. Ford vetoed it.

Congress approved the nomination of Nelson A. Rockefeller as vice president. It also overrode presidential vetoes of two bills—one broadening the Freedom of Information Act, a second authorizing educational benefits for Korean War and Vietnam-era veterans.

1980. The lame-duck session of the 96th Congress was productive, at least until Dec. 5, the original adjournment date set by congressional leaders. By that date a budget had been approved, along with a budget-reconciliation measure. Ten regular appropriations bills had cleared, though one subsequently was vetoed. Congress had approved two major environmental measures—an Alaskan lands bill and toxic waste "superfund" legislation—as well as a three-year extension of general revenue sharing.

After Dec. 5, however, the legislative pace slowed noticeably. Action on a continuing appropriations resolution for those departments

Recent Lame-Duck Sessions

Year	Congress	Dates
1948	80th	Dec. 31, 1948 (2-hour session)
1950	81st	Nov. 27, 1950—Jan. 2, 1951
1954	83rd	Nov. 8, 1954—Dec. 2, 1954
1970	91st	Nov. 16, 1970—Jan. 2, 1971 (Senate)
1974	93rd	Nov. 18, 1974—Dec. 20, 1974
1980	96th	Nov. 12, 1980—Dec. 16, 1980
1982	97th	Nov. 29, 1982—Dec. 23, 1982 (Senate)
		Nov. 29, 1982—Dec. 21, 1982 (House)
1994	103rd	Nov. 29, 1994 (House)
		Nov. 30, 1994—Dec. 1, 1994 (Senate)
1998	105th	Dec. 17, 1998—Dec. 19, 1998 (House)
2000	106th	Nov. 13, 2000—Dec. 15, 2000

and agencies whose regular funding had not been cleared was delayed, first by a filibuster on a fair housing bill and later by more than 100 "Christmas tree" amendments, including a $10,000-a-year pay raise for members. After the conference report failed in the Senate and twice was rewritten, the bill was shorn of virtually all its "ornaments" and finally cleared by both chambers on Dec. 16.

1982. Despite the reluctance of congressional leaders, President Ronald Reagan urged the convening of a postelection session at the end of the 97th Congress, principally to pass remaining appropriations bills.

Rising unemployment—and Democratic election gains in the House—made job creation efforts the focus of the lame-duck Congress, however. Overriding the objections of Republican conservatives, Congress passed Reagan-backed legislation raising the federal gasoline tax from 4 cents to 9 cents a gallon to pay for highway repairs and mass transit. Supporters said the legislation would help alleviate unemployment by creating 300,000 jobs.

Congress eventually cleared four additional appropriations bills, packaging the remaining six in a continuing appropriations resolution that also included a pay raise for House members. Conferees dropped funding for emergency jobs programs to avert a threatened veto of the resolution.

The lame-duck session also was highlighted by Congress's refusal to fund production and procurement of the first five MX intercontinental missiles. This was the first time in recent history that either house of Congress had denied a president's request to fund production of a strategic weapon.

1994. Congress reconvened to reconsider, and ultimately approve, the Uruguay Round pact strengthening the General Agreement on Tariffs and Trade (GATT). The bill had been submitted Sept. 27, 1994, by President Clinton under fast-track rules for trade legislation, which allowed each chamber only an up-or-down vote on the bill without amendments. But the rules also allowed every chairman with jurisdiction to take up to 45 days to review the bill. Sen. Ernest F. Hollings, D-S.C., demanded his forty-five days, forcing the Senate leadership to schedule a two-day lame-duck session.

Clinton asked the House to approve the bill before the October adjournment, but the Democratic leadership delayed consideration. The House reconvened for a one-day session Nov. 29 and passed the GATT bill by a wide margin.

Following a twenty-hour debate Nov. 30 and Dec. 1, the Senate gave overwhelming approval to the bill.

1998. The House reconvened in December for a remarkable, historic event: to vote on the impeachment of a president. After a tumultuous political year, House Republicans pushed through articles of impeachment for what they believe was President Clinton's lying under oath. The event was characterized by a year-long political chasm between House Republicans, who led the effort for impeachment, and Democrats in both chambers. It also was characterized by charges of sexual misconduct involving Clinton and release of a controversial and in places graphic report about sexual conduct of the president that Republicans defended as necessary to prove their case. The report was prepared by Independent Counsel Kenneth Starr. In the short time the House was in session, it voted—largely along party lines—in favor of impeachment charges, which would be tried—and rejected—by the Senate early in the following year. *(Story, pp. 797, 813)*

2000. Congress returned after the 2000 elections largely to complete action of appropriations measures that had remained unfinished as President Clinton continued to wrestle with his Republican adversaries in Congress over spending priorities. Partisan fighting over spending and taxes had been one of the principal matters that divided the White House and Capitol Hill during the latter years of Clinton's presidency. The year 2000 was no exception as Congress was unable to avert its annual pileup of appropriations bills at the end of the session. The pileup was exacerbated in 2000 because of the controversial presidential elections that were not decided until a Supreme Court decision in December awarding contested Florida electoral votes to Republican George W. Bush. With the GOP about to reclaim the White House, its party members in Congress suddenly had new leverage in the final bargaining over appropriations. The lame-duck session lumbered into mid-December when an omnibus package was used to close the books on four spending bills and move other unrelated legislation. *(Story, p. 81)*

Senate Cloture Votes, 1917–2000

The filibuster, identified by the public primarily as nonstop speech, has been an enshrined Senate tradition throughout the chamber's history but became a focus of increasing criticism in the twentieth century as a device to thwart majority decisions. It was not until 1917 that the Senate adopted a rule, known as cloture, that allowed a majority—albeit a supermajority—to end a filibuster and bring a measure to a vote. The number of votes required to invoke cloture has varied over the years, standing at 60 in early 2002 if there are no Senate vacancies. (The actual rule requires a three-fifths majority of members to invoke cloture; the Senate has 100 members.)

Even with the rule in place, however, the number of filibusters and attempts to invoke cloture was limited until the 92nd Congress in 1971–1973. From that time on, and especially during the 1990s, cloture attempts expanded greatly as the character of the Senate changed from what one scholar called "communitarian" and deliberative to individualistic, increasingly partisan, and media-driven. In the ten Congresses during the twenty years from 1971 to 1991, cloture was attempted no less than thirteen times in each two-year period, and on the average twenty-five times each Congress. As dramatic as that growth was, it paled against the expansion in the following five Congresses from 1991 to 2001. In that ten-year period cloture attempts averaged fifty a Congress. (*Table, p. 971*)

During President Bill Clinton's second term, a particularly partisan period from 1997 to 2001, a substantial number of cloture votes—more than 35 percent—were decided by a majority of 70 to 100 votes in favor. This higher success rate (than during previous decades) suggested that cloture was used less in connection with debates on far-reaching national issues—as was often the case in the past—and more for political and legislative maneuvering. For example, cloture, if invoked, requires amendments to be germane to the legislation being considered. Under normal procedures, senators may offer nongermane amendments to get a vote on proposals blocked in committee or advocated only by a few senators. In other cases a nongermane amendment may be intended to advance a political party's agenda in the media or to require senators to take a position that will be used against them in the next election. Much of this can be prevented by invoking cloture even if a true filibuster is not expected. Thus, increasingly cloture votes have been used by the majority party—Republican during Clinton's second term—to control the Senate's agenda.

CHANGES IN THE RULE

The Senate's ultimate check on the filibuster is the provision for cloture, or limitation of debate, contained in Rule 22 of its Standing Rules. The original Rule 22 was adopted in 1917 following a furor over the "talking to death" of a proposal by President Woodrow Wilson for arming American merchant ships before the United States entered World War I. The new cloture rule required the votes of two-thirds of all the senators present and voting to invoke cloture. In 1949, during a parliamentary skirmish preceding scheduled consideration of a Fair Employment Practices Commission bill, the requirement was raised to two-thirds of the entire Senate membership.

A revision of the rule in 1959 provided for limitation of debate by a vote of two-thirds of the senators present and voting, two days after a cloture petition was submitted by sixteen senators. If cloture was adopted by the Senate, further debate was limited to one hour for each senator on the bill itself and on all amendments affecting it. No new amendments could be offered except by unanimous consent. Amendments that were not germane to the pending business and dilatory motions were out of order. The rule applied both to regular legislation and to motions to change the Standing Rules.

Rule 22 was revised significantly in 1975 by lowering the vote needed for cloture to three-fifths of the Senate membership (sixty if there were no vacancies). That revision applied to any matter except proposed rules changes, for which the old requirement of a two-thirds majority of senators present and voting still applied.

In a further revision of the rule, the Senate in 1979 limited postcloture delaying tactics by providing that once cloture was invoked, a final vote had to be taken after no more than 100 hours of debate. All time spent on quorum calls, roll-call votes, and other parliamentary procedures was to be included in the 100-hour limit.

When the Senate decided to televise its floor proceedings in 1986, it further tightened up the time on postcloture debate. Rule 22 was revised to reduce to thirty hours, from 100, the time allowed for debate, procedural moves, and roll-call votes after the Senate had invoked cloture to end a filibuster.

Following is a list of the 545 cloture votes taken between 1917, when Senate Rule 22 was adopted, and the end of 2000; 193 of the votes (in **bold type**) were successful.

Issue	Date	Vote	Yeas needed
Versailles Treaty	Nov. 15, 1919	78–16	63
Emergency tariff	Feb. 2, 1921	36–35	48
Tariff bill	July 7, 1922	45–35	54
World Court	Jan. 25, 1926	68–26	63
Migratory birds	June 1, 1926	46–33	53
Branch banking	Feb. 15, 1927	65–18	56
Disabled officers	Feb. 26, 1927	51–36	58
Colorado River	Feb. 26, 1927	32–59	61
D.C. buildings	Feb. 28, 1927	52–31	56
Prohibition Bureau	Feb. 28, 1927	55–27	55
Banking Act	Jan. 19, 1933	58–30	59
Anti-lynching	Jan. 27, 1938	37–51	59
Anti-lynching	Feb. 16, 1938	42–46	59
Anti-poll tax	Nov. 23, 1942	37–41	52
Anti-poll tax	May 15, 1944	36–44	54
Fair Employment Practices Commission	Feb. 9, 1946	48–36	56
British loan	May 7, 1946	41–41	55
Labor disputes	May 25, 1946	3–77	54
Anti-poll tax	July 31, 1946	39–33	48

Issue	Date	Vote	Yeas needed
Fair Employment	May 19, 1950	52–32	64
Fair Employment	July 12, 1950	55–33	64
Atomic Energy Act	July 26, 1954	44–42	64
Civil Rights Act	March 10, 1960	42–53	64
Amend Rule 22	Sept. 19, 1961	37–43	54
Literacy tests	May 9, 1962	43–53	64
Literacy tests	May 14, 1962	42–52	63
Comsat Act	Aug. 14, 1962	63–27	60
Amend Rule 22	Feb. 7, 1963	54–42	64
Civil Rights Act	June 10, 1964	71–29	67
Legislative reapportionment	Sept. 10, 1964	30–63	62
Voting Rights Act	May 25, 1965	70–30	67
Right-to-work repeal	Oct. 11, 1965	45–47	62
Right-to-work repeal	Feb. 8, 1966	51–48	66
Right-to-work repeal	Feb. 10, 1966	50–49	66
Civil Rights Act	Sept. 14, 1966	54–42	64
Civil Rights Act	Sept. 19, 1966	52–41	62
D.C. home rule	Oct. 10, 1966	41–37	52
Amend Rule 22	Jan. 24, 1967	53–46	66

Issue	Date	Vote	Yeas needed
Open housing	Feb. 20, 1968	55–37	62
Open housing	Feb. 26, 1968	56–36	62
Open housing	March 1, 1968	59–35	63
Open housing	March 4, 1968	65–32	65
Abe Fortas nomination	Oct. 1, 1968	45–43	59
Amend Rule 22	Jan. 16, 1969	51–47	66
Amend Rule 22	Jan. 28, 1969	50–42	62
Electoral College	Sept. 17, 1970	54–36	60
Electoral College	Sept. 29, 1970	53–34	58
Supersonic transport	Dec. 19, 1970	43–48	61
Supersonic transport	Dec. 22, 1970	42–44	58
Amend Rule 22	Feb. 18, 1971	48–37	57
Amend Rule 22	Feb. 23, 1971	50–36	58
Amend Rule 22	March 2, 1971	48–36	56
Amend Rule 22	March 9, 1971	55–39	63
Military draft	June 23, 1971	65–27	62
Lockheed loan	July 26, 1971	42–47	60
Lockheed loan	July 28, 1971	59–39	66
Lockheed loan	July 30, 1971	53–37	60
Military draft	Sept. 21, 1971	61–30	61
William Rehnquist nomination	Dec. 10, 1971	52–42	63
Equal job opportunity	Feb. 1, 1972	48–37	57
Equal job opportunity	Feb. 3, 1972	53–35	59
Equal job opportunity	Feb. 22, 1972	71–23	63
U.S.-Soviet arms pact	Sept. 14, 1972	76–15	61
Consumer Agency	Sept. 29, 1972	47–29	51
Consumer Agency	Oct. 3, 1972	55–32	58
Consumer Agency	Oct. 5, 1972	52–30	55
School busing	Oct. 10, 1972	45–37	55
School busing	Oct. 11, 1972	49–39	59
School busing	Oct. 12, 1972	49–38	58
Voter registration	April 30, 1973	56–31	58
Voter registration	May 3, 1973	60–34	63
Voter registration	May 9, 1973	67–32	66
Public campaign financing	Dec. 2, 1973	47–33	54
Public campaign financing	Dec. 3, 1973	49–39	59
Rhodesian chrome ore	Dec. 11, 1973	59–35	63
Rhodesian chrome ore	Dec. 13, 1973	62–33	64
Legal services program	Dec. 13, 1973	60–36	64
Legal services program	Dec. 14, 1973	56–29	57
Rhodesian chrome ore	Dec. 18, 1973	63–26	60
Legal services program	Jan. 30, 1974	68–29	65
Genocide Treaty	Feb. 5, 1974	55–36	61
Genocide Treaty	Feb. 6, 1974	55–36	62
Government pay raise	March 6, 1974	67–31	66
Public campaign financing	April 4, 1974	60–36	64
Public campaign financing	April 9, 1974	64–30	63
Public debt ceiling	June 19, 1974	50–43	62
Public debt ceiling	June 19, 1974	45–48	62
Public debt ceiling	June 26, 1974	48–50	66
Consumer Agency	July 30, 1974	56–42	66
Consumer Agency	Aug. 1, 1974	59–39	66
Consumer Agency	Aug. 20, 1974	59–35	63
Consumer Agency	Sept. 19, 1974	64–34	66
Export-Import Bank	Dec. 3, 1974	51–39	60
Export-Import Bank	Dec. 4, 1974	48–44	62
Trade reform	Dec. 13, 1974	71–19	60
FY 1975 supplemental funds	Dec. 14, 1974	56–27	56
Export-Import Bank	Dec. 14, 1974	49–35	56
Export-Import Bank	Dec. 16, 1974	54–34	59
Social services programs	Dec. 17, 1974	70–23	62
Tax law changes	Dec. 17, 1974	67–25	62
Rail Reorganization Act	Feb. 26, 1975	86–8	63
Amend Rule 22	March 5, 1975	73–21	63
Amend Rule 22	March 7, 1975	73–21	63
Tax reduction	March 20, 1975	59–38	60
Tax reduction	March 21, 1975	83–13	60
Agency for Consumer Advocacy	May 13, 1975	71–27	60
Senate staffing	June 11, 1975	77–19	64
New Hampshire Senate seat	June 24, 1975	57–39	60
New Hampshire Senate seat	June 25, 1975	56–41	60
New Hampshire Senate seat	June 26, 1975	54–40	60
New Hampshire Senate seat	July 8, 1975	57–38	60
New Hampshire Senate seat	July 9, 1975	57–38	60
New Hampshire Senate seat	July 10, 1975	54–38	60
Voting Rights Act	July 21, 1975	72–19	60
Voting Rights Act	July 23, 1975	76–20	60
Oil price decontrol	July 30, 1975	54–38	60
Anti-school busing amendments	Sept. 23, 1975	46–48	60
Anti-school busing amendments	Sept. 24, 1975	64–33	60
Common-site picketing	Nov. 11, 1975	66–30	60
Common-site picketing	Nov. 14, 1975	58–31	60
Common-site picketing	Nov. 18, 1975	62–37	60
Rail reorganization	Dec. 4, 1975	61–27	60
New York City aid	Dec. 5, 1975	70–27	60
Rice Production Act	Feb. 3, 1976	70–19	60
Antitrust amendments	June 3, 1976	67–22	60
Antitrust amendments	Aug. 31, 1976	63–27	60
Civil Rights attorneys' fees	Sept. 23, 1976	63–26	60
Draft resisters pardons	Jan. 24, 1977	53–43	60
Campaign financing	July 29, 1977	49–45	60
Campaign financing	Aug. 1, 1977	47–46	60
Campaign financing	Aug. 2, 1977	52–46	60
Natural gas pricing	Sept. 26, 1977	77–17	60
Labor law revision	June 7, 1978	42–47	60
Labor law revision	June 8, 1978	49–41	60
Labor law revision	June 13, 1978	54–43	60
Labor law revision	June 14, 1978	58–41	60
Labor law revision	June 15, 1978	58–39	60
Labor law revision	June 22, 1978	53–45	60
Revenue Act of 1978	Oct. 9, 1978	62–28	60
Energy taxes	Oct. 14, 1978	71–13	60
Windfall profits tax	Dec. 12, 1979	53–46	60
Windfall profits tax	Dec. 13, 1979	56–40	60
Windfall profits tax	Dec. 14, 1979	56–39	60
Windfall profits tax	Dec. 17, 1979	84–14	60
William Lubbers nomination	April 21, 1980	46–60	60
William Lubbers nomination	April 22, 1980	62–34	60
Rights of institutionalized	April 28, 1980	44–39	60
Rights of institutionalized	April 29, 1980	56–34	60
Rights of institutionalized	April 30, 1980	53–35	60
Rights of institutionalized persons	May 1, 1980	60–34	60
Bottlers' antitrust immunity	May 15, 1980	86–6	60
Draft registration funding	June 10, 1980	62–32	60
Don Zimmerman nomination	Aug. 1, 1980	51–35	60
Don Zimmerman nomination	Aug. 4, 1980	45–31	60
Don Zimmerman nomination	Aug. 5, 1980	63–31	60
Alaska lands	Aug. 18, 1980	63–25	60
Vessel tonnage/strip mining	Aug. 21, 1980	61–32	60
Fair housing amendments	Dec. 3, 1980	51–39	60
Fair housing amendments	Dec. 4, 1980	62–32	60
Fair housing amendments	Dec. 9, 1980	54–43	60
Breyer nomination	Dec. 9, 1980	68–28	60
Justice Department authorization	July 10, 1981	38–48	60
Justice Department authorization	July 13, 1981	54–32	60
Justice Department authorization	July 29, 1981	59–37	60
Justice Department authorization	Sept. 10, 1981	57–33	60
Justice Department authorization	Sept. 16, 1981	61–36	60
Justice Department authorization	Dec. 10, 1981	64–35	60
State, Justice, Commerce funds	Dec. 11, 1981	59–35	60
Justice Department authorization	Feb. 9, 1982	63–33	60
Broadcast Senate proceedings	April 20, 1982	47–51	60
Criminal Code Reform Act	April 27, 1982	45–46	60
1982 supplemental funds	May 27, 1982	95–2	60
Voting Rights Act	June 15, 1982	86–8	60
Debt limit increase	Sept. 9, 1982	41–47	60
Debt limit increase	Sept. 13, 1982	45–35	60
Debt limit increase	Sept. 15, 1982	50–44	60
Debt limit increase	Sept. 20, 1982	50–39	60
Debt limit increase	Sept. 21, 1982	53–47	60
Debt limit increase	Sept. 22, 1982	54–46	60
Debt limit increase	Sept. 23, 1982	53–45	60
Antitrust Equal Enforcement Act	Dec. 2, 1982	38–58	60
Antitrust Equal Enforcement Act	Dec. 2, 1982	44–51	60
Transportation Assistance Act	Dec. 13, 1982	75–13	60
Transportation Assistance Act	Dec. 16, 1982	48–50	60
Transportation Assistance Act	Dec. 16, 1982	5–93	60
Transportation Assistance Act	Dec. 19, 1982	89–5	60
Transportation Assistance Act	Dec. 20, 1982	87–8	60
Transportation Assistance Act	Dec. 23, 1982	81–5	60
Jobs funding/interest withholding	March 16, 1983	50–48	60
Jobs funding/interest withholding	March 16, 1983	59–39	60
International trade/interest withholding	April 19, 1983	34–53	60
International trade/interest withholding	April 19, 1983	39–59	60
Defense authorizations, 1984	July 21, 1983	55–41	60
Radio broadcasting to Cuba	Aug. 3, 1983	62–33	60
National Gas Policy Act	Nov. 3, 1983	86–7	60
Capital punishment	Feb. 9, 1984	65–26	60
Hydroelectric power plants	July 30, 1984	60–28	60
J. Harvie Wilkinson nomination	July 31, 1984	57–39	60
Agriculture funds, FY 1985	Aug. 6, 1984	54–31	60
Agriculture funds, FY 1985	Aug. 8, 1984	68–30	60
J. Harvie Wilkinson nomination	Aug. 9, 1984	65–32	60
Financial Services Act	Sept. 10, 1984	89–3	60

Issue	Date	Vote	Yeas needed
Financial Services Act	Sept. 13, 1984	92–6	60
Broadcasting Senate procedures	Sept. 18, 1984	73–26	60
Broadcasting Senate procedures	Sept. 21, 1984	37–44	60
Surface Transportation Act	Sept. 24, 1984	70–12	60
Continuing funds	Sept. 29, 1984	92–4	60
Anti-apartheid	July 10, 1985	88–8	60
Line-item veto	July 18, 1985	57–42	60
Line-item veto	July 23, 1985	57–41	60
Line-item veto	July 24, 1985	58–40	60
Anti-apartheid	Sept. 9, 1985	53–34	60
Anti-apartheid	Sept. 11, 1985	57–41	60
Anti-apartheid	Sept. 12, 1985	11–88	60
Debt limit/balanced budget	Oct. 6, 1985	57–38	64
Debt limit/balanced budget	Oct. 9, 1985[1]	53–39	62
Conrail sale	Jan. 23, 1986	90–7	60
Conrail sale	Jan. 30, 1986	70–27	60
Marlin Fitzwater nomination	March 18, 1986	64–33	60
Washington airports transfer	March 21, 1986	50–39	60
Washington airports transfer	March 25, 1986	66–32	60
Hobbs Act amendments	April 16, 1986	44–54	60
Defense authorization, FY 1987	Aug. 6, 1986	53–46	60
Aid to Nicaraguan contras	Aug. 13, 1986	59–40	60
South Africa sanctions	Aug. 13, 1986	89–11	60
Aid to Nicaraguan contras	Aug. 13, 1986	62–37	60
William Rehnquist nomination	Sept. 17, 1986	68–31	60
Product liability reform	Sept. 25, 1986	97–1	60
Omnibus drug bill	Oct. 15, 1986	58–38	60
Immigration reform	Oct. 17, 1986	69–21	60
Contra aid moratorium	March 23, 1987	46–45	60
Contra aid moratorium	March 24, 1987	50–50	60
Contra aid moratorium	March 25, 1987	54–46	60
Relief for the homeless	April 9, 1987	68–29	60
Defense authorization, FY 1988	May 15, 1987	52–36	60
Defense authorization, FY 1988	May 19, 1987	58–41	60
Defense authorization, FY 1988	May 20, 1987	59–39	60
Campaign finance	June 9, 1987	52–47	60
Campaign finance	June 16, 1987	49–46	60
Campaign finance	June 17, 1987	51–47	60
Campaign finance	June 18, 1987	50–47	60
Campaign finance	June 19, 1987	45–43	60
Kuwaiti tanker reflagging	July 9, 1987	57–42	60
Kuwaiti tanker reflagging	July 14, 1987	53–40	60
Kuwaiti tanker reflagging	July 15, 1987	54–44	60
Melissa Wells nomination	Sept. 9, 1987	65–24	60
Campaign finance	Sept. 10, 1987	53–42	60
Campaign finance	Sept. 15, 1987	51–44	60
Kuwaiti tanker escort	Oct. 1, 1987	54–45	60
Defense authorization, FY 1988	Oct. 1, 1987	41–58	60
C. William Verity nomination	Oct. 13, 1987	85–8	60
War powers compliance	Oct. 20, 1987	67–28	60
Energy and water funds (Nuclear waste depository)	Nov. 10, 1987	87–0	60
Campaign finance	Feb. 26, 1988	53–41	60
Polygraph protection	March 3, 1988	77–19	60
Intelligence oversight	March 15, 1988	73–18	60
Risk notification	March 23, 1988	33–59	60
Risk notification	March 24, 1988	2–93	60
Risk notification	March 28, 1988	41–44	60
Risk notification	March 29, 1988	42–52	60
Campaign spending limitations	April 21, 1988	52–42	60
Campaign spending limitations	April 22, 1988	53–37	60
Extend immigration legalization program	April 28, 1988	40–56	60
Death penalty, drug-related killings	June 9, 1988	70–26	60
Great Smoky Mountain Wilderness Act	June 20, 1988	49–35	60
Great Smoky Mountain Wilderness Act	June 21, 1988	54–42	60
Plant-closing notification	June 29, 1988	58–39	60
Plant-closing notification	July 6, 1988	88–5	60
Textile import quotas	Sept. 7, 1988	68–29	60
Minimum wage restoration	Sept. 22, 1988	53–43	60
Minimum wage restoration	Sept. 23, 1988	56–35	60
Parental and medical leave	Oct. 3, 1988	85–6	60
Parental and medical leave	Oct. 7, 1988	50–46	60
Defense authorization, FY 1990	Aug. 2, 1989	84–13	60
Airline smoking ban	Sept. 14, 1989	77–21	60
Eastern Airlines strike commission	Oct. 3, 1989	61–36	60
Nicaraguan election aid	Oct. 13, 1989	52–42	60
Nicaraguan election aid	Oct. 17, 1989	74–25	60
Eastern Airlines strike commission	Oct. 26, 1989	62–38	60
Capital gains tax cut	Nov. 14, 1989	51–47	60
Capital gains tax cut	Nov. 15, 1989	51–47	60
Government pay-and-ethics package	Nov. 17, 1989	90–9	60
Armenian genocide day	Feb. 22, 1990	49–49	60
Armenian genocide day	Feb. 27, 1990	48–51	60
Hatch Act revisions	May 1, 1990	70–28	60
AIDS emergency relief	May 15, 1990	95–3	60
Chemical weapons sanctions	May 17, 1990	87–4	60
Omnibus crime package	June 5, 1990	54–37	60
Omnibus crime package	June 7, 1990	57–37	60
Air travel rights for the blind	June 12, 1990	56–44	60
Civil Rights Act of 1990	July 17, 1990	62–38	60
FY 1991 defense authorization	Aug. 3, 1990	58–41	60
Motor vehicle fuel efficiency	Sept. 14, 1990	68–28	60
Motor vehicle fuel efficiency	Sept. 25, 1990	57–42	60
Title X family planning amendments	Sept. 26, 1990	50–46	60
National motor-voter registration	Sept. 26, 1990	55–42	60
FY 1991 foreign operations funds	Oct. 12, 1990	51–38	60
Vertical price fixing	May 7, 1991	61–37	60
Vertical price fixing	May 8, 1991	63–35	60
Crime bill	June 28, 1991	41–58	60
Crime bill	July 10, 1991	56–43	60
Crime bill	July 10, 1991	71–27	60
National motor-voter registration	July 18, 1991	57–41	60
FY 1992 VA-HUD funds	July 18, 1991	57–40	60
National motor-voter registration	July 18, 1991	59–40	60
Foreign aid authorization	July 24, 1991	87–10	60
Foreign aid authorization	July 25, 1991	52–44	60
Foreign aid authorization	July 25, 1991	63–33	60
Extended unemployment benefits	July 29, 1991	96–1	60
FY 1992 defense authorization	Aug. 2, 1991	58–40	60
FY 1992 interior funds	Sept. 19, 1991	55–41	60
Federal Facility Compliance Act	Oct. 17, 1991	85–14	60
Civil Rights Act	Oct. 22, 1991	93–4	60
National energy policy	Nov. 1, 1991	50–44	60
Banking reform	Nov. 13, 1991	76–19	60
Iranian hostage release investigation	Nov. 22, 1991	51–43	60
Crime conference report	Nov. 27, 1991	49–38	60
School improvement bill	Jan. 21, 1992	93–0	60
National energy strategy	Feb. 4, 1992	90–5	60
Joint ventures antitrust	Feb. 25, 1992	98–0	60
Lumbee Tribe recognition	Feb. 27, 1992	58–39	60
Corp. for Public Broadcasting	March 3, 1992	87–7	60
Crime bill	March 19, 1992	54–43	60
Defense/domestic spending walls	March 26, 1992	50–48	60
NIH/fetal tissue research	March 31, 1992	98–2	60
Motor-voter bill	May 7, 1992	61–38	60
Motor-voter bill	May 12, 1992	58–40	60
Drug abuse mental health	June 9, 1992	84–9	60
Striker replacement	June 11, 1992	55–41	60
Striker replacement	June 16, 1992	57–42	60
Balanced budget amendment	June 30, 1992	56–39	60
Balanced budget amendment	July 1, 1992	56–39	60
National energy strategy	July 23, 1992	58–33	60
National energy strategy	July 28, 1992	93–3	60
Edward Carnes nomination	Sept. 9, 1992	66–30	60
Product liability	Sept. 10, 1992	57–39	60
Product liability	Sept. 10, 1992	58–38	60
School improvement bill	Sept. 15, 1992	85–6	60
Labor/HHS/education funds	Sept. 16, 1992	56–38	60
START treaty	Sept. 29, 1992	87–6	60
School improvement bill	Oct. 2, 1992	59–40	60
Crime bill	Oct. 2, 1992	55–43	60
NIH/fetal tissue research	Oct. 2, 1992	85–12	60
National energy strategy	Oct. 8, 1992	84–8	60
Tax bill	Oct. 8, 1992	80–10	60
Motor-voter bill	March 5, 1993	52–36	60
Motor-voter bill	March 9, 1993	62–38	60
Motor-voter bill	March 16, 1993	59–41	60
Stimulus package	April 2, 1993	55–43	60
Stimulus package	April 3, 1993	52–37	60
Stimulus package	April 5, 1993	49–29	60
Stimulus package	April 21, 1993	56–43	60
Motor-voter bill	May 11, 1993	63–37	60
Campaign finance	June 10, 1993	53–41	60
Campaign finance	June 15, 1993	52–45	60
Campaign finance	June 16, 1993	62–37	60
National service	July 29, 1993	59–41	60
Walter Dellinger confirmation	Oct. 7, 1993	59–39	60
Interior funds	Oct. 21, 1993	53–41	60
Interior funds	Oct. 26, 1993	51–45	60
Interior funds	Oct. 28, 1993	54–44	60
State Department nominations	Nov. 3, 1993	58–42	60
Brady gun bill	Nov. 19, 1993	57–42	60
Janet Ann Napolitano confirmation	Nov. 19, 1993	72–26	60
Brady gun bill	Nov. 19, 1993	57–41	60

Issue	Date	Vote	Yeas needed	Issue	Date	Vote	Yeas needed
Competitiveness bill	March 15, 1994	56–42	60	FY 1998 District of Columbia funds	Sept. 30, 1997	58–41	60
Federal worker retirement buyout	March 24, 1994	58–41	60	Campaign finance legislation	Oct. 7, 1997	52–48	60
Federal worker retirement buyout	March 26, 1994	63–36	60	Campaign finance legislation	Oct. 7, 1997	53–47	60
Education goals 2000	March 26, 1994	62–23	60	**FY 1998 District of Columbia funds**	Oct. 7, 1997	99–1	60
Derek Shearer nomination	May 24, 1994	63–35	60	Campaign finance legislation	Oct. 8, 1997	52–47	60
Sam Brown, Jr. nomination	May 24, 1994	54–44	60	Campaign finance legislation	Oct. 9, 1997	52–47	60
Sam Brown, Jr. nomination	May 25, 1994	56–42	60	Campaign finance legislation	Oct. 9, 1997	51–48	60
Product liability	June 28, 1994	54–44	60	Highway and transit reauthorization	Oct. 23, 1997	48–52	60
Product liability	June 29, 1994	57–41	60	Highway and transit reauthorization	Oct. 23, 1997	48–50	60
Striker replacement	July 12, 1994	53–47	60	Highway and transit reauthorization	Oct. 24, 1997	43–49	60
Striker replacement	July 13, 1994	53–46	60	Highway and transit reauthorization	Oct. 28, 1997	52–48	60
Crime bill	Aug. 25, 1994	61–38	60	Education savings accounts	Oct. 31, 1997	56–41	60
Campaign finance	Sept. 22, 1994	96–2	60	**FY 1998 defense authorization**	Oct. 31, 1997	93–2	60
California desert protection	Sept. 23, 1994	73–20	60	Education savings accounts	Nov. 4, 1997	56–44	60
Campaign finance	Sept. 27, 1994	57–43	60	**Fast track trade procedures**	Nov. 4, 1997	69–31	60
Campaign finance	Sept. 30, 1994	52–46	60	**David Satcher confirmation**	Feb. 10, 1998	75–23	60
Ricki Tigert nomination	Oct. 3, 1994	63–32	60	Ban human cloning research	Feb. 11, 1998	42–54	60
H. Lee Sarokin nomination	Oct. 4, 1994	85–12	60	Restrict political use of union dues	Feb. 26, 1998	51–48	60
Elementary and secondary education	Oct. 5, 1994	75–24	60	Restrict political use of union dues	Feb. 26, 1998	45–54	60
Lobbying disclosure/gift ban	Oct. 6, 1994	52–46	66	**Highway and mass transit programs**	March 11, 1998	96–3	60
Lobbying disclosure/gift ban	Oct. 7, 1994	55–42	65	**Education savings accounts**	March 17, 1998	74–24	60
California desert protection	Oct. 8, 1994	68–23	60	Expand education savings accounts	March 19, 1998	55–44	60
Unfunded mandates	Jan. 19, 1995	54–44	60	Expand education savings accounts	March 26, 1998	58–42	60
Balanced-budget amendment	Feb. 16, 1995	57–42	60	U.S. anti-missile defense policy	May 13, 1998	59–41	60
Striker replacement	March 15, 1995	58–39	60	Create nuclear waste storage in Nevada	June 2, 1998	56–39	60
Health insurance tax deduction	April 3, 1995	83– 0	60	Set federal policies to curb smoking	June 9, 1998	42–56	60
Supplemental funds, rescissions	April 6, 1995	56–44	60	Set federal policies to curb smoking	June 10, 1998	43–55	60
Product liability	May 4, 1995	46–53	60	Set federal policies to curb smoking	June 11, 1998	43–56	60
Product liability	May 4, 1995	47–52	60	Set federal policies to curb smoking	June 17, 1998	57–42	60
Product liability	May 8, 1995	43–49	60	**Limit product liability suits**	July 7, 1998	71–24	60
Product liability	May 9, 1995	60–38	60	Limit punitive damages in product liability suits	July 9, 1998	51–47	60
Interstate waste	May 12, 1995	50–47	60	U.S. court review, local zoning decisions	July 13, 1998	52–42	60
Telecommunications	June 14, 1995	89–11	60	**FY 1999 legislative branch funds**	July 21, 1998	83–16	60
Henry Foster nomination	June 21, 1995	57–43	60	U.S. anti-missile defense policy	Sept. 9, 1998	59–41	60
Henry Foster nomination	June 22, 1995	57–43	60	**Consumer bankruptcy laws**	Sept. 9, 1998	99–1	60
Regulatory overhaul	July 17, 1995	48–46	60	Campaign finance	Sept. 10, 1998	52–48	60
Regulatory overhaul	July 18, 1995	53–47	60	**Parental consent abortion bill**	Sept. 11, 1998	97–0	60
Regulatory overhaul	July 20, 1995	58–40	60	Limit union organizing	Sept. 14, 1998	52–42	60
State Department authorization	Aug. 1, 1995	55–45	60	Evading parental consent abortion laws	Sept. 22, 1998	54–45	60
State Department authorization	Aug. 1, 1995	55–45	60	**Limit presidential appointment powers**	Sept. 24, 1998	96–1	60
Cuba sanctions	Oct. 12, 1995	56–37	60	Limit presidential appointment powers	Sept. 28, 1998	53–38	60
Cuba sanctions	Oct. 17, 1995	59–36	60	**Ban Internet sales taxes**	Sept. 29, 1998	89–6	60
Cuba sanctions	Oct. 18, 1995	98–0	60	**Banking regulation revision**	Oct. 5, 1998	93–0	60
Farm bill	Feb. 1, 1996	53–45	60	**Ban Internet sales taxes for two years**	Oct. 7, 1998	94–4	60
Farm bill	Feb. 6, 1996	59–34	60	Waive federal education spending rules	March 8, 1999	54–41	60
District of Columbia funds	Feb. 27, 1996	54–44	60	Waive federal education spending rules	March 9, 1999	55–39	60
District of Columbia funds	Feb. 29, 1996	52–42	60	Authorize $11.4 billion for new teacher hirings	March 10, 1999	44–55	60
District of Columbia funds	March 5, 1996	53–43	60	Special education funding	March 10, 1999	55–44	60
District of Columbia funds	March 12, 1996	56–44	60	U.S. troops in Kosovo	March 23, 1999	55–44	60
Whitewater committee extension	March 12, 1996	53–47	60	Social Security "lockbox" and debt limit	April 22, 1999	54–45	60
Whitewater committee extension	March 13, 1996	53–47	60	**Y2K liability limits**	April 26, 1999	94–0	60
Whitewater committee extension	March 14, 1996	51–46	60	Y2K liability limits	April 29, 1999	52–47	60
Product liability	March 20, 1996	60–40	60	Social Security "lockbox," debt limit	April 30, 1999	49–44	60
Whitewater committee extension	March 20, 1996	53–47	60	Y2K liability limits	May 18, 1999	53–45	60
Whitewater committee extension	March 21, 1996	52–46	60	Social Security "lockbox," debt limit	June 15, 1999	53–46	60
Presidio Park management	March 27, 1996	51–49	60	**Steel, oil, gas loan guarantee**	June 15, 1999	70–29	60
Presidio Park management	March 28, 1996	55–45	60	Social Security "lockbox"	June 16, 1999	55–44	60
Whitewater committee extension	April 16, 1996	51–46	60	Steel import quotas	June 22, 1999	42–57	60
Term Limits constitutional amendment	April 23, 1996	58–42	60	FY 2000 agriculture funds	June 28, 1999	50–37	60
Immigration revision	April 29, 1996	91–0	60	FY 2000 transportation funds	June 28, 1999	49–40	60
Immigration revision	May 2, 1996	100–0	60	FY 2000 commerce, state, justice funds	June 28, 1999	49–39	60
White House Travel Office reimbursement	May 7, 1996	52–44	60	FY 2000 foreign operations funds	June 28, 1999	49–41	60
White House Travel Office reimbursement	May 8, 1996	53–45	60	**Budget procedures**	July 1, 1999	99–1	60
White House Travel Office reimbursement	May 9, 1996	52–44	60	Social Security "lockbox," debt limit	July 16, 1999	52–43	60
White House Travel Office reimbursement	May 14, 1996	54–43	60	**FY 2000 intelligence authorization**	July 20, 1999	99–0	60
Missile defense	June 4, 1996	53–46	60	**Juvenile justice programs**	July 28, 1999	77–22	60
Campaign finance overhaul	June 25, 1996	54–46	60	FY 2000 agriculture funds/milk marketing	Aug. 4, 1999	53–47	60
Defense authorization	June 26, 1996	52–46	60	FY 2000 transportation funds	Sept. 9, 1999	49–49	60
Defense authorization	June 28, 1996	53–43	60	**Puerto Rican nationalists' clemency**	Sept. 13, 1999	93–0	60
Right-to-work legislation	July 10, 1996	31–68	60	Oil royalty valuation system	Sept. 13, 1999	55–40	60
Nuclear waste storage	July 16, 1996	65–34	60	Bankruptcy law revision	Sept. 21, 1999	53–45	60
Federal Aviation Administration Reauthorization	Oct. 3, 1996	66–31	60	Brian Stewart nomination	Sept. 21, 1999	55–44	60
Volunteer liability limitation	April 29, 1997	53–46	60	**Oil royalty valuation system**	Sept. 23, 1999	60–39	60
Volunteer liability limitation	April 30, 1997	55–44	60	**FY 2000 agriculture funds**	Oct. 12, 1999	79–20	60
Supplemental funds	May 7, 1997	100–0	60	Campaign finance soft money ban	Oct. 19, 1999	52–48	60
Compensatory time, flexible credit	May 15, 1997	53–47	60	Campaign finance soft money, union dues	Oct. 19, 1999	53–47	60
Compensatory time, flexible credit	June 4, 1997	51–47	60	**Trade with Sub-Saharan Africa**	Oct. 26, 1999	90–8	60
FY 1998 defense authorization	July 8, 1997	46–45	60	Trade with Sub-Saharan Africa, Caribbean	Oct. 29, 1999	45–46	60
Joel Klein nomination	July 14, 1997	78–11	60	**Trade with Sub-Saharan Africa, Caribbean**	Nov. 2, 1999	74–23	60
Food and Drug Administration overhaul	Sept. 5, 1997	89–5	60	**FY 2000 omnibus funds**	Nov. 19, 1999	87–9	60
Food and Drug Administration overhaul	Sept. 16, 1997	94–4	60				

Issue	Date	Vote	Yeas needed	Issue	Date	Vote	Yeas needed
Nuclear waste storage	Feb. 8, 2000	94–3	60	**Estate tax repeal**	July 11, 2000	99–1	60
Marsha Berzon nomination	March 8, 2000	86–13	60	**FY 2001 treasury funds**	July 26, 2000	97–0	60
Richard Paez nomination	March 8, 2000	85–14	60	**FY 2001 intelligence authorization**	July 26, 2000	96–1	60
Flag desecration constitutional amendment	March 29, 2000	100–0	60	**FY 2001 energy, water funds**	July 27, 2000	100–0	60
Federal gas tax suspension	March 30, 2000	86–11	60	**Trade with China**	July 27, 2000	86–12	60
Federal gas tax suspension	April 11, 2000	43–56	60	**High technology visas**	Sept. 19, 2000	97–1	60
Marriage penalty tax	April 13, 2000	53–45	60	**High technology visas**	Sept. 26, 2000	94–3	60
Marriage penalty tax	April 13, 2000	53–45	60	**High technology visas**	Sept. 28, 2000	92–3	60
Victims' rights	April 25, 2000	82–12	60	**FY 2001 interior funds**	Oct. 5, 2000	89–8	60
Marriage penalty tax	April 27, 2000	51–44	60	Bankruptcy law revision conference report	Nov. 1, 2000	53–30	60
Africa trade agreement	May 11, 2000	76–18	60	**Bankruptcy law revision conference report**	Dec. 5, 2000	67–31	60

1. Vote was taken after midnight in the session that began Oct. 8, 1985.

Attempted and Successful Cloture Votes, 1919–2001

Congress		Attempted cloture votes	Successful cloture votes	Congress		Attempted cloture votes	Successful cloture votes
66th	(1919–1921)	1	1	91st	(1969–1971)	6	0
67th	(1921–1923)	1	0	92nd	(1971–1973)	20	4
68th	(1923–1925)	0	0	93rd	(1973–1975)	31	9
69th	(1925–1927)	5	2	94th	(1975–1977)	27	17
70th	(1927–1929)	0	0	95th	(1977–1979)	13	3
71st	(1929–1931)	0	0	96th	(1979–1981)	21	10
72nd	(1931–1933)	1	0	97th	(1981–1983)	27	9
73rd	(1933–1935)	0	0	98th	(1983–1985)	19	11
74th	(1935–1937)	2	0	99th	(1985–1987)	23	10
75th	(1937–1939)	0	0	100th	(1987–1989)	43	11
76th	(1939–1941)	0	0	101st	(1989–1991)	24	11
77th	(1941–1943)	1	0	102nd	(1991–1993)	48	23
78th	(1943–1945)	1	0	103rd	(1993–1995)	42	13
79th	(1945–1947)	4	0	104th	(1995–1997)	50	9
80th	(1947–1949)	0	0	105th	(1997–1999)	53	18
81st	(1949–1951)	2	0	106th	(1999–2001)	58	28
82nd	(1951–1953)	0	0	TOTALS		545	193
83rd	(1953–1955)	1	0				
84th	(1955–1957)	0	0				
85th	(1957–1959)	0	0				
86th	(1959–1961)	1	0				
87th	(1961–1963)	4	1				
88th	(1963–1965)	3	1				
89th	(1965–1967)	7	1				
90th	(1967–1969)	6	1				

NOTE: The number of votes required to invoke cloture was changed March 7, 1975, from two-thirds of those present and voting, to three-fifths of the total Senate membership, as Rule xxii of the standing rules of the Senate was amended.

SOURCES: *Congress and the Nation,* selected volumes (Washington, D.C.: Congressional Quarterly, selected years); *CQ Almanac,* selected volumes (Washington, D.C.: Congressional Quarterly, selected years); Richard S. Beth, Congressional Research Service, Library of Congress.

House Discharge Petitions since 1931

The discharge petition is a little-used but dramatic House device that enables a majority of representatives to bring to the floor legislation blocked in committee. The following table shows the frequency with which the discharge petition has been used since the present discharge procedure was adopted in 1931 through the second session of the 106th Congress. While the procedure obviously is rarely used and even more rarely successful, it may on occasion indirectly succeed by impelling a legislative committee, the Rules Committee, or the leadership to act on a measure and thereby avoid the discharge.

Congress		Discharge petitions filed	Discharge motion		Committee discharged	Underlying measure[3]	
			Entered[1]	Called up[2]		Passed House	Received final approval[4]
72nd	(1931–1933)	12	5	5	1	1	–
73rd	(1933–1935)	31	6	1	1	1	–
74th	(1935–1937)	33	3	2	2	–	–
75th	(1937–1939)	43	4	4	3[5]	2	1
76th	(1939–1941)	37[5]	2	2	2	2	–
77th	(1941–1943)	15	1	1	1	1	–
78th	(1943–1945)	21	3	3	3	3	1[6]
79th	(1945–1947)	35	3	1	1	1	–
80th	(1947–1949)	20	1	1	1	1	–
81st	(1949–1951)	34	3[7]	1	1	1	–
82nd	(1951–1953)	14	–	–	–	–	–
83rd	(1953–1955)	10	1	1	1	1	–
84th	(1955–1957)	6	–	–	–	–	–
85th	(1957–1959)	7	1	1	1	1	–
86th	(1959–1961)	7	1	1	1	1	1
87th	(1961–1963)	6	–	–	–	–	–
88th	(1963–1965)	5	–	–	–	–	–
89th	(1965–1967)	6	1	1	1	1	–
90th	(1967–1969)	4	–	–	–	–	–
91st	(1969–1971)	12	1	1	1	1	–
92nd	(1971–1973)	15	1	1	1	–	–
93rd	(1973–1975)	10	–	–	–	–	–
94th	(1975–1977)	15	–	–	–	–	–
95th	(1977–1979)	11	–	–	–	–	–
96th	(1979–1981)	14	2	1	1	–	–
97th	(1981–1983)	24	1	–	–	–	–
98th	(1983–1985)	13	1	–	–	–	–
99th	(1985–1987)	10	1	–	–	–	–
100th	(1987–1989)	5[8]	–	–	–	–	–
101st	(1989–1991)	8	1	–	–	–	–
102nd	(1991–1993)	8	1[9]	1[9]	1[9]	–	–
103rd	(1993–1995)	26	2[9]	2[9]	2[9]	1	1[6]
104th	(1995–1997)	15	–	–	–	–	–
105th	(1997–1999)	8	–	–	–	–	–
106th	(1999–2001)	11	–	–	–	–	–
	TOTALS	551	46	31	26	19	4

1. A discharge motion is "entered" when the petition receives sufficient signatures for it to be entered on the Calendar of Motions to Discharge Committees. This number was 145 in the 72nd and 73rd Congresses, 219 in the 86th and 87th Congresses, and 218 for all other Congresses in the table.

2. A discharge motion may be offered on the floor on any second or fourth Monday falling at least seven legislative days after the discharge petition is entered. Each day on which the House convenes is usually a legislative day.

3. A discharge petition may be filed to bring to the floor either a substantive measure in committee or a "special rule" from the Committee on Rules providing for House consideration of such a measure that is either in committee or previously reported. The last two columns of this table reflect action on the underlying, substantive measure, not on the special rule, if any, on which discharge was directly sought.

4. Includes bills and joint resolutions becoming law; constitutional amendments submitted to the states for ratification; resolutions agreed to by the House; and concurrent resolutions finally agreed to by both chambers.

5. During this Congress, the Rules Committee was discharged from a special rule for consideration of one measure, and the measure was taken up but then recommitted. Subsequently, the Rules Committee was discharged from a second special rule for consideration of the measure. This measure accordingly appears twice under "Committee discharged" and earlier columns, but only once under "Passed House" and subsequently.

6. Resolution attempting to change House Rules.

7. Includes one petition entered with respect to a special rule on a measure and another on the same measure directly.

8. Includes one petition filed on a special rule for considering two measures.

9. Includes one measure in the 102nd Congress and two in the 103rd from which the committee was discharged, and which were brought to the floor, by unanimous consent after the discharge petition was entered.

SOURCE: Richard S. Beth, "The Discharge Rule in the House: Recent Use in Historical Context," Congressional Research Service, Library of Congress, September 15, 1997; updates provided by CRS, September 1999 and April 2002.

Congressional Apportionment, 1789–2000

State	Constitution (1789)[2]	Year of census[1]																			
		1790	1800	1810	1820	1830	1840	1850	1860	1870	1880	1890	1900	1910	1930[3]	1940	1950	1960	1970	1980	1990	2000
Alabama				1[4]	3	5	7	7	6	8	8	9	9	10	9	9	9	8	7	7	7	7
Alaska																	1[4]	1	1	1	1	1
Arizona														1[4]	1	2	2	3	4	5	6	8
Arkansas					1[4]	1	2	3	4	5	6	7	7	7	7	6	4	4	4	4	4	
California						2[4]	2	3	4	6	7	8	11	20	23	30	38	43	45	52	53	
Colorado									1[4]	1	2	3	4	4	4	4	4	5	6	6	7	
Conn.	5	7	7	7	6	6	4	4	4	4	4	4	5	5	6	6	6	6	6	6	6	5
Delaware	1	1	1	2	1	1	1	1	1	1	1	1	1	1	1	1	1	1	1	1	1	1
Florida						1[4]	1	1	2	2	2	3	4	5	6	8	12	15	19	23	25	
Georgia	3	2	4	6	7	9	8	8	7	9	10	11	11	12	10	10	10	10	10	10	11	13
Hawaii																	1[4]	2	2	2	2	2
Idaho										1[4]	1	1	2	2	2	2	2	2	2	2	2	
Illinois				1[4]	1	3	7	9	14	19	20	22	25	27	27	26	25	24	24	22	20	19
Indiana				1[4]	3	7	10	11	11	13	13	13	13	13	12	11	11	11	11	10	10	9
Iowa						2[4]	2	6	9	11	11	11	11	9	8	8	7	6	6	5	5	
Kansas								1	3	7	8	8	8	7	6	6	5	5	5	4	4	
Kentucky		2	6	10	12	13	10	10	9	10	11	11	11	11	9	9	8	7	7	7	6	6
Louisiana				1[4]	3	3	4	4	5	6	6	6	7	8	8	8	8	8	8	8	7	7
Maine				7[4]	7	8	7	6	5	5	4	4	4	4	3	3	3	2	2	2	2	2
Maryland	6	8	9	9	9	8	6	6	5	6	6	6	6	6	6	6	7	8	8	8	8	8
Massachusetts	8	14	17	13[5]	13	12	10	11	10	11	12	13	14	16	15	14	14	12	12	11	10	10
Michigan					1[4]	3	4	6	9	11	12	12	13	17	17	18	19	19	18	16	15	
Minnesota							2[4]	2	3	5	7	9	10	9	9	9	8	8	8	8	8	
Mississippi				1[4]	1	2	4	5	5	6	7	7	8	8	7	7	6	5	5	5	5	4
Missouri					1	2	5	7	9	13	14	15	16	16	13	13	11	10	10	9	9	9
Montana										1[4]	1	1	2	2	2	2	2	2	2	2	1	1
Nebraska.								1[4]	1	3	6	6	6	5	4	4	3	3	3	3	3	
Nevada								1[4]	1	1	1	1	1	1	1	1	1	1	1	2	2	3
New Hampshire	3	4	5	6	6	5	4	3	3	3	2	2	2	2	2	2	2	2	2	2	2	2
New Jersey	4	5	6	6	6	6	5	5	5	7	7	8	10	12	14	14	14	15	15	14	13	13
New Mexico														1[4]	1	2	2	2	2	3	3	3
New York	6	10	17	27	34	40	34	33	31	33	34	34	37	43	45	45	43	41	39	34	31	29
North Carolina	5	10	12	13	13	13	9	8	7	8	9	9	10	10	11	12	12	11	11	11	12	13[7]
North Dakota										1[4]	1	2	3	2	2	2	2	1	1	1	1	
Ohio			1[4]	6	14	19	21	21	19	20	21	21	21	22	24	23	23	24	23	21	19	18
Oklahoma													5[4]	8	9	8	6	6	6	6	6	5
Oregon				–				1[4]	1	1	1	2	2	3	3	4	4	4	4	5	5	5
Pennsylvania	8	13	18	23	26	28	24	25	24	27	28	30	32	36	34	33	30	27	25	23	21	19
Rhode Island	1	2	2	2	2	2	2	2	2	2	2	2	2	3	2	2	2	2	2	2	2	2
South Carolina	5	6	8	9	9	9	7	6	4	5	7	7	7	7	6	6	6	6	6	6	6	6
South Dakota										2[4]	2	2	3	2	2	2	2	2	1	1	1	
Tennessee		1[4]	3	6	9	13	11	10	8	10	10	10	10	10	9	10	9	9	8	9	9	9
Texas						2[4]	2	4	6	11	13	16	18	21	21	22	23	24	27	30	32	
Utah										1[4]	1	2	2	2	2	2	2	2	3	3	3[7]	
Vermont		2	4	6	5	5	4	3	3	3	2	2	2	2	1	1	1	1	1	1	1	1
Virginia	10	19	22	23	22	21	15	13	11	9	10	10	10	10	9	9	10	10	10	10	11	11
Washington										1[4]	2	3	5	6	6	7	7	7	8	9	9	
West Virginia									3	4	4	5	6	6	6	6	5	4	4	3	3	
Wisconsin						2[4]	3	6	8	9	10	11	11	10	10	10	10	9	9	9	8	
Wyoming										1[4]	1	1	1	1	1	1	1	1	1	1	1	
TOTAL	65	106	142	186	213	242	232	237	243	293	332	357	391	435	435	435	437[6]	435	435	435	435	435

1. Apportionment effective with congressional election two years after census.
2. Original apportionment made in Constitution, pending first census.
3. No apportionment was made in 1920.
4. These figures are not based on any census, but indicate the provisional representation accorded newly admitted states by Congress, pending the next census.
5. Twenty members were assigned to Massachusetts, but seven of these were credited to Maine when that area became a state.
6. Normally 435, but temporarily increased two seats by Congress when Alaska and Hawaii became states.
7. In a case pending before the U.S. Supreme Court in April 2002, Utah was challenging a device used by the Census Bureau in taking the 2000 census that Utah claimed wrongly deprived the state of an additional seat in Congress. If Utah's claim prevailed, that state would have four seats rather than three. The state that was expected to forfeit a seat was North Carolina, which had gained one seat, for a total of thirteen, as a result of the 2000 census. The Court had not decided the case as of April 12, 2002.

SOURCES: *Biographical Directory of the American Congress* and Bureau of the Census.

The Presidency

Clinton Appointments
to Major Posts   977

Presidential Vetoes, 1997–2001   994

Clinton Appointments to Major Posts

President Clinton's second term began with a flurry of cabinet changes, as he named replacements to lead seven of the fourteen cabinet departments: Commerce, Defense, Energy, Housing and Urban Development, Labor, State, and Transportation. By term's end, there had been four additional turnovers in department heads—at Commerce and Energy again, as well as at Treasury and Veterans Affairs. Only Attorney General Janet Reno, Secretary of Education Richard W. Riley, Secretary of Health and Human Services Donna Shalala, and Secretary of the Interior Bruce Babbitt stayed at their posts for both terms.

A few of the second-term cabinet nominees received quick Senate confirmation. The new secretaries of state, defense, commerce, and housing and urban development were sworn in to coincide with the resignations of their successors. (*Clinton cabinet box, p. 978; Clinton appointments 1993–1996, Congress and the Nation IX, p. 1109*)

Other nominations went less smoothly. Clinton's choice for secretary of labor, Alexis Herman, and secretary of energy, Federico F. Peña, had their confirmations held for several months. Herman was investigated for alleged fund-raising improprieties, and Peña was thought inexperienced for the position. Peña stayed in the Energy job for about fifteen months and then was succeeded by Bill Richardson. Richardson's swearing in was held up for several weeks after his Senate confirmation while an "informal inquiry" was conducted into allegations that he had created a job for former White House intern Monica S. Lewinsky, as part of a cover-up of a White House sex scandal. Treasury secretary nominee Lawrence H. Summers's confirmation was never in jeopardy, but it was delayed by senators trying to use it as leverage on health care issues and in protest against a controversial ambassadorial appointment.

After the Republican takeover of Congress in 1995, the Senate delayed or killed dozens of the president's appointees to federal judgeships. Sen. John Ashcroft, R-Mo., emerged as a powerful adversary, waging a war on virtually all of Clinton's choices. The most controversial example was in 1999, when the Senate rejected the nomination of Ronnie L. White—the first African American on Missouri's Supreme Court—for a U.S. District Court judgeship. He was the first judicial nominee to be rejected since the defeat of Robert H. Bork was blocked for a seat on the Supreme Court in 1987.

With the switch of control of the Senate, Republican Sen. Jesse Helms of North Carolina gained the chairmanship of the Foreign Relations Committee and waged battle against many of the Clinton nominees for diplomatic posts. He actively opposed several nominations and held captive the nominations of those whose positions did not agree with his conservative views. He single-handedly scuttled the nomination of former Massachusetts Gov. William F. Weld, a moderate Republican, to an ambassadorship and gave his fellow senators a history lesson on failed nominations in the process.

Below are profiles of cabinet members and others who were confirmed to serve in key executive branch positions during the second Clinton administration, followed by brief accounts of major controversial nominations.

Cabinet, 1997–2001

COMMERCE

William M. Daley was confirmed Jan. 30, 1997, to become Clinton's third secretary of commerce. Daley succeeded Mickey Kantor, who was returning to California to practice law. While the Daley nomination met with little dissent, the Senate vote, 95–2, yielded the first "no" votes of any confirmation at the start of the Clinton's second term. The Commerce, Science, and Transportation Committee had approved Daley's nomination, 19–1, on Jan. 29.

Although he had never run for public office, Daley was regarded as a skilled politician. He ran the fund-raising effort for the 1996 Democratic National Convention and helped Clinton win a near landslide in Illinois in the general election. He was a member of a prominent political family: his father, Richard J. Daley, dominated as mayor of Chicago from 1955 to 1976, and his brother, Richard M. Daley, was the current mayor of Chicago.

Daley, a partner at the Chicago law firm Mayer, Brown & Platt and a former bank president, had been associated with Clinton since the 1992 presidential campaign. Daley had been seen as a front-runner for secretary of transportation in Clinton's first term but was passed over for former Denver mayor Federico F. Peña. Clinton instead appointed Daley to the board of the Federal National Mortgage Association (Fannie Mae), a government-sponsored enterprise. He also gave him a more public role as special counsel on the North American Free Trade Agreement.

Declaring at his Jan. 22 confirmation hearing that he would eschew partisanship, Daley promised to keep the troubled Commerce Department free of political activity during his tenure. The pledge was a successful preemptive strike that quelled any intention of Republicans on the Senate Commerce, Science, and Transportation Committee to voice their allegations that the Clinton administration had turned the Commerce Department into a Democratic political operation.

To some conservative Republicans, the issue of partisan politics at Commerce was secondary to a larger theme: whether the department should exist at all. In the previous Congress, the Commerce Department had emerged as one of the top targets of Republicans interested in eliminating departments they saw as wasteful. Although such efforts failed, some members remained determined to dismantle Commerce, scrapping some of its functions and dispersing the rest to other agencies.

Despite this backdrop, the hearing went relatively easily. Even Republican senators Spencer Abraham of Michigan and Sam Brownback of Kansas—the department's most severe critics on the committee—took a gentle approach in questioning the nominee. While acknowledging that some changes needed to be made, Daley defended the department, saying it remained a vital advocate for U.S. businesses facing global competition.

Daley had received a lucrative income from his work as a lobbyist and corporate adviser, earning nearly $1 million in 1996. He also served on boards of directors of a handful of companies. Sen. Wendell H. Ford, D-Ky., asked Daley to respond to questions that had been raised about his service as a board member on Fannie Mae that coincided with work that his law firm had done for the federally chartered corporation. Daley denied that there were any ties between his position at Fannie Mae and the work his law firm had done for the corporation. He said if his law firm was not qualified to work for Fannie Mae, "we wouldn't be representing them." Responding to concerns that Chicago might benefit disproportionately from his position at the helm of Commerce, Daley promised to recuse himself from specific matters in which Chicago was a party.

CLINTON ADMINISTRATION CABINET

Following is a list of cabinet officers who served in the administration of President Bill Clinton during his eight years in office between Jan. 20, 1993, and Jan. 20, 2001. The list does not include acting secretaries.

Dates given are for actual service in office, beginning with the cabinet officers' swearing-in date, which may vary from date of confirmation by the Senate. *(Presidents and their cabinets, 1933–1980, Congress and the Nation Vol. V., p. 1111; Reagan cabinet, 1981–1989, Congress and the Nation Vol. VII, p. 1045; Bush cabinet, 1989–1993, Congress and the Nation Vol. VIII, p. 1171)*

Secretary of State
Warren M. Christopher—Jan. 22, 1993–Jan. 20, 1997
Madeleine K. Albright—Jan. 23, 1997–Jan. 20, 2001

Secretary of the Treasury
Lloyd M. Bentsen—Jan. 22, 1993–Dec. 22, 1994
Robert E. Rubin—Jan. 10, 1995–July 2, 1999
Lawrence H. Summers—July 2, 1999–Jan. 20, 2001

Secretary of Defense
Les Aspin—Jan. 20, 1993–Feb. 2, 1994
William J. Perry—Feb. 3, 1994–Jan. 24, 1997
William S. Cohen—Jan. 24, 1997–Jan. 20, 2001

Attorney General
Janet Reno—March 12, 1993–Jan. 20, 2001

Secretary of the Interior
Bruce Babbitt—Jan. 22, 1993–Jan. 2, 2001

Secretary of Agriculture
A. Michael Espy—Jan. 22, 1993–Dec. 31, 1994
Daniel R. Glickman—March 30, 1995–Jan. 19, 2001

Secretary of Commerce
Ronald H. Brown—Jan. 22, 1993–April 3, 1996
Mickey Kantor[1]—April 12, 1996–Jan. 21, 1997
William M. Daley—Jan. 30, 1997–July 19, 2000
Norman Y. Mineta—July 21, 2000–Jan. 19, 2001

Secretary of Labor
Robert B. Reich—Jan. 22, 1993–Jan. 10, 1997
Alexis M. Herman—May 1, 1997–Jan. 20, 2001

Secretary of Health and Human Services
Donna E. Shalala—Jan. 22, 1993–Jan. 20, 2001

Secretary of Education
Richard W. Riley—Jan. 22, 1993–Jan. 20, 2001

Secretary of Housing and Urban Development
Henry G. Cisneros—Jan. 22, 1993–Jan. 19, 1997
Andrew M. Cuomo—Jan. 29, 1997–Jan. 20, 2001

Secretary of Transportation
Federico F. Peña—Jan. 22, 1993–Feb. 14, 1997
Rodney E. Slater—Feb. 14, 1997–Jan. 20, 2001

Secretary of Energy
Hazel R. O'Leary—Jan. 22, 1993–Jan. 20, 1997
Federico F. Peña —March 12, 1997–June 30, 1998
Bill Richardson—Aug. 18, 1998–Jan. 20, 2001

Secretary of Veterans Affairs
Jesse Brown—Jan. 22, 1993–July 1, 1997
Togo D. West, Jr.—May 5, 1998–July 24, 2000

1. Kantor served as a recess appointment; Senate confirmation was not constitutionally required until the end of 1997.

Daley specifically vowed to reduce the number of political appointees at Commerce from 256 to 156 and defer all overseas trade missions by department officials pending a thirty-day review into the rules and criteria governing such missions. Some GOP lawmakers had accused the administration of turning department-sponsored missions into junkets to reward businesses that contributed to the Democratic Party.

Sam Brownback, R-Kan., voted against Daley in committee and on the floor. Brownback, who favored dismantling the Commerce Department, said Daley had not suggested sufficient program cuts. Also voting "no" on the floor was James M. Inhofe, R-Okla. But otherwise, Daley won praise. "He's an experienced, talented individual," said Commerce Committee Chairman John McCain, R-Ariz., who ran Daley's confirmation hearing.

On July 20, 2000, the Senate confirmed former representative **Norman Y. Mineta,** D-Calif., to become Clinton's fourth secretary of

commerce. He was approved by voice vote and without debate. Mineta became the first person of Asian-Pacific descent to hold a cabinet post. He succeeded William M. Daley, who resigned July 19 to head Vice President Al Gore's presidential campaign, in the waning months of the Clinton administration.

Mineta served in the House from 1975 to 1995 and was known for his interest in aviation and consumer issues. He was also a driving force behind the 1988 Civil Liberties Act (PL 100-383), which compensated Japanese Americans interned in relocation camps in the United States during World War II. He and his family were interned in Wyoming.

When he first won the presidency in 1993, Clinton had tried to interest Mineta in becoming the secretary of transportation, but Mineta wanted to stay in the 103rd Congress and become chairman of the Public Works and Transportation Committee. Ten months after the GOP assumed control of the House, Mineta resigned in October

1995 to be a top executive for a growing transportation technology business at Lockheed Martin IMS, a branch of one of the nation's largest defense contractors.

"Some might say that the months remaining in this administration [are] not a lot of time to make a difference," Mineta said when he was nominated. "But I disagree. Six months is a virtual eternity in the new economy."

Mineta said in a Senate Commerce, Science, and Transportation Committee hearing July 19 that he would focus on free and fair trade, economic growth, and "digital inclusion" for people left out of the nation's technology boom. The committee approved his nomination the following day.

Mineta was respected by his former colleagues from both parties and his nomination was well received. "His entire track record . . . has been one of consensus building," said a former aide.

"I want to make sure that there's nothing that he's been involved in since he left the Congress that would be a problem," said Majority Leader Trent Lott, R-Miss. "But I think generally there's going to be a positive reaction. We all know him and knew him to be an effective legislator." Commerce Committee Chairman John McCain, R-Ariz., called Mineta "highly qualified."

At the conclusion of the Clinton administration, Mineta was the only Democrat chosen to be in the in-coming Bush administration cabinet, but he would move to transportation secretary.

DEFENSE

President Clinton reached across party lines to nominate Republican **William S. Cohen,** a former senator from Maine, to be secretary of defense. Cohen replaced William J. Perry, who resigned to spend more time with his grandchildren.

Cohen was questioned by his former colleagues on the Senate Armed Services Committee, unanimously approved, and then confirmed by the full Senate without dissent—all in one day. The 99–0 vote Jan. 22, 1997, came after a brief debate in which senators lauded their just-retired colleague as a thoughtful and independent-minded voice for bipartisanship in defense policy. The Armed Services panel had approved Cohen's nomination by a vote of 18–0.

Cohen won a vacant U.S. House seat in 1972 and served six years (1973–1979) before moving in 1979 to the Senate, where he was a member of the Armed Services and Governmental Affairs committees. On Jan. 16, 1996, Cohen announced his intention to retire after three terms in the U.S. Senate (1979–1997).

Twice in his career the fiercely independent Cohen resisted strong political pressure from other Republicans and mounted high-profile challenges to presidents of his party over what he saw as intolerable deceptions of Congress. In 1974, while still a House freshman, he was a key member of the centrist coalition that backed impeachment of President Richard Nixon in the wake of the Watergate scandal and cover-up. During 1987 hearings, he blasted high-ranking members of President Ronald Reagan's administration for lawbreaking in connection with the Iran-contra scandal in which Reagan associates secretly sold arms to Iran and used some of the profits to fund "contra" rebels fighting the leftist government of Nicaragua.

Though one of the Senate's most liberal Republicans on domestic issues, Cohen's record on defense questions was solidly in the GOP mainstream. He had vigorously criticized the Clinton administration for not accelerating the antimissile defense program, deferring increases in the weapons procurement budget, and refusing to obtain congressional approval of overseas troop deployments. He had consistently supported higher military budgets than his Democratic colleagues or the administration and generally favored a more assertive foreign policy.

But Cohen assured the committee that he could work effectively within the Clinton team. "My record is one of bridging differences—not papering them over, but building consensus behind reasonable and responsible compromises," he said. "Uniformity of opinion within an administration is not an imperative, or even an ideal to be sought."

"My presumption is that [Cohen] has . . . pledged his loyalty, as is appropriate," said John McCain, R-Ariz., a fellow Armed Services Committee member and a close friend. "But he has also made it clear to the president that he will act in what he thinks is the best interest of the United States."

ENERGY

The Senate voted 99–1 on March 12, 1997, to confirm **Federico F. Peña** as energy secretary. Peña, who had been transportation secretary in Clinton's first term, replaced Hazel R. O'Leary, who retired Jan. 20.

Peña's nomination was clouded initially by widespread speculation that Clinton picked him mainly to preserve the cabinet's ethnic diversity. Clinton had been leaning toward Elizabeth Moler, chairman of the Federal Energy Regulatory Commission, for the energy post, and Peña had planned to leave the government. But with Housing and Urban Development Secretary Henry G. Cisneros retiring, Peña's departure would have left the cabinet with no Hispanic members. Clinton asked Peña to stay as energy secretary.

The nomination became enmeshed in the controversy over nuclear waste disposal and Peña was not confirmed until three months after his nomination.

At the Senate Energy and Natural Resources Committee hearing Jan. 30 on his nomination, Peña faced a barrage of pointed questions. The tough reception signaled strong dissatisfaction not with the nominee, but with the department he was asked to lead. Committee members raised issues—such as nuclear waste disposal, a nuclear weapons test ban, oil drilling in the Arctic, and the future of federally owned power plants—that vexed the energy department in recent years and led critics to argue it should be eliminated. Even the committee's ranking Democrat, Dale Bumpers of Arkansas, challenged Peña on the administration's approach to deregulating the electric power industry.

Some senators questioned whether his last-minute nomination meant that the administration viewed the job, in the words of Energy Committee Chairman Frank H. Murkowski, R-Alaska, as a "throwaway" position. Yet Peña was regarded as a strong administrator at transportation, and his lack of experience on energy and nuclear weapons issues did not emerge as a major obstacle to his nomination. At the hearing, Peña largely reiterated the administration's standing energy policies, carried out by retiring Secretary O'Leary. But many in Congress criticized O'Leary's stewardship of the department, and Peña was warned that inertia at Energy would not be tolerated.

The long-stymied effort to establish a central repository for the nation's nuclear waste spurred heated discussion at the hearing. Sens. Murkowski, Larry E. Craig of Idaho, and Rod Grams of Minnesota blasted the administration's opposition to construction of a temporary storage site at Yucca Mountain, Nevada, for the waste products piling up at civilian nuclear reactors and government facilities. "This administration struts around the country saying they're the No. 1 environmental administration ever," Craig said. "Yet they have flatly stuck their heads in the sand" on nuclear waste, which he declared the most critical environmental issue facing the nation.

Murkowski and a handful of other Republicans on the Energy Committee tried to use Peña's confirmation to pressure the White House to drop a veto threat against proposed nuclear waste legislation. Murkowski twice canceled committee action on the nomination in February.

"It's patently unfair to hold a perfectly good man hostage to a particular issue," said Bumpers. On March 6 the committee finally voted, 19–0, to send the nomination to the Senate floor. Committee member Grams voted "present" to protest the White House's nuclear policies and then blocked the full Senate from moving quickly under unanimous consent rules to approve Peña. Grams was the only senator to vote against Peña.

Bill Richardson was confirmed as energy secretary by a voice vote of the Senate July 31, 1998, succeeding Peña, who resigned to return to private life. Two days earlier the Senate Energy and Natural Resources Committee voted 18–0 to approve his nomination.

But committee chairman Frank H. Murkowski, R-Alaska, took the unusual step Aug. 7 of asking President Clinton to delay swearing in Richardson while the Energy Committee conducted "an informal inquiry" to resolve questions about whether Richardson told the truth about his dealings with former White House intern Monica S. Lewinsky.

Murkowski's request was prompted by a *Washington Times* article contending that Richardson did not have an opening on his staff when he offered to hire Lewinsky in 1997, contrary to what he told the committee under oath at his confirmation hearing. Independent Counsel Kenneth W. Starr was investigating whether Clinton had a sexual relationship with Lewinsky and tried to cover it up, in part by finding a job for her. The article quoted unidentified sources who said that Richardson planned to create a position to accommodate Lewinsky's wish to work in New York. The article said that when allegations of a sexual relationship between Lewinsky and Clinton became public, Richardson looked for a job he could say had existed before he interviewed Lewinsky. "This article raises serious questions that are the obligation of this committee to explore," Murkowski said in a statement.

After the article appeared, Richardson issued a statement denying the allegation. A bipartisan Energy Committee staff report issued Aug. 17 found "clear and convincing evidence corroborating" his testimony. Richardson was sworn in on Aug. 18.

In addition to the Lewinsky matter, Richardson had also faced tough questioning from Republicans senators on nuclear waste disposal. At a July 22 confirmation hearing, Larry E. Craig, R-Idaho, repeatedly pressed Richardson to negotiate an agreement to build a temporary storage site for high-level waste generated by nuclear power plants. The House and Senate passed bills in 1997 requiring the department to build such a facility near Yucca Mountain, Nevada, 100 miles northwest of Las Vegas. But Clinton vowed to veto any bill to establish a site.

Craig threatened to delay a vote on Richardson until he received assurances from the president that Richardson would have the authority to negotiate on nuclear waste storage issues. Committee members from both parties countered that Richardson's nomination should not be held hostage for political purposes. Craig relented after Murkowski received a letter from Clinton in which the president said Richardson must oversee the department's assessment of the Nevada's site long-term storage potential.

Richardson had served as Clinton's ambassador to the United Nations since 1997. Before that he had been a member of the House of Representatives from New Mexico's Third District, serving from 1983 to 1997 and rising to the leadership post of chief deputy whip. (*U.N. Representative, p. 984*)

As ambassador, Richardson extended his role as an international negotiator, working with Congress to hammer out an agreement to pay the U.S. debt to the United Nations. A member of the National Security Council, he also helped construct American policy on Iraq's refusal to comply with U.N. resolutions. But Richardson was eager to move to the Energy Department, in part because the department oversaw nuclear issues and his native New Mexico was home to nuclear research facilities.

Richardson was born in California to a Mexican mother and American father, and was raised in Mexico City. With the departure of Peña, Richardson became the only Hispanic American in the cabinet.

HOUSING AND URBAN DEVELOPMENT

Andrew M. Cuomo received Senate confirmation, 99–0, on Jan. 29, 1997, to become President Clinton's second secretary of housing and urban development (HUD). Cuomo replaced Henry G. Cisneros, who retired in the face of an investigation by an independent counsel for allegedly concealing information about payments to a former mistress.

Cuomo's nomination was approved unanimously Jan. 28 by the Senate Banking, Housing and Urban Affairs Committee. At his Jan. 22 confirmation hearing, Cuomo had drawn bipartisan praise for his experience and commitment to making housing affordable, particularly for the poor and elderly. "I commend my fellow New Yorker for his record of public service," said Committee Chairman Alfonse M. D'Amato, R-N.Y. "He has shown innovation, insight, and tireless efforts to serve our cities, suburbs, and rural areas."

The son of former Democratic New York governor Mario M. Cuomo, the nominee previously served as assistant HUD secretary for community planning and development (1993–1996) and had been involved in housing issues in New York prior to that.

Paul S. Sarbanes of Maryland, the panel's ranking Democrat, noted that Cuomo in 1986 founded a New York organization that provided transitional housing for the homeless. "It's clear," Sarbanes said, "that Mr. Cuomo is an excellent choice at this time."

Committee members did make clear that their kind words for Cuomo did not extend to the department itself, which many conservative Republicans considered to be a bloated and poorly run bureaucracy. Some had recommended the elimination of the department.

"HUD has failed," said Lauch Faircloth, R-N.C. "In many instances, it's lost sight of its mission. Management is the problem. HUD has become a massive Washington bureaucracy."

In response to such concerns, Cuomo said he was committed to continuing streamlining efforts initiated by Cisneros, while also finding ways to meet the housing needs of low-income families and senior citizens. "We have to balance the budget and meet our responsibilities," he said. "We have to do both. I don't think the two are mutually inconsistent."

A key architect of federal "empowerment zones" and HUD's restructuring, Cuomo pledged continued reforms, including a public housing overhaul.

LABOR

The Senate confirmed **Alexis M. Herman** as secretary of labor April 30, 1997, on a bipartisan vote of 85–13. She replaced Robert B. Reich, who left Jan. 10 to return to Harvard University and his family in Boston. Herman was the first African American in the post. Her nomination had been approved by voice vote April 10 by the Senate Labor and Human Resources Committee.

Herman waited several months for her chance to testify before the Labor Committee. The confirmation hearing was delayed because of questions about whether she engaged in improper fund-raising activities while serving as director of the White House Office of Public Liaison during President Clinton's first term.

Herman was greeted at the March 18 hearing by a supportive, standing-room-only audience that included prominent African Americans, such as Children's Defense Fund president Marian Wright Edelman; NAACP president Kweisi Mfume, a former House member (D-Md., 1987–1996); newly confirmed Transportation Secretary Rodney Slater; and more than a dozen members of the Congressional Black Caucus. Recalling the failed nominations of African American law Professor Lani Guinier in 1993 to head the Justice Department's civil rights division and of black physician Henry W. Foster Jr. in 1995 to be surgeon general, many of those on hand sought to demonstrate their support for Herman.

In more than four hours of testimony, Herman responded to questions about her management philosophy, her activities in the Clinton White House, her experiences in the Labor Department in the 1970s, and her work as a private consultant on diversity before she returned to government in 1993. Few panel members delved deeply into allegations about Herman's involvement in White House political fund-raising, the topic that initially threatened to derail the nomination.

Before the hearing, Herman had been asked by the Labor panel to respond to written questions about her tenure as director of the Office of Public Liaison. At the hearing, committee Chairman James M. Jeffords, R-Vt., pointedly criticized the White House for alleged fund-raising improprieties. Herman reluctantly said that administration officials had apparently made some mistakes. Hoping to change the line of questioning, she repeatedly said that her top priority would be to address the needs of working families.

After her testimony, Jeffords praised Herman for her knowledge of labor issues, which stemmed from stints as a union organizer and as director of the Labor Department's Women's Bureau during the Carter administration. "Too many people lack the skills they need to find jobs," Jeffords said. "This is not news to anyone, particularly the nominee, who has spent much of her life trying to attack these problems."

Herman was also lauded by committee Democrats, who noted that she honed her political skills while growing up under segregation in Mobile, Alabama, in the early 1960s.

But the wait for Herman was still not over. The GOP leadership delayed floor action, using Herman's confirmation as a bargaining chip in an escalating dispute over administration plans to issue an executive order giving priority to unionized companies in federal contract bids on large, long-term projects. Senate Democrats responded by refusing to allow legislation to reach the floor until Herman's nomination was allowed to proceed. Clinton ultimately agreed to issue a "presidential memorandum" that would have the same effect as an executive order except that it would expire when Clinton left office. Both sides claimed victory and Herman was quickly confirmed.

STATE

Madeleine K. Albright was confirmed Jan. 22, 1997, on a 99–0 vote, to replace Warren M. Christopher and become the nation's first female secretary of state. The Senate Foreign Relations Committee approved her nomination on Jan. 20, Inauguration Day, on an 18–0 vote.

Foreign Relations Committee Chairman Jesse Helms, R-N.C., warmly praised Albright, who had served as U.S. representative to the United Nations during President Clinton's first term. "She's a strong lady," Helms said. "She's a courageous lady." Helms added that his support for Albright "should in no way be misconstrued as an endorsement of the Clinton foreign policy."

During her day-long confirmation hearing Jan. 8 Albright was praised as a trailblazer for women's rights, lauded as a "role model for the country," credited for ousting an unpopular U.N. secretary-general, and even referred to as "cool."

While Helms and his GOP colleagues were taken with Albright as a messenger, they were less impressed with her message. Helms slammed Clinton's policies toward Haiti, Iraq, and Cuba and charged that the administration in general had been "too often vacillating and insecure."

Like any cabinet nominee, Albright was mostly interested in surviving the hearing without any major gaffes. She succeeded and was able to turn the hearing's only unscripted moment—a protest against U.S. policy toward Iraq by members of a left-wing religious group—to her advantage by using it to launch an off-the-cuff attack on Iraqi leader Saddam Hussein.

Albright's deft handling of that incident confirmed her reputation as an effective, if sometimes unpredictable, advocate for U.S. interests abroad. On that count, she would represent a dramatic contrast to the cautious, lawyerly Christopher. "I have been known for my plain-speaking," she told the panel. "I'm going to tell it like it is."

Albright indicated she would closely follow the course set by Christopher on the major international issues facing the United States—Russia, China, Bosnia, and the Middle East. She began making the case for increased funding for foreign aid and other international programs and for the Senate to approve a treaty banning the development and deployment of chemical weapons.

"We are the world's richest, strongest, most respected nation," she said. "We are also the largest debtor to the United Nations and the international financial institutions. We provide a smaller percentage of our wealth to support democracy and growth in the developing world than any other industrialized nation."

Helms was unmoved by Albright's plea that paying off U.S. debts to the U.N. was necessary to restore U.S. global credibility. "I'm growing a little tired of the wailing and gnashing of teeth" over the U.S. arrearages, he said.

The Foreign Relations Committee seemed eager to make history by confirming a woman as the nation's top diplomat. But Albright earned plaudits for her record as well as for her gender. Helms expressed admiration for Albright's lead role in denying a second term for UN Secretary-General Boutros Boutros-Ghali of Egypt. She helped orchestrate Boutros-Ghali's ouster and his replacement by Kofi Annan of Ghana, the Clinton administration's choice for the post.

Although Albright was cautious in her policy pronouncements, she pledged to work with the committee on a plan to reorganize the foreign affairs bureaucracy, a cherished goal of Helms.

Albright was born in Prague, Czechoslovakia, and emigrated to the United States with her family in 1948, fleeing the communist takeover. She was fluent in French and Czech, with good speaking and reading abilities in Russian and Polish. Albright's appointment led to discoveries about her family's heritage and to revelations about the deaths of more than a dozen Jewish relatives, including three of her grandparents, in the Holocaust.

TRANSPORTATION

The nomination of **Rodney E. Slater** to become secretary of transportation was confirmed by the Senate Feb. 6, 1997, by a 98–0 vote. He succeeded Federico F. Peña, who was slated to become the next energy secretary. A unanimous Senate Commerce, Science, and Transportation Committee approved the nomination on Feb. 5.

Slater breezed through the confirmation process. He came to the job with nearly ten years of experience in transportation oversight. He previously ran Arkansas's highway program under then-governor Bill Clinton and headed the Federal Highway Administration from 1993 to 1997.

At a two-hour hearing on Jan. 29, Slater pledged to make transportation safety his top priority. With recent passenger airline disasters causing widespread public concern, Slater said that ensuring safety would be "the true North Star that guides our moral compass."

No senator spoke against Slater. However, committee Chairman John McCain, R-Ariz., chided him about his role in a 1996 Clinton campaign strategy group. A planning memo by the African American Working Group—headed by Alexis Herman, the White House director of public liaison at the time—suggested highlighting key black officials in the administration as a means of promoting voter turnout. The memo also took an apparent slap at Republicans by labeling opponents of Democrats as "enemies of civil rights." Slater, who was a member of the working group, described the civil rights language as "unfortunate." Apparently mollified, McCain called the response "important."

In written testimony submitted to the committee, Slater rejected a proposal by House Budget Committee Chairman John R. Kasich, R-Ohio, and others to turn over responsibility for most transportation projects to the states. "The federal government can play—indeed, must play—an important role in helping each state in a diverse union create the national [transportation] network," Slater contended.

TREASURY

Lawrence H. Summers was confirmed July 1, 1999, by a 97–2 vote of the Senate, to become the third Treasury secretary of the Clinton administration. He succeeded Robert E. Rubin, for whom he had been deputy since 1995. The Senate Finance Committee had approved the nomination, 13–0, on June 22, without debate.

Summers had received a mostly warm welcome at a Finance Committee hearing June 17. Members of both parties praised his intellect and grasp of national and international financial issues. He assured committee members that there would be no significant policy shifts, if he were allowed to succeed Rubin, who was widely credited with helping sustain a thriving economy. "We share a common orientation with respect to economic policy," Summers said.

Summers faced some tough questions on trade issues, international monetary policy, taxes, and entitlement programs. In one of the sharpest exchanges, Bob Kerrey, D-Neb., pressed Summers on Social Security's looming budget crisis. Kerrey said that because the administration had ruled out a payroll tax increase, the only way to make up the expected shortfall would be to use general revenues from individual and corporate income taxes to repay the debt owed to the Social Security trust fund. When Summers hesitated to concede that point, Kerrey insisted that the administration's positions left no alternative and at one point threatened to withdraw his support for Summers's nomination. Ultimately Summers agreed that income taxes would be needed to repay the debt.

Summers reiterated the administration's position that budget surpluses should be used to pay down the national debt, not for tax cuts. "When you reduce public debt, you are reducing future taxes," Summers said.

Summers also retracted a comment he previously made in which he described efforts to reduce estate taxes—a Republican priority—as "selfishness." He said he agreed it could be difficult for heirs, especially small-business owners and farmers, to pay estate taxes when they inherited a business that could not be easily converted to cash.

Although the Finance Committee had sole jurisdiction over Summers's confirmation, the Senate Banking, Housing, and Urban Affairs Committee held a hearing on Summers while the Finance Committee was voting June 22. Chairman Phil Gramm, R-Texas, said he had little problem with Clinton's nominee. Treasury secretaries had "really been the highlight of their administration," he said.

Summers's confirmation was never in much doubt, but it was delayed by senators trying to use it as leverage on other issues. James M. Inhofe, R-Okla., blocked votes on Summers and all other nominations for a week over the president's recess appointment of gay philanthropist James C. Hormel as ambassador to Luxembourg, but he yielded when Clinton promised to warn Congress of his plans to make future recess appointments.

The confirmation then became entangled in debate over health care. Democrats said Majority Leader Trent Lott, R-Miss., used the nomination as a bargaining chip to get Democrats to agree to drop a health care amendment to an agricultural spending bill (S 1233).

Summers had established himself as the intellectual powerhouse of the Clinton administration's economic team by the time he came to the position. He spent most of his career in policy making and academia. Summers had been Treasury's deputy secretary since August 1995 and under secretary for international affairs from 1993 to 1995. He was a former chief economist at the World Bank and an economics professor at Harvard.

VETERANS AFFAIRS

By voice vote, the Senate on April 28, 1998, confirmed the nomination of former Army Secretary **Togo D. West Jr.** to be secretary of veterans affairs (VA). West had served as acting secretary since Jan. 2. The previous secretary, Jesse Brown, resigned July 1, 1997, to take a private-sector job. Clinton's initial choice to replace him, Deputy Secretary Hershel W. Gober, withdrew his nomination in October in the face of questions about his personal conduct. *(Gober nomination, p. 986)*

Confirmation was delayed by questions about infighting among factions within the army and about sexual harassment scandals that rocked the Army during West's tenure as secretary. The Senate Veterans' Affairs Committee delayed consideration of West's nomination after Michael B. Enzi, R-Wyo., wrote to the committee expressing concern about the complaints.

West addressed these issues during a Feb. 24, 1998, hearing. He was questioned on other topics as well, including a VA proposal to deny compensation for treatment of some veterans for smoking-related illnesses if their tobacco use was not confined to their years of military service.

West was also questioned about the way exceptions were granted for the interment of people who would not normally be accorded burial at Arlington National Cemetery. Republicans in Congress suggested that burial plots were awarded to Democratic Party donors, but the criticisms receded after West made public a list of the waivers he had granted and explained the basis for each one. The General Accounting Office later found that waivers were not proved to be linked to political considerations.

Satisfied that West had addressed his concerns, Enzi withdrew his opposition shortly before the committee unanimously approved West's nomination on April 22.

West was a former member of the U.S. Army Field Artillery Corps, served as general counsel for the Navy, and later held that same position for the Department of Defense. He went on to become senior vice president for defense contractor Northrop Grumman Corp. West had been Army secretary since 1993.

West resigned as VA secretary July 24, 2000. Gober served as acting secretary until the end of the Clinton administration.

Other Key Positions

CENTRAL INTELLIGENCE AGENCY

George J. Tenet was confirmed July 10, 1997, by the Senate as director of central intelligence, four months after he was nominated and nearly eight months after the job fell vacant when John M. Deutch resigned in December 1996. He was confirmed by voice vote, with little debate, just hours after the Senate Intelligence Committee, in a closed session, voted unanimously in favor of his nomination. Tenet became the fifth CIA director in the 1990s.

Tenet was nominated in March after President Clinton's first choice, former national security adviser Anthony Lake, withdrew when his nomination became entangled in partisan controversy over foreign policy and political fund-raising practices. *(Lake nomination, p. 987)*

Tenet had been acting director of central intelligence since Deutch's resignation. He served under Lake at the National Security Council (NSC) before becoming deputy director of central intelligence in 1995. He began his career in government in 1982 when he went to work for Sen. John Heinz, R-Pa., as a legislative assistant focused mainly on energy, defense, and foreign affairs issues. Before joining the White House in 1993, Tenet served as staff director of the Senate Intelligence Committee from 1988 to 1993 and was introduced at his confirmation hearing by his old boss, former senator David L. Boren, D-Okla. (1979–1994), who had been chairman of the committee at the time.

Tenet received a generally favorable reception from the committee during his May 6 confirmation hearing. He met with the panel behind closed doors May 7 to discuss classified issues.

Senators delved into Tenet's views on how he would lead the nation's intelligence community, which included the CIA and several other intelligence agencies, most of which are part of the Defense Department. Tenet was asked by several senators about what reforms were still needed in the wake of the devastating Aldrich H. Ames spy scandal, which had become public in 1994. He said he would continue implementing reforms begun under Deutch and noted that several important steps had already been taken to beef up the CIA's counter-intelligence efforts. He also expressed his strong support for using people, not just satellites and electronic eavesdropping, to collect intelligence.

The committee vote on Tenet's nomination was put on hold while the Justice Department investigated his failure to disclose until 1994 his ownership of real estate in Greece and U.S. telephone companies' stocks he inherited after his father died in 1983. He said he was unaware of the holdings until his family discovered the paperwork in a safe deposit box in 1994. Tenet, who at the time was working for the NSC, informed White House ethics officials. He subsequently was nominated and confirmed to be deputy director of central intelligence.

The Justice Department cleared him of any wrongdoing and his nomination to head the CIA was approved by the Senate.

COUNCIL OF ECONOMIC ADVISERS

Janet Yellen won confirmation Feb. 13, 1997, to serve as chairman of President Clinton's Council of Economic Advisers (CEA), one day after she received a 17–0 endorsement from the Senate Banking Committee. Senate approval was by voice vote.

Yellen, a former economics professor at the University of California at Berkeley, replaced Joseph E. Stiglitz. By accepting the nomination Yellen gave up the seat on the Board of Governors of the Federal Reserve that she had held since 1994.

"I am tremendously pleased you will be taking on this assignment," Banking Committee Chairman Alfonse M. D'Amato, R-N.Y., told Yellen at her Feb. 5 confirmation hearing. GOP committee members pressed for her views on the balanced-budget amendment, taxes, and economic growth.

In response to a question from Lauch Faircloth, R-N.C., Yellen said she strongly opposed amending the Constitution to require balanced budgets. Echoing the president and other administration officials, Yellen said the amendment could precipitate a recession or depression by eliminating the government's ability to lower taxes or increase spending during economic downturns.

Responding to another question from Faircloth, Yellen said she would not give "high priority" to a broad-based capital gains tax cut advocated by many Republicans.

Yellen also told the committee that she considered it a "very important priority" to promote policies that would improve the economy's current 2.5 percent annual growth rate. "I am not satisfied with 2.5 percent growth, and I don't think any of us should be satisfied with 2.5 percent growth," Yellen said.

Republicans encouraged her to press that view in the White House. "Many people, including President Clinton, now consider a growth rate of 2.5 percent to be acceptable, even laudable," said Sen. Connie Mack, R-Fla. "We should not accept such mediocrity."

Yellen resigned in August 1999 to return to teaching at Berkeley.

Martin N. Baily was confirmed by voice vote of the Senate on Aug. 5, 1999, as chairman of the Council of Economic Advisers, replacing Janet Yellen. The Senate Banking Committee held a hearing and approved Baily's nomination a day earlier.

Baily had served as one of the three members of the CEA from October 1994 until August 1996. From September 1996 to July 1999 Baily was a principal at McKinsey & Company at the Global Institute in Washington, D.C.

Previously, Baily had taught at the Massachusetts Institute of Technology, Yale, and the University of Maryland. He also had been a senior fellow at the Brookings Institution and served as an academic advisor to the Congressional Budget Office and the Federal Reserve Board.

FEDERAL RESERVE BOARD

Alan Greenspan was confirmed in 2000 for a fourth term as chairman of the Federal Reserve Board of Governors, amid a bipartisan chorus that gave him much of the credit for an economic expansion of record duration. His nomination was approved by a voice vote of the Senate Banking Committee on Feb. 1, 2000, and confirmed by an 89–4 vote of the full Senate on Feb. 3.

Confirmation came one day after the Fed raised the federal funds interest rate—what banks charged one another for overnight loans—for the fourth time since June 1999, in an effort to temper the pace of the economy's growth and thereby keep inflation in check. The action gave fresh ammunition to the small cadre of Greenspan critics in the Senate, who said his moves against inflation had an unwelcome trickle-down effect, by making it more difficult for many people to obtain financing for new home purchases or business expenses.

"My farmers, who are already hurting enough," lamented Tom Harkin, D-Iowa, "are going to get hit again." Byron L. Dorgan, D-N.D., called the rate increases "a tax on every single American." But fewer sided with their view this time than the detractors had predicted, and fewer than when Greenspan was last confirmed, in 1996.

Greenspan, a lifelong Republican, was first nominated as chairman in 1987 by President Ronald Reagan. He was nominated to a second term in 1992 by President George Bush and to a third term in 1996 by President Clinton. His new term would begin in June 2000 and run to June 2004. *(Congress and the Nation Vol. VII, p. 1049; Congress and the Nation Vol. VIII, p. 1176; Congress and the Nation Vol. IX, p. 1116.)*

OFFICE OF MANAGEMENT AND BUDGET

Jacob J. Lew was confirmed by voice vote by the Senate on July 31, 1998, to become director of the Office of Management and Budget (OMB). Lew, who had been deputy OMB director since August 1995, took over the top position at OMB when Franklin D. Raines left to become chairman of the Federal National Mortgage Association (Fannie Mae).

The Senate Governmental Affairs Committee held a hearing on Lew's nomination June 22, 1998, and approved it July 15.

Lew, an attorney, had been a special assistant to Clinton from February 1993 through October 1994, before moving to OMB. Earlier in his career he had served as principal domestic policy adviser to House Speaker Thomas P. "Tip" O'Neill Jr., D-Mass. He also spent nearly eight years as assistant director and then executive director of the House Democratic Steering and Policy Committee.

"Only a handful of people in Washington have Jack Lew's profound knowledge of the federal budget and the legislative process," Clinton said. "Almost none of them has his ability to explain it in plain English."

OFFICE OF U.S. TRADE REPRESENTATIVE

The Senate voted 99–1 on March 5, 1997, to confirm **Charlene Barshefsky** as U.S. trade representative. Barshefsky took over from Mickey Kantor, who became secretary of commerce. Barshefsky had been the acting trade representative since April 1996 and deputy trade representative from 1993 to 1996.

Barshefsky enjoyed support from lawmakers in both chambers, who praised her steely demeanor at the bargaining table, her hard-nosed negotiating style, and her dedication to enhancing U.S. trade opportunities and protecting American exports from unfair foreign competition. The Senate Finance Committee recommended Barshefsky's confirmation by voice vote on Jan. 30.

But to assume the job, she also needed both chambers of Congress to approve a waiver of provisions in a 1995 lobbying law (PL 104-65) that prohibited anyone who had represented a foreign government from being appointed U.S. trade representative. When Barshefsky was in private practice as a trade lawyer, she had briefly advised the government of Canada and the province of Quebec on a trade dispute. The White House asked Congress to waive the law in the most limited way possible by making an exception only for Barshefsky. The Finance Committee reported a waiver resolution (S J Res 5—no written report) on Feb. 3.

The waiver was particularly troubling to Senate Majority Leader Trent Lott, R-Miss., who said repeatedly that he did "not like waiving laws. The law is on the books." Lott and Wayne Allard, R-Colo., were the only two senators to vote against the waiver. Allard was also the lone vote against Barshefsky's nomination.

The Senate approved the waiver after a proposed amendment was handily defeated. The amendment, offered by Ernest F. Hollings,

D-S.C., had posed the most serious threat to Barshefsky's nomination, because it would have required Congress to vote on all international trade agreements that would "in effect" amend or repeal U.S. laws. The Clinton administration was adamantly opposed to the Hollings amendment, saying it would completely hamstring U.S. trade policy.

Finance Committee Chairman William V. Roth Jr., R-Del., a strong Barshefsky supporter, argued that the Hollings amendment could "immobilize our ability to negotiate trade agreements, even on relatively minor issues, as Congress would be required to approve tens if not hundreds of such agreements. . . . All of these agreements would also be fully amendable," Roth said.

In the end, Hollings's proposal won some warm words but few votes. It was tabled (killed) March 5 by an 84–16 vote. Democrats who might have supported his approach in the abstract wanted to avoid hurting a Clinton nominee, and, on the Republican side, free-trade lawmakers objected to the amendment on principle. Nine Democrats and seven Republicans supported Hollings's amendment, including Republican conference chairman Larry E. Craig of Idaho and Democratic Whip Byron L. Dorgan of North Dakota.

The arguments in the House over the waiver were brief and relatively calm. Ways and Means Chairman Bill Archer, R-Texas, said he supported the waiver because Barshefsky had only "a minimal advisory role to the Canadian government a number of years ago."

The Senate approved the waiver by a vote of 98–2 on March 5; the House gave voice vote approval March 11. Clinton signed S J Res 5 (PL 105-5) into law on March 17, the day before Barshefsky was sworn in as trade representative.

SOLICITOR GENERAL

Seth P. Waxman, President Clinton's nominee for solicitor general, was confirmed by the Senate by voice vote on Nov. 7, 1997. Waxman thus became the nation's chief litigator, representing the government before the Supreme Court and deciding which cases to appeal.

Waxman had been the acting solicitor general since Sept. 1 and previously was deputy solicitor general. Before joining the government, he had worked for a Washington law firm.

Waxman won praise from all sides at his Nov. 5 confirmation hearing before the Senate Judiciary Committee. Chairman Orrin G. Hatch, R-Utah, commended Waxman's "very distinguished career," and Sen. Joseph I. Lieberman, D-Conn., said Waxman was "a merit appointment."

In the wake of controversy surrounding Clinton's nomination of Bill Lann Lee to be assistant attorney general for civil rights, Hatch asked Waxman if he would fight to preserve possible future laws banning affirmative action. Waxman said he would support the constitutionality of any law for which "a reasonable argument" could be made. "I don't think anybody can deny that there are reasonable arguments on both sides," Waxman said, adding that a decision not to defend a law "should be very, very rare." *(Lee nomination, p. 986)*

UNITED NATIONS REPRESENTATIVE

Bill Richardson won unanimous Senate approval Feb. 11, 1997, to become the new U.S. representative to the United Nations. He replaced Madeleine K. Albright, who resigned to become secretary of state. *(Albright nomination, p. 981)*

The vote on Richardson, who had served more than fourteen years (1983–1997) as a Democratic representative from New Mexico, was 100–0. The Senate Foreign Relations Committee had approved his nomination earlier that day on an 18–0 vote.

During the brief committee debate, Foreign Relations Chairman Jesse Helms, R-N.C., and other Republicans warned that congressional approval of a Clinton administration request for more than $1 billion to clear U.S. debts to the U.N. would hinge on the world body implementing major reforms.

Richardson garnered attention while in Congress as something of a roving envoy to some of the world's harshest, most anti-American dictatorships. He worked to secure the release of prisoners and hostages in Cuba, Iraq, Bangladesh, North Korea, and Sudan. He also traveled to Haiti for peace negotiations in 1994.

Richardson resigned in 1998 to become secretary of energy. *(Richardson nomination, p. 980)*

Richard C. Holbrooke was confirmed Aug. 5, 1999, by the Senate, on a vote of 81–16, to become permanent representative to the United Nations. He replaced Bill Richardson, who left in 1998 to become energy secretary. The Senate Foreign Relations Committee approved the nomination by voice vote June 30—more than a year after his nomination and only after extensive committee hearings.

Holbrooke's nomination was initially held up pending a Justice Department investigation into allegations that he violated federal ethics rules by improperly trading on his government contacts after leaving the State Department for the private sector in 1996. Clinton sent his name to the Senate on Feb. 10 after Holbrooke agreed to pay $5,000 to settle civil charges stemming from the allegations, while still denying their veracity.

After leaving his job in Clinton's first term as assistant secretary of state for European and Canadian affairs, Holbrooke returned to investment banking as a vice chairman of CS First Boston Group, but he continued to take diplomatic assignments from Clinton. Holbrooke, a renowned diplomatic trouble-shooter, served as the chief negotiator of the 1995 Bosnian peace settlement. He was an assistant secretary of state for Asian affairs in the Carter administration.

Before the final vote, Holbrooke underwent an eight-month administration investigation, a four-month investigation by the Senate Foreign Relations Committee, and four hearings before that committee—an extraordinary number for an ambassadorial nominee. Then the vote on his nomination was delayed for more than a month because senators imposed holds in an effort to pressure the Clinton administration on unrelated issues. The vote finally came after Senate Majority Leader Trent Lott, R-Miss., and Sen. Charles E. Grassley, R-Iowa, removed the last holds.

"I don't know if there has been an individual who has been more probed and investigated," said Chuck Hagel, R-Neb., in urging his colleagues to confirm Holbrooke. "We have allowed bipartisanship in foreign policy and national security to erode."

Joseph R. Biden Jr. of Delaware, ranking Democrat on the Foreign Relations Committee, railed against Lott and Grassley for holding up the nomination since June 30. Biden said the Republican lawmakers were guilty of "abuse of power" and said, "This is a bad, bad, bad practice and this is a good, good, good nominee."

In the debate on Holbrooke's nomination, the only objections came from Republicans opposed to the Clinton administration's policy in Bosnia and Kosovo.

Controversial Nominations

1997

Pete Peterson. Former representative Pete Peterson (D-Fla., 1991–1997), who spent more than six years as a prisoner of war in Vietnam, had been nominated by President Clinton in May 1996 to become the first American ambassador to Vietnam since the United

States normalized relations with its former adversary in 1995. But the Senate Foreign Relations Committee refused to act on his nomination in 1996 after senior Republicans on the committee contended that the appointment would violate a rarely invoked constitutional provision of the Constitution barring members of Congress from serving in offices created, or for which the pay was increased, during their terms.

"The reason for the postponement . . . is the White House's failure to meet the constitutional requirements for the nomination," Craig Thomas, R-Wyo., chairman of the Foreign Relations Subcommittee on East Asian and Pacific Affairs, said in a floor speech Sept. 4, 1996. "It has nothing to do with Pete Peterson as a nominee."

Under the committee's interpretation of the Constitution, Peterson's nomination would have to be resubmitted after the 105th Congress convened in January 1997.

The Clinton administration disagreed with the decision, as did Peterson, who expressed disappointment. "I regret the delay," he said in an interview. "It's essentially shut down bilateral relations between the U.S. and Vietnam at a crucial period."

Peterson's confirmation hearing was finally held Feb. 13, 1997. But then New Hampshire Republican Robert C. Smith, a leading critic of Clinton's decision to restore diplomatic ties with Vietnam, blocked the nomination from proceeding because of GOP concerns that the administration's Vietnam policy might have been influenced by financial contributions made to Democrats by the Riady family of Indonesia, which had been at the center of controversy over Democratic fund-raising practices in the 1996 presidential campaign. "If we're going to hold up other people for other things, we should at least wait until we get some answers on that issue," Smith said. He emphasized that he had no reservations about Peterson's qualifications.

Arizona Republican Sen. John McCain, who helped lead congressional efforts in behalf of normalizing relations with Hanoi, tried to put to rest speculation that campaign contributions played a role in the decision to normalize relations. "Let me say as strongly as I can that this rumor is entirely unsubstantiated by fact," McCain told the committee.

Smith also pressed the White House to consult with the intelligence community before declaring that Hanoi was fully cooperating in the search for clues to the fate of servicemen still listed as missing from the Vietnam War. He removed his hold after receiving written assurances that the president would consult with a variety of defense and intelligence officials in determining whether Vietnam was cooperating to the fullest extent. Sen. John Kerry, D-Mass., who helped lead a Senate investigation into cases of missing servicemen, said Peterson's presence in Hanoi would "enhance our credibility and greatly facilitate our ability to get those answers."

The Senate Foreign Relations Committee approved Peterson's nomination March 4 by voice vote. The full Senate approved the nomination by voice vote April 10.

Roger Ferguson and **Edward Gramlich.** President Clinton nominated Roger Ferguson and Edward Gramlich on July 10, 1997, to fill open seats on the Federal Reserve Board of Governors. Ferguson was a New York-based partner at the international consulting firm McKinsey & Co. Gramlich was dean of the University of Michigan's School of Public Policy, where he had been an economics professor for more than twenty years.

The nominations were approved by the Senate Banking Committee without objection on Oct. 8, but then Democratic critics of the Federal Reserve Board's monetary policy, led by Iowa Sen. Tom Harkin, put a hold on the nominations. Harkin said the Federal Reserve Board, under Chairman Alan Greenspan, had allowed interest rates to remain too high for working Americans, on the belief that higher rates were keeping inflation in check. Harkin said the nominees' positions were "too much in line with the present thinking at the Fed. . . . And I think that is going to cost us dearly in the years ahead."

Byron L. Dorgan, D-N.D., joined Harkin, saying the board would not gain new perspective with these nominees. The governors "all come from the same area. They all look the same. They all wear the same suits. They all have the same educational background," Dorgan said. "If you put them in a barrel and shake it up, the same person winds up on top—gray suit, Ivy League background."

Harkin allowed the confirmation to proceed after Majority Leader Trent Lott, R-Miss., agreed to give Harkin ninety minutes of floor time.

The two nominees were confirmed by the Senate by voice vote on Oct. 30. Ferguson filled the unexpired term of Lawrence Lindsey, who left the board to join the American Enterprise Institute. Ferguson's term would expire Jan. 31, 2000. Gramlich took the seat vacated by Janet Yellen, who became chairman of the president's Council of Economic Advisers. Gramlich's term would expire on Jan. 31, 2008.

William F. Weld. Former Massachusetts governor William F. Weld, a moderate Republican, was nominated July 23, 1997, by President Clinton to become ambassador to Mexico. Weld resigned his governorship July 29 to accept the appointment but then faced unrelenting opposition from Jesse Helms, R-N.C., the chairman of the Senate Foreign Relations Committee. Helms charged that Weld was unqualified for the Mexico post because of his record on narcotics issues, including support for the medical use of marijuana and policies to supply needles to heroin addicts. Helms also criticized Weld's record in gaining drug convictions when he was a U.S. attorney.

As chairman, Helms held the power to stop Weld's nomination simply by refusing to hold a confirmation hearing—and that is what Helms vowed to do. Weld was thought to have hurt his chances for confirmation by directly attacking Helms and his control over the committee process. On July 15 Weld had urged Clinton not to give in to Helms's "ideological extortion" and claimed that his nomination fight "has everything to do with the future of the Republican Party."

Weld visited the Capitol July 31 seeking support. Senate Majority Leader Trent Lott, R-Miss., said Weld should take another post "or look for work." Lott also suggested that Weld might improve his prospects by apologizing to Helms.

Helms steadfastly refused to hold a committee hearing on the nomination. On Aug. 7 Richard G. Lugar of Indiana, second-ranking Republican on the Foreign Relations Committee, threatened to attack tobacco and peanut subsidies unless Helms held a hearing on Weld. Lugar had not indicated how he would vote on the Weld nomination but said he thought it was important to hold a hearing. The relationship between Helms and Lugar had been chilly since 1995, when Helms exercised his seniority to assume the chairmanship of the Foreign Relations Committee and deprive Lugar, a leading GOP voice on foreign policy, of the post.

On Sept. 5 Lugar and three other members of the Foreign Relations Committee made use of a rarely used Senate rule to convene a special committee meeting. Helms scheduled the meeting for Sept. 12 but would not put the nomination on the agenda. "The sole purpose of this meeting will be to discuss the history of countless failed nominations," Helms stated.

At the thirty-minute hearing, Helms used oversized charts that had been compiled by the Congressional Research Service to detail how 154 nominees over the previous ten years never got confirmation hearings because senators blocked their selections. He attacked his critics, singling out Lugar and Delaware Sen. Joseph R. Biden Jr., the ranking Democrat on the panel, who he said had thwarted numerous nominations.

"The distinguished senator from Indiana decided to challenge my authority as a committee chairman and, by implication, challenge the authority of all other committee chairmen, now and in the future," Helms said. "I have felt obliged to state this morning, in detail, for the record, the true facts."

With Weld and his wife watching from the back of the committee room, Helms also made it clear that he would continue to block the nomination. However, he had indicated in an Aug. 1 letter to Clinton, which was released at the hearing, that he would consider the moderate Republican for another diplomatic post. "You deserve a better nominee, and the nation needs an ambassador in Mexico with a proven record as a drug fighter," Helms wrote.

The end of the Weld nomination came after Lott, in a phone call with Clinton on Sept. 13, indicated that a prolonged fight with Helms could spill into other foreign policy issues. "We need the chairman's cooperation, if not outright support" on other issues, Lott said Sept. 15.

Weld withdrew his name Sept. 15. Speaking in the White House briefing room, Weld—unbowed to the end—delivered a statement entitled, "How I Spent My Summer Vacation," in which he assailed Helms, the Senate, and Washington. "You know what I found out?" he asked. "In Washington, the rule is, all the senators don't have to advise and consent, even though the Constitution says they do. And in Washington, you do have to go on bended knee, even if you only want the government to do what the Constitution says."

Weld's approach throughout the process left several GOP chairmen and a good number of senior Democrats, though they would not admit it publicly, secretly rooting for Helms.

Hershel W. Gober. Hershel W. Gober, deputy director of veterans affairs and a veteran of both the Army and Marine Corps, was President Clinton's first choice to succeed Jesse Brown Jr., who resigned July 1, 1997, as head of the Department of Veterans Affairs. But Clinton withdrew the nomination at Gober's request on Oct. 24, 1997.

The nomination was withdrawn amid reports of sexual harassment allegations against Gober and questions about how the VA had investigated the case. In addition, news reports surfaced in September that Gober and his wife, VA general counsel Mary Lou Keener, had accumulated thousands of dollars in unjustified travel expenses attending conferences and meetings, including a 1994 trip to finalize a lease on a VA building in Paris. Gober denied any improprieties.

Gober, a longtime ally of the president, had been director of veterans affairs in Arkansas when Clinton was governor. Gober said he could best serve the administration by remaining in the post of deputy secretary.

Wyche Fowler Jr. Wyche Fowler Jr. received Senate confirmation Oct. 27, 1997, to serve as ambassador to Saudi Arabia. The vote was 90–0. The Senate Foreign Relations Committee approved the nomination by voice vote Oct. 8.

Fowler, a Democrat from Georgia, served in the House from 1977 to 1987 and in the Senate from 1987 to 1993. Fowler had been in Saudi Arabia since August 1996, when Clinton appointed him while Congress was in recess.

Committee action on Fowler's nomination had been temporarily delayed when Sen. John Ashcroft, R-Mo., put a hold on it. Ashcroft said that while he did not oppose the nomination, he would not release it until the administration answered several questions on U.S.-Saudi relations.

Bill Lann Lee. Bill Lann Lee, a lawyer for the NAACP Legal Defense and Education Fund, was nominated in 1997 to become assistant attorney general for civil rights, to replace D. L. Patrick.

The nomination was controversial from the start. Democrats portrayed Lee as a pragmatist who favored settling cases out of court and making reasonable accommodations to his adversaries. But conservatives said he was a liberal ideologue wedded to views of affirmative action that were increasingly being struck down by courts.

In nominating Lee, President Clinton had presented Republicans with a dilemma: allowing him to be confirmed threatened to upset party regulars who opposed affirmative action. But challenging Lee—a Chinese American with a compelling background of overcoming humble origins—worried GOP moderates who feared the party would alienate Asian Americans, an increasingly important swing vote.

At Lee's confirmation hearing on Oct. 22, 1997, Republicans on the Senate Judiciary Committee alternated between questioning him and apologizing for having to do so. "I like you very much personally, there is no doubt of that," said Chairman Orrin G. Hatch, R-Utah. "But you're going to have to answer some of these questions."

Lee declined to give substantive answers to questions about his views on busing and on what he believed his role in the administration would be on Proposition 209—a 1996 California ballot initiative ending affirmative action in state hiring, contracting, and university admissions. He cited several reasons for deflecting questions: some issues, he said, might come before him in his capacity as assistant attorney general; others would be better addressed to people higher in the administration.

When it became clear that Republicans on the Senate Judiciary Committee had the votes to keep the nomination from reaching the floor, Democrats, struggling to keep his nomination alive, prevented the panel from taking a formal vote.

Hatch reminded Democrats that in 1989 they had blocked William Lucas, a Bush nominee for the same job as Lee, who lost in committee on a tie vote. Hatch then said he was not calling for a quid pro quo.

Clinton announced Dec. 15, 1997, that he would make Lee acting assistant attorney general for civil rights. Clinton decided against a recess appointment to avoid angering senators of both parties who closely guarded their prerogatives.

"While he will have the full authority and support to carry out the duties of the assistant attorney for civil rights," Clinton said, "I still look forward to striking the word 'acting' from his title."

In early 1999 the battle heated up again. Hatch asked Clinton Feb. 16 to find "a confirmable candidate" for the post, saying that "during Lee's tenure, the Justice Department has advocated the same policies that initially led to his failure to be confirmed as assistant attorney general." Instead, the White House signaled the next day that Clinton would formally resubmit Lee's nomination.

And on Feb. 18 Deputy Attorney General Eric H. Holder Jr. said that Lee could stay in his post indefinitely because he was not subject to the 210-day limit on most "acting" appointments that Republicans had included in the fiscal 1999 omnibus spending law (PL 105-277). Hatch said the language was meant to cover Lee.

Clinton finally issued a recess appointment Aug. 3, 2000, naming Lee to head the Justice Department's civil rights division.

"While he is well within his legal rights to make recess appointments," said Hatch, "it would be better if the president would send us a nominee who could get the support of the Senate Judiciary Committee."

Daryl Jones. Daryl Jones, a Florida state senator, lieutenant colonel in the Air Force Reserve, and former fighter pilot, was nominated in October 1997 to be Air Force secretary, but the nomination was ultimately blocked in 1998 by a tie vote of the Senate Armed Services Committee.

Jones's nomination was met with a barrage of criticism from fellow officers, who contended he was a mediocre pilot who won a coveted assignment to one of the squadron's F-16s because of political

favoritism and that he sought preferential treatment because he was African American.

When the Armed Services panel held its first hearing on the nomination June 16, 1998, the allegations had started to mount. At a second confirmation hearing July 16, his former squadron mates urged the committee to reject the nomination, charging that Jones exaggerated his flying record, shaded the truth about his business dealings, and even pressured subordinates to buy Amway household products. At the contentious, nine-hour July 16 hearing, the committee also interrogated a panel of officers who supported Jones, and finally the nominee himself.

"I believe there are serious questions about Daryl Jones's personal integrity," Col. Thomas Dyches, a former commander of the 93rd Fighter Squadron, told the panel. "His life, in my opinion, is governed by his own personal goals."

Dyches testified that he grounded Jones because his handling of F-16 fighters became unsafe. Jones had told the committee he stepped down as a pilot because of other demands on his time. His supporters contended that he had not lied, but rather had given up his pilot status after being told that if he did not, he would be grounded.

Besides enjoying apparently solid support among Senate Democrats, Jones also had some important backing among GOP heavyweights, including Armed Services Chairman Strom Thurmond of South Carolina, Florida's Connie Mack, and Thad Cochran of Mississippi, who appointed Jones to the Air Force Academy in 1973.

Thurmond and most Democrats said that some of the charges against Jones involved innocent oversights on his part or administrative errors by the Air Force, while other allegations turned out to be unsubstantiated. "Sometimes when there's smoke, there's only smoke," said ranking committee Democrat Carl Levin of Michigan.

In a letter to Thurmond, Defense Secretary William S. Cohen called Jones "a man of proven ability who understands the challenges of public service."

But some Republicans insisted that Jones's responses to the allegations revealed a pattern of trying to evade responsibility for misdeeds, acknowledging them only when confronted with clear evidence. The issue, they insisted, was not whether Jones had been proved guilty of wrongdoing, but whether, in the wake of a long and turbulent confirmation, he could give the Air Force strong leadership.

On July 22, by a vote of 9–9, the committee blocked the nomination. The vote came on a motion that the committee report the nomination to the Senate without the usual recommendation that it be confirmed. Chairman Thurmond joined all eight committee Democrats to support the motion, but the panel's nine other Republicans voted no.

After that motion was rejected, Levin proposed that the committee report the nomination with an unfavorable recommendation, giving Clinton and Jones a chance to fight for the nomination in the Senate as a whole. But committee Republicans indicated they would oppose Levin's proposal, so he withdrew it without putting it to a formal vote.

Tony Lake. Following the resignation of John M. Deutch, National Security Advisor Tony Lake was nominated Dec. 5, 1996, to head the Central Intelligence Agency. In the weeks that followed, Lake became ensnared in a partisan dispute that ranged from questions on his role in Iran-Bosnia arms transfers and alleged improprieties in White House and Democratic fundraising practices, to his stock holdings and ability to remain independent of the administration. In reaction, on March 17, 1997, Lake asked that his nomination be withdrawn. The Senate approved Clinton's nomination of George Tenet to the CIA post in July. Tenet had been Lake's chief intelligence adviser at the National Security Council. *(Tenet nomination, p. 983)*

Lake had an extensive background in foreign affairs, including work in government and academia. He was named Clinton's national security adviser in 1993 after serving as a senior foreign policy adviser to Clinton's 1992 presidential campaign. Lake also served in the Nixon and Carter administrations.

Lake's surprise decision to withdraw his nomination came after three days of testimony, March 11–13, before the Intelligence Committee. An additional round of hearings had been set for March 18–20. Earlier his confirmation hearings had been postponed twice.

In a letter to Clinton, Lake complained that the nomination process had become a "political football in a game with constantly moving goalposts." Although Lake believed he had the votes to be confirmed, he said he was concerned that his nomination would be subjected to an "endless" series of delays. "I have gone through the past three months and more with patience and, I hope, dignity. But I have lost the former and could lose the latter as this political circus continues indefinitely," Lake wrote.

During the first week of hearings, questions for Lake included: his role in a 1994 decision by the Clinton administration to give tacit approval to the shipment of arms from Iran to the Muslim-dominated Bosnian government; why he was not informed by his staffers about an FBI briefing detailing an alleged plan by the Chinese government to influence U.S. elections; and whether he could provide objective intelligence information given his background in helping to formulate foreign policy.

Lake's nomination was further complicated when the *Wall Street Journal* on March 17 reported allegations that Donald Fowler, former chairman of the Democratic National Committee, had attempted to persuade NSC officials to change a recommendation that controversial businessman Roger Tamraz, a heavy donor to the party, not be invited to White House meetings. The story alleged that Fowler arranged to have a favorable CIA report on Tamraz sent to the NSC and, despite warnings against it, Tamraz was subsequently permitted to attend some White House events. The allegations raised questions about why Lake's subordinates did not bring the matter to his attention and about possible interference of politics at the CIA.

Senate Intelligence Committee Vice Chairman Bob Kerrey, D-Neb., who had been expected to support Lake, expressed deep concern about the allegations in the *Journal* story and said Lake's failure to ensure that NSC staff members would bring such a matter to his attention was a "potentially disqualifying mistake." Kerrey said he communicated his concern to Lake and to the White House on March 17, leading to speculation that the potential loss of Kerrey's support added to Lake's decision to withdraw.

Congressional Democrats and White House officials accused Senate Republicans of politicizing the confirmation process and waging personal attacks against Lake's integrity. White House Press Secretary Mike McCurry, at a March 18 briefing, said the confirmation process Lake went through was "inexcusably flawed." Later that day during a news conference, Clinton declared that "the cycle of political destruction must end."

Senate Minority Leader Tom Daschle, D-S.D., said the hearings amounted to "character assassination," and he called on the committee to apologize to Lake. Kerrey also criticized those who had made "innuendos" that Lake had broken the law in the Iran-Bosnia matter. A Justice Department investigation into whether Lake and other administration officials made false statements to a House committee found Lake did not commit any criminal wrongdoing.

Even some Republicans criticized the way in which Lake's nomination was handled. Sen. Richard G. Lugar, R-Ind., an Intelligence Committee member, described the confirmation process for Lake as "another example of Borking," a reference to the rough time Democrats gave Robert H. Bork before defeating his nomination to the Supreme Court in 1987.

Other Republicans argued that the process worked exactly as it was supposed to. Sen. Jon Kyl, R-Ariz., said, "This is a tough job. I didn't think the hearings were that tough at all."

"The process worked. In the end, he didn't stand up," said Sen. Phil Gramm, R-Texas, who threatened to keep Lake's nomination from coming to the floor if senators were not given access to the nominee's FBI file. "He was the wrong person for the wrong job."

It was the second time a Clinton nominee had bowed out of consideration for the intelligence job. In 1995 retired Air Force Gen. Michael P. C. Carns withdrew after being picked to succeed R. James Woolsey as director of Central Intelligence. Carns was forced to step aside amid revelations that he had broken immigration laws when he brought a Philippine domestic worker to the United States. (*Congress and the Nation Vol. IX, pp. 1120–1121*)

1998

David Satcher. On Feb. 10, 1998, the Senate approved the nomination of David Satcher to be both U.S. surgeon general and assistant secretary of health in the Department of Health and Human Services. The vote was 63–35.

Nineteen Republicans joined forty-four Democrats to support the confirmation, filling a post that had been vacant since 1994, when Surgeon General Joycelyn Elders was forced to resign for controversial remarks about human sexuality. The nomination of President Clinton's initial choice to succeed her, Nashville obstetrician/gynecologist Henry W. Foster Jr., was derailed in 1995 by questions about the number of abortions he had performed. (*Controversial nominations, Congress and the Nation Vol. IX, p. 1121*)

Senate confirmation followed a 75–23 cloture vote that broke a filibuster by GOP conservatives. Sens. John Ashcroft, R-Mo., and Daniel R. Coats, R-Ind., had led the battle to defeat Satcher. But Satcher found support from many Republicans, including Orrin G. Hatch of Utah and Bill Frist of Tennessee, the chamber's only physician.

Satcher, like both Elders and Foster, was an African American physician. He had served as director of the Centers for Disease Control and Prevention (CDC) since 1993. Before that, he had been president of Meharry Medical College in Nashville, Tenn.

Questions were raised about Satcher's participation, while he served as CDC head, in controversial AIDS studies conducted in Africa in which some women infected with the AIDS virus were given placebos instead of medication that could have treated the disease. Some senators—and many antiabortion groups—criticized him for opposing a ban on an abortion procedure opponents called "partial-birth abortions." Ashcroft also criticized Satcher for his support of needle exchange programs intended to help protect drug users from contracting HIV, the virus that causes AIDS.

Five Republicans on the Labor and Human Resources Committee had voted against Satcher's nomination on Oct. 22, 1997, citing the abortion and AIDS issues. While the panel approved the nomination by a 12–5 vote, consideration by the full Senate was delayed until 1998 because, according to Senate Majority Leader Trent Lott, R-Miss., several senators had requested floor time to debate the nomination fully.

In the end, Satcher was aided by the near-unanimous support of the medical community, including the American Medical Association, as well as the backing of two conservative Republican physicians in Congress, Sen. Frist and Rep. Tom Coburn of Oklahoma.

Frederica Massiah-Jackson. On March 16, 1998, Frederica Massiah-Jackson gave up her more than seven-month effort to join the federal bench by asking that her nomination be withdrawn, thereby ending one of the more acrimonious battles in the ongoing war over judicial appointments. Facing a host of critics who called her soft on crime and hostile to police and prosecutors, Massiah-Jackson likely would have been rejected by the Senate the following day.

For the previous two years, President Clinton and the Republican-controlled Senate had been skirmishing over who should serve in the prestigious and powerful federal courts. But until the Massiah-Jackson fight, Republicans had never been poised to actually defeat a nomination. Rather, they had tried to wear nominees down by keeping their nominations bottled up in committee.

Massiah-Jackson's July 31, 1997, nomination to a district judgeship based in Philadelphia had initially appeared ready for approval. A local judge, Massiah-Jackson had never been a major target of conservative groups. Her nomination had been endorsed by her state's two Republican senators, Arlen Specter and Rick Santorum, and initially there were no complaints from local groups. The Senate Judiciary Committee held a hearing on the nomination Oct. 29, 1997, and approved it on a 12–6 vote on Nov. 6.

But opposition began to form in late December 1997. Prosecutors and police groups in the Philadelphia area started coming forward to oppose her. She was cited by these groups for two incidents in court: one in which she used profanity, and one in which she ordered undercover agents to identify themselves. She was also criticized for a series of rulings characterized as inappropriately lenient.

At an unusual second hearing convened by the committee on March 11, 1998, she began to address fifty such cases only to be confronted with twenty more from Philadelphia-area prosecutors.

After the criticisms surfaced, Specter continued to support her while Santorum was poised to vote against her. Specter and Santorum were put in a difficult position during the fight. The two had worked out a deal with the White House in which they had agreed to give tentative support to every three of Clinton's picks from Pennsylvania in return for making each fourth pick themselves. They reserved the right to quash a potential nominee at the outset, if a vetting committee they created found reason to object. In this case, none of the people who eventually came forward to oppose Massiah-Jackson did so to the vetting committee. After supporting her, the two senators watched as Philadelphia politicians seemed to come out of the woodwork to complain about her record.

The controversy played right into the hands of Sen. John Ashcroft, R-Mo., and others who had been waging a war on virtually all the president's choices. In a Feb. 10 speech, Ashcroft said Massiah-Jackson was a good example of why the Senate should resist growing pressure from the White House, moderate Republicans, Chief Justice William H. Rehnquist, and others who had urged Congress and Clinton to end the judicial battles and fill some of the eighty-three vacancies on the federal bench.

"Some would point to this as unnecessary delay," said Ashcroft. "But we will create an actual crisis, not an imagined one, if we send individuals of this caliber into America's courtrooms."

At the announcement of her withdrawal, Massiah-Jackson said: "I have been a fighter . . . all my life, but allowing still more and more selective, one-sided, and unsubstantiated charges to go unanswered in this politicized environment is not acceptable to me after my long journey."

William A. Fletcher. After a delay of more than three years and a pair of unusual political maneuvers, the Senate on Oct. 8, 1998, voted 57–41 to confirm the nomination of William A. Fletcher to be a judge on the Ninth U.S. Circuit Court of Appeals.

Fletcher, a law professor at the University of California at Berkeley and a friend of President Clinton's, was nominated for the judgeship in 1995. His nomination immediately drew fire from conservatives, who criticized him as another liberal judge on an activist Ninth Circuit court. John Ashcroft, R-Mo., leader of those who sought to block consideration of Fletcher's nomination, said the Ninth Circuit—which served nine western states, Guam, and the Northern Mariana Islands—was the "epicenter of judicial activism in this country."

The nomination was among the hardest fought of the 105th Congress. To get Fletcher to the bench, Clinton and congressional Democrats had to agree to GOP terms on two other matters.

The Clinton administration made a deal with Sen. Slade Gorton, R-Wash., to nominate Barbara Durham, conservative chief justice on the Washington state Supreme Court, to the Ninth Circuit in exchange for Fletcher's confirmation. Democratic critics said the deal set a terrible precedent that would encourage other Republican senators to follow suit. (*Durham nomination, below*)

In another deal, Senate Democrats agreed to support a GOP-backed antinepotism measure (S 1892). The bill, which prohibited close relatives from sitting on the same federal appellate or trial court, was passed by the Senate two days before it confirmed Fletcher. The measure (PL 105-300) was signed into law Oct. 27, even though some Democrats warned that it was unconstitutional. The nepotism issue had been raised because Betty Binns Fletcher, the mother of the nominee, had served since 1979 on the Ninth Circuit. But, at age seventy-five and facing GOP objections to a mother and son sitting on the same court, she had already served notice that she would be taking semiretirement, known as senior status, if her son was confirmed.

S 1892 would not have affected the Fletchers in any event; it applied only to nominations made after it became law. The bill's sponsor, Sen. Jon Kyl, R-Ariz., introduced the legislation to clarify the intent of a little-known antinepotism law that had been on the books since 1922. He said the possibility of a mother-son team in the circuit courts was not a good idea.

After the Durham agreement, Judiciary Chairman Orrin Hatch, R-Utah, pressed for a committee vote in early May. "This has been held up for far too long," the chairman said. While Fletcher was liberal, the traditionally conservative Hatch said, he "appears to be about as apolitical a person as you can find." With one of the committee's ten Republicans objecting anonymously to a vote, the committee on May 7 decided to delay action on Fletcher. At the same time, Hatch delayed marking up S 1892 amid signs that the bill had also become linked to the Fletcher-Durham swap.

The Judiciary Committee finally approved the Fletcher nomination May 21 by a 12–6 vote. The panel reported S 1892 that same day.

1999

Barbara Durham. In 1998 President Clinton agreed to nominate Barbara Durham, a conservative Republican jurist in Washington state, for the influential Ninth U.S. Circuit Court of Appeals, which reviewed trial court decisions in California, eight other western states, and two Pacific territories. Durham was serving as chief judge of the Washington state Supreme Court. Her nomination was part of a deal that the White House had struck with Republican senator Slade Gorton of Washington under which Durham would be nominated in exchange for Senate confirmation to the same court of William A. Fletcher and two other nominees. (*Fletcher nomination, above*).

Judiciary Committee Chairman Orrin G. Hatch, R-Utah, indicated that while he supported Fletcher, he was under no obligation to honor the nomination-for-a-confirmation deal.

Democrats made clear their displeasure that Clinton decided to negotiate with Republicans who had stalled many of his nominees, some for as long as three years.

"As Russell Long used to say when he was chairman of the Finance Committee: 'I ain't for any deal I ain't a part of,'" said Joseph R. Biden Jr., D-Del. Clearly miffed at the deal, Biden said the administration had "caved." "It's bad policy. It's bad politics," he said. "It makes no sense."

Fletcher was confirmed in October 1998, and one of the other two nominees was ultimately confirmed, but Durham ran into opposition once she was nominated Jan. 26, 1999. On May 27 she said she was withdrawing her nomination because her husband was seriously ill.

J. Brian Atwood. J. Brian Atwood, administrator of the Agency for International Development (AID) since 1993, was nominated Jan. 6, 1999, by President Clinton to become U.S. ambassador to Brazil. The nomination stalled when Senate Foreign Relations Committee Chairman Jesse Helms, R-N.C., refused to act on it. For years Atwood had clashed with Helms over Helms's attempts to abolish AID as part of his reorganization of the foreign affairs bureaucracy. Helms reportedly chafed at what he viewed as Atwood's personal attacks against him.

AID's foes and supporters alike credited Atwood's lobbying with saving AID as an independent agency while two other independent foreign affairs agencies had been merged into the State Department by the fiscal 1999 omnibus spending bill (PL 105-277). Atwood's feat was even more remarkable given that the authors of the legislation—Helms and House International Relations Committee Chairman Benjamin A. Gilman, R-N.Y.—wanted to eliminate AID.

With Helms unwilling to act on his nomination, Atwood was unable to win Senate confirmation, and he withdrew his name from consideration May 18, 1999. Atwood said in a statement that Helms apparently "believes that I pursued this administration's position too vigorously. I regret that he feels this way, but I do not regret fighting for the independence of USAID."

Atwood resigned his AID post on July 9.

James C. Hormel. On June 4, 1999, President Clinton appointed businessman and philanthropist James C. Hormel to be ambassador to Luxembourg, making the appointment during the Memorial Day recess. This would allow Hormel to serve until the end of 2000 without Senate confirmation.

Clinton first sent Hormel's name to the Senate in 1997. In November 1997 the Senate Foreign Relations Committee, chaired by conservative Sen. Jesse Helms, R-N.C., had reported the nomination favorably among some thirty other ambassadorial and State Department selections. But the nomination went no further because of stiff opposition from several conservative Senate Republicans, who said they worried that, because Hormel was homosexual, he would push a gay agenda in a diplomatic post.

Two Republican senators who were Mormons, Gordon H. Smith of Oregon and Orrin G. Hatch of Utah, joined Democrats in a letter February 1998 to colleagues expressing their support for the nomination and their hope for a favorable Senate vote. "He's a gentleman and a gentle man, academically distinguished and philanthropically generous. He would be an honorable ambassador," Smith said March 9. The senator said his meeting with Hormel and the nominee's response to a series of questions convinced Smith that he would not be an activist on homosexual issues if confirmed.

But Tim Hutchinson of Arkansas, one of several Republicans senators who put a hold on the nomination, urged Clinton to withdraw the nomination and choose another candidate for the posting. Hutchinson argued that, since the populace of Luxembourg was 97 percent Roman Catholic, a homosexual ambassador would be an affront to the country. The White House, meanwhile, stepped up its campaign for the nominee, distributing to senators a packet of material in support of Hormel.

Majority Leader Trent Lott, R-Miss., who had called Clinton's choice of Hormel a "payoff" to the homosexual community, on July 20 said that it was "not practical" for the nomination to be considered in 1998.

Clinton nominated Hormel again in 1999. But when Helms showed little inclination to have his committee consider the nomination a second time, Clinton gave Hormel a recess appointment. In response, Sen. James M. Inhofe, R-Okla., announced June 8, 1999, that he would put a hold on all nonmilitary nominations moving through the Senate, including the nomination of a new Treasury secretary. The hold stayed in place for a week, until Clinton agreed to alert the Senate in advance of any future recess appointments.

Hormel, heir to the meatpacking company's fortune, had served as alternate representative on the U.S. delegation to the Fifty-First Session of the United Nations General Assembly and was a member of the U.S. delegation to the U.N. Human Rights Commission in 1995. He also had served on several civic and nonprofit boards in the San Francisco area.

Carol J. Parry. Former Chase Manhattan Bank executive Carol J. Parry was nominated on Aug. 5, 1999, to fill a seat on the Federal Reserve Board of Governors. The seat had been vacated in 1998 by Susan M. Phillips, and the Clinton administration waited more than a year to nominate Parry for the position.

Among other senior management duties at Chase, Parry had been director of the community development division, where she oversaw the bank's compliance with the 1977 Community Reinvestment Act (PL 95-128), an antiredlining law. At the time of Parry's nomination, reinvestment provisions were a controversial part of a pending bill (S 900) to overhaul the financial services industry. Parry had been endorsed by a key community group that supported the reinvestment act.

Phil Gramm, R-Texas, chairman of the Senate Banking, Housing and Urban Affairs Committee, which had jurisdiction over Federal Reserve Board nominees, was an ardent critic of the 1977 law. Gramm declined to proceed with Parry's confirmation hearings. In reaction, the Clinton administration refused to send Congress a nominee for a second vacancy that had opened on the board until Parry's nomination was confirmed.

After more than a year, Gram announced on October 2000, that no more Fed appointments would be considered until the next administration in 2001. "We're done. We're pretty much finished with appointments," Gramm said. "It's too late in the session."

"This is a crazy way to do business around here," said Minority Whip Harry Reid, D-Nev. "I don't think they should be held up. The Federal Reserve Board has been an untouchable."

Ted Stewart. Conservative judicial nominee Ted Stewart, chief of staff to Republican governor Michael O. Leavitt of Utah, was confirmed by the Senate Oct. 5, 1999, by a vote of 94–5, to fill a vacant federal judgeship in Utah. The Senate Judiciary Committee favorably reported the nomination July 29, with only Democratic Sens. Edward M. Kennedy of Massachusetts and Russell D. Feingold of Wisconsin voting against.

President Clinton and Senate Judiciary Committee Chairman Orrin G. Hatch, R-Utah, had reportedly reached an agreement in which Stewart, a political ally of the senator's, would be nominated in exchange for Hatch holding hearings on other Clinton nominees. Hatch had not scheduled any hearings on judicial nominations since the start of the 106th Congress and threatened not to as long as Stewart's nomination was in limbo.

Environmental groups, who were sharply critical of Stewart's record while director of Utah's Department of Natural Resources, were outraged that Clinton might name Stewart. And Hatch was outraged that the president might not. "I'm not going to like that," Hatch told television station KSL in Salt Lake City when asked how he would react if Stewart was not selected by the president. "Things can get rough around here."

Hatch told the *Deseret News* of Salt Lake City on June 15 that the president intended to nominate Stewart. The next day, the Judiciary Committee held its first confirmation hearing of the year, for six nominees to the U.S. District courts and two nominees for U.S. Courts of Appeal vacancies.

Stewart received his nomination July 27. While Hatch had never explicitly acknowledged that Stewart's nomination was his price for reengaging the confirmation process, the timing of the developments was more than coincidental.

Following Stewart's nomination, Hatch threw his support behind two Clinton nominees to the U.S. Court of Appeals for the Ninth Circuit, federal district judge Richard Paez and attorney Marsha Berzon. He moved their nominations through his committee, spoke on their behalf, and cast the deciding vote that reported the nominations to the full Senate. *(Paez nomination, p. 992; Berzon nomination, p. 992)*

But Stewart, having cleared the committee vote, ran into opposition in the full Senate. The Democrats kept blocking a Senate vote, going so far as to filibuster the nomination. An attempt to cut off debate was rejected on Sept. 21, 1999, 55–44—five votes short of the sixty votes needed for cloture. The Democrats wanted confirmation of three judges to the Ninth Circuit, Paez and Berzon among them. But after Hatch said he would shut down nominations for the year, they agreed on Oct. 1 to a floor vote on Stewart, in return for votes on six other judicial nominees.

In the end, Stewart had been nominated, approved by committee, and confirmed by the Senate in less than three months. "All one has to do is look at the terrible unfairness of someone having to wait 1,300 days, twenty-five times longer than Ted Stewart . . . to see how unfair this system is," Minority Leader Tom Daschle, D-S.D., said.

Ronnie L. White. President Clinton first nominated Ronnie L. White—the first black on Missouri's Supreme Court—for a U.S. District Court judgeship in Missouri in June 1997. On May 21, 1998, the Senate Judiciary Committee reported his nomination favorably, 13–3. Republican Sen. Christopher S. Bond of Missouri had spoken enthusiastically of the nominee at his hearing on May 14. But the Senate did not act on the nomination before the end of the 105th Congress.

Clinton renominated White in January 1999, at the beginning of the 106th Congress. His nomination was approved by the Judiciary Committee on July 22, with six Republicans voting against reporting it favorably. The nomination was brought to the Senate floor Oct. 4, as part of a deal in which Democrats agreed to allow a vote on the nomination of Ted Stewart in exchange for floor consideration of several other nominees, including White. *(Stewart nomination, above.)*

Sen. John Ashcroft, R-Mo., one of the most vehement critics of Clinton's nominees, argued against the nomination. Ashcroft cited White's dissents in three Missouri Supreme Court decisions to illustrate what he called the nominee's "procriminal jurisprudence."

"I believe Judge White's opinions have been, and if confirmed his opinions on the federal bench will continue to be, pro-criminal and activist, with a slant toward criminals and defendants against prosecutors and the culture in terms of maintaining order," Ashcroft said. "He will use his lifetime appointment to push law in a procriminal direction consistent with his own personal political agenda, rather than defer to the legislative will of the people and interpret the law rather than expand it or redirect the law."

Ashcroft said White "has been the champion of those dissenting in death penalty cases and has dissented in ways which, very frankly, have occasioned an outcry from the law enforcement community in

Missouri." The day of the vote, Ashcroft sent a letter to his colleagues urging defeat of White, citing dissents White wrote in state Supreme Court cases that upheld death sentences.

Patrick J. Leahy of Vermont, the ranking Democrat on the Judiciary Committee, countered during the floor debate that White was "far more apt to affirm a death penalty decision" than to reverse it, asserting that White had voted to affirm forty-one times and reverse seventeen times.

The nomination was defeated by a party-line vote of 45–54 on Oct. 5. Several Republicans who supported White in the Judiciary Committee, including committee Chairman Orrin G. Hatch, R-Utah, switched on the floor. Despite publicly supporting White in the past, Bond, Missouri's other Republican senator, voted against the nominee.

White was the first judicial nominee to be rejected by the full Senate since Robert H. Bork was blocked from taking a seat on the Supreme Court in 1987. *(Congress and the Nation Vol. VII, p. 786)*

"I am hoping . . . the United States has not reverted to a time in its history when there was a color test on nominations," Leahy said after White's defeat.

Clinton leveled his own charges against Senate Republicans the next day. "The Republican-controlled Senate is adding credence to the perceptions that they treat minority and women judicial nominees unfairly and unequally," he said. Clinton added that the vote created "a real doubt about the Senate's ability to fairly perform its constitutional duty to advise and consent."

Clinton's comments capped months of Democratic complaints that the Republican-controlled Senate had unfairly delayed confirmation votes on his nominees, especially women and minorities. Republicans, in turn, accused Clinton of intentionally nominating unqualified minorities and women to the bench in hopes of painting the GOP as bigoted. Conservative Republicans also said Clinton was nominating judges who were too liberal, and they vowed to continue delaying confirmations until more "mainstream" nominees were sent to the Senate.

Carol Moseley-Braun. Overcoming the highly publicized opposition of Senate Foreign Relations Committee Chairman Jesse Helms, R-N.C., Carol Moseley-Braun on Nov. 10, 1999, easily won confirmation, 96–2, as U.S. ambassador to New Zealand and Samoa. The Illinois Democrat had been the first black woman to serve in the Senate (1993–1999).

Only Helms and Peter G. Fitzgerald, R-Ill., who had defeated Moseley-Braun in her reelection bid in 1998, voted against her confirmation. The Foreign Relations Committee's approved her nomination Nov. 8, 17–1, with only Helms opposing her.

Initially, Moseley-Braun's confirmation appeared to be a long shot, with Helms saying, "She's got so many problems that I would not suggest you hold your breath waiting for her to be reported out" by the committee. Former senators nominated to serve as U.S. ambassadors usually received a warm embrace, a quick hearing, and easy approval from their former colleagues. In fact, Senate Minority Leader Tom Daschle, D-S.D., pointed out Oct. 20 that the last time a former senator was rejected for an ambassadorship was 1835.

The controversy allowed Democrats to allege that Helms's attack was part of a general pattern of racial insensitivity on the part of Republicans. Backing down, Helms agreed to hold hearings if the administration provided the panel with documents he said were needed to probe a series of charges that Moseley-Braun was guilty of ethical violations. After those documents were produced, Helms's colleagues on the committee agreed that they were not of sufficient weight to deny Moseley-Braun the nomination.

Helms did not even attend the Nov. 5 confirmation hearing. Craig Thomas, R-Wyo., chairman of the East Asian and Pacific Affairs Subcommittee, who chaired the hearing, left questions about Moseley-Braun's ethics to Paul Coverdell, R-Ga., who gently gave her several opportunities to address allegations about her campaign finances and travel while in office.

At the outset of the hearing, Joseph R. Biden Jr. of Delaware, the committee's ranking Democrat, said that there was not "any shred of evidence, any single scintilla of evidence, that would disqualify Senator . . . Moseley-Braun from serving as the United States ambassador to New Zealand."

The allegations were that she had used as much as $200,000 in campaign funds for personal expenses and had received inappropriate financing for a visit to Nigeria when that country was ruled by a military dictator.

Regarding the allegation that she misused campaign funds, Moseley-Braun said the Federal Election Commission (FEC) and other agencies had cleared her of wrongdoing. She said an FEC audit found evidence that only $311 in 1992 campaign funds was unaccounted for. "I don't know what it takes to put a stake in the heart of that nasty rumor," she said. "Seven years of being smeared with this has not been fun."

Moseley-Braun also told committee members that the two trips she took to Nigeria during her term as a senator were paid for with private money, not out of her Senate budget. She said the visits were "personal in nature" and not intended as missions on behalf of the U.S. government. "At no time have I ever taken a position or taken an action that was in any way contradictory or contravened U.S. policy," she said.

Although Helms sparred with the White House over the Moseley-Braun documents, he came under increasing pressure from Democrats who said his stand smacked of racism and from a group of members, predominantly black women, who marched to his office Nov. 3 to argue their case. The group cited Moseley-Braun's pioneering role as the first and only black woman in the Senate.

Moseley-Braun's nomination also renewed a personal quarrel with Helms that began with her 1993 campaign against extending a design patent for the United Daughters of the Confederacy. Helms was managing the bill on the floor at the time of her filibuster.

Speaking on the Senate floor Nov. 9, Helms accused the Clinton administration of laying a political trap for him. "Perhaps the folks in the administration knew exactly what they were doing," Helms said. "Perhaps they hoped the spectacle of a public dispute between Jesse Helms and Carol Moseley-Braun would serve the base political interests of the Clinton administration."

2000

Richard A. Paez. Richard A. Paez, a federal district court judge in California, was nominated in January 1996 for a seat on the Ninth Circuit Court of Appeals. GOP opponents held up final approval of his nomination for four years.

The Senate Judiciary Committee held a hearing on Paez's nomination Feb. 25, 1998, and favorably reported it March 19. Paez had not been confirmed by the end of the 105th Congress, so Clinton resubmitted the nomination at the start of the 106th Congress. The Senate Judiciary Committee approved his nomination, 10–8, on July 29, 1999, but an attempt to call up the nomination for floor action was rejected, 45–53, on Sept. 21. Paez's nomination was finally confirmed on March 9, 2000, by a 59–39 vote. He had waited 1505 days—longer than any nominee in history, according to Democrats—for his confirmation.

Democrats cited the long delays on Paez, who was Hispanic, and another nominee to that circuit—Marsha L. Berzon, who had been nominated in 1998—to back their contention that Republicans were less inclined to vote to confirm minority and female appointees. To make the point, Vice President Al Gore began a press conference after the March 9 vote by saying, in Spanish, "Friends, today we've finally achieved justice." *(Berzon nomination, below)*

Republicans angrily denied the charge, saying the problem with Paez and Berzon was their liberal activism—a trait they said was shared by judges on the Ninth Circuit. They had raised objections to Paez on several fronts, including his handling of a trial dealing with abortion protesters and his ruling in a case dealing with human rights in Burma.

The nominations of Paez and Berzon had lingered on the calendar until Senate Majority Leader Trent Lott, R-Miss., finally agreed in November 1999, to bring the pair up for a vote before March 15, 2000. Lott made the promise in order to end a Democratic hold on a home-state ally of his, Tupelo Mayor Glenn McCullough, who had been nominated for a six-year term on the Tennessee Valley Authority board. "I do not think it is reasonable to try to hold up one six-year term nominee to try to get two lifetime nominees to the Ninth Circuit Court of Appeals, a circuit that already has too many activist judges in it, a circuit that is the most liberal in this country, . . . a circuit basically that is out of control," Lott had said on the floor Oct. 28.

During the March 9 debate, Lott said he opposed Paez because of "highly questionable rulings and political statements while sitting on the bench. . . . When you go on the bench, your political involvement, your personal preferences, should remain private. You should assume the bench and keep your mouth shut until you rule appropriately."

But the majority leader took steps to block procedural tactics by other opponents. First, he discouraged a filibuster by conservative Republican Robert C. Smith, N.H., who emerged as the fiercest critic of Paez, Berzon, and the Ninth Circuit. Debate on Paez was cut off by an 85–14 cloture vote on March 8.

Lott also said he would not support a motion to indefinitely postpone a vote on Paez's nomination. Jeff Sessions, R-Ala., had pushed for a postponement so the Senate could look into Paez's handling of a criminal fraud case against Democratic fundraiser John Huang. Paez had sentenced Huang to one year of probation following a guilty plea in August 1999. Lott agreed that "there is something not right about that. It does not pass the smell test." But he still opposed the motion to postpone, which fell on a 31–67 vote.

Vice President Al Gore, who had rushed to Washington from the presidential campaign trail in case he was needed to break a tie vote, urged the Senate to act more rapidly on future nominations. "When it comes to our judiciary, justice delayed is still justice denied. So today I say to the Senate majority once again, stop holding our justice system hostage," Gore said.

On the final vote, Paez won the support of Judiciary Committee Chairman Orrin G. Hatch, R-Utah, as well as thirteen other Republicans who crossed party lines to vote for him.

Marsha L. Berzon. On March 9, 2000, the Senate approved Marsha L. Berzon for a seat on the Ninth Circuit Court of Appeals by a vote of 64–34. Berzon, a San Francisco labor lawyer, had first been nominated in January 1998.

The Senate Judiciary Committee had held a hearing on the nomination July 30, 1998. But Republican conservatives, complaining that Berzon was too liberal to receive a lifetime appointment, blocked further action in the 105th Congress.

Berzon was renominated in January 1999. Another hearing was held June 16, 1999, and the Judiciary Committee reported it, 10–8, on July 1. But an attempt to bring the nomination to the floor was rejected, 45–54, on Sept. 21.

Her confirmation had been paired with that of Richard A. Paez, whose nomination to the Ninth Circuit had been held since January

1996. In late 1999 Senate Majority Leader Trent Lott, R-Miss., finally reached agreement with the Democrats to schedule a vote on Berzon and Paez, in exchange for a vote on a nominee he favored. *(Paez nomination, p. 992)*

Berzon had specialized in employment discrimination cases and had prepared many briefs for the Supreme Court, including four she personally argued before the justices. Although critics focused on her legal work on behalf of labor unions, Berzon seemed to be more a victim of the GOP's antipathy toward the Ninth Circuit than anything specific she had done. Although many Republicans included her with Paez, their objections generally had to do with Paez's statements and rulings. They contended that appointing Berzon and Paez to the Ninth Circuit would continue that panel's leftward drift.

Sen. Jim Bunning, R-Ky., said on March 8 that he opposed Berzon's nomination because "looking at her past and the causes which she has pushed show that, if confirmed, she is not going to help steer the Ninth Circuit toward the judicial mainstream."

"This is a renegade circuit out of the mainstream of American jurisprudence," said Republican Robert C. Smith, N.H., on March 9, adding that the circuit had "an abysmal record" of being overturned by the Supreme Court. He and other senators called for an overhaul of the circuit, which served about 50 million people.

Democrats charged that Republicans were merely opposed to the nominations of women and members of racial minorities, a charge they angrily denied.

Debate on Berzon was cut off by an 86–13 cloture vote on March 8 and the final vote to confirm was taken the next day. In the end a group of nineteen mostly moderate Republican senators crossed party lines, rejected their party leaders' position, and joined with all the Senate's Democrats to support her confirmation.

Presidential Vetoes, 1997–2001

President Bill Clinton vetoed a total of twenty bills (all public measures) during his second term in office. In his first four years, he vetoed seventeen (also all public bills), for a total of thirty-seven during his two terms in office. The number is relatively low compared to veto totals of other presidents since 1953 who faced a Congress in the control of the opposition party. Democrats controlled Congress only during the first two years (103rd Congress) of Clinton's presidency. He did not cast any vetoes during that two-year period, making him the first president since 1853 to go an entire Congress without vetoing a single bill. The last president to do that was Millard Fillmore during the 32nd Congress (1851–1853).

Grover Cleveland issued the most vetoes in one term, 414. Franklin Roosevelt, who served as president for a little more than three terms, vetoed the most measures, 635. Seven presidents vetoed no bills.

Clinton was overridden only twice during his tenure, and one of those was to restore line-item vetoes he struck from a military construction bill—one of Congress's most parochial pieces of regular legislation because of the dollars it pours into congressional districts and states.

Vetoes, 1953–2001

President (Congresses)	Regular Vetoes	Pocket Vetoes	Total Vetoes	Overridden
Dwight D. Eisenhower (83rd–86th)	73	108	181	2
John F. Kennedy (87th–88th)	12	9	21	0
Lyndon B. Johnson (88th–90th)	16	14	30	0
Richard M. Nixon (91st–93rd)	26	17	43	7
Gerald R. Ford (93rd–94th)	48	18	66	12
Jimmy Carter (95th–96th)	13	18	31	2

President (Congresses)	Regular Vetoes	Pocket Vetoes	Total Vetoes	Overridden
Ronald Reagan (97th–100th)	39	39	78	9
George Bush[1] (101st–102nd)	29	15	44	1
Bill Clinton[2] (103rd–106th)	36	1	37	2

1. President Bush attempted to pocket-veto two bills during recess periods. Congress considered the two bills enacted into law because of the President's failure to return the legislation. The bills are not counted as pocket vetoes in this table.

2. Does not include line-item vetoes, which were permitted under a 1996 law that was struck down by the Supreme Court.

Following is a list of bills vetoed by Clinton during his second term, 1997–2001. *(Clinton vetoes 1993–1997, Congress and the Nation Vol. IX, p. 1122)*

1997

1. HR 1469
   (Emergency appropriations for disaster relief containing policy riders)
   Vetoed: June 9, 1997
   No override attempt.
   (Story, p. 58)

2. HR 1122
   (Banning partial birth abortions)
   Vetoed: Oct. 10, 1997
   House overrode July 23, 1998: 296–132.
   Senate sustained veto Sept. 18, 1998: 64–36.
   (Story, p. 455)

3. HR 2631
   (Restore thirty-eight projects in FY 1998 military constructions appropriations bill (HR 2016—PL 105-45) vetoed under line-item veto authority in effect at the time)
   Vetoed: Nov. 13, 1997
   House overrode Feb. 5, 1998: 347–69.
   Senate overrode Feb. 25, 1998: 78–20.
   (Story, p. 64)

1998

1. S 1502
   (School vouchers in the District of Columbia)
   Vetoed: May 20, 1998
   No override attempt.
   (Story, p. 528)

2. HR 2709
   (Russia sanctions for technical assistance to Iran's missile program)
   Vetoed: June 23, 1998
   No override attempt.
   (Story, p. 195)

3. HR 2646
   (Expand tax benefits of education savings accounts)
   Vetoed: July 21, 1998
   No override attempt.
   (Story, p. 518)

4. HR 4101
   (Agriculture and nutrition programs fiscal 1999 appropriations)
   Vetoed: Oct. 7, 1998
   No override attempt.
   (Story, p. 63)

5. HR 1757
   (Reauthorize and reorganize the State Department)
   Vetoed: Oct. 21, 1998
   No override attempt.
   (Story, p. 189)

1999

1. HR 2488
   (Reduce federal income, gift, estate, capital gains and other taxes)
   Vetoed: Sept. 23, 1999
   No override attempt.
   (Story, p. 87)

2. HR 2587
   (District of Columbia fiscal 2000 appropriations)
   Vetoed: Sept. 28, 1999
   No override attempt.
   (Story, p. 73)

3. HR 2606
   (Foreign operations fiscal 2000 appropriations)
   Vetoed: Oct. 18, 1999

No override attempt.
(Story, pp. 75, 210)

4. HR 2670
   (Commerce, State, Justice fiscal 2000
      appropriations)
   Vetoed: Oct. 25, 1999
   No override attempt.
   (Story, p. 74)

5. HR 3064
   (D.C., Labor, HHS, Education fiscal
      2000 appropriations)
   Vetoed: Nov. 3, 1999
   No override attempt.
   (Story, p. 73)

2000

1. S 1287
   (Nevada nuclear waste storage site)
   Vetoed: April 25, 2000

Senate sustained veto May 2, 2000:
   64–35.
(Story, p. 407)

2. HR 4810
   (Marriage status tax cut)
   Vetoed: Aug. 5, 2000
   House sustained veto Sept. 13, 2000:
      270–158.
   (Story, p. 113)

3. HR 8
   (Repeal of taxes on estates, gifts, and
      trusts)
   Vetoed: Aug. 31, 2000
   House sustained veto Sept. 7, 2000:
      274–157.
   (Story, p. 115)

4. HR 4733
   (Energy and water fiscal 2001
      appropriations)
   Vetoed: Oct. 7, 2000

House overrode Oct. 11, 2000: 315–98.
No override attempt in Senate.
(Story, p. 83)

5. HR 4516
   (Treasury, postal, legislative fiscal 2001
      appropriations)
   Vetoed: Oct. 30, 2000
   No override attempt.
   (Story, p. 81)

6. HR 4392
   (Intelligence authorization for fiscal
      2001)
   Vetoed: Nov. 4, 2000
   No override attempt.
   (Story, p. 227)

7. HR 2415
   (Consumer bankruptcy overhaul)
   Pocket-vetoed Dec. 19, 2000
   No override attempt.
   (Story, p. 142)

Selected Texts, 1997–2000

The Presidency   999

Clinton Impeachment   1017

Congress   1022

Campaigns and Elections   1032

President Clinton's Second Inaugural Address

Following is the text of President Clinton's second inaugural address, delivered on Jan. 20, 1997.

My fellow citizens, at this last presidential inauguration of the 20th century, let us lift our eyes toward the challenges that await us in the next century.

It is our great good fortune that time and chance have put us not only at the edge of a new century in a new millennium, but on the edge of a bright new prospect in human affairs: a moment that will define our course and our character for decades to come.

We must keep our old democracy forever young.

Guided by the ancient vision of a promised land, let us set our sights upon a land of new promise.

The promise of America was born in the 18th century out of the bold conviction that we are all created equal. It was extended and preserved in the 19th century, when our nation spread across the continent, saved the union and abolished the awful scourge of slavery.

Then, in turmoil and triumph, that promise exploded on to the world stage to make this the American Century—and what a century it has been.

America became the world's mightiest industrial power, saved the world from tyranny in two world wars and a long Cold War, and time and again reached out across the globe to millions who, like us, longed for the blessings of liberty.

Along the way, Americans produced a great middle class and security in old age; built unrivaled centers of learning and opened public schools to all; split the atom and explored the heavens; invented the computer and the microchip; and deepened the wellspring of justice by making a revolution in civil rights for African-Americans and all minorities, and extending the circle of citizenship, opportunity and dignity to women.

Now, for the third time, a new century is upon us and another time to choose. We began the 19th century with a choice to spread our nation from coast to coast.

We began the 20th century with a choice to harness the industrial revolution to our values of free enterprise, conservation and human decency. Those choices made all the difference.

At the dawn of the 21st century, a free people must now choose to shape the forces of the Information Age and the global society; to unleash the limitless potential of all our people; and, yes, to form a more perfect union.

When last we gathered, our march to this new future seemed less certain than it does today. We vowed then to set a clear course to renew our nation.

In these four years, we have been touched by tragedy, exhilarated by challenge, strengthened by achievement.

America stands alone as the world's indispensable nation. Once again, our economy is the strongest on earth. Once again, we are building stronger families, thriving communities, better educational opportunities, a cleaner environment.

Problems that once seemed destined to deepen now bend to our efforts. Our streets are safer and record numbers of our fellow citizens have moved from welfare to work.

And once again, we have resolved for our time a great debate over the role of government. Today, we can declare government is not the problem and government is not the solution. We, the American people, we are the solution.

Our Founders understood that well and gave us a democracy strong enough to endure for centuries, flexible enough to face our common challenges and advance our common dreams in each new day.

THE ROLE OF GOVERNMENT

As times change, so government must change. We need a new government for a new century: humble enough not to try to solve all our problems for us, but strong enough to give us the tools to solve our problems for ourselves; a government that is smaller, lives within its means and does more with less.

Yet, where it can stand up for our values and interests around the world, and where it can give Americans the power to make a real difference in their everyday lives, government should do more, not less.

The preeminent mission of our new government is to give all Americans an opportunity—not a guarantee—but a real opportunity to build better lives.

Beyond that, my fellow citizens, the future is up to us. Our Founders taught us that the preservation of our liberty and our union depends upon responsible citizenship, and we need a new sense of responsibility for our new century.

There is work to do, work that government alone cannot do: teaching children to read, hiring people off welfare rolls, coming out from behind locked doors and shuttered windows to help reclaim our streets from drugs and gangs and crime, taking time out of our own lives to serve others.

Each and every one of us in our own way must assume personal responsibility, not only for ourselves and our families, but for our neighbors and our nation.

Our greatest responsibility is to embrace a new spirit of community for a new century. For any one of us to succeed, we must succeed as one America. The challenge of our past remains the challenge of our future.

Will we be one nation, one people, with one common destiny—or not?

Will we all come together or come apart?

The divide of race has been America's constant curse, and each new wave of immigrants gives new targets to old prejudices. Prejudice and contempt cloaked in the pretense of religious or political convictions are no different.

These forces have nearly destroyed our nation in the past. They plague us still. They fuel the fanaticism of terror. And they torment the lives of millions in fractured nations all around the world.

These obsessions cripple both those who hate and, of course, those who are hated, robbing both of what they might become. We cannot, we will not succumb to the dark impulses that lurk in the far regions of the soul everywhere. We shall overcome them.

And we shall replace them with a generous spirit of a people who feel at home with one another.

Our rich texture of racial, religious and political diversity will be a godsend in the 21st century. Great rewards will come to those who can live together, learn together, work together, forge new ties that bind together.

THE SHAPE OF AN ERA TO COME

As this new era approaches, we can already see its broad outlines.

Ten years ago, the Internet was the mystical province of physicists. Today, it is a commonplace encyclopedia for millions of school children.

Scientists now are decoding the blueprint of human life. Cures for our most feared illnesses seem close at hand. The world is no longer divided into two hostile camps.

Instead, now we are building bonds with nations that once were our adversaries. Growing connections of commerce and culture give us a chance to lift the fortunes and spirits of people the world over.

And for the very first time in all of history, more people on this planet live under democracy than dictatorship.

My fellow Americans, as we look back at this remarkable century, we may ask, can we hope not just to follow, but even to surpass the achievements of the 20th century in America and to avoid the awful bloodshed that stained its legacy?

To that question, every American here and every American in our land today must answer a resounding yes.

'A NEW LAND OF PROMISE'

This is the heart of our task. With a new vision of government, a new sense of responsibility, a new spirit of community, we will sustain America's journey. The promise we sought in a new land, we will find again in a land of new promise.

In this new land, education will be every citizen's most prized possession. Our schools will have the highest standards in the world, igniting the spark of possibility in the eyes of every girl and every boy. And the doors of higher education will be opened to all.

The knowledge and power of the Information Age will be within reach not just of the few but of every classroom, every library, every child.

Parents and children will have time not only to work but to read and play together. And the plans they make at their kitchen table will be those of a better home, a better job, the certain chance to go to college.

Our streets will echo again with the laughter of our children, because no one will try to shoot them or sell them drugs anymore.

Everyone who can work will work, with today's permanent underclass part of tomorrow's growing middle class.

New miracles of medicine at last will reach not only those who can claim care now but the children and hard-working families too long denied.

We will stand mighty for peace and freedom, and maintain a strong defense against terror and destruction. Our children will sleep free from the threat of nuclear, chemical or biological weapons.

Ports and airports, farms and factories will thrive with trade and innovation and ideas. And the world's greatest democracy will lead a whole world of democracies.

Our land of new promise will be a nation that meets its obligations; a nation that balances its budget, but never loses the balance of its values; a nation where . . . a nation where our grandparents have secure retirement and health care, and their grandchildren know we have made the reforms necessary to sustain those benefits for their time; a nation that fortifies the world's most productive economy, even as it protects the great natural bounty of our water, air and majestic land.

And in this land of new promise, we will have reformed our politics so that the voice of the people will always speak louder than the din of narrow interests, regaining the participation and deserving the trust of all Americans.

Fellow citizens, let us build that America: a nation ever moving forward toward realizing the full potential of all its citizens. Prosperity and power—yes, they are important, and we must maintain them. But let us never forget the greatest progress we have made and the greatest progress we have yet to make is in the human heart.

In the end, all the world's wealth and a thousand armies are no match for the strength and decency of the human spirit.

EVOKING KING'S DREAM

Thirty-four years ago, the man whose life we celebrate today spoke to us down there at the other end of this mall in words that moved the conscience of a nation. Like a prophet of old, he told of his dream that one day America would rise up and treat all its citizens as equals before the law and in the heart.

Martin Luther King's dream was the American Dream. His quest is our quest: the ceaseless striving to live out our true creed. Our history has been built on such dreams and labors. And by our dreams and labors, we will redeem the promise of America in the 21st century.

To that effort, I pledge all my strength and every power of my office. I ask the members of Congress here to join in that pledge.

The American people returned to office a president of one party and a Congress of another. Surely, they did not do this to advance the politics of petty bickering and extreme partisanship they plainly deplore.

No. They call on us instead to be repairers of the breach and to move on with America's mission. America demands and deserves big things from us, and nothing big ever came from being small.

Let us remember the timeless wisdom of Cardinal Bernardin when facing the end of his own life.

He said it is wrong to waste the precious gift of time on acrimony and division.

Fellow citizens, we must not waste the precious gift of this time, for all of us are on that same journey of our lives. And our journey, too, will come to an end. But the journey of our America must go on.

And so, my fellow Americans, we must be strong, for there is much to dare. The demands of our time are great, and they are different. Let us meet them with faith and courage, with patience and a grateful, happy heart.

Let us shape the hope of this day into the noblest chapter in our history. Yes, let us build our bridge . . . a bridge wide enough and strong enough for every American to cross over to a blessed land of new promise.

May those generations whose faces we cannot yet see—whose names we may never know—say of us here that we led our beloved land into a new century with the American dream alive for all her children, with the American promise of a more perfect union a reality for all her people, with America's bright flame of freedom spreading throughout all the world.

From the height of this place and the summit of this century, let us go forth.

May God strengthen our hands for the good work ahead and always, always bless our America.

President Clinton's 1997 State of the Union Address

Following is President Clinton's State of the Union address delivered to Congress on Feb. 4, 1997.

Mr. Speaker, Mr. Vice President, members of the 105th Congress, distinguished guests, my fellow Americans:

I think I should start by saying thanks for inviting me back.

I come before you tonight with a challenge as great as any in our peacetime history—and a plan of action to meet that challenge, to prepare our people for the bold new world of the 21st century.

We have much to be thankful for. With four years of growth, we have won back the basic strength of our economy. With crime and welfare rolls declining, we are winning back our optimism, the enduring faith that we can master any difficulty. With the Cold War receding and global commerce at record levels, we are helping to win an unrivaled peace and prosperity all across the world.

My fellow Americans, the state of our union is strong, but now we must rise to the decisive moment, to make a nation and a world better than any we have ever known.

The new promise of the global economy, the Information Age, unimagined new work, life-enhancing technology—all these are ours to seize. That is our honor and our challenge. We must be shapers of events, not observers, for if we do not act, the moment will pass and we will lose the best possibilities of our future.

We face no imminent threat, but we do have an enemy. The enemy of our time is inaction.

So tonight I issue a call to action—action by this Congress, action by our states, by our people to prepare America for the 21st century; action to keep our economy and our democracy strong and working for all our people; action to strengthen education and harness the forces of technology and science; action to build stronger families and stronger communities and a safer environment; action to keep America the world's strongest force for peace, freedom and prosperity; and above all, action to build a more perfect union here at home.

The spirit we bring to our work will make all the difference.

We must be committed to the pursuit of opportunity for all Americans, responsibility from all Americans in a community of all Americans. And we must be committed to a new kind of government: not to solve all our problems for us, but to give our people—all our people—the tools they need to make the most of their own lives. And we must work together.

The people of this nation elected us all. They want us to be partners, not partisans. They put us all right here in the same boat. They gave us all oars, and they told us to row. Now, here is the direction I believe we should take.

BALANCED BUDGET

First, we must move quickly to complete the unfinished business of our country: to balance the budget, renew our democracy and finish the job of welfare reform.

Over the last four years, we have brought new economic growth by investing in our people, expanding our exports, cutting our deficits, creating over 11 million new jobs, a four-year record.

Now we must keep our economy the strongest in the world. We here tonight have an historic opportunity. Let this Congress be the Congress that finally balances the budget.

In two days I will propose a detailed plan to balance the budget by 2002. This plan will balance the budget and invest in our people while protecting Medicare, Medicaid, education and the environment. It will balance the budget and build on the vice president's efforts to make our government work better—even as it costs less.

It will balance the budget and provide middle-class tax relief to pay for education and health care, to help to raise a child, to buy and sell a home.

Balancing the budget requires only your vote and my signature. It does not require us to rewrite our Constitution. I believe, I believe it is both unnecessary and unwise to adopt a balanced-budget amendment that could cripple our country in time of economic crisis and force unwanted results such as judges halting Social Security checks or increasing taxes.

Let us at least agree we should not pass any measure, no measure should be passed that threatens Social Security. We don't need, whatever your view on that, we all must concede we don't need a constitutional amendment, we need action. Whatever our differences, we should balance the budget now, and then, for the long-term health of our society, we must agree to a bipartisan process to preserve Social Security and reform Medicare for the long run, so that these fundamental programs will be as strong for our children as they are for our parents.

And let me say something that's not in my script tonight. I know this is not going to be easy. But I really believe one of the reasons the American people gave me a second term was to take the tough decisions in the next four years that will carry our country through the next 50 years. I know it is easier for me than for you to say or do. But another reason I was elected is to support all of you, without regard to party, to give you what is necessary to join in these decisions. We owe it to our country and to our future.

CAMPAIGN FINANCE REFORM

Our second piece of unfinished business requires us to commit ourselves tonight, before the eyes of America, to finally enacting bipartisan campaign finance reform.

Now, Senators [John] McCain [R-Ariz.] and [Russell D.] Feingold [D-Wis.], Representatives [Christopher] Shays [R-Conn.] and [Martin T.] Meehan [D-Mass.] have reached across party lines here to craft tough and fair reform. Their proposal would curb spending, reduce the role of special interests, create a level playing field between challengers and incumbents, and ban contributions from non-citizens, all corporate sources, and the other large soft-money contributions that both parties receive.

You know and I know that this can be delayed, and you know and I know that delay will mean the death of reform.

So let's set our own deadline. Let's work together to write bipartisan campaign finance reform into law and pass McCain-Feingold by the day we celebrate the birth of our democracy, July the 4th.

FROM WELFARE TO WORK

There is a third piece of unfinished business. Over the last four years, we moved a record two and a quarter million people off the welfare roles. Then last year Congress enacted landmark welfare reform legislation demanding that all able-bodied recipients assume the responsibility of moving from welfare to work. Now each and every one of us has to fulfill our responsibility, indeed our moral obligation, to make sure that people who now must work can work. And now we must act to meet a new goal: 2 million more people off the welfare rolls by the year 2000.

Here is my plan: tax credits and other incentives for businesses that hire people off welfare; incentives for job placement firms in states to create more jobs for welfare recipients; training, transportation and child care to help people go to work.

Now I challenge every state—turn those welfare checks into private sector paychecks. I challenge every religious congregation, every community nonprofit, every business to hire someone off welfare. And I'd like to say especially to every employer in our country who ever criticized the old welfare system, you can't blame that old system anymore; we have torn it down. Now, do your part. Give someone on welfare the chance to go to work.

Tonight I am pleased to announce that five major corporations—Sprint, Monsanto, UPS, Burger King and United Airlines—will be the first to join in a new national effort to marshal America's businesses large and small to create jobs so that people can move from welfare to work.

We passed welfare reform. All of you know I believe we were right to do it. But no one can walk out of this chamber with a clear conscience unless you are prepared to finish the job.

And we must join together to do something else, too, something both Republican and Democratic governors have asked us to do: to restore basic health and disability benefits when misfortune strikes immigrants who came to this country legally, who work hard, pay taxes and obey the law. To do otherwise is simply unworthy of a great nation of immigrants.

EDUCATION

Now, looking ahead, the greatest step of all, the high threshold to the future we must now cross, and my No. 1 priority for the next four years, is to ensure that all Americans have the best education in the world.

Let's work together to meet these three goals: every 8-year-old must be able to read, every 12-year-old must be able to log on to the Internet, every 18-year-old must be able to go to college and every adult American must be able to keep on learning for a lifetime.

My balanced budget makes an unprecedented commitment to these goals—$51 billion next year—but far more than money is required. I have a plan, a call to action for American education based on these 10 principles:

First, a national crusade for education standards—not federal government standards, but national standards, representing what all our students must know to succeed in the knowledge economy of the 21st century. Every state and school must shape the curriculum to reflect these standards and train teachers to lift students up to them. To help schools meet the standards and measure their progress, we will lead an effort over the next two years to develop national tests of student achievement in reading and math.

Tonight I issue a challenge to the nation. Every state should adopt high national standards, and by 1999, every state should test every fourth-grader in reading and every eighth-grader in math to make sure these standards are met.

Raising standards will not be easy, and some of our children will not be able to meet them at first. The point is not to put our children down, but to lift them up. Good tests will show us who needs help, what changes in teaching to make, and which schools need to improve. They can help us end social promotion, for no child should move from grade school to junior high or junior high to high school until he or she is ready.

Last month our secretary of Education, Dick Riley, and I visited northern Illinois, where eighth-grade students from 20 school districts, in a project aptly called First in the World, took the third International Math and Science Study.

That's a test that reflects the world-class standards our children must meet for the new era. And those students in Illinois tied for first in the world in science and came in second in math. Two of them, Kristen Tanner and Chris Getsla, are here tonight along with their teacher, Sue Winski. They're up there with the first lady, and they prove that when we aim high and challenge our students, they will be the best in the world. Let's give them a hand. Stand up, please.

Second, to have the best schools, we must have the best teachers. Most of us in this chamber would not be here tonight without the help of those teachers. I know that I wouldn't be here.

For years many of our educators, led by North Carolina's [Democratic] governor, Jim Hunt, and the National Board for Professional Teaching Standards, have worked very hard to establish nationally accepted credentials for excellence in teaching.

Just 500 of these teachers have been certified since 1995. My budget will enable 100,000 more to seek national certification as master teachers. We should reward and recognize our best teachers. And as we reward them, we should quickly and fairly remove those few who don't measure up, and we should challenge more of our finest young people to consider teaching as a career.

Third, we must do more to help all our children read. Forty percent—40 percent—of our 8-year-olds cannot read on their own. That's why we have just launched the America Reads initiative, to build a citizen army of 1 million volunteer tutors to make sure every child can read independently by the end of the 3rd grade. We will use thousands of AmeriCorps volunteers to mobilize this citizen army. We want at least 100,000 college students to help.

And tonight I'm pleased that 60 college presidents have answered my call, pledging that thousands of their work-study students will serve for one year as reading tutors.

This is also a challenge to every teacher and every principal.

You must use these tutors to help your students read. And it is especially a challenge to our parents. You must read with your children every night.

This leads to the fourth principle: Learning begins in the first days of life. Scientists are now discovering how young children develop emotionally and intellectually from their very first days and how important it is for parents to begin immediately talking, singing, even reading to their infants. The first lady has spent years writing about this issue, studying it. And she and I are going to convene a White House conference on early learning and the brain this spring to explore how parents and educators can best use these startling new findings.

We already know we should start teaching children before they start school. That's why this balanced budget expands Head Start to 1 million children by 2002. And that is why the vice president and Mrs. Gore will host their annual family conference this June on what we can do to make sure that parents are an active part of their children's learning all the way through school.

They've done a great deal to highlight the importance of family in our life, and now they're turning their attention to getting more parents involved in their children's learning all the way through school. I thank you, Mr. Vice President, and I thank you especially, Tipper, for what you're doing.

Fifth, every state should give parents the power to choose the right public school for their children. Their right to choose will foster competition and innovation that can make public schools better. We should also make it possible for more parents and teachers to start charter schools, schools that set and meet the highest standards and exist only as long as they do.

Our plan will help America to create 3,000 of these charter schools by the next century, nearly seven times as many as there are in the country today, so that parents will have even more choices in sending their children to the best schools.

Sixth, character education must be taught in our schools. We must teach our children to be good citizens. And we must continue to promote order and discipline; supporting communities that introduce school uniforms, impose curfews, enforce truancy laws, remove disruptive students from the classroom, and have zero tolerance for guns and drugs in schools.

Seventh, we cannot expect our children to raise themselves up in schools that are literally falling down. With the student population at an all-time high, and record numbers of school buildings falling into disrepair, this has now become a serious national concern. Therefore, my budget includes a new initiative: $5 billion to help communities finance $20 billion in school construction over the next four years.

Eighth, we must make the 13th and 14th years of education—at least two years of college—just as universal in America by the 21st century as a high school education is today, and we must open the doors of college to all Americans.

To do that, I propose America's Hope Scholarship, based on Georgia's pioneering program—two years of a $1,500 tax credit for college tuition, enough to pay for the typical community college. I also propose a tax deduction of up to $10,000 a year for all tuition after high school, an expanded IRA you can withdraw from tax free for education, and the largest increase in Pell grant scholarships in 20 years.

Now this plan will give most families the ability to pay no taxes on money they save for college tuition. I ask you to pass it and give every American who works hard the chance to go to college.

Ninth, in the 21st century we must expand the frontiers of learning across a lifetime. All our people, of whatever age, must have the chance to learn new skills.

Most Americans live near a community college. The roads that take them there can be paths to a better future. My GI bill for America's workers will transform the confusing tangle of federal training programs into a simple skill grant to go directly into eligible workers' hands.

For too long this bill has been sitting on that desk there, without action. I ask you to pass it now. Let's give more of our workers the ability to learn and to earn for a lifetime.

Tenth, we must bring the power of the Information Age into all our schools.

Last year, I challenged America to connect every classroom and library to the Internet by the year 2000, so that for the first time in our history, children in the most isolated rural town, the most comfortable suburbs, the poorest inner-city schools will have the same access to the same universe of knowledge.

That is my plan—a call to action for American education. Some may say that it is unusual for a president to pay this kind of attention to education. Some may say it is simply because the president and his wonderful wife have been obsessed with this subject for more years than they can recall. That is not what is driving these proposals. We must understand the significance of this endeavor.

One of the greatest sources of our strength throughout the Cold War was a bipartisan foreign policy. Because our future was at stake, politics stopped at the water's edge. Now I ask you, and I ask all our nation's governors, I ask parents, teachers and citizens all across America, for a new nonpartisan commitment to education, because education is a critical national security issue for our future and politics must stop at the schoolhouse door.

HARNESSING TECHNOLOGY

To prepare America for the 21st century, we must harness the powerful forces of science and technology to benefit all Americans. This is the first State of the Union carried live in video over the Internet, but we've only begun to spread the benefits of a technology revolution that should become the modern birthright of every citizen.

Our effort to connect every classroom is just the beginning. Now we should connect every hospital to the Internet so that doctors can instantly share data about their patients with the best specialists in the field.

And I challenge the private sector tonight to start by connecting every children's hospital as soon as possible so that a child in bed can stay in touch with school, family and friends. A sick child need no longer be a child alone.

We must build the second generation of the Internet so that our leading universities and national laboratories can communicate in speeds a thousand times faster than today to develop new medical treatments, new sources of energy, new ways of working together. But we cannot stop there.

As the Internet becomes our new town square, a computer in every home—a teacher of all subjects, a connection to all cultures—this will no longer be a dream, but a necessity. And over the next decade, that must be our goal.

We must continue to explore the heavens, pressing on with the Mars probes and the International Space Station, both of which will have practical applications for our everyday living.

We must speed the remarkable advances in medical science. The human genome project is now decoding the genetic mysteries of life. American scientists have discovered genes linked to breast cancer and ovarian cancer and medication that stops a stroke in progress and begins to reverse its effects, and treatments that dramatically lengthen the lives of people with HIV and AIDS.

Since I took office, funding for AIDS research at the National Institutes of Health has increased dramatically to $1.5 billion. With new resources, NIH will now become the most powerful discovery engine for an AIDS vaccine, working with other scientists, to finally end the threat of AIDS. Remember that every year, every year we move up the discovery of an AIDS vaccine we'll save millions of lives around the world. We must reinforce our commitment to medical science.

To prepare America for the 21st century, we must build stronger families. Over the past four years, the Family and Medical Leave Law has helped millions of Americans to take time off to be with their families.

With new pressures on people and the way they work and live, I believe we must expand family leave so that workers can take time off for teacher conferences and a child's medical checkup. We should pass flex time so workers can choose to be paid for overtime in income or trade it in for time off to be with their families.

We must continue, step by step, to give more families access to affordable quality health care. Forty million Americans still lack health insurance. Ten million children still lack health insurance. Eighty percent of them have working parents who pay taxes. That is wrong.

My balanced budget will extend health coverage to up to 5 million of those children. Since nearly half of all children who lose their insurance do so because their parents lose or change a job, my budget will also ensure that people who temporarily lose their jobs can still afford to keep their health insurance. No child should be without a doctor just because a parent is without a job.

My Medicare plan modernizes Medicare, increases the life of the trust fund to 10 years, provides support for respite care for the many families with loved ones afflicted with Alzheimer's, and, for the first time, it would fully pay for annual mammograms.

Just as we ended drive-through deliveries of babies last year, we must now end the dangerous and demeaning practice of forcing women home from the hospital only hours after a mastectomy.

I ask your support for bipartisan legislation to guarantee that a woman can stay in the hospital for 48 hours after a mastectomy. With us tonight is Dr. Kristen Zarfos, a Connecticut surgeon whose outrage at this practice spurred a national movement and inspired this legislation. I'd like her to stand so we can thank her for her efforts. Dr. Zarfos, thank you.

In the last four years, we have increased child support collections by 50 percent. Now we should go further and do better by making it a felony for any parent to cross a state line in an attempt to flee from this, his or her most sacred obligation.

Finally, we must also protect our children by standing firm in our determination to ban the advertising and marketing of cigarettes that endanger their lives.

BUILDING STRONGER COMMUNITIES

To prepare America for the 21st century, we must build stronger communities. We should start with safe streets. Serious crime has dropped five years in a row. The key has been community policing. We must finish the job of putting 100,000 community police on the streets of the United States.

We should pass the Victims' Rights Amendment to the Constitution, and I ask you to mount a full-scale assault on juvenile crime, with legislation that declares war on gangs with new prosecutors and tougher penalties, extends the Brady bill so violent teen criminals will not be able to buy handguns, requires child safety locks on handguns to prevent unauthorized use, and helps to keep our schools open after hours, on weekends and in the summer so our young people will have someplace to go and something to say yes to.

This balanced budget includes the largest anti-drug effort ever—to stop drugs at their source; punish those who push them; and teach our young people that drugs are wrong, drugs are illegal, and drugs will kill them. I hope you will support it.

Our growing economy has helped to revive poor urban and rural neighborhoods, but we must do more to empower them to create the conditions in which all families can flourish and to create jobs through investment by business and loans by banks.

We should double the number of empowerment zones. They've already brought so much hope to communities like Detroit, where the unemployment rate has been cut in half in four years. We should restore contaminated urban land and buildings to constructive use. We should expand the network of community development banks.

And together, we must pledge tonight that we will use this empowerment approach, including private sector tax incentives, to renew our capital city so that Washington is a great place to work and live—and once again the proud face America shows the world.

We must protect our environment in every community. In the last four years, we cleaned up 250 toxic waste sites, as many as in the previous 12. Now we should clean up 500 more so that our children grow up next to parks, not poison. I urge you to pass my proposal to make big polluters live by a simple rule: If you pollute our environment, you should pay to clean it up.

In the last four years, we strengthened our nation's safe food and clean drinking water laws; we protected some of America's rarest, most beautiful land in Utah's Red Rocks region; created three new national parks in the California desert; and began to restore the Florida Everglades.

Now we must be as vigilant with our rivers as we are with our lands. Tonight I announce that this year I will designate 10 American Heritage Rivers to help communities alongside them revitalize their waterfronts and clean up pollution in the rivers, proving once again that we can grow the economy as we protect the environment.

We must also protect our global environment, working to ban the worst toxic chemicals and to reduce the greenhouse gases that challenge our health even as they change our climate.

Now, we all know that in all of our communities some of our children simply don't have what they need to grow and learn in their own homes or schools or neighborhoods. And that means the rest of us must do more, for they are our children, too. That's why [former] President [George] Bush, General Colin Powell [former chairman of the Joint Chiefs of Staff], former Housing Secretary Henry Cisneros will join the vice president and me to lead the President's Summit of Service in Philadelphia in April.

Our national service program, AmeriCorps, has already helped 70,000 young people to work their way through college as they serve America. Now we intend to mobilize millions of Americans to serve in thousands of ways. Citizen service is an American responsibility which all Americans should embrace. And I ask your support for that endeavor.

I'd like to make just one last point about our national community. Our economy is measured in numbers and statistics. And it's very important. But the enduring worth of our nation lies in our shared values and our soaring spirit. So instead of cutting back on our modest efforts to support the arts and humanities, I believe we should stand by them and challenge our artists, musicians and writers, challenge our museums, libraries and theaters.

We should challenge all Americans in the arts and humanities to join with their fellow citizens to make the year 2000 a national celebration of the American spirit in every community, a celebration of our common culture in the century that is past and in the new one to come in a new millennium so that we can remain the world's beacon not only of liberty but of creativity long after the fireworks have faded.

WORLD LEADERSHIP

To prepare America for the 21st century, we must master the forces of change in the world and keep American leadership strong and sure for an uncharted time.

Fifty years ago, a farsighted America led in creating the institutions that secured victory in the Cold War and built a growing world economy. As a result, today more people than ever embrace our ideals and share our interests. Already we have dismantled many of the blocks and barriers that divided our parents' world. For the first time, more people live under democracy than dictatorship, including every nation in our own hemisphere but one, and its day, too, will come.

Now we stand at another moment of change and choice, and another time to be farsighted, to bring America 50 more years of security and prosperity.

In this endeavor, our first task is to help to build for the very first time an undivided, democratic Europe. When Europe is stable, prosperous, and at peace, America is more secure.

To that end, we must expand NATO by 1999, so that countries that were once our adversaries can become our allies. At the special NATO summit this summer, that is what we will begin to do. We must strengthen NATO's Partnership for Peace with non-member allies. And we must build a stable partnership between NATO and a democratic Russia.

An expanded NATO is good for America, and a Europe in which all democracies define their future not in terms of what they can do to each other, but in terms of what they can do together for the good of all—that kind of Europe is good for America.

Second, America must look to the East no less than to the West.

Our security demands it. Americans fought three wars in Asia in this century.

Our prosperity requires it. More than 2 million American jobs depend upon trade with Asia. There, too, we are helping to shape an Asian Pacific community of cooperation, not conflict.

But let our progress there not mask the peril that remains. Together with South Korea, we must advance peace talks with North Korea and bridge the Cold War's last divide. And I call on Congress to fund our share of the agreement under which North Korea must continue to freeze and then dismantle its nuclear weapons program.

We must pursue a deeper dialogue with China for the sake of our interests and our ideals. An isolated China is not good for America. A China playing its proper role in the world is. I will go to China, and I have invited China's president to come here, not because we agree on everything, but because engaging China is the best way to work on our common challenges, like ending nuclear testing, and to deal frankly with our fundamental differences, like human rights.

The American people must prosper in the global economy. We've worked hard to tear down trade barriers abroad so that we can create good jobs at home. I'm proud to say that today America is once again the most competitive nation and the No. 1 exporter in the world.

Now we must act to expand our exports, especially to Asia and Latin America, two of the fastest-growing regions on earth, or be left behind as these emerging economies forge new ties with other nations. That is why we need the authority now to conclude new trade agreements that open markets to our goods and services even as we preserve our values.

We need not shrink from the challenge of the global economy. After all, we have the best workers and the best products. In a truly open market, we can out-compete anyone, anywhere on earth.

But this is about more than economics. By expanding trade, we can advance the cause of freedom and democracy around the world. There is no better example of this truth than Latin America, where democracy and open markets are on the march together. That is why I will visit there in the spring to reinforce our important ties.

We should all be proud that America led the effort to rescue our neighbor, Mexico, from its economic crisis. And we should all be proud that last month Mexico repaid the United States, three full years ahead of schedule, with half a billion-dollar profit to us.

America must continue to be an unrelenting force for peace. From the Middle East to Haiti, from Northern Ireland to Africa, taking reasonable risks for peace keeps us from being drawn into far more costly conflicts later. With American leadership, the killing has stopped in Bosnia. Now the habits of peace must take hold.

The new NATO force will allow reconstruction and reconciliation to accelerate. Tonight I ask Congress to continue its strong support of our troops. They are doing a remarkable job there for America, and America must do right by them.

Fifth, we must move strongly against new threats to our security. In the past four years, we agreed to ban—we led the way to a worldwide agreement to ban nuclear testing.

With Russia, we dramatically cut nuclear arsenals and we stopped targeting each other's citizens. We are acting to prevent nuclear materials from falling into the wrong hands, and to rid the world of land mines.

We are working with other nations with renewed intensity to fight drug traffickers and to stop terrorists before they act and hold them fully accountable if they do.

Now we must rise to a new test of leadership—ratifying the Chemical Weapons Convention. Make no mistake about it, it will make our troops safer from chemical attack. It will help us to fight terrorism. We have no more important obligations, especially in the wake of what we now know about the Gulf War.

This treaty has been bipartisan from the beginning, supported by Republican and Democratic administrations, and Republican and Democratic members of Congress, and already approved by 68 nations. But if we do not act by April the 29th, when this convention goes into force—with or without us—we will lose the chance to have Americans leading and enforcing this effort. Together we must make

the Chemical Weapons Convention law so that at last we can begin to outlaw poisoned gas from the earth.

Finally, we must have the tools to meet all these challenges. We must maintain a strong and ready military. We must increase funding for weapons modernization by the year 2000. And we must take good care of our men and women in uniform. They are the world's finest.

We must also renew our commitment to America's diplomacy and pay our debts and dues to international financial institutions like the World Bank—and to a reforming United Nations. Every dollar—every dollar we devote to preventing conflicts, to promoting democracy, to stopping the spread of disease and starvation brings a sure return in security and savings. Yet international affairs spending today is just 1 percent of the federal budget, a small fraction of what America invested in diplomacy to choose leadership over escapism at the start of the Cold War.

If America is to continue to lead the world, we here who lead America simply must find the will to pay our way. A farsighted America moved the world to a better place over these last 50 years. And so it can be for another 50 years. But a shortsighted America will soon find its words falling on deaf ears all around the world.

Almost exactly 50 years ago in the first winter of the Cold War, President [Harry S] Truman stood before a Republican Congress and called upon our country to meet its responsibilities of leadership. This was his warning. He said, "If we falter, we may endanger the peace of the world, and we shall surely endanger the welfare of this nation."

That Congress, led by Republicans like Senator Arthur Vandenberg [of Michigan], answered President Truman's call. Together, they made the commitments that strengthened our country for 50 years. Now let us do the same. Let us do what it takes to remain the indispensable nation, to keep America strong, secure and prosperous for another 50 years.

STRENGTH THROUGH DIVERSITY

In the end, more than anything else, our world leadership grows out of the power of our example here at home, out of our ability to remain strong as one America.

All over the world people are being torn asunder by racial, ethnic and religious conflicts that fuel fanaticism and terror. We are the world's most diverse democracy, and the world looks to us to show that it is possible to live and advance together across those kinds of differences. America has always been a nation of immigrants.

From the start, a steady stream of people in search of freedom and opportunity have left their own lands to make this land their home. We started as an experiment in democracy fueled by Europeans. We have grown into an experiment in democratic diversity fueled by openness and promise.

My fellow Americans, we must never, ever believe that our diversity is a weakness; it is our greatest strength.

Americans speak every language, know every country. People on every continent can look to us and see the reflection of their own great potential, and they always will, as long as we strive to give all our citizens, whatever their background, an opportunity to achieve their own greatness.

We're not there yet. We still see evidence of a biting bigotry and intolerance in ugly words and awful violence, in burned churches and bombed buildings. We must fight against this in our country and in our hearts.

Just a few days before my second inauguration, one of our country's best-known pastors, Reverend Robert Schuller, suggested that I read Isaiah 58:12. Here's what it says: "Thou shalt raise up the foundations of many generations, and thou shalt be called the repairer of the breach, the restorer of paths to dwell in."

I placed my hand on that verse when I took the oath of office, on behalf of all Americans, for no matter what our differences in our faiths, our backgrounds, our politics, we must all be repairers of the breach.

I want to say a word about two other Americans who show us how. Congressman Frank Tejeda [D-Texas] was buried yesterday, a proud American whose family came from Mexico. He was only 51 years old. He was awarded the Silver Star, the Bronze Star and the Purple Heart fighting for his country in Vietnam. And he went on to serve Texas and America fighting for our future here in this chamber.

We are grateful for his service and honored that his mother, Lillie Tejeda, and his sister, Mary Alice, have come from Texas to be with us here tonight. And we welcome you. Thank you.

Gary Locke, the newly elected governor of Washington state, is the first Chinese-American governor in the history of our country. He's the proud son of two of the millions of Asian-American immigrants who strengthened America with their hard work, family values and good citizenship.

He represents the future we can all achieve. Thank you, governor, for being here. Please stand up.

Reverend Schuller, Congressman Tejeda, Governor Locke, along with Kristen Tanner and Chris Getsla, Sue Winski and Dr. Kristen Zarfos—they're all Americans from different roots whose lives reflect the best of what we can become when we are one America.

We may not share a common past, but we surely do share a common future. Building one America is our most important mission, the foundation for many generations of every other strength we must build for this new century. Money cannot buy it, power cannot compel it, technology cannot create it. It can only come from the human spirit.

America is far more than a place; it is an idea—the most powerful idea in the history of nations, and all of us in this chamber, we are now the bearers of that idea, leading a great people into a new world.

A child born tonight will have almost no memory of the 20th century. Everything that child will know about America will be because of what we do now to build a new century. We don't have a moment to waste.

Tomorrow there will be just over 1,000 days until the year 2000. One thousand days to prepare our people. One thousand days to work together. One thousand days to build a bridge to a land of new promise.

My fellow Americans, we have work to do. Let us seize those days and the century.

Thank you. God bless you. And God bless America.

President Clinton's Address to the United Nations

Following is President Clinton's Sept. 22, 1997, address to the United Nations.

Mr. President [Hennadiy Vdovenko], Mr. Secretary General [Kofi Annan], distinguished guests: Five years ago, when I first addressed this Assembly, the Cold War had only just ended and the transition to a new era was beginning. Now, together, we are making that historic transition.

Behind us we leave a century full of humanity's capacity for the worst and its genius for the best. Before us, at the dawn of a new mil-

lennium, we can envision a new era that escapes the 20th century's darkest moments, fulfills its most brilliant possibilities and crosses frontiers yet unimagined.

We are off to a promising start. For the first time in history, more than half the people represented in this Assembly freely choose their own governments. Free markets are growing, spreading individual opportunity and national well-being. Early in the 21st century, more than 20 of this Assembly's members, home to half the Earth's population, will lift themselves from the ranks of low-income nations.

Powerful forces are bringing us closer together, profoundly changing the way we work and live and relate to each other. Every day, millions of our citizens on every continent use laptops and satellites to send information, products and money across the planet in seconds. Bit by bit, the information age is chipping away at the barriers—economic, political and social—that once kept people locked in and ideas locked out. Science is unraveling mysteries in the tiniest of human genes and the vast cosmos.

Never in the course of human history have we had a greater opportunity to make our people healthier and wiser, to protect our planet from decay and abuse, to reap the benefits of free markets without abandoning the social contract and its concern for the common good. Yet today's possibilities are not tomorrow's guarantees. We have work to do.

The forces of global integration are a great tide, inexorably wearing away the established order of things. But we must decide what will be left in its wake. People fear change when they feel its burdens but not its benefits. They are susceptible to misguided protectionism, to the poisoned appeals of extreme nationalism, and ethnic, racial and religious hatred. New global environmental challenges require us to find ways to work together without damaging legitimate aspirations for progress. We're all vulnerable to the reckless acts of rogue states and to an unholy axis of terrorists, drug traffickers and international criminals. These 21st-century predators feed on the very free flow of information and ideas and people we cherish. They abuse the vast power of technology to build black markets for weapons, to compromise law enforcement with huge bribes of illicit cash, to launder money with the keystroke of a computer. These forces are our enemies. We must face them together because no one can defeat them alone.

NEW STRATEGY OF SECURITY

To seize the opportunities and move against the threats of this new global era, we need a new strategy of security. Over the past five years, nations have begun to put that strategy in place through a new network of institutions and arrangements with distinct missions but a common purpose—to secure and strengthen the gains of democracy and free markets while turning back their enemies.

We see this strategy taking place on every continent—expanded military alliances like NATO, its Partnership for Peace, its partnerships with a democratic Russia and a democratic Ukraine; free-trade arrangements like the WTO [World Trade Organization] and the Global Information Technology Agreement; and the move toward free-trade areas by nations in the Americas, the Asia-Pacific region and elsewhere around the world; strong arms control regimes like the Chemical Weapons Convention and the Nonproliferation Treaty; multinational coalitions with zero tolerance for terrorism, corruption, crime and drug trafficking; binding international commitments to protect the environment and safeguard human rights.

Through this web of institutions and arrangements, nations are now setting the international ground rules for the 21st century, laying a foundation for security and prosperity for those who live within them, while isolating those who challenge them from the outside. This system will develop and endure only if those who follow the rules of peace and freedom fully reap their rewards. Only then will our people believe that they have a stake in supporting and shaping the emerging international system.

CORE MISSIONS

The United Nations must play a leading role in this effort, filling in the fault lines of the new global era. The core missions it has pursued during its first half-century will be just as relevant during the next half-century: the pursuit of peace and security, promoting human rights and moving people from poverty to dignity and prosperity through sustainable development.

Conceived in the caldron of war, the United Nations' first task must remain the pursuit of peace and security. For 50 years the U.N. has helped prevent world war and nuclear holocaust. Unfortunately, conflicts between nations and within nations had endured. From 1945 until today, they have cost 20 million lives. Just since the end of the Cold War, each year there have been more than 30 armed conflicts in which more than a thousand people have lost their lives, including, of course, a quarter of a million killed in the former Yugoslavia and more than half a million in Rwanda. Millions of personal tragedies the world over are a warning that we dare not be complacent or indifferent. Trouble in a far corner can become a plague on everyone's house.

People the world over cheered the hopeful developments in Northern Ireland, grieved over the innocent loss of life and the stalling of the peace process in the Middle East and longed for a resolution of the differences on the Korean Peninsula, or between Greece and Turkey, or between the great nations of India and Pakistan as they celebrate the 50th anniversaries of their birth.

The United Nations continues to keep many nations away from bloodshed: in El Salvador and Mozambique, in Haiti and Namibia, in Cyprus and in Bosnia, where so much remains to be done but can still be done because the bloodshed has ended.

The record of service of the United Nations has left a legacy of sacrifice. Just last week, we lost some of our finest sons and daughters in a crash of a U.N. helicopter in Bosnia. Five were Americans, five were Germans, one Polish and one British; all citizens of the world we are trying to make, each a selfless servant of peace. And the world is poorer for their passing.

At this very moment, the United Nations is keeping the peace in 16 countries, often in partnership with regional organizations like NATO, the OAS [Organization of American States], ASEAN [Association of Southeast Asian Nations] and ECOWAS [Economic Community of West African States], avoiding wider conflicts and even greater suffering. Our shared commitment to more realistic peacekeeping training for U.N. troops, a stronger role for civilian police, better integration between military and civilian agencies—all these will help the United Nations to meet these missions in the years ahead.

At the same time, we must improve the U.N.'s capabilities, after a conflict ends, to help peace become self-sustaining. The U.N. cannot build nations, but it can help nations to build themselves by fostering legitimate institutions of government, monitoring elections and laying a strong foundation for economic reconstruction.

This week, the Security Council will hold an unprecedented ministerial meeting on African security, which our secretary of State is proud to chair, and which President [Robert] Mugabe, chairman of the Organization of African Unity, will address. It will highlight the role the United Nations can and should play in preventing conflict on a continent where amazing progress toward democracy and de-velopment is occurring alongside still too much discord, disease and distress.

In the 21st century, our security will be challenged increasingly by interconnected groups that traffic in terror, organized crime and drug smuggling. Already these international crime and drug syndicates drain up to $750 billion a year from legitimate economies. That sum exceeds the combined GNP of more than half the nations in this room. These groups threaten to undermine confidence in fragile new democracies and market economies that so many of you are working so hard to see endure.

Two years ago I called upon all the members of this Assembly to join in the fight against these forces. I applaud the U.N.'s recent resolution calling on its members to join the major international antiterrorism conventions, making clear the emerging international consensus that terrorism is always a crime and never a justifiable political act. As more countries sign on, terrorists will have fewer places to run or hide.

I also applaud the steps that members are taking to implement the declaration on crime and public security that the United States proposed two years ago, calling for increased cooperation to strengthen every citizen's right to basic safety, through cooperation on extradition and asset forfeiture, shutting down gray markets for guns and false documents, attacking corruption and bringing higher standards to law enforcement in new democracies.

The spread of these global criminal syndicates also has made all the more urgent our common quest to eliminate weapons of mass destruction. We cannot allow them to fall or to remain in the wrong hands. Here, too, the United Nations must lead, and it has, from UNSCOM [U.N. Special Commission] in Iraq to the International Atomic Energy Agency, now the most expansive global system ever devised to police arms control agreements.

When we met here last year, I was honored to be the first of 146 leaders to sign the Comprehensive Test Ban Treaty [CTBT], our commitment to end all nuclear tests for all time—the longest-sought, hardest-fought prize in the history of arms control. It will help to prevent the nuclear powers from developing more advanced and more dangerous weapons. It will limit the possibilities for other states to acquire such devices.

I am pleased to announce that today I am sending this crucial treaty to the United States Senate for ratification. Our common goal should be to enter the CTBT into force as soon as possible, and I ask for all of you to support that goal.

DEFENDING HUMAN RIGHTS

The United Nations' second core mission must be to defend and extend universal human rights and to help democracy's remarkable gains endure. Fifty years ago the U.N.'s Universal Declaration of Human Rights stated the international community's conviction that people everywhere have the right to be treated with dignity, to give voice to their opinions, to choose their leaders; that these rights are universal—not American rights, not Western rights, not rights for the developed world only, but rights inherent in the humanity of people everywhere.

Over the past decade, these rights have become a reality for more people than ever—from Asia to Africa, from Europe to the Americas. In a world that links rich and poor, North and South, city and countryside, in an electronic network of shared images in real time, the more these universal rights take hold, the more people who do not enjoy them will demand them.

Armed with photocopiers and fax machines, e-mail and the Internet, supported by an increasingly important community of nongovernmental organizations, they will make their demands known, spreading the spirit of freedom, which as the history of the last 10 years has shown us, ultimately will prevail.

The United Nations must be prepared to respond, not only by setting standards but by implementing them. To deter abuses, we should strengthen the U.N.'s field operations and early warning systems. To strengthen democratic institutions, the best guarantors of human rights, we must pursue programs to help new legal, parliamentary and electoral institutions get off the ground. To punish those responsible for crimes against humanity and to promote justice so that peace endures, we must maintain our strong support for the U.N.'s war crime tribunals and truth commissions. And before the century ends, we should establish a permanent international court to prosecute the most serious violations of humanitarian law.

The United States welcomes the Secretary General's efforts to strengthen the role of human rights within the U.N. system and his splendid choice of Mary Robinson as the new High Commissioner. We will work hard to make sure that she has the support she needs to carry out her mandate.

Finally, the United Nations has a special responsibility to make sure that as the global economy creates greater wealth, it does not produce growing disparities between the haves and have-nots, or threaten the global environment—our common home.

Progress is not yet everyone's partner. More than half the world's people are two days' walk from a telephone, literally disconnected from the global economy. Tens of millions lack the education, the training, the skills they need to make the most of their God-given abilities.

The men and women of the United Nations have expertise across the entire range of humanitarian and development activities. Every day they are making a difference. We see it in nourished bodies of once-starving children, in the full lives of those immunized against disease, in the bright eyes of children exposed to education through the rich storehouse of human knowledge, in refugees cared for and returned to their homes, in the health of rivers and lakes restored.

The United Nations must focus even more on shifting resources from handouts to hand-ups, on giving people the tools they need to make the most of their own destinies. Spreading ideas in education and technology, the true wealth of nations, is the best way to give people a chance to succeed.

And the United Nations must continue to lead in ensuring that today's progress does not come at tomorrow's expense. When the nations of the world gather again next December in Kyoto from the U.N. Climate Change Conference, all of us, developed and developing nations, must seize the opportunity to turn back the clock on greenhouse gas emissions so that we can leave a healthy planet to our children.

In these efforts, the U.N. no longer can and no longer need go it alone. Innovative partnerships with the private sector, NGOs [nongovernment organizations] and the international financial institutions can leverage its effectiveness many times over. Last week, a truly visionary American, Ted Turner, made a remarkable donation to strengthen the U.N.'s development and humanitarian programs. His gesture highlights the potential for partnership between the U.N. and the private sector in contributions of time, resources and expertise. And I hope more will follow his lead.

In this area and others, the Secretary General is aggressively pursuing the most far-reaching reform of the United Nations in its history—not to make the U.N. smaller as an end in itself, but to make it better. The United States strongly supports his leadership. We should pass the Secretary General's reform agenda this session.

U.N. DUES

On every previous occasion I have addressed this assembly, the issue of our country's dues has brought the commitment of the United States to the United Nations into question. The United States was a founder of the U.N. We are proud to be its host. We believe in its ideals. We continue to be, as we have been, its largest contributor. We are committed to seeing the United Nations succeed in the 21st century.

This year, for the first time since I have been president, we have an opportunity to put the questions of debts and dues behind us once and for all, and to put the United Nations on a sounder financial footing for the future. I have made it a priority to work with our Congress on comprehensive legislation that would allow us to pay off the bulk of our arrears and assure full financing of America's assessment in the years ahead. Our Congress' actions to solve this problem reflects a strong bipartisan commitment to the United Nations and to America's role within it.

At the same time, we look to member states to adopt a more equitable scale of assessment. Let me say that we also strongly support expanding the Security Council to give more countries a voice in the most important work of the U.N. In more equitably sharing responsibility for its successes, we can make the U.N. stronger and more democratic than it is today. I ask the General Assembly to act on these proposals this year so that we can move forward together.

At the dawn of a new century, so full of hope, but not free of peril, more than ever we need a United Nations where people of reason can work through shared problems and take action to combat them, where nations of good will can join in the struggle for freedom and prosperity, where we can shape a future of peace and progress and the preservation of our planet.

We have the knowledge, we have the intelligence, we have the energy, we have the resources for the work before us. We are building the necessary networks of cooperation. The great question remaining is whether we have the vision and the heart necessary to imagine a future that is different from the past, necessary to free ourselves from destructive patterns of relations with each other and within our own nations and live a future that is different.

A new century and a new millennium is upon us. We are literally present at the future, and it is the great gift that is our obligation to leave our children.

Thank you very much.

President Clinton's 2000 State of the Union Address

Following is President Clinton's State of the Union address delivered to Congress on Jan. 27, 2000.

Mr. Speaker, Mr. Vice President, members of Congress, honored guests, my fellow Americans: We are fortunate to be alive at this moment in history.

Never before has our nation enjoyed, at once, so much prosperity and social progress with so little internal crisis and so few external threats. Never before have we had such a blessed opportunity—and, therefore, such a profound obligation—to build the more perfect union of our founders' dreams.

We begin the new century with over 20 million new jobs. The fastest economic growth in more than 30 years. The lowest unemployment rates in 30 years. The lowest poverty rates in 20 years. The lowest African-American and Hispanic unemployment on record; the first back-to-back surpluses in 42 years; and next month America will achieve the longest period of economic growth in our entire history.

We have built a new economy, and our economic revolution has been matched by a revival of the American spirit: crime down by 20 percent to its lowest level in 25 years; teen births down seven years in a row; adoptions up by 30 percent; welfare rolls cut in half to their lowest levels in 30 years.

My fellow Americans, the state of our union is the strongest it has ever been.

REINVENTING AMERICA

As always, the real credit belongs to the American people. My gratitude also goes to those of you in this chamber who have worked with us to put progress over partisanship. Eight years ago, it was not so clear to most Americans there would be much to celebrate in the year 2000. Then our nation was gripped by economic distress, social decline, political gridlock. The title of a best-selling book that year asked: "America: What Went Wrong?"

In the best traditions of our nation, Americans determined to set things right. We restored the vital center, replacing outdated ideologies with a new vision anchored in basic, enduring values: opportunity for all, responsibility from all, a community of all Americans.

We reinvented government, transforming it into a catalyst for new ideas that stress both opportunity and responsibility, and give our people the tools to solve their own problems.

With the smallest federal work force in 40 years, we turned record deficits into record surpluses and doubled our investment in education. We cut crime with 100,000 community police and the Brady law, which has kept guns out of the hands of half a million criminals.

We ended welfare as we knew it, requiring work while protecting health care and nutrition for children, and investing more in child care, transportation and housing to help their parents go to work.

We've helped parents to succeed at home and at work, with family leave, which 20 million Americans have now used to care for a newborn child or a sick loved one. We have engaged 150,000 young Americans in citizen service through AmeriCorps, while helping them earn money for college.

In 1992, we just had a road map. Today, we have results.

But even more important, America again has the confidence to dream big dreams. But we must not let this confidence drift into complacency, for we, all of us, will be judged by the dreams and deeds we pass on to our children. And on that score, we will be held to a high standard indeed, because our chance to do good is so great.

21ST CENTURY REVOLUTION

My fellow Americans, we have crossed the bridge we built to the 21st century. Now we must shape a 21st century American revolution of opportunity, responsibility and community. We must be now, as we were in the beginning, a new nation.

At the dawn of the last century, Theodore Roosevelt said, "The one characteristic more essential than any other is foresight. It should be the growing nation with a future that takes the long look ahead."

So tonight, let us take our long look ahead and set great goals for our nation. To 21st century America, let us pledge these things: Every child will begin school ready to learn and graduate ready to succeed . . . every family will be able to succeed at home and at work, and no child will be raised in poverty.

We will meet the challenge of the aging of America. We will assure quality affordable health care at last for all Americans.

We will make America the safest big country on Earth.

We will pay off our national debt for the first time since 1835.

We will bring prosperity to every American community. We will reverse the course of climate change and leave a safer, cleaner planet. America will lead the world toward shared peace and prosperity, and the far frontiers of science and technology. And we will become at last what our founders pledged us to be so long ago: one nation, under God, indivisible, with liberty and justice for all.

GREAT GOALS

These are great goals, worthy of a great nation. We will not reach them all this year. Not even in this decade. But we will reach them.

Let us remember that the first American revolution was not won with a single shot. The continent was not settled in a single year. The lesson of our history, and the lesson of the last seven years, is that great goals are reached step by step, always building on our progress, always gaining ground. Of course, you can't gain ground if you're standing still. For too long, this Congress has been standing still on some of our most pressing national priorities. So let's begin tonight with them.

Again, I ask you to pass a real patients' bill of rights.

I ask you to pass common-sense gun-safety legislation.

I ask you to pass campaign finance reform.

I ask you to vote up or down on judicial nominations and other important appointees.

And again I ask you—I implore you—to raise the minimum wage.

Now, two years ago . . . as we reached across party lines to reach our first balanced budget, I asked that we meet our responsibility to the next generation by maintaining our fiscal discipline. Because we refused to stray from that path, we are doing something that would have seemed unimaginable seven years ago. We are actually paying down the national debt. If we stay on this path, we can pay down the debt entirely in just 13 years now and make America debt-free for the first time since Andrew Jackson was president in 1835.

In 1993, we began to put our fiscal house in order with the Deficit Reduction Act, which you'll all remember won passage in both houses by just a single vote. Your former colleague, my first secretary of the Treasury, led that effort and sparked our long boom. He's here with us tonight.

Lloyd Bentsen, you have served America well, and we thank you.

Beyond paying off the debt, we must ensure that the benefits of debt reduction go to preserving two of the most important guarantees we make to every American: Social Security and Medicare.

Tonight—tonight, I ask you to work with me to make a bipartisan down payment on Social Security reform, by crediting the interest savings from debt reduction to the Social Security trust fund so that it will be strong and sound for the next 50 years.

But this is just the start of our journey. We must also take the right steps toward reaching our great goals.

EDUCATION GOALS

First and foremost, we need a 21st century revolution in education, guided by our faith that every single child can learn.

Because education is more important than ever, more than ever the key to our children's future, we must make sure all our children have that key. That means quality preschool and after-school, the best-trained teachers in the classroom and college opportunities for all our children.

For seven years now, we've worked hard to improve our schools with opportunity and responsibility, investing more but demanding more in turn. Reading, math, college entrance scores are up. Some of the most impressive gains are in schools in very poor neighborhoods.

But all successful schools have followed the same proven formula: higher standards, more accountability and extra help so children who need it can get it to reach those standards.

I have sent Congress a reform plan based on that formula. It holds states and school districts accountable for progress and rewards them for results.

Each year, our national government invests more than $15 billion in our schools. It is time to support what works and stop supporting what doesn't.

Now, as we demand more from our schools, we should also invest more in our schools.

Let's double our investment to help states and districts turn around their worst-performing schools or shut them down.

Let's double our investments in after-school and summer school programs, which boost achievement and keep people off the street and out of trouble. If—if we do this, we can give every single child in every failing school in America—everyone—the chance to meet high standards.

Since 1993, we've nearly doubled our investment in Head Start and improved its quality. Tonight, I ask you for another $1 billion for Head Start, the largest increase in the history of the program.

We know that children learn best in smaller classes with good teachers. For two years in a row, Congress has supported my plan to hire 100,000 new, qualified teachers to lower class sizes in the early grades. I thank you for that, and I ask you to make it three in a row.

And to make sure all teachers know the subjects they teach, tonight I propose a new teacher quality initiative to recruit more talented people into the classroom, reward good teachers for staying there and give all teachers the training they need.

We know charter schools provide real public school choice. When I became president, there was just one independent public charter school in all America. Today, thanks to you, there are 1,700. I ask you now to help us meet our goal of 3,000 charter schools by next year.

We know we must connect all our classrooms to the Internet. And we're getting there. In 1994, only 3 percent of our classrooms were connected. Today, with the help of the vice president's E-rate program, more than half of them are, and 90 percent of our schools have at least one Internet connection.

But we cannot finish the job when a third of all our schools are in serious disrepair.

Many of them have walls and wires so old they're too old for the Internet.

So tonight, I propose to help 5,000 schools a year make immediate and urgent repairs, and again, to help build or modernize 6,000 more to get students out of trailers and into high-tech classrooms.

I ask all of you to help me double our bipartisan GEAR-UP program, which provides mentors for disadvantaged young people. If we double it, we can provide mentors for 1.4 million of them.

Let's also offer these kids from disadvantaged backgrounds the same chance to take the same college test prep courses wealthier students use to boost their test scores. To make the American dream achievable for all, we must make college affordable for all. For seven years, on a bipartisan basis, we have taken action toward that goal: larger Pell grants, more-affordable student loans, education IRAs and our HOPE scholarships, which have already benefited 5 million young people. Now, 67 percent of high school graduates are going on to college. That's up 10 percent since 1993. Yet millions of families still strain to pay college tuition. They need help.

TAX CUTS FOR EDUCATION

So I propose a landmark, $30 billion college opportunity tax cut, a middle-class tax deduction for up to $10,000 in college tuition costs.

The previous actions of this Congress have already made two years of college affordable for all. It's time to make four years of college affordable for all.

If we take all these steps, we will move a long way toward making sure every child starts school ready to learn and graduates ready to succeed.

We also need a 21st century revolution to reward work and strengthen families by giving every parent the tools to succeed at work and at the most important work of all: raising children.

HEALTH CARE

That means making sure every family has health care and the support to care for aging parents, the tools to bring their children up right, and that no child grows up in poverty. From my first days as president, we've worked to give families better access to better health care. In 1997, we passed the Children's Health Insurance Program, CHIP, so that workers who don't have coverage through their employers at least can get it for their children.

So far, we've enrolled 2 million children. We're well on our way to our goal of 5 million. But there are still more than 40 million of our fellow Americans without health insurance—more than there were in 1993.

Tonight, I propose that we follow Vice President Gore's suggestion to make low-income parents eligible for the insurance that covers their children.

Together with our children's initiative—think of this—together with our children's initiative, this action would enable us to cover nearly a quarter of all the uninsured people in America.

Again, I want to ask you to let people between the ages of 55 and 65, the fastest-growing group of uninsured, buy into Medicare.

And this year I propose to give them a tax credit to make that choice an affordable one. I hope you will support that as well.

When the Baby Boomers retire, Medicare will be faced with caring for twice as many of our citizens, yet it is far from ready to do so. My generation must not ask our children's generation to shoulder our burden. We simply must act now to strengthen and modernize Medicare.

My budget includes a comprehensive plan to reform Medicare, to make it more efficient and more competitive. And it dedicates nearly $400 billion of our budget surplus to keep Medicare solvent past 2025.

And at long last, it also provides funds to give every senior a voluntary choice of affordable coverage for prescription drugs.

Life-saving drugs are an indispensable part of modern medicine. No one creating a Medicare program today would even think of excluding coverage for prescription drugs. Yet more than three in five of our seniors now lack dependable drug coverage, which can lengthen and enrich their lives. The millions of older Americans who need prescription drugs the most pay the highest prices for them.

In good conscience, we cannot let another year pass without extending to all our seniors this lifeline of affordable prescription drugs.

Record numbers of Americans are providing for aging or ailing loved ones at home. It's a loving but a difficult and often very expensive choice. Last year, I proposed a $1,000 tax credit for long-term care. Frankly, it wasn't enough. This year, let's triple it to $3,000.

But this year, let's pass it. We also have to make needed investments to expand access to mental health care. I want to take a moment to thank the person who led our first White House conference on mental health last year, and who, for seven years, has led all our efforts to break down the barriers to decent treatment of people with mental illness. Thank you, Tipper Gore.

Taken together, these proposals would mark the largest investment in health care in the 35 years since Medicare was created—the largest investment in 35 years. That would be a big step toward assuring quality health care for all Americans, young and old. And I ask you to embrace them and pass them.

EARNING THE TAX CREDIT

We must also make investments that reward work and support families. Nothing does that better than the earned income tax credit, the EITC. The "E" in the "EITC" is about earning, working, taking responsibility and being rewarded for it.

In my very first address to you, I asked Congress to greatly expand this credit, and you did. As a result, in 1998 alone, the EITC helped more than 4.3 million Americans work their way out of poverty toward the middle class. That's double the number in 1993.

Tonight, I propose another major expansion of the EITC, to reduce the marriage penalty, to make sure it rewards marriage as it rewards work and also to expand the tax credit for families that have more than two children.

It punishes people with more than two children today.

Our proposal would allow families with three or more children to get up to $1,100 more in tax relief. These are working families, their children should not be in poverty. We also can't reward work and family unless men and women get equal pay for equal work.

Today—today, the female unemployment rate is the lowest it has been in 46 years. Yet women still only earn about 75 cents for every dollar men earn. We must do better by providing the resources to enforce present equal pay laws, training more women for high-paying, high-tech jobs, and passing the Paycheck Fairness Act. Many working parents spend up to a quarter, a quarter of their income on child care. Last year, we helped parents provide child care for about 2 million children. My child care initiative before you now along with funds already secured in welfare reform would make child care better, safer and more affordable for another 400,000 children. I ask you to pass that. They need it out there in America.

For hard-pressed middle-income families, we should also expand the child care tax credit. And I believe strongly we should take the next big step and make that tax credit refundable for low-income families.

For those—for people making under $30,000 a year, that could mean up to $2,400 for child care costs.

You know, we all say we're pro-work and pro-family. Passing this proposal would prove it.

Tens of millions of Americans live from paycheck to paycheck.

As hard as they work, they still don't have the opportunity to save. Too few can make use of IRAs and 401(k) plans. We should do more to help all working families save and accumulate wealth.

That's the idea behind the individual development accounts, the IDAs. I ask you to take that idea to a new level, with new retirement savings accounts that enable every low- and moderate-income family in America to save for retirement, a first home, a medical emergency or a college education. I propose to match their contributions, however small, dollar for dollar, every year they save. And I propose to give a major new tax credit to any small business that will provide a meaningful pension to its workers. Those people ought to have retirement as well as the rest of us.

Nearly one in three American children grows up without a father. These children are five times more likely to live in poverty than children with both parents at home. Clearly, demanding and supporting responsible fatherhood is critical to lifting all our children out of poverty.

We've doubled child support collections since 1992, and I am proposing to you tough new measures to hold still more fathers responsible. But we should recognize that a lot of fathers want to do right by their children but need help to do it.

A FATHER'S RESPONSIBILITY

Carlos Rosas of St. Paul, Minn., wanted to do right by his son, and he got the help to do it. Now, he's got a good job and he supports his little boy. My budget will help 40,000 more fathers make the same choices Carlos Rosas did. And I thank him for being here tonight.

Stand up, Carlos. Thank you.

If there is any single issue on which we should be able to reach across party lines, it is in our common commitment to reward work and strengthen families. Just remember what we did last year: We came together to help people with disabilities keep their health insurance when they go to work, and I thank you for that.

Thanks to overwhelming bipartisan support from this Congress, we have improved foster care. We've helped those young people who leave it when they turn 18. And we have dramatically increased the number of foster care children going into adoptive homes. I thank all of you for all of that.

Of course, I am forever grateful to the person who has led our efforts from the beginning and who has worked so tirelessly for children and families for 30 years now, my wife Hillary. And I thank her. If we take the steps I've just discussed, we can go a long, long way toward empowering parents to succeed at home and at work and ensuring that no child is raised in poverty.

We can make these vital investments in health care, education, support for working families, and still offer tax cuts to help pay for college, for retirement, to care for aging parents, to reduce the marriage penalty.

We can do these things without forsaking the path of fiscal discipline that got us to this point here tonight.

Indeed, we must make these investments and these tax cuts in the context of a balanced budget that strengthens and extends the life of Social Security and Medicare and pays down the national debt.

Crime in America has dropped for the past seven years—that's the longest decline on record—thanks to a national consensus we helped to forge on community police, sensible gun safety and effective prevention. But nobody, nobody here, nobody in America believes we're safe enough. So again, I ask you to set a higher goal. Let's make this country the safest big country in the world.

Now, last fall, Congress supported my plan to hire, in addition to the 100,000 community police we've already funded, 50,000 more, concentrated in high-crime neighborhoods. I ask your continued support for that.

GUN CONTROL

Soon after the Columbine tragedy, Congress considered common-sense gun legislation to require Brady background checks at the gun shows, child safety locks for new handguns, and a ban on the importation of large-capacity ammunition clips. With courage, and a tie-breaking vote by the vice president, the Senate faced down the gun lobby, stood up to the American people and passed this legislation. But the House failed to follow suit.

Now, we have all seen what happens when guns fall into the wrong hands. Daniel Mauser was only 15 years old when he was gunned down at Columbine. He was an amazing kid, a straight-A student, a good skier.

Like all parents who lose their children, his father, Tom, has borne unimaginable grief. Somehow he has found the strength to honor his son by transforming his grief into action. Earlier this month, he took a leave of absence from his job to fight for tougher gun safety laws. I pray that his courage and wisdom will at long last move this Congress to make common-sense gun legislation the very next order of business.

Tom Mauser, stand up. We thank you for being here tonight.

We must strengthen our gun laws and enforce those already on the books better.

Federal gun crime prosecutions are up 16 percent since I took office, but we must do more. I propose to hire more federal and local gun prosecutors and more ATF [Bureau of Alcohol, Tobacco and Firearms] agents to crack down on illegal gun traffickers and bad-apple dealers. And we must give them the enforcement tools that they need—tools to trace every gun and every bullet used in every gun crime in the United States. I ask you to help us do that.

Every state in this country already requires hunters and automobile drivers to have a license. I think they ought to do the same thing for handgun purchases.

Now, specifically—specifically, I propose a plan to ensure that all new handgun buyers must first have a photo license from their state showing they passed a Brady background check and a gun safety course before they get the gun. I hope you'll help me pass that in this Congress.

Listen to this. Listen to this. The accidental gun rate—the accidental gun death rate of children under 15 in the United States is nine times higher than in the other 25 industrialized countries combined.

Now, technologies now exist that could lead to guns that can only be fired by the adults who own them. I ask Congress to fund research into smart-gun technology to save these children's lives. I ask responsible leaders in the gun industry to work with us on smart guns and other steps to keep guns out of the wrong hands to keep our children safe.

You know, every parent I know worries about the impact of violence in the media on their children. I want to begin by thanking the entertainment industry for accepting my challenge to put voluntary ratings on TV programs and video and Internet games. But frankly, the ratings are too numerous, diverse and confusing to be really useful to parents.

So tonight, I ask the industry to accept the first lady's challenge: to develop a single, voluntary rating system for all children's entertainment that is easier for parents to understand and enforce.

The steps I outline will take us well on our way to make America the safest big country in the world.

Now, to keep our historic economic expansion going—the subject of a lot of discussion in this community and others—I believe we need a 21st-century revolution to open new markets, start new businesses, hire new workers right here in America: in our inner cities, poor rural areas and Native American reservations.

Our nation's prosperity hasn't yet reached these places. Over the last six months, I have traveled to a lot of them—joined by many of you and many farsighted business people—to shine a spotlight on the enormous potential in communities from Appalachia to the Mississippi Delta, from Watts to the Pine Ridge Reservation. Everywhere I go, I meet talented people eager for opportunity and able to work. Tonight, I ask you, let's put them to work.

I also—because empowerment zones have been creating these opportunities for five years now, I also ask you to increase incentives to invest in them and to create more of them.

A COMMON GOAL

And let me say to all of you again, what I have tried to say at every turn. This is not a Democratic or a Republican issue. Giving people a chance to live their dreams is an American issue. Mr. Speaker, it was a powerful moment last November when you joined the Rev. Jesse Jackson and me in your home state of Illinois and committed to working toward our common goal, by combining the best ideas from both sides of the aisle. I want to thank you again and to tell you, Mr. Speaker, I look forward to working with you. This is a worthy joint endeavor.

I also ask you to make special efforts to address the areas of our nation with the highest rates of poverty: our Native American reservations and the Mississippi Delta. My budget includes a $110 million initiative to promote economic development in the Delta and a billion dollars to increase economic opportunity, health care, education and law enforcement for our Native American communities.

We should begin this new century by honoring our historic responsibility to empower the first Americans. And I want to thank tonight the leaders and the members from both parties who have expressed to me an interest in working with us on these efforts. They are profoundly important.

FARMING AND HIGH-TECH FUTURE

There's another part of our American community in trouble tonight: our family farmers. When I signed the Farm Bill in 1996, I said there was great danger it would work well in good times but not in bad. Well, droughts, floods and historically low prices have made these times very bad for the farmers. We must work together to strengthen the farm safety net, invest in land conservation, and create some new markets for them by expanding our programs for bio-based fuels and products. Please, they need help. Let's do it together.

Opportunity for all requires something else today: having access to a computer and knowing how to use it. That means we must close the digital divide between those who've got the tools and those who don't.

Now, connecting classrooms and libraries to the Internet is crucial, but it's just a start. My budget ensures that all new teachers are trained to teach 21st century skills, and it creates technology centers in 1,000 communities to serve adults.

This spring, I'll invite high-tech leaders to join me on another "new markets tour" to close the digital divide and open opportunity for our people. I want to thank the high-tech companies that already are doing so much in this area, and I hope the new tax incentives I have proposed will get all the rest of them to join us. This is a national crusade. We have got to do this and do it quickly.

Now, again I say to you, these are steps. But step by step we can go a long way toward our goal of bringing opportunity to every community.

To realize the full possibilities of this economy, we must reach beyond our own borders, to shape the revolution that is tearing down barriers and building new networks among nations and individuals, and economies and cultures: globalization.

It is the central reality of our time. Of course, change this profound is both liberating and threatening to people. But there is no turning back. And our open, creative society stands to benefit more than any other if we understand, and act on the realities of interdependence. We have to be at the center of every vital global network as a good neighbor and a good partner. We have to recognize that we cannot build our future without helping others to build theirs.

TRADE INITIATIVES

The first thing we have got to do is to forge a new consensus on trade.

Now those of us who believe passionately in the power of open trade, we have to ensure that it lifts both our living standards and our values, never tolerating abusive child labor or a race to the bottom on the environment and worker protection.

But others must recognize that open markets and rules-based trade are the best engines we know for raising living standards, reducing global poverty and environmental destruction, and assuring the free flow of ideas. I believe as strongly as I did the first day I got here the only direction forward for America on trade, the only direction for America on trade, is to keep going forward. I ask you to help me forge that consensus. Now, we have to make developing economies our partners in prosperity. That's why I would like to ask you again to finalize our groundbreaking African and Caribbean Basin Trade Initiatives.

But globalization is about more than economics. Our purpose must be to bring together the world around freedom and democracy and peace, and to oppose those who would tear it apart.

Here are the fundamental challenges I believe America must meet to shape the 21st century world:

WORLD ECONOMICS

First, we must continue to encourage our former adversaries, Russia and China, to emerge as stable, prosperous, democratic nations. Both are being held back today from reaching their full potential—Russia by the legacy of communism, an economy in turmoil, a cruel and self-defeating war in Chechnya; China by the illusion that it can buy stability at the expense of freedom.

But think how much has changed in the past decade: 5,000 former Soviet nuclear weapons taken out of commission; Russian soldiers actually serving with ours in the Balkans; Russian people electing their leaders for the first time in 1,000 years; and in China, an economy more open to the world than ever before.

Of course, no one—not a single person in this chamber tonight—can know for sure what direction these great nations will take, but we do know for sure that we can choose what we do. And we should do everything in our power to increase the chance that they will choose wisely to be constructive members of our global community.

That's why we should support those Russians who are struggling for a democratic, prosperous future; continue to reduce both our nuclear arsenals; and help Russia to safeguard weapons and materials that remain. And that's why I believe Congress should support the agreement we negotiated to bring China into the WTO by passing permanent normal trade relations as soon as possible this year.

I think you ought to do it for two reasons. First of all, our markets are already open to China. This agreement will open China's markets to us.

And second, it will plainly advance the cause of peace in Asia and promote the cause of change in China. No, we don't know where it's going. All we can do is decide what we're going to do. But when all is said and done, we need to know we did everything we possibly could to maximize the chance that China will choose the right future. A second challenge we've got is to protect our own security from conflicts that pose the risk of wider war and threaten our common humanity. We can't prevent every conflict or stop every outrage, but where our interests are at stake and we can make a difference, we should be and we must be peace-makers.

We should be proud of our role in bringing the Middle East closer to a lasting peace; building peace in Northern Ireland; working for peace in East Timor and Africa; promoting reconciliation between Greece and Turkey and in Cyprus; working to defuse these crises between India and Pakistan; and defending human rights and religious freedom.

And we should be proud of the men and women of our armed forces and those of our allies who stopped the ethnic cleansing in Kosovo, enabling a million people to return to their homes.

When Slobodan Milosevic unleashed his terror on Kosovo, Capt. John Cherrey was one of the brave airmen who turned the tide. And when another American plane was shot down over Serbia, he flew into the teeth of enemy air defenses to bring his fellow pilot home.

Thanks to our armed forces' skill and bravery, we prevailed in Kosovo without losing a single American in combat.

I want to introduce Capt. Cherrey to you. We honor Capt. Cherrey and we promise you, captain, we'll finish the job you began. Stand up so we can see you.

SAFE TECHNOLOGY

A third challenge we have is to keep this inexorable march of technology from giving terrorists and potentially hostile nations the means to undermine our defenses. Keep in mind, the same technological advances that have shrunk cell phones to fit in the palms of our hands, can also make weapons of terror easier to conceal and easier to use.

We must meet this threat by making effective agreements to restrain nuclear and missile programs in North Korea, curbing the flow of lethal technology to Iran, preventing Iraq from threatening its neighbors, increasing our preparedness against chemical and biological attack, protecting our vital computer systems from hackers and criminals, and developing a system to defend against new missile threats while working to preserve our ABM [Anti-ballistic missile] missile treaty with Russia. We must do all these things.

I predict to you, when most of us are long gone, but some time in the next 10 to 20 years, the major security threat this country will face will come from the enemies of the nation-state: the narco-traffickers, and the terrorists, and the organized criminals who will be organized together—working together with increasing access to ever more sophisticated chemical and biological weapons.

And I want to thank the Pentagon and others for doing what they're doing right now to try to help protect us and plan for that so that our defenses will be strong. I ask for your support so they can succeed.

I also want to ask you for a constructive bipartisan dialogue this year to work to build a consensus which I hope will eventually lead to the ratification of the Comprehensive Nuclear Test Ban Treaty.

I hope we can also have a constructive effort to meet the challenge that is presented to our planet by the huge gulf between rich and poor. We cannot accept a world in which part of humanity lives on the cutting edge of a new economy and the rest lives on the bare edge of survival. I think we have to do our part to change that with expanded trade, expanded aid and the expansion of freedom.

This is interesting: From Nigeria to Indonesia, more people got the right to choose their leaders in 1999 than in 1989 when the Berlin Wall fell. We've got to stand by these democracies, including and especially tonight Colombia, which is fighting narco-traffickers for its own people's lives and for our children's lives. I have proposed a strong two-year package to help Colombia win this fight. I want to thank the leaders in both parties, in both houses for listening to me and the president of Colombia about it.

We have got to pass this. I want to ask your help. A lot is riding on this. And it's so important for the long-term stability of our country and for what happens in Latin America.

I also want you to know I'm going to send you new legislation to go after what these drug barons value the most: their money. And I hope you will pass that as well. In a world where over a billion people live on less than a dollar a day, we also have got to do our part in the global endeavor to reduce the debts of the poorest countries so they can invest in education, health care and economic growth. That's what the pope and other religious leaders have urged us to do, and last year Congress made a down payment on America's share. I ask you to continue that. I thank you for what you did and ask you to stay the course.

FINAL CHALLENGES AND THANKS

I also want to say that America must help more nations to break the bonds of disease. Last year in Africa, 10 times as many people died from AIDS as were killed in wars. Ten times. The budget I give you invests $150 million more in the fight against this and other infectious killers. And today I propose a tax credit to speed the development of vaccines for diseases like malaria, TB and AIDS.

I ask the private sector and our partners around the world to join us in embracing this cause. We can save millions of lives together and we ought to do it.

I also want to mention our final challenge which, as always, is the most important. I ask you to pass a national security budget that keeps our military the best trained and best equipped in the world, with heightened readiness and 21st century weapons; which raises salaries for our servicemen and women; which protects our veterans; which fully funds the diplomacy that keeps our soldiers out of war; which makes good on our commitment to our U.N. dues and arrears. I ask you to pass this budget.

I also want to say something, if I might, very personal tonight.

The American people watching us at home, with the help of all the commentators, can tell from who stands and who sits and who claps and who doesn't, that there are still modest differences of opinion in this room. But I want to thank you for something, every one of you. I want to thank you for the extraordinary support you have given, Republicans and Democrats alike, to our men and women in uniform. I thank you for that.

And I also want to thank especially two people. First, I want to thank our secretary of Defense, Bill Cohen, for symbolizing our bipartisan commitment to national security. Thank you, sir. Even more, I want to thank his wife, Janet, who more than any other American citizen has tirelessly traveled this world to show the support we all feel for our troops. Thank you, Janet Cohen. I appreciate it.

These are the challenges we have to meet so that we can lead the world toward peace and freedom in an era of globalization.

ENVIRONMENTAL COMMITMENT

I want to tell you that I am very grateful for many things as president. But one of the things I'm grateful for is the opportunities that the vice president and I have had to finally put to rest the bogus idea that you cannot grow the economy and protect the environment at the same time.

Now, as our economy has grown, we have rid more than 500 neighborhoods of toxic waste; ensured cleaner air and water for millions of people; in the past three months alone, we've helped preserve more than 40 million acres of roadless lands in our national forests; created three new national monuments.

But as our communities grow, our commitment to conservation must continue to grow. Tonight, I propose creating a permanent conservation fund to restore our wildlife, protect coastlines, save natural treasures, from the California redwoods to the Everglades.

This Lands Legacy endowment would represent by far the most enduring investment in land preservation ever proposed in this house. I hope we can get together with all the people with different ideas and do this. This is a gift we should give to our children and our children for all time, across party lines.

We can make an agreement to do this. Last year, the vice president launched a new effort to make communities more liberal—livable.

Liberal—no. No. (Laughter)

Wait a minute. I got a punchline now.

That's this year's agenda. Last year it was livable, right? (Laughter)

That's what Sen. Lott's going to say in the commentary afterward. (Laughter)

To make our communities more livable—this is big business. This is a big issue. What does that mean?

You ask anybody that lives in an unlivable community and they'll tell you. They want their kids to grow up next to parks, not parking lots. The parents don't want to have to spend all their time stalled in traffic when they could be home with their children.

Tonight I ask you to support new funding for the following things to make American communities more liberal—livable. (Laughter)

One—I've done pretty well with this speech, but I can't say that. One, I want you to help us to do three things. We need more funding for advanced transit systems.

We need more funding for saving open spaces in places of heavy development.

And we need more funding—this ought to have bipartisan appeal—we need more funding for helping major cities around the Great Lakes protect their waterways and enhance their quality of life. We need these things, and I want you to help.

Now, the greatest environmental challenge of the new century is global warming. The scientists tell us the 1990s were the hottest decade of the entire millennium. If we fail to reduce the emission of greenhouse gases, deadly heat waves and droughts will become more frequent, coastal areas will flood and economies will be disrupted.

That is going to happen unless we act. Many people in the United States, some people in this chamber, and lots of folks around the world still believe you cannot cut greenhouse gas emissions without slowing economic growth.

In the Industrial Age that may well have been true. But in this digital economy, it is not true anymore. New technologies make it possible to cut harmful emissions and provide even more growth.

For example, just last week, automakers unveiled cars that get 70 to 80 miles a gallon, the fruits of a unique research partnership between government and industry. And before you know it, efficient production of biofuels will give us the equivalent of hundreds of miles from a gallon of gasoline.

To speed innovation in these kinds of technologies, I think we should give a major tax incentive to business for the production of clean energy, and to families for buying energy-saving homes and appliances and the next generation of super-efficient cars when they hit the showroom floor. And I also ask the auto industry to use available technologies to make all new cars more fuel efficient right away.

And I ask this Congress to do something else: Please help us make more of our clean-energy technology available to the developing world. That will create cleaner growth abroad and a lot more new jobs here in the United States of America.

Now, in this new century—in this new century innovations in science and technology will be key not only to the health of the environment but to miraculous improvements in the quality of our lives and advances in the economy.

Later this year, researchers will complete the first draft of the entire human genome: the very blueprint of life. It is important for all our fellow Americans to recognize that federal tax dollars have funded much of this research, and that this and other wise investments in science are leading to a revolution in our ability to detect, treat and prevent disease.

For example, researchers have identified genes that cause Parkinson's, diabetes and certain kinds of cancer. They are designing precision therapies that will block the harmful effect of these genes for good. Researchers already are using this new technique to target and destroy cells that cause breast cancer. Soon we may be able to use it to prevent the onset of Alzheimer's.

Scientists are also working on an artificial retina to help many blind people to see; and, listen to this, microchips that would actually directly stimulate damaged spinal cords in a way that could allow people now paralyzed to stand up and walk.

These kinds of innovations are also propelling our remarkable prosperity. Information technology only includes 8 percent of our employment, but now accounts for a third of our economic growth—along with jobs that pay, by the way, about 80 percent above the private sector average.

Again, we ought to keep in mind government-funded research brought supercomputers, the Internet and communications satellites into being.

Soon researchers will bring us devices that can translate foreign languages as fast as you can talk, materials 10 times stronger than steel at a fraction of the weight, and—this is unbelievable to me—molecular computers the size of a teardrop with the power of today's fastest supercomputers.

To accelerate the march of discovery across all these disciplines of science and technology, I ask you to support my recommendation of an unprecedented $3 billion in the 21st Century Research Fund, the largest increase in civilian research in a generation.

We owe it to our future.

TECHNOLOGY WITH VALUES

Now, these new breakthroughs have to be used in ways that reflect our values. First and foremost, we have to safeguard our citizens' privacy. Last year, we proposed to protect every citizen's medical records. This year, we will finalize those rules. We have also taken the first steps to protect the privacy of bank and credit card records and other financial statements. Soon I will send legislation to you to finish that job.

We must also act to prevent any genetic discrimination whatever by employers or insurers. I hope you will support that.

These steps will allow us to lead toward the far frontiers of science and technology. They will enhance our health, the environment, the economy in ways we can't even imagine today.

But we all know that at a time when science, technology and the forces of globalization are bringing so many changes into all our lives, it's more important than ever that we strengthen the bonds that root us in our local communities and in our national community.

No tie binds different people together like citizen service. There is a new spirit of service in America, a movement we have tried to support with AmeriCorps, expanded Peace Corps, unprecedented new partnerships with businesses, foundations, community groups.

Partnerships, for example, like the one that enlisted 12,000 companies which have now moved 650,000 of our fellow citizens from welfare to work. Partnerships to battle drug abuse, AIDS, teach young people to read, save America's treasures, strengthen the arts, fight teen pregnancy, prevent violence among young people, promote racial healing. The American people are working together.

But we should do more to help Americans help each other. First, we should help faith-based organizations to do more to fight poverty and drug abuse and help people get back on the right track with initiatives like Second Chance Homes that do so much to help unwed teen mothers.

Second, we should support Americans who tithe and contribute to charities but don't earn enough to claim a tax deduction for it.

Tonight, I propose new tax incentives that would allow low- and middle-income citizens who don't itemize to get that deduction. It's nothing but fair, and it will get more people to give.

We should do more—thank you.

We should do more to help new immigrants to fully participate in our community. That's why I recommend spending more to teach them civics and English. And since everybody in our community counts, we've got to make sure everyone is counted in this year's census.

Now, within 10 years, just 10 years, there will be no majority race in our largest state of California. In a little more than 50 years, there'll be no majority race in America. In a more interconnected world, this diversity can be our greatest strength. Just look around this chamber. Look around. We have members in this Congress from virtually every racial, ethnic and religious background. And I think you would agree that America is stronger because of it.

But you also have to agree that all those differences you just clapped for all too often spark hatred and division even here at home.

Just in the last couple of years, we've seen a man dragged to death in Texas just because he was black. We saw a young man murdered in Wyoming just because he was gay. Last year, we saw the shootings of African-Americans, Asian-Americans and Jewish children just because of who they were.

This is not the American way and we must draw the line.

I ask you—I ask you to draw that line by passing without delay the Hate Crimes Prevention Act and the Employment Non-Discrimination Act.

And I ask you to reauthorize the Violence Against Women Act.

CIVIL RIGHTS PROTECTION

Finally, tonight I propose the largest ever investment in our civil rights laws for enforcement, because no American should be subjected to discrimination in finding a home, getting a job, going to school or securing a loan.

Protections in law should be protections in fact.

Last February, because I thought this was so important, I created the White House Office of One America to promote racial reconciliation. That's what one of my personal heroes, Hank Aaron, has done all his life. From his days as our all-time home run king to his recent acts of healing, he has always brought people together. We should follow his example and we're honored to have him with us tonight.

Stand up, Hank Aaron.

I just want to say one more thing about this, and I want everyone of you to think about this next time you get mad at one of your colleagues on the other side of the aisle. This fall at the White House, Hillary had one of her millennium dinners, and we had a very distinguished scientist there. He was an expert in this whole work on the human genome. And he said that we are all, regardless of race, genetically 99.9 percent the same.

Now, you may find that uncomfortable when you look around here.

But it's—it is worth remembering. We can laugh about this, but you think about it. Modern science has confirmed what ancient faiths have always taught. The most important fact of life is our common humanity.

Therefore, we should do more than just tolerate our diversity. We should honor it and celebrate it.

My fellow Americans, every time I prepare for the State of the Union, I approach it with hope and expectation and excitement for our nation. But tonight is very special because we stand on the mountain top of a new millennium. Behind us we can look back and see the great expanse of American achievement, and before us we can see even greater, grander frontiers of possibility.

We should all of us be filled with gratitude and humility for our present progress and prosperity. We should be filled with awe and joy at what lies over the horizon. And we should be filled with absolute determination to make the most of it.

You know, when the framers finished crafting our Constitution in Philadelphia, Benjamin Franklin stood in Independence Hall and he reflected on the carving of the sun that was on the back of a chair he saw.

The sun was low on the horizon. So he said this: He said, "I've often wondered whether that sun was rising or setting. Today," Franklin said, "I have the happiness to know it's a rising sun."

Today, because each succeeding generation of Americans has kept the fire of freedom burning brightly, lighting those frontiers of possibility, we all still bask in the glow and the warmth of Mr. Franklin's rising sun.

After 224 years, the American Revolution continues. We remain a new nation. As long as our dreams outweigh our memories, America will be forever young. That is our destiny. And this is our moment.

Thank you, God bless you, and God bless America.

Selected Texts on the Impeachment of President Clinton

For just the second time in the nation's history, Congress debated the removal of a president from office through impeachment. In late 1998 the House—by a largely partisan division—charged that President Clinton committed perjury and obstructed justice in an effort to cover up an affair with a young White House intern, Monica Lewinsky. On separate votes the House considered four articles of impeachment, approving two, and sent them to the Senate for trial as provided in the Constitution. However, the Senate in early 1999 rejected both articles, thereby acquitting the president. Following are several documents relating to the events. *(Impeachment, p. 813)*

Clinton: 'Critical Lapse in Judgment'

Following is the text of President Clinton's Aug. 17, 1998, address to the nation in which the president acknowledged a relationship with White House intern Monica Lewinsky that was "not appropriate" and was "wrong." He said his conduct was "a critical lapse in judgment."

Good evening.

This afternoon, in this room, from this chair, I testified before the Office of Independent Counsel and the grand jury.

I answered their questions truthfully, including questions about my private life, questions no American citizen would ever want to answer.

Still, I must take complete responsibility for all my actions, both public and private. And that is why I am speaking to you tonight.

As you know, in a deposition in January, I was asked questions about my relationship with Monica Lewinsky. While my answers were legally accurate, I did not volunteer information.

Indeed, I did have a relationship with Ms. Lewinsky that was not appropriate. In fact, it was wrong. It constituted a critical lapse in judgment and a personal failure on my part for which I am solely and completely responsible.

But I told the grand jury today, and I say to you now that at no time did I ask anyone to lie, to hide or destroy evidence or to take any other unlawful action.

I know that my public comments and my silence about this matter gave a false impression. I misled people, including even my wife. I deeply regret that.

I can only tell you I was motivated by many factors. First, by a desire to protect myself from the embarrassment of my own conduct.

I was also very concerned about protecting my family. The fact that these questions were being asked in a politically inspired lawsuit, which has since been dismissed, was a consideration too.

In addition, I had real and serious concerns about an independent counsel investigation that began with private business dealings 20 years ago, dealings, I might add, about which an independent federal agency found no evidence of any wrongdoing by me or my wife over two years ago.

The independent counsel investigation moved on to my staff and friends, then into my private life. And now the investigation itself is under investigation.

This has gone on too long, cost too much and hurt too many innocent people.

Now, this matter is between me, the two people I love most—my wife and our daughter—and our God. I must put it right, and I am prepared to do whatever it takes to do so.

Nothing is more important to me personally. But it is private, and I intend to reclaim my family life for my family. It's nobody's business but ours.

Even presidents have private lives. It is time to stop the pursuit of personal destruction and the prying into private lives and get on with our national life.

Our country has been distracted by this matter for too long, and I take my responsibility for my part in all of this. That is all I can do.

Now it is time—in fact, it is past time—to move on.

We have important work to do—real opportunities to seize, real problems to solve, real security matters to face.

And so tonight, I ask you to turn away from the spectacle of the past seven months, to repair the fabric of our national discourse and to return our attention to all the challenges and all the promise of the next American century.

Thank you for watching. And good night.

Democratic Senators' Comments

Although Democrats generally supported Clinton throughout the proceedings, some were sharply critical of his conduct. Following are excerpts of comments by four Democrats made in the Senate.

SEN. JOSEPH I. LIEBERMAN

The following is from the Sept. 3, 1998, statement of Sen. Joseph I. Lieberman, D-Conn.

Whether he or we think it fair or not, the reality is in 1998 that a president's private life is public. . . . The president is not just the elected leader of our country. He is, as presidential scholar Clinton Rossiter observed, "the one-man distillation of the American people. . . ." The president is a role model who, because of his prominence and the moral authority that emanates from his office, sets standards of behavior for the people he serves. . . .

In this case, the president apparently had extramarital relations with an employee half his age and did so in the workplace, in the vicinity of the Oval Office. Such behavior is not just inappropriate. It is immoral. And it is harmful, for it sends a message of what is acceptable behavior to the larger American family, particularly to our children, which is as influential as the negative message that is communicated by the entertainment culture. . . .

I believe that the president could have lessened the harm his relationship with Ms. Lewinsky has caused if he had acknowledged his mistake and spoken with candor about it to the American people shortly after it became public in January. But, as we now know, he chose not to do this.

This deception is particularly troubling because it was not just a reflexive and, in many ways, understandable human act of concealment to protect himself and his family from what he called the embarrassment of his own conduct . . . but rather it was the intentional and premeditated decision to do so. . . .

The transgressions the president has admitted to are too consequential for us to walk away and leave the impression for our children today and for our posterity tomorrow that what he acknowledges he did within the White House is acceptable behavior for our nation's leader. On the contrary, as I have said, it is wrong and unacceptable, and should be followed by some measure of public rebuke and accountability.

We in Congress, elected representatives of all the American people, are surely capable institutionally of expressing such disapproval through a resolution of reprimand or censure of the president for his misconduct. But it is premature to do so, as my colleagues of both parties seem to agree, until we have received the report of the independent counsel and the White House's response to it.

In the same way, it seems to me that talk of impeachment and resignation at this time is unjust and unwise. . . .

SEN. BOB KERRY

The following is from the speech of Sen. Bob Kerrey, D-Neb., immediately after Lieberman's speech.

I wish to join him and say that the president has got to go far further than he did in his speech to the nation. This is not just inappropriate behavior. This is not a private matter.

SEN. DANIEL PATRICK MOYNIHAN

The following is from the speech of Sen. Daniel Patrick Moynihan, D-N.Y., following Kerrey's speech.

In the aftermath of the president's speech on Aug. 17, I commented that it was not adequate. But it was not until just this moment that the full measure of that inadequacy was presented to us in the context of the needs of the nation, of the profound moral consequences that will arise not just from what has happened but from what might happen if we do not proceed with the measure of moral compass, but also with a capacity to understand we are all sinners.

President Clinton was asked at a photo opportunity Sept. 4 in Dublin, Ireland, if he had any comments on Lieberman's remarks. His response:

"I've been briefed on them, and basically I agree with what he said. I've already said that I made a bad mistake, it was indefensible, and I'm sorry about it. So I have nothing else to say except that I can't disagree with anyone else who wants to be critical of what I have already acknowledged was indefensible."

SEN. ROBERT C. BYRD

The following are remarks by Sen. Robert C. Byrd, D-W.Va., on Sept. 9, 1998.

The pressure on the Congress is escalating. Talk of impeachment is in the air, along with suggestions of resolutions of reprimand and censure. Some have even suggested that we ought to get on with impeachment and get this thing behind us.

There had to come a time sooner or later when the boil would be lanced. The problem is that with the lancing a hemorrhaging may be only one of those continuing symptoms of an even greater lancing, perhaps even an amputation, that still lurks in the shadows up ahead.

There is no question but that the president himself has sown the wind and he is reaping the whirlwind. His televised speech of Aug. 17 heaped hot coals upon himself—coals causing wounds that continue to inflame and burn ever more deeply. Coming as the speech did so soon after the president's appearance before the grand jury, his words were ill-timed, ill-formed and ill-advised. . . .

In this instance, the president himself has by his own actions and his own words thrown the first stone at himself, and thus, made himself vulnerable to the stoning by others.

What a sorrowful spectacle!

To maintain that presidents have private lives is, of course, not to be denied. But the Oval Office of the White House is not a private office. It is where much of the business of the nation is conducted daily. . . .

Former President Nixon, in an earlier tragedy for the nation and for all of us who were here and lived through it, tried the same thing—delay, delay, delay and counterattack, attack, attack. . . . Time seems to be turning backwards in its flight. And many of the mistakes that President Nixon made are being made all over again.

As we find ourselves being brought nearer and nearer, as it would seem, to a yawning abyss, I urge that we all step back, and give ourselves and the country a little pause in which to reflect and meditate before we cast ourselves headlong over the precipice. To say we ought to get on with impeachment and get this thing behind us is a bold thing to say. But boldness to the point of cavalierness can come back to haunt us. . . .

I also suggest that putting this thing behind us is not going to be an easy thing to do. If Congress reaches that stage of voting on articles of impeachment, it is going to be a traumatic experience for all of us, both here in this city and throughout the country. . . .

There is a constitutional process in place. We should let it work. It is my suggestion that everyone should exercise some self-restraint against calling for impeachment or censure or for the president's resignation. Who knows? I may do that before it's all over. But not now. . . .

Let us, as senators, remember that if the House ultimately votes to impeach this president, then we all should be careful not to attempt to influence the other body—and when I say we all, I have reference to ourselves and to the executive branch and to the media. . . .

We must not compromise any final decision by rushing to judgment in advance. I trust that we all will weigh carefully in our own minds and hearts the possible consequences to the nation of our words and actions and judgments if that duty ultimately should beckon us. . . .

And so I respectfully urge everyone in this town to calm down for a little while and contemplate with seriousness the impact that our actions may have on the well-being of the nation—your children, my grandchildren, our children, our grandchildren—and the paralysis we may be spawning if we continue to be mesmerized with each new rumor and each new titillating whisper.

Independent Counsel's Report

At the center of the impeachment action was the office of Independent Counsel Kenneth W. Starr who had been investigating various charges against the president. The House's impeachment actions in the fall of 1998 were precipitated by release of the primary report by Starr. Following are excerpts from the report submitted to the House on Sept. 9, 1998, and released Sept. 11, 1998. The excerpts are taken from the introductory section laying out "eleven possible grounds for impeachment" of President Clinton.

Pursuant to Section 595(c) of Title 28, the Office of Independent Counsel hereby submits substantial and credible information that President Clinton obstructed justice during the *Jones v. Clinton* sexual harassment lawsuit by lying under oath and concealing evidence of his relationship with a young White House intern and federal employee, Monica Lewinsky.

After a federal criminal investigation of the President's actions began in January 1998, the President lied under oath to the grand jury and obstructed justice during the grand jury investigation. There also is substantial and credible information that the President's actions with respect to Monica Lewinsky constitute an abuse of authority inconsistent with the President's constitutional duty to faithfully execute the laws.

There is substantial and credible information supporting the following eleven possible grounds for impeachment:

1. President Clinton lied under oath in his civil case when he denied a sexual affair, a sexual relationship, or sexual relations with Monica Lewinsky.

2. President Clinton lied under oath to the grand jury about his sexual relationship with Ms. Lewinsky.

3. In his civil deposition, to support his false statement about the sexual relationship, President Clinton also lied under oath about being alone with Ms. Lewinsky and about the many gifts exchanged between Ms. Lewinsky and him.

4. President Clinton lied under oath in his civil deposition about his discussions with Ms. Lewinsky concerning her involvement in the *Jones* case.

5. During the *Jones* case, the President obstructed justice and had an understanding with Ms. Lewinsky to jointly conceal the truth about their relationship by concealing gifts subpoenaed by Ms. Jones's attorneys.

6. During the *Jones* case, the President obstructed justice and had an understanding with Ms. Lewinsky to jointly conceal the truth of their relationship from the judicial process by a scheme that included the following means: (i) Both the President and Ms. Lewinsky understood that they would lie under oath in the *Jones* case about their sexual relationship; (ii) the President suggested to Ms. Lewinsky that she prepare an affidavit that, for the President's purposes, would memorialize her testimony under oath and could be used to prevent questioning of both of them about their relationship; (iii) Ms. Lewinsky signed and filed the false affidavit; (iv) the President used Ms. Lewinsky's false affidavit at his deposition in an attempt to head off questions about Ms. Lewinsky; and (v) when that failed, the President lied under oath at his civil deposition about the relationship with Ms. Lewinsky.

7. President Clinton endeavored to obstruct justice by helping Ms. Lewinsky obtain a job in New York at a time when she would have been a witness harmful to him were she to tell the truth in the *Jones* case.

8. President Clinton lied under oath in his civil deposition about his discussions with Vernon Jordan concerning Ms. Lewinsky's involvement in the *Jones* case.

9. The President improperly tampered with a potential witness by attempting to corruptly influence the testimony of his personal secretary, Betty Currie, in the days after his civil deposition.

10. President Clinton endeavored to obstruct justice during the grand jury investigation by refusing to testify for seven months and lying to senior White House aides with knowledge that they would relay the President's false statements to the grand jury—and did thereby deceive, obstruct, and impede the grand jury.

11. President Clinton abused his constitutional authority by (i) lying to the public and the Congress in January 1998 about his relationship with Ms. Lewinsky; (ii) promising at that time to cooperate fully with the grand jury investigation; (iii) later refusing six invitations to testify voluntarily to the grand jury; (iv) invoking Executive Privilege; (v) lying to the grand jury in August 1998; and (vi) lying

again to the public and Congress on August 17, 1998—all as part of an effort to hinder, impede, and deflect possible inquiry by the Congress of the United States.

The first two possible grounds for impeachment concern the President's lying under oath about the nature of his relationship with Ms. Lewinsky. The details associated with those grounds are, by their nature, explicit. The President's testimony unfortunately has rendered the details essential with respect to those two grounds, as will be explained in those grounds.

WHITE HOUSE RESPONSE TO STARR REPORT

Following are excerpts from the preliminary response issued by the White House Sept. 11, 1998, shortly after a House vote to release Independent Counsel Kenneth W. Starr's report:

The President has acknowledged a serious mistake—an inappropriate relationship with Monica Lewinsky. He has taken responsibility for his actions, and he has apologized to the country, to his friends, leaders of his party, the cabinet and most importantly, his family.

This private mistake does not amount to an impeachable action. A relationship outside one's marriage is wrong—and the President admits that. It is not a high crime or misdemeanor. The Constitution specifically states that Congress shall impeach only for "treason, bribery or other high crimes and misdemeanors." . . .

"High crimes and misdemeanors" had a fixed meaning to the Framers of our Constitution—it meant wrongs committed against our system of government. The impeachment clause was designed to protect our country against a President who was using his official powers against the nation, against the American people, against our society. It was never designed to allow a political body to force a President from office for a very personal mistake. . . .

[Starr's] report is based entirely on allegations obtained by a grand jury . . . that would never be admitted in court, that has never been seen by the President or his lawyers, and that was not subject to cross-examination or any other traditional safeguards to ensure its credibility. . . .

The President did not commit perjury. Most of the illegal leaks suggesting his testimony was perjurious falsely describe his testimony. First of all, the President never testified in the Jones deposition that he was not alone with Ms. Lewinsky. The President never testified that his relationship with Ms. Lewinsky was the same as with any other intern. To the contrary, he admitted exchanging gifts with her, knowing about her job search, receiving cards and notes from her, and knowing other details of her personal life that made it plain he had a special relationship with her.

The President has admitted he had an improper sexual relationship with Ms. Lewinsky. In a civil deposition, he gave narrow answers to ambiguous questions. As a matter of law, those answers could not give rise to a criminal charge of perjury. In the face of the President's admission of his relationship, the disclosure of lurid and salacious allegations can only be intended to humiliate the President and force him from office.

There was no obstruction of justice. We believe [Clinton personal secretary] Betty Currie testified that Ms. Lewinsky asked her to hold the gifts and that the President never talked to her about the gifts. The President admitted giving and receiving gifts from Ms. Lewinsky when he was asked about it. The President never asked Ms. Lewinsky to get rid of the gifts and he never asked Ms. Currie to get them. We believe that Ms. Currie's testimony supports the President's.

The President never tried to get Ms. Lewinsky a job after she left the White House in order to influence her testimony in the Paula

Jones case. The President knew Ms. Lewinsky was unhappy in her Pentagon job after she left the White House and did ask the White House personnel office to treat her fairly in her job search. He never instructed anyone to hire her, or even indicated that he very much wanted it to happen. . . .

The President did not facilitate Ms. Lewinsky's interview with [cabinet member] Bill Richardson, or her discussions with [Clinton friend and adviser] Vernon Jordan. Betty Currie asked [Deputy Chief of Staff] John Podesta if he could help her with her New York job search which led to an interview with Bill Richardson, and Ms. Currie also put her in touch with her longtime friend, Mr. Jordan. Mr. Jordan has made it clear that this is the case, and, as a private individual, he is free to offer job advice wherever he sees fit.

There was no witness tampering. Betty Currie was not supposed to be a witness in the Paula Jones case. If she was not called or going to be called, it was impossible for any conversations the President had with her to be witness tampering. The President testified that he did not in any way attempt to influence her recollection. . . .

Invocation of privileges was not an abuse of power. The President's lawful assertion of privileges in a court of law was only made on the advice of his Counsel, and was in significant measure validated by the courts. The legal claims were advanced sparingly and as a last resort after all attempts at compromise by the White House Counsel's office were rejected to protect the core constitutional and institutional interests of this and future presidencies.

Neither the President nor the White House played a role in the Secret Service's lawful efforts to prevent agents from testifying to preserve its protective function. The President never asked, directed or participated in any decision regarding the protective function privilege. Neither did any White House official. The Treasury and Justice departments independently decided to respond to the historically unprecedented subpoenas of Secret Service personnel and to pursue the privilege to ensure the protection of this and future presidents.

The President did not abuse his power by permitting White House staff to comment on the investigation. The President has acknowledged misleading his family, staff and the country about the nature of his relationship with Ms. Lewinsky. . . . However, this personal failing does not constitute a criminal abuse of power. If allowing aides to repeat misleading statements is a crime, then any number of public officials are guilty of misusing their office for as long as they fail to admit wrongdoing in response to any allegation about their activities.

The actions of White House attorneys were completely lawful. The White House Counsel attorneys provided the President and White House officials with informed, candid advice on issues raised during this investigation that affected the President's official duties. This was especially necessary given the fact that impeachment proceedings against the President were a possible result of the OIC's [Office of the Independent Counsel] investigation from Day One. . . .

This means that the OIC report is left with nothing but the details of a private sexual relationship. . . . Given the flimsy and unsubstantiated basis for the accusations, there is a complete lack of any credible evidence to initiate an impeachment inquiry concerning the President. . . .

Where's Whitewater? The OIC's allegations reportedly include no suggestion of wrongdoing by the President in any of the areas which Mr. Starr spent four years investigating: Whitewater, the FBI files and the White House travel office. What began as an inquiry into a 24-year-old land deal in Arkansas has ended as an inquest into brief, improper personal encounters between the President and Monica Lewinsky. Despite the exhaustive nature of the OIC's investigation into the Whitewater, FBI files and travel office matters . . . to this day the OIC has never exonerated the President or the First Lady of wrongdoing.

Articles of Impeachment

Following is the text of H Res 611, the articles of impeachment against President Clinton, that the Judiciary Committee presented to the full House. Articles I and III were approved by the House on Dec. 19, 1998; articles II and IV were rejected. (1998 key votes, p. 883)

Resolution, Impeaching William Jefferson Clinton, President of the United States, for high crimes and misdemeanors.

Resolved, that William Jefferson Clinton, President of the United States, is impeached for high crimes and misdemeanors, and that the following articles of impeachment be exhibited to the United States Senate:

Articles of impeachment exhibited by the House of Representatives of the United States of America in the name of itself and of the people of the United States of America, against William Jefferson Clinton, President of the United States of America, in maintenance and support of its impeachment against him for high crimes and misdemeanors.

ARTICLE I

In his conduct while President of the United States, William Jefferson Clinton, in violation of his constitutional oath faithfully to execute the office of the President of the United States, and to the best of his ability, preserve, protect, and defend the Constitution of the United States, and in violation of his constitutional duty to take care that the laws be faithfully executed, has willfully corrupted and manipulated the judicial process of the United States for his personal gain and exoneration, impeding the administration of justice, in that:

On August 17, 1998, William Jefferson Clinton swore to tell the truth, the whole truth and nothing but the truth before a Federal grand jury of the United States. Contrary to that oath, William Jefferson Clinton willfully provided perjurious, false and misleading testimony to the grand jury concerning one or more of the following: (1) the nature and details of his relationship with a subordinate government employee; (2) prior perjurious, false and misleading testimony he gave in a Federal civil rights action brought against him; (3) prior false and misleading statements he allowed his attorney to make to a Federal judge in that civil rights action; and (4) his corrupt efforts to influence the testimony of witnesses and to impede the discovery of evidence in that civil rights action.

In doing this, William Jefferson Clinton has undermined the integrity of his office, has brought disrepute on the Presidency, has betrayed his trust as President, and has acted in a manner subversive of the rule of law and justice, to the manifest injury of the people of the United States.

Wherefore, William Jefferson Clinton, by such conduct, warrants impeachment and trial, and removal from office and disqualification to hold and enjoy any office of honor, trust or profit under the United States.

ARTICLE II

In his conduct while President of the United States, William Jefferson Clinton, in violation of his constitutional oath faithfully to execute the office of President of the United States, and, to the best of his ability, preserve, protect, and defend the Constitution of the United States, and in violation of his constitutional duty to take care that the laws be faithfully executed, has willfully corrupted and manipulated the judicial process of the United States for his personal gain and exoneration, impeding the administration of justice, in that:

(1) On December 23, 1997, William Jefferson Clinton, in sworn answers to written questions asked as part of a Federal civil rights action brought against him, willfully provided perjurious, false and misleading testimony in response to questions deemed relevant by a Federal judge concerning conduct and proposed conduct with subordinate employees.

(2) On January 17, 1998, William Jefferson Clinton swore under oath to tell the truth, the whole truth, and nothing but the truth in a deposition given as part of a Federal civil rights action brought against him. Contrary to that oath, William Jefferson Clinton willfully provided perjurious, false and misleading testimony in response to questions deemed relevant by a Federal judge concerning the nature and details of his relationship with a subordinate government employee, his knowledge of that employee's involvement and participation in the civil rights action brought against him, and his corrupt efforts to influence the testimony of that employee.

In all of this, William Jefferson Clinton has undermined the integrity of his office, has brought disrepute on the Presidency, has betrayed his trust as president, and has acted in a manner subversive of the rule of law and justice, to the manifest injury of the people of the United States.

Wherefore William Jefferson Clinton, by such conduct, warrants impeachment and trial, and removal from office and disqualification to hold and enjoy any office of honor, trust or profit under the United States.

ARTICLE III

In his conduct, while President of the United States, William Jefferson Clinton, in violation of his constitutional oath faithfully to execute the office of President of the United States and, to the best of his ability, preserve, protect, and defend the Constitution of the United States, and in violation of his constitutional duty to take care that the laws be faithfully executed, has prevented, obstructed, and impeded the administration of justice, and has to that end engaged personally, and through his subordinates and agents, in a course of conduct or scheme designed to delay, impede, cover up, and conceal the existence of evidence and testimony related to a Federal civil rights action brought against him in a duly instituted judicial proceeding.

The means used to implement this course of conduct or scheme included one or more of the following acts:

(1) On or about December 17, 1997, William Jefferson Clinton corruptly encouraged a witness in a Federal civil rights action brought against him to execute a sworn affidavit in that proceeding that he knew to be perjurious, false and misleading.

(2) On or about December 17, 1997, William Jefferson Clinton corruptly encouraged a witness in a Federal civil rights action brought against him to give perjurious, false and misleading testimony if and when called to testify personally in that proceeding.

(3) On or about December 28, 1997, William Jefferson Clinton corruptly engaged in, encouraged, or supported a scheme to conceal evidence that had been subpoenaed in a Federal civil rights action brought against him.

(4) Beginning on or about December 7, 1997, and continuing through and including January 14, 1998, William Jefferson Clinton intensified and succeeded in an effort to secure job assistance to a witness in a Federal civil rights action brought against him in order to corruptly prevent the truthful testimony of that witness in that proceeding at a time when the truthful testimony of that witness would have been harmful to him.

(5) On January 17, 1998, at his deposition in a Federal civil rights action brought against him, William Jefferson Clinton corruptly allowed his attorney to make false and misleading statements to a Federal judge characterizing an affidavit, in order to prevent questioning deemed relevant by the judge. Such false and misleading statements were subsequently acknowledged by his attorney in a communication to that judge.

(6) On or about January 18 and January 20–21, 1998, William Jefferson Clinton related a false and misleading account of events relevant to a Federal civil rights action brought against him to a potential witness in that proceeding, in order to corruptly influence the testimony of that witness.

(7) On or about January 21, 23, and 26, 1998, William Jefferson Clinton made false and misleading statements to potential witnesses in a Federal grand jury proceeding in order to corruptly influence the testimony of those witnesses. The false and misleading statements made by William Jefferson Clinton were repeated by witnesses to the grand jury, causing the grand jury to receive false and misleading information.

In all of this, William Jefferson Clinton has undermined the integrity of his office, has brought disrepute on the Presidency, has betrayed his trust as President, and has acted in a manner subversive to the rule of law and justice, to the manifest injury to the people of the United States.

Wherefore, William Jefferson Clinton, by such conduct, warrants impeachment and trial, and removal from office and disqualification to hold and enjoy any office of honor, trust or profit under the United States.

ARTICLE IV

Using the powers and influence of the office of the President of the United States, William Jefferson Clinton, in violation of his constitutional oath faithfully to execute the office of President of the United States and, to the best of his ability, preserve, protect, and defend the Constitution of the United States, and in disregard of his constitutional duty to take care that the laws be faithfully executed, has engaged in conduct that resulted in misuse and abuse of his high office, impaired the due and proper administration of justice and the conduct of lawful inquiries, and contravened the authority of the legislative branch and the truth-seeking purpose of a coordinate investigative proceeding, in that, as President, William Jefferson Clinton refused and failed to respond to certain written requests for admission and willfully made perjurious, false and misleading sworn statements in response to certain written requests for admission propounded to him as part of the impeachment inquiry authorized by the House of Representatives of the Congress of the United States.

William Jefferson Clinton, in refusing and failing to respond and in making perjurious, false and misleading statements, assumed to himself functions and judgments necessary to the exercise of the sole power of impeachment vested by the Constitution in the House of Representatives and exhibited contempt for the inquiry.

In doing this, William Jefferson Clinton has undermined the integrity of his office, has brought disrepute on the Presidency, has betrayed his trust as President, and has acted in a manner subversive of the rule of law and justice, to the manifest injury of the people of the United States.

Wherefore, William Jefferson Clinton, by such conduct, warrants impeachment and trial, and removal from office and disqualification to hold and enjoy any office of honor, trust or profit under the United States.

Rep. Newt Gingrich's Comments on Reelection as House Speaker

Following is text of the remarks by House Speaker Newt Gingrich, R-Ga., Jan. 7, 1997, after his reelection to the Speakership. (Story p. 757)

Let me say to those who voted for me, from the bottom of my heart, thank you. To those who voted for someone else, I hope that I can work with you in such a way that you feel that I am capable of being Speaker of the whole House and representing everyone.

To the freshmen and their families and all the young people who are here today, you are part of a wonderful experience. Just as in less than two weeks we will welcome the president for an inaugural, we here in the legislative branch also celebrate a remarkable moment which the entire world watches; a time when an entire nation voluntarily decides how to govern itself and does so in such a manner that there is a sense among the entire country that freedom is secure and that every citizen can participate.

This is the 105th time we've done this as a country—every two years. The first one actually did not occur until April the 1st, 1789, because while everyone was supposed to show up in March for the brand new Congress, they couldn't find a quorum. And then they all came together. And there are wonderful stories by people who were there written in their diaries and their letters about the fact that they were just folks from all over, of many different backgrounds. Back then they would all have been male and they would all have been white and they would all have been property holders.

Today we have extended democracy and freedom to levels that the Founding Fathers could not have imagined. And any citizen anywhere on the planet watching through C-SPAN and through the networks and seeing this room and its diversity can appreciate the degree to which America opens its doors and its hearts to all people of all backgrounds to have a better future.

In addition to the elected members, we are very fortunate to have a professional staff on both sides of the aisle and a professional staff serving on a nonpartisan basis. And let me say that I think that Robin Carle stood well as the clerk of the House in representing all of us establishing the dignity.

And I thought that in the interchanges between she and Chairman [Vic] Fazio [D-Calif.] that the world could see legitimate partisanship engaged in legitimacy—legitimately, exactly the way it should be; in a professional, in a courteous, in a firm way on both sides. And I think that's part of what we have to teach the world.

In just a few moments, my dear friend John [D.] Dingell [D-Mich.], who represents a tradition in his district, who has fought all these years for all that he believes in, who in the last Congress served so ably in helping pass the telecommunications bill, is going to swear me in. And I am going to ask—then I will have a chance to swear you in. But before that, if I might, I'd say to my dear friend—let me say my wife is here and my mother and my relatives.

And two years ago, they were here with my father. He is not here today, as I think all of you know. He was an infantryman. He served this country. He believed in honor, duty, country.

Let me say to the entire House that two years ago, when I became the first Republican Speaker in 40 years, to the degree I was too brash, too self-confident or too pushy, I apologize. To whatever degree, in

any way, that I brought controversy or inappropriate attention to the House, I apologize.

It is my intention to do everything I can to work with every member of this Congress. And I would just say, as with telecommunication in Congressman Dingell's case, on welfare reform, on line item veto, on telecommunications reform, on steps towards a balanced budget, again and again we found a bipartisan majority willing to pass significant legislation, willing to work together.

There's much work to be done. I've asked Chairman Henry [J.] Hyde [R-Ill.] of the Judiciary Committee to look at the issue of judicial activism. He has agreed to hold hearings looking at that issue.

I think all of us should focus on increasing American jobs through world sales. And I have asked Chairman [Bill] Archer [R-Texas] to look at the whole issue of taxation and how it affects American job creation.

I've also asked the Ways and Means Committee to look at oversight on NAFTA, on the World Trade Organization, because the fact is, we have to move the legislative branch into the information age. If there are going to be continuing bodies around the world, then Chairman [Benjamin A.] Gilman [R-N.Y.] in International Relations and Chairman Archer and others have to get in the habit, I think, of a kind of aggressive oversight, reporting to the nation on whether or not our interests are being protected.

I've also asked Chairman Archer to prepare a series of hearings looking at the entire issue of how we revise the entire tax code; whether we go towards a flat tax or whether we replace the income tax with a sales tax, or what we do; but to begin a process that, frankly, may take four to six years, but is the right direction for the right reason.

Finally, I've asked Chairman [Floyd D.] Spence [R-S.C.] on the National Security Committee, both to look at the issue of national missile defense and to look at the question of military reform.

And let me say to all of my friends on both sides of the aisle, we have every opportunity through reform to shrink the Pentagon to a triangle; we have every opportunity to apply the lessons of downsizing, the lessons of the information age. And just because something is in uniform doesn't mean it has to be saluted, but instead, we should be getting every penny for our taxpayers, and we in the Congress should be looking at long-term contracting as one way to dramatically lower the cost of defense.

But I want to talk about one other area. And here I just want to say there's something more than legislation. Each of us is a leader back home. And I want to just talk very briefly about three topics, and it's about these children and their America, children on both sides of the aisle, children from all backgrounds in every state.

I think we have to ask the question, as leaders, beyond legislation: How do we continue to create one nation under God, indivisible, with liberty and justice for all? I believe most Americans, whether native-born or immigrant, still desire for us to be one nation. So let me briefly talk about three areas that I think are vital.

Let me say first, I think—I'm going to talk just for a second about race, drugs and ignorance. First, let me ask all you: Do we not need to rethink our whole approach to race? And let me draw the parallel to Dick Fosbury. He was a high jumper. In the 1968 Olympics in Mexico City, he developed an entire new approach which is now used by everyone. Yet for six years, the U.S. Olympic Committee rejected it.

My point is very simple. I don't believe any rational American can be comfortable with where we are on the issue of race. And I think all of us ought to take on the challenge as leaders, beyond legislation, beyond our normal jobs, of asking some new questions in some new ways. After all, what does race mean when, if based on merit alone, ethnic Asians would make up a clear majority at the University of California at Berkeley? What does race mean when colleges recruit minorities in the name of inclusiveness and diversity and then segregate them in their own dormitories? What does race mean when many Americans cannot fill out their census forms because they're an amalgam of races? And furthermore, if those of us who are conservative say that bureaucracy and compulsion is not the answer, then what are we going to say to a child born in a poor neighborhood with a broken home and no one to help them rise, who has no organic contact to prosperity and has no organic contact to a better future?

Now, I mentioned this in passing two years ago, and one of the failures that I would take some of the responsibility for is that we did not follow up. But I want to put it right on the table today that every one of us, as a leader, has an obligation to reach out beyond party and beyond ideology and, as Americans, to say, "One of the highest values we're going to spend the next two years on is openly dealing with the challenge of meaning that when we say in our declaration that we are endowed by our Creator with certain unalienable rights, including life, liberty and the pursuit of happiness, that every child in every neighborhood, of every background, is endowed by God.

"And every time America fails to meet that, we are failing to meet God's test for the country we should be."

Let me say second about drugs; I think we have to redefine and rethink our approach to drugs. One of my close friends had her 19-year-old sister overdose, and her 19-year-old sister today is in a coma and celebrated her 20th birthday in that coma. Drugs aren't statistics. As Charlie Rangel [D-N.Y.] told me at breakfast just two years ago, drugs are real human beings being destroyed. Drugs are real violence. If we did not have drugs in this country, the amount of spouse abuse, the amount of child abuse, the amount of violence would drop dramatically. And so I want to suggest that we should take seriously reaching across all barriers and establishing an all-out effort.

You know, the Columbia University Center for Addiction and Substance Abuse has done a fascinating study. The center found that one of the best predictors of whether a child will stay free of drugs is whether he or she practices a religion. Joe Califano, Lyndon Johnson's former adviser and Jimmy Carter's secretary of Health and Human Services [formerly Health, Education and Welfare], says that religion is part of the solution to our drug problems and to drug treatment itself. Alcoholics Anonymous refers to a "higher power." I don't know what all the answers are. But I do know that if we love these children, in addition to fighting racism and reaching out to every child, we need to decide that we are prepared to have the equivalent of an abolitionist movement against drugs and to do what it takes so that none of these children end up in a coma celebrating their birthday or end up dead.

Lastly, we need to pay closer attention to a word you don't hear much anymore: ignorance. Traditionally, ignorance ranked with pestilence, hunger, war as abominations upon humanity. But in recent years, the word ignorance has been cleaned up and refined into some aspect of educational failure. I mean by ignorance something deeper. It's not about geography in the third grade. It's about learning the work ethic. It's about learning to be a citizen. It's about learning to save. It's about all the things that make us functional. It's about the things that allow virtually everybody in this room to get up each morning and have a good life.

There are too many places in America where people are born into dysfunction, educated into dysfunction and live in dysfunction, and we should find a way to reach out in this modern era and use every tool at our fingertips, from computers to television to radio to personal volunteerism, so that every family that today happens to be dysfunctional has a chance within the next few years to learn to be functional.

And I think we should take ignorance as serious a problem as drugs or race.

We in the Congress have one place; we have an obligation beyond any other, and that's this city. And I want to commend [Delegate] Eleanor Holmes Norton [D-D.C.] for the leadership she has shown and the courage she has shown day after day and week after week. She and Tom Davis [R-Va.] and Jim Walsh [R-N.Y.] worked their hearts out over the last two years, and I believe it is fair to say that in some ways, we have begun to make progress. It is not easy. It has to be done carefully. It cannot violate the right of the citizens of this city. But let's be candid; first, this is our national capital. We have a unique obligation on both sides of the aisle, to care about Washington, because we are today to Washington what a state government would be back home to your town. We have an unusual obligation to Washington.

Second, it is our national capital. And people looked at me as though I'd lost my mind a year and a half ago when I met with [Washington, D.C.] Mayor [Marion S.] Barry and I said, "You know, our vision ought to be the finest capital city in the world." And that ought to be our vision.

And furthermore, if we're going to talk honestly about race and we're going to talk honestly about drugs and we're going to talk honestly about ignorance, we owe it to every citizen of this District, every child in this District, to have a decent chance to grow up and go to a school that succeeds, in a neighborhood that is drug-free and safe, with an expectation of getting a job in a community that actually cares about them and provides a better future. And we should take on as a capital—as a Congress, our responsibilities to the District of Columbia, and we should do it proudly. And we should not be ashamed to go back home and say, "You're darn right we're helping our national capital because we want you to visit it with pride, and we want you to know that you can say to anyone anywhere in the world: Come to America and visit Washington, it is a great city."

Let me close with this final thought—and I appreciate my friend John [Dingell] standing there. And I apologize for having drawn you forward, particularly since you're standing on one foot.

But this has been a very difficult time. And to those who agonized and ended up voting for me, I thank you. Some of this difficulty, frankly, I brought on myself. We will deal with that in more detail later. And I apologize to the House and the country for having done so. Some of it is part of the natural process of partisan competition.

This morning, a very dear friend of mine said that he was going to pray to God that I would win today, and I asked him not to. I asked him to pray to God that whatever happens is what God wants, and then we would try to understand it and learn from it.

Let me put that forward in the same thing for all of us as we approach the next two years. I was really struck about a month ago when I walked down to the Lincoln Memorial and I read the Second Inaugural, which is short enough to be on the wall. And 12 times in that inaugural, Lincoln refers to God. I went back and read Washington's first inaugural, which is replete with reference to America existing within God's framework. I read Jefferson's first inaugural—since he's often described as a Deist—which refers to the importance and the power of Providence. All of you can visit the Jefferson Memorial where he says—around the top it is inscribed—"I have sworn upon the altar of God Almighty eternal hostility against all forms of tyranny over the minds of men."

We have much to be proud of as Americans.

This is a great and a wonderful system. We have much to be ashamed of as Americans; from drug addiction to spouse and child abuse; to children living in ignorance and poverty surrounded by the greatest, wealthiest nation in the world; to a political system that clearly has to be overhauled from the ground up if it is going to be worthy of the respect we want and cherish.

I would just suggest to all of you that until we learn in a non-sectarian way—not Baptist, not Catholic, not Jewish—in a non-sectarian way—until we learn to re-establish the authority that we are endowed by our Creator, that we owe it to our Creator, and that we need to seek divine guidance in what we are doing, we are not going to solve this country's problems. In that spirit, with your prayers and help, I will seek to be worthy of being Speaker of the House, and I will seek to work with every member sent by their constituents to represent them in the United States Congress.

Excerpts of Findings in Gingrich Ethics Case

Following are excerpts of the report, released Jan. 17, 1997, by special counsel James M. Cole about the alleged ethics violations of House Speaker Newt Gingrich, R-Ga. The excerpts include the summary of the House ethics subcommittee's findings and the analysis and conclusion of the charges. (Story, p. 761)

C. SUMMARY OF THE SUBCOMMITTEE'S FACTUAL FINDINGS

The Subcommittee found that in regard to two projects, Mr. Gingrich engaged in activity involving 501(c)(3) organizations that was substantially motivated by partisan, political goals. The Subcommittee also found that Mr. Gingrich provided the Committee with material information about one of those projects that was inaccurate, incomplete, and unreliable.

1. AOW/ACTV

The first project was a television program called the American Opportunities Workshop (AOW). It took place in May 1990. The idea for this project came from Mr. Gingrich and he was principally responsible for developing its message. AOW involved broadcasting a television program on the subject of various governmental issues. Mr. Gingrich hoped that this program would help create a "citizens' movement." Workshops were set up throughout the country where people could gather to watch the program and be recruited for the citizens' movement. While the program was educational, the citizens' movement was also considered a tool to recruit non-voters and people who were apolitical to the Republican Party. The program was deliberately free of any references to Republicans or partisan politics because Mr. Gingrich believed such references would dissuade the target audience of non-voters from becoming involved.

AOW started out as a project of GOPAC, a political action committee dedicated to, among other things, achieving Republican control of the United States House of Representatives.

Its methods for accomplishing this goal included the development and articulation of a political message and the dissemination of that message as widely as possible. One such avenue of dissemination was AOW. The program, however, consumed a substantial portion of GOPAC's revenues. Because of the expense, Mr. Gingrich and others at GOPAC decided to transfer the project to a 501(c)(3) organization in order to attract tax-deductible funding. The 501(c)(3) organization chosen was the Abraham Lincoln Opportunity Foundation (ALOF).

ALOF was dormant at the time and was revived to sponsor AOW's successor, American Citizens' Television (ACTV). ALOF operated out of GOPAC's offices. Virtually all its officers and employers were simultaneously GOPAC officers or employees. ACTV had the same educational aspects and partisan, political goals as AOW. The principal difference between the two was that ACTV used approximately $260,000 in tax-deductible contributions to fund its operations. ACTV broadcast three television programs in 1990 and then ceased operations. The last program was funded by a 501(c)(4) organization because the show's content was deemed to be too political for a 501(c)(3) organization.

2. Renewing American Civilization

The second project utilizing 501(c)(3) organizations involved a college course taught by Mr. Gingrich called Renewing American Civilization. Mr. Gingrich developed the course as a subset to and tool of a larger political and cultural movement also called Renewing American Civilization. The goal of this movement, as stated by Mr. Gingrich, was the replacement of the "welfare state" with an "opportunity society." A primary means of achieving this goal was the development of the movement's message and the dissemination of that message as widely as possible. Mr. Gingrich intended that a "Republican majority" would be the heart of the movement and that the movement would "professionalize" House Republicans. A method for achieving these goals was to use the movement's message to "attract voters, resources, and candidates." According to Mr. Gingrich, the course was, among other things, a primary and essential means to develop and disseminate the message of the movement.

The core message of the movement and the course was that the welfare state had failed, that it could not be repaired but had to be replaced, and that it had to be replaced with an opportunity society based on what Mr. Gingrich called the "Five Pillars of American Civilization." These were: 1) personal strength; 2) entrepreneurial free enterprise; 3) the spirit of invention; 4) quality as defined by Edwards Deming; and 5) the lessons of American history. The message also concentrated on three substantive areas. These were: 1) jobs and economic growth; 2) health; and 3) saving the inner city.

This message was also Mr. Gingrich's main campaign theme in 1993 and 1994 and Mr. Gingrich sought to have Republican candidates adopt the Renewing American Civilization message in their campaigns. In the context of political campaigns, Mr. Gingrich used the term "welfare state" as a negative label for Democrats and the term "opportunity society" as a positive label for Republicans.

As General Chairman of GOPAC, Mr. Gingrich decided that GOPAC would use Renewing American Civilization as its political message and theme during 1993–1994. GOPAC, however, was having financial difficulties and could not afford to disseminate its political messages as it had in past years. GOPAC had a number of roles in regard to the course. For example, GOPAC personnel helped develop, manage, promote, and raise funds for the course.

GOPAC Charter Members helped develop the idea to teach the course as a means for communicating GOPAC's message. GOPAC Charter Members at Charter Meetings helped develop the content of the course. GOPAC was "better off" as a result of the nationwide dissemination of the Renewing American Civilization message via the course in that the message GOPAC had adopted and determined to be the one that would help it achieve its goals was broadcast widely and at no cost to GOPAC.

The course was taught at Kennesaw State College (KSC) in 1993 and at Reinhardt College in 1994 and 1995. Each course consisted of ten lectures and each lecture consisted of approximately four hours of classroom instruction, for a total of forty hours. Mr. Gingrich taught twenty hours of each course and his co-teacher, or occasionally a guest lecturer, taught twenty hours. Students from each of the colleges as well as people who were not students attended the lectures. Mr. Gingrich's 20-hour portion of the course was taped and distributed to remote sites, referred to as "site hosts," via satellite, videotape and cable television. As with AOW/ACTV, Renewing American Civilization involved setting up workshops around the country where people could gather to watch the course. While the course was educational, Mr. Gingrich intended that the workshops would be, among other things, a recruiting tool for GOPAC and the Republican Party.

The major costs for the Renewing American Civilization course were for dissemination of the lectures. This expense was primarily paid for by tax-deductible contributions made to the 501(c)(3) organizations that sponsored the course. Over the three years the course was broadcast, approximately $1.2 million was spent on the project. The Kennesaw State College Foundation (KSCF) sponsored the course the first year. All funds raised were turned over to KSCF and dedicated exclusively for the use of the Renewing American Civilization course.

KSCF did not, however, manage the course and its role was limited to depositing donations into its bank account and paying bills from that account that were presented to it by the Dean of the KSC Business School. KSCF contracted with the Washington Policy Group, Inc. (WPG) to manage and raise funds for the course's development, production and distribution. Jeffrey Eisenach, GOPAC's Executive Director from June 1991 to June 1993, was the president and sole owner of WPG. WPG and Mr. Eisenach played similar roles with respect to AOW/ACTV.

When the contract between WPG and KSCF ended in the fall of 1993, the Progress and Freedom Foundation (PFF) assumed the role WPG had with the course at the same rate of compensation. Mr. Eisenach was PFF's founder and president. Shortly after PFF took over the management of the course, the Georgia Board of Regents passed a resolution prohibiting any elected official from teaching at a Georgia state educational institution. This was the culmination of a controversy that had arisen around the course at KSC. A group of KSC faculty had objected to the course being taught on the campus because of a belief that it was an effort to use the college to disseminate a political message. Because of the Board of Regents' decision and the controversy, it was decided that the course would be moved to a private college.

The course was moved to Reinhardt for the 1994 and 1995 sessions. While there, PFF assumed full responsibility for the course. PFF no longer received payments to run the course but, instead, took in all contributions to the course and paid all the bills, including paying Reinhardt for the use of the college's video production facilities. All funds for the course were raised by and expended by PFF under its tax-exempt status.

3. Failure to Seek Legal Advice

Under the Internal Revenue Code, a 501(c)(3) organization must be operated exclusively for exempt purposes. The presence of a single non-exempt purpose, if more than insubstantial in nature, will destroy the exemption regardless of the number or importance of truly exempt purposes. Conferring a benefit on private interests is a non-exempt purpose. Under the Internal Revenue Code, a 501(c)(3) organization is also prohibited from intervening in a political campaign or providing any support to a political action committee. These prohibitions reflect congressional concerns that taxpayer funds not be used to subsidize political activity.

During the Preliminary Inquiry, the Subcommittee consulted with an expert in the law of tax-exempt organizations and read materials on the subject. Mr. Gingrich's activities on behalf of AOW/ACTV and Renewing American Civilization, as well as the activities of others on behalf of those projects done with Mr. Gingrich's knowledge and approval, were reviewed by the expert. The expert concluded that those activities violated the status of the organizations under section 501(c)(3) in that, among other things, those activities were intended to confer more than insubstantial benefits on GOPAC, Mr. Gingrich, and Republican entities and candidates, and provided support to GOPAC.

At Mr. Gingrich's request, the Subcommittee also heard from tax counsel retained by Mr. Gingrich for the purposes of the Preliminary Inquiry. While that counsel is an experienced tax attorney with a sterling reputation, he has less experience in dealing with tax-exempt organizations law than does the expert retained by the Subcommittee. According to Mr. Gingrich's tax counsel, the type of activity involved in the AOW/ACTV and Renewing American Civilization projects would not violate the status of the relevant organizations under section 501(c)(3). He opined that once it was determined that an activity was "educational," as defined by the IRS, and did not have the effect of benefiting a private interest, it did not violate the private benefit prohibition. In the view of Mr. Gingrich's tax counsel, motivation on the part of an organization's principals and agents is irrelevant. Further, he opined that a 501(c)(3) organization does not violate the private benefit prohibition or political campaign prohibition through close association with or support of a political action committee unless it specifically calls for the election or defeat of an identifiable political candidate.

Both the Subcommittee's tax expert and Mr. Gingrich's tax counsel, however, agreed that had Mr. Gingrich sought their advice before embarking on activities of the type involved in AOW/ACTV and the Renewing American Civilization course, each of them would have advised Mr. Gingrich not to use a 501(c)(3) organization as he had in regard to those activities. The Subcommittee's tax expert said that doing so would violate 501(c)(3). During his appearance before the Subcommittee, Mr. Gingrich's tax counsel said that he would not have recommended the use of 501(c)(3) organizations to sponsor the course because the combination of politics and 501(c)(3) organizations is an "explosive mix" almost certain to draw the attention of the IRS.

Based on the evidence, it was clear that Mr. Gingrich intended that the AOW/ACTV and Renewing American Civilization projects have substantial partisan, political purposes. In addition, he was aware that political activities in the context of 501(c)(3) organizations were problematic. Prior to embarking on these projects, Mr. Gingrich had been involved with another organization that had direct experience with the private benefit prohibition in a political context, the American Campaign Academy. In a 1989 Tax Court opinion issued less than a year before Mr. Gingrich set the AOW/ACTV project into motion, the Academy was denied its exemption under 501(c)(3) because, although educational, it conferred an impermissible private benefit on Republican candidates and entities. Close associates of Mr. Gingrich were principals in the American Campaign Academy, Mr. Gingrich taught at the Academy, and Mr. Gingrich had been briefed at the time on the tax controversy surrounding the Academy. In addition, Mr. Gingrich stated publicly that he was taking a very aggressive approach to the use of 501(c)(3) organizations in regard to, at least, the Renewing American Civilization course.

Taking into account Mr. Gingrich's background, experience, and sophistication with respect to tax-exempt organizations, and his status as a Member of Congress obligated to maintain high ethical standards, the Subcommittee concluded that Mr. Gingrich should have known to seek appropriate legal advice to ensure that his conduct in regard to the AOW/ACTV and Renewing American Civilization projects was in compliance with 501(c)(3). Had he sought and followed such advice—after having set out all the relevant facts, circumstances, plans, and goals described above—501(c)(3) organizations would not have been used to sponsor Mr. Gingrich's ACTV and Renewing American Civilization projects.

4. Mr. Gingrich's Statements to the Committee

In responding to the complaints filed against him concerning the Renewing American Civilization course, Mr. Gingrich submitted several letters to the Committee. His first letter, dated October 4, 1994, did not address the tax issues raised in Mr. Jones' complaint, but rather responded to the part of the complaint concerning unofficial use of official resources.

In it Mr. Gingrich stated that GOPAC, among other organizations, paid people to work on the course. After this response, the Committee wrote Mr. Gingrich and asked him specifically to address issues related to whether the course had a partisan, political aspect to it and, if so, whether it was appropriate for a 501(c)(3) organization to be used to sponsor the course. The Committee also specifically asked whether GOPAC had any relationship to the course. Mr. Gingrich's letter in response, dated December 8, 1994, was prepared by his attorney, but it was read, approved, and signed by Mr. Gingrich. It stated that the course had no partisan, political aspects to it, that his motivation for teaching the course was not political, and that GOPAC neither was involved in nor received any benefit from any aspect of the course. In his testimony before the Subcommittee, Mr. Gingrich admitted that these statements were not true.

When the amended complaint was filed with the Committee in January 1995, Mr. Gingrich's attorney responded to the complaint on behalf of Mr. Gingrich in a letter dated March 27, 1995. His attorney addressed all the issues in the amended complaint, including the issues related to the Renewing American Civilization course. The letter was signed by Mr. Gingrich's attorney, but Mr. Gingrich reviewed and approved it prior to its being delivered to the Committee. In an interview with Mr. Cole, Mr. Gingrich stated that if he had seen anything inaccurate in the letter he would have instructed his attorney to correct it. Similar to the December 8, 1994, letter, the March 27, 1995, letter stated that the course had no partisan, political aspects to it, that Mr. Gingrich's motivation for teaching the course was not political, and that GOPAC had no involvement in nor received any benefit from any aspect of the course. In his testimony before the Subcommittee, Mr. Gingrich admitted that these statements were not true.

The goal of the letters was to have the complaints dismissed. Of the people involved in drafting or editing the letters, or reviewing them for accuracy, only Mr. Gingrich had personal knowledge of the facts contained in the letters regarding the course. The facts in the letters that were inaccurate, incomplete, and unreliable were material to the Committee's determination on how to proceed with the tax questions contained in the complaints.

D. STATEMENT OF ALLEGED VIOLATION

On December 21, 1996, the Subcommittee issued a Statement of Alleged Violation (SAV) stating that Mr. Gingrich had engaged in conduct that did not reflect creditably on the House of Representatives in that by failing to seek and follow legal advice, Mr. Gingrich failed to take appropriate steps to ensure that activities with respect to the AOW/ACTV project and the Renewing American Civilization project were in accordance with section 501(c)(3); and that on or about December 8, 1994, and on or about March 27, 1995, information was transmitted to the Committee by and on behalf of Mr. Gingrich that was material to matters under consideration by the Committee, which information, as Mr. Gingrich should have known, was inaccurate, incomplete, and unreliable.

On December 21, 1996, Mr. Gingrich filed an answer with the Subcommittee admitting to this violation of House Rules. . . .

IX. ANALYSIS AND CONCLUSION

A. Tax Issues

In reviewing the evidence concerning both the AOW/ACTV project and the Renewing American Civilization project, certain patterns became apparent. In both instances, GOPAC had initiated the use of the messages as part of its political program to build a Republican majority in Congress. In both instances there was an effort to have the material appear to be nonpartisan on its face, yet serve as a partisan, political message for the purpose of building the Republican Party.

Under the "methodology test" set out by the Internal Revenue Service, both projects qualified as educational. However, they both had substantial partisan, political aspects. Both were initiated as political projects and both were motivated, at least in part, by political goals.

The other striking similarity is that, in both situations, GOPAC was in need of a new source of funding for the projects and turned to a 501(c)(3) organization for that purpose.

Once the projects had been established at the 501(c)(3) organizations, however, the same people continued to manage it as had done so at GOPAC, the same message was used as when it was at GOPAC, and the dissemination of the message was directed toward the same goal as when the project was at GOPAC—building the Republican Party. The only significant difference was that the activity was funded by a 501(c)(3) organization.

This was not a situation where one entity develops a message through a course or a television program for purely educational purposes and then an entirely separate entity independently decides to adopt that message for partisan, political purposes. Rather, this was a coordinated effort to have the 501(c)(3) organization help in achieving a partisan, political goal. In both instances the idea to develop the message and disseminate it for partisan, political use came first. The use of the 501(c)(3) came second as a source of funding.

This factual analysis was accepted by all Members of the Subcommittee and the Special Counsel. However, there was a difference of opinion as to the result under 501(c)(3) when applying the law to these facts. Ms. Roady, the Subcommittee's tax expert, was of the opinion that the facts presented a clear violation of 501(c)(3) because the evidence showed that the activities were intended to benefit Mr. Gingrich, GOPAC, and other Republican candidates and entities. Mr. Holden, Mr. Gingrich's tax attorney, disagreed. He found that the course was non-partisan in its content, and even though he assumed that the motivation for disseminating it involved partisan, political goals, he did not find a sufficiently narrow targeting of the dissemination to conclude that it was a private benefit to anyone.

Some Members of the Subcommittee and the Special Counsel agreed with Ms. Roady and concluded that there was a clear violation of 501(c)(3) with respect to AOW/ACTV and Renewing American Civilization. Other Members of the Subcommittee were troubled by reaching this conclusion and believed that the facts of this case presented a unique situation that had not previously been addressed by the legal authorities.

As such, they did not feel comfortable supplanting the functions of the Internal Revenue Service or the Tax Court in rendering a ruling on what they believed to be an unsettled area of the law.

B. Statements Made to the Committee

The letters Mr. Gingrich submitted to the Committee concerning the Renewing American Civilization complaint were very troubling to the Subcommittee. They contained definitive statements about facts that went to the heart of the issues placed before the Committee. In the case of the December 8, 1994, letter, it was in response to a direct request from the Committee for specific information relating to the partisan, political nature of the course and GOPAC's involvement in it.

Both letters were efforts by Mr. Gingrich to have the Committee dismiss the complaints without further inquiry. In such situations, the Committee does and should place great reliance on the statements of Members. The letters were prepared by Mr. Gingrich's lawyers.

After the Subcommittee deposed the lawyers, the reasons for the statements being in the letters was not made any clearer. The lawyers did not conduct any independent factual research.

Looking at the information the lawyers used to write the letters, the Subcommittee was unable to find any factual basis for the inaccurate statements contained therein. A number of exhibits attached to the complaint were fax transmittal sheets from GOPAC.

While this did not on its face establish anything more than GOPAC's fax machine having been used for the project, it certainly should have put the attorneys on notice that there was some relationship between the course and GOPAC that should have been examined before saying that GOPAC had absolutely no involvement in the course.

The lawyers said they relied on Mr. Gingrich and his staff to ensure that the letters were accurate; however, none of Mr. Gingrich's staff had sufficient knowledge to be able to verify the accuracy of the facts. While Mr. Gaylord and Mr. Eisenach did have sufficient knowledge to verify many of the facts, they were not asked to do so. The only person who reviewed the letters for accuracy, with sufficient knowledge to verify those facts, was Mr. Gingrich.

The Subcommittee considered the relevance of the reference to GOPAC in Mr. Gingrich's first letter to the Committee dated October 4, 1994. In that letter he stated that GOPAC was one of the entities that paid people to work on the course. Some Members of the Subcommittee believed that this was evidence of lack of intent to deceive the Committee on Mr. Gingrich's part because if he had planned to hide GOPAC's involvement, he would not have made such an inconsistent statement in the subsequent letters. Other Members of the Subcommittee and the Special Counsel appreciated this point, but believed the first letter was of little value. The statement in that letter was only directed to establishing that Mr. Gingrich had not used congressional resources in developing the course.

The first letter made no attempt to address the tax issues, even though it was a prominent feature of the complaint. When the Committee specifically focused Mr. Gingrich's attention on that issue and questions concerning GOPAC's involvement in the course, his response was not accurate.

During his testimony before the Subcommittee, Mr. Gingrich stated that he did not intend to mislead the Committee and apologized for his conduct. This statement was a relevant consideration for some Members of the Subcommittee, but not for others.

The Subcommittee concluded that because these inaccurate statements were provided to the Committee, this matter was not resolved as expeditiously as it could have been. This caused a controversy over the matter to arise and last for a substantial period of time, it disrupted the operations of the House, and it cost the House a substantial amount of money in order to determine the facts.

C. Statement of Alleged Violation

Based on the information described above, the Special Counsel proposed a Statement of Alleged Violations (SAV) to the Subcommittee on December 12, 1996. The SAV contained three counts:

1) Mr. Gingrich's activities on behalf of ALOF in regard to AOW/ACTV, and the activities of others in that regard with his knowledge and approval, constituted a violation of ALOF's status under section 501(c)(3);

2) Mr. Gingrich's activities on behalf of Kennesaw State College Foundation, the Progress and Freedom Foundation, and Reinhardt College in regard to the Renewing American Civilization course, and the activities of others in that regard with his knowledge and approval, constituted a violation of those organizations' status under section 501(c)(3); and

3) Mr. Gingrich had provided information to the Committee, directly or through counsel, that was material to matters under consideration by the Committee, which Mr. Gingrich knew or should have known was inaccurate, incomplete, and unreliable.

1. DELIBERATIONS ON THE TAX COUNTS

There was a difference of opinion regarding whether to issue the SAV as drafted on the tax counts. Concern was expressed about deciding this tax issue in the context of an ethics proceeding. This led the discussion to the question of the appropriate focus for the Subcommittee. A consensus began to build around the view that the proper focus was on the conduct of the Member, rather than a resolution of issues of tax law. From the beginning of the Preliminary Inquiry, there was a desire on the part of each of the Members to find a way to reach a unanimous conclusion in this matter. The Members felt it was important to confirm the bipartisan nature of the ethics process.

The discussion turned to what steps Mr. Gingrich had taken in regard to these two projects to ensure they were done in accord with the provisions of 501(c)(3). In particular, the Subcommittee was concerned with the fact that:

1) Mr. Gingrich had been "very well aware" of the American Campaign Academy case prior to embarking [on this] project;

2) he had been involved with 501(c)(3) organizations to a sufficient degree to know that politics and tax-deductible contributions are, as his tax counsel said, an "explosive mix";

3) he was clearly involved in a project that had significant partisan, political goals, and he had taken an aggressive approach to the tax laws in regard to both AOW/ACTV; and

4) Renewing American Civilization projects. Even Mr. Gingrich's own tax lawyer told the Subcommittee that if Mr. Gingrich had come to him before embarking on these projects, he would have advised him to not use a 501(c)(3) organization for the dissemination of AOW/ACTV or Renewing American Civilization.

Had Mr. Gingrich sought and followed this advice, he would not have used the 501(c)(3) organizations, would not have had his projects subsidized by taxpayer funds, and would not have created this controversy that has caused significant disruption to the House. The Subcommittee concluded that there were significant and substantial warning signals to Mr. Gingrich that he should have heeded prior to embarking on these projects. Despite these warnings, Mr. Gingrich did not seek any legal advice to ensure his conduct conformed with the provisions of 501(c)(3).

In looking at this conduct in light of all the facts and circumstances, the Subcommittee was faced with a disturbing choice. Either Mr. Gingrich did not seek legal advice because he was aware that it would not have permitted him to use a 501(c)(3) organization for his projects, or he was reckless in not taking care that, as a Member of Congress, he made sure that his conduct conformed with the law in an area where he had ample warning that his intended course of action was fraught with legal peril.

The Subcommittee decided that regardless of the resolution of the 501(c)(3) tax question, Mr. Gingrich's conduct in this regard was improper, did not reflect creditably on the House, and was deserving of sanction.

2. DELIBERATIONS CONCERNING THE LETTERS

The subcommittee's deliberation concerning the letters provided to the Committee centered on the question of whether Mr. Gingrich intentionally submitted inaccurate information. There was a belief that the record developed before the Subcommittee was not conclusive on this point. The Special Counsel suggested that a good argument could be made, based on the record, that Mr. Gingrich did act intentionally, however it would be difficult to establish that with a high degree of certainty.

The culmination of the evidence on this topic again left the Subcommittee with a disturbing choice. Either Mr. Gingrich intentionally made misrepresentations to the Committee, or he was again reckless in the way he provided information to the Committee concerning a very important matter.

The standard applicable to the Subcommittee's deliberations was whether there is reason to believe that Mr. Gingrich had acted as charged in this count of the SAV. All felt that this standard had been met in regard to the allegation that Mr. Gingrich "knew" that the information he provided to the Committee was inaccurate.

However, there was considerable discussion to the effect that if Mr. Gingrich wanted to admit to submitting information to the Committee that he "should have known" was inaccurate, the Subcommittee would consider deleting the allegation that he knew the information was inaccurate.

The Members were of the opinion that if there were to be a final adjudication of the matter, taking into account the higher standard of proof that is involved at that level, "should have known" was an appropriate framing of the charge in light of all the facts and circumstances.

3. DISCUSSIONS WITH MR. GINGRICH'S COUNSEL AND RECOMMENDED SANCTION

On December 13, 1996, the Subcommittee issued an SAV charging Mr. Gingrich with three counts of violations of House Rules. Two counts concerned the failure to seek legal advice in regard to the 501(c)(3) projects, and one count concerned providing the Committee with information which he knew or should have known was inaccurate.

At the time the Subcommittee voted this SAV, the Members discussed the matter among themselves and reached a consensus that it would be in the best interests of the House for the matter to be resolved without going through a disciplinary hearing. It was estimated that such a hearing could take up to three months to complete and would not begin for several months.

Because of this, it was anticipated that the House would have to deal with this matter for another six months. Even though the Subcommittee Members felt that it would be advantageous to the House to avoid a disciplinary hearing, they all were committed to the proposition that any resolution of the matter had to reflect adequately the seriousness of the offenses.

To this end, the Subcommittee Members discussed and agreed upon a recommended sanction that was fair in light of the conduct reflected in this matter, but explicitly recognized that the full Committee would make the ultimate decision as to the recommendation to the full House as to the appropriate sanction.

In determining what the appropriate sanction should be in this matter, the Subcommittee and Special Counsel considered the seriousness of the conduct, the level of care exercised by Mr. Gingrich, the disruption caused to the House by the conduct, the cost to the House in having to pay for an extensive investigation, and the repetitive nature of the conduct.

As is noted above, the Subcommittee was faced with troubling choices in each of the areas covered by the Statement of Alleged Violation. Either Mr. Gingrich's conduct in regard to the 501(c)(3) organizations and the letters he submitted to the Committee was intentional or it was reckless. Neither choice reflects creditably on the House.

While the Subcommittee was notable to reach a comfortable conclusion on these issues, the fact that the choice was presented is a factor in determining the appropriate sanction. In addition, the violation does not represent only a single instance of reckless conduct.

Rather, over a number of years and in a number of situations, Mr. Gingrich showed a disregard and lack of respect for the standards of conduct that applied to his activities.

Under the Rules of the Committee, a reprimand is the appropriate sanction for a serious violation of House Rules and a censure is appropriate for a more serious violation of House Rules. *Rule 20(g), Rules of the Committee on Standards of Official Conduct.*

It was the opinion of the Subcommittee that this matter fell somewhere in between. Accordingly, the Subcommittee and the Special Counsel recommend that the appropriate sanction should be a reprimand and a payment reimbursing the House for some of the costs of the investigation in the amount of $300,000.

Mr. Gingrich has agreed that this is the appropriate sanction in this matter.

Beginning on December 15, 1996, Mr. Gingrich's counsel and the Special Counsel began discussions directed toward resolving the matter without a disciplinary hearing. The discussions lasted through December 20, 1996.

At that time an understanding was reached by both Mr. Gingrich and the Subcommittee concerning this matter. That understanding was put on the record on December 21, 1996 by Mr. Cole [as] follows:

Mr. Cole: The subcommittee has had an opportunity to review the facts in this case, and has had extensive discussion about the appropriate resolution of this matter.

Mr. Cardin: If I might just add here to your next understanding, the Members of the subcommittee, prior to the adoption of the Statement of Alleged Violation, were concerned that the nonpartisan deliberations of the subcommittee continue beyond the findings of the subcommittee. Considering the record of the full Ethics Committee in the 104th Congress and the partisan environment in the full House, the Members of the subcommittee felt that it was important to exercise bipartisan leadership beyond the workings of the subcommittee.

Mr. Cole: It was the opinion of the Members of the subcommittee and the Special Counsel, that based on the facts of this case as they are currently known, the appropriate sanction for the conduct described in the original Statement of Alleged Violations is a reprimand and the payment of $300,000 toward the cost of the preliminary inquiry.

In light of this opinion, the subcommittee Members and the Special Counsel intend to recommend to the full committee that this be the sanction recommended by the full committee to the House. The Members also intend to support this as the sanction in the committee and on the Floor of the House.

However, if new facts are developed or brought to the attention of the Members of the subcommittee, they are free to change their opinions.

The Subcommittee, through its counsel, has communicated this to Mr. Gingrich, through his counsel. Mr. Gingrich has agreed that if the subcommittee will amend the Statement of Alleged Violations to be one count, instead of three counts, however, still including all of the conduct described in the original Statement of Alleged Violations, and will allow the addition of some language which reflects aspects of the record in this matter concerning the involvement of Mr. Gingrich's counsel in the preparation of the letters described in the original Count 3 of the Statement of Alleged Violations, he will admit to the entire Statement of Alleged Violation and agree to the view of the subcommittee Members and the Special Counsel as to the appropriate sanction.

In light of Mr. Gingrich's admission to the Statement of Alleged Violation, the subcommittee is of the view that the rules of the committee will not require that an adjudicatory hearing take place; however, a sanction hearing will need to be held under the rules.

The subcommittee and Mr. Gingrich desire to have the sanction hearing concluded as expeditiously as possible, but it is understood that this will not take place at the expense of orderly procedure and a full and fair opportunity for the full committee to be informed of any information necessary for each Member of the full committee to be able to make a decision at the sanction hearing.

After the subcommittee has voted a new Statement of Alleged Violation, Mr. Gingrich will file his answer admitting to it. The subcommittee will seek the permission of the full committee to release the Statement of Alleged Violation, Mr. Gingrich's answer, and a brief press release which has been approved by Mr. Gingrich's counsel. At the same time, Mr. Gingrich will release a brief press release that has been approved by the subcommittee's Special Counsel.

Both the subcommittee and Mr. Gingrich agree that no public comment should be made about this matter while it is still pending. This includes having surrogates sent out to comment on the matter and attempt to mischaracterize it.

Accordingly, beyond the press statements described above, neither Mr. Gingrich nor any Member of the subcommittee may make any further public comment. Mr. Gingrich understands that if he violates this provision, the subcommittee will have the option of reinstating the original Statement of Alleged Violations and allowing Mr. Gingrich an opportunity to withdraw his answer.

And I should note that it is the intention of the subcommittee that "public comments" refers to press statements; that, obviously, we are free and Mr. Gingrich is free to have private conversations with Members of Congress about these matters.

After the Subcommittee voted to issue the substitute SAV, the Special Counsel called Mr. Gingrich's counsel and read to him what was put on the record concerning this matter. Mr. Gingrich's counsel then delivered to the Subcommittee Mr. Gingrich's answer admitting to the Statement of Alleged Violation. . . .

D. POST-DECEMBER 21, 1996, ACTIVITY

Following the release of this Statement of Alleged Violation, numerous press accounts appeared concerning this matter. In the opinion of the Subcommittee Members and the Special Counsel, a number of the press accounts indicated that Mr. Gingrich had violated the agreement concerning statements about the matter. Mr. Gingrich's counsel was notified of the Subcommittee's concerns and the Subcommittee met to consider what action to take in light of this apparent violation. The Subcommittee determined that it would not nullify the agreement.

While there was serious concern about whether Mr. Gingrich had complied with the agreement, the Subcommittee was of the opinion that the best interests of the House still lay in resolving the matter without a disciplinary hearing and with the recommended sanction that its Members had previously determined was appropriate. However, Mr. Gingrich's counsel was informed that the Subcommittee believed a violation of the agreement had occurred and retained the right to withdraw from the agreement with appropriate notice to Mr. Gingrich. To date no such notice has been given.

Election of Dennis Hastert as House Speaker

Following are remarks by House Minority Leader Richard A. Gephardt, D-Mo., and J. Dennis Hastert, R-Ill., before Hastert was sworn in as the new Speaker of the House of Representatives on Jan. 6, 1999. Hastert succeeded Newt Gingrich, R-Ga., who resigned from Congress. (Story, p. 757)

Richard A. Gephardt: Mr. Speaker and members of the House, before I hand the gavel over to our new Speaker, let me say to him simply, let's bury the hatchet.

First, I want to say to the new Speaker that Jane Gephardt and I would like to invite him and his wife Jean to our congressional district in Missouri, and I hope that in the days ahead Jane and I can come to your congressional district in Illinois.

The only problem I have with this new Speaker is that, as I understand it, he's a Chicago Cubs fan and—

J. Dennis Hastert: But my wife's a Cardinals fan.

Gephardt: And all of you know that I'm a St. Louis Cardinals fan—and he tells me his wife is a St. Louis Cardinals fan, which gives me real hope. But if Sammy Sosa and Mark McGwire can figure it out, so can we.

Now, Mr. Speaker, you know that over the next two years I am going to work hard to win a majority back for Democratic values and ideas. But I want to shift the focus today away from politics to other ideas, to other efforts that we can make together to do us all proud. Let's put to rest finally the poisonous politics that has infected this place.

Let's join together, not only in words but in deeds, to do right by the people to live up to our oaths, and to move our nation forward into a new century of prosperity. This is hallowed ground. This is a precious place where we have nurtured and protected for generations our democracy. We have a burden—all of us—and we have a responsibility to live up to those who have gone before us, and today and in the future to reach toward the sky and to listen to our better angels. It is in this spirit that I am proud to hand the gavel to the new Speaker of the House, to our new Speaker of the House, the gentleman from Illinois, Dennis Hastert.

Hastert: Thank you, Mr. Speak—Mr. Leader—for your kind and thoughtful remarks. I'm going to break tradition, and at this point I am going to ask you to hold the gavel so that I may go down to the floor.

Customarily a new Speaker gives his first remarks from the Speaker's chair. And while I have great respect for the traditions of this House and this institution, I am breaking tradition this once because my legislative home is here on the floor with you, and so is my heart.

To you, the members of the 106th Congress, to my family and friends and constituents, I say thank you. This is not a job that I sought, but one that I embrace with determination and enthusiasm. In the next few minutes I will share with you how I plan to carry out the job that you have given me.

But first I think we need to take a moment—and I want to say goodbye to a member of this House who made history. Newt [Gingrich], this institution has been forever transformed by your presence, and for years to come all Americans will benefit from the changes that you've championed—a balanced budget, welfare reform, tax relief. And in fact this week families all over America are beginning to calculate their taxes. And to help them they'll find a child tax credit made possible by the Congress that you led. Thank you, Newt, good luck, and God bless you in your new endeavors.

Those of you here in this House know me. But Hastert is not exactly a household name across America. So our fellow citizens deserve to know who I am and what I am going to do. What I am is a former high school teacher, a wrestling and football coach, a small businessman and a state legislator. And for the last 12 years I've been a member of this House. I am indebted to the people of the 14th congressional district of Illinois who continue to send me here to represent them.

I believe in limited government. But when government does act it must be for the good of the people. And serving in this body is a privilege—it is not a right—and each of us was sent here to conduct the people's business. And I intend to get down to business. That means formulating, debating and voting on legislation that addresses the problems that the American people want solved.

In the turbulent days behind us, debate on merits often gave way to personal attacks. Some have felt slighted, insulted or ignored. That is wrong, and that will change. Solutions to problems cannot be found in a pool of bitterness. They can be found in an environment in which we trust one another's word, where we generate heat and passion, but where we recognize that each member is equally important to our overall mission of improving life for the American people. In short, I believe all of us, regardless of party, can respect one another, and even as fiercely as we disagree on particular issues.

And speaking of people who find ways to work together across the political fence, let me bring an analogy to a personal level. Two good Illinois friends of mine—George Ryan, the Republican governor-elect and Richard Daley, the Democratic mayor of Chicago—are in the visitors' gallery side by side, and I will ask them to stand to be recognized.

Those who know me well will tell you that I am true to my word. To me a commitment is a commitment, and what you see and hear today is what you will see and hear tomorrow.

Nobody knows me better than my family. My wife Jean and our sons Josh and Ethan are here today. They are my reason for being, and Jean, she keeps me—helps me keep my feet on the ground. And she and the boys are my daily reminder that home is on the Fox River and not the Potomac River. To Jean, Josh and Ethan, thank you for everything, and I love you.

As a teacher I explained the story of America year after year, and I soon came to realize that it was a story, but a story that keeps changing, for we Americans are restless people, and we like to tackle and solve problems. And we are constantly renewing our nation, experimenting and creating new ways of doing things. And I like to work against the backdrop of American basics—freedom, liberty, responsibility and opportunity. You can count on me to be a workhorse.

My experience as a football and wrestling coach taught me some other lessons that apply here. A good coach knows when to step back and let others shine in the spotlight.

President [Ronald] Reagan for years had a plaque in his office that said it all: "There is no limit to what can be accomplished if you don't mind who gets the credit." A good coach doesn't rely on only a few star players, and everyone on the squad has something to offer. And you never get to the finals without a well-rounded team, and above all, a coach worth his salt will instill in his team a sense of fair play, camaraderie, respect for the game and for the opposition. Without those, victory is hollow and defeat represents opportunities lost. I found that to be true around here too.

So where do we go from here? Some media pundits say that we'll have two years of stalemate because the Republican majority is too small. And some say that the White House, bent on revenge, will not give us a moment's peace. And some say the minority in this House will prevent passage of serious legislation so that they can later claim this was a do-nothing Congress. Washington is a town of rumors and guesses and speculation. So none of this comes as a surprise. But none of it needs to come true—that is, if we really respect the voters that sent us here.

To my Republican colleagues, I say it's time to put forward the major elements of our legislative program. We will succeed or fail depending upon how sensible a program we offer. And to my Democratic colleagues, I will say I will meet you halfway—maybe more so on occasion. But cooperation is a two-way street, and I expect you to meet me halfway, too.

The president and a number of Democrats here in the House have been saying it's time to address several issues head-on. I'll buy that. But I think we should agree that stalemate is not an option; solutions are.

And to all my colleagues I say, we must get our job done, and done now. And we have an obligation to pass all the appropriations bills by this summer, and we will not leave this chamber until we do.

I intend to be a good listener, but I want to hear ideas and the debate that flows from them. And I will have a low tolerance for campaign speeches masquerading as debate, whatever the source.

Our country faces four big challenges which we must address. And not next month or next year or the year after that, but now. And each challenge involves an element of our security. And first is retirement and health security.

Both our Social Security and Medicare programs will run into brick walls in a few years if we don't do something about them now. And we must make sure that Social Security is there for those who depend on it and those who expect to. We also must consider options for younger workers, so that they can look forward to an even brighter retirement.

Nearly a year ago, President Clinton came here to give his State of the Union address. He called for reform of Social Security. This year I invite him to return to give us his reform plan. And he has my assurance that it will be taken seriously.

Second, we must ensure a secure future for America's children by insisting that every child has a good school and a safe, drug-free environment. In my 16 years as a teacher I learned that most of the decisions having to do with education are best left to the people closest to the situation—parents, teachers, school board members. What should the federal government's role be? It should be to see that as many education dollars go directly to the classroom where they will do the most good.

And the next is economic security. In the early '80s we adopted policies that lay the foundations for long-term growth. And except for one brief period, that growth has continued ever since. And we want our economy to keep on growing. Well, toward that end it's time for us in Congress to put a microscope to the ways that government takes money from our fellow citizens and how it spends it.

There is a culture here in Washington that has grown unchallenged for too long. It combines three notions. One is that government has prior claim to the earnings of all Americans, as if they work for the government and not the other way around. Another notion is that a government program once it's begun will never end. And a third notion is that every program must grow each passing year. Well, to borrow a musical line, it just ain't necessarily so—at least it won't be as long as I am around here and have something to say about it.

We must measure every dollar we spend by this criterion: Is it really necessary? This is important. For most Americans money doesn't come easy. When I was a kid, to make ends meet my dad had a feed business, and he worked nights in a restaurant. My mom raised chickens and sold the eggs. And I still remember when tax time came around, our family really felt it. What we need is a leaner, more efficient government, along with tax policies that spur and sustain growth by giving tax relief to all working Americans.

And finally there's the challenge of America's security in a world of danger and uncertainty. Without it, other elements of our security won't be possible. And we no longer worry about Soviet nuclear bombs raining down on us. Today there are different worries: the sudden violence of a terrorist bomb, the silent threat of biological weapons, or the rogue state that aims a deadly missile at one of our cities. We need a defense capability that matches these turn-of-the-century threats. And we have asked the men and women of our armed forces to take on assignments in many corners of the earth, yet we have not given them the best equipment or preparation that they need to match those assignments. That must be corrected.

These are not Democratic or Republican issues. They are American issues. We should be able to reach agreement quickly on the goals. And, yes, we are going to argue about the means. But if we are in earnest about our responsibilities, we will find common ground to get the job done. In the process we will build the people's faith in this great United States Congress.

As a classroom teacher and a coach I learned the value of brevity. I learned that it's work, not talk, that wins championships. In closing, I want you to know just how proud I am to be chosen to be your Speaker. And there's a big job ahead for all of us. And so I ask that God bless this House as we move forward together.

Thank you very much.

Controversy swirled about fund-raising tactics used to fund re-election campaigns during the period, particularly the activities of Vice President Al Gore in the run-up to the 1996 presidential elections. Republican charges of improper and possible illegal activities dogged Gore throughout his last four years as vice president and as the Democratic presidential nominee in 2000. *(Story p. 807)*

Gore Discusses Fund-Raising Activities

Following is a transcript of a March 3, 1997, news conference in which Vice President Al Gore discussed his role in Democratic fund-raising:

Gore: Good afternoon. Thank you all for coming. Mike was out here a little bit earlier and I noticed you had a number of questions for him about my role in the campaign, so I thought it would be a good idea for me to come down and answer your questions.

I want to make a short opening statement, and then I'll be happy to take your questions.

First of all, I want to spell out the facts of my role in the campaign. First of all, to state the obvious, I was a candidate for reelection in the campaign. I worked very hard for the reelection of President Clinton and myself. I'm very proud that I was able to be effective in helping to reelect President Clinton. And I was very proud that I was able to also in—as part of that effort—to help raise campaign funds.

Everything that I did I understood to be lawful. I attended campaign—traditional campaign fund-raising events as a principal speaker in many locations all around the country. The vast majority of the campaign funds that I've been given credit for raising came in that form.

I also made telephone calls to ask people to host events and to ask people to make lawful contributions to the campaign.

On a few occasions, I made some telephone calls from my office in the White House using a DNC [Democratic National Committee] credit card. I was advised there was nothing wrong with that practice.

The Hatch Act has a specific provision saying that, while federal employees are prohibited from requesting campaign contributions, the president and the vice president are not covered by that act because, obviously, we are candidates.

The separate question of whether or not campaign contributions can be asked for from somebody who is in a federal office or in a room that is used for official business is part of a law that was intended to prohibit putting pressure on federal employees and soliciting from federal employees.

I've never solicited a contribution from any federal employee, nor would I. Nor did I ever ask for a campaign contribution from anyone who was in a government office or on federal property.

Now all of the charges related to telephone calls were made to the Democratic National Committee. There were a few occasions in which I made such calls. The first was in December of 1995. As we continue our review of this, we have found the first session in December of 1995. There were a few other sessions during which I made telephone calls in the spring of 1996.

My counsel—Charles Burson is my counsel here—my counsel advises me that there is no controlling legal authority or case that says that there was any violation of law whatsoever in the manner in which I asked people to contribute to our reelection campaign.

I have decided to adopt a policy of not making any such calls ever again, notwithstanding the fact that they are charged to the Democratic National Committee as a matter of policy. We're continuing our review of this matter and I think the entire episode constitutes further reasons why there should be campaign finance reform.

The president and I strongly support campaign finance reform, and we hope it is adopted.

Now . . . Helen?

Question: *. . . are you saying that there—that you never did any fund-raising from a government office or building or . . .*

Gore: I never asked for a campaign contribution from anyone who was in a government office. I never did anything that I thought was wrong.

If there had been a shred of doubt in my mind that anything I did was a violation of law, I assure you I would not have done that. And my counsel advises me, let me repeat, that there is no controlling legal authority that says that any of these activities violated any law.

Question: *Mr. Vice President, but given the fact that you now have changed your policy, I'm sure you can understand the appearance, whether or not it was technically legal, the appearance wasn't very good, and that one of these people you apparently solicited told Bob Woodward and The* Washington Post *that it amounted to, in his opinion, at least, a shakedown—that when you were soliciting funds from him, given his nature of his business, you were shaking him down.*

Gore: Well, I cannot explain to you what some anonymous source wants to say. I can tell you this, that I never, ever said or did anything that would have given rise to a feeling like that on the part of someone who was asked to support our campaign. I never did that, and I never would do that.

Question: *There's a memo from the White House counsel written in 1995 that very simply says, no solicitation can be made from the White House—no phone calls, no mail. How can you say that that was OK for you to do it?*

Gore: That memo, authored by former White House Counsel Ab Mikva, was addressed to White House employees other than the president and vice president. All White House employees, just like all other federal employees, are prohibited from asking for campaign contributions. There is an exemption for the president and vice president.

But that particular memo was not designed to address either the president or the vice president, because there is a different section of law that applies to the president and vice president as candidates, as opposed to the White House staff.

Question: *So you're saying that you were exempt from any proscriptions, from raising money right there in the White House. That was OK for you to do?*

Gore: That particular—No, no. No, no. I'd never ask anyone in the White House for a campaign contribution.

Question: *You sat in the White House. You called people and asked them for contributions.*

Gore: Well, let me—I stated the fax situation earlier.

And I described it in some detail. I never have asked a federal employee for a contribution, never would, never will. I have never asked anyone in the White House or on federal property for a campaign contribution.

Now—and all calls that I made were charged to the Democratic National Committee. I was advised there was nothing wrong with that. My counsel tells me there is no controlling legal authority that says was any violation of any law. Yes?

Question: *Mr. Vice President, excuse me, there was a little discrepancy in the Buddhist temple. Can you clear that up? I mean, because certain statements were made, denied, and then actually accepted.*

Gore: Well, that's a separate matter and I've dealt with it, and I don't really want to go back into that now.

We can come back to it at the end of this if you want to.

Question: *You said that there were only a few instances where you did . . .*

Gore: Correct.

Question: *. . . ask people for money. Could you say why in those instances you did? Were you told that you would make the difference? Or was it for a particular sum? Did someone in the campaign say, "We need you to close this"? Can you explain the circumstances under which you . . .*

Gore: I participated in meetings of our top campaign advisers where it became clear that, in order to achieve the president's goals of getting a balanced budget, passing these measures to protect Medicare and Medicaid and education and the environment and so forth, that the DNC needed a larger budget to put advertisements on television.

And I volunteered to raise—to help in the effort to raise money for the Democratic National Committee.

Question: *Mr. Vice President, I'm confused on one point. I've heard what you said. And as picayune as it may seem, there seems to be conflict over whether or not you're saying the law allows you, as vice president, to sit in your office and to use a federal phone credit card or not, to make a call to someone outside. You're saying that the law does allow you to be in, basically, federal property and use federal property, although it's being reimbursed to some degree, that that—that is OK?*

Gore: As a matter of policy, I decided that I'm not going to do that. As a matter of law, there is no—according to my counsel—there is no controlling legal authority, no case ever brought, ever decided that says that is a violation of law.

The intent of the statute—let me repeat—was to prevent a supervisor from talking to a federal employee and saying, "We want you to contribute money." I've never done that.

Secondly, I have never asked anyone who was on federal property or in the White House for a campaign contribution.

Question: *But you're . . .*

Gore: A follow-up here and then I'll go to you.

Question: *But if you're in the clear on it, then why shift policy, if you're in the clear on that?*

Gore: Well, because it's aroused a great deal of concern and comment, and it's not—it's not something that I want to continue if it's going to raise this kind of concern.

Question: *Just to follow up on that, are you basically then admitting that you made a mistake or made mistakes?*

Gore: No.

What I am saying—I mean implicit in the decision to change the policy and say I'm not going to make such calls again is an acknowledgment that if—you know—if I had realized in advance that this would cause such concern, then I wouldn't have done it in the first place.

But let me repeat—I understood what I did to be legal and appropriate. I felt like I was doing the right thing. I am proud that I was able to do a lot of effective work to help reelect Bill Clinton and keep this country moving in the right direction.

I'll spare you the rhetoric about the results of what we have been able to do, but I want you to know that I'm very proud to be a part of that effort.

Question: *What is your position on the—on the elimination of soft money from campaigns?*

Gore: Oh, I favor—I favor the so-called McCain-Feingold bill which would do that. The president and I strongly favor campaign finance reform legislation that would accomplish that objective, and we hope that it will pass.

Question: *Vice President Gore, there has been a lot written about your impregnable reputation for a—for being above the fray and for being ethically someone who really hasn't been questioned on these issues. Does this shatter that, and does it hurt you for the year 2000?*

Gore: Well, on the second part of it, I'm—I've told you before that I'm not focused on a political campaign in the future. I'm focused on doing everything I can to help this president be the best president he's capable of being and to move this country in the right direction. And he's doing a terrific job. I'm very proud to be a part of his team.

On the first part of the question, I'll say again, I never did anything that I felt was wrong, much less illegal. And again, I am advised that there is no controlling legal authority that says this was in violation of law.

Question: *Vice President Gore, did you feel any discomfort at all as you called these individuals and asked them for donations? And did you ask for specific amounts of money when you spoke with them?*

Gore: Yes, I did. On the first part of your question—you know, I served eight years in the House and eight years in the Senate, and I was used to calling people to ask them to help with the campaign.

I introduced legislation some years ago to call for complete public financing of campaigns and to prevent the contributions that are now legal, over and above, the public financing of the presidential campaigns.

The legislation that I sponsored and supported did not have enough support to pass. I still favor that legislation, but it didn't pass. There's probably even less support for it now.

So we have a system of campaign finance here in the United States that says candidates who are running for office ought to go out and ask people to contribute to their campaigns and to have fundraisers. And so I was used to doing that as a candidate for the House, as a candidate for the Senate.

I would be surprised if all—if all 100 members of the United States Senate and all 435—well, there are probably some House members who don't, because they have safe seats and don't raise any money. But I would be surprised if all senators and most all House members did not, as a matter of routine, call people up and ask them to hold fundraisers and ask them to help raise money.

That is the standard way that we finance campaigns. So I was used to that. Does it make one uncomfortable to do that? Why, sure. But if you believe in what you're doing, in balancing the budget and moving this country forward, and you know that the only way you can be successful in achieving the agenda you believe is right for the country, is to play by the rules as they exist and raise campaign funds, then you do that.

And typically, what happens to members of the House and Senate is they'll put it off and put it off until the election year comes and then the people helping them will say, you've got to devote time to raise money. And they say, oh, I hate this, I don't want to do it. And then they get into it and they start making the calls and they raise the money.

I'm exactly the same way.

Question: *Mr. Vice President, if there's nothing coy about the year 2000, anyone who expects to run for president in 2000 has to start very* *early thinking about money. Predecessors of yours have started PACs, political action committees or fund-raising arms. What are you going to do between now and 19...*

Gore: I've made no decision about that whatsoever. And I really am focused on my work as vice president and doing everything I can to help this president.

If the time comes when I become a candidate, I'll be glad to answer such questions and talk about such matters at that time. But we're not there yet.

Question: *So you're going to raise no money at all? You will raise no money at all for a political action committee or anything else that would...*

Gore: I have not set up a political action committee and I've made no decision to do so. Whether I will in the future or not, I really haven't decided.

Question: *Mr. Vice President—something that I'm just a little confused about. You said there was only just a handful of incidents when you used the White House.*

Gore: Correct.

Question: *So we can assume the preponderance of calls were made from the DNC or your residence? Is that...*

Gore: No, no, there were a handful of incidents, period.

Question: *Oh, these are the only incidents that you raised money, period.*

Gore: That's correct. I went to the DNC on one occasion in, I believe, October of 1994 to help raise money for the party. You know, the impression was created that I went out and raised all this money and then they talked about me calling people on the telephone, and the two things were put together to give the impression that I raised all this money by calling people on the telephone.

Question: *So you're saying...*

Gore: That is not an accurate impression. Most all of the money for the campaign that I'm given credit for raising came in the form of traditional events where I was the main speaker at fund-raising events.

There were a few occasions, as I said at the very outset, where I did make telephone calls and I have described those.

But that was the minor part of what I did in raising funds.

Question: *... solicitor-in-chief. Could we get clear on this?...*

Gore: I never heard such a phrase. I never heard such a phrase until I read it in the paper.

Question: *Mr. Vice President, you said that the president and vice president were covered under the Hatch Act and that part—in that way, you two were different.*

Gore: Yes.

Question: *But the other part of the statute seems to set up federal buildings as a sanctuary from fund-raising. Were you unaware of that part of the statute?*

Gore: No, I was not. And let me repeat—I never asked for a contribution from anyone who was in a federal building. And all of the calls that I made were charged to the DNC. I was advised that was proper. In reviewing the matter, my counsel advises me there's no case. There's no controlling legal authority that says that violated the law.

Question: *Well, then the question—is it possible that the absence of case law on this means that reasonable people could differ about what parts of the statute mean, applied to different activities in which you may have taken part at different times?*

Gore: Well, that's not a question for me to determine. I'm advised that it is—that there is no case or no controlling legal authority that says it is a violation of the law. And I never did anything that I felt was wrong, much less a violation of the law.

Question: *Mr. Vice President, also, did you know about—did the president know about any of these calls you made? Did you discuss it? Did he ever ask you to make any calls? Was he aware of your...*

Gore: No, he never asked me to make calls. I'm sure that he was aware that I was helping to raise funds for the campaign. It's—well, I won't comment on what other vice presidents have or have not done.

But I don't think it is surprising to people that when a president and vice president are running for reelection that the vice president helps to raise funds for the campaign.

And anybody who wants to create the impression that that is something brand new in American politics, I would invite to take another look at that question.

Question: *Mr. Vice President, when the Clinton-Gore election agreed to take public funds, it also agreed to spending caps. And yet you're referring to the DNC's soft money operation as "our campaign." Doesn't this operation show that, as a practical matter, there was no distinction between the Clinton-Gore campaign and the DNC's soft money operation?*

Gore: No, there was a clear distinction. There was a separate message. There were separate legal requirements. It was—it was separate in most all respects.

Now, the fact that the agenda supported by the Democratic National Committee's advertisements was similar to and overlapping with the agenda that was being pressed by the incumbent Democratic president should not be surprising.

And again, it's hardly unique in American political history for an incumbent president to be supported by the political party of which he is the titular head. That is commonplace.

Question: *Mr. Vice President, was there any particular urgency to the calls the few occasions that you did make calls from the White House. Were they—could not have waited until you were in a setting away from your office in the White House?*

Gore: Well, first of all, as I said before, I was advised there was nothing wrong with it.

So the question did not occur in that form. So there was not a sense of urgency in that sense.

We felt, as we were preparing for our campaign, a general sense that, you know, we wanted to make sure that we had the ability to compete.

Let me remind you that the—our opponents raised over all, I believe, what, 40 percent more than we did? And so we knew that they had a big head start and that they had a huge collection of resources, so we felt that—we felt the need to move on with it.

Question: *To follow up on that, you also could have made these very same calls from somewhere else?*

Gore: One more, and then I'm going to have to go.

Question: *You have said that this is not unique in American politics, but judging from the comments of your predecessors, it would appear that direct solicitation by the vice president had not been done in the past. Were you aware of that?*

Gore: No.

Question: *And also the fact that the president himself refused to make these phone calls. Were you aware of that, and why did you think perhaps a different sort of standard applied to you?*

Gore: No, I was not aware of the latter. On the first part of your question, what I said was not unique was the practice of incumbent vice presidents running for reelection, going out to help raise money for the campaign and for the political party of which they were a part.

And I will leave it to you all to determine whether that's totally unique or not. I'm not—I don't want to get into what any other vice president has done. I'm proud of what I did.

I do not feel like I did anything wrong, much less illegal. I—I am proud to have done everything I possibly could to help support the reelection of this president and to help move his agenda forward. It is helping this country.

Our economy is roaring. Inflation is low. Crime is down. Investments in education and protecting the environment are going up.

Social trends are favorable. Economic trends are favorable. We are moving in the right direction.

Let me tell you. One of the principal reasons we are is that we have a president and a group of people who are proud to support his efforts, who are willing to go out there every day and fight hard, sometimes against powerful odds, to make sure that we pass this agenda and move forward. And I am very proud to continue to play a role in that.

Thank you very much.

Attorney General Rejects Call for Counsel

Following is the full text of Attorney General Janet Reno's letter, released April 14, 1997, to Senate Judiciary Committee Chairman Orrin G. Hatch, R-Utah, explaining her office's decision not to appoint an independent counsel to investigate White House and Democratic campaign fund-raising:

Dear Mr. Chairman:

On March 13, 1997, you and nine other majority party members of the Committee on the Judiciary of the United States Senate wrote to me requesting the appointment of an independent counsel to investigate possible fundraising violations in connection with the 1996 campaign. You made that request pursuant to a provision of the Independent Counsel Act, 28 U.S.C. Section 592(g)(1), which provides that "a majority of majority party members (of the Committee on the Judiciary) . . . may request in writing that the Attorney General apply for the appointment of an independent counsel." The act requires me to respond within 30 days, setting forth the reasons for my decision on each of the matters with respect to which your request is made. 28 U.S.C. Section 592(g)(2).

I am writing to inform you that I have not initiated a "preliminary investigation" (as that term is defined in the Independent Counsel Act) of any of the matters mentioned in your letter. Rather, as you know, matters relating to campaign financing in the 1996 Federal elections have been under active investigation since November by a task force of career Justice Department prosecutors and Federal Bureau of Investigation [FBI] agents. This task force is pursuing the investigation vigorously and diligently, and it will continue to do so. I can assure you that I have given your views and your arguments careful thought, but at this time, I am unable to agree, based on the facts and the law, that an independent counsel should be appointed to handle this investigation.

1. THE INDEPENDENT COUNSEL ACT

In order to explain my reasons, I would like to outline briefly the relevant provisions of the Independent Counsel Act. The Act can be invoked in two circumstances that are relevant here:

First, if there are sufficient allegations (as further described below) of criminal activity by a covered person, defined as the President and Vice President, cabinet officers, certain other enumerated high Federal officials, or certain specified officers of the President's election campaign (not party officials), see 28 U.S.C. Section 591(b), I must seek appointment of an independent counsel.

Second, if there are sufficient allegations of criminal activity by a person other than a covered person, and I determine that "an investigation or prosecution of (that) person by the Department of Justice may result in a personal, financial or political conflict of interest," see 28 U.S.C. Section 591(c)(1), I may seek appointment of an independent counsel.

In either case, I must follow a two-step process to determine whether the allegations are sufficient. First I must determine whether the allegations are sufficiently specific and credible to constitute grounds to investigate whether an individual may have violated Federal criminal law. 28 U.S.C. Section 591(d). If so, the Department commences a "preliminary investigation" for up to 90 days (which can be extended an additional 60 days upon a showing of good cause). 28 U.S.C. Section 592(a). If, at the conclusion of this "preliminary investigation," I determine further investigation of the matters is warranted, I must seek an independent counsel.

Certain important features of the Act are critical to my decision in this case:

First, the Act sets forth the only circumstances in which I may seek an independent counsel pursuant to its provisions. I may not invoke its procedures unless the statutory requirements are met.

Second, the Act does not permit or require me to commence a preliminary investigation unless there is specific and credible evidence that a crime may have been committed. In your letter, you suggest that it is not the responsibility of the Department of Justice to determine whether a particular set of facts suggests a potential Federal crime, but that such legal determinations should be left to an independent counsel. I do not agree. Under the Independent Counsel Act, it is the Department's obligation to determine in the first instance whether particular conduct potentially falls within the scope of a particular criminal statute such that criminal investigation is warranted. If it is our conclusion that the alleged conduct is not criminal, then there is no basis for appointment of an independent counsel, because there would be no specific and credible allegation of a violation of criminal law. See 28 U.S.C. Section 592(a)(1).

Third, there is an important difference between the mandatory and discretionary provisions of the Act. Once I have received specific and credible allegations of criminal conduct by a covered person, I must commence a preliminary investigation and, if further investigation is warranted at the end of the preliminary investigation, seek appointment of an independent counsel. If, on the other hand, I receive specific and credible evidence that a person not covered by the mandatory provisions of the Act has committed a crime, and I determine that a conflict of interest exists with respect to the investigation of that person, I may but need not commence a preliminary investigation pursuant to the provisions of the Act. This provision gives me the flexibility to decide whether, overall, the national interest would be best served by appointment of an independent counsel in such a case, or whether it would be better for the Department of Justice to continue a vigorous investigation of the matter.

Fourth, even this discretionary provision is not available unless I find a conflict of interest of the sort contemplated by the Act. The Congress has made it very clear that this provision should be invoked only in certain narrow circumstances. Under the Act, I must conclude that there is a potential for an actual conflict of interest, rather than merely an appearance of a conflict of interest. The Congress expressly adopted this higher standard to ensure that the provision would not be invoked unnecessarily. See 128 Cong. Rec. H 9507 (daily ed. Dec. 13, 1982) (statement of Rep. Hall.) Moreover, I must find that there is a potential for such an actual conflict with respect to the investigation of a particular person, not merely with respect to the overall matter. Indeed, when the Act was reauthorized in 1994, Congress considered a proposal for a more flexible standard for invoking the discretionary clause, which would have permitted its use to refer any "matter" to an Independent Counsel when the purposes of the Act would be served. Congress rejected this suggestion, explaining that such a standard would "substantially lower the threshold for use of the general discretionary provision." H.R. Conf. Rep. No. 511, 103rd Cong., 2nd Sess. 9 (1994).

2. COVERED PERSONS: THE MANDATORY PROVISIONS OF THE ACT.

Let me now turn to the specific allegations in your letter. You assert that there are "new questions of possible wrongdoing by senior White House officials themselves," and you identify a number of particular types of conduct in support of this claim. While all of the specific issues you mention are under review or active investigation by the task force, at this time we have no specific, credible evidence that any covered White House official may have committed a Federal crime in respect to any of these issues. Nevertheless, I will discuss separately each area that you raise.

First, you suggest that "federal officials may have illegally solicited and/or received contributions on federal property." The conduct you describe could be a violation of 18 U.S.C. Section 607. We are aware of a number of allegations of this sort; all are being evaluated, and where appropriate, investigations have been commenced. The Department takes allegations of political fundraising by Federal employees on Federal property seriously, and in appropriate cases would not hesitate to prosecute such matters. Indeed, the Public Integrity Section, which is overseeing the work of the campaign financing task force, recently obtained a number of guilty pleas from individuals who were soliciting and accepting political contributions within the Department of Agriculture.

The analysis of a potential section 607 violation is a fact-specific inquiry. A number of different factors must be considered when reviewing allegations that this law may have been violated:

First, the law specifically applies only to contributions as technically defined by the Federal Election Campaign Act (FECA) funds commonly referred to as "hard money." The statute originally applied broadly to any political fundraising, but in 1979, over the objection of the Department of Justice, Congress narrowed the scope of section 607 to render it applicable only to FECA contributions. Before concluding that section 607 may have been violated, we must have evidence that a particular solicitation involved a "contribution" within the definition of the FECA.

Second, there are private areas of the White House that, as a general rule, fall outside the scope of the statute, because of the statutory requirement that the particular solicitation occur in an area "occupied in the discharge of official duties." 3 Op. Off. Legal Counsel 31 (1979). The distinction recognizes that while the Federal Government provides a residence to the president, similar to the housing that it might provide to foreign service officers, this residence is still the personal home of an individual within which restrictions that might validly apply to the Federal workplace should not be imposed. Before we can conclude that section 607 may have been violated, we must have evidence that fundraising took place in locations covered by the provisions of the statute.

With respect to coordinated media advertisements by political parties (an area that has received much attention of late), the proper characterization of a particular expenditure depends not on the degree of coordination, but rather on the content of the message. Indeed, just last year the FEC [Federal Election Commission] and the Department of Justice took this position in a brief filed before the Supreme Court, in a case decided on other grounds. See generally, Brief for the Respondent, *Colorado Republican Federal Campaign Committee v. FEC*, (S. Ct. No. 95-489) at 2-3, 18 n.15, 23-24. In this connection, the FEC has concluded that party media advertisements that focus on "national legislative activity" and that do not contain an "electioneering message" may be financed, in part, using "soft" money, i.e., money that does not comply with FECA's contribution limits. FEC Advisory Op. 1995-25, 2 Fed. Elec. Camp. Fin. Guide (CCH) Paragraph 6162, at 12, 109-12,110 (August 24, 1995); FEC Advisory Op. 1985-14, 2 Fed. Elec. Camp. Fin. Guide (CCH) Paragraph 5819, at 11,185-11,186 (May 30, 1985). Moreover, such advertisements are not subject to any applicable limitations on coordinated expenditures by the party on behalf of its candidates. AO 1985-14 at 11-185-11,186.

We recognize that there are allegations that both presidential candidates and both national political parties engaged in a concerted effort to take full advantage of every funding option available to them under the law, to craft advertisements that took advantage of the lesser regulation quantities of soft political funding to finance these ventures. However, at the present time, we lack specific and credible evidence suggesting that these activities violated the FECA. Moreover, even assuming that, after a thorough investigation, the FEC were to conclude that regulatory violations occurred, we presently lack specific and credible evidence suggesting that any covered person participated in any such violations.

3. CONFLICT OF INTEREST: THE DISCRETIONARY PROVISIONS OF THE ACT.

In urging me to conclude that the investigation poses the type of potential conflict of interest contemplated by the Act, you rely heavily on my testimony before the Senate Committee on Government Affairs in 1993 in support of reauthorization of the Independent Counsel Act. I stand by those views and continue to support the overall concept underlying the Act. My decisions pursuant to the Act have been, I believe, fully consistent with those views.

The remarks you quote from my testimony should be interpreted within the context of the statutory language I was discussing. When, for example, I referred to the need for the Act to deal with the inherent conflict of interest when the Department of Justice investigates "high-level Executive Branch officials," I was referring to persons covered under the mandatory provisions of the Act. With respect to the conflict of interest provision, my testimony expressed the conviction that the Act "would in no way pre-empt this Department's authority to investigate public corruption," and that the Department was clearly capable of "vigorous investigation of wrongdoing by public officials, whatever allegiance or stripes they may wear. I will vigorously defend and continue this tradition." While I endorsed the concept of the discretionary clause to deal with unforeseeable situations, I strongly emphasized that "it is part of the Attorney General's job to make difficult decisions in tough cases. I have no intention of abdicating that responsibility."

These principles continue to guide my decision making today.

These are times when reliance on the discretionary clause is appropriate, and indeed, as you point out, I have done so myself on a few occasions. However, in each of those cases, I considered the particular factual context in which the allegations against those persons arose and the history of the matter. Moreover, even after finding the existence of a potential conflict, I must consider whether under all the circumstances discretionary appointment of an independent counsel is appropriate. In each case, therefore, the final decision has been an exercise of my discretion, as provided for under the act.

I have undertaken the same examination here. Based on the facts as we know them now, I have not concluded that any conflict of interest would ensue from our vigorous and thorough investigation of the allegations contained in your letter.

Your letter relies upon press reports, certain documents and various public statements which you assert demonstrate that "officials at the highest level of the White House were involved in formulating, coordinating and implementing the Democratic National Committee's (DNC's) Fundraising efforts for the 1996 presidential campaign." You suggest that a thorough investigation of "fundraising improprieties" will therefore necessarily include an inquiry into the "knowledge and/or complicity of very senior White House officials," and that the Department of Justice would therefore have a conflict of interest investigating these allegations.

To the extent that "improprieties" comprise crimes, they are being thoroughly investigated by the agents and prosecutors assigned to the task force. Should that investigation develop at any time specific and credible evidence that any covered person may have committed a crime, the Act will be triggered, and I will fulfill my responsibilities under the Act. In addition, should that investigation develop specific and credible evidence that a crime may have been committed by a "very senior" White House official who is not covered by the Act, I will decide whether investigation of that person by the Department might result in a conflict of interest, and, if so, whether the discretionary clause should be invoked. Until then, however, the mere fact that employees of the White House and the DNC worked closely together in the course of President Clinton's re-election campaign does not warrant appointment of an independent counsel. As I have stated above, the Department has a long history of investigating allegations of criminal activity by high-ranking Government officials without fear or favor, and will do so in this case.

I also do not accept the suggestion that there will be widespread public distrust of the actions and conclusions of the Department if it continues to investigate this matter, creating a conflict of interest warranting the appointment of an independent counsel. First, unless I find that the investigation of a particular person against whom specific and credible allegations have been made would pose a conflict, I have no authority to utilize the procedures of the Act. Moreover, I have confidence that the career professionals in the Department will investigate this matter in a fashion that will satisfy the American people that justice has been done.

Finally, even were I to determine that a conflict of interest of the sort contemplated by the statute exists in this case, and as noted above I do not find such a conflict at this time, there would be a number of weighty considerations that I would have to consider in determining whether to exercise my discretion to seek an independent counsel at this time. Because invocation of the conflict of interest provision is discretionary, it would still be my responsibility in that circumstance to weigh all the factors and determine whether appointment of an independent counsel would best serve the national interest. If in the future this investigation reveals evidence indicating that a conflict of interest exists, these factors will continue to weigh heavily in my evaluation of whether or not to invoke the discretionary provisions of the Act.

I assure you, once again, that allegations of violations of Federal criminal law with respect to campaign financing in the course of the 1996 Federal elections will be thoroughly investigated and, if appropriate, prosecuted. At this point it appears to me that that task should be performed by the Department of Justice and its career investigators

and prosecutors. I want to emphasize, however, that the task force continues to receive new information (much has been discovered even since I received your letter), and I will continue to monitor the investigation closely in light of my responsibilities under the Independent Counsel Act. Should future developments make it appropriate to invoke the procedures of the Act, I will do so without hesitation.

Sincerely,

Janet Reno

Presidential Nominating Conventions, 1996

1996 REPUBLICAN PLATFORM

The Republican Party on Aug. 12–15, 1996, showcased GOP presidential nominee Bob Dole, the former Senate majority leader from Kansas, and his vice-presidential selection, former New York representative Jack F. Kemp, at the party's nominating convention in San Diego, California. Seeking to energize loyalists while also expanding its base, the convention's carefully orchestrated moments melded the twin themes of compassion and conservatism.

Following are excerpts from the Republican platform of 1996.

Tax Relief. American families are suffering from the twin burdens of stagnant incomes and near-record taxes. . . . American families deserve better. They should be allowed to keep more of their hard-earned money so they can spend on their priorities. . . .

In response to this unprecedented burden confronting America, we support an across-the-board, 15-percent tax cut to marginal tax rates. . . . To remove impediments to job creation and economic growth, we support reducing the top tax rate on capital gains by 50 percent. . . . The income tax on Social Security benefits . . . must be repealed. . . .

To protect the American people from those who would undo their forthcoming victory over big government, we support legislation requiring a super-majority vote in both houses of Congress to raise taxes. . . .

Balancing the Budget. . . . Republicans support a Balanced Budget Amendment to the Constitution, phased in over a short period and with appropriate safeguards for national emergencies. . . .

Homeownership. . . . We support transforming public housing into private housing, converting low-income families into proud homeowners. Resident management of public housing is a first step toward that goal, which includes eliminating the Department of Housing and Urban Development (HUD). HUD's core functions will be turned over to the states. . . .

Changing Washington from the Ground Up. . . . We support elimination of the Departments of Commerce, Housing and Urban Development, Education, and Energy, and the elimination, defunding or privatization of agencies which are obsolete, redundant, of limited value, or too regional in focus. Examples of agencies . . . .are the National Endowment for the Arts, the National Endowment for the Humanities, the Corporation for Public Broadcasting and the Legal Services Corporation. . . .

Government Reform. . . . True reform is indeed needed: ending taxpayer subsidies for campaigns, strengthening party structures to guard against rogue operations, requiring full and immediate disclosure of all contributions, and cracking down on the indirect support, or "soft money," by which special interest groups underwrite their favored candidates. . . .

Regulatory Reform. . . . A Republican administration will require periodic review of existing regulations to ensure they are effective and do away with obsolete and conflicting rules. We will encourage civil servants to find ways to reduce regulatory burdens on the public and will require federal agencies to disclose the costs of new regulations on individuals and small businesses. . . . We will require agencies to conduct cost-benefit analyses of their regulations. . . .

Restoring Justice to the Courts. . . . The federal judiciary, including the U.S. Supreme Court, has overstepped its authority under the Constitution. It has usurped the right of citizen legislators and popularly elected executives to make law by declaring duly enacted laws to be "unconstitutional" through the misapplication of the principle of judicial review. . . . A Republican president will ensure that a process is established to select for the federal judiciary nominees who understand that their task is first and foremost to be faithful to the Constitution and to the intent of those who framed it. . . .

The Nation's Capital. . . . We reaffirm the constitutional status of the District of Columbia as the seat of government of the United States and reject calls for statehood for the District. . . . We call for structural reform of the city's government and its education system. . . .

Upholding the Rights of All. . . . We oppose discrimination based on sex, race, age, creed, or national origin and will vigorously enforce anti-discrimination statutes. We reject the distortion of those laws to cover sexual preference, and we endorse the Defense of Marriage Act to prevent states from being forced to recognize same-sex unions. Because we believe rights inhere in individuals, not in groups, we will attain our nation's goal of equal rights without quotas or other forms of preferential treatment. . . .

The unborn child has a fundamental individual right to life which cannot be infringed. We support a human life amendment to the Constitution and we endorse legislation to make clear that the Fourteenth Amendment's protections apply to unborn children. Our purpose is to have legislative and judicial protection of that right against those who perform abortions. . . .

We applaud Bob Dole's commitment to revoke the Clinton executive orders concerning abortion and to sign into law an end to partial-birth abortions. . . .

We defend the **constitutional right to keep and bear arms**. . . .

A Sensible Immigration Policy. . . . Illegal aliens should not receive public benefits other than emergency aid, and those who become parents while illegally in the United States should not be qualified to claim benefits for their offspring. Legal immigrants should depend for assistance on their sponsors, who are legally responsible for their financial well-being, not the American taxpayers. . . .

From Many, One. . . . While we benefit from our differences, we must also strengthen the ties that bind us to one another. Foremost among those is the flag. Its deliberate desecration is not "free speech," but an assault against our history and our hopes. We support a constitutional amendment that will restore to the people, through their elected representatives, their right to safeguard Old Glory. . . .

We support the official recognition of English as the nation's common language. . . .

Improving Education. . . . The federal government has no constitutional authority to be involved in school curricula or to control jobs in the workplace. That is why we will abolish the Department of Education, end federal meddling in our schools and promote family choice at all levels of learning. . . .

We will continue to work for the return of voluntary prayer to our schools. . . .

Health Care. Our goal is to maintain the quality of America's health care—the best in the world, bar none—while making health care and health insurance more accessible and more affordable. . . .

We reaffirm our determination to protect Medicare. We will ensure a significant annual expansion in Medicare. That isn't "cutting Medicare." It's a projected average annual rate of growth of 7.1 percent a year—more than twice the rate of inflation—to ensure coverage for those who need it now and those who will need it in the future . . .

The Middle East. . . . We applaud the Republican Congress for enacting legislation to recognize Jerusalem as the undivided capital of Israel. A Republican administration will ensure that the U.S. Embassy is moved to Jerusalem by May 1999. . . .

The Men and Women of Defense. . . . We affirm that homosexuality is incompatible with military service. . . . We reaffirm our support for the exemption of women from ground combat units and are concerned about the current policy of involuntarily assigning women to combat or near-combat units. . . .

1996 DEMOCRATIC PLATFORM

Meeting in Chicago for the eleventh time in the party's history, the Democratic Party on August 26–29, 1996, jubilantly renominated President Bill Clinton and Vice President Al Gore. Democratic officials produced a convention designed to stir the viewing public's emotions. Speakers and videos highlighted the party's racial and ethnic diversity while drawing attention to Clinton's efforts to ease the burdens on middle-class families.

Following are excerpts from the Democratic platform of 1996.

Balancing the Budget. . . . In 1992, we promised to cut the deficit in half over four years. We did. Our 1993 economic plan cut spending by over a quarter trillion dollars in five years. . . . Now the Democratic Party is determined to finish the job and balance the budget. President Clinton has put forward a plan to balance the budget by 2002 while living up to our commitments to our elderly and our children and maintaining strong economic growth. . . . Today's Democratic Party believes we have a duty to care for our parents, so they can live their lives in dignity. That duty includes securing Medicare and Medicaid, finding savings without reducing quality or benefits, and protecting Social Security for future generations. . . .

Tax Relief. . . . Today's Democratic Party is committed to targeted tax cuts that help working Americans invest in their future, and we insist that any tax cuts are completely paid for, because we are determined to balance the budget. . . .

Foreign Trade. We believe that if we want the American economy to continue strong growth, we must continue to expand trade, and not retreat from the world. . . . We must continue to work to lower foreign trade barriers. . . .

Education. . . . In the next four years, we must do even more to make sure America has the best public schools on earth. . . . We must hold students, teachers, and schools to the highest standards. Every child should be able to read by the end of the third grade. Students should be required to demonstrate competency and achievement for promotion or graduation. Teachers should be required to meet high standards for professional performance and be rewarded for the good jobs they do—and there should be a fair, timely, cost-effective process to remove those who do not measure up. . . . We should expand public school choice, but we should not take American tax dollars from public schools and give them to private schools. We should promote public charter schools that are held to the highest standards of accountability and access. . . .

Health Care. The Democratic Party is committed to ensuring that Americans have access to affordable, high-quality health care. . . . In the next four years, we must take further steps to ensure that Americans have access to quality, affordable health care. We should start by making sure that people get help paying premiums so they do not lose health care while they're looking for a new job. We support expanded coverage of home care, hospice, and community-based services, so the elderly and people with disabilities of all ages can live in their own communities and as independently as possible. We . . . believe health insurance coverage for mental health care is vitally important and we support parity for mental health care.

Retirement. . . . We want . . . to make sure people can carry their pensions with them when they change jobs, protect pensions even further, and expand the number of workers with pension coverage. Democrats created Social Security, we oppose efforts to dismantle it, and we will fight to save it. We must ensure that it is on firm financial footing well into the next century. . . .

Fighting Crime. . . . President Clinton beat back fierce Republican opposition . . . .to answer the call of America's police officers and pass the toughest Crime Bill in history. . . . And it is making a difference. In city after city and town after town, crime rates are finally coming down. . . . Any attempt to repeal the Brady Bill or assault weapons ban will be met with a veto. We must do everything we can to stand behind our police officers, and the first thing we should do is pass a ban on cop-killer bullets. . . .

Immigration. . . . We support a legal immigration policy that is pro-family, pro-work, pro-responsibility, and pro-citizenship, and we deplore those who blame immigrants for economic and social problems. . . . We cannot tolerate illegal immigration and we must stop it. . . .

We deplore those who use the need to stop illegal immigration as a pretext for discrimination. And we applaud the wisdom of Republicans . . . who oppose the mean-spirited and shortsighted effort of Republicans in Congress to bar the children of illegal immigrants from schools. . . .

Welfare Reform. . . . Over the past four years, President Clinton has dramatically transformed the welfare system. . . . Welfare rolls are finally coming down—there are 1.3 million fewer people on welfare today than there were when President Clinton took office in January 1993.

. . . . Thanks to President Clinton and the Democrats, the new welfare bill includes the health care and child care people need so they can go to work confident their children will be cared for. Thanks to President Clinton and the Democrats, the new welfare bill imposes time limits and real work requirements. . . . Thanks to President Clinton and the Democrats, the new welfare bill cracks down on deadbeat parents and requires minor mothers to live at home with their parents or with another responsible adult. . . .

We know the new bill passed by Congress is far from perfect— parts of it should be fixed because they go too far and have nothing to do with welfare reform. . . .

Abortion. The Democratic Party stands behind the right of every woman to choose, consistent with *Roe v. Wade,* and regardless of ability to pay. President Clinton took executive action to make sure that the right to make such decisions is protected for all Americans. Over the last four years, we have taken action to end the gag rule and ensure safety at family planning and women's health clinics. We believe it is a fundamental constitutional liberty that individual Americans— not government—can best take responsibility for making the most difficult and intensely personal decisions regarding reproduction. . . .

Political Reform. . . . The President and the Democratic Party support the bipartisan McCain-Feingold campaign finance reform bill. It will limit campaign spending, curb the influence of PACs and lobbyists, and end the soft money system. Perhaps most important of all, this bill provides free TV time for candidates, so they can talk directly to citizens about real issues and real ideas. . . . It is time to take the reins of democracy away from big money and put them back in the hands of the American people, where they belong. We applaud efforts by broadcasters and private citizens alike, to increase candidates' direct access to voters through free TV. . . .

The Middle East. . . . Jerusalem is the capital of Israel and should remain an undivided city accessible to people of all faiths. We are also committed to working with our Arab partners for peace to build a brighter, more secure and prosperous future for all the people of the Middle East. . . .

Protecting Our Environment. . . . We are committed to protecting the majestic legacy of our National Parks. . . . We will be good stewards of our old-growth forests, oppose new offshore oil drilling and mineral exploration and production in our nation's many environmentally critical areas, and protect our oceans from oil spills and the dumping of toxic and radioactive waste. . . .

Fighting Discrimination. Today's Democratic Party knows we must renew our efforts to stamp out discrimination and hatred of every kind, wherever and whenever we see it. . . . We believe everyone in America should learn English so they can fully share in our daily life, but we strongly oppose divisive efforts like English-only legislation. . . .

Religious Freedom. Today's Democratic Party understands that all Americans have a right to express their faith. . . . Americans have a right to express their love of God in public, and we applaud the President's work to ensure that children are not denied private religious expression in school. . . .

Presidential Nominating Conventions, 2000

2000 REPUBLICAN PLATFORM

Meeting July 31–August 3, 2000, in Philadelphia, the Republican Party made history of its own by naming George W. Bush, the son of a president, as the GOP standard-bearer for 2000. The proud father, former president George Bush, was among the many family members applauding the party's choice. Delegates hoped a victory by Texas governor Bush would give the nation its second father-son presidential pair. The first was Federalist John Adams (1797–1801) and Democrat John Quincy Adams (1825–1829). Both were one-term presidents, as was the senior Bush, who lost to Democrat Bill Clinton in 1992. The party's 32,000-word platform was replete with references to prosperity and ways to use it, chiefly through tax cuts, which Bush said would benefit all taxpayers and not just the rich. *(Story, p. 22)*

Following are excerpts from the Republican platform of 2000.

Taxes and Budget. . . . When the average American family has to work more than four months out of every year to fund all levels of government, it's time to change the tax system, to make it simpler, flatter, and fairer for everyone. It's time for an economics of inclusion that will let people keep more of what they earn and accelerate movement up the opportunity ladder.

We therefore enthusiastically endorse the principles of Governor Bush's Tax Cut with a Purpose:

Replace the five current tax brackets with four lower ones, ensuring all taxpayers significant tax relief while targeting it especially toward low-income workers.

• Help families by doubling the child tax credit to $1,000, making it available to more families, and eliminating the marriage penalty.

• Encourage entrepreneurship and growth by capping the top marginal rate, ending the death tax, and making permanent the Research and Development credit.

• Promote charitable giving and education. Foster capital investment and savings to boost today's dangerously low personal savings rate. . . .

Family Matters. We support the traditional definition of "marriage" as the legal union of one man and one woman, and we believe that federal judges and bureaucrats should not force states to recognize other living arrangements as marriages. . . . We do not believe sexual preference should be given special legal protection or standing in law.

Education. . . . Raise academic standards through increased local control and accountability to parents, shrinking a multitude of federal programs into five flexible grants in exchange for real, measured progress in student achievement.

Assist states in closing the achievement gap and empower needy families to escape persistently failing schools by allowing federal dollars to follow their children to the school of their choice.

. . . . We recognize that. . . . the role of the federal government must be progressively limited as we return control to parents, teachers, and local school boards. . . . The Republican Congress rightly opposed attempts by the Department of Education to establish federal testing that would set the stage for a national curriculum. We believe it's time to test the Department, and each of its programs, instead. . . .

Abortion. . . . The Supreme Court's recent decision, prohibiting states from banning partial-birth abortions—a procedure denounced by a committee of the American Medical Association and rightly branded as four-fifths infanticide—shocks the conscience of the nation. As a country, we must keep our pledge to the first guarantee of the Declaration of Independence. That is why we say the unborn child has a fundamental individual right to life which cannot be infringed. We support a human life amendment to the Constitution and we endorse legislation to make clear that the Fourteenth Amendment's protections apply to unborn children. . . .

Gun Laws. . . . We defend the constitutional right to keep and bear arms, and we affirm the individual responsibility to safely use and store firearms.

Because self-defense is a basic human right, we will promote training in their safe usage, especially in federal programs for women and the elderly. A Republican administration will vigorously enforce current gun laws, neglected by the Democrats, especially by prosecuting dangerous offenders identified as felons in instant background checks. Although we support background checks to ensure that guns do not fall into the hands of criminals, we oppose federal licensing of law-abiding gun owners and national gun registration as a violation of the Second Amendment and an invasion of privacy of honest citizens. . . .

New Americans. . . . Our country's ethnic diversity within a shared national culture is unique in all the world. We benefit from our differences, but we must also strengthen the ties that bind us to one another. Foremost among those is the flag. Its deliberate desecration is not "free speech" but an assault against both our proud history and our greatest hopes. We therefore support a constitutional amendment that will restore to the people, through their elected representatives, their right to safeguard Old Glory.

Another sign of our unity is the role of English as our common language. . . . For newcomers, it has always been the fastest route to the mainstream of American life. English empowers. That is why fluency in English must be the goal of bilingual education programs. We support the recognition of English as the nation's common language. At the same time, mastery of other languages is important for America's competitiveness in the world market. . . .

As a nation of immigrants, we welcome all new Americans who have entered lawfully and are prepared to follow our laws and provide for themselves and their families. In their search for a better life, they strengthen our economy, enrich our culture, and defend the nation in war and in peace. To ensure fairness for those wishing to reside in this country, and to meet the manpower needs of our expanding economy, a total overhaul of the immigration system is sorely needed. . . .

Saving Social Security. . . . Anyone currently receiving Social Security, or close to being eligible for it, will not be impacted by any changes. Key changes should merit bipartisan agreement so any reforms will be a win for the American people rather than a political victory for any one party.

Real reform does not require, and will not include, tax increases.

Personal savings accounts must be the cornerstone of restructuring. Each of today's workers should be free to direct a portion of their payroll taxes to personal investments for their retirement future. . . . Today's financial markets offer a variety of investment options, including some that guarantee a rate of return higher than the current Social Security system with no risk to the investor. Choice is the key. Any new options for retirement security should be voluntary, so workers can choose to remain in the current system or opt for something different. . . .

Health Care. . . . Medicare, at age 35, needs a new lease on life. It's time to bring this program, so critical for 39 million seniors and individuals with disabilities, into the Twenty-first Century. It's time to modernize the benefit package to match current medical science, improve the program's financial stability, and cut back the bureaucratic jungle that is smothering it. It's time to give older Americans access to the same health insurance plan the Congress has created for itself, so that seniors will have the same choices and security as Members of Congress, including elimination of all current limitations and restrictions that prevent the establishment of medical savings accounts. . . .

Medicare, the bedrock of care for our elderly, is suffocating under more than 130,000 pages of federal rules, three times the size of the entire IRS code. It pays for only 53 percent of seniors' care, provides no outpatient prescription drugs, and does not cover real long-term care, and it is still headed for bankruptcy in the near future. The doctor-patient relationship has been eroded, and in some instances replaced, by external decision-making and managed care bureaucracy.

We intend to save this beleaguered system with a vision of health care adapted to the changing demands of a new century. It is as simple, and yet as profound, as this: All Americans should have access to high-quality and affordable health care. . . . In achieving that goal, we will promote a health care system that supports, not supplants, the private sector; that promotes personal responsibility in health care decision-making; and that ensures the least intrusive role for the federal government. . . .

Women's Health. . . . Across this country, and at all levels of government, Republicans are at the forefront in aggressively developing health care initiatives targeted specifically at the needs of women. The enormous increases in the NIH [National Institutes of Health] budget brought about by the Republican Congress will make possible aggressive new research and clinical trials into diseases and health issues that disproportionately affect women as well as into conditions that affect the elderly, the majority of whom are women. And we are leading efforts to reach out to underserved and minority female populations, where disparities persist in life expectancy, infant mortality and death rates from cancer, heart disease, and diabetes. . . .

Energy. . . . By any reasonable standard, the Department of Energy has utterly failed in its mission to safeguard America's energy security. The Federal Energy Regulatory Commission has been no better, and the Environmental Protection Agency (EPA) has been shutting off America's energy pipeline with a regulatory blitz that has only just begun. In fact, 36 oil refineries have closed in just the last eight years, while not a single new refinery has been built in this country in the last quarter-century. EPA's patchwork of regulations has driven fuel prices higher in some areas than in others. . . .

A Military for the Twenty-first Century. . . . Over the past seven years, a shrunken American military has been run ragged by a deployment tempo that has eroded its military readiness. Many units have seen their operational requirements increased four-fold, wearing out both people and equipment. Only last fall the Army certified two of its premier combat divisions as unready for war because of underfunding, mismanagement, and overcommitment to peacekeeping missions around the globe. More Army units and the other armed services report similar problems. It is a national scandal that almost one quarter of our Army's active combat strength is unfit for wartime duty. . . .

The new Republican government will renew the bond of trust between the Commander-in-Chief, the American military, and the American people. The military is not a civilian police force or a political referee. We believe the military must no longer be the object of social experiments. We affirm traditional military culture. We affirm that homosexuality is incompatible with military service. . . .

The Middle East and Persian Gulf. . . . It is important for the United States to support and honor Israel, the only true democracy in the Middle East. We will ensure that Israel maintains a qualitative edge in defensive technology over any potential adversaries. We will not pick sides in Israeli elections. The United States has a moral and legal obligation to maintain its Embassy and Ambassador in Jerusalem. Immediately upon taking office, the next Republican president will begin the process of moving the U. S. Embassy from Tel Aviv to Israel's capital, Jerusalem. . . .

GEORGE W. BUSH'S ACCEPTANCE SPEECH

Following are excerpts of Texas Gov. George W. Bush's Aug. 3, 2000, speech to the Republican National Convention in Philadelphia.

Mr. Chairman, delegates and my fellow citizens, I proudly accept your nomination.

Thank you for this honor. Together, we will renew America's purpose.

Our founders first defined that purpose here in Philadelphia. Ben Franklin was here, Thomas Jefferson and, of course, George Washington, or, as his friends called him, George W.

I am proud to have Dick Cheney by my side. He is a man—he is a man of integrity and sound judgment who has proven that public service can be noble service. America will be proud to have a leader of such character to succeed Al Gore as vice president of the United States.

I'm grateful for Sen. John McCain. I appreciate so very much his speech two nights ago. I appreciate his friendship. I love his spirit for America. And I want to thank the other candidates who sought this office, as well. Their convictions have strengthened our party.

I'm especially grateful tonight to my family. . . . My father was the last president of a great generation, a generation of Americans who stormed beaches, liberated concentration camps and delivered us from evil. Some never came home. Those who did put their medals in drawers, went to work and built on a heroic scale highways and universities, suburbs and factories, great cities and grand alliances, the strong foundations of an American century. Now the question comes to the sons and daughters of this achievement: What is asked of us?

This is a remarkable moment in the life of our nation. Never has the promise of prosperity been so vivid. But times of plenty like times of crises are tests of American character. Prosperity can be a tool in our hands used to build and better our country, or it can be a drug in our system dulling our sense of urgency, of empathy, of duty. Our opportunities are too great, our lives too short, to waste this moment.

So tonight, we vow to our nation we will seize this moment of American promise. We will use these good times for great goals. We will confront the hard issues, threats to our national security, threats to our health and retirement security, before the challenges of our time become crises for our children.

And we will extend the promise of prosperity to every forgotten corner of this country: to every man and woman, a chance to succeed; to every child, a chance to learn; and to every family, a chance to live with dignity and hope.

For eight years, the Clinton-Gore administration has coasted through prosperity. The path of least resistance is always downhill. But America's way is the rising road. This nation is daring and decent and ready for change.

Our current president embodied the potential of a generation—so many talents, so much charm, such great skill. But in the end, to what end? So much promise to no great purpose.

Little more than a decade ago, the Cold War thawed, and with the leadership of Presidents Reagan and Bush, that wall came down.

But instead of seizing this moment, the Clinton-Gore administration has squandered it. We have seen a steady erosion of American power and an unsteady exercise of American influence. Our military is low on parts, pay and morale. If called on by the commander in chief today, two entire divisions of the Army would have to report, "Not ready for duty, sir."

This administration had its moment, they had their chance. They have not led. We will.

This generation was given the gift of the best education in American history, yet we do not share that gift with everyone. Seven of 10 fourth-graders in our highest poverty schools cannot read a simple children's book. And still this administration continues on the same old path, the same old programs, while millions are trapped in schools where violence is common and learning is rare. This administration had its chance. They have not led. We will.

America has a strong economy and a surplus. We have the public resources and the public will, even the bipartisan opportunities to strengthen Social Security and repair Medicare. But this administration, during eight years of increasing need, did nothing. They had their moment. They have not led. We will.

Our generation has a chance to reclaim some essential values, to show we have grown up before we grow old. But when the moment for leadership came, this administration did not teach our children, it disillusioned them. They had their chance. They have not led. We will.

And now they come asking for another chance, another shot. Our answer: Not this time, not this year. This is not the time for third chances; it is the time for new beginnings.

The rising generations of this country have our own appointment with greatness. It does not rise or fall with the stock market. It cannot be bought with our wealth. Greatness is found when American character and American courage overcome American challenges.

When Lewis Morris of New York was about to sign the Declaration of Independence, his brother advised against it, warning he would lose all his property. But Morris, a plain-spoken founder, responded, "Damn the consequences, give me the pen."

That is the eloquence of American action. . . . An American president must call upon that character.

Tonight in this hall, we resolve to be the party not of repose but of reform. We will write not footnotes but chapters in the American story. We will add the work of our hands to the inheritance of our fathers and mothers and leave this nation greater than we found it. . . . We know the test of leadership. The issues are joined. We will strengthen Social Security and Medicare for the greatest generation and for generations to come. Medicare does more than meet the needs of our elderly; it reflects the values of our society. We will set it on firm financial ground and make prescription drugs available and affordable for every senior who needs them. Social Security has been called the third rail of American politics, the one you're not supposed to touch because it might shock you. But if you don't touch it, you cannot fix it. And I intend to fix it.

To the seniors in this country, you earned your benefits, you made your plans, and President George W. Bush will keep the promise of Social Security, no changes, no reductions, no way. . . . Now is the time for Republicans and Democrats to end the politics of fear and save Social Security together. For younger workers, we will give you the option, your choice, to put part of your payroll taxes into sound, responsible investments. When this money is in your name, in your account, it's just not a program, it's your property. . . .

One size does not fit all when it comes to educating our children, so local people should control local schools. And those who spend your tax dollars must be held accountable. When a school district receives federal funds to teach poor children, we expect them to learn. And if they don't, parents should get the money to make a different choice.

Now is the time to make Head Start an early learning program to teach all our children to read and renew the promise of America's public schools.

Another test of leadership is tax relief. The last time taxes were this high as a percentage of our economy, there was a good reason: We were fighting World War II. Today our high taxes fund a surplus. . . . The surplus is not the government's money; the surplus is the people's money.

I will use this moment of opportunity to bring common sense and fairness to the tax code. And I will act on principle. On principle, every family, every farmer and small-business person should be free to pass on their life's work to those they love, so we will abolish the death tax.

On principle, no one in America should have to pay more than a third of their income to the federal government, so we will reduce tax rates for everyone in every bracket.

On principle, those with the greatest need should receive the greatest help, so we will lower the bottom rate from 15 percent to 10 percent and double the child credit. . . .

The world needs America's strength and leadership. And America's armed forces need better equipment, better training and better pay. We will give our military the means to keep the peace, and we will give it one thing more: a commander in chief who respects our men and women in uniform and a commander in chief who earns their respect. A generation shaped by Vietnam must remember the lessons of Vietnam: When America uses force in the world, the cause must be just, the goal must be clear, and the victory must be overwhelming.

I will work to reduce nuclear weapons and nuclear tension in the world, to turn these years of influence into decades of peace. And at the earliest possible date, my administration will deploy missile defenses to guard against attack and blackmail. Now is the time not to defend outdated treaties but to defend the American people.

A time of prosperity is a test of vision, and our nation today needs vision. That's a fact. Or as my opponent might call it, a risky truth scheme.

Every one of the proposals I've talked about tonight he's called a risky scheme over and over again. It is the sum of his message, the

politics of the roadblock, the philosophy of the stop sign. . . . He now leads the party of Franklin Delano Roosevelt, but the only thing he has to offer is fear itself. That outlook is typical of many in Washington, always seeing the tunnel at the end of the light.

But I come from a different place and it has made me a different leader. In Midland, Texas, where I grew up, the town motto was, "The sky's the limit," and we believed it. There was a restless energy, a basic conviction that with hard work, anybody could succeed and everybody deserved a chance. . . .

This background leaves more than an accent, it leaves an outlook: optimistic, impatient with pretense, confident that people can chart their own course in life. That background may lack the polish of Washington. Then again, I don't have a lot of things that come with Washington. I don't have enemies to fight. I have no stake in the bitter arguments of the last few years. I want to change the tone of Washington to one of civility and respect. . . .

As governor, I've made difficult decisions and stood by them under pressure. I've been where the buck stops in business and in government. I've been a chief executive who sets an agenda, sets big goals, and rallies people to believe and achieve them. I am proud of this record, and I am prepared for the work ahead.

If you give me your trust, I will honor it. Grant me a mandate, I will use it. Give me the opportunity to lead this nation, and I will lead.

And we need a leader to seize the opportunities of this new century: the new cures of medicine, the amazing technologies that will drive our economy and keep the peace. But our new economy must never forget the old, unfinished struggle for human dignity. . . .

Big government is not the answer, but the alternative to bureaucracy is not indifference. It is to put conservative values and conservative ideas into the thick of the fight for justice and opportunity. This is what I mean by compassionate conservatism. And on this ground, we will lead our nation.

We will give low-income Americans tax credits to buy the private health insurance they need and deserve. We will transform today's housing rental program to help hundreds of thousands of low-income families find stability and dignity in a home of their own. And in the next bold step of welfare reform, we will support the heroic work of homeless shelters and hospices, food [pantries] and crisis pregnancy centers, people reclaiming their communities block by block and heart by heart. . . . My administration will give taxpayers new incentives to donate to charity, encourage after-school programs that build character, and support mentoring groups that shape and save young lives.

I will lead our nation toward a culture that values life—the life of the elderly and sick, the life of the young and the life of the unborn. Good people can disagree on this issue, but surely we can agree on ways to value life by promoting adoption, parental notification. And when Congress sends me a bill against "partial birth" abortion, I will sign it into law.

Behind every goal I've talked about tonight is a great hope for our country. A hundred years from now this must not be remembered as an age rich in possession and poor in ideals. . . .

2000 DEMOCRATIC PLATFORM

Declaring himself "my own man," Vice President Al Gore stepped from the shadow of President Bill Clinton and accepted the Democratic Party's nomination for president on the final night of the party's August 14–17, 2000, convention at Los Angeles's Staples Center. Reinforcing the independence he sought to portray, Gore earlier had taken a gamble unprecedented in American politics. He chose as his running mate Sen. Joseph Lieberman of Connecticut, making him the first Jew to run on a major party's national ticket. Besides being of a religious minority, Lieberman had at times broken with his party on economic issues and had sternly deplored Clinton's sexual affair with Monica Lewinsky. Gore's speech and the party platform stressed the prosperity and budget surpluses achieved during Clinton's two terms. *(Story, p. 23)*

Following are excerpts from the Democratic platform of 2000.

Fiscal Discipline. . . . Today, for most families, the federal tax burden is the lowest it has been in twenty years. The Bush tax slash takes a different course. It is bigger than any cut Newt Gingrich ever dreamed of. It would let the richest one percent of Americans afford a new sports car and middle class Americans afford a warm soda. It is so out-of-step with reality that the Republican Congress refused to enact it. It would undermine the American economy and undercut our prosperity. . . . Democrats seek the right kind of tax relief—tax cuts that are specifically targeted to help those who need them the most.

These tax cuts would let families live their values by helping them save for college, invest in their job skills and lifelong learning, pay for health insurance, afford child care, eliminate the marriage penalty for working families, care for elderly or disabled loved ones, invest in clean cars and clean homes, and build additional security for their retirement.

Retirement Security. . . . The choice for Americans on this vital part of our national heritage has never been more clear: Democrats believe in using our prosperity to save Social Security; the Republicans' tax cut would prevent America from ensuring our senior citizens have a secure retirement. We owe it to America's children and their children to make the strength and solvency of Social Security a major national priority.

That's why Al Gore is committed to making Social Security safe and secure for more than half a century by using the savings from our current unprecedented prosperity to strengthen the Social Security Trust Fund in preparation for the retirement of the Baby Boom generation. . . .

To build on the success of Social Security, Al Gore has proposed the creation of Retirement Savings Plus—voluntary, tax-free, personally-controlled, privately-managed savings accounts with a government match that would help couples build a nest egg of up to $400,000. . . .

Education. . . . George W. Bush and the Republican Party offer neither real accountability nor reasonable investment [in education]. . . . Their version of accountability relies on private school vouchers that would offer too few dollars to too few children to escape their failing schools. These vouchers would pass the buck on accountability while pulling bucks out of the schools that need them most. . . .

By the end of the next presidential term, we should have a fully qualified, well trained teacher in every classroom in every school in every part of this country and every teacher should pass a rigorous test to get there.

By the end of the next presidential term, every failing school in America should be turned around—or shut down and reopened under new public leadership.

By the end of the next presidential term, we should ensure that no high school student graduates unless they have mastered the basics of reading and math—so that the diploma they receive really means something.

By the end of the next presidential term, parents across the nation ought to be able to choose the best public school for their children. . . .

We should make a college education as universal as high school is today. Al Gore has proposed a new National Tuition Savings program to tie together state tuition savings programs in more than 30 states so that parents can save for college tax-free and inflation-free. We propose a tax cut for tuition and fees for post-high school education and training that allows families to choose either a $10,000 a year tax deduction or a $2,800 tax credit. . . .

Fighting Crime. . . . Strong and Sensible Gun Laws. . . . Democrats believe that we should fight gun crime on all fronts—with stronger laws and stronger enforcement. That's why Democrats fought and passed the Brady Law and the Assault Weapons Ban. We increased federal, state, and local gun crime prosecution by 22 percent since 1992. Now gun crime is down by 35 percent.

Now we must do even more. We need mandatory child safety locks, to protect our children. We should require a photo license I.D., a full background check, and a gun safety test to buy a new handgun in America. We support more federal gun prosecutors, ATF agents and inspectors, and giving states and communities another 10,000 prosecutors to fight gun crime.

Hate Crimes. . . . Hate crimes are more than assaults on people, they are assaults on the very idea of America. They should be punished with extra force. Protections should include hate violence based on gender, disability or sexual orientation. And the Republican Congress should stop standing in the way of this pro-civil rights, anti-crime legislation. . . .

Valuing Families. . . . Responsible Entertainment. . . . Parents and the entertainment industry must accept more responsibility. Many parents are not aware of the resources available to them, such as the V-chip technology in television sets and Internet filtering devices, that can help them shield children from violent entertainment. The entertainment industry must accept more responsibility and exercise more self-restraint, by strictly enforcing movie ratings, by taking a close look at violence in its own advertising, and by determining whether the ratings systems are allowing too many children to be exposed to too much violence and cruelty.

Health Care. Universal Health Coverage. There is much more left to do. We must redouble our efforts to bring the uninsured into coverage step-by-step and as soon as possible. We should guarantee access to affordable health care for every child in America. We should expand coverage to working families, including more Medicaid assistance to help with the transition from welfare to work. . . . In addition, Americans aged 55 to 65—the fastest growing group of uninsured—should be allowed to buy into the Medicare program to get the coverage they need. By taking these steps, we can move our nation closer to the goal of providing universal health coverage for all Americans.

. . . . A Real Patients' Bill of Rights. Medical decisions should be made by patients and their doctors and nurses, not accountants and bureaucrats at the end of a phone line a thousand miles away. . . . Americans need a real, enforceable Patients' Bill of Rights with the right to see a specialist, the right to appeal decisions to an outside board, guaranteed coverage of emergency room care, and the right to sue when they are unfairly denied coverage. . . .

Protecting and Strengthening Medicare. It is time we ended the tragedy of elderly Americans being forced to choose between meals and medication. It is time we modernized Medicare with a new prescription drug benefit. This is an essential step in making sure that the best new cures and therapies are available to our seniors and disabled Americans. We cannot afford to permit our seniors to receive only part of the medical care they need. . . .

Abortion. Choice. The Democratic Party stands behind the right of every woman to choose, consistent with *Roe v. Wade,* and regardless of ability to pay. We believe it is a fundamental constitutional liberty that individual Americans—not government—can best take responsibility for making the most difficult and intensely personal decisions regarding reproduction. This year's Supreme Court rulings show to us all that eliminating a woman's right to choose is only one justice away. That's why the stakes in this election are as high as ever. . . .

Campaign Finance Reform. . . . The big-time lobbyists and special interest were so eager [in 2000] to invest in George W. Bush and deliver campaign cash to him hand-over-fist that he became the first major party nominee to pull out of the primary election financing structure and refuse to abide by campaign spending limits.

In this year's presidential primaries it became clear that the Republican establishment is violently opposed to John McCain's call for reforming our democracy. Al Gore supports John McCain's campaign for political reform. In fact, the McCain-Feingold bill is the very first piece of legislation that a President Al Gore will submit to Congress—and he will fight for it until it becomes the law of the land.

Then he will go even further—much further. He will insist on tough new lobbying reform, publicly-guaranteed TV time for debates and advocacy by candidates, and a crackdown on special interest issue ads. . . .

Transforming the Military. . . . The Democratic Party understands that, good as they are, the armed forces must continue to evolve. They must not only remain prepared for conventional military action, but must sharpen their ability to deal with new missions and new kinds of threats. They must become more agile, more versatile, and must more completely incorporate the revolutionary implications and advantages of American supremacy in information technology.

. . . . A high-tech fighting force must recruit, train, and retain a professional all-volunteer force of the highest caliber. . . . While the number of soldiers and families on food stamps is down by two-thirds over the past decade, it is unacceptable that any member of our armed forces should have to rely on food stamps. Al Gore is committed to equal treatment of all service members and believes all patriotic Americans be allowed to serve their country without discrimination, persecution, and violence. . . .

Middle East. . . . Jerusalem is the capital of Israel and should remain an undivided city accessible to people of all faiths. In view of the government of Israel's courageous decision to withdraw from Lebanon, we believe special responsibility now resides with Syria to make a contribution toward peace. The recently-held Camp David summit, while failing to bridge all the gaps between Israel and the Palestinians, demonstrated President Clinton's resolve to do all the United States could do to bring an end to that long conflict. Al Gore, as president, will demonstrate the same resolve. . . .

AL GORE'S ACCEPTANCE SPEECH

Following are excerpts of Vice President Al Gore's Aug. 17, 2000, speech at the Democratic National Convention in Los Angeles.

I speak tonight of gratitude, achievement and high hopes for our country. . . .

I'm honored tonight by the support of a leader of high ideals and fundamental decency, who will be an important part of our country's future—[former] Sen. Bill Bradley [D-N.J.].

There's someone else who will shape that future—a leader of character and courage. A defender of the environment and working families—the next vice president of the United States, [Sen.] Joe Lieberman [D-Conn.]. I picked him for one simple reason: He's the best person for the job.

For almost eight years now, I've been the partner of a leader who moved us out of the valley of recession and into the longest period of prosperity in American history. I say to you tonight: Millions of Americans will live better lives for a long time to come because of the job that's been done by President Bill Clinton.

Instead of the biggest deficits in history, we now have the biggest surpluses. The highest home ownership ever. The lowest inflation in a generation. Instead of losing jobs, we have 22 million new jobs. Above all, our success comes from you, the people who have worked hard for your families. Let's not forget that a few years ago you were also working hard. But your hard work was undone by a government that didn't work, didn't put people first, and wasn't on your side.

Together, we changed things to help unleash your potential, and innovation and investment in the private sector, the engine that drives our economic growth. And our progress on the economy is a good chapter in our history.

But now we turn the page and write a new chapter. . . . This election is not an award for past performance. I'm not asking you to vote for me on the basis of the economy we have. Tonight, I ask for your support on the basis of the better, fairer, more prosperous America we can build together. Together, let's make sure that our prosperity enriches not just the few, but all working families. Let's invest in health care, education, a secure retirement, and middle class tax cuts.

I'm happy that the stock market has boomed and so many businesses and new enterprises have done well. This country is richer and stronger. But my focus is on working families—people trying to make house payments and car payments, working overtime to save for college and do right by their kids. . . .

To all the families in America who have to struggle to afford the right education and the skyrocketing cost of prescription drugs, I want you to know this: I've taken on the powerful forces. And as president, I'll stand up to them, and I'll stand up for you.

To all the families who are struggling with things that money can't measure—like trying to find a little more time to spend with your children, or protecting your children from entertainment that you think glorifies violence and indecency—I want you to know: I believe we must challenge a culture with too much meanness and not enough meaning. And as president, I will stand with you for a goal that we share: to give more power back to the parents, to choose what your own children are exposed to, so you can pass on your family's basic lessons of responsibility and decency. . . .

We could squander this moment, but our country would be the poorer for it. Instead, let's lift our eyes and see how wide the American horizon has become. We're entering a new time, we're electing a new president, and I stand here tonight as my own man, and I want you to know me for who I truly am. I grew up in a wonderful family. I have a lot to be thankful for. And the greatest gift my parents gave me was love. When I was a child, it never once occurred to me that the foundation upon which my security depended would ever shake. And of all the lessons my parents taught me, the most powerful one was unspoken: the way they loved one another. . . . My parents taught me that the real values in life aren't material but spiritual. They include faith and family, duty and honor, and trying to make the world a better place.

I finished college at a time when all that seemed to be in doubt, and our nation's spirit was being depleted. We saw the assassination of our best leaders, appeals to racial backlash and the first warning signs of Watergate. I remember the conversations I had with Tipper back then and the doubts we had about the Vietnam War. But I enlisted in the Army because I knew if I didn't go, someone else in the small town of Carthage, Tenn., would have to go in my place. I was an Army reporter in Vietnam. When I was there, I didn't do the most, or run the gravest danger. But I was proud to wear my country's uniform.

When I came home, running for office was the very last thing I ever thought I would do. I studied religion at Vanderbilt and worked nights as a police reporter at the Nashville Tennesseean. And I saw more of what could go wrong in America—not only on the police beat, but as an investigative reporter covering local government. I also saw so much of what could go right—citizens lifting up local communities, family by family, block by block, neighborhood by neighborhood, in churches and charities, on school boards and city councils.

And then, Tipper and I started our own family. And when our first daughter, Karenna, was born, I began to see the future through a fresh set of eyes. . . . And I decided that I could not turn away from service at home—any more than I could have turned away from service in Vietnam.

That's why I ran for Congress. In my first term, a family in Hardeman County, Tenn., wrote a letter and told how worried they were about toxic waste that had been dumped near their home. I held some of the first hearings on the issue. And ever since, I've been there in the fight against the big polluters. . . . On the issue of the environment, I've never given up, I've never backed down, and I never will. And I say it again tonight: We must reverse the silent, rising tide of global warming.

In the Senate and as vice president, I fought for welfare reform. . . . Others talked about welfare reform. We actually reformed welfare and set time limits. Instead of handouts, we gave people training to go from welfare to work. And we have cut the welfare rolls in half and moved millions into good jobs.

For almost 25 years now, I've been fighting for people. And for all that time, I've been listening to people, holding open meetings in the places where they live and work. And you know what? I've learned a lot. . . . I've learned that the issues before us, the problems and the policies, all have names. And I don't mean the big fancy names that we put on programs and legislation. I'm talking about family names like Nystel, Johnson, Gutierrez, and Malone—people and families I've met in the last year, all across this country. . . . And so here tonight, in the name of all the working families who are the strength and soul of America, I accept your nomination for president of the United States.

I'm here to talk seriously about the issues. I believe people deserve to know specifically what a candidate proposes to do. . . . If you entrust me with the presidency, I will put our democracy back in your hands, and get all the special-interest money—all of it—out of our democracy by enacting campaign finance reform. I feel so strongly about this, I promise you that campaign finance reform will be the very first bill that Joe Lieberman and I send to Congress.

Let others try to restore the old guard. We come to this convention as the change we wish to see in America. And what are those changes?

At a time when most Americans will live to know even their great-grandchildren, we will save and strengthen Social Security and Medicare—not only for this generation, but for generations to come.

At a time of almost unimaginable medical breakthroughs, we will fight for affordable health care for all—so patients and ordinary people are not left powerless and broke. We will move toward universal health coverage, step by step, starting with all children. Let's get all children covered by the year 2004. And let's move to the day when we end the stigma of mental illness and treat it like every other illness, everywhere in this nation. Within the next few years, scientists will identify the genes that cause every type of cancer. We need a national commitment equal to the promise of this unequalled moment. So we will double the federal investment in medical research. We will find new medicines and new cures—not just for cancer, but for everything from diabetes to HIV/AIDS.

At a time when there is more computer power in a Palm Pilot than in the spaceship that took Neil Armstrong to the moon, we will offer all our people lifelong learning and new skills for the higher paying jobs of the future.

At a time when the amount of human knowledge is doubling every five years, we will do bold things to make our schools the best in the world. I will fight for the single greatest commitment to education since the G.I. Bill: for revolutionary improvements in our schools. For higher standards and more accountability. To put a fully qualified teacher in every classroom, test all new teachers, and give teachers the training and professional development they deserve. It's time to treat and reward teachers like the professionals they are.

It's not just about more money. It's about higher standards, accountability, new ideas. But we can't do it without new resources. And that's why I will invest far more in our schools—in the long run, a second-class education always costs more than a first-class education. And I will not go along with any plan that would drain taxpayer money away from our public schools and give it to private schools in the form of vouchers. This nation was a pioneer of universal public education. Now let's set a specific new goal for the first decade of the 21st century: high-quality universal pre-school. . . .

We also have to give middle class families help in paying for college with tax-free college savings, and by making most college tuition tax-deductible. Open the doors of learning to all. And all of this—all of this—is the change we wish to see in America.

Not so long ago, a balanced budget seemed impossible. Now our budget surpluses make it possible to give a full range of targeted tax cuts to working families. Not just to help you save for college, but to pay for health insurance or child care. To reform the estate tax, so people can pass on a small business or a family farm. And to end the marriage penalty—the right way, the fair way—because we shouldn't force couples to pay more in income taxes just because they're married.

But let me say it plainly: I will not go along with a huge tax cut for the wealthy at the expense of everyone else and wreck our good economy in the process. Under the tax plan the other side has proposed, for every 10 dollars that goes to the wealthiest 1 percent, middle-class families would get one dime. And lower-income families would get one penny. In fact, if you add it up, the average family would get about enough money to buy one extra Diet Coke a day, about 62 cents in change. Let me tell you: that's not the kind of change I'm working for. . . .

I'll fight for a new, tax-free way to help you save and build a bigger nest egg for your retirement. I'm talking about something extra that you can save and invest for yourself. Something that will supplement Social Security, not be subtracted from it. . . .

In the next four years, we will pay off all the national debt this nation accumulated in our first 200 years. This will put us on the path to completely eliminating the debt by 2012, keeping America prosperous far into the future.

But there's something at stake in this election that's even more important than economic progress. Simply put, it's our values; it's our responsibility to our loved ones, to our families. . . .

Putting both Social Security and Medicare in an iron-clad lock box where the politicians can't touch them—to me, that kind of common sense is a family value.

Getting cigarettes out of the hands of kids before they get hooked is a family value. I will crack down on the marketing of tobacco to our children, no matter how hard the tobacco companies lobby, no matter how much they spend.

A new prescription drug benefit under Medicare for all our seniors—that's a family value. And let me tell you: I will fight for it, and the other side will not. . . .

There's one other word we've heard a lot of in this campaign, and that word is honor. To me, honor is not just a word, but an obligation. And you have my word: We will honor hard work by raising the minimum wage so that work always pays more than welfare.

We will honor families by expanding child care and after-school care and family and medical leave so working parents have the help they need to care for their children—because one of the most important jobs of all is raising our children. And we'll support the right of parents to decide that one of them will stay home longer with their babies if that's what they believe is best for their families.

We will honor the ideal of equality by standing up for civil rights and defending affirmative action.

We will honor equal rights and fight for an equal day's pay for an equal day's work.

And let there be no doubt: I will protect and defend a woman's right to choose. The last thing this country needs is a Supreme Court that overturns *Roe v. Wade.*

We will remove all the old barriers so that those who are called disabled can develop all their abilities. And we will also widen the circle of opportunity for all Americans and enforce all our civil rights laws. We will pass the Employment Non-Discrimination Act.

And we will honor the memory of Matthew Shepard, Joseph Ileto and James Byrd, whose families all joined us this week, by passing a law against hate crimes.

We will honor the hard work of raising a family by doing all we can to help parents protect their children. Parents deserve the simple security of knowing that their children are safe whether they're walking down the street, surfing the World Wide Web or sitting behind a desk in school.

To make families safer, we passed the toughest crime bill in history, and we're putting 100,000 new community police on our streets. Crime has fallen in every major category for seven years in a row. But there's still too much danger and there's still too much fear. So tonight I want to set another new, specific goal: to cut the crime rate year after year, every single year throughout this decade. That's why I'll fight to add another 50,000 new community police [officers]. . . .

I will fight for a crime victims' bill of rights, including a constitutional amendment to make sure that victims, and not just criminals, are guaranteed rights in our justice system.

I'll fight to toughen penalties on those who misuse the Internet to prey on our children and violate our privacy. And I'll fight to make every school in this nation drug-free and gun-free. I believe in the right of sportsmen and hunters and law-abiding citizens to own firearms. But I want mandatory background checks to keep guns away from criminals and mandatory child safety locks to protect our children. . . .

I'm excited about America's prospects and full of hope for America's future. Our country has come a long way, and I've come a long way since that long ago time when I went to Vietnam. I've never forgotten what I saw there and the bravery of so many young Americans. The price of freedom is sometimes high, but I never believed that America should turn inward.

As a senator, I broke with many in our party and voted to support the Gulf War when Saddam Hussein invaded Kuwait because I believed America's vital interests were at stake.

Early in my public service, I took up the issue of nuclear arms control and nuclear weapons because nothing is more fundamental than protecting our national security.

Now I want to lead America because I love America. I will keep America's defenses strong. I will make sure our armed forces continue

to be the best-equipped, best-trained and best-led in the entire world. . . . We must always have the will to defend our enduring interests—from Europe to the Middle East, to Japan and Korea. We must strengthen our partnerships with Africa, Latin America and the rest of the developing world.

We must welcome and promote truly free trade. But I say to you: It must be fair trade. We must set standards to end child labor, to prevent the exploitation of workers and the poisoning of the environment. Free trade can and must be—and if I'm president, will be—a way to lift everyone up, not bring anyone down to the lowest common denominator.

So those are the issues, and that's where I stand. . . . Sometimes in this campaign, when I visit a school and see a hardworking teacher trying to change the world one child at a time—I see the face of my father. And I know that teaching our children well is not just the teacher's job; it's everyone's job. And it has to be our national mission.

I've shaken hands in diners and coffee shops all across this country. And sometimes when I see a waitress working hard and thanking someone for a tip, I see the face of my mother. And I know for that waitress carrying trays, or a construction worker in the winter cold, I will never agree to raise the retirement age to 70, or threaten the promise of Social Security.

I say to you tonight: We've got to win this election because every hardworking American family deserves to open the door to their dream. In our democracy, the future is not something that just happens to us; it is something we make for ourselves—together.

So to the young people watching tonight, I say: This is your time to make new the life of our world. We need your help to rekindle the spirit of America.

And I ask all of you, my fellow citizens: From this city that marked both the end of America's journey westward and the beginning of the New Frontier, let us set out on a new journey to the best America. A new journey on which we advance not by the turning of wheels, but by the turning of our minds, the reach of our vision, the daring grace of the human spirit.

Yes, we have our problems. But the United States of America is the best country ever created—and still, as ever, the hope of humankind. Yes, we're all imperfect. But as Americans we all share in the privilege and challenge of building a more perfect union.

I know my own imperfections. I know that sometimes people say I'm too serious, that I talk too much substance and policy. Maybe I've done that tonight.

But the presidency is more than a popularity contest. It's a day-by-day fight for people. Sometimes, you have to choose to do what's difficult or unpopular. Sometimes, you have to be willing to spend your popularity in order to pick the hard right over the easy wrong.

There are big choices ahead, and our whole future is at stake. . . . If you entrust me with the presidency, I know I won't always be the most exciting politician. But I pledge to you tonight: I will work for you every day, and I will never let you down.

Supreme Court's *Bush v. Gore* Decision

The 2000 presidential election was the most contentious of the twentieth century. The outcome hinged on a mass of disputed votes in Florida and on efforts to determine how many voters had cast their ballots. In the end, the dispute was resolved by the U.S. Supreme Court, by a narrow 5–4 decision, that in effect gave the election to George W. Bush. (*Story, p. 25*)

Following are excerpts from the unsigned majority opinion, a concurring opinion, and four dissenting opinions, in the case of Bush v.

Gore, in which the Supreme Court by a vote of 5–4 ruled on Dec. 12, 2000, that the Florida Supreme Court had failed to guarantee equal protection of the laws when it ordered a manual count of several thousand disputed votes cast in the presidential election and ruled further that the error could not be remedied in time to meet a Dec.12 deadline for selecting electors. The decision had the effect of naming Republican George W. Bush, governor of Texas, the president-elect of the United States.

MAJORITY OPINION

On December 8, 2000, the Supreme Court of Florida ordered that the Circuit Court of Leon County tabulate by hand 9,000 ballots in Miami-Dade County. It also ordered the inclusion in the certified vote totals of 215 votes identified in Palm Beach County and 168 votes identified in Miami-Dade County for Vice President Albert Gore, Jr., and Senator Joseph Lieberman, Democratic Candidates for President and Vice President. The Supreme Court noted that petitioner, Governor George W. Bush asserted that the net gain for Vice President Gore in Palm Beach County was 176 votes, and directed the Circuit Court to resolve that dispute on remand. The court further held that relief would require manual recounts in all Florida counties where so-called "undervotes" had not been subject to manual tabulation. The court ordered all manual recounts to begin at once. Governor Bush and Richard Cheney, Republican Candidates for the Presidency and Vice Presidency, filed an emergency application for a stay of this mandate. On December 9, we granted the application, treated the application as a petition for a writ of certiorari, and granted certiorari.

... On November 8, 2000, the day following the Presidential election, the Florida Division of Elections reported that petitioner, Governor Bush, had received 2,909,135 votes, and respondent, Vice President Gore, had received 2,907,351 votes, a margin of 1,784 for Governor Bush. Because Governor Bush's margin of victory was less than "one-half of a percent . . . of the votes cast," an automatic machine recount was conducted under . . . the Florida Election Code, the results of which showed Governor Bush still winning the race but by a diminished margin. Vice President Gore then sought manual recounts in Volusia, Palm Beach, Broward, and Miami-Dade Counties, pursuant to Florida's election protest provisions. A dispute arose concerning the deadline for local county canvassing boards to submit their returns to the Secretary of State (Secretary). The Secretary declined to waive the November 14 deadline imposed by statute. The Florida Supreme Court, however, set the deadline at November 26. We granted certiorari and vacated the Florida Supreme Court's decision, finding considerable uncertainty as to the grounds on which it was based. On December 11, the Florida Supreme Court issued a decision on remand reinstating that date. On November 26, the Florida Elections Canvassing Commission certified the results of the election and declared Governor Bush the winner of Florida's 25 electoral votes. On November 27, Vice President Gore, pursuant to Florida's contest provisions, filed a complaint in Leon County Circuit Court contesting the certification. He sought relief pursuant to §102.168 (3) (c), which provides that "[r]eceipt of a number of illegal votes or rejection of a number of legal votes sufficient to change or place in doubt the result of the election" shall be grounds for a contest. The Circuit Court denied relief, stating that Vice President Gore failed to meet his burden of proof. He appealed to the First District Court of Appeal, which certified the matter to the Florida Supreme Court.

Accepting jurisdiction, the Florida Supreme Court affirmed in part and reversed in part. The court held that the Circuit Court had been correct to reject Vice President Gore's challenge to the results certified in Nassau County and his challenge to the Palm Beach County Canvassing Board's determination that 3,300 ballots cast in that county were not, in the statutory phrase, "legal votes." The Supreme Court held that Vice President Gore had satisfied his burden of proof . . . with respect to his challenge to Miami-Dade County's failure to tabulate, by manual count, 9,000 ballots on which the machines had failed to detect a vote for President ("undervotes"). Noting the closeness of the election, the Court explained that "[o]n this record, there can be no question that there are legal votes within the 9,000 uncounted votes sufficient to place the results of this election in doubt." A "legal vote," as determined by the Supreme Court, is "one in which there is a 'clear indication of the intent of the voter.' " The court therefore ordered a hand recount of the 9,000 ballots in Miami-Dade County. Observing that the contest provisions vest broad discretion in the circuit judge to "provide any relief appropriate under such circumstances," the Supreme Court further held that the Circuit Court could order "the Supervisor of Elections and the Canvassing Boards, as well as the necessary public officials, in all counties that have not conducted a manual recount or tabulation of the undervotes . . . to do so forthwith, said tabulation to take place in the individual counties where the ballots are located." The Supreme Court also determined that Palm Beach County and Miami-Dade County, in their earlier manual recounts, had identified a net gain of 215 and 168 legal votes, respectively, for Vice President Gore. Rejecting the Circuit Court's conclusion that Palm Beach County lacked the authority to include the 215 net votes submitted past the November 26 deadline, the Supreme Court explained that the deadline was not intended to exclude votes identified after that date through ongoing manual recounts. As to Miami-Dade County, the Court concluded that although the 168 votes identified were the result of a partial recount, they were "legal votes [that] could change the outcome of the election." The Supreme Court therefore directed the Circuit Court to include those totals in the certified results, subject to resolution of the actual vote total from the Miami-Dade partial recount.

The petition presents the following questions: whether the Florida Supreme Court established new standards for resolving Presidential election contests, thereby violating Art. II, §1, cl. 2, of the United States Constitution and failing to comply with 3 U.S.C. §5, and whether the use of standardless manual recounts violates the Equal Protection and Due Process Clauses. With respect to the equal protection question, we find a violation of the Equal Protection Clause. . . .

The individual citizen has no federal constitutional right to vote for electors for the President of the United States unless and until the state legislature chooses a statewide election as the means to implement its power to appoint members of the Electoral College. This is the source for the statement in *McPherson v. Blacker* (1892) that the State legislature's power to select the manner for appointing electors is plenary; it may, if it so chooses, select the electors itself, which indeed was the manner used by State legislatures in several States for many years after the Framing of our Constitution. History has now favored the voter, and in each of the several States the citizens themselves vote for Presidential electors. When the state legislature vests the right to vote for President in its people, the right to vote as the legislature has prescribed is fundamental; and one source of its fundamental nature lies in the equal weight accorded to each vote and the equal dignity owed to each voter. The State, of course, after granting the franchise in the special context of Article II, can take back the power to appoint electors. . . .

The right to vote is protected in more than the initial allocation of the franchise. Equal protection applies as well to the manner of its exercise. Having once granted the right to vote on equal terms, the State may not, by later arbitrary and disparate treatment, value one person's vote over that of another. . . .

There is no difference between the two sides of the present controversy on these basic propositions. Respondents say that the very purpose of vindicating the right to vote justifies the recount procedures now at issue. The question before us, however, is whether the recount procedures the Florida Supreme Court has adopted are consistent with its obligation to avoid arbitrary and disparate treatment of the members of its electorate.

Much of the controversy seems to revolve around ballot cards designed to be perforated by a stylus but which, either through error or deliberate omission, have not been perforated with sufficient precision for a machine to count them. In some cases a piece of the card—a chad—is hanging, say by two corners. In other cases there is no separation at all, just an indentation. The Florida Supreme Court has ordered that the intent of the voter be discerned from such ballots. For purposes of resolving the equal protection challenge, it is not necessary to decide whether the Florida Supreme Court had the authority under the legislative scheme for resolving election disputes to define what a legal vote is and to mandate a manual recount implementing that definition. The recount mechanisms implemented in response to the decisions of the Florida Supreme Court do not satisfy the minimum requirement for nonarbitrary treatment of voters necessary to secure the fundamental right. Florida's basic command for the count of legally cast votes is to consider the "intent of the voter." This is unobjectionable as an abstract proposition and a starting principle. The problem inheres in the absence of specific standards to ensure its equal application. The formulation of uniform rules to determine intent based on these recurring circumstances is practicable and, we conclude, necessary.

. . . The want of those rules here has led to unequal evaluation of ballots in various respects. As seems to have been acknowledged at oral argument, the standards for accepting or rejecting contested ballots might vary not only from county to county but indeed within a single county from one recount team to another. . . .

The State Supreme Court ratified this uneven treatment. It mandated that the recount totals from two counties, Miami-Dade and Palm Beach, be included in the certified total. The court also appeared to hold *sub silentio* that the recount totals from Broward County, which were not completed until after the original November 14 certification by the Secretary of State, were to be considered part of the new certified vote totals even though the county certification was not contested by Vice President Gore. Yet each of the counties used varying standards to determine what was a legal vote. Broward County used a more forgiving standard than Palm Beach County, and uncovered almost three times as many new votes, a result markedly disproportionate to the difference in population between the counties. In addition, the recounts in these three counties were not limited to so-called undervotes but extended to all of the ballots. The distinction has real consequences. A manual recount of all ballots identifies not only those ballots which show no vote but also those which contain more than one, the so-called overvotes. Neither category will be counted by the machine. This is not a trivial concern.

At oral argument, respondents estimated there are as many as 110,000 overvotes statewide. As a result, the citizen whose ballot was not read by a machine because he failed to vote for a candidate in a way readable by a machine may still have his vote counted in a manual recount; on the other hand, the citizen who marks two candidates in a way discernable by the machine will not have the same opportunity to have his vote count, even if a manual examination of the ballot would reveal the requisite indicia of intent. Furthermore, the citizen who marks two candidates, only one of which is discernable by the machine, will have his vote counted even though it should have been read as an invalid ballot. The State Supreme Court's inclusion of vote counts based on these variant standards exemplifies concerns with the remedial processes that were under way.

That brings the analysis to yet a further equal protection problem. The votes certified by the court included a partial total from one county, Miami-Dade. The Florida Supreme Court's decision thus gives no assurance that the recounts included in a final certification must be complete. Indeed, it is respondent's submission that it would be consistent with the rules of the recount procedures to include whatever partial counts are done by the time of final certification, and we interpret the Florida Supreme Court's decision to permit this. . . . The press of time does not diminish the constitutional concern. A desire for speed is not a general excuse for ignoring equal protection guarantees.

In addition to these difficulties the actual process by which the votes were to be counted under the Florida Supreme Court's decision raises further concerns. That order did not specify who would recount the ballots. The county canvassing boards were forced to pull together ad hoc teams comprised of judges from various Circuits who had no previous training in handling and interpreting ballots. Furthermore, while others were permitted to observe, they were prohibited from objecting during the recount.

The recount process, in its features here described, is inconsistent with the minimum procedures necessary to protect the fundamental right of each voter in the special instance of a statewide recount under the authority of a single state judicial officer. Our consideration is limited to the present circumstances, for the problem of equal protection in election processes generally presents many complexities.

The question before the Court is not whether local entities, in the exercise of their expertise, may develop different systems for implementing elections. Instead, we are presented with a situation where a state court with the power to assure uniformity has ordered a statewide recount with minimal procedural safeguards. When a court orders a statewide remedy, there must be at least some assurance that the rudimentary requirements of equal treatment and fundamental fairness are satisfied. Given the Court's assessment that the recount process underway was probably being conducted in an unconstitutional manner, the Court stayed the order directing the recount so it could hear this case and render an expedited decision. The contest provision, as it was mandated by the State Supreme Court, is not well calculated to sustain the confidence that all citizens must have in the outcome of elections. The State has not shown that its procedures include the necessary safeguards. . . .

Upon due consideration of the difficulties identified to this point, it is obvious that the recount cannot be conducted in compliance with the requirements of equal protection and due process without substantial additional work. It would require not only the adoption (after opportunity for argument) of adequate statewide standards for determining what is a legal vote, and practicable procedures to implement them, but also orderly judicial review of any disputed matters that might arise. . . .

The Supreme Court of Florida has said that the legislature intended the State's electors to "participat[e] fully in the federal electoral process," as provided in 3 U.S.C. §5.

That statute, in turn, requires that any controversy or contest that is designed to lead to a conclusive selection of electors be completed by December 12. That date is upon us, and there is no recount procedure in place under the State Supreme Court's order that comports with minimal constitutional standards. Because it is evident that any recount seeking to meet the December 12 date will be unconstitutional for the reasons we have discussed, we reverse the judgment of the Supreme Court of Florida ordering a recount to proceed. Seven Justices of the Court agree that there are constitutional problems with the recount ordered by the Florida Supreme Court that demand a remedy. The only disagreement is as to the remedy.

Because the Florida Supreme Court has said that the Florida Legislature intended to obtain the safe-harbor benefits of 3 U.S.C. §5, JUSTICE BREYER's proposed remedy—remanding to the Florida Supreme Court for its ordering of a constitutionally proper contest until December 18—contemplates action in violation of the Florida election code, and hence could not be part of an "appropriate" order authorized by Fla. Stat. §102.168 (8) (2000). . . .

None are more conscious of the vital limits on judicial authority than are the members of this Court, and none stand more in admiration of the Constitution's design to leave the selection of the President to the people, through their legislatures, and to the political sphere. When contending parties invoke the process of the courts, however, it becomes our unsought responsibility to resolve the federal and constitutional issues the judicial system has been forced to confront. The judgment of the Supreme Court of Florida is reversed, and the case is remanded for further proceedings not inconsistent with this opinion.

Pursuant to this Court's Rule 45.2, the Clerk is directed to issue the mandate in this case forthwith.

It is so ordered.

CONCURRING OPINION

We join the per curiam opinion. We write separately because we believe there are additional grounds that require us to reverse the Florida Supreme Court's decision.

I

We deal here not with an ordinary election, but with an election for the President of the United States. . . .

In most cases, comity and respect for federalism compel us to defer to the decisions of state courts on issues of state law. That practice reflects our understanding that the decisions of state courts are definitive pronouncements of the will of the States as sovereigns. Of course, in ordinary cases, the distribution of powers among the branches of a State's government raises no questions of federal constitutional law, subject to the requirement that the government be republican in character. . . . But there are a few exceptional cases in which the Constitution imposes a duty or confers a power on a particular branch of a State's government. This is one of them.

Article II, §1, cl. 2, provides that "[e]ach State shall appoint, in such Manner as the Legislature thereof may direct," electors for President and Vice President. Thus, the text of the election law itself, and not just its interpretation by the courts of the States, takes on independent significance. . . . A significant departure from the legislative scheme for appointing Presidential electors presents a federal constitutional question.

3 U.S.C. §5 informs our application of Art. II, §1, cl. 2, to the Florida statutory scheme, which, as the Florida Supreme Court acknowledged, took that statute into account. Section 5 provides that the State's selection of electors "shall be conclusive, and shall govern in the counting of the electoral votes" if the electors are chosen under laws enacted prior to election day, and if the selection process is completed six days prior to the meeting of the electoral college. . . .

If we are to respect the legislature's Article II powers, therefore, we must ensure that postelection state-court actions do not frustrate the legislative desire to attain the "safe harbor" provided by §5.

In Florida, the legislature has chosen to hold statewide elections to appoint the State's 25 electors. Importantly, the legislature has delegated the authority to run the elections and to oversee election disputes to the Secretary of State (Secretary), and to state circuit courts. Isolated sections of the code may well admit of more than one inter-

pretation, but the general coherence of the legislative scheme may not be altered by judicial interpretation so as to wholly change the statutorily provided apportionment of responsibility among these various bodies. In any election but a Presidential election, the Florida Supreme Court can give as little or as much deference to Florida's executives as it chooses, so far as Article II is concerned, and this Court will have no cause to question the court's actions. But, with respect to a Presidential election, the court must be both mindful of the legislature's role under Article II in choosing the manner of appointing electors and deferential to those bodies expressly empowered by the legislature to carry out its constitutional mandate.

In order to determine whether a state court has infringed upon the legislature's authority, we necessarily must examine the law of the State as it existed prior to the action of the court. Though we generally defer to state courts on the interpretation of state law . . . there are of course areas in which the Constitution requires this Court to undertake an independent, if still deferential, analysis of state law. . . .

This inquiry does not imply a disrespect for state courts but rather a respect for the constitutionally prescribed role of state legislatures. To attach definitive weight to the pronouncement of a state court, when the very question at issue is whether the court has actually departed from the statutory meaning, would be to abdicate our responsibility to enforce the explicit requirements of Article II.

II

Acting pursuant to its constitutional grant of authority, the Florida Legislature has created a detailed, if not perfectly crafted, statutory scheme that provides for appointment of Presidential electors by direct election. Under the statute, "[v]otes cast for the actual candidates for President and Vice President shall be counted as votes cast for the presidential electors supporting such candidates." The legislature has designated the Secretary of State as the "chief election officer," with the responsibility to "[o]btain and maintain uniformity in the application, operation, and interpretation of the election laws."

The state legislature has delegated to county canvassing boards the duties of administering elections. Those boards are responsible for providing results to the state Elections Canvassing Commission, comprising the Governor, the Secretary of State, and the Director of the Division of Elections. . . .

After the election has taken place, the canvassing boards receive returns from precincts, count the votes, and in the event that a candidate was defeated by .5% or less, conduct a mandatory recount. The county canvassing boards must file certified election returns with the Department of State by 5 p. m. on the seventh day following the election. The Elections Canvassing Commission must then certify the results of the election. The state legislature has also provided mechanisms both for protesting election returns and for contesting certified election results. . . . Any protest must be filed prior to the certification of election results by the county canvassing board. Once a protest has been filed, "the county canvassing board may authorize a manual recount." If a sample recount . . . "indicates an error in the vote tabulation which could affect the outcome of the election," the county canvassing board is instructed to: "(a) Correct the error and recount the remaining precincts with the vote tabulation system; (b) Request the Department of State to verify the tabulation software; or (c) Manually recount all ballots." In the event a canvassing board chooses to conduct a manual recount of all ballots, [state law] prescribes procedures for such a recount.

. . . The grounds for contesting an election include "[r]eceipt of a number of illegal votes or rejection of a number of legal votes sufficient to change or place in doubt the result of the election." Any contest must be filed in the appropriate Florida circuit court, and the canvassing board or election board is the proper party defendant. [Florida law] provides that "[t]he circuit judge to whom the contest is presented may fashion such orders as he or she deems necessary to ensure that each allegation in the complaint is investigated, examined, or checked, to prevent or correct any alleged wrong, and to provide any relief appropriate under such circumstances." In Presidential elections, the contest period necessarily terminates on the date set by 3 U.S.C. §5 for concluding the State's "final determination" of election controversies.

In its first decision . . . , the Florida Supreme Court extended the 7-day statutory certification deadline established by the legislature. This modification of the code, by lengthening the protest period, necessarily shortened the contest period for Presidential elections. Underlying the extension of the certification deadline and the short-changing of the contest period was, presumably, the clear implication that certification was a matter of significance: The certified winner would enjoy presumptive validity, making a contest proceeding by the losing candidate an uphill battle. In its latest opinion, however, the court empties certification of virtually all legal consequence during the contest, and in doing so departs from the provisions enacted by the Florida Legislature. The court determined that canvassing boards' decisions regarding whether to recount ballots past the certification deadline (even the certification deadline established by Harris I) are to be reviewed de novo, although the election code clearly vests discretion whether to recount in the boards, and sets strict deadlines subject to the Secretary's rejection of late tallies and monetary fines for tardiness. . . . Moreover, the Florida court held that all late vote tallies arriving during the contest period should be automatically included in the certification regardless of the certification deadline (even the certification deadline established by Harris I), thus virtually eliminating both the deadline and the Secretary's discretion to disregard recounts that violate it.

Moreover, the court's interpretation of "legal vote," and hence its decision to order a contest-period recount, plainly departed from the legislative scheme. Florida statutory law cannot reasonably be thought to require the counting of improperly marked ballots. Each Florida precinct before election day provides instructions on how properly to cast a vote, §101.46; each polling place on election day contains a working model of the voting machine it uses, §101.5611; and each voting booth contains a sample ballot, §101.46. In precincts using punch-card ballots, voters are instructed to punch out the ballot cleanly. . . .

No reasonable person would call it "an error in the vote tabulation," or a "rejection of legal votes," when electronic or electromechanical equipment performs precisely in the manner designed, and fails to count those ballots that are not marked in the manner that these voting instructions explicitly and prominently specify. The scheme that the Florida Supreme Court's opinion attributes to the legislature is one in which machines are required to be "capable of correctly counting votes," but which nonetheless regularly produces elections in which legal votes are predictably not tabulated, so that in close elections manual recounts are regularly required. This is of course absurd. The Secretary of State, who is authorized by law to issue binding interpretations of the election code, rejected this peculiar reading of the statutes. . . . The Florida Supreme Court, although it must defer to the Secretary's interpretations, . . . rejected her reasonable interpretation and embraced the peculiar one.

But as we indicated in our remand of the earlier case, in a Presidential election the clearly expressed intent of the legislature must prevail. And there is no basis for reading the Florida statutes as requiring the counting of improperly marked ballots, as an examination of the Florida Supreme Court's textual analysis shows. . . . The

State's Attorney General (who was supporting the Gore challenge) confirmed in oral argument here that never before the present election had a manual recount been conducted on the basis of the contention that "undervotes" should have been examined to determine voter intent. For the court to step away from this established practice, prescribed by the Secretary of State, the state official charged by the legislature with "responsibility to . . . [o]btain and maintain uniformity in the application, operation, and interpretation of the election laws," §97.012 (1), was to depart from the legislative scheme.

III

The scope and nature of the remedy ordered by the Florida Supreme Court jeopardizes the "legislative wish" to take advantage of the safe harbor provided by 3 U.S.C. §5. December 12, 2000, is the last date for a final determination of the Florida electors that will satisfy §5. Yet in the late afternoon of December 8th—four days before this deadline—the Supreme Court of Florida ordered recounts of tens of thousands of so-called "undervotes" spread through 64 of the State's 67 counties. This was done in a search for elusive—perhaps delusive—certainty as to the exact count of 6 million votes. But no one claims that these ballots have not previously been tabulated; they were initially read by voting machines at the time of the election, and thereafter reread by virtue of Florida's automatic recount provision. No one claims there was any fraud in the election. The Supreme Court of Florida ordered this additional recount under the provision of the election code giving the circuit judge the authority to provide relief that is "appropriate under such circumstances."

Surely when the Florida Legislature empowered the courts of the State to grant "appropriate" relief, it must have meant relief that would have become final by the cut-off date of 3 U.S.C. §5. In light of the inevitable legal challenges and ensuing appeals to the Supreme Court of Florida and petitions for certiorari to this Court, the entire recounting process could not possibly be completed by that date. . . .

As the dissent noted: "In [the four days remaining], all questionable ballots must be reviewed by the judicial officer appointed to discern the intent of the voter in a process open to the public. Fairness dictates that a provision be made for either party to object to how a particular ballot is counted. Additionally, this short time period must allow for judicial review. I respectfully submit this cannot be completed without taking Florida's presidential electors outside the safe harbor provision, creating the very real possibility of disenfranchising those nearly 6 million voters who are able to correctly cast their ballots on election day." . . . Given all these factors, and in light of the legislative intent identified by the Florida Supreme Court to bring Florida within the "safe harbor" provision of 3 U.S.C. §5, the remedy prescribed by the Supreme Court of Florida cannot be deemed an "appropriate" one as of December 8.

It significantly departed from the statutory framework in place on November 7, and authorized open-ended further proceedings which could not be completed by December 12, thereby preventing a final determination by that date.

For these reasons, in addition to those given in the per curiam, we would reverse.

CHIEF JUSTICE REHNQUIST, with whom JUSTICE SCALIA and JUSTICE THOMAS join, concurring.

STEVENS'S DISSENT

The Constitution assigns to the States the primary responsibility for determining the manner of selecting the Presidential electors. . . . When questions arise about the meaning of state laws, including election laws, it is our settled practice to accept the opinions of the highest courts of the States as providing the final answers. On rare occasions, however, either federal statutes or the Federal Constitution may require federal judicial intervention in state elections. This is not such an occasion.

The federal questions that ultimately emerged in this case are not substantial. Article II provides that "[e]ach State shall appoint, in such Manner as the Legislature thereof may direct, a Number of Electors." It does not create state legislatures out of whole cloth, but rather takes them as they come—as creatures born of, and constrained by, their state constitutions. Lest there be any doubt, we stated over 100 years ago in *McPherson v. Blacker* (1892), that "[w]hat is forbidden or required to be done by a State" in the Article II context "is forbidden or required of the legislative power under state constitutions as they exist." In the same vein, we also observed that "[t]he [State's] legislative power is the supreme authority except as limited by the constitution of the State." The legislative power in Florida is subject to judicial review pursuant to Article V of the Florida Constitution, and nothing in Article II of the Federal Constitution frees the state legislature from the constraints in the state constitution that created it. Moreover, the Florida Legislature's own decision to employ a unitary code for all elections indicates that it intended the Florida Supreme Court to play the same role in Presidential elections that it has historically played in resolving electoral disputes. The Florida Supreme Court's exercise of appellate jurisdiction therefore was wholly consistent with, and indeed contemplated by, the grant of authority in Article II.

It hardly needs stating that Congress, pursuant to 3 U.S.C. §5, did not impose any affirmative duties upon the States that their governmental branches could "violate." Rather, §5 provides a safe harbor for States to select electors in contested elections "by judicial or other methods" established by laws prior to the election day. Section 5, like Article II, assumes the involvement of the state judiciary in interpreting state election laws and resolving election disputes under those laws. Neither §5 nor Article II grants federal judges any special authority to substitute their views for those of the state judiciary on matters of state law.

Nor are petitioners correct in asserting that the failure of the Florida Supreme Court to specify in detail the precise manner in which the "intent of the voter," is to be determined rises to the level of a constitutional violation. We found such a violation when individual votes within the same State were weighted unequally . . . but we have never before called into question the substantive standard by which a State determines that a vote has been legally cast. And there is no reason to think that the guidance provided to the fact-finders, specifically the various canvassing boards, by the "intent of the voter" standard is any less sufficient—or will lead to results any less uniform—than, for example, the "beyond a reasonable doubt" standard employed everyday by ordinary citizens in courtrooms across this country.

Admittedly, the use of differing substandards for determining voter intent in different counties employing similar voting systems may raise serious concerns. Those concerns are alleviated—if not eliminated—by the fact that a single impartial magistrate will ultimately adjudicate all objections arising from the recount process. Of course, as a general matter, "[t]he interpretation of constitutional principles must not be too literal. We must remember that the machinery of government would not work if it were not allowed a little play in its joints." *Bain Peanut Co. of Tex. v. Pinson* (1931) (Holmes, J.). If it were otherwise, Florida's decision to leave to each county the determination of what balloting system to employ—despite enormous differences in accuracy—might run afoul of equal protection. So, too, might the similar decisions of the vast majority of state legislatures to delegate to local authorities certain decisions with respect to voting systems and ballot design. Even assuming that aspects of the remedial scheme might ultimately be found to violate the Equal Protection Clause, I could not subscribe to the majority's disposition of the case. As the majority explicitly holds, once a state legislature determines to select electors through a popular vote, the right to have one's vote counted is of constitutional stature. As the majority further acknowledges, Florida law holds that all ballots that reveal the intent of the voter constitute valid votes. Recognizing these principles, the majority nonetheless orders the termination of the contest proceeding before all such votes have been tabulated. Under their own reasoning, the appropriate course of action would be to remand to allow more specific procedures for implementing the legislature's uniform general standard to be established.

In the interest of finality, however, the majority effectively orders the disenfranchisement of an unknown number of voters whose ballots reveal their intent—and are therefore legal votes under state law—but were for some reason rejected by ballot-counting machines. It does so on the basis of the deadlines set forth in Title 3 of the United States Code. But, as I have already noted, those provisions merely provide rules of decision for Congress to follow when selecting among conflicting slates of electors. They do not prohibit a State from counting what the majority concedes to be legal votes until a bona fide winner is determined. Indeed, in 1960, Hawaii appointed two slates of electors and Congress chose to count the one appointed on January 4, 1961, well after the Title 3 deadlines. . . . Thus, nothing prevents the majority, even if it properly found an equal protection violation, from ordering relief appropriate to remedy that violation without depriving Florida voters of their right to have their votes counted. As the majority notes, "[a] desire for speed is not a general excuse for ignoring equal protection guarantees." Finally, neither in this case, nor in its earlier opinion in *Palm Beach County Canvassing Bd. v. Harris,* did the Florida Supreme Court make any substantive change in Florida electoral law. Its decisions were rooted in long-established precedent and were consistent with the relevant statutory provisions, taken as a whole. It did what courts do—it decided the case before it in light of the legislature's intent to leave no legally cast vote uncounted. In so doing, it relied on the sufficiency of the general "intent of the voter" standard articulated by the state legislature, coupled with a procedure for ultimate review by an impartial judge, to resolve the concern about disparate evaluations of contested ballots. If we assume—as I do—that the members of that court and the judges who would have carried out its mandate are impartial, its decision does not even raise a colorable federal question.

What must underlie petitioners' entire federal assault on the Florida election procedures is an unstated lack of confidence in the impartiality and capacity of the state judges who would make the critical decisions if the vote count were to proceed. Otherwise, their position is wholly without merit. The endorsement of that position by the majority of this Court can only lend credence to the most cynical appraisal of the work of judges throughout the land. It is confidence in the men and women who administer the judicial system that is the true backbone of the rule of law. Time will one day heal the wound to that confidence that will be inflicted by today's decision. One thing, however, is certain. Although we may never know with complete certainty the identity of the winner of this year's Presidential election, the identity of the loser is perfectly clear. It is the Nation's confidence in the judge as an impartial guardian of the rule of law. I respectfully dissent.

JUSTICE STEVENS, with whom JUSTICE GINSBURG AND JUSTICE BREYER join, dissenting.

SOUTER'S DISSENT

The Court should not have reviewed either *Bush v. Palm Beach County Canvassing Bd.* or this case, and should not have stopped Florida's attempt to recount all undervote ballots by issuing a stay of the Florida Supreme Court's orders during the period of this review. If this Court had allowed the State to follow the course indicated by the opinions of its own Supreme Court, it is entirely possible that there would ultimately have been no issue requiring our review, and political tension could have worked itself out in the Congress following the procedure provided in 3 U.S.C. §15. The case being before us, however, its resolution by the majority is another erroneous decision.

As will be clear, I am in substantial agreement with the dissenting opinions of JUSTICE STEVENS, JUSTICE GINSBURG and JUSTICE BREYER. I write separately only to say how straightforward the issues before us really are.

There are three issues: whether the State Supreme Court's interpretation of the statute providing for a contest of the state election results somehow violates 3 U.S.C. §5; whether that court's construction of the state statutory provisions governing contests impermissibly changes a state law from what the State's legislature has provided, in violation of Article II, §1, cl. 2, of the national Constitution; and whether the manner of interpreting markings on disputed ballots failing to cause machines to register votes for President (the undervote ballots) violates the equal protection or due process guaranteed by the Fourteenth Amendment. None of these issues is difficult to describe or to resolve.

A

The 3 U.S.C. §5 issue is not serious. That provision sets certain conditions for treating a State's certification of Presidential electors as conclusive in the event that a dispute over recognizing those electors must be resolved in the Congress under 3 U.S.C. §15. Conclusiveness requires selection under a legal scheme in place before the election, with results determined at least six days before the date set for casting electoral votes. But no State is required to conform to §5 if it cannot do that (for whatever reason); the sanction for failing to satisfy the conditions of §5 is simply loss of what has been called its "safe harbor." And even that determination is to be made, if made anywhere, in the Congress.

B

The second matter here goes to the State Supreme Court's interpretation of certain terms in the state statute governing election "contests." The issue is whether the judgment of the state supreme court has displaced the state legislature's provisions for election contests: is the law as declared by the court different from the provisions made by the legislature, to which the national Constitution commits responsibility for determining how each State's Presidential electors are chosen? . . .

Bush does not, of course, claim that any judicial act interpreting a statute of uncertain meaning is enough to displace the legislative provision and violate Article II; statutes require interpretation, which does not without more affect the legislative character of a statute within the meaning of the Constitution. What Bush does argue, as I understand the contention, is that the interpretation of §102.168 was so unreasonable as to transcend the accepted bounds of statutory interpretation, to the point of being a nonjudicial act and producing new law untethered to the legislative act in question.

The starting point for evaluating the claim that the Florida Supreme Court's interpretation effectively rewrote §102.168 must be the language of the provision on which Gore relies to show his right to raise this contest: that the previously certified result in Bush's favor was produced by "rejection of a number of legal votes sufficient to change or place in doubt the result of the election."

None of the state court's interpretations is unreasonable to the point of displacing the legislative enactment quoted. As I will note below, other interpretations were of course possible, and some might have been better than those adopted by the Florida court's majority; the two dissents from the majority opinion of that court and various briefs submitted to us set out alternatives. But the majority view is in each instance within the bounds of reasonable interpretation, and the law as declared is consistent with Article II.

The statute does not define a "legal vote," the rejection of which may affect the election. The State Supreme Court was therefore required to define it, and in doing that the court looked to another election statute, dealing with damaged or defective ballots, which contains a provision that no vote shall be disregarded "if there is a clear indication of the intent of the voter as determined by a canvassing board." The court read that objective of looking to the voter's intent as indicating that the legislature probably meant "legal vote" to mean a vote recorded on a ballot indicating what the voter intended.

It is perfectly true that the majority might have chosen a different reading. . . . But even so, there is no constitutional violation in following the majority view; Article II is unconcerned with mere disagreements about interpretive merits.

The Florida court next interpreted "rejection" to determine what act in the counting process may be attacked in a contest. Again, the statute does not define the term. The court majority read the word to mean simply a failure to count. That reading is certainly within the bounds of common sense, given the objective to give effect to a voter's intent if that can be determined. . . .

The same is true about the court majority's understanding of the phrase "votes sufficient to change or place in doubt" the result of the election in Florida. The court held that if the uncounted ballots were so numerous that it was reasonably possible that they contained enough "legal" votes to swing the election, this contest would be authorized by the statute. While the majority might have thought (as the trial judge did) that a probability, not a possibility, should be necessary to justify a contest, that reading is not required by the statute's text, which says nothing about probability. Whatever people of good will and good sense may argue about the merits of the Florida court's reading, there is no warrant for saying that it transcends the limits of reasonable statutory interpretation to the point of supplanting the statute enacted by the "legislature" within the meaning of Article II. . . .

C

It is only on the third issue before us that there is a meritorious argument for relief, as this Court's Per Curiam opinion recognizes. It is an issue that might well have been dealt with adequately by the Florida courts if the state proceedings had not been interrupted, and if not disposed of at the state level it could have been considered by the Congress in any electoral vote dispute. But because the course of state proceedings has been interrupted, time is short, and the issue is before us, I think it sensible for the Court to address it.

Petitioners have raised an equal protection claim (or, alternatively, a due process claim . . . in the charge that unjustifiably disparate standards are applied in different electoral jurisdictions to otherwise identical facts. It is true that the Equal Protection Clause does not forbid the use of a variety of voting mechanisms within a jurisdiction, even though different mechanisms will have different levels of effectiveness in recording voters' intentions; local variety can be justified by concerns about cost, the potential value of innovation, and so on. But evidence in the record here suggests that a different order of disparity obtains under rules for determining a voter's intent that have been applied (and could continue to be applied) to identical types of ballots used in identical brands of machines and exhibiting identical physical characteristics (such as "hanging" or "dimpled" chads).

I can conceive of no legitimate state interest served by these differing treatments of the expressions of voters' fundamental rights. The differences appear wholly arbitrary. In deciding what to do about this, we should take account of the fact that electoral votes are due to be cast in six days. I would therefore remand the case to the courts of Florida with instructions to establish uniform standards for evaluating the several types of ballots that have prompted differing treatments, to be applied within and among counties when passing on such identical ballots in any further recounting (or successive recounting) that the courts might order.

Unlike the majority, I see no warrant for this Court to assume that Florida could not possibly comply with this requirement before the date set for the meeting of electors, December 18.

. . . To recount these [ballots] manually would be a tall order, but before this Court stayed the effort to do that the courts of Florida were ready to do their best to get that job done. There is no justification for denying the State the opportunity to try to count all disputed ballots now. I respectfully dissent.

JUSTICE SOUTER, with whom JUSTICE BREYER joins and with whom JUSTICE STEVENS and JUSTICE GINSBURG join with regard to all but Part C, dissenting.

GINSBURG'S DISSENT

I

THE CHIEF JUSTICE acknowledges that provisions of Florida's Election Code "may well admit of more than one interpretation." But instead of respecting the state high court's province to say what the State's Election Code means, THE CHIEF JUSTICE maintains that Florida's Supreme Court has veered so far from the ordinary practice of judicial review that what it did cannot properly be called judging. . . . I might join THE CHIEF JUSTICE were it my commission to interpret Florida law. But disagreement with the Florida court's interpretation of its own State's law does not warrant the conclusion that the justices of that court have legislated. There is no cause here to believe that the members of Florida's high court have done less than "their mortal best to discharge their oath of office," and no cause to upset their reasoned interpretation of Florida law. . . .

The extraordinary setting of this case has obscured the ordinary principle that dictates its proper resolution: Federal courts defer to state high courts' interpretations of their State's own law. This principle reflects the core of federalism, on which all agree. . . .

THE CHIEF JUSTICE's solicitude for the Florida Legislature comes at the expense of the more fundamental solicitude we owe to the legislature's sovereign.

Were the other members of this Court as mindful as they generally are of our system of dual sovereignty, they would affirm the judgment of the Florida Supreme Court.

II

I agree with JUSTICE STEVENS that petitioners have not presented a substantial equal protection claim. Ideally, perfection would be the appropriate standard for judging the recount. But we live in an imperfect world, one in which thousands of votes have not been counted. I cannot agree that the recount adopted by the Florida court, flawed as it may be, would yield a result any less fair or precise than the certification that preceded that recount. . . .

Even if there were an equal protection violation, I would agree with JUSTICE STEVENS, JUSTICE SOUTER, and JUSTICE BREYER that the Court's concern about the December 12 date is misplaced. Time is short in part because of the Court's entry of a stay on December 9, several hours after an able circuit judge in Leon County had begun to superintend the recount process. More fundamentally, the Court's reluctance to let the recount go forward . . . ultimately turns on its own judgment about the practical realities of implementing a recount, not the judgment of those much closer to the process.

. . . In sum, the Court's conclusion that a constitutionally adequate recount is impractical is a prophecy the Court's own judgment will not allow to be tested. Such an untested prophecy should not decide the Presidency of the United States.

I dissent.

JUSTICE GINSBURG, with whom JUSTICE STEVENS joins, and with whom JUSTICE SOUTER and JUSTICE BREYER join as to Part I, dissenting.

BREYER'S DISSENT

The Court was wrong to take this case. It was wrong to grant a stay. It should now vacate that stay and permit the Florida Supreme Court to decide whether the recount should resume.

I

The political implications of this case for the country are momentous. But the federal legal questions presented, with one exception, are insubstantial.

The majority raises three Equal Protection problems with the Florida Supreme Court's recount order: first, the failure to include overvotes in the manual recount; second, the fact that all ballots, rather than simply the undervotes, were recounted in some, but not all, counties; and third, the absence of a uniform, specific standard to guide the recounts. As far as the first issue is concerned, petitioners presented no evidence, to this Court or to any Florida court, that a manual recount of overvotes would identify additional legal votes. The same is true of the second, and, in addition, the majority's reasoning would seem to invalidate any state provision for a manual recount of individual counties in a statewide election.

The majority's third concern does implicate principles of fundamental fairness. The majority concludes that the Equal Protection Clause requires that a manual recount be governed not only by the uniform general standard of the "clear intent of the voter," but also by uniform subsidiary standards. . . . I agree that, in these very special circumstances, basic principles of fairness should have counseled the adoption of a uniform standard to address the problem. In light of the majority's disposition, I need not decide whether, or the extent to which, as a remedial matter, the Constitution would place limits upon the content of the uniform standard.

Nonetheless, there is no justification for the majority's remedy, which is simply to reverse the lower court and halt the recount entirely. An appropriate remedy would be, instead, to remand this case with instructions that, even at this late date, would permit the Florida Supreme Court to require recounting all undercounted votes in Florida, including those from Broward, Volusia, Palm Beach, and Miami-Dade Counties, whether or not previously recounted prior to the end of the protest period, and to do so in accordance with a single-uniform substandard.

The majority justifies stopping the recount entirely on the ground that there is no more time. In particular, the majority relies on the lack of time for the Secretary to review and approve equipment needed to separate undervotes. But the majority reaches this conclusion in the absence of any record evidence that the recount could not have been completed in the time allowed by the Florida Supreme Court. The majority finds facts outside of the record on matters that state courts are in a far better position to address. Of course, it is too late for any such recount to take place by December 12, the date by which election disputes must be decided if a State is to take advantage of the safe harbor provisions of 3 U.S.C. §5.

Whether there is time to conduct a recount prior to December 18, when the electors are scheduled to meet, is a matter for the state courts to determine. And whether, under Florida law, Florida could or could not take further action is obviously a matter for Florida courts, not this Court, to decide. . . .

By halting the manual recount, and thus ensuring that the uncounted legal votes will not be counted under any standard, this Court crafts a remedy out of proportion to the asserted harm. And that remedy harms the very fairness interests the Court is attempting to protect. The manual recount would itself redress a problem of unequal treatment of ballots. As JUSTICE STEVENS points out, the ballots of voters in counties that use punch-card systems are more likely to be disqualified than those in counties using optical-scanning systems. According to recent news reports, variations in the undervote rate are even more pronounced. . . . Thus, in a system that allows counties to use different types of voting systems, voters already arrive at the polls with an unequal chance that their votes will be counted. I do not see how the fact that this results from counties' selection of different voting machines rather than a court order makes the outcome any more fair. Nor do I understand why the Florida Supreme Court's recount order, which helps to redress this inequity, must be entirely prohibited based on a deficiency that could easily be remedied.

The remainder of petitioners' claims, which are the focus of the CHIEF JUSTICE's concurrence, raise no significant federal questions. I cannot agree that the CHIEF JUSTICE's unusual review of state law in this case is justified by reference either to Art. II, §1, or to 3 U.S.C. §5.

Moreover, even were such review proper, the conclusion that the Florida Supreme Court's decision contravenes federal law is untenable. . . .

II

Despite the reminder that this case involves "an election for the President of the United States," no preeminent legal concern, or practical concern related to legal questions, required this Court to hear this case, let alone to issue a stay that stopped Florida's recount process in its tracks. With one exception, petitioners' claims do not ask us to vindicate a constitutional provision designed to protect a basic human right. Petitioners invoke fundamental fairness, namely, the need for procedural fairness, including finality. But with the one "equal protection" exception, they rely upon law that focuses, not upon that basic need, but upon the constitutional allocation of power. Respondents invoke a competing fundamental consideration—the need to determine the voter's true intent. But they look to state law, not to federal constitutional law, to protect that interest.

Neither side claims electoral fraud, dishonesty, or the like. And the more fundamental equal protection claim might have been left to the state court to resolve if and when it was discovered to have mattered. It could still be resolved through a remand conditioned upon issuance of a uniform standard; it does not require reversing the Florida Supreme Court. Of course, the selection of the President is of fundamental national importance. But that importance is political, not legal. And this Court should resist the temptation unnecessarily to resolve tangential legal disputes, where doing so threatens to determine the outcome of the election.

The Constitution and federal statutes themselves make clear that restraint is appropriate. They set forth a road map of how to resolve disputes about electors, even after an election as close as this one. That road map foresees resolution of electoral disputes by state courts. See 3 U.S.C. §5 (providing that, where a "State shall have provided, by laws enacted prior to [election day], for its final determination of any controversy or contest concerning the appointment of . . . electors . . . by judicial or other methods," the subsequently chosen electors enter a safe harbor free from congressional challenge). But it nowhere provides for involvement by the United States Supreme Court. To the contrary, the Twelfth Amendment commits to Congress the authority and responsibility to count electoral votes. A federal statute, the Electoral Count Act, enacted after the close 1876 Hayes-Tilden Presidential election, specifies that, after States have tried to resolve disputes (through "judicial" or other means), Congress is the body primarily authorized to resolve remaining disputes. . . .

Given this detailed, comprehensive scheme for counting electoral votes, there is no reason to believe that federal law either foresees or requires resolution of such a political issue by this Court. Nor, for that matter, is there any reason to . . . think [that] the Constitution's Framers would have reached a different conclusion. Madison, at least, believed that allowing the judiciary to choose the presidential electors "was out of the question." The decision by both the Constitution's Framers and the 1886 Congress to minimize this Court's role in resolving close federal presidential elections is as wise as it is clear.

However awkward or difficult it may be for Congress to resolve difficult electoral disputes, Congress, being a political body, expresses the people's will far more accurately than does an unelected Court. And the people's will is what elections are about.

. . . I think it not only legally wrong, but also most unfortunate, for the Court simply to have terminated the Florida recount. Those who caution judicial restraint in resolving political disputes have described the quintessential case for that restraint as a case marked, among other things, by the "strangeness of the issue," its "intractability to principled resolution," its "sheer momentousness . . . which tends to unbalance judicial judgment," and "the inner vulnerability, the self-doubt of an institution which is electorally irresponsible and has no earth to draw strength from." Those characteristics mark this case.

At the same time, as I have said, the Court is not acting to vindicate a fundamental constitutional principle, such as the need to protect a basic human liberty. No other strong reason to act is present. Congressional statutes tend to obviate the need. And, above all, in this highly politicized matter, the appearance of a split decision runs the risk of undermining the public's confidence in the Court itself. That confidence is a public treasure. It has been built slowly over many years, some of which were marked by a Civil War and the tragedy of segregation. It is a vitally necessary ingredient of any successful effort to protect basic liberty and, indeed, the rule of law itself. We run no risk of returning to the days when a President (responding to this Court's efforts to protect the Cherokee Indians) might have said, "John Marshall has made his decision; now let him enforce it!" But we do risk a self-inflicted wound—a wound that may harm not just the Court, but the Nation.

I fear that in order to bring this agonizingly long election process to a definitive conclusion, we have not adequately attended to that necessary "check upon our own exercise of power," "our own sense of self-restraint." *United States v. Butler* (1936) (Stone, J., dissenting). Justice Brandeis once said of the Court, "The most important thing we do is not doing." What it does today, the Court should have left undone. I would repair the damage as best we now can, by permitting the Florida recount to continue under uniform standards. I respectfully dissent.

JUSTICE BREYER, with whom JUSTICE STEVENS and JUSTICE GINSBURG join except as to Part I–A–1, and with whom JUSTICE SOUTER joins as to Part I, dissenting.

Al Gore's Concession Speech

Following is a transcript of Vice President Al Gore's Dec. 13, 2000, televised address conceding the presidency to Texas Gov. George W. Bush. Gore spoke from the Old Executive Office Building in Washington, D.C.

Just moments ago, I spoke with George W. Bush and congratulated him on becoming the 43rd president of the United States. And I promised I wouldn't call him back this time.

I offered to meet with him as soon as possible, so that we can start to heal the divisions of the campaign, and the contest through which we have just passed.

Almost a century and a half ago, Sen. Stephen Douglas told Abraham Lincoln, who had just defeated him for the presidency, "Partisan feeling must yield to patriotism. I am with you, Mr. President, and God bless you."

In that same spirit, I say to President-elect Bush that what remains of partisan rancor must now be put aside. And may God bless his stewardship of this country.

Neither he nor I anticipated this long and difficult road. Certainly, neither of us wanted it to happen. Yet it came. And now it has ended, resolved as it must be resolved—through the honored institutions of our democracy.

Over the library of one of our great law schools is inscribed the motto: "Not under man but under God and law." It is the ruling principle of American freedom, the source of our democratic liberties; I have tried to make it my guide throughout this contest, as it has guided America's deliberations of all the complex issues of the past five weeks.

Now the U.S. Supreme Court has spoken. Let there be no doubt: While I strongly disagree with the court's decision, I accept it. I accept the finality of this outcome, which will be ratified next Monday in the Electoral College. And tonight, for the sake of our unity as a people and the strength of our democracy, I offer my concession.

I also accept my responsibility, which I will discharge unconditionally—to honor the new president-elect, and do everything possible to help him bring Americans together in fulfillment of the great vision that our Declaration of Independence defines, and that our Constitution affirms and defends.

Let me say how grateful I am to all those who supported me—and supported the cause for which we have fought.

Tipper and I feel a deep gratitude to Joe and Hadassah Lieberman, who brought passion and high purpose to our partnership—and opened new doors not just for our campaign, but for our country.

This has been an extraordinary election. But in one of God's unforeseen paths, this belatedly broken impasse can point us all to a new common ground. For its very closeness can serve to remind us that we are one people, with a shared history and a shared destiny.

Indeed, that history gives us many examples of contests as hotly debated, as fiercely fought, with their own challenges to the popular will.

Other disputes have dragged on for weeks before reaching resolution. And each time, both the victor and the vanquished have accepted the result peacefully, and in a spirit of reconciliation.

So let it be with us.

I know that many of my supporters are disappointed. I am, too. But our disappointment must be overcome by our love of country.

And I say to our fellow members of the world community: Let no one see this contest as a sign of American weakness. The strength of American democracy is shown most clearly through the difficulties it can overcome.

Some have expressed concern that the unusual nature of this election might hamper the next president in the conduct of his office. I do not believe it need be so.

President-elect Bush inherits a nation whose citizens will be ready to assist him in the conduct of his large responsibilities. I personally will be at his disposal.

And I call on all Americans—I particularly urge all who stood with us—to unite behind our next president.

This is America. Just as we fight hard when the stakes are high, we close ranks and come together when the contest is done.

And while there will be time enough to debate our continuing differences, now is the time to recognize that that which unites us is greater than that which divides us.

While we yet hold and do not yield our opposing beliefs, there is a higher duty than the one we owe to political party.

This is America, and we put country before party. We will stand together behind our new president.

As for what I'll do next, I don't know the answer to that one yet. Like many of you, I'm looking forward to spending the holidays with family and old friends. I know I'll spend time in Tennessee and mend some fences—literally and figuratively.

Some have asked whether I have any regrets, and I do have one regret: that I didn't get the chance to stay and fight for the American people for the next four years. Especially for those who need burdens lifted and barriers removed. Especially for those who feel their voices have not been heard.

I heard you—and I will not forget.

I've seen America in this campaign. And I like what I see. It's worth fighting for. And that's a fight I'll never stop.

As for the battle that ends tonight, I do believe, as my father once said, that no matter how hard the loss, defeat may serve as well as victory to shake the soul and let the glory out.

So for me, this campaign ends as it began: with the love of Tipper and our family; with faith in God and in the country I have been so proud to serve, from Vietnam to the vice presidency; and with gratitude to our truly tireless campaign staff and volunteers, including all those who worked so hard in Florida for the last 36 days.

Now the political struggle is over. And we turn again to the unending struggle for the common good of all Americans, and for those multitudes around the world who look to us for leadership in the cause of freedom.

In the words of our great hymn, "America, America, let us crown thy good with brotherhood, from sea to shining sea."

And now, my friends, in a phrase I once addressed to others—it is time for me to go.

Thank you, and good night. And God bless America.

George W. Bush's Acceptance Speech

Following is a transcript of President-elect George W. Bush's Dec. 13, 2000, televised speech after the concession of Vice President Al Gore. Bush spoke from the chamber of the state House of Representatives in Austin, Texas.

Thank you all. Thank you very much. Good evening, my fellow Americans. I appreciate so very much the opportunity to speak with you tonight.

Mr. Speaker, Lieutenant Governor, friends, distinguished guests, our country has been through a long and trying period, with the outcome of the presidential election not finalized for longer than any of us could ever imagine.

Vice President Gore and I put our hearts and hopes into our campaigns. We both gave it our all. We shared similar emotions, so I understand how difficult this moment must be for Vice President Gore and his family.

He has a distinguished record of service to our country as a congressman, a senator and a vice president.

This evening I received a gracious call from the vice president. We agreed to meet early next week in Washington, and we agreed to do our best to heal our country after this hard-fought contest.

Tonight I want to thank all the thousands of volunteers and campaign workers who worked so hard on my behalf.

I also salute the vice president and his supporters for waging a spirited campaign. And I thank him for a call that I know was difficult to make. Laura and I wish the vice president and Sen. [Joseph I.] Lieberman and their families the very best.

I have a lot to be thankful for tonight. I'm thankful for America, and thankful that we were able to resolve our electoral differences in a peaceful way.

I'm thankful to the American people for the great privilege of being able to serve as your next president.

I want to thank my wife and our daughters for their love. Laura's active involvement as first lady has made Texas a better place, and she will be a wonderful first lady of America.

I am proud to have Dick Cheney by my side, and America will be proud to have him as our next vice president.

Tonight I chose to speak from the chamber of the Texas House of Representatives because it has been a home to bipartisan cooperation. Here in a place where Democrats have the majority, Republicans and Democrats have worked together to do what is right for the people we represent.

We've had spirited disagreements. And in the end, we found constructive consensus. It is an experience I will always carry with me, an example I will always follow.

I want to thank my friend, House Speaker Pete Laney, a Democrat, who introduced me today. I want to thank the legislators from both political parties with whom I've worked.

Across the hall in our Texas capitol is the state Senate. And I cannot help but think of our mutual friend, the former Democrat lieutenant governor, Bob Bullock. His love for Texas and his ability to work in a bipartisan way continue to be a model for all of us.

The spirit of cooperation I have seen in this hall is what is needed in Washington, D.C. It is the challenge of our moment. After a difficult election, we must put politics behind us and work together to make the promise of America available for every one of our citizens.

I am optimistic that we can change the tone in Washington, D.C.

I believe things happen for a reason, and I hope the long wait of the last five weeks will heighten a desire to move beyond the bitterness and partisanship of the recent past.

Our nation must rise above a house divided. Americans share hopes and goals and values far more important than any political disagreements.

Republicans want the best for our nation, and so do Democrats. Our votes may differ, but not our hopes.

I know America wants reconciliation and unity. I know Americans want progress. And we must seize this moment and deliver.

Together, guided by a spirit of common sense, common courtesy and common goals, we can unite and inspire the American citizens.

Together, we will work to make all our public schools excellent, teaching every student of every background and every accent, so that no child is left behind.

Together we will save Social Security and renew its promise of a secure retirement for generations to come.

Together we will strengthen Medicare and offer prescription drug coverage to all of our seniors.

Together we will give Americans the broad, fair and fiscally responsible tax relief they deserve.

Together we'll have a bipartisan foreign policy true to our values and true to our friends, and we will have a military equal to every challenge and superior to every adversary.

Together we will address some of society's deepest problems one person at a time, by encouraging and empowering the good hearts and good works of the American people.

This is the essence of compassionate conservatism, and it will be a foundation of my administration.

These priorities are not merely Republican concerns or Democratic concerns; they are American responsibilities.

During the fall campaign, we differed about the details of these proposals, but there was remarkable consensus about the important issues before us: excellent schools, retirement and health security, tax relief, a strong military, a more civil society.

We have discussed our differences. Now it is time to find common ground and build consensus to make America a beacon of opportunity in the 21st century.

I'm optimistic this can happen. Our future demands it, and our history proves it. Two hundred years ago, in the election of 1800, America faced another close presidential election. A tie in the Electoral College put the outcome into the hands of Congress.

After six days of voting and 36 ballots, the House of Representatives elected Thomas Jefferson the third president of the United States. That election brought the first transfer of power from one party to another in our new democracy.

Shortly after the election, Jefferson, in a letter titled "Reconciliation and Reform," wrote this: "The steady character of our countrymen is a rock to which we may safely moor; unequivocal in principle, reasonable in manner. We should be able to hope to do a great deal of good to the cause of freedom and harmony."

Two hundred years have only strengthened the steady character of America. And so as we begin the work of healing our nation, tonight I call upon that character: respect for each other; respect for our differences; generosity of spirit, and a willingness to work hard and work together to solve any problem.

I have something else to ask you, to ask every American. I ask for you to pray for this great nation. I ask for your prayers for leaders from both parties. I thank you for your prayers for me and my family, and I ask you to pray for Vice President Gore and his family.

I have faith that with God's help we as a nation will move forward together as one nation, indivisible. And together we will create an America that is open, so every citizen has access to the American dream; an America that is educated, so every child has the keys to realize that dream; and an America that is united in our diversity and our shared American values that are larger than race or party.

I was not elected to serve one party, but to serve one nation.

The president of the United States is the president of every single American, of every race and every background.

Whether you voted for me or not, I will do my best to serve your interests and I will work to earn your respect.

I will be guided by President Jefferson's sense of purpose, to stand for principle, to be reasonable in manner, and above all, to do great good for the cause of freedom and harmony.

The presidency is more than an honor. It is more than an office. It is a charge to keep, and I will give it my all.

Thank you very much and God bless America.

Political Charts

Summary of Presidential Elections, 1789–2000	1059
Victorious Party in Presidential Races, 1860–2000	1062
1996 Presidential Election	1064
1996 Electoral Votes	1065
2000 Presidential Election	1066
2000 Electoral Votes	1067
2000 Republican Convention Balloting	1068
2000 Democratic Convention Balloting	1069
Distribution of House Seats and Electoral Votes	1070
Party Affiliations in Congress and the Presidency, 1789–2001	1071
105th Congress Special Elections, 1997 Gubernatorial Returns	1073
1998 Elections Returns for Governor, Senate, and House	1074
106th Congress Special Elections, 1999 Gubernatorial Returns	1081
2000 Elections Returns for Governor, Senate, and House	1082
Results of House Elections, 1928–2000	1090
Governors, 1997–2001	1094

Summary of Presidential Elections, 1789–2000

Year	No. of states	Candidates	Party	Electoral vote	Popular vote
1789[1]	10	**George Washington**	**Fed.**	**69**	—[2]
		John Adams	Fed.	34	
1792[1]	15	**George Washington**	**Fed.**	**132**	—[2]
		John Adams	Fed.	77	
1796[1]	16	**John Adams**	**Fed.**	**71**	—[2]
		Thomas Jefferson	Dem.-Rep.	68	
1800[1]	16	**Thomas Jefferson**	**Dem.-Rep.**	**73**	—[2]
		Aaron Burr	Dem.-Rep.	73	
		John Adams	Fed.	65	
		Charles Cotesworth Pinckney	Fed.	64	
1804	17	**Thomas Jefferson**	**Dem.-Rep.**	**162**	—[2]
		George Clinton			
		Charles Cotesworth Pinckney	Fed.	64	
		Rufus King			
1808	17	**James Madison**	**Dem.-Rep.**	**122**	—[2]
		George Clinton			
		Charles Cotesworth Pinckney	Fed.	64	
		Rufus King			
1812	18	**James Madison**	**Dem.-Rep.**	**128**	—[2]
		Elbridge Gerry			
		George Clinton	Fed.	89	
		Jared Ingersoll			
1816	19	**James Monroe**	**Dem.-Rep.**	**183**	—[2]
		Daniel D. Tompkins			
		Rufus King	Fed.	34	
		John Howard			
1820	24	**James Monroe**	**Dem.-Rep.**	**231[3]**	—[2]
		Daniel D. Tompkins			
1824[4]	24	**John Quincy Adams**	**Dem.-Rep.**	**99**	**113,122 (30.9%)**
		John C. Calhoun			
		Andrew Jackson	Dem.-Rep.	84	151,271 (41.3%)
		Nathan Sanford			
1828	24	**Andrew Jackson**	**Dem.-Rep.**	**178**	**642,553 (56.0%)**
		John C. Calhoun			
		John Quincy Adams	Nat.-Rep.	83	500,897 (43.6%)
		Richard Rush			
1832[5]	24	**Andrew Jackson**	**Dem.**	**219**	**701,780 (54.2%)**
		Martin Van Buren			
		Henry Clay	Nat.-Rep.	49	484,205 (37.4%)
		John Sergeant			
1836[6]	26	**Martin Van Buren**	**Dem.**	**170**	**764,176 (50.8%)**
		Richard M. Johnson			
		William Henry Harrison	Whig	73	550,816 (36.6%)
		Francis Granger			
1840	26	**William Henry Harrison**	**Whig**	**234**	**1,275,390 (52.9%)**
		John Tyler			
		Martin Van Buren	Dem.	60	1,128,854 (46.8%)
		Richard M. Johnson			
1844	26	**James K. Polk**	**Dem.**	**170**	**1,339,494 (49.5%)**
		George M. Dallas			
		Henry Clay	Whig	105	1,300,004 (48.1%)
		Theodore Frelinghuysen			
1848	30	**Zachary Taylor**	**Whig**	**163**	**1,361,393 (47.3%)**
		Millard Fillmore			
		Lewis Cass	Dem.	127	1,223,460 (42.5%)
		William O. Butler			
1852	31	**Franklin Pierce**	**Dem.**	**254**	**1,607,510 (50.8%)**
		William R. King			
		Winfield Scott	Whig	42	1,386,942 (43.9%)
		William A. Graham			
1856[7]	31	**James Buchanan**	**Dem.**	**174**	**1,836,072 (45.3%)**
		John C. Breckinridge			
		John C. Fremont	Rep.	114	1,342,345 (33.1%)
		William L. Dayton			
1860[8]	33	**Abraham Lincoln**	**Rep.**	**180**	**1,865,908 (39.8%)**
		Hannibal Hamlin			
		Stephen A. Douglas	Dem.	12	1,380,202 (29.5%)
		Herschel V. Johnson			
1864[9]	36	**Abraham Lincoln**	**Rep.**	**212**	**2,218,388 (55.0%)**
		Andrew Johnson			
		George B. McClellan	Dem.	21	1,812,807 (45.0%)
		George H. Pendleton			
1868[10]	37	**Ulysses S. Grant**	**Rep.**	**214**	**3,013,650 (52.7%)**
		Schuyler Colfax			
		Horatio Seymour	Dem.	80	2,708,744 (47.3%)
		Francis P. Blair Jr.			
1872	37	**Ulysses S. Grant**	**Rep.**	**286**	**3,598,235 (55.6%)**
		Henry Wilson			
		Horace Greeley	Dem.	—[11]	2,834,761 (43.8%)
		Benjamin Gratz Brown			
1876	38	**Rutherford B. Hayes**	**Rep.**	**185**	**4,034,311 (47.9%)**
		William A. Wheeler			
		Samuel J. Tilden	Dem.	184	4,288,546 (51.0%)
		Thomas A. Hendricks			
1880	38	**James A. Garfield**	**Rep.**	**214**	**4,446,158 (48.3%)**
		Chester A. Arthur			
		Winfield S. Hancock	Dem.	155	4,444,260 (48.2%)
		William H. English			
1884	38	**Grover Cleveland**	**Dem.**	**219**	**4,874,621 (48.5%)**
		Thomas A. Hendricks			
		James G. Blaine	Rep.	182	4,848,936 (48.2%)
		John A. Logan			

(table continues)

Year	No. of states	Candidates	Party	Electoral vote	Popular vote	Year	No. of states	Candidates	Party	Electoral vote	Popular vote
1888	38	**Benjamin Harrison** *Levi P. Morton*	**Rep.**	**233**	**5,443,892 (47.8%)**	1940	48	**Franklin D. Roosevelt** *Henry A. Wallace*	**Dem.**	**449**	**27,263,448 (54.7%)**
		Grover Cleveland *Allen G. Thurman*	Dem.	168	5,534,488 (48.6%)			Wendell L. Willkie *Charles L. McNary*	Rep.	82	22,336,260 (44.8%)
1892[12]	44	**Grover Cleveland** *Adlai E. Stevenson*	**Dem.**	**277**	**5,551,883 (46.1%)**	1944	48	**Franklin D. Roosevelt** *Harry S. Truman*	**Dem.**	**432**	**25,611,936 (53.4%)**
		Benjamin Harrison *Whitelaw Reid*	Rep.	145	5,179,244 (43.0%)			Thomas E. Dewey *John W. Bricker*	Rep.	99	22,013,372 (45.9%)
1896	45	**William McKinley** *Garret A. Hobart*	**Rep.**	**271**	**7,108,480 (51.0%)**	1948[15]	48	**Harry S. Truman** *Alben W. Barkley*	**Dem.**	**303**	**24,105,587 (49.5%)**
		William J. Bryan *Arthur Sewall*	Dem.	176	6,511,495 (46.7%)			Thomas E. Dewey *Earl Warren*	Rep.	198	21,970,017 (45.1%)
1900	45	**William McKinley** *Theodore Roosevelt*	**Rep.**	**292**	**7,218,039 (51.7%)**	1952	48	**Dwight D. Eisenhower** *Richard M. Nixon*	**Rep.**	**442**	**33,936,137 (55.1%)**
		William J. Bryan *Adlai E. Stevenson*	Dem.	155	6,358,345 (45.5%)			Adlai E. Stevenson II *John J. Sparkman*	Dem.	89	27,314,649 (44.4%)
1904	45	**Theodore Roosevelt** *Charles W. Fairbanks*	**Rep.**	**336**	**7,626,593 (56.4%)**	1956[16]	48	**Dwight D. Eisenhower** *Richard M. Nixon*	**Rep.**	**457**	**35,585,245 (57.4%)**
		Alton B. Parker *Henry G. Davis*	Dem.	140	5,028,898 (37.6%)			Adlai E. Stevenson II *Estes Kefauver*	Dem.	73	26,030,172 (42.0%)
1908	46	**William Howard Taft** *James S. Sherman*	**Rep.**	**321**	**7,676,258 (51.6%)**	1960[17]	50	**John F. Kennedy** *Lyndon B. Johnson*	**Dem.**	**303**	**34,221,344 (49.7%)**
		William J. Bryan *John W. Kern*	Dem.	162	6,406,801 (43.0%)			Richard Nixon *Henry Cabot Lodge*	Rep.	219	34,106,671 (49.5%)
1912[13]	48	**Woodrow Wilson** *Thomas R. Marshall*	**Dem.**	**435**	**6,293,152 (41.8%)**	1964	50*	**Lyndon B. Johnson** *Hubert H. Humphrey*	**Dem.**	**486**	**43,126,584 (61.1%)**
		William Howard Taft *James S. Sherman*	Rep.	8	3,486,333 (23.2%)			Barry Goldwater *William E. Miller*	Rep.	52	27,177,838 (38.5%)
1916	48	**Woodrow Wilson** *Thomas R. Marshall*	**Dem.**	**277**	**9,126,300 (49.2%)**	1968[18]	50*	**Richard Nixon** *Spiro T. Agnew*	**Rep.**	**301**	**31,785,148 (43.4%)**
		Charles E. Hughes *Charles W. Fairbanks*	Rep.	254	8,546,789 (46.1%)			Hubert H. Humphrey *Edmund S. Muskie*	Dem.	191	31,274,503 (42.7%)
1920	48	**Warren G. Harding** *Calvin Coolidge*	**Rep.**	**404**	**16,133,314 (60.3%)**	1972[19]	50*	**Richard Nixon** *Spiro T. Agnew*	**Rep.**	**520**	**47,170,179 (60.7%)**
		James M. Cox *Franklin D. Roosevelt*	Dem.	127	9,140,884 (34.2%)			George McGovern *Sargent Shriver*	Dem.	17	29,171,791 (37.5%)
1924[14]	48	**Calvin Coolidge** *Charles G. Dawes*	**Rep.**	**382**	**15,717,553 (54.1%)**	1976[20]	50*	**Jimmy Carter** *Walter F. Mondale*	**Dem.**	**297**	**40,830,763 (50.1%)**
		John W. Davis *Charles W. Bryan*	Dem.	136	8,386,169 (28.8%)			Gerald R. Ford *Robert Dole*	Rep.	240	39,147,793 (48.0%)
1928	48	**Herbert C. Hoover** *Charles Curtis*	**Rep.**	**444**	**21,411,991 (58.2%)**	1980	50*	**Ronald Reagan** *George Bush*	**Rep.**	**489**	**43,904,153 (50.7%)**
		Alfred E. Smith *Joseph T. Robinson*	Dem.	87	15,000,185 (40.8%)			Jimmy Carter *Walter F. Mondale*	Dem.	49	35,483,883 (41.0%)
1932	48	**Franklin D. Roosevelt** *John N. Garner*	**Dem.**	**472**	**22,825,016 (57.4%)**	1984	50*	**Ronald Reagan** *George Bush*	**Rep.**	**525**	**54,455,074(58.8%)**
		Herbert C. Hoover *Charles Curtis*	Rep.	59	15,758,397 (39.6%)			Walter F. Mondale *Geraldine Ferraro*	Dem.	13	37,577,137 (40.6%)
1936	48	**Franklin D. Roosevelt** *John N. Garner*	**Dem.**	**523**	**27,747,636 (60.8%)**	1988[21]	50*	**George Bush** *Dan Quayle*	**Rep.**	**426**	**48,881,278 (53.4%)**
		Alfred M. Landon *Frank Knox*	Rep.	8	16,679,543 (36.5%)			Michael S. Dukakis *Lloyd Bentsen*	Dem.	111	41,805,374 (45.6%)

Year	No. of states	Candidates	Party	Electoral vote	Popular vote	Year	No. of states	Candidates	Party	Electoral vote	Popular vote
1992	50*	**Bill Clinton** *Al Gore*	**Dem.**	**370**	**44,908,233 (43.0%)**	2000[22]	50*	**George W. Bush** *Richard B. Cheney*	**Rep.**	**271**	**50,455,156 (47.9%)**
		George Bush *Dan Quayle*	Rep.	168	39,102,282 (37.4%)			Al Gore *Joseph I. Lieberman*	Dem.	266	50,992,335 (48.4%)
1996	50*	**Bill Clinton** *Al Gore*	**Dem.**	**379**	**47,402,357 (49.2%)**						
		Bob Dole *Jack Kemp*	Rep.	159	39,198,755 (40.7%)						

SOURCES: Harold W. Stanley and Richard G. Niemi, *Vital Statistics on American Politics,* 5th ed. (Washington, D.C.: CQ Press, 1995), table 3-13; Richard M. Scammon, Alice V. McGillivray, and Rhodes Cook, *America Votes 24* (Washington, D.C.: CQ Press, 2001), 9, 13.

NOTES: Bold indicates victors. In the elections of 1789, 1792, 1796, and 1800, each candidate ran for the office of president. The candidate with the second highest number of electoral votes became vice president. For elections after 1800, italic indicates vice-presidential candidates. Dem.-Rep.—Democratic-Republican; Fed.—Federalist; Nat.-Rep.—National-Republican; Dem.—Democratic; Rep.—Republican.   1. Elections of 1789–1800 were held under rules that did not allow separate voting for president and vice president.   2. Popular vote returns are not shown before 1824 because consistent, reliable data are not available.   3. Monroe ran unopposed. One electoral vote was cast for John Adams and Richard Stockton, who were not candidates.   4. 1824: All four candidates represented Democratic-Republican factions. William H. Crawford received 41 electoral votes, and Henry Clay received 37 votes. Since no candidate received a majority, the election was decided (in Adams's favor) by the House of Representatives.   5. 1832: Two electoral votes were not cast.   6. 1836: Other Whig candidates receiving electoral votes were Hugh L. White, who received 26 votes, and Daniel Webster, who received 14 votes.   7. 1856: Millard Fillmore, Whig-American, received 8 electoral votes.   8. 1860: John C. Breckinridge, Southern Democrat, received 72 electoral votes. John Bell, Constitutional Union, received 39 electoral votes.   9. 1864: Eighty-one electoral votes were not cast.   10. 1868: Twenty-three electoral votes were not cast.   11. 1872: Horace Greeley, Democrat, died after the election. In the electoral college, Democratic electoral votes went to Thomas Hendricks, 42 votes; Benjamin Gratz Brown, 18 votes; Charles J. Jenkins, 2 votes; and David Davis, 1 vote. Seventeen electoral votes were not cast.   12. 1892: James B. Weaver, People's Party, received 22 electoral votes.   13. 1912: Theodore Roosevelt, Progressive Party, received 86 electoral votes.   14. 1924: Robert M. La Follette, Progressive Party, received 13 electoral votes.   15. 1948: J. Strom Thurmond, States' Rights Party, received 39 electoral votes.   16. 1956: Walter B. Jones, Democrat, received 1 electoral vote.   17. 1960: Harry Flood Byrd, Democrat, received 15 electoral votes.   18. 1968: George C. Wallace, American Independent Party, received 46 electoral votes.   19. 1972: John Hospers, Libertarian Party, received 1 electoral vote.   20. 1976: Ronald Reagan, Republican, received 1 electoral vote.   21. 1988: Lloyd Bentsen, the Democratic vice-presidential nominee, received 1 electoral vote for president.   22. 2000: One District of Columbia elector did not vote.   *Fifty states plus the District of Columbia.

Victorious Party in Presidential Races, 1860–2000

State	1860	1864	1868	1872	1876	1880	1884	1888	1892	1896	1900	1904	1908	1912	1916	1920	1924	1928
Alabama	SD	[2]	R	R	D	D	D	D	D	D	D	D	D	D	D	D	D	D
Alaska																		
Arizona														D	D	R	R	R
Arkansas	SD	[2]	R	[4]	D	D	D	D	D	D	D	D	D	D	D	D	D	D
California	R	R	R	R	R	D[6]	R	R	D[7]	R[12]	R	R	R	PR	D	R	R	R
Colorado					R	R	R	R	PP	D	D	R	D	D	D	R	R	R
Connecticut	R	R	R	R	D	R	D	D	D	R	R	R	R	D	R	R	R	R
Delaware	SD	D	D	D	D	D	D	D	D	R	R	R	R	D	R	R	R	R
Dist. of Columbia																		
Florida	SD	[2]	R	R	D	D	D	D	D	D	D	D	D	D	D	D	D	R
Georgia	SD	[2]	D	D[5]	D	D	D	D	D	D	D	D	D	D	D	D	D	D
Hawaii																		
Idaho									PP	D	D	R	R	D	D	R	R	R
Illinois	R	R	R	R	R	R	R	R	D	R	R	R	R	D	R	R	R	R
Indiana	R	R	R	R	D	R	D	R	D	R	R	R	R	D	R	R	R	R
Iowa	R	R	R	R	R	R	R	R	R	R	R	R	R	D	R	R	R	R
Kansas		R	R	R	R	R	R	R	PP	D	R	R	R	D	D	R	R	R
Kentucky	CU	D	D	D	D	D	D	D	D	R[13]	D	D	D	D	D	D	R	R
Louisiana	SD	[2]	D	[4]	R	D	D	D	D	D	D	D	D	D	D	D	D	D
Maine	R	R	R	R	R	R	R	R	R	R	R	R	R	D	R	R	R	R
Maryland	SD	R	D	D	D	D	D	D	D	R	R	D[14]	D[15]	D	D	R	R	R
Massachusetts	R	R	R	R	R	R	R	R	R	R	R	R	R	D	R	R	R	D
Michigan	R	R	R	R	R	R	R	R	R[8]	R	R	R	R	PR	R	R	R	R
Minnesota	R	R	R	R	R	R	R	R	R	R	R	R	R	PR	R	R	R	R
Mississippi	SD	[2]	[3]	R	D	D	D	D	D	D	D	D	D	D	D	D	D	D
Missouri	D	R	R	D	D	D	D	D	D	D	D	R	R	D	D	R	R	R
Montana									R	D	D	R	R	D	D	R	R	R
Nebraska		R	R	R	R	R	R	R	R	D	R	R	R	D	D	R	R	R
Nevada		R	R	R	R	R	D	R	PP	D	D	R	D	D	D	R	R	R
New Hampshire	R	R	R	R	R	R	R	R	R	R	R	R	R	D	R	R	R	R
New Jersey	R[1]	D	D	R	D	D	D	D	D	R	R	R	R	D	R	R	R	R
New Mexico														D	D	R	R	R
New York	R	R	D	R	D	R	D	R	D	R	R	R	R	D	R	R	R	D
North Carolina	SD	[2]	R	R	D	D	D	D	D	D	D	D	D	D	D	D	D	R
North Dakota									[9]	R	R	R	R	D	D	R	R	R
Ohio	R	R	R	R	R	R	R	R	R[10]	R	R	R	R	D	D	R	R	R
Oklahoma													D	D	D	R	D	R
Oregon	R	R	D	R	R	R	R	R	R[11]	R	R	R	R	D	R	R	R	R
Pennsylvania	R	R	R	R	R	R	R	R	R	R	R	R	R	PR	R	R	R	R
Rhode Island	R	R	R	R	R	R	R	R	R	R	R	R	R	D	R	R	R	R
South Carolina	SD	[2]	R	R	D	D	D	D	D	D	D	D	D	D	D	D	D	D
South Dakota									R	D	R	R	R	PR	D	R	R	R
Tennessee	CU	[2]	R	D	D	D	D	D	D	D	D	D	D	D	D	R	D	R
Texas	SD	[2]	[3]	D	D	D	D	D	D	D	D	D	D	D	D	D	D	R
Utah										D	D	R	R	R	D	R	R	R
Vermont	R	R	R	R	R	R	R	R	R	R	R	R	R	R	R	R	R	R
Virginia	CU	[2]	[3]	R	D	D	D	D	D	D	D	D	D	D	D	D	D	R
Washington									R	D	R	R	R	PR	D	R	R	R
West Virginia		R	R	R	D	D	D	D	D	R	R	R	R	D	D	R	R	R
Wisconsin	R	R	R	R	R	R	R	R	D	R	R	R	R	D	R[16]	R	PR	R
Wyoming									R	D	R	R	R	D	D	R	R	R
Winning Party	R	R	R	R	R	R	D	R	D	R	R	R	R	D	D	R	R	R

NOTE: With the exception of the District of Columbia, blanks indicate states not yet admitted to the Union. The District of Columbia received the presidential vote in 1961.

KEY: AI-American Independent Party; CU-Constitutional Union Party; D-Democratic Party; PP-People's Party; PR-Progressive (Bull Moose) Party; R-Republican Party; SD-Southern Democratic Party; SR-States' Rights Democratic Party.
1. Four electors voted Republican; three, Democratic.
2. Confederate states did not vote in 1864.
3. Did not vote in 1868.
4. Votes were not counted.
5. Three votes for Greeley not counted.
6. Five electors voted Democratic; one, Republican.
7. Eight electors voted Democratic; one, Republican.
8. Nine electors voted Republican; five, Democratic.
9. One vote each for Democratic, Republican and People's parties.
10. Twenty-two electors voted Republican; one, Democratic.

																		Number of times parties won		
1932	1936	1940	1944	1948	1952	1956	1960	1964	1968	1972	1976	1980	1984	1988	1992	1996	2000	Dems.	Reps.	Other
D	D	D	D	SR	D	D[18]	D[19]	R	AI	R	D	R	R	R	R	R	R	22	10	3
							R	D	R	R	R	R	R	R	R	R	R	1	10	0
D	D	D	D	D	R	R	R	R	R	R	R	R	R	R	R	D	R	8	15	0
D	D	D	D	D	D	D	D	D	AI	R	R	R	R	R	D	D	R	26	6	2
D	D	D	D	D	R	R	R	D	R	R	R	R	R	R	D	D	D	12	23	1
D	D	R	R	D	R	R	R	D	R	R	R	R	R	R	D	R	R	10	21	1
R	D	D	D	R	R	R	D	D	D	R	R	R	R	R	D	D	D	14	22	0
R	D	D	D	R	R	R	D	D	R	R	D	R	R	R	D	D	D	17	18	1
								D	D	D	D	D	D	D	D	D	D[26]	10	0	0
D	D	D	D	D	R	R	R	D	R	R	D	R	R	R	R	D	R	20	14	1
D	D	D	D	D	D	D	D	R	AI	R	D	D	R	R	R	D	R	27	6	2
							D	D	D	R	D	D	R	D	D	D	D	9	2	0
D	D	D	D	D	R	R	R	D	R	R	R	R	R	R	R	R	R	10	17	1
D	D	D	D	D	R	R	D	D	R	R	R	R	R	D	D	D	D	12	24	0
D	D	R	R	R	R	R	R	D	R	R	R	R	R	R	R	R	R	7	29	0
D	D	R	D	D	R	R	R	D	R	R	R	R	D	D	D	D	D	9	27	0
R	R	R	R	R	R	R	R	D	R	R	R	R	R	R	R	R	R	6	28	1
D	D	D	D	D	D	R	D	D	R	D	R	R	R	D	D	D	R	24	11	1
D	D	D	D	SR	D	D	[20]	R	AI	R	D	R	R	R	R	R	R	21	9	4
D	D	D	D	D	R	R	D	D	R	R	D	R	R	R	R	D	R	22	14	0
D	D	D	D	D	R	R	R	D	R	R	R	R	R	R	R	D	R	11	17	0
D	D	R	R	R	R	R	D	R	R	R	R	R	R	R	R	R	R	7	27	0
D	D	D	D	D	R	R	D	D	R	R	R	R	R	R	D	D	R	15	19	1
R	D	D	D	D	R	R	R	D	R	R	R	R	R	R	D	D	R	8	28	0
D	D	D	D	D	R	R	D	D	R	R	R	R	R	R	D	D	D	17	19	0
D	D	D	D	D	R	R	D	D	R	D	R	R	R	R	D	D	D	12	11	0
D	D	D	D	D	R	R	D	D	D	R	R	R	R	R	D	D	D	17	19	0
D	D	D	D	D	D	D	D	D	R[22]	R	D	R	R	R	R	R	R	23	11	1
D	D	R	R	R	R	R	R	D	R	R	R	R	R	R	R	R	R	5	22	1
D	D	D	R	D	R	R	R	D	R	R	R	D	R	R	D	D	D	10	26	0
D	D	D	D	D	R	R	R[21]	D	R	R	R	R	R	R	R	R	R	10	14	0
D	D	D	D	D	R	R	R	D	R	R	R	R	R	D	D	D	D	11	25	0
R	D	D	D	R	R	R	D	D	D	R	D	R	R	R	D	D	D	10	25	1
D	D	D	D	D	D	R	D	D	R	R	D	R	D	D	D	D	D	16	20	0
D	D	D	D	SR	D	D	D	R	R	R	D	R	R	R	R	R	R	21	12	2
D	D	R	R	SR	R	R	R	D	R	R	R	R	R	R	R	R	R	4	23	1
D	D	D	D	D[17]	R	R	R	D	R	R	R	R	R	R	R	R	R	22	12	1
D	D	D	D	D	R	R	R	D	D	R	R	R	R	R	R	R	R	23	10	1
D	D	D	D	D	R	R	D	D	R	R	R	R	R	R	R	R	R	8	19	0
R	R	R	R	R	R	R	R	D	R	R	R	R	R	D	D	D	D	4	32	0
D	D	D	D	D	R	D	D	D	D	R[23]	R	R	R	R	R	R	R	19	14	1
D	D	D	D	D	R	R	R	D	D	R[24]	R	D	D	D	D	D	D	13	14	1
D	D	D	D	D	D	R	D	D	D	R	R	D	R	D[25]	D	D	R	20	15	0
D	D	D	D	D	R	R	D	D	R	R	D	R	R	R	D	D	D	12	23	1
D	D	D	R	D	R	R	D	D	R	R	D	R	R	R	R	R	R	8	20	0
D	D	D	D	D	R	R	D	D	R	R	D	R	R	R	R	R	R	14	22	0

11. Three electors voted Republican; one, People's Party.
12. Eight electors voted Republican; one, Democratic.
13. Twelve electors voted Republican; one, Democratic.
14. Seven electors voted Democratic; one, Republican.
15. Six electors voted Democratic; two, Republican.
16. Seven electors voted Republican; one, Democratic.
17. Eleven electors voted Democratic; one, States' Rights.
18. One elector voted for Walter B. Jones.

19. Six of eleven electors voted for Harry F. Byrd.
20. Eight independent electors voted for Byrd.
21. One vote cast for Byrd.
22. Twelve electors voted Republican; one, American Independent.
23. One elector voted Libertarian.
24. One elector voted for Ronald Reagan.
25. One elector voted for Lloyd Bentsen.
26. One elector did not vote.

1996 Presidential Election

State	Total vote	Bill Clinton (Democrat) Votes	%	Bob Dole (Republican) Votes	%	Ross Perot (Reform) Votes	%	Ralph Nader (Green) Votes	%	Other[1] Votes	%	Plurality	
Alabama	1,534,349	662,165	43.2	769,044	50.1	92,149	6.0	—		10,991	0.7	106,879	R
Alaska	241,620	80,380	33.3	122,746	50.8	26,333	10.9	7,597	3.1	4,564	1.9	42,366	R
Arizona	1,404,405	653,288	46.5	622,073	44.3	112,072	8.0	2,062	0.1	14,910	1.1	31,215	D
Arkansas	884,262	475,171	53.7	325,416	36.8	69,884	7.9	3,649	0.4	10,142	1.1	149,755	D
California	10,019,484	5,119,835	51.1	3,828,380	38.2	697,847	7.0	237,016	2.4	136,406	1.4	1,291,455	D
Colorado	1,510,704	671,152	44.4	691,848	45.8	99,629	6.6	25,070	1.7	23,005	1.5	20,696	R
Connecticut	1,392,614	735,740	52.8	483,109	34.7	139,523	10.0	24,321	1.7	9,921	0.7	252,631	D
Delaware	271,084	140,355	51.8	99,062	36.5	28,719	10.6	156	0.1	2,792	1.0	41,293	D
Florida	5,303,794	2,546,870	48.0	2,244,536	42.3	483,870	9.1	4,101	0.1	24,417	0.5	302,334	D
Georgia	2,299,071	1,053,849	45.8	1,080,843	47.0	146,337	6.4	—		18,042	0.8	26,994	R
Hawaii	360,120	205,012	56.9	113,943	31.6	27,358	7.6	10,386	2.9	3,421	0.9	91,069	D
Idaho	491,719	165,443	33.6	256,595	52.2	62,518	12.7	—		7,163	1.5	91,152	R
Illinois	4,311,391	2,341,744	54.3	1,587,021	36.8	346,408	8.0	1,447		34,771	0.8	754,723	D
Indiana	2,135,842	887,424	41.5	1,006,693	47.1	224,299	10.5	895		16,531	0.8	119,269	R
Iowa	1,234,075	620,258	50.3	492,644	39.9	105,159	8.5	6,550	0.5	9,464	0.8	127,614	D
Kansas	1,074,300	387,659	36.1	583,245	54.3	92,639	8.6	914	0.1	9,843	0.9	195,586	R
Kentucky	1,388,708	636,614	45.8	623,283	44.9	120,396	8.7	701	0.1	7,714	0.6	13,331	D
Louisiana	1,783,959	927,837	52.0	712,586	39.9	123,293	6.9	4,719	0.3	15,524	0.9	215,251	D
Maine	605,897	312,788	51.6	186,378	30.8	85,970	14.2	15,279	2.5	5,482	0.9	126,410	D
Maryland	1,780,870	966,207	54.3	681,530	38.3	115,812	6.5	2,606	0.1	14,715	0.8	284,677	D
Massachusetts	2,556,785	1,571,763	61.5	718,107	28.1	227,217	8.9	4,565	0.2	35,133	1.4	853,656	D
Michigan	3,848,844	1,989,653	51.7	1,481,212	38.5	336,670	8.7	2,322	0.1	38,987	1.0	508,441	D
Minnesota	2,192,640	1,120,438	51.1	766,476	35.0	257,704	11.8	24,908	1.1	23,114	1.1	353,962	D
Mississippi	893,857	394,022	44.1	439,838	49.2	52,222	5.8	—		7,775	0.9	45,816	R
Missouri	2,158,065	1,025,935	47.5	890,016	41.2	217,188	10.1	534		24,392	1.1	135,919	D
Montana	407,261	167,922	41.2	179,652	44.1	55,229	13.6	—		4,458	1.1	11,730	R
Nebraska	677,415	236,761	35.0	363,467	53.7	71,278	10.5	—		5,909	0.9	126,706	R
Nevada	464,279	203,974	43.9	199,244	42.9	43,986	9.5	4,730	1.0	12,345	2.7	4,730	D
New Hampshire	499,175	246,214	49.3	196,532	39.4	48,390	9.7	—		8,039	1.6	49,682	D
New Jersey	3,075,807	1,652,329	53.7	1,103,078	35.9	262,134	8.5	32,465	1.1	25,801	0.8	549,251	D
New Mexico	556,074	273,495	49.2	232,751	41.9	32,257	5.8	13,218	2.4	4,353	0.8	40,744	D
New York	6,316,129	3,756,177	59.5	1,933,492	30.6	503,458	8.0	75,956	1.2	47,046	0.7	1,822,685	D
North Carolina	2,515,807	1,107,849	44.0	1,225,938	48.7	168,059	6.7	2,108	0.1	11,853	0.4	118,089	R
North Dakota	266,411	106,905	40.1	125,050	46.9	32,515	12.2	—		1,941	0.7	18,145	R
Ohio	4,534,434	2,148,222	47.4	1,859,883	41.0	483,207	10.7	2,962	0.1	40,160	0.9	288,339	D
Oklahoma	1,206,713	488,105	40.4	582,315	48.3	130,788	10.8	—		5,505	0.5	94,210	R
Oregon	1,377,760	649,641	47.2	538,152	39.1	121,221	8.8	49,415	3.6	19,331	1.4	111,489	D
Pennsylvania	4,506,118	2,215,819	49.2	1,801,169	40.0	430,984	9.6	3,086	0.1	55,060	1.2	414,650	D
Rhode Island	390,284	233,050	59.7	104,683	26.8	43,723	11.2	6,040	1.5	2,788	0.7	128,367	D
South Carolina	1,151,689	506,283	44.0	573,458	49.8	64,386	5.6	—		7,562	0.7	67,175	R
South Dakota	323,826	139,333	43.0	150,543	46.5	31,250	9.7	—		2,700	0.8	11,210	R
Tennessee	1,894,105	909,146	48.0	863,530	45.6	105,918	5.6	6,427	0.3	9,084	0.4	45,616	D
Texas	5,611,644	2,459,683	43.8	2,736,167	48.8	378,537	6.7	4,810	0.1	32,447	0.6	276,484	R
Utah	665,629	221,633	33.3	361,911	54.4	66,461	10.0	4,615	0.7	11,009	1.7	140,278	R
Vermont	258,449	137,894	53.4	80,352	31.1	31,024	12.0	5,585	2.2	3,594	1.4	57,542	D
Virginia	2,416,642	1,091,060	45.1	1,138,350	47.1	159,861	6.6	—		27,371	1.1	47,290	R
Washington	2,253,837	1,123,323	49.8	840,712	37.3	201,003	8.9	60,322	2.7	28,477	1.3	282,611	D
West Virginia	636,459	327,812	51.5	233,946	36.8	71,639	11.3	—		3,062	0.5	93,866	D
Wisconsin	2,196,169	1,071,971	48.8	845,029	38.5	227,339	10.4	28,723	1.3	23,107	1.1	226,942	D
Wyoming	211,571	77,934	36.8	105,388	49.8	25,928	12.3	—		2,321	1.1	27,454	R
Dist. of Col.	185,726	158,220	85.2	17,339	9.3	3,611	1.9	4,780	2.6	1,776	1.0	140,881	D
Total	96,277,872	47,402,357	49.2	39,198,755	40.7	8,085,402	8.4	685,040	0.7	906,318	0.9	8,203,602	D

1. Others receiving votes: Harry Browne (Libertarian), 485,798; Howard Phillips (U.S. Taxpayers), 184,658; John Hagelin (Natural Law), 113,668; Monica Moorehead (Workers World), 29,083; Marsha Feinland (Peace and Freedom), 25,332; Charles E. Collins (Independent), 8,930; James E. Harris (Socialist Workers), 8,476; Dennis Peron, (Grassroots) 5,378; Mary Cal Hollis (Socialist), 4,706; Jerome White (Socialist Equality), 2,438; Diane Beall Templin (American), 1,847; Earl F. Dodge (Prohibition), 1,298; A. Peter Crane (Independent Party of Utah), 1,101; Ralph Forbes (America First), 932; John Birrenbach (Independent Grassroots), 787; Isabell Masters (Looking Back), 752; Steve Michael (Independent), 408; "None of These Candidates," 5,608; scattered write-ins, 25,118.

1996 Electoral Votes

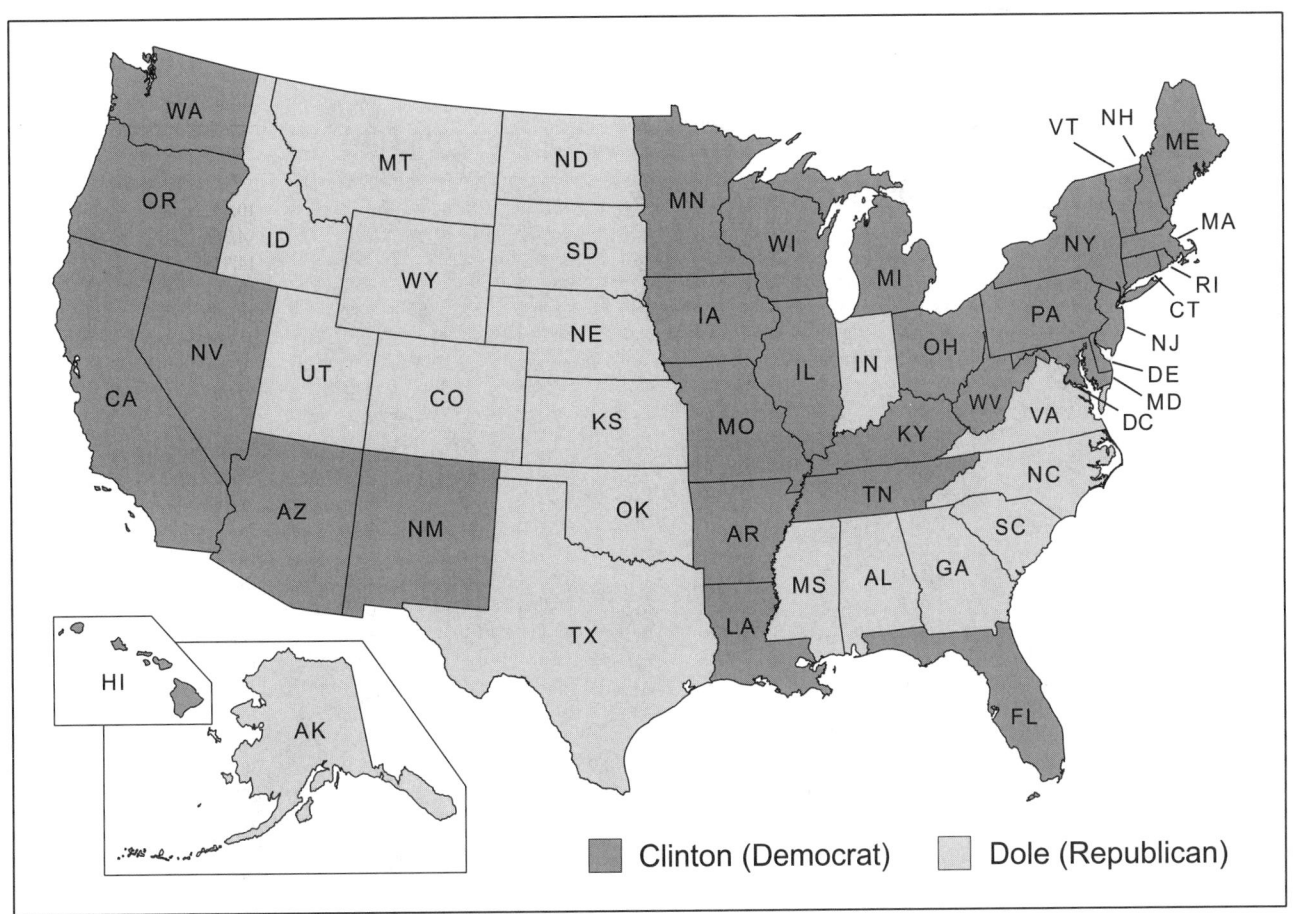

Clinton (Democrat) Dole (Republican)

States	Electoral votes	Clinton	Dole	States	Electoral votes	Clinton	Dole
Alabama	(9)	–	9	Nebraska	(5)	–	5
Alaska	(3)	–	3	Nevada	(4)	4	–
Arizona	(8)	8	–	New Hampshire	(4)	4	–
Arkansas	(6)	6	–	New Jersey	(15)	15	–
California	(54)	54	–	New Mexico	(5)	5	–
Colorado	(8)	–	8	New York	(33)	33	–
Connecticut	(8)	8	–	North Carolina	(14)	–	14
Delaware	(3)	3	–	North Dakota	(3)	–	3
District of Columbia	(3)	3	–	Ohio	(21)	21	–
Florida	(25)	25	–	Oklahoma	(8)	–	8
Georgia	(13)	–	13	Oregon	(7)	7	–
Hawaii	(4)	4	–	Pennsylvania	(23)	23	–
Idaho	(4)	–	4	Rhode Island	(4)	4	–
Illinois	(22)	22	–	South Carolina	(8)	–	8
Indiana	(12)	–	12	South Dakota	(3)	–	3
Iowa	(7)	7	–	Tennessee	(11)	11	–
Kansas	(6)	–	6	Texas	(32)	–	32
Kentucky	(8)	8	–	Utah	(5)	–	5
Louisiana	(9)	9	–	Vermont	(3)	3	–
Maine	(4)	4	–	Virginia	(13)	–	13
Maryland	(10)	10	–	Washington	(11)	11	–
Massachusetts	(12)	12	–	West Virginia	(5)	5	–
Michigan	(18)	18	–	Wisconsin	(11)	11	–
Minnesota	(10)	10	–	Wyoming	(3)	–	3
Mississippi	(7)	–	7				
Missouri	(11)	11	–	Totals	(538)	379	159
Montana	(3)	–	3				

2000 Presidential Election

State	Total vote	George W. Bush (Republican) Votes	%	Al Gore (Democrat) Votes	%	Ralph Nader (Green) Votes	%	Patrick J. Buchanan (Reform) Votes	%	Other Votes	%	Plurality	
Alabama	1,666,272	941,173	56.5	692,611	41.6	18,323	1.1	6,351	0.4	7,814	0.5	248,562	R
Alaska	285,560	167,398	58.6	79,004	27.7	28,747	10.1	5,192	1.8	5,219	1.8	88,394	R
Arizona	1,532,016	781,652	51.0	685,341	44.7	45,645	3.0	12,373	0.8	7,005	0.5	96,311	R
Arkansas	921,781	472,940	51.3	422,768	45.9	13,421	1.5	7,358	0.8	5,294	0.6	50,172	R
California	10,965,856	4,567,429	41.7	5,861,203	53.4	418,707	3.8	44,987	0.4	75,530	0.7	1,293,774	D
Colorado	1,741,368	883,748	50.8	738,227	42.4	91,434	5.3	10,465	0.6	17,494	1.0	145,521	R
Connecticut	1,459,525	561,094	38.4	816,015	55.9	64,452	4.4	4,731	0.3	13,233	0.9	254,921	D
Delaware	327,622	137,288	41.9	180,068	55.0	8,307	2.5	777	0.2	1,182	0.4	42,780	D
Florida	5,963,110	2,912,790	48.8	2,912,253	48.8	97,488	1.6	17,484	0.3	23,095	0.4	537	R
Georgia	2,596,645	1,419,720	54.7	1,116,230	43.0	13,273	0.5	10,926	0.4	36,496	1.4	303,490	R
Hawaii	367,951	137,845	37.5	205,286	55.8	21,623	5.9	1,071	0.3	2,126	0.6	67,441	D
Idaho	501,621	336,937	67.2	138,637	27.6	12,292	2.5	7,615	1.5	6,140	1.2	198,300	R
Illinois	4,742,123	2,019,421	42.6	2,589,026	54.6	103,759	2.2	16,106	0.3	13,811	0.3	569,605	D
Indiana	2,199,302	1,245,836	56.6	901,980	41.0	18,531	0.8	16,959	0.8	15,996	0.7	343,856	R
Iowa	1,315,563	634,373	48.2	638,517	48.5	29,374	2.2	5,731	0.4	7,568	0.6	4,144	D
Kansas	1,072,218	622,332	58.0	399,276	37.2	36,086	3.4	7,370	0.7	7,154	0.7	223,056	R
Kentucky	1,544,187	872,492	56.5	638,898	41.4	23,192	1.5	4,173	0.3	5,432	0.4	233,594	R
Louisiana	1,765,656	927,871	52.6	792,344	44.9	20,473	1.2	14,356	0.8	10,612	0.6	135,527	R
Maine	651,817	286,616	44.0	319,951	49.1	37,127	5.7	4,443	0.7	3,680	0.6	33,335	D
Maryland	2,020,480	813,797	40.3	1,140,782	56.5	53,768	2.7	4,248	0.2	7,885	0.4	326,985	D
Massachusetts	2,702,984	878,502	32.5	1,616,487	59.8	173,564	6.4	11,149	0.4	23,282	0.9	737,985	D
Michigan	4,232,711	1,953,139	46.1	2,170,418	51.3	84,165	2.0	2,061	0.0	22,928	0.5	217,279	D
Minnesota	2,438,685	1,109,659	45.5	1,168,266	47.9	126,696	5.2	22,166	0.9	11,898	0.5	58,607	D
Mississippi	994,184	572,844	57.6	404,614	40.7	8,122	0.8	2,265	0.2	6,339	0.6	168,230	R
Missouri	2,359,892	1,189,924	50.4	1,111,138	47.1	38,515	1.6	9,818	0.4	10,497	0.4	78,786	R
Montana	410,997	240,178	58.4	137,126	33.4	24,437	5.9	5,697	1.4	3,559	0.9	103,052	R
Nebraska	697,019	433,862	62.2	231,780	33.3	24,540	3.5	3,646	0.5	3,191	0.5	202,082	R
Nevada	608,970	301,575	49.5	279,978	46.0	15,008	2.5	4,747	0.8	7,662	1.3	21,597	R
New Hampshire	569,081	273,559	48.1	266,348	46.8	22,198	3.9	2,615	0.5	4,361	0.8	7,211	R
New Jersey	3,187,226	1,284,173	40.3	1,788,850	56.1	94,554	3.0	6,989	0.2	12,660	0.4	504,677	D
New Mexico	598,605	286,417	47.8	286,783	47.9	21,251	3.6	1,392	0.2	2,762	0.5	366	D
New York	6,821,999	2,403,374	35.2	4,107,697	60.2	244,030	3.6	31,599	0.5	35,299	0.5	1,704,323	D
North Carolina	2,911,262	1,631,163	56.0	1,257,692	43.2	—	0.0	8,874	0.3	13,533	0.5	373,471	R
North Dakota	288,256	174,852	60.7	95,284	33.1	9,486	3.3	7,288	2.5	1,346	0.5	79,568	R
Ohio	4,701,998	2,350,363	50.0	2,183,628	46.4	117,799	2.5	26,721	0.6	23,484	0.5	166,735	R
Oklahoma	1,234,229	744,337	60.3	474,276	38.4	—	0.0	9,014	0.7	6,602	0.5	270,061	R
Oregon	1,533,968	713,577	46.5	720,342	47.0	77,357	5.0	7,063	0.5	15,629	1.0	6,765	D
Pennsylvania	4,913,119	2,281,127	46.4	2,485,967	50.6	103,392	2.1	16,023	0.3	26,610	0.5	204,840	D
Rhode Island	409,047	130,555	31.9	249,508	61.0	25,052	6.1	2,273	0.6	1,659	0.4	118,953	D
South Carolina	1,382,717	785,937	56.8	565,561	40.9	20,200	1.5	3,519	0.3	7,500	0.5	220,376	R
South Dakota	316,269	190,700	60.3	118,804	37.6	—	0.0	3,322	1.1	3,443	1.1	71,896	R
Tennessee	2,076,181	1,061,949	51.1	981,720	47.3	19,781	1.0	4,250	0.2	8,481	0.4	80,229	R
Texas	6,407,637	3,799,639	59.3	2,433,746	38.0	137,994	2.2	12,394	0.2	23,864	0.4	1,365,893	R
Utah	770,754	515,096	66.8	203,053	26.3	35,850	4.7	9,319	1.2	7,436	1.0	312,043	R
Vermont	294,308	119,775	40.7	149,022	50.6	20,374	6.9	2,192	0.7	2,945	1.0	29,247	D
Virginia	2,739,447	1,437,490	52.5	1,217,290	44.4	59,398	2.2	5,455	0.2	19,814	0.7	220,200	R
Washington	2,487,433	1,108,864	44.6	1,247,652	50.2	103,002	4.1	7,171	0.3	20,744	0.8	138,788	D
West Virginia	648,124	336,475	51.9	295,497	45.6	10,680	1.6	3,169	0.5	2,303	0.4	40,978	R
Wisconsin	2,598,607	1,237,279	47.6	1,242,987	47.8	94,070	3.6	11,446	0.4	12,825	0.5	5,708	D
Wyoming	218,351	147,947	67.8	60,481	27.7	4,625	2.1	2,724	1.2	2,574	1.2	87,466	R
Dist. of Col.	201,894	18,073	9.0	171,923	85.2	10,576	5.2	—	0.0	1,322	0.7	153,850	D
Total	105,396,627	50,455,156	47.9	50,992,335	48.4	2,882,738	2.7	449,077	0.4	617,321	0.6	537,179	D

2000 Electoral Votes

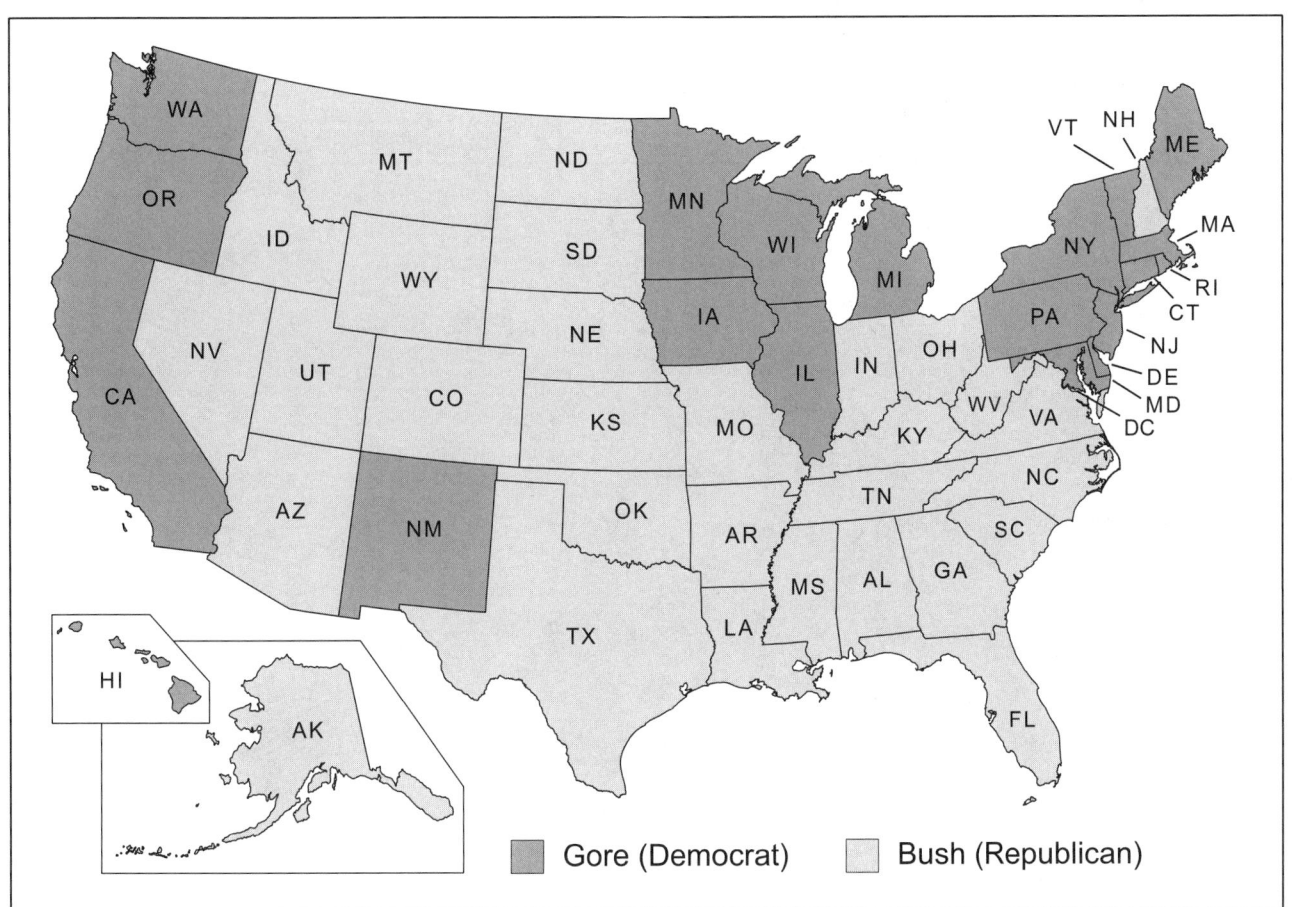

Gore (Democrat)   Bush (Republican)

States	Electoral votes	Bush	Gore	States	Electoral votes	Bush	Gore
Alabama	(9)	9	–	Nebraska	(5)	5	–
Alaska	(3)	3	–	Nevada	(4)	4	–
Arizona	(8)	8	–	New Hampshire	(4)	4	–
Arkansas	(6)	6	–	New Jersey	(15)	–	15
California	(54)	–	54	New Mexico	(5)	–	5
Colorado	(8)	8	–	New York	(33)	–	33
Connecticut	(8)	–	8	North Carolina	(14)	14	–
Delaware	(3)	–	3	North Dakota	(3)	3	–
District of Columbia[1]	(3)	–	2	Ohio	(21)	21	–
Florida	(25)	25	–	Oklahoma	(8)	8	–
Georgia	(13)	13	–	Oregon	(7)	–	7
Hawaii	(4)	–	4	Pennsylvania	(23)	–	23
Idaho	(4)	4	–	Rhode Island	(4)	–	4
Illinois	(22)	–	22	South Carolina	(8)	8	–
Indiana	(12)	12	–	South Dakota	(3)	3	–
Iowa	(7)	–	7	Tennessee	(11)	11	–
Kansas	(6)	6	–	Texas	(32)	32	–
Kentucky	(8)	8	–	Utah	(5)	5	–
Louisiana	(9)	9	–	Vermont	(3)	–	3
Maine	(4)	–	4	Virginia	(13)	13	–
Maryland	(10)	–	10	Washington	(11)	–	11
Massachusetts	(12)	–	12	West Virginia	(5)	5	–
Michigan	(18)	–	18	Wisconsin	(11)	–	11
Minnesota	(10)	–	10	Wyoming	(3)	3	–
Mississippi	(7)	7	–				
Missouri	(11)	11	–	Totals	(538)	271	266
Montana	(3)	3	–				

1. Barbara Lett-Simmons, a Gore elector in Washington, D.C., withheld her vote from Gore as a symbolic protest over the political status of the district.

2000 Republican Convention Balloting

Delegation	Total votes	First presidential ballot Bush
Alabama	44	44
Alaska	23	23
Arizona	30	30
Arkansas	24	24
California	162	162
Colorado	40	40
Connecticut	25	25
Delaware	12	12
Florida	80	80
Georgia	54	54
Hawaii	14	14
Idaho	28	28
Illinois	74	74
Indiana	55	55
Iowa	25	25
Kansas	35	35
Kentucky	31	31
Louisiana	29	29
Maine	14	14
Maryland	31	31
Massachusetts	37	37
Michigan	58	58
Minnesota	34	34
Mississippi	33	33
Missouri	35	35
Montana	23	23
Nebraska	30	30
Nevada	17	17
New Hampshire	17	17
New Jersey	54	54
New Mexico	21	21
New York	101	101
North Carolina	62	62
North Dakota	19	19
Ohio	69	69
Oklahoma	38	38
Oregon	24	24
Pennsylvania	78	78
Rhode Island	14	14
South Carolina	37	37
South Dakota	22	22
Tennessee	37	37
Texas	124	124
Utah	29	29
Vermont	12	12
Virginia	56	56
Washington	37	37
West Virginia	18	18
Wisconsin	37	37
Wyoming	22	22
District of Columbia	15	15
Puerto Rico	14	14
Virgin Islands	4	4
American Samoa	4	4
Guam	4	4
Total	2,066	2,066

2000 Democratic Convention Balloting

Delegation	Total votes	First presidential ballot[1] Gore
Alabama	64	64
Alaska	19	19
Arizona	55	55
Arkansas	47	47
California	435	435
Colorado	61	61
Connecticut	67	67
Delaware	22	22
Florida	186	186
Georgia	92	92
Hawaii	33	33
Idaho	23	23
Illinois	190	190
Indiana	88	88
Iowa	57	57
Kansas	42	42
Kentucky	58	58
Louisiana	73	73
Maine	33	33
Maryland	95	95
Massachusetts	118	118
Michigan	157	157
Minnesota	91	91
Mississippi	48	48
Missouri	92	92
Montana	24	24
Nebraska	32	32
Nevada	29	29
New Hampshire	29	29
New Jersey	124	124
New Mexico	35	35
New York	294	294
North Carolina	103	103
North Dakota	22	22
Ohio	170	170
Oklahoma	52	52
Oregon	58	58
Pennsylvania	191	191
Rhode Island	33	33
South Carolina	52	52
South Dakota	22	22
Tennessee	81	81
Texas	231	231
Utah	29	29
Vermont	22	22
Virginia	95	95
Washington	94	94
West Virginia	42	42
Wisconsin	93	93
Wyoming	18	18
District of Columbia	33	33
Puerto Rico	58	58
Virgin Islands	6	6
American Samoa	6	6
Guam	6	6
Democrats Abroad	9	9
Total	4,339	4,339

1. Unofficial total. There may have been several delegates not voting.

Distribution of House Seats and Electoral Votes

State	U.S. House Seats									Electoral Votes					
	1963–1973	1970 Census Changes	1973–1983	1980 Census Changes	1983–1993	1990 Census Changes	1993–2003	2000 Census Changes	2003–2013	1952, 1956, 1960	1964, 1968	1972, 1976, 1980	1984, 1988	1992, 1996, 2000	2004, 2008
Alabama	8	−1	7	—	7	—	7	—	7	11	10	9	9	9	9
Alaska	1	—	1	—	1	—	1	—	1	3	3	3	3	3	3
Arizona	3	+1	4	+1	5	+1	6	+2	8	4	5	6	7	8	10
Arkansas	4	—	4	—	4	—	4	—	4	8	6	6	6	6	6
California	38	+5	43	+2	45	+7	52	+1	53	32	40	45	47	54	55
Colorado	4	+1	5	+1	6	—	6	+1	7	6	6	7	8	8	9
Connecticut	6	—	6	—	6	—	6	−1	5	8	8	8	8	8	7
Delaware	1	—	1	—	1	—	1	—	1	3	3	3	3	3	3
Dist. of Col.	—	—	—	—	—	—	—	—	—	—	3	3	3	3	3
Florida	12	+3	15	+4	19	+4	23	+2	25	10	14	17	21	25	27
Georgia	10	—	10	—	10	+1	11	+2	13	12	12	12	12	13	15
Hawaii	2	—	2	—	2	—	2	—	2	3	4	4	4	4	4
Idaho	2	—	2	—	2	—	2	—	2	4	4	4	4	4	4
Illinois	24	—	24	−2	22	−2	20	−1	19	27	26	26	24	22	21
Indiana	11	—	11	−1	10	—	10	−1	9	13	13	13	12	12	11
Iowa	7	−1	6	—	6	−1	5	—	5	10	9	8	8	7	7
Kansas	5	—	5	—	5	−1	4	—	4	8	7	7	7	6	6
Kentucky	7	—	7	—	7	−1	6	—	6	10	9	9	9	8	8
Louisiana	8	—	8	—	8	−1	7	—	7	10	10	10	10	9	9
Maine	2	—	2	—	2	—	2	—	2	5	4	4	4	4	4
Maryland	8	—	8	—	8	—	8	—	8	9	10	10	10	10	10
Massachusetts	12	—	12	−1	11	−1	10	—	10	16	14	14	13	12	12
Michigan	19	—	19	−1	18	−2	16	−1	15	20	21	21	20	18	17
Minnesota	8	—	8	—	8	—	8	—	8	11	10	10	10	10	10
Mississippi	5	—	5	—	5	—	5	−1	4	8	7	7	7	7	6
Missouri	10	—	10	−1	9	—	9	—	9	13	12	12	11	11	11
Montana	2	—	2	—	2	−1	1	—	1	4	4	4	4	3	3
Nebraska	3	—	3	—	3	—	3	—	3	6	5	5	5	5	5
Nevada	1	—	1	+1	2	—	2	+1	3	3	3	3	4	4	5
New Hampshire	2	—	2	—	2	—	2	—	2	4	4	4	4	4	4
New Jersey	15	—	15	−1	14	−1	13	—	13	16	17	17	16	15	15
New Mexico	2	—	2	+1	3	—	3	—	3	4	4	4	5	5	5
New York	41	−2	39	−5	34	−3	31	−2	29	45	43	41	36	33	31
North Carolina	11	—	11	—	11	+1	12	+1	13*	14	13	13	13	14	15
North Dakota	2	−1	1	—	1	—	1	—	1	4	4	3	3	3	3
Ohio	24	−1	23	−2	21	−2	19	−1	18	25	26	25	23	21	20
Oklahoma	6	—	6	—	6	—	6	−1	5	8	8	8	8	8	7
Oregon	4	—	4	+1	5	—	5	—	5	6	6	6	7	7	7
Pennsylvania	27	−2	25	−2	23	−2	21	−2	19	32	29	27	25	23	21
Rhode Island	2	—	2	—	2	—	2	—	2	4	4	4	4	4	4
South Carolina	6	—	6	—	6	—	6	—	6	8	8	8	8	8	8
South Dakota	2	—	2	−1	1	—	1	—	1	4	4	4	3	3	3
Tennessee	9	−1	8	+1	9	—	9	—	9	11	11	10	11	11	11
Texas	23	+1	24	+3	27	+3	30	+2	32	24	25	26	29	32	34
Utah	2	—	2	+1	3	—	3	—	3*	4	4	4	5	5	5
Vermont	1	—	1	—	1	—	1	—	1	3	3	3	3	3	3
Virginia	10	—	10	—	10	+1	11	—	11	12	12	12	12	13	13
Washington	7	—	7	+1	8	+1	9	—	9	9	9	9	10	11	11
West Virginia	5	−1	4	—	4	−1	3	—	3	8	7	6	6	5	5
Wisconsin	10	−1	9	—	9	—	9	−1	8	12	12	11	11	11	10
Wyoming	1	—	1	—	1	—	1	—	1	3	3	3	3	3	3

NOTE: Table is based on the censuses of 1960, 1970, 1980, 1990, and 2000.

* In a case pending before the U.S. Supreme Court in April 2002, Utah was challenging a device used by the Census Bureau in taking the 2000 census that Utah claimed wrongly deprived the state of an additional seat in Congress. If Utah's claim prevailed, that state would have four seats rather than three. The state that was expected to forfeit a seat was North Carolina, which had gained one seat, for a total of thirteen, as a result of the 2000 census. The Court had not decided the case as of April 12, 2002.

Party Affiliations in Congress and the Presidency, 1789–2001

Year	Congress	House		Senate		President
		Majority party	Principal minority party	Majority party	Principal minority party	
1789–1791	1st	AD-38	Op-26	AD-17	Op-9	F (Washington)
1791–1793	2nd	F-37	DR-33	F-16	DR-13	F (Washington)
1793–1795	3rd	DR-57	F-48	F-17	DR-13	F (Washington)
1795–1797	4th	F-54	DR-52	F-19	DR-13	F (Washington)
1797–1799	5th	F-58	DR-48	F-20	DR-12	F (J. Adams)
1799–1801	6th	F-64	DR-42	F-19	DR-13	F (J. Adams)
1801–1803	7th	DR-69	F-36	DR-18	F-13	DR (Jefferson)
1803–1805	8th	DR-102	F-39	DR-25	F-9	DR (Jefferson)
1805–1807	9th	DR-116	F-25	DR-27	F-7	DR (Jefferson)
1807–1809	10th	DR-118	F-24	DR-28	F-6	DR (Jefferson)
1809–1811	11th	DR-94	F-48	DR-28	F-6	DR (Madison)
1811–1813	12th	DR-108	F-36	DR-30	F-6	DR (Madison)
1813–1815	13th	DR-112	F-68	DR-27	F-9	DR (Madison)
1815–1817	14th	DR-117	F-65	DR-25	F-11	DR (Madison)
1817–1819	15th	DR-141	F-42	DR-34	F-10	DR (Monroe)
1819–1821	16th	DR-156	F-27	DR-35	F-7	DR (Monroe)
1821–1823	17th	DR-158	F-25	DR-44	F-4	DR (Monroe)
1823–1825	18th	DR-187	F-26	DR-44	F-4	DR (Monroe)
1825–1827	19th	AD-105	J-97	AD-26	J-20	DR (J.Q. Adams)
1827–1829	20th	J-119	AD-94	J-28	AD-20	DR (J.Q. Adams)
1829–1831	21st	D-139	NR-74	D-26	NR-22	DR (Jackson)
1831–1833	22nd	D-141	NR-58	D-25	NR-21	D (Jackson)
1833–1835	23rd	D-147	AM-53	D-20	NR-20	D (Jackson)
1835–1837	24th	D-145	W-98	D-27	W-25	D (Jackson)
1837–1839	25th	D-108	W-107	D-30	W-18	D (Van Buren)
1839–1841	26th	D-124	W-118	D-28	W-22	D (Van Buren)
1841–1843	27th	W-133	D-102	W-28	D-22	W (W. Harrison); W (Tyler)
1843–1845	28th	D-142	W-79	W-28	D-25	W (Tyler)
1845–1847	29th	D-143	W-77	D-31	W-25	D (Polk)
1847–1849	30th	W-115	D-108	D-36	W-21	D (Polk)
1849–1851	31st	D-112	W-109	D-35	W-25	W (Taylor); W (Fillmore)
1851–1853	32nd	D-140	W-88	D-35	W-24	W (Fillmore)
1853–1855	33rd	D-159	W-71	D-38	W-22	D (Pierce)
1855–1857	34th	R-108	D-83	D-40	R-15	D (Pierce)
1857–1859	35th	D-118	R-92	D-36	R-20	D (Buchanan)
1859–1861	36th	R-114	D-92	D-36	R-26	D (Buchanan)
1861–1863	37th	R-105	D-43	R-31	D-10	R (Lincoln)
1863–1865	38th	R-102	D-75	R-36	D-9	R (Lincoln)
1865–1867	39th	U-149	D-42	U-42	D-10	R (Lincoln); D (A. Johnson)
1867–1869	40th	R-143	D-49	R-42	D-11	D (A. Johnson)
1869–1871	41st	R-149	D-63	R-56	D-11	R (Grant)
1871–1873	42nd	R-134	D-104	R-52	D-17	R (Grant)
1873–1875	43rd	R-194	D-92	R-49	D-19	R (Grant)
1875–1877	44th	D-169	R-109	R-45	D-29	R (Grant)
1877–1879	45th	D-153	R-140	R-39	D-36	R (Hayes)
1879–1881	46th	D-149	R-130	D-42	R-33	R (Hayes)
1881–1883	47th	R-147	D-135	R-37	D-37	R (Garfield); R (Arthur)
1883–1885	48th	D-197	R-118	R-38	D-36	R (Arthur)
1885–1887	49th	D-183	R-140	R-43	D-34	D (Cleveland)
1887–1889	50th	D-169	R-152	R-39	D-37	D (Cleveland)
1889–1891	51st	R-166	D-159	R-39	D-37	R (B. Harrison)
1891–1893	52nd	D-235	R-88	R-47	D-39	R (B. Harrison)
1893–1895	53rd	D-218	R-127	D-44	R-38	D (Cleveland)
1895–1897	54th	R-244	D-105	R-43	D-39	D (Cleveland)
1897–1899	55th	R-204	D-113	R-47	D-34	R (McKinley)
1899–1901	56th	R-185	D-163	R-53	D-26	R (McKinley)

(table continues)

Year	Congress	House Majority party	House Principal minority party	Senate Majority party	Senate Principal minority party	President
1901–1903	57th	R-197	D-151	R-55	D-31	R (McKinley); R (T. Roosevelt)
1903–1905	58th	R-208	D-178	R-57	D-33	R (T. Roosevelt)
1905–1907	59th	R-250	D-136	R-57	D-33	R (T. Roosevelt)
1907–1909	60th	R-222	D-164	R-61	D-31	R (T. Roosevelt)
1909–1911	61st	R-219	D-172	R-61	D-32	R (Taft)
1911–1913	62nd	D-228	R-161	R-51	D-41	R (Taft)
1913–1915	63rd	D-291	R-127	D-51	R-44	D (Wilson)
1915–1917	64th	D-230	R-196	D-56	R-40	D (Wilson)
1917–1919	65th	D-216	R-210	D-53	R-42	D (Wilson)
1919–1921	66th	R-240	D-190	R-49	D-47	D (Wilson)
1921–1923	67th	R-301	D-131	R-59	D-37	R (Harding)
1923–1925	68th	R-225	D-205	R-51	D-43	R (Coolidge)
1925–1927	69th	R-247	D-183	R-56	D-39	R (Coolidge)
1927–1929	70th	R-237	D-195	R-49	D-46	R (Coolidge)
1929–1931	71st	R-267	D-167	R-56	D-39	R (Hoover)
1931–1933	72nd	D-220	R-214	R-48	D-47	R (Hoover)
1933–1935	73rd	D-310	R-117	D-60	R-35	D (F. Roosevelt)
1935–1937	74th	D-319	R-103	D-69	R-25	D (F. Roosevelt)
1937–1939	75th	D-331	R-89	D-76	R-16	D (F. Roosevelt)
1939–1941	76th	D-261	R-164	D-69	R-23	D (F. Roosevelt)
1941–1943	77th	D-268	R-162	D-66	R-28	D (F. Roosevelt)
1943–1945	78th	D-218	R-208	D-58	R-37	D (F. Roosevelt)
1945–1947	79th	D-242	R-190	D-56	R-38	D (F. Roosevelt); D (Truman)
1947–1949	80th	R-245	D-188	R-51	D-45	D (Truman)
1949–1951	81st	D-263	R-171	D-54	R-42	D (Truman)
1951–1953	82nd	D-234	R-199	D-49	R-47	D (Truman)
1953–1955	83rd	R-221	D-211	R-48	D-47	R (Eisenhower)
1955–1957	84th	D-232	R-203	D-48	R-47	R (Eisenhower)
1957–1959	85th	D-233	R-200	D-49	R-47	R (Eisenhower)
1959–1961	86th	D-283	R-153	D-64	R-34	R (Eisenhower)
1961–1963	87th	D-263	R-174	D-65	R-35	D (Kennedy)
1963–1965	88th	D-258	R-177	D-67	R-33	D (Kennedy); D (L. Johnson)
1965–1967	89th	D-295	R-140	D-68	R-32	D (L. Johnson)
1967–1969	90th	D-247	R-187	D-64	R-36	D (L. Johnson)
1969–1971	91st	D-243	R-192	D-57	R-43	R (Nixon)
1971–1973	92nd	D-254	R-180	D-54	R-44	R (Nixon)
1973–1975	93rd	D-239	R-192	D-56	R-42	R (Nixon); R (Ford)
1975–1977	94th	D-291	R-144	D-60	R-37	R (Ford)
1977–1979	95th	D-292	R-143	D-61	R-38	D (Carter)
1979–1981	96th	D-276	R-157	D-58	R-41	D (Carter)
1981–1983	97th	D-243	R-192	R-53	D-46	R (Reagan)
1983–1985	98th	D-269	R-165	R-54	D-46	R (Reagan)
1985–1987	99th	D-252	R-182	R-53	D-47	R (Reagan)
1987–1989	100th	D-258	R-177	D-55	R-45	R (Reagan)
1989–1991	101st	D-259	R-174	D-55	R-45	R (Bush)
1991–1993	102nd	D-267	R-167	D-56	R-44	R (Bush)
1993–1995	103rd	D-258	R-176	D-57	R-43	D (Clinton)
1995–1997	104th	R-230	D-204	R-53	D-47	D (Clinton)
1997–1999	105th	R-227	D-207	R-55	D-45	D (Clinton)
1999–2001	106th	R-222	D-211	R-55	D-45	D (Clinton)
2001–	107th	R-222	D-211	D-50[1]	R-49	R (G.W. Bush)

SOURCES: *CQ Weekly*, various issues; U.S. Bureau of the Census, *Historical Statistics of the United States, Colonial Times to 1970* (Washington, D.C.: Government Printing Office, 1975); and U.S. Congress, Joint Committee on Printing, *Official Congressional Directory* (Washington, D.C.: Government Printing Office, 1967–).

NOTE: Figures are for the beginning of the first session of each Congress except for Senate in 2001 (see footnote). Key to abbreviations: AD—Administration; AM—Anti-Masonic; D—Democratic; DR—Democratic-Republican; F—Federalist; J—Jacksonian; NR—National Republican; Op—Opposition; R—Republican; U—Unionist; W—Whig.

1. The November 2000 Senate elections resulted in a 50–50 split between Republicans and Democrats in that chamber. On June 5, 2001, Republican Sen. James Jeffords of Vermont left the Republican Party to become an Independent. However, he caucused with the Democrats, giving them—in effect—a 51-49 controlling majority in the Senate.

1997 Gubernatorial Elections

	Vote total	Percent		Vote total	Percent
New Jersey—Nov. 4, 1997			**Virginia—Nov. 4, 1997**		
Christine Todd Whitman (R)	1,133,394	46.9	James S. Gilmore III (R)	969,062	55.8
James McGreevey (D)	1,107,968	45.8	Donald S. Beyer Jr. (D)	738,971	42.6

Special House Elections, 105th Congress

Texas 28th CD—April 12, 1997

Ciro D. Rodriguez (D)	19,992	66.7
Juan F. Solis III (D)	9,990	33.3

New Mexico 3rd CD—May 13, 1997

Bill Redmond (R)	43,559	42.7
Eric P. Serna (D)	40,542	39.8
Carol A. Miller (GREEN)	17,101	16.8
Edward D. Nagel (LIBERT)	393	0.4
Daniel J. Pearlman (REF)	304	0.3
John Bishop (WI)	36	—
Michael A. Guss (WI)	5	—
Orlin G. Cole (WI)	2	—

New York 13th CD—Nov. 4, 1997

Vito J. Fossella (R)	79,838	61.3
Eric N. Vitaliano (D)	50,373	38.7

New York 6th CD—Feb. 3, 1998

Gregory W. Meeks (D)	14,224	56.5
Alton R. Waldon Jr. (Conservative, Independence)	5,229	20.8
Barbara M. Clark (21st Century)	3,305	13.1
Celestine V. Miller (R)	2,209	8.8
Mary Cronin (RTL)	206	0.8

California 22nd CD—March 10, 1998

Lois Capps (D)	93,392	53.5
Tom J. Bordonaro Jr. (R)	78,224	44.8
Robert Bakhaus (LIBERT)	3,079	1.8

California 9th CD All-Party Primary—April 7, 1998

Barbara Lee (D)	33,497	66.8
Greg Harper (D)	8,048	16.1
Claiborne (Clay) Sanders (R)	6,114	12.2
Randal Stewart (D)	2,481	4.9

California 44th CD All-Party Primary—April 7, 1998

Mary Bono (R)	53,755	64.0
Ralph Waite (D)	24,228	28.8
Anna Nevenich (D)	2,415	2.9
John W. J. Overman (R)	1,435	1.7
Tom Harney (R)	1,235	1.5
Bud Mathewson (R)	946	1.1

Pennsylvania 1st CD—May 19, 1998

Robert A. Brady (D)	13,923	73.6
William M. Harrison (R)	2,436	12.9
Juanita Norwood (REF)	1,993	10.5
John J. Featherman (LIBERT)	558	3.0

New Mexico 1st CD—June 23, 1998

Heather Wilson (R)	54,853	44.6
Phillip Maloof (D)	48,747	39.6
Robert Anderson (GREEN)	18,108	14.7
Bruce Bush (LIBERT)	1,337	1.1
Orlin Cole (WI)	10	—

Special Senate Elections, 105th Congress

None

NOTE: D—Democrat, GREEN—Green, I—Independent, LIBERT—Libertarian, R—Republican, REF—Reform, RTL—Right to Life, WI—write-in

1998 Elections Returns for Governor, Senate, and House

Following are the official vote returns for the gubernatorial, Senate, and House races compiled by Congressional Quarterly from the figures supplied by the 50 state election boards.

Vote totals are included for all candidates listed on the ballot who received 5 percent or more of the total vote. (For candidates who received under 5 percent, consult *America Votes 23* (1999), published by CQ Press.)

An asterisk (*) indicates an incumbent.

An "X" denotes candidates without major-party opposition; no votes were tallied.

An "AL" indicates an at-large member of Congress in a state with a single congressional district.

See p. 1073 for special elections and 1997 gubernatorial elections.

	Vote total	Percent
Alabama		
Governor		
Don Siegelman (D)	760,155	57.7
Forrest H. "Fob" James Jr. (R)*	554,746	42.1
Senate		
Richard C. Shelby (R)*	817,973	63.2
Clayton Suddith (D)	474,568	36.7
House		
1 Sonny Callahan (R)*	112,872	100.0
2 Terry Everett (R)*	131,428	69.3
Joe Fondren (D)	58,136	30.7
3 Bob Riley (R)*	101,731	58.1
Joe Turnham (D)	73,357	41.9
4 Robert B. Aderholt (R)*	106,297	56.4
Donald Bevill (D)	82,065	43.5
5 Robert E. "Bud" Cramer (D)*	134,819	69.7
Gil Aust (R)	58,536	30.3
6 Spencer Bachus (R)*	154,761	71.8
Donna Wesson Smalley (D)	60,657	28.1
7 Earl F. Hilliard (D)*	136,431	100.0
Alaska		
Governor		
Tony Knowles (D)*	112,879	51.3
John Lindauer (R)	39,331	17.9
Ray Metcalfe (MOD R)	13,540	6.2
Senate		
Frank H. Murkowski (R)*	165,227	74.5
Joseph Sonneman (D)	43,743	19.7
House		
AL Don Young (R)*	139,676	62.6
James W. "Jim" Duncan (D)	77,232	34.6

	Vote total	Percent
Arizona		
Governor		
Jane Dee Hull (R)*	620,188	60.9
Paul Johnson (D)	361,552	35.5
Senate		
John McCain (R)*	696,577	68.7
Ed Ranger (D)	275,224	27.2
House		
1 Matt Salmon (R)*	98,840	64.6
David Mendoza (D)	51,108	35.4
2 Ed Pastor (D)*	57,178	67.6
Edward Clyde "Ed" Barron (R)	23,628	28.0
3 Bob Stump (R)*	137,618	67.3
Stuart Marc Starky (D)	66,979	32.7
4 John Shadegg (R)*	102,722	64.7
Eric Ehst (D)	49,538	31.2
5 Jim Kolbe (R)*	103,952	51.6
Thomas John Volgy (D)	91,030	45.2
6 J. D. Hayworth (R)*	106,891	53.0
Steve Owens (D)	88,001	43.7
Arkansas		
Governor		
Mike Huckabee (R)*	421,989	59.8
Bill Bristow (D)	272,923	38.7
Senate		
Blanche Lincoln (D)	385,878	55.1
Fay Boozman (R)	295,870	42.2
House		
1 Marion Berry (D)*	X	X
2 Vic Snyder (D)*	100,334	58.0
Phil Wyrick (R)	72,737	42.0
3 Asa Hutchinson (R)*	154,780	80.8

	Vote total	Percent
Ralph Forbes (REF)	36,917	19.3
4 Jay Dickey (R)*	92,346	57.5
Judy Smith (D)	68,194	42.5
California		
Governor		
Gray Davis (D)	4,860,702	58.0
Dan Lungren (R)	3,218,030	38.4
Senate		
Barbara Boxer (D)*	4,411,705	53.1
Matt Fong (R)	3,576,351	43.0
House		
1 Mike Thompson (D)	121,713	61.9
Mark Luce (R)	64,622	32.8
2 Wally Herger (R)*	128,372	62.5
Roberts "Rob" Braden (D)	70,837	34.5
3 Doug Ose (R)	100,621	52.4
Sandie Dunn (D)	86,471	45.0
4 John T. Doolittle (R)*	155,306	62.6
David Shapiro (D)	85,394	34.4
5 Robert T. Matsui (D)*	130,715	71.9
Robert S. Dinsmore (R)	47,307	26.0
6 Lynn Woolsey (D)*	158,446	68.0
Ken McAuliffe (R)	69,295	29.7
7 George Miller (D)*	125,842	76.7
Norman H. Reece (R)	38,290	23.3
8 Nancy Pelosi (D)*	148,027	85.8
David J. Martz (R)	20,781	12.0
9 Barbara Lee (D)*	140,722	82.8
Claiborne "Clay" Sanders (R)	22,431	13.2
10 Ellen O. Tauscher (D)*	127,134	53.5
Charles Ball (R)	103,299	43.4
11 Richard W. Pombo (R)*	95,496	61.4
Robert L. Figueroa (D)	56,345	36.2
12 Tom Lantos (D)*	128,135	74.0
Robert H. Evans Jr. (R)	36,562	21.1
13 Pete Stark (D)*	101,671	71.2
James R. Goetz (R)	38,050	26.6
14 Anna G. Eshoo (D)*	129,663	68.6
John C. "Chris" Haugen (R)	53,719	28.4
15 Tom Campbell (R)*	111,876	60.5
Dick Lane (D)	70,059	37.9
16 Zoe Lofgren (D)*	85,503	72.8
Horace Eugene Thayn (R)	27,494	23.4
17 Sam Farr (D)*	103,719	64.5
Bill McCampbell (R)	52,470	32.7
18 Gary A. Condit (D)*	118,842	86.8
Linda M. DeGroat (LIBERT)	18,089	13.2
19 George P. Radanovich (R)*	131,105	79.4
Jonathan Richter (LIBERT)	34,044	20.6
20 Cal Dooley (D)*	60,599	60.7
Cliff Unruh (R)	39,183	39.3

ABBREVIATIONS FOR PARTY DESIGNATIONS

AMH	American Heritage	L	Liberal
AMI	American Independent	LIBERT	Libertarian
C	Conservative	MOD R	Moderate Republican
CONSTL	Constitutional	NL	Natural Law
D	Democratic	R	Republican
DFL	Democratic Farmer-Labor	REF	Reform
GREEN	Green	RTL	Right to Life
I	Independent	S	Socialist
IA	Independent American	TAX	Taxpayers
IND	Independence (New York)	WF	Working Families
INDEP	Independence		

		Vote total	Percent
21	William Thomas (R)*	115,989	78.9
	John Evans (REF)	30,994	21.1
22	Lois Capps (D)*	111,388	55.1
	Tom Bordonaro (R)	86,921	43.0
23	Elton W. Gallegly (R)*	96,362	60.1
	Daniel Gonzalez (D)	64,068	39.9
24	Brad Sherman (D)*	103,491	57.3
	Randy Hoffman (R)	69,501	38.5
25	Howard P. "Buck" McKeon (R)*	114,013	74.7
	Bruce Acker (LIBERT)	38,669	25.3
26	Howard L. Berman (D)*	69,000	82.5
	Juan Carlos Ros (LIBERT)	6,556	7.8
	Maria Armoudian (GREEN)	4,858	5.8
27	James E. Rogan (R)*	80,702	50.7
	Barry Gordon (D)	73,875	46.4
28	David Dreier (R)*	90,607	57.6
	Janice Nelson (D)	61,721	39.3
29	Henry A. Waxman (D)*	131,561	73.9
	Mike Gottlieb (R)	40,282	22.6
30	Xavier Becerra (D)*	58,230	81.2
	Patricia Jean Parker (R)	13,441	18.8
31	Matthew G. Martinez (D)*	61,173	70.0
	Frank Moreno (R)	19,786	22.6
	Krista Lieberg-Wong (GREEN)	4,377	5.0
32	Julian C. Dixon (D)*	112,253	86.7
	Laurence Ardito (R)	14,622	11.3
33	Lucille Roybal-Allard (D)*	43,310	87.2
	Wayne Miller (R)	6,364	12.8
34	Grace Napolitano (D)	76,471	67.6
	Ed Perez (R)	32,321	28.6
35	Maxine Waters (D)*	78,732	89.3
	Gordon Michael Mego (AMI)	9,413	10.7
36	Steve Kuykendall (R)	88,843	48.9
	Janice Hahn (D)	84,624	46.6
37	Juanita Millender-McDonald (D)*	70,026	85.1
	Saul E. Lankster (R)	12,301	14.9
38	Steve Horn (R)*	71,386	52.9
	Peter Mathews (D)	59,767	44.3
39	Ed Royce (R)*	97,366	62.6
	A. R. Groom (D)	52,815	34.0
40	Jerry Lewis (R)*	97,406	64.9
	Robert Conaway (D)	47,897	31.9
41	Gary Miller (R)	68,310	53.2
	Eileen Ansari (D)	52,264	40.7
42	George E. Brown Jr. (D)*	62,207	55.3
	Elia Pirozzi (R)	45,328	40.3
43	Ken Calvert (R)*	83,012	55.7
	Mike Rayburn (D)	56,373	37.8
44	Mary Bono (R)*	97,013	60.1
	Ralph Waite (D)	57,697	35.7
45	Dana Rohrabacher (R)*	94,296	58.7
	Patricia Neal (D)	60,022	37.3
46	Loretta Sanchez (D)*	47,964	56.4
	Robert Dornan (R)	33,388	39.3
47	Christopher Cox (R)*	132,711	67.6
	Christina Avalos (D)	57,938	29.5
48	Ron Packard (R)*	138,948	76.9
	Sharon Miles (NL)	23,262	12.9
	Daniel Muhe (LIBERT)	18,509	10.2
49	Brian P. Bilbray (R)*	90,516	48.8
	Christine Kehoe (D)	86,400	46.6
50	Bob Filner (D)*	77,354	99.2
51	Randy "Duke" Cunningham (R)*	126,229	61.0
	Dan Kripke (D)	71,706	34.7

		Vote total	Percent
52	Duncan Hunter (R)*	116,251	75.7
	Lynn Badler (LIBERT)	21,933	14.3
	Adrienne Pelton (NL)	15,380	10.0

Colorado

Governor

	Vote total	Percent
Bill Owens (R)	648,202	49.1
Gail Schoettler (D)	639,905	48.4

Senate

	Vote total	Percent
Ben Nighthorse Campbell (R)*	829,370	62.5
Dottie Lamm (D)	464,754	35.0

House

		Vote total	Percent
1	Diana DeGette (D)*	116,628	66.9
	Nancy McClanahan (R)	52,452	30.1
2	Mark Udall (D)	113,946	49.9
	Bob Greenlee (R)	108,385	47.4
3	Scott McInnis (R)*	156,501	66.1
	Robert Reed Kelley (D)	74,479	31.5
4	Bob Schaffer (R)*	131,318	59.3
	Susan Kirkpatrick (D)	89,973	40.7
5	Joel Hefley (R)*	155,790	72.7
	Ken Alford (D)	55,609	26.0
6	Tom Tancredo (R)	111,374	55.9
	Henry L. Strauss (D)	82,662	41.5

Connecticut

Governor

	Vote total	Percent
John G. Rowland (R)*	628,707	62.9
Barbara B. Kennelly (D)	354,187	35.4

Senate

	Vote total	Percent
Christopher J. Dodd (D)*	628,306	65.1
Gary A. Franks (R)	312,177	32.4

House

		Vote total	Percent
1	John B. Larson (D)	97,681	58.1
	Kevin O'Connor (R)	69,668	41.4
2	Sam Gejdenson (D)*	99,567	61.0
	Gary M. Koval (R)	57,860	35.5
3	Rosa DeLauro (D)*	109,726	71.3
	Martin Reust (R)	42,090	27.4
4	Christopher Shays (R)*	94,767	69.1
	Jonathan Kantrowitz (D)	40,988	29.9
5	Jim Maloney (D)*	78,394	49.9
	Mark Nielsen (R)	76,051	48.4
6	Nancy L. Johnson (R)*	101,630	58.1
	Charlotte Koskoff (D)	69,201	39.6

Delaware

House

		Vote total	Percent
AL	Michael N. Castle (R)*	119,811	66.4
	Dennis E. Williams (D)	57,446	31.8

Florida

Governor

	Vote total	Percent
Jeb Bush (R)	2,191,105	55.3
Buddy MacKay (D)	1,773,054	44.7

Senate

	Vote total	Percent
Bob Graham (D)*	2,436,407	62.5
Charlie Crist (R)	1,463,755	37.5

House

		Vote total	Percent
1	Joe Scarborough (R)*	140,525	99.5
2	Allen Boyd (D)*	138,440	95.2
3	Corrine Brown (D)*	66,621	55.4
	Bill Randall (R)	53,530	44.6
4	Tillie Fowler (R)*	X	X
5	Karen L. Thurman (D)*	132,005	66.3
	Jack "THRO" Gargan (REF)	67,147	33.7
6	Cliff Stearns (R)*	X	X

		Vote total	Percent
7	John L. Mica (R)*	X	X
8	Bill McCollum (R)*	104,298	65.8
	Al Krulick (D)	54,245	34.2
9	Michael Bilirakis (R)*	X	X
10	C. W. Bill Young (R)*	X	X
11	Jim Davis (D)*	85,262	64.9
	Joe Chillura (R)	46,176	35.1
12	Charles T. Canady (R)*	X	X
13	Dan Miller (R)*	X	X
14	Porter J. Goss (R)*	X	X
15	Dave Weldon (R)*	129,278	63.1
	David R. Golding (D)	75,654	36.9
16	Mark Foley (R)*	X	X
17	Carrie P. Meek (D)*	X	X
18	Ileana Ros-Lehtinen (R)*	X	X
19	Robert Wexler (D)*	X	X
20	Peter Deutsch (D)*	X	X
21	Lincoln Diaz-Balart (R)*	84,018	74.8
	Patrick Cusack (D)	28,378	25.2
22	E. Clay Shaw Jr. (R)*	X	X
23	Alcee L. Hastings (D)*	X	X

Georgia

Governor

	Vote total	Percent
Roy E. Barnes (D)	941,076	52.5
Guy Millner (R)	790,201	44.1

Senate

	Vote total	Percent
Paul Coverdell (R)*	918,540	52.4
Michael Coles (D)	791,904	45.2

House

		Vote total	Percent
1	Jack Kingston (R)*	92,229	100.0
2	Sanford D. Bishop (D)*	77,953	56.8
	Joe McCormick (R)	59,305	43.2
3	Mac Collins (R)*	123,064	100.0
4	Cynthia A. McKinney (D)*	100,622	61.1
	Sunny Warren (R)	64,146	38.9
5	John Lewis (D)*	109,177	78.5
	John H. Lewis Sr. (R)	29,877	21.5
6	Newt Gingrich (R)*	164,996	70.7
	Gary "Bats" Pelphrey (D)	68,366	29.3
7	Bob Barr (R)*	85,982	55.4
	James F. Williams (D)	69,293	44.6
8	Saxby Chambliss (R)*	87,993	62.4
	Ronald L. Cain (D)	53,079	37.6
9	Nathan Deal (R)*	122,713	100.0
10	Charlie Norwood (R)*	88,527	59.6
	Marion Spencer "Denise" Freeman (D)	60,004	40.4
11	John Linder (R)*	120,909	69.3
	Vincent Littman (D)	53,510	30.7

Hawaii

Governor

	Vote total	Percent
Benjamin J. Cayetano (D)*	204,206	50.1
Linda Lingle (R)	198,952	48.8

Senate

	Vote total	Percent
Daniel K. Inouye (D)*	315,252	79.2
Crystal Young (R)	70,964	17.8

House

		Vote total	Percent
1	Neil Abercrombie (D)*	116,693	61.6
	Gene Ward (R)	68,905	36.3
2	Patsy T. Mink (D)*	144,254	69.4
	Carol J. Douglass (R)	50,423	24.3

Idaho

Governor

	Vote total	Percent
Dirk Kempthorne (R)	258,095	67.7
Robert C. Huntley (D)	110,815	29.1

	Vote total	Per cent
Senate		
Michael D. Crapo (R)	262,966	69.5
Bill Mauk (D)	107,375	28.4
House		
1 Helen Chenoweth (R)*	113,231	55.3
Dan Williams (D)	91,653	44.7
2 Mike Simpson (R)	91,337	52.5
Richard H. Stallings (D)	77,736	44.7

Illinois

	Vote total	Per cent
Governor		
George H. Ryan (R)	1,714,094	51.0
Glenn Poshard (D)	1,594,191	47.5
Senate		
Peter G. Fitzgerald (R)	1,709,041	47.4
Carol Moseley-Braun (D)*	1,610,496	50.3
House		
1 Bobby L. Rush (D)*	151,890	87.1
Marlene White Ahimaz (R)	18,429	10.6
2 Jesse L. Jackson Jr. (D)*	148,985	89.4
Robert Gordon III (R)	16,075	9.6
3 William O. Lipinski (D)*	115,887	72.5
Robert Marshall (R)	44,012	27.5
4 Luis V. Gutierrez (D)*	54,244	81.7
John Birch (R)	10,529	15.9
5 Rod R. Blagojevich (D)*	95,738	74.0
Alan Spitz (R)	33,687	26.0
6 Henry J. Hyde (R)*	111,603	67.3
Thomas A. Cramer (D)	49,906	30.1
7 Danny K. Davis (D)*	130,984	92.9
Dorn E. Van Cleave III (LIBERT)	9,984	7.1
8 Philip M. Crane (R)*	104,242	68.6
Mike Rothman (D)	47,614	31.4
9 Janice D. "Jan" Schakowsky (D)	107,878	74.6
Herbert Sohn (R)	33,448	23.1
10 John E. Porter (R)	138,429	100.0
11 Gerald C. "Jerry" Weller (R)*	100,597	58.8
Gary S. Mueller (D)	70,458	41.2
12 Jerry F. Costello (D)*	99,665	60.4
Bill Price (R)	65,409	39.6
13 Judy Biggert (R)	121,889	61.0
Susan W. Hynes (D)	77,878	39.0
14 J. Dennis Hastert (R)*	117,304	69.8
Robert A. Cozzi Jr. (D)	50,844	30.2
15 Thomas W. Ewing (R)*	104,255	61.6
Laurel Lunt Prussing (D)	65,054	38.4
16 Donald Manzullo (R)*	143,868	100.0
17 Lane Evans (D)*	100,128	51.6
Mark Baker (R)	94,072	48.4
18 Ray LaHood (R)*	158,175	100.0
19 David Phelps (D)	122,430	58.3
Brent Winters (R)	87,614	41.7
20 John M. Shimkus (R)*	121,103	61.3
Rick Verticchio (D)	76,475	38.7

Indiana

	Vote total	Per cent
Senate		
Evan Bayh (D)	1,012,244	63.7
Paul Helmke (R)	552,732	34.8
House		
1 Peter J. Visclosky (D)*	92,634	72.5
Michael Petyo (R)	33,503	26.2
2 David M. McIntosh (R)*	99,608	60.6
Sherman A. Boles (D)	62,452	38.0
3 Tim Roemer (D)*	84,625	58.1
Daniel A. Holtz (R)	61,041	41.9
4 Mark E. Souder (R)*	93,671	63.3

	Vote total	Per cent
Mark J. Wehrle (D)	54,286	36.7
5 Steve Buyer (R)*	101,567	62.5
David F. Steele III (D)	58,504	36.0
6 Dan Burton (R)*	135,240	72.0
Bob Kern (D)	31,472	16.8
Joe Hauptmann (LIBERT)	21,015	11.2
7 Edward A. Pease (R)*	109,712	68.9
Samuel "Dutch" Hillenberg (D)	44,823	28.1
8 John N. Hostettler (R)*	92,785	52.1
Gail Riecken (D)	81,871	46.0
9 Baron Hill (D)	92,973	50.8
Jean Leising (R)	87,797	47.9
10 Julia M. Carson (D)*	69,682	58.3
Gary A. Hofmeister (R)	47,017	39.4

Iowa

	Vote total	Per cent
Governor		
Tom Vilsack (D)	500,231	52.3
Jim Ross Lightfoot (R)	444,787	46.5
Senate		
Charles E. Grassley (R)*	648,480	68.4
David Osterberg (D)	289,049	30.5
House		
1 Jim Leach (R)*	106,419	56.5
Bob Rush (D)	79,529	42.3
2 Jim Nussle (R)*	104,613	55.2
Rob Tully (D)	83,405	44.0
3 Leonard L. Boswell (D)*	107,947	56.9
Larry McKibben (D)	78,063	41.1
4 Greg Ganske (R)*	129,942	65.2
Jon Dvorak (D)	67,550	33.9
5 Tom Latham (R)*	132,730	99.2

Kansas

	Vote total	Per cent
Governor		
Bill Graves (R)*	544,882	73.4
Tom Sawyer (D)	168,243	22.7
Senate		
Sam Brownback (R)*	474,639	65.3
Paul Feleciano Jr. (D)	229,718	31.6
House		
1 Jerry Moran (R)*	152,775	80.7
Jim Phillips (D)	36,618	19.3
2 Jim Ryun (R)*	108,527	61.0
Jim Clark (D)	69,521	39.0
3 Dennis Moore (D)	103,376	52.4
Vince Snowbarger (R)*	93,938	47.6
4 Todd Tiahrt (R)*	94,785	58.3
Jim Lawing (D)	62,737	38.6

Kentucky

	Vote total	Per cent
Senate		
Jim Bunning (R)	569,817	49.7
Scotty Baesler (D)	563,051	49.2
House		
1 Edward Whitfield (R)*	95,308	55.2
Tom Barlow (D)	77,402	44.8
2 Ron Lewis (R)*	113,285	63.7
Bob Evans (D)	62,848	35.3
3 Anne Meagher Northup (R)*	100,690	51.5
Chris Gorman (D)	92,865	47.5
4 Ken Lucas (D)	93,485	53.4
Gex Williams (R)	81,547	46.6
5 Harold Rogers (R)*	142,215	78.2
Sidney Bailey-Bamer (D)	39,585	21.8
6 Ernie Fletcher (R)	104,046	53.1
Ernesto Scorsone (D)	90,033	46.0

Louisiana

	Vote total	Per cent
Senate		
John B. Breaux (D)*	620,502	64.0
Jim Donelon (R)	306,616	31.6
House		
1 Robert L. Livingston (R)*	X	X
2 William J. Jefferson (D)*	102,247	86.0
David Reed (D)	10,803	9.1
Don-Terry Veal (D)	5,899	5.0
3 W. J. "Billy" Tauzin (R)*	X	X
4 Jim McCrery (R)*	X	X
5 John C. Cooksey (R)*	X	X
6 Richard H. Baker (R)*	97,044	50.7
Marjorie McKeithen (D)	94,201	49.3
7 Chris John (D)*	X	X

Maine

	Vote total	Per cent
Governor		
Angus King (I)*	246,772	58.6
James B. Longley Jr. (R)	79,716	18.9
Thomas J. Connolly (D)	50,506	12.0
Patricia H. LaMarche (GREEN)	28,722	6.8
House		
1 Tom Allen (D)*	134,335	60.3
Ross J. Connelly (R)	79,160	35.5
2 John Baldacci (D)*	146,202	76.2
Jonathan Reisman (R)	45,674	23.8

Maryland

	Vote total	Per cent
Governor		
Parris N. Glendening (D)*	846,972	55.1
Ellen R. Sauerbrey (R)	688,357	44.8
Senate		
Barbara A. Mikulski (D)*	1,062,810	70.5
Ross Z. Pierpont (R)	444,637	29.5
House		
1 Wayne T. Gilchrest (R)*	135,771	69.2
Irving Pinder (D)	60,450	30.8
2 Robert L. Ehrlich Jr. (R)*	145,711	69.3
Kenneth T. Bosley (D)	64,474	30.7
3 Benjamin L. Cardin (D)*	137,501	77.6
Colin Felix Harby (R)	39,667	22.4
4 Albert R. Wynn (D)*	129,139	85.7
John B. Kimble (R)	21,518	14.3
5 Steny H. Hoyer (D)*	126,792	65.4
Robert B. Ostrom (R)	67,176	34.6
6 Roscoe G. Bartlett (R)*	127,802	63.4
Timothy D. McCown (D)	73,728	36.6
7 Elijah E. Cummings (D)*	112,699	85.7
Kenneth Kondner (R)	18,742	14.3
8 Constance A. Morella (R)*	133,145	60.3
Ralph G. Neas (D)	87,497	39.6

Massachusetts

	Vote total	Per cent
Governor		
Paul Cellucci (R)*	967,160	50.8
Scott Harshbarger (D)	901,843	47.4
House		
1 John W. Olver (D)*	121,863	71.7
Gregory L. Morgan (R)	48,055	28.3
2 Richard E. Neal (D)*	130,550	99.0
3 James McGovern (D)*	108,613	56.9
Matthew J. Amorello (R)	79,174	41.5
4 Barney Frank (D)*	148,340	98.4
5 Martin T. Meehan (D)*	127,418	70.7
David E. Coleman (R)	52,725	29.3
6 John F. Tierney (D)*	117,132	54.6

		Vote total	Per cent
	Peter G. Torkildsen (R)	90,986	42.4
7	Edward J. Markey (D)*	137,178	70.6
	Patricia H. Long (R)	56,977	29.3
8	Michael E. Capuano (D)	99,603	81.7
	Philip Hyde III (R)	14,125	11.6
9	Joe Moakley (D)*	150,667	99.4
10	Bill Delahunt (D)*	164,917	70.0
	Eric V. Bleicken (R)	70,466	29.9

Michigan

Governor

		Vote total	Per cent
	John Engler (R)*	1,883,005	62.2
	Geoffrey Fieger (D)	1,143,574	37.8

House

1	Bart Stupak (D)*	130,129	58.7
	Michelle A. McManus (R)	87,630	39.5
2	Peter Hoekstra (R)*	146,854	68.7
	Bob Shrauger (D)	63,573	29.8
3	Vernon Ehlers (R)*	146,364	73.1
	John Ferguson Jr. (D)	49,489	24.7
4	Dave Camp (R)*	155,343	91.3
	Dan Marsh (LIBERT)	10,404	6.1
5	James A. Barcia (D)*	135,254	71.2
	Donald W. Brewster (R)	51,442	27.1
6	Fred Upton (R)*	113,292	70.1
	Clarence J. Annen (D)	45,358	28.1
7	Nick Smith (R)*	104,656	57.7
	Jim Berryman (D)	72,998	40.1
8	Debbie Stabenow (D)*	125,169	57.4
	Susan Grimes Munsell (R)	84,254	38.6
9	Dale E. Kildee (D)*	105,457	55.9
	Tom McMillin (R)	79,062	41.9
10	David E. Bonior (D)*	108,770	52.4
	Brian Palmer (R)	94,027	45.3
11	Joe Knollenberg (R)*	144,264	63.9
	Travis M. Reeds (D)	76,107	33.7
12	Sander Levin (D)*	105,824	55.9
	Leslie A. Touma (R)	79,619	42.0
13	Lynn Nancy Rivers (D)*	99,935	58.1
	Tom Hickey (R)	68,328	39.8
14	John Conyers Jr. (D)*	126,321	86.9
	Vendella M. Collins (R)	16,140	11.1
15	Carolyn Cheeks Kilpatrick (D)*	108,582	87.0
	Chrysanthea D. Boyd-Fields (R)	12,887	10.3
16	John D. Dingell (D)*	116,145	66.6
	William Morse (R)	54,121	31.0

Minnesota

Governor

	Jesse Ventura (REF)	773,403	37.0
	Norm Coleman (R)	716,880	34.3
	Hubert H. Humphrey III (DFL)	587,060	28.1

House

1	Gil Gutknecht (R)*	131,233	54.7
	Tracy L. Beckman (D)	108,420	45.2
2	David Minge (D)*	148,933	57.0
	Craig Duehring (R)	99,490	38.1
3	Jim Ramstad (R)*	203,731	71.9
	Stanley J. Leino (D)	66,505	23.5
4	Bruce Vento (D)*	128,726	53.7
	Dennis R. Newinski (R)	95,388	39.8
5	Martin Olav Sabo (D)*	145,535	66.9
	Frank Taylor (R)	60,035	27.6
6	William P. "Bill" Luther (D)*	148,728	50.0
	John Kline (R)	136,866	46.0

		Vote total	Per cent
7	Collin C. Peterson (D)*	169,907	71.7
	Aleta Edin (R)	66,562	28.1
8	James L. Oberstar (D)*	173,734	66.0
	Jerry Shuster (R)	69,667	26.5
	Stan "The Man" Estes (REF)	15,137	6.4

Mississippi

House

1	Roger Wicker (R)*	66,738	67.2
	Rex Weathers (D)	30,438	30.6
2	Bennie Thompson (D)*	80,507	71.2
	Will Chipman (LIBERT)	32,533	28.8
3	Charles W. "Chip" Pickering Jr. (R)*	84,785	84.6
	C. T. Scarborough (LIBERT)	15,465	15.4
4	Ronnie Shows (D)	73,252	53.4
	Delbert Hosemann (R)	61,551	44.9
5	Gene Taylor (D)*	78,661	77.8
	Randy McDonnell (R)	19,341	19.1

Missouri

Senate

	Christopher S. Bond (R)*	830,625	52.7
	Jeremiah W. Nixon (D)	690,208	43.8

House

1	William L. Clay (D)*	90,840	72.6
	Richmond A. Soulade Sr. (R)	30,635	24.5
2	James M. Talent (R)*	142,313	70.0
	John Ross (D)	57,565	28.3
3	Richard A. Gephardt (D)*	98,287	55.8
	William J. Federer (R)	74,005	42.0
4	Ike Skelton (D)*	133,173	71.0
	Cecilia D. Noland (R)	51,005	27.2
5	Karen McCarthy (D)*	101,313	65.9
	Penny Bennett (R)	47,582	31.0
6	Pat Danner (D)*	136,774	70.9
	Jeff Bailey (R)	51,679	26.8
7	Roy Blunt (R)*	129,746	72.6
	Marc Perkel (D)	43,416	24.3
8	Jo Ann Emerson (R)*	104,271	62.6
	Anthony J. "Tony" Heckemeyer (D)	59,426	35.7
9	Kenny Hulshof (R)*	117,196	62.2
	Linda Vogt (D)	66,861	35.5

Montana

House

AL	Rick Hill (R)*	175,748	53.0
	Robert "Dusty" Deschamps (D)	147,073	44.4

Nebraska

Governor

	Mike Johanns (R)`	293,910	53.9
	Bill Hoppner (D)	250,678	46.0

House

1	Doug Bereuter (R)*	136,058	73.5
	Don Eret (D)	48,826	26.4
2	Lee Terry (R)	106,782	65.5
	Michael Scott (D)	55,722	34.2
3	Bill Barrett (R)*	149,896	84.3
	Jerry Hickman (LIBERT)	27,278	15.3

Nevada

Governor

	Kenny Guinn (R)	223,892	51.6
	Jan Laverty Jones (D)	182,281	42.0

Senate

	Harry Reid (D)*	208,650	47.9

		Vote total	Per cent
	John Ensign (R)	208,222	47.8

House

1	Shelley Berkley (D)	79,315	49.2
	Don Chairez (R)	73,540	45.7
2	Jim Gibbons (R)*	201,623	81.1
	Christopher Horne (IA)	20,738	8.3
	Louis R. Tomburello (LIBERT)	18,561	7.5

New Hampshire

Governor

	Jeanne Shaheen (D)*	210,769	66.1
	Jay Lucas (R)	98,473	30.9

Senate

	Judd Gregg (R)*	213,477	67.8
	George Condodemetraky (D)	88,883	28.2

House

1	John E. Sununu (R)*	104,430	66.8
	Peter Flood (D)	51,783	33.1
2	Charles Bass (R)*	85,740	53.1
	Mary Rauh (D)	72,217	44.8

New Jersey

House

1	Robert E. Andrews (D)*	90,279	73.2
	Ronald L. Richards (R)	27,855	22.6
2	Frank A. LoBiondo (R)*	93,248	65.9
	Derek Hunsberger (D)	43,563	30.8
3	H. James Saxton (R)*	97,508	62.0
	Steven J. Polansky (D)	55,248	35.1
4	Christopher H. Smith (R)*	92,991	62.0
	Larry Schneider (D)	52,281	35.0
5	Marge Roukema (R)*	106,304	63.7
	Mike Schneider (D)	55,487	33.3
6	Frank Pallone Jr. (D)*	78,102	57.0
	Michael Ferguson (R)	55,180	40.3
7	Bob Franks (R)*	77,751	52.5
	Maryanne S. Connelly (D)	65,776	44.4
8	Bill Pascrell Jr. (D)*	81,068	62.1
	Matthew J. Kirnan (R)	46,289	35.4
9	Steven R. Rothman (D)*	91,330	64.6
	Steve Lonegan (R)	47,817	33.8
10	Donald M. Payne (D)*	82,244	83.5
	William Stanley Wnuck (R)	10,678	10.8
11	Rodney Frelinghuysen (R)*	100,910	67.7
	John P. Scollo (D)	44,160	29.6
12	Rush Holt (D)	92,528	50.1
	Michael Pappas (R)*	87,221	47.2
13	Robert Menendez (D)*	70,308	80.1
	Theresa de Leon (R)	14,615	16.6

New Mexico

Governor

	Gary E. Johnson (R)*	271,948	54.5
	Martin J. Chavez (D)	226,755	45.5

House

1	Heather A. Wilson (R)*	86,784	48.3
	Phillip J. Maloof (D)	75,040	41.9
	Robert L. Anderson (GREEN)	17,266	9.6
2	Joe Skeen (R)*	85,077	57.9
	E. Shirley Baca (D)	61,796	42.1
3	Tom Udall (D)	91,248	53.2
	Bill Redmond (R)*	74,266	43.3

New York

Governor

	George E. Pataki (R, C)*	2,571,991	54.3

	Vote total	Percent
Peter F. Vallone (D, WF)	1,570,317	33.2
Tom Golisano (IND)	364,056	7.7

Senate

	Vote total	Percent
Charles E. Schumer (D)	2,551,065	54.6
Alfonse M. D'Amato (R)*	2,058,988	44.1

House

		Vote total	Percent
1	Michael P. Forbes (R, RTL, C)*	99,460	64.1
	William G. Holst (D)	55,630	35.9
2	Rick A. Lazio (R, C)*	85,089	66.2
	John C. Bace (D)	37,949	29.5
3	Peter T. King (R, RTL)*	117,258	64.3
	Kevin N. Langberg (D)	63,628	34.9
4	Carolyn McCarthy (D)*	90,256	52.6
	Gregory R. Becker (R)	79,984	46.6
5	Gary L. Ackerman (D, INDEP, L)*	97,404	65.0
	David C. Pinzon (R, C)	49,586	33.1
6	Gregory W. Meeks (D)*	76,122	100.0
7	Joseph Crowley (D)	50,924	69.0
	James J. Dillon (R)	18,896	25.6
	Richard Retcho (C)	3,960	5.4
8	Jerrold Nadler (D, L)*	112,948	86.0
	Ted Howard (R)	18,383	14.0
9	Anthony Weiner (D, INDEP)	69,439	66.4
	Louis Telano (R)	24,486	23.4
	Melinda Katz (L)	5,698	5.5
10	Edolphus Towns (D, L)*	83,528	92.3
	Ernestine M. Brown (R)	5,577	6.2
11	Major R. Owens (D, L)*	75,773	90.0
	David Greene (R, C)	7,284	8.7
12	Nydia M. Velázquez (D)*	53,269	83.6
	Rosemarie Markgraf (R)	7,405	11.6
13	Vito J. Fossella (R, C, RTL)*	76,138	64.8
	Eugene V. "Gene" Prisco (D, L)	40,167	34.2
14	Carolyn B. Maloney (D, L, INDEP)*	111,072	77.4
	Stephanie Kupferman (R)	32,458	22.6
15	Charles B. Rangel (D, L)*	90,424	93.1
	David E. Cunningham (R)	5,633	5.8
16	Jose E. Serrano (D, L)*	67,367	95.4
17	Eliot L. Engel (D, L)*	80,947	88.0
	Peter Fiumefreddo (R, C, INDEP)	11,037	12.0
18	Nita M. Lowey (D)*	91,623	82.8
	Daniel McMahon (C)	12,594	11.4
19	Sue W. Kelly (R, C)*	98,512	62.5
	Dick Collins (D)	52,503	33.3
20	Benjamin A. Gilman (R)*	98,546	58.3
	Paul J. Feiner (D, INDEP, L)	65,589	38.8
21	Michael R. McNulty (D, C, INDEP)*	146,639	74.2
	Lauren Ayers (R)	50,931	25.8
22	John E. Sweeney (R, C, INDEP)	106,919	55.3
	Jean Parvin Bordewich (D)	81,296	42.1
23	Sherwood L. Boehlert (R)*	111,242	80.8
	David Vickers (C, INDEP)	26,493	19.2
24	John M. McHugh (R, C)*	116,682	79.0
	Neil P. Tallon (D)	31,011	21.0
25	James T. Walsh (R, C)*	121,204	69.4
	Yvonne Rothenberg (D, L, GREEN)	53,461	30.6
26	Maurice D. Hinchey (D, INDEP, L)*	108,204	61.8
	William H. "Bud" Walker (R, C)	54,776	31.2

		Vote total	Percent
	Randall Terry (RTL)	12,160	6.9
27	Thomas M. Reynolds (R, C)	102,042	57.3
	Bill Cook (D, INDEP, RTL)	75,978	42.7
28	Louise Slaughter (D)*	118,856	64.8
	Richard A. "Dick" Kaplan (R, INDEP)	56,443	30.8
29	John J. LaFalce (D, INDEP, L)*	97,235	57.0
	Chris Collins (R, C)	69,481	40.7
30	Jack Quinn (R, C, INDEP)*	116,093	67.8
	Crystal D. Peoples (D)	55,199	32.2
31	Amo Houghton (R, C)*	107,615	68.1
	Caleb Rossiter (D)	40,091	25.3
	James R. Pierce Sr. (RTL)	10,546	6.7

North Carolina

Senate

	Vote total	Percent
John Edwards (D)	1,029,237	51.2
Lauch Faircloth (R)*	945,943	47.0

House

		Vote total	Percent
1	Eva Clayton (D)*	85,125	62.2
	Ted Tyler (R)	50,578	37.0
2	Bob Etheridge (D)*	100,550	57.4
	Dan Page (R)	72,997	41.7
3	Walter B. Jones (R)*	83,529	61.9
	Jon Williams (D)	50,041	37.1
4	David E. Price (D)*	129,157	57.4
	Tom Roberg (R)	93,469	41.6
5	Richard M. Burr (R)*	119,103	67.6
	Mike Robinson (D)	55,806	31.7
6	Howard Coble (R)*	112,740	88.6
	Jeffrey D. Bentley (LIBERT)	14,454	11.4
7	Mike McIntyre (D)*	124,366	91.3
	Paul Meadows (LIBERT)	11,924	8.7
8	Robin Hayes (R)	67,505	50.7
	Mike Taylor (D)	64,127	48.2
9	Sue Myrick (R)*	120,570	69.3
	Rory Blake (D)	51,345	29.5
10	Cass Ballenger (R)*	118,541	85.6
	Deborah Garrett Eddins (LIBERT)	19,970	14.4
11	Charles H. Taylor (R)*	112,908	56.6
	David Young (D)	84,256	42.2
12	Melvin Watt (D)*	82,305	56.0
	Scott Keadle (R)	62,070	42.2

North Dakota

Senate

	Vote total	Percent
Byron L. Dorgan (D)*	134,747	63.2
Donna Nalewaja (R)	75,013	35.2

House

		Vote total	Percent
AL	Earl Pomeroy (D)*	119,668	56.2
	Kevin Cramer (R)	87,511	41.1

Ohio

Governor

	Vote total	Percent
Robert A. Taft II (R)	1,678,721	50.0
Lee Fisher (D)	1,498,956	44.7

Senate

	Vote total	Percent
George V. Voinovich (R)	1,922,087	56.5
Mary O. Boyle (D)	1,482,054	43.5

House

		Vote total	Percent
1	Steve Chabot (R)*	92,421	53.0
	Roxanne Qualls (D)	82,003	47.0
2	Rob Portman (R)*	154,344	75.8
	Charles W. Sanders (D)	49,293	24.2
3	Tony P. Hall (D)*	114,198	69.3
	John Shondel (R)	50,544	30.7

		Vote total	Percent
4	Michael G. Oxley (R)*	112,011	63.8
	Paul A. McClain (D)	63,529	36.2
5	Paul E. Gillmor (R)*	123,979	66.7
	Susan Davenport Darrow (D)	61,926	33.3
6	Ted Strickland (D)*	102,852	57.0
	Nancy P. Hollister (R)	77,711	43.0
7	David L. Hobson (R)*	120,765	67.2
	Donald E. Minor Jr. (D)	49,780	27.7
	James Schrader (LIBERT)	9,146	5.1
8	John A. Boehner (R)*	127,979	70.7
	John W. Griffin (D)	52,912	29.3
9	Marcy Kaptur (D)*	130,793	81.1
	Edward Emery (R)	30,312	18.8
10	Dennis Kucinich (D)*	110,552	66.8
	Joe Slovenic (R)	55,537	33.2
11	Stephanie Tubbs Jones (D)	115,226	80.4
	James D. Hereford (R)	18,592	13.0
	Jean Murrell Capers (I)	9,477	6.6
12	John R. Kasich (R)*	124,197	67.2
	Edward S. Brown (D)	60,694	32.8
13	Sherrod Brown (D)*	116,309	61.5
	Grace L. Drake (R)	72,666	38.5
14	Thomas C. Sawyer (D)*	106,046	62.7
	Tom Watkins (R)	63,027	37.3
15	Deborah Pryce (R)*	113,846	65.7
	Adam Clay Miller (D)	49,334	28.5
	Kevin Nestor (I)	9,996	5.7
16	Ralph Regula (R)*	117,426	64.0
	Peter D. Ferguson (D)	66,047	36.0
17	James A. Traficant Jr. (D)*	123,718	68.2
	Paul H. Alberty (R)	57,703	31.8
18	Bob Ney (R)*	113,119	60.3
	Robert Burch (D)	74,571	39.7
19	Steven C. LaTourette (R)*	126,786	66.4
	Elizabeth Kelley (D)	64,090	33.6

Oklahoma

Governor

	Vote total	Percent
Frank Keating (R)*	505,498	57.9
Laura Boyd (D)	357,552	40.9

Senate

	Vote total	Percent
Don Nickles (R)*	570,682	66.4
Don E. Carroll (D)	268,898	31.3

House

		Vote total	Percent
1	Steve Largent (R)*	91,031	61.8
	Howard Plowman (D)	56,309	38.2
2	Tom Coburn (R)*	85,581	57.7
	Kent Pharaoh (D)	59,042	39.8
3	Wes Watkins (R)*	89,832	62.0
	Walt Roberts (D)	55,163	38.0
4	J. C. Watts Jr. (R)*	83,272	61.5
	Ben Odom (D)	52,107	38.5
5	Ernest Istook (R)*	103,217	68.2
	Mary Catherine "M. C." Smothermon (D)	48,182	31.8
6	Frank D. Lucas (R)*	85,261	65.0
	Paul M. Barby (D)	43,555	33.2

Oregon

Governor

	Vote total	Percent
John Kitzhaber (D)*	717,061	64.4
Bill Sizemore (R)	334,001	30.0

Senate

	Vote total	Percent
Ron Wyden (D)*	682,425	61.1
John Lim (D)	377,739	33.8

House

		Vote total	Percent
1	David Wu (D)	119,993	50.1

		Vote total	Per-cent
	Molly Bordonaro (R)	112,827	47.1
2	Greg Walden (R)	132,316	61.5
	Kevin M. Campbell (D)	74,924	34.8
3	Earl Blumenauer (D)*	153,889	83.9
	Bruce Alexander Knight (LIBERT)	16,930	9.2
	Walter F. "Walt" Brown (S)	10,199	5.6
4	Peter A. DeFazio (D)*	157,524	70.1
	Steve J. Webb (R)	64,143	28.6
5	Darlene Hooley (D)*	124,916	54.9
	Marylin Shannon (R)	92,215	40.5

Pennsylvania

Governor

		Vote total	Per-cent
	Tom J. Ridge (R)*	1,736,844	57.4
	Ivan Itkin (D)	938,745	31.0
	Peg Luksik (CONSTL)	315,761	10.4

Senate

	Vote total	Per-cent
Arlen Specter (R)*	1,814,180	61.3
Bill Lloyd (D)	1,028,839	34.8

House

		Vote total	Per-cent
1	Robert A. Brady (D)*	77,788	81.2
	William M. Harrison (R)	15,898	16.6
2	Chaka Fattah (D)*	102,763	86.5
	Anne Marie Mulligan (R)	16,001	13.5
3	Robert A. Borski (D)*	66,270	59.3
	Charles F. Dougherty (R)	45,390	40.7
4	Ron Klink (D)*	103,183	63.8
	Mike Turzai (R)	58,485	36.2
5	John E. Peterson (R)*	99,502	84.8
	William M. Belitskus (GREEN)	17,734	15.1
6	Tim Holden (D)*	83,374	61.0
	John Meckley (R)	54,579	39.0
7	Curt Weldon (R)*	119,491	71.8
	Martin J. D'Urso (D)	46,920	28.2
8	Jim Greenwood (R)*	93,697	63.3
	Bill Tuthill (D)	48,320	32.6
9	Bud Shuster (R)*	125,409	99.5
10	Donald L. Sherwood (R)	84,275	48.7
	Patrick Casey (D)	83,760	48.4
11	Paul E. Kanjorski (D)*	88,933	66.8
	Stephen A. Urban (R)	44,123	33.2
12	John P. Murtha (D)*	100,528	68.5
	Timothy E. Holloway (R)	46,239	31.5
13	Joseph M. Hoeffel III (D)	95,105	51.6
	Jon D. Fox (R)*	85,915	46.6
14	William J. Coyne (D)*	83,355	60.5
	Bill Ravotti (R)	52,745	38.3
15	Pat Toomey (R)	81,755	55.0
	Roy C. Afflerbach (D)	66,930	45.0
16	Joseph E. Pitts (R)*	95,979	70.5
	Robert S. Yorczyk (D)	40,092	29.5
17	George W. Gekas (R)*	114,931	99.8
18	Mike Doyle (D)*	98,363	67.7
	Dick Walker (R)	46,945	32.3
19	Bill Goodling (R)*	96,284	67.6
	Linda G. Ropp (D)	40,674	28.5
20	Frank Mascara (D)*	97,885	99.8
21	Phil English (R)*	94,518	63.4
	Larry Klemens (D)	54,591	36.6

Rhode Island

Governor

		Vote total	Per-cent
	Lincoln C. Almond (R)*	156,180	51.0
	Myrth York (D)	129,105	42.1
	Robert J. Healey Jr. (I)	19,250	6.3

House

		Vote total	Per-cent
1	Patrick J. Kennedy (D)*	92,788	66.8
	Ronald G. Santa (R)	38,460	27.7
2	Bob Weygand (D)*	110,917	72.0
	John O. Matson (R)	38,170	24.8

South Carolina

Governor

	Vote total	Per-cent
James H. Hodges (D)	570,070	53.2
David Beasley (R)*	484,088	45.2

Senate

	Vote total	Per-cent
Ernest F. Hollings (D)*	562,791	52.7
Robert D. Inglis (R)	488,132	45.7

House

		Vote total	Per-cent
1	Mark Sanford (R)*	118,414	91.0
	Joseph F. Innella (NL)	11,586	8.9
2	Floyd D. Spence (R)*	119,583	57.8
	Jane Frederick (D)	84,864	41.0
3	Lindsey Graham (R)*	129,047	99.7
4	Jim DeMint (R)	105,264	57.7
	Glenn Gilbert Reese (D)	73,314	40.2
5	John M. Spratt (D)*	95,105	57.9
	Mike Burkhold (R)	66,299	40.4
6	James "Jim" Clyburn (D)*	116,507	72.6
	Gary McLeod (R)	41,421	25.8

South Dakota

Governor

	Vote total	Per-cent
William J. Janklow (R)*	166,621	64.0
Bernie Hunhoff (D)	85,473	32.9

Senate

	Vote total	Per-cent
Thomas Daschle (D)*	162,884	62.1
Ron Schmidt (R)	95,431	36.4

House

		Vote total	Per-cent
AL	John Thune (R)*	194,157	75.1
	Jeff Moser (D)	64,433	24.9

Tennessee

Governor

	Vote total	Per-cent
Don Sundquist (R)*	669,973	68.6
John J. Hooker (D)	287,750	29.5

House

		Vote total	Per-cent
1	Bill Jenkins (R)*	68,904	69.1
	Kay C. White (D)	30,710	30.8
2	John J. "Jimmy" Duncan Jr. (R)*	90,860	88.6
3	Zach Wamp (R)*	75,100	66.0
	James D. "Jim" Lewis Jr. (D)	37,144	32.6
4	Van Hilleary (R)*	62,829	59.6
	Jerry W. Cooper (D)	42,627	40.4
5	Bob Clement (D)*	74,611	82.8
	William M. Lancaster (I)	6,162	6.8
	Al Borgman (I)	4,983	5.5
6	Bart Gordon (D)*	75,055	54.6
	Walt R. Massey Jr. (R)	62,277	45.3
7	Ed Bryant (R)*	91,980	99.5
8	John Tanner (D)*	76,803	100.0
9	Harold E. Ford Jr. (D)*	75,428	78.7
	Claude Burdikoff (R)	18,078	18.9

Texas

Governor

	Vote total	Per-cent
George W. Bush (R)*	2,551,454	68.2
Gary Mauro (D)	1,165,444	31.2

House

		Vote total	Per-cent
1	Max Sandlin (D)*	80,788	59.4
	Dennis Boerner (R)	55,191	40.6
2	Jim Turner (D)*	81,556	58.4

		Vote total	Per-cent
	Brian Babin (R)	56,891	40.8
3	Sam Johnson (R)*	106,690	91.2
	Ken Ashby (LIBERT)	10,288	8.8
4	Ralph M. Hall (D)*	82,989	57.6
	Jim Lohmeyer (R)	58,954	40.9
5	Pete Sessions (R)*	61,714	55.8
	Victor M. Morales (D)	48,073	43.4
6	Joe Barton (R)*	112,957	72.9
	Ben B. Boothe (D)	40,112	25.9
7	Bill Archer (R)*	111,010	93.3
	Drew Parks (LIBERT)	7,889	6.6
8	Kevin Brady (R)*	123,372	92.8
	Don L. Richards (LIBERT)	9,576	7.2
9	Nick Lampson (D)*	86,055	63.7
	Tom Cottar (R)	49,107	36.3
10	Lloyd Doggett (D)*	116,127	85.2
	Vincent J. May (LIBERT)	20,155	14.8
11	Chet Edwards (D)*	71,142	82.4
	Vince Hanke (LIBERT)	15,161	17.6
12	Kay Granger (R)*	66,740	61.9
	Tom Hall (D)	39,084	36.3
13	William M. "Mac" Thornberry (R)*	81,141	67.9
	Mark Harmon (D)	37,027	31.0
14	Ron Paul (R)*	84,459	55.3
	Loy Sneary (D)	68,014	44.5
15	Rubén Hinojosa (D)*	47,957	59.4
	Tom Haughey (R)	34,221	41.6
16	Silvestre Reyes (D)*	67,486	87.9
	Stu Nance (LIBERT)	5,329	6.9
	Lorenzo Morales (I)	3,952	5.1
17	Charles W. Stenholm (D)*	75,367	53.6
	Rudy Izzard (R)	63,700	45.3
18	Sheila Jackson-Lee (D)*	82,091	89.9
	James Galvan (LIBERT)	9,176	10.1
19	Larry Combest (R)*	108,266	83.6
	Sidney Blankenship (D)	21,162	16.4
20	Charlie Gonzalez (D)	50,356	63.2
	James Walker (R)	28,347	35.6
21	Lamar Smith (R)*	165,047	91.4
	Jeffrey C. Blunt (LIBERT)	15,561	8.6
22	Tom DeLay (R)*	87,840	65.2
	Hill Kemp (D)	45,386	33.7
23	Henry Bonilla (R)*	73,177	63.8
	Charlie Urbina Jones (D)	40,281	35.1
24	Martin Frost (D)*	56,321	57.5
	Shawn Terry (R)	40,105	40.9
25	Ken Bentsen (D)*	58,591	57.9
	John Sanchez (R)	41,848	41.3
26	Dick Armey (R)*	120,332	88.1
	Joe Turner (LIBERT)	16,182	11.9
27	Solomon P. Ortiz (D)*	61,638	63.3
	Erol A. Stone (R)	34,284	35.2
28	Ciro D. Rodriguez (D)*	71,849	90.5
	Edward Elmer (LIBERT)	7,504	9.5
29	Gene Green (D)*	44,179	92.8
30	Eddie Bernice Johnson (D)*	57,603	72.2
	Carrie Kelleher (R)	21,338	27.0

Utah

Senate

	Vote total	Per-cent
Robert F. Bennett (R)*	316,652	64.0
Scott Leckman (D)	163,172	33.0

House

		Vote total	Per-cent
1	James V. Hansen (R)*	109,708	67.7
	Steve Beierlein (D)	49,307	30.4
2	Merrill Cook (R)*	93,718	52.8
	Lily Eskelsen (D)	77,198	43.5
3	Christopher B. Cannon (R)*	100,830	76.9

	Vote total	Per-cent
Will Christensen (IA)	20,720	15.8
Kitty K. Burton (LIBERT)	9,553	7.3

Vermont

Governor

Howard Dean (D)*	121,425	55.7
Ruth Dwyer (R)	89,726	41.1

Senate

Patrick J. Leahy (D)*	154,567	72.2
Fred H. Tuttle (R)	48,051	22.4

House

AL	Bernard Sanders (I)*	136,403	63.4
	Mark Candon (R)	70,740	32.9

Virginia

House

1	Herbert H. Bateman (R)*	76,474	77.1
	Bradford L. Phillips (I)	13,235	13.2
	Josh Billings (I)	9,492	9.5
2	Owen B. Pickett (D)*	67,975	94.3
3	Robert C. Scott (D)*	48,129	76.0
	Robert S. "Bob" Barnett (I)	14,453	22.8
4	Norman Sisisky (D)*	64,563	97.0
5	Virgil H. Goode Jr. (D)*	73,097	98.9
6	Robert W. Goodlatte (R)*	89,177	69.3
	David Bowers (D)	39,487	30.7
7	Thomas J. Bliley Jr. (R)*	77,044	78.7
	Bradley E. Evans (I)	20,293	20.7
8	James P. Moran (D)*	97,545	66.7
	Demaris Miller (R)	48,352	33.1
9	Rick Boucher (D)*	87,163	60.9
	Joe Barta (R)	55,918	39.1
10	Frank R. Wolf (R)*	103,648	71.6
	Cornell W. Brooks (D)	36,476	25.2
11	Thomas M. Davis III (R)*	91,603	81.7
	C. W. Levi Levy (I)	18,807	16.8

Washington

Senate

Patty Murray (D)*	1,103,184	58.6
Linda Smith (R)	785,377	41.6

House

1	Jay Inslee (D)	112,726	49.8
	Rick White (R)*	99,919	44.1
	Bruce Craswell (AMH)	13,837	6.1
2	Jack Metcalf (R)*	124,125	55.2
	Grethe Cammermeyer (D)	100,776	44.8
3	Brian Baird (D)	120,364	54.7
	Don Benton (R)	99,855	45.3
4	Richard "Doc" Hastings (R)*	121,684	69.1
	Gordon Allen Pross (D)	43,043	24.4
	Peggy McKerlie (REF)	11,363	6.5
5	George Nethercutt (R)*	110,040	56.9
	Brad Lyons (D)	73,545	38.1
	John Beal (AMH)	9,673	5.0
6	Norm Dicks (D)*	143,308	68.4
	Bob Lawrence (R)	66,291	31.6
7	Jim McDermott (D)*	183,076	88.2
	Stan Lippmann (REF)	19,545	9.4
8	Jennifer Dunn (R)*	135,539	59.7
	Heidi Behrens-Benedict (D)	91,371	40.3
9	Adam Smith (D)*	111,948	64.7
	Ron Taber (R)	61,108	35.3

West Virginia

House

1	Alan B. Mollohan (D)*	105,101	84.7
	Richard Kerr (LIBERT)	19,013	15.3
2	Bob Wise (D)*	99,357	73.0
	Sally Anne Kay (R)	29,136	21.4
	John Brown (LIBERT)	7,660	5.6
3	Nick J. Rahall II (D)*	78,814	86.6
	Joe Whelan (LIBERT)	12,196	13.4

Wisconsin

Governor

Tommy G. Thompson (R)*	1,047,716	59.7
Edward R. Garvey (D)	679,553	38.7

Senate

Russell D. Feingold (D)*	890,059	50.5
Mark W. Neumann (R)	852,272	48.4

House

1	Paul Ryan (R)	108,475	57.1
	Lydia Spottswood (D)	81,164	42.7
2	Tammy Baldwin (D)	116,377	52.5
	Josephine Musser (R)	103,528	46.7
3	Ron Kind (D)*	128,256	71.5
	Troy A. Brechler (R)	51,001	28.4
4	Gerald D. Kleczka (D)*	105,841	57.9
	Tom Reynolds (R)	76,666	42.0
5	Thomas M. Barrett (D)*	121,129	78.2
	Jack Melvin (R)	33,506	21.6
6	Tom Petri (R)*	144,144	92.6
	Timothy Farness (TAX)	11,267	7.2
7	David R. Obey (D)*	115,613	60.6
	Scott West (R)	75,049	39.3
8	Mark Green (R)	112,418	54.6
	Jay Johnson (D)*	93,441	45.4
9	F. James Sensenbrenner Jr. (R)*	175,533	91.3
	Jeffrey M. Gonyo (INDEP)	16,419	8.5

Wyoming

Governor

Jim Geringer (R)*	97,235	55.6
John P. Vinich (D)	70,754	40.5

House

AL	Barbara Cubin (R)*	100,687	57.8
	Scott Farris (D)	67,399	38.7

1999 Gubernatorial Elections

	Vote total	Percent		Vote total	Percent
Louisiana—Oct. 23, 1999			**Mississippi—Nov. 2, 1999**		
Mike Foster (R)	805,203	62.2	Ronnie Musgrove (D)	379,034	49.6
William J. Jefferson (D)	382,445	29.5	Mike Parker (R)	370,691	48.5
Kentucky—Nov. 2, 1999					
Paul E. Patton (D)	352,099	60.7			
Peppy Martin (R)	128,788	22.2			

Special House Elections, 106th Congress

	Vote total	Percent		Vote total	Percent
Georgia 6th CD—Feb. 23, 1999			**California 42nd CD—Nov. 16, 1999**		
Johnny Isakson (R)	51,548	65.1	Joe Baca (D)	23,690	50.6
Christina Jeffrey (R)	20,115	25.4	Elia Pirozzi (R)	21,018	44.9
Gary "Bats" Pelphry (D)	4,014	5.1	Rick Simon (REF)	1,198	2.6
Barry Doublestein (R)	1,593	2.0	John "Scott" Ballard (LIBERT)	956	2.0
A. Leigh Baier (I)	1,459	1.8			
Marco Longo (R)	478	0.6			
Kelly Brown (I, WI)	6	—			
Louisiana 1st CD (runoff)—May 29, 1999					
David Vitter (R)	61,661	50.7			
David Conner Treen (D)	59,849	49.3			

Senate, 106th Congress

Rhode Island

John H. Chafee (R) died Oct. 24, 1999. His son, Lincoln D. Chafee (R), was appointed Nov. 2, 1999, to fill the vacancy.

Georgia

Paul Coverdell (R) died July 18, 2000. Former Gov. Zell Miller (D) was appointed July 24, 2000, to fill the vacancy.

NOTE: D—Democrat, I—Independent, LIBERT—Libertarian, R—Republican, REF—Reform, WI—write-in

2000 Elections Returns for Governor, Senate, and House

Following are the official vote returns for the gubernatorial, Senate, and House races compiled by Congressional Quarterly from the figures supplied by the 50 state election boards.

Vote totals are included for all candidates listed on the ballot who received 5 percent or more of the total vote. (For candidates who received under 5 percent, consult *America Votes 24* (2001), published by CQ Press.)

An asterisk (*) indicates an incumbent.

An "X" denotes candidates without major-party opposition; no votes were tallied.

An "AL" indicates an at-large member of Congress in a state with a single congressional district.

See p. 1081 for special elections and 1999 gubernatorial elections.

		Vote total	Percent
Alabama			
House			
1	Sonny Callahan (R)*	151,188	91.3
	Richard M. "Dick" Coffee (LIBERT)	14,031	8.5
2	Terry Everett (R)*	151,830	68.2
	Charles Woods (D)	64,958	29.2
3	Bob Riley (R)*	147,317	86.9
	John P. Sophocleus (LIBERT)	21,119	12.4
4	Robert B. Aderholt (R)*	140,009	60.6
	Marsha Folsom (D)	86,400	37.4
5	Robert E. "Bud" Cramer (D)*	186,059	88.8
	Alan Fulton Barksdale (LIBERT)	22,110	10.6
6	Spencer Bachus (R)*	212,751	87.9
	Terry Reagin Sr. (LIBERT)	28,189	11.7
7	Earl F. Hilliard (D)*	148,243	74.6
	Ed Martin (R)	46,134	23.2
Alaska			
House			
AL	Don Young (R)*	190,862	69.6
	Clifford Mark Greene (D)	45,372	16.5
	Anna C. Young (GREEN)	22,440	8.2
Arizona			
Senate			
	Jon Kyl (R)*	1,108,196	79.3
	William Toel (I)	109,230	7.8
	Vance Hansen (GREEN)	108,926	7.8
	Barry J. Hess II (LIBERT)	70,724	5.1
House			
1	Jeff Flake (R)	123,289	53.6
	David Mendoza (D)	97,455	42.4

		Vote total	Percent
2	Ed Pastor (D)*	84,034	68.5
	Bill Barenholtz (R)	32,990	26.9
3	Bob Stump (R)*	198,367	65.7
	Gene Scharer (D)	94,676	31.4
4	John Shadegg (R)*	140,396	64.0
	Ben Jankowski (D)	71,803	32.7
5	Jim Kolbe (R)*	172,986	60.1
	George Cunningham (D)	101,564	35.3
6	J. D. Hayworth (R)*	186,687	61.4
	Larry Nelson (D)	108,317	35.6
Arkansas			
House			
1	Marion Berry (D)*	120,266	60.1
	Susan Myshka (R)	79,437	39.7
2	Vic Snyder (D)*	126,957	57.5
	Bob Thomas (R)	93,692	42.5
3	Asa Hutchinson (R)*		100.0
4	Mike Ross (D)	108,143	51.0
	Jay Dickey (R)*	104,017	49.0
California			
Senate			
	Dianne Feinstein (D)*	5,932,522	55.8
	Tom Campbell (R)	3,886,853	36.6
House			
1	Mike Thompson (D)*	155,638	65.0
	Russell J. "Jim" Chase (R)	66,987	28.0
2	Wally Herger (R)*	168,172	65.7
	Stan Morgan (D)	72,075	28.2
3	Doug Ose (R)*	129,254	56.2
	Bob Kent (D)	93,067	40.4
4	John T. Doolittle (R)*	197,503	63.4
	Mark Norberg (D)	97,974	31.5
5	Robert T. Matsui (D)*	147,025	68.7
	Ken Payne (R)	55,945	26.1

		Vote total	Percent
6	Lynn Woolsey (D)*	182,116	64.3
	Ken McAuliffe (R)	80,169	28.3
7	George Miller (D)*	159,692	76.5
	Christopher Hoffman (R)	44,154	21.1
8	Nancy Pelosi (D)*	181,847	84.4
	Adam Sparks (R)	25,298	11.7
9	Barbara Lee (D)*	182,352	85.0
	Arneze Washington (R)	21,033	9.8
10	Ellen O. Tauscher (D)*	160,429	52.6
	Claude B. Hutchison Jr. (R)	134,863	44.2
11	Richard W. Pombo (R)*	120,635	57.8
	Tom Santos (D)	79,539	38.1
12	Tom Lantos (D)*	158,404	74.5
	Mike Garza (R)	44,162	20.8
13	Pete Stark (D)*	129,012	70.4
	James Goetz (R)	44,99	24.3
14	Anna G. Eshoo (D)*	161,720	70.2
	Bill Quraishi (R)	59,338	25.8
15	Mike Honda (D)	128,545	54.3
	Jim Cunneen (R)	99,866	42.2
16	Zoe Lofgren (D)*	115,118	72.1
	Horace Thayn (R)	37,213	23.3
17	Sam Farr (D)*	143,219	68.6
	Clint Engler (R)	51,557	24.7
18	Gary A. Condit (D)*	121,003	67.1
	Steve Wilson (R)	56,465	31.3
19	George P. Radanovich (R)*	144,517	64.9
	Daniel Rosenberg (D)	70,578	31.7
20	Cal Dooley (D)*	66,235	52.3
	Rich Rodriguez (R)	57,563	45.5
21	Bill Thomas (R)*	142,539	71.6
	Pedro Martinez (D)	49,318	24.8
22	Lois Capps (D)*	135,538	53.1
	Mike Stoker (R)	113,094	44.3
23	Elton Gallegly (R)*	119,479	54.1
	Michael Case (D)	89,918	40.7
24	Brad Sherman (D)*	155,398	66.0
	Jerry Doyle (R)	70,169	29.8
25	Howard P. "Buck" McKeon (R)*	138,628	62.2
	Sid Gold (D)	73,921	33.2
26	Howard L. Berman (D)*	96,500	84.1
	Bill Farley (LIBERT)	13,052	11.4
27	Adam Schiff (D)	113,708	52.7
	James E. Rogan (R)*	94,518	43.8
28	David Dreier (R)*	116,557	56.8
	Janice M. Nelson (D)	81,804	39.9
29	Henry A. Waxman (D)*	180,295	75.7
	Jim Scileppi (R)	45,784	19.2
30	Xavier Becerra (D)*	83,223	83.3
	Tony Goss (R)	11,788	11.8
31	Hilda Solis (D)	89,600	79.4

		Vote total	Percent
	Krista Lieberg-Wong (GREEN)	10,294	9.1
	Michael McGuire (LIBERT)	7,138	6.3
	Richard Griffin (NL)	5,882	5.2
32	Julian C. Dixon (D)*	137,447	83.5
	Kathy Williamson (R)	19,924	12.1
33	Lucille Roybal-Allard (D)*	60,510	84.5
	Wayne Miller (R)	8,260	11.5
34	Grace F. Napolitano (D)*	105,980	71.3
	Robert Arthur Canales (R)	33,445	22.5
	Julia F. Simon (NL)	9,262	6.2
35	Maxine Waters (D)*	100,569	86.5
	Carl McGill (R)	12,582	10.8
36	Jane Harman (D)	115,651	48.4
	Steven T. Kuykendall (R)*	111,199	46.5
37	Juanita Millender-McDonald (D)*	93,269	82.3
	Vernon Van (R)	12,762	11.3
38	Steve Horn (R)*	87,266	48.4
	Gerrie Schipske (D)	85,498	47.5
39	Ed Royce (R)*	129,294	62.7
	Gill G. Kanel (D)	64,938	31.5
40	Jerry Lewis (R)*	151,069	79.9
	Frank Schmit (NL)	19,029	10.1
	Jay Lindberg (LIBERT)	18,924	10.0
41	Gary G. Miller (R)*	104,695	58.9
	Rodolfo "Rudy" Favila (D)	66,361	37.4
42	Joe Baca (D)*	90,585	59.8
	Elia Pirozzi (R)	53,239	35.1
43	Ken Calvert (R)*	140,201	73.7
	Bill Reed (LIBERT)	29,755	15.6
	Nathaniel Adam (NL)	20,376	10.7
44	Mary Bono (R)*	123,738	59.2
	Ron Oden (D)	79,302	37.9
45	Dana Rohrabacher (R)*	136,275	62.1
	Ted Crisell (D)	71,066	32.4
46	Loretta Sanchez (D)*	70,381	60.2
	Gloria Matta Tuchman (R)	40,928	35.0
47	Christopher Cox (R)*	181,365	65.6
	John L. Graham (D)	83,186	30.1
48	Darrell Issa (R)	160,627	61.4
	Peter Kouvelis (D)	74,073	28.3
49	Susan A. Davis (D)	113,400	49.6
	Brian P. Bilbray (R)*	105,515	46.2
50	Bob Filner (D)*	95,191	68.3
	Bob Divine (R)	38,526	27.6
51	Randy "Duke" Cunningham (R)*	172,291	64.3
	George "Jorge" Barraza (D)	81,408	30.4
52	Duncan Hunter (R)*	131,345	64.7
	Craig B. Barkacs (D)	63,537	31.3

Colorado

House

1	Diana DeGette (D)*	141,831	68.7
	Jesse L. Thomas (R)	56,291	27.3
2	Mark Udall (D)*	155,725	55.0
	Carolyn Cox (R)	109,338	38.6
3	Scott McInnis (R)*	199,204	65.8
	Curtis Imrie (D)	87,921	29.1
4	Bob Schaffer (R)*	209,078	79.5
	Dan Sewell Ward (NL)	19,721	7.5
	Kordon Baker (LIBERT)	19,713	7.5
5	Joel Hefley (R)*	253,330	82.7
	Kerry Kantor (LIBERT)	37,719	12.3
	Randy MacKenzie (NL)	15,260	5.0
6	Tom Tancredo (R)*	141,410	53.9
	Ken Toltz (D)	110,568	42.1

Connecticut

Senate

	Joseph I. Lieberman (D)*	828,902	63.2
	Philip A. Giordano (R)	448,077	34.2

House

1	John B. Larson (D)*	151,932	71.9
	Bob Backlund (R)	59,331	28.1
2	Rob Simmons (R)	114,380	50.6
	Sam Gejdenson (D)*	111,520	49.4
3	Rosa DeLauro (D)*	156,910	71.9
	June Gold (R)	60,037	27.5
4	Christopher Shays (R)*	119,155	57.6
	Stephanie Sanchez (D)	84,472	40.9
5	Jim Maloney (D)*	118,932	53.6
	Mark D. Nielsen (R)	98,229	44.3
6	Nancy L. Johnson (R)*	143,698	62.6
	Paul Vincent Valenti (D)	75,471	32.9

Delaware

Governor

	Ruth Ann Minner (D)	191,695	59.2
	John M. Burris (R)	128,603	39.7

Senate

	Thomas R. Carper (D)	181,566	55.5
	William V. Roth Jr. (R)*	142,891	43.7

House

AL	Michael N. Castle (R)*	211,797	67.6
	Mike Miller (D)	96,488	30.8

Florida

Senate

	Bill Nelson (D)	2,989,487	51.0
	Bill McCollum (R)	2,705,348	46.2

House

1	Joe Scarborough (R)*	226,473	99.5
2	Allen Boyd (D)*	185,579	72.1
	Doug Dodd (R)	71,754	27.9
3	Corrine Brown (D)*	102,143	57.6
	Jennifer Carroll (R)	75,228	42.4
4	Ander Crenshaw (R)	203,090	67.0
	Tom Sullivan (D)	94,587	31.2
5	Karen L. Thurman (D)*	180,338	64.3
	Peter C. K. "Pete" Enwall (R)	100,244	35.7
6	Cliff Stearns (R)*	178,789	99.9
7	John L. Mica (R)*	171,018	63.2
	Daniel Vaughen (D)	99,531	36.8
8	Richard "Ric" Keller (R)	125,253	50.8
	Linda Chapin (D)	121,295	49.2
9	Michael Bilirakis (R)*	210,318	81.9
	Jon Scott Duffey (REF)	46,474	18.1
10	C. W. Bill Young (R)*	146,799	75.7
	Josette Green (NL)	26,908	13.9
	Randy Heine (NP)	20,296	10.5
11	Jim Davis (D)*	149,465	84.6
	Charlie Westlake (LIBERT)	27,197	15.4
12	Adam Putnam (R)	125,224	57.0
	Michael Stedem (D)	94,395	43.0
13	Dan Miller (R)*	175,918	63.8
	Daniel E. Dunn (D)	99,568	36.1
14	Porter J. Goss (R)*	242,614	85.2
	Sam Farling (NL)	41,988	14.8
15	Dave Weldon (R)*	176,189	58.8
	Patsy Ann Kurth (D)	117,511	39.2
16	Mark Foley (R)*	176,153	60.2
	Jean Elliott Brown (D)	108,782	37.2
17	Carrie P. Meek (D)*	100,715	100.0
18	Ileana Ros-Lehtinen (R)*	112,968	100.0

19	Robert Wexler (D)*	171,080	71.6
	Morris Kent Thompson (R)	67,789	28.4
20	Peter Deutsch (D)*	156,765	99.9
21	Lincoln Diaz-Balart (R)*	132,317	100.0
22	E. Clay Shaw Jr. (R)*	105,855	50.1
	Elaine Bloom (D)	105,256	49.9
23	Alcee L. Hastings (D)*	89,179	76.3
	Bill Lambert (R)	27,630	23.7

Georgia

Senate

	Zell Miller (D)*	1,413,224	58.2
	Matt Mattingly (R)	920,478	37.9

House

1	Jack Kingston (R)*	131,684	69.1
	Joyce Marie Griggs (D)	58,776	30.9
2	Sanford D. Bishop Jr. (D)*	96,430	53.5
	Dylan Glenn (R)	83,870	46.5
3	Mac Collins (R)*	150,200	63.5
	Gail Notti (D)	86,309	36.5
4	Cynthia A. McKinney (D)*	139,579	60.7
	Sunny Warren (R)	90,277	39.3
5	John Lewis (D)*	137,333	77.2
	Hank Schwab (R)	40,606	22.8
6	Johnny Isakson (R)*	256,595	74.8
	Brett DeHart (D)	86,666	25.2
7	Bob Barr (R)*	126,312	55.3
	Roger Kahn (D)	102,272	44.7
8	Saxby Chambliss (R)*	113,380	58.9
	Jim Marshall (D)	79,051	41.1
9	Nathan Deal (R)*	183,171	75.2
	James Harrington (D)	60,360	24.8
10	Charlie Norwood (R)*	122,590	63.2
	Marion Spencer "Denise" Freeman (D)	71,309	36.8
11	John Linder (R)*	199,652	100.0

Hawaii

Senate

	Daniel K. Akaka (D)*	251,215	72.7
	John S. Carroll (R)	84,701	24.5

House

1	Neil Abercrombie (D)*	108,517	69.0
	Philip L. Meyers (R)	44,989	28.6
2	Patsy T. Mink (D)*	112,856	61.6
	Russell R. Francis (R)	65,906	36.0

Idaho

House

1	C. L. "Butch" Otter (R)	173,743	64.8
	Linda Pall (D)	84,080	31.4
2	Mike Simpson (R)*	158,912	70.7
	Craig Williams (D)	58,265	25.9

Illinois

House

1	Bobby L. Rush (D)*	172,271	87.8
	Raymond G. Wardingley (R)	23,915	12.2
2	Jesse L. Jackson Jr. (D)*	175,995	89.8
	Robert Gordon III (R)	19,906	10.2
3	William O. Lipinski (D)*	145,498	75.6
	Karl Groth (R)	47,005	24.4
4	Luis V. Gutierrez (D)*	89,487	88.6
	Stephanie Sailor (LIBERT)	11,476	11.4
5	Rod R. Blagojevich (D)*	142,161	87.3
	Matthew Joseph Beauchamp (LIBERT)	20,728	12.7
6	Henry J. Hyde (R)*	133,327	58.9

		Vote total	Per-cent
	Brent Christensen (D)	92,880	41.1
7	Danny K. Davis (D)*	164,155	85.9
	Robert Dallas (R)	26,872	14.1
8	Philip M. Crane (R)*	141,918	61.0
	Lance Pressl (D)	90,777	39.0
9	Jan Schakowsky (D)*	147,002	76.4
	Dennis J. Driscoll (R)	45,344	23.6
10	Mark Steven Kirk (R)	121,582	51.2
	Lauren Beth Gash (D)	115,924	48.8
11	Jerry Weller (R)*	132,384	56.4
	James P. Stevenson (D)	102,485	43.6
12	Jerry F. Costello (D)*	183,208	100.0
13	Judy Biggert (R)*	193,250	66.2
	Thomas Mason (D)	98,768	33.8
14	J. Dennis Hastert (R)*	188,597	74.0
	Vern Deljonson (D)	66,309	26.0
15	Timothy V. Johnson (R)	125,943	53.2
	Mike Kelleher (D)	110,679	46.8
16	Donald Manzullo (R)*	178,174	66.7
	Charles W. Hendrickson (D)	88,781	33.2
17	Lane Evans (D)*	132,494	54.9
	Mark Baker (R)	108,853	45.1
18	Ray LaHood (R)*	173,706	67.1
	Joyce Harant (D)	85,317	32.9
19	David D. Phelps (D)*	155,101	64.6
	James E. "Jim" Eatherly (R)	85,137	35.4
20	John Shimkus (R)*	161,393	63.1
	Jeffrey Cooper (D)	94,382	36.9

Indiana

Governor

	Vote total	Per-cent
Frank L. O'Bannon (D)*	1,232,525	56.6
David M. McIntosh (R)	908,285	41.7

Senate

	Vote total	Per-cent
Richard G. Lugar (R)*	1,427,944	66.6
David L. Johnson (D)	683,273	31.9

House

		Vote total	Per-cent
1	Peter J. Visclosky (D)*	148,683	71.6
	Jack Reynolds (R)	56,200	27.0
2	Mike Pence (R)	106,023	50.9
	Bob Rock (D)	80,885	38.8
	William G. Frazier (I)	19,077	9.2
3	Tim Roemer (D)*	107,438	51.6
	Chris Chocola (R)	98,822	47.4
4	Mark Souder (R)*	131,051	62.3
	Mike Foster (D)	74,492	35.4
5	Steve Buyer (R)*	132,051	60.9
	Greg Goodnight (D)	81,427	37.5
6	Dan Burton (R)*	199,207	70.3
	Darin Patrick Griesey (D)	74,881	26.4
7	Brian D. Kerns (R)	135,869	64.8
	Michael Graf (D)	66,764	31.8
8	John Hostettler (R)*	116,879	52.7
	Paul Perry (D)	100,488	45.3
9	Baron P. Hill (D)*	126,420	54.2
	Michael Everett Bailey (R)	102,219	43.8
10	Julia Carson (D)*	91,689	58.5
	Marvin B. Scott (R)	62,233	39.7

Iowa

House

		Vote total	Per-cent
1	Jim Leach (R)*	164,972	61.8
	Bob Simpson (D)	96,283	36.1
2	Jim Nussle (R)*	139,906	55.4
	Donna L. Smith (D)	110,327	43.7
3	Leonard L. Boswell (D)*	156,327	62.8
	Jay B. Marcus (R)	83,810	33.7
4	Greg Ganske (R)*	169,267	61.4
	Michael L. Huston (D)	101,112	36.7

		Vote total	Per-cent
5	Tom Latham (R)*	159,367	68.8
	Mike Palecek (D)	67,593	29.2

Kansas

House

		Vote total	Per-cent
1	Jerry Moran (R)*	216,484	89.3
	Jack W. Warner (LIBERT)	25,843	10.7
2	Jim Ryun (R)*	164,951	67.4
	Stanley Wiles (D)	71,709	29.3
3	Dennis Moore (D)*	154,505	50.0
	Phill Kline (R)	144,672	46.9
4	Todd Tiahrt (R)*	131,871	54.4
	Carlos Nolla (D)	101,980	42.0

Kentucky

House

		Vote total	Per-cent
1	Edward Whitfield (R)*	132,115	58.0
	Brian Roy (D)	95,806	42.0
2	Ron Lewis (R)*	160,800	67.7
	Brian Pedigo (D)	74,537	31.4
3	Anne M. Northup (R)*	142,106	52.9
	Eleanor Jordan (D)	118,875	44.2
4	Ken Lucas (D)*	125,872	54.3
	Don Bell (R)	100,943	43.5
5	Harold Rogers (R)*	145,980	73.6
	Sidney "Jane" Bailey-Bamer (D)	52,495	26.4
6	Ernie Fletcher (R)*	142,971	52.8
	Scotty Baesler (D)	94,167	34.8
	Gatewood Galbraith (I)	32,436	12.0

Louisiana

House

		Vote total	Per-cent
1	David Vitter (R)*	191,379	80.5
	Michael A. Armato (D)	40,917	17.2
2	William J. Jefferson (D)*	X	X
3	W. J. "Billy" Tauzin (R)*	143,446	78.0
	Edwin J. "Eddie" Albares (I)	16,908	9.2
	Anita Rosenthal (NL)	13,488	7.3
	Dion Bourque (LIBERT)	10,118	5.5
4	Jim McCrery (R)*	122,678	70.5
	Phillip R. Green (D)	43,600	25.1
5	John Cooksey (R)*	123,975	69.1
	Roger Beall (D)	50,163	28.0
6	Richard H. Baker (R)*	165,637	68.0
	Kathy J. Rogillio (D)	72,192	29.7
7	Chris John (D)*	152,796	83.3
	Michael P. Harris (LIBERT)	30,687	16.7

Maine

Senate

	Vote total	Per-cent
Olympia J. Snowe (R)*	437,689	68.9
Mark Lawrence (D)	197,183	31.1

House

		Vote total	Per-cent
1	Tom Allen (D)*	202,823	59.8
	Jane Amero (R)	123,915	36.5
2	John Baldacci (D)*	219,783	73.4
	Richard Campbell (R)	79,522	26.6

Maryland

Senate

	Vote total	Per-cent
Paul S. Sarbanes (D)*	1,230,013	63.2
Paul Rappaport (R)	715,178	36.7

House

		Vote total	Per-cent
1	Wayne T. Gilchrest (R)*	165,293	64.4
	Bennett Bozman (D)	91,022	35.5
2	Robert L. Ehrlich Jr. (R)*	178,556	68.6
	Kenneth T. Bosley (D)	81,591	31.3

		Vote total	Per-cent
3	Benjamin L. Cardin (D)*	169,347	75.7
	Colin Harby (R)	53,827	24.0
4	Albert R. Wynn (D)*	172,624	87.2
	John B. Kimble (R)	24,973	12.6
5	Steny H. Hoyer (D)*	166,231	65.1
	Thomas E. "Tim" Hutchins (R)	89,019	34.9
6	Roscoe G. Bartlett (R)*	168,624	60.6
	Donald DeArmon (D)	109,136	39.3
7	Elijah E. Cummings (D)*	134,066	87.1
	Kenneth Kondner (R)	19,773	12.8
8	Constance A. Morella (R)*	156,241	52.0
	Terry Lierman (D)	136,840	45.5

Massachusetts

Senate

	Vote total	Per-cent
Edward M. Kennedy (D)*	1,889,494	72.7
Jack E. Robinson (R)	334,341	12.9

House

		Vote total	Per-cent
1	John W. Olver (D)*	169,375	68.2
	Pete Abair (R)	73,580	29.6
2	Richard E. Neal (D)*	196,670	98.9
3	Jim McGovern (D)*	213,065	98.8
4	Barney Frank (D)*	200,638	74.9
	Martin D. Travis (R)	56,553	21.1
5	Martin T. Meehan (D)*	199,601	98.0
6	John F. Tierney (D)*	205,324	71.0
	Paul McCarthy (R)	83,501	28.9
7	Edward J. Markey (D)*	211,543	98.9
8	Michael E. Capuano (D)*	144,031	99.3
9	Joe Moakley (D)*	193,020	77.6
	Janet E. Jeghelian (R)	48,672	19.6
10	Bill Delahunt (D)*	234,675	74.1
	Eric V. Bleichen (R)	81,192	25.6

Michigan

Senate

	Vote total	Per-cent
Debbie Stabenow (D)	2,061,952	49.5
Spencer Abraham (R)*	1,994,693	47.9

House

		Vote total	Per-cent
1	Bart Stupak (D)*	169,649	58.4
	Chuck Yob (R)	117,300	40.4
2	Peter Hoekstra (R)*	186,762	64.4
	Bob Shrauger (D)	96,370	33.2
3	Vernon J. Ehlers (R)*	179,539	65.0
	Tim Steele (D)	91,309	33.1
4	Dave Camp (R)*	182,128	68.0
	Lawrence D. Hollenbeck (D)	78,019	29.1
5	James A. Barcia (D)*	184,048	74.3
	Ronald G. Actis (R)	59,274	23.9
6	Fred Upton (R)*	159,373	67.9
	James Bupp (D)	68,532	29.2
7	Nick Smith (R)*	147,369	61.1
	Jennie Crittendon (D)	86,080	35.7
8	Mike Rogers (R)	145,190	48.8
	Dianne Byrum (D)	145,079	48.7
9	Dale E. Kildee (D)*	158,184	61.1
	Grant Garrett (R)	92,926	35.9
10	David E. Bonior (D)*	181,818	64.4
	Thomas Turner (R)	93,713	33.2
11	Joe Knollenberg (R)*	170,790	55.8
	Matthew Frumin (D)	124,053	40.5
12	Sander M. Levin (D)*	157,720	64.3
	Bart Baron (R)	78,795	32.1
13	Lynn Rivers (D)*	160,084	64.7
	Carl F. Barry (R)	79,445	32.1
14	John Conyers Jr. (D)*	168,982	89.3
	William A. Ashe (R)	17,582	9.3

		Vote total	Per-cent
15	Carolyn Cheeks Kilpatrick (D)*	140,609	88.6
	Chrysanthea D. Boyd-Fields (R)	14,336	9.0
16	John D. Dingell (D)*	167,142	71.0
	William Morse (R)	62,469	26.5

Minnesota

Senate

	Vote total	Per-cent
Mark Dayton (D)	1,181,553	48.8
Rod Grams (R)*	1,047,474	43.3
James Gibson (INDEP)	140,583	5.8

House

		Vote total	Per-cent
1	Gil Gutknecht (R)*	159,835	56.4
	Mary Rieder (D)	117,946	41.6
2	Mark Kennedy (R)	138,957	48.1
	David Minge (D)*	138,802	48.0
3	Jim Ramstad (R)*	222,571	67.6
	Sue Shuff (D)	98,219	29.8
4	Betty McCollum (D)	130,403	48.0
	Linda Runbeck (R)	83,852	30.9
	Tom Foley (INDEP)	55,899	20.6
5	Martin Olav Sabo (D)*	176,629	69.2
	Frank Taylor (R)	58,191	22.8
6	Bill Luther (D)*	176,340	49.6
	John Kline (R)	170,900	48.0
7	Collin C. Peterson (D)*	185,771	68.7
	Glen Menze (R)	79,175	29.3
8	James L. Oberstar (D)*	210,094	67.8
	Robert Lemen (R)	79,890	25.8

Mississippi

Senate

	Vote total	Per-cent
Trent Lott (R)*	654,941	65.9
Troy Brown (D)	314,090	31.6

House

		Vote total	Per-cent
1	Roger Wicker (R)*	145,967	69.8
	Joey Grist (D)	59,763	28.6
2	Bennie Thompson (D)*	112,777	65.1
	Hardy Caraway (R)	54,090	31.2
3	Charles W. "Chip" Pickering Jr. (R)*	153,899	73.2
	William Clay Thrash (D)	54,151	25.7
4	Ronnie Shows (D)*	115,732	58.1
	Dunn Lampton (R)	79,218	39.8
5	Gene Taylor (D)*	153,264	78.8
	Randy McDonnell (R)	35,309	18.2

Missouri

Governor

	Vote total	Per-cent
Bob Holden (D)	1,152,752	49.1
James M. Talent (R)	1,131,307	48.2

Senate

	Vote total	Per-cent
Mel Carnahan (D)[1]	1,191,812	50.5
John Ashcroft (R)*	1,142,852	48.4

House

		Vote total	Per-cent
1	William Lacy Clay Jr. (D)	149,173	75.2
	Zellner Dwight Billingsly (R)	42,730	21.5
2	Todd Akin (R)	164,926	55.3
	Ted House (D)	126,441	42.4
3	Richard A. Gephardt (D)*	147,222	57.8
	William J. Federer (R)	100,967	39.7
4	Ike Skelton (D)*	180,634	66.9
	James A. Noland Jr. (R)	84,406	31.3
5	Karen McCarthy (D)*	159,826	68.8
	Steve Gordon (R)	66,439	28.6
6	Sam Graves (R)	138,925	50.9
	Steve Danner (D)	127,792	46.8

		Vote total	Per-cent
7	Roy Blunt (R)*	202,305	73.9
	Charles Christrup (D)	65,510	23.9
8	Jo Ann Emerson (R)*	162,239	69.3
	Bob Camp (D)	67,760	28.9
9	Kenny Hulshof (R)*	172,787	59.3
	Steven R. Carroll (D)	111,662	38.3

Montana

Governor

	Vote total	Per-cent
Judy Martz (R)	209,135	51.0
Mark O'Keefe (D)	193,131	47.1

Senate

	Vote total	Per-cent
Conrad Burns (R)*	208,082	50.6
Brian Schweitzer (D)	194,430	47.2

House

		Vote total	Per-cent
AL	Denny Rehberg (R)	211,418	51.5
	Nancy Keenan (D)	189,971	46.3

Nebraska

Senate

	Vote total	Per-cent
Ben Nelson (D)	353,097	51.0
Don Stenberg (R)	337,967	48.8

House

		Vote total	Per-cent
1	Doug Bereuter (R)*	155,485	66.2
	Alan Jacobsen (D)	72,859	31.0
2	Lee Terry (R)*	148,911	65.8
	Shelley Kiel (D)	70,268	31.1
3	Tom Osborne (R)	182,117	82.0
	Rollie Reynolds (D)	34,944	15.7

Nevada

Senate

	Vote total	Per-cent
John Ensign (R)	330,687	55.1
Ed Bernstein (D)	238,260	39.7

House

		Vote total	Per-cent
1	Shelley Berkley (D)*	118,469	51.7
	Jon Porter (R)	101,276	44.2
2	Jim Gibbons (R)*	229,608	64.5
	Tierney Cahill (D)	106,379	29.9

New Hampshire

Governor

	Vote total	Per-cent
Jeanne Shaheen (D)*	275,038	48.7
Gordon Humphrey (R)	246,952	43.7
Mary Brown (I)	35,904	6.4

House

		Vote total	Per-cent
1	John E. Sununu (R)*	150,609	52.9
	Martha Fuller Clark (D)	128,387	45.1
2	Charles Bass (R)*	152,581	56.2
	Barney Brannen (D)	110,367	40.6

New Jersey

Senate

	Vote total	Per-cent
Jon Corzine (D)	1,511,237	50.1
Bob Franks (R)	1,420,267	47.1

House

		Vote total	Per-cent
1	Robert E. Andrews (D)*	167,327	76.2
	Charlene Cathcart (R)	46,455	21.2
2	Frank A. LoBiondo (R)*	155,187	66.4
	Edward G. Janosik (D)	74,632	31.9
3	H. James Saxton (R)*	157,053	57.3
	Susan Bass Levin (D)	112,848	41.2
4	Christopher H. Smith (R)*	158,515	63.2
	Reed Gusciora (D)	87,956	35.1
5	Marge Roukema (R)*	175,546	65.4
	Linda Mercurio (D)	81,715	30.4
6	Frank Pallone Jr. (D)*	141,698	67.5
	Brian T. Kennedy (R)	62,454	29.8
7	Mike Ferguson (R)	128,434	51.6

		Vote total	Per-cent
	Maryanne S. Connelly (D)	113,479	45.6
8	Bill Pascrell Jr. (D)*	134,074	67.0
	Anthony Fusco Jr. (R)	60,606	30.3
9	Steven R. Rothman (D)*	140,462	67.9
	Joseph Tedeschi (R)	61,984	30.0
10	Donald M. Payne (D)*	133,073	87.5
	Dirk B. Weber (R)	18,436	12.1
11	Rodney Frelinghuysen (R)*	186,140	68.0
	John P. Scollo (D)	80,958	29.6
12	Rush D. Holt (D)*	146,162	48.7
	Dick Zimmer (R)	145,511	48.5
13	Robert Menendez (D)*	117,856	78.7
	Theresa de Leon (R)	27,849	18.6

New Mexico

Senate

	Vote total	Per-cent
Jeff Bingaman (D)*	363,744	61.7
Bill Redmond (R)	225,517	38.3

House

		Vote total	Per-cent
1	Heather A. Wilson (R)*	107,296	50.3
	John Kelly (D)	92,187	43.3
	Daniel Kerlinsky (GREEN)	13,656	6.4
2	Joe Skeen (R)*	100,742	58.1
	Michael A. Montoya (D)	72,614	41.9
3	Tom Udall (D)*	135,040	67.2
	Lisa L. Lutz (R)	65,979	32.8

New York

Senate

	Vote total	Per-cent
Hillary Rodham Clinton (D)	3,747,310	55.3
Rick A. Lazio (R)	2,915,730	43.0

House

		Vote total	Per-cent
1	Felix J. Grucci Jr. (R, INDEP, C, RTL)	133,020	55.5
	Regina Seltzer (D)	97,299	40.6
2	Steven Israel (D)	90,438	47.9
	Joan B. Johnson (R)	65,880	34.9
	Robert T. Walsh Sr. (RTL)	11,224	6.0
	Richard Thompson (C)	10,824	5.7
	David Bishop (INDEP, GREEN, WF)	10,266	5.4
3	Peter T. King (R, INDEP, C, RTL)*	143,126	59.5
	Dal LaMagna (D, GREEN, WF)	95,787	39.8
4	Carolyn McCarthy (D, INDEP, WF)*	136,703	60.6
	Greg R. Becker (R, C, RTL)	87,830	38.9
5	Gary L. Ackerman (D, INDEP, L, WF)*	137,684	68.0
	Edward Elkowitz (R, C)	61,084	30.1
6	Gregory W. Meeks (D, WF)*	120,818	100.0
7	Joseph Crowley (D)*	78,207	71.7
	Rose Robles Birtley (R)	24,592	22.5
8	Jerrold Nadler (D, L, WF)*	150,273	81.2
	Marian S. Henry (R)	27,057	14.6
9	Anthony Weiner (D, L)*	98,983	68.4
	Noach Dear (R, C)	45,649	31.6
10	Edolphus Towns (D, L)*	120,700	90.2
	Ernestine M. Brown (R)	6,852	5.1
11	Major R. Owens (D, WF)*	112,050	87.0
	Susan Cleary (R)	8,406	6.5
	Una Clarke (D, L)	7,366	5.7
12	Nydia M. Velazquez (D, WF)*	86,288	87.1
	Rosemary Markgraf (R)	10,052	10.1
13	Vito J. Fossella (R, C, RTL)*	109,806	64.6
	Katina M. Johnstone (D, WF)	57,603	33.9

		Vote total	Percent
14	Carolyn B. Maloney (D, L)*	148,080	73.9
	Carla Rhodes (R)	45,453	22.7
15	Charles B. Rangel (D, L, WF)*	130,161	91.9
	Jose A. Suero (R)	7,346	5.2
16	Jose E. Serrano (D, L)*	103,041	95.8
17	Eliot L. Engel (D, L)*	115,093	89.7
	Patrick McManus (C, R)	13,201	10.3
18	Nita M. Lowey (D)*	126,878	67.3
	John G. Vonglis (R, C)	58,022	30.8
19	Sue W. Kelly (R, C)*	145,532	60.9
	Larry Otis Graham (D, L, WF)	85,871	35.9
20	Benjamin A. Gilman (R)*	136,016	57.6
	Paul J. Feiner (D, L, GREEN, WF)	94,646	40.1
21	Michael R. McNulty (D, INDEP, C)*	175,339	74.4
	Thomas G. Pillsworth (R)	60,333	25.6
22	John E. Sweeney (R, C)*	167,368	67.9
	Kenneth F. McCallion (D, GREEN, WF)	79,111	32.1
23	Sherwood Boehlert (R, INDEP)*	124,132	60.5
	David Vickers (C, RTL)	42,854	20.9
	Richard W. Englebrecht (D)	38,049	18.6
24	John M. McHugh (R, C)*	138,322	74.3
	Neil P. Tallon (D)	42,698	22.9
25	James T. Walsh (R, INDEP, C)*	151,880	69.0
	Francis J. Gavin (D)	64,533	29.3
26	Maurice D. Hinchey (D, INDEP, WF, L)*	140,395	62.0
	Bob Moppert (R, C)	83,856	37.0
27	Thomas M. Reynolds (R, C)*	157,694	69.3
	Thomas W. Pecoraro (D)	69,870	30.7
28	Louise M. Slaughter (D)*	151,688	65.7
	Mark C. Johns (R, C)	75,348	32.6
29	John J. LaFalce (D, INDEP, L)*	128,328	61.3
	Brett M. Sommer (R, C, RTL)	81,159	38.7
30	Jack Quinn (R, C, INDEP)*	138,452	67.1
	John Fee (D, L, WF)	67,819	32.9
31	Amory Houghton (R, C)*	154,238	77.3
	Kisun J. Peters (D)	45,193	22.7

North Carolina

Governor

	Vote total	Percent
Mike Easley (D)	1,530,324	52.0
Richard Vinroot (R)	1,360,960	46.3

House

		Vote total	Percent
1	Eva Clayton (D)*	124,171	65.6
	Duane E. Kratzer Jr. (R)	62,198	32.9
2	Bob Etheridge (D)*	146,733	58.3
	Doug Haynes (R)	103,011	40.9
3	Walter B. Jones Jr. (R)*	121,940	61.4
	Leigh Harvey McNairy (D)	74,058	37.3
4	David E. Price (D)*	200,885	61.6
	Jess Ward (R)	119,412	36.6
5	Richard M. Burr (R)*	172,489	92.8
	Steven Francis LeBoeuf (LIBERT)	13,366	7.2
6	Howard Coble (R)*	195,727	91.0
	Jeffrey D. Bentley (LIBERT)	18,726	8.7
7	Mike McIntyre (D)*	160,185	69.7
	James Adams (R)	66,463	28.9
8	Robin Hayes (R)*	111,950	55.0

		Vote total	Percent
	Mike Taylor (D)	89,505	44.0
9	Sue Myrick (R)*	264,220	68.6
	Ed McGuire (D)	79,382	30.0
10	Cass Ballenger (R)*	164,182	68.2
	Delmas Parker (D)	70,877	29.5
11	Charles H. Taylor (R)*	146,677	55.1
	Sam Neill (D)	112,234	42.1
12	Melvin Watt (D)*	135,570	64.8
	Joshua "Chad" Mitchell (R)	69,596	33.3

North Dakota

Governor

	Vote total	Percent
John Hoeven (R)	159,255	55.0
Heidi Heitkamp (D)	130,144	45.0

Senate

	Vote total	Percent
Kent Conrad (D)*	176,470	61.4
Duane Sand (R)	111,069	38.6

House

		Vote total	Percent
AL	Earl Pomeroy (D)*	151,173	52.9
	John Dorso (R)	127,251	44.5

Ohio

Senate

	Vote total	Percent
Mike DeWine (R)*	2,665,512	59.9
Ted Celeste (D)	1,595,066	35.9

House

		Vote total	Percent
1	Steve Chabot (R)*	116,768	53.0
	John Cranley (D)	98,328	44.6
2	Rob Portman (R)*	204,184	73.6
	Charles W. Sanders (D)	64,091	23.1
3	Tony P. Hall (D)*	177,731	83.0
	Regina Burch (NL)	36,516	17.0
4	Michael G. Oxley (R)*	156,510	67.4
	Daniel L. Dickman (D)	67,330	29.0
5	Paul E. Gillmor (R)*	169,857	69.8
	Dannie Edmon (D)	62,138	25.5
6	Ted Strickland (D)*	138,849	57.7
	Michael Azinger (R)	96,966	40.3
7	David L. Hobson (R)*	163,646	67.6
	Donald E. Minor Jr. (D)	60,755	25.1
	John R. Mitchel (I)	13,983	5.8
8	John A. Boehner (R)*	179,756	71.0
	John G. Parks (D)	66,293	26.2
9	Marcy Kaptur (D)*	168,547	74.8
	Dwight E. Bryan (R)	49,446	21.9
10	Dennis J. Kucinich (D)*	167,063	75.0
	Bill Smith (R)	48,930	22.0
11	Stephanie Tubbs Jones (D)*	164,134	84.8
	James Sykora (R)	21,630	11.2
12	Pat Tiberi (R)	39,242	52.9
	Maryellen O'Shaughnessy (D)	115,432	43.8
13	Sherrod Brown (D)*	170,058	64.6
	Rick H. Jeric (R)	84,295	32.0
14	Tom Sawyer (D)*	149,184	64.8
	Rick Wood (R)	71,432	31.0
15	Deborah Pryce (R)*	156,792	67.5
	Bill Buckel (D)	64,805	27.9
16	Ralph Regula (R)*	162,294	69.2
	William Smith (D)	62,709	26.8
17	James A. Traficant Jr. (D)*	120,333	50.0
	Paul Alberty (R)	54,751	22.7
	Randy D. Walter (I)	51,793	21.5
18	Bob Ney (R)*	152,325	64.4
	Marc D. Guthrie (D)	79,232	33.5
19	Steven C. LaTourette (R)*	174,262	69.2
	Dale Virgil Blanchard (D)	70,429	28.0

Oklahoma

House

		Vote total	Percent
1	Steve Largent (R)*	138,528	69.3
	Dan Lowe (D)	58,493	29.2
2	Brad Carson (D)	107,273	54.9
	Andy Ewing (R)	81,672	41.8
3	Wes Watkins (R)*	137,826	86.6
	Argus W. Yandell Jr. (I)	14,660	9.2
4	J. C. Watts Jr. (R)*	114,000	64.9
	Larry Weatherford (D)	54,808	31.2
5	Ernest Istook (R)*	134,159	68.4
	Garland McWatters (D)	53,275	27.2
6	Frank D. Lucas (R)*	95,635	59.3
	Randy Beutler (D)	63,106	39.2

Oregon

House

		Vote total	Percent
1	David Wu (D)*	176,902	58.3
	Charles Starr (R)	115,303	38.0
2	Greg Walden (R)*	220,086	73.6
	Walter A. Ponsford (D)	78,101	26.1
3	Earl Blumenauer (D)*	181,049	66.8
	Jeffrey L. Pollock (R)	64,128	23.6
4	Peter A. DeFazio (D)*	197,998	68.0
	John Lindsey (R)	88,950	30.6
5	Darlene Hooley (D)*	156,315	56.8
	Brian Boquist (R)	118,631	43.1

Pennsylvania

Senate

	Vote total	Percent
Rick Santorum (R)*	2,481,962	52.4
Ron Klink (D)	2,154,908	45.5

House

		Vote total	Percent
1	Robert A. Brady (D)*	149,621	88.3
	Steven N. Kush (R)	19,920	11.7
2	Chaka Fattah (D)*	180,021	98.0
3	Robert A. Borski (D)*	130,528	68.7
	Charles F. Dougherty (R)	59,343	31.3
4	Melissa Hart (R)	145,390	59.0
	Terry Van Horne (D)	100,995	41.0
5	John E. Peterson (R)*	147,570	85.5
	William M. Belitskus (GREEN)	13,857	8.0
	Thomas A. Martin (LIBERT)	11,020	6.4
6	Tim Holden (D)*	140,084	66.3
	Thomas G. Kopel (R)	71,227	33.7
7	Curt Weldon (R)*	172,569	64.8
	Peter A. Lennon (D)	93,687	35.2
8	James C. Greenwood (R)*	154,090	59.1
	Ron Strouse (D)	100,617	38.6
9	Bud Shuster (R)*	184,401	99.4
10	Donald L. Sherwood (R)*	124,830	52.6
	Patrick Casey (D)	112,580	47.4
11	Paul E. Kanjorski (D)*	131,948	66.4
	Stephen A. Urban (R)	66,699	33.6
12	John P. Murtha (D)*	145,538	70.8
	Bill Choby (R)	56,575	27.5
13	Joseph M. Hoeffel (D)*	146,026	52.8
	Stewart Greenleaf (R)	126,501	45.7
14	William J. Coyne (D)*	147,533	99.9
15	Patrick J. Toomey (R)*	118,307	53.2
	Ed O'Brien (D)	103,864	46.7
16	Joseph R. Pitts (R)*	162,403	66.9
	Robert S. Yorczyk (D)	80,177	33.1
17	George W. Gekas (R)*	166,236	71.5
	Leslye Hess Herrmann (D)	66,190	28.5
18	Mike Doyle (D)*	156,131	69.4

	Vote total	Per-cent
Craig C. Stephens (R)	68,798	30.6
19 Todd Platts (R)	168,722	72.5
Jeff Sanders (D)	61,538	26.5
20 Frank R. Mascara (D)*	145,131	64.4
Ronald J. Davis (R)	80,312	35.6
21 Phil English (R)*	135,164	60.8
Mark Flitter (D)	87,018	39.2

Rhode Island

Senate

Lincoln Chafee (R)*	222,588	56.8
Bob Weygand (D)	161,023	41.1

House

1 Patrick J. Kennedy (D)*	123,442	66.7
Steve Cabral (R)	61,522	33.2
2 Jim Langevin (D)	123,805	62.2
Rodney D. Driver (I)	42,625	21.4
Robert G. "Bob" Tingle (R)	27,932	14.0

South Carolina

House

1 Henry Brown (R)	139,597	60.3
Andy Brack (D)	82,622	35.7
2 Floyd D. Spence (R)*	154,338	57.0
Jane Frederick (D)	110,672	40.8
3 Lindsey Graham (R)*	150,176	67.8
George Brightharp (D, UC)	67,174	30.3
4 Jim DeMint (R)*	150,436	79.6
Ted Adams (CONST)	16,532	8.7
April Bishop (LIBERT)	12,757	6.7
5 John M. Spratt Jr. (D)*	126,877	58.8
Carl Gullick (R)	85,247	39.5
6 James E. Clyburn (D)*	138,053	71.8
Vince Ellison (R)	50,005	26.0

South Dakota

House

AL John Thune (R)*	231,083	73.4
Curt M. Hohn (D)	78,321	24.9

Tennessee

Senate

Bill Frist (R)*	1,255,444	65.1
Jeff Clark (D)	621,152	32.2

House

1 Bill Jenkins (R)*	157,828	100.0
2 John J. "Jimmy" Duncan Jr. (R)*	187,154	89.3
Kevin J. Rowland (LIBERT)	22,304	10.6
3 Zach Wamp (R)*	139,840	63.9
Will Callaway (D)	75,785	34.6
4 Van Hilleary (R)*	133,622	65.8
David H. Dunaway (D)	67,165	33.1
5 Bob Clement (D)*	149,277	72.5
Stan Scott (R)	50,386	24.5
6 Bart Gordon (D)*	168,861	62.1
David Charles (R)	97,169	35.7
7 Ed Bryant (R)*	171,056	69.6
Richard P. Sims (D)	71,587	29.1
8 John Tanner (D)*	143,127	72.3
Billy Yancy (R)	54,929	27.7
9 Harold E. Ford Jr. (D)*	143,298	100.0

Texas

Senate

Kay Bailey Hutchison (R)*	4,082,091	65.0
Gene Kelly (D)	2,030,315	32.2

House

1 Max Sandlin (D)*	118,157	55.8
Noble Willingham (R)	91,912	43.4
2 Jim Turner (D)*	162,891	91.1
Gary Lyndon Dye (LIBERT)	15,939	8.9
3 Sam Johnson (R)*	187,486	71.6
Billy Wayne Zachary (D)	67,233	25.7
4 Ralph M. Hall (D)*	145,887	60.3
Jon Newton (R)	91,574	37.9
5 Pete Sessions (R)*	100,487	54.0
Regina Montoya Coggins (D)	82,629	44.4
6 Joe L. Barton (R)*	222,685	88.1
Frank Brady (LIBERT)	30,056	11.9
7 John Culberson (R)	183,712	73.9
Jeff Sell (D)	60,694	24.4
8 Kevin Brady (R)*	233,848	91.6
Gil Guillory (LIBERT)	21,368	8.4
9 Nick Lampson (D)*	130,143	59.2
Paul Williams (R)	87,165	39.7
10 Lloyd Doggett (D)*	203,628	84.6
Michael Davis (LIBERT)	37,203	15.4
11 Chet Edwards (D)*	105,782	54.8
Ramsey W. Farley (R)	85,546	44.3
12 Kay Granger (R)*	67,612	36.0
13 William M. "Mac" Thornberry (R)*	117,995	67.6
Curtis Clinesmith (D)	54,343	31.1
14 Ron Paul (R)*	137,370	59.7
Loy Sneary (D)	92,689	40.3
15 Ruben Hinojosa (D)*	106,570	88.5
Frank L. Jones (LIBERT)	13,167	10.9
16 Silvestre Reyes (D)*	92,649	68.3
Daniel Power (R)	40,921	30.2
17 Charles W. Stenholm (D)*	120,670	59.0
Darrell Clements (R)	72,535	35.5
Debra Monde (LIBERT)	11,180	5.5
18 Sheila Jackson-Lee (D)*	131,857	76.5
Bob Levy (R)	38,191	22.2
19 Larry Combest (R)*	170,319	91.6
John M. Turnbow (LIBERT)	15,579	8.4
20 Charlie Gonzalez (D)*	107,487	87.7
Alejandro "Alex" DePena (LIBERT)	15,087	12.3
21 Lamar Smith (R)*	251,049	75.9
Jim Green (D)	73,326	22.2
22 Tom DeLay (R)*	154,662	60.4
Jo Ann Matranga (D)	92,645	36.2
23 Henry Bonilla (R)*	119,679	59.3
Isidro Garza Jr. (D)	78,274	38.8
24 Martin Frost (D)*	103,152	61.8
Bryndan Wright (R)	61,235	36.7
25 Ken Bentsen (D)*	106,112	60.1
Phil Sudan (R)	68,010	38.5
26 Dick Armey (R)*	214,025	72.5
Steve Love (D)	75,601	25.6
27 Solomon P. Ortiz (D)*	102,088	63.4
Pat Ahumada (R)	54,660	33.9
28 Ciro D. Rodriguez (D)*	123,104	89.0
William A. "Bill" Stallknecht (LIBERT)	15,156	11.0
29 Gene Green (D)*	84,665	73.3
Joe Vu (R)	29,606	25.6
30 Eddie Bernice Johnson (D)*	109,163	91.8
Kelly Rush (LIBERT)	9,798	8.2

Utah

Governor

Michael O. Leavitt (R)*	424,837	55.8
Bill Orton (D)	321,979	42.3

Senate

Orrin G. Hatch (R)*	504,803	65.6
Scott N. Howell (D)	242,569	31.5

House

1 James V. Hansen (R)*	180,591	69.0
Kathleen Collinwood (D)	71,229	27.2
2 Jim Matheson (D)	145,021	55.9
Derek W. Smith (R)	107,114	41.3
3 Christopher B. Cannon (R)*	138,943	58.5
Donald Dunn (D)	88,547	37.3

Vermont

Governor

Howard Dean (D)*	148,059	50.5
Ruth Dwyer (R)	111,359	37.9
Anthony Pollina (PROG)	28,116	9.6

Senate

James M. Jeffords (R)*	189,133	65.6
Ed Flanagan (D)	73,352	25.4

House

AL Bernard Sanders (I)*	196,118	69.2
Karen Kerin (R)	51,977	18.3
Peter Diamondstone (D)	14,918	5.3

Virginia

Senate

George F. Allen (R)	1,420,460	52.3
Charles S. Robb (D)*	1,296,093	47.7

House

1 Jo Ann Davis (R)	151,344	57.5
Lawrence Davies (D)	97,399	37.0
2 Edward L. Schrock (R)	97,856	52.0
Jody Wagner (D)	90,328	48.0
3 Robert C. Scott (D)*	137,527	97.7
4 Norman Sisisky (D)*	189,787	98.9
5 Virgil H. Goode Jr. (I)*	143,312	67.3
John Boyd (D)	65,387	30.7
6 Robert W. Goodlatte (R)*	153,338	99.3
7 Eric I. Cantor (R)	192,652	66.9
Warren A. Stewart (D)	94,935	33.0
8 James P. Moran (D)*	164,178	63.3
Demaris Miller (R)	88,262	34.1
9 Rick Boucher (D)*	137,488	69.8
Michael D. "Oz" Osborne (R)	59,335	30.1
10 Frank R. Wolf (R)*	238,817	84.2
Brian M. Brown (LIBERT)	28,107	9.9
Marc A. Rossi (I)	16,031	5.7
11 Thomas M. Davis III (R)*	150,395	61.9
Mike Corrigan (D)	83,455	34.3

Washington

Governor

Gary Locke (D)*	1,441,973	58.4
John Carlson (R)	980,060	39.7

Senate

Maria Cantwell (D)	1,199,437	48.7
Slade Gorton (R)*	1,197,208	48.6

House

1 Jay Inslee (D)*	155,820	54.6
Dan McDonald (R)	121,823	42.6
2 Rick Larsen (D)	146,617	50.0
John Koster (R)	134,660	45.9
3 Brian Baird (D)*	159,428	56.4
Trent Matson (R)	114,861	40.6

		Vote total	Percent
4	Richard "Doc" Hastings (R)*	143,259	60.9
	Jim Davis (D)	87,585	37.3
5	George Nethercutt (R)*	144,038	57.3
	Tom Keefe (D)	97,703	38.9
6	Norm Dicks (D)*	164,853	64.7
	Bob Lawrence (R)	79,215	31.1
7	Jim McDermott (D)*	193,470	72.8
	Joe Szwaja (GREEN)	52,142	19.6
	Joel Grus (LIBERT)	20,197	7.6
8	Jennifer Dunn (R)*	183,255	62.2
	Heidi Behrens-Benedict (D)	104,944	35.6
9	Adam Smith (D)*	135,452	61.7
	Chris Vance (R)	76,766	35.0

West Virginia

Governor

	Vote total	Percent
Bob Wise (D)	324,822	50.1
Cecil H. Underwood (R)*	305,926	47.2

Senate

	Vote total	Percent
Robert C. Byrd (D)*	469,215	77.8
David T. Gallaher (R)	121,635	20.2

House

		Vote total	Percent
1	Alan B. Mollohan (D)*	170,974	87.8
	Richard Kerr (LIBERT)	23,797	12.2
2	Shelley Moore Capito (R)	108,769	48.5
	Jim Humphreys (D)	103,003	45.9
	John Brown (LIBERT)	12,543	5.6
3	Nick J. Rahall II (D)*	146,807	91.3
	Jeff Robinson (LIBERT)	13,979	8.7

Wisconsin

Senate

	Vote total	Percent
Herb Kohl (D)*	1,563,238	61.5
John Gillespie (R)	940,744	37.0

House

		Vote total	Percent
1	Paul D. Ryan (R)*	177,612	66.6
	Jeffrey C. Thomas (D)	88,885	33.3
2	Tammy Baldwin (D)*	163,534	51.4
	John Sharpless (R)	154,632	48.6
3	Ron Kind (D)*	173,505	63.7
	Susan Tully (R)	97,741	35.9
4	Gerald D. Kleczka (D)*	163,622	60.8
	Tim Riener (R)	101,811	37.8

		Vote total	Percent
5	Thomas M. Barrett (D)*	173,893	77.7
	Jonathan Smith (R)	49,296	22.0
6	Tom Petri (R)*	179,205	65.0
	Daniel Flaherty (D)	96,125	34.9
7	David R. Obey (D)*	173,007	63.3
	Sean Cronin (R)	100,264	36.7
8	Mark Green (R)*	211,388	74.6
	Dean Reich (D)	71,575	25.3
9	F. James Sensenbrenner Jr. (R)*	239,498	74.0
	Mike Clawson (D)	83,720	25.9

Wyoming

Senate

	Vote total	Percent
Craig Thomas (R)*	157,622	73.8
Mel Logan (D)	47,087	22.0

House

		Vote total	Percent
AL	Barbara Cubin (R)*	141,848	66.8
	Michael Allen Green (D)	60,638	28.6

1. Carnahan died three weeks before the election but his name remained on the ballot. Following the election, his widow, Jean Carnahan, was appointed to the seat by the governor. The appointment was for a two-year period with an election in 2002 to fill the remaining four years of the term.

Results of House Elections, 1928–2000

	1928	1930	1932	1934	1936	1938	1940	1942	1944	1946	1948	1950	1952	1954	1956	1958	1960	1962	1964
Totals																			
Democrats	165	217	313	322	334	262	268	222	242	188	263	235	213	232	234	283	263	259	295
Republicans	269	217	117	103	88	169	162	209	191	246	171	199	221	203	201	153	174	176	140
Alabama																			
Democrats	10	10	9[1]	9	9	9	9	9	9	9	9	9	9	9	9	9	9	8[1]	3
Republicans	0	0	0	0	0	0	0	0	0	0	0	0	0	0	0	0	0	0	5
Alaska																			
Democrats	—	—	—	—	—	—	—	—	—	—	—	—	—	—	—	1	1	1	1
Republicans	—	—	—	—	—	—	—	—	—	—	—	—	—	—	—	0	0	0	0
Arizona																			
Democrats	1	1	1	1	1	1	1	2[2]	2	2	2	2	1	1	1	1	1	2[2]	2
Republicans	0	0	0	0	0	0	0	0	0	0	0	0	1	1	1	1	1	1	1
Arkansas																			
Democrats	7	7	7	7	7	7	7	7	7	7	7	7	6[1]	6	6	6	6	4[1]	4
Republicans	0	0	0	0	0	0	0	0	0	0	0	0	0	0	0	0	0	0	0
California																			
Democrats	1	1	11[2]	13	15	12	11	12[2]	16	9	10	10	11[2]	11	13	16	16	25[2,3]	23
Republicans	10	10	9	7	4	8	9	11	7	14	13	13	19	19	17	14	14	13	15
Colorado																			
Democrats	1	1	4	4	4	4	2	1	0	1	3	2	2	2	2	3	2	2	4
Republicans	3	3	0	0	0	0	2	3	4	3	1	2	2	2	2	1	2	2	0
Connecticut																			
Democrats	0	2	2[2]	4	6	2	6	0	4	0	3	2	1	1	0	6	4	5	6
Republicans	5	3	4	2	0	4	0	6	2	6	3	4	5	5	6	0	2	1	0
Delaware																			
Democrats	0	0	1	0	1	0	1	0	1	0	0	0	0	1	0	1	1	1	1
Republicans	1	1	0	1	0	1	0	1	0	1	1	0	1	0	0	0	0	0	0
Florida																			
Democrats	4	4	5[2]	5	5	5	5	6[2]	6	6	6	6	8[2]	7	7	7	7	10[2]	10
Republicans	0	0	0	0	0	0	0	0	0	0	0	0	0	1	1	1	1	2	2
Georgia																			
Democrats	12	12	10[1]	10	10	10	10	10	10	10	10	10	10	10	10	10	10	10	9
Republicans	0	0	0	0	0	0	0	0	0	0	0	0	0	0	0	0	0	0	1
Hawaii																			
Democrats	—	—	—	—	—	—	—	—	—	—	—	—	—	—	—	—	1	2[2]	2
Republicans	—	—	—	—	—	—	—	—	—	—	—	—	—	—	—	—	0	0	0
Idaho																			
Democrats	0	0	2	2	2	1	1	1	1	0	1	0	1	1	1	1	2	2	1
Republicans	2	2	0	0	0	1	1	1	1	2	1	2	1	1	1	1	0	0	1
Illinois																			
Democrats	6	13[4]	19	21	21	17	11	7[1]	11	6	12	8	9[1]	12	11	14	14	12[1]	13
Republicans	21	14	8	6	6	10	16	19	15	20	14	18	16	13	14	11	11	12	11
Indiana																			
Democrats	3	9	12[1]	11	11	5	4	2[1]	2	2	7	2	1	2	2	8	4[4]	4	6
Republicans	10	4	0	1	1	7	8	9	9	9	4	9	10	9	9	3	7	7	5
Iowa																			
Democrats	0	1	6[1]	6	5	2	2	0[1]	0	0	0	0	0	0	1	4	2	1[1]	6
Republicans	11	10	3	3	4	7	7	8	8	8	8	8	8	8	7	4	6	6	1
Kansas																			
Democrats	1	1	3[1]	3	2	1	1	0[1]	0	0	0	0	1	0	1	3	1	0[1]	0
Republicans	7	7	4	4	5	6	6	6	6	6	6	6	5	6	5	3	5	5	5
Kentucky																			
Democrats	2	9	9[1]	8	8	8	8	8	8	6	7	7	6[1]	6	6	7	7	5[1]	6
Republicans	9	2	0	1	1	1	1	1	1	3	2	2	2	2	2	1	1	2	1
Louisiana																			
Democrats	8	8	8	8	8	8	8	8	8	8	8	8	8	8	8	8	8	8	8
Republicans	0	0	0	0	0	0	0	0	0	0	0	0	0	0	0	0	0	0	0
Maine																			
Democrats	0	0	2[1]	2	0	0	0	0	0	0	0	0	0	0	1	2	0	0[1]	1
Republicans	4	4	1	1	3	3	3	3	3	3	3	3	3	3	2	1	3	2	1
Maryland																			
Democrats	4	6	6	6	6	6	6	4	5	4	4	3	3[2]	4	4	7	6	6[2]	6
Republicans	2	0	0	0	0	0	0	2	1	2	2	3	4	3	3	0	1	2	2
Massachusetts																			
Democrats	3	4	5[1]	7	5	5	6	4[1]	4	5	4	6	6	7	7	8	8	7[1]	7
Republicans	13	12	10	8	10	10	9	10	10	9	8	8	8	7	7	6	6	5	5
Michigan																			
Democrats	0	0	10[2]	6	8	5	6	5	6	3	5	5	5[2]	7	6	7	7	8[2]	12
Republicans	13	13	7	11	9	12	11	12	11	14	12	12	13	11	12	11	11	11	7
Minnesota																			
Democrats	0	0	1[1]	1	1	1	0	0	2	1	4	4	4	5	5	4	3	4[1]	4
Republicans	9	9	3	5	3	7	8	8	7	8	5	5	5	4	4	5	6	4	4
Mississippi																			
Democrats	8	8	7[1]	7	7	7	7	7	7	7	7	7	6[1]	6	6	6	6	5[1]	4
Republicans	0	0	0	0	0	0	0	0	0	0	0	0	0	0	0	0	0	0	1
Missouri																			
Democrats	6	12	13[1]	12	12	12	10	5	7	4	12	10	7	9	10	10	9	8[1]	8
Republicans	10	4	0	1	1	1	3	8	6	9	1	3	4	2	1	1	2	2	2

1. State lost seats due to reapportionment.
2. State gained seats due to reapportionment.
3. Alaska 1972, California 1962, and Louisiana 1972: national and state totals reflect the reelection of a Democrat who died before the election but whose name remained on the ballot.
4. Illinois 1930, Indiana 1960 and 1984, and New Hampshire 1936: national and state totals reflect the final outcome of a contested election in which a Republican was first certified the winner, but the House decided to seat the Democrat.

	1966	1968	1970	1972	1974	1976	1978	1980	1982	1984	1986	1988	1990	1992	1994	1996	1998	2000
Totals																		
Democrats	248	243	255	243	291	292	277	243	269	253	258	260	267	258	204	207	211	212
Republicans	187	192	180	192	144	143	158	192	166	182	177	175	167	176	230	227	223	221
Alabama																		
Democrats	5	5	5	4[1]	4	4	4	4	5	5	5	5	5	4	4	2	2	2
Republicans	3	3	3	3	3	3	3	3	2	2	2	2	2	3	3	5	5	5
Alaska																		
Democrats	0	0	1	1[3]	0	0	0	0	0	0	0	0	0	0	0	0	0	0
Republicans	1	1	0	0	1	1	1	1	1	1	1	1	1	1	1	1	1	1
Arizona																		
Democrats	1	1	1	1[2]	1	2	2	2	2[2]	1	1	1	1	3[2]	1	1	1	1
Republicans	2	2	2	3	3	2	2	2	3	4	4	4	4	3	5	5	5	5
Arkansas																		
Democrats	3	3	3	3	3	3	2	2	2	3	3	3	3	2	2	2	2	3
Republicans	1	1	1	1	1	1	2	2	2	1	1	1	1	2	2	2	2	1
California																		
Democrats	21	21	20	23[2]	28	29	26	22	28[2]	27	27	27	26	30[2]	27	29	28	32
Republicans	17	17	18	20	15	14	17	21	17	18	18	18	19	22	25	23	24	20
Colorado																		
Democrats	3	3	2	2[2]	3	3	3	3	3[2]	2	3	3	3	2	2	2	2	2
Republicans	1	1	2	3	2	2	2	2	3	4	3	3	3	4	4	4	4	4
Connecticut																		
Democrats	5	4	3	3	4	4	5	4	4	3	3	3	3	3	3	4	4	3
Republicans	1	2	2	3	2	2	1	2	2	3	3	3	3	3	3	2	2	3
Delaware																		
Democrats	0	0	0	0	0	0	0	0	1	1	1	1	1	0	0	0	0	0
Republicans	1	1	1	1	1	1	1	1	0	0	0	0	0	1	1	1	1	1
Florida																		
Democrats	9	9	9	11[2]	10	10	12	11	13[2]	12	12	10	9	10[2]	8	8	8	8
Republicans	3	3	3	4	5	5	3	4	6	7	7	9	10	13	15	15	15	15
Georgia																		
Democrats	8	8	8	9	10	10	9	9	9	8	8	9	9	7[2]	4	3	3	3
Republicans	2	2	2	1	0	0	1	1	1	2	2	1	1	4	7	8	8	8
Hawaii																		
Democrats	2	2	2	2	2	2	2	2	2	2	1	1	2	2	2	2	2	2
Republicans	0	0	0	0	0	0	0	0	0	0	1	1	0	0	0	0	0	0
Idaho																		
Democrats	0	0	0	0	0	0	0	0	0	1	1	1	2	1	0	0	0	0
Republicans	2	2	2	2	2	2	2	2	2	1	1	1	0	1	2	2	2	2
Illinois																		
Democrats	12	12	12	10	13	12	11	10	12[1]	13	13	14	15	12[1]	10	10	10	10
Republicans	12	12	12	14	11	12	13	14	10	9	9	8	7	8	10	10	10	10
Indiana																		
Democrats	5	4	5	4	9	8	7	6	5[1]	5[4]	6	6	8	7	4	4	4	4
Republicans	6	7	6	7	2	3	4	5	5	5	4	4	2	3	6	6	6	6
Iowa																		
Democrats	2	2	2	3[1]	5	4	3	3	3	2	2	2	2	1[1]	0	1	1	1
Republicans	5	5	5	3	1	2	3	3	3	4	4	4	4	4	5	4	4	4
Kansas																		
Democrats	0	0	1	1	1	2	1	1	2	2	2	2	2	2[1]	0	0	1	1
Republicans	5	5	4	4	4	3	4	4	3	3	3	3	3	2	4	4	3	3
Kentucky																		
Democrats	4	4	5	5	5	5	4	4	4	4	4	4	4	4[1]	2	1	1	1
Republicans	3	3	2	2	2	2	3	3	3	3	3	3	3	2	4	5	5	5
Louisiana																		
Democrats	8	8	8	7[3]	6[5]	6	5	6	6	6	5	4	4	4[1]	4	2	2	2
Republicans	0	0	0	1	2	2	3	2	2	2	3	4	4	3	3	5	5	5
Maine																		
Democrats	2	2	2	1	0	0	0	0	0	0	1	1	1	1	1	2	2	2
Republicans	0	0	0	1	2	2	2	2	2	2	1	1	1	1	1	0	0	0
Maryland																		
Democrats	5	4	5	4	5	5	6	7	7	6	6	6	5	4	4	4	4	4
Republicans	3	4	3	4	3	3	2	1	1	2	2	2	3	4	4	4	4	4
Massachusetts																		
Democrats	7	7	8	9[6]	10	10	10	10	10[1]	10	10	10	10	8[1]	8	10	10	10
Republicans	5	5	4	3	2	2	2	2	1	1	1	1	1	2	2	0	0	0
Michigan																		
Democrats	7	7	7	7	12	11	13	12	12[1]	11	11	11	11	10[1]	9	10	10	9
Republicans	12	12	12	12	7	8	6	7	6	7	7	7	7	6	7	6	6	7
Minnesota																		
Democrats	3	3	4	4	5	5	4	3	5	5	5	5	6	6	6	6	6	5
Republicans	5	5	4	4	3	3	4	5	3	3	3	3	2	2	2	2	2	3
Mississippi																		
Democrats	5	5	5	3	3	3	3	3	3	3	4	4	5	5	4	2	3	3
Republicans	0	0	0	2	2	2	2	2	2	2	1	1	0	0	1	3	2	2
Missouri																		
Democrats	8	9	9	9	9	8	8	6	6[1]	6	5	5	6	6	6	5	5	4
Republicans	2	1	1	1	1	2	2	4	3	3	4	4	3	3	3	4	4	5

5. Louisiana 1974: national and state totals reflect the final outcome of a contested election in which no winner was declared, followed by a special election won by the Republican.

6. Massachusetts 1972 and Pennsylvania 1980: national and state Democratic totals reflect the election of an Independent candidate who previously announced he would serve as a Democrats.

	1928	1930	1932	1934	1936	1938	1940	1942	1944	1946	1948	1950	1952	1954	1956	1958	1960	1962	1964
Montana																			
Democrats	1	1	2	2	2	1	1	2	1	1	1	1	1	1	2	2	1	1	1
Republicans	1	1	0	0	0	1	1	0	1	1	1	1	1	1	0	0	1	1	1
Nebraska																			
Democrats	2	4	5¹	4	4	2	2	0¹	0	0	1	0	0	0	0	2	0	0¹	1
Republicans	4	2	0	1	1	3	3	4	4	4	3	4	4	4	4	2	4	3	2
Nevada																			
Democrats	0	0	1	1	1	1	1	1	1	0	1	1	0	0	1	1	1	1	1
Republicans	1	1	0	0	0	0	0	0	0	1	0	0	1	1	0	0	0	0	0
New Hampshire																			
Democrats	0	0	1	1	1⁴	0	0	0	0	0	0	0	0	0	0	0	0	0	1
Republicans	2	2	1	1	1	2	2	2	2	2	2	2	2	2	2	2	2	2	1
New Jersey																			
Democrats	2	3	4²	4	7	3	4	3	2	2	5	5	5	6	4	5	6	7²	11
Republicans	10	9	10	10	7	11	10	11	12	12	9	9	9	8	10	9	8	8	4
New Mexico																			
Democrats	0	1	1	1	1	1	1	2²	2	2	2	2	2	2	2	2	2	2	2
Republicans	1	0	0	0	0	0	0	0	0	0	0	0	0	0	0	0	0	0	0
New York																			
Democrats	23	23	29²	29	29	25	25	23	22	16	24	23	16¹	17	17	19	22	20¹	27
Republicans	20	20	16	16	16	19	19	21	22	28	20	22	27	26	26	24	21	21	14
North Carolina																			
Democrats	8	10	11²	11	11	11	11	12²	12	12	12	12	11	11	11	11	11	9¹	9
Republicans	2	0	0	0	0	0	0	0	0	0	0	0	1	1	1	1	1	2	2
North Dakota																			
Democrats	0	0	0¹	0	0	0	0	0	0	0	0	0	0	0	0	1	0	0	1
Republicans	3	3	2	2	2	2	2	2	2	2	2	2	2	2	2	1	2	2	1
Ohio																			
Democrats	3	9	18²	18	22	9	12	3¹	6	4	12	7	6	6	6	9	7	6²	10
Republicans	19	13	6	6	2	15	12	20	17	19	11	15	16	17	17	14	16	18	14
Oklahoma																			
Democrats	5	7	9²	9	9	9	8	7¹	6	6	8	6	5¹	5	5	5	5	5	5
Republicans	3	1	0	0	0	0	1	1	2	2	0	2	1	1	1	1	1	1	1
Oregon																			
Democrats	0	1	2	1	2	1	1	0²	0	0	0	0	0	1	3	3	2	3	3
Republicans	3	2	1	2	1	2	2	4	4	4	4	4	4	3	1	1	2	1	1
Pennsylvania																			
Democrats	1	3	11¹	23	27	15	19	14¹	15	5	16	13	11¹	14	13	16	14	13¹	15
Republicans	35	33	23	11	7	9	15	19	18	28	19	20	19	16	17	14	16	14	12
Rhode Island																			
Democrats	1	1	2¹	2	2	0	2	2	2	2	2	2	2	2	2	2	2	2	2
Republicans	2	2	0	0	0	2	0	0	0	0	0	0	0	0	0	0	0	0	0
South Carolina																			
Democrats	7	7	6¹	6	6	6	6	6	6	6	6	6	6	6	6	6	6	6	6
Republicans	0	0	0	0	0	0	0	0	0	0	0	0	0	0	0	0	0	0	0
South Dakota																			
Democrats	0	0	2¹	2	1	0	0	0	0	0	0	0	0	0	1	1	0	0	0
Republicans	3	3	0	0	1	2	2	2	2	2	2	2	2	2	1	1	2	2	2
Tennessee																			
Democrats	8	8	7¹	7	7	7	7	8²	8	8	8	8	7¹	7	7	7	7	6	6
Republicans	2	2	2	2	2	2	2	2	2	2	2	2	2	2	2	2	2	3	3
Texas																			
Democrats	17	17	21²	21	21	21	21	21	21	21	21	21	22²	21	21	21	21	21²	23
Republicans	1⁷	1	0	0	0	0	0	0	0	0	0	0	0	1	1	1	1	2	0
Utah																			
Democrats	0	0	2	2	2	2	2	2	2	1	2	2	0	0	0	1	2	0	1
Republicans	2	2	0	0	0	0	0	0	0	1	0	0	2	2	2	1	0	2	1
Vermont																			
Democrats	0	0	0¹	0	0	0	0	0	0	0	0	0	0	0	0	1	0	0	0
Republicans	2	2	1	1	1	1	1	1	1	1	1	1	1	1	1	0	1	1	1
Virginia																			
Democrats	8	9	9¹	9	9	9	9	9	9	9	9	9	7²	8	8	8	8	8	8
Republicans	2	1	0	0	0	0	0	0	0	0	0	0	3	2	2	2	2	2	2
Washington																			
Democrats	1	1	6²	6	6	6	6	3	4	1	2	2	1²	1	1	1	2	1	5
Republicans	4	4	0	0	0	0	0	3	2	5	4	4	6	6	6	6	5	6	2
West Virginia																			
Democrats	1	2	6	6	6	5	6	3	5	2	6	6	5	6	4	5	5	4¹	4
Republicans	5	4	0	0	0	1	0	3	1	4	0	0	1	0	2	1	1	1	1
Wisconsin																			
Democrats	0	1	5¹	3	3	0	1	3	2	0	2	1	1	3	3	5	4	4	5
Republicans	11	10	5	0	0	8	6	5	7	10	8	9	9	7	7	5	6	6	5
Wyoming																			
Democrats	0	0	0	1	1	0	1	0	0	0	0	0	0	0	0	0	1	1	0
Republicans	1	1	1	0	0	1	0	1	1	1	1	1	1	1	1	1	0	0	0

Notes: State totals reflect the number of Democrats and Republicans in each House delegation at the start of each Congress. The above totals do not include "other" representatives elected as independent or third-party candidates. Those numbers are California: Progressive 1936 (1). (No formal party. The representative became a Democrat in 1938.) Minnesota: Farmer-Labor 1928–1930 (1), 1932 (5), 1934 (3), 1936 (5), 1938–1942 (1). (Merged with D in 1944.) New York: American Labor 1938–1948 (1). (Party disbanded after 1954.) Ohio: Independent 1950–1952 (1). (Defeated by Democrat in 1954.) Wisconsin: Progressive 1934 (7), 1936–1938 (2), 1940 (3), 1942 (2) and 1944 (1). (Disbanded after 1944. The last Progressive became a Republican in 1946.) Vermont: Independent 1990–2000 (1). Virginia: Independent 2000 (1). National totals: 1928–1930 (1), 1932 (5), 1934 (10), 1936 (13), 1938 (4), 1940 (5), 1942 (4), 1944 (2), 1946–1952 (1), 1990–1998 (1), and 2000 (2).

	1966	1968	1970	1972	1974	1976	1978	1980	1982	1984	1986	1988	1990	1992	1994	1996	1998	2000
Montana																		
Democrats	1	1	1	1	2	1	1	1	1	1	1	1	1	1[1]	1	1	0	0
Republicans	1	1	1	1	0	1	1	1	1	1	1	1	1	0	0	0	1	1
Nebraska																		
Democrats	0	0	0	0	0	1	1	0	0	0	0	1	1	1	0	0	0	0
Republicans	3	3	3	3	3	2	2	3	3	3	3	2	2	2	3	3	3	3
Nevada																		
Democrats	1	1	1	0	1	1	1	1	1[2]	1	1	1	1	1	0	0	1	1
Republicans	0	0	0	1	0	0	0	0	1	1	1	1	1	1	2	2	1	1
New Hampshire																		
Democrats	0	0	0	0	1	1	1	1	1	0	0	0	1	1	0	0	0	0
Republicans	2	2	2	2	1	1	1	1	1	2	2	2	1	1	2	2	2	2
New Jersey																		
Democrats	9	9	9	8	12	11	10	8	9[1]	8	8	8	8	7[1]	5	6	7	7
Republicans	6	6	6	7	3	4	5	7	5	6	6	6	6	6	8	7	6	6
New Mexico																		
Democrats	2	0	1	1	1	1	1	0	1[2]	1	1	1	1	1	1	1	1	1
Republicans	0	2	1	1	1	1	1	2	2	2	2	2	2	2	2	2	2	2
New York																		
Democrats	26	26	24	22[1]	27	28	26	22	20[1]	19	20	21	21	18[1]	17	18	18	19
Republicans	15	15	17	17	12	11	13	17	14	15	14	13	13	13	14	13	13	12
North Carolina																		
Democrats	8	7	7	7	9	9	9	7	9	6	8	8	7	8[2]	4	6	5	5
Republicans	3	4	4	4	2	2	2	4	2	5	3	3	4	4	8	6	7	7
North Dakota																		
Democrats	0	0	1	0[1]	0	0	0	1	1	1	1	1	1	1	1	1	1	1
Republicans	2	2	1	1	1	1	1	0	0	0	0	0	0	0	0	0	0	0
Ohio																		
Democrats	5	6	7	7[1]	8	10	10	11	10[1]	11	11	11	11	10[1]	6	8	8	8
Republicans	19	18	17	16	15	13	13	12	11	10	10	10	10	9	13	11	11	11
Oklahoma																		
Democrats	4	4	4	5	6	5	5	5	5	5	4	4	4	4	1	0	0	1
Republicans	2	2	2	1	0	1	1	1	1	1	2	2	2	2	5	6	6	5
Oregon																		
Democrats	2	2	2	2	4	4	4	3	3[2]	3	3	3	4	4	3	4	4	4
Republicans	2	2	2	2	0	0	0	1	2	2	2	2	1	1	2	1	1	1
Pennsylvania																		
Democrats	14	14	14	13[1]	14	17	15	13[6]	13[1]	13	12	12	11	11[1]	11	11	11	10
Republicans	13	13	13	12	11	8	10	12	10	10	11	11	12	10	10	10	10	11
Rhode Island																		
Democrats	2	2	2	2	2	2	2	1	1	1	1	0	1	1	2	2	2	2
Republicans	0	0	0	0	0	0	0	1	1	1	1	2	1	1	0	0	0	0
South Carolina																		
Democrats	5	5	5	4	5	5	4	2	3	3	4	4	4	3	2	2	2	2
Republicans	1	1	1	2	1	1	2	4	3	3	2	2	2	3	4	4	4	4
South Dakota																		
Democrats	0	0	2	1	0	0	1	1	1[1]	1	1	1	1	1	1	0	0	0
Republicans	2	2	0	1	2	2	1	1	0	0	0	0	0	0	0	1	1	1
Tennessee																		
Democrats	5	5	5	3[1]	5	5	5	5	6[2]	6	6	6	6	6	4	4	4	4
Republicans	4	4	4	5	3	3	3	3	3	3	3	3	3	3	5	5	5	5
Texas																		
Democrats	21	20	20	20[2]	21	22	20	19	22[2]	17	17	19	19	21[2]	19	17	17	17
Republicans	2	3	3	4	3	2	4	5	5	10	10	8	8	9	11	13	13	13
Utah																		
Democrats	0	0	1	2	2	1	1	0	0[2]	0	1	1	2	2	1	0	0	1
Republicans	2	2	1	0	0	1	1	2	3	3	2	2	1	1	2	3	3	2
Vermont																		
Democrats	0	0	0	0	0	0	0	0	0	0	0	0	0	0	0	0	0	0
Republicans	1	1	1	1	1	1	1	1	1	1	1	1	0	0	0	0	0	0
Virginia																		
Democrats	6	5	4	3	5	4	4	1	4	4	5	5	6	7[2]	6	6	6	4
Republicans	4	5	6	7	5	6	6	9	6	6	5	5	4	4	5	5	5	6
Washington																		
Democrats	5	5	6	6	6	6	6	5	5[2]	5	5	5	5	8[2]	2	3	5	6
Republicans	2	2	1	1	1	1	1	2	3	3	3	3	3	1	7	6	4	3
West Virginia																		
Democrats	4	5	5	4[1]	4	4	4	2	4	4	4	4	4	3[1]	3	3	3	2
Republicans	1	0	0	0	0	0	0	2	0	0	0	0	0	0	0	0	0	1
Wisconsin																		
Democrats	3	3	5	5[1]	7	7	6	5	5	5	5	5	4	4	3	5	4	5
Republicans	7	7	5	4	2	2	3	4	4	4	4	4	5	5	6	4	5	4
Wyoming																		
Democrats	0	1	1	1	1	0	0	0	0	0	0	0	0	0	0	0	0	0
Republicans	1	1	0	0	0	0	1	1	1	1	1	1	1	1	1	1	1	1

7. Texas 1928: national and state totals reflect the final outcome of a contested election in which a Democrats was at first certified the winner, but the House decided to seat the Republican.

Governors, 1997–2001

Following is a list of governors who served during the period of President Bill Clinton's second term, 1997–2001. Dates of service for a governor in office between 1997 and 2001 include any terms served by the individual before this period. All governors serve four-year terms except those representing New Hampshire and Vermont; they serve two-year terms.

Party designation appears in parentheses following the governor's name. The following abbreviations were used: (D) Democrat; (I) Independent; (R) Republican; (REF) Reform. *(Governors, 1981–1984, Congress and the Nation Vol. VI, p. 1122; 1985–1988, Congress and the Nation Vol. VII, p. 1143; 1989–1992, Congress and the Nation Vol. VIII, p. 1259; 1993–1996, Congress and the Nation Vol. IX, p. 1211.)*

	Dates of service
Alabama	
Forrest H. "Fob" James (R)	Jan. 16, 1995–Jan. 18, 1999
Don Siegelman (D)	Jan. 18, 1999–
Alaska	
Tony Knowles (D)	Dec. 5, 1994–
Arizona	
Fife Symington (R)	March 6, 1991–Sept. 5, 1997
Jane D. Hull (R)	Sept. 5, 1997–
Arkansas	
Mike Huckabee (R)	July 15, 1996–
California	
Pete Wilson (R)	Jan. 7, 1991–Jan. 4, 1999
Gray Davis (D)	Jan. 4, 1999–
Colorado	
Roy R. Romer (D)	Jan. 13, 1987–Jan. 12, 1999
Bill Owens (R)	Jan. 12, 1999–
Connecticut	
John G. Rowland (R)	Jan. 4, 1995–
Delaware	
Thomas R. Carper (D)	Jan. 19, 1993–Jan. 3, 2001
Ruth Ann Miner (D)	Jan. 3, 2001–
Florida	
Lawton Chiles (D)	Jan. 8, 1991–Dec. 12, 1998
Buddy MacKay (D)	Dec. 12, 1998–Jan. 5, 1999
Jeb Bush (R)	Jan. 5, 1999–
Georgia	
Zell Miller (D)	Jan. 14, 1991–Jan. 11, 1999
Roy Barnes (D)	Jan. 11, 1999–
Hawaii	
Benjamin J. Cayetano (D)	Dec. 5, 1994–
Idaho	
Philip E. Batt (R)	Jan. 2, 1995–Jan. 8, 1999
Dirk Kempthorne (R)	Jan. 8, 1999–

	Dates of service
Illinois	
Jim Edgar (R)	Jan. 14, 1991–Jan. 11, 1999
George Ryan (R)	Jan. 11, 1999–
Indiana	
Frank L. O'Bannon (D)	Jan. 13, 1997–
Iowa	
Terry E. Branstad (R)	Jan. 14, 1983–Jan. 15, 1999
Tom Vilsack (D)	Jan. 15, 1999–
Kansas	
Bill Graves (R)	Jan. 9, 1995–
Kentucky	
Paul E. Patton (D)	Dec. 12, 1995–
Louisiana	
Mike Foster (R)	Jan. 8, 1996–
Maine	
Angus King Jr. (I)	Jan. 5, 1995–
Maryland	
Parris N. Glendening (D)	Jan. 18, 1995–
Massachusetts	
William F. Weld (R)	Jan. 3, 1991–July 29, 1997
Argeo "Paul" Cellucci (R)	July 29, 1997–
Michigan	
John Engler (R)	Jan. 1, 1991–
Minnesota	
Arne H. Carlson (R)	Jan. 7, 1991–Jan. 5, 1999
Jesse Ventura (REF)	Jan. 5, 1999–
Mississippi	
Kirk Fordice (R)	Jan. 14, 1992–Jan. 11, 2000
Ronnie Musgrove (D)	Jan. 11, 2000–
Missouri	
Mel Carnahan (D)	Jan. 11, 1993–Oct. 15, 2000
Roger B. Wilson (D)	Oct. 16, 2000–Jan. 8, 2001
Bob Holden (D)	Jan. 8, 2001–

	Dates of service
Montana	
Marc Racicot (R)	Jan. 4, 1993–Jan. 2, 2001
Judy Martz (R)	Jan. 2, 2001–
Nebraska	
Earl "Ben" Nelson (D)	Jan. 9, 1991–Jan. 7, 1999
Mike Johanns (R)	Jan. 7, 1999–
Nevada	
Bob J. Miller (D)	Jan. 3, 1989–Jan. 4, 1999
Kenny Guinn (R)	Jan. 4, 1999–
New Hampshire	
Jeanne Shaheen (D)	Jan. 9, 1997–
New Jersey	
Christine Todd Whitman (R)	Jan. 18, 1994–
New Mexico	
Gary E. Johnson (R)	Jan. 1, 1995–
New York	
George E. Pataki (R)	Jan. 1, 1995–
North Carolina	
James B. Hunt Jr. (D)	Jan. 8, 1977–Jan. 5, 1985
	Jan. 9, 1993–Jan. 6, 2001
Michael Easley (D)	Jan. 6, 2001–
North Dakota	
Edward T. Schafer (R)	Jan. 5, 1993–Dec. 15, 2000
John Hoeven (R)	Dec. 15, 2000–
Ohio	
George V. Voinovich (R)	Jan. 14, 1991–Dec. 31, 1998
Nancy Hollister (R)	Dec. 31, 1998–Jan. 11, 1999
Robert A. Taft II (R)	Jan. 11, 1999–
Oklahoma	
Frank Keating (R)	Jan. 9, 1995–
Oregon	
John Kitzhaber (D)	Jan. 9, 1995–

	Dates of service
Pennsylvania	
Tom Ridge (R)	Jan. 17, 1995–
Rhode Island	
Lincoln C. Almond (R)	Jan. 3, 1995–
South Carolina	
David Beasley (R)	Jan. 11, 1995–Jan. 13, 1999
Jim Hodges (D)	Jan. 13, 1999–
South Dakota	
William J. Janklow (R)	Jan. 1, 1979–Jan. 6, 1987
	Jan. 7, 1995–
Tennessee	
Don Sundquist (R)	Jan. 21, 1995–
Texas	
George W. Bush (R)	Jan. 17, 1995–Dec. 21, 2000
Rick Perry (R)	Dec. 21, 2000–
Utah	
Mike O. Leavitt (R)	Jan. 3, 1993–
Vermont	
Howard Dean (D)	Aug. 14, 1991–
Virginia	
George F. Allen (R)	Jan. 15, 1994–Jan. 17, 1998
James S. Gilmore (R)	Jan. 17, 1998–
Washington	
Gary Locke (D)	Jan. 15, 1997–
West Virginia	
Cecil H. Underwood (R)	Jan. 14, 1957–Jan. 16, 1961
	Jan. 13, 1997–Jan. 15, 2001
Bob Wise (D)	Jan. 15, 2001–
Wisconsin	
Tommy G. Thompson (R)	Jan. 5, 1987–
Wyoming	
Jim Geringer (R)	Jan. 2, 1995–

Public Laws 1997–2001

105th Congress—1997   1099

105th Congress—1998   1106

106th Congress—1999   1117

106th Congress—2000   1125

105th Congress—1997

PL 105-1 (H J Res 25) Make technical corrections to the Omnibus Consolidated Appropriations Act of 1997 (PL 104-208). Introduced by Livingston, R-La., Jan. 9, 1997. House passed Jan. 9. Senate passed Jan. 21. President signed Feb. 3, 1997.

PL 105-2 (HR 668) Amend the Internal Revenue Code of 1986 to reinstate the Airport and Airway Trust Fund excise taxes. Introduced by Archer, R-Texas, Feb. 11, 1997. House Ways and Means reported Feb. 13 (H Rept 105-5). House passed, under suspension of the rules, Feb. 26. Senate passed Feb. 27. President signed Feb. 28, 1997.

PL 105-3 (H J Res 36) Approve the presidential finding that the limitation on obligations imposed by section 518A(a) of the Foreign Operations Export Financing and Related Programs Appropriations Act of 1997, is having a negative impact on the proper functioning of the population planning program. Introduced by Armey, R-Texas, Feb. 4, 1997. House Appropriations discharged Feb. 10. House passed Feb. 13. Senate passed Feb. 25. President signed Feb. 28, 1997.

PL 105-4 (HR 499) Designate the facility of the United States Postal Service under construction at 7411 Barlite Blvd. in San Antonio, Texas, as the "Frank M. Tejeda Post Office Building." Introduced by Bonilla, R-Texas, Feb. 4, 1997. House passed, under suspension of the rules, Feb. 5. Senate passed Feb. 26. President signed March 3, 1997.

PL 105-5 (S J Res 5) Wave certain provisions of the Trade Act of 1974 relating to the appointment of the U.S. Trade Representative. Introduced by Roth, R-Del., Jan. 21, 1997. Senate Finance reported Feb. 3 (no written report). Senate passed March 5. House passed, under suspension of the rules, March 11. President signed March 17, 1997.

PL 105-6 (HR 924) Amend Title 18, U.S. Code, to give further assurance to victims of crime of their right to attend and observe the trials of those accused of the crime. Introduced by McCollum, R-Fla., March 5, 1997. House Judiciary reported, amended, March 17 (H Rept 105-28). House passed, as amended, under suspension of the rules, March 18. Senate passed March 19. President signed March 19, 1997.

PL 105-7 (HR 514) Permit the waiver of District of Columbia residency requirements for certain employees of the Office of the Inspector General of the District of Columbia. Introduced by Davis, R-Va., Feb. 4, 1997. House Government Reform and Oversight reported, amended, March 17 (H Rept 105-29). House passed, as amended, under suspension of the rules, March 18. Senate passed March 20. President signed March 25, 1997.

PL 105-8 (S 410) Extend the effective date of the Investment Advisers Supervision Coordination Act. Introduced by D'Amato, R-N.Y., March 6, 1997. Senate passed March 12. House passed March 18. President signed March 31, 1997.

PL 105-9 (HR 412) Approve a settlement agreement between the Bureau of Reclamation and the Oroville-Tonasket Irrigation District. Introduced by Hastings, R-Wash., Jan. 9, 1997. House Resources reported, amended, March 10 (H Rept 105-8). House passed, amended, March 18. Senate passed April 8. President signed April 14, 1997.

PL 105-10 (HR 785) Designate the J. Phil Campbell Sr. Natural Resource Conservation Center. Introduced by Norwood, R-Ga., Feb. 13, 1997. House Agriculture reported March 20 (H Rept 105-36). House passed, under suspension of the rules, April 8. Senate passed April 10. President signed April 24, 1997.

PL 105-11 (HR 1225) Make a technical correction to Title 28, U.S. Code, relating to jurisdiction for lawsuits against terrorist states. Introduced by Hyde, R-Ill., April 8, 1997. House Judiciary reported April 10 (H Rept 105-48). House passed, under suspension of the rules, April 15. Senate passed April 24. President signed April 25, 1997.

PL 105-12 (HR 1003) Clarify federal law with respect to restricting the use of federal funds in support of assisted suicide. Introduced by Hall, D-Texas, March 11, 1997. House Commerce reported, amended, April 8 (H Rept 105-46, Pt. 1). House passed, as amended, under suspension of the rules, April 10. Senate passed April 16. President signed April 18, 1997.

PL 105-13 (HR 1001) Extend the term of appointment of certain members of the Prospective Payment Assessment Commission and the Physician Payment Review Commission. Introduced by Thomas, R-Calif., March 10, 1997. House Ways and Means reported April 10 (H Rept 105-49, Pt. 1). House Commerce reported April 14 (H Rept 105-49, Pt. 2). House passed, under suspension of the rules, April 15. Senate passed April 30. President signed May 14, 1997.

PL 105-14 (S 305) Authorize the president to award a gold medal on behalf of the Congress to Francis Albert "Frank" Sinatra in recognition of his outstanding and enduring contributions through his entertainment career and humanitarian activities. Introduced by D'Amato, R-N.Y., Feb. 12, 1997. Senate passed Feb. 26. House passed April 29. President signed May 14, 1997.

PL 105-15 (HR 968) Amend Title XVIII and XIX of the Social Security Act to permit a waiver of the prohibition of offering nurse aide training and competency evaluation programs in certain nursing facilities. Introduced by Ehrlich, R-Md., March 6, 1997. House Ways and Means reported, amended, March 13 (H Rept 105-23, Pt. 1). House Commerce reported, amended, March 18 (H Rept 105-23, Pt. 2). House passed, amended, April 8. Senate passed April 30. President signed May 15, 1997.

PL 105-16 (HR 1650) Authorize the president to award a gold medal on behalf of the Congress to Mother Teresa of Calcutta in recognition of her outstanding and enduring contributions through humanitarian and charitable activities. Introduced by Christensen, R-Neb., May 16, 1997. House passed, under suspension of the rules, May 20. Senate passed May 21. President signed June 2, 1997.

PL 105-17 (HR 5) Amend the Individuals with Disabilities Education Act to reauthorize and make improvements to that Act. Introduced by Goodling, R-Pa., Jan. 7, 1997. House Education and the Workforce reported, amended, May 13 (H Rept 105-95). House passed as amended, under suspension of the rules, May 13. Senate passed May 14. President signed June 4, 1997.

PL 105-18 (HR 1871) Make emergency supplemental appropriations for recovery from natural disasters, and for overseas peacekeeping efforts, including those in Bosnia, for the fiscal year ending Sept. 30, 1997. Introduced by Livingston, R-La., June 12, 1997. House Appropriations and Budget discharged. House passed June 12. Senate passed June 12. President signed June 12, 1997.

PL 105-19 (S 543) Provide certain protections to volunteers, nonprofit organizations, and governmental entities in lawsuits based on the activities of volunteers. Introduced by Coverdell, R-Ga., April 9, 1997. Senate passed, amended, May 1. House Judiciary discharged. House passed, with amendment, May 21. Senate agreed to House amendment May 21. President signed June 18, 1997.

PL 105-20 (HR 956) Amend the National Narcotics Leadership Act of 1988 to establish and encourage local communities that first demonstrate a comprehensive, long-term commitment to reduce substance abuse among youth. Introduced by Portman, R-Ohio, March 5, 1997. House Government Reform and Oversight reported, amended, May 20 (H Rept 105-105, Pt. 1). House Commerce discharged. House passed as amended, under suspension of the rules, May 22. Senate passed June 18. President signed June 27, 1997.

PL 105-21 (H J Res 32) Consent to certain amendments enacted by the legislature of the state of Hawaii to the Hawaiian Homes Commission Act of 1920. Introduced by Abercrombie, D-Hawaii, Jan. 21, 1997. House Resources reported March 11 (H Rept 105-16). House passed, under suspension of the rules, March 11. Senate Energy and Natural Resources reported May 16 (S Rept 105-19). Senate passed June 12. President signed June 27, 1997.

PL 105-22 (S 342) Extend certain privileges, exemptions, and immunities to Hong Kong Economic and Trade Offices. Introduced by Thomas, R-Wyo., Feb. 24, 1997. Senate Foreign Relations reported May 8 (no written report). Senate passed May 20. House passed, under suspension of the rules, June 17. President signed June 27, 1997.

PL 105-23 (HR 363) Amend section 2118 of the Energy Policy Act of 1992 to extend the Electric and Magnetic Fields Research and Public Information Dissemination Program. Introduced by Towns, D-N.Y., Jan. 7, 1997. House Commerce reported, amended, April 21 (H Rept 105-60, Pt. 1). House Science reported, amended, April 21 (H Rept 105-60, Pt. 2). House passed, as amended, under suspension of the rules, April 29. Senate Energy and Natural Resources reported June 12 (S Rept 105-27). Senate passed June 20. President signed July 3, 1997.

PL 105-24 (HR 1306) Amend the Federal Deposit Insurance Act to clarify the applicability of host state laws to any branch in such state of an out-of-state bank. Introduced by Roukema, R-N.J., April 10, 1997. House passed, amended, under suspension of the rules, May 21. Senate passed with amendments June 12. House agreed to Senate amendments June 24. President signed July 3, 1997.

PL 105-25 (HR 1553) Amend the President John F. Kennedy Assassination Records Collection Act of 1992 to extend the authorization of the Assassination Records Review Board until Sept. 30, 1998. Introduced by Burton, R-Ind., May 8, 1997. House Government Reform and Oversight reported June 19 (H Rept 105-138, Pt. 1). House Judiciary discharged. House passed, under suspension of the rules, June 23. Senate passed June 25. President signed July 3, 1997.

PL 105-26 (HR 1902) Immunize donations made in the form of charitable gift annuities and charitable remainder trusts from the antitrust laws and state laws similar to the antitrust laws. Introduced by Hyde, R-Ill., June 17, 1997. House Judiciary reported June 23 (H Rept 105-146). House passed, under suspension of the rules, June 23. Senate passed June 24. President signed July 3, 1997.

PL 105-27 (HR 173) Amend the Federal Property and Administrative Services Act of 1949 to authorize donation of surplus federal law enforcement canines to their handlers. Introduced by Gallerly, R-Calif., Jan. 7, 1997. House passed, amended, under suspension of the rules, April 16. Senate Governmental Affairs reported June 26 (no written report). Senate passed June 27. President signed July 18, 1997.

PL 105-28 (HR 649) Amend sections of the Department of Energy Organization Act that are obsolete or inconsistent with other statutes and to repeal a related section of the Federal Energy Administration Act of 1974. Introduced by Schaefer, R-Colo., Feb. 6, 1997. House Commerce reported June 11 (H Rept 105-11). House passed, under suspension of the rules, March 11. Senate Energy and Natural Resources reported March 12 (S Rept 105-26). Senate passed June 27. President signed July 18, 1997.

PL 105-29 (S J Res 29) Direct the secretary of the interior to design and construct a permanent addition to the Franklin D. Roosevelt Memorial in Washington, D.C. Introduced by Inouye, D-Hawaii, May 1, 1997. Senate passed May 1. House Resources reported July 8 (H Rept 105-167). House passed, under suspension of the rules, July 8. President signed July 24, 1997.

PL 105-30 (HR 1901) Clarify that the protections of the Federal Tort Claims Act apply to the members and personnel of the National Gambling Impact Study Commission. Introduced by Hyde, R-Ill., June 17, 1997. House Judiciary reported June 23 (H Rept 105-145). House passed, under suspension of the rules, June 23. Senate passed July 9. President signed July 25, 1997.

PL 105-31 (HR 2018) Waive temporarily the Medicaid enrollment composition rule for the Better Health Plan of Amherst, N.Y. Introduced by Paxon, R-N.Y., June 24, 1997. House Commerce reported, amended, July 8 (H Rept 105-165). House passed, as amended, under suspension of the rules, July 8. Senate passed July 11. President signed July 25, 1997.

PL 105-32 (H J Res 90) Waive certain enrollment requirements with respect to two specified bills of the 105th Congress. Introduced by Diaz-Balart, R-Fla., July 31, 1997. House passed July 31. Senate passed July 31. President signed Aug. 1, 1997.

PL 105-33 (HR 2015) Provide for reconciliation pursuant to subsections (b)(1) and (c) of section 105 of the concurrent resolution on the budget for fiscal year 1998 (H Con Res 84) to balance the federal budget. Introduced by Kasich, R-Ohio, June 23, 1997. House Budget reported June 24 (H Rept 105-149). House passed, amended, June 25. Senate passed, with amendment, June 25. Conference report filed in the House July 29 (H Rept 105-217). House agreed to conference report July 30. Senate cleared July 31. President signed Aug. 5, 1997.

PL 105-34 (HR 2014) Provide for reconciliation pursuant to subsections (b)(2) and (d) of section 105 of the concurrent resolution on the budget for fiscal year 1998 (H Con Res 84) to reduce taxes. Introduced by Kasich, R-Ohio, June 23, 1997. House Budget reported June 24 (H Rept 105-148). House passed, amended, June 26. Senate passed, with amendment, June 27. Conference report filed in the House July 30 (H Rept 105-220). House agreed to conference report July 31. Senate cleared July 31. President signed Aug. 5, 1997.

PL 105-35 (HR 1226) Amend the Internal Revenue Code of 1986 to prevent the unauthorized inspection of tax returns or tax return information. Introduced by Archer, R-Texas, April 8, 1997. House Ways and Means reported, amended, April 14 (H Rept 105-51). House passed, as amended, under suspension of the rules, April 15. Senate passed July 23. President signed Aug. 5, 1997.

PL 105-36 (HR 709) Reauthorize and amend the National Geologic Mapping Act of 1992. Introduced by Cubin, R-Wyo., Feb. 12, 1997. House Resources reported, amended, March 11 (H Rept 105-17). House passed, as amended, under suspension of the rules, March 11. Senate Energy and Natural Resources discharged. Senate passed July 23. President signed Aug. 5, 1997.

PL 105-37 (S 430) Amend the Act of June 20, 1910, to protect the permanent trust funds of the state of New Mexico from erosion because of inflation and modify the basis on which distributions are made from those funds. Introduced by Domenici, R-N.M., March 12, 1997. Energy and Natural Resources reported May 15 (S Rept 105-18). Senate passed May 21. House passed, under suspension of the rules, July 28. President signed Aug. 7, 1997.

PL 105-38 (S 670) Amend the Immigration and Nationality Technical Corrections Act of 1994 to eliminate the special transition rule for issuance of a certificate of citizenship for certain children born outside the United States. Introduced by Abraham, R-Mich., April 30, 1997. Senate Judiciary reported May 8 (no written report). Senate passed May 14. House Judiciary discharged. House passed July 28. President signed Aug. 8, 1997.

PL 105-39 (HR 1198) Direct the secretary of the interior to convey certain land to Grants Pass, Ore. Introduced by Smith, R-Ore., March 20, 1997. House Resources reported, amended, July 8 (H Rept 105-166). House passed, amended, under suspension of the rules, July 8. Senate Energy and Natural Resources reported July 30 (no written report). Senate passed July 31. President signed Aug. 11, 1997.

PL 105-40 (HR 1944) Provide for a land exchange involving the Warner Canyon Ski Area and other land in Oregon. Introduced by Smith, R-Ore., June 17, 1997. House Resources reported July 21 (H Rept 105-193). House passed, under suspension of the rules, July 22. Senate Energy and Natural Resources reported July 30 (no written report). Senate passed July 31. President signed Aug. 11, 1997.

PL 105-41 (HR 1585) Allow postal patrons to contribute to funding for breast cancer research through the voluntary purchase of certain specially issued U.S. postage stamps. Introduced by Molinari, R-N.Y., May 13, 1997. House passed, amended, under suspension of the rules, July 22. Senate passed July 24. President signed Aug. 13, 1997.

PL 105-42 (HR 408) Amend the Marine Mammal Protection Act of 1972 to support the International Dolphin Conservation Program in the eastern tropical Pacific Ocean. Introduced by Gilchrest, R-Md., Jan. 9, 1997. House Resources reported, amended, April 24 (H Rept 105-74, Pt. 1). House Ways and Means reported May 1 (H Rept 105-74, Pt. 2). House passed, amended, May 21. Senate Commerce, Science and Transportation discharged. Senate passed, with amendment, July 30. House agreed to Senate amendment July 31. President signed Aug. 15, 1997.

PL 105-43 (HR 1866) Continue favorable treatment for need-based educational aid under the antitrust laws. Introduced by Smith, R-Texas, June 11, 1997. House Judiciary reported June 23 (H Rept 105-144). House passed, under suspension of the rules, June 23. Senate passed, with amendment, July 30. House agreed to Senate amendment, under suspension of the rules, Sept. 8. President signed Sept. 17, 1997.

PL 105-44 (HR 63) Designate the reservoir created by Trinity Dam in the Central Valley project in California as "Trinity Lake." Introduced by Herger, R-Calif., Jan. 7, 1997. House Resources reported March 10 (H Rept 105-9). House passed, under suspension of the rules, March 11. Senate Energy and Natural Resources reported Sept. 2 (S Rept 105-70). Senate passed Sept. 16. President signed Sept. 30, 1997.

PL 105-45 (HR 2016) Make appropriations for military construction, family housing, and base realignment and closure for the Department of Defense for the fiscal year ending Sept. 30, 1998. Introduced by Packard, R-Calif., June 24, 1997. House Appropriations reported June 24 (H Rept 105-150). House passed July 8. Senate Appropriations reported, amended, July 17 (S Rept 105-52). Senate passed, with amendments, July 22. Conference report filed in the House Sept. 9 (H Rept 105-247). House agreed to conference report Sept. 16. Senate cleared Sept. 17. President signed Sept. 30, 1997. President exercised line-item veto authority (H Doc 105-147), Oct. 6, 1997.

PL 105-46 (H J Res 94) A joint resolution making continuing appropriations for fiscal year 1998. Introduced by Livingston, R-La., Sept. 26, 1997. House Appropriations discharged. House passed Sept. 29. Senate passed Sept. 30. President signed Sept. 30, 1997.

PL 105-47 (S 910) Authorize appropriations for carrying out the Earthquake Hazards Reduction Act of 1977 for fiscal years 1998 and 1999. Introduced by Frist, R-Tenn., June 16, 1997. Senate Commerce, Science and Transportation reported, amended, July 30 (S Rept 105-59). Senate passed, amended, July 31. House passed, under suspension of the rules, Sept. 16. President signed Oct. 1, 1997.

PL 105-48 (S 1211) Provide permanent authority for the administration of au pair programs. Introduced by Helms, R-N.C., Sept. 24. Senate Foreign Relations reported Sept. 24 (no written report). Senate passed Sept. 25. House passed, under suspension of the rules, Sept. 29. President signed Oct. 1, 1997.

PL 105-49 (HR 111) Authorize the secretary of agriculture to convey a parcel of unused agricultural land in Dos Palos, Calif., to the Dos Palos Ag Boosters for use as a farm school. Introduced by Condit, D-Calif., Jan. 7, 1997. House Agriculture reported March 20 (H Rept 105-34). House passed, amended, under suspension of the rules, April 16. Senate Agriculture, Nutrition, and Forestry discharged. Senate passed Sept. 23. President signed Oct. 6, 1997.

PL 105-50 (HR 680) Amend the Federal Property and Administrative Services Act of 1949 to authorize the transfer to states of surplus personal property for donation to nonprofit providers of necessaries to impoverished families and individuals. Introduced by Hamilton, D-Ind., Feb. 11, 1997. House passed, amended, under suspension of the rules April 29. Senate Governmental Affairs reported June 26 (no written report). Senate passed, with amendments, July 9. House agreed to Senate amendments Sept. 18. President signed Oct. 6, 1997.

PL 105-51 (HR 2248) Authorize the president to award a gold medal on behalf of the Congress to Ecumenical Patriarch Bartholomew in recognition of his outstanding and enduring contributions toward religious understanding and peace. Introduced by Leach, R-Iowa, July 24, 1997. House Banking and Financial Services discharged. House passed Sept. 17. Senate passed Sept. 24. President signed Oct. 6, 1997.

PL 105-52 (HR 2443) Designate the federal building at 601 Fourth St., N.W., in the District of Columbia, as the "Federal Bureau of Investigation, Washington Field Office Memorial Building," in honor of William H. Christian Jr., Martha Dixon Martinez, Michael J. Miller, Anthony Palmisano and Edwin R. Woodriffe. Introduced by Norton, D-D.C., Sept. 9, 1997. House Transportation and Infrastructure discharged. House passed Sept. 18. Senate Environment and Public Works reported Sept. 24 (no written report). Senate passed Sept. 24. President signed Oct. 6, 1997.

PL 105-53 (S 996) Provide for the authorization of appropriations in each fiscal year for arbitration in U.S. district courts. Introduced by Grassley, R-Iowa, July 8, 1997. Senate Judiciary discharged. Senate passed, amended, July 31. House passed, with amendments, under suspension of the rules, Sept. 23. Senate agreed to House amendments Sept. 30. President signed Oct. 6, 1997.

PL 105-54 (S 1198) Amend the Immigration and Nationality Act to extend the special immigrant religious worker program; to amend the Illegal Immigration Reform and Immigrant Responsibility Act of 1996 to extend the deadline for designation of an effective date for paperwork changes in the employer sanctions program; and to require the secretary of state to waive or reduce the fee for application and issuance of a nonimmigrant visa for aliens coming to the United States for certain charitable purposes. Introduced by Abraham, R-Mich., Sept. 18. Senate passed, amended, Sept. 18. House passed, with amendments, under suspension of the rules, Oct. 1. Senate agreed to House amendments Oct. 1. President signed Oct. 6, 1997.

PL 105-55 (HR 2209) Make appropriations for the legislative branch for the fiscal year ending Sept. 30, 1998. Introduced by Walsh, R-N.Y., July 22. House Appropriations reported July 22 (H Rept 105-196). House passed, amended, July 28. Senate passed, with amendment, July 29. Conference report filed in the House Sept. 18 (H Rept 105-254). House agreed to conference report Sept. 24. Senate agreed to conference report Sept. 24. President signed Oct. 7, 1997.

PL 105-56 (HR 2266) Make appropriations for the Department of Defense for the fiscal year ending Sept. 30, 1998. Introduced by Young, R-Fla., July 25, 1997. House Appropriations reported July 25 (H Rept 105-206). House passed, amended, July 29. Senate passed, with amendment, July 29. Conference report filed in the House Sept. 23 (H Rept 105-265). House agreed to conference report Sept. 25. Senate agreed to conference report Sept. 25. President signed Oct. 8, 1997. President exercised line-item veto authority (H Doc 105-155), Oct. 14, 1997.

PL 105-57 (HR 1420) Amend the National Wildlife Refuge System Administration Act of 1966 to improve the management of the National Wildlife Refuge System. Introduced by Young, R-Alaska, April 23, 1997. House Resources reported April 23 (H Rept 105-106). House passed, amended, under suspension of the rules June 3. Senate passed, with amendments, Sept. 10. House agreed to Senate amendments, under suspension of the rules, Sept. 23. President signed Oct. 9, 1997.

PL 105-58 (S 871) To establish the Oklahoma City National Memorial as a unit of the National Park System and to designate the Oklahoma City Memorial Trust. Introduced by Nickles, R-Okla., June 10, 1997. Senate Energy and Natural Resources reported July 30 (S Rept 105-71). Senate passed July 31. House passed, with amendment, under suspension of the rules, Sept. 23. Senate agreed to House amendment Sept. 25. President signed Oct. 9, 1997.

PL 105-59 (HR 394) Provide for the release of the reversionary interest held by the United States in certain property located in the county of Iosco, Mich. Introduced by Barcla, D-Mich., Jan. 9, 1997. House Agriculture reported March 20 (H Rept 105-35). House passed, under suspension of the rules, April 8. Senate Agriculture, Nutrition, and Forestry discharged. Senate passed, Sept. 30. President signed Oct. 10, 1997.

PL 105-60 (HR 1948) Provide for the exchange of lands within Admiralty Island National Monument. Introduced by Young, R-Alaska, June 17, 1997. House Resources reported, amended, Sept. 23 (H Rept 105-261). House passed, amended, under suspension of the rules, Sept. 23. Senate passed Sept. 30. President signed Oct. 10, 1997.

PL 105-61 (HR 2378) Make appropriations for the Treasury Department, the Postal Service, the Executive Office of the President, and certain independent agencies, for the fiscal year ending Sept. 30, 1998. Introduced by Kolbe, R-Ariz., Sept. 3, 1997. House Appropriations reported draft bill Aug. 5 (H Rept 105-240, Pts. 1, 2 and 3). House passed, amended, Sept. 17. Senate passed, with amendment, Sept. 17. Conference report filed in the House Sept. 29 (H Rept 105-284). House agreed to conference report Sept. 30. Senate agreed to conference report Oct. 1. President signed Oct. 10, 1997. President exercised line-item veto authority (H Doc 105-156), Oct. 16, 1997.

PL 105-62 (HR 2203) Make appropriations for energy and water development for the fiscal year ending Sept. 30, 1998. Introduced by McDade, R-Pa., July 21, 1997. House Appropriations reported July 21 (H Rept 105-190). House passed, amended, July 25. Senate passed, with amendment, July 28. Conference report filed in the House Sept. 26 (H Rept 105-271). House agreed to conference report Sept. 30. Senate agreed to conference report Sept. 30. President signed Oct. 13, 1997. President exercised line-item veto authority (H Doc 105-157), Oct. 16, 1997.

PL 105-63 (S 1000) To designate the U.S. courthouse at 500 State Ave. in Kansas City, Kan., as the "Robert J. Dole United States Courthouse." Introduced by Roberts, R-Kan., July 10, 1997. Senate Environment and Public Works reported July 24 (no written report). Senate passed July 25. House passed, under suspension of the rules, Sept. 23. President signed Oct. 22, 1997.

PL 105-64 (H J Res 97) Make further continuing appropriations for the fiscal year 1998. Introduced by Livingston, R-La., Oct. 21, 1997. House passed Oct. 22. Senate passed Oct. 23. President signed Oct. 23, 1997.

PL 105-65 (HR 2158) Make appropriations for the Departments of Veterans Affairs and Housing and Urban Development, and for various independent agencies, commissions, corporations, and offices for the fiscal year ending Sept. 30, 1998. Introduced by Lewis, R-Calif., July 11, 1997. House Appropriations reported July 11 (H Rept 105-175). House passed, amended, July 16. Senate passed, with amendment, July 22. Conference report filed in the House Oct. 6 (H Rept 105-297). House agreed to conference report Oct. 8. Senate agreed to conference report Oct. 9. President signed Oct. 27, 1997. President exercised line-item veto authority (H Doc 105-167), Nov. 1, 1997.

PL 105-66 (HR 2169) Make appropriations for the Department of Transportation and related agencies for the fiscal year ending Sept. 30, 1998. Introduced by Wolf, R-Va., July 16, 1997. House Appropriations reported July 16 (H Rept 105-188). House passed, amended, July 23. Senate passed, with amendment, July 30. Conference report filed in the House Oct. 7 (H Rept 105-313). House agreed to conference report Oct. 9. Senate agreed to conference report Oct. 9. President signed Oct. 27, 1997. President exercised line-item veto authority (H Doc 105-168), Nov. 1, 1997.

PL 105-67 (H J Res 75) A joint resolution to confer status as an honorary veteran of the U.S. Armed Forces on Leslie Townes "Bob" Hope. Introduced by Stump, R-Ariz., April 30, 1997. House Veterans' Affairs reported June 3 (H Rept 105-109). House passed, under suspension of the rules, June 3. Senate Veterans' Affairs reported Sept. 4 (no written report). Senate passed Sept. 9. President signed Oct. 30, 1997.

PL 105-68 (H J Res 101) A joint resolution making further continuing appropriations for the fiscal year 1998. Introduced by Livingston, R-La., Nov. 7, 1997. House Appropriations discharged. House passed Nov. 7. Senate passed Nov. 7. President signed Nov. 7, 1997.

PL 105-69 (H J Res 104) A joint resolution making further continuing appropriations for the fiscal year 1998. Introduced by Livingston, R-La., Nov. 9, 1997. House Appropriations discharged. House passed Nov. 9. Senate passed Nov. 9. President signed Nov. 9, 1997.

PL 105-70 (HR 2013) Designate the facility of the U.S. Postal Service located at 551 Kingstown Rd. in South Kingstown, R.I., as the "David B. Champagne Post Office Building." Introduced by Weygand, D-R.I., June 23, 1997. House passed, under suspension of the rules, Oct. 21. Senate passed Oct. 24. President signed Nov. 10, 1997.

PL 105-71 (H J Res 105) A joint resolution making further continuing appropriations for the fiscal year 1998. Introduced by Livingston, R-La., Nov. 10, 1997. House Appropriations discharged. House passed Nov. 10 (legislative day of Nov. 9). Senate passed Nov. 10. President signed Nov. 10, 1997.

PL 105-72 (S 1227) Amend Title I of the Employee Retirement Income Security Act of 1974 to clarify treatment of investment managers under such title. Introduced by Jeffords, R-Vt., Sept. 26, 1997. Senate passed Sept. 26. House passed, under suspension of the rules, Oct. 28. President signed Nov. 10, 1997.

PL 105-73 (HR 2464) Amend the Immigration and Nationality Act to exempt internationally adopted children under age ten from the immunization requirement. Introduced by McCollum, R-Fla., Sept. 11, 1997. House Judiciary reported, amended, Oct. 1 (H Rept 105-289). House passed, amended, under suspension of the rules, Oct. 21. Senate passed Nov. 4. President signed Nov. 12, 1997.

PL 105-74 (S 587) Require the secretary of the interior to exchange certain lands located in Hinsdale County, Colo. Introduced by Campbell, R-Colo., April 16, 1997. Senate Energy and Natural Resources reported, amended, Oct. 6 (S Rept 105-96). Senate passed, amended, Oct. 9. House passed, under suspension of the rules, Nov. 4. President signed Nov. 12, 1997.

PL 105-75 (S 588) Provide for the expansion of the Eagles Nest Wilderness within the Arapaho National Forest and the White River National Forest, Colo., to include land known as the Slate Creek Addition. Introduced by Campbell, R-Colo., April 16, 1997. Senate Energy and Natural Resources reported, amended, Oct. 6 (S Rept 105-97). Senate passed, amended, Oct. 9. House passed, under suspension of the rules, Nov. 4. President signed Nov. 12, 1997.

PL 105-76 (S 589) Provide for a boundary adjustment and land conveyance involving the Raggeds Wilderness, White River National Forest, Colo., to correct the effects of earlier erroneous land surveys. Introduced by Campbell, R-Colo., April 16, 1997. Senate Energy and Natural Resources reported, amended, Oct. 6 (S Rept 105-98). Senate passed, amended, Oct. 9. House passed, under suspension of the rules, Nov. 4. President signed Nov. 12, 1997.

PL 105-77 (S 591) Transfer the Dillon Ranger District in the Arapaho National Forest to the White River National Forest in Colorado. Introduced by Campbell, R-Colo., April 16, 1997. Senate Energy and Natural Resources reported, amended, Oct. 6 (S Rept 105-99). Senate passed, amended, Oct. 9. House passed, under suspension of the rules, Nov. 4. President signed Nov. 12, 1997.

PL 105-78 (HR 2264) Make appropriations for the departments of Labor, Health and Human Services, and Education, and related agencies for the fiscal year ending Sept. 30, 1998. Introduced by Porter, R-Ill., July 25, 1997. House Appropriations reported July 25 (H Rept 105-205). House passed, amended, Sept. 17. Senate passed, with amendment, Sept. 17. Conference report filed in the House Nov. 7 (H Rept 105-390). House agreed to conference report Nov. 7. Senate cleared Nov. 8. President signed Nov. 13, 1997.

PL 105-79 (HR 79) Provide for the conveyance of certain land in the Six Rivers National Forest in California for the benefit of the Hoopa Valley Tribe. Introduced by Riggs, R-Calif., Jan. 7, 1997. House Resources reported, amended, June 3 (H Rept 105-110). House passed, amended, under suspension of the rules, June 3. Senate Indian Affairs reported Oct. 29 (S Rept 105-117). Senate passed Nov. 4. President signed Nov. 13, 1997.

PL 105-80 (HR 672) Make technical amendments to certain provisions of Title 17, U.S. Code. Introduced by Coble, R-N.C., Feb. 11, 1997. House Judiciary reported, amended, March 17 (H Rept 105-25). House passed, amended, under suspension of the rules, March 18. Senate Judiciary discharged. Senate passed, with amendments, Oct. 30. House agreed to Senate amendments, under suspension of the rules, Nov. 4. President signed Nov. 13, 1997.

PL 105-81 (HR 708) Require the secretary of the interior to conduct a study concerning grazing use of certain land within and adjacent to Grand Teton National Park, Wyo., and to extend temporarily certain grazing privileges. Introduced by Cubin, R-Wyo., Feb. 12, 1997. House Resources reported, amended, Oct. 6 (H Rept 105-300). House passed, amended, under suspension of the rules, Oct. 21. Senate passed Nov. 4. President signed Nov. 13, 1997.

PL 105-82 (S 931) Designate the Marjory Stoneman Douglas Wilderness and the Ernest F. Coe Visitor Center. Introduced by Graham, D-Fla., June 18, 1997. Senate Energy and Natural Resources reported Sept. 2 (S Rept 105-68). Senate passed Sept. 16. House passed, under suspension of the rules, Nov. 4. President signed Nov. 13, 1997.

PL 105-83 (HR 2107) Make appropriations for the Department of the Interior and related agencies for the fiscal year ending Sept. 30, 1998. Introduced by Regula, R-Ohio, July 1, 1997. House Appropriations reported July 1 (H Rept 105-163). House passed, amended, July 15. Senate Appropriations reported, amended, July 22 (S Rept 105-56). Senate passed, with amendments, Sept. 18. Conference report filed in the House Oct. 22 (H Rept 105-337). House agreed to conference report Oct. 24. Senate agreed to conference report Oct. 28. President signed Nov. 14, 1997.

PL 105-84 (H J Res 106) A joint resolution making further continuing appropriations for the fiscal year 1998. Introduced by Livingston, R-La., Nov. 13, 1997. House Appropriations discharged. House passed Nov. 13. Senate passed Nov. 13. President signed Nov. 14, 1997.

PL 105-85 (HR 1119) Authorize appropriations for fiscal year 1998 for military activities of the Department of Defense, and to prescribe military personnel strengths for fiscal years 1998 and 1999. Introduced by Spence, R-S.C., March 19, 1997. House National Security reported, amended, June 16 (H Rept 105-132). House passed, amended, June 25. Senate passed, with amendments, July 11. Conference report filed in the House Oct. 23 (H Rept 105-340). House agreed to conference report Oct. 28. Senate agreed to conference report Nov. 6. President signed Nov. 18, 1997.

PL 105-86 (HR 2160) Make appropriations for Agriculture, Rural Development, Food and Drug Administration, and related agencies programs for the fiscal year ending Sept. 30, 1998. Introduced by Skeen, R-N.M., July 14, 1997. House Appropriations reported July 14 (H Rept 105-178). House passed, amended, July 24. Senate passed, with amendment, Sept. 3. Conference report filed in the House Sept. 17 (H Rept 105-252). House agreed to conference report Oct. 6. Senate agreed to conference report Oct. 29. President signed Nov. 18, 1997.

PL 105-87 (HR 282) Designate the U.S. Post Office building located at 153 East 110th St. in New York as the "Oscar Garcia Rivera Post Office Building." Introduced by Serrano, D-N.Y., Jan. 7, 1997. House passed, under suspension of the rules, Oct. 21. Senate Governmental Affairs reported Nov. 6 (no written report). Senate passed Nov. 9. President signed Nov. 19, 1997.

PL 105-88 (HR 681) Designate the U.S. Post Office building at 313 East Broadway in Glendale, Calif., as the "Carlos J. Moorhead Post Office Building." Introduced by Hyde, R-Ill., Feb. 11, 1997. House passed, under suspension of the rules, Oct. 21. Senate Governmental Affairs reported Nov. 6 (no written report). Senate passed Nov. 9. President signed Nov. 19, 1997.

PL 105-89 (HR 867) Promote the adoption of children in foster care. Introduced by Camp, R-Mich., Feb. 27, 1997. House Ways and Means reported, amended, April 28 (H Rept 105-77). House passed, amended, April 30. Senate passed, with amendment, Nov. 8. House agreed to Senate amendment, with amendment, pursuant to H Res 327 Nov. 13. Senate agreed to House amendment to Senate amendment Nov. 13. President signed Nov. 19, 1997.

PL 105-90 (HR 1057) Designate the building in Indianapolis that houses the operations of the Circle City Station Post Office as the "Andrew Jacobs Jr. Post Office Building." Introduced by Burton, R-Ind., March 13, 1997. House passed, under suspension of the rules, June 17. Senate Governmental Affairs discharged. Senate passed Nov. 9. President signed Nov. 19, 1997.

PL 105-91 (HR 1058) Designate the facility of the U.S. Postal Service under construction at 150 West Margaret Dr. in Terre Haute, Ind., as the "John T. Myers Post Office Building." Introduced by Burton, R-Ind., March 13, 1997. House passed, under suspension of the rules, June 17. Senate Governmental Affairs discharged. Senate passed Nov. 9. President signed Nov. 19, 1997.

PL 105-92 (HR 1377) Amend Title I of the Employee Retirement Income Security Act of 1974 to encourage retirement income savings. Introduced by Fawell, R-Ill., April 17, 1997. House Education and the Workforce reported, amended, May 20 (H Rept 105-104). House passed, amended, under suspension of the rules, May 21. Senate Labor and Human Resources discharged. Senate passed, with amendment, Nov. 7. House agreed to Senate amendment, under suspension of the rules, Nov. 9. President signed Nov. 19, 1997.

PL 105-93 (HR 1479) Designate the federal building and U.S. Courthouse at 300 Northeast First Ave. in Miami as the "David W. Dyer Federal Courthouse." Introduced by Hastings, D-Fla., April 29, 1997. House Transportation and Infrastructure reported, amended, July 31 (H Rept 105-227). House passed, amended, under suspension of the rules, Oct. 29. Senate Environment and Public Works discharged. Senate passed Nov. 9. President signed Nov. 19, 1997.

PL 105-94 (HR 1484) Redesignate the Dublin Federal Courthouse building in Dublin, Ga., as the "J. Roy Rowland Federal Courthouse." Introduced by Norwood, R-Ga., April 29, 1997. House Transportation and Infrastructure reported, amended, July 31 (H Rept 105-226). House passed, amended, under suspension of the rules, Oct. 29. Senate Environment and Public Works discharged. Senate passed Nov. 9. President signed Nov. 19, 1997.

PL 105-95 (HR 1747) Amend the John F. Kennedy Center Act to authorize the design and construction of additions to the parking garage and certain site improvements. Introduced by Shuster, R-Pa., May 22, 1997. House Transportation and Infrastructure reported, amended, June 12 (H Rept 105-130). House passed, amended, under suspension of the rules, June 17. Senate passed Nov. 7. President signed Nov. 19, 1997.

PL 105-96 (HR 1787) Assist in the conservation of Asian elephants by supporting and providing financial resources for the conservation programs of nations within the range of Asian elephants and projects of persons with demonstrated expertise in the conservation of Asian elephants. Introduced by Saxton, R-N.J., June 4, 1997. House Resources reported, amended, Sept. 23 (H Rept 105-266, Pt. 1). House International Relations discharged. House passed, amended, under suspension of the rules, Oct. 21. Senate Environment and Public Works reported Nov. 7 (no written report). Senate passed Nov. 8. President signed Nov. 19, 1997.

PL 105-97 (HR 2129) Designate the U.S. Post Office located at 150 North 3rd St. in Steubenville, Ohio, as the "Douglas Applegate Post Office." Introduced by Traficant, D-Ohio, July 9, 1997. House passed, under suspension of the rules, Oct. 21. Senate Governmental Affairs reported Nov. 6 (no written report). Senate passed Nov. 9. President signed Nov. 19, 1997.

PL 105-98 (HR 2367) Increase, effective Dec. 1, 1997, the rates of compensation for veterans with service-connected disabilities and the rates of dependency and indemnity compensation for the survivors of certain disabled veterans. Introduced by Stump, R-Ariz., July 31, 1997. House Veterans' Affairs reported Oct. 9 (H Rept 105-320). House passed, amended, Oct. 31. Senate passed Nov. 5. President signed Nov. 19, 1997.

PL 105-99 (HR 2564) Designate the U.S. Post Office located at 450 North Centre St. in Pottsville, Pa., as the "Peter J. McCloskey Postal Facility." Introduced by Holden, D-Pa., Sept. 26, 1997. House passed, under suspension of the rules, Oct. 21. Senate Governmental Affairs reported Nov. 6 (no written report). Senate passed Nov. 9. President signed Nov. 19, 1997.

PL 105-100 (HR 2607) Make appropriations for the government of the District of Columbia and other activities chargeable in whole or in part against the revenues of said District for the fiscal year ending Sept. 30, 1998. Introduced by Taylor, R-N.C., Oct. 6, 1997. House Appropriations reported Oct. 6 (H Rept 105-298). House passed, amended, Oct. 9. Senate passed, with amendments, Nov. 9. House agreed to the Senate amendment to the text, with an amendment, and disagreed to the Senate amendment to the title, Nov. 12. Senate receded from its amendment to the title Nov. 13. Senate agreed to the House amendment to the Senate amendment to the text Nov. 13. President signed Nov. 19, 1997.

PL 105-101 (S 813) Amend Chapter 91 of Title 18, U.S. Code, to provide criminal penalties for theft and willful vandalism at national cemeteries. Introduced by Thurmond, R-S.C., May 23, 1997. Senate Judiciary reported, amended, Oct. 23 (no written report). Senate passed, amended, Nov. 4. House passed, under suspension of the rules, Nov. 8. President signed Nov. 19, 1997.

PL 105-102 (HR 1086) Codify without substantive change laws related to transportation and to improve the U.S. Code. Introduced by Hyde, R-Ill., March 17, 1997. House Judiciary reported, amended, June 25 (H Rept 105-153). House passed, amended, under suspension of the rules, July 8. Senate Judiciary reported Sept. 18 (no written report). Senate passed Nov. 8. President signed Nov. 20, 1997.

PL 105-103 (HR 2813) Waive time limitations specified by law in order to allow the Medal of Honor to be awarded to Robert R. Ingram of Jacksonville, Fla., for acts of valor while a Navy Hospital Corpsman in the republic of Vietnam during the Vietnam War. Introduced by Fowler, R-Fla., Nov. 4, 1997. House passed, under suspension of the rules, Nov. 8. Senate passed Nov. 10. President signed Nov. 20, 1997.

PL 105-104 (H J Res 91) A joint resolution granting the consent of Congress to the Apalachicola-Chattahoochee-Flint River Basin Compact. Introduced by Barr, R-Ga., July 31, 1997. House Judiciary reported, amended, Oct. 31 (H Rept 105-369). House passed, amended, under suspension of the rules, Nov. 4. Senate passed Nov. 7. President signed Nov. 20, 1997.

PL 105-105 (H J Res 92) A joint resolution granting the consent of Congress to the Alabama-Coosa-Tallapoosa River Basin Compact. Introduced by Callahan, R-Ala., July 31, 1997. House Judiciary reported Oct. 31 (H Rept 105-370). House passed, amended, under suspension of the rules, Nov. 4. Senate passed Nov. 7. President signed Nov. 20, 1997.

PL 105-106 (S 669) Provide for the acquisition of the Plains Railroad Depot at the Jimmy Carter National Historic Site. Introduced by Coverdell, R-Ga., April 30, 1997. Senate Energy and Natural Resources reported June 26 (S Rept 105-39). Senate passed July 11. House passed, under suspension of the rules, Nov. 9. President signed Nov. 20, 1997.

PL 105-107 (S 858) Authorize appropriations for fiscal year 1998 for intelligence and intelligence-related activities of the federal government, the Community Management Account and the Central Intelligence Agency Retirement and Disability System. Introduced by Shelby, R-Ala., June 9, 1997. Senate Intelligence reported June 9 (S Rept 105-24). Senate Armed Services reported June 18 (no written report). Senate passed, amended, June 19. House passed with amendment July 17. Conference report filed in the House Oct. 28

(H Rept 105-350). Senate agreed to conference report Nov. 6. House agreed to conference report Nov. 7. President signed Nov. 20, 1997.

PL 105-108 (S 1231) Authorize appropriations for fiscal years 1998 and 1999 for the U.S. Fire Administration. Introduced by Frist, R-Tenn., Sept. 26, 1997. Senate Commerce, Science and Transportation reported Oct. 30 (S Rept 105-124). Senate passed Nov. 4. House passed, under suspension of the rules, Nov. 9. President signed Nov. 20, 1997.

PL 105-109 (S 1347) Permit the city of Cleveland to convey certain lands that the United States conveyed to the city. Introduced by Glenn, D-Ohio, Oct. 30, 1997. Senate Commerce, Science and Transportation discharged. Senate passed Nov. 8. House passed, under suspension of the rules, Nov. 9. President signed Nov. 20, 1997.

PL 105-110 (S 1377) Amend the act incorporating the American Legion to make a technical correction. Introduced by Hatch, R-Utah, Nov. 5, 1997. Senate passed Nov. 5. House passed, under suspension of the rules, Nov. 8. President signed Nov. 20, 1997.

PL 105-111 (HR 1090) Amend Title 38, U.S. Code, to allow revision of veterans benefits decisions based on clear and unmistakable error. Introduced by Evans, D-Ill., March 18, 1997. House Veterans' Affairs reported April 14 (H Rept 105-52). House passed, under suspension of the rules, April 16. Senate Veterans' Affairs discharged. Senate passed Nov. 10. President signed Nov. 21, 1997.

PL 105-112 (HR 1840) Provide a law enforcement exception to the prohibition on the advertising of certain electronic devices. Introduced by McCollum, R-Fla., June 10, 1997. House Judiciary reported June 26 (H Rept 105-162). House passed, under suspension of the rules, July 8. Senate Judiciary discharged. Senate passed Nov. 10. President signed Nov. 21, 1997.

PL 105-113 (HR 2366) Transfer to the secretary of agriculture the authority to conduct the census of agriculture. Introduced by Stenholm, D-Texas, July 31, 1997. House Agriculture reported Oct. 2 (H Rept 105-296, Pt. 1). House passed, under suspension of the rules, Oct. 21. Senate Governmental Affairs reported Nov. 7 (S Rept 105-141). Senate passed Nov. 10. President signed Nov. 21, 1997.

PL 105-114 (S 714) Extend and improve the Native American Veteran Housing Loan Pilot Program of the Department of Veterans Affairs, to extend certain authorities of the secretary of veterans affairs relating to services for homeless veterans, and to extend certain other authorities of the secretary. Introduced by Akaka, D-Hawaii, May 7, 1997. Senate Veterans' Affairs reported, amended, Oct. 30 (S Rept 105-123). Senate passed, amended, Nov. 5. House passed, with amendments, under suspension of the rules, Nov. 9. Senate agreed to House amendments Nov. 10. President signed Nov. 21, 1997.

PL 105-115 (S 830) Amend the Federal Food, Drug, and Cosmetic Act and the Public Health Service Act to improve the regulation of food, drugs, devices, and biological products. Introduced by Jeffords, R-Vt., June 5, 1997. Senate Labor and Human Resources reported, amended, July 1 (S Rept 105-43). Senate passed, amended, Sept. 24. House passed, with amendments, Oct. 7. Conference report filed in the House Nov. 9 (H Rept 105-399). Senate agreed to conference report Nov. 9. House agreed to conference report, under suspension of the rules, Nov. 9. President signed Nov. 21, 1997.

PL 105-116 (S 923) Amend Title 38, U.S. Code, to prohibit interment or memorialization in certain cemeteries of persons committing federal or state capital crimes. Introduced by Specter, R-Pa., June 17, 1997. Senate Veterans' Affairs discharged. Senate passed, amended, June 18. House Veterans' Affairs reported, with amendments, Oct. 9 (H Rept 105-319). House passed, with amendments, Oct. 31. Senate agreed to House amendments Nov. 10. President signed Nov. 21, 1997.

PL 105-117 (S 1258) Amend the Uniform Relocation Assistance and Real Property Acquisition Policies Act of 1970 to prohibit an alien who is not lawfully present in the United States from receiving assistance under that Act. Introduced by Bennett, R-Utah, Oct. 6, 1997. Senate Environment and Public Works reported, amended, Nov. 4 (no written report). Senate passed, amended, Nov. 8. House passed, under suspension of the rules, Nov. 9. President signed Nov. 21, 1997.

PL 105-118 (HR 2159) Make appropriations for foreign operations, export financing, and related programs for the fiscal year ending Sept. 30, 1998. Introduced by Callahan, R-Ala., July 14, 1997. House Appropriations reported

July 14 (H Rept 105-176). House passed, amended, Sept. 4. Senate passed, with amendment, Sept. 5. Conference report filed in the House Nov. 12 (H Rept 105-401). House agreed to conference report Nov. 13 (legislative day of Nov. 12). Senate agreed to conference report Nov. 13. President signed Nov. 26, 1997.

PL 105-119 (HR 2267) Make appropriations for the departments of Commerce, Justice, and State, the judiciary, and related agencies for the fiscal year ending Sept. 30, 1998. Introduced by Rogers, R-Ky., July 25, 1997. House Appropriations reported July 25 (H Rept 105-207). House passed, amended, Sept. 30. Senate passed, with amendment, Oct. 1. Conference report filed in the House Nov. 13 (H Rept 105-405). House agreed to conference report Nov. 13. Senate agreed to conference report Nov. 13. President signed Nov. 26, 1997. President exercised line-item veto authority, Dec. 2, 1997.

PL 105-120 (H J Res 103) A joint resolution waiving certain enrollment requirements with respect to certain specified bills of the 105th Congress. Introduced by Armey, R-Texas, Nov. 8, 1997. House Oversight discharged. House passed Nov. 10 (legislative day of Nov. 9). Senate passed Nov. 13. President signed Nov. 26, 1997.

PL 105-121 (S 1026) Reauthorize the Export-Import Bank of the United States. Introduced by Grams, R-Minn., July 17, 1997. Senate Banking, Housing, and Urban Affairs reported, amended, Sept. 10 (S Rept 105-76). Senate passed, amended, Sept. 16. House passed, with amendment, Oct. 6. Conference report filed in the House Nov. 7 (H Rept 105-392). Senate agreed to conference report Nov. 8. House agreed to conference report, under suspension of the rules, Nov. 9. President signed Nov. 26, 1997.

PL 105-122 (S 819) Designate the U.S. Courthouse at 200 South Washington St. in Alexandria, Va., as the "Martin V. B. Bostetter Jr. United States Courthouse." Introduced by Warner, R-Va., June 2, 1997. Senate Environment and Public Works reported June 5 (no written report). Senate passed June 12. House passed, under suspension of the rules, Nov. 13. President signed Dec. 1, 1997.

PL 105-123 (S 833) Designate the federal building courthouse at Public Square and Superior Ave. in Cleveland as the "Howard M. Metzenbaum United States Courthouse." Introduced by Lautenberg, D-N.J., June 5, 1997. Senate Environment and Public Works reported June 26 (no written report). Senate passed July 25. House passed, under suspension of the rules, Nov. 13. President signed Dec. 1, 1997.

PL 105-124 (S 1228) Provide for a ten-year circulating commemorative coin program to commemorate each of the fifty states. Introduced by Chafee, R-R.I., Sept. 26, 1997. Senate Banking, Housing, and Urban Affairs reported, amended, Oct. 31 (S Rept 105-130). Senate passed, amended, Nov. 9. House passed, under suspension of the rules, Nov. 13. President signed Dec. 1, 1997.

PL 105-125 (S 1354) Amend the Communications Act of 1934 to provide for the designation of common carriers not subject to the jurisdiction of a state commission as eligible telecommunications carriers. Introduced by McCain, R-Ariz., Oct. 31, 1997. Senate Commerce, Science and Transportation reported Nov. 8 (no written report). Senate passed Nov. 9. House passed, under suspension of the rules, Nov. 13. President signed Dec. 1, 1997.

PL 105-126 (S 1378) Extend the authorization of use of official mail in the location and recovery of missing children. Introduced by Warner, R-Va., Nov. 5, 1997. Senate passed Nov. 5. House passed, under suspension of the rules, Nov. 12. President signed Dec. 1, 1997.

PL 105-127 (S 1417) Provide for the design, construction, furnishing, and equipping of a Center for Performing Arts within the complex known as the New Mexico Hispanic Cultural Center. Introduced by Domenici, R-N.M., Nov. 7, 1997. Senate passed Nov. 7. House passed, under suspension of the rules, Nov. 13. President signed Dec. 1, 1997.

PL 105-128 (S 1505) Make technical and conforming amendments to the Museum and Library Services Act. Introduced by Jeffords, R-Vt., Nov. 9, 1997. Senate passed Nov. 9. House passed, under suspension of the rules, Nov. 13. President signed Dec. 1, 1997.

PL 105-129 (S 1507) Amend the National Defense Authorization Act for fiscal year 1998 to make certain technical corrections. Introduced by Thurmond, R-S.C., Nov. 9, 1997. Senate passed Nov. 9. House passed, under suspension of the rules, Nov. 12. President signed Dec. 1, 1997.

PL 105-130 (S 1519) Provide a six-month extension of highway, highway safety, and transit programs pending enactment of a law reauthorizing the Intermodal Surface Transportation Efficiency Act of 1991. Introduced by Bond, R-Mo., Nov. 10, 1997. Senate passed Nov. 10. House passed, under suspension of the rules, Nov. 12. President signed Dec. 1, 1997.

PL 105-131 (HR 1254) Designate the U.S. Post Office building located at 1919 West Bennett St. in Springfield, Mo., as the "John N. Griesemer Post Office Building." Introduced by Blunt, R-Mo., April 9, 1997. House passed, amended, under suspension of the rules, Sept. 16. Senate Governmental Affairs discharged. Senate passed Nov. 13. President signed Dec. 2, 1997.

PL 105-132 (S 156) Provide certain benefits of the Pick-Sloan Missouri River Basin program to the Lower Brule Sioux Tribe. Introduced by Daschle, D-S.D., Jan. 21, 1997. Senate Energy and Natural Resources discharged. Senate Indian Affairs reported Nov. 8 (S Rept 105-146). Senate passed, amended, Nov. 9. House Resources discharged. House passed Nov. 13. President signed Dec. 2, 1997.

PL 105-133 (S 476) Provide for the establishment of not less than 2,500 Boys and Girls Clubs of America facilities by the year 2000. Introduced by Hatch, R-Utah, March 19, 1997. Senate Judiciary reported May 1 (no written report). Senate passed May 15. House Judiciary discharged. House passed, with amendment, Nov. 13. Senate agreed to House amendment Nov. 13. President signed Dec. 2, 1997.

PL 105-134 (S 738) Reform the statutes relating to Amtrak, and to authorize appropriations for Amtrak. Introduced by Hutchison, R-Texas, May 14, 1997. Senate Commerce, Science and Transportation reported, amended, Sept. 24 (S Rept 105-85). Senate passed, amended, Nov. 7. House passed, with amendment, under suspension of the rules, Nov. 13. Senate agreed to House amendment Nov. 13. President signed Dec. 2, 1997.

PL 105-135 (S 1139) Reauthorize the programs of the Small Business Administration. Introduced by Bond, R-Mo., Aug. 19, 1997. Senate Small Business reported Aug. 19 (S Rept 105-62). Senate passed, amended, Sept. 9. House passed, with amendments, Sept. 29. Senate agreed to House amendment, with amendment, Oct. 31. House agreed to Senate amendment to House amendment, under suspension of the rules, Nov. 9. President signed Dec. 2, 1997.

PL 105-136 (S 1161) Amend the Immigration and Nationality Act to authorize appropriations for refugee and entrant assistance for fiscal years 1998 and 1999. Introduced by Abraham, R-Mich., Sept. 10, 1997. Senate passed Sept. 10. House failed to pass, under suspension of the rules, Oct. 1 (two-thirds required). House passed, under suspension of the rules, Nov. 13. President signed Dec. 2, 1997.

PL 105-137 (S 1193) Amend Chapter 443 of Title 49, U.S. Code, to extend the authorization of the aviation insurance program. Introduced by Gorton, R-Wash., Sept. 18, 1997. Senate Commerce, Science and Transportation reported, amended, Nov. 6 (S Rept 105-140). Senate passed, amended, Nov. 8. House passed Nov. 13. President signed Dec. 2, 1997.

PL 105-138 (S 1559) Provide for the design, construction, furnishing, and equipping of a Center for Historically Black Heritage within Florida A&M University. Introduced by Mack, R-Fla., Nov. 13, 1997. Senate passed Nov. 13. House passed Nov. 13. President signed Dec. 2, 1997.

PL 105-139 (S 1565) Make technical corrections to the Nicaraguan Adjustment and Central American Relief Act. Introduced by Abraham, R-Mich., Nov. 13, 1997. Senate passed Nov. 13. House passed Nov. 13. President signed Dec. 2, 1997.

PL 105-140 (S J Res 39) Provide for the convening of the second session of the 105th Congress. Introduced by Lott, R-Miss., Nov. 13, 1997. Senate passed Nov. 13. House passed Nov. 13. President signed Dec. 2, 1997.

PL 105-141 (HR 1493) Require the attorney general to establish a program in local prisons to identify, prior to arraignment, criminal aliens and aliens who are unlawfully present in the United States. Introduced by Gallegly, R-Calif., April 30, 1997. House Judiciary reported, amended, Oct. 23 (H Rept 105-338). House passed, under suspension of the rules, Nov. 4. Senate Judiciary discharged. Senate passed Nov. 13. President signed Dec. 5, 1997.

PL 105-142 (HR 2626) Clarify the Pilot Records Improvement Act of 1996. Introduced by Duncan, R-Tenn., Oct. 7, 1997. House Transportation and Infrastructure reported, amended, Oct. 31 (H Rept 105-372). House

passed, amended, under suspension of the rules, Nov. 9. Senate passed Nov. 13. President signed Dec. 5, 1997.

PL 105-143 (HR 1604) Provide for the division, use, and distribution of judgment funds of the Ottawa and Chippewa Indians of Michigan pursuant to dockets numbered 18-E, 58, 364 and 18-R before the Indian Claims Commission. Introduced by Kildee, D-Mich., May 14, 1997. House Resources reported, amended Oct. 28 (H Rept 105-352). House passed, amended, under suspension of the rules, Nov. 4. Senate passed, with amendments, Nov. 9. House agreed to Senate amendments Nos. 1-60, 62, and 63 and disagreed to Senate amendment No. 61, under suspension of the rules Nov. 13. Senate receded from its amendment No. 61 Nov. 13. President signed Dec. 15, 1997.

PL 105-144 (HR 2979) Authorize acquisition of certain real property for the Library of Congress. Introduced by Thomas, R-Calif., Nov. 9, 1997. House passed, amended, under suspension of the rules. Nov. 12. Senate passed Nov. 13. President signed Dec. 15, 1997.

PL 105-145 (H J Res 95) Grant the consent of Congress to the Chickasaw Trail Economic Development Compact. Introduced by Bryant, R-Tenn., Oct. 6, 1997. House Judiciary reported Nov. 7 (H Rept 105-389). House passed, under suspension of the rules, Nov. 12. Senate passed Nov. 13. President signed Dec. 15, 1997.

PL 105-146 (HR 1658) Reauthorize and amend the Atlantic Striped Bass Conservation Act and related laws. Introduced by Saxton, R-N.J., May 16, 1997. House Resources reported, amended, July 8 (H Rept 105-169). House passed, amended, under suspension of the rules, July 8. Senate Commerce, Science and Transportation reported, with amendments, Nov. 8 (S Rept 105-149). Senate passed, with amendments, Nov. 10. House agreed to Senate amendments, under suspension of the rules, Nov. 13. President signed Dec. 16, 1997.

PL 105-147 (HR 2265) Amend the provisions of Titles 17 and 18, U.S. Code, to provide greater copyright protection by amending criminal copyright infringement provisions. Introduced by Goodlatte, R-Va., July 25, 1997. House Judiciary reported, amended, Oct. 23 (H Rept 105-339). House passed, amended, under suspension of the rules, Nov. 4. Senate Judiciary discharged. Senate passed Nov. 13. President signed Dec. 16, 1997.

PL 105-148 (HR 2476) Amend Title 49, U.S. Code, to require the National Transportation Safety Board and individual foreign air carriers to address the needs of families of passengers involved in aircraft accidents involving foreign air carriers. Introduced by Underwood, D-Guam, Sept. 15, 1997. House Transportation and Infrastructure reported, amended, Oct. 31 (H Rept 105-371). House passed, amended, under suspension of the rules, Nov. 9. Senate passed Nov. 13. President signed Dec. 16, 1997.

PL 105-149 (HR 3025) Amend the federal charter for Group Hospitalization and Medical Services, Inc. Introduced by Davis, R-Va., Nov. 12, 1997. House passed, under suspension of the rules, Nov. 13. Senate passed Nov. 13. President signed Dec. 16, 1997.

PL 105-150 (HR 3034) Amend section 13031 of the Consolidated Omnibus Budget Reconciliation Act of 1985, relating to customs user fees, to allow the use of such fees to provide for customs inspection personnel in connection with the arrival of passengers in Florida. Introduced by Shaw, R-Fla., Nov. 12, 1997. House passed, under suspension of the rules, Nov. 13. Senate passed Nov. 13. President signed Dec. 16.

PL 105-151 (H J Res 96) Grant the consent and approval of Congress for Maryland, Virginia, and the District of Columbia to amend the Washington Metropolitan Area Transit Regulation Compact. Introduced by Davis, R-Va., Oct. 9, 1997. House Judiciary reported Nov. 8 (H Rept 105-396). House passed, under suspension of the rules, Nov. 12. Senate passed Nov. 13. President signed Dec. 16, 1997.

PL 105-152 (HR 2796) Authorize the reimbursement of members of the Army deployed to Europe in support of operations in Bosnia for certain out-of-pocket expenses incurred by the members during the period beginning on Oct. 1, 1996, and ending on May 31, 1997. Introduced by Clayton, D-N.C., Nov. 4, 1997. House passed, amended, under suspension of the rules, Nov. 13. Senate passed Nov. 13. President signed Dec. 17, 1997.

PL 105-153 (HR 2977) Amend the Federal Advisory Committee Act to clarify public disclosure requirements that are applicable to the National

Academy of Sciences and the National Academy of Public Administration. Introduced by Horn, R-Calif., Nov. 9, 1997. House passed, under suspension of the rules, Nov. 10 (legislative day of Nov. 9). Senate passed Nov. 13. President signed Dec. 17, 1997.

105th Congress—1998

PL 105-154 (S 1575) Rename the Washington National Airport located in the District of Columbia and Virginia as the "Ronald Reagan Washington National Airport." Introduced by Coverdell, R-Ga., Jan. 27, 1998. Senate passed Feb. 4. House passed Feb. 5. President signed Feb. 6, 1998.

PL 105-155 (HR 1271) Authorize the Federal Aviation Administration's research, engineering, and development programs for fiscal years 1998 through 2000, and for other purposes. Introduced by Morella, R-Md., April 10, 1997. House Science reported, amended, April 21 (H Rept 105-61). House passed, amended, April 29. Senate Commerce, Science and Transportation reported, amended, Nov. 9 (S Rept 105-152). Senate passed, amended, Nov. 13. House agreed to amendments, under suspension of the rules, Feb. 3, 1998. President signed Feb. 11, 1998.

PL 105-156 (HR 3042) Amend the Morris K. Udall Scholarship and Excellence in National Environmental and Native American Public Policy Act of 1992 to establish the United States Institute for Environmental Conflict Resolution to conduct environmental conflict resolution and training, and for other purposes. Introduced by Kolbe, R-Ariz., on Nov. 13, 1997. House Education and the Workforce and Resources discharged. House passed Nov. 13. Senate passed Jan. 29, 1998. President signed Feb. 11, 1998.

PL 105-157 (S 1349) Authorize the secretary of transportation to issue a certificate of documentation with appropriate endorsement for employment in the coastwise trade for the vessel Prince Nova, and for other purposes. Introduced by Dodd, D-Conn., on Oct. 30, 1997. Senate Commerce, Science and Transportation discharged. Senate passed Nov. 13. House passed Feb. 3, 1998. President signed Feb. 11, 1998.

PL 105-158 (S 1564) Provide redress for inadequate restitution of assets, seized by the U.S. government during World War II, which belonged to victims of the Holocaust, and for other purposes. Introduced by D'Amato, R-N.Y., on Nov. 13, 1997. Senate passed Nov. 13. House International Relations discharged. House passed Jan. 27, 1998. President signed Feb. 13, 1998.

PL 105-159 (HR 2631) Disapprove the cancellations transmitted by the president Oct. 6, 1997, regarding PL 105-45, fiscal 1998 military construction appropriations. Introduced by Skeen, R-N.M., on Oct. 7, 1997. House passed, under suspension of the rules, Nov. 8. Senate passed Nov. 9. President vetoed Nov. 13, 1997. House Appropriations discharged Feb. 5, 1998. House overrode president's veto Feb. 5. Senate overrode president's veto Feb. 25. Bill became law Feb. 25, 1998.

PL 105-160 (S 927) Reauthorize the Sea Grant Program. Introduced by Snowe, R-Maine, on June 17, 1997. Senate Commerce, Science and Transportation reported Nov. 8 (S Rept 105-150). Senate passed, amended, Nov. 13. House passed, amended, under suspension of the rules, Feb. 11, 1998. Senate agreed to House amendment Feb. 12. President signed March 6, 1998.

PL 105-161 (S 916) Designate the U.S. Post Office building located at 750 Highway 28 East in Taylorsville, Miss., as the "Blaine H. Eaton Post Office Building." Introduced by Cochran, R-Miss., on June 17, 1997. Senate Government Affairs discharged. Senate passed Oct. 9. House passed, under suspension of the rules, Feb. 24, 1998. President signed March 9, 1998.

PL 105-162 (S 985) Designate the post office located at 194 Ward St. in Patterson, N.J., as the "Larry Doby Post Office." Introduced by Torricelli, D-N.J., on June 27, 1997. Senate Governmental Affairs discharged. Senate passed, amended, Oct. 9. House passed, under suspension of the rules, Feb. 24, 1998. President signed March 9, 1998.

PL 105-163 (HR 595) Designate the federal building and U.S. courthouse located at 475 Mulberry St. in Macon, Ga., as the "William Augustus Bootle Federal Building and United States Courthouse." Introduced by Chambliss, R-Ga., on Feb. 5, 1997. House Transportation and Infrastructure reported July 31 (H Rept 105-233). House passed, under suspension of the rules, Nov. 13. Senate passed March 6, 1998. President signed March 20, 1998.

PL 105-164 (HR 3116) Address the Year 2000 computer problems with regard to financial institutions, to extend examination parity to the Director of the Office of Thrift Supervision and the National Credit Union Administration, and for other purposes. Introduced by Leach, R-Iowa, on Jan. 28, 1998. House Banking and Financial Services reported, amended, Feb. 24 (H Rept 105-417). Senate passed March 6. President signed March 20, 1998.

PL 105-165 (S 347) Designate the federal building located at 61 Forsyth St. S.W., in Atlanta, Ga., as the "Sam Nunn Atlanta Federal Center." Introduced by Cleland, D-Ga., on Feb. 24, 1997. Senate Environment and Public Works reported June 5 (no written report). Senate passed June 12. House Transportation and Infrastructure discharged. House passed, amended, March 3, 1998. Senate agreed to House amendments March 6. President signed March 20, 1998.

PL 105-166 (S 758) Make certain technical corrections to the Lobbying Disclosure Act of 1995. Introduced by Levin, D-Mich., on May 16, 1997. Senate Governmental Affairs reported Nov. 8, 1997 (S Rept 105-147). Senate passed Nov. 13. House passed, under suspension of the rules, March 18, 1998. President signed April 6, 1998.

PL 105-167 (S 750) Consolidate certain mineral interests in the National Grasslands in Billings County, N.D., through the exchange of federal and private mineral interests to enhance land management capabilities and environmental and wildlife protection, and for other purposes. Introduced by Dorgan, D-N.D., on May 15, 1997. Senate Energy and Natural Resources reported, amended, Sept. 30 (S Rept 105-92). Senate passed, amended, Oct. 6. House passed, under suspension of the rules, March 30, 1998. President signed April 13, 1998.

PL 105-168 (S 419) Provide surveillance, research, and services aimed at prevention of birth defects, and for other purposes. Introduced by Bond, R-Mo., on March 11, 1997. Senate Labor and Human Resources discharged. Senate passed, amended, June 12. House passed, under suspension of the rules, March 10, 1998. President signed April 21, 1998.

PL 105-169 (HR 1116) Provide for the conveyance of the reversionary interest of the United States in certain lands to the Clint Independent School District and the Fabens Independent School District. Introduced by Reyes, D-Texas, on March 18, 1997. House passed, under suspension of the rules, Sept. 29. Senate Foreign Relations reported March 3, 1998 (no written report). Senate passed April 1. President signed April 24, 1998.

PL 105-170 (HR 2843) Direct the administrator of the Federal Aviation Administration to reevaluate the equipment in medical kits carried on, and to make a decision regarding requiring automatic external defibrillators to be carried on, aircraft operated by air carriers, and for other purposes. Introduced by Duncan, R-Tenn., on Nov. 6, 1997. House Transportation and Infrastructure reported March 20, 1998 (H Rept 105-456). House passed, amended, under suspension of the rules, March 24. Senate Commerce, Science and Transportation discharged. Senate passed April 3. President signed April 24, 1998.

PL 105-171 (HR 3226) Authorize the secretary of agriculture to convey certain lands and improvements in the state of Virginia, and for other purposes. Introduced by Goodlatte, R-Va., on Feb. 12, 1998. House passed under suspension of the rules, March 24. Senate passed April 3. President signed April 24, 1998.

PL 105-172 (S 493) Amend Title 18, U.S. Code, with respect to scanning receivers and similar devices. Introduced by Kyl, R-Ariz., on March 20, 1997. Senate Judiciary reported, amended, Sept. 18 (no written report). Senate passed, amended, Nov. 10. House Judiciary discharged. House passed, amended, Feb. 26, 1998. Senate agreed to House amendments April 1. President signed April 24, 1998.

PL 105-173 (S 1178) Amend the Immigration and Nationality Act to modify and extend the visa waiver pilot program, and to provide for the collection of data with respect to the number of nonimmigrants who remain in the United States after the expiration of the period of stay authorized by the attorney general. Introduced by Abraham, R-Mich., on Sept. 15, 1997. Senate passed, amended, Sept. 26. House passed, amended, March 25, 1998. Senate agreed to House amendments April 1. President signed April 27, 1998.

PL 105-174 (HR 3579) Make emergency supplemental appropriations for the fiscal year ending Sept. 30, 1998, and for other purposes. Introduced by Livingston, R-La., on March 27, 1998. Appropriations reported March 27

(H Rept 105-469). House passed, amended, March 31. Senate passed, amended, March 31. Senate asked for conference March 31. House agreed to conference April 23. Conference report filed in the House on April 30 (H Rept 105-504). House agreed to conference report April 30. Senate agreed to conference report April 30. President signed May 1, 1998.

PL 105-175 (H J Res 102) Express the sense of the Congress on the occasion of the 50th anniversary of the founding of the modern state of Israel and reaffirming the bonds of friendship and cooperation between the United States and Israel. Introduced by Lantos, D-Calif., on Nov. 7, 1997. House passed, under suspension of the rules, April 28, 1998. Senate passed April 29. President signed May 11, 1998.

PL 105-176 (HR 3301) Amend Chapter 51 of Title 31, U.S. Code, to allow the secretary of the Treasury greater discretion with regard to the placement of the required inscriptions on quarter dollars issued under the Fifty States Commemorative Coin Program. Introduced by Castle, R-Del., on March 2, 1998. House Banking and Financial Services discharged. House passed March 27. Senate passed May 19. President signed May 29, 1998.

PL 105-177 (HR 2472) Extend certain programs under the Energy Policy and Conservation Act. Introduced by Schaffer, R-Colo., on Sept. 15, 1997. Commerce reported Sept. 26 (H Rept 105-275). House passed, under suspension of the rules, Sept. 29. Senate passed, amended, Sept. 30. House agreed to Senate amendment Nov. 9. Senate agreed to House amendment Feb. 12, 1998. Senate insisted on its amendment and asked for conference Feb. 12. House agreed to Senate amendment, under suspension of the rules, May 19. President signed June 1, 1998.

PL 105-178 (HR 2400) Authorize funds for federal-aid highways, highway safety programs, and transit programs, and for other purposes. Introduced by Shuster, R-Pa., on Sept. 4, 1997. House Transportation and Infrastructure reported, amended, March 25, 1998 (H Rept 105-467, Pt. I). House Transportation and Infrastructure filed supplemental report March 27 (Part II). House Ways and Means reported, amended, March 27 (Part III). House Budget discharged. House passed, amended, April 1. Senate passed, amended, April 2. Senate asked for conference April 2. House disagreed with Senate amendment and agreed to conference April 3. Conference report filed May 22 (H Rept 105-550). House agreed to conference report May 22. Senate agreed to conference report May 22. President signed June 9, 1998.

PL 105-179 (HR 824) Redesignate the federal building located at 717 Madison Place, N.W., in the District of Columbia, as the "Howard T. Markey National Courts Building," introduced by Hyde, R-Ill., on Feb. 25, 1997. House Transportation and Infrastructure reported July 28, 1997 (H Rept 105-211). House passed, under suspension of the rules, Sept. 23, 1997. Senate Environment and Public Works reported May 21, 1998 (no written report). Senate passed June 2. President signed June 16, 1998.

PL 105-180 (HR 3565) Amend Part L of the Omnibus Crime Control and Safe Streets Act of 1968. Introduced by McCollum, R-Fla., on March 26, 1998. House Judiciary reported April 21 (H Rept 105-486). House passed, under suspension of the rules, April 21. Senate passed May 15. President signed June 16, 1998.

PL 105-181 (S 1605) Establish a matching grant program to help state and local jurisdictions purchase armor vests for use by law enforcement departments. Introduced by Campbell, R-Colo., on Feb. 4, 1998. Senate Judiciary reported, amended, Feb. 26 (no written report). Senate passed, amended, March 11. House Judiciary discharged. House passed, amended, May 12. Senate agreed to House amendments May 15. President signed June 16, 1998.

PL 105-182 (S 423) Extend the legislative authority for the Board of Regents of Gunston Hall to establish a memorial to honor George Mason. Introduced by Robb, D-Va., on March 11, 1997. Senate Energy and Natural Resources reported June 26 (S Rept 105-38). Senate passed July 11. House Resources reported Oct. 31 (H Rept 105-363). House passed, under suspension of the rules, June 9, 1998. President signed June 19, 1998.

PL 105-183 (S 1244) Amend Title 11, U.S. Code, to protect certain charitable contributions, and for other purposes. Introduced by Grassley, R-Iowa, on Oct. 1, 1997. House Judiciary reported, amended, Feb. 26, 1998 (no written report). Senate passed, amended, May 13. House passed June 3. President signed June 19, 1998.

PL 105-184 (HR 1847) Improve the criminal law relating to fraud against consumers. Introduced by Goodlatte, R-Va., on June 10, 1997. House Judiciary

reported, amended, June 26 (H Rept 105-158). House passed, amended, under suspension of the rules, July 8. Senate Judiciary reported, amended, Oct. 9 (no written report). Senate passed, amended, Nov. 9. House agreed to Senate amendment, under suspension of the rules, June 16, 1998. President signed June 23, 1998.

PL 105-185 (S 1150) Ensure that federally funded agricultural research, extension, and education address high-priority concerns with national or multistate significance, to reform, extend, and eliminate certain agricultural research programs, and for other purposes. Introduced by Lugar, R-Ind., on Sept. 5, 1997. Senate Agriculture, Nutrition and Forestry reported Sept. 5 (S Rept 105-73). Senate passed, amended, Oct. 29. House passed, amended, Feb. 24, 1998. House asked for conference Feb. 24. Senate disagreed with House amendment and agreed to conference Feb. 27. Conference report filed April 22 (H Rept 105-492). Senate agreed to conference report May 12. House agreed to conference report June 4. President signed June 23, 1998.

PL 105-186 (S 1900) Establish a commission to examine issues pertaining to the disposition of Holocaust-era assets in the United States before, during, and after World War II, and to make recommendations to the president on further action, and for other purposes. Introduced by D'Amato, R-N.Y., on April 1, 1998. Senate Banking, Housing and Urban Affairs reported, amended, April 30 (no written report). Senate passed, amended, May 1. House passed, amended, June 9. Senate agreed to House amendment June 10. President signed June 23, 1998.

PL 105-187 (HR 3811) Establish felony violations for the failure to pay legal child support obligations, and for other purposes. Introduced by Hyde, R-Ill., on May 7, 1998. House passed, under suspension of the rules, May 12. Senate passed June 5. President signed June 24, 1998.

PL 105-188 (S 2069) Permit the mineral leasing of Native American land located within the Fort Berthold Indian Reservation in any case in which there is consent from a majority interest in the parcel of land under consideration for lease. Introduced by Dorgan, D-N.D., on May 12, 1998. Senate Indian Affairs reported, amended, June 5 (S Rept 105-205). Senate passed, amended, June 10. House passed June 24. President signed July 7, 1998.

PL 105-189 (HR 651) Extend the deadline under the Federal Power Act for the construction of a hydroelectric project located in the state of Washington, and for other purposes. Introduced by White, R-Wash., on Feb. 6, 1997. House Commerce reported March 11 (H Rept 105-12). House passed, under suspension of the rules, March 11. Senate Energy and Natural Resources reported Nov. 4 (S Rept 105-133). Senate passed June 25, 1998. President signed July 14, 1998.

PL 105-190 (HR 652) Extend the deadline under the Federal Power Act for the construction of a hydroelectric project located in the state of Washington, and for other purposes. Introduced by White, R-Wash., on Feb. 6, 1997. House Commerce reported March 11 (H Rept 105-13). House passed, under suspension of the rules, March 11. Senate Energy and Natural Resources reported Nov. 4 (S Rept 105-134). Senate passed June 25, 1998. President signed July 14, 1998.

PL 105-191 (HR 848) Extend the deadline under the Federal Power Act applicable to the construction of the AuSable Hydroelectric Project in New York, and for other purposes. Introduced by McHugh, R-N.Y., on Feb. 26, 1997. House Commerce reported June 7 (H Rept 105-122). House passed, under suspension of the rules, June 10. Senate Energy and Natural Resources reported Nov. 4 (S Rept 105-135). Senate passed June 25, 1998. President signed July 14, 1998.

PL 105-192 (HR 1184) Extend the deadline under the Federal Power Act for the construction of the Bear Creek Hydroelectric Project in the state of Washington, and for other purposes. Introduced by Metcalf, R-Wash., on March 20, 1997. House Commerce reported June 7 (H Rept 105-123). House passed, amended, under suspension of the rules, June 10. Senate Energy and Natural Resources reported Nov. 4 (S Rept 105-136). Senate passed June 25, 1998. President signed July 14, 1998.

PL 105-193 (HR 1217) Extend the deadline under the Federal Power Act for the construction of a hydroelectric project located in the state of Washington, and for other purposes. Introduced by Metcalf, R-Wash., on March 21, 1997. House Commerce reported June 7 (H Rept 105-124). House passed, under suspension of the rules, June 10. Senate Energy and Natural Resources reported Nov. 4 (S Rept 105-137). Senate passed June 25, 1998. President signed July 14, 1998.

PL 105-194 (S 2282) Amend the Arms Export Control Act, and for other purposes. Introduced by McConnell, R-Ky., on July 9, 1998. Senate passed, amended, July 9. House passed, amended, under suspension of the rules, July 14. Senate agreed to House amendment July 14. President signed July 14, 1998.

PL 105-195 (HR 960) Validate certain conveyances in the City of Tulare, Tulare County, Calif., and for other purposes. Introduced by Thomas, R-Calif., March 5, 1997. House passed, amended, July 8. Senate Energy and Natural Resources reported Oct. 31. Senate passed June 25, 1998. President signed July 16, 1998.

PL 105-196 (HR 2202) Amend the Public Health Service Act to revise and extend the bone marrow donor program, and for other purposes. Introduced by Young, R-Fla., July 17, 1997. House Commerce reported, amended, May 18, 1998 (H Rept 105-538). House passed, amended, May 19. Senate Labor and Human Resources discharged. Senate passed June 24. President signed July 16, 1998.

PL 105-197 (HR 2864) Require the secretary of labor to establish a program under which employers may consult with state officials respecting compliance with occupational safety and health requirements. Introduced by Ballenger, R-N.C., Nov. 7, 1997. House Education and the Workforce reported, amended, March 17, 1998 (H Rept 105-444). House passed, amended, March 17. Senate passed June 24. President signed July 16, 1998.

PL 105-198 (HR 2877) Amend the Occupational Safety and Health Act of 1970. Introduced by Ballenger, R-N.C., Nov. 7, 1997. House Education and the Workforce reported, amended, March 17, 1998 (H Rept 105-445). House passed, amended, March 17. Senate passed June 24. President signed July 16, 1998.

PL 105-199 (HR 3035) Establish an advisory commission to provide advice and recommendations on the creation of an integrated, coordinated federal policy designed to prepare for and respond to serious drought emergencies. Introduced by Skeen, R-N.M., Nov. 12, 1997. House Transportation and Infrastructure reported, amended, May 22, 1998 (H Rept 105-554, Pt. 1). House Resources discharged. House Agriculture discharged. House passed, amended, under suspension of the rules June 16. Senate passed June 24. President signed July 16, 1998.

PL 105-200 (HR 3130) Provide for an alternative penalty procedure for states that fail to meet federal child support data processing requirements, to reform federal incentive payments for effective child support performance, and to provide for a more flexible penalty procedure for states that violate interjurisdictional adoption requirements. Introduced by Shaw, R-Fla., Jan. 28, 1998. House Ways and Means reported, amended, Feb. 27 (H Rept 105-422). House passed, amended, March 5. Senate Finance discharged. Senate passed, amended, April 2. House agreed to Senate amendments, with amendments, June 25. Senate agreed to House amendments to Senate amendments June 26. President signed July 16, 1998.

PL 105-201 (H J Res 113) Approve the location of a Martin Luther King Jr. memorial in the nation's capital. Introduced by Morella, R-Md., March 4, 1998. House Resources reported June 22 (H Rept 105-589). House passed June 22. Senate passed June 25. President signed July 16, 1998.

PL 105-202 (S 731) Extend the legislative authority for construction of the National Peace Garden memorial, and for other purposes. Introduced by Bumpers, D-Ark., May 8, 1997. Senate Energy and Natural Resources reported June 26, 1997 (S Rept 105-40). Senate passed July 11. House Resources reported Oct. 31 (H Rept 105-362). House passed, amended, Nov. 13. Senate agreed to House amendment June 25, 1998. President signed July 16, 1998.

PL 105-203 (HR 1635) Establish within the U.S. National Park Service the National Underground Railroad Network to Freedom program, and for other purposes. Introduced by Stokes, D-Ohio, May 15, 1997. House Resources reported, amended, June 3, 1998 (H Rept 105-559). House passed, amended, under suspension of the rules June 9. Senate Energy and Natural Resources discharged. Senate passed June 25. President signed July 21, 1998.

PL 105-204 (S 2316) Require the secretary of energy to submit to Congress a plan to ensure that all amounts accrued on the books of the U.S. Enrichment Corp. for the disposition of depleted uranium hexafluoride will be used to treat and recycle depleted uranium hexafluoride. Introduced by McConnell, R-Ky., July 15, 1998. Senate passed, amended, July 16. House passed by unanimous consent July 20. President signed July 21, 1998.

PL 105-205 (HR 1316) Amend Chapter 87 of Title 5, U.S. Code, with respect to the order of precedence to be applied in the payment of life insurance benefits. Introduced by Collins, R-Ga., April 14, 1997. House Government Reform and Oversight reported, amended, June 18 (H Rept 105-134). House passed, amended, June 24. Senate Governmental Affairs reported Nov. 6 (no written report). Senate passed June 18, 1998. President signed July 22, 1998.

PL 105-206 (HR 2676) Amend the Internal Revenue Code of 1986 to restructure and reform the IRS, and for other purposes. Introduced by Archer, R-Texas, Oct. 21, 1997. House Ways and Means reported, amended, Oct. 31 (H Rept 105-364, Pt. 1). House Government Reform and Oversight discharged. House Rules discharged. House passed, amended, Nov. 5. Senate Finance reported, amended, April 22, 1998 (S Rept 105-174). Senate passed, amended, May 7. Conference report filed in House June 24 (H Rept 105-599). House agreed to conference report June 25. Senate agreed to conference report July 9. President signed July 22, 1998.

PL 105-207 (HR 1273) Authorize appropriations for fiscal years 1998 and 1999 for the National Science Foundation. Introduced by Schiff, R-N.M., April 10, 1997. House Science reported, amended, April 21 (H Rept 105-63). House passed, amended, April 24. Senate Labor and Human Resources discharged. Senate passed, amended, May 12, 1998. House agreed to Senate amendment, under suspension of the rules, July 14. President signed July 29, 1998.

PL 105-208 (HR 1439) Facilitate the sale of certain land in Tahoe National Forest, in the state of California, to Placer County, California. Introduced by Doolittle, R-Calif., April 24, 1997. House Resources reported, amended, June 3 (H Rept 105-114). House passed, amended, under suspension of the rules, June 3. Senate Energy and Natural Resources reported June 26, 1998 (S Rept 105-231). Senate passed July 17. President signed July 29, 1998.

PL 105-209 (HR 1460) Allow for election of the delegate from Guam by other than separate ballot. Introduced by Underwood, D-Guam, April 24, 1997. House Resources reported, amended, Sept. 18 (H Rept 105-253). House passed, amended, under suspension of the rules, Sept. 23. Senate Energy and Natural Resources reported June 5, 1998 (S Rept 105-203). Senate passed July 17. President signed July 29, 1998.

PL 105-210 (HR 1779) Make a minor adjustment in the exterior boundary of the Devil's Backbone Wilderness in the Mark Twain National Forest, Missouri, to exclude a small parcel of land containing improvements. Introduced by Blunt, R-Mo., June 4, 1997. House Agriculture reported Oct. 2 (H Rept 105-295, Pt. 1). House Resources discharged Oct. 2. House passed, under suspension of the rules, Oct. 21. Senate Energy and Natural Resources reported June 26, 1998 (S Rept 105-232). Senate passed July 17. President signed July 29, 1998.

PL 105-211 (HR 2165) Extend the deadline under the Federal Power Act applicable to the construction of FERC Project Number 3862 in the state of Iowa. Introduced by Leach, R-Iowa, July 15, 1997. House Commerce reported Sept. 26 (H Rept 105-273). House passed, under suspension of the rules, Nov. 13. Senate Energy and Natural Resources reported July 2, 1998 (S Rept 105-237). Senate passed July 17. President signed July 29, 1998.

PL 105-212 (HR 2217) Extend the deadline under the Federal Power Act applicable to the construction of FERC Project Number 9248 in the state of Colorado. Introduced by McInnis, R-Colo., July 22, 1997. House Commerce reported May 6, 1998 (H Rept 105-509). House passed, under suspension of the rules, May 12. Senate Energy and Natural Resources reported July 2 (S Rept 105-238). Senate passed July 17. President signed July 29, 1998.

PL 105-213 (HR 2841) Extend the time required for the construction of a hydroelectric project. Introduced by Bunning, R-Ky., Nov. 6, 1997. House Commerce reported May 6, 1998 (H Rept 105-510). House passed, amended, under suspension of the rules, May 12. Senate Energy and Natural Resources reported July 2 (S Rept 105-239). Senate passed July 17. President signed July 29, 1998.

PL 105-214 (HR 2870) Amend the Foreign Assistance Act of 1961 to facilitate protection of tropical forests through debt reduction with developing countries with tropical forests. Introduced by Portman, R-Ohio, Nov. 7, 1997. House International Relations reported, amended, March 13, 1998 (H Rept 105-443). House passed, amended, March 19. Senate Foreign Relations discharged. Senate passed, amended, July 14. House agreed to Senate amendment July 15. President signed July 29, 1998.

PL 105-215 (HR 3156) Present a congressional gold medal to Nelson Rolihlahla Mandela. Introduced by Houghton, R-N.Y., Feb. 4, 1998. House passed, under suspension of the rules, June 16. Senate passed July 14. President signed July 29, 1998.

PL 105-216 (S 318) Require automatic cancellation and notice of cancellation rights with respect to private mortgage insurance, which is required as a condition for entering into a residential mortgage transaction, to abolish the Thrift Depositor Protection Oversight Board, and for other purposes. Introduced by D'Amato, R-N.Y., Feb. 12, 1997. House Banking, Housing, and Urban Affairs reported, amended, Oct. 31 (H Rept 105-129). Senate passed, amended, Nov. 9. Senate passed, amended, Nov. 9. House passed, amended, under suspension of the rules, July 14, 1998. Senate agreed to House amendments, with amendment, July 15. House agreed to Senate amendments, amended, July 16. President signed July 29, 1998.

PL 105-217 (HR 39) Reauthorize the African Elephant Conservation Act. Introduced by Young, R-Alaska, Jan. 7, 1997. House Resources reported April 21 (H Rept 105-59). House passed, under suspension of the rules, April 23. Senate Environment and Public Works reported June 25, 1998 (no written report). Senate passed July 23. President signed Aug. 5, 1998.

PL 105-218 (HR 643) Designate the United States courthouse to be constructed at the corner of Superior and Huron Rds., in Cleveland, Ohio, as the "Carl B. Stokes United States Courthouse." Introduced by LaTourette, R-Ohio, Feb. 6, 1997. House Transportation and Infrastructure reported July 31 (H Rept 105-231). House passed, under suspension of the rules, Sept. 23. Senate Environment and Public Works reported July 22, 1998 (no written report). Senate passed July 31. President signed Aug. 7, 1998.

PL 105-219 (HR 1151) Amend the Federal Credit Union Act to clarify existing law and ratify the longstanding policy of the National Credit Union Administration Board with regard to field of membership of federal credit unions. Introduced by LaTourette, R-Ohio, March 20, 1997. House Banking and Financial Services reported, amended, March 30, 1998 (H Rept 105-472). House passed, amended, under suspension of the rules, April 1. Senate Banking, Housing, and Urban Affairs reported, amended, May 21 (S Rept 105-193). Senate passed, amended, July 28. House agreed to Senate amendment under suspension of the rules Aug. 4. President signed Aug. 7, 1998.

PL 105-220 (HR 1385) Consolidate, coordinate, and improve employment, training, literacy, and vocational rehabilitation programs in the United States. Introduced by McKeon, R-Calif., April 17, 1997. House Education and the Workforce reported, amended, May 8 (H Rept 105-93). House passed, amended, May 16. Senate Labor and Human Resources discharged May 1, 1998. Senate passed, amended, May 5. House disagreed to Senate amendment and agreed to a conference May 22. Conference report filed in House July 29 (H Rept 105-659). Senate agreed to conference report July 30. House agreed to conference report July 31. President signed Aug. 7, 1998.

PL 105-221 (HR 3152) Provide that certain volunteers at private nonprofit food banks are not employees for purposes of the Fair Labor Standards Act of 1938. Introduced by Campbell, R-Calif., Feb. 4, 1998. House Education and the Workforce discharged. House passed, amended, June 25. Senate Labor and Human Resources discharged. Senate passed July 29. President signed Aug. 7, 1998.

PL 105-222 (HR 3731) Designate the auditorium located within the Sandia Technology Transfer Center in Albuquerque, N.M., as the "Steve Schiff Auditorium." Introduced by Skeen, R-N.M., April 23, 1998. National Security discharged July 15. House passed July 16. Senate passed July 30. President signed Aug. 7, 1998.

PL 105-223 (HR 4354) Establish the United States Capitol Police Memorial Fund on behalf of the families of Detective John Michael Gibson and Private First Class Jacob Joseph Chestnut of the United States Capitol Police. Introduced by Gingrich, R-Ga., July 30, 1998. House Oversight and Ways and Means discharged. House passed, amended, July 31. Senate passed July 31. President signed Aug. 7, 1998.

PL 105-224 (HR 434) Provide for the conveyance of small parcels of land in the Carson National Forest and the Santa Fe National Forest, New Mexico, to the village of El Rito and the town of Jemez Springs, N.M. Introduced by Richardson, D-N.M., Jan. 9, 1997. House Resources reported, amended, Oct. 30 (H Rept 105-359). House passed, amended, under suspension of the rules, Nov. 4. Senate Energy and Natural Resources reported, amended, July 2, 1998 (S Rept 105-236). Senate passed, amended, July 17. House agreed to Senate amendment under suspension of the rules Aug. 3. President signed Aug. 12, 1998.

PL 105-225 (HR 1085) Revise, codify, and enact without substantive change certain general and permanent laws, related to patriotic and national observances, ceremonies, and organizations, as Title 36, U.S. Code, "Patriotic and National Observances, Ceremonies and Organizations." Introduced by Hyde, R-Ill., March 17, 1997. House Judiciary reported, amended, Oct. 21 (H Rept 105-326). House passed, amended, Feb. 3, 1998. Senate Judiciary reported July 16 (no written report). Senate passed July 30. President signed Aug. 12, 1998.

PL 105-226 (HR 3504) Amend the John F. Kennedy Center Act to authorize appropriations for the John F. Kennedy Center for the Performing Arts and to further define the criteria for capital repair and operation and maintenance. Introduced by Shuster, R-Pa., March 19, 1998. Transportation and Infrastructure reported, amended, May 13 (H Rept 105-533). House passed, amended, under suspension of the rules, June 3. Senate Environment and Public Works reported July 22 (no written report). Senate passed July 31. President signed Aug. 12, 1998.

PL 105-227 (HR 4237) Amend the District of Columbia Convention Center and Sports Arena Authorization Act of 1995 to revise the revenues and activities covered under such act. Introduced by Norton, D-D.C., July 16, 1998. House Government Reform and Oversight and Rules discharged. House passed July 30. Senate passed July 31. President signed Aug. 4, 1998.

PL 105-228 (S 2344) Amend the Agricultural Market Transition Act to provide for the advance payment, in full, of the fiscal year 1999 payments otherwise required under production flexibility contracts. Introduced by Coverdell, R-Ga., July 22, 1998. Senate Agriculture, Nutrition and Forestry discharged. Senate passed July 30. House passed, under suspension of the rules, Aug. 3. President signed Aug. 12, 1998.

PL 105-229 (HR 765) Ensure maintenance of a herd of wild horses in Cape Lookout National Seashore. Introduced by Jones, R-N.C., Feb. 13, 1997. House Resources reported July 14 (H Rept 105-179). House passed, under suspension of the rules, July 22. Senate Energy and Natural Resources reported, amended, Oct. 28 (S Rept 105-115). Senate passed, amended, July 17, 1998. House agreed to Senate amendment, under suspension of the rules, Aug. 3. President signed Aug. 13, 1998.

PL 105-230 (HR 872) Establish rules governing product liability actions against raw materials and bulk component suppliers to medical device manufacturers. Introduced by Gekas, R-Pa., Feb. 27, 1997. House Judiciary reported, amended, May 22, 1998 (H Rept 105-549, Pt. 1). House Commerce reported, amended, July 14 (Part 2). House passed, amended, July 30. Senate passed July 30. President signed Aug. 13, 1998.

PL 105-231 (S 1759) Grant a federal charter to the American GI Forum of the United States. Introduced by Hatch, R-Utah, March 13, 1998. Senate Judiciary discharged. Senate passed, amended, July 31. House passed, under suspension of the rules, Aug. 3. President signed Aug. 13, 1998.

PL 105-232 (S 1800) Designate the federal building and U.S. courthouse located at 85 Marconi Boulevard in Columbus, Ohio, as the "Joseph P. Kinneary United States Courthouse." Introduced by Glenn, D-Ohio, March 19, 1998. Senate Environment and Public Works reported May 21 (no written report). Senate passed June 2. House Transportation and Infrastructure reported July 14 (H Rept 105-619). House passed, under suspension of the rules, Aug. 4. President signed Aug. 13, 1998.

PL 105-233 (S 2143) Amend Chapter 45 of Title 28, U.S. Code to authorize the administrative assistant to the Chief Justice to accept voluntary services. Introduced by Hatch, R-Utah, June 9, 1998. Senate Judiciary reported, amended, July 9 (no written report). Senate passed, amended, July 16. House passed, amended, under suspension of the rules, Aug. 3. President signed Aug. 13, 1998.

PL 105-234 (HR 3824) Amend the Fastener Quality Act to exempt from its coverage certain fasteners approved by the Federal Aviation Administration for use in aircraft. Introduced by Sensenbrenner, R-Wis., May 11, 1998. House Science reported, amended, June 9 (H Rept 105-574, Pt. 1). House Commerce discharged. House passed, amended, under suspension of the rules, June 16. Senate Commerce, Science and Transportation reported, amended, July 27 (S Rept 105-267). Senate passed, amended, July 31. House agreed to Senate amendments Aug. 6. President signed Aug. 14, 1998.

PL 105-235 (S J Res 54) Find the government of Iraq in unacceptable and material breach of its international obligations. Introduced by Lott, R-Miss.,

June 25, 1998. Senate Foreign Relations reported July 27 (no written report). Senate passed, amended, July 31. House passed, under suspension of the rules, Aug. 3. President signed Aug. 14, 1998.

PL 105-236 (HR 629) Grant the consent of the Congress to the Texas Low-Level Radioactive Waste Disposal Compact. Introduced by Barton, R-Texas, Feb. 6, 1997. House Commerce reported July 15 (H Rept 105-181). House passed, amended, Oct. 7. Senate passed, amended, April 1, 1998. Conference report filed in the House July 16 (H Rept 105-630). House agreed to conference report July 29. Senate agreed to conference report Sept. 2. President signed Sept. 20, 1998.

PL 105-237 (HR 4059) Make appropriations for military construction, family housing, and base realignment and closure for the Department of Defense for the fiscal year ending September 30, 1999. Introduced by Packard, R-Calif., June 16, 1998. House Appropriations reported June 16 (H Rept 105-578). House passed June 22. Senate passed, amended, June 25. Conference report filed in the House on July 24 (H Rept 105-647). House agreed to conference report July 29. Senate agreed to conference report Sept. 1. President signed Sept. 20, 1998.

PL 105-238 (S 1683) Transfer administrative jurisdiction over part of the Lake Chelan National Recreation Area from the secretary of the interior to the secretary of agriculture for inclusion in the Wenatchee National Forest. Introduced by Gorton, R-Wash., Feb. 26, 1998. Senate Energy and Natural Resources reported, amended, June 10 (S Rept 105-228). Senate passed, amended, July 17. House passed, under suspension of the rules, Sept. 9. President signed Sept. 23, 1998.

PL 105-239 (S 1883) Direct the secretary of the interior to convey the Marion National Fish Hatchery and the Claude Harris National Aquacultural Research Center to the state of Alabama. Introduced by Shelby, R-Ala., March 31, 1998. Senate Environment and Public Works reported, amended, July 24 (S Rept 105-263). Senate passed, amended, July 31. House passed, under suspension of the rules, Sept. 9. President signed Sept. 23, 1998.

PL 105-240 (H J Res 128) Make continuing appropriations for fiscal year 1999. Introduced by Livingston, R-La., Sept. 16, 1998. House passed Sept. 17. Senate passed Sept. 17. President signed Sept. 25, 1998.

PL 105-241 (S 2112) Make the Occupational Safety and Health Act of 1970 applicable to the United States Postal Service in the same manner as any other employer. Introduced by Enzi, R-Wyo., May 22, 1998. Senate Labor and Human Resources reported July 28 (no written report). Senate passed July 31. House passed, under suspension of the rules, Sept. 14. President signed Sept. 28, 1998.

PL 105-242 (HR 1856) Amend the Fish and Wildlife Act of 1956 to direct the secretary of the interior to conduct a volunteer pilot project at one national wildlife refuge in each U.S. Fish and Wildlife Service region. Introduced by Saxton, R-N.J., June 10, 1997. House Resources reported, amended, Oct. 21 (H Rept 105-329). House passed, amended, under suspension of the rules, Nov. 4. Senate Environment and Public Works reported, amended, July 28, 1998 (no written report). Senate passed, amended, Sept. 11. House agreed to Senate amendments Sept. 18. President signed Oct. 5, 1998.

PL 105-243 (S 1695) Authorize the secretary of the interior to study the suitability and feasibility of designating the Sand Creek Massacre National Historic Site in the state of Colorado as a unit of the National Park System. Introduced by Campbell, R-Colo., March 2, 1998. Senate Energy and Natural Resources reported, amended, July 10 (S Rept 105-244). Senate passed, amended, July 17. House Resources reported Sept. 9 (H Rept 105-687). House passed Sept. 18. President signed Oct. 6, 1998.

PL 105-244 (HR 6) Extend the authorization of programs under the Higher Education Act of 1965. Introduced by McKeon, R-Calif., on Jan. 7, 1997. House Education and the Workforce reported, amended, April 17, 1998 (H Rept 105-481). House passed, amended, May 6. Senate Labor and Human Resources discharged May 7. Senate passed, amended, July 9. Conference report filed in the House on Sept. 25 (H Rept 105-750). House agreed to conference report Sept. 28. Senate agreed to conference report Sept. 29. President signed Oct. 7, 1998.

PL 105-245 (HR 4060) Make appropriations for energy and water development for the fiscal year ending Sept. 30, 1999. Introduced by McDade, R-Pa., June 16, 1998. House Appropriations reported June 16 (H Rept 105-581). House passed, amended, June 22. Senate passed, amended, June 23. Con-

ference report filed in the House on Sept. 25 (H Rept 105-749). House agreed to conference report Sept. 28. Senate agreed to conference report Sept. 29. President signed Oct. 7, 1998.

PL 105-246 (S 1379) Amend Section 552 of Title 5, U.S. Code, and the National Security Act of 1947 to require disclosure under the Freedom of Information Act regarding certain persons and to disclose Nazi war criminal records without impairing any investigation or prosecution conducted by the Department of Justice or certain intelligence matters. Introduced by DeWine, R-Ohio, Nov. 5, 1997. Senate Judiciary reported, amended, March 5, 1998 (no written report). Senate passed, amended, June 19. House passed Aug. 6. President signed Oct. 8, 1998.

PL 105-247 (HR 3096) Correct a provision relating to termination of benefits for convicted persons. Introduced by Greenwood, R-Pa., Jan. 27, 1998. House Education and the Workforce reported March 17 (H Rept 105-446). House passed March 24. Senate Governmental Affairs reported Aug. 25 (S Rept 105-296). Senate passed Sept. 28. President signed Oct. 9, 1998.

PL 105-248 (HR 4382) Amend the Public Health Service Act to revise and extend the program for mammography quality standards. Introduced by Bliley, R-Va., Aug. 3, 1998. House Commerce reported, amended, Sept. 14 (H Rept 105-713). House passed, amended, under suspension of the rules, Sept. 15. Senate passed Sept. 25. President signed Oct. 9, 1998.

PL 105-249 (H J Res 133) Make further continuing appropriations for fiscal year 1999. Introduced by Livingston, R-La., Oct. 9, 1998. House Appropriations discharged. House passed Oct. 9. Senate passed Oct. 9. President signed Oct. 9, 1998.

PL 105-250 (S 1355) Designate the United States courthouse located at 141 Church St. in New Haven, Conn. as the "Richard C. Lee United States Courthouse." Introduced by Lieberman, D-Conn., Oct. 31, 1997. Senate Environment and Public Works reported May 21, 1998 (no written report). Senate passed June 2. House passed, amended, under suspension of the rules, Sept. 23. Senate agreed to House amendments Sept. 30. President signed Oct. 9, 1998.

PL 105-251 (S 2022) Provide for the improvement of interstate criminal justice identification, information, communications, and forensics. Introduced by DeWine, R-Ohio, April 3, 1998. Senate Judiciary reported, amended, May 21 (no written report). Senate passed, amended, July 13. House passed, amended, under suspension of the rules, Oct. 7. Senate agreed to House amendments Oct. 8. President signed Oct. 9, 1998.

PL 105-252 (S 2071) Extend a quarterly financial report program administered by the secretary of commerce. Introduced by Thompson, R-Tenn., May 13, 1998. Senate Governmental Affairs reported July 8 (S Rept 105-241). Senate passed Sept. 10. House Government Reform and Oversight discharged. House passed Sept. 28. President signed Oct. 9, 1998.

PL 105-253 (H J Res 131) Waive certain enrollment requirements for the remainder of the 105th Congress with respect to any bill or joint resolution making general or continuing appropriations for fiscal year 1999. Introduced by Solomon, R-N.Y., Oct. 7, 1998. House Oversight discharged. House passed Oct. 8. Senate passed Oct. 9. President signed Oct. 12, 1998.

PL 105-254 (H J Res 134) Make further continuing appropriations for fiscal year 1999. Introduced by Livingston, R-La., Oct. 12, 1998. House Appropriations discharged. House passed Oct. 12. Senate passed Oct. 12. President signed Oct. 12, 1998.

PL 105-255 (HR 3007) Establish the Commission on the Advancement of Women in Science, Engineering, and Technology Development. Introduced by Morella, R-Md., Nov. 9, 1997. House Science reported, amended, June 3, 1998 (H Rept 105-562, Pt. 1). House passed, amended, under suspension of the rules, Sept. 14. Senate passed Oct. 1. President signed Oct. 14, 1998.

PL 105-256 (HR 4068) Make certain technical corrections in laws relating to Native Americans. Introduced by Young, R-Alaska, June 16, 1998. House Resources reported, amended, Sept. 18 (H Rept 105-733). House passed, amended, under suspension of the rules, Sept. 23. Senate passed Oct. 1. President signed Oct. 14, 1998.

PL 105-257 (H J Res 135) Make further continuing appropriations for fiscal year 1999. Introduced by Livingston, R-La., Oct. 14, 1998. Appropriations discharged. House passed Oct. 14. Senate passed Oct. 14. President signed Oct. 14, 1998.

PL 105-258 (S 414) Amend the Shipping Act of 1984 to encourage competition in international shipping and growth of United States exports. Introduced by Hutchison, R-Texas, March 10, 1997. Senate Commerce, Science and Transportation reported, amended, July 31 (S Rept 105-61). Senate passed, amended, April 22, 1998. House passed, amended, under suspension of the rules, Aug. 4. Senate agreed to House amendment Oct. 1. President signed Oct. 14, 1998.

PL 105-259 (HR 4658) Extend the date by which an automated entry-exit control system must be developed. Introduced by Smith, R-Texas, Oct. 1, 1998. House Judiciary discharged. House passed Oct. 1. Senate passed Oct. 8. President signed Oct. 15, 1998.

PL 105-260 (H J Res 136) Make further continuing appropriations for fiscal year 1999. Introduced by Livingston, R-La., Oct. 16, 1998. House Appropriations discharged. House passed Oct. 16. Senate passed Oct. 16. President signed Oct. 16, 1998.

PL 105-261 (HR 3616) Authorize appropriations for fiscal year 1999 for military activities of the Department of Defense and prescribe military personnel strengths for fiscal year 1999. Introduced by Spence, R-S.C., April 1, 1998. House National Security reported, amended, May 12 (H Rept 105-532). House passed, amended, May 21. Senate passed, with amendments, June 25. Conference report filed in the House on Sept. 22 (H Rept 105-736). House agreed to conference report Sept. 24. Senate agreed to conference report Oct. 1. President signed Oct. 17, 1998.

PL 105-262 (HR 4103) Make appropriations for the Department of Defense for the fiscal year ending Sept. 30, 1999. Introduced by Young, R-Fla., June 22, 1998. House Appropriations reported June 22 (H Rept 105-591). House passed, amended, June 24. Senate passed, amended, July 30. Conference report filed in the House Sept. 25 (H Rept 105-746). House agreed to conference report Sept. 28. Senate agreed to conference report Sept. 29. President signed Oct. 17, 1998.

PL 105-263 (HR 449) Provide for the orderly disposal of certain federal lands in Clark County, Nevada, and provide for the acquisition of environmentally sensitive lands in the state of Nevada. Introduced by Ensign, R-Nev., Jan. 20, 1997. House Resources reported, amended, April 23 (H Rept 105-68). House passed, amended, under suspension of the rules April 23. Senate Energy and Natural Resources reported Aug. 25, 1998 (S Rept 105-291). Senate passed Oct. 2. President signed Oct. 19, 1998.

PL 105-264 (HR 930) Require federal employees to use federal travel charge cards for all payments of expenses of official government travel; amend Title 31, U.S. Code, to establish requirements for prepayment audits of federal agency transportation expenses; authorize reimbursement of federal agency employees for taxes incurred on travel or transportation reimbursements; and authorize test programs for the payment of federal employee travel and relocation expenses. Introduced by Horn, R-Calif., March 5, 1997. House passed, amended, under suspension of the rules, April 16. Senate Governmental Affairs reported, amended, Aug. 25, 1998 (S Rept 105-295). Senate passed, with amendments, Sept. 1. House agreed to Senate amendments under suspension of the rules Oct. 5. President signed Oct. 19, 1998.

PL 105-265 (HR 1481) Amend the Great Lakes Fish and Wildlife Restoration Act of 1990 to provide for implementation of recommendations of the U.S. Fish and Wildlife Service contained in the Great Lakes Fishery Restoration Study Report. Introduced by LaTourette, R-Ohio, on April 29, 1997. House Resources reported, amended, Sept. 15, 1998 (H Rept 105-715). House passed, amended, under suspension of the rules Sept. 23. Senate passed Oct. 2. President signed Oct. 19, 1998.

PL 105-266 (HR 1836) Amend Chapter 89 of Title 5, U.S. Code, to improve administration of sanctions against unfit health care providers under the Federal Employees Health Benefits Program. Introduced by Burton, R-Ind., June 10, 1997. House Government Reform and Oversight reported, amended, Nov. 4 (H Rept 105-374). House passed, amended, under suspension of the rules Nov. 4. Senate Governmental Affairs reported, amended, July 21, 1998 (S Rept 105-257). Senate passed, amended, Sept. 30. House agreed to Senate amendments under suspension of the rules Oct. 5. President signed Oct. 19, 1998.

PL 105-267 (HR 3381) Direct the secretaries of agriculture and the interior to exchange land and other assets with Big Sky Lumber Co. Introduced by

Hill, R-Mont., March 5, 1998. House Resources reported, amended, Sept. 16 (H Rept 105-723, Pt. 1). House Agriculture discharged. House passed, amended, under suspension of the rules, Sept. 23. Senate passed Oct. 2. President signed Oct. 19, 1998.

PL 105-268 (HR 3790) Require the secretary of the Treasury to mint coins in commemoration of the bicentennial of the Library of Congress. Introduced by Thomas, R-Calif., May 5, 1998. House passed under suspension of the rules Aug. 4. Senate Banking, Housing, and Urban Affairs discharged. Senate passed Oct. 6. President signed Oct. 19, 1998.

PL 105-269 (HR 4248) Authorize the use of receipts from the sale of the Migratory Bird Hunting and Conservation Stamp to promote additional stamp purchases. Introduced by Cunningham, R-Calif., July 16, 1998. House passed, amended, under suspension of the rules, Sept. 28. Senate passed Oct. 6. President signed Oct. 19, 1998.

PL 105-270 (S 314) Provide a process for identifying the functions of the federal government that are not inherently governmental. Introduced by Thomas, R-Wyo., Feb. 12, 1997. Senate Governmental Affairs reported, amended, July 28, 1998 (S Rept 105-269). Senate passed, amended, July 30. House passed under suspension of the rules Oct. 5. President signed Oct. 19, 1998.

PL 105-271 (S 2392) Encourage the disclosure and exchange of information about computer processing problems, solutions, test practices and test results in connection with the transition to the year 2000. Introduced by Bennett, R-Utah, July 30, 1998. Senate Judiciary reported, amended, Sept. 17 (no written report). Senate passed, amended, Sept. 28. House passed Oct. 1. President signed Oct. 19, 1998.

PL 105-272 (HR 3694) Authorize appropriations for fiscal year 1999 for intelligence and intelligence-related activities of the U.S. government, the Community Management Account, and the Central Intelligence Agency Retirement and Disability System. Introduced by Gross, R-Fla., April 21, 1998. House Intelligence reported, amended, May 5 (H Rept 105-508). House passed, amended, May 7. Senate Intelligence discharged. Senate passed, with amendment, June 26. Conference report filed in the House Oct. 5 (H Rept 105-780). House agreed to conference report Oct. 7. Senate agreed to conference report Oct. 8. President signed Oct. 20, 1998.

PL 105-273 (H J Res 137) Make further continuing appropriations for the fiscal year 1999. Introduced by Livingston, R-La., Oct. 19, 1998. House Appropriations discharged. House passed Oct. 19. Senate passed Oct. 20. President signed Oct. 20, 1998.

PL 105-274 (HR 4566) Make technical and clarifying amendments to the National Capital Revitalization and Self-Government Improvement Act of 1997. Introduced by Davis, R-Va., Sept. 15, 1998. House passed, amended, Oct. 10, under suspension of the rules. Senate passed Oct. 14. President signed Oct. 21, 1998.

PL 105-275 (HR 4112) Make appropriations for the legislative branch for the fiscal year ending Sept. 30, 1999. Introduced by Walsh, R-N.Y., June 23, 1998. House Appropriations reported June 23 (H Rept 105-595). House passed, amended, June 25. Senate passed, amended, July 21. Conference report filed in the House Sept. 22 (H Rept 105-734). House agreed to conference report Sept. 24. Senate agreed to conference report Sept. 25. President signed Oct. 21, 1998.

PL 105-276 (HR 4194) Make appropriations for the departments of Veterans Affairs and Housing and Urban Development, and for sundry independent agencies, boards, commissions, corporations, and offices for the fiscal year ending Sept. 30, 1999. Introduced by Lewis, R-Calif., July 8, 1998. House Appropriations reported July 8, 1998 (H Rept 105-610). House passed, amended, July 29. Senate passed, amended, July 30. Conference report filed in the House Oct. 5 (H Rept 105-769). House agreed to conference report Oct. 6. Senate agreed to conference report Oct. 8. President signed Oct. 21, 1998.

PL 105-277 (HR 4328) Make appropriations for the Department of Transportation and related agencies for the fiscal year ending Sept. 30, 1999. Introduced by Wolf, R-Va., July 24, 1998. House Appropriations reported July 24 (H Rept 105-648). House passed, amended, July 30. Senate passed, amended, July 30. Conference report filed in the House Oct. 19 (H Rept 105-825). House agreed to conference report Oct. 20. Senate agreed to conference report Oct. 21. President signed Oct. 21, 1998.

PL 105-278 (HR 2616) Amend Titles VI and X of the Elementary and Secondary Education Act of 1965 to improve and expand charter schools. Introduced by Riggs, R-Calif., Oct. 6, 1997. House Education and the Workforce reported, amended, Oct. 14 (H Rept 105-321). House passed, amended, Nov. 7. Senate Labor and Human Resources discharged. Senate passed, amended, Oct. 8, 1998. House agreed to Senate amendment, under suspension of the rules, Oct. 10. President signed Oct. 22, 1998.

PL 105-279 (HR 1659) Provide for the expeditious completion of the acquisition of private mineral interests within the Mount St. Helens National Volcanic Monument mandated by the 1982 act that established the monument. Introduced by Smith, R-Wash., May 16, 1997. House Resources reported, amended, Sept. 11, 1998 (H Rept 105-704). House passed, amended, under suspension of the rules, Sept. 23. Senate passed Oct. 7. President signed Oct. 23, 1998.

PL 105-280 (HR 2411) Provide for a land exchange involving the Cape Cod National Seashore and extend the authority for the Cape Cod National Seashore Advisory Commission. Introduced by Delahunt, D-Mass., Sept. 5, 1997. House Resources reported, amended, June 5, 1998 (H Rept 105-568). House passed, amended, June 22, under suspension of the rules. Senate Energy and Natural Resources reported Sept. 25 (S Rept 105-392). Senate passed Oct. 7. President signed Oct. 26, 1998.

PL 105-281 (HR 2886) Provide for a demonstration project in the Stanislaus National Forest, Calif., under which a private contractor will perform multiple resource management activities for that unit of the National Forest System. Introduced by Doolittle, R-Calif., on Nov. 7, 1997. House Resources reported, amended, May 12, 1998 (H Rept 105-527). House passed, amended, under suspension of the rules May 12. Senate Energy and Natural Resources reported, amended, Aug. 25 (S Rept 105-292). Senate passed, amended, Oct. 2. House agreed to Senate amendment Oct. 10. President signed Oct. 26, 1998.

PL 105-282 (HR 3796) Authorize the secretary of agriculture to convey the administrative site for the Rogue River National Forest and use the proceeds for the construction or improvement of offices and support buildings for the Rogue River National Forest and the Bureau of Land Management. Introduced by Smith, R-Ore., on May 5, 1998. House Resources reported June 3 (H Rept 105-561). House passed June 16 under suspension of the rules. Senate Energy and Natural Resources reported, with amendment, Aug. 25 (S Rept 105-293). Senate passed, amended, Oct. 2. House agreed to Senate amendment Oct. 10. President signed Oct. 26, 1998.

PL 105-283 (HR 4081) Extend the deadline under the Federal Power Act applicable to the construction of a hydroelectric project in the state of Arkansas. Introduced by Hutchinson, R-Ark., on June 18, 1998. House Commerce reported Sept. 25 (H Rept 105-748). House passed Sept. 28 under suspension of the rules. Senate passed Oct. 7. President signed Oct. 26, 1998.

PL 105-284 (HR 4284) Authorize the government of India to establish a memorial to honor Mahatma Gandhi in the District of Columbia. Introduced by McCollum, R-Fla., on July 21, 1998. House Resources reported July 31 (H Rept 105-666). House passed Sept. 15, under suspension of the rules. Senate Energy and Natural Resources discharged. Senate passed Oct. 8. President signed Oct. 26, 1998.

PL 105-285 (S 2206) Amend the Head Start Act, the Low-Income Home Energy Assistance Act of 1981, and the Community Services Block Grant Act to reauthorize and make improvements to those acts and to establish demonstration projects that provide an opportunity for persons with limited means to accumulate assets. Introduced by Coats, R-Ind., on June 23, 1998. Senate Labor and Human Resources reported, amended, July 21 (S Rept 105-256). Senate passed, amended, July 27. House passed, with amendment, under suspension of the rules, Sept. 14. Conference report filed in the House Oct. 6, (H Rept 105-788). Senate agreed to conference report Oct. 8. House agreed to conference report, under suspension of the rules, Oct. 9. President signed Oct. 27, 1998.

PL 105-286 (HR 8) Amend the Clean Air Act to deny entry into the United States of certain foreign motor vehicles that do not comply with state laws governing motor vehicles emissions. Introduced by Bilbray, R-Calif., on Jan. 7, 1997. House Commerce reported, amended, July 20, 1998 (H Rept 105-634). House passed, amended, under suspension of the rules, July 20. Senate Environment and Public Works reported Sept. 28 (S Rept 105-355). Senate passed, with amendment, Oct. 5. House agreed to Senate amendment under suspension of the rules, Oct. 7. President signed Oct. 27, 1998.

PL 105-287 (HR 624) Amend the Armored Car Industry Reciprocity Act of 1993 to clarify certain requirements and to improve the flow of interstate commerce. Introduced by Whitfield, R-Ky., on Feb. 6, 1997. House Commerce reported Feb. 25 (H Rept 105-6). House passed Feb. 26 under suspension of the rules. Senate Commerce, Science and Transportation reported Sept. 1, 1998 (S Rept 105-297). Senate passed Oct. 9. President signed Oct. 27, 1998.

PL 105-288 (HR 1021) Provide for a land exchange involving certain National Forest System lands within the Routt National Forest in the state of Colorado. Introduced by McInnis, R-Colo., on March 11, 1997. House Resources reported May 5, 1998 (H Rept 105-506). House passed May 12 under suspension of the rules. Senate passed Oct. 9. President signed Oct. 27, 1998.

PL 105-289 (HR 1197) Amend Title 35, U.S. Code, to protect patent owners against the unauthorized sale of plant parts taken from plants illegally reproduced. Introduced by Smith, R-Ore., on March 20, 1997. House passed Oct. 9, 1998, under suspension of the rules. Senate passed, with amendment, Oct. 15. House agreed to Senate amendment under suspension of the rules Oct. 16. President signed Oct. 27, 1998.

PL 105-290 (HR 2186) Authorize the secretary of the interior to provide assistance to the National Historic Trails Interpretive Center in Casper, Wyo. Introduced by Cubin, R-Wyo., on July 17, 1997. House Resources reported March 24, 1998 (H Rept 105-459). House passed March 30 under suspension of the rules. Senate Energy and Natural Resources reported Sept. 9 (S Rept 105-323). Senate passed, with amendments, Oct. 2. House agreed to Senate amendments Oct. 10. President signed Oct. 27, 1998.

PL 105-291 (HR 2370) Amend the Organic Act of Guam for the purposes of clarifying the local judicial structure and the Office of Attorney General. Introduced by Underwood, D-Guam, on July 31, 1997. House Resources reported, amended, Sept. 24, 1998 (H Rept 105-742). House passed, amended, under suspension of the rules Oct. 5. Senate passed Oct. 15. President signed Oct. 27, 1998.

PL 105-292 (HR 2431) Establish an Office of Religious Persecution Monitoring and provide for the imposition of sanctions against countries engaged in a pattern of religious persecution. Introduced by Wolf, R-Va., Sept. 8, 1997. House International Relations reported, amended, April 1, 1998 (H Rept 105-480, Pt. 1). House Ways and Means reported, amended, May 8 (Part 2). House Judiciary reported, amended, May 8 (Part 3). House Banking and Financial Services and House Rules discharged. House passed, amended, May 14. Senate passed, with amendments, Oct. 9. House agreed to Senate amendments under suspension of the rules Oct. 10. President signed Oct. 27, 1998.

PL 105-293 (HR 2795) Extend certain contracts between the Bureau of Reclamation and irrigation water contractors in Wyoming and Nebraska that receive water from Glendo Reservoir. Introduced by Barrett, R-Neb., Nov. 4, 1997. House Resources reported, amended, June 25, 1998 (H Rept 105-604). House passed, amended, under suspension of the rules Sept. 15. Senate passed Oct. 7. President signed Oct. 27, 1998.

PL 105-294 (HR 3069) Extend the Advisory Council on California Indian Policy to allow it to advise Congress on the implementing of the council's proposals and recommendations. Introduced by Miller, D-Calif., Nov. 13, 1997. House Resources reported June 9, 1998 (H Rept 105-571). House passed under suspension of the rules June 16, 1998. Senate Indian Affairs reported, with amendment, Sept. 22 (S Rept 105-342). Senate passed Oct. 9. President signed Oct. 27, 1998.

PL 105-295 (HR 4079) Authorize the construction of temperature control devices at Folsom Dam in California. Introduced by Doolittle, R-Calif., June 18, 1998. House Resources reported Sept. 15 (H Rept 105-717). House passed, amended, under suspension of the rules Sept. 15. Senate Energy and Natural Resources reported Sept. 25 (S Rept 105-378). Senate passed Oct. 7. President signed Oct. 27, 1998.

PL 105-296 (HR 4166) Amend the Idaho Admission Act regarding the sale or lease of school land. Introduced by Crapo, R-Idaho, June 25, 1998. House Resources reported Sept. 11 (H Rept 105-705). House passed under suspension of the rules Sept. 15. Senate Energy and Natural Resources reported Sept. 25 (S Rept 105-393). Senate passed Oct. 7. President signed Oct. 27, 1998.

PL 105-297 (S 53) Require the general application of the antitrust laws to major league baseball. Introduced by Hatch, R-Utah, Jan. 21, 1997. Senate Judiciary reported, amended, Oct. 29 (S Rept 105-118). Senate passed, amended,

July 30, 1998. House passed Oct. 7 under suspension of the rules. President signed Oct. 27, 1998.

PL 105-298 (S 505) Amend the provisions of Title 17, U.S. Code, with respect to the duration of copyright. Introduced by Hatch, R-Utah, March 20, 1997. Senate Judiciary discharged. Senate passed, amended, Oct. 7, 1998. House passed under suspension of the rules Oct. 7. House passed under suspension of the rules Oct. 7. President signed Oct. 27, 1998.

PL 105-299 (S 1298) Designate a federal building located in Florence, Ala., as the "Justice John McKinley Federal Building." Introduced by Shelby, R-Ala., Oct. 20, 1997. Senate Environment and Public Works reported May 21, 1998 (no written report). Senate passed June 2. House passed, under suspension of the rules, Oct. 9. President signed Oct. 27, 1998.

PL 105-300 (S 1892) Provide that a person closely related to a judge of a court exercising judicial power under article III of the U.S. Constitution (other than the Supreme Court) may not be appointed as a judge of the same court. Introduced by Kyl, R-Ariz., March 31, 1998. Senate Judiciary reported May 21 (no written report). Senate passed Oct. 6. House passed, under suspension of the rules, Oct. 7. President signed Oct. 27, 1998.

PL 105-301 (S 1976) Increase public awareness of the plight of victims of crime with developmental disabilities, collect data to measure the magnitude of the problem, and develop strategies to address the safety and justice needs of victims of crime with developmental disabilities. Introduced by DeWine, R-Ohio, April 23, 1998. Senate Judiciary reported, amended, June 25 (no written report). Senate passed, amended, July 13. House passed, under suspension of the rules, Oct. 7. President signed Oct. 27, 1998.

PL 105-302 (S 2235) Amend Part Q of the Omnibus Crime Control and Safe Streets Act of 1968 to encourage the use of school resource officers. Introduced by Campbell, R-Colo., June 25, 1998. Senate Judiciary reported Sept. 24 (no written report). Senate passed Oct. 7. House passed, under suspension of the rules, Oct. 9. President signed Oct. 27, 1998.

PL 105-303 (HR 1702) Encourage the development of a commercial space industry in the United States. Introduced by Sensenbrenner, R-Wis., May 22, 1997. House Science reported, amended, Oct. 24 (H Rept 105-347). House passed, amended, Nov. 4. Senate Commerce, Science and Transportation reported, amended, June 2, 1998 (S Rept 105-198). Senate passed, amended, July 30. House agreed to Senate amendment with an amendment pursuant to H. Res. 572 Oct. 5. Senate agreed to House amendment to Senate amendment Oct. 8. President signed Oct. 28, 1998.

PL 105-304 (HR 2281) Amend Title 17, U.S. Code, to implement the World Intellectual Property Organization Copyright Treaty and Performances and Phonograms Treaty. Introduced by Coble, R-N.C., July 29, 1997. House Judiciary reported, amended, May 22, 1998 (H Rept 105-551, Pt. 1). House Commerce reported, amended, July 22 (Part 2). House Ways and Means discharged. House passed, amended, under suspension of the rules, Aug. 4. Senate passed, amended, Sept. 17. Conference report filed in the House Oct. 8 (H Rept 105-796). Senate agreed to conference report Oct. 8. House agreed to conference report under suspension of the rules Oct. 12. President signed Oct. 28, 1998.

PL 105-305 (HR 3332) Amend the High-Performance Computing Act of 1991 to authorize appropriations for fiscal years 1999 and 2000 for the Next Generation Internet program, to require the Advisory Committee on High-Performance Computing and Communications, Information Technology, and the Next Generation Internet to monitor and give advice concerning the development and implementation of the Next Generation Internet program and report to the president and the Congress on its activities. Introduced by Sensenbrenner, R-Wis., March 4, 1998. House passed, amended, under suspension of the rules, Sept. 14. Senate Commerce, Science and Transportation discharged. Senate passed Oct. 8. President signed Oct. 28, 1998.

PL 105-306 (HR 4558) Make technical amendments to clarify the provision of benefits for noncitizens, and to improve the provision of unemployment insurance, child support, and supplemental security income benefits. Introduced by Shaw, R-Fla., Sept. 14, 1998. House Ways and Means reported, amended, Sept. 22 (H Rept 105-735, Pt. 1). House passed, amended, under suspension of the rules, Sept. 23. Senate passed Oct. 8. President signed Oct. 28, 1998.

PL 105-307 (S 2468) Designate the Biscayne National Park Visitor Center as the Dante Fascell Visitor Center. Introduced by Graham, D-Fla., Sept. 14, 1998. Senate Energy and Natural Resources reported, amended, Sept. 25 (S Rept 105-407). Senate passed, amended, Oct. 7. House Resources discharged. House passed Oct. 10. President signed Oct. 29, 1998.

PL 105-308 (HR 700) Remove the restriction on the distribution of certain revenues from the Mineral Springs parcel to certain members of the Agua Caliente Band of Cahuilla Indians. Introduced by S. Bono, R-Calif., Feb. 12, 1997. House Resources reported, amended, Sept. 3 (H Rept 105-241). House passed, amended, under suspension of the rules Sept. 8. Senate Indian Affairs reported, with amendment, Sept. 28, 1998 (S Rept 105-349). Senate passed, amended, Oct. 12. House agreed to Senate amendment under suspension of the rules Oct. 15. President signed Oct. 30, 1998.

PL 105-309 (HR 1274) Authorize appropriations for the National Institute of Standards and Technology for fiscal years 1998 and 1999. Introduced by Morella, R-Md., April 10, 1997. House Science reported, amended, April 21 (H Rept 105-64). House passed, amended, April 24. Senate Commerce, Science and Transportation discharged. Senate passed, with amendment, Oct. 9, 1998. House agreed to Senate amendment under suspension of the rules Oct. 13. President signed Oct. 30, 1998.

PL 105-310 (HR 1756) Amend Chapter 53 of Title 31, U.S. Code, to require the development and implementation by the secretary of the Treasury of a national strategy to combat money laundering and related financial crimes. Introduced by Velazquez, D-N.Y., June 3, 1997. House Banking and Financial Services reported, amended, June 25, 1998 (H Rept 105-608, Pt. 1). House Judiciary discharged. House passed, amended, under suspension of the rules Oct. 5. Senate passed, with amendment, Oct. 15. House agreed to Senate amendment under suspension of the rules Oct. 16. President signed Oct. 30, 1998.

PL 105-311 (HR 2675) Require that the Office of Personnel Management submit proposed legislation under which group universal life insurance and group variable universal life insurance would be available under Chapter 87 of Title 5, U.S. Code. Introduced by Mica, R-Fla., Oct. 21, 1997. House Government Reform and Oversight reported, amended, Nov. 4. (H Rept 105-373). House passed, amended, under suspension of the rules, Nov. 4. Senate Governmental Affairs reported, with amendments, Sept. 21, 1998 (S Rept 105-337). Senate passed, with amendments, Oct. 5. House agreed to Senate amendments under suspension of the rules Oct. 8. President signed Oct. 30, 1998.

PL 105-312 (HR 2807) Amend the Rhinoceros and Tiger Conservation Act of 1994 to prohibit the selling, importing, or exporting of products labeled as containing substances derived from rhinoceros or tiger. Introduced by Saxton, R-N.J., Nov. 4, 1997. House Resources reported, amended, April 28, 1998 (H Rept 105-495). House passed, amended, under suspension of the rules April 28. Senate Environment and Public Works discharged. Senate passed, with amendment, Oct. 13. House agreed to Senate amendment, with amendments, Oct. 14. Senate agreed to House amendments to Senate amendment Oct. 15. President signed Oct. 30, 1998.

PL 105-313 (HR 3055) Deem the activities of the Miccosukee Tribe on the Tamiami Indian Reservation to be consistent with the purposes of the Everglades National Park. Introduced by Hastings, D-Fla., Nov. 13, 1997. House Resources reported, amended, Sept. 11, 1998 (H Rept 105-708, Pt. 1). House passed, amended, under suspension of the rules, Oct. 12. Senate passed Oct. 15. President signed Oct. 30, 1998.

PL 105-314 (HR 3494) Amend Title 18, U.S. Code, with respect to violent sex crimes against children. Introduced by McCollum, R-Fla., March 18, 1998. House Judiciary reported, amended, June 3 (H Rept 105-557). House passed, amended, June 11. Senate Judiciary reported, with amendments, Sept. 17 (no written report). Senate passed, with amendments, Oct. 9. House agreed to Senate amendments under suspension of the rules Oct. 12. President signed Oct. 30, 1998.

PL 105-315 (HR 3528) Amend Title 28, U.S. Code, with respect to the use of alternative dispute resolution processes in United States district courts. Introduced by Coble, R-N.C., March 23, 1998. House Judiciary reported, amended, April 21 (H Rept 105-487). House passed, amended, under suspension of the rules April 21. Senate Judiciary reported, with amendments, July 30 (no written report). Senate passed, with amendments, Oct. 7. House agreed to Senate amendments under suspension of the rules Oct. 10. President signed Oct. 30, 1998.

PL 105-316 (HR 3687) Authorize prepayment of amounts due under a water reclamation project contract for the Canadian River Project, Texas. Introduced by Thornberry, R-Texas, April 1, 1998. House Resources discharged. House passed, amended, Aug. 7. Senate Energy and Natural Resources reported, with amendment, Sept. 25 (S Rept 105-410). Senate passed Oct. 14. President signed Oct. 30, 1998.

PL 105-317 (HR 3903) Provide for an exchange of lands located near Gustavus, Alaska. Introduced by Young, R-Alaska, May 19, 1998. House Resources reported, amended, Sept. 11 (H Rept 105-706, Pt. 1). House Commerce discharged. House passed, amended, under suspension of the rules Sept. 15. Senate passed Oct. 2. Senate passed, amended, Oct. 8. House agreed to Senate amendments Oct. 10. President signed Oct. 30, 1998.

PL 105-318 (HR 4151) Amend Chapter 47 of Title 18, U.S. Code, relating to identity fraud. Introduced by Shadegg, R-Ariz., June 25, 1998. House passed, amended, under suspension of the rules, Oct. 7. Senate passed Oct. 14. President signed Oct. 30, 1998.

PL 105-319 (HR 4293) Establish a cultural and training program for disadvantaged individuals from Northern Ireland and the Republic of Ireland. Introduced by Walsh, R-N.Y., July 21, 1998. House passed, amended, under suspension of the rules Oct. 7. Senate passed Oct. 8. President signed Oct. 30, 1998.

PL 105-320 (HR 4309) Provide a comprehensive program of support for victims of torture. Introduced by Smith, R-N.J., July 22, 1998. House International Relations reported, amended, Sept. 14 (H Rept 105-709, Pt. 1). House Commerce discharged. House passed, amended, under suspension of the rules Sept. 14. Senate passed, amended, Oct. 8. House agreed to Senate amendment under suspension of the rules Oct. 10. President signed Oct. 30, 1998.

PL 105-321 (HR 4326) Transfer administrative jurisdiction over certain federal lands located within or adjacent to the Rogue River National Forest and to clarify the authority of the Bureau of Land Management to sell and exchange other federal lands in Oregon. Introduced by Smith, R-Ore., July 24, 1998. House Resources reported Oct. 12 (H Rept 105-810). House passed, amended, Oct. 12. Senate passed Oct. 14. President signed Oct. 30, 1998.

PL 105-322 (HR 4337) Authorize the secretary of the interior to provide financial assistance to the state of Maryland for a pilot program to develop measures to eradicate or control nutria and restore marshland damaged by nutria. Introduced by Gilchrest, R-Md., July 27, 1998. House passed under suspension of the rules Sept. 28. Senate passed Oct. 9. President signed Oct. 30, 1998.

PL 105-323 (HR 4660) Amend the State Department Basic Authorities Act of 1956 to provide rewards for information leading to the arrest or conviction of any individual for the commission of an act, or conspiracy to commit an act, of international terrorism, narcotics-related offenses, or for serious violations of international humanitarian law relating to the former Yugoslavia. Introduced by Gilman, R-N.Y., Oct. 1, 1998. House passed, amended, under suspension of the rules Oct. 8. Senate passed, with amendment, Oct. 14. House agreed to Senate amendment under suspension of the rules Oct. 15. President signed Oct. 30, 1998.

PL 105-324 (HR 4679) Amend the Federal Food, Drug, and Cosmetic Act to clarify the circumstances in which a substance is considered to be a pesticide chemical for purposes of such act. Introduced by Bliley, R-Va., Oct. 2, 1998. House passed under suspension of the rules Oct. 7. Senate passed Oct. 9. President signed Oct. 30, 1998.

PL 105-325 (S 231) Establish the National Cave and Karst Research Institute in the state of New Mexico. Introduced by Bingaman, D-N.M., Jan. 29, 1997. Senate Energy and Natural Resources reported June 26 (S Rept 105-37). Senate passed July 11. House Resources reported April 28, 1998 (H Rept 105-496). House passed Oct. 10. President signed Oct. 30, 1998.

PL 105-326 (S 890) Dispose of certain federal properties located in Dutch John, Utah, and assist the local government in the interim delivery of basic services to the Dutch John community. Introduced by Bennett, R-Utah, June 12, 1997. Senate Energy and Natural Resources reported, amended, July 27, 1998 (S Rept 105-264). Senate passed, amended, Oct. 2. House passed Oct. 8. President signed Oct. 30, 1998.

PL 105-327 (S 1333) Amend the Land and Water Conservation Fund Act of 1965 to allow national park units that cannot charge an entrance or admission fee to retain other fees and charges. Introduced by Frist, R-Tenn., Oct. 29, 1997. Senate Energy and Natural Resources reported, amended, Sept. 8, 1998 (S Rept 105-311). Senate passed, amended, Oct. 2. House Resources discharged. House passed Oct. 10. President signed Oct. 30, 1998.

PL 105-328 (S 2094) Amend the Fish and Wildlife Improvement Act of 1978 to enable the secretary of the interior to more effectively use the proceeds of sales of certain items. Introduced by Allard, R-Colo., May 20, 1998. Senate Environment and Public Works reported, amended, July 31 (S Rept 105-285). Senate passed, amended, Sept. 11. House passed under suspension of the rules Oct. 9. President signed Oct. 30, 1998.

PL 105-329 (S 2106) Expand the boundaries of Arches National Park, Utah, to include portions of certain drainages that are under the jurisdiction of the Bureau of Land Management, and to include a portion of Fish Seep Draw owned by the state of Utah. Introduced by Bennett, R-Utah, May 21, 1998. Senate Energy and Natural Resources reported, amended Sept. 14 (S Rept 105-330). Senate passed, amended Oct. 2. House passed Oct. 10, 1998. President signed Oct. 30, 1998.

PL 105-330 (S 2193) Implement the provisions of the Trademark Law Treaty. Introduced by Hatch, R-Utah, June 18, 1998. Senate Judiciary reported July 16 (no written report). Senate passed, amended, Sept. 17. House passed, under suspension of the rules, Oct. 9. President signed Oct. 30, 1998.

PL 105-331 (HR 678) Require the secretary of the Treasury to mint coins in commemoration of the sesquicentennial of the birth of Thomas Alva Edison and to redesign the half dollar circulating coin for 1997 to commemorate Edison. Introduced by Gillmor, R-Ohio, Feb. 11, 1997. House passed, amended, under suspension of the rules Sept. 9, 1998. Senate passed Oct. 7. President signed Oct. 31, 1998.

PL 105-332 (HR 1853) Amend the Carl D. Perkins Vocational and Applied Technology Education Act. Introduced by Riggs, R-Calif., June 10, 1997. House Education and the Workforce reported, amended, July 14 (H Rept 105-177). House passed, amended, July 22. Senate Labor and Human Resources discharged. Senate passed, with amendment, June 12, 1998. Senate agreed to conference report (H Rept 105-800) Oct. 8. House agreed to conference report Oct. 9. President signed Oct. 31, 1998.

PL 105-333 (HR 2000) Amend the Alaska Native Claims Settlement Act to make certain clarifications to the land bank protection provisions. Introduced by Young, R-Alaska, June 19, 1997. House Resources reported, amended, Aug. 5, 1998 (H Rept 105-677). House passed, amended, under suspension of the rules Sept. 23. Senate passed Oct. 7. President signed Oct. 31, 1998.

PL 105-334 (HR 2327) Provide for a change in the exemption from the child labor provisions of the Fair Labor Standards Act of 1938 for minors between sixteen and eighteen years of age who engage in the operation of automobiles and trucks. Introduced by Combest, R-Texas, July 31, 1997. House passed, amended, under suspension of the rules Sept. 28, 1998. Senate passed, with amendment, Oct. 12. House agreed to Senate amendment under suspension of the rules Oct. 13. President signed Oct. 31, 1998.

PL 105-335 (HR 3830) Provide for the exchange of certain lands within the state of Utah. Introduced by Hansen, R-Utah, May 12, 1998. House Resources reported June 24 (H Rept 105-598). House passed June 24. Senate Energy and Natural Resources reported Sept. 14 (S Rept 105-331). Senate passed Oct. 9. President signed Oct. 31, 1998.

PL 105-336 (HR 3874) Amend the Child Nutrition Act of 1966 to make improvements to the special supplemental nutrition program for women, infants, and children and to extend the authority of that program through fiscal year 2003. Introduced by Castle, R-Del., May 14, 1998. House Education and the Workforce reported, amended, July 20 (H Rept 105-633). House passed, amended, under suspension of the rules July 20. Senate passed, amended, Sept. 17. Conference report filed in the House Oct. 6 (H Rept 105-786). Senate agreed to conference report Oct. 7. House agreed to conference report under suspension of the rules Oct. 9. President signed Oct. 31, 1998.

PL 105-337 (HR 4259) Allow Haskell Indian Nations University and the Southwestern Indian Polytechnic Institute each to conduct a demonstration project to test the feasibility and desirability of new personnel management policies and procedures. Introduced by Snowbarger, R-Kan., July 16, 1998. House Government Reform and Oversight reported Sept. 9 (H Rept 105-700, Pt. 1). House passed Oct. 6. Senate passed Oct. 14. President signed Oct. 31, 1998.

PL 105-338 (HR 4655) Establish a program to support a transition to democracy in Iraq. Introduced by Gilman, R-N.Y., Sept. 29, 1998. House passed under suspension of the rules Oct. 5. Senate passed Oct. 7. President signed Oct. 31, 1998.

PL 105-339 (S 1021) Amend Title 5, U.S. Code, to provide that consideration may not be denied to preference eligibles applying for certain positions in the competitive service. Introduced by Hagel, R-Neb., July 16, 1997. Senate Veterans' Affairs reported, amended, Sept. 21, 1998 (S Rept 105-340). Senate passed, amended, Oct. 5. House passed under suspension of the rules Oct. 8. President signed Oct. 31, 1998.

PL 105-340 (S 1722) Amend the Public Health Service Act to revise and extend certain programs with respect to women's health research and prevention activities at the National Institutes of Health and the Centers for Disease Control and Prevention. Introduced by Frist, R-Tenn., March 6, 1998. Senate Labor and Human Resources discharged. Senate passed, amended, Oct. 12. House passed under suspension of the rules Oct. 13. President signed Oct. 31, 1998.

PL 105-341 (S 2285) Establish a commission, in honor of the 150th Anniversary of the Seneca Falls Convention, to further protect sites of historic importance in the efforts to secure equal rights for women. Introduced by Dodd, D-Conn., July 10, 1998. Senate Energy and Natural Resources reported Sept. 25 (S Rept 105-396). Senate passed Oct. 7. House Resources discharged. House passed Oct. 10. President signed Oct. 31, 1998.

PL 105-342 (S 2240) Establish the Adams National Historical Park in the Commonwealth of Massachusetts. Introduced by Murkowski, R-Alaska, June 26, 1998. Senate Energy and Natural Resources reported, amended, Sept. 25 (S Rept 105-404). Senate passed, amended, Oct. 7. House Resources discharged. House passed Oct. 10. President signed Nov. 2, 1998.

PL 105-343 (S 2246) Amend the act that established the Frederick Law Olmsted National Historic Site, in the Commonwealth of Massachusetts, by modifying the boundary. Introduced by Murkowski, R-Alaska, June 26, 1998. Senate Energy and Natural Resources reported Sept. 25 (S Rept 105-405). Senate passed Oct. 7. House Resources discharged. House passed Oct. 10. President signed Nov. 2, 1998.

PL 105-344 (S 2413) Prohibit the conveyance of Woodland Lake Park tract in Apache-Sitgreaves National Forest in Arizona unless the conveyance is made to the town of Pinetop-Lakeside or authorized by act of Congress. Introduced by McCain, R-Ariz., July 31, 1998. Senate Energy and Natural Resources reported, amended, Oct. 6 (S Rept 105-384). Senate passed, amended, Oct. 9. House passed Oct. 10. President signed Nov. 2, 1998.

PL 105-345 (S 2427) Amend the Omnibus Parks and Public Lands Management Act of 1996 to extend the legislative authority for the Black Patriots Foundation to establish a commemorative work. Introduced by Campbell, R-Colo., Aug. 31, 1998. Senate Energy and Natural Resources discharged. Senate passed Oct. 8. House Resources discharged. House passed Oct. 10. President signed Nov. 2, 1998.

PL 105-346 (S 2505) Direct the secretary of the interior to convey title to the Tunnison Lab Hagerman Field Station in Gooding County, Idaho, to the University of Idaho. Introduced by Craig, R-Idaho, Sept. 21, 1998. Senate Environment and Public Works reported, amended, Sept. 28 (S Rept 105-354). Senate passed, amended, Oct. 5. House passed under suspension of the rules Oct. 9. President signed Nov. 2, 1998.

PL 105-347 (S 2561) Amend the Fair Credit Reporting Act with respect to furnishing and using consumer reports for employment purposes. Introduced by Nickles, R-Okla., Oct. 6, 1998. Senate passed Oct. 6. House passed Oct. 9. President signed Nov. 2, 1998.

PL 105-348 (S J Res 51) Grant the consent of Congress to the Potomac Highlands Airport Authority Compact entered into between the states of Maryland and West Virginia. Introduced by Sarbanes, D-Md., June 10, 1998. Senate Judiciary reported July 30 (no written report). Senate passed July 31. House passed under suspension of the rules Oct. 9. President signed Nov. 2, 1998.

PL 105-349 (S J Res 58) Recognize the accomplishments of inspectors general since their creation in 1978 in preventing and detecting waste, fraud, abuse, and mismanagement, and in promoting economy, efficiency, and effectiveness in the federal government. Introduced by Glenn, D-Ohio, Oct. 1,

1998. Senate passed Oct. 1. House passed under suspension of the rules Oct. 10. President signed Nov. 2, 1998.

PL 105-350 (H J Res 138) Appoint the day for the convening of the first session of the 106th Congress. Introduced by Solomon, R-N.Y., Oct. 20, 1998. House passed Oct. 20. Senate passed Oct. 21. President signed Nov. 3, 1998.

PL 105-351 (S 538) Authorize the secretary of the interior to convey certain facilities of the Minidoka project to the Burley Irrigation District. Introduced by Craig, R-Idaho, April 9, 1997. Senate Energy and Natural Resources reported, amended, Nov. 3 (S Rept 105-131). Senate passed, amended June 25, 1998. House passed Oct. 12. President signed Nov. 3, 1998.

PL 105-352 (S 744) Authorize the construction of the Fall River Water Users District Rural Water System and authorize financial assistance to the Fall River Water Users District, a nonprofit corporation, in the planning and construction of the water supply system. Introduced by Johnson, D-S.D., May 14, 1997. Senate Energy and Natural Resources reported, amended, Sept. 25, 1998 (S Rept 105-369). Senate passed, amended Oct. 7. House Resources discharged. House passed Oct. 12. President signed Nov. 3, 1998.

PL 105-353 (S 1260) Amend the Securities Act of 1933 and the Securities Exchange Act of 1934 to limit the conduct of securities class actions under state law. Introduced by Gramm, R-Texas, Oct. 7, 1997. Senate Banking, Housing, and Urban Affairs reported, amended, May 4, 1998 (S Rept 105-182). Senate passed, amended, May 13. House passed, amended, July 22. Conference report filed in House Oct. 9 (H Rept 105-803). Senate agreed to conference report Oct. 13. House agreed to conference report, under suspension of the rules, Oct. 13. President signed Nov. 3, 1998.

PL 105-354 (S 2524) Clarify without substantive change laws related to Patriotic and National Observances, Ceremonies, and Organizations and to improve the U.S. Code. Introduced by Hatch, R-Utah, Sept. 28, 1998. Senate Judiciary reported Oct. 1 (no written report). Senate passed Oct. 8. House passed, under suspension of the rules, Oct. 12. President signed Nov. 3, 1998.

PL 105-355 (HR 3910) Authorize the Automobile National Heritage Area. Introduced by Dingell, D-Mich., May 20, 1998. House Resources discharged. House passed, amended, Oct. 10. Senate passed Oct. 14. President signed Nov. 6, 1998.

PL 105-356 (S 2232) Establish the Little Rock Central High School National Historic Site in the state of Arkansas. Introduced by Bumpers, D-Ark., June 25, 1998. Senate Energy and Natural Resources reported, amended, Sept. 8 (S Rept 105-307). Senate passed, amended, Oct. 2. House Resources discharged. House passed Oct. 8. President signed Nov. 6, 1998.

PL 105-357 (HR 3633) Amend the Controlled Substances Import and Export Act to place limitations on controlled substances brought into the United States from Mexico. Introduced by Chabot, R-Ohio, April 1, 1998. House Judiciary reported July 16 (H Rept 105-629, Pt. 1). House Commerce discharged. House passed, amended, under suspension of the rules, Aug. 3. Senate passed Oct. 20. President signed Nov. 10, 1998.

PL 105-358 (HR 3723) Authorize funds for the payment of salaries and expenses of the Patent and Trademark Office. Introduced by Coble, R-N.C., April 23, 1998. House Judiciary reported, amended, May 12 (H Rept 105-528). House passed, amended, under suspension of the rules, May 12. Senate Judiciary discharged. Senate passed Oct. 14. President signed Nov. 10, 1998.

PL 105-359 (HR 4501) Require the secretary of agriculture and the secretary of the interior to conduct a study to improve the access for persons with disabilities to outdoor recreational opportunities made available to the public. Introduced by Schaffer, R-Colo., Aug. 6, 1998. House passed, under suspension of the rules, Oct. 14. Senate passed Oct. 20. President signed Nov. 10, 1998.

PL 105-360 (HR 4821) Extend into fiscal year 1999 the visa processing period for diversity applicants whose visa processing was suspended during fiscal year 1998 due to embassy bombings. Introduced by Smith, R-Texas, Oct. 13, 1998. House passed, under suspension of the rules, Oct. 15. Senate passed Oct. 21. President signed Nov. 10, 1998.

PL 105-361 (S 459) Amend the Native American Programs Act of 1974 to extend certain authorizations. Introduced by Campbell, R-Colo., March 18, 1997. Senate Indian Affairs reported, amended, May 21 (S Rept 105-20). Senate passed, amended, Sept. 29. House Education and the Workforce discharged. House passed with amendments Oct. 9, 1998. Senate agreed to House amendments Oct. 14. President signed Nov. 10, 1998.

PL 105-362 (S 1364) Eliminate unnecessary and wasteful federal reports. Introduced by McCain, R-Ariz., Nov. 4, 1997. Senate Governmental Affairs reported, amended, May 11, 1998 (S Rept 105-187). Senate passed, amended June 10. House passed with amendment, under suspension of the rules, Oct. 13. Senate agreed to House amendment with amendment Oct. 21. House agreed to Senate amendment to House amendment Oct. 21. President signed Nov. 10, 1998.

PL 105-363 (S 1718) Amend the Weir Farm National Historic Site Establishment Act of 1990 to authorize the acquisition of additional acreage for the historic site to permit the development of visitor and administrative facilities and to authorize the appropriation of additional amounts for the acquisition of real and personal property. Introduced by Lieberman, D-Conn., March 5, 1998. Senate Energy and Natural Resources reported, amended, Sept. 14 (S Rept 105-328). Senate passed, amended Oct. 2. House Resources discharged. House passed with amendments Oct. 10. Senate agreed to House amendments Oct. 14. President signed Nov. 10, 1998.

PL 105-364 (S 2241) Provide for the acquisition of lands formerly occupied by the Franklin D. Roosevelt family at Hyde Park, N.Y. Introduced by Murkowski, R-Alaska, June 26, 1998. Senate Energy and Natural Resources reported Sept. 25 (S Rept 105-400). Senate passed Oct. 7. House Resources discharged. House passed Oct. 15. President signed Nov. 10, 1998.

PL 105-365 (S 2272) Amend the boundaries of Grant-Kohrs Ranch National Historic Site in the state of Montana. Introduced by Burns, R-Mont., July 8, 1998. Senate Energy and Natural Resources reported Sept. 9 (S Rept 105-324). Senate passed Oct. 2. House passed, under suspension of the rules, Oct. 15. President signed Nov. 10, 1998.

PL 105-366 (S 2375) Amend the Securities Exchange Act of 1934 and the Foreign Corrupt Practices Act of 1977, to strengthen prohibitions on international bribery and other corrupt practices. Introduced by D'Amato, R-N.Y., July 30, 1998. Senate Banking, Housing, and Urban Affairs reported July 30, 1998 (S Rept 105-277). Senate passed July 31. House passed with amendments Oct. 9. Senate agreed to House amendments with amendments Oct. 14. House disagreed to Senate amendments Nos. 2 through 6 and agreed to Senate amendment No. 1, with an amendment Oct. 20. Senate receded from its amendments Nos. 2 through 6 Oct. 21. Senate agreed to House amendment to Senate amendment No. 1 Oct. 21. President signed Nov. 10, 1998.

PL 105-367 (S 2500) Protect the sanctity of contracts and leases entered into by surface patent holders with respect to coalbed methane gas. Introduced by Enzi, R-Wyo., Sept. 18, 1998. Senate Energy and Natural Resources reported amended Sept. 25 (S Rept 105-408). Senate passed, amended, Oct. 9. House passed, under suspension of the rules, Oct. 15. President signed Nov. 10, 1998.

PL 105-368 (HR 4110) Provide a cost of living adjustment in rates of compensation paid to veterans with service-connected disabilities and to make various improvements in education, housing, and cemetery programs of the Department of Veterans Affairs. Introduced by Stump, R-Ariz., June 23, 1998. House Veterans' Affairs reported July 15 (H Rept 105-627). House passed, amended under suspension of the rules, Aug. 3. Senate Veterans' Affairs discharged. Senate passed with amendment, Sept. 30. House agreed to Senate amendment with amendments Oct. 10. Senate agreed to House amendments to Senate amendment Oct. 21. President signed Nov. 11, 1998.

PL 105-369 (HR 1023) Provide for compassionate payments with regard to individuals with blood-clotting disorders, such as hemophilia, who contracted human immunodeficiency virus due to contaminated blood products. Introduced by Goss, R-Fla., March 11, 1997. House Judiciary reported, amended, March 25, 1998 (H Rept 105-465, Pt. 1). House Ways and Means reported, amended May 7 (Pt. 2). House Commerce discharged. House passed, amended, under suspension of the rules, May 19. Senate Labor and Human Resources reported Oct. 7 (no written report). Senate passed Oct. 21. President signed Nov. 12, 1998.

PL 105-370 (HR 2070) Amend Title 18, U.S. Code, to provide for the mandatory testing for serious transmissible diseases of incarcerated persons whose bodily fluids come into contact with corrections personnel and notice to those persons of the results of the tests. Introduced by Solomon, R-N.Y., June 25, 1997. House Judiciary reported, amended, July 31, 1998 (H Rept 105-665). House passed, amended, under suspension of the rules Aug. 3. Senate

Judiciary discharged. Senate passed, amended, Oct. 20. House agreed to Senate amendment Oct. 21. President signed Nov. 12, 1998.

PL 105-371 (HR 2263) Authorize and request the president to award the Medal of Honor posthumously to Theodore Roosevelt for his gallant and heroic actions in the attack on San Juan Heights, Cuba, during the Spanish-American War. Introduced by McHale, D-Pa., July 25, 1997. House passed, under suspension of the rules, Oct. 8, 1998. Senate passed Oct. 21, 1998. President signed Nov. 12, 1998.

PL 105-372 (HR 3267) Direct the secretary of the interior, acting through the Bureau of Reclamation, to conduct a feasibility study and construct a project to reclaim the Salton Sea. Introduced by Hunter, R-Calif., Feb. 25, 1998. House Resources reported, amended, July 14 (H Rept 105-621, Pt. 1). House Transportation and Infrastructure discharged. House passed, amended July 15. Senate passed, amended Oct. 13. House agreed to Senate amendments Oct. 21. President signed Nov. 12, 1998.

PL 105-373 (HR 4083) Make available to the Ukrainian Museum and Archives the USIA television program "Window on America." Introduced by Kucinich, D-Ohio, June 18, 1998. House passed, amended, under suspension of the rules Sept. 14. Senate Foreign Relations discharged. Senate passed Oct. 21. President signed Nov. 12, 1998.

PL 105-374 (HR 4164) Amend Title 28, U.S. Code, with respect to the enforcement of child custody and visitation orders. Introduced by Coble, R-N.C., June 25, 1998. House passed, under suspension of the rules, July 14. Senate Judiciary discharged. Senate passed, amended, Oct. 21. House agreed to Senate amendment Oct. 21. President signed Nov. 12, 1998.

PL 105-375 (S 759) Amend the State Department Basic Authorities Act of 1956 to require the secretary of state to submit an annual report to Congress concerning diplomatic immunity. Introduced by Coverdell, R-Ga., May 16, 1997. Senate Foreign Relations reported, amended, Nov. 4 (no written report). Senate passed, amended, Nov. 8. House passed, under suspension of the rules, Oct. 14, 1998. President signed Nov. 12, 1998.

PL 105-376 (S 1132) Modify the boundaries of the Bandelier National Monument to include the lands within the headwaters of the Upper Alamo Watershed that drain into the monument and that are not currently within the jurisdiction of a federal land management agency, to authorize purchase or donation of those lands. Introduced by Bingaman, D-N.M., July 31, 1997. Senate Energy and Natural Resources reported, amended April 29, 1998 (S Rept 105-178). Senate passed, amended, July 17. House passed Oct. 20. President signed Nov. 12, 1998.

PL 105-377 (S 1134) Grant the consent and approval of Congress to an interstate forest fire protection compact. Introduced by Murray, D-Wash., July 31, 1997. Senate Judiciary reported July 16, 1998 (no written report). Senate passed July 30. House passed, under suspension of the rules, Oct. 15. President signed Nov. 12, 1998.

PL 105-378 (S 1408) Establish the Lower East Side Tenement National Historic Site. Introduced by D'Amato, R-N.Y., Nov. 7, 1997. Senate Energy and Natural Resources reported Sept. 8, 1998 (S Rept 105-303). Senate passed Oct. 2. House Resources discharged. House passed, amended, Oct. 10. Senate agreed to House amendment Oct. 14. President signed Nov. 12, 1998.

PL 105-379 (S 1733) Amend the Food Stamp Act of 1977 to require food stamp state agencies to take certain actions to ensure that food stamp coupons are not issued for deceased individuals, and to require the secretary of agriculture to conduct a study of options for the design, development, implementation, and operation of a national database to track participation in federal means-tested public assistance programs. Introduced by Lugar, R-Ind., March 10, 1998. Senate Agriculture, Nutrition, and Forestry discharged. Senate passed, amended, Oct. 14. House passed, under suspension of the rules, Oct. 15. President signed Nov. 12, 1998.

PL 105-380 (S 2129) Eliminate restrictions on the acquisition of certain land contiguous to Hawaii Volcanoes National Park. Introduced by Akaka, D-Hawaii, June 2, 1998. Senate Energy and Natural Resources reported Sept. 8 (S Rept 105-313). Senate passed Oct. 2. House Resources discharged. House passed Oct. 14. President signed Nov. 12, 1998.

PL 105-381 (S J Res 35) Grant the consent of Congress to the Pacific Northwest Emergency Management Arrangement. Introduced by Craig, R-Idaho, July 21, 1997. Senate Judiciary reported July 16, 1998 (no written report). Senate passed July 31. House passed, under suspension of the rules, Oct. 15. President signed Nov. 12, 1998.

PL 105-382 (HR 633) Amend the Foreign Service Act of 1980 to provide that the annuities of certain special agents and security personnel of the Department of State be computed in the same way as applies generally with respect to federal law enforcement officers. Introduced by Davis, R-Va., Feb. 6, 1997. House International Relations reported, amended, Sept. 28, 1998 (H Rept 105-755, Pt. 1). House Government Reform and Oversight discharged. House passed, amended, under suspension of the rules Oct. 5. Senate passed Oct. 20. President signed Nov. 13, 1998.

PL 105-383 (HR 2204) Authorize appropriations for fiscal years 1998 and 1999 for the Coast Guard. Introduced by Shuster, R-Pa., July 24, 1997. House Transportation and Infrastructure reported, amended, July 31 (H Rept 105-236). House passed, amended Oct. 21. Senate passed, amended, Oct. 12, 1998. House agreed to Senate amendment with an amendment Oct. 15. Senate agreed to House amendment to Senate amendment Oct. 21. President signed Nov. 13, 1998.

PL 105-384 (HR 3461) Approve a governing international fishery agreement between the United States and the Republic of Poland. Introduced by Saxton, R-N.J., March 12, 1998. House Resources discharged. House passed, amended, Oct. 12. Senate passed Oct. 21. President signed Nov. 13, 1998.

PL 105-385 (HR 4283) Support sustainable and broad-based agricultural and rural development in sub-Saharan Africa. Introduced by Bereuter, R-Neb., July 21, 1998. House International Relations reported Aug. 6 (H Rept 105-681, Pt. 1). House Agriculture discharged. House passed, under suspension of the rules, Sept. 28. Senate passed, amended, Oct. 20. House agreed to Senate amendment Oct. 20. President signed Nov. 13, 1998.

PL 105-386 (S 191) Throttle criminal use of guns. Introduced by Helms, R-N.C., Jan. 22, 1997. Senate Judiciary reported, amended, Nov. 6 (no written report). Senate passed, amended, Nov. 13. House passed, amended, under suspension of the rules, Oct. 9, 1998. Senate agreed to House amendment Oct. 15. President signed Nov. 13, 1998.

PL 105-387 (S 391) Provide for the disposition of certain funds appropriated to pay judgment in favor of the Mississippi Sioux Indians. Introduced by Dorgan, D-N.D., March 4, 1997. Senate Indian Affairs reported, amended Oct. 7, 1998 (S Rept 105-379). Senate passed, amended, Oct. 9. House passed, amended, under suspension of the rules, Oct. 10. Senate agreed to House amendment Oct. 14. President signed Nov. 13, 1998.

PL 105-388 (S 417) Extend energy conservation programs under the Energy Policy and Conservation Act through Sept. 30, 2002. Introduced by Murkowski, R-Alaska, March 10, 1997. Senate Energy and Natural Resources reported, amended, June 11 (S Rept 105-25). Senate passed, amended, June 27. House passed, amended, Sept. 28, 1998. Senate agreed to House amendments, with amendment, Oct. 8. House agreed to Senate amendment to House amendments under suspension of the rules, Oct. 15. President signed Nov. 13, 1998.

PL 105-389 (S 1397) Establish a commission to assist in commemoration of the centennial of powered flight and the achievements of the Wright brothers. Introduced by Helms, R-N.C., Nov. 7, 1997. Senate Governmental Affairs reported, amended, Aug. 25, 1998 (S Rept 105-294). Senate passed, amended, Sept. 22. House passed under suspension of the rules, Oct. 14. President signed Nov. 13, 1998.

PL 105-390 (S 1525) Provide financial assistance for higher education to the dependents of federal, state, and local public safety officers who are killed or permanently and totally disabled as the result of a traumatic injury sustained in the line of duty. Introduced by Specter, R-Pa., Nov. 12, 1997. Senate Judiciary reported May 7, 1998 (no written report). Senate passed May 15. House Judiciary discharged. House passed, amended, Oct. 10. Senate agreed to House amendment Oct. 15. President signed Nov. 13, 1998.

PL 105-391 (S 1693) Provide for improved management and increased accountability for certain National Park Service programs. Introduced by Thomas, R-Wyo., Feb. 27, 1998. Senate Energy and Natural Resources reported, amended, June 5 (S Rept 105-202). Senate passed, amended, June 11. House Resources reported, amended, Oct. 2 (H Rept 105-767). House passed, under suspension of the rules, Oct. 13. Senate agreed to House amendment Oct. 14. President signed Nov. 13, 1998.

PL 105-392 (S 1754) Amend the Public Health Service Act to consolidate and reauthorize health professions and minority and disadvantaged health professions and disadvantaged health education programs. Introduced by Frist, R-Tenn., March 12, 1998. Senate Labor and Human Resources reported, amended June 23 (S Rept 105-220). Senate passed, amended July 31. House passed, amended, under suspension of the rules, Oct. 13. Senate agreed to House amendment Oct. 14. President signed Nov. 13, 1998.

PL 105-393 (S 2364) Reauthorize and make reforms to programs authorized by the Public Works and Economic Development Act of 1965 and the Appalachian Regional Development Act of 1965. Introduced by Chafee, R-R.I., July 28, 1998. Senate Environment and Public Works reported Sept. 14 (S Rept 105-332). Senate passed, amended, Oct. 12. House passed, under suspension of the rules, Oct. 13. President signed Nov. 13, 1998.

PL 105-394 (S 2432) Support programs of grants to states to address the assistive technology needs of individuals with disabilities. Introduced by Jeffords, R-Vt., Sept. 2, 1998. Senate Labor and Human Resources reported, amended, Sept. 15 (S Rept 105-334). Senate passed, amended, Oct. 5. House passed, amended, under suspension of the rules, Oct. 9. Senate agreed to House amendment Oct. 14. President signed Nov. 13, 1998.

106th Congress—1999

PL 106-1 (HR 433) Restore the management and personnel authority of the mayor of the District of Columbia. Introduced by Davis, R-Va., on Feb. 2, 1999. House Government Reform discharged. House passed Feb. 9. Senate passed Feb. 23. President signed March 5, 1999.

PL 106-2 (HR 882) Nullify any reservation of funds during fiscal year 1999 for guaranteed loans under the Consolidated Farm and Rural Development Act for qualified beginning farmers or ranchers. Introduced by Combest, R-Texas, on March 1, 1999. House passed, under suspension of the rules, March 2. Senate passed March 8. President signed March 15, 1999.

PL 106-3 (S 447) Deem the applications submitted by the Dodson School Districts for certain Impact Aid payments for fiscal year 1999 as filed on time, and process for payment. Introduced by Burns, R-Mont., on Feb. 23, 1999. Senate Health, Education, Labor and Pensions discharged. Senate passed March 2. House passed March 10. President signed March 23, 1999.

PL 106-4 (HR 540) Amend Title XIX of the Social Security Act to prohibit transfers or discharges of residents of nursing facilities as a result of a voluntary withdrawal from participation in the Medicaid program. Introduced by Davis, D-Fla., on Feb. 3, 1999. House Commerce reported March 8 (H Rept 106-44). House passed, under suspension of the rules, March 10. Senate passed March 15. President signed March 25, 1999.

PL 106-5 (HR 808) Extend for three additional months the period for which Chapter 12 of Title 11 of the U.S. Code is reenacted. Introduced by Smith, R-Mich., on Feb. 23, 1999. House Judiciary reported, amended, March 9 (H Rept 106-45). House passed, amended, under suspension of the rules, March 11. Senate passed March 24. President signed March 30, 1999.

PL 106-6 (S 643) Authorize the Airport Improvement Program for two months. Introduced by McCain, R-Ariz., on March 17, 1999. Senate passed, amended, March 17. House passed March 24. President signed March 31, 1999.

PL 106-7 (HR 1212) Protect producers of agricultural commodities who applied for a Crop Revenue Coverage PLUS supplemental endorsement for the 1999 crop year. Introduced by Combest, R-Texas, on March 22, 1999. House passed, amended, under suspension of the rules, March 23. Senate passed March 25. President signed April 1, 1999.

PL 106-8 (S 314) Provide for a loan guarantee program to address the Year 2000 computer problems of small businesses. Introduced by Bond, R-Mo., on Jan. 27, 1999. Senate Small Business reported Feb. 23 (S Rept 106-5). Senate passed March 2. House passed, under suspension of the rules, March 23. President signed April 2, 1999.

PL 106-9 (HR 68) Amend Section 20 of the Small Business Act and make technical corrections in Title III of the Small Business Investment Act. Introduced by Talent, R-Mo., on Jan. 6, 1999. House Small Business reported Jan.

19 (H Rept 106-1). House passed, amended, under suspension of the rules, Feb. 2. Senate Small Business discharged. Senate passed, with amendment, March 22. House agreed to Senate amendment, under suspension of the rules, March 23. President signed April 5, 1999.

PL 106-10 (HR 92) Designate the federal building and U.S. courthouse at 251 N. Main St. in Winston-Salem, N.C., as the "Hiram H. Ward Federal Building and United States Courthouse." Introduced by Coble, R-N.C., on Jan. 6, 1999. House Transportation and Infrastructure reported Feb. 23 (H Rept 106-20). House passed, under suspension of the rules, Feb. 23. Senate Environment and Public Works reported March 17 (no written report). Senate passed March 23. President signed April 5, 1999.

PL 106-11 (HR 158) Designate the federal courthouse at 316 N. 26th St. in Billings, Mont., as the "James F. Battin Federal Courthouse." Introduced by Hill, R-Mont., on Jan. 6, 1999. House Transportation and Infrastructure reported, amended, Feb. 23 (H Rept 106-21). House passed, amended, under suspension of the rules, Feb. 23. Senate Environment and Public Works reported March 17 (no written report). Senate passed March 23. President signed April 5, 1999.

PL 106-12 (HR 233) Designate the federal building at 700 E. San Antonio St. in El Paso, Texas, as the "Richard C. White Federal Building." Introduced by Reyes, D-Texas, on Jan. 6, 1999. House Transportation and Infrastructure reported Feb. 23 (H Rept 106-22). House passed, under suspension of the rules, Feb. 23. Senate Environment and Public Works reported March 17 (no written report). Senate passed March 23. President signed April 5, 1999.

PL 106-13 (HR 396) Designate the federal building located at 1301 Clay St. in Oakland, Calif., as the "Ronald V. Dellums Federal Building." Introduced by Miller, D-Calif., on Jan. 19, 1999. House Transportation and Infrastructure reported Feb. 23 (H Rept 106-23). House passed, under suspension of the rules, Feb. 23. Senate Environment and Public Works reported March 17 (no written report). Senate passed March 23. President signed April 5, 1999.

PL 106-14 (H J Res 26) Provide for the reappointment of Barber B. Conable Jr. as a citizen regent of the Board of Regents of the Smithsonian Institution. Introduced by Johnson, R-Texas, on Feb. 9, 1999. House Administration discharged. House passed March 23. Senate passed March 24. President signed April 6, 1999.

PL 106-15 (H J Res 27) Provide for the reappointment of Dr. Hanna H. Gray as a citizen regent of the Board of Regents of the Smithsonian Institution. Introduced by Johnson, R-Texas, on Feb. 9, 1999. House Administration discharged. House passed March 23. Senate passed March 24. President signed April 6, 1999.

PL 106-16 (H J Res 28) Provide for the reappointment of Wesley S. Williams Jr. as a citizen regent of the Board of Regents of the Smithsonian Institution. Introduced by Johnson, R-Texas, on Feb. 9, 1999. House Administration discharged. House passed March 23. Senate passed March 24. President signed April 6, 1999.

PL 106-17 (HR 774) Amend the Small Business Act to change the conditions of participation and authorize appropriations for the women's business center program. Introduced by Velazquez, D-N.Y., on Feb. 23, 1999. House Small Business reported March 10 (H Rept 106-47). House passed, amended, under suspension of the rules, March 16. Senate passed March 24. President signed April 6, 1999.

PL 106-18 (HR 171) Authorize appropriations for the Coastal Heritage Trail Route in New Jersey. Introduced by LoBiondo, R-N.J., on Jan. 6, 1999. House Resources reported Feb. 11 (H Rept 106-16). House passed, under suspension of the rules, Feb. 23. Senate Energy and Natural Resources reported March 17 (S Rept 106-24). Senate passed March 25. President signed April 8, 1999.

PL 106-19 (HR 705) Make technical corrections with respect to the monthly reports submitted by the Postmaster General on official mail of the House of Representatives. Introduced by Thomas, R-Calif., on Feb. 11, 1999. House Administration discharged. House passed Feb. 11. Senate Governmental Affairs discharged. Senate passed March 25. President signed April 8, 1999.

PL 106-20 (HR 193) Designate a portion of the Sudbury, Assabet, and Concord Rivers as a component of the National Wild and Scenic Rivers System. Introduced by Meehan, D-Mass., on Jan. 6, 1999. House Resources re-

ported Feb. 8 (H Rept 106-10). House passed, amended, under suspension of the rules, Feb. 23. Senate Energy and Natural Resources reported March 17 (S Rept 106-25). Senate passed March 25. President signed April 9, 1999.

PL 106-21 (HR 1376) Extend the tax benefits available with respect to services performed in a combat zone to services performed in the Federal Republic of Yugoslavia (Serbia/Montenegro) and certain other areas. Introduced by Archer, R-Texas, on April 13, 1999. House Ways and Means reported, amended, April 13 (H Rept 106-90). House passed, amended, April 15. Senate passed April 15. President signed April 19, 1999.

PL 106-22 (HR 440) Make technical corrections to the Microloan Program. Introduced by Talent, R-Mo., on Feb. 2, 1999. House Small Business reported Feb. 8 (H Rept 106-12). House passed, amended, under suspension of the rules, Feb. 9. Senate Small Business discharged. Senate passed, amended, March 25. House agreed to Senate amendment, under suspension of the rules, April 12. President signed April 27, 1999.

PL 106-23 (HR 911) Designate the federal building at 310 New Bern Ave., Raleigh, N.C., as the "Terry Sanford Federal Building." Introduced by Etheridge, D-N.C., on March 2, 1999. House passed, amended, under suspension of the rules, April 12. Senate passed April 15. President signed April 27, 1999.

PL 106-24 (S 388) Authorize the establishment of a disaster mitigation pilot program in the Small Business Administration. Introduced by Cleland, D-Ga., on Feb. 8, 1999. Senate Small Business discharged. Senate passed March 25. House passed, under suspension of the rules, April 12. President signed April 27, 1999.

PL 106-25 (HR 800) Provide for education flexibility partnerships. Introduced by Castle, R-Del., on Feb. 23, 1999. House Education and the Workforce reported, amended, March 8 (H Rept 106-43). House passed, amended, March 11. Senate passed, amended, March 11. Conference report filed in the House April 20 (H Rept 106-100). House agreed to conference report April 21. Senate agreed to conference report April 21. President signed April 29, 1999.

PL 106-26 (S 531) Authorize the president to award a gold medal on behalf of the Congress to Rosa Parks in recognition of her contributions to the nation. Introduced by Abraham, R-Mich., on March 4, 1999. Senate Banking, Housing and Urban Affairs discharged. Senate passed April 19. House passed April 20. President signed May 4, 1999.

PL 106-27 (S 453) Designate the federal building at 709 W. 9th St. in Juneau, Alaska, as the "Hurff A. Saunders Federal Building." Introduced by Murkowski, R-Alaska, on Feb. 24, 1999. Senate Environment and Public Works reported March 17 (no written report). Senate passed March 23. House Transportation and Infrastructure reported April 27 (H Rept 106-113). House passed, under suspension of the rules, May 4. President signed May 13, 1999.

PL 106-28 (S 460) Designate the U.S. courthouse at 401 S. Michigan St. in South Bend, Ind., as the "Robert K. Rodibaugh United States Bankruptcy Courthouse." Introduced by Lugar, R-Ind., on Feb. 24, 1999. Senate Environment and Public Works reported March 17 (no written report). Senate passed March 23. House Transportation and Infrastructure reported March 24 (H Rept 106-114). House passed, under suspension of the rules, May 4. President signed May 13, 1999.

PL 106-29 (HR 432) Designate the North/South Center at the University of Miami as the "Dante B. Fascell North-South Center." Introduced by Gilman, R-N.Y., on Feb. 2, 1999. House passed Feb. 2, under suspension of the rules. Senate Foreign Relations reported March 23 (no written report). Senate passed May 5. President signed May 21, 1999.

PL 106-30 (HR 669) Amend the Peace Corps Act to authorize appropriations for fiscal 2000 through 2003. Introduced by Campbell, R-Calif., on Feb. 10, 1999. House International Relations reported Feb. 16 (H Rept 106-18). House passed March 3. Senate Foreign Relations reported May 11 (S Rept 106-46). Senate passed May 12. President signed May 21, 1999.

PL 106-31 (HR 1141) Make emergency supplemental appropriations for the fiscal year ending Sept. 30, 1999. Introduced by Young, R-Fla., on March 17, 1999. House Appropriations reported March 17 (H Rept 106-64). House passed March 24. Senate passed, amended, March 25. Conference report filed in the House May 14 (H Rept 106-143). House agreed to conference report May 18. Senate agreed to conference report May 20. President signed May 21, 1999.

PL 106-32 (HR 1034) Declare a portion of the James River and Kanawha Canal in Richmond, Va., to be nonnavigable waters of the United States for purposes of Title 46, U.S. Code, and the other maritime laws of the U.S. Introduced by Bliley, R-Va., on March 9, 1999. House Transportation and Infrastructure reported, amended, under suspension of the rules, April 27 (H Rept 106-107). House passed, amended, April 27. Senate Commerce, Science and Transportation reported May 18 (no written report). Senate passed May 26. President signed June 1, 1999.

PL 106-33 (HR 1121) Designate the federal building and U.S. courthouse at 18 Greenville St. in Newnan, Ga., as the "Lewis R. Morgan Federal Building and United States Courthouse." Introduced by Collins, R-Ga., March 16, 1999. House Transportation and Infrastructure reported April 27 (H Rept 106-111). House passed, under suspension of the rules, May 4. Senate Environment and Public Works discharged. Senate passed May 26. President signed June 7, 1999.

PL 106-34 (HR 1183) Amend the Fastener Quality Act to strengthen protections against the sale of mismarked, misrepresented, and counterfeit fasteners and eliminate unnecessary requirements. Introduced by Sensenbrenner, R-Wis., March 18, 1999. House Science reported, amended, April 29 (H Rept 106-121, Pt. 1). House Commerce discharged. House passed, amended, under suspension of the rules, May 11. Senate passed May 25. President signed June 8, 1999.

PL 106-35 (HR 1379) Amend the Omnibus Consolidated and Emergency Supplemental Appropriations Act of 1999 to make a technical correction relating to an emergency supplemental appropriation for international narcotics control and law enforcement assistance. Introduced by Gilman, R-N.Y., April 13, 1999. House passed, amended, April 20. Senate Foreign Relations discharged. Senate passed May 27. President signed June 15, 1999.

PL 106-36 (HR 435) Make miscellaneous and technical changes to various trade laws. Introduced by Archer, R-Texas, Feb. 2, 1999. House passed, under suspension of the rules, Feb. 9. Senate passed, with amendment, May 27. House agreed to Senate amendment, under suspension of the rules, June 7. President signed June 25, 1999.

PL 106-37 (HR 775) Establish certain procedures for civil actions brought for damages relating to the failure of any device or system to process or otherwise deal with the transition from the year 1999 to the year 2000. Introduced by Davis, R-Va., Feb. 23, 1999. House Judiciary reported, amended May 7 (H Rept 106-131, Pt. 1). Small Business discharged. Commerce discharged. House passed, amended, May 12. Senate passed, with amendment, June 15. Conference report filed in the House on June 29 (H Rept 106-212). House agreed to conference report July 1. Senate agreed to conference report July 1. President signed July 20, 1999.

PL 106-38 (HR 4) Declare it to be the policy of the United States to deploy a national missile defense. Introduced by Weldon, R-Pa., Feb. 4, 1999. House Armed Services reported March 2 (H Rept 106-39, Pt. 1). International Relations discharged. House passed March 18. Senate passed, with amendment, May 18. House agreed to Senate amendment May 20. President signed July 22, 1999.

PL 106-39 (HR 2035) Correct errors in the authorizations of certain programs administered by the National Highway Traffic Safety Administration. Introduced by Tauzin, R-La., June 8, 1999. House Commerce reported June 25 (H Rept 106-200). House passed, amended, under suspension of the rules, July 12. Senate passed July 15. President signed July 28, 1999.

PL 106-40 (S 880) Amend the Clean Air Act to remove flammable fuels from the list of substances with respect to which reporting and other activities are required under the risk management plan program. Introduced by Inhofe, R-Okla., April 26, 1999. Senate Environment and Public Works reported, amended, June 9 (S Rept 106-70). Senate passed June 23. House passed, amended, July 21. Senate agreed to House amendment Aug. 2. President signed Aug. 5, 1999.

PL 106-41 (S 604) Direct the secretary of agriculture to complete a land exchange with Georgia Power Co. Introduced by Coverdell, R-Ga., March 15, 1999. Senate Agriculture, Nutrition and Forestry reported June 21 (no written report). Senate passed June 28. House passed, under suspension of the rules, July 26. President signed Aug. 5, 1999.

PL 106-42 (S 1258) Authorize funds for the payment of salaries and expenses of the Patent and Trademark Office. Introduced by Hatch, R-Utah,

June 22, 1999. Senate Judiciary reported July 1 (no written report). Senate passed July 1. House passed, under suspension of the rules, July 26. President signed Aug. 5, 1999.

PL 106-43 (S 1259) Amend the Trademark Act of 1946 relating to dilution of famous marks. Introduced by Hatch, R-Utah, June 22, 1999. Senate Judiciary reported July 1 (no written report). Senate passed July 1. House passed, under suspension of the rules, July 26. President signed Aug. 5, 1999.

PL 106-44 (S 1260) Make technical corrections to Title 17, U.S. Code, and other laws. Introduced by Hatch, R-Utah, June 22, 1999. Senate Judiciary reported July 1 (no written report). Senate passed July 1. House passed, under suspension of the rules, July 26. President signed Aug. 5, 1999.

PL 106-45 (HR 66) Preserve the cultural resources of the Route 66 corridor and authorize the secretary of the interior to provide assistance. Introduced by Wilson, R-N.M., Jan. 6, 1999. House Resources reported, amended May 13 (H Rept 106-137). House passed, amended, June 30. Senate passed July 27. President signed Aug. 10, 1999.

PL 106-46 (HR 2565) Clarify the quorum requirement for the board of directors of the Export-Import Bank of the United States. Introduced by Leach, R-Iowa, July 20, 1999. House passed, amended, under suspension of the rules, July 26. Senate Banking, Housing and Urban Affairs discharged Aug. 5. Senate passed Aug. 5. President signed Aug. 11, 1999.

PL 106-47 (S 1543) Amend the Agricultural Adjustment Act of 1938 to provide for the release of tobacco production and marketing information. Introduced by McConnell, R-Ky., Aug. 5, 1999. Senate passed Aug. 5. House passed Aug. 5. President signed Aug. 13, 1999

PL 106-48 (HR 211) Designate the federal building and U.S. courthouse at West 920 Riverside Ave. in Spokane, Wash., as the "Thomas S. Foley Federal Building and United States Courthouse," and the plaza at the south entrance of such building and courthouse as the "Walter F. Horan Plaza." Introduced by Nethercutt, R-Wash., Jan. 6, 1999. House passed, amended, under suspension of the rules, Aug. 2. Senate passed Aug. 5. President signed Aug. 17, 1999.

PL 106-49 (HR 1219) Amend the Office of Federal Procurement Policy Act and the Miller Act, relating to payment protections for persons providing labor and materials for federal construction projects. Introduced by Maloney, D-N.Y., March 23, 1999. House Government Reform reported, amended, July 30 (H Rept 106-277, Pt. 1). House passed, amended, under suspension of the rules, Aug. 2. Senate passed Aug. 5. President signed Aug. 17, 1999.

PL 106-50 (HR 1568) Provide technical, financial, and procurement assistance to veteran-owned small businesses. Introduced by Talent, R-Mo., April 27, 1999. House Small Business reported, amended, June 29 (H Rept 106-206, Pt. 1). House Veterans' Affairs discharged June 29. House passed, amended, under suspension of the rules, June 29. Senate Small Business reported, amended, Aug. 4 (S Rept 106-136). Senate passed, amended, Aug. 5. House agreed to Senate amendment Aug. 6. President signed Aug. 17, 1999.

PL 106-51 (HR 1664) Make emergency supplemental appropriations for military operations, refugee relief, and humanitarian assistance relating to the conflict in Kosovo, and for military operations in southwest Asia for the fiscal year ending Sept. 30, 1999. Introduced by Young, R-Fla., May 4, 1999. House Appropriations reported May 4 (H Rept 106-125). House passed, amended, May 6. Senate Appropriations reported, amended, May 25 (no written report). Senate passed, with amendments, June 18. House agreed to Senate amendments Aug. 4. President signed Aug. 17, 1999.

PL 106-52 (HR 2465) Make appropriations for military construction, family housing, and base realignment and closure for the Department of Defense for the fiscal year ending Sept. 30, 2000. Introduced by Hobson, R-Ohio, July 2, 1999. House Appropriations reported July 2, 1999 (H Rept 106-221). House passed July 13. Senate passed, with amendment, July 14. Conference report filed in the House on July 27 (H Rept 106-266). House agreed to conference report July 29. Senate agreed to conference report Aug. 3. President signed Aug. 17, 1999.

PL 106-53 (S 507) Provide for the conservation and development of water and related resources, and authorize the Army Corps of Engineers to construct various projects for improvements to rivers and harbors of the United States. Introduced by Warner, R-Va., March 2, 1999. Senate Environment and Public Works reported, amended, March 23 (S Rept 106-34). Senate passed, amended, April 19. House passed, with amendment, July 22. Conference report filed in the House on Aug. 5 (H Rept 106-298). Senate agreed to conference report Aug. 5. House agreed to conference report Aug. 5. President signed Aug. 17, 1999.

PL 106-54 (S 606) Direct the secretary of the Treasury to pay specified funds to the Global Exploration and Development Corp., Kerr-McGee Corp., and Kerr-McGee Chemical LLC, in settlement and compromise of claims. Introduced by Nickles, R-Okla., March 15, 1999. Senate Judiciary reported, amended, June 10 (no written report). Senate passed, amended, July 1. House passed, amended, under suspension of the rules, Aug. 2. Senate agreed to House amendment Aug. 4. President signed Aug. 17, 1999.

PL 106-55 (S 1546) Amend the International Religious Freedom Act of 1998 to provide additional administrative authority to the U.S. Commission on International Religious Freedom, and to make technical corrections to that act. Introduced by Nickles, R-Okla., Aug. 5, 1999. Senate passed Aug. 5. House passed Aug. 5. President signed Aug. 17, 1999.

PL 106-56 (HR 457) Amend Title 5, U.S. Code, to increase the amount of leave time available to a federal employee in any year in connection with serving as an organ donor. Introduced by Cummings, D-Md., on Feb. 2, 1999. House Government Reform reported June 8 (H Rept 106-174). House passed, under suspension of the rules, July 26. Senate Governmental Affairs reported Aug. 27 (S Rept 106-143). Senate passed Sept. 8. President signed Sept. 24, 1999.

PL 106-57 (HR 1905) Make appropriations for the legislative branch for the fiscal year ending Sept. 30, 2000. Introduced by Taylor, R-N.C., on May 24, 1999. House Appropriations reported May 21 (H Rept 106-156). House passed, amended, June 10. Senate passed, with amendments, June 16. Conference report filed in the House on Aug. 4 (H Rept 106-290). House agreed to conference report Aug. 5. Senate agreed to conference report Aug. 9. President signed Sept. 29, 1999.

PL 106-58 (HR 2490) Make appropriations for the Treasury Department, the U.S. Postal Service, the Executive Office of the President, and certain independent agencies for the fiscal year ending Sept. 30, 2000. Introduced by Kolbe, R-Ariz., on July 13, 1999. House Appropriations reported July 13 (H Rept 106-231). House passed, amended, July 15. Senate passed, with amendment, July 19. Conference report filed in the House on Sept. 14 (H Rept 106-319). House agreed to conference report Sept. 15. Senate agreed to conference report Sept. 16. President signed Sept. 29, 1999.

PL 106-59 (S 1637) Extend through the end of the current fiscal year certain expiring Federal Aviation Administration authorizations. Introduced by Lott, R-Miss., on Sept. 24, 1999. Senate passed Sept. 24. House passed, under suspension of the rules, Sept. 27. President signed Sept. 29, 1999.

PL 106-60 (HR 2605) Make appropriations for energy and water development for the fiscal year ending Sept. 30, 2000. Introduced by Packard, R-Calif., July 23, 1999. House Appropriations reported July 23, 1999 (H Rept 106-253). House passed, amended, July 27. Senate passed, with amendment, July 28. Conference report filed in the House Sept. 27 (H Rept 106-336). House agreed to conference report Sept. 27. Senate agreed to conference report Sept. 28. President signed Sept. 29, 1999.

PL 106-61 (H J Res 34) Congratulate and commend the veterans of foreign wars. Introduced by Stump, R-Ariz., on Feb. 25, 1999. House Veterans' Affairs reported June 29 (H Rept 106-205). House passed, under suspension of the rules, June 29. Senate passed Sept. 28. President signed Sept. 29, 1999.

PL 106-62 (H J Res 68) Make continuing appropriations for fiscal year 2000. Introduced by Young, R-Fla., on Sept. 27, 1999. House passed Sept. 28. Senate passed Sept. 28. President signed Sept. 30, 1999.

PL 106-63 (S 380) Reauthorize the Congressional Award Act. Introduced by Craig, R-Idaho, on Feb. 4, 1999. Senate Governmental Affairs reported March 26 (S Rept 106-38). Senate passed April 13. House passed, under suspension of the rules, Sept. 13. President signed Oct. 1, 1999.

PL 106-64 (HR 2981) Extend energy conservation programs under the Energy Policy and Conservation Act through March 31, 2000. Introduced by Bliley, R-Va., on Sept. 30, 1999. House Commerce discharged. House passed Sept. 30. Senate passed Sept. 30. President signed Oct. 5, 1999.

PL 106-65 (S 1059) Authorize appropriations for fiscal year 2000 for military activities of the Department of Defense, for military construction, for defense activities of the Department of Energy, and to prescribe personnel strengths for the Armed Forces. Introduced by Warner, R-Va., on May 17, 1999. Senate Armed Services reported May 17 (S Rept 106-50). Senate passed, amended, May 27. House passed, with amendment, June 14. Conference report filed in the House on Aug. 6 (H Rept 106-301). House agreed to conference report Sept. 15. Senate agreed to conference report Sept. 22. President signed Oct. 5, 1999.

PL 106-66 (S 293) Direct the secretaries of agriculture and interior to convey certain lands in San Juan County, N.M., to San Juan College. Introduced by Domenici, R-N.M., on Jan. 21, 1999. Senate Energy and Natural Resources reported March 16 (S Rept 106-17). Senate passed, amended, March 25. House passed, under suspension of the rules, Sept. 27. President signed Oct. 6, 1999.

PL 106-67 (S 944) Amend Public Law 105-188 to provide for the mineral leasing of certain Native American lands in Oklahoma. Introduced by Inhofe, R-Okla., on May 3, 1999. Senate Indian Affairs reported Aug. 2 (S Rept 106-132). Senate passed Aug. 5. House Resources reported Sept. 27 (H Rept 106-338). House passed, under suspension of the rules, Sept. 27. President signed Oct. 6, 1999.

PL 106-68 (S 1072) Make certain technical and other corrections relating to the Centennial of Flight Commemoration Act. Introduced by DeWine, R-Ohio, on May 18, 1999. Senate Governmental Affairs reported July 8 (S Rept 106-105). Senate passed, amended, Aug. 5. House passed, under suspension of the rules, Sept. 27. President signed Oct. 6, 1999.

PL 106-69 (HR 2084) Make appropriations for the Department of Transportation and related agencies for the fiscal year ending Sept. 30, 2000. Introduced by Wolf, R-Va., on June 9, 1999. House Appropriations reported June 9 (H Rept 106-180). House passed, amended, June 23. Senate passed, with amendment, Sept. 16. Conference report filed in the House Sept. 30 (H Rept 106-355). House agreed to conference report Oct. 1. Senate agreed to conference report Oct. 4. President signed Oct. 9, 1999.

PL 106-70 (S 1606) Extend for nine additional months the period for which Chapter 12 of Title 11, U.S. Code, is enacted. Introduced by Grassley, R-Iowa, on Sept. 21, 1999. Senate passed, amended, Sept. 30. House passed, under suspension of the rules, Oct. 4. President signed Oct. 9, 1999.

PL 106-71 (S 249) Provide funding for the National Center for Missing and Exploited Children and reauthorize the Runaway and Homeless Youth Act. Introduced by Hatch, R-Utah, on Jan. 19, 1999. Senate Judiciary reported, amended, March 4 (no written report). Senate passed, amended, April 19. House passed, with amendment, under suspension of the rules, May 25. Senate agreed to House amendment Sept. 28. President signed Oct. 12, 1999.

PL 106-72 (S 559) Designate the federal building located at 33 East 8th St. in Austin, Texas, as the "J. J. 'Jake' Pickle Federal Building." Introduced by Gramm, R-Texas, on March 8, 1999. Senate Environment and Public Works reported May 12 (no written report). Senate passed June 16. House passed, under suspension of the rules, Oct. 5. President signed Oct. 19, 1999.

PL 106-73 (HR 3036) Provide for interim continuation of administration of motor carrier functions by the Federal Highway Administration. Introduced by Shuster, R-Pa., on Oct. 7, 1999. House passed, amended, under suspension of the rules, Oct. 12. Senate passed Oct. 14. President signed Oct. 19, 1999.

PL 106-74 (HR 2684) Make appropriations for the departments of Veterans Affairs and Housing and Urban Development, and for various independent agencies, boards, commissions, corporations, and offices for fiscal 2000. Introduced by Walsh, R-N.Y., on Aug. 3, 1999. House Appropriations reported Aug. 3 (H Rept 106-286). House passed, amended, Sept. 9. Senate Appropriations discharged. Senate passed, with amendment, Sept. 24. Conference report filed in the House Oct. 13 (H Rept 106-379). House agreed to conference report Oct. 14. Senate agreed to conference report Oct. 15. President signed Oct. 20, 1999.

PL 106-75 (H J Res 71) Make further continuing appropriations for fiscal 2000. Introduced by Young, R-Fla., on Oct. 18, 1999. House passed Oct. 19. Senate passed Oct. 19. President signed Oct. 21, 1999.

PL 106-76 (S 323) Redesignate the Black Canyon of the Gunnison National Monument as a national park and establish the Gunnison Gorge National Conservation Area. Introduced by Campbell, R-Colo., on Jan. 28, 1999. Senate Energy and Natural Resources reported, amended, June 8 (S Rept 106-69). Senate passed, amended, July 1. House Resources reported, amended, Sept. 8 (H Rept 106-307). House passed, with amendment, under suspension of the rules, Sept. 27. Senate agreed to House amendment Oct. 1. President signed Oct. 21, 1999.

PL 106-77 (HR 560) Designate the federal building located at 300 Recinto Sur St. in Old San Juan, Puerto Rico, as the "Jose V. Toledo United States Post Office and Courthouse." Introduced by Romero-Barcelo, D-P.R., on Feb. 3, 1999. House Transportation and Infrastructure reported, amended, April 27 (H Rept 106-108). House passed, amended, under suspension of the rules, May 4. Senate Environment and Public Works reported Sept. 29 (no written report). Senate passed Oct. 8. President signed Oct. 22, 1999.

PL 106-78 (HR 1906) Make appropriations for agriculture, rural development, the Food and Drug Administration, and related agencies for fiscal 2000. Introduced by Skeen, R-N.M., on May 24, 1999. House Appropriations reported May 21 (H Rept 106-157). House passed, amended, June 8. Senate Appropriations discharged. Senate passed, with amendment, Aug. 4. Conference report filed in the House on Sept. 30 (H Rept 106-354). House agreed to conference report Oct. 1. Senate agreed to conference report Oct. 13. President signed Oct. 22, 1999.

PL 106-79 (HR 2561) Make appropriations for the Department of Defense for fiscal 2000. Introduced by Lewis, R-Calif., on July 20, 1999. House Appropriations reported July 20 (H Rept 106-244). House passed, amended, July 22. Senate passed, with amendment, July 28. Conference report filed in the House Oct. 8 (H Rept 106-371). House agreed to conference report Oct. 13. Senate agreed to conference report Oct. 14. President signed Oct. 25, 1999.

PL 106-80 (S 322) Amend Title 4, U.S. Code, to add the Martin Luther King Jr. holiday to the list of days on which the flag should especially be displayed. Introduced by Campbell, R-Colo., on Jan. 28, 1999. Senate Judiciary reported April 29 (no written report). Senate passed June 14. House passed Oct. 12. President signed Oct. 25, 1999.

PL 106-81 (S 800) Promote and enhance public safety through the use of 911 as the universal emergency assistance number, further deploy wireless 911 service, support states in upgrading 911 capabilities, and encourage construction and operation of seamless, ubiquitous, and reliable networks for personal wireless services. Introduced by Burns, R-Mont., on April 14, 1999. Senate Commerce, Science and Transportation reported Aug. 4 (S Rept 106-138). Senate passed, amended, Aug. 5. House passed, under suspension of the rules, Oct. 12. President signed Oct. 26, 1999.

PL 106-82 (HR 356) Provide for the conveyance of certain property from the United States to Stanislaus County, Calif. Introduced by Condit, D-Calif., on Jan. 19, 1999. House passed, under suspension of the rules, Oct. 4. Senate passed Oct. 13. President signed Oct. 27, 1999.

PL 106-83 (HR 1663) Designate as a national memorial the memorial being built at the Riverside National Cemetery in Riverside, Calif., to honor recipients of the Medal of Honor. Introduced by Calvert, R-Calif., on May 4, 1999. House Veterans' Affairs reported, amended, Sept. 30 (H Rept 106-351). House passed, amended, under suspension of the rules, Oct. 5. Senate Armed Services discharged. Senate passed Oct. 20. President signed Oct. 28, 1999.

PL 106-84 (HR 2841) Amend the Revised Organic Act of the Virgin Islands to provide for greater fiscal autonomy consistent with other United States jurisdictions. Introduced by Christensen, D-Virgin Is., on Sept. 13, 1999. House Resources reported Sept. 27 (H Rept 106-337). House passed, amended, under suspension of the rules, Sept. 27. Senate Energy and Natural Resources discharged. Senate passed Oct. 19. President signed Oct. 28, 1999.

PL 106-85 (H J Res 73) Make further continuing appropriations for fiscal 2000. Introduced by Young, R-Fla., on Oct. 27, 1999. House passed Oct. 28. Senate passed Oct. 28. President signed Oct. 29, 1999.

PL 106-86 (HR 659) Authorize appropriations for the protection of the Paoli and Brandywine Battlefields in Pennsylvania, direct the National Park Service to conduct a special resource study of the Paoli and Brandywine Battlefields, and authorize the Valley Forge Museum of the American Revolution at Valley Forge National Historical Park. Introduced by Weldon, R-Pa., on Feb. 9, 1999. House Resources reported May 13 (H Rept 106-139). House passed, amended, June 22. Senate Energy and Natural Resources discharged. Senate passed, with amendments, Oct. 14. House agreed to Senate amendments, under suspension of the rules, Oct. 18. President signed Oct. 31, 1999.

PL 106-87 (HR 2367) Reauthorize a comprehensive program of support for victims of torture. Introduced by Smith, R-N.J., on June 29, 1999. House passed, amended, under the suspension of the rules, Sept. 21. Senate passed Oct. 21. President signed Nov. 3, 1999.

PL 106-88 (H J Res 75) Make further continuing appropriations for fiscal 2000. Introduced by Young, R-Fla., on Nov. 3, 1999. House passed Nov. 4. Senate passed Nov. 4. President signed Nov. 5, 1999.

PL 106-89 (HR 1175) Locate and secure the return of Zachary Baumel, an American citizen, and other Israeli soldiers missing in action. Introduced by Lantos, D-Calif., on March 18, 1999. House passed, amended, under suspension of the rules, June 22. Senate Foreign Relations reported with amendment June 30 (no written report). Senate passed, with amendments, Aug. 5. House agreed to Senate amendments, under suspension of the rules, Oct. 26. President signed Nov. 8, 1999.

PL 106-90 (H J Res 62) Grant the consent of Congress to the boundary change between Georgia and South Carolina. Introduced by Linder, R-Ga., on July 22, 1999. House Judiciary reported Sept. 8 (H Rept 106-304). House passed, under suspension of the rules, Sept. 21. Senate Judiciary reported Oct. 21 (no written report). Senate passed Oct. 26. President signed Nov. 8, 1999.

PL 106-91 (S 437) Designate the U.S. courthouse under construction at 338 Las Vegas Blvd. South in Las Vegas, Nev., as the "Lloyd D. George United States Courthouse." Introduced by Reid, D-Nev., on Feb. 22, 1999. Senate Environment and Public Works reported March 17 (no written report). Senate passed March 23. House passed, under suspension of the rules, Oct. 26. President signed Nov. 9, 1999.

PL 106-92 (S 1652) Designate the Old Executive Office Building at 17th St. and Pennsylvania Ave. N.W., in Washington, D.C., as the Dwight D. Eisenhower Executive Office Building. Introduced by Chafee, R-R.I., on Sept. 28, 1999. Senate Environment and Public Works reported Sept. 29 (no written report). Senate passed Oct. 19. House passed, under suspension of the rules, Oct. 26. President signed Nov. 9, 1999.

PL 106-93 (H J Res 76) Waive certain enrollment requirements for the remainder of the first session of the 106th Congress with respect to any bill or joint resolution making general appropriations or continuing appropriations for fiscal 2000. Introduced by Thomas, R-Calif., on Nov. 8, 1999. House Administration discharged. House passed Nov. 9. Senate passed Nov. 9. President signed Nov. 10, 1999.

PL 106-94 (H J Res 78) Make further continuing appropriations for fiscal 2000. Introduced by Young, R-Fla., on Nov. 9, 1999. House Appropriations discharged. House passed Nov. 9. Senate passed Nov. 10. President signed Nov. 10, 1999.

PL 106-95 (HR 441) Amend the Immigration and Nationality Act with respect to the requirements for the admission of nonimmigrant nurses who will practice in health profession shortage areas. Introduced by Rush, D-Ill., on Feb. 2, 1999. House Judiciary reported May 12 (H Rept 106-135). House passed, under suspension of the rules, May 24. Senate Judiciary reported June 24 (no written report). Senate passed with amendments Oct. 22. House agreed to Senate amendment, under suspension of the rules, Nov. 2. President signed Nov. 12, 1999.

PL 106-96 (HR 609) Amend the Export Apple and Pear Act to limit the applicability of the act to apples. Introduced by Walden, R-Ore., on Feb. 4, 1999. House Agriculture reported March 2 (H Rept 106-36). House passed, under suspension of the rules, March 2. Senate Banking, Housing and Urban Affairs discharged. Senate passed Nov. 3. President signed Nov. 12, 1999.

PL 106-97 (HR 915) Authorize a cost of living adjustment in the pay of administrative law judges. Introduced by Gekas, R-Pa., on March 2, 1999. House Government Reform reported, amended, Oct. 18 (H Rept 106-387). House passed, amended, under suspension of the rules, Oct. 25. Senate Governmental Affairs reported Nov. 4 (no written report). Senate passed Nov. 8. President signed Nov. 12, 1999.

PL 106-98 (HR 974) Establish a program to afford high school graduates from the District of Columbia the benefits of in-state tuition at state colleges and universities outside the District of Columbia. Introduced by Davis, R-Va., on March 4, 1999. House Government Reform reported, amended, May 24 (H Rept 106-158, Pt. 1). House Ways and Means discharged. House passed, amended, under suspension of the rules, May 24. Senate Governmental Affairs reported, amended, Sept. 9 (S Rept 106-154). Senate passed, with amendment, Oct. 19. House agreed to Senate amendment, under suspension of the rules, Nov. 1. President signed Nov. 12, 1999.

PL 106-99 (HR 2303) Direct the Librarian of Congress to prepare the history of the House of Representatives. Introduced by Larson, D-Conn., on June 22, 1999. House passed, amended, under suspension of the rules, Oct. 25. Senate Rules and Administration discharged. Senate passed Oct. 29. President signed Nov. 12, 1999.

PL 106-100 (HR 3122) Permit the enrollment in the House of Representatives Child Care Center of children of federal employees who are not employees of the legislative branch. Introduced by Thomas, R-Calif., on Oct. 21, 1999. House passed, under suspension of the rules, Oct. 25. Senate Rules and Administration discharged. Senate passed Nov. 4. President signed Nov. 12, 1999.

PL 106-101 (H J Res 54) Grant the consent of Congress to the Missouri-Nebraska Boundary Compact. Introduced by Danner, D-Mo., on May 12, 1999. House Judiciary reported Sept. 8 (H Rept 106-303). House passed, under suspension of the rules, Sept. 21. Senate Judiciary reported Nov. 4 (no written report). Senate passed Nov. 5. President signed Nov. 12, 1999.

PL 106-102 (S 900) Enhance competition in the financial services industry by providing a framework for the affiliation of banks, securities firms, and other financial service providers. Introduced by Gramm, R-Texas, on April 28, 1999. Senate Banking, Housing and Urban Affairs reported April 28 (S Rept 106-44). Senate passed, amended, May 6. House passed, with amendments, July 20. Conference report filed in the House Nov. 2 (H Rept 106-434). Senate agreed to conference report Nov. 4. House agreed to conference report Nov. 4. President signed Nov. 12, 1999.

PL 106-103 (HR 348) Authorize the construction of a monument to honor those who have served the nation's civil defense and emergency management programs. Introduced by Bartlett, R-Md., on Jan. 19, 1999. House Resources reported Oct. 27 (H Rept 106-416). House passed, under suspension of the rules, Nov. 1. Senate passed Nov. 8. President signed Nov. 13, 1999.

PL 106-104 (HR 3061) Amend the Immigration and Nationality Act to extend for an additional two years the period for admission of an alien as a nonimmigrant under section 101(a)(15)(S), and authorize appropriations for the refugee assistance program under Chapter 2 of Title IV of the act. Introduced by Smith, R-Texas, on Oct. 12, 1999. House passed, under suspension of the rules, Oct. 26. Senate passed Nov. 8. President signed Nov. 13, 1999.

PL 106-105 (H J Res 80) Make further continuing appropriations for fiscal 2000. Introduced by Dreier, R-Calif., on Nov. 16, 1999. House passed Nov. 17. Senate passed Nov. 17. President signed Nov. 18, 1999.

PL 106-106 (H J Res 83) Make further continuing appropriations for fiscal 2000. Introduced by Young, R-Fla., on Nov. 17, 1999. House passed, amended, Nov. 18. Senate passed Nov. 18. President signed Nov. 19, 1999.

PL 106-107 (S 468) Improve the effectiveness and performance of federal financial assistance programs, simplify the application and reporting requirements, and improve the delivery of services to the public. Introduced by Voinovich, R-Ohio, Feb. 25. Senate Governmental Affairs reported, amended, July 1 (S Rept 106-103). Senate passed, amended, July 15. House passed, with amendment, under suspension of the rules, Nov. 2. Senate agreed to House amendment Nov. 4. President signed Nov. 20, 1999.

PL 106-108 (HR 2454) Assure the long-term conservation of midcontinent light geese and the biological diversity of the ecosystem upon which many North American migratory birds depend, by directing the secretary of the interior to implement rules to reduce the overabundant population of midcontinent light geese. Introduced by Saxton, R-N.J., July 1, 1999. House Resources reported, amended, July 29 (H Rept 106-271). House passed, amended, under suspension of the rules, Aug. 2. Senate Environment and Public Works reported, with amendments, Oct. 14 (S Rept 106-188). Senate passed, with amendments, Nov. 8. House agreed to Senate amendments, under suspension of the rules, Nov. 10. President signed Nov. 24, 1999.

PL 106-109 (HR 2724) Make technical corrections to the Water Resources Development Act of 1999. Introduced by Shuster, R-Pa., Aug. 5, 1999. House passed Aug. 5. Senate Environment and Public Works reported, amended, Oct. 13 (S Rept 106-183). Senate passed, with amendment, Nov. 8. House agreed to Senate amendment, under suspension of the rules, Nov. 10. President signed Nov. 24, 1999.

PL 106-110 (S 1235) Amend Part G of Title I of the Omnibus Crime Control and Safe Streets Act of 1968 to allow railroad police officers to attend the Federal Bureau of Investigation National Academy for law enforcement training. Introduced by Leahy, D-Vt., on June 17, 1999. Senate Judiciary reported Oct. 21 (no written report). Senate passed Oct. 26. House passed, under suspension of the rules, Nov. 17. President signed Nov. 24, 1999.

PL 106-111 (HR 100) Establish designations for U.S. Postal Service buildings in Philadelphia. Introduced by Fattah, D-Pa., on Jan. 6, 1999. House passed, under suspension of the rules, May 24. Senate Governmental Affairs reported Nov. 4 (no written report). Senate passed Nov. 19. President signed Nov. 29, 1999.

PL 106-112 (HR 197) Designate the building of the U.S. Postal Service at 410 North 6th St. in Garden City, Kan., as the "Clifford R. Hope Post Office." Introduced by Moran, R-Kan., on Jan. 6, 1999. House passed, under suspension of the rules, May 24. Senate Governmental Affairs reported Nov. 4 (no written report). Senate passed Nov. 19. President signed Nov. 29, 1999.

PL 106-113 (HR 3194) Make appropriations for the government of the District of Columbia for fiscal 2000. Introduced by Istook, R-Okla., on Nov. 2, 1999. House passed Nov. 3. Senate passed, with amendment, Nov. 3. Conference report filed in the House Nov. 18 (H Rept 106-479). House agreed to conference report Nov. 18. Senate agreed to conference report Nov. 19. President signed Nov. 29, 1999.

PL 106-114 (S 278) Direct the secretary of the interior to convey certain lands to the county of Rio Arriba, N.M. Introduced by Domenici, R-N.M., on Jan. 21, 1999. Senate Energy and Natural Resources reported March 16 (S Rept 106-16). Senate passed March 25. House Resources reported Oct. 27 (H Rept 106-418). House passed, under suspension of the rules, Nov. 17. President signed Nov. 29, 1999.

PL 106-115 (S 382) Establish the Minuteman Missile National Historic Site in South Dakota. Introduced by Johnson, D-S.D., on Feb. 4, 1999. Senate Energy and Natural Resources reported March 17 (S Rept 106-23). Senate passed March 25. House Resources reported Oct. 18 (H Rept 106-391). House passed, under suspension of the rules, Nov. 17. President signed Nov. 29, 1999.

PL 106-116 (S 1398) Clarify certain boundaries on maps relating to the Coastal Barrier Resources System. Introduced by Helms, R-N.C., on July 20, 1999. Senate Environment and Public Works reported, amended, Oct. 6 (S Rept 106-171). Senate passed, amended, Nov. 8. House passed, under suspension of the rules, Nov. 17. President signed Nov. 29, 1999.

PL 106-117 (HR 2116) Amend Title 38, U.S. Code, to establish a program of extended care services for veterans and to make other improvements in health care programs of the Department of Veterans Affairs. Introduced by Stearns, R-Fla., on June 9, 1999. House Veterans' Affairs reported, amended, July 16 (H Rept 106-237). House passed, amended, under suspension of the rules, Sept. 21. Senate Veterans' Affairs discharged. Senate passed, with amendments, Nov. 5. Conference report filed in the House Nov. 16 (H Rept 106-470). House agreed to conference report, under suspension of the rules, Nov. 16. Senate agreed to conference report Nov. 19. President signed Nov. 30, 1999.

PL 106-118 (HR 2280) Amend Title 38, U.S. Code, to provide a cost of living adjustment in compensation rates paid for service-connected disabilities, enhance the compensation, memorial affairs, and housing programs of the Department of Veterans Affairs, and improve retirement authorities applicable to judges of the U.S. Court of Appeals for Veterans Claims. Introduced by Stump, R-Ariz., June 18, 1999. House Veterans' Affairs reported, amended, June 25 (H Rept 106-202). House passed, amended, under suspension of the rules, June 29. Senate Veterans' Affairs discharged. Senate passed, with amendment, July 26. House agreed to Senate amendment with amendments pursuant to H Res 368 on Nov. 9. Senate agreed to House amendments to Senate amendment Nov. 19. President signed Nov. 30, 1999.

PL 106-119 (HR 20) Authorize the secretary of the interior to construct and operate a visitor center for the Upper Delaware Scenic and Recreational

River on land owned by the state of New York. Introduced by Gilman, R-N.Y., on Jan. 6, 1999. House Resources reported Oct. 4 (H Rept 106-361). House passed, under suspension of the rules, Oct. 12. Senate Energy and Natural Resources reported, with amendment, Nov. 2 (S Rept 106-211). Senate passed Nov. 19. President signed Dec. 3, 1999.

PL 106-120 (HR 1555) Authorize appropriations for fiscal 2000 for intelligence and intelligence-related activities of the U.S. government, the Community Management Account, and the Central Intelligence Agency Retirement and Disability System. Introduced by Goss, R-Fla., on April 26, 1999. House Intelligence reported, amended, May 7 (H Rept 106-130, Pt. 1). House Armed Services discharged. House passed, amended, May 13. Senate passed, with amendment, July 21. Conference report filed in the House Nov. 5 (H Rept 106-457). House agreed to conference report Nov. 9. Senate agreed to conference report Nov. 19. President signed Dec. 3, 1999.

PL 106-121 (HR 459) Extend the deadline under the Federal Power Act for FERC Project No. 9401, the Mount Hope Waterpower Project. Introduced by Frelinghuysen, R-N.J., on Feb. 2, 1999. House Commerce reported April 28 (H Rept 106-119). House passed, under suspension of the rules, May 4. Senate Energy and Natural Resources reported June 24 (S Rept 106-97). Senate passed Nov. 19. President signed Dec. 6, 1999.

PL 106-122 (HR 1094) Amend the Federal Reserve Act to broaden the range of discount window loans that may be used as collateral for federal reserve notes. Introduced by Leach, R-Iowa, on March 11, 1999. House passed, amended, under suspension of the rules, Aug. 2. Senate Banking, Housing and Urban Affairs discharged. Senate passed Nov. 19. President signed Dec. 6, 1999.

PL 106-123 (HR 1191) Designate certain facilities of the U.S. Postal Service in Chicago. Introduced by Davis, D-Ill., on March 18, 1999. House passed, under suspension of the rules, May 24. Senate Governmental Affairs reported Nov. 4 (no written report). Senate passed Nov. 19. President signed Dec. 6, 1999.

PL 106-124 (HR 1251) Designate the U.S. Postal Service building at 8850 South 700 East, Sandy, Utah, as the "Noal Cushing Bateman Post Office Building." Introduced by Cook, R-Utah, on March 24, 1999. House passed, under suspension of the rules, May 24. Senate Governmental Affairs reported Nov. 4 (no written report). Senate passed Nov. 19. President signed Dec. 6, 1999.

PL 106-125 (HR 1327) Designate the U.S. Postal Service building at 34480 Highway 101 South in Cloverdale, Ore., as the "Maurine B. Neuberger United States Post Office." Introduced by Hooley, D-Ore., on March 25, 1999. House passed, under suspension of the rules, June 29. Senate Governmental Affairs reported Nov. 4 (no written report). Senate passed Nov. 19. President signed Dec. 6, 1999.

PL 106-126 (HR 3373) Require the secretary of the Treasury to mint coins in conjunction with the minting of coins by the Republic of Iceland in commemoration of the millennium of the discovery of the New World by Leif Ericson. Introduced by Leach, R-Iowa, on Nov. 16, 1999. House passed, under suspension of the rules, Nov. 16. Senate passed Nov. 19. President signed Dec. 6, 1999.

PL 106-127 (H J Res 85) Appoint the day for the convening of the second session of the 106th Congress. Introduced by Armey, R-Texas, on Nov. 18, 1999. House passed Nov. 18. Senate passed Nov. 19. President signed Dec. 6, 1999.

PL 106-128 (S 574) Direct the secretary of the interior to make corrections to a map relating to the Coastal Barrier Resources System. Introduced by Biden, D-Del., on March 10, 1999. Senate Environment and Public Works reported March 26 (S Rept 106-39). Senate passed April 22. House Resources discharged. House passed Nov. 18. President signed Dec. 6, 1999.

PL 106-129 (S 580) Amend Title IX of the Public Health Service Act to revise and extend the Agency for Healthcare Policy and Research. Introduced by Frist, R-Tenn., on March 10, 1999. Senate Health, Education, Labor and Pensions discharged. Senate passed, amended, Nov. 3. House passed Nov. 18. President signed Dec. 6, 1999.

PL 106-130 (S 1418) Provide for the holding of court at Natchez, Miss., in the same manner as court is held at Vicksburg, Miss. Introduced by Cochran, R-Miss., on July 22, 1999. Senate Judiciary reported Nov. 4 (no written report). Senate passed Nov. 5. House passed, with amendment, under suspension of the rules, Nov. 17. Senate agreed to House amendment Nov. 19. President signed Dec. 6, 1999.

PL 106-131 (HR 449) Authorize the Gateway Visitor Center at Independence National Historical Park. Introduced by Borski, D-Pa., Feb. 22, 1999. House Resources reported March 17 (H Rept 106-66). House passed, under suspension of the rules, April 12. Senate Energy and Natural Resources reported June 7 (S Rept 106-68). Senate passed Nov. 19. President signed Dec. 7, 1999.

PL 106-132 (HR 592) Redesignate Great Kills Park in the Gateway National Recreation Area as "World War II Veterans Park at Great Kills." Introduced by Fossella, R-N.Y., on Feb. 4, 1999. House Resources reported, amended June 16 (H Rept 106-188). House passed, amended, June 30. Senate Energy and Natural Resources reported Nov. 2 (S Rept 106-212). Senate passed Nov. 19. President signed Dec. 7, 1999.

PL 106-133 (HR 747) Protect the permanent trust funds of the state of Arizona from erosion due to inflation and modify the basis on which distributions are made from those funds. Introduced by Stump, R-Ariz., on Feb. 11. House Resources reported May 13 (H Rept 106-140). House passed, under suspension of the rules, Aug. 2. Senate passed Nov. 19. President signed Dec. 7, 1999.

PL 106-134 (HR 748) Amend the act that established the Keweenaw National Historical Park to require the secretary of the interior to consider nominees of various local interests in appointing members of the Keweenaw National Historical Parks Advisory Commission. Introduced by Stupak, D-Mich., on Feb. 11, 1999. House Resources reported, amended, Oct. 7 (H Rept 106-367). House passed, amended, under suspension of the rules, Oct. 12. Senate Energy and Natural Resources discharged. Senate passed Nov. 19. President signed Dec. 7, 1999.

PL 106-135 (HR 791) Amend the National Trails System Act to designate the route of the War of 1812 British invasion of Maryland and Washington, D.C., and the route of the American defense, for study for potential addition to the national trails system. Introduced by Gilchrest, R-Md., on Feb. 23, 1999. House Resources reported, amended, June 17 (H Rept 106-189). House passed, amended, June 30. Senate passed Nov. 19. President signed Dec. 7, 1999.

PL 106-136 (HR 970) Authorize the secretary of the interior to provide assistance to the Perkins County Rural Water System Inc. for the construction of water supply facilities in Perkins County, S.D. Introduced by Thune, R-S.D., on March 3, 1999. House Resources reported, amended, Oct. 20 (H Rept 106-405). House passed, amended, under suspension of the rules, Oct. 26. Senate passed Nov. 19. President signed Dec. 7, 1999.

PL 106-137 (HR 1794) Require the secretary of state to report to Congress on efforts to more actively support Taiwan's participation in the World Health Organization. Introduced by Brown, D-Ohio, on May 13, 1999. House passed, amended, under suspension of the rules, Oct. 4. Senate Foreign Relations reported Nov. 3 (no written report). Senate passed Nov. 19. President signed Dec. 7, 1999.

PL 106-138 (HR 2079) Provide for the conveyance of certain National Forest System lands in the state of South Dakota. Introduced by Thune, R-S.D., on June 8, 1999. House Resources reported July 26 (H Rept 106-261). House passed, under suspension of the rules, Sept. 21. Senate Energy and Natural Resources discharged. Senate passed Nov. 19. President signed Dec. 7, 1999.

PL 106-139 (HR 2886) Amend the Immigration and Nationality Act to provide that an adopted alien who is less than eighteen years of age may be considered a child under the act if adopted with or after a sibling who is a child under the act. Introduced by Horn, R-Calif., on Sept. 21, 1999. House Judiciary reported Oct. 14 (H Rept 106-383). House passed, under suspension of the rules, Oct. 18. Senate Judiciary discharged. Senate passed Nov. 19. President signed Dec. 7, 1999.

PL 106-140 (HR 2889) Amend the Central Utah Project Completion Act to provide for acquisition of water and water rights for Central Utah Project purposes, completion of Central Utah project facilities, and implementation of water conservation measures. Introduced by Cannon, R-Utah, Sept. 21, 1999. House Resources reported Oct. 27 (H Rept 106-417). House passed, under suspension of the rules, Nov. 1. Senate passed Nov. 19. President signed Dec. 7, 1999.

PL 106-141 (HR 3257) Amend the Congressional Budget Act of 1974 to assist the Congressional Budget Office with the scoring of state and local mandates. Introduced by Reynolds, R-N.Y., on Nov. 8, 1999. House passed, amended, under suspension of the rules, Nov. 16. Senate passed Nov. 19. President signed Dec. 7, 1999.

PL 106-142 (H J Res 65) Commend the World War II veterans who fought in the Battle of the Bulge. Introduced by Smith, R-N.J., on Aug. 5, 1999. House Veterans' Affairs reported, amended, Sept. 30 (H Rept 106-352, Pt. 1). House passed, amended, under suspension of the rules, Oct. 5. Senate Judiciary reported Nov. 2 (no written report). Senate passed Nov. 19. President signed Dec. 7, 1999.

PL 106-143 (S 28) Authorize an interpretive center and related visitor center within the Four Corners Monument Tribal Park. Introduced by Hatch, R-Utah, on Jan. 19, 1999. Senate Indian Affairs reported, amended, Aug. 27 (S Rept 106-144). Senate passed, amended, Sept. 9. House passed Nov. 18. President signed Dec. 7, 1999.

PL 106-144 (S 416) Direct the secretary of agriculture to convey the city of Sisters, Ore., a certain parcel of land for use in connection with a sewage treatment plant. Introduced by Smith, R-Ore., on Feb. 11, 1999. Senate Energy and Natural Resources reported, amended, June 2 (S Rept 106-60). Senate passed, amended, July 1. House Resources reported, with amendment, Nov. 5 (H Rept 106-453). House passed, with amendment, under suspension of the rules, Nov. 17. Senate agreed to House amendment Nov. 19. President signed Dec. 7, 1999.

PL 106-145 (HR 15) Designate a portion of the Otay Mountain region of California as wilderness. Introduced by Bilbray, R-Calif., on Jan. 6, 1999. House Resources reported March 17 (H Rept 106-65). House passed, under suspension of the rules, April 12. Senate Energy and Natural Resources reported July 21 (S Rept 106-116). Senate passed Nov. 19. President signed Dec. 9, 1999.

PL 106-146 (HR 658) Establish the Thomas Cole National Historic Site in New York as an affiliated area of the National Park System. Introduced by Sweeney, R-N.Y., on Feb. 9, 1999. House Resources reported, amended, May 13 (H Rept 106-138). House passed, amended, under suspension of the rules, Sept. 13. Senate passed Nov. 19. President signed Dec. 9, 1999.

PL 106-147 (HR 1104) Authorize the secretary of the interior to transfer administrative jurisdiction over land within the boundaries of the Home of Franklin D. Roosevelt National Historic Site to the Archivist of the United States for the construction of a visitor center. Introduced by Sweeney, R-N.Y., on March 11, 1999. House Resources reported May 13 (H Rept 106-141). House passed, under suspension of the rules, Aug. 2. Senate passed Nov. 19. President signed Dec. 9, 1999.

PL 106-148 (HR 1528) Reauthorize and amend the National Geologic Mapping Act of 1992. Introduced by Cubin, R-Wyo., on April 22, 1999. House Resources reported Oct. 18 (H Rept 106-389). House passed, under suspension of the rules, Oct. 26. Senate passed Nov. 19. President signed Dec. 9, 1999.

PL 106-149 (HR 1619) Amend the Quinebaug and Shetucket Rivers Valley National Heritage Corridor Act of 1994 to expand the boundaries of the Corridor. Introduced by Gejdenson, D-Conn., on April 29, 1999. House Resources reported, amended, Sept. 8 (H Rept 106-306). House passed, amended, under suspension of the rules, Sept. 13. Senate Energy and Natural Resources reported Nov. 2 (S Rept 106-213). Senate passed Nov. 19. President signed Dec. 9, 1999.

PL 106-150 (HR 1665) Allow the National Park Service to acquire certain land for addition to the Wilderness Battlefield in Virginia, as previously authorized by law, by purchase, or by exchange as well as by donation. Introduced by Bateman, R-Va., on May 4, 1999. House Resources reported, amended, Oct. 4 (H Rept 106-362). House passed, amended, under suspension of the rules, Oct. 12. Senate passed Nov. 19. President signed Dec. 9, 1999.

PL 106-151 (HR 1693) Amend the Fair Labor Standards Act of 1938 to clarify the overtime exemption for employees engaged in fire protection activities. Introduced by Ehrlich, R-Md., on May 5, 1999. House passed, under suspension of the rules, Nov. 4. Senate passed Nov. 19. President signed Dec. 9, 1999.

PL 106-152 (HR 1887) Amend Title 18, U.S. Code, to punish the depiction of animal cruelty. Introduced by Gallegly, R-Calif., on May 20, 1999. House

Judiciary reported, amended, Oct. 19 (H Rept 106-397). House passed, amended, under suspension of the rules, Oct. 19. Senate passed Nov. 19. President signed Dec. 9, 1999.

PL 106-153 (HR 1932) Authorize the president to award a gold medal on behalf of Congress to Father Theodore M. Hesburgh in recognition of his outstanding and enduring contributions to civil rights, higher education, the Catholic Church, the nation, and the global community. Introduced by Roemer, D-Ind., on May 25, 1999. House passed, under suspension of the rules, Oct. 12. Senate passed Nov. 19. President signed Dec. 9, 1999.

PL 106-154 (HR 2140) Improve protection and management of the Chattahoochee River National Recreation Area in the state of Georgia. Introduced by Deal, R-Ga., on June 10, 1999. House Resources reported, amended, Oct. 7 (H Rept 106-369). House passed, amended, under suspension of the rules, Oct. 18. Senate passed Nov. 19. President signed Dec. 9, 1999.

PL 106-155 (HR 2401) Amend the U.S. Holocaust Assets Commission Act of 1998 to extend the period by which the final report is due and to authorize additional funding. Introduced by Lazio, R-N.Y., on June 30, 1999. House passed, under suspension of the rules, Oct. 4. Senate Banking, Housing and Urban Affairs discharged. Senate passed Nov. 19. President signed Dec. 9, 1999.

PL 106-156 (HR 2632) Designate certain federal lands in the Talladega National Forest in the state of Alabama as the Dugger Mountain Wilderness. Introduced by Riley, R-Ala., on July 29, 1999. House Resources reported Oct. 28 (H Rept 106-422, Pt. 1). House Agriculture discharged. House passed, under suspension of the rules, Nov. 1. Senate passed Nov. 19. President signed Dec. 9, 1999.

PL 106-157 (HR 2737) Authorize the secretary of the interior to convey to the state of Illinois certain federal land associated with the Lewis and Clark National Historic Trail to be used as a historic and interpretive site along the trail. Introduced by Costello, D-Ill., on Aug. 5, 1999. House Resources reported, amended, Nov. 1 (H Rept 106-427). House passed, amended, under suspension of the rules, Nov. 1. Senate passed Nov. 19. President signed Dec. 9, 1999.

PL 106-158 (HR 3381) Reauthorize the Overseas Private Investment Corporation and the Trade and Development Agency. Introduced by Manzullo, R-Ill., on Nov. 16, 1999. House passed, under suspension of the rules, Nov. 17. Senate passed Nov. 19. President signed Dec. 9, 1999.

PL 106-159 (HR 3419) Amend Title 49, U.S. Code, to establish the Federal Motor Carrier Safety Administration. Introduced by Shuster, R-Pa., on Nov. 17, 1999. House Transportation and Infrastructure discharged. House passed Nov. 18. Senate passed Nov. 19. President signed Dec. 9, 1999.

PL 106-160 (HR 3456) Amend statutory damages provisions of Title 17, U.S. Code. Introduced by Coble, R-N.C., on Nov. 18, 1999. House Judiciary discharged. House passed Nov. 18. Senate passed Nov. 19. President signed Dec. 9, 1999.

PL 106-161 (H J Res 46) Confer status as an honorary veteran of the U.S. Armed Forces on Zachary Fisher. Introduced by Maloney, D-N.Y. on April 28, 1999. House passed, under suspension of the rules, Nov. 2. Senate passed Nov. 19. President signed Dec. 9, 1999.

PL 106-162 (S 67) Designate the headquarters building of the Department of Housing and Urban Development in Washington, D.C., as the "Robert C. Weaver Federal Building." Introduced by Moynihan, D-N.Y., on Jan. 19, 1999. Senate Environment and Public Works reported March 17 (no written report). Senate passed March 23. House passed Nov. 18. President signed Dec. 9, 1999.

PL 106-163 (S 438) Provide for the settlement of the water rights claims of the Chippewa Cree Tribe of the Rocky Boy's Reservation. Introduced by Burns, R-Mont., on Feb. 22, 1999. Senate Indian Affairs reported July 22 (S Rept 106-200). Senate Energy and Natural Resources discharged. Senate passed, amended, Nov. 4. House passed Nov. 18. President signed Dec. 9, 1999.

PL 106-164 (S 548) Establish the Fallen Timbers Battlefield and Fort Miamis National Historical Site in the state of Ohio. Introduced by DeWine, R-Ohio, on March 4, 1999. Senate Energy and Natural Resources reported, amended, June 7 (S Rept 106-64). Senate passed, amended, Oct. 14. House Resources discharged. House passed Nov. 18. President signed Dec. 9, 1999.

PL 106-165 (S 791) Amend the Small Business Act with respect to the women's business center program. Introduced by Kerry, D-Mass., on April 14, 1999. Senate Small Business reported, amended, Nov. 2 (S Rept 106-214). Senate passed, amended, Nov. 5. House passed Nov. 18. President signed Dec. 9, 1999.

PL 106-166 (S 1595) Designate the U.S. courthouse at 401 West Washington St. in Phoenix as the "Sandra Day O'Connor United States Courthouse." Introduced by Kyl, R-Ariz., on Sept. 16, 1999. Senate Environment and Public Works reported Sept. 29 (no written report). Senate passed Oct. 8. House Transportation and Infrastructure discharged. House passed Nov. 18. President signed Dec. 9, 1999.

PL 106-167 (S 1866) Redesignate the Coastal Barrier Resources System as the "John H. Chafee Coastal Barrier Resources System." Introduced by Smith, R-N.H., on Nov. 4, 1999. Senate passed Nov. 4. House Resources discharged. House passed Nov. 18. President signed Dec. 9, 1999.

PL 106-168 (S 335) Amend Chapter 30 of Title 39, U.S. Code, to provide for the nonmailability of certain deceptive matter relating to sweepstakes, skill contests, facsimile checks, administrative procedures, orders, and civil penalties relating to such matter. Introduced by Collins, R-Maine, on Feb. 3, 1999. Senate Governmental Affairs reported, amended, July 1 (S Rept 106-102). Senate passed, amended, Aug. 2. House passed, with amendment, under suspension of the rules, Nov. 9. Senate agreed to House amendment Nov. 19. President signed Dec. 12, 1999.

PL 106-169 (HR 3443) Amend Part E of Title IV of the Social Security Act to provide states with more funding and greater flexibility in carrying out programs designed to help children make the transition from foster care to self-sufficiency. Introduced by Johnson, R-Conn., on Nov. 18, 1999. House Ways and Means, House Commerce discharged. House passed Nov. 18. Senate passed Nov. 19. President signed Dec. 14, 1999.

PL 106-170 (HR 1180) Amend the Social Security Act to expand the availability of health care coverage for working individuals with disabilities, and establish a Ticket to Work and Self-Sufficiency Program in the Social Security Administration to provide meaningful opportunities to work. Introduced by Lazio, R-N.Y., on March 18. House Commerce reported, amended, July 1 (H Rept 106-220, Pt. 1). House passed, amended, under suspension of the rules, Oct. 19. Senate passed, with amendment, Oct. 21. Conference report filed in the House Nov. 17 (H Rept 106-478). House agreed to conference report Nov. 18. Senate agreed to conference report Nov. 19. President signed Dec. 17, 1999.

106th Congress—2000

PL 106-171 (S 1733) Amend the Food Stamp Act of 1977 to provide for a national standard of interoperablity and portability applicable to electronic food stamp benefit transactions. Introduced by Fitzgerald, R-Ill., on Oct. 14, 1999. Senate Agriculture, Nutrition, and Forestry discharged. Senate passed, amended, Nov. 19. House passed, under suspension of the rules, Jan. 31, 2000. President signed Feb. 11, 2000.

PL 106-172 (HR 2130) Amend the Controlled Substances Act to direct the emergency scheduling of gamma hydroxybutyric acid and provide for a national awareness campaign. Introduced by Upton, R-Mich., on June 10, 1999. House Commerce reported, amended, Sept. 27 (H Rept 106-340, Pt. 1). House Judiciary discharged. House passed, amended, under suspension of the rules, Oct. 12. Senate passed, with amendments, Nov. 19. House agreed to Senate amendments under suspension of the rules, Jan. 31, 2000. President signed Feb. 18, 2000.

PL 106-173 (HR 1451) Establish the Abraham Lincoln Bicentennial Commission. Introduced by Lahood, R-Ill., on April 15, 1999. House passed, amended, under suspension of the rules, Oct. 4. Senate Judiciary discharged. Senate passed, with amendment, Nov. 19. House agreed to Senate amendment, under suspension of the rules, Feb. 8, 2000. President signed Feb. 25, 2000.

PL 106-174 (S 632) Provide assistance for poison prevention and stabilize the funding of regional poison control centers. Introduced by DeWine, R-Ohio, on March 16, 1999. Senate Health, Education, Labor and Pensions reported, amended, Aug. 4 (no written report). Senate passed, amended, Aug. 5.

House passed, under suspension of the rules, Feb. 8, 2000. President signed Feb. 25, 2000.

PL 106-175 (HR 3557) Authorize the president to award a gold medal on behalf of the Congress to Cardinal John O'Connor, archbishop of New York, in recognition of his accomplishments as a priest, a chaplain, and a humanitarian. Introduced by Fossella, R-N.Y. , on Jan. 31, 2000. House passed, under suspension of the rules, Feb. 15. Senate Banking, Housing and Urban Affairs discharged. Senate passed March 1. President signed March 5, 2000.

PL 106-176 (HR 149) Make technical corrections to the Omnibus Parks and Public Lands Management Act of 1996. Introduced by Hansen, R-Utah, on Jan. 6, 1999. House Resources reported, amended, Feb. 12 (H Rept 106-17). House passed, amended, under suspension of the rules, Feb. 23. Senate Energy and Natural Resources reported, with amendments, July 28 (S Rept 106-125). Senate passed, amended, Nov. 19. House agreed to Senate amendments, under suspension of the rules, Feb. 15, 2000. President signed March 10, 2000.

PL 106-177 (HR 764) Reduce the incidence of child abuse and neglect. Introduced by Pryce, R-Ohio, on Feb. 12, 1999. House Judiciary reported Oct. 1 (H Rept 106-360). House passed, amended, Oct. 5. Senate Judiciary reported, with amendment, Oct. 28 (no written report). Senate passed, with amendment, Nov. 19. House agreed to Senate amendment, under suspension of the rules, Feb. 1, 2000. President signed March 10, 2000.

PL 106-178 (HR 1883) Provide for the application of measures to foreign persons who transfer certain goods, services, or technology to Iran. Introduced by Gilman, R-N.Y., on May 20, 1999. House International Relations reported, amended, Sept. 14 (H Rept 106-315, Pt. 1). House Science discharged. House passed, amended, under suspension of the rules, Sept. 14. Senate passed, with amendment, Feb. 24, 2000. House agreed to Senate amendments March 1. President signed March 14, 2000.

PL 106-179 (S 613) Encourage Native American economic development and provide for the disclosure of Native American tribal sovereign immunity in contracts involving Native American tribes. Introduced by Campbell, R-Colo., on March 15, 1999. Senate Indian Affairs reported, amended, Sept. 8 (S Rept 106-150). Senate passed, amended, Sept. 15. House Resources reported Feb. 29, 2000 (H Rept 106-501). House passed, under suspension of the rules, Feb. 29. President signed March 14, 2000.

PL 106-180 (S 376) Amend the Communications Satellite Act of 1962 to promote competition and privatization in satellite communications. Introduced by Burns, R-Mont. on Feb. 4, 1999. Senate Commerce, Science and Transportation reported, amended, June 30 (S Rept 106-100). Senate passed, amended, July 1. House Commerce discharged. House passed, with amendment, Nov. 10. Conference report filed in the House March 2, 2000 (H Rept 106-509). Senate agreed to conference report March 2. House agreed to conference report March 9. President signed March 17, 2000.

PL 106-181 (HR 1000) Amend Title 49, U.S. Code, to reauthorize programs of the Federal Aviation Administration. Introduced by Shuster, R-Pa., on March 4, 1999. House Transportation and Infrastructure reported, amended, May 28 (H Rept 106-167, Pt. 1). House Transportation and Infrastructure filed supplemental report June 9 (H Rept 106-167, Pt. 2). House Budget and Rules discharged. House passed, amended, June 15. Senate Commerce, Science and Transportation discharged. Senate passed, with amendment, Oct. 5. Conference report filed in the House March 8, 2000 (H Rept 106-513). Senate agreed to conference report March 8. House agreed to conference report March 15. President signed April 5, 2000.

PL 106-182 (HR 5) Amend Title II of the Social Security Act to eliminate the earnings test for individuals who have attained retirement age. Introduced by Johnson, R-Texas, on March 1, 1999. House Ways and Means reported, amended, March 1, 2000 (H Rept 106-507). House passed, amended, March 1. Senate passed with amendment, March 22. House agreed to Senate amendment March 28. President signed April 7, 2000.

PL 106-183 (HR 1374) Designate the U.S. Post Office building located at 680 U.S. Highway 130 in Hamilton, N.J., as the "John K. Rafferty Hamilton Post Office Building." Introduced by Smith, R-N.J., on April 12, 1999. House passed, amended, under suspension of the rules, Oct. 12. Senate Governmental Affairs reported March 27, 2000 (no written report). Senate passed April 3. President signed April 13, 2000.

PL 106-184 (HR 3189) Designate the U.S. Post Office located at 14071 Peyton Dr. in Chino Hills, Calif., as the "Joseph Ileto Post Office." Introduced by Miller, R-Calif., on Nov. 1, 1999. House passed, under suspension of the rules, Nov. 8. Senate Governmental Affairs reported March 27, 2000 (no written report). Senate passed April 3. President signed April 14, 2000.

PL 106-185 (HR 1658) Provide a more just and uniform procedure for federal civil forfeitures. Introduced by Hyde, R-Ill., on May 4, 1999. House Judiciary reported, amended, June 18 (H Rept 106-192). House passed, amended, June 24. Senate Judiciary reported, with amendment, March 23, 2000 (no written report). Senate passed, with amendment, March 27. House agreed to Senate amendment, under suspension of the rules, April 11. President signed April 25, 2000.

PL 106-186 (S J Res 43) Express the sense of Congress that the president of the United States should encourage free and fair elections and respect for democracy in Peru. Introduced by Coverdell, R-Ga., on March 28, 2000. Senate passed, amended, April 7. House International Relations discharged. House passed April 11. President signed April 25, 2000.

PL 106-187 (HR 1231) Direct the secretary of agriculture to convey certain National Forest lands to Elko County, Nev., for continued use as a cemetery. Introduced by Gibbons, R-Nev., on March 23, 1999. House Resources reported, amended, Sept. 8 (H Rept 106-308). House passed, under suspension of the rules, Sept. 21. Senate Energy and Natural Resources reported March 9 (S Rept 106-238). Senate passed April 13. President signed April 28, 2000.

PL 106-188 (HR 2368) Assist in the resettlement and relocation of the people of Bikini Atoll by amending the terms of the trust fund established during the U.S. administration of the Trust Territory of the Pacific Islands. Introduced by Young, R-Alaska, on June 29, 1999. House Resources reported July 27 (H Rept 106-267). House passed, under suspension of the rules, Sept. 13. Senate Energy and Natural Resources reported March 9, 2000 (S Rept 106-240). Senate passed April 13. President signed April 28, 2000.

PL 106-189 (HR 2862) Direct the secretary of the interior to release reversionary interests held by the United States in certain parcels of land in Washington County, Utah, to facilitate an anticipated land exchange. Introduced by Hansen, R-Utah, on Sept. 14, 1999. House passed, under suspension of the rules, Nov. 16. Senate Energy and Natural Resources reported March 9, 2000 (S Rept 106-241). Senate passed April 13. President signed April 28, 2000.

PL 106-190 (HR 2863) Clarify the legal effect on the United States of the acquisition of a parcel of land in the Red Cliffs Desert Reserve in Utah. Introduced by Hansen, R-Utah, on Sept. 14, 1999. House passed, under suspension of the rules, Nov. 16. Senate Energy and Natural Resources reported March 9, 2000 (S Rept 106-242). Senate passed April 13. President signed April 28, 2000.

PL 106-191 (HR 3063) Amend the Mineral Leasing Act to increase the maximum acreage of federal leases for sodium that may be held by an entity in any one state. Introduced by Cubin, R-Wyo., on Oct. 13, 1999. House Resources reported Nov. 15 (H Rept 106-469). House passed, under suspension of the rules, Nov. 16. Senate Energy and Natural Resources reported April 12, 2000 (S Rept 106-270). Senate passed April 13. President signed April 28, 2000.

PL 106-192 (HR 1615) Amend the Wild and Scenic Rivers Act to extend the designation of a portion of the Lamprey River in New Hampshire as a recreational river to include an additional river segment. Introduced by Sununu, R-N.H., on April 28, 1999. House Resources reported Oct. 7 (H Rept 106-368). House passed, under suspension of the rules, Oct. 12. Senate Energy and Natural Resources reported April 12, 2000 (S Rept 106-269). Senate passed April 13. President signed May 2, 2000.

PL 106-193 (HR 1753) Promote the research, identification, assessment, exploration, and development of methane hydrate resources. Introduced by Doyle, D-Pa., on May 11, 1999. House Science reported, amended, Oct. 13 (H Rept 106-377, Pt. 1). House Resources reported, amended, Oct. 18 (H Rept 106-377, Pt. 2). House passed, under suspension of the rules, Oct. 26. Senate passed, with amendment, Nov. 19. House agreed to Senate amendment, with an amendment pursuant to H Res 453, April 3, 2000. Senate agreed to House amendment to Senate amendment April 13. President signed May 2, 2000.

PL 106-194 (HR 3090) Amend the Alaska Native Claims Settlement Act to restore certain lands to the Elim Native Corporation. Introduced by Young, R-Alaska, on Oct. 18, 1999. House Resources reported, amended, Nov. 5 (H Rept 106-452). House passed, under suspension of the rules, Nov. 9. Senate Energy and Natural Resources reported April 10, 2000 (S Rept 106-258). Senate passed April 13. President signed May 2, 2000.

PL 106-195 (H J Res 86) Recognize the 50th anniversary of the Korean War and the service by members of the armed forces during that war. Introduced by Ewing, R-Ill., on Feb. 1, 2000. House passed, under suspension of the rules, March 8. Senate Judiciary reported April 12 (no written report). Senate passed April 13. President signed May 2, 2000.

PL 106-196 (S 1567) Designate the U.S. courthouse located at 223 Broad St. in Albany, Ga., as the "C. B. King U.S. Courthouse." Introduced by Coverdell, R-Ga., on Sept. 8, 1999. Senate Environment and Public Works reported Sept. 29 (no written report). Senate passed Oct. 8. House Transportation and Infrastructure reported, with amendments, March 29, 2000 (H Rept 106-552). House passed, under suspension of the rules, April 3. Senate agreed to House amendments April 13. President signed May 2, 2000.

PL 106-197 (S 1769) Continue reporting requirements of Section 2519 of Title 18, U.S. Code, beyond Dec. 21, 1999. Introduced by Leahy, D-Vt., on Oct. 22, 1999. Senate Judiciary reported, amended, Oct. 28 (no written report). Senate passed, amended, Nov. 5. House Judiciary discharged. House passed, with amendments, Nov. 18. Senate agreed to House amendments April 13, 2000. President signed May 2, 2000.

PL 106-198 (S J Res 40) Provide for the appointment of Alan G. Spoon as a citizen regent of the Board of Regents of the Smithsonian Institution. Introduced by Cochran, R-Miss., on Feb. 29, 2000. Senate Rules and Administration discharged. Senate passed April 12. House passed, under suspension of the rules, May 2. President signed May 5, 2000.

PL 106-199 (S J Res 42) Provide for the reappointment of Manuel L. Ibanez as a citizen regent of the Board of Regents of the Smithsonian Institution. Introduced by Cochran, R-Miss., on Feb. 29, 2000. Senate Rules and Administration discharged. Senate passed April 12. House passed, under suspension of the rules, May 2. President signed May 5, 2000.

PL 106-200 (HR 434) Authorize a new trade and investment policy for sub-Saharan Africa. Introduced by Crane, R-Ill., on Feb. 2, 1999. House International Relations reported, amended, Feb. 16 (H Rept 106-19, Pt. 1). House Ways and Means reported, amended, June 17 (H Rept 106-19, Pt. 2). House Banking and Financial Services discharged. House passed, amended, July 16. Senate passed, with amendments, Nov. 3. Conference report filed in the House May 4 (H Rept 106-606). House agreed to conference report May 4. Senate agreed to conference report May 11. President signed May 18, 2000.

PL 106-201 (S 1744) Amend the Endangered Species Act of 1973 to provide that certain species conservation reports shall continue to be submitted. Introduced by Chafee, R-R.I., on Oct. 18, 1999. Senate Environment and Public Works reported Oct. 18 (S Rept 106-194). Senate passed March 27, 2000. House passed, under suspension of the rules, May 3. President signed May 18, 2000.

PL 106-202 (S 2323) Amend the Fair Labor Standards Act of 1938 to clarify the treatment of stock options under the act. Introduced by McConnell, R-Ky., on March 29, 2000. Senate passed April 12. House passed, under suspension of the rules, May 3. President signed May 18, 2000.

PL 106-203 (HR 2412) Designate the federal building and U.S. courthouse located at 1300 South Harrison St. in Fort Wayne, Ind., as the "E. Ross Adair Federal Building and U.S. Courthouse." Introduced by Souder, R-Ind., on June 30, 1999. House Transportation and Infrastructure reported March 23, 2000 (H Rept 106-540). House passed, under suspension of the rules, March 28. Senate Environment and Public Works reported April 13 (no written report). Senate passed May 4. President signed May 22, 2000.

PL 106-204 (S 2370) Designate the federal building located at 500 Pearl St. in New York City as the "Daniel Patrick Moynihan U.S. Courthouse." Introduced by Schumer, D-N.Y., on April 6, 2000. Senate Environment and Public Works reported April 13 (no written report). Senate passed May 4. House passed, under suspension of the rules, May 15. President signed May 23, 2000.

PL 106-205 (S J Res 44) Support the Day of Honor 2000 to honor and recognize the service of minority veterans in the U.S. armed forces during World War II. Introduced by Kennedy, D-Mass., on April 6, 2000. Senate Judiciary discharged. Senate passed May 18. House passed May 23. President signed May 26, 2000.

PL 106-206 (HR 154) Provide for the collection of fees for the making of motion pictures, television productions, and sound tracks in National Park System and National Wildlife Refuge System units. Introduced by Hefley, R-Colo., on Jan. 6, 1999. House Resources reported, amended, March 23 (H Rept 106-75). House passed, under suspension of the rules, April 12. Senate Energy and Natural Resources reported, with amendments, June 7 (S Rept 106-67). Senate passed, with amendments, Nov. 19. House agreed to Senate amendments, under suspension of the rules, May 22, 2000. President signed May 26, 2000.

PL 106-207 (HR 371) Expedite the naturalization of aliens who served with special guerrilla units in Laos. Introduced by Vento, D-Minn., on Jan. 19, 1999. House Judiciary reported, amended, April 6 (H Rept 106-563). House passed, under suspension of the rules, May 2, 2000. Senate Judiciary reported, with amendment, May 18 (no written report). Senate passed, with amendment, May 18. House agreed to Senate amendment May 23. President signed May 26, 2000.

PL 106-208 (HR 834) Extend the authorization for the Historic Preservation Fund. Introduced by Hefley, R-Colo., on Feb. 24, 1999. House Resources reported, amended, July 20 (H Rept 106-241). House passed, under suspension of the rules, Sept. 21. Senate Energy and Natural Resources reported, with amendments, March 9, 2000 (S Rept 106-237). Senate passed, with amendments, April 13. House agreed to Senate amendments, under suspension of the rules, May 22. President signed May 26, 2000.

PL 106-209 (HR 1377) Designate the facility of the U.S. Postal Service at 9308 S. Chicago Ave. in Chicago, Ill., as the "John J. Buchanan Post Office Building." Introduced by Weller, R-Ill., on April 13, 1999. House passed, under suspension of the rules, May 24. Senate Governmental Affairs reported, with amendments, Nov. 4 (no written report). Senate passed, with amendments, Nov. 19. House agreed to Senate amendments, under suspension of the rules, May 15, 2000. President signed May 26, 2000.

PL 106-210 (HR 1832) Reform unfair and anticompetitive practices in the professional boxing industry. Introduced by Oxley, R-Ohio, on May 17, 1999. House Commerce reported, amended, Nov. 4 (H Rept 106-449, Pt. 1). House Education and the Workforce discharged Nov. 4. House passed, under suspension of the rules, Nov. 8. Senate passed, with amendments, April 7, 2000. House agreed to Senate amendments, under suspension of the rules, May 22. President signed May 26, 2000.

PL 106-211 (HR 3629) Amend the Higher Education Act of 1965 to improve the program for American Indian Tribal Colleges and Universities under Part A of Title III. Introduced by Green, R-Wis., on Feb. 10, 2000. House passed, under suspension of the rules, May 2. Senate passed May 18. President signed May 26, 2000.

PL 106-212 (HR 3707) Authorize funds for the site selection and construction of a facility in Taipei, Taiwan, suitable for the mission of the American Institute in Taiwan. Introduced by Bereuter, R-Neb., on Feb. 29, 2000. House passed, under suspension of the rules, March 28. Senate Foreign Relations reported, with amendment, April 20 (no written report). Senate passed, with amendment, May 2. House agreed to Senate amendment May 18. President signed May 26, 2000.

PL 106-213 (S 1836) Extend the deadline for starting construction of a hydroelectric project in Alabama. Introduced by Hollings, D-S.C., on Nov. 1, 1999. Senate Energy and Natural Resources reported April 12, 2000 (S Rept 106-265). Senate passed April 13. House Commerce discharged. House passed May 22. President signed May 26, 2000.

PL 106-214 (HR 3293) Amend the law that authorized the Vietnam Veterans Memorial to authorize the placement within the site of the memorial of a plaque to honor those Vietnam veterans who died after their service in the Vietnam War, but as a direct result of that service. Introduced by Gallegly, R-Calif., on Nov. 10, 1999. House Resources reported, amended April 13, 2000 (H Rept 106-585). House passed, amended, under suspension of the rules May 9. Senate Energy and Natural Resources discharged. Senate passed May 25. President signed June 15, 2000.

PL 106-215 (HR 4489) Amend Section 110 of the Illegal Immigration Reform and Immigrant Responsibility Act of 1996. Introduced by Smith, R-Texas, on May 18, 2000. House passed, under suspension of the rules, May 23. Senate passed May 25. President signed June 15, 2000.

PL 106-216 (HR 1953) Authorize leases for terms not to exceed ninety-nine years on land held in trust for the Torres Martinez Desert Cahuilla Indians and the Guidiville Band of Pomo Indians of the Guidiville Indian Rancheria. Introduced by Bono, R-Calif., on May 26, 1999. House passed, amended, under suspension of the rules, Nov. 17. Senate Indian Affairs reported May 18, 2000 (no written report). Senate passed June 8. President signed June 20, 2000.

PL 106-217 (HR 2484) Provide that land owned by the Lower Sioux Indian Community in the state of Minnesota but not held in trust by the United States for the Community may be leased or transferred by the Community without further approval by the United States. Introduced by Minge, D-Minn., on July 12, 1999. House Resources reported Feb. 29, 2000 (H Rept 106-502). House passed, under suspension of the rules, Feb. 29. Senate Indian Affairs reported May 18 (no written report). Senate passed June 8. President signed June 20, 2000.

PL 106-218 (HR 3639) Designate the federal building located at 2201 C St., N.W., in the District of Columbia, currently headquarters for the Department of State, as the "Harry S Truman Federal Building." Introduced by Skelton, D-Mo., on Feb. 10, 2000. House passed, amended, under suspension of the rules, May 23. Senate passed June 8. President signed June 20, 2000.

PL 106-219 (HR 4542) Designate the Washington Opera in Washington, D.C., as the National Opera. Introduced by Goodling, R-Pa., on May 25, 2000. House passed, under suspension of the rules, June 6. Senate passed June 7. President signed June 20, 2000.

PL 106-220 (S 291) Convey certain real property within the Carlsbad Project in New Mexico to the Carlsbad Irrigation District. Introduced by Domenici, R-N.M., on Jan. 21, 1999. Senate Energy and Natural Resources reported March 17, 2000 (S Rept 106-19). Senate passed March 25. House passed, under suspension of the rules, June 7. President signed June 20, 2000.

PL 106-221 (S 356) Authorize the secretary of the interior to convey certain works, facilities, and titles of the Gila Project, and designated lands within or adjacent to the Gila Project, to the Wellton-Mohawk Irrigation and Drainage District. Introduced by Kyl, R-Ariz., on Feb. 3, 1999. Senate Energy and Natural Resources reported March 17 (S Rept 106-21). Senate passed March 25. House passed, under suspension of the rules, June 7, 2000. President signed June 20, 2000.

PL 106-222 (S 777) Require the secretary of agriculture to establish an electronic filing and retrieval system to enable farmers and other persons to file all required paperwork electronically with selected Agriculture Department agencies and to access public information on programs administered by these agencies. Introduced by Fitzgerald, R-Ill., on April 13, 1999. Senate Agriculture discharged. Senate passed, amended, Nov. 4. House passed, amended, under suspension of the rules, April 10, 2000. Senate agreed to House amendments, with amendments, May 18. House agreed to Senate amendments to House amendments June 6. President signed June 20, 2000.

PL 106-223 (S 2722) Authorize the award of the Medal of Honor to Ed W. Freeman, James K. Okubo, and Andrew J. Smith. Introduced by Akaka, D-Hawaii, on June 13, 2000. Senate passed June 13. House passed June 16. President signed June 20, 2000.

PL 106-224 (HR 2559) Amend the Federal Crop Insurance Act to strengthen the safety net for agricultural producers by providing greater access to more affordable risk management tools and improved protection from production and income loss. Introduced by Combest, R-Texas, on July 20, 1999. House Agriculture reported, amended, Aug. 5 (H Rept 106-300, Pt. 1). Supplemental report filed Sept. 22 (H Rept 106-300, Pt. 2). House passed, amended, Sept. 29. Senate passed amended, March 23, 2000. Conference report filed in the House on May 29 (H Rept 106-639). House agreed to conference report May 25. Senate agreed to conference report May 25. President signed June 20, 2000.

PL 106-225 (HR 3642) Authorize the president to award posthumously a gold medal on behalf of the Congress to Charles M. Schulz in recognition of his lasting artistic contributions to the nation and the world. Introduced by Thompson, D-Calif., on Feb. 10, 2000. House passed, under suspension of the rules, Feb. 15. Senate Banking, Housing, and Urban Affairs discharged. Senate passed, with amendments, May 2. House agreed to Senate amendments June 6. President signed June 20, 2000.

PL 106-226 (HR 4387) Provide that the School Governance Charter Amendment Act of 2000 take effect on the date it is ratified by the voters of the District of Columbia. Introduced by Norton, D-D.C., on May 4, 2000. House Government Reform reported June 12 (H Rept 106-664). House passed, under suspension of the rules, June 12. Senate passed June 14. President signed June 27, 2000.

PL 106-227 (H J Res 101) Recognize the 225th birthday of the U.S. Army. Introduced by Spence, R-S.C., on June 8, 2000. House passed, under suspension of the rules, June 13. Senate Judiciary discharged. Senate passed June 15. President signed June 29, 2000.

PL 106-228 (S 1967) Make technical corrections to the status of certain land held in trust for the Mississippi Band of Choctaw Indians, and take certain land into trust for that band. Introduced by Cochran, R-Miss., on Nov. 18, 1999. Senate Indian Affairs reported June 13, 2000 (S Rept 106-307). Senate passed June 14. House passed, under suspension of the rules, June 19. President signed June 29, 2000.

PL 106-229 (S 761) Regulate interstate commerce by electronic means (including electronic signatures) and permit and encourage the continued expansion of electronic commerce through the operation of free-market forces. Introduced by Abraham, R-Mich., on March 25, 1999. Senate Commerce, Science and Transportation reported, with amendments, July 30 (S Rept 106-131). Senate passed, amended, Nov. 19. House passed, amended, Feb. 16, 2000. Conference report filed in the House on June 8 (H Rept 106-661). House agreed to conference report June 14. Senate agreed to conference report June 16. President signed June 30, 2000.

PL 106-230 (HR 4762) Amend the Internal Revenue Code of 1986 to require "527" organizations to disclose their political activities. Introduced by Houghton, R-N.Y., on June 27, 2000. House passed, under suspension of the rules, June 28. Senate passed June 29. President signed July 1, 2000.

PL 106-231 (HR 642) Redesignate the federal building located at 701 South Santa Fe Ave. in Compton, Calif., known as the Compton Main Post Office, as the "Mervyn Malcolm Dymally Post Office Building." Introduced by Millender-McDonald, D-Calif., on Feb. 9, 1999. House Government Reform discharged. House passed Nov. 18. Senate Governmental Affairs reported June 21, 2000 (no written report). Senate passed June 23. President signed July 6, 2000.

PL 106-232 (HR 643) Redesignate the federal building located at 10301 South Compton Ave. in Los Angeles, Calif., known as the Watts Finance Office, as the "Augustus F. Hawkins Post Office Building." Introduced by Millender-McDonald, D-Calif., on Feb. 9, 1999. House passed, under suspension of the rules, Oct. 12. Senate Governmental Affairs reported June 21, 2000 (no written report). Senate passed June 23. President signed July 6, 2000.

PL 106-233 (HR 1666) Designate the facility of the U.S. Postal Service at 200 East Pinckney St. in Madison, Fla., as the "Captain Colin P. Kelly Jr. Post Office." Introduced by Boyd, D-Fla., on May 4, 1999. House passed, under suspension of the rules, March 21, 2000. Senate Governmental Affairs reported June 21 (no written report). Senate passed June 23. President signed July 6, 2000.

PL 106-234 (HR 2307) Designate the building of the U.S. Postal Service located at 5 Cedar St. in Hopkinton, Mass., as the "Thomas J. Brown Post Office Building." Introduced by McGovern, D-Mass., on June 22, 1999. House passed, under suspension of the rules, Nov. 8. Senate Governmental Affairs reported June 21, 2000 (no written report). Senate passed June 23. President signed July 6, 2000.

PL 106-235 (HR 2357) Designate the U.S. Post Office located at 3675 Warrensville Center Rd. in Shaker Heights, Ohio, as the "Louis Stokes Post Office." Introduced by Traficant, D-Ohio, on June 24, 1999. House passed, under suspension of the rules, Oct. 12. Senate Governmental Affairs reported June 21, 2000 (no written report). Senate passed June 23. President signed July 6, 2000.

PL 106-236 (HR 2460) Designate the U.S. Post Office located at 125 Border Ave. West in Wiggins, Miss., as the "Jay Hanna 'Dizzy' Dean Post Office." Introduced by Taylor, D-Miss., on July 1, 1999. House passed, under suspension of the rules, Oct. 12. Senate Governmental Affairs reported June 21, 2000 (no written report). Senate passed June 23. President signed July 6, 2000.

PL 106-237 (HR 2591) Designate the United States Post Office located at 713 Elm St. in Wakefield, Kan., as the "William H. Avery Post Office." Introduced by Moran, R-Kan., on July 22, 1999. House passed, under suspension of

the rules, Oct. 12. Senate Governmental Affairs reported June 21, 2000 (no written report). Senate passed June 23. President signed July 6, 2000.

PL 106-238 (HR 2952) Redesignate the facility of the U.S. Postal Service located at 100 Orchard Park Dr. in Greenville, S.C., as the "Keith D. Oglesby Station." Introduced by DeMint, R-S.C., on Sept. 27, 1999. House passed, under suspension of the rules, March 8, 2000. Senate Governmental Affairs reported June 21 (no written report). Senate passed June 23. President signed July 6, 2000.

PL 106-239 (HR 3018) Designate the U.S. Post Office located at 557 East Bay St. in Charleston, S.C., as the "Marybelle H. Howe Post Office." Introduced by Clyburn, D-S.C., on Oct. 5, 1999. House passed, amended, under suspension of the rules, March 8, 2000. Senate Governmental Affairs reported June 21 (no written report). Senate passed June 23. President signed July 6, 2000.

PL 106-240 (HR 3699) Designate the facility of the U.S. Postal Service located at 8409 Lee Highway in Merrifield, Va., as the "Joel T. Broyhill Postal Building." Introduced by Wolf, R-Va., on Feb. 29, 2000. House passed, under suspension of the rules, March 14. Senate Governmental Affairs reported June 21 (no written report). Senate passed June 23. President signed July 6, 2000.

PL 106-241 (HR 3701) Designate the facility of the U.S. Postal Service located at 3118 Washington Blvd. in Arlington, Va., as the "Joseph L. Fisher Post Office Building." Introduced by Wolf, R-Va., on Feb. 29, 2000. House passed, under suspension of the rules, March 14. Senate Governmental Affairs reported June 21 (no written report). Senate passed June 23. President signed July 6, 2000.

PL 106-242 (HR 4241) Designate the facility of the U.S. Postal Service located at 1818 Milton Ave. in Janesville, Wis., as the "Les Aspin Post Office Building." Introduced by Ryan, R-Wis., on April 11, 2000. House passed, under suspension of the rules, June 6. Senate Governmental Affairs reported June 21 (no written report). Senate passed June 23. President signed July 6, 2000.

PL 106-243 (HR 3051) Direct the secretary of the interior and the Bureau of Reclamation to conduct a feasibility study on the Jicarilla Apache Reservation in the state of New Mexico. Introduced by Udall, D-N.M., on Oct. 7, 1999. House passed, amended, under suspension of the rules, Nov. 17. Senate Indian Affairs reported June 22, 2000 (no written report). Senate passed June 28. President signed July 10, 2000.

PL 106-244 (S 1309) Amend Title I of the Employee Retirement Income Security Act of 1974 and provide for the preemption of state law in certain cases relating to certain church plans. Introduced by Sessions, R-Ala., on June 30, 1999. Senate Health, Education, Labor, and Pensions discharged. Senate passed, amended, Nov. 19. House passed, under suspension of the rules, June 26, 2000. President signed July 10, 2000.

PL 106-245 (S 1515) Amend the Radiation Exposure Compensation Act. Introduced by Hatch, R-Utah, on Aug. 5, 1999. Senate Health, Education, Labor, and Pensions discharged. Senate Judiciary reported, amended, Nov. 2 (no written report). Senate passed Nov. 19. House Judiciary reported, with amendments, June 26, 2000 (H Rept 106-697). House passed, under suspension of the rules, June 27. Senate agreed to House amendments June 28. President signed July 10, 2000.

PL 106-246 (HR 4425) Make appropriations for military construction, family housing, and base realignment and closure for the Department of Defense for the fiscal year ending September 30, 2001. Introduced by Hobson, R-Ohio, on May 11, 2000. House Appropriations reported May 11 (H Rept 106-614). House passed, amended, May 16. Senate passed, with amendment, May 18. Conference report filed in the House on June 29 (H Rept 106-710). House agreed to conference report June 29. Senate agreed to conference report June 30. President signed July 13, 2000.

PL 106-247 (S 148) Require the secretary of the interior to establish a program to provide assistance in the conservation of neotropical migratory birds. Introduced by Abraham, R-Mich., on Jan. 19, 1999. Senate Environment and Public Works reported March 26 (S Rept 106-36). Senate passed April 13. House passed, amended, under suspension of the rules, June 26, 2000. Senate agreed to House amendment June 29. President signed July 20, 2000.

PL 106-248 (S 1892) Authorize the acquisition of the Valles Caldera and provide for an effective land and wildlife management program for this resource within the Department of Agriculture. Introduced by Domenici, R-N.M., on Nov. 9, 1999. Senate Energy and Natural Resources reported, amended, April 12, 2000 (S Rept 106-267). Senate passed, amended, April 13. House Resources reported July 11 (H Rept 106-724). House passed, under suspension of the rules, July 12. President signed July 25, 2000.

PL 106-249 (S 986) Direct the secretary of the interior to convey the Griffith Project to the Southern Nevada Water Authority. Introduced by Reid, D-Nev., on May 6, 1999. Senate Energy and Natural Resources reported, amended, Oct. 6 (S Rept 106-173). Senate passed, amended, Nov. 19. House Resources reported July 10, 2000 (H Rept 106-717). House passed, under suspension of the rules, July 10. President signed July 26, 2000.

PL 106-250 (HR 3544) Authorize a gold medal to be awarded on behalf of the Congress to Pope John Paul II in recognition of his many and enduring contributions to peace and religious understanding. Introduced by Leach, R-Iowa, on Jan. 27, 2000. House passed, amended, under suspension of the rules, May 23. Senate passed July 13. President signed July 27, 2000.

PL 106-251 (HR 3591) Provide for the award of a gold medal on behalf of the Congress to former President Ronald Reagan and his wife Nancy Reagan in recognition of their service to the nation. Introduced by Gibbons, R-Nev., on Feb. 8, 2000. House passed, under suspension of the rules, April 3. Senate passed July 13. President signed July 27, 2000.

PL 106-252 (HR 4391) Amend Title 4 of the U.S. Code to establish sourcing requirements for state and local taxation of mobile telecommunication services. Introduced by Hyde, R-Ill., on May 4, 2000. House Judiciary reported, amended, July 10 (H Rept 106-719). House passed, amended, under suspension of the rules, July 11. Senate passed July 14. President signed July 28, 2000.

PL 106-253 (HR 4437) Grant to the U.S. Postal Service the authority to issue semipostals. Introduced by McHugh, R-N.Y., on May 11, 2000. House Government Reform reported, amended, July 17 (H Rept 106-734). House Commerce and House Armed Services discharged. House passed, amended, under suspension of the rules, July 17. Senate passed July 26. President signed July 28, 2000.

PL 106-254 (HR 1791) Amend Title 18, U.S. Code, to provide penalties for harming animals used in federal law enforcement. Introduced by Weller, R-Ill., on May 13, 1999. House Judiciary reported, amended, Oct. 12 (H Rept 106-372). House passed, amended, under suspension of the rules, Oct. 12. Senate Judiciary discharged. Senate passed July 19, 2000. President signed Aug. 2, 2000.

PL 106-255 (HR 4249) Foster cross-border cooperation and environmental cleanup in Northern Europe. Introduced by Gejdenson, D-Conn., on April 12, 2000. House passed, amended, under suspension of the rules, May 15. Senate Foreign Relations reported June 28 (no written report). Senate passed July 19. President signed Aug. 2, 2000.

PL 106-256 (S 2327) Establish a Commission on Ocean Policy. Introduced by Hollings, D-S.C., on March 29, 2000. Senate Commerce, Science and Transportation reported May 23 (S Rept 106-301). Senate passed, amended, June 26. House passed, under suspension of the rules, July 25. President signed Aug. 7, 2000.

PL 106-257 (S 1629) Provide for the exchange of certain land in the state of Oregon. Introduced by Smith, R-Ore., on Sept. 23, 1999. Senate Energy and Natural Resources reported, amended, March 22, 2000 (S Rept 106-248). Senate passed, amended, April 13. House Resources reported July 17 (H Rept 106-747). House passed, under suspension of the rules, July 25. President signed Aug. 8, 2000.

PL 106-258 (S 1910) Amend the act establishing the Women's Rights National Historical Park to permit the secretary of the interior to acquire title in fee simple to the Hunt House located in Waterloo, N.Y. Introduced by Moynihan, D-N.Y., on Nov. 10, 1999. Senate Energy and Natural Resources reported, amended, April 12, 2000 (S Rept 106-268). Senate passed, amended, April 13. House passed, under suspension of the rules, July 25. President signed Aug. 8, 2000.

PL 106-259 (HR 4576) Make appropriations for the Department of Defense for the fiscal year ending Sept. 30, 2001. Introduced by Lewis, R-Calif., on June 1, 2000. House Appropriations reported June 1 (H Rept 106-644). House passed June 7. Senate passed, with amendment, June 13. House disagreed to Senate amendment July 12. Conference report filed in the House on

July 17 (H Rept 106-754). House agreed to conference report July 19. Senate agreed to conference report July 27. President signed Aug. 9, 2000.

PL 106-260 (HR 1167) Amend the Indian Self-Determination and Education Assistance Act to provide for further self-governance by Native American tribes. Introduced by Miller, D-Calif., on March 17, 1999. House Resources reported, amended, Nov. 17 (H Rept 106-477). House passed, amended, under suspension of the rules, Nov. 17. Senate passed, with amendment, April 4, 2000. House agreed to Senate amendment with amendments pursuant to H Res 562 on July 24. Senate agreed to House amendments to Senate amendment July 26. President signed Aug. 18, 2000.

PL 106-261 (HR 1749) Designate Wilson Creek in Avery and Caldwell counties, N.C., as a component of the National Wild and Scenic Rivers System. Introduced by Ballenger, R-N.C., on May 11, 1999. House Resources reported, amended, Feb. 29, 2000 (H Rept 106-500). House passed, amended, under suspension of the rules, Feb. 29. Senate Energy and Natural Resources reported June 27 (S Rept 106-320). Senate passed July 27. President signed Aug. 18, 2000.

PL 106-262 (HR 1982) Name the Department of Veterans Affairs outpatient clinic located at 125 Brookley Dr., Rome, N.Y., as the "Donald J. Mitchell Department of Veterans Affairs Outpatient Clinic." Introduced by Boehlert, R-N.Y., on May 27, 1999. House passed, amended, under suspension of the rules, July 25, 2000. Senate Veterans' Affairs discharged. Senate passed July 27. President signed Aug. 18, 2000.

PL 106-263 (HR 3291) Provide for the settlement of the water rights claims of the Shivwits Band of the Paiute Indian Tribe of Utah. Introduced by Hansen, R-Utah, on Nov. 10, 1999. House Resources reported, amended, July 17, 2000 (H Rept 106-743). House passed, amended, under suspension of the rules, July 25. Senate passed July 27. President signed Aug. 18, 2000.

PL 106-264 (HR 3519) Provide for negotiations for the creation of a trust fund to be administered by the International Bank for Reconstruction and Development of the International Development Association to combat the AIDS epidemic. Introduced by Leach, R-Iowa, on Jan. 24, 2000. House Banking and Financial Services reported, amended, March 28 (H Rept 106-548). House passed, amended, under suspension of the rules, May 15. Senate Foreign Relations discharged. Senate passed, with amendment, July 26. House agreed to Senate amendment July 27. President signed Aug. 19, 2000.

PL 106-265 (HR 4040) Amend Title 5, U.S. Code, to provide for the establishment of a program under which long-term care insurance is made available to federal employees, members of the uniformed services, and civilian and military retirees, and to correct certain retirement coverage errors. Introduced by Scarborough, R-Fla., on March 21, 2000. House Government Reform reported, amended, May 8 (H Rept 106-610, Pt. 1). House Armed Services discharged. House passed, amended, under suspension of the rules, May 9. Senate Governmental Affairs discharged. Senate passed, amended, July 25. House agreed to Senate amendments with amendments July 27. Senate agreed to House amendments July 27. President signed Sept. 19, 2000.

PL 106-266 (HR 1729) Designate the federal facility at 1301 Emmet St. in Charlottesville, Va., as the "Pamela B. Gwin Hall." Introduced by Goode, I-Va., on May 6, 1999. House Transportation and Infrastructure reported April 13, 2000 (H Rept 106-587). House passed, under suspension of the rules, May 3. Senate Environment and Public Works reported July 26 (no written report). Senate passed Sept. 13. President signed Sept. 22, 2000.

PL 106-267 (HR 1901) Designate the U.S. border station in Pharr, Texas, as the "Kika de la Garza United States Border Station." Introduced by Traficant, D-Ohio, on May 20, 1999. House Transportation and Infrastructure reported April 13, 2000 (H Rept 106-586). House passed, under suspension of the rules, May 3. Senate Environment and Public Works reported July 26 (no written report). Senate passed Sept. 13. President signed Sept. 22, 2000.

PL 106-268 (HR 1959) Designate the federal building at 743 East Durango Blvd. in San Antonio, Texas, as the "Adrian A. Spears Judicial Training Center." Introduced by Gonzalez, D-Texas, on May 26, 1999. House Transportation and Infrastructure reported, amended, June 22, 2000 (H Rept 106-688). House passed, amended, under suspension of the rules, June 27. Senate Environment and Public Works reported July 26 (no written report). Senate passed Sept. 13. President signed Sept. 22, 2000.

PL 106-269 (HR 4608) Designate the U.S. courthouse at 220 West Depot St. in Greeneville, Tenn., as the "James H. Quillen United States Courthouse."

Introduced by Jenkins, R-Tenn., on June 8, 2000. House Transportation and Infrastructure reported June 22 (H Rept 106-689). House passed, under suspension of the rules, June 27. Senate Environment and Public Works reported July 26 (no written report). Senate passed Sept. 13. President signed Sept. 22, 2000.

PL 106-270 (S 1027) Reauthorize the participation of the Bureau of Reclamation in the Deschutes Resources Conservancy. Introduced by Smith, R-Ore., on May 12, 1999. Senate Energy and Natural Resources reported June 24 (S Rept 106-96). Senate passed July 1. House Resources reported Sept. 6, 2000 (H Rept 106-805). House passed, under suspension of the rules, Sept. 12. President signed Sept. 22, 2000.

PL 106-271 (S 1117) Establish the Corinth Unit of Shiloh National Military Park, in the vicinity of the city of Corinth, Miss., and in the state of Tennessee. Introduced by Lott, R-Miss., on May 25, 1999. Senate Energy and Natural Resources reported, amended, Oct. 14 (S Rept 106-186). Senate passed, amended, Nov. 19. House passed, under suspension of the rules, Sept. 12, 2000. President signed Sept. 22, 2000.

PL 106-272 (S 1374) Authorize the development and maintenance of a multiagency campus project in the town of Jackson, Wyo. Introduced by Thomas, R-Wyo., on July 15, 1999. Senate Energy and Natural Resources reported, amended, Nov. 5 (S Rept 106-215). Senate passed, amended, Nov. 19. House Resources reported July 17, 2000 (H Rept 106-748). House passed, under suspension of the rules, Sept. 12. President signed Sept. 22, 2000.

PL 106-273 (S 1937) Amend the Pacific Northwest Electric Power Planning and Conservation Act to provide for electricity sales by the Bonneville Power Administration to joint operating entities. Introduced by Craig, R-Idaho, on Nov. 17, 1999. Senate Energy and Natural Resources discharged. Senate passed Nov. 19. House Resources reported Sept. 6, 2000 (H Rept 106-820, Pt. 1). House Commerce discharged. House passed, under suspension of the rules, Sept. 12. President signed Sept. 22, 2000.

PL 106-274 (S 2869) Protect religious liberty. Introduced by Hatch, R-Utah, on July 13, 2000. Senate passed July 27. House passed July 27. President signed Sept. 22, 2000.

PL 106-275 (H J Res 109) Make continuing appropriations for fiscal 2001. Introduced by Young, R-Fla., on Sept. 25, 2000. House passed Sept. 26. Senate passed Sept. 28. President signed Sept. 29, 2000.

PL 106-276 (S 1638) Amend the Omnibus Crime Control and Safe Streets Act of 1968 to extend the retroactive eligibility dates for financial assistance for higher education for spouses and dependent children of federal, state, and local law enforcement officers who are killed in the line of duty. Introduced by Ashcroft, R-Mo., on Sept. 24, 1999. Senate Judiciary reported Feb. 10, 2000 (no written report). Senate passed, amended, May 15. House passed, under suspension of the rules, Sept. 19. President signed Oct. 2, 2000.

PL 106-277 (S 2460) Authorize the payment of rewards to individuals furnishing information relating to persons subject to indictment for serious violations of international humanitarian law in Rwanda. Introduced by Feingold, D-Wis., on April 25, 2000. Senate Foreign Relations reported June 12 (no written report). Senate passed June 23. House passed, under suspension of the rules, Sept. 19. President signed Oct. 2, 2000.

PL 106-278 (HR 940) Designate the Lackawanna Valley and Schuykill River National Heritage Area. Introduced by Sherwood, R-Pa., on March 2, 1999. House Resources reported, amended, Aug. 3, 1999 (H Rept 106-285). House passed, amended, under suspension of the rules, Sept. 13. Senate Energy and Natural Resources reported, amended, July 12, 2000 (S Rept 106-342). Senate passed, with amendments, July 27. Proceedings vacated July 27. Senate passed, with amendments, Sept. 18. House agreed to Senate amendments Sept. 21. President signed Oct. 6, 2000.

PL 106-279 (HR 2909) Provide for implementation by the United States of the Hague Convention on Protection of Children and Cooperation in Respect of Intercountry Adoption. Introduced by Gilman, R-N.Y., on Sept. 22, 1999. House International Relations reported, amended, June 22, 2000 (H Rept 106-691, Pt. 1). House Judiciary discharged. House Education and the Workforce discharged. House Ways and Means discharged. House passed, amended, under suspension of the rules, July 18. Senate passed, with amendment, July 27. House agreed to Senate amendment, with amendment, Sept. 18. Senate agreed to House amendment Sept. 20. President signed Oct. 6, 2000.

PL 106-280 (HR 4919) Amend the Foreign Assistance Act of 1961 and the Arms Export Control Act to make improvements to defense and security assistance provisions under those Acts and authorize the transfer of naval vessels to certain foreign countries. Introduced by Gilman, R-N.Y., on July 24, 2000. House passed, under suspension of the rules, July 24. Senate Foreign Relations discharged. Senate passed, with amendment, Sept. 7. Conference report filed in the House Sept. 19 (H Rept 106-868). House agreed to conference report Sept. 21. Senate agreed to conference report Sept. 22. President signed Oct. 6, 2000.

PL 106-281 (HR 5193) Amend the National Housing Act to temporarily extend the applicability of the down payment simplification provisions for the FHA single family housing mortgage insurance program. Introduced by Lazio, R-N.Y., on Sept. 18, 2000. House passed, amended, under suspension of the rules Sept. 19. Senate Banking, Housing and Urban Affairs discharged. Senate passed Sept. 28. President signed Oct. 6, 2000.

PL 106-282 (H J Res 110) Make further continuing appropriations for fiscal 2001. Introduced by Young, R-Fla., on Oct. 2, 2000. House passed Oct. 3. Senate passed Oct. 5. President signed Oct. 6, 2000.

PL 106-283 (S 430) Amend the Alaska Native Claims Settlement Act and provide for a land exchange between the secretary of agriculture and the Kake Tribal Corporation. Introduced by Murkowski, R-Alaska, on Feb. 22, 1999. Senate Energy and Natural Resources reported, amended, March 22 (S Rept 106-31). Senate passed, amended, April 19. House Resources reported, with amendment, Jan. 27, 2000 (H Rept 106-489). House passed, with amendment, under suspension of the rules, May 22. Senate agreed to House amendment Sept. 22. President signed Oct. 6, 2000.

PL 106-284 (HR 999) Amend the federal Water Pollution Control Act to improve the quality of coastal recreation waters. Introduced by Bilbray, R-Calif., on March 4, 1999. House Transportation and Infrastructure reported, amended, April 19, 1999 (H Rept 106-98). House passed, amended, April 22. Senate Environment and Public Works reported Aug. 25, 2000 (no written report). Senate passed, with amendment, Sept. 21. House agreed to Senate amendment, under suspension of the rules, Sept. 26. President signed Oct. 10, 2000.

PL 106-285 (HR 2647) Amend the act entitled "An Act relating to the water rights of the Ak-Chin Indian Community" to clarify certain provisions concerning the leasing of such water rights. Introduced by Shadegg, R-Ariz., on July 29, 1999. House Resources reported May 2, 2000 (H Rept 106-598). House passed May 9, under suspension of the rules. Senate Indian Affairs reported Sept. 19 (S Rept 106-415). Senate passed Sept. 27. President signed Oct. 10, 2000.

PL 106-286 (HR 4444) Authorize extension of nondiscriminatory treatment (normal trade relations treatment) to the People's Republic of China. Introduced by Archer, R-Texas, May 15, 2000. House Ways and Means reported, amended, May 22 (H Rept 106-632). House passed, amended, May 24. Senate passed Sept. 19. President signed Oct. 10, 2000.

PL 106-287 (HR 4700) Grant the consent of the Congress to the Kansas and Missouri Metropolitan Culture District Compact. Introduced by McCarthy, D-Mo., June 20, 2000. House Judiciary reported July 20 (H Rept 106-769). House passed, under suspension of the rules, July 24. Senate passed Sept. 26. President signed Oct. 10, 2000.

PL 106-288 (H J Res 72) Grant the consent of the Congress to the Red River Boundary Compact. Introduced by Thornberry, R-Texas, on Oct. 19, 1999. House Judiciary reported, amended, July 20, 2000 (H Rept 106-770). House passed, amended, under suspension of the rules, July 24. Senate passed Sept. 26. President signed Oct. 10, 2000.

PL 106-289 (S 1295) Designate the U.S. Post Office at 3813 Main St. in East Chicago, Indiana, as the "Lance Corporal Harold Gomez Post Office." Introduced by Lugar, R-Ind., on June 28, 1999. Senate Governmental Affairs reported Nov. 4 (no written report). Senate passed Nov. 19. House passed, under suspension of the rules, Sept. 27, 2000. President signed Oct. 10, 2000.

PL 106-290 (S 1324) Expand the boundaries of the Gettysburg National Military Park to include Wills House. Introduced by Santorum, R-Pa., on July 1, 1999. Senate Energy and Natural Resources reported Oct. 14 (S Rept 106-187). Senate passed Nov. 19. House passed, under suspension of the rules, Sept. 26, 2000. President signed Oct. 10, 2000.

PL 106-291 (HR 4578) Make appropriations for the Department of the Interior and related agencies for the fiscal year ending Sept. 30, 2001. Introduced by Regula, R-Ohio, on June 1, 2000. House Appropriations reported June 1 (H Rept 106-646). House passed, amended, June 16. Senate Appropriations reported, amended, June 19 (S Rept 106-312). Senate passed, amended, July 18. Conference report filed in the House Sept. 29 (H Rept 106-914). House agreed to conference report Oct. 3. Senate agreed to conference report Oct. 5. President signed Oct. 11, 2000.

PL 106-292 (HR 4115) Authorize appropriations for the U.S. Holocaust Memorial Museum. Introduced by Cannon, R-Utah, on March 29, 2000. House Resources reported, amended, July 17 (H Rept 106-751). House passed, amended, Sept. 7. Senate Energy and Natural Resources reported Sept. 28 (S Rept 106-436). Senate passed Sept. 28. President signed Oct. 12, 2000.

PL 106-293 (HR 4931) Provide for the training or orientation of individuals, during a presidential transition, who the president intends to appoint to certain top-level positions and provide for a study and report on improving the financial disclosure process for certain presidential nominees. Introduced by Horn, R-Calif., on July 24, 2000. House Government Reform discharged. House passed Sept. 13. Senate passed Sept. 28. President signed Oct. 12, 2000.

PL 106-294 (S 704) Amend Title 18, U.S. Code, to combat the overuse of prison health care services and control rising prisoner health care costs. Introduced by Kyl, R-Ariz., on March 24, 1999. Senate Judiciary reported, amended, April 29 (no written report). Senate passed, amended, May 27. House Judiciary discharged. House passed, with amendment, Sept. 19, 2000. Senate agreed to House amendment Sept. 28. President signed Oct. 12, 2000.

PL 106-295 (HR 1162) Designate the bridge on U.S. Route 231 that crosses the Ohio River between Maceo, Ky., and Rockport, Ind., as the "William H. Natcher Bridge." Introduced by Lewis, R-Ky., on March 17, 1999. House Transportation and Infrastructure reported April 27 (H Rept 106-112). House passed, under suspension of the rules, May 4. Senate Environment and Public Works reported Sept. 28, 2000 (no written report). Senate passed Oct. 4. President signed Oct. 13, 2000.

PL 106-296 (HR 1605) Designate the U.S. courthouse building at 402 N. Walnut St. and Prospect Ave. in Harrison, Ark., as the "J. Smith Henley Federal Building." Introduced by Hutchinson, R-Ark., April 28, 1999. House Transportation and Infrastructure reported, amended, March 23, 2000 (H Rept 106-536). House passed, amended, under suspension of the rules, April 3. Senate Environment and Public Works reported Sept. 28 (no written report). Senate passed Oct. 4. President signed Oct. 13, 2000.

PL 106-297 (HR 1800) Amend the Violent Crime Control and Law Enforcement Act of 1994 to ensure that certain information regarding prisoners is reported to the attorney general. Introduced by Hutchinson, R-Ark., on May 13, 1999. House passed, amended, under suspension of the rules, July 24, 2000. Senate Judiciary discharged. Senate passed Oct. 3. President signed Oct. 13, 2000.

PL 106-298 (HR 2752) Give Lincoln County, Nev., the right to purchase at fair market value certain public land within that county. Introduced by Gibbons, R-Nev., on Aug. 5, 1999. House Resources reported, amended, Sept. 14, 2000 (H Rept 106-847). House passed, amended, under suspension of the rules, Sept. 26. Senate passed Oct. 3. President signed Oct. 13, 2000.

PL 106-299 (HR 2773) Amend the Wild and Scenic Rivers Act to designate the Wekiva River and its tributaries of Rock Springs Run and Black Water Creek in the state of Florida as components of the national wild and scenic rivers system. Introduced by McCollum, R-Fla., on Aug. 5, 1999. House Resources reported, amended, July 17, 2000 (H Rept 106-739). House passed, amended, under suspension of the rules, July 24. Senate passed Oct. 3. President signed Oct. 13, 2000.

PL 106-300 (HR 4318) Establish the Red River National Wildlife Refuge. Introduced by McCrery, R-La., on April 13, 2000. House Resources reported, amended, Sept. 6 (H Rept 106-809). House passed, amended, under suspension of the rules, Sept. 12. Senate Environment and Public Works reported Oct. 2 (S Rept 106-462). Senate passed Oct. 4. President signed Oct. 13, 2000.

PL 106-301 (HR 4579) Provide for the exchange of certain lands within the state of Utah. Introduced by Hansen, R-Utah, on June 6, 2000. House passed, amended, under suspension of the rules, July 11. Senate Energy and

Natural Resources reported Oct. 2 (S Rept 106-463). Senate passed Oct. 3. President signed Oct. 13, 2000.

PL 106-302 (HR 4583) Extend the authorization for the Air Force Memorial Foundation to establish a memorial in the District of Columbia or its environs. Introduced by Hansen, R-Utah, on June 6, 2000. House Resources reported Sept. 6 (H Rept 106-817). House passed, under suspension of the rules, Sept. 12. Senate Energy and Natural Resources discharged. Senate passed Oct. 3. President signed Oct. 13, 2000.

PL 106-303 (HR 4642) Make certain personnel flexibilities available with respect to the General Accounting Office. Introduced by Burton, R-Ind., on June 13, 2000. House passed, amended, under suspension of the rules, Sept. 19. Senate Governmental Affairs discharged. Senate passed Oct. 4. President signed Oct. 13, 2000.

PL 106-304 (HR 4806) Designate the federal building at 1710 Alabama Ave. in Jasper, Ala., as the "Carl Elliott Federal Building." Introduced by Aderholt, R-Ala., on June 29, 2000. House passed, under suspension of the rules, July 25. Senate Environment and Public Works reported Sept. 28 (no written report). Senate passed Oct. 4. President signed Oct. 13, 2000.

PL 106-305 (HR 5284) Designate the U.S. customhouse at 101 East Main St. in Norfolk, Va., as the "Owen B. Pickett United States Customhouse." Introduced by Scott, D-Va., on Sept. 25, 2000. House Transportation and Infrastructure reported Oct. 2 (H Rept 106-922). House passed, under suspension of the rules, Oct. 2. Senate passed Oct. 4. President signed Oct. 13, 2000.

PL 106-306 (H J Res 111) Make further continuing appropriations for fiscal 2001. Introduced by Young, R-Fla., on Oct. 11, 2000. House passed Oct. 12. Senate passed Oct. 12. President signed Oct. 13, 2000.

PL 106-307 (S 366) Amend the National Trails System Act to designate El Camino Real de Tierra Adentro as a National Historic Trail. Introduced by Bingaman, D-N.M., on Feb. 4, 1999. Senate Energy and Natural Resources reported, amended, March 17 (S Rept 106-22) Senate passed, amended, Nov. 19. House passed, under suspension of the rules, Oct. 3, 2000. President signed Oct. 13, 2000.

PL 106-308 (S 1794) Designate the federal courthouse at 145 East Simpson Ave. in Jackson, Wyo., as the "Clifford P. Hansen Federal Courthouse." Introduced by Thomas, R-Wyo., on Oct. 26, 1999. Senate Environment and Public Works reported Feb. 9, 2000 (no written report). Senate passed March 2. House Transportation and Infrastructure reported Sept. 7 (H Rept 106-828). House passed, under suspension of the rules, Oct. 2. President signed Oct. 13, 2000.

PL 106-309 (HR 1143) Establish a program to provide assistance for programs of credit and other financial services for microenterprises in developing countries. Introduced by Gilman, R-N.Y., on March 17, 1999. House International Relations reported April 12 (H Rept 106-82). House passed, amended, April 13. Senate Foreign Relations discharged. Senate passed, amended, Oct. 3, 2000. House agreed to Senate amendment Oct. 5. President signed Oct. 17, 2000.

PL 106-310 (HR 4365) Amend the Public Health Service Act with respect to children's health. Introduced by Bilirakis, R-Fla., on May 3, 2000. House passed, amended, under suspension of the rules, May 9. Senate Health, Education, Labor, and Pensions discharged. Senate passed, with amendment, Sept. 22. House agreed to Senate amendment Sept. 27. President signed Oct. 17, 2000.

PL 106-311 (HR 5362) Increase the fees charged to employers who are petitioners for the employment of H-1B nonimmigrant workers. Introduced by Dreier, R-Calif., on Oct. 3, 2000. House Judiciary discharged. House passed Oct. 6. Senate passed Oct. 10. President signed Oct. 17, 2000.

PL 106-312 (S 1198) Establish a three-year pilot project for the General Accounting Office to report to Congress on economically significant agency regulatory actions. Introduced by Shelby, R-Ala., on June 9, 1999. Senate Governmental Affairs reported, amended, Dec. 7 (S Rept 106-225). Senate passed, amended, May 9, 2000. House passed, under suspension of the rules, Oct. 3. President signed Oct. 17, 2000.

PL 106-313 (S 2045) Amend the Immigration and Nationality Act with respect to H-1B nonimmigrant aliens. Introduced by Hatch, R-Utah, on Feb. 9,

2000. Senate Judiciary reported, amended, April 11 (S Rept 106-260). Senate passed, amended, Oct. 3. House passed, under suspension of the rules, Oct. 3. President signed Oct. 17, 2000.

PL 106-314 (S 2272) Improve the administrative efficiency and effectiveness of the nation's abuse and neglect courts. Introduced by DeWine, R-Ohio, on March 22, 2000. Senate Judiciary reported July 27 (no written report). Senate passed, amended, Sept. 26. House passed, under the suspension of the rules, Oct. 3. President signed Oct. 17, 2000.

PL 106-315 (HR 2302) Designate the building of the U.S. Postal Service at 307 Main St. in Johnson City, N.Y., as the "James W. McCabe Sr. Post Office Building." Introduced by Hinchey, D-N.Y., on June 22, 1999. House passed, under suspension of the rules, Sept. 6, 2000. Senate Governmental Affairs reported Sept. 29 (no written report). Senate passed Oct. 6. President signed Oct. 19, 2000.

PL 106-316 (HR 2496) Reauthorize the Junior Duck Stamp Conservation and Design Program Act of 1994. Introduced by Ortiz, D-Texas, on July 13, 1999. House Resources reported, amended, Oct. 18 (H Rept 106-390). House passed, amended, under suspension of the rules, Oct. 26. Senate Environment and Public Works reported Oct. 2, 2000 (S Rept 106-457). Senate passed Oct. 5. President signed Oct. 19, 2000.

PL 106-317 (HR 2641) Make technical corrections to Title X of the Energy Policy Act of 1992. Introduced by Cubin, R-Wyo., on July 29, 1999. House Commerce reported, amended, Sept. 25, 2000 (H Rept 106-886). House passed, amended, under suspension of the rules, Sept. 27. Senate passed Oct. 5. President signed Oct. 19, 2000.

PL 106-318 (HR 2778) Amend the Wild and Scenic Rivers Act to designate segments of the Taunton River in the Commonwealth of Massachusetts for study for potential addition to the National Wild and Scenic Rivers System. Introduced by Moakley, D-Mass., on Aug. 5, 1999. House Resources reported, amended, June 19, 2000 (H Rept 106-678). House passed, amended, under suspension of the rules, June 19. Senate Energy and Natural Resources discharged. Senate passed Oct. 5. President signed Oct. 19, 2000.

PL 106-319 (HR 2833) Establish the Yuma Crossing National Heritage Area. Introduced by Pastor, D-Ariz., on Sept. 9, 1999. House Resources reported, amended, July 17, 2000 (H Rept 106-740). House passed, amended, under suspension of the rules, July 25. Senate passed Oct. 5, 2000. President signed Oct. 19, 2000.

PL 106-320 (HR 2938) Designate the facility of the U.S. Postal Service at 424 S. Michigan St. in South Bend, Ind., as the "John Brademas Post Office." Introduced by Roemer, D-Ind., on Sept., 23 1999. House passed, under suspension of the rules, June 20, 2000. Senate Governmental Affairs discharged. Senate passed Oct. 6. President signed Oct. 19, 2000.

PL 106-321 (HR 3030) Designate the facility of the U.S. Postal Service at 757 Warren Rd. in Ithaca, N.Y., as the "Matthew F. McHugh Post Office." Introduced by Hinchey, D-N.Y., on Oct. 6, 1999. House passed, under suspension of the rules, June 6, 2000. Senate Governmental Affairs reported Sept. 29 (no written report). Senate passed Oct. 6. President signed Oct. 19, 2000.

PL 106-322 (HR 3454) Designate the U.S. post office at 451 College St. in Macon, Ga., as the "Henry McNeal Turner Post Office." Introduced by Chambliss, R-Ga., on Nov. 18, 1999. House passed, under suspension of the rules, Sept. 6, 2000. Senate Governmental Affairs reported Sept. 29 (no written report). Senate passed Oct. 6. President signed Oct. 19, 2000.

PL 106-323 (HR 3745) Authorize the addition of certain parcels to the Effigy Mounds National Monument in Iowa. Introduced by Nussle, R-Iowa, on Feb. 29, 2000. House Resources reported, amended, Sept. 7 (H Rept 106-826). House passed, amended, under suspension of the rules, Sept. 26. Senate passed Oct. 5. President signed Oct. 19, 2000.

PL 106-324 (HR 3817) Redesignate the Big South Trail in the Comanche Peak Wilderness Area of Roosevelt National Forest in Colorado as the "Jaryd Atadero Legacy Trail." Introduced by Tancredo, R-Colo., on March 1, 2000. House Resources reported, amended, July 17 (H Rept 106-738). House passed, amended, under suspension of the rules, July 25. Senate Energy and Natural Resources discharged. Senate passed Oct. 5. President signed Oct. 19, 2000.

PL 106-325 (HR 3909) Designate the facility of the U.S. Postal Service at 4601 S. Cottage Grove Ave. in Chicago, Ill., as the "Henry W. McGee Post Of-

fice Building." Introduced by Rush, D-Ill., on March 14, 2000. House passed, under suspension of the rules, July 11. Senate Governmental Affairs reported Sept. 29 (no written report). Senate passed Oct. 6. President signed Oct. 19, 2000.

PL 106-326 (HR 3985) Designate the facility of the U.S. Postal Service located at 14900 S.W. 30th St. in Miramar City, Fla., as the "Vicki Coceano Post Office Building." Introduced by Hastings, D-Fla., on March 15, 2000. House passed, amended, under suspension of the rules, July 17. Senate Governmental Affairs reported Sept. 29 (no written report). Senate passed Oct. 6. President signed Oct. 19, 2000.

PL 106-327 (HR 4157) Designate the facility of the U.S. Postal Service located at 600 Lincoln Ave. in Pasadena, Calif., as the "Matthew 'Mack' Robinson Post Office Building." Introduced by Rogan, R-Calif., on April 3, 2000. House passed, under suspension of the rules, July 18. Senate Governmental Affairs reported Sept. 29 (no written report). Senate passed Oct. 6. President signed Oct. 19, 2000.

PL 106-328 (HR 4169) Designate the facility of the U.S. Postal Service located at 2000 Vassar St. in Reno, Nev., as the "Barbara F. Vucanovich Post Office Building." Introduced by Gibbons, R-Nev., on April 4, 2000. House passed, under suspension of the rules, July 12. Senate Governmental Affairs reported Sept. 29 (no written report). Senate passed Oct. 6. President signed Oct. 19, 2000.

PL 106-329 (HR 4226) Authorize the secretary of agriculture to sell or exchange all or part of certain administrative sites and other land in the Black Hills National Forest, and use funds derived from the sale or exchange to acquire replacement sites and to acquire or construct administrative improvements in connection with the Black Hills National Forest. Introduced by Thune, R-S.D., on April 10, 2000. House Resources reported, amended, Sept. 6 (H Rept 106-816). House passed, amended, under suspension of the rules, Sept. 18. Senate passed Oct. 5. President signed Oct. 19, 2000.

PL 106-330 (HR 4285) Authorize the secretary of agriculture to convey certain administrative sites for National Forest System lands in Texas and to convey certain National Forest System land to the New Waverly Gulf Coast Trades Center. Introduced by Turner, D-Texas, on April 13, 2000. House Agriculture discharged. House passed July 27. Senate Energy and Natural Resources reported Sept. 29 (S Rept 106-447). Senate passed Oct. 5. President signed Oct. 19, 2000.

PL 106-331 (HR 4286) Provide for the establishment of the Cahaba River National Wildlife Refuge in Bibb County, Ala. Introduced by Bachus, R-Ala., on April 13, 2000. House Resources reported, amended, July 10 (H Rept 106-713). House passed, amended, under suspension of the rules, July 10. Senate Environment and Public Works reported Oct. 2 (S Rept 106-461). Senate passed Oct. 5. President signed Oct. 19, 2000.

PL 106-332 (HR 4435) Clarify certain boundaries on the map relating to Unit NC01 of the Coastal Barrier Resources System. Introduced by Jones, R-N.C., on May 11, 2000. House Resources reported June 6 (H Rept 106-648). House passed, amended, under suspension of the rules, June 7. Senate Environment and Public Works reported Oct. 3 (S Rept 106-473). Senate passed Oct. 5. President signed Oct. 19, 2000.

PL 106-333 (HR 4447) Designate the facility of the U.S. Postal Service located at 919 W. 34th St. in Baltimore, Md., as the "Samuel H. Lacy Sr. Post Office Building." Introduced by Cummings, D-Md., on May 15, 2000. House passed, under suspension of the rules, July 12. Senate Governmental Affairs reported Sept. 29 (no written report). Senate passed Oct. 6. President signed Oct. 19, 2000.

PL 106-334 (HR 4448) Designate the facility of the U.S. Postal Service located at 3500 Dolfield Ave. in Baltimore, Md., as the "Judge Robert Bernard Watts Sr. Post Office Building." Introduced by Cummings, D-Md., on May 15, 2000. House passed, under suspension of the rules, Sept. 6. Senate Governmental Affairs reported Sept. 29 (no written report). Senate passed Oct. 6. President signed Oct. 19, 2000.

PL 106-335 (HR 4449) Designate the facility of the U.S. Postal Service located at 1908 N. Ellamont St. in Baltimore, Md., as the "Dr. Flossie McClain Dedmond Post Office Building." Introduced by Cummings, D-Md., on May 15, 2000. House passed, under suspension of the rules, Sept. 6. Senate Governmental Affairs reported Sept. 29 (no written report). Senate passed Oct. 6. President signed Oct. 19, 2000.

PL 106-336 (HR 4484) Designate the facility of the U.S. Postal Service located at 500 N. Washington St. in Rockville, Md., as the "Everett Alvarez Jr. Post Office Building." Introduced by Morella, R-Md., on May 17, 2000. House passed, under suspension of the rules, Sept. 6. Senate Governmental Affairs reported Sept. 29 (no written report). Senate passed Oct. 6. President signed Oct. 19, 2000.

PL 106-337 (HR 4517) Designate the facility of the U.S. Postal Service located at 24 Tsienneto Rd. in Derry, N.H., as the "Alan B. Shepard Jr. Post Office Building." Introduced by Sununu, R-N.H., on May 23, 2000. House passed, under suspension of the rules, July 18. Senate Governmental Affairs reported Sept. 29 (no written report). Senate passed Oct. 6. President signed Oct. 19, 2000.

PL 106-338 (HR 4534) Designate the facility of the U.S. Postal Service located at 114 Ridge St. in Lenoir, N.C., as the "James T. Broyhill Post Office Building." Introduced by Burr, R-N.C., on May 24, 2000. House passed, amended, under suspension of the rules, Sept. 6. Senate Governmental Affairs reported Sept. 29 (no written report). Senate passed Oct. 6. President signed Oct. 19, 2000.

PL 106-339 (HR 4554) Redesignate the facility of the U.S. Postal Service located at 1602 Frankford Ave. in Philadelphia, Pa., as the "Joseph F. Smith Post Office Building." Introduced by Borski, D-Pa., on May 25, 2000. House passed, under suspension of the rules, July 18. Senate Governmental Affairs reported Sept. 29 (no written report). Senate passed Oct. 6. President signed Oct. 19, 2000.

PL 106-340 (HR 4615) Redesignate the facility of the U.S. Postal Service located at 3030 Meredith Ave. in Omaha, Neb., as the "Reverend J.C. Wade Post Office." Introduced by Terry, R-Neb., on June 8, 2000. House passed, under suspension of the rules, Sept. 6. Senate Governmental Affairs reported Sept. 29 (no written report). Senate passed Oct. 6. President signed Oct. 19, 2000.

PL 106-341 (HR 4658) Designate the facility of the U.S. Postal Service located at 301 Green St. in Fayetteville, N.C., as the "J.L. Dawkins Post Office Building." Introduced by Hayes, R-N.C., on June 14, 2000. House passed, under suspension of the rules, July 11. Senate Governmental Affairs reported Sept. 29 (no written report). Senate passed Oct. 6. President signed Oct. 19, 2000.

PL 106-342 (HR 4884) Redesignate the facility of the U.S. Postal Service located at 200 W. 2nd St. in Royal Oak, Mich., as the "William S. Broomfield Post Office Building." Introduced by Knollenberg, R-Mich., on July 19, 2000. House passed, under suspension of the rules, Sept. 6. Senate Governmental Affairs reported Sept. 29 (no written report). Senate passed Oct. 6. President signed Oct. 19, 2000.

PL 106-343 (S 1236) Extend the deadline under the Federal Power Act for commencement of the construction of the Arrowrock Dam Hydroelectric Project in Idaho. Introduced by Craig, R-Idaho, on June 17, 1999. Senate Energy and Natural Resources reported Oct. 4 (S Rept 106-170). Senate passed Nov. 19. House Commerce reported, with amendment, May 19, 2000 (H Rept 106-630). House passed, with amendment, under suspension of the rules, May 22. Senate agreed to House amendment Oct. 5. President signed Oct. 19, 2000.

PL 106-344 (H J Res 114) Make further continuing appropriations for fiscal 2001. Introduced by Young, R-Fla., on Oct. 18, 2000. House passed Oct. 19. Senate passed Oct. 19. President signed Oct. 20, 2000.

PL 106-345 (S 2311) Revise and extend the Ryan White CARE Act programs under Title XXVI of the Public Health Service Act, to improve access to health care and the quality of health care under such programs and to provide for the development of increased capacity to provide health care and related support services to individuals and families with HIV disease. Introduced by Jeffords, R-Vt., on March 29, 2000. Senate Health, Education, Labor, and Pensions reported May 15 (S Rept 106-294). Senate passed, amended, June 6. House passed, with amendments, Oct. 5. Senate agreed to House amendments Oct. 5. President signed Oct. 20, 2000.

PL 106-346 (HR 4475) Make appropriations for the Department of Transportation and related agencies for fiscal 2001. Introduced by Wolf, R-Va., on May 17, 2000. House Appropriations reported May 17 (H Rept 106-622). House passed, amended, May 19. Senate Appropriations discharged. Senate passed, with amendment, June 15. Conference report filed in the House Oct. 5

(H Rept 106-940). House agreed to conference report Oct. 6. Senate agreed to conference report Oct. 6. President signed Oct. 23, 2000.

PL 106-347 (HR 4975) Designate the post office and courthouse located at 2 Federal Square, Newark, N.J., as the "Frank R. Lautenberg Post Office and Courthouse." Introduced by Lobiondo, R-N.J., on July 26, 2000. House passed, under suspension of the rules, Sept. 19. Senate passed Oct. 6. President signed Oct. 23, 2000.

PL 106-348 (HR 1509) Authorize the Disabled Veterans' LIFE Memorial Foundation to establish a memorial in the District of Columbia or its environs to honor veterans who became disabled while serving in the Armed Forces of the United States. Introduced by Johnson, R-Texas, on April 21, 1999. House Resources reported April 13, 2000 (H Rept 106-583). House passed, under suspension of the rules, May 3. Senate Energy and Natural Resources discharged. Senate passed Oct. 5. President signed Oct. 24, 2000.

PL 106-349 (HR 3201) Authorize the secretary of the interior to study the suitability and feasibility of designating the Carter G. Woodson Home in the District of Columbia as a National Historic Site. Introduced by Norton, D-D.C., on Nov. 2, 1999. House passed, under suspension of the rules, Feb. 15, 2000. Senate Energy and Natural Resources reported June 27 (S Rept 106-322). Senate passed Oct. 5. President signed Oct. 24, 2000.

PL 106-350 (HR 3632) Revise the boundaries of the Golden Gate National Recreation Area. Introduced by Lantos, D-Calif., on Feb. 10, 2000. House Resources reported, amended, Sept. 7 (H Rept 106-825). House passed, amended, under suspension of the rules, Sept. 12. Senate passed Oct. 5. President signed Oct. 24, 2000.

PL 106-351 (HR 3676) Establish the Santa Rosa and San Jacinto Mountains National Monument in California. Introduced by Bono, R-Calif., on Feb. 16, 2000. House Resources reported, amended, July 17 (H Rept 106-750). House passed, amended, under suspension of the rules, July 25. Senate Energy and Natural Resources discharged. Senate passed Oct. 5. President signed Oct. 24, 2000.

PL 106-352 (HR 4063) Establish the Rosie the Riveter-World War II Home Front National Historical Park in the State of California. Introduced by Miller, D-Calif., on March 22, 2000. House Resources reported, amended, July 11 (H Rept 106-723). House passed, amended, under suspension of the rules, July 11. Senate Energy and Natural Resources reported, with amendments, Sept. 29 (S Rept 106-446). Senate passed Oct. 5. President signed Oct. 24, 2000.

PL 106-353 (HR 4275) Establish the Colorado Canyons National Conservation Area and the Black Ridge Canyons Wilderness. Introduced by McInnis, R-Colo., on April 13, 2000. House passed, amended, under suspension of the rules, July 25. Senate Energy and Natural Resources reported Oct. 2 (S Rept 106-460). Senate passed Oct. 5. President signed Oct. 24, 2000.

PL 106-354 (HR 4386) Amend Title XIX of the Social Security Act to provide medical assistance for certain women screened and found to have breast or cervical cancer under a federally funded screening program and amend the Public Health Service Act and the Federal Food, Drug, and Cosmetic Act with respect to surveillance and information concerning the relationship between cervical cancer and the human papillomavirus (HPV). Introduced by Myrick, R-N.C., on May 4, 2000. House passed, amended, under suspension of the rules, May 9. Senate passed, with amendment, Oct. 4. House agreed to Senate amendment Oct. 12. President signed Oct. 24, 2000.

PL 106-355 (HR 4613) Amend the National Historic Preservation Act to establish a national historic lighthouse preservation program. Introduced by Sounder, R-Ind., on June 8, 2000. House Resources reported, amended, Sept. 26 (H Rept 106-890). House passed, amended, under suspension of the rules, Sept. 26. Senate passed Oct. 5. President signed Oct. 24, 2000.

PL 106-356 (HR 5036) Amend the Dayton Aviation Heritage Preservation Act of 1992 to clarify the areas included in the Dayton Aviation Heritage National Historical Park and authorize appropriations for that park. Introduced by Hall, D-Ohio, on July 27, 2000. House Resources reported Sept. 26 (H Rept 106-896). House passed, amended, under suspension of the rules, Sept. 26. Senate passed Oct. 5. President signed Oct. 24, 2000.

PL 106-357 (S 1849) Designate segments and tributaries of White Clay Creek, Del. and Pa., as a component of the National Wild and Scenic Rivers

System. Introduced by Biden, D-Del., on Nov. 3, 1999. Senate Energy and Natural Resources reported, amended, April 12, 2000 (S Rept 106-266). Senate passed, amended, April 13. House passed, with amendment, under suspension of the rules, Sept. 18. Senate agreed to House amendment Oct. 5. President signed Oct. 24, 2000.

PL 106-358 (H J Res 115) Make further continuing appropriations for fiscal 2001. Introduced by Young, R-Fla., on Oct. 24, 2000. House passed Oct. 25. Senate passed Oct. 25. President signed Oct. 26, 2000.

PL 106-359 (H J Res 116) Make further continuing appropriations for fiscal 2001. Introduced by Young, R-Fla., on Oct. 24, 2000. House passed Oct. 26. Senate passed Oct. 26. President signed Oct. 26, 2000.

PL 106-360 (HR 34) Direct the secretary of the interior to make technical corrections to a map relating to the Coastal Barrier Resources System. Introduced by Goss, R-Fla., on Jan. 6, 1999. House Resources discharged. House passed Nov. 18. Senate Environment and Public Works reported, with amendments, Oct. 3, 2000 (S Rept 106-471). Senate passed, with amendments, Oct. 5. House agreed to Senate amendments, under suspension of the rules, Oct. 12. President signed Oct. 27, 2000.

PL 106-361 (HR 208) Amend Title 5, U.S. Code, to allow for the contribution of certain rollover distributions to accounts in the Thrift Savings Plan and eliminate certain waiting-period requirements for participating in the plan. Introduced by Morella, R-Md., on Jan. 6, 1999. House Government Reform reported, amended, April 13 (H Rept 106-87). House passed, amended, under suspension of the rules, April 20. Senate Governmental Affairs reported, with amendments, July 13, 2000 (S Rept 106-343). Senate passed, with amendments, July 21. House agreed to Senate amendments, under suspension of the rules, Oct. 10. President signed Oct. 27, 2000.

PL 106-362 (HR 1695) Provide for the conveyance of certain federal public lands in the Ivanpah Valley, Nev., to Clark County, Nev., for the development of an airport facility. Introduced by Gibbons, R-Nev., on May 5, 1999. House Resources reported, amended, Nov. 16 (H Rept 106-471). House passed, amended, March 9, 2000. Senate Energy and Natural Resources reported, with amendments, Aug. 25 (S Rept 106-394). Senate passed, with amendments, Oct. 5. House agreed to Senate amendments, under suspension of the rules, Oct. 17. President signed Oct. 27, 2000.

PL 106-363 (HR 1715) Extend the expiration date of the Defense Production Act of 1950. Introduced by Bachus, R-Ala., on May 6, 1999. House passed, amended, under suspension of the rules, Sept. 18, 2000. Senate passed Oct. 12. President signed Oct. 27, 2000.

PL 106-364 (HR 2296) Amend the Revised Organic Act of the Virgin Islands to provide that the number of members on the legislature of the Virgin Islands and the number of such members constituting a quorum shall be determined by the laws of the Virgin Islands. Introduced by Christensen, D-Virgin Is., on June 22, 1999. House Resources reported Sept. 6 (H Rept 106-807). House passed, under suspension of the rules, Sept. 12, 2000. Senate Energy and Natural Resources discharged. Senate passed Oct. 17. President signed Oct. 27, 2000.

PL 106-365 (HR 2879) Provide for the placement at the Lincoln Memorial of a plaque commemorating the speech of the Rev. Dr. Martin Luther King Jr., known as the "I Have a Dream" speech. Introduced by Northup, R-Ky., on Sept. 15, 1999. House Resources reported Nov. 4 (H Rept 106-448). House passed, under suspension of the rules, Nov. 9. Senate Energy and Natural Resources reported, with amendment, July 10, 2000 (S Rept 106-334). Senate passed, with amendment, Oct. 5. House agreed to Senate amendment, under suspension of the rules, Oct. 10. President signed Oct. 27, 2000.

PL 106-366 (HR 2984) Direct the secretary of the interior, through the Bureau of Reclamation, to convey the assets of the Middle Loup Division of the Missouri River Basin Project in Nebraska to the Loup Basin Reclamation District, the Sargent River Irrigation District, and the Farwell Irrigation District, all in Nebraska. Introduced by Barrett, R-Neb., on Sept. 30, 1999. House Resources reported, amended, Sept. 7, 2000 (H Rept 106-829). House passed, amended, under suspension of the rules, Sept. 18. Senate Energy and Natural Resources discharged. Senate passed Oct. 13. President signed Oct. 27, 2000.

PL 106-367 (HR 3235) Improve academic and social outcomes for youth and reduce both juvenile crime and the risk that youth will become victims of crime by providing productive activities conducted by law enforcement personnel during nonschool hours. Introduced by Barrett, D-Wis., on Nov. 5, 1999. House Judiciary reported, amended, Sept. 18, 2000 (H Rept 106-859). House passed, amended, under suspension of the rules, on Oct. 2. Senate passed Oct. 13. President signed Oct. 27, 2000.

PL 106-368 (HR 3236) Authorize the secretary of the interior to enter into contracts with the Weber Basin Water Conservancy District, Utah, to use Weber Basin Project facilities for the impounding, storage, and carriage of nonproject water for domestic, municipal, industrial, and other purposes. Introduced by Cannon, R-Utah, on Nov. 5, 1999. House Resources reported, amended, July 17, 2000 (H Rept 106-742). House passed, amended, under suspension of the rules, July 25. Senate Energy and Natural Resources reported Sept. 28 (S Rept 106-434). Senate passed Oct. 13. President signed Oct. 27, 2000.

PL 106-369 (HR 3292) Provide for the establishment of the Cat Island National Wildlife Refuge in West Feliciana Parish, La. Introduced by Baker, R-La., on Nov. 10, 1999. House Resources reported, amended, June 8, 2000 (H Rept 106-659). House passed, amended, under suspension of the rules, June 19. Senate Environment and Public Works reported, with amendments, Oct. 2 (S Rept 106-459). Senate passed, with amendments, Oct. 5. House agreed to Senate amendments, under suspension of the rules, Oct. 12. President signed Oct. 27, 2000.

PL 106-370 (HR 3468) Direct the secretary of the interior to convey certain water rights to Duchesne City, Utah. Introduced by Cannon, R-Utah, on Nov. 18, 1999. House Resources reported July 17, 2000 (H Rept 106-737). House passed, amended, under suspension of the rules, July 25. Senate passed Oct. 13. President signed Oct. 27, 2000.

PL 106-371 (HR 3577) Increase the amount authorized to be appropriated for the north side pumping division of the Minidoka reclamation project, Idaho. Introduced by Simpson, R-Idaho, on Feb. 3, 2000. House Resources reported May 2 (H Rept 106-599). House passed, under suspension of the rules, May 8. Senate Energy and Natural Resources reported Sept. 28 (S Rept 106-435). Senate passed Oct. 13. President signed Oct. 27, 2000.

PL 106-372 (HR 3986) Provide for a study of the engineering feasibility of a water exchange in lieu of electrification of the Chandler Pumping Plant at Prosser Diversion Dam, Wash. Introduced by Hastings, R-Wash., on March 15, 2000. House Resources reported, amended, Sept. 19 (H Rept 106-864). Failed passage under suspension of the rules (two-thirds required) Sept. 19. House passed, amended, Sept. 20. Senate Energy and Natural Resources discharged. Senate passed Oct. 13. President signed Oct. 27, 2000.

PL 106-373 (HR 4002) Amend the Foreign Assistance Act of 1961 to revise and improve provisions relating to famine prevention and freedom from hunger. Introduced by Brady, R-Texas, on March 16, 2000. House passed, amended, under suspension of the rules, July 24. Senate Foreign Relations reported, amended, Oct. 2 (no written report). Senate passed, amended, Oct. 4. House agreed to Senate amendment Oct. 12. President signed Oct. 27, 2000.

PL 106-374 (HR 4132) Reauthorize grants for water resources research and technology institutes established under the Water Resources Research Act of 1984. Introduced by Doolittle, R-Calif., on March 30, 2000. House Resources reported July 10 (H Rept 106-714). House passed, under suspension of the rules, July 10. Senate Environment and Public Works discharged. Senate passed Oct. 18. President signed Oct. 27, 2000.

PL 106-375 (HR 4259) Require the secretary of the Treasury to mint coins in commemoration of the National Museum of the American Indian of the Smithsonian Institution. Introduced by Lucas, R-Okla., on April 12, 2000. House passed, under suspension of the rules, Sept. 26. Senate passed Oct. 11. President signed Oct. 27, 2000.

PL 106-376 (HR 4389) Direct the secretary of the interior to convey certain water distribution facilities to the Northern Colorado Water Conservancy District. Introduced by Schaffer, R-Colo., on May 4, 2000. House Resources reported, amended, Sept. 6 (H Rept 106-812). House passed, amended, under suspension of the rules, Oct. 3. Senate passed Oct. 13. President signed Oct. 27, 2000.

PL 106-377 (HR 4635) Make appropriations for the departments of Veterans Affairs and Housing and Urban Development, and for sundry independent agencies, boards, commissions, corporations, and offices for fiscal 2001. Introduced by Walsh, R-N.Y., on June 12, 2000. House Appropriations reported June 12 (H Rept 106-674). House passed, amended, June 21. Senate

Appropriations reported, with amendment, Sept. 13 (S Rept 106-410). Senate passed, with amendment, Oct. 12. Conference report filed in the House Oct. 18 (H Rept 106-988). House agreed to conference report Oct. 19. Senate agreed to conference report Oct. 19. President signed Oct. 27, 2000.

PL 106-378 (HR 4681) Provide for the adjustment of status of certain Syrian nationals. Introduced by Lazio, R-N.Y., on June 15, 2000. House passed, amended, under suspension of the rules, July 11. Senate passed Oct. 13. President signed Oct. 27, 2000.

PL 106-379 (HR 5107) Make certain corrections in copyright law. Introduced by Coble, R-N.C., on Sept. 6, 2000. House Judiciary reported Sept. 18 (H Rept 106-861). House passed, amended, under suspension of the rules, Sept. 19. Senate passed Oct. 12. President signed Oct. 27, 2000.

PL 106-380 (HR 5212) Direct the American Folklife Center at the Library of Congress to establish a program to collect video and audio recordings of personal histories and testimonials of American war veterans. Introduced by Kind, D-Wis., on Sept. 19, 2000. House passed, amended, under suspension of the rules, Oct. 4. Senate passed Oct. 17. President signed Oct. 27, 2000.

PL 106-381 (H J Res 117) Make further continuing appropriations for fiscal 2001. Introduced by Young, R-Fla., on Oct. 24, 2000. House passed Oct. 27. Senate passed Oct. 27. President signed Oct. 27, 2000.

PL 106-382 (S 624) Authorize construction of the Fort Peck Reservation Rural Water System in Montana. Introduced by Burns, R-Mont., on March 16, 1999. Senate Energy and Natural Resources reported, amended, Oct. 20 (S Rept 106-198). Senate passed, amended, Nov. 19. House Resources reported, with amendment, Sept. 7, 2000 (H Rept 106-823) House passed, with amendment, under suspension of the rules, Sept. 12. Senate agreed to House amendment Oct. 13. President signed Oct. 27, 2000.

PL 106-383 (S 2498) Authorize the Smithsonian Institution to plan, design, construct, and equip laboratory, administrative, and support space to house base operations for the Smithsonian Astrophysical Observatory Submillimeter Array on Mauna Kea at Hilo, Hawaii. Introduced by Moynihan, D-N.Y., on May 2, 2000. Senate Rules and Administration discharged. Senate passed June 14. House passed, under suspension of the rules, Oct. 17. President signed Oct. 27, 2000.

PL 106-384 (S 2686) Amend Chapter 36 of Title 39, U.S. Code, to modify rates relating to reduced rate mail matter. Introduced by Cochran, R-Miss., on June 7, 2000. Senate Governmental Affairs reported Oct. 3 (S Rept 106-468). Senate passed Oct. 6. House Government Reform discharged. House passed Oct. 11. President signed Oct. 27, 2000.

PL 106-385 (S 3201) Rename the National Museum of American Art the Smithsonian American Art Museum. Introduced by Frist, R-Tenn., on Oct. 12, 2000. Senate passed Oct. 12. House passed, under suspension of the rules, Oct. 17. President signed Oct. 27, 2000.

PL 106-386 (HR 3244) Combat trafficking of persons, especially into the sex trade, slavery, and slavery-like conditions in the United States and countries around the world through prevention, through prosecution and enforcement against traffickers, and through protection and assistance to victims of trafficking. Introduced by Smith, R-N.J., on Nov. 8, 1999. House International Relations reported, amended, Nov. 22 (H Rept 106-487, Pt. 1). House Judiciary reported, amended, April 13, 2000 (H Rept 106-487, Pt. 2). House Banking and Financial Services discharged. House passed, amended, under suspension of the rules, May 9. Senate passed, with amendment, July 27. Conference report filed in the House Oct. 5 (H Rept 106-939). House agreed to conference report Oct. 6. Senate agreed to conference report Oct. 11. President signed Oct. 28, 2000.

PL 106-387 (HR 4461) Make appropriations for Agriculture, Rural Development, Food and Drug Administration, and related agencies programs for fiscal 2001. Introduced by Skeen, R-N.M., on May 16, 2000. House Appropriations reported May 16 (H Rept 106-619). House passed, amended, July 11. Senate passed, with amendment, July 20. Conference report filed in the House Oct. 6 (H Rept 106-948). House agreed to conference report Oct. 11. Senate agreed to conference report Oct. 18. President signed Oct. 28, 2000.

PL 106-388 (H J Res 118) Make further continuing appropriations for fiscal 2001. Introduced by Young, R-Fla., on Oct. 24, 2000. House passed Oct. 28. Senate passed Oct. 28. President signed Oct. 28, 2000.

PL 106-389 (H J Res 119) Make further continuing appropriations for fiscal 2001. Introduced by Young, R-Fla., on Oct. 24, 2000. House passed Oct. 29. Senate passed Oct. 29. President signed Oct. 29, 2000.

PL 106-390 (HR 707) Amend the Robert T. Stafford Disaster Relief and Emergency Assistance Act to authorize a program for predisaster mitigation, to streamline the administration of disaster relief, and to control the federal costs of disaster assistance. Introduced by Fowler, R-Fla., on Feb. 11, 1999. House Transportation and Infrastructure reported, amended, March 3 (H Rept 106-40). House passed, amended, March 4. Senate Environment and Public Works reported May 16 (no written report). Senate passed, with amendment, July 19, 2000. House agreed to Senate amendment, with amendment, Oct. 3. Senate agreed to House amendment, with amendment, Oct. 5. House agreed to Senate amendment, under suspension of the rules, Oct. 10. President signed Oct. 30, 2000.

PL 106-391 (HR 1654) Authorize appropriations for the National Aeronautics and Space Administration for fiscal years 2000, 2001, and 2002. Introduced by Rohrabacher, R-Calif., on May 3, 1999. House Science reported, amended, May 18 (H Rept 106-145). House passed, amended, May 19. Senate passed, with amendment, Nov. 5. Conference report filed in the House Sept. 12, 2000 (H Rept 106-843). House agreed to conference report Sept. 14. Senate agreed to conference report Oct. 13. President signed Oct. 30, 2000.

PL 106-392 (HR 2348) Authorize the Bureau of Reclamation to provide cost sharing for the endangered fish recovery implementation programs for the Upper Colorado and San Juan River Basins. Introduced by Hansen, R-Utah, on June 24, 1999. House Resources reported, amended, July 25, 2000 (H Rept 106-791). House passed, amended, under suspension of the rules, July 25. Senate passed Oct. 13. President signed Oct. 30, 2000.

PL 106-393 (HR 2389) Restore stability and predictability to the annual payments made to states and counties containing National Forest System lands and public domain lands managed by the Bureau of Land Management for use by the counties for the benefit of public schools and roads. Introduced by Deal, R-Ga., on June 30, 1999. House Agriculture reported, amended, Oct. 18. (H Rept 106-392, Pt. 1). House Resources discharged. House passed, amended, Nov. 3. Senate Energy and Natural Resources discharged. Senate passed, with amendment, Oct. 6, 2000. House agreed to Senate amendment, under suspension of the rules, Oct. 10. President signed Oct. 30, 2000.

PL 106-394 (HR 2842) Amend Chapter 89 of Title 5, U.S. Code, concerning the Federal Employees Health Benefits Program, to enable the federal government to enroll an employee and his or her family in the program when a state court orders the employee to provide health insurance coverage for a child of the employee but the employee fails to provide the coverage. Introduced by Cummings, D-Md., on Sept. 13, 1999. House Government Reform reported, amended, July 24, 2000 (H Rept 106-779). House passed, amended, under suspension of the rules, Sept. 19. Senate Governmental Affairs discharged Sept. 20. Senate passed Oct. 13. President signed Oct. 30, 2000.

PL 106-395 (HR 2883) Amend the Immigration and Nationality Act to confer U.S. citizenship automatically and retroactively on certain foreign-born children adopted by citizens of the United States. Introduced by Smith, R-Texas, on Sept. 21, 1999. House Judiciary reported, amended, Sept. 14, 2000 (H Rept 106-852). House passed, amended, under suspension of the rules, Sept. 19. Senate passed Oct. 12. President signed Oct. 30, 2000.

PL 106-396 (HR 3767) Amend the Immigration and Nationality Act to make improvements to, and permanently authorize, the visa waiver pilot program under section 217. Introduced by Smith, R-Texas on March 1, 2000. House Judiciary reported, amended, April 6 (H Rept 106-564). House passed, amended, under the suspension of the rules, April 11. Senate passed, with amendments, Oct. 3. House agreed to Senate amendments, under suspension of the rules, Oct. 10. President signed Oct. 30, 2000.

PL 106-397 (HR 3995) Establish procedures governing the responsibilities of court-appointed receivers who administer departments, offices, and agencies of the District of Columbia government. Introduced by Norton, D-D.C., on March 15, 2000. House Government Reform reported, amended, June 12 (H Rept 106-663). House passed, amended, under suspension of the rules, June 12. Senate Governmental Affairs reported Oct. 6 (S Rept 106-493). Senate passed Oct. 12. President signed Oct. 30, 2000.

PL 106-398 (HR 4205) Authorize appropriations for fiscal 2001 for military activities of the Department of Defense, for military construction and for defense activities of the Department of Energy, and prescribe military personnel strengths for fiscal 2001. Introduced by Spence, R-S.C., on April 6, 2000. House Armed Services reported, amended, May 12 (H Rept 106-616). House passed, amended, May 18. Senate passed, with amendment, July 13. Conference report filed in the House Oct. 6 (H Rept 106-945). House agreed to conference report Oct. 11. Senate agreed to conference report Oct. 12. President signed Oct. 30, 2000.

PL 106-399 (HR 4828) Designate wilderness areas and a cooperative management and protection area in the vicinity of Steens Mountain in Harney County, Ore. Introduced by Walden, R-Ore., on July 12, 2000. House Resources reported, amended, Oct. 3 (H Rept 106-929, Pt. 1). House Agriculture discharged. House passed, amended, Oct. 4. Senate passed Oct. 12. President signed Oct. 30, 2000.

PL 106-400 (HR 5417) Rename the Stewart B. McKinney Homeless Assistance Act as the "McKinney-Vento Homeless Assistance Act." Introduced by LaFalce, D-N.Y., on Oct. 6, 2000. House Banking and Financial Services discharged. House passed Oct. 11. Senate passed Oct. 13. President signed Oct. 30, 2000.

PL 106-401 (H J Res 120) Make further continuing appropriations for fiscal 2001. Introduced by Young, R-Fla., on Oct. 24, 2000. House passed Oct. 30. Senate passed Oct. 30. President signed Oct. 30, 2000.

PL 106-402 (S 1809) Improve service systems for individuals with developmental disabilities. Introduced by Jeffords, R-Vt., on Oct. 27, 1999. Senate Health, Education, Labor, and Pensions reported, amended, Nov. 4 (no written report). Senate passed, amended, Nov. 8. House Education and the Workforce, House Commerce discharged. House passed Oct. 11, 2000. President signed Oct. 30, 2000.

PL 106-403 (H J Res 121) Make further continuing appropriations for fiscal 2001. Introduced by Young, R-Fla., on Oct. 29, 2000. Senate passed Oct. 31. House passed Oct. 31. President signed Nov. 1, 2000.

PL 106-404 (HR 209) Improve the ability of federal agencies to license federally owned inventions. Introduced by Morella, R-Md., on Jan. 6, 1999. House Science reported, amended, May 6 (H Rept 106-129, Pt. 1). House Judiciary discharged. House passed, amended, under suspension of the rules, May 11. Senate Commerce, Science and Transportation discharged. Senate passed, with amendment, Oct. 5, 2000. House agreed to Senate amendment, under suspension of the rules, Oct. 17. President signed Nov. 1, 2000.

PL 106-405 (HR 2607) Promote the development of the commercial space transportation industry, and authorize appropriations for the Office of the Associate Administrator for Commercial Space Transportation and for the Office of Space Commercialization. Introduced by Rohrabacher, R-Calif., on July 26, 1999. House passed, amended, under suspension of the rules, Oct. 4. Senate Commerce, Science and Transportation discharged. Senate passed, with amendment, Oct. 13, 2000. House agreed to Senate amendment, under suspension of the rules, Oct. 17. President signed Nov. 1, 2000.

PL 106-406 (HR 2961) Amend the Immigration and Nationality Act to authorize a three-year pilot program under which the attorney general may extend the period during which certain nonimmigrant aliens who require medical treatment in the United States and were admitted under the Visa Waiver Pilot Program may remain in the United States. Introduced by Bentsen, D-Texas, on Sept. 28, 1999. House Judiciary reported July 11, 2000 (H Rept 106-721). House passed, amended, under suspension of the rules, July 18. Senate Judiciary discharged. Senate passed Oct. 19. President signed Nov. 1, 2000.

PL 106-407 (HR 3069) Authorize the administrator of General Services to provide for redevelopment of the Southeast Federal Center in the District of Columbia. Introduced by Franks, R-N.J., on Oct. 13, 1999. House Transportation and Infrastructure reported, amended, April 13, 2000 (H Rept 106-591). House passed, amended, under suspension of the rules, May 8. Senate Governmental Affairs reported, with amendments, Oct. 2 (S Rept 106-458). Senate passed, with amendments, Oct. 11. House agreed to Senate amendments, under suspension of the rules, Oct. 17. President signed Nov. 1, 2000.

PL 106-408 (HR 3671) Amend the Pittman-Robertson Wildlife Restoration Act and the Dingell-Johnson Sport Fish Restoration Act to enhance the funds available for grants to states for fish and wildlife conservation projects, to reauthorize and amend the National Fish and Wildlife Foundation Establishment Act, and to commemorate the centennial of the establishment of the first national wildlife refuge in the United States on March 14, 1903. Introduced by Young, R-Alaska, on Feb. 16, 2000. House Resources reported, amended, March 30 (H Rept 106-554). House passed, amended, April 5. Senate Environment and Public Works reported, with amendment, Oct. 10 (S Rept 106-495). Senate passed, with amendments, Oct. 12. House agreed to Senate amendments, under suspension of the rules, Oct. 18. President signed Nov. 1, 2000.

PL 106-409 (HR 4068) Amend the Immigration and Nationality Act to extend for an additional three years the special immigrant religious worker program. Introduced by Pease, R-Ind., on March 23, 2000. House passed, under suspension of the rules, Sept. 19. Senate passed Oct. 19. President signed Nov. 1, 2000.

PL 106-410 (HR 4110) Amend Title 44, U.S. Code, to authorize appropriations for the National Historical Publications and Records Commission for fiscal years 2002 through 2005. Introduced by Horn, R-Calif., on March 29, 2000. House Government Reform reported July 20 (H Rept 106-768). House passed, amended, under suspension of the rules, July 24. Senate Governmental Affairs reported Oct. 3 (S Rept 106-466). Senate passed Oct. 19. President signed Nov. 1, 2000.

PL 106-411 (HR 4320) Assist in the conservation of great apes by supporting and providing financial resources for the conservation programs of countries within the range of great apes and projects of persons with demonstrated expertise in the conservation of great apes. Introduced by Miller, D-Calif., on April 13, 2000. House Resources reported, amended, July 25 (H Rept 106-792). House passed, amended, under suspension of the rules, July 25. Senate Environment and Public Works reported Oct. 3 (S Rept 106-472). Senate passed Oct. 19. President signed Nov. 1, 2000.

PL 106-412 (HR 4835) Authorize the exchange of land between the secretary of the interior and the director of Central Intelligence at the George Washington Memorial Parkway in McLean, Va. Introduced by Moran, D-Va., on July 12, 2000. House Resources reported Sept. 26 (H Rept 106-895, Pt. 1). House passed, under suspension of the rules, Sept. 26. Senate Energy and Natural Resources discharged. Senate passed Oct. 19. President signed Nov. 1, 2000.

PL 106-413 (HR 4850) Increase, effective Dec. 1, 2000, the rates of compensation for veterans with service-connected disabilities and the rates of dependency and indemnity compensation for the survivors of certain disabled veterans. Introduced by Stump, R-Ariz., on July 13, 2000. House Veterans' Affairs reported July 24 (H Rept 106-783). House passed, under suspension of the rules, July 25. Senate Veterans' Affairs discharged. Senate passed, with amendments, Oct. 12. House agreed to Senate amendments, under suspension of the rules, Oct. 17. President signed Nov. 1, 2000.

PL 106-414 (HR 5164) Amend Title 49, U.S. Code, to require reports concerning defects in motor vehicles, tires, or other motor vehicle equipment in foreign countries. Introduced by Upton, R-Mich., on Sept. 13, 2000. House Commerce reported, amended, Oct. 10 (H Rept 106-954). House passed, amended, under suspension of the rules, Oct. 11. Senate passed Oct. 11. President signed Nov. 1, 2000.

PL 106-415 (HR 5234) Amend the Hmong Veterans' Naturalization Act of 2000 to extend the applicability of that Act to certain former spouses of deceased Hmong veterans. Introduced by Radanovich, R-Calif., on Sept. 20, 2000. House passed, under suspension of the rules, Sept. 25. Senate passed Oct. 19. President signed Nov. 1, 2000.

PL 106-416 (H J Res 122) Make further continuing appropriations for fiscal 2001. Introduced by Young, R-Fla, on Oct. 29, 2000. House passed Nov. 1. Senate passed Nov. 1. President signed Nov. 1, 2000.

PL 106-417 (S 406) Amend the Indian Health Care Improvement Act to make permanent the demonstration program that allows for direct billing of Medicare, Medicaid, and other third-party payers, and to expand the eligibility under such program to other tribes and tribal organizations. Introduced by Murkowski, R-Alaska, on Feb. 10, 1999. Senate Indian Affairs reported, amended, Sept. 8 (S Rept 106-152). Senate passed, amended, Sept. 15. House Resources reported Sept. 6, 2000 (S Rept 106-818, Pt. 1). House Ways and Means, House Commerce discharged. House passed, under suspension of the rules, Oct. 17. President signed Nov. 1, 2000.

PL 106-418 (S 1296) Designate portions of the lower Delaware River and associated tributaries as a component of the National Wild and Scenic Rivers

System. Introduced by Lautenberg, D-N.J., on June 28, 1999. Senate Energy and Natural Resources reported, amended, Nov. 2 (S Rept 106-207). Senate passed, amended, Nov. 19. House passed, under suspension of the rules, Oct. 17, 2000. President signed Nov. 1, 2000.

PL 106-419 (S 1402) Amend Title 38, U.S. Code, to increase amounts of education assistance for veterans under the Montgomery GI Joe Bill and to enhance programs providing education benefits for veterans. Introduced by Specter, R-Pa., on July 20, 1999. Senate Veterans' Affairs reported July 20 (S Rept 106-114). Senate passed July 26. House passed, amended, under suspension of the rules, May 23, 2000. Senate agreed to House amendments with amendments Oct. 12. House agreed to Senate amendments, under suspension of the rules, Oct. 17. President signed Nov. 1, 2000.

PL 106-420 (S 1455) Enhance protections against fraud in the offering of financial assistance for college education. Introduced by Abraham, R-Mich., on July 28, 1999. Senate Judiciary reported, amended, Oct. 29 (no written report). Senate passed, amended, Nov. 4. House passed, under suspension of the rules, Sept. 25, 2000. President signed Nov. 1, 2000.

PL 106-421 (S 1705) Direct the secretary of the interior to enter into land exchanges to acquire from the private owner and to convey to the state of Idaho approximately 1,240 acres of land near the City of Rocks National Reserve, Idaho. Introduced by Craig, R-Idaho, on Oct. 7, 1999. Senate Energy and Natural Resources reported April 12, 2000 (S Rept 106-262). Senate passed April 13. House Resources reported July 17 (H Rept 106-749). House passed, under suspension of the rules, Oct. 17. President signed Nov. 1, 2000.

PL 106-422 (S 1707) Amend the Inspector General Act of 1978 (5 U.S.C. App.) to provide that certain designated federal entities shall be establishments under the act. Introduced by Thompson, R-Tenn., on Oct. 7, 1999. Senate Governmental Affairs reported, amended, Nov. 8 (S Rept 106-218). Senate passed, amended, Nov. 19. House passed, under suspension of the rules, Oct. 17, 2000. President signed Nov. 1, 2000.

PL 106-423 (S 2102) Provide to the Timbisha Shoshone Tribe a permanent land base within its aboriginal homeland. Introduced by Inouye, D-Hawaii, on Feb. 24, 2000. Senate Indian Affairs reported, amended, June 30 (S Rept 106-327). Senate passed, amended, July 19. House passed, under suspension of the rules, Oct. 17. President signed Nov. 1, 2000.

PL 106-424 (S 2412) Amend Title 49, U.S. Code, to authorize appropriations for the National Transportation Safety Board for fiscal years 2000, 2001, 2002, and 2003. Introduced by McCain, R-Ariz., on April 12, 2000. Senate Commerce, Science and Transportation reported Aug. 25 (S Rept 106-386). Senate passed, amended, Oct. 3. House passed, under suspension of the rules, Oct. 17. President signed Nov. 1, 2000.

PL 106-425 (S 2917) Settle the land claims of the Pueblo of Santo Domingo. Introduced by Domenici, R-N.M., on July 25, 2000. Senate Indian Affairs discharged. Senate passed Oct. 11. House passed, under suspension of the rules, Oct. 17. Senate Indian Affairs reported Oct. 18 (S Rept 106-506). President signed Nov. 1, 2000.

PL 106-426 (H J Res 123) Make further continuing appropriations for fiscal 2001. Introduced by Young, R-Fla., on Oct. 29, 2000. House passed, amended, Nov. 2. Senate passed Nov. 2. President signed Nov. 3, 2000.

PL 106-427 (H J Res 124) Make further continuing appropriations for fiscal 2001. Introduced by Young, R-Fla., on Oct. 29, 2000. House passed Nov. 3. Senate passed Nov. 3. President signed Nov. 4, 2000.

PL 106-428 (H J Res 84) Make further continuing appropriations for fiscal 2001. Introduced by Young, R-Fla., on Nov. 18, 1999. House passed Nov. 18. Senate passed, with amendments, Nov. 1, 2000. House agreed to Senate amendments Nov. 3. President signed Nov. 4, 2000.

PL 106-429 (HR 4811) Make appropriations for foreign operations, export financing, and related programs for fiscal 2001. Introduced by Callahan, R-Ala., on July 10, 2000. House Appropriations reported July 10 (H Rept 106-720). House passed, amended, July 13. Senate passed, with amendment, July 18. Conference report filed in the House Oct. 24 (H Rept 106-997). House agreed to conference report Oct. 25. Senate agreed to conference report Oct. 25. President signed Nov. 6, 2000.

PL 106-430 (HR 5178) Require changes in the blood-borne pathogens standard in effect under the Occupational Safety and Health Act of 1970.

Introduced by Ballenger, R-N.C., on Sept. 14, 2000. House passed, amended, under suspension of the rules, Oct. 3. Senate passed Oct. 26. President signed Nov. 6, 2000.

PL 106-431 (HR 468) Establish the Saint Helena Island National Scenic Area. Introduced by Kildee, D-Mich., on Feb. 2, 1999. House Resources reported, amended, July 26 (H Rept 106-255). House passed, amended, under suspension of the rules, Sept. 21. Senate Energy and Natural Resources reported, amended, Aug. 25, 2000 (S Rept 106-392). Senate passed, amended, Oct. 5. House failed to agree to Senate amendment, under suspension of the rules, Oct. 12. House agreed to Senate amendment Oct. 24. President signed Nov. 6, 2000.

PL 106-432 (HR 1725) Provide for the conveyance by the Bureau of Land Management to Douglas County, Ore., of a county park and certain adjacent land. Introduced by DeFazio, D-Ore., on May 6, 1999. House Resources reported Nov. 4 (H Rept 106-446). House passed, under suspension of the rules, March 21, 2000. Senate passed, amended, Oct. 5. House agreed to Senate amendments, under suspension of the rules, Oct. 23. President signed Nov. 6, 2000.

PL 106-433 (HR 3218) Amend Title 31, U.S. Code, to prohibit the appearance of Social Security account numbers on or through unopened mailings of checks or other drafts issued on public money in the Treasury. Introduced by Calvert, R-Calif., on Nov. 4, 1999. House passed, under suspension of the rules, Oct. 18, 2000. Senate passed Oct. 25. President signed Nov. 6, 2000.

PL 106-434 (HR 3657) Provide for the conveyance of a small parcel of public domain land in the San Bernardino National Forest in California. Introduced by Bono, R-Calif., on Feb. 15, 2000. House Resources reported, amended, July 17 (H Rept 106-744). House passed, amended, under suspension of the rules, Sept. 12. Senate Energy and Natural Resources discharged. Senate passed, amended, Oct. 19. House agreed to Senate amendment, under suspension of the rules, Oct. 23. President signed Nov. 6, 2000.

PL 106-435 (HR 3679) Provide for the minting of commemorative coins to support the 2002 Salt Lake Olympic Winter Games and the programs of the U.S. Olympic Committee. Introduced by Cook, R-Utah, on Feb. 16, 2000. House passed, amended, under suspension of the rules, Sept. 19. Senate passed Oct. 23. President signed Nov. 6, 2000.

PL 106-436 (HR 4315) Designate the facility of the U.S. Postal Service at 3695 Green Rd. in Beachwood, Ohio, as the "Larry Small Post Office Building." Introduced by LaTourette, R-Ohio, on April 13, 2000. House passed, under suspension of the rules, Oct. 2. Senate passed Oct. 24. President signed Nov. 6, 2000.

PL 106-437 (HR 4404) Permit the payment of medical expenses incurred by the U.S. Park Police in the performance of duty to be made directly by the National Park Service and allow for waiver and indemnification in mutual law enforcement agreements between the National Park Service and a state or political subdivision when required by state law. Introduced by Hansen, R-Utah, on May 9, 2000. House Resources reported, amended, Sept. 14 (H Rept 106-854, Pt. 1). House Government Reform discharged. House passed, amended, under suspension of the rules, Oct. 17. Senate passed Oct. 26. President signed Nov. 6, 2000.

PL 106-438 (HR 4450) Designate the facility of the U.S. Postal Service at 900 E. Fayette St. in Baltimore, Md., as the "Judge Harry Augustus Cole Post Office Building." Introduced by Cummings, D-Md., on May 15, 2000. House passed, under suspension of the rules, Sept. 19. Senate Governmental Affairs discharged. Senate passed Oct. 24. President signed Nov. 6, 2000.

PL 106-439 (HR 4451) Designate the facility of the U.S. Postal Service at 1001 Frederick Rd. in Baltimore, Md., as the "Frederick L. Dewberry Jr. Post Office Building." Introduced by Cummings, D-Md., on May 15, 2000. House passed, under suspension of the rules, on Sept. 25. Senate Governmental Affairs discharged. Senate passed Oct. 24. President signed Nov. 6, 2000.

PL 106-440 (HR 4625) Designate the facility of the U.S. Postal Service at 2108 E. 38th St. in Erie, Pa., as the "Gertrude A. Barber Post Office Building." Introduced by English, R-Pa., on June 9, 2000. House passed, under suspension of the rules, Sept. 19. Senate Governmental Affairs discharged. Senate passed Oct. 24. President signed Nov. 6, 2000.

PL 106-441 (HR 4786) Designate the facility of the U.S. Postal Service at 110 Postal Way in Carrollton, Ga., as the "Samuel P. Roberts Post Office Building." Introduced by Barr, R-Ga., on June 29, 2000. House passed, under suspension of the rules, Sept. 19. Senate Governmental Affairs discharged. Senate passed Oct. 24. President signed Nov. 6, 2000.

PL 106-442 (HR 4957) Amend the Omnibus Parks and Public Lands Management Act of 1996 to extend the legislative authority for the Black Patriots Foundation to establish a commemorative work. Introduced by Rangel, D-N.Y., on July 25, 2000. House passed, under suspension of the rules, Sept. 12. Senate passed Oct. 26. President signed Nov. 6, 2000.

PL 106-443 (HR 5083) Extend the authority of the Los Angeles Unified School District to use certain park lands in the city of South Gate, Calif., which were acquired with amounts provided from the land and water conservation fund, for elementary school purposes. Introduced by Roybal-Allard, D-Calif., on July 27, 2000. House passed, under suspension of the rules, Oct. 12. Senate passed Oct. 26. President signed Nov. 6, 2000.

PL 106-444 (HR 5157) Amend Title 44, U.S. Code, to ensure preservation of the records of the Freedmen's Bureau. Introduced by Millender-McDonald, D-Calif., on Sept. 12, 2000. House Government Reform discharged. House passed, amended, Oct. 19. Senate passed Oct. 26. President signed Nov. 6, 2000.

PL 106-445 (HR 5273) Clarify the intention of the Congress with regard to the authority of the U.S. Mint to produce numismatic coins. Introduced by Bachus, R-Ala., on Sept. 25, 2000. House passed, under suspension of the rules, Sept. 26. Senate Banking, Housing, and Urban Affairs discharged. Senate passed Oct. 24. President signed Nov. 6, 2000.

PL 106-446 (HR 5314) Require the immediate termination of the Department of Defense practice of euthanizing military working dogs at the end of their useful working life, and facilitate the adoption of retired military working dogs by law enforcement agencies, former handlers of these dogs, and other persons capable of caring for them. Introduced by Bartlett, R-Md., on Sept. 27, 2000. House passed, amended, under suspension of the rules, Oct. 10. Senate passed, with amendment, Oct. 24. House agreed to Senate amendment, under suspension of the rules, Oct. 26. President signed Nov. 6, 2000.

PL 106-447 (S 614) Provide for regulatory reform in order to encourage investment, business, and economic development with respect to activities conducted on Native American lands. Introduced by Campbell, R-Colo., on March 15, 1999. Senate Indian Affairs reported, amended, Sept. 8 (S Rept 106-151). Senate passed, amended, Sept. 15. House passed, under suspension of the rules, Oct. 23, 2000. President signed Nov. 6, 2000.

PL 106-448 (S 2812) Amend the Immigration and Nationality Act to provide a waiver of the oath of renunciation and allegiance for naturalization of aliens having certain disabilities. Introduced by Hatch, R-Utah, on June 29, 2000. Senate Judiciary reported July 20 (no written report). Senate passed July 21. House Judiciary discharged. House passed, with amendment, Oct. 10. Senate agreed to House amendment Oct. 19. President signed Nov. 6, 2000.

PL 106-449 (S 3062) Modify the date on which the mayor of the District of Columbia submits a performance accountability plan to Congress. Introduced by Voinovich, R-Ohio, on Sept. 18, 2000. Senate Governmental Affairs reported Oct. 3 (S Rept 106-469). Senate passed Oct. 6. House Government Reform discharged. House passed Oct. 19. President signed Nov. 6, 2000.

PL 106-450 (HR 1651) Amend the Fishermen's Protective Act of 1967 to extend the period during which reimbursement may be provided to owners of U.S. fishing vessels for costs incurred when the vessel is seized and detained by a foreign country. Introduced by Young, R-Alaska, on April 29, 1999. House Resources reported June 23 (H Rept 106-197). House passed, amended, under suspension of the rules, Sept. 13. Senate Commerce, Science and Transportation reported, with amendment, May 23, 2000 (S Rept 106-302). Senate passed, with amendment, June 26. House failed to agree to Senate amendment, under suspension of the rules, July 25. House agreed to Senate amendment, with an amendment, Sept. 18. Senate agreed to House amendment Oct. 25. President signed Nov. 7, 2000.

PL 106-451 (HR 2442) Provide for the preparation of a government report detailing injustices suffered by Italian Americans during World War II and a formal acknowledgment of such injustices by the president. Introduced by Lazio, R-N.Y., on July 1, 1999. House passed, under suspension of the rules, Nov. 10. Senate Judiciary reported, amended, Sept. 28, 2000 (no written report). Senate passed, with amendments, Oct. 19. House agreed to Senate

amendments, under suspension of the rules, Oct. 24. President signed Nov. 7, 2000.

PL 106-452 (HR 4831) Redesignate the facility of the U.S. Postal Service at 2339 N. California St. in Chicago, Ill., as the "Roberto Clemente Post Office." Introduced by Gutierrez, D-Ill., on July 12, 2000. House passed, amended, under suspension of the rules, Oct. 10. Senate passed Oct. 24. President signed Nov. 7, 2000.

PL 106-453 (HR 4853) Redesignate the facility of the U.S. Postal Service at 1568 S. Glen Rd. in South Euclid, Ohio, as the "Arnold C. D'Amico Station." Introduced by Jones, D-Ohio, on July 13, 2000. House Government Reform discharged. House passed, amended, Oct. 12. Senate passed Oct. 24. President signed Nov. 7, 2000.

PL 106-454 (HR 5229) Designate the facility of the U.S. Postal Service at 219 S. Church St. in Odum, Ga., as the "Ruth Harris Coleman Post Office." Introduced by Kingston, R-Ga., on Sept. 20, 2000. House passed, under suspension of the rules, Oct. 10. Senate passed Oct. 24. President signed Nov. 7, 2000.

PL 106-455 (S 501) Address resource management issues in Glacier Bay National Park, Alaska. Introduced by Murkowski, R-Alaska, on March 2, 1999. Senate Energy and Natural Resources reported, amended, July 29 (S Rept 106-128). Senate passed, amended, Nov. 19. House passed, under suspension of the rules, Oct. 23, 2000. President signed Nov. 7, 2000.

PL 106-456 (S 503) Designate certain land in the San Isabel National Forest in Colorado as the "Spanish Peaks Wilderness." Introduced by Allard, R-Colo., on March 2, 1999. Senate Energy and Natural Resources reported, amended, March 9, 2000 (S Rept 106-233). Senate passed, amended, April 13. House passed, under suspension of the rules, Oct. 23. President signed Nov. 7, 2000.

PL 106-457 (S 835) Encourage the restoration of estuary habitat through more efficient project financing and enhanced coordination of federal and nonfederal restoration programs. Introduced by Chafee, R-R.I., on April 20, 1999. Senate Environment and Public Works reported, amended, Oct. 14 (S Rept 106-189). Senate passed, amended, March 30, 2000. House passed, with amendment, under suspension of the rules, Sept. 12. Senate agreed to conference report Oct. 23. Conference report filed in the House on Oct. 24 (H Rept 106-995). House agreed to conference report Oct. 25. President signed Nov. 7, 2000.

PL 106-458 (S 1088) Authorize the secretary of agriculture to convey certain administrative sites in national forests in Arizona and to convey certain land to the City of Sedona, Ariz., for a wastewater treatment facility. Introduced by Kyl, R-Ariz., on May 20, 1999. Senate Energy and Natural Resources reported July 21 (S Rept 106-115). Senate passed, amended, Nov. 19. House passed, under suspension of the rules, Oct. 23, 2000. President signed Nov. 7, 2000.

PL 106-459 (S 1211) Amend the Colorado River Basin Salinity Control Act to authorize additional measures to carry out the control of salinity upstream of Imperial Dam in a cost-effective manner. Introduced by Bennett, R-Utah, on June 10, 1999. Senate Energy and Natural Resources reported, amended, Oct. 6 (S Rept 106-175). Senate passed, amended, Nov. 19. House Resources reported Sept. 6, 2000 (H Rept 106-814). House passed, under suspension of the rules, Oct. 23. President signed Nov. 7, 2000.

PL 106-460 (S 1218) Direct the secretary of the interior to issue to the Landusky School District, without consideration, a patent for the surface and mineral estates of certain lots. Introduced by Burns, R-Mont., on June 14, 1999. Senate Energy and Natural Resources reported, amended, March 20, 2000 (S Rept 106-245). Senate passed, amended, April 13. House passed, under suspension of the rules, Oct. 23. President signed Nov. 7, 2000.

PL 106-461 (S 1275) Authorize the secretary of the interior to produce and sell products and to sell publications relating to the Hoover Dam and to deposit revenues generated from the sales into the Colorado River Dam fund. Introduced by Kyl, R-Ariz., on June 24, 1999. Senate Energy and Natural Resources reported Oct. 18 (S Rept 106-195). Senate passed Nov. 19. House Resources reported Sept. 6, 2000 (H Rept 106-808). House passed, under suspension of the rules, Oct. 23. President signed Nov. 7, 2000.

PL 106-462 (S 1586) Reduce the fractionated ownership of Native American lands. Introduced by Campbell, R-Colo., on Sept. 15, 1999. Senate Indian

Affairs reported, amended, July 26, 2000 (S Rept 106-361). Senate passed, amended, July 26. House passed, under suspension of the rules, Oct. 23. President signed Nov. 7, 2000.

PL 106-463 (S 2300) Amend the Mineral Leasing Act to increase the maximum acreage of federal leases for coal that may be held by an entity in any one state. Introduced by Thomas, R-Wyo., on March 28, 2000. Senate Energy and Natural Resources reported Aug. 25 (S Rept 106-378). Senate passed Oct. 5. House passed, under suspension of the rules, Oct. 23. President signed Nov. 7, 2000.

PL 106-464 (S 2719) Provide for business development and trade promotion for Native Americans. Introduced by Campbell, R-Colo., on June 13, 2000. Senate Indian Affairs reported June 26 (no written report). Senate passed June 28. House passed, under suspension of the rules, Oct. 23. President signed Nov. 7, 2000.

PL 106-465 (S 2950) Authorize the secretary of the interior to establish the Sand Creek Massacre Historic Site in Colorado. Introduced by Campbell, R-Colo., on July 27, 2000. Senate Energy and Natural Resources reported, amended, Sept. 25 (S Rept 106-418). Senate passed, amended, Oct. 5. House passed, under suspension of the rules, Oct. 23. President signed Nov. 7, 2000.

PL 106-466 (S 3022) Direct the secretary of the interior to convey certain irrigation facilities to the Nampa and Meridian Irrigation District. Introduced by Craig, R-Idaho, on Sept. 8, 2000. Senate Energy and Natural Resources reported, amended, Oct. 3 (S Rept 106-480). Senate passed, amended, Oct. 13. House passed, under suspension of the rules, Oct. 23. President signed Nov. 7, 2000.

PL 106-467 (HR 1235) Authorize the secretary of the interior to enter into contracts with the Solano County Water Agency, Calif., to use Solano Project facilities for impounding, storage, and carriage of nonproject water for domestic, municipal, and industrial purposes. Introduced by Miller, D-Calif., on March 23, 1999. House Resources reported Nov. 1 (H Rept 106-426). House passed, under suspension of the rules, Nov. 1. Senate Energy and Natural Resources reported Sept. 28, 2000 (S Rept 106-433). Senate passed Oct. 27. President signed Nov. 9, 2000.

PL 106-468 (HR 2780) Authorize the attorney general to provide grants for organizations to find missing adults. Introduced by Myrick, R-N.C., on Aug. 5, 1999. House passed, under suspension of the rules, Oct. 19, 2000. Senate passed Oct. 26. President signed Nov. 9, 2000.

PL 106-469 (HR 2884) Extend energy conservation programs under the Energy Policy and Conservation Act through fiscal 2003. Introduced by Bliley, R-Va., on Sept. 21, 1999. House Commerce reported, amended, Oct. 1 (H Rept 106-359). House passed, amended, under suspension of the rules, April 12, 2000. Senate passed, with amendment, Oct. 19. House agreed to Senate amendment, under suspension of the rules, Oct. 24. President signed Nov. 9, 2000.

PL 106-470 (HR 4312) Direct the secretary of the interior to conduct a study of the suitability and feasibility of establishing an Upper Housatonic Valley National Heritage Area in Connecticut and Massachusetts. Introduced by Johnson, R-Conn., on April 13, 2000. House passed, under suspension of the rules, Oct. 17. Senate passed Oct. 27. President signed Nov. 9, 2000.

PL 106-471 (HR 4646) Designate certain National Forest System lands within the boundaries of Virginia as wilderness areas. Introduced by Goode, I-Va., on June 13, 2000. House passed, amended, under suspension of the rules, Oct. 17. Senate passed Oct. 27. President signed Nov. 9, 2000.

PL 106-472 (HR 4788) Amend the United States Grain Standards Act to extend the authority of the secretary of agriculture to collect fees to cover the cost of services performed under the act, to extend the authorization of appropriations for the act, and to improve the administration of the act. Introduced by Barrett, R-Neb., on June 29, 2000. House passed, amended, under suspension of the rules, Oct. 10. Senate passed, with amendment, Oct. 12. House agreed to Senate amendment, with an amendment, Oct. 17. Senate agreed to House amendment Oct. 24. President signed Nov. 9, 2000.

PL 106-473 (HR 4794) Require the secretary of the interior to complete a resource study of the 600-mile route through Connecticut, Delaware, Maryland, Massachusetts, New Jersey, New York, Pennsylvania, Rhode Island, and Virginia used by George Washington and Gen. Rochambeau during the American Revolutionary War. Introduced by Larson, D-Conn., on June 29, 2000.

House passed, under suspension of the rules, Oct. 23. Senate passed Oct. 27. President signed Nov. 9, 2000.

PL 106-474 (HR 4846) Establish the National Recording Registry in the Library of Congress to maintain and preserve sound recordings and recording collections that are culturally, historically, or aesthetically significant. Introduced by Thomas, R-Calif., on July 13, 2000. House passed, amended, under suspension of the rules, July 25. Senate passed, with amendments, Oct. 25. House disagreed to Senate amendments Nov. 1. Senate receded from its amendments Nov. 1. President signed Nov. 9, 2000.

PL 106-475 (HR 4864) Amend Title 38, U.S. Code, to reaffirm and clarify the duty of the secretary of veterans affairs to assist claimants for benefits under laws administered by the secretary. Introduced by Stump, R-Ariz., on July 17, 2000. House Veterans' Affairs reported, amended, July 24 (H Rept 106-781). House passed, amended, under suspension of the rules, July 25. Senate Veterans' Affairs discharged. Senate passed, with amendment, Sept. 25. House agreed to Senate amendment, under suspension of the rules, Oct. 17. President signed Nov. 9, 2000.

PL 106-476 (HR 4868) Amend the Harmonized Tariff Schedule of the United States to modify temporarily certain rates of duty and make other technical amendments to the trade laws. Introduced by Crane, R-Ill., on July 18, 2000. House Ways and Means reported, amended, July 25 (H Rept 106-789). House passed, amended, under suspension of the rules, July 25. Senate Finance reported, with amendment, Oct. 12 (S Rept 106-503). Senate passed, with amendment, Oct. 13. House agreed to Senate amendment, with amendment, Oct. 24. Senate agreed to House amendment Oct. 26. President signed Nov. 9, 2000.

PL 106-477 (HR 5110) Designate the U.S. courthouse at 3470 12th St. in Riverside, Calif., as the "George E. Brown Jr. United States Courthouse." Introduced by Calvert, R-Calif., on Sept. 6, 2000. House passed, under suspension of the rules, Oct. 17. Senate passed Nov. 1. President signed Nov. 9, 2000.

PL 106-478 (HR 5302) Designate the U.S. courthouse at 1010 Fifth Ave. in Seattle, Wash., as the "William Kenzo Nakamura United States Courthouse." Introduced by McDermott, D-Wash., on Sept. 26, 2000. House passed, under suspension of the rules, Oct. 17. Senate passed Nov. 1. President signed Nov. 9, 2000.

PL 106-479 (HR 5331) Authorize the Frederick Douglass Gardens, Inc., to establish a memorial and gardens on Department of the Interior lands in the District of Columbia or its environs in honor and commemoration of Frederick Douglass. Introduced by Davis, D-Ill., on Sept. 28, 2000. House passed, under suspension of the rules, Oct. 3. Senate passed Oct. 26. President signed Nov. 9, 2000.

PL 106-480 (HR 5388) Designate a building proposed to be located within the boundaries of the Chincoteague National Wildlife Refuge in Virginia, as the "Herbert H. Bateman Educational and Administrative Center." Introduced by Young, R-Alaska, on Oct. 4, 2000. House Resources discharged. House passed Oct. 24. Senate passed Nov. 1. President signed Nov. 9, 2000.

PL 106-481 (HR 5410) Establish revolving funds for the operation of certain programs and activities of the Library of Congress. Introduced by Thomas, R-Calif., on Oct. 6, 2000. House passed, amended, under suspension of the rules, Oct. 17. Senate passed Oct. 31. President signed Nov. 9, 2000.

PL 106-482 (HR 5478) Authorize the secretary of the interior to acquire by donation suitable land to serve as the new location for the home of Alexander Hamilton, commonly known as the Hamilton Grange, and to authorize the relocation of the Hamilton Grange to the acquired land. Introduced by Rangel, D-N.Y., on Oct. 17, 2000. House passed, under suspension of the rules, Oct. 24. Senate passed Oct. 27. President signed Nov. 9, 2000.

PL 106-483 (H J Res 102) Recognize that the Birmingham Pledge has made a significant contribution in fostering racial harmony and reconciliation in the United States and around the world. Introduced by Bachus, R-Ala., on June 14, 2000. House passed, under suspension of the rules, Sept. 12. Senate Judiciary discharged. Senate passed, with amendments, Oct. 26. House agreed to Senate amendments, under suspension of the rules, Oct. 30. President signed Nov. 9, 2000.

PL 106-484 (S 484) Provide for the granting of refugee status in the United States to nationals of certain foreign countries in which American Vietnam

War POW/MIAs or American Korean War POW/MIAs may be present, if those nationals assist in the return to the United States of those POW/MIAs alive. Introduced by Campbell, R-Colo., on Feb. 25, 1999. Senate Judiciary reported May 18, 2000 (no written report). Senate passed, amended, May 24. House International Relations, House Judiciary discharged. House passed Oct. 24. President signed Nov. 9, 2000.

PL 106-485 (S 610) Direct the secretary of the interior to convey certain land under the jurisdiction of the Bureau of Land Management in Washakie County and Big Horn County, Wyo., to the Westside Irrigation District, Wyo. Introduced by Enzi, R-Wyo., on March 15, 1999. Senate Energy and Natural Resources reported, amended, June 27, 2000 (S Rept 106-313). Senate passed, amended, July 27. House passed, under suspension of the rules, Oct. 23. President signed Nov. 9, 2000.

PL 106-486 (S 698) Review the suitability and feasibility of recovering costs of high altitude rescues at Denali National Park and Preserve in Alaska. Introduced by Murkowski, R-Alaska, on March 24, 1999. Senate Energy and Natural Resources reported June 9 (S Rept 106-71). Senate passed Nov. 19. House passed, under suspension of the rules, Oct. 24, 2000. President signed Nov. 9, 2000.

PL 106-487 (S 710) Authorize a feasibility study on the preservation of certain Civil War battlefields along the Vicksburg Campaign Trail. Introduced by Lott, R-Miss., on March 24, 1999. Senate Energy and Natural Resources reported, amended, Oct. 14 (S Rept 106-184). Senate passed, amended, Nov. 19. House passed, under suspension of the rules, Oct. 23, 2000. President signed Nov. 9, 2000.

PL 106-488 (S 748) Improve Native American hiring and contracting by the federal government in Alaska. Introduced by Murkowski, R-Alaska, on March 25, 1999. Senate Energy and Natural Resources reported, amended, June 9, 1999 (S Rept 106-72). Senate passed, amended, Nov. 19. House passed, under suspension of the rules, Oct. 23, 2000. President signed Nov. 9, 2000.

PL 106-489 (S 893) Amend Title 46, U.S. Code, to provide equitable treatment with respect to state and local income taxes for certain individuals who perform duties on vessels. Introduced by Gorton, R-Wash., on April 27, 1999. Senate Commerce, Science and Transportation reported Sept. 26, 2000 (S Rept 106-421). Senate passed Sept. 28. House passed, under suspension of the rules, Oct. 24. President signed Nov. 9, 2000.

PL 106-490 (S 1030) Provide that the conveyance by the Bureau of Land Management of the surface estate to certain land in Wyoming in exchange for certain private land will not result in the removal of the land from operation of the mining laws. Introduced by Enzi, R-Wyo., on May 13, 1999. Senate Energy and Natural Resources reported, amended, Oct. 6 (S Rept 106-174). Senate passed, amended, Nov. 19. House Resources reported Sept. 26, 2000 (H Rept 106-898). House passed, under suspension of the rules, Oct. 23. President signed Nov. 9, 2000.

PL 106-491 (S 1367) Amend the act that established the Saint-Gaudens Historic Site in New Hampshire, by modifying the boundary. Introduced by Murkowski, R-Alaska, on July 14, 1999. Senate Energy and Natural Resources reported, amended, June 27, 2000 (S Rept 106-314). Senate passed, amended, Oct. 5. House passed, under suspension of the rules, Oct. 23. President signed Nov. 9, 2000.

PL 106-492 (S 1438) Establish the National Law Enforcement Museum on federal land in the District of Columbia. Introduced by Campbell, R-Colo., on July 27, 1999. Senate Energy and Natural Resources reported, amended, July 10, 2000 (S Rept 106-330). Senate passed, amended, Sept. 28. House passed, under suspension of the rules, Oct. 24. President signed Nov. 9, 2000.

PL 106-493 (S 1778) Provide for equal exchanges of land around the Cascade Reservoir. Introduced by Craig, R-Idaho, on Oct. 25, 1999. Senate Energy and Natural Resources reported, amended, April 13, 2000 (S Rept 106-271). Senate passed, amended, April 13. House Resources reported Sept. 20 (H Rept 106-871). House passed, under suspension of the rules, Oct. 23. President signed Nov. 9, 2000.

PL 106-494 (S 1894) Provide for the conveyance of certain land to Park County, Wyo. Introduced by Thomas, R-Wyo., on Nov. 9, 1999. Senate Energy and Natural Resources reported, amended, June 27, 2000 (S Rept 106-315). Senate passed, amended, July 27. House passed, under suspension of the rules, Oct. 23. President signed Nov. 9, 2000.

PL 106-495 (S 2069) Permit the conveyance of certain land in Powell, Wyo. Introduced by Enzi, R-Wyo., on Feb. 10, 2000. Senate Energy and Natural Resources reported Sept. 7 (S Rept 106-402). Senate passed Oct. 5. House passed, under suspension of the rules, Oct. 23. President signed Nov. 9, 2000.

PL 106-496 (S 2425) Authorize the Bureau of Reclamation to participate in the planning, design, and construction of the Bend Feed Canal Pipeline Project in Oregon. Introduced by Smith, R-Ore., on April 13, 2000. Senate Energy and Natural Resources reported, amended, July 24 (S Rept 106-359). Senate passed, amended, Oct. 13. House passed, under suspension of the rules, Oct. 23. President signed Nov. 9, 2000.

PL 106-497 (S 2872) Improve the cause of action for misrepresentation of Native American arts and crafts. Introduced by Campbell, R-Colo., on July 14, 2000. Senate Indian Affairs reported Oct. 2 (S Rept 106-452). Senate passed Oct. 5. House passed, under suspension of the rules, Oct. 23. President signed Nov. 9, 2000.

PL 106-498 (S 2882) Authorize the Bureau of Reclamation to conduct certain feasibility studies to augment water supplies for the Klamath Project in Oregon and California. Introduced by Smith, R-Ore., on July 17, 2000. Senate Energy and Natural Resources reported, amended, Oct. 4 (S Rept 106-489). Senate passed, amended, Oct. 13. House passed, under suspension of the rules, Oct. 23. President signed Nov. 9, 2000.

PL 106-499 (S 2951) Authorize the secretary of the interior to conduct a study to investigate opportunities to better manage the water resources in the Salmon Creek watershed of the upper Columbia River. Introduced by Gorton, R-Wash., on July 27, 2000. Senate Energy and Natural Resources reported, amended, Sept. 28 (S Rept 106-431). Senate passed, amended, Oct. 13. House passed, under suspension of the rules, Oct. 23. President signed Nov. 9, 2000.

PL 106-500 (S 2977) Assist in the establishment of an interpretive center and museum in the vicinity of the Diamond Valley Lake in southern California to ensure the protection and interpretation of the paleontology discoveries made at the lake and develop a trail system for the lake for use by pedestrians and nonmotorized vehicles. Introduced by Feinstein, D-Calif., on July 27, 2000. Senate Energy and Natural Resources reported Oct. 2 (S Rept 106-455). Senate passed Oct. 5. House passed, under suspension of the rules, Oct. 23. President signed Nov. 9, 2000.

PL 106-501 (HR 782) Amend the Older Americans Act of 1965 to authorize appropriations for fiscal years 2000 through 2003. Introduced by Barrett, R-Neb., on Feb. 23, 1999. House Education and the Workforce reported, amended, Sept. 28 (H Rept 106-343). House passed, amended, under suspension of the rules, Oct. 25, 2000. Senate passed Oct. 26. President signed Nov. 13, 2000.

PL 106-502 (HR 1444) Authorize the secretary of the interior to establish a program to plan, design, and construct facilities to mitigate adverse impacts associated with irrigation system water diversions by local governmental entities in Oregon, Washington, Montana, and Idaho. Introduced by DeFazio, D-Ore., on April 15, 1999. House Resources reported, amended, Nov. 5 (H Rept 106-454, Pt. 1). House passed, amended, under suspension of the rules, Nov. 9. Senate Energy and Natural Resources reported, with amendments, March 9, 2000 (S Rept 106-239). Senate passed, with amendments, April 13. House agreed to Senate amendments with amendments Oct. 17. Senate agreed to House amendments Oct. 27. President signed Nov. 13, 2000.

PL 106-503 (HR 1550) Authorize appropriations for the United States Fire Administration for fiscal years 2000 and 2001. Introduced by Smith, R-Mich., on April 26, 1999. House Science reported, amended, May 10 (H Rept 106-133). House passed, amended, under suspension of the rules, May 11. Senate Commerce, Science and Transportation discharged. Senate passed, with amendment, Oct. 18, 2000. House agreed to Senate amendment with amendments Oct. 27. Senate agreed to House amendments Oct. 31. President signed Nov. 13, 2000.

PL 106-504 (HR 2462) Amend the Organic Act of Guam. Introduced by Underwood, D-Guam, on July 1, 1999. House Resources reported, amended, July 25, 2000 (H Rept 106-787). House passed, amended, under suspension of the rules, July 25. Senate Energy and Natural Resources discharged. Senate passed, with amendment, Oct. 24. House agreed to Senate amendment, under suspension of the rules, Oct. 31. President signed Nov. 13, 2000.

PL 106-505 (HR 2498) Amend the Public Health Service Act to provide for recommendations of the secretary of health and human services regarding the placement of automatic external defibrillators in federal buildings to improve survival rates of individuals who experience cardiac arrest, and to establish protections from civil liability arising from the emergency use of the devices. Introduced by Stearns, R-Fla., on July 13, 1999. House Commerce reported, amended, May 23, 2000 (H Rept 106-634). House passed, amended, under suspension of the rules, May 23. Senate passed, with amendment, Oct. 26. House agreed to Senate amendment, under suspension of the rules, Oct. 27. President signed Nov. 13, 2000.

PL 106-506 (HR 3388) Promote environmental restoration around the Lake Tahoe basin. Introduced by Doolittle, R-Calif., on Nov. 16, 1999. House Resources reported, amended, Sept. 7, 2000 (H Rept 106-833, Pt. 1). House Agriculture, House Transportation and Infrastructure discharged. House passed, amended, under suspension of the rules, Oct. 23. Senate passed Oct. 27. President signed Nov. 13, 2000.

PL 106-507 (HR 3621) Provide for the posthumous promotion of William Clark of the Commonwealth of Virginia and the Commonwealth of Kentucky, co-leader of the Lewis and Clark Expedition, to the grade of captain in the Regular Army. Introduced by Bereuter, R-Neb., on Feb. 10, 2000. House passed, under suspension of the rules, Oct. 10. Senate passed Oct. 27. President signed Nov. 13, 2000.

PL 106-508 (HR 5239) Provide for increased penalties for violations of the Export Administration Act of 1979. Introduced by Gilman, R-N.Y., on Sept. 21, 2000. House passed, amended, under suspension of the rules, Sept. 25. Senate Banking, Housing, and Urban Affairs discharged. Senate passed, with amendment, Oct. 11. House agreed to Senate amendment, under suspension of the rules, Oct. 30. President signed Nov. 13, 2000.

PL 106-509 (S 700) Amend the National Trails System Act to designate the Ala Kahakai Trail as a National Historic Trail. Introduced by Akaka, D-Hawaii, on March 24, 1999. Senate Energy and Natural Resources reported, amended, June 7 (S Rept 106-65). Senate passed, amended, July 1. House passed, under suspension of the rules, Oct. 24, 2000. President signed Nov. 13, 2000.

PL 106-510 (S 938) Eliminate restrictions on the acquisition of certain land contiguous to Hawaii Volcanoes National Park. Introduced by Akaka, D-Hawaii, on May 3, 1999. Senate Energy and Natural Resources reported June 24 (S Rept 106-92). Senate passed, amended, Oct. 14. House passed, under suspension of the rules, Oct. 24, 2000. President signed Nov. 13, 2000.

PL 106-511 (S 964) Provide for equitable compensation for the Cheyenne River Sioux Tribe. Introduced by Daschle, D-S.D., on May 5, 1999. Senate Indian Affairs reported, amended, Nov. 8 (S Rept 106-217). Senate passed, amended, Nov. 19. House Resources reported Oct. 6, 2000 (H Rept 106-944). House passed, with amendment, under suspension of the rules, Oct. 18. Senate agreed to House amendment Oct. 24. President signed Nov. 13, 2000.

PL 106-512 (S 1474) Provide conveyance of the Palmetto Bend project to the state of Texas. Introduced by Hutchison, R-Texas, on Aug. 2, 1999. Senate Energy and Natural Resources reported, amended, July 24, 2000 (S Rept 106-358). Senate passed, amended, Oct. 13. House passed, under suspension of the rules, Oct. 24. President signed Nov. 13, 2000.

PL 106-513 (S 1482) Amend the National Marine Sanctuaries Act. Introduced by Snowe, R-Maine, on Aug. 4, 1999. Senate Commerce, Science and Transportation reported, amended, July 21, 2000 (S Rept 106-353). Senate passed, amended, Oct. 17. House passed, under suspension of the rules, Oct. 24. President signed Nov. 13, 2000.

PL 106-514 (S 1752) Reauthorize and amend the Coastal Barrier Resources Act. Introduced by Chafee, R-R.I., on Oct. 20, 1999. Senate Environment and Public Works reported, amended, April 4, 2000 (S Rept 106-252). Senate passed, amended, Sept. 27. House passed, under suspension of the rules, Oct. 24. President signed Nov. 13, 2000.

PL 106-515 (S 1865) Provide grants to establish demonstration mental health courts. Introduced by DeWine, R-Ohio, on Nov. 4, 1999. Senate Judiciary reported, amended, July 27, 2000 (no written report). Senate passed, amended, Sept. 26. House passed, under suspension of the rules, Oct. 24. President signed Nov. 13, 2000.

PL 106-516 (S 2345) Direct the secretary of the interior to conduct a special resource study concerning the preservation and public use of sites associated with Harriet Tubman in Auburn, N.Y. Introduced by Schumer, D-N.Y., on April 4, 2000. Senate Energy and Natural Resources reported, amended,

Sept. 29 (S Rept 106-440). Senate passed, amended, Oct. 5. House passed, under suspension of the rules, Oct. 24. President signed Nov. 13, 2000.

PL 106-517 (S 2413) Amend the Omnibus Crime Control and Safe Streets Act of 1968 to clarify the procedures and conditions for the award of matching grants for the purchase of armor vests. Introduced by Campbell, R-Colo., on April 12, 2000. Senate Judiciary reported June 29 (no written report). Senate passed, amended, Oct. 10. House passed Oct. 25. President signed Nov. 13, 2000.

PL 106-518 (S 2915) Make improvements in the operation and administration of the federal courts. Introduced by Grassley, R-Iowa, on July 25, 2000. Senate Judiciary reported, amended, Sept. 28 (no written report). Senate passed, amended, Oct. 19. House passed, with amendments, Oct. 25. Senate agreed to House amendments Oct. 27. President signed Nov. 13, 2000.

PL 106-519 (HR 4986) Amend the Internal Revenue Code of 1986 to repeal the provisions relating to foreign sales corporations (FSCs) and to exclude extraterritorial income from gross income. Introduced by Archer, R-Texas, on July 27, 2000. House Ways and Means reported, amended, Sept. 13 (H Rept 106-845). House passed, amended, under suspension of the rules, Sept. 13. Senate Finance reported, with amendments, Sept. 20 (S Rept 106-416). Senate passed, with amendment, Nov. 1. House agreed to Senate amendment, under suspension of the rules, Nov. 14. President signed Nov. 15, 2000.

PL 106-520 (H J Res 125) Make further continuing appropriations for fiscal 2001. Introduced by Young, R-Fla., on Nov. 13, 2000. House Appropriations discharged. House passed Nov. 13. Senate passed Nov. 14. President signed Nov. 15, 2000.

PL 106-521 (HR 2346) Authorize the enforcement by state and local governments of certain Federal Communications Commission regulations regarding use of citizens band radio equipment. Introduced by Ehlers, R-Mich., on June 24, 1999. House Commerce reported Sept. 22, 2000 (H Rept 106-883). House passed, under suspension of the rules, Sept. 27. Senate passed, with amendment, Oct. 31. House agreed to Senate amendment, under suspension of the rules, Nov. 13. President signed Nov. 22, 2000.

PL 106-522 (HR 5633) Make appropriations for the government of the District of Columbia and other activities chargeable in whole or in part against the revenues of the District for the fiscal year ending September 30, 2001. Introduced by Istook, R-Okla., on Nov. 14, 2000. House Appropriations discharged. House passed Nov. 14. Senate passed Nov. 14. President signed Nov. 22, 2000.

PL 106-523 (S 768) Establish court-martial jurisdiction over civilians serving with the armed forces during contingency operations, and establish federal jurisdiction over crimes committed outside the United States by former members of the armed forces and civilians accompanying them. Introduced by Sessions, R-Ala., on April 13, 1999. Senate Judiciary reported, amended, June 24 (no written report). Senate passed, with amendments, July 1. House Armed Services and House Judiciary discharged. House passed, with amendments, July 25, 2000. Senate agreed to House amendments Oct. 26. President signed Nov. 22, 2000.

PL 106-524 (S 1670) Revise the boundary of Fort Matanzas National Monument. Introduced by Graham, D-Fla., on Sept. 30, 1999. Senate Energy and Natural Resources reported July 10, 2000 (S Rept 106-331). Senate passed Oct. 5. House passed, under suspension of the rules, Oct. 31. President signed Nov. 22, 2000.

PL 106-525 (S 1880) Amend the Public Health Service Act to improve the health of minority individuals. Introduced by Kennedy, D-Mass., on Nov. 8, 1999. Senate Health, Education, Labor, and Pensions discharged. Senate passed Oct. 26, 2000. House passed, under suspension of the rules, Oct. 31. President signed Nov. 22, 2000.

PL 106-526 (S 1936) Authorize the secretary of agriculture to sell or exchange all or part of certain administrative sites and other National Forest System land in Oregon and use the resulting proceeds for National Forest System purposes. Introduced by Wyden, D-Ore., on Nov. 16, 1999. Senate Energy and Natural Resources reported, amended, April 6, 2000 (S Rept 106-256). Senate passed July 27. House Resources reported, with amendment, Oct. 5 (H Rept 106-938). House passed, amended, under suspension of the rules, Oct. 17. Senate agreed to House amendment Oct. 27. President signed Nov. 22, 2000.

PL 106-527 (S 2020) Adjust the boundary of the Natchez Trace Parkway in Mississippi. Introduced by Cochran, R-Miss., on Feb. 1, 2000. Senate Energy and Natural Resources reported July 10 (S Rept 106-332). Senate passed July 27. House passed, under suspension of the rules, Oct. 31. President signed Nov. 22, 2000.

PL 106-528 (S 2440) Amend Title 49, U.S. Code, to improve airport security. Introduced by Hutchison, R-Texas, on April 13, 2000. Senate Commerce, Science and Transportation reported, amended, Aug. 25 (S Rept 106-388). Senate passed, amended, Oct. 3. House passed, with amendment, under suspension of the rules, Oct. 23. Senate agreed to House amendment Oct. 25. President signed Nov. 22, 2000.

PL 106-529 (S 2485) Direct the secretary of the interior to provide assistance in planning and constructing a regional heritage center in Calais, Maine. Introduced by Collins, R-Maine, on April 27, 2000. Senate Energy and Natural Resources reported, amended, June 27 (S Rept 106-319). Senate passed, amended, Oct. 5. House passed Oct. 30. President signed Nov. 22, 2000.

PL 106-530 (S 2547) Provide for the establishment of the Great Sand Dunes National Park and Preserve and the Baca National Wildlife Refuge in Colorado. Introduced by Allard, R-Colo., on May 11, 2000. Senate Energy and Natural Resources reported, amended, Oct. 3 (S Rept 106-479). Senate passed, amended, Oct. 5. House passed, under suspension of the rules, Oct. 25. President signed Nov. 22, 2000.

PL 106-531 (S 2712) Amend Chapter 35 of Title 31, U.S. Code, to authorize the consolidation of certain financial and performance management reports required of federal agencies. Introduced by Thompson, R-Tenn., on June 12, 2000. Senate Governmental Affairs reported July 11 (S Rept 106-337). Senate passed July 19. House passed, under suspension of the rules, Oct. 27. President signed Nov. 22, 2000.

PL 106-532 (S 2773) Amend the Agricultural Marketing Act of 1946 to enhance dairy markets through dairy product mandatory reporting. Introduced by Feingold, D-Wis., on June 22, 2000. Senate Agriculture, Nutrition and Forestry discharged. Senate passed, amended, Oct. 25. House passed Oct. 25. President signed Nov. 22, 2000.

PL 106-533 (S 2789) Amend the Congressional Award Act to establish a Congressional Recognition for Excellence in Arts Education Board. Introduced by Cochran, R-Miss., on June 26, 2000. Senate Governmental Affairs discharged. Senate passed, amended, Oct. 27. House passed, under suspension of the rules, Oct. 31. President signed Nov. 22, 2000.

PL 106-534 (S 3164) Protect seniors from fraud. Introduced by Bayh, D-Ind., on Oct. 5, 2000. Senate Judiciary discharged. Senate passed Oct. 24. House passed, under suspension of the rules, Oct. 30. President signed Nov. 22, 2000.

PL 106-535 (S 3194) Designate the facility of the U.S. Postal Service at 431 George St. in Millersville, Pa., as the "Robert S. Walker Post Office." Introduced by Santorum, R-Pa., on Oct. 12, 2000. Senate Governmental Affairs discharged. Senate passed Oct. 24. House passed, under suspension of the rules, Oct. 27. President signed Nov. 22, 2000.

PL 106-536 (S 3239) Amend the Immigration and Nationality Act to provide special immigrant status for certain U.S. international broadcasting employees. Introduced by Helms, R-N.C., on Oct. 25, 2000. Senate passed Oct. 25. House passed, under suspension of the rules, Oct. 31. President signed Nov. 22, 2000.

PL 106-537 (H J Res 126) Make further continuing appropriations for fiscal 2001. Introduced by Young, R-Fla., on Dec. 4, 2000. House passed Dec. 5. Senate passed Dec. 5. President signed Dec. 5, 2000.

PL 106-538 (HR 2941) Establish the Las Cienegas National Conservation Area in Arizona. Introduced by Kolbe, R-Ariz., on Sept. 24, 1999. House Resources reported, amended, Oct. 4, 2000 (H Rept 106-934). House passed, amended, Oct. 5. Senate passed Oct. 27. President signed Dec. 6, 2000.

PL 106-539 (H J Res 127) Make further continuing appropriations for fiscal 2001. Introduced by Young-R-Fla., on Dec. 6, 2000. House passed Dec. 7. Senate passed Dec. 7. President signed Dec. 7, 2000.

PL 106-540 (H J Res 128) Make further continuing appropriations for fiscal 2001. Introduced by Young, R-Fla., on Dec. 7, 2000. House passed Dec. 8. Senate passed Dec. 8. President signed Dec. 8, 2000.

PL 106-541 (S 2796) Provide for the conservation and development of water and related resources and authorize the secretary of the Army to construct various projects for improvements to U.S. rivers and harbors. Introduced by Voinovich, R-Ohio, on June 27, 2000. Senate Environment and Public Works reported, amended, July 27 (S Rept 106-362). Senate passed, with amendments, Sept. 25. House passed, with amendments, Oct. 19. Conference report filed in the House on Oct. 31 (H Rept 106-1020). Senate agreed to conference report Oct. 31. House agreed to conference report Nov. 3. President signed Dec. 11, 2000.

PL 106-542 (H J Res 129) Make further continuing appropriations for fiscal 2001. Introduced by Young, R-Fla., on Dec. 7, 2000. House passed Dec. 11. Senate passed Dec. 11. President signed Dec. 11, 2000.

PL 106-543 (H J Res 133) Make further continuing appropriations for fiscal 2001. Introduced by Young, R-Fla., on Dec. 14, 2000. House Appropriations discharged. House passed Dec. 15. Senate passed Dec. 15. President signed Dec. 15, 2000.

PL 106-544 (HR 3048) Amend section 879 of Title 18, U.S. Code, to clarify the authority of the Secret Service regarding threats against former presidents and members of their families. Introduced by McCollum, R-Fla., on Oct. 7, 1999. House Judiciary reported, amended, June 12, 2000 (H Rept 106-669). House passed, amended, under suspension of the rules, June 26. Senate passed, with amendments, Oct. 13. House disagreed to some Senate amendments and added an amendment, Oct. 25. Senate receded and agreed to the House amendment Dec. 6. President signed Dec. 19, 2000.

PL 106-545 (HR 4281) Establish, where feasible, guidelines, recommendations, and regulations that promote the regulatory acceptance of new and revised toxicological tests that protect human and animal health and the environment while reducing, refining, or replacing animal tests and ensuring human safety and product effectiveness. Introduced by Calvert, R-Calif., on April 13, 2000. House Commerce reported, amended, Oct. 16 (H Rept 106-980). House passed, amended, under suspension of the rules, Oct. 17. Senate passed Dec. 6. President signed Dec. 19, 2000.

PL 106-546 (HR 4640) Authorize grants to states for carrying out DNA analyses for use in the FBI's Combined DNA Index System, and provide for the collection and analysis of DNA samples from certain violent and sexual offenders for use in such system. Introduced by McCollum, R-Fla., on June 12, 2000. House Judiciary reported, amended, Sept. 26 (H Rept 106-900, Pt. 1). House Armed Services discharged. House passed, amended, under suspension of the rules, Oct. 2. Senate passed, with amendment, Dec. 6. House agreed to Senate amendment Dec. 7. President signed Dec. 19, 2000.

PL 106-547 (HR 4827) Amend Title 18, U.S. Code, to prevent entry by false pretenses to any U.S. property, vessel, or aircraft or to secure area of any airport, and to prevent the misuse of genuine and counterfeit police badges by those seeking to commit a crime. Introduced by Horn, R-Calif., on July 12, 2000. House Judiciary reported, amended, Sept. 28 (H Rept 106-913). House passed, amended, under suspension of the rules, Oct. 2. Senate passed Dec. 6. President signed Dec. 19, 2000.

PL 106-548 (S 1972) Direct the secretary of agriculture to convey to the town of Dolores, Colo., the current site of the Joe Rowell Park. Introduced by Allard, R-Colo., on Nov. 19, 1999. Senate Energy and Natural Resources reported, amended, Aug. 25, 2000 (S Rept 106-375). Senate passed, amended, Oct. 5. House failed to pass, under suspension of the rules, Nov. 13. House Resources discharged. House passed Dec. 4. President signed Dec. 19, 2000.

PL 106-549 (S 2594) Authorize the secretary of the interior to contract with the Mancos Water Conservancy District to use the Mancos Project facilities for impounding, storing, diverting, and carrying nonproject water for irrigation, domestic, municipal, industrial, and any other beneficial purposes. Introduced by Allard, R-Colo., on May 18, 2000. Senate Energy and Natural Resources reported, amended, Sept. 28 (S Rept 106-427). Senate passed, amended, Oct. 13. House Resources discharged. House passed Dec. 4. President signed Dec. 19, 2000.

PL 106-550 (S 3137) Establish a commission to commemorate the 250th anniversary of the birth of James Madison. Introduced by Sessions, R-Ala., on Sept. 28, 2000. Senate passed Oct. 25. House passed, under suspension of the rules, Dec. 4. President signed Dec. 19, 2000.

PL 106-551 (HR 3514) Amend the Public Health Service Act to provide for a system of sanctuaries for chimpanzees that have been designated as no longer needed in research conducted or supported by the Public Health Service. Introduced by Greenwood, R-Pa., on Nov. 22, 1999. House passed, amended, under suspension of the rules, Oct. 24, 2000. Senate passed Dec. 6. President signed Dec. 20, 2000.

PL 106-552 (HR 5016) Redesignate the facility of the U.S. Postal Service located at 514 Express Center Dr. in Chicago, Ill., as the "J. T. Weeker Service Center." Introduced by Blagojevich, D-Ill., on July 27, 2000. House passed, amended, under suspension of the rules, Oct. 17. Senate passed Dec. 14. President signed Dec. 20, 2000.

PL 106-553 (HR 4942) Make appropriations for the government of the District of Columbia and other activities chargeable in whole or in part against the revenues of the District for fiscal 2001. Introduced by Istook, R-Okla., on July 25, 2000. House Appropriations reported July 25 (H Rept 106-786). House passed, amended, Sept. 14. Senate passed, with amendment, Sept. 27. Conference report filed in the House Oct. 26 (H Rept 106-1005). House agreed to conference report Oct. 26. Senate agreed to conference report Oct. 27. President signed Dec. 21, 2000.

PL 106-554 (HR 4577) Make appropriations for the departments of Labor, Health and Human Services, Education, and related agencies for fiscal 2001. Introduced by Porter, R-Ill., on June 1, 2000. House Appropriations reported June 1 (H Rept 106-645). House passed, amended, June 14. Senate passed, with amendment, June 30. Conference report filed in the House Dec. 15 (H Rept 106-1033). House agreed to conference report Dec. 15. Senate agreed to conference report Dec. 15. President signed Dec. 21, 2000.

PL 106-555 (HR 2903) Reauthorize the Striped Bass Conservation Act. Introduced by Saxton, R-N.J., on Sept. 21, 1999. House passed, amended, under suspension of the rules, Oct. 31, 2000. Senate passed Dec. 8. President signed Dec. 21, 2000.

PL 106-556 (HR 5210) Designate the facility of the U.S. Postal Service at 200 S. George St. in York, Pa., as the "George Atlee Goodling Post Office Building." Introduced by Goodling, R-Pa., on Sept. 19, 2000. House passed, under suspension of the rules, Oct. 17. Senate passed Dec. 14. President signed Dec. 21, 2000.

PL 106-557 (HR 5461) Amend the Magnuson-Stevens Fishery Conservation and Management Act to eliminate the wasteful and unsportsmanlike practice of shark finning. Introduced by Cunningham, R-Calif., on Oct. 12, 2000. House passed, under suspension of the rules, Oct. 30. Senate passed Dec. 7. President signed Dec. 21, 2000.

PL 106-558 (S 439) Amend the National Forest and Public Lands of Nevada Enhancement Act of 1988 to adjust the boundary of the Toiyabe National Forest, Nev., and amend Chapter 55 of Title 5, U.S. Code, to authorize equal overtime pay provisions for all federal employees engaged in wildland fire suppression operations. Introduced by Bryan, D-Nev., on Feb. 22, 1999. Senate Energy and Natural Resources reported Nov. 2 (S Rept 106-205). Senate passed Nov. 19. House Resources reported July 17, 2000 (H Rept 106-746). House passed, as amended, under suspension of the rules, Oct. 23. Senate agreed to House amendments Dec. 7. President signed Dec. 21, 2000.

PL 106-559 (S 1508) Provide technical and legal assistance for tribal justice systems and members of Native American tribes. Introduced by Campbell, R-Colo., on Aug. 5, 1999. Senate Indian Affairs reported, amended, Nov. 8 (S Rept 106-219). Senate passed, amended, Nov. 19. House Resources reported Sept. 6, 2000 (H Rept 106-819, Pt. 1). House Judiciary discharged. House passed, with amendment, under suspension of the rules, Oct. 23. Senate agreed to House amendment Dec. 11. President signed Dec. 21, 2000.

PL 106-560 (S 1898) Provide protection against the risks to the public inherent in the interstate transportation of violent prisoners. Introduced by Dorgan, D-N.D., on Nov. 9, 1999. Senate Judiciary reported, amended, Sept. 28, 2000 (no written report). Senate passed, amended, Oct. 25. House Judiciary discharged. House passed Dec. 7. President signed Dec. 21, 2000.

PL 106-561 (S 3045) Improve the quality, timeliness, and credibility of forensic science services for criminal justice purposes. Introduced by Sessions, R-Ala., on Sept. 14, 2000. Senate Judiciary discharged. Senate passed, amended, Oct. 26. House Judiciary discharged. House passed Dec. 7. President signed Dec. 21, 2000.

PL 106-562 (HR 1653) Approve a governing international fishery agreement between the United States and the Russian Federation. Introduced by Young, R-Alaska, on April 29, 1999. House Resources reported June 22

(H Rept 106-195). House passed, amended, under suspension of the rules, Oct. 31, 2000. Senate passed Dec. 14. President signed Dec. 23, 2000.

PL 106-563 (HR 2570) Require the secretary of the interior to undertake a study of ways to commemorate the national significance of the U.S. roadways that comprise the Lincoln Highway. Introduced by Regula, R-Ohio, on July 20, 1999. House Resources reported Sept. 28, 2000 (H Rept 106-912). House passed, under suspension of the rules, Oct. 17. Senate passed Dec. 15. President signed Dec. 23, 2000.

PL 106-564 (HR 3756) Establish a standard time zone for Guam and the Commonwealth of the Northern Mariana Islands. Introduced by Underwood, D-Guam, on Feb. 29, 2000. House passed, under suspension of the rules, Oct. 10. Senate passed Dec. 15. President signed Dec. 23, 2000.

PL 106-565 (HR 4907) Establish the Jamestown 400th Commemoration Commission. Introduced by Bateman, R-Va., on July 20, 2000. House passed, under suspension of the rules Oct. 30. Senate passed Dec. 15. President signed Dec. 23, 2000.

PL 106-566 (S 1694) Direct the secretary of the interior to conduct a study on the reclamation and reuse of water and wastewater in Hawaii. Introduced by Akaka, D-Hawaii, on Oct. 6, 1999. Senate Energy and Natural Resources reported, amended, March 9, 2000 (S Rept 106-234). Senate passed, amended, April 13. House Resources reported, with amendment, Sept. 18 (H Rept 106-857) House passed, with amendments, under suspension of rules, Oct. 24. Senate agreed to House amendments Dec. 7. President signed Dec. 23, 2000.

PL 106-567 (HR 5630) Authorize appropriations for fiscal 2001 for intelligence and intelligence-related activities, the Community Management Account, and the Central Intelligence Agency Retirement and Disability System. Introduced by Goss, R-Fla., on Nov. 13, 2000. House Select Intelligence discharged. House passed Nov. 13. Senate passed, with amendments, Dec. 6. House agreed to Senate amendments Dec. 11. President signed Dec. 27, 2000.

PL 106-568 (HR 5528) Authorize the construction of a Wakpa Sica Reconciliation Place in Fort Pierre, S.D. Introduced by Thune, R-S.D., on Oct. 24, 2000. House passed, amended, under suspension of the rules, Oct. 26. Senate passed Dec. 11. President signed Dec. 27, 2000.

PL 106-569 (HR 5640) Expand home ownership in the United States. Introduced by Leach, R-Iowa, on Dec. 5, 2000. House passed, under suspension of the rules, Dec. 5. Senate passed Dec. 7. President signed Dec. 27, 2000.

PL 106-570 (S 2943) Authorize additional assistance for international malaria control. Introduced by Helms, R-N.C., on July 27, 2000. Senate Foreign Relations reported July 27 (no written report). Senate passed Oct. 19. House passed, amended, under suspension of the rules, Oct. 27. Senate agreed to House amendments, with amendment, Dec. 14. House agreed to Senate amendment Dec. 15. President signed Dec. 27, 2000.

PL 106-571 (HR 207) Amend Title 5, U.S. Code, to provide that physicians' comparability allowances be treated as part of basic pay for retirement purposes. Introduced by Morella, R-Md., on Jan. 6, 1999. House passed, amended, under suspension of the rules, Oct. 31, 2000. Senate passed Dec. 15. President signed Dec. 28, 2000.

PL 106-572 (HR 2816) Establish a grant program to assist state and local law enforcement in deterring, investigating, and prosecuting computer crimes. Introduced by Salmon, R-Ariz., on Sept. 8, 1999. House Judiciary discharged. House passed, amended, Dec. 15, 2000. Senate passed Dec. 15. President signed Dec. 28, 2000.

PL 106-573 (HR 3594) Repeal revisions to the tax code related to the installment method of accounting. Introduced by Herger, R-Calif., on Feb. 8, 2000. House passed, under suspension of the rules, Dec. 15. Senate passed Dec. 15. President signed Dec. 28, 2000.

PL 106-574 (HR 4020) Authorize an expansion of the boundaries of Sequoia National Park to include Dillonwood Giant Sequoia Grove. Introduced by Radanovich, R-Calif., on March 16, 2000. House passed, amended, under suspension of the rules, Oct. 31. Senate passed, with amendment, Dec. 15. House agreed to Senate amendment Dec. 15. President signed Dec. 28, 2000.

PL 106-575 (HR 4656) Authorize the Forest Service to convey certain lands in the Lake Tahoe Basin to the Washoe County School District for use as an elementary school site. Introduced by Gibbons, R-Nev., on June 14, 2000. House Resources reported Sept. 22 (H Rept 106-885). House failed to pass, under suspension of the rules, Oct. 12. House passed Oct. 24. Senate passed Dec. 15. President signed Dec. 28, 2000.

PL 106-576 (S 1761) Direct the secretary of the interior, through the Bureau of Reclamation, to conserve and enhance the water supplies of the Lower Rio Grande Valley. Introduced by Hutchison, R-Texas, on Oct. 21, 1999. Senate Energy and Natural Resources discharged. Senate passed, amended, Oct. 27, 2000. House passed, with amendment, under suspension of the rules, Dec. 4. Senate agreed to House amendment Dec. 15. President signed Dec. 28, 2000.

PL 106-577 (S 2749) Establish the California Trail Interpretive Center in Elko, Nev., to facilitate the interpretation of the development and use of trails in the settling of the western portion of the United States. Introduced by Reid, D-Nev., on June 19, 2000. Senate Energy and Natural Resources reported Sept. 29 (S Rept 106-441). Senate passed Oct. 5. House passed, with amendment, under suspension of the rules, Oct. 24. Senate agreed to House amendment Dec. 15. President signed Dec. 28, 2000.

PL 106-578 (S 2924) Strengthen the enforcement of federal statutes relating to false identification. Introduced by Collins, R-Maine, on July 26, 2000. Senate Judiciary reported, amended, Sept. 28 (no written report). Senate passed, amended, Oct. 31. House Judiciary discharged. House passed, with amendment, Dec. 15. Senate agreed to House amendment Dec. 15. President signed Dec. 28, 2000.

PL 106-579 (S 3181) Establish the White House Commission on the National Moment of Remembrance. Introduced by Hagel, R-Neb., on Oct. 10, 2000. Senate Judiciary discharged. Senate passed Oct. 27. House passed Dec. 15. President signed Dec. 28, 2000.

PL 106-580 (HR 1795) Amend the Public Health Service Act to establish the National Institute of Biomedical Imaging and Engineering. Introduced by Burr, R-N.C., on May 13, 1999. House Commerce reported, amended, Sept. 26, 2000 (H Rept 106-889). House passed, amended, under suspension of the rules, Sept. 27. Senate passed Dec. 15. President signed Dec. 29, 2000.

Index

Index

A

AARP
  fraud against the elderly, 675
  jobs for older Americans, 496
  physicians' non-Medicare contracts, 437
  Social Security earnings limit, 583–584
Abercrombie, Neil, D-Hawaii
  shark protection, 396
ABM treaty. See Anti-Ballistic Missile Treaty
Abortion
  action
    1997–1998, 455–459
    1999–2000, 472–474
    summary, 7, 16, 19, 20, 429, 430–431
  adoption counseling, 482
  bankruptcy of violent protesters, 143–144
  clinic leafleting, 689
  federal employee health plan, 68, 455, 458
  Fitzgerald election, 11
  health policy leadership, 435 (box)
  human cloning, 460, 745–746
  Hyde amendment bans
    children's health insurance, 436, 443, 459
    Medicaid, 458–459
  international family planning, 194–195,
    457–458, 473–474
    foreign aid appropriations, 59, 66, 75, 83, 184,
      185, 186, 187, 188, 210–217
    IMF dues, 194
    State Department authorization, 74, 189–192,
      217–219
    summary, 173, 175, 177, 204, 431, 455
    U.N. debt repayment, 192–193, 220
  military hospitals, 242, 243, 255, 256, 278, 279,
    292
  parental consent circumvention, 431, 455,
    456–457, 474, 662
  "partial-birth" procedure, 7, 430–431, 455–456,
    472, 473, 662
    Supreme Court decision, 455, 684, 686–687
  physician collective bargaining ban, 481
  religious health plans conscience exemptions,
    442, 458
  Republican convention, 23
  Roe v. Wade endorsement, 473
  RU486, 63, 431, 455, 482
  Supreme Court decisions, 689, 716–717
  unborn victims of violence, 474–475, 591,
    661–662
  Violence Against Women Act, 631
  visa ban for coercers, 182, 183, 260
**Abraham Lincoln Birthplace National Historic
  Site,** 359
Abraham, Spencer, R-Mich.
  border controls, 676
  children born abroad, 619
  election defeat, 28
  ESEA authorization, 539
  foreign aid, 210, 229, 230
  high-tech visas, 617, 618
  Lee nomination, 626
  migratory birds, 389
  NEA funding, 739

ACDA. See Arms Control and Disarmament
  Agency
Acid rain, 383
Ackerman, Gary L., D-N.Y.
  flag desecration, 667
Acquired immune deficiency syndrome (AIDS)
  ape conservation, 379
  discrimination against HIV positive, 688
  foreign aid appropriations, 176, 214, 215, 217
  hemophiliacs, 459
  HIV testing
    newborns, 483
    prison inmates, 600
    sex offenders, 644
  needle-exchange program ban, 74
  partner notification, 483
  prevention, treatment programs
    appropriations, 67
    authorization, 483
  prisoner health care, 653
ADA. See Americans with Disabilities Act
Adams, John Quincy, 22
Aderholt, Robert B., D-Ala.
  juvenile crime, 636
Administrative Office of the U.S. Court System,
  669
Administrative Procedures Act of 1946,
  226–227, 394
Administrative subpoenas, 651, 656
Adolescents and youth. See also Colleges and
  universities; Elementary and secondary education;
  Juvenile crime
  alcohol use
    sales to minors, 337, 635
    underage drinking prevention, 482
  drug testing for driver's license applicants, 602
  employment
    Amish exceptions, 584–585
    job training overhaul, 574
    work opportunity tax credits, 99
  gun ownership limits
    assault weapons ban, 641
    minimum age, 638
  health
    medical privacy, 479
    smoking reduction, 59, 316, 318, 322, 323
    tobacco regulation, 482
  parental consent to birth control, 67
  sexual, violent materials access, 16, 636–637
    Internet, 684, 688
  social services, 491
    after-school snacks, 431, 494
    Police Athletic League, 650
    post-foster care aid, 496
    teen parents in welfare-to-work, 490, 512
Adoption
  abortion alternative counseling, 482
  D.C. unmarried couples, 66
  foster children, 431, 493–494
  international treaty, 231
  orphaned immigrant siblings, 673
Adoption and Safe Families Act, 493
Adult day care, 502
Adult education. See also Literacy programs
  ed-flex plan, 540

Adult Education and Literacy Grant, 574
**Adult Employment and Training Opportunities
  Grant,** 574
Advanced Technology Program, 745
Advertising. See also Political advertising
  casino gambling, 689
  national parks filming fees, 356, 358, 387
  space ads, 752–753
**Advisory Commission on Drug-Free
  Communities,** 602
Aegis radar defense systems
  appropriations, 246, 262, 288, 300
  authorization, 242–243, 245, 258, 282, 295
Affirmative action
  Clinton term summary, 591, 593
  colleges, universities, 511, 616
  federal contractors, 615–616
  Lee nomination, 616, 624–627, 800
  Supreme Court decisions, 717
Afghanistan
  "Silk Road" trade, 169
  U.S. air strikes, 1998, 196, 267
AFL-CIO
  asbestos compensation, 665
  farmworker visas, 674
  fast track for trade pacts, 154
  high-tech visas, 618
Africa
  AIDS control, 215, 230
  elephant conservation, 369
  U.S. relations, 803
    travel visas, 677
  U.S. trade, 16, 156, 158
    clothing exports initiative, 149, 160, 167–168
    conflict diamonds, 82
    Export-Import Bank, 157
African Americans
  Agriculture Department discrimination, 422
  asbestos compensation, 666
  Clinton appointments, 799, 800
    judicial nominations, 678–679
  Clinton race initiative, 798
  employment rates, 35
  lupus research, 481
  members of Congress
    Moseley-Braun defeat, 11
    totals, 1947–2001 (table), 29
  racial profiling in traffic stops, 608, 652
  Republican convention, 23
  school vouchers, 528
African Elephant Conservation Act of 1988, 369
African Elephant Conservation Fund, 369
Age
  juvenile criminal trials as adults, 593–597,
    633–637
  Medicare eligibility, 50, 52, 433, 435, 436, 437,
    464
  minimum age for gun purchases, 638
  Social Security eligibility, 582 (box)
Age discrimination
  Supreme Court decisions, 717
Age Discrimination in Employment Act, 685
Aged persons. See Elderly persons
Agency for Health Care Policy and Research,
  453, 476, 477–478

Agency for Healthcare Research and Quality (AHRQ)
authorization, 477–478
minority health, 484
patient safety, 478
Agency for International Development (AID)
foreign policy agency reorganization, 69, 190, 191, 192, 193–194
international family planning programs, 473
Agency for Nuclear Stewardship, 305
Aging Committee, Senate Special
jurisdiction, leadership, 760, 956
Agricultural exports and imports
China trade agreement, 161, 163
economic sanctions reform, 170
food sanctions, 83, 223–224, 418, 419, 420–421, 424, 426
summary, 417
WTO Seattle meeting, 148
Agricultural labor
immigration rules, 629, 673–674
Agricultural price supports and income subsidies. *See also Crop insurance*
appropriations, 75–76, 76, 77, 85, 425
budget outlays, FY 1987–2001 (graph), 418
budget resolution, FY 2000, 73
dairy pricing, 424–425
farm tax breaks, 88, 98, 101, 419, 422–423, 565
research, 421–422
summary, 417
suspense accounts, 104
Agriculture and farming. *See also Agricultural exports and imports; Agricultural price supports and income subsidies; Crop insurance; Livestock and ranching*
alternative fuels, 356
bankruptcy law overhaul, 144
family farm estate taxes, 91, 94, 95, 99, 115–116
FHLB changes, 140
summary, 417–418, 419, 424
Treasury Department credit study, 140
water resources
California project, 381–382
Everglades restoration, 375
runoff pollution, 382
Agriculture Committee, House
jurisdiction, leadership, 760, 770, 956–957
Agriculture Department, U.S. (USDA)
appropriations, 59, 63, 75
Conservation Reserve Program, 420
dairy pricing, 75, 424–425
economic sanctions, 200
federal lands
California national monument, 403
damaged tree removal, 387–388
northern spotted owl, 392
swaps, 403
watershed dams, 385
homeless programs, 561
leadership (box), 420
racial discrimination remedies, 422
rural TV loans, 338
Agriculture, Nutrition and Forestry Committee, Senate
jurisdiction, leadership, 760, 951
AHRQ. *See Agency for Healthcare Research and Quality*
AID. *See Agency for International Development*
Aid to Families with Dependent Children, 486, 490
AIDS. *See Acquired immune deficiency syndrome*
Aiken, Ann L., 623
"Aimee's Law," 590, 631–633
Air Force One, 789
Air Force, U.S.
antimissile defenses, 244, 258, 261, 294

B-2 bomber, 240
B-52 fleet, 299
cargo planes, 288, 300
combat aircraft
appropriations, 247, 249, 261–262, 284, 288, 300
authorization, 241, 244–245, 258, 281–282, 294–295
F-22 funding, 76, 286–287 (box)
hurricane hunters, 248
laser weapons, 258, 261, 294
maintenance depots, 239–245
military construction appropriations, 252–253 (box), 289
personnel
levels, 240, 287
pilot retention, 285
senior commander travel, 284, 289
Quadrennial Defense Review, 264
Air Force Reserve, 248
Air National Guard, 248
Air pollution
Clean Air Act, 351, 382
Clinton term summary, 341, 344, 372, 799
D.C. clean air fee, 56
EPA research, 747
gasoline additive MTBE, 390–391
highway projects funding, 382
ozone standard, 84
vehicle emissions, 365, 382
Air safety
FAA authorization, 321
Supreme Court decisions, 728
Air security
counterfeit police badges, 644–645
Air-traffic control
controllers on Reagan airport, 741
FAA authorization, 321
system modernization, 331
Air transportation. *See also Air safety; Air security; Air-traffic control; Airline ticket taxes; Airports*
aviation fuel taxes, 102
budget outlays, 1987–2001 (graph), 316
FAA authorization, 331–332
Aircraft carriers
appropriations, 246, 247, 249, 262
authorization, 241, 282, 295
Nimitz overhaul, 245, 249
Airline ticket taxes
passenger fees, 48, 154, 321, 331–332
tax cuts, 1997, 92, 93, 101–102
Airport and Airway Trust Fund, 315, 331–332
Airports
border security controls, 676
Clinton term summary, 315
congestion relief, 331
construction, 72–73, 331–332
improvement grants, 321
noise abatement, 752
Reagan National, 741–742
AK-47 machine guns, 163
Akaka, Daniel, D-Hawaii
China trade agreement, 165
methane research, 388–389
Al Qaeda, 803
Alabama
weather station, 162
Alamo River, Calif., 365
Alaska
antimissile defenses, 294
development bills, 379
federal lands, 366–367, 391–392
Tongass forest logging, 67, 395
national wildlife refuges, 67, 348–349
ANWR oil drilling, 413

ocean policy panel, 364
offshore oil revenue, 376
Steller sea lion protection, 82, 393–394
subsistence fishing, 388
Alaska National Interest Lands Conservation Act of 1980, 342, 413
Albania
U.S. trade status, 168
U.S. troop deployment ban, 260, 261, 262
Albanian Kosovars, 178, 179, 204–208, 277, 802–803
Albo Pest Control Co., 773
Albright, Madeleine K.
Azerbaijan aid ban, 187 (box)
chemical weapons treaty, 269
foreign aid appropriations, 186
foreign policy leadership, 179 (box), 799
Kosovo policy, 205
NATO expansion, 273
North Korea missile moratorium, 803
Russia sanctions, 196
State Department authorization, 217
State Department leadership, 978 (box), 981
U.N. debt repayment, 219
Ukraine reform certification, 185
Alcohol abuse and alcoholism
college prevention programs, 513
drunken driving, 84, 319
public housing ban, 560
treatment programs, 564, 565
underage drinking prevention, 482
Alcoholic beverages
Internet sales, 317, 331, 337, 629, 631, 632, 633
interstate shipments to minors, 635
Alex Brown Inc., 123
Alexander, Lamar, 22
Aliens. *See Foreign nationals; Illegal immigrants*
Allard, Wayne, R-Colo.
Barshefsky nomination, 152 (box)
intelligence authorization, 228
new national parks, 381
Allen, George F., 28
Allen, Susan Au, 625
Allen, Tom, D-Maine
antimissile defenses, 307
campaign finance reform, 781, 782
Allied Signal, 282
Alternative fuels. *See also Ethanol*
excise taxes, 100
federal biodiesel use, 356
gasoline additive MTBE, 390–391
global warming, 355–356
methane research, 388–389
sanctions for oil producers, 414
Alternative minimum tax
budget resolution adjustment, 80
businesses, 91–92, 94, 95, 98
personal credits, 106, 112, 113, 114
standard deductions, 102
Alternative sentencing, 644, 656
Alternative water resource programs, 387
Altman, Stuart H., 465
Alvarez, Aida, 320 (box)
Ambulance services, 440
Amchem Products, 665
"America Reads" program, 529
American Airlines, 321
American Association of Health Plans, 436, 462
American Association of Mechanical Instrumentation, 450
American Bankers Association, 125
American Bar Association
judicial nominations, 624
juvenile crime, 597
American Civil Liberties Union
civil assets forfeiture, 648

Internet content regulation, 688
judicial activism, 621
Molloway nomination, 623
racial profiling, 652
terrorism response, 309
American Classic Voyages Co., 246
American College of Obstetricians and Gynecologists, 456, 472
American Community Renewal Act, 564
American Discovery Trail, 359, 400
American Enterprise Institute, 663
American Express, 126
American Farm Bureau Federation, 425
American Hawaii Cruises, 246
American Heart Association, 746
American Heritage Rivers Initiative, 370
American Hospital Association, 462, 479, 480
American Insurance Association, 397
American Legion, 611, 667
American Lung Association, 390
American Medical Association
assisted suicide, 607, 658
malpractice database access, 482
partial-birth abortion, 456, 473
patients' rights, 455, 482
physician antitrust, 480
American Petroleum Institute, 390
American River, 373
American Samoa
campaign finance reform, 789
American Society of Pain Management Nurses, 607
Americans for Economic Growth, 773
Americans for Tax Reform, 741
Americans with Disabilities Act (ADA) of 1990
Civil Rights Commission, 609
Supreme Court decisions, 688
AmeriCorps, 84
Amish teen workers, 584–585
Amphibious landing transport ships
appropriations, 247–248, 249, 288, 300
authorization, 245, 282, 295
Amtrak
authorization, 738
Clinton term summary, 6, 315, 318
restructuring, 101, 320–321
Amway, 101
Amy Boyer's Law, 82
Amyotrophic lateral sclerosis, 463, 464
Anaheim, Calif., 620
Anderson, E. Ratcliffe, 480
Anderson, Margo J., 733
Andrews, Robert E., D-N.J.
foreign aid appropriations, 211
OPIC authorization, 169
student loans, 510, 526
teacher training, 533
Animal and Plant Health Inspection Service, 384
Animals. *See also Endangered species; Invasive species; Livestock and ranching; Veterinary medicine; Wildlife protection*
animal cruelty videos, 650–651
pets in public housing, 558, 561
police dogs, horses, 650
Annan, Kofi
Iraq confrontations, 197 (box)
U.S. dues for U.N., 218
Anthrax
military immunization program, 289
Anti-Ballistic Missile (ABM) Treaty of 1972
antimissile defenses, 238, 265–266, 306
CFE treaty amendment, 274–275
chemical weapons treaty negotiations, 268
Clinton term summary, 175, 239

Antibiotics
appropriate use, 481
patents, 449
Antimissile defense systems
action
1997–1998, 265–267
1999–2000, 306–308
chronology (box), 307
summary, 175, 235, 276
appropriations, 68, 248, 249, 259, 261, 262, 266, 287, 297, 299, 301
authorization, 241–242, 244, 257–258, 281, 294
long-term defense planning, 264
Taiwan protection, 182
testing, 257, 292
Antimissile satellites, 258, 261
Antipersonnel land mines. *See Land mines*
Antipoverty programs
Clinton domestic policies, 798
community development initiatives, 564–565
Community Reinvestment Act, 130, 132, 136
education
Head Start, 491–493
literacy programs, 529–530
student loans for teachers, 509–513, 519–520, 545
Title 1 education aid, 507, 531
microenterprise aid, 140
Antiquities Act of 1906, 341, 343, 365–366, 389–390, 393
Anti-Terrorism and Effective Death Penalty Act of 1996, 676, 690
Antitrust law
baseball exemption, 316, 324
health professionals, 480–481
international energy programs, 356
Microsoft case, 38
ocean shipping, 322
Supreme Court decisions, 692
tobacco regulation, 316
ANWR. *See Arctic National Wildlife Refuge*
Apache helicopters
appropriations, 248, 261, 288
authorization, 244, 258, 281
Ape conservation, 379–380
Appalachian region
highway projects, 319
Appeals. *See also Habeas corpus appeals*
Supreme Court decisions, 695, 697–698
Appeals courts, U.S.
judicial nominations, 627–628, 677–678, 679–680
rulings
clean air standards, 382
FDA tobacco regulation, 323
financial services modernization, 138, 139
nuclear waste storage, 363
trial attendance by victims, 609
Appropriations
bills
FY 1998, 58–60
FY 1999, 62–70, 76–77
FY 2000, 73–76, 84–85
FY 2001, 81–84
budget process reform, 77
CARA automatic funding, 207–211
Clinton term summary, 4, 5, 11, 19, 20, 42
veto use, 810–811
contingent allocations, 54
dual-track procedures, 538
incremental defense funding, 289
line-item veto, 64–65, 691
off-budget programs, 332
Appropriations Committee, House
jurisdiction, leadership, 191, 770, 957

Appropriations Committee, Senate
jurisdiction, leadership, 759, 951
Aquifers, 382
Arafat, Yasser, 190 (box), 216 (box), 802
Arbitration
federal courts, 607–608
Supreme Court decisions, 689, 721
Archer, Bill, R-Texas
China-U.S. trade, 152, 163
community development, 564–565
education savings accounts, 518
fast track for trade pacts, 155
health policy
disabled workers' insurance, 470–471
Medicare drug benefits, 466
railroad pensions, 581
Social Security surplus protection, 78
superfund overhaul, 352, 397
tax policy, 88
corporate income earned abroad, 118
tax cuts, 1997, 92
tax cuts, 1999, 110–111
Arctic areas
bird population control, 384
Arctic National Wildlife Refuge (ANWR)
oil exploration drilling, 409–410, 413
budget resolution, FY 2001, 80
Clinton term summary, 799
system management, 348
Argentina
financial crisis, 39, 147, 156, 801
Arizona
casino income taxes, 92
Las Cienegas conservation area, 394
NASA Origins project, 742–743
national monuments, 389, 390
sex offender registries, 604
Arkansas
congressional elections, 29
term limits, 784
Arkansas Committee on Professional Conduct, 827
Arlington National Cemetery, 283, 502
Armed Services Committee, House
jurisdiction, leadership, 770, 957
Armed Services Committee, Senate
jurisdiction, leadership, 760, 769, 951–952
Armenia
genocide resolution, 231
"Silk Road" trade, 169
U.S. aid appropriations, 185, 187, 189, 210
Azerbaijan ban, 169, 187 (box)
Armey, Dick, R-Texas
asbestos compensation, 665
China trade agreement, 162
congressional pay, 791
education
school vouchers, 528
teacher training, 532
FALN clemency, 681
foreign aid appropriations, 188, 212
gun control, 640
hate crimes, 644
House ethics overhaul, 766
House leadership, 7 (box), 760, 769
on Clinton, 15
Gingrich coup attempt, 762–763 (box)
Gingrich reprimand, 761–762
House chaplain, 775
IMF issues, 194, 213
tax policy, 89, 112
Arms control. *See also Anti-Ballistic Missile Treaty; Chemical Weapons Convention; Comprehensive Test Ban Treaty; Nuclear weapons proliferation; Nunn-Lugar program*
antimissile defenses, 306–307

CFE treaty, 239, 268, 274–275
land mine ban, 274
NATO "Founding Act," 802
Russia-U.S. monitoring, 223
underground stockpiles destruction, 295
unilateral reduction authority, 277, 278, 292
**Arms Control and Disarmament Agency
(ACDA)**
export controls, 242, 245
foreign policy agency reorganization, 68, 190,
191, 192, 193–194
Arms Export Control Act of 1994
economic sanctions, 159, 170, 223, 288–289, 421
Glenn amendment, 200
Arms sales. *See also Missile technology transfer;
Nuclear weapons proliferation*
economic sanctions reform, 169
Export-Import Bank financing, 157
resale of controlled exports, 229
Taiwan missile defense, 182
Army Corps of Engineers
Everglades restoration, 372–375
ocean policy panel, 364
salmon project, 395
water projects appropriations, 76
Army National Guard, 244
Army, U.S.
air, sea transport, 245, 249, 282, 300
antimissile defenses, 244, 248, 257–258, 259,
261, 266
arsenal privatization, 261
digital communications network, 240, 244, 248,
258, 261
foreign military training, 211, 230, 291, 296
ground combat weapons
appropriations, 248–249, 261, 287–288,
299–300
authorization, 244, 247, 258, 281, 294
land mine treaty, 274
military construction appropriations, 252–253
(box)
mobile force transformation, 290, 292, 294,
297–300
personnel
force level, 248
recruiting benefits, 280, 285
sexual harassment remedies, 275
West VA leadership, 499 (box)
Arnold Air Force Base, Tenn., 253 (box)
Arsenal ships, 245
Arsenic, 84
Arts education award, 531, 546–547
Arts programs
NEA funding, 59, 738–739, 750–751
Republican platform, 23
Asbestos, 664–666
Asbestos Compensation, Office of, 665
Ashcroft, John, R-Mo.
abortion, 458
asbestos compensation, 665
assisted suicide, 606
budget resolution, FY 1999, 61
economic sanctions reform, 170, 224
education savings accounts, 519–520
election defeat, 28
flag desecration, 666–667
judicial activism, 621
judicial nominations, 623
Fletcher, 627
White, 678, 800
law enforcement
crime victims' rights, 668–669
juvenile crime, 635, 636
methamphetamine traffic, 602
NATO expansion, 273
NEA funding, 739

Asian Americans
Clinton appointments, 799
Lee nomination, 624–627
Asian countries
financial crisis, 39, 66, 147, 156, 801
"Silk Road" trade, 169
Asian Pacific Center, 252 (box)
Aspin, Les, 978 (box)
Assassination Records Review Board, 613
Assisted-living facilities
Section 8 project conversion, 567
veterans pilot program, 502
Association of Trial Lawyers of America, 665, 786
Association health plans, 468, 469 (box)
Asteroids, 249
Asthma
Clean Air Act, 351
research, 482
AT&T, 330
Atlanta, Ga.
clean air standards, 382
school shootings, 638, 640
Atlantic Striped Bass Conservation Act of 1984,
380
ATMs. *See Automated teller machines*
Attorney general. *See Justice Department, U.S.*
Attorney's fees
civil assets forfeiture, 649
IDEA disputes, 516
labor law enforcement, 585
Supreme Court decisions, 695
Atwood, J. Brian, 990
Australia
U.S. export controls, 229
Australia Group, 270
Authorizing committees
off-budget programs, 332
Autism research, 482
Automated electronic defibrillators, 481
Automated teller machines (ATMs), 137
Automobile Heritage Area, 359
Automobile safety
airbags, 686
Clinton term summary, 315–316
tire defects, rollovers, 331, 333
rollover ratings, 84
Automobiles and auto industry. *See also
Traffic law*
accounting methods, 105
commuting
D.C. clean air fee, 56
parking or cash, 104
emissions standards, 365, 382
fuel efficiency standards, 16, 67, 84, 333 (box),
410
global warming treaty, 355
vehicle theft program, 613
Aviation. *See Air transportation*
Avondale Industries, 288
Azerbaijan
CFE treaty changes, 274
U.S. aid appropriations, 169, 185, 187, 188, 189,
210
ban summary, 187 (box)

B

B-2 bombers
appropriations, 58, 246, 247, 249, 262
authorization, 240–245, 258, 281
B-52 bombers
appropriations, 248
fleet retention, 299
improvements, 281
Babbitt, Bruce
Antiquities Act, 366

campaign finance investigation, 779
grazing advisory panels, fees, 419–420, 357
Interior Department leadership, 347 (box), 978
(box)
national wildlife refuges, 349
Baca, Joe, D-Calif.
special election, 7
Baca Ranch, Colo., 381
Bachus, Spencer R-Ala.
high-tech visas, 671
Hilliard ethics probe, 766
veterans burial rights, 499
Backpacker magazine, 400
Badlands National Park, 387
Baesler, Scotty, 12
Bail bondsmen, 599
Baily, Martin N., 35 (box), 983
Baker, Howard H. Jr., 303 (box)
Baker, James A. III, 25
Baker, Nancy Kassebaum, 252–253
Baker Resource Area, 403
Baker, Richard H., R-La.
Cat Island wildlife refuge, 402
community development, 564
Balanced Budget Act of 1997, 17, 48–56
Balanced budget amendment, 56–58
Balanced Budget Refinement Act, 461
Baldwin, Tammy, D-Wis.
Violence Against Women Act, 631
Balkan countries. *See also Albania; Bosnia;
Kosovo; Yugoslavia*
U.S. aid appropriations, 210, 211, 214, 215, 217
U.S. military operations, 299
Ballenger, Cass, R-N.C.
bilingual education, 517–518
compensatory time, 576
OSHA overhaul bills, 577
physician antitrust, 481
Ballet companies, 739
Ballistic Missile Defense Organization, 294
Ballot access, 707
Bananas, 168
BancOne, 125
Bank for International Settlements, 189
Bank Holding Company Act of 1956, 122, 124
(box), 130, 135
Bankers Trust New York Corp., 123
**Banking and Financial Services Committee,
House**
jurisdiction, leadership, 770, 957–958
**Banking, Housing and Urban Affairs
Committee, Senate**
jurisdiction, leadership, 769, 952
Bankruptcy
Amtrak restructuring, 320–321
federal contractors, 749–750
gun manufacturers, 143, 642
judgeships expansion, 608
minimum wage proposals, 579–580
student loans, 512
Supreme Court decisions, 692–693
system overhaul, 121, 126–128, 130, 142–144
Banks and banking
bankruptcy overhaul, 126–128
CFTC regulation exemption, 142
China trade agreement, 161
civil assets forfeiture, 649
Clinton term summary, 15, 120–121
credit union expansion, 128
electronic signatures, 335–336
encryption exports, 327
financial services modernization, 122–126,
130–141
competing interests (box), 131
earlier reform attempts (box), 124
key rulings (box), 123

interstate banking, 129
money laundering, 605
savings account subsidies for poor, 565
student loans, 508, 509–510, 511–512, 526
Supreme Court decisions, 692
Y2K glitch, 330
Barak, Ehud, 801–802
Baran, Jan, 763
Barbour, Haley, 126, 778
Barnes, Roy, 30
Barr, Bob, R-Ga.
  campaign finance reform, 782
  defense appropriations, 284
  electronic information access, 656
  ethics probe, 774
  farmworker visas, 674
  Hilliard ethics probe, 766
  intelligence authorization, 202
  law enforcement
    bulletproof vests, 600
    civil assets forfeiture, 605, 648
    DNA evidence, 655
    gun control, 640
  Puerto Rico status, 741
Barrett, Bill, R-Neb.
  teacher training, 511
Barrett, Thomas M., D-Wis.
  drug czar authorization, 603
Barrier islands, 383
Barry, Marion S. Jr., 740
Barshefsky, Charlene
  fast track for trade pacts, 154
  trade leadership, 152 (box), 984
Barstow, Calif., 261
Bartlett, Roscoe G., R-Md.
  defense authorization, 295
  sexual material on military posts, 275
Barton, Joe L., R-Texas
  electric deregulation, 404–407
  energy research and development, 746–747
  FDA overhaul, 446
  nuclear waste storage, 407
    low-level waste, 360
  Strategic Petroleum Reserve, 409
  term limits, 784
Baseball
  antitrust exemption, 316, 324
Bath Iron Works, 288
Battered women. *See Domestic violence*
Baucus, Max, D-Mont.
  China trade agreement, 163
  endangered species, 386
  ethics probe, 771
  gun control, 640
  Medicare changes, 436
Bauer, Robert F., 784
Baumgarten, Jane, 584
Bayh, Birch E., 12
Bayh, Evan, 12
Beaches
  stranded marine mammals, 380–381
  water quality standards, 380
Bears
  meat, organs import ban, 381
Beckwith, Samira, 607
Becton, Julius W. Jr., 528
Beef. *See Meat*
Begala, Paul, 750
Bell Helicopter, 288
Bello, Judy, 484
Beneficiary Improvement and Protection Act, 463
Bennett, Pamela, 607
Bennett, Robert F., R-Utah
  campaign finance reform, 789
  Clinton impeachment, 827

defense authorization, 293
flag desecration, 611
public housing reform, 558
Bentsen, Ken, D-Texas
  financial services modernization, 133
Bentsen, Lloyd M., 34 (box), 126, 978 (box)
Bereuter, Doug, R-Neb.
  campaign finance reform, 789
  China policy, 209
  China trade agreement, 161, 162 (box), 163, 164
  defense authorization, 254
  foreign aid appropriations, 215
  sanctions for oil producers, 414
Berman, Howard L., D-Calif.
  farmworker visas, 674
  Gingrich reprimand, 762–763
  high-tech visas, 671
  House leadership, 760
  judicial activism, 622
Berman, Robert A., 775
Bernstein, Ed, 28
Berzon, Marcia L., 677–678, 679–680, 800, 992
Beyer, Donald S. Jr., 8
Bhutto, Benazir, 765
Biden, Joseph R. Jr., D-Del.
  assisted suicide, 659
  chemical weapons treaty, 268, 270, 271
  China policy, 208–209
  "dolphin-safe" tuna, 346
  education savings accounts, 519
  flag desecration, 611
  foreign aid authorization, 228
  foreign policy agencies reorganization, 175, 177, 193
  juvenile crime, 596, 635
  Senate leadership, 760
  State Department authorization, 190, 191, 192, 217–218
  Third World debt/forest protection, 369
  U.N. debt repayment, 192–193, 219–220
  violence against women, 590, 631
"Big Dig," 772
Bilbray, Brian P., R-Calif.
  coastal water quality, 380
  election defeat, 29
  Otay mountain wilderness, 401
  vehicle emissions, 365
Bilingual education, 508, 509, 516–518
Bilingual Education and Minority Languages Affairs, Office of, 517
Bilirakis, Michael, R-Fla.
  date-rape drugs, 654
  health policy research, 478
  organ transplants, 476
  patients' rights, 469
Bin Laden, Osama, 267, 309, 803
Bingaman, Jeff, D-N.M.
  conservation lands acquisition, 378
  defense policy
    authorization, 293
    NATO expansion, 273
    nuclear security, 305
  education
    dropout prevention, 541
    education savings accounts, 519, 545
  electric deregulation, 404, 406
  energy supplies, 410
  national monuments, 390
  nuclear waste storage, 361–362, 408
  Senate leadership, 769
Biodiesel fuel, 356
Biodiversity
  Everglades restoration, 341
  national wildlife refuges, 349
Biological products
  FDA overhaul, 444, 445, 448

Biological weapons
  antimissile defenses, 267
  Iraq policy, 196–198
  long-term defense planning, 264
  terrorism countermeasures, 267, 295, 308–309, 481
  underground stockpile destruction, 295
  vaccines, 481
Biology. *See Medical research*
Biomass fuel, 565
Biomaterials liability, 322
Biosphere reserves, 368, 401
Biotechnology companies
  human cloning, 460
Bipartisanship
  budget and tax policy, 43, 48–49, 87–88
  China trade agreement, 162
  health care policy, 433
  law enforcement bills, 589, 590–591
Bird Drive Basin, Fla., 375
Birds
  Cat Island wildlife refuge, 402
  habitat conservation, 389
  migratory bird hunting, 358
  nutria eradication, 363
  population control, 384–385
Birth control
  China-U.S. trade, 151
  condom warnings on HPV, 470–471
  federal health insurance coverage, 10, 68, 455, 458, 792–793
  international family planning programs, 194–195, 457–458, 473–474
    foreign aid appropriations, 59, 66, 75, 83, 184–186, 188, 189, 210–214, 216–217
    State Department authorization, 74, 189–192, 217
    summary, 175, 204, 431
    U.N. debt repayment, 192–193
  parental consent, 67
Birth defects, 482
Biscayne Bay, 375
Biscayne National Park, 375
Bittman, Robert, 816
BJA. *See Justice Assistance, Bureau of*
Black Canyon of the Gunnison National Park, 381
Black Ridge Canyons Wilderness, 403–404
Blackwater National Wildlife Refuge, 363
Blair, Tony, 273, 308
Blankenship, Robert, 773
"Blanket primaries," 688
Bliley, Thomas J. Jr., R-Va.
  electric deregulation, 404–407
  electronic signatures, 335–336
  environmental protection
    Clean Air Act, 351
    superfund overhaul, 352–353, 396
    underground storage tanks, 370
  financial services modernization, 134
  health policy
    assisted suicide, 606
    child health bills, 482
    disabled workers' insurance, 470–471
    health policy research agency, 478
    medical malpractice, 482
    minority health programs, 485
    organ transplants, 475–476
    patients' rights, 468
    nuclear security, 306
Blinder, Alan S., 34 (box)
Block grants. *See also Community Development Block Grants*
  day-care services, 482
  education, 507, 509, 517, 519, 520, 527, 531–539
  teacher training, 511, 512

homeless programs, 561–562
juvenile crime prevention, 594, 595, 634
law enforcement, 654
  bulletproof vests, 599–600
  forensics labs, 657
public housing reform, 555–561
social services, 615
welfare reform, 486, 490
Blood
hemophiliacs with HIV, 459
Blue Cross/Blue Shield, 104
"Blue Dog" Democrats
budget resolution, FY 2000, 73
superfund overhaul, 396
tax cuts, 1997, 93
Blumenauer, Earl, D-Ore.
superfund overhaul, 397
Blumenthal, Sidney, 824
Blunt, Roy, R-Mo.
China trade agreement, 162 (box)
Boats and boating
coastal zone protection, 384
jetboats in Hells Canyon, 367
Minnesota wilderness, 367
Bobcats, 402
Body armor, 645
Boehlert, Sherwood, R-N.Y.
Antiquities Act, 366
education savings accounts, 546
endangered species, 351
energy research and development, 747
grazing fees, 357
national parks projects, 359
property rights, 738
superfund overhaul, 353, 396–398
Boehner, John A., R-Ohio
financial services modernization, 125
House leadership, 7 (box), 760, 769
  Gingrich coup attempt, 763 (box)
  McDermott ethics probe, 765, 774
patients' rights, 468–469
Title I education authorization, 534
Boeing 747 aircraft
laser weapons, 261
Boeing Corp.
F-15 procurement, 284, 288, 295, 296, 297, 300
F/A-18 procurement, 288, 294
helicopter upgrades, 282
Joint Strike Fighter, 290, 297
Osprey, 288
satellite launches, 180
space station, 743, 753
Boies, David, 25, 687 (box)
Bombs, 635
Bond, Christopher S., R-Mo.
Clean Air Act, 382
defense appropriations, 284, 296
gasoline additive MTBE, 391
human cloning, 460, 746
White nomination, 678
Bone density tests, 50
Bonilla, Henry, R-Texas
low-level nuclear waste, 360
Bonior, David E., D-Mich.
China trade agreement, 161, 162 (box), 164
congressional pay, 791
credit union expansion, 128
"dolphin-safe" tuna, 346
financial services modernization, 134
House leadership, 760, 769
secret evidence in deportation, 664
Bonneville Power Administration, 406
Bono (U2 band member), 176, 216
Bono, Mary, R-Calif.
California national monument, 403

election, 13
Salton Sea rehabilitation, 364
Bono, Sonny, R-Calif.
death, successor, 13
Salton Sea rehabilitation, 364
Bonobo protection, 379–380
Boone, Pat, 668
Boozman, Fay, 12
Border Patrol, U.S., 613
Borders. *See also Canada-U.S. border;
Mexico-U.S. border*
entry, exit monitoring, 675–676
Boren amendment, 50, 434, 436, 441–442
Bork, Robert H., 622–623, 818
Borski, Robert A., D-Pa.
water projects, 374
Bosnia
Kosovo refugees, 205
NATO expansion, 273
U.S. peacekeeping
  appropriations, 58, 62, 68, 69, 246–247, 249,
  250, 259, 260, 262, 298
  authorization, 240, 242, 243, 245, 252–257,
  277, 281
  congressional-executive relations, 198, 260
  summary, 174, 802
Boston, Mass., 772
Boundary Waters Act of 1978, 367
Boundary Waters Canoe Area Wilderness, 367
Bounty hunters, 599
Bowles, Erskine, 62, 63
Boxer, Barbara, D-Calif.
defense appropriations, 284, 298
ed-flex plan, 541
environmental protection
  Arctic wildlife refuge drilling, 413
  conservation lands acquisition, 377
  "dolphin-safe" tuna, 345–347
  forest health, 369
gun violence in schools, 545
partial-birth abortion, 456, 473
Strategic Petroleum Reserve, 409
Boy Scouts, 689
Boyd, Allen, D-Fla.
compensatory time, 576
Boyer, Amy, 82
Boyle, Mary O., 12
Boys and Girls Clubs of America, 595
Bradley, Bill, 22, 311
Bradley troop carriers, 248, 281
**Brady Handgun Violence Protection Act of
1993,** 635, 639–640, 685
Brady, James S., 638–639
Brady, Robert A., 14
Branch Davidians, 680–681
Brazil
financial crisis, 39, 147, 801
space station, 743
**Breast and Cervical Cancer Mortality
Prevention Act of 1990,** 472
Breast cancer
charity stamps, 751
mammogram coverage by Medicare, 45, 433,
435, 437, 441
Medicaid coverage, 431, 471–472
patients' rights, 467
reconstructive surgery, 454
research appropriations, 247, 289
Breaux, John B., D-La.
education savings accounts, 544
Landrieu election, 785
Medicare commission, 464–465
Medicare drug benefits, 465
Senate leadership, 760
Breyer, Stephen
abortion, 686

assisted suicide, 687
cable TV regulation, 688
Florida presidential vote, 26, 687 (box)
freedom of speech, 688
president's immunity in civil suits, 691
Supreme Court summary, 684, 689 (box)
Bribery
gratuities law ruling, 792 (box)
Bridges
penalties for blocking, 55
Bridgestone/Firestone Inc., 333
"Brilliant Pebbles," 307 (box)
Brokerages. *See Securities dealers*
Brooke Amendment, 555, 559
Brookings Institution, 663
Broward County, Fla., 25, 26 (box), 686 (box)
Brown, Corrine, D-Fla.
ethics probe, 765, 773
Brown, George E. Jr., D-Calif.
death, successor, 17
NSF authorization, 745
space station, 743
Brown, Jesse, 499 (box), 978 (box)
Brown, Lee P., 594 (box)
Brown, Marta Macias, 17
Brown, Ronald H.
Commerce leadership, 152 (box), 320 (box),
626, 978 (box)
DeLay ethics probe, 764
Brown, Sherrod, D-Ohio
children's health insurance, 435
Brownback, Sam, R-Kan.
congressional pay, 791
defense appropriations, 284
defense authorization, 256
federal-D.C. ties, 740
foreign aid appropriations, 187, 210
  Azerbaijan ban, 187 (box)
Browner, Carol
Clean Air Act, 351
clean water regulation, 383
electric deregulation, 404
EPA leadership, 344, 347 (box)
gasoline additive MTBE, 391
superfund overhaul, 353, 397, 398
Brownfields cleanup
summary, 345
superfund overhaul, 352, 354, 396–398
tax cuts, 1997, 100
Bryan, Richard H., D-Nev.
financial services modernization, 135
flag desecration, 668
nuclear waste storage, 361, 363
successor, 28
Bryant, Ed, R-Tenn.
civil assets forfeiture, 648
Justice Department authorization, 613
Buchanan, Patrick, 25, 27
Buddhists
campaign finance scandals, 778–779, 808
Budget Act of 1921, 44 (box)
Budget, Bureau of the, 44 (box)
Budget Committee, House
budget enforcement, 53
jurisdiction, leadership, 760, 958
Budget Committee, Senate
budget enforcement, 53
jurisdiction, leadership, 952
Budget, U.S. *See also Appropriations; Taxes*
budget process
  balanced budget amendment, 56–58
  budget law history (box), 44
  discretionary spending caps, 53
  enhanced rescissions, 64
  firewalls, 53
  line-item veto, 64–65

off-budget programs, 331–332
PAYGO rules, 48, 53–54, 77–78
reform proposals, 77–78
rules extension (box), 52
Senate procedures task force, 54
sequestration, 53
budget reconciliation
FY 1997, 48–56
budget resolution
FY 1998, 43–48
FY 1999, 60–61
FY 2000, 71–73
FY 2001, 79–81
5-year rule, 54
Gingrich coup attempt, 762 (box)
Clinton term summary, 4, 6, 11, 16–17, 19, 36,
    40–42, 43, 71, 798
debt limit, 51,54
debt reduction proposals
budget resolution, FY 1999, 60
budget resolution, FY 2000, 71–73
gasoline tax, 315, 319
90–10 plan, 86
Social Security surplus protection, 78–79
space station cuts, 754
surplus use, 85–86, 87, 88, 111
deficit, debt, 1980–2000 (graph), 41
deficit history, 1929–2000 (table), 36
deficit reduction, 51
budget resolution, FY 1998, 44
defense appropriations, FY 1998, 247
Republican goals, 49
glossary (box), 46
revenue, 51
offshore oil royalties, 375–379
radio spectrum auctions, 325–326
revenue, outlays, 1993–2000 (table), 41
surplus (box), 39
Bulgaria
U.S. military aid authorization, 230
Bulletproof vests, 599–600, 645
Bumpers, Dale L., D-Ark.
Clinton impeachment, 826
high-tech visas, 617
Minnesota wilderness, 367
Senate leadership, 760, 769
space station, 743–744
successor, 12
Bunning, Jim, R-Ky.
China-U.S. trade, 152
House ethics overhaul, 766
Senate election, 12
Bureau. *See other part of name*
Burns, Conrad, R-Mont.
asbestos compensation, 664
conservation lands acquisition, 378
NASA authorization, 752
Senate leadership, 759
Burr, Richard M., R-N.C.
electric deregulation, 405
Burton, Dan, R-Ind.
campaign finance reform, 779
ethics probe, 765
FALN clemency, 682
House leadership, 760
Puerto Rico status, 741
Bus transportation
safety, 331, 332–333
driver shift regulation, 84
Bush, George H.W.
abortion, 175, 177, 190, 211, 216, 217
Cabinet picks, 28
CIA headquarters name, 203
defense and foreign policy
antimissile defenses, 307 (box)
chemical weapons treaty, 268

China satellite launches, 181
China-U.S. trade, 153
defense spending, 235
Iraq confrontations, 197 (box)
Middle East, 802
Persian Gulf War, 174
Yugoslavia, 178, 802
economic conditions, 33
budgets, 40–41
policy leadership, 34 (box)
environmental policy, 342
African elephant conservation, 369
Third World debt forgiveness, 369
Iran-contra pardons, 808
judicial nominations, 623, 624, 680
presidential election, 2000, 23, 24
presidential library, 155
veto use, 811
voter guides ruling, 790 (box)
Bush, George W.
economic conditions, 33
Justice Department Kennedy building, 742
low-level nuclear waste, 360
nuclear test ban treaty, 311
presidential election, 2000, 21–27
acceptance speech (text), 1055–1056
China trade agreement, 160
environmental issues, 344
military deployments, 20
popular, electoral vote by region (table), 21
Social Security privatization, 583 (box)
summary, 4, 20
Supreme Court decision, 684, 686–687 (box)
tax policy, 89, 117
Texas gubernatorial election, 13
U.S. Kosovo policy, 208
Bush, Jeb
Florida gubernatorial election, 13
Florida presidential vote, 21
Bush, Laura, 23
Business and industry. *See also Business taxes;
Competition and monopoly; Employment and unemployment; Enterprise zones; Federal contractors; Foreign trade; Small business; Stocks, bonds,
and securities*
campaign finance reform, 780, 789
Clinton term summary, 315–317, 318
consumer privacy, 121
education issues
computer donations, 523
enterprise zones, 523
entrepreneurship education, 533
vocational education, 513, 514, 515
environmental issues
Clean Air Act, 351
superfund overhaul, 352
government-related ventures
federal lab licensing, 747
NASA projects, 753
NIST authorization, 745
Internet commerce
address registration, 746 (box)
electronic signatures, 335–336
Y2K liability, 330, 336
product liability, 322
religious expression, 660–661
Supreme Court decisions, 692–695, 715
Business Roundtable, 161
Business taxes
bankruptcy overhaul bill, 142–144
budget receipts, 1980–2000 (graph), 88
budget resolution, FY 2000, 72
capital gains, losses, 97, 102, 117
Clinton term summary, 15
corporate alternative minimum tax, 91–92,
    95, 98

credits
carry-back, -forward periods, 104–105
appropriations bill, 63
global warming remedies, 355
orphan drug development, 99
research and development, 99, 106, 111, 113
retirement accounts, 582
satellite launch industry, 304 (box)
welfare-to-work, 100
work opportunity, 99
deductions
brownfields cleanup, 100
meals, child education, 580
severance pay, 158
depreciation calculations, 104
economic development incentives, 82, 117
business enterprise zones, 99–100, 740
community development, 564–565
empowerment zones, 100
education
computer donations, 96, 523, 545
employee tuition aid, 544, 545
job training partnerships, 96
foreign income, 117, 118
incentives for energy producers, 409
Indian tribes, 92
inventory accounting, 100–101
involuntary property loss conversions, 104
minimum wage proposals, 579–580
percentage of GDP, 1935–2000 (table), 91
superfund overhaul, 352, 396, 397
Supreme Court decisions, 694–695
tax cuts, 1997, 90–105
unrelated business income, 105
Butler, Richard, 196
"Butterfly" ballots, 25, 27 (box)
"Buy American" concept, 149
Buyer, Steve, R-Ind.
affirmative action, 615–616
Army sexual harassment, 275
defense authorization, 242, 278, 291, 293
religious expression, 612
Byrd, Robert C., D-W.Va.
antidumping fee redirection, 83
Central American refugees, 619
China trade agreement, 164
Clinton impeachment, 823
comments (text), 1018
defense
appropriations, 260
authorization, 256
Kosovo operations, 208, 301
nuclear lab security, 412–413
nuclear test ban treaty, 311
flag desecration, 668
global warming treaty, 355
law enforcement
crime victims' rights, 669
hate crimes, 643
juvenile crime, 635
line-item veto, 64, 252 (box)
partial-birth abortion, 456
steel industry loans, 77
surface transportation authorization, 319
Byrd rule, 52, 78, 111
Byrne grants, 603–604, 644

C

C-17 cargo aircraft
appropriations, 246, 247, 249, 262, 288, 300
authorization, 245, 258
C-130 cargo aircraft
appropriations, 247, 248, 259, 260, 288, 300
artillery, 281, 288

authorization, 257, 258, 282, 295
tanker version, 284
Cabinet
agriculture leadership, 420 (box)
Clinton appointments (profiles), 977–993
commerce, transportation, small business leadership, 320 (box)
defense policy leadership, 241 (box)
economic leadership, 34–35 (box)
education leadership, 510 (box)
energy, environmental policy leadership, 347 (box)
foreign policy leadership, 179 (box)
health leadership, 435 (box)
housing leadership, 556 (box)
labor leadership, 575 (box)
law enforcement leadership, 594 (box)
trade leadership, 152 (box)
Cable television
Clinton term summary, 317
"must carry" local stations, 689
rate regulation, 331
ratings system, 327
retransmission fees, 329
rural area coverage, 338
satellite TV, 75, 338
sexually explicit programming, 688
Supreme Court decisions, 689
CAFE. *See Corporate average fuel economy standards*
Calderon, Sila, 30
CALFED, 374
California
Air Force maintenance depot, 239–240, 241, 242, 245
bankruptcy judges, 608
bilingual education, 516–518
"blanket primaries," 688
child support enforcement, 495
congressional elections, 13, 17, 29
environmental issues
conservation lands acquisition, 376, 377
national forest logging, 67, 368–369, 399–400
national monuments, 389, 390, 403
northern spotted owl, 392
Otay Mountain wilderness, 401
Sequoia National Park, 401–402
vehicle emissions, 365
gubernatorial election, 11, 13
illegal immigrants, 671
Internet alcohol sales, 337
mortgage insurance, 563
Proposition 209, 511, 624, 626
school vouchers, 30
term limits (box), 783
water resources
coastal water quality, 380
fish screens, 395
gasoline additive MTBE, 390–391
groundwater restoration, 383
Lake Tahoe restoration, 402–403
Salton Sea rehabilitation, 364–365
water projects, 373, 374, 381–382
welfare benefits, 619, 688
Calista Native Regional Corporation, 367
Callahan, Sonny, R-Ala.
foreign aid appropriations, 211–212
Middle East summit, 190 (box)
Caloosahatchee estuary, 375
Calvert, Ken, R-Calif.
campaign finance reform, 782, 788
energy research and development, 746
NOAA authorization, 745
Cambodia
U.S. aid appropriations, 186
Camp David. *See Middle East peace process*

Camp Dawson, W.Va., 253 (box)
Camp Williams, Utah, 252 (box)
Campaign finance
Chinese contributions, 152, 153
investigations, 180, 181–182
Clinton scandals, 807–808
Rich pardon, 808
ethics probes
Barr, 774
DeLay, 764, 773
Hilliard, 772–773
Kim, 764
Shuster, 771
FEC term limits, 68
527 PACs, 293, 786–787
presidential election, 2000, 25
reform action
1997–1998, 776–783
1999–2000, 788–790
flag desecration amendment, 668
highway bill, 319
summary, 11, 15–16, 19–20
Senate, House investigations (box), 778–779
Supreme Court decisions, 684, 688, 708
texts, 1032–1035
Campbell, Ben Nighthorse, R-Colo.
bulletproof vests, 599
compensatory time, 577
ethics probe, 770–771
new national parks, 381
school resource officers, 530
Senate leadership, 759
union "salting," 575
Campbell, Tom, R-Calif.
Bosnia war powers test, 198
Kosovo policy, 206
physician antitrust, 480–481
State Department authorization, 218
Canada
Barshefsky nomination, 152 (box)
bird population control, 384
space station, 743
U.S. ambassador, 30
U.S. trade
air, ship passenger fees, 154
drug reimports, 484
export controls, 229
Canada-U.S. border area
highway projects, 319
Minnesota wilderness, 367
security controls, 676
vehicle emissions, 365
Canady, Charles T., R-Fla.
abortion, 457
affirmative action, 615–616
assisted suicide, 607, 658–659
electronic information access, 656
flag desecration, 667
judicial activism, 591, 622
religious expression, 612, 660
sex trafficking, 630
Cancer. *See also Breast cancer; Carcinogens; Cervical cancer; Prostate cancer*
asbestos compensation, 664–666
chemotherapy drugs, 465
colorectal screenings, 45, 433, 437, 441, 463
gasoline additive MTBE, 390
Canfield, William B. III, 784
Cannon, Christopher B., R-Utah
asbestos compensation, 666
San Rafael Swell, 402
Cantwell, Maria, D-Wash.
Senate election, 28
Capital gains taxes
budget reconciliation, 1997, 48, 49
business installment sales, 117

business property in enterprise zones, 100
community development initiatives, 564
extraordinary dividends, 103
holding period, 107, 108, 109
primary residence exclusion, 91, 97
rate changes, 90–91, 92, 94, 95, 97, 110, 112
short sales, 102
small business rollover, 97
tax cuts, 1997, 87, 89, 90–94
Capital Management Services, 805 (box)
Capital punishment. *See Death penalty*
Capitol Police
appropriations, 69
Capitol shootings, 455
Capitol, U.S.
security appropriations, 69
volunteer tour guides, 616
Capps, Lois D., 13
Capps, Walter, D-Calif.
death, successor, 13
Capuano, Michael E., D-Mass.
home ownership aid, 566
CARA. *See Conservation and Reinvestment Act*
Carbon dioxide emissions, 354–356
Cardiac Arrest Survival Act, 481
Cardin, Benjamin, D-Md.
China trade agreement, 163
estate taxes, 116
Medicare payments, 461
pension changes, 582
Carey, Ron, 578 (box)
Caribbean Basin Initiative, 156, 158
Caribbean countries
hurricane disaster relief, 77
U.S. trade, 16
air, ship passenger fees, 154
tariffs, 149, 156, 157–158, 160, 167–168
U.S. visas, 677
Carl D. Perkins Vocational and Applied Technology Education Act of 1990, 513
Carl D. Perkins Vocational and Technical Education Act of 1998, 543
Carl Mullican Communications, 784
Carnahan, Jean, 28
Carnahan, Mel, 28
Carnivore surveillance system, 337
Carper, Thomas R., 28
Carter, Jimmy
budget policy, 40
China trade agreement, 151, 161
veto use, 811
Caspian Sea region
foreign aid appropriations, 210
Cassell, Paul, 689
Cassidy, Butch, 402
Castle, Michael N., R-Del.
education
block grants, 527
ed-flex plan, 539
education research academy, 549
hate crimes prevention, 536
Straight A's funding flexibility, 535
teacher training, 533
Export-Import Bank, 157
527 PACs, 787
food assistance programs, 495
public housing reform, 556
Castro, Fidel
Elián González case, 225 (box)
U.S. trade with Cuba
economic sanctions, 224, 225
food sales, 418, 424, 426
travel restrictions, 211
Cat Island, La., 402
Caterpillar Inc., 118
Catfish, 384

Caucasus region
"Silk Road" trade, 169
Cellular telephones
criminal investigations, 656
fraudulent cloning, 329
Celucci, Paul, 30
Cemex, 764
Censure
impeachment alternative, 820, 822, 827
Census Act Amendments of 1976, 748 (box), 691
Census Bureau, 63, 66, 74, 736–737, 748 (box)
Census sampling issue
appropriations, 59, 63, 66, 74
legislative action, 736–737, 748–749
summary, 733–734
Supreme Court case, 690, 691, 710–711, 748 (box)
Center for Marine Conservation, 346
Center for New Black Leadership, 625
Center for Patient Study, 478
Center for Strategic and International Studies, 309
Centers for Disease Control and Prevention (CDC)
asbestos compensation, 666
breast, cervical cancer screenings, 431, 472
food labeling, 444, 445, 452
lab modernization, 481
prostate cancer detection, 481
Central American countries
immigrants, refugees in U.S., 619–620, 671–673
U.S. aid
disaster relief, 77, 189
military training, 211
U.S. tariffs, 149, 156, 157–158, 160, 167–168
Central Intelligence Agency (CIA)
authorizations, 200–202, 226–228
missile technology transfer, 153, 181
Jeremiah panel report, 262
leadership, 179 (box), 799
Deutch pardon, 808
terrorism countermeasures, 309
Wye River accords, 190 (box)
Central Oregon Resource Area, 403
Central Valley Water Project, 381–382
Cervical cancer
condom warning labels, 472
Medicaid, Medicare coverage
Pap test screening, 433, 437, 441, 462
treatment, 431, 441, 462, 471–472
CFE. *See Conventional Forces in Europe Treaty*
CFTC. *See Commodity Futures Trading Commission*
Chabot, Steve, R-Ohio
concealed weapons, 598
judicial activism, 622
violence against women, 630
Chabrow, Jay W., 743
Chad, 25
Chafee, John H., R-R.I.
death, successor, 17, 470, 472
education savings accounts, 544
environmental protection
Clean Air Act, 351, 382
coastal barrier resources, 383
endangered species, 385
superfund overhaul, 397
flag desecration, 667
foster children
adoption, 494
post-care aid, 496
health policy
breast, cervical cancer, 472
medical savings accounts, 467
Medicare changes, 435–436, 437
patients' rights, 468

Chafee, Lincoln R-R.I.
minimum wage, 580
patients' rights, 470
Senate election, 17
Challenger **space shuttle,** 180
Chamber of Commerce of the United States
China trade agreement, 161
education block grants, 527
high-tech visas, 618
Paez nomination, 679–680
superfund overhaul, 398
Chaplains
House of Representatives, 775
Charities and nonprofit organizations
debt limits, 96–97, 523
drug-free workplace programs, 602
federal grants/election role, 761, 773
527 PACs, 786–787
gifts to severely ill children, 491
Head Start preference, 492
jobs for older Americans, 496
mileage deductions, 98
missing adults, children, 656–657
nonimmigrant visas, 619
prison labor, 603
semipostal stamps, 751
stock donations, 99, 106
tax-exemption appeal for commercial
insurance, 104
violence against women, 631
volunteer liability shield, 615
Charlotte, N.C., 613
Charter schools, 525–526, 799
Chechnya
Clinton term summary, 175
U.S. aid to Russia, 216, 222, 223
Cheese. *See Milk and dairy products*
Chemical Manufacturers Association, 268
Chemical weapons. *See also Chemical Weapons Convention*
antimissile defenses, 267
Iraq policy, 196–198
long-term defense planning, 264
Russia disposal aid, 282, 286, 291, 292, 295, 299
terrorism countermeasures, 267, 308–309
Chemical Weapons Convention of 1993
Senate approval, 62, 69, 177, 239, 268–272
foreign policy agencies reorganization, 193
Russia sanctions, 195
"understandings," 271
summary (box), 269
Chemicals and chemical industry
chemical weapons treaty, 268
China trade agreement, 161
superfund overhaul, 396–397
Cheney, Richard
chemical weapons treaty, 269
vice presidential election, 2000, 21–22, 23
Chenoweth, Helen, R-Idaho
American Heritage Rivers, 370
Antiquities Act, 366
conservation lands acquisition, 377
migratory birds, 389
Minnesota wilderness, 367
national forests, 387–388
northern spotted owl, 392
NSF authorization, 744–745
U.N. lands designation, 401
Chesapeake Bay, 386–387
Chicago Board of Trade, 141
Chicago, Ill.
airports, 67, 321, 332
Chicago Mercantile Exchange, 141
Child abuse. *See also Child pornography; Child sexual abuse*
foster child adoption, 6, 494

juvenile crime prevention, 595
prevention, treatment programs, 646–647
violence against women, 630–631, 632
volunteer liability, 615
Child care
after-school programs, 528
budget resolution, FY 1999, 60
day-care services grants, 482
for-profit Head Start providers, 491–493
low-income student aid, 513
military posts, 250, 251, 301
welfare-to-work needs, 491
Child care tax credit, 60, 72, 110
Child custody and visitation
grandparents' rights, 688, 710
Child Custody Protection Act, 431, 455, 456–457
Child health and safety. *See also Child abuse; Children's Health Insurance Program; Child nutrition programs; Disabled children*
Amish work exceptions, 584–585
Clean Air Act, 351
crime
prevention, 530
school transfers, 534
witness to violence, 482
drug abuse prevention, 602
foreign development aid, 186, 188, 214
foster child adoption, 493
gun safety locks, 594, 595, 637–642
HIV-testing for newborns, 483
pediatric drug studies, 444, 447–448
pediatrics training, 478
research, 482–483
tax cuts, 1997, 93, 94, 95
unintentional injury, 482
Child labor
Caribbean trade, 158
China-U.S. trade, 256
Export-Import Bank, 157
Child nutrition programs
after-school snacks, 431, 494
school breakfast/lunch program, 471, 494–495
summer meals, 494
WIC program, 431, 494–495
Child pornography
Internet distribution, 329
online reporting, 657
wiretaps, 646
Child sexual abuse. *See also Child pornography*
deportation, 676
DNA evidence, 655
mandatory sentences, 647
missing children, 657
offender registries, 603–604
prematurely released offenders, 631–632
sex trafficking, 590, 629–630
wiretaps on offenders, 646
Child support
bank privacy rules, 132, 137
IRS access to HHS registry, 103
state enforcement programs, 495
Supreme Court decisions, 710
violence against women, 632
Child tax credit
budget reconciliation, 1997, 48, 49
tax cuts, 1997, 87, 90, 92–94, 95–96
tax cuts, 1999, 111
Child welfare
child abuse prevention, 647
foster care, 493–495
post-care aid, 496
gifts to severely ill children, 491
immigrant food stamp benefits, 421
poverty report, 545
Child Welfare Act of 1980, 493

Children. *See also Adolescents and youth; Adoption; Child health and safety; Child labor; Child support; Child welfare; Elementary and secondary education; Family issues; Foster care; Juvenile crime; Parental rights and issues*
  AIDS orphan assistance, 230
  citizenship if born abroad, 619
  Internet data collection, 68
    pornography access, 68, 82
  orphaned immigrant siblings, 673
  sexual materials access
    Internet, 68, 82, 329, 684, 688
    television ratings, 327
Children's Defense Fund, 597, 637
Children's Health Insurance Program (CHIP)
  abortion ban, 458–459
  budget reconciliation, 1997, 48, 49, 50–51
  budget resolution, FY 1998, 43, 45, 48
  community development initiatives, 565
  Medicaid, Medicare changes, 117, 432, 433, 436–437, 438, 442–443
    givebacks bill, 462, 463, 464
  summary, 6, 429
Children's hospitals, 478
Children's Welfare League of America, 637
Chile
  NASA Origins project, 742
Chimpanzee protection, 379–380
China
  arms control
    antimissile defenses, 182, 308
    chemical weapons treaty, 270
    Cox report, 302, 304 (box)
    missile technology from Canada, 229
    missile technology from Russia, 157, 222, 223, 242
    missile technology from satellite launches, 180–182, 254–255, 277
    missile technology to Iran, 180, 181, 182
    missile technology to Pakistan, 153, 164, 180, 181, 182
    nuclear espionage, 166, 208, 226, 276, 279, 282, 292, 302, 303 (box), 304 (box), 410, 411
    reporting requirement, 282
    sanctions proposed in trade bill, 164–165, 209
  economic conditions, 39
  global warming treaty, 354
  Hong Kong reversion, 152–153
  human rights issues, 162 (box), 165, 182–183, 208, 209
  population control programs
    foreign aid appropriations, 184, 186, 188, 210, 214, 217
    State Department authorization, 191, 218, 219
  U.S. relations, 180–183, 208–210
    Belgrade embassy bombing, 166, 209, 226
    campaign finance scandals, 152, 180, 181–182, 808
    Clinton term summary, 173, 174–175, 177
    intelligence activities monitoring, 201
    Jiang, Clinton state visits, 153, 182, 183, 183 (box), 254, 256
    military visit limits, 279, 282
    Taiwan support, 182, 183, 209–210
    visa denials, 182, 183, 260
  U.S. trade, 151–153, 160–166
    China Army companies, 182, 256
    clean coal technology, 164, 746
    computer restrictions, 243, 304 (box)
    Export-Import Bank preferences, 157
    Hong Kong ties, 158
    news broadcasts, 163, 166, 182
    prison labor, 157, 165, 182, 209
    "safeguards," 162 (box)

    satellite launches, 166, 180–182, 209, 254, 255, 256, 277, 279, 282, 302, 304 (box), 752
    "Silk Road" trade, 169
    status, 6, 19, 20, 147, 151, 184, 204, 209
    summary, 148–149, 166, 174, 800–801
    WTO membership, 160
China Investigation Committee, House, 958
Chincoteague National Wildlife Refuge, 348
Chinook helicopters, 282
CHIP. *See Children's Health Insurance Program*
Chippewa Indians, 779
Chirac, Jacques, 273
Chiropractic services, 440
Christensen, John W., R-Neb.
  appropriations, FY 1999, 63
Christian Coalition
  education savings accounts, 518
  marriage income tax penalty, 111
  religious expression, 611
  voter guides ruling, 790 (box)
Christopher, Warren M., 25, 179 (box), 193, 978 (box)
Chugach Alaska Corp., 379
Chugach National Forest, 379
Chung, Johnny, 181–182
Church-state separation
  community development block grants, 566–567
  literacy programs, 535
  parochial school aid, 689
  religious expression, 611–612
  Supreme Court decisions, 688, 689, 714–715
  Ten Commandments display, 636
Churches and religious organizations. *See also Private and parochial schools*
  AIDS assistance, 230
  Amish work exceptions, 584–585
  China trade agreement, 161
  community development, 564–565, 566–567
  community services block grants, 491, 492
  globalization opposition, 148
  health plan conscience exemptions, 68, 442, 458
  House chaplain, 775
  literacy programs, 535
  Supreme Court decisions, 685
  visas for religious workers, 675
  zoning enforcement, 591, 660–661
CIA. *See Central Intelligence Agency*
Cigarette and tobacco taxes
  budget reconciliation, 1997, 48, 49, 50
  budget resolution, FY 1998, 48
  budget resolution, FY 2000, 72
  budget resolution, FY 2001, 80
  children's health insurance, 318, 433, 436, 438, 442
  tax cuts, 1997, 93, 94, 95
  tobacco settlement, 323
Circuit courts. *See Appeals courts, U.S.*
Cisneros, Henry G., 554, 556 (box), 809, 978 (box)
Citizens Flag Alliance, 611, 667
Citizens for Independent Courts, 678
Citizens Progressive Alliance, 770–771
Citizenship
  children born abroad, 618
  disabled applicants, 676
  investors in U.S. companies, 617
  Puerto Rico status, 740–741
  Supreme Court decisions, 716
  verification for voter registration, 780, 782
Civil Justice Reform Act of 1990, 608
Civil Rights Act of 1957, 608
Civil Rights Act of 1964, 536
Civil rights and liberties. *See also Discrimination; First Amendment*
  China trade agreement, 165
  crime victims' rights, 609

    Lee nomination, 624–627
    roving wiretaps, 202
    Supreme Court decisions, 684, 686–689
Civil Rights Commission Amendments Act of 1994, 608
Civil Rights Commission, U.S., 608–609
Civil service. *See Federal employees*
Civil Service Retirement System, 56
Clark County, Nev., 401
Clark, Russell, 621
Clark, Vernon A., 772
Clark, Wesley K., 241 (box)
Clarke, Richard A., 308
Class action suits, 696
Clay, William L., D-Mo.
  education
    ed-flex plan, 541
    federal funds shifting, 536
    student loans, 511, 526
    Title I authorization, 534
  juvenile crime, 597
Clean Air Act of 1970
  action, 1999–2000, 382
  gasoline additive MTBE, 390
  regulations implementation, 342, 351
  vehicle emissions, 365
Clean coal technology, 164, 409, 746, 750
Clean Lakes Program, 383
Clean water act, 341, 342, 372, 382–383, 799
Clean Water Action Plan, 66
Cleland, Max, D-Ga.
  balanced budget amendment, 57
  defense authorization, 256
  defense leadership, 241 (box)
  gun control, 640
Clemency
  Puerto Rican FALN activists, 669, 681–683
Clementine program, 249
Cleveland, Grover, 22
Clinger, William F., 760
Clinical Pharmacology Training Program, 449
Clinical Research Enhancement Act, 481
Clinton, Bill. *See also Clinton impeachment*
  abortion
    Mexico City policy, 195, 211, 217, 457–458, 473–474
    parental consent circumvention, 457, 474
    partial-birth procedure, 455–456, 472
    summary, 430–431, 455
  agriculture policy, 419
  budget policy
    appropriations, 58–60, 62–70, 73–75, 81–84
    budget reconciliation, 1997, 48–50
    budget resolutions, 43–47, 60–61, 71–72, 79–80
    debt reduction, 85
    Gingrich coup attempt, 762 (box)
    summary, 36, 40–42, 43, 71
  business policy
    product liability, 322
    tobacco settlement, 323
  census sampling, 736–737
  community development, 564–565
  congressional relations
    campaign finance reform, 776–779
    line-item veto, 64–65, 251, 811
    summary, 3–5, 6–8, 10–11, 15–17, 19–20, 809–812
    veto use (box), 810–811
    vetoes, 1997–2001 (list), 994–995
  defense policy
    antimissile defenses, 235, 238, 265–267, 276, 294, 306–308
    appropriations, 245–248, 259–261, 283–285, 296–300
    chemical weapons treaty, 268–270

defense authorizations, 239–243, 252–257, 276–280, 290–296
F-22 funding, 286 (box)
land mine treaty, 274
military construction, 251, 252 (box), 289–290, 300–301
NATO expansion, 272–273
nuclear security, 302, 306
nuclear test ban treaty, 310–311
summary, 235–238, 239, 276
terrorism, 267
domestic policy summary, 798–799
economic policy summary, 33–39, 798
education policy
bilingual education, 517
block grants, 527
charter schools, 525
class-size reduction, 543–544
ed-flex plan, 539, 540
education savings accounts, 518–520, 544–545
ESEA authorization, 531–533, 538
literacy programs, 529
national testing, 523–525
school construction bonds, 544
school vouchers, 528–529
student loan consolidation, 526
summary, 507–508, 509
tax incentives, 520–522
elections and politics
Clinton-Lazio race, 471, 808
congressional candidates, 29
presidential election, 1996, 21
presidential election, 2000, 23–24
energy policy
energy supplies, 409–410
nuclear lab security, 410–411
Strategic Petroleum Reserve, 409
summary, 341, 344
environmental policy
Alaska development, 379
American Heritage Rivers, 370
Arctic refuge drilling, 413
clean water regulation, 382
conservation lands acquisition, 376, 378
coral reef protection, 393
"dolphin-safe" tuna, 346
forest logging roads, 394–395
global warming treaty, 354–355
grazing fees, 357
Minnesota wilderness, 367
national monument designation, 365–366, 389–390
northern spotted owl, 392
nuclear waste storage, 362, 407–409
summary, 341–344, 345
federal-D.C. ties, 740
federal Y2K fix, 330
flag desecration, 667
financial services regulation
banking modernization, 132, 133
bankruptcy law revision, 121, 142, 144
credit union expansion, 128
securities fraud lawsuits, 128–129
summary, 120–121, 130
foreign policy
Armenia resolution, 231
Bosnia, 198
China, 180–183, 208–210
Colombian antidrug aid, 220
economic sanctions, 200, 223–225
Elián González case, 225 (box)
federal agencies reorganization, 193–194
foreign aid appropriations, 184, 185, 186–189, 210–213, 214–216
IMF dues, 194

intelligence authorizations, 200–201, 226–228
Iraq, 196–198
Kosovo, 177–180, 204–208
Mexico antidrug certification, 203
Middle East summits, 190 (box), 216 (box)
Peace Corps, 230
Russia sanctions, 195–196
sanctions for religious persecution, 199
State Department authorization, 189–192, 217–218
summary, 173–177, 204, 800–803
U.N. debt repayment, 220
health policy
assisted suicide, 459
breast, cervical cancer, 472
budget surplus for Medicare, 464
disabled worker's insurance, 431, 470–471
human cloning, 460
medical privacy, 480
Medicare drug benefits, 465
Medicare, Medicaid payments, 430, 433, 434, 462–464
organ transplants, 476
patients' rights, 430, 454, 467, 468
summary, 429
immigration, 619, 672
judicial activism, 622
labor policy
minimum wage, 579, 580
summary, 571–572
union "salting," 576
law enforcement
civil assets forfeiture, 647
clemency for Puerto Ricans, 669, 681–683
gun control, 638–639, 641, 642
hate crimes, 643, 644
juvenile crime, 593–594, 595, 597, 637
racial profiling, 652
summary, 589–593
violence against women, 631
nominations and appointments, 592, 799–800
Cabinet, key posts (profiles), 977–983
controversial nominations, 985–993
judicial nominations, 622–624, 627–628, 629, 677–680
Lee nomination, 624–627
recess appointments, 680
scandals and pardons, 804–809
campaign finance, 807–808
FBI files use, 805 (box)
Jones harassment suit, 684, 690, 691, 805–807
pardons, 808–809
White House Travel Office firings, 805 (box)
Whitewater, 804–805
Social Security, 582–583 (box)
space programs
Glenn in space, 742 (box)
NASA authorization, 742–743
private space shuttles, 744
satellite launches, 752
space station, 744
summary, 735
speeches (text), 999–1017
tax policy
catchall package, 2000, 117
estate taxes, 115–117
IRS overhaul, 106
marriage status, 113–115
Republican plans, 105–106, 110
summary, 87–89, 90, 110
tax cuts, 1997, 90, 93–94
trade policy
African initiative, 167–168
China status, agreement, 151–153, 160–165, 166
fast-track procedures, 153–156

leadership, 152 (box)
steel import quotas, 169–170
summary, 147–150, 151
Vietnam status, 158–159, 167
transportation, 319
veterans' disability claims, 498
welfare policy
foster child adoption, 493
Head Start, 491
immigrant food stamp benefits, 421
summary, 431, 486
welfare law revisions, 486–488
Clinton, Hillary Rodham
campaign finance issues, 779, 788
Clinton impeachment, 815, 823
FALN clemency, 681
Glenn in space, 742 (box)
Senate election, 28, 471, 806–807 (box)
Rich campaign donations, 808
travel office firings, 805 (box)
Whitewater scandal, 804–805, 813, 827
Clinton impeachment
articles of impeachment
summaries (box), 821
text, 1020–1021
background, 804
censure alternative, 820, 822, 827
Democratic senators' comments (text), 1017–1018
House actions, 758, 818–823
Iraq air strikes, 173, 780, 822 (box)
Jones harassment suit, 691, 813–816
legislative effects
appropriations, 62
budget resolution, FY 1999, 61
ed-flex bill markup, 540
fast track for trade pacts, 156
independent counsel law, 663
summary, 15
tax policy, 88, 110
transportation, commerce agenda, 318
political effects
House elections, 13, 28, 29
presidential election, 2000, 24
postverdict developments, 827
Senate trial, 823–827
Starr report, 816–818
excerpts (text), 1018–1021
summary, 3, 4, 10, 813
Clinton, Roger, 809
Cloning, 459–460, 745–746
Clothing
tariffs, 149, 157–158, 160
African trade initiative, 168
Cloture
Senate cloture votes, 1917–2000 (list), 967–971
Clyburn, James E., D-S.C.
ed-flex plan, 541
Coal
clean-coal technology, 164, 409, 746, 750
federal leases, 413–414
global warming treaty, 355
Coalition to Preserve Religious Liberty, 612
Coalitions for America, 792
Coast Guard, U.S.
appropriations, 85, 263, 302
terrorism countermeasures, 605
Coastal areas
beached marine mammals, 380–381
development restrictions, 383–384
estuary restoration, 386
marine sanctuaries, 388
NOAA authorization, 745
ocean policy panel, 364, 392
offshore oil revenue, 376–378
water quality, 372, 375, 380

Coastal Barrier Resources Act, 383
Coastal Barrier Resources System, 383
Coastal Zone Management Act, 383–384
Coats, Daniel R., R-Ind.
  charter schools, 525
  defense authorization, 243
  education savings accounts, 520
  FDA overhaul, 447
  successor, 12
Coburn, Tom, R-Okla.
  AIDS programs, 483
  breast, cervical cancer, 471–472
  drug reimports, 484
  fetal tissue regulation, 482
  Medicare changes, 434
  NSF authorization, 744
  patients' rights, 468–469
  physician antitrust, 481
Cocaine
  Colombia antidrug aid, 221
  drug czar targets, 603
Cochran, Thad, R-Miss.
  antimissile defenses, 307
  arts education award, 547
  defense appropriations, 297
  defense authorization, 243
  drug reimports, 484
  Senate leadership, 759
Cod fishing, 82
Cohen, William S.
  antimissile defenses, 307
  antiterrorist air strikes, 267
  defense cost-cutting plan, 264, 265
  defense leadership, 235, 240, 241 (box), 978
    (box), 979
  F-22 funding, 286–287 (box)
  military base closings, 253–254, 277
  military base jobs privatization, 261
  NATO expansion, 273
  Quadrennial Defense Review, 264
  satellite launches, 752
  Senate leadership, 760
  sex-integrated military training, 253
  U.S. Bosnia policy, 260
Coins
  commemorative state quarters, 129
  dollar coin, 129
U.S.S. Cole, 217, 293, 309, 803, 807 (box)
Cole, James M., 761, 774
Coleman, Norm, 13
Colleges and universities. *See also Student aid*
  affirmative action, 616, 511
  alcohol abuse prevention, 513
  clinical pharmacology training, 449
  crime
    juvenile records access, 637
    missing persons investigations, 547
    prevention, 513
    sex offender registries, 547
  debt limits, 96–97
  FAA research grants, 321
  federal outlays, 1987–2001 (graph), 508
  fire protection, 547
  foreign students, 309
  high-tech visas, 670
  historic preservation at women's colleges, 547
  merchandise licensing codes, 511
  methane research, 389
  NASA grants, 752
    minority program, 742
  national parks resource research, 359
  sports programs, 511
  student organization fees, 689
  teacher training, 545
Collins, Barbara-Rose, 766
Collins, Cardiss, 760

Collins, Susan, R-Maine
  false IDs, 657
  patients' rights, 467
  teachers' tax breaks, 545
Colombia
  antidrug initiative, 20, 84–85, 173, 176, 204,
    215, 219, 220–221, 300, 301
  U.S. aid appropriations, 211
  U.S. troop limits, 291
Colorado
  conservation areas, 403–404
  gun show background checks, 30
  initiative petitions, 688
  national parks, monuments, 372, 381, 390
  term limits, 784
Colorado Canyons National Conservation Area,
  403–404
Colorado River
  salinity control, 402
  Salton Sea rehabilitation, 365
Colorectal cancer screening, 45, 433, 437, 441,
  463
**Columbia Basin Ecosystem Management
Plan,** 67
Columbia River, 67, 395
Columbia University, 85
Columbine High School. *See Littleton, Colo.,
school shootings*
Comanche helicopters
  appropriations, 248, 261, 287
  authorization, 244, 258, 281
Combest, Larry, R-Texas
  House leadership, 760, 770
  watershed dams, 385
Combined DNA Index System, 655
Commerce Committee, House
  jurisdiction, leadership, 746–747, 958–959
Commerce Department, U.S.
  appropriations, 63, 73, 74, 82
  census sampling, 736
  China trade agreement, 161, 162, 165
  "dolphin-safe" tuna, 346, 348
  export controls, 167, 180, 181
    encryption technology, 336
    satellite launches, 254, 256–257, 259, 302
    supercomputers, 242, 245
  leadership, 152 (box), 320 (box)
  patent overhaul, 324
  sea lion protection, 393
  space launches, 754
**Commerce, Science and Transportation
Committee, Senate**
  jurisdiction, leadership, 759, 952–953
Commercial Space Transportation, Office of,
  754
Commission on Civil Rights, U.S., 608–609
Commission on Ocean Policy, 392
**Commission on Protecting and Reducing
Government Secrecy,** 201
Commodities Exchange Act of 1936, 120, 130,
  141
Commodity Credit Corporation, 219
Commodity Futures Modernization Act,
  141–142
Commodity Futures Trading Commission, 82,
  141–142
Common Cause, 663
Commonwealth Party (Puerto Rico), 741
Communications. *See also Telecommunications*
  Clinton term summary, 316–317
  electromagnetic pulse vulnerability, 295
  Navy, Marine systems privatization, 296
Communications Decency Act of 1996, 688
Communism and communist countries
  China trade agreement, 160–166
  collapse effects on trade, 147

  U.S. trade limits, 149, 151, 158
  sanctions reform, 169
Community-action groups
  drug control grants, 602
Community colleges
  vocational education, 513, 514
Community development
  budget outlays, 1987–2001 (graph), 554
  initiatives, 564–565
Community Development Block Grants
  home ownership aid, 566
  public housing reform, 556, 558
**Community Oriented Policing Services (COPS)
program**
  appropriations, 74
  community services grants, 491
  law enforcement grants, 654
  school resource officers, 530
**Community Partnership Against Crime
program,** 556
Community Reinvestment Act of 1977, 122, 123,
  126, 128, 130–136
Community service
  jobs for older Americans, 496
  public housing tenants, 555–560
  welfare-to-work grants, 489
Community Services Block Grant programs,
  486, 491–493
Competition and monopoly. *See also
Antitrust law*
  airlines, 332
  electric deregulation, 404–407
  Medicare bidding, 441
  prison industries, 652–653
  satellite TV, 329, 338
  telecommunications "slamming," 330
Competitiveness
  high-tech export controls, 167
    encryption technology, 326
  ocean shipping, 321–322
  patent system overhaul, 334
  space launches, 754
**Comprehensive Environmental Response,
Compensation, and Liability Act.** *See Superfund*
Comprehensive Test Ban Treaty
  foreign aid appropriations, 187, 210
  provisions (box), 311
  Senate rejection, 310–311
  summary, 16, 173, 204, 276, 803
  underground stockpiles destruction, 295
Comptroller of the Currency, Office of the, 122,
  123 (box), 139
Computers. *See also Internet; Year 2000 (Y2K)
computer problem*
  cyber-crimes, 656
  education savings account use, 518, 519, 520,
    544
  federal upgrades, 62
    Defense Department, 259
  foreign trade, 147
    China trade agreement, 161
    export controls, 166, 242, 243, 245, 304 (box)
    software sales, 101
  high-tech visas, 616–619
  school programs
    classroom use, 536
    computer literacy, 538
    donations, 96, 523, 545
    loans to religious schools, 689
    training, 671
  software copyright, 15, 316, 331, 334
  terrorism countermeasures, 267, 605
Conflict diamonds, 82
Confrontation of accusers, 699
Congo
  U.S. trade exclusion, 168

Congress, members of. *See also Congressional elections; Congressional ethics; Congressional pay; Term limits*
 African Americans, 1947–2000 (table), 29
 age structure of Congress, 1949–2001 (table), 17
 drug-testing policy, 761
 Hispanics, 1947–2001 (table), 30
 list, 1997–2001, 942–950
 women, 1947–2001 (table), 28
Congress, U.S. *See also Congress, members of; Congressional committees; Congressional districts; Congressional employees; Congressional-executive relations; Congressional votes; House of Representatives, U.S.; Legislative process; Senate, U.S.*
 leadership, 1997–2000 (table), 7
 legislative branch appropriations, 58, 69, 75, 81
 party affiliations in Congress, presidency, 1789–2001 (table), 1071–1072
 session statistics (boxes), 6, 10, 15, 19
  postelection sessions, 1948–2000, 965–966
Congressional Accountability Act, 771
Congressional Accountability Project
 congressional ethics probes
  DeLay, 764
  Shuster, 765, 771
 congressional pay, 792
Congressional Award Act, 546
Congressional Black Caucus
 budget proposals, 47
 China trade agreement, 162
 foreign aid appropriations, 215
 Haitian refugee deportations, 618
 presidential electoral vote, 27 (box)
 student loans, 511
 Title I education waivers, 541
Congressional Budget and Impoundment Control Act of 1974, 44 (box), 53, 54
Congressional Budget Office (CBO)
 budget enforcement, 53
 budget law history, 44 (box)
 estimates and reports
  appropriations caps, 17
  aviation trust fund, 331
  B-2 bombers, 242
  breast, cervical cancer, 472
  budgets, 39 (box), 40, 45, 47, 79–81
  defense appropriations, 285
  federal rules impact analysis, 749
  forest revenue sharing, 399
  foster child adoption, 484
  hospital patient discharge timing, 434–435
  Medicare payments, 461
  military base closures, 243
  military health care, 292
  patients' rights, 455
  physician antitrust, 480
  prescription drug user fees, 447
  radio spectrum auctions, 56, 285, 325–326
  rural TV subsidy, 338
  Social Security trust fund, 73
  student loans, 510
  superfund overhaul, 352
Congressional committees. *See also specific committees*
 House funding, 762 (box), 767
  contingency funds, 761
 House rules, 770
 jurisdiction, leadership, subcommittees, 105th, 106th Cong. (tables), 951–964
 work sessions while House meets, 761
Congressional districts
 House apportionment, 691, 708–709, 733–734, 748 (box)
 minority districts ruling (box), 788
 racial redistricting, 688

Congressional elections
 campaign finance reform, 776–783, 788–790
 House results, 1928–2000 (table), 1090–1093
 Supreme Court decisions, 708
Congressional elections, 1880, 28
Congressional elections, 1994, 3, 41, 43, 757, 797–798
Congressional elections, 1996
 budget policy effects, 49
 contested seats
  Landrieu, 784–785
  Sanchez, 785
 results summary, 6
Congressional elections, 1997
 special elections, 8–9
  returns (table), 1073
Congressional elections, 1998
 Clinton impeachment, 813, 819
 House races, 12–13
 returns (table), 1074–1080
 Senate races, 11–12
 special elections, 13–14
 summary, 10, 11, 758
Congressional elections, 1999
 special elections, 17
  returns (table), 1081
Congressional elections, 2000
 House races, 29–30
 returns (table), 1082–1088
 Senate races, 28–29
 summary, 3–4, 21, 28–30
Congressional employees
 drug-testing policy, 761
 House administrative officer, 768
 Shuster ethics case, 771–772
 veterans job preference, 501
Congressional ethics
 book advances, 807 (box)
 Gingrich reprimand, 761–764
 gratuities law ruling, 792 (box)
 House committee rules overhaul, 766–767
 investigations
  105th Congress, 764–766
  106th Congress, 770–774
 physicians' outside income, 767–768
 Senate rules overhaul, 774–775
Congressional-executive relations
 budget process, 41–42, 77
 clemency, 681–682
 Clinton term summary, 3–5, 809–812
 environmental policy, 372
  CARA funding, 375–379
  global warming treaty, 354
  national monument designations, 344, 365–366, 389–390
  U.N. lands designation, 401
 foreign policy
  Bosnia/war powers, 198, 259–261
  government secrecy, 201, 202
  Iraq-U.S. relations, 196–197
  Kosovo policy, 205–208
  president's travel, 183 (box)
  sanctions for religious persecution, 199
  troop deployments, 174, 277–278
 independent counsel law, 662
 line-item veto, 7–8, 43, 64–65
 trade policy
  China agreement, 161
  fast-track procedures, 155–156
Congressional Gold Medals, 751
Congressional-judicial relations
 judicial activism, 620–622
 judicial nominations, 622–624, 677–680
  Fletcher, 627–628
 Supreme Court decisions, 684

Congressional mail
 campaign finance reform, 782
 franking privilege, 771, 789
Congressional pay
 action
  1997–1998, 791–793
  1999–2000, 794
 appropriations, 59, 76
 gifts, 770
 gratuities law ruling, 792 (box)
 physicians' outside income, 767–768
 presidential pay raise, 751
 salary history, 1789–2001 (chart), 794
Congressional Recognition for Excellence in Arts Education Awards Board, 546–547
Congressional Research Service
 ed-flex plan, 540
 flag desecration study, 667
Congressional Review Act, 584
Congressional staff. *See Congressional employees*
Congressional votes
 House pairs, 770
 key votes, 1997–2000, 865–932
 recorded vote totals, 1950–2000 (table), 12
 Senate cloture votes, 1917–2000 (list), 967–971
 two-thirds for tax hikes, 761
 vote-a-thons, 54
Connecticut
 congressional elections, 29
 F-22 funding, 286 (box)
 mortgage insurance, 563
Connecticut River, 370
Conrad, Kent, D-N.D.
 education savings accounts, 544
 fast track for trade pacts, 154, 156
 flag desecration, 611, 667–668
 NATO expansion, 274
Conservation. *See also Energy conservation; National parks and monuments; Soil conservation; Water conservation; Wetlands protection; Wilderness areas; Wildlife protection*
 budget outlays, FY 1987–2001 (graph), 342
 Colorado, Utah areas, 403–404
 community development initiatives, 565
 estate taxes, 99
 federal lands acquisition, 83, 375–379
 forest health, 368
 Third World debt forgiveness, 369
 U.N. lands designation, 367–368, 401, 744–745
Conservation and Reinvestment Act (CARA), 375–379
Conservation Reserve Program, 419, 420
Conservative Action Team
 budget alternative, FY 1998, 47
 budget resolution, FY 1999, 61
 minority health, 484–485
Constantine, Thomas A., 477, 606
Constitution, U.S. *See also specific amendments*
 census procedures, 733–734, 736
 commerce clause, in hate crimes, 643
 impeachment procedures, 823
 line-item veto, 64–65
 presidential misbehavior, 820
 presidential pay, 751
 proposed amendments
  balanced budget, 56–58
  campaign finance reform, 781
  crime victims rights, 591, 609, 668–669
  flag desecration, 591, 593, 610–611, 629, 666–668
  religious expression, 591, 593, 611–612
  term limits, 6, 783–784
 recess appointments, 626
 retroactive punishment, 633
Consumer protection
 auto safety, 333

bankruptcy overhaul, 126–128
cell phone fraud, 329
Clinton term summary, 316–317
"dolphin-safe" tuna labels, 348
drug reimports, 483–484
electronic signatures, 335
FDA overhaul, 444–446
federal rules impact analysis, 749
fraud against the elderly, 675
gun safety locks, 596
long-distance service "slamming," 330
managed health care, 434, 454
manufactured housing, 566
privacy issues, 121
   financial services modernization, 130–137
   Internet, 331, 337
   medical records, 479–480
radio spectrum auctions, 326
student aid fraud, 546
Contempt of Congress
POGO citation, 775
Contempt of court, 669, 699
Continuing resolutions
budget process reform, 77–78
Contraceptives. *See Birth control*
"Contract with America"
Clinton term summary, 797, 818
Democrat votes, 92
highway bill, 319
line-item veto, 64
tax cuts, 1997, 94
Controlled foreign corporations, 101
Controlled Substances Act of 1970, 477, 606, 654
**Conventional Forces in Europe (CFE) Treaty of
1990,** 223, 239, 268, 274–275
Conyers, Ga., school shootings, 76
Conyers, John Jr., D-Mich.
asbestos compensation, 666
bankruptcy law overhaul, 143
Clinton impeachment, 816, 819
flag desecration, 667
intelligence authorization, 201
Justice Department authorization, 613
law enforcement
   assisted suicide, 606, 659
   civil assets forfeiture, 648
   electronic information access, 656
   fetal rights, 662
   gun control, 641
   hate crimes, 642
   juvenile crime, 595
   racial profiling in traffic stops, 608, 652
   sex trafficking, 630
   violence against women, 631
   witness intimidation, 601
physician antitrust, 480
visas, 671, 677
volunteer liability shield, 615
Cook, Rhodes, 27
Cooley, Wes, 766
Cooperative Threat Reduction program, 282
Coordinated expenditures,
campaign finance reform, 783, 789
voter guides ruling, 790 (box)
Copper River, 379
COPS. *See Community Oriented Policing Services
program*
Copyright
computer software, 331, 334
digital works, 315, 316, 318, 328
satellite TV broadcasts, 329, 338
Supreme Court decisions, 693
Copyright Office, U.S., 329
Coral Reef Task Force, 393
Cormorants, 384
Corn, 391

Coronado Naval Amphibious Base, Calif.,
252 (box)
**Corporate average fuel economy (CAFE)
standards,** 67, 84
Corzine, John, 29
Cosmetics
health warning labels, 445, 446, 453
Cost bonds, 648, 649
Coughlin, Daniel P., 775
Council of Economic Advisers, 35 (box)
Council of Environmental Quality, 387
Counterfeiting
computer software, 334
police badges, 644–645
Court of Appeals for Veterans Claims, 502
Court of Federal Claims, U.S.
nuclear waste storage, 363
property rights, 738
Courts. *See also Federal courts*
Supreme Court decisions, 695–697
Coverdell, Paul, R-Ga.
death, successor, 19, 30
education savings accounts, 508, 518, 519, 521,
545
FALN clemency, 682
forensics labs, 657
property rights, 738
Reagan National airport, 741
Senate leadership, 7 (box), 759, 769
Cox, Archibald, 662
Cox, Christopher, R-Calif.
House leadership, 760, 769
Internet taxes, 327
missile, nuclear security, 180, 215, 279, 302,
303, 304
   China espionage report (box), 304
Russia policy task force, 175
Craig, Gregory B., 825
Craig, Larry E., R-Idaho
conservation lands acquisition, 378
forest revenues, 399–400
forest roadless areas, 394
foster child adoption, 494
gun control, 639–640
hate crimes, 643
Hells Canyon jetboats, 367
Kosovo policy, 208
national monuments, 390
NATO expansion, 273
Richardson nomination, 347 (box)
Cramer, Robert E. "Bud," D-Ala.
China trade agreement, 162
superfund overhaul, 396
Crane Naval Surface Warfare Center, Ind.,
253 (box)
Crane, Philip M., R-Ill.
NEA funding, 738
"Crank." *See Methamphetamine*
Crapo, Michael D., R-Idaho
bear parts import ban, 381
clean water regulation, 383
Senate election, 12
Credit card companies
bankruptcy law revision, 121, 126–128, 142–143
identity theft, 600
interest on debt obligations, 102
Credit cards
Defense Department purchases, 245
Credit unions
bankruptcy overhaul, 126
financial services modernization, 125
membership expansion, 128
Crime and criminals. *See also Crime prevention
programs; Crime victims; Criminal background
checks; Drug trafficking; Felons; Fraud; Hate
crimes; Juvenile crime; Police and law enforcement*

*agencies; Prisons and prisoners; Sentencing; Sex
crimes; Terrorism and counterterrorism*
animal cruelty, 650–651
body armor use, 645
bounty hunters, 599
cemetery vandalism, 604
child support evasion, 495
civil assets forfeiture, 604–605, 647–649
Clinton term summary, 589, 593, 799
D.C. justice system reorganization, 55
defendants' confessions, 689
deportation, 676–677
diplomatic immunity, 203
DNA evidence, 654–655
electronic information access, 655–656
encryption technology, 336
federal spending firewalls, 53
fetal rights, 474–475, 661
forensics labs, 657
gun-related crime, 594–597
   penalties, 597–598, 633, 635, 636, 639, 642
Internet gambling, 328–329
Justice Department authorization, 613
money laundering, 605–606
overseas crimes, 649
public housing standards, 556, 560
Supreme Court decisions, 684, 689–690,
   697–707
violence against women, 630–631, 632
witness intimidation, 601
Crime prevention programs
college programs, 513
hate crimes education, 536
juvenile crime, 593–596, 633
law enforcement block grants, 654
Police Athletic League, 650
school resource officers, 530
Crime victims
aid
   child abuse, 646–647
   sex trafficking, 629–630, 632
   violence against women, 630–631, 632
constitutional amendment proposal, 591, 609,
   668–669
disabled persons, 601
impact statements, 609–610
notification of pardon, 682
restitution from prisoner health care fees, 653
school transfers, 534
Crime Victims' Fund, 646, 653
Criminal background checks
adoptive, foster parents, 494
explosives purchases, 638
gun purchasers, 598, 631, 685
   armored car guards, 598
   gun shows, 30, 538, 629, 635, 637, 639–641
   pawnshops, 635, 639–640
private security officers, 599, 657
SBA loan applicants, 324
U.S. marshal nominees, 614
Croatia
U.S. policies, 802
Crop insurance
appropriations, 59
authorization, 421–422
federal subsidy, 425–426
summary, 417–418, 419, 424
Crowe, William J. Jr., 217
Crowell, Craven, 371
Crowley, Joseph, D-N.Y.
drug reimports, 483
home ownership aid, 567
Cruise missiles
authorization, 294–295
Russian sales to China, 157, 242
submarine weapons, 277

Cruise ships, 246
Crusader weapon, 248, 261, 281, 287–288, 299–300
Cuba
  refugees in U.S., 490, 619–620
  Russian intelligence facility, 222, 223
  terrorism victims' suits, 632
  U.S. relations study commission, 292
  U.S. trade
    Clinton term summary, 16, 173, 204
    economic sanctions, 76, 81, 83, 170, 223–226, 421, 424, 426
    encryption export ban, 336
    travel limits, 83, 210–211
Cuban Americans
  Cuba sanctions, 224
  Elián González case, 225 (box)
Cunningham, Randy "Duke," R-Calif.
  shark protection, 396
  union "salting," 575
Cuomo, Andrew M.
  HUD leadership, 554, 556 (box), 978 (box), 980
  public housing reform, 558
Currency. *See also Coins*
  export limits, 689
  IMF rules, 189
Currie, Betty, 817, 818, 821 (box), 822
Curtis, Charles B., 412
Customs Service, U.S.
  firearms training center, 85
  foreign travelers to U.S., 677
  terrorism countermeasures, 605
  vehicle emissions, 365
CVN-77 carrier, 258
Cypress trees, 402
Cystic Fibrosis Foundation, 746
Czech Republic
  NATO expansion, 189, 230, 272–274, 802

D

Dairy Indemnity Program, 420
Dairy products. *See Milk and dairy products*
Daley, Richard J., 320 (box)
Daley, Richard M., 320 (box)
Daley, William M.
  China trade agreement, 161
  Commerce leadership, 320 (box), 977, 978 (box)
Dallas, TX, 162
Damage suits, 718–719
D'Amato, Alphonse M., R-N.Y.
  American Heritage Rivers, 370
  compensatory time, 577
  education savings accounts, 520
  electoral defeat, 11–12
  financial services modernization, 122, 125–126, 132
  patients' rights, 454
  Senate leadership, 769
  welfare law revisions, 487
Dams
  Snake River salmon project, 395
  watershed dam restoration, 385
Danforth, John C., 680–681
Danner, Pat, D-Mo.
  breast, cervical cancer, 472
Danzig, Richard, 295
Daschle, Tom, D-S.D.
  appropriations, 63, 69–70
  budget resolution, FY 2000, 71
  campaign finance reform, 790
  Clinton impeachment, 818
  Cuba sanctions, 224
  defense policy
    authorization, 256, 277, 293

    military construction appropriations, 251
    nuclear test ban treaty, 311
  education savings accounts, 519
  fast track for trade pacts, 154
  gun control, 638
  health policy
    Medicare drug benefits, 466
    partial-birth abortion, 456
    patients' rights, 455
  judicial nominations, 624, 678, 679
  juvenile crime, 635
  Landrieu election, 784–785
  Lee nomination, 625
  Reagan National airport, 741
  Senate leadership, 7 (box), 759, 769
  Social Security surplus protection, 79
  superfund overhaul, 353
  tax policy
    marriage status, 114
    Republican tax cuts, 1999, 112
Date rape, 631, 632, 654
David, Susan, 29
Davidson, Dick, 462
Davis-Bacon Act of 1931, 374, 492–493
Davis, Danny K., D-Ill.
  public housing reform, 557
Davis, Jim, D-Fla.
  nursing home evictions, 485
Davis, Thomas M. III, R-Va.
  campaign finance reform, 777
  D.C. student aid, 548
  House leadership, 769
  Reagan National airport, 742
  Y2K liability, 336
Dayton, Mark, 28
DD-21-class destroyers, 300
DEA. *See Drug Enforcement Administration*
Deafness
  pediatric hearing loss research, 482
Deal, Nathan, R-Ga.
  forest revenues, 399
Death penalty
  DNA evidence, 655
  Edwards election, 12
  gun control, 638
  habeas corpus appeals, 622, 690
  juvenile crime, 594, 596, 634
  military burial denial in capital crime, 498–499
  Supreme Court decisions, 698
  White nomination, 678
  witness intimidation, 601
DeFazio, Peter A., D-Ore.
  defense appropriations, 297
  forest revenues, 399
  Reagan National airport, 741–742
  superfund overhaul, 396
Defenders of Wildlife, 346
Defense Airborne Reconnaissance Office, 201
Defense contractors
  Air Force maintenance depots, 240–243, 245
  Defense Department purchasing, 245
  innovative thinking, 277, 282–283
  military administrative jobs, 261, 264–265
  payment rate, 285
Defense Department, U.S.
  antimissile defenses, 265–267, 307, 308
  appropriations, 58, 62, 68, 69, 73, 76, 77, 84–85
    FY 1997 supplemental, 250
    FY 1998, 245–249
    FY 1998 military construction, 250–251, 252–253 (box)
    FY 1998 supplemental, 250
    FY 1999, 259–262
    FY 1999 military construction, 263
    FY 1999 supplemental (first), 262
    FY 1999 supplemental (second), 263

    FY 2000, 283–289
    FY 2000 military construction, 289–290
    FY 2000 supplemental, 300–302
    FY 2001, 296–300
    FY 2001 military construction, 300–302
    incremental funding, 289
  arms control, 278
  authorization
    FY 1998, 239–245
    FY 1999, 252–259
    FY 2000, 276–283
    FY 2001, 290–296
  budget resolutions, 72, 80
  cemetery vandalism, 604
  Colombia antidrug aid, 220
  contractor payments, 285
  export controls, 167, 181, 242, 245
  F-22 funding, 286–287 (box)
  foreign military training, 211
  Joint Strike fighter, 290
  land mine treaty, 274
  military pay review, 261
  nuclear lab security, 411
  Pentagon name proposal, 741
  private space shuttles, 744
  radio spectrum use, 283
  satellite launch security, 180, 304 (box)
  school impact aid, 535
  Strategic Petroleum Reserve, 409
  terrorism preparedness, 295, 308–309, 481
  U.S. troops in Kosovo, 207
  underground weapons destruction study, 295
Defense Institute for Hemispheric Security Cooperation, 296
Defense policy. *See also Arms control; Defense Department; Military personnel; Nuclear weapons; Terrorism and counterterrorism; specific armed services*
  budget outlays national defense, 1987–2001 (graph), 236
  Clinton term summary, 16, 20, 173–174, 235–238, 239, 276
  federal spending firewalls, 53
  high-tech export controls, 166–167
  innovative thinking, 282–283
  leadership, 241 (box)
  long-term assessment, 263–265, 295
  national security study panels, 262
  post–Cold War missions, 286–287
  readiness reporting, 257
Defense Programs, Office of (DOE), 305
Defibrillators, 481
DeGette, Diana, D-Colo.
  China trade agreement, 162 (box)
de la Garza, E. "Kika," 760
Delahunt, Bill, D-Mass.
  gun-related crime, 597
  judicial activism, 621, 622
  methamphetamine traffic, 602
  sanctions for oil producers, 414
DeLauro, Rosa, D-Conn.
  House leadership, 769–770
Delaware
  bankruptcy judges, 608
  congressional elections, 28
Delaware plan, 23
DeLay, Randy, 764
DeLay, Tom, R-Texas
  asbestos compensation, 665
  campaign finance reform, 781, 782, 788
    527 PACs, 787
  China summits, 183 (box)
  China-U.S. trade, 20, 152, 162
  congressional pay, 791–792
  Cuba sanctions, 83, 225
  defense authorization, 279

ethics investigation, 759, 764, 773
gun control, 16, 640
House leadership, 7 (box), 760, 769
  Gingrich coup attempt, 763 (box)
judicial activism, 621, 622
juvenile crime, 637
Kosovo policy, 205
NASA authorization, 753
post–foster care aid, 496
Dellums, Ron, D-Calif.
defense authorization, 242
House leadership, 770
successor, 13
Delta Airlines, 321
DeMint, Jim, R-S.C.
China trade agreement, 162 (box)
Democratic Congressional Campaign Committee
DeLay lawsuit, 773
Democratic National Committee (DNC)
campaign finance
  Chinese contributions, 182
  issue advocacy ads, 780 (box)
  reform action, 778–779
Teamsters probe, 578 (box)
Democratic Party
presidential election, 1996
  platform (text), 1038–1039
presidential election, 2000, 22, 23–24
  convention balloting (table), 1069
  platform (text), 1042–1044
Dentists
VA pay, 502
Depleted uranium, 365
Deportation
Central American refugees, 619
judicial activism, 621
Justice Department authorization, 613
removal appeals, 676–677
secret evidence, 663–664
Supreme Court decisions, 716
terrorism, 605
travelers in U.S., 677
violence against women, 631, 632
Deposit insurance
financial services modernization, 123
wholesale institutions exclusion, 132
Deposit Insurance Act of 1996, 140
Deregulation. *See Regulation and deregulation*
Derivatives, 141–142
Desalinization projects, 402
Detainers, 700
Detroit River, 370
Deutch, John M., 179 (box), 808–809
Developing countries
debt relief
  foreign aid appropriations, 73, 75, 83, 210–217
  foreign aid authorization, 229
  IMF gold reserves, 75, 176, 213 (box), 228
  summary, 20, 173, 204
  tropical forest protection, 369
environmental protection, 215
  global warming treaty, 354, 355
U.S. development aid, 186
  authorization, 228–229
  microenterprises, 230
U.S. trade, 147, 159
  African trade initiative, 167–168
  Caribbean countries, 158
  GSP extension, 105, 169
  OPIC authorization, 169
Developmental disabilities, 601
Devil's Tower National Monument, 387
DeWine, Mike, R-Ohio
compensatory time, 576–577
crimes against disabled, 601

fetal rights, 662
Fletcher nomination, 628
job training overhaul, 573, 574
Lee nomination, 625
prisoner mental health, 656
Diabetes
pediatric research, 482
prevention, treatment
  Medicare coverage, 45, 437, 441, 443
  Native Americans, 443, 751
  nutritional therapy, 463
Diamonds, 82
Diaz-Balart, Lincoln, R-Fla.
Central American refugees, 619
Cuba sanctions, 83
Dickey, Jay, R-Ark.
election defeat, 29
Dicks, Norm, D-Wash.
House leadership, 770
national monuments, 390
NEA funding, 750
nuclear security, 279, 304
Diesel fuel
biodiesel, 356
taxes, 580
Digital communications networks
Army battlefield links, 240, 244, 248, 258, 261
Navy system, 245, 249, 262
Digital divide, 119
Digital television, 325–326
Dillonwood Grove, Calif., 402
Dingell, John D., D-Mich.
defense authorization, 279
environmental protection
  conservation lands acquisition, 376, 378
  national wildlife refuges, 349
  superfund overhaul, 353, 396–398
financial services modernization, 125
gun control, 641
health policy
  drug-abuse prevention, treatment, 602
  drug reimports, 484
  Medicare changes, 434
  organ transplants, 476–477
  patients' rights, 454, 467, 468
nuclear security, 305–306
term limits, 784
Dingell-Johnson Act of 1950, 393
Diplomacy. *See Foreign service and diplomacy*
Disabled American Veterans, 503
Disabled children
education
  appropriations, 82
  charter schools, 525
  discipline for weapons at school, 516, 538, 544, 636, 637, 639
  ed-flex plan, 539, 540
  education savings accounts bill, 545
  IDEA authorization, 508, 515–516
  intensive medical care, 541
  national test exemptions, 532
  special education instructors, 533
health insurance for adopted children, 494
Medicaid coverage, 51, 117, 442, 464, 487, 565
SSI benefits, 490
Disabled persons. *See also Disabled children; Disabled veterans*
citizenship applicants, 676
crime victims, 601
  hate crimes, 20, 629, 642–644
  violence against women, 631, 632
discrimination, 661
ergonomics standards, 584
health insurance for employed, 431, 442, 470–471
housing
  affordable housing, 567

caretaker tax breaks, 110
home ownership aid, 566–567
Supreme Court decisions, 688, 719–720
welfare benefits for disabled immigrants, 48
  food stamps, 421–422
  Medicaid, 45, 442, 464, 487–488
  SSI, 43, 45, 49, 51, 52, 53, 487–488, 490
Disabled veterans
benefit appeals, 499
benefit COLAs, 498, 500, 503
job preference, 501
long-term health care, 502
Persian Gulf War compensation, 497–498
Disadvantaged Youth Employment and Training Opportunities Grant, 574
Disaster relief
appropriations, 58, 59, 68, 76–77, 84–85, 300, 301–302
budget outlays, 1987–2001 (graph), 554
budget process reform, 78
census controversies, 736
congressional-executive relations, 4, 7
crop insurance, 424
foreign aid appropriations, 189
military missions, 299
Discharge petitions, 972
Discovery, 742 (box)
Discovery (law), 700–701
Discrimination. *See also Discrimination in employment; Hate crimes; Racial discrimination; Religious discrimination*
age discrimination, 717
Civil Rights Commission, 608–609
Export-Import Bank loans, 157
health insurers, 480
insurance "redlining," 143
low-level nuclear waste site, 360
sexual orientation, 30, 689
U.S. visa refusals, 677
World War II minorities, 664
Discrimination in employment
affirmative action, 615–616
Baucus ethics probe, 771
disabled persons, 688
faith-based programs, 535, 536, 565
federal gender, race rules, 7
sexual harassment, 687
Supreme Court decisions, 688, 720–721
union "salting," 573, 575, 584–585
VA rulings, 497
welfare-to-work jobs, 489
Displaced homemakers, 514, 574
District attorneys, U.S.
prosecutor guidelines, 66
District courts, U.S.
arbitration, 607–608
dispute resolution program, 613–614
DNA evidence, 655
judicial nominations, 623, 678–679
recess appointments, 680
rulings
  census procedures, 736
  Internet address registration fees, 746 (box)
  sexual material on military posts, 275
District of Columbia
airports, 67, 321, 332, 741–742
appropriations, 59, 66, 73, 619
bridge-blocking penalties, 55
budget reconciliation, FY 1997, 54–56
education
  school vouchers, 528–529
  tuition aid, 531, 547–548
employees
  pensions, 54
  residence rule, 66
enterprise zones, 99–100

federal relationship, 54, 55, 739–740
Gandhi memorial, 359
law enforcement
    court appropriations, 55
    criminal justice system reorganization, 55
    DNA evidence, 655
    penal system transfer, 54–55
    truth in sentencing, 55
management changes, 54
presidential electoral vote, 27
Union Station air rights, 51, 56
wage garnisheeing rules, 55
Divided government
budget policy effects, 41–42, 63
Clinton term summary, 3, 20
veto use, 811
Dixon, Julian C., D-Calif.
death, 29
House leadership, 770
DNA records
evidence database, 654–655
unidentified persons, 646
DNC. *See Democratic National Committee*
Dodd, Christopher J., D-Conn.
defense authorization, 292
economic sanctions, 200
education
    disabled students, 545
    ed-flex plan, 528
    Head Start, 492
FDA overhaul, 445
foreign aid appropriations, 184, 210–211
handgun safety locks, 598
medical errors, 479
Senate leadership, 769
DOE. *See Energy Department, U.S.*
Dog race betting, 337
Dogs
police animals, 650
Doggett, Lloyd, D-Texas
527 PACs, 786, 787
low-level nuclear waste, 360
State Department authorization, 219
Dolan, Michael P., 107
Dole, Bob, R-Kan.
balanced budget amendment, 57
chemical weapons treaty, 268
disabled workers' insurance, 470
Gingrich reprimand, 762–763
independent counsel law, 663
Kosovo policy, 178–179
NATO expansion, 272
popular, electoral vote by region, 1996 (table),
    21
radio spectrum auctions, 325
Dole, Elizabeth, 22
Dolphin protection treaty, 341, 344, 346–348
Dombeck, Mike, 394
Domenici, Pete V., R-N.M.
budget resolution, FY 1999, 61
budget resolution, FY 2000, 72
energy supplies, 410
military construction appropriations, 251
nuclear lab security, 76, 305, 411
nuclear test ban treaty, 310
Richardson nomination, 347 (box)
Social Security surplus protection, 78
Domestic violence
charity postal stamps, 751
child witness aid, 636
Justice Department authorization, 613
restrictions for those convicted
    gun ownership, 638
    prisoner transport employment, 654
Violence against Women Act, 630–631, 632

Dooley, Cal, D-Calif.
California water project, 382
House chaplain, 775
House leadership, 770
Doolittle, John T., R-Calif.
campaign finance reform, 782, 788–789
gun control, 642
water resources, 373
Dorgan, Byron L., D-N.D.
assisted suicide, 606
Cuba sanctions, 224
defense authorization, 243
drug reimports, 484
flag desecration, 611, 667–668
Senate leadership, 760
Doris Day Animal League, 651
Dornan, Robert K., R-Calif.
Sanchez contested election, 785
DoubleClick Inc., 337
Double-crested cormorants, 384
Double jeopardy, 701
Dow Chemical Co., 334
Dreier, David, R-Calif.
defense authorization, 291
high-tech visas, 618, 671
House leadership, 770
Drill sergeants, 244, 275
Drinking water safety
Alaska watershed protection, 379, 392
Colorado River salinity, 402
EPA research, 747
gasoline additive MTBE, 390–391
Driver Privacy Protection Act of 1994, 685
Driver's licenses
drug testing for teenage applicants, 602
Drug abuse
needle-exchange programs, 62, 66, 67, 74
public housing reform, 560
prevention programs, 602
    after-school programs, 536
    community-group grants, 602
    federal coordination, 602–603
    methamphetamine, Ecstasy, 482
treatment programs, 602
    alternative sentencing, 644
    Colombia antidrug aid, 221
    community development initiatives, 564, 565
    juvenile crime, 595, 596, 635
Drug czar. *See National Drug Control Policy,
Office of*
Drug Enforcement Administration (DEA)
assisted suicide, 477, 606–607, 658
date-rape drugs, 654
methamphetamine traffic, 602
off-duty officers, 614
**Drug-Free Communities, Advisory
Commission on,** 602
Drug-free schools
disabled student discipline, 515
ESEA authorization, 532, 536
school resource officers, 530
Drug testing
Congress members, staff, 761
federal employees, 602
state election candidates, 720
teenage driver's license applicants, 602
U.S. marshal nominees, 614
Drug trafficking
date-rape drugs, 654
drug courts, 654
drug-related crime, 603
    civil assets forfeiture, 604, 647
    gun penalties, 597, 635, 642
    juvenile crime, 595, 596, 634
    WIC program fraud, 494
    witness intimidation, 601

interdiction
    defense appropriations, 262
    Otay Mountain wilderness, 401
    railroad officer training, 652
    tobacco settlement, 322
international narcotics control
    Colombia initiative, 20, 84–85, 173, 176, 204,
        215, 300, 301–302
    debt forgiveness, 369
    foreign aid appropriations, 184
    intelligence authorizations, 226, 227–228
    Mexico certification, 203
    State Department authorization, 219
    terrorism countermeasures, 605
methamphetamine, 593, 601–602
money laundering, 605–606
student loan penalties, 510, 547
Supreme Court decisions, 701
Drug treatment. *See Drug abuse*
Drugs and pharmaceutical industry
addiction therapy development, 602
antibiotics, 449, 481
assisted suicide, 459, 477, 605–606, 658–660,
    687
clinical trials database, 448, 467
Columbia University patent extension, 85
discontinuance notice, 446, 450
economic benefits, 448
experimental, unapproved treatments, 444,
    452–453
fast-track approvals, 448
FDA overhaul, 429, 431, 444–450, 452–454
GHB for sleep disorders, 654
foreign trade
    income earned abroad, 118
    reimports, 83, 483–484
    standards, 453
immunosuppressive drugs, 462, 463, 465
labeling, 449
manufacturing changes, 448
Medicaid benefit for degenerative conditions,
    471
Medicare coverage
    action, 1999–2000, 465–466
    budget resolution, FY 2000, 79–81
    China trade pact, 164
    marriage tax cut, 115
    Medicare commission, 464
    Medicare "givebacks" bill, 462, 463
    Republican tax cuts, 110–111, 113
    summary, 20
medicine exemption in trade sanctions, 76, 83,
    170, 200, 223–226
military retirees' prescription benefit, 290, 291,
    294, 297, 298, 299
orphan drug tax credit, 99
over-the-counter drug warning labels, 445, 453
pharmacy regulation, 449
postmarketing studies, 449–450
veterans' prescriptions, 500
Drunken driving, 84, 319
Dual-use technologies
defense appropriations, 247
export controls, 166–167
terrorism, 309
Dulles International Airport, 741
Dunn, Jennifer, R-Wash.
estate taxes, 116
House leadership, 769
Durbin, Richard J., D-Ill.
bankruptcy overhaul, 127
defense appropriations, 260
defense authorization, 243, 292
FDA overhaul, 446
violence prevention, 545
Durham, Barbara, 627–628, 989

Dvorak, Bob, 775
Dwyer, William, 627
Dyer, James W., 65
Dyess Air Force Base, Tex., 252 (box)

E

E-mail
  access in criminal investigations, 656
Eagen, James M. "Jay" III, 768
Eagle Forum, 574
Early Head Start, 491, 492
Earmarks
  appropriations, 85, 298
    military construction, 250–251, 252–253
      (box)
  budget process reform, 77
  surface transportation authorization, 319
Earned income tax credit (EITC)
  disabled workers' insurance, 471
  fraud prevention, 53, 103
  marriage status tax cut, 114, 115
  program expansion, 798
Earth
  image from space, 752
East Timor
  independence, 213
Eastern states
  presidential vote, 1996, 2000 (table), 21
Ebola, 379
Economic and Educational Opportunities
  Committee, House
  renaming, 761
Economic development. See also Developing
  countries; Enterprise zones
  business tax breaks, 82, 117
  community development
    initiatives package, 564–565
    outlays, 1987–2001 (graph), 554
  domestic aid/China trade link, 161
  environmental regulation, 341
    Alaska development, 379
    Arctic wildlife refuge drilling, 413
    coastal areas, 383
    endangered species protection, 350, 385
    federal lands acquisition, 74
    global warming treaty, 355
    national monuments, 389
    San Rafael Swell, 402
    U.N. lands designation, 368
  federal rules impact analysis, 749
  property rights, 737–738
Economic policy. See also Budget, U.S.; Business
  and industry; Economic development; Employment and unemployment; Foreign trade; Labor
  unions; Taxes
  Clinton term summaries, 33–39, 147–149,
    417–418, 571, 798
  growth, 1980–2000 (graph), 37
  inflation, 1980–2000 (graph), 37
  leadership (box), 34–35
  "new economy," 34–36
  presidential campaign issue, 23, 24, 33, 42
Economic sanctions. See Foreign trade sanctions
Ecstasy, 482
Edison Electric Institute, 405
Education. See also Adult education; Colleges and
  universities; Education savings accounts; Elementary and secondary education; Literacy programs;
  Vocational education
  business tax deductions, 580
  Clinton term summary, 798, 799
  Head Start, 11, 486, 489–493, 798
  NASA videos, 753
  research academy, 548–549
  tax incentives, 48, 49, 87, 90, 94, 96–97
Education Amendments of 1972, 511

Education and the Workforce Committee,
  House
  jurisdiction, leadership, 959
  renaming, 761
Education Department, U.S.
  appropriations, 59–60, 67, 73–74, 81–82, 810,
    812
  audits, 548
  bilingual education, 517
  budget resolution, FY 2001, 79
  charter schools, 525
  ed-flex plan, 527–528, 542–543
  educational research academy, 548–549
  ESEA authorization, 532, 535, 537
  hate crime prevention, 507, 538
  Head Start, 493
  homeless programs, 561
  IDEA authorization, 515
  leadership (box), 510
  literacy programs, 529
  national testing, 524
  Republican platform, 23
  student loans
    consolidation, 526
    program monitoring, 509, 510, 512, 513
    scams, 546
Education Flexibility Partnership
  Demonstration Act, 539
Education for All Handicapped Children Act of
  1975, 515
Education savings accounts
  action, 1998–1999, 518–520
  budget reconciliation, 522
  Republican tax cuts, 1999, 112
  summary, 507–508
  tax cuts, 1997, 90, 94, 96
Education Trust, 540
Edwards, Chet, D-Texas
  community development block grants,
    566–567
Edwards, Edwin W., 18
Edwards, George C., 810
Edwards, John, D-N.C.
  election, 12
  nuclear waste storage, 409
Edwards, Mickey, 679
Egypt
  U.S. aid
    appropriations, 66, 184, 185, 186, 189, 214,
      216
    military aid authorization, 229
Ehlers, Vernon J., R-Mich.
  NEA funding, 738
  Sanchez election, 785
Ehrlich, Robert L. Jr., R-Md.
  electric deregulation, 405
Eighth Amendment, 690
Eisenbach, Jeffrey, 763
Eisenhower, Dwight D.
  presidential commemoratives, 751
  veto use, 811
Eisenhower Professional Development
  Program, 533, 540, 543
EITC. See Earned-income tax credit
El Salvador
  immigrants, refugees in U.S., 619–620, 671–672
Elderly persons. See also Medicare; Pensions and
  retirement income
  aging research, 742 (box)
  clean air, 351
  crime
    female victims aid, 632
    fraud, 675
  housing
    affordable housing, 567
    caretaker tax breaks, 110, 112
    home ownership aid, 567

  reverse mortgages, 561, 566, 567
  immigrant welfare benefits
    food stamps, 421–422
    SSI, 490
  Older Americans Act authorization, 496
  PACE benefits, 442
Elders, Joycelyn, 435 (box)
Elections. See also Campaign finance;
  Congressional elections; Presidential elections
  "blanket primaries," 688
  initiative petitions, 688
  nonprofit organization role, 761
  Supreme Court decisions, 688, 707–710
Electoral college, 21–22
Electoral vote
  distribution of House seats, votes 1952–2000
    (table), 1070
Electoral Vote Count Act of 1887, 22, 27 (box)
Electric Boat Corp., 245
Electric power
  biomass tax credit, 565
  deregulation proposals, 315, 316, 318, 331, 341,
    344, 372, 404–407
  national grid reliability, 406
  TVA federal subsidy, 69, 370–371
Electric Power Supply Association, 406
Electric Reliability Organization, 406
Electricity Restructuring Stakeholders, 406
Electromagnetic pulses, 295
Electronic Communications Privacy Act, 765
Electronic Data Services, 296
Electronic Industries Alliance, 773
Electronic signatures, 108, 316, 331, 335–336
Elementary and secondary education. See also
  Literacy programs; Private and parochial schools;
  School vouchers; Schools; Teachers
  accountability standards, 532
  after-school programs, 539, 540, 541
  Amish apprenticeships, 584–585
  arts education award, 546–547
  bilingual education, 508, 509, 516–518
  charter schools, 525–526, 799
  class-size reduction
    appropriations, 67, 74, 82
    budget resolution, 60
    ed-flex plan, 540, 541–542, 543–544
    ESEA authorization, 532–533, 537
    overseas military bases, 301
    summary, 798, 810
  Clinton term summary, 507–508, 531
  college prep for middle-schoolers, 509, 511, 513
  computer donations, 96, 523, 545
  computer training, 671
  defense spending alternative, 298
  dropout prevention, 517, 519, 539, 540, 541
  entrepreneurship clearinghouse, 533
  federal education aid
    appropriations, 73, 74, 82
    block grants, 527, 531
    budget resolution, FY 2000, 73
    ESEA authorization, 531–539
    flexibility, 507, 508, 527–528, 534–535
    funds shifting, 536–537
    impact aid, 531, 535–536
    outlays, 1987–2001 (graph), 508
    summary, 16–17, 20
  home schooling, 574
  IDEA authorization, 515–516
  job training overhaul, 573, 574
  national assessment testing, 59, 60, 62, 67, 508,
    509, 519, 520, 523–525, 799
  remedial education, 541
  ROTC programs, 280, 285, 294
  school choice, 20, 536
  school libraries, 82, 538
  social promotion, 532, 539, 540, 541, 545
  Supreme Court decisions, 689

vocational education, 513–515
Elementary and Secondary Education Act (ESEA) of 1965
authorization, 507, 531–539
Title I
authorization, 531, 534, 537–538
background, 531–532
charter schools, 525
ed-flex waivers, 539–544
Title II, 539, 540, 543
Title III, 543
Title IV, 543
Title VI
ed-flex waivers, 543
vouchers, 528
Title VII, 543
Elephant conservation, 369
Eleventh Amendment, 685
Elim, Alaska, 391–392
Elim Native Corp., 391
Emergency Immigrant Education Program, 543
Emergency medical care
patients' rights, 430, 433, 437, 439, 454, 467–468, 469
terrorism response training, 295
Emery County, Utah, 402
Emory University, 647
Employee Retirement Income Security Act (ERISA) of 1974, 430
Employee stock ownership plans, 105
Employment and unemployment. *See also Child labor; Congressional employees; Discrimination in employment; Federal employees; Labor standards; Military personnel; Minimum wage; Occupational health and safety; Pensions and retirement income; Prison labor; Salaries and wages*
Clinton term summary, 33, 35, 571, 798
immigrant workers, 620
farm labor, 673–674
high-tech visas, 69, 616–619, 670–672
nurses, 674–675
job training
budget reconciliation, FY 1997, 51
business-school partnerships, 96
federal programs overhaul, 572, 573–575
foreign trade dislocation, 154, 155
math, computer students, 618
prison industries, 652–653
public housing tenants, 558, 559
veterans programs, 498 (graph)
vocational education, 513
welfare law revisions, 488, 489
women, 514
jobs programs
depressed communities, 82
older Americans, 496
summer jobs, 67
tax credits for disadvantaged workers, 99, 106
welfare-to-work credits, 100
Supreme Court decisions, 721–724
unemployment, 1980–2000 (graph), 37
union "salting," 575–576, 584–585
Employment Discrimination Complaint Adjudication Office (VA), 497
Empowerment zones, 100, 529, 564–565
Encryption technology
copyright protection, 328
export controls, 326–327, 336
Endangered species
ape protection, 379–380
federal protection, 349–351, 385–386
migratory birds, 389
national wildlife refuges, 348
new national parks, 381
northern spotted owl, 392
salmon, 67, 395
sea lions, 82, 393–394

shark protection, 348, 372, 395–396
Supreme Court decisions, 710
tuna fishing bycatch, 348
Endangered Species Act of 1973
authorization, 349–351, 385–386
summary, 341, 342, 343, 345, 372, 799
Energy and Natural Resources Committee, Senate
jurisdiction, leadership, 760, 769, 953
Energy assistance
appropriations, 67
authorization, 486
Head Start bill, 491, 492, 493
Energy conservation
appropriations, 67
authorization, 356
budget resolution, FY 1999, 60
electric deregulation, 405
energy research and development, 746, 754
fuel economy standards, 67
sanctions for oil producers, 414
tax break for home devices, 110
Energy Conservation and Production Act of 1976, 356
Energy Department, U.S. (DOE)
appropriations, 58, 69, 76, 83, 262
clean coal technology, 750
employees
leadership, 347 (box)
nuclear security "dual-hatting," 292, 296, 306
nuclear weapons workers' compensation, 293, 296
polygraph tests, 290, 296, 303 (box), 304, 306
export controls, 242, 245
methane research, 388–389
nuclear lab security, 226–227, 302–306, 344, 372, 410–413
Chinese espionage, 208, 226, 276
counterintelligence, 302, 304 (box), 306
defense authorization, 276, 277, 279–280, 282, 292
Lee investigation (box), 303
nuclear sales, 255
nuclear weapons
authorization, 258
explosive test alternative, 310
next generation Internet, 746
nuclear waste storage, 361–363, 407–408
POGO contempt of Congress, 775
Republican platform, 23
research and development, 746–747, 754
Russia arms reduction, 282
underground weapons destruction study, 295
uranium cleanup, 365
Energy policy
budget outlays, FY 1987–2001 (graph), 343
cabinet leadership, 347 (box)
summary, 341, 344, 345, 372
Energy Policy and Conservation Act of 1992, 356, 400, 409
Energy resources. *See also Alternative fuels; Coal; Electric power; Natural gas; Nuclear energy; Oil*
fossil fuel research, 754
OTC derivatives, 142
tax breaks, 565
research and development, 746–747, 754
English Language Acquisition, Office of, 517
English-language issues
bilingual education, 516–518
immigrant education, 508
Puerto Rico status, 741
Supreme Court decisions, 721
voting materials, 782
English, Phil, R-Pa.
campaign finance reform, 782
Enhanced rescissions, 64

Enrichment Corporation, U.S., 365
Ensign, John, R-Nev.
election defeat, 28
nuclear waste storage, 361–363
Enterprise zones
business-school partnerships, 605
District of Columbia, 99–100, 740
empowerment zones, 100, 529, 564–565
literacy programs, 529
school bonds tax credit, 96
small business loans for HUBZones, 324
Environment and Public Works Committee, Senate
jurisdiction, leadership, 953
Environmental protection. *See also Conservation; Environmental Protection Agency; Global climate change; Pollution control; Toxic waste cleanup*
action
1997–1998, 345–370
1999–2000, 372–404
summary, 20, 341–344, 799
appropriations, 59, 66–67, 73, 74
cabinet leadership, 347 (box)
China trade agreement, 164
energy policy conflicts, 410
federal land grazing fees, 419–420
federal rules impact analysis, 749
NASA Earth monitoring, 742
Supreme Court decisions, 691, 710
trade agreements, 154, 155
U.N. programs, 367–368, 401, 744–745
Environmental Protection Agency (EPA)
appropriations, 59, 70
Clean Air Act, 351, 382
clean water regulations, 382–383
coastal water quality, 380
gasoline additive MTBE, 390–391
global warming treaty, 70, 355
leadership, 347 (box)
nuclear waste storage, 362, 407–408
research and development, 747
space station bill, 754
superfund overhaul, 352–354, 396–399
underground storage tanks, 370
vehicle emissions, 365
Enzi, Michael, R-Wyo.
Export-Import Bank, 157
high-tech export controls, 167
OSHA overhaul, 577
EPA. *See Environmental Protection Agency*
Epilepsy research, 482
Eppard, Ann, 765, 771–772
Equal Employment Opportunity Commission, 688
Ergonomic standards, 584
ESEA. *See Elementary and Secondary Education Act*
Eshoo, Anna G., D-Calif.
AIDS programs, 483
breast, cervical cancer, 472
FDA overhaul, 446
Medicare payments, 461
Espionage
China technology transfer, 166, 180–182, 208, 226, 276, 302
House committee report, 304 (box)
DOE nuclear lab security, 279, 302–306, 344, 410–414
Lee investigation, 303 (box)
intelligence authorizations, 202, 227
Espy, Mike, 420 (box), 792 (box), 978 (box)
Establishment clause. *See Church-state separation*
Estate taxes
budget reconciliation, 1997, 49
community development bill, 565
repeal effort, 115–117

Republican tax cuts, 1999, 110, 112
  summary, 19, 20
  tax cuts, 1997, 87, 89, 91–94, 95, 98–99
Estonia
  U.S. military aid, 189, 230
Estuary Habitat Restoration Council, 386
Estuary protection, 386–387
Ethanol
  gasoline additive MTBE, 390–391
  price supports, 425
  tax credit, 92
Ethics Committee, House. *See Standards of Official Conduct Committee*
Ethics Committee, Senate Select
  ethics process changes, 774–775
  jurisdiction, leadership, 759–760, 955
"Ethnic cleansing," 178, 204–205
European Union (EU)
  China trade agreement, 160
  U.S. trade
    disputes, 118, 168
    drug reimports, 484
  U.S. troop deployments, 279
Euthanasia, 606, 658
Evans, Lane, D-Ill.
  Export-Import Bank, 157
  House leadership, 760
  land mine limits, 254, 274
Even Start program
  authorization, 82, 529, 531, 535–536
  ed-flex waivers, 543
Everett, Terry, R-Ala.
  defense authorization, 242
Everglades, 341, 344, 372–375
Everglades National Park, 375, 376
Evidence, 696, 701
Ewing, Thomas W., R-Ill.
  campaign finance reform, 788
Ex post facto laws, 701
Excise taxes. *See also Airline ticket taxes; Cigarette and tobacco taxes; Gasoline and motor fuel taxes*
  fish, wildlife conservation, 393
  percentage of GDP, 1935–2000 (table), 91
  tax cuts, 1997, 100, 101–102
  telephones, 102, 116, 118–119, 334–335
  trucks, tires, 102
  vaccines, 100
Executive Office of the President
  advisers' financial disclosure, 750
  appropriations, 68
Executive privilege
  clemency for Puerto Ricans, 669, 682
  Starr investigation, 815
Executive Salary Cost of Living Adjustment Act of 1975, 751
Exit polling, 25
Experimental Program to Stimulate Competitive Research, 752
Expert testimony, 696
Explosive taggants, 267
Export Administration Act, 166–167, 209, 229, 304 (box)
Export Bank, U.S., 157
Export-Import Bank
  authorization, 156–157
  Gazprom aid ban, 186
Exports. *See Foreign trade*
Extradition, 701

F

F-15 aircraft
  appropriations, 249, 284, 288, 296, 297, 300
  authorization, 245, 281, 290, 292, 295
  F-22 funding controversy, 286–287 (box)

F-16 aircraft
  appropriations, 249, 262, 284, 300
  authorization, 245, 258, 281, 290, 292, 295
F-22 aircraft
  appropriations, 76, 237–238, 247, 249, 261, 283, 288, 297, 300
  authorization, 241, 244, 258, 277, 281, 290, 294
  defense policy assessment, 264
  House funding denial (box), 286–287
  test facility, 253 (box)
F/A-18 aircraft
  appropriations, 247, 249, 259, 260, 261, 284, 288, 300
  authorization, 241, 244, 258, 278, 281, 290, 294
  defense policy assessment, 264
  F-22 funding controversy, 286 (box)
FAA. *See Federal Aviation Administration*
Fair Labor Standards Act of 1938
  compensatory time, 576
  employee stock options, 581
  minimum wage, 579
Faircloth, Lauch, R-N.C.
  electoral defeat, 12
  federal-D.C. ties, 740
Fairfax County, Va., 55
Faith-based organizations. *See Churches and religious organizations*
Faleomavaega, Eni F.H., D-Am. Samoa
  beached marine mammals, 380–381
  bird population control, 384
False claims, 696
False Claims Act, 685
False Pass, Alaska, 374
Falun Gong, 209
Family issues. *See also Adoption; Children; Domestic violence; Marriage and divorce; Parental rights and issues*
  business property losses, 104
  compensatory time, 576
  court nepotism ban, 627
  drug abuse prevention, 602
  estate taxes, 99, 116
  immigration, 617, 630, 673
  literacy programs, 82, 491–493, 529
  slain police officers, 614–615, 651
  social services to troubled families, 494
Family Preservation Act, 494
Family Research Council, 527, 574
Family Support Act of 1988, 495
Farias, Hillory J., 654
Farm Service Agency, 420
Farming. *See Agriculture and farming*
Farmworker Justice Fund, 674
Farr, Sam, D-Calif.
  forest revenue, 399
  Salton Sea rehabilitation, 364
Fast-track procedures
  FDA drug review, 448
  high-tech visas, 672
  trade agreements, 7, 147, 151, 153–156, 163
    line-item veto, 65
Fattah, Chaka, D-Pa.
  student loans, 511
Faulkner, Scot M., 768
Fazio, Vic, D-Calif.
  House leadership, 7 (box), 760, 769
FBI. *See Federal Bureau of Investigation*
FCC. *See Federal Communications Commission*
FDA. *See Food and Drug Administration*
FEC. *See Federal Election Commission*
Fed. *See Federal Reserve Board*
Federal Advisory Committee Act, 394
Federal Aviation Administration (FAA)
  appropriations, 67
  authorization, 315, 321, 331–332

  Las Vegas airport, 401
  private space shuttles, 744
Federal budget. *See Budget, U.S.*
Federal buildings
  counterfeit police badges, 644–645
  name-change proposals, 741–742
  security force, 657–658
Federal Bureau of Investigation (FBI)
  armored car robberies, 598
  background checks for gun purchasers, 641
  campaign finance scandals, 808
  DNA evidence, 654–655
  encryption technology, 326, 336
  FALN clemency, 682
  gun registry funding, 598
  Hoover Building name, 741–742
  intelligence authorization, 226
  Internet privacy, 337
  Landrieu election, 784–785
  leadership, 594 (box)
  nuclear lab security, 303 (box), 411
  presidential protection authority, 613
  railroad officer training, 652
  sex offender registries, 604
  terrorism, 267, 309, 605, 646
  unidentified persons, 646
  Waco investigation, 680–681
  White House files use, 804, 805 (box)
Federal Bureau of Prisons
  D.C. system transfer, 54–55, 740
  HIV testing, 600
  prison labor, 603
  prisoner health care, 653
Federal Communications Commission (FCC)
  Internet taxes, 328
  long-distance service "slamming," 330
  satellite TV, 338
  spectrum auctions, 51, 56, 285, 325–326
  television ratings, 327
Federal contractors. *See also Defense contractors*
  affirmative action, 591, 615–616
  competitive bids for park concessions, 358
  Davis-Bacon wage rules, 492–493
  federal source provision, 652–653
  intelligence whistleblowers, 201
  public housing tenant hires, 557
  small business competitiveness, 324–325
  subcontractor protection in bankruptcy, 749–750
  Supreme Court decisions, 712
  transport of prisoners, 653–654
  union preference, 799–800
  VA job discrimination complaints, 497
Federal court judges
  assault penalties, 613, 656
  civil suit assignment, 621, 622
  concealed weapons permits, 669
  judicial activism, 591–592, 593, 620–622, 637
  nepotism ban, 627
  nominations, 622–624, 677–680
    Clinton term summary, 592, 593, 629, 799, 800
    Fletcher, 627–628
  pay, 621, 622, 791
Federal courts. *See also Appeals courts, U.S.; District courts, U.S.; Federal court judges; Supreme Court, U.S.*
  jurisdiction
    habeas corpus appeals, 690
    health care lawsuits, 430, 454
    Internet alcohol sales, 631, 633
    juvenile crime, 593–597, 636
    money laundering, 605–606
    private suits against states, 685
    property rights, 737–738
    secret evidence in deportation, 664

securities fraud lawsuits, 128–129
Y2K liability, 336
operations
appropriations, 63, 74
budget outlays, 1987–2001 (graph), 590
D.C. system, 55
delay list publication, 608
system housekeeping changes, 669
televised proceedings, 622, 669
transferee courts, 669–670
veterans job preference, 501
Supreme Court decisions, 696–697
Federal debt. *See Budget, U.S.*
Federal Election Commission (FEC)
campaign finance reform, 782, 783, 788–790
527 PACs, 786
issue advocacy ads, 780 (box)
Rich donations, 809
voter guides ruling, 790 (box)
congressional ethics investigations
Barr, 774
Gingrich reprimand, 764
McDermott, 765
staff term limits, 68
Supreme Court decisions, 708
Federal Emergency Management Agency
appropriations, FY 1998, 59
terrorism preparedness, 309, 481
Federal employee health insurance
abortion, 68
assisted suicide, 459, 606
contraceptives, 68, 455, 458, 792–793
government share formula, 56
Federal employee pay and benefits. *See also*
Federal employee health insurance
cost-of-living adjustments, 68
retirement plans, 51, 56
D.C. courts, 55
Federal employees. *See also Federal employee pay*
and benefits; Military personnel
D.C. clean air fees, 56
drug testing, 602
ethics office, 750
intelligence whistleblowers, 201
job discrimination, 688
military administration privatization, 265
Supreme Court decisions, 711, 721
tax record snooping ban, 106 (box)
veterans job preference, 500–501
Federal Employees Health Benefits Program,
56, 464
Federal Employees Retirement System, 56
Federal Energy Regulatory Commission (FERC)
electric deregulation, 404–407
Federal government (general). *See also Federal*
buildings; Federal employees; Federal lands; Waste
and abuse in government programs; specific
departments and agencies
alternative fuel use, 356
appropriations, FY 1998, 59
budget outlays, 1987–2001 (graph), 733
campaign use of vehicles, 788, 789
computer upgrades, 62
D.C. relationship, 739–740
document access, 739
invention licensing, 747
ocean policy panel, 364
radio spectrum auctions, 325, 326
regulation review, 749
rulemaking process, 737
rules impact analysis, 749
school impact aid, 531, 535–536
Supreme Court decisions, 710–714
terrorism preparedness, 645–646
Y2K fix, 330, 793
Federal Highway Administration, 67, 332

Federal Home Loan Bank (FHLB) system, 140
Federal Housing Administration (FHA)
affordable housing for elderly, disabled, 567
foreclosure relief, 51, 562–563
loan limits, 563
reverse mortgages, 567
Federal lands. *See also National forests; National*
parks and monuments; National wildlife refuges
acquisition
appropriations, 74, 83–84
Arizona conservation area, 394
CARA, 375–379
GAO study, 403
"no net loss" amendment, 378
Oregon swaps, 403
summary, 17, 20, 372
Alaska swaps, 366–367
budget outlays, FY 1987–2001 (graph), 342
cemetery vandalism, 604
Clinton term summary, 343
coal leases, 413–414
Colorado, Utah conservation areas, 403–404
filming
fees, 356, 387
violent content, 635
grazing leases, 67, 419–420, 356–357
hate crimes, 642, 643
highways and roads
appropriations, 84
closing procedures, 388
projects authorization, 319
Lake Tahoe basin, 402–403
oil drilling revenues, 74, 409
sales
Governors Island, 51, 56
Las Vegas airport, 401
timber harvests, 67, 359
revenue sharing, 399–400
U.N. protection designation, 368, 401
Utah wilderness, 366
Federal Maritime Commission
merger proposal, 322
ocean shipping rates, 322
Federal Motor Carrier Administration, 332
Federal Prison Industries, Inc., 652–653
Federal Protective Service (FPS), 657–658
Federal Reserve Board
audits, 140
chair, on loan fund board, 334
Clinton term summary, 33
financial services modernization, 122–123,
130–136
GAO study, 140
IMF reforms, 66
leadership, 34–35 (box)
monetary policy summary, 38
stock futures, 142
Federal Savings and Loan Insurance
Corporation, 124 (box)
Federal-state relations
assisted suicide, 658–660
Clinton term summary, 5
criminal background checks, 599
juvenile crime, 596
Supreme Court decisions, 684, 685–686
Federal Trade Commission
financial services modernization, 137
identity theft, 600
parental consent to Internet data collection, 68
student aid scams, 546
Federal Trade Commission Act, 348
Federation for American Immigration Reform,
670
Federation of American Hospital Systems, 461
Federation of American Scientists, 200

Feingold, Russell D., D-Wis.
campaign finance reform, 777, 783, 789–790
527 PACs, 786
Clinton impeachment, 823
crime victims' rights, 668
defense policy
appropriations, 260
authorization, 278, 293
flag desecration, 667
methamphetamine traffic, 602
organ transplants, 477
State Department authorization, 191
World War II minorities, 664
Feinstein, Dianne, D-Calif.
balanced budget amendment, 57
Clinton impeachment, 827
education
ed-flex plan, 541
social promotion, 545
flag desecration, 611, 667
Fletcher nomination, 628
gasoline additive MTBE, 391
health
human cloning, 460, 746
"partial birth" abortion, 456
high-tech visas, 591, 617, 671
law enforcement
body armor, 645
crime victims rights, 609, 668
gun control, 640
juvenile crime, 635
Lee nomination, 626
Felons. *See also Criminal background checks;*
Sex offenders
body armor sales ban, 645
employment restriction
Medicaid providers, 442
prisoner transport, 654
gun ownership ban, 635, 642
juveniles, 595, 635, 637, 638, 642
mandatory sentences, 642
work opportunity tax credits, 99
Female genital mutilation, 183, 260
FERC. *See Federal Energy Regulatory Commission*
Ferguson, Roger W. Jr., 34–35 (box), 985
Fetal tissue regulation, 482
FHA. *See Federal Housing Administration*
FHLB. *See Federal Home Loan Bank*
Fifth Amendment
property rights, 737
Filner, Bob, D-Calif.
deportation, 677
Finance Committee, Senate
jurisdiction, leadership, 953
Finn, Chester E. Jr., 524
Fire control and prevention
college dorm systems, 547
firefighters
college aid for slain officers' family, 651
D.C. pensions, 740
home ownership aid, 566
terrorism response training, 295
forest fires, 83, 368, 403
Firearms. *See also Hunting*
AK-47 imports, 163
armored car employees, 598
concealed weapons permits, 598–599, 650
federal judges, 669
criminal background checks for purchasers,
631
domestic violence offenders, 631
gun shows, 30, 538, 629, 635, 636, 637,
639–641
pawnshops, 635, 639–640
Supreme Court decisions, 685
FBI registry, 598

gun control
action, 1999–2000, 637–642
appropriations bills, 76, 81, 301
Clinton term summary, 16, 19, 20, 589–590, 629
ESEA authorization, 531, 536, 538
juvenile crime bill, 633–637
gun manufacturers
bankruptcy, 143, 642
liability suits, 322, 642
gun-related crime
assaults on judges, 613
juvenile offenders, 594–597, 629, 633, 635, 636, 639
mandatory sentences, 597–598, 642
owner liability, 633
WIC voucher fraud, 494
handgun wait period, 638–639
high-capacity ammo clips, 637, 638, 640, 641, 642
maximum number of purchases, 638
merchant storage requirements, 595
minimum age to purchase, 638
nondealer sales at gun shows, 639
ownership ban
assault weapons for minors, 641
domestic violence offenders, 588, 638
felons, 635, 642
violent juveniles, 595, 635, 637, 638, 642
proficiency
Customs Service training center, 85
U.S. marshals, 614
safety locks, 536, 593, 594–596, 598, 633, 634, 635, 637, 638, 640–642
schools
disabled student discipline, 516, 538, 544
restrictions, 545, 636, 637, 639, 641
shootings statistics collection, 536
semi-automatic weapons, 635
Firestone tire recall, 331, 333
First Amendment. See also Church-state separation; Freedom of association; Freedom of religion; Freedom of speech
California term limits, 783 (box)
campaign finance reform, 789
527 PACs, 787
classified information leaks, 204, 227, 228
McDermott ethics probe, 765, 774
NEA funding, 738 (box)
religious expression, 612
Supreme Court decisions, 688–689, 714–716
Fish and fisheries
Alaska land swaps, 367
bird population control, 384
conservation programs, 376
coral reef protection, 393
dolphin protection treaty, 341, 344, 345–348
estuary restoration, 386–387
Fish and Wildlife Service spending, 392–393
fishing in wildlife refuges, 348–349
Great Lakes restoration projects, 357
marine sanctuaries, 388
ocean policy panel, 364
Oregon wilderness, 403
salmon project, 395
sea lion protection, 82, 393–394
shark protection, 348, 372, 395–396
striped bass moratorium, 380
subsistence fishing, 388
Fish and Wildlife Service, U.S.
bird population control, 384–385
endangered species protection, 350, 385
filming fees, 387
Fish and Wildlife Foundation board, 356
Great Lakes restoration projects, 357–358
migratory bird hunting, 358

national wildlife refuges, 348
ocean policy panel, 364
revenue from seized items, 369–370
salmon project, 395
spending restrictions, 392–393
Fiske, Robert B., 804
Fitzgerald, Peter G., R-Ill.
election, 11
patients' rights, 468, 470
Fitzsimmons, Ron, 456
Fitzwater, Marlin, 805 (box)
Flag, U.S.
desecration ban amendment, 591, 593, 610–611, 629, 666–668
King birthday display, 751–752
Flake, Floyd H., 14
Fletcher, Betty Binns, 627–628
Fletcher, William A., 623, 627–628, 989
Flood control projects
Endangered Species Act waivers, 351
Everglades restoration, 372–373, 375
watershed dams, 385
Flood insurance, 561
Floods
disaster relief appropriations, 58
Florida
bankruptcy judges, 608
bankruptcy overhaul, 127, 143
children's health insurance, 438, 443
college savings plan, 685
congressional elections, 28
Everglades restoration, 341, 344, 372–375
financial services modernization, 123 (box)
gubernatorial election, 1998, 13
Internet gambling, 337
presidential election, 2000, 21–22, 25
chronology (box), 26–27
summary, 20
Supreme Court decisions, 684, 686–687 (box)
space programs, 735
welfare benefits for immigrants, 619
Florida Bay, 375
Florida Supreme Court, 21, 25, 26 (box), 686 (box)
Florio, James J., 8
Flunitrazepam, 654
Foglietta, Thomas M., 14
Foley, Mark, R-Fla.
hate crimes, 642
student loans, 511
Food and Agriculture Organization, 219
Food and Drug Administration (FDA)
drug reimports, 483–484
overhaul, 444–454
mission statement, 453
summary, 6, 429, 431
RU486, 63, 431, 455, 482
tobacco regulation, 316, 323–324, 482, 690, 691
Food and nutrition. See also Food assistance programs; Food safety; Meat; Milk and dairy products
China trade agreement, 161
food exemption in sanctions, 76, 83, 159, 170, 200, 223–226
foreign trade sanctions, 418, 424, 426
labeling, 444, 445, 446, 452
Medicare coverage
diet counseling, 50
nutritional therapy, 463
Food assistance programs. See also Child nutrition programs; Food stamps
Meals on Wheels, 431, 496
outlays, FY 1987–2001 (graph), 488
WIC authorization, 431, 494–495
Food safety
agricultural research authorization, 422

dairy recalls, 420
irradiation, 446, 452
packaging standards, 446, 452
Food stamps
authorization, 421–422
budget reconciliation, FY 1997, 51
budget resolution, FY 1998, 45
immigrant benefits, 419, 421, 422, 486, 490
military qualifiers, 293
prisoners, 489, 495
welfare law revisions, 486–490
Footwear imports, 158
Ford, Gerald R.
budget policy, 40
China trade agreement, 161
environmental policy, 342
fast track for trade pacts, 155
Nixon pardon, 808
veto use, 811
Ford, James D., 775
Ford Motor Co., 333
Ford, Wendell H., D-Ky.
nuclear waste storage, 361
Senate leadership, 7 (box), 759, 769
successor, 12
telecommunications "slamming," 330
Fordice, Kirk, 18
Foreign aid
agency reorganization, 191
AIDS assistance, 230
appropriations
FY 1998, 183–186
FY 1999, 66, 186–189
FY 2000, 73, 75, 210–214
FY 2001, 83, 214–217
authorization proposal, 228–229
budget outlays, 1987–2001 (chart), 174
Clinton term summary, 173, 176, 177, 204
Colombia antidrug initiative, 220–221
military aid authorization, 229–230
military humanitarian missions, 247
Peace Corps, 230
sanctions
oil producers, 414
Pakistan, 224
policy reform, 169
Russia, 222, 223
sex trafficking, 629–630, 632
State Department authorization, 191–192, 218
Foreign currency exchange
dollar strength, 149–150
stability, in trade talks, 156
Foreign Intelligence Advisory Board, 269, 279, 302, 303, 305
Foreign languages
bilingual education, 516–518
Foreign nationals
campaign finance
investigations, 181–182
reform action, 781, 788, 789
military, nuclear lab visits, 279
professional licenses, 491
Sanchez election, 785
Foreign policy. See also Defense policy; Foreign aid; Foreign service and diplomacy; Foreign trade; Immigration and emigration; State Department
appropriations, FY 1998, 59
budget outlays, 1987–2001 (chart), 174
campaign finance investigations, 778
Clinton administration leadership, 179 (box)
Clinton term summary, 6, 16, 20, 173–176, 204, 800–803
economic sanctions reform, 169–170
federal agency reorganization, 68–69, 185, 189–192, 193–194
food sanctions, 426

Foreign Relations Committee, Senate
  jurisdiction, leadership, 760, 953–954
  prestige, 176, 228
Foreign sales corporations, 118
Foreign service and diplomacy
  Clinton term summary, 173, 175, 177
  diplomatic immunity, 203
  embassy security, 75, 144, 217–218, 219, 262,
    267, 803
    Marine guards, 280
  Hong Kong trade offices, 158
  nominations delay, 222, 800
  sanctions for religious persecution, 198–199
  U.S. embassy in Jerusalem, 191, 192, 218, 219
Foreign trade. *See also Agricultural exports and*
  imports; Arms sales; Export-Import Bank; Foreign
  trade sanctions; Oil; Ships and shipping; Tariffs;
  Trade agreements
  action
    1997–1998, 151–159
    1999–2000, 160–170
    summary, 16, 39, 147–150, 151, 173, 175,
      800–801
  banking, 123 (box), 140
  Canadian border controls, 676
  China status, 151–153
    army affiliates, 182
  "dolphin-safe" tuna, 345–348
  drugs, medical devices, 453, 483–484
  dumping, 163, 333
    antidumping fee redirection, 83
  export assistance
    appropriations, 66
    energy conservation, 356
    foreign aid appropriations, 188
  export controls, 302, 305
    China policy, 180, 181, 209
    dual-use technology, 166–167
    encryption technology, 318, 326–327, 336
    military aid authorization, 229
    missile technology, 254, 256–257, 259, 282
    supercomputers, 242, 243, 245, 291, 293, 304
      (box)
  import duties waivers, 105
  import restrictions
    bear parts ban, 381
    exported prescription drugs, 83
    high-capacity ammo clips, 640
    ivory ban, 369
    prison labor, 182
    steel quotas, 168–169
  import "surges," 162 (box), 163, 165
  foreign investment in U.S., 150
    immigrant status, 617
    land acquisition, 401
  job retraining aid, 154, 155
  mergers with foreign firms, 304 (box)
  ocean shipping, 321–322
  OPIC authorization, 159, 169
  patent overhaul, 324, 334
  satellite launches, 180–181, 254–255
  status nomenclature, 108, 109
  Supreme Court decisions, 693
  trade balance, 1985–2000 (graph), 148
    U.S. deficit, 149–150
  U.S. tax law changes, 106
    credits holding period, 104
    income earned abroad, 117, 118
    interest expenses, 112
    joint ventures, 101
    passive investment accounts, 101
    software sales, 101
Foreign trade sanctions
  action
    1997–1998, 199–200
    1999–2000, 223–226

  summary, 204
  African elephant conservation, 369
  agricultural exports, 420–421, 424, 426
  arms sales, 164–165
  China, 182, 209
  Cuba, 223–226
    agricultural exports, 421, 424, 426
    appropriations bills, 76, 81, 83, 170
    summary, 16, 173, 204
  food, medicine exemptions, 83, 159, 170, 424
  India, Pakistan for nuclear tests
    agricultural exports, 159, 421
    defense bills, 284, 288–289
    summary, 204
    waiver authority, 170, 200, 223–224
  Iraq, 803
  oil price-fixing, 414
  policy reform, 169–170
  religious persecution, 198–199
  Russia, 195–196, 221–223, 268, 270
  Serbia, 208
  state powers, 686
  Yugoslavia, 178, 180
Forensics labs, 657
Forest Counties Payment Committee, 399
Forest Service, U.S.
  Alaska road development, 379
  California logging, 368
  filming fees, 387
  Hells Canyon jetboats, 367
  Lake Tahoe water studies, 402–403
  revenue sharing, 399–400
  road closing procedures, 388
  roadless areas, 394–395
Forests and forest products. *See also National*
  forests
  Alaska development bills, 379
  China trade agreement, 161
  clean water regulations, 382–383
  northern spotted owl, 392
  timber harvests on federal lands, 359
  tropical rain forest protection, 369
  wildfire prevention, 83, 368, 403
Forfeiture. *See also Search and seizure*
  civil assets in crime, 590–591, 604–605, 629,
    647–649
    drug-trafficking, 226–227
  Supreme Court decisions, 701–702
Fort Atkinson, Neb., 285
Fort Bliss, Tex., 253 (box)
Fort Bragg, N.C., 253 (box)
Fort Campbell, Ky., 253 (box)
Fort Carson, Colo., Rail Yard, 252 (box)
Fort Davis National Historic Site, 359
Fort Derussey, Hawaii, 252 (box)
Fort Douglas, Utah, 252 (box)
Fort Drum, N.Y., 253 (box)
Fort Irwin, Calif., 248, 252 (box)
Fort Knox, Ky., 253 (box)
Fossella, Vito J., R-N.Y.
  election, 9
  FALN clemency, 682
Foster care
  adoption, 431, 493–494
  earned income tax credit rules, 471
  post-care aid for older teenagers, 496
Foster, Henry W. Jr., 435 (box), 678
Foster, Murphy J. "Mike," 17, 784
Foster, Vincent W. Jr., 813
401(k) pension plans
  contribution limits, 105, 112, 117, 119, 582
  military personnel, 280
Fourteenth Amendment
  California term limits, 783 (box)
  Supreme Court decisions, 685, 688
  welfare benefits, 688

Fourth Amendment, 271, 690
Fowler, Tillie, R-Fla.
  Kosovo policy, 205
  term limits, 784
Fowler, Wyche Jr., 986
Fox, Jon D., R-Pa.
  electoral defeat, 13
Fox, Sarah, 679
FPS. *See Federal Protective Service*
France
  NATO expansion, 273
Frank, Barney, D-Mass.
  asbestos compensation, 665
  bankruptcy law overhaul, 142
  civil assets forfeiture, 648
  defense policy
    appropriations, 247
    authorization, 279
  home ownership aid, 566
  intelligence authorization, 201
  judicial activism, 621
  public housing reform, 556, 557
  religious expression, 660
  term limits, 783
Frank, Steve, 787
Franking privilege
  campaign finance reform, 789
  McCain ethics complaint, 771
Franks, Bob, R-N.J.
  election defeat, 29
Fraud. *See also Consumer protection; Waste and*
  abuse in government programs
  cell phone cloning, 329
  elderly victims, 675
  election fraud
    Landrieu investigation, 784
    Sanchez election, 785
  electronic signatures, 335–336
  false IDs, 657
  identity theft, 600
  "pretext" telephoning, 132, 137
  securities fraud lawsuits, 128–129
  sex trafficking, 629
  student aid scams, 531, 546
  Teamsters probe, 578 (box)
  Whitewater scandal, 805 (box)
  WIC vouchers, 494–495
Free Congress Research and Education
  Foundation, 623
Free Trade Area of the Americas, 148, 153, 158
Freedom of association
  "blanket primaries," 688
  Boy Scouts gay exclusion, 689, 715
Freedom of Information Act
  Civil Rights Commission, 609
  Supreme Court decisions, 712
Freedom of religion
  China policy, 182, 183, 209
    trade agreement, 162 (box), 165
    trade status, 149, 166
    summits, 183 (box)
  religious expression, 660–661
    amendment, 591, 593, 611–612
  sanctions for foreign persecution, 177, 198–199
  visa denial, 183, 260
Freedom of speech
  animal cruelty videos, 651
  campaign finance reform, 780, 781
  flag desecration, 610–611, 666–667
  Supreme Court decisions, 684, 715–716
  voter guides ruling, 790 (box)
Freedom of the press
  classified information disclosure, 228
Freedom to Farm Act of 1996, 417
Freeh, Louis J.
  campaign finance scandals, 808

FBI leadership, 594 (box)
Landrieu election, 785
nuclear security, 303 (box)
Frelinghuysen, Rodney, R-N.J.
partial-birth abortion, 456
Frist, Bill, R-Tenn.
education
ed-flex plan, 527–528, 539
Title 1 authorization, 537
health policy
child health bills, 482
health policy research agency, 478
human cloning, 460, 746
medical errors, 479
Medicare commission, 465
Medicare drug benefits, 465–466
organ transplants, 475–477
patients' rights, 467
NASA authorization, 752
space station, 753
tobacco regulation, 324
TVA federal subsidy, 371
Frost, Martin, D-Texas
China trade agreement, 162
House leadership, 7 (box), 769
Fund for Rural America, 421
Furse, Elizabeth, D-Ore.
nuclear waste storage, 362

G

GAF Corp., 665
Galbraith, Gatewood, 18
Gallagher, Neil, 682
Gallegly, Elton, R-Calif.
affirmative action, 616
animal cruelty, 651
high-tech visas, 671
immigration 245(i) provision, 620
Galvez Letona, Gustavo, 676
Galvin, Matthew, 736
Gambling
bankruptcy overhaul, 126, 127, 608
casino advertising, 688
casino income taxes, 92
Internet regulation, 316, 328–329, 331, 337
loss tax deductions, 520
lump sum payments, 443
Gamma hydroxybutyric acid (GHB), 654
Gandhi, Mohandas K.
D.C. memorial, 359
Gangs
antiloitering law, 690, 704
juvenile crime, 593–597, 634, 635
prevention programs, 491
school resource officers, 530
witness intimidation, 601
Ganske, Greg, R-Iowa
FDA tobacco regulation, 482
Medicare changes, 434
patients' rights, 455, 468
superfund overhaul, 396
GAO. See General Accounting Office
Garfield, James A., 28
Gasoline
fuel efficiency standards, 333 (box)
MTBE additive ban, 390–391
sulfur levels, 382
Gasoline and motor fuel taxes
aviation fuel, 102
diesel taxes, 580
federal tax, 372, 409–410
budget resolution, FY 2001, 80
summary, 315
surface transportation authorization, 319
tax cuts, 1997, 92, 93, 100

kerosene, 102
underground tank cleanup, 102, 370
Gates, Bill, 38
GATT. See General Agreement on Tariffs and Trade
Gaylord, Joseph, 763
Gazprom, 186
"GEAR UP" program, 513
Geese, 358, 384–385
Gejdenson, Sam, D-Conn.
election defeat, 29
House leadership, 760, 770
State Department authorization, 218
Gekas, George W., R-Pa.
affirmative action, 616
bankruptcy overhaul, 127, 143
judgeships expansion, 608
Clean Air Act, 351
Gender-based hate crimes, 642–644
General Accounting Office (GAO)
budget law history, 44 (box)
Civil Rights Commission regulations, 608
Education Department audit, 548
estimates and studies
Amtrak debt, 321
anthrax immunization, 289
ATM fees, 137
census sampling, 733, 736
community development, 564
counterfeit police badges, 645
drug economic benefits, 448
ed-flex plan, 540
export controls on computers, 243
F-22 aircraft, 247
FDA review time, 445
federal land swaps, 403
Federal Reserve roles, 140
Fish and Wildlife Service spending, 393
global warming treaty, 354, 355
home inspections for FHA loans, 563
job training overhaul, 573
Joint Strike Fighter, 290
Landrieu election, 784
Medicare payments, 462–463
military base closings, 243
military weapons warranties, 245
NASA programs, 734, 753
North Korea nuclear capability, 186
nuclear lab security, 412
S corporations, 140–141
vehicle emissions, 365
federal rules impact analysis, 749
IRS oversight, 109
veterans job preference, 501
General Agreement on Tariffs and Trade (GATT)
China trade agreement, 160
U.S. trade policy summary, 147, 148, 151
General Dynamics, 245, 288
General Electric, 120, 125
General Services Administration, 657–658
Generalized System of Preferences (GSP), 105, 159, 168, 169
Genetic engineering, 422
Genetics
medical privacy, 480
Geneva Protocol of 1925, 269 (box)
Genocide
Armenia resolution, 231
Saddam indictment proposal, 197
Geological Survey, U.S.
coastal water quality, 380
methane research, 389
Georgia (Republic)
CFE treaty changes, 274
"Silk Road" trade, 169
U.S. aid appropriations, 185, 189

Georgia (State)
Air Force maintenance depots, 240, 243
congressional elections, 17, 30
F-22 funding controversy, 286 (box)
redistricting, 688
Georgia College and State University, 547
Gephardt, Richard A., D-Mo.
appropriations, 63
Clinton impeachment, 816, 818, 822
congressional pay, 791
defense appropriations, 296
FALN clemency, 681
financial services modernization, 134
health
drug reimports, 483
Medicare changes, 433
Medicare drug benefits, 466
partial-birth abortion, 456
House ethics overhaul, 766
House leadership
Gingrich coup attempt, 763 (box)
Gingrich reprimand, 762
House chaplain, 775
House organization, 760, 769
remarks on election (text), 1029–1031
Sanchez election, 785
summary, 7 (box), 757, 758
IRS overhaul, 107
Kosovo policy, 205
nuclear waste storage, 408
Reagan National airport, 742
superfund overhaul, 352
trade policy
China-U.S. trade, 152, 164
fast track procedures, 153, 156
Russia sanctions, 196
German Americans, 664
Germany
economic conditions, 39
Gerrymanders, 788 (box)
GHB. See Gamma hydroxybutyric acid
Gibbon protection, 379–380
Gibbons, Jim, R-Nev.
Las Vegas airport, 401
nuclear waste storage, 362
Gibbons, Sam M., 760
Gift taxes, 91, 98–99, 110, 116
Gilchrest, Wayne T., R-Md.
"dolphin-safe" tuna, 346
estuary restoration, 386
Gilman, Benjamin A., R-N.Y.
China policy, 208
defense authorization, 254, 255
foreign aid appropriations, 184
Kosovo policy, 205
overseas study grants, 549
sanctions for oil producers, 414
State Department authorization, 190–191, 192, 218
Gilmore, James S. III, 8, 309
Gingrich, Newt, R-Ga.
appropriations omnibus bill, 11, 63
budget reconciliation, 1997, 49–50, 53
campaign finance reform, 776, 780–781
scandals, 808
voter guides ruling, 790 (box)
census controversies, 736
China-U.S. trade, 152–153
congressional pay, 791–792
defense policy
appropriations, 247, 259
authorization, 258
education tax incentives, 522
ethics reprimand, 757–758, 759, 761–764, 774
book advance, 807 (box)
committee rules overhaul, 766

McDermott ethics probe, 765, 774
  report excerpts (text), 1024–1029
fast track for trade pacts, 154, 349, 350
federal-D.C. ties, 740
financial services regulation
  credit union expansion, 128
  modernization, 122, 125
foreign policy
  Iraq, 197
  Russia sanctions, 196
  State Department authorization, 192
grazing fees, 420
health policy
  Medicare commission, 464
  patients' rights, 454
House leadership
  attempted coup, 50, 94–95, 762–763 (box)
  cell phone interception, 329
  Clinton veto use, 810
  committee funding, 767
  House elections, 1998, 13
  House organization, 760
  House rules, 760
  remarks on election (text), 1022–1024
  resignation, 10, 15, 17, 24, 769, 813, 819
  successor, 17
  summary, 3, 6, 7 (box), 11, 757–758
HUD cost reductions, 562
NEA funding, 738
nuclear waste storage, 361, 363
religious expression, 612
school vouchers, 528–529
space programs, 735
surface transportation authorization, 319
tax cuts, 1997, 94–95
tobacco settlement, 322
Ginsburg, Ruth Bader
  assisted suicide, 687
  Florida presidential vote, 26, 687 (box)
  initiative petitions, 688
  Supreme Court summary, 684, 685, 689 (box)
Giuliani, Rudolph W., 9, 28, 806–807 (box)
Glacier Bay National Park, 367, 388
Glass-Steagall Act of 1933, 122, 123, 124 (box), 130, 135
Glaucoma screening, 463
Glenn Amendment, 200
Glenn, John, D-Ohio
  Senate leadership, 769
  space shuttle mission (box), 742
  successor, 12
Glickman, Dan, 420 (box), 422, 978 (box)
Global climate change
  appropriations, 67
  Clinton term summary, 799
  Kyoto protocol, 70, 354–356, 341, 344, 345
  Triana project, 752
Global Climate Coalition, 187
Global Environment Facility, 188, 189, 214, 216, 217
Global Positioning Satellites, 282
Globalization, 39, 147–149, 800–801
"Go Girl" program, 537
Goals 2000 program, 527, 532
Gober, Hershel W., 986
Gold
  IMF reserves for debt relief, 213 (box)
Goldin, Daniel S., 734–735, 744
Goldman, Sheldon, 621
González, Elián, 83, 204, 225 (box), 426, 592
Gonzalez, Henry B., D-Texas
  House leadership, 770
  public housing reform, 556
Goodlatte, Robert W., R-Va.
  campaign finance reform, 782

forest revenues, 399
Y2K liability, 336
Goodling, Bill, R-Pa.
  compensatory time, 576
  education
    block grants, 527
    ed-flex plan, 540, 541
    ESEA authorization, 532–536
    Even Start program, 535
    federal funds shifting, 536
    Head Start, 491–493
    IDEA authorization, 515
    national testing, 524
    teacher training, 511, 533
    Title I, 534
    vocational education, 514
  union "salting," 585
GOPAC, 763–764
Gordon, Bart, D-Tenn.
  superfund overhaul, 398
Gordon, John A., 306, 412
Gore, Al
  campaign finance scandals, 807–808
    news conference (text), 1032–1035
  Clinton impeachment, 823
  energy supplies, 410
  global climate change, 799
  hate crimes, 643
  National Performance Review, 193
  nuclear test ban treaty, 311
  Paez nomination, 679
  presidential election, 2000, 21–27
    China trade agreement, 160, 162
    Clinton role, 798, 804, 813
    concession speech (text), 1055
    Cuba sanctions, 224
    debt reduction, 85
    effect on Clinton-Lazio race, 807 (box)
    environmental issues, 344, 372
    foreign policy summary, 175
    popular, electoral vote by region (table), 21
    Russia expertise, 222, 223
    summary, 4, 20
    Supreme Court decisions, 684, 686–687 (box)
    vice presidential candidates, 412
  Senate votes as vice president
    electoral vote challenge, 22
    gun control, 16, 634, 635, 637, 639, 640
    Republican deterrence, 143
  space shuttle, 744
  student loans, 509
  Triana project, 752
  TVA subsidy, 69
Gorilla protection, 379–380
Gorton, Slade, R-Wash.
  Colombia antidrug aid, 221
  education
    block grants, 517, 519, 520
    IDEA authorization, 516
    school vouchers, 539
  election defeat, 28
  electric deregulation, 406
  judicial nominations, 624
    Fletcher, 627
  NEA funding, 750
  product liability, 322
Goshute Indian reservation, 366
Goss, Porter J., R-Fla.
  defense authorization, 279
  House leadership, 760
  intelligence authorization, 226
  Russia sanctions, 223
Government ethics. See also Congressional ethics
  Export-Import Bank, 157
  federal prosecutors, 66
  gratuities law ruling, 792 (box)

outside advisers, 750
Tenet, Holbrooke inquiries, 179 (box)
trade representative restrictions, 152 (box)
Government Ethics, Office of, 750
Government Printing Office (GPO), 739
Government Reform and Oversight Committee, House
  funding, 767
  jurisdiction, leadership, 760, 959
Governmental Affairs Committee, Senate
  campaign finance reform, 776–777, 778
  jurisdiction, leadership, 759, 769, 954
Governors. See National Governors' Association
  1997 elections, 8
    returns, 1073
  1998 elections, 11, 13
    returns, 1074–1080
  1999 elections, 18
    returns, 1081
  2000 elections, 21, 30
    returns, 1082–1088
  list, 1997–2001, 1094–1095
Governors Island, N.Y., 51, 56
GPO. See Government Printing Office
Graduate education
  employer-provided tuition aid, 544, 545
  pediatrics, 478
Graham, Bob, D-Fla.
  Central American refugees, 619
  education
    education savings accounts, 544, 545
    student loans, 512
  health policy
    Medicare drug benefits, 466
    Medicare payments, 435, 462, 463
    nursing home evictions, 485
  nuclear waste storage, 363
Graham, Lindsey, R-S.C.
  asbestos compensation, 666
  Clinton impeachment, 820
  fetal rights, 474, 662
  job training overhaul, 574
  student loans, 510
  surface transportation authorization, 319
Gramlich, Edward, 35 (box), 985
Gramm, Phil, R-Texas
  budget resolution, FY 2001, 80
  China trade agreement, 163
  commodities law overhaul, 141
  credit union expansion, 128
  defense appropriations, 298
  disabled workers' insurance, 471
  education savings accounts, 544–545
  electronic signatures, 335
  farmworker visas, 674
  fast track for trade pacts, 154
  financial services modernization, 121, 122, 126, 130, 132–135
  foreign aid authorization, 228–229
  judicial nominations, 623, 624
  railroad pensions, 581
  rural TV, 338
  Senate leadership, 769
  surface transportation authorization, 319
  tax cuts, 1997, 93
Gramm-Rudman-Hollings Act of 1985, 44 (box)
Grams, Rod, R-Minn.
  defense authorization, 243
  election defeat, 28
  Export-Import Bank, 157
  Minnesota wilderness, 367
  Peña nomination, 347 (box)
Grand Staircase-Escalante National Monument, 365–366, 389, 799
Grapes, 161
Grapes of Wrath, 394

Grassley, Charles E., R-Iowa
  arbitration in federal courts, 607
  bankruptcy overhaul, 127
  corporate income earned abroad, 118
  health policy
    Medicaid for disabled children, 565
    medical errors, 479
    Medicare changes, 436
  juvenile crime, 597
  off-duty police officers, 614
  Senate leadership, 760
Grazing
  Clinton term summary, 341, 343, 345
  fees, 356–357, 419–420
  lease renewal, 67, 74–75
  national park provision, 381
Great apes, 379–380
Great Britain
  antimissile defenses, 308
  Hong Kong reversion, 152–153, 158
  Iraq weapons programs, 803
  military reconnaissance vehicle, 299
  U.S. export controls, 229
Great Lakes
  coastal water quality, 380
  ocean policy panel, 392
  restoration projects, 357–358
Great Plains
  bird population control, 384
Great Sand Dunes National Park and Preserve,
  381
Greece
  U.S. aid appropriations, 66, 186
Green, Gene, D-Texas
  low-level nuclear waste, 360
Green, Joyce Hens, 790 (box)
Green, Mark, R-Wis.
  child molesters, 647
Green Party, 22
Green, Pincus, 808
Greenhouse gases, 354–356
Greenpeace, 346
Greenspan, Alan
  balanced budget amendment, 57
  commodities regulation, 141
  economic policy leadership, 33, 34 (box),
    983–984
  financial services modernization, 131–134
  monetary policy summary, 38
Greenwood, James C., R-Pa.
  abortion, 474
  foreign aid appropriations, 211, 215
  juvenile crime, 636
  superfund overhaul, 396, 398
Gregg, Judd, R-N.H.
  defense appropriations, 283
  disabled education
    IDEA authorization, 516
    literacy bill, 529
  education
    ed-flex plan, 540
    teacher liability protection, 539
    Title I authorization, 537
  FDA overhaul, 445
  juvenile crime, 633
  supplemental appropriations, 85
  terrorism, 308
Grissom Air Reserve Base, Ind., 253 (box)
Grizzly bears, 356, 377
Groundwater
  California projects, 374, 383
  Everglades restoration, 375
  gasoline additive MTBE, 390–391
  superfund overhaul, 352, 397
Grove, Andy, 616
GSP. See Generalized System of Preferences

Guatemala
  congressional access to intelligence, 202
  immigrants, refugees in U.S., 619–620, 671–672
  international adoptions, 231
Gubernatorial elections. See Governors
Guilty pleas, 702
Gulf War. See Persian Gulf War
Gun control. See Firearms
Gun Owners of America, 594, 597, 639
Gunnison River, 381
Gutierrez, Luis V., D-Ill.
  homeless programs, 561
  public housing reform, 556
  Puerto Rico status, 741

H

H-1B visas, 68, 591, 593, 616–619, 629
H-2A visas, 673–674
H-60 helicopters, 280, 288, 295, 300
Habeas corpus appeals, 621, 622, 690, 702–703
Habiger, Eugene E., 303
Habitat conservation, 350
Hagel, Chuck, R-Neb.
  527 PACs, 786
  land mines, 274
**Hague Convention on Protection of Children
  and Cooperation in Respect of Intercountry
  Adoption,** 231
Haiti
  immigrants, refugees in U.S., 68, 490, 619, 671,
    672, 673
  U.S. military deployments, 174, 277, 279, 281
  war criminals, 646
Hall, Ralph M., D-Texas
  assisted suicide, 606
  low-level nuclear waste, 360
  Medicare changes, 434
  superfund overhaul, 398
Hamilton, Lee H., D-Ind.
  House leadership, 770
  nuclear security, 303 (box)
  State Department authorization, 191, 192
Hansen, James V., R-Utah
  Gingrich reprimand, 762–763
  House leadership, 760, 770
  national parks
    national monuments designation, 390
    operations, 358
    projects, 359
Harkin, Tom, D-Iowa
  defense appropriations, 284, 298
  juvenile crime, 636
  medical errors, 479
  NATO expansion, 274
  school construction, 538
  Senate leadership, 760
  visas for high-tech workers, 591, 618
Harman, Jane, D-Calif.
  defense authorization, 242
  election, 29
Harrah's Entertainment, 785
Harris, Eric, 633
Harris, Katherine, 25, 26 (box), 686 (box)
Harrison, Benjamin, 22
Hartford, Rosa, 457, 474
Hastert, J. Dennis, R-Ill.
  appropriations, 73, 82, 85
  budget process, 16–17
  budget resolution, FY 2000, 72–73
  business investment incentives, 82
  China trade agreement, 161
  community development, 564–565
  drug czar authorization, 603
  education
    college sports, 511

    teacher training, 532
  ethanol plant, 425
  Everglades restoration, 374
  financial services modernization, 134
  527 PACs, 787
  foreign policy
    Armenia genocide resolution, 231
    Colombia antidrug aid, 85, 220
    foreign aid appropriations, 212, 215
    international narcotics control, 176
    Kosovo policy, 205
    Russia policy task force, 175
  gun control, 640–641
  health policy
    Medicare drug benefits, 466
    Medicare payments, 462, 463
    patients' rights, 468
    physician antitrust, 480
  House leadership
    House audit, 770 (box)
    House chaplain, 775
    remarks on election (text), 1029–1031
    summary, 7 (box), 758, 769, 809, 812
  minimum wage, 580
  Republican tax cuts, 1999, 111
  Strategic Petroleum Reserve, 409
Hastings, Richard "Doc," R-Wash.
  salmon project, 395
Hatch, Orrin G., R-Utah
  assisted suicide, 477, 659
  bankruptcy law overhaul, 143
  baseball antitrust exemption, 324
  budget resolution, FY 1998, 48
  China trade agreement, 163
  civil assets forfeiture, 648
  congressional pay, 791
  disabled citizenship applicants, 676
  drug reimports, 484
  education savings accounts, 545
  FALN clemency, 682
  FBI building name, 742
  flag desecration, 610–611, 668
  high-tech visas, 670–672
  immigration relief, 673
  Internet privacy, 337
  judicial nominations, 623, 624, 678
    Fletcher, 627–628
  law enforcement
    alternative sentencing, 644
    assisted suicide, 607
    civil assets forfeiture, 591
    gun control, 642
    handgun safety locks, 598
    hate crimes, 643
    juvenile crime, 595, 596, 634, 635, 637
    pardon process, 682–683
    U.S. marshals, 614
    Waco investigation, 681
  Lee nomination, 625–627
  Medicare changes, 436
  religious expression, 660–661
  tax cuts, 1997, 93
  Supreme Court volunteers, 616
Hate crimes
  definition expansion, 20, 293, 629, 642–644
  Education Department prevention programs,
    507, 536, 538
  federal prosecution, 74
  flag desecration, 610
  Supreme Court decisions, 690
Hawaii
  coral reef protection, 393
  Native Hawaiian education, 534
  unexploded bomb removal, 248
Hawn, Goldie, 161
Hayden, Michael V., 227

Hayes, Rutherford B., 22
Hayworth, J.D., R-Ariz.
  casino income taxes, 92
  congressional pay, 792
Hazardous substances. *See also Air pollution; Food safety; Nuclear waste disposal; Radiation; Tobacco; Toxic waste cleanup; Waste disposal; Water pollution*
  asbestos compensation, 664–666
  gasoline additive MTBE, 390
  mercury study, 453
  Persian Gulf War veterans, 497
Head Start, 11, 486, 491–493, 798
Health and Human Services Department, U.S.
  appropriations, 59–60, 67, 73–74, 81–82
  health
    bioterrorism, 481
    breast, cervical cancer, 472
    date-rape drugs, 654
    drug, medical device regulation, 446–453, 483–484
    medical records privacy, 20, 479
    Medicare changes, 439, 441
    organ transplants, 475–477, 481
  information availability to VA, 499
  leadership, 435 (box)
  welfare and social services
    child poverty report, 545
    child support order registry, 103
    fraud against the elderly, 675
    Head Start, 491
    homeless programs, 561
    international adoptions, 231
  welfare law revisions, 490
Health care. *See also Child health and safety; Food and nutrition; Hazardous substances; Health care providers; Health care; Health insurance; Hospitals; Immunizations; Long-term health care; Medical devices and equipment; Medical research; Mental health and illness; Military health care; Nursing homes; Organ transplants; Rural health care; Veterans health care; Women's health; specific diseases*
  assisted suicide, 606–607
  budget outlays, 1987–2001 (graph), 434
  clinical practice guidelines, 478
  Clinton term summary, 19, 20
  federal prisoners, 653
  medical errors, 429, 478–479
  public health emergencies, 481–482
  quality measurement, 477–478
  Republican platform, 23
  smokers' costs, 323
Health Care Financing Administration
  home health care, 443
  Medicare "givebacks," 461
  tobacco settlement, 323
Health care providers. *See also Nurses; Physicians*
  antitrust, 480–481
  clinical research education, 481
  dentists' VA pay, 502
  medical errors, 478–479
  medical privacy, 479
  Medicare payments, 429, 461
  physical therapist visas, 671
  whistleblower protections, 470
Health, Education, Labor and Pensions Committee, Senate
  jurisdiction, leadership, 954
Health insurance. *See also Children's Health Insurance Program; Federal employee health insurance; Health maintenance organizations (HMOs); Managed health care plans; Medicaid; Medicare; Medical savings accounts*
  deductibility for self-employed, 98, 105, 106, 112, 115, 422–423, 580

disabled workers, 15, 470–471
medical records privacy, 479–480
Medigap policies, 439
patients' rights, 430, 454, 466–470
physician antitrust, 480–481
prescription drug benefits, 465–466
Health Insurance Association of America, 466
Health Insurance Portability and Accountability Act, 479
Health maintenance organizations (HMOs)
  Clinton term summary, 15
  Medicare payments, 430, 432, 434, 438, 463
  patients' rights, 454
Health Marts, 468, 469 (box)
Heart disease
  defibrillator liability shield, 481
Hefley, Joel, R-Colo.
  campaign finance reform, 782
  defense authorization, 254
  national parks
    filming fees, 356, 387
    new Colorado parks, 381
    operations, 358
Hefner, W.G. "Bill," D-N.C.
  congressional pay, 793
Helicopter carriers
  appropriations, 262, 283, 284, 285, 288, 296, 297, 300
  authorization, 255, 257, 258, 276, 277, 282, 292, 295
Hells Canyon National Recreation Area, 367
Helmke, Paul, 12
Helms, Jesse, R-N.C.
  China trade agreement, 164, 165
  defense policy
    chemical weapons treaty, 239, 268, 270, 271
    nuclear test ban treaty, 310–311
  foreign policy
    AIDS assistance, 230
    Albright confirmation, 179 (box)
    China summits, 183 (box)
    Clinton term summary, 173, 175, 176, 177
    economic sanctions, 224, 421
    federal agency reorganization, 59, 193
    foreign aid appropriations, 210
    foreign aid authorization, 228–229
    international adoptions, 231
    military aid authorization, 229
    NATO expansion, 273
    nominations, 800
    nuclear test ban treaty, 187
    Russia sanctions, 222, 223
    State Department authorization, 189–192, 217–219
    U.N. debt repayment, 192–193, 219–220
  Higher Education Act, 512
  NEA funding, 739
  U.S. visa refusals, 677
  welfare law revisions, 488
Helping Empower Low-Income Parents (HELP) scholarships, 528
Hemophiliacs, 459
Hepatitis
  pediatric research, 482
  testing for prison inmates, 600
Herger, Wally, R-Calif.
  Social Security surplus protection, 78
Heritage Foundation, 532
Herman, Alexis
  jobs for older Americans, 496
  Labor leadership, 575 (box), 615, 799, 978 (box), 980
Hermandad Mexicana Nacional, 785
Heroin, 603
Heslin, Sheila, 779
High-energy physics, 746, 754

Higher Education Act of 1965
  authorization, 507, 508, 509, 509–513, 616
  technical corrections, 547
Highway Trust Fund, 92, 93, 100, 315
Highways and roads
  appropriations, 59, 67, 84
  budget resolution, FY 1999, 60, 61
  clean air standards, 382
  Clinton term summary, 6, 11, 315, 318
  federal lands
    Alaska development, 67, 379
    road closing procedures, 388
  food stamp authorization, 422
  national forest roads
    forest health bills, 368
    national parks projects, 359
    roadless areas, 394–395
    summary, 341, 343, 344, 799
  Route 66 preservation, 394
  surface transportation authorization, 318–320
Hiking, 400
The Hill, 772–773
Hilleary, Van, R-Tenn.
  defense authorization, 242
Hilliard, Earl F., D-Ala.
  ethics probes, 765–766, 772–773
Hinojosa, Rubén, D-Texas
  student loans, 511
Hispanic Americans
  Agriculture Department discrimination, 422
  bilingual education, 516–518
  citizenship verification for voter registration, 780
  employment rates, 35
  FALN clemency, 681
  low-level nuclear waste site, 359–361
  members of Congress, 29
    totals, 1947–2001 (table), 30
  Paez nomination, 679
  racial profiling in traffic stops, 652
  Republican convention, 23
  Sanchez contested election, 785
  student loans, 511
Hispanic Caucus
  immigration relief, 673
  student loans, 511
Historic preservation programs
  Ft. Atkinson cemetery, 285
  King personal papers, 752
  offshore oil revenue, 377, 378
  Route 66, 394
  women's colleges, 547
HIV. *See Acquired immune deficiency syndrome (AIDS)*
Hoeffel, Joseph M., D-Pa.
  federal rules impact analysis, 749
Hoekstra, Peter, R-Mich.
  Education Department audit, 548
  prison industries, 652–653
  school choice, 536
Hoffa, James P., 578 (box)
Hogan, Thomas F., 65 (box), 765
Holbrooke, Richard C., 178, 179 (box), 985
Holidays
  King birthday flag code, 751–752
Hollings, Ernest F., D-S.C.
  campaign finance reform, 668
  financial services modernization, 132
  high-tech visas, 672
  juvenile crime, 635
  nuclear waste storage, 363
  ocean policy panel, 392
  partial-birth abortion, 456
  space launches, 754
Hollywood. *See Motion pictures*

Holt, Rush D., D-N.J.
teacher training, 533
Holtzman, Elizabeth, 12
Home equity conversion mortgages, 561
Home health care
Medicare payments, 50, 52, 68, 75, 430, 441,
443–444, 461, 462
patient copayments, 433, 435, 436, 437
Older Americans Act, 496
HOME Investment Partnerships Program, 556,
558, 566
Home mortgages
FHA loans
foreclosure relief, 562–563
limits, 563
Section 8 opt-outs, 567
FHLB changes, 140
mortgage insurance, 563, 567
reverse mortgages, 561, 566, 567
VA fees, 499, 500
Home Rule Flexibility grants, 556, 560
Home schooling, 574
Homeless
program consolidation, 561–562
Title I education grants, 534
veterans programs, 500
Homicide. *See Murder*
Homosexuals
Boy Scout leader ban, 689
discrimination, 661
hate crime definition, 20, 629, 642–644
international adoptions, 231
Republican convention, 23
same-sex marriage, 30
Honduras
immigrants in U.S., 672
Honey production, 421, 422
Hong Kong
China-U.S. trade, 152, 158
economic conditions, 801
Hoover, Herbert, 391
Hoover, J. Edgar, 741–742
HOPE education tax credit, 90, 94, 95, 96, 508,
521, 522, 526
HOPE VI housing program, 560
Hoppe, David, 515
HOPWA. *See Housing Opportunities for Persons
with AIDS*
Hormel, James C., 990
Horn, Steve, R-Calif.
campaign finance reform, 782
counterfeit police badges, 645
Horse race betting, 337
Horses
police animals, 650
Hospices
assisted suicide, 659
Medicare payments, 462
Hospitals. *See also Military hospitals; Veterans
hospitals*
clinical research aid, 481
energy conservation, 356
foreign nurses, 674–675
low-level nuclear waste, 360
Medicaid, Medicare payments, 45, 50, 75, 82,
430, 433, 439–440, 441–442, 461–464
disproportionate share poor patients, 432,
434, 436, 440, 442
specialty hospitals, 440
teaching hospitals, 434, 436, 437, 439, 440,
462, 478
nurse training for sex crime treatment, 630
organ transplants, 475–477
patient discharge timing, 434
religious expression, 661

Houghton, Amo, R-N.Y.
527 PACs, 787
House Administration (Oversight) Committee
jurisdiction, leadership, 760, 770, 959–960
House of Representatives, U.S.
administrative officer, 768
apportionment
apportionment, 1789–2000 (chart), 973
census issues, 691, 708–709, 733–734, 748
(box)
distribution of seats, electoral votes,
1952–2000 (table), 1070
audit (box), 770
chaplain, 775
committee funding, 767
discharge petitions, 1931–2001 (chart), 972
elections, 1998, 12–13
elections, 2000, 29–30
leadership, organization, 7 (box)
105th Congress, 760
106th Congress, 770–771
members
105th Congress, 936–937, 938
106th Congress, 938, 940–941
political committees, 963
presidential election role, 22
rules
105th Congress, 760–761
106th Congress, 771
Speaker's salary, 751
standing committees, 105th, 106th Congress,
951–964
House Post Office scandal, 764 (box)
House Rule 45, 763
House-Senate relations
China trade agreement, 164
Clinton term summary, 5, 15–16
Housing. *See also Home mortgages; Housing assistance; Military housing*
energy saving devices, 110
home energy aid, 67, 356, 405
homestead exemption in bankruptcy, 126,
127–128, 142–144
low-flow toilets, 400
mobile home standards, 563, 566
**Housing and Urban Development Department,
U.S. (HUD)**
appropriations, 59, 75, 84
Clinton term summary, 553–554
community development, 564–565
costs reduction, 562–563
home ownership aid, 563
homeless programs, 561
leadership (box), 556
manufactured housing, 563, 566
public housing reform, 556–561
Housing assistance
affordable housing for elderly, disabled, 567
appropriations, 59, 84
budget outlays, FY 1987–2001 (graph), 488
budget reconciliation, FY 1997, 51
community development, 565
D.C. tax credits, 740
domestic violence victims, 632
FHA loans
foreclosure relief, 562–563
limits, 563
home ownership aid, 565–566
homeless programs, 561
HUD cost reductions, 562–563
immigrant farm workers, 674
public housing reform, 11, 69, 553–561
veterans programs, 498 (graph), 499
Housing Evaluation and Accreditation Board,
557

**Housing Opportunities for Persons with AIDS
(HOPWA),** 567
Hoyer, Steny H., D-Md.
congressional pay, 792
House leadership, 770
military construction appropriations, 251
Sanchez election, 785
HPV. *See Human papillomavirus*
Hu Yaobang, 208
Huang, John, 679, 778
Hubbell, Webster L., 779, 809
HUBZones, 324
HUD. *See Housing and Urban Development
Department, U.S.*
Hudson River, 370
Hughes Electronics Corp., 180, 181, 302
Hulshof, Kenny, R-Mo.
disabled workers' insurance, 470
Human embryo creation, 67, 74, 459–460,
745–746
Human papillomavirus (HPV), 472
Human rights
Chechnya, 223
China-U.S. relations, 175, 180, 182–183,
208–209
defense authorization, 256
trade agreement, 161–166
trade status, 149, 151–153, 166
Colombia, 220, 221
congressional access to intelligence, 202
economic sanctions reform, 169
Export-Import Bank, 157
Indonesia aid, 213
military training participants, 211, 230, 291,
296
Serbia, 214, 216
sex trafficking, 629
Third World debt forgiveness, 369
U.S. trade policy summary, 148
war criminals, 646
Human Rights and Labor, Office of, 629
Humane Society of the United States, 346, 384
Humphrey, Hubert, 22
Humphrey, Hubert III, 13
"Humvees," 244
Hungary
NATO expansion, 189, 230, 272–274, 802
Hunsicker, Lawrence, 475
Hunter, Duncan, R-Calif.
defense authorization, 254–255
Hunting
Arizona conservation area, 394
bear parts import ban, 381
bird population control, 384–385
Fish and Wildlife Service programs, 392–393
migratory birds, 358
national wildlife refuges, 348–349
nutria eradication, 363
Hurricanes
disaster relief, 68, 76–77, 189
hurricane hunter aircraft, 248
military damage repair, 263
Huse, James G., 657
Hussein (King of Jordan), 189
Hutchinson, Asa, R-Ark.
asbestos compensation, 666
bounty hunters, 599
campaign finance reform, 781, 782, 788
China trade agreement, 162 (box)
civil assets forfeiture, 648
Clinton impeachment, 825
college aid for slain officers' families, 651
religious expression, 612
secret evidence in deportation, 664
term limits, 783
violence against women, 631

Hutchinson, Tim, R-Ark.
  China-U.S. trade, 153
  Clinton impeachment, 825
  defense appropriations, 260, 261
  defense authorization, 256
  foreign aid appropriations, 184
  NEA funding, 739
  organ transplants, 477
Hutchison, Kay Bailey, R-Texas
  defense appropriations, 260
    F-22 funding, 287 (box)
  education
    education savings accounts, 520
    teacher training, 545
  gasoline additive MTBE, 391
  judicial nominations, 623
  NATO expansion, 274
  NEA funding, 739
  Senate leadership, 7 (box)
Hyde amendment
  children's health insurance, 436, 443, 459
  Medicaid, 458–459
Hyde, Henry J., R-Ill.
  affirmative action, 616
  asbestos compensation, 664–666
  balanced budget amendment, 58
  bankruptcy law overhaul, 143
    judgeships expansion, 608
  child support enforcement, 495
  Clinton impeachment, 816, 818–819, 823, 824
  farmworker visas, 674
  flag desecration, 610–611
  health
    abortion funding ban, 458
    assisted suicide, 477
    fetal rights, 662
    physician antitrust, 480
  high-tech visas, 671
  judicial pay, 622
  Justice Department authorization, 613
  Kosovo policy, 205
  law enforcement
    assisted suicide, 606, 658, 659
    civil assets forfeiture, 590–591, 604–605, 629,
      647–649
    gun control, 640–642
    juvenile crime, 636, 637
    racial profiling, 652
    witness intimidation, 601
  religious expression, 612
  term limits, 783
Hydropower, 410

I

IBM Corp., 334
Ice Harbor Dam, 395
Ickes, Harold M., 779
Idaho
  conservation lands acquisition, 377
  damaged tree removal, 387
  forest revenue, 399
  Hells Canyon jetboats, 367
  salmon project, 395
  term limits, 784
IDEA. *See Individuals with Disabilities
  Education Act*
Identification documents
  counterfeit police badges, 644–645
  false IDs, 657
  immigrant workers, 674
  unidentified persons, 646
  voting, 782
Identity theft, 600–601
Ignagni, Karen, 436

Illegal immigrants
  amnesty, 82, 671, 672–673
  emergency medical services, 442
  identification before arraignment, 620
  overstayed tourist limits, 677
  provision 245(i), 620
  railroad officer training, 652
  smuggling penalties, 675
  temporary farm workers, 673–674
**Illegal Immigration Reform and Immigration
  Responsibility Act of 1996,** 676
IMF. *See International Monetary Fund*
Immigration and emigration. *See also
  Deportation; Illegal immigrants; Political asylum;
  Refugees*
  border controls, 675–676
  census undercount, 748 (box)
  Clinton term summary, 589, 591, 629
  education programs
    bilingual education, 508, 516–518
    ed-flex plan, 540, 541
  food stamps, 419, 421–422, 486, 490
  Medicaid, SSI benefits, 43, 45
    budget reconciliation, 1997, 48, 49, 50–53
    Medicaid changes, 442, 464
  Republican platform, 23
  Supreme Court decisions, 716
  violence against women, 631, 632
  visas for high-tech workers, 68, 616–619,
    670–672
  war criminals, 646
  welfare benefits, 431
    welfare law revisions, 486–488, 490
Immigration and Naturalization Service (INS)
  amnesty for illegal aliens, 673
  border controls, 676
  Elián González case, 225 (box), 592
  field office upgrades, 613
  foreign students, 309
  foreign travelers, 677
  high-tech visas, 671
  illegal aliens in prisons, 620
  juvenile crime, 595
  terrorism deportations, 605
    secret evidence, 663–664
Immigration Overhaul Law of 1996, 619
Immunity
  Shuster ethics case, 772
  Starr investigation of Clinton, 815
Immunizations
  biological weapons vaccine development, 481
  children's health insurance, 443
  Medicare coverage, 45
  military anthrax program, 289
  vaccine excise tax, 100
  vaccine production halt notice, 446
Immunosuppressive drugs, 462, 463, 465
Imports. *See Foreign trade*
Income taxes. *See also Capital gains taxes; Child
  tax credit; Earned-income tax credit*
  averaging for farmers, 101
  budget receipts, 1980–2000 (graph), 88
  child care credit, 60, 72, 110
  compliance
    estimated taxes, 102
    IRS levy on benefits, 103
  D.C. home-buyers credits, 740
  deductions and exclusions
    business meals, 101
    charity mileage, 98
    employer-paid tuition, 520, 523
    health insurance premiums, 112, 468
    home offices, 98
    IRAs, 98
    school supplies, for teachers, 545
    standard, for dependents, 102

    standard, for married couples, 111, 114
    stock donations to charity, 99
  education incentives, 90, 95, 96, 508, 520–523
    education savings accounts, 90, 96, 518, 522,
      544–546
    prepaid tuition plans, 546
  electronic return filing, 108
  farm tax breaks, 422–423
  federal unemployment tax, 102
  foreign credits holding period, 104
  IRA contribution limits, 581–582
  joint filers
    disproportionate income, 107, 113
    innocent spouses, 106, 108
    "marriage penalty," 19, 20, 60, 61, 79–80, 88,
      89, 110–112, 113–115, 565
  military personnel in Kosovo, 206
  percentage of GDP, 1935–2000 (table), 91
  rate reduction, 110–111, 112
  tax cuts, 1997, 90–105
  tax cuts, 1999, 110–112
  tax liability
    employer-provided meals, 109
    parking compensation, 104
    partnership sales, appreciation, 104
    tuition assistance, 96
    U.S. citizens overseas, 101
    workers' compensation, 101
  tax record snooping ban, 106 (box)
  two-thirds vote to increase, 761
Independent Counsel, Office of, 813
Independent counsels
  authorization, 662–663, 813
  campaign finance scandals, 808
  ethics guidelines, 66
  Whitewater investigation, 804–805
Independent Insurance Agents of America,
  123 (box)
Independent Living Program, 496
India
  Gandhi memorial in D.C., 359
  global warming treaty, 354
  nuclear tests
    antimissile defenses, 308
    test ban treaty, 310, 311
    U.S. intelligence failure, 262
  U.S. trade sanctions, 200, 204, 223–224, 284,
    288–289
    food exemptions, 159, 170, 421
    nuclear sales, 255
Indian Affairs, Bureau of, 546
Indian Affairs Committee, Senate
  jurisdiction, leadership, 759, 954
Indian Health Service, 751
U.S.S. *Indianapolis*, 296
Indians/Native Americans
  bulletproof vests, 599
  business taxes, 92
  casinos/campaign contributions, 779
  Everglades restoration, 372
  Great Lakes restoration projects, 357
  health
    diabetes prevention, treatment, 443
    uranium miners compensation, 296
  Internet gambling, 337
  juvenile crime, 595
  land conservation, 377
  school construction, 546
  Supreme Court decisions, 713–714
  Title I education grants, 534
  welfare-to-work grants, 489
Individual development accounts, 491, 492, 564,
  565
Individual retirement accounts (IRAs)
  contribution limits, 98, 111, 112, 117, 119,
    581–582

educational use, 94, 95, 96, 521, 522
minimum wage bill, 580
Roth IRAs, 91, 97–98
  conversions, 107, 112
  tax cuts, 1997, 87, 90, 97–98
Individual rights
  Supreme Court decisions, 716–721
Individuals with Disabilities Education Act (IDEA)
  authorization, 508, 509, 515–516
  charter schools, 525
  student discipline, 544
Indonesia
  financial crisis, 801
  Huang campaign contributions, 778
  U.S. aid appropriations, 213
Infants
  Early Head Start, 491, 492
  WIC authorization, 431, 494–495
Information access and disclosure. *See also Criminal background checks*
  Clinton impeachment news leaks, 825–826
  consumer protection
    ATM fees, 137
    bank-community group agreements, 132, 136
    bank insurance activities, 139
    credit card interest rates, 143
    fraud against the elderly, 675
    managed health care plan gag clauses, 432, 433, 437, 439, 442
    manufactured housing defects, 566
    medical malpractice database, 482
    Medicare+Choice plan services, 439
    school performance, 538, 541, 543
  government operations
    federal court delays, 608
    GPO documents, 739
    IMF budget, 212
    IRS access to federal registries, 103
    IRS records, audits, 106 (box), 108
    Kennedy assassination records, 613
    VA, for means testing, 499
  House ethics overhaul, 767
  law enforcement
    bomb construction, 635
    child abuse prevention, 647
    college investigations of missing persons, 547
    crime victims rights, 609
    electronic information in crime investigations, 655–656
    grand jury access for state banks, 140
    HIV status of sex offenders, 644
    juvenile crime records, 594–595, 637
    school records of violent offenders, 511, 538
    sex offender registries, 547, 556, 603–604
    unidentified persons, 646
  privacy
    financial information, 121
    Internet privacy, 337
    medical records, 479–480
    PBS donor lists, 338
    Social Security numbers, 337
  security classified information
    Chinese espionage, 208
    criminal penalties, 204
    intelligence authorizations, 200–201, 202, 227–228
    nuclear secrets, 290, 296, 303 (box)
Information Agency, U.S. (USIA)
  foreign policy agency reorganization, 68–69, 193–194
  State Department authorization, 190, 191, 192
Inglis, Bob, R-S.C.
  term limits, 783
  volunteer liability, 615

Inhofe, James M., R-Okla.
  antimissile defenses, 267
  Clean Air Act, 351, 382
  defense authorization, 256
  endangered species protection, 351
  Everglades restoration, 373, 374
  gasoline additive MTBE, 391
  judicial nominations, 679
  NEA funding, 751
  recess appointments, 680
Initiative petitions, 688, 708
Injunctions, 697
Innovative Education Program Strategies, 543
Inouye, Daniel K., D-Hawaii
  defense appropriations, 246, 248, 283
Inslee, Jay, D-Wash.
  financial services modernization, 133
Institute of Medicine
  medical errors, 478–479
  organ transplants, 476, 477
Insulin patents, 449
Insurance. *See also Health insurance; Liability issues and insurance*
  financial services modernization, 120–126, 130–141
  flood insurance, 561
  mortgage insurance, 563, 567
  tax treatment of life insurance contracts, 104
  title insurance, 139
Intel Corp., 616
Intellectual property
  depreciation calculations, 104
  digital copyright, 328
  patent overhaul, 324
  software copyright, 334
Intelligence activities. *See also Central Intelligence Agency; Espionage*
  appropriations, 262
  authorizations, 204
    FY 1998, 200–201
    FY 1999, 201–203
    FY 2000, 226–227
    FY 2001, 227–228
  chemical weapons treaty verification, 269, 270
  defense authorization, 277
  encryption exports, 326
  nuclear security, 302–306
  Russian facility in Cuba, 222, 223
  terrorism, 309
  weapons detection, 262, 267
Intelligence Committee, House Select
  jurisdiction, leadership, 760, 770, 962
Intelligence Committee, Senate Select
  jurisdiction, leadership, 760, 955
Intelsat, 254
Interagency Council on the Homeless, 561
Interior Department, U.S.
  African elephant conservation, 369
  Alaska land swaps, 367
  appropriations, 59, 66–67, 73–75, 83–84
  California national monument, 403
  cemetery vandalism, 604
  coastal barrier resources, 383
  conservation areas, 394, 403–404
  damaged tree removal, 387–388
  endangered species protection, 350
  Everglades restoration, 373
  Indian casino/campaign contributions, 779
  King plaque at Lincoln Memorial, 752
  Las Vegas airport, 401
  leadership, 347 (box)
  Lorton Prison transfer, 55
  migratory birds, 389
  national parks
    filming fees, 356, 387
    operations, 358–359

  national wildlife refuges, 348–349, 363, 402
  northern spotted owl, 392
  POGO contempt of Congress, 775
  Salton Sea rehabilitation, 364–365
  U.N. lands designation, 401
  water projects appropriations, 76
Intermodal Surface Transportation Efficiency Act of 1991, 318–320
Intermodal Transportation Board, 322
Internal Revenue Service (IRS)
  appropriations, 76, 81, 84
  benefits levy, 103
  business inventory accounting, 100–101
  527 PACs, 786–787
  gift reevaluation limits, 99
  Gingrich ethics probe, 774
  information access to HHS, VA, 103, 499
  overhaul, 90, 106–109, 319
  tax record snooping ban, 106 (box)
International Association of Chiefs of Police, 648, 675
International Atomic Energy Agency, 196, 219
International Brotherhood of Teamsters, 578 (box)
International Commission on Missing Persons in Bosnia, 178–179
International Covenant on Civil and Political Rights, 183
International Criminal Tribunal, 208, 217
International development banks
  foreign aid appropriations, 186, 187
International Emergency Economic Powers Act of 1977, 414
International Energy Program, 356
International financial organizations. *See also International Monetary Fund; World Bank*
  China loans, 182
  multilateral debt relief, 215
  Yugoslav sanctions, 208
International Labor Organization, 155, 219
International Monetary Fund (IMF)
  anti-globalization protests, 148
  Clinton term summary, 11, 173, 175, 176, 177
  financial crises, 39, 801
  gold revaluation for debt relief, 75, 212, 213 (box), 214, 216, 217
  U.S. contributions
    abortion controversies, 458
    appropriations, 59, 62, 66, 184, 185, 186–189
    authorization, 192, 194
    budget caps exemption, 53
    foreign aid authorization, 228–229
International Red Cross, 274
International Relations Committee, House
  jurisdiction, leadership, 191, 770, 960
  prestige, 176
International Space Station, 222
International Trade Commission, U.S., 165
Internet
  access regulation, 328
  address registration fees, 746 (box)
  alcohol sales, 337, 629, 631, 632
  bomb construction information, 635
  campaign finance reform, 788
  Clinton term summary, 315, 316–317, 318, 331
  consumer protection, 331
  copyright infringement, 328, 334
  cyber-stalking, 632, 645
  data collection on children, 68
  domain names, 336–337
  electronic signatures, 335–336
  false IDs, 657
  gambling, 328–329, 337
  GPO document access, 739
  information access in criminal investigations, 656

international trade, 147
next generation network, 746, 747
parental controls, 635
pornography, sexual material, 68, 82, 329, 684, 688
  online reporting, 657
privacy, 82, 337
sales taxes, 68, 327–328, 335
shipping rates disclosure, 322
student aid fraud, 546
telephone excise tax, 119, 334
Triana space project, 752
Interstate Commerce Commission, 332
Interstate compacts
low-level nuclear waste, 360
Invasive species
bird population control, 384–385
Great Lakes restoration projects, 357
nutria eradication, 363–364
Inventions
federal lab licenses, 747
filings abroad, 334
patent system overhaul, 324, 334
Investment Advisors Act of 1940, 138
Investment trusts, 138
Iowa
bankruptcy law overhaul, 143
Iran
missile technology, 238, 276, 307
  Canada, 229
  China, 181, 182, 183 (box)
  Russia, 69, 175, 177, 184, 185, 189, 195–196, 204, 216, 221–223, 268, 270
natural gas development, 186
U.S. relations, 222
  antimissile defenses, 265, 266
  terrorism victims' suits, 632
U.S. trade
  encryption exports ban, 336
  food sanctions, 83, 223, 224, 424, 426
  "Silk Road" trade, 169
Iran-contra affair, 808, 818
Iran-Iraq Arms Non-Proliferation Act of 1992, 182
Iraq
U.S. antimissile defenses, 266, 307 (box)
U.S. military operations
  air strikes, 10, 173, 235, 287, 821, 822 (box)
  appropriations, 263, 299
  authorization, 277, 281
  no-fly zone enforcement, 58, 250
U.S. relations, 196–198
  confrontation chronology (box), 197
  economic sanctions, 224, 225
  encryption exports ban, 336
  frozen assets in U.S., 219
  intelligence authorization, 202
  Saddam opposition funding, 192, 214, 217
  summary, 803
Iraq Liberation Act, 197–198
IRAs. *See Individual retirement accounts*
Ireland
U.S. aid, 192
Irrigation projects
Colorado River salinity control, 402
fish screens, 395
IRS. *See Internal Revenue Service*
Isakson, Johnny, R-Ga.
election, 17
Isotope manufacturing, 747
Israel
Camp David summit, 2000, 216 (box)
Russia sanctions, 195–196, 222
U.S. aid, 176
  appropriations, FY 1998, 184, 185
  appropriations, FY 1999, 66, 186, 189

appropriations, FY 2000, 75, 211, 214
appropriations, FY 2001, 216
military aid authorization, 229
U.S. relations
  Pollard case, 190 (box)
  summary, 801–802
  U.S. embassy in Jerusalem, 191, 192, 218, 219
U.S. trade
  export controls on supercomputers, 243
Wye River summit, 1998, 190 (box)
Issue advocacy ads
campaign finance reform, 777–783, 789
FEC ruling, 780 (box)
527 PACs, 786–787
tobacco settlement, 323
Istook, Ernest, R-Okla.
Kosovo policy, 207
organ transplants, 476
religious expression, 611–612
Italian Americans, 664
Ivey, William J., 750
Ivory Coast
U.S. trade exclusion, 168
Ivory import ban, 369
Izembek National Wildlife Refuge, 67

J

Jackson, Andrew, 22, 811
Jackson, Jesse, 616
Jackson, Jesse L. Jr., D-Ill.
homeless programs, 561
public housing reform, 556, 557
Jackson-Lee, Sheila, D-Texas
assisted suicide, 659
date-rape drugs, 654
immigration
  alien smuggling, 677
  deportation restrictions, 677
  farm worker visas, 674
  high-tech visas, 671
  sex trafficking victims, 630
NASA authorization, 742
public housing reform, 557
term limits, 783
war criminals, 646
Jackson-Vanik amendment
Albania, Kyrgyzstan trade, 168
China-U.S. trade, 149, 151, 161, 165
Vietnam trade status, 159
Jai alai betting, 337
Janitors for Justice, 55
Japan
economic conditions, 39
U.S. trade policy summary, 147, 150
Jaworski, Leon, 662
Jefferson, William J., D-La.
fast track for trade pacts, 155
Jeffords, James M., R-Vt.
campaign finance reform, 777, 780
  527 PACs, 787
China trade agreement, 163
education policy
  ed-flex plan, 541–542
  education savings accounts, 544
  ESEA authorization, 537
  IDEA authorization, 515–516
  literacy programs, 529
  student loans, 512
  vocational education, 514
hate crimes, 642
health policy
  disabled workers' insurance, 470
  drug reimports, 484
  FDA overhaul, 445–446
  medical errors, 479

medical privacy, 480
patients' rights, 467
job training overhaul, 574
minimum wage, 580
Senate leadership, 759
workplace teams, 578
Jenkins, Louis "Woody," 784–785
Jennifer's Law, 646
Jennings, Chris, 462
Jeremiah, David, 262
Jerusalem, Israel
U.S. embassy, 191, 192, 218, 219
Jetboats, 367, 384
Jews
hate crimes, 642
"JFK" (1992 film), 613
Jiang Zemin, 182, 183 (box)
Jipping, Thomas L., 623
Jobs. *See Employment and unemployment*
John Deere, 105
John Paul II, 176, 216
Johnson, Andrew, 15, 813, 814 (box)
Johnson, Jay, D-Wis.
election, defeat, 13
Johnson, Lyndon B.
budget policy, 40
Elementary and Secondary Education Act, 531
Head Start, 496
veto use, 811
Johnson, Nancy L., R-Conn.
education savings accounts, 546
Gingrich reprimand, 762
House leadership, 760
NEA funding, 739
pediatrics training, 478
Johnson, Norma Holloway, 764
Johnson, Randy, 618
Johnson, Sam, R-Texas
union "salting," 575
Johnson, Tim, R-Ill.
balanced budget amendment, 56, 57
defense authorization, 292
Johnston, J. Bennett, 760
Johnstown, Pa., 252 (box)
Joint Budget Committee, 44
Joint Chiefs of Staff
antimissile defenses, 267
chemical weapons treaty, 271
leadership, 241 (box)
military base closings, 277
military spending, 235–237
National Guard, reserves seat, 244
Joint Committee on Printing, 739, 965
Joint Committee on Taxation
community development, 565
education savings accounts, 518, 544
estate taxes, 116
IRS oversight, 109
jurisdiction, leadership, 964
tax provisions cost estimates, 45
Joint Committee on the Library, 964
Joint Economic Committee, 963
Joint STARS radar plane, 262, 281–282, 288
Joint Strike Fighter
appropriations, 249, 261, 284, 288, 297, 298, 300
authorization, 241, 244, 258, 281, 290, 292, 294
F-22 funding controversy, 286–287 (box)
long-range defense planning, 264
test facility, 253 (box)
Jones, Daryl, 987
Jones, Donald, 763
Jones, Paula Corbin, 691, 804, 805–807, 813–818, 821 (box), 822, 827
Jones, Stephanie Tubbs, D-Ohio
child abuse programs, 647

Jordan
U.S. aid, 176
appropriations, FY 1998, 185
appropriations, FY 1999, 189
appropriations, FY 2000, 75, 211, 215
appropriations, FY 2001, 216
military aid authorization, 229
Wye River summit, 190 (box)
Jordan, Vernon E. Jr., 817, 824
Joshua Tree National Monument, 387
Joyner, Carlotta C., 540
Judicial activism, 620–622, 627–628, 678, 679
Judicial Conference of the United States
crime victims' rights, 668
federal court system changes, 669
Judicial Selection Monitoring Project, 623
Judiciary Committee, House
Clinton impeachment, 816–822
jurisdiction, leadership, 960
Judiciary Committee, Senate
jurisdiction, leadership, 613, 760, 954–955
Waco investigation, 681
Jury trial
hate crimes, 690
Supreme Court decisions, 696, 704
Justice Assistance, Bureau of (BJA), 614
Justice Department, U.S.
antitrust for physicians, 480
appropriations, 63, 73, 74, 82, 85
asbestos compensation, 665
authorization, 613
campaign finance investigations, 779, 808
China missile technology transfer, 181, 254
classified information disclosure, 227, 228
congressional ethics probes
Burton, 765
Shuster, 765, 772
Traficant, 774
congressional issues
GPO documents, 739
Landrieu election, 784–785
criminal law enforcement
alternative sentencing, 644
assisted suicide, 606–607, 659
background checks for security officers, 599
bulletproof vests, 599
civil assets forfeiture, 647–649
confessions, 689
crime victims rights, 668–669
crimes against disabled, 601
cyberstalking, 645
date-rape drugs, 654
D.C. sentencing guidelines, 55, 740
DNA evidence, 655
FALN clemency, 682
false IDs, 657
forensics labs, 657
Internet pornography, 329
juvenile crime, 595
law enforcement grants, 654
methamphetamine traffic, 602
money laundering, 605
pardon process, 682–683
prisoner deaths, 653
prisoner mental health, 656
racial profiling in traffic stops, 608, 652
school resource officers, 530
seizure of civil assets, 591, 604–605
sex offender registries, 603
student aid fraud, 546
transport of prisoners, 653
Waco investigation, 680–681
government ethics inquiries
Holbrooke, 179 (box)
Tenet, 179 (box)
immigration

border controls, 676
disabled citizenship applicants, 676
foreign travelers, 677
illegal aliens, 620
independent counsel law, 662
Italian Americans, 664
Kennedy building, 742
minority health programs, 485
nuclear security, 303 (box)
organ transplants, 476
personnel
leadership, 7, 594 (box), 800
Lee nomination, 624–627
medals of valor, 614
U.S. marshals nominees, 614
terrorism, 309, 481, 605
tobacco suit, 85
Justis, Marty, 611
Juvenile arthritis research, 482
Juvenile crime
action
1997–1998, 593–597
1999–2000, 633–637
summary, 589–590, 629
gun control, 16, 637–642
law enforcement grants, 654
Police Athletic League, 650
released offender aid, 482
school records disclosure, 511, 538
violence prevention grants, 482
Juvenile Delinquency Prevention Block Grant Program, 595, 634
Juvenile Justice and Delinquency Prevention Act, 634
Juvenile Justice and Delinquency Prevention, Office of, 595, 636

K

Kahn, Chip, 466
Kake Tribal Corp., 379, 392
Kanka, Megan, 603, 639
Kansas
bankruptcy law overhaul, 143
sex offenders
mental hospital commitment, 690
registries, 604
tornado disaster aid, 77
Kantor, Mickey
commerce leadership, 320 (box), 626, 978 (box)
DeLay ethics probe, 764
trade leadership, 152 (box)
Kaptur, Marcy, D-Ohio
campaign finance reform, 782
Kashmir
India, Pakistan sanctions, 159
Kasich, John R., R-Ohio
budget resolution, FY 1999, 61
defense authorization, 242, 291
FAA authorization, 332
Kosovo policy, 207–208
Kassebaum Baker, Nancy Landon, 252–253, 445, 759
Katzmann, Robert A., 623
Kazakhstan
satellite launches, 229
"Silk Road" trade, 169
Keck Observatory, 743
Keesler Air Force Base, Miss., 248
Kelly Air Logistics Center, 241, 242
Kelly, Sue W., R-N.Y.
partial-birth abortion, 456
Kempthorne, Dirk, R-Idaho
endangered species protection, 350–351
successor, 12
Kendall, David E., 805 (box), 816, 827

Kennedy airport, 321, 332
Kennedy, Anthony M.
cable TV regulation, 688
First Amendment cases, 688
Florida presidential vote, 26, 687 (box)
Supreme Court decisions, 684
Supreme Court summary, 689 (box)
Kennedy, Edward M., D-Mass.
budget resolution, FY 1998, 48
Central American refugees, 619
defense authorization, 293
education
education savings accounts, 519–520, 545
ESEA authorization, 537, 538, 539
student loans, 512, 526
teacher training, 545
employment
compensatory time, 576–577
high-tech visas, 617, 670–671
job training overhaul, 574
minimum wage, 580
workplace teams, 578
health policy
child health bills, 482
disabled workers' insurance, 470
FDA overhaul, 445–447
human cloning, 460
Medicaid for disabled children, 565
medical errors, 478–479
Medicare changes, 52, 436
organ transplants, 477
patients' rights, 454, 467, 470
law enforcement
crime victims rights, 609
gun control, 638
hate crimes, 642–643
juvenile crime, 636
methamphetamine traffic, 602
religious expression, 660–661
Kennedy, John F.
assassination documents review, 613
Peace Corps, 230
popular vote, 1960, 22
veto use, 811
Kennedy, Joseph P. II, D-Mass.
public housing reform, 556, 557
vocational education, 514
Kennedy, Mark, 29
Kennedy, Robert F., 638, 742
Kennelly, Barbara B., D-Conn.
House leadership, 760, 770
Kennesaw State College, 774
Kentucky
gubernatorial election, 18
uranium cleanup, 365
Kenya
U.S. embassy bombing, 217, 267, 803
Kerosene taxes, 102
Kerrey, Bob, D-Neb.
Clinton impeachment comments (text), 1018
crop insurance, 426
defense authorization, 278, 292, 293
education savings accounts, 544
IRS overhaul, 107
Medicare changes, 436
Medicare commission, 464
Kerry, John, D-Mass.
global warming treaty, 355
Senate leadership, 760
Kessler, David, 445, 691
Ketamine, 654
Khatami, Mohammad, 196
Kidney disease
dialysis, 429, 463
nutritional therapy, 463
Kidsave IRA, 521

Kildee, Dale, D-Mich.
  ed-flex plan, 540, 541
  student loans, 508, 509–510, 526
Kilpatrick, Carolyn Cheeks
  public housing reform, 556
Kim Dae Jung, 803
Kim il-Jong, 803
Kim, Jay C., R-Calif.
  ethics probe, 764–765
Kim, June, 764, 765
Kimbell, Jeffrey J., 445
Kimmel, Husband E., 296
Kind, Ron, D-Wis.
  ESEA authorization, 536
King, Angus, 13
King, Martin Luther Jr.
  commemorative actions, 751–752
  gun control, 638
Kingston, Jack, R-Ga.
  judicial activism, 621
  nuclear lab security, 412
Kiowa helicopters, 247, 248
Kirtland Air Force Base, N.M., 252 (box)
Kissinger, Henry A., 161
Kit Carson Peak, Colo., 381
U.S.S. Kitty Hawk, 241
Klebold, Dylan, 633
Klein, Joel, 480
Klink, Ron, R-Pa.
  Clean Air Act, 351
Knollenberg, Joe, R-Mich.
  low-flow toilets, 400
Knowles, Tony, 413
Koger, Frank, 608
Kohl, Herb, D-Wis.
  congressional pay, 793
  high-tech visas, 617
  juvenile crime, 596
  organ transplants, 477
Kolbe, Jim, R-Ariz.
  congressional pay, 792
  Republican convention, 23
Kolter, Joe, 764 (box)
**Korean Peninsula Energy Development
  Organization,** 186–187, 188, 189, 214, 217
Koresh, David, 680
Kosovo
  action
    1997–1998, 177–180
    1999–2000, 204–208
    summary, 16, 20, 173, 174, 177, 204, 802–803
  Army effectiveness, 290
  defense authorization, 277, 278–279, 281, 291,
    293
  foreign aid appropriations, 211, 214, 215
  military operations appropriations, 76–77,
    84–85, 189, 260, 263, 283, 298, 300, 301
  NATO campaign analysis, 287
  refugee relief, 283
Kosovo Liberation Army, 178, 205
Kostunica, Vojislav, 205
Kristen's Act, 657
Ku Klux Klan, 615
Kucinich, Dennis J., D-Ohio
  defense appropriations, 297
  federal rules impact analysis, 749
  nuclear waste storage, 362
  teacher training, 533
Kuhn, Thomas R., 405
Kuykendall, Steven T., R-Calif.
  election defeat, 29
Kyl, Jon, R-Ariz.
  chemical weapons treaty, 268, 269–271
  crime victims rights, 609, 668–669
  Fletcher nomination, 627–628
  foreign aid appropriations, 186

  IMF dues, 194
  intelligence authorization, 226
  Internet gambling, 328–329
  Medicare changes, 436–437
  military construction appropriations, 250
  nepotism in judgeships, 627
  nuclear lab security, 305, 411
  nuclear test ban treaty, 311
  prisoner health care, 653
  terrorism, 309
Kyoto protocol on global warning
  action, 1997–98, 354–356
  appropriations, 67, 70
  summary, 341, 344, 345, 799
Kyrgyzstan
  U.S. trade, 168, 169

L

Labeling
  condom warnings of HPV, 471–472
  cosmetic, nonprescription drug warnings, 445,
    446, 453
  "dolphin-safe" tuna, 345–348
  food health, nutrient claims, 444, 445, 446, 452
  food packaging safety, 452
  prescription drugs, 449, 454
**Labor and Human Resources Committee,
  Senate**
  jurisdiction, leadership, 759, 955
Labor Department, U.S.
  appropriations, 59–60, 67, 73–74, 81–82
  China trade agreement, 165
  employee stock options, 581
  homeless programs, 561
  immigration
    high-tech visas, 616–618
    provision 245(i), 620
  job training overhaul, 574
  leadership, 575 (box), 799
  minimum wage exception, 51
  veterans' job preference, 501
  welfare-to-work grants, 487, 489–490
Labor disputes
  baseball antitrust exemption, 324
Labor Relations Act of 1935
  workplace teams, 578
Labor standards
  Caribbean trade, 158
  China trade agreement, 162 (box), 164, 165
  college merchandise, 511
  fast track for trade pacts, 154, 155
  welfare-to-work jobs, 487, 490
Labor unions
  Amtrak restructuring, 320–321
  antidumping fee redirection, 83
  auto fuel efficiency standards, 333 (box)
  balanced budget amendment, 56
  Berzon nomination, 680
  campaign finance reform, 777, 780, 789
    527 PACs, 786–787
  China trade agreement, 161, 162
  Clinton term summary, 571–572
  Export-Import Bank, 157
  federal contracts, 799–800
  foreign trade policy
    China status, 149
    fast-track procedures, 148, 153–156
    summary, 147, 801
    U.S. deficit, 149
  high-tech visas, 618
  prison industries, 652
  railroad pensions, 581
  "salting" ban, 573, 575–576, 584–585
  school vouchers, 528
  superfund overhaul, 396

  Supreme Court decisions, 721, 723
  Teamsters probe (box), 578
  welfare law revisions, 487
  workplace teams, 578
LaFalce, John J., D-N.Y.
  China trade agreement, 162 (box)
  Export-Import Bank, 157
  financial services modernization, 133
  House leadership, 770
Lafferty, Andrea, 644
LaGuardia airport, 321, 332
LaHood, Ray, R-Ill.
  Clinton impeachment, 821
  organ transplants, 476
Lake, Anthony C. "Tony," 179 (box), 799, 987
Lake Okeechobee, 375
Lake Tahoe, Calif., 391, 402–403
Lame duck sessions, 965–966
Land and Water Conservation Fund, 66–67, 376,
  377
Land Management, Bureau of
  Colorado national parks, 381
  forest revenue sharing, 399–400
  grazing fees, 357
  Native Alaskan lands, 391
  Oregon land swaps, 403
  road closing procedures, 388
Land mines
  defense authorization, 254, 255, 256, 259
  treaty to ban, 274
Land use
  property rights, 737–738
  Supreme Court decisions, 724
  U.N. lands designation, 368, 401, 745
  zoning, 591, 660–661, 737
Landrieu, Mary L., D-La.
  antimissile defenses, 307
  balanced budget amendment, 57
  conservation lands acquisition, 376
  contested election, 784–785
  international adoptions, 231
Lands Legacy initiative, 74
LaPierre, Wayne, 638
Large Hadron Collider, 746
Largent, Steve, R-Okla.
  electric deregulation, 404
  House leadership, 769
Las Cienegas National Conservation Area, 394
Las Vegas, Nev., 401
Lasers
  antimissile satellites, weapons, 248, 258, 261,
    294
Lassen National Forest, 368
Latin America
  debt forgiveness/forest protection, 369
  "dolphin-safe" tuna, 345
  migratory bird conservation, 389
  U.S. military training, 211, 230, 291, 296
Latvia
  NATO aid, 189
Laughlin Air Force Base, Tex., 253 (box)
Lautenberg, Frank R., D-N.J.
  gun control, 538, 638, 639, 640
  juvenile crime, 635
  successor, 29
  welfare law revisions, 488
Lawyers and law practice. See also Attorney's fees
  Clinton suspension, 827
  military recruiting benefits, 280
  product liability, 322
  Supreme Court decisions, 695–696
  Y2K liability, 336
Lazio, Rick A., R-N.Y.
  health policy
    breast, cervical cancer, 471
    disabled workers' insurance, 470–471

homeless programs, 561
HUD cost reductions, 562
Italian Americans, 664
minimum wage, 579
public housing reform, 554, 556, 557, 558
Senate defeat, 28, 806–807 (box)
unidentified persons, 646
Leach, Jim, R-Iowa
community development, 564
financial services modernization, 120, 122, 124, 130, 133–134
HUD cost reductions, 562
public housing reform, 556, 558
State Department authorization, 192
Leadership Conference on Civil Rights, 661
League of United Latin American Citizens, 360
Leahy Amendments, 221
Leahy, Patrick J., D-Vt.
assisted suicide, 607
baseball antitrust exemption, 324
defense policy
land mine limits, 254, 274
flag desecration, 667
Fletcher nomination, 628
foreign aid appropriations, 213
Colombia antidrug aid, 221
judicial nominations, 623, 678, 679
law enforcement
civil assets forfeiture, 648
crime victims rights, 609
DNA evidence, 655
juvenile crime, 635
pardon process, 683
methamphetamine traffic, 602
partial-birth abortion, 456
Senate leadership, 760
Waco investigation, 681
Leaking Underground Storage Tank Trust Fund, 370
Leather imports, 158
Leavitt, Michael O., 678
Lee, Barbara, D-Calif.
election, 13
foreign aid appropriations, 215
Lee, Bill Lann, 7, 592, 593, 616, 623, 624–627, 680, 800, 986
Lee, Wen Ho, 303 (box), 411
Leesburg, S.C., Training Site, 253 (box)
Legislative branch. See Congress, U.S.
Legislative process
budget policy summary, 42
glossary, 831–856
how a bill becomes a law (chart), 859
legislative process in brief, 857–861
Legislative vetoes
GPO documents, 739
Lend-Lease program, 222
Lepping, Erica, 548
Lethal Drug Abuse Prevention Act, 477
Lett-Simmons, Barbara, 27 (box)
Levin, Carl, D-Mich.
defense authorization, 242, 243, 277, 279, 292
federal rule making, 737
gun manufacturer bankruptcy, 642
intelligence authorization, 226–227
nuclear security, 305
nuclear waste storage, 363
Russia sanctions, 196
Senate leadership, 760
Levin, Sander M., D-Mich.
China policy, 209
China trade agreement, 161, 162 (box), 163, 164
Lew, Jacob J.
appropriations bills, 63, 463
economic policy leadership, 35 (box), 984

foreign aid appropriations, 212
Medicare "givebacks," 463
nuclear security, 305
Lewinsky sex scandal
Clinton address (text), 1017
Clinton impeachment, 691, 814–827
Clinton term summary, 797, 804, 806–807
foreign policy effects, 173, 196–197
political effects, 10
Lieberman nomination, 23, 24
Richardson nomination, 347 (box)
Lewis, Jerry, R-Calif.
defense appropriations, 261, 284, 297
F-22 funding, 237, 286–287 (box)
Lewis, John, D-Ga.
affirmative action in college admissions, 511
Lewis Spacecraft mission, 94
Lewis, Terry P., 26 (box)
Liability issues and insurance
Amtrak injuries, 321
asbestos compensation, 664–666
donated body armor, 645
"good Samaritan" use of defibrillators, 481
gun manufacturers, 642
gun owners, 633, 641
gun show sellers, 639
off-duty police officers, 614
patients' rights, 467–470
product liability law, 316, 322
sexual harassment, 687–688
space launches, 754
teachers in school discipline, 539
tobacco settlement, 322–323
volunteers, 615
Y2K computer glitch, 330, 331, 336
Libby, Mont., 85, 664–665
Liberia
immigration relief, 673
Libraries
digital copyright, 328
Internet pornography filters, 82
school collections, 538
Libya
Hilliard ethics probe, 765–766
U.S. antimissile defenses, 266
U.S. food sanctions, 83, 223–225, 424, 426
Lieberman, Joseph I., D-Conn.
China trade agreement, 165
Clinton impeachment, 827
remarks (text), 1017
ESEA authorization, 539
527 PACs, 786
flag desecration, 611
medical errors, 479
Senate leadership, 769
vice presidential election, 2000, 21, 23, 24
Life insurance
tax treatment of contracts, 104
Lifetime Learning tax credit, 90, 96, 508, 522
Limited-purpose banks, 140
Lincoln, Abraham
birth centennial, 751
birthplace historic site, 359
Lincoln, Blanche L., D-Ark.
election, 12
Lincoln Memorial, 752
Linder, John, R-Ga.
House leadership, 760, 769
Line-item veto
Clinton use, 7–8, 43, 811
defense appropriations, 249–250
HUD, agencies appropriations, 59
military construction appropriations, 58, 251, 252–253 (box)
NASA appropriations, 742–743
transportation appropriations, 59

summary (box), 64–65
Supreme Court decision, 11, 690, 691, 811
Lippo Group, 778
Liquid ecstasy, 654
Liquified natural gas taxes, 100
Literacy programs
adults, 574
appropriations, 67
authorization, 529–530
community services family programs, 491, 492, 493
Even Start, 82, 529, 531, 535–536
public housing tenants, 558
Lithuania
NATO aid, 189
Little Goose Dam, 395
Little Rock, Ark.
Central High historic site, 359
Littleton, Colo., school shootings
congressional condolences, 638
gun control, 76, 638–642
gun violence at schools resolution, 545
juvenile crime bill, 589–590, 629, 633–634, 636
Litton Industries
cargo ship contract, 288
helicopter carrier, 245, 249, 255, 258, 262, 276, 282, 283, 295, 296, 300
Livestock and ranching. See also Grazing; Meat; Milk and dairy products
endangered species protection, 349
feed aid, 423
feedlot pollution, 382–383
income tax averaging, 423
price supports, 425
Livingston, Robert L., R-La.
appropriations bills, 59, 63
foreign aid, 187–188
bilingual education, 517
Clinton impeachment, 820, 822
defense appropriations, 248
House leadership, 13, 758, 769, 770
resignation, 10, 17, 24, 821
organ transplants, 475
Local Educational Agency Grants, 534
Local Law Enforcement Block Grant, 74
Lockhart, Joe
China trade agreement, 164
flag desecration, 667
Lockheed Martin Corp.
cargo planes, 257, 258, 259, 282, 288, 295, 300
F-16 production, 249, 288, 295, 300
F-22 procurement, 286–287 (box), 294, 297
Joint Strike Fighter, 290, 297
satellite launches, 180
Lofgren, Zoe, D-Calif.
alien smuggling, 675
electronic information access, 656
fetal rights, 475, 662
flag desecration, 610
gun control, 641
high-tech visas, 670, 671
Internet alcohol sales, 632
juvenile crime, 595
Logging. See Forests; National forests
Loitering, 690, 704
Long Island Sound, 387
Long March missiles, 180, 181
Long-term health care
insurance, 469 (box)
PACE benefits, 442
reverse mortgages, 566, 567
tax credit proposal, 72
veterans benefits, 502
Longbow radar systems, 244, 248, 258, 261, 281, 288

Loral Space and Communications, 153, 180–182, 254, 302

Lorton prison, 54–55, 740

Los Alamos National Laboratory, 303 (box), 305, 410, 412

Los Angeles, Calif.
  airport as al Qaeda target, 803

Lott, Trent, R-Miss.
  asbestos compensation, 665
  assisted suicide, 659
  bankruptcy law overhaul, 143
  budget process
    balanced budget amendment, 57
    budget reconciliation, 1997, 49–50
    budget resolution, FY 1998, 48
    Social Security surplus protection, 79
    supplemental appropriations, 84–85
  campaign finance reform, 777, 780, 790
    527 PACs, 786
  Clinton impeachment, 821
    Iraq air strikes, 822 (box)
  community development, 565
  compensatory time, 576
  dairy pricing, 425
  defense policy
    antimissile defenses, 266
    appropriations, 247, 249, 262, 283, 285, 296, 297
    chemical weapons treaty, 268, 269–270
    defense authorization, 245, 255, 258, 276, 277, 292
    military construction appropriations, 301
    NATO expansion, 273
    nuclear security, 305
    nuclear test ban treaty, 310–311
  education
    ed-flex plan, 540, 541
    ESEA authorization, 531, 538, 539
    IDEA authorization, 515
    savings accounts, 519–520
    tax incentives, 521
  energy supplies, 409–410
  environmental protection
    conservation lands acquisition, 378
    Everglades restoration, 374
    nuclear waste storage, 363, 409
    superfund overhaul, 396, 398
  FAA authorization, 332
  federal-D.C. ties, 740
  financial services modernization, 126, 134
  flag desecration, 611
  food stamp authorization, 422
  foreign policy
    Colombia antidrug aid, 221
    economic sanctions task force, 200
    foreign aid appropriations, 215
    Iraq, 197
    Kosovo, 179, 206
    Russia sanctions, 222
  gun control, 638, 640
  hate crimes, 643
  health policy
    disabled workers' insurance, 470
    human cloning, 460
    organ transplants, 476
    patients' rights, 15, 467
  high-tech visas, 616, 618, 672
  immigration relief, 673
  judicial nominations, 624, 678–679
  minimum wage, 580
  NASA authorization, 752
  nuclear lab security, 411
  Senate leadership, 7 (box), 19, 759, 769
    Clinton election, 807 (box)
    Gingrich coup attempt, 762–763 (box)
    Landrieu election, 784–785

tax policy
  catchall tax package, 117
  estate taxes, 116
  marriage status tax cut, 114, 115
  tax cuts, 1997, 95
  tax cuts, 1998, 106
  tax cuts, 1999, 111, 112
  tobacco settlement, 322, 323
  trade policy
    Barshefsky nomination, 152 (box)
    China trade agreement, 163, 164
    fast track for trade pacts, 156
  Waco investigation, 681

Lotteries, 337

Lou Gehrig's disease, 463, 464

Louisiana
  Cat Island wildlife refuge, 402
  congressional elections, 17
  gubernatorial elections, 18
  nutria eradication, 363
  offshore oil revenue, 376
  organ transplants, 475–476
  sex offender registries, 604

Louisiana Independent Federation of Electors, 785

Low-Income Home Energy Assistance Program (LIHEAP), 67, 491, 492, 493

Low-Level Radioactive Waste Policy Act of 1980, 360

Lower Granite Dam, 395

Lower Monument Dam, 395

Lowey, Nita M., D-N.Y.
  abortion, 255, 458
  health insurance for birth control, 10, 458

LPD transports
  appropriations, 247–248, 249, 300
  authorization, 295

Lugar, Richard G., R-Ind.
  economic sanctions, 200
  food sanctions, 420–421
  Conservation Reserve Program, 420
  crop insurance, 425–426
  nuclear test ban treaty, 310
  nuclear weapons reduction aid, 242, 243
  State Department authorization, 191
  Third World debt/forest protection, 369
  U.N. debt repayment, 193

Lung cancer
  asbestos compensation, 664–666

Lungren, Dan, 517

Lupus Research Act, 481

M

M-1 tanks
  appropriations, 248, 261, 288
  authorization, 244, 258, 281

M-113 troop carriers, 294

Ma, Seokuk, 765

Macedonia
  U.S. Kosovo policy, 205, 802
  U.S. peacekeeping role, 260, 261, 262

Mack, Connie, R-Fla.
  education savings accounts, 520, 545
  ESEA authorization, 539
  federal-D.C. ties, 740
  HUD cost reductions, 562
  public housing reform, 554, 558
  Senate leadership, 7 (box), 759, 769
  successor, 28

MacKay, Kenneth H. "Buddy," 13

Madison Guaranty Savings and Loan, 804, 805 (box)

Maine
  ballot initiatives, 30
  gubernatorial election, 13

low-level nuclear waste, 359–361
  prison guard overtime, 685

Make-a-Wish Foundation, 491

Malheur National Forest, 387, 403

Malmstrom Air Force Base, Mont., 253 (box)

Maloof, Phillip J., 14

Mammograms, 45, 433, 435, 437, 441

Man and Biosphere program, 401, 744

Managed health care plans. *See also Health maintenance organizations (HMOs)*
  child patients, 482
  Medicaid enrollees, 442
    abortion funding ban, 458–459
  Medicare payments, 54, 82, 430, 432, 434, 436, 437, 438–439, 461–464
  patients' rights, 69–70, 429, 454–455, 466–470
    bill comparison (box), 469
    defense authorization bill, 293
    emergency care, 432, 433, 437, 439
    hospital discharge timing, 434
    physicians' gag clauses, 433, 437, 439
    rural areas, 432, 437

Management and Budget, Office of (OMB)
  budget enforcement, 53
  budget estimates, 39 (box), 45
  budget law history, 44 (box)
  D.C. courts appropriations, 55
  defense appropriations, 297, 298
  education savings accounts, 545
  ergonomics standards, 584
  federal rules impact analysis, 749
  intelligence authorization, 202
  leadership, 35 (box)
  line-item veto, 249–250
  military construction appropriations, 250, 251
  military humanitarian missions, 299
  NASA authorization, 743
  nuclear security, 305

Manion, Daniel, 627

Mann, Thomas E., 626

Manufactured housing, 563, 566

Manzullo, Donald, R-Ill.
  homeless programs, 561
  judicial activism, 622

Marijuana
  drug-czar targets, 603
  legalization issue, 603
  Weld nomination, 800

Marine Corps, U.S.
  air, sea transport
    appropriations, 249, 261, 262, 288
    authorization, 258, 282, 295
  communications privatization, 296
  embassy guards, 280
  ground combat weapons, 244
  helicopter carrier, 255, 276
  long-range defense planning, 264
  tanker aircraft, 258

Marine Mammal Protection Act of 1972, 345, 380

Marine mammals
  beached mammals, 380–381
  dolphin protection, 341, 344, 346–348
  sea lion protection, 82, 393–394

Marine Protection, Research and Sanctuaries Act of 1972, 388

Markey, Edward J., D-Mass.
  electric deregulation, 404, 405
  financial services modernization, 133–134
  nuclear waste storage, 362, 408
  State Department authorization, 218

Marriage and divorce
  civil assets forfeiture, 648, 649
  income taxes
    disproportionate income, 107, 113
    innocent spouses, 106, 108

"marriage penalty," 19, 20, 60, 61, 79–80, 88, 89, 110–112, 113–115, 565
same-sex unions, 30
unmarried couple adoptions, 66
Mars Climate Orbiter Mission, 734
Mars Pathfinder, 734
Marshals Service, U.S.
appointments, 614
authorization, 613
juvenile crime, 595
Martin, Peppy, 18
Martinez, Matthew G., R-Calif.
bilingual education, 517
school vouchers, 528
teacher training, 533
vocational education, 514
Maryland
bankruptcy judges, 608
D.C. student aid, 547–548
mortgage insurance, 563
nutria eradication, 363–364
Mass transit
appropriations, 59, 67
authorization, 318–320
Clinton term summary, 11, 315
Massachusetts
gubernatorial elections, 30
mortgage insurance, 563
Myanmar sanctions, 686
Massiah-Jackson, Frederica, 988
Mathematics education
"Go Girl" program, 537
high-tech workers, 670–672
national testing, 523–525
teacher training, 533
Matsui, Robert T., D-Calif.
China-U.S. trade, 162, 166
fast track for trade pacts, 155, 156
Medicare drug benefits, 466
Mattingly, Mack, 30
Mauritius
U.S. trade, 168
Mayport, Fla., Naval Station, 252 (box)
McCaffrey, Barry, 594 (box)
McCain, John, R-Ariz.
auto safety, 333
campaign finance reform, 777, 783, 789–790
527 PACs, 786
defense policy
appropriations, 246, 283, 298
defense authorization, 243, 278, 292, 293
military construction appropriations, 250, 289
encryption exports, 336
ethics probe, 771
FAA authorization, 321, 332
foreign aid appropriations, 184, 186–187
high-tech visas, 616
Internet sales taxes, 335
Kosovo policy, 206
patients' rights, 468, 470
presidential election, 2000, 22
satellite TV, 338
Senate leadership, 759
space launches, 754
space station, 743, 753
tobacco settlement, 322, 323
truck safety, 332–333
Y2K liability, 336
McCarran-Ferguson Act of 1945, 138
McCarthy, Carolyn, D-N.Y.
gun control, 638, 639, 641
ESEA authorization, 536
vocational education, 514
McClellan Air Logistics Center, 241, 242

McCollum, Bill, R-Fla.
economic sanctions, 199
election defeat, 28
Justice Department authorization, 613
law enforcement
animal cruelty, 650–651
bounty hunters, 599
bulletproof vests, 599–600
DNA evidence, 655
gun control, 640–641
gun-related crime, 597
juvenile crime, 594, 596–597, 633, 636
money laundering, 605
prison labor, 603, 652
prisoner health care, 653
Secret Service authority, 651
sex offender registries, 603–604
stalking, 645
violence against women, 631
witness intimidation, 601
military construction appropriations, 250
term limits, 783–784
U.S. marshal nominees, 614
McConnell Air Force Base, Kans., 253 (box)
McConnell, Mitch, R-Ky.
bear parts import ban, 381
campaign finance reform, 780, 789–790
FEC term limits, 68
527 PACs, 786
employee stock options, 581
flag desecration, 668
foreign aid appropriations, 184, 210
juvenile crime, 635
Russia aid ban, 223
Senate leadership, 760, 769
uranium cleanup, 365
McCrery, Jim, R-La.
SSI benefits for immigrants, 487
McCullough, Glenn, 679
McCurdy, Dave, 773
McCurry, Mike
fast track for trade pacts, 156
Lee nomination, 626
McDade, Joseph M., R-Pa.
gratuities law ruling, 792 (box)
prosecutor guidelines, 66
McDermott, Jim, D-Wash.
assisted suicide, 606
ethics probe, 765, 774
fast track for trade pacts, 155
Gingrich reprimand, 761–762
House leadership, 760
McDonnell Douglas, 241, 249
McDougal, James B., 804, 805 (box)
McDougal, Susan, 804, 805 (box), 809
McGovern, Jim, D-Mass.
student loans, 511
McGreevey, James, 8
McHugh, John M., R-N.Y.
ethics office authorization, 750
McInnis, Scott, R-Colo.
campaign finance reform, 781
new national parks, 381
tobacco settlement, 323
McIntosh, David M., R-Ind.
campaign finance reform, 782
congressional pay, 792
federal rules impact analysis, 749
McKeon, Howard P. "Buck," R-Calif.
job training overhaul, 574
student loans, 508, 509–510, 526
McKinney, Cynthia A., D-Ga.
sex trafficking, 629
McVay, Charles III, 296
McVeigh, Timothy, 498, 609–610
MEADS, 258

Meals on Wheels, 431, 496
Meat
ape protection, 379–380
bear parts import ban, 381
beef exports to EU, 168
China trade agreement, 161
irradiation, 446, 452
market price disclosure, 423
Medal of Honor, 500
Medicaid
abortion funding ban, 458–459
action, 1997–1998, 432–433, 436, 438, 441–442
assisted suicide, 459, 606
breast, cervical cancer, 471–472
budget reconciliation, 1997, 48, 50, 54
budget resolution
FY 1998, 45, 46, 47
FY 1999, 60
FY 2000, 72
children's health insurance, 50–51, 436, 438, 443
Clinton term summary, 6, 429–430, 431
disabled children, 51, 117, 442, 464, 487, 565
disabled workers, 442, 470–471
federal-D.C. ties, 740
fraud prevention, 442
immigrant eligibility, 45, 442, 464, 487, 488
line-item veto of NY provision, 64
managed care plans, 442
Medicare "givebacks" bill, 462–464
nursing home evictions, 485
outlays, 1987–2001 (graph), 430
post-foster care aid, 496
smokers' health costs, 66, 72, 323
veteran nursing home patients, 500
welfare recipients entering workforce, 464
Medical Advisory Board on Pain Relief, 607
Medical Care Collections Fund, 500
Medical-Care Cost Recovery Fund, 500
Medical Device Manufacturers Association, 445
Medical devices and equipment
China trade agreement, 161
FDA overhaul, 431, 444–447, 450–453
Medicare payments, 440
supplier liability, 316, 322
Medical education and training
armed forces school, 249
clinical pharmacology, 449
clinical research student aid, 481
Medicare payments to teaching hospitals, 434, 436, 437, 439, 440
pediatrics training, 478
Medical ethics
human cloning, 459–460
organ transplants, 475–477
Medical laboratories
construction grants, 481
Medicare payments, 441
Medical malpractice
damage award caps, 433–434, 438, 454
database access, 482
Medical records
privacy, 20, 429, 479–480
Internet privacy, 337
veterans' benefit appeals, 502
Medical research
appropriations, 73, 289
federal agencies, 453, 477–478
Glenn in space, 742 (box)
human embryo creation, 67, 74
cloning, 459–460, 745–746
lab construction grants, 481
lupus, 481
medical privacy, 479
minority health, 484–485
pediatrics initiative, 482

Persian Gulf War illnesses, 497, 500
prostate cancer, 481
student aid, 481, 484
zero-gravity projects, 753
Medical savings accounts (MSAs)
budget reconciliation, FY 1997, 50, 54
Medicare changes, 432, 433–434, 435, 437, 438
patients' rights bill, 467, 468
Medicare
action
1997–1998, 432–443
1999–2000, 461–464
summary, 6, 15, 429–430, 431
age of eligibility, 50, 52, 433, 435, 436, 437, 464
appropriations, 73, 75, 82
assisted suicide, 459, 606
beneficiary "lock-in," 437
budget outlays, FY1987–2001 (graph), 430, 572
budget reconciliation, 1997, 48, 49, 50–54
budget resolution
FY 1998, 43, 45
FY 1999, 60–61
FY 2000, 71–73
FY 2001, 79–81
CARA funding, 377, 378
catchall tax package, 117
disabled workers, 470–471
fraud, abuse control, 441
home health care, 68, 441, 443–444
patient copayments, 433, 435, 436, 437
long-term solvency issue, 433, 437
budget surplus use to bolster, 110, 464, 465
commission for future planning, 441, 464–465
means test, 50, 52, 435–436, 437
military retirees, 291, 294
payroll taxes as percentage of GDP, 1935–2000 (table), 91
premium payment aid, 434
prescription drug coverage, 20, 79–81, 110–111, 113, 115, 164, 465–466
Medicare commission, 463
payment "givebacks" bill, 462
reimportation bill, 483, 484
preventive care initiatives, 441
tobacco settlement, 61
trust fund surplus for debt reduction, 86
Medicare Catastrophic Coverage Act of 1988, 465
Medicare+Choice plans, 438–439, 462–463
Medicare Payment Advisory Commission, 441, 461, 462
Medicine. *See Drugs and pharmaceutical industry*
Medigap insurance policies, 439, 465
Meehan, Martin T., D-Mass.
campaign finance reform, 780–782, 788–789
527 PACs, 787
Meek, Carrie P., D-Fla.
defense authorization, 279
Meeks, Gregory W., D-N.Y.
election, 14
Megan's Law, 547, 603, 639
Melatonin, 742 (box)
Memphis, Tenn., 613
Menendez, Robert, D-N.J.
House leadership, 770
Sanchez election, 785
Mental health and illness
child witnesses to violence, 482
community placement, 688
confinement for sex offenders, 690
drill sergeant screening, 244, 275
gun control, 639
juvenile crime, 634
medical privacy, 479
Medicare payments to psychiatric facilities, 440
prison inmates, 656

Supreme Court decisions, 688, 690
veterans services, 502
Mental retardation
citizenship applicants, 676
crime victims, 601
criminal offenders, 656
Fragile X research, 482
Merchant banking, 125, 135
Mercury, 453
Merit System Protection Board, 501
Methamphetamine
drug-czar targets, 603
prevention program authorization, 482
trafficking penalties, 593, 601–602
transportation bill, 602
Methane research, 388–389
Methanol taxes, 100
Methyl tertiary butyl ether (MTBE), 390–391
Metropolitan Washington Airports Authority, 741–742
Mexico
financial crisis, 66, 147
NAFTA effects, 148, 154
narcotics control, 184, 203
U.S. trade, 158
air, ship passenger fees, 154
"dolphin-safe" tuna, 345, 346
drug reimports, 484
U.S. visas for farm workers, 673–674
Weld nomination, 7, 173, 623, 624, 800
Mexico City policy, 175, 184, 190, 192, 195, 211, 431, 457–458, 472, 473–474
Mexico-U.S. border
highway projects, 319
low-level nuclear waste site, 360
Otay Mountain wilderness, 401
vehicle emissions, 365
Meyer, Lawrence H., 35 (box)
Meyers, Jan, 760
Miami-Dade County, Fla., 26–27 (box), 686 (box)
Michigan
bankruptcy judges, 608
child support enforcement, 495
congressional elections, 28
school vouchers, 30
Microenterprise aid, 140, 229, 230
Microsoft Corp., 38, 101, 616
Middle East peace process
Camp David summit, 2000, 216 (box)
Clinton term summary, 801–802
Wye River accords, 1998, 190 (box)
U.S. aid appropriations, 73, 75, 176, 189, 210–214
Midwestern states
Clean Air Act, 351
crop insurance, 415–426
dairy pricing, 75, 76, 424–425
presidential vote, 1996, 2000 (table), 21
Migrant workers
immigration relief, 672–673
Migratory Bird Treaty Act of 1918, 358, 384
Migratory birds
habitat conservation, 389
hunting, 358
Mikulski, Barbara A., D-Md.
computer literacy, 538
FDA overhaul, 445
Medicare changes, 436
Senate leadership, 7 (box), 759, 769
Military courts
civilian crimes overseas, 650
Supreme Court decisions, 712–713
Military dependents
abortion, 242, 243, 255, 256, 278, 279, 292
health care, 257, 294

Military health care. *See also Military hospitals*
anthrax immunization, 289
antimissile defense alternative, 297
appropriations, 85, 249, 301
assisted suicide, 459, 606
dependents, 257, 294
retirees, 255, 257, 276, 290–294, 297–299
Military hospitals
abortion, 242, 243, 256, 257, 278, 279, 292
military retirees, 291
Military housing
appropriations, 250, 251, 263, 289, 300, 301
barracks improvements, 301
facilities authorization, 257
off-base allowances, 244, 285, 293
sex-integration of recruits, 252–253, 256
Military pay. *See also Military retirement*
appropriations, 76, 77, 260, 261, 263, 283, 284, 285, 296, 298, 299
defense authorization, 239, 244, 256, 277, 279, 280, 290, 293
401(k) plans, 280
officers' pay, 280
recruiting benefits, 277, 280
review, 261
Military personnel. *See also Military health care; Military pay; Military retirement; Military training; Overseas deployments of U.S. troops; Women in military service*
force levels
appropriations, 248
authorization, 240, 244, 257
remains, from Vietnam War, 158–159
Military posts
administrative jobs privatization, 264–265
base closings
Air Force maintenance depots, 239–243, 245
appropriations, 251, 263, 289, 290, 301
cost-cutting plan, 265
defense authorization, 240–241, 243, 253–254, 255, 256, 277, 278, 292
long-range defense planning, 264
summary, 276
Chinese visit limits, 279, 282
construction appropriations, 58, 65, 69, 75, 84, 85, 250–251, 261, 300–302
vetoes provisions, 252–253 (box)
day-care centers, 250, 251, 301
facilities authorization, 257
schools, 301
sexual materials sales, 275
Military recruiting
authorization, 257
benefits, 277, 280, 285, 293, 299
fitness levels, 244, 280
Military reserves. *See also National Guard*
appropriations, 248–249, 263
military construction, 250–251
defense authorization, 242, 244, 258
Military retirement. *See also Veterans benefits*
career change to teaching, 545
health care, 255, 257, 276, 290–294, 297–299
minimum service, 244, 248, 280, 285
pensions, 280
Military training
Army changes, 275
School of the Americas, 211, 230, 291, 296
sex-integration, 243, 244, 252–253, 254, 255, 256
Vieques exercises, 290–291, 296
Milk and dairy products
China trade agreement, 161
dairy pricing, 17, 73, 75, 76, 212, 418, 424–425
recall indemnity, 420, 423
Miller, Carol A., 9

Miller, Dan, R-Fla.
2000 census, 748
Miller, George, D-Calif.
compensatory time, 576
education
ed-flex plan, 540, 541
student loans, 511
teacher training, 533
environmental protection
conservation lands acquisition, 376–378
"dolphin-safe" tuna, 346
endangered species protection, 351, 386
forest health, 368
national parks operations, 358
national wildlife refuges, 349
ocean policy panel, 364
Salton Sea rehabilitation, 364–365
U.N. lands designation, 368
Puerto Rico status, 741
Miller, Thomas "Papa Bear," 784
Miller, Zell, D-Ga.
election, 30
Million Mom March, 538
Mills, Cheryl D., 825
Milosevic, Slobodan
U.S. Kosovo policy, 178–180, 204–208
U.S. Russia sanctions, 222, 223
U.S. Yugoslavia policy, 278, 803
reconstruction aid ban, 210, 283, 286
Minerals and mining
conflict diamonds, 82
U.N. lands designation, 368
waste sites on public lands, 74
Mineta, Norman Y., 343, 978, 978 (box)
Minge, David, D-Mich.
election defeat, 29
Minimum wage
community service, 557
increase proposals, 15, 20, 572, 579–580
bankruptcy overhaul bill, 142–144
budget resolutions, 73, 80
catchall tax package, 117
welfare-to-work jobs, 51, 487, 488
Mink, 402
Mink, Patsy T., D-Hawaii
education
school counselors, 537
teacher training, 533
Title I benefits for Native Hawaiians, 534
vocational education, 596
Lee nomination, 626
Minnesota
congressional elections, 28, 29
dairy pricing, 424
gubernatorial election, 13
mortgage insurance, 563
wilderness areas, 367
Minorities. *See also African Americans; Hispanic Americans*
census methods, 733–734, 736, 748
financial services modernization, 126
hate crimes, 642
judicial nominations, 678, 679
juvenile crime, 634, 636
NASA education, research programs, 742
redistricting ruling, 788 (box)
religious expression, 661
World War II treatment, 664
Minority business
estate taxes, 115–117
Minority health
clinical trials of drugs, 448
lupus research, 481
organ transplants, 476
programs authorization, 484–485

Minority Health and Health Disparities Research and Education Act, 484
Minority voting rights
Supreme Court decisions, 689
Mint, U.S., 129
Mir **space station,** 754
Missile Technology Control Regime, 195, 304 (box)
Missile technology transfer
China sales to Iran, 181, 182, 183 (box)
China sales to Pakistan, 153, 164, 181, 182, 183 (box)
China satellite launches, 153, 180–182, 254–255, 259, 282, 302, 304 (box), 752
Russia sales to China, 157, 222, 223
Russia sales to Iran, 69, 175, 185, 195–196, 204, 216, 221–223, 270
U.S. sanctions, 169, 268
Missiles. *See also Antimissle defense systems; Missile technology transfer*
appropriations, 248
defense authorization, 277, 282, 293
North Korean program, 186, 188, 803
Missing-in-action military personnel
Vietnam trade status, 158–159
Missing Person File, 646
Missing persons. *See also Missing-in-action military personnel*
college investigations, 547
missing adults, 656–657
missing children, 657
unidentified persons, 646
Mission to Planet Earth, 742
Missionaries' visas, 675
Mississippi
bankruptcy judges, 608
gubernatorial elections, 18
helicopter carrier production, 282, 288, 297
lake dredging, 65
offshore oil revenue, 378
sex offender registries, 604
shipbuilding, 249
Mississippi River, 370
Mississippi University for Women, 547
Missouri
congressional elections, 28
F-15 appropriations, 297
judicial nominations, 677–679
mortgage insurance, 563
term limits, 784
Missouri River, 83, 84, 370
Mitchell Air Reserve Station, Wis., 253 (box)
Mitchell, George J., 663
Moakley, Joe, D-Mass.
defense authorization, 291
foreign aid appropriations, 211
State Department authorization, 218
Mobil Oil Co., 775
Mobile homes, 563, 566
Modafferi, Kristen, 657
Mojave National Preserve, 376, 401
Molinari, Susan, R-N.Y.
successor, 9
Mollohan, Alan B., D-W.Va.
census sampling, 736–737
Molloway, Susan Oki, 623
Money. *See Coins; Currency*
Money laundering, 604, 605–606
Montana
forest revenue, 399
salmon project, 395
Montenegro
Kosovo refugees, 205, 207
U.S. aid appropriations, 214
U.S. trade, 180
Montgomery GI bill, 500, 502–503, 512

Montgomery, G.V. "Sonny," 500, 760
Moody Air Force Base, Ga., 252 (box)
Moran, James P., D-Va.
Reagan National airport, 742
superfund overhaul, 396
Moran, Jerry, R-Kan.
Cuba sanctions, 225–226
Morella, Constance A., R-Md.
federal invention licensing, 747
home ownership aid, 567
Reagan National airport, 742
violence against women, 630
vocational education, 514
Morial, Marc, 785
Morris, Dick, 750
Mosbacher, Robert A., 733
Moseley-Braun, Carol, D-Ill.
ambassadorship nomination, 991
Central American refugees, 619
education savings accounts, 520
election defeat, 11
fast track for trade pacts, 156
flag desecration, 611
Lee nomination, 626
Medicare changes, 436
Moskit missiles, 223
Most-favored-nation trade status, 151
Mothers Against Drunk Driving, 668
Motion Picture Association of America, 329, 387
Motion pictures and videotapes
animal cruelty, 650–651
digital copyright, 328
national parks filming fees, 356, 358, 387
sexual material on military posts, 275
violence, 635, 636
Motor Carriers, Office of, 67, 332
Motor voter law, 781
Mountain Home Air Force Base, Idaho, 252–253 (box)
Moynihan, Daniel Patrick, D-N.Y.
Clinton impeachment remarks (text), 1017
health policy
disabled workers' insurance, 470
Medicare changes, 436
partial-birth abortion, 456
intelligence authorization, 201
NATO expansion, 274
nuclear test ban treaty, 311
pension changes, 582
successor, 28, 806 (box)
MSAs. *See Medical savings accounts*
MTBE. *See Methyl tertiary butyl ether*
Mullins, David W. Jr., 34 (box)
Municipal bonds, 140
Murder
fetal rights, 661–662
juvenile crime, 594
repeat offenses on premature release, 590, 631–633, 635
witness intimidation, 601
Murdoch, Rupert, 254
Murkowski, Frank H., R-Alaska
Alaska land swaps, 367, 379
Arctic wildlife refuge drilling, 413
conservation lands acquisition, 376, 378
electric deregulation, 404–406
energy conservation, 356
energy supplies, 410
forest roadless areas, 395
global warming treaty, 354, 355
national monuments, 390
nuclear lab security, 305, 411
nuclear waste storage, 361–363, 407–408
Richardson nomination, 347 (box)
Strategic Petroleum Reserve, 409
subsistence fishing, 388

Murrah Building, 657–658
Murray, Patty, D-Wash.
  defense authorization, 243, 256, 278, 292
  ed-flex plan, 540
  ESEA authorization, 537, 539
  FDA overhaul, 445
Murtha, John P., D-Pa.
  F-22 funding, 287 (box)
  House ethics overhaul, 766
  military construction appropriations, 251
Musgrove, Ronnie, 18
Music
  digital copyright, 328
  video violence, 637
Muslims
  U.S. Kosovo policy, 178
Mutual funds
  financial services modernization, 120, 138
  tax rules, 105
Mutual of America, 104
Myanmar
  Massachusetts economic sanctions, 686
Myrick, Sue, R-N.C.
  breast, cervical cancer, 472
  gun-related crime, 597

N

NACARA parity, 673
Nader, Ralph. *See also Congressional Accountability Project*
  presidential election, 2000, 22, 27
    popular, electoral vote by region, 21
Nadler, Jerrold, D-N.Y.
  bankruptcy law overhaul, 143
  Clinton impeachment, 822
  defense appropriations, 247
  home ownership aid, 567
  religious expression, 660–661
  space station, 754
  television in federal courts, 622
  term limits, 783
  witness intimidation, 601
NAFTA. *See North American Free Trade Agreement*
Nagorno-Karabakh
  U.S. aid to Azerbaijan, 169, 187, 189, 210
    summary, 187 (box)
NASA. *See National Aeronautics and Space Administration*
Nashville, Tenn., 613
Nassau County, Fla., 26 (box)
National Abortion Federation, 456, 662
National Academy for Education Research, Statistics, Evaluation and Information, 548–549
National Academy of Sciences
  auto rollover ratings, 84
  census sampling, 736
  food labeling, 445, 452
  fuel efficiency standards, 84, 333 (box)
  national educational testing, 524, 525
  national monuments, 390
  northern spotted owl, 392
  nuclear waste storage, 408
  organ transplants, 476
  Persian Gulf War illnesses, 500
  Triana space project, 753
National Aeronautics and Space Administration (NASA)
  appropriations, FY 1998, 59
  authorization, 331, 742–743, 752–753
  Clinton term summary, 734–735
  Glenn in space, 742 (box)
  next generation Internet, 746
  Russia sanctions, 222

  space station, 743–744, 753–754
National Agricultural Workers Survey, 673
National Air Traffic Controllers Association, 741
National Archives
  document declassification, 201
  Kennedy assassination documents, 613
National Assessment Governing Board, 524, 525, 549
National Assessment of Educational Progress, 524, 525, 532, 549
National Association for Home Care, 443
National Association for the Advancement of Colored People, 422
National Association of Broadcasters, 325
National Association of Criminal Defense Lawyers, 597, 605
National Association of Insurance Commissioners, 139
National Association of Realtors, 397
National Association of Registered Agents and Brokers, 139–140
National Audubon Society, 384
National Automobile Dealers Association, 397
National Bank Act of 1916, 123 (box)
National Bankruptcy Review Commission, 126–127
National Bipartisan Commission on the Future of Medicare, 464–465
National cemeteries
  Arlington eligibility, expansion, 283, 502
  Ft. Atkinson preservation, 285
  theft, vandalism, 604
National Center for Education Statistics, 536
National Center for Minority Health and Health Disparities, 82, 484
National Center for Missing and Exploited Children, 594, 597, 657, 668
National Commission on Restructuring the Internal Revenue Service, 107
National Commission on Retirement Policy, 582 (box)
National Commission on Terrorism, 267, 309
National Conference of Bankruptcy Judges, 608
National Coordinator for Security, Infrastructure Protection and Counterterrorism, 267
National Credit Union Administration, 128
National Crime Information Center, 646
National Crime Victims Survey, 601
National Council of Senior Citizens, 496
National Defense Panel, 240
National Discovery Trails, 400
National District Attorneys Association, 597
National Domestic Preparedness Office, 646
National Drug Control Policy, Office of
  community group grants, 602
  leadership, 594 (box)
  overhaul plan, 593, 602–603
National Economic Council, 35 (box)
National Education Association, 545
National Endowment for the Arts (NEA)
  elimination proposal, 7
  funding, 59, 738–739, 750–751
  Supreme Court ruling, 738 (box)
National Energy Marketers Association, 406
National Environmental Policy Act of 1970, 342, 387, 401
National Estuarine Reserve System, 388
National Federation of Independent Business
  chemical weapons treaty, 268
  superfund overhaul, 397, 398
National Federation of Republican Assemblies, 787
National Fish and Wildlife Foundation, 356, 393
National forests. *See also Forest Service, U.S.*
  Alaska road easement, 379

  Clinton term summary, 341
  conservation easement acquisition, 378
  damaged tree removal, 387–388
  forest health, 368–369
  logging
    revenue sharing, 399–400
    roads, 343, 344, 359, 372, 378, 394–395, 799
    Tongass, 67
  Supreme Court decisions, 710
National Governors' Association
  crime victims' rights, 668
  ed-flex plan, 528, 539–540
  Internet taxes, 327
  juvenile crime, 597
  welfare law revisions, 487
National Guard
  appropriations, 248–249
    military construction, 250–251, 252–253 (box), 263, 289
  Bradley upgrades, 281
  defense authorization, 242, 244, 257, 258
  Joint Chiefs post, 244
  long-term defense planning, 264
  terrorism preparedness, 295, 308–309
  VA home loans, 500
National Guard Association of the United States, 244
National Head Start Association, 492
National Highway Traffic Safety Administration
  drug testing for teenage driver's license applicants, 602
  truck safety, 67
National Historic Preservation Fund, 547
National Hospice Organization, 607, 658
National Imagery and Mapping Agency, 226
National Instant Criminal Background Check system, 631
National Institute for Occupational Safety and Health, 666
National Institute of Corrections, 613
National Institute of Standards and Technology (NIST), 745, 746
National Institutes of Health
  appropriations, 67, 74, 82
  clinical trials database, 448
  lab construction aid, 481
  lupus research, 481
  minority health, 484
  next generation Internet, 746
  pediatric research, 482
  prostate cancer research, 481
National Labor Relations Board, 585, 679
National League of Cities
  bulletproof vests, 600
  Internet taxes, 327
  religious expression, 660
National Marine Fisheries Service, 393
National marine sanctuaries, 388
National Memorial Cemetery of the Pacific, 604
National monuments. *See National parks and monuments*
National Nuclear Security Administration, 276, 279, 282, 292, 296, 302, 306, 411
National Ocean Service, 745
National Oceanic and Atmospheric Administration (NOAA)
  authorization, 745
  coastal water quality, 380
  coral reef protection, 393
  estuary restoration, 386
  Fish and Wildlife Foundation board, 356
  ocean policy panel, 364, 392
National Organ Transplant Act of 1984, 476
National Park Service
  filming fees, 387
  long-distance trails, 400

operations overhaul, 358–359
subsistence fishing, 388
Utah wilderness, 366
National Park Service Concessions Management Advisory Board, 359
National parks and monuments
appropriations, 84
CARA funding priorities, 377–378
Clinton term summary, 799
coral reef protection, 393
Everglades restoration, 372, 375
filming fees, 356, 387
King speech commemorative, 752
management overhaul, 358
new designations
California, 403
Colorado parks, 381
presidential authority, 20, 341, 344, 365–366, 389–390
projects, 359
Sequoia addition, 401–402
National Performance Review, 193
National Policy Forum (NPF), 778
National Practitioner Data Bank, 482
National Railroad Passenger Corporation. *See Amtrak*
National Reconnaissance Office, 200, 201, 227, 228
National Research Council of the National Academy of Sciences, 392
National Rifle Association (NRA)
civil assets forfeiture, 648
527 PACs, 786–787
gun control, 16, 638–641
juvenile crime bill, 633
National Right to Life Committee
527 PACs, 786
human cloning, 460
National Science Foundation (NSF)
appropriations, 59
authorization, 744–745
Internet address registration fees, 746 (box)
next generation Internet, 746
National Security Agency (NSA), 227
National Security and Military/Commercial Concerns with the People's Republic of China, House Select Committee on U.S., 180–182, 302, 958
National Security Committee, House
jurisdiction, leadership, 960–961
National Security Council
terrorism, 267, 308
National service
literacy programs, 529
National Sheriffs Association, 675
National Smokers Alliance, 771
National Steel and Shipbuilding Co., 288
National Victims Center, 609
National Weather Service, 745
National Wildlife Property Repository, 369
National Wildlife Refuge System, 344, 345, 348–349
National Wildlife Refuge System Administration Act of 1966, 348–349
National Wildlife Refuge System Centennial Commission, 393
National wildlife refuges
Alaska road, 67
ANWR oil drilling, 413
Cat Island acquisition, 402
Clinton term summary, 341
filming fees, 387
management overhaul, 348–349
nutria eradication, 363
Salton Sea rehabilitation, 364
NationsBank, 125

Native Alaskans
Alaska development, 379
land claims, 391–392
subsistence fishing, 388
Native Americans. *See Indians*
NATO. *See North Atlantic Treaty Organization*
Natural gas
Arctic wildlife refuge drilling, 413
Clinton term summary, 372
energy supplies, 410
federal offshore revenue, 375–379
federal subsidies, 316
Iran development, 186
methane research, 388–389
"Silk Road" trade, 169
stripper well loans, 333–334
Turkmenistan aid, 189
Natural Resources Defense Council
coastal water quality, 380
gasoline additive MTBE, 390
Nature reserves. *See also National wildlife refuges; Wilderness areas*
coral reef protection, 393
Navajo Indians
reservation lands, 366
uranium miner compensation, 296
Naval Research Laboratory, 389
Navy, U.S.
aircraft and ships
appropriations, 246, 247, 249, 261, 288, 300
authorization, 241, 243, 245, 258, 278, 281–282, 294–295
antimissile defenses, 244, 248, 257, 261, 294
Cole attack, 293
communications privatization, 296
digital communications networks, 245, 249, 262
long-term defense planning, 264
military construction appropriations, 252–253 (box), 289
Northrop Grumman location, 162
personnel levels, 240
recruiting benefits, 280, 299
Vieques exercises, 290–291, 296
NEA. *See National Endowment for the Arts*
Nebraska
"partial-birth" abortion, 431, 455, 473, 686
same-sex marriage, 30
term limits, 784
Nellis Air Force Base, Nev., 253 (box)
Nelson, Bill, 28
Nelson, John C., 473
Neotropical migratory birds, 385
Nepotism
federal court judgeships, 627
Nerve gas, 299
Netanyahu, Benjamin, 190 (box)
Nethercutt, George, R-Wash.
Cuba sanctions, 83, 224–225, 426
NASA authorization, 752
NEA funding, 751
Network Solutions Inc., 746 (box)
Neumann, Mark W., R-Wis.
House committee funding, 767
Nevada
congressional elections, 28
nuclear waste storage, 344, 361–363, 407–408
same-sex marriage, 30
term limits, 784
New Jersey
bankruptcy judges, 608
Boy Scout gay ban, 649
congressional elections, 29
gasoline additive MTBE, 390
gubernatorial election, 8
hate crimes, 690
racial profiling in traffic stops, 652

New Markets initiative, 564
New Mexico
congressional elections, 8, 9, 14
nuclear security, 305
New River, Calif., 365
New York
assisted suicide, 687
bankruptcy judges, 608
children's health insurance, 438, 443
congressional elections, 8, 9, 14, 28
Clinton Senate race, 806–807 (box)
gasoline additive MTBE, 390
Medicaid changes, 438
mortgage insurance, 563
New York, N.Y.
airports, 67, 321, 332
Governors Island sale, 51, 56
line-item veto of Medicaid provision, 64, 65
treated sewage disposal, 361
New York Stock Exchange, 138 (box), 141
New York Times
Clinton impeachment, 825–826
Newport News Shipbuilding and Dry Dock Co., 245, 249
News Corp., 254
News media
child abuse programs, 647
China trade agreement, 163
cross-ownership rules, 326
presidential campaign coverage, 2000, 24, 25
Newton, Wayne, 668
Ney, Bob, R-Ohio
China trade agreement, 162 (box)
Sanchez election, 785
Ng Lap Seng, 778
Niagara Falls, N.Y., International Airport, 253 (box)
Nicaragua
refugees in U.S., 619–620
Nicaraguan and Cuban Adjustment and Relief Act, 673
Nichols, Terry, 609
Nickles, Don, R-Okla.
asbestos compensation, 665
conservation lands acquisition, 378
defense appropriations, 283
education savings accounts, 544
health policy
assisted suicide, 477, 606–607, 658–660
disabled workers' insurance, 470, 471
organ transplants, 476
Kosovo policy, 207
Lee nomination, 625
Medicare changes, 436
patients' rights, 467, 470
railroad pensions, 581
sanctions for religious persecution, 199
Senate leadership, 7 (box), 759, 769
"Silk Road" trade, 169
tax cuts, 1997, 93
Waco investigation, 680–681
welfare law revisions, 488
Niedermeier, Christine M., 771
Nigeria
U.S. relations, 803
Nikko Enterprises, 765
U.S.S. *Nimitz*, 245, 249
NIST. *See National Institute of Standards and Technology*
Nitze, Paul, 273
Nixon, Richard
budget policy, 40
Clinton comparison, 797
environmental policy, 342
financial services modernization, 124 (box)
popular vote, 1960, 1968, 22

veto use, 811
Watergate scandal, 813
Ford pardon, 808
independent counsel law, 662
NOAA. *See National Oceanic and Atmospheric Administration*
Noise abatement, 752
Nominations and appointments. *See also Cabinet*
Clinton term summary, 7, 592, 799–800, 977–993
judicial appointments, 593, 622–624, 677–680
recess appointments, 679, 680
U.S. marshals, 614
Nonprofits. *See Charities and nonprofit organizations*
Norfolk, Va., Naval Air Station, 253 (box)
Norfolk, Va., Naval Shipyard, 252 (box)
North American Electric Reliability Council, 406
North American Free Trade Agreement (NAFTA)
adverse impact aid, 324
Caribbean trade, 158
"dolphin-safe" tuna, 346
results, 153–154
summary, 147, 148, 151
North Atlantic Treaty Organization (NATO)
Bosnia operations, 243, 245, 246, 247, 255
Clinton term summary, 10, 173, 174, 177
expansion, 189, 191, 192, 230, 239, 246, 272–274, 802
Kosovo policy, 177–178, 204–208, 291, 802–803
U.S. appropriations, 84–85, 263, 283
treaty excerpts, 272 (box)
U.S. antimissile defenses, 308
U.S. appropriations for infrastructure, 251, 263, 289, 301
U.S. commanders, 241 (box)
Yugoslavia operations, 278–279
campaign analysis, 287
Chinese embassy bombing, 166, 209, 226
North Carolina
minority districts, 788 (box)
North Dakota
B-52 fleet, 299
flag desecration, 667–668
North Korea
nuclear proliferation issues, 175
China technology transfer, 164
missile technology, 238, 276
nuclear test ban treaty, 311
State Department authorization, 218, 219
U.S. aid appropriations, 66, 186–189, 214, 215, 217
U.S. antimissile defenses, 265, 266, 267, 306, 307
U.S. aid ban, 289
U.S. land mines, 254, 274
U.S. relations, 803
U.S. trade
encryption exports ban, 336
food sanctions, 83, 223–225, 424, 426
North, Oliver L., 790 (box)
Northeast Interstate Dairy Compact, 75, 76, 424–425
Northern spotted owl, 392
Northrop Grumman Corp., 162
Northup, Anne M., R-Ky.
campaign finance reform, 782
Northwest Forest Plan, 392
Northwestern Hawaiian Island Coral Reef Reserve, 393
Norton, Eleanor Holmes, D-D.C.
federal-D.C. ties, 740
school vouchers, 529
vocational education, 514

Norwood, Charlie, R-Ga.
juvenile crime, 637
Medicare drug benefits, 465
nuclear waste storage, 407
patients' rights, 434, 454
NPF. *See National Policy Forum*
NRA. *See National Rifle Association*
NRO. *See National Reconnaissance Office*
NSA. *See National Security Agency*
NSF. *See National Science Foundation*
Nuccio, Richard A., 202
Nuclear energy. *See Nuclear power plants; Nuclear waste disposal; Nuclear weapons*
neutron production, 754
Nuclear power plants. *See also Nuclear waste disposal*
decommissioning, 406
Nuclear Power Propulsion Training Center, 250
Nuclear-powered aircraft carriers
appropriations, 262, 288
authorization, 241, 242–243, 245, 258, 282
Nuclear Regulatory Commission
nuclear waste storage, 407–408
utility decommissioning, 406
Nuclear submarines
appropriations, 249, 262, 288
authorization, 241, 242, 245, 295
Nuclear waste disposal
Clinton term summary, 341, 344, 345, 372
Energy Department nominations, 347 (box)
high-level interim site, 361–363, 407
long-term storage, 361, 407–409
low-level Texas site, 359–361
uranium enrichment plant cleanup, 365
Nuclear Waste Fund, 361
Nuclear Waste Policy Act of 1982, 361
Nuclear weapons. *See also Arms control; Nuclear weapons proliferation*
appropriations, 58, 76
electromagnetic pulse vulnerability, 295
tritium production, 256
U.S. intelligence detection, 262, 267
worker compensation, 290, 293, 296
Nuclear weapons proliferation. *See also Arms control; Comprehensive Test Ban Treaty; Missile technology transfer; Nunn-Lugar program*
DOE lab security, 277
Chinese espionage, 166, 208, 226, 276, 279, 282, 302, 303 (box), 304 (box), 410, 411
overhaul, 226–227, 276, 279, 292, 302–306, 410–414
Iraq program, 196–198, 803
North Korean development, 186, 188
China sales, 164
U.S. transfer ban, 215, 218
Russian materials disposal, 69, 76, 262
ex-Soviet brain-drain, 210, 214, 282
supercomputer export controls, 242
terrorists, 308–309
U.S. sales to India, 255
U.S. sanctions on India, Pakistan, 159, 170, 200, 223–224, 284, 288–299
Nude dancing, 688
Nunn-Lugar program
appropriations, 246, 247, 286, 299
chemical weapons facility exemption, 282, 291, 292, 295
defense authorization, 242, 243, 282, 295
Nunn, Sam, 242, 273, 760
Nurses
training to treat sex crimes, 630
VA pay, 502
visas, 674–675
Nursing homes
debt limits, 96–97

Medicaid, Medicare payments, 50, 75, 82, 430, 433, 437, 441–442, 461–464
Medicaid patients
eviction ban, 485
veterans, 500
religious expression, 661
Nussbaum, Bernard W., 805 (box)
Nussle, Jim, R-Iowa
fast track for trade pacts, 155
Nutria, 363–364
Nutrition. *See Food and nutrition*
Nutritional Labeling and Education Act of 1990, 445

O

Oakar, Mary Rose, 766
Oakdale, Pa., 253 (box)
Oberg, James, 744
Oberstar, James L., D-Minn.
Minnesota wilderness, 367
Reagan National airport, 742
superfund overhaul, 397
Obey, David R., D-Wis.
Colombia antidrug aid, 220–221
defense appropriations, 247, 285
NEA funding, 739
Social Security surplus protection, 79
O'Brien, Timothy, 775
Obscenity and pornography. *See also Child pornography; Sexually explicit material*
animal cruelty videos, 650
cemetery vandalism, 604
Internet regulation, 68, 317, 329, 688
school, library filters, 82
NEA funding standards, 738 (box)
Occupational safety and health
Amish work exceptions, 584–585
drug-free workplaces, 602
ergonomics standards, 584
nuclear weapons workers' compensation, 290, 293, 296
OSHA overhaul, 577
Postal Service workers' compensation, 56
repetitive stress injury, 81–82
state consultants, 577
workplace safety, 20
workplace teams, 578
Occupational Safety and Health Act, 572
Occupational Safety and Health Administration (OSHA)
attorney's fees, 585
ergonomics standards, 584
overhaul plans, 573, 577–578
repetitive stress injury, 82
Oceans. *See also Coastal areas; Fish and fisheries*
coral reef protection, 393
environmental policy panel, 364, 392
NOAA authorization, 745
oceanographic research ship, 245, 247
shipping law revision, 321–322
Ochsner Health Plan, 462
O'Connor, Sandra Day
abortion, 686
assisted suicide, 687
census sampling, 691, 748 (box)
federal-state relations, 685
Florida presidential vote, 26, 687 (box)
Internet content regulation, 688
property rights, 691
Supreme Court summary, 684, 689 (box)
tobacco regulation, 691
Odeen, Philip A., 264
Official English, 517, 721, 741
O'Hare International Airport, 321, 332

Ohio
mental health courts, 656
uranium cleanup, 365
Ohio-class submarines, 277
Oil
Arctic wildlife refuge drilling, 80, 413
Azerbaijan aid ban, 187 (box), 210
Clinton term summary, 372
energy supplies, 409–410
federal offshore drilling revenues, 74, 344, 375–379
federal subsidies, 316
gasoline additive MTBE, 391
home heating oil reserve, 409
sanctions for price-fixing, 414
shortage remedies, 356
"Silk Road" trade, 169
Strategic Petroleum Reserve, 409
foreign leases, 56
stripper well loans, 333–334
superfund overhaul, 396–397
tariffs, 156, 158
U.S. budget policy, 40
underground storage tanks, 102, 370
Oklahoma
Air Force maintenance depots, 240, 243
tornado disaster aid, 77
Oklahoma City, Okla., bombings
counterterrorism legislation, 267
Federal Protective Service, 657–658
gun control, 638
McVeigh burial rights, 498
trial attendance by victims, 609–610
unborn victims, 474
Old Executive Office Building, 751
Older Americans Act, 431, 496
O'Leary, Hazel R., 347 (box), 978 (box)
Olson, Theodore, 25, 686 (box)
Olympic games infrastructure, 252 (box), 319, 789
OMB. *See Management and Budget, Office of*
O'Nesti, Charles, 774
Opera companies, 739
Operation Safe Home, 558
OPIC. *See Overseas Private Investment Corporation*
Oracle Co., 101
Orangutan protection, 379–380
Oregon
assisted suicide, 16, 117, 429, 477, 606, 658–659
federal land exchanges, 403
gun show background checks, 30
Hells Canyon jetboats, 367
national forests
damaged tree removal, 387
northern spotted owl, 392
revenue sharing, 399–400
national monuments, 390
nuclear waste storage, 362
salmon project, 395
wilderness areas, 403
Organ Procurement and Transplantation Network Act of 2000, 477
Organ Procurement Organization Certification Act, 481
Organ transplants
China trade agreement, 165
immunosuppressive drugs, 462, 463, 465
marriage status tax cut, 113
national allocation regulation, 67, 74, 471, 475–477, 478
procurement organization certification, 481
Organization for the Prohibition of Chemical Weapons, 269 (box)
Organization of Petroleum Exporting Countries (OPEC), 409–410, 414

Organized labor. *See Labor unions*
Origins project, 742–743
Ornstein, Norman, 21
OSHA. *See Occupational Safety and Health Administration*
Osteoporosis screening, 437, 441
Otay Mountain wilderness, 401
OTC derivatives, 141–142
Ottoman Empire
Armenia genocide resolution, 231
Overseas deployments of U.S. forces
Bosnia
appropriations, 246–247, 249, 250, 259, 260
defense authorization, 240, 243, 245, 252–256, 277, 281
War Powers Act test, 198
Clinton term summary, 178
Colombia, 221, 291
congressional-executive relations, 198, 259–261, 277–278
Europe, 279
Haiti, 174, 277, 279, 281
humanitarian missions, 299
Iraq, Persian Gulf
appropriations, 250, 263, 298, 299
defense authorization, 277, 281
Kosovo
action, 1999–2000, 204–208
appropriations, 283, 286, 300, 301
background, 178–180
defense authorization, 277, 278–279, 281, 291
president's authority, 20, 178
summary, 204
Republican platform, 23
service benefits, 280
Yugoslavia, 278–279, 299
Overseas Private Investment Corporation (OPIC)
authorization, 159, 169
foreign aid appropriations, 211
political risk insurance, 185
Oxley, Michael G., R-Ohio
decimal pricing of stocks, 138 (box)
EPA research, 747
superfund overhaul, 353, 396, 398
Oysters, 386
Ozone
Clean Air Act, 351
pollution standard, 84

P

PACE. *See Programs of All-Inclusive Care for the Elderly*
Pacific Ocean
"dolphin-safe" tuna, 345–348
Packard, Ron, R-Calif.
nuclear lab security, 411
PACs. *See Political action committees*
Paez, Richard A., 592, 629, 677–678, 679–680, 764, 800, 992
Pain treatment, 477, 606–607, 658–660, 687
Pakistan
Burton ethics probe, 765
China missile technology, 153, 164, 181, 182, 183 (box)
nuclear tests, 310, 311
antimissile defenses, 308
U.S. aid, 224
U.S. trade sanctions, 200, 204, 223–224, 284, 288–289
food exemptions, 159, 170, 421
wheat sale, 200
Palestine Liberation Organization, 190 (box)
Palestinian Authority
Camp David summit, 2000, 216 (box)

U.S. aid, 75, 176, 185, 214
Wye River summit, 190 (box)
Palestinians
Middle East peace process, 801–802
U.S. aid appropriations, 211
Wye River summit, 190 (box)
Palliative medical care, 658
Pallone, Frank Jr., D-N.J.
"dolphin-safe" tuna, 347
drug-abuse prevention, treatment, 602
electric deregulation, 405
FDA overhaul, 446
superfund overhaul, 398
Palm Beach County, Fla., 25, 26–27 (box), 686 (box)
Pan Asian Chamber of Commerce, U.S., 625
Panama Declaration, 346
Panetta, Leon E., 35 (box)
Pap tests, 433, 437, 441, 462
Paper
China trade agreement, 161
Pappas, Michael, R-N.J.
electoral defeat, 13
Paralyzed Veterans of America, 503
Pardons
Clinton scandals, 808–809
crime victims' rights, 668–669, 682
FALN clemency, 669, 681–683
Parental rights and issues
abortion
circumvention of consent, 431, 455, 456–457
fathers' suits, 456
college safety, 547
community services parenting programs, 491
consent, notification of birth control, 67
consent to Internet data collection, 68
consent to medical research on children, 482
grandparents' visitation rights, 688
gun control, 638
Internet filters, 635
juvenile crime, 633
medical records of children, 479
paternity establishment, 493–494
teens in welfare-to-work, 512
Parole and probation
juvenile crime, 595
Supreme Court decisions, 690, 704
Parole Commission, U.S., 55
Parry, Carol J., 990
"Partial-birth" abortion. *See Abortion*
Partial Birth Abortion Ban Act, 473
Particulate matter, 351
Partisanship
Clinton impeachment, 813–827
Clinton term summary, 3–5, 15, 809
education policy, 507–508
law enforcement issues, 589
punitive legislative actions, 773
Passive foreign investment companies, 101
Passports, 677
Pastrana, Andres, 220
Pataki, George E., 487
Patent and Trademark Office, U.S., 75, 324, 334
Patents
Clinton term summary, 316
insulin and antibiotics, 449
patent system overhaul, 75, 324, 334
pediatric prescription drugs, 444, 447–448
Supreme Court decisions, 685, 693–694
Paternity establishment, 492–493
Patient Access to Responsible Care Act, 454
Patients' Bill of Rights Plus Act, 467, 478
Patrick Air Force Base, Fla., 252 (box)
Patrick, Deval L., 625
Patriot missiles, 301
Patten, Chris, 152–153

Patterson, Andrew C., 625
Patton, Paul E., 18
Paul, Ron, R-Texas
  campaign finance reform, 782
  ESEA authorization, 536
  Hong Kong-U.S. trade, 158
  national wildlife refuges, 349
Pawnshops, 635
Paxon, Bill, R-N.Y.
  campaign finance reform, 781
  Gingrich coup attempt, 763 (box)
  House leadership, 760
Pay. *See Salaries and wages*
"Paycheck Protection Act," 777
PAYGO rules, 48, 52, 53–54
Payne, Donald M., D-N.J.
  Davis-Bacon wage rules, 492
  education
    hate crime prevention, 536
    sex offenders on campus, 547
    Title I waivers, 541
    vocational education, 514
PCBs, 397
Peace Corps, 230
Pearl Harbor attack, 296
Pease, Ed, R-Ind.
  affirmative action, 616
  asbestos compensation, 666
Pediatric medical care
  children's health insurance, 443
  drug studies, patents, 444, 447–448
  patients' rights, 470
Pediatric Research Initiative, 482
Pelicans, 384
Pell, Claiborne, 760
Pell grants, 509–513, 526, 545
Pelosi, Nancy, D-Calif.
  bilingual education, 518
  China trade agreement, 163
  drug treatment programs, 221
  foreign aid appropriations, 184
Peña, Federico F., 320 (box), 347 (box), 978
  (box), 979
Pennsylvania
  bankruptcy judges, 608
  children's health insurance, 438, 443
  congressional elections, 14
  organ transplants, 475
Pensions and retirement income. *See also 401(k)*
  pension plans; Individual retirement accounts
  (IRAs); Military retirement; Social Security
  basis recovery formula, 104
  Clinton term summary, 572, 579
  contribution limits, 112, 116, 117, 119, 581–582
  creditor access in bankruptcy, 144
  D.C. public workers, 54, 740
  defined-benefit plan limits, 105
  employer stock in 401(k) plans, 105
  federal employees, 51, 56
  railroad workers, 580–581
  Social Security supplement account proposal,
    72, 79, 583 (box)
  state, local government employees, 105
  Supreme Court decisions, 722
  tax incentives for savings, 117, 119
Pentagon. *See Defense Department, U.S.*
Peonage, 629
People's Republic of China. *See China*
Perchlorates, 383
Peregrine falcons, 381
Perkins vocational education grants, 513–515,
  523
Perot, Ross, 21 (table)
Perry, William J., 241 (box), 978 (box)
Persian Gulf
  U.S. military missions, 281, 298, 299

Persian Gulf War, 174, 197, 237
Persian Gulf War veterans
  health care, 497–498, 500
  Iraqi frozen assets, 219
Personnel Management, Office of, 56
Peru
  Colombia antidrug aid, 220
Pest eradication, 557
Peterson, Collin C., D-Minn.
  tax cuts, 1997, 93
Peterson, John E., R-Penn.
  campaign finance reform, 782
Peterson, Pete, 985
Pets
  public housing tenants, 558, 561
Pharmaceutical Research and Manufacturers of
  America, 483
Pharmaceuticals. *See Drugs and pharmaceutical*
  industry
Phonics, 520
Physical fitness
  military recruits, 244
Physical therapists, 461, 671
Physician assistants, 502
Physician Payment Review Commission, 441
Physicians
  antitrust law, 480–481
  assisted suicide, 16, 30, 117, 459, 477, 606–607,
    658–660, 686, 687, 717–718
  fetal rights, 661
  hospital patient discharge timing, 434
  malpractice database, 482
  managed care plan "gag clauses," 432, 433, 437,
    439, 442, 469
  medical devices for rare conditions, 450
  medical necessity determinations, 469, 470
  Medicare payments, 50, 439, 440–441
    private contracts, 436, 437, 438–439
  members of Congress, 430, 434, 460, 468, 472,
    475
    outside income, 767–768
  partial-birth abortion, 456, 473
  patients' access to specialists, 467, 469–470
  prisoner health care, 653
Physicians for Human Rights, 422
Pickering, Charles W. "Chip," 781
Pine River Irrigation District, 771
Pipelines
  Endangered Species Act waivers, 351
Pittman-Robertson Act of 1937, 393
Pitts, Joseph R., R-Pa.
  Amish work exceptions, 584
  education block grants, 527
Plan Colombia, 220–221
Planetary research, 742–743
Planning boards, 737
Plants. *See also Agriculture and farming;*
  Endangered species
  national wildlife refuges, 349
Pledge of allegiance
  disabled citizenship applicants, 676
Plouffe, David, 29
Plumas National Forest, 368
Plutonium, 69
Podesta, John, 408, 462
POGO. *See Project on Government Oversight*
Poland
  NATO expansion, 189, 230, 272–274, 802
Police and law enforcement agencies. *See also*
  Federal Bureau of Investigation
  animals in law enforcement, 650
  appropriations, FY 1998, 59
  bank privacy rules, 132, 137
  budget outlays, 1987–2001 (graph), 590
  bulletproof vests, 599–600, 645
  civil assets forfeiture, 647–649

  Clinton term summary, 589
  counterfeit badges, 644–645
  criminal use of body armor, 645
  electronic information access, 655–656
  encryption exports, 326
  handgun safety locks, 598
  illegal immigrants, 620
  missing adults, 656–657
  police officers
    assault penalties, 613, 656
    concealed weapons, 598–599, 650
    D.C. pensions, 740
    Federal Protective Service, 657–658
    home ownership aid, 566, 567
    medals of valor, 614
    new hires appropriations, 73, 74
    off-duty liability, 614
    private security personnel, 599
    railroad officers, 652
    school resource officers, 530
    slain officers, 614–615, 651
    U.S. marshal nominees, 614
  prisoner deaths, 653
  racial profiling in traffic stops, 608, 652
  sex offender registries, 603–604
  Supreme Court decisions, 689–690
  terrorism
    investigative tools, 267
    response training, 295
  unidentified persons, 646
  violence against women, 632
  wiretaps, 646
  witness intimidation, 601
Police Athletic League, 650
Political action committees (PACs)
  Section 527 groups, 786–787
Political advertising
  campaign finance reform, 776–783, 789
  527 PACs, 786–787
Political asylum
  food stamp benefits, 422
  religious persecution victims, 198–199
Political parties and interest groups. *See also*
  Political action committees; specific parties
  campaign finance reform, 776–783, 788–790
  527 PACs, 786
  party affiliations in Congress, presidency,
    1789–2001 (table), 1071–1072
Political prisoners
  China policy, 165, 208, 209
Political risk insurance, 159, 169, 185
Pollard, Jonathan Jay, 190 (box)
Pollock fishing, 82, 393
Pollution control. *See also Air pollution; Water*
  pollution
  budget outlays, FY 1987–2001 (graph), 342
  Clinton term summary, 342–343
  global warming treaty, 354–356
  mining waste, 74
  superfund overhaul, 353–354
  underground storage tanks, 370
Polygraph tests, 290, 296, 303 (box), 304, 306
Pombo, Richard W., R-Calif.
  coastal management plans, 384
  National Discovery Trails, 400
  national parks projects, 359
Pomeroy, Earl, D-N.D.
  House chaplain, 775
Pork. *See Meat*
Pork-barrel projects
  line-item veto, 64
  surface transportation authorization, 319
Pornography. *See Obscenity and pornography*
Porter, John Edward, R-Ill.
  China trade agreement, 163
  foreign aid appropriations, 188

Portman, Rob, R-Ohio
  antidrug grants, 602
  drug abuse prevention, 602
  IRS overhaul, 107
  pension changes, 582
  retirement savings tax incentives, 119
  Third World debt/forest protection, 369
Positron emission tomography, 449
Posse Comitatus Act, 309
Postal Service, U.S.
  appropriations, 59, 68, 76, 81
  charity stamps, 751
  OSHA standards, 577–578
  workers' compensation, 56
Postsecondary education. See also Colleges and
  universities; Vocational education
  welfare recipients, 512
Potomac River, 370
Poultry
  China trade agreement, 161
  electric power from waste, 565
Powell, Colin L., 23
Pregnancy. See also Abortion; Birth control
  adoption counseling, 482
  educational aid for pregnant women, 514
  fetal rights, 474–475, 591, 661–662
  prenatal care
    research, 482
    prisoners, 653
Preschool education. See Head Start
Prescription Drug User Fee Act of 1992, 444,
  447
Prescription drugs. See Drugs and
  pharmaceutical industry
Presidential election, 1992
  voter guides ruling, 790 (box)
Presidential election, 1996
  economic issues, 33, 41–42
  electoral vote by state (map, table), 1065
  issue advocacy ads, 780 (box)
  party platforms (text), 1037–1039
  popular, electoral vote by region (table), 21
  popular vote by state (table), 1064
Presidential election, 2000
  campaign, 24–25
  Clinton role, 804
  economic issues, 33
  effect on appropriations bills, 81–82
  electoral vote by state (map, table), 1067
  Florida role, 13, 25–27
    chronology (box), 26–27
  foreign policy issues, 175, 222
  Gore Senate tie-breakers, 143
  nominations, 22
    Democratic convention, 23–24, 1069
    Republican convention, 22–23, 1068
  popular, electoral vote by region (table), 21
  popular vote by state (table), 1066
  summary, 3–4, 20, 21–22
  Supreme Court decisions, 684, 686–687 (box)
    opinions (texts), 1046–1055
Presidential elections. See also Campaign
  finance; specific elections
  Delaware plan for primaries, 23
  popular winners, electoral losers, 22
  victorious party, 1860–2000 (table), 1062–1063
  vote summary, 1789–2000 (table), 1059–1061
Presidential Legal Expense Fund, 778
President's Foreign Intelligence Advisory
  Board, 302, 303, 305, 410–411
President's Task Force on National Health Care
  Reform, 806 (box)
Presidents, U.S. See also Congressional-executive
  relations; Executive Office of the President;
  Presidential elections
  commemorative designations, 751

party affiliations in Congress, presidency,
  1789–2001 (table), 1071–1072
protection authority, 613, 651
salary, 17, 76, 751
Pressler, Larry, 759
Preventive medical care. See also Immunizations
  children's health insurance, 443
  Medicare coverage, 45, 50, 433, 437, 441
  prisoner health care, 653
Primary elections
  "blanket primaries," 688
  Delaware plan, 23
  Supreme Court decisions, 708
Prince William Sound, 379
Prison labor
  bulletproof vest production, 600
  China imports ban, 164, 165, 182, 209, 256
  Export-Import Bank, 157
  market expansion, 652
  state, local governments, nonprofits, 603
Prisons and prisoners. See also Felons;
  Sentencing
  boot camps, 595, 634
  construction ban in juvenile crime grants, 596
  D.C. system transfer, 54–55, 740
  DNA evidence, 655
  food stamps, 489, 495
  habeas corpus appeals, 621, 622, 690
  health care, 653
    drug treatment, 602
    HIV testing, 600
  housing of juveniles, 596, 634–635, 636
  illegal immigrants, 620
  inmate deaths, 653
  inmate mental health, 656
  releases due to overcrowding, 622, 637
  religious expression, 660–661
  Supreme Court decisions, 704–705
  transport of prisoners, 653–654
Privacy
  electronic information access, 655–656
  encryption technology, 318, 326–327
  financial services modernization, 121, 130–137
  identity theft, 600–601
  Internet protections, 82, 337
  medical records, 429, 479–480
  Supreme Court decisions, 685–687
  tax record snooping ban, 106 (box)
  wiretaps, 646
Private and parochial schools
  education savings accounts, 518–520, 544–546
  IRA use for tuition, 95, 507–508
  public aid
    computer loans, 689
    federal funds shifting, 536
    remedial education services, 689
    Title I benefits, 534
    vouchers, 6–7, 528–529, 537, 539
  religious expression amendment benefits
    clause, 611
  Supreme Court decisions, 684, 689
Privatization
  military base administrative jobs, 264–265
  military housing, 301
  Navy, Marine communications, 296
  Social Security, 583 (box)
Pro-Life Caucus, House, 473
Probation. See Parole and probation
Product liability, 316, 322, 336
Programs of All-Inclusive Care for the Elderly
  (PACE), 442
Progress and Freedom Foundation, 774
Project Exile, 642
Project on Government Oversight (POGO), 775
"Project Scholarscam," 546

Promoting Safe and Stable Families program,
  494
Propane taxes, 100
Property rights. See also Intellectual property
  rights
  Alaska land swaps, 367
  civil assets forfeiture, 589–590, 604–605,
    647–649
  conservation lands acquisition, 376–378
  environmental protection, 343–344, 345, 372
    American Heritage Rivers, 370
    Antiquities Act, 366
    California monument, 403
    coastal management plans, 383–384
    endangered species protection, 67, 349–351,
      385–386
    migratory birds, 389
    National Discovery Trails, 400
  federal court access, 737–738
  Supreme Court decisions, 691, 697, 724
Prosecutors. See also District attorneys, U.S.;
  Independent counsels
  student loan forgiveness, 547
Prospective Payment Assessment Commission,
  441, 465
Prostate cancer
  charity stamps, 751
  Defense Department research appropriations,
    289
  Medicare coverage of screenings, 50, 433, 437,
    441
  NIH, CDC research, 481
Prostate Cancer Research and Protection Act,
  481
Prostitution
  immigrant smuggling, 675
  sex trafficking, 590, 629
Prowler aircraft, 281, 287, 288
Pryce, Deborah, R-Ohio
  child abuse programs, 647
  compensatory time, 576
  tobacco settlement, 323
Pryor, David, 760
Public broadcasting
  donor list sales, 338
  spectrum auctions, 325
  Supreme Court decisions, 716
Public defenders, 547, 669
Public health
  action, 1999–2000, 481–482
  Clean Air Act, 351
  coastal water quality, 380
  federal rules impact analysis, 749
  tobacco settlement, 323
Public Health Improvement Act of 2000, 481
Public Health Service
  food labels, 445
Public Health Threats and Emergencies Act, 481
Public housing block grants, 559
Public laws
  list, 1997–2001, 1099–1144
  totals enacted, 1975–2000 (table), 11
Public safety
  food, drug product review, 445
  law enforcement block grants, 654
  officers
    medals of valor, 614
    student aid for dependents, if slain, 614–615
  radio spectrum allocation, 326
Public Utilities Holding Company Act
  (PUHCA) of 1935, 404–407
Puerto Rico
  clemency for FALN activists, 669, 681–683
  gubernatorial election, 30
  status, 740–741
  Vieques naval exercises, 290–291, 296

Putin, Vladimir V., 222, 801

Q

Quadrennial Defense Review, 237, 239, 240, 244, 248, 263–264
Qualified Zone Academy Bonds, 546
Quayle, Dan, 22
Quincy Library Group, 368
Quinn, Jack, R-N.Y.
  land mines, 274
  Title I education authorization, 534

R

Raben, Robert, 683
Racial discrimination
  Agriculture Department programs, 422
  minority districts ruling, 688, 788 (box)
  minority health programs, 484–485
  traffic stops, 608, 652
  voting rights, 688
  U.S. visa refusals, 677
Racketeer-Influenced and Corrupt Organizations Act (RICO)
  DeLay ethics probe, 773
  juvenile crime, 594, 595, 597
  Supreme Court decisions, 728–729
Radanovich, George P., R-Calif.
  national monuments, 389
Radiation
  nuclear worker exposure, 290, 293, 296
Radio
  China trade agreement, 166
  spectrum allocations
    auctions, 48, 50, 51, 56, 72, 285, 325–326
    defense use, 283
  U.S. foreign broadcasting, 191, 198
Radio Free Asia, 166, 182, 191
Radio Free Europe, 191
Radiopharmaceuticals, 449
Rail Passenger Service Act of 1970, 320
Railroads. *See also* Amtrak
  highway crossings, 686
  law officer training, 652
  safety postage stamps, 751
  workers' pensions, 580–581
Raines, Franklin D.
  economic policy leadership, 35 (box)
  federal-D.C. ties, 740
  military construction appropriations, 250
Ralston, Joseph W., 241 (box)
Ramstad, Jim, R-Minn.
  Colombia antidrug aid, 220
Ranching. *See* Grazing; Livestock and ranching; Meat
Rangel, Charles, D-N.Y.
  China trade agreement, 162
  Cuba sanctions, 226
  education savings accounts, 519–520, 546
  estate taxes, 116
  House leadership, 760
  minimum wage, 580
  tax cuts, 1997, 92–93
Rape. *See* Sex crimes
Rapid City, S.D., 253 (box)
Ravitch, Diane, 524
Ray, Ricky, 459
Ray, Robert W., 804, 805 (box), 827
Reading instruction
  children's literacy programs, 529
  national testing, 523–525
  teacher training, 520
Reagan Legacy Project, 741
Reagan, Nancy, 751
Reagan, Ronald

abortion, 175, 177, 190, 211, 217
airport renaming, 741–742
antimissile defenses, 265, 307 (box)
budget policy, 40
Caribbean trade, 158
Clinton comparison, 797
Congressional Gold Medal, 751
economic policy leadership, 34 (box)
environmental policy, 342
  grazing fees, 357
financial services modernization, 124 (box)
foreign satellite launches, 180–181
housing policy, 553
independent counsel law, 663
nominations, 626
  judicial posts, 622–623, 627
recess appointments, 680
Peace Corps, 230
tax policy, 110
veto use, 811
Real estate
  capital gains taxes, 93, 97
  financial services modernization, 135
Real estate investment trusts, 106
Recess appointments, 626–627, 679, 680
Reclamation, Bureau of, 395
Reclamation projects
  Salton Sea rehabilitation, 364–365
Recorded votes
  totals, 1950–2000 (table), 12
Recreation. *See also* Sports
  budget outlays, FY 1987–2001 (graph), 342
  coastal areas, 380, 384
  conservation lands acquisition, 376–378
  Hells Canyon jetboats, 367
  Minnesota wilderness, 367
  national wildlife refuges, 348–349
Recycling
  superfund exemption, 396–398
Red Carpet Motel, 647
Redband trout, 403
Redmond, Bill, R-N.M.
  election, 9
  electoral defeat, 13
Reed, Jack, D-R.I.
  education
    ed-flex plan, 528
    ESEA authorization, 538
  FDA overhaul, 446
  OSHA overhaul, 577
  public housing reform, 558
Reform Party, 22
Refuge Recreation Act of 1962, 348
Refugees
  Central Americans in U.S., 619–620
  food stamp benefits, 422
  foreign aid appropriations, 185, 189
  Haitians in U.S., 68, 619
  Kosovars, 178, 205, 283
  sanctions for religious persecution, 199
  State Department authorization, 219
  welfare aid, 490
  World War II treatment, 664
Regional transmission organization (RTOs), 404
Regula, Ralph, R-Ohio
  conservation lands acquisition, 377
  NEA funding, 738–739
Regulation and deregulation
  commodities law overhaul, 141–142
  community development, 564–565
  D.C. government, 55
  electric power, 318, 404–407
  elementary and secondary education, 527–528, 539–544
  environmental protection, 341, 342–343

FDA overhaul, 431, 444–454
federal rulemaking, 737
federal rules impact analysis, 749
federal-state relations, 685
financial services, 121–126, 130–141
GAO rules review, 749
gun control, 637–642
housing impact analysis, 563
Internet, 316–317
local education, 508
manufactured housing, 566
national forest roads, 799
organ transplants, 475–477
Supreme Court decisions, 711–712
tobacco products, 316, 323–324
transportation, commerce summary, 315, 316
Regulatory Flexibility Act, 351
Regulatory Right-to-Know Act, 749
Rehabilitation services
  disabled workers' insurance, 471
  veterans, 498 (graph)
Rehnquist, William
  assisted suicide, 687
  background checks on gun purchasers, 685
  Clinton impeachment, 823, 826
  defendants' confessions, 689
  Florida presidential vote, 26, 687 (box)
  Internet content regulation, 688
  judicial confirmation delays, 593, 622, 624, 678
  Supreme Court summary, 684, 689 (box)
  violence against women, 685
Reich, Robert B., 978 (box)
Reid, Harry, D-Nev.
  balanced budget amendment, 58
  campaign finance reform, 790
  contraceptive coverage by health insurance, 458
  defense authorization, 293
  election, 28
  federal building names, 741–742
  nuclear waste storage, 361, 363, 409
  Senate leadership, 7 (box), 760, 769
Reid, Samantha, 654
Reimer, Dennis L., 249
Reinhardt College, 774
Reischauer, Robert D., 62
Religion. *See* Church-state separation; Churches and religious organizations; Freedom of religion; Religious discrimination
Religious discrimination
  China trade agreement, 164
  community development grants, 567
  immigration ban for persecutors, 646
  Ireland aid, 192
  juvenile services grants, 636, 637
  literacy programs, 535
  religious expression, 660–661
  Russia aid ban, 184, 185, 216, 223
Religious Freedom Restoration Act of 1993, 660, 685
Remote-sensing satellites, 744
Renaudin, George, 462
Renewable energy resources
  appropriations, 67
  electric deregulation, 331, 405
  energy research and development, 746
  global warming treaty, 356
  technology export aid, 356
Renewal communities, 564–565
Reno, Janet
  assisted suicide, 477, 606, 658, 659
  campaign finance investigations, 779, 808
    rejection of independent counsel (text), 1035
  civil assets forfeiture, 648
  crime victims rights, 609
  Elián González case, 225 (box), 592
  FALN clemency, 682

gun control, 639
independent counsel law, 662–663
Justice leadership, 594 (box), 799, 978 (box)
Landrieu election, 785
Lee nomination, 625
nuclear security, 303 (box)
seizure of civil assets, 591
Starr investigation, 815
terrorism, 267, 308
Waco investigation, 680–681
Whitewater investigation, 804
Repetitive motion injury, 81–82, 584
Republican Conference, Senate
judicial nominations, 624
Republican Majority Issues Committee, 773
Republican National Committee (RNC)
campaign finance reform, 778
issue advocacy ads, 780 (box)
Delaware plan for primaries, 23
Republican Party
Clinton term summary, 3–5
presidential election, 1996
platforms (text), 1037–1039
presidential election, 2000, 22–23
convention balloting (table), 1068
platforms (text), 1039–1046
Republicans for Clean Air, 786
Rescissions
line-item veto, 64
Reserve Officer Training Corps (ROTC)
programs, 280, 285, 294
Resolution Trust Corporation, 563
Resources Committee, House
jurisdiction, leadership, 961
Respite care, 496
Retirement. *See Pensions and retirement income*
Reverse mortgages, 561, 566, 567
Reyes, Silvestre, D-Texas
low-level nuclear waste, 360
Reynolds, Gladys A., 625
Reynolds, William Bradford, 626
Rezendes, Victor S., 355
Rich, Denise, 808
Rich, Mark, 808
Richard, Barry, 25
Richards, Ann W., 360
Richardson, William B.
electric deregulation, 404, 406
Energy department leadership, 347 (box), 978
(box), 980
energy supplies, 410
foreign policy leadership, 179 (box)
House successor, 9
nuclear lab security, 276, 279–280, 292,
302–306, 410–413
nuclear waste storage, 407–408
nuclear workers' compensation, 293
sanctions for oil producers, 414
U.N. debt repayment, 193
U.N. representative, 984
Ricky Ray Hemophilia Relief Fund Act, 459
RICO. *See Racketeer-Influenced and Corrupt*
Organizations Act
Riggs, Frank, R-Calif.
affirmative action, 511, 616
bilingual education, 517–518
Head Start, 492
school vouchers, 528
Right to counsel
juvenile crime, 596
Supreme Court decisions, 705
Riley, Richard W.
bilingual education, 517
ed-flex plan, 541
education block grants, 527
Education leadership, 510 (box), 978 (box)

education savings accounts, 519
ESEA authorization, 538
national educational testing, 524
school vouchers, 529
student loans, 510, 512
Rio Grande, 370
Ritter, Scott, 198
Rivers and streams. *See also specific rivers*
Alaska development, 379
American Heritage Rivers Initiative, 370
clean water regulations, 382–383
estuary restoration, 386–387
fish screens, 395
non-point pollution, 384
Oregon wilderness, 403
Salton Sea rehabilitation, 364–365
Riverside National Cemetery, 604
Rivlin, Alice M., 34–35 (box)
RNC. *See Republican National Committee*
Robb, Charles S., D-Va.
defense authorization, 243
education savings accounts, 544–545
election defeat, 28
high-tech visas, 670
nuclear waste storage, 363
voter guides ruling, 790 (box)
Robbery
armored cars, 598
Roberts, Pat, R-Kan.
crop insurance, 426
defense policy
appropriations, 260, 261
authorization, 278
House leadership, 760
Robot aircraft and vehicles, 294
Rockefeller, John D. IV, D-W.Va.
manufactured housing, 566
Medicare changes, 435–436, 437
NASA authorization, 752
product liability, 322
Rodriguez, Ciro D., 8
Roemer, Tim, D-Ind.
education
ed-flex plan, 539
student loans, 511
teacher training, 533
Title I authorization, 534
intelligence authorization, 227
space station, 743, 753–754
Rogan, James E., D-Calif.
alien smuggling, 675
Armenia genocide resolution, 231
election defeat, 29
high-tech visas, 617
judicial activism, 622
space station, 754
Rohrabacher, Dana, R-Calif.
campaign finance reform, 782
China-U.S. trade, 152, 166
Clinton impeachment, 822
defense authorization, 242
immigration 245(i) provision, 620
NASA authorization, 742, 752
Russia sanctions, 223
Vietnam-U.S. trade, 159, 167
Rohypnol, 654
Roll Call
Livingston extramarital affairs, 758
Roman Catholics
House chaplain, 775
Romania
international adoptions, 231
NATO expansion, 273
U.S. military aid authorization, 230
Romero-Barceló, Carlos A., D-P.R.
bilingual education, 517

FALN clemency, 682
Puerto Rico status, 741
Ronald Reagan Washington National Airport,
321, 332, 741–742
Roosevelt, Eleanor, 806 (box)
Roosevelt, Franklin D.
banking reform, 124 (box)
Clinton comparison, 797
TVA history, 371
veto use, 811
Ros-Lehtinen, Ileana, R-Fla.
Cuba trade sanctions, 83
disabled citizenship applicants, 676
Rose Law Firm, 779, 805 (box)
Rosner, Jeremy, 273
Ross' geese, 384
Ross, Mike, 29
Ross, Murray, 461
Rossello, Pedro, 290
Rostenkowski, Dan, 764 (box)
Rota, Robert V., 764 (box)
Roth IRAs, 91, 97–98, 107
Roth, William V. Jr., R-Del.
Arctic wildlife refuge drilling, 413
China trade agreement, 164
community development, 565
education savings accounts, 519, 545
election defeat, 28
fast track for trade pacts, 156
health policy
disabled workers' insurance, 470
Medicare payments, 435–436, 461–463
individual retirement accounts, 91, 97, 107
Social Security
outside earnings limit, 584
surplus protection, 78–79
tax policy
estate taxes, 116
marriage status tax cut, 115
tax cuts, 1997, 93
tax cuts, 1999, 111
tax extenders, 1999, 113
welfare law revisions, 488
Rothman, Steven R., D-N.J.
flag desecration, 610
Roukema, Marge, R-N.J.
school vouchers, 528
Roybal-Allard, Lucille, D-Calif.
homeless programs, 561
RTOs. *See Regional transmission organizations*
RU486, 63, 431, 455, 482
Rubin, Robert E.
economic policy leadership, 34–35 (box), 978
(box)
IRS overhaul, 107
Social Security surplus protection, 78
Rudman, Warren B., 302–303, 410
Ruff, Charles F.C., 825
Rules and Administration Committee, Senate
jurisdiction, leadership, 769, 955
Rules Committee, House
jurisdiction, leadership, 770, 961
State Department authorization, 191
Rumsfeld, Donald H.
antimissile defenses, 238, 266–267, 307
chemical weapons treaty, 268–269
weapons intelligence, 262
Runaway and Homeless Youth Act, 657
Rural Access to Emergency Devices Act, 481
Rural areas. *See also Rural health care*
aid authorization, 421, 422
census undercount, 748
development aid, 161
tax breaks, 117
domestic violence prevention, 613
education

ed-flex plan, 544
teachers' loan forgiveness, 510–511, 513
Title I grants, 534
vocational education, 513–515
electric deregulation, 404–406
empowerment zones, 100
Export-Import Bank, 157
forest revenues, 399–400
NASA research grants, 752
satellite television, 331, 338
Rural health care
defibrillator acquisition, 481
managed care plans, 436, 437
Medicare payments, 430, 462
nurses visas, 674–675
organ transplants, 476
telemedicine, 435, 441
Rural Utilities Service, 338
Russia
arms control agreements
antimissile defenses, 265–266, 306–308
CFE treaty, 223, 274–275
chemical weapons treaty, 270
START II reductions, 277, 292
Chechnya, 222, 223
financial crisis, 39, 66, 147, 156, 801
IMF loans, 188
intelligence facility in Cuba, 223
international adoptions, 231
Kosovo, Yugoslavia policy, 205, 222, 223
NATO expansion, 272–274, 802
religious persecution issue, 185
sex trafficking, 629
space station, 222, 734, 743–744, 753–754
technology transfer issues
brain-drain prevention, 210, 214, 282
missile sales to China, 222, 223
reporting requirement, 282
sanctions for sales to Iran, 69, 185, 195–196, 204, 221–223, 270
U.S. aid
appropriations, FY 1998, 184, 185–186
appropriations, FY 1999, 69, 186, 188, 189
appropriations, FY 2000, 210, 214
appropriations, FY 2001, 214, 215, 216
authorization, 228
debt write-off, 222
limitations, 185, 196, 222, 223
U.S. relations summary, 173, 174, 175, 177, 801
U.S. trade
export controls on computers, 243
Export-Import Bank limits, 157
satellite launches, 229
"Silk Road" trade, 169
weapons capacity reduction
chemical weapons destruction plant, 282, 291, 292, 295
Nunn-Lugar appropriations, 246, 247, 286, 299
Nunn-Lugar authorization, 242, 243, 282, 295
plutonium, uranium disposal, 69, 76, 262
Ryan, Paul D., R-Wis.
community development, 564
Ryan White AIDS programs, 67, 483
Ryun, Jim, R-Kan.
defense authorization, 279
homeless programs, 561
nuclear security, 304

S

S-CHIP. See Children's Health Insurance Program
Sabo, Martin Olav, D-Minn.
House leadership, 760
Sacramento, Calif., 391
Sacramento River, 373

Saddam Hussein
Iraq-U.S. relations, 192, 196–198, 803
intelligence authorization, 202
U.S. air strikes, 821, 822 (box)
Safe and Drug-Free Schools and Communities Program, 536, 543
Safe Drinking Water Act of 1974, 342, 343
Safe Medical Devices Act of 1990, 451–452
Salaries and wages. See also Congressional pay; Federal employee pay; Military pay; Minimum wage; Pensions and retirement income; Unemployment compensation
alien farm workers, 673–674
compensatory time, 7, 573, 576–577
D.C. garnishee rules, 55
Davis-Bacon rules, 492–493
employer-provided meals, 109
federal rules impact analysis, 749
federal unemployment taxes, 102
high-tech visas, 671
prison industries, 652
stock options, 581
Supreme Court decisions, 685, 722
tuition assistance, 96, 520
U.S. presidents, 751
Sales taxes
Internet commerce, 68, 316, 327–328, 331, 335
Sallie Mae, 510
Salmon, 67, 395
Salmon, Matt, R-Ariz.
juvenile crime, 637
sex offenders on campus, 547
Salon, 819
Salt Lake City, Utah
sewer project funding, 789
transit projects, 319
Salton Sea National Wildlife Refuge, 364–365
San Francisco, Calif.
AIDS programs, 483
San Gabriel Basin, Calif., 374, 383
San Jose, Calif., 613
San Rafael Swell, Utah, 402
Sanchez, Loretta, D-Calif.
contested election, 785
defense authorization, 292
Sanctions. See Foreign trade sanctions
Sanders, Bernard, I-Vt.
defense authorization, 242
Export-Import Bank, 157
FALN clemency, 681
homeless programs, 561
intelligence authorization, 201, 226
Sandia National Laboratory, 305
Sanford, Mark, R-S.C.
Cuba travel, 225
space station, 754
Sanitation workers, 55, 566
Santa Monica, Calif., 391
Santa Rosa and San Jacinto Mountains National Monument, 403
Santorum, Rick, R-Pa.
community development, 565
juvenile crime, 635
partial-birth abortion, 456, 473
Sarbanes, Paul S., D-Md.
financial services modernization, 132
public housing reform, 558
Satcher, David, 7, 435 (box), 988
Satellite television
action, 329, 338
appropriations, 73, 75
summary, 15, 317, 331
Satellites
antimissile defenses, 248
antisatellite missile research, 249
domestic launch industry

expansion stimulation, 304 (box)
launch vehicles, 744, 754
liability risk-sharing, 754
foreign launches
DOD security, 304 (box)
China security breach, 153, 180–182, 209, 254–255, 259, 277, 279, 282, 302, 304 (box), 752
licensing authority, 180–181, 254, 256–257, 259, 304 (box)
review period for ex-Soviet launches, 229
intelligence collection, 226, 227
NRO contracting, 228
NASA authorization, 752–753
satellite-guided weapons, 294–295
Saudi Arabia
U.S. Iraq policy, 197
Sauls, N. Samuel, 26–27 (box)
Save-the-Redwoods League, 402
Savings and loan associations
financial services modernization, 123 (box), 125, 130, 131, 137, 140
RTC dissolution, 563
Whitewater investigation, 804, 805 (box)
Savings Association Insurance Fund, 140
Sawyer, Tom, D-Ohio
China trade agreement, 162 (box)
Saxton, H. James, R-N.J.
bird population control, 384–385
coastal management plans, 384
ocean policy panel, 364
SBA. See Small Business Administration
Scalia, Antonin
abortion clinic leafleting, 689
defendants' confessions, 689
Florida presidential vote, 26, 687 (box)
hate crimes, 690
sexual harassment, 687
Supreme Court summary, 689 (box)
Scanlon, William, 462–463
Scarborough, Joe, R-Fla.
asbestos compensation, 666
organ transplants, 476
Schaefer, Dan, R-Colo.
low-level nuclear waste, 360
nuclear waste storage, 362
underground storage tanks, 370
Schaffer, Bob, R-Colo.
congressional pay, 794
Title I educational authorization, 534
Schakowsky, Jan, D-Ill.
home ownership aid, 566
Schattman, Michael D., 623
Schiff, Adam, 29
Schiff, Steven H., R-N.M.
death, successor, 14
Schlafly, Phyllis, 574
Schlesinger, James R., 268
School choice, 20, 536. See also School vouchers
School lunch/breakfast program, 471, 494–495
School of the Americas, 211, 230, 291, 296
School prayer
memorial services, 635
religious expression amendment, 591, 593, 611–612
Supreme Court decisions, 684, 689
School vouchers
appropriations, FY 1998, 59
ballot issues, 2000, 30
District of Columbia, 528–529
ESEA authorization, 536, 537, 539
federal funding, 528–529
Head Start alternative child care, 492–493
religious expression amendment, 611
summary, 6–7, 507, 509

Schools
construction
appropriations, 81
bonds, 60, 72, 97, 111, 117, 519, 520, 523, 544, 546
emergency repairs, 798
federal impact aid, 535
grants, loan authorization, 538
renovation grants, 82
counselors, 537
energy conservation, 356
forest revenues, 399–400
Internet porn filters, 82
law enforcement
block grants, 654
crime prevention programs, 595, 635, 636
drug abuse prevention, 536, 602
law enforcement resource officers, 530
security equipment, 635, 637
shooting statistics collection, 536
violence prevention programs, 545
weapons possession penalties, 516, 538, 544, 636, 637, 639, 641
sexual harassment, 687–688
Schumer, Charles, D-N.Y.
bankruptcy law overhaul, 143
civil assets forfeiture, 648
juvenile crime, 595, 597, 637
Senate election, 11–12
sex offender registries, 604
Schwartz, Bernard L., 153, 180–181
Schwitz, Randy, 741
Science and technology. *See also Medical research; Space programs; Technology transfer*
budget outlays, 1987–2001 (graph), 734
energy research and development, 746–747, 754
environmental protection research
"dolphin-safe" tuna, 348
endangered species, 350, 386
Fish and Wildlife Foundation, 356
global warming, 354–355
marine sanctuaries, 388
national park resources, 359
nuclear waste storage, 361
ocean policy, 364
federal lab licensing, 747
methane research, 388–389
next generation Internet, 746
NIST authorization, 745
NSF authorization, 744–745
research and development tax credits, 63, 113
visas for high-tech workers, 68, 616–619, 670–672
Science Committee, House
jurisdiction, 746–747, 760, 961–962
Science education
"Go Girl" program, 537
teacher training, 533
visas for high-tech workers, 670–672
Scientists
advisory panels
drug approvals, 449
organ transplant policy, 477
Russian brain-drain prevention, 210
Scott, Robert C., D-Va.
alien smuggling, 675
animal cruelty, 651
asbestos compensation, 666
Clinton impeachment, 820
education
faith-based literacy programs, 535
hate crime prevention, 536
Title I waivers, 541
flag desecration, 610
HIV testing, 644

law enforcement
bounty hunters, 599
civil assets forfeiture, 605
DNA evidence, 655
juvenile crime, 633, 634
police animals, 650
prisoner deaths, 653
prisoner health care, 653
wiretaps, 646
religious expression, 612
term limits, 783–784
Scowcroft, Brent, 269, 804 (box)
Scripps Institution of Oceanography, 752
Scully, Tom, 461
Sea Gull Lake, Minn., 367
Sea lions, 82, 393–394
Sea turtles, 348
Search and seizure. *See also Forfeiture*
automobile searches, 690
chemical weapons treaty inspections, 271
IRS collections, 109
Supreme Court decisions, 690, 705–706
wildlife items, 369–370
Seattle Post-Intelligencer, 664–665
SEC. *See Securities and Exchange Commission*
Second Amendment, 640, 641–642
Secret Service, U.S.
FBI files use, 805 (box)
off-duty officers, 614
presidential protection authority, 613, 651
Section 8 housing vouchers
affordable housing for elderly, disabled, 567
appropriations, 84
authorization, 556, 558, 559, 560
home ownership aid, 566–567
homeless programs, 562
HUD cost reductions, 562–563
Section 527 PACs, 786–787
Securities and Exchange Commission (SEC)
chair, on loan fund board, 334
financial services modernization, 131 (box), 135–138
stock futures contracts, 141–142
Securities dealers
financial services modernization, 120–126, 130–141
securities fraud lawsuits, 128–129
stock futures, 141
Securities holding companies, 138
Seed, Richard, 460
Self-employed persons
health insurance, 98, 105, 106, 115, 422–423, 468, 580
tax breaks, 88
unemployment compensation, 490–491
Self-incrimination, 689, 706
Semiconductors, 161
Semipostals, 751
Senate, U.S.
budget procedures task force, 54
cloture votes, 1917–2000 (list), 967–971
elections, 1998, 11–12
elections, 2000, 28–29
judicial nominations, 622–624
leadership, organization, 7 (box)
105th Congress, 759–760
106th Congress, 769
members
105th Congress, 935
106th Congress, 938, 939
political committees, 956
standing committees, 105th, 106th Congress, 951–956
Sensenbrenner, F. James Jr., R-Wis.
Clinton impeachment, 825
House leadership, 760

judicial pay, 622
NASA authorization, 735, 752
nuclear security, 306
space station, 743, 753
Sentencing
alien smuggling, 675
alternative sentencing, 644, 656
assaults on federal officers, 613, 656
child molesters, 647
D.C., 55, 740
date-rape drugs, 654
fetal rights, 662
gun-related convictions, 597–598, 642
juvenile offenders, 641
hate crimes, 690
identity theft, 600
juvenile crime, 596
methamphetamine trafficking, 601–602
software piracy, 334
Supreme Court decisions, 706–707
victims impact statements, 609–610
Sentencing Commission, U.S.
alien smuggling, 675
assault on federal officers, 613
FALN clemency, 682
gun-related crime, 597
identity theft, 600
methamphetamine traffic, 601–602
new member confirmation, 334
student aid fraud, 546
Separation of powers
judicial activism, 620–622
line-item veto, 64–65
Supreme Court decisions, 690, 691, 714
Sequoia National Park, 391, 401–402
Serbia
U.S. aid, 214, 216, 229
U.S. Kosovo policy
action, 1997–1998, 177–180
action, 1999–2000, 204–208
aid ban, 210, 214
China embassy bombing, 209
Clinton term summary, 173, 174, 177, 204, 802–803
defense appropriations, 284
Serna, Eric P., 8
Serrano, Jose E., D-N.Y.
Puerto Rico status, 741
Service Employees International Union, 55
Sessions, Jeff, R-Ala.
law enforcement
civil assets forfeiture, 648, 649
forensics labs, 657
hate crimes prevention, 538
juvenile crime, 635
Paez nomination, 679
organ transplants, 477
prepaid tuition plans, 544
TVA federal subsidy, 371
Sessions, Pete, R-Texas
sanctions for oil producers, 414
Sewage
coastal water quality, 380
low-flow toilets, 400
NYC treated sewage, 361
Sex crimes. *See also Child sexual abuse; Sex offenders*
date rape, 631, 632, 654
gender-based hate crimes, 643
rape as abortion ban exemption, 278
sex trafficking, 590, 629–630, 632
training for hospital nurses, 630
Sex offenders
consenting adults, 604
deportation, 677
DNA evidence, 654–655

HIV testing, 644
mental hospital commitment, 690, 707
public housing ban, 556, 557, 560
registries and neighborhood notification, 593, 603–604, 639
college campuses, 547
repeat offenses on premature release, 590, 631–633, 635
STD tests for juveniles, 597
Sexual harassment
Baucus ethics probe, 771
cyber-stalking, 632
Jones charges against Clinton, 684, 804, 813–814
military training, 243, 252–253, 275
Supreme Court decisions, 684, 686, 687–688
VA procedures, 497
Sexual misconduct
Clinton-Lewinsky affair, 10, 23, 815–827
congressional-executive relations summary, 3, 10
Fordice scandal, 18
Hyde admission, 819
Livingston resignation, 758, 821
Tower nomination, 818
Sexual orientation
discrimination, 30, 689
hate crimes definition, 629, 642–644
Sexually explicit material. *See also Obscenity and pornography*
cable TV, 688
Internet regulation, 684, 688
military posts, 275
sales to minors, 16, 636–637
television ratings, 327
Sexually transmitted diseases. *See also Acquired immune deficiency syndrome (AIDS)*
medical privacy, 479
tests for juvenile offenders, 597
Shadegg, John, R-Ariz.
conservation lands acquisition, 378
identity theft, 600
patients' rights, 468–469
Shalala, Donna E.
disabled workers' insurance, 471
drug reimports, 483
FDA overhaul, 446, 447
Head Start, 492
health policy leadership, 435 (box), 978 (box)
Medicare payments, 463
organ transplants, 475, 476
Shalikashvili, John M.
defense leadership, 241 (box)
defense procurement budget, 237, 240, 264
Sharks, 348, 372, 395–396
Shaw, E. Clay Jr., R-Fla.
campaign finance reform, 782
Shaw, Patricia Hearst, 809
Shays, Christopher, R-Conn.
campaign finance reform, 780–782, 788–789
527 PACs, 787
defense appropriations, 247
defense authorization, 279
home ownership aid, 567
"partial-birth" abortion, 456
Shelby, Richard C., R-Ala.
China summits, 183 (box)
credit union expansion, 128
financial services modernization, 132–133, 135
intelligence authorization, 228
manufactured housing, 566
Middle East summit, 190 (box)
nuclear security, 303 (box)
Senate leadership, 760
TVA federal subsidy, 371

Shelton, Henry H.
antimissile defenses, 267
defense leadership, 241 (box)
U.S. troops in Bosnia, 260
Shepard, Matthew, 642
Sherman, Brad, D-Calif.
foreign aid appropriations, 215
Shinseki, Eric K., 299
Shipping Act of 1984, 321–322
Ships and shipping
budget outlays for water transportation, FY 1987–2001 (graph), 316
ocean shipping law revision, 321–322
passenger fees, 154
Supreme Court decisions, 693
vessel tonnage fees, 51, 56
Short, Walter C., 296
Shuster, Bill, 772
Shuster, "Bud," R-Pa.
Amtrak restructuring, 321
budget resolution, FY 1998, 47
budget resolution, FY 2000, 72–73
ethics probe, 765, 771–772
Everglades restoration, 373, 374
FAA authorization, 331–332
railroad pensions, 581
superfund overhaul, 353
surface transportation authorization, 319–320
transportation summary, 315
truck safety, 332–333
Siegel, Mark A., 765
Sierra Blanca, Tex., 359–361
Sierra Club, 405, 787
Sierra Leone
U.S. trade, 168
Sikorsky helicopters, 282, 288, 295, 300
Silk Road, 210, 214
Silk Road Strategy Act, 187 (box)
Simmons, Bob, 29
Simon and Schuster, 807 (box)
Simpson, Alan K., 760
Single parents
education aid, 514
Head Start authorization, 491
Sissoko, Fountanga Dit Babari, 773
Skaggs, David E., D-Colo.
defense appropriations, 260, 261
flag desecration, 611
Skelton, Ike, D-Mo.
defense authorization, 278–279, 291
House leadership, 770
Kosovo policy, 207
"Slamming," 330
Slater, Rodney, 320 (box), 978 (box), 981
Slaughter, Louise, D-N.Y.
NEA funding, 750–751
sex trafficking, 629
Slave labor and slavery
China trade agreement, 161, 165
crime bill, 629, 632
immigrant smuggling, 675
sex trafficking, 590, 629
Sleep disorders, 654
Slovenia
NATO expansion, 273
Small business
alternative minimum tax, 95, 98
bankruptcy overhaul, 126
capital gains taxes, 97
chemical weapons treaty, 268
community development, 564
environmental issues
Clean Air Act, 351
summary, 342–343
superfund overhaul, 354, 396–398
estate taxes, 91, 94, 95, 99, 115–116

Export-Import Bank, 157
federal rules impact analysis, 749
FHLB changes, 140
health insurance, 454, 468
microenterprise aid, 140
foreign aid, 229, 230
patent system overhaul, 324, 334
product liability, 322
SBA programs authorization, 324–325
tax incentives for retirement plans, 119, 582
Treasury Department credit study, 140
union "salting," 575
Y2K liability, 336
Small Business Administration (SBA)
authorization, 82, 324–325
drug-free workplaces, 602
leadership, 320 (box)
microenterprise aid, 140
Small Business Committee, House
jurisdiction, leadership, 760, 770, 962
Small Business Committee, Senate
jurisdiction, leadership, 760, 955
Small Business Regulatory Enforcement Fairness Act, 351
Smart bombs, 294–295
Smith, Adam, D-Wash.
national forests, 388
northern spotted owl, 392
Smith, Benjamin Nathaniel, 642
Smith, Bob, R-Ore.
Conservation Reserve Program, 420
grazing fees, 357
House leadership, 760, 770
Smith, Christopher H., R-N.J.
contraceptive coverage by health insurance, 458
foreign aid appropriations, 184, 211
international adoptions, 231
Mexico City policy, 473
"partial-birth" abortion, 473
sex trafficking, 590, 629–630
State Department authorization, 191, 217, 218
Smith, Gordon H., R-Ore.
antimissile defense system, 238
Arctic wildlife refuge drilling, 413
assaults on federal judges, 613
527 PACs, 786
foreign aid appropriations, 184, 185
gun control, 639
hate crimes, 642
Smith-Hughes Vocational Education Act of 1917, 522
Smith, Lamar, R-Texas
House leadership, 770
immigration
border controls, 676
high-tech visas, 590, 617–618, 670–672
provision 245(i), 620
sex trafficking victims, 630
war criminals, 646
Smith, Linda, R-Wash.
campaign finance reform, 782
congressional pay, 791–792
Smith, Robert C., R-N.H.
China trade agreement, 165
clean water regulations, 391
defense authorization, 256, 278
Everglades restoration, 373, 374
gasoline additive MTBE, 391
IDEA authorization, 516
judicial nominations, 623, 679
juvenile crime, 637
Kosovo policy, 207
NATO expansion, 273
NEA funding, 750
Senate leadership, 759–760
superfund overhaul, 353

Smoking
adolescent reduction, 59, 316, 318, 322, 323
smokers' health costs, 316, 323
Smullens, Stanton, 479
Snake River, 367, 395
Snake River Potato Growers Inc., 65
Snow geese, 384
Snowbarger, Vincent, R-Kan.
electoral defeat, 13
Snowe, Olympia J., R-Maine
campaign finance reform, 777, 780
527 PACs, 787
defense authorization, 256, 278, 292
"dolphin-safe" tuna, 347
low-level nuclear waste, 360
minimum wage, 580
Social Security. *See also Social Security numbers*
balanced budget amendment, 56–58
benefits
bankruptcy law overhaul, 143
eligibility age, 582 (box)
IRS levy, 103
outside earnings limit, 20, 572, 583–584
budget outlays, FY 1987–2001 (graph), 572
CARA funding priorities, 377, 378
Clinton term summary, 11, 15, 17, 572
directed federal investment, 583 (box)
long-term prospects, 48, 572, 582–583 (box)
using budget surplus to "save," 36, 39 (box),
60–61, 71–73, 87, 88, 105–106, 110
payroll taxes, 583 (box)
budget receipts, 1980–2000 (graph), 88
percentage of GDP, 1935–2000 (table), 91
privatization proposal, 583 (box)
Supreme Court decisions, 714
surplus protection "lockbox," 71, 73, 78–79
budget process reform, 77
budget resolution, FY 2001, 79
debt reduction plans, 86
Social Security Act
Medicaid expense recovery, 323
welfare law revisions, 490
Social Security Administration
information availability to VA, 499
Social Security Disability Insurance (SSDI),
470–471
Social Security numbers
EITC fraud prevention, 103
false IDs, 657
identity theft, 600
Internet privacy, 82, 337
Sodomy, 604
Soft money
campaign finance reform, 776–777, 781–783,
788–790
Clinton-Lazio race, 807 (box)
FEC term limits, 68
Soil conservation
appropriations, 66–67
Clinton term summary, 341
conservation lands acquisition, 377
grazing regulations, 357
reserve program enrollment, 419, 420
Solar energy
electric deregulation, 405
energy supplies, 410
Solis, Juan F. III, 8
Solomon, Gerald B.H., R-N.Y.
Clinton impeachment, 821
Iraq air strikes, 822 (box)
encryption exports, 326
Export-Import Bank, 157
financial services modernization, 125
flag desecration, 610–611
House leadership, 770

Puerto Rico status, 741
State Department authorization, 191
Somalia
U.S. military deployments, 174
Somatic cell nuclear transfer, 745–746
**Sonny Bono Salton Sea National Wildlife
Refuge,** 364–365
Souder, Mark, R-Ind.
community development block grants,
566–567
education
religious school programs, 535, 536
spending flexibility, 534–535
student loan ban for drug offense, 510
juvenile crime, 636
Souter, David
asbestos compensation, 665
campaign finance limits, 688
Florida presidential vote, 26, 687 (box)
Supreme Court summary, 689 (box)
South Africa
U.S. trade, 168
South American countries. *See also Latin
America*
U.S. aid
military training, 211
narcotics control, 215, 219
U.S. trade, 155
South Carolina
fetal rights, 662
sex offender registries, 604
South Dakota
bankruptcy law overhaul, 143
term limits, 784
South Florida Ecosystem Task Force, 375
South Florida Water Management District, 375
South Korea
financial crisis, 801
land mine treaty, 274
North Korean relations, 803
Southeastern Legal Foundation, 736
Southern states
African trade initiative, 168
dairy pricing, 424–425
presidential vote, 1996, 2000 (table), 21
Senate leadership, 759
Southwest Airlines, 321
Soviet Union, former. *See also specific countries*
arms reduction aid, 282, 286, 295, 299
refugees in U.S., 620
"Silk Road" trade, 169
technology transfer prevention, 230
U.S. aid appropriations, 75, 214, 216
Space-Based Infra-Red System, Low-altitude,
294
Space Commercialization, Office of, 754
Space programs. *See also Satellites; Space shuttle*
advertising, 752–753
appropriations, FY 1998, 59
asteroid tracking, 249
budget outlays, 1987–2001 (graph), 734
Clinton term summary, 734–735
NASA authorization, 742–743, 752–753
Space Reconnaissance, Office of, 228
Space shuttle
Clinton team summary, 734
Glenn mission, 742 (box)
NASA authorization, 752–754
private licenses, 744
space station assembly, 754
Space station, 743–744, 752, 753–754
Spallation Neutron Source, 754
Special education. *See Disabled children*
Special prosecutors. *See Independent counsels*
Specter, Arlen, R-Pa.
Arctic wildlife refuge drilling, 413

on Clinton congressional relations, 811
compensatory time, 577
defense authorization, 277–278
flag desecration, 611
Fletcher nomination, 628
foreign aid appropriations, 187
health policy
assisted suicide, 659
medical errors, 479
organ transplants, 475
"partial-birth" abortion, 456
patients' rights, 468
juvenile crime, 596
Kosovo policy, 207
Lee nomination, 625–626, 800
minimum wage, 580
sanctions for religious persecution, 198
Senate leadership, 760
veterans burial rights, 498
Waco investigation, 681
Speir, Robert A., 775
Spence, Floyd D., R-S.C.
defense authorization, 242, 254, 279
nuclear security, 304
Sperling, Gene B., 35 (box)
Spitzer, Robert J., 810 (box)
Sport Fish Restoration Act of 1950, 393
Sport utility vehicles
emissions standards, 382
fuel efficiency standards, 333 (box)
rollover dangers, 333
Sports. *See also Baseball; Recreation*
college programs, 511
Police Athletic League, 650
Spratt, John M. Jr., D-S.C.
House leadership, 760
SR-71 blackbird aircraft, 248, 249
SSI. *See Supplemental Security Income*
SS-N-22 missiles, 157
**St. Inigoes, Md., Naval Electronic Systems
Engineering Activity,** 253 (box)
St. Lucie estuary, 375
Stabenow, Debbie, D-Mich.
election, 28
NIST authorization, 745
Stalking
cyber-stalking, 632, 645
Stamps. *See Postal Service*
**Standards of Official Conduct Committee,
House**
jurisdiction, leadership, 760, 770
McDermott ethics probe, 765
rules overhaul, 760, 766–767
Stanton, Edwin M., 814 (box)
Stark, Pete, D-Calif.
China trade agreement, 163
Medicare payments, 461
Starr, Kenneth W.
Clinton impeachment, 10, 691, 813–827
independent counsel law, 66, 663
Whitewater investigation, 804
START II treaty, 266, 277, 278, 292
State and local government. *See also
Federal-state relations; Governors*
arts funding, 738–739
boundary disputes, 716–725
business
electronic signatures, 335
telecommunications "slamming," 330
census 2000, 748
education
bilingual programs, 508
block grants, 16, 527, 531, 537, 539
charter schools, 525
disabled students, 515–516
ESEA authorization, 531–539

literacy programs, 529–530
prepaid tuition programs, 96, 523
regulation flexibility, 527–528, 534–535, 539–544
school construction, 546
teacher training, 532–533
vocational education, 513–515
elections
campaign finance reform, 782, 783
minority voting rights, 688
electric deregulation, 316, 404–407
employee pension plans, 105
environmental protection
American Heritage Rivers, 370
bird population control, 384–385
Clean Air Act, 351
clean water regulations, 383
coastal management plans, 383–384
coastal water quality, 380
conservation lands acquisition, 376–378, 394
endangered species, 351
energy conservation, 356
estuary restoration, 386–387
Everglades restoration, 373–375
Fish and Wildlife Service spending, 392–393
forest revenue sharing, 399–400
Great Lakes restoration, 357
national monuments, 389–390
ocean policy panel, 364
superfund overhaul, 352–354, 396–398
underground storage tanks, 370
watershed dams, 385
wildlife refuges, 349
federal-D.C. ties, 739–740
federal rules impact analysis, 749
financial services regulation
bankruptcy overhaul, 127
financial services modernization, 131 (box), 135, 137–140
interstate banking, 129
municipal bonds, 140
private activity bonds, 565
securities fraud lawsuits, 128
health policy
breast, cervical cancer, 472
children's health insurance, 50, 432, 438, 442–443
cosmetics warning labels, 445–446, 453
day care services, 482
disabled workers' insurance, 471
HIV partner notification, 483
Medicaid, 50, 54, 432–433, 438, 441–442, 463–464
medical privacy, 479
patients' rights, 467
tobacco settlement, 316, 318, 323
housing
home ownership aid, 566–567
homeless programs, 561–562
public housing reform, 555–561
Section 8 contracts, 562
labor policy
job training overhaul, 573–575
workplace safety, 577
law enforcement
adult entertainment, 688
alternative sentencing, 644
armored car gun permits, 598
assisted suicide, 606–607, 658–659
background checks for firearms, 685
block grants, 654
bounty hunters, 599
bulletproof vests, 599–600, 645
child abuse programs, 646–647
college aid for officers' family, 651–652
concealed weapons permits, 598–599, 650

crime victims' rights, 668
DNA evidence, 654–655
federal prison labor, 603
fetal rights, 661–662
flag desecration, 610
forensics labs, 657
gun-related crime, 642
hate crimes, 643
HIV testing, 644
Internet alcohol sales, 337, 631, 633
juvenile crime, 589–590, 593–597, 633–636
money laundering, 605
prison disease control, 600
prisoner deaths, 653
prisoner mental health, 656
released offenders, 631–633, 637
sex offender registries, 603–604
terrorism preparedness, 308, 309, 645–646
trial attendance by victims, 609
unidentified persons, 646
violence against women, 630–631, 632
volunteers liability, 615
zoning, 591, 660–661
property rights, 737
religious expression amendment, 611–612
taxes and revenue
grazing fees, 419–420
interest on trust accounts, 691
Internet commerce, 316, 318, 327–328, 335
private activity bonds, 106
Supreme Court decisions, 727–728
tobacco settlement, 323
transportation, 315, 318–320
water projects cost-sharing, 373–375
welfare
benefits, 688, 486–491
child support enforcement, 495
foster care, 493–494
Head Start, 491
Older Americans Act, 496
State Children's Health Insurance Program.
See Children's Health Insurance Program
State Department, U.S.
appropriations, 63, 73, 74, 82
authorization, 75, 189–192, 217–219
China satellite launches, 180
China trade agreement, 165
Colombia antidrug aid, 220
diplomatic immunity, 203
economic sanctions, 199, 200
religious persecution, 198–199
export controls, 180, 181
high-tech exports, 167
satellite launches, 254, 256–257, 259, 302, 304 (box)
supercomputers, 242, 245
foreign policy agency reorganization, 69, 190, 191, 193–194
foreign policy leadership, 179 (box)
foreign travelers, 677
immigration provision, 620
intelligence leak to Congress, 201, 202
international adoptions, 231
NATO expansion, 273
North Korea missile, nuclear program, 188
overseas study grants, 549
private space shuttles, 744
sex trafficking, 590, 629–630, 632
tuna fishing bycatch, 348
State Farm Insurance Co., 333
State Justice Institute, 55
Statehood
Puerto Rico status, 740–741
Statue of Liberty, 401
Stearns, Cliff, R-Fla.
campaign finance reform, 781, 782

Steel
antidumping fees redirection, 83
China trade agreement, 163
federal subsidies, 77, 316, 333–334
import quotas, 16, 168–169
Steens Mountain Cooperative Management and Protection Area, 403
Stein, Dan, 670
Steinbeck, John, 394
Steller sea lions, 82, 393–394
Stenholm, Charles W., D-Texas
House leadership, 760
Stevens, John Paul
abortion clinic leafleting, 689
background checks for guns, 685
federal-state relations, 685
Florida presidential vote, 26, 687 (box)
Internet content regulation, 688
line-item veto, 65
presidential immunity in civil suits, 691
school prayer, 689
Supreme Court summary, 684, 689 (box)
Stevens, Ted, R-Alaska
budget resolution, FY 2001, 80
China trade agreement, 164
congressional pay, 793
defense policy
appropriations, 243, 246, 260, 297, 298
military construction, 301
NATO expansion, 274
nuclear test ban treaty, 310–311
organ transplants, 476
sea lion protection, 82, 393–394
Senate leadership, 759
Stewart, Ted, 678, 990
Stiglitz, Joseph E., 35 (box)
Stocks, bonds, and securities. *See also Securities dealers; Treasury securities*
business tax provisions, 102–103
capital gains tax on short sales, 102
debt instruments, 103
decimal pricing, 138 (box)
donations to charity, 99, 106
employee stock options, 581
401(k) plan limits, 105
futures contracts, 141–142
investment company limitations, 105
railroad pensions, 581
Social Security proposals, 583 (box)
state, local government, 106, 565
stock market summary, 38–39
Stone, Oliver, 613
"Straight A's" program, 507, 534–535, 537
Strategic Defense Initiative, 249, 265, 307 (box)
Strategic Petroleum Reserve, 56, 356, 409
Strossen, Nadine, 621
Student aid
bankruptcy overhaul, 127
budget reconciliation, FY 1997, 51
Clinton term summary, 799
D.C. students, 547–548
debt cancellation, 523
dependents of slain police officers, 614–615, 651–652
drug crime restrictions, 510, 547
Education Department oversight, 509, 510, 513
education savings accounts, 7, 518–520, 544–546
education tax incentives, 90, 94, 96, 520–523
deductions for interest, 522
employer assistance, 96, 520, 523, 544, 545
guaranty agencies, 523
high-tech visa fees, 618, 671–672
Higher Education Act authorization, 508, 509–513
Hispanic colleges, 511

interest rates, 509–510, 511–512
loan consolidation, 526–527
medical research, 481, 484
military recruiting, 257, 280, 285
  ROTC programs, 294
overseas programs, 549
prepaid tuition plans, 520, 523, 544, 546
scams, 531, 546
teachers, 509–513, 519–520, 545
veterans, 498 (graph), 500, 502–503, 512
women entering workforce, 513, 514
Subchapter S corporations, 105, 140–141
Submarines
appropriations, 300
defense authorization, 258, 277, 282
female crew, 295
Substance abuse. *See Alcohol abuse and alcoholism; Drug abuse; Smoking*
Substance Abuse and Mental Health Services Administration, 482
Sudan
U.S. air strikes, 1998, 172, 267
U.S. trade sanctions
  encryption exports ban, 336
  food, 83, 223–225, 424, 426
  religious persecution, 199
  terrorism, 199
Suicide
physician assistance, 16, 30, 117, 429, 459, 463, 477, 593, 606–607, 658–660
  Supreme Court decisions, 459, 686, 687, 717–718
prevention programs, 482
Suma Ching Hai Meditation Association, 778
Summers, Lawrence H.
commodities regulation, 141
economic policy leadership, 34 (box), 978 (box), 982
financial services modernization, 135
Sun Diamond Growers, 792 (box)
Sundance Kid, 402
Sunscreens, 449
Superconducting supercollider, 746–747
Superfund
Clinton term summary, 341–344, 345, 799
overhaul plan, 352–354, 396–399
Supplemental Security Income (SSI)
budget reconciliation, 1997, 49, 51–53
budget resolution, FY 1998, 43, 45
disabled children, 490
disabled workers' insurance, 470
Medicaid changes, 442
welfare law revision, 486, 487, 488, 490
work opportunity tax credits, 99
Supreme Court cases
AT&T v. Central Office Telephone, 711
AT&T v. Iowa Utilities Board, 711
Abrams v. Johnson, 708
Adarand Constructors v. Slater, 717
Agostini v. Felton, 714
Air Line Pilots Assn. v. Miller, 721
Alaska v. Native Village of Venetie Tribal Government, 713
Albertson's v. Kirkingburg, 720
Alden v. Maine, 725–726
Allentown Mack Sales and Service v. National Labor Relations Board, 721–722
Almendarez-Torres v. U.S., 707
Amchem Products v. Windsor, 665, 696
American Manufacturers Mutual Insurance Co. v. Sullivan, 724
Amoco Production Co. v. Southern Ute Indian Tribe, 713
Apprendi v. New Jersey, 707
Arizona v. California, 728

Arizona Department of Revenue v. Blaze Construction Co., 727
Arizonans for Official English v. Arizona, 721
Arkansas v. Farm Credit Services of Central Arkansas, 727
Arkansas Educational Television Commission v. Forbes, 716
Associates Commercial Corp. v. Rash, 692
Atherton v. Federal Deposit Insurance Corp., 692
Atlantic Mutual Insurance v. Commissioner of Internal Revenue, 694
Auer v. Robbins, 722
Babbitt v. Youpee, 713
Bailey v. U.S., 597
Baker v. General Motors, 697
Bank of America v. 203 N. LaSalle St. Partnership, 693
Baral v. U.S., 695
Barnett Bank v. Nelson, 123 (box), 139
Bates v. U.S., 699
Bay Area Laundry and Dry Cleaning Pension Trust Fund v. Ferbar Corp. of California, 722
Beach v. Ocwen Federal Bank, 692
Beck v. Prupis, 729
Bennett v. Spear, 710
Bibles v. Oregon Natural Desert Assn., 712
Blessing v. Freestone, 710
Board of County Commissioners of Bryan County, Oklahoma v. Brown, 718
Board of Regents, University of Wisconsin System v. Southworth, 715
Bogan v. Scott-Harris, 718
Boggs v. Boggs, 722
Bond v. U.S., 706
Bousley v. U.S., 702
Boy Scouts of America v. Dale, 715
Bracy v. Gramley, 702
Bragdon v. Abbott, 719
Brogan v. U.S., 699
Bryan v. U.S., 700
Buchanan v. Angelone, 698
Buckley v. American Constitutional Law Assn., 708
Buckley v. Valeo, 688, 786, 787
Burlington Industries v. Ellerth, 720–721
Bush v. Gore, 21, 25–26, 686–687 (box)
  opinions (texts), 1046–1055
Bush v. Palm Beach Canvassing Board, 686–687 (box)
Byrd v. Raines, 64
Calderon v. Ashmus, 703
Calderon v. Coleman, 703
Calderon v. Thompson, 702
California v. Deep Sea Research Inc., 725
California v. Roy, 702
California Democratic Party v. Jones, 708
California Dental Assn. v. Federal Trade Commission, 711
California Division of Labor Standards Enforcement v. Dillingham Construction, 722
California Public Employees' Retirement System v. Felzen, 694
Campbell v. Louisiana, 704
Camps Newfound/Owatonna Inc. v. Town of Harrison, 727
Carmell v. Texas, 701
Caron v. U.S., 700
Carter v. U.S., 700
Cass County, Minnesota v. Leech Lake Band of Chippewa Indians, 713
Castillo v. U.S., 700
Caterpillar v. Lewis, 695
Cedar Rapids Community School District v. Garret F., 719–720

Central State University v. American Association of University Professors, Central State University Chapter, 723
Chadha v. Immigration and Naturalization Service, 739
Chandler v. Miller, 720
Christensen v. Harris County, 723
City of Boerne v. Flores, 660, 714
City of Chicago v. International College of Surgeons, 696
City of Chicago v. Morales, 704
City of Erie v. Pap's A.M., 715–716
City of Monroe v. U.S., 709
City of Monterey v. Del Monte Dunes at Monterey, 724
City of West Covina v. Perkins, 705
Cleveland v. Policy Management Systems Corp., 720
Clinton v. City of New York, 65, 714
Clinton v. Goldsmith, 713
Clinton v. Jones, 714
Cohen v. De La Cruz, 693
College Savings Bank v. Florida Prepaid Postsecondary Education Expense Fund, 726
Colorado Republican Federal Campaign Committee v. Federal Election Commission, 776
Commissioner v. Solliman, 98
Commissioner of Internal Revenue v. Estate of Hubert, 694
Conn v. Gabbert, 695
Cortez Byrd Chips v. Bill Harbert Construction, 695
County of Sacramento v. Lewis, 718
Crawford-El v. Britton, 718
Crosby v. National Foreign Trade Council, 712
Cunningham v. Hamilton County, 696
Davis v. Monroe County Board of Education, 719
De Buono v. NYSA-ILA Medical and Clinical Services Fund, 727
Department of Commerce v. U.S. House of Representatives, 710–711, 748 (box)
Department of the Army v. Blue Fox Inc., 712
Dickerson v. U.S., 706
Dickinson v. Zurko, 694
Dooley v. Korean Air Lines, 728
Drye v. U.S., 695
Dunn v. Commodity Futures Trading Commission, 711
Eastern Enterprises v. Apfel, 722
Edmond v. U.S., 712–713
Edwards v. Balisok, 718
Edwards v. Carpenter, 703
Edwards v. U.S., 707
El Al Israel Airlines v. Tsui Yuan Tseng, 729
El Paso Natural Gas v. Neztsosie, 697
Employment Division v. Smith, 660
Faragher v. City of Boca Raton, 721
Federal Election Commission v. Akins, 708
Feltner v. Columbia Pictures Television, 693
Fidelity Financial Services v. Fink, 692
Fiore v. White, 703
Fischer v. U.S., 700
Flippo v. West Virginia, 706
Florida v. J.L., 706
Florida v. White, 706
Florida Prepaid Postsecondary Education Expense Fund v. College Savings Bank, 726
Food and Drug Administration v. Brown & Williamson Tobacco, 712
Foreman v. Dallas County, Texas, 709
Forney v. Apfel, 714
Foster v. Love, 708
Free v. Abbott Laboratories, 696
Friends of the Earth v. Laidlaw Environmental Services, 710
Garner v. Jones, 704

Gebser v. Lago Vista Independent School District, 718

Geier v. American Honda Motor Co., 712

Geissal v. Moore Medical Corp., 722

General Electric v. Joiner, 696

General Motors v. Tracy, 727

Gilbert v. Homar, 723

Glickman v. Wileman Brothers & Elliott, 711

Gray v. Maryland, 701

Greater New Orleans Broadcasting Assn. v. U.S., 715

Greene v. Georgia, 698

Grupo Mexicano de Desarrollo v. Alliance Bond Fund, 697

Gutierrez v. Ada, 709

Haddle v. Garrison, 718–719

Hanlon v. Berger, 719

Harbor Tug & Barge Co. v. Papai, 723

Harris Trust and Savings Bank v. Salomon Smith Barney, 722

Hartford Underwriters Insurance v. Union Planters Bank, 693

Hetzel v. Prince William County, 697

Hill v. Colorado, 716

Hohn v. U.S., 703

Holloway v. U.S., 700

Hopkins v. Reeves, 698

Hudson v. U.S., 701

Hughes Aircraft v. Jacobson, 722

Hughes Aircraft v. U.S. ex rel. Schumer, 696

Humana Inc. v. Forsyth, 729

Hunt v. Cromartie, 709, 788 (box)

Hunt-Wesson v. Franchise Tax Board of California, 728

Idaho v. Coeur d'Alene Tribe of Idaho, 725

Illinois v. Wardlow, 706

Immigration and Naturalization Service v. Aguirre-Aguirre, 716

Immigration and Naturalization Service v. Yueh-Shaio Yang, 716

Ingalls Shipbuilding Inc. v. Department of Labor, 723

Inter-Modal Rail Employees Assn. v. Atchison, Topeka & Santa Fe Railway Co., 722

Jefferson v. City of Tarrant, Alabama, 718

Jefferson County, Alabama v. Acker, 727–728

Johnson v. Fankell, 718

Johnson v. U.S., 697, 707

Jones v. U.S. (527 U.S. 373), 698

Jones v. U.S. (529 U.S. 848), 700

Kalina v. Fletcher, 718

Kansas v. Hendricks, 707

Kawaauhau v. Geiger, 692–693

Kimel v. Florida Board of Regents, 726

Kiowa Tribe of Oklahoma v. Manufacturing Technologies Inc., 713

Klehr v. A.O. Smith Corp., 728

Knowles v. Iowa, 705

Kolstad v. American Dental Assn., 721

Kumbo Tire v. Carmichael, 696

LaChance v. Erickson, 711

Lambert v. Wicklund, 717

Lambrix v. Singletary, 702

Lau v. Nichols, 517

Lawyer v. Department of Justice, 709

Lewis v. U.S., 699

Lexecon v. Milberg Weiss Bershad Hynes & Lerach, 670, 696–697

Lilly v. Virginia, 699

Lindh v. Murphy, 702

Lopez v. Monterey County, California, 709

Los Angeles Police Dept. v. United Reporting Publishing Corp., 715

Lunding v. New York Tax Appeals Tribunal, 727

Lynce v. Mathis, 704

M.L.B. v. S.L.J., 695

Marquez v. Screen Actors Guild, 723

Martin v. Hadix, 695

Martinez v. Court of Appeal of California, 697–698

Maryland v. Dyson, 706

Maryland v. Wilson, 705

Mazurek v. Armstrong, 717

McMillian v. Monroe County, Alabama, 718

Metro-North Commuter Railroad Co. v. Buckley, 723

Metropolitan Stevedore Co. v. Rambo, 723–724

Miller v. Albright, 716

Miller v. French, 704–705

Minnesota v. Carter, 705

Minnesota v. Mille Lac Band of Chippewa Indians, 713–714

Miranda, 689

Missouri v. Jenkins, 621

Mitchell v. Helms, 714–715

Mitchell v. U.S., 706

Mobil Oil Exploration and Producing Southeast v. U.S., 712

Monge v. California, 701

Montana v. Crow Tribe of Indians, 713

Murphy v. United Parcel Service, 720

Murphy Brothers v. Michett Pipe Stringing, 697

Muscarello v. U.S., 699–700

NAACP v. Alabama, 786

Nader v. U.S., 704

National Aeronautics and Space Administration v. Federal Labor Relations Authority, 721

National Collegiate Athletic Assn. v. Smith, 719

National Credit Union Administration v. First National Bank & Trust, 692

National Endowment for the Arts v. Finley, 715, 738 (box)

National Federation of Federal Employees, Local 1309 v. Department of the Interior, 721

National Labor Relations Board v. Town & Country Electric, 575

Nelson v. Adams USA, 697

New Jersey v. New York, 725

New Mexico ex rel. Ortiz v. Reed, 701

New York v. Hill, 700

Newsweek v. Florida Department of Revenue, 727

Nixon v. Shrink Missouri Government PAC, 708

Norfolk Southern Railway v. Shanklin, 712

Nynex v. Discon, 692

O'Dell v. Netherland, 702

O'Gilvie v. U.S., 694

Ohio v. Robinette, 705

Ohio Adult Parole Authority v. Woodard, 698

Ohio Forestry Assn. v. Sierra Club, 710

Ohler v. U.S, 698

Old Chief v. U.S., 701

Olmstead v. L.C., 720

Oncale v. Sundowner Offshore Services, 720

Ortiz v. Fibreboard, 665, 696

O'Sullivan v. Boerckel, 703

Oubre v. Entergy Operations Inc., 717

Pegram v. Herdrich, 722

Peguero v. U.S., 703

Pennsylvania Board of Probation and Parole v. Scott, 704

Pennsylvania Department of Corrections v. Yeskey, 719

Pfaff v. Wells Electronics, 693–694

Phillips v. Washington Legal Foundation, 724

Portuondo v. Agard, 707

Pounders v. Watson, 699

Printz v. U.S., 711

Public Lands Council v. Babbitt, 712

Quality King Distributors v. L'Anza Research International, 693

Raines v. Byrd, 714

Raleigh v. Illinois Department of Revenue, 693

Ramdass v. Angelone, 698

Reeves v. Sanderson Plumbing Products, 717

Regents of the University of California v. Doe, 725

Regions Hospital v. Shalala, 711

Reno v. American-Arab Anti-Discrimination Committee, 716

Reno v. American Civil Liberties Union, 715

Reno v. Bossier Parish School Board, 709, 710

Reno v. Condon, 712

Rice v. Cayetano, 710

Richards v. Wisconsin, 705

Richardson v. McKnight, 718

Richardson v. U.S., 701

Rivet v. Regions Bank of Louisiana, 696

Roberts v. Galen of Virginia, 711

Robinson v. Shell Oil Co., 720

Roe v. Flores-Ortega, 705

Roe v. Wade, 16, 455, 473, 661–662

Rotella v. Wood, 729

Ruhrgas v. Marathon Oil, 697

Saenz v. Roe, 721

Salinas v. U.S., 699

Santa Fe Independent School District v. Doe, 714

Saratoga Fishing v. J.M. Martinac, 693

Schenck v. Pro-Choice Network of Western New York, 716–717

Shalala v. Illinois Council on Long Term Care, 712

Sims v. Apfel, 714

Slack v. Daniel, 703

Smith v. Robbins, 698

Snake River Potato Growers v. Rubin, 65

South Central Bell Telephone Co. v. Alabama, 727

South Dakota v. Yankton Sioux Tribe, 713

Spencer v. Kemma, 702

State Oil v. Khan, 692

Steel Co. v. Citizens for a Better Environment, 710

Stenberg v. Carhart, 473, 717

Stewart v. Martinez-Villareal, 702

Strate v. A-1 Contractors, 713

Strickler v. Greene, 700–701

Suitum v. Tahoe Regional Planning Agency, 724

Sutton v. United Air Lines, 720

Swidler & Berlin v. U.S., 695

Texas v. Johnson, 667

Texas v. Lesage, 717

Texas v. U.S., 709

Textron Lycoming Reciprocating Engine Division, AVCO Corp. v. United Automobile, Aerospace and Agricultural Implement Workers of America, 723

Timmons v. Twin Cities Area New Party, 707–708

Trest v. Cain, 702

Troxel v. Granville, 710

Turner Broadcasting System v. Federal Communications Commission, 716

UNUM Life Insurance Co. of America v. Ward, 722

U.S. v. Alaska, 724–725

U.S. v. Bajakajian, 701–702

U.S. v. Balsys, 706

U.S. v. Beggerly, 697

U.S. v. Bestfoods, 710

U.S. v. Brockamp, 694

U.S. v. Cabrales, 707

U.S. v. Estate of Romani, 695

U.S. v. Gonzales, 707

U.S. v. Haggar Apparel, 693

U.S. v. Hubbell, 706

U.S. v. Hyde, 702

U.S. v. Johnson, 704

U.S. v. Jose, 694
U.S. v. LaBonte, 707
U.S. v. Lanier, 699
U.S. v. Locke, 712
U.S. v. Martinez, 704
U.S. v. Morrison, 630–631, 643, 719
U.S. v. O'Hagan, 699
U.S. v. Playboy Entertainment Group, 716
U.S. v. Ramirez, 705
U.S. v. Rodriguez-Moreno, 707
U.S. v. Scheffer, 701
U.S. v. Sun-Diamond Growers of California, 700, 792 (box)
U.S. v. U.S. Shoe Corp., 694
U.S. v. Watts, 706–707
U.S. v. Wells, 699
Vacco v. Quill, 459
Vermont Agency of Natural Resources v. U.S., 726–727
Village of Willowbrook v. Olech, 719
Wal-Mart Stores v. Samara Brothers, 695
Walters v. Metropolitan Educational Enterprises, 720
Warner-Jenkinson v. Hilton Davis Chemical, 693
Washington v. Glucksberg, 459, 717–718
Weeks v. Angelone, 698
Weisgram v. Marley, 695
West v. Gibson, 721
Williams v. Taylor, 703
Wilson v. Layne, 719
Wisconsin v. City of New York, 733
Wisconsin Department of Corrections v. Schacht, 697
Wright v. Universal Maritime Service Corp., 721
Wyoming v. Houghton, 705
Young v. Fordice, 709
Young v. Harper, 704
Your Home Visiting Nurse Services v. Shalala, 711
Supreme Court decisions
abortion, 16, 431, 455, 472, 473, 661–662, 716–717
asbestos compensation, 665
assisted suicide, 459, 606, 717–718
bilingual education, 517
business law, 692–695
   antitrust, 692
   banking, 122, 123 (box), 139, 692
   bankruptcy, 692–693
   baseball antitrust exemption, 324
   business taxes, 694–695
   copyright, 693
   credit unions, 125, 128
   foreign trade, 693
   maritime law, 693
   patents, 693–694
   shareholder suits, 694
   telecommunications, 716
   trademarks, 695
civil rights and liberties
   church-state separation, 714–715
   drug testing, 720
   First Amendment, 688–689, 714–716
   flag desecration, 610–611, 666, 667
   freedom of association, 715
   freedom of speech, 715–716
   religious expression, 591, 660–661
commerce clause, 643
Congress
   campaign finance, 776, 708
   elections, 708
   Federal Election Commission, 708
   pay raises, 794
   primary elections, 708
   reapportionment, redistricting, 708–709, 788 (box)

court procedures, 695–697
   appeals, 695
   arbitration, 695
   attorney fees, 695
   attorneys, 695–696
   class actions, 696
   evidence, 696
   expert testimony, 696
   false claims, 696
   federal courts, 696–697
   injunctions, 697
   judgments, 697
   jury trial, 697
   removal, 697
   state courts, 697
criminal law and procedure, 689–691, 697–707
   appeals, 697–698
   capital punishment, 698
   contempt of court, 699
   discovery, 700–701
   double jeopardy, 701
   drug offenses, 701
   evidence, 701
   ex post facto laws, 701
   extradition, 701
   forfeiture, 701–702
   guilty pleas, 702
   habeas corpus appeals, 702–703
   harmless error, 704
   hate crimes, 643
   jury selection, 704
   loitering, 704
   mandatory gun penalties, 597
   parole and probation, 704
   prisons, 704–705
   right to counsel, 705
   search and seizure, 705–706
   self-incrimination, 706
   sentencing, 706–707
   sex offenders, 707
   trials, 707
   venue, 707
   Violence Against Women Act, 590, 630–631
   witnesses, 699
damage suits, 718–719
disability rights, 541, 719–720
discrimination
   affirmative action, 717
   age discrimination, 717
   employment, 720–721
election law, 707–710
   Florida presidential vote, 20, 21, 25–27, 684, 686–687 (box)
   issue advocacy ad, 786, 787
   voting rights, 709–710
environmental protection
   endangered species, 710
   fines, 710
   national forests, 710
   nuclear waste storage, 363
   "right to know," 710
   toxic waste, 710
family law
   child support enforcement, 710
   child visitation, 710
   Elian González, 225 (box)
federal courts, 696
   transferee courts, 669–670
federal government
   census, 63, 74, 710–711, 733, 734, 748 (box)
   contracts, 712
   federal employees, 711, 721
   freedom of information, 712
   NEA funding standards, 738 (box)
   regulation, 711–712, 724
federal-state relations, 685–686

gifts to public officials, 792 (box)
immigration law, 716
individual rights, 686–688, 716–721
labor law, 721–724
   arbitration, 721
   labor unions, 723
   pensions and benefits, 722
   Social Security, 714
   union "salting," 575
   workers' compensation, 723–724
military affairs, 712–713
Native Americans, 713–714
official English, 721
pardon power, 683
presidents in civil suits, 690, 691, 804, 806, 814
property rights, 597, 724
   water rights, 728
public television, 716
separation of powers, 690, 691, 714
   judicial tax decisions, 621
   legislative veto, 739
   line-item veto, 8, 11, 43, 64, 65, 690, 691, 743, 811
state and local government
   employees, 723
   immunity, 725–726
   land use, 724
   state boundaries, 724–725
   state courts, 697
   taxes, 327, 727–728
taxation
   home office deductions, 98
torts, 728–600
welfare, 721
Supreme Court Historical Society, 616
Supreme Court, U.S. *See also Supreme Court cases; Supreme Court decisions*
   caseload, 685, 690 (table)
   chief justice's salary, 751
   Clinton term summary, 684–691
   justices, 684–685, 689 (box)
   volunteer tour guides, 616
Surface Transportation Board, 322
Surgeon general, 435 (box), 636
Sweeney, John E., R-N.Y.
   campaign finance reform, 789
   civil assets forfeiture, 648
Sweepstakes fraud, 675
Swift, Jane, 30
Switzerland
   energy research and development, 746–747
Syria
   economic sanctions, 199
   encryption exports ban, 336

T

T-visas, 590, 630, 632
Tahoe National Forest, 368
Taiwan
   China-U.S. relations, 175, 180, 183, 209–210
      trade agreement, 163, 165
   missile defense, 182
Taiwan Relations Act of 1979, 183, 209
Tajikistan
   "Silk Road" trade, 169
Takings clause, 724
Talent, James M., R-Mo.
   House leadership, 760
   patients' rights, 468
Tamraz, Roger, 779
TANF. *See Temporary Assistance for Needy Families*
Tanks
   vehicle development, 281, 288, 292, 294, 299

Tanner, John, D-Tenn.
  estate taxes, 116
  fast track for trade pacts, 155
Tanzania
  U.S. embassy bombing, 217, 267, 803
Tariffs
  Caribbean trade, 157–158
  China policy, 209
  China trade agreement, 160, 161, 163
  clothing and textile imports, 149
  Generalized System of Preferences, 159
  trade policy summary, 147
  Vietnam trade, 167
Tauscher, Ellen O., D-Calif.
  superfund overhaul, 397
Tauzin, W.J. "Billy," R-La.
  armored car gun permits, 598
  auto safety, 333
  conservation lands acquisition, 378
  electric deregulation, 407
  House ethics overhaul, 766
  nuclear waste storage, 408
  ocean policy panel, 364
  Puerto Rico status, 741
Tax Court, U.S., 108
Taxes. *See also Business taxes; Estate taxes; Excise taxes; Income taxes; Internal Revenue Service; Sales taxes*
  appropriations, FY 1999, 62, 68
  budget reconciliation, FY 1997, 48–50
  budget resolutions
    FY 1998, 43–48
    FY 1999, 60–61
    FY 2000, 71–73
    FY 2001, 79–81
  budget surplus, 39 (box)
  Clinton term summary, 4, 11, 15, 19, 20, 36, 71, 87–89, 90, 110
  debt reduction, 86
  527 PACs, 786–787
  Gingrich coup attempt, 762 (box)
  health-related changes, 467–469
  judicial activism, 621, 622
  line-item veto, 64–65
  minimum wage proposals, 579–580
  presidential campaign issue, 24, 25
  tax credit extensions, 105–106, 113
  tax cuts, 1997, 90–105
  tax cuts, 1999, 110–112
  tax cuts, 2000, 117
  tax receipts, 1980–2001 (graph), 88
  taxes as percentage of GDP, 1935–2000 (table), 91
  two-thirds vote to raise, 761
Taxpayer Advocate, Office of the, 107
Taxpayer Bill of Rights, 107–108
Taxpayer Relief Act of 1997, 48
Taylor, Gene, D-Miss.
  defense authorization, 291
  drug abuse prevention, 602
  Reagan National airport, 741
Taylor Grazing Act of 1934, 357
TB. *See Tuberculosis*
Teachers
  certification requirements, 532
  competency tests, 520, 539, 544
  D.C. pensions, 740
  discipline liability, 539
  Head Start instructors, 491, 492
  high-tech visas, 671
  home ownership aid, 566
  late vocation, 545
  merit pay, 520, 539, 544
  new hires
    appropriations, 62, 67, 73, 74, 81, 82, 810 (box)
    ed-flex plan, 540, 541

  education block grants, 527
  ESEA authorization, 532–533, 537, 539
  professional development, 74
  recruitment, training grants, 508, 509–512, 520
    ed-flex plan, 540–544
    ESEA authorization, 531, 532–534, 537, 539
    technology use, 533
  sabbatical leave, 533
  student loan forgiveness, 509, 510, 513, 519–520
  tax deductions for school supplies, 545
Teachers Insurance Annuity Association-College Retirement Equity Fund, 104
TEAM Act, 578
Teamsters union, 578 (box)
Tear gas, 269 (box), 271
Technical schools, 513, 515
Technology in education
  computer donations, 96, 523, 545
  ed-flex plan, 541, 543
  federal funds shifting, 536
  teacher training, 533
Technology Literacy Challenge Fund, 536
Technology transfer. *See also Missile technology transfer; Nuclear weapons proliferation*
  clean-coal tech to China, 164
  federal lab licensing, 747
  renewable energy export aid, 356
  reporting requirements, 282
  supercomputer export controls, 304 (box)
Teenagers. *See Adolescents and youth*
Tejeda, Frank M., D-Texas
  death, successor, 8
Telecommunications. *See also Telephone communications*
  China trade agreement, 161
  Clinton term summary, 317, 318
  encryption exports, 326–327
  high-tech visas, 616
  rural health care, 435, 441
  Supreme Court decisions, 716
Telecommunications Act of 1996, 327, 338
Tele-Communications Inc., 254
Telemarketing fraud, 675
Telephone communications
  cell phone fraud, 329
  criminal investigations, 656
  encryption technology, 336
  excise taxes, 116, 118–119, 334–335
    prepaid phone cards, 102
  roving wiretaps, 202
  "slamming" restrictions, 330
  toll-free "vanity" numbers, 325
  universal service, 325, 326, 327
Telescopes, 742–743
Television. *See also Cable television*
  antidrug ads, 602
  casino gambling ads, 689
  Clinton term summary, 317, 318
  federal court proceedings, 622, 669
  issue advocacy ads, 777
  low power TV, 338
  media cross-ownership rules, 326
  national parks filming fees, 356, 358, 387
  ratings system, 327
  satellite broadcasts, 73, 75, 329, 331, 338
  spectrum auctions, 325–326
  uniform ratings, 637
  violent programming, 635, 636
Temporary Assistance for Needy Families (TANF) block grant, 490, 495
Ten Commandments, 636
Tenet, George J.
  CIA leadership, 179 (box), 799, 983
  intelligence authorizations, 200, 201, 227
  terrorism, 267, 309

Tennessee
  bankruptcy judges, 608
  presidential election, 2000, 27
  TVA subsidy, 69
Tennessee Valley Authority (TVA)
  board nomination, 679
  electric deregulation, 406
  federal subsidy, 69, 370–371
Tenure of Office Act of 1867, 814 (box)
Term limits
  action, 1997–1998, 783–784
  California law (box), 783
  summary, 6
Territories, U.S.
  Supreme Court decisions, 709
Terrorism and counterterrorism
  action
    1997–1998, 267–268, 605
    1999–2000, 308–310
    summary, 803
  Afghanistan, Sudan air strikes, 1998, 196, 267
  border controls, 676
  China technology sales, 180
  Cole attack, 217, 293, 309, 803, 807 (box)
  counterterrorism appropriations, 62, 68, 84, 262
  Defense Department coordination, 295
  defense leadership, 241 (box)
  economic sanctions, 199–200
  FALN clemency, 681–683
  gun control, 638
  Iran sanctions, 222
  Justice Department authorization, 613
  long-term defense planning, 264
  military aid authorization, 229–230
  National Security Council office, 267
  preparedness, 645–646
    bioterrorism, 481
    response training, 295
  roving wiretaps, 202
  secret evidence in deportation, 663–664
  technology transfer reports, 282
  Third World debt forgiveness, 369
  U.S. aid to Yemen, 217
  U.S. embassy security, 75, 217–218, 219
  victims aid, 629, 631, 632, 633
  Wye River accords, 190 (box)
Terrorism Preparedness, Office of, 645–646
Texas
  Air Force maintenance depots, 239–242, 245
  bankruptcy overhaul, 127, 143
  congressional elections, 8
  ed-flex plan, 540, 541
  F-22 funding, 286–287 (box)
  interest on trust accounts, 691
  low-level nuclear waste, 359–361
  Medicaid, 438
  mortgage insurance, 563
  Republican convention, 23
  space programs, 735
Texas Women's University, 547
Textiles
  African trade initiative, 168
  tariffs, 156, 157–158, 160
Textron, 288
THAAD. *See Theater High-Altitude Area Defense*
Theater companies, 739
Theater High-Altitude Area Defense (THAAD)
  antimissile defenses, 266
  appropriations, 248, 259, 261
  authorization, 244, 257
Third International Mathematics and Science Study, 524
Thirteenth Amendment
  community service, 557
  hate crimes, 643

Thomas, Bill, R-Calif.
campaign finance reform, 777, 780, 781, 788–789
House administrative officer, 768
House audit, 770 (box)
Medicare commission, 464
Medicare drug benefits, 465–466
Medicare payments, 433, 461–463
Sanchez election, 785
Thomas, Clarence
abortion, 687
campaign finance, 688
defendants' confessions, 689
Florida presidential vote, 26, 687 (box)
forfeiture, 690
hate crimes, 690
minority districts, 788 (box)
nomination controversy, 622, 626
sexual harassment, 687
Supreme Court summary, 689 (box)
Thomas, Craig, R-Wyo.
conservation lands acquisition, 378
endangered species protection, 350–351
national parks operations, 358
Thomason, Harry, 750
Thompson, Fred, R-Tenn.
Aimee's law, 632
campaign finance reform, 776–777, 778
China policy, 209
China trade agreement, 164–165
crime victims rights, 609
defense authorization, 293
federal rulemaking, 737
Fletcher nomination, 628
independent counsel law, 663
juvenile crime, 596
Lee nomination, 626
nuclear lab security, 412
Senate leadership, 759
TVA federal subsidy, 371
volunteer liability, 615
Thompson, Tommy G., 477
Thornberry, William M. "Mac," R-Texas
conservation lands acquisition, 378
nuclear lab security, 412
Thrift Depositor Protection Oversight Board, 563
Thrifts. *See Savings and loan associations*
Thurman, Karen, D-Fla.
organ transplants, 476
Thurmond, Strom, R-S.C.
American Heritage Rivers, 370
defense authorization, 255, 256
Lee nomination, 626
Senate leadership, 7 (box), 759, 769
Tiananmen Square crackdown, 151
Tibet
China trade agreement, 165
Tied-Aid Credit Fund, 157
Tierney, John F., D-Mass
charter schools, 525
defense appropriations, 297
Tilden, Samuel J., 22
Title insurance, 139
Tobacco. *See also Cigarette and tobacco taxes; Smoking*
Clinton term summary, 11, 315, 316, 318
farm price supports, 59, 425
FDA regulation, 323–324, 454, 482, 690, 691
income earned abroad, 118
industry-states settlement
congressional ratification, 322–324
D.C. exemption, 66
federal costs recoupment, 60–61, 72
tax cuts, 1997, 95

Iraqi frozen assets, 219
Justice Department suit, 85
Tomahawk missiles, 282
Tongass National Forest, 67, 379, 395
Tonkin Gulf resolution of 1964, 197
Tornadoes, 77
Torricelli, Robert F., D-N.J.
balanced budget amendment, 56, 57
China trade agreement, 164–165
economic sanctions, 200, 224
education savings accounts, 520, 545
intelligence leak incident, 201, 202
Lee nomination, 626
veterans burial rights, 498
Torts, 728–729
Torture
China trade agreement, 165
Tower, John, 818
Towers, Barbara, 625
Towns, Edolphus, D-N.Y.
public housing reform, 557
superfund overhaul, 398
Toxic waste cleanup. *See also Nuclear waste disposal*
Clinton term summary, 341, 372
brownfields, 100, 352, 354, 396–398
energy research and development, 747
superfund overhaul, 352–354, 396–398
Supreme Court decisions, 710
underground storage tanks, 102, 370
waterway dredging, 84
Trade Act of 1974. *See Jackson-Vanik amendment*
Trade agreements. *See also General Agreement on Tariffs and Trade; North American Free Trade Agreement; World Trade Organization*
China-U.S. trade, 160–166
drugs, medical devices, food, 453
fast-track procedures, 7, 148, 151, 153–156, 163
Vietnam-U.S. trade, 149, 158–159
Trade representatives, U.S.
biomedical, food issues, 453
China trade agreement, 165
trade leadership, 152 (box), 984
Trademarks
Internet addresses, 336–337
Supreme Court decisions, 685, 695
Traditional Values Coalition, 644
Traffic law
auto searches, 690
racial profiling, 608, 652
Traficant, James A. Jr., D-Ohio
ethics probe, 774
minimum wage, 580
Youngstown community development, 566
Transferee courts, 669–670
TransHub, 753–754
Transportation. *See also Air transportation; Automobiles and auto industry; Bus transportation; Highways and roads; Railroads; Ships and shipping; Trucks and trucking*
budget outlays, FY 1987–2001 (graph), 316
Clinton term summary, 315–316
nuclear waste storage, 362
Transportation and Infrastructure Committee, House
jurisdiction, leadership, 962–963
Transportation Department, U.S. (DOT)
appropriations, 67, 75, 84
fuel efficiency standards, 84, 333 (box), 410
leadership, 320 (box)
space launches, 754
truck, bus safety, 84, 332
Transportation Equity Act for the 21st Century, 367
Travel and tourism
Cuba restrictions, 83, 210–211, 223–225, 426

Las Vegas airport, 401
Minnesota wilderness, 367
national parks admissions fees, 358–359
national wildlife refuges, 348
visa authorization, 677
Treasury Department, U.S.
appropriations, 59, 66, 68, 76, 81
China trade agreement, 165
coin designs, 129
corporate income earned abroad, 118
economic sanctions for terrorism, 199
education savings accounts, 518
EITC fraud, 103
endangered species conservation fund, 389
estate taxes, 116
false IDs, 657
financial services modernization, 123, 130–141
forest revenues, 399–400
frozen assets of drug-traffickers, 226–227
gun show regulation, 639
IRS overhaul, 107–109
leadership, 34 (box)
money laundering, 605
offshore oil revenue, 377–378
savings and loan bailout, 563
student loans, 509
tax provisions cost estimates, 45
terrorism countermeasures, 605
VA funding, 499, 500
World Bank AIDS assistance, 230
Treasury securities
Clinton term summary, 38
interest rates, 1980–2000 (graph), 37
railroad pensions, 581
Treaties and international agreements. *See also Arms control; Kyoto protocol on global warming; Trade agreements*
civil assets forfeiture, 649
digital copyright, 328
dolphin protection, 341, 344, 345–348
energy market information sharing, 356
international adoptions, 231
U.N. lands designation, 368
war criminals, 646
Treen, Dave, 17
Triana space project, 752–753
Tribe, Laurence, 25, 687 (box)
Tricare health program, 257, 291
Trident II missiles
appropriations, 246, 248
authorization, 277, 282, 293
Trie, Charlie Yah din, 778
Tripp, Linda R., 814–815
Tritium, 256, 258
Truancy prevention, 528
Trucks and trucking
Army, Marine authorization, 244
emissions standards, 382
excise taxes on trucks, tires, 102
fuel efficiency standards, 333 (box)
Minnesota wilderness, 367
safety, 67, 84, 331, 332–333
Truman, Harry S.
national parks filming fees, 356, 387
veto use, 811
Truth in Regulating Act, 749
Truth in sentencing, 55
Tuberculosis
foreign aid, 217, 229, 230
testing for prison inmates, 600
Tucker, Jim Guy, 805
Tudjman, Franjo, 802
Tuition tax credit, 94
Tuna
dolphin protection, 341, 344, 345–348
tariffs, 156, 158

Tunisia
U.S. aid appropriations, 189
Turkey
Armenia genocide resolution, 231
"Silk Road" trade, 169
U.S. aid appropriations, 66, 186
Turkmenistan
"Silk Road" trade, 169
U.S. aid appropriations, 189
Tuskegee Airmen National Historic Site, 359
TVA. *See Tennessee Valley Authority*
21st Century Community Learning Centers, 536
Twenty-first Century Research Laboratories Act, 481
Tyson, Laura D'Andrea, 35 (box), 464–465

U

U-2 reconnaissance planes, 287
U.S. Bankcorp, 121
U.S. Conference of Mayors, 396
U.S. Family Network, 773
U.S. Public Housing Act of 1937, 553, 555, 558
U.S. Term Limits, 783–784
Udall, Mark, D-Colo.
forest revenues, 399
San Rafael Swell, 402
Udall, Thomas, D-N.M.
election, 9
Ukraine
CFE treaty changes, 274
U.S. aid appropriations, 185, 189
U.S. satellite launches, 229
Umatilla National Forest, 403
Underground storage tanks
cleanup funding, 102, 370
gasoline additive MTBE, 390
superfund overhaul, 397
Underwood, Cecil H., 30
Unemployment. *See Employment and unemployment*
Unemployment compensation
FUTA surtax extension, 102
outlays, FY 1987–2001 (graph), 488
self-employed persons, 490–491
Unfunded Mandates Act, 351
UNICOR, 652–653
Unidentified Persons File, 646
Unitary thrifts, 133
United Auto Workers, 618
United Defense Corp., 294
United Nations
Clinton term summary, 173, 175, 176, 177
environmental protection, 367–368, 401, 744–745
Iraq weapons inspection, 196–197, 803, 822 (box)
peacekeeping
funding, 219
Kosovo, 205, 803
U.S. budget share, 219
U.S. debt repayment
abortion controversies, 458, 473–474
action, 1997–1998, 192–193
action, 1999–2000, 219–220
appropriations, 59, 66, 74
budget cap exemption, 53
foreign aid appropriations, 185, 188, 210, 212–213
State Department authorization, 189–192, 217–219
summary, 7, 16, 175, 204, 803
U.S. representatives, 179 (box)
United Nations Commission on Human Rights, 182–183, 208

United Nations Educational, Scientific and Cultural Organization (UNESCO), 368, 401
United Nations Population Fund (UNFPA)
State Department authorization, 191, 218, 219
U.S. aid appropriations, 184, 186, 188, 189
FY 2000, 210, 212, 214
FY 2001, 216–217
United Nations General Assembly
jeopardized U.S. seat, 74, 193, 212
United Nations Security Council
Iraq weapons inspection, 198
U.S. support of resolutions, 287
United Network for Organ Sharing, 475–477
United Technologies Corp., 282, 288, 295, 300
Universal Savings Accounts, 72
Universal Service Fund, 325, 326
University of Arizona, 743
University of Montevallo, 547
University of North Carolina at Greensboro, 547
University of Pittsburgh, 475
University of Science and Arts of Oklahoma, 547
Universities. *See Colleges and universities*
Upper Tier missile defense system, 244
Upton, Fred, R-Mich.
education savings accounts, 546
Uranium
energy research and development, 747
enrichment plant cleanup, 365
Navajo miner compensation, 296
U.S. aid to Russia, 69
Urban areas
census undercount, 748 (box)
conservation lands acquisition, 376, 377, 378
development aid, 117, 161
empowerment zones, 100
health care
Medicare payments, 430
nurses visas, 674
Uruguay Round. *See General Agreement on Tariffs and Trade*
USA Engage, 200
USDA. *See Agriculture Department, U.S.*
User fees
FDA reviews, 429, 431, 444–445, 447
national parks
admissions, 358–359
filming, 356, 387
patent overhaul, 324
radio spectrum auctions, 325
USIA. *See Information Agency, U.S.*
Utah
Air Force maintenance depots, 240, 243
conservation areas, 403–404
national monument designation, 365–366
San Rafael Swell, 402
wilderness area, 366
Utah School and Institutional Trust Lands Administration, 366
Utah Schools and Lands Improvement Act of 1993, 366
Utility companies
Clean Air Act, 351
D.C. mergers, 56
directors on bank boards, 140
electric deregulation, 404–407
Uzbekistan
"Silk Road" trade, 169

V

V-22 Osprey aircraft
appropriations, 249, 262, 288
authorization, 258, 282
V-chips, 327

VA. *See Veterans Affairs Department, U.S.*
Vacancies Act, 627
Vaccine Injury Compensation Trust Fund, 100
Vaccines. *See Immunizations*
Vaginal cancer screening, 441
Vallecito Reservoir and Dam, 770–771
Vandalism at national cemeteries, 604
Vandenberg, Arthur, 196
Velázquez, Nydia M., D-N.Y.
FALN clemency, 681
House leadership, 770
money laundering, 605
public housing reform, 556
Velleco, John, 639
Vencor Inc., 485
Venezuela
"dolphin-safe" tuna, 345
Vento, Bruce F., D-Minn.
Antiquities Act, 366
asbestos compensation, 664
Export-Import Bank, 157
financial services modernization, 133
grazing fees, 357
homeless programs, 562
Minnesota wilderness, 367
national parks operations, projects, 358, 359
public housing reform, 556, 557
U.N. lands designation, 368
Ventura County, Calif., 651
Ventura, Jesse, 13, 161
Venue, 707
Vermont
low-level nuclear waste, 359–361
Vertol, 288
Veterans. *See Persian Gulf War veterans; Veterans Affairs Department; Veterans benefits*
Veterans' Affairs Committee, House
jurisdiction, leadership, 760, 963
Veterans' Affairs Committee, Senate
jurisdiction, leadership, 760, 956
Veterans Affairs Department, U.S.
appropriations, 59, 75, 84
benefit appeals, 499, 502
cemetery vandalism, 604
cost-saving programs, 499–500
health insurance payments, 499
homeless programs, 561
IRS information access, 103
leadership, 499 (box)
long-term health care, 502
nurses' pay, 502
sexual harassment complaints, 497
Veterans benefits. *See also Veterans health care*
action, 1997–1998, 497–501
action, 1999–2000, 502–503
appeals, 499, 502
appropriations, FY 1998, 59
budget outlays, FY 1987–2001 (graph), 498
budget reconciliation, FY 1997, 51
burial rights, 283, 499–500
disability COLA adjustments, 498, 500, 503
education aid, 500, 502–503, 512
employment
federal job preference, 500–501
work opportunity tax credit, 99
homeless programs, 500
means test for VA programs, 103
pension limits for Medicaid patients, 500
Veterans health care
appropriations, 73
benefits expansion, 502–503
budget resolution, FY 2000, 73
Clinton term summary, 431
copayments, 500
long-term care services, 502
non-VA hospitals, 503

Persian Gulf War illnesses, 497, 500
space station bill, 754
Veterans hospitals
construction authorization, 502
nurse, dentists pay, 502
Persian Gulf War veterans, 497
Veterans of Foreign Wars, 503
Veterans Preference Act of 1944, 501
Veterinary medicine
animal tranquilizers, 654
drug manufacture, 448, 449
Vetoes. *See also Legislative veto; Line-item veto*
Clinton term summary, 4, 7, 42, 810–811
Clinton vetoes, 1997–2001, 994–995
Washington's first veto, 733
Vice presidents, U.S.
salary, 751
Secret Service protection, 651
terrorism, 309
vice presidential candidates, 2000, 23, 24
Video game violence, 635–636
Videotapes. *See Motion pictures and videotapes*
Vieques, 290–291, 292, 296
Vietnam
U.S. trade, 149, 158–159, 167, 801
Vietnam Veterans of America Foundation, 274
Vietnam War
missing service personnel, remains, 158–159
Vietnamese immigrants, 517
Violence
entertainment media, 635, 636
gun-related crime, 597, 639
juvenile crime, 593–597, 633–637
prevention
grants to cities, 482
school programs, 530, 538, 545
television ratings, 327
Violence Against Women Act, 590, 629, 630–631, 632, 685
Virgin Islands
coral reef protection, 393
Virginia
bankruptcy judges, 608
congressional elections, 28
D.C. student aid, 547–548
death penalty appeals, 690
federal-D.C. ties, 740
prison system transfer, 54–55
gubernatorial elections, 8
Visa U.S.A., 126
Visas
agricultural workers, 673–674
bans
abortion coercers, 182, 183, 260
religious persecutors, 183, 260
fees, 619, 672
foreign investors in U.S. business, 617
high-tech workers, 68, 591, 593, 616–619, 629, 670–672
nurses, 674–675
religious workers, 675
sex-trafficking victims, 590, 630, 632
tourists, 677
Vitaliano, Eric N., 9
Vitter, David, R-La.
election, 17
Vocational education
budget outlays, 1987–2001 (graph), 508
ed-flex plan, 540, 541, 542
job training overhaul, 573–575
program overhaul, 508, 509, 513–515
Smith-Hughes repeal, 523
welfare work requirement, 512
Voice of America, 166
Voinovich, George V., R-Ohio
Senate election, 12

Volunteers
liability protection, 615
literacy programs, 529
Supreme Court tours, 616
Volusia County, Fla., 26 (box), 686 (box)
Voter guides
campaign finance reform, 788
court ruling, 790 (box)
gifts to public officials, 792 (box)
Voter News Service, 25
Voter participation
House elections, 1998, 13
Voter registration
citizenship verification, 782
soft money ban, 789
Voting
English-only materials, 782
exit polling, 25
hate crimes, 642, 643
photo ID, 782
voting systems, 21, 22
Voting fraud
Landrieu election, 784–785
Sanchez election, 785
Voting rights
Supreme Court decisions, 709–710
Voting Rights Act, 710

W

Waco, Tex., shootout, 680–681
Wade, Benjamin, 814 (box)
Wag the Dog, 196
Wages. *See Salaries and wages*
Wakefield, Mary, 479
Walker, Robert S., 760
Wall Street Journal, 57
Wallowa-Whitman National Forest, 403
Waltman, Jim, 349
Wamp, Zach, R-Tenn.
juvenile crime, 637
War crimes
Bosnia, 246
Chechnya, 216, 222, 223
immigration restrictions, 646
Serbia and Yugoslavia, 214, 216, 217
Milosevic indictment, 208
War Powers Resolution of 1973
Bosnia test, 198
Kosovo policy, 206–207, 277
Warner, John W., R-Va.
Cuba sanctions, 224
defense policy
authorization, 277, 292, 293, 294
military construction, 301
NATO expansion, 273
nuclear test ban treaty, 310–311
terrorism, 309
Everglades restoration, 373, 374
Landrieu election, 784–785
Senate leadership, 769
Warsaw Convention, 729
Washington, D.C. *See District of Columbia*
Washington, George
census-related veto, 733
Reagan National airport renaming, 741
Washington Post
Lewinsky scandal, 815
Washington (State)
assisted suicide, 687
congressional elections, 28
damaged tree removal, 387
F-22 funding, 286 (box)
forest revenues, 399
grandparents' rights, 688

national monuments, 390
northern spotted owl, 392
salmon project, 395
Waste and abuse in federal programs. *See also Whistleblowers*
bankruptcy overhaul, 126–128, 142–144
Education Department audit, 548
EITC fraud, 53, 103
House committee funding, 767
IRS overhaul, 106–109
job training overhaul, 573
Medicaid, Medicare fraud, 429, 437–438, 441, 442
WIC fraud, 494–495
Waste disposal. *See also Nuclear waste disposal; Sewage; Toxic waste cleanup*
mining sites on public lands, 74
superfund exemptions, 397, 398
Water conservation
alternative water resource program, 387
low-flow toilets, 400
Water pollution. *See also Drinking water safety*
arsenic standard, 84
Clinton term summary, 343, 344, 372
coastal areas, 380, 383
EPA regulations, 382–383
gasoline additive MTBE, 390–391
Great Lakes projects, 357–358
non-point runoff, 66, 382–383, 384
ocean policy panel, 364
superfund overhaul, 353
Water Pollution Control Act of 1972, 383
Water projects
appropriations, 58, 69, 76, 83, 84
California projects, 373, 374, 381–382
conservation area ban, 404
estuary restoration, 387
Everglades restoration, 372–375
hazardous waste dredging, 84
salmon screens, 395
watershed dams, 385
Water resources. *See also Fish and fisheries; Groundwater; Oceans; Rivers and streams; Water conservation; Water pollution; Water projects; Wetlands protection*
budget outlays, FY 1987–2001 (graph), 342
Water Resources Development Act of 2000, 373, 374
Water rights
Supreme Court decisions, 728
Water supply systems
alternative water resource program, 387
Everglades restoration, 372–373, 375
Water transportation. *See Ships and shipping*
Watergate scandal, 662, 813, 819
Waters, Maxine, D-Calif.
asbestos compensation, 666
foreign aid appropriations, 215
home ownership aid, 566
immigrant smuggling, 675
juvenile crime, 595
public housing reform, 556
Watershed and Flood Prevention Act, 385
Waterways. *See Rivers and streams; Water projects*
Watt, Melvin, D-N.C.
asbestos compensation, 666
assisted suicide, 658
flag desecration, 667
high-tech visas, 618
juvenile crime, 595, 636
public housing reform, 556, 557
religious expression, 612, 660
witness intimidation, 601
Watts, J.C. Jr., R-Okla.
affirmative action in college admissions, 511

community development, 565
House leadership, 7 (box), 769
Waxman, Henry A., D-Calif.
ethics office authorization, 750
FALN clemency, 682
health policy
AIDS programs, 483
FDA overhaul, 446
Medicare changes, 434
House leadership, 760
Waxman, Seth P., 984
Ways and Means Committee, House
jurisdiction, leadership, 760, 963
Weapons. *See Arms control; Firearms; Nuclear weapons*
Weather
NOAA authorization, 745
Weather stations, 162
Web sites. *See Internet*
Weinberger, Caspar W., 269
Weiner, Anthony, D-N.Y.
asbestos compensation, 666
civil assets forfeiture, 648
electronic information access, 656
NASA authorization, 752
secret evidence in deportation, 664
violence against women, 630
Weld, William F., 7, 173, 623, 624, 800, 986
Weldon, Dave, R-Fla.
HIV testing for sex offenders, 644
home ownership aid, 566
NASA authorization, 752
public housing reform, 557
veterans health care, 503
Welfare and social services. *See also Food stamps; Medicaid; Supplemental Security Income (SSI)*
budget reconciliation, 1997, 48, 51–52, 54
budget resolution, FY 1998, 45
Clinton term summary, 429, 431, 486, 798–799
commuter aid, 67
education, for work requirements, 512
effects of 1996 reform
disabled children, 51
food stamp authorization, 419, 421
Head Start, 491–492
job training overhaul, 575
law revisions, 486–491
homeless programs, 561–562
immigrants, 619
small business loans, 324
Supreme Court decisions, 688, 721
welfare-to-work grants, 487, 489–490
work opportunity tax credits, 99, 100
workfare wages for EITC, 103
Wellstone, Paul, D-Minn.
child poverty report, 545
China trade agreement, 164, 165
Colombia antidrug aid, 221
defense appropriations, 297
ed-flex plan, 528, 541, 542
education for welfare work requirements, 512
FDA overhaul, 445
juvenile crime, 636
low-level nuclear waste, 360
Medicare changes, 52, 436
West Bank
Wye River summit, 190 (box)
West, Togo D. Jr., 499 (box), 978 (box), 982
West Virginia
Customs Service training facility, 85
gubernatorial election, 30
Western Caucus
national monuments, 389
Western states
environmental policy, 343, 345
conservation lands acquisition, 376–378

endangered species, 350–351
forest revenues, 399
grazing fees, 357
national monument designation, 365–366, 389–390
presidential vote, 1996, 2000 (table), 21
property rights, 737–738
Westlands Water District, 381
Wetlands protection
Cat Island wildlife refuge, 402
Everglades restoration, 372–375
nutria eradication, 363–364
Salton Sea rehabilitation, 364–365
Wexler, Robert, D-Fla.
flag desecration, 610
Weyrich, Paul M., 623, 792
Whales
sea lion protection, 394
Wharton Econometric Forecasting Associates, 355
Wheat
food sanctions, 421
Pakistan sale, 200
Whistleblowers
classified information, 204
intelligence authorizations, 200–201, 202, 227, 228
money laundering, 605
patients' rights, 470
Whistleblowers Protection Act, 202
White House. *See also Executive Office of the President*
fund-raising use, 789, 807–808
White House Travel Office, 750, 805 (box), 813
White, Rick, R-Wash.
campaign finance reform, 781
electoral defeat, 13
White, Ronnie L., 592, 629, 677, 678–679, 800, 991
White, Ryan, 483
White Sands, N.M., Missile Range, 253 (box)
White Sands National Monument, 387
Whitewater investigation, 804–805, 809, 813, 815, 827
Whitfield, Edward, R-Ky.
campaign finance reform, 782, 788
Whiting Field, Fla., 252 (box)
Whitman, Christine Todd, 8, 30
Wholesale financial institutions, 123, 131–132
WIC. *See Women, Infants, and Children program*
Wicker, Roger, R-Miss.
campaign finance reform, 781, 782
Wild and scenic rivers, 381, 403
Wilderness areas
Hells Canyon jetboats, 367
Minnesota truck restrictions, 367
national parks projects, 359
national wildlife refuges, 348
Oregon region, 403
Otay Mountain region, 401
roadless forest areas, 394–395
San Rafael Swell, 402
Utah national monument, 366
Wilderness Society, 349
Wildflowers, 403
Wildlife protection. *See also Endangered species; Invasive species; National wildlife refuges*
African elephants, 369
ape protection, 379–380
beached marine mammals, 380–381
bear parts import ban, 381
bird population control, 384–385
"dolphin-safe" tuna, 345–348
Fish and Wildlife Foundation, 356
Fish and Wildlife Service spending, 392–393
Great Lakes projects, 357–358

migratory birds, 358, 389
offshore oil revenue, 376–378
Otay Mountain wilderness, 401
Salton Sea rehabilitation, 364–365
sea lion protection, 393–394
Wildlife Restoration Act of 1937, 393
Wilensky, Gail, 462
Wilhelm, Charles E., 279
Wilkinson, J. Harvie, 623
Will, George, 668
Willamette River, 370
Willard, Aimee, 632
Wilson, Heather, R-N.M.
election, 14
Wind energy, 405
Wine
China trade agreement, 161
Internet sales, 337, 631
Winthrop University, 547
Wiretaps
child-sex offenders, 646
encryption technology, 336
intelligence authorization, 201, 202
Internet privacy, 337
Justice Department authorization, 613
terrorism countermeasures, 267, 605
Wisconsin
child molesters, 647
dairy pricing, 424
organ transplants, 475, 477
Wise, Bob, D-W.Va.
gubernatorial election, 30
Wisenberg, Solomon L., 816
Wolf, Frank R., R-Va.
bankruptcy judges, 608
sanctions for religious persecution, 198–199
Wolves, 356
Women. *See also Abortion; Domestic violence; Pregnancy; Sex crimes; Women in military service; Women's health*
college sports, 511
crime
college campus crime, 513
sex trafficking, 590, 629–630, 632
Violence Against Women Act, 590, 630–631, 632, 685
education
math, science classes, 537
single-sex schools, 520
elections and politics
Clinton appointments, 678, 679, 799
governors, 30
members of Congress, 12, 28 (table), 29
New Jersey, 8
Republican convention, 23
employment
education aid, 513, 514
job training overhaul, 574
Women in military service
abortion, 242, 243, 255, 256, 278, 279, 292
sex-integrated training, 252–253, 254, 255, 256
sexual harassment remedies, 275
submarine crews, 295
Women, Infants, and Children (WIC) program, 431, 494–495
Women's colleges
historic preservation, 547
Women's health. *See also Abortion; Pregnancy*
clinical trials of drugs, 448
insurance coverage for cancers, 431
lupus research, 481
patients' rights, 467, 469–470
Republican platform, 23
Wood. *See Forests and forest products*
"Woofies." *See Wholesale financial institutions*
Wool, 168

Woolsey, Lynn, D-Calif.
ESEA authorization, 537
Work Incentives Improvement Act, 470–471, 476
Work study aid, 513
Workers' compensation
injured Postal Service employees, 56
Supreme Court decisions, 723–724
tax treatment, 101
Workforce Development Boards, 575
World Bank
AIDS assistance, 230
anti-globalization protests, 148
U.S. aid appropriations, 75, 188, 189, 216
World Health Organization, 219
World Heritage sites, 368, 401
World Intellectual Property Organization, 328
World Trade Organization (WTO)
advisory commission, 189
anti-globalization protests, 148
China membership, 149, 160–166, 202
trade agreements, 155
U.S. compliance, 117, 118
U.S. trade policy summary, 39, 147, 800–801
World War II
Italian Americans, 664
officers' exoneration, 296
Wrestling, 511
Wright, Charles Parker, 775
Wright, Susan Webber, 815, 827
Wrongful convictions, 655
WTO. *See World Trade Organization*
Wu, David, D-Ore.
ed-flex plan, 540, 541
Title I education authorization, 534
Wyden, Ron, D-Ore.
assisted suicide, 117, 463, 477, 607, 658–660
ed-flex plan, 539
endangered species, 351

forest revenues, 400
Hells Canyon jetboats, 367
Wye River. *See Middle East peace process*
Wynn, Albert R., D-Md.
House leadership, 770

X

X-33 space launch vehicle, 734

Y

Yates, Sidney R., D-Ill.
NEA funding, 738
Year 2000 (Y2K) computer problem
defense appropriations, 259, 262
FAA authorization, 321
federal agency fix, 68, 330, 793
high-tech visas, 616
liability issue, 330, 331, 336
summary, 316
Year 2000 Technology Problem, Special Senate Committee on, 956
Yellen, Janet, 35 (box), 983
Yellowfin tuna, 345
Yellowstone National Park, 368, 401
Yeltsin, Boris, 188, 801
Yemen
Cole attack, 293, 803
U.S. aid appropriations, 217
Yorktown, Va., Naval Weapons Station, 253 (box)
Young, Ambrous Tung, 778
Young Brothers Development Co., 778
Young, C.W. Bill, R-Fla.
Clinton veto power, 810–811
defense appropriations, 261
Everglades restoration, 374
FAA authorization, 332

House leadership, 770
organ transplants, 476
Young, Don, R-Alaska
Alaska development, 379
native lands, 391
conservation lands acquisition, 376–378
"dolphin-safe" tuna, 346
endangered species, 386
forest health, 368
national wildlife refuges, 348–349
NOAA authorization, 745
nuclear waste storage, 362
ocean policy panel, 364
offshore oil drilling revenues, 344
U.N. lands designation, 368
Young, Nina, 346
Youngstown, Ohio, 85, 566
Youth. *See Adolescents and youth*
Youth Violence Task Force, 639
Yucca Mountain, Nev., 361–363, 407–409
Yugoslavia. *See also Bosnia; Kosovo; Serbia*
Chinese embassy bombing, 166, 209, 226
Russian loans, 222
U.S. aid appropriations, 216, 217
reconstruction aid ban, 283, 286
U.S. Kosovo policy, 177–178, 204–208
U.S. relations, 802–803
U.S. troop presence, 260, 261, 262, 278–279
Yukon Delta National Wildlife Refuge, 367

Z

Zaire. *See Congo*
Zero-gravity research, 753
Zimbabwe
U.S. trade exclusion, 168
Zinni, Anthony C., 198
Zoning, 591, 660–661, 737
Zumwalt, Elmo, 269